Constitutional Law

ASPEN CASEBOOK SERIES

CONSTITUTIONAL LAW: CASES, MATERIALS, AND PROBLEMS

FIFTH EDITION

RUSSELL L. WEAVER

PROFESSOR OF LAW & DISTINGUISHED UNIVERSITY SCHOLAR
UNIVERSITY OF LOUISVILLE
LOUIS D. BRANDEIS SCHOOL OF LAW

STEVEN I. FRIEDLAND

PROFESSOR OF LAW AND SENIOR SCHOLAR
ELON UNIVERSITY SCHOOL OF LAW

RICHARD D. ROSEN

GLENN D. WEST ENDOWED RESEARCH PROFESSOR OF LAW
TEXAS TECH UNIVERSITY SCHOOL OF LAW

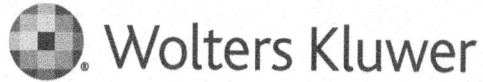

Published by Wolters Kluwer in New York.

Wolters Kluwer Legal & Regulatory U.S. serves customers worldwide with CCH, Aspen Publishers, and Kluwer Law International products. (www.WKLegaledu.com)

To contact Customer Service, e-mail customer.service@wolterskluwer.com, call 1-800-234-1660, fax 1-800-901-9075, or mail correspondence to:

> Wolters Kluwer
> Attn: Order Department
> PO Box 990
> Frederick, MD 21705

Printed in the United States of America.

1 2 3 4 5 6 7 8 9 0

ISBN: 978-1-5438-3044-6

Library of Congress Cataloging-in-Publication Data

Names: Weaver, Russell L., 1952- author. | Friedland, Steven I., author. | Rosen, Richard, 1948- author.
Title: Constitutional law : cases, materials, and problems / Russell L. Weaver, Professor of Law & Distinguished University Scholar, University of Louisville, Louis D. Brandeis School of Law; Steven I. Friedland, Professor of Law and Senior Scholar, Elon University School of Law; Richard D. Rosen, Glenn D. West Endowed Research Professor of Law, Texas Tech University School of Law.
Description: Fifth edition. | New York : Wolters Kluwer Legal & Regulatory U.S./Aspen Publishers, 2021. | Series: Aspen casebook series | Includes bibliographical references and index. | Summary: "This is a casebook on Constitutional Law for law students"—Provided by publisher.
Identifiers: LCCN 2020048852 (print) | LCCN 2020048853 (ebook) | ISBN 9781543830446 (hardcover) | ISBN 9781543830453 (ebook)
Subjects: LCSH: Constitutional law—United States. | LCGFT: Casebooks (Law)
Classification: LCC KF4550 .C59366 2021 (print) | LCC KF4550 (ebook) | DDC 342.73—dc23
LC record available at https://lccn.loc.gov/2020048852
LC ebook record available at https://lccn.loc.gov/2020048853

About Wolters Kluwer Legal & Regulatory U.S.

Wolters Kluwer Legal & Regulatory U.S. delivers expert content and solutions in the areas of law, corporate compliance, health compliance, reimbursement, and legal education. Its practical solutions help customers successfully navigate the demands of a changing environment to drive their daily activities, enhance decision quality and inspire confident outcomes.

Serving customers worldwide, its legal and regulatory portfolio includes products under the Aspen Publishers, CCH Incorporated, Kluwer Law International, ftwilliam.com and MediRegs names. They are regarded as exceptional and trusted resources for general legal and practice-specific knowledge, compliance and risk management, dynamic workflow solutions, and expert commentary.

SUMMARY OF CONTENTS

CONTENTS

VI.

STATE ACTION

557

VII.

PROCEDURAL DUE PROCESS

625

VIII.

SUBSTANTIVE PROTECTION OF ECONOMIC RIGHTS

663

IX.

SUBSTANTIVE DUE PROCESS: MODERN FUNDAMENTAL RIGHTS

739

X.

EQUAL PROTECTION 883

XI.

FREEDOM OF SPEECH

1127

XII.

THE RELIGION CLAUSES

1735

XIII.

THE RIGHT TO KEEP AND BEAR ARMS

1915

This new edition continues our inclusion in Wolters Kluwer's Connected Casebook series. This move provides a number of advantages to student users because the book includes a number of important components, including the following:

- an ebook component which allows students to read, search, highlight, and annotate the text of their casebook;
- a study center component which provides students was access to thousands of video and text explanations of difficult concepts, assessment questions, practice essays, as well as hypothetical and issue-spotting exercises; and
- an outline component which allows students to quickly create effective course-long outlines, directly integrating excerpts and notes from the textbook.

In addition, some of the less used materials have been moved online, including the campaign finance materials and the Second Amendment materials. Professors who prefer these sections will have traditional chapter materials (that include cases, notes and problems) available to them. Those who prefer a more limited approach can use the textual materials that will be included in the hard cover version of the book.

This new edition continues and refines the pedagogical approach adopted in earlier editions. Historically, most constitutional law casebooks have been written like mini-treatises. In addition to including the landmark constitutional law cases, they have included detailed notes that discuss every highway and byway of the law. Most of these books have a tendency to overload rather than facilitate the learning process. Students are reluctant to read 1,900 pages of constitutional law, much less to pore over the details. Moreover, because most constitutional law casebooks include so many decisions (in mini-treatise fashion), casebook authors have been forced to severely edit the decisions that they do include.

In creating this fifth edition of the book, our primary goal was to produce an accessible and teachable book that will help students understand constitutional theory, lead students to greater insights, generate classroom interactivity, and provide a platform for inspired learning. One way that we accomplish these objectives is through the inclusion of problems. In this book, because of the nature of constitutional law, we do not use a single type of problem but instead use many different models and formats. Many problems are factual in nature and are designed to encourage students to think about how constitutional doctrine might apply in particular contexts. In some instances, these fact-based problems are premised upon actual cases, including United States Supreme Court cases. Other problems are theoretical in nature and are simply designed to help students better understand constitutional doctrine.

With a given problem, we might be trying to achieve any one of several objectives. For example, we use problems to illustrate and clarify doctrinal principles and conflicts, place students in real-life situations and ask them how they would respond, help students view constitutional law issues in modern and historical context, or prepare students for actual practice. Some problems probe divisions in the law, while others ask students to apply existing doctrine to new situations. Some problems place students in the position of a lawyer and ask them to explain how they might argue a particular case (e.g., what facts or arguments might they use in support of their positions). In other words, the user should not expect to see a single, monolithic approach to problems.

In using problems, we accept the criticisms of the Realists and Critical Legal Theory movement. In other words, one of our goals is to encourage students to think critically and to develop arguments and theory, rather than to view law as simply a "deductive process." As a result, even if the Court has rendered a decision in a particular case, we might present that case as a "problem" because we want students to critically analyze the issues involved. Even if a student responds, "I read the decided case and the Court held . . . ," the professor can respond with questions designed to stimulate thought. "Ok, fair enough. Now, do you think that the Court got it right? Did it give sufficient weight to this consideration? How could the Court possibly have reached that conclusion?" Such analysis helps students become better lawyers.

In any constitutional law casebook, tradeoffs are necessary, and we have made a number of intentional ones. First, although we include the landmark cases, we do not attempt to catalog every decision (even every United States Supreme Court) decision in each of the relevant areas. Over the past half-century, constitutional case law has multiplied to the extent that it is impossible to thoroughly discuss every decision and do justice to each one. As a result, constitutional law casebooks authors are necessarily forced to include some decisions and to exclude others. Otherwise, our book would be too long. Although this book is designed to give students a thorough grounding in constitutional law, students can always consult secondary sources if they desire more treatise-like discussions. In this book, we have chosen cases for a variety of reasons. Some were chosen because they are modern cases that reflect the current state of the law. Others were chosen because they are "landmarks" that students need to read and understand. In some cases, we have included older cases that help students understand and evaluate the modern approach.

Because we present fewer cases overall, we are generally able to include more of the cases that we do include. In other words, we allow students to read the Court's own words and decide for themselves what the decisions mean. Other cases may come in through questions, problems, or hypotheticals.

We give thanks to the many people who assisted us in the creation and revision of this book, including our research assistants and secretaries. We are particularly grateful to students who helped us find and correct errors. Finally, we are thankful to our spouses, significant others, and children who supported us through the various stages of this project.

RLW, SIF, and RDR

THE CONSTITUTION OF THE UNITED STATES

We the People of the United States, in Order to form a more perfect Union, establish justice, insure domestic Tranquility, provide for the common defence, promote the general Welfare, and secure the Blessings of Liberty to ourselves and our Posterity, do ordain and establish this Constitution for the United States of America.

ARTICLE I

Section 1. All legislative Powers herein granted shall be vested in a Congress of the United States which shall consist of a Senate and House of Representatives.

Section 2. [1] The House of Representatives shall be composed of Members chosen every second Year by the People of the several States, and the Electors in each State shall have the Qualifications requisite for Electors of the most numerous Branch of the State Legislature.

[2] No Person shall be a Representative who shall not have attained to the Age of twenty five Years, and been seven Years a Citizen of the United States, and who shall not, when elected, be an Inhabitant of that State in which he shall be chosen.

[3] Representatives and direct Taxes shall be apportioned among the several States which may be included within this Union, according to their respective Numbers, which shall be determined by adding to the whole Number of free Persons, including those bound to Service for a Term of Years, and excluding Indians not taxed, three fifths of all other Persons. The actual Enumeration shall be made within three Years after the first meeting of the Congress of the United States, and within every subsequent Term of ten Years, in such Manner as they shall by Law direct. The Number of Representatives shall not exceed one for every thirty Thousand, but each State shall have at Least One Representative; and until such enumeration shall be made, the State of New Hampshire shall be entitled to chuse three, Massachusetts eight, Rhode Island and Providence Plantations one, Connecticut five, New York six, New Jersey four, Pennsylvania eight, Delaware one, Maryland six, Virginia ten, North Carolina five, South Carolina five, and Georgia three.

[4] When vacancies happen in the Representation from any State, the Executive Authority thereof shall issue Writs of Election to fill such Vacancies.

[5] The House of Representatives shall chuse their Speaker and other Officers; and shall have the sole Power of Impeachment.

Section 3. [1] The Senate of the United States shall be composed of two Senators from each State, chosen by the Legislature thereof, for six Years; and each Senator shall have one Vote.

[2] Immediately after they shall be assembled in Consequence of the first Election, they shall be divided as equally as may be into three Classes. The Seats of the Senators of the first Class shall be vacated at the Expiration of the second Year, of the second Class at the Expiration of the fourth Year, and of the third Class at the Expiration of the sixth Year, so that one third may be chosen every second Year; and if Vacancies happen by Resignation, or otherwise, during the Recess of the Legislature of any State, the Executive thereof may make temporary Appointments until the next Meeting of the Legislature, which shall then fill such Vacancies.

[3] No Person shall be a Senator who shall not have attained to the Age of thirty Years, and been nine Years a Citizen of the United States, and who shall not, when elected, be an Inhabitant of that State for which he shall be chosen.

[4] The Vice President of the United States shall be President of the Senate, but shall have no Vote, unless they be equally divided.

[5] The Senate shall chuse their other Officers, and also a President pro tempore, in the absence of the Vice President, or when he shall exercise the Office of President of the United States.

[6] The Senate shall have the sole Power to try all Impeachments. When sitting for that Purpose, they shall be on Oath or Affirmation. When the President of the United States is tried, the Chief Justice shall preside: And no Person shall be convicted without the Concurrence of two thirds of the Members present.

[7] Judgment in Cases of Impeachment shall not extend further than to removal from Office, and disqualification to hold and enjoy any Office of honor, Trust or Profit under the United States: but the Party convicted shall nevertheless be liable and subject to Indictment, Trial, judgment and Punishment, according to Law.

Section 4. [1] The Times, Places and Manner of holding Elections for Senators and Representatives, shall be prescribed in each State by the Legislature thereof; but the Congress may at any time by law make or alter such Regulations, except as to the Places of chusing Senators.

[2] The Congress shall assemble at least once in every Year, and such Meeting shall be on the first Monday in December, unless they shall by Law appoint a different Day.

Section 5. [1] Each house shall be the Judge of the Elections, Returns and Qualifications of its own members, and a Majority of each shall constitute a Quorum to do Business; but a smaller Number may adjourn from day to day, and may be authorized to compel the Attendance of absent members, in such Manner, and under such Penalties as each House may provide.

[2] Each House may determine the Rules of its Proceedings, punish its Members for disorderly Behavior, and, with the Concurrence of two thirds, expel a Member.

[3] Each House shall keep a Journal of its Proceedings, and from time to time publish the same, excepting such Parts as may in their Judgment require Secrecy; and the Yeas and Nays of the Members of either House on any question shall, at the Desire of one fifth of those Present, be entered on the Journal.

[4] Neither House, during the Session of Congress, shall, without the Consent of the other, adjourn for more than three days, nor to any other Place than that in which the two Houses shall be sitting.

Section 6. [1] The Senators and Representatives shall receive a Compensation for their Services, to be ascertained by Law, and paid out of the Treasury of the United

States. They shall in all Cases, except Treason, Felony and Breach of the Peace, be privileged from Arrest during their Attendance at the Session of their respective Houses, and in going to and returning from the same; and for any Speech or Debate in either House, they shall not be questioned in any other Place.

[2] No Senator or Representative shall, during the time for which he was elected, be appointed to any civil Office under the Authority of the United States, which shall have been created, or the Emoluments whereof shall have been encreased during such time; and no Person holding any office under the United States, shall be a Member of either House during his Continuance in Office.

Section 7. [1] All Bills for raising Revenue shall originate in the House of Representatives; but the Senate may propose or concur with Amendments as on other Bills.

[2] Every Bill which shall have passed the House of Representatives and the Senate, shall, before it becomes a Law, be presented to the President of the United States; If he approve he shall sign it, but if not he shall return it, with his Objections to the House in which it shall have originated, who shall enter the Objections at large on their Journal, and proceed to reconsider it. If after such Reconsideration two thirds of that House shall agree to pass the Bill, it shall be sent, together with the Objections, to the other House, by which it shall likewise be reconsidered, and if approved by two thirds of that House, it shall become a Law. But in all such Cases the Votes of both Houses shall be determined by Yeas and Nays, and the Names of the Persons voting for and against the Bill shall be entered on the Journal of each House respectively. If any Bill shall not be returned by the President within ten Days (Sundays excepted) after it shall have been presented to him, the Same shall be a Law, in like Manner as if he had signed it, unless the Congress by their Adjournment prevents its Return, in which Case it shall not be a Law.

[3] Every Order, Resolution, or Vote to Which the Concurrence of the Senate and House of Representatives may be necessary (except on a question of Adjournment) shall be presented to the President of the United States; and before the Same shall take Effect, shall be approved by him, or being disapproved by him, shall be repassed by two thirds of the Senate and House of Representatives, according to the Rules and Limitations prescribed in the Case of a Bill.

Section 8. [1] The Congress shall have Power To lay and collect Taxes, Duties, Imposts and Excises, to pay the Debts and provide for the common Defence and general Welfare of the United States; but all Duties, Imposts and Excises shall be uniform throughout the United States;

[2] To borrow money on the credit of the United States;

[3] To regulate Commerce with foreign Nations, and among the several States, and with the Indian Tribes;

[4] To establish an uniform Rule of Naturalization, and uniform Laws on the subject of Bankruptcies throughout the United States;

[5] To coin Money, regulate the Value thereof, and of foreign Coin, and fix the Standard of Weights and Measures;

[6] To provide the Punishment of counterfeiting the Securities and current Coin of the United States;

[7] To establish Post Offices and post Roads;

[8] To promote the Progress of Science and useful Arts, by securing for limited Times to Authors and Inventors the exclusive Right to their respective Writings and Discoveries;

[9] To constitute Tribunals inferior to the supreme Court;

[10] To define and punish Piracies and Felonies committed on the high Seas, and Offenses against the Law of Nations;

[11] To declare War, grant Letters of Marque and Reprisal, and make Rules concerning Captures on Land and Water;

[12] To raise and support Armies, but no Appropriation of Money to that Use shall be a longer Term than two Years;

[13] To provide and maintain a Navy;

[14] To make Rules for the Government and Regulation of the land and naval Forces;

[15] To provide for calling forth the Militia to execute the Laws of the Union, suppress Insurrections and repel Invasions;

[16] To provide for organizing, arming, and disciplining, the Militia, and for governing such Part of them as may be employed in the Service of the United States, reserving to the States respectively, the Appointment of the Officers, and the Authority of training the Militia according to the discipline prescribed by Congress;

[17] To exercise exclusive Legislation in all Cases whatsoever, over such District (not exceeding ten Miles square) as may, by Cession of particular States, and the Acceptance of Congress, become the Seat of the Government of the United States, and to exercise like Authority over all Places purchased by the Consent of the Legislature of the State in which the Same shall be, for the Erection of Forts, Magazines, Arsenals, dock-Yards, and other needful Buildings;—And

[18] To make all Laws which shall be necessary and proper for carrying into Execution the foregoing Powers, and all other Powers vested by this Constitution in the Government of the United States, or in any Department or Officer thereof.

Section 9. [1] The Migration or Importation of such Persons as any of the States now existing shall think proper to admit, shall not be prohibited by the Congress prior to the Year one thousand eight hundred and eight, but a Tax or duty may be imposed on such Importation, not exceeding ten dollars for each Person.

[2] The privilege of the Writ of Habeas Corpus shall not be suspended, unless when in Cases of Rebellion or Invasion the public Safety may require it.

[3] No Bill of Attainder or ex post facto Law shall be passed.

[4] No Capitation, or other direct, Tax shall be laid, unless in Proportion to the Census or Enumeration herein before directed to be taken.

[5] No Tax or Duty shall be laid on articles exported from any State.

[6] No Preference shall be given by any Regulation of Commerce or Revenue to the Ports of one State over those of another: nor shall Vessels bound to, or from, one State, be obliged to enter, clear, or pay Duties in another.

[7] No Money shall be drawn from the Treasury, but in Consequence of Appropriations made by Law; and a regular Statement and Account of the Receipts and Expenditures of all public Money shall be published from time to time.

[8] No title of Nobility shall be granted by the United States: And no Person holding any Office of Profit or Trust under them, shall, without the Consent of the Congress, accept of any present, Emolument, Office, or Title, of any kind whatever, from any King, Prince, or foreign State.

Section 10. [1] No State shall enter into any Treaty, Alliance, or Confederation; grant Letters of Marque and Reprisal; coin Money; emit Bills of Credit; make any Thing but gold and silver Coin a Tender in Payment of Debts; pass any Bill of

Attainder, ex post facto Law, or Law impairing the Obligation of Contracts, or grant any title of Nobility.

[2] No State shall, without the Consent of the Congress, lay any Imposts or Duties on Imports or Exports, except what may be absolutely necessary for executing its inspection Laws: and the net Produce of all Duties and Imposts, laid by any State on Imports or Exports, shall be for the Use of the Treasury of the United States; and all such Laws be subject to the Revision and Controul of the Congress.

[3] No State shall, without the Consent of Congress, lay any Duty of Tonnage, keep Troops, or Ships of War in time of Peace, enter into any Agreement or Compact with another State, or with a foreign Power, or engage in War, unless actually invaded, or in such imminent Danger as will not admit of delay.

ARTICLE II

Section 1. [1] The executive Power shall be vested in a President of the United States of America. He shall hold his Office during the Term of four Years, and, together with the Vice President, chosen for the same Term, be elected, as follows: [2] Each State shall appoint, in such Manner as the Legislature thereof may direct, a Number of Electors, equal to the whole Number of Senators and Representatives to which the State may be entitled in the Congress: but no Senator or Representative, or Person holding an Office of Trust or Profit under the United States, shall be appointed an Elector.

[3] The Electors shall meet in their respective States, and vote by Ballot for two Persons, of whom one at least shall not be an Inhabitant of the same State with themselves. And they shall make a List of all the Persons voted for, and of the Number of Votes for each; which List they shall sign and certify, and transmit sealed to the Seat of the Government of the United States, directed to the President of the Senate. The President of the Senate shall, in the Presence of the Senate and House of Representatives, open all the Certificates, and the Votes shall then be counted. The Person having the greatest Number of Votes shall be the President, if such Number be a Majority of the whole Number of Electors appointed; and if there be more than one who have such Majority, and have an equal Number of Votes, then the House of Representatives shall immediately chuse by Ballot one of them for President; and if no Person have a Majority, then from the five highest on the List the said House shall in like Manner chuse the President. But in chusing the President, the Votes shall be taken by States, the Representation from each State having one vote; a quorum for this Purpose shall consist of a Member or Members from two thirds of the States, and a Majority of all the States shall be necessary to a Choice. In every Case, after the Choice of the President, the Person having the Greatest Number of Votes of the Electors shall be the Vice President. But if there should remain two or more who have equal Votes, the Senate shall chuse from them by Ballot the Vice President.

[4] The Congress may determine the Time of chusing the Electors, and the Day on which they shall give their Votes; which Day shall be the same throughout the United States.

[5] No person except a natural born Citizen, or a Citizen of the United States, at the time of the Adoption of this Constitution, shall be eligible to the Office of

President; neither shall any Person be eligible to that Office who shall not have attained to the Age of thirty five Years, and been fourteen Years a Resident within the United States.

[6] In case of the removal of the President from Office, or of his Death, Resignation, or Inability to discharge the Powers and Duties of the said Office, the Same shall devolve on the Vice President, and the Congress may by Law provide for the Case of Removal, Death, Resignation or Inability, both of the President and Vice President, declaring what Officer shall then act as President, and such Officer shall act accordingly, until the Disability be removed, or a President shall be elected.

[7] The President shall, at stated Times, receive for his Services, a Compensation, which shall neither be increased nor diminished during the Period for which he shall have been elected, and he shall not receive within that Period any other Emolument from the United States, or any of them.

[8] Before he enter on the Execution of his Office, he shall take the following Oath or Affirmation: "I do solemnly swear (or affirm) that I will faithfully execute the Office of President of the United States, and will to the best of my Ability, preserve, protect and defend the Constitution of the United States."

Section 2. [1] The President shall be Commander in Chief of the Army and Navy of the United States, and of the Militia of the several States, when called into the actual Service of the United States; he may require the Opinion, in writing, of the principal Officer in each of the executive Departments, upon any subject relating to the Duties of their respective Offices, and he shall have Power to grant Reprieves and Pardons for Offenses against the United States, except in Cases of Impeachment.

[2] He shall have Power, by and with the Advice and Consent of the Senate, to make Treaties, provided two thirds of the Senators present concur; and he shall nominate, and by and with the Advice and Consent of the Senate, shall appoint Ambassadors, other public Ministers and Consuls, Judges of the supreme Court, and all other Officers of the United States, whose Appointments are not herein otherwise provided for, and which shall be established by Law: but the Congress may by Law vest the Appointment of such inferior Officers, as they think proper, in the President alone, to the Courts of Law, or in the Heads of Departments.

[3] The President shall have Power to fill up all Vacancies that may happen during the Recess of the Senate by granting Commissions which shall expire at the End of their next Session.

Section 3. He shall from time to time give to the Congress Information of the State of the Union, and recommend to their Consideration such Measures as he shall judge necessary and expedient; he may, on extraordinary Occasions, convene both Houses, or either of them, and in Case of Disagreement between them, with Respect to the time of Adjournment, he may adjourn them to such Time as he shall think proper; he shall receive Ambassadors and other public Ministers; he shall take Care that the Laws be faithfully executed, and shall Commission all the Officers of the United States.

Section 4. The President, Vice President and all civil Officers of the United States, shall be removed from Office on Impeachment for, and Conviction of, Treason, Bribery, or other high Crimes and Misdemeanors.

ARTICLE III

Section 1. The judicial Power of the United States, shall be vested in one supreme Court, and in such inferior Courts as the Congress may from time to time ordain and establish. The Judges, both of the supreme and inferior Courts, shall hold their Offices during good Behaviour, and shall, at stated Times, receive for their Services a Compensation, which shall not be diminished during their Continuance in Office.

Section 2. [1] The Judicial Power shall extend to all Cases, in Law and Equity, arising under this Constitution, the Laws of the United States, and Treaties made, or which shall be made, under their Authority; — to all Cases affecting Ambassadors, other public Ministers and Consuls; — to all Cases of admiralty and maritime Jurisdiction; — to Controversies to which the United States shall be a Party; — to Controversies between two or more States; between a State and Citizens of another State; — between Citizens of different States; — between Citizens of the same State claiming Lands under Grants of different States, and between a State, or the Citizens thereof, and foreign States, Citizens or Subjects.

[2] In all cases affecting Ambassadors, other public Ministers and Consuls, and those in which a State shall be Party, the supreme Court shall have original Jurisdiction. In all the other Cases before mentioned, the supreme Court shall have appellate Jurisdiction, both as to Law and Fact, with such Exceptions, and under such Regulations as the Congress shall make.

[3] The trial of all Crimes, except in Cases of Impeachment, shall be by Jury; and such Trial shall be held in the State where the said Crimes shall have been committed; but when not committed within any State, the Trial shall be at such Place or Places as the Congress may by Law have directed.

Section 3. [1] Treason against the United States, shall consist only in levying War against them, or in adhering to their Enemies, giving them Aid and Comfort. No person shall be convicted of Treason unless on the Testimony of two Witnesses to the same over Act, or on Confession in open Court.

[2] The Congress shall have Power to declare the Punishment of Treason, but no Attainder of Treason shall work Corruption of Blood, or Forfeiture except during the Life of the Person attainted.

ARTICLE IV

Section 1. Full Faith and Credit shall be given in each State to the public Acts, Records, and judicial Proceedings of every other State. And the Congress may by general Laws prescribe the Manner in which such Acts, Records and Proceedings shall be proved, and the Effect thereof.

Section 2. [1] The Citizens of each State shall be entitled to all Privileges and Immunities of Citizens in the several States.

[2] A Person charged in any State with Treason, Felony, or other Crime, who shall flee from Justice, and be found in another State, shall on demand of the executive

Authority of the State from which he fled, be delivered up, to be removed to the State having Jurisdiction of the Crime.

[3] No Person held to Service or Labour in one State, under the Laws thereof, escaping into another, shall, in Consequence of any Law or Regulation therein, be discharged from such Service or Labour, but shall be delivered up on Claim of the Party to whom such Service or Labour may be due.

Section 3. [1] New States may be admitted by the Congress into this Union; but no new State shall be formed or erected within the Jurisdiction of any other State; nor any State be formed by the Junction of two or more States, or Parts of States, without the Consent of the Legislatures of the States concerned as well as of the Congress.

[2] The Congress shall have Power to dispose of and make all needful Rules and Regulations respecting the Territory or other Property belonging to the United States; and nothing in this Constitution shall be so construed as to Prejudice any Claims of the United States, or of any particular State.

Section 4. The United States shall guarantee to every State in this Union a Republican Form of Government, and shall protect each of them against Invasion; and on Application of the Legislature, or of the Executive (when the Legislature cannot be convened) against domestic Violence.

ARTICLE V

The Congress, whenever two thirds of both Houses shall deem it necessary, shall propose Amendments to this Constitution, or, on the Application of the Legislatures of two thirds of the several States, shall call a Convention for proposing Amendments, which, in either Case, shall be valid to all Intents and Purposes, as part of this Constitution, when ratified by the Legislatures of three fourths of the several States, or by Conventions in three fourths thereof, as the one or the other Mode of Ratification may be proposed by the Congress; Provided that no Amendment which may be made prior to the Year One thousand eight hundred and eight shall in any Manner affect the first and fourth Clauses in the Ninth Section of the first Article; and that no State, without its Consent, shall be deprived of its equal Suffrage in the Senate.

ARTICLE VI

[1] All Debts contracted and Engagements entered into, before the Adoption of this Constitution, shall be as valid against the United States under this Constitution, as under the Confederation.

[2] This Constitution, and the Laws of the United States which shall be made in Pursuance thereof; and all Treaties made, or which shall be made, under the Authority of the United States, shall be the supreme Law of the Land; and the Judges in every State shall be bound thereby, any Thing in the Constitution or Laws of any State to the Contrary notwithstanding.

[3] The Senators and Representatives before mentioned, and the Members of the several State Legislatures, and all executive and judicial Officers, both of the United

States and of the several States, shall be bound by Oath or Affirmation, to support this Constitution; but no religious Test shall ever be required as a Qualification to any Office or public Trust under the United States.

ARTICLE VII

The Ratification of the Conventions of nine States shall be sufficient for the Establishment of this Constitution between the States so ratifying the Same.

Done in Convention by the Unanimous Consent of the States present the Seventeenth Day of September in the Year of our Lord one thousand seven hundred and Eighty seven and of the Independence of the United States of America the Twelfth.

ARTICLES IN ADDITION TO, AND AMENDMENT OF, THE CONSTITUTION OF THE UNITED STATES OF AMERICA, PROPOSED BY CONGRESS, AND RATIFIED BY THE LEGISLATURES OF THE SEVERAL STATES, PURSUANT TO THE FIFTH ARTICLE OF THE ORIGINAL CONSTITUTION.

AMENDMENT I [1791]

Congress shall make no law respecting an establishment of religion, or prohibiting the free exercise thereof; or abridging the freedom of speech, or of the press; or the right of the people peaceably to assemble, and to petition the Government for a redress of grievances.

AMENDMENT II [1791]

A well regulated Militia, being necessary to the security of a free State, the right of the people to keep and bear Arms, shall not be infringed.

AMENDMENT III [1791]

No Soldier shall, in time of peace be quartered in any house, without the consent of the Owner, nor in time of war, but in a manner to be prescribed by law.

AMENDMENT IV [1791]

The right of the people to be secure in their persons, houses, papers, and effects, against unreasonable searches and seizures, shall not be violated, and no Warrants shall issue, but upon probable cause, supported by Oath or affirmation, and particularly describing the place to be searched, and the persons or things to be seized.

AMENDMENT V [1791]

No person shall be held to answer for a capital, or otherwise infamous crime, unless on a presentment or indictment of a Grand Jury, except in cases arising in the land or naval forces, or in the Militia, when in actual service in time of War or public danger; nor shall any person be subject for the same offence to be twice put in jeopardy of life or limb; nor shall be compelled in any criminal case to be a witness against himself, nor be deprived of life, liberty, or property, without due process of law; nor shall private property be taken for public use, without just compensation.

AMENDMENT VI [1791]

In all criminal prosecutions, the accused shall enjoy the right to a speedy and public trial, by an impartial jury of the State and district wherein the crime shall have been committed, which district shall have been previously ascertained by law, and to be informed of the nature and cause of the accusation; to be confronted with the witnesses against him; to have compulsory process for obtaining witnesses in his favor, and to have the Assistance of Counsel for his defence.

AMENDMENT VII [1791]

In Suits at common law, where the value in controversy shall exceed twenty dollars, the right of trial by jury shall be preserved, and no fact tried by a jury, shall be otherwise reexamined in any Court of the United States, than according to the rules of the common law.

AMENDMENT VIII [1791]

Excessive bail shall not be required, nor excessive fines imposed, nor cruel and unusual punishments inflicted.

AMENDMENT IX [1791]

The enumeration in the Constitution, of certain rights, shall not be construed to deny or disparage others retained by the people.

AMENDMENT X [1791]

The powers not delegated to the United States by the Constitution, nor prohibited by it to the States, are reserved to the States respectively, or to the people.

AMENDMENT XI [1798]

The Judicial power of the United States shall not be construed to extend to any suit in law or equity, commenced or prosecuted against one of the United States by Citizens of another State, or by Citizens or Subjects of any Foreign State.

AMENDMENT XII [1804]

The Electors shall meet in their respective states and vote by ballot for President and Vice-President, one of whom, at least, shall not be an inhabitant of the same state with themselves; they shall name in their ballots the person voted for as President, and in distinct ballots the person voted for as Vice-President, and they shall make distinct lists of all persons voted for as President, and of all persons voted for as Vice-President, and of the number of votes for each, which lists they shall sign and certify, and transmit sealed to the seat of the government of the United States, directed to the President of the Senate;—The President of the Senate shall, in the presence of the Senate and House of Representatives, open all the certificates and the votes shall then be counted;—The person having the greatest number of votes for President, shall be the President, if such number be a majority of the whole number of Electors appointed; and if no person have such majority, then from the persons having the highest numbers not exceeding three on the list of those voted for as President, the House of Representatives shall choose immediately, by ballot, the President. But in choosing the President, the votes shall be taken by states, the representation from each state having one vote; a quorum for this purpose shall consist of a member or members from two-thirds of the states, and a majority of all the states shall be necessary to a choice. And if the House of Representatives shall not choose a President whenever the right of choice shall devolve upon them, before the fourth day of March next following, then the Vice-President shall act as President, as in the case of the death or other constitutional disability of the President.—The person having the greatest number of votes as Vice-President, shall be the Vice-President, if such number be a majority of the whole number of Electors appointed, and if no person have a majority, then from the two highest numbers on the list, the Senate shall choose the Vice-President; a quorum for the purpose shall consist of two-thirds of the whole number of Senators, and a majority of the whole number shall be necessary to a choice. But no person constitutionally ineligible to the office of President shall be eligible to that of Vice-President of the United States.

AMENDMENT XIII [1865]

Section 1. Neither slavery nor involuntary servitude, except as a punishment for crime whereof the party shall have been duly convicted, shall exist within the United States, or any place subject to their jurisdiction.

Section 2. Congress shall have power to enforce this article by appropriate legislation.

AMENDMENT XIV [1868]

Section 1. All persons born or naturalized in the United States, and subject to the jurisdiction thereof, are citizens of the United States and of the State wherein they reside. No State shall make or enforce any law which shall abridge the privileges or immunities of citizens of the United States; nor shall any State deprive any person of life, liberty, or property, without due process of law; nor deny to any person within its jurisdiction the equal protection of the laws.

Section 2. Representatives shall be apportioned among the several States according to their respective numbers, counting the whole number of persons in each State, excluding Indians not taxed. But when the right to vote at any election for the choice of electors for President and Vice-President of the United States, Representatives in Congress, the Executive and Judicial officers of a State, or the members of the Legislature thereof, is denied to any of the male inhabitants of such State, being twenty-one years of age, and citizens of the United States, or in any way abridged, except for participation in rebellion, or other crime, the basis of representation therein shall be reduced in the proportion which the number of such male citizens shall bear to the whole number of male citizens twenty-one years of age in such State.

Section 3. No person shall be a Senator or Representative in Congress, or elector of President and Vice-President, or hold any office, civil or military, under the United States, or under any State, who, having previously taken an oath, as a member of Congress, or as an officer of the United States, or as a member of any State legislature, or as an executive or judicial officer of any State, to support the Constitution of the United States, shall have engaged in insurrection or rebellion against the same, or given aid or comfort to the enemies thereof. But Congress may by a vote of two-thirds of each House, remove such disability.

Section 4. The validity of the public debt of the United States, authorized by law, including debts incurred for payment of pensions and bounties for services in suppressing insurrection or rebellion, shall not be questioned. But neither the United States nor any State shall assume or pay any debt or obligation incurred in aid of insurrection or rebellion against the United States, or any claim for the loss of emancipation of any slave; but all such debts, obligations and claims shall be held illegal and void.

Section 5. The Congress shall have power to enforce, by appropriate legislation, the provisions of this article.

AMENDMENT XV [1870]

Section 1. The right of citizens of the United States to vote shall not be denied or abridged by the United States or by any State on account of race, color, or previous condition of servitude.

Section 2. The Congress shall have power to enforce this article by appropriate legislation.

AMENDMENT XVI [1913]

The Congress shall have power to lay and collect taxes on incomes, from whatever source derived, without apportionment among the several States, and without regard to any census or enumeration.

AMENDMENT XVII [1913]

[1] The Senate of the United States shall be composed of two Senators from each State, elected by the people thereof, for six years, and each Senator shall have one vote. The electors in each State shall have the qualifications requisite for electors of the most numerous branch of the State legislatures.

[2] When vacancies happen in the representation of any State in the Senate, the executive authority of such State shall issue writs of election to fill such vacancies: *Provided,* That the legislature of any State may empower the executive thereof to make temporary appointments until the people fill the vacancies by election as the legislature may direct.

[3] This amendment shall not be so construed as to affect the election or term of any Senator chosen before it becomes valid as part of the Constitution.

AMENDMENT XVIII [1919]

Section 1. After one year from the ratification of this article the manufacture, sale, or transportation of intoxicating liquors within, the importation thereof into, or the exportation thereof from the United States and all territory subject to the jurisdiction thereof for beverage purposes is hereby prohibited.

Section 2. The Congress and the several States shall have concurrent power to enforce this article by appropriate legislation.

Section 3. This article shall be inoperative unless it shall have been ratified as an amendment to the Constitution by the legislatures of the several States, as provided in the Constitution, within seven years from the date of the submission hereof to the States by the Congress.

AMENDMENT XIX [1920]

[1] The right of citizens of the United States to vote shall not be denied or abridged by the United States or by any State on account of sex.

[2] Congress shall have power to enforce this article by appropriate legislation.

AMENDMENT XX [1933]

Section 1. The terms of the President and Vice President shall end at noon on the 20th day of January, and the terms of Senators and Representatives at noon on the 3d day of January, of the years in which such terms would have ended if this article had not been ratified; and the terms of their successor shall then begin.

Section 2. The Congress shall assemble at least once in every year, and such meeting shall begin at noon on the 3d day of January, unless they shall by law appoint a different day.

Section 3. If, at the time fixed for the beginning of the term of the President, the President elect shall have died, the Vice President elect shall become President. If a President shall not have been chosen before the time fixed for the beginning of his term, or if the President elect shall have failed to qualify, then the Vice President elect shall act as President until a President shall have qualified; and the Congress may by law provide for the case wherein neither a President elect nor a Vice President elect shall have qualified, declaring who shall then act as President, or the manner in which one who is to act shall be selected, and such person shall act accordingly until a President or Vice President shall have qualified.

Section 4. The Congress may by law provide for the case of the death of any of the persons from whom the House of Representatives may choose a President whenever the right of choice shall have devolved upon them, and for the case of the death of any of the persons from whom the Senate may choose a Vice President whenever the right of choice shall have devolved upon them.

Section 5. Sections 1 and 2 shall take effect on the 15th day of October following the ratification of this article.

Section 6. This article shall be inoperative unless it shall have been ratified as an amendment to the Constitution by the legislatures of three-fourths of the several States within seven years from the date of its submission.

AMENDMENT XXI [1933]

Section 1. The eighteenth article of amendment to the Constitution of the United States is hereby repealed.

Section 2. The transportation or importation into any State, Territory, or possession of the United States for delivery or use therein of intoxicating liquors, in violation of the laws thereof, is hereby prohibited.

Section 3. This article shall be inoperative unless it shall have been ratified as an amendment to the Constitution by conventions in the several States, as provided in the Constitution, within seven years from the date of the submissions hereof to the States by the Congress.

AMENDMENT XXII [1951]

Section 1. No person shall be elected to the office of the President more than twice, and no person who has held the office of President, or acted as President, for more than two years of a term to which some other person was elected President shall be elected to the office of the President more than once. But this Article shall not apply to any person holding the office of President when this Article was proposed by the Congress, and shall not prevent any person who may be holding the office of President, or acting as President, during the term within which the Article becomes operative from holding the office of President or acting as President during the remainder of such term.

Section 2. This article shall be inoperative unless it shall have been ratified as an amendment to the Constitution by the legislatures of three-fourths of the several States within seven years from the date of its submission to the States by the Congress.

AMENDMENT XXIII [1961]

Section 1. The District constituting the seat of Government of the United States shall appoint in such manner as the Congress may direct:

A number of electors of President and Vice President equal to the whole number of Senators and Representatives in Congress to which the District would be entitled if it were a State, but in no event more than the least populous State; they shall be in addition to those appointed by the States, but they shall be considered, for the purposes of the election of President and Vice President, to be electors appointed by a State; and they shall meet in the District and perform such duties as provided by the twelfth article of amendment.

Section 2. The Congress shall have power to enforce this article by appropriate legislation.

AMENDMENT XXIV [1964]

Section 1. The right of citizens of the United States to vote in any primary or other election for President or Vice President for electors for President or Vice President, or for Senator or Representative in Congress, shall not be denied or abridged by the United States or any State by reason of failure to pay any poll tax or other tax.

Section 2. The Congress shall have power to enforce this article by appropriate legislation.

AMENDMENT XXV [1967]

Section 1. In case of the removal of the President from office or of his death or resignation, the Vice President shall become President.

Section 2. Whenever there is a vacancy in the office of the Vice President, the President shall nominate a Vice President who shall take office upon confirmation by a majority vote of both Houses of Congress.

Section 3. Whenever the President transmits to the President pro tempore of the Senate and the Speaker of the House of Representatives his written declaration that he is unable to discharge the powers and duties of his office, and until he transmits to them a written declaration to the contrary, such powers and duties shall be discharged by the Vice President as Acting President.

Section 4. Whenever the Vice President and a Majority of either the principal officers of the executive departments or of such other body as Congress may by law provide, transmit to the President pro tempore of the Senate and the Speaker of the House of Representatives their written declaration that the President is unable to discharge the powers and duties of his office, the Vice President shall immediately assume the powers and duties of the office as Acting President.

Thereafter, when the President transmits to the President pro tempore of the Senate and the Speaker of the House of Representatives his written declaration that no inability exists, he shall resume the powers and duties of his office unless the Vice President and a majority of either the principal officers of the executive department or of such other body as Congress may by law provide, transmit within four days to the President pro tempore of the Senate and the Speaker of the House of Representatives their written declaration that the President is unable to discharge the powers and duties of his office. Thereupon Congress shall decide the issue, assembling within forty-eight hours for that purpose if not in session. If the Congress, within twenty-one days after receipt of the latter written declaration, or, if Congress is not in session, within twenty-one days after Congress is required to assemble, determined by two-thirds vote of both Houses that the President is unable to discharge the powers and duties of his office, the Vice President shall continue to discharge the same as Acting President; otherwise, the President shall resume the powers and duties of his office.

AMENDMENT XXVI [1971]

Section 1. The right of citizens of the United States, who are eighteen years of age or older, to vote shall not be denied or abridged by the United States or by any State on account of age.

Section 2. The Congress shall have power to enforce this article by appropriate legislation.

AMENDMENT XXVII [1992]

Section 1. No law, varying the Compensation for the services of the Senators and Representatives, shall take effect, unless an election of Representatives shall have intervened.

Constitutional Law

1

Judicial Review

U.S. CONSTITUTION, ARTICLE III

Section 1. The judicial Power of the United States, shall be vested in one supreme Court, and in such inferior Courts as the Congress may from time to time ordain and establish. The Judges, both of the supreme and inferior Courts, shall hold their offices during good Behaviour, and shall at stated Times, receive for their Services, a Compensation, which shall not be diminished during their Continuance in Office.

Section 2. [1] The judicial Power shall extend to all Cases, in Law and Equity, arising under this Constitution, the Laws of the United States, and Treaties made, or which shall be made, under their Authority;—to all Cases affecting Ambassadors, other public Ministers and Consuls;—to all Cases of admiralty and maritime Jurisdiction;—to Controversies to which the United States shall be a Party;—to Controversies between two or more States;—between a State and Citizens of another State;—between Citizens of different States;—between Citizens of the same State claiming Lands under Grants of different States, and between a State or the Citizens thereof, and foreign States, Citizens or Subjects.

[2] In all Cases affecting Ambassadors, other public Ministers and Consuls, and those in which a State shall be Party, the supreme Court shall have original Jurisdiction. In all the other Cases before mentioned, the supreme Court shall have appellate Jurisdiction, both as to Law and Fact, with such Exceptions, and under such Regulations as the Congress shall make.

[Roadmap for Chapter 1 is contained in online file.]

∾ PROBLEM: THE HISTORIC PRESERVATION ACT ∾

Congress recently passed the Historic Preservation Act (HPA) to help provide for the upkeep and renovation of historic sites. Because of the 2008 economic downturn, donations and visits to private historical organizations declined. As a result, some nonfederal historic properties were falling into disrepair. Faced with the possible loss of the "nation's historic buildings," or at least their deterioration, Congress decided that it needed to take immediate action to help support "historic preservation" and help "preserve the nation's culture and history." The HPA made money available not only to governmental entities, but also to private entities that owned or controlled historic sites.

During enactment of the HPA, there was considerable debate regarding whether Congress should provide funding to help preserve historic religious sites. Supporters of the legislation argued that there are a number of very historic religious buildings, including the National Cathedral (1907) in the District of Columbia, St. Patrick's Cathedral (1858) and Trinity Church (1698) in New York City, the Old North Church (1723, associated with Paul Revere) in Boston, and even ancient Native American sites (e.g., Pe' Sla, Black Hills, South Dakota) that had been used for religious purposes. Supporters noted that, in addition to their religious purposes, these sites have cultural and historic value, attract tourists, and bring a much-needed economic stimulus to their communities.

Congress ultimately decided to make religious institutions eligible for funding under the HPA. In the Act, Congress emphasized the nation's "religious traditions" and its obligation to "accommodate" religious groups under the Free Exercise Clause. Nevertheless, because Congress was concerned about the possible Establishment Clause implications of funding religious organizations, it decided to provide less funding for historic religious sites than for other historic sites. In particular, while Congress authorized payment for the entire cost of renovating most public and private sites, it provided that religious groups could be compensated for only 50% of the cost of renovating churches or church-related buildings. Because of budgetary constraints, Congress was not able to allocate as much money under the Act as it would have liked. Although $2 billion was needed to fully renovate all historic properties, Congress was able to allocate only $1 billion. The Act established a new governmental agency, the Historic Preservation Agency (HPA), and authorized it to consider and approve applications for funding under the Act.

The new legislation generated much controversy. Some claimed that the HPA violates the First Amendment to the United States Constitution. In particular, Citizens Opposed to Religious Funding (CORF) claimed that the legislation runs afoul of the Establishment Clause. They were joined by foundations that owned other historic properties who believed that religious sites should not be allowed to share in the limited pool of historic preservation funds. By contrast, some religious groups claimed that the law discriminates against religion, by providing less funding to religiously oriented properties, and therefore violates the Free Exercise Clause.

As you work your way through this chapter, you will be asked to consider whether any of these groups can challenge the HPA.

A. *MARBURY* AND "THE POWER TO SAY WHAT THE LAW IS"

Constitutions inevitably address fundamental issues regarding governmental structure and the status of (and relationships between) the branches of government.

In some instances, the rights and responsibilities of the various branches are clearly defined. In other instances, they are not so clearly defined. In this chapter, we examine questions relating to the U.S. Supreme Court's authority to interpret the Constitution in the face of conflicting interpretations by Congress and the executive branch.

Marbury v. Madison

5 U.S. (1 Cranch) 137 (1803)

Mr. Chief Justice MARSHALL delivered the opinion of the court.

After the Federalists were defeated in the election of 1800, but before Thomas Jefferson assumed the presidency, the Federalists sought to retain a measure of power by creating new federal judgeships and filling them with Federalist appointees. William Marbury was confirmed as a magistrate in the District of Columbia, and his commission was signed by President John Adams and sealed by Secretary of State James Madison. Unfortunately for Marbury, his commission was not delivered before Jefferson assumed office. Jefferson ordered that all undelivered commissions be withheld. Marbury sought a writ of mandamus to compel Madison to deliver the commission in an original action in the U.S. Supreme Court. He did so pursuant to Section 13 of the Judiciary Act of 1789, which gave the Court the "power to issue writs of *mandamus,* in cases warranted by the principles and usages of law, to any persons holding office, under the authority of the United States." The present motion is for a mandamus.

1st. Has the applicant a right to the commission he demands? Since Marbury's commission was signed by the President, and sealed by the secretary of state, he was appointed; and as the law creating the office, gave the officer a right to hold for five years, independent of the executive, the appointment was not revocable. To withhold his commission is violative of a vested legal right.

2dly. If he has a right, and that right has been violated, do the laws of this country afford him a remedy? The very essence of civil liberty certainly consists in the right of every individual to claim the protection of the laws, whenever he receives an injury. The government of the United States has been emphatically termed a government of laws, and not of men. It will certainly cease to deserve this high appellation, if the laws furnish no remedy for the violation of a vested legal right. Where a specific duty is assigned by law, and individual rights depend upon the performance of that duty, it seems equally clear that the individual who considers himself injured, has a right to resort to the laws of his country for a remedy.

It remains to be inquired whether, 3dly. He is entitled to the remedy for which he applies. This depends on, 1st. The nature of the writ applied for, and, 2dly. The power of this court.

1st. The nature of the writ. This writ, if awarded, would be directed to an officer of government, and its mandate to him would be, to use the words of Blackstone, "to do a particular thing therein specified, which appertains to his office and duty and which the court has previously determined, or at least supposes, to be consonant to right and justice." To render the mandamus a proper remedy, the officer to whom it is to be directed, must be one to whom, on legal principles, such writ may be directed; and the person applying for it must be without any other specific and legal remedy.

1st. With respect to the officer to whom it would be directed. The province of the court is, solely, to decide on the rights of individuals, not to inquire how the executive, or executive officers, perform duties in which they have a discretion. This, then, is a plain case of a mandamus, either to deliver the commission, or a copy of it from the record; and it only remains to be inquired,

Whether it can issue from this court. The act to establish the judicial courts of the United States authorizes the supreme court "to issue writs of mandamus, in cases warranted by the principles and usages of law, to any courts appointed, or persons holding office, under the authority of the United States." The secretary of state, being a person, holding an office under the authority of the United States, is precisely within the letter of the description; and if this court is not authorized to issue a writ of mandamus to such an officer, it must be because the law is unconstitutional, and therefore absolutely incapable of conferring the authority, and assigning the duties which its words purport to confer and assign.

The constitution vests the whole judicial power of the United States in one supreme court, and such inferior courts as congress shall, from time to time, ordain and establish. It is declared that "the supreme court shall have original jurisdiction in all cases affecting ambassadors, other public ministers and consuls, and those in which a state shall be a party. In all other cases, the supreme court shall have appellate jurisdiction."

When an instrument organizing fundamentally a judicial system, divides it into one supreme, and so many inferior courts as the legislature may ordain and establish; then enumerates its powers, and proceeds so far to distribute them, as to define the jurisdiction of the supreme court by declaring the cases in which it shall take original jurisdiction, and that in others it shall take appellate jurisdiction, the plain import of the words seems to be, that in one class of cases its jurisdiction is original, and not appellate; in the other it is appellate, and not original. To enable this court then to issue a mandamus, it must be shown to be an exercise of appellate jurisdiction, or to be necessary to enable them to exercise appellate jurisdiction. It is the essential criterion of appellate jurisdiction, that it revises and corrects the proceedings in a cause already instituted, and does not create that case. Although, therefore, a mandamus may be directed to courts, yet to issue such a writ to an officer for the delivery of a paper, is in effect the same as to sustain an original action for that paper, and therefore seems not to belong to appellate, but to original jurisdiction. Neither is it necessary in such a case as this, to enable the court to exercise its appellate jurisdiction.

The authority, therefore, given to the supreme court, by the act establishing the judicial courts of the United States, to issue writs of mandamus to public officers, appears not to be warranted by the constitution; and it becomes necessary to inquire whether a jurisdiction, so conferred, can be exercised.

That the people have an original right to establish, for their future government, such principles as, in their opinion, shall be most conducive to their own happiness, is the basis on which the whole American fabric has been erected. The principles, therefore, so established are deemed fundamental. As the authority, from which they proceed, is supreme, and can seldom act, they are designed to be permanent. This original and supreme will organizes the government, and assigns to different departments their respective powers. It may either stop here; or establish certain limits not to be transcended by those departments.

The government of the United States is of the latter description. The powers of the legislature are defined and limited; and that those limits may not be mistaken or forgotten, the constitution is written. The distinction between a government with limited and unlimited powers is abolished, if those limits do not confine the persons on whom they are imposed, and if acts prohibited and acts allowed are of equal obligation. It is a proposition too plain to be contested, that the constitution controls any legislative act repugnant to it; or, that the legislature may alter the constitution by an ordinary act.

The constitution is either a superior, paramount law, unchangeable by ordinary means, or it is on a level with ordinary legislative acts, and like other acts, is alterable when the legislature shall please to alter it. If the former part of the alternative be true, then a legislative act contrary to the constitution is not law: if the latter part be true, then written constitutions are absurd attempts, on the part of the people, to limit a power in its own nature illimitable. Certainly all those who have framed written constitutions contemplate them as forming the fundamental and paramount law of the nation, and consequently the theory of every such government must be, that an act of the legislature repugnant to the constitution is void. This theory is consequently to be considered by this court as one of the fundamental principles of our society.

If an act of the legislature, repugnant to the constitution, is void, does it, notwithstanding its invalidity, bind the courts and oblige them to give it effect? Does it constitute a rule as operative as if it was a law? This would be to overthrow in fact what was established in theory; and would seem, at first view, an absurdity too gross to be insisted on.

It is emphatically the province and duty of the judicial department to say what the law is. Those who apply the rule to particular cases, must of necessity expound and interpret that rule. If two laws conflict with each other, the courts must decide on the operation of each. If a law be in opposition to the constitution: if both the law and the constitution apply to a particular case, so that the court must either decide that case conformably to the law, disregarding the constitution; or conformably to the constitution, disregarding the law: the court must determine which of these conflicting rules governs the case. This is of the very essence of judicial duty.

If the courts are to regard the constitution; and the constitution is superior to any ordinary act of the legislature; the constitution, and not such ordinary act, must govern the case to which they both apply. Those who controvert the principle that the constitution is to be considered, in court, as a paramount law, are reduced to the necessity of maintaining that courts must close their eyes on the constitution, and see only the law. This doctrine would subvert the very foundation of all written constitutions. It would declare that an act, which, according to the principles and theory of our government, is entirely void, is yet, in practice, completely obligatory. That it thus reduces to nothing what we have deemed the greatest improvement on political institutions—a written constitution, would of itself be sufficient for rejecting the construction. But the peculiar expressions of the constitution of the United States furnish additional arguments in favor of its rejection.

The judicial power of the United States is extended to all cases arising under the constitution. Could it be the intention of those who gave this power, to say that, in using it, the constitution should not be looked into? That a case arising under the constitution should be decided without examining the instrument under which it arises? This is too extravagant to be maintained.

There are many other parts of the constitution which serve to illustrate this subject. It is declared that "no tax or duty shall be laid on articles exported from any state." Suppose a duty on the export of cotton, of tobacco, or of flour; and a suit instituted to recover it. Ought the judges to close their eyes on the constitution, and only see the law? The constitution declares that "no bill of attainder or ex post facto law shall be passed." If, however, such a bill should be passed and a person should be prosecuted under it, must the court condemn to death those victims whom the constitution endeavors to preserve? "No person," says the constitution, "shall be convicted of treason unless on the testimony of two witnesses to the same overt act, or on confession in open court." Here the language of the constitution is addressed especially to the courts. It prescribes, directly for them, a rule of evidence not to be departed from. If the legislature should change that rule, and declare one witness, or a confession out of court, sufficient for conviction, must the constitutional principle yield to the legislative act? From these and many other selections which might be made, it is apparent, that the framers of the constitution contemplated that instrument as a rule for the government of courts, as well as of the legislature. Why otherwise does it direct the judges to take an oath to support it? This oath certainly applies, in an especial manner, to their conduct in their official character. How immoral to impose it on them, if they were to be used as the instruments, and the knowing instruments, for violating what they swear to support!

The oath of office, too, imposed by the legislature, is completely demonstrative of the legislative opinion on this subject. It is in these words: "I do solemnly swear that I will administer justice without respect to persons, and do equal right to the poor and to the rich; and that I will faithfully and impartially discharge all the duties incumbent on me as according to the best of my abilities and understanding, agreeably to the constitution and laws of the United States." Why does a judge swear to discharge his duties agreeably to the constitution of the United States, if that constitution forms no rule for his government, if it is closed upon him and cannot be inspected by him. If such be the real state of things, this is worse than solemn mockery. To prescribe, or to take this oath, becomes equally a crime.

In declaring what shall be the supreme law of the land, the constitution itself is first mentioned; and not the laws of the United States generally, but those only which shall be made in pursuance of the constitution, have that rank. The particular phraseology of the constitution of the United States confirms and strengthens the principle, supposed to be essential to all written constitutions, that a law repugnant to the constitution is void, and that courts, as well as other departments, are bound by that instrument.

The rule must be discharged.

BACKGROUND
Conflict of Interest?

Chief Justice Marshall was President Adams's secretary of state and was the official charged with delivering Marbury's commission to him. As a result, some questioned whether Marshall should have participated in the Court's resolution of the case.

Food for Thought

The United Kingdom functions without a written constitution, and its courts have historically refused to exercise judicial review over acts of Parliament (although they have exercised review authority over the actions of administrative agencies). Nevertheless, with certain exceptions (e.g., Britain is a signatory to the European Convention on Human Rights, which applies to acts of Parliament), British courts assume that a parliamentary enactment is constitutional. Is the British approach preferable to that of the United States? Is Britain regarded as any less respectful of human rights than the United States? Can we assume that Congress will act in good faith and will not enact an unconstitutional law? Under such a system, what would be the remedy if, for example, Congress enacted a law abridging freedom of speech? *See* Russell L. Weaver & Geoffrey J.G. Bennett, *The Northern Ireland Media Ban: Some Reflections on Judicial Review*, 22 VAND. J. TRANSNAT'L L. 1119 (1989).

Enforcement of Judicial Decrees and Practical Constraints on Judicial Authority

In the *Marbury* case, suppose that the Court did not strike down the Judiciary Act, and instead ordered Madison to give Marbury his commission. Suppose also that Madison refused to do so. How would the Court have enforced its decree against Madison? If we look at the matter purely from a "power perspective," the executive branch has control of the police and the armed forces. Does the judiciary have comparable sources of power at its disposal? If not, how does the judiciary enforce its decrees?

∽ PROBLEMS: JUDICIAL REVIEW ∽

1. *Does the Constitution Really Make It "Emphatically the Province and Duty of the Judiciary to Say What the Law Is"?* Even if the courts may exercise judicial review, questions might be raised regarding whether other branches of government also have the power to "say what the law is." In particular, are there contexts in which Congress's or the President's interpretation of the Constitution should prevail over the Court's interpretation? President Jefferson once posed a hypothetical question about an individual who is convicted of a crime and appeals on the basis that the conviction is unconstitutional. The U.S. Supreme Court considers the case, interprets and applies the law, and decides that the conviction is constitutional. The individual, now a convict, applies to you (the President of the United States) for a pardon. As President, you are free to pardon the convict whether or not the conviction was validly obtained, but you are particularly troubled by what you regard as an invalid conviction. If you believe that the conviction was unconstitutional, notwithstanding the Supreme Court's conclusions, should you take that into account in deciding whether to pardon? In other words, should you accept the Court's conclusions regarding the validity of the conviction?

2. *Must the Judiciary Retain the Authority to Decide All Legal Questions?* Suppose that Congress enacts the Nuclear Regulatory Act (NRA), which vests the Nuclear Regulatory Commission (NRC) with the power to oversee the development and operation of nuclear reactors in the United States. The NRA also provides the NRC with the authority to promulgate "reasonable" regulations governing the disposal of nuclear waste that are designed to serve the "public interest." Suppose that the NRC promulgates a regulation prohibiting the storage of nuclear waste "in or near" major metropolitan areas. An association of power companies seeks to challenge the regulation on the basis that it does not serve the "public interest." You are the judge assigned to hear the case. How should you go about deciding whether the regulation is "reasonable" and whether it serves the "public interest"? Must you resolve those questions independently, or is it appropriate for you to defer to the NRC's recommendation if it is "reasonable"? In other words, what are the role and scope of your judicial review authority? *See Chevron v. Natural Resources Defense Council, Inc.*, 467 U.S. 837 (1984).

Martin v. Hunter's Lessee

14 U.S. (1 Wheat.) 304 (1816)

STORY, J., delivered the opinion of the court.

The Court of Appeals of Virginia refused to comply with a mandate of the U.S. Supreme Court. The case came back to the U.S. Supreme Court on the issue of whether that Court could review the judgment of a Virginia court.

The third article of the constitution provides that the supreme court shall have *appellate jurisdiction*, both as to law and fact, with such exceptions, and under such regulations, as the congress shall make. The framers contemplated that cases within the judicial cognizance of the United States not only might but would arise in the state courts. The sixth article declares, that "this constitution, and the laws of the United States which shall be made in pursuance thereof, and all treaties made, or which shall be made, under the authority of the United States, shall be the supreme law of the land, and the judges in every state shall be bound thereby, anything in the constitution or laws of any state to the contrary notwithstanding." This obligation is imperative upon the state judges in their official, and not merely in their private, capacities. Judges were not to decide merely according to the laws or constitution of the state, but according to the constitution, laws and treaties of the United States—"the supreme law of the land." To all these cases the judicial power, by the very terms of the constitution, is to extend. It cannot extend by original jurisdiction if that was already rightfully and exclusively attached in the state courts, which may occur; it must, therefore, extend by appellate jurisdiction, or not at all.

It has been argued that such an appellate jurisdiction over state courts is inconsistent with the genius of our governments, and the spirit of the constitution. The Constitution is crowded with provisions which restrain or annul the sovereignty of the states in some of the highest branches of their prerogatives. The tenth section of the first article contains a long list of disabilities and prohibitions imposed upon the states. The language of the constitution is also imperative upon the states as to the performance of many duties. It is imperative upon the state legislatures to make laws prescribing the time, places, and manner of holding elections for senators and representatives, and for electors of president and vice-president. It is certainly difficult to support the argument that the appellate power over the decisions of state courts is contrary to the genius of our institutions.

Nor can such a right be deemed to impair the independence of state judges. They are expressly bound to obedience by the letter of the constitution. From the very nature of things, the absolute right of decision, in the last resort, must rest somewhere—wherever it may be vested it is susceptible of abuse. In all questions of jurisdiction the inferior, or appellate court, must pronounce the final judgment; and common sense, as well as legal reasoning, has conferred it upon the latter.

A motive of another kind, perfectly compatible with the most sincere respect for state tribunals, might induce the grant of appellate power over their decisions. That motive is the importance, and even necessity of *uniformity* of decisions throughout the whole United States, upon all subjects within the purview of the constitution. Judges of equal learning and integrity, in different states, might differently interpret a statute, or a treaty of the United States, or even the constitution itself: If there were no revising authority to control these jarring and discordant judgments, and harmonize them into uniformity, the laws, the treaties, and the constitution of the United States would be different in different states, and might, perhaps, never have precisely the same construction, obligation, or efficacy, in any two states. The public mischiefs that would attend such a state of things would be truly deplorable.

The appellate power of the United States does extend to cases pending in the state courts and this is supported by the letter and spirit of the constitution. It is the opinion of the court that the judgment of the court of appeals of Virginia, rendered on the mandate in this cause, be reversed, and the judgment of the district court, held at Winchester, be, and the same is, hereby affirmed.

The Relationship Between the Federal Constitution and State Constitutions

In *Martin*, the Court recognizes that the U.S. Constitution is the supreme law of the land. The individual states also have their own constitutions, and some provide for more rights than are permitted under the U.S. Constitution. Suppose that you are a state supreme court justice who wishes to interpret your state constitution more expansively than the U.S. Supreme Court interprets the U.S. Constitution. For example, in *California v. Greenwood*, 486 U.S. 35 (1988), the Court held that there is no "search" or "seizure" under the Fourth Amendment to the U.S. Constitution when police arrange to obtain a citizen's garbage from trash collectors. In *State v. Hempele*, 120 N.J. 182, 576 A.2d 793 (N.J. 1990), the New Jersey Supreme Court held that similar conduct violates the New Jersey Constitution. Does New Jersey have the authority to interpret similar language in its state constitution differently than the way the U.S. Supreme Court interprets the U.S. Constitution? More importantly, can you choose to follow *Hempele* rather than *Greenwood* in interpreting your state constitution?

Cooper v. Aaron

358 U.S. 1 (1958)

Opinion of the Court by THE CHIEF JUSTICE, Mr. Justice BLACK, Mr. Justice FRANKFURTER, Mr. Justice DOUGLAS, Mr. Justice BURTON, Mr. Justice CLARK, Mr. Justice HARLAN, Mr. Justice BRENNAN, and Mr. Justice WHITTAKER.

This case raises questions of the highest importance to the maintenance of our federal system of government. It involves a claim by the Governor and Legislature of a State that there is no duty on state officials to obey federal court orders resting on this Court's considered interpretation of the United States Constitution. Specifically, the Governor and Legislature of Arkansas claim that they are not bound by our holding in *Brown v. Board of Education*, 347 U.S. 483. That holding was that the Fourteenth Amendment forbids States to use their governmental powers to bar children on racial grounds from attending schools where there is state participation through any arrangement, management, funds or property.

Following the holding in *Brown*, the Little Rock, Arkansas, School Board was going forward with its preparation for desegregating the Little Rock school system, other state authorities were actively pursuing a program designed to perpetuate in Arkansas the system of racial segregation in violation of *Brown*. First came, in November 1956, an amendment to the State Constitution flatly commanding the Arkansas General Assembly to oppose "in every Constitutional manner the unconstitutional-constitutional desegregation decisions of the U.S. Supreme Court." Then, a law relieving school children from compulsory attendance at racially mixed schools, and a law establishing a State Sovereignty Commission, were enacted by the General Assembly.

The School Board and the Superintendent of Schools nevertheless continued with preparations to desegregate. Nine Negro children were scheduled for admission to Central High School. On September 2, 1957, the day before these students were to enter, the school authorities were met with drastic opposing action on the part of the Governor of Arkansas, who dispatched units of the Arkansas National Guard and placed the school "off limits" to colored students. The Governor's action had not been requested by the school authorities. As the Negro children attempted to enter the high school, units of the Arkansas National Guard "acting pursuant to the Governor's order, stood shoulder to shoulder at the school grounds and thereby forcibly prevented the 9 Negro students from entering," as they did every school day during the following three weeks.

On February 20, 1958, the School Board and the Superintendent of Schools filed a petition in the District Court seeking a postponement of their program for desegregation. Their position was that because of extreme public hostility, which they stated had been engendered largely by the official attitudes and actions of the Governor and the Legislature, the maintenance of a sound educational program at Central High School, with the Negro students in attendance, would be impossible. The Board therefore proposed that the Negro students already admitted to the school be withdrawn and sent to segregated schools, and that all further steps to carry out the Board's desegregation program be postponed for two and one-half years.

The constitutional rights of respondents are not to be sacrificed or yielded to the violence and disorder which have followed upon the actions of the Governor and Legislature. As this Court said some 41 years ago in a unanimous opinion in a case involving another aspect of racial segregation: Law and order are not here to be preserved by depriving the Negro children of their constitutional rights. The constitutional rights of children not to be discriminated against in school admission on grounds of race or color can neither be nullified openly and directly by state legislators or state executive or judicial officers, nor nullified indirectly by them through evasive schemes for segregation.

We should answer the premise of the actions of the Governor and Legislature that they are not bound by our holding in the *Brown* case. It is necessary only to recall basic constitutional propositions which are settled doctrine. Article VI of the Constitution makes the Constitution the "supreme Law of the Land." In 1803, Chief Justice Marshall, speaking for a unanimous Court, referring to the Constitution as "the fundamental and paramount law of the nation," declared in the notable case of *Marbury v. Madison*, 1 Cranch 137 that "It is emphatically the province and duty of the judicial department to say what the law is." This decision declared the basic principle that the federal judiciary is supreme in the exposition of the law of the Constitution, and that principle has ever since been respected by this Court and the Country as a permanent and indispensable feature of our constitutional system. It follows that the interpretation of the Fourteenth Amendment enunciated by this Court in the *Brown* case is the supreme law of the land, and Art. VI of the Constitution makes it of binding effect on the States. Every state legislator and executive and judicial officer is solemnly committed by oath taken pursuant to Art. VI, ¶3 "to support this Constitution." Chief Justice Taney, speaking for a unanimous Court in 1859, said that this requirement reflected the framers' "anxiety to preserve the Constitution in full force, in all its powers, and to guard against resistance to or evasion of its authority, on the part of a State."

No state legislator or executive or judicial officer can war against the Constitution without violating his undertaking to support it. Chief Justice Marshall spoke for a unanimous Court in saying that: "If the legislatures of the several states may, at will, annul the judgments of the courts of the United States, and destroy the rights acquired under those judgments, the constitution itself becomes a solemn mockery." *United States v. Peters*, 5 Cranch 115 1809. A Governor who asserts a power to nullify a federal court order is similarly restrained. If he had such power, said Chief Justice Hughes, in 1932, also for a unanimous Court, "it is manifest that the fiat of a state Governor, and not the Constitution of the United States, would be the supreme law of the land; that the restrictions of the Federal Constitution upon the exercise of state power would be but impotent phrases."

Note: Brown, Cooper, *and Judicial Legitimacy*

Cases like *Cooper* suggest the importance of legitimacy to the Court's effectiveness. The Court needs public acceptance and respect for its decisions, and it needs the support of officials in the executive branch (at least to the extent that such officials will be called upon to enforce the Court's decisions). This need for respect limits the Court's autonomy. Although the Court often provides special protections for minority groups (also known as the Court's counter-majoritarian function), the Court is often forced to rely on the support of elected officials to enforce its judgments. If the Court becomes too far out of step with public opinion, the Court risks noncompliance or public resistance. As *Cooper* dramatically illustrates, there was widespread opposition to the Court's decision in *Brown v. Board of Education* which mandated desegregation. Indeed, there is evidence that the Court anticipated societal opposition and deliberately chose a "go slow" approach to implementing *Brown*. In other words, rather than demanding an immediate end to segregation, the Court ordered that desegregation take place with "all deliberate speed." In fact, because of the opposition, the Court did little to enforce its mandate for many years. When the Court did move to end segregation, it still encountered significant opposition and ultimately depended on elected officials to enforce its mandate. In Little Rock, federal officials in the executive branch ultimately moved to force compliance.

The Supreme Court and Life Tenure

Proponents of judicial review often point out that federal judges are appointed for life and therefore have the independence to follow their consciences free of the sways and influences of the times or the prevailing political winds. But does life tenure also have disadvantages? Some justices serve for very long periods of time, spanning multiple presidential administrations. For example, Justice William O. Douglas was appointed to the Supreme Court in 1939 and served until 1972. Do justices become out of touch after such a long stint on the Court? Is it good for judges to have life tenure and never have to face the electorate? But are there political checks even on life appointees? If the Court gets too far out of step with the electorate, do the President and Congress have ways to bring them back into line? If so, what are they?

B. RESTRAINTS ON JUDICIAL AUTHORITY

Even if we accept Justice Marshall's assertion that it is "emphatically the province and duty of the judiciary to say what the law is," there are numerous restraints on judicial authority. Some of these restraints are self-imposed, while others are imposed by the Constitution or other sources. In the remainder of this chapter, we consider the nature and impact of the various restraints.

1. Practical Limitations on Judicial Authority

There are a number of intensely practical limitations on the U.S. Supreme Court's ability to declare "what the law is." Because the Court can hear only a limited number of cases per year, the Court has always regarded its jurisdiction as discretionary rather than mandatory. As Rule 10 of the Court's rules make clear, even if the Court perceives that a lower court has erred, the Court can (and often does) decline to review the case. The Court tends to focus on important federal questions.

Rule 10. Considerations Governing Review on Certiorari

Review on a writ of certiorari is not a matter of right, but of judicial discretion. A petition for a writ of certiorari will be granted only for compelling reasons. The following, although neither controlling nor fully measuring the Court's discretion, indicate the character of the reasons the Court considers:

(a) a United States court of appeals has entered a decision in conflict with the decision of another United States court of appeals on the same important matter; has decided an important federal question in a way that conflicts with a decision by a state court of last resort; or has so far departed from the accepted and usual course of judicial proceedings, or sanctioned such a departure by a lower court, as to call for an exercise of this Court's supervisory power;

(b) a state court of last resort has decided an important federal question in a way that conflicts with the decision of another state court of last resort or of a United States court of appeals;

(c) a state court or a United States court of appeals has decided an important question of federal law that has not been, but should be, settled by this Court, or has decided an important federal question in a way that conflicts with relevant decisions of this Court.

A petition for a writ of certiorari is rarely granted when the asserted error consists of erroneous factual findings or the misapplication of a properly stated rule of law.

The discretionary nature of the Court's authority is revealed in its case statistics. Over the last two-plus centuries of the Court's existence, it has been presented with more and more cases. For example, compared with only 51 cases on the Court's docket in 1853, the number had risen to 8,000 cases by the mid-1990s. Despite the dramatic increase, the Court is able to hear only a very small percentage of the cases presented to it. In fact, the number of cases actually heard and decided by the Court on the merits has been declining. Although the Court decided 150 to 200 cases per year during much of the twentieth century, it now issues only about 80 decisions per year. *See* Ryan J. Owens & David A. Simon, *Explaining the Supreme Court's Shrinking Docket*, 53 Wm. & Mary L. Rev. 2019 (2012).

2. Congressional Control over Federal Court Jurisdiction

An additional limitation on the Court's authority comes from the Constitution itself, and in particular Article III, which defines the Court's jurisdiction. Article III,

Section 2, Clause 2 gives the Supreme Court original jurisdiction over cases involving "Ambassadors, other Public Ministers and Consuls, and those in which a State shall be a Party," and also gives the Court appellate jurisdiction "with such Exceptions, and under such Regulations as the Congress shall make." Given that most cases arrive at the Court by appeal, Congress's control over the Court's appellate jurisdiction represents a potentially significant restraint on the Court's power and prestige.

From a congressional perspective, the "with such Exceptions and under such Regulations" language represents a potentially significant restraint on the U.S. Supreme Court's jurisdiction. In recent decades, members of Congress have introduced bills designed to strip the Court of its jurisdiction over such controversial issues as school prayer, abortion, school busing, and the exclusionary evidence rule. During his tenure in the U.S. Senate, the late Senator Jesse Helms was distressed by the Court's decisions on school prayer (stating that state-sponsored prayer in the public schools violated the Establishment Clause of the First Amendment). In an effort to overturn those decisions, Helms proposed a constitutional amendment allowing state-sponsored prayer in public schools. When the amendment effort failed, he proposed to strip all federal courts, including the U.S. Supreme Court, of their jurisdiction over school prayer cases. As you read the following cases, think about the constitutionality of such a court-stripping bill.

Ex Parte McCardle

74 U.S. 506 (1868)

THE CHIEF JUSTICE delivered the opinion of the court.

William McCardle was charged with libel and other offenses for publishing newspaper articles about the post–Civil War military government in Mississippi. He sought a writ of habeas corpus from a federal court, but the writ was denied. McCardle then appealed to the U.S. Supreme Court. While the case was pending, Congress passed an act repealing the Court's jurisdiction over the case.

The first question necessarily is that of jurisdiction; for, if the act of March, 1868, takes away the jurisdiction defined by the act of February, 1867, it is useless, if not improper, to enter into any discussion of other questions. It is quite true, as argued by petitioner, that the appellate jurisdiction of this court is not derived from acts of Congress. It is conferred by the Constitution. But it is conferred "with such exceptions and under such regulations as Congress shall make." It is unnecessary to consider whether, if Congress had made no exceptions and no regulations, this court might have exercised general appellate jurisdiction under rules prescribed by itself. For among the earliest acts of the first Congress was the act to establish the judicial courts of the United States. That act provided for the organization of this court, and prescribed regulations for the exercise of its jurisdiction.

The principle that the affirmation of appellate jurisdiction implies the negation of all such jurisdiction not affirmed having been thus established, it was an almost necessary consequence that acts of Congress, providing for the exercise of jurisdiction, should come to be spoken of as acts granting jurisdiction, and not as acts making exceptions to the constitutional grant of it. The exception to appellate jurisdiction in the case before us, however, is not an inference from the affirmation of other appellate jurisdiction. It is made in terms. The provision of the act of 1867, affirming the appellate jurisdiction of this court in cases of habeas corpus, is expressly repealed. It is hardly possible to imagine a plainer instance of positive exception.

We are not at liberty to inquire into the motives of the legislature. We can only examine its power under the Constitution; and the power to make exceptions to the appellate jurisdiction of this court is given by express words.

What, then, is the effect of the repealing act upon the case before us? Without jurisdiction the court cannot proceed at all in any cause. Jurisdiction is power to declare the law, and when it ceases to exist, the only function remaining to the court is that of announcing the fact and dismissing the cause. This is not less clear upon authority than upon principle. It is quite clear, therefore, that this court cannot proceed to pronounce judgment in this case, for it has no longer jurisdiction of the appeal; and judicial duty is not less fitly performed by declining ungranted jurisdiction than in exercising firmly that which the Constitution and the laws confer.

Counsel seem to have supposed, if effect be given to the repealing act in question, that the whole appellate power of the court, in cases of habeas corpus, is denied. But this is an error. The act of 1868 does not except from that jurisdiction any cases but appeals from Circuit Courts under the act of 1867. It does not affect the jurisdiction which was previously exercised.

The appeal of the petitioner in this case must be

Dismissed for Want of Jurisdiction.

Notes: **Klein** *and* **Plaut**

1. *The* Klein *Decision.* Just three years after *McCardle*, the Court decided *United States v. Klein*, 80 U.S. 128 (1871), involving a law that authorized the government to seize abandoned or captured property from those who had aided, countenanced, and abetted the Confederacy during the Civil War. Pursuant to this law, the United States seized V.F. Wilson's cotton, sold it, and placed the proceeds in the U.S. Treasury. Prior to his death, Wilson took advantage of a presidential proclamation offering a "full pardon" with restoration of all rights to those who agreed to "take and keep inviolate a prescribed oath" to support the Constitution of the United States and the union of the states thereunder. After Wilson's death, Klein, the administrator of Wilson's estate, sued to recover proceeds from the sale of the cotton, claiming that the pardon had restored Wilson's rights and property.

Klein won in the Court of Claims, and the government appealed. While the appeal was pending, Congress passed a statute declaring that a presidential pardon shall not be admissible in the Court of Claims to support a claim for recovery. The statute also provided that, to the extent that the Court of Claims has ruled in favor of a claimant based on a presidential pardon: "The Supreme Court, on appeal, shall have no further jurisdiction of the cause, and shall dismiss for want of jurisdiction. It is further provided that whenever any pardon, granted to any suitor in the Court of Claims, for the proceeds of captured and abandoned property, shall recite in substance that the person pardoned took part in the late rebellion, or was guilty of any act of rebellion or disloyalty, and shall have been accepted in writing without express disclaimer and protestation against the fact, such pardon or acceptance shall be taken as conclusive evidence in the Court of Claims, and on appeal, that the claimant did give aid to the rebellion; and on proof of such pardon, or acceptance, which proof may be made summarily on motion or otherwise, the jurisdiction of the court shall cease, and the suit shall be forthwith dismissed." The Court ruled the statute unconstitutional and refused to apply it:

> The language of the proviso shows plainly that it does not intend to withhold appellate jurisdiction except as a means to an end. Its great and controlling purpose is to deny to pardons granted by the President the effect which this court had adjudged them to have. The proviso declares that pardons shall not be considered by this court on appeal. We had already decided that it was our duty to consider them and give them effect, in cases like the present, as equivalent to proof of loyalty. This is not an exercise of the acknowledged power of Congress to make exceptions and prescribe regulations to the appellate power. The court is required to ascertain the existence of certain facts and thereupon to declare that its jurisdiction on appeal has ceased, by dismissing the bill. What is this but to prescribe a rule for the decision of a cause in a particular way? In the case before us, the Court of Claims has rendered judgment for the claimant and an appeal has been taken to this court. We are directed to dismiss the appeal, if we find that the judgment must be affirmed, because of a pardon granted to the intestate of the claimants. Can we do so without allowing one party to the controversy to decide it in its own favor? Can we do so without allowing that the legislature may prescribe rules of decision to the Judicial Department of the government in cases pending before it? We think not. Congress has inadvertently passed the limit which separates the legislative from the judicial power. Congress has already provided that the Supreme Court shall have jurisdiction of the judgments of the Court of Claims on appeal. Can it prescribe a rule in conformity with which the court must deny to itself the jurisdiction thus conferred, because and only because its decision, in accordance with settled law, must be adverse to the government and favorable to the suitor? This question seems to us to answer itself.

See also Ex Parte Yerger, 75 U.S. (8 Wall.) 75 (1869).

2. *The* Plaut *Decision.* In *Plaut v. Spendthrift Farm, Inc.*, 514 U.S. 211 (1995), petitioners brought a civil action for fraud and deceit in the sale of stock in violation of Section 10(b) of the Securities Exchange Act of 1934 and Rule 10b-5 of the Securities and Exchange Commission. In prior cases, the Court had held that Section 10(b) and Rule 10b-5 litigation must be commenced within one year after the discovery of the facts constituting the violation and within three years after such violation. These prior holdings were applied to the petitioner's suit and led to dismissal. Subsequently, Congress passed the Federal Deposit Insurance

Corporation Improvement Act of 1991. Section 476 of the Act became Section 27A of the Securities Exchange Act of 1934, which provided that, when an action was commenced prior to a certain date, that "would have been timely filed under the limitation period provided by the laws applicable in the jurisdiction, including principles of retroactivity, as such laws existed on June 19, 1991." Because petitioners had filed their case prior to June 19, 1991, they moved to reinstate the action previously dismissed with prejudice. The Court held that Congress exceeded its authority: "The Act offends a postulate of Article III deeply rooted in our law. Article III establishes a 'judicial department' with the 'province and duty to say what the law is' in particular cases and controversies. 'A judgment conclusively resolves the case' because a 'judicial Power' is one to render dispositive judgments. By retroactively commanding the federal courts to reopen final judgments, Congress has violated this fundamental principle and effects a clear violation of the separation-of-powers principle. When retroactive legislation requires its own application in a case already finally adjudicated, it does no more and no less than 'reverse a determination once made, in a particular case.'" Justice Stevens, joined by Justice Ginsburg, dissented: "A large class of investors reasonably and in good faith thought they possessed rights of action before the surprising announcement of the *Lampf* rule on June 20, 1991. Congress' decision to extend that rule and procedure to 10b-5 actions dismissed during the brief period between this Court's law-changing decision in *Lampf* and Congress' remedial action is not a sufficient reason to hold the statute unconstitutional."

McCardle*'s Precedential Value*

Some have questioned whether *McCardle* retains vitality after *Klein*. Consider Justice Douglas's dissent in *Glidden v. Zdanok*, 370 U.S. 530, 605 n.11 (1962) (Douglas, J., dissenting), which flatly stated that there "is serious question whether the *McCardle* case could command a majority view today." Former Yale professor, and rejected U.S. Supreme Court nominee, Robert Bork stated that "*McCardle* is a rather enigmatic precedent. If it stands for the proposition that Congress may take away any category of the Supreme Court's jurisdiction, it obviously is capable of destroying the entire institution of judicial review since *Marbury v. Madison*. So read, there is good reason to doubt *McCardle*'s vitality as a precedent today." Robert Bork, *Constitutionality of the President's Busing Proposals* 7 (American Enterprise Institute 1972).

Notes and Questions: Congressional Regulation of Judicial Power

1. *Does Congress Have Plenary Authority over the Supreme Court's Appellate Jurisdiction?* During the 1970s and 1980s, some members of Congress, unhappy with the Court's decisions on controversial issues like school prayer, abortion,

and school busing, sought to remove the Court's appellate authority over those issues. In recent years, some have suggested that the Court should be deprived of the authority to hear appeals involving the Pledge of Allegiance (and the claim that the Pledge involves an unconstitutional establishment of religion). Suppose that Congress decides to pass a law stripping the Court of its review authority over issues like school prayer and busing. Would such a law be constitutional?

2. *Can Congress Take Away the Supreme Court's Original Jurisdiction?* McCardle recognizes that Congress has broad power to limit the Supreme Court's appellate jurisdiction. But what about the Supreme Court's original jurisdiction? Article III, Section 2 read in its entirety states as follows: "In all Cases affecting Ambassadors, other public Ministers and Consuls, and those in which a State shall be a Party, the supreme Court shall have original Jurisdiction. In all the other Cases before mentioned i.e., mentioned in §1, the supreme Court shall have appellate jurisdiction, both as to Law and Fact, with such Exceptions and under such Regulations as the Congress shall make." Section 2 clearly provides Congress leeway to make "exceptions and regulations" to the Court's appellate jurisdiction. Does it also allow Congress to strip the Court of both its original jurisdiction and its appellate authority over issues like busing and school prayer?

3. *Does the Supreme Court Have an "Essential Constitutional Role"?* Some commentators have argued that, even though Congress may make "exceptions" to the Supreme Court's appellate jurisdiction, as well as "regulate" that jurisdiction, Congress cannot "destroy the *essential role* of the Supreme Court in the constitutional plan." Henry M. Hart, *The Power of Congress to Limit the Jurisdiction of Federal Courts: An Exercise in Dialectic,* 66 HARV. L. REV. 1362, 1365 (1953) (emphasis added). A second commentator agrees: "It is not reasonable to conclude that the Constitution gave Congress the power to destroy that role. Reasonably interpreted the clause means 'With such exceptions and under such regulations as Congress may make,' not inconsistent with the essential functions of the Supreme Court under this Constitution." Leonard G. Ratner, *Congressional Power over the Appellate Jurisdiction of the Supreme Court,* 109 U. PA. L. REV. 157 (1960). At least one commentator disagrees with these assessments: "The courts do not pass on constitutional questions because there is a special function vested in them to enforce the Constitution or police the other agencies of government. They do so rather for the reason that they must decide a litigated case that is otherwise within their jurisdiction and in doing so must give effect to the supreme law of the land." Herbert Wechsler, *The Courts and the Constitution,* 65 COLUM. L. REV. 1001, 1005-1006 (1965). Which of these views is more consistent with *Marbury?* Does *Marbury* really make it "the province and duty of the judicial department to say what the law is," or does the judiciary share this authority with other branches? If Congress strips the Court of its review authority over controversial issues, who will decide those issues? What is the ultimate effect on constitutional interpretation? Is it relevant that Congress has gradually eliminated the categories of cases in which the Court must hear an appeal, and expanded the scope of the Court's discretionary jurisdiction, to the point where the Court's appellate docket consists almost

entirely of cases it has chosen to hear? Is it relevant that thousands of cert. petitions are filed with the Court every year, but the Court typically grants fewer than 100? Thus, a case that comes up through the state system will probably be heard only by a state court, even if a federal question is involved.

4. *If the Court Has an "Essential Role," What Is That Role?* Consider the statements of one commentator: "The supremacy clause of Article VI mandates one supreme federal law throughout the land, and Article III establishes the Supreme Court as the constitutional instrument for implementing that clause. Its essential functions under the Constitution are: 1) ultimately to resolve inconsistent or conflicting interpretations of federal law, and particularly of the Constitution, by state and federal courts; 2) to maintain the supremacy of federal law, and particularly the Constitution, when it conflicts with state law or is challenged by state authority." Ratner, *supra*. Do you agree? Is there a preferable way to define that role?

5. *Must Some Federal Court Be Available to Hear All Federal Questions?* In *McCardle*, the habeas plaintiff's case could have been heard in the lower federal courts. Can Congress go further and deprive all federal courts of the authority to hear particular types of federal question claims? This question is not completely hypothetical. Over the last hundred years, Congress has considered bills designed to accomplish exactly this result. For example, Congress has considered bills that would have stripped all federal courts of jurisdiction over cases involving busing and abortion. Moreover, Article III, Section 1 authorizes the creation of the lower federal courts: "The judicial Power of the United States, shall be vested in one supreme Court, and in such inferior Courts as the Congress may from time to time ordain and establish." Since Congress has the power to "ordain and establish" inferior federal courts, it also has the power to abolish them as well as to limit their jurisdiction. *See Yakus v. United States*, 321 U.S. 414 (1944); *Lockerty v. Phillips*, 319 U.S. 182 (1943).

Despite Congress's authority, may it strip the lower federal courts of their jurisdiction over an issue (e.g., school prayer or busing) and simultaneously strip the Supreme Court of its appellate jurisdiction over that same issue? If such bills had passed, would they be constitutional? Consider the following perspectives: A) "To remove or permit the removal from the entire federal judiciary, including the Supreme Court, of the constitutional review of state conduct would be to alter the balance of federal authority fundamentally and dangerously." Lawrence Gene Sager, *Foreword: Constitutional Limitations on Congress' Authority to Regulate the Jurisdiction of the Federal Courts*, 95 HARV. L. REV. 17, 55 (1981); B) The Constitution does not prohibit this sort of comprehensive stripping of jurisdiction. The Framers considered the state courts to have played a crucial role in the protection of federal constitutional rights, and thus should not be viewed as having required federal court jurisdiction over all federal question cases. *See* Henry M. Hart, *The Power of Congress to Limit the Jurisdiction of the Federal Courts: An Exercise in Dialectic*, 66 HARV. L. REV. 1363 (1953); C) Joseph Story, a Supreme Court Justice in the early nineteenth century, believed not only that some federal court must be available to hear every federal question case, but also that some federal question cases should be heard *only* by a federal court. Which perspective is preferable? Does it matter that some state judges lack the life tenure provisions granted to federal judges? In some states, in fact, judges must stand for election. Also, does it or should it matter that most appeals to the Supreme Court stand only a very small chance of being heard?

6. *More on the Historic Preservation Act.* Now let's think about the Historic Preservation Act problem described at the beginning of the chapter. Suppose that, after various Establishment Clause and Free Exercise Clause challenges are filed against the law, Congress passes a law prohibiting the U.S. Supreme Court from exercising jurisdiction over cases challenging the legislation. Would such a law be constitutional? As you think about that issue, consider the questions set forth in the following sections.

3. The Political Question Doctrine

Even though the Court may have the authority to say what the law is, are there situations in which the Court should decline to exercise its authority? For example, should the Court decline to exercise its review authority out of respect for coordinate branches of government, for the individual states, or for the political process? In this section, we examine the so-called "political question" doctrine, which operates as a limitation on judicial authority.

Baker v. Carr

369 U.S. 186 (1962)

Justice BRENNAN delivered the opinion of the court.

Tennessee's legislature apportioned legislative districts in 1901 but refused to do so again for more than 60 years. During the intervening period, Tennessee's legislative districts became so malapportioned that 37% of Tennessee voters elected 20 of the 33 senators and 40% of the voters elected 60 of the 99 House members. Plaintiffs challenged Tennessee's system for electing its state legislature, alleging that the state legislative districts were so grossly malapportioned with respect to population that the apportionment scheme denied plaintiffs' constitutional rights to equal protection. The district court dismissed the lawsuit on the ground that it presented a nonjusticiable political question. We hold that this challenge to an apportionment presents no nonjusticiable "political question." Of course the mere fact that the suit seeks protection of a political right does not mean it presents a political question.

Our discussion requires review of a number of political question cases. It is the relationship between the judiciary and the coordinate branches of the Federal Government, and not the federal judiciary's relationship to the States, which gives rise to the "political question." "In determining whether a question falls within (the political question) category, the appropriateness under our system of government of attributing finality to the action of the political departments and also the lack of satisfactory criteria for a judicial determination are dominant considerations." The nonjusticiability of a political question is primarily a function of the separation of powers. Much confusion results from the capacity of the "political question" label to obscure the need for case-by-case inquiry. Deciding whether a matter has been committed by the Constitution to another branch of government, or whether the action of that branch exceeds whatever authority has been committed, is a delicate exercise in constitutional interpretation, and is a responsibility of this Court as ultimate interpreter of the Constitution. To demonstrate this requires no less than to analyze representative cases and to infer from them the analytical threads that make up the political question doctrine.

Foreign relations: There are sweeping statements to the effect that questions touching foreign relations are political questions. Resolution of such issues frequently turn on standards that defy judicial application, or involve the exercise of a discretion demonstrably committed to the executive or legislature; but many such questions uniquely demand single-voiced statement of the Government's views. Yet it is error to suppose that every case or controversy which touches foreign relations lies beyond judicial cognizance. Our cases show a discriminating analysis of the particular question posed, in terms of the history of its management by the political branches, of its susceptibility to judicial handling in the light of its nature and posture in the specific case, and of the possible consequences of judicial action. For example, though a court will not ordinarily inquire whether a treaty has been terminated, since on that question "governmental action must be regarded as of controlling importance," if there has been no conclusive "governmental action" then a court can construe a treaty and may find it provides the answer. Though a court will not undertake to construe a treaty in a manner inconsistent with a subsequent federal statute, no similar hesitancy obtains if the asserted clash is with state law. While recognition of foreign governments so strongly defies judicial treatment that without executive recognition a foreign state has been called "a republic of whose existence we know nothing," and the judiciary ordinarily follows the executive as to which nation has sovereignty over disputed territory, once sovereignty over an area is politically determined and declared, courts may examine the resulting status and decide independently whether a statute applies to that area. Similarly, recognition of belligerency abroad is an executive responsibility, but if the executive proclamations fall short of an explicit answer, a court may construe them seeking, for example, to determine whether the situation is such that statutes designed to assure American neutrality have become operative.

Dates of duration of hostilities: Though it has been stated broadly that "the power which declared the necessity is the power to declare its cessation, and what the cessation requires," here too analysis reveals isolable reasons for the presence of political questions, underlying this Court's refusal to review the political departments' determination of when or whether a war has ended. Dominant is the need for finality in the political determination, for emergency's nature demands "A prompt and unhesitating obedience." But deference rests on reason, not habit. The question in a particular case may not seriously implicate considerations of finality—e.g., a public program of importance (rent control) yet not central to the emergency effort. Further, clearly definable criteria for decision may be available. In such case the political question barrier falls away: "On the other hand, even in private litigation which directly implicates no feature of separation of powers, lack of judicially discoverable standards and the drive for even-handed application may impel reference to the political departments' determination of dates of hostilities" beginning and ending.

Validity of enactments: In *Coleman v. Miller* 307 U.S. 433 (1939), this Court held that the questions of how long a proposed amendment to the Federal Constitution remained open to ratification, and what effect a prior rejection had on a subsequent ratification, were committed to congressional resolution and involved criteria of decision that necessarily escaped the judicial grasp. Similar considerations apply to the enacting process: "The respect due to coequal and independent departments," and the need for finality and certainty about the status of a statute contribute to judicial reluctance to inquire whether, as passed, it complied with all requisite formalities. But it is not true that courts will never delve into a legislature's records: If the enrolled statute lacks an effective date, a court will not hesitate to seek it in the legislative journals. The political question doctrine, a tool for maintenance of governmental order, will not be applied to promote only disorder.

We come to the ultimate inquiry whether our precedents as to what constitutes a nonjusticiable "political question" bring the case before us under the umbrella of that doctrine. A natural beginning is to note whether any of the common characteristics which we have been able to identify and label descriptively are present. We find none: The question is the consistency of state action with the Federal Constitution. We have no question decided, or to be decided, by a political branch of government coequal with this Court. Nor do we risk embarrassment of our government abroad, or grave disturbance at home if we take issue with Tennessee as to the constitutionality of her action here challenged. Nor need the appellants, in order to succeed in this action, ask the Court to enter upon policy determinations for which judicially manageable standards are lacking. Judicial standards under the Equal Protection Clause are well developed and familiar, and it has been open to courts since the enactment of the Fourteenth Amendment to determine, if on the particular facts they must, that a discrimination reflects no policy, but simply arbitrary and capricious action. We conclude that the complaint's allegations of a denial of equal protection present a justiciable constitutional cause of action upon which appellants are entitled to a trial and a decision. The right asserted is within the reach of judicial protection under the Fourteenth Amendment.

The judgment of the District Court is reversed and the case is remanded for further proceedings consistent with this opinion.

Rucho v. Common Cause
_____

139 S.Ct. 2484 (2019)

Chief Justice ROBERTS delivered the opinion of the Court.

Plaintiffs challenged their States' congressional districting maps as unconstitutional partisan gerrymanders. The North Carolina plaintiffs complained that the State's districting plan discriminated against Democrats; the Maryland plaintiffs complained that their State's plan discriminated against Republicans. These cases require us to consider again whether claims of excessive partisanship in districting are "justiciable."

The first case involves a challenge to the congressional redistricting plan enacted by the Republican-controlled North Carolina General Assembly in 2016. Republican legislators instructed their mapmaker to use political data to draw a map that would produce a congressional delegation of ten Republicans and three Democrats. One Democratic state senator objected because, as recently as 2012, "Democratic congressional candidates had received more votes on a statewide basis than Republican candidates." The General Assembly approved the 2016 Plan by a party-line vote. In 2016, North Carolina conducted congressional elections using the Plan, and Republican candidates won 10 of the 13 congressional districts. Plaintiffs challenged the Plan on multiple constitutional grounds. [A] three-judge District Court unanimously concluded that the 2016 Plan violated the Equal Protection Clause and Article I of the Constitution [and] the First Amendment. Defendants appealed. While that appeal was pending, we decided *Gill v. Whitford*, 138 S.Ct. 1916 (2018). In that case, we held that a plaintiff asserting a partisan gerrymandering claim based on a theory of vote dilution must establish standing by showing he lives in an allegedly "cracked" or "packed" district. A "cracked" district is one in which a party's supporters are divided among multiple districts, so that they fall short of a majority in each; a "packed" district is one in which a party's supporters are highly concentrated, so they win that district by a large margin, "wasting" many votes that would improve their chances in others. After deciding *Gill*, we remanded. On remand, the District Court again struck down the 2016 Plan.

The second case is *Lamone v. Benisek*. In 2011, the Maryland Legislature—dominated by Democrats—undertook to redraw the lines of that State's eight congressional districts. The Governor, Democrat Martin O'Malley, appointed a redistricting committee to redraw the map. The Governor's aim was to "use redistricting to change the overall composition of Maryland's congressional delegation to 7 Democrats and 1 Republican by flipping" one district. The Plan reduced the number of registered Republicans in the Sixth District by about 66,000 and increased the number of registered Democrats by about 24,000. The map was adopted by a party-line vote. It was used in the 2012 election and succeeded in flipping the Sixth District. A Democrat has held the seat ever since. Three Maryland voters filed this lawsuit. The District Court entered summary judgment for plaintiffs. Defendants appealed directly to this Court under 28 U.S.C. §1253.

Article III of the Constitution limits federal courts to deciding "Cases" and "Controversies." Federal courts can address only questions "historically viewed as capable of resolution through the judicial process." *Flast v. Cohen*, 392 U.S. 83, 95 (1968). Chief Justice Marshall famously wrote that it is "the province and duty of the judicial department to say what the law is." *Marbury v. Madison*, 5 U.S. 137 (1803). Sometimes, "the judicial department has no business entertaining the claim of unlawfulness—because the question is entrusted to one of the political branches or involves no judicially enforceable rights." *Vieth v. Jubelirer*, 541 U.S. 267, 277 (2004) (plurality opinion). In such a case the claim is said to present a "political question" and to be nonjusticiable—outside the courts' competence and therefore beyond the courts' jurisdiction. *Baker v. Carr*, 369 U.S. 186 (1962). Among the political question cases are those that lack "judicially discoverable and manageable standards for resolving them." The question is whether there is an "appropriate role for the Federal Judiciary" in remedying the problem of partisan gerrymandering—whether such claims are claims of *legal* right, resolvable according to *legal* principles, or political questions that must find their resolution elsewhere.

Partisan gerrymandering is nothing new. Nor is frustration with it. The practice was known in the Colonies prior to Independence, and the Framers were familiar with it at the time of the drafting and ratification of the Constitution. The Framers addressed the election of Representatives to Congress in the Elections Clause. Art. I, §4, cl. 1. That provision assigns to state legislatures the power to prescribe the "Times, Places and Manner of holding Elections" for Members of Congress, while giving Congress the power to "make or alter" any such regulations. Congress has regularly exercised its Elections Clause power, including to address partisan gerrymandering. The Apportionment Act of 1842, which required single-member districts for the first time, specified that those districts be "composed of contiguous territory" in "an attempt to forbid the practice of the gerrymander." Later statutes added requirements of compactness and equality of population. Congress also used its Elections Clause power in 1870, enacting the first comprehensive federal statute dealing with elections as a way to enforce the Fifteenth Amendment. In the 1950s, Congress enacted a series of laws to protect the right to vote through measures such as the suspension of literacy tests and the prohibition of English-only elections.

In two areas—one-person, one-vote and racial gerrymandering—there is a role for the courts with respect to at least some issues that could arise from a State's drawing of congressional districts. But the Framers were aware of electoral districting problems. They settled on a characteristic approach, assigning the issue to the state legislatures, expressly checked and balanced by the Federal Congress. At no point was there a suggestion that the federal courts had a role to play. Nor was there any indication that the Framers had heard of courts doing such a thing. Courts have been called upon to resolve a variety of questions surrounding districting. *See Wood v. Broom*, 287 U.S. 1 (1932); *Colegrove v. Green*, 328 U.S. 549 (1946). In *Baker v. Carr*, voters in Tennessee complained that the State's districting plan for state representatives "debased" their votes, because the plan was predicated on a 60-year-old census that no longer reflected the distribution of population in the State. Plaintiffs argued that votes of people in overpopulated districts held less value than those of people in less-populated districts, and that this inequality violated the Equal Protection Clause of the Fourteenth Amendment. The District Court dismissed on the ground that the claim was not justiciable. This Court reversed. It identified various considerations relevant to determining whether a claim is a nonjusticiable political question, including whether there is "a lack of judicially discoverable and manageable standards for resolving it." The claim of population inequality among districts did not fall into that category, because such a claim could be decided under basic equal protection principles. In *Wesberry v. Sanders*, the Court extended its ruling to malapportionment of congressional districts, holding that Article I, §2, required that "one man's vote in a congressional election be worth as much as another's." Another line of challenges to districting plans has focused on race. Laws that explicitly discriminate on the basis of race, as well as those that are race neutral on their face but are unexplainable on grounds other than race, are presumptively invalid. The Court applied those principles to electoral boundaries in *Gomillion v. Lightfoot*, concluding that a challenge to an "uncouth twenty-eight sided" municipal boundary line that excluded black voters from city elections stated a constitutional claim. In *Wright v. Rockefeller*, 376 U.S. 52 (1964), the Court extended the reasoning of *Gomillion* to congressional districting.

Partisan gerrymandering claims have proved far more difficult to adjudicate. While it is illegal for a jurisdiction to depart from the one-person, one-vote rule, or to engage in racial discrimination in districting, "a jurisdiction may engage in constitutional political gerrymandering." *Hunt v. Cromartie*, 526 U.S. 541, 551 (1999); *Shaw v. Hunt*, 517 U.S. 899 (1996). To hold that legislators cannot take partisan interests into account when drawing district lines would essentially countermand the Framers' decision to entrust districting to political entities. The "central problem" is not determining whether a jurisdiction has engaged in partisan gerrymandering. It is "determining when political gerrymandering has gone too far." *Vieth*, 541 U.S. at 296 (plurality opinion).

We first considered a partisan gerrymandering claim in *Gaffney v. Cummings* in 1973. There we rejected an equal protection challenge to Connecticut's redistricting plan, which "aimed at a rough scheme of proportional representation of the two major political parties" by "wiggling and joggling boundary lines" to create the appropriate number of safe seats for each party. In upholding the plan, we reasoned that districting "inevitably has and is intended to have substantial political consequences." Thirteen years later, in *Davis v. Bandemer*, we addressed a claim that Indiana Republicans had cracked and packed Democrats in violation of the Equal Protection Clause. 478 U.S. 109 (1986) (plurality opinion). A majority agreed that the case was justiciable, but the Court splintered over the proper standard to apply. The Court held that plaintiffs failed to show that the plan violated the Constitution. Eighteen years later, in *Vieth*, the plaintiffs complained that Pennsylvania's legislature "ignored all traditional redistricting criteria, including the preservation of local government boundaries," in order to benefit Republican congressional candidates. Once again a majority could not find a justiciable standard for resolving the plaintiffs' partisan gerrymandering claims.

Any standard for resolving such claims must be grounded in a "limited and precise rationale" and be "clear, manageable, and politically neutral." An expansive standard requiring "the correction of all election district lines drawn for partisan reasons would commit federal and state courts to unprecedented intervention in the American political process," *Vieth,* 541 U.S. at 306 (Kennedy, J.). If federal courts are to "inject themselves into the most heated partisan issues" by adjudicating partisan gerrymandering claims, they must be armed with a standard that can reliably differentiate unconstitutional from "constitutional political gerrymandering." *Cromartie,* 526 U.S. at 551.

Partisan gerrymandering claims rest on an instinct that groups with a certain level of political support should enjoy a commensurate level of political power and influence. A districting map is alleged to be unconstitutional because it makes it too difficult for one party to translate statewide support into seats in the legislature. Partisan gerrymandering claims invariably sound in a desire for proportional representation. The Founders certainly did not think proportional representation was required. For more than 50 years after ratification of the Constitution, many States elected their congressional representatives through at-large or "general ticket" elections. Such States typically sent single-party delegations to Congress. That meant that a party could garner nearly half of the vote statewide and wind up without any seats in the congressional delegation. The Whigs in Alabama suffered that fate in 1840. Unable to claim that the Constitution requires proportional representation, plaintiffs ask the courts to make their own political judgment about how much representation particular political parties *deserve*—based on the votes of their supporters—and to rearrange the challenged districts to achieve that end. But federal courts are not equipped to apportion political power as a matter of fairness, nor is there any basis for concluding that they were authorized to do so.

The difficulty in settling on a "clear, manageable and politically neutral" test for fairness is that it is not clear what fairness looks like. There is "unfairness" in any winner-take-all system. Fairness may mean a greater number of competitive districts. Such a claim seeks to undo packing and cracking so that supporters of the disadvantaged party have a better shot at electing their preferred candidates. But making as many districts as possible competitive could be a disaster for the disadvantaged party. "A narrow statewide preference for either party would produce an overwhelming majority for the winning party in the state legislature." *Bandemer,* 478 U.S. at 130 (plurality). Perhaps the ultimate objective of a "fairer" share of seats in the congressional delegation is most readily achieved by yielding to the gravitational pull of proportionality and engaging in cracking and packing, to ensure each party its "appropriate" share of "safe" seats. Such an approach comes at the expense of competitive districts and of individuals in districts allocated to the opposing party. Or perhaps fairness should be measured by adherence to "traditional" districting criteria, such as maintaining political subdivisions, keeping communities of interest together, and protecting incumbents. But protecting incumbents enshrines a particular partisan distribution. And the "natural political geography" of a State—such as the fact that urban electoral districts are often dominated by one political party—can itself lead to inherently packed districts. Traditional criteria such as compactness and contiguity "cannot promise political neutrality. A decision under these standards would unavoidably have significant political effect, whether intended or not." *Vieth,* 541 U.S. at 308 (Kennedy concurring). There are no legal standards discernible in the Constitution for making such judgments, let alone limited and precise standards that are clear, manageable, and politically neutral. Any judicial decision on what is "fair" in this context would be an "unmoored determination" of the sort characteristic of a political question beyond the competence of the federal courts.

Only after determining how to define fairness can [one] begin to answer the determinative question: "How much is too much?" If compliance with traditional districting criteria is the touchstone, how much deviation from those criteria is constitutionally acceptable and how should mapdrawers prioritize competing criteria? Should a court "reverse gerrymander" other parts of a State to counteract "natural" gerrymandering caused by the urban concentration of one party? If a districting plan protected half of the incumbents but redistricted the rest into head to head races, would that be constitutional? A court would have to rank the relative importance of traditional criteria and weigh how much deviation to allow. If a court focused on the respective number of seats in the legislature, it would have to decide the ideal number of seats for each party and determine at what point deviation from that balance went too far. If a 5–3 allocation corresponds most closely to statewide vote totals, is a 6–2 allocation permissible, given that legislatures have the authority to engage in a degree of partisan gerrymandering? Which seats should be packed and which cracked? Or if the goal is as many competitive districts as possible, how close does the split need to be for the district to be considered competitive? Even assuming the court knew which version of fairness to be looking for, there are no discernible and manageable standards for deciding whether there has been a violation. The questions are "unguided and ill-suited to the development of judicial standards," *Vieth,* 541 U.S. at 296 (plurality opinion), and "results from one gerrymandering case to the next would likely be disparate and inconsistent."

Appellees contend that if we can adjudicate one-person, one-vote claims, we can also assess partisan gerrymandering claims. But the one-person, one-vote rule is relatively easy to administer as a matter of math. The same cannot be said of partisan gerrymandering claims, because the Constitution supplies no objective measure for assessing whether a districting map treats a political party fairly. The Court's constitutionally prescribed role is to vindicate the individual rights of the people appearing before it." Nor do our racial gerrymandering cases provide an appropriate standard for assessing partisan gerrymandering. A racial gerrymandering claim does not ask for a fair share of political power and influence, with all the justiciability conundrums that entails. It asks for the elimination of a racial classification. A partisan gerrymandering claim cannot ask for the elimination of partisanship.

Appellees and the dissent propose a number of "tests" for evaluating partisan gerrymandering claims, but none meets the need for a limited and precise standard that is judicially discernible and manageable. And none provides a solid grounding for judges to take the extraordinary step of reallocating power and influence between political parties. The *Common Cause* District Court required plaintiffs to prove "that a legislative mapdrawer's predominant purpose in drawing the lines of a particular district was to 'subordinate adherents of one political party and entrench a rival party in power.'" The District Court next required a showing "that the dilution of the votes of supporters of a disfavored party in a particular district—by virtue of cracking or packing—is likely to persist in subsequent elections such that an elected representative from the favored party in the district will not feel a need to be responsive to constituents who support the disfavored party." Finally, after a prima facie showing of partisan vote dilution, the District Court shifted the burden to defendants to prove that the discriminatory effects are "attributable to a legitimate state interest or other neutral explanation." In racial gerrymandering cases, we rely on a "predominant intent" inquiry to determine whether race was, in fact, the reason particular district boundaries were drawn the way they were. If district lines were drawn for the purpose of separating racial groups, then they are subject to strict scrutiny because "race-based decisionmaking is inherently suspect." *Miller*, 515 U.S. at 915. But determining that lines were drawn on the basis of partisanship does not indicate that the districting was improper. A permissible intent—securing partisan advantage—does not become constitutionally impermissible, like racial discrimination, when that permissible intent "predominates." Appellees assure us that "the persistence of a party's advantage may be shown through probing how a plan would perform under other plausible electoral conditions." Experience proves that accurately predicting electoral outcomes is not so simple, either because the plans are based on flawed assumptions about voter preferences and behavior or because demographics and priorities change over time. In our two leading partisan gerrymandering cases, the predictions of durability proved to be dramatically wrong. In 1981, Republicans controlled both houses of the Indiana Legislature as well as the governorship. Democrats challenged the state legislature districting map enacted by the Republicans. *Bandemer* rejected that challenge, and just months later the Democrats increased their share of House seats in the 1986 elections. Two years later the House was split 50–50 between Democrats and Republicans, and the Democrats took control of the chamber in 1990. Democrats also challenged the Pennsylvania congressional districting plan at issue in *Vieth*. Two years after that challenge failed, they gained four seats in the delegation, going from a 12–7 minority to an 11–8 majority. At the next election, they flipped another Republican seat. Even the most sophisticated districting maps cannot reliably account for some of the reasons voters prefer one candidate over another, or why their preferences may change. Voters elect individual candidates in individual districts, and their selections depend on the issues that matter to them, the quality of the candidates, the tone of the candidates' campaigns, the performance of an incumbent, national events or local issues that drive voter turnout, and other considerations. Many voters split their tickets. Others never register with a political party, and vote for candidates from both major parties at different points. Asking judges to predict how a particular districting map will perform in future elections risks basing constitutional holdings on unstable ground outside judicial expertise. It is hard to see what the District Court's third prong — providing the defendant an opportunity to show that the discriminatory effects were due to a "legitimate redistricting objective" — adds to the inquiry. The first prong already requires the plaintiff to prove that partisan advantage predominates.

The District Courts also found partisan gerrymandering claims justiciable [focusing on] proof of intent to burden individuals based on their voting history or party affiliation; an actual burden on political speech or associational rights; and a causal link between the invidious intent and actual burden. Both District Courts concluded that the districting plans at issue violated the plaintiffs' First Amendment right to association. The District Court in North Carolina relied on testimony that, after the 2016 Plan, the plaintiffs faced "difficulty raising money, attracting candidates, and mobilizing voters to support the political causes and issues such Plaintiffs sought to advance." Similarly, the District Court in Maryland examined testimony that "revealed a lack of enthusiasm, indifference to voting, a sense of disenfranchisement, a sense of disconnection, and confusion," and concluded that Republicans "were burdened in fundraising, attracting volunteers, campaigning, and generating interest in voting." There are no restrictions on speech, association, or any other First Amendment activities in the districting plans at issue. Plaintiffs are free to engage in those activities no matter what the effect of a plan may be on their district. Plaintiffs' argument is that partisanship in districting should be regarded as discrimination against supporters of the opposing party on the basis of political viewpoint. Under that theory, any level of partisanship in districting would constitute an infringement of First Amendment rights. But the First Amendment test simply describes the act of districting for partisan advantage. It provides no standard for determining when partisan activity goes too far. How much of a decline in voter engagement is enough to constitute a First Amendment burden? How many petitions unsigned? How many calls for volunteers unheeded? The *Common Cause* District Court held that a partisan gerrymander places an unconstitutional burden on speech if it has more than a "*de minimis*" "chilling effect or adverse impact" on First Amendment activity. But the First Amendment analysis offers no "clear" and "manageable" way of distinguishing permissible from impermissible partisan motivation. The *Common Cause* court [concluded] that "a judicially manageable framework for evaluating partisan gerrymandering claims need not distinguish an 'acceptable' level of partisan gerrymandering from 'excessive' partisan gerrymandering" because "the Constitution does not authorize state redistricting bodies to engage in such partisan gerrymandering." The decisions prove the prediction of the *Vieth* plurality that "a First Amendment claim, if sustained, would render unlawful *all* consideration of political affiliation in districting" contrary to our established precedent.

The dissent proposes using a State's own districting criteria as a neutral baseline from which to measure a partisan gerrymander. The dissent would have us line up all the possible maps drawn using those criteria according to the partisan distribution they would produce. Distance from the "median" map would indicate whether a particular districting plan harms supporters of one party to an unconstitutional extent. As an initial matter, it does not make sense to use criteria that will vary from State to State and year to year as the baseline for determining whether a gerrymander violates the Federal Constitution. The degree of partisan advantage that the Constitution tolerates should not turn on criteria offered by the gerrymanderers themselves. The same map could be constitutional or not depending solely on what the mapmakers said they set out to do. Even if we were to accept the dissent's baseline, it would return us to "the original unanswerable question (How much political motivation and effect is too much?)." *Vieth*, 541 U.S. at 296 (plurality opinion). Would twenty percent from the median map be okay? Forty percent? Sixty percent? The dissent argues that there are other instances in law where matters of degree are left to the courts. True enough. But those instances typically involve constitutional or statutory provisions or common law confining and guiding the exercise of judicial discretion. Here, the Constitution provides no basis to guide the exercise of judicial discretion. Common experience gives content to terms such as "substantial risk" or "substantial harm," but the same cannot be said of substantial deviation from a median map. There is no way to tell whether the prohibited deviation from that map should kick in at 25 percent or 75 percent or some other point. The only provision in the Constitution that specifically addresses the matter assigns it to the political branches. See Art. I, §4, cl. 1.

The North Carolina District Court concluded that the 2016 Plan exceeded the North Carolina General Assembly's Elections Clause authority because, among other reasons, "the Elections Clause did not empower State legislatures to disfavor the interests of supporters of a particular candidate or party in drawing congressional districts." The court further held that partisan gerrymandering infringes the right of "the People" to select their representatives. The plurality in *Vieth* concluded that neither §2 nor §4 of Article I "provides a judicially enforceable limit on the political considerations that the States and Congress may take into account when districting." The District Court nevertheless asserted that partisan gerrymanders violate "the core principle of our republican government" preserved in Art. I, §2, "namely, that the voters should choose their representatives, not the other way around." That seems like an objection more properly grounded in the Guarantee Clause of Article IV, §4, which "guarantees to every

State in the Union a Republican Form of Government." This Court has several times concluded that the Guarantee Clause does not provide the basis for a justiciable claim. See, *e.g.*, *Pacific States Telephone & Telegraph Co. v. Oregon*, 223 U.S. 118 (1912).

Excessive partisanship in districting leads to results that reasonably seem unjust. But the fact that gerrymandering is "incompatible with democratic principles," does not mean that the solution lies with the federal judiciary. Partisan gerrymandering claims present political questions beyond the reach of the federal courts. Federal judges have no license to reallocate political power between the two major political parties, with no plausible grant of authority in the Constitution, and no legal standards to limit and direct their decisions. "Judicial action must be governed by *standard*, by *rule*," and must be "principled, rational, and based upon reasoned distinctions" found in the Constitution or laws. *Vieth*, 541 U.S. at 278 (plurality opinion). Judicial review of partisan gerrymandering does not meet those basic requirements. The dissent essentially embraces the argument that "this Court *can* address the problem of partisan gerrymandering because it *must*." That is not the test of our authority under the Constitution; that document "confines the federal courts to a properly judicial role." *Town of Chester v. Laroe Estates, Inc.*, 137 S.Ct. 1645, 1650 (2017). Appellees and dissent seek an unprecedented expansion of judicial power. We have never struck down a partisan gerrymander as unconstitutional. The expansion of judicial authority would be into one of the most intensely partisan aspects of American political life. That intervention would be unlimited in scope and duration—it would recur over and over around the country with each new round of districting, for state as well as federal representatives. Consideration of the impact of today's ruling on democratic principles cannot ignore the effect of the unelected and politically unaccountable branch of the Federal Government assuming such an extraordinary and unprecedented role.

Our conclusion does not condone excessive partisan gerrymandering. The States are actively addressing the issue on a number of fronts. In 2015, the Supreme Court of Florida struck down that State's congressional districting plan as a violation of the Fair Districts Amendment to the Florida Constitution. The dissent wonders why we can't do the same. The answer is that there is no "Fair Districts Amendment" to the Federal Constitution. Numerous other States are restricting partisan considerations in districting through legislation. Voters in Colorado and Michigan approved constitutional amendments creating multi-member commissions that will be responsible in whole or in part for creating and approving district maps for congressional and state legislative districts. [In] Missouri, voters overwhelmingly approved the creation of a state demographer to draw state legislative district lines. Other States have mandated some of the traditional districting criteria for their mapmakers. Some have outright prohibited partisan favoritism in redistricting.

The Framers gave Congress the power to do something about partisan gerrymandering in the Elections Clause. The first bill introduced in the 116th

Congress would require States to create 15-member independent commissions
to draw congressional districts and would establish certain redistricting criteria,
including protection for communities of interest, and ban partisan gerrymandering. Dozens of other bills have been introduced to limit reliance on political
considerations in redistricting. In 2010, H. R. 6250 would have required States to
follow standards of compactness, contiguity, and respect for political subdivisions
in redistricting. It also would have prohibited the establishment of congressional
districts "with the major purpose of diluting the voting strength of any person,
or group, including any political party," except when necessary to comply with
the Voting Rights Act of 1965. We express no view on any of these proposals. We
simply note that the avenue for reform established by the Framers, and used by
Congress in the past, remains open.

   We have no commission to allocate political power and influence in the
absence of a constitutional directive or legal standards to guide us in the exercise
of such authority. "It is emphatically the province and duty of the judicial department to say what the law is." *Marbury v. Madison*, 1 Cranch at 177. In this rare
circumstance, that means our duty is to say "this is not law."

   The judgments of the United States District Court for the Middle District of
North Carolina and the United States District Court for the District of Maryland
are vacated, and the cases are remanded with instructions to dismiss for lack of
jurisdiction.

   It is so ordered.

Justice KAGAN, with whom Justice GINSBURG, Justice BREYER, and Justice SOTOMAYOR
join, dissenting.

   The partisan gerrymanders in these cases deprived citizens of the most fundamental of their constitutional rights: the rights to participate equally in the
political process, to join with others to advance political beliefs, and to choose
their political representatives. In so doing, the gerrymanders debased and dishonored our democracy, turning upside-down the core American idea that all
governmental power derives from the people. These gerrymanders enabled politicians to entrench themselves in office against voters' preferences. They promoted partisanship. They encouraged a politics of polarization and dysfunction.
If left unchecked, gerrymanders irreparably damage our system of government.
Courts across the country have coalesced around manageable judicial standards to
resolve partisan gerrymandering claims. The standards allow judicial intervention
in the worst-of-the-worst cases of democratic subversion, causing blatant constitutional harms. In giving such gerrymanders a pass from judicial review, the majority
goes tragically wrong. By drawing districts to maximize the power of some voters
and minimize the power of others, a party in office can entrench itself for a decade
or more, no matter what the voters would prefer. Partisan gerrymandering turns it
around. Politicians can cherry-pick voters to ensure their reelection.

   Big data and modern technology—of the kind that the mapmakers in
North Carolina and Maryland used—make today's gerrymandering altogether

different from the crude linedrawing of the past. County-level voting data has given way to precinct-level or city-block-level data; and mapmakers avail themselves of data sets providing wide-ranging information about even individual voters. While bygone mapmakers may have drafted three or four districting plans, today's mapmakers can generate thousands of possibilities at the touch of a key—and then choose the one giving their party maximum advantage (while still meeting traditional districting requirements). The 2010 redistricting cycle produced some of the most extreme partisan gerrymanders in this country's history. Someplace along this road, "we the people" become sovereign no longer. The Fourteenth Amendment "guarantees the opportunity for equal participation by all voters in the election" of legislators. *Reynolds v. Sims*, 377 U.S. 533, 566 (1964). That opportunity "can be denied by a debasement or dilution of the weight of a citizen's vote just as effectively as by wholly prohibiting the free exercise of the franchise." Id., at 555. Partisan gerrymandering implicates the First Amendment too. That Amendment gives its greatest protection to political beliefs, speech, and association. Yet partisan gerrymanders subject certain voters to "disfavored treatment"—counting their votes for less—precisely because of "their voting history and their expression of political views." *Vieth*, 541 U.S. at 314 (Kennedy, J.). Representative democracy is "unimaginable without the ability of citizens to band together in support of candidates who espouse their political views." *California Democratic Party v. Jones*, 530 U.S. 567, 574 (2000).

The majority declines to provide any remedy. Federal courts across the country have converged on a standard for adjudicating partisan gerrymandering claims. The standard does not use any judge-made conception of electoral fairness—either proportional representation or any other; instead, it takes as its baseline a State's *own* criteria of fairness, apart from partisan gain. The standard invalidates the most extreme partisan gerrymanders. Gerrymandering is anti-democratic in the most profound sense. In our government, "all political power flows from the people." That means, as Alexander Hamilton said, "that the people should choose whom they please to govern them." 2 Debates on the Constitution 257 (J. Elliot ed. 1891). In Maryland and North Carolina they cannot. The practices challenged in these cases imperil our system of government. Part of the Court's role in that system is to defend its foundations. None is more important than free and fair elections. With respect but deep sadness, I dissent.

Notes: The Political Question Doctrine

1. *The Rhode Island Constitution.* Following the American Revolution, Rhode Island continued to function under a royal charter issued by Charles II in 1663. In the 1840s, Rhode Island citizens called a constitutional convention to draft a state constitution. Although the resulting constitution was ratified by a vote of the people, and elections were held, the charter government refused to recognize the constitution or the elected officials. When the charter government

declared a state of martial law and used force to put down what it perceived as a "rebellion" by sending soldiers to search Martin Luther's house, and Luther sued for trespass, defendants claimed that they were acting pursuant to governmental authority, thus presenting the question of whether the charter government or the constitutionally elected government constituted the legitimate authority. In *Luther v. Borden*, 48 U.S. (7 How.) 1 (1849), the Court held that the case presented a nonjusticiable political question and refused to decide whether the charter government was legitimate: "The fourth section of the fourth article of the Constitution of the United States provides that the United States shall guarantee to every State in the Union a republican form of government. Under this article it rests with Congress to decide what government is the established one in a State. Its decision is binding on every other department of the government, and could not be questioned in a judicial tribunal. It is true that Congress was not called upon to decide the controversy. Yet the right to decide is placed there, and not in the courts. This tribunal should be the last to overstep its own jurisdiction. While it should always be ready to meet any question confided to it by the Constitution, it is its duty not to pass beyond its appropriate sphere of action, and to take care not to involve itself in discussions which properly belong to other forums."

2. *Termination of the Taiwan Treaty.* In *Goldwater v. Carter*, 444 U.S. 996 (1979), the Court held that President Carter's decision to terminate a treaty with Taiwan, and to recognize instead the People's Republic of China, constituted a political question. The decision was challenged by members of Congress who claimed that, since the Constitution requires Congress to ratify treaties, it implicitly requires that treaty terminations be ratified as well. Carter responded that the Constitution's silence regarding treaty termination gave him unilateral authority to decide whether to terminate. A concurring Justice Powell disagreed with the Court's decision to dismiss: "The Constitution does not unquestionably commit the power to terminate treaties to the President alone. We are asked to decide whether the President may terminate a treaty without congressional approval. Resolution of the question may not be easy, but only requires us to apply normal principles of interpretation to the constitutional provisions at issue. The case involves neither review of the President's activities as Commander in Chief nor impermissible interference in the field of foreign affairs. Interpretation of the Constitution does not imply lack of respect for a coordinate branch. If the President and the Congress had reached irreconcilable positions, final disposition of the question would eliminate multiple constitutional interpretations. The suggestion that this case presents a political question is incompatible with this Court's willingness on previous occasions to decide whether one branch of our Government has impinged upon the power of another."

3. *Blocking the Elected Candidate.* In *Powell v. McCormack*, 395 U.S. 486 (1969), the Court rejected the argument that only the House of Representatives could decide whether to seat Adam Clayton Powell, Jr. After Powell was duly elected to the U.S. House of Representatives, the House refused to seat him because he had engaged in misconduct. The Court concluded that Article I, Section 5

of the Constitution (which provides that "each House shall be the Judge of the Elections, Returns, and Qualifications of its own Members") creates a "'textually demonstrable constitutional commitment' to the House of the 'adjudicatory power' to determine Powell's qualifications." However, the Court concluded that this textual commitment extended only to the question of "the qualifications expressly set forth in the Constitution," and Powell had met those requirements: "The 'textual commitment' formulation of the political question doctrine does not bar federal courts from adjudicating petitioners' claims that he was improperly expelled for other reasons. Therefore, since Powell was duly elected by the voters of the 18th Congressional District of New York and was not ineligible to serve under any provision of the Constitution, the House was without power to exclude him from its membership."

∽ PROBLEMS & QUESTIONS: THE POLITICAL QUESTION DOCTRINE ∽

1. *The Scope of the Judicial Function.* Following the Court's decision in *Baker*, suppose that a federal court concludes that Tennessee's apportionment system violates the Equal Protection Clause of the U.S. Constitution. Once the court makes that declaration, what is the judicial role? The plaintiffs in *Baker* asked the Court to declare the 1901 legislation unconstitutional, and to order statewide elections for legislators without regard to counties or districts. Should a federal court enter such an order? Alternatively, does *Marbury* suggest that the federal court has the power to reapportion Tennessee's districts itself? Should a court do that?

2. *The Historic Preservation Act and the Political Question Doctrine.* Again, suppose that the Historic Preservation Act is challenged on Establishment Clause and Free Exercise grounds by the groups listed in the problem. Would the case be regarded as a "political question" so that the federal courts should refuse to hear it?

3. *The Disputed Presidential Election.* The presidential election of 2000 hinged on the question of which candidate received the most popular votes in the State of Florida and thereby captured that state's electoral votes. Based on the initial tally, then-Governor Bush was thought to have won Florida by a margin of 1,784 votes. After litigation in the Florida courts, including ballot recounts, the case was brought before the Court with Bush seeking to challenge the Florida Supreme Court's decision to order another ballot recount. Two questions were presented: 1) whether the Florida Supreme Court established new standards for resolving presidential election contests, thereby violating Article II, Section 1, Clause 2 of the U.S. Constitution, and failing to comply with 3 U.S.C. §5; and 2) whether the use of a standardless manual recount violates the Equal Protection and Due Process clauses. In effect, the Court's decision would (and did) determine the outcome of the presidential election. Should the U.S. Supreme Court have dismissed the

challenge on the basis of the political question doctrine? In thinking about this issue, what weight do you give to the fact that the "Constitution assigns to the States the primary responsibility for determining the manner of selecting the Presidential electors"?

4. *Combat Operations.* During the Vietnam War, a congresswoman and some Air Force officers sought to challenge the validity of combat operations being conducted in Cambodia. Article I, Section 8 of the U.S. Constitution provides that Congress shall have the power to declare war. By contrast, Article II, Section 2 provides that the President is the "Commander in Chief of the Army and Navy of the United States, and of the militia of the several States, when called into the actual service of the United States." Suppose that plaintiffs point to various congressional enactments regarding the declaration and cessation of hostilities, and claim that the President is not in compliance. Defendants respond by pointing to congressional funding appropriations which they believe authorized the war. Is it appropriate for a court to rule on whether a military action constitutes a "war" and whether congressional approval is required (or has been given)? If the court answers both of these questions in the affirmative, is it appropriate for the court to issue an order prohibiting further combat operations in Cambodia? If the courts are unwilling to intervene, how will these issues be resolved? *Compare Holtzman v. Schlesinger,* 361 F. Supp. 553 (D.C.N.Y. 1973), *with Holtzman v. Schlesinger,* 484 F.2d 1307 (2d Cir. 1973); *see also DaCasta v. Laird,* 471 F.2d 1146 (2d Cir. 1973); *Sarnoff v. Connally,* 457 F.2d 809 (9th Cir. 1972); *Orlando v. Laird,* 443 F.2d 1039 (2d Cir. 1971). Other decisions dealing with undeclared wars include *Crockett v. Reagan,* 720 F.2d 1355 (D.C. Cir. 1983); *Campbell v. Clinton,* 203 F.3d 19 (D.C. Cir. 2000); *Ange v. Bush,* 752 F. Supp. 509 (D.D.C. 1990).

C. THE CASE OR CONTROVERSY REQUIREMENT

Article III, Section 2 of the U.S. Constitution contains perhaps the most important limitation on judicial power: the "case" and "controversy" requirement. This limitation has spawned multiple restrictions on the scope of judicial authority, including the prohibition against advisory opinions, the ripeness and mootness doctrines, and the standing requirement.

1. The Prohibition Against Advisory Opinions

The prohibition against advisory opinions is of long standing. In 1793, Secretary of State Thomas Jefferson solicited input from the U.S. Supreme Court regarding whether "it would be available in the solution of important questions of the construction of treaties, laws of nations and laws of the land, which the Secretary said might be presented under circumstances which 'do not give a cognizance of them to the tribunals of the country.'" *See Muskrat v. United States*, 219 U.S. 346 (1911). Chief Justice Jay and his associates responded that "'the lines of separation drawn by the Constitution between the three departments of government afford strong arguments against the propriety of extrajudicially deciding the questions alluded to, and expressing the view that the power given by the Constitution to the President, of calling on heads of departments for opinions, seems to have been purposely, as well as expressly, united to the executive departments.' *Correspondence & Public Papers of John Jay*, vol. 3, p. 486." *Id.* The justices noted that "by the express terms of the Constitution, the exercise of the judicial power is limited to 'cases' and 'controversies.' Beyond this it does not extend, and unless it is asserted in a case or controversy within the meaning of the Constitution, the power to exercise it is nowhere conferred."

What constitutes a "case" or "controversy"? In *Muskrat*, the Court suggested that the phrase "cases and controversies" refers to "the claims of litigants brought before the courts for determination by such regular proceedings as are established by law or custom for the protection or enforcement of rights, or the prevention, redress, or punishment of wrongs. Whenever the claim of a party under the Constitution, laws, or treaties of the United States takes such a form that the judicial power is capable of acting upon it, then it has become a case. The term implies the existence of present or possible adverse parties, whose contentions are submitted to the court for adjudication."

BACKGROUND
Declaratory Judgments

In *Piedmont & Northern Railway Co. v. United States*, 280 U.S. 469 (1930), the Court held that the federal courts did not have jurisdiction to entertain a declaratory judgment action: "What plaintiffs are seeking is, therefore, in substance, a declaratory judgment. Such a remedy is not within either the statutory or the equity jurisdiction of federal courts." In later decisions, the Court recognized the power of the federal courts to render declaratory judgments provided that the litigation actually involves a case or controversy.

Food for Thought: Advisory Opinions

1. *More on the Historic Preservation Act.* Let's return to the Historic Preservation Act, and assume that lawsuits are filed immediately after the law is enacted, but before awards have been made. The lawsuits raise both Establishment Clause and

Free Exercise Clause challenges. If you are the judge assigned to hear the cases, do they present just "hypothetical" or "abstract" injury? Is it permissible for you to hear and decide the constitutional issues?

    2. *The Protestors and the Mayor.* Suppose that a protestor demonstrates daily against the mayor on the sidewalk in front of City Hall in Louisville, Kentucky. Police officers inform the protestor that he will be arrested unless he ceases his protest and leaves the area. The protestor seeks a declaratory judgment that the police officers' actions violate his First Amendment right to freedom of speech. The protestor vows to resume his protest if he receives a favorable ruling in the declaratory judgment action. If he does not receive a favorable ruling, he will not resume his protest for fear of arrest. Can a federal court consider the protestor's request for declaratory relief, or does the case involve an impermissible request for an advisory opinion? *See Steffel v. Thompson,* 415 U.S. 452 (1974); *Samuels v. Mackell,* 401 U.S. 66 (1971).

2. *Ripeness*

The federal courts have insisted that lawsuits be brought at the "right" time. A case that is brought too early is held to be not "ripe" for adjudication. As you read the following cases, ask yourself whether the Court's decision is based on prudential or constitutional requirements, or on a combination of the two. Ripeness issues have been extensively litigated over the last half-century. In its early decision in *United Public Workers of America (C.I.O.) v. Mitchell,* 330 U.S. 75 (1947), the Court concluded that a challenge to the Hatch Act (which prohibited certain political activities by federal employees) was not "ripe" for review. The Court emphasized that a "hypothetical threat" is not sufficient, and that it could only speculate as to the kinds of political activity the appellants desired to engage in or as to the contents of their proposed statements or the circumstances of their publication. However, by 1967, in its holding in *Abbott Laboratories v. Gardner,* 387 U.S. 136 (1967), the Court took a more expansive approach to justiciability issues.

Susan B. Anthony List v. Driehaus

573 U.S. 149 (2014)

Justice THOMAS delivered the opinion of the Court.

    Petitioners challenge an Ohio statute that prohibits certain "false statements" "during the course of any campaign for nomination or election to public office or office of a political party." Ohio Rev. Code Ann. §3517.21(B). As relevant here, the statute makes it a crime for any person to "make a false statement concerning the voting record of a candidate or public official," or to "post, publish, circulate, distribute, or otherwise disseminate a false statement concerning a candidate, either knowing the same to be false or with reckless disregard of whether it was false or not."[1]

"Any person" may file a complaint with the Ohio Elections Commission alleging a violation of the statute. If filed within 60 days of a primary election or 90 days of a general election, the complaint is referred to a panel for an expedited hearing, generally within two business days, to determine whether there is probable cause to believe the violation occurred. Upon a finding of probable cause, the full Commission must, within 10 days, hold a hearing. The Commission may subpoena witnesses and compel production of documents. At the hearing, the parties may make opening and closing statements and present evidence. If the Commission determines by "clear and convincing evidence" that a party has violated the law, the Commission "shall" refer the matter to the relevant county prosecutor. Alternatively, the Commission may issue a reprimand. Violation of the statute is a first-degree misdemeanor punishable by up to six months of imprisonment, a fine up to $5,000, or both. A second conviction is a fourth-degree felony that carries a mandatory penalty of disfranchisement.

Petitioner Susan B. Anthony List (SBA) is a "pro-life advocacy organization." During the 2010 election cycle, SBA publicly criticized various Members of Congress who voted for the Patient Protection and Affordable Care Act (ACA). It issued a press release announcing its plan to "educate voters that their representative voted for a health care bill that includes taxpayer-funded abortion." The press release listed then-Congressman Steve Driehaus, respondent, who voted for the ACA. SBA also sought to display a billboard in Driehaus' district condemning that vote. The billboard would have read: "Shame on Steve Driehaus! Driehaus voted FOR taxpayer-funded abortion." The advertising company that owned the billboard space refused to display that message after Driehaus threatened legal action. Driehaus filed a complaint with the Ohio Elections Commission alleging that SBA had violated §§3517.21(B)(9) and (10) by falsely stating that he had voted for "taxpayer-funded abortion." Because Driehaus filed his complaint 29 days before the general election, a Commission panel held an expedited hearing and found probable cause that a violation had been committed. SBA filed suit, seeking declaratory and injunctive relief based on the First and Fourteenth Amendments of the United States Constitution. The District Court stayed the action pending the Commission proceedings. The Sixth Circuit denied SBA's motion for an injunction pending appeal. Driehaus and SBA agreed to postpone the hearing until after the election.

---

1. Section 3517.21(B) provides in relevant part: "No person, during the course of any campaign for nomination or election to public office or office of a political party, by means of campaign materials, including sample ballots, an advertisement on radio or television or in a newspaper or periodical, a public speech, press release, or otherwise, shall knowingly and with intent to affect the outcome of such campaign do any of the following: (9) Make a false statement concerning the voting record of a candidate or public official; (10) Post, publish, circulate, distribute, or otherwise disseminate a false statement concerning a candidate, either knowing the same to be false or with reckless disregard of whether it was false or not, if the statement is designed to promote the election, nomination, or defeat of the candidate."

When Driehaus lost the election, he moved to withdraw his complaint against SBA. The District Court lifted the stay. The amended complaint alleged that Ohio Rev. Code Ann. §§3517.21 (B) (9) and (10) are unconstitutional both facially and as applied. Specifically, the complaint alleged that SBA's speech about Driehaus had been chilled; that SBA "intends to engage in substantially similar activity in the future"; and that it "faced the prospect of its speech and associational rights again being chilled and burdened," because "any complainant can bring it before the Commission, forcing it to expend time and resources defending itself." The District Court consolidated SBA's suit with a suit brought by Coalition Opposed to Additional Spending and Taxes (COAST), an advocacy organization that alleged that the same Ohio false statement provisions are unconstitutional both facially and as applied. COAST intended to disseminate e-mail and other materials criticizing Driehaus' vote for the ACA as a vote "to fund abortions with tax dollars," but refrained because of the proceedings against SBA. COAST alleged that it "desires to make the same or similar statements about other federal candidates who voted for" the ACA, but that fear "of finding itself subject to the same fate" as SBA has deterred it from doing so. The District Court dismissed both suits as non-justiciable. The Sixth Circuit affirmed. We granted certiorari and reverse.

Article III of the Constitution limits the jurisdiction of federal courts to "Cases" and "Controversies." U.S. Const., Art. III, §2. The doctrine of standing gives meaning to these constitutional limits by "identifying those disputes which are appropriately resolved through the judicial process." *Lujan v. Defenders of Wildlife*, 504 U.S. 555, 560 (1992). "Article III standing, which is built on separation-of-powers principles, serves to prevent the judicial process from being used to usurp the powers of the political branches." *Clapper v. Amnesty Int'l USA*, 568 U.S. ___ (2013) (slip op., at 9). To establish Article III standing, plaintiff must show an "injury in fact," a sufficient "causal connection between the injury and the conduct complained of," and a "likelihood" that the injury "will be redressed by a favorable decision." *Lujan, supra*, at 560-561.

This case concerns the injury-in-fact requirement, which helps to ensure that the plaintiff has a "personal stake in the outcome of the controversy." *Warth v. Seldin*, 422 U.S. 490 (1975). An injury sufficient to satisfy Article III must be "concrete and particularized" and "actual or imminent, not 'conjectural' or 'hypothetical.'" *Lujan, supra*, at 560. An allegation of future injury may suffice if the threatened injury is "certainly impending," or there is a "'substantial risk' that the harm will occur." *Clapper*, 568 U.S., at ___, n.5. "'The party invoking federal jurisdiction bears the burden of establishing' standing." *Id.* "Each element must be supported in the same way as any other matter on which the plaintiff bears the burden of proof, *i.e.*, with the manner and degree of evidence required at the successive stages of the litigation." *Lujan, supra*, at 561.

One recurring issue is determining when the threatened enforcement of a law creates an Article III injury. When an individual is subject to a threat, an actual arrest, prosecution, or other enforcement action is not a prerequisite to challenging the law. *See Steffel v. Thompson*, 415 U.S. 452 (1974). A plaintiff satisfies

the injury-in-fact requirement where he alleges "an intention to engage in a
course of conduct arguably affected with a constitutional interest, but proscribed
by a statute, and there exists a credible threat of prosecution." *Babbitt v. Farm
Workers*, 442 U.S. 289, 298 (1979). In *Steffel*, police officers threatened to arrest
petitioner and his companion for distributing handbills protesting the Vietnam
War. Petitioner left to avoid arrest; his companion remained and was arrested and
charged with criminal trespass. Petitioner sought a declaratory judgment that the
trespass statute was unconstitutional as applied to him. We determined that petitioner had alleged a credible threat of enforcement: He had been warned to stop
handbilling and threatened with prosecution if he disobeyed; he stated his desire
to continue handbilling (an activity he claimed was constitutionally protected);
and his companion's prosecution showed that his "concern with arrest" was not
"chimerical." Under those circumstances, "it is not necessary that petitioner first
expose himself to actual arrest or prosecution to be entitled to challenge a statute that he claims deters the exercise of his constitutional rights." In *Babbitt*, we
considered a pre-enforcement challenge to a statute that made it an unfair labor
practice to encourage consumers to boycott an "agricultural product by the use of
dishonest, untruthful and deceptive publicity." Plaintiffs contended that the law
"unconstitutionally penalized inaccuracies inadvertently uttered in the course of
consumer appeals." We explained that a plaintiff could bring a pre-enforcement
suit when he "has alleged an intention to engage in a course of conduct arguably
affected with a constitutional interest, but proscribed by statute, and there exists
a credible threat of prosecution." Plaintiffs had "actively engaged in consumer
publicity campaigns in the past" and alleged "an intention to continue" those
campaigns in the future. Although they did not "plan to propagate untruths,"
"erroneous statement is inevitable in free debate." We concluded that plaintiffs'
fear of prosecution was not "imaginary or wholly speculative," and their challenge
to the consumer publicity provision presented an Article III case or controversy.

Here, SBA and COAST contend that the threat of enforcement of the false
statement statute amounts to an Article III injury in fact. We agree: Petitioners
have alleged a credible threat of enforcement. First, petitioners have alleged "an
intention to engage in a course of conduct arguably affected with a constitutional
interest." Petitioners have pleaded specific statements they intend to make in
future election cycles. SBA has already stated that representatives who voted for
the ACA supported "taxpayer-funded abortion," and it has alleged an "intent to
engage in substantially similar activity in the future." COAST has alleged that it
previously intended to disseminate materials criticizing a vote for the ACA as a
vote "to fund abortions with tax dollars," and that it "desires to make the same
or similar statements about other federal candidates who voted for the ACA."
Because petitioners' intended future conduct concerns political speech, it is certainly "affected with a constitutional interest." *Babbitt, supra*, at 298. Petitioners'
intended future conduct is "arguably proscribed by the statute" they wish to challenge. The Ohio false statement law sweeps broadly, and covers the subject matter
of petitioners' intended speech. A Commission panel already found probable

cause to believe that SBA violated the statute when it stated that Driehaus had supported "taxpayer-funded abortion"—the same sort of statement petitioners plan to disseminate in the future. Under these circumstances, we have no difficulty concluding that petitioners' intended speech is "arguably proscribed" by the law. As long as petitioners continue to engage in comparable electoral speech, that speech will remain arguably proscribed by Ohio's false statement statute.

Respondents contend that SBA's fears of enforcement are misplaced because SBA has not said it "plans to lie or recklessly disregard the veracity of its speech." SBA's insistence that the allegations in its press release were true did not prevent the Commission from finding probable cause to believe that SBA had violated the law. There is every reason to think that similar speech will result in similar proceedings. Nothing requires a plaintiff who wishes to challenge the constitutionality of a law to confess that he will in fact violate that law. The threat of future enforcement of the statute is substantial. Past enforcement against the same conduct is good evidence that the threat of enforcement is not "chimerical." The threat is more substantial given that the Commission panel found probable cause to believe that SBA's speech violated the false statement statute. Future complainants may well "invoke the prior probable-cause finding to prove that SBA *knowingly* lied." The statute allows "any person" with knowledge of the purported violation to file a complaint. Because the universe of potential complainants is not restricted to state officials who are constrained by explicit guidelines or ethical obligations, there is a real risk of complaints from political opponents. Finally, Commission proceedings are not a rare occurrence. The Commission "handles about 20 to 80 false statement complaints per year," and the Commission frequently fields complaints alleging violations of the statute. Moreover, respondents have not disavowed enforcement if petitioners make similar statements in the future. The specter of enforcement is so substantial that the owner of the billboard refused to display SBA's message after receiving a letter threatening Commission proceedings. The prospect of future enforcement is far from "imaginary or speculative." *Babbitt, supra*, at 298.

Administrative action, like arrest or prosecution, may give rise to harm sufficient to justify pre-enforcement review. The "practical effect" of the Ohio false statement scheme is "to permit a private complainant to gain a campaign advantage without ever having to prove the falsity of a statement." "Complainants may time their submissions to achieve maximum disruption of their political opponents while calculating that an ultimate decision on the merits will be deferred until after the election." The target of a false statement complaint may be forced to divert significant time and resources to hire legal counsel and respond to discovery requests in the crucial days leading up to an election. Where a Commission panel issues a pre-election probable-cause finding, "such a determination itself may be viewed by the electorate as a sanction by the State."

Although the threat of Commission proceedings is substantial, Commission proceedings are backed by the additional threat of criminal prosecution. The combination of those two threats suffices to create an Article III injury. See

Babbitt, supra, at 302. Both SBA and COAST have alleged a credible threat of enforcement. We need not resolve the continuing vitality of the prudential ripeness doctrine because the "fitness" and "hardship" factors are easily satisfied here. First, petitioners' challenge to the statute presents an issue that is "purely legal, and will not be clarified by further factual development." *Thomas v. Union Carbide Agricultural Products Co.,* 473 U.S. 568 (1985). Denying prompt judicial review would impose a substantial hardship on petitioners, forcing them to choose between refraining from core political speech or engaging in that speech and risking costly Commission proceedings and criminal prosecution.

Petitioners have demonstrated an injury in fact sufficient for Article III standing. We reverse the judgment and remand the case for further proceedings consistent with this opinion, including a determination whether the remaining Article III standing requirements are met.

It is so ordered.

Notes and Questions: Ripeness

1. *Connecticut's Anti-Contraception Law. Poe v. Ullman,* 367 U.S. 497 (1961), decided before the Court's landmark decisions in *Griswold* and *Roe,* involved a Connecticut statute that prohibited the use of contraceptive devices, and also prohibited doctors from giving medical advice regarding the use of such devices. Plaintiff's three pregnancies had produced infants with multiple congenital abnormalities and all died shortly after birth. Doctors concluded that the abnormalities were genetic. Both plaintiffs (husband and wife) claimed that the possibility of an additional pregnancy placed them under great emotional stress, was damaging to their physical and mental health, that they wanted to use contraceptive devices to prevent conception, and claimed that the wife was unable to obtain contraceptive information because of the Connecticut law. Even though plaintiffs were joined by doctors who claimed that they feared prosecution for giving advice regarding the use of contraceptive devices, the Court held that the case was not justiciable. Even though Connecticut's attorney general had stated that he intended to prosecute violations of the law, including the use of or advice concerning contraceptives, the Court noted that Connecticut's law had not been enforced since 1879: "During more than three-quarters of a century, a prosecution for its violation seems never to have been initiated, save in [one case]. The circumstances of that case, decided in 1940, only prove the abstract character of what is before us. There, a test case was brought to determine the constitutionality of the Act as applied against two doctors and a nurse who had allegedly disseminated contraceptive information. We were [also] advised that contraceptives are commonly and notoriously sold in Connecticut drug stores. 'The best teaching of this Court's experience admonishes us not to entertain constitutional questions in advance of the strictest necessity.' To pass on these statutes now, in order to protect appellants from the hazards of prosecution, would be to close our eyes to reality."

2. *The Loyalty Oath.* Ohio enacted a statute that required candidates for public office to take a loyalty oath stating that the candidate's party is not engaged in an attempt to overthrow the government by force or violence, is not associated with a group making such an attempt, and does not involve itself in sedition or treason. In *Socialist Labor Party v. Gilligan*, 406 U.S. 583 (1972), in which the Socialist Party challenged the loyalty oath requirement as unconstitutional, the Court held that the case was not justiciable: "Nothing shows that appellants have suffered any injury thus far, and the law's future effect remains wholly speculative. Notwithstanding that appellants have in the past executed the required affidavit without injury, it is possible that at some future time they may be able to demonstrate injury as a result of the application of the provision challenged here. Our adjudication of the merits of such a challenge will await that time."

3. *Radioactive Waste. New York v. United States*, 505 U.S. 144 (1992), involved a congressional enactment that required the states to deal with the problem of low-level radioactive waste no later than 2016, or assume title to the waste which was previously owned by private individuals and companies. When individual states challenged the law as an infringement of the Tenth Amendment to the U.S. Constitution, the United States objected that the case was not ripe for review. The Court disagreed, noting that low-level radioactive waste is unlikely to disappear by 2016, and emphasizing that it takes many years to develop a new disposal site, and therefore the state must take immediate action in order to avoid the consequences.

∽ PROBLEMS: RIPENESS ∽

1. *More on the Historic Preservation Act.* Again assume that legal challenges are filed soon after the law is enacted, but before any applications for funding have been submitted. Again the challenges raise Free Exercise Clause and Establishment Clause challenges. Is the Act ripe for judicial review? Would it matter whether any religious organizations have indicated an intent to apply for funding?

2. *The (First) Persian Gulf War.* In the early 1990s, President George H.W. Bush deployed 230,000 U.S. troops to the Persian Gulf region in preparation for an invasion of Iraq. The President's stated objective was to provide "an adequate *offensive* military option" should that be necessary to achieve such goals as the withdrawal of Iraqi forces from Kuwait. At about the same time, Secretary of Defense Richard Cheney (later Vice President Cheney) stated that the additional military forces would give the United States the ability "to conduct *offensive* military operations." In November 1990, plaintiffs (all members of Congress) sued, claiming that the initiation of offensive U.S. military action was imminent, that such action would be unlawful in the absence of a declaration of war by Congress,

and that a war without concurrence by Congress would deprive plaintiffs of the voice to which they are entitled under the Constitution. The Department of Justice claimed that the case was not ripe for review because no offensive action had been initiated. If you are the judge assigned to hear the case, how would you rule? Is the case ripe for decision? If not, what additional facts must be shown in order to make the case ripe? Must the plaintiffs wait until the President commits troops to military action? If so, won't it then be too late? *See Dellums v. Bush*, 752 F. Supp. 1141 (D.D.C. 1990).

3. *Department of Homeland Security (DHS) Searches.* DHS has always exercised broad authority to search persons and goods that enter the United States. Recently, DHS announced new policies regarding searches of electronic devices, including iPhones, laptops, and other electronic equipment, at the U.S. border. The new rules give DHS broad authority to search the entire content of electronic devices, as well as to copy information found on those devices. Plaintiff, who frequently travels outside the country with his laptop, is worried that DHS may seize and copy his laptop on a future occasion. Can plaintiff challenge the DHS rule now, or does plaintiff have to wait until one of his electronic devices is actually seized? If his laptop is seized, plaintiff will clearly have standing to challenge that seizure. However, will he then have standing to seek injunctive relief against future seizures? *See Abidor v. Napolitano*, 990 F. Supp.2d 260 (E.D.N.Y. 2013).

3. Mootness

The mootness doctrine also involves timing. But when that doctrine applies, the claim is that a case is presented too late. Even though the claim may have been ripe at one point, subsequent events have rendered it "moot."

DeFunis v. Odegaard

416 U.S. 312 (1974)

PER CURIAM.

Petitioner Marco DeFunis, Jr., applied for admission at the University of Washington Law School, a state-operated institution. DeFunis was denied admission and sought a mandatory injunction commanding respondents to admit him as a member of the first-year class, on the ground that the Law School admissions policy had resulted in the unconstitutional denial of his application for admission. The trial court granted the requested relief. DeFunis was admitted to the Law School and began his legal studies in the fall of 1971. The Washington Supreme Court reversed the judgment when DeFunis was in his second year at the Law School. DeFunis petitioned this Court for a writ of certiorari, and the Washington Supreme Court's judgment was stayed. By virtue of this stay, DeFunis has remained in law school, and was in the first term of his third and final year when this Court considered his certiorari petition. Respondents indicated that, if the decision of the Washington Supreme Court were permitted to stand, petitioner could complete the term for which he was then enrolled but would have to apply to the faculty for permission to continue in the school before he could register for another term. Respondents made clear that the Law School will not in any way seek to abrogate this registration.

The inability of the federal judiciary "to review moot cases derives from the requirement of Art. III of the Constitution under which the exercise of judicial power depends upon the existence of a case or controversy." *Liner v. Jafco, Inc.,* 375 U.S. 301 (1964). Under Art. III "even in cases arising in the state courts, the question of mootness is a federal one which a federal court must resolve before it assumes jurisdiction." *North Carolina v. Rice, supra,* 404 U.S. at 246.

Since DeFunis has now registered for his final term, he will be given an opportunity to complete all academic and other requirements for graduation, and will receive his diploma regardless of any decision this Court might reach on the merits of this case. A determination by this Court is no longer necessary to compel that result, and could not serve to prevent it. DeFunis did not cast his suit as a class action, and the only remedy he requested was an injunction commanding his admission to the Law School. He was not only accorded that remedy, but he now has been irrevocably admitted to the final term of the final year of Law School. The controversy between the parties has thus clearly ceased to be "definite and concrete" and no longer "touches the legal relations of parties having adverse legal interests." *Aetna Life Ins. Co. v. Haworth,* 300 U.S. 227 (1937).

It has been the settled practice of the Court, in contexts no less significant, to accept representations such as these as parameters for decision. A voluntary cessation of the admissions practices complained of could make this case moot only if it could be said with assurance "that there is no reasonable expectation that the wrong will be repeated." *W.T. Grant Co., supra,* 345 U.S. at 633. Otherwise, "the defendant is free to return to his old ways," and there would be a "public interest in having the legality of the practices settled." But mootness in the present case depends upon the simple fact that DeFunis is now in the final quarter of the final year of his course of study, and the policy of the Law School to permit him to complete the term for which he is now enrolled.

It might be suggested that this case presents a question that is "capable of repetition, yet evading review," and is thus amenable to federal adjudication even though it might otherwise be moot. But DeFunis will never again be required to run the gauntlet of the Law School's admission process, and so the question is certainly not "capable of repetition" so far as he is concerned. It hardly follows that the issue he raises will in the future evade review. If the admissions procedures of the Law School remain unchanged, there is no reason to suppose that a subsequent case attacking those procedures will not come with relative speed to this Court.

The Court cannot, consistently with the limitations of Art. III of the Constitution, consider the substantive constitutional issues tendered by the parties. Accordingly, the judgment of the Supreme Court of Washington is vacated, and the cause is remanded for such proceedings as by that court may be deemed appropriate.

It is so ordered.

Vacated and remanded.

Justice BRENNAN, with whom Justice DOUGLAS, Justice WHITE, and Justice MARSHALL *concur, dissenting.*

Many weeks of the school term remain, and petitioner may not receive his degree despite respondents' assurances that petitioner will be allowed to complete this term's schooling. Any number of unexpected events—illness, economic necessity, even academic failure—might prevent his graduation. Were that misfortune to befall, respondents warn that "DeFunis would have to request continued admission for the remainder of his law school education, and discretionary action by the University would have to be taken." Thus, petitioner might once again have to run the gauntlet of the University's allegedly unlawful admissions policy. Because the University's position implies no concession that its admissions policy is unlawful, this controversy falls squarely within the Court's long line of decisions holding that the "mere voluntary cessation of allegedly illegal conduct does not moot a case." *United States v. Concentrated Phosphate Export Assn.*, 393 U.S. 199 (1968).

While we must be vigilant to require that litigants maintain a personal stake in the outcome of a controversy, there is no want of an adversary contest in this case. The Court concedes that, if petitioner has lost his stake in this controversy, he did so only when he registered for the spring term. But appellant took that action only after the case had been fully litigated in the state courts, briefs had been filed in this Court, and oral argument had been heard. The case is thus ripe for decision on a fully developed factual record with sharply defined and fully canvassed legal issues. The constitutional issues avoided today concern vast numbers of people. Few constitutional questions in recent history have stirred as much debate. They must inevitably return to the federal courts and to this Court. Because avoidance of repetitious litigation serves the public interest, that inevitability counsels against mootness determinations not compelled by the record.

Notes and Questions: Mootness

1. *"Capable of Repetition, Yet Evading Review." Roe v. Wade*, 410 U.S. 113 (1973), involved a Texas statute that criminalized abortion. Jane Roe, a single unmarried pregnant woman, claimed that she wanted to terminate her pregnancy by an abortion "performed by a competent, licensed physician, under safe, clinical conditions." However, she was unable to obtain a "legal" abortion in Texas because her life was not threatened by the pregnancy, and she could not afford

to travel to another state to obtain an abortion. By the time the Court heard the case, Roe was no longer pregnant, and the state moved to dismiss the case on mootness grounds. The Court held that the case was not moot: "When pregnancy is a significant fact in the litigation, the normal 266-day human gestation period is so short that the pregnancy will come to term before the usual appellate process is complete. If that termination makes a case moot, pregnancy litigation seldom will survive much beyond the trial stage, and appellate review will be effectively denied. Pregnancy often comes more than once to the same woman, and will always be with us. Pregnancy provides a classic justification for a conclusion of nonmootness. It truly could be 'capable of repetition, yet evading review.' *Southern Pacific Terminal Co. v. ICC*, 219 U.S. 498 (1911). We agree that Jane Roe had standing to undertake this litigation, that she presented a justiciable controversy, and that the termination of her 1970 pregnancy has not rendered her case moot."

2. *More on "Capable of Repetition."* In *United States v. Sanchez-Gomez*, 138 S.Ct. 1532 (2018), four criminal defendants objected to the fact that they were bound by full restraints during their pretial proceedings. However, by the time that their cases reached the appellate courts those cases had ended with defendants decisions to plead guilty. Two defendants, who had been charged with illegal entry into the U.S. claimed that their cases were not moot because their claims were "capable of repetition, yet evading review." The Court rejected the argument, noting that a dispute qualifies for that exception only "if (1) the challenged action is in its duration too short to be fully litigated prior to its cessation or expiration, and (2) there is a reasonable expectation that the same complaining party will be subjected to the same action again." Defendants claimed that they met both prongs because they will again violate the law, be apprehended, and be returned to pretrial custody. The Court rejected those arguments, noting that it has "assumed that litigants will conduct their activities within the law and so avoid prosecution and conviction as well as exposure to the challenged course of conduct." The Court rejected the idea that the nature of their offense (illegal entry into the US) made it extremely likely that they would make another illegal entry and again be subjected to pretrial detention.

3. *Jurisdictional or Prudential?* When the Court applies doctrines like mootness or ripeness, it sometimes dismisses because there is no "case" or "controversy" within the meaning of Article III. At other times, even though a case or controversy may exist, the Court simply decides that it is not prudent to hear the case because it is not sufficiently ripe or is nearly moot. Some complain that the Court effectively uses these doctrines to slam the courthouse door in the faces of litigants. In *DeFunis*, the Court suggests that it "cannot, consistently with the limitations of Art. III of the Constitution, consider the substantive constitutional issues tendered by the parties." Was this statement true? Was the dismissal in that case really jurisdictional? What if DeFunis had become sick and was forced to postpone the conclusion of his studies for a year? Is it clear that the law school would have allowed him to complete his studies and graduate?

∿ PROBLEMS: MOOTNESS ∿

1. *Police Chokeholds.* Los Angeles police use chokeholds on some suspects and arrestees. Plaintiff complains that two citizens have died from the chokeholds, and he fears that police will use a chokehold on him in the future (as they have done before). While the case is pending, the police impose a six-month moratorium on the use of chokeholds except under circumstances where deadly force is authorized. Based on the moratorium, the city moves to dismiss the case as moot. Plaintiff objects, claiming that the moratorium is not permanent and may be lifted at any time. Is the case moot? *See City of Los Angeles v. Lyons,* 461 U.S. 95 (1983).

2. *Challenging the Permit.* Laidlaw Environmental Services, Inc., bought a hazardous waste incinerator facility that included a wastewater treatment plant. Shortly after Laidlaw acquired the facility, the South Carolina Department of Health and Environmental Control (DHEC) granted Laidlaw a permit to discharge treated water into a nearby river. The permit placed limits on Laidlaw's discharge of various pollutants, including mercury, regulated the flow, temperature, toxicity, and pH of effluent from the facility, and imposed monitoring and reporting obligations. When Laidlaw's discharges exceed the limits specified in the permit, Friends of the Earth files suit. Is the suit moot if Laidlaw agrees to terminate its violations and to make "every effort" to comply with its permit obligations? What if it permanently closes the incinerator facility, starts dismantling it, puts the site up for sale, and ceases all discharges from the facility permanently? *See Friends of the Earth, Inc. v. Laidlaw Environmental Services,* 528 U.S. 167 (2000).

3. *Mootness and the Sex Offender Registry.* In *United States v. Juvenile Male,* 564 U.S. 932 (2011), a convicted sex offender challenged a trial court order requiring him to register under the Sex Offender Registration and Notification Act. After he turned 21, and was no longer subject to the jurisdiction of the juvenile court, the special order expired. Since state law would have required him to register as a sex offender anyway, the Court dismissed his challenge to the special order as moot: "When defendant challenges his underlying *conviction,* this Court's cases have presumed the existence of collateral consequences. But when a defendant challenges only an expired *sentence,* no such presumption applies and the defendant must bear the burden of identifying some ongoing 'collateral consequence' that is 'traceable' to the challenged portion of the sentence and 'likely to be redressed by a favorable judicial decision.'" The Court found no injury even though state law required him to register, and the obligation continued to apply regardless of the outcome in this case.

4. Standing

Standing focuses on whether plaintiff has "alleged such a personal stake in the outcome of a controversy to warrant invocation of federal-court jurisdiction." As a general rule, plaintiff must be suffering an "injury in fact" that is both concrete and particularized, and the injury must be "actual and imminent" as opposed to conjectural or hypothetical, must be fairly traceable to the defendant's challenged action, and it must be likely that a favorable judicial decision will prevent or redress the injury. Although standing is related to ripeness and mootness, because plaintiff may lack sufficient interest when a case is not yet ripe or has become moot, standing cases do not always involve questions of timing.

The cases cited below involve suits by individuals who seek to challenge governmental action. Some base their standing claims on their status as citizens or taxpayers. Others rely on congressional authorization in the sense that there is a federal statute that authorizes those "adversely affected or aggrieved" by agency action to sue. Still others attempt to sue on behalf of third parties. In each of these contexts, the Court has developed special standing rules.

a. Taxpayer and Citizen Standing

Do citizens and taxpayers have the right to enforce the U.S. Constitution? Some have argued that citizens and taxpayers should have automatic standing to enforce constitutional limits on governmental authority.

In two cases decided together in the 1920s, *Frothingham v. Mellon* and *Massachusetts v. Mellon*, 262 U.S. 447 (1923), the Court considered challenges to the Maternity Act, which appropriated money for the purpose of reducing maternal and infant mortality as well as for protecting the health of mothers and infants. The State of Massachusetts sued, claiming that its rights as a sovereign state and the rights of its citizens had been "invaded and usurped" by the Act. The Court concluded that Massachusetts's "rights" had not been invaded: "The powers of the state are not invaded since the statute imposes no obligation but simply extends an option which the state is free to accept or reject." The Court also rejected the idea that Massachusetts could bring suit on behalf of its citizens: "Citizens of Massachusetts are also citizens of the United States. It cannot be conceded that a state, as *parens patriae*, may institute judicial proceedings to protect citizens of the United States from the operation of the statutes thereof. It is the United States, and not the state, which represents them as *parens patriae*, when such representation becomes appropriate; and to the former, and not to the latter, they must look for such protective measures as flow from that status."

Food for Thought

In 2020, there were extensive protests for racial justice in Portland, Oregon. President Trump referred to the protests as "riots" because of damage to buildings and businesses. Believing that Oregon officials were not doing enough to quell the protests, President Trump decided to send in the Department of Homeland

Security. Oregon officials sued, claiming that President Trump is acting unlawfully, and that they have standing to represent the interests of their citizens. Do
Oregon officials have the right to maintain the action?

———————————

The *Frothingham* Court also held that she could not establish standing to sue
based on her status as a citizen and a federal taxpayer even though she argued
that her tax burden would be increased by the appropriations:

> A taxpayer's interest in the moneys of the treasury—partly realized from
> taxation and partly from other sources—is shared with millions of others, is
> comparatively minute and indeterminable, and the effect upon future taxa-
> tion, of any payment out of the funds, so remote, fluctuating and uncertain,
> that no basis is afforded for an appeal to the preventive powers of a court of
> equity. The administration of any statute, likely to produce additional taxation
> to be imposed upon a vast number of taxpayers, the extent of whose several
> liability is indefinite and constantly changing, is essentially a matter of public
> and not individual concern. If one taxpayer may champion and litigate such
> a cause, then every other taxpayer may do the same in respect of every other
> appropriation act and statute whose administration requires the outlay of pub-
> lic money, and whose validity may be questioned.

The Court went on to note that "the functions of government under our system are apportioned. To the legislative department has been committed the duty
of making laws, to the executive the duty of executing them, and to the judiciary
the duty of interpreting and applying them in cases properly brought before the
courts. The general rule is that neither department may invade the province of
the other and neither may control, direct, or restrain the action of the other. We
have no power *per se* to review and annul acts of Congress on the ground that
they are unconstitutional. That question may be considered only when the justification for some direct injury suffered or threatened, presenting a justiciable
issue, is made to rest upon such an act." *Frothingham* left open the possibility that
a municipal taxpayer might be able to establish standing to challenge municipal
expenditures on the theory that the taxpayer's interest in a municipal treasury is
more substantial.

DaimlerChrysler Corp. v. Cuno

547 U.S. 332 (2006)

Justice ROBERTS delivered the opinion of the Court.

Jeeps were mass-produced in 1941 for the U.S. Army in Toledo, Ohio. Nearly
60 years later, the city of Toledo and State of Ohio sought to encourage the current
manufacturer of Jeeps—DaimlerChrysler to expand its Jeep operation in Toledo,
by offering local and state tax benefits for new investment. Taxpayers in Toledo
sued, alleging that their local and state tax burdens were increased by the tax

breaks, tax breaks that they asserted violated the Commerce Clause. We are obligated before reaching this Commerce Clause question to determine whether the taxpayers who objected to the credit have standing to press their complaint in federal court. We conclude that they do not, and we therefore can proceed no further.

Ohio levies a franchise tax "upon corporations for the privilege of doing business in the state, owning or using a part or all of its capital or property in the state, or holding a certificate of compliance authorizing it to do business in the state." Ohio Rev. Code Ann. §5733.01. A taxpayer that purchases "new manufacturing machinery and equipment" and installs it at sites in the State receives a credit against the franchise tax. Municipalities may also offer partial property tax waivers to businesses that agree to invest in qualifying areas. With consent from local school districts, the partial property tax waiver can be increased to a complete exemption.

In 1998, DaimlerChrysler entered into a contract under which it agreed to expand its Jeep assembly plant in Toledo. In exchange, the city agreed to waive the property tax for the plant, with the consent of the two school districts in which the plant is located. Because DaimlerChrysler undertook to purchase and install "new manufacturing machinery and equipment," it was also entitled to a credit against the state franchise tax.

Most of the plaintiffs were residents of Toledo, who paid taxes to both the city of Toledo and State of Ohio. They claimed that they were injured because the tax breaks for DaimlerChrysler diminished the funds available to the city and State, imposing a "disproportionate burden" on plaintiffs. The District Court held that, "at the bare minimum, the Plaintiffs who are taxpayers have standing to object to the property tax exemption and franchise tax credit statutes under the 'municipal taxpayer standing' rule articulated in *Massachusetts v. Mellon*, 262 U.S. 447 (1923)." On the merits, the District Court found that neither tax benefit violated the Commerce Clause. The Court of Appeals for the Sixth Circuit agreed as to the municipal property tax exemption, but held that the state franchise tax credit violated the Commerce Clause.

Chief Justice Marshall, in *Marbury v. Madison*, 1 Cranch 137, 2 L. Ed. 60 (1803), grounded the Federal Judiciary's authority to exercise judicial review and interpret the Constitution on the necessity to do so in the course of carrying out the judicial function of deciding cases. Determining that a matter before the federal courts is a proper case or controversy under Article III therefore assumes particular importance in ensuring that the Federal Judiciary respects "'the proper—and properly limited—role of the courts in a democratic society,'" *Allen v. Wright*, 468 U.S. 737, 750 (1984) (quoting *Warth v. Seldin*, 422 U.S. 490, 498 (1975)). If a dispute is not a proper case or controversy, the courts have no business deciding it, or expounding the law in the course of doing so.

This case-or-controversy limitation is crucial in maintaining the "tripartite allocation of power" set forth in the Constitution. *Valley Forge Christian College v. Americans United for Separation of Church and State, Inc.*, 454 U.S. 464 (1982). The "core component" of the requirement that a litigant have standing to invoke the authority of a federal court "is an essential and unchanging part of the case-or-controversy requirement of Article III." *Lujan v. Defenders of Wildlife*, 504 U.S. 555, 560 (1992). The requisite elements of this "core component derived directly from the Constitution" are familiar: "A plaintiff must allege personal injury fairly traceable to the defendant's allegedly unlawful conduct and likely to be redressed by the requested relief." *Allen, supra,* at 751. We have been asked to decide an important question of constitutional law concerning the Commerce Clause. Before we do so, we must find that the question is presented in a "case" or "controversy" that is, in James Madison's words, "of a Judiciary Nature." 2 RECORDS OF THE FEDERAL CONVENTION OF 1787, p. 430 (M. Farrand ed. 1966). That requires plaintiffs to carry the burden of establishing their standing under Article III.

Plaintiffs claim standing by virtue of their status as Ohio taxpayers, alleging that the franchise tax credit "depletes the funds of the State of Ohio to which the Plaintiffs contribute through their tax payments" and thus "diminishes the total funds available for lawful uses and imposes disproportionate burdens on" them. On several occasions, this Court has denied *federal* taxpayers standing under Article III to object to a particular expenditure of federal funds simply because they are taxpayers. Thus the alleged "deprivation of the fair and constitutional use of a federal taxpayer's tax dollar" cannot support a challenge to the conveyance of Government land to a private religious college, *Valley Forge, supra,* at 476, and "the interest of a taxpayer in the moneys of the federal treasury furnishes no basis" to argue that a federal agency's loan practices are unconstitutional.

The animating principle behind these cases was announced in *Frothingham v. Mellon,* decided with *Massachusetts v. Mellon,* 262 U.S. 447 (1923). The logic of those decisions is equally applicable to taxpayer challenges to expenditures that deplete the treasury, and to taxpayer challenges to so-called "tax expenditures," which reduce amounts available to the treasury by granting tax credits or exemptions. In either case, the alleged injury is based on the asserted effect of the allegedly illegal activity on public revenues, to which the taxpayer contributes. Standing has been rejected in such cases because the alleged injury is not "concrete and particularized," but instead a grievance the taxpayer "suffers in some indefinite way in common with people generally," *Frothingham, supra,* at 488. In addition, the injury is not "actual or imminent," but instead "conjectural or hypothetical." *Defenders of Wildlife, supra,* at 560. It is unclear that tax breaks at issue here deplete the treasury: The very point of tax benefits is to spur economic activity, which in turn *increases* government revenues. In this very action, the Michigan plaintiffs claimed that they were injured because they lost out on the added revenues that would have accompanied DaimlerChrysler's decision to expand facilities in Michigan.

Plaintiffs' alleged injury is "conjectural or hypothetical" in that it depends on how legislators respond to a reduction in revenue, if that is the consequence of the credit. Establishing injury requires speculating that elected officials will increase a taxpayer-plaintiff's tax bill to make up a deficit; establishing redressability requires speculating that abolishing the challenged credit will redound to the benefit of the taxpayer because legislators will pass along the supposed increased revenue in the form of tax reductions. Neither sort of speculation suffices to support standing. A taxpayer plaintiff has no right to insist that the government dispose of any increased revenue it might experience as a result of his suit by decreasing his tax liability or bolstering programs that benefit him. The decision of how to allocate any such savings is the very epitome of a policy judgment committed to the "broad and legitimate discretion" of lawmakers, which "the courts cannot presume either to control or to predict." *ASARCO, supra,* at 615 (opinion of Kennedy, J.). Under such circumstances, we have no assurance that the asserted injury is "imminent"—that it is "certainly impending."

The rationale for rejecting federal taxpayer standing applies with undiminished force to state taxpayers. In *Doremus v. Board of Ed. of Hawthorne,* 342 U.S. 429 (1952), we noted that "the interests of a taxpayer in the moneys of the federal treasury are too indeterminable, remote, uncertain and indirect" to support standing to challenge "their manner of expenditure." We then "reiterated" what we had said in rejecting a federal taxpayer challenge to a federal statute "as equally true when a state Act is assailed: 'The taxpayer must be able to show that he has sustained some direct injury and not merely that he suffers in some indefinite way in common with people generally.'" The allegations of injury that plaintiffs make furnish no better basis for finding standing than those made in cases where federal taxpayer standing was denied. Plaintiffs claim that DaimlerChrysler's tax credit depletes the Ohio fisc and "imposes disproportionate burdens on them." This is no different from similar claims by federal taxpayers we have already rejected under Article III as insufficient to establish standing. State policymakers, no less than their federal counterparts, retain broad discretion to make "policy decisions" concerning state spending "in different ways depending on their perceptions of wise state fiscal policy and myriad other circumstances." *ASARCO, supra,* at 615 (opinion of Kennedy, J.). A party seeking federal jurisdiction cannot rely on such "speculative inferences to connect his injury to the challenged actions of the defendant," *Simon,* 426 U.S. at 45. Indeed, because state budgets frequently contain an array of tax and spending provisions, any number of which may be challenged on a variety of bases, affording state taxpayers standing to press such challenges simply because their tax burden gives them an interest in the state treasury would interpose the federal courts as "virtually continuing monitors of the wisdom and soundness" of state fiscal administration, contrary to the more modest role Article III envisions for federal courts. *See id.,* at 760 (quoting *Laird v. Tatum,* 408 U.S. 1, 15 (1972)). For the foregoing reasons, we hold that state taxpayers have no standing under Article III to challenge state tax or spending decisions simply by virtue of their status as taxpayers.

Plaintiffs also claim that their status as *municipal* taxpayers gives them standing to challenge the *state* franchise tax credit. In plaintiffs' challenge to the state franchise tax credit, however, they identify no municipal action contributing to any claimed injury. Instead, they try to leverage the notion of municipal taxpayer standing beyond challenges to municipal action. First, plaintiffs claim that because state law requires revenues from the franchise tax to be distributed to local governments, the award of a credit to DaimlerChrysler reduced such distributions and thus depleted the funds of "local governments to which Respondents pay taxes." But plaintiffs' challenge is still to the state law and state decision, not those of their municipality. Any effect that enjoining DaimlerChrysler's credit will have on municipal funds, therefore, will not result from automatic operation of a statutory formula, but from a hypothesis that the state government will choose to direct the supposed revenue from the restored franchise tax to municipalities. This is the sort of conjecture we may not entertain in assessing standing. The second way plaintiffs seek to leverage their standing is by relying on *Mine Workers v. Gibbs*, 383 U.S. 715 (1966). *Gibbs* held that federal-question jurisdiction over a claim may authorize a federal court to exercise jurisdiction over state-law claims that may be viewed as part of the same case because they "derive from a common nucleus of operative fact" as the federal claim. Plaintiffs' reading of *Gibbs* would have remarkable implications. The doctrines of mootness, ripeness, and political question all originate in Article III's "case" or "controversy" language, no less than standing does. Yet if *Gibbs'* "common nucleus" formulation announced a new definition of "case" or "controversy" for all Article III purposes, a federal court would be free to entertain moot or unripe claims, or claims presenting a political question, if they "derived from" the same "operative facts" as another federal claim suffering from none of these defects. Plaintiffs failed to establish Article III injury with respect to their *state* taxes, and even if they did with respect to their *municipal* taxes, that injury does not entitle them to seek a remedy as to the state taxes.

Because plaintiffs have no standing to challenge that credit, the lower courts erred by considering their claims on the merits. The judgment of the Sixth Circuit is therefore vacated in part, and the cases are remanded for dismissal of plaintiffs' challenge to the franchise tax credit.

It is so ordered.

BACKGROUND
Taxpayer Challenges to Bible Readings

In *Doremus v. Board of Education*, 342 U.S. 429 (1952), taxpayers filed an Establishment Clause challenge against Bible readings in the New Jersey public schools. The Court held that the plaintiffs could not establish standing: "There is no allegation that this activity is supported by any separate tax or paid for from any particular appropriation or that it adds any sum whatever to the cost of conducting the school. No information is given as to what kind of taxes are paid by appellants and there is no averment that the Bible reading increases any tax they do pay or that as taxpayers they are, will, or possibly can be out of pocket because of it."

Notes and Questions: Standing

1. *More on Taxpayer Status.* Taxpayers always have standing to challenge the validity of a *tax* (as opposed to an expenditure) that they are forced to pay. As a result, in *Baldwin v. G.A.F. Seelig, Inc.*, 294 U.S. 511 (1935), milk sellers in the State of New York had standing to challenge a tax on them equivalent to 5 cents per gallon sold.

2. *Leasing Public Lands.* In *ASARCO, Inc. v. Kadish*, 490 U.S. 605 (1989), an Arizona statute that authorized the state land department to lease minerals and school trust lands at a prescribed rate was challenged by taxpayers who claimed that the statute did not comply with congressionally imposed standards for leasing or selling lands. Plaintiffs were joined by a teachers' association and its members. The Court concluded that all of the plaintiffs lacked standing: "Respondents asserted that the statute governing mineral leases has 'deprived the school trust funds of millions of dollars thereby resulting in unnecessarily higher taxes.' Even if the first part of that assertion were correct, it is pure speculation whether the lawsuit would result in any actual tax relief for respondents. If they were to prevail, it is conceivable that more money might be devoted to education; but since education in Arizona is not financed solely from the school trust fund, the State might reduce its supplement from the general funds to provide for other programs. The same flaw defeats the claim that the teachers association would have had standing to bring this suit. The claims raised here are the kind of generalized grievances brought by concerned citizens that we have consistently held are not cognizable in the federal courts." Nevertheless, the Court decided that leaseholders had standing to challenge the law: "Petitioners hold mineral leases granted under the state law the Arizona Supreme Court invalidated. Although no accounting of sums remains at issue in this particular case, the decision to be reviewed poses a serious and immediate threat to the continuing validity of those leases by virtue of its holding that they were granted under improper procedures and an invalid law. The state proceedings ended in a declaratory judgment adverse to petitioners, an adjudication of legal rights which constitutes the kind of injury cognizable in this Court on review from the state courts." Chief Justice Rehnquist, joined by Justice Scalia, dissented, arguing that the original plaintiffs lacked standing and that the "subsequent proceedings in the state court have obviously not cured this defect."

3. *Citizens and Tenth Amendment Claims.* In *Bond v. United States*, 564 U.S. 211 (2011), a defendant in a criminal case alleged that Congress did not have the power to enact the Chemical Weapons Convention Implementation Act, under which she was being prosecuted. Her argument was based on the Tenth Amendment and the premise that Congress enacted the law in violation of basic federalism principles. The Court held that she had standing to raise the Tenth Amendment claims: "Article III's prerequisites are met. Bond seeks to vindicate her own constitutional interests. The individual, in a proper case, can assert injury from governmental action taken in excess of the authority that federalism

defines. Her rights do not belong to a State. Federalism is more than an exercise in setting the boundary between different institutions of government for their own integrity. Federalism also protects the liberty of all persons within a State by ensuring that laws enacted in excess of delegated governmental power cannot direct or control their actions." Justice Ginsburg, joined by Justice Breyer, concurred: "Bond, like any other defendant, has a personal right not to be convicted under a constitutionally invalid law."

∽ PROBLEMS: *FROTHINGHAM*, TAXPAYER STANDING, AND CITIZEN STANDING ∽

1. *The Historic Preservation Act and Citizenship Standing.* Why shouldn't plaintiffs be able to establish standing to raise Establishment Clause and Free Exercise Clause claims against the HPA based solely on their status as citizens of the United States? Suppose that they think that the Historic Preservation Act is "bad policy" because local and state governments, and historic preservation organizations, should be required to pay for the upkeep of their own properties, and should not be allowed to shift their costs to the U.S. government. Why shouldn't such allegations sufficient to establish standing?

2. Frothingham *and Municipal Taxpayers.* Suppose that a municipality decides to adopt a maternity program like the one at issue in *Frothingham.* A municipal taxpayer wishes to challenge the program as illegitimate and claims that expenditures under the program will increase her taxes. In light of *Frothingham* and *Cuno,* does the municipal taxpayer have standing? Does it matter how large the municipality is or how large the municipal budget? How much the taxpayer pays annually in taxes? How much of the municipal budget the program consumes?

3. *More on* Doremus *and Bible Readings.* In *Doremus,* the Court held that taxpayers did not have standing to challenge Bible readings in the public schools. What would the plaintiff taxpayers have needed to allege to establish standing to challenge the readings? Would it be enough to allege that the public schools spent public money purchasing copies of the Bible? Would they have to allege something more? If so, what? Would it make a difference that one of the plaintiffs has a child in the school where the Bible readings are being conducted? What would the parent have to allege to establish standing?

4. *Army Surveillance.* Plaintiffs claim that the Department of the Army has engaged in "surveillance of lawful and peaceful civilian political activity" and that the surveillance has a "chilling" effect on the exercise of their First Amendment rights. Plaintiffs sue claiming that such information gathering is inappropriate to the army's role under the U.S. Constitution, is inherently dangerous, and that the army may misuse the information in a way that would cause direct harm to them. Are these allegations of injury sufficient to establish standing? Would it matter that most, if not all, of the plaintiffs and/or the organizations of which they are

members have previously been the subject of army surveillance reports and their names have appeared in the army's records? *See Laird v. Tatum,* 408 U.S. 1 (1972).

Clapper v. Amnesty International USA

568 U.S. 398 (2013)

Justice Alito delivered the opinion of the Court.

In 1978, Congress enacted the Foreign Intelligence Surveillance Act (FISA) to authorize and regulate certain governmental electronic surveillance of communications for foreign intelligence purposes. See 50 U.S.C. §1801 *et seq.* Congress legislated against the backdrop of our decision in *United States v. United States Dist. Court for Eastern Dist. of Mich.,* 407 U.S. 297 (1972), in which we explained that the standards and procedures that law enforcement officials must follow when conducting "surveillance of 'ordinary crime'" might not be required in the context of surveillance conducted for domestic national-security purposes. *Keith* suggested that a special framework for foreign intelligence surveillance might be constitutionally permissible. Congress created two specialized courts. Congress authorized judges of the Foreign Intelligence Surveillance Court (FISC) to approve electronic surveillance for foreign intelligence purposes if there is probable cause to believe that "the target of electronic surveillance is a foreign power or an agent of a foreign power," and each of the specific "facilities or places at which the electronic surveillance is directed is being used, or is about to be used, by a foreign power or an agent of a foreign power." §105(a)(3). Additionally, Congress vested the Foreign Intelligence Surveillance Court of Review with jurisdiction to review any denials by the FISC of applications for electronic surveillance. §103(b).

In wake of the September 11th attacks, President George W. Bush authorized the National Security Agency (NSA) to conduct warrantless wiretapping of telephone and e-mail communications where one party to the communication was located outside the United States and a participant in "the call was reasonably believed to be a member or agent of al Qaeda or an affiliated terrorist organization," In 2007, the FISC issued orders authorizing the Government to target international communications into or out of the United States where there was probable cause to believe that one participant to the communication was a member or agent of al Qaeda or an associated terrorist organization. These FISC orders subjected any electronic surveillance that was then occurring under the NSA's program to the approval of the FISC. After a FISC Judge subsequently narrowed the FISC's authorization of such surveillance, the Executive asked Congress to amend FISA so that it would provide the intelligence community with additional authority to meet the challenges of modern technology and international terrorism.

When Congress enacted the FISA Amendments Act of 2008, it left much of FISA intact, but it "established a new and independent source of intelligence collection authority, beyond that granted in traditional FISA." 1 Kris & Wilson

§9:11, at 349. §702 of FISA, which was enacted as part of the FISA Amendments Act, supplements FISA authority by creating a new framework under which the Government may seek the FISC's authorization of certain foreign intelligence surveillance targeting the communications of non-U.S. persons located abroad. Unlike traditional FISA surveillance, §1881a does not require the Government to demonstrate probable cause that the target of the electronic surveillance is a foreign power or agent of a foreign power. Unlike traditional FISA, §1881a does not require the Government to specify the nature and location of each of the particular facilities or places at which the electronic surveillance will occur.

Surveillance under §1881a is subject to statutory conditions, judicial authorization, congressional supervision, and compliance with the Fourth Amendment. Section 1881a provides that, upon the issuance of an order from the Foreign Intelligence Surveillance Court, "the Attorney General and the Director of National Intelligence may authorize jointly, for a period of up to 1 year, the targeting of persons reasonably believed to be located outside the United States to acquire foreign intelligence information." §1881a(a). Surveillance under §1881a may not be intentionally targeted at any person known to be in the United States or any U.S. person reasonably believed to be located abroad. §1881a(b)(1)–(3). Additionally, acquisitions under §1881a must comport with the Fourth Amendment. §1881a(b)(5). Moreover, surveillance under §1881a is subject to congressional oversight and several types of Executive Branch review.

Section 1881a mandates that the Government obtain the Foreign Intelligence Surveillance Court's approval of "targeting" procedures, "minimization" procedures, and a governmental certification regarding proposed surveillance. §1881a(a), (c)(1), (i)(2), (i)(3). Among other things, the Government's certification must attest that (1) procedures are in place "that have been approved, have been submitted for approval, or will be submitted with the certification for approval by the [FISC] that are reasonably designed" to ensure that an acquisition is "limited to targeting persons reasonably believed to be located outside" the United States; (2) minimization procedures adequately restrict the acquisition, retention, and dissemination of nonpublic information about unconsenting U.S. persons, as appropriate; (3) guidelines have been adopted to ensure compliance with targeting limits and the Fourth Amendment; and (4) the procedures and guidelines referred to above comport with the Fourth Amendment. §1881a(g)(2).

The Foreign Intelligence Surveillance Court's role includes determining whether the Government's certification contains the required elements. The Court assesses whether the targeting procedures are "reasonably designed" (1) to "ensure that an acquisition is limited to targeting persons reasonably believed to be located outside the United States" and (2) to "prevent the intentional acquisition of any communication as to which the sender and all intended recipients are known to be located in the United States." §1881a(i)(2)(B). The Court analyzes whether the minimization procedures "meet the definition of minimization procedures under section 1801(h), as appropriate." §1881a(i)(2)(C). The Court also assesses whether the targeting and minimization procedures are consistent with the statute and the Fourth Amendment.

Respondents are attorneys and human rights, labor, legal, and media organizations whose work allegedly requires them to engage in sensitive and sometimes privileged telephone and e-mail communications with colleagues, clients, sources, and other individuals located abroad. Respondents believe that some of the people with whom they exchange foreign intelligence information are likely targets of surveillance under §1881a. Respondents claim that they communicate by telephone and e-mail with people the Government "believes or believed to be associated with terrorist organizations," "people located in geographic areas that are a special focus" of the Government's counterterrorism or diplomatic efforts, and activists who oppose governments that are supported by the United States Government. Respondents claim that §1881a compromises their ability to locate witnesses, cultivate sources, obtain information, and communicate confidential information to their clients. Respondents also assert that they "have ceased engaging" in certain telephone and e-mail conversations. According to respondents, the threat of surveillance will compel them to travel abroad in order to have in-person conversations. In addition, respondents declare that they have undertaken "costly and burdensome measures" to protect the confidentiality of sensitive communications.

Respondents filed this action seeking (1) a declaration that §1881a, on its face, violates the Fourth Amendment, the First Amendment, Article III, and separation-of-powers principles and (2) a permanent injunction against the use of §1881a. Respondents assert two separate theories of Article III standing. First, they claim that there is an objectively reasonable likelihood that their communications will be acquired under §1881a at some point in the future, thus causing them injury. Second, respondents maintain that the risk of surveillance under §1881a is so substantial that they have been forced to take costly and burdensome measures to protect the confidentiality of their international communications. The District Court held that respondents do not have standing. The Second Circuit reversed. We granted certiorari.

Article III of the Constitution limits federal courts' jurisdiction to certain "Cases" and "Controversies." "One element of the case-or-controversy requirement" is that plaintiffs "must establish that they have standing to sue." *Raines v. Byrd,* 521 U.S. 811, 818 (1997). Article III standing, built on separation-of-powers principles, serves to prevent the judicial process from being used to usurp the powers of the political branches. *Valley Forge Christian College v. Americans United for Separation of Church and State, Inc.,* 454 U.S. 464, 471 (1982). In keeping with the purpose of this doctrine, "our standing inquiry has been especially rigorous when reaching the merits of the dispute would force us to decide whether an action taken by one of the other two branches of the Federal Government was unconstitutional." *Raines, supra,* at 819. We have often found a lack of standing in cases in which the Judiciary has been requested to review actions of the political branches in the fields of intelligence gathering and foreign affairs, see, *e.g.,*

Richardson, supra, at 167; *Laird v. Tatum,* 408 U.S. 1, 11 (1972). To establish Article III standing, an injury must be "concrete, particularized, and actual or imminent; fairly traceable to the challenged action; and redressable by a favorable ruling." *Monsanto Co. v. Geertson Seed Farms,* 130 S. Ct. 2743, 2752 (2010). "Threatened injury must be *certainly impending* to constitute injury in fact," and "allegations of *possible* future injury" are not sufficient. *Whitmore,* 495 U.S. at 158.

Respondents assert that they can establish injury in fact that is fairly traceable to §1881a because there is an objectively reasonable likelihood that their communications with their foreign contacts will be intercepted under §1881a at some point in the future. This argument fails. The "objectively reasonable likelihood" standard is inconsistent with our requirement that "threatened injury must be certainly impending to constitute injury in fact." *Whitmore, supra,* at 158. Respondents' argument rests on their highly speculative fear that: (1) the Government will decide to target the communications of non-U.S. persons with whom they communicate; (2) in doing so, the Government will choose to invoke its authority under §1881a rather than utilizing another method of surveillance; (3) the Article III judges who serve on the Foreign Intelligence Surveillance Court will conclude that the Government's proposed surveillance procedures satisfy §1881a's many safeguards and are consistent with the Fourth Amendment; (4) the Government will succeed in intercepting the communications of respondents' contacts; and (5) respondents will be parties to the communications that the Government intercepts. Respondents' theory of standing, which relies on a highly attenuated chain of possibilities, does not satisfy the requirement that threatened injury must be certainly impending. Even if respondents could demonstrate injury in fact, the second link in the above-described chain of contingencies—which amounts to mere speculation about whether surveillance would be under §1881a or some other authority—shows that respondents cannot satisfy the requirement that any injury in fact must be fairly traceable to §1881a.

First, it is speculative whether the Government will imminently target communications to which respondents are parties. Section 1881a expressly provides that respondents, who are U.S. persons, cannot be targeted under §1881a. Respondents fail to offer evidence that their communications have been monitored. Respondents' theory rests on their assertion that the Government will target *other individuals*—namely, their foreign contacts. Respondents speculate and make assumptions about whether their communications with their foreign contacts will be acquired under §1881a. "The party invoking federal jurisdiction bears the burden of establishing" standing—and, at the summary judgment stage, a party "can no longer rest on 'mere allegations,' but must 'set forth' by affidavit or other evidence 'specific facts.'" *Defenders of Wildlife,* 504 U.S. at 561. Respondents have set forth no specific facts demonstrating that the communications of their foreign contacts will be targeted. Because §1881 *authorizes*—but does not *mandate* or *direct*—the surveillance that respondents fear, respondents' allegations are conjectural. Respondents can only speculate as to how the Attorney General and the Director of National Intelligence will exercise their discretion in determining which communications to target.[4]

Second, even if respondents could demonstrate that the targeting of their foreign contacts is imminent, respondents can only speculate as to whether the Government will use §1881a-authorized surveillance rather than other methods. Even after enactment of the FISA Amendments Act, the Government may still conduct electronic surveillance of persons abroad under the older provisions of FISA so long as it satisfies the applicable requirements, including a demonstration of probable cause to believe that the person is a foreign power or agent of a foreign power. The Government may also obtain information from the intelligence services of foreign nations. The Government contends that it can conduct FISA-exempt human and technical surveillance programs that are governed by Executive Order 12333. Even if respondents could demonstrate that their foreign contacts will imminently be targeted—indeed, that interception of their own communications will imminently occur—they would still need to show that their injury is fairly traceable to §1881a. Third, even if respondents could show that the Government will seek the Foreign Intelligence Surveillance Court's authorization to acquire the communications of respondents' foreign contacts under §1881a, respondents can only speculate as to whether that court will authorize such surveillance. In the past, we have been reluctant to endorse standing theories that require guesswork as to how independent decisionmakers will exercise their judgment.

Fourth, even if the Government were to obtain the Foreign Intelligence Surveillance Court's approval to target respondents' foreign contacts under §1881a, it is unclear whether the Government would succeed in acquiring the communications of respondents' foreign contacts.

Fifth, even if the Government were to conduct surveillance of respondents' foreign contacts, respondents can only speculate as to whether *their own communications* with their foreign contacts would be incidentally acquired. In sum, respondents' speculative chain of possibilities does not establish that injury based on potential future surveillance is certainly impending or is fairly traceable to §1881a.[5]

---

4. The Government could resolve the standing inquiry by disclosing to a court, perhaps *in camera*, (1) whether it is intercepting respondents' communications and (2) what targeting or minimization procedures it is using. It is *respondents'* burden to prove standing by pointing to specific facts, *Lujan v. Defenders of Wildlife*, 504 U.S. 555 (1992), not the Government's burden to disprove standing. This type of hypothetical disclosure proceeding would allow a terrorist to determine whether he is currently under U.S. surveillance simply by filing a lawsuit challenging the Government's surveillance program. The court's postdisclosure decision about whether to dismiss the suit for lack of standing would signal to the terrorist whether his name was on the list of surveillance targets.

5. Our cases do not require plaintiffs to demonstrate that it is literally certain that the harms they identify will come about. We have found standing based on a "substantial risk" that the harm will occur, which may prompt plaintiffs to reasonably incur costs to mitigate or avoid that harm. But plaintiffs bear the burden of pleading and proving concrete facts showing that defendant's actual action has caused the substantial risk of harm. Plaintiffs cannot rely on speculation about "the unfettered choices made by independent actors not before the court." *Defenders of Wildlife*, 504 U.S. at 562.

Respondents assert that they are suffering ongoing injuries that are fairly traceable to §1881a because the risk of surveillance under §1881a requires them to take costly and burdensome measures to protect the confidentiality of their communications. The threat of surveillance sometimes compels them to avoid certain e-mail and phone conversations, to "talk in generalities rather than specifics," or to travel so that they can have in-person conversations. Respondents cannot manufacture standing by inflicting harm on themselves based on their fears of hypothetical future harm that is not certainly impending. Any ongoing injuries that respondents are suffering are not fairly traceable to §1881a. If the law were otherwise, an enterprising plaintiff would be able to secure a lower standard for Article III standing simply by making an expenditure based on a nonparanoid fear. Even before §1881a was enacted, they had a similar incentive to engage in many of the countermeasures that they are now taking. For instance, respondent Scott McKay's declaration describes "knowledge" that thousands of communications involving one of his clients were monitored in the past. But this surveillance was conducted pursuant to FISA authority that predated §1881a. Because respondents do not face a threat of certainly impending interception under §1881a, the costs that they have incurred to avoid surveillance are simply the product of their fear of surveillance, and *Laird* makes clear that such a fear is insufficient to create standing.

Respondents also suggest that they should be held to have standing because otherwise the constitutionality of §1881a could not be challenged. Our holding today by no means insulates §1881a from judicial review. Congress created a comprehensive scheme in which the Foreign Intelligence Surveillance Court evaluates the Government's certifications, targeting procedures, and minimization procedures—including assessing whether the targeting and minimization procedures comport with the Fourth Amendment. Additionally, if the Government intends to use or disclose information obtained or derived from a §1881a acquisition in judicial or administrative proceedings, it must provide advance notice of its intent, and the affected person may challenge the lawfulness of the acquisition. Thus, if the Government were to prosecute one of respondent-attorney's foreign clients using §1881a-authorized surveillance, the Government would be required to make a disclosure. Although the foreign client might not have a viable Fourth Amendment claim, it is possible that the monitoring of the target's conversations with his or her attorney would provide grounds for a claim of standing on the part of the attorney. Unlike the present case, it would be clear that the Government had acquired the foreign client's communications using §1881a-authorized surveillance. Finally, any electronic communications service provider that the Government directs to assist in §1881a surveillance may challenge the lawfulness of that directive before the FISC.

Respondents lack Article III standing because they cannot demonstrate that the future injury they purportedly fear is certainly impending and because they cannot manufacture standing by incurring costs in anticipation of non-imminent harm. We therefore reverse the judgment of the Second Circuit and remand the case for further proceedings consistent with this opinion.

It is so ordered.

JUSTICE BREYER, with whom JUSTICE GINSBURG, JUSTICE SOTOMAYOR, and JUSTICE KAGAN join, dissenting.

The Government's interception of a private telephone or e-mail conversation amounts to an injury that is "concrete and particularized." Plaintiffs seek as relief a judgment declaring unconstitutional (and enjoining enforcement of) a statutory provision authorizing those interceptions; and, such a judgment would redress the injury by preventing it. Thus, the question is whether the injury is "actual or imminent."

The addition of §1881a in 2008 changed prior law in three important ways. First, it eliminated the requirement that the Government describe to the court each specific target and identify each facility at which its surveillance would be directed, thus permitting surveillance on a programmatic, not necessarily individualized, basis. §1881a(g). Second, it eliminated the requirement that a target be a "foreign power or an agent of a foreign power." Third, it diminished the court's authority to insist upon, and eliminated its authority to supervise, instance-specific privacy-intrusion minimization procedures (though the Government still must use court-approved general minimization procedures). Thus, using the authority of §1881a, the Government can obtain court approval for its surveillance of electronic communications between places within the United States and targets in foreign territories by showing the court (1) that "a significant purpose of the acquisition is to obtain foreign intelligence information," and (2) that it will use general targeting and privacy-intrusion minimization procedures of a kind that the court had previously approved. §1881a(g).

Several considerations, along with commonsense, convince me that there is a very high likelihood that Government, *acting under §1881a,* will intercept at least some of the communications. First, plaintiffs have engaged, and continue to engage, in electronic communications of a kind that the 2008 amendment, but not the prior Act, authorizes the Government to intercept. These communications include discussions with family members of those detained at Guantanamo, friends and acquaintances of those persons, and investigators, experts and others with knowledge of circumstances related to terrorist activities. These persons are foreigners located outside the United States. Plaintiffs exchange with these persons "foreign intelligence information," defined to include information that "relates to" "international terrorism" and "the national defense or the security of the United States." Second, plaintiffs have a strong *motive* to engage in, and the Government has a strong *motive* to listen to, conversations of the kind described. A fair reading of the affidavit of Scott McKay indicates that [he] will engage in conversations that concern what suspected foreign terrorists, such as his client, have done; in conversations that concern his clients' families, colleagues, and contacts; in conversations that concern what those persons (or those connected to them) have said and done, at least in relation to terrorist activities; in conversations that concern the political, social, and commercial environments in which the suspected terrorists have lived and worked. Journalists and human rights workers have strong similar motives to conduct conversations of this kind. The Government has a strong motive to learn as much as it can reasonably learn about suspected terrorists (such as those detained at Guantanamo), as well as about their contacts and activities, along with those of friends and family members. The Government is motivated by the critical, overriding need to protect America from terrorism. Third, the Government's *past behavior* shows that it has sought, and will in all likelihood continue to seek, information about alleged terrorists and detainees through means that include surveillance of electronic communications. McKay states that the Government (under the pre-2008 law) "intercepted some 10,000 telephone calls and 20,000 email communications involving his client Mr. Al-Hussayen." Fourth, the Government has the *capacity* to conduct electronic surveillance of the kind at issue.

Of course, to exercise this capacity the Government must have intelligence court authorization. But the Government rarely files requests that fail to meet the statutory criteria. There is no reason to believe that the communications described would fail to meet the conditions necessary for approval. Compared with prior law, §1881a simplifies and thus expedites the approval process, making it more likely that the Government will use §1881a to obtain the necessary approval. Nothing suggests the presence of some special factor here that might support a contrary conclusion. Ordinarily a party that seeks to defeat a strong natural inference must bear the burden of showing that some such special circumstance exists. We need only assume that the Government is doing its job (to find out about, and combat, terrorism) in order to conclude that there is a high probability that the Government will intercept at least some electronic communication to which some of the plaintiffs are parties. The majority is wrong when it describes the harm threatened plaintiffs as "speculative."

The majority says that the plaintiffs have failed to show that the threatened harm is "*certainly impending.*" But *certainty* is not, and never has been, the touchstone of standing. Federal courts frequently entertain actions for injunctions and for declaratory relief aimed at preventing future activities that are reasonably likely or highly likely to take place. That degree of certainty is all that is needed to support standing here. Courts have often found *probabilistic* injuries sufficient to support standing. Plaintiff McKay points out that, when he communicates abroad about, or in the interests of, a client (*e.g.,* a client accused of terrorism), he must "make an assessment" whether his "client's interests would be compromised" should the Government "acquire the communications." If so, he must either forgo the communication or travel abroad. Since travel is expensive, since forgoing communication can compromise the client's interests, McKay's assessment itself takes time and effort. I dissent, with respect, from the majority's contrary conclusion.

Note: **Lance v. Coffman**

Lance v. Coffman, 549 U.S. 437 (2007), involved a challenge to a state redistricting plan. After Colorado legislators were unable to redraw congressional districts following the 2000 census, to accommodate an additional representative, a state court did it for them. When the legislature was finally able to agree on a plan in 2003, Colorado voters sued claiming that Colorado's Constitution only permits redistricting once per census, and therefore the court drawn plan must remain in effect until the next census. The Court held that the voters lacked standing to sue:

> Our refusal to serve as a forum for generalized grievances has a lengthy pedigree. In *United States v. Richardson*, 418 U.S. 166 (1974), a federal taxpayer challenged the Government's failure to disclose certain CIA expenditures as a violation of the Constitution's Accounts Clause, which requires that "a regular Statement and Account of the Receipts and Expenditures of all public Money shall be published from time to time." Art. I, §9, cl. 7. This Court dismissed the claim as a "generalized grievance" that is "plainly undifferentiated and 'common to all members of the public.'" The same day, in *Schlesinger v. Reservists Comm. to Stop the War*, 418 U.S. 208 (1974), we addressed standing to bring a challenge under the Constitution's Incompatibility Clause, which provides that "no Person holding any Office under the United States, shall be a Member of either House during his Continuance in Office." Art. I, §6, cl. 2. Citizen-taxpayers brought a lawsuit contending that Members of Congress who were also members of the military Reserves violated the Incompatibility Clause. This Court dismissed for lack of standing. Standing to sue may not be predicated upon an interest of the kind alleged here which is held in common by all members of the public, because of the necessarily abstract nature of the injury all citizens share." Refusing to entertain generalized grievances ensures that "there is a real need to exercise the power of judicial review" in a particular case, and it helps guarantee that courts fashion remedies "no broader than required by the precise facts to which the court's ruling would be applied." In short, it ensures that courts exercise power that is judicial in nature.

Plaintiffs here are four Colorado voters. "The only injury plaintiffs allege is that the law—specifically the Elections Clause—has not been followed. This injury is precisely the kind of undifferentiated, generalized grievance about the conduct of government that we have refused to countenance in the past. Because plaintiffs assert no particularized stake in the litigation, we hold that they lack standing to bring their Elections Clause claim.

Notes: Legislator Standing

1. *Legislator Standing.* In *Raines v. Byrd*, 521 U.S. 811 (1997), members of Congress who had voted against the Line Item Veto Act sought to challenge that Act, which gave the President the authority to "cancel" certain spending and tax benefit measures after he had signed them into law. The Members claimed that the Act adversely affected "their constitutionally prescribed lawmaking powers." The Court disagreed, noting that "the injury claimed by the

Members of Congress is not claimed in any private capacity but solely because they are Members of Congress. The claimed injury thus runs (in a sense) with the Member's seat, a seat which the Member holds as trustee for his constituents, not as a prerogative of personal power." As a result, the Court held that "these individual members of Congress do not have a sufficient 'personal stake' in this dispute and have not alleged a sufficiently concrete injury to have established Article III standing."

2. *More on Legislator Standing. Raines* can be contrasted with the holding in *Coleman v. Miller*, 307 U.S. 433 (1939), which involved the Kansas secretary of state's decision to endorse a resolution ratifying a proposed amendment to the U.S. Constitution with the notation that it had been "passed" by the legislature. Plaintiffs, members of the Kansas Senate, sued to force the secretary of state to change his endorsement to "not passed" on the basis that the lieutenant governor had, without authority, cast the deciding vote. All 21 plaintiffs had voted against the amendment, claiming that it was not ratified within a reasonable period of time. The Court held that the legislators had standing to bring the case: "plaintiffs include senators, whose votes against ratification have been overridden and virtually held for naught although if they are right in their contentions their votes would have been sufficient to defeat ratification. These senators have a plain, direct and adequate interest in maintaining the effectiveness of their votes. Petitioners have set up and claimed a right and privilege under the Constitution of the United States to have their votes given effect and the state court has denied that right and privilege." Justice Frankfurter, joined by justices Black and Douglas, argued that the plaintiffs lacked standing to bring the case: "What is their distinctive claim not possessed by every Kansan? The fact that these legislators are part of the ratifying mechanism while the ordinary citizen of Kansas is not, is irrelevant. We can only adjudicate an issue as to which there is a claimant who has a special, individualized stake in it. One who is merely the self-constituted spokesman of a constitutional point of view cannot ask us to pass on it. The Kansas legislators could not bring suit on behalf of the people of the United States to determine whether Kansas could still vote for the Child Labor Amendment. They cannot gain standing by having brought a suit in their own names. None of the petitioners can here raise questions concerning the power of the Kansas legislature to ratify the Amendment."

∾ PROBLEMS: CITIZEN STANDING TO CHALLENGE CONSTITUTIONAL AMENDMENTS ∾

1. *Standing to Challenge Constitutional Amendments.* Would citizens ever have standing to challenge the validity of a constitutional amendment? Suppose that an amendment is adopted prohibiting child labor. Which of the following groups could establish standing to sue: 1) All Kansas citizens on the basis that it is a common concern of every citizen of the United States whether the Amendment is

still alive, or whether Kansas can be included among the necessary three-fourths of the several States? 2) Citizens of other states (if Kansas's ratification vote put the amendment "over the top" in terms of ratification)? 3) Parent who want their child to be able to work? 4) A business owner who employs children? *See Coleman v. Miller*, 307 U.S. 433 (1939).

2. *The Emoluments Clause.* Article I, Section 9, Clause 8 of the United States Constitution contains the "Emoluments Clause" which restricts members of the government from receiving gifts, emoluments, offices, or titles from foreign states without the consent of the United States Congress. Following President Trump's inauguration, questions have been raised regarding whether he has violated the clause, in particular because foreign governments are paying for their employees to stay at Trump hotels. Do congressional Democrats have the right to challenge President Trump under the clause? Does a citizen and taxpayer have standing to challenge President Trump's alleged violation of the Emoluments Clause? Would a competitor hotel have standing? A city's business and convention bureau who believes that foreign governments are directing convention business to Trump hotels? What about members of Congress? Consider the following argument: "By accepting emoluments without 'the Consent of the Congress,' Defendant has violated the Foreign Emoluments Clause. In the process, Defendant has deprived Plaintiffs of their ability to vote on which emoluments he, as a federal office-holder, may accept. When legislators' votes are 'completely nullified' or 'deprived of all validity,' they may seek judicial redress to 'have their votes given effect.' Such nullification occurs both where a previously cast vote has been unlawfully disregarded and where, as here, legislators are unlawfully denied an 'opportunity to cast a binding vote' in the first place. By refusing to seek Plaintiffs' consent as constitutionally required, 'the President's action has deprived them of this opportunity completely, in the sense that they have no legislative power to exercise an equivalent voting opportunity.' Plaintiffs thus have 'a plain, direct and adequate interest in maintaining the effectiveness of their votes' on whether consent should be given to Defendant's acceptance of foreign emoluments."

Hein v. Freedom From Religion Foundation, Inc.

551 U.S. 587 (2007)

Justice ALITO announced the judgment of the Court and delivered an opinion in which THE CHIEF JUSTICE and Justice KENNEDY join.

This is a lawsuit in which it was claimed that conferences held as part of the President's Faith-Based and Community Initiatives program violated the Establishment Clause of the First Amendment because, among other things, President Bush and former Secretary of Education Paige gave speeches that used "religious imagery" and praised the efficacy of faith-based programs in delivering social services. Plaintiffs contend that they meet the standing requirements of Article III of the Constitution because they pay federal taxes.

In 2001, the President issued an executive order creating the White House Office of Faith-Based and Community Initiatives within the Executive Office of the President. Exec. Order No. 13199, 3 CFR 752. The purpose of this new office was to ensure that "private and charitable community groups, including religious ones have the fullest opportunity permitted by law to compete on a level playing field, so long as they achieve valid public purposes" and adhere to "the bedrock principles of pluralism, nondiscrimination, evenhandedness, and neutrality." The office was specifically charged with eliminating unnecessary bureaucratic, legislative, and regulatory barriers that could impede such organizations' effectiveness and ability to compete equally for federal assistance. By separate executive orders, the President created Executive Department Centers for Faith-Based and Community Initiatives within several federal agencies and departments. These centers were given the job of ensuring that faith-based community groups would be eligible to compete for federal financial support without impairing their independence or autonomy, as long as they did "not use direct Federal financial assistance to support any inherently religious activities, such as worship, religious instruction, or proselytization." Exec. Order No. 13279, 3 CFR §2(f), p. 260. The President directed that "no organization should be discriminated against on the basis of religion or religious belief in the administration or distribution of Federal financial assistance under social service programs," and that "all organizations that receive Federal financial assistance under social services programs should be prohibited from discriminating against beneficiaries or potential beneficiaries of the social services programs on the basis of religion or religious belief." Petitioners, who have been sued in their official capacities, are the directors of the White House Office and various Executive Department Centers. No congressional legislation specifically authorized the creation of the White House Office or the Executive Department Centers. Rather, they were "created entirely within the Executive Branch by Presidential executive order." Nor has Congress enacted any law specifically appropriating money for these entities' activities. Instead, their activities are funded through general Executive Branch appropriations. For example, the Department of Education's Center is funded from money appropriated for the Office of the Secretary of Education, while the Department of Housing and Urban Development's Center is funded through that Department's salaries and expenses account.

Respondents are Freedom From Religion Foundation, Inc., a nonstock corporation "opposed to government endorsement of religion," and three of its members. Respondents brought suit in federal court, alleging that petitioners violated the Establishment Clause by organizing conferences at which faith-based organizations allegedly "are singled out as being particularly worthy of federal funding, and the belief in God is extolled as distinguishing the claimed effectiveness of faith-based social services." Respondents further alleged that the content of these conferences sent a message to religious believers "that they are insiders

and favored members of the political community" and that the conferences sent
the message to nonbelievers "that they are outsiders" and "not full members of
the political community." In short, respondents alleged that the conferences
were designed to promote, and had the effect of promoting, religious community
groups over secular ones. The asserted basis for standing was that the individual
respondents are federal taxpayers who are "opposed to the use of Congressional
taxpayer appropriations to advance and promote religion." Respondents sought
to challenge Executive Branch expenditures for these conferences, which, they
contended, violated the Establishment Clause. The District Court dismissed the
claims for lack of standing. A divided panel of the United States Court of Appeals
for the Seventh Circuit reversed. We granted certiorari and reverse.

Article III of the Constitution limits the judicial power of the United States to
the resolution of "Cases" and "Controversies," and "Article III standing enforces
the Constitution's case-or-controversy requirement." *DaimlerChrysler Corp. v. Cuno,*
547 U.S. 332, 342 (2006). The elements of Article III standing are well established: "A plaintiff must allege personal injury fairly traceable to the defendant's
allegedly unlawful conduct and likely to be redressed by the requested relief."
Allen v. Wright, 468 U.S. 737, 751 (1984).

"The judicial power of the United States defined by Art. III is not an uncon-
ditioned authority to determine the constitutionality of legislative or executive
acts." *Valley Forge Christian College v. Americans United for Separation of Church and
State, Inc.,* 454 U.S. 464, 471 (1982). The federal courts are not empowered to
seek out and strike down any governmental act that they deem to be repugnant
to the Constitution. Rather, federal courts sit "solely, to decide on the rights of
individuals," *Marbury v. Madison,* 1 Cranch 137, 170, 2 L. Ed. 60 (1803), and must
"refrain from passing upon the constitutionality of an act unless obliged to do so
in the proper performance of our judicial function, when the question is raised
by a party whose interests entitle him to raise it." *Valley Forge, supra,* at 474.

As a general matter, the interest of a federal taxpayer in seeing that Treasury
funds are spent in accordance with the Constitution does not give rise to the
kind of redressable "personal injury" required for Article III standing. Of course,
a taxpayer has standing to challenge the *collection* of a specific tax assessment as
unconstitutional; being forced to pay such a tax causes a real and immediate economic injury to the individual taxpayer. *See, e.g., Follett v. Town of McCormick,* 321
U.S. 573 (1944). But that is not the interest respondents assert here. Rather, their
claim is that, having paid lawfully collected taxes into the Federal Treasury, they
have a continuing, legally cognizable interest in ensuring that those funds are not
used by the Government in a way that violates the Constitution.

We have consistently held that this type of interest is too generalized and
attenuated to support Article III standing. In *Flast v. Cohen,* 392 U.S. 83 (1968),
the Court carved out a narrow exception to the general constitutional prohibition
against taxpayer standing. The taxpayer-plaintiff in that case challenged the distribution of federal funds to religious schools under the Elementary and Secondary

Education Act of 1965, alleging that such aid violated the Establishment Clause. The Court set out a two-part test for determining whether a federal taxpayer has standing to challenge an allegedly unconstitutional expenditure:

> First, the taxpayer must establish a logical link between that status and the type of legislative enactment attacked. Thus, a taxpayer will be a proper party to allege the unconstitutionality only of exercises of congressional power under the taxing and spending clause of Art. I, §8, of the Constitution. It will not be sufficient to allege an incidental expenditure of tax funds in the administration of an essentially regulatory statute. Secondly, the taxpayer must establish a nexus between that status and the precise nature of the constitutional infringement alleged. Under this requirement, the taxpayer must show that the challenged enactment exceeds specific constitutional limitations imposed upon the exercise of the congressional taxing and spending power and not simply that the enactment is generally beyond the powers delegated to Congress by Art. I, §8.

Flast, 392 U.S. at 102. The Court held that the taxpayer-plaintiff in *Flast* had satisfied both prongs of this test: The plaintiff's "constitutional challenge was made to an exercise by Congress of its power under Art. I, §8, to spend for the general welfare," and she alleged a violation of the Establishment Clause, which "operates as a specific constitutional limitation upon the exercise by Congress of the taxing and spending power conferred by Art. I, §8."

Respondents argue that this case falls within the *Flast* exception. But this broad reading fails to observe "the rigor with which the *Flast* exception ought to be applied." *Valley Forge,* 454 U.S. at 481. Given that the alleged Establishment Clause violation in *Flast* was funded by a specific congressional appropriation and was undertaken pursuant to an express congressional mandate, the Court concluded that the taxpayer-plaintiffs had established the requisite "logical link between their taxpayer status and the type of legislative enactment attacked." "Their constitutional challenge was made to an exercise by Congress of its power under Art. I, §8, to spend for the general welfare." As this Court later noted, *Flast* "limited taxpayer standing to challenges directed 'only at exercises of congressional power'" under the Taxing and Spending Clause. *Valley Forge,* 454 U.S. at 479. The link between congressional action and constitutional violation is missing here. Congress provided general appropriations to the Executive Branch to fund its day-to-day activities. These appropriations did not expressly authorize, direct, or even mention the expenditures of which respondents complain. Those expenditures resulted from executive discretion, not congressional action.

We have never found taxpayer standing under such circumstances. In *Valley Forge,* we held that a taxpayer lacked standing to challenge "a decision by the federal Department of Health, Education and Welfare to transfer a parcel of federal property" to a religious college because this transfer was "not a congressional action." In fact, the connection to congressional action was closer in *Valley Forge* because the "particular Executive Branch action" being challenged was "arguably authorized" by the Federal Property and Administrative Services Act of 1949, which permitted federal agencies to transfer surplus property to private entities.

Nevertheless, we found that plaintiffs lacked standing because *Flast* "limited tax-payer standing to challenges directed 'only at exercises of congressional power'" under the Taxing and Spending Clause.[1] *Bowen v. Kendrick*, 487 U.S. 589 (1988), is not to the contrary. In that case, we held that the taxpayer-plaintiffs had standing to mount an as-applied challenge to the Adolescent Family Life Act (AFLA), which authorized federal grants to private community service groups including religious organizations. The Court found "a sufficient nexus between the taxpayer's standing as a taxpayer and the congressional exercise of taxing and spending power," notwithstanding the fact that "the funding authorized by Congress had flowed through and been administered" by an Executive Branch official. But the key was the Court's recognition that AFLA was "at heart a program of disbursement of funds pursuant to Congress' taxing and spending powers," and that plaintiffs' claims "called into question how the funds authorized by Congress were being disbursed *pursuant to the AFLA's statutory mandate.*" Unlike this case, *Kendrick* involved a "program of disbursement of funds pursuant to Congress' taxing and spending powers" that "Congress had created," "authorized," and "mandated." Respondents cite no statute whose application they challenge. The best they can do is to point to unspecified, lump-sum "Congressional budget appropriations" for the general use of the Executive Branch—the allocation of which "is an administrative decision traditionally regarded as committed to agency discretion." *Lincoln v. Vigil*, 508 U.S. 182, 192 (1993). It cannot be that every legal challenge to a discretionary Executive Branch action implicates the constitutionality of the underlying congressional appropriation.[3]

Respondents argue that it is "arbitrary" to distinguish between money spent pursuant to congressional mandate and expenditures made in the course of executive discretion, because "the injury to taxpayers in both situations is the very injury targeted by the Establishment Clause and *Flast*—the expenditure for the support of religion of funds exacted from taxpayers." But *Flast* focused on congressional action, and we decline this invitation to extend its holding to encompass discretionary Executive Branch expenditures. We have repeatedly emphasized that the *Flast* exception has a "narrow application in our precedent," that only "slightly lowered" the bar on taxpayer standing, and that must be applied with "rigor," *Valley Forge, supra*, at 481. In the four decades since its creation, the *Flast* exception has largely been confined to its facts. We have declined

---

1. *Valley Forge* also relied on a [claim] that the authorizing Act was an exercise of Congress' power under the Property Clause of Art. IV, §3, cl. 2, and not the Taxing and Spending Clause of Art. I, §8. But this conclusion merely provided an additional basis for denying a claim of standing that was already foreclosed because it was not based on any congressional action.

3. Nor is it relevant that Congress may have informally "earmarked" portions of its general Executive Branch appropriations to fund the offices and centers whose expenditures are at issue. "Where 'Congress merely appropriates lump-sum amounts without statutorily restricting what can be done with those funds, a clear inference arises that it does not intend to impose legally binding restrictions, and indicia in committee reports and other legislative history as to how the funds should or are expected to be spent do not establish any legal requirements on' the agency." *Lincoln*, 508 U.S. at 192.

to lower the taxpayer standing bar in suits alleging violations of any constitutional provision apart from the Establishment Clause. *See Tilton v. Richardson*, 403 U.S. 672 (1971) (Free Exercise Clause); *Richardson*, 418 U.S. at 175 (Statement and Account Clause of Art. I); *Schlesinger*, 418 U.S. at 228 (Incompatibility Clause of Art. I); *Cuno, supra* (Commerce Clause). We have similarly refused to extend *Flast* to permit taxpayer standing for Establishment Clause challenges that do not implicate Congress' taxing and spending power. *See Valley Forge, supra*, at 479-482. We have "limited the expansion of federal taxpayer and citizen standing in the absence of specific statutory authorization to an outer boundary drawn by the *results* in *Flast*."

Because almost all Executive Branch activity is funded by some congressional appropriation, extending *Flast* to purely executive expenditures would effectively subject every federal action—be it a conference, proclamation or speech—to Establishment Clause challenge by any taxpayer in federal court. It would also raise serious separation-of-powers concerns. By framing the standing question solely in terms of whether the dispute would be presented in an adversary context and in a form traditionally viewed as capable of judicial resolution, *Flast* "failed to recognize that this doctrine has a separation-of-powers component, which keeps courts within certain traditional bounds vis-a-vis the other branches, concrete adverseness or not." *Lewis v. Casey*, 518 U.S. 343 (1996).

The constitutional requirements for federal-court jurisdiction—including the standing requirements and Article III—"are an essential ingredient of separation and equilibration of powers." *Steel Co. v. Citizens for Better Environment*, 523 U.S. 83 (1998). "Relaxation of standing requirements is directly related to the expansion of judicial power," and lowering the taxpayer standing bar to permit challenges of purely executive actions "would significantly alter the allocation of power at the national level, with a shift away from a democratic form of government." *Richardson*, 418 U.S. at 188 (Powell, J., concurring). This would "be quite at odds with *Flast*'s own promise that it would not transform federal courts into forums for taxpayers' 'generalized grievances'" about the conduct of government, and would "open the Judiciary to an arguable charge of providing 'government by injunction,'" *Schlesinger*, 418 U.S. at 222. It would deputize federal courts as "virtually continuing monitors of the wisdom and soundness of Executive action." *Allen*, 468 U.S. at 760. Neither the Court of Appeals nor respondents has identified a workable limitation.

Respondents set out a parade of horribles that they claim could occur if *Flast* is not extended to discretionary Executive Branch expenditures. For example, they say, a federal agency could use its discretionary funds to build a house of worship or to hire clergy of one denomination and send them out to spread their faith. Or an agency could use its funds to make bulk purchases of Stars of David, crucifixes, or depictions of the star and crescent for use in its offices or for distribution to the employees or the general public. In the unlikely event that any of these executive actions did take place, Congress could quickly step in. Respondents make no effort to show that these improbable abuses could not be challenged in federal court by plaintiffs who would possess standing based on grounds other than taxpayer standing.

The Court of Appeals did not apply *Flast*; it extended *Flast*. It is a necessary concomitant of the doctrine of *stare decisis* that a precedent is not always expanded to the limit of its logic. We leave *Flast* as we found it. For these reasons, the judgment of the Court of Appeals for the Seventh Circuit is reversed.

It is so ordered.

Justice SCALIA, with whom Justice THOMAS joins, *concurring in the judgment.*

Flast is wholly irreconcilable with the Article III restrictions on federal-court jurisdiction that this Court has repeatedly confirmed are embodied in the doctrine of standing. Wallet Injury is the type of concrete and particularized injury one would expect to be asserted in a *taxpayer* suit, namely, a claim that the plaintiff's tax liability is higher than it would be, but for the allegedly unlawful government action. The stumbling block for suits challenging government expenditures based on this type of injury is that plaintiff cannot satisfy the traceability and redressability prongs of standing. It is uncertain what the plaintiff's tax bill would have been had the allegedly forbidden expenditure not been made, and it is even more speculative whether the government will, in response to an adverse court decision, lower taxes rather than spend the funds in some other manner.

Psychic Injury has nothing to do with the plaintiff's tax liability. The injury consists of the taxpayer's *mental displeasure* that money extracted from him is being spent in an unlawful manner. Psychic Injury is directly traceable to the improper *use* of taxpayer funds, and it is redressed when the improper use is enjoined, regardless of whether that injunction affects the taxpayer's purse. *Flast* and the cases following its teaching have invoked a peculiarly restricted version of Psychic Injury, permitting taxpayer displeasure over unconstitutional spending to support standing *only if* the constitutional provision allegedly violated is a specific limitation on the taxing and spending power. This conceptualizing of injury in fact in purely mental terms conflicts squarely with the familiar proposition that a plaintiff lacks a concrete and particularized injury when his only complaint is the generalized grievance that the law is being violated.

Flast relied on Psychic Injury to support standing, describing the "injury" as the taxpayer's allegation that "his tax money is being extracted and spent in violation of specific constitutional protections against such abuses of legislative power." The criteria in *Flast*'s two-part test are *entirely unrelated* to the purported goal of ensuring that the plaintiff has a sufficient "stake in the outcome of the controversy." If taxpayers upset with the government's giving money to parochial schools had standing to sue, so should the taxpayers who disapproved of the government's paying public-school teachers to read the Bible. I cannot fathom why Article III standing should turn on whether the government enables a religious organization to obtain real estate by giving it a check drawn from general tax revenues or instead by buying the property itself and then transferring title.

Is a taxpayer's purely psychological displeasure that his funds are being spent in an allegedly unlawful manner sufficiently concrete and particularized to support Article III standing? The answer is no. Nor does *Flast*'s two-pronged "nexus" test cure the Article III deficiency. The taxpayer seeks "relief that no more directly and tangibly benefits him than it does the public at large." *Lujan, supra,* at 573-574. It is of no conceivable relevance whether the Establishment Clause was originally conceived of as a specific limitation on the taxing and spending power. Once a proper understanding of the relationship of standing to the separation of powers is brought to bear, Psychic Injury, even as limited in *Flast,* is revealed for what it is: a contradiction of the basic propositions that the function of the judicial power "is, solely, to decide on the rights of individuals," *Marbury v. Madison,* 1 Cranch 137, 170, 2 L. Ed. 60 (1803), and generalized grievances affecting the public at large have their remedy in the political process. It is time—past time—to call an end. *Flast* should be overruled.

Justice SOUTER, with whom Justice STEVENS, Justice GINSBURG, and Justice BREYER join, *dissenting.*

We held in *Flast* that the "'injury' alleged in Establishment Clause challenges to federal spending" is "the very 'extraction and spending' of 'tax money' in aid of religion." *DaimlerChrysler Corp. v. Cuno,* 547 U.S. 332 (2006) (quoting *Flast, supra,* at 106). The right of conscience and the expenditure of an identifiable three pence raised by taxes for the support of a religious cause are not to be split off from one another. The three pence implicates the conscience, and the injury from Government expenditures on religion is not accurately classified with the "Psychic Injury" that results whenever a congressional appropriation or executive expenditure raises hackles of disagreement with the policy supported. "Every taxpayer can claim a personal constitutional right not to be taxed for the support of a religious institution," and thus distinguished the case from one in which a taxpayer sought only to air a generalized grievance in federal court. Here, there is no dispute that taxpayer money in identifiable amounts is funding conferences, and these are alleged to have the purpose of promoting religion. When executive agencies spend identifiable sums of tax money for religious purposes, no less than when Congress authorizes the same thing, taxpayers suffer injury. The plurality points to separation of powers to explain its distinction between legislative and executive spending decisions, but there is no difference between Judicial Branch review of an executive decision and judicial evaluation of a congressional one. We owe respect to each of the other branches, and no one has suggested that the Establishment Clause lacks applicability to executive uses of money.

In the case of economic or physical harms, the "injury in fact" question is straightforward. Once one strays from these obvious cases, the enquiry can turn subtle. Are esthetic harms sufficient for Article III standing? What about being forced to compete on an uneven playing field based on race (without showing that an economic loss resulted), or living in a racially gerrymandered electoral district? These injuries are no more concrete than seeing one's tax dollars spent on religion, but we have recognized each one as enough for standing. *See Friends of Earth, Inc. v. Laidlaw Environmental Services (TOC), Inc.,* 528 U.S. 167 (2000) (esthetic injury). This is not to say that any sort of alleged injury will satisfy Article III, but only that intangible harms must be evaluated case by case. *Flast* speaks for this Court's recognition (shared by a majority of the Court) that when the Government spends money for religious purposes a taxpayer's injury is serious and concrete enough to be "judicially cognizable." The judgment of sufficient injury takes account of the Madisonian relationship of tax money and conscience, but it equally reflects the Founders' pragmatic "conviction that individual religious liberty could be achieved best under a government which was stripped of all power to tax, to support, or otherwise to assist any or all religions," *Everson v. Board of Ed. of Ewing,* 330 U.S. 1, 11 (1947), and the realization continuing to the modern day that favoritism for religion sends the message to nonadherents that they are outsiders, not full members of the political community. *McCreary County v. American Civil Liberties Union of Ky.,* 545 U.S. 844, 860 (2005).[4] Because the taxpayers in this case have alleged the type of injury this Court has seen as sufficient for standing, I would affirm.

Note: **Flast** *and the Commerce Clause*

In *DaimlerChrysler Corp. v. Cuno,* 547 U.S. 332 (2006), the Court rejected the argument that *Flast* authorizes a special exception for Commerce Clause challenges: "Plaintiffs' reliance on *Flast* is misguided: Whatever rights plaintiffs have under the Commerce Clause, they are fundamentally unlike the right not to "contribute three pence for the support of any one religious establishment" (quoting 2 WRITINGS OF JAMES MADISON 186 (G. Hunt ed. 1901)). "Even if the two Clauses are similar in that they implicate governments' fiscal decisions, a finding that the Commerce Clause satisfies the *Flast* test would leave no principled way of distinguishing those other constitutional provisions that we have recognized constrain governments' taxing and spending decisions. Such a broad application of *Flast*'s exception to the general prohibition on taxpayer standing would be quite at odds with its narrow application in our precedent and *Flast*'s own promise that it would not transform federal courts into forums for taxpayers' 'generalized grievances.' *Flast* discerned in the history of the Establishment Clause 'the specific evils feared by its drafters that the taxing and spending power would be used to favor one religion over another or to support religion in general.' The Court understood the 'injury' alleged in Establishment Clause challenges to federal spending to be the 'extraction and spending' of 'tax money' in aid of religion alleged by a plaintiff. An injunction against the spending would redress *that* injury, regardless

---

4. There will not always be competitors for the funds who would make better plaintiffs (and indeed there appears to be no such competitor here), so after accepting the importance of the injury there is no reason to refuse standing as a prudential matter.

of whether lawmakers would dispose of the savings in a way that would benefit the taxpayer-plaintiffs personally."

Note: Standing in Gerrymandering Cases

In *Gill v. Whitford,*138 S. Ct. 1916 (2018), the Court defined the requirements to establish standing in cases involving claims that political boundaries had been gerrymandered. Some of the plaintiffs alleged that they lived in districts that had been "packed" (packing a party's members into a district that they will win by an overwhelming margin) or "cracked" (splitting a party's members so that they routinely fall just short of a majority in both districts), thereby diluting their votes, and they sought to submit a substitute redistricting plan that was perfectly balanced between the political parties. Wisconsin's political geography, particularly the high concentration of Democratic voters in urban centers, afforded the Republican Party a natural, but modest, advantage in the districting process. The Court held that "a plaintiff who alleges that he is the object of a racial gerrymander—a drawing of district lines on the basis of race—has standing to assert only that his own district has been gerrymandered." Those who do not live in gerrymandered districts are only to assert "a generalized grievance against governmental conduct of which he or she does not approve." The Court rejected the idea that voters have a state-wide interest in avoiding gerrymandered districts. The Court remanded the case so that plaintiffs could try to prove that they lived in packed or cracked districts. Justice Kagan's concurrence set forth a roadmap for making that showing.

Flast *and Tax Credits*

In *Arizona Christian School Tuition Organization v. Winn,* 563 U.S. 125 (2011), the Court refused to allow plaintiffs to use *Flast* to challenge an Arizona law that provided tax credits for scholarships to students attending private schools, including sectarian schools. The Court rejected the idea that taxpayers had standing to challenge the tax credit, as well as the idea that they could establish standing under *Flast.* The Court noted that *Flast* "provides a 'narrow exception' to 'the general rule against taxpayer standing,'" and the Court refused to apply that narrow exception in this case: "The STO tax credit is not tantamount to a religious tax or to a tithe and does not visit the injury identified in *Flast.* It follows that respondents have neither alleged an injury for standing purposes under general rules nor met the *Flast* exception." Justice Scalia argued that *Flast* is an "anomaly" which should be repudiated. Justice Kagan disagreed, arguing that "This novel distinction between appropriations and tax expenditures has as little basis in principle as it has in our precedent. Cash grants and targeted tax breaks are means of accomplishing the same government objective—to provide financial support to select individuals or organizations. From now on, government need follow just one simple rule—subsidize through the tax system—to preclude taxpayer challenges to state funding of religion."

Food For Thought

After *Hein*, can it be said that any other constitutional limitations operate as a specific limitation on Article I, Section 8 expenditures? If so, which ones? In other words, is *Flast* essentially limited to its facts?

∼ PROBLEMS ∼

1. *Challenging Presidential Action.* When we examined challenges to undeclared wars, we saw that such suits are usually dismissed as involving political questions (or perhaps on ripeness grounds). Should such suits also be dismissed on standing grounds? After *Frothingham, Flast,* and *Valley Forge,* suppose that the President masses troops in a foreign country in preparation for a possible invasion of a third country. Which of the following individuals have standing to challenge the President's action: A citizen who wants to challenge the action as an undeclared war? A citizen who wants to argue that the President's action constitutes an undeclared war in violation of Congress's power to declare war? A soldier, about to be shipped to the theater of operations, who claims that she is illegally being placed in harm's way? Members of Congress who claims that the President's actions constitute a violation of their right to vote on whether to go to war? *See Holtzman v. Schlesinger,* 484 F.2d 1307 (2d Cir. 1973); *Dellums v. Bush,* 752 F. Supp. 1141 (D.D.C. 1990).

2. *"Birther" Lawsuits.* Even though President Barack Obama released a birth certificate showing that he was born in Hawaii, members of the "Birther Movement" claimed that he was not born in the United States, and therefore was not eligible to be President of the United States. Does an individual have standing to assert such a claim based on his status as a citizen and taxpayer of the United States? What if plaintiff was a candidate for the presidency of the United States (competing against Obama)? A write-in candidate for President? A member of the United States military who has been ordered to deploy to Iraq who claims that the order is invalid because Obama is not legitimately in office? *See Berg v. Obama,* 586 F.3d 234 (3d Cir. 2009); *Sibley v. Obama,* 866 F. Supp. 2d 17 (D.D.C. 2012); *Rhodes v. McDonald,* 2009 WL 2997605 (M.D. Ga. 2012).

3. *Challenging Science Curriculum Standards.* A state board of education adopts science standards for use in public schools. The standards establish performance expectations for students, but vest local school districts with the authority to determine their own curricula. Citizens for Objective Public Education (COPE) seeks to challenge the standards on the basis that they establish a non-religious

world view that breaches parental trust and fosters anti-religious instruction. If local school districts retain the authority to implement their own standards, do parents have standing to challenge the state standards? *See COPE v. Kansas State Board of Education*, 821 F.3d 1215 (10th Cir. 2016).

4. *More on the Historic Preservation Act.* In light of *Flast* and the Court's other standing decisions, can any of the groups seeking to challenge the Historic Preservation Act establish standing? Under *Flast*? On some other ground? On what basis?

b. Causation

The Court has held that the "irreducible constitutional minimum" of standing contains three elements: 1) the plaintiff must have suffered an "injury in fact"—an invasion of a legally protected interest that is a) concrete and particularized and b) actual or imminent, not conjectural or hypothetical; 2) there must be a causal connection between the injury and the conduct complained of; and 3) it must be likely, as opposed to merely speculative, that the injury will be redressed by a favorable decision. *See Lujan v. Defenders of Wildlife*, 504 U.S. 555 (1992). The Court has also held that it will not entertain a "generalized grievance against allegedly illegal governmental conduct." *See, e.g., Schlesinger v. Reservists Committee to Stop the War*, 418 U.S. 208 (1974). "It is the burden of the party who seeks the exercise of jurisdiction in his favor" "clearly to allege facts demonstrating that he is a proper party to invoke judicial resolution of the dispute."

Standing cases can involve both constitutional (Article III "case and controversy") and "prudential" components. "Prudential" means that, although the case may present enough of a case and controversy so that Article III allows a federal court to hear the case, the Court might decline to hear it for discretionary (so-called "prudential") reasons.

Lujan v. Defenders of Wildlife

504 U.S. 555 (1992)

Justice SCALIA delivered the opinion of the Court with respect to Parts I, II, III-A, and IV, and an opinion with respect to Part III-B, in which THE CHIEF JUSTICE, Justice WHITE, and Justice THOMAS join.

This case involves a challenge to a rule promulgated by the Secretary of the Interior interpreting §7 of the Endangered Species Act of 1973 (ESA), in such fashion as to render it applicable only to actions within the United States or on the high seas. The preliminary issue, and the only one we reach, is whether respondents, plaintiffs below, have standing to seek judicial review of the rule.

I

The ESA seeks to protect species of animals against threats to their continuing existence caused by man. The ESA instructs the Secretary of the Interior to promulgate by regulation a list of those species which are either endangered or threatened under enumerated criteria, and to define the critical habitat of these species. Section 7(a)(2) of the Act then provides, in pertinent part:

> Each Federal agency shall, in consultation with and with the assistance of the Secretary of the Interior, insure that any action authorized, funded, or carried out by such agency is not likely to jeopardize the continued existence of any endangered species or threatened species or result in the destruction or adverse modification of habitat of such species which is determined by the Secretary, after consultation as appropriate with affected States, to be critical.

In 1978, the Fish and Wildlife Service (FWS) and the National Marine Fisheries Service (NMFS), on behalf of the Secretary of the Interior and the Secretary of Commerce respectively, promulgated a joint regulation stating that the obligations imposed by §7(a)(2) extend to actions taken in foreign nations. The next year, however, the Interior Department began to reexamine its position. A revised joint regulation, reinterpreting §7(a)(2) to require consultation only for actions taken in the United States or on the high seas, was proposed in 1983, and promulgated in 1986. Thereafter, respondents, organizations dedicated to wildlife conservation and other environmental causes, filed this action against the Secretary of the Interior, seeking a declaratory judgment that the new regulation is in error as to the geographic scope of §7(a)(2) and an injunction requiring the Secretary to promulgate a new regulation restoring the initial interpretation.

Our cases have established that the irreducible constitutional minimum of standing contains three elements. First, the plaintiff must have suffered an "injury in fact"—an invasion of a legally protected interest which is (a) concrete and particularized, and (b) "actual or imminent, not 'conjectural' or 'hypothetical.'" Second, there must be a causal connection between the injury and the conduct complained of—the injury has to be "fairly traceable to the challenged action of the defendant, and not the result of the independent action of some third party not before the court." Third, it must be "likely," as opposed to merely "speculative," that the injury will be "redressed by a favorable decision."

III

We think the Court of Appeals failed to apply the foregoing principles in denying the Secretary's motion for summary judgment. Respondents had not made the requisite demonstration of (at least) injury and redressability.

A

Respondents' claim to injury is that the lack of consultation with respect to certain funded activities abroad "increases the rate of extinction of endangered and threatened species." Of course, the desire to use or observe an animal species, even for purely esthetic purposes, is undeniably a cognizable interest for purpose of standing. "But the 'injury in fact' test requires more than an injury to a cognizable interest. It requires that the party seeking review be himself among the injured." To survive the Secretary's summary judgment motion, respondents had to submit affidavits or other evidence showing, through specific facts, not only that listed species were in fact being threatened by funded activities abroad, but also that one or more of respondents' members would thereby be "directly" affected apart from their "'special interest' in the subject."

Ms. Joyce Kelly stated that she traveled to Egypt in 1986 and "observed the traditional habitat of the endangered Nile crocodile, intends to do so again, and hopes to observe the crocodile directly," and that she "will suffer harm in fact as the result of the American role in overseeing the rehabilitation of the Aswan High Dam on the Nile and in developing Egypt's Master Water Plan." Ms. Amy Skilbred averred that she traveled to Sri Lanka in 1981 and "observed the habitat" of "endangered species such as the Asian elephant and the leopard" at what is now the site of the Mahaweli project funded by the Agency for International Development (AID), although she "was unable to see any of the endangered species"; "this development project," she continued, "will seriously reduce endangered, threatened, and endemic species habitat including areas that I visited, which may severely shorten the future of these species"; that threat, she concluded, harmed her because she "intends to return to Sri Lanka in the future and hopes to be more fortunate in spotting at least the endangered elephant and leopard." When Ms. Skilbred was asked when she had plans to return to Sri Lanka, she reiterated that "I intend to go back to Sri Lanka," but confessed that she had no current plans: "I don't know when. There is a civil war going on right now. I don't know. Not next year, I will say. In the future."

We shall assume for the sake of argument that certain agency-funded projects threaten listed species—though that is questionable. The affidavits plainly contain no facts showing how damage to the species will produce "imminent" injury to Mses. Kelly and Skilbred. That the women "had visited" the areas of the projects before the projects commenced proves nothing." 'Past exposure to illegal conduct does not in itself show a present case or controversy regarding injunctive relief if unaccompanied by any continuing, present adverse effects.'" And the affiants' profession of an "intent" to return to the places they had visited before—where they will presumably, this time, be deprived of the opportunity to observe animals of the endangered species—is simply not enough. Such "some day" intentions—without any description of concrete plans, or indeed even any specification of when the some day will be—do not support a finding of the "actual or imminent" injury that our cases require.

Respondents propose a series of novel standing theories. The first, inelegantly styled "ecosystem nexus," proposes that any person who uses any part of a "contiguous ecosystem" adversely affected by a funded activity has standing even if the activity is located a great distance away. This approach is inconsistent with our opinion in *National Wildlife Federation,* which held that a plaintiff claiming injury from environmental damage must use the area affected by the challenged activity and not an area roughly "in the vicinity" of it. It makes no difference that the general-purpose section of the ESA states that the Act was intended in part "to provide a means whereby the ecosystems upon which endangered species and threatened species depend may be conserved," 16 U.S.C. §1531(b). To say that the Act protects ecosystems is not to say that the Act creates (if it were possible) rights of action in persons who have not been injured in fact, that is, persons who use portions of an ecosystem not perceptibly affected by the unlawful action in question.

Respondents' other theories are called the "animal nexus" approach, whereby anyone who has an interest in studying or seeing the endangered animals anywhere on the globe has standing; and the "vocational nexus" approach, under which anyone with a professional interest in such animals can sue. Under these theories, anyone who goes to see Asian elephants, and anyone who is a keeper of Asian elephants, has standing to sue because the Director of the Agency for International Development (AID) did not consult with the Secretary regarding the AID-funded project in Sri Lanka. This is beyond reason. Standing is not "an ingenious academic exercise in the conceivable," but, at the summary judgment stage, a factual showing of perceptible harm. The person who observes or works with a particular animal threatened by a federal decision is facing perceptible harm, since the very subject of his interest will no longer exist. It is even plausible—though it goes to the outermost limit—to think that a person who observes or works with animals of a particular species in the very area of the world where that species is threatened by a federal decision is facing such harm, since some animals that might have been the subject of his interest will no longer exist. It goes beyond the limit, however, and into pure speculation and fantasy, to say that anyone who observes or works with an endangered species, anywhere in the world, is appreciably harmed by a single project affecting some portion of that species with which he has no more specific connection.

B

Besides failing to show injury, respondents failed to demonstrate redressability. Instead of attacking the separate decisions to fund particular projects allegedly causing them harm, respondents chose to challenge a more generalized level of Government action (rules regarding consultation), the invalidation of which would affect all overseas projects. This programmatic approach has obvious practical advantages, but also obvious difficulties insofar as proof of causation or redressability is concerned. As we have said in another context, "suits challenging, not specifically identifiable Government violations of law, but the particular programs agencies establish to carry out their legal obligations are, even when premised on allegations of several instances of violations of law, rarely if ever appropriate for federal-court adjudication." *Allen,* 468 U.S. at 759-760.

The most obvious problem in the present case is redressability. Since the agencies funding the projects were not parties to the case, the District Court could accord relief only against the Secretary: He could be ordered to revise his regulation to require consultation for foreign projects. But this would not remedy respondents' alleged injury unless the funding agencies were bound by the Secretary's regulation, which is very much an open question. When the Secretary promulgated the regulation at issue here, he thought it was binding on the agencies. The Solicitor General, however, repudiated that position and the agencies themselves apparently deny the Secretary's authority.

A further impediment to redressability is the fact that the agencies supply only a fraction of the funding for a foreign project. AID, for example, has provided less than 10% of the funding for the Mahaweli project. Respondents have produced nothing to indicate that the projects they have named will either be suspended, or do less harm to listed species, if that fraction is eliminated. It is entirely conjectural whether the nonagency activity that affects respondents will be altered or affected by the agency activity they seek to achieve. There is no standing.

Respondents lack standing to bring this action and the Court of Appeals erred in denying the summary judgment motion filed by the United States. The opinion of the Court of Appeals is hereby reversed, and the cause is remanded for proceedings consistent with this opinion.

It is so ordered.

Justice KENNEDY, with whom Justice SOUTER joins, *concurring in part* and *concurring in the judgment.*

As Government programs and policies become more complex and far-reaching, we must be sensitive to the articulation of new rights of action that do not have clear analogs in our common-law tradition. Modern litigation has progressed far from the paradigm of Marbury suing Madison to get his commission, or Ogden seeking an injunction to halt Gibbons' steamboat operations. Congress has the power to define injuries and articulate chains of causation that will give rise to a case or controversy where none existed before. In exercising this power, however, Congress must at the very least identify the injury it seeks to vindicate and relate the injury to the class of persons entitled to bring suit. The citizen-suit provision of the Endangered Species Act does not meet these minimal requirements, because while the statute purports to confer a right on "any person to enjoin the United States and any other governmental instrumentality or agency who is alleged to be in violation of any provision of this chapter," it does not of its own force establish that there is an injury in "any person" by virtue of any "violation." 16 U.S.C. §1540(g)(1)(A).

Notes and Questions: Causation

1. *Environmental Organization Standing.* In *Sierra Club v. Morton*, 405 U.S. 727 (1972), the Sierra Club challenged the U.S. Forest Service's decision to build a 20-mile road in the Sierra Nevada Mountains in California. The area was "quasi-wilderness" with "great natural beauty," but its "relative inaccessibility and lack of development" limited the number of tourists who could visit. In order to increase usage, USFS authorized the construction of a resort and an access road. The Sierra Club, which wanted to maintain the area unchanged, sought a declaratory judgment that various aspects of the proposed development contravened federal laws and regulations. The Sierra Club tried to claim standing based on its status as an organization with "a special interest in the conservation and maintenance of the national parks, game refuges and forests of the country." The Court held that the Sierra Club lacked standing:

> The complaint alleged that the development 'would destroy or adversely affect the scenery, natural and historic objects and wildlife of the park and would impair the enjoyment of the park for future generations.' This type of harm may amount to an 'injury in fact' sufficient to lay the basis for standing under §10 of the APA. Aesthetic and environmental well-being, like economic well-being, are important ingredients of the quality of life in our society, and the fact that environmental interests are shared by the many does not make them less deserving of legal protection. But the 'injury in fact' test requires more than an injury to a cognizable interest. It requires that the party seeking review be himself injured. The impact of the proposed road will not fall indiscriminately upon every citizen. The alleged injury will be felt directly only by those who use the park, and for whom the aesthetic and recreational values of the area will be lessened by the highway and ski resort. The Sierra Club failed to allege that it or its members would be affected in any of their activities or pastimes by the development. If any group with a bona fide 'special interest' could initiate litigation, it is difficult to perceive why any individual citizen with the same bona fide special interest would not also be entitled to do so." In order to establish standing, the Sierra Club would be required to demonstrate that one of its members would actually be injured by the development.

Justice Blackmun dissented: "I would hold that an organization such as the Sierra Club, possessed, as it is, of pertinent, bona fide, and well-recognized attributes and purposes in the area of environment, to litigate environmental issues. This incursion need only recognize the interest of one who has a provable, sincere, dedicated, and established status. We need not fear that there will be no limit to the number of those who desire to participate in environmental litigation. The courts will exercise appropriate restraints."

2. *SCRAP and Article III's Standing Requirements.* An older decision, *United States v. SCRAP*, 412 U.S. 669 (1973), took a much more expansive view of causation and redressability. That case involved a challenge to the Interstate Commerce Commission's failure to suspend a surcharge of 2.5% that various railroads had imposed on freight shipments because of increasing costs and inadequate resources. The suit was brought by certain environmental groups, including Students Challenging Regulatory Agency Procedures (SCRAP), an

unincorporated group of five law students, and the Environmental Defense Fund (EDF), to challenge the ICC's failure to suspend the surcharge, claiming that the rate increase would lead to less recycling, as well as more litter, and therefore would cause "economic, recreational and aesthetic harm." The Court held that the plaintiffs could establish standing:

> All persons who utilize the scenic resources of the country, and all who breathe its air, could claim harm similar to that alleged by the environmental groups here. But standing is not to be denied simply because many people suffer the same injury. The injury alleged here is different from that at issue in *Sierra Club*. Petitioner there complained about the construction of a specific project that would directly affect the Mineral King Valley. Here, the Court was asked to follow a far more attenuated line of causation to the eventual injury—a general rate increase would allegedly cause increased use of nonrecyclable commodities as compared to recyclable goods, thus resulting in the need to use more natural resources to produce such goods, some of which resources might be taken from the Washington area, and resulting in more refuse that might be discarded in national parks in the Washington area. The railroads protest that the appellees could never prove that a general increase in rates would have this effect. Of course, pleadings must be something more than an ingenious academic exercise in the conceivable. Plaintiff must allege that he has been or will in fact be perceptibly harmed by the challenged agency action, not that he can imagine circumstances in which he could be affected by the agency's action. And the allegations must be true and capable of proof at trial. But we deal here simply with pleadings in which appellees alleged a specific and perceptible harm that distinguished them from other citizens who had not used the natural resources that were claimed to be affected; their allegations, if proved, would place them squarely among those persons injured in fact by the Commission's action, and entitled under the clear import of Sierra Club to seek review.

Justice Douglas agreed: "Where a river is polluted and a person is dependent on it for drinking water, there would not be the slightest doubt that he would have standing to present his claim. When smog settles on a city, any person who must breathe that air or feel the sulphuric acid forming in his eyes, would have standing. It is equally obvious that any resident of an area whose paths are strewn with litter, whose parks, or picnic grounds are defaced by it has standing to tender his complaint to the court." Justice White, joined by two other justices, dissented in part: "The majority acknowledges that these allegations reflect an 'attenuated line of causation,' but is willing to suspend judgment in the dim hope that proof at trial will flesh them out and establish the necessary nexus between appellees and the rate increase. The alleged injuries are so remote, speculative, and insubstantial that they fail to confer standing. They become no more concrete, real, or substantial when it is added that materials will cost more at the marketplace and that somehow the freight rate increase will increase air pollution."

4. *Tax-Exempt Discriminatory Schools.* In *Allen v. Wright*, 468 U.S. 737 (1984), the parents of African American children sought to compel the IRS to deny tax-exempt status to racially discriminatory private schools. Plaintiffs claimed

that the "deductions facilitated the raising of funds to organize new schools and expand existing schools in order to accommodate white students avoiding attendance in desegregating public school districts," thereby interfering with the ability of plaintiffs' children to be educated in desegregated public schools. The Court concluded that plaintiffs' "children's diminished ability to receive an education in a racially integrated school" was "not only judicially cognizable but one of the most serious injuries recognized in our legal system." However, the Court found that the injury alleged was not traceable to the Government conduct that was being challenged as unlawful: the IRS's grant of tax exemptions to racially discriminatory schools: "It is uncertain how many racially discriminatory private schools are receiving tax exemptions. Moreover, it is entirely speculative whether withdrawal of a tax exemption from any particular school would lead the school to change its policies. It is just as speculative whether a parent of a child attending such a private school would transfer the child to public school if the private school was threatened with loss of tax-exempt status. It is also pure speculation whether, in a particular community, a large enough number of the relevant school officials and parents would reach decisions that collectively would have a significant impact on the racial composition of the public schools. The links in the chain of causation are far too weak for the chain as a whole to sustain respondents' standing." Justice Brennan dissented: "Elimination of tax-exempt status for racially discriminatory private schools would lessen the impact that those institutions have in defeating efforts to desegregate the public schools." Justice Stevens, joined by Justice Blackmun, also dissented: "Without tax-exempt status, private schools will either not be competitive in terms of cost, or have to change their admissions policies, reducing their competitiveness for parents seeking 'a racially segregated alternative' to public schools. Considerations of tax policy, economics, and pure logic all confirm the conclusion that respondents' injury in fact is fairly traceable to the Government's allegedly wrongful conduct."

5. *Gender Discrimination.* In *Heckler v. Mathews*, 465 U.S. 728 (1984), a male challenged the Social Security Act because it contained a gender-based classification that discriminated against him. However, the law contained a severability provision that would have prevented the plaintiff from obtaining additional benefits even if he prevailed in the lawsuit. The most that he could have hoped for was to prevent women from obtaining a discriminatorily high level of benefits. The Court held that the plaintiff had standing to challenge the discrimination:

> Appellee claims a type of personal injury we have recognized as judicially cognizable. He alleges that the pension offset exception subjects him to unequal treatment in the provision of his Social Security benefits solely because of his gender; specifically, as a nondependent man, he receives fewer benefits than he would if he were a similarly situated woman. Although the severability clause would prevent a court from increasing the benefits payable

to appellee, a court may either declare the statute a nullity and order that its benefits not extend to the class that the legislature intended to benefit, or it may extend the coverage of the statute to include those who are aggrieved by the exclusion. The injury caused by the unequal treatment may 'be redressed by a favorable decision,' and he therefore has standing to prosecute this action.

6. *Standing to Challenge Police Misconduct.* In *City of Los Angeles v. Lyons,* 461 U.S. 95 (1983), plaintiffs brought a civil rights action that sought preliminary and permanent injunctive relief barring the police from using chokeholds. Plaintiffs, who alleged that the city routinely encouraged its police to use chokeholds and that numerous individuals had been injured or killed by this practice, sought a court order prohibiting the practice "except in situations where the victim reasonably appears to be threatening the immediate use of deadly force." The Court held that plaintiffs lacked standing to sue:

> That Lyons may have been illegally choked by the police, while presumably affording Lyons standing to claim damages against the individual officers and perhaps against the City, does nothing to establish a real and immediate threat that he would again be stopped for a traffic violation, or for any other offense, by an officer or officers who would illegally choke him into unconsciousness without any provocation or resistance on his part. The allegation that the police in Los Angeles routinely apply chokeholds in situations where they are not threatened by the use of deadly force falls far short of the allegations necessary to establish a case or controversy. Lyons would have to credibly allege that he faced a realistic threat from the future application of the City's policy. Absent a sufficient likelihood that he will again be wronged in a similar way, Lyons is no more entitled to an injunction than any other citizen of Los Angeles; and a federal court may not entertain a claim by any or all citizens who no more than assert that certain practices of law enforcement officers are unconstitutional." Justice Marshall dissented: "Chokeholds pose a high and unpredictable risk of serious injury or death. Because Lyons has a claim for damages against the City, and because he cannot prevail on that claim unless he demonstrates that the City's chokehold policy violates the Constitution, his personal stake in the outcome of the controversy adequately assures an adversary presentation of his challenge to the constitutionality of the policy. Moreover, resolution of this challenge will be largely dispositive of his requests for declaratory and injunctive relief. No doubt the requests raise additional questions. But these questions involve familiar issues relating to the appropriateness of particular forms of relief, and have never been thought to implicate a litigant's standing to sue.

Food for Thought

SCRAP *Reconsidered.* In the *SCRAP* decision, *supra,* the Court held that plaintiffs had standing. However, *SCRAP* was decided in the 1970s. In light of more recent decisions, in particular *Wright* and *Lyons,* both decided in the 1980s, is *SCRAP* still good law? If *SCRAP* arose today, and you were asked to argue that it is no longer good law, what would you argue? How might the other side respond?

∼ PROBLEMS: CAUSATION ∼

1. *Causation and the Historic Preservation Act.* Consider the HPA, described in the problem at the beginning of the chapter. If the trial court concludes that any of the plaintiffs have standing, is it likely to conclude that causation exists? In other words, if the plaintiffs prevail, is the injury "redressable"? Why or why not?

2. *Racial Steering.* Plaintiffs allege that defendants are engaged in "racial steering" at two apartment complexes in violation of Section 804 of the Fair Housing Act of 1968. The complaint identified Coles as a Black "renter plaintiff" who attempted to rent an apartment from Havens and was falsely told that no apartments were available. The other two individual plaintiffs, Coleman and Willis, were "tester plaintiffs," who were employed by an independent organization to determine whether Havens practiced racial steering. Coleman (who is Black) was told more than once that no apartments were available, whereas Willis (who is white) was told that there were vacancies. The three plaintiffs, who at the time the complaint was filed were all residents of the City of Richmond or the adjacent county, averred that they were injured by the discriminatory acts. Coles, the Black renter, claimed that he had been "denied the right to rent real property." He and the two tester plaintiffs alleged that Havens's practices deprived them of the "important social, professional, business and economic, political and aesthetic benefits of interracial associations that arise from living in integrated communities free from discriminatory housing practices." Coleman, the Black tester, alleged that the misinformation given her by Havens had caused her "specific injury." Do both Coleman and Willis have standing to serve as plaintiffs if they have no intention of moving into the apartment complex but were acting solely as testers? Does it matter that no misrepresentations were made to Willis? Would it matter that, in passing the Fair Housing Act, Congress "intended standing under §812 to extend to the full limits of Art. III" and stated that courts should not apply prudential barriers in deciding standing questions under that section? *See Havens Realty Corp. v. Coleman*, 455 U.S. 363 (1982).

Massachusetts v. Environmental Protection Agency

549 U.S. 497 (2007)

Justice STEVENS delivered the opinion of the Court.

Nineteen private organizations filed a rulemaking petition asking EPA to regulate "greenhouse gas emissions from new motor vehicles under §202 of the Clean Air Act." Petitioners maintained that 1998 was the "warmest year on record"; that carbon dioxide, methane, nitrous oxide, and hydrofluorocarbons are "heat trapping greenhouse gases"; that greenhouse gas emissions have significantly accelerated climate change; and that a 1995 report warned that "carbon dioxide remains the most important contributor to man-made forcing of climate change." The petition further alleged that climate change will have serious adverse effects on human health and the environment. As to EPA's statutory authority, the petition observed that the agency itself had already confirmed that it had the power to regulate carbon dioxide.

Fifteen months after the petition's submission, EPA requested public comment on "all the issues raised in the petition," adding a "particular" request for comments on "any scientific, technical, legal, economic or other aspect of these issues that may be relevant to EPA's consideration of this petition." 66 Fed. Reg. 7486, 7487 (2001). Before the close of the comment period, the White House sought "assistance in identifying the areas in the science of climate change where there are the greatest certainties and uncertainties" from the National Research Council, asking for a response "as soon as possible." The result was a 2001 report titled Climate Change Science: An Analysis of Some Key Questions (NRC Report), which, drawing heavily on an earlier report, concluded that "greenhouse gases are accumulating in Earth's atmosphere as a result of human activities, causing surface air temperatures and subsurface ocean temperatures to rise. Temperatures are, in fact, rising."

EPA entered an order denying the rulemaking petition. The agency gave two reasons for its decision: (1) the Clean Air Act does not authorize EPA to issue mandatory regulations to address global climate change; and (2) even if the agency had the authority to set greenhouse gas emission standards, it would be unwise to do so at this time. The agency began by recognizing that the concentration of greenhouse gases has dramatically increased as a result of human activities, and acknowledged the increase in global surface air temperatures. EPA nevertheless gave controlling importance to the NRC Report's statement that a causal link between the two "cannot be unequivocally established." Given that uncertainty, EPA concluded that regulating greenhouse gas emissions would be unwise. The agency furthermore characterized any EPA regulation of motor-vehicle emissions as a "piecemeal approach" to climate change, and stated that such regulation would conflict with the President's "comprehensive approach" to the problem. According to EPA, unilateral EPA regulation of motor-vehicle greenhouse gas emissions might also hamper the President's ability to persuade key developing countries to reduce greenhouse gas emissions. Petitioners, joined by intervenor States and local governments, sought review of EPA's order in the United States Court of Appeals for the District of Columbia Circuit. Two judges agreed "that the EPA Administrator properly exercised his discretion."

Article III of the Constitution limits federal-court jurisdiction to "Cases" and "Controversies." Those two words confine "the business of federal courts to questions presented in an adversary context and in a form historically viewed as capable of resolution through the judicial process." Flast v. Cohen, 392 U.S. 83 (1968). No justiciable "controversy" exists when parties seek adjudication of a political question, when they ask for an advisory opinion, or when the question sought to be adjudicated has been mooted by subsequent developments. This case suffers from none of these defects.

"The gist of standing" is whether petitioners have "such a personal stake in the outcome of the controversy as to assure that concrete adverseness which sharpens the presentation of issues upon which the court so largely depends for illumination." *Baker v. Carr*, 369 U.S. 186, 204 (1962). To ensure the proper adversarial presentation, *Lujan* holds that a litigant must demonstrate that it has suffered a concrete and particularized injury that is either actual or imminent, that the injury is fairly traceable to the defendant, and that it is likely that a favorable decision will redress that injury. Only one of the petitioners needs to have standing to permit us to consider the petition for review. It is of considerable relevance that the party seeking review here is a sovereign State and not, as it was in *Lujan,* a private individual. States are not normal litigants for the purposes of invoking federal jurisdiction. As Justice Holmes explained in *Georgia v. Tennessee Copper Co.*, 206 U.S. 230, 237 (1907), a case in which Georgia sought to protect its citizens from air pollution originating outside its borders: "The State owns very little of the territory alleged to be affected, and the damage to it capable of estimate in money, possibly, at least, is small. This is a suit by a State for an injury to it in its capacity of *quasi*-sovereign. In that capacity the State has an interest independent of and behind the titles of its citizens, in all the earth and air within its domain. It has the last word as to whether its mountains shall be stripped of their forests and its inhabitants shall breathe pure air." That Massachusetts does in fact own a great deal of the "territory alleged to be affected" only reinforces the conclusion that its stake in the outcome of this case is sufficiently concrete to warrant the exercise of federal judicial power.

When a State enters the Union, it surrenders certain sovereign prerogatives. Massachusetts cannot invade Rhode Island to force reductions in greenhouse gas emissions, it cannot negotiate an emissions treaty with China or India, and in some circumstances the exercise of its police powers to reduce in-state motor-vehicle emissions might well be pre-empted. These sovereign prerogatives are now lodged in the Federal Government, and Congress has ordered EPA to protect Massachusetts (among others) by prescribing standards applicable to the "emission of any air pollutant from any class or classes of new motor vehicle engines, which in the Administrator's judgment cause, or contribute to, air pollution which may reasonably be anticipated to endanger public health or welfare." 42 U.S.C. §7521(a)(1). Congress has moreover recognized a concomitant procedural right to challenge the rejection of its rulemaking petition as arbitrary and capricious. Given that procedural right and Massachusetts' stake in protecting its quasi-sovereign interests, the Commonwealth is entitled to special solicitude in our standing analysis.

We held in *Georgia v. Pennsylvania R. Co.*, 324 U.S. 439, 447 (1945), that there is a critical difference between allowing a State "to protect her citizens from the operation of federal statutes" (which *Mellon* prohibits) and allowing a State to assert its rights under federal law (which it has standing to do). Massachusetts does not dispute that the Clean Air Act *applies* to its citizens; it rather seeks to assert its rights under the Act. EPA's steadfast refusal to regulate greenhouse gas emissions presents a risk of harm to Massachusetts that is both "actual" and "imminent." There is a "substantial likelihood that the judicial relief requested" will prompt EPA to take steps to reduce that risk. *Duke Power Co. v. Carolina Environmental Study Group, Inc.*, 438 U.S. 59 (1978).

The Injury. The harms associated with climate change are serious and well recognized. The NRC Report itself—which EPA regards as an "objective and independent assessment of the relevant science," identifies a number of environmental changes that have already inflicted significant harms, including "the global retreat of mountain glaciers, reduction in snow-cover extent, the earlier spring melting of ice on rivers and lakes, and the accelerated rate of rise of sea levels during the 20th century relative to the past few thousand years." NRC Report 16. Petitioners allege that this only hints at the environmental damage yet to come. According to climate scientist Michael MacCracken, "qualified scientific experts involved in climate change research" have reached a "strong consensus" that global warming threatens (among other things) a precipitate rise in sea levels by the end of the century, MacCracken Decl. ¶15, Stdg. App. 207, "severe and irreversible changes to natural ecosystems," a "significant reduction in water storage in winter snowpack in mountainous regions with direct and important economic consequences," and an increase in the spread of disease. He also observes that rising ocean temperatures may contribute to the ferocity of hurricanes.

That these climate-change risks are "widely shared" does not minimize Massachusetts' interest in the outcome of this litigation. According to petitioners' unchallenged affidavits, global sea levels rose somewhere between 10 and 20 centimeters over the 20th century as a result of global warming. These rising seas have already begun to swallow Massachusetts' coastal land. Because the Commonwealth "owns a substantial portion of the state's coastal property," it has alleged a particularized injury in its capacity as a landowner. If sea levels continue to rise as predicted, one Massachusetts official believes that a significant fraction of coastal property will be "either permanently lost through inundation or temporarily lost through periodic storm surge and flooding events." Remediation costs alone, petitioners allege, could run well into the hundreds of millions of dollars.

Causation. EPA does not dispute the existence of a causal connection between man-made greenhouse gas emissions and global warming. At a minimum, EPA's refusal to regulate such emissions "contributes" to Massachusetts' injuries. EPA nevertheless maintains that its decision not to regulate greenhouse gas emissions from new motor vehicles contributes so insignificantly to petitioners' injuries that the agency cannot be hauled into federal court. For the same reason, EPA does not believe that any realistic possibility exists that the relief petitioners seek would mitigate global climate change and remedy their injuries. That is especially so because predicted increases in greenhouse gas emissions from developing nations, particularly China and India, are likely to offset any marginal domestic decrease. But EPA overstates its case. Its argument rests on the erroneous assumption that a small incremental step, because it is incremental, can never be attacked in a federal judicial forum. Accepting that premise would doom most challenges to regulatory action. Agencies, like legislatures, do not generally resolve massive problems in one fell regulatory swoop. They instead whittle away at them over time, refining their preferred approach as circumstances change and as they develop a more-nuanced understanding of how best to proceed. That a first step might be tentative does not itself support the notion that federal courts lack jurisdiction to determine whether that step conforms to law.

Reducing domestic automobile emissions is hardly a tentative step. Even leaving aside other greenhouse gases, the United States transportation sector emits an enormous quantity of carbon dioxide into the atmosphere—more than 1.7 billion metric tons in 1999 alone. That accounts for more than 6% of worldwide carbon dioxide emissions. Considering just emissions from the transportation sector, which represent less than one-third of this country's total carbon dioxide emissions, the United States would still rank as the third-largest emitter of carbon dioxide in the world. Judged by any standard, U.S. motor-vehicle emissions make a meaningful contribution to greenhouse gas concentrations and hence, according to petitioners, to global warming.

The Remedy. While regulating motor-vehicle emissions will not by itself *reverse* global warming, it by no means follows that we lack jurisdiction to decide whether EPA has a duty to take steps to *slow* or *reduce* it. Because of the enormity of the potential consequences associated with man-made climate change, the fact that the effectiveness of a remedy might be delayed during the (relatively short) time it takes for a new motor-vehicle fleet to replace an older one is essentially irrelevant. Nor is it dispositive that developing countries such as China and India are poised to increase greenhouse gas emissions substantially over the next century: A reduction in domestic emissions would slow the pace of global emissions increases, no matter what happens elsewhere.

We attach considerable significance to EPA's "agreement with the President that 'we must address the issue of global climate change,'" and to EPA's ardent support for various voluntary emission-reduction programs. As Judge Tatel observed in dissent below, "EPA would presumably not bother with such efforts if it thought emissions reductions would have no discernable impact on global warming." In sum, the rise in sea levels associated with global warming has already harmed and will continue to harm Massachusetts. The risk of catastrophic harm, though remote, is nevertheless real. That risk would be reduced to some extent if petitioners received the relief they seek. We hold that petitioners have standing to challenge the EPA's denial of their rulemaking petition.

The judgment of the Court of Appeals is reversed, and the case is remanded for further proceedings consistent with this opinion.

It is so ordered.

Chief Justice ROBERTS, with whom Justice SCALIA, Justice THOMAS, and Justice ALITO join, *dissenting.*

The status of Massachusetts as a State cannot compensate for petitioners' failure to demonstrate injury in fact, causation, and redressability. The Court focuses on the Commonwealth's asserted loss of coastal land as the injury in fact. If petitioners' particularized injury is loss of coastal land, it is also that injury that must be "actual or imminent, not conjectural or hypothetical," "real and immediate," and "certainly impending," One of petitioners' declarants predicts global warming will cause sea level to rise by 20 to 70 centimeters *by the year 2100.* Accepting a century-long time horizon and a series of compounded estimates renders requirements of imminence and immediacy utterly toothless. "Allegations of possible future injury do not satisfy the requirements of Art. III. A threatened injury must be *certainly impending* to constitute injury in fact."

Petitioners' reliance on Massachusetts's loss of coastal land as their injury in fact for standing purposes creates insurmountable problems for them with respect to causation and redressability. Because local greenhouse gas emissions disperse throughout the atmosphere and remain there for anywhere from 50 to 200 years, it is global emissions data that are relevant. Domestic motor vehicles contribute about 6 percent of global carbon dioxide emissions and 4 percent of global greenhouse gas emissions. The amount of global emissions at issue here is smaller still; the Clean Air Act covers only *new* motor vehicles and *new* motor vehicle engines, so petitioners' desired emission standards might reduce only a fraction of 4 percent of global emissions. As EPA explained in its denial of petitioners' request for rulemaking, "predicting future climate change necessarily involves a complex web of economic and physical factors including: our ability to predict future global anthropogenic emissions of greenhouse gases and aerosols; the fate of these emissions once they enter the atmosphere (e.g., what percentage are absorbed by vegetation or are taken up by the oceans); the impact of those emissions that remain in the atmosphere on the radiative properties of the atmosphere; changes in critically important climate feedbacks (e.g., changes in cloud cover and ocean circulation); changes in temperature characteristics (e.g., average temperatures, shifts in daytime and evening temperatures); changes in other climatic parameters (e.g., shifts in precipitation, storms); and ultimately the impact of such changes on human health and welfare (e.g., increases or decreases in agricultural productivity, human health impacts)."

Petitioners are never able to trace their alleged injuries back through this complex web to the fractional amount of global emissions that might have been limited with EPA standards. Redressability is even more problematic. To the tenuous link between petitioners' alleged injury and the indeterminate fractional domestic emissions at issue here, add the fact that petitioners cannot meaningfully predict what will come of the 80 percent of global greenhouse gas emissions that originate outside the United States. As the Court acknowledges, "developing countries such as China and India are poised to increase greenhouse gas emissions substantially over the next century," so the domestic emissions at issue here may become an increasingly marginal portion of global emissions, and any decreases produced by petitioners' desired standards are likely to be overwhelmed many times over by emissions increases elsewhere in the world. When the existence of an element of standing "depends on the unfettered choices made by independent actors not before the courts and whose exercise of broad and legitimate discretion the courts cannot presume either to control or to predict," a party must present facts supporting an assertion that the actor will proceed in such a manner. *Defenders of Wildlife*, 504 U.S. at 562 (quoting ASARCO Inc. v. Kadish, 490 U.S. 605, 615 (1989) (opinion of Kennedy, J.).

Limitation of the judicial power to cases and controversies "is crucial in maintaining the tripartite allocation of power set forth in the Constitution." *DaimlerChrysler*, 547 U.S. at 341. The Court today—addressing Article III's "core component of standing," fails to take this limitation seriously. Today's decision recalls the previous high-water mark of diluted standing requirements, *SCRAP* involved "probably the most attenuated injury conferring Art. III standing" and "surely went to the very outer limit of the law." *SCRAP* made standing seem a lawyer's game, rather than a fundamental limitation ensuring that courts function as courts and not intrude on the politically accountable branches. Today's decision is *SCRAP* for a new generation.

Justice SCALIA, with whom THE CHIEF JUSTICE, Justice THOMAS, and Justice ALITO join, *dissenting.*

This Court has no jurisdiction to decide this case because petitioners lack standing.

Food for Thought

Can the potential plaintiffs challenging the Historic Preservation Act satisfy the causation and redressability requirements?

c. Congressionally Authorized Standing

Can Congress authorize plaintiffs to bring suit when standing would not otherwise exist? As previously noted, there is a constitutional aspect to the standing doctrine as well as a prudential aspect. The constitutional aspect stems from Article III's case and controversy requirement and cannot be waived by Congress. The prudential aspect is a limitation imposed by the Court on itself. In some instances, even when a case or controversy exists, the Court refuses to hear a case in deference to a coordinate branch of government. If Congress has invited the Court to hear a particular type of case, do prudential restraints diminish or disappear?

In *Association of Data Processing Service Organizations, Inc. v. Camp*, 397 U.S. 150 (1970), the Court examined congressional authorization in the context of a suit brought by sellers of data-processing services who challenged a ruling by the comptroller of the currency. Under the ruling, national banks were allowed to provide data-processing services to banks and to bank customers. Petitioners alleged that they would lose profits to national banks, and that at least one national bank was performing or preparing to perform such services. The suit was brought not only against the bank, but also against the comptroller of the currency, who was alleged to have caused petitioners injury in fact by his ruling. In holding that plaintiffs had standing, the Court articulated a two-part test for establishing standing to sue under congressional enactments:

> The first question is whether the plaintiff alleges that the challenged action has caused him injury in fact, economic or otherwise. There can be no doubt that petitioners have satisfied this test. Petitioners allege that competition by national banks in the business of providing data processing services might entail future loss of profits for the petitioners, and that respondents had previously agreed or negotiated to perform such services. The "legal interest" test goes to the merits. The question of standing is different. It concerns, apart from the "case" or "controversy" test, the question whether the interest sought to be protected by the complainant is arguably within the zone of interests to be protected or regulated by the statute or constitutional guarantee in question. Thus the Administrative Procedure Act grants standing to a person "aggrieved by agency action within the meaning of a relevant statute." 5 U.S.C. §702 (1964 ed., Supp. IV). That interest, at times, may reflect "aesthetic, conservational, and recreational" as well as economic values. We mention these noneconomic values to emphasize that standing may stem from them as well as from the economic injury in which petitioners rely here.

Lujan v. Defenders of Wildlife

504 U.S. 555 (1992)

The facts and other parts of the Court's opinion are set forth *on page 80.*

IV

The Court of Appeals found that respondents had standing because they had suffered a "procedural injury." The so-called "citizen-suit" provision of the ESA provides, in pertinent part, that "any person may commence a civil suit on his own behalf (A) to enjoin any person, including the United States and any other governmental instrumentality or agency who is alleged to be in violation of any provision of this chapter." The court held that, because §7(a)(2) requires interagency consultation, the citizen-suit provision creates a "procedural right" to consultation in all "persons"—so that anyone can file suit in federal court to challenge the Secretary's (or presumably any other official's) failure to follow the assertedly correct consultative procedure, notwithstanding his or her inability to allege any discrete injury flowing from that failure. This is not a case where plaintiffs are seeking to enforce a procedural requirement the disregard of which could impair a separate concrete interest of theirs (e.g., the procedural requirement for a hearing prior to denial of their license application, or the procedural requirement for an environmental impact statement before a federal facility is constructed next door to them). Nor is it a case where concrete injury has been suffered by many persons, as in mass fraud or mass tort situations. Nor, finally, is it the unusual case in which Congress has created a concrete private interest in the outcome of a suit against a private party for the government's benefit, by providing a cash bounty for the victorious plaintiff. Rather, the court held that the injury-in-fact requirement had been satisfied by congressional conferral upon all persons of an abstract, self-contained, noninstrumental "right" to have the Executive observe the procedures required by law. We reject this view.

A plaintiff raising only a generally available grievance about government — claiming only harm to his and every citizen's interest in proper application of the Constitution and laws, and seeking relief that no more directly and tangibly benefits him than it does the public at large — does not state an Article III case or controversy. *See Schlesinger v. Reservists Comm. to Stop the War*, 418 U.S. 208 (1974). Standing to sue may not be predicated upon an interest of this kind. To be sure, our generalized-grievance cases have typically involved Government violation of procedures assertedly ordained by the Constitution rather than the Congress. But there is absolutely no basis for making the Article III inquiry turn on the source of the asserted right. Whether courts act on their own, or at the invitation of Congress, in ignoring the concrete injury requirement described in our cases, they would be discarding a principle fundamental to the separate and distinct constitutional role of the Third Branch — one of the essential elements that identifies those "Cases" and "Controversies" that are the business of the courts rather than of the political branches. "The province of the court," as Chief Justice Marshall said in Marbury v. Madison, "is, solely, to decide the rights of individuals." Vindicating the public interest (including the public interest in Government observance of the Constitution and laws) is the function of Congress and the Chief Executive. The question presented here is whether the public interest in proper administration of the laws (specifically, in agencies' observance of a particular, statutorily prescribed procedure) can be converted into an individual right by a statute that denominates it as such, and that permits all citizens (or a subclass of citizens who suffer no distinctive concrete harm) to sue. If the concrete injury requirement has separation-of-powers significance, the answer must be obvious: To permit Congress to convert the undifferentiated public interest in executive officers' compliance with the law into an "individual right" vindicable in the courts is to permit Congress to transfer from the President to the courts the Chief Executive's most important constitutional duty, to "take Care that the Laws be faithfully executed," Art. II, §3. It would enable the courts, with the permission of Congress, "to assume a position of authority over the governmental acts of another and co-equal department." We have rejected that vision of our role.

"The injury required by Art. III may exist solely by virtue of 'statutes creating legal rights, the invasion of which creates standing.'" *Warth* (quoting Linda R. S. v. Richard D., 410 U.S. 614 (1973)). As we said in *Sierra Club*, "Statutory broadening of the categories of injury that may be alleged in support of standing is a different matter from abandoning the requirement that the party seeking review must himself have suffered an injury." Whether or not *Warth* can be extended beyond that distinction, it is clear that in suits against the Government, at least, the concrete injury requirement must remain.

Notes: More on Congressional Authorization

1. *Congressional Authorization and Procedural Rights.* In *Massachusetts v. Environmental Protection Agency*, 549 U.S. 497 (2007), in addition to finding causation and redressability, the Court emphasized congressional authorization, noting that "authorization is of critical importance to the standing inquiry:

> "Congress has the power to define injuries and articulate chains of causation that will give rise to a case or controversy where none existed before." *Lujan*, 504 U.S. at 580 (Kennedy, J., concurring). "In exercising this power, Congress must at the very least identify the injury it seeks to vindicate and relate the injury to the class of persons entitled to bring suit." We will not "entertain citizen suits to vindicate the public's nonconcrete interest in the proper administration of the laws." Notwithstanding authorization, the litigant must still "demonstrate that it has suffered a concrete and particularized injury that is actual or imminent, that the injury is fairly traceable to the defendant, and that it is likely that a favorable decision will redress that injury." Nevertheless, "a litigant to whom Congress has 'accorded a procedural right to protect his concrete interests,'—here, the right to challenge agency action unlawfully withheld—'can assert that right without meeting all the normal standards for redressability and immediacy.' When a litigant is vested with a procedural right, that litigant has standing if there is some possibility that the requested relief will prompt the injury-causing party to reconsider the decision that allegedly harmed the litigant."

2. *The Individuals with Disabilities Education Act (IDEA).* Winkelman v. Parma City School District, 550 U.S. 516 (1992), involved whether the IDEA gave an autistic child's parents the right to file suit to enforce a school district's obligations toward their child. The Court examined the IDEA to determine Congress's intent, and concluded that the "parents enjoy enforceable rights at the administrative stage, and it would be inconsistent with the statutory scheme to bar them from continuing to assert these rights in federal court." The Court noted that the "Act does not *sub silentio* or by implication bar parents from seeking to vindicate the rights accorded to them. Through its provisions for expansive review and extensive parental involvement, the statute leads to the opposite result." The Court held that the parents had a sufficient interest to justify a grant of standing: "A parent of a child with a disability has a particular and personal interest in fulfilling 'our national policy of ensuring equality of opportunity, full participation, independent living, and economic self-sufficiency for individuals with disabilities.'" As a result, parents could seek review on a broad range of issues, including "any matter relating to the identification, evaluation, or educational placement of the child, or the provision of a free appropriate public education to such child."

3. *Tax Discrimination.* In *CSX Transportation, Inc. v. Alabama Department of Revenue*, 562 U.S. 277 (2011), the Court construed the Railroad Revitalization and Regulatory Reform Act of 1976. In doing so, the Court held that a railroad

may invoke the statute to challenge sales and use taxes that apply to rail carriers (among others) but exempt their competitors in the transportation industry.

Summers v. Earth Island Institute

555 U.S. 988 (2009)

Justice SCALIA delivered the opinion of the Court.

Respondents are a group of organizations dedicated to protecting the environment collectively "Earth Island". They seek to prevent the United States Forest Service from enforcing regulations that exempt small fire-rehabilitation and timber-salvage projects from the notice, comment, and appeal process used by the Forest Service for more significant land management decisions. We must determine whether respondents have standing to challenge the regulations in the absence of a live dispute over a concrete application of those regulations.

In 1992, Congress enacted the Forest Service Decisionmaking and Appeals Reform Act (Appeals Reform Act or Act), 106 Stat. 1419. This required the Forest Service to establish a notice, comment, and appeal process for "proposed actions of the Forest Service concerning projects and activities implementing land and resource management plans developed under the Forest and Rangeland Renewable Resources Planning Act of 1974." The Forest Service's regulations implementing the Act provided that certain of its procedures would not be applied to projects that the Service considered categorically excluded from the requirement to file an environmental impact statement (EIS) or environmental assessment (EA). Later amendments to the Forest Service's manual of implementing procedures, adopted by rule after notice and comment, provided that fire-rehabilitation activities on areas of less than 4,200 acres, and salvage-timber sales of 250 acres or less, did not cause a significant environmental impact and thus would be categorically exempt from the requirement to file an EIS or EA. 68 Fed. Reg. 33824 (2003). This had the effect of excluding these projects from the notice, comment, and appeal process.

In the summer of 2002, fire burned a significant area of the Sequoia National Forest. In September 2003, the Service issued a decision memo approving the Burnt Ridge Project, a salvage sale of timber on 238 acres damaged by that fire. Pursuant to its categorical exclusion of salvage sales of less than 250 acres, the Forest Service did not provide notice in a form consistent with the Appeals Reform Act, did not provide a period of public comment, and did not make an appeal process available. Respondents filed a complaint challenging the failure of the Forest Service to apply to the Burnt Ridge Project §215.4(a) of its regulations implementing the Appeals Reform Act (requiring prior notice and comment), and §215.12(f) of the regulations (setting forth an appeal procedure). The complaint also challenged six other Forest Service regulations implementing the Act that were not applied to the Burnt Ridge Project. They are irrelevant to this appeal.

The District Court granted a preliminary injunction against the Burnt Ridge salvage-timber sale. Thereafter, the parties settled their dispute. The Government argued that, with the Burnt Ridge dispute settled, and with no other project before the court in which respondents were threatened with injury in fact, respondents lacked standing to challenge the regulations; and that absent a concrete dispute over a particular project a challenge to the regulations would not be ripe. The District Court proceeded, however, to adjudicate the merits of Earth Island's challenges. It invalidated five regulations. The Ninth Circuit held that Earth Island's challenges were not ripe for adjudication. It affirmed, however, the District Court's determination that §§215.4(a) and 215.12(f), which were applicable to the Burnt Ridge Project, were contrary to law, and upheld the nationwide injunction against their application. We granted certiorari.

In limiting the judicial power to "Cases" and "Controversies," Article III of the Constitution restricts it to the traditional role of Anglo-American courts, which is to redress or prevent actual or imminently threatened injury to persons caused by private or official violation of law. Except when necessary in the execution of that function, courts have no charter to review and revise legislative and executive action. *See Lujan v. Defenders of Wildlife,* 504 U.S. 555 (1992). This limitation "is founded in concern about the proper—and properly limited—role of the courts in a democratic society." *Warth v. Seldin,* 422 U.S. 490 (1975). Standing is one of several doctrines that reflect this fundamental limitation. It requires federal courts to satisfy themselves that "the plaintiff has 'alleged such a personal stake in the outcome of the controversy' as to warrant *his* invocation of federal-court jurisdiction." 422 U.S. at 498-499. He bears the burden of showing that he has standing for each type of relief sought. To seek injunctive relief, plaintiff must show that he is under threat of suffering "injury in fact" that is concrete and particularized; the threat must be actual and imminent, not conjectural or hypothetical; it must be fairly traceable to the challenged action of the defendant; and it must be likely that a favorable judicial decision will prevent or redress the injury. *Friends of Earth, Inc. v. Laidlaw Environmental Services (TOC), Inc.,* 528 U.S. 167 (2000). This requirement assures that "there is a real need to exercise the power of judicial review in order to protect the interests of the complaining party," *Schlesinger v. Reservists Comm. to Stop the War,* 418 U.S. 208, 221 (1974). Where that need does not exist, allowing courts to oversee legislative or executive action "would significantly alter the allocation of power away from a democratic form of government." *Richardson, supra,* at 188 (Powell, J., concurring).

The regulations under challenge here neither require nor forbid any action on the part of respondents. The standards and procedures that they prescribe for Forest Service appeals govern only the conduct of Forest Service officials engaged in project planning. "When the plaintiff is not himself the object of the government action or inaction he challenges, standing is not precluded, but it is ordinarily 'substantially more difficult' to establish." *Defenders of Wildlife, supra,* at 562. Respondents can demonstrate standing only if application of the regulations by the Government will affect *them* in the manner described above. Respondent organizations can assert the standing of their members. To establish the concrete and particularized injury that standing requires, respondents point to their members' recreational interests in the National Forests. While generalized harm to the forest or the environment will not alone support standing, if that harm in fact affects the recreational or even the mere esthetic interests of the plaintiff, that will suffice. *Sierra Club v. Morton*, 405 U.S. 727 (1972).

Affidavits alleged that organization member Ara Marderosian had repeatedly visited the Burnt Ridge site, that he had imminent plans to do so again, and that his interests in viewing the flora and fauna of the area would be harmed if the Burnt Ridge Project went forward without incorporation of the ideas he would have suggested if the Forest Service had provided him an opportunity to comment. This was sufficient to establish Article III standing with respect to Burnt Ridge. However, the parties settled their differences. Marderosian's injury in fact has been remedied, and is "not at issue in this case." Respondents have identified no other application of the invalidated regulations that threatens imminent and concrete harm to the interests of their members. The only other affidavit relied on was that of Jim Bensman. He asserted that he had suffered injury in the past from development on Forest Service land. That does not suffice because it was not tied to application of the challenged regulations, does not identify any particular site, and relates to past injury rather than imminent future injury. Bensman's affidavit further asserts that he has visited many National Forests and plans to visit several unnamed National Forests in the future. The affidavit fails to allege that *any* particular timber sale or other project claimed to be unlawfully subject to the regulations will impede a specific and concrete plan of Bensman's to enjoy the National Forests. National Forests occupy more than 190 million acres. There may be a chance, but is hardly a likelihood, that Bensman's wanderings will bring him to a parcel affected by a project unlawfully subject to the regulations. Indeed, without further specification it is impossible to tell *which* projects are (in respondents' view) unlawfully subject to the regulations. We are asked to assume not only that Bensman will stumble across a project tract unlawfully subject to the regulations, but that the tract is about to be developed by the Forest Service in a way that harms his recreational interests, and that he would have commented on the project but for the regulation. Accepting an intention to visit the National Forests as adequate to confer standing to challenge any Government action affecting any portion of those forests would be tantamount to eliminating the requirement of concrete, particularized injury in fact.

The Bensman affidavit does refer specifically to a series of projects in the Allegheny National Forest that are subject to the challenged regulations. It does not assert, however, any firm intention to visit their locations, saying only that Bensman "wants to" go there. This vague desire to return is insufficient to satisfy the requirement of imminent injury: "Such 'some day' intentions—without any description of concrete plans, or indeed any specification of *when* the some day will be—do not support a finding of the 'actual or imminent' injury that our cases require." *Defenders of Wildlife*, 504 U.S. at 564.

Respondents argue that they have standing to bring their challenge because they have suffered procedural injury, namely that they have been denied the ability to file comments on some Forest Service actions and will continue to be so denied. But deprivation of a procedural right without some concrete interest that is affected by the deprivation—a procedural right *in vacuo*—is insufficient to create Article III standing. Only a "person who has been accorded a procedural right to protect *his concrete interests* can assert that right without meeting all the normal standards for redressability and immediacy." Respondents alleged such injury in their challenge to the Burnt Ridge Project, claiming that but for the allegedly unlawful abridged procedures they would have been able to oppose the project that threatened to impinge on their concrete plans to observe nature in that specific area. But Burnt Ridge is now off the table.

It makes no difference that the procedural right has been accorded by Congress. That can loosen the strictures of the redressability prong of our standing inquiry. Unlike redressability, the requirement of injury in fact is a hard floor of Article III jurisdiction that cannot be removed by statute. "It would exceed Article III's limitations if, at the behest of Congress and in the absence of any showing of concrete injury, we were to entertain citizen suits to vindicate the public's nonconcrete interest in the proper administration of the laws. The party bringing suit must show that the action injures him in a concrete and personal way."

The dissent proposes a hitherto unheard-of test for organizational standing: whether, accepting the organization's description of the activities of its members, there is a statistical probability that some of those members are threatened with concrete injury. Since the Sierra Club asserts that it has more than "700,000 members nationwide, including thousands of members in California" who "use and enjoy the Sequoia National Forest," it is probable (according to the dissent) that some (unidentified) members have planned to visit some (unidentified) small parcels affected by the Forest Service's procedures and will suffer (unidentified) concrete harm as a result. This novel approach to the law of organizational standing would make a mockery of our prior cases, which have required plaintiff-organizations to make specific allegations establishing that at least one identified member had suffered or would suffer harm. The court has an independent obligation to assure that standing exists, regardless of whether it is challenged by the parties. "Standing," we have said, "is not 'an ingenious academic exercise in the conceivable' but requires a factual showing of perceptible harm." Because of the difficulty of verifying the facts upon which such probabilistic standing depends, the Court has required plaintiffs claiming an organizational standing to identify members who have suffered the requisite harm—surely not a difficult task here, when so many thousands are alleged to have been harmed.

The dissent would have us replace the requirement of "imminent" harm, which it acknowledges our cases establish, with the requirement of " 'a *realistic* threat' that reoccurrence of the challenged activity would cause the plaintiff harm in the reasonably near future." The problem for the dissent is that the timely affidavits no more meet that requirement than they meet the usual formulation.

They fail to establish that the affiants' members will *ever* visit one of the small parcels at issue.

The judgment of the Court of Appeals is reversed in part and affirmed in part.

It is so ordered.

Justice KENNEDY, *concurring.*

This case would present different considerations if Congress had sought to provide redress for a concrete injury "giving rise to a case or controversy where none existed before." Nothing in the statute at issue here, however, indicates Congress intended to identify or confer some interest separate and apart from a procedural right.

Justice BREYER, with whom Justice STEVENS, Justice SOUTER, and Justice GINSBURG join, *dissenting.*

Imagine that Congress enacted a *statutory* provision that expressly permitted environmental groups like respondents to bring cases like the present one, provided that the group has members who have used salvage-timber parcels in the past and are likely to do so in the future, and that the group's members have opposed Forest Service timber sales in the past (using notice, comment, and appeal procedures to do so) and will likely use those procedures to oppose salvage-timber sales in the future. The majority cannot, and does not, claim that such a statute would be unconstitutional. How then can it find the present case constitutionally unauthorized?

How can the majority credibly claim that salvage-timber sales, and similar projects, are unlikely to harm the asserted interests of the members of these environmental groups? Where the Court has directly focused upon the matter, *i.e.,* a plaintiff has *already* been subject to the injury it wishes to challenge, the Court has asked whether there is a *realistic likelihood* that the challenged future conduct will, in fact, recur and harm the plaintiff. Would courts deny *standing* to a landowner who complains that a neighbor's upstream dam constitutes a nuisance — even if the harm to his downstream property (while bound to occur) will not occur for several years? A threat of future harm may be realistic even where the plaintiff cannot specify precise times, dates, and GPS coordinates. Thus, we recently held that Massachusetts has *standing* to complain of a procedural failing, namely, EPA's failure properly to determine whether to restrict carbon dioxide emissions, even though that failing would create Massachusetts-based harm which (though likely to occur) might not occur for several decades.

The Forest Service admits that it intends to conduct thousands of further salvage-timber sales and other projects exempted under the challenged regulations "in the reasonably near future." How then can the Court deny that the plaintiffs have shown a "realistic" threat that the Forest Service will continue to authorize (without the procedures claimed necessary) salvage-timber sales, and other Forest Service projects, that adversely affect the recreational, aesthetic, and environmental interests of the plaintiffs' members? Respondents allege, and the Government has conceded, that the Forest Service took wrongful actions (such as selling salvage timber) "thousands" of times in the two years prior to suit. The organizations, the Sierra Club for example, have hundreds of thousands of members who use forests regularly across the Nation for recreational, scientific, aesthetic, and environmental purposes. These organizations (and their members), believing that actions such as salvage-timber sales harm those interests, regularly oppose salvage-timber sales (and similar actions) in proceedings before the agency. The organizations intend to continue to express their opposition to such actions in those proceedings in the future. With respect, I dissent.

Notes: More on Congressional Authorization

1. *Standing and Federal Election Laws.* In *Federal Election Commission v. Akins,* 524 U.S. 11 (1998), respondents challenged the Federal Election Commission's (FEC) conclusion that the American Israel Public Affairs Committee (AIPAC) was not a "political committee" within the meaning of the Federal Election Campaign Act of 1971 (FECA), and therefore did not have to make disclosures regarding its membership, contributions, and expenditures under federal election laws. Respondents relied on federal election laws which provided that "any party aggrieved by an order of the Commission dismissing a complaint filed by such party may file a petition" in federal court seeking review of that dismissal. The Court held that the voters had standing to challenge the FEC's determination: "Prudential standing is satisfied when the injury asserted by a plaintiff 'arguably falls within the zone of interests to be protected or regulated by the statute in question.' Given the language of the statute and the nature of the injury, Congress, intending to protect voters such as respondents from suffering the kind of injury here at issue, intended to authorize this kind of suit. The 'injury in fact' that respondents have suffered consists of their inability to obtain information—lists of AIPAC donors, and campaign-related contributions and expenditures—that, on respondents' view of the law, the statute requires that AIPAC make public. There is no reason to doubt their claim that the information would help them to evaluate candidates for public office, especially candidates who received assistance from AIPAC, and to evaluate the role that AIPAC's financial assistance might play in a specific election. Where large numbers of Americans suffer alike, the political process, rather than the judicial process, may provide the more appropriate remedy for a widely shared grievance. The informational injury at issue here, directly related to voting, the most basic of political rights, is sufficiently concrete and specific such that the fact that it is widely shared does not deprive Congress of constitutional power to authorize its vindication in the federal courts." Justice Scalia, joined by Justices O'Connor and Thomas, dissented: "The interpretation that the Court gives the statutory provision deprives it of almost all its limiting force. *Any voter* can sue to compel the agency to require registration of an entity as a political committee, even though the 'aggrievement'

consists of nothing more than the deprivation of access to information whose
public availability would have been one of the consequences of registration."

2. Qui Tam *Actions.* In *Vermont Agency of Natural Resources v. United States ex
rel. Stevens*, 529 U.S. 765 (2000), the Court interpreted a federal *qui tam* statute that provided that "a person may bring a civil action *for the person and for
the United States Government*," and also provided that the plaintiff shall receive
a bounty *out of the United States' recovery* for filing and/or prosecuting a successful action on behalf of the government. The statute gave a private citizen "the
right to continue as a party to the action" even when the government itself has
assumed "primary responsibility" for prosecuting the action, entitled the citizen
to a hearing before the government's voluntary dismissal of the suit, and prohibited the government from settling the suit over the citizen's objection without
a judicial determination of "fairness, adequacy and reasonableness." Plaintiff
brought a *qui tam* action against the Vermont Agency of Natural Resources
(VANR), his former employer, alleging that it had submitted false claims to the
Environmental Protection Agency (EPA) in connection with various federal
grant programs administered by the EPA. Specifically, he claimed that the VANR
had overstated the amount of time its employees spent on the federally funded
projects, thereby inducing the government to disburse more grant money than
the VANR was entitled to receive. The Court held that Stevens had standing to
bring the action: "As to this portion of the recovery—the bounty he will receive
if the suit is successful—a *qui tam* relator has a 'concrete private interest in the
outcome of the suit.' But the same might be said of someone who has placed a
wager upon the outcome. An interest unrelated to injury in fact is insufficient
to give a plaintiff standing. The interest must consist of obtaining compensation
for, or preventing, the violation of a legally protected right. A *qui tam* relator has
suffered no such invasion—indeed, the 'right' he seeks to vindicate does not
even fully materialize until the litigation is completed and the relator prevails.
We believe, however, that adequate basis for the relator's suit for his bounty is
to be found in the doctrine that the assignee of a claim has standing to assert
the injury in fact suffered by the assignor. The FCA can reasonably be regarded
as effecting a partial assignment of the Government's damages claim. Although
we have never expressly recognized 'representational standing' on the part of
assignees, we have routinely entertained their suits, and also suits by subrogees,
who have been described as 'equitable assignees.' The United States' injury in
fact suffices to confer standing on respondent Stevens."

∾ PROBLEMS: STANDING AND CONGRESSIONAL
AUTHORIZATION ∾

1. *More on the Historic Preservation Act.* In regard to the Historic Preservation
Act, described at the beginning of the chapter, Congress did not explicitly authorize any of the plaintiffs to challenge the legislation. Indeed, to the contrary,

Congress reached a political compromise adverse to their interests. How does the absence of congressional authorization affect the various plaintiffs' abilities to file suit?

2. Lujan *Reconsidered.* What could the plaintiffs in *Lujan* have done differently that would have helped them establish standing? For example, would they have had standing if they had purchased airplane tickets to travel to Sri Lanka for three months hence and had every intention of going at that time? Would it matter that the environmental effects might not have occurred by that time? If so, would the plaintiffs be required to purchase tickets for an even later trip? Could the plaintiff organizations have substituted different individuals who had a stronger claim of injury? What types of individuals might have satisfied that requirement?

Monsanto Co. v. Geerston Seed Farms

561 U.S. 139 (2010)

Justice ALITO delivered the opinion of the Court.

This case arises out of a decision by the Animal and Plant Health Inspection Service (APHIS) to deregulate a variety of genetically engineered alfalfa. The District Court held that APHIS violated the National Environmental Policy Act of 1969 (NEPA), by issuing its deregulation decision without first completing a detailed assessment of the environmental consequences of its proposed course of action. The District Court vacated the agency's decision completely deregulating the alfalfa variety in question; ordered APHIS not to act on the deregulation petition until it had completed a detailed environmental review; and enjoined almost all future planting of the genetically engineered alfalfa pending the completion of that review. The Court of Appeals affirmed. The main issue concerns the breadth of that relief. We reverse and remand.

The Plant Protection Act (PPA), 7 U.S.C. §7701 *et seq.,* provides that the Secretary of the Department of Agriculture (USDA) may issue regulations "to prevent the introduction of plant pests into the United States or the dissemination of plant pests within the United States." The Secretary has delegated that authority to APHIS, a division of the USDA. Acting pursuant to that delegation, APHIS has promulgated regulations governing "the introduction of organisms and products altered or produced through genetic engineering that are plant pests or are believed to be plant pests." Under those regulations, certain genetically engineered plants are presumed to be "plant pests"—and thus "regulated articles" under the PPA—until APHIS determines otherwise. However, any person may petition APHIS for a determination that a regulated article does not present a plant pest risk and therefore should not be subject to the applicable regulations. APHIS may grant such a petition in whole or in part.

In deciding whether to grant nonregulated status to a genetically engineered plant variety, APHIS must comply with NEPA, which requires federal agencies "to the fullest extent possible" to prepare an environmental impact statement (EIS) for "every recommendation or report on proposals for legislation and other major Federal action significantly affecting the quality of the human environment." 42 U.S.C. §4332(2)(c). The statutory text "speaks solely in terms of *proposed* actions; it does not require an agency to consider the possible environmental impacts of less imminent actions when preparing the impact statement on proposed actions." Kleppe v. Sierra Club, 427 U.S. 390 (1976). An agency need not complete an EIS for a proposal if it finds, on the basis of a shorter "environmental assessment" (EA), that the proposed action will not have a significant impact on the environment. Even if a particular agency proposal requires an EIS, applicable regulations allow the agency to take at least some action in furtherance of that proposal while the EIS is being prepared.

This case involves Roundup Ready Alfalfa (RRA), an alfalfa crop that has been genetically engineered to be tolerant of glyphosate, the active ingredient of the herbicide Roundup. Petitioner Monsanto Company owns the intellectual property rights to RRA. Monsanto licenses those rights to Forage Genetics International (FGI), the exclusive developer of RRA seed. APHIS initially classified RRA as a regulated article, but petitioners sought nonregulated status for two strains of RRA. APHIS prepared a draft EA assessing the likely environmental impact of the requested deregulation. It then published a notice in the Federal Register advising the public of the deregulation petition and soliciting public comments on its draft EA. After considering the public comments that it received, APHIS issued a Finding of No Significant Impact and decided to deregulate RRA unconditionally without preparing an EIS. Prior to this decision, APHIS had authorized almost 300 field trials of RRA conducted over a period of eight years.

After APHIS granted RRA nonregulated status, respondents (two conventional alfalfa seed farms and environmental groups concerned with food safety) filed this action against the Secretary of Agriculture and certain other officials in Federal District Court, challenging APHIS's decision to completely deregulate RRA. Their complaint alleged violations of NEPA, the Endangered Species Act of 1973 (ESA), and the PPA. Respondents did not seek preliminary injunctive relief pending resolution of those claims. Hence, RRA enjoyed nonregulated status for approximately two years. During that period, more than 3,000 farmers in 48 States planted an estimated 220,000 acres of RRA.

The District Court accepted APHIS's determination that RRA does not have any harmful health effects on humans or livestock. Nevertheless, the District Court held that APHIS violated NEPA by deregulating RRA without first preparing an EIS. The Ninth Circuit affirmed. We granted certiorari.

Respondents contend that petitioners lack standing to seek our review of the lower court rulings. We disagree. Standing under Article III of the Constitution requires that an injury be concrete, particularized, and actual or imminent; fairly traceable to the challenged action; and redressable by a favorable ruling. Petitioners here satisfy all three criteria. Petitioners are injured by their inability to sell or license RRA to prospective customers until such time as APHIS completes the required EIS. Because that injury is caused by the order that petitioners challenge on appeal, it would be redressed by a favorable ruling from this Court.

Respondents do not dispute that petitioners would have standing to contest the District Court's permanent injunction order if they had pursued a different litigation strategy. Instead, respondents argue that the injury of which petitioners complain is independently caused by a part of the District Court's order that petitioners failed to challenge, namely, the vacatur of APHIS's deregulation decision. The practical consequence of the vacatur, respondents contend, was to restore RRA to the status of a regulated article; and, subject to certain exceptions, federal regulations ban the growth and sale of regulated articles. Because petitioners did not specifically challenge the District Court's vacatur, respondents reason, they lack standing to challenge a part of the District Court's order (*i.e.*, the injunction) that does not cause petitioners any injury not also caused by the vacatur.

Respondents' argument fails for two reasons. First, although petitioners did not challenge the vacatur directly, they adequately preserved their objection that the vacated deregulation decision should have been replaced by APHIS's proposed injunction. Throughout the remedial phase of this litigation, one of the main disputes between the parties has been whether the District Court was required to adopt APHIS's proposed judgment. That judgment would have replaced the vacated deregulation decision with an order expressly allowing continued planting of RRA subject to certain limited conditions. Accordingly, if the District Court had adopted the agency's suggested remedy, there would still be authority for the continued planting of RRA, because there would, in effect, be a new deregulation decision. Second, petitioners have standing to challenge the part of the District Court's order enjoining partial deregulation. Respondents focus their argument on the part of the judgment enjoining the planting of RRA, but the judgment also states that "before granting Monsanto's deregulation petition, *even in part,* the federal defendants shall prepare an environmental impact statement." That part of the judgment goes beyond the vacatur of APHIS's deregulation decision.

Respondents contended that the restriction on APHIS's ability to effect a partial deregulation of RRA does not cause petitioners "an actual or an imminent harm." In order for a partial deregulation to occur, respondents argued, the case would have to be remanded to the agency, and APHIS would have to prepare an EA "that may or may not come out in favor of a partial deregulation." Because petitioners cannot prove that those two events would happen, respondents contended, the asserted harm is too speculative to satisfy the actual or imminent injury requirement. We reject this argument. If the injunction were lifted, we do not see why the District Court would have to remand the matter to the agency in order for APHIS to effect a partial deregulation. Even if a remand were required, we perceive no basis on which the District Court could decline to remand the matter to the agency so that it could determine whether to pursue a partial deregulation during the pendency of the EIS process. It is undisputed that petitioners have submitted a deregulation petition and that a partial deregulation of the kind embodied in the agency's proposed judgment would afford petitioners much of the relief that they seek; it is also undisputed that, absent the District Court's order, APHIS could attempt to effect such a partial deregulation pending its completion of the EIS. For purposes of resolving the standing question, we need not decide whether or to what extent a party challenging an injunction that bars an agency from granting certain relief must show that the agency would be likely to afford such relief if it were free to do so. The agency takes the view that a partial deregulation reflecting its proposed limitations is in the public interest. Thus, there is more than a strong likelihood that APHIS would partially deregulate RRA were it not for the District Court's injunction. The District Court's elimination of that likelihood is sufficient to establish a constitutionally cognizable injury. That injury would be redressed by a favorable decision here, since "vacating the current injunction will allow petitioners to go back to the agency, to seek a partial deregulation," even if the District Court's vacatur of APHIS's deregulation decision is left intact. We therefore hold that petitioners have standing to seek this Court's review.[2]

We next consider petitioners' contention that respondents lack standing to seek injunctive relief. *See DaimlerChrysler Corp. v. Cuno*, 547 U.S. 332, 352 (2006). Petitioners argue that respondents have failed to show that any of the respondents is likely to suffer a constitutionally cognizable injury absent injunctive relief. We disagree. Respondents include conventional alfalfa farmers. Emphasizing "the undisputed concentration of alfalfa seed farms," the District Court found that those farmers had "established a 'reasonable probability' that their organic and conventional alfalfa crops will be infected with the engineered gene" if RRA is completely deregulated.[3] A substantial risk of gene flow injures respondents in several ways. For example, respondents represent that, in order to continue marketing their product to consumers who wish to buy non-genetically-engineered alfalfa, respondents would have to conduct testing to find out whether and to what extent their crops have been contaminated. Respondents also allege that the risk of gene flow will cause them to take measures to minimize the likelihood of potential contamination and to ensure an adequate supply of non-genetically-engineered alfalfa.

Such harms, which respondents will suffer even if their crops are not actually infected with the Roundup ready gene, are sufficiently concrete to satisfy the injury-in-fact prong of the constitutional standing analysis. Those harms are attributable to APHIS's deregulation decision which gives rise to a significant risk of gene flow to non-genetically-engineered varieties of alfalfa. A judicial order prohibiting the growth and sale of all or some genetically engineered alfalfa

2. Even if the District Court's order prohibiting a partial deregulation applies only to "the *particular* partial deregulation order proposed to the court by APHIS," petitioners would still have standing to challenge that aspect of the order.

3. One of the respondents specifically alleges that he owns an alfalfa farm in a prominent seed-growing region and faces a significant risk of contamination from RRA. Other declarations provide support for the conclusion that deregulation of RRA poses a significant risk of contamination to respondents' crops.

would remedy respondents' injuries by eliminating or minimizing the risk of gene flow to conventional and organic alfalfa crops. We conclude that respondents have constitutional standing to seek injunctive relief from the complete deregulation order at issue here.

Petitioners suggest that respondents fail to satisfy the "zone of interests" test we have articulated as a prudential standing requirement in cases challenging agency compliance with particular statutes. That argument is unpersuasive because respondents' injury has an environmental as well as an economic component. The risk that the RRA gene conferring glyphosate resistance will infect conventional and organic alfalfa is a significant environmental effect within the meaning of NEPA. Petitioners did not appeal that ruling. Respondents now seek injunctive relief to avert the risk of gene flow to their crops—the very same effect determined to be a significant environmental concern for purposes of NEPA. The mere fact that respondents also seek to avoid economic harms that are tied to the risk of gene flow does not strip them of prudential standing.

In short, respondents have standing to seek injunctive relief, and petitioners have standing to seek this Court's review of the Ninth Circuit's judgment affirming the entry of such relief. We therefore proceed to the merits of the case.

The judgment of the Ninth Circuit is reversed, and the case is remanded for further proceedings consistent with this opinion.

It is so ordered.

d. *Jus Tertii* (Third-Party) Standing

To what extent do litigants have standing to raise the rights of others who are not parties to a federal court proceeding? In *Singleton v. Wulff*, 428 U.S. 106 (1976), physicians brought a constitutional challenge against a Missouri statute that excluded abortions that are not "medically indicated" from Medicaid benefits available to needy persons. The doctors showed that they performed non-medically indicated abortions and that they would suffer financial injury (the loss of payments) if the statute remained in effect. However, the doctors also wanted to assert the rights of their patients. The Court began by articulating the general rule that courts do not allow individuals to assert the rights of third parties (individuals who are not parties to the case before the court):

> Federal courts must hesitate before resolving a controversy, even one within their constitutional power, on the basis of the rights of third persons not parties to the litigation. First, courts should not adjudicate such rights unnecessarily, and it may be that the holders of those rights either do not wish to assert them, or will be able to enjoy them regardless of whether the in-court litigant is successful. Second, third parties themselves usually will be the best proponents of their own rights. The courts depend on effective advocacy, and therefore should prefer to construe legal rights only when the most effective advocates of those rights are before them. The holders of the rights may have a like preference, to the extent they will be bound by the courts' decisions under the doctrine of *Stare decisis*.

Despite the general rule, the Court suggested that third-party standing might be appropriate in some cases: "This Court has looked to two factual elements to determine whether the rule should apply in a case. The first is the relationship of the litigant to the person whose right he seeks to assert. If the enjoyment of the right is inextricably bound up with the activity the litigant wishes to pursue, the court's construction of the right is not unnecessary in the sense that the right's enjoyment will be unaffected by the outcome of the suit. Furthermore, the relationship between the litigant and the third party may be such that the former is fully, or very nearly, as effective a proponent of the right as the latter."

In *Singleton,* relying on *Griswold v. Connecticut,* 381 U.S. 479 (1965), the Court held that a licensed physician could assert the privacy rights of married patients to receive contraceptive advice, and that abortion providers had standing to represent their patients: "A woman cannot safely secure an abortion without the aid of a physician, and an impecunious woman cannot easily secure an abortion without the physician being paid by the State. The constitutionally protected abortion decision is one in which the physician is intimately involved. Aside from the woman herself, the physician is uniquely qualified to litigate the constitutionality of the State's interference with, or discrimination against, that decision. As to the woman's assertion of her own rights, there are several obstacles. She may be chilled by a desire to protect the very privacy of her decision from the publicity of a court suit. A second obstacle is the imminent mootness, at least in the technical sense, of any individual woman's claim. Only a few months after the maturing of the decision to undergo an abortion, her right will have been irrevocably lost, assuming that unless the impecunious woman can establish Medicaid eligibility she must forgo abortion. These obstacles are not insurmountable. Suit may be brought under a pseudonym. A woman who is no longer pregnant may nonetheless retain the right to litigate the point because it is 'capable of repetition yet evading review.' *Roe v. Wade,* 410 U.S. at 124-125. It may be that a class could be assembled, whose fluid membership included some women with live claims. But if assertion of the right is to be 'representative' to such an extent, there seems little loss of effective advocacy from allowing its assertion by a physician."

In *Elk Grove Unified School District v. Newdow,* 542 U.S. 1 (2004), a father, an atheist, sought to challenge recitation of the Pledge of Allegiance in his daughter's school. He objected on the basis that the Pledge contains the words "under God," which he viewed as an establishment of religion. When the daughter's mother, the custodial parent, intervened in opposition to the father's suit, the Court concluded that the father lacked standing to represent his daughter's interests: "The interests of the affected persons are in many respects antagonistic. Of course, legal disharmony in family relations is not uncommon, and in many instances that disharmony poses no bar to federal-court adjudication of proper federal questions. What makes this case different is that Newdow's standing derives entirely from his relationship with his daughter, but he lacks the right to litigate as her next friend. In marked contrast to our case law on *jus tertii,* the interests of this parent and this child are not parallel and, indeed, are potentially in conflict."

∾ PROBLEMS: EXCEPTIONS TO *JUS TERTII* ∾

1. *The Historic Preservation Act and* Jus Tertii. To the extent that any of the parties seeking to challenge the Historic Preservation Act (described in the problem at the beginning of the chapter) lack standing in their own right, can they assert the rights of others? Who? On what basis?

2. *Contraception Bans.* Assume that the Court's privacy decisions had not been rendered, and that a Massachusetts statute makes it a crime to give "away any drug, medicine, instrument or article whatever for the prevention of conception." The statute distinguishes between married persons (who can obtain contraceptives to prevent pregnancy, but only from doctors or druggists by prescription) and single persons (who are not allowed to obtain contraceptives from anyone). In addition, the law prohibits both married and single persons from obtaining contraceptives for the purpose of preventing the spread of disease. William Baird was convicted of "exhibiting contraceptive articles while delivering a lecture on contraception to a group of students at a college and for giving a woman a package of Emko vaginal foam at the end of his address." Does Baird have standing to raise the rights of unmarried persons who are denied access to contraceptives? Does his status as an "authorized distributor of contraceptives" allow him to assert the interests of the users of his products? *See Eisenstadt v. Baird,* 405 U.S. 438 (1972).

3. *The Murderer's Mother.* Gary Gilmore was convicted of murder and sentenced to death. He waived his rights and agreed to submit to execution. His mother, acting as "next friend," applied for a stay of execution. Gilmore opposed the stay. Does Gilmore's mother have standing to act as his "next friend" and seek an application for a stay? Should it matter that Gilmore objects to the application? Would it matter whether Gilmore is competent and made a knowing waiver of his rights? What if he is incompetent? *See Gilmore v. Utah,* 429 U.S. 1012 (1976).

4. *The Alleged Terrorist's Father.* Following the 9/11 attack on the World Trade Center in New York City, Yaser Easm Hamdi was detained as an enemy combatant. He was a U.S. citizen, detained on U.S. soil, but was denied access to an attorney and therefore was effectively denied access to the courts. Hamdi's father, as "next friend," sought a writ of habeas corpus on his son's behalf. Under such circumstances, may the father assert his son's right to habeas corpus? *See Hamdi v. Rumsfeld,* 542 U.S. 507 (2004).

5. *Beer Sales.* An Oklahoma statute provides that males between the ages of 18 and 21 cannot purchase 3.2% beer, but that females can purchase the beer when they reach the age of 18. Plaintiff was less than 21 years old when the suit was filed, but turned 21 before the case was decided. Does plaintiff still have standing

to bring the suit? Could the suit be maintained by anyone else (e.g., a beer distributor that sells 3.2% beer)? *See Craig v. Boren*, 429 U.S. 190 (1976).

6. *Challenging Restrictive Covenants.* A state statute permits restrictive covenants that prohibit covenanted property from being sold to members of specified minority groups. Everyone agrees that the minority groups would have standing to challenge the covenant in an appropriate case, and that members of minority groups cannot be required to pay damages for breach of the covenant. However, plaintiffs seek damages from those who sell the real property in violation of the covenants. May defendant sellers assert the rights of minority groups in defense of the damage actions? Do defendants have standing to challenge the covenants? How would you argue the case for defendants? How might plaintiffs respond? *See Barrows v. Jackson*, 346 U.S. 249 (1953).

7. *The Association.* An Alabama statute requires foreign corporations to report the names and addresses of its members to Alabama's attorney general. The National Association for the Advancement of Colored People (NAACP) refuses to comply with the reporting requirement, and the State of Alabama files suit to prohibit the NAACP from conducting further activities within the state. The NAACP responds by challenging the reporting requirements as a violation of the First Amendment's speech and assembly provisions. In particular, the NAACP claims that its members may be harassed or discriminated against if their identities are disclosed. The NAACP seeks to challenge the requirements on its own behalf as well as on behalf of its members. May the NAACP assert the constitutional rights of its members? What must it show in order to do so? Can the NAACP bring the suit in it own right? *See NAACP v. Alabama*, 357 U.S. 449 (1958).

[Points to Remember for Chapter 1 is contained in online file.]

2

National Legislative Power

U.S. CONSTITUTION, ARTICLE I

Section 1. All legislative Powers herein granted shall be vested in a Congress of the United States, which shall consist of a Senate and House of Representatives.

Section 8. The Congress shall have Power to lay and collect Taxes, Duties, Imposts and Excises, to pay the Debts and provide for the common Defence and general Welfare of the United States, but all Duties, Imposes and Excises shall be uniform throughout the United States;

To borrow Money on the credit of the United States;

To regulate Commerce with foreign Nations, and among the several States, and with the Indian Tribes;

To establish an uniform Rule of Naturalization, and uniform Laws on the subject of Bankruptcies throughout the United States;

To coin Money; regulate the Value thereof, and of foreign Coin, and fix the Standard of Weights and Measures;

To provide for the Punishment of counterfeiting the Securities and current Coin of the United States;

To establish Post Offices and post Roads;

To promote the Progress of Science and useful Arts, by securing for limited Times to Authors and Inventors the exclusive Right to their respective Writings and Discoveries;

To constitute Tribunals inferior to the supreme Court;

To define and punish Piracies and Felonies committed on the high Seas, and Offenses against the Law of Nations;

To declare War, grants Letters of Marque and Reprisal, and make Rules concerning Captures on Land and Water;

To raise and support Armies, but no Appropriation of Money to that Use shall be for a longer Term than two years;

To provide and maintain a Navy;

To make Rules for the Government and Regulation of the land and naval Forces;

To provide for calling forth the Militia to execute the Laws of the Union, suppress Insurrections and repel Invasions;

To provide for organizing, arming, and disciplining, the Militia, and for governing such Part of them as may be employed in the Service of the United States respectively, the

Appointment of the Officers, and the Authority of training the Militia according to the discipline prescribed by Congress.

To exercise exclusive Legislation in all Cases whatsoever, over such District (not exceeding ten Miles square) as may, by Cession of Particular States, and the Acceptance of Congress, become the Seat of the Government of the United States, and to exercise like Authority over all Places purchased by the Consent of the Legislature of the State in which the Same shall be, for the Erection of Forts, Magazines, Arsenals, dock-Yards and other needful Buildings;—And

To make all Laws which shall be necessary and proper for carrying into Execution the foregoing Powers, and all other Powers vested by this Constitution in the Government of the United States, or in any Department or Officer thereof.

U.S. CONSTITUTION, ARTICLE IV

Section 3. The Congress shall have Power to dispose of and make all needful Rules and Regulations respecting the Territory or other Property belonging to the United States; and nothing in this Constitution shall be so construed as to Prejudice any Claims of the United States, or of any particular State.

U.S. CONSTITUTION, FOURTEENTH AMENDMENT

[1] All persons born or naturalized in the United States, and subject to the jurisdiction thereof, are citizens of the United States and of the State wherein they reside. No State shall make or enforce any law which shall abridge the privileges or immunities of citizens of the United States; nor shall any State deprive any person of life, liberty, or property, without due process of law; nor deny to any person within its jurisdiction the equal protection of the laws.

[Roadmap for Chapter 2 is contained in online file.]

✑ PROBLEM: THE EDUCATION FOR A BETTER AMERICA ACT ✑

Congress, concerned about the quality of education in the United States, is considering adopting the Education for a Better America Act. The reasons for Congress's concerns are well documented. For decades, American children have been falling behind their peers in other countries in math and science as well as in other critical subjects. In addition, too many children drop out of school, and suffer various negative effects as a result: reduced employment prospects, much higher rates of alcoholism and drug abuse, higher incarceration rates, and an increased tendency toward domestic violence. At the same time, society is becoming more technological and more international in character and needs a more highly qualified work force. Also, Congress believes that many existing schools are failing. Too many teachers are unqualified or incompetent. Schools are rife with drugs and other distracting influences. Lots of kids come from broken and dysfunctional homes. The net effect is that too many schools are not effectively educating kids. In order to compete in a modern business environment, Congress believes that students need to be better educated, and therefore that educational reform is vital to the health and well-being of the U.S. economy.

Suppose that you are counsel to a congressional committee that is considering how to "reform" and "reshape" the U.S. educational system. A number of suggestions have been offered regarding how the Education for a Better America Act should be structured. Some believe that the Act should provide financial incentives to local schools that meet stated educational goals and objectives. Others believe that the Act should include mandates that impose requirements and obligations on local schools. As you work your way through this chapter, you will be asked to advise Congress about how it should structure the legislation, and about what types of provisions should (or should not) be included in the final legislation.

As powerful as the U.S. Supreme Court may have become over the past two centuries, primary legislative power rests with Congress. In this chapter, we focus on the parameters of national legislative power.

Under the Articles of Confederation, the federal government was given limited legislative power as the states retained that power for themselves. However, under the Articles, the country did not function well. The individual states imposed barriers against trade, including tariffs and embargos, which made interstate commerce difficult. In addition, there were concerns regarding whether the federal government had sufficient power to provide for foreign affairs and the national defense. In an effort to deal with these problems, a convention was called in the mid-1780s to amend the Articles of Confederation. That call ultimately led to the constitutional convention that produced the present Constitution.

During the constitutional convention, much debate focused on the scope of federal power. Alexander Hamilton pushed for a broad conception of federal power, arguing that Congress should be given the "power to pass all laws which it shall judge necessary to the common defense and general welfare of the Union." Others argued for a more limited conception of federal power. Framing the debate was a recognition by the states that any powers given to the federal government would diminish their own power. Even though the states were reluctant to give too much power to the federal government, they recognized the need to create a stronger federal government than had existed under the Articles of Confederation.

The Framers ultimately decided to create a federal government with limited powers. Instead of giving Congress the power to legislate on any matter it deems appropriate, the Framers created a government of limited, enumerated powers. Article I, Section 8 gives Congress "all legislative powers herein granted." This limited conception of federal powers was also reflected in the Tenth Amendment, which provides that "The powers not delegated to the United States by the

Constitution, nor prohibited by it to the States, are reserved to the States respectively, or to the people."

Despite giving the federal government limited powers, Article I, Section 8 of the new Constitution granted Congress several important powers, including the right to borrow money, to establish uniform rules on naturalization and bankruptcy, to coin money, to provide punishment for counterfeiting, to establish post offices and roads, to provide for the protection of scientists and artists through rules governing rights to writings and discoveries, to provide and maintain a navy, to raise and support armies, and to define and punish piracies.

Given the Constitution's plan of enumerated powers, two separate and distinct questions tend to arise in congressional power cases. First, does Congress have the power to pass a given piece of legislation? In other words, do any of the enumerated powers give it that authority? For example, does the Commerce Clause give Congress the power to pass the law in question? If not, does Congress have implied powers that permit it to adopt the legislation? Second, does the law violate a limitation on that authority (e.g., free speech or equal protection)?

In this chapter, we will see that the scope of congressional power has ebbed and flowed during the last two centuries as the Court's interpretation of Article I has shifted. As you read the following cases, think about the broad issues in historical context. Has the federal system remained faithful to its roots, or has it morphed and expanded into a system that goes beyond the one contemplated by the Framers of the Constitution? If the scope of federal power has expanded, was this expansion necessary, inevitable or even desirable?

A. THE NECESSARY AND PROPER CLAUSE

One of the most important enumerated powers is found in Article I, Section 8, Paragraph 18, the so-called "Necessary and Proper" Clause. It provides that Congress shall have the power to "make all Laws which shall be necessary and proper for carrying into Execution the foregoing Powers, and all other Powers vested by this Constitution in the Government of the United States, or in any Department of Officer thereof."

The Necessary and Proper Clause is important because it expands the scope of the enumerated powers. For example, since Article I, Section 8 explicitly gives Congress the power to "provide and maintain a Navy," Paragraph 18 allows Congress to do those things that are "necessary and proper" to the maintenance of a navy.

There has been much debate regarding the scope and meaning of the Necessary and Proper Clause. Thomas Jefferson preferred a strict construction of the clause, arguing that it should be interpreted to mean "absolutely necessary." In other words, in providing for and maintaining a navy, Congress could only do those things that were "absolutely necessary" to the provision and maintenance of a navy. Alexander Hamilton, by contrast, preferred a "helpful" or "convenience" standard. In other words, Congress could do anything that was "helpful" or "convenient" to the provision and maintenance of a navy.

The following case arose in the early nineteenth century during a period of economic upheaval. Some believed that the Bank of the United States, far from being a passive player, had actually created the upheaval by providing easy credit which led to a speculative boom. As a result, there was a movement (that ultimately failed) to revoke the bank's charter. As you read *McCulloch*, think about whether Chief Justice Marshall implicitly endorses either the "absolutely necessary" or the "convenience" test, or whether he opts for some other test.

McCulloch v. Maryland

17 U.S. (4 Wheat.) 316 (1819)

Chief Justice MARSHALL delivered the opinion of the Court.

A Maryland statute taxed the operations of all banks that had not been charted by the state itself. The Bank of the United States, a bank chartered by Congress and owned by the federal government, refused, through James McCulloch, its cashier, to pay the tax, arguing that the state did not have the power to tax a federal government instrumentality. The Maryland Supreme Court upheld the tax, and the United States appealed.

The first question is—has congress power to incorporate a bank? This can scarcely be considered an open question. The principle was introduced at a very early period of our history, has been recognized by successive legislatures, and has been acted upon by the judicial department, in cases of peculiar delicacy, as a law of undoubted obligation.

Counsel for the state of Maryland deemed it of some importance, in the construction of the constitution, to consider that instrument, not as emanating from the people, but as the act of sovereign and independent states. The powers of the general government, it has been said, are delegated by the states, who alone are truly sovereign; and must be exercised in subordination to the states, who alone possess supreme dominion. It would be difficult to sustain this proposition. The convention which framed the constitution was indeed elected by state legislatures. But the instrument, when it came from their hands, was a mere proposal, without obligation, or pretensions. It was reported to the then existing congress of the United States, with a request that it "be submitted to a convention of delegates, chosen in each state by the people thereof, under the recommendation of its legislature, for their assent and ratification."

From these conventions, the constitution derives its whole authority. The government proceeds directly from the people; is "ordained and established," in the name of the people. It required not the affirmance, and could not be negatived, by the state governments. The constitution, when thus adopted, was of complete obligation, and bound the state sovereignties. It has been said, that the people had already surrendered all their powers to the state sovereignties, and had nothing more to give. But, surely, the question whether they may resume and modify the powers granted to government, does not remain to be settled. When, "in order to form a more perfect union," it was deemed necessary to change this alliance into an effective government, possessing great and sovereign powers, and acting directly on the people, the necessity of referring it to the people, and of deriving its powers directly from them, was felt and acknowledged by all. The government of the Union, then is, emphatically and truly, a government of the people. In form, and in substance, it emanates from them. Its powers are granted by them, and are to be exercised directly on them, and for their benefit.

If any proposition could command the universal assent of mankind, we expect it would be that the government of the Union, though limited in its powers, is supreme within its sphere of action. It is the government of all; its powers are delegated by all; it represents all, and acts for all. This question is not left to mere reason: the people have, in express terms, decided it, by saying, "this constitution, and the laws of the United States, which shall be made in pursuance thereof," "shall be the supreme law of the land," and by requiring that the members of the state legislatures, and the officers of the executive and judicial departments of the states, shall take the oath of fidelity to it. The government of the United States, though limited in its powers, is supreme; and its laws, when made in pursuance of the constitution, form the supreme law of the land, "anything in the constitution or laws of any state to the contrary notwithstanding."

Among the enumerated powers, we do not find that of establishing a bank or creating a corporation. But there is no phrase in the instrument which, like the articles of confederation, excludes incidental or implied powers; and which requires that everything granted shall be expressly and minutely described. A constitution, to contain an accurate detail of all the subdivisions of which its great powers will admit, and of all the means by which they may be carried into execution, would partake of the prolixity of a legal code, and could scarcely be embraced by the human mind. Its nature, therefore, requires that only its great outlines should be marked, its important objects designated, and the minor ingredients which compose those objects, be deduced from the nature of the objects themselves. In considering this question, then, we must never forget that it is a constitution we are expounding.

Although, among the enumerated powers of government, we do not find the word "bank" or "incorporation," we find the great powers, to lay and collect taxes; to borrow money; to regulate commerce; to declare and conduct a war; and to raise and support armies and navies. The sword and the purse, all the external relations, and no inconsiderable portion of the industry of the nation, are intrusted to its government. It may with great reason be contended, that a government, intrusted with such ample powers, on the due execution of which the happiness and prosperity of the nation so vitally depends, must also be intrusted with ample means for their execution. The power being given, it is the interest of the nation to facilitate its execution. Throughout this vast republic,

revenue is to be collected and expended, armies are to be marched and supported. The exigencies of the nation may require, that the treasure raised in the
north should be transported to the south, that raised in the east, conveyed to the
west, or that this order should be reversed. Is that construction of the constitution to be preferred, which would render these operations difficult, hazardous
and expensive? Can we adopt that construction (unless the words imperiously
require it), which would impute to the framers, when granting these powers
for the public good, the intention of impeding their exercise, by withholding a
choice of means? If, indeed, such be the mandate of the constitution, we have
only to obey; but that instrument does not profess to enumerate the means by
which the powers it confers may be executed; nor does it prohibit the creation
of a corporation, if the existence of such a being be essential, to the beneficial
exercise of those powers.

The power of creating a corporation, though appertaining to sovereignty, is
not, like the power of making war, or levying taxes or of regulating commerce, a
great substantive and independent power, which cannot be implied as incidental to other powers, or used as a means of executing them. It is never the end
for which other powers are exercised, but a means by which other objects are
accomplished. No sufficient reason is, therefore, perceived, why it may not pass
as incidental to those powers which are expressly given, if it be a direct mode of
executing them.

But the constitution of the United States has not left the right of congress to
employ the necessary means, for the execution of the powers conferred on the
government, to general reasoning. To its enumeration of powers is added, that of
making "all laws which shall be necessary and proper, for carrying into execution
the foregoing powers, and all other powers vested by this constitution, in the
government of the United States, or in any department thereof." Counsel for the
state of Maryland have urged various arguments, to prove that this clause, though,
in terms a grant of power, is really restrictive of the general right, which might
otherwise be implied, of selecting means for executing the enumerated powers.
The argument is drawn from that peculiar language of this clause. Congress is
not empowered by it to make all laws, which may have relation to the powers conferred on the government, but such only as may be "necessary and proper" for
carrying them into execution. The word "necessary" is considered as controlling
the whole sentence, and as limiting the right to pass laws for the execution of the
granted powers, to such as are indispensable, and without which the power would
be nugatory. That it excludes the choice of means, and leaves to congress, in each
case, that only which is most direct and simple. Is it true, that this is the sense in
which the word "necessary" is used? Does it import an absolute physical necessity, so strong, that one thing to which another may be termed necessary, cannot
exist without that other? We think it does not. If reference be had to its use, in
the common affairs of the world, or approved authors, it frequently imports no
more than that one thing is convenient, or useful, or essential to another. This

word, like others, is used in various senses; and, in its construction, the subject, the context, the intention of the person using them, are all to be taken into view.

Let this be done in the case under consideration. The subject is the execution of those great powers on which the welfare of a nation essentially depends. It must have been the intention of those who gave these powers, to insure, so far as human prudence could insure, their beneficial execution. This could not be done, by confiding the choice of means to such narrow limits as not to leave it in the power of congress to adopt any which might be appropriate, and which were conducive to the end. This provision is made in a constitution, intended to endure for ages to come, and consequently, to be adapted to the various crises of human affairs. To have prescribed the means by which government should, in all future time, execute its powers, would have been to change, entirely, the character of the instrument, and give it the properties of a legal code. It would have been an unwise attempt to provide, by immutable rules, for exigencies which, if foreseen at all, must have been seen dimly, and which can be best provided for as they occur. To have declared, that the best means shall not be used, but those alone, without which the power given would be nugatory, would have been to deprive the legislature of the capacity to avail itself of experience, to exercise its reason, and to accommodate its legislation to circumstances.

We admit that the powers of the government are limited, and that its limits are not to be transcended. But the sound construction of the constitution must allow to the national legislature that discretion, with respect to the means by which the powers it confers are to be carried into execution, which will enable that body to perform the high duties assigned to it, in the manner most beneficial to the people. Let the end be legitimate, let it be within the scope of the constitution, and all means which are appropriate, which are plainly adapted to that end, which are not prohibited, but consist with the letter and spirit of the constitution, are constitutional.

Food for Thought

1. *Reclaiming Arid Land.* In *Kansas v. Colorado*, 206 U.S. 46 (1907), Congress sought to divert water from the Arkansas River to reclaim arid land in Colorado. The Constitution provides Congress with the power to regulate interstate commerce, as well as the power to regulate navigation. Although the Arkansas River is navigable, it was not navigable in the place where the diversion occurred, and water was not being diverted for navigability purposes. The Court held that Congress had exceeded its authority under the Constitution: "If the national government was asserting that the appropriation for irrigation was affecting the navigability of the stream, it would become our duty to determine the truth of the charge. But the government makes no such contention. That raises the question whether the reclamation of arid lands is one of the powers granted to

the general government. Turning to the enumeration of the powers granted to Congress by the 8th section of the 1st article of the Constitution, no one of them, by any implication, refers to the reclamation of arid lands. The last paragraph of the section which authorizes Congress to make all laws which shall be necessary or proper for carrying into execution the foregoing powers, and all other powers vested by this Constitution in the government of the United States, or in any department or officer thereof, is not the delegation of a new and independent power, but simply provision for making effective the powers theretofore mentioned. This construction of the Constitution is made absolutely certain by the 10th Amendment. This Amendment disclosed the widespread fear that the national government might, under the pressure of a supposed general welfare, attempt to exercise powers which had not been granted. Powers affecting the internal affairs of the states not granted to the United States by the Constitution, nor prohibited by it to the states, are reserved to the states respectively, and all powers of a national character which are not delegated to the national government by the Constitution are reserved to the people of the United States. We have within our borders extensive tracts of arid lands which ought to be reclaimed, and it may well be that no power is adequate for their reclamation other than that of the national government. But, if no such power has been granted, none can be exercised." Note the Court's construction of the Tenth Amendment. Does it comport with either Jefferson or Hamilton's views? As you read the rest of this chapter, consider whether the Court continues to construe the clause consistently with this decision.

2. *Is the Necessary and Proper Clause Implicit in the Constitution?* Some argue that, if the Constitution had not contained the Necessary and Proper Clause, the Court would have been forced to imply its existence. For example, Madison argued in *The Federalist No. 44*: "Had the Constitution been silent on this head, there can be no doubt that all the particular powers requisite as means of executing the general powers would have resulted to the government, by unavoidable implication." If Madison is right, should the Clause be regarded as a *limitation* on the scope of federal power rather than as an expansion?

3. *The Louisiana Purchase.* During his presidency, Thomas Jefferson made the Louisiana Purchase, which added a large section of land to the new country. Under Jefferson's construction of the Necessary and Proper Clause, can the purchase be justified? As you examine Article I, Section 8 (or, for that matter, other provisions of the Constitution), do you find any provision that explicitly authorizes the purchase? If not, how can the purchase be justified? Under his construction of the Clause, was Jefferson required to seek and obtain a constitutional amendment authorizing the purchase?

4. *The Limits of Implied Powers.* If the concept of implicit power is accepted, where does it end? Consider these comments of President Jefferson: "Congress is authorized to defend the nation. Ships are necessary for defense; copper is necessary for ships; mines, necessary for copper; a company necessary to work

the mines; and who can doubt this reasoning who has ever played at 'This is the House that Jack Built'? Under such a process of filiation of necessities the sweeping clause makes clean work." Do you agree? Does Jefferson's logic suggest that the Necessary and Proper Clause should be more neatly cabined? By what standard? An "absolutely necessary" standard?

5. *"We Must Never Forget"* In deciding *McCulloch*, Chief Justice Marshall made his famous statement: "We must, never forget that it is a *Constitution* we are expounding." In the context of the case, Marshall's statement argues for a broader interpretation of the Constitution. Consider the following responses: a) Justice Frankfurter, who stated that "precisely '*because* it is a *constitution* we are expounding,' we ought not to take liberties with it." *National Marine Ins. Co. v. Tidewater Transfer Co.*, 337 U.S. 582, 647 (1949) (Frankfurter, J., dissenting); b) Professor Kurland, who stated that "whenever a judge quotes this passage, you can be sure that the court will be throwing the constitutional text, its history, and its structure to the winds in reaching its conclusion." Philip B. Kurland, *Curia Regis: Some Comments on the Divine Rights of Kings and Courts to Say What the Law Is*, 23 ARIZ. L. REV. 582, 591 (1981). Who is correct, and what are the implications for constitutional interpretation?

United States v. Comstock

560 U.S. 126 (2010)

Justice BREYER delivered the opinion of the Court.

A federal civil-commitment statute authorizes the Department of Justice to detain a mentally ill, sexually dangerous federal prisoner beyond the date the prisoner would otherwise be released. We ask whether the Federal Government has the authority under Article I of the Constitution to enact this federal civil-commitment program or whether its doing so falls beyond the reach of a government of "enumerated powers." *McCulloch v. Maryland*, 4 Wheat. 316, 405 (1819). We conclude that the Constitution grants Congress the authority to enact §4248 as "necessary and proper for carrying into Execution" the powers "vested by" the "Constitution in the Government of the United States." Art. I, §8, cl. 18.

The statute allows a court to order the civil commitment of an individual who is currently "in the custody of the Federal Bureau of Prisons," if that individual (1) has previously "engaged or attempted to engage in sexually violent conduct or child molestation," (2) currently "suffers from a serious mental illness, abnormality, or disorder," and (3) "as a result of" that mental illness, abnormality, or disorder is "sexually dangerous to others," in that "he would have serious difficulty in refraining from sexually violent conduct or child molestation if released." §§4247(a)(5)(6). In order to detain a person, the Government (acting through the Department of Justice) must certify to a federal district judge that the prisoner meets the conditions just described. When a certification is filed, the statute automatically stays the individual's release from prison, thereby giving the Government an opportunity to prove its claims at a hearing through psychiatric (or other) evidence. The prisoner "shall be represented by counsel" and shall have "an opportunity" at the hearing "to testify, to present evidence, to subpoena witnesses on his behalf, and to confront and cross-examine" the Government's witnesses. If the Government proves its claims by "clear and convincing evidence," the court will order the prisoner's continued commitment in "the custody of the Attorney General," who must "make all reasonable efforts to cause" the State where that person was tried, or the State where he is domiciled, to "assume responsibility for his custody, care, and treatment." If either State is willing to assume that responsibility, the Attorney General "shall release" the individual "to the appropriate official" of that State. If neither State will assume responsibility," the "Attorney General shall place the person for treatment in a suitable federal facility." Confinement in the federal facility will last until either (1) the person's mental condition improves to the point where he is no longer dangerous (with or without appropriate ongoing treatment), in which case he will be released; or (2) a State assumes responsibility for his custody, care, and treatment, in which case he will be transferred to the custody of that State. The statute establishes a system for ongoing psychiatric and judicial review of the individual's case, including judicial hearings at the request of the confined person at six-month intervals.

In 2006, the Government instituted proceedings against the respondents in this case. Three had previously pleaded guilty in federal court to possession of child pornography, and the fourth to sexual abuse of a minor. The fifth respondent had been charged with aggravated sexual abuse of a minor, but was found mentally incompetent to stand trial. Each respondent moved to dismiss. Among other things, they claimed that, in enacting the statute, Congress exceeded the powers granted to it by Art. I, §8 of the Constitution, including those granted by the Commerce Clause and the Necessary and Proper Clause. The District Court granted their motion to dismiss and the Court of Appeals for the Fourth Circuit upheld the dismissal. We granted certiorari.

The question is whether the Necessary and Proper Clause, Art. I, §8, cl. 18, grants Congress authority to enact the statute before us. We assume, but do not decide, that other provisions of the Constitution, such as the Due Process Clause, do not prohibit civil commitment in these circumstances. We ask solely whether the Federal Government, exercising its enumerated powers, may enact such a statute. We conclude that the Constitution grants Congress legislative power sufficient to enact §4248. We base this conclusion on five considerations.

First, the Necessary and Proper Clause grants Congress broad authority to enact federal legislation. The Federal "Government is acknowledged to be one of enumerated powers," *McCulloch*, 4 Wheat. at 405, which means that "every law enacted by Congress must be based on one or more of" those powers, *United States v. Morrison*, 529 U.S. 598, 607 (2000). But "a government, entrusted with such" powers, "must also be entrusted with ample means for their execution." *McCulloch*, 4 Wheat. at 408. The Necessary and Proper Clause makes clear that the Constitution's grants of specific federal legislative authority are accompanied by broad power to enact laws that are "convenient, or useful" or "conducive" to the authority's "beneficial exercise." The word "necessary" does not mean "absolutely necessary." "Let the end be legitimate, let it be within the scope of the constitution, and all means which are appropriate, which are plainly adapted to that end, which are not prohibited, but consist with the letter and spirit of the constitution, are constitutional." In determining whether the Necessary and Proper Clause grants Congress the legislative authority to enact a particular statute, we look to see whether the statute constitutes a means that is rationally related to the implementation of a constitutionally enumerated power. *Sabri v. United States*, 541 U. S. 600 (2004). As Chief Justice Marshall stated, a federal statute, in addition to being authorized by Art. I, §8, must also "not be prohibited" by the Constitution. *McCulloch, supra,* at 421. The Constitution leaves the "choice of means primarily to the judgment of Congress. If the means adopted are really calculated to attain the end, the degree of their necessity, the extent to which they conduce to the end, the closeness of the relationship between the means adopted and the end to be attained, are matters for congressional determination alone." *Burroughs v. United States*, 290 U. S. 534, 547 (1934).

The Constitution, which nowhere speaks explicitly about the creation of federal crimes beyond those related to "counterfeiting," "treason," or "Piracies and Felonies committed on the high Seas" or "against the Law of Nations," Art. I, §8, cls. 6, 10; Art. III, §3, nonetheless grants Congress broad authority to create such crimes. Congress routinely exercises its authority to enact criminal laws in furtherance of its enumerated powers to regulate interstate and foreign commerce, to enforce civil rights, to spend funds for the general welfare, to establish federal courts, to establish post offices, to regulate bankruptcy, to regulate naturalization, and so forth. *See, e.g., Lottery Case, supra.* Similarly, Congress, in order to ensure the enforcement of federal criminal laws enacted in furtherance of its enumerated powers, can cause a prison to be erected within the jurisdiction of the United States, and direct that all persons sentenced to imprisonment under the laws of the United States shall be confined there. *Ex parte Karstendick*, 93 U.S. 396 (1876). Moreover, Congress, having established a prison system, can enact laws that ensure that system's safe and responsible administration by, for example, requiring prisoners to receive medical care and educational training, and can ensure the safety of the prisoners, prison workers and visitors, and those in surrounding communities by creating further criminal laws governing entry, exit, and smuggling, and by employing prison guards to ensure discipline and security. *See, e.g.,* §1791. Neither Congress' power to criminalize conduct, nor its power to imprison individuals who engage in that conduct, nor its power to enact laws governing prisons and prisoners, is explicitly mentioned in the Constitution.

But Congress nonetheless possesses broad authority to do each of those things in the course of "carrying into Execution" the enumerated powers "vested by" the "Constitution in the Government of the United States," Art. I, §8, cl. 18 authority granted by the Necessary and Proper Clause.

Second, the civil-commitment before us constitutes a modest addition to a set of federal prison related mental-health statutes that have existed for decades. We recognize that even a longstanding history of related federal action does not demonstrate a statute's constitutionality. A history of involvement, however, can be "helpful in reviewing the substance of a congressional statutory scheme," *Gonzales*, 545 U.S. at 21, and the reasonableness of the relation between the new statute and pre-existing federal interests. Here, Congress has long been involved in the delivery of mental health care to federal prisoners, and has long provided for their civil commitment. Over three decades, Congress created a national, federal civil-commitment program under which any person who was either charged with or convicted of any federal offense in any federal court could be confined in a federal mental institution. These statutes did not raise the question presented here, for they all provided that commitment in a federal hospital would end upon completion of the relevant "terms" of federal "imprisonment" as set forth in the underlying criminal sentence or statute. But between 1948 and 1949, Congress modified the law to provide for the civil commitment of individuals who are, or who become, mentally incompetent at any time after their arrest and before the expiration of their sentence, and it set forth various procedural safeguards, including proof that the person if released "will probably endanger the safety of the officers, the property, or other interests of the United States." This precondition was interpreted by the Judiciary to mean that "release would endanger the safety of persons, property or the public interest in general — not merely interests peculiar to the United States." *United States v. Curry*, 410 F.2d 1372, 1374 (CA4 1969). In 1984, Congress modified these statutes to authorize (explicitly) civil commitment if, in addition to the other conditions, the prisoner's "release would create a substantial risk of bodily injury to another person or serious damage to the property of another." §4246(d). Congress also elaborated upon the condition "that suitable arrangements are not otherwise available" by directing the Attorney General to seek alternative placement in state facilities. In 2006, Congress enacted the statute before us. It differs from earlier statutes in that it focuses directly upon persons who, due to a mental illness, are sexually dangerous. Many of these individuals were likely already subject to civil commitment under §4246, which, since 1949, has authorized the postsentence detention of federal prisoners who suffer from a mental illness and who are thereby dangerous (sexually or otherwise). Aside from its focus on sexually dangerous persons, §4248 is similar to the provisions first enacted in 1949. In that respect, it is a modest addition to a longstanding federal statutory framework, which has been in place since 1855.

Third, Congress reasonably extended its longstanding civil-commitment system to cover mentally ill and sexually dangerous persons who are already in federal custody, even if doing so detains them beyond the termination of their criminal sentence. For one thing, the Federal Government is the custodian of its prisoners. As custodian, it has the constitutional power to protect nearby (and other) communities from the danger federal prisoners may pose. At common law, one "who takes charge of a third person" is "under a duty to exercise reasonable care to control" that person to prevent him from causing reasonably foreseeable "bodily harm to others." RESTATEMENT (SECOND) OF TORTS §319, p. 129 (1963, 1969). If a federal prisoner is infected with a communicable disease that threatens others, surely it would be "necessary and proper" for the Federal Government to take action, pursuant to its role as custodian, to refuse (at least until the threat diminishes) to release that individual among the general public, where he might infect others (even if not threatening an interstate epidemic. "If confinement of such an individual is a "necessary and proper" thing to do, then how could it not be similarly "necessary and proper" to confine an individual whose mental illness threatens others to the same degree?

Section 4248 is "reasonably adapted" to Congress' power to act as a responsible federal custodian (a power that rests, in turn, upon federal criminal statutes that legitimately implement constitutionally enumerated authority). Congress could have reasonably concluded that federal inmates who suffer from a mental illness that causes them to "have serious difficulty in refraining from sexually violent conduct," would pose an especially high danger to the public if released. Congress could also have reasonably concluded that a reasonable number of such individuals would likely *not* be detained by the States if released from federal custody, in part because the Federal Government itself severed their claim to "legal residence in any State" by incarcerating them in remote federal prisons. Congress' desire to address the specific challenges, taken together with its responsibilities as a custodian, supports the conclusion that §4248 satisfies "review for means-end rationality," i.e., it satisfies the Constitution's insistence that a federal statute represent a rational means for implementing a constitutional grant of legislative authority.

Fourth, the statute properly accounts for state interests. Respondents and the dissent contend that §4248 violates the Tenth Amendment because it "invades the province of state sovereignty" in an area typically left to state control. The powers "delegated to the United States by the Constitution" include those specifically enumerated powers listed in Article I along with the implementation authority granted by the Necessary and Proper Clause. Virtually by definition, these powers are not powers that the Constitution "reserved to the States." *See New York, supra,* at 159. Nor does this statute invade state sovereignty or improperly limit the scope of "powers that remain with the States." To the contrary, it requires *accommodation* of state interests: The Attorney General must inform the State in which the federal prisoner "is domiciled or was tried" that he is detaining someone with respect to whom those States may wish to assert authority, and he must encourage those States to assume custody of the individual. He must also immediately "release" that person "to the appropriate official of" either State "if such State will assume responsibility." Either State has the right, at any time, to assert its authority over the individual, which will prompt the immediate transfer to State custody. "The Federal Government would have no appropriate role" once "the transfer to State responsibility and State control has occurred."

Fifth, the links between §4248 and an enumerated Article I power are not too attenuated. Neither is the statutory provision too sweeping in its scope. Invoking the cautionary instruction that we may not "pile inference upon inference" in order to sustain congressional action under Article I, respondents argue that, when legislating pursuant to the Necessary and Proper Clause, Congress' authority can be no more than one step removed from a specifically enumerated power. But this argument is irreconcilable with our precedents. As Chief Justice Marshall recognized in *McCulloch*, "the power 'to establish post offices and post roads' is executed by the single act of *making* the establishment. From this has been inferred the power and duty of *carrying* the mail along the post road, from one post office to another. From this *implied* power, has been inferred the right to *punish* those who steal letters from the post office, or rob the mail." Our necessary and proper jurisprudence contains multiple examples of similar reasoning. Even the dissent acknowledges that Congress has the implied power to criminalize any conduct that might interfere with the exercise of an enumerated power, and the additional power to imprison people who violate those (inferentially authorized) laws, and the power to provide for the safe and reasonable management of prisons, and the additional power to regulate the prisoners' behavior even after their release. Of course, each of those powers is ultimately "derived from" an enumerated power. That enumerated power is "the enumerated power that justifies the defendant's statute of conviction." Every such statute must be legitimately predicated on an enumerated power. The same enumerated power that justifies the creation of a federal criminal statute, and that justifies the additional implied federal powers that the dissent considers legitimate, justifies civil commitment under §4248.

Nor need we fear that our holding confers on Congress a general "police power, which the Founders denied the National Government and reposed in the States." *Morrison*, 529 U.S. at 618. Section 4248 is narrow in scope. It has been applied to only a small fraction of federal prisoners. Its reach is limited to individuals already "in the custody of the" Federal Government. Indeed, the Solicitor General argues that "the Federal Government would not have the power to commit a person who has been released from prison and whose period of supervised release is completed." Far from a "general police power," §4248 is a reasonably adapted and narrowly tailored means of pursuing the Government's legitimate interest as a custodian in the responsible administration of its prison system.

To be sure, "the Federal Government undertakes activities today that would have been unimaginable to the Framers in two senses; first, because the Framers would not have conceived that *any* government would conduct such activities; and second, because the Framers would not have believed that the *Federal* Government, rather than the States, would assume such responsibilities. Yet the powers conferred upon the Federal Government by the Constitution were phrased in language broad enough to allow for expansion of the Federal Government's role." *New York*, 505 U.S. at 157. The Framers demonstrated foresight in drafting a Constitution capable of such resilience through time. As Chief Justice Marshall observed nearly 200 years ago, the Necessary and Proper Clause is part of "a constitution intended to endure for ages to come, and, consequently, to be adapted to the various crises of human affairs." *McCulloch*, 4 Wheat. at 415.

The statute is a "necessary and proper" means of exercising the federal authority that permits Congress to create federal criminal laws, to punish their violation, to imprison violators, to provide appropriately for those imprisoned, and to maintain the security of those who are not imprisoned but who may be affected by the federal imprisonment of others. The Constitution consequently authorizes Congress to enact the statute. We do not reach or decide any claim that the statute or its application denies equal protection of the laws, procedural or substantive due process, or any other rights guaranteed by the Constitution. Respondents are free to pursue those claims on remand.

The judgment of the Court of Appeals for the Fourth Circuit with respect to Congress' power to enact this statute is reversed, and the case is remanded for further proceedings consistent with this opinion.

It is so ordered.

Justice KENNEDY, *concurring in the judgment.*

Under the Necessary and Proper Clause, application of a "rational basis" test should be at least as exacting as it has been in the Commerce Clause cases, if not more so. *Raich, Lopez,* and *Hodel* require a tangible link to commerce, not a mere conceivable rational relation. Congress has acted within its powers to ensure that an abrupt end to the federal detention of prisoners does not endanger third parties. Having acted within its constitutional authority to detain the person, the National Government can acknowledge a duty to ensure that an abrupt end to the detention does not prejudice the States and their citizens.

Justice ALITO, *concurring in the judgment.*

The term "necessary" requires an "appropriate" link between a power conferred by the Constitution and the law enacted by Congress. Here, there is a substantial link to Congress' constitutional powers.

Justice THOMAS, *dissenting.*

No enumerated power expressly delegates to Congress the power to enact a civil-commitment regime for sexually dangerous persons, nor does any other provision in the Constitution vest Congress or the other branches of the Federal Government with such a power. Section 4248 can be a valid exercise of congressional authority only if it is "necessary and proper for carrying into Execution" one or more of those federal powers enumerated in the Constitution. The Government identifies no specific enumerated power or powers as a constitutional predicate, and none are readily discernable. This Court has recognized that the power to care for the mentally ill and, where necessary, the power "to protect the community from the dangerous tendencies of some" mentally ill persons, are among the numerous powers that remain with the States. *Addington v. Texas*, 441 U.S. 418 (1979).

Instead of asking what enumerated power §4248 "carries into Execution," the Court surveys other laws Congress has enacted and concludes that, because §4248 is related to those laws, the "links" between §4248 and an enumerated power are not "too attenuated"; hence, §4248 is a valid exercise of Congress' Necessary and Proper Clause authority. This unnecessarily confuses the analysis and, followed to its logical extreme, would result in an unwarranted expansion of federal power. The Necessary and Proper Clause does not provide Congress with authority to enact any law simply because it furthers *other laws* Congress has enacted in the exercise of its incidental authority; the Clause plainly requires a showing that every federal statute "carries into Execution" one or more of the Federal Government's *enumerated* powers. The statute's definition of a "sexually dangerous person" does not require a federal court to find any connection between the reasons supporting civil commitment and the enumerated power with which that person's criminal conduct interfered. Section 4248 allows a court to civilly commit an individual without finding that he was ever charged with or convicted of a federal crime involving sexual violence. Section 4248 permits the term of federal civil commitment to continue beyond the date on which a convicted prisoner's sentence expires or the date on which the statute of limitations on an untried defendant's crime has run, and the definition of a "sexually dangerous person" does not require evidence that this sexually dangerous condition will manifest itself in a way that interferes with a federal law that executes an enumerated power or in a geographic location over which Congress has plenary authority. Once the Federal Government's criminal jurisdiction over a prisoner ends, so does any "special relationship" between the Government and the former prisoner. The fact that the Federal Government has the authority to imprison a person for the purpose of punishing him for a federal crime—sex-related or otherwise—does not provide the Government with the additional power to exercise indefinite civil control over that person.

Note: National Federation v. Sebelius

In *National Federation of Independent Business v. Sebelius*, 567 U.S. 519 (2012), the Court construed the Necessary and Proper Clause as applied to the Patient Protection and Affordable Care Act of 2010. In an opinion set forth in the Commerce Clause section, the Court concluded that the individual mandate could not be upheld under the Commerce Clause authority, and then held that it could not be justified under the Necessary and Proper Clause either.

**FOOD FOR THOUGHT: MORE ON THE EDUCATION
FOR A BETTER AMERICA ACT**

Congress wants to know whether it can justify passage of the Act under the Necessary and Proper Clause, or whether the Act must be based on another clause (possibly in conjunction with the Necessary and Proper Clause). Which other clause might be used (other than the Commerce Clause, which we examine shortly)?

B. THE COMMERCE CLAUSE

Article I, Section 8, Paragraph 3 contains perhaps the most potent federal power, the Commerce Clause: "The Congress shall have Power to regulate Commerce with foreign Nations, and among the several States, and with the Indian Tribes."

The U.S. Constitution differs markedly from the Articles of Confederation in regard to commerce. Under the Articles, the states reserved the commerce power to themselves and denied it to Congress. Moreover, although the Articles gave Congress some control over foreign affairs, one provision of the Articles specifically prohibited Congress from entering into treaties limiting the states' power over commerce or their right to tax imports and exports.

The Articles of Confederation did not provide the basis for a sound economy. The states used their powers to protect their own economies at the expense of the economies of neighboring states, and there "grew up a conflict of commercial regulations, destructive to the harmony of the States, and fatal to their commercial interests abroad." *Gibbons v. Ogden*, 22 U.S. (9 Wheat.) 1 (1824) (Johnson, J., concurring). Many states imposed economic sanctions, including taxes and tariffs, on trade from other states. By 1785–1786, the nation was mired in a recession caused by "a high national debt, increasing trade deficits, and economic infighting." DANIEL A. FARBER & SUZANNA SHERRY, A HISTORY OF THE AMERICAN CONSTITUTION 25 (West 1990).

As the economic situation worsened, many called for a convention to amend the Articles of Confederation. The initial convention was supposed to propose amendments to the Articles that would give the federal government increased power over commerce. However, not enough states sent delegates. When the delegates finally did meet, they quickly realized that more drastic change was needed, and they called for a subsequent convention to make more sweeping changes. This subsequent convention, which ultimately became known as the Constitutional Convention, produced our present Constitution and the current version of the Commerce Clause.

Under the Commerce Clause, a number of questions arise. How much power did Congress receive? Does Congress have "exclusive" power, or are the states allowed to exercise "concurrent" power? If concurrent power exists, where does federal power end and state power begin?

1. Early Cases

The Constitution did not define the phrase "among the several states." That task was left to the courts, and a number of cases came before the Court in the nineteenth century.

Gibbons v. Ogden

22 U.S. 1 (1824)

Mr. Chief Justice MARSHALL delivered the opinion of the Court, and, after stating the case, proceeded as follows:

In 1803, New York granted Robert Livingston a long-term monopoly on steamship operations in New York waters. Livingston subsequently assigned to Aaron Ogden the exclusive right to run steamships between New York City and Elizabethtown, New Jersey. When Thomas Gibbons, who held a federal license, began operations on a similar route, Ogden sued.

Appellant contends that the New York laws which purport to give Ogden an exclusive privilege are repugnant to the constitution and laws of the United States. They are said to be repugnant—

> 1st. To that clause in the constitution which authorizes Congress to regulate commerce. 2d. To that which authorizes Congress to promote the progress of science and useful arts.

Reference has been made to the political situation of these States, anterior to its formation. It has been said, that they were sovereign, completely independent, and connected with each other only by a league. This is true. But, when these allied sovereigns converted their league into a government, empowered to enact laws, the character in which the States appear, underwent a change, the extent of which must be determined by a fair consideration of the instrument by which that change was effected. This instrument contains an enumeration of powers expressly granted by the people to their government. It has been said, that these powers ought to be construed strictly. But why ought they to be so construed? In the last of the enumerated powers, that which grants, expressly, the means for carrying all others into execution, Congress is authorized "to make all laws which shall be necessary and proper" for the purpose. But this limitation on the means which may be used, is not extended to the powers which are conferred; nor is there one sentence in the constitution, which prescribes this rule.

The words are, "Congress shall have power to regulate commerce with foreign nations, and among the several States, and with the Indian tribes." The subject to be regulated is commerce. Counsel for appellee would limit it to traffic, to buying and selling, or the interchange of commodities, and do not admit that it comprehends navigation. This would restrict a general term, applicable to many objects, to one of its significations. Commerce, undoubtedly, is traffic, but it is something more: it is intercourse. It describes the commercial intercourse between nations, and parts of nations, in all its branches, and is regulated by prescribing rules for carrying on that intercourse. The mind can scarcely conceive a system for regulating commerce between nations, which shall exclude laws concerning navigation, which shall be silent on the admission of vessels, and be confined to prescribing rules for the conduct of individuals, in the actual employment of buying and selling, or of barter.

If commerce does not include navigation, the government of the Union has no direct power over that subject, and can make no law prescribing what shall constitute American vessels, or requiring that they shall be navigated by American seamen. America understands, and has uniformly understood, the word "commerce," to comprehend navigation. It was so understood when the constitution was framed. The power over commerce, including navigation, was one of the primary objects for which the people of America adopted their government. The word used in the constitution comprehends, and has been understood to comprehend, navigation within its meaning; and a power to regulate navigation, is as expressly granted, as if that term had been added to the word "commerce."

To what commerce does this power extend? The constitution informs us, to commerce "with foreign nations, and among the several States, and with the Indian tribes." These words comprehend every species of commercial intercourse between the United States and foreign nations. No trade can be carried on between this country and any other, to which this power does not extend. Commerce, as the word is used in the constitution, is a unit, every part of which is indicated by the term. The subject to which the power is next applied, is to commerce "among the several States." The word "among" means intermingled with. A thing which is intermingled with them. Commerce among the States, cannot stop at the external boundary line of each State, but may be introduced into the interior. It is not intended that these words comprehend that commerce, which is completely internal, which is carried on between man and man in a State, or between different parts of the same State, and which does not extend to or affect other States.

Comprehensive as the word "among" is, it may very properly be restricted to commerce which concerns more States than one. The enumeration presupposes something not enumerated; and that something, if we regard the language or the subject of the sentence, must be the exclusively internal commerce of a State. The genius and character of the whole government seem to be, that its action is to be applied to all the external concerns of the nation, and to those internal concerns which affect the States generally; but not to those which are completely within a particular State, which do not affect other States, and with which it is not necessary to interfere, for the purpose of executing some of the general powers of the government. The completely internal commerce of a State, then, may be considered as reserved for the State itself.

In regulating commerce with foreign nations, the power of Congress does not stop at the jurisdictional lines of the several States. It would be a very useless power, if it could not pass those lines. If Congress has the power to regulate, that power must be exercised whenever the subject exists. If it exists within the States, if a foreign voyage may commence or terminate at a port within a State, then the power of Congress may be exercised within a State. This principle is, if possible, still more clear, when applied to commerce "among the several States." Can a trading expedition between two adjoining States, commence and terminate outside of each? If the trading intercourse be between two States remote from each other, must it not commence in one, terminate in the other, and probably pass through a third? Commerce among the States must, of necessity, be commerce with the States. The power of Congress, whatever it may be, must be exercised within the territorial jurisdiction of the several States.

What is this power? It is the power to regulate; that is, to prescribe the rule by which commerce is to be governed. This power, like all others vested in Congress, is complete in itself, may be exercised to its utmost extent, and acknowledges no limitations, other than are prescribed in the constitution. The wisdom and the discretion of Congress, their identity with the people, and the influence which their constituents possess at elections, are, as in many other instances, as for example, of declaring war, the sole restraints on which they have relied, to secure them from its abuse. They are the restraints on which the people must often rely solely, in all representative governments.

The power of Congress comprehends navigation, within the limits of every State in the Union; so far as that navigation may be, in any manner, connected with "commerce with foreign nations, or among the several States, or with the Indian tribes." It may, of consequence, pass the jurisdictional line of New York, and act upon the very waters to which the prohibition now under consideration applies.

It has been urged with great earnestness that the States may severally exercise the same power, within their respective jurisdictions. It is said, that they possessed it as an inseparable attribute of sovereignty, before the formation of the constitution, and still retain it, except so far as they have surrendered it by that instrument; that this principle results from the nature of the government, and is secured by the tenth amendment; that an affirmative grant of power is not exclusive, unless in its own nature it be such that the continued exercise of it by the former possessor is inconsistent with the grant, and that this is not of that description. Appellant contends that full power to regulate a particular subject, implies the whole power, and leaves no residuum; that a grant of the whole is incompatible with the existence of a right in another to any part of it.

The power to lay and collect taxes is, like the power to regulate commerce, made in general terms, and has never been understood to interfere with the exercise of the same power by the State. Although many powers formerly exercised by the States, are transferred to the government of the Union, State governments remain, and constitute a most important part of our system. The power of taxation is indispensable to their existence, and is a power which is capable of residing in, and being exercised by, different authorities at the same time. When each government exercises the power of taxation, neither is exercising the power of the other. But, when a State proceeds to regulate commerce with foreign nations, or among the several States, it is exercising the very power granted to Congress, and is doing the very thing which Congress is authorized to do. There is no analogy between the power of taxation and the power of regulating commerce.

Inspection laws are said to be regulations of commerce, and are recognised in the constitution, as being passed in the exercise of a power remaining with the States. That inspection laws may have a remote and considerable influence on commerce, will not be denied; but that a power to regulate commerce is the source from which the right to pass them is derived, cannot be admitted. The object of inspection laws, is to improve the quality of articles produced by the labour of a country; to fit them for exportation; or for domestic use. They act upon the subject before it becomes an article of foreign commerce, or of commerce among the States, and prepare it for that purpose. They form a portion of that immense mass of legislation, which embraces everything within the territory of a State, not surrendered to the general government: all which can be most advantageously exercised by the States themselves. Inspection laws, quarantine laws, health laws of every description, as well as laws regulating the internal commerce of a State, and those which respect turnpike roads, ferries, &c., are component parts of this mass.

No direct general power over these objects is granted to Congress; and they remain subject to State legislation. If the legislative power of the Union can reach them, it must be for national purposes; it must be where the power is expressly given for a special purpose, or is clearly incidental to some power which is expressly given. The government of the Union, in the exercise of its express powers, of regulating commerce with foreign nations and among the States, may use means that may also be employed by a State, in the exercise of its acknowledged powers; that of regulating commerce within the State. If Congress license vessels to sail from one port to another, in the same State, the act is supposed to be, necessarily, incidental to the power expressly granted to Congress, and implies no claim of a direct power to regulate the purely internal commerce of a State, or to act directly on its system of police. If a State, in passing laws on subjects acknowledged to be within its control, shall adopt a measure of the same character with one which Congress may adopt, it does not derive its authority from the particular power which has been granted, but from some other, which remains with the State, and may be executed by the same means. Experience shows, that the same measures, or measures scarcely distinguishable from each other, may flow from distinct powers; but this does not prove that the powers themselves are identical.

It has been contended that, as the word "to regulate" implies in its nature, full power over the thing to be regulated, it excludes, necessarily, the action of all others that would perform the same operation on the same thing. That regulation is designed for the entire result, applying to those parts which remain as they were, as well as to those which are altered. It produces a uniform whole, which is as much disturbed and deranged by changing what the regulating power designs to leave untouched, as that on which it has operated. There is great force in this argument, and the Court is not satisfied that it has been refuted. Since, in exercising the power of regulating their own purely internal affairs, whether of trading or police, the States may sometimes enact laws, the validity of which depends on their interfering with, and being contrary to, an act of Congress passed in pursuance of the constitution, the Court will enter upon the inquiry, whether the laws of New York have, in their application to this case, come into collision with an act of Congress, and deprived a citizen of a right to which that act entitles him. Should this collision exist, it will be immaterial whether those laws were passed in virtue of a concurrent power "to regulate commerce with foreign nations and among the several States," or, in virtue of a power to regulate their domestic trade and police. The acts of New York must yield to the law of Congress; and the decision sustaining the privilege they confer, against a right given by a law of the Union, must be erroneous.

It has been contended, that if a law passed by a State, in the exercise of its acknowledged sovereignty, comes into conflict with a law passed by Congress in pursuance of the constitution, they affect the subject, and each other, like equal opposing powers. But the framers of our constitution foresaw this state of things, and provided for it, by declaring the supremacy not only of itself, but of the laws made in pursuance of it. The constitution is the supreme law. The appropriate application of that part of the clause which confers supremacy on laws and treaties, is to such acts of the State Legislatures as do not transcend their powers, but, though enacted in the execution of acknowledged State powers, interfere with, or are contrary to the laws of Congress, made in pursuance of the constitution, or some treaty made under the authority of the United States. In every such case, the act of Congress, or the treaty, is supreme; and the law of the State, though enacted in the exercise of powers not controverted, must yield to it.

Notes: The Nineteenth-Century Commerce Clause

1. Gibbons's *Impact.* "The effects of the decision were at once felt in the waters of New York and the other States." CHARLES WARREN, THE SUPREME COURT IN UNITED STATES HISTORY vol. 2, 75 (Little, Brown 1922):

> The newspapers of the North carried this item: "Yesterday the Steamboat *United States,* entered New York in triumph, with streamers flying, and a large company of passengers exulting in the decision of the United States Supreme Court against the New York monopoly. She fired a salute which was loudly returned by huzzas from the wharves." A representative Southern paper spoke of "the immense public advantages that flow from the decision. The fare in the steamboats that ply between New York and New Haven has been reduced from five to three dollars." A year after the decision, *Niles Register* reported that the number of steamboats plying from New York had increased from six to forty-three. The importance of the case in the eyes

of the public was its effect in shattering the great monopoly against which they had been struggling for fifteen years.

2. *Insurance Policies as Commerce.* Despite *Gibbons*'s expansive language, the Court did not always construe the Commerce Clause broadly during the nineteenth century. *Paul v. Virginia,* 75 U.S. (8 Wall.) 168 (1868), involved a Virginia statute that discriminated against insurance companies incorporated in other states. The statute was challenged as repugnant to the federal commerce power. In an opinion delivered by Justice Field, the Court rejected the challenge, concluding that "issuing a policy of insurance is not a transaction of commerce" so the Commerce Clause does not reach it.

3. *Internal Commerce.* In some early decisions, the Court held that the states retained control over their internal commerce. *Kidd v. Pearson,* 128 U.S. 1 (1888), involved an Iowa statute that prohibited the manufacture of liquor as applied to an Iowa company that sold its product in other states. The Court upheld the law: "Congress's power over commerce does not comprehend the purely internal domestic commerce of a state, which is carried on or between different parts of the same state. It does not follow that, because the products of a domestic manufacture may ultimately become the subjects of interstate commerce, at the pleasure of the manufacturer, the legislation of the state respecting such manufacture is an attempted exercise of the power to regulate commerce exclusively conferred upon congress."

4. *Interstate Steamers.* Some nineteenth-century decisions took a more expansive view regarding the scope of the Commerce Clause. *The Daniel Ball,* 77 U.S. 557 (1870), involved a steamer that traveled wholly within the State of Michigan, but that carried merchandise being transported to and from other states. The Court held that a federal safety regulation could be applied to the steamer: "We are unable to draw any clear and distinct line between the authority of Congress to regulate an agency employed in commerce between the States, when that agency extends through two or more States, and when it is confined entirely within the limits of a single State. If its authority does not extend to an agency in such commerce, when that agency is confined within the limits of a State, its authority over interstate commerce may be defeated. Several agencies combining, each taking up the commodity transported at the boundary line at one end of a State, and leaving it at the boundary line at the other end, the Federal jurisdiction would be entirely ousted, and the constitutional provision would become a dead letter."

∾ PROBLEM: MORE ON THE EDUCATION FOR A BETTER AMERICA ACT ∾

Under *Gibbons*'s conception of Congress's Commerce Clause power, does Congress have the power to pass the Act? Could Congress provide financial incentives to local school districts to encourage them to reform? Could it also mandate various actions (e.g., the administration of student performance tests or special training for teachers)?

2. *Early Twentieth-Century Cases*

When the Constitution was ratified, the United States was a largely agrarian society. By the end of the nineteenth century, the economy was in a period of dramatic and rapid transition to an industrialized society. Industrialization produced profound changes in the U.S. economy. The development of railroads, and eventually cars, allowed people and goods to move freely across state borders. Although many commercial problems may have been local in nature at one time, the evolution of society and commerce meant that many issues were increasingly becoming national problems. As a result, Congress began to assume a more active regulatory role, passing the Interstate Commerce Act, the Sherman Act, and a host of other regulatory legislation. Congress's more aggressive posture forced the Court to confront difficult questions regarding the scope of Congress's power. It did so in several cases decided early in the twentieth century. In some of these cases, the Court took an expansive view of federal power. In other cases, it took a more restrictive view.

Champion v. Ames

188 U.S. 321 (1903)

(THE LOTTERY CASE)

Mr. Justice HARLAN delivered the opinion of the court:

Appellant Champion was indicted for conspiring to transport lottery tickets across state lines in violation of federal law. Champion sought a writ of habeas corpus on the basis that the law prohibiting the transportation of lottery tickets was unconstitutional. Appellant insists that the carrying of lottery tickets from one state to another state by an express company engaged in carrying freight and packages, although such tickets may be contained in a box or package, does not constitute, and cannot by any act of Congress be legally made to constitute, commerce among the states within the meaning of the Constitution; consequently Congress cannot make it an offense to cause such tickets to be carried from one state to another.

Commerce among the states embraces navigation, intercourse, communication, traffic, the transit of persons, and the transmission of messages by telegraph. The power to regulate commerce among the several states is vested in Congress as absolutely as it would be in a single government, having in its constitution the same restrictions on the exercise of the power as are found in the Constitution of the United States; that such power is plenary, complete in itself, and may be exerted by Congress to its utmost extent, subject only to such limitations as the

Constitution imposes upon the exercise of the powers; and that in determining the character of the regulations to be adopted Congress has a large discretion which is not to be controlled by the courts, simply because, in their opinion, such regulations may not be the best or most effective that could be employed.

It was argued that lottery tickets are not of any real or substantial value in themselves, and therefore are not subjects of commerce. We cannot accept the broad statement that such tickets are of no value. The lottery company offered a large capital prize, to be paid to the holder of the ticket winning the prize at the drawing. We are of opinion that lottery tickets are subjects of traffic, and therefore are subjects of commerce, and the regulation of the carriage of such tickets from state to state, at least by independent carriers, is a regulation of commerce among the several states.

But it is said that the statute in question does not regulate the carrying of lottery tickets from state to state, but by punishing those who cause them to be so carried Congress in effect prohibits such carrying; that in respect of the carrying from one state to another of articles or things that are, in fact, or according to usage in business, the subjects of commerce, the authority given Congress was not to *prohibit*, but only to *regulate*.

The Constitution does not define what is to be deemed a legitimate regulation of interstate commerce. In *Gibbons v. Ogden* it was said that the power to regulate such commerce is the power to prescribe the rule by which it is to be governed. While our government be one of enumerated powers, the Constitution does not attempt to set forth all the means by which such powers may be carried into execution. It leaves to Congress a large discretion as to the means that may be employed in executing a given power. Let the end be legitimate, let it be within the scope of the Constitution, and all means which are appropriate, which are plainly adapted to that end, which are not prohibited, but consist with the letter and spirit of the Constitution, are constitutional. 4 Wheat. 421.

We have said that the carrying from state to state of lottery tickets constitutes interstate commerce, and that the regulation of such commerce is within the power of Congress under the Constitution. Are we prepared to say that a provision which is a *prohibition* of the carriage of such articles from state to state is not a fit or appropriate mode for the *regulation* of that particular kind of commerce? If lottery traffic, *carried on through interstate commerce*, is a matter of which Congress may take cognizance and over which its power may be exerted, can it be possible that it must tolerate the traffic, and simply regulate the manner in which it may be carried on? Or may not Congress, for the protection of the people of all the states, and under the power to regulate interstate commerce, devise such means, within the scope of the Constitution, and not prohibited by it, as will drive that traffic out of commerce among the states?

In determining whether regulation may under some circumstances properly take the form or have the effect of prohibition, the nature of the interstate traffic which it sought to suppress cannot be overlooked. If a state, when considering legislation for the suppression of lotteries within its own limits, may properly take into view the evils that inhere in the raising of money, in that mode, why may not Congress, invested with the power to regulate commerce among the several states, provide that such commerce shall not be polluted by the carrying of lottery tickets from one state to another? The power of Congress to regulate commerce among the states is plenary, is complete in itself, and is subject to no limitations except such as may be found in the Constitution. Surely it will not be said to be a part of anyone's liberty that he shall be allowed to introduce into commerce among the states an element that will be confessedly injurious to the public morals.

If it be said that the act of 1894 is inconsistent with the 10th Amendment, reserving to the states respectively, or to the people, the powers not delegated to the United States, the answer is that the power to regulate commerce among the states has been expressly delegated to Congress. Congress does not assume to interfere with traffic or commerce in lottery tickets carried on exclusively within the limits of any state, but has in view only commerce of that kind among the several states. As a state may, for the purpose of guarding the morals of its own people, forbid all sales of lottery tickets within its limits, so Congress, for the purpose of guarding the people of the United States against the "widespread pestilence of lotteries" and to protect the commerce which concerns all the states, may prohibit the carrying of lottery tickets from one state to another. Congress only supplemented the action of those states which, for the protection of the public morals, prohibit the drawing of lotteries, as well as the sale or circulation of lottery tickets, within their respective limits. We should hesitate long before adjudging that an evil of such appalling character, carried on through interstate commerce, cannot be met and crushed by the only power competent to that end. Congress alone has the power to occupy, by legislation, the whole field of interstate commerce.

That regulation may sometimes appropriately assume the form of prohibition is also illustrated by the case of diseased cattle, transported from one state to another. Such cattle may have, notwithstanding their condition, a value in money for some purposes, and yet it cannot be doubted that Congress, under its power to regulate commerce, may either provide for their being inspected before transportation begins, or, in its discretion, may prohibit their being transported from one state to another.

We decide nothing more than that lottery tickets are subjects of traffic among those who choose to sell or buy them; that the carriage of such tickets by independent carriers from one state to another is therefore interstate commerce; that under its power to regulate commerce among the several states Congress — subject to the limitations imposed by the Constitution upon the exercise of the powers granted — has plenary authority over such commerce, and may prohibit the carriage of such tickets from state to state; and that legislation to that end, and of that character, is not inconsistent with any limitation or restriction imposed upon the exercise of the powers granted to Congress.

The judgment is affirmed.

Mr. Chief Justice FULLER, with whom *concur* Mr. Justice BREWER, Mr. Justice SHIRAS, and Mr. Justice PECKHAM, *dissenting*:

An act prohibiting the carriage of lottery matter would be necessary and proper to the execution of a power to suppress lotteries; but that power belongs to the states and not to Congress. To hold that Congress has general police power would be to hold that it may accomplish objects not intrusted to the general government, and to defeat the operation of the 10th Amendment.

Does the grant to Congress of the power to regulate interstate commerce import the absolute power to prohibit it? The power to prohibit the transportation of diseased animals and infected goods over railroads or on steamboats is an entirely different thing, for they would be in themselves injurious to the transaction of interstate commerce, and are essentially commercial in their nature. The exclusion of diseased persons rests on different ground, for nobody would pretend that persons could be kept off the trains because they were going from one state to another to engage in the lottery business. However enticing that business may be, we do not understand these pieces of paper themselves can communicate bad principles by contact. I regard this decision as inconsistent with the views of the framers of the Constitution, and of Marshall, its great expounder.

∾ PROBLEM: MORE ON THE EDUCATION FOR A BETTER AMERICA ACT ∾

Does *Champion* offer insights into whether (and how) Congress can pass the Act? Also, note the Court's conception of the Tenth Amendment. If Congress passes this legislation, does it have to worry about running afoul of that Amendment?

Houston, East & West Texas Railway Co. v. United States

234 U.S. 342 (1914)

Mr. Justice HUGHES delivered the opinion of the court:

These suits were brought in the commerce court by the Houston, East & West Texas Railway Company and the Houston & Shreveport Railroad Company, and by the Texas & Pacific Railway Company, respectively, to set aside an order of the Interstate Commerce Commission upon the ground that it exceeded the Commission's authority.

The Interstate Commerce Commission found that the interstate class rates out of Shreveport to named Texas points were unreasonable, and it established maximum class rates for this traffic. These rates were substantially the same as the class rates fixed by the Railroad Commission of Texas, and charged by the carriers, for transportation for similar distances in that state. The Interstate Commerce Commission also found that the carriers maintained "higher rates from Shreveport to points in Texas" than were in force "from cities in Texas to such points under substantially similar conditions and circumstances," and that thereby "an unlawful and undue preference and advantage" was given to the Texas cities, and a "discrimination" that was "undue and unlawful" was effected against Shreveport. In order to correct this discrimination, the carriers were directed to desist from charging higher rates for the transportation of any commodity from Shreveport to Dallas and Houston, respectively, and intermediate than were contemporaneously charged for the carriage of such commodity from Dallas and Houston toward Shreveport for equal distances, as the Commission found that relation of rates to be reasonable.

Appellants object that, as the discrimination found by the Commission to be unjust arises out of the relation of intrastate rates, maintained under state authority, to interstate rates that have been upheld as reasonable, its correction was beyond the Commission's power. The order might be complied with, and the discrimination avoided, either by reducing the interstate rates from Shreveport to the level of the competing intrastate rates, or by raising these intrastate rates to the level of the interstate rates, or by such reduction in the one case and increase in the other. But it is urged that, so far as the interstate rates were sustained by the Commission as reasonable, the Commission was without authority to compel their reduction in order to equalize them with the lower intrastate rates.

It is unnecessary to repeat what has frequently been said with respect to the complete and paramount character of the power confided to Congress to regulate commerce among the several states. It is the essence of this power that, where it exists, it dominates. Interstate trade was not left to be destroyed or impeded by the rivalries of local government. The purpose was to make impossible the recurrence of the evils which had overwhelmed the Confederation, and to provide the necessary basis of national unity by insuring "uniformity of regulation against conflicting and discriminating state legislation." By virtue of the comprehensive terms of the grant, the authority of Congress is at all times adequate to meet the varying exigencies that arise, and to protect the national interest by securing the freedom of interstate commercial intercourse from local control. *Gibbons v. Ogden*, 9 Wheat. 1.

Congress is empowered to regulate, — that is, to provide the law for interstate commerce; to enact "all appropriate legislation" for its "protection and advancement," to adopt measures "to promote its growth and insure its safety," "to foster, protect, control, and restrain." Its authority, extending to these interstate carriers as instruments of interstate commerce, necessarily embraces the right to control their operations in all matters having such a close and substantial relation to interstate traffic that the control is essential or appropriate to the security of that traffic, to the efficiency of the interstate service, and to the maintenance of conditions under which interstate commerce may be conducted upon fair terms and without molestation or hindrance. As it is competent for Congress to legis-late to these ends, it may seek their attainment by requiring that the agencies of interstate commerce shall not be used in such manner as to cripple, retard, or destroy it. The fact that carriers are instruments of intrastate commerce, as well as of interstate commerce, does not derogate from the complete and paramount authority of Congress over the latter, or preclude the Federal power from being exerted to prevent the intrastate operations of carriers from being made a means of injury to that which has been confided to Federal care. Wherever the inter-state and intrastate transactions of carriers are so related that the government of the one involves the control of the other, it is Congress, and not the state, that is entitled to prescribe the final and dominant rule, for otherwise Congress would be denied the exercise of its constitutional authority, and the state, and not the nation, would be supreme within the national field.

Congress, in the exercise of its paramount power, may prevent the com-mon instrumentalities of interstate and intrastate commercial intercourse from being used in their intrastate operations to the injury of interstate commerce. This is not to say that Congress possesses the authority to regulate the internal commerce of a state, as such, but that it does possess the power to foster and protect interstate commerce, and to take all measures necessary or appropriate to that end, although intrastate transactions of interstate carriers may thereby be controlled.

We find no reason to doubt that Congress is entitled to keep the highways of interstate communication open to interstate traffic upon fair and equal terms. That an unjust discrimination in the rates of a common carrier, by which one person or locality is unduly favored as against another under substantially sim-ilar conditions of traffic, constitutes an evil, is undeniable; and where this evil consists in the action of an interstate carrier in unreasonably discriminating against interstate traffic over its line, the authority of Congress to prevent it is equally clear. It is immaterial, so far as the protecting power of Congress is concerned, that the discrimination arises from intrastate rates as compared with interstate rates. The use of the instrument of interstate commerce in a discrimi-natory manner so as to inflict injury upon that commerce, or some part thereof, furnishes abundant ground for Federal intervention. Nor can the attempted exercise of state authority alter the matter, where Congress has acted, for a state may not authorize the carrier to do that which Congress is entitled to forbid and has forbidden.

The decree of the Commerce Court is affirmed in each case.

Affirmed.

Note

Although the *Lottery Case* involved an expansion of federal power, the follow-ing case makes clear that the trend during this era was not uniformly expansionist.

Hammer v. Dagenhart

247 U.S. 251 (1918)

Mr. Justice DAY delivered the opinion of the Court.

Is it within the authority of Congress in regulating commerce among the states to prohibit the transportation in interstate commerce of manufactured goods, the product of a factory in which, within thirty days prior to their removal therefrom, children under the age of fourteen have been employed or permitted to work, or children between the ages of fourteen and sixteen years have been employed or permitted to work more than eight hours in any day, or more than six days in any week, or after the hour of 7 o'clock p.m., or before the hour of 6 o'clock a.m.?

The power essential to the passage of this act, the government contends, is found in the commerce clause of the Constitution which authorizes Congress to regulate commerce with foreign nations and among the states. In *Gibbons v. Ogdon*, 9 Wheat. 1, Chief Justice Marshall, in defining the extent and nature of the commerce power, said, "It is the power to regulate; that is, to prescribe the rule by which commerce is to be governed." In other words, the power is one to control the means by which commerce is carried on, which is the contrary of the assumed right to forbid commerce from moving and thus destroying it as to particular commodities. But it is insisted that cases establish the doctrine that the power to regulate given to Congress incidentally includes the authority to prohibit the movement of ordinary commodities. The cases demonstrate the contrary. They rest upon the character of the particular subjects dealt with and the fact that the scope of governmental authority, state or national, is such that the authority to prohibit is as to them but the exertion of the power to regulate.

The first of these cases is *Champion v. Ames*, 188 U.S. 321, the so-called *Lottery Case*, in which it was held that Congress might pass a law having the effect to keep the channels of commerce free from use in the transportation of tickets used in the promotion of lottery schemes. In *Hipolite Egg Co. v. United States*, 220 U.S. 45, this court sustained the power of Congress to pass the Pure Food and Drug Act, which prohibited the introduction into the states by means of interstate commerce of impure foods and drugs. In each of these instances the use of interstate transportation was necessary to the accomplishment of harmful results. Although the power over interstate transportation was to regulate, that could only be accomplished by prohibiting the use of the facilities of interstate commerce to effect the evil intended.

This element is wanting in the present case. The thing intended by this statute is the denial of the facilities of interstate commerce to manufacturers in states who employ children within the prohibited ages. The act does not regulate transportation among the states, but aims to standardize the ages at which children may be employed in mining and manufacturing within the states. The goods shipped are themselves harmless. The act permits them to be freely shipped after thirty days from the time of their removal from the factory. When offered for shipment, and before transportation begins, production is over, and the mere fact that they were intended for interstate commerce transportation does not make their production subject to federal control under the commerce power. Commerce "consists of intercourse and traffic and includes the transportation of persons and property, as well as the purchase, sale and exchange of commodities." The making of goods and the mining of coal are not commerce, nor does the fact that these things are to be afterwards shipped, or used in interstate commerce, make their production part thereof. Over interstate transportation, or its incidents, the regulatory power of Congress is ample, but the production of articles, intended for interstate commerce, is a matter of local regulation. If it were otherwise, all manufacture intended for interstate shipment would be brought under federal control to the practical exclusion of the authority of the states, a result not contemplated by the framers of the Constitution when they vested in Congress the authority to regulate commerce among the States. *Kidd v. Pearson,* 128 U.S. 1.

It is contended that the authority of Congress may be exerted to control interstate commerce in the shipment of childmade goods because of the effect of the circulation of such goods in other states where the evil of this class of labor has been recognized by local legislation, and the right to employ child labor has been more rigorously restrained than in the state of production. In other words, unfair competition may be controlled by closing the channels of interstate commerce to manufacturers in those states where the local laws do not meet what Congress deems to be the more just standard of other states.

There is no power vested in Congress to require the states to exercise their police power so as to prevent possible unfair competition. Many causes may cooperate to give one state, by reason of local laws or conditions, an economic advantage over others. The commerce clause was not intended to give Congress a general authority to equalize such conditions. In some states laws have been passed fixing minimum wages for women, in others the local law regulates the hours of labor of women in various employments. Business done in such states may be at an economic disadvantage when compared with states which have no such regulations; surely, this fact does not give Congress the power to deny transportation in interstate commerce to those who carry on business where the hours of labor and the rate of compensation for women have not been fixed by a standard in use in other states and approved by Congress. The grant of power of Congress over the subject of interstate commerce was to enable it to regulate such commerce, and not to give it authority to control the states in their exercise of the police power over local trade and manufacture.

The grant of authority over a purely federal matter was not intended to destroy the local power always existing and carefully reserved to the states in the Tenth Amendment to the Constitution. Police regulations relating to the internal trade and affairs of the states have been uniformly recognized as within such control. In the judgment which established the broad power of Congress over interstate commerce, Chief Justice Marshall said: "Inspection laws act upon the subject, before it becomes an article of foreign commerce, or of commerce among the states, and prepare it for that purpose. They form a portion of that immense mass of legislation, which embraces everything within the territory of a state, not surrendered to the general government; all of which can be most advantageously exercised by the states themselves. Inspection laws, quarantine laws, health laws of every description, as well as laws for regulating the internal commerce of a state, and those which respect turnpike roads, ferries, etc., are component parts of this mass."

That there should be limitations upon the right to employ children in mines and factories in the interest of their own and the public welfare, all will admit. That such employment is generally deemed to require regulation is shown by the fact that every state in the Union has a law upon the subject. In North Carolina, the state wherein is located the factory in the present case, no child under twelve years of age is permitted to work. It may be desirable that such laws be uniform, but our federal government is one of enumerated powers; "this principle," declared Chief Justice Marshall in *McCulloch v. Maryland,* 4 Wheat. 316, "is universally admitted."

A statute must be judged by its natural and reasonable effect. Control by Congress over interstate commerce cannot authorize the exercise of authority not entrusted to it by the Constitution. The maintenance of the authority of the states over matters purely local is as essential to the preservation of our institutions as is the conservation of the supremacy of the federal power in all matters entrusted to the nation by the federal Constitution.

In interpreting the Constitution it must never be forgotten that the nation is made up of states to which are entrusted the powers of local government. To them and to the people the powers not expressly delegated to the national government are reserved. The power of the states to regulate their purely internal affairs by such laws as seem wise to the local authority is inherent and has never been surrendered to the general government. *Slaughter House Cases,* 16 Wall. 36. To sustain this statute would sanction an invasion by the federal power of the control of a matter purely local in its character, and over which no authority has been delegated to Congress in conferring the power to regulate commerce among the states.

We have neither authority nor disposition to question the motives of Congress in enacting this legislation. The purposes must be attained consistently with constitutional limitations and not by an invasion of the powers of the states. This court has no more important function than that which devolves upon it the obligation to preserve inviolate the constitutional limitations upon the exercise of authority federal and state to the end that each may continue to discharge, harmoniously with the other, the duties entrusted to it by the Constitution. The necessary effect of this act is a prohibition against the movement in interstate commerce of ordinary commercial commodities to regulate the hours of labor of children in factories and mines within the states, a purely state authority. The act is repugnant to the Constitution. It not only transcends the authority delegated to Congress over commerce but also exerts power as to a purely local matter to which the federal authority does not extend. The far reaching result of upholding the act cannot be more plainly indicated than by pointing out that if Congress can thus regulate matters entrusted to local authority by prohibition of the movement of commodities in interstate commerce, all freedom of commerce will be at an end, and the power of the states over local matters may be eliminated, and thus our system of government be practically destroyed.

For these reasons we hold that this law exceeds the constitutional authority of Congress. It follows that the decree of the District Court must be
   Affirmed.

Mr. Justice HOLMES, *dissenting.*

The statute confines itself to prohibiting the carriage of certain goods in interstate or foreign commerce. Congress is given power to regulate such commerce in unqualified terms. Regulation means the prohibition of something, and when interstate commerce is the matter to be regulated the regulation may prohibit any part of such commerce that Congress sees fit to forbid. It is established by the *Lottery Case* that a law is not beyond the regulative power of Congress merely because it prohibits certain transportation out and out. The Act does not meddle with anything belonging to the states. They may regulate their internal affairs and their domestic commerce as they like. But when they seek to send their products across the state line they are no longer within their rights. The public policy of the United States is shaped with a view to the benefit of the nation as a whole. The national welfare as understood by Congress may require a different attitude within its sphere from that of some self-seeking State. It seems entirely constitutional for Congress to enforce its understanding by all the means at its command.

∾ PROBLEM: MORE ON THE EDUCATION FOR A BETTER AMERICA ACT ∾

What insights does *Hammer* offer regarding whether Congress can pass the Act and how it should structure the Act? Does the Tenth Amendment explicitly limit the scope of Congress's authority and the content of the legislation?

3. The Constitutional Crisis

In 1929, the stock market crashed. Following the crash, the country settled into a prolonged period of economic depression. In 1932, President Franklin Delano Roosevelt (FDR) was elected on the promise of a "New Deal." The situation facing FDR and the country was grim. In 1931, the year before he was elected, more than 2,000 banks had failed. By the winter of 1932–1933, shortly before Roosevelt assumed office, "one-fourth of the nation's work force was unemployed," and the price of wheat had dropped by "nearly 90 percent." Industrial output had fallen by 60 percent. *See* ROBERT S. MCELVAINE, THE GREAT DEPRESSION: AMERICA 1929–1941 137 (Times Books 1984).

Roosevelt took office demanding "action, and action now," calling an extraordinary session of Congress to begin five days after his inauguration. During this session, the House passed 11 major bills with only 40 hours of debate. During his first hundred days, Roosevelt pushed through Congress bills regulating financial markets, creating federal works programs, and regulating prices and wages. Congress passed the Agricultural Adjustment Act, the Bituminous Coal Act, the Farm Relief Act, the Emergency Farm Mortgage Act, the National Industrial Recovery Act, the Railway Pension Act, and the Truth-in-Securities Act. The federal courts were hostile to these acts.

Carter v. Carter Coal Co.

298 U.S. 238 (1936)

Mr. Justice SUTHERLAND delivered the opinion of the Court.

The purposes of the "Bituminous Coal Conservation Act of 1935" are to stabilize the bituminous coal-mining industry and promote its interstate commerce; to provide for co-operative marketing of bituminous coal; to levy a tax on such coal and provide for a drawback under certain conditions; to declare the production, distribution, and use of such coal to be affected with a national public interest; to conserve the national resources of such coal; to provide for the general welfare, and for other purposes. The constitutional validity of the act is challenged in each of the suits.

Section 1, among other things, declares that the production and distribution by producers of coal bear upon and directly affect interstate commerce, and render regulation of production and distribution imperative for the protection of such commerce; that certain features connected with the production, distribution, and marketing have led to waste of the national coal resources, disorganization of interstate commerce in such coal, and burdening and obstructing interstate commerce therein; that practices prevailing in the production of such coal directly affect interstate commerce and require regulation for the protection of that commerce; and that the right of mine workers to organize and collectively bargain for wages, hours of labor, and conditions of employment should be guaranteed in order to prevent constant wage cutting and disparate labor costs detrimental to fair interstate competition, and in order to avoid obstructions to interstate commerce that recur in industrial disputes over labor relations at the mines. These declarations constitute not enactments of law, but legislative averments by way of inducement to the enactment which follows.

Section 3 provides: "There is hereby imposed upon the sale or other disposal of all bituminous coal produced within the United States an excise tax of 15 per centum on the sale price at the mine. Provided that any coal producer who has filed with the National Bituminous Coal Commission his acceptance of the code provided for in section 4 of this Act, and who acts in compliance with the provisions of such code, shall be entitled to a drawback in the form of a credit upon the amount of such tax payable hereunder, equivalent to 90 per centum of the amount of such tax." Section 4 provides that the commission shall formulate the elaborate provisions contained therein into a working agreement to be known as the Bituminous Coal Code.

The act confers the power to fix the minimum price of coal at every coal mine in the United States. The labor provisions of the code require that in order to effectuate the purposes of the act the district boards and code members shall accept specified conditions contained in the code, among which are the following: "Employees to be given the right to organize and bargain collectively. Such employees have the right of peaceable assemblage for the discussion of the principles of collective bargaining."

The question is whether the labor provisions of the act can be upheld as an exercise of the power to regulate interstate commerce. As used in the Constitution, the word "commerce" is the equivalent of the phrase "intercourse for the purposes of trade," and includes transportation, purchase, sale, and exchange of commodities between the citizens of the different states. The power to regulate commerce embraces the instruments by which commerce is carried on. In *Adair v. United States*, 208 U.S. 161, the phrase "Commerce among the several states" was defined as comprehending "traffic, intercourse, trade, navigation, communication, the transit of persons, and the transmission of messages by telegraph, — indeed, every species on commercial intercourse among the several states."

The distinction between manufacture and commerce was discussed in *Kidd v. Pearson*, 128 U.S. 1, 20 (1888), where it was said:

> No distinction is more clearly expressed in economic and political literature, than that between manufactures and commerce. Manufacture is transformation — the fashioning of raw materials into a change of form for use. The functions of commerce are different. If it be held that the term includes the regulation of all such manufactures as are intended to be the subject of commercial transactions in the future, it is impossible to deny that it would also include all productive industries that contemplate the same thing. The result would be that congress would be invested, to the exclusion of the states, with the power to regulate, not only manufacture, but also agriculture, horticulture, stock-raising, domestic fisheries, mining, — in short, every branch of human industry. For is there one of them that does not contemplate, more or less clearly, an interstate or foreign market? Does not the wheat-grower of the northwest, and the cotton-planter of the south, plant, cultivate, and harvest his crop with an eye on the prices at Liverpool, New York, and Chicago?

One who produces or manufactures a commodity, subsequently sold and shipped by him in interstate commerce, whether such sale and shipment were originally intended or not, has engaged in two distinct and separate activities. So far as he produces or manufactures a commodity, his business is purely local. So far as he sells and ships, or contracts to sell and ship, the commodity to customers in another state, he engages in interstate commerce. In respect of the former, he is subject only to regulation by the state; in respect of the latter, to regulation only by the federal government.

The word "commerce" is the equivalent of the phrase "intercourse for the purposes of trade." Plainly, the incidents leading up to and culminating in the mining of coal do not constitute such intercourse. The employment of men, the fixing of their wages, hours of labor, and working conditions, the bargaining in respect of these things—whether carried on separately or collectively—each and all constitute intercourse for the purposes of production, not of trade. The latter is a thing apart from the relation of employer and employee, which in all producing occupations is purely local in character. Extraction of coal from the mine is the aim and the completed result of local activities. Commerce in the coal mined is not brought into being by force of these activities, but by negotiations, agreements and circumstances entirely apart from production. Mining brings the subject-matter of commerce into existence. Commerce disposes of it.

Another group of cases rest upon the circumstance that the acts in question constituted direct interferences with the "flow" of commerce among the states. In the *Swift Case*, livestock was consigned and delivered to stockyards—not as a place of final destination, but as "a throat through which the current flows." The sales which ensued merely changed the private interest in the subject of the current without interfering with its continuity. It was nowhere suggested that the interstate commerce power extended to the growth or production of the things which, after production, entered the flow. If the court had held that the raising of the cattle, including the wages paid to and working conditions of the herders and others employed in the business, could be regulated by Congress, that decision and decisions holding similarly would be in point; for it is that situation, and not the one with which the court actually dealt, which here concerns us.

Section 1 of the act now under review declares that all production and distribution of bituminous coal "bear upon and directly affect its interstate commerce"; and that regulation thereof is imperative for the protection of such commerce. That the production of every commodity intended for interstate sale and transportation has some effect upon interstate commerce may be freely granted; and we are brought to the final and decisive inquiry, whether here that effect is direct, as the "Preamble" recites, or indirect. The distinction is not formal, but substantial in the highest degree, as we pointed out in *Schechter*, "If the commerce clause were construed to reach all enterprises and transactions which could be said to have an indirect effect upon interstate commerce, the federal authority would embrace practically all activities of the people, and the authority of the state over domestic concerns would exist only by sufferance of the federal government."

Whether the effect of a given activity or condition is direct or indirect is not always easy to determine. The word "direct" implies that the activity or condition invoked shall operate proximately—not remotely, or collaterally—to produce the effect. It connotes the absence of an efficient intervening agency or condition. The extent of the effect bears no logical relation to its character. The distinction between a direct and an indirect effect turns, not upon the magnitude of the cause or the effect, but entirely upon the manner in which the effect has been brought about. If the production of a single ton of coal intended for interstate sale and shipment, and actually so sold and shipped, affects interstate commerce indirectly, the effect does not become direct by multiplying the tonnage, or increasing the number of men employed, or adding to the expense or complexities of the business. Rules of law are sometimes qualified by considerations of degree. But the matter of degree has no bearing upon the question since that question is not—What is the extent of the local activity or condition, or the extent of the effect produced upon interstate commerce? but—What is the relation between the activity or condition and the effect?

Much stress is put upon the evils which come from the struggle between employers and employees over the matter of wages, working conditions, the right of collective bargaining, etc., and the resulting strikes, curtailment, and irregularity of production and effect on prices; and it is insisted that interstate commerce is greatly affected thereby. But, in addition to what has just been said, the answer is that the evils are all local evils over which the federal government has no legislative control. The relation of employer and employee is a local relation. The wages are paid for the doing of local work. Working conditions are obviously local conditions. The employees are not engaged in or about commerce, but exclusively in producing a commodity. The controversies and evils, which it is the object of the act to regulate and minimize, are local controversies and evils affecting local work undertaken to accomplish that local result. Such effect as they may have upon commerce, however extensive it may be, is secondary and indirect. An increase in the greatness of the effect adds to its importance. It does not alter its character.

The want of power on the part of the federal government is the same whether the wages, hours of service, and working conditions, and the bargaining about them, are related to production before interstate commerce has begun, or to sale and distribution after it has ended. The decrees in Nos. 636, 649, and 650 must be reversed and the causes remanded for further consideration in conformity with this opinion. The decree in No. 651 will be affirmed.

It is so ordered.

Notes: The Constitutional Crisis

1. *Other Setbacks. Carter* involved only one of many setbacks for FDR's "New Deal." In *Panama Refining Co. v. Ryan*, 293 U.S. 388 (1935), the Court struck down Section 9(c) of the National Industrial Recovery Act (NIRA) of 1933 on unlawful delegation grounds. Then, in *A.L.A. Schechter Poultry Corp. v. United States*, 295 U.S. 495 (1935), the Court struck down other sections of the NIRA. In all, the Court struck down four major pieces of legislation (the National Industrial Recovery Act, the Bituminous Coal Act, the Agricultural Adjustment Act, and the Railway Pension Act). In addition, the federal courts issued hundreds of injunctions against New Deal legislation.

2. *The Court Packing Plan.* Decisions like *Panama Refining* and *Schechter*, coupled with the Court's restrictive interpretation of the Commerce Clause in cases like *Carter*, upset President Roosevelt, who viewed the Court as an obstacle to his reform program. At the time, several major pieces of legislation had not been ruled on by the courts, including the National Labor Relations Act, the Social Security Act, and the Public Utility Holding Act. FDR was worried that the Court would strike them down, too. Following his landslide reelection victory in 1936, President Roosevelt decided to move against the Court by proposing his now infamous "Court Packing Plan." The Plan would have altered the Court's membership (and, presumably, its decisions) by adding more members to the Court. When a judge or justice of any federal court reached the age of 70 without availing himself of the opportunity to retire on a pension, a new member could be appointed by the President. The appointment would be made in the manner prescribed by the Constitution: nomination by the President with confirmation by the Senate. *See* William E. Leuchtenburg, *The Origins of Franklin D. Roosevelt's "Court Packing" Plan*, 1966 SUP. CT. REV. 347-394. At the time, 6 justices were 70 or older. If the plan had passed, the Court's membership would have expanded to 15 members, probably giving Roosevelt a majority of members sympathetic to his position.

Despite FDR's popularity, and the popularity of his New Deal, many opposed the legislation. Everyone agreed that Congress was constitutionally authorized to control the number of Supreme Court justices, and that the number of justices had not remained static at nine. Nevertheless, many felt that it was inappropriate for FDR to manipulate the Court's membership in an effort to control the Court's decisions. Interestingly, the court packing plan never came to a vote. While the legislation was pending, the Court decided the following case.

∽ PROBLEM: MORE ON THE EDUCATION FOR A BETTER AMERICA ACT ∽

Does education have such a "direct" effect on interstate commerce that *Carter* would allow Congress to regulate it? In light of *Carter*, are you concerned about how the Tenth Amendment might affect your ability to pass or to structure the legislation?

NLRB v. Jones & Laughlin Steel Corp.

301 U.S. 1 (1937)

Mr. Chief Justice HUGHES delivered the opinion of the Court.

The National Labor Relations Board (NLRB) concluded that Jones & Laughlin Steel Corp. had engaged in the unfair labor practice of discharging employees in order to interfere with their union organizing activities. The NLRB ordered Jones & Laughlin to cease and desist from such practices, to offer reinstatement to ten of the employees named, to make good their losses in pay, and to post notices that it would not discharge or discriminate against members or prospective members of the union. The court of appeals refused to enforce the order, holding that it lay beyond the scope of federal power.

Respondent argues that the act can have no application to respondent's relations with its production employees because they are not subject to regulation by the federal government. The Labor Board concluded that the works in Pittsburgh and Aliquippa "might be likened to the heart of a self-contained, highly integrated body. They draw in the raw materials from Michigan, Minnesota, West Virginia, Pennsylvania through arteries and by means controlled by the respondent; they transform the materials and then pump them out to the nation through the vast mechanism which the respondent has elaborated." To carry on the activities of the entire steel industry, 33,000 men mine ore, 44,000 men mine coal, 4,000 men quarry limestone, 16,000 men manufacture coke, 343,000 men manufacture steel, and 83,000 men transport its product. Respondent has about 10,000 employees in its Aliquippa plant, which is located in a community of about 30,000 persons.

The act is challenged as an attempt to regulate all industry, thus invading the reserved powers of the States over their local concerns. It is asserted that references in the act to interstate and foreign commerce are colorable at best; that the act is not a true regulation of such commerce or of matters which directly affect it, but on the contrary has the fundamental object of placing under the compulsory supervision of the federal government all industrial labor relations within the nation.

There can be no question that the commerce thus contemplated by the act is interstate and foreign commerce in the constitutional sense. The act also defines the term "affecting commerce" section 2(7), 29 U.S.C.A. §152(7): "The term 'affecting commerce' means in commerce, or burdening or obstructing commerce or the free flow of commerce, or having led or tending to lead to a labor dispute burdening or obstructing commerce or the free flow of commerce."

This definition is one of exclusion as well as inclusion. The grant of authority to the Board does not extend to the relationship between all industrial employees and employers. It purports to reach only what may be deemed to burden or obstruct commerce and it must be construed as contemplating the exercise of control within constitutional bounds. Acts which directly burden or obstruct interstate or foreign commerce, or its free flow, are within the reach of the congressional power. Acts having that effect are not immune because they grow out of labor disputes. It is the effect upon commerce, not the source of the injury, which is the criterion. Whether or not particular action does affect commerce in such a close and intimate fashion as to be subject to federal control, and hence to lie within the authority conferred upon the Board, is left to be determined as individual cases arise. We thus inquire whether the constitutional boundary has been passed.

The congressional authority to protect interstate commerce from burdens and obstructions is not limited to transactions which can be deemed to be an essential part of a "flow" of interstate or foreign commerce. The fundamental principle is that the power to regulate commerce is the power to enact "all appropriate legislation" for its "protection or advancement"; to adopt measures "to promote its growth and insure its safety"; "to foster, protect, control, and restrain." That power is plenary and may be exerted to protect interstate commerce "no matter what the source of the dangers which threaten it." *Second Employers' Liability Cases,* 223 U.S. 1, 51 (1912). Although activities may be intrastate in character when separately considered, if they have such a close and substantial relation to interstate commerce that their control is essential or appropriate to protect that commerce from burdens and obstructions, Congress cannot be denied the power to exercise that control. Undoubtedly the scope of this power must be considered in light of our dual system of government and may not be extended to embrace effects upon interstate commerce so indirect and remote that to embrace them, in view of our complex society, would effectually obliterate the distinction between what is national and what is local and create a completely centralized government.

The fact that the employees here concerned were engaged in production is not determinative. The question remains as to the effect upon interstate commerce of the labor practice involved. In *Schechter,* the effect there was so remote as to be beyond the federal power. To find "immediacy or directness" there was to find it "almost everywhere," a result inconsistent with our federal system. In *Carter,* the Court was of the opinion that the provisions of the statute relating to production were invalid upon several grounds.

Giving full weight to respondent's contention with respect to a break in the continuity of the "stream of commerce" by reason of respondent's manufacturing operations, the stoppage of those operations by industrial strife would have a most serious effect upon interstate commerce. In view of respondent's far-flung activities, it is idle to say that the effect would be indirect or remote. It would be immediate and might be catastrophic. We are asked to shut our eyes to the plainest facts of our national life and to deal with the question of direct and indirect effects in an intellectual vacuum. Because there may be but indirect and remote effects upon interstate commerce in connection with a host of local enterprises throughout the country, it does not follow that other industrial activities do not have such a close and intimate relation to interstate commerce as to make the presence of industrial strife a matter of the most urgent national concern. When industries organize themselves on a national scale, making their relation to interstate commerce the dominant factor in their activities, how can it be maintained that their industrial labor relations constitute a forbidden field into which Congress may not enter when it is necessary to protect interstate commerce from the paralyzing consequences of industrial war?

Experience has demonstrated that recognition of the right of employees to self-organization and to have representatives of their own choosing for the purpose of collective bargaining is often an essential condition of industrial peace.

Refusal to confer and negotiate has been one of the most prolific causes of strife. These questions have engaged the attention of Congress and have been the subject of many inquiries. The steel industry is one of the great industries of the United States, with activities affecting interstate commerce at every point. The Government refers to the steel strike of 1919–1920 with its far-reaching consequences. The fact that there appears to have been no major disturbance in that industry in the more recent period did not dispose of the possibilities of future and like dangers to interstate commerce which Congress was entitled to foresee and to exercise its power to forestall. It is not necessary to detail the facts as to respondent's enterprise. It presents in a most striking way the close and intimate relation which a manufacturing industry may have to interstate commerce and we have no doubt that Congress had constitutional authority to safeguard the right of respondent's employees to self-organization and freedom in the choice of representatives for collective bargaining.

Our conclusion is that the order of the Board was within its competency and that the act is valid as here applied.

Reversed and remanded.

Mr. Justice McReynolds delivered the following *dissenting* opinion which was joined by Justices Van Devanter, Sutherland, and Butler.

The Court departs from well-established principles followed in *Schechter Poultry Corporation* and *Carter Coal Co.* The power of Congress under the commerce clause does not extend to relations between employers and their employees engaged in manufacture. Any effect on interstate commerce by the discharge of employees would be indirect and remote in the highest degree. The immediate effect may be to create discontent among all those employed and a strike may follow, which, in turn, may result in reducing production, which ultimately may reduce the volume of goods moving in interstate commerce. By this chain of indirect and progressively remote events we finally reach the evil with which it is said the legislation under consideration undertakes to deal. A more remote and indirect interference with interstate commerce or a more definite invasion of the powers reserved to the states is difficult, if not impossible, to imagine.

Notes

1. *The "Switch That Saved Nine."* Justice Roberts, who voted to strike down federal action in *Carter Coal*, voted to sustain it in *Jones & Laughlin*.

2. *The Aftermath.* Following the *Jones & Laughlin* decision, support for the court packing plan waned. Senator Joseph Robinson developed a modified plan that appeared to have a good chance of passage. But when he died suddenly of a heart attack, the plan was voted down. *See* William E. Leuchtenberg, *The Origins of Franklin D. Roosevelt's "Court-Packing" Plan*, 1966 Sup. Ct. Rev. 347.

∾ PROBLEM: MORE ON THE EDUCATION FOR A BETTER AMERICA ACT ∾

Does *Jones & Laughlin* alter your perspective on whether Congress can pass the legislation? Does it matter whether Congress includes spending incentives (designed to encourage school officials to act in particular ways), or whether it also includes specific mandates regarding how education reform is to be achieved? How does the Tenth Amendment come into play after this decision?

4. Post-Switch Expansion of Federal Power: A Half-Century of Deference

Jones & Laughlin ushered in a half-century during which the Court upheld essentially every assertion of federal regulatory power under the Commerce Clause. This post-1937 deferential approach is illustrated in the following cases.

United States v. Darby

312 U.S. 100 (1941)

Mr. Justice STONE delivered the opinion of the Court.

The principal questions raised in this case are whether Congress has constitutional power to prohibit the shipment in interstate commerce of lumber manufactured by employees whose wages are less than a prescribed minimum or whose weekly hours of labor at that wage are greater than a prescribed maximum, and whether it has power to prohibit the employment of workmen in the production of goods "for interstate commerce" at other than prescribed wages and hours. A subsidiary question is whether in connection with such prohibitions Congress can require the employer subject to them to keep records showing the hours worked each day and week by each of his employees including those engaged "in the production and manufacture of goods, lumber, for 'interstate commerce.'"

While manufacture is not of itself interstate commerce, the shipment of manufactured goods interstate is commerce and the prohibition of such shipment by Congress is indubitably a regulation of commerce. The power to regulate commerce is the power "to prescribe the rule by which commerce is to be governed." It extends not only to those regulations which aid, foster and protect commerce, but those which prohibit it.

The power of Congress over interstate commerce "is complete in itself, may be exercised to its utmost extent, and acknowledges no limitations, other than are prescribed by the constitution." *Gibbons v. Ogden.* Congress, following its own conception of public policy concerning the restrictions which may appropriately be imposed on interstate commerce, is free to exclude from commerce articles whose use in the states for which they are destined it may conceive to be injurious to the public health, morals or welfare, even though the state has not sought to regulate their use. Such regulation is not a forbidden invasion of state power merely because its motive or its consequence is to restrict the use of articles of commerce within the states of destination and is not prohibited unless by other Constitutional provisions. It is no objection to the assertion of the power to regulate interstate commerce that its exercise is attended by the same incidents which attend the exercise of the police power of the states.

The motive and purpose of the present regulation are plainly to make effective the Congressional conception of public policy that interstate commerce should not be made the instrument of competition in the distribution of goods produced under substandard labor conditions, which competition is injurious to the commerce and to the states from and to which the commerce flows. The motive and purpose of a regulation of interstate commerce are matters for the legislative judgment upon the exercise of which the Constitution places no restriction and over which the courts are given no control.

In the more than a century which has elapsed since *Gibbons*, these principles of constitutional interpretation have been so long and repeatedly recognized by this Court as applicable to the Commerce Clause, that there would be little occasion for repeating them now were it not for the decision of this Court twenty-two years ago in *Hammer v. Dagenhart*, 247 U.S. 251 (1918). In that case it was held that Congress was without power to exclude the products of child labor from interstate commerce. *Hammer* has not been followed. The distinction on which the decision was rested that Congressional power to prohibit interstate commerce is limited to articles which in themselves have some harmful or deleterious property—a distinction which was novel when made and unsupported by any provision of the Constitution—has long since been abandoned. The thesis of the opinion that the motive of the prohibition or its effect to control in some measure the use or production within the states of the article thus excluded from the commerce can operate to deprive the regulation of its constitutional authority has long since ceased to have force. *Hammer* was a departure from the principles which have prevailed in the interpretation of the commerce clause both before and since the decision and such vitality, as a precedent, as it then had has long since been exhausted. It should be and now is overruled.

There remains the question whether such restriction on the production of goods for commerce is a permissible exercise of the commerce power. The power of Congress over interstate commerce is not confined to the regulation of commerce among the states. It extends to those activities intrastate which so affect interstate commerce or the exercise of the power of Congress over it as to make regulation of them appropriate means to the attainment of a legitimate end, the exercise of the granted power of Congress to regulate interstate commerce. *McCulloch v. Maryland.*

While this Court has found state regulation of interstate commerce, when uniformity of regulation is of national concern, to be incompatible with the

Commerce Clause even though Congress has not legislated on the subject, the Court has never implied such restraint on state control over matters intrastate not deemed to be regulations of interstate commerce or its instrumentalities even though they affect the commerce. In the absence of Congressional legislation state laws which are not regulations of commerce itself or its instrumentalities are not forbidden even though they affect interstate commerce. But it does not follow that Congress may not by appropriate legislation regulate intrastate activities where they have a substantial effect on interstate commerce. *See National Labor Relations Board v. Jones & Laughlin Steel Corp.* This Court has held that the power to regulate interstate commerce extends to the regulation of activities intrastate which have a substantial effect on the commerce or the exercise of the Congressional power over it.

The means adopted by §15(a)(2) for the protection of interstate commerce by the suppression of the production of the condemned goods for interstate commerce is so related to the commerce and so affects it as to be within the reach of the commerce power. Congress, to attain its objective in the suppression of nationwide competition in interstate commerce by goods produced under substandard labor conditions, has made no distinction as to the volume or amount of shipments in commerce or production for commerce by any particular shipper or producer. It recognized that in present day industry, competition by a small part may affect the whole and that the total effect of many small producers may be great. The legislation aimed at a whole embraces all its parts.

Our conclusion is unaffected by the Tenth Amendment which provides: "The powers not delegated to the United States by the Constitution, nor prohibited by it to the States, are reserved to the States respectively, or to the people." The amendment states but a truism that all is retained which has not been surrendered. There is nothing in the history of its adoption to suggest that it was more than declaratory of the relationship between the national and state governments as it had been established by the Constitution before the amendment or that its purpose was other than to allay fears that the new national government might seek to exercise powers not granted, and that the states might not be able to exercise fully their reserved powers.

Question

Note the dramatic shift in the Court's views on the scope of the Commerce Clause and on the Tenth Amendment as a limitation on federal power. Not only does the Court overrule *Hammer*, which treated the Tenth Amendment as an independent limitation on federal power, but the Court flatly states that the Tenth Amendment is a "truism." What does it mean to say that the Tenth Amendment is a "truism"?

Wickard v. Filburn

317 U.S. 111 (1942)

Mr. Justice JACKSON delivered the opinion of the Court.

Appellee sought to enjoin enforcement against himself of the marketing penalty imposed by amendments to the Agricultural Adjustment Act of 1938, upon that part of his 1941 wheat crop which was available for marketing in excess of the marketing quota established for his farm. He also sought a declaratory judgment that the wheat marketing quota provisions of the Act were unconstitutional because they were not sustainable under the Commerce Clause or consistent with the Due Process Clause of the Fifth Amendment.

The general scheme of the Agricultural Adjustment Act of 1938 as related to wheat is to control the volume moving in interstate and foreign commerce in order to avoid surpluses and shortages and the consequent abnormally low or high wheat prices and obstructions to commerce. Within prescribed limits and by prescribed standards the Secretary of Agriculture is directed to ascertain and proclaim each year a national acreage allotment for the next crop of wheat, which is then apportioned to the states and their counties, and is eventually broken up into allotments for individual farms.

Appellee has owned and operated a small farm in Ohio, maintaining a herd of dairy cattle, selling milk, raising poultry, and selling poultry and eggs. It has been his practice to raise a small acreage of winter wheat, to sell a portion of the crop; to feed part to poultry and livestock on the farm, some of which is sold; to use some in making flour for home consumption; and to keep the rest for seeding. Appellee's 1941 wheat allotment was 11.1 acres, and he was allowed a yield of 20.1 bushels of wheat per acre. He sowed 23 acres, and harvested 11.9 acres of excess acreage, 239 bushels, which, under the Act, constituted farm marketing excess, subject to a penalty of 49 cents a bushel, or $ 117.11.

It is urged that under the Commerce Clause of the Constitution, Article I, §8, clause 3, Congress does not possess the power it has sought to exercise. The question would merit little consideration except for the fact that this Act extends federal regulation to production not intended in any part for commerce but wholly for consumption on the farm. The sum of this is that the Federal Government fixes a quota including all that the farmer may harvest for sale or for his own farm needs, and declares that wheat produced on excess acreage may neither be disposed of nor used except upon payment of the penalty or except it is stored as required by the Act or delivered to the Secretary of Agriculture.

Appellee says that this is a regulation of production and consumption of wheat. Such activities are, he urges, beyond the reach of Congressional power under the Commerce Clause, since they are local in character, and their effects upon interstate commerce are at most "indirect." The Government argues that the statute regulates neither production nor consumption, but only marketing; and that if the Act does go beyond the regulation of marketing it is sustainable as a "necessary and proper" implementation of the power of Congress over interstate commerce.

The Government's concern lest the Act be held to be a regulation of production or consumption rather than of marketing is attributable to a few dicta and decisions of this Court which might be understood to lay it down that activities such as "production," "manufacturing," and "mining" are strictly "local" and, except in special circumstances, cannot be regulated under the commerce power because their effects upon interstate commerce are, as matter of law, only "indirect." Today, when this power has been held to have great latitude, there is no decision that such activities may be regulated where no part of the product is intended for interstate commerce or intermingled with the subjects thereof. A review of the course of decision under the Commerce Clause will make plain, that questions of the power of Congress are not to be decided by reference to any formula which would give controlling force to nomenclature such as "production" and "indirect" and foreclose consideration of the actual effects of the activity in question upon interstate commerce.

In the *Shreveport Rate Cases*, this Court held that railroad rates of an intrastate character and fixed by authority of the state might, nevertheless, be revised by the Federal Government because of the economic effects which they had upon interstate commerce. The opinion found federal intervention constitutionally authorized because of "matters having such a close and substantial relation to interstate traffic that the control is essential or appropriate to the security of that traffic, to the efficiency of the interstate service, and to the maintenance of the conditions under which interstate commerce may be conducted upon fair terms and without molestation or hindrance."

The Court's recognition of the relevance of economic effects in the application of the Commerce Clause has made the mechanical application of legal formulas no longer feasible. Questions of federal power cannot be decided simply by finding the activity to be "production" nor can consideration of its economic effects be foreclosed by calling them "indirect." Even if appellee's activity be local and though it may not be regarded as commerce, it may still, whatever its nature, be reached by Congress if it exerts a substantial economic effect on interstate commerce and this irrespective of whether such effect is what might at some earlier time have been defined as "direct" or "indirect."

Commerce among the states in wheat is large and important. Although wheat is raised in every state but one, production in most states is not equal to consumption. Sixteen states on average have had a surplus of wheat above their own requirements for feed, seed, and food. Thirty-two states and the District of Columbia, where production has been below consumption, have looked to these surplus-producing states for their supply as well as for wheat for export and carry-over. The wheat industry has been a problem industry for some years. The effect of consumption of homegrown wheat on interstate commerce is due to the fact that it constitutes the most variable factor in the disappearance of the wheat crop. Consumption on the farm appears to vary in an amount greater than 20 per cent of average production. The total amount of wheat consumed as food varies but relatively little, and use as seed is relatively constant.

The maintenance by government regulation of a price for wheat can be accomplished as effectively by sustaining or increasing the demand as by limiting the supply. The effect of the statute before us is to restrict the amount which may be produced for market and the extent to which one may forestall resort to the market by producing to meet his own needs. That appellee's contribution to the demand for wheat may be trivial by itself is not enough to remove him from the scope of federal regulation where, as here, his contribution, taken together with that of many others similarly situated, is far from trivial.

It is well established that the power to regulate commerce includes the power to regulate the prices at which commodities in that commerce are dealt in and practices affecting such prices. One of the primary purposes of the Act in question was to increase the market price of wheat and to that end to limit the volume that could affect the market. It can hardly be denied that a factor of such volume and variability as home-consumed wheat would have a substantial influence on price and market conditions. This may arise because being in marketable condition such wheat overhangs the market and if induced by rising prices tends to flow into the market and check price increases. If it is never marketed, it supplies a need of the man who grew it which would otherwise be reflected by purchases in the open market. Home-grown wheat in this sense competes with wheat in commerce. The stimulation of commerce is a use of the regulatory function quite as definitely as prohibitions or restrictions thereon. Congress may properly have considered that wheat consumed on the farm where grown if wholly outside the scheme of regulation would have a substantial effect in defeating and obstructing its purpose to stimulate trade therein at increased prices.

It is said that this Act, forcing some farmers into the market to buy what they could provide for themselves, is an unfair promotion of the markets and prices of specializing wheat growers. It is the essence of regulation that it lays a restraining hand on the self-interest of the regulated and that advantages from the regulation commonly fall to others. The conflicts of economic interest between the regulated and those who advantage by it are wisely left under our system to resolution by the Congress under its legislative process. Such conflicts rarely lend themselves to judicial determination. With the wisdom, workability, or fairness, of the plan of regulation we have nothing to do.

Reversed.

Notes

1. Paul *Overturned.* Two years later, in *United States v. South-Eastern Underwriters Assn,* 322 U.S. 533 (1944), the Court overturned *Paul v. Virginia*'s holding that insurance policies do not constitute commerce within the meaning of the

Commerce Clause. In *South-Eastern*, appellees were indicted for violating the Sherman Act. Since the indictments were based on conduct involving insurance policies, appellees argued that the Sherman Act could not be applied to them because "the business of fire insurance is not commerce." The Court disagreed: "It would be difficult to hold that no activities of any insurance company can ever constitute interstate commerce so as to make it subject to such regulation;— activities which, as part of the conduct of a legitimate and useful commercial enterprise, may embrace integrated operations in many states and involve the transmission of great quantities of money, documents, and communications across dozens of state lines."

2. *Expansion of Federal Power.* In the wake of decisions like *Darby* and *Wickard*, the federal government's power over the U.S. economy increased dramatically. The federal government began to assert control over such diverse matters as consumer safety, energy, agriculture, aviation travel, civil rights, drugs, labor, commerce, securities, and banking.

∾ PROBLEM: MORE ON THE EDUCATION FOR A BETTER AMERICA ACT ∾

After *Wickard*, does it appear that Congress can enact this legislation? Can it include both incentives and mandates? Does the Tenth Amendment seem to limit the scope of Congress's authority?

Heart of Atlanta Motel, Inc. v. United States

379 U.S. 241 (1964)

Mr. Justice CLARK delivered the opinion of the Court.

This is a declaratory judgment action, attacking the constitutionality of Title II of the Civil Rights Act of 1964. Appellant owns and operates the Heart of Atlanta Motel which has 216 rooms available to transient guests. The motel is located two blocks from downtown Peachtree Street. It is readily accessible to interstate highways 75 and 85 and state highways 23 and 41. Appellant solicits patronage from outside the State of Georgia through various national advertising media, including magazines of national circulation; it maintains over 50 billboards and highway signs within the State, soliciting patronage for the motel; it accepts convention trade from outside Georgia and approximately 75% of its registered guests are from out of State. Prior to passage of the Act the motel had followed a practice of refusing to rent rooms to Negroes, and it alleged that it intended to continue to do so.

Appellant contends that Congress in passing this Act exceeded its power to regulate commerce under Art. I, §8, cl. 3, of the Constitution of the United States. This Title is divided into seven sections beginning with §201(a) which provides that: "All persons shall be entitled to the full and equal enjoyment of the goods, services, facilities, privileges, advantages, and accommodations of any place of public accommodation, as defined in this section, without discrimination or segregation on the ground of race, color, religion, or national origin." There are listed in §201(b) four classes of business establishments, each of which "serves the public" and "is a place of public accommodation" within the meaning of §201(a) "if its operations affect commerce, or if discrimination or segregation by it is supported by State action." The covered establishments are: "(1) any inn, hotel, motel, or other establishment which provides lodging to transient guests."

It is admitted that the operation of the motel brings it within the provisions of §201(a) of the Act and that appellant refused to provide lodging for transient Negroes because of their race or color and that it intends to continue that policy unless restrained. The sole question is, therefore, the constitutionality of the Civil Rights Act of 1964 as applied to these facts. The legislative history of the Act indicates that Congress based the Act on §5 and the Equal Protection Clause of the Fourteenth Amendment as well as its power to regulate interstate commerce under Art. I, §8, cl. 3, of the Constitution. The Senate Commerce Committee made it clear that the fundamental object of Title II was to vindicate "the deprivation of personal dignity that accompanies denials of equal access to public establishments." It noted that such an objective has been and could be readily achieved "by congressional action based on the commerce power of the Constitution." S. Rep. No. 872, *supra,* at 16-17.

While the Act as adopted carried no congressional findings, the record of its passage through each house is replete with evidence of the burdens that discrimination by race or color places upon interstate commerce. This testimony included the fact that people have become increasingly mobile with millions of people of all races traveling from State to State; that Negroes in particular have been the subject of discrimination in transient accommodations, having to travel great distances to secure the same; that often they have been unable to obtain accommodations and have had to call upon friends to put them up overnight, and that these conditions had become so acute as to require the listing of available lodging for Negroes in a special guidebook which was itself "dramatic testimony to the difficulties" Negroes encounter in travel.

The power of Congress to deal with these obstructions depends on the meaning of the Commerce Clause. Its meaning was first enunciated 140 years ago by the great Chief Justice John Marshall in *Gibbons v. Ogden.* The determinative test of the exercise of power by the Congress under the Commerce Clause is simply whether the activity sought to be regulated is "commerce which concerns more States than one" and has a real and substantial relation to the national interest. That Congress was legislating against moral wrongs in many of these areas rendered its enactments no less valid. In framing Title II of this Act Congress was also dealing with what it considered a moral problem. But that does not detract from the overwhelming evidence of disruptive effect that racial discrimination has had on commercial intercourse. It was this burden which empowered Congress to enact appropriate legislation, and, given this basis for the exercise of its power, Congress was not restricted by the fact that the particular obstruction to interstate commerce was also deemed a moral and social wrong.

It is said that the operation of the motel here is of a purely local character. As Chief Justice Stone put it in *United States v. Darby*: "The power of Congress over interstate commerce is not confined to the regulation of commerce among the states. It extends to those activities intrastate which so affect interstate commerce or the exercise of the power of Congress over it as to make regulation of them appropriate means to the attainment of a legitimate end, the exercise of the granted power of Congress to regulate interstate commerce."

Thus the power of Congress to promote interstate commerce also includes the power to regulate the local incidents thereof, including local activities in both the States of origin and destination, which might have a substantial and harmful effect upon that commerce. One need only examine the evidence which we have discussed above to see that Congress may—as it has—prohibit racial discrimination by motels serving travelers, however "local" their operations may appear.

The action of Congress in adoption of the Act as applied to a motel which concededly serves interstate travelers is within the power granted it by the Commerce Clause of the Constitution. Congress could have pursued other methods to eliminate the obstructions it found in interstate commerce caused by racial discrimination. But this is a matter of policy that rests entirely with Congress not with the courts. How obstructions in commerce may be removed—what means are to be employed—is within the sound and exclusive discretion of Congress. It is subject only to one caveat—the means chosen must be reasonably adapted to the end permitted by the Constitution. We cannot say that its choice here was not so adapted. The Constitution requires no more.

Affirmed.

Notes

1. *Ollie's Barbecue.* Consistent with *Heart of Atlanta, Katzenbach v. McClung,* 379 U.S. 294 (1964), upheld a federal law prohibiting discrimination as applied to a family-owned restaurant in Birmingham, Alabama, that specialized in barbecued meats and homemade pies and could seat 220 customers. The restaurant catered to family and white-collar trade and maintained only a take-out service for African Americans; two-thirds of its 36 employees were African American. In upholding the Act, the Court stated:

> The record is replete with testimony of the burdens placed on interstate commerce by racial discrimination in restaurants. A comparison of per capita spending by Negroes in restaurants, theaters, and like establishments indicated less spending, after discounting income differences, in areas where discrimination is widely practiced. This condition, which was especially aggravated in the South, was due to racial segregation. This diminutive spending has a close connection to interstate commerce. The fewer customers a restaurant enjoys the less

food it sells and consequently the less it buys. Moreover, discrimination in restaurants had a direct and highly restrictive effect upon interstate travel by Negroes. Discriminatory practices prevent Negroes from buying prepared food served on premises while on a trip, except in isolated and unkempt restaurants and under most unsatisfactory and often unpleasant conditions. Established restaurants in such areas sold less interstate goods because of the discrimination, interstate travel was obstructed directly by it, business in general suffered, and many new businesses refrained from establishing as a result. The volume of food purchased by Ollie's Barbecue from out of state was insignificant when compared with the total foodstuffs moving in commerce. But the Commerce Power "extends to those activities intrastate which so affect interstate commerce, or the exertion of the power of Congress over it, as to make regulation appropriate to the attainment of a legitimate end, the effective execution of the power to regulate interstate commerce." *United States v. Wrightwood Dairy Co.*, 315 U.S. 110 (1942). Commerce "may, whatever its nature, be reached by Congress if it exerts a substantial economic effect on interstate commerce." *Wickard v. Filburn, supra*, at 125. Confronted with the facts before Congress, we conclude that it had a rational basis for finding that racial discrimination in restaurants had a direct and adverse effect on the free flow of interstate commerce. The Civil Rights Act of 1964, we find to be plainly appropriate in the resolution of what the Congress found to be a national commercial problem of the first magnitude.

2. *Federal Criminal Legislation.* Historically, the states have been responsible for virtually all basic criminal legislation, including the crimes of murder, robbery, rape, and assault. Congress has passed some criminal statutes, but most of these crimes have involved crimes against the federal government (filing a false tax return) or criminal activity that crossed state lines (e.g., *The Lottery Case*). In *Perez v. United States*, 402 U.S. 146 (1971), the Court upheld the Consumer Credit Protection Act, which made it illegal to engage in "extortionate credit transactions," and defined "extortionate" as those characterized by the use or threat of the use of "violence or other criminal means" in enforcement. The law was applied to a "loan shark" (Perez) who used threats of violence as a method of collection. In upholding the Act, the Court concluded: "Extortionate credit transactions, though purely intrastate, may in the judgment of Congress affect interstate commerce. In the present case there is a tie between local loan sharks and interstate crime. The legislation grew out of reports and studies that supplied Congress with knowledge that the loan shark racket provides organized crime with its second most lucrative source of revenue, exacts millions from people, coerces its victims into the commission of crimes against property, and causes the takeover by racketeers of legitimate businesses. It appears that loan sharking is one way organized interstate crime holds guns to the heads of the poor and the rich alike and syphons funds from numerous localities to finance its national operations." Justice Stewart dissented: "Congress surely has power under the Commerce Clause to enact criminal laws to protect the instrumentalities of interstate commerce, to prohibit the misuse of the channels or facilities of interstate commerce, and to prohibit or regulate those intrastate activities that have a demonstrably substantial effect on interstate commerce. But under the statute before us a man can be convicted without any proof of interstate movement, of the use of the facilities of interstate commerce, or of facts showing that his conduct affected interstate commerce. The Framers of

the Constitution never intended that the National Government might define as a crime and prosecute such wholly local activity through the enactment of federal criminal laws."

3. *Environmental Regulation.* In *Hodel v. Virginia Surface Mining and Reclamation Association, Inc.*, 452 U.S. 264 (1981), the Court upheld the Surface Mining Control and Reclamation Act, a comprehensive statute designed to "establish a nation-wide program to protect society and the environment from the adverse effects of surface coal mining operations." Among other things, the Act required: restoration of land after mining to its prior condition, restoration of land to its approximate original contour, segregation and preservation of topsoil, minimization of disturbance to the hydrologic balance, construction of coal mine waste piles used as dams and embankments, revegetation of mined areas, and spoil disposal. In upholding the Act, the Court stated:

> When Congress has determined that an activity affects interstate commerce, the courts need inquire only whether the finding is rational. The Act recites the congressional finding that many surface mining operations result in disturbances of surface areas that burden and adversely affect commerce and the public welfare by destroying or diminishing the utility of land for commercial, industrial, residential, recreational, agricultural, and forestry purposes, by causing erosion and landslides, by contributing to floods, by polluting the water, by destroying fish and wildlife habitats, by impairing natural beauty, by damaging the property of citizens, by creating hazards dangerous to life and property, by degrading the quality of life in local communities, and by counteracting governmental programs and efforts to conserve soil, water, and other natural resources. Similarly, the House Committee documented the adverse effects of surface coal mining on interstate commerce. In light of the evidence available to Congress and the detailed consideration that the legislation received, we cannot say that Congress did not have a rational basis for concluding that surface coal mining has substantial effects on interstate commerce. The commerce power "extends to those activities intrastate which so affect interstate commerce, or the exertion of the power of Congress over it, as to make regulation of them appropriate means to the attainment of a legitimate end, the effective execution of the granted power to regulate interstate commerce." *United States v. Wrightwood Dairy Co.*, 315 U.S. at 119. Here, Congress rationally determined that regulation of surface coal mining is necessary to protect interstate commerce from adverse effects that may result from that activity. This congressional finding is sufficient to sustain the Act as a valid exercise of Congress' power under the Commerce Clause. Moreover, the Act responds to a congressional finding that nationwide "surface mining and reclamation standards are essential in order to insure that competition in interstate commerce among sellers of coal produced in different States will not be used to undermine the ability of the several States to improve and maintain adequate standards on coal mining operations within their borders."

∾ PROBLEMS ∾

1. *Comprehensive Criminal Legislation.* If Congress can regulate extortionate credit transactions, is Congress free to pass comprehensive criminal legislation? Could it, for example, enact general federal crimes on such topics as murder, robbery, and rape? Can you argue that crimes like murder, robbery, and rape

have a substantial impact on interstate commerce? How might you respond to these arguments?

2. *Domestic Relations.* Historically, the states have exercised power over domestic relations, including such issues as marriage and divorce. Based on decisions like *Darby, Jones & Laughlin, Wickard,* and *Heart of Atlanta,* could Congress pass a comprehensive statute dealing with domestic relations? How would you argue that a comprehensive federal domestic relations law is constitutional?

3. *Are There Limits to the Commerce Power?* Following decisions like *Darby, Wickard,* and *Heart of Atlanta,* is there anything that Congress cannot reach under its Commerce Clause power? For example, take a look around your classroom. Do you see anything that is beyond Congress' Commerce Clause power? The blackboard? The desks? The chairs? The computer technology?

Note: Growth of the Modern Administrative State

The constitutional crisis of the 1930s brought with it the demise of the nondelegation doctrine—the idea that congressional power could not be delegated to executive branch officials or agencies. Decisions like *Panama Refining* and *Schechter,* which limited Congress's power to delegate, were effectively overruled. In later cases, the Court sustained increasingly broad assertions of power. Consider the following language from *INS v. Chadha,* 462 U.S. 919, 985 (1983): "In practice, restrictions on the scope of the power that could be delegated diminished and all but disappeared. The 'intelligible principle' through which agencies have attained enormous control over the economic affairs of the country was held to include such formulations as 'just and reasonable,' '*public interest,*' 'public convenience, interest, or necessity,' and 'unfair methods of competition.'"

In recent decades, Congress has delegated more and more power to administrative agencies. As the District of Columbia Circuit noted, "administrative agencies may well have a more far-reaching effect on the daily lives of all citizens than do the combined actions of the executive, legislative and Judicial Branches." *Ballerina Pen Co. v. Kunzig,* 433 F.2d 1204, 1207 (D.C. Cir. 1970), *cert. denied,* 401 U.S. 950 (1971). The growth of agency power is reflected in the size of the Code of Federal Regulations, which has grown dramatically in size.

In *Gundy v. United States,* 136 S. Ct. 2216 (2019), the Court rejected a claim that Congress had unconstitutionally delegated authority under the Sex Offender Registration and Notification Act (SORNA). Under SORNA, Congress gave the Attorney General "the authority to specify the applicability of the requirements of this subchapter to sex offenders convicted before the enactment of this chapter . . . and to prescribe rules for the registration of any such sex offenders and for other categories of sex offenders who are unable to comply with subsection (b)." Under that delegated authority, the Attorney General issued an interim rule specifying that SORNA's registration requirements apply in full to "sex offenders convicted of the offense for which registration is required prior to the enactment of that Act." The Court upheld the delegation: "Congress may 'obtain the assistance of its coordinate Branches'—and in particular, may confer substantial discretion on executive agencies to implement and enforce the laws." A "statutory delegation is constitutional as long as Congress 'lays down by legislative act an intelligible principle to which the person or body authorized to exercise the delegated authority is directed to conform.'" "The text, considered alongside its context, purpose, and history, makes clear that the Attorney General's discretion extends only to considering and addressing feasibility issues. Given that statutory meaning, Gundy's constitutional claim must fail."

Although the growth of administrative power may have been necessary, and perhaps inevitable, that growth has not been without costs. Justice Jackson stated that "the rise of administrative bodies probably has been the most significant legal trend of the last century. They have become a veritable fourth branch of the Government, which has deranged our three-branch legal theories." *Federal Trade Commission v. Ruberoid Co.*, 343 U.S. 470, 487 (1952) (Jackson, J., dissenting).

5. Revolution and Retreat?

For half a century, the Court interpreted the Commerce Clause expansively in decisions like *Wickard* and *Heart of Atlanta*. There were few limits to Congress's authority under the Commerce Clause, and the Tenth Amendment had little impact on Congress's authority. Then the Court decided the following case.

United States v. Lopez

514 U.S. 549 (1995)

Chief Justice REHNQUIST delivered the opinion of the Court.

In the Gun-Free School Zones Act of 1990, Congress made it a federal offense "for any individual knowingly to possess a firearm at a place that the individual knows, or has reasonable cause to believe, is a school zone." 18 U.S.C. §922(q)(1)(A). The Act neither regulates a commercial activity nor contains a requirement that the possession be connected in any way to interstate commerce. We hold that the Act exceeds the authority of Congress "to regulate Commerce among the several States." U.S. Const., Art. I, §8, cl. 3.

Respondent, who was then a 12th-grade student, arrived at Edison High School in San Antonio, Texas, carrying a concealed .38 caliber handgun and five bullets. He was arrested and charged with violating the Gun-Free School Zones Act of 1990.

We start with first principles. The Constitution creates a Federal Government of enumerated powers. *See* U.S. Const., Art. I, §8. As James Madison wrote, "the powers delegated by the proposed Constitution to the federal government are few and defined. Those which remain in the State governments are numerous and indefinite." *The Federalist No. 45*, pp. 292-293 (C. Rossiter ed. 1961). The Court, through Chief Justice Marshall, first defined the nature of Congress' commerce power in *Gibbons v. Ogden*, 9 Wheat. 1, 6 L. Ed. 23 (1824). For nearly a century thereafter, the Court's Commerce Clause decisions dealt rarely with the extent of Congress' power. In 1887, Congress enacted the Interstate Commerce Act, and in 1890, Congress enacted the Sherman Antitrust Act. These laws ushered in a new era of federal regulation under the commerce power. When cases involving these laws reached this Court, we imported from our negative Commerce Clause cases the approach that Congress could not regulate activities such as "production," "manufacturing," and "mining." *See, e.g., Carter v. Carter Coal Co.,* 298 U.S. 238 (1936). Simultaneously, the Court held that, where the interstate and intrastate aspects of commerce were so mingled together that full regulation of interstate commerce required incidental regulation of intrastate commerce, the Commerce Clause authorized such regulation. *See Houston, E. & W.T.R. Co. v. United States*, 234 U.S. 342 (1914).

Jones & Laughlin Steel, Darby, and *Wickard* ushered in an era of Commerce Clause jurisprudence that greatly expanded the previously defined authority of Congress. In part, this was a recognition of the great changes that had occurred in the way business was carried on in this country. Enterprises that had once been local or at most regional in nature had become national in scope. But the doctrinal change also reflected a view that earlier Commerce Clause cases artificially had constrained the authority of Congress to regulate interstate commerce. But even these modern-era precedents confirmed that this power is subject to outer limits.

We have identified three broad categories of activity that Congress may regulate under its commerce power. First, Congress may regulate the use of the channels of interstate commerce. Second, Congress is empowered to regulate and protect the instrumentalities of interstate commerce, or persons or things in interstate commerce, even though the threat may come only from intrastate activities. *See, e.g., Shreveport Rate Cases*, 234 U.S. 342 (1914). Finally, Congress' commerce authority includes the power to regulate those activities having a substantial relation to interstate commerce, i.e., those activities that substantially affect interstate commerce. *Maryland v. Wirtz*, 392 U.S. 183 (1968). Within this final category, our case law has not been clear whether an activity must "affect" or "substantially affect" interstate commerce in order to be within Congress' power to regulate it under the Commerce Clause. We conclude, consistent with the great weight of our case law, that the proper test requires an analysis of whether the regulated activity "substantially affects" interstate commerce.

We now consider the power of Congress to enact §922(q). The first two categories of authority may be quickly disposed of: §922(q) is not a regulation of the use of the channels of interstate commerce, nor is it an attempt to prohibit the interstate transportation of a commodity through the channels of commerce; nor can §922(q) be justified as a regulation by which Congress has sought to protect an instrumentality of interstate commerce or a thing in interstate commerce.

Thus, if §922(q) is to be sustained, it must be under the third category. We have upheld a wide variety of congressional Acts regulating intrastate economic activity where the activity substantially affected interstate commerce. Examples include the regulation of intrastate coal mining, intrastate extortionate credit transactions, restaurants utilizing substantial interstate supplies, and hotels catering to interstate guests, and production and consumption of home-grown wheat. Even *Wickard*, perhaps the most far reaching example of Commerce Clause authority over intrastate activity, involved economic activity in a way that the possession of a gun in a school zone does not.

Section 922(q) is a criminal statute that has nothing to do with "commerce" or any sort of economic enterprise, however broadly one might define those terms. Section 922(q) is not an essential part of a larger regulation of economic activity, in which the regulatory scheme could be undercut unless the intrastate activity were regulated. It cannot, therefore, be sustained under our cases upholding regulations of activities that arise out of or are connected with a commercial transaction, which viewed in the aggregate, substantially affects interstate commerce.

Section 922(q) contains no jurisdictional element which would ensure, through case-by-case inquiry, that the firearm possession in question affects interstate commerce. For example, in *United States v. Bass*, 404 U.S. 336 (1971), the Court interpreted former 18 U.S.C. §1202(a), which made it a crime for a felon to "receive, possess, or transport in commerce or affecting commerce any firearm." The Court interpreted the possession component of §1202(a) to require an additional nexus to interstate commerce because the statute was ambiguous and because "unless Congress conveys its purpose clearly, it will not be deemed to have significantly changed the federal-state balance." Section 922(q) has no express jurisdictional element which might limit its reach to a discrete set of firearm possessions that have an explicit connection with or effect on interstate commerce.

"Neither the statute nor its legislative history contains express congressional findings regarding the effects upon interstate commerce of gun possession in a school zone." Congress normally is not required to make formal findings as to the substantial burdens that an activity has on interstate commerce. But to the extent that congressional findings would enable us to evaluate the legislative judgment that the activity in question substantially affected interstate commerce, even though no such substantial effect was visible to the naked eye, they are lacking here. The Government argues that Congress has accumulated institutional expertise regarding the regulation of firearms through previous enactments. Importation of previous findings to justify §922(q) is especially inappropriate here because the "prior federal enactments or Congressional findings do not speak to the subject matter of section 922(q) or its relationship to interstate commerce."

The Government argues that possession of a firearm in a school zone may result in violent crime and that violent crime can affect the functioning of the national economy. First, the costs of violent crime are substantial, and, through the mechanism of insurance, those costs are spread throughout the population. Second, violent crime reduces the willingness of individuals to travel to areas that are perceived to be unsafe. The Government argues that the presence of guns in schools poses a substantial threat to the educational process by threatening the learning environment. A handicapped educational process, in turn, will result in a less productive citizenry. That would have an adverse effect on the Nation's economic well-being. As a result, the Government argues that Congress could rationally have concluded that §922(q) substantially affects interstate commerce.

The Government admits, under its "costs of crime" reasoning, that Congress could regulate not only all violent crime, but all activities that might lead to violent crime, regardless of how tenuously they relate to interstate commerce. Similarly, under the Government's "national productivity" reasoning, Congress could regulate any activity that it found was related to the economic productivity of individual citizens: family law (including marriage, divorce, and child custody), for example. Under the theories that the Government presents, it is difficult to perceive any limitation on federal power, even in areas such as criminal law enforcement or education where States historically have been sovereign. Thus, if we were to accept the Government's arguments, we are hard-pressed to posit any activity that Congress is without power to regulate. If Congress can, pursuant to its Commerce Clause power, regulate activities that adversely affect the learning environment, then it also can regulate the educational process directly. Congress could determine that a school's curriculum has a "significant" effect on the extent of classroom learning. As a result, Congress could mandate a federal curriculum for local elementary and secondary schools because what is taught in local schools has a significant "effect on classroom learning," and that has a substantial effect on interstate commerce.

The possession of a gun in a local school zone is in no sense an economic activity that might, through repetition, substantially affect interstate commerce. Respondent was a local student at a local school; there is no indication that he had recently moved in interstate commerce, and there is no requirement that his possession of the firearm have any concrete tie to interstate commerce. To uphold the Government's contentions, we would have to pile inference upon inference in a manner that would convert congressional authority under the Commerce Clause to a general police power of the sort retained by the States. Admittedly, some of our cases have taken long steps down that road, giving great deference to congressional action. The broad language in these opinions has suggested the possibility of additional expansion, but we decline to proceed any further. To do so would require us to conclude that the Constitution's enumeration of powers does not presuppose something not enumerated and that there never will be a distinction between what is truly national and what is truly local. This we are unwilling to do.

For the foregoing reasons the judgment of the Court of Appeals is
Affirmed.

Justice KENNEDY, with whom Justice O'CONNOR joins, *concurring.*

The statute upsets the federal balance to a degree that renders it an unconstitutional assertion of the commerce power. Neither the actors nor their conduct have a commercial character, and neither the purposes nor the design of the statute have an evident commercial nexus. The statute makes the simple possession of a gun within 1,000 feet of the grounds of the school a criminal offense. In a sense any conduct in this interdependent world has an ultimate commercial origin or consequence, but we have not yet said the commerce power may reach so far. If Congress attempts that extension, then we must inquire whether the exercise of national power seeks to intrude upon an area of traditional state concern. While it is doubtful that any State, or indeed any reasonable person, would argue that it is wise policy to allow students to carry guns on school premises, considerable disagreement exists about how best to accomplish that goal. In this circumstance, the States may perform their role as laboratories for experimentation to devise solutions. Indeed, over 40 States already have criminal laws outlawing the possession of firearms on or near school grounds. The statute before us forecloses the States from experimenting and exercising their own judgment in an area to which States lay claim by right of history and expertise, and it does so by regulating an activity beyond the realm of commerce in the ordinary and usual sense of that term.

Justice THOMAS, *concurring.*

Our case law has drifted far from the original understanding of the Commerce Clause. I believe that we must further reconsider our "substantial effects" test with an eye toward constructing a standard that reflects the text and history of the Commerce Clause without totally rejecting our more recent Commerce Clause jurisprudence. The aggregation principle is clever, but has no stopping point.

Justice STEVENS, *dissenting.*

Guns are articles of commerce and articles that can be used to restrain commerce. Their possession is the consequence, either directly or indirectly, of commercial activity. Congress' power to regulate commerce in firearms includes the power to prohibit possession of guns at any location because of their potentially harmful use; Congress may also prohibit their possession in particular markets. The market for handguns by school-age children is, distressingly, substantial. Whether or not the national interest in eliminating that market would have justified federal legislation in 1789, it surely does today.

Justice SOUTER, *dissenting.*

The practice of deferring to rationally based legislative judgments "is a paradigm of judicial restraint." In judicial review under the Commerce Clause, it reflects our respect for the institutional competence of the Congress on a subject expressly assigned to it by the Constitution and our appreciation of the legitimacy that comes from Congress's political accountability in dealing with matters open to a wide range of possible choices. It seems fair to ask whether the step taken by the Court today does anything but portend a return to the untenable jurisprudence from which the Court extricated itself almost 60 years ago. The answer is not reassuring. The suggestion is either that a connection between commerce and these subjects is remote, or that the commerce power is weaker when it touches subjects on which the States have historically been the primary legislators. Neither suggestion is tenable. As for remoteness, the commercial prospects of an illiterate State or Nation are not rosy. As for the notion that the commerce power diminishes the closer it gets to customary state concerns, that idea has been flatly rejected, and not long ago. The commerce power, we have often observed, is plenary.

Justice BREYER, with whom Justice STEVENS, Justice SOUTER, and Justice GINSBURG join, *dissenting*.

Reports, hearings, and literature make clear that the problem of guns in and around schools is widespread and extremely serious. Violence in schools significantly interferes with the quality of education. Congress obviously could have thought that guns and learning are mutually exclusive. Congress could therefore have found a substantial educational problem—teachers unable to teach, students unable to learn—and concluded that guns near schools contribute substantially to the size and scope of that problem. Having found that guns in schools significantly undermine the quality of education in our Nation's classrooms, Congress could have found that gun-related violence in and around schools is a commercial, as well as a human, problem. Education, although far more than economics, has long been inextricably intertwined with the Nation's economy. Nearly a quarter of America's economic growth in the early years of this century is traceable directly to increased schooling. In recent years the link between secondary education and business has strengthened. Increasing global competition has made primary and secondary education economically more important. Firms base their location decisions upon the presence of a work force with a basic education. The Court's holding threatens legal uncertainty in an area of law that seemed reasonably well settled. Congress has enacted many statutes including criminal statutes, that use the words "affecting commerce" to define their scope, and other statutes contain no jurisdictional language at all.

∾ PROBLEMS ∾

1. *More on the Gun-Free School Zones Act.* In passing the Gun-Free School Zones Act, could Congress have done anything differently that would have resulted in the law being upheld? If so, what? If you had been counsel to the relevant committees, what would you have advised?

2. *More on the Education for a Better America Act.* Does *Lopez* suggest that Congress might have difficulty passing the proposed legislation? In light of *Lopez*, what might Congress be allowed to do (or precluded from doing) in this Act? How does the Tenth Amendment come into play?

United States v. Morrison

529 U.S. 598 (2000)

Chief Justice REHNQUIST delivered the opinion of the Court.

We consider the constitutionality of 42 U.S.C. §13981, which provides a federal civil remedy for the victims of gender-motivated violence. The United States Court of Appeals for the Fourth Circuit, sitting en banc, struck down §13981. We affirm.

Petitioner Christy Brzonkala enrolled at Virginia Polytechnic Institute (Virginia Tech) in 1994. Brzonkala met respondents Morrison and Crawford, who were students at Virginia Tech and members of its varsity football team. Brzonkala alleges that Morrison and Crawford assaulted and repeatedly raped her. After the attack, Morrison told Brzonkala, "You better not have any diseases." In the months following the rape, Morrison allegedly announced in the dormitory's dining room that he "liked to get girls drunk and." The omitted portions consist of boasting, debased remarks about what Morrison would do to women, vulgar remarks that cannot fail to shock and offend. Brzonkala alleges that this attack caused her to become severely emotionally disturbed and depressed. She sought assistance from a university psychiatrist, who prescribed antidepressant medication. Shortly after the rape Brzonkala stopped attending classes and withdrew from the university. In early 1995, Brzonkala filed a complaint against respondents under Virginia Tech's Sexual Assault Policy. Morrison was found guilty of sexual assault and suspended for two semesters. The University later reopened the case and found Morrison guilty only of "using abusive language," but this finding was set aside. Virginia Tech did not inform Brzonkala of this decision. After learning from a newspaper that Morrison would be returning to Virginia Tech for the fall 1995 semester, she dropped out of the university again. In December 1995, Brzonkala sued Morrison, Crawford, and Virginia Tech in the United States District Court for the Western District of Virginia alleging a violation of §13981. The District Court dismissed the complaint. A divided panel of the Court of Appeals reversed, but the full Court of Appeals concluded that Congress lacked constitutional authority to enact §13981's civil remedy. We granted certiorari.

Section 13981 was part of the Violence Against Women Act of 1994. It states that "all persons within the United States shall have the right to be free from crimes of violence motivated by gender." To enforce that right, subsection (c) declares: "A person (including a person who acts under color of any statute, ordinance, regulation, custom, or usage of any State) who commits a crime of violence motivated by gender and thus deprives another of the right declared in subsection (b) of this section shall be liable to the party injured, in an action for the recovery of compensatory and punitive damages, injunctive and declaratory relief, and such other relief as a court may deem appropriate." Section 13981 defines a "crime of violence motivated by gender" as "a crime of violence committed because of gender or on the basis of gender, and due, at least in part, to an animus based on the victim's gender." §13981(d)(1). It also provides that the term "crime of violence" includes any

> (A) act or series of acts that would constitute a felony against the person or that would constitute a felony against property if the conduct presents a serious risk of physical injury to another, and that would come within the meaning of State or Federal offenses described in section 16 of Title 18, whether or not those acts have actually resulted in criminal charges, prosecution, or conviction and whether or not those acts were committed in the special maritime, territorial, or prison jurisdiction of the United States; and
> (B) includes an act or series of acts that would constitute a felony described in subparagraph (A) but for the relationship between the person who takes such action and the individual against whom such action is taken.

Further clarifying the broad scope of §13981's civil remedy, subsection (e)(2) states that "nothing in this section requires a prior criminal complaint, prosecution, or conviction to establish the elements of cause of action under subsection (c) of this section." Subsection (e)(3) provides a §13981 litigant with choice of forums: Federal and state courts "shall have concurrent jurisdiction" over complaints brought under the section.

Although the language of §13981 covers a wide swath of criminal conduct, Congress placed some limitations on the section's federal civil remedy. Subsection (e)(1) states that "nothing in this section entitles a person to a cause of action under subsection (c) of this section for random acts of violence unrelated to gender or for acts that cannot be demonstrated, by a preponderance of the evidence, to be motivated by gender." Subsection (e)(4) further states that §13981 shall not be construed "to confer on the courts of the United States jurisdiction over any State law claim seeking the establishment of a divorce, alimony, equitable distribution of marital property, or child custody decree."

Every law enacted by Congress must be based on one or more of its powers enumerated in the Constitution. Congress explicitly identified the sources of federal authority on which it relied in enacting §13981. It said that a "Federal civil rights cause of action" is established "pursuant to the affirmative power of Congress under section 5 of the Fourteenth Amendment to the Constitution, as well as under section 8 of Article I of the Constitution." We address Congress' authority to enact this remedy under each of these constitutional provisions.

Due respect for the decisions of a coordinate branch of Government demands that we invalidate a congressional enactment only upon a plain showing that Congress has exceeded its constitutional bounds. *See United States v. Lopez*, 514 U.S. at 568 (Kennedy, J., concurring). As discussed in *Lopez*, our interpretation of the Commerce Clause has changed as our Nation has developed. In the years since *NLRB v. Jones & Laughlin Steel Corp.*, 301 U.S. 1 (1937), Congress has had considerably greater latitude in regulating conduct and transactions under the Commerce Clause than our previous case law permitted. *Lopez* emphasized, however, that even under our modern, expansive interpretation of the Commerce Clause, Congress' regulatory authority is not without effective bounds. Modern Commerce Clause jurisprudence has "identified three broad categories of activity that Congress may regulate under its commerce power." "First, Congress may regulate the use of the channels of interstate commerce." "Second, Congress is empowered to regulate and protect the instrumentalities of interstate commerce, or persons or things in interstate commerce, even though the threat may come only from intrastate activities." "Finally, Congress' commerce authority includes the power to regulate those activities having a substantial relation to interstate commerce, i.e., those activities that substantially affect interstate commerce."

Petitioners do not contend that these cases fall within either of the first two of these categories of Commerce Clause regulation. They seek to sustain §13981 as a regulation of activity that substantially affects interstate commerce. Under *Lopez*, the proper resolution of the present cases is clear. Gender-motivated crimes of violence are not, in any sense of the phrase, economic activity. While we need not adopt a categorical rule against aggregating the effects of any non-economic activity in order to decide these cases, thus far our cases have upheld Commerce Clause regulation of intrastate activity only where that activity is economic in nature. §13981 contains no jurisdictional element establishing that the federal cause of action is in pursuance of Congress' power to regulate interstate commerce. Section 13981 *is* supported by numerous findings regarding the serious impact that gender-motivated violence has on victims and their families. But the existence of congressional findings is not sufficient, by itself, to sustain the constitutionality of Commerce Clause legislation. As we stated in *Lopez*, "whether particular operations affect interstate commerce sufficiently to come under the constitutional power of Congress to regulate them is ultimately a judicial rather than a legislative question, and can be settled finally only by this Court."

In these cases, Congress' findings are weakened by the fact that they rely so heavily on a method of reasoning that we have rejected as unworkable if we are to maintain the Constitution's enumeration of powers. Congress found that gender-motivated violence affects interstate commerce "by deterring potential victims from traveling interstate, from engaging in employment in interstate business, and from transacting with business, and in places involved in interstate commerce; by diminishing national productivity, increasing medical and other costs, and decreasing the supply of and the demand for interstate products." Given these findings, the concern that we expressed in *Lopez* that Congress might use the Commerce Clause to completely obliterate the Constitution's distinction between national and local authority seems well founded. The reasoning that petitioners advance seeks to follow the but-for causal chain from the initial occurrence of violent crime (the suppression of which has been the prime object of the States' police power) to every attenuated effect upon interstate commerce. If accepted, petitioners' reasoning would allow Congress to regulate any crime as long as the nationwide, aggregated impact of that crime has substantial effects on employment, production, transit, or consumption. If Congress may regulate gender-motivated violence, it would be able to regulate murder or any other type of violence since gender-motivated violence, as a subset of all violent crime, is certain to have lesser economic impacts than the larger class of which it is a part.

Petitioners' reasoning will not limit Congress to regulating violence but may be applied equally as well to family law and other areas of traditional state regulation since the aggregate effect of marriage, divorce, and childrearing on the national economy is undoubtedly significant. Congress may have recognized this specter when it expressly precluded §13981 from being used in the family law context. Under our Constitution, the limitation of congressional authority is not solely a matter of legislative grace.

The political branches have a role in interpreting and applying the Constitution, but since *Marbury* this Court has remained the ultimate expositor of the constitutional text. We reject the argument that Congress may regulate non-economic, violent criminal conduct based solely on that conduct's aggregate effect on interstate commerce. The Constitution requires a distinction between what is truly national and what is truly local. The regulation and punishment of intrastate violence that is not directed at the instrumentalities, channels, or goods involved in interstate commerce has always been the province of the States. Indeed, we can think of no better example of the police power, which the Founders denied the National Government and reposed in the States, than the suppression of violent crime and vindication of its victims. *See, e.g., Lopez,* 514 U.S. at 566.

Petitioners argue that the section's civil remedy should be upheld as an exercise of Congress' remedial power under §5 of the Fourteenth Amendment. Section 5 states that Congress may " 'enforce' by 'appropriate legislation' the constitutional guarantee that no State shall deprive any person of 'life, liberty, or property, without due process of law,' nor deny any person 'equal protection of the laws.' " *City of Boerne v. Flores,* 521 U.S. 507 (1997). Petitioners' §5 argument is founded on an assertion that there is pervasive bias in various state justice systems against victims of gender-motivated violence. Congress concluded that discriminatory stereotypes often result in insufficient investigation and prosecution of gender-motivated crime, inappropriate focus on the behavior and credibility of the victims of that crime, and unacceptably lenient punishments for those actually convicted of gender-motivated violence. Petitioners contend that this bias denies victims of gender-motivated violence the equal protection of the laws and that Congress therefore acted appropriately in enacting a private civil remedy against the perpetrators of gender-motivated violence to both remedy the States' bias and deter future instances of discrimination in the state courts. It is a time-honored principle that the Fourteenth Amendment, by its very terms, prohibits only state action. Section 13981 is not aimed at any State or state actor, but at individuals who have committed criminal acts motivated by gender bias.

Petitioner Brzonkala's complaint alleges that she was the victim of a brutal assault. But Congress' effort in §13981 to provide a federal civil remedy can be sustained neither under the Commerce Clause nor under §5 of the Fourteenth Amendment. If the allegations here are true, no civilized system of justice could fail to provide her a remedy for the conduct of respondent Morrison. But under our federal system that remedy must be provided by the Commonwealth of Virginia, and not by the United States. The judgment of the Court of Appeals is
   Affirmed.

Justice THOMAS, *concurring.*

The "substantial effects" test under the Commerce Clause is inconsistent with the original understanding of Congress' powers and with this Court's early Commerce Clause cases. Until this Court replaces its Commerce Clause jurisprudence with a standard more consistent with the original understanding, we will continue to see Congress appropriating state police powers under the guise of regulating commerce.

Justice SOUTER, with whom Justice STEVENS, Justice GINSBURG, and Justice BREYER join, *dissenting.*

One difference from *Lopez* is the mountain of data assembled by Congress showing the effects of violence against women on interstate commerce. Passage of the Act was preceded by four years of hearings, which included testimony from physicians and law professors; from survivors of rape and domestic violence; and from representatives of state law enforcement and private business. The record includes reports on gender bias from task forces in 21 States, and we have the benefit of factual findings in the Reports issued by Congress and its committees over the long course leading to enactment.

With respect to domestic violence, Congress received evidence for the following findings: three out of four American women will be victims of violent crimes sometime during their life; violence is the leading cause of injuries to women ages 15 to 44; as many as 50 percent of homeless women and children are fleeing domestic violence; since 1974, the assault rate against women has outstripped the rate for men by at least twice for some age groups and far more for others; battering "is the single largest cause of injury to women in the United States"; an estimated 4 million American women are battered each year by their husbands or partners; over 1 million women in the United States seek medical assistance each year for injuries sustained from their husbands or other partners; between 2,000 and 4,000 women die every year from domestic abuse; arrest rates may be as low as 1 for every 100 domestic assaults; partial estimates show that violent crime against women costs this country at least 3 billion—not million, but billion—dollars a year; estimates suggest that we spend $ 5 to $ 10 billion a year on health care, criminal justice, and other social costs of domestic violence; the evidence as to rape was similarly extensive, supporting these conclusions; the incidence of rape rose four times as fast as the total national crime rate over the past 10 years; according to one study, close to half a million girls now in high school will be raped before they graduate; one hundred twenty-five thousand college women can expect to be raped during this—or any—year; three-quarters of women never go to the movies alone after dark because of the fear of rape and nearly 50 percent do not use public transit alone after dark for the same reason; forty-one percent of judges surveyed believed that juries give sexual assault victims less credibility than other crime victims; less than 1 percent of all rape victims have collected damages; an individual who commits rape has only about 4 chances in 100 of being arrested, prosecuted, and found guilty of any offense; almost one-quarter of convicted rapists never go to prison and another quarter received sentences in local jails where the average sentence is 11 months; almost 50 percent of rape victims lose their jobs or are forced to quit because of the crime's severity.

Based on the data thus partially summarized, Congress found that: crimes of violence motivated by gender have a substantial adverse effect on interstate commerce, by deterring potential victims from traveling interstate, from engaging in employment in interstate business, and from transacting with business, and in places involved, in interstate commerce, by diminishing national productivity, increasing medical and other costs, and decreasing the supply of and the demand for interstate products.

Congress explicitly stated the predicate for the exercise of its Commerce Clause power. The sufficiency of the evidence cannot seriously be questioned. The legislative record here is far more voluminous than the record compiled by Congress and found sufficient in two prior cases upholding Title II of the Civil Rights Act of 1964 against Commerce Clause challenges. The Act would have passed muster at any time between *Wickard* in 1942 and *Lopez* in 1995, a period in which the law enjoyed a stable understanding that congressional power under the Commerce Clause, complemented by the authority of the Necessary and Proper Clause, extended to all activity that, when aggregated, has a substantial effect on interstate commerce. The fact that the Act does not pass muster before today is proof, to a degree that *Lopez* was not, that the Court's nominal adherence to the substantial effects test is merely that. Some congressional conclusions about obviously substantial, cumulative effects on commerce are being assigned lesser values than the once-stable doctrine would assign them.

One might reasonably have doubted that Members of this Court would ever again toy with a return to the days before *NLRB v. Jones & Laughlin Steel Corp.*, 301 U.S. 1 (1937), which brought the earlier and nearly disastrous experiment to an end. Today's revival of a distinction between commercial and noncommercial conduct is at odds with *Wickard*, and the enquiry into commercial purpose, first intimated by the *Lopez* concurrence is cousin to the intent-based analysis employed in *Hammer*, but rejected for Commerce Clause purposes in *Heart of Atlanta* and *Darby*.

The Court finds it relevant that the statute addresses conduct traditionally subject to state prohibition under domestic criminal law, a fact said to have some heightened significance when the violent conduct in question is not aimed directly at interstate commerce or its instrumentalities. History seems to be recycling, for the theory of traditional state concern as grounding a limiting principle has been rejected previously. All of this convinces me that today's ebb of the commerce power rests on error, and at the same time leads me to doubt that the majority's view will prove to be enduring law.

Justice BREYER, with whom Justice STEVENS joins, and with whom Justice SOUTER and Justice GINSBURG join as to Part I-A, *dissenting.*

The "economic/noneconomic" distinction is not easy to apply. The Court would permit Congress to aggregate, hence regulate, "noneconomic" activity taking place at economic establishments. *See Heart of Atlanta Motel, Inc. v. United States,* 379 U.S. 241 (1964). It would permit Congress to regulate where that regulation is "an essential part of a larger regulation of economic activity, in which the regulatory scheme could be undercut unless the intrastate activity were regulated." Given the former exception, can Congress simply rewrite the present law and limit its application to restaurants, hotels, perhaps universities, and other places of public accommodation? Given the latter exception, can Congress save the present law by including it, or much of it, in a broader "Safe Transport" or "Workplace Safety" act?

Notes and Questions

1. *Rewriting the Act.* At the end of his dissent, Justice Breyer asks: can Congress "simply rewrite the present law and limit its application to restaurants, hotels, perhaps universities, and other places of public accommodation?" Given the latter exception, can Congress save the present law by including it, or much of it, in a broader 'Safe Transport' or 'Workplace Safety' act?" May it?

2. *Impact on Prior Decisions.* How much do *Lopez* and *Morrison* impact the Court's Commerce Clause jurisprudence? In light of those decisions, should the Court overrule *Heart of Atlanta,* in which the Court applied the 1964 Civil Rights Act to racial discrimination by hotels? Should it overrule *United States v. Darby,* in which Congress prohibited the employment of workmen in the production of goods "for interstate commerce" at other than prescribed wages and hours?

3. *Has the Governing Test Changed?* At first blush, it seemed that the decision in *Heart of Atlanta* had broadly defined the term *commerce* as well as the reach of Congress's power under the Commerce Clause, to focus on whether "the activity sought to be regulated is 'commerce which concerns more States than one' and has *a real and substantial relation to the national interest."* *Heart of Atlanta,* 379 U.S. at 255. Is this still the determinative test after *Lopez* and *Morrison?*

4. *Marijuana Use and Cultivation. Gonzales v. Raich,* 545 U.S. 1 (2005), involved the federal Controlled Substances Act (CSA), 21 U.S.C. §§801 *et seq.,* which made it illegal to possess, obtain, or manufacture cannabis even for personal use. In

contrast to the CSA, California law provided for the "compassionate use" of mari-juana by seriously ill residents. The CSA was challenged by two women who were using marijuana for medical reasons under the California law, one of whom was growing her own marijuana and the other of whom was receiving it free from other local growers, and neither of whom was involved in interstate commerce of marijuana. The Court upheld the CSA on Commerce Clause grounds, conclud-ing that the activity had a "substantial relationship" to interstate commerce. The Court noted that the "similarities between this case and *Wickard* are striking. Like the farmer in *Wickard,* respondents are cultivating, for home consumption, a fun-gible commodity for which there is an established, albeit illegal, interstate market. Just as the Agricultural Adjustment Act was designed 'to control the volume of wheat moving in interstate and foreign commerce in order to avoid surpluses' and consequently control the market price, a primary purpose of the CSA is to control the supply and demand of controlled substances in both lawful and unlawful drug markets." The Court concluded that "leaving home-consumed marijuana outside federal control would similarly affect price and market conditions. Production of the commodity meant for home consumption, be it wheat or marijuana, has a sub-stantial effect on supply and demand in the national market for that commodity."

5. *The Hobbs Act.* In *Taylor v. United States,* 136 S. Ct. 2074 (2016), defendant was charged with violating the Hobbs Act for breaking into the homes of two drug dealers. The question was whether the conduct had a sufficient relationship to interstate commerce to justify the federal law. In both cases, Taylor and other gang members broke into the homes, confronted the residents, demanded the location of drugs and money, found neither, and left relatively empty handed. Nevertheless, the Court held "that the Commerce Clause gives Congress author-ity to regulate the national market for marijuana, including the authority to pro-scribe the purely intrastate production, possession, and sale of this controlled substance. Because Congress may regulate these intrastate activities based on their aggregate effect on interstate commerce, it follows that Congress may also regulate intrastate drug *theft.* Since the Hobbs Act criminalizes robberies and attempted robberies that affect any commerce 'over which the United States has jurisdiction,' §1951(b)(3), the prosecution in a Hobbs Act robbery case satisfies the Act's commerce element if it shows that the defendant robbed or attempted to rob a drug dealer of drugs or drug proceeds. By targeting a drug dealer in this way, a robber necessarily affects or attempts to affect commerce over which the United States has jurisdiction."

∾ PROBLEMS ∾

1. *General Criminal Legislation.* In an earlier problem, you were asked to think about whether cases like *Darby* and *Wickard* could be construed as authorizing Congress to pass a comprehensive criminal statute. After *Lopez,* do you reach the

same conclusions regarding Congress's power over these issues? Similarly, do you have additional thoughts about whether Congress may pass a comprehensive law governing divorce? After reading *Gonzales*, do you see Congress's power differently?

2. *More on the Education for a Better America Act.* How does *Morrison* affect your analysis of whether Congress can pass this legislation? Can Congress include specific mandates (e.g., requiring school tests and specific types of teacher training) as well as just spending incentives?

National Federation of Independent Business v. Sebelius

567 U.S. 519 (2012)

Chief Justice ROBERTS announced the judgment of the Court and delivered the opinion of the Court with respect to Parts I, II, and III-C, an opinion with respect to Part IV, in which Justice BREYER and Justice KAGAN join, and an opinion with respect to Parts III-A, III-B, and III-D.

Today we resolve constitutional challenges to the Patient Protection and Affordable Care Act of 2010 (ACA). We do not consider whether the Act embodies sound policies. That judgment is entrusted to the Nation's elected leaders. We ask only whether Congress has the power under the Constitution to enact the challenged provisions. In our federal system, the National Government possesses limited powers; the States and the people retain the remainder. *McCulloch v. Maryland*, 4 Wheat. 316, 405, 4 L. Ed. 579 (1819). We must determine whether the Constitution grants Congress powers it now asserts, but which many believe it does not possess. Resolving this controversy requires us to examine the limits of the Government's power, and our own role in policing those boundaries.

Rather than granting general authority to perform all conceivable functions of government, the Constitution lists, or enumerates, the Federal Government's powers. Congress may, for example, "coin Money," "establish Post Offices," and "raise and support Armies." Art. I, §8, cls. 5, 7, 12. The Constitution's express conferral of some powers makes clear that it does not grant others. The Federal Government "can exercise only the powers granted to it." *McCulloch, supra*, at 405. The restrictions on government power foremost in many Americans' minds are likely to be affirmative prohibitions, such as contained in the Bill of Rights. If no enumerated power authorizes Congress to pass a certain law, that law may not be enacted, even if it would not violate any of the express prohibitions in the Bill of Rights or elsewhere in the Constitution. "The powers not delegated to the United States by the Constitution are reserved to the States respectively, or to the people." U.S. CONST., AMDT. 10. The Federal Government has expanded dramatically over the past two centuries, but it still must show that a constitutional grant of power authorizes its actions. *See, e.g., United States v. Comstock*, 130 S.Ct. 1949 (2010). The Constitution may restrict state governments. But where prohibitions do not apply, state governments do not need constitutional authorization to act. The States can perform many of the vital functions of modern government—punishing street crime, running public schools, and zoning property—even though the Constitution's text does not authorize any government to do so. We refer to this power possessed by the States but not by the Federal Government, as the "police power." *See, e.g., United States v. Morrison,* 529 U.S. 598 (2000).

"State sovereignty is not an end in itself: Rather, federalism secures to citizens the liberties that derive from the diffusion of sovereign power." *New York v. United States,* 505 U.S. 144, 181 (1992). Because the police power is controlled by 50 different States instead of one national sovereign, the Framers ensured that powers which "in the ordinary course of affairs, concern the lives, liberties, and properties of the people" were held by governments more local and more accountable than a distant federal bureaucracy. The Federalist No. 45, at 293 (J. Madison). The independent power of the States serves as a check on the power of the Federal Government: "By denying any one government complete jurisdiction over all the concerns of public life, federalism protects the liberty of the individual from arbitrary power." *Bond v. United States,* 131 S.Ct. 2355, 2364 (2011).

This case concerns two powers that the Constitution does grant the Federal Government, but which must be read carefully to avoid creating a general federal authority akin to the police power. The Constitution authorizes Congress to "regulate Commerce with foreign Nations, and among the several States, and with the Indian Tribes." Art. I, §8, cl. 3. Our precedents read that to mean that Congress may regulate "the channels of interstate commerce," "persons or things in interstate commerce," and "those activities that substantially affect interstate commerce." *Morrison, supra,* at 609. This power can be expansive and has been held to authorize federal regulation of such seemingly local matters as a farmer's decision to grow wheat for himself and his livestock. *See Wickard v. Filburn,* 317 U.S. 111 (1942).

Congress may also "lay and collect Taxes, Duties, Imposts and Excises, to pay the Debts and provide for the common Defence and general Welfare of the United States." U.S. Const., Art. I, §8, cl. 1. Put simply, Congress may tax and spend. This grant gives the Federal Government considerable influence even in areas where it cannot directly regulate. *See, e.g., License Tax Cases,* 5 Wall. 462, 471, 18 L. Ed. 497 (1867). In exercising its spending power, Congress may offer funds to the States, and may condition those offers on compliance with specified conditions. These offers may induce the States to adopt policies that the Federal Government could not impose. *See, e.g., South Dakota v. Dole,* 483 U.S. 203 (1987).

The reach of the Federal Government's enumerated powers is broader still because the Constitution authorizes Congress to "make all Laws which shall be necessary and proper for carrying into Execution the foregoing Powers." Art. I, §8, cl. 18. We have long read this provision to give Congress great latitude in exercising its powers: "Let the end be legitimate, let it be within the scope of the constitution, and all means which are appropriate, which are plainly adapted to that end, which are not prohibited, but consist with the letter and spirit of the constitution, are constitutional." *McCulloch,* 4 Wheat. at 421, 4 L. Ed. 579.

"Proper respect for a coordinate branch of the government" requires that we strike down an Act of Congress only if "the lack of constitutional authority to pass the act in question is clearly demonstrated." *United States v. Harris*, 106 U.S. 629, 635 (1883). This Court is vested with the authority to interpret the law; we possess neither the expertise nor the prerogative to make policy judgments. Those decisions are entrusted to our Nation's elected leaders, who can be thrown out of office if the people disagree with them. It is not our job to protect the people from the consequences of their political choices.

Deference in matters of policy cannot, however, become abdication in matters of law. "The powers of the legislature are defined and limited; and those limits may not be mistaken, or forgotten." *Marbury v. Madison*, 1 Cranch 137, 176, 2 L. Ed. 60 (1803). Our respect for Congress's policy judgments can never extend so far as to disavow restraints on federal power that the Constitution carefully constructed. It is the responsibility of this Court to enforce the limits on federal power by striking down acts of Congress that transgress those limits. *Marbury v. Madison, supra,* at 175–176.

I

In 2010, Congress enacted the ACA. The Act aims to increase the number of Americans covered by health insurance and decrease the cost of health care. The Act's 10 titles stretch over 900 pages and contain hundreds of provisions. This case concerns constitutional challenges to two key provisions, commonly referred to as the individual mandate and the Medicaid expansion. The individual mandate requires most Americans to maintain "minimum essential" health insurance coverage. 26 U.S.C. §5000A. The mandate does not apply to some individuals, such as prisoners and undocumented aliens. Many individuals will receive the required coverage through their employer, or from a government program such as Medicaid or Medicare. But for individuals who are not exempt and do not receive health insurance through a third party, the means of satisfying the requirement is to purchase insurance from a private company.

Beginning in 2014, those who do not comply with the mandate must make a "shared responsibility payment" to the Federal Government. That payment, which the Act describes as a "penalty," is calculated as a percentage of household income, subject to a floor based on a specified dollar amount and a ceiling based on the average annual premium the individual would have to pay for qualifying private health insurance. In 2016, the penalty will be 2.5 percent of an individual's household income, but no less than $695 and no more than the average yearly premium for insurance that covers 60 percent of the cost of 10 specified services (*e.g.,* prescription drugs and hospitalization). The Act provides that the penalty will be paid to the Internal Revenue Service with an individual's taxes, and "shall be assessed and collected in the same manner" as tax penalties. 26 U.S.C. §5000A(g)(1). The Act, however, bars the IRS from using several of its normal enforcement tools, such as criminal prosecutions and levies. Some individuals who are subject to the mandate are nonetheless exempt from the penalty—for example, those with income below a certain threshold and members of Indian tribes.

Plaintiffs, including various states, individuals, and the National Federation of Independent Business, alleged that the individual mandate exceeded Congress's powers under Article I of the Constitution. The District Court agreed and the Court of Appeals for the Eleventh Circuit affirmed.

II

The Court held that the Anti-Injunction Act, which precludes the Court from enjoining, did not preclude it from hearing the case because the Court viewed the mandate as imposing a "penalty" rather than a tax.

III

The Government advances two theories for the proposition that Congress had constitutional authority to enact the individual mandate. First, the Government argues that Congress had the power to enact the mandate under the Commerce Clause. Under that theory, Congress may order individuals to buy health insurance because the failure to do so affects interstate commerce, and could undercut the ACA's other reforms. Second, the Government argues that we should uphold it as an exercise of Congress's power to tax.

A

The Government's first argument is that the individual mandate is a valid exercise of Congress's power under the Commerce Clause and the Necessary and Proper Clause. According to the Government, the health care market is characterized by a significant cost-shifting problem. Everyone will eventually need health care at a time and to an extent they cannot predict, but if they do not have insurance, they often will not be able to pay for it. Because state and federal laws require hospitals to provide a degree of care without regard to the ability to pay, hospitals end up receiving compensation for only a portion of the services they provide. To recoup the losses, hospitals pass on the cost to insurers through higher rates, and insurers pass on the cost to policy holders in the form of higher premiums. Congress estimated that uncompensated care raises family health insurance premiums, on average, by over $1,000 per year. Congress addressed the problem of those who cannot obtain insurance coverage because of preexisting conditions or other health issues through the Act's "guaranteed-issue" and "community-rating" provisions, which prohibit insurance companies from denying coverage to those with such conditions or charging unhealthy individuals higher premiums than healthy individuals.

The guaranteed-issue and community-rating reforms do not address the issue of healthy individuals who choose not to purchase insurance to cover potential health care needs. In fact, the reforms exacerbate that problem, by providing an incentive for individuals to delay purchasing health insurance until they become sick, relying on the promise of guaranteed and affordable coverage. The reforms also threaten to impose massive new costs on insurers, who are required to accept unhealthy individuals but prohibited from charging them rates necessary to pay for their coverage. This will lead insurers to significantly increase premiums on everyone. By requiring that individuals purchase health insurance, the mandate prevents cost-shifting by those who would otherwise go without it. In addition, the mandate forces into the insurance risk pool more healthy individuals, whose premiums subsidize the costs of covering the unhealthy individuals the reforms require insurers to accept. The Government contends that the individual mandate is within Congress's power because the failure to purchase insurance "has a substantial and deleterious effect on interstate commerce" by creating the cost-shifting problem.

"The power of Congress over interstate commerce is not confined to the regulation of commerce among the states," but extends to activities that "have a substantial effect on interstate commerce." *United States v. Darby*, 312 U.S. 100, 118-119 (1941). Congress's power is not limited to regulation of an activity that by itself substantially affects interstate commerce, but also extends to activities that do so only when aggregated with similar activities of others. *See Wickard*, 317 U.S. at 127. Given its expansive scope, Congress has employed the commerce power in a variety of ways to address the pressing needs of the time. But Congress has never attempted to rely on that power to compel individuals not engaged in commerce to purchase an unwanted product.[3]

The Constitution grants Congress the power to "*regulate* Commerce." Art. I, §8, cl. 3. The power to *regulate* presupposes the existence of commercial activity to be regulated. For example, the Constitution gives Congress the power to "coin Money," in addition to the power to "regulate the Value thereof." *Id.*, cl. 5. It gives Congress the power to "raise and support Armies" and to "provide and maintain a Navy," in addition to the power to "make Rules for the Government and Regulation of the land and naval Forces." *Id.*, cls. 12-14. If the power to regulate the armed forces or the value of money included the power to bring the subject of the regulation into existence, the specific grant of such powers would have been unnecessary. The language of the Constitution reflects the natural understanding that the power to regulate assumes there is already something to be regulated. *See, e.g., Lopez, supra,* at 560; *Wickard, supra,* at 125.

The individual mandate does not regulate existing commercial activity. It instead compels individuals to *become* active in commerce by purchasing a product, on the ground that their failure to do so affects interstate commerce. Construing the Commerce Clause to permit Congress to regulate individuals *because* they are

---

3. Other congressional mandates—to report for jury duty, to register for the draft, to purchase firearms in anticipation of militia service, to exchange gold currency for paper currency, and to file a tax return—are based on constitutional provisions other than the Commerce Clause.

doing nothing would open a new and potentially vast domain to congressional authority. Every day individuals do not do an infinite number of things. Allowing Congress to justify federal regulation by pointing to the effect of inaction on commerce would bring countless decisions an individual could *potentially* make within the scope of federal regulation, and empower Congress to make those decisions for him.

The farmer in *Wickard* was actively engaged in the production of wheat, and the Government could regulate that activity because of its effect on commerce. The Government's theory here would establish that individuals may be regulated under the Commerce Clause whenever enough of them are not doing something the Government would have them do. The Government's logic would justify a mandatory purchase to solve almost any problem. Many Americans do not eat a balanced diet. The failure to have a healthy diet increases health care costs, to a greater extent than the failure to purchase insurance. Those increased costs are borne in part by other Americans who must pay more, just as the uninsured shift costs to the insured. Under the Government's theory, Congress could address the diet problem by ordering everyone to buy vegetables. People often fail to do things that would be good for them or good for society. Those failures—joined with the similar failures of others—can have a substantial effect on interstate commerce.

That is not the country the Framers of our Constitution envisioned. The Federalist No. 45, at 293. While Congress's authority under the Commerce Clause has expanded with the growth of the national economy, our cases have "always recognized that the power to regulate commerce, though broad indeed, has limits." *Maryland v. Wirtz,* 392 U.S. 183, 196 (1968). The Government's theory would erode those limits. The Federalist No. 48, at 309 (J. Madison). Congress already enjoys vast power to regulate much of what we do. Accepting the Government's theory would give Congress license to regulate what we do not do, fundamentally changing the relation between the citizen and the Federal Government.[6]

The Government argues that because sickness and injury are unpredictable but unavoidable, "the uninsured as a class are active in the market for health care, which they regularly seek and obtain." The individual mandate "merely regulates how individuals finance and pay for that active participation—requiring that they do so through insurance, rather than through attempted self-insurance with the back-stop of shifting costs to others." The phrase "active in the market" cannot obscure the fact that most of those regulated by the individual mandate are not currently engaged in any commercial activity involving health care, and that fact is fatal to the Government's effort to "regulate the uninsured as a class." Our precedents recognize Congress's power to regulate "classes of *activities,*" *Gonzales v. Raich,* 545 U.S. 1, 17 (2005), not classes of *individuals,* apart from any activity in which they are engaged.

---

6. Justice GINSBURG suggests that "an individual who opts not to purchase insurance can be seen as actively selecting self-insurance." But "self-insurance" is nothing more than a failure to purchase insurance.

The individual mandate's regulation of the uninsured as a class is divorced from any link to existing commercial activity. The mandate primarily affects healthy, often young adults who are less likely to need significant health care and have other priorities for spending their money. It is because these individuals, as an actuarial class, incur relatively low health care costs that the mandate helps counter the effect of forcing insurance companies to cover others who impose greater costs than their premiums are allowed to reflect. The individual mandate is targeted at a class whose commercial inactivity is its defining feature.

The Government regards it as sufficient to trigger Congress's authority that almost all those who are uninsured will, at some unknown point in the future, engage in a health care transaction. The proposition that Congress may dictate the conduct of an individual today because of prophesied future activity finds no support in our precedent. Congress can anticipate the *effects* on commerce of an economic activity. *See, e.g., Heart of Atlanta Motel, Inc. v. United States*, 379 U.S. 241 (1964). We have never permitted Congress to anticipate that activity in order to regulate individuals not currently engaged in commerce. Our cases involve preexisting economic activity. *See, e.g., Wickard*, 317 U.S. at 127. Everyone will likely participate in the markets for food, clothing, transportation, shelter, or energy; that does not authorize Congress to direct them to purchase particular products. The Commerce Clause is not a license to regulate an individual from cradle to grave, simply because he will predictably engage in particular transactions. Any police power to regulate individuals, as opposed to activities, remains vested in the States.

The Government argues that health insurance is a unique product, and that upholding the mandate would not justify mandatory purchases of items such as cars or broccoli because, "health insurance is not purchased for its own sake; it is a means of financing health-care consumption and covering universal risks." But cars and broccoli are purchased for transportation and food.

The Government says that health insurance and health care financing are "inherently integrated." But that does not mean the compelled purchase of the first is properly regarded as a regulation of the second. No matter how "inherently integrated," they involve different transactions, entered into at different times, with different providers. For most of those targeted by the mandate, significant health care needs will be years, or even decades, away. The proximity and degree of connection between the mandate and the subsequent commercial activity is too lacking. The individual mandate forces individuals into commerce precisely because they elected to refrain from commercial activity. Such a law cannot be sustained under a clause authorizing Congress to "regulate Commerce."

The Government contends that Congress has the power under the Necessary and Proper Clause to enact the individual mandate because it is an "integral part of a comprehensive scheme of economic regulation." Under this argument, it is enough that Congress regulate commercial activity in a way that requires regulation of inactivity to be effective. The power to "make all Laws which shall be necessary and proper for carrying into Execution" the powers enumerated in the Constitution, Art. I, §8, cl. 18, vests Congress with authority to enact provisions "incidental to the enumerated power, and conducive to its beneficial exercise," *McCulloch,* 4 Wheat. at 418, 4 L. Ed. 579. The Clause does not provide "great substantive and independent powers" beyond those specifically enumerated. The Clause is " 'merely a declaration that the means of carrying into execution those powers otherwise granted are included in the grant.' " *Kinsella v. United States ex rel. Singleton,* 361 U.S. 234, 247 (1960) (quoting VI WRITINGS OF JAMES MADISON 383 (G. Hunt ed. 1906)).

We have been deferential to Congress's determination that a regulation is "necessary." We have thus upheld laws that are " 'convenient, or useful' or 'conducive' to the authority's 'beneficial exercise.' " *Comstock,* 130 S.Ct. at 1965 (quoting *McCulloch, supra,* at 413). But we have declared unconstitutional laws that undermine the structure of government established by the Constitution. Such laws are not "*proper* means for carrying into Execution" Congress's enumerated powers. Rather, they are " 'merely acts of usurpation' which 'deserve to be treated as such.' " *Printz v. United States,* 521 U.S. 898, 924 (1997) (quoting The Federalist No. 33, at 204 (A. Hamilton)).

The individual mandate cannot be sustained under the Necessary and Proper Clause as an essential component of the insurance reforms. Cases upholding laws under that Clause involved exercises of authority derivative of, and in service to, a granted power. We have upheld provisions permitting continued confinement of those *already in federal custody* when they could not be safely released, *Comstock, 130 S.Ct. at 1954*; criminalizing bribes involving organizations receiving federal *funds, Sabri v. United States,* 541 U.S. 600 (2004); and tolling state statutes of limitations while cases are pending in federal court, *Jinks v. Richland County,* 538 U.S. 456 (2003). The individual mandate vests Congress with the extraordinary ability to create the necessary predicate to the exercise of an enumerated power. This is in no way an authority that is "narrow in scope," or "incidental" to the exercise of the commerce power, *McCulloch, supra,* at 418. Such a conception of the Necessary and Proper Clause would work a substantial expansion of federal authority. No longer would Congress be limited to regulating under the Commerce Clause those who by some preexisting activity bring themselves within the sphere of federal regulation. Instead, Congress could draw within its regulatory scope those who otherwise would be outside of it. Even if the individual mandate is "necessary" to the Act's insurance reforms, such an expansion of federal power is not a "proper" means for making those reforms effective.

The Government relies on our decision in *Gonzales v. Raich* involving "comprehensive legislation to regulate the interstate market" in marijuana. Congress's attempt to regulate the interstate market for marijuana would have been substantially undercut if it could not also regulate intrastate possession and consumption. Just as the individual mandate cannot be sustained as a law regulating the substantial effects of the failure to purchase health insurance, neither can it be upheld as a "necessary and proper" component of the insurance reforms. The commerce power thus does not authorize the mandate.

B

[The Court went on to hold that the individual mandate could be upheld under Congress's enumerated power to "lay and collect Taxes." Art. I, §8, cl. 1. This section of the opinion is set forth in the section on Congress's power to tax.]

IV

[The Court then discussed the validity of the Medicaid expansion under the spending power. That portion of the opinion is discussed in the section on Congress' power to spend.]

The Affordable Care Act is constitutional in part and unconstitutional in part. The Framers created a Federal Government of limited powers, and assigned to this Court the duty of enforcing those limits. The Court does so today. But the Court does not express any opinion on the wisdom of the Affordable Care Act. Under the Constitution, that judgment is reserved to the people.

The judgment of the Court of Appeals for the Eleventh Circuit is affirmed in part and reversed in part.

It is so ordered.

Justice GINSBURG, with whom Justice SOTOMAYOR joins, and with whom Justice BREYER and Justice KAGAN join as to Parts I, II, III, and IV, *concurring in part, concurring in the judgment in part*, and *dissenting in part*.

The Commerce Clause authorizes Congress to enact the minimum coverage provision.

I

Since 1937, our precedent has recognized Congress' authority to set the Nation's course in the economic and social welfare realm. *See NLRB v. Jones & Laughlin Steel Corp.*, 301 U.S. 1, 37 (1937). The Chief Justice's crabbed reading of the Commerce Clause harks back to the era in which the Court routinely thwarted Congress' efforts to regulate the national economy in the interest of those who labor to sustain it. It should not have staying power. States cannot resolve the problem of the uninsured on their own. An individual state's universal health-care system would bring an influx of unhealthy individuals into the State and result in increased spending on medical services. A State would have to raise taxes, and health-insurance companies would have to increase premiums, which would, in turn, encourage businesses and healthy individuals to leave the State. Aware that a national solution was required, Congress had to require that individuals obtain private health insurance coverage, and the mandate gives them a financial incentive to acquire insurance. The mandate serves a purpose vital to Congress' plan. Because individuals with preexisting medical conditions cost insurance companies significantly more than those without such conditions, insurers refused to insure these individuals, charged them substantially higher premiums, or offered only limited coverage that did not include the preexisting illness. Congress passed the mandate to deal with this problem.

II

Until today, whether Congress validly exercised its commerce power was guided by two familiar principles. First, Congress has the power to regulate economic activities "that substantially affect interstate commerce." *Gonzales v. Raich,* 545 U.S. 1 (2005). This power extends even to local activities that, viewed in the aggregate, have a substantial impact on interstate commerce. Second, we owe a large measure of respect to Congress when it frames and enacts economic and social legislation. Congress had a rational basis for concluding that the uninsured, as a class, substantially affect interstate commerce. Given the far-reaching effects on interstate commerce, the decision to forgo insurance is an economic decision Congress has the authority to address under the Commerce Clause. The minimum coverage provision, furthermore, bears a "reasonable connection" to Congress' goal of protecting the health-care market from the disruption caused by individuals who fail to obtain insurance. "Where legislators have a rational basis for finding a chosen regulatory scheme necessary to the protection of commerce, our investigation is at an end." *Katzenbach,* 379 U.S. at 303-304. Congress' enactment of the minimum coverage provision, which addresses a specific interstate problem in a practical, experience-informed manner, easily meets this criterion.

The commerce power does not, the Chief Justice announces, permit Congress to "compel individuals to become active in commerce by purchasing a product." Everyone will, at some point, consume health-care products and services. Congress could reasonably have viewed the market from a long-term perspective, encompassing all transactions virtually certain to occur over the next decade, not just those occurring here and now. Congress' authority, under the Commerce Clause, to direct the conduct of an individual today (the farmer in *Wickard,* stopped from growing excess wheat) because of a prophesied future transaction (the eventual sale of that wheat in the interstate market). Congress' actions are even more rational in this case, where the future activity (the consumption of medical care) is certain to occur, the sole uncertainty being the time the activity will take place. Congress is merely defining the terms on which individuals pay for an interstate good they consume.

The Chief Justice calls the minimum coverage provision an illegitimate effort to make young, healthy individuals subsidize insurance premiums paid by the less hale and hardy. Over a lifespan, the costs and benefits even out: The young who pay more than their fair share currently will pay less than their fair share when they become senior citizens. Even if some will pay more for health insurance than they receive in health services, that is how insurance works. Every insured person receives protection against a catastrophic loss, even though only a subset of the covered class will ultimately need that protection. Nothing in the Commerce Clause implies that Congress' commerce power is limited to regulating those actively engaged in commercial transactions.

The Chief Justice's view is premised on a fear that the commerce power would otherwise know no limits. Congress would remain unable to regulate non-economic conduct that has only an attenuated effect on interstate commerce and is traditionally left to state law. Congress, the Chief Justice posits, might mandate that an individual's failure to eat a healthy diet, like the failure to purchase health insurance, imposes costs on others. The Court would have to believe that individuals forced to buy vegetables would then eat them (instead of throwing or giving them away), would prepare the vegetables in a healthy way (steamed or raw, not deep-fried), would cut back on unhealthy foods, and would not allow other factors (such as lack of exercise or little sleep) to trump the improved diet. Such "piling of inference upon inference" is just what the Court refused to do in *Lopez* and *Morrison*.

III

One of Congress' goals in enacting the ACA was to eliminate the industry's practice of charging higher prices or denying coverage to individuals with preexisting medical conditions. Without the mandate, guaranteed-issue and community-rating requirements would trigger an adverse-selection death-spiral in the health-insurance market. The provisions are " 'reasonably adapted' to the attainment of a legitimate end under the commerce power": the elimination of pricing and sales practices that take an applicant's medical history into account.

The mandate is not "proper" legislation, the Chief Justice urges, because it "undermines the structure of government established by the Constitution." The Chief Justice does not explain *why* the power to direct either the purchase of health insurance or the payment of a penalty collectible as a tax is more far-reaching than other implied powers this Court has found permissible under the Necessary and Proper Clause. These powers include the power to enact criminal laws, to imprison, including civil imprisonment, and to create a national bank; *see McCulloch, supra.*[10] The ACA addresses the very sort of interstate problem that made the commerce power essential in our federal system. The statutory provision need only be "conducive" and "reasonably adapted" to the goal Congress seeks to achieve. The minimum coverage provision meets this requirement.

IV

In the early 20th century, this Court regularly struck down economic regulation. The Chief Justice's Commerce Clause opinion, and even more so the joint dissenters' reasoning, bear a disquieting resemblance to those long-overruled decisions.

---

10. Congress regularly requires individuals who are "doing nothing" to take action. Examples include federal requirements to report for jury duty, to register for selective service, to purchase firearms and gear in anticipation of service in the Militia, to turn gold currency over to the Federal Government in exchange for paper currency.

V

[In this section, Ginsberg stated that she would have upheld the Medicaid expansion.]

Justice SCALIA, Justice KENNEDY, Justice THOMAS, and Justice ALITO, *dissenting*.

There are structural limits upon federal power—upon what it can prescribe with respect to private conduct, and upon what it can impose upon the sovereign States. The Act before us exceeds federal power. The Government claims that the mandate is "integral to the ACA's reforms" and "necessary to make effective the Act's core reforms." Here, Congress has impressed into service third parties, healthy individuals who could be but are not customers of the relevant industry, to offset the undesirable consequences of the regulation. If Congress can command even those furthest removed from an interstate market to participate in the market, then the Commerce Clause becomes a font of unlimited power. The Federalist No. 33, p. 202 (C. Rossiter ed.1961). The Government argues that the Individual Mandate is a "regulation of activities having a substantial relation to interstate commerce. The problem is that the mandate focuses on goods and services that people *do not purchase.* They are not participants in that market, and cannot be made so (and thereby subjected to regulation) by defining participants to include all those who will, later in their lifetime, probably purchase the goods or services. All of us consume food, and when we do so the Federal Government can prescribe what its quality must be and even how much we must pay. But the Government cannot say when and what we will buy. Justice Ginsburg claims that Congress needs only a " 'rational basis' for concluding that the *regulated activity* substantially affects interstate commerce." But it must be *activity* affecting commerce that is regulated.

Justice THOMAS, *dissenting.*

"A 'substantial effects' test under the Commerce Clause is inconsistent with the original understanding of Congress' powers and with this Court's early Commerce Clause cases." *Morrison,* 529 U.S. at 627 (Thomas, J., concurring). The Court's continued use of that test "has encouraged the Federal Government to persist in its view that the Commerce Clause has virtually no limits." *Morrison, supra,* at 627. The Government's unprecedented claim in this suit is a case in point.

⌐ PROBLEM: *SEBELIUS* AND THE EDUCATION FOR A BETTER AMERICA ACT ⌐

After *Sebelius,* can one conclude that the Education for a Better America Act is sufficiently related to "commerce" so that Congress has the power to pass this broad-based educational reform legislation?

C. THE TAXING POWER

Article I, Section 8 also gives Congress the power to impose taxes: "The Congress shall have Power To lay and collect Taxes, Duties, Imposes and Excises." Most of the litigation under this clause has focused on Congress's power to regulate conduct by imposing taxes. This so-called "regulation by taxation" is generally unobjectionable if Congress seeks to tax something that it otherwise has the power to regulate (e.g., something within its Art. I, §8 power). However, what happens if Congress tries to regulate through taxation something that it does not have the power to regulate?

Bailey v. Drexel Furniture Co.

259 U.S. 20 (1922)

(Child Labor Tax Case)

Mr. Chief Justice Taft delivered the opinion of the Court.

This case presents the question of the constitutional validity of the Child Labor Tax Law. Plaintiff Drexel Furniture Company is engaged in the manufacture of furniture in the Western district of North Carolina. It received a notice from the Internal Revenue Service indicating that it had been assessed $ 6,312.79 for having during 1919 employed and permitted to work in its factory a boy under 14 years of age, thus incurring the tax of 10 per cent on its net profits for that year. The company paid the tax under protest, and, after rejection of its claim for a refund, brought this suit. On demurrer, judgment was entered for the company against the collector for the full amount, with interest.

The Child Labor Tax Law is attacked on the ground that it is a regulation of the employment of child labor in the states — an exclusively state function under the federal Constitution and within the reservations of the Tenth Amendment. Defendant claims that it is a mere excise tax levied by Congress under its broad power of taxation conferred by section 8, article 1, of the federal Constitution. We must construe the law and interpret the intent and meaning of Congress from the language of the act. Does this law impose a tax with only that incidental restraint and regulation which a tax must inevitably involve? Or does it regulate by the use of the so-called tax as a penalty? If it were an excise on a commodity or other thing of value, we might not be permitted under previous decisions of this court to infer solely from its heavy burden that the act intends a prohibition instead of a tax. But this act is more. It provides a heavy exaction for a departure from a detailed and specified course of conduct in business. That course of business is that employers shall employ in mines and quarries, children of an age greater than 16 years; in mills and factories, children of an age greater than 14 years, and shall prevent children of less than 16 years in mills and factories from working more than 8 hours a day or 6 days in the week. If an employer departs from this prescribed course of business, he is to pay to the government one-tenth of his entire net income in the business for a full year. The amount is not to be proportioned to the extent or frequency of the departures, but is to be paid by the employer in full measure whether he employs 500 children for a year, or employs only one for a day. In the light of these features, a court must be blind not to see that the so-called tax is imposed to stop the employment of children within the age limits prescribed. Its prohibitory and regulatory effect and purpose are palpable.

It is the duty and function of this court in cases regularly brought to its bar to decline to recognize or enforce seeming laws of Congress, dealing with subjects not intrusted to Congress, but left or committed by the supreme law of the land to the control of the states. We cannot avoid the duty, even though it requires us to refuse to give effect to legislation designed to promote the highest good. Out of proper respect for the acts of a co-ordinate branch of the government, this court has gone far to sustain taxing acts as such, even though there has been ground for suspecting, from the weight of the tax, it was intended to destroy its subject. But in the act before us the presumption of validity cannot prevail, because proof of the contrary is found on the very face of its provisions. Grant the validity of this law, all that Congress would need to do, hereafter, in seeking to take over to its control any one of the great number of subjects of public interest, jurisdiction of which the states have never parted with, and which are reserved to them by the Tenth Amendment, would be to enact a detailed measure of complete regulation of the subject and enforce it by a so-called tax upon departures from it. To give such magic to the word "tax" would be to break down all constitutional limitation of the powers of Congress and completely wipe out the sovereignty of the states.

The difference between a tax and a penalty is sometimes difficult to define, and yet the consequences in the required method of collection often are important. Where the sovereign enacting the law has power to impose both tax and penalty, the difference between revenue production and regulation may be immaterial, but not so when one sovereign can impose a tax only, and the power of regulation rests in another. Taxes are occasionally imposed in the discretion of the Legislature on proper subjects with the motive of obtaining revenue and with the incidental motive of discouraging them by making their continuance onerous. They do not lose their character as taxes because of the incidental motive. But there comes a time in the extension of the penalizing features of the so-called tax when it loses its character as such and becomes a mere penalty, with the characteristics of regulation and punishment. Such is the law before us. Although Congress does not invalidate the contract of employment or declare that employment within the mentioned ages is illegal, it does exhibit its intent to achieve the latter result by adopting the criteria of wrongdoing and imposing its consequence on those who transgress its standard.

This case cannot be distinguished from *Hammer v. Dagenhart*, 247 U.S. 251. Congress there enacted a law to prohibit transportation in interstate commerce of goods made at a factory in which there was employment of children within the ages and for the same number of hours a day and days in a week as are penalized by the act in this case. This court held the law to be void. In the case at bar, Congress in the name of a tax which is penalty seeks to do the same thing, and the effort must be equally futile. The analogy of *Dagenhart* is clear. The congressional power over interstate commerce is, within its proper scope, just as complete and unlimited as the congressional power to tax, and the legislative motive in its exercise is just as free from judicial suspicion and inquiry. Yet when Congress threatened to stop interstate commerce in ordinary and necessary commodities, unobjectionable as subjects of transportation, and to deny the same to the people of a state in order to coerce them into compliance with Congress' regulation of state concerns, the court said this was not regulation of interstate commerce, but rather that of state concerns and was invalid. Here the so-called tax is a penalty to coerce people of a state to act as Congress wishes them to act in respect of a matter completely the business of the state government under the federal Constitution.

For the reasons given, we must hold the Child Labor Tax Law invalid and the judgment of the District Court is
Affirmed.

Notes and Questions

1. *More on the Police Power.* Following the *Child Labor Tax Case*, the Court rendered a similar holding in *United States v. Constantine*, 296 U.S. 287 (1935). In *Constantine*, the Court struck down a law that imposed a much higher tax on liquor businesses found to be operating in violation of state law. The Court concluded that the law violated the police power of the state.

2. *Is* Dagenhart *Still Valid?* In *Bailey*, note the Court's reliance on *Dagenhart* and that decision's interpretation of the Commerce Clause and the Tenth Amendment. Does the Court still adhere to that interpretation? If not, how have the Court's attitudes changed? How would this change affect the Court's analysis today?

United States v. Sanchez

340 U.S. 42 (1950)

Mr. Justice CLARK delivered the opinion of the Court.

This is a direct appeal from dismissal of a suit for recovery of $ 8,701.65 in taxes and interest alleged to be due under §7(a)(2) of the Marihuana Tax Act, 26 U.S.C. §2590(a)(2), 26 U.S.C.A. §2590(a)(2). In their motion to dismiss, which was granted without opinion, defendants attacked the constitutionality of this subsection on the ground that it levied a penalty, not a tax. The validity of this levy is the issue here.

In enacting the Marihuana Tax Act, the Congress had two objectives: "The development of a plan of taxation which will raise revenue and at the same time render extremely difficult the acquisition of marihauna by persons who desire it for illicit uses, and the development of an adequate means of publicizing dealings in marihuana in order to tax and control the traffic effectively." S. Rep. No. 900, 75th Cong., 1st Sess., p. 3. Pursuant to these objectives, §3230 of the Code imposes a special tax ranging from $ 1 to $ 24 on "every person who imports, manufactures, produces, compounds, sells, deals in, dispenses, prescribes, administers, or gives away marihuana." For purposes of administration, §3231 requires such persons to register at the time of the payment of the tax with the Collector of the District in which their businesses are located. The Code then makes it unlawful—with certain exceptions not pertinent here—for any person to transfer marihuana except in pursuance of a written order of the transferee on a blank form issued by the Secretary of the Treasury. Section 2590 requires the transferee at the time he applies for the order form to pay a tax on such transfer of $ 1 per ounce or fraction thereof if he has paid the special tax and registered, or $ 100 per ounce or fraction thereof if he has not paid the special tax and registered. §2590(a)(2). The transferor is also made liable for the tax so imposed, in the event the transfer is made without an order form and without the payment of the tax by the transferee. Defendants in this case are transferors.

It is obvious that §2590, by imposing a severe burden on transfers to unregistered persons, implements the congressional purpose of restricting traffic in marihuana to accepted industrial and medicinal channels. Hence the attack rests on the regulatory character and prohibitive burden of the section as well as the penal nature of the imposition. Despite the regulatory effect and the close resemblance to a penalty, it does not follow that the levy is invalid.

First. It is beyond question that a tax does not cease to be valid merely because it regulates, discourages, or even deters the activities taxed. The principle applies even though the revenue obtained is negligible, or the revenue purpose of the tax may be secondary. Nor does a tax statute necessarily fall because it touches on activities which Congress might not otherwise regulate. As pointed out in *Magnano Co. v. Hamilton*, 292 U.S. 40 (1934) "From the beginning of our government, the courts have sustained taxes although imposed with the collateral intent of effecting ulterior ends which, considered apart, were beyond the constitutional power of the lawmakers to realize by legislation directly addressed to their accomplishment." The tax in question is a legitimate exercise of the taxing power despite its collateral regulatory purpose and effect.

Second. The tax levied by §2590(a)(2) is not conditioned upon commission of a crime. The tax is on the transfer of marihuana to a person who has not paid the special tax and registered. Such a transfer is not made unlawful under the statute. Liability for the tax rests primarily with the transferee; but if he fails to pay, then the transferor becomes liable. It is thus the failure of the transferee to pay the tax that gives rise to the liability of the transferor. Since his tax liability does not rest on criminal conduct, the tax can be properly called a civil rather than a criminal sanction. The fact Congress provided civil procedure for collection indicates its intention that the tax be treated as such. *Helvering v. Mitchell*, 303 U.S. 391 (1938). Moreover, the Government is seeking to collect the levy by a judicial proceeding with its attendant safeguards.

Nor is the civil character of the tax imposed by §2590(a)(2) altered by its severity in relation to that assessed by §2590(a)(1). The difference has a rational foundation. Unregistered persons are not likely to procure the required order form prior to transfer or pay the required tax. Free of sanctions, dealers would be prone to accommodate such persons in their unlawful activity. The imposition of equally severe tax burdens on such transferors is reasonably adapted to secure payment of the tax by transferees or stop transfers to unregistered persons, as well as to provide an additional source from which the expense of unearthing clandestine transfers can be recovered. *Cf. Helvering v. Mitchell, supra.*

The judgment below must be reversed and the cause remanded for further proceedings in conformity with this opinion.

Reversed.

Notes and Questions

Since *Constantine* was decided in 1935, the Court has routinely upheld federal laws imposing taxes. *See, e.g., United States v. Kahriger*, 345 U.S. 22 (1953) (tax on firearms); *Sonzinsky v. United States*, 300 U.S. 506 (1937) (tax on wagering). In part, the Court's post-1935 position has been driven by its expanded interpretation of the Commerce Clause. In other words, as Congress's Commerce Clause power expanded during the period of deference, Congress has had little need to use taxes for regulatory purposes. As the Court begins to place limitations on Congress's Commerce Clause authority, in decisions like *Lopez* and *Morrison*, should the Court be less deferential to Congress's decision to regulate through taxation?

National Federation of Independent Business v. Sebelius

567 U.S. 519 (2012)

[The first part of this decision is set forth in the Commerce Clause Section B.]

Chief Justice ROBERTS announced the judgment of the Court and delivered the opinion of the Court with respect to Parts I, II, and III-C, an opinion with respect to Part IV, in which Justice BREYER and Justice KAGAN join, and an opinion with respect to Parts III-A, III-B, and III-D.

Today we resolve constitutional challenges to two provisions of the Patient Protection and Affordable Care Act of 2010: the individual mandate, which requires individuals to purchase a health insurance policy providing a minimum level of coverage; and the Medicaid expansion, which gives funds to the States on the condition that they provide specified health care to all citizens whose income falls below a certain threshold.

I

The individual mandate requires most Americans to maintain "minimum essential" health insurance coverage. 26 U.S.C. §5000A. Those who do not comply with the mandate must make a "shared responsibility payment" to the Federal Government. That payment, which the Act describes as a "penalty," is calculated as a percentage of household income, subject to a floor based on a specified dollar amount and a ceiling based on the average annual premium the individual would have to pay for qualifying private health insurance. In 2016, for example, the penalty will be 2.5 percent of an individual's household income, but no less than $ 695 and no more than the average yearly premium for insurance that covers 60 percent of the cost of 10 specified services (*e.g.*, prescription drugs and hospitalization). The penalty will be paid to the Internal Revenue Service with an individual's taxes, and "shall be assessed and collected in the same manner" as tax penalties, such as the penalty for claiming too large an income tax refund. 26 U.S.C. §5000A(g)(1). The Act bars the IRS from using several of its normal enforcement tools, such as criminal prosecutions and levies. Some individuals who are subject to the mandate are nonetheless exempt from the penalty—those with income below a certain threshold and members of Indian tribes. We granted certiorari to review the judgment of the Court of Appeals for the Eleventh Circuit.

II

The Anti-Injunction Act provides that "no suit for the purpose of restraining the assessment or collection of any tax shall be maintained in any court by any person, whether or not such person is the person against whom such tax was assessed." 26 U.S.C. §7421(a). This statute protects the Government's ability to collect a consistent stream of revenue, by barring litigation to enjoin or otherwise obstruct the collection of taxes. Because of the Anti-Injunction Act, taxes can ordinarily be challenged only after they are paid, by suing for a refund. *See Enochs v. Williams Packing & Nav. Co.*, 370 U.S. 1 (1962). The penalty for not complying with the individual mandate first becomes enforceable in 2014. The present challenge seeks to restrain the penalty's future collection on the basis that the Internal Revenue Code treats the penalty as a tax, and that the Anti-Injunction Act bars this suit. The Court concluded that the individual mandate is a penalty, rather than a tax, and is not subject to the Anti-Injunction Act.

III

The Government argues that if the commerce power does not support the mandate, we should nonetheless uphold it as an exercise of Congress's power to tax.

According to the Government, even if Congress lacks the power to direct individuals to buy insurance, the only effect of the individual mandate is to raise taxes on those who do not do so, and thus the law may be upheld as a tax.

A

[In this section, the Court concluded that the individual mandate could not be upheld under the Commerce Clause even when coupled with the Necessary and Proper Clause.]

B

Because the Commerce Clause does not support the individual mandate, it is necessary to turn to the Government's second argument: that the mandate may be upheld as within Congress's enumerated power to "lay and collect Taxes." Art. I, §8, cl. 1. In making its Commerce Clause argument, the Government defended the mandate as a regulation requiring individuals to purchase health insurance. The Government does not claim that the taxing power allows Congress to issue such a command. Instead, the Government asks us to read the mandate as imposing a tax on those who do not buy that product.

If a statute has two meanings, one of which violates the Constitution, courts should adopt the meaning that does not do so. *Blodgett v. Holden*, 275 U.S. 142 (1927) (concurring opinion). The most straightforward reading of the mandate is that it commands individuals to purchase insurance. But the Commerce Clause does not give Congress that power. It is therefore necessary to ask whether the Government's alternative reading of the statute—that it only imposes a tax on those without insurance—is reasonable.

Under the mandate, if an individual does not maintain health insurance, the only consequence is that he must make an additional payment to the IRS when he pays his taxes. That, according to the Government, means the mandate can be regarded as establishing a condition that triggers a tax—the required payment to the IRS. Under that theory, the mandate is not a legal command to buy insurance. Rather, it makes going without insurance just another thing the Government taxes, like buying gasoline or earning income. If the mandate is in effect just a tax on those who do not have health insurance, it may be within Congress's constitutional power to tax. The question is not whether that is the most natural interpretation of the mandate, but only whether it is a "fairly possible" one. "Every reasonable construction must be resorted to, in order to save a statute from unconstitutionality." *Hooper v. California*, 155 U.S. 648, 657 (1895).

C

The exaction the ACA imposes on those without health insurance looks like a tax. The "shared responsibility payment" is paid into the Treasury by "taxpayers" when they file their tax returns. It does not apply to individuals who do not pay income taxes because their household income is less than the filing threshold. For taxpayers who owe the payment, its amount is determined by such familiar factors as taxable income, number of dependents, and joint filing status. The requirement to pay is found in the Internal Revenue Code and enforced by the IRS, which must assess and collect it "in the same manner as taxes." This process yields the essential feature of any tax: it produces at least some revenue for the Government. Indeed, the payment is expected to raise about $ 4 billion per year by 2017. It is true that the Act describes the payment as a "penalty," not a "tax." But while that label is fatal to the application of the Anti-Injunction Act, it does not determine whether the payment may be viewed as an exercise of Congress's taxing power. It is up to Congress whether to apply the Anti-Injunction Act to any particular statute. That choice does not control whether an exaction is within Congress's constitutional power to tax.

We have held that exactions not labeled taxes nonetheless were authorized by Congress's power to tax. In the *License Tax Cases,* 5 Wall. 462, 471, 18 L. Ed. 497 (1867), we held that federal licenses to sell liquor and lottery tickets—for which the licensee had to pay a fee—could be sustained as exercises of the taxing power. In *New York v. United States* we upheld as a tax a "surcharge" on out-of-state nuclear waste shipments, a portion of which was paid to the Federal Treasury. 505 U.S., at 171. We thus ask whether the shared responsibility payment falls within Congress's taxing power, "disregarding the designation of the exaction, and viewing its substance and application." *United States v. Constantine,* 296 U.S. 287, 294 (1935).

Our cases confirm this functional approach. In *Drexel Furniture,* we focused on three practical characteristics of the so-called tax on employing child laborers that convinced us the "tax" was actually a penalty. First, the tax imposed an exceedingly heavy burden—10 percent of a company's net income—on those who employed children, no matter how small their infraction. Second, it imposed that exaction only on those who knowingly employed underage laborers. Such scienter requirements are typical of punitive statutes, because Congress often wishes to punish only those who intentionally break the law. Third, this "tax" was enforced in part by the Department of Labor, an agency responsible for punishing violations of labor laws, not collecting revenue.

The shared responsibility payment may for constitutional purposes be considered a tax, not a penalty: For most Americans the amount due will be far less than the price of insurance, and it can never be more. It may often be a reasonable financial decision to make the payment rather than purchase insurance, unlike the "prohibitory" financial punishment in *Drexel Furniture.* Second, the individual mandate contains no scienter requirement. Third, the payment is collected solely by the IRS through the normal means of taxation—except that the Service is *not* allowed to use those means most suggestive of a punitive sanction, such as criminal prosecution. The fact that exaction here is paid like a tax, to the agency that collects taxes—rather than exacted by Department of Labor inspectors after ferreting out willful malfeasance—suggests that this exaction may be viewed as a tax.

Although the payment will raise considerable revenue, it is designed to expand health insurance coverage. But taxes that seek to influence conduct are nothing new. Some of our earliest federal taxes sought to deter the purchase of imported manufactured goods in order to foster the growth of domestic industry. Today, federal and state taxes can compose more than half the retail price of cigarettes, not just to raise more money, but to encourage people to quit smoking. We have upheld such regulatory measures as taxes on selling marijuana and sawed-off shotguns. *See United States v. Sanchez,* 340 U.S. 42 (1950). "Every tax is in some measure regulatory. It interposes an economic impediment to the activity taxed as compared with others not taxed." *Sonzinsky v. United States,* 300 U.S. 506, 513 (1937). That §5000A seeks to shape decisions about whether to buy health insurance does not mean that it cannot be a valid exercise of the taxing power.

In distinguishing penalties from taxes, this Court has explained that "if the concept of penalty means anything, it means punishment for an unlawful act or omission." *United States v. Reorganized CF & I Fabricators of Utah, Inc.,* 518 U.S. 213, 224 (1996). While the individual mandate aims to induce the purchase of health insurance, neither the Act nor any other law attaches negative legal consequences to not buying health insurance, beyond requiring a payment to the IRS. If someone chooses to pay rather than obtain health insurance, they have fully complied with the law. Indeed, it is estimated that four million people each year will choose to pay the IRS rather than buy insurance. That Congress regards such extensive failure to comply with the mandate as tolerable suggests that Congress did not think it was creating outlaws. Plaintiffs contend that Congress's choice of language—stating that individuals "shall" obtain insurance or pay a "penalty"—requires reading §5000A as punishing unlawful conduct. We have rejected a similar argument before. *New York,* 505 U.S. at 152-153.

The dissenters argue that we cannot uphold §5000A as a tax because Congress did not "frame" it as such. They contend that even if the Constitution permits Congress to do exactly what we interpret this statute to do, the law must be struck down because Congress used the wrong labels. Our precedent demonstrates that Congress had the power to impose the exaction in §5000A under the taxing power, and that §5000A need not be read to do more than impose a tax. That is sufficient to sustain it.

Even if the taxing power enables Congress to impose a tax on not obtaining health insurance, any tax must comply with other requirements in the Constitution. Plaintiffs argue that the shared responsibility payment does not do so, citing Article I, §9, clause 4. That clause provides: "No Capitation, or other direct, Tax shall be laid, unless in Proportion to the Census or Enumeration herein before directed to be taken." This requirement means that any "direct Tax" must be apportioned so that each State pays in proportion to its population. Even when the Direct Tax Clause was written it was unclear what else, other than a capitation (also known as a "head tax" or "poll tax"), might be a direct tax.

Soon after the framing, Congress passed a tax on ownership of carriages, over James Madison's objection that it was an unapportioned direct tax. This Court upheld the tax, in part reasoning that apportioning such a tax would make little sense, because it would have required taxing carriage owners at dramatically different rates depending on how many carriages were in their home State. *See Hylton v. United States,* 3 Dall. 171, 174, 1 L. Ed. 556 (1796). That view of what a direct tax might be persisted for a century.

A tax on going without health insurance does not fall within any recognized category of direct tax. It is not a capitation. Capitations are taxes paid by every person, "without regard to property, profession, or *any other circumstance.*" *Hylton, supra,* at 175. The whole point of the shared responsibility payment is that it is triggered by specific circumstances—earning a certain amount of income but not obtaining health insurance. The payment is also plainly not a tax on the ownership of land or personal property. The shared responsibility payment is thus not a direct tax that must be apportioned. Even if only a tax, the payment under §5000A(b) remains a burden that the Federal Government imposes for an omission, not an act. If it is troubling to interpret the Commerce Clause as authorizing Congress to regulate those who abstain from commerce, it should be similarly troubling to permit Congress to impose a tax for not doing something. Three considerations allay this concern. First, the Constitution does not guarantee that individuals may avoid taxation through inactivity. A capitation is a tax that everyone must pay simply for existing, and capitations are expressly contemplated by the Constitution. Sustaining the mandate as a tax depends only on whether Congress *has* properly exercised its taxing power to encourage purchasing health insurance, not whether it *can.* Upholding the individual mandate under the Taxing Clause thus does not recognize any new federal power. It determines that Congress has used an existing one.

Congress's ability to use its taxing power to influence conduct is not without limits. A few of our cases invalidated punitive exactions obviously designed to regulate behavior otherwise regarded at the time as beyond federal authority. See, *e.g., United States v. Butler,* 297 U.S. 1 (1936); *Drexel Furniture,* 259 U.S. 20. More often, we have declined to closely examine the regulatory motive or effect of revenue-raising measures. *See Kahriger,* 345 U.S. at 27-31. We have nonetheless maintained that "there comes a time in the extension of the penalizing features of the tax when it loses its character as such and becomes a mere penalty with the characteristics of regulation and punishment." *Kurth Ranch,* 511 U.S. at 779. We have explained that the shared responsibility payment's practical characteristics pass muster as a tax under our narrowest interpretations of the taxing power. We need not decide the precise point at which an exaction becomes so punitive that the taxing power does not authorize it. The "power to tax is not the power to destroy while this Court sits." *Oklahoma Tax Comm'n v. Texas Co.,* 336 U.S. 342, 364 (1949).

Although the breadth of Congress's power to tax is greater than its power to regulate commerce, the taxing power does not give Congress the same degree of control over individual behavior. Once we recognize that Congress may regulate a particular decision under the Commerce Clause, the Federal Government can bring its full weight to bear. Congress may simply command individuals to do as it directs. An individual who disobeys may be subjected to criminal sanctions, including not only fines and imprisonment, but all the consequences of being branded a criminal: deprivation of civil rights, such as the right to bear arms or vote in elections; loss of employment opportunities; social stigma; and severe disabilities in controversies such as custody or immigration disputes. Congress's authority under the taxing power is limited to requiring an individual to pay money into the Federal Treasury.[11]

The ACA's requirement that individuals pay a financial penalty for not obtaining health insurance may reasonably be characterized as a tax. Because the Constitution permits such a tax, it is not our role to forbid it, or to pass upon its wisdom or fairness.

D

Justice GINSBURG questions the necessity of rejecting the Government's commerce power argument, given that §5000A can be upheld under the taxing power. Section 5000A would be unconstitutional if read as a command.

The ACA is constitutional in part and unconstitutional in part. The judgment of the Court of Appeals for the Eleventh Circuit is affirmed in part and reversed in part.

It is so ordered.

Justice GINSBURG, with whom Justice SOTOMAYOR joins, and with whom Justice BREYER and Justice KAGAN join as to Parts I, II, III, and IV, *concurring in part, concurring in the judgment in part,* and *dissenting in part.*

I would hold that the Commerce Clause authorizes Congress to enact the minimum coverage provision.

Justice SCALIA, Justice KENNEDY, Justice THOMAS, and Justice ALITO, *dissenting.*

Congress has attempted to regulate beyond the scope of its Commerce Clause authority. The fact that Congress "imposed a penalty" for failure to buy insurance is sufficient to render that failure unlawful. What counts is what the statute says, and that is clear. To say that the Individual Mandate merely imposes a tax is not to interpret the statute but to rewrite it. Imposing a tax through judicial legislation inverts the constitutional scheme, and places the power to tax in the branch of government least accountable to the citizenry.

---

11. Individuals do not have a choice not to pay a tax due, and may face prosecution for failing to do so (although not for the shared responsibility payment). That does not show that the tax restricts the lawful choice whether to undertake or forgo the activity on which the tax is predicated.

Note: More on the ACA

Subsequent to the decision in *Sebelius,* Congress eliminated the "tax" imposed as part of the ACA mandate. Since the tax provided the basis for upholding the Act, new litigation has ensued regarding whether the ACA is constitutional. The case is now pending before the U.S. Supreme Court.

∾ PROBLEM: PRIVATE SCHOOLS AND THE EDUCATION FOR A BETTER AMERICA ACT ∾

Now, let's think about the Education for a Better America Act from another perspective. If Congress can require everyone to purchase health insurance, on pain of a tax if they fail to do so, can it also use its taxing power to control educational choices? Suppose that Congress believes that private schools have an adverse impact on the quality of public education. While there is evidence suggesting that private schools have a beneficial impact on public education (because governmental entities do not have to spend money educating children who attend private schools), there is also a negative effect in that private schools involve a "brain drain" from the public school system. In other words, many of the best and brightest students are sent to private schools, resulting in lower educational attainment levels in public schools. Could Congress impose a $ 2,000 tax on families who choose to "purchase" private school educations for their children?

D. POWER TO SPEND FOR THE GENERAL WELFARE

Article I, Section 8, which contains the power to tax, also contains the power to spend for the general welfare: "The Congress shall have Power To lay and collect Taxes, Duties, Imposes and Excises, to pay the Debts and provide for the common Defence and general Welfare of the United States."

From cases like *Dagenhart* and *Bailey,* we know that Congress was initially unable to impose its child labor laws through either its Commerce Clause power or its taxing power. Does Congress have greater power to control or regulate conduct under its power to spend for the general welfare? In *United States v. Butler,* 297 U.S. 1 (1935), the Court concluded that there were limits on the scope of Congress to spend for the general welfare. The Court refused to precisely define the phrase "general welfare of the United States." The Court held that the Act transgressed the reserved rights of the states because the Act was "a matter beyond the powers delegated to the federal government." The Court rejected the argument that the Act should be upheld "because the end is accomplished by voluntary co-operation." The Court concluded that the program was not really voluntary because "the amount offered is intended to be sufficient to exert pressure on the participants to force them to agree to the proposed regulation." The Court noted that a refusal to participate may result in financial ruin because "those who receive payments will be able to undersell him." Moreover, the Court viewed the Act as "a scheme for purchasing with federal funds submission to federal regulation of a subject reserved to the states." "Congress may not indirectly accomplish those ends by taxing and spending to purchase compliance." However, in the Court's later decision in *South Dakota v. Dole*, 483 U.S. 203 (1987), the Court upheld a conditional spending program. In that case, the Court upheld a congressional act which prohibited states from receiving certain federal highway funds if they allowed individuals under 21 years of age to purchase or possess alcoholic beverages. *Dole* is discussed more fully below.

In *Pennhurst State School & Hospital v. Halderman*, 451 U.S. 1 (1981), the Court upheld the Developmentally Disabled Assistance and Bill of Rights Act of 1975, which provided financial assistance for the creation of programs to care for and treat the developmentally disabled. The Act was voluntary, and the states were given the choice of complying with the conditions set forth in the Act or forgoing federal funding. However, if they chose to participate, they were subject to the Act's "bill of rights" provision, which granted mentally retarded persons a right to "appropriate treatment, services, and habilitation" in "the setting that is least restrictive of personal liberty." Pennsylvania accepted the federal funding. When a mentally retarded resident of a Pennsylvania hospital brought suit claiming that conditions were unsanitary, inhumane, and dangerous, and asserting that the Act provided him with a right to adequate habilitation in the least restrictive environment, Pennsylvania claimed that the Act exceeded Congress's power under the Spending Clause. In upholding the Act, the Court noted that

> Legislation enacted pursuant to the spending power is in the nature of a contract: in return for federal funds, the States agree to comply with federally imposed conditions. Legitimacy under the spending power thus rests on whether the State voluntarily and knowingly accepts the terms of the 'contract.' There can, of course, be no knowing acceptance if a State is unaware of the conditions or is unable to ascertain what is expected. Accordingly, if Congress intends to impose a condition on the grant of federal moneys, it must do so unambiguously. Applying those principles we find nothing in the Act or its legislative history to suggest that Congress intended to require the States to assume the high cost of providing 'appropriate treatment' in the 'least restrictive environment' to their mentally retarded citizens. The court below failed to recognize the distinction between congressional 'encouragement' of state programs and the imposition of binding obligations on the States.

Justice White, joined by Justices Brennan and Marshall, dissented in part: "I agree that §6010 was enacted pursuant to Congress' spending power, and not pursuant to its power under §5 of the Fourteenth Amendment. Accordingly, the Act was not intended to place duties on States independent of their participation in the program established by the Act."

National Federation of Independent Business v. Sebelius

567 U.S. 519 (2012)

Chief Justice ROBERTS announced the judgment of the Court and delivered the opinion of the Court with respect to Parts I, II, and III-C, an opinion with respect to Part IV, in which Justice BREYER and Justice KAGAN join, and an opinion with respect to Parts III-A, III-B, and III-D.

Today we resolve constitutional challenges to two provisions of the Patient Protection and Affordable Care Act of 2010: the individual mandate, which requires individuals to purchase a health insurance policy providing a minimum level of coverage; and the Medicaid expansion, which gives funds to the States on the condition that they provide specified health care to all citizens whose income falls below a certain threshold. The individual mandate is discussed in the Commerce Clause, Necessary and Proper, and Taxing portions of this opinion which are set for in those sections.

Enacted in 1965, Medicaid offers federal funding to States to assist pregnant women, children, needy families, the blind, the elderly, and the disabled in obtaining medical care. *See* 42 U.S.C. §1396a(a)(10). In order to receive that funding, States must comply with federal criteria governing matters such as who receives care and what services are provided at what cost. By 1982 every State had chosen to participate in Medicaid. Federal funds received through the Medicaid program have become a substantial part of state budgets, now constituting over 10 percent of most States' total revenue.

The Affordable Care Act expands the scope of the Medicaid program and increases the number of individuals the States must cover. For example, the Act requires state programs to provide Medicaid coverage to adults with incomes up to 133 percent of the federal poverty level, whereas many States now cover adults with children only if their income is considerably lower, and do not cover childless adults at all. The Act increases federal funding to cover the States' costs in expanding Medicaid coverage, although States will bear a portion of the costs on their own. If a State does not comply with the Act's new coverage requirements, it may lose not only the federal funding for those requirements, but all of its federal Medicaid funds.

The state plaintiffs argued that the Medicaid expansion exceeds Congress's constitutional powers. The Court of Appeals held that the Medicaid expansion is a valid exercise of Congress's power under the Spending Clause. U.S. Const., Art. I, §8, cl. 1. We granted certiorari.

IV

The States contend that the Medicaid expansion exceeds Congress's authority under the Spending Clause. There is no doubt that the Act dramatically increases state obligations under Medicaid. The current Medicaid program requires States to cover only certain discrete categories of needy individuals — pregnant women, children, needy families, the blind, the elderly, and the disabled. There is no mandatory coverage for most childless adults, and the States typically do not offer such coverage. The States also enjoy flexibility with respect to the coverage levels for parents of needy families. On average States cover only those unemployed parents who make less than 37 percent of the federal poverty level, and only those employed parents who make less than 63 percent of the poverty line. The Medicaid provisions of the ACA require States to expand their Medicaid programs to cover *all* individuals under the age of 65 with incomes below 133 percent of the federal poverty line. The Act also establishes a new "essential health benefits" package, which States must provide to all new Medicaid recipients — a level sufficient to satisfy a recipient's obligations under the individual mandate. The Federal Government will pay 100 percent of the costs of covering these newly eligible individuals through 2016. In the following years, the federal payment level gradually decreases, to a minimum of 90 percent. The Federal Government estimates that its Medicaid spending will increase by approximately $ 100 billion per year, nearly 40 percent above current levels.

The Spending Clause grants Congress the power "to pay the Debts and provide for the general Welfare of the United States." U.S. CONST., ART. I, §8, cl. 1. Congress may use this power to grant federal funds to the States, and may condition a grant upon the States' "taking certain actions that Congress could not require them to take." *College Savings Bank,* 527 U.S. at 686. Such measures "encourage a State to regulate in a particular way, and influence a State's policy choices." *New York, supra,* at 166. The conditions ensure that the funds are used by the States to "provide for the general Welfare" in the manner Congress intended.

Our cases have recognized limits on Congress's power under the Spending Clause to secure state compliance with federal objectives. "Spending Clause legislation is 'much in the nature of a *contract.*'" *Barnes v. Gorman,* 536 U.S. 181, 186 (2002) (quoting *Pennhurst State School and Hospital v. Halderman,* 451 U.S. 1, 17 (1981)). The legitimacy of Congress's exercise of the spending power "thus rests on whether the State voluntarily and knowingly accepts the terms of the 'contract.'" *Pennhurst, supra,* at 17. Respecting this limitation is critical to ensuring that Spending Clause legislation does not undermine the status of the States as independent sovereigns in our federal system. For this reason, "the Constitution has never been understood to confer upon Congress the ability to require the States to govern according to Congress' instructions." *New York, supra,* at 162. Otherwise the two-government system established by the Framers would give way to a system that vests power in one central government, and individual liberty would suffer.

That insight has led this Court to strike down federal legislation that commandeers a State's legislative or administrative apparatus for federal purposes. *See, e.g., Printz,* 521 U.S. at 933; *New York, supra,* at 174-175. We also scrutinize

Spending Clause legislation to ensure that Congress is not using financial induce-
ments to exert a "power akin to undue influence." *Steward Machine Co. v. Davis,*
301 U.S. 548, 590 (1937). Congress may use its spending power to create incentives for States to act in accordance with federal policies. But when "pressure
turns into compulsion," the legislation runs contrary to our system of federalism.
That is true whether Congress directly commands a State to regulate or indirectly
coerces a State to adopt a federal regulatory system as its own.

Permitting the Federal Government to force the States to implement a
federal program would threaten the political accountability key to our federal
system. "Where the Federal Government directs the States to regulate, it may
be state officials who will bear the brunt of public disapproval, while the federal
officials who devised the regulatory program may remain insulated from the
electoral ramifications of their decision." Spending Clause programs do not
pose this danger when a State has a legitimate choice whether to accept the federal conditions in exchange for federal funds. In such a situation, state officials
can fairly be held politically accountable for choosing to accept or refuse the
federal offer. But when the State has no choice, the Federal Government can
achieve its objectives without accountability. This danger is heightened when
Congress acts under the Spending Clause, because Congress can use that power
to implement federal policy it could not impose directly under its enumerated
powers.

We look to the States to defend their prerogatives by adopting "the simple
expedient of not yielding" to federal blandishments when they do not want to
embrace the federal policies as their own. *Massachusetts v. Mellon,* 262 U.S. 447
(1923). The States, however, object that Congress has "crossed the line distinguishing encouragement from coercion," *New York, supra,* at 175, in the way it has
structured the funding: Instead of simply refusing to grant new funds to States
that will not accept the new conditions, Congress has threatened to withhold
those States' existing Medicaid funds. The States claim that this threat serves no
purpose other than to force unwilling States to sign up for the dramatic expansion in health care coverage effected by the Act.

We have upheld Congress's authority to condition the receipt of funds on
the States' complying with restrictions on the use of those funds, because that is
the means by which Congress ensures that the funds are spent according to its
view of the "general Welfare." Conditions that do not govern the use of the funds,
however, cannot be justified. When, such conditions take the form of threats to
terminate other significant independent grants, the conditions are properly
viewed as a means of pressuring the States to accept policy changes. In *South
Dakota v. Dole,* we considered a challenge to a federal law that threatened to withhold five percent of a State's federal highway funds if the State did not raise its
drinking age to 21. The Court found that the condition was "directly related to
one of the main purposes for which highway funds are expended—safe interstate travel." At the same time, the condition was not a restriction on how the
highway funds—set aside for specific highway improvement and maintenance

efforts—were to be used. We accordingly asked whether "the financial inducement offered by Congress" was "so coercive as to pass the point at which 'pressure
turns into compulsion.' " By "financial inducement" the Court meant the threat
of losing five percent of highway funds; no new money was offered to the States
to raise their drinking ages. We found that the inducement was not impermissibly
coercive, because Congress was offering only "relatively mild encouragement to
the States." The federal funds constituted less than half of one percent of South
Dakota's budget at the time and "the encouragement was a valid use of the spending power." Whether to accept the drinking age change "remained the prerogative of the States not merely in theory but in fact."

In this case, the financial "inducement" Congress has chosen is much
more than "relatively mild encouragement"—it is a gun to the head. If a State's
Medicaid plan does not comply with the Act's requirements, the Secretary of
Health and Human Services may declare that "further payments will not be
made to the State." 42 U.S.C. §1396c. A State that opts out thus stands to lose not
merely "a relatively small percentage" of its existing Medicaid funding, but *all* of
it. Medicaid spending accounts for over 20 percent of the average State's total
budget, with federal funds covering 50 to 83 percent of those costs. The threatened loss of over 10 percent of a State's overall budget, in contrast, is economic
dragooning that leaves the States with no real option but to acquiesce in the
Medicaid expansion.[12]

The States contend that the expansion is in reality a new program and
that Congress is forcing them to accept it by threatening funds for the existing
Medicaid program. We cannot agree that existing Medicaid and the expansion
dictated by the Affordable Care Act are all one program simply because "Congress
styled" them as such. The Government claims that the Medicaid expansion is
properly viewed as a modification of the existing program because the States
agreed that Congress could change the terms of Medicaid when they signed on in
the first place. A State confronted with statutory language reserving the right to
"alter" or "amend" the pertinent provisions of the Social Security Act might reasonably assume that Congress was entitled to make adjustments to the Medicaid
program. The Medicaid expansion, however, accomplishes a shift in kind, not
merely degree. The original program was designed to cover medical services
for four particular categories of the needy: the disabled, the blind, the elderly,
and needy families with dependent children. Previous amendments to Medicaid
merely altered and expanded the boundaries of these categories. Under the
ACA, Medicaid is transformed into a program to meet the health care needs of
the entire non-elderly population with income below 133 percent of the poverty
level. It is no longer a program to care for the neediest among us, but rather an
element of a comprehensive national plan to provide universal health insurance

---

12. Justice GINSBURG observes that state Medicaid spending will increase by only 0.8 percent after the
expansion. That not only ignores increased state administrative expenses, but also assumes that the Federal
Government will continue to fund the expansion at the current statutorily specified levels.

coverage.[14] While Congress may have styled the expansion a mere alteration of Medicaid, it was enlisting the States in a new health care program. Congress created a separate funding provision to cover the costs of providing services to any person made newly eligible by the expansion. While Congress pays 50 to 83 percent of the costs of covering individuals currently enrolled in Medicaid, once the expansion is fully implemented Congress will pay 90 percent of the costs for newly eligible persons. Conditions on use of the funds are also distinct. Congress mandated that newly eligible persons receive coverage that is less comprehensive than the traditional Medicaid benefit package.

"Though Congress' power to legislate under the spending power is broad, it does not include surprising participating States with postacceptance or 'retroactive' conditions." *Pennhurst, supra,* at 25. A State could hardly anticipate that Congress's reservation of the right to "alter" or "amend" the Medicaid program included the power to transform it so dramatically. Justice Ginsburg claims that this expansion is no different from previous changes to Medicaid. The amendment requiring States to cover pregnant women and increasing the number of eligible children can hardly be described as a major change in a program that provided health care for "families with dependent children."

The Court in *Steward Machine* did not attempt to "fix the outermost line" where persuasion gives way to coercion. It is enough for today that wherever that line may be, this statute is surely beyond it. Congress may not simply "conscript state agencies into the national bureaucratic army," FERC v. Mississippi, 456 U.S. 742, 775 (1982) (O'Connor, J., concurring and dissenting), and that is what it is attempting to do with the Medicaid expansion.

Nothing precludes Congress from offering funds to expand the availability of health care, and requiring that States accepting such funds comply with the conditions on their use. What Congress is not free to do is to penalize States that choose not to participate in that new program by taking away their existing Medicaid funding. Section 1396c gives the Secretary of Health and Human Services the authority to do just that. In light of the Court's holding, the Secretary cannot apply §1396c to withdraw existing Medicaid funds for failure to comply with the requirements set out in the expansion. That fully remedies the constitutional violation. The chapter of the United States Code that contains §1396c includes a severability clause confirming that we need go no further. Today's holding does not affect the continued application of §1396c to the existing Medicaid program. Nor does it affect the Secretary's ability to withdraw funds provided under the ACA if a State that has chosen to participate in the expansion fails to comply with the requirements of that Act.

---

14. Justice Ginsburg suggests that "Congress could have repealed Medicaid and enacted a new program combining the pre-2010 coverage with the expanded coverage required by the ACA." Practical constraints would inhibit, if not preclude, the Federal Government from repealing the existing program and putting every feature of Medicaid on the table for political reconsideration.

This is not to say, as the dissent suggests, that we are "rewriting the Medicaid Expansion." Section 1396c is unconstitutional when applied to withdraw existing Medicaid funds from States that decline to comply with the expansion. We then follow Congress's explicit textual instruction to leave unaffected "the remainder of the chapter, and the application of the challenged provision to other persons or circumstances." When we invalidate an application of a statute because that application is unconstitutional, we are not "rewriting" the statute; we are merely enforcing the Constitution.

The question remains whether today's holding affects other provisions of the ACA. The question is whether Congress would have wanted the rest of the Act to stand, had it known that States would have a genuine choice whether to participate in the new Medicaid expansion. Unless it is "evident" that the answer is no, we must leave the rest of the Act intact. *Champlin Refining Co. v. Corporation Comm'n of Okla.*, 286 U.S. 210 (1932). We are confident that Congress would have wanted to preserve the rest of the Act. Congress assumed that every State would participate in the Medicaid expansion, given that States had no real choice. The Court today limits the financial pressure the Secretary may apply to induce States to accept the terms of the Medicaid expansion. As a practical matter, that means States may now choose to reject the expansion. Some States may decline to participate. Other States may voluntarily sign up, finding the idea of expanding Medicaid coverage attractive, particularly given the funding the Act offers. We have no way of knowing how many States will accept the terms of the expansion, but we do not believe Congress would have wanted the whole Act to fall, simply because some may choose not to participate. The other reforms Congress enacted will remain "fully operative," and will still function "consistent with Congress' basic objectives in enacting the statute," *Booker, supra,* at 259. Confident that Congress would not have intended anything different, the rest of the Act need not fall in light of our constitutional holding.

The ACA is constitutional in part and unconstitutional in part. The Framers created a Federal Government of limited powers, and assigned to this Court the duty of enforcing those limits. The Court does so today. But the Court does not express any opinion on the wisdom of the ACA. Under the Constitution, that judgment is reserved to the people.

The judgment of the Court of Appeals for the Eleventh Circuit is affirmed in part and reversed in part.

It is so ordered.

Justice GINSBURG, with whom Justice SOTOMAYOR joins, and with whom Justice BREYER and Justice KAGAN join as to Parts I, II, III, and IV, *concurring in part, concurring in the judgment in part,* and *dissenting in part.*

The Commerce Clause authorizes Congress to enact the minimum coverage provision. The Spending Clause permits the Medicaid expansion exactly as Congress enacted it.

V

The spending power permits Congress to define the contours of programs financed with federal funds. A ritualistic requirement that Congress repeal and reenact spending legislation in order to enlarge the population served by a federally funded program would advance no constitutional principle and would scarcely serve the interests of federalism. The Chief Justice acknowledges that Congress may "condition the receipt of federal funds on the States' complying with restrictions on the use of those funds," but concludes that the 2010 expansion is unduly coercive. Any fair appraisal of Medicaid would require acknowledgment of the considerable autonomy States enjoy.

This Court has respected Congress' prescription of spending conditions, and has required States to abide by them. *See, e.g., Pennhurst,* 451 U.S. at 17. We have recognized Congress' prerogative to condition a State's receipt of Medicaid funding on compliance with the terms Congress set for participation in the program. *See, e.g., Harris,* 448 U.S. at 301. There are federalism-based limits on the use of Congress' conditional spending power. In the leading decision, *South Dakota v. Dole,* the Court identified four criteria. The conditions placed on federal grants to States must (a) promote the "general welfare," (b) "unambiguously" inform States what is demanded of them, (c) be germane "to the federal interest in particular national projects or programs," and (d) not "induce the States to engage in activities that would themselves be unconstitutional." *Dole* also mentioned, but did not adopt, a further limitation: Congress might be prohibited from offering a "financial inducement so coercive as to pass the point at which 'pressure turns into compulsion.'" Prior to today's decision, the Court has never ruled that the terms of any grant crossed the indistinct line between temptation and coercion. *Pennhurst*'s rule demands that conditions on federal funds be unambiguously clear at the time a State receives and uses the money—not at the time, perhaps years earlier, when Congress passed the law establishing the program. From the start, the Medicaid Act put States on notice that the program could be changed. The statute allows states to withdraw from the program.

THE CHIEF JUSTICE asks whether "the financial inducement offered by Congress passed the point at which pressure turns into compulsion." The financial inducement Congress employed here, he concludes, is "a gun to the head" that forces States to acquiesce. When future Spending Clause challenges arrive, as they likely will in the wake of today's decision, how will litigants and judges assess whether "a State has a legitimate choice whether to accept the federal conditions in exchange for federal funds"? The coercion inquiry appears to involve political judgments that defy judicial calculation. In view of The Chief Justice's disposition, I agree that the Medicaid Act's severability clause determines the appropriate remedy. When a court confronts an unconstitutional statute, its endeavor must be to conserve, not destroy, the legislature's dominant objective.

Justice SCALIA, Justice KENNEDY, Justice THOMAS, and Justice ALITO, *dissenting*.

There are structural limits upon federal power—upon what it can prescribe with respect to private conduct, and upon what it can impose upon the sovereign States. As for the constitutional power to tax and spend for the general welfare: The Court has long since expanded that beyond (what Madison thought it meant) taxing and spending for those aspects of the general welfare that were within the Federal Government's enumerated powers. The principal practical obstacle that prevents Congress from using the tax-and-spend power to assume all the general-welfare responsibilities traditionally exercised by the States is the sheer impossibility of managing a Federal Government large enough to administer such a system. That obstacle can be overcome by granting funds to the States, allowing them to administer the program. That is fair and constitutional enough when the States freely agree to have their powers employed and their employees enlisted in the federal scheme. But it is a blatant violation of the constitutional structure when the States have no choice. The Act before us here exceeds federal power both in mandating the purchase of health insurance and in denying nonconsenting States all Medicaid funding. These parts of the Act are central to its design and operation, and all the Act's other provisions would not have been enacted without them. In our view it must follow that the entire statute is inoperative.

The power to make any expenditure that furthers "the general welfare" is obviously very broad. *See Helvering,* 301 U.S. at 640-641. While Congress may seek to induce States to accept conditional grants, Congress may not cross the "point at which pressure turns into compulsion, and ceases to be inducement." *Steward Machine,* 301 U.S. at 590. The Federal Government suggests that it is sufficient if States are "free, *as a matter of law,* to turn down" federal funds. When a heavy federal tax is levied to support a federal program that offers large grants to the States, States may, as a practical matter, be unable to refuse to participate in the federal program and to substitute a state alternative. Even if a State believes that the federal program is ineffective and inefficient, withdrawal would likely force the State to impose a huge tax increase on its residents, and this new state tax would come on top of the federal taxes already paid by residents to support subsidies to participating States. Any State that refuses to expand its Medicaid programs in this way is threatened with a severe sanction: the loss of all its federal Medicaid funds. The States devote a larger percentage of their budgets to Medicaid than to any other item. A State forced out of the Medicaid program would face burdens in addition to the loss of federal Medicaid funding. For example, a nonparticipating State might be found to be ineligible for other major federal funding sources. Congress clearly expressed its informed view that no State could possibly refuse the offer that the ACA extends. The Medicaid Expansion therefore exceeds Congress' spending power and cannot be implemented. The most natural remedy would be to invalidate the Medicaid Expansion. We should not accept the Government's invitation to attempt to solve a constitutional problem by rewriting the Medicaid Expansion so as to allow States that reject it to retain their pre-existing Medicaid funds.

∾ PROBLEMS ∾

1. Butler *Revisited.* Following *Dole* and *Sebelius,* suppose that Congress wants to reimpose the provisions of the Agricultural Adjustment Act that it tried to impose in *United States v. Butler.* As you may recall, in *Butler,* Congress concluded that an economic emergency existed because of a disparity between the prices of agricultural and other commodities. This disparity affected both farmers' purchasing power and transactions in agricultural commodities. In an effort to deal with this disparity, Congress tried to reduce farm acreage "through agreements with producers or by other voluntary methods," and to provide for rental or benefit payments to be made in exchange for the reduction. In order to finance the benefits payments, Congress levied processing taxes on various commodities. Would the Act be valid if enacted today?

2. *Child Labor Tax Case Revisited.* In *Hammer v. Dagenhart* and the *Child Labor Tax Case,* Congress tried unsuccessfully to restrict child labor. In *Hammer,* the Court tried to achieve that objective under the Commerce Clause. In the *Child Labor Tax Case,* it tried to do so under its taxing power. Obviously, in light of the Court's subsequent interpretations of the Commerce Clause, *Hammer* has been overruled, and Congress can now regulate child labor under the Commerce Clause. After *Dole,* can it also do so under the Spending Clause through conditional grants to the states or by threatening to withhold federal funds unless the states restrict child labor?

3. *Removing Federal Funding from Sanctuary Cities.* As part of his effort to arrest and deport undocumented immigrants, President Trump issued an executive order declaring that so-called sanctuary cities have caused "immeasurable harm to the American people and to the very fabric of our republic," and threatens those cities with the loss of federal funds. Under the federal spending authority, may the federal government require state and local officials to arrest and detain undocumented immigrants? May it require them to notify the federal government regarding the existence of undocumented aliens? Can it remove federal funding from state and local governments that refuse to cooperate?

4. *More on the Education for a Better America Act.* Now, let's think about the impact of *Sebelius* on Congress's power under the Spending Clause. Suppose that Congress provides a substantial amount of funding for K–12 education, which Congress decides that students would be better educated if they attended year-round schools (in other words, they did not take a summer vacation), and if the school day was extended by an hour per day. Accordingly, in the Act, Congress is thinking about mandating year-round education and nine-hour school days as

a condition of obtaining federal funding for education. Can Congress mandate these changes after *Sebelius*?

E.   THE WAR POWER AND TREATY POWER

Article I also gives Congress a number of powers relating to war and foreign affairs. Included is the power to declare war and to regulate commerce with foreign states. This power is, in some respects, shared with the President, who also has substantial authority over foreign affairs. For example, under Article II, Section 2, the President is the Commander in Chief of the army and the navy, and has the power to appoint ambassadors and consuls. In addition, as noted, he has the power to make treaties.

In Chapter 3, we examine the scope of presidential power as well as the intersection between congressional power and executive power, especially with regard to the war power. In this section, we focus primarily on congressional powers, including the war power and the treaty power. However, it is important to remember that the Constitution also gives Congress the power to "regulate foreign affairs." In *Perez v. Brownell*, 356 U.S. 44 (1958), the Court upheld a congressional enactment that mandated a loss of U.S. citizenship for "voting in a political election in a foreign state."

1.   *The War Power*

The war power gives Congress the authority not only to declare war but also to pass legislation necessary to the conduct of the war. Few dispute that the war power applies to military contexts. The power is more controversial, however, when it is applied to controlling the conduct of U.S. citizens within the United States.

Woods v. Cloyd W. Miller Co.

333 U.S. 138 (1948)

Mr. Justice DOUGLAS delivered the opinion of the Court.

Title II of the Housing and Rent Act of 1947, which imposed maximum rents, became effective on July 1, 1947, and the following day the appellee demanded increases of 40% and 60% for rental accommodations in the Cleveland Defense-Rental Area, and admitted violation of the Act and regulations adopted pursuant thereto. Appellant instituted this proceeding under §206(b) of the Act to enjoin the violations. A preliminary injunction issued. After a hearing it was dissolved and a permanent injunction denied.

The District Court was of the view that the authority of Congress to regulate rents by virtue of the war power ended with the Presidential Proclamation terminating hostilities since that proclamation inaugurated "peace-in-fact." The District Court expressed the further view that rent control is not within the war power because "the emergency created by housing shortage came into existence long before the war."

We conclude that the war power sustains this legislation. The Court said in *Hamilton v. Kentucky Distilleries and Warehouse Co.*, 251 U.S. 146, that the war power includes the power "to remedy the evils which have arisen from its rise and progress" and continues for the duration of that emergency. Whatever may be the consequences when war is officially terminated, the war power does not necessarily end with the cessation of hostilities. Those cases followed the reasoning of *Stewart v. Kahn*, 11 Wall. 493, 20 L. Ed. 176, which held that Congress had the power to toll the statute of limitations of the States during the period when the process of their courts was not available to litigants due to the conditions obtaining in the Civil War.

The constitutional validity of the present legislation follows *a fortiori* from those cases. The legislative history of the Act makes clear that there has not yet been eliminated the deficit in housing which was caused by the heavy demobilization of veterans and by the cessation or reduction in residential construction during the period of hostilities due to the allocation of building materials to military projects. Since the war effort contributed heavily to that deficit, Congress has the power even after the cessation of hostilities to control the forces that a short supply of the needed article created. If that were not true, the Necessary and Proper Clause, Art. I, §8, cl. 18, would be drastically limited in its application to the war powers. It would render Congress powerless to remedy conditions the creation of which followed from the mobilization of men and materials for successful prosecution of the war. So to read the Constitution would be to make it self-defeating.

We recognize that the effects of war under modern conditions may be felt in the economy for years and years, and that if the war power can be used in days of peace to treat wounds which war inflicts on our society, it may not only swallow up all other powers of Congress but largely obliterate the Ninth and the Tenth Amendments. There are no such implications in today's decision. We deal here with the consequences of a housing deficit intensified during the period of hostilities by the war effort. Whether the war power has been properly employed in cases such as this is open to judicial inquiry. The constitutionality of action taken by Congress does not depend on recitals of the power which it undertakes to exercise. Here it is plain from the legislative history that Congress was invoking its war power to cope with a current condition of which the war was a direct and immediate cause. Its judgment on that score is entitled to the respect granted like legislation enacted pursuant to the police power.

Under the present Act the Housing Expediter is authorized to remove the rent controls in any defense-rental area if in his judgment the need no longer exists by reason of new construction or satisfaction of demand in other ways. Nor is there here a grant of unbridled administrative discretion. The standards prescribed pass muster under our decisions. The fact that the property regulated suffers a decrease in value is no more fatal to the exercise of the war power than it is where the police power is invoked to the same end.

Reversed.

Mr. Justice JACKSON, *concurring.*

The "war power" is the most dangerous one to free government in the whole catalogue of powers. It usually is invoked in haste and excitement when calm legislative consideration of constitutional limitation is difficult. It is executed in a time of patriotic fervor that makes moderation unpopular. Worst of all, it is interpreted by Judges under the influence of the same passions and pressures. As in this case, the Government urges hasty decision to forestall some emergency or serve some purpose and pleads that paralysis will result if its claims to power are denied or their confirmation delayed. Particularly when the war power is invoked to do things to the liberties of people, or to their property or economy that only indirectly affect conduct of the war and do not relate to the management of the war itself, the constitutional basis should be scrutinized with care. We still are technically in a state of war. I would not be willing to hold that war powers may be indefinitely prolonged merely by keeping legally alive a state of war that had in fact ended. But I find no reason to conclude that we could find that the present state of war is merely technical. We have armies abroad exercising our war power and have made no peace terms with our allies not to mention our principal enemies. The conclusion that the war power has been applicable during the lifetime of this legislation is unavoidable.

Note: The War Power and Domestic Regulation

During World War I, Congress passed the War-Time Prohibition Act, which authorized the President to prohibit the use of grains, cereals, fruits, or other food products in the manufacture or production of wine, beer, other intoxicating malt, or vinous liquor for beverage purposes. The legislation authorized the President to continue the prohibition until the end of the war and thereafter until demobilization. In two decisions, the Court upheld the prohibition as applied to alcoholic beverages produced after the war ended. In *Ruppert v. Caffey,* 251 U.S. 264 (1920), the Court stated: "Since Congress has power to increase war efficiency by prohibiting liquor traffic, no reason appears why it should be denied the power to make its prohibition effective." Justice McReynolds, joined by two other justices, dissented: "When active hostilities have ended and demobilization has been completed, I can see no reasonable relationship between the war declared in 1917, or the demobilization following, or restoration of peace and destruction of the value of complainant's beverage." Likewise, in *Hamilton v. Kentucky Distilleries Co.*, 251 U.S. 146 (1919), the Court held: "The mere cessation of hostilities under the armistice did not abridge or suspend the power of Congress to resort to prohibition of the liquor traffic as a means of increasing our war efficiency, that the support and care of the army and navy during demobilization was within the war emergency, and that the act was valid when passed." The Court went on to note that demobilization was continuing at the time.

∾ PROBLEM: A PEACETIME DRAFT? ∾

Under Congress's power to wage war, Congress arguably has the authority to authorize a military draft. Such power probably also exists because of Article I, Section 8, which gives Congress the power to "raise and support Armies" and to "provide and maintain a Navy." No one doubts Congress's authority to impose a draft during periods of war. Would it also be permissible for Congress to impose a peacetime draft? Suppose Congress decided that a period of military service would help inculcate a sense of public service and commitment in youth. Or it would help the nation be prepared for future wars. Is a peacetime draft permissible?

2. *The Treaty Power*

Although Article II, Section 2 gives the President the power to make treaties, it provides that a two-thirds vote of the Senate is required for ratification. In this section, we examine the scope of the treaty power and its impact on domestic law.

Missouri v. Holland

252 U.S. 416 (1920)

Mr. Justice HOLMES delivered the opinion of the Court.

This is a bill in equity brought by the State of Missouri to prevent a game warden of the United States from attempting to enforce the Migratory Bird Treaty Act of July 3, 1918, and the regulations made by the Secretary of Agriculture in pursuance of the same. The ground is that the statute is an unconstitutional interference with the rights reserved to the States by the Tenth Amendment, and that the acts of the defendant done and threatened under that authority invade the sovereign right of the State and contravene its will manifested in statutes.

On December 8, 1916, a treaty between the United States and Great Britain was proclaimed by the President. It recited that many species of birds in their annual migrations traversed many parts of the United States and Canada, that they were of great value as a source of food and in destroying insects injurious to vegetation, but were in danger of extermination through lack of adequate protection. It therefore provided for closed seasons and protection in other forms, and agreed that the two powers would take or propose to their lawmaking bodies the necessary measures for carrying the treaty out. The act of July 3, 1918, entitled an act to give effect to the convention, prohibited the killing, capturing or selling any of the migratory birds included in the terms of the treaty except as permitted by regulations compatible with those terms, to be made by the Secretary of Agriculture. Regulations were proclaimed. The question is whether the treaty and statute are void as an interference with the rights reserved to the States.

It is not enough to refer to the Tenth Amendment, reserving the powers not delegated to the United States, because by Article 2, Section 2, the power to make treaties is delegated expressly, and by Article 6 treaties made under the authority of the United States, along with the Constitution and laws of the United States made in pursuance thereof, are declared the supreme law of the land. If the treaty is valid there can be no dispute about the validity of the statute under Article 1, Section 8, as a necessary and proper means to execute the powers of the Government.

Acts of Congress are the supreme law of the land only when made in pursuance of the Constitution, while treaties are declared to be so when made under the authority of the United States. It is open to question whether the authority of the United States means more than the formal acts prescribed to make the convention. There may be matters of the sharpest exigency for the national well-being that an act of Congress could not deal with but that a treaty followed by such an act could, and it is not lightly to be assumed that, in matters requiring national action, "a power which must belong to and somewhere reside in every civilized government" is not to be found. The treaty in question does not contravene any prohibitory words found in the Constitution. The question is whether it is forbidden by some invisible radiation from the general terms of the Tenth Amendment. We must consider what this country has become in deciding what that amendment has reserved.

As most of the laws of the United States are carried out within the States and as many of them deal with matters which in the silence of such laws the State might regulate, such general grounds are not enough to support Missouri's claim. Valid treaties "are as binding within the territorial limits of the States as they are elsewhere throughout the dominion of the United States." No doubt the great body of private relations usually fall within the control of the State, but a treaty may override its power. This proposition was recognized as early as *Hopkirk v. Bell*, 3 Cranch, 454, 2 L. Ed. 497, with regard to statutes of limitation, and as to confiscation, in *Ware v. Hylton*, 3 Dall. 199, 1 L. Ed. 568.

Here a national interest of very nearly the first magnitude is involved. It can be protected only by national action in concert with that of another power. The subject matter is only transitorily within the State and has no permanent habitat therein. But for the treaty and statute there soon might be no birds for any powers to deal with. We see nothing in the Constitution that compels the Government to sit by while a food supply is cut off and the protectors of our forests and our crops are destroyed. It is not sufficient to rely upon the States. We are of opinion that the treaty and statute must be upheld.

Decree affirmed.

Note: The Impact of Treaties on Local Law

In *DeGeofroy v. Riggs*, 133 U.S. 258 (1890), a U.S. citizen died intestate but owning valuable real property. A treaty between the United States and France provided that citizens of one country could inherit property in the other country. However, local law made it illegal for foreign citizens to own property in that jurisdiction. Riggs's sister, who was married to a Frenchman, and her children (who claimed French citizenship) sought to inherit the property. The Court held that the treaty controlled over the local law:

> That the treaty power extends to all proper subjects of negotiation between our government and the governments of other nations is clear. The protection which should be afforded to the citizens of one country owning property in another, and the manner in which that property may be transferred, devised, or inherited, are fitting subjects for such negotiation, and of regulation by mutual stipulations between the two countries. As commercial intercourse increases between countries, the residence of citizens of one country within the territory of the other naturally follows; and the removal of their disability from alienage to hold, transfer, and inherit property, in such cases, tends to promote amicable relations. The treaty power as expressed in the constitution, is in terms unlimited, except by restraints which are found in that instrument against the action of the government, or of its departments, and those arising from the nature of the government itself, and of that of the states. It would not be contended that it extends so far as to authorize what the constitution forbids, or a change in the character of the government, or in that of one of the states, or a cession of any portion of the territory of the latter, without its consent. But, with these exceptions, it is not perceived that there is any limit to the questions which can be adjusted touching any matter which is properly the subject of negotiation with a foreign country.

See also Hauenstein v. Lynham, 100 U.S. 483 (1880); *Ware v. Hylton*, 3 U.S. (3 Dall.) 199 (1796).

∾ PROBLEM: RESTRICTING CITIZEN RIGHTS ∾

A country, an influential trading partner of the United States, engages in abusive labor practices and mistreats its citizens. Within the United States, human rights organizations have banded together to oppose trade with this partner and to conduct protests designed to pressure the partner. Under pressure from the trading partner, the President agrees to a treaty that restricts the right of U.S. citizens to criticize the trading partner. The treaty is ratified by the Senate. Is the treaty valid?

Whitney v. Robertson

124 U.S. 190 (1888)

FIELD, J.

Plaintiffs are merchants, doing business in the city of New York who imported a large quantity of "centrifugal and molasses sugars" from the island of San Domingo. These goods were similar in kind to sugars produced in the Hawaiian islands, which are admitted free of duty under the treaty with the king of those islands, and the act of congress passed to carry the treaty into effect. They were duly entered at the custom-house at the port of New York; the plaintiffs claiming that, by the treaty with the republic of San Domingo, the goods should be admitted on the same terms, that is, free of duty, as similar articles, the produce and manufacture of the Hawaiian islands. The defendant, who was at the time collector of the port, refused to allow this claim, treated the goods as dutiable articles under the acts of congress, and exacted duties on them to the amount of $ 21,936. Plaintiffs paid, under protest, the duties exacted, and brought the present action to recover the amount. Defendant demurred and final judgment was entered in his favor.

Plaintiffs rely for an exemption upon the ninth article of the treaty with the Dominican republic: "No higher or other duty shall be imposed on the importation into the United States of any article, the growth, produce, or manufacture of the Dominican republic, or of her fisheries; and no higher or other duty shall be imposed on the importation into the Dominican republic of any article, the growth, produce, or manufacture of the United States, or their fisheries, than are or shall be payable on the like articles, the growth, produce, or manufacture of any other foreign country, or its fisheries."

The act of congress under which the duties were collected, authorized their exaction. It is of general application, making no exception in favor of goods of any country. It was passed after the treaty with the Dominican republic, and, if there be any conflict between the stipulations of the treaty and the requirements of the law, the latter must control. A treaty is primarily a contract between two or more independent nations. For the infraction of its provisions a remedy must be sought by the injured party through reclamations upon the other. When the stipulations are not self-executing, they can only be enforced pursuant to legislation to carry them into effect, and such legislation is as much subject to modification and repeal by congress as legislation upon any other subject. If the treaty contains stipulations which are self-executing, that is, require no legislation to make them operative, to that extent they have the force and effect of a legislative enactment. Congress may modify such provisions, so far as they bind the United States, or supersede them altogether. By the constitution, a treaty is placed on the same footing, and made of like obligation, with an act of legislation. Both are declared by that instrument to be the supreme law of the land, and no superior efficacy is given to either over the other. When the two relate to the same subject, the courts will always endeavor to construe them so as to give effect to both, if that can be done without violating the language of either; but, if the two are inconsistent, the one last in date will control the other: provided, always, the stipulation of the treaty on the subject is self-executing. If the country with which the treaty is made is dissatisfied with the action of the legislative department, it may present its complaint to the executive head of the government, and take such other measures as it may deem essential for the protection of its interests. The courts can afford no redress. Whether the complaining nation has just cause of complaint, or our country was justified in its legislation, are not matters for judicial cognizance. *Taylor v. Morton*, 2 Curt. 454, 459.

When a law is clear in its provisions, its validity cannot be assailed before the courts for want of conformity to stipulations of a previous treaty not already executed. Considerations of that character belong to another department of the government. The duty of the courts is to construe and give effect to the latest expression of the sovereign will.

Judgment affirmed.

Notes

1. *More on the Scope of the Treaty Power.* In *Reid v. Covert*, 354 U.S. 1 (1957), the Court offered further insight into the meaning of the treaty power:

> No agreement with a foreign nation can confer power on the Congress, or on any other branch of Government, which is free from the restraints of the Constitution. Article VI, the Supremacy Clause of the Constitution, declares: 'This Constitution, and the Laws of the United States which shall be made in Pursuance thereof; and all Treaties made, or which shall be made, under the Authority of the United States, shall be the supreme Law of the Land.' There is nothing in this language which intimates that treaties and laws enacted pursuant to them do not have to comply with the provisions of the Constitution. Nor is there anything in the debates which accompanied the drafting and ratification of the Constitution which suggests such a result. These debates as well as the history that surrounds the adoption of the treaty provision in Article VI make it clear that the reason treaties were not limited to those made in 'pursuance' of the Constitution was so that agreements made by the United States under the Articles of Confederation, including the important peace treaties which concluded the Revolutionary War, would remain in effect. It would be manifestly contrary to the objectives of those who created the Constitution, as well as those who were responsible for the Bill of Rights—let alone alien to our entire constitutional history and tradition—to construe Article VI as permitting the United States to exercise power under an international agreement without observing constitutional prohibitions. In effect, such construction would permit amendment of that document in a manner not sanctioned by Article V. The prohibitions of the Constitution were designed to apply to all branches of the National Government and they cannot be nullified by the Executive or by the Executive and the Senate combined."

2. *Seizure of the British Vessel.* In *Cook v. United States*, 288 U.S. 102 (1933), the Court upheld a treaty limiting the government's ability to seize vessels. Under Section 581 of the Tariff Act, officers of the Coast Guard were authorized to stop

and board any vessel at any place within 12 miles of the coast of the United States "to examine the manifest and to inspect, search, and examine" the vessel and any merchandise in it. If it appeared that any violation of any law of the United States had been committed, the vessel or merchandise was subject to forfeiture. The collector of customs, pursuant to the Tariff Act, assessed against Frank Cook, master of the *Mazel Tov*, a penalty for failure to include liquor in the manifest. Cook challenged the penalty, alleging that, because of a treaty between the United States and Great Britain, the seizure was unlawful. He argued that the 12-mile limit was, with respect to British vessels, modified by the treaty so as to substitute for four leagues from "our" coast, the distance that "can be traversed in one hour by the vessel suspected of endeavoring to commit the offense." In the case, the Court held that the "Treaty, being later in date than the act of 1922, superseded, so far as inconsistent with the act, the authority which had been conferred by section 581 upon officers of the Coast Guard to board, search, and seize beyond our territorial waters. *Whitney v. Robertson*, 124 U.S. 190. For in a strict sense the Treaty was self-executing, in that no legislation was necessary to authorize executive action pursuant to its provisions."

3. *The Rhodesian Embargo.* In *Diggs v. Shultz*, 470 F.2d 461 (D.C. Cir. 1972), the United Nations Security Council adopted Resolution 232, directing that all member states impose an embargo on trade with Southern Rhodesia. In compliance, the President of the United States issued executive orders providing criminal sanctions for violation of the embargo. Later, Congress adopted the "Byrd Amendment" to the Strategic and Critical Materials Stock Piling Act, 50 U.S.C. §98-98h, which provided in part: "Sec. 10. Notwithstanding any other provision of law, the President may not prohibit or regulate the importation into the United States of any material determined to be strategic and critical pursuant to the provisions of this Act, if such material is the product of any foreign country or area not listed as a Communist-dominated country or area for so long as the importation into the United States of material of that kind which is the product of such Communist-dominated countries or areas is not prohibited by any provision of law." Since Southern Rhodesia was not a Communist-controlled country, and as the United States imported from Communist countries substantial quantities of metallurgical chromite and other materials available from Rhodesia, the Byrd Amendment contemplated the resumption of trade between the United States and Southern Rhodesia. It was argued that the Byrd Amendment could not authorize the issuance of a license contrary to the country's treaty obligations. The Court held: "Alleging that the Byrd Amendment did not and could not authorize issuance of a license contrary to this country's treaty obligations, appellants sought to enjoin further importation, to require official seizure, and to restrain use, of materials already imported under the General License, and to declare the General License null and void. Under our constitutional scheme, Congress can denounce treaties if it sees fit to do so, and there is nothing the other branches of government can do about it. We consider that this is precisely what Congress has done in this case."

∾ PROBLEMS ∾

1. *Immigration, Treaties, and Statutes.* Plaintiff sought a writ of habeas corpus to obtain release from an allegedly unlawful detention by Captain Walker, master of the steamship *Belgic*, lying in the harbor of San Francisco. Plaintiff is a Chinese laborer who resided in San Francisco for 12 years before he traveled to China. When he left, he possessed a certificate issued by the collector of customs entitling him to return to the United States. While he was gone, Congress passed an act annulling such certificates and abrogating the right to land. The validity of the act is assailed as being in effect an expulsion from the country of Chinese laborers, in violation of existing treaties between the United States and China, and of rights vested in them under the laws of Congress. Is plaintiff entitled to the writ? *See Chae Chan Ping v. United States,* 130 U.S. 581 (1889).

2. *More on the Education for a Better America Act.* Could the President and Congress enter into a treaty on education that would allow for the imposition of educational requirements that Congress could not impose directly?

F. CONGRESSIONAL POWER TO ENFORCE CIVIL RIGHTS

U.S. CONSTITUTION, THIRTEENTH AMENDMENT (1865)

Section 1. Neither slavery nor involuntary servitude, except as punishment for crime whereof the party shall have been duly convicted, shall exist within the United States, or any place subject to their jurisdiction.

Section 2. Congress shall have power to enforce the article by appropriate legislation.

U.S. CONSTITUTION, FOURTEENTH AMENDMENT (1868)

Section 1. All persons born or naturalized in the United States and subject to the jurisdiction thereof, are citizens of the United States and of the State wherein they reside. No State shall make or enforce any law which shall abridge the privileges or immunities of citizens of the United States; nor shall any State deprive any person of life, liberty, or property, without due process of law; nor deny to any person within its jurisdiction the equal protection of the laws.

Section 2. Representatives shall be apportioned among the several States according to their respective numbers, counting the whole number of persons in each State, excluding Indians not taxed. But when the right to vote at any election for the choice of electors for President and Vice President of the United States, Representatives in Congress, the Executive and Judicial officers of a State, or the members of the Legislature thereof, is denied to any of the male inhabitants of such State, being twenty-one years of age, and citizens of the United States, or in any way abridged, except for participation in rebellion, or other crime, the basis of representation therein shall be reduced in the proportion which the number of such male citizens shall bear to the whole number of male citizens twenty-one years of age in such State.

Section 3. No person shall be a Senator or Representative in Congress, or elector of President and Vice President, or hold any office, civil or military, under the United States, or under any State, who, having previously taken an oath, as a member of Congress, or as an officer of the United States, or as a member of any State legislature, or as an executive or judicial officer of any State, to support the Constitution of the United States, shall have engaged in insurrection or rebellion against the same, or given aid or comfort to the enemies thereof. But Congress may by a vote of two-thirds of each House, remove such disability.

Section 4. The validity of the public debt of the United States, authorized by law, including debts incurred for payment of pensions and bounties for services in suppressing insurrection or rebellion, shall not be questioned. But neither the United States nor any State shall assume or pay any debt or obligation incurred in aid of insurrection or rebellion against the United States, or any claim for the loss or emancipation of any slave; but all such debts, obligations and claims shall be held illegal and void.

Section 5. The Congress shall have power to enforce, by appropriate legislation, the provisions of this article.

U.S. CONSTITUTION, FIFTEENTH AMENDMENT (1870)

Section 1. The right of citizens of the United States to vote shall not be denied or abridged by the United States or by any State on account of race, color, or previous condition of servitude.

Section 2. The Congress shall have power to enforce this article by appropriate legislation.

∾ PROBLEM: SECOND FLOOR ∾

A criminal defendant and a court reporter suffering from mobility impairments sued the State of Tennessee, claiming that the state failed to provide access to the courts for individuals with disabilities, especially to the upper floors of local courthouses. The suit was brought under Title II of the Americans with Disabilities Act (ADA), seeking damages despite the state's position that it had sovereign immunity from suit.

∾ PROBLEM: CRITICAL CONFINEMENT ∾

Meanwhile, in nearby Georgia, a paraplegic inmate brought suit against the state, its department of corrections, and state prison officials, claiming his rights were violated under Title II of the ADA. The man, John Smith, was serving a sentence of 14 years for drug smuggling. Smith claims he is confined 23 hours a day in a 12-foot by 3-foot cell, where there is not enough room to turn his wheelchair around. Furthermore, the prison is not outfitted with facilities that permit him to use the toilet or shower without help, causing him to suffer injuries when he is forced to attempt such use on his own. The legal questions in Smith's case include the following: 1) Can Congress, pursuant to its Section 5 power to enforce the Fourteenth Amendment, create private remedies against the states for violations of the Fourteenth Amendment? 2) Can the remedies created by Congress be prophylactic remedial legislation beyond racial discrimination? 3) Can Congress abrogate state sovereign immunity from suit to enforce the provisions of the Reconstruction Amendments? 4) Can Congress authorize prospective injunctive relief against a state pursuant to Section 5 of the Fourteenth Amendment? (*See, e.g., Tennessee v. Lane*, 541 U.S. 509 (2004); *United States v. Georgia*, 546 U.S. 151 (2006).)

Prior to the end of the Civil War, Congress proposed the Thirteenth Amendment, abolishing slavery and involuntary servitude. The vote in Congress approving the Amendment barely surpassed the two-thirds majority vote required under Article V. Many believed that the Amendment implicitly made slaves citizens, effectively overruling *Dred Scott v. Sandford*, 60 U.S. 393 (1857). Within a year of the Amendment's ratification, Congress enacted the Civil Rights Act of 1866, providing Black citizens with "the same right in every state to make and enforce contracts, to sue, be parties, to inherit, purchase, sell and convey real and personal property; and to the full and equal benefit of all laws and proceedings for the security of person and property as is enjoyed by white citizens."After the Thirteenth Amendment was ratified, the 15-member Joint Congressional Committee on Reconstruction designed and proposed the Fourteenth Amendment in December of 1865. Led by a conservative Republican senator, William Fessenden of Maine, and a radical Republican Senator, Thaddeus Stevens of Pennsylvania, the Amendment was a product not only of the Civil War but of the politics of the times as well. The Fourteenth Amendment expressly transformed all former slaves into citizens and offered them a variety of protections. The Amendment produced considerable litigation, particularly dealing with its meaning and reach.

Congress proposed the Fifteenth Amendment in 1869, and it was ratified in 1870. This Amendment gave Congress the power to ensure that voting rights were administered fairly and equally.

These three Reconstruction Amendments gave Congress the power to protect the rights of Blacks in America. It has been argued that Congress gave itself the power because it did not trust the judicial branch to do the same. In fact, after *Dred Scott v. Sandford*, Congress might have become leery of courts putting aside regional, popular, or cultural leanings to enforce civil rights.

Over time, the limited power of the federal government was expanded by the Thirteenth, Fourteenth, and Fifteenth Amendments, empowering the federal government to grant and protect the citizenship of former slaves. *The Slaughterhouse Cases*, 83 U.S. (16 Wall.) 36 (1873). The legislative debates and congressional record relating to the passage and ratification of the Reconstruction Amendments were inconclusive as to the nature and scope of Congress's power to enforce the Amendment's substantive provisions. These issues were left to the courts, where early cases examined congressional efforts to remove the "badges and incidents of slavery" in public accommodations, transportation, and voting. *The Civil Rights Acts of 1866*, 1870, 1871, and 1875 survive in various forms today.

Modern congressional legislation protecting rights covers the spectrum of interests and include the Civil Rights Act of 1964 and most of the Voting Rights Act of 1965. There are also acts prohibiting firearms within so many feet of a schoolyard and protecting patent rights, the rights of women, the disabled, and the expression of religious views. The following cases and notes suggest that the balance of power between the Court and Congress has been as difficult to determine as the balance of power between the states and the federal government.

1. Early Developments

Relatively few cases dealt with the meaning of the Thirteenth Amendment after its ratification. Those cases that were brought often dealt with the scope of its coverage, especially the meaning of "involuntary servitude."

∼ PROBLEM: PUBLIC SERVICE ∼

An Arizona man, Peter Mast, brought suit against a division of the State of Arizona, claiming that an Arizona law requiring all able-bodied persons between the ages of 21 and 25 to complete at least one weekend of public service appropriate to the person's skills, age, and circumstances is unconstitutional. The law has limited opt-out provisions and defines a weekend as "at most 48 hours at a time." Mast was prosecuted for refusing to comply with several requests for service and was sentenced to serve two days in jail for failing to comply with the duty requirement. Mast contends that the law requires "involuntary servitude" in violation of the Thirteenth Amendment. Who should win this lawsuit? How does Mast's claim differ from the claims in the two enforcement of civil rights problems, *Second Floor* and *Critical Confinement?*

The Civil Rights Cases

109 U.S. 3 (1883)

BRADLEY, J.
These cases involve a challenge to the constitutionality of the Civil Rights Act of 1875. Four cases appeal indictments for denying to persons of color the accommodations and privileges of an inn or a theater. The fifth case was brought by a husband and wife when a railway conductor refused to allow the wife to ride in the ladies' car because she was a person of African descent.

The essence of the Civil Rights Act of 1875 is to declare that, in the enjoyment of the accommodations and privileges of inns, public conveyances, theatres, and other places of public amusement, no distinction shall be made between citizens of different race or color, or between those who have, and those who have not, been slaves. The second section makes it a penal offence to deny to any citizen of any race or color, regardless of previous servitude, any of the accommodations or privileges mentioned in the first section.

Has Congress constitutional power to make such a law? No one will contend that the power to pass it was contained in the Constitution before the adoption of the last three amendments. The power is sought in the Fourteenth Amendment. The last section of the amendment invests Congress with power to enforce it by appropriate legislation. To enforce what? To enforce the prohibition. To adopt appropriate legislation for correcting the effects of such prohibited State laws and State acts, and thus to render them effectually null, void, and innocuous. This is the legislative power conferred upon Congress, and this is the whole of it. It does not authorize Congress to create a code of municipal law for the regulation of private rights. Positive rights and privileges are undoubtedly secured by the Fourteenth Amendment; but they are secured by way of prohibition against State laws and State proceedings affecting those rights and privileges, and by power given to Congress to legislate for the purpose of carrying such prohibition into effect. *United States v. Cruikshank*, 92 U.S. 542.

Until some State law has been passed, or some State action through its officers or agents has been taken, adverse to the rights of citizens sought to be protected by the Fourteenth Amendment, no legislation of the United States under said amendment, nor any proceeding under such legislation, can be called into activity: for the prohibitions of the amendment are against State laws and acts done under State authority. Congress cannot properly cover the whole domain of rights appertaining to life, liberty and property, defining them and providing for their vindication. That would be to establish a code of municipal law regulative of all private rights between man and man in society. If this legislation is appropriate for enforcing the prohibitions of the amendment, it is difficult to see where it is to stop. Why may not Congress with equal show of authority enact a code of laws for the enforcement and vindication of all rights of life, liberty, and property? If it is supposable that the States may deprive persons of life, liberty, and property without due process of law, why should not Congress proceed at once to prescribe due process of law for the protection of every one of these fundamental rights?

This is not corrective legislation; it is primary and direct. It supercedes and displaces State legislation on the same subject or only allows it permissive force. It ignores such regulation and assumes that the matter is one that belongs to the domain of national regulation. Whether it would not have been a more effective protection of the rights of citizens to have clothed Congress with plenary power over the whole subject, is not now the question. What we have to decide is, whether such plenary power has been conferred upon Congress by the Fourteenth Amendment; and, in our judgment, it has not. No countenance of authority for the passage of the law in question can be found in either the Thirteenth or Fourteenth Amendment of the Constitution; and no other ground of authority for its passage being suggested, it must necessarily be declared void, at least so far as its operation in the several States is concerned.

The first and second sections of the act of congress of March 1, 1875, entitled 'An act to protect all citizens in their civil and legal rights,' are unconstitutional and void, and that judgment should be rendered upon the several indictments in those cases accordingly. And it is so ordered.

Justice HARLAN, *dissenting.*

The opinion proceeds upon grounds too narrow and artificial. Before considering the language and scope of these amendments it will be proper to recall the relations subsisting, prior to their adoption, between the national government and the institution of slavery. Harlan then discussed how the Court upheld Congress's power to enact the Fugitive Slave Laws pursuant to Section 2, Article 4 and direct states to act affirmatively to protect the property interest of slaveholders in fugitive slaves. We have seen that the power of Congress, by legislation, to enforce the master's right to have his slave delivered up on claim was implied from the recognition of that right in the national Constitution. But the power conferred by the Thirteenth Amendment does not rest upon implication or inference. Those who framed it were not ignorant of the discussion, covering many years of our country's history, as to the constitutional power of Congress to enact the Fugitive Slave Laws of 1793 and 1850. When, therefore, it was determined, by a change in the fundamental law, to uproot the institution of slavery wherever it existed in the land, and to establish universal freedom, there was a fixed purpose to place the authority of Congress in the premises beyond the possibility of a doubt. Therefore power to enforce the Thirteenth Amendment, by appropriate legislation, was expressly granted.

The assumption that this amendment consists wholly of prohibitions upon State laws and State proceedings in hostility to its provisions, is unauthorized by its language. If any right was created by that amendment, the grant of power, through appropriate legislation, to enforce its provisions, authorizes Congress, by means of legislation, operating throughout the entire Union, to guard, secure, and protect that right. If, then, exemption from discrimination, in respect of civil rights, is a new constitutional right, secured by the grant of State citizenship to colored citizens of the United States, why may not the nation, by means of its own legislation of a primary direct character, guard, protect and enforce that right? It is a right and privilege, which the nation conferred. This court has always given a broad and liberal construction to the Constitution, so as to enable Congress to enforce rights secured by that instrument.

∼ PROBLEM: OLLIE'S BBQ RANCH ∼

Ollie owns a roadside barbeque stand in Memphis, called Ollie's BBQ Ranch. The stand is located on Ollie's private property. The business is readily accessible to people traveling on the interstate highway going to Atlanta. By word of mouth and in-state advertising, the business has grown such that Ollie is thinking about opening another stand in northern Tennessee. On the front door, a prominently placed large sign reads, "Whites Only." After *The Civil Rights Cases,* can Congress address Ollie's practice of excluding Black customers? How are the problems *Second Floor* and *Critical Confinement* useful here?

2. *Modern Civil Rights Cases*

Congress did not enact any civil rights laws between 1875 and 1957. When Congress finally began to respond to growing political pressure for racial equality in the 1960s, Congress was not forced to rely solely on its authority under Section 5 of the Fourteenth Amendment, which had been severely restricted in *The Civil Rights Cases.* Instead, in passing the 1964 Civil Rights Act, it was able to rely on the now-expanded interpretation of Congress's spending and commerce powers. This avenue was not foreclosed by *The Civil Rights Cases,* which raised but did not reach the issue of whether the Commerce Clause authorized Congress to enact civil rights legislation to protect African Americans. In 1964, in *Heart of Atlanta Motel v. United States,* 379 U.S. 241 (1964), the Court upheld Title II of the Civil Rights Act of 1964 as applied to a motel that serves interstate passengers: "Title II is carefully limited to enterprises having a direct and substantial relation to the interstate flow of goods and people."

Two years later, in *United States v. Guest,* 383 U.S. 745 (1966), the Court ruled that Section 5 of the Fourteenth Amendment authorized Congress to make it a crime for white supremacists to conspire to deprive African Americans of their civil rights. While Justice Stewart's majority opinion rested on a finding of state action (defendants had acted in concert with state officials), six justices were prepared to overrule *The Civil Rights Cases,* arguing that Section 5 empowered Congress to punish all conspiracies to interfere with the exercise of rights conferred under Section 1, "whether or not state officers or others acting under the color of state law are implicated in the conspiracy."

In *United States v. Morrison,* 529 U.S. 598 (2000), involving the Violence Against Women Act and its federal civil remedy for the victims of gender-motivated violence, the Court finally put the question of whether Congress could reach private action under Section 5 to rest. In a five-to-four majority decision, Chief Justice Rehnquist concluded for the majority that the law could not be upheld under the Fourteenth Amendment:

> Section 5 is "a positive grant of legislative power," that includes authority to "prohibit conduct which is not itself unconstitutional and to intrude into 'legislative spheres of autonomy

previously reserved to the States.'" Nevertheless, the majority concluded that the congressional enforcement power is not unlimited, and that several limitations inherent in §5's text and constitutional context. Petitioners' §5 argument is founded on an assertion that there is pervasive bias in various state justice systems against victims of gender-motivated violence. This assertion is supported by a voluminous congressional record. Petitioners contend that this bias denies victims of gender-motivated violence the equal protection of the laws and that Congress therefore acted appropriately in enacting a private civil remedy against the perpetrators of gender-motivated violence to both remedy the States' bias and deter future instances of discrimination in the state courts. As our cases have established, state-sponsored gender discrimination violates equal protection unless it serves "important governmental objectives and the discriminatory means employed" are "substantially related to the achievement of those objectives." However, the language and purpose of the Fourteenth Amendment place certain limitations on the manner in which Congress may attack discriminatory conduct. These limitations are necessary to prevent the Fourteenth Amendment from obliterating the Framers' carefully crafted balance of power between the States and the National Government. That Amendment erects no shield against merely private conduct, however discriminatory or wrongful. In *The Civil Rights Cases* we held that the public accommodation provisions of the Civil Rights Act of 1875, which applied to purely private conduct, were beyond the scope of the §5 enforcement power. Petitioners contend that two more recent decisions have in effect overruled this longstanding limitation on Congress' §5 authority. They rely on *United States v. Guest* for the proposition that the rule laid down in *The Civil Rights Cases* is no longer good law. In *Guest*, three Members of the Court, in a separate opinion by Justice Brennan, expressed the view that *The Civil Rights Cases* were wrongly decided, and that Congress could under §5 prohibit actions by private individuals. Three other Members of the Court, who joined the opinion of the Court, joined a separate opinion by Justice Clark which in two or three sentences stated the conclusion that Congress could punish all conspiracies that interfere with Fourteenth Amendment rights. Though these three Justices saw fit to opine on matters not before the Court in *Guest*, the Court had no occasion to revisit *The Civil Rights Cases*. To accept petitioners' argument, one must add to the three Justices joining Justice Brennan's reasoned explanation for his belief that *The Civil Rights Cases* were wrongly decided, the three Justices joining Justice Clark's opinion who gave no explanation whatever for their similar view. This is simply not the way that reasoned constitutional adjudication proceeds. We accordingly have no hesitation in saying that it would take more than the naked dicta contained in Justice Clark's opinion, when added to Justice Brennan's opinion, to cast any doubt upon the enduring vitality of *The Civil Rights Cases*. For these reasons, we conclude that Congress' power under §5 does not extend to the enactment of §13981.

As previously noted, the Court also concluded that the law could not be sustained under the Commerce Clause.

In *Jones v. Alfred H. Mayer Co.*, 392 U.S. 409 (1968), the Court rejected the view in *The Civil Rights Cases* that Congress's power under Section 2 of the Thirteenth Amendment to prohibit private discrimination is limited. Although the majority acknowledged that the Thirteenth Amendment has no state action requirement, the Court narrowly defined the terms "badges and incidents of slavery" to exclude discrimination by hotels, transportation companies, and other public accommodations. *Cf. Plessy v. Ferguson. Jones* upheld Congress's power to prohibit private and public discrimination in the sale and rental of property under 42 U.S.C. 1982, a portion of the Civil Rights Act of 1866.

BACKGROUND

In 1967, the United States charged 18 men with involvement in a Ku Klux Klan plot to murder three young civil rights workers, Michael Schwerner, James Chaney, and Andrew Goodman, in Philadelphia, Mississippi. It was alleged that on June 21, 1964, the three men were let out of a county jail at night, and were allegedly picked up by a sheriff's police car later that night, transported to a remote road, and intentionally murdered to punish them for their behavior. The bodies were taken to an earthen dam under construction and buried. The conspiracy charge was not based on assault and murder, but rather the deprivation, under color of state law, of the three men's Fourteenth Amendment due process rights to life, liberty, or property. The case led to one of the most famous criminal trials in the twentieth century, called the *Mississippi Burning Case* in the popular vernacular. Defendants appealed their indictments in *United States v. Price*, 383 U.S. 787 (1966), which was argued in the U.S. Supreme Court by Solicitor General Thurgood Marshall, who later became a Supreme Court Justice. The Court observed, "we have no doubt of 'the power of Congress to enforce by appropriate criminal sanction every right guaranteed by the Due Process Clause of the Fourteenth Amendment.'" The Court held that the federal statutes in question criminalized the conduct subject to the indictment and that "under color of state law" could include private individuals acting in concert with state officials. Seven of the 18 defendants were convicted, including Cecil Price, the chief deputy sheriff of Neshoba County. One of the defendants who was not convicted, Edgar Ray Killen, was eventually found guilty in 2005 of three counts of manslaughter.

～ PROBLEMS ～

1. *Family Medical Leave Act.* Congress decides to respond to the growing effort of state legislatures and courts to provide employment security for people forced to choose between their jobs and taking time off to recuperate from an extended illness or care for a sick family member. In 2009, Congress enacted the Family Medical Leave Act pursuant to its power under the Commerce Clause and Section 5 of the Fourteenth Amendment, providing for private injunctive relief and damages if states deprive individuals of the right to a family leave to care for family members under specific circumstances. You are the staff attorney for the congressional committee that promoted the law. You anticipate that a state will challenge the law when a new father seeks to assert his right to family leave to care for his newborn child. How should the United States defend such a claim? What should be included in the congressional record to help defend against such a claim?

2. *1866 Civil Rights Act—Take II.* As part of the Civil Rights Act of 1866, Congress provided that "all citizens within the jurisdiction of the United States

have the same rights to make and enforce contracts." A group of African American parents sued a private school that denied admission to their children solely on the basis of race. Does Congress have the power to prohibit this form of discrimination pursuant to the power granted under the Thirteenth Amendment?

3. *Competing Interpretations.* As between the Congress and the Executive Branch, whose interpretation of existing constitutional law should prevail? Suppose Congress enacts a law that requires the Executive Branch to get a warrant for all communications gathered by United States companies involving foreign nationals outside of the United States who are communicating with persons located in the United States. If the National Security Agency (NSA) applies the law to include warrantless surveillance if a foreign national is "of interest," but Congress objects, which interpretation governs? How does the congressional power to enforce civil rights apply here, if at all? Some commentators have strong opinions about such questions. *See,* e.g., W. Huhn, *Congress Has the Power to Enforce the Bill of Rights Against the Federal Government; Therefore FISA Is Constitutional and the President's Terrorist Surveillance Program Is Illegal,* 16 WILLIAM & MARY BILL OF RIGHTS J. 537 (2007).

4. *NSA Surveillance.* Congress enacts a law that requires the Executive Branch to get a warrant for all communications gathered by United States companies involving foreign nationals outside of the United States who are communicating with persons located in the United States. If the National Security Agency (NSA) applies the law to include warrantless surveillance of a foreign national "of interest," but Congress objects, which interpretation governs, Congress's or the Executive's? How does the congressional power to enforce civil rights apply here, if at all? As between the Congress and the Executive Branch, whose interpretation of existing constitutional law should prevail? Some commentators have strong opinions about such questions. *See,* e.g., W. Huhn, *Congress Has the Power to Enforce the Bill of Rights Against the Federal Government; Therefore FISA Is Constitutional and the President's Terrorist Surveillance Program Is Illegal,* 16 WILLIAM & MARY BILL OF RIGHTS J. 537 (2007).

3. Congressional Enforcement of the Right to Vote

In the prior cases, the Court grappled with the line between the power of the state over "local matters" and the exercise of federal government power in these same areas under the Reconstruction Amendments and the Commerce Clause. The following cases examine the roles of Congress and the Court in declaring and responding to violations of the Constitution.

Katzenbach v. Morgan

384 U.S. 641 (1966)

BRENNAN, J.

These cases concern the constitutionality of §4(e) of the Voting Rights Act of 1965, which provides that no person who has successfully completed the

sixth primary grade in a public school in, or a private school accredited by, the
Commonwealth of Puerto Rico in which the language of instruction was other
than English shall be denied the right to vote in any election because of his inability to read or write English. Appellees brought this suit to challenge the constitutionality of §4(e) insofar as it prohibits the enforcement of the election laws of
New York requiring an ability to read and write English as a condition of voting.
Under these laws many of the several hundred thousand New York City residents
who have migrated there from the Commonwealth of Puerto Rico had previously been denied the right to vote, and appellees attack §4(e) insofar as it would
enable many of these citizens to vote. We hold that, in the application challenged
in these cases, §4(e) is a proper exercise of the powers granted to Congress by
§5 of the Fourteenth Amendment and that by force of the Supremacy Clause the
New York English literacy requirement cannot be enforced to the extent that it is
inconsistent with §4(e).

The Attorney General of the State of New York argues that an exercise of
congressional power under §5 of the Fourteenth Amendment that prohibits the
enforcement of a state law can only be sustained if the Judicial Branch determines
that the state law is prohibited by the provisions of the Amendment that Congress
sought to enforce. More specifically, he urges that §4(e) cannot be sustained as
appropriate legislation to enforce the Equal Protection Clause unless the judiciary decides—even with the guidance of a congressional judgment—that the
application of the English literacy requirement prohibited by §4(e) is forbidden
by the Equal Protection Clause itself. We disagree. Neither the language nor history of §5 supports such a construction. As was said with regard to §5 in Ex parte
Virginia, "It is the power of Congress which has been enlarged."

Thus our task is limited to determining whether such legislation is, as
required by §5, appropriate legislation to enforce the Equal Protection Clause.
There can be no doubt that §4(e) may be regarded as an enactment to enforce
the Equal Protection Clause. Congress explicitly declared that it enacted §4(e)
"to secure the rights under the fourteenth amendment of persons educated in
American-flag schools in which the predominant classroom language was other
than English." The persons referred to include those who have migrated from
the Commonwealth of Puerto Rico to New York and who have been denied
the right to vote because of their inability to read and write English, and the
Fourteenth Amendment rights referred to include those emanating from the
Equal Protection Clause. More specifically, §4(e) may be viewed as a measure to
secure for the Puerto Rican community residing in New York nondiscriminatory
treatment by government—both in the imposition of voting qualifications and
the provision or administration of governmental services, such as public schools,
public housing and law enforcement.

Section 4(e) may be readily seen as "plainly adapted" to furthering these aims
of the Equal Protection Clause. It was for Congress to assess and weigh the various conflicting considerations—the risk or pervasiveness of the discrimination

in governmental services, the effectiveness of eliminating the state restriction on the right to vote as a means of dealing with the evil, the adequacy or availability of alternative remedies, and the nature and significance of the state interests that would be affected by the nullification of the English literacy requirement. It is not for us to review the congressional resolution of these factors. We conclude that §4(e) is appropriate legislation to enforce the Equal Protection Clause and reverse the judgment of the District Court.

Note

Four years after *Morgan*, the Court held in *Oregon v. Mitchell*, 400 U.S. 112 (1970), that a federal voting rights statute could lower the age for voting in federal elections to 18 from 21. Five justices (Black, Burger, Harlan, Stewart, and Blackmun) held that Congress could not interfere with the voting age set by individual states for state and local elections. Writing for those opposed to allowing Congress to set the age for state and local elections, Justice Black wrote: "There are at least three limitations upon Congress' power to enforce the guarantees of the Civil War Amendments. First, Congress may not by legislation repeal other provisions of the Constitution. Second, the power granted to Congress was not intended to strip the States of their power to govern themselves or to convert our national government of enumerated powers into a central government of unrestrained authority over every inch of the whole Nation. Third, Congress may only 'enforce' the provisions of the amendments and may do so only by 'appropriate legislation.' Congress has no power under the enforcement sections to undercut the amendments' guarantees of personal equality and freedom from discrimination, or to undermine those protections of the Bill of Rights which we have held the Fourteenth Amendment made applicable to the States. Of course, we have upheld congressional legislation under the Enforcement Clauses in some cases where Congress has interfered with state regulation of the local electoral process. *Katzenbach v. Morgan*. But division of power between state and national governments, like every provision of the Constitution, was expressly qualified by the Civil War Amendments' ban on racial discrimination. Where Congress attempts to remedy racial discrimination under its enforcement powers, its authority is enhanced by the avowed intention of the framers of the Thirteenth, Fourteenth, and Fifteenth Amendments." The Court unanimously upheld the legislative suspension of literacy testing in both state and federal elections as a qualification for voting: "In imposing a nationwide ban on literacy tests, Congress has recognized a national problem for what it is—a serious *national* dilemma that touches every corner of our land. Congress has decided that the way to solve the problems of racial discrimination is to deal with nationwide discrimination with nationwide legislation." Subsequent to this decision, the Twenty-sixth Amendment to the U.S. Constitution lowered the minimum voting age to 18 for all elections.

City of Rome v. United States

446 U.S. 156 (1980)

Mr. Justice MARSHALL delivered the opinion of the Court.

At issue in this case is the constitutionality of the Voting Rights Act of 1965 and its applicability to electoral changes and annexations made by the city of Rome, Ga.

It is clear that under §2 of the Fifteenth Amendment Congress may prohibit practices that in and of themselves do not violate §1 of the Amendment, so long as the prohibitions attacking racial discrimination in voting are "appropriate," as that term is defined in *McCulloch v. Maryland* and *Ex parte Virginia*. In the present case, we hold that the Act's ban on electoral changes that are discriminatory in effect is an appropriate method of promoting the purposes of the Fifteenth Amendment, even if it is assumed that §1 of the Amendment prohibits only intentional discrimination in voting. Congress could rationally have concluded that, because electoral changes by jurisdictions with a demonstrable history of intentional racial discrimination in voting create the risk of purposeful discrimination, it was proper to prohibit changes that have a discriminatory impact. We find no reason, then, to disturb Congress' considered judgment that banning electoral changes that have a discriminatory impact is an effective method of preventing States from "'undoing or defeating the rights recently won' by Negroes."

The judgment of the District Court is affirmed.

Justice REHNQUIST, with whom Justice STEWART joins, *dissenting.*

The facts of this case signal the necessity for this Court to carefully scrutinize the alleged source of congressional power to intrude so deeply in the governmental structure of the municipal corporations created by some of the 50 States. There are three theories of congressional enforcement power relevant to this case. First, it is clear that if the proposed changes would violate the Constitution, Congress could certainly prohibit their implementation. It has never been seriously maintained, however, that Congress can do no more than the judiciary to enforce the Amendments' commands. Thus, if the electoral changes in issue do not violate the Constitution, as judicially interpreted, it must be determined whether Congress could nevertheless appropriately prohibit these changes under the other two theories of congressional power. Under the second theory, Congress can act remedially to enforce the judicially established substantive prohibitions of the Amendments. If not properly remedial, the exercise of this power could be sustained only if this Court accepts the premise of the third theory that Congress has the authority under its enforcement powers to determine, without more, that electoral changes with a disparate impact on race violate the Constitution, in which case Congress by a legislative Act could effectively amend the Constitution.

Neither of the first two theories for sustaining the exercise of congressional power supports this application of the Voting Rights Act. The result reached by the Court today can be sustained only upon the theory that Congress was empowered to determine that structural changes with a disparate impact on a minority group's ability to elect a candidate of their race violates the Fourteenth or Fifteenth Amendment. This construction of the Fourteenth Amendment was rejected in *The Civil Rights Cases*. The Court today fails to heed this prior precedent. To permit congressional power to prohibit the conduct challenged in this case requires state and local governments to cede far more of their powers to the Federal Government than the Civil War Amendments ever envisioned; and it requires the judiciary to cede far more of its power to interpret and enforce the Constitution than ever envisioned. The intrusion is all the more offensive to our constitutional system when it is recognized that the only values fostered are debatable assumptions about political theory which should properly be left to the local democratic process.

∾ PROBLEM: PRECLEARANCE ∾

Congress decides to extend the "preclearance" requirements of the Voting Rights Act of 1965, based on Section 2, the enforcement provision of the Fifteenth Amendment, for another 25 years. The preclearance provisions, in Section 5 of the Act, require states to obtain federal permission before election procedures can be changed in those jurisdictions that have a history of minority voter disenfranchisement. Does Congress have the power to extend Section 5 of the Act if there is currently no evidence of voter disenfranchisement or any other unconstitutional voting rights deprivations? Can Congress justify the extension if there is a credible argument that the Act will deter future violations? *See Northwest Austin Municipal Utility District Number One v. Holder,* 557 U.S. 193 (2009). Do the voting rights enforcement cases parallel the enforcement of the Fourteenth Amendment cases, such as the sample problems *Second Floor* and *Critical Confinement* above?

4. *Religious Freedom and Congressional Fourteenth Amendment Enforcement Power*

City of Boerne v. Flores

521 U.S. 507 (1997)

KENNEDY, J.

A local zoning authority's denial to a church of a building permit was challenged under the Religious Freedom Restoration Act of 1993. The case calls into question the authority of Congress to enact RFRA. We conclude the statute exceeds Congress' power.

Congress enacted RFRA in direct response to the Court's decision in *Employment Div., Dept. of Human Resources of Ore. v. Smith.* There, we considered a Free Exercise Clause claim brought by members of the Native American Church who were denied unemployment benefits when they lost their jobs because they had used peyote. Many in Congress criticized the Court's reasoning, and this disagreement resulted in the passage of RFRA.

RFRA prohibits "government" from "substantially burdening" a person's exercise of religion even if the burden results from a rule of general applicability unless the government can demonstrate the burden "(1) is in furtherance of a compelling governmental interest; and (2) is the least restrictive means of furthering that compelling governmental interest." §2000bb-1.

Congress relied on its Fourteenth Amendment enforcement power in enacting the most far reaching and substantial of RFRA's provisions, those which impose its requirements on the States. The parties disagree over whether RFRA is a proper exercise of Congress' §5 power "to enforce" by "appropriate legislation" the constitutional guarantee that no State shall deprive any person of "life, liberty, or property, without due process of law" nor deny any person "equal protection of the laws."

In defense of the Act respondent contends that RFRA is permissible enforcement legislation. Congress is only protecting one of the liberties guaranteed by the Fourteenth Amendment's Due Process Clause, the free exercise of religion, beyond what is necessary under *Smith.* It is said the congressional decision to dispense with proof of deliberate or overt discrimination and instead concentrate on a law's effects accords with the settled understanding that §5 includes the power to enact legislation designed to prevent as well as remedy constitutional violations. It is further contended that Congress' §5 power is not limited to remedial or preventive legislation.

"As broad as the congressional enforcement power is, it is not unlimited." *Oregon v. Mitchell.* In assessing the breadth of §5's enforcement power, we begin with its text. Congress has been given the power "to enforce" the "provisions of this article." We agree with respondent, of course, that Congress can enact legislation under §5 enforcing the constitutional right to the free exercise of religion.

Congress' power under §5, however, extends only to "enforcing" the provisions of the Fourteenth Amendment. The Court has described this power as "remedial," *South Carolina v. Katzenbach.* The design of the Amendment and the text of §5 are inconsistent with the suggestion that Congress has the power to decree the substance of the Fourteenth Amendment's restrictions on the States. Legislation which alters the meaning of the Free Exercise Clause cannot be said to be enforcing the Clause. Congress does not enforce a constitutional right by changing what the right is. It has been given the power "to enforce," not the power to determine what constitutes a constitutional violation. Were it not so, what Congress would be enforcing would no longer be, in any meaningful sense, the "provisions of the Fourteenth Amendment."

While the line between measures that remedy or prevent unconstitutional actions and measures that make a substantive change in the governing law is not easy to discern, and Congress must have wide latitude in determining where it lies, the distinction exists and must be observed. There must be a congruence and proportionality between the injury to be prevented or remedied and the means adopted to that end. Lacking such a connection, legislation may become substantive in operation and effect. History and our case law support drawing the distinction, one apparent from the text of the Amendment.

The Fourteenth Amendment's history confirms the remedial, rather than substantive, nature of the Enforcement Clause. The design of the Fourteenth Amendment has proved significant also in maintaining the traditional separation of powers between Congress and the Judiciary. The first eight Amendments to the Constitution set forth self-executing prohibitions on governmental action, and this Court has had primary authority to interpret those prohibitions. As enacted, the Fourteenth Amendment, Section 1, confers substantive rights against the States which, like the provisions of the Bill of Rights, are self-executing. The power to interpret the Constitution in a case or controversy remains in the Judiciary.

The remedial and preventive nature of Congress' enforcement power, and the limitation inherent in the power, were confirmed in our earliest cases on the Fourteenth Amendment. *Civil Rights Cases.* Although the specific holdings of these early cases might have been superseded or modified, *see, e.g., Heart of Atlanta Motel, Inc. v. United States; United States v. Guest,* their treatment of Congress' §5 power as corrective or preventive, not definitional, has not been questioned.

Any suggestion that Congress has a substantive, non-remedial power under the Fourteenth Amendment is not supported by our case law. There is language in our opinion in *Katzenbach v. Morgan,* which could be interpreted as acknowledging a power in Congress to enact legislation that expands the rights contained in §1 of the Fourteenth Amendment. This is not a necessary interpretation, however, or even the best one. The Court perceived a factual basis on which Congress could have concluded that New York's literacy requirement "constituted an invidious discrimination in violation of the Equal Protection Clause." As Justice Stewart explained in *Oregon v. Mitchell,* interpreting *Morgan* to give Congress the power to interpret the Constitution "would require an enormous extension of that decision's rationale."

If Congress could define its own powers by altering the Fourteenth Amendment's meaning, no longer would the Constitution be "superior paramount law, unchangeable by ordinary means." It would be "on a level with ordinary legislative acts, and, like other acts, alterable when the legislature shall please to alter it." Marbury v. Madison. Under this approach, it is difficult to conceive of a principle that would limit congressional power. Shifting legislative majorities could change the Constitution and effectively circumvent the difficult and detailed amendment process contained in Article V.

We now turn to consider whether RFRA can be considered enforcement legislation under §5 of the Fourteenth Amendment. Respondent contends that RFRA is a proper exercise of Congress' remedial or preventive power. If Congress can prohibit laws with discriminatory effects in order to prevent racial discrimination in violation of the Equal Protection Clause, *see Fullilove v. Klutznick* (plurality opinion); *City of Rome,* then it can do the same, respondent argues, to promote religious liberty.

While preventive rules are sometimes appropriate remedial measures, there must be a congruence between the means used and the ends to be achieved. The appropriateness of remedial measures must be considered in light of the evil presented. Strong measures appropriate to address one harm may be an unwarranted response to another, lesser one.

A comparison between RFRA and the Voting Rights Act is instructive. In contrast to the record which confronted Congress and the judiciary in the voting rights cases, RFRA's legislative record lacks examples of modern instances of generally applicable laws passed because of religious bigotry. The history of persecution in this country detailed in the hearings mentions no episodes occurring in the past 40 years. It is difficult to maintain that the evidence presented in legislative hearings are examples of legislation enacted or enforced due to animus or hostility to the burdened religious practices or that they indicate some widespread pattern of religious discrimination in this country. This lack of support in the legislative record, however, is not RFRA's most serious shortcoming. Judicial deference, in most cases, is based not on the state of the legislative record Congress compiles but "on due regard for the decision of the body constitutionally appointed to decide." *Oregon v. Mitchell.* As a general matter, it is for Congress to determine the method by which it will reach a decision.

Regardless of the state of the legislative record, RFRA cannot be considered remedial, preventive legislation, if those terms are to have any meaning. RFRA is so out of proportion to a supposed remedial or preventive object that it cannot be understood as responsive to, or designed to prevent, unconstitutional behavior. It appears, instead, to attempt a substantive change in constitutional protections. Preventive measures prohibiting certain types of laws may be appropriate when there is reason to believe that many of the laws affected by the congressional enactment have a significant likelihood of being unconstitutional. Remedial legislation under §5 "should be adapted to the mischief and wrong which the Fourteenth Amendment was intended to provide against." *Civil Rights Cases.*

RFRA is not so confined. Sweeping coverage ensures its intrusion at every level of government, displacing laws and prohibiting official actions of almost every description and regardless of subject matter. RFRA's restrictions apply to every agency and official of the Federal, State, and local Governments. RFRA applies to all federal and state law, statutory or otherwise, whether adopted before or after its enactment. RFRA has no termination date or termination mechanism. Any law is subject to challenge at any time by any individual who alleges a substantial burden on his or her free exercise of religion.

The stringent test RFRA demands of state laws reflects a lack of proportionality or congruence between the means adopted and the legitimate end to be achieved. If an objector can show a substantial burden on his free exercise, the State must demonstrate a compelling governmental interest and show that the law is the least restrictive means of furthering its interest. Claims that a law substantially burdens someone's exercise of religion will often be difficult to contest. Requiring a State to demonstrate a compelling interest and show that it has adopted the least restrictive means of achieving that interest is the most demanding test known to constitutional law. If " 'compelling interest' really means what it says many laws will not meet the test. The test would open the prospect of constitutionally required religious exemptions from civic obligations of almost every conceivable kind." This is a considerable congressional intrusion into the States' traditional prerogatives and general authority to regulate for the health and welfare of their citizens.

The substantial costs RFRA exacts, both in practical terms of imposing a heavy litigation burden on the States and in terms of curtailing their traditional general regulatory power, far exceed any pattern or practice of unconstitutional conduct under the Free Exercise Clause as interpreted in *Smith*. Simply put, RFRA is not designed to identify and counteract state laws likely to be unconstitutional because of their treatment of religion. RFRA was designed to control cases and controversies, such as the one before us; but as the provisions of the federal statute here invoked are beyond congressional authority, it is this Court's precedent, not RFRA, which must control.

It is for Congress in the first instance to "determine whether and what legislation is needed to secure the guarantees of the Fourteenth Amendment," and its conclusions are entitled to much deference. *Katzenbach v. Morgan*. Congress' discretion is not unlimited, however, and the courts retain the power to determine if Congress has exceeded its authority under the Constitution. Broad as the power of Congress is under the Enforcement Clause of the Fourteenth Amendment, RFRA contradicts vital principles necessary to maintain separation of powers and the federal balance. The judgment of the Court of Appeals sustaining the Act's constitutionality is reversed.

It is so ordered.

∾ PROBLEMS ∾

1. *The Boerne Supremacy.* Assume that Congress decides after the *City of Boerne* decision that Section 1 of the Thirteenth Amendment prohibits states from engaging in the practice of enticing unpaid interns to work at state offices with the expectation that the internship might lead to paid employment. Congress views such internships as "involuntary servitude." If the courts disagree with Congress's position, is Congress's conclusion at all relevant to the Court's determination of what constitutes a violation of Section 1? Explain.

2. *Creating Individual Remedies.* In *Fitzpatrick v. Bitzer*, 427 U.S. 445 (1976), the Court held that Congress could use the power granted to it under the Fourteenth Amendment to create individual remedies against the states. Has *Fitzpatrick* been overruled?

[Points to Remember for Chapter 2 is contained in online file.]

3

The Federal Executive Powers

U.S. CONSTITUTION, ARTICLE II

Section 1. The executive Power shall be vested in a President of the United States of America. He shall hold his Office during the Term of four Years, and, together with the Vice President, chosen for the same Term, be elected.

Section 1, Clause 5. No person except a natural born Citizen, or a Citizen of the United States, at the time of the Adoption of this Constitution, shall be eligible to the Office of President; neither shall any person be eligible to that Office who shall not have attained to the Age of thirty five Years, and been fourteen Years a Resident within the United States.

Section 2. The President shall be Commander in Chief of the Army and Navy of the United States, and of the Militia of the several States, when called into the actual Service of the United States; he may require the Opinion, in writing, of the principal Officer in each of the executive Departments, upon any Subject relating to the Duties of their respective Offices, and he shall have Power to Grant Reprieves and Pardons for Offences against the United States, except in Cases of Impeachment. He shall have Power, by and with the Advice and Consent of the Senate, to make Treaties, provided two thirds of the Senators present concur; and he shall nominate, and by and with the Advice and Consent of the Senate, shall appoint Ambassadors, other public Ministers and Consuls, Judges of the Supreme Court, and all other Officers of the United States, whose Appointments are not herein otherwise provided for, and which shall be established by Law: but the Congress may by Law vest the Appointment of such inferior Officers, as they think proper, in the President alone, in the Courts of Law, or in the Heads of Departments. The President shall have Power to fill up all Vacancies that may happen during the Recess of the Senate, by granting Commissions which shall expire at the End of their next Session.

Section 3. He shall from time to time give to the Congress Information on the State of the Union, and recommend to their Consideration such Measures as he shall judge necessary and expedient; he may, on extraordinary Occasions, convene both Houses, or either of them, and in Case of Disagreement between them, with Respect to the Time of Adjournment, he may adjourn them to such Time as he shall think proper; he shall receive Ambassadors and other public Ministers; he shall take Care that the Laws be faithfully executed, and shall Commission all the Officers of the United States.

Section 4. The President, Vice President and all Civil Officers of the United States, shall be removed from Office on Impeachment for and Conviction of, Treason, Bribery, or other high Crimes and Misdemeanors.

U.S. CONSTITUTION, TWELFTH AMENDMENT

The person having the greatest number of votes for President, shall be the President, if such number be a majority of the whole number of electors appointed.

[Roadmap for Chapter 3 is contained in online file.]

∾ PROBLEM: NO DRILLING ZONES ∾

The President decides that no oil, gas, or mineral exploration should be allowed in certain public lands and sea areas, despite a law enacted by Congress four years earlier declaring those public lands "free and open" to oil exploration and purchase by private companies. In making this decision, the President concluded that he, as the chief executive, has an obligation to act in the public interest to save the natural state of these public places. The President bases the creation of "no drilling" zones on: 1) precedent—since early in the country's history, there have been more than 200 such presidential "withdrawal" orders in the face of contrary legislation; 2) preservation of the environment—the Deepwater Horizon oil rig explosion and leak into the Gulf of Mexico off the coast of Louisiana created an emergency the country can ill afford again; and 3) national security—the President has been informed that oil drilling on these lands is particularly susceptible to a terrorist attack and has had some intelligence that drilling operations will be infiltrated by Taliban sympathizers from the Middle East. Consequently, the President prepares to issue Executive Order 4049, which has two primary parts: a) no drilling or exploration for oil, natural gas, or other minerals that would upset the ecology and environment as defined by a series of benchmarks; and b) no entry into these lands, similar to the "no-fly" list, of certain persons, including those in this country unlawfully or with expired visas, within designated, publicized areas, with "knowing" violations to be subject to deportation, if applicable, and criminal penalties.

As you go through this chapter, you will be asked to serve as White House counsel and to advise the President about whether he has the power to take such action without the express authorization of Congress, or whether he can justify his actions on other grounds. You will also be asked to think about whether the President's creation of "no drilling zones" is subject to judicial review, and how it might be received by the courts.

EXECUTIVE POWERS BY THE NUMBERS

1. To become President, a majority of electors is required by the Twelfth Amendment. Given the current number of electors, 538, a person must receive the votes of at least 270 electors to become President.

2. A President can be elected twice or only once if he or she has served more than half of another President's term. See the Twenty-second Amendment.

3. A President must be at least 35 years of age, a resident of the United States for at least 14 years, and a natural born citizen.

4. The separation of powers doctrine, often used as a limit on executive action, is not mentioned anywhere in the Constitution. Instead, it is implied by the constitutional structure created by the Framers.

BACKGROUND
Who Was Our First President?

Most people are aware that the first President of the United States was George Washington, but some historians offer a footnote about John Hanson of Maryland, who was elected the first president of the Congress after the ratification of the Articles of Confederation, our first unifying Constitution. That document governed the 13 states from its ratification in 1781 through 1789, when it was replaced by the current Constitution. The Articles of Confederation were revised and essentially rewritten at the Constitutional Convention in Philadelphia in 1787, in no small measure because of the lack of an independent and fully functioning chief executive.

The chief executive of the United States, the President, might not earn as much money as other chief executives, especially those who toil in the private sector, but the President has an unparalleled job description. The President is the Commander in Chief of the U.S. armed forces, the diplomatic representative of the country, and the so-called "leader of the free world." In addition, unlike Article I of the Constitution, which vests legislative power in a bicameral Congress, the President is given the entirety of the Executive Branch's powers: "The Executive Power shall be vested in a President of the United States of America." U.S. CONST. art. II, §1.

Even though the Framers vested all executive power in a single person, it is debatable whether the Framers intended for the President to exercise far-ranging powers. After the Revolutionary War, it was logical to expect the colonists to viscerally move away from a strong central government for fear of replicating British rule. Indeed, in the years following the Declaration of Independence, the reaction of the new Americans against the strong grip of colonial British governors led to weak chief executives in most state constitutions and the national Articles of Confederation alike. *See* DANIEL A. FARBER AND SUZANNA SHERRY, A HISTORY OF THE AMERICAN CONSTITUTION 79-80 (West 1990). In the nascent days of America, then, the pendulum of centralized executive power had swung far in the other direction—too far, at least, for those who distrusted the Legislative Branch, a beneficiary of many of the powers stripped from the executive. With the distrust of executive governance increasingly tempered by the disarray caused by a weak centralized government, the U.S. Constitution replaced the Articles of Confederation in March 1789 and forged a more neutral balance of powers. Despite the lack of transparency of the Framers' intent regarding the scope of Executive Branch powers, it could readily be argued based on the historical context that the Executive Branch was designed to play a forceful, if complementary, role in directing the nation.

A perspective that assists in understanding the contours of executive authority is the notion that many of the boundaries between the branches are not defined in the Constitution and have ebbed and flowed over time, particularly when the nation is at war or peace. Although the Judicial Branch has set some of the boundaries, many are unsettled or indeterminate, such as where the President's Commander in Chief power ends and Congress's power to declare war begins. These areas, though, have found their way into the mainstream culture. Some of the most prominent issues have included the appointment of federal judges; the role of the President in domestic lawmaking, foreign affairs, and war; vetoes; and the scope of executive immunity and privilege. In fact, the President is likely to be in the center of the most vexing issues of the day, from the economy, to health care, to the conflicts in Iraq and Afghanistan.

A. IMPLIED PRESIDENTIAL POWERS

A recurring theme concerning the boundaries of executive power is whether the Constitution grants the President implied powers in addition to those enumerated in Article II. Judicial analysis has raised numerous questions, including: 1) If there are implied powers, what is the scope of those powers? and 2) If the President has implied powers, are those powers derived from the express powers in the Constitution, the inherent powers lying outside of the affirmative grant of powers in the Constitution, or both?

Of particular note in the debate over implied powers is the comparative treatment of such powers in Articles I and II. Article II lacks a clause authorizing the executive to exercise implied powers that are "necessary and proper" to carrying out his express powers. By contrast, Article I, Section 8, Clause 18 supplies Congress with the power to enact those laws "necessary and proper" to carrying out its express powers. As interpreted by Chief Justice John Marshall in *McCulloch v. Maryland*, 17 U.S. (4 Wheat.) 316 (1819), the Necessary and Proper Clause provides an affirmative recognition of implied legislative powers. Nevertheless, the President historically has chosen to assume that he possesses implied powers as well. For example, President George Washington issued a Proclamation of Neutrality when the United States was asked to take sides during the French Revolution. He issued the proclamation despite congressional inaction and lack of constitutional authorization. *See Youngstown Sheet & Tube Co. v. Sawyer*, 343 U.S.

579, 683-684 (1952) (Vinson, J., dissenting). Justice Vinson, in *Youngstown Sheet & Tube Co.*, offered additional examples of implied executive actions: "Without declaration of war, President Lincoln . . . summoned troops and paid them . . . proclaimed a naval blockade of the Confederacy and seized ships violating the blockade without prior Congressional approval." *Id.* at 685. Lincoln also suspended the writ of Habeas Corpus, even though the constitution creates this as an Article I, legislative power and not an Article II, executive power. He did so even over the admonition against doing so by Supreme Court Justice Taney. Further, President John Adams issued an arrest warrant for a person to promote the execution of a treaty.

One of the earliest illustrations of judicial recognition of implied executive powers can be found in *In re Neagle*, 135 U.S. 1 (1890). There, a federal marshal was assigned by the attorney general to protect a U.S. Supreme Court Justice following threats of harm to the Justice. When the assigned marshal succeeded in stopping an attack on the Justice and killing the attacker, the marshal was arrested and charged with murder on the basis that the attorney general did not have express constitutional authority to offer such protection. It appears the California authorities who initiated the arrest reasoned that the Constitution does not contain a "bodyguard power." The Supreme Court responded to the marshal's petition for habeas corpus by holding that an express constitutional authority to appoint a bodyguard was not required. Instead, the Court recognized an inherent power of the Executive Branch to assure the safety of the government, including the Supreme Court, arising out of its "take care" enforcement powers.

Several presidents, most notably Teddy Roosevelt, have argued that the President possesses a reservoir of implied powers. These arguments were both philosophical and pragmatic, related to the fact that presidents were required to deal with pressing and immediate international problems. The arguments centered around the Constitution's text—asserting that implied powers were not formally rejected by the text of the Constitution—and, on a much broader plane, policy that the President is the necessary leader of the country. President Roosevelt stated:

> My view was that every executive officer, and above all every executive officer in high position, was a steward to the people bound actively and affirmatively to do all he could for the people, and not to content himself with the negative merit of keeping his talents undamaged in a napkin. I declined to adopt the view that what was imperatively necessary for the Nation could not be done by the President unless he could find some specific authorization to do it. My belief was that it was not only his right but his duty to do anything that the needs of the Nation demanded unless such action was forbidden by the Constitution or by the laws. Under this interpretation of executive power I did and caused to be done many things not previously done by the President and the heads of the departments. I did not usurp power, but I did greatly broaden the use of executive power. In other words, I acted for the public welfare, I acted for the common well-being of all our people, whenever and in whatever manner was necessary, unless prevented by direct constitution or legislative prohibition.

THEODORE ROOSEVELT, THEODORE ROOSEVELT, AN AUTOBIOGRAPHY (vol. 20
of THE WORKS OF THEODORE ROOSEVELT, national ed.), chap. 10, 347-348
(Scribner's 1926).

∾ PROBLEMS ∾

1. *"The Little Rock 9."* After the decision in *Brown v. Board of Education*, 347 U.S.
483 (1954), several states decided to resist the directive to dismantle intentionally
segregated schools. In Arkansas, nine African American children signed up to
attend the all-white Little Rock High School for the 1956-1957 school year. The
state's strategy was to provide only half-hearted protection for the children, even
in the face of angry mobs. If Congress had not authorized the use of protective
force to protect the nine schoolchildren, could the President still provide protection from National Guard and Army troops in a matter concerning a single state
high school? For background, *see, e.g.,* J. WILLIAMS, EYES ON THE PRIZE: AMERICA'S
CIVIL RIGHTS YEARS, *1954–1965* (Penguin 1988).

2. *The Memorandum.* Assume that your assistant at the Office of Legal Counsel
writes a memorandum titled "Inherent Powers of the Executive Branch." The
memorandum states, in pertinent part, "The Executive has implied powers, independent of the positive grants provided in the Constitution, to protect its citizenry. This includes obtaining information about threats to the well-being of
the polity and individuals. In this century, combating terrorism requires use of
these inherent powers in several different ways, from rendition and aggressive
tactics used to extract information from terrorist captives to conducting warrantless searches in order to obtain foreign intelligence information. The Foreign
Intelligence Surveillance Act (FISA) cannot interfere with this inherent constitutional power." How would you critique the accuracy of the memorandum's evaluation of the constitutional power of the President? Explain.

BACKGROUND
Are There Inherent Executive Powers?

While most scholars do not believe the executive has broad or even any
inherent powers—although implied powers are a different story—there
have been some adherents of this view, including scholars tapped to serve
in recent administrations. The Foreign Intelligence Surveillance Court of
Review, in a *per curiam* opinion, wrote, "we take for granted that the President
does have inherent authority to conduct warrantless searches to obtain
foreign intelligence information and, assuming that is so, FISA (Foreign
Intelligence Surveillance Act) could not encroach on the President's constitutional power."

B. THE VOLATILE BOUNDARY BETWEEN EXECUTIVE AND
LEGISLATIVE POWERS: SEPARATION OF POWERS ISSUES

The interface between the powers of Congress and the powers of the President is one of the more volatile boundaries in American government and has given rise to many separation of powers issues. Conflicts have arisen in both the foreign and domestic policy arenas, with the residue of these conflicts creating accepted roles and traditions.

A scoreboard of sorts has resulted, with the courts tending to favor Congress's powers in domestic disputes and the President's powers in international disputes. This oversimplification does not explain the genius of the Constitution, which involves not a complete "separation of powers" but rather a weave of interdependent powers. Much like an assembly line that requires each component to function smoothly for the overall efficiency of the line, governance of the United States requires legislative action (bicameral approval and presentment to the President) as well as executive approval (veto power) and implementation (the Take Care Clause).

Many of the following cases represent conflicts between the branches of government, in which the executive, the legislature, and even the judiciary lay claim to legitimacy in the exercise of power. A significant subtext to these claims is formalism versus functionalism: Should the President, who is vested with the entire executive power under Article II, ever be limited by the other branches in exercising that power and controlling enforcement of the federal law, particularly in national security matters? This subtext is exemplified by today's debate about the unitary presidency: How extensive and strong are a President's powers under the Constitution?

The first case, *Youngstown Sheet & Tube Co. v. Sawyer*, 343 U.S. 579 (1952), provides a seminal illustration of the tensions that run the length of the boundaries between the Executive and Legislative branches. In that case, the Supreme Court mediated power claims by the President and Congress, illustrating the Supreme Court's vision of a domestic boundary between the two branches and, more pragmatically, how to avoid a stand-off between the President and Congress when tackling pressing domestic problems. Often called the *Steel Seizure Case*, it could be considered the "Power Seizure Case" instead, because President Truman believed expedient Executive Branch action required him to seize domestic power during the Korean War to avoid a steel strike and maintain the continuity of military operations in Korea. Congress apparently did not share the President's view of the necessity for action, especially action by the executive.

The issues in the case focused on whether the President had implied powers to act domestically without any purported authority from the Congress. The Court was faced with a variety of possible analytical approaches — that the President's conduct was justified by the "theater of war," by a more general "pressing public importance," by the "dormancy" of Congress, or was simply not justified at all.

As in many other Supreme Court cases, the context of *Youngstown Sheet &*
Tube Co. is important to the legal issues in the case. Prior to the time President
Truman took control of the major steel production plants in the United States,
steel was a significant ingredient in the creation of weapons supplying the war
effort in Korea. In the early 1950s, defense spending increased exponentially, with
much of it earmarked to fund the action in Korea. *See Youngstown Sheet & Tube Co.*,
343 U.S., at 671 (Vinson, J., dissenting). Steel was a very important commodity
in the defense effort. After the issues could not be resolved through negotiations, the President of the United Steelworkers called a general strike. The night
before the strike was to commence, Truman gave a radio address to the country
and then issued Executive Order 10340, authorizing the Secretary of Commerce,
Charles Sawyer, to take possession of and operate the steel mills. The President
stated in the Order that the threatened strike created "the existence of a national
emergency" because "steel is an indispensable component of substantially all of

President Truman announcing the seizure of the steel mills.

such weapons and materials." Because no labor settlement had been reached, "to assure the continued availability of steel and steel products during the existing emergency, it is necessary that the United States take possession of and operate the steel plants." Exec. Order No. 10340, 17 Fed. Reg. 3139 (1952).

Of the seven different opinions written in the case, Justice Jackson's classic concurrence has best withstood the test of time. Jackson's concurrence resonates with both scholars and pragmatists alike in capturing the dynamic nature of the boundaries between executive and legislative powers.

Youngstown Sheet & Tube Co. v. Sawyer

343 U.S. 579 (1952)

BLACK, J.

We are asked to decide whether President Truman was acting within his constitutional power when he issued an order directing the Secretary of Commerce Sawyer to take possession of and operate most of the Nation's steel mills. The mill owners argue that the President's order amounts to lawmaking, a legislative function which the Constitution has expressly confided to the Congress and not to the President. The Government's position is that the order was made on findings of the President that his action was necessary to avert a national catastrophe which would inevitably result from a stoppage of steel production, and that in meeting this grave emergency the President was acting within the aggregate of his constitutional powers as the Nation's Chief Executive and the Commander in Chief of the Armed Forces of the United States.

The issue emerges here from the following series of events: While the Korean War was occurring in the latter part of 1951, a dispute arose between the steel companies and their employees over terms and conditions that should be included in new collective bargaining agreements. Long-continued conferences failed to resolve the dispute. On December 18, 1951, the employees' representative, United Steelworkers of America, C.I.O., gave notice of an intention to strike when the existing bargaining agreements expired on December 31. On April 4, 1952, the Union gave notice of a nation-wide strike called to begin at 12:01 a.m. April 9. The indispensability of steel as a component of substantially all weapons and other war materials led the President to believe that the proposed work stoppage would immediately jeopardize our national defense and that governmental seizure of the steel mills was necessary in order to assure the continued availability of steel. Reciting these considerations for his action, the President, a few hours before the strike was to begin, issued Executive Order 10340. The order directed the Secretary of Commerce to take possession of most of the steel mills and keep them running. The Secretary immediately issued his own possessory orders, calling upon the presidents of the various seized companies to serve as operating managers for the United States. They were directed to carry on their activities in accordance with regulations and directions of the Secretary. The next morning the President sent a message to Congress reporting his action. Congress has taken no action. Obeying the Secretary's orders under protest, the companies brought proceedings against him in the District Court. Their complaints charged that the seizure was not authorized by an act of Congress or by any constitutional provisions. The District Court was asked to declare the orders of the President and the Secretary invalid and to issue preliminary and permanent injunctions restraining their enforcement. Opposing the motion for preliminary injunction, the United States asserted that a strike disrupting steel production for even a brief period would so endanger the well-being and safety of the Nation that the President had 'inherent power' to do what he had done—power "supported by the Constitution, by historical precedent, and by court decisions."

Two crucial issues have developed: First. Should final determination of the constitutional validity of the President's order be made in this case which has proceeded no further than the preliminary injunction stage? Second. If so, is the seizure order within the constitutional power of the President?

The President's power, if any, to issue the order must stem either from an act of Congress or from the Constitution itself. There is no statute that expressly authorizes the President to take possession of property as he did here. Nor is there any act of Congress to which our attention has been directed from which such a power can fairly be implied. Indeed, we do not understand the Government to rely on statutory authorization for this seizure.

Moreover, the use of the seizure technique to solve labor disputes in order to prevent work stoppages was not only unauthorized by any congressional enactment; prior to this controversy, Congress had refused to adopt that method of settling labor disputes.

The indispensability of steel as a component of substantially all weapons and other war materials led the President to believe that the proposed work stoppage would immediately jeopardize our national defense and that governmental seizure of the steel mills was necessary in order to assure the continued availability of steel. Reciting these considerations for his action, the President, a few hours before the strike was to begin, issued Executive Order 10340.

It is clear that if the President had authority to issue the order he did, it must be found in some provisions of the Constitution. And it is not claimed that express constitutional language grants this power to the President. The contention is that presidential power should be implied from the aggregate of his powers under the Constitution. Particular reliance is placed on provisions in Article II which says that "the executive Power shall be vested in a President"; that "he shall take Care that the Laws be faithfully executed"; and that he "shall be Commander in Chief of the Army and Navy of the United States."

The order cannot properly be sustained as an exercise of the President's military power as Commander in Chief of the Armed Forces. The Government attempts to do so by citing a number of cases upholding broad powers in military commanders engaged in day-to-day fighting in a theater of war. Such cases need not concern us here. Even though "theater of war" be an expanding concept, we cannot with faithfulness to our constitutional system hold that the Commander in Chief of the Armed Forces has the ultimate power as such to take possession of private property in order to keep labor disputes from stopping production. This is a job for the Nation's lawmakers, not for its military authorities.

Nor can the seizure order be sustained because of the several constitutional provisions that grant executive power to the President. In the framework of our Constitution, the President's power to see that the laws are faithfully executed refutes the idea that he is to be a lawmaker. The Constitution limits his functions in the lawmaking process to the recommending of laws he thinks wise and the vetoing of laws he thinks bad.

The President's order does not direct that a congressional policy be executed in a manner prescribed by Congress—it directs that a presidential policy be executed in a manner prescribed by the President. The power of Congress to adopt such public policies as those proclaimed by the order is beyond question. It can authorize the taking of private property for public use. It can make laws regulating the relationships between employers and employees, prescribing rules designed to settle labor disputes, and fixing wages and working conditions in certain fields of our economy. The Constitution did not subject this law-making power of Congress to presidential or military supervision or control.

It is said that other Presidents without congressional authority have taken possession of private business enterprises in order to settle labor disputes. But even if this be true, Congress has not thereby lost its exclusive constitutional authority to make laws necessary and proper to carry out the powers vested by the Constitution "in the Government of the United States, or in any Department or Officer thereof."

Even though "theater of war" be an expanding concept, we cannot with faithfulness to our constitutional system hold that the Commander in Chief of the Armed Forces has the ultimate power as such to take possession of private property in order to keep labor disputes from stopping production. This is a job for the Nation's lawmakers, not for its military authorities. In the framework of our Constitution, the President's power to see that the laws are faithfully executed refutes the idea that he is to be a lawmaker. The Constitution limits his functions in the lawmaking process to the recommending of laws he thinks wise and the vetoing of laws he thinks bad.

The Founders of this Nation entrusted the law-making power to the Congress alone in both good and bad times. It would do no good to recall the historical events, the fears of power and the hopes for freedom that lay behind their choice. Such a review would but confirm our holding that this seizure order cannot stand.

The judgment of the District Court is affirmed.

Mr. Justice JACKSON, *concurring* in the judgment and opinion of the Court.

That comprehensive and undefined presidential powers hold both practical advantages and grave dangers for the country will impress anyone who has served as legal adviser to a President in time of transition and public anxiety.

A judge, like an executive adviser, may be surprised at the poverty of really useful and unambiguous authority applicable to concrete problems of executive power as they actually present themselves. Just what our forefathers did envision, or would have envisioned had they foreseen modern conditions, must be divined from materials almost as enigmatic as the dreams Joseph was called upon to interpret for Pharaoh. A century and a half of partisan debate and scholarly speculation yields no net result but only supplies more or less apt quotations from respected sources on each side of any question.

Presidential powers are not fixed but fluctuate, depending upon their disjunction or conjunction with those of Congress. We may well begin by a somewhat over-simplified grouping of practical situations in which a President may doubt, or others may challenge his powers, and by distinguishing roughly the legal consequences of this factor of relativity.

1. When the President acts pursuant to an express or implied authorization of Congress, his authority is at its maximum, for it includes all that he possesses in his own right plus all that Congress can delegate. In these circumstances, and in these only, may he be said (for what it may be worth), to personify the federal sovereignty. If his act is held unconstitutional under these circumstances, it usually means that the Federal Government as an undivided whole lacks power. A seizure executed by the President pursuant to an Act of Congress would be supported by the strongest of presumptions and the widest latitude of judicial interpretation, and the burden of persuasion would rest heavily upon any who might attack it.

2. When the President acts in absence of either a congressional grant or denial of authority, he can only rely upon his own independent powers, but there is a zone of twilight in which he and Congress may have concurrent authority, or in which its distribution is uncertain. Therefore, congressional inertia, indifference or quiescence may sometimes, at least as a practical matter, enable, if not invite, measures on independent presidential responsibility. In this area, any actual test of power is likely to depend on the imperatives of events and contemporary imponderables rather than on abstract theories of law.

3. When the President takes measures incompatible with the expressed or implied will of Congress, his power is at its lowest ebb, for then he can rely only upon his own constitutional powers, minus any constitutional powers of Congress over the matter. Courts can sustain exclusive Presidential control in such a case only by disabling the Congress from acting upon the subject. Presidential claim to a power at once so conclusive and preclusive must be scrutinized with caution, for what is at stake is the equilibrium established by our constitutional system.

Into which of these classifications does this executive seizure of the steel industry fit? It is eliminated from the first by admission, for it is conceded that no congressional authorization exists for this seizure. That takes away also the support of the many precedents and declarations which made in relation, and must be confined, to this category.

Can it then be defended under flexible tests available to the second category? It seems clearly eliminated from that class because Congress has not left seizure of private property an open field but has covered it by three statutory policies inconsistent with this seizure. In cases where the purpose is to supply needs of the Government itself, two courses are provided: one, seizure of a plant which fails to comply with obligatory orders placed by the Government, another, condemnation of facilities, including temporary use under the power of eminent domain. The third is applicable where it is the general economy of the country that is to be protected rather than exclusive governmental interests. None of these were invoked.

This leaves the current seizure to be justified only by the severe tests under the third grouping, where it can be supported only by any remainder of executive power after subtraction of such powers as Congress may have over the subject. In short, we can sustain the President only by holding that seizure of such strike-bound industries is within his domain and beyond control by Congress. Thus, this Court's first review of such seizures occurs under circumstances which leave Presidential power most vulnerable to attack and in the least favorable of possible constitutional postures.

The clause on which the Government next relies is that "the President shall be Commander in Chief of the Army and Navy of the United States." These cryptic words have given rise to some of the most persistent controversies in our constitutional history.

Assuming that we are in a war de facto, whether it is or is not a war de jure, does that empower the Commander-in-Chief to seize industries he thinks necessary to supply our army? The Constitution expressly places in Congress power "to raise and support Armies" and "to provide and maintain a Navy." (Emphasis supplied.) This certainly lays upon Congress primary responsibility for supplying the armed forces. Congress alone controls the raising of revenues and their appropriation and may determine in what manner and by what means they shall be spent for military and naval procurement. I suppose no one would doubt that Congress can take over war supply as a Government enterprise.

But I have no illusion that any decision by this Court can keep power in the hands of Congress if it is not wise and timely in meeting its problems. A crisis that challenges the President equally, or perhaps primarily, challenges Congress. If not good law, there was worldly wisdom in the maxim attributed to Napoleon that "the tools belong to the man who can use them." We may say that power to legislate for emergencies belongs in the hands of Congress, but only Congress itself can prevent power from slipping through its fingers.

Mr. Justice CLARK, *concurring* in the judgment of the Court.

The limits of presidential power are obscure. However, Article II, no less than Article I, is part of "a constitution intended to endure for ages to come, and, consequently, to be adapted to the various crises of human affairs." Some of our Presidents, such as Lincoln, "felt that measures otherwise unconstitutional might become lawful by becoming indispensable to the preservation of the Constitution through the preservation of the nation." Others, such as Theodore

Roosevelt, thought the President to be capable, as a "steward" of the people, of exerting all power save that which is specifically prohibited by the Constitution or the Congress. In my view—taught me not only by the decision of Chief Justice Marshall in *Little v. Barreme*, 2 Cranch 170, 2 L.Ed. 243, but also by a score of other pronouncements of distinguished members of this bench—the Constitution does grant to the President extensive authority in times of grave and imperative national emergency. In fact, to my thinking, such a grant may well be necessary to the very existence of the Constitution itself. As Lincoln aptly said, "(is) it possible to lose the nation and yet preserve the Constitution?" In describing this authority I care not whether one calls it "residual," "inherent," "moral," "implied," "aggregate," "emergency," or otherwise. I am of the conviction that those who have had the gratifying experience of being the President's lawyer have used one or more of these adjectives only with the utmost of sincerity and the highest of purpose.

I conclude that where Congress has laid down specific procedures to deal with the type of crisis confronting the President, he must follow those procedures in meeting the crisis; but that in the absence of such action by Congress, the President's independent power to act depends upon the gravity of the situation confronting the nation.

Mr. Chief Justice VINSON, with whom Mr. Justice REED and Mr. Justice MINTON join, *dissenting*.

In passing upon the question of Presidential powers in this case, we must first consider the context in which those powers were exercised. Those who suggest that this is a case involving extraordinary powers should be mindful that these are extraordinary times. A world not yet recovered from the devastation of World War II has been forced to face the threat of another and more terrifying global conflict.

Congress also directed the President to build up our own defenses. Congress, recognizing the "grim fact that the United States is now engaged in a struggle for survival" and that "it is imperative that we now take those necessary steps to make our strength equal to the peril of the hour," granted authority to draft men into the armed forces. As a result, we now have over 3,500,000 men in our armed forces. One is not here called upon even to consider the possibility of executive seizure of a farm, a corner grocery store or even a single industrial plant. Such considerations arise only when one ignores the central fact of this case—that the Nation's entire basic steel production would have shut down completely if there had been no Government seizure. Even ignoring for the moment whatever confidential information the President may possess as "the Nation's organ for foreign affairs," the uncontroverted affidavits in this record amply support the finding that "a work stoppage would immediately jeopardize and imperil our national defense."

In passing upon the grave constitutional question presented, we must never forget, as Chief Justice Marshall admonished, that the Constitution is "intended to endure for ages to come, and consequently, to be adapted to the various crises of human affairs," and that "(i)ts means are adequate to its ends." Cases do arise presenting questions which could not have been foreseen by the Framers. In such cases, the Constitution has been treated as a living document adaptable to new situations. In 1941, President Roosevelt acted to protect Iceland from attack by Axis powers when British forces were withdrawn by sending our forces to occupy Iceland. Congress was informed of this action on the same day that our forces reached Iceland. The occupation of Iceland was but one of "at least 125 incidents" in our history in which Presidents, "without Congressional authorization, and in the absence of a declaration of war, have ordered the Armed Forces to take action or maintain positions abroad."

No basis for claims of arbitrary action, unlimited powers or dictatorial usurpation of congressional power appears. On the contrary, judicial, legislative and executive precedents throughout our history demonstrate that the President acted in full conformity with his duties under the Constitution. Accordingly, we would reverse the order of the District Court.

BACKGROUND
Justice Robert H. Jackson

Robert H. Jackson served as an Associate Justice on the Supreme Court from 1941 until 1954, shortly after *Brown v. Board of Education* was decided. He was a former attorney general and the lead prosecutor at the Nuremburg trials, taking a leave of absence from the Supreme Court to serve in this role. He also was the last Justice to be appointed to the Supreme Court without having graduated from a law school.

BACKGROUND
Justice Tom Clark

Justice Tom Clark served under President Harry Truman as his attorney general. This relationship did not interfere with Justice Clark's decision in *Youngstown Sheet & Tube Co.*, in light of the fact that Clark ruled against his former boss. *See* David McCulloch, *Truman* 896-902 (Touchstone 1992).

Case Postscript

After the Supreme Court declared the President's seizure of the steel mills unconstitutional, a strike indeed occurred. Shortly thereafter, however, by July 24, 1952, a settlement was reached, quelling the fear of a significant disruption in the steel supply. In announcing the settlement, President Truman stated that, "I was just advised that six major steel companies and the United Steel Workers of America (CIO) have reached agreement on important basic issues. The union is calling its National Wage Policy Committee to meet in Washington for the purpose of ratifying the agreement. This should lead to a speedy resumption of steel production." Statement by President Truman on the Settlement of the Steel Strike on July 24, 1952.

∽ PROBLEMS ∽

1. *Sailin' Away.* After significant deterioration of relations with France, Congress enacted a law authorizing the President to apprehend American ships "sailing to ports of call in France." In response to this law, five ships were detained, three of which were sailing to France and two from France. The ship captains who detained the five ships were sued. Did the President comply with the legislature's directive? What are the best arguments for both sides?

2. *Tariffs.* The President enters into an executive agreement with Canada concerning tariffs associated with the importation of certain vegetables. This international agreement between the President and Canada followed a law enacted by Congress providing for higher tariffs on the importation of the same vegetables. *See* 18 U.S.C. §2432. Can the President constitutionally lower the tariffs on the vegetables below the floor for tariffs set by Congress in its earlier law, 18 U.S.C. §2432? Explain.

3. *The President's Memorandum.* A Mexican national was convicted in Texas of gang rape and murder and given the death sentence. The petitioner appealed, claiming the state courts ignored a memorandum from the President describing his constitutional rights to include not only the *Miranda* warnings but also an opportunity to confer with the Mexican consulate based on a prior treaty. The President had issued the memorandum in question stating that pursuant to a treaty, a decision by the International Court of Justice requires state courts to first inform the defendants of their right to contact their embassy concerning their detention prior to their conviction or else the United States will provide reconsideration. The President's use of a treaty to create domestic law was not supported by an enabling statute enacted by Congress, and the treaty did not state it was "self-executing" as domestic law. Can the President, through the memorandum, unilaterally make the treaty apply domestically? Why or why not? *See Medellin v. Texas,* 552 U.S. 491 (2008).

4. *Whalers.* To combat world whaling practices, Congress enacts a law giving the President the discretionary power to refuse entry into the United States of any fish products from countries that fail to follow international whaling limits. The law was designed to protect the world's whales through an indirect sanctioning system, particularly the aggressive whaling practiced by Japanese fishermen. While whaling violations were documented after the enactment

of the law, especially by Japan, the President used his discretion to do nothing, and suit was filed claiming the President did not follow the law to protect whales internationally. a) Is this challenge a question of foreign relations — specifically, Japan's whaling practices — and consequently a nonjusticiable political question? b) If the question is justiciable, did the President properly enforce the law? c) Assume Congress amended the law to remove all of the President's discretion in enforcing the law. If the President still refuses to exclude any fish products from importation, how should a court rule on this issue?

5. *No Drilling Zones.* In the introductory problem at the beginning of the chapter, if the Supreme Court upheld the President's creation of no drilling zones under *Youngstown Sheet & Tube Co.*, what is the most likely rationale of the Court? Do you agree with that rationale? Explain.

C. ADDITIONAL SEPARATION OF POWERS ISSUES

Interactions among the legislature, the executive, and the courts often involve "separation of powers" issues. These questions concern more than the literal separation of branches and often involve either the interdependence or usurpation of powers.

Separation of powers problems can be compartmentalized either as one branch of government delegating powers to a coordinate branch of government or administrative agencies, or as one branch of government taking powers away from another branch of government. Delegation of powers questions generally arise from the doctrine prohibiting one branch of government from sharing its powers with other branches or administrative agencies. "Power grabs" by one branch from another arise in certain contexts — namely, veto, appointment, and removal situations.

While the separation of powers doctrine is universally recognized as a bedrock constitutional doctrine, it cannot be found anywhere in the text of the Constitution. Scholars and pragmatists alike infer the doctrine from the structural framework of the first three Articles, which divide the powers of government among three well-defined branches. The lack of textual recognition, however, has contributed to the doctrine's imprecise purpose and reach, with its invocation having a wide variety of meanings, often dependent on the branch that is doing the invoking and in consideration of circumstances in which the dispute arose. *See, e.g.,* Gerhard Casper, *An Essay in Separation of Powers: Some Early Versions and Practices,* 30 WM. & MARY L. REV. 211 (1989).

There is as much evidence of the Constitution's efforts to intertwine the powers of the three branches as there is to keep them sequestered or buffered. *See, e.g.,* Philip Kurland, *The Rise and Fall of the Doctrine of Separation of Powers,* 85 MICH. L. REV. 592 (1986). For example, treaties require both presidential and Senate action. Legislation requires the approval of the President, unless two thirds of the Congress overrides the President's veto. In a now-famous passage from *Youngstown Sheet & Tube Co. v. Sawyer*, 343 U.S. 579 (1952), Justice Jackson declared: "While the Constitution diffuses power the better to secure liberty, it also contemplates that practice will integrate the dispersed powers into a workable government. It enjoins upon its branches a separateness but interdependence, autonomy but reciprocity." Thus, instead of a hermetically sealed lining between the branches, the separation of powers doctrine creates "a carefully crafted system of checked and balanced power within each Branch to avoid tyranny in a Branch." *Mistretta v. United States*, 488 U.S. 361, 381 (1989). The three branches are like the legs on a three-legged stool, "each leg must be approximately the same length if the stool is not to tip over." *Id.*

1. The "Nondelegation" of Powers Doctrine

The "nondelegation" of powers doctrine is potentially applicable when one branch of government (usually Congress) attempts to delegate its powers directly to another branch or to an administrative agency in another branch. The courts have held in some instances that such delegations are unconstitutional in violation of the separation of powers doctrine. The doctrine has been strongly influenced by historical developments.

As you may recall from Chapter 2, during the 1930s the nation suffered through the Great Depression. When President Franklin Roosevelt was elected on the promise of a "New Deal," Congress enacted an array of bills designed to pull the country out of the economic malaise. The Court began to question how much power Congress could delegate to administrative agencies. Important questions were involved. At what point did Congress delegate its own lawmaking function and not just leave "the details" to agency determination or, conversely, usurp the powers vested in another branch? The answers were left to the courts and the courts' contours of the nondelegation doctrine.

The courts were faced with a dilemma, however. The framework of nondelegation was not expressly contained in the Constitution and was left to judicial interpretation through precedent, the Framers' intent, and pragmatism. While pragmatic justifications for delegation were apparent, whether the courts would uphold the doctrine against a formalistic constitutional challenge was not.

The doctrine reached its apex in 1935, when the Court struck down two statutes as unconstitutional delegations of power. The cases of *A.L.A. Schecter Poultry Corp. v. United States*, 295 U.S. 495 (1935), and *Panama Refining Co. v. Ryan*, 293 U.S. 388 (1935), stood for the proposition that delegation without sufficient standards for implementing congressional policy—without an "intelligible principle to which the person or body authorized to exercise the delegated authority is directed to conform," *J.W. Hampton, Jr., & Co. v. United States*, 276 U.S. 394 (1928)—was unconstitutional.

Since 1935, the nondelegation doctrine has retained its formal status but has lost most of its teeth. The demise of the doctrine, coupled with the Court's expanded interpretation of the Commerce Clause (which, as we know from Chapter 2, also resulted from the constitutional crisis of the 1930s), led to a dramatic expansion of the size and scope of the federal government. Because of the change in the Court's Commerce Clause jurisprudence, Congress was able to assume control over even larger parts of the nation and the economy. Likewise, as it became possible for Congress to delegate more and more power to administrative agencies, Congress began to create large federal bureaucracies. The net effect of these developments was a significant increase in the number of federal administrative agencies, including such entities as the Federal Aviation Administration, the Internal Revenue Service, the Federal Communications Commission, and the Environmental Protection Agency, which were charged with refining and implementing the government agenda. In addition, those agencies began to promulgate lots of regulations. Indeed, Congress began to articulate legislation in broad terms, and essentially left it to agencies to fill in the broad outlines of the regulation. As the Supreme Court observed: "In an increasingly complex society, Congress obviously could not perform its functions if it were obliged to find all the facts subsidiary to the basic conclusions which support the defined legislative policy."

The complete demise of the nondelegation doctrine, however, is premature, since it still retains vitality as a limit, especially on legislative action. As noted by Justice Breyer, "The 'nondelegation' doctrine represents an added constitutional check upon Congress's authority to delegate power to the Executive Branch." *Clinton v. New York*, 524 U.S. 417, 484 (1998) (dissenting opinion). Many of the cases in the following sections, while labeled "appointments" or "removal" or "veto" issues, also could be viewed through the prism of nondelegation.

In *Buckley v. Valeo*, 424 U.S. 1 (1976), a case involving freedom of speech and separation of powers challenges to the Federal Election Campaign Act of 1971, 2 U.S.C. §§431 *et seq.*, the Supreme Court struck down provisions of the Act that restructured the Federal Election Commission. The Court found that Congress had appropriated executive powers to itself by creating a commission with rule-making and enforcement powers, while at the same time reserving the appointment power for four of the eight commission members to certain officers of Congress alone. Although the Court held that the provisions violated the Appointments Clause, the violation that occurred could be viewed as the improper delegation of powers from one branch to another. The Court noted:

> Insofar as the powers confided in the Commission are essentially of an investigative and informative nature, falling in the same general category as those powers which Congress

might delegate to one of its own committees, there can be no question that the Commission as presently constituted may exercise them. But when we go beyond this type of authority to the more substantial powers exercised by the Commission, we reach a different result. The Commission's enforcement power, exemplified by its discretionary power to seek judicial relief, is authority that cannot possibly be regarded as merely in aid of the legislative function of Congress.

In *Mistretta v. United States*, 488 U.S. 361 (1989), the Supreme Court considered another nondelegation question, this time involving the constitutionality of the sentencing guidelines created by the U.S. Sentencing Commission. The commission was instituted by Congress in the Sentencing Reform Act of 1984. In upholding the creation of the commission and the guidelines against a separation of powers challenge, Justice Blackmun, for the Court, justified the porous nature of the modern doctrine by alluding to the pragmatic importance of delegation. He wrote:

The nondelegation doctrine is rooted in the principle of separation of powers that underlies our tripartite system of Government. The Constitution provides that "all legislative Powers herein granted shall be vested in a Congress of the United States," U.S. Const., Art. I, §1, and we long have insisted that "the integrity and maintenance of the system of government ordained by the Constitution" mandate that Congress generally cannot delegate its legislative power to another Branch. *Field v. Clark*, 143 U.S. 649, 692 (1892). In a passage now enshrined in our jurisprudence, Chief Justice Taft, writing for the Court, explained our approach to such cooperative ventures: "In determining what Congress may do in seeking assistance from another branch, the extent and character of that assistance must be fixed according to common sense and the inherent necessities of the government co-ordination." *J.W. Hampton, Jr., & Co. v. United States*, 276 U.S. 394, 406 (1928). So long as Congress "shall lay down by legislative act an intelligible principle to which the person or body authorized to exercise the delegated authority is directed to conform, such legislative action is not a forbidden delegation of legislative power." *Id.*, at 409. Applying this "intelligible principle" test to congressional delegations, our jurisprudence has been driven by a practical understanding that in our increasingly complex society, replete with ever changing and more technical problems, Congress simply cannot do its job absent an ability to delegate power under broad general directives. *See Opp Cotton Mills, Inc. v. Administrator*, 312 U.S. 126 (1941).

In light of our approval of these broad delegations, we harbor no doubt that Congress's delegation of authority to the Sentencing Commission is sufficiently specific and detailed to meet constitutional requirements.

Congress provided even more detailed guidance to the Commission about categories of offenses and offender characteristics. Congress directed that guidelines require a term of confinement at or near the statutory maximum for certain crimes of violence.

Developing proportionate penalties for hundreds of different crimes by a virtually limitless array of offenders is precisely the sort of intricate, labor-intensive task for which delegation to an expert body is especially appropriate. Although Congress has delegated significant discretion to the Commission to draw judgments from its analysis of existing sentencing practice and alternative sentencing models, "Congress is not confined to that method of executing its policy which involves the least possible delegation of discretion to administrative officers." *Yakus v. United States*, 321 U.S. at 425-426.

<h2 align="center">∾ PROBLEMS ∾</h2>

1. *Delegation of Authority to Regulate Organic Products.* Congress enacts a law providing for the regulation of organic products in the United States, mandating different labels for distinctive methods of farming or, in the case of animal products, feeding. In part of the law, Congress directs the U.S. Department of Agriculture "to create uniform and effective standards by which to further categorize the products sold, including the nature and substance of federal seals affixed to each of the products." Does this legislation violate the nondelegation doctrine? Explain.

2. *D.C. National Airport Governance.* Congress seeks smoother ingress and egress to Reagan Washington National Airport, which lies just across the Potomac River and minutes away from Washington, D.C. To this end, it enacts a law, "D.C. National Airport Governance," that creates a congressional subcommittee to oversee and operate the airport. The subcommittee would consist of ten members of Congress, five from each house, who would supervise the operation of the airport, including parking, security, personnel, and most other governance decisions. Is this subcommittee constitutional? *See Metropolitan Washington Airport Authority v. Citizens for Abatement of Aircraft Noise, Inc.,* 501 U.S. 252 (1991).

3. *Farm Subsidies.* Congress, after observing the increasing competition American farmers face from farmers in other countries, enacts a protectionist law. The law provides that any American farmer who goes bankrupt and has been the subject of a judgment regarding the payment of creditors can petition a special congressional committee drawn equally from each house for redress. The committee has been given the power to reduce the creditor payments and make a more favorable resolution for the bankrupt farmer. Is this law constitutional? Explain.

4. *Unreviewable Discretion.* Congress entered into the United States–China Relations Act in 2006, a wide-ranging trade agreement. Section 421 gave the President discretion to increase tariffs on Chinese imports if "market disruptions" occur. An American business that imported devices modifying the heights of wheelchairs and motorized scooters, Skootr, Inc., brought suit, claiming that the increased tariffs on scooter and wheelchair imports unilaterally imposed by the President due to an alleged market disruption were unconstitutional. How should a court rule?

2. The Veto Power

The veto power vested in the President is described in the Constitution as the "disapproval" of legislation: "Every Order, Resolution or Vote to which the Concurrence of the Senate and House of Representatives may be necessary (except on a question of Adjournment) shall be presented to the President of the United States; and before the Same shall take Effect, shall be approved by him, or being disapproved by him, shall be repassed by two thirds of the Senate and House of Representatives." Art. I, §7, cl. 3. Constitutional veto issues have arisen in two distinct contexts. One context involved the so-called "legislative veto," exercised by Congress or one of its two houses. The other involved the so-called "line item veto," exercised by the President. These veto contexts raise issues about who has the final say on legislation and whether any of the legislative powers can be held in reserve, like a rebuttal in an oral argument.

a. The Legislative Veto

Can Congress reserve a form of veto power to itself in otherwise properly enacted legislation? This is not merely an academic question. As noted by Justice Powell in his concurrence in the following case, *Immigration and Naturalization Service v. Chadha,* 462 U.S. 919 (1983), "Congress has included the veto in literally hundreds of statutes, dating back to the 1930s."

BACKGROUND
A Legislative Veto That Paved the Way of Note

One of the most significant legislative vetoes occurred in 1932, when President Herbert Hoover agreed with Congress that legislation giving the President the power to reconfigure part of the Executive Branch could be subject to a congressional override by either the House of Representatives or the Senate. After this pragmatic arrangement was rolled out, many subsequent laws contained similar veto provisions.

Immigration and Naturalization Service v. Chadha

462 U.S. 919 (1983)

Chief Justice BURGER delivered the opinion of the Court.

We granted certiorari to consider the constitutionality of §244(c)(2) of the Immigration and Naturalization Act, which authorized one house of Congress to invalidate the decision of the Executive Branch.

Chadha is an East Indian who was born in Kenya and holds a British passport. He was lawfully admitted to the United States in 1966 on a nonimmigrant student visa. His visa expired on June 30, 1972. On October 11, 1973, the District Director of the Immigration and Naturalization Service ordered Chadha to show cause why he should not be deported for having "remained in the United States for a longer time than permitted." Pursuant to §242(b) of the Immigration and Nationality Act (Act), 8 U.S.C. §1252(b), a deportation hearing was held before an immigration judge on January 11, 1974. Chadha conceded that he was deportable for overstaying his visa and the hearing was adjourned to enable him to file an application for suspension of deportation under §244(a)(1) of the Act, 8 U.S.C. §1254(a)(1). The immigration judge found that Chadha met the requirements of §244(a)(1): he had resided continuously in the United States for over seven years, was of good moral character, and would suffer "extreme hardship" if deported. Pursuant to §244(c)(1) of the Act, 8 U.S.C. §1254(c)(1), the immigration judge suspended Chadha's deportation and a report of the suspension was transmitted to Congress.

On December 12, 1975, Representative Eilberg, Chairman of the Judiciary Subcommittee on Immigration, Citizenship, and International Law, introduced a resolution opposing "the granting of permanent residence in the United States to six aliens," including Chadha. The resolution was passed without debate or recorded vote. Since the House action was pursuant to §244(c)(2), the resolution was not treated as an Article I legislative act; it was not submitted to the Senate or presented to the President for his action. After the House veto of the Attorney General's decision to allow Chadha to remain in the United States, the immigration judge reopened the deportation proceedings to implement the House order deporting Chadha. Chadha moved to terminate the proceedings on the ground that §244(c)(2) is unconstitutional.

We granted certiorari and turn now to the question whether action of one House of Congress under §244(c)(2) violates strictures of the Constitution. We begin, of course, with the presumption that the challenged statute is valid. Its wisdom is not the concern of the courts; if a challenged action does not violate the Constitution, it must be sustained.

Justice White undertakes to make a case for the proposition that the one-House veto is a useful "political invention" and we need not challenge that assertion.

The Presentment Clauses. The records of the Constitutional Convention reveal that the requirement that all legislation be presented to the President before becoming law was uniformly accepted by the Framers.

The decision to provide the President with a limited and qualified power to nullify proposed legislation by veto was based on the profound conviction of the Framers that the powers conferred on Congress were the powers to be most carefully circumscribed.

The President's role in the lawmaking process also reflects the Framers' careful efforts to check whatever propensity a particular Congress might have to enact oppressive, improvident, or ill-considered measures.

Bicameralism. The bicameral requirement of Art. I, §1, cl. 7 was of scarcely less concern to the Framers than was the Presidential veto and indeed the two concepts are interdependent. Beginning with this presumption, we must nevertheless establish that the challenged action under §244(c)(2) is of the kind to which the procedural requirements of Art. I, §7 apply. Not every action taken by either House is subject to the bicameralism and presentment requirements of Art. I.

The legislative character of the one-House veto in this case is confirmed by the character of the Congressional action it supplants. Neither the House of Representatives nor the Senate contends that, absent the veto provision in §244(c)(2), either of them, or both of them acting together, could effectively require the Attorney General to deport an alien once the Attorney General, in the exercise of legislatively delegated authority, had determined the alien should remain in the United States.

The nature of the decision implemented by the one-House veto in this case further manifests its legislative character. After long experience with the clumsy, time consuming private bill procedure, Congress made a deliberate choice to delegate to the Executive Branch, and specifically to the Attorney General, the authority to allow deportable aliens to remain in this country in certain specified circumstances.

Finally, we see that when the Framers intended to authorize either House of Congress to act alone and outside of its prescribed bicameral legislative role, they narrowly and precisely defined the procedure for such action. There are but four provisions in the Constitution, explicit and unambiguous, by which one House may act alone with the unreviewable force of law, not subject to the President's veto: (a) The House of Representatives alone was given the power to initiate impeachments. Art. I, §2, cl. 6; (b) The Senate alone was given the power to conduct trials following impeachment on charges initiated by the House and to convict following trial. Art. I, §3, cl. 5; (c) The Senate alone was given final unreviewable power to approve or to disapprove presidential appointments. Art. II, §2, cl. 2; (d) The Senate alone was given unreviewable power to ratify treaties negotiated by the President. Art. II, §2, cl. 2. Clearly, when the Draftsmen sought to confer special powers on one House, independent of the other House, or of the President, they did so in explicit, unambiguous terms. These carefully defined exceptions from presentment and bicameralism underscore the difference between the legislative functions of Congress and other unilateral but important and binding one-House acts provided for in the Constitution.

The veto authorized by §244(c)(2) doubtless has been in many respects a convenient shortcut; the "sharing" with the Executive by Congress of its authority over aliens in this manner is, on its face, an appealing compromise.

But it is crystal clear from the records of the Convention, contemporaneous writings and debates, that the Framers ranked other values higher than efficiency. We hold that the Congressional veto provision in §244(c)(2) is severable from the Act and that it is unconstitutional. Accordingly, the judgment of the Court of Appeals is *Affirmed*.

Justice POWELL, *concurring* in the judgment.

The Court's decision, based on the Presentment Clauses, Art. I, §7, cls. 2 and 3, apparently will invalidate every use of the legislative veto. The breadth of this holding gives one pause. Congress has included the veto in literally hundreds of statutes, dating back to the 1930s. Congress clearly views this procedure as essential to controlling the delegation of power to administrative agencies. The history of the Immigration Act makes clear that §244(c)(2) did not alter the division of actual authority between Congress and the Executive. At all times, whether through private bills, or through affirmative concurrent resolutions, or through the present one-House veto, a permanent change in a deportable alien's status could be accomplished only with the agreement of the Attorney General, the House, and the Senate.

The central concern of the presentation and bicameralism requirements of Article I is that when a departure from the legal status quo is undertaken, it is done with the approval of the President and both Houses of Congress—or, in the event of a presidential veto, a two-thirds majority in both Houses. This interest is fully satisfied by the operation of §244(c)(2). The President's approval is found in the Attorney General's action in recommending to Congress that the deportation order for a given alien be suspended. The House and the Senate indicate their approval of the Executive's action by not passing a resolution of disapproval within the statutory period. Thus, a change in the legal status quo—the deportability of the alien—is consummated only with the approval of each of the three relevant actors. The disagreement of any one of the three maintains the alien's pre-existing status: the Executive may choose not to recommend suspension; the House and Senate may each veto the recommendation. Thus understood, §244(c)(2) fully effectuates the purposes of the bicameralism and presentation requirements.

The Court of Appeals struck §244(c)(2) as violative of the constitutional principle of separation of powers. It is true that the purpose of separating the authority of government is to prevent unnecessary and dangerous concentration of power in one branch. But the history of the separation of powers doctrine is also a history of accommodation and practicality.

I regret that I am in disagreement with my colleagues on the fundamental questions that this case presents. But even more I regret the destructive scope of the Court's holding.

Today's decision strikes down in one fell swoop provisions in more laws enacted by Congress than the Court has cumulatively invalidated in its history. I fear it will now be more difficult "to insure that the fundamental policy decisions in our society will be made not by an appointed official but by the body immediately responsible to the people," *Arizona v. California,* 373 U.S. 546, 626 (1963).

∾ PROBLEMS ∾

1. *Funding for Remodeling.* Congress enacts a law requiring monies to be allocated for the remodeling of federal courthouses around the country. The law stipulates that "if the remodeling cannot be done for the amount allocated, the bookkeeper at the courthouse in question shall petition the House of

Representatives for additional sums, with detailed explanations for the requests. The House of Representatives, through a special subcommittee of eight representatives from eight different geographical areas of the country (e.g., North, South, East, West, Southeast, etc.), can then decide either to grant the request or to cancel the allocation to that courthouse altogether." Is this law constitutional?

2. *Congressional Action by Majority Vote.* Congress enacted legislation providing that an independent commission, composed of three persons selected by the head of the U.S. Immigration and Customs Enforcement (ICE), shall determine whether a deportable alien can remain in the United States, subject to a veto by the entire Congress based on a majority vote. The commission approved the immigration status of an alien, Kandinsky, but that approval was vetoed by Congress. The result is that Kandinsky will soon be deported. Kandinsky brought suit, claiming the law is unconstitutional in light of the Presentment Clauses in Article I, Section 7, Clauses 2 and 3. How should a court rule on this claim?

b. The "Line Item Veto"

The Constitution does not expressly answer the question of whether Congress can authorize the President to veto a single "line item" of legislation. In light of the constitutional silence, arguments exist on both sides. On the one hand, if the President can veto legislation in its entirety, shouldn't the President be able to veto any of its component parts? Furthermore, if the President can fail to spend when authorized by Congress to do so, why can't the President similarly fail to execute a line item authorized by Congress? On the other hand, does the text of the Constitution and the Framers' intent confine the veto power to the entire four corners of legislation and not lesser parts of it?

These questions were answered generally in *Clinton v. New York*, 524 U.S. 417 (1998). On August 11, 1997, President Clinton vetoed two line items contained in legislation enacted by Congress pursuant to the Line Item Veto Act, 2 U.S.C. §§691 *et seq.*, which became effective on the first day of 1997. That Act allowed the President to "cancel" certain parts or "line items" of legislation and not just the legislation in its entirety. The two canceled line items involved congressional spending. The President stated that his motive was an attempt to reduce the federal budget deficit. One line item involved a waiver of tax recoupment included in §4722(c) of the Balanced Budget Act of 1997, which could have amounted to as much as $2.6 billion in returned taxes from the State of New York. The other line item was a tax credit issued in the Taxpayer Relief Act of 1997, allowing some sellers of food processing facilities to farmers to receive preferential tax treatment.

The case elicited divergent perspectives on the separation of powers. Justice Stevens, for the majority, took a formalistic approach, concluding that the textual limits of the Constitution, requiring approval of both houses of Congress and then the President for a bill to become law, dictate the outcome of the case. The President, in performing a line item veto, had effectively changed the bill that had been approved by both houses of Congress and, consequently, was creating new legislation improperly. By contrast, Justice Breyer, in dissent, recalled Justice Marshall's words in *McCulloch v. Maryland,* 17 U.S. 316, (4 Wheat.) (1819), denying the propriety of "immutable rules," that would have marginalized the Constitution and given it "the properties of a legal code."

Clinton v. New York

524 U.S. 417 (1998)

Justice STEVENS delivered the opinion of the Court.

The Line Item Veto Act (Act), 2 U.S.C. §§691 *et seq.* (1994 ed., Supp. II), was enacted in April 1996 and became effective on January 1, 1997. Reaching the merits, we agree that the cancellation procedures set forth in the Act violate the Presentment Clause, Art. I, §7, cl. 2, of the Constitution.

The Line Item Veto Act gives the President the power to "cancel in whole" three types of provisions that have been signed into law: "(1) any dollar amount of discretionary budget authority; (2) any item of new direct spending; or (3) any limited tax benefit." 2 U.S.C. §691(a) (1994 ed., Supp. II). It is undisputed that the New York case involves an "item of new direct spending" and that the Snake River case involves a "limited tax benefit" as those terms are defined in the Act. It is also undisputed that each of those provisions had been signed into law pursuant to Article I, §7, of the Constitution before it was canceled.

The Act requires the President to adhere to precise procedures whenever he exercises his cancellation authority. In identifying items for cancellation he must consider the legislative history, the purposes, and other relevant information about the items. *See* 2 U.S.C. §691(b) (1994 ed., Supp. II). A cancellation takes effect upon receipt by Congress of the special message from the President.

In both legal and practical effect, the President has amended two Acts of Congress by repealing a portion of each. "Repeal of statutes, no less than enactment, must conform with Art. I." *INS v. Chadha,* 462 U.S. 919, 954 (1983). There is no provision in the Constitution that authorizes the President to enact, to amend, or to repeal statutes. Moreover, after a bill has passed both Houses of Congress, but "before it becomes a Law," it must be presented to the President. If he approves it, "he shall sign it, but if not he shall return it, with his Objections to that House in which it shall have originated, who shall enter the Objections at large on their Journal, and proceed to reconsider it." Art. I, §7, cl. 2. His "return" of a bill, which is usually described as a "veto," is subject to being overridden by a two-thirds vote in each House. There are important differences between the President's "return" of a bill pursuant to Article I, §7, and the exercise of the President's cancellation authority pursuant to the Line Item Veto Act. The constitutional return takes place before the bill becomes law; the statutory cancellation occurs after the bill becomes law. The constitutional return is of the entire bill; the statutory cancellation is of only a part. Although the Constitution expressly authorizes the President to play a role in the process of enacting statutes, it is silent on the subject of unilateral Presidential action that either repeals or amends parts of duly enacted statutes. There are powerful reasons for construing constitutional silence on this profoundly important issue as equivalent to an express prohibition. The procedures governing the enactment of statutes set forth in the text of Article I were the product of the great debates and compromises that produced the Constitution itself. Familiar historical materials provide abundant support for the conclusion that the power to enact statutes may only "be exercised in accord with a single, finely wrought and exhaustively considered, procedure." *Chadha*, 462 U.S., at 951. Our first President understood the text of the Presentment Clause as requiring that he either "approve all the parts of a Bill, or reject it in total." What has emerged in these cases from the President's exercise of his statutory cancellation powers, however, are truncated versions of two bills that passed both Houses of Congress. They are not the product of the "finely wrought" procedure that the Framers designed.

First, relying primarily on *Field v. Clark*, 143 U.S. 649 (1892), the Government contends that the cancellations were merely exercises of discretionary authority granted to the President by the Balanced Budget Act and the Taxpayer Relief Act read in light of the previously enacted Line Item Veto Act. Second, the Government submits that the substance of the authority to cancel tax and spending items "is, in practical effect, no more and no less than the power to "decline to spend" specified sums of money, or to "decline to implement" specified tax measures." Neither argument is persuasive.

In *Field v. Clark*, the Court upheld the constitutionality of the Tariff Act of 1890. Act of Oct. 1, 1890, 26 Stat. 567. That statute contained a "free list" of almost 300 specific articles that were exempted from import duties "unless otherwise specially provided for in this act." Section 3 was a special provision that directed the President to suspend that exemption for sugar, molasses, coffee, tea, and hides "whenever, and so often" as he should be satisfied that any country producing and exporting those products imposed duties on the agricultural products of the United States that he deemed to be "reciprocally unequal and unreasonable."

There are three critical differences between the power to suspend the exemption from import duties and the power to cancel portions of a duly enacted statute. First, the exercise of the suspension power was contingent upon a condition that did not exist when the Tariff Act was passed: the imposition of "reciprocally unequal and unreasonable" import duties by other countries. In contrast, the exercise of the cancellation power within five days after the enactment of the Balanced Budget and Tax Reform Acts necessarily was based on the same conditions that Congress evaluated when it passed those statutes. Second, under the Tariff Act, when the President determined that the contingency had arisen, he had a duty to suspend; in contrast, while it is true that the President was required by the Act to make three determinations before he canceled a provision, *see* 2 U.S.C. §691(a)(A) (1994 ed., Supp. II), those determinations did not qualify his discretion to cancel or not to cancel. Finally, whenever the President suspended an exemption under the Tariff Act, he was executing the policy that Congress had embodied in the statute. In contrast, whenever the President cancels an item of new direct spending or a limited tax benefit he is rejecting the policy judgment made by Congress and relying on his own policy judgment.

The Government's reliance upon other tariff and import statutes, discussed in *Field*, that contain provisions similar to the one challenged in *Field*, *is* unavailing for the same reasons. Some of those statutes authorized the President to "suspend and discontinue" statutory duties upon his determination that discriminatory duties imposed by other nations had been abolished. Further, the cited statutes all relate to foreign trade, and this Court has recognized that in the foreign affairs arena, the President has "a degree of discretion and freedom from statutory restriction which would not be admissible were domestic affairs alone involved." *United States v. Curtiss-Wright Export Corp.*, 299 U.S. 304, 320 (1936).

The critical difference between this statute and all of its predecessors, however, is that unlike any of them, this Act gives the President the unilateral power to change the text of duly enacted statutes. None of the Act's predecessors could even arguably have been construed to authorize such a change.

Our decision rests on the narrow ground that the procedures authorized by the Line Item Veto Act are not authorized by the Constitution.

If there is to be a new procedure in which the President will play a different role in determining the final text of what may "become a law," such change must come not by legislation but through the amendment procedures set forth in Article V of the Constitution.

The judgment of the District Court is affirmed.

Justice KENNEDY, *concurring.*

To say the political branches have a somewhat free hand to reallocate their own authority would seem to require acceptance of two premises: first, that the public good demands it, and second, that liberty is not at risk. The former premise is inadmissible. The Constitution's structure requires a stability which transcends the convenience of the moment. The latter premise, too, is flawed. Liberty is always at stake when one or more of the branches seek to transgress the separation of powers.

The principal object of the statute, it is true, was not to enhance the President's power to reward one group and punish another, to help one set of taxpayers and hurt another, to favor one State and ignore another. Yet these are its undeniable effects. The law establishes a new mechanism which gives the President the sole ability to hurt a group that is a visible target, in order to disfavor the group or to extract further concessions from Congress. The law is the functional equivalent of a line item veto and enhances the President's powers beyond what the Framers would have endorsed.

Justice SCALIA, with whom Justice O'CONNOR joins, and with whom Justice BREYER joins as to Part III, *concurring in part* and *dissenting in part.*

As much as the Court goes on about Art. I, §7, therefore, that provision does not demand the result the Court reaches. It no more categorically prohibits the Executive *reduction* of congressional dispositions in the course of implementing statutes that authorize such reduction, than it categorically prohibits the Executive *augmentation* of congressional dispositions in the course of implementing statutes that authorize such augmentation—generally known as substantive rulemaking.

I turn, then, to the crux of the matter: whether Congress's authorizing the President to cancel an item of spending gives him a power that our history and traditions show must reside exclusively in the Legislative Branch. Insofar as the degree of political, "lawmaking" power conferred upon the Executive is concerned, there is not a dime's worth of difference between Congress's authorizing the President to *cancel* a spending item, and Congress's authorizing money to be spent on a particular item at the President's discretion. And the latter has been done since the founding of the Nation. From 1789-1791, the First Congress made lump-sum appropriations for the entire Government—"sums not exceeding" specified amounts for broad purposes.

The short of the matter is this: had the Line Item Veto Act authorized the President to "decline to spend" any item of spending contained in the Balanced Budget Act of 1997, there is not the slightest doubt that authorization would have been constitutional. What the Line Item Veto Act does instead—authorizing the President to "cancel" an item of spending—is technically different. But the technical difference does *not* relate to the technicalities of the Presentment Clause, which have been fully complied with; and the doctrine of unconstitutional delegation, which *is* at issue here, is preeminently *not* a doctrine of technicalities. The title of the Line Item Veto Act, which was perhaps designed to simplify for public comprehension, or perhaps merely to comply with the terms of a campaign pledge, has succeeded in faking out the Supreme Court. The President's action it authorizes in fact is not a line-item veto and thus does not offend Art. I, §7; and insofar as the substance of that action is concerned, it is no different from what Congress has permitted the President to do since the formation of the Union.

For the foregoing reasons, I respectfully *dissent.*

Justice BREYER, with whom Justice O'CONNOR and Justice SCALIA join as to Part III, *dissenting.*

Chief Justice Marshall, in a well-known passage, explained, "To have prescribed the means by which government should, in all future time, execute its powers, would have been to change, entirely, the character of the instrument, and give it the properties of a legal code. It would have been an unwise attempt to provide, by immutable rules, for exigencies which, if foreseen at all, must have been seen dimly, and which can be best provided for as they occur." *McCulloch v. Maryland*, 4 Wheat. 316, 415, 4 L.Ed. 579 (1819). This passage, like the cases I have just mentioned, calls attention to the genius of the Framers' pragmatic vision, which this Court has long recognized in cases that find constitutional room for necessary institutional innovation.

The Court believes that the Act violates the literal text of the Constitution. A simple syllogism captures its basic reasoning: Major Premise: The Constitution sets forth an exclusive method for enacting, repealing, or amending laws. Minor Premise: The Act authorizes the President to "repeal or amend" laws in a different way, namely by announcing a cancellation of a portion of a previously enacted law. Conclusion: The Act is inconsistent with the Constitution.

I find this syllogism unconvincing, however, because its Minor Premise is faulty. When the President "canceled" the two appropriation measures now before us, he did not *repeal* any law nor did he *amend* any law. He simply *followed* the law, leaving the statutes, as they are literally written, intact.

Because I disagree with the Court's holding of literal violation, I must consider whether the Act nonetheless violates separation-of-powers principles — principles that arise out of the Constitution's vesting of the "executive Power" in "a President," U.S. Const., Art. II, §1, and "all legislative Powers" in "a Congress," Art. I, §1. There are three relevant separation-of-powers questions here: (1) Has Congress given the President the wrong kind of power, i.e., "non-Executive" power? (2) Has Congress given the President the power to "encroach" upon Congress's own constitutionally reserved territory? (3) Has Congress given the President too much power, violating the doctrine of "nondelegation"? These three limitations help assure "adequate control by the citizen's Representatives in Congress," upon which Justice Kennedy properly insists. And with respect to *this* Act, the answer to all these questions is "no."

Viewed conceptually, the power the Act conveys is the right kind of power. It is "executive." As explained above, an exercise of that power "executes" the Act. Conceptually speaking, it closely resembles the kind of delegated authority — to spend or not to spend appropriations, to change or not to change tariff rates — that Congress has frequently granted the President, any differences being differences in degree, not kind.

In addition, one cannot say that the Act "encroaches" upon Congress's power, when Congress retained the power to insert, by simple majority, into any future appropriations bill, into any section of any such bill, or into any phrase of any section, a provision that says the Act will not apply. Congress also retained the power to "disapprove," and thereby reinstate, any of the President's cancellations. Thus *this* Act is not the sort of delegation "without sufficient check" that concerns Justice Kennedy. Indeed, the President acts only in response to, and on the terms set by, the Congress. Consequently, with respect, I *dissent*.

∼ PROBLEMS ∼

1. *Legal Aid.* Congress enacts legislation providing funds for a near-Asian country in the throes of natural disasters, most recently, flooding from a monsoon.

As part of the legislation, Congress states: "The funding shall be administered in three distinct subsets, going to different agencies and parts of the country. These subsets are severable and distinguishable. The President has the power under this Act to determine if funding is necessary under each of the parts and may decide not to utilize any or all of the funds in each part. If the President forgoes the use of any of the funds, however, there must be detailed and written advance notice given to Congress, describing the reasons for doing so. In the alternative, the President can simply veto any one of the three subsets prior to signing the Act into law." Is this legislation constitutional? Explain.

2. *Condition Precedent.* Congress enacts a law stating, "In the event of a health care pandemic or disaster of such significant proportions that it interferes with the normal operation of a state, the President is empowered to spend up to $50 million to ameliorate that health care problem." Can the President refuse to spend any money? Is the law constitutional? Explain.

3. The President's Signing Statements

From the days of George Washington onward, presidents have used a variety of methods to strengthen and broadcast their powers. One of these methods is the signing statement, a written comment by a President as he approves a bill. The signing statement was allegedly first used by President James Monroe, and then continued by other notable presidents, such as Andrew Jackson and Ulysses S. Grant. In the past, the statements were often ceremonial, offering a rhetorical flourish to a bill's approval. In recent times, these statements have taken on a decidedly political tone, meeting a variety of goals. First, by issuing a signing statement about a law the President finds disagreeable, the President is able to voice displeasure about the law short of exercising a veto. The President also influences the shape of the law by declaring its constitutional boundaries—creating an "executive" history of sorts, similar to a legislative history. Further, a signing statement can influence how the law will operate by creating advance expectations about the law's implementation. In addition, the signing statement stakes out the President's turf and promotes the theory of a "unitary President," noting where the President finds the law constitutionally repugnant.

On one hand, signing statements do not have the force of law and reside in the shadows of the presidency. On the other hand, the statements dictate the position of the executive and can be used to diminish legislation and influence a court's review of that legislation. *See, e.g., Ameron Inc. v. U.S. Corps of Engineers,* 787 F.2d 878 (3d Cir. 1986).

During the past several decades, presidents have favored the signing statement. Under President George W. Bush, for example, the practice of issuing signing statements flourished, with a total of at least 150 signing statements. In 2001 alone, Bush issued 23 signing statements. The number climbed to 34 in 2002, but leveled off somewhat in 2003 to 27 and to 23 in 2004. *See* Phillip Cooper, *By*

Order of the President: The Use and Abuse of Direct Presidential Action (University Press of Kansas 2002) (describing a variety of tools used by presidents to wield power, from executive orders to signing statements). The signing statements presented numerous constitutional challenges, numbering 505 according to one commentator. *Id.* Whether signing statements will take on greater significance in coming years remains to be seen. At a minimum, however, these statements provide a glimpse of the President's conceptualization of the role of the Executive Branch in implementing government policy.

Because of the significance and proliferation of signing statements, the American Bar Association convened a task force to consider the matter. After much deliberation and dialogue, the Task Force reached several conclusions. Some of these are reprinted below.

A.B.A. Taskforce on Presidential Signing Statements and the Separation of Powers — Recommendations 2006

If our constitutional system of separation of powers is to operate as the framers intended, the President must accept the limitations imposed on his office by the Constitution itself. The use of presidential signing statements to have the last word as to which laws will be enforced and which will not is inconsistent with those limitations and poses a serious threat to the rule of law. It is this threat which the Task Force recommendations seek to address.

A.

Signing Statements Must Respect the Rule of Law and Our Constitutional System of Separation of Powers

As noted above, the first Recommendation urges that the President and those who succeed him cease the practice of using presidential signing statements to state his intention to disregard or decline to enforce a law or to interpret it in a manner inconsistent with the will of Congress. One of the most fundamental innovations of the American Constitution was to separate the executive from the legislative power. The Framers regarded this separation of powers as "essential to the preservation of liberty." James Madison, *The Federalist No. 51.*

In particular, the Framers sought to prevent in our new government the abuses that had arisen from the exercise of prerogative power by the Crown. Their device for doing so was to vest lawmaking power in the Congress and enforcement power in the President, and to provide in Article II §3 that the President "shall take Care that the Laws be faithfully executed." As the Supreme Court stated in holding that President Truman could not seize the nation's steel mills during the Korean war without congressional authorization, "In the framework of our Constitution, the President's power to see that the laws are faithfully executed refutes the idea that he is to be a lawmaker." *Youngstown Sheet & Tube Co. v. Sawyer*, 343 U.S. 579 (1952).

B.

Presidential Concerns Regarding Constitutionality of Pending Bills Should Be Communicated to Congress Prior to Passage

The White House and each of the 15 major executive departments maintain large and sophisticated legislative or congressional affairs offices and routinely and closely track the progress of bills introduced in the Congress. Moreover, much legislation considered by Congress each session emanates initially from the Executive Branch. For that reason, it is unlikely that important legislation would be considered and passed without the opportunity for full and fair input by the Administration.

Therefore, our second recommendation urges the President, if he believes that any provision of a bill pending before Congress would be unconstitutional if enacted, to communicate such concerns to Congress prior to passage. It is reasonable to expect the President to work cooperatively with Congress to identify and ameliorate any constitutional infirmities during the legislative process, rather than waiting until after passage of legislation to express such concerns in a signing statement.

C.

Signing Statements Should Not Be a Substitute for a Presidential Veto

The third Recommendation urges the President to confine signing statements to the meaning, purpose, or significance of bills he has signed into law, which he then must faithfully execute. For example, it is entirely appropriate for the President to praise a bill as a landmark in civil rights or environmental law and applaud its legislative sponsors, or to provide his views as to how the enactment of the law will affect the welfare of the nation.

When Congress enacted the Sarbanes-Oxley Act, President Bush wrote in his signing statement that it contained "the most far-reaching reforms of American business practices since the time of Franklin Delano Roosevelt." And when President Carter signed the Foreign Intelligence Surveillance Act of 1978, he wrote in his signing statement:

> The bill requires, for the first time, a prior judicial warrant for *all* electronic surveillance for foreign intelligence or counterintelligence purposes in the United States in which communications of U.S. persons might be intercepted. It clarifies the Executive's authority to gather foreign intelligence by electronic surveillance in the United States. It will remove any doubt about the legality of those surveillances which are conducted to protect our country against

espionage and international terrorism. It will assure FBI field agents and others involved in intelligence collection that their acts are authorized by statute and, if a U.S. person's communications are concerned, by a court order. And it will protect the privacy of the American people. *Id.*

Such statements contribute to public dialogue and accountability.

However, these Recommendations urge the President not to use signing statements in lieu of compliance with his constitutional obligation to veto any bill that he believes violates the Constitution in whole or in part. That obligation follows from the original intent and practice of the Founding Fathers, including President George Washington.

To sign a bill and refuse to enforce some of its provisions because of constitution a qualms is tantamount to exercising the line-item veto power held unconstitutional by the Supreme Court in *Clinton v. New York, supra.* By honoring his obligation to veto any bill he believes would violate the Constitution in any respect the President honors his oath to defend the Constitution. That obligation ensures that both Congress and the President will be politically accountable for their actions and that the law the President enforces will not be different from the one Congress enacted.

4. Executive Orders and Actions

Since he took office, President Trump has issued dozens of directives about how he will lead the Executive Branch and carry out the law. While there is no definition for the various types of presidential directives in the Constitution, Presidents since George Washington have issued Executive Orders, Executive Actions, and Proclamations. These directives are done unilaterally, without the approval of Congress.

President Trump has issued more than fifty executive orders, which generally have the force of law concerning how the executive branch will execute the law. He also has taken numerous executive actions, which concern executive policy in "faithfully executing the law." Some of the more significant Executive Orders include:

- Executive Order 13820: Termination of Presidential Advisory Commission on Election Integrity, in effect revoking Executive Order 13799 (establishment of Presidential Advisory Commission on Election Integrity).
- Executive Order 13823: Protecting America Through Lawful Detention of Terrorists. This Executive Order dealt with the detention of alleged terrorists at Guantanamo Bay Camp in Cuba, and whether that detention is legal and when the Secretary of Defense may transfer persons to that facility.

Note that President Trump's orders on immigration, restricting immigration from various countries, such as Iran, Libya, Somalia, Sudan, Syria, and Yemen, have led to various challenges and to the Supreme Court. *See, e.g., Trump v.*

International Refugee Assistance Project, 582 U.S. ___ (2017). The case of *Hawai'i v. Trump (2018),* also about the immigration restrictions, is discussed *infra.*

Note

In the first alleged Executive Order in 1789, George Washington sent a request to the federal department heads, "to impress me with a full, precise, and distinct general idea of the affairs of the United States." In 1948, President Truman issued an executive order to desegregate the armed forces. In 1957, President Eisenhower issued an executive order to desegregate the public schools in Little Rock, Arkansas.

5. Executive Power in the Pandemic Era

There have been many areas of executive powers triggered by the spreading of the novel coronavirus. Questions about the limits of executive branch authority, particularly in ordering closures and the wearing of masks, have led to litigation and commentary. *See, e.g.,* Bart Jansen, ""Draconian?" "House Arrest?" Coronavirus Lockdowns Prompt Raft of Lawsuits Against States," *USA Today* (May 25, 2020). Found at: https://www.usatoday.com/story/news/politics/2020/05/25/coronoavirus-lockdowns-prompt-raft-lawsuits-against-states/5231533002/

In the spring of 2020, most governors issued orders involving quarantines, closures of businesses and the wearing of masks indoors or in places where people cannot stay physically distant. One issue that recurred was the power of the executive to determine which institutions and businesses were "essential" and thus could keep operating. A lawsuit by a church in Nevada to reopen—just like the casinos—illustrates the constitutional questions that are associated with such a suit. The lawsuit, *Calvary Chapel Dayton Valley v. Sisolak,* sought injunctive relief to allow the church to hold services. The constitutional basis for the suit was the First Amendment, with the claim that allowing the casinos to open up to 50% capacity, but not places of worship, denied the free exercise of religion and the freedom of speech. The Supreme Court denied the request for an injunction while on appeal on July 24, 2020. Justice Alito dissented, arguing that the church had safeguards in place that met CDC standards—and would be as good if not better than the casinos in maintaining safety. Justice Alito stated:

> The Constitution guarantees the free exercise of religion. It says nothing about the freedom to play craps or blackjack, to feed tokens into a slot machine, or to engage in any other game of chance. But the Governor of Nevada apparently has different priorities. Claiming virtually unbounded power to restrict constitutional rights during the COVID-19 pandemic, he has issued a directive that severely limits attendance at religious services. A church, synagogue, or mosque, regardless of its size, may not admit more than 50 persons, but casinos and certain other favored facilities may admit 50% of their maximum occupancy—and in the case of gigantic Las Vegas casinos, this means that thousands of patrons are allowed.

≈ PROBLEMS ≈

1. *Game of Chance.* How would you rule if you were on the Court? What would your view be if you were a casino employee? Gambler? City bus driver?

2. *Meatpacking.* Can an employer at a meatpacking plant raise an executive order related to Covid-19 as a defense to a negligence action brought by employees? In this case, the plaintiff claimed that the defendant did not warn the employees about Covid-19 infection in the workplace. If the employer argues that it was protected by the president's executive order to keep meatpacking operations running, should it win? *See Requena v. Pilgrim's Pride of New Hampshire,* (E.D. Texas 2020). For additional information, see https://www .pacermonitor.com/public/case/35078627/Requena_et_al_v_Pilgrims_Pride_ Corporation.

≈ PROBLEM: NO DRILLING ZONES II ≈

In the introductory problem on no drilling zones, would it have made a difference in the outcome of the dispute if the President had proffered a signing statement articulating the President's position that the creation of no drilling zones was constitutional under the law? What should the President have included in the statement? Explain.

6. *The President and Immigration*

A. The Constitution

In Article I, Section 8, Congress is given the power to make laws over immigration, specifically, "To establish an uniform Rule of Naturalization . . ." But Congress does not reside in this arena alone. Article II gives the President the power to "take Care that the Laws be faithfully executed . . ." Article II, Section 3. In recent decades, the president has become increasingly active in the immigration area based on this Article II enforcement power.

B. *Trump v. Hawai'i*

Trump v. Hawai'i concerned a September 2017 Executive Order by President Trump. The Order limited travel to the United States by foreign nationals from certain countries, including Libya, Iran, Venezuela, Chad, Syria, Yemen, and Somalia. The Order was preceded by two similar orders. All were challenged in the federal courts. The State of Hawaii argued that the Executive Order exceeded the president's immigration power and violated the Establishment Clause by favoring one religion over another. The Supreme Court various issues, including justiciability, the scope of Executive Branch power, national security, and the Establishment Clause. The following excerpt focuses on the issue involving the powers of the Executive Branch.

Trump v. Hawai'i

138 S. Ct. 2392 (2018)

Chief Justice ROBERTS delivered the opinion of the Court.

Under the Immigration and Nationality Act, foreign nationals seeking entry into the United States undergo a vetting process to ensure that they satisfy the numerous requirements for admission. The Act also vests the President with authority to restrict the entry of aliens whenever he finds that their entry "would be detrimental to the interests of the United States." 8 U. S. C. §1182(f). Relying on that delegation, the President concluded that it was necessary to impose entry restrictions on nationals of countries that do not share adequate information for an informed entry determination, or that otherwise present national security risks. Presidential Proclamation No. 9645, 82 Fed. Reg. 45161 (2017). The plaintiffs in this litigation, respondents here, challenged the application of those entry restrictions to certain aliens abroad. We now decide whether the President had authority under the Act to issue the Proclamation, and whether the entry policy violates the Establishment Clause of the First Amendment.

Shortly after taking office, President Trump signed Executive Order No. 13769, Protecting the Nation from Foreign Terrorist Entry into the United States. 82 Fed. Reg. 8977 (2017) (EO–1). EO–1 directed the Secretary of Homeland Security to conduct a review to examine the adequacy of information provided by foreign governments about their nationals seeking to enter the United States. Pending that review, the order suspended for 90 days the entry of foreign nationals from seven countries—Iran, Iraq, Libya, Somalia, Sudan, Syria, and Yemen — that had been previously identified by Congress or prior administrations as posing heightened terrorism risks. The District Court for the Western District of Washington entered a temporary restraining order blocking the entry restrictions, and the Court of Appeals for the Ninth Circuit denied the Government's request to stay that order. In response, the President revoked EO–1, replacing it with Executive Order No. 13780, which again directed a worldwide review. 82 Fed. Reg. 13209 (2017) (EO–2). Citing investigative burdens on agencies and the need to diminish the risk that dangerous individuals would enter without adequate vetting, EO–2 also temporarily restricted the entry (with case-by-case waivers) of foreign nationals from six of the countries covered by EO–1: Iran, Libya, Somalia, Sudan, Syria, and Yemen. The order explained that those countries had been selected because each "is a state sponsor of terrorism, has been significantly compromised by terrorist organizations, or contains active conflict zones." The entry restriction was to stay in effect for 90 days, pending completion of the worldwide review.

These interim measures were immediately challenged in court. The District Courts for the Districts of Maryland and Hawaii entered nationwide preliminary injunctions barring enforcement of the entry suspension, and the respective Courts of Appeals upheld those injunctions, albeit on different grounds. This Court granted certiorari and stayed the injunctions—allowing the entry suspension to go into effect—with respect to foreign nationals who lacked a "credible claim of a bona fide relationship" with a person or entity in the United States. The temporary restrictions in EO–2 expired before this Court took any action, and we vacated the lower court decisions as moot.

On September 24, 2017, after completion of the worldwide review, the President issued the Proclamation before us—Proclamation No. 9645, Enhancing Vetting Capabilities and Processes for Detecting Attempted Entry into the United States by Terrorists or Other Public-Safety Threats. 82 Fed. Reg. 45161. The Proclamation (as its title indicates) sought to improve vetting procedures by identifying ongoing deficiencies in the information needed to assess whether nationals of particular countries present "public safety threats." To further that purpose, the Proclamation placed entry restrictions on the nationals of eight foreign states whose systems for managing and sharing information about their nationals the President deemed inadequate. The Proclamation described how foreign states were selected for inclusion based on the review undertaken pursuant to EO–2. As part of that review, the Department of Homeland Security (DHS), in consultation with the State Department and several intelligence agencies, developed a "baseline" for the information required from foreign governments to confirm the identity of individuals seeking entry into the United States, and to determine whether those individuals pose a security threat. The baseline included three components. The first, "identity-management information," focused on whether a foreign government ensures the integrity of travel documents by issuing electronic passports, reporting lost or stolen passports, and making available additional identity related information. Second, the agencies considered the extent to which the country discloses information on criminal history and suspected terrorist links, provides travel document exemplars, and facilitates the U.S. Government's receipt of information about airline passengers and crews traveling to the United States. Finally, the agencies weighed various indicators of national security risk, including whether the foreign state is a known or potential terrorist safe haven and whether it regularly declines to receive returning nationals following final orders of removal from the United States.

After consulting with multiple Cabinet members and other officials, the President adopted the Acting Secretary's recommendations and issued the Proclamation. Invoking his authority under 8 U.S.C. §§1182(f) and 1185(a), the President determined that certain entry restrictions were necessary to "prevent the entry of those foreign nationals about whom the United States Government lacks sufficient information"; "elicit improved identity management and information-sharing protocols and practices from foreign governments"; and otherwise "advance the foreign policy, national security, and counterterrorism objectives" of the United States. The President explained that these restrictions would be the "most likely to encourage cooperation" while "protecting the United States until such time as improvements occur."

The Proclamation imposed a range of restrictions that vary based on the "distinct circumstances" in each of the eight countries. For countries that do not cooperate with the United States in identifying security risks (Iran, North Korea, and Syria), the Proclamation suspends entry of all nationals, except for Iranians seeking nonimmigrant student and exchange-visitor visas. For countries that have information-sharing deficiencies but are nonetheless "valuable counterterrorism partners" (Chad, Libya, and Yemen), it restricts entry of nationals seeking immigrant visas and nonimmigrant business or tourist visas. Because Somalia generally satisfies the baseline standards but was found to present special risk factors, the Proclamation suspends entry of nationals seeking immigrant visas and requires additional scrutiny of nationals seeking nonimmigrant visas. And for Venezuela, which refuses to cooperate in information sharing but for which alternative means are available to identify its nationals, the Proclamation limits entry only of certain government officials and their family members on nonimmigrant business or tourist visas. The Proclamation exempts lawful permanent residents and foreign nationals who have been granted asylum. It also provides for case-by-case waivers when a foreign national demonstrates undue hardship, and that his entry is in the national interest and would not pose a threat to public safety. §3(c)(i). The Proclamation further directs DHS to assess on a continuing basis whether entry restrictions should be modified or continued, and to report to the President every 180 days. Upon completion of the first such review period, the President, on the recommendation of the Secretary of Homeland Security, determined that Chad had sufficiently improved its practices, and he accordingly lifted restrictions on its nationals. Presidential Proclamation No. 9723, 83 Fed. Reg. 15937 (2018).

Plaintiffs are the State of Hawaii, three individuals (Dr. Ismail Elshikh, John Doe #1, and John Doe #2), and the Muslim Association of Hawaii. The State operates the University of Hawaii system, which recruits students and faculty from the designated countries. The three individual plaintiffs are U.S. citizens or lawful permanent residents who have relatives from Iran, Syria, and Yemen applying for immigrant or nonimmigrant visas. The Association is a nonprofit organization that operates a mosque in Hawaii. Plaintiffs challenged the Proclamation—except as applied to North Korea and Venezuela—on several grounds. As relevant here, they argued that the Proclamation contravenes provisions in the Immigration and Nationality Act (INA). Plaintiffs further claimed that the Proclamation violates the Establishment Clause of the First Amendment, because it was motivated not by concerns pertaining to national security but by animus toward Islam. The District Court granted a nationwide preliminary injunction barring enforcement of the entry restrictions. The court concluded that the Proclamation violated two provisions of the INA: §1182(f), because the President did not make sufficient findings that the entry of the covered foreign nationals would be detrimental to the national interest, and §1152(a)(1)(A), because the policy discriminates against immigrant visa applicants on the basis of nationality. The Court of Appeals affirmed. The court first held that the Proclamation exceeds the President's authority under §1182(f). In its view, that provision authorizes only a "temporary" suspension of entry in response to "exigencies" that "Congress would be ill-equipped to address." The court further reasoned that the Proclamation "conflicts with the INA's finely reticulated regulatory scheme" by addressing "matters of immigration already passed upon by Congress." The Ninth Circuit then turned to §1152(a)(1)(A) and determined that the entry restrictions also contravene the prohibition on nationality-based discrimination in the issuance of immigrant visas. The court did not reach plaintiffs' Establishment Clause claim. We granted certiorari.

[The Court considered an initial question of justiciability here, which it called a "difficult question." The Court assumed that the statutory claims are reviewable.]

Plaintiffs argue that the Proclamation is not a valid exercise of the President's authority under the INA. In their view, §1182(f) confers only a residual power to temporarily halt the entry of a discrete group of aliens engaged in harmful conduct. They also assert that the Proclamation violates another provision of the INA—8 U.S.C. §1152(a)(1)(A) —because it discriminates on the basis of nationality in the issuance of immigrant visas. By its plain language, §1182(f) grants the President broad discretion to suspend the entry of aliens into the United States. The President lawfully exercised that discretion based on his findings— following a worldwide, multi-agency review—that entry of the covered aliens would be detrimental to the national interest. And plaintiffs' attempts to identify a conflict with other provisions in the INA, and their appeal to the statute's purposes and legislative history, fail to overcome the clear statutory language.

The text of §1182(f) states: "Whenever the President finds that the entry of any aliens or of any class of aliens into the United States would be detrimental to the interests of the United States, he may by proclamation, and for such period as he shall deem necessary, suspend the entry of all aliens or any class of aliens as immigrants or nonimmigrants, or impose on the entry of aliens any restrictions he may deem to be appropriate."

By its terms, §1182(f) exudes deference to the President in every clause. It entrusts to the President the decisions whether and when to suspend entry ("whenever he finds that the entry" of aliens "would be detrimental" to the national interest); whose entry to suspend ("all aliens or any class of aliens"); for how long ("for such period as he shall deem necessary"); and on what conditions ("any restrictions he may deem to be appropriate"). It is therefore unsurprising that we have previously observed that §1182(f) vests the President with "ample power" to impose entry restrictions in addition to those elsewhere enumerated in the INA. *Sale*, 509 U. S., at 187 (finding it "perfectly clear" that the President could "establish a naval blockade" to prevent illegal migrants from entering the United States).

The Proclamation falls well within this comprehensive delegation. The sole prerequisite set forth in §1182(f) is that the President "find" that the entry of the covered aliens "would be detrimental to the interests of the United States." The President has undoubtedly fulfilled that requirement here. He first ordered DHS and other agencies to conduct a comprehensive evaluation of every single country's compliance with the information and risk assessment baseline. The President then issued a Proclamation setting forth extensive findings describing how deficiencies in the practices of select foreign governments—several of which are state sponsors of terrorism—deprive the Government of "sufficient information to assess the risks [those countries' nationals] pose to the United States." Based on that review, the President found that it was in the national interest to restrict entry of aliens who could not be vetted with adequate information—both to protect national security and public safety, and to induce improvement by their home countries. The Proclamation therefore "crafted country-specific restrictions that would be most likely to encourage cooperation given each country's distinct circumstances," while securing the Nation "until such time as improvements occur."

Plaintiffs believe that these findings are insufficient. They argue, as an initial matter, that the Proclamation fails to provide a persuasive rationale for why nationality alone renders the covered foreign nationals a security risk. And they further discount the President's stated concern about deficient vetting because the Proclamation allows many aliens from the designated countries to enter on nonimmigrant visas. Such arguments are grounded on the premise that §1182(f) not only requires the President to make a finding that entry "would be detrimental to the interests of the United States," but also to explain that finding with sufficient detail to enable judicial review. That premise is questionable. But even assuming that some form of review is appropriate, plaintiffs' attacks on the sufficiency of the President's findings cannot be sustained. The 12-page Proclamation—which thoroughly describes the process, agency evaluations, and recommendations underlying the President's chosen restrictions—is more detailed than any prior order a President has issued under §1182(f). Moreover, plaintiffs' request for a searching inquiry into the persuasiveness of the President's justifications is inconsistent with the broad statutory text and the deference traditionally accorded the President in this sphere. "Whether the President's chosen method" of addressing perceived risks is justified from a policy perspective is "irrelevant to the scope of his §1182(f) authority." *Sale*, 509 U. S., at 187. And when the President adopts "a preventive measure in the context of international affairs and national security," he is "not required to conclusively link all of the pieces in the puzzle before courts grant weight to his empirical conclusions." *Holder v. Humanitarian Law Project*, 561 U.S. 1, 35 (2010).

Like its predecessors, the Proclamation makes clear that its "conditional restrictions" will remain in force only so long as necessary to "address" the identified "inadequacies and risks" within the covered nations. Proclamation Preamble, and §1(h). To that end, the Proclamation establishes an ongoing process to engage covered nations and assess every 180 days whether the entry restrictions should be modified or terminated. Indeed, after the initial review period, the President determined that Chad had made sufficient improvements to its identity management protocols, and he accordingly lifted the entry suspension on its nationals.

Finally, the Proclamation properly identifies a "class of aliens"—nationals of select countries—whose entry is suspended. Plaintiffs argue that "class" must refer to a well-defined group of individuals who share a common "characteristic" apart from nationality. But the text of §1182(f), of course, does not say that, and the word "class" comfortably encompasses a group of people linked by nationality. Plaintiffs also contend that the class cannot be "overbroad." But that simply amounts to an unspoken tailoring requirement found nowhere in Congress's grant of authority to suspend entry of not only "any class of aliens" but "all aliens." In short, the language of §1182(f) is clear, and the Proclamation does not exceed any textual limit on the President's authority.

Confronted with this "facially broad grant of power," plaintiffs focus their attention on statutory structure and legislative purpose. They seek support in, first, the immigration scheme reflected in the INA as a whole, and, second, the legislative history of §1182(f) and historical practice. Neither argument justifies departing from the clear text of the statute. Plaintiffs' structural argument starts with the premise that §1182(f) does not give the President authority to countermand Congress's considered policy judgments. The President, they say, may supplement the INA, but he cannot supplant it. And in their view, the Proclamation falls in the latter category because Congress has already specified a two-part solution to the problem of aliens seeking entry from countries that do not share sufficient information with the United States. First, Congress designed an individualized vetting system that places the burden on the alien to prove his admissibility. Second, instead of banning the entry of nationals from particular countries, Congress sought to encourage information sharing through a Visa Waiver Program offering fast-track admission for countries that cooperate with the United States.

We may assume that §1182(f) does not allow the President to expressly override particular provisions of the INA. But plaintiffs have not identified any conflict between the statute and the Proclamation that would implicitly bar the President from addressing deficiencies in the Nation's vetting system.

To the contrary, the Proclamation supports Congress's individualized approach for determining admissibility. The INA sets forth various inadmissibility grounds based on connections to terrorism and criminal history, but those provisions can only work when the consular officer has sufficient (and sufficiently reliable) information to make that determination. One of the key objectives of the Proclamation is to encourage foreign governments to improve their practices, thus facilitating the Government's vetting process overall.

Nor is there a conflict between the Proclamation and the Visa Waiver Program. The Program allows travel without a visa for short-term visitors from 38 countries that have entered into a "rigorous security partnership" with the United States. DHS, U. S. Visa Waiver Program (Apr. 6, 2016). Eligibility for that partnership involves "broad and consequential assessments of the country's foreign security standards and operations." A foreign government must (among other things) undergo a comprehensive evaluation of its "counterterrorism, law enforcement, immigration enforcement, passport security, and border management capabilities," often including "operational site inspections of airports, seaports, land borders, and passport production and issuance facilities." The Visa Waiver Program creates a special exemption for citizens of countries that maintain exemplary security standards and offer "reciprocal [travel] privileges" to United States citizens. 8 U.S.C. §1187(a)(2)(A). But in establishing a select partnership covering less than 20% of the countries in the world, Congress did not address what requirements should govern the entry of nationals from the vast majority of countries that fall short of that gold standard—particularly those nations presenting heightened terrorism concerns. Nor did Congress attempt to determine—as the multi-agency review process did—whether those high risk countries provide a minimum baseline of information to adequately vet their nationals. Once again, this is not a situation where "Congress has stepped into the space and solved the exact problem." Given the clarity of the text, we need not consider such extratextual evidence. At any rate, plaintiffs' evidence supports the plain meaning of the provision.

Plaintiffs' final statutory argument is that the President's entry suspension violates §1152(a)(1)(A), which provides that "no person shall be discriminated against in the issuance of an immigrant visa because of the person's race, sex, nationality, place of birth, or place of residence." They contend that we should interpret the provision as prohibiting nationality-based discrimination throughout the entire immigration process, despite the reference in §1152(a)(1)(A) to the act of visa issuance alone. Specifically, plaintiffs argue that §1152(a)(1)(A) applies to the predicate question of a visa applicant's eligibility for admission and the subsequent question whether the holder of a visa may in fact enter the country. Any other conclusion, they say, would allow the President to circumvent the protections against discrimination enshrined in §1152(a)(1)(A). As an initial matter, this argument challenges only the validity of the entry restrictions on immigrant travel. Section 1152(a)(1)(A) is expressly limited to the issuance of "immigrant visas" while §1182(f) allows the President to suspend entry of "immigrants or nonimmigrants." At a minimum, then, plaintiffs' reading would not affect any of the limitations on nonimmigrant travel in the Proclamation. In any event, we reject plaintiffs' interpretation because it ignores the basic distinction between admissibility determinations and visa issuance that runs throughout the INA.

[The Court proceeded to address the issue of whether the Proclamation was "issued for the unconstitutional purpose of excluding Muslims." In doing so, the

Court first considered whether standing requirements were met and then dealt with the merits, considering how the Establishment Clause and presidential powers intersected in the area of the admission of foreign nationals to the United States.] The First Amendment provides, in part, that "Congress shall make no law respecting an establishment of religion, or prohibiting the free exercise thereof." Our cases recognize that "the clearest command of the Establishment Clause is that one religious denomination cannot be officially preferred over another." *Larson v. Valente*, 456 U. S. 228, 244 (1982). Plaintiffs believe that the Proclamation violates this prohibition by singling out Muslims for disfavored treatment. The entry suspension, they contend, operates as a "religious gerrymander," in part because most of the countries covered by the Proclamation have Muslim-majority populations.

The case before us differs in numerous respects from the conventional Establishment Clause claim. Unlike the typical suit involving religious displays or school prayer, plaintiffs seek to invalidate a national security directive regulating the entry of aliens abroad. Their claim accordingly raises a number of delicate issues regarding the scope of the constitutional right and the manner of proof. The Proclamation, moreover, is facially neutral toward religion. Plaintiffs therefore ask the Court to probe the sincerity of the stated justifications for the policy by reference to extrinsic statements—many of which were made before the President took the oath of office. These various aspects of plaintiffs' challenge inform our standard of review.

For more than a century, this Court has recognized that the admission and exclusion of foreign nationals is a "fundamental sovereign attribute exercised by the Government's political departments largely immune from judicial control." *Fiallo v. Bell*, 430 U. S. 787, 792 (1977). Because decisions in these matters may implicate "relations with foreign powers," or involve "classifications defined in the light of changing political and economic circumstances," such judgments "are frequently of a character more appropriate to either the Legislature or the Executive." *Mathews v. Diaz*, 426 U. S. 67, 81 (1976). Nonetheless, although foreign nationals seeking admission have no constitutional right to entry, this Court has engaged in a circumscribed judicial inquiry when the denial of a visa allegedly burdens the constitutional rights of a U. S. citizen. In *Kleindienst v. Mandel*, the Attorney General denied admission to a Belgian journalist and self described "revolutionary Marxist," Ernest Mandel, who had been invited to speak at a conference at Stanford University. 408 U. S., at 756–757. The professors who wished to hear Mandel speak challenged that decision under the First Amendment, and we acknowledged that their constitutional "right to receive information" was implicated. But we limited our review to whether the Executive gave a "facially legitimate and bona fide" reason for its action. Given the authority of the political branches over admission, we held that "when the Executive exercises this [delegated] power negatively on the basis of a facially legitimate and bona fide reason, the courts will neither look behind the exercise of that discretion, nor test it by balancing its justification" against the asserted constitutional interests of

U.S. citizens. The principal dissent suggests that *Mandel* has no bearing on this case, but our opinions have reaffirmed and applied its deferential standard of review across different contexts and constitutional claims. In *Din,* Justice Kennedy reiterated that "respect for the political branches' broad power over the creation and administration of the immigration system" meant that the Government need provide only a statutory citation to explain a visa denial. Likewise in *Fiallo,* we applied *Mandel* to a "broad congressional policy" giving immigration preferences to mothers of illegitimate children. Even though the statute created a "categorical" entry classification that discriminated on the basis of sex and legitimacy, the Court concluded that "it is not the judicial role in cases of this sort to probe and test the justifications" of immigration policies.

For one, "judicial inquiry into the national-security realm raises concerns for the separation of powers" by intruding on the President's constitutional responsibilities in the area of foreign affairs. *Ziglar v. Abbasi,* 582 U. S. ___, ___ (2017). For another, "when it comes to collecting evidence and drawing inferences" on questions of national security, "the lack of competence on the part of the courts is marked." The upshot of our cases in this context is clear: "Any rule of constitutional law that would inhibit the flexibility" of the President "to respond to changing world conditions should be adopted only with the greatest caution," and our inquiry into matters of entry and national security is highly constrained. We need not define the precise contours of that inquiry in this case. A conventional application of *Mandel,* asking only whether the policy is facially legitimate and bona fide, would put an end to our review. But the Government has suggested that it may be appropriate here for the inquiry to extend beyond the facial neutrality of the order. For our purposes, we assume that we may look behind the face of the Proclamation to the extent of applying rational basis review. That standard of review considers whether the entry policy is plausibly related to the Government's stated objective to protect the country and improve vetting processes. As a result, we may consider plaintiffs' extrinsic evidence, but will uphold the policy so long as it can reasonably be understood to result from a justification independent of unconstitutional grounds.

Given the standard of review, it should come as no surprise that the Court hardly ever strikes down a policy as illegitimate under rational basis scrutiny. On the few occasions where we have done so, a common thread has been that the laws at issue lack any purpose other than a "bare desire to harm a politically unpopular group." *Department of Agriculture v. Moreno,* 413 U. S. 528, 534 (1973). In one case, we invalidated a local zoning ordinance that required a special permit for group homes for the intellectually disabled, but not for other facilities such as fraternity houses or hospitals. The Proclamation is expressly premised on legitimate purposes: preventing entry of nationals who cannot be adequately vetted and inducing other nations to improve their practices. The text says nothing about religion. Plaintiffs and the dissent nonetheless emphasize that five of the seven nations currently included in the Proclamation have Muslim-majority populations. Yet that fact alone does not support an inference of religious hostility, given that the policy covers just 8% of the world's Muslim population and is limited to countries that were previously designated by Congress or prior administrations as posing national security risks. As for Iraq, the Secretary of Homeland Security determined that entry restrictions were not warranted in light of the close cooperative relationship between the U. S. and Iraqi Governments and the country's key role in combating terrorism in the region.

The policy permits nationals from nearly every covered country to travel to the United States on a variety of nonimmigrant visas. See, e.g., §§2(b)–(c), (g), (h) (permitting student and exchange visitors from Iran, while restricting only business and tourist nonimmigrant entry for nationals of Libya and Yemen, and imposing no restrictions on nonimmigrant entry for Somali nationals). These carveouts for nonimmigrant visas are substantial: On its face, this program is similar to the humanitarian exceptions set forth in President Carter's order during the Iran hostage crisis. See Exec. Order No. 12206, 3 CFR 249.

Finally, the dissent invokes *Korematsu v. United States*, 323 U.S. 214 (1944). Whatever rhetorical advantage the dissent may see in doing so, *Korematsu* has nothing to do with this case. The forcible relocation of U. S. citizens to concentration camps, solely and explicitly on the basis of race, is objectively unlawful and outside the scope of Presidential authority. But it is wholly inapt to liken that morally repugnant order to a facially neutral policy denying certain foreign nationals the privilege of admission. The entry suspension is an act that is well within executive authority and could have been taken by any other President—the only question is evaluating the actions of this particular President in promulgating an otherwise valid Proclamation. The dissent's reference to *Korematsu*, however, affords this Court the opportunity to make express what is already obvious: *Korematsu* was gravely wrong the day it was decided, has been overruled in the court of history, and—to be clear—"has no place in law under the Constitution." 323 U.S., at 248 (Jackson, J., dissenting). Under these circumstances, the Government has set forth a sufficient national security justification to survive rational basis review. We express no view on the soundness of the policy. We simply hold today that plaintiffs have not demonstrated a likelihood of success on the merits of their constitutional claim.

Because plaintiffs have not shown that they are likely to succeed on the merits of their claims, we reverse the grant of the preliminary injunction as an abuse of discretion. *Winter v. Natural Resources Defense Council, Inc.*, 555 U. S. 7, 32 (2008). The case now returns to the lower courts for such further proceedings as may be appropriate. Our disposition of the case makes it unnecessary to consider the propriety of the nationwide scope of the injunction issued by the District Court. The judgment of the Court of Appeals is reversed, and the case is remanded for further proceedings consistent with this opinion.

It is so ordered.

Justice KENNEDY, concurring.

I join the Court's opinion in full. There may be some common ground between the opinions in this case, in that the Court does acknowledge that in some instances, governmental action may be subject to judicial review to determine whether or not it is "inexplicable by anything but animus," *Romer v. Evans*, 517 U.S. 620, 632 (1996), which in this case would be animosity to a religion. Whether judicial proceedings may properly continue in this case, in light of the substantial deference that is and must be accorded to the Executive in the conduct of foreign affairs, and in light of today's decision, is a matter to be addressed in the first instance on remand. And even if further proceedings are permitted, it would be necessary to determine that any discovery and other preliminary matters would not themselves intrude on the foreign affairs power of the Executive.

There are numerous instances in which the statements and actions of Government officials are not subject to judicial scrutiny or intervention. That does not mean those officials are free to disregard the Constitution and the rights it proclaims and protects. The oath that all officials take to adhere to the Constitution is not confined to those spheres in which the Judiciary can correct or even comment upon what those officials say or do. Indeed, the very fact that an official may have broad discretion, discretion free from judicial scrutiny, makes it all the more imperative for him or her to adhere to the Constitution and to its meaning and its promise. The First Amendment prohibits the establishment of religion and promises the free exercise of religion. From these safeguards, and from the guarantee of freedom of speech, it follows there is freedom of belief and expression. It is an urgent necessity that officials adhere to these constitutional guarantees and mandates in all their actions, even in the sphere of foreign affairs. An anxious world must know that our Government remains committed always to the liberties the Constitution seeks to preserve and protect, so that freedom extends outward, and lasts.

THOMAS, J., concurring.

Section 1182(f) does not set forth any judicially enforceable limits that constrain the President. Nor could it, since the President has inherent authority to exclude aliens from the country. Further, the Establishment Clause does not create an individual right to be free from all laws that a "reasonable observer" views as religious or antireligious. Plaintiffs cannot raise any other First Amendment claim, since the alleged religious discrimination in this case was directed at aliens abroad. *See United States v. Verdugo-Urquidez*, 494 U.S. 259, 265 (1990). And, even on its own terms, the plaintiffs' proffered evidence of anti-Muslim discrimination is unpersuasive. Merits aside, I write separately to address the remedy that the plaintiffs sought and obtained in this case. The District Court imposed an injunction that barred the Government from enforcing the President's Proclamation against anyone, not just the plaintiffs. Injunctions that prohibit the Executive Branch from applying a law or policy against anyone — often called "universal" or "nationwide" injunctions — have become increasingly common. District courts, including the one here, have begun imposing universal injunctions without considering their authority to grant such sweeping relief. These injunctions are beginning to take a toll on the federal court system — preventing legal questions from percolating through the federal courts, encouraging forum shopping, and making every case a national emergency for the courts and for the Executive Branch. I am skeptical that district courts have the authority to enter universal injunctions. These injunctions did not emerge until a century and a half after the founding. And they appear to be inconsistent with longstanding limits on equitable relief and the power of Article III courts. If their popularity continues, this Court must address their legality.

Justice BREYER, with whom Justice KAGAN joins, dissenting.

The question before us is whether Proclamation No. 9645 is lawful. If its promulgation or content was significantly affected by religious animus against Muslims, it would violate the relevant statute or the First Amendment itself. *Church of Lukumi Babalu Aye, Inc. v. Hialeah,* 508 U. S. 520 (1993). If, however, its sole *ratio decidendi* was one of national security, then it would be unlikely to violate either the statute or the Constitution. Which is it? Members of the Court principally disagree about the answer to this question, i.e., about whether or the extent to which religious animus played a significant role in the Proclamation's promulgation or contenting my view, the Proclamation's elaborate system of exemptions and waivers can and should help us answer this question. That system provides for case-by-case consideration of persons who may qualify for visas despite the Proclamation's general ban. Those persons include lawful permanent residents, asylum seekers, refugees, students, children, and numerous others. There are likely many such persons, perhaps in the thousands.

The Solicitor General asked us to consider the Proclamation "as" it is "written" and "as" it is "applied," waivers and exemptions included. On the one hand, if the Government is applying the exemption and waiver provisions as written, then its argument for the Proclamation's lawfulness is strengthened. For one thing, the Proclamation then resembles more closely the two important Presidential precedents on point, President Carter's Iran order and President Reagan's Cuba proclamation, both of which contained similar categories of persons authorized to obtain case-by-case exemptions.

Further, since the case-by-case exemptions and waivers apply without regard to the individual's religion, application of that system would help make clear that the Proclamation does not deny visas to numerous Muslim individuals (from those countries) who do not pose a security threat. And that fact would help to rebut the First Amendment claim that the Proclamation rests upon anti-Muslim bias rather than security need. Finally, of course, the very fact that Muslims from those countries would enter the United States (under Proclamation-provided exemptions and waivers) would help to show the same thing.

On the other hand, if the Government is not applying the system of exemptions and waivers that the Proclamation contains, then its argument for the Proclamation's lawfulness becomes significantly weaker. For one thing, the relevant precedents—those of Presidents Carter and Reagan—would bear far less resemblance to the present Proclamation. Indeed, one might ask, if those two

Presidents thought a case-by-case exemption system appropriate, what is different about present circumstances that would justify that system's absence? For another thing, the relevant statute requires that there be "findings" that the grant of visas to excluded persons would be "detrimental to the interests of the United States." Yet there would be no such findings in respect to those for whom the Proclamation itself provides case-by-case examination (followed by the grant of a visa in appropriate cases).

And, perhaps most importantly, if the Government is not applying the Proclamation's exemption and waiver system, the claim that the Proclamation is a "Muslim ban," rather than a "security-based" ban, becomes much stronger. How could the Government successfully claim that the Proclamation rests on security needs if it is excluding Muslims who satisfy the Proclamation's own terms? At the same time, denying visas to Muslims who meet the Proclamation's own security terms would support the view that the Government excludes them for reasons based upon their religion.

Unfortunately there is evidence that supports the second possibility, i.e., that the Government is not applying the Proclamation as written. The Proclamation provides that the Secretary of State and the Secretary of Homeland Security "shall coordinate to adopt guidance" for consular officers to follow when deciding whether to grant a waiver. §3(c)(ii). Yet, to my knowledge, no guidance has issued. The only potentially relevant document I have found consists of a set of State Department answers to certain Frequently Asked Questions, but this document simply restates the Proclamation in plain language for visa applicants. It does not provide guidance for consular officers as to how they are to exercise their discretion.

An examination of publicly available statistics also provides cause for concern. The State Department reported that during the Proclamation's first month, two waivers were approved out of 6,555 eligible applicants. In its reply brief, the Government claims that number increased from 2 to 430 during the first four months of implementation. That number, 430, however, when compared with the number of pre-Proclamation visitors, accounts for a minuscule percentage of those likely eligible for visas, in such categories as persons requiring medical treatment, academic visitors, students, family members, and others belonging to groups that, when considered as a group (rather than case by case), would not seem to pose security threats.

Amici have suggested that there are numerous applicants who could meet the waiver criteria. For instance, the Proclamation anticipates waivers for those with "significant business or professional obligations" in the United States, §3(c)(iv)(C), and amici identify many scholars who would seem to qualify. The Proclamation also anticipates waivers for those with a "close family member (e.g., a spouse, child, or parent)" in the United States,§3(c)(iv)(D), and amici identify many such individuals affected by the Proclamation. The Pars Equality Center identified 1,000 individuals—including parents and children of U.S. citizens—who sought and were denied entry under the Proclamation, hundreds of whom seem to meet the waiver criteria. Other data suggest the same. The Proclamation does not apply to asylum seekers or refugees. §§3(b)(vi), 6(e). Yet few refugees have been admitted since the Proclamation took effect. While more than 15,000 Syrian refugees arrived in the United States in 2016, only 13 have arrived since January 2018.

Similarly few refugees have been admitted since January from Iran (3), Libya (1), Yemen (0), and Somalia (122). The Proclamation also exempts individuals applying for several types of nonimmigrant visas: lawful permanent residents, parolees, those with certain travel documents, dual nationals of non-covered countries, and representatives of governments or international organizations. §§3(b)(i)–(v). It places no restrictions on the vast majority of student and exchange visitors, covering only those from Syria, which provided 8 percent of student and exchange visitors from the five countries in 2016. §§2(b)–(h). Visitors from Somalia are eligible for any type of nonimmigrant visa, subject to "additional scrutiny." §2(h)(ii). If nonimmigrant visa applications under the Proclamation resemble those in 2016, 16 percent of visa applicants would be eligible for exemptions. In practice, however, only 258 student visas were issued to applicants from Iran (189), Libya (29), Yemen (40), and Somalia (0) in the first three months of 2018. This is less than a quarter of the volume needed to be on track for 2016 student visa levels. And only 40 nonimmigrant visas have been issued to Somali nationals, a decrease of 65 percent from 2016. While this is but a piece of the picture, it does not provide grounds for confidence.

Finally, in a pending case in the Eastern District of New York, a consular official has filed a sworn affidavit asserting that he and other officials do not, in fact, have discretion to grant waivers. According to the affidavit, consular officers "were not allowed to exercise that discretion" and "the waiver process is merely 'window dressing.'" Another report similarly indicates that the U. S. Embassy in Djibouti, which processes visa applications for citizens of Yemen, received instructions to grant waivers "only in rare cases of imminent danger," with one consular officer reportedly telling an applicant that "'even for infants, we would need to see some evidence of a congenital heart defect or another medical issue of that degree of difficulty that would likely lead to the child's developmental harm or death.'" Declarations, anecdotal evidence, facts, and numbers taken from amicus briefs are not judicial fact findings. The government has not had an opportunity to respond, and a court has not had an opportunity to decide. But, given the importance of the decision in this case, the need for assurance that the Proclamation does not rest upon a "Muslim ban," and the assistance in deciding the issue that answer to the "exemption and waiver" questions may provide, I would send this case back to the District Court for further proceedings. And, I would leave the injunction in effect while the matter is litigated. Regardless, the Court's decision today leaves the District Court free to explore these issues on remand. If this Court must decide the question without this further litigation, I would, on balance, find the evidence of antireligious bias, including statements on a website taken down only after the President issued the two executive orders preceding the Proclamation, along with the other statements also set forth in Justice Sotomayor's opinion, a sufficient basis to set the Proclamation aside. And for these reasons, I respectfully dissent.

Justice SOTOMAYOR, with whom Justice GINSBURG joins, dissenting.

[Justice Sotomayor dissented, stating, "Based on the evidence in the record, a reasonable observer would conclude that the Proclamation was motivated by anti-Muslim animus. That alone suffices to show that plaintiffs are likely to succeed on the merits of their Establishment Clause claim." For the rest of Justice Sotomayor's dissent, see the First Amendment part of the Supplement, *infra*.]

Notes

1. *Immigration Policy.* In the May and early June of 2018, the Federal Government adopted a policy separating and detaining parents and children at the border who apparently were attempting to enter the United States either unlawfully or to attempt lawful asylum. A so-called "zero tolerance" policy was adopted, where those who attempted to enter without a lawful basis would be prosecuted. On June 20, 2018, President Trump signed an Executive Order to keep undocumented families from being separated at the border. The President might be limited in what happens to undocumented children based on a consent decree filed in *Central District of California, Jenny L. Flores, v. Reno* (1991), creating standards and limits on the detention of undocumented minors.

2. *DACA.* In 2012, President Barak Obama announced through an executive memorandum a temporary program called "Deferred Action for Childhood Arrivals" or DACA. This program defers deportation for two years to qualified people who were brought to the United States unlawfully as children. The two-year deferral is renewable. Individuals in the program can become eligible for a work permit, but not citizenship. Qualifications for the program include being in school, graduating from high school, or being honorably discharged from the military. No felony or serious misdemeanor convictions are permitted. There have been approximately 700,000 approved DACA applications.

In 2017, the then-Attorney General, Jefferson Sessions, advised the acting secretary of the Department of Homeland Security, Elaine Duke, to rescind the DACA program, claiming it was an unconstitutional exercise of executive authority. The Trump administration thereafter announced that the program would be wound down — first, by not accepting new applications, and second, by limiting renewals. The decision to wind down the program led to a lawsuit that claimed the government decision was "arbitrary and capricious" in violation of the Administrative Procedure Act (APA).

In its 2019-2020 term, the Supreme Court agreed to hear the case, *Department of Homeland Security v. Regents of California*. The outcome was a 5-4 decision, with Chief Justice John Roberts Jr. writing the opinion for a plurality of the court. The

Chief Justice found that there was no reasoned basis for the decision as required by the APA and thus the Administration violated the procedural requirements set up by law. While the justices agreed that the Trump Administration had the power to terminate DACA, it was the way they went about it that led five justices to conclude the decision ran afoul of federal law.

Dept. of Homeland Security v. Regents of California

591 U.S.___ (2020)

Chief Justice ROBERTS delivered the opinion of the Court, except as to Part IV.

In the summer of 2012, the Department of Homeland Security (DHS) announced an immigration program known as Deferred Action for Childhood Arrivals, or DACA. That program allows certain unauthorized aliens who entered the United States as children to apply for a two-year forbearance of removal. Those granted such relief are also eligible for work authorization and various federal benefits. Some 700,000 aliens have availed themselves of this opportunity.

Five years later, the Attorney General advised DHS to rescind DACA, based on his conclusion that it was unlawful. The Department's Acting Secretary issued a memorandum terminating the program on that basis. The termination was challenged by affected individuals and third parties who alleged, among other things, that the Acting Secretary had violated the Administrative Procedure Act (APA) by failing to adequately address important factors bearing on her decision. For the reasons that follow, we conclude that the Acting Secretary did violate the APA, and that the rescission must be vacated.

I

In June 2012, the Secretary of Homeland Security issued a memorandum announcing an immigration relief program for "certain young people who were brought to this country as children." Known as DACA, the program applies to childhood arrivals who were under age 31 in 2012; have continuously resided here since 2007; are current students, have completed high school, or are honorably discharged veterans; have not been convicted of any serious crimes; and do not threaten national security or public. DHS concluded that individuals who meet these criteria warrant favorable treatment under the immigration laws because they "lacked the intent to violate the law," are "productive" contributors to our society, and "know only this country as home."

"[T]o prevent [these] low priority individuals from being removed from the United States," the DACA Memorandum instructs Immigration and Customs Enforcement to "exercise prosecutorial discretion[] on an individual basis . . . by deferring action for a period of two years, subject to renewal." Id., at 100a. In addition, it directs U. S. Citizenship and Immigration Services (USCIS) to "accept applications to determine whether these individuals qualify for work authorization during this period of deferred action," id., at 101a, as permitted under regulations long predating DACA's creation. Pursuant to other regulations, deferred action recipients are considered "lawfully present" for purposes of, and therefore eligible to receive, Social Security and Medicare benefits.

In November 2014, two years after DACA was promulgated, DHS issued a memorandum announcing that it would expand DACA eligibility by removing the age cap, shifting the date-of-entry requirement from 2007 to 2010, and extending the deferred action and work authorization period to three years. In the same memorandum, DHS created a new, related program known as Deferred Action for Parents of Americans and Lawful Permanent Residents, or DAPA. That program would have authorized deferred action for up to 4.3 million parents whose children were U. S. citizens or lawful permanent residents. These parents were to enjoy the same forbearance, work eligibility, and other benefits as DACA recipients.

Before the DAPA Memorandum was implemented, 26 States, led by Texas, filed suit in the Southern District of Texas. The States contended that DAPA and the DACA expansion violated the APA's notice and comment requirement, the Immigration and Nationality Act (INA), and the Executive's duty under the Take Care Clause of the Constitution. The District Court found that the States were likely to succeed on the merits of at least one of their claims and entered a nationwide preliminary injunction barring implementation of both DAPA and the DACA expansion.

A divided panel of the Court of Appeals for the Fifth Circuit affirmed the preliminary injunction. *Texas v. United States,* 809 F. 3d 134, 188 (2015). In opposing the injunction, the Government argued that the DAPA Memorandum reflected an unreviewable exercise of the Government's enforcement discretion. The Fifth Circuit majority disagreed.

The majority . . . upheld the injunction on two grounds. It first concluded the States were likely to succeed on their procedural claim that the DAPA Memorandum was a substantive rule that was required to undergo notice and comment. It then held that the APA required DAPA to be set aside because the program was "manifestly contrary" to the INA, which "expressly and carefully provides legal designations allowing defined classes" to "receive the benefits" associated with "lawful presence" and to qualify for work.

This Court affirmed the Fifth Circuit's judgment by an equally divided vote, which meant that no opinion was issued. *United States v. Texas,* 579 U. S. ___ (2016) (per curiam). For the next year, litigation over DAPA and the DACA expansion continued in the Southern District of Texas, while implementation of those policies remained enjoined.

Then, in June 2017, following a change in Presidential administrations, DHS rescinded the DAPA Memorandum. In explaining that decision, DHS cited the preliminary injunction and ongoing litigation in Texas, the fact that DAPA had never taken effect, and the new administration's immigration enforcement priorities.

Three months later, in September 2017, Attorney General Jefferson B. Sessions III sent a letter to Acting Secretary of Homeland Security Elaine C. Duke, "advis[ing]" that DHS "should rescind" DACA as well. Citing the Fifth Circuit's opinion and this Court's equally divided affirmance, the Attorney General concluded that DACA shared the "same legal . . . defects that the courts recognized as to DAPA" and was "likely" to meet a similar fate. "In light of the costs and burdens" that a rescission would "impose[] on DHS," the Attorney General urged DHS to "consider an orderly and efficient wind-down process." Ibid.

The next day, Duke acted on the Attorney General's advice. In her decision memorandum, Duke summarized the history of the DACA and DAPA programs, the Fifth Circuit opinion and ensuing affirmance, and the contents of the Attorney General's letter. "Taking into consideration the Supreme Court's and the Fifth Circuit's rulings" and the "letter from the Attorney General," she concluded that the "DACA program should be terminated."

II

The dispute before the Court is not whether DHS may rescind DACA. All parties agree that it may. The dispute is instead primarily about the procedure the agency followed in doing so.

The APA "sets forth the procedures by which federal agencies are accountable to the public and their actions subject to review by the courts," and directs that agency actions be "set aside" if they are "arbitrary" or "capricious," 5 U.S.C. §706(2)(A). Under this "narrow standard of review, . . . a court is not to substitute its judgment for that of the agency," *FCC v. Fox Television Stations, Inc.,* 556 U.S. 502, 513 (2009), but instead to assess only whether the decision was "based on a consideration of the relevant factors and whether there has been a clear error of judgment," *Citizens to Preserve Overton Park, Inc. v. Volpe,* 401 U. S. 402, 416 (1971).

But before determining whether the rescission was arbitrary and capricious, we must first address the Government's contentions that DHS's decision is unreviewable under the APA and outside this Court's jurisdiction.

[The Court then found that the APA "establishes a "basic presumption of judicial review or one 'suffering legal wrong because of agency action'" and that the claim in this case was reviewable.]

III [The Merits]

Deciding whether agency action was adequately explained requires, first, knowing where to look for the agency's explanation. The natural starting point here is the explanation provided by Acting Secretary Duke when she announced the rescission in September 2017. But the Government urges us to go on and consider the June 2018 memorandum submitted by Secretary Nielsen as well. That memo was prepared after the D. C. District Court vacated the Duke rescission and gave DHS an opportunity to "reissue a memorandum rescinding DACA, this time providing a fuller explanation for the determination that the program lacks statutory and constitutional authority." 298 F. Supp. 3d, at 245. According to the Government, the Nielsen Memorandum is properly before us because it was invited by the District Court and reflects the views of the Secretary of Homeland Security—the official responsible for immigration policy. Respondents disagree, arguing that the Nielsen Memorandum, issued nine months after the rescission, impermissibly asserts prudential and policy reasons not relied upon by Duke.

It is a "foundational principle of administrative law" that judicial review of agency action is limited to "the grounds that the agency invoked when it took the action." *Michigan*, 576 U. S., at 758. If those grounds are inadequate, a court may remand for the agency to do one of two things: First, the agency can offer "a fuller explanation of the agency's reasoning at the time of the agency action." *Pension Benefit Guaranty Corporation v. LTV Corp.*, 496 U. S. 633, 654 (1990). This route has important limitations. When an agency's initial explanation "indicate[s] the determinative reason for the final action taken," the agency may elaborate later on that reason (or reasons) but may not provide new ones. *Camp v. Pitts*, 411 U. S. 138, 143 (1973) (per curiam). Alternatively, the agency can "deal with the problem afresh" by taking new agency action. *SEC v. Chenery Corp.*, 332 U. S. 194, 201 (1947) (Chenery II). An agency taking this route is not limited to its prior reasons but must comply with the procedural requirements for new agency action.

The District Court's remand thus presented DHS with a choice: rest on the Duke Memorandum while elaborating on its prior reasoning, or issue a new rescission bolstered by new reasons absent from the Duke Memorandum. Secretary Nielsen took the first path. Rather than making a new decision, she "decline[d] to disturb the Duke memorandum's rescission" and instead "provide[d] further explanation" for that action. Indeed, the Government's subsequent request for reconsideration described the Nielsen Memorandum as "additional explanation for [Duke's] decision" and asked the District Court to "leave in place [Duke's] September 5, 2017 decision to rescind the DACA policy." Contrary to the position of the Government before this Court, and of Justice Kavanaugh in dissent, (opinion concurring in judgment in part and dissenting in part), the Nielsen Memorandum was by its own terms not a new rule implementing a new policy.

Because Secretary Nielsen chose to elaborate on the reasons for the initial rescission rather than take new administrative action, she was limited to the agency's original reasons, and her explanation "must be viewed critically" to ensure that the rescission is not upheld on the basis of impermissible "post hoc rationalization." But despite purporting to explain the Duke Memorandum, Secretary Nielsen's reasoning bears little relationship to that of her predecessor. Acting Secretary Duke rested the rescission on the conclusion that DACA is unlawful. Period. By contrast, Secretary Nielsen's new memorandum offered three "separate and independently sufficient reasons" for the rescission, only the first of which is the conclusion that DACA is illegal.

Her second reason is that DACA is, at minimum, legally questionable and should be terminated to maintain public confidence in the rule of law and avoid burdensome litigation. No such justification can be found in the Duke Memorandum. Legal uncertainty is, of course, related to illegality. But the two justifications are meaningfully distinct, especially in this context. While an agency might, for one reason or another, choose to do nothing in the face of uncertainty, illegality presumably requires remedial action of some sort.

The policy reasons that Secretary Nielsen cites as a third basis for the rescission are also nowhere to be found in the Duke Memorandum. That document makes no mention of a preference for legislative fixes, the superiority of case-by-case decision-making, the importance of sending a message of robust enforcement, or any other policy consideration. Nor are these points included in the legal analysis from the Fifth Circuit and the Attorney General. They can be viewed only as impermissible post hoc rationalizations and thus are not properly before us.

The Government, echoed by Justice Kavanaugh, protests that requiring a new decision before considering Nielsen's new justifications would be "an idle and useless formality." *NLRB v. Wyman-Gordon Co.*, 394 U. S. 759, 766. Procedural requirements can often seem such. But here the rule serves important values of administrative law. Requiring a new decision before considering new reasons promotes "agency accountability" by ensuring that parties and the public can respond fully and in a timely manner to an agency's exercise of authority. Considering only contemporaneous explanations for agency action also instills confidence that the reasons given are not simply "convenient litigating position[s]." *Christopher v. SmithKline Beecham Corp.*, 567 U. S. 142, 155 (2012). Permitting agencies to invoke belated justifications, on the other hand, can upset "the orderly functioning of the process of review," *SEC v. Chenery Corp.*, 318 U. S. 80, 94 (1943), forcing both litigants and courts to chase a moving target. Each of these values would be markedly undermined were we to allow DHS to rely on reasons offered nine months after Duke announced the rescission and after three different courts had identified flaws in the original explanation.

The functional reasons for requiring contemporaneous explanations apply with equal force regardless whether post hoc justifications are raised in court by those appearing on behalf of the agency or by agency officials themselves. Justice Holmes famously wrote that "[m]en must turn square corners when they deal with the Government." *Rock Island, A. & L. R. Co. v. United States*, 254 U. S. 141, 143 (1920). But it is also true, particularly when so much is at stake, that "the Government should turn square corners in dealing with the people." St. *Regis Paper Co. v. United States*, 368 U. S. 208, 229 (1961) (Black, J., dissenting). The basic rule here is clear: An agency must defend its actions based on the reasons it gave when it acted. This is not the case for cutting corners to allow DHS to rely upon reasons absent from its original decision.

We turn, finally, to whether DHS's decision to rescind DACA was arbitrary and capricious. As noted earlier, Acting Secretary Duke's justification for the rescission was succinct: "Taking into consideration" the Fifth Circuit's conclusion that DAPA was unlawful because it conferred benefits in violation of the INA, and the Attorney General's conclusion that DACA was unlawful for the same reason, she concluded—without elaboration—that the "DACA program should be terminated."

Respondents maintain that this explanation is deficient for three reasons. Their first and second arguments work in tandem, claiming that the Duke Memorandum does not adequately explain the conclusion that DACA is unlawful, and that this conclusion is, in any event, wrong. While those arguments carried the day in the lower courts, in our view they overlook an important constraint on Acting Secretary Duke's decision making authority—she was bound by the Attorney General's legal determination.

The same statutory provision that establishes the Secretary of Homeland Security's authority to administer and enforce immigration laws limits that authority, specifying that, with respect to "all questions of law," the determinations of the Attorney General "shall be controlling." Respondents are aware of this constraint. Indeed they emphasized the point in the reviewability sections of their briefs. But in their merits arguments, respondents never addressed whether or how this unique statutory provision might affect our review. They did not discuss whether Duke was required to explain a legal conclusion that was not hers to make. Nor did they discuss whether the current suits challenging Duke's rescission decision, which everyone agrees was within her legal authority under the INA, are proper vehicles for attacking the Attorney General's legal conclusion.

Because of these gaps in respondents' briefing, we do not evaluate the claims challenging the explanation and correctness of the illegality conclusion. Instead we focus our attention on respondents' third argument—that Acting Secretary Duke "failed to consider . . . important aspect[s] of the problem" before her.

Whether DACA is illegal is, of course, a legal determination, and therefore a question for the Attorney General. But deciding how best to address a finding of illegality moving forward can involve important policy choices, especially when the finding concerns a program with the breadth of DACA. Those policy choices are for DHS.

Acting Secretary Duke plainly exercised such discretionary authority in winding down the program. Among other things, she specified that those DACA recipients whose benefits were set to expire within six months were eligible for two-year renewals.

But there is more to DAPA (and DACA) than such benefits. The defining feature of deferred action is the decision to defer removal (and to notify the affected alien of that decision). And the Fifth Circuit was careful to distinguish that forbearance component from eligibility for benefits. As it explained, the "challenged portion of DAPA's deferred-action program" was the decision to make DAPA recipients eligible for benefits. The other "[p]art of DAPA," the court noted, "involved the Secretary's decision—at least temporarily—not to enforce the immigration laws as to a class of what he deem[ed] to be low-priority illegal aliens." Id., at 166. Borrowing from this Court's prior description of deferred action, the Fifth Circuit observed that "the states do not challenge the Secretary's decision to 'decline to institute proceedings, terminate proceedings, or decline to execute a final order of deportation.'" And the Fifth Circuit underscored that nothing in its decision or the preliminary injunction "requires the Secretary to remove any alien or to alter" the Secretary's class-based "enforcement priorities." *Texas*, 809 F. 3d, at 166, 169. In other words, the Secretary's forbearance authority was unimpaired.

In short, the Attorney General neither addressed the forbearance policy at the heart of DACA nor compelled DHS to abandon that policy. Thus, removing benefits eligibility while continuing forbearance remained squarely within the discretion of Acting Secretary Duke, who was responsible for "[e]stablishing national immigration enforcement policies and priorities." 6 U.S.C. 202(5). But Duke's memo offers no reason for terminating forbearance. She instead treated the Attorney General's conclusion regarding the illegality of benefits as sufficient to rescind both benefits and forbearance, without explanation.

That reasoning repeated the error we identified in one of our leading modern administrative law cases, *Motor Vehicle Manufacturers Association of the United States, Inc. v. State Farm Mutual Automobile Insurance Co.* There, the National Highway Traffic Safety Administration (NHTSA) promulgated a requirement that motor vehicles produced after 1982 be equipped with one of two passive restraints: airbags or automatic seatbelts. Four years later, before the requirement went into effect, NHTSA concluded that automatic seatbelts, the restraint of choice for most manufacturers, would not provide effective protection. Based on that premise, NHTSA rescinded the passive restraint requirement in full. We concluded that the total rescission was arbitrary and capricious. As we explained, NHTSA's justification supported only "disallow[ing] compliance by means of" automatic seatbelts. It did "not cast doubt" on the "efficacy of airbag technology" or upon "the need for a passive restraint standard." Given NHTSA's prior judgment that "airbags are an effective and cost-beneficial lifesaving technology," we held that "the mandatory passive restraint rule [could] not be abandoned without any consideration whatsoever of an airbags-only requirement."

While the factual setting is different here, the error is the same. Even if it is illegal for DHS to extend work authorization and other benefits to DACA recipients, that conclusion supported only "disallow[ing]" benefits. It did "not cast doubt" on the legality of forbearance or upon DHS's original reasons for extending forbearance to childhood arrivals. Thus, given DHS's earlier judgment that forbearance is "especially justified" for "productive young people" who were brought here as children and "know only this country as home," the DACA Memorandum could not be rescinded in full "without any consideration whatsoever" of a forbearance-only policy.

The Government acknowledges that "[d]eferred action coupled with the associated benefits are the two legs upon which the DACA policy stands." It insists, however, that "DHS was not required to consider whether DACA's illegality could be addressed by separating" the two. According to the Government, "It was not

arbitrary and capricious for DHS to view deferred action and its collateral benefits as importantly linked." Perhaps. But that response misses the point. The fact
that there may be a valid reason not to separate deferred action from benefits
does not establish that DHS considered that option or that such consideration
was unnecessary.

The lead dissent acknowledges that forbearance and benefits are legally
distinct and can be decoupled. It contends, however, that we should not "dis-
sect" agency action "piece by piece." The dissent instead rests on the Attorney
General's legal determination—which considered only benefits—"to supply the
'reasoned analysis'" to support rescission of both benefits and forbearance (quoting *State Farm*). But *State Farm* teaches that when an agency rescinds a prior policy
its reasoned analysis must consider the "alternative[s]" that are "within the ambit
of the existing [policy]." Here forbearance was not simply "within the ambit of
the existing [policy]," it was the centerpiece of the policy: DACA, after all, stands
for "*Deferred Action* for Childhood Arrivals." But the rescission memorandum
contains no discussion of forbearance or the option of retaining forbearance
without benefits. Duke "entirely failed to consider [that] important aspect of the
problem." *State Farm*.

That omission alone renders Acting Secretary Duke's decision arbitrary
and capricious. But it is not the only defect. Duke also failed to address whether
there was "legitimate reliance" on the DACA Memorandum. *Smiley v. Citibank
(South Dakota), N. A.*, 517 U.S. 735, 742 (1996). When an agency changes course,
as DHS did here, it must "be cognizant that longstanding policies may have
'engendered serious reliance interests that must be taken into account.'" *Encino
Motorcars, LLC v. Navarro*, 579 U.S. ___, ___ (2016) (quoting *Fox Television*, 556
U.S., at 515). "It would be arbitrary and capricious to ignore such matters." *Id.*, at
515. Yet that is what the Duke Memorandum did.

For its part, the Government does not contend that Duke considered potential reliance interests; it counters that she did not need to. In the Government's
view, shared by the lead dissent, DACA recipients have no "legally cognizable
reliance interests" because the DACA Memorandum stated that the program
"conferred no substantive rights" and provided benefits only in two-year incre-
ments. But neither the Government nor the lead dissent cites any legal authority
establishing that such features automatically preclude reliance interests, and we
are not aware of any. These disclaimers are surely pertinent in considering the
strength of any reliance interests, but that consideration must be undertaken by
the agency in the first instance, subject to normal APA review. There was no such
consideration in the Duke Memorandum.

The dissent is correct that DACA was rescinded because of the Attorney
General's illegality determination. But nothing about that determination foreclosed or even addressed the options of retaining forbearance or accommodating particular reliance interests. Acting Secretary Duke should have considered
those matters but did not. That failure was arbitrary and capricious in violation
of the APA.

IV

Lastly, we turn to respondents' claim that the rescission violates the equal protection guarantee of the Fifth Amendment.

The parties dispute the proper framing of this claim. The Government contends that the allegation that the Executive, motivated by animus, ended a program that disproportionately benefits certain ethnic groups is a selective enforcement claim. Such a claim, the Government asserts, is barred by our decision in *Reno v. American-Arab AntiDiscrimination Committee.* Respondents counter that their claim falls outside the scope of that precedent because they are not challenging individual enforcement proceedings. We need not resolve this debate because, even if the claim is cognizable, the allegations here are insufficient.

To plead animus, a plaintiff must raise a plausible inference that an "invidious discriminatory purpose was a motivating factor" in the relevant decision. *Arlington Heights v. Metropolitan Housing Development Corp.*, 429 U.S. 252, 256 (1977). Possible evidence includes disparate impact on a particular group, "[d]epartures from the normal procedural sequence," and "contemporary statements by members of the decision making body." Id., at 266-268. Tracking these factors, respondents allege that animus is evidenced by (1) the disparate impact of the rescission on Latinos from Mexico, who represent 78% of DACA recipients; (2) the unusual history behind the rescission; and (3) pre- and post-election statements by President Trump. Brief for New York 54-55.

None of these points, either singly or in concert, establishes a plausible equal protection claim. First, because Latinos make up a large share of the unauthorized alien population, one would expect them to make up an outsized share of recipients of any cross-cutting immigration relief program. See B. Baker, DHS, Office of Immigration Statistics, Population Estimates, Illegal Alien Population Residing in the United States: January 2015, Table 2 (Dec. 2018). Were this fact sufficient to state a claim, virtually any generally applicable immigration policy could be challenged on equal protection grounds.

We do not decide whether DACA or its rescission are sound policies. "The wisdom" of those decisions "is none of our concern." *Chenery II*, 332 U.S., at 207. We address only whether the agency complied with the procedural requirement that it provide a reasoned explanation for its action. Here the agency failed to consider the conspicuous issues of whether to retain forbearance and what if anything to do about the hardship to DACA recipients. That dual failure raises doubts about whether the agency appreciated the scope of its discretion or exercised that discretion in a reasonable manner.

The appropriate recourse is therefore to remand to DHS so that it may consider the problem anew. The judgment in NAACP, is affirmed. The judgment in Regents, is vacated in part and reversed in part. And in *Batalla Vidal*, No. 18–589, the February 13, 2018 order granting respondents' motion for a preliminary injunction is vacated, the November 9, 2017 order partially denying the Government's motion to dismiss is affirmed in part, and the March 29, 2018 order partially denying the balance of the Government's motion to dismiss is reversed in part. All three cases are remanded for further proceedings consistent with this opinion. It is so ordered.

Justice SOTOMAYOR, J., Concurring in part, Concurring in the judgment in part, and Dissenting in part.

The majority rightly holds that the Department of Homeland Security (DHS) violated the Administrative Procedure Act in rescinding the Deferred Action for Childhood Arrivals (DACA) program. But the Court forecloses any challenge to the rescission under the Equal Protection Clause. I believe that determination is unwarranted on the existing record and premature at this stage of the litigation. I would instead permit respondents to develop their equal protection claims on remand.

Respondents' equal protection challenges come to us in a preliminary posture. All that respondents needed to do at this stage of the litigation was state sufficient facts that would "allo[w a] court to draw the reasonable inference that [a] defendant is liable for the misconduct alleged." *Ashcroft v. Iqbal*, 556 U.S. 662, 678 (2009). The three courts to evaluate respondents' pleadings below held that they cleared this modest threshold. *See also Batalla Vidal v. Nielsen*, 291 F.Supp. 3d 260, 274 (EDNY 2018).

I too would permit respondents' claims to proceed on remand. The complaints each set forth particularized facts that plausibly allege discriminatory animus. The plurality disagrees, reasoning that "[n]one of these points, either singly or in concert, establishes a plausible equal protection claim." But it reaches that conclusion by discounting some allegations altogether and by narrowly viewing the rest.

First, the plurality dismisses the statements that President Trump made both before and after he assumed office. The *Batalla Vidal* complaints catalog then-candidate Trump's declarations that Mexican immigrants are "people that have lots of problems," "the bad ones," and "criminals, drug dealers, [and] rapists." 291 F. Supp. 3d, at 276. The Regents complaints additionally quote President Trump's 2017 statement comparing undocumented immigrants to "animals" responsible for "the drugs, the gangs, the cartels, the crisis of smuggling and trafficking, [and] MS13." 298 F. Supp. 3d 1304, 1314 (ND Cal. 2018). The plurality brushes these aside as "unilluminating," "remote in time," and having been "made in unrelated contexts."

But "nothing in our precedent supports [the] blinkered approach" of disregarding any of the campaign statements as remote in time from later-enacted policies. *Trump* v. *Hawaii*, 585 U. S. ___, ___, n. 3 (2018) (Sotomayor, J., dissenting). Nor did any of the statements arise in unrelated contexts. They bear on unlawful migration from Mexico—a keystone of President Trump's campaign and a policy priority of his administration—and, according to respondents, were an animating force behind the rescission of DACA. Cf. *ibid.* (noting that Presidential Proclamation No. 9645, 82 Fed. Reg. 45161 (2017), which barred entry of individuals from several Muslim-majority countries, was an outgrowth of the President's campaign statements about Muslims). Taken together, "the words of the President" help to "create the strong perception" that the rescission decision was "contaminated by impermissible discriminatory animus." 585 U.S., at ___ (opinion of Sotomayor, J.). This perception provides respondents with grounds to litigate their equal protection claims further.

Next, the plurality minimizes the disproportionate impact of the rescission decision on Latinos after considering this point in isolation. *Ante*, at 28 ("Were this fact sufficient to state a claim, virtually any generally applicable immigration policy could be challenged on equal protection grounds"). But the impact of the policy decision must be viewed in the context of the President's public statements on and off the campaign trail. At the motion-to-dismiss stage, I would not so readily dismiss the allegation that an executive decision disproportionately harms the same racial group that the President branded as less desirable mere months earlier.

Finally, the plurality finds nothing untoward in the "specific sequence of events leading up to the challenged decision." *Arlington Heights v. Metropolitan Housing Development Corp.*, 429 U.S. 252, 267 (1977). I disagree. As late as June 2017, DHS insisted it remained committed to DACA, even while rescinding a related program, the Deferred Action for Parents of Americans and Lawful Permanent Residents. App. 718-720. But a mere three months later, DHS terminated DACA without, as the plurality acknowledges, considering important aspects of the termination. The abrupt change in position plausibly suggests that something other than questions about the legality of DACA motivated the rescission decision. Accordingly, it raises the possibility of a "significant mismatch between the decision . . . made and the rationale . . . provided." *Department of Commerce v. New York*, 588 U. S. ___, ___ (2019). Only by bypassing context does the plurality conclude otherwise.

The facts in respondents' complaints create more than a "sheer possibility that a defendant has acted unlawfully." *Iqbal*, 556 U.S., at 678. Whether they ultimately amount to actionable discrimination should be determined only after factual development on remand. Because the Court prematurely disposes of respondents' equal protection claims by overlooking the strength of their complaints, I join all but Part IV of the opinion and do not concur in the corresponding part of the judgment.

Justice THOMAS, with whom Justice ALITO and Justice GORSUCH join, concurring in the judgment in part and dissenting in part.

Between 2001 and 2011, Congress considered over two dozen bills that would have granted lawful status to millions of aliens who were illegally brought to this country as children. Each of those legislative efforts failed. In the wake of this impasse, the Department of Homeland Security (DHS) under President Barack Obama took matters into its own hands. Without any purported delegation of authority from Congress and without undertaking a rulemaking, DHS unilaterally created a program known as Deferred Action for Childhood Arrivals (DACA). The three-page DACA memorandum made it possible for approximately 1.7 million illegal aliens to qualify for temporary lawful presence and certain federal and state benefits. When President Donald Trump took office in 2017, his Acting Secretary of Homeland Security, acting through yet another memorandum, rescinded the DACA memorandum. To state it plainly, the Trump administration rescinded DACA the same way that the Obama administration created it: unilaterally, and through a mere memorandum.

Today the majority makes the mystifying determination that this rescission of DACA was unlawful. In reaching that conclusion, the majority acts as though it is engaging in the routine application of standard principles of administrative law. On the contrary, this is anything but a standard administrative law case.

DHS created DACA during the Obama administration without any statutory authorization and without going through the requisite rulemaking process. As a result, the program was unlawful from its inception. The majority does not even attempt to explain why a court has the authority to scrutinize an agency's policy reasons for rescinding an unlawful program under the arbitrary and capricious microscope. The decision to countermand an unlawful agency action is clearly reasonable. So long as the agency's determination of illegality is sound, our review should be at an end.

Today's decision must be recognized for what it is: an effort to avoid a politically controversial but legally correct decision. The Court could have made clear that the solution respondents seek must come from the Legislative Branch. Instead, the majority has decided to prolong DHS' initial overreach by providing a stopgap measure of its own. In doing so, it has given the green light for future political battles to be fought in this Court rather than where they rightfully belong—the political branches. Such timidity forsakes the Court's duty to apply the law according to neutral principles, and the ripple effects of the majority's error will be felt throughout our system of self-government.

Perhaps even more unfortunately, the majority's holding creates perverse incentives, particularly for outgoing administrations. Under the auspices of today's decision, administrations can bind their successors by unlawfully adopting significant legal changes through Executive Branch agency memoranda. Even if the agency lacked authority to effectuate the changes, the changes cannot be undone by the same agency in a successor administration unless the successor provides sufficient policy justifications to the satisfaction of this Court. In other words, the majority erroneously holds that the agency is not only permitted, but required, to continue administering unlawful programs that it inherited from a previous administration. I respectfully dissent in part.

Justice KAVANAUGH, concurring in the judgment in part and dissenting in part.

For the last 20 years, the country has engaged in consequential policy, religious, and moral debates about the legal status of millions of young immigrants who, as children, were brought to the United States and have lived here ever since.

Those young immigrants do not have legal status in the United States under current statutory law. They live, go to school, and work here with uncertainty about their futures. Despite many attempts over the last two decades, Congress has not yet enacted legislation to afford legal status to those immigrants.

In 2012, exercising its view of the Executive's prosecutorial discretion under Article II and the immigration laws, President Obama's administration unilaterally instituted a program known as Deferred Action for Childhood Arrivals, or DACA. Under DACA, eligible young immigrants may apply for and receive deferred action. They must renew their DACA status every two years. Under the program, the Executive Branch broadly forbears from enforcing certain immigration removal laws against DACA recipients. And by virtue of the forbearance, DACA recipients also become eligible for work authorization and other benefits.

Since 2017, President Trump's administration has sought to rescind DACA based on its different and narrower understanding of the Executive's prosecutorial discretion under Article II and the immigration laws. In its view, the Executive Branch legally may not, and as a policy matter should not, *unilaterally* forbear from enforcing the immigration laws against such a large class of individuals. The current administration has stated that it instead wants to work with Congress to enact comprehensive legislation that would address the legal status of those immigrants together with other significant immigration issues.

The question before the Court is whether the Executive Branch acted lawfully in ordering rescission of the ongoing DACA program. To begin with, all nine Members of the Court accept, as do the DACA plaintiffs themselves, that the Executive Branch possesses the legal authority to rescind DACA and to resume pre-DACA enforcement of the immigration laws enacted by Congress. Having previously adopted a policy of prosecutorial discretion and nonenforcement with respect to a particular class of offenses or individuals, the Executive Branch has the legal authority to rescind such a policy and resume enforcing the law enacted by Congress. The Executive Branch's exercise of that rescission authority is subject to constitutional constraints and may also be subject to statutory constraints. The narrow legal dispute here concerns a statutory constraint—namely, whether the Executive Branch's action to rescind DACA satisfied the general arbitrary-and-capricious standard of the Administrative Procedure Act, or APA.

The APA's arbitrary-and-capricious standard requires that agency action be reasonable and reasonably explained. As the Court has long stated, judicial review under that standard is deferential to the agency. The Court may not substitute its policy judgment for that of the agency. The Court simply ensures that the agency has acted within a broad zone of reasonableness and, in particular, has reasonably considered the relevant issues and reasonably explained the decision. See *FCC v. Fox Television Stations, Inc.*, 556 U.S. 502 (2009); *Motor Vehicle Mfrs. Assn. of United States, Inc. v. State Farm Mut. Automobile Ins. Co.*, 463 U.S. 29 (1983).

The Executive Branch explained its decision to rescind DACA in two sequential memorandums by successive Secretaries of Homeland Security: the

2017 Duke Memorandum and the 2018 Nielsen Memorandum. The Duke Memorandum focused on DACA's perceived legal flaws. The Court today finds the Duke Memorandum insufficient under the APA's arbitrary-and-capricious standard.

But regardless of whether the Court is correct about the Duke Memorandum, the Nielsen Memorandum more fully explained the Department's legal reasons for rescinding DACA, and clarified that even if DACA were lawful, the Department would still rescind DACA for a variety of policy reasons. The Nielsen Memorandum also expressly addressed the reliance interests of DACA recipients. The question under the APA's deferential arbitrary-and-capricious standard is not whether we agree with the Department's decision to rescind DACA. The question is whether the Nielsen Memorandum reasonably explained the decision to rescind DACA. Under ordinary application of the arbitrary-and-capricious standard, the Nielsen Memorandum—with its alternative and independent rationales and its discussion of reliance—would pass muster as an explanation for the Executive Branch's action.

The Nielsen Memorandum was issued nine months after the Duke Memorandum. Under the Administrative Procedure Act, the Nielsen Memorandum is itself a "rule" setting forth "an agency statement of general . . . applicability and future effect designed to implement policy." 5 U.S.C. 551(4). Because it is a rule, the Nielsen Memorandum constitutes "agency action." §551(13). As the Secretary of Homeland Security, Secretary Nielsen had the authority to decide whether to stick with Secretary Duke's decision to rescind DACA, or to make a different decision. Like Secretary Duke, Secretary Nielsen chose to rescind DACA, and she provided additional explanation. Her memorandum was akin to common forms of agency action that follow earlier agency action on the same subject—for example, a supplemental or new agency statement of policy, or an agency order with respect to a motion for rehearing or reconsideration. Courts often consider an agency's additional explanations of policy or additional explanations made, for example, on agency rehearing or reconsideration, or on remand from a court, even if the agency's bottom-line decision itself does not change.

Yet the Court today jettisons the Nielsen Memorandum by classifying it as a *post hoc* justification for rescinding DACA. Under our precedents, however, the *post hoc* justification doctrine merely requires that courts assess agency action based on the official explanations of the agency decision makers, and not based on after-the-fact explanations advanced *by agency lawyers during litigation* (or by judges). As the D. C. Circuit has explained, the *post hoc* justification doctrine "is not a time barrier which freezes an agency's exercise of its judgment after an initial decision has been made and bars it from further articulation of its reasoning. It is a rule directed at reviewing courts which forbids judges to uphold agency action on the basis of rationales offered by anyone other than the proper decision makers." *Alpharma, Inc. v. Leavitt*, 460 F.3d 1, 6 (2006) (Garland, J.).

Indeed, the ordinary judicial remedy for an agency's insufficient explanation is to remand for further explanation by the relevant agency personnel. It would make little sense for a court to exclude official explanations by agency personnel such as a Cabinet Secretary simply because the explanations are purportedly *post hoc*, and then to turn around and remand for further explanation by those same agency personnel. Yet that is the upshot of the Court's application of the *post hoc* justification doctrine today. The Court's refusal to look at the Nielsen Memorandum seems particularly mistaken, moreover, because the Nielsen Memorandum shows that the Department, back in 2018, considered the policy issues that the Court today says the Department did not consider. *Ante*, at 20-26.

To be sure, cases such as *Overton Park* and *Camp v. Pitts* suggest that courts reviewing certain agency *adjudications* may in some circumstances decline to examine an after-the-fact agency explanation. See *Camp v. Pitts*, 411 U.S. 138 (1973) (*per curiam*); *Citizens to Preserve Overton Park, Inc. v. Volpe*, 401 U.S 402 (1971). But agency adjudications are "concerned with the determination of past and present rights and liabilities," Attorney General's Manual on the Administrative Procedure Act 14 (1947), and implicate the due process interests of the individual parties to the adjudication. Judicial review of an adjudication therefore ordinarily focuses on what happened during the agency's adjudication process of deciding that individual case.

Even if certain agency adjudications have a slightly more stringent restriction on *post hoc* explanations, the APA is "based upon a dichotomy between rule making and adjudication," *ibid.*, and this case involves an ongoing agency rule that has future effect—the rescission of DACA. The Nielsen Memorandum implements and explains the rescission of DACA. I am aware of no case from this Court, and the Court today cites none, that has employed the *post hoc* justification doctrine to exclude an agency's official explanation of an agency rule. For purposes of arbitrary-and-capricious review, it does not matter whether the latest official explanation was two years ago or three years ago. What matters is whether the explanation was reasonable and followed the requisite procedures. In my view, the Court should consider the Nielsen Memorandum in deciding whether the Department's rescission of DACA satisfies the APA's arbitrary-and-capricious standard.

Because the Court excludes the Nielsen Memorandum, the Court sends the case back to the Department of Homeland Security for further explanation. Although I disagree with the Court's decision to remand, the only practical consequence of the Court's decision to remand appears to be some delay. The Court's decision seems to allow the Department on remand to relabel and reiterate the substance of the Nielsen Memorandum, perhaps with some elaboration as suggested in the Court's opinion.

The Court's resolution of this narrow APA issue of course cannot eliminate the broader uncertainty over the status of the DACA recipients. That uncertainty is a result of Congress's inability thus far to agree on legislation, which in turn has forced successive administrations to improvise, thereby triggering many rounds of relentless litigation with the prospect of more litigation to come. In contrast to those necessarily short-lived and stopgap administrative measures, the Article I legislative process could produce a sturdy and enduring solution to this issue, one way or the other, and thereby remove the uncertainty that has persisted for years for these young immigrants and the Nation's immigration system. In the meantime, as to the narrow APA question presented here, I appreciate the Court's careful analysis, but I ultimately disagree with its treatment of the Nielsen Memorandum. I therefore respectfully dissent from the Court's judgment on plaintiffs' APA claim, and I concur in the judgment insofar as the Court rejects plaintiffs' equal protection claim.

D. THE PRESIDENT'S APPOINTMENT AND REMOVAL POWERS

Even though the President's appointment and removal powers are often lumped together, each is a distinct power, with its own set of rules. The President has the power to appoint and remove various government officials, some located within the Executive Branch and some in the other branches. The application of these powers is not always intuitive, particularly in light of the way the Supreme Court has carved out the Separation of Powers doctrine over the years. The powers vary, depending on whether the official is appointed or removed, designated "principal" or "inferior," or engaged in executive, judicial, or legislative types of activities.

The scope of the President's appointment and removal powers can be seen to rest as much on the conceptualization of the separation of powers among the three branches as on pragmatism. Much depends on whether one believes there is elegant simplicity in placing a single person in charge of executing federal law, or whether there ought to be a less sharply defined interdependence among the branches, characterized by dynamic change over time. *See, e.g.,* Peter M. Shane, *Independent Policymaking and Presidential Power: A Constitutional Analysis,* 57 Geo. Wash. L. Rev. 596 (1989); and Peter L. Strauss, *Formal and Functional Approaches to Separation-of-Powers Questions—A Foolish Inconsistency?,* 72 Cornell L. Rev. 488 (1987). This tension often has played out on a field divided by those advancing a strong unitary theory of the executive and those opposing such a position.

These appointment and removal powers often intersect with and complement the powers of Congress. As a necessary and proper derivative of its legislative power, Congress holds the power to create offices and agencies to carry out its laws. Art. I, §8, cl. 18 (the Necessary and Proper Clause). Congress is simply precluded from creating an agency and then inserting officials to run the agency and execute the law. Such consolidated authority would belie the separation of powers principle.

Appointments Power. The Constitution states: "The President shall nominate, and by and with the Advice and Consent of the Senate, shall appoint Ambassadors, other public Ministers and Consuls, Judges of the Supreme Court, and all other Officers of the United States, whose Appointments are not herein otherwise provided for, and which shall be established by Law: but the Congress may by Law vest the Appointment of such inferior Officers, as they think proper, in the President alone, in the Courts of Law, or in the Heads of Departments." Art. II, §2, cl. 2. While the appointment of officers of the United States is based on a carefully described process, which officials are viewed as "Officers of the United States" and which are viewed as "inferior," as well as the meaning of "as they think proper," have been subject to judicial scrutiny and interpretation.

The Constitution effectively divides the appointment of government officials subject to constitutional limitations into two categories—those high-ranking officials considered officers of the United States, or "principal" officers, and officers considered "inferior" (although still wielding considerable power). The principal officers include the heads of departments, such as the secretary of state, other cabinet positions, ambassadors, and federal judges. Inferior officers include many remaining government officials, who often wield considerable policy power.

The process for appointing officers of the United States is prescribed by the Constitution. Art. II, §2, cl. 2. The President has the power to nominate these persons and, "by and with the advice and consent of the Senate," to appoint these individuals to their posts. *Id.* A notable example involves the appointment of a new federal judge, such as Sonia Sotomayor. She was nominated by President Obama to become an Associate Justice of the U.S. Supreme Court, sat for confirmation hearings before the Senate Judiciary Committee, and then was approved by the full Senate. The process for inferior officers is not articulated in the Constitution and has been left to judicial interpretation. A critical appointments issue often involves how much control must be ceded to the President in appointing members of the Executive Branch.

The President's power to nominate judges and other officers has become embroiled in politics in recent years. Two dangers have arisen. The first is the lack of movement of nominees. The Constitution does not require that a person nominated by the President receive a hearing or even a vote on a hearing once taken, and some nominees have languished for long periods of time. In fact, since 1980, the time has doubled for judicial confirmations. This has led to a second consequence—a reluctance to become a nominee, not just because of the potential time delay, but also because of the disclosure requirements and likely media scrutiny that occurs in the modern 24/7 media cycle. According to statistics, there are 59 vacancies as of June 2015 in the federal district courts, appellate courts, and courts of international trade. *See http://www.uscourts.gov/judges-judgeships/judicial-vacancies.* Further, of these 59 vacancies, there are only a total of 15 positions with nominations pending. *Id.*

Several cases in the 1970s and 1980s developed the appointments power doctrine. *Buckley v. Valeo*, 424 U.S. 1 (1976), which follows, was one of several cases shaping the boundaries of the President's appointment powers (and constituted a seminal case in the landscape of campaign finance laws for many years).

Buckley v. Valeo

424 U.S. 1 (1976)

Per Curiam

These appeals present constitutional challenges to the key provisions of the Federal Election Campaign Act of 1971 (Act), and related provisions of the Internal Revenue Code of 1954, all as amended in 1974.

The Court of Appeals, in sustaining the legislation in large part against various constitutional challenges, viewed it as "by far the most comprehensive reform legislation (ever) passed by Congress concerning the election of the President, Vice-President, and members of Congress."

The statutes at issue, summarized in broad terms, contain the following provisions: (a) individual political contributions are limited to $1,000 to any single candidate per election; independent expenditures by individuals and groups "relative to a clearly identified candidate" are limited to $1,000 a year; campaign spending by candidates for various federal offices and spending for national conventions by political parties are subject to prescribed limits; (b) contributions and expenditures above certain threshold levels must be reported and publicly disclosed; (c) a system for public funding of Presidential campaign activities is established and (d) a Federal Election Commission is established to administer and enforce the legislation.

The Federal Election Commission

The 1974 amendments to the Act create an eight-member Federal Election Commission (Commission), and vest in it primary and substantial responsibility for administering and enforcing the Act. The question that we address in this portion of the opinion is whether, in view of the manner in which a majority of its members are appointed, the Commission may under the Constitution exercise the powers conferred upon it.

Chapter 14 of Title 2 makes the Commission the principal repository of the numerous reports and statements which are required by that chapter to be filed by those engaging in the regulated political activities. Its duties under Section 438(a) with respect to these reports and statements include filing and indexing, making them available for public inspection, preservation, and auditing and field investigations.

Beyond these recordkeeping, disclosure, and investigative functions, however, the Commission is given extensive rulemaking and adjudicative powers. Its duty is "to prescribe suitable rules and regulations to carry out the provisions of chapter (14)." Section 437d(a)(9) authorizes it to "formulate general policy with respect to the administration of this Act" and enumerated sections of Title 18's Criminal Code, as to all of which provisions the Commission "has primary jurisdiction with respect to (their) civil enforcement." Section 437c(b). The Commission is authorized under Section 437f(a) to render advisory opinions with respect to activities possibly violating the Act, the Title 18 sections, or the campaign funding provisions of Title 26.

The Commission's enforcement power is both direct and wide-ranging. It may institute a civil action for (i) injunctive or other relief against "any acts or practices which constitute or will constitute a violation of this Act," (ii) declaratory or injunctive relief "as may be appropriate to implement or con(s)true any provisions" governing administration of funds for Presidential election campaigns and national party conventions, and (iii) "such injunctive relief as is appropriate to implement any provision" governing the payment of matching funds for Presidential primary campaigns. In no respect do the foregoing civil actions require the concurrence of or participation by the Attorney General; conversely, the decision not to seek judicial relief in the above respects would appear to rest solely with the Commission.

The body in which this authority is reposed consists of eight members. The Secretary of the Senate and the Clerk of the House of Representatives are ex officio members of the Commission without the right to vote. Two members are appointed by the President pro tempore of the Senate "upon the recommendations of the majority leader of the Senate and the minority leader of the Senate." Two more are to be appointed by the Speaker of the House of Representatives, likewise upon the recommendations of its respective majority and minority leaders. The remaining two members are appointed by the President. Each of the six voting members of the Commission must be confirmed by the majority of both Houses of Congress, and each of the three appointing authorities is forbidden to choose both of their appointees from the same political party.

Appellants urge that since Congress has given the Commission wide-ranging rulemaking and enforcement powers with respect to the substantive provisions of the Act, Congress is precluded under the principle of separation of powers from vesting in itself the authority to appoint those who will exercise such authority. Their argument is based on the language of Art. II, §2, cl. 2, of the Constitution, which provides in pertinent part as follows:

"(The President) shall nominate, and by and with the Advice and Consent of the Senate, shall appoint all other Officers of the United States, whose Appointments are not herein otherwise provided for, and which shall be established by Law: but the Congress may by Law vest the Appointment of such inferior Officers, as they think proper, in the President alone, in the Courts of Law, or in the Heads of Departments."

Appellants' argument is that this provision is the exclusive method by which those charged with executing the laws of the United States may be chosen. Congress, they assert, cannot have it both ways. If the Legislature wishes the Commission to exercise all of the conferred powers, then its members are in fact "Officers of the United States" and must be appointed under the Appointments Clause. But if Congress insists upon retaining the power to appoint, then the members of the Commission may not discharge those many functions of the

Commission which can be performed only by "Officers of the United States," as that term must be construed within the doctrine of separation of powers.

James Madison, writing in *The Federalist No. 47,* defended the work of the Framers against the charge that these three governmental powers were not entirely separate from one another in the proposed Constitution. He asserted that while there was some admixture, the Constitution was nonetheless true to Montesquieu's well-known maxim that the legislative, executive, and judicial departments ought to be separate and distinct.

Yet it is also clear from the provisions of the Constitution itself, and from the Federalist Papers, that the Constitution by no means contemplates total separation of each of these three essential branches of Government. The President is a participant in the law-making process by virtue of his authority to veto bills enacted by Congress. The Senate is a participant in the appointive process by virtue of its authority to refuse to confirm persons nominated to office by the President.

We think that the term "Officers of the United States" as used in Art. II, defined to include "all persons who can be said to hold an office under the government" in *United States v. Germaine, supra,* is a term intended to have substantive meaning. We think its fair import is that any appointee exercising significant authority pursuant to the laws of the United States is an "Officer of the United States," and must, therefore, be appointed in the manner prescribed by §2, cl. 2, of that Article.

Although two members of the Commission are initially selected by the President, his nominations are subject to confirmation not merely by the Senate, but by the House of Representatives as well. The remaining four voting members of the Commission are appointed by the President pro tempore of the Senate and by the Speaker of the House. While the second part of the Clause authorizes Congress to vest the appointment of the officers described in that part in "the Courts of Law, or in the Heads of Departments," neither the Speaker of the House nor the President pro tempore of the Senate comes within this language.

The phrase "Heads of Departments," used as it is in conjunction with the phrase "Courts of Law," suggests that the Departments referred to are themselves in the Executive Branch or at least have some connection with that branch. While the Clause expressly authorizes Congress to vest the appointment of certain officers in the "Courts of Law," the absence of similar language to include Congress must mean that neither Congress nor its officers were included within the language "Heads of Departments" in this part of cl. 2. Thus with respect to four of the six voting members of the Commission, neither the President, the head of any department, nor the Judiciary has any voice in their selection.

Insofar as the powers confided in the Commission are essentially of an investigative and informative nature, falling in the same general category as those powers which Congress might delegate to one of its own committees, there can be no question that the Commission as presently constituted may exercise them.

But when we go beyond this type of authority to the more substantial powers exercised by the Commission, we reach a different result. The Commission's enforcement power, exemplified by its discretionary power to seek judicial relief, is authority that cannot possibly be regarded as merely in aid of the legislative function of Congress. A lawsuit is the ultimate remedy for a breach of the law, and it is to the President, and not to the Congress, that the Constitution entrusts the responsibility to "take Care that the Laws be faithfully executed." Art. II, §3.

We hold that these provisions of the Act, vesting in the Commission primary responsibility for conducting civil litigation in the courts of the United States for vindicating public rights, violate Art. II, §2, cl. 2, of the Constitution. Such functions may be discharged only by persons who are "Officers of the United States" within the language of that section.

Notes

1. *Wide-Ranging.* The significant scope and sweeping nature of *Buckley* generated considerable attention in its aftermath. As one commentator noted, "Almost everyone who has commented on *Buckley* in the quarter-century since it was decided agrees with at least part of the Court's decision. There is strong disagreement, however, about which part of the decision is correct." P. Bender, *The Constitutionality of Campaign Finance Legislation: After* Buckley v. Valeo, 34 A.S.U. L. J. 1105 (2002).

2. *Mistretta v. United States. Mistretta,* 488 U.S. 361 (1989), further developed the understanding of the President's appointment power. In this case, the Supreme Court considered a challenge to the Sentencing Reform Act of 1984, which tasked the U.S. Sentencing Commission with creating sentencing guidelines for defendants convicted of federal crimes. A key issue was how the commission members were to be appointed under the law. The Act provided the President with the power to appoint members, subject to the advice and consent of the Senate. The persons to be appointed to the commission were to come from the Judicial Branch. Could the President control appointments involving a commission composed of judges? Justice Blackmun, writing for the Court, concluded that the President's appointment powers under the Act did not improperly interfere with the independence of the Judicial Branch. Justice Blackmun stated: "The mere fact that the President within his appointment portfolio has positions that may be attractive to federal judges does not, of itself, corrupt the integrity of the Judiciary. Were the impartiality of the Judicial Branch so easily subverted, our constitutional system of tripartite Government would have failed long ago." Justice Scalia dissented: "While the products of the Sentencing Commission's labors have been given the modest name, 'Guidelines,' they have the force and effect of laws, prescribing the sentences criminal defendants are to receive. A judge who disregards them will be reversed. I dissent from today's decision because I can find no place within our constitutional system for an agency created by Congress to exercise no governmental power other than the making of laws."

~ **PROBLEMS** ~

1. *Crack Cocaine Commission.* Congress enacted the Crack Cocaine Sentencing Reform Act of 1995, which created a Sentencing Commission composed of seven voting members appointed by a committee made up of the President and two federal appellate judges. The appointed members must be approved by the Senate. Does this commission, located in the Judicial Branch, violate the separation of powers requirements of the Constitution?

2. *Reprise of No Drilling Zones.* Suppose Congress permits the no drilling zones proposed by the President in the introductory problem, but decides to create a commission to oversee those zones. The commission is designed to have five members, all to be appointed by the judiciary. Is this process constitutional?

Morrison v. Olson, 487 U.S. 654 (1988), deals with several constitutional issues. One issue involved the appointment of inferior executive officers outside of the Executive Branch.

The case owed its origins to the constitutional crisis caused by the Watergate break-in and resulting cover-up, leading to President Nixon's resignation in 1974. Following that period, Congress enacted the Ethics in Government Act of 1978. The Act included a provision for the appointment of an "independent counsel" (sometimes referred to as a "special prosecutor"), imbued with the authority to investigate, report, and prosecute government conduct in violation of the law. The independent counsel was to be appointed by a special panel of three federal judges.

Morrison arose as a result of Independent Counsel Alexia Morrison's investigation of Ted Olson, who was then head of the Justice Department's Office of Legal Counsel.

Morrison v. Olson

487 U.S. 654 (1988)

Chief Justice REHNQUIST delivered the opinion of the Court.

This case presents us with a challenge to the independent counsel provisions of the Ethics in Government Act of 1978. We hold today that these provisions of the Act do not violate the Appointments Clause of the Constitution, Art. II, §2, cl. 2, or the limitations of Article III, nor do they impermissibly interfere with the President's authority under Article II in violation of the constitutional principle of separation of powers.

Briefly stated, Title VI of the Ethics in Government Act (Title VI or the Act), allows for the appointment of an "independent counsel" to investigate and, if appropriate, prosecute certain high-ranking Government officials for violations of federal criminal laws. The Act requires the Attorney General, upon receipt of information that he determines is "sufficient to constitute grounds to investigate whether any person covered by the Act may have violated any Federal criminal law," to conduct a preliminary investigation of the matter. When the Attorney General has completed this investigation, or 90 days has elapsed, he is required to report to a special court (the Special Division) created by the Act "for the purpose of appointing independent counsels." 28 U.S.C. §49 (1982 ed., Supp. V). If the Attorney General determines that "there are no reasonable grounds to believe that further investigation is warranted," then he must notify the Special Division of this result. In such a case, "the division of the court shall have no power to appoint an independent counsel." §592(b)(1). If, however, the Attorney General has determined that there are "reasonable grounds to believe that further investigation or prosecution is warranted," then he "shall apply to the division of the court for the appointment of an independent counsel." The Attorney General's application to the court "shall contain sufficient information to assist the court in selecting an independent counsel and in defining that independent counsel's prosecutorial jurisdiction." §592(d). Upon receiving this application, the Special Division "shall appoint an appropriate independent counsel and shall define that independent counsel's prosecutorial jurisdiction." §593(b).

With respect to all matters within the independent counsel's jurisdiction, the Act grants the counsel "full power and independent authority to exercise all investigative and prosecutorial functions and powers of the Department of Justice, the Attorney General, and any other officer or employee of the Department of Justice." §594(a). The functions of the independent counsel include "conducting grand jury proceedings and other investigations, participating in civil and criminal court proceedings and litigation, and appealing any decision in any case in which the counsel participates in an official capacity." §594(a)(1)-(3). Under §594(a)(9), the counsel's powers include "initiating and conducting prosecutions in any court of competent jurisdiction, framing and signing indictments, filing informations, and handling all aspects of any case, in the name of the United States." The counsel may appoint employees, §594(c), may request and obtain assistance from the Department of Justice, §594(d), and may accept referral of matters from the Attorney General if the matter falls within the counsel's jurisdiction as defined by the Special Division, §594(e). The Act also states that an independent counsel "shall, except where not possible, comply with the written or other established policies of the Department of Justice respecting enforcement of the criminal laws." §594(f). In addition, whenever a matter has been referred to an independent counsel under the Act, the Attorney General and the Justice Department are required to suspend all investigations and proceedings regarding the matter. §597(a). Two statutory provisions govern the length of an independent counsel's tenure in office. The first defines the procedure for removing an independent counsel. Section 596(a)(1) provides: "An independent counsel appointed under this chapter may be removed from office, other than by impeachment and conviction, only by the personal action of the Attorney General and only for good cause, physical disability, mental incapacity, or any other condition that substantially

impairs the performance of such independent counsel's duties." The other provision governing the tenure of the independent counsel defines the procedures
for "terminating" the counsel's office. Under §596(b)(1), the office of an independent counsel terminates when he or she notifies the Attorney General that
he or she has completed or substantially completed any investigations or prosecutions undertaken pursuant to the Act. In addition, the Special Division, acting
either on its own or on the suggestion of the Attorney General, may terminate
the office of an independent counsel at any time if it finds that "the investigation
of all matters within the prosecutorial jurisdiction of such independent counsel
have been completed or so substantially completed that it would be appropriate
for the Department of Justice to complete such investigations and prosecutions."
§596(b)(2). Finally, the Act provides for congressional oversight of the activities
of independent counsel. An independent counsel may from time to time send
Congress statements or reports on his or her activities. §595(a)(2).

The proceedings in this case provide an example of how the Act works in
practice. In 1982, two Subcommittees of the House of Representatives issued
subpoenas directing the Environmental Protection Agency (EPA) to produce
certain documents relating to the efforts of the EPA and the Land and Natural
Resources Division of the Justice Department to enforce the "Superfund Law."
Acting on the advice of the Justice Department, the President ordered the
Administrator of EPA to invoke executive privilege to withhold certain of the
documents on the ground that they contained "enforcement sensitive information." The Administrator obeyed this order and withheld the documents. In
response, the House voted to hold the Administrator in contempt, after which
the Administrator and the United States together filed a lawsuit against the
House. The conflict abated in March 1983, when the administration agreed to
give the House Subcommittees limited access to the documents. The following year, the House Judiciary Committee began an investigation into the Justice
Department's role in the controversy over the EPA documents. During this
investigation, appellee Olson testified before a House Subcommittee on March
10, 1983.

After consulting with other Department officials, however, the Attorney
General chose to apply to the Special Division for the appointment of an independent counsel solely with respect to appellee Olson. The Attorney General
accordingly requested appointment of an independent counsel to investigate
whether Olson's March 10, 1983, testimony "regarding the completeness of
OLC's response to the Judiciary Committee's request for OLC documents, and
regarding his knowledge of EPA's willingness to turn over certain disputed documents to Congress, violated 18 U.S.C. §1505, §1001, or any other provision of
federal criminal law." Attorney General Report, at 2-3.

The Appointments Clause of Article II reads as follows: "The President shall
nominate, and by and with the Advice and Consent of the Senate, shall appoint
Ambassadors, other public Ministers and Consuls, Judges of the Supreme
Court, and all other Officers of the United States, whose Appointments are not

herein otherwise provided for, and which shall be established by Law: but the Congress may by Law vest the Appointment of such inferior Officers, as they think proper, in the President alone, in the Courts of Law, or in the Heads of Departments." U.S. Const., Art. II, §2, cl. 2. The parties do not dispute that "the Constitution for purposes of appointment divides all its officers into two classes." *United States v. Germaine*, 99 U.S. (9 Otto) 508, 509 (1879). As we stated in *Buckley v. Valeo*, 424 U.S. 1, 132 (1976): "Principal officers are selected by the President with the advice and consent of the Senate. Inferior officers Congress may allow to be appointed by the President alone, by the heads of departments, or by the Judiciary." The initial question is, accordingly, whether appellant is an "inferior" or a "principal" officer. If she is the latter, as the Court of Appeals concluded, then the Act is in violation of the Appointments Clause. The line between "inferior" and "principal" officers is one that is far from clear, and the Framers provided little guidance into where it should be drawn. We need not attempt here to decide exactly where the line falls between the two types of officers, because in our view appellant clearly falls on the "inferior officer" side of that line. Several factors lead to this conclusion. First, appellant is subject to removal by a higher Executive Branch official that indicates that she is to some degree "inferior" in rank and authority. Second, appellant is empowered by the Act to perform only certain, limited duties. An independent counsel's role is restricted primarily to investigation and, if appropriate, prosecution for certain federal crimes.

Third, appellant's office is limited in jurisdiction. Not only is the Act itself restricted in applicability to certain federal officials suspected of certain serious federal crimes, but an independent counsel can only act within the scope of the jurisdiction that has been granted by the Special Division pursuant to a request by the Attorney General. Finally, appellant's office is limited in tenure. There is concededly no time limit on the appointment of a particular counsel. Nonetheless, the office of independent counsel is "temporary" in the sense that an independent counsel is appointed essentially to accomplish a single task, and when that task is over the office is terminated, either by the counsel herself or by action of the Special Division.

This does not, however, end our inquiry under the Appointments Clause. Appellees argue that even if appellant is an "inferior" officer, the Clause does not empower Congress to place the power to appoint such an officer outside the Executive Branch. The relevant language of the Appointments Clause admits of no limitation on interbranch appointments. Indeed, the inclusion of "as they think proper" seems clearly to give Congress significant discretion to determine whether it is "proper" to vest the appointment of, for example, executive officials in the "courts of Law."

We also note that the history of the Clause provides no support for appellees' position. Throughout most of the process of drafting the Constitution, the Convention concentrated on the problem of who should have the authority to appoint judges.

We do not mean to say that Congress's power to provide for interbranch appointments of "inferior officers" is unlimited. *Siebold* itself suggested that Congress's decision to vest the appointment power in the courts would be improper if there was some "incongruity" between the functions normally performed by the courts and the performance of their duty to appoint. In the light of the Act's provision making the judges of the Special Division ineligible to participate in any matters relating to an independent counsel they have appointed, 28 U.S.C. §49(f) (1982 ed., Supp. V) we do not think that appointment of the independent counsel by the court runs afoul of the constitutional limitation on "incongruous" interbranch appointments.

Justice SCALIA, *dissenting.*

It is the proud boast of our democracy that we have "a government of laws and not of men." Many Americans are familiar with that phrase; not many know its derivation. It comes from Part the First, Article XXX, of the Massachusetts Constitution of 1780, which reads in full as follows: "In the government of this Commonwealth, the legislative department shall never exercise the executive and judicial powers, or either of them: The executive shall never exercise the legislative and judicial powers, or either of them: The judicial shall never exercise the legislative and executive powers, or either of them: to the end it may be a government of laws and not of men." The Framers of the Federal Constitution similarly viewed the principle of separation of powers as the absolutely central guarantee of a just Government. In No. 47 of *The Federalist,* Madison wrote that "no political truth is certainly of greater intrinsic value, or is stamped with the authority of more enlightened patrons of liberty." *The Federalist No. 47,* p. 301 (C. Rossiter ed. 1961).

That is what this suit is about. Power. The allocation of power among Congress, the President, and the courts in such fashion as to preserve the equilibrium the Constitution sought to establish—so that "a gradual concentration of the several powers in the same department." *The Federalist No. 51,* p. 321 (J. Madison).

The Court concedes that "there is no real dispute that the functions performed by the independent counsel are 'executive,'" though it qualifies that concession by adding "in the sense that they are law enforcement functions that typically have been undertaken by officials within the Executive Branch."

As for the second question, whether the statute before us deprives the President of exclusive control over that quintessentially executive activity: The Court does not, and could not possibly, assert that it does not. That is indeed the whole object of the statute.

As I have said, however, it is ultimately irrelevant *how much* the statute reduces Presidential control. The case is over when the Court acknowledges, as it must, that "it is undeniable that the Act reduces the amount of control or supervision that the Attorney General and, through him, the President exercises over the investigation and prosecution of a certain class of alleged criminal activity."

This Court extends into the very heart of our most significant constitutional function the "totality of the circumstances" mode of analysis that this Court has in recent years become fond of. Taking all things into account, we conclude that the power taken away from the President here is not really *too* much.

BACKGROUND
Implications of the Independent Counsel Law

The independent counsel law has had a significant impact on the country's political history. Kenneth Starr was a special prosecutor appointed under the independent counsel law to investigate the apparent suicide of Deputy White House Counsel Vince Foster and President Bill Clinton's Whitewater land investments. Starr's investigation led him to disclosures by Monica Lewinsky about an affair she had with President Clinton. Starr left the independent counsel's office to become the dean of Pepperdine Law School and then the president of Baylor University.

∾ PROBLEMS ∾

1. *The Commish.* Congress creates a new commission to oversee Major League Baseball, finding that the organization requires governmental oversight. The commission is given the power to veto team relocation, ticket price increases, and player salaries. The law states "the Commission shall be composed of three members of Congress, two members chosen by the President, and one member chosen by the Chief Justice of the United States." Is this commission's appointment process constitutional? Explain.

2. *Newly Discovered Evidence.* Suppose a special prosecutor has been appointed to explore allegations of wrongdoing in one area of an executive officer's conduct, and the prosecutor uncovers evidence suggesting wrongdoing in another area. What are the limits of the prosecutor's pursuit of the newly discovered area, if any? Can the prosecution recommend impeachment for the wrongdoing if it was done by the President?

3. *The Special Prosecutor's Report.* If a special prosecutor intends to file a report about the President's conduct, what level of detail should be included in the report? If the report includes alleged sexual misconduct, how graphic should the report be? Can Congress impose limits on a special prosecutor's report? If so, what?

In the following case, the Court considered the constitutionality of various aspects of the Public Company Accounting Oversight Board (Oversight Board), which was created pursuant to the Sarbanes-Oxley Act to impose greater oversight on the auditing process of public companies. The Act called on members of the Securities and Exchange Commission (SEC) to appoint the members of the Oversight Board. It also contained removal restrictions for members of the board, limiting removal on dual levels "for cause."

Free Enterprise Fund v. Public Company Accounting Oversight Board

561 U.S. 477 (2010)

Chief Justice ROBERTS delivered the opinion of the court.

Since 1789, the Constitution has been understood to empower the President to keep these officers accountable by removing them from office, if necessary. See generally *Myers v. United States,* 272 U.S. 52 (1926). This Court has determined, however, that this authority is not without limit. In *Humphrey's Executor v. United States,* 295 U.S. 602 (1935), we held that Congress can, under certain circumstances, create independent agencies run by principal officers appointed by the President, whom the President may not remove at will but only for good cause. Likewise, in *United States v. Perkins,* 116 U.S. 483 (1886), and *Morrison v. Olson,* 487 U.S. 654 (1988), the Court sustained similar restrictions on the power of principal executive officers—themselves responsible to the President—to remove their own inferiors. The parties do not ask us to reexamine any of these precedents. The question here is whether these separate layers of protection may be combined. May the President be restricted in his ability to remove a principal officer, who is in turn restricted in his ability to remove an inferior officer, even though that inferior officer determines the policy and enforces the laws of the United States? We hold that such multilevel protection from removal is contrary to Article II's vesting of the executive power in the President. The President cannot "take Care that the Laws be faithfully executed" if he cannot oversee the faithfulness of the officers who execute them. Here the President cannot remove an officer who enjoys more than one level of good-cause protection, even if the President determines that the officer is neglecting his duties or discharging them improperly. That judgment is instead committed to another officer, who may or may not agree with the President's determination, and whom the President cannot remove simply because that officer disagrees with him. This contravenes the President's "constitutional obligation to ensure the faithful execution of the laws." *Id.,* at 693.

After a series of celebrated accounting debacles, Congress enacted the Sarbanes-Oxley Act of 2002 (or Act), 116 Stat. 745. Among other measures, the Act introduced tighter regulation of the accounting industry under a new Public Company Accounting Oversight Board. The Board is composed of five members, appointed to staggered 5- year terms by the Securities and Exchange Commission. It was modeled on private self-regulatory organizations in the securities industry—such as the New York Stock Exchange—that investigate and discipline their own members subject to Commission oversight. Congress created the Board as a private "nonprofit corporation," and Board members and employees are not considered Government "officers or employees" for statutory purposes. The Board can thus recruit its members and employees from the private sector by paying salaries far above the standard Government pay scale. Unlike the self-regulatory organizations, however, the Board is a Government-created, Government-appointed entity, with expansive powers to govern an entire industry. Every accounting firm—both foreign and domestic—that participates in auditing public companies under the securities laws must register with the Board, pay it an annual fee, and comply with its rules and oversight. The Board is charged with enforcing the Sarbanes-Oxley Act, the securities laws, the Commission's rules, its own rules, and professional accounting standards. To this end, the Board may regulate every detail of an accounting firm's practice, including hiring and professional development, promotion, supervision of audit work, the acceptance of new business and the continuation of old, internal inspection procedures, professional ethics rules, and "such other requirements as the Board may prescribe."

Despite the provisions specifying that Board members are not Government officials for statutory purposes, the parties agree that the Board is "part of the Government" for constitutional purposes, *Lebron v. National Railroad Passenger Corporation,* 513 U.S. 374, 397 (1995), and that its members are " 'Officers of the United States' " who "exercise significant authority pursuant to the laws of the United States," *Buckley v. Valeo,* 424 U.S. 1, 125-126 (1976) (*per curiam*) (quoting Art. II, §2, cl. 2).

The Act places the Board under the SEC's oversight, particularly with respect to the issuance of rules or the imposition of sanctions (both of which are subject to Commission approval and alteration). But the individual members of the Board—like the officers and directors of the self-regulatory organizations—are substantially insulated from the Commission's control. The Commission cannot remove Board members at will, but only "for good cause shown," "in accordance with" certain procedures. Those procedures require a Commission finding, "on the record" and "after notice and opportunity for a hearing," that the Board member "(A) has willfully violated any provision of the Act, the rules of the Board, or the securities laws; "(B) has willfully abused the authority of that member; or "(C) without reasonable justification or excuse, has failed to enforce compliance with any such provision or rule, or any professional standard by any registered public accounting firm or any associated person thereof." Removal of a Board member requires a formal Commission order and is subject to judicial review. Similar procedures govern the Commission's removal of officers and directors of the private self-regulatory organizations. The parties agree that the Commissioners cannot themselves be removed by the President except under the

Humphrey's Executor standard of "inefficiency, neglect of duty, or malfeasance in office," and we decide the case with that understanding.

Beckstead and Watts, LLP, is a Nevada accounting firm registered with the Board. The Board inspected the firm, released a report critical of its auditing procedures, and began a formal investigation. Beckstead and Watts and the Free Enterprise Fund, a nonprofit organization of which the firm is a member, then sued the Board and its members, seeking (among other things) a declaratory judgment that the Board is unconstitutional and an injunction preventing the Board from exercising its powers. The District Court granted summary judgment to respondents. A divided Court of Appeals affirmed. We granted certiorari. We hold that the dual for-cause limitations on the removal of Board members contravene the Constitution's separation of powers.

The landmark case of *Myers v. United States* reaffirmed the principle that Article II confers on the President "the general administrative control of those executing the laws." It is *his* responsibility to take care that the laws be faithfully executed. The buck stops with the President, in Harry Truman's famous phrase. As we explained in *Myers,* the President therefore must have some "power of removing those for whom he can not continue to be responsible."

Nearly a decade later in *Humphrey's Executor,* this Court held that *Myers* did not prevent Congress from conferring good—cause tenure on the principal officers of certain independent agencies. That case concerned the members of the Federal Trade Commission, who held 7-year terms and could not be removed by the President except for "inefficiency, neglect of duty, or malfeasance in office." The Court distinguished *Myers* on the ground that *Myers* concerned "an officer who is merely one of the units in the executive department and, hence, inherently subject to the exclusive and illimitable power of removal by the Chief Executive, whose subordinate and aid he is." By contrast, the Court characterized the FTC as "quasi-legislative and quasi-judicial" rather than "purely executive," and held that Congress could require it "to act independently of executive control." Because "one who holds his office only during the pleasure of another, cannot be depended upon to maintain an attitude of independence against the latter's will," the Court held that Congress had power to "fix the period during which the Commissioners shall continue in office, and to forbid their removal except for cause in the meantime."

Humphrey's Executor did not address the removal of inferior officers, whose appointment Congress may vest in heads of departments. If Congress does so, it is ordinarily the department head, rather than the President, who enjoys the power of removal. See *Myers, supra,* at 119; *Hennen, supra,* at 259-260. This Court has upheld for-cause limitations on that power as well.

We again considered the status of inferior officers in *Morrison.* That case concerned the Ethics in Government Act, which provided for an independent counsel to investigate allegations of crime by high executive officers. The counsel was appointed by a special court, wielded the full powers of a prosecutor, and was removable by the Attorney General only " 'for good cause.' We recognized that the independent counsel was undoubtedly an executive officer, rather than "'quasi-legislative'" or "'quasi-judicial,'" but we stated as "our present considered view" that Congress had power to impose good-cause restrictions on her removal. The Court noted that the statute "gave the Attorney General," an officer directly responsible to the President and "through whom" the President could act, "several means of supervising or controlling" the independent counsel-"most importantly the power to remove the counsel for good cause." Under those circumstances, the Court sustained the statute. *Morrison* did not, however, address the consequences of more than one level of good-cause tenure-leaving the issue, as both the court and dissent below recognized, "a question of first impression" in this Court.

We have previously upheld limited restrictions on the President's removal power. In those cases, however, only one level of protected tenure separated the President from an officer exercising executive power. It was the President—or a subordinate he could remove at will—who decided whether the officer's conduct merited removal under the good-cause standard.

The Act before us does something quite different. It not only protects Board members from removal except for good cause, but withdraws from the President any decision on whether that good cause exists. That decision is vested instead in other tenured officers—the Commissioners—none of whom is subject to the President's direct control. The result is a Board that is not accountable to the President, and a President who is not responsible for the Board.

The added layer of tenure protection makes a difference. Without a layer of insulation between the Commission and the Board, the Commission could remove a Board member at any time, and therefore would be fully responsible for what the Board does. The President could then hold the Commission to account for its supervision of the Board, to the same extent that he may hold the Commission to account for everything else it does.

A second level of tenure protection changes the nature of the President's review. Now the Commission cannot remove a Board member at will. The President therefore cannot hold the Commission fully accountable for the Board's conduct, to the same extent that he may hold the Commission accountable for everything else that it does. The Commissioners are not responsible for the Board's actions.

This novel structure does not merely add to the Board's independence, but transforms it. Neither the President, nor anyone directly responsible to him, nor even an officer whose conduct he may review only for good cause, has full control over the Board. The President is stripped of the power our precedents have preserved, and his ability to execute the laws—by holding his subordinates accountable for their conduct—is impaired.

That arrangement is contrary to Article II's vesting of the executive power in the President. Without the ability to oversee the Board, or to attribute the Board's failings to those whom he *can* oversee, the President is no longer the judge of the Board's conduct. He is not the one who decides whether Board members are abusing their offices or neglecting their duties. He can neither ensure that the laws are faithfully executed, nor be held responsible for a Board member's breach of faith. This violates the basic principle that the President "cannot delegate ultimate responsibility or the active obligation to supervise that goes with it," because Article II "makes a single President responsible for the actions of the Executive Branch." *Clinton v. Jones,* 520 U.S. 681, 712-713 (1997) (BREYER, J., *concurring* in judgment).

Indeed, if allowed to stand, this dispersion of responsibility could be multiplied. If Congress can shelter the bureaucracy behind two layers of good-cause tenure, why not a third?

Without a clear and effective chain of command, the public cannot "determine on whom the blame or the punishment of a pernicious measure, or series of pernicious measures ought really to fall." That is why the Framers sought to ensure that "those who are employed in the execution of the law will be in their proper situation, and the chain of dependence be preserved; the lowest officers, the middle grade, and the highest, will depend, as they ought, on the President, and the President on the community." 1 Annals of Cong., at 499 (J. Madison). By granting the Board executive power without the Executive's oversight, this Act subverts the President's ability to ensure that the laws are faithfully executed—as well as the public's ability to pass judgment on his efforts. The Act's restrictions are incompatible with the Constitution's separation of powers.

No one doubts Congress's power to create a vast and varied federal bureaucracy. But where, in all this, is the role for oversight by an elected President?

In fact, the multilevel protection that the dissent endorses "provides a blueprint for extensive expansion of the legislative power." *MWAA, supra,* at 277. In a system of checks and balances, "power abhors a vacuum," and one branch's handicap is another's strength. 537 F.3d, at 695, n. 4 (KAVANAUGH, J., *dissenting*).

The Court went on to hold that the Sarbanes-Oxley Act was still "fully operative" without the tainted provisions and that the unconstitutional provisions were severable from the remaining law.

The judgment of the United States Court of Appeals for the District of Columbia Circuit is affirmed in part and reversed in part, and the case is remanded for further proceedings consistent with this opinion.

It is so ordered.

Justice BREYER, with whom Justice STEVENS, Justice GINSBURG, and Justice SOTOMAYOR join, *dissenting.*

I agree that the Accounting Board members are inferior officers. But in my view the statute does not significantly interfere with the President's "executive Power." Art. II, §1. It violates no separation-of-powers principle. And the Court's contrary holding threatens to disrupt severely the fair and efficient administration of the laws. I consequently dissent.

The legal question before us arises at the intersection of two general constitutional principles. On the one hand, Congress has broad power to enact statutes "necessary and proper" to the exercise of its specifically enumerated constitutional authority. Art. I, §8, cl. 18. As Chief Justice Marshall wrote for the Court nearly 200 years ago, the Necessary and Proper Clause reflects the Framers' efforts to create a Constitution that would "endure for ages to come." *McCulloch v. Maryland*, 17 U.S. 316 (1819). Thus the Necessary and Proper Clause affords Congress broad authority to "create" governmental " 'offices' " and to structure those offices "as it chooses." *Buckley v. Valeo*, 424 U.S. 1, 138 (1976) *(per curiam)*. On the other hand, the opening sections of Articles I, II, and III of the Constitution separately and respectively vest "all legislative Powers" in Congress, the "executive Power" in the President, and the "judicial Power" in the Supreme Court (and such "inferior Courts as Congress may from time to time ordain and establish"). In doing so, these provisions imply a structural separation-of-powers principle. See, *e.g.*, *Miller v. French*, 530 U.S. 327, 341-342 (2000). And that principle, along with the instruction in Article II, §3 that the President "shall take Care that the Laws be faithfully executed," limits Congress' power to structure the Federal Government. See, *e.g.*, *INS v. Chadha*, 462 U.S. 919, 946 (1983). Indeed, this Court has held that the separation-of-powers principle guarantees the President the authority to dismiss certain Executive Branch officials at will. *Myers v. United States*, 272 U.S. 52 (1926). But neither of these two principles is absolute in its application to removal cases.

In short, the question presented lies at the intersection of two sets of conflicting, broadly framed constitutional principles. And no text, no history, perhaps no precedent provides any clear answer. When previously deciding this kind of non-textual question, the Court has emphasized the importance of examining how a particular provision, taken in context, is likely to function.

To what extent then is the Act's "for cause" provision likely, as a practical matter, to limit the President's exercise of executive authority? In practical terms no "for cause" provision can, in isolation, define the full measure of executive power. This is because a legislative decision to place ultimate administrative authority in, say, the Secretary of Agriculture rather than the President, the way in which the statute defines the scope of the power the relevant administrator can exercise, the decision as to who controls the agency's budget requests and funding, the relationships between one agency or department and another, as well as more purely political factors (including Congress' ability to assert influence) are more likely to affect the President's power to get something done.

But even if we put all these other matters to the side, we should still conclude that the "for cause" restriction before us will not restrict presidential power significantly. For one thing, the restriction directly limits, not the President's power, but the power of an already independent agency.

In other words, the Court fails to show why *two* layers of "for cause" protection—Layer One insulating the Commissioners from the President, and Layer Two insulating the Board from the Commissioners—impose any more serious limitation upon the *President's* powers than *one* layer.

At the same time, Congress and the President had good reason for enacting the challenged "for cause" provision. First and foremost, the Board adjudicates cases. This Court has long recognized the appropriateness of using "for cause" provisions to protect the personal independence of those who even only sometimes engage in adjudicatory functions. *Humphrey's Executor, supra,* at 623-628.

Where a "for cause" provision is so unlikely to restrict presidential power and so likely to further a legitimate institutional need, precedent strongly supports its constitutionality.

One last question: How can the Court simply *assume* without deciding that the SEC Commissioners themselves are removable only "for cause"? I do not need to decide whether the Commissioners are in fact removable only "for cause" because I would uphold the Accounting Board's removal provision as constitutional regardless. But were that not so, a determination that the silent SEC statute means no more than it says would properly avoid the determination of unconstitutionality that the Court now makes.

In my view the Court's decision is wrong—very wrong. If the Court were to look to the proper functional and contextual considerations, it would find the Accounting Board provision constitutional. With respect I dissent.

1. The President's Recess Appointment Power

A little-known but significant power of the President lies in Article II, Section 2, Clause 3. That provision states: "The President shall have the power to fill up all vacancies that may happen during the Recess of the Senate, by granting commissions which shall expire at the End of their next session."

Presidents, beginning with George Washington, have used this provision to fill hundreds of governmental vacancies, mostly federal judgeships that might not have been approved by the Senate. Presidents have sometimes appointed controversial nominees, many of whom have served for a limited time, only until the expiration of Congress's following session. Yet, for all of the nominees whose appointments expired in this way, there were many judges who used the limited term as a positive "tryout" and subsequently received full approval. Perhaps the best known of the judges in this category was Thurgood Marshall, who was a recess appointment to the Court of Appeals for the Second Circuit. Several of the other Supreme Court Justices, including Earl Warren and William Brennan, were recess appointees.

In recent years, the President's recess power has not been used quite as often as in times past, in part because of the political fallout such appointments create between a Congress on recess and a sitting President. In January 2004, for example, President George W. Bush named Charles Pickering to the Court of Appeals for the Fifth Circuit as a recess appointment. As is sometimes the case, the President pursued Pickering's approval as a nonrecess appointment, but Pickering ended the confirmation battle by retiring from the federal bench. President Bush also used his recess appointment power to name John Bolton as ambassador to the United Nations. President Obama has made multiple recess appointments as well.

The Supreme Court resolved a split in the circuits about the meaning of the Recess Appointments Clause in *N.L.R.B. v. Canning*, 573 U.S. 513 (2014). In a unanimous decision, the Court, through Justice Breyer, found that the President's appointments to the N.L.R.B. were unconstitutional. In so finding, the Court waded through weighty separation of powers issues as well as the interpretation of the word "the."

National Labor Relations Board v. Canning

573 U.S. 513 (2014)

Justice BREYER delivered the opinion of the Court.

Ordinarily the President must obtain "the Advice and Consent of the Senate" before appointing an "Officer of the United States." U.S. Const. Art. II, §II, cl. 2. But the Recess Appointments Clause creates an exception. It gives the President alone the power "to fill up all Vacancies that may happen during the Recess of the Senate, by granting Commissions which shall expire at the End of their next Session." Art. II, §2, cl. 3. We here consider three questions about the application of this Clause.

The first concerns the scope of the words "recess of the Senate." Does that phrase refer only to an intersession recess (*i.e.,* a break between formal sessions of Congress), or does it also include an intra-session recess, such as a summer recess in the midst of a session? We conclude that the Clause applies to both kinds of recess.

The second question concerns the scope of the words "vacancies that may happen." Does that phrase refer only to vacancies that first come into existence during a recess, or does it also include vacancies that arise prior to a recess but continue to exist during the recess? We conclude that the Clause applies to both kinds of vacancy.

The third question concerns calculation of the length of a "recess." The President made the appointments here at issue on January 4, 2012. At that time the Senate was in recess pursuant to a December 17, 2011, resolution providing for a series of brief recesses punctuated by "*pro forma* sessions," with "no business transacted," every Tuesday and Friday through January 20, 2012. S. J., 112th Cong., 1st Sess., 923 (2011) (hereinafter 2011 S. J.). In calculating the length of a recess are we to ignore the *pro forma* sessions, thereby treating the series of brief recesses as a single, month-long recess? We conclude that we cannot ignore these *pro forma* sessions.

Our answer to the third question means that, when the appointments before us took place, the Senate was in the midst of a 3-day recess. Three days is too short a time to bring a recess within the scope of the Clause. Thus we conclude that the President lacked the power to make the recess appointments here at issue.

The case before us arises out of a labor dispute. The National Labor Relations Board (NLRB) found that a Pepsi-Cola distributor, Noel Canning, had unlawfully refused to reduce to writing and execute a collective-bargaining agreement with a labor union. The Board ordered the distributor to execute the agreement and to make employees whole for any losses. *Noel Canning,* 358 N. L. R. B. No. 4 (2012).

The Pepsi-Cola distributor subsequently asked the Court of Appeals for the District of Columbia Circuit to set the Board's order aside. It claimed that three of the five Board members had been invalidly appointed, leaving the Board without the three lawfully appointed members necessary for it to act. See 29 U.S.C. Section 160(f) (providing for judicial review); Section 153(a) (providing for a 5-member Board); Section 153(b) (providing for a 3-member quorum); *New Process Steel, L. P. v. NLRB,* 560 U.S. 674 (2010) (in the absence of a lawfully appointed quorum, the Board cannot exercise its powers).

The three members in question were Sharon Block, Richard Griffin, and Terence Flynn. In 2011 the President had nominated each of them to the Board. As of January 2012, Flynn's nomination had been pending in the Senate awaiting confirmation for approximately a year. The nominations of each of the other two had been pending for a few weeks. On January 4, 2012, the President, invoking the Recess Appointments Clause, appointed all three to the Board.

The distributor argued that the Recess Appointments Clause did not authorize those appointments. It pointed out that on December 17, 2011, the Senate, by unanimous consent, had adopted a resolution providing that it would take a series of brief recesses beginning the following day. See 2011 S. J. 923. Pursuant to that resolution, the Senate held *pro forma* sessions every Tuesday and Friday until it returned for ordinary business on January 23, 2012. The President's January 4 appointments were made between the January 3 and January 6 *pro forma* sessions. In the distributor's view, each *pro forma* session terminated the immediately preceding recess.

The Court of Appeals agreed that the appointments fell outside the scope of the Clause. But the court set forth different reasons. It held that the Clause's words "the recess of the Senate" do not include recesses that occur *within* a formal session of Congress, *i.e.,* intra-session recesses. Rather those words apply only to recesses *between* those formal sessions, *i.e.,* inter-session recesses. Since the second session of the 112th Congress began on January 3, 2012, the day before the President's appointments, those appointments occurred during an intra-session recess, and the appointments consequently fell outside the scope of the Clause.

The Court of Appeals added that, in any event, the phrase "vacancies that may happen during the recess" applies only to vacancies that come into existence during a recess. The vacancies that Members Block, Griffin, and Flynn were appointed to fill had arisen before the beginning of the recess during which they were appointed.

We shall answer all three questions presented. We recognize that the President has nominated others to fill the positions once occupied by Members Block, Griffin, and Flynn, and that the Senate has confirmed these successors. But, as the parties recognize, the fact that the Board now unquestionably has a quorum does not moot the controversy about the validity of the previously entered Board order. And there are pending before us petitions from decisions in other cases involving challenges to the appointment of Board Member Craig Becker. The President appointed Member Becker during an intra-session recess that was not punctuated by *pro forma* sessions, and the vacancy Becker filled had come into existence prior to the recess.

Before turning to the specific questions presented, we shall mention two background considerations that we find relevant to all three. First, *the Recess Appointments Clause sets forth a subsidiary, not a primary, method for appointing officers of the United States.* The immediately preceding Clause Article II, Section 2, Clause 2 provides the primary method of appointment. It says that the President "shall nominate, *and by and with the Advice and Consent of the Senate,* shall appoint Ambassadors, other public Ministers and Consuls, Judges of the Supreme Court, and all other Officers of the United States" (emphasis added).

The Federalist Papers make clear that the Founders intended this method of appointment, requiring Senate approval, to be the norm (at least for principal officers). Alexander Hamilton wrote that the Constitution vests the power of *nomination* in the President alone because "one man of discernment is better fitted to analise and estimate the peculiar qualities adapted to particular offices, than a body of men of equal, or perhaps even of superior discernment." The Federalist No. 76, p. 510 (J. Cooke ed. 1961). At the same time, the need to secure Senate approval provides "an excellent check upon a spirit of favoritism in the President, and would tend greatly to preventing the appointment of unfit characters from State prejudice, from family connection, from personal attachment, or from a view to popularity." *Id.,* at 513.

Thus the Recess Appointments Clause reflects the tension between, on the one hand, the President's continuous need for "the assistance of subordinates," *Myers v. United States,* 272 U.S. 52, 117 (1926), and, on the other, the Senate's practice, particularly during the Republic's early years, of meeting for a single brief session each year, see Art. I, §4, cl. 2; Amdt. 20, §2 (requiring the Senate to "assemble" only "once in every year"). We seek to interpret the Clause as granting the President the power to make appointments during a recess but not offering the President the authority routinely to avoid the need for Senate confirmation.

Second, *in interpreting the Clause, we put significant weight upon historical practice.* For one thing, the interpretive questions before us concern the allocation of power between two elected branches of Government. Long ago Chief Justice Marshall wrote that "a doubtful question, one on which human reason may pause, and the human judgment be suspended, in the decision of which the great principles of liberty are not concerned, but the respective powers of those who are equally the representatives of the people, are to be adjusted; if not put at rest by the practice of the government, ought to receive a considerable impression from that practice." *McCulloch v. Maryland,* 4 Wheat. 316, 401 (1819).

There is a great deal of history to consider here. Presidents have made recess appointments since the beginning of the Republic. Their frequency suggests that the Senate and President have recognized that recess appointments can be both necessary and appropriate in certain circumstances. We have not previously interpreted the Clause, and, when doing so for the first time in more than 200 years, we must hesitate to upset the compromises and working arrangements that the elected branches of Government themselves have reached.

The first question concerns the scope of the phrase "*the recess* of the Senate." Art. II, §2, cl. 3 (emphasis added). The Constitution provides for congressional elections every two years. And the 2-year life of each elected Congress typically consists of two formal 1-year sessions, each separated from the next by an "inter-session recess." Congressional Research Service, H. Hogue, Recess Appointments: Frequently Asked Questions 2 (2013). The Senate or the House of Representatives announces an inter-session recess by approving a resolution stating that it will "adjourn *sine die,*" *i.e.,* without specifying a date to return (in which case Congress will reconvene when the next formal session is scheduled to begin).

The Senate and the House also take breaks in the midst of a session. The Senate or the House announces any such "intra-session recess" by adopting a resolution stating that it will "adjourn" to a fixed date, a few days or weeks or even months later. All agree that the phrase "the recess of the Senate" covers inter-session recesses. The question is whether it includes intra-session recesses as well.

In our view, the phrase "the recess" includes an intra-session recess of substantial length. Its words taken literally can refer to both types of recess. Founding-era dictionaries define the word "recess," much as we do today, simply as "a period of cessation from usual work." 13 The Oxford English Dictionary 322-323 (2d ed. 1989) (hereinafter OED) (citing 18th- and 19th-century sources for that definition of "recess"); 2 N. Webster, An American Dictionary of the English Language (1828) ("remission or suspension of business or procedure").

We recognize that the word "the" in "*the* recess" might suggest that the phrase refers to the single break separating formal sessions of Congress. That is because the word "the" frequently (but not always) indicates "a particular thing." 2 Johnson 2003. But the word can also refer "to a term used generically or universally." 17 OED 879. The Constitution, for example, directs the Senate to choose a President *pro tempore* "in *the* Absence of the Vice-President." Art. I, §3, cl. 5 (emphasis added). And the Federalist Papers refer to the chief magistrate of an ancient Achaean league who "administered the government in *the* recess of the Senate." The Federalist No. 18, at 113 (J. Madison) (emphasis added). Reading "the" generically in this way, there is no linguistic problem applying the Clause's phrase to both kinds of recess. And, in fact, the phrase "the recess" was used to refer to intra-session recesses at the time of the founding. See, *e.g.,* 3 Farrand 76 (letter from Washington to Jay); New Jersey Legislative-Council Journal, 5th Sess., 1st Sitting 70, 2d Sitting 9 (1781) (twice referring to a 4-month, intra-session break as "the Recess").

The constitutional text is thus ambiguous. And we believe the Clause's purpose demands the broader interpretation. The Clause gives the President authority to make appointments during "the recess of the Senate" so that the President can ensure the continued functioning of the Federal Government when the

Senate is away. The Senate is equally away during both an inter-session and an intra-session recess, and its capacity to participate in the appointments process has nothing to do with the words it uses to signal its departure.

History also offers strong support for the broad interpretation. In 1867 and 1868, Congress for the first time took substantial, nonholiday intra-session breaks, and President Andrew Johnson made dozens of recess appointments. The Federal Court of Claims upheld one of those specific appointments, writing "we have *no doubt* that a vacancy occurring while the Senate was thus temporarily adjourned" during the "first session of the Fortieth Congress" was "legally filled by appointment of the President alone." *Gould v. United States*, 19 Ct. Cl. 593, 595-596 (1884) (emphasis added). Attorney General Evarts also issued three opinions concerning the constitutionality of President Johnson's appointments, and it apparently did not occur to him that the distinction between intra-session and inter-session recesses was significant. Similarly, though the 40th Congress impeached President Johnson on charges relating to his appointment power, he was not accused of violating the Constitution by making intra-session recess appointments. Hartnett, Recess Appointments of Article III Judges: Three Constitutional Questions, 26 Cardozo L. Rev. 377, 409 (2005).

In all, between the founding and the Great Depression, Congress took substantial intra-session breaks (other than holiday breaks) in four years: 1867, 1868, 1921, and 1929. And in each of those years the President made intra-session recess appointments.

Since 1929, and particularly since the end of World War II, Congress has shortened its inter-session breaks as it has taken longer and more frequent intra-session breaks; if we include military appointments, Presidents have made thousands of intra-session recess appointments. *Id.,* at 11a-64a. President Franklin Roosevelt, for example, commissioned Dwight Eisenhower as a permanent Major General during an intra-session recess; President Truman made Dean Acheson Under Secretary of State; and President George H. W. Bush reappointed Alan Greenspan as Chairman of the Federal Reserve Board.

Not surprisingly, the publicly available opinions of Presidential legal advisers that we have found are nearly unanimous in determining that the Clause authorizes these appointments. In 1921, for example, Attorney General Daugherty advised President Harding that he could make intra-session recess appointments. He reasoned: "If the President's power of appointment is to be defeated because the Senate takes an adjournment to a specified date, the painful and inevitable result will be measurably to prevent the exercise of governmental functions. I can not bring myself to believe that the framers of the Constitution ever intended such a catastrophe to happen." 33 Op. Atty. Gen. 20, 23.

We must note one contrary opinion authored by President Theodore Roosevelt's Attorney General Philander Knox. Knox advised the President that the Clause did not cover a 19-day intra-session Christmas recess. 23 Op. Atty. Gen. 599 (1901). But in doing so he relied heavily upon the use of the word "the," a linguistic point that we do not find determinative. See *supra,* at 10.

What about the Senate? We recognize that the Senate cannot easily register opposition as a body to every governmental action that many, perhaps most, Senators oppose. But the Senate has not been silent or passive regarding the meaning of the Clause: A Senate Committee did register opposition to President Theodore Roosevelt's use of the Clause, and the Senate as a whole has legislated in an effort to discourage certain kinds of recess appointments. And yet we are not aware of any formal action it has taken to call into question the broad and functional definition of "recess" first set out in the 1905 Senate Report and followed by the Executive Branch since at least 1921. Nor has Justice Scalia identified any. All the while, the President has made countless recess appointments during intra-session recesses.

The upshot is that restricting the Clause to inter-session recesses would frustrate its purpose. It would make the President's recess-appointment power dependent on a formalistic distinction of Senate procedure. Moreover, the President has consistently and frequently interpreted the word "recess" to apply to intra-session recesses, and has acted on that interpretation. The Senate as a body has done nothing to deny the validity of this practice for at least three-quarters of a century. And three-quarters of a century of settled practice is long enough to entitle a practice to "great weight in a proper interpretation" of the constitutional provision. *The Pocket Veto Case*, 279 U.S. at 689.

Some argue that the Founders would likely have intended the Clause to apply only to inter-session recesses, for they hardly knew any other. The problem with this argument, however, is that it does not fully describe the relevant founding intent. The question is not: Did the Founders at the time think about intra-session recesses? Perhaps they did not. The question is: Did the Founders intend to restrict the scope of the Clause to the form of congressional recess then prevalent, or did they intend a broader scope permitting the Clause to apply, where appropriate, to somewhat changed circumstances? The Founders knew they were writing a document designed to apply to ever-changing circumstances over centuries. After all, a Constitution is "intended to endure for ages to come," and must adapt itself to a future that can only be "seen dimly," if at all. *McCulloch*, 4 Wheat., at 415. We therefore think the Framers likely did intend the Clause to apply to a new circumstance that so clearly falls within its essential purposes, where doing so is consistent with the Clause's language.

The greater interpretive problem is determining how long a recess must be in order to fall within the Clause. Is a break of a week, or a day, or an hour too short to count as a "recess"? The Clause itself does not say. And Justice Scalia claims that this silence itself shows that the Framers intended the Clause to apply only to an inter-session recess.

We disagree. For one thing, the most likely reason the Framers did not place a textual floor underneath the word "recess" is that they did not foresee the *need* for one. They might have expected that the Senate would meet for a single session lasting at most half a year. The Federalist No. 84, at 596 (A. Hamilton). And they might not have anticipated that intra-session recesses would become lengthier and more significant than inter-session ones. The Framers' lack of clairvoyance on that point is not dispositive. Unlike Justice Scalia, we think it most consistent with our constitutional structure to presume that the Framers would have allowed intra-session recess appointments where there was a long history of such practice.

Moreover, the lack of a textual floor raises a problem that plagues *both* interpretations—Justice Scalia's and ours. Today a brief inter-session recess is just as possible as a brief intra-session recess. And though Justice Scalia says that the "notion that the Constitution empowers the President to make unilateral appointments every time the Senate takes a half-hour lunch break is *so absurd as to be self-refuting*," he must immediately concede (in a footnote) that the President "can make recess appointments during any break *between* sessions, *no matter how short*."

Even the Solicitor General, arguing for a broader interpretation, acknowledges that there is a lower limit applicable to both kinds of recess. He argues that the lower limit should be three days by analogy to the Adjournments Clause of the Constitution. That Clause says: "Neither House, during the Session of Congress, shall, without the Consent of the other, adjourn for more than three days." Art. I, §5, cl. 4.

We agree with the Solicitor General that a 3-day recess would be too short. The Adjournments Clause reflects the fact that a 3-day break is not a significant interruption of legislative business. As the Solicitor General says, it is constitutionally *de minimis.* A Senate recess that is so short that it does not require the consent of the House is not long enough to trigger the President's recess-appointment power.

That is not to say that the President may make recess appointments during any recess that is "more than three days." Art. I, §5, cl. 4. The Recess Appointments Clause seeks to permit the Executive Branch to function smoothly when Congress is unavailable. And though Congress has taken short breaks for almost 200 years, and there have been many thousands of recess appointments in that time, we have not found a single example of a recess appointment made during an intra-session recess that was shorter than 10 days.

There are a few historical examples of recess appointments made during inter-session recesses shorter than 10 days. But when considered against 200 years of settled practice, we regard these few scattered examples as anomalies. We therefore conclude, in light of historical practice, that a recess of more than 3 days but less than 10 days is presumptively too short to fall within the Clause. We add the word "presumptively" to leave open the possibility that some very unusual circumstance—a national catastrophe, for instance, that renders the Senate unavailable but calls for an urgent response—could demand the exercise of the recess-appointment power during a shorter break. (It should go without saying—except that Justice Scalia compels us to say it—that political opposition in the Senate would not qualify as an unusual circumstance.)

In sum, we conclude that the phrase "the recess" applies to both intra-session and inter-session recesses. If a Senate recess is so short that it does not require the consent of the House, it is too short to trigger the Recess Appointments Clause.

See Art. I, §5, cl. 4. And a recess lasting less than 10 days is presumptively too short as well.

The second question concerns the scope of the phrase "vacancies *that may happen* during the recess of the Senate." Art. II, §2, cl. 3 (emphasis added). All agree that the phrase applies to vacancies that initially occur during a recess. But does it also apply to vacancies that initially occur before a recess and continue to exist during the recess? In our view the phrase applies to both kinds of vacancy. We believe that the Clause's language, read literally, permits, though it does not naturally favor, our broader interpretation.

In any event, the linguistic question here is not whether the phrase can be, but whether it must be, read more narrowly. And the broader reading, we believe, is at least a permissible reading of a "doubtful" phrase. We consequently go on to consider the Clause's purpose and historical practice. In light of some linguistic ambiguity, the basic purpose of the Clause, and the historical practice we have described, we conclude that the phrase "all vacancies" includes vacancies that come into existence while the Senate is in session.

The third question concerns the calculation of the length of the Senate's "recess." On December 17, 2011, the Senate by unanimous consent adopted a resolution to convene "*pro forma* sessions" only, with "no business transacted," on every Tuesday and Friday from December 20, 2011, through January 20, 2012. 2011 S. J. 923. At the end of each *pro forma* session, the Senate would "adjourn until" the following *pro forma* session. *Ibid.* During that period, the Senate convened and adjourned as agreed. It held *pro forma* sessions on December 20, 23, 27, and 30, and on January 3, 6, 10, 13, 17, and 20; and at the end of each *pro forma* session, it adjourned until the time and date of the next.

The President made the recess appointments before us on January 4, 2012, in between the January 3 and the January 6 *pro forma* sessions. We must determine the significance of these sessions — that is, whether, for purposes of the Clause, we should treat them as periods when the Senate was in session or as periods when it was in recess. If the former, the period between January 3 and January 6 was a 3-day recess, which is too short to trigger the President's recess-appointment power. If the latter, however, then the 3-day period was part of a much longer recess during which the President did have the power to make recess appointments.

The Solicitor General argues that we must treat the *pro forma* sessions as periods of recess. He says that these "sessions" were sessions in name only because the Senate was in recess as a *functional* matter. In our view, however, the *pro forma* sessions count as sessions, not as periods of recess. We hold that, for purposes of the Recess Appointments Clause, the Senate is in session when it says it is, provided that, under its own rules, it retains the capacity to transact Senate business. The Senate met that standard here.

The standard we apply is consistent with the Constitution's broad delegation of authority to the Senate to determine how and when to conduct its business. The Constitution explicitly empowers the Senate to "determine the Rules of its Proceedings." Art. I, §5, cl. 2. And we have held that "all matters of method are open to the determination" of the Senate, as long as there is "a reasonable relation between the mode or method of proceeding established by the rule and the result which is sought to be attained" and the rule does not "ignore constitutional restraints or violate fundamental rights." *United States v. Ballin*, 144 U.S. 1, 5 (1892).

In addition, the Constitution provides the Senate with extensive control over its schedule. There are only limited exceptions. See Amdt. 20, §2 (Congress must meet once a year on January 3, unless it specifies another day by law); Art. II, §3 (Senate must meet if the President calls it into special session); Art. I, §5, cl. 4 (neither House may adjourn for more than three days without consent of the other). The Constitution thus gives the Senate wide latitude to determine whether and when to have a session, as well as how to conduct the session.

For these reasons, we conclude that we must give great weight to the Senate's own determination of when it is and when it is not in session. But our deference to the Senate cannot be absolute. When the Senate is without the *capacity* to act, under its own rules, it is not in session even if it so declares. Accordingly, we conclude that when the Senate declares that it is in session and possesses the capacity, under its own rules, to conduct business, it is in session for purposes of the Clause.

Applying this standard, we find that the *pro forma* sessions were sessions for purposes of the Clause. First, the Senate said it was in session. The Journal of the Senate and the Congressional Record indicate that the Senate convened for a series of twice-weekly "sessions" from December 20 through January 20. And these reports of the Senate "must be assumed to speak the truth." *Ballin.*

Second, the Senate's rules make clear that during its *pro forma* sessions, despite its resolution that it would conduct no business, the Senate retained the power to conduct business. During any *pro forma* session, the Senate could have conducted business simply by passing a unanimous consent agreement. See Riddick's 1313. The Senate in fact conducts much of its business through unanimous consent. Senate rules presume that a quorum is present unless a present Senator questions it. And when the Senate has a quorum, an agreement is unanimously passed if, upon its proposal, no present Senator objects. It is consequently unsurprising that the Senate *has* enacted legislation during *pro forma* sessions even when it has said that no business will be transacted. Indeed, the Senate passed a bill by unanimous consent during the second *pro forma* session after its December 17 adjournment. 2011 S. J. 924. And that bill quickly became law.

By way of contrast, we do not see how the Senate could conduct business during a recess. It could terminate the recess and then, when in session, pass a bill. But in that case, of course, the Senate would no longer be in recess. It would be in session. And that is the crucial point. Senate rules make clear that, once in session, the Senate can act even if it has earlier said that it would not.

The Recess Appointments Clause responds to a structural difference between the Executive and Legislative Branches: The Executive Branch is perpetually in operation, while the Legislature only acts in intervals separated by recesses. The purpose of the Clause is to allow the Executive to continue operating while the Senate is unavailable. We believe that the Clause's text, standing alone, is ambiguous. It does not resolve whether the President may make appointments during intra-session recesses, or whether he may fill pre-recess vacancies. But the broader reading better serves the Clause's structural function. Moreover, that broader reading is reinforced by centuries of history, which we are hesitant to disturb. We thus hold that the Constitution empowers the President to fill any existing vacancy during any recess—intra-session or inter-session—of sufficient length.

Justice Scalia would render illegitimate thousands of recess appointments reaching all the way back to the founding era. More than that: Calling the Clause an "anachronism," he would basically read it out of the Constitution. He performs this act of judicial excision in the name of liberty. We fail to see how excising the Recess Appointments Clause preserves freedom. In fact, Alexander Hamilton observed in the very first Federalist Paper that "the vigour of government is essential to the security of liberty." The Federalist No. 1, at 5. And the Framers included the Recess Appointments Clause to preserve the "vigour of government" at times when an important organ of Government, the United States Senate, is in recess. Justice Scalia's interpretation of the Clause would defeat the power of the Clause to achieve that objective.

The foregoing discussion should refute Justice Scalia's claim that we have "embraced" an "adverse-possession theory of executive power." Instead, as in all cases, we interpret the Constitution in light of its text, purposes, and "our whole experience" as a Nation. *Missouri v. Holland*, 252 U.S. 416, 433 (1920). And we look to the actual practice of Government to inform our interpretation.

Given our answer to the last question before us, we conclude that the Recess Appointments Clause does not give the President the constitutional authority to make the appointments here at issue. Because the Court of Appeals reached the same ultimate conclusion (though for reasons we reject), its judgment is *affirmed*.

Justice SCALIA, with whom THE CHIEF JUSTICE, Justice THOMAS, and Justice ALITO join, *concurring* in the judgment.

Except where the Constitution or a valid federal law provides otherwise, all "Officers of the United States" must be appointed by the President "by and with the Advice and Consent of the Senate." U.S. Const., Art. II, §2, cl. 2. That general rule is subject to an exception: "The President shall have Power to fill up all Vacancies that may happen during the Recess of the Senate, by granting Commissions which shall expire at the End of their next Session." *Id.*, §2, cl. 3.

To prevent the President's recess-appointment power from nullifying the Senate's role in the appointment process, the Constitution cabins that power in two significant ways. First, it may be exercised only in "the Recess of the Senate," that is, the intermission between two formal legislative sessions. Second, it may be used to fill only those vacancies that "happen during the Recess," that is, offices that become vacant during that intermission. Both conditions are clear from the Constitution's text and structure, and both were well understood at the founding.

The Court of Appeals correctly held that the appointments here at issue are invalid because they did not meet either condition.

Today's majority disregards two overarching principles that ought to guide our consideration of the questions presented here. First, the Constitution's core, government-structuring provisions are no less critical to preserving liberty than are the later adopted provisions of the Bill of Rights. Indeed, "so convinced were the Framers that liberty of the person inheres in structure that at first they did not consider a Bill of Rights necessary." *Clinton v. City of New York*, 524 U.S. 417, 450 (1998) (KENNEDY, J., *concurring*). Second and relatedly, when questions involving the Constitution's government-structuring provisions are presented in a justiciable case, it is the solemn responsibility of the Judicial Branch "'to say what the law is.'" *Zivotofsky v. Clinton*, 566 U.S. ___, ___ (2012) (quoting *Marbury v. Madison*, 1 Cranch 137 , 177 (1803)). This Court does not defer to the other branches' resolution of such controversies; as Justice Kennedy has previously written, our role is in no way "lessened" because it might be said that "the two political branches are adjusting their own powers between themselves." *Clinton.*

The first question presented is whether "the Recess of the Senate," during which the President's recess-appointment power is active, is (a) the period between two of the Senate's formal sessions, or (b) any break in the Senate's proceedings. I would hold that "the Recess" is the gap between sessions and that the appointments at issue here are invalid because they undisputedly were made *during* the Senate's session. The Court's contrary conclusion—that "the Recess" includes "breaks in the midst of a session"—is inconsistent with the Constitution's text and structure, and it requires judicial fabrication of vague, unadministrable limits on the recess-appointment power (thus defined) that overstep the judicial role. The majority's methodology thus all but guarantees the continuing aggrandizement of the Executive Branch.

The second question presented is whether vacancies that "happen during the Recess of the Senate," which the President is empowered to fill with recess appointments, are (a) vacancies that *arise* during the recess, or (b) all vacancies that *exist* during the recess, regardless of when they arose. I would hold that the recess-appointment power is limited to vacancies that arise during the recess in which they are filled, and I would hold that the appointments at issue here—which undisputedly filled pre-recess vacancies—are invalid for that reason as well as for the reason that they were made during the session. The Court's contrary conclusion is inconsistent with the Constitution's text and structure, and it further undermines the balance the Framers struck between Presidential and Senatorial power. Historical practice also fails to support the majority's conclusion on this issue.

What the majority needs to sustain its judgment is an ambiguous text and a clear historical practice. What it has is a clear text and an at-best-ambiguous historical practice. Even if the Executive could accumulate power through adverse possession by engaging in a *consistent* and *unchallenged* practice over a long period of time, the oft-disputed practices at issue here would not meet that standard.

Nor have those practices created any justifiable expectations that could be disappointed by enforcing the Constitution's original meaning. There is thus no ground for the majority's deference to the unconstitutional recess-appointment practices of the Executive Branch.

The majority replaces the Constitution's text with a new set of judge-made rules to govern recess appointments. Henceforth, the Senate can avoid triggering the President's now-vast recess-appointment power by the odd contrivance of never adjourning for more than three days without holding a *pro forma* session at which it is understood that no business will be conducted.

The real tragedy of today's decision is not simply the abolition of the Constitution's limits on the recess-appointment power and the substitution of a novel framework invented by this Court. It is the damage done to our separation-of-powers jurisprudence more generally. Sad, but true: The Court's embrace of the adverse-possession theory of executive power (a characterization the majority resists but does not refute) will be cited in diverse contexts, including those presently unimagined, and will have the effect of aggrandizing the Presidency beyond its constitutional bounds and undermining respect for the separation of powers. I *concur.*

∾ PROBLEM: RECESS? ∾

Suppose the Senate declares an 11-day break in one of its regular sessions. Based on an event in Iraq, it curtails the break after seven days. During those days, the President appoints a person to the N.L.R.B. Is the appointment valid under *Canning?*

2. Removal Powers

While it might be assumed that if the President has the power to appoint government officials, there is also an associated power to remove them, the actual rules are more complicated than that based on the conceptualization of the three branches as interdependent and not absolutely separate. Generally, Congress cannot reserve to itself the power to remove officials who are executive officers. The Court grappled with this rule in early cases such as *Myers v. United States*, 272 U.S. 52 (1925), where the Court struck down a law providing that some postmasters of the United States could not be removed without Congress's consent, and *Humphrey's Executor v. United States*, 295 U.S. 602 (1935), where the Court upheld a provision in the Federal Trade Commission (FTC) Act, permitting presidential removal of Federal Trade Commissioners, but only for certain reasons. The Court in *Humphrey's Executor* distinguished the law in *Myers,* finding that the FTC did not lie purely within the executive realm like *Myers,* because it exercised "quasi-legislative or quasi-judicial powers."

Just who is an "executive official" and what is the executive function can be difficult, if not insuperable, questions to resolve. The Supreme Court has leaned toward permitting congressional limitations on removal and even shared responsibility for the removal of officials who are considered "hybrid," in that they have some responsibilities outside of enforcement of the law, such as judicial responsibilities. These officials generally do not serve "at the pleasure of the President."

In *Bowsher v. Synar*, 478 U.S. 714 (1986), the Supreme Court considered whether Congress's law directing the comptroller general to help balance the federal budget, the "Gramm-Rudman-Hollings Act," was consistent with separation of powers limitations. A key issue was whether the comptroller general is an executive officer or a legislative actor who could be controlled by Congress, particularly in removal matters. The Supreme Court affirmed the lower court decision, striking down the law as a violation of the separation of powers.

The background of the case is instructive. Congress enacted the Balanced Budget and Emergency Deficit Act of 1985 to promote a balanced federal budget. To ensure that deficits did not continue to increase, the Act called for the comptroller general of the General Accounting Office, an agency under the auspices of Congress, to assist with cutting the budget in a manner prescribed by the Act. The comptroller was removable under the Act only by Congress, not by the President or any other official.

Shortly after the President approved the Act, Congressman Synar and other members of Congress filed suit. They claimed the law was unconstitutional and sought a declaratory judgment of their rights.

Bowsher v. Synar

478 U.S. 714 (1986)

Chief Justice BURGER delivered the opinion of the Court.

The question presented by these appeals is whether the assignment by Congress to the Comptroller General of the United States of certain functions under the Balanced Budget and Emergency Deficit Control Act of 1985 violates the doctrine of separation of powers.

On December 12, 1985, the President signed into law the Balanced Budget and Emergency Deficit Control Act of 1985, 2 U.S.C. §901 *et seq.* (1982 ed., Supp. III), popularly known as the "Gramm-Rudman-Hollings Act." The purpose of the Act is to eliminate the federal budget deficit. To that end, the Act sets a "maximum deficit amount" for federal spending for each of fiscal years 1986 through 1991. The size of that maximum deficit amount progressively reduces to zero in fiscal year 1991. These "automatic" reductions are accomplished through a rather complicated procedure, spelled out in §251, the so-called "reporting provisions" of the Act. Each year, the Directors of the Office of Management and Budget (OMB) and the Congressional Budget Office (CBO) independently estimate the amount of the federal budget deficit for the upcoming fiscal year. If that deficit exceeds the maximum targeted deficit amount for that fiscal year by more than a specified amount, the Directors of OMB and CBO independently calculate, on a program-by-program basis, the budget reductions necessary to ensure that the deficit does not exceed the maximum deficit amount. The Act then requires the Directors to report jointly their deficit estimates and budget reduction calculations to the Comptroller General. The Comptroller General, after reviewing the Directors' reports, then reports his conclusions to the President. §251(b). The President in turn must issue a "sequestration" order mandating the spending reductions specified by the Comptroller General. §252. There follows a period during which Congress may by legislation reduce spending to obviate, in whole or in part, the need for the sequestration order. If such reductions are not enacted, the sequestration order becomes effective and the spending reductions included in that order are made.

We noted recently that "the Constitution sought to divide the delegated powers of the new Federal Government into three defined categories, Legislative, Executive, and Judicial." *INS v. Chadha*, 462 U.S. 919, 951 (1983). The declared purpose of separating and dividing the powers of government, of course, was to "diffuse power the better to secure liberty." *Youngstown Sheet & Tube Co. v. Sawyer*, 343 U.S. 579, 635 (1952) (Jackson, J., concurring). Justice Jackson's words echo the famous warning of Montesquieu, quoted by James Madison in *The Federalist No. 47*, that "there can be no liberty where the legislative and executive powers are united in the same person, or body of magistrates." *The Federalist No. 47*, p. 325 (J. Cooke ed. 1961).

Other, more subtle, examples of separated powers are evident as well. Unlike parliamentary systems such as that of Great Britain, no person who is an officer of the United States may serve as a Member of the Congress. Art. I, §6. Moreover, unlike parliamentary systems, the President, under Article II, is responsible not to the Congress but to the people, subject only to impeachment proceedings which are exercised by the two Houses as representatives of the people. Art. II, §4.

The Constitution does not contemplate an active role for Congress in the supervision of officers charged with the execution of the laws it enacts. The President appoints "Officers of the United States" with the "Advice and Consent of the Senate." Art. II, §2. Once the appointment has been made and confirmed, however, the Constitution explicitly provides for removal of Officers of the United States by Congress only upon impeachment by the House of Representatives and conviction by the Senate. A direct congressional role in the removal of officers charged with the execution of the laws beyond this limited one is inconsistent with separation of powers. This was made clear in debate in the First Congress in 1789.

This Court first directly addressed this issue in *Myers v. United States*, 272 U.S. 52 (1925). At issue in *Myers* was a statute providing that certain postmasters could be removed only "by and with the advice and consent of the Senate." The

President removed one such Postmaster without Senate approval, and a lawsuit ensued. Chief Justice Taft, writing for the Court, declared the statute unconstitutional on the ground that for Congress to "draw to itself, or to either branch of it, the power to remove or the right to participate in the exercise of that power would be to infringe the constitutional principle of the separation of governmental powers."

A decade later, in *Humphrey's Executor v. United States,* 295 U.S. 602 (1935), relied upon heavily by appellants, a Federal Trade Commissioner who had been removed by the President sought back pay. *Humphrey's Executor* involved an issue not presented either in the *Myers* case or in this case—i.e., the power of Congress to limit the President's powers of removal of a Federal Trade Commissioner. The relevant statute permitted removal "by the President," but only "for inefficiency, neglect of duty, or malfeasance in office." Justice Sutherland, speaking for the Court, upheld the statute, holding that "illimitable power of removal is not possessed by the President with respect to Federal Trade Commissioners." The Court distinguished *Myers,* reaffirming its holding that congressional participation in the removal of executive officers is unconstitutional.

The Court reached a similar result in *Wiener v. United States,* 357 U.S. 349 (1958), concluding that, under *Humphrey's Executor,* the President did not have unrestrained removal authority over a member of the War Claims Commission. In light of these precedents, we conclude that Congress cannot reserve for itself the power of removal of an officer charged with the execution of the laws except by impeachment.

Our decision in *INS v. Chadha,* 462 U.S. 919 (1983), supports this conclusion. In *Chadha,* we struck down a one-House "legislative veto" provision by which each House of Congress retained the power to reverse a decision Congress had expressly authorized the Attorney General to make: "Congress must abide by its delegation of authority until that delegation is legislatively altered or revoked."

With these principles in mind, we turn to consideration of whether the Comptroller General is controlled by Congress. Appellants urge that the Comptroller General performs his duties independently and is not subservient to Congress. We agree with the District Court that this contention does not bear close scrutiny. The critical factor lies in the provisions of the statute defining the Comptroller General's office relating to removability. Although the Comptroller General is nominated by the President from a list of three individuals recommended by the Speaker of the House of Representatives and the President *pro tempore* of the Senate, *see* 31 U.S.C. §703(a)(2), and confirmed by the Senate, he is removable only at the initiative of Congress. He may be removed not only by impeachment but also by joint resolution of Congress "at any time" resting on any one of the following bases: "(i) permanent disability;" "(ii) inefficiency;" "(iii) neglect of duty;" "(iv) malfeasance;" or "(v) a felony or conduct involving moral turpitude." This provision was included, as one Congressman explained in urging passage of the Act, because Congress "felt that the Comptroller General should be brought under the sole control of Congress, so that Congress at any moment when it found he was inefficient and was not carrying on the duties of his office as he should and as the Congress expected, could remove him without the long, tedious process of a trial by impeachment." 61 Cong. Rec. 1081 (1921).

Justice White contends: "The statute does not permit anyone to remove the Comptroller at will; removal is permitted only for specified cause, with the existence of cause to be determined by Congress following a hearing. Any removal under the statute would presumably be subject to post-termination judicial review to ensure that a hearing had in fact been held and that the finding of cause for removal was not arbitrary." *Post.* That observation by the dissenter rests on at least two arguable premises: (a) that the enumeration of certain specified causes of removal excludes the possibility of removal for other causes; and (b) that any removal would be subject to judicial review, a position that appellants were unwilling to endorse.

Glossing over these difficulties, the dissent's assessment of the statute fails to recognize the breadth of the grounds for removal. The statute permits removal for "inefficiency," "neglect of duty," or "malfeasance." These terms are very broad and, as interpreted by Congress, could sustain removal of a Comptroller General for any number of actual or perceived transgressions of the legislative will. The Constitutional Convention chose to permit impeachment of executive officers only for "Treason, Bribery, or other high Crimes and Misdemeanors." It rejected language that would have permitted impeachment for "maladministration," with Madison arguing that "so vague a term will be equivalent to a tenure during pleasure of the Senate." 2 M. Farrand, *Records of the Federal Convention of 1787,* 550 (1911).

The executive nature of the Comptroller General's functions under the Act is revealed in §252(a)(3) which gives the Comptroller General the ultimate authority to determine the budget cuts to be made. Indeed, the Comptroller General commands the President himself to carry out, without the slightest variation (with exceptions not relevant to the constitutional issues presented), the directive of the Comptroller General as to the budget reductions. Congress of course initially determined the content of the Balanced Budget and Emergency Deficit Control Act; and undoubtedly the content of the Act determines the nature of the executive duty. However, as *Chadha* makes clear, once Congress makes its choice in enacting legislation, its participation ends. Congress can thereafter control the execution of its enactment only indirectly—by passing new legislation. *Chadha,* 462 U.S., at 958. By placing the responsibility for execution of the Balanced Budget and Emergency Deficit Control Act in the hands of an officer who is subject to removal only by itself, Congress in effect has retained control over the execution of the Act and has intruded into the executive function. The Constitution does not permit such intrusion.

We conclude that the District Court correctly held that the powers vested in the Comptroller General under Section 251 violate the command of the

Constitution that the Congress play no direct role in the execution of the laws. Accordingly, the judgment and order of the District Court are affirmed.

∾ PROBLEM: THE PRESIDENT'S POWER TO FIRE A SPECIAL COUNSEL ∾

Could the President of the United States have fired special counsel Robert Mueller? While this question remains unanswered, it garnered considerable attention during Mr. Mueller's time as special prosecutor. Mr. Mueller was appointed special counsel on May 17, 2017, to investigate "Russian interference with the 2016 presidential election and related matters" by the Acting Attorney General, Rod Rosenstein. If the President asked for your opinion on the matter, what would you have said? If the answer is yes, under what circumstances could such a removal occur?

There are those commentators who claim that since the President under the Constitution must "take care that the laws be faithfully executed," he is charged with being the chief law enforcement officer, responsible for all prosecutions and investigations. *Myers v. United States*, 272 U.S. 52, 118 (1926) ("The association of removal with appointment of executive officers is not incompatible with our republican form of Government"). Consequently, the President can fire prosecutors or halt any such investigations or prosecutions that are occurring. Other commentators have differing viewpoints. Some assert that the Department of Justice has regulations that protect Mr. Mueller from firing without reason. Others assert that while no safeguards in the law existed to protect Mr. Mueller's employment in his position, Congress could have adopted safeguards for the special prosecutor, ensuring that he cannot be fired without cause.

∾ PROBLEM: THE AUDIT ∾

Congress enacts a law requiring audits of all government agency books on a rotating schedule, every four years. The law states that auditing shall occur by individuals appointed by and operating out of the General Accounting Office. These individuals shall provide detailed written reports to Congress. Removal of these officials shall occur by a committee appointed jointly by Congress and a specially appointed panel of federal judges. Is the auditing law, particularly its procedure for removing committee members, constitutional? Explain.

E. FOREIGN AFFAIRS AND COMMANDER-IN-CHIEF POWERS

The President has broad powers over foreign affairs. The powers extend from acting as the chief diplomat and representative of the United States, to participating in appointing ambassadors, to entering into relationships and agreements with foreign countries, and to protecting U.S. citizens as the Commander in Chief. Some of these powers are shared with Congress, which also exercises constitutional power in the international sphere. Congress's powers include regulating foreign commerce under the Commerce Clause, spending on the armed forces, and declaring war. The Senate's advice and consent also is required for treaties.

1. Foreign Affairs Powers

The President has wide-ranging powers over foreign policy and international affairs. As the chief executive, the President is by virtue of office the representative of the United States in a myriad of activities, from political visits to and from other heads of state, to a wide variety of agreements with other countries and international organizations, such as the United Nations. A significant question that arises in the foreign affairs arena is whether the President has powers as head of state that are independent of those powers derived from the Constitution.

The case of *United States v. Curtiss Wright Export Corporation*, 299 U.S. 304 (1936), provided a seminal opportunity for the Court to delineate the source and scope of the foreign affairs powers. In *Curtiss Wright Export Corporation*, the Court was faced with an issue asking whether there was a duality in the executive's exercise of domestic powers and foreign powers. The Court concluded that there was a distinction—and that where the President was operating indeed mattered. The Court found that the President's role in foreign affairs was both plenary and inherent, with the President serving as the representative of the entire nation.

United States v. Curtiss Wright Export Corporation

299 U.S. 304 (1936)

Mr. Justice SUTHERLAND delivered the opinion of the Court.

On January 27, 1936, the Curtiss Wright Export Corporation was indicted for conspiring to sell military weapons to the nation of Bolivia. At the time, Bolivia was engaged in a military conflict. Curtiss Wright's action allegedly violated both a joint resolution of Congress and a proclamation issued by the President the same day. The resolution granted the President authority to prohibit the sale of arms to nations engaged in conflict in the Chaco, and President Franklin Roosevelt's proclamation prohibited such action. Then, on November 29, 1935, President Roosevelt issued a new proclamation revoking the earlier one, but leaving in place any existing violation. An issue in the case was the effect of the President's "revocation."

Not only, as we have shown, is the federal power over external affairs in origin and essential character different from that over internal affairs, but participation in the exercise of the power is significantly limited. In this vast external realm, with its important, complicated, delicate and manifold problems, the President alone has the power to speak or listen as a representative of the nation. He makes treaties with the advice and consent of the Senate; but he alone negotiates. Into the field of negotiation the Senate cannot intrude; and Congress itself is power-less to invade it. As Marshall said in his great argument of March 7, 1800, in the House of Representatives, "The President is the sole organ of the nation in its external relations, and its sole representative with foreign nations." Annals, 6th Cong., col. 613. The Senate Committee on Foreign Relations at a very early day in our history (February 15, 1816), reported to the Senate, among other things, as follows: "The President is the constitutional representative of the United States with regard to foreign nations. He manages our concerns with foreign nations and must necessarily be most competent to determine when, how, and upon what subjects negotiation may be urged with the greatest prospect of success. For his conduct he is responsible to the Constitution." 8 U.S. Sen. Reports Comm. on Foreign Relations, p. 24.

It is important to bear in mind that we are here dealing not alone with an authority vested in the President by an exertion of legislative power, but with such an authority plus the very delicate, plenary and exclusive power of the President as the sole organ of the federal government in the field of interna-tional relations—a power which does not require as a basis for its exercise an act of Congress, but which, of course, like every other governmental power, must be exercised in subordination to the applicable provisions of the Constitution.

The marked difference between foreign affairs and domestic affairs in this respect is recognized by both houses of Congress in the very form of their req-uisitions for information from the executive departments. In the case of every department except the Department of State, the resolution directs the official to furnish the information. In the case of the State Department, dealing with for-eign affairs, the President is requested to furnish the information "if not incom-patible with the public interest."

Practically every volume of the United States Statutes contains one or more acts or joint resolutions of Congress authorizing action by the President in respect of subjects affecting foreign relations, which either leave the exercise of the power to his unrestricted judgment, or provide a standard far more general than that which has always been considered requisite with regard to domestic affairs.

In *Field v. Clark*, 143 U.S. 649, 691, this court declared that "the practical con-struction of the constitution, as given by so many acts of Congress, and embrac-ing almost the entire period of our national existence, should not be overruled, unless upon a conviction that such legislation was clearly incompatible with the supreme law of the land." The rule is one which has been stated and applied many times by this court.

The Executive proclamation recites, "I have found that the prohibition of the sale of arms and munitions of war in the United States to those countries now engaged in armed conflict in the Chaco may contribute to the reestablishment of peace between those countries, and that I have consulted with the governments of other American Republics and have been assured of the cooperation of such governments as I have deemed necessary as contemplated by the said joint resolution." This finding satisfies every requirement of the Joint Resolution. There is no suggestion that the resolution is fatally uncertain or indefinite; and a finding which follows its language, as this finding does, cannot well be challenged as insufficient.

It was not within the power of the President to repeal the Joint Resolution; and his second proclamation did not purport to do so. It "revoked" the first proclamation; and the question is, did the revocation of the proclamation have the effect of abrogating the resolution or of precluding its enforcement in so far as that involved the prosecution and punishment of offenses committed during the life of the first proclamation? We are of opinion that it did not.

∽ PROBLEMS ∽

1. *Russian Republic.* A former Soviet republic establishes its own government. The President of the United States agrees to meet with the new leader of the republic. During the meeting, the leaders agree to meet again and engage in a trade relationship, as detailed in the agreement. The agreement, generally referred to as the Litinov Agreement after the republic's leader, is challenged by the Senate as violating the treaty power requiring the Senate's consent. Was the President's action constitutional? *See United States v. Pink*, 315 U.S. 203 (1942).

2. *China.* The Executive Branch, through the Department of the Treasury, issued a travel restriction to China. The restriction stated: "No tourist or business travel to China will be permitted unless a showing of reasonable and compelling need is demonstrated." Is this travel restriction constitutional? If yes, what is the constitutional basis for the Treasury Department's actions?

What country contains the city of Jerusalem? This geography question is one of longstanding conflict and discussion. The question also provided the backdrop for a significant interbranch dispute regarding the scope of the President's recognition power and whether it is exclusive or shared to a certain extent with Congress.

Zivotofsky v. Kerry

576 U.S. ___ (2015)

Justice KENNEDY delivered the opinion of the Court.

A delicate subject lies in the background of this case. That subject is Jerusalem. Questions touching upon the history of the ancient city and its present legal and international status are among the most difficult and complex in international affairs.

The Court addresses two questions to resolve the interbranch dispute now before it. First, it must determine whether the President has the exclusive power to grant formal recognition to a foreign sovereign. Second, if he has that power, the Court must determine whether Congress can command the President and his Secretary of State to issue a formal statement that contradicts the earlier recognition. The statement in question here is a congressional mandate that allows a United States citizen born in Jerusalem to direct the President and Secretary of State, when issuing his passport, to state that his place of birth is "Israel."

Jerusalem's political standing has long been, and remains, one of the most sensitive issues in American foreign policy, and indeed it is one of the most delicate issues in current international affairs. In 1948, President Truman formally recognized Israel in a signed statement of "recognition." That statement did not recognize Israeli sovereignty over Jerusalem. Over the last 60 years, various actors have sought to assert full or partial sovereignty over the city, including Israel, Jordan, and the Palestinians. Yet, in contrast to a consistent policy of formal recognition of Israel, neither President Truman nor any later United States President has issued an official statement or declaration acknowledging any country's sovereignty over Jerusalem. Instead, the Executive Branch has maintained that "the status of Jerusalem should be decided not unilaterally but in consultation with all concerned." United Nations Gen. Assembly Official Records.

The President's position on Jerusalem is reflected in State Department policy regarding passports and consular reports of birth abroad. Understanding that passports will be construed as reflections of American policy, the State Department's Foreign Affairs Manual instructs its employees, in general, to record the place of birth on a passport as the "country having present sovereignty over the actual area of birth." Dept. of State, 7 Foreign Affairs Manual (FAM) §1383.4 (1987). If a citizen objects to the country listed as sovereign by the State Department, he or she may list the city or town of birth rather than the country. See *id.*, §1383.6. The FAM, however, does not allow citizens to list a sovereign that conflicts with Executive Branch policy. See generally *id.*, §1383. Because the United States does not recognize any country as having sovereignty over Jerusalem, the FAM instructs employees to record the place of birth for citizens born there as "Jerusalem." *Id.*, §1383.5-6 (emphasis deleted).

In 2002, Congress passed the Act at issue here, the Foreign Relations Authorization Act, Fiscal Year 2003, 116 Stat. 1350. Section 214 of the Act is titled

"United States Policy with Respect to Jerusalem as the Capital of Israel." The subsection that lies at the heart of this case, §214(d), addresses passports. That subsection seeks to override the FAM by allowing citizens born in Jerusalem to list their place of birth as "Israel." Titled "Record of Place of Birth as Israel for Passport Purposes," §214(d) states "for purposes of the registration of birth, certification of nationality, or issuance of a passport of a United States citizen born in the city of Jerusalem, the Secretary shall, upon the request of the citizen or the citizen's legal guardian, record the place of birth as Israel."

When he signed the Act into law, President George W. Bush issued a statement declaring his position that §214 would, "if construed as mandatory rather than advisory, impermissibly interfere with the President's constitutional authority to formulate the position of the United States, speak for the Nation in international affairs, and determine the terms on which recognition is given to foreign states." Statement on Signing the Foreign Relations Authorization Act, Fiscal Year 2003, Public Papers of the Presidents, George W. Bush, Vol. 2, Sept. 30, 2002, p. 1698 (2005). The President concluded, "U. S. policy regarding Jerusalem has not changed."

Some parties were not reassured by the President's statement. A cable from the United States Consulate in Jerusalem noted that the Palestine Liberation Organization Executive Committee, Fatah Central Committee, and the Palestinian Authority Cabinet had all issued statements claiming that the Act "undermines the role of the U. S. as a sponsor of the peace process." In the Gaza Strip and elsewhere residents marched in protest. In response the Secretary of State advised diplomats to express their understanding of "Jerusalem's importance to both sides and to many others around the world." He noted his belief that America's "policy towards Jerusalem" had not changed.

In 2002, petitioner Menachem Binyamin Zivotofsky was born to United States citizens living in Jerusalem. In December 2002, Zivotofsky's mother visited the American Embassy in Tel Aviv to request both a passport and a consular report of birth abroad for her son. *Id.,* at 25. She asked that his place of birth be listed as "Jerusalem, Israel." The Embassy clerks explained that, pursuant to State Department policy, the passport would list only "Jerusalem." Zivotofsky's parents objected and, as his guardians, brought suit on his behalf in the United States District Court for the District of Columbia, seeking to enforce §214(d). Pursuant to §214(d), Zivotofsky claims the right to have "Israel" recorded as his place of birth in his passport. After Zivotofsky brought suit, the District Court dismissed his case, reasoning that it presented a nonjusticiable political question and that Zivotofsky lacked standing. The Court of Appeals for the District of Columbia Circuit reversed on the standing issue, but later affirmed the District Court's political question determination. This Court granted certiorari, vacated the judgment, and remanded the case. Whether §214(d) is constitutional, the Court held, is not a question reserved for the political branches. In reference to Zivotofsky's claim the Court observed "the Judiciary must decide if Zivotofsky's interpretation of the statute is correct, and whether the statute is constitutional" — not whether

Jerusalem is, in fact, part of Israel. *Zivotofsky* v. *Clinton*. On remand the Court of Appeals held the statute unconstitutional. It determined that "the President exclusively holds the power to determine whether to recognize a foreign sovereign," and that "section 214(d) directly contradicts a carefully considered exercise of the Executive branch's recognition power." This Court again granted certiorari.

In considering claims of Presidential power this Court refers to Justice Jackson's familiar tripartite framework from *Youngstown Sheet & Tube Co.* v. *Sawyer*, 343 U. S. 579-638 (1952) (concurring opinion). The framework divides exercises of Presidential power into three categories: First, when "the President acts pursuant to an express or implied authorization of Congress, his authority is at its maximum, for it includes all that he possesses in his own right plus all that Congress can delegate." Second, "in absence of either a congressional grant or denial of authority" there is a "zone of twilight in which he and Congress may have concurrent authority," and where "congressional inertia, indifference or quiescence may" invite the exercise of executive power. Finally, when "the President takes measures incompatible with the expressed or implied will of Congress he can rely only upon his own constitutional powers minus any constitutional powers of Congress over the matter." To succeed in this third category, the President's asserted power must be both "exclusive" and "conclusive" on the issue.

In this case the Secretary contends that §214(d) infringes on the President's exclusive recognition power by "requiring the President to contradict his recognition position regarding Jerusalem in official communications with foreign sovereigns." Brief for Respondent 48. In so doing the Secretary acknowledges the President's power is "at its lowest ebb." *Youngstown*, 343 U. S., at 637. Because the President's refusal to implement §214(d) falls into Justice Jackson's third category, his claim must be "scrutinized with caution," and he may rely solely on powers the Constitution grants to him alone.

To determine whether the President possesses the exclusive power of recognition the Court examines the Constitution's text and structure, as well as precedent and history bearing on the question. Recognition is a "formal acknowledgement" that a particular "entity possesses the qualifications for statehood" or "that a particular regime is the effective government of a state." Restatement (Third) of Foreign Relations Law of the United States §203, Comment *a*, p. 84 (1986). It may also involve the determination of a state's territorial bounds. See 2 M. Whiteman, Digest of International Law §1, p. 1 (1963). Recognition is often effected by an express "written or oral declaration." 1 J. Moore, Digest of International Law §27, p. 73 (1906). It may also be implied—for example, by concluding a bilateral treaty or by sending or receiving diplomatic agents.

In practice, then, the President's recognition determination is just one part of a political process that may require Congress to make laws. The President's exclusive recognition power encompasses the authority to acknowledge, in a formal sense, the legitimacy of other states and governments, including their territorial bounds. Albeit limited, the exclusive recognition power is essential to the conduct of Presidential duties. The formal act of recognition is an executive power that Congress may not qualify. If the President is to be effective in negotiations over a formal recognition determination, it must be evident to his counterparts abroad that he speaks for the Nation on that precise question.

A clear rule that the formal power to recognize a foreign government subsists in the President therefore serves a necessary purpose in diplomatic relations. All this, of course, underscores that Congress has an important role in other aspects of foreign policy, and the President may be bound by any number of laws Congress enacts. In this way ambition counters ambition, ensuring that the democratic will of the people is observed and respected in foreign affairs as in the domestic realm. See The Federalist No. 51, p. 322 (J. Madison).

No single precedent resolves the question whether the President has exclusive recognition authority and, if so, how far that power extends. In part that is because, until today, the political branches have resolved their disputes over questions of recognition. The relevant cases, though providing important instruction, address the division of recognition power between the Federal Government and the States, see, *e.g., Pink*, 315 U. S. 203, or between the courts and the political branches, see, *e.g., Banco Nacional de Cuba*, 376 U.S., at 410 — not between the President and Congress. As the parties acknowledge, some isolated statements in those cases lend support to the position that Congress has a role in the recognition process. In the end, however, a fair reading of the cases shows that the President's role in the recognition process is both central and exclusive.

During the administration of President Van Buren, in a case involving a dispute over the status of the Falkland Islands, the Court noted that "when the executive branch of the government" assumes "a fact in regard to the sovereignty of any island or country, it is conclusive on the judicial department." *Williams*, 13 Pet., at 420.

Having examined the Constitution's text and this Court's precedent, it is appropriate to turn to accepted understandings and practice. In separation-of-powers cases this Court has often "put significant weight upon historical practice." *NLRB* v. *Noel Canning*, 573 U. S. ___, ___ (2014). Here, history is not all on one side, but on balance it provides strong support for the conclusion that the recognition power is the President's alone. As the power to recognize foreign states resides in the President alone, the question becomes whether §214(d) infringes on the Executive's consistent decision to withhold recognition with respect to Jerusalem.

Section 214(d) requires the President, through the Secretary, to identify citizens born in Jerusalem who so request as being born in Israel. But according to the President, those citizens were not born in Israel. As a matter of United States policy, neither Israel nor any other country is acknowledged as having sovereignty over Jerusalem. In this way, §214(d) "directly contradicts" the "carefully calibrated and longstanding Executive branch policy of neutrality toward Jerusalem."

If the power over recognition is to mean anything, it must mean that the President not only makes the initial, formal recognition determination but also that he may maintain that determination in his and his agent's statements. This conclusion is a matter of both common sense and necessity. If Congress could command the President to state a recognition position inconsistent with his own, Congress could override the President's recognition determination. Thus, if Congress could alter the President's statements on matters of recognition or force him to contradict them, Congress in effect would exercise the recognition power.

If Congress may not pass a law, speaking in its own voice, that effects formal recognition, then it follows that it may not force the President himself to contradict his earlier statement. That congressional command would not only prevent the Nation from speaking with one voice but also prevent the Executive itself from doing so in conducting foreign relations.

Although the statement required by §214(d) would not itself constitute a formal act of recognition, it is a mandate that the Executive contradict his prior recognition determination in an official document issued by the Secretary of State. As a result, it is unconstitutional. This is all the more clear in light of the longstanding treatment of a passport's place-of-birth section as an official executive statement implicating recognition. See 725 F. 3d, at 224 (Tatel, J., concurring). The Secretary's position on this point has been consistent: He will not place information in the place-of-birth section of a passport that contradicts the President's recognition policy. See 7 FAM §1383.

The flaw in §214(d) is further underscored by the undoubted fact that the purpose of the statute was to infringe on the recognition power—a power the Court now holds is the sole prerogative of the President. The statute is titled "United States Policy with Respect to Jerusalem as the Capital of Israel." §214, 116 Stat. 1365. The House Conference Report proclaimed that §214 "contains four provisions related to the recognition of Jerusalem as Israel's capital." H. R. Conf. Rep. No. 107-671, p. 123 (2002). From the face of §214, from the legislative history, and from its reception, it is clear that Congress wanted to express its displeasure with the President's policy by, among other things, commanding the Executive to contradict his own, earlier stated position on Jerusalem. This Congress may not do.

It is true, as Zivotofsky notes, that Congress has substantial authority over passports. See *Haig* v. *Agee*, 453 U. S. 280 (1981); *Zemel* v. *Rusk*, 381 U. S. 1 (1965). The Court does not question the power of Congress to enact passport legislation of wide scope.

The problem with §214(d), however, lies in how Congress exercised its authority over passports. To allow Congress to control the President's communication in the context of a formal recognition determination is to allow Congress to exercise that exclusive power itself. As a result, the statute is unconstitutional.

In holding §214(d) invalid the Court does not question the substantial powers of Congress over foreign affairs in general or passports in particular. This case is confined solely to the exclusive power of the President to control recognition determinations, including formal statements by the Executive Branch acknowledging the legitimacy of a state or government and its territorial bounds.

Congress cannot command the President to contradict an earlier recognition determination in the issuance of passports.

The judgment of the Court of Appeals for the District of Columbia Circuit is *Affirmed*.

Justice SCALIA, with whom THE CHIEF JUSTICE and Justice ALITO join, *dissenting*.

This case arises out of a dispute between the Executive and Legislative Branches about whether the United States should treat Jerusalem as a part of Israel. The Constitution contemplates that the political branches will make policy about the territorial claims of foreign nations the same way they make policy about other international matters: The President will exercise his powers on the basis of his views, Congress its powers on the basis of its views. That is just what has happened here.

The political branches of our Government agree on the real-world fact that Israel controls the city of Jerusalem. See Jerusalem Embassy Act of 1995, 109 Stat. 398; Brief for Respondent 3. They disagree, however, about how official documents should record the birthplace of an American citizen born in Jerusalem. The Executive does not accept any state's claim to sovereignty over Jerusalem, and it maintains that the birthplace designation "Israel" would clash with this stance of neutrality. But the National Legislature has enacted a statute that provides: "For purposes of the registration of birth, certification of nationality, or issuance of a passport of a United States citizen born in the city of Jerusalem, the Secretary of State shall, upon the request of the citizen or the citizen's legal guardian, record the place of birth as Israel." Foreign Relations Authorization Act, Fiscal Year 2003, §214(d), 116 Stat. 1366. Menachem Zivotofsky's parents seek enforcement of this statutory right in the issuance of their son's passport and consular report of birth abroad. They regard their son's birthplace as a part of Israel and insist as "a matter of conscience" that his Israeli nativity "not be erased" from his identity documents. App. 26.

Before turning to Presidential power under Article II, I think it well to establish the statute's basis in congressional power under Article I. Congress's power to "establish an uniform Rule of Naturalization," Art. I, §8, cl. 4, enables it to grant American citizenship to someone born abroad. *United States* v. *Wong Kim Ark*, 169 U. S. 649-703 (1898). The naturalization power also enables Congress to furnish the people it makes citizens with papers verifying their citizenship — say a consular report of birth abroad (which certifies citizenship of an American born outside the United States) or a passport (which certifies citizenship for purposes of international travel). As the Necessary and Proper Clause confirms, every congressional power "carries with it all those incidental powers which are necessary to its complete and effectual execution." *Cohens* v. *Virginia*, 6 Wheat. 264, 429 (1821). Even on a miserly understanding of Congress's incidental authority, Congress may make grants of citizenship "effectual" by providing for the issuance of certificates authenticating them.

One would think that if Congress may grant Zivotofsky a passport and a birth report, it may also require these papers to record his birthplace as "Israel." The birthplace specification promotes the document's citizenship-authenticating function by identifying the bearer, distinguishing people with similar names but different birthplaces from each other, helping authorities uncover identity fraud, and facilitating retrieval of the Government's citizenship records. See App. 70. To be sure, recording Zivotovsky's birthplace as "Jerusalem" rather than "Israel" would fulfill these objectives, but when faced with alternative ways to carry its powers into execution, Congress has the "discretion" to choose the one it deems "most beneficial to the people." *McCulloch* v. *Maryland*, 4 Wheat. 316, 421 (1819). It thus has the right to decide that recording birthplaces as "Israel" makes for better foreign policy. Or that regardless of international politics, a passport or birth report should respect its bearer's conscientious belief that Jerusalem belongs to Israel.

No doubt congressional discretion in executing legislative powers has its limits; Congress's chosen approach must be not only "necessary" to carrying its powers into execution, but also "proper." History does not even support an exclusive Presidential power to make what the Court calls "formal statements" about "the legitimacy of a state or government and its territorial bounds,"

In the final analysis, the Constitution may well deny Congress power to recognize—the power to make an international commitment accepting a foreign entity as a state, a regime as its government, a place as a part of its territory, and so on. But whatever else §214(d) may do, it plainly does not make (or require the President to make) a commitment accepting Israel's sovereignty over Jerusalem. I *dissent*.

PROBLEMS

1. *The Jerusalem Connection.* Suppose the next President of the United States takes a new position in a speech, saying that Jerusalem ought to be at recognized as a shared capital of Israel. Can Mr. Zivotofsky seek a passport change once again?

2. *I am from the Spratly Islands.* A small Filipino community lives in the Spratly Islands, an area claimed by both the Philippines and China. If a person born in the islands wishes to have her passport indicate that she is Chinese, but the President has not agreed with China's claims, can Congress still authorize the inclusion of China on her passport? Explain.

Notes

1. The United States Embassy in Israel. In 1995, Congress enacted the Jerusalem Embassy Act, proclaiming that Jerusalem is the capital of Israel and that the US Embassy should be moved there by May 31, 1999. Despite the target date, the Act also allowed the President to use a waiver to keep the US embassy in Tel Aviv for a six-month period if it was "necessary to protect the national security interests of the United States." https://www.congress.gov/104/plaws/publ45/PLAW-104publ45.pdf

The waiver was continued every six months, maintaining the embassy in Tel Aviv, until December 2017, when President Trump declared his intent to change the location of the Embassy. On May 14, 2018, an interim Embassy was opened in Jerusalem. The diplomatic staff is still transitioning to the new location, as is the Ambassador. https://www.haaretz.com/us-news/.premium-why-did-trump-sign-a-waiver-postponing-u-s-embassy-move-this-week-1.6156839

2. North Korea. President Trump met with the leader of North Korea, Kim Jong-un, on June 12, 2018, in Singapore to get North Korea to agree to nuclear disarmament. At the summit, President Trump agreed to suspend a joint military exercise with South Korea and both leaders pledged their commitment to denuclearization of the Korean peninsula.

∾ PROBLEM ∾

Suppose President Trump meets again with Kim Jong-un and agrees to supply North Korea with planes and computer programs for every nuclear device North Korea destroys instead of detonates. You are an advisor to the President. Please advise the President on whether he has the power to unilaterally enter into such an agreement and how he can go about this endeavor.

2. War and the Commander-in-Chief Power — Formalism Versus Functionalism

The Executive Branch does not have the power to declare war. That power is firmly fixed within the domain of the legislature. Art. I, §8, cl. 11 ("The Congress shall have Power To declare War"). Over the past two centuries, the President has wielded an equally formidable tool, the "Commander-in-Chief" power. This power has permitted the Executive Branch to commit troops abroad and to engage in a wide variety of military actions involving weapons, ships, and airplanes. At times, the exercise of the commander's power appears to be equivalent to declaring war, and frames the tension between formalism and functionalism. Although Congress holds the formal power to declare war, the President holds the power to engage in it — and its subdivisions often labeled military actions or conflicts. The military actions in Korea in the 1950s, Vietnam from the 1950s through the 1970s, and Iraq in the 1990s and in 2003 through the present, for example, are effectively indistinguishable from a formal war. Each of these military engagements was fought with a panoply of weapons and considerable personnel, some of whom suffered injuries and death. While Congress often offered express support for military enterprises, as evidenced by the Gulf of Tonkin Resolution, Joint

Resolution of Congress, H.J. Res. 1145 (Aug. 7, 1964), viewed as supporting the deployment of combat forces in Vietnam, the analytical key to these enterprises is that they still were thought to be within the Executive Branch's power to protect U.S. citizens and interests abroad.

Congress's power to declare war, when placed side by side with the executive power to commit troops abroad, underscores the tension between formal and pragmatic approaches to the Constitution. The Congress formally holds the power, but as a functional matter, the executive has wielded it most often.

∾ PROBLEMS ∾

1. *Send in the Troops.* The President decides to help protect an ally from invasion by sending in troops to protect that country. No American citizens are directly in danger. The President notifies Congress about his decision to send troops the same day the troops are sent, without seeking approval or authorization of any kind. Is the President's action constitutional? *See, e.g., Youngstown Sheet & Tube Co. v. Sawyer,* 343 U.S. at 671 (Vinton, J., dissenting).

2. *No Nukes.* Congress enacts the following law: "Prior to initiating a preemptive strike using nuclear weapons, the President must obtain approval by the Congress, since such a strike is the equivalent of a Declaration of War." Is enacting the law within the power of Congress?

3. *No First Strikes.* Congress enacts the same law as in Problem 2, except that the law prohibits all first strikes with conventional weapons as well as nuclear ones, except in "self-defense" or the equivalent. Is this law constitutional?

The War Powers Resolution

In 1973, after an accumulation of executive military actions without an accompanying declaration of war, Congress attempted to reassert its participation in the Constitution's balance of war powers by enacting the War Powers Resolution. The Resolution was adopted over presidential veto, 50 U.S.C.A. §1541 *et seq.*, and placed various limitations on the executive's use of force abroad.

The courts have not ruled on the constitutionality of the Resolution, and its constitutional status remains in question. The Resolution permits the President, acting as Commander in Chief of the armed forces, to deploy combat troops in hostile situations, but only if there is "(1) a declaration of war, (2) specific statutory authorization, or (3) a national emergency created by attack upon the United States, its territories or possessions, or its armed forces." 50 U.S.C.A. §1541(c) (1973). The Resolution adds:

> the President shall submit within 48 hours to the Speaker of the House of Representatives and to the President Pro Tempore of the Senate a report, in writing, setting forth;

(A) the circumstances necessitating the introduction of United States Armed Forces;

(B) the constitutional and legislative authority under which such introduction took place; and

(C) the estimated scope and duration of the hostilities or involvement. *Id.* at §1543(a)(3)(c).

Within sixty calendar days after a report is submitted or is required to be submitted the President shall terminate any use of United States Armed Forces unless the Congress (1) has declared war (2) has extended by law such sixty-day period §1544(b).

(A) *NATO.* The President of the United States, in coordination with the North Atlantic Treaty Organization (NATO), directs American troops in Croatia. Assume Congress deadlocked 213-213 on a vote to authorize the use of American troops in the NATO operation for air strikes. The President contends that the use of troops in Croatia was based on his authority as Commander in Chief and that the strikes were necessary to protect U.S. trading interests in Europe. The action in Croatia lasted 79 days, past the 60-day general limit (without congressional approval of an extension) imposed by the War Powers Resolution. The President was required by the same Resolution to submit a report to Congress within 48 hours of committing troops in actual or imminent hostilities. Assuming the President did not comply with the requirements of the War Powers Resolution, were the President's actions permissible? If the answer is no, what penalty should result? Should members of Congress be allowed to bring suit against the President to enforce the War Powers Resolution? *See Campbell v. Clinton,* 203 F.3d 19 (D.C. Cir. 2000).

(B) *The Roland Amendment.* Suppose Congress enacts a law with an amendment named for its sponsor, Representative Roland. The Roland Amendment prohibits any expenditures of U.S. government funds that have the "purpose or effect" of aiding the rebel fighters in the Bolivian Mountains, known as the Bolivian Freedom Revolutionary Nation (BFRN). Representative Roland stated, "Let me make very clear that this prohibition applies to all funds available in the coming fiscal year regardless of any accounting procedure at any agency. It clearly prohibits any expenditure, including those for salaries or all support costs." Subsequently, officials of the National Security Council, an executive agency, secretly sold some surplus supplies and arms from the air force and navy to several European nations at a profit. The National Security Council officials, led by a staff member named Ollie East, donated the profits from the sales to the BFRN. Ollie claimed that these actions were within the executive's power as Commander in Chief and the President's proper role in foreign policy. He further contended that the conduct did not violate the Roland Amendment. What arguments would you make on Ollie's behalf that his actions were in compliance with the Roland Amendment and were constitutional? What arguments would you make that his actions were in violation of the Amendment? Which arguments are more persuasive? Why?

(C) *Rogues.* The dictator of a rogue state in Asia goes on the nation's television to denounce the West. At the close of his speech, he threatens to fire a nuclear missile at an "occupied North American target" if the United States does not promptly withdraw from Iraq. Can the President unilaterally attack that country without Congress's approval? Why or why not? What would be the impact if Congress passes a resolution opposing such an attack, including a vow not to fund it?

(D) *Presidential Care Packages?* Suppose the President of the United States learns in 2012 that the rebels in Syria are in great need of guns and food. The President gives a speech saying it is America's duty to aid the rebels in a time of need and that innocent men, women and children are being killed by Syria President Bashar al-Assad's regime. Can the American President unilaterally supply food to the rebels without Congress' approval? Guns? Military advisors? Explain.

(E) *Hostilities.* What counts as "hostilities" triggering the War Powers Resolution in light of the continuing unrest in various areas of the world? Can a more explicit and transparent definition be crafted? In the spring of 2011, President Obama committed United States troops to the NATO military air operation in Libya. If the actions involving United States support rose to the level of "hostilities" against Libya, the President was required under the War Powers Resolution to limit American participation or get the permission of Congress to continue such a mission. Instead, the President chose to interpret United States participation action that did not rise to the level of "hostilities" — apparently adopting the view of some of his advisors, and not the contrary view shared by other advisors. See, e.g., C. Savage, "2 Top Lawyers Lose Argument on War Power," P. 1 Col. 2 (June 18, 2011). Should all supportive military actions be considered "hostilities"? Is there any way to distinguish some military engagements from others in a predictive and bright-line manner?

F.   THE PRESIDENT'S POWER TO FIGHT TERRORISM

After the September 11, 2001, terrorist attacks on the United States, Americans attempted to create a security system to prevent future terrorist incursions. The security measures included the creation of a new cabinet-level agency, the Department of Homeland Security; the enactment of a law, called the USA PATRIOT Act;[*] and other significant tools, from enhanced airport security to extended border searches and antiterrorist training. One important measure was the attempt to detain indefinitely, without constitutional limitation, those persons participating in or supporting terrorist activities or groups. The detainees were considered to be "enemy combatants" by President Bush, leading to scrutiny by the courts over whether the detentions were constitutional. Although President

---

[*] The name "USA PATRIOT" is an acronym for Uniting and Strengthening America by Providing Appropriate Tools Required to Intercept and Obstruct Terrorism Act of 2001, USA Patriot Act, Pub. L. No. 107-56, 115 Stat. 272 (2001).

Obama's administration no longer calls the detainees "enemy combatants," there are still people who hold a similar status.

1. The President's Powers to Detain Alleged Terrorists

One week after the September 11 attacks, Congress enacted the Authorization for Use of Military Force (AUMF), 115 Stat. 224, allowing the Executive Branch to use all "necessary and appropriate force" against the al Qaeda terrorist network, the Taliban, other terrorists, and any nation harboring the same. Two months later, in November 2001, the President issued an order directing the military to identify and detain "enemy combatants," those persons fighting for or supporting terrorist organizations opposing the United States. Those persons were considered to be different from enemy soldiers who were part of a nation's fighting force in uniform and on the battlefield.

Numerous persons believed to be agents of terror were captured in Afghanistan and Iraq. Most of these persons were relocated to a detention facility at the U.S. Naval Base at Guantanamo Bay, Cuba, while some were detained within the United States. These detainees were thought to be foreign nationals. By June 2004, nearly 600 alleged members of the Taliban and the al Qaeda terrorist organization were detained at Guantanamo.

According to the Executive Branch, the combatants violated the law of war and thus fell outside of the requirements set forth by the Geneva Conventions for prisoners of war. By designating the detainees as enemy combatants, the President intended to create for them a distinctive and entirely military judicial process. The new model collapsed the traditional division of responsibilities in criminalizing nonmilitary conduct: definition by the Legislative Branch, prosecution by the Executive Branch, and trial by the judiciary. The President's model instead concentrated the responsibilities solely in the Executive Branch and omitted constitutional safeguards, such as the right to be charged, the right to meet with an attorney, the right not to be held indefinitely, and the right to contest the designation of enemy combatant status in court. In justifying this approach, the administration claimed the Executive Branch had inherent power to detain enemy combatants and the authorization to do so by Congress when it enacted the AUMF.

The legal issues involving the detention of enemy combatants intersect at several different levels of analysis. On one level, the cases raise a threshold question of jurisdiction: Can the civil courts, including the Supreme Court, exercise jurisdiction over a matter involving warfare on foreign soil? While courts had previously adopted a posture of deference toward the Legislative and Executive branches in times of armed conflict, *see, e.g., United States v. Korematsu*, 323 U.S. 214 (1944), the federal courts indicated that the Judicial Branch was not ready to cede total control to the Executive Branch during pressing times of combat.

On another analytical level, bedrock separation of powers issues emerged. The detainees' claims revealed the tension between the President's Article II power as Commander in Chief and Congress's Article I power to declare war. The lack of clarity at the intersection between the two powers was strikingly evident.

Further, the cases illuminated the tension underlying the structure of checks and balances. If the power to authorize the detention of American citizens on American soil or American-held territory usually emanates from the Legislative Branch, while the prosecution of these detentions is typically within the province of the Executive Branch, when is it permissible to merge these distinctive roles?

Similarly, the cases focused attention on the uneasy coexistence between power and its limits. Even if the Executive Branch possessed the power to indefinitely detain enemy combatants, what safeguards of the Constitution apply, if any, to protect detainees from imprisonment without an endpoint—particularly if the detainee is an American citizen being detained on American soil?

Last, the fundamental societal conflict between the right to security and the right to freedom of action percolated to the surface in these cases. This basic dichotomy is particularly nettlesome in times of crisis, when the relative openness of American society receives increasing scrutiny and heightened challenges.

2. Detention of U.S. Citizens as Alleged Terrorists

While all of the enemy combatant detainees were assumed to have been foreign nationals, some, in fact, were American citizens. The detention of Americans as enemy combatants raised delicate and complex questions. At a minimum, are U.S. citizen detainees protected to a greater extent by the Constitution than foreign national detainees?

As various detention cases filtered through the federal court system, the Supreme Court agreed to hear several of the cases during its 2003-2004 term. *Hamdi v. Rumsfeld,* 542 U.S. 507 (2004), presented the question of whether an American citizen captured in a war zone, Afghanistan, and labeled an enemy combatant could be detained indefinitely in the United States without constitutional protections, such as the right to be heard and the right to counsel. In a second case, *Rumsfeld v. Padilla,* 542 U.S. 426 (2004), the issue was whether the indefinite detention of an American citizen apprehended on a suspicion of terrorist activities in the United States was constitutional. The citizen, Jose Padilla, was not charged with a crime, but was instead held as an enemy combatant.

WORLD WAR II AS PRECEDENT: EX PARTE QUIRIN

World War II provided a useful backdrop for a Supreme Court charged with deciding various types of enemy combatant cases. During the war, courts were confronted with questions about the status of enemy combatants and whether they deserved prisoner of war status under the Geneva Conventions. *Ex parte Quirin,* 317 U.S. 1 (1942), provided seminal analysis about the status of enemy combatants captured on American soil. In *Quirin,* the Supreme Court ruled on the constitutionality of the President's appointment of a military commission to try German agents captured on American soil. The Court ruled that the agents, even one claiming U.S. citizenship, could be tried by a military tribunal in lieu of the civil courts and safeguards of the Constitution. The Court's decision had both theoretical and pragmatic consequences. Within days of the Court's ruling, six of the petitioners had been put to death pursuant to the military commission's sentence.

Ex Parte Quirin

317 U.S. 1 (1942)

Petitioners Burger, Heinck and Quirin, together with Dasch, boarded a German submarine which proceeded across the Atlantic to Amagansett Beach on Long Island, New York. The four were there landed from the submarine in the hours of darkness, on or about June 13, 1942, carrying with them a supply of explosives, fuses and incendiary and timing devices. While landing, they wore German Marine Infantry uniforms or parts of uniforms. Immediately after landing, they buried their uniforms and related articles and proceeded in civilian dress to New York City. Other Petitioners landed, including one named Haupt, who alleged he was an American citizen. All were taken into custody in New York or Chicago by agents of the Federal Bureau of Investigation.

The President, as President and Commander in Chief of the Army and Navy, by Order of July 2, 1942, appointed a Military Commission and directed it to try petitioners for offenses against the law of war and the Articles of War, and prescribed regulations for the procedure on the trial and for review of the record of the trial and of any judgment or sentence of the Commission. On the same day, by Proclamation, the President declared that "all persons who are subjects, citizens or residents of any nation at war with the United States or who give obedience to or act under the direction of any such nation, and who during time of war enter or attempt to enter the United States through coastal or boundary defenses, and are charged with committing or attempting or preparing to commit sabotage, espionage, hostile or warlike acts, or violations of the law of war, shall be subject to the law of war and to the jurisdiction of military tribunals."

The Constitution thus invests the President as Commander in Chief with the power to wage war which Congress has declared, and to carry into effect all laws passed by Congress for the conduct of war and for the government and regulation of the Armed Forces, and all laws defining and punishing offences against the law of nations, including those which pertain to the conduct of war.

From the very beginning of its history this Court has recognized and applied the law of war as including that part of the law of nations which prescribes, for the conduct of war, the status, rights and duties of enemy nations as well as of enemy individuals. By the Articles of War, and especially Article 15, Congress has explicitly provided, so far as it may constitutionally do so, that military tribunals shall have jurisdiction to try offenders or offenses against the law of war in appropriate cases. Congress, in addition to making rules for the government of our Armed Forces, has thus exercised its authority to define and punish offenses against the law of nations by sanctioning, within constitutional limitations, the jurisdiction of military commissions to try persons for offenses which, according to the rules and precepts of the law of nations, and more particularly the law of war, are cognizable by such tribunals. And the President, as Commander in Chief, by his Proclamation in time of war his invoked that law. By his Order creating the present Commission he has undertaken to exercise the authority conferred upon him by Congress, and also such authority as the Constitution itself gives the Commander in Chief, to direct the performance of those functions which may constitutionally be performed by the military arm of the nation in time of war.

By universal agreement and practice the law of war draws a distinction between the armed forces and the peaceful populations of belligerent nations and also between those who are lawful and unlawful combatants. Lawful combatants are subject to capture and detention as prisoners of war by opposing military forces. Unlawful combatants are likewise subject to capture and detention, but in addition they are subject to trial and punishment by military tribunals for acts which render their belligerency unlawful. The spy who secretly and without uniform passes the military lines of a belligerent in time of war, seeking to gather military information and communicate it to the enemy, or an enemy combatant who without uniform comes secretly through the lines for the purpose of waging war by destruction of life or property, are familiar examples of belligerents who are generally deemed not to be entitled to the status of prisoners of war, but to be offenders against the law of war subject to trial and punishment by military tribunals. *See* Winthrop, *Military Law,* 2d Ed., pp. 1196-1197, 1219-1221.

Petitioners stress the pronouncement of this Court in the Milligan case, 4 Wall. page 121, 18 L.Ed. 281, that the law of war "can never be applied to citizens in states which have upheld the authority of the government, and where the courts are open and their process unobstructed." Elsewhere in its opinion, the Court was at pains to point out that Milligan, a citizen twenty years resident in Indiana, who had never been a resident of any of the states in rebellion, was not an enemy belligerent either entitled to the status of a prisoner of war or subject to the penalties imposed upon unlawful belligerents. We construe the Court's statement as to the inapplicability of the law of war to Milligan's case as having particular reference to the facts before it. From them the Court concluded that Milligan, not being a part of or associated with the armed forces of the enemy, was a non-belligerent, not subject to the law of war save as—in circumstances found not there to be present and not involved here—martial law might be constitutionally established.

Affirmed.

Notes

1. *Non-Detention Act.* In 1971, Congress enacted the Non-Detention Act, 18 U.S.C. §4001(a), which limited the power of the President to detain individuals unless authorized by the Legislative Branch. This Act attempted to rein in the powers of the Executive Branch. A sponsor of the Act, Abner Mikva, noted that its purpose was to avoid the creation of internment camps for citizens, such as the camps created during World War II and described in cases such as *Korematsu v. United States. See* A. Mikva, *Dangerous Executive Power,* The Washington Post, July 16, 2004, at A21.

2. *AUMF.* Through the AUMF, the President could "use all necessary and appropriate force against those nations, organizations, or persons he determines planned, authorized, committed, or aided the terrorist attacks," and could also use such force against any persons or groups that "harbored such organizations or persons." In addition, the President was given the power "to prevent any future acts of international terrorism against the United States by such nations, organizations or persons."

The Act did not specify whether the detention of persons was contemplated and, if it was, how the detention should be governed or the length of time permitted. The Act did not contain pertinent legislative history to help resolve such questions. Instead, case law was used to interpret the parameters of the law.

3. *Rumsfeld v. Padilla.* 542 U.S. 426 (2004). This case involving U.S. citizen Jose Padilla, received perhaps the most attention of the detention cases because of its factual posture. After Padilla was arrested at Chicago's O'Hare Airport, it was reported that he was going to ignite a radiological or so-called "dirty" bomb on behalf of terrorists on American soil. While the facts provided fodder for publicity, the case turned out to be a lesson in jurisdictional jurisprudence—specifically, the importance of following proper procedures in habeas corpus claims. The petitioner had been detained in New York before being moved to a Navy brig located in Charleston, South Carolina. While in South Carolina, Padilla was not permitted to communicate with family, counsel, or others. Chief Justice Rehnquist, for the Court, dismissed the case prior to reaching the merits of the detention. The Court found that Padilla failed to file his habeas corpus petition in the right court. Padilla's attorney had filed the claim in the Southern District of New York, pursuant to New York's long-arm statute. The Chief Justice held that the appropriate respondent under the applicable federal statute was his custodian—the commander of the South Carolina brig. 28 U.S.C. §§2241-2243. Thus, he ruled that the federal court in New York did not have jurisdiction and dismissed the case.

Subsequently, Padilla filed a second petition for certiorari with the U.S. Supreme Court. Padilla attempted to jump over the intermediate appellate court by filing the petition prior to the Court of Appeals for the Fourth Circuit hearing the case. On June 13, 2005, the Supreme Court rejected Padilla's petition for certiorari, allowing the Fourth Circuit to move forward with oral arguments on July 19, 2005.

Hamdi v. Rumsfeld

542 U.S. 507 (2004)

O'CONNOR, J.

Yaser Esam Hamdi, a U.S. citizen born in Louisiana, grew up in Saudi Arabia. He later traveled to Afghanistan, where he was detained by American forces and labeled an enemy combatant. After first being held at the naval base in Guantanamo Bay, Cuba, he was transferred to the continental United States, without formal charges or access to counsel. Hamdi's father filed a habeas corpus petition on his son's behalf, claiming his son was a victim of circumstance and challenging the U.S. government's ability to hold Hamdi indefinitely without charges or proceedings.

At this difficult time in our Nation's history, we are called upon to consider the legality of the Government's detention of a United States citizen on United States soil as an "enemy combatant" and to address the process that is constitutionally owed to one who seeks to challenge his classification as such. The United States Court of Appeals for the Fourth Circuit held that petitioner's detention was legally authorized and that he was entitled to no further opportunity to challenge his enemy-combatant label. We now vacate and remand. We hold that although Congress authorized the detention of combatants in the narrow circumstances alleged here, due process demands that a citizen held in the United States as an enemy combatant be given a meaningful opportunity to contest the factual basis for that detention before a neutral decision maker.

On September 11, 2001, the al Qaeda terrorist network used hijacked commercial airliners to attack prominent targets in the United States. Approximately 3,000 people were killed in those attacks. One week later, in response to these "acts of treacherous violence," Congress passed a resolution authorizing the President to "use all necessary and appropriate force against those nations, organizations, or persons he determines planned, authorized, committed, or aided the terrorist attacks" or "harbored such organizations or persons, in order to prevent any future acts of international terrorism against the United States by such nations, organizations or persons." Authorization for Use of Military Force ("the AUMF"), 115 Stat. 224. Soon thereafter, the President ordered United States Armed Forces to Afghanistan, with a mission to subdue al Qaeda and quell the Taliban regime that was known to support it.

Hamdi was seized as an "enemy combatant" and his father sought a writ of habeas corpus on his behalf, arguing that, "as an American citizen, Hamdi enjoys the full protections of the Constitution," and that Hamdi's detention in the United States without charges, access to an impartial tribunal, or assistance of counsel "violated and continues to violate the Fifth and Fourteenth Amendments to the United States Constitution." The District Court appointed the federal public defender as counsel for the petitioners, and ordered that counsel be given access to Hamdi. The United States Court of Appeals for the Fourth Circuit reversed.

On remand, the Government filed a response and a motion to dismiss the petition. It attached to its response a declaration from one Michael Mobbs ("Mobbs Declaration"), who identified himself as Special Advisor to the Under Secretary of Defense for Policy. Mobbs set forth what remains the sole evidentiary support that the Government has provided to the courts for Hamdi's detention. The declaration states that Hamdi "traveled to Afghanistan" in July or August 2001, and that he thereafter "affiliated with a Taliban military unit and received weapons training." It asserts that Hamdi "remained with his "Taliban unit following the attacks of September 11" and that, during the time when Northern Alliance forces were "engaged in battle with the Taliban," "Hamdi's Taliban unit surrendered" to those forces, after which he "surrendered his Kalishnikov assault rifle" to them. Mobbs also states that, because al Qaeda and the Taliban "were and are hostile forces engaged in armed conflict with the armed forces of the United States," "individuals associated with" those groups "were and continue to be enemy combatants." The Fourth Circuit rejected Petitioner's claims and denied rehearing en banc and we granted certiorari. We now vacate the judgment below and remand.

The threshold question before us is whether the Executive has the authority to detain citizens who qualify as "enemy combatants." The Government has never provided any court with the full criteria that it uses in classifying individuals as such. It has made clear, however, that, the "enemy combatant" that it is seeking to detain in this case is an individual who, it alleges, was "'part of or supporting forces hostile to the United States or coalition partners'" in Afghanistan and who "'engaged in an armed conflict against the United States'" there. We therefore answer only the narrow question before us: whether the detention of citizens falling within that definition is authorized.

The AUMF authorizes the President to use "all necessary and appropriate force" against "nations, organizations, or persons" associated with the September 11, 2001, terrorist attacks. There can be no doubt that individuals who fought against the United States in Afghanistan as part of the Taliban, an organization known to have supported the al Qaeda terrorist network responsible for those attacks, are individuals Congress sought to target in passing the AUMF. We conclude that detention of individuals falling into the limited category we are considering, for the duration of the particular conflict in which they were captured, is so fundamental and accepted an incident to war as to be an exercise of the "necessary and appropriate force" Congress has authorized the President to use.

The capture and detention of lawful combatants and the capture, detention, and trial of unlawful combatants, by "universal agreement and practice," are "important incidents of war." *Ex parte Quirin,* 317 U.S., at 28. The purpose of detention is to prevent captured individuals from returning to the field of battle and taking up arms once again.

There is no bar to this Nation's holding one of its own citizens as an enemy combatant. In *Quirin,* one of the detainees, Haupt, alleged that he was a naturalized United States citizen. We held that "citizens who associate themselves with the military arm of the enemy government, and with its aid, guidance and direction enter this country bent on hostile acts, are enemy belligerents within the meaning of the law of war." While Haupt was tried for violations of the law of war, nothing in *Quirin* suggests that his citizenship would have precluded his mere detention for the duration of the relevant hostilities. A citizen, no less than an alien, can be "part of or supporting forces hostile to the United States or coalition partners" and "engaged in an armed conflict against the United States." Such a citizen, if released, would pose the same threat of returning to the front during the ongoing conflict.

Hamdi objects, nevertheless, that Congress has not authorized the *indefinite* detention to which he is now subject. It is a clearly established principle of the law of war that detention may last no longer than active hostilities. *See* Article 118 of the Geneva Convention (III) Relative to the Treatment of Prisoners of War, Aug. 12, 1949 1955. The United States may detain, for the duration of these hostilities, individuals legitimately determined to be Taliban combatants who "engaged in an armed conflict against the United States." If the record establishes that United States troops are still involved in active combat in Afghanistan, those detentions are part of the exercise of "necessary and appropriate force," and therefore are authorized by the AUMF.

Ex parte Milligan, 4 Wall. 2, 125, 18 L.Ed. 281 (1866), does not undermine our holding. Milligan was not a prisoner of war, but a resident of Indiana arrested while at home. The Court in *Ex parte Quirin,* 317 U.S. 1 (1942), dismissed the language of *Milligan* that the petitioners citizenship prevented them from being subject to military process. *Quirin* was a unanimous opinion.

Justice Scalia argues that *Quirin* cannot guide our inquiry here because "in *Quirin* it was uncontested that the petitioners were members of enemy forces," while Hamdi challenges his classification as an enemy combatant. But it is unclear why such a concession should have any relevance. Our opinion only finds legislative authority to detain under the AUMF once it is sufficiently clear that the individual is, in fact, an enemy combatant; whether that is established by concession or by some other process that verifies this fact with sufficient certainty seems beside the point.

Justice Scalia largely ignores the context of this case: a United States citizen captured in a *foreign* combat zone. Justice Scalia refers to only one case involving this factual scenario—a case in which a United States citizen-POW (a member of the Italian army) from World War II was seized on the battlefield in Sicily and then held in the United States. The court in that case held that the military detention of that United States citizen was lawful. *See In re Territo,* 156 F.2d, at 148.

Even in cases in which the detention of enemy combatants is legally authorized, there remains the question of what process is constitutionally due to a citizen who disputes his enemy-combatant status. All parties agree that, absent suspension, the writ of habeas corpus remains available to every individual detained within the United States. U.S. Const., Art. I, §9, cl. 2. Only in the rarest of circumstances has Congress seen fit to suspend the writ. At all other times, it has remained a critical check on the Executive, ensuring that it does not detain individuals except in accordance with law. *See INS v. St. Cyr*, 533 U.S. 289 (2001). Most notably, section 2243 provides that "the person detained may, under oath, deny any of the facts set forth in the return or allege any other material facts," and section 2246 allows the taking of evidence in habeas proceedings by deposition, affidavit, or interrogatories.

The simple outline of section 2241 makes clear both that Congress envisioned that habeas petitioners would have some opportunity to present and rebut facts and that courts in cases like this retain some ability to vary the ways in which they do so as mandated by due process. The Government recognizes the basic procedural protections required by the habeas statute, but asks us to hold that, given both the flexibility of the habeas mechanism and the circumstances presented in this case, the presentation of the Mobbs Declaration to the habeas court completed the required factual development.

The "facts" that constitute the alleged concession are insufficient to support Hamdi's detention. Under the definition of enemy combatant that we accept today as falling within the scope of Congress's authorization, Hamdi would need to be "part of or supporting forces hostile to the United States or coalition partners" and "engaged in an armed conflict against the United States" to justify his detention in the United States for the duration of the relevant conflict. The habeas petition states only that "when seized by the United States Government, Mr. Hamdi resided in Afghanistan." We reject any argument that Hamdi has made concessions that eliminate any right to further process.

The Government's second argument is that further factual exploration is unwarranted and inappropriate in light of the extraordinary constitutional interests at stake. The Government argues courts should review its determination that a citizen is an enemy combatant under a very deferential "some evidence" standard.

The ordinary mechanism that we use for balancing such serious competing interests, and for determining the procedures that are necessary to ensure that a citizen is not "deprived of life, liberty, or property, without due process of law," U.S. Const., Amdt. 5, is the test that we articulated in *Mathews v. Eldridge*. *Mathews* dictates that the process due in any given instance is determined by weighing "the private interest that will be affected by the official action" against the Government's asserted interest, "including the function involved" and the burdens the Government would face in providing greater process. The *Mathews* calculus then contemplates a judicious balancing of these concerns, through an analysis of "the risk of an erroneous deprivation" of the private interest if the process were reduced and the "probable value, if any, of additional or substitute safeguards." We take each of these steps in turn.

"In our society liberty is the norm," and detention without trial "is the carefully limited exception." Nor is the weight on this side of the *Mathews* scale offset by the circumstances of war or the accusation of treasonous behavior, for "it is clear that commitment for *any* purpose constitutes a significant deprivation of liberty that requires due process protection," and at this stage in the *Mathews* calculus, we consider the interest of the *erroneously* detained individual. *Carey v. Piphus,* 435 U.S. 247 (1978). Moreover, an unchecked system of detention carries the potential to become a means for oppression and abuse of others who do not present that sort of threat. *See Ex parte Milligan,* 4 Wall., at 125. The Founders knew the nation they were founding would be involved in war and that unlimited power, wherever lodged at such a time, was especially hazardous to freemen. We reaffirm today the fundamental nature of a citizen's right to be free from involuntary confinement by his own government without due process of law, and we weigh the opposing governmental interests against the curtailment of liberty that such confinement entails.

On the other side of the scale are the weighty and sensitive governmental interests in ensuring that those who have in fact fought with the enemy during a war do not return to battle against the United States. The law of war and the realities of combat may render such detentions both necessary and appropriate, and our due process analysis need not blink at those realities. It is during our most challenging and uncertain moments that our Nation's commitment to due process is most severely tested; and it is in those times that we must preserve our commitment at home to the principles for which we fight abroad.

We therefore hold that a citizen-detainee seeking to challenge his classification as an enemy combatant must receive notice of the factual basis for his classification, and a fair opportunity to rebut the Government's factual assertions before a neutral decision maker. The exigencies of the circumstances may demand that, aside from these core elements, enemy combatant proceedings may be tailored to alleviate their uncommon potential to burden the Executive at a time of ongoing military conflict. Hearsay, for example, may need to be accepted as the most reliable available evidence from the Government in such a proceeding. Likewise, the Constitution would not be offended by a presumption in favor of the Government's evidence, so long as that presumption remained a rebuttable one and fair opportunity for rebuttal were provided. Thus, once the Government puts forth credible evidence that the habeas petitioner meets the enemy-combatant criteria, the onus could shift to the petitioner to rebut that evidence with more persuasive evidence that he falls outside the criteria. A burden-shifting scheme of this sort would meet the goal of ensuring that the errant tourist, embedded journalist, or local aid worker has a chance to prove military error while giving due regard to the Executive once it has put forth meaningful support for its conclusion that the detainee is in fact an enemy combatant. We think it unlikely that this basic process will have the dire impact on the central functions of war making that the Government forecasts.

In sum, while the full protections that accompany challenges to detentions in other settings may prove unworkable and inappropriate in the enemy-combatant setting, the threats to military operations posed by a basic system of independent review are not so weighty as to trump a citizen's core rights to challenge meaningfully the Government's case and to be heard by an impartial adjudicator.

We have long since made clear that a state of war is not a blank check for the President when it comes to the rights of the Nation's citizens. *Youngstown Sheet & Tube Co.*, 343 U.S., at 587. Whatever power the United States Constitution envisions for the Executive in its exchanges with other nations or with enemy organizations in times of conflict, it most assuredly envisions a role for all three branches when individual liberties are at stake.

Because we conclude that due process demands some system for a citizen detainee to refute his classification, the proposed "some evidence" standard is inadequate. Any process in which the Executive's factual assertions go wholly unchallenged or are simply presumed correct without any opportunity for the alleged combatant to demonstrate otherwise falls constitutionally short. We have utilized the "some evidence" standard in the past as a standard of review, not as a standard of proof.

Aside from unspecified "screening" processes, and military interrogations in which the Government suggests Hamdi could have contested his classification, Hamdi has received no process. Plainly, the "process" Hamdi has received is not that to which he is entitled under the Due Process Clause.

There remains the possibility that the standards we have articulated could be met by an appropriately authorized and properly constituted military tribunal. Indeed, it is notable that military regulations already provide for such process in related instances, dictating that tribunals be made available to determine the status of enemy detainees who assert prisoner-of-war status under the Geneva Convention. As we have discussed, a habeas court in a case such as this may accept affidavit evidence like that contained in the Mobbs Declaration, so long as it also permits the alleged combatant to present his own factual case to rebut the Government's return. We anticipate that a District Court would proceed with the caution that we have indicated is necessary in this setting, engaging in a factfinding process that is both prudent and incremental.

Since our grant of certiorari in this case, Hamdi has been appointed counsel, with whom he has met for consultation purposes on several occasions, and with whom he is now being granted unmonitored meetings. He unquestionably has the right to access to counsel in connection with the proceedings on remand. No further consideration of this issue is necessary at this stage of the case.

The judgment of the United States Court of Appeals for the Fourth Circuit is vacated, and the case is remanded for further proceedings.

It is so ordered.

Justice SOUTER, with whom Justice GINSBURG joins, *concurring in part, dissenting in part,* and *concurring* in the judgment.

The plurality accepts the Government's position that if Hamdi's designation as an enemy combatant is correct, his detention (at least as to some period) is authorized by an Act of Congress as required by §4001(a), that is, by the Authorization for Use of Military Force. Here, I disagree and respectfully dissent. The Government has failed to demonstrate that the Force Resolution authorizes the detention complained of here.

On the record in front of us, the Government has not made out a case on any theory. The issue is how broadly or narrowly to read the Non-Detention Act, the tone of which is severe: "No citizen shall be imprisoned or otherwise detained by the United States except pursuant to an Act of Congress." Should the severity of the Act be relieved when the Government's stated factual justification for incommunicado detention is a war on terrorism, so that the Government may be said to act "pursuant" to congressional terms that fall short of explicit authority to imprison individuals? With one possible though important qualification, the answer has to be no. For a number of reasons, the prohibition within §4001(a) has to be read broadly to accord the statute a long reach and to impose a burden of justification on the Government.

It is instructive to recall Justice Jackson's observation that the President is not Commander in Chief of the country, only of the military. *Youngstown Sheet & Tube Co. v. Sawyer,* 343 U.S. 579 (1952) (concurring opinion). There may be room for one qualification to Justice Jackson's statement, however: in a moment of genuine emergency, when the Government must act with no time for deliberation, the Executive may be able to detain a citizen if there is reason to fear he is an imminent threat to the safety of the Nation and its people.

I find Hamdi's detention forbidden by §4001(a) and unauthorized by the Force Resolution. Subject to these qualifications, I join with the plurality in a judgment of the Court vacating the Fourth Circuit's judgment and remanding the case.

Justice SCALIA, with whom Justice STEVENS joins, *dissenting.*

Where the Government accuses a citizen of waging war against it, our constitutional tradition has been to prosecute him in federal court for treason or some other crime. Where the exigencies of war prevent that, the Constitution's Suspension Clause, Art. I, §9, cl. 2, allows Congress to relax the usual protections temporarily. Absent suspension, however, the Executive's assertion of military exigency has not been thought sufficient to permit detention without charge. No one contends that the congressional Authorization for Use of Military Force, on which the Government relies to justify its actions here, is an implementation of the Suspension Clause. Accordingly, I would reverse the decision below.

The allegations here, of course, are no ordinary accusations of criminal activity. Hamdi has been imprisoned because the Government believes he participated in the waging of war against the United States. The relevant question, then, is whether there is a different, special procedure for imprisonment of a citizen accused of wrongdoing *by aiding the enemy in wartime.*

Justice O'Connor, writing for a plurality of this Court, asserts that captured enemy combatants (other than those suspected of war crimes) have traditionally been detained until the cessation of hostilities and then released. That is probably an accurate description of wartime practice with respect to enemy *aliens.* The tradition with respect to American citizens, however, has been quite different. Citizens aiding the enemy have been treated as traitors subject to the criminal process. There are times when military exigency renders resort to the traditional criminal process impracticable. But the happiness of our Constitution is, that it is not left to the executive power to determine when the danger of the state is so great, as to render this measure expedient. For the parliament only, or legislative power, whenever it sees proper, can authorize the crown, by suspending the *habeas corpus* act for a short and limited time, to imprison suspected persons without giving any reason for so doing.

Our Federal Constitution contains a provision explicitly permitting suspension, but limiting the situations in which it may be invoked: "The privilege of the Writ of Habeas Corpus shall not be suspended, unless when in Cases of Rebellion or Invasion the public Safety may require it." Art. I, §9, cl. 2. Although this provision does not state that suspension must be effected by, or authorized by, a legislative act, it has been so understood, consistent with English practice and the Clause's placement in Article I. *See Ex parte Bollman,* 4 Cranch 75, 101, 2 L.Ed. 554 (1807).

The absence of military authority to imprison citizens indefinitely in wartime—whether or not a probability of treason had been established by means less than jury trial—was confirmed by three cases decided during and immediately after the War of 1812. In the first, *In re Stacy,* 10 Johns, 328 (N.Y. 1813), a citizen was taken into military custody on suspicion that he was "carrying provisions and giving information to the enemy." Stacy petitioned for a writ of habeas corpus, and, after the defendant custodian attempted to avoid complying, Chief Justice Kent ordered attachment against him.

Two other cases, later cited with approval by this Court in *Ex parte Milligan,* 4 Wall. 2, 18 L.Ed. 281 (1866), upheld verdicts for false imprisonment against military officers. In *Smith v. Shaw,* 12 Johns. 257 (N.Y. 1815), the court affirmed an award of damages for detention of a citizen on suspicion that he was, among other things, "an enemy's spy in time of war." Finally, in *M'Connell v. Hampton,* 12 Johns. 234 (N.Y. 1815), a jury awarded $9,000 for false imprisonment after a military officer confined a citizen on charges of treason.

President Lincoln, when he purported to suspend habeas corpus without congressional authorization during the Civil War, apparently did not doubt that suspension was required if the prisoner was to be held without criminal trial.

Further evidence comes from this Court's decision in *Ex parte Milligan, supra.* There, the Court issued the writ to an American citizen who had been tried by military commission for offenses that included conspiring to overthrow the Government, seize munitions, and liberate prisoners of war. The Court rejected in no uncertain terms the Government's assertion that military jurisdiction was proper "under the 'laws and usages of war'": "It can serve no useful purpose to inquire what those laws and usages are, whence they originated, where found, and on whom they operate; they can never be applied to citizens in states which have upheld the authority of the government, and where the courts are open and their process unobstructed."

The Government places primary reliance upon *Ex parte Quirin,* 317 U.S. 1 (1942), a World War II case upholding the trial by military commission of eight German saboteurs, one of whom, Hans Haupt, was a U.S. citizen.

In *Quirin* it was uncontested that the petitioners were members of enemy forces. They were "*admitted* enemy invaders," and it was "undisputed" that they had landed in the United States in service of German forces. The specific holding of the Court was only that, "upon the *conceded* facts," the petitioners were "plainly within the boundaries" of military jurisdiction. But where those jurisdictional facts are *not* conceded—where the petitioner insists that he is *not* a belligerent—*Quirin* left the pre-existing law in place: Absent suspension of the writ, a citizen held where the courts are open is entitled either to criminal trial or to a judicial decree requiring his release.

It follows from what I have said that Hamdi is entitled to a habeas decree requiring his release unless (1) criminal proceedings are promptly brought, or (2) Congress has suspended the writ of habeas corpus. A suspension of the writ could, of course, lay down conditions for continued detention, similar to those that today's opinion prescribes under the Due Process Clause.

The plurality finds justification for Hamdi's imprisonment in the Authorization for Use of Military Force. This is not remotely a congressional suspension of the writ, and no one claims that it is.

Several limitations give my views in this matter a relatively narrow compass. They apply only to citizens, accused of being enemy combatants, who are detained within the territorial jurisdiction of a federal court. This is not likely to be a numerous group; currently we know of only two, Hamdi and Jose Padilla. Where the citizen is captured outside and held outside the United States, the constitutional requirements may be different.

Because the Court has proceeded to meet the current emergency in a manner the Constitution does not envision, I respectfully dissent.

Justice THOMAS, *dissenting.*

The Executive Branch, acting pursuant to the powers vested in the President by the Constitution and with explicit congressional approval, has determined that Yaser Hamdi is an enemy combatant and should be detained. This detention falls squarely within the Federal Government's war powers, and we lack the expertise and capacity to second-guess that decision. As such, petitioners' habeas challenge should fail, and there is no reason to remand the case.

Notes

1. *Post-Decision Actions.* After the detention rulings, the Pentagon decided to give all detainees at the Guantanamo Bay base hearings to determine whether they were indeed enemy combatants. The hearings were to be conducted by newly constituted combatant status review tribunals. *See* John Mintz, *Pentagon Sets Hearings for 595 Detainees*, The Washington Post, July 8, 2004. Section A.

2. *Hamdi's Fate.* Less than two months after the *Hamdi* decision, it was reported that the government and the petitioner's lawyers were working out a plan to release Hamdi. *See* David G. Savage, *"Enemy Combatant" May Soon Be Freed*, L.A. Times (Aug. 14, 2004), *http://articles.latimes.com/2004/aug/12/nation/na-hamdi12*. The government agreed to release Hamdi and deport him to Saudi Arabia in October 2004. One condition of his release was that Hamdi renounce his U.S. citizenship. There also were travel restrictions, including a requirement to notify the Saudi Arabian government of plans to travel and the prohibition of travel to the United States, Israel, Gaza Strip, Syria, Iraq, Afghanistan, and Pakistan. Hamdi also made a promise not to sue the U.S. government for a violation of his rights.

❧ PROBLEMS ❧

1. *Burden of Proof.* Suppose the military tribunal trying enemy combatants after the *Hamdi* decision places the burden of proof squarely on the defendant to prove beyond a reasonable doubt that the designation of "enemy combatant" was in error. Is this allocation of the burden of proof unconstitutional? a) Suppose the same military tribunal decides that hearsay evidence—regardless of its alleged reliability—is admissible in any hearing to determine enemy combatant status. Is the inclusion of hearsay evidence constitutional? b) Suppose the same military tribunal decides that the opportunity for refutation approved by the Supreme Court in *Hamdi* meant only that the petitioner would have two hours to argue and/or present evidence that the government erred in designating the petitioner an enemy combatant and that no discovery by the petitioner would be allowed. Permissible?

2. *The Charity Donor.* Suppose Jeffrey Morris contributed to the Human Action Front, a charity providing aid to injured and sick persons in war zones around the world. It was subsequently discovered that the charity also funneled money to the al Qaeda network. Morris, a major contributor, was arrested and held as an enemy combatant. Morris's family asks you to represent him. What would you argue on his behalf? What are his rights?

3. *The War on Drugs.* The President declares that the United States is at war against a nefarious enemy—drug lords importing illegal drugs into the country in great amounts. As part of an executive order implementing legislation cracking

down on illegal drug importation, the President also declares that special military tribunals shall be instituted to try the major offenders. Are such tribunals constitutional? If the tribunals are constitutional and the detainees can be held as enemy combatants, could they be held until the "war on drugs" is officially declared over? Explain.

4. *Terrorist Pins.* The Johnson-Smith terrorist network adopts special "pins" that can be placed on jacket lapels as a uniform feature of dress. A member of the group, captured undercover in northern Indiana, Anwar Jones, was found to be wearing the special pin and openly carrying a firearm. Should Jones, a U.S. citizen raised in Afghanistan, be considered a lawful or unlawful belligerent? Explain.

The national security issues permeating the courts and society in recent years have emphasized a central dichotomy between the right to freedom of action and the right to security. These two values often conflict in the context of court intervention in executive action to fight terrorism.

The Court in *Boumediene v. Bush,* 553 U.S. 723 (2008), held that a provision of the Military Commissions Act of 2006 was unconstitutional insofar as it denied detainees challenging their detentions the right to bring habeas corpus claims in U.S. federal courts. The five-to-four decision effectively found that the U.S. Constitution reached the base in Guantanamo Bay, Cuba, and that the Executive Branch was overreaching in its approach to detaining people it designated as enemy combatants. Justice Kennedy, writing for the Court, noted:

> In deciding the constitutional questions now presented we must determine whether petitioners are barred from seeking the writ or invoking the protections of the Suspension Clause either because of their status, i.e., petitioners' designation by the Executive Branch as enemy combatants, or their physical location, i.e., their presence at Guantanamo Bay. The Government contends that noncitizens designated as enemy combatants and detained in territory located outside our Nation's borders have no constitutional rights and no privilege of habeas corpus. Petitioners contend they do have cognizable constitutional rights and that Congress, in seeking to eliminate recourse to habeas corpus as a means to assert those rights, acted in violation of the Suspension Clause.

The Court went on to hold that the privilege of habeas corpus applied to the base in Guantanamo Bay:

> We hold that Art. I, §9, cl. 2, of the Constitution has full effect at Guantanamo Bay. If the privilege of habeas corpus is to be denied to the detainees now before us, Congress must act in accordance with the requirements of the Suspension Clause. *Cf. Hamdi,* 542 U.S., at 564 (Scalia, J., dissenting) ("Indefinite imprisonment on reasonable suspicion is not an available option of treatment for those accused of aiding the enemy, absent a suspension of the writ"). This Court may not impose a *de facto* suspension by abstaining from these controversies. *See Hamdan,* 548 U.S., at 585, n.16. The MCA does not purport to be a formal suspension of the writ; and the Government, in its submissions to us, has not argued that it is. Petitioners, therefore, are entitled to the privilege of habeas corpus to challenge the legality of their detention.

Significantly, the Court proceeded to a second question, whether the government's procedures provided an adequate substitute for the writ of habeas corpus. The Court concluded that the procedures were not an equivalency because of the "considerable risk of error" in the decisions of the Combat Status Review Tribunals (CSRT).

How the outcome of the case will affect the approximately 270 detainees at Guantanamo is unclear because the case left the particulars of the habeas corpus claims to the federal district courts. Nevertheless, the ruling has both legal and practical implications. On the practical side, there are countries that might not prosecute detainee nationals if such nationals end up being returned to their home countries. Also, the ruling raises questions about the future of Guantanamo as a holding camp for detainees. On the legal side, upon the retirement of Justice O'Connor and the appointment of Justice Alito, it was thought that Justice Kennedy would be entrenched firmly in the middle of the Court's close decisions. While there have been fewer close decisions than predicted in 2008, this one left Justice Kennedy centrally positioned, at least to the extent that he wrote the decision for the majority.

Notes

1. *Financing Terrorist Organizations.* In *Holder v. Humanitarian Law Project*, 561 U.S. 1 (2010), the Court considered whether a federal law banning the knowing provision of material support for organizations designated as foreign terrorist organizations was constitutional. The law had banned personnel and training support, as well as "expert advice and assistance" to organizations that are indelibly "tainted" by criminal activity. The contributing organizations wished to offer assistance only for the lawful aspects of two organizations falling within the terrorist label, and they challenged the law as vague in violation of the Fifth Amendment and a violation of the freedom of speech and right to associate under the First Amendment. The Court found that the law was not unconstitutionally vague and did not violate any First Amendment rights, either. The Court found that the statutory line dividing permissible "general knowledge" assistance from "specific" skill training was sufficiently understandable and workable. The Court also concluded that the "knowledge" requirement of the statute did not pertain to the defendant furthering any illegal terrorism, just that the organization had a nexus to unlawful terrorism activities.

2. *Boumediene's Legacy: The Scope of U.S Court Jurisdiction Over Detained Suspects.* In *Boumediene,* the Court provided the detainees with a "meaningful opportunity" to challenge the Government's rationale for detaining them. Courts have struggled with the scope and meaning of *Boumediene* since that time. In 2009, in *Al Maqaleh v. Gates,* 604 F.Supp.2d 205 (D.D.C. 2009), a U.S. district court applied the *Boumediene* multifactor test to four petitions for habeas corpus by foreign national detainees in a large Afghanistan prison, the Bagram Theater Internment

Prison located at Bagram Airfield near Kabul, Afghanistan. The Court held that habeas corpus review should apply to three of the four petitions. (The fourth was a citizen of Afghanistan, arguing against creating friction with the host country by allowing a challenge to detention.)

What if an American organization, Aid to Sri Lanka, Inc., wanted to provide a Sri Lankan group, New Sri Lankan World, listed as a foreign terrorist organization under the law, with a geography and topography course? Would that course qualify as general knowledge assistance and be permitted or specific skill training, and be prohibited?

∾ PROBLEM: NO TERRORISM ZONES ∾

In addition to the no drilling zones created by the President in the introductory problem, assume the President designates several persons as "enemy combatants" after receiving a threat related to drilling operations in Alaska, near an area already considered a no drilling zone. Several of the persons so designated are captured in northern Canada preparing to enter the United States. If these persons are held at an American base in northern Canada, what rights must the detainees be accorded? Why? Does it matter whether the persons were apparently entering the United States unlawfully? Or whether they had contact with other persons on the no-entry list?

3. The War on Terror's Impact on Privacy

A particular right that is often involved in matters of national security is the right to privacy. It was revealed in the spring of 2006 that the National Security Agency (NSA) had been conducting warrantless wiretapping and mining telephone conversations and recording data involving American citizens. The government mined data about international phone calls, including those originating in the United States. The resulting controversy left two polarized groups. Those opposed to the government conduct contended that the phone taps were not authorized by current laws and were anathema to constitutional protections against government overreaching, particularly the Fourth Amendment prohibition against unreasonable searches and seizures. Supporters of the executive action argued that the phone taps were consistent with and authorized by laws against terrorism and essential presidential powers to fight terrorism.

The issue remains murky, given that there has been no ruling directly on point from the Supreme Court, especially in the post–9/11 era. In a decision in the Eastern District of Michigan more than 30 years ago, a federal judge found that wiretapping of U.S. citizens without a warrant in the interest of national security violated the constitutional requirements of the Fourth Amendment. The judge's decision was eventually upheld by the U.S. Supreme Court in *United States v. United States District Court*, 407 U.S. 297 (1972). That case, however, did not involve foreign terrorism issues.

The closest legislation on point, the Foreign Intelligence Surveillance Act of 1978 (FISA), requires a warrant based on probable cause for wiretapping and does not include an exception for domestic spying for terrorism prevention purposes. The question remains, however, whether the 1978 Surveillance Act was impliedly superseded by an Act passed by Congress shortly after the September 11, 2001, attacks, the Authorization of Use of Military Force (AUMF). In addition, some argue that the 1978 Surveillance Act impermissibly limits the President's Commander in Chief powers.

After the warrantless surveillance program was uncovered and then vetted in the media, a variety of lawsuits were filed, often concerning the interception of telephonic communications. The NSA was not the only defendant. For example, in In re: National Security Agency Telecommunications Records Litigation, 483 F. Supp. 2d 934 (N.D. Ca. 2007), California customers of telephone companies brought suit against those companies to enjoin them from sharing telephone calling records with the NSA. The suit was filed under state privacy law. In *Hepting v. AT&T Corp.*, 439 F. Supp. 2d 974 (N.D. Ca. 2006), the AT&T company was sued by its own customers for violating the customers' privacy rights by participating in the warrantless surveillance program. And in *A.C.L.U. v. N.S.A.*, 438 F. Supp. 2d 754 (E.D. Mich. 2006), the American Civil Liberties Union brought suit seeking injunctive relief against the NSA's secret program with reference to intercepted international telephone and Internet communications.

4. Use of Drones

The United States has utilized drones to strike various terrorist targets in the past decade. Recently, the federal government released a statement indicating that as a result of the 473 counterterrorist strikes, 116 civilians have been killed. Deb Riechmann, *U.S. Says Up to 116 Civilians Killed in Counterterror Strikes*, NY Times, June 30, 2016. *See also*, Kevin Liptak, *White House reveals number of civilian deaths from drone strikes*, CNN, (July 1, 2016, 4:39 PM), *http://www.cnn.com/2016/07/01/politics/white-house-drone-civilian-death-report/*. Is the use of drones justified in light of his information?

G. THE TREATY POWER

The treaty power, shared between Congress and the President, is one of the most useful tools of American foreign policy. While the Constitution prescribes how treaties are formed, the document does not delineate the relationships between treaties and domestic laws, or between laws enacted pursuant to treaties and laws based on state powers. Both separation of powers and federalism issues are implicated.

As between treaties and congressional acts, where both are seen as having equal status, generally the most recent of actions is considered valid. For many years, the question of whether federal treaties superseded state law remained unanswered. In *Missouri v. Holland*, 252 U.S. 416 (1920), however, the Court confronted just such an issue. Also, *Holland* opens up a proverbial "can of worms," raising a question unanswered by the text of the Constitution: Does the treaty power reside independent of the Constitution? (And if so, can the power be sustained without constitutional conformity?)

Missouri v. Holland

252 U.S. 416 (1920)

Mr. Justice HOLMES delivered the opinion of the Court.

This is a bill in equity brought by the State of Missouri to prevent a game warden of the United States from attempting to enforce the Migratory Bird Treaty Act of July 3, 1918, c. 128, 40 Stat. 755, and the regulations made by the Secretary of Agriculture in pursuance of the same. The ground of the bill is that the statute is an unconstitutional interference with the rights reserved to the States by the Tenth Amendment, and that the acts of the defendant done and threatened under that authority invade the sovereign right of the State and contravene its will manifested in statutes.

On December 8, 1916, a treaty between the United States and Great Britain was proclaimed by the President. It recited that many species of birds in their annual migrations traversed many parts of the United States and of Canada, that they were of great value as a source of food and in destroying insects injurious to vegetation, but were in danger of extermination through lack of adequate protection. It therefore provided for specified closed seasons and protection in other forms, and agreed that the two powers would take or propose to their lawmaking bodies the necessary measures for carrying the treaty out. 39 Stat. 1702.

To answer this question of constitutionality of the treaty, it is not enough to refer to the Tenth Amendment, reserving the powers not delegated to the United States, because by Article 2, Section 2, the power to make treaties is delegated expressly, and by Article 6 treaties made under the authority of the United States, along with the Constitution and laws of the United States made in pursuance thereof, are declared the supreme law of the land. If the treaty is valid there can be no dispute about the validity of the statute under Article 1, Section 8, as a necessary and proper means to execute the powers of the Government. The language of the Constitution as to the supremacy of treaties being general, the question before us is narrowed to an inquiry into the ground upon which the present supposed exception is placed.

It is said that a treaty cannot be valid if it infringes the Constitution, that there are limits, therefore, to the treaty-making power, and that one such limit is that what an act of Congress could not do unaided, in derogation of the powers reserved to the States, a treaty cannot do. An earlier act of Congress that attempted by itself and not in pursuance of a treaty to regulate the killing of migratory birds within the States had been held bad in the District Court. *United States v. Shauver*, 214 Fed. 154. Those decisions were supported by arguments that migratory birds were owned by the States in their sovereign capacity for the benefit of their people, and that under cases like *Geer v. Connecticut*, 161 U.S. 519, this control was one that Congress had no power to displace. The same argument is supposed to apply now with equal force.

Whether the two cases cited were decided rightly or not they cannot be accepted as a test of the treaty power. Acts of Congress are the supreme law of the land only when made in pursuance of the Constitution, while treaties are declared to be so when made under the authority of the United States. It is open to question whether the authority of the United States means more than the formal acts prescribed to make the convention. We do not mean to imply that there are no qualifications to the treaty-making power; but they must be ascertained in a different way. The treaty in question does not contravene any prohibitory words to be found in the Constitution. The only question is whether it is forbidden by some invisible radiation from the general terms of the Tenth Amendment.

Here a national interest of very nearly the first magnitude is involved. It can be protected only by national action in concert with that of another power. The subject matter is only transitorily within the state and has no permanent habitat therein. But for the treaty and the statute there soon might be no birds for any powers to deal with. We see nothing in the Constitution that compels the Government to sit by while a food supply is cut off and the protectors of our forests and our crops are destroyed. It is not sufficient to rely upon the States. The reliance is vain, and were it otherwise, the question is whether the United States is forbidden to act. We are of opinion that the treaty and statute must be upheld.

Decree *affirmed*.

Note

The Scope of Treaties. In *Medellin v. Texas*, 552 U.S. 491 (2008), a Mexican national convicted of murder in Texas state court filed a habeas corpus petition seeking the protection of a treaty entered into by the United States. The Supreme Court, in an opinion written by Chief Justice Roberts, denied the petitioner relief under the treaty. The Court found that the treaty, which would have benefited the petitioner if it applied domestically, did not create binding federal law that displaced existing state law. In his opinion, Justice Roberts noted the difference between treaties that have an effect internationally and those that also extend their reach to domestic matters. Justice Roberts first laid out the general framework of analysis: that treaties can be self-executing and automatically binding domestically, or not self-executing, requiring implementation statutes by Congress. He then analyzed the treaty in question, finding that the Vienna Convention was not automatically applicable domestically and had not been made binding to domestic law by Congress. Justice Roberts summarized the legal principle by stating, "In sum, while treaties 'may comprise international commitments they are not domestic law unless Congress has either enacted implementing statutes or the treaty itself conveys an intention that it be "self-executing" and is ratified on these terms.'" *Igartua-De La Rosa v. United States*, 417 F.3d 145, 150 (C.A.1 2005) (en banc).

PROBLEM: ALIEN INHERITANCE LAWS

West Virginia enacted a law in 1982 stating that aliens could not inherit property in the state. In 1990, the United States entered into a treaty with Australia, permitting Australians to sell inherited land and recover the proceeds. In 1992, Congress passed a law permitting aliens to keep two thirds of the proceeds from land inherited in the United States and then sold. If M. Dundee, an Australian, inherits property located in Virginia worth $1 million in 1994, what are her legal rights?

H. EXECUTIVE AGREEMENTS

Executive agreements are agreements negotiated by the President with other countries. These agreements have constitutional status despite the lack of express congressional assent. The wide variety and necessity of agreements on all sorts of issues, from where heads of state will sit during meetings to when the next meeting will take place, provide implicit support for such agreements.

Perhaps the most well-known executive agreements resulted from a dark moment in American history, the taking of American hostages by Iran. On November 4, 1979, Americans were taken hostage in the U.S. Embassy by Iranian students during an uprising. President Carter was unsuccessful in negotiating the release of the hostages, and the crisis continued for 444 days. The crisis lasted until the very end of President Carter's term and the beginning of President Reagan's presidency. At that time, a deal was struck for the hostages' release. The deal involved several executive agreements, the constitutionality of which was the subject of the next case.

Dames & Moore v. Regan

453 U.S. 654 (1981)

Justice REHNQUIST delivered the opinion of the Court.

We are confined to a resolution of the dispute presented to us. That dispute involves various Executive Orders and regulations by which the President nullified attachments and liens on Iranian assets in the United States, directed that these assets be transferred to Iran, and suspended claims against Iran that may be presented to an International Claims Tribunal. This action was taken in an effort to comply with an Executive Agreement between the United States and Iran.

On November 4, 1979, the American Embassy in Tehran was seized and our diplomatic personnel were captured and held hostage. In response to that crisis, President Carter, acting pursuant to the International Emergency Economic Powers Act, 91 Stat. 1626, 50 U.S.C. §§1701-1706 (1976 ed., Supp. III) (hereinafter IEEPA), declared a national emergency on November 14, 1979, and blocked the removal or transfer of "all property and interests in property of the Government of Iran, its instrumentalities and controlled entities and the Central Bank of Iran which are or become subject to the jurisdiction of the United States" Exec. Order No. 12170, 3 CFR 457 (1980). President Carter authorized the Secretary of the Treasury to promulgate regulations carrying out the blocking order. On November 15, 1979, the Treasury Department's Office of Foreign Assets Control issued a regulation providing that "unless licensed or authorized any attachment, judgment, decree, lien, execution, garnishment, or other judicial process is null and void with respect to any property in which on or since November 14, 1979, there existed an interest of Iran." 31 CFR §535.203(e) (1980).

On December 19, 1979, petitioner Dames & Moore filed suit in the United States District Court for the Central District of California against the Government of Iran, the Atomic Energy Organization of Iran, and a number of Iranian banks. In its complaint, petitioner alleged that its wholly owned subsidiary, Dames & Moore International, was a party to a written contract with the Atomic Energy Organization, and that the subsidiary's entire interest in the contract had been assigned to petitioner. Under the contract, the subsidiary was to conduct site studies for a proposed nuclear power plant in Iran. As provided in the terms of the contract, the Atomic Energy Organization terminated the agreement for its own convenience on June 30, 1979. Petitioner contended, however, that it was owed $3,436,694.30 plus interest for services performed under the contract prior to the date of termination. The District Court issued orders of attachment directed against property of the defendants, and the property of certain Iranian banks was then attached to secure any judgment that might be entered against them.

On January 20, 1981, the Americans held hostage were released by Iran pursuant to an Agreement entered into the day before and embodied in two Declarations of the Democratic and Popular Republic of Algeria. The Agreement stated that "it is the purpose of the United States and Iran to terminate all litigation as between the Government of each party and the nationals of the other, and to bring about the settlement and termination of all such claims through binding arbitration." In furtherance of this goal, the Agreement called for the establishment of an Iran-United States Claims Tribunal which would arbitrate any claims not settled within six months. Awards of the Claims Tribunal are to be "final and binding" and "enforceable in the courts of any nation in accordance with its laws."

On January 19, 1981, President Carter issued a series of Executive Orders implementing the terms of the agreement. Exec. Order Nos. 12276-12285, 46 Fed. Reg. 7913-7932. On February 24, 1981, President Reagan issued an Executive Order in which he "ratified" the January 19th Executive Orders. Exec. Order No. 12294, 46 Fed. Reg. 14111. Moreover, he "suspended" all "claims which may be presented to the Tribunal" and provided that such claims "shall have no legal effect in any action now pending in any court of the United States."

The parties and the lower courts, confronted with the instant questions, have all agreed that much relevant analysis is contained in *Youngstown Sheet & Tube Co. v. Sawyer*, 343 U.S. 579 (1952). Justice Black's opinion for the Court in that case, involving the validity of President Truman's effort to seize the country's steel mills in the wake of a nationwide strike, recognized that "the President's power, if any, to issue the order must stem either from an act of Congress or from the Constitution itself."

In nullifying post-November 14, 1979, attachments and directing those persons holding blocked Iranian funds and securities to transfer them to the Federal Reserve Bank of New York for ultimate transfer to Iran, President Carter cited five sources of express or inherent power. The Government, however, has principally relied on §203 of the IEEPA, 91 Stat. 1626, 50 U.S.C. §1702(a)(1) (1976 ed., Supp. III), as authorization for these actions. Section 1702(a)(1) provides in part: "At the times and to the extent specified in section 1701 of this title, the President may, under such regulations as he may prescribe, by means of instructions, licenses, or otherwise—" (A) investigate, regulate, or prohibit—"(i) any transactions in foreign exchange," (ii) transfers of credit or payments between, by, through, or to any banking institution, to the extent that such transfers or payments involve any interest of any foreign country or a national thereof, "(iii) the importing or exporting of currency or securities, and" (B) investigate, regulate, direct and compel, nullify, void, prevent or prohibit, any acquisition, holding, withholding, use, transfer, withdrawal, transportation, importation or exportation of, or dealing in, or exercising any right, power, or privilege with respect to, or transactions involving, any property in which any foreign country or a national thereof has any interest; "by any person, or with respect to any property, subject to the jurisdiction of the United States." The Government contends that the acts of "nullifying" the attachments and ordering the "transfer" of the frozen assets are specifically authorized by the plain language of the above statute. The two Courts of Appeals that have considered the issue agreed with this contention.

Petitioner contends that we should ignore the plain language of this statute because an examination of its legislative history as well as the history of §5(b) of the Trading With the Enemy Act (hereinafter TWEA), 40 Stat. 411, as amended, 50 U.S.C. App. §5(b) (1976 ed. and Supp. III), from which the pertinent language of §1702 is directly drawn, reveals that the statute was not intended to give the President such extensive power over the assets of a foreign state during times of national emergency.

We do not agree and refuse to read out of §1702 all meaning to the words "transfer," "compel," or "nullify." Nothing in the legislative history of either §1702 or §5(b) of the TWEA requires such a result. To the contrary, we think both the legislative history and cases interpreting the TWEA fully sustain the broad authority of the Executive when acting under this congressional grant of power. *See Orvis v. Brownell,* 345 U.S. 183 (1953).

This Court has previously recognized that the congressional purpose in authorizing blocking orders is "to put control of foreign assets in the hands of the President." *Propper v. Clark,* 337 U.S. 472, 493 (1949).

Because the President's action in nullifying the attachments and ordering the transfer of the assets was taken pursuant to specific congressional authorization, it is "supported by the strongest of presumptions and the widest latitude of judicial interpretation, and the burden of persuasion would rest heavily upon any who might attack it." *Youngstown,* 343 U.S., at 637 (Jackson, J., concurring). Under the circumstances of this case, we cannot say that petitioner has sustained that heavy burden.

Although we have concluded that the IEEPA constitutes specific congressional authorization to the President to nullify the attachments and order the transfer of Iranian assets, there remains the question of the President's authority to suspend claims pending in American courts. Such claims have, of course, an existence apart from the attachments which accompanied them. In terminating these claims through Executive Order No. 12294 the President purported to act under authority of both the IEEPA and 22 U.S.C. §1732, the so-called "Hostage Act." 46 Fed. Reg. 14111 (1981).

We conclude that although the IEEPA authorized the nullification of the attachments, it cannot be read to authorize the suspension of the claims.

The Hostage Act, passed in 1868, provides: "Whenever it is made known to the President that any citizen of the United States has been unjustly deprived of his liberty by or under the authority of any foreign government, it shall be the duty of the President forthwith to demand of that government the reasons of such imprisonment; and if it appears to be wrongful and in violation of the rights of American citizenship, the President shall forthwith demand the release of such citizen, and if the release so demanded is unreasonably delayed or refused, the President shall use such means, not amounting to acts of war, as he may think necessary and proper to obtain or effectuate the release; and all the facts and proceedings relative thereto shall as soon as practicable be communicated by the President to Congress."

Although the broad language of the Hostage Act suggests it may cover this case, there are several difficulties with such a view. The legislative history indicates that the Act was passed in response to a situation unlike the recent Iranian crisis. Congress in 1868 was concerned with the activity of certain countries refusing to recognize the citizenship of naturalized Americans traveling abroad, and repatriating such citizens against their will. The legislative history is also somewhat ambiguous on the question whether Congress contemplated Presidential action such as that involved here or rather simply reprisals directed against the offending foreign country and *its* citizens.

Although we have declined to conclude that the IEEPA or the Hostage Act directly authorizes the President's suspension of claims for the reasons noted, we cannot ignore the general tenor of Congress's legislation in this area in trying to determine whether the President is acting alone or at least with the acceptance of Congress.

Crucial to our decision today is the conclusion that Congress has implicitly approved the practice of claim settlement by executive agreement. This is best demonstrated by Congress's enactment of the International Claims Settlement Act of 1949.

Over the years Congress has frequently amended the International Claims Settlement Act to provide for particular problems arising out of settlement agreements, thus demonstrating Congress's continuing acceptance of the President's claim settlement authority.

In addition to congressional acquiescence in the President's power to settle claims, prior cases of this Court have also recognized that the President does have some measure of power to enter into executive agreements without obtaining the advice and consent of the Senate. In *United States v. Pink*, 315 U.S. 203 (1942), for example, the Court upheld the validity of the Litvinov Assignment, which was part of an Executive Agreement whereby the Soviet Union assigned to the United States amounts owed to it by American nationals so that outstanding claims of other American nationals could be paid.

Similarly, Judge Learned Hand recognized: The constitutional power of the President extends to the settlement of mutual claims between a foreign government and the United States, at least when it is an incident to the recognition of that government; and it would be unreasonable to circumscribe it to such controversies.

Petitioner asserts that Congress divested the President of the authority to settle claims when it enacted the Foreign Sovereign Immunities Act of 1976 (hereinafter FSIA), 28 U.S.C. §§1330, 1602 *et seq.* The FSIA granted personal and subject-matter jurisdiction in the federal district courts over commercial suits brought by claimants against those foreign states which have waived immunity. 28 U.S.C. §1330. Petitioner thus insists that the President, by suspending its claims, has circumscribed the jurisdiction of the United States courts in violation of Art. III of the Constitution.

We disagree. In the first place, we do not believe that the President has attempted to divest the federal courts of jurisdiction. Executive Order No. 12294 purports only to "suspend" the claims, not divest the federal court of "jurisdiction."

As we read the Executive Order, those claims not within the jurisdiction of the Claims Tribunal will "revive" and become judicially enforceable in United States courts.

In light of all of the foregoing—the inferences to be drawn from the character of the legislation Congress has enacted in the area, such as the IEEPA and the Hostage Act, and from the history of acquiescence in executive claims settlement—we conclude that the President was authorized to suspend pending claims pursuant to Executive Order No. 12294.

~ PROBLEM: NULLIFY ~

Congress enacted a law in 2009 authorizing "the President to nullify judgments in United States courts providing for attachments of assets of foreign countries when significant foreign policy concerns require such a nullification." After North Korea took several journalists hostage in 2010 and attempts at negotiation failed, the President negotiated a window of release of the hostages, but only if the President nullified several attachments placed on North Korean–owned property and suspended several claims pending against North Korea in U.S. courts. Would the nullifications be considered constitutional?

I. EXECUTIVE PRIVILEGE AND IMMUNITY FROM SUIT

Executive privilege from disclosure of information and immunity from suit are two executive powers that can be treated as defenses against the powers of the other branches of government. These executive powers are considered necessary to promote the free and unfettered performance of the executive function, without a chilling effect caused by forced disclosure or the threat of litigation.

1. Executive Privilege

Perhaps the most noteworthy executive privilege case of its generation was precipitated by the Watergate scandal that led to the downfall of the Nixon presidency. On June 17, 1972, burglars broke into the offices of the Democratic National Committee located at the Watergate Complex in Washington, D.C. This petty burglary soon became a smoking cauldron of political intrigue. The burglary was instigated by President Nixon's Committee to Re-Elect the President (CREEP) for political reasons. Knowledge of the burglary and its cover-up was eventually traced to the President himself.

President Nixon had secretly taped all conversations in the Oval Office, including his own. These tapes were the subject of *United States v. Nixon*, 418

U.S. 683 (1974), the next case, in which the Court decided whether executive privilege shielded the President from forced disclosure. The tapes turned out to be significant, not only to the Watergate burglary trial but also to the survival of Nixon's presidency. They connected the President to the cover-up of the Watergate burglary.

United States v. Nixon

418 U.S. 683 (1974)

Mr. Chief Justice BURGER delivered the opinion of the Court.

This litigation presents for review the denial of a motion, filed in the District Court on behalf of the President of the United States, in the case of *United States v. Mitchell et al.* (D.C. Crim. No. 74-110), to quash a third-party subpoena *duces tecum* issued by the United States District Court for the District of Columbia, pursuant to Fed. Rule Crim. Proc. 17(c). The subpoena directed the President to produce certain tape recordings and documents relating to his conversations with aides and advisers. The court rejected the President's claims of absolute executive privilege, of lack of jurisdiction, and of failure to satisfy the requirements of Rule 17(c). The President appealed to the Court of Appeals. We granted both the United States' petition for certiorari before judgment (No. 73-1766), and also the President's cross-petition for certiorari before judgment (No. 73-1834), because of the public importance of the issues presented and the need for their prompt resolution.

On March 1, 1974, a grand jury of the United States District Court for the District of Columbia returned an indictment charging seven named individuals with various offenses, including conspiracy to defraud the United States and to obstruct justice. Although he was not designated as such in the indictment, the grand jury named the President, among others, as an unindicted coconspirator. On April 18, 1974, upon motion of the Special Prosecutor, *see* n.8, *infra*, a subpoena *duces tecum* was issued pursuant to Rule 17(c) to the President by the United States District Court and made returnable on May 2, 1974. This subpoena required the production, in advance of the September 9 trial date, of certain tapes, memoranda, papers, transcripts or other writings relating to certain precisely identified meetings between the President and others. The Special Prosecutor was able to fix the time, place, and persons present at these discussions because the White House daily logs and appointment records had been delivered to him. On April 30, the President publicly released edited transcripts of 43 conversations; portions of 20 conversations subject to subpoena in the present case were included. On May 1, 1974, the President's counsel, filed a 'special appearance' and a motion to quash the subpoena under Rule 17(c). This motion was accompanied by a formal claim of privilege.

The Claim of Privilege. We turn to the claim that the subpoena should be quashed because it demands 'confidential conversations between a President and his close advisors that it would be inconsistent with the public interest to produce.' App. 48a. The first contention is a broad claim that the separation of powers doctrine precludes judicial review of a President's claim of privilege. The second contention is that if he does not prevail on the claim of absolute privilege, the court should hold as a matter of constitutional law that the privilege prevails over the subpoena *duces tecum*.

In the performance of assigned constitutional duties each branch of the Government must initially interpret the Constitution, and the interpretation of its powers by any branch is due great respect from the others. The President's counsel, as we have noted, reads the Constitution as providing an absolute privilege of confidentiality for all Presidential communications. Many decisions of this Court, however, have unequivocally reaffirmed the holding of *Marbury v. Madison*, 1 Cranch, 137, 2 L.Ed. 60 (1803), that "(i)t is emphatically the province and duty of the judicial department to say what the law is."

No holding of the Court has defined the scope of judicial power specifically relating to the enforcement of a subpoena for confidential Presidential communications for use in a criminal prosecution, but other exercises of power by the Executive Branch and the Legislative Branch have been found invalid as in conflict with the Constitution.

The Watergate Complex in Washington, D.C., where the break-in occurred.

However, neither the doctrine of separation of powers, nor the need for confidentiality of high-level communications, without more, can sustain an absolute, unqualified Presidential privilege of immunity from judicial process under all circumstances. The President's need for complete candor and objectivity from advisers calls for great deference from the courts. However, when the privilege depends solely on the broad, undifferentiated claim of public interest in the confidentiality of such conversations, a confrontation with other values arises. Absent a claim of need to protect military, diplomatic, or sensitive national security secrets, we find it difficult to accept the argument that even the very important interest in confidentiality of Presidential communications is significantly diminished by production of such material for in camera inspection with all the protection that a district court will be obliged to provide.

The impediment that an absolute, unqualified privilege would place in the way of the primary constitutional duty of the Judicial Branch to do justice in criminal prosecutions would plainly conflict with the function of the courts under Art. III. In designing the structure of our Government and dividing and allocating the sovereign power among three co-equal branches, the Framers of the Constitution sought to provide a comprehensive system, but the separate powers were not intended to operate with absolute independence.

"While the Constitution diffuses power the better to secure liberty, it also contemplates that practice will integrate the dispersed powers into a workable government. It enjoins upon its branches separateness but interdependence, autonomy but reciprocity." *Youngstown Sheet & Tube Co. v. Sawyer*, 343 U.S., at 635 (Jackson, J., concurring). To read the Art. II powers of the President as providing an absolute privilege as against a subpoena essential to enforcement of criminal statutes on no more than a generalized claim of the public interest in confidentiality of nonmilitary and nondiplomatic discussions would upset the constitutional balance of "a workable government" and gravely impair the role of the courts under Art. III.

Since we conclude that the legitimate needs of the judicial process may outweigh Presidential privilege, it is necessary to resolve those competing interests in a manner that preserves the essential functions of each branch. The right and indeed the duty to resolve that question does not free the Judiciary from according high respect to the representations made on behalf of the President. *United States v. Burr*, 25 F. Cas. p. 187 (C.C. Va. 1807).

The expectation of a President to the confidentiality of his conversations and correspondence, like the claim of confidentiality of judicial deliberations, for example, has all the values to which we accord deference for the privacy of all citizens and, added to those values, is the necessity for protection of the public interest in candid, objective, and even blunt or harsh opinions in Presidential decision making. A President and those who assist him must be free to explore alternatives in the process of shaping policies and making decisions and to do so in a way many would be unwilling to express except privately. These are the considerations justifying a presumptive privilege for Presidential communications. The privilege is fundamental to the operation of Government and inextricably rooted in the separation of powers under the Constitution. In *Nixon v. Sirica*, 159 U.S. App. D.C. 58, 487 F.2d 700 (1973), the Court of Appeals held that such Presidential communications are "presumptively privileged," and this position is accepted by both parties in the present litigation.

But this presumptive privilege must be considered in light of our historic commitment to the rule of law. This is nowhere more profoundly manifest than in our view that the twofold aim (of criminal justice) is that guilt shall not escape or innocence suffer.

In this case the President challenges a subpoena served on him as a third party requiring the production of materials for use in a criminal prosecution; he does so on the claim that he has a privilege against disclosure of confidential communications. He does not place his claim of privilege on the ground they are military or diplomatic secrets. As to these areas of Art. II duties the courts have traditionally shown the utmost deference to Presidential responsibilities.

In this case we must weigh the importance of the general privilege of confidentiality of Presidential communications in performance of the President's responsibilities against the inroads of such a privilege on the fair administration of criminal justice. The interest in preserving confidentiality is weighty indeed and entitled to great respect. However, we cannot conclude that advisers will be moved to temper the candor of their remarks by the infrequent occasions of disclosure because of the possibility that such conversations will be called for in the context of a criminal prosecution.

On the other hand, the allowance of the privilege to withhold evidence that is demonstrably relevant in a criminal trial would cut deeply into the guarantee of due process of law and gravely impair the basic function of the courts. A President's acknowledged need for confidentiality in the communications of his office is general in nature, whereas the constitutional need for production of relevant evidence in a criminal proceeding is specific and central to the fair adjudication of a particular criminal case in the administration of justice.

We conclude that when the ground for asserting privilege as to subpoenaed materials sought for use in a criminal trial is based only on the generalized interest in confidentiality, it cannot prevail over the fundamental demands of due process of law in the fair administration of criminal justice. The generalized assertion of privilege must yield to the demonstrated, specific need for evidence in a pending criminal trial.

Upon receiving a claim of privilege from the Chief Executive, it became the further duty of the District Court to treat the subpoenaed material as presumptively privileged and to require the Special Prosecutor to demonstrate that the Presidential material was "essential to the justice of the (pending criminal) case." *United States v. Burr*, 25 Fed. Cas., at 192. Here the District Court treated the material as presumptively privileged, proceeded to find that the Special Prosecutor had made a sufficient showing to rebut the presumption, and ordered an in camera examination of the subpoenaed material.

On the basis of our examination of the record we are unable to conclude that the District Court erred in ordering the inspection. Accordingly we affirm the order of the District Court that subpoenaed materials be transmitted to that court.

We have no doubt that the District Judge will at all times accord to Presidential records that high degree of deference suggested in *United States v. Burr, supra,* and will discharge his responsibility to see to it that until released to the Special Prosecutor no in camera material is revealed to anyone.

Affirmed.

Note: A Privilege for the Vice President?

Executive privilege questions that remain open include who can claim executive privilege and, when claims are permitted, under what circumstances they are allowed. In *Cheney v. United States District Court,* 542 U.S. 367 (2004), for example, the Supreme Court reaffirmed a partial executive privilege. This case involved a civil suit against then Vice President Cheney, seeking the disclosure of information about several meetings the vice president had with members of private industry. The Supreme Court remanded, permitting the lower court to rule on the discovery requests after balancing the interests involved.

∾ PROBLEMS ∾

1. *Leak.* During an independent counsel investigation of the disclosure of the identity of a Central Intelligence Agency secret agent, destroying the possibility of her future participation in secret operations, the President of the United States, the vice president, and several of the President's senior staff were interviewed. The reports of these interviews, conducted by the Department of Justice, were subpoenaed by a congressional committee also investigating the disclosure. a) Can the President refuse to submit the documents relating to his interview, which was led by the FBI? b) Can the President refuse to submit the documents relating to the vice president's interview by the Justice Department based on executive privilege? c) Can the President refuse to submit the documents relating to the senior staff interviews by the Justice Department based on executive privilege?

2. *More on No Drilling Zones.* In the introductory problem, the President had intelligence that al Qaeda sympathizers would infiltrate drilling operations in no drilling areas. If the President decided to engage in secret operations to detect such infiltrations, would the President have to turn over this information upon a subpoena by the courts or Congress?

2. *Immunity from Suit*

Executive immunity from suit has been a recurring issue stretching back to the early days of our government. The Executive Branch's amenability to suit was affirmed early in our history in the famous case of *Marbury v. Madison*, 5 U.S. 137 (1803), where the Court permitted a claimant, William Marbury, to sue the Secretary of State, James Madison, for failing to deliver a judicial commission. Although immunity from suit centers around official acts while the executive is in office, the Supreme Court has refused to broadly extend the immunity to conduct taking place prior to the President serving as chief executive.

In *Clinton v. Jones*, 520 U.S. 681 (1997), the Supreme Court allowed a civil suit against President Clinton to proceed after balancing the interests at hand. The suit was based on alleged acts occurring prior to the time Clinton became President.

Clinton v. Jones

520 U.S. 681 (1997)

Justice STEVENS delivered the opinion of the Court.

This case raises a constitutional and a prudential question concerning the Office of the President of the United States. Respondent, a private citizen, seeks to recover damages from the current occupant of that office based on actions allegedly taken before his term began. The President submits that in all but the most exceptional cases the Constitution requires federal courts to defer such litigation until his term ends and that, in any event, respect for the office warrants such a stay. Despite the force of the arguments supporting the President's submissions, we conclude that they must be rejected.

Petitioner, William Jefferson Clinton, was elected to the Presidency in 1992, and re-elected in 1996. His term of office expires on January 20, 2001. In 1991 he was the Governor of the State of Arkansas. Respondent, Paula Corbin Jones, is a resident of California. In 1991 she lived in Arkansas, and was an employee of the Arkansas Industrial Development Commission.

In response to the complaint, petitioner promptly advised the District Court that he intended to file a motion to dismiss on grounds of Presidential immunity.

The District Judge denied the motion to dismiss on immunity grounds and ruled that discovery in the case could go forward, but ordered any trial stayed until the end of petitioner's Presidency.

Both parties appealed. A divided panel of the Court of Appeals affirmed the denial of the motion to dismiss, but because it regarded the order postponing the trial until the President leaves office as the "functional equivalent" of a grant of temporary immunity, it reversed that order.

Petitioner's principal submission—that "in all but the most exceptional cases," Brief for Petitioner i, the Constitution affords the President temporary immunity from civil damages litigation arising out of events that occurred before he took office—cannot be sustained on the basis of precedent. Only three sitting Presidents have been defendants in civil litigation involving their actions prior to taking office. Complaints against Theodore Roosevelt and Harry Truman had been dismissed before they took office; the dismissals were affirmed after their respective inaugurations. Two companion cases arising out of an automobile accident were filed against John F. Kennedy in 1960 during the Presidential campaign. After taking office, he unsuccessfully argued that his status as Commander in Chief gave him a right to a stay under the Soldiers' and Sailors' Civil Relief Act of 1940. The motion for a stay was denied by the District Court, and the matter was settled out of court. Thus, none of those cases sheds any light on the constitutional issue before us.

The principal rationale for affording certain public servants immunity from suits for money damages arising out of their official acts is inapplicable to unofficial conduct. In cases involving prosecutors, legislators, and judges we have repeatedly explained that the immunity serves the public interest in enabling such officials to perform their designated functions effectively without fear that a particular decision may give rise to personal liability. That rationale provided the principal basis for our holding that a former President of the United States was "entitled to absolute immunity from damages liability predicated on his official acts," *Fitzgerald*, 457 U.S., at 749.

Moreover, when defining the scope of an immunity for acts clearly taken *within* an official capacity, we have applied a functional approach. "Frequently our decisions have held that an official's absolute immunity should extend only to acts in performance of particular functions of his office." Hence, for example, a judge's absolute immunity does not extend to actions performed in a purely administrative capacity.

As a starting premise, petitioner contends that he occupies a unique office with powers and responsibilities so vast and important that the public interest demands that he devote his undivided time and attention to his public duties. He submits that—given the nature of the office—the doctrine of separation of powers places limits on the authority of the Federal Judiciary to interfere with the Executive Branch that would be transgressed by allowing this action to proceed. It does not follow, however, that separation-of-powers principles would be violated by allowing this action to proceed.

As a factual matter, petitioner contends that this particular case—as well as the potential additional litigation that an affirmance of the Court of Appeals judgment might spawn—may impose an unacceptable burden on the President's time and energy, and thereby impair the effective performance of his office.

We disagree. As we have already noted, in the more than 200-year history of the Republic, only three sitting Presidents have been subjected to suits for their private actions. If the past is any indicator, it seems unlikely that a deluge of such litigation will ever engulf the Presidency. As for the case at hand, if properly managed by the District Court, it appears to us highly unlikely to occupy any substantial amount of petitioner's time.

It is also settled that the President is subject to judicial process in appropriate circumstances. Although Thomas Jefferson apparently thought otherwise, Chief Justice Marshall, when presiding in the treason trial of Aaron Burr, ruled that a subpoena *duces tecum* could be directed to the President. *United States v. Burr*, 25 F. Cas. 30 (No. 14,692d) (C.C. Va. 1807). We unequivocally and emphatically endorsed Marshall's position when we held that President Nixon was obligated to comply with a subpoena commanding him to produce certain tape recordings of his conversations with his aides. *United States v. Nixon*, 418 U.S. 683 (1974). In sum, "it is settled law that the separation-of-powers doctrine does not bar every exercise of jurisdiction over the President of the United States."

The reasons for rejecting such a categorical rule apply as well to a rule that would require a stay "in all but the most exceptional cases." Brief for Petitioner i. Indeed, if the Framers of the Constitution had thought it necessary to protect the President from the burdens of private litigation, we think it far more likely that they would have adopted a categorical rule than a rule that required the President to litigate the question whether a specific case belonged in the "exceptional case" subcategory. In all events, the question whether a specific case should receive exceptional treatment is more appropriately the subject of the exercise of judicial discretion than an interpretation of the Constitution. Accordingly, we turn to the question whether the District Court's decision to stay the trial until after petitioner leaves office was an abuse of discretion.

We add a final comment on two matters that are discussed at length in the briefs: the risk that our decision will generate a large volume of politically motivated harassing and frivolous litigation, and the danger that national security concerns might prevent the President from explaining a legitimate need for a continuance.

We are not persuaded that either of these risks is serious. Most frivolous and vexatious litigation is terminated at the pleading stage or on summary judgment, with little if any personal involvement by the defendant. *See* Fed. Rules Civ. Proc. 12, 56. Moreover, the availability of sanctions provides a significant deterrent to litigation directed at the President in his unofficial capacity.

The Federal District Court has jurisdiction to decide this case. Like every other citizen who properly invokes that jurisdiction, respondent has a right to an orderly disposition of her claims. Accordingly, the judgment of the Court of Appeals is affirmed.

It is so ordered.

Justice BREYER, *concurring* in the judgment.

I agree with the majority that the Constitution does not automatically grant the President an immunity from civil lawsuits based upon his private conduct. Nor does the "doctrine of separation of powers require federal courts to stay" virtually "all private actions against the President until he leaves office." In my view, however, once the President sets forth and explains a conflict between judicial proceeding and public duties, the matter changes. At that point, the Constitution permits a judge to schedule a trial in an ordinary civil damages action (where postponement normally is possible without overwhelming damage to a plaintiff) only within the constraints of a constitutional principle — a principle that forbids a federal judge in such a case to interfere with the President's discharge of his public duties. I have no doubt that the Constitution contains such a principle applicable to civil suits, based upon Article II's vesting of the entire "Executive Power" in a single individual, implemented through the Constitution's structural separation of powers, and revealed both by history and case precedent.

J. THE PARDON POWER

The President enjoys broad discretionary power to pardon people for their misconduct. For example, shortly after taking office, Gerald Ford, in Presidential Proclamation 4311, pardoned his predecessor. The proclamation stated: "The prospects of such a trial of former President Richard M. Nixon will cause prolonged and divisive debate over the propriety of exposing to further punishment and degradation a man who has already paid the unprecedented penalty of resigning the highest elective office of the United States."

Despite the breadth of presidential discretion, presidential use of the pardon power has not been without controversy. For example, President Bill Clinton ignited a firestorm when he pardoned Marc Rich, an international fugitive wanted on tax evasion, just prior to leaving office. The pardon was not warranted in the eyes of many of the President's political opponents and even some supporters were puzzled as to the President's reasoning. The pardon could not be challenged, however, because it was a political act solely committed to the President of the United States in Article II.

1. Commutation of Sentences

In *United States v. I. Lewis Libby*, 495 F. Supp. 2d 49 (D.D.C. 2007), the issue involved the relationship between the President's executive clemency power and federal statutory sentencing requirements. Specifically, the case presented the question of whether a President could commute the sentence of a criminal defendant while maintaining a term of supervised release in derogation of a statute that required incarceration prior to any supervised release. The district court held that the executive clemency power was bound only by the requirements of the Constitution, not the statute.

The defendant, Lewis "Scooter" Libby, was convicted of obstruction of justice and perjury and sentenced to a period of 30 months of incarceration, followed by a two-year term of supervised release. Pursuant to statute, 18 U.S.C. §3583, supervised release is intended to follow a term of incarceration. The defendant had been an aide to Vice President Dick Cheney when the underlying conduct occurred. President George W. Bush issued a Grant of Executive Clemency on July 2, 2007, for the prison term, stating that the sentence was "excessive." (Statement by the President on Executive Clemency for Lewis Libby at 1.) The two-year supervised release term, however, was not modified by the clemency.

Article II, Section 2 of the U.S. Constitution gives the executive the power to grant clemency in relation to criminal prosecutions. This pardon power is not subject to standards and is generally free from judicial review. The District Court agreed with the Government in finding that the President could "disregard established statutory requirements in commuting the sentence of a criminal defendant, so long as the conditions placed upon the commutation 'do not otherwise offend the Constitution.' *Schick v. Reed*, 419 U.S. 256 (1974)." *Libby* at 52-53. Thus, the Constitution trumps the otherwise lawful statutory requirement.

Note: More on the Pardon Power

State governors, as well as the President, have the power to pardon convicted criminals or others who are or will be prosecuted for criminal conduct. This power has been wielded in some states for decades as an executive prerogative. Is this an outdated power? Since a jury of one cannot convict a person, should a single person be able to undo what a jury has done and grant clemency? Keep these questions in mind with the following situation.

In the waning months of his second term as Governor of Mississippi, Haley Barbour exercised his pardon power in the same manner as many governors preceding him. It was the number and nature of pardons by Governor Barbour that caught people's attention. Barbour pardoned more than 200 people, including several murderers, although the large majority of people pardoned had already served out their sentences. The pardons made the national news and created headlines due to their breadth and nature. The ex-governor explained why he pardoned so many individuals:

The pardons were intended to allow them to find gainful employment or acquire professional licenses as well as hunt and vote. My decision about clemency was based upon the recommendation of the parole board in more than 90% of the cases. The people were not threats to society, but if any of them commits an offense—even a misdemeanor—they'll be returned to custody to serve out their term.[15]

Did Governor Barbour abuse the pardon power? If yes, what should be done to limit such powers, if anything?

[Points to Remember for Chapter 3 is contained in online file.]

---

15. Richard Fausset, *Outgoing Governor Haley Barbour's Pardons Shock Mississippi*, U.S. Section, Los Angeles Times, January 12, 2012.

4

The Relationship Between the States and the Federal Government

[Roadmap for Chapter 4 is contained in online file.]

∾ PROBLEM: THE EDUCATION FOR A BETTER AMERICA (EBA) ACT, CONTINUED ∾

Congress is considering enacting a new law, the Education for a Better America (EBA) Act, to promote a uniform level of education in this country, free of charge. Congress is inclined to enact this law for a variety of reasons. For decades, American children have been falling behind children in other countries in math and science as well as in other critical subjects. More troubling, too many children drop out of school, and dropouts suffer lower employment prospects, higher rates of alcoholism, drug abuse, and incarceration, and are more likely to be involved in domestic violence. Even when children stay in school, the accessibility of drugs and weapons diminishes what schools aim to accomplish. Moreover, today's society is becoming more technological and more international in character, and Congress believes students need a revised and more sophisticated education in order to compete in today's environment.

You work for a new member of Congress, Julia St. James, who believes that the states are not doing an adequate job in educating children. She wants to engineer a federal takeover of education because she is not particularly enthusiastic about the results of the "No Child Left Behind" Act. The congresswoman gives you the task of creating several different options related to offering states incentives and requiring mandatory directives as riders to the Education for a Better America Act. Here are her three primary themes, accompanied by some specific ideas: 1) *Reward Teacher Quality.* The congresswoman has suggested that states abolish tenure for teachers and substitute a merit pay system and more limited job security protections; 2) *Adopt Stay-in-School Initiatives.* The congresswoman would like for the Act to include incentives and mandatory directives (e.g., loss of driving privileges for dropouts); 3) *Promote Civics and Language Arts as well as Math and Science.* The congresswoman wants to consider how to best promote a fundamentally sound education.

In this chapter, you will be asked to advise the congresswoman about the permissible scope of federal government interactions with the states on a constitutional level and what specific initiatives she should propose to ameliorate these profound education problems.

————————

The Constitution does not treat the states as subdivisions of the federal government. Instead, the Constitution creates a system of dual sovereignty that allocates some powers to the federal government and the remaining powers to state governments or to the people. Whereas Chapter 5 focuses on the power of the states to regulate commerce, this chapter focuses on so-called "intergovernmental immunities," meaning the right by another government (federal or state) to be free of the regulation or taxes of the other government. In earlier times, both sovereigns tested these boundaries, but in recent decades, the federal government is usually alleged to be the transgressor.

In *National Federation of Independent Business v. Sebelius*, 567 U.S. 519 (2012), as part of a landmark decision regarding the constitutionality of the Patient Protection and Affordable Care Act (PPACA), the Court touched on cooperative federalism. Cooperative federalism involves achieving federal goals through the cooperative use of states and their employees in a form of federal-state partnership, allowing states to play a meaningful role in the process, including an exercise of state discretion.

This idea of cooperative federalism contrasts with federal preemption, where the federal government takes on implementation in its entirety and effectively prohibits states from participating in the process. In *Sebelius*, the Court concluded that the cooperative relationship structure of the PPACA did not comport with the Constitution. The Court found in part that the PPACA exceeded the Congress's spending powers by granting the Secretary of Health and Human Services (HHS) the power to impose a penalty on states choosing through their discretion to opt out of participation in the PPACA's expansion of the Medicaid programs administered by states. This excess power correlatively violated the power of states and the doctrine of federalism.

A. STATE POWER TO TAX THE FEDERAL GOVERNMENT

Do the states have the power to tax entities of the federal government? The power to tax raises important and controversial issues because it is an essential element of sovereignty and can impose significant burdens on the taxed entity. Questions regarding the power of the states to tax the federal government were resolved very early in U.S. history.

BACKGROUND OF MCCULLOCH V. MARYLAND
The Showdown over the Second National Bank

The twenty-year run of the First National Bank was terminated in 1811 due to a lack of congressional support. A perceived need for a new bank to regulate currency prompted the creation of the Second National Bank in 1816. Many opposed the bank on policy and constitutionality grounds. The bank was challenged in Maryland by the placement of a tax on its Maryland branch. The bank refused to pay the Maryland tax and the federal-state showdown was on in *McCulloch v. Maryland*, 17 U.S. (4 Wheat.) 316 (1819).

BACKGROUND
The Oral Argument in McCulloch

McCulloch featured prominent attorneys arguing the case. Daniel Webster was one of the attorneys who represented the cashier of the federal bank, James McCulloch. Luther Martin was one of the attorneys representing Maryland. In those days, the duration of oral arguments was not limited, and the argument in this case is reputed to have lasted for six days.

McCulloch v. Maryland

17 U.S. (4 Wheat.) 316 (1819)

MARSHALL, C. J., delivered the opinion of the court.

In 1816, Congress chartered the Second Bank of the United States, which ultimately included a Maryland branch. Maryland passed a statute taxing all banks established "without authority from the State." Banks subject to the law must pay an annual fee of $15,000 or could issue notes only on stamped paper provided by the state. The state charged differing fees for the stamped paper based on the denomination of the note. The statute was enforceable through criminal penalties as well as statutory penalties. The cashier was liable for a penalty of $500 per offense. John James, acting on his own behalf as well as on behalf of the State of Maryland, sued McCulloch, cashier of the Maryland branch, claiming that McCulloch was operating a bank without statutory authority as well as failing to comply with the Maryland law. When James won in the Maryland courts, McCulloch sought review in the U.S. Supreme Court. [The section of the opinion that discusses the federal government's authority to establish a national bank is omitted].

Whether the state of Maryland may, without violating the constitution, tax that branch? That the power of taxation is one of vital importance; that it is retained by the states; that it is not abridged by the grant of a similar power to the government of the Union; that it is to be concurrently exercised by the two governments—are truths which have never been denied. But such is the paramount character of the constitution, that its capacity to withdraw any subject from the action of even this power is admitted. The states are expressly forbidden to lay any duties on imports or exports, except what may be absolutely necessary for executing their inspection laws. If the obligation of this prohibition must be conceded—if it may restrain a state from the exercise of its taxing power on imports and exports—the same paramount character would seem to restrain, as it certainly may restrain, a state from such other exercise of this power, as is in its nature incompatible with, and repugnant to, the constitutional laws of the Union. A law, absolutely repugnant to another, as entirely repeals that other as if express terms of repeal were used.

Counsel for the bank place its claim to be exempted from the power of a state to tax its operations. There is no express provision for the case, but the claim has been sustained on a principle which so entirely pervades the constitution, is so intermixed with the materials which compose it, so interwoven with its web, so blended with its texture, as to be incapable of being separated from it, without rending it into shreds. This great principle is, that the constitution and the laws made in pursuance thereof are supreme; that they control the constitution and laws of the respective states, and cannot be controlled by them. From this, which may be almost termed an axiom, other propositions are deduced as corollaries, on the truth or error of which, and on their application to this case, the cause has been supposed to depend. These are, 1st. That a power to create implies a power to preserve: 2d. That a power to destroy, if wielded by a different hand, is hostile to, and incompatible with these powers to create and to preserve: 3d. That where this repugnancy exists, that authority which is supreme must control, not yield to that over which it is supreme.

The states have no power, by taxation or otherwise, to retard, impede, burden, or in any manner control, the operations of the constitutional laws enacted by congress to carry into execution the powers vested in the general government. This is, we think, the unavoidable consequence of that supremacy which the constitution has declared. We are unanimously of opinion, that the law passed by the legislature of Maryland, imposing a tax on the Bank of the United States, is unconstitutional and void.

∾ PROBLEMS ∾

1. *State Strategy #1: Taxing Interest Received From Federal Banks.* An attorney for the State of Maryland, Tania Tanner, went to her boss shortly after the *McCulloch* case was decided and said, "After *McCulloch,* the states seem to be limited in their ability to impose taxes. But, suppose that we want to impose our state income taxes on interest received by private customers of the national bank? As I read *McCulloch,* it does not prohibit us from taxing such income." Do you agree? Why might the federal government be reluctant to allow the states to tax this income? What state taxation might be permissible? *See Graves v. New York,* 306 U.S. 466 (1939).

2. *State Strategy #2: A Neutral Tax on Land.* The same Maryland attorney, Tania Tanner, thought of another creative way to impose a tax while galloping to work on her horse. She decided to propose a neutral tax on all property within the state—including the vast federal landholdings outside of Baltimore as well as the land on which the federal bank sat. Would this new law be constitutional? *See Van Brocklin v. Anderson,* 117 U.S. 151 (1886). Should it matter whether the land is owned by a private citizen and leased to the United States? What if federal land is leased to a private business? *See United States v. County of Fresno,* 429 U.S. 452 (1977). What if Tania also proposed taxing the interest on federal bonds held by Maryland residents? *See Weston v. City Council of Charleston,* 27 U.S. (2 Pet.) 449 (1829).

3. *More on the Education for a Better America Act.* Now, let's return to the problem presented at the beginning of the chapter. If the federal government raises the bar for educational goals in state public schools, as suggested in that problem, does the analysis of whether the states can tax federal entities, property, or bonds change affect the analysis?

Dawson v. Steager

139 S. Ct. 698 (2019)

Justice GORSUCH delivered the opinion of the Court.

If you spent your career as a state law enforcement officer in West Virginia, you're likely to be eligible for a generous tax exemption when you retire. But if you served in federal law enforcement, West Virginia will deny you the same benefit. The question is whether a State may discriminate against federal retirees in that way. For most of his career, James Dawson worked in the U. S. Marshals Service. After he retired, he began looking into the tax treatment of his pension. It turns out that his home State, West Virginia, doesn't tax the pension benefits of certain former state law enforcement employees. But it does tax the benefits of all former federal employees. So Mr. Dawson brought this lawsuit alleging that West Virginia violated 4 U. S. C. §111. In that statute, the United States has consented to state taxation of the "pay or compensation" of "officers or employees of the United States," but only if the "taxation does not discriminate against the officer or employee because of the source of the pay or compensation."

Section 111 codifies a legal doctrine almost as old as the Nation. In *McCulloch v. Maryland*, 4 Wheat. 316 (1819), this Court invoked the Constitution's Supremacy Clause to invalidate Maryland's effort to levy a tax on the Bank of the United States. Chief Justice Marshall explained that "the power to tax involves the power to destroy," and he reasoned that if States could tax the Bank they could "defeat" the federal legislative policy establishing it. For the next few decades, this Court interpreted *McCulloch* "to bar most taxation by one sovereign of the employees of another." *Davis v. Michigan Dept. of Treasury*, 489 U.S. 803, 810 (1989). In time, the Court softened its stance and upheld neutral income taxes—those that treated federal and state employees with an even hand. So eventually the intergovernmental tax immunity doctrine came to be understood to bar only *discriminatory* taxes. It was this understanding that Congress "consciously drew upon" when adopting §111 in 1939. This understanding has animated our application of §111. Since the statute's adoption, we have upheld an Alabama income tax that did not discriminate on the basis of the source of the employees' compensation. But we invalidated a Michigan tax that discriminated "in favor of retired state employees and against retired federal employees." *Davis*, 489 U. S., at 814. We struck down a Kansas law that taxed the retirement benefits of federal military personnel at a higher rate than state and local government retirement benefits. *Barker v. Kansas*, 503 U.S. 594 (1992). And we have rejected a Texas scheme that imposed a property tax on a private company operating on land leased from the federal government, but a "less burdensome" tax on property leased from the State. *Phillips Chemical Co. v. Dumas Independent School Dist.*, 361 U.S. 376 (1960). A West Virginia trial court found that the State's statute represented "precisely the type of favoritism" §111 prohibits. *Id.*, at 23a. But the West Virginia Supreme Court of Appeals saw it differently. We granted certiorari.

We believe the state trial court had it right. A State violates §111 when it treats retired state employees more favorably than retired federal employees and no "significant differences between the two classes" justify the differential treatment. *Davis*, 489 U. S., at 814–816 (1989). Here, West Virginia expressly affords state law enforcement retirees a tax benefit that federal retirees cannot receive. And before us everyone accepts the trial court's factual finding that there aren't any "significant differences" between Mr. Dawson's former job responsibilities and those of the tax-exempt state law enforcement retirees. We have little difficulty concluding that West Virginia's law unlawfully "discriminates" against Mr. Dawson "because of the source of his pay or compensation," just as §111 forbids.

West Virginia accepts that its statute distinguishes between persons based on their former job duties. It accepts, too, the finding that Mr. Dawson's former job responsibilities are materially identical to those of state retirees who qualify for its tax exemption. But, the State submits, Mr. Dawson's former job responsibilities are *also* similar to those of other state law enforcement retirees who *don't* qualify for its tax exemption. And, the State insists, the fact that it treats federal retirees no worse than (some) similarly situated state employees should be enough to save its statute. But this mistakes the nature of our inquiry. Under §111, the question isn't whether federal retirees are similarly situated to state retirees who *don't* receive a tax benefit; the relevant question is whether they are similarly situated to those who *do*. The State says the real distinction its statute draws isn't based on former job duties at all. Maybe its statute actually favors certain state law enforcement retirees only because their pensions are less generous than those of their federal law enforcement counterparts. The State suggests we should remand the case to the West Virginia courts to explore this possibility.

While the State was free to draw whatever classifications it wished, the statute it enacted does not classify persons or groups based on the relative generosity of their pension benefits. Instead, it extends a special tax benefit to retirees who served as West Virginia police officers, firefighters, or deputy sheriffs—and it categorically denies that same benefit to retirees who served in similar federal law enforcement positions. Even if Mr. Dawson's pension turned out to be *identical* to a state law enforcement officer's pension, the law as written would deny him a tax exemption. West Virginia's law thus discriminates "because of the source of compensation or pay" in violation of §111. Whether the unlawful classification found in the text of a statute might serve as some sort of proxy for a lawful classification hidden behind it is neither here nor there. No more than a beneficent legislative intent, an implicit but lawful distinction cannot save an express and unlawful one.

Because West Virginia's statute unlawfully discriminates against Mr. Dawson, we reverse the judgment of the West Virginia Supreme Court of Appeals and remand the case for further proceedings not inconsistent with this opinion, including the determination of an appropriate remedy.

It is so ordered.

B. FEDERAL POWER TO TAX THE STATES

Given that states lack the power to tax the federal government, does the federal government likewise lack the power to tax the states? In several early cases, the Court held that the federal government had limited power to tax the states. For example, in *Collector v. Day*, 78 U.S. (11 Wall.) 113 (1871), the Court held that the salary of a state judicial officer, in that case a probate judge, was immune from federal income tax. The Court emphasized that the officer was engaged in the performance of a function that pertained to state governments at the time the Constitution was adopted. But, in the 1930s, the Court overruled *Day* and held that the salaries of state employees were subject to federal tax. *See Helvering v. Gerhardt*, 304 U.S. 405 (1938). The Court's current approach to the federal taxing power is reflected in the next two cases.

Massachusetts v. United States

435 U.S. 444 (1978)

Mr. Justice BRENNAN delivered the opinion of the Court.

Congress imposed an annual registration tax on all civil aircraft that fly in the navigable airspace of the United States. The State of Massachusetts challenged the tax as applied to a helicopter which the Commonwealth uses exclusively for patrolling highways and other police functions. The Commonwealth claims that the United States may not constitutionally impose a tax that directly affects the essential and traditional state function of operating a police force.

The immunity of the Federal Government from state taxation is bottomed on the Supremacy Clause, but the States' immunity from federal taxes was judicially implied from the States' role in the constitutional scheme. *Collector v. Day*, 78 U.S. (11 Wall.) 113 (1871), emphasized that the States were independent sovereigns when the Constitution was adopted, and that the Constitution presupposes and guarantees the continued existence of the States as governmental bodies performing traditional sovereign functions. To implement this aspect of the constitutional plan, *Collector v. Day* concluded that it was imperative absolutely to prohibit any federal taxation that directly affected a traditional state function, quoting Mr. Chief Justice Marshall's aphorisms that "the power of taxing may be exercised so far as to destroy," and "a right to tax, in its nature, acknowledges no limits." The Court has more recently remarked that these maxims refer primarily to two attributes of the taxing power. First, in imposing a tax to support the services a government provides to the public at large, a legislature need not consider the value of particular benefits to a taxpayer, but may assess the tax solely on the basis of taxpayers' ability to pay. Second, a tax is a powerful regulatory device; a legislature can discourage or eliminate an activity within its regulatory jurisdiction simply by imposing a heavy tax on its exercise. *Collector v. Day*, like *McCulloch*, reflected the view that the taxing power required a flat and absolute prohibition against a tax implicating an essential state function because the ability of the federal courts to determine whether particular revenue measures would destroy such an essential function was to be doubted.

"Cogent reasons" were recognized for narrowly limiting the immunity of the States from federal imposts. The first is that any immunity for the protection of state sovereignty is at the expense of the sovereign power of the National

Government to tax. Therefore, when the scope of the States' constitutional immunity is enlarged beyond that necessary to protect the continued ability of the States to deliver traditional governmental services, the burden of the immunity is thrown upon the National Government without any corresponding promotion of the constitutionally protected values. The second, also recognized by Mr. Chief Justice Marshall in *McCulloch*, is that the political process is uniquely adapted to accommodating the competing demands "for national revenue, on the one hand, and for reasonable scope for the independence of state action, on the other," *Helvering v. Gerhardt.* The Congress, composed as it is of members chosen by state constituencies, constitutes an inherent check against the possibility of abusive taxing of the States by the National Government.

In recognition of these considerations, decisions of the Court either have declined to enlarge the scope of state immunity or have in fact restricted its reach. Typical of this trend are decisions holding that the National Government may tax revenue-generating activities of the States that are of the same nature as those traditionally engaged in by private persons. It is true that some of the opinions speak of the state activity taxed as "proprietary" and thus not an immune essential governmental activity, but *New York v. United States* rejected the governmental-proprietary distinction as untenable. The majority reasoned that a nondiscriminatory tax may be applied to a state business activity where the recognition of immunity would "accomplish a withdrawal from the taxing power of the nation a subject of taxation of a nature which has been traditionally within that power from the beginning. Its exercise by a nondiscriminatory tax, does not curtail the business of the state government more than it does the like business of the citizen."

Illustrative of decisions actually restricting the scope of the immunity is the line of cases that culminated in the overruling of *Collector v. Day* in *Graves v. New York*, 306 U.S. 466 (1939). *Day* involved a nondiscriminatory tax that was imposed not directly on the State but rather on the salary earned by a judicial officer. Neither *Day* itself nor its progeny or precursors made clear how such a taxing measure could be employed to preclude the States from performing essential functions. In any case, in the line of decisions that culminated in *Graves*, the Court demonstrated that immunity for the salaries paid key state officials is not justifiable. Although key state officials are agents of the State, they are also citizens of the United States, so their income is a natural subject for income taxation.

More significantly, because the taxes imposed were nondiscriminatory and thus also applicable to income earned by persons in private employment, the risk was virtually nonexistent that such revenue provisions could significantly impede a State's ability to hire able persons to perform its essential functions. The only advantage conceivably to be lost by denying the States such immunity is that essential state functions might be obtained at a lesser cost because employees exempt from taxation might be willing to work for smaller salaries. But that was regarded as an inadequate ground for sustaining the immunity and preventing the National Government from requiring these citizens to support its activities. The purpose of the implied constitutional restriction on the national taxing power is not to give an advantage to the States by enabling them to engage employees at a lower charge than those paid by private entities, but rather is solely to protect the States from undue interference with their traditional governmental functions. While a tax on the salary paid key state officers may increase the cost of government, it will no more preclude the States from performing traditional functions than it will prevent private entities from performing their missions.

These two lines of decisions illustrate the "practical construction" that the Court now gives the limitation the existence of the States constitutionally imposes on the national taxing power; "that limitation cannot be so varied or extended as seriously to impair either the taxing power of the government imposing the tax or the appropriate exercise of the functions of the government affected by it." Where the subject of tax is a natural and traditional source of federal revenue and where it is inconceivable that such a revenue measure could ever operate to preclude traditional state activities, the tax is valid. While the Court has by no means abandoned its doubts concerning its ability to make particularized assessments of the impact of revenue measures on essential state operations, it has recognized that some generic types of revenue measures could never seriously threaten the continued functioning of the States and hence are outside the scope of the implied tax immunity.

A nondiscriminatory taxing measure that operates to defray the cost of a federal program by recovering a fair approximation of each beneficiary's share of the cost is surely no more offensive to the constitutional scheme than is either a tax on the income earned by state employees or a tax on a State's sale of bottled water. The National Government's interest in being compensated for its expenditures is only too apparent. Such revenue measures by their very nature cannot possess the attributes that led Mr. Chief Justice Marshall to proclaim that the power to tax is the power to destroy. There is no danger that such measures will not be based on benefits conferred or that they will function as regulatory devices unduly burdening essential state activities. A revenue provision that forces a State to pay its own way when performing an essential function will increase the cost of the state activity. But *Graves*, and its precursors teach that an economic burden on traditional state functions without more is not a sufficient basis for sustaining a claim of immunity. Since the Constitution explicitly requires States to bear similar economic burdens when engaged in essential operations, it cannot be seriously contended that federal exactions from the States of their fair share of the cost of specific benefits they receive from federal programs offend the constitutional scheme.

Our decisions implementing these constitutional provisions have consistently recognized that the interests protected by these Clauses are not offended by revenue measures that operate only to compensate a government for benefits supplied. A governmental body has an obvious interest in making those who specifically benefit from its services pay the cost and, provided that the charge is structured to compensate the government for the benefit conferred, there can be no danger of the kind of interference with constitutionally valued activity that the Clauses were designed to prohibit.

Applying these principles to this case demonstrates that the Commonwealth's claim of constitutional immunity is particularly insubstantial. First, there is no question but that the tax imposed by §4491 is nondiscriminatory. It applies not only to private users of the airways but also to civil aircraft operated by the United States—facts which minimize, if not eliminate entirely, the basis for a conclusion that §4491 might be an abusive exercise of the taxing power. Indeed, the Revenue Act discriminates in favor of the States since it retains the States' exemption from the 7-cent-per-gallon fuel tax that applies to private noncommercial general aviation—a fact that illustrates the manner in which the political process is peculiarly adapted to the protection of state interests.

Second, the tax satisfies the requirement that it be a fair approximation of the cost of the benefits civil aircraft receive from the federal activities. Congress believed that four measures, taken together, would fairly reflect some of the cost of the benefits that redound to the noncommercial general aircraft that fly in the navigable airspace of the United States: a 7-cent-per-gallon fuel tax, a 5-cent-per-pound tax on aircraft tires, a 10-cent-per-pound tax on tubes and the annual aircraft registration tax. The formula contained in these four measures taken together does not give weight to every factor affecting appropriate compensation for airport and airway use. A probable deficiency in the formula arises because not all aircraft make equal use of the federal navigational facilities or of the airports that have been planned or constructed with federal assistance. But the present scheme nevertheless is a fair approximation of the cost of the benefits each aircraft receives. Every aircraft that flies in the navigable airspace of the United States has available to it the navigational assistance and other special services supplied by the United States. Even those aircraft that have never received specific services from the National Government benefit from them in the sense that the services are available for their use if needed and in that the services makes the airways safer for all users. The four taxes, taken together, fairly reflect the benefits received, since three are geared directly to use, whereas the fourth, the aircraft registration tax, is designed to give weight to factors affecting the level of use of the navigational facilities. A more precisely calibrated formula—which would include landing fees, charges for specific services received, and less reliance on annual flat fees would be administratively more costly.

It follows that a State may not complain of the application of §4491 on the ground it is not a fair approximation of use. Since the fuel tax, tire and tube tax, and annual registration fee together constitute an appropriate means of recovering the amount of the federal investment, a State, being exempt from the fuel, tire, and tube taxes, can have no constitutional objection to the application of the registration fee alone.

Finally, the tax is not excessive in relation to the cost of the Government benefits supplied. When Congress enacted the Revenue Act, it contemplated that the user fees imposed on civil aircraft would not be sufficient to cover the federal expenditures on civil aviation in any one year, and the actual experience during the first years of operation was that the revenues fell far short of covering the annual civil aviation outlays. Since the Commonwealth pays far less than private noncommercial users of the airways, there therefore is no basis for a conclusion that the application of the registration tax to the States produces revenues in excess of the costs incurred by the Federal Government.

Affirmed.

A Related Case: New York v. United States

New York v. United States, 326 U.S. 572 (1946), discussed in *Massachusetts v. United States,* involved a tax on mineral waters that was applied to sales by a state-owned entity. The Court upheld the tax: "When States sought to control the liquor traffic by going into the liquor business, they were denied immunity from federal taxes upon the liquor business. We certainly see no reason for putting soft drinks in a different constitutional category from hard drinks. We reject limitations upon the taxing power of Congress derived from such untenable criteria as 'proprietary' against 'governmental' activities of the States, or historically sanctioned activities of Government or activities conducted merely for profit, and find no restriction upon Congress to include the States in levying a tax exacted equally from private persons upon the same subject matter." Justice Douglas dissented:

> Can it be that a general federal tax on the issuance of securities would be constitutional if applied to the issuance of municipal securities or of state bonds or of the securities of public utility districts organized by the States? Could the States be classified with farmers, business men, industrial workers, judges and other ordinary citizens and required to pay an income tax to the federal government? It is said that a federal income tax on the tax revenues of a State would not be sustained because such a tax would interfere with a sovereign function of the State. But can it be that a federal income tax on state revenues derived not from taxes but from the sale of mineral water, liquor, lumber and the like, would be sustained?
>
> A tax is a powerful, regulatory instrument. Local government does not exist for itself. The fact that local government may enter the domain of private enterprise and operate a project for profit does not put it in the class of private business enterprise for tax purposes. Local government exists to provide for the welfare of its people, not for a limited group of stockholders. If the federal government can place the local governments on its tax collector's list, their capacity to serve the needs of their citizens is at once hampered or curtailed. The field of federal excise taxation alone is practically without limits. Many state activities are in marginal enterprises where private capital refuses to venture. Add to the cost of these projects a federal tax and the social program may be destroyed before it can be launched. In any case, the repercussions of such a fundamental change on the credit of the States and on their programs to take care of the needy and to build for the future would be considerable. To say the present tax will be sustained because it does not impair the State's functions of government is to conclude either that the sale by the State of its mineral water is not a function of government or that the present tax is so slight as to be no burden. The former obviously is not true. The latter overlooks the fact that the power to tax lightly is the power to tax severely. The power to tax is indeed one of the most effective forms of regulation. And no

more powerful instrument for centralization of government could be devised. For with the federal government immune and the States subject to tax, the economic ability of the federal government to expand its activities at the expense of the States is at once apparent. That is the result whether the rule of *State of South Carolina v. United States* be perpetuated or a new rule of discrimination be adopted.

∽ PROBLEMS ∽

1. *Additional Tax Revenues.* Congress knows that education is costly, and that improving education will cost a lot of money. To raise money for its education initiatives, such as the EBA, Congress is interested in finding new ways to tax. Can Congress tax the following items to raise funds to pay for the EBA Act: a) operations of state-owned utilities, b) public guided tours for tourists in state parks, c) private donations to state universities, and d) soda sales from machines in state office buildings?

2. *Interest on Bonds.* Suppose the federal government wishes to tax the interest received by private parties on state and local bonds. Does it have the power to do so? What are the best arguments for each side? *See Willcuts v. Bunn,* 282 U.S. 216 (1931). *See also Group No. 1 Oil Corporation v. Bass,* 283 U.S. 279 (1931); *Metcalf & Eddy v. Mitchell,* 269 U.S. 514 (1926); *Pollock v. Farmers' Loan & Trust Co.,* 157 U.S. 429 (1895).

3. *Salaries of State Employees.* The states may not tax the federal government itself, but are permitted to tax the salaries of federal employees. Since many states have decided to do so, the federal government decides to reciprocate and tax the salaries of state employees. Is this tax permissible? *See Helvering v. Therrell,* 303 U.S. 218 (1938); *McLoughlin v. Commissioner,* 303 U.S. 218 (1938).

4. *A State's Income.* Most states impose an income tax on their citizens. The receipts derived from these taxes are considered revenue to the state. In light of the issue raised by Justice Douglas in his dissent in *New York,* above, can the federal government impose a tax on a state's income from its own taxes? Rely on the majority decision in *New York* as well as the majority opinion in *Massachusetts.*

5. *Corporate Franchises.* The federal government also wishes to impose a tax on the privilege of exercising corporate franchises granted by a state to public service companies. Would such a tax be permissible? *See Flint v. Stone Tracy Co.,* 220 U.S. 107 (1911).

C. STATE IMMUNITY FROM FEDERAL REGULATION

Can the federal government regulate state governments? Prior to the 1930s, few commentators would have bothered to ask such a question. At that time, the Court regarded the Tenth Amendment as a significant independent limitation on congressional power. In addition, prior to the 1930s, the Court construed the scope of federal power, particularly the power of the Commerce Clause, more restrictively. As we have seen, in decisions like *Hammer v. Dagenhart*, 247 U.S. 251 (1918), the Court struck down restrictions on child labor. During this period, it was highly doubtful whether Congress could regulate in such areas as the wages and hours of private-sector workers, much less the wages and hours of state workers.

In the post-1937 period, as the Court gave great deference to Congress in the use of its Commerce Clause power, federal assertions of authority expanded dramatically. In *United States v. Darby*, 312 U.S. 100 (1941), the Court upheld wage and hour restrictions on employees. Emboldened by these favorable decisions, Congress began to impose more and more restrictions on wages and hours. In the cases that follow, Congress has gone beyond trying to regulate the wages and hours of private employees and is directly regulating the wages and hours of state employees.

BACKGROUND
The National League of Cities

The National League of Cities (NLC) was founded in 1924 and has more than 1,600 cities, municipalities, towns, and villages as members. With headquarters in Washington, D.C., the organization works in conjunction with forty-nine equivalent state "league of cities" organizations. The NLC sometimes engages in litigation on behalf of its members, as the following case illustrates.

National League of Cities v. Usery

426 U.S. 833 (1976)

Mr. Justice REHNQUIST delivered the opinion of the Court.

Nearly 40 years ago Congress enacted the Fair Labor Standards Act, and required employers covered by the Act to pay their employees a minimum hourly wage and to pay them at one and one-half times their regular rate of pay for hours worked in excess of 40 during a work week. Covered employers were required to keep records to aid in the enforcement of the Act, and to comply with specified child labor standards. This Court unanimously upheld the Act as a valid exercise of congressional authority under the commerce power.

The original Fair Labor Standards Act specifically excluded the States and their political subdivisions from its coverage. In 1974, Congress extended the minimum wage and maximum hour provisions to almost all public employees employed by the States and by their various political subdivisions. The Act did make some provision for public employment relationships that are without counterpart in the private sector, such as those presented by fire protection and law enforcement personnel. Appellants include individual cities and States, the National League of Cities, who challenge the validity of the 1974 amendments. Their contention is that when Congress seeks to regulate directly the activities of States as public employers, it transgresses an affirmative limitation on the exercise of its power.

In *Lane County v. Oregon,* 7 Wall. 71 (1869), Chief Justice Chase said: "In many articles of the Constitution the necessary existence of the States, and, within their proper spheres, the independent authority of the States, is distinctly recognized." Appellee Secretary argues that the cases in which this Court has upheld sweeping exercises of authority by Congress have already curtailed the sovereignty of the States quite as much as the 1974 amendments. We do not agree. It is one thing to recognize the authority of Congress to enact laws regulating individual businesses. It is quite another to uphold a similar exercise of congressional authority directed to the States as States. There are attributes of sovereignty attaching to every state government which may not be impaired by Congress, not because Congress may lack an affirmative grant of legislative authority to reach the matter, but because the Constitution prohibits it from exercising the authority in that manner. In *Coyle v. Oklahoma,* 221 U.S. 559 (1911), the Court gave this example of such an attribute: "The power to locate its own seat of government, and to determine when and how it shall be changed from one place to another, and to appropriate its own public funds for that purpose, are essentially and peculiarly state powers. That one of the original thirteen states could now be shorn of such powers by an act of Congress would not be for a moment entertained."

One undoubted attribute of state sovereignty is the States' power to determine the wages which shall be paid to those whom they employ in order to carry out their governmental functions, what hours those persons work, and what compensation will be provided where these employees may be called upon to work overtime. The question we must resolve is whether these determinations are "functions essential to separate and independent existence," so that Congress may not abrogate the States' otherwise plenary authority to make them.

Appellants advanced estimates of substantial costs which will be imposed upon them by the 1974 amendments. The Metropolitan Government of Nashville and Davidson County, Tenn., for example, asserted that the Act will increase its costs of providing essential police and fire protection, without any increase in service or in current salary levels, by $938,000 per year. Cape Girardeau, Mo., estimated that its annual budget for fire protection may have to be increased by anywhere from $250,000 to $400,000 over the current figure of $350,000.

The Act displaces state policies regarding the manner in which they will structure delivery of those governmental services which their citizens require. The Act, speaking directly to the States qua States, requires that they shall pay all but an extremely limited minority of their employees the minimum wage rates currently chosen by Congress. It may well be that as a matter of economic policy it would be desirable that States comply with these minimum wage requirements. But the federal requirement directly supplants the considered policy choices of the States' elected officials and administrators as to how they wish to structure pay scales in state employment.

This dilemma presented by the minimum wage restrictions may seem not immediately different from that faced by private employers. The difference, however, is that a State is not merely a factor in the "shifting economic arrangements" of the private sector of the economy, but is itself a coordinate element in the system established by the Framers for governing our Federal Union. This congressionally imposed displacement of state decisions may substantially restructure traditional ways in which the local governments have arranged their affairs. The requirement imposing premium rates upon any employment in excess of what Congress has decided is appropriate for a workweek appears likely to coerce the States to structure work periods in some employment areas, such as police and fire protection, in a manner substantially different from practices which have long been commonly accepted among local governments. Provisions such as these contemplate a significant reduction of traditional volunteer assistance which has been in the past drawn on to complement the operation of many local governmental functions.

Our examination of the effect of the 1974 amendments satisfies us that both the minimum wage and the maximum hour provisions will impermissibly interfere with the integral governmental functions of these bodies. Their application will significantly alter or displace the States' abilities to structure employer-employee relationships in such areas as fire prevention, police protection, sanitation, public health, and parks and recreation. These activities are typical of those performed by state and local governments in discharging their dual functions of administering the public law and furnishing public services. Indeed, it is functions such as these which governments are created to provide, services such as these which the States have traditionally afforded their citizens. If Congress may withdraw from the States the authority to make those fundamental employment decisions upon which their systems for performance of these functions must rest, we think there would be little left of the States' "separate and independent existence." The dispositive factor is that Congress has attempted to exercise its Commerce Clause authority to prescribe minimum wages and maximum hours to be paid by the States in their capacities as sovereign governments. In so doing, Congress has sought to wield its power in a fashion that would impair the States' "ability to function effectively in a federal system." This exercise of congressional authority does not comport with the federal system of government embodied in the Constitution. Insofar as the challenged amendments operate to directly displace the States' freedom to structure integral operations in areas of traditional governmental functions, they are not within the authority granted Congress by Art. I, §8, cl. 3.

The States as States stand on a quite different footing from an individual or a corporation when challenging the exercise of Congress' power to regulate commerce. Congress may not exercise its power so as to force directly upon the States its choices as to how essential decisions regarding the conduct of integral governmental functions are to be made. Such assertions of power if unchecked, would, as Mr. Justice Douglas cautioned, allow "the National Government to devour the essentials of state sovereignty," and would therefore transgress the bounds of the authority granted Congress under the Commerce Clause.

The judgment of the District Court is accordingly *reversed*, and the cases are *remanded* for further proceedings consistent with this opinion.

So ordered.

Mr. Justice BRENNAN, with whom Mr. Justice WHITE and Mr. Justice MARSHALL join, *dissenting.*

One hundred fifty-two years ago Mr. Chief Justice Marshall enunciated that principle to which, until today, his successors on this Court have been faithful. "The power over commerce is vested in Congress as absolutely as it would be in a single government, having in its constitution the same restrictions on the exercise of the power as are found in the constitution of the United States. The wisdom and the discretion of Congress, their identity with the people, and the influence which their constituents possess at elections, are the sole restraints on which they have relied, to secure them from its abuse. They are the restraints on which the people must often rely solely, in all representative governments." *Gibbons v. Ogden*, 9 Wheat. 1, 197 (1824). Congress is constituted of representatives in both the Senate and House Elected from the States. Decisions upon the extent of federal intervention under the Commerce Clause into the affairs of the States are in that sense decisions of the States themselves.

Garcia v. San Antonio Metropolitan Transit Authority

469 U.S. 528 (1985)

Justice BLACKMUN delivered the opinion of the Court.

We revisit in these cases an issue raised in *National League of Cities v. Usery*. In that litigation, this Court, by a sharply divided vote, ruled that the Commerce Clause does not empower Congress to enforce the minimum-wage and overtime provisions of the Fair Labor Standards Act (FLSA) against the States "in areas of traditional governmental functions." Although *National League of Cities* supplied some examples of "traditional governmental functions," it did not offer a general explanation of how a "traditional" function is to be distinguished from a "nontraditional" one. Since then, federal and state courts have struggled with the task of identifying a traditional function for purposes of state immunity under the Commerce Clause. In the present cases, a lower federal court held that municipal ownership and operation of a mass-transit system is a traditional governmental function and thus is exempt from FLSA. Other lower courts reached the opposite conclusion. Our examination of this "function" standard applied in these and other cases over the last eight years persuades us that the attempt to draw the boundaries of state regulatory immunity in terms of "traditional governmental function" is not only unworkable but is also inconsistent with established principles of federalism and with those very federalism principles on which *National League of Cities* purported to rest. That case, accordingly, is overruled.

The history of public transportation in San Antonio, Tex., is characteristic of the history of local mass transit in the United States generally. Passenger transportation for hire was originally provided on a private basis subject to governmental regulation. In 1959, the city purchased a private transit company and replaced it with a public authority that eventually became known as the San Antonio Metropolitan Transit Authority (SAMTA), a public mass-transit authority organized on a countywide basis.

Under *National League of Cities*, four conditions must be satisfied before a state activity may be deemed immune from a particular federal regulation under the Commerce Clause. First, the federal statute must regulate "the 'States as States.'" Second, the statute must "address matters that are indisputably 'attributes of state sovereignty.'" Third, state compliance with the federal obligation must "directly impair the States' ability 'to structure integral operations in areas of traditional governmental functions.'" Finally, the relation of state and federal interests must not be such that "the nature of the federal interest justifies state submission."

The controversy in the present cases has focused on the third requirement — that the challenged federal statute trench on "traditional governmental functions." The District Court voiced a common concern: "Despite the abundance of adjectives, identifying which particular state functions are immune remains difficult." Just how troublesome the task has been is revealed by the results reached in other federal cases. Courts have held that regulating ambulance services, licensing automobile drivers, operating a municipal airport, performing solid waste disposal, and operating a highway authority, are functions protected under *National League of Cities*. At the same time, courts have held that issuance of industrial development bonds, regulation of intrastate natural gas sales, regulation of traffic on public roads, regulation of air transportation, operation of a telephone system, leasing and sale of natural gas, operation of a mental health facility, and provision of in-house domestic services for the aged and handicapped, are not entitled to immunity. We find it difficult, if not impossible, to identify an organizing principle that places each of the cases in the first group on one side of a line and each of the cases in the second group on the other side. The constitutional distinction is elusive.

This Court itself has made little headway in defining the scope of the governmental functions deemed protected under *National League of Cities*. That case set forth examples of protected and unprotected functions, but provided no explanation of how those examples were identified. It might be fair to assume that case-by-case development would lead to a workable standard for resolving this issue. A cautionary note is sounded, however, by the Court's experience in the related field of state immunity from federal taxation. In *South Carolina v. United States*, 199 U.S. 437 (1905), the Court held that the state tax immunity extended only to the "ordinary" and "strictly governmental" instrumentalities of state governments and not to instrumentalities "used by the State in the carrying on of an ordinary private business." While the Court applied this distinction for the following 40 years, at no time did the Court develop a consistent formulation of the kinds of governmental functions that were entitled to immunity. These tax-immunity attempted to distinguish between "governmental" and "proprietary" functions. To say that the distinction proved to be stable would be an overstatement. In 1911, the Court declared that a municipal water supply "is no part of the essential governmental functions of a State." Later, the Court decided that the provision of a municipal water supply was immune from federal taxation as an essential governmental function, even though municipal water-works long had been operated for profit by private industry. It was this uncertainty and instability that led the Court, in *New York v. United States*, 326 U.S. 572 (1946), to conclude that the distinction between "governmental" and "proprietary" functions was "untenable" and must be abandoned.

The distinction the Court discarded as unworkable in the field of tax immunity has proved no more fruitful in the field of regulatory immunity under the Commerce Clause. Neither do any of the alternative standards appear manageable. We rejected the possibility of making immunity turn on a standard of "tradition." The most obvious defect of a historical approach is that it prevents a court from accommodating changes in the historical functions of States, changes that have resulted in a number of once-private functions like education being assumed by the States. The only apparent virtue of a rigorous historical standard, namely, its promise of a reasonably objective measure for state immunity, is illusory. Reliance on history as an organizing principle results in line-drawing of the most arbitrary sort; the genesis of state governmental functions stretches over a historical continuum from before the Revolution to the present, and courts would have to decide how longstanding a pattern of state involvement had to be for federal regulatory authority to be defeated.

A nonhistorical standard for selecting immune governmental functions is likely to be just as unworkable. The goal of identifying "uniquely" governmental functions, for example, has been rejected by the Court in the field of governmental tort liability in part because the notion of a "uniquely" governmental function is unmanageable. Another possibility would be to confine immunity to "necessary" governmental services, that is, services that would be provided inadequately or not at all unless the government provided them. The set of services that fits into this category, however, may well be negligible. The fact that an unregulated market produces less of some service than a State deems desirable does not mean that the State itself must provide the service; in most if not all cases, the State can "contract out" by hiring private firms to provide the service or simply by providing subsidies to existing suppliers.

There is a more fundamental problem that explains why the Court was never able to provide a basis for the governmental-proprietary distinction and why an attempt to draw such distinctions is unlikely to succeed. Neither the governmental-proprietary distinction nor any other that purports to separate out important governmental functions can be faithful to the role of federalism in a democratic society. The essence of our federal system is that within the realm of authority left open to them under the Constitution, the States must be equally free to engage in any activity that their citizens choose for the common weal, no matter how unorthodox or unnecessary anyone else deems state involvement to be. Any rule that looks to the "traditional," "integral," or "necessary" nature of governmental functions inevitably invites an unelected federal judiciary to make decisions about which state policies it favors and which ones it dislikes. In the words of Justice Black: "There is not, and there cannot be, any unchanging line of demarcation between essential and non-essential governmental functions. Many governmental functions have at some time in the past been non-governmental. The genius of our government provides that, within the sphere of constitutional action, the people—acting not through the courts but through their elected legislative representatives—have the power to determine as conditions demand, what services and functions the public welfare requires." *Helvering v. Gerhardt*, 304 U.S., at 427 (concurring opinion).

We therefore reject, as unsound in principle and unworkable in practice, a rule of state immunity from federal regulation that turns on a judicial appraisal of whether a particular governmental function is "integral" or "traditional." Any such rule leads to inconsistent results at the same time that it disserves principles of democratic self-governance, and it breeds inconsistency precisely because it is divorced from those principles. If there are limits on the Federal Government's power to interfere with state functions, we must look elsewhere to find them. The central theme of *National League of Cities* was that the States occupy a special position in our constitutional system and that the scope of Congress' authority under the Commerce Clause must reflect that position. *National League of Cities* reflected the general conviction that the Constitution precludes "the National Government from devouring the essentials of state sovereignty." In order to be faithful to the underlying federal premises of the Constitution, courts must look for the "postulates which limit and control."

What has proved problematic is not the perception that the Constitution's federal structure imposes limitations on the Commerce Clause, but rather the nature and content of those limitations. One approach to defining the limits on Congress' authority to regulate the States under the Commerce Clause is to identify certain underlying elements of political sovereignty that are deemed essential to the States' "separate and independent existence." This approach obviously underlay the Court's use of the "traditional governmental function" concept. It also has led to the separate requirement that the challenged federal statute "address matters that are indisputably 'attributes of state sovereignty.'" In *National League of Cities* itself, for example, the Court concluded that decisions by a State concerning the wages and hours of its employees are an "undoubted attribute of state sovereignty." The opinion did not explain what aspects of such decisions made them such an "undoubted attribute," and the Court since then has remarked on the uncertain scope of the concept.

We doubt that courts ultimately can identify principled constitutional limitations on the scope of Congress' Commerce Clause powers over the States merely by relying on a priori definitions of state sovereignty. In part, this is because of the elusiveness of objective criteria for "fundamental" elements of state sovereignty, a problem we have witnessed in the search for "traditional governmental functions." There is, however, a more fundamental reason: the sovereignty of the States is limited by the Constitution itself. A variety of sovereign powers, for example, are withdrawn from the States by Article I, §10. Section 8 of the same Article works an equally sharp contraction of state sovereignty by authorizing Congress to exercise a wide range of legislative powers and (in conjunction with the Supremacy Clause of Article VI) to displace contrary state legislation. By providing for final review of questions of federal law in this Court, Article III curtails the sovereign power of the States' judiciaries to make authoritative determinations of law. Finally, the developed application, through the Fourteenth Amendment, of the greater part of the Bill of Rights to the States limits the sovereign authority that States otherwise would possess to legislate with respect to their citizens and to conduct their own affairs.

The States unquestionably do "retain a significant measure of sovereign authority." They do so, however, only to the extent that the Constitution has not divested them of their original powers and transferred those powers to the Federal Government. To say that the Constitution assumes the continued role of the States is to say little about the nature of that role. With rare exceptions, like the guarantee, in Article IV, §3, of state territorial integrity, the Constitution does not carve out express elements of state sovereignty that Congress may not employ its delegated powers to displace.

When we look for the States' "residuary and inviolable sovereignty," in the shape of the constitutional scheme, a different measure of state sovereignty emerges. Apart from the limitation on federal authority inherent in the delegated nature of Congress' Article I powers, the principal means chosen by the Framers to ensure the role of the States in the federal system lies in the structure of the Federal Government itself. The Federal Government was designed in large part to protect the States from overreaching by Congress. The Framers thus gave the States a role in the selection both of the Executive and the Legislative Branches of the Federal Government. The States were vested with indirect influence over the House of Representatives and the Presidency by their control of electoral qualifications and their role in Presidential elections. They were given more direct influence in the Senate, where each State received equal representation and each Senator was to be selected by the legislature of his State. The significance attached to the States' equal representation in the Senate is underscored by the prohibition of any constitutional amendment divesting a State of equal representation without the State's consent. James Madison explained that the Federal Government "will partake sufficiently of the spirit of the States, to be disinclined to invade the rights of the individual States, or the prerogatives of their governments."

The effectiveness of the federal political process in preserving the States' interests is apparent in the course of federal legislation. The States have been able to direct a substantial proportion of federal revenues into their own treasuries in the form of general and program-specific grants in aid. In the past quarter-century, federal grants to States and localities have grown from $7 billion to $96 billion. The States have obtained federal funding for such services as police and fire protection, education, public health and hospitals, parks and recreation, and sanitation. Moreover, at the same time, the States have been able to exempt themselves from a wide variety of obligations imposed by Congress under the Commerce Clause. For example, the Federal Power Act, the National Labor Relations Act, the Labor-Management Reporting and Disclosure Act, the Occupational Safety and Health Act, the Employee Retirement Income Security Act, and the Sherman Act all contain express or implied exemptions for States and their subdivisions. Against this background, we are convinced that the fundamental limitation that the constitutional scheme imposes on the Commerce Clause to protect the "States as States" is one of process rather than one of result. Any substantive restraint on the exercise of Commerce Clause powers must find its justification in the procedural nature of this basic limitation, and it must be tailored to compensate for possible failings in the national political process rather than to dictate a "sacred province of state autonomy."

Insofar as the present cases are concerned, we need go no further than to state that we perceive nothing in the overtime and minimum-wage requirements of the FLSA that is destructive of state sovereignty or violative of any constitutional provision. The status of public mass transit simply underscores the extent to which the structural protections of the Constitution insulate the States from federally imposed burdens. Congress has not simply placed a financial burden on the shoulders of States and localities that operate mass-transit systems, but has provided substantial countervailing financial assistance that may leave individual mass-transit systems better off than they would have been had Congress never intervened in the area. Congress's treatment of public mass transit reinforces our conviction that the national political process systematically protects States from the risk of having their functions in that area handicapped by Commerce Clause regulation. In affording SAMTA employees the protections of the wage and hour provisions of the FLSA contravened no affirmative limit on Congress's power under the Commerce Clause.

We continue to recognize that the States occupy a special and specific position in our constitutional system and that the scope of Congress' authority under the Commerce Clause must reflect that position. But the principal and basic limit on the federal commerce power is that inherent in all congressional action — the built-in restraints that our system provides through state participation in federal governmental action. The political process ensures that laws that unduly burden the States will not be promulgated. In these cases the internal safeguards of the political process have performed as intended. We do not lightly overrule recent precedent. We have not hesitated, however, when it has become apparent that a prior decision has departed from a proper understanding of congressional power under the Commerce Clause. Due respect for the reach of congressional power within the federal system mandates that we do so now. *National League of Cities v. Usery* is overruled. The judgment of the District Court is reversed, and these cases are remanded to that court for further proceedings consistent with this opinion.

It is so ordered.

Justice POWELL, with whom THE CHIEF JUSTICE, Justice REHNQUIST, and Justice O'CONNOR join, *dissenting.*

Today's decision effectively reduces the Tenth Amendment to meaningless rhetoric when Congress acts pursuant to the Commerce Clause. Today's opinion does not explain how the States' role in the electoral process guarantees that particular exercises of the Commerce Clause power will not infringe on residual state sovereignty. Members of Congress are elected from the various States, but once in office they are Members of the Federal Government. Although the States participate in the Electoral College, this is hardly a reason to view the President as a representative of the States' interest against federal encroachment. The States' role in our system of government is a matter of constitutional law, not of legislative grace. More troubling than the logical infirmities in the Court's reasoning is the result of its holding, i.e., that federal political officials, invoking the Commerce Clause, are the sole judges of the limits of their own power. This result is inconsistent with the fundamental principles of our constitutional system. At least since *Marbury*, it has been the settled province of the federal judiciary "to say what the law is" with respect to the constitutionality of Acts of Congress.

Much of the initial opposition to the Constitution was rooted in the fear that the National Government would be too powerful and eventually would eliminate the States as viable political entities. This concern was voiced repeatedly until proponents of the Constitution made assurances that a Bill of Rights, including a provision explicitly reserving powers in the States, would be among the first business of the new Congress. So strong was the concern that the proposed Constitution was seriously defective without a specific bill of rights, including a provision reserving powers to the States, that in order to secure the votes for ratification, the Federalists eventually conceded that such provisions were necessary. The Bill of Rights were proposed and adopted early in the first session of the First Congress. The Framers believed that the separate sphere of sovereignty reserved to the States would ensure that the States would serve as an effective "counterpoise" to the power of the Federal Government. The harm to the States that results from federal overreaching under the Commerce Clause is not simply a matter of dollars and cents. By usurping functions traditionally performed by the States, federal overreaching under the Commerce Clause undermines the constitutionally mandated balance of power between the States and the Federal Government, a balance designed to protect our fundamental liberties.

The Court today propounds a view of federalism that pays only lipservice to the role of the States. Although it says that the States "unquestionably do 'retain a significant measure of sovereign authority,'" it fails to recognize the broad, yet specific areas of sovereignty that the Framers intended the States to retain. The Court barely acknowledges that the Tenth Amendment exists and recasts it to say that the States retain their sovereign powers "only to the extent that the Constitution has not divested them of their original powers and transferred those powers to the Federal Government." This rephrasing reflects the Court's unprecedented view that Congress is free under the Commerce Clause to assume a State's traditional sovereign power, and to do so without judicial review of its action. The Court's view of federalism appears to relegate the States to precisely the trivial role that opponents of the Constitution feared.

In overruling *National League of Cities,* today's opinion apparently authorizes federal control over the terms and conditions of employment of all state and local employees. The Court's action reflects a serious misunderstanding, if not an outright rejection, of the history of our country and the intention of the Framers of the Constitution. Although the Court's opinion purports to recognize that the States retain some sovereign power, it does not identify even a single aspect of state authority that would remain when the Commerce Clause is invoked to justify federal regulation. As I view the Court's decision today as rejecting the basic precepts of our federal system and limiting the constitutional role of judicial review, I dissent.

Justice O'CONNOR, with whom Justice POWELL and Justice REHNQUIST join, *dissenting.*

The true "essence" of federalism is that the States as States have legitimate interests which the National Government is bound to respect even though its laws are supreme. If federalism is to remain meaningful, this Court cannot abdicate its constitutional responsibility to oversee the Federal Government's compliance with its duty to respect the legitimate interests of the States.

The Framers perceived the interstate commerce power to be important but limited, and expected that it would be used primarily if not exclusively to remove interstate tariffs and to regulate maritime affairs and large-scale mercantile enterprise. In an era when interstate commerce represented a tiny fraction of economic activity and most goods and services were produced and consumed close to home, the interstate commerce power left a broad range of activities beyond the reach of Congress. In the decades since ratification of the Constitution, interstate economic activity has steadily expanded. Industrialization, coupled with advances in transportation and communications, has created a national economy in which virtually every activity occurring within the borders of a State plays a part. Because virtually every state activity, like virtually every activity of a private individual, arguably "affects" interstate commerce, there is now a real risk that

Congress will gradually erase the diffusion of power between State and Nation on which the Framers based their faith in the efficiency and vitality of our Republic.

It is not enough that the "end be legitimate"; the means to that end chosen by Congress must not contravene the spirit of the Constitution. Congress might rationally conclude that the location a State chooses for its capital may affect interstate commerce, but Congress would nevertheless be barred from dictating that location because such an exercise of a delegated power would undermine the state sovereignty inherent in the Tenth Amendment. Similarly, Congress in the exercise of its taxing and spending powers can protect federal savings and loan associations, but if it chooses to do so by converting quasi-public state savings and loan associations into federal associations, it contravenes the reserved powers of the States because the conversion is not a reasonably necessary exercise of power to reach the desired end. State autonomy is a relevant factor in assessing the means by which Congress exercises its powers. This principle requires the Court to enforce affirmative limits on federal regulation of the States to complement the judicially crafted expansion of the interstate commerce power. *National League of Cities* represented an attempt to define such limits. The Court today washes its hands of all efforts to protect the States.

A proper resolution lies in weighing state autonomy as a factor in the balance when interpreting the means by which Congress can exercise its authority on the States as States. It is insufficient to ask only whether the same regulation would be valid if enforced against a private party. That reasoning is inconsistent with the spirit of our Constitution. It remains relevant that a State is being regulated. The autonomy of a State is an essential component of federalism. I respectfully *dissent*.

∽ PROBLEMS ∽

1. *All In.* Congress enacts a law after *Garcia* that is similar, but includes the following provision: "All state or local employees are subject to the FLSA, including fire protection personnel, police employees, state legislators, and judges." The legislative history of the law acknowledges Justice Powell's dissent, particularly where he stated, "today's opinion apparently authorizes federal control over the terms and conditions of employment of all state and local employees." Is the law constitutional?

2. *Capital Relocation Program.* Suppose that Congress decides that the location a state has chosen for its state capital negatively affects interstate commerce (by affecting how far people have to drive). Despite Justice O'Connor's dissent, could Congress dictate a change in a state capital's location? Would the political process solve this problem? How?

3. *Mandatory Retirement Age.* After *Garcia*, suppose that Congress imposes a mandatory retirement age for all law enforcement officers, including those employed by states and their subdivisions. Is this law constitutional?

4. *The Education for a Better America Act.* To ensure that the teaching profession attracts highly qualified applicants, Congress considers adding a provision to the EBA that would require all public school teachers in the United States be paid equal to or more than the average pay for all professionals. The pay scale would be based on a special scaffolding correlated to recognized and high-paying professions, accounting for experience, educational advancement, and other relevant factors. Would such a requirement be constitutional? Would the requirement be good policy? Explain your conclusions.

D. FEDERAL COMMANDEERING OF STATE RESOURCES

Since Congress has broad regulatory power, including the power to regulate the states, can it tell the states what laws to enact? Consider the following case.

New York v. United States

505 U.S. 144 (1992)

Justice O'CONNOR delivered the opinion of the Court.

We live in a world full of low level radioactive waste. Radioactive material is present in luminous watch dials, smoke alarms, measurement devices, medical fluids, research materials, and the protective gear and construction materials used by workers at nuclear power plants. Low level radioactive waste is generated by the Government, by hospitals, by research institutions, and by various industries. The waste must be isolated from humans for long periods of time, often for hundreds of years. Millions of cubic feet of low level radioactive waste must be disposed of each year.

Although there were five sites for disposal of low-level radioactive waste in the early 1970s, only three remained in existence by 1979. The problem reached crisis proportions when two of those sites shut down temporarily and then announced plans to close permanently, and the state with the only remaining site (South Carolina) announced a 50 percent reduction in the quantity of waste that would be accepted. Faced with the possibility that the Nation would be left with no disposal sites, Congress enacted the Low-Level Radioactive Waste Policy Act. Congress declared a federal policy of holding each State "responsible for providing for the availability of capacity either within or outside the State for the disposal of low-level radioactive waste generated within its borders," and found that such waste could be disposed of "most safely and efficiently on a regional basis." The 1980 Act authorized States to enter into regional compacts that, once ratified by Congress, would have the authority to restrict the use of their disposal facilities to waste generated within member States. There were no penalties for States that failed to participate in this plan.

By 1985, only three approved regional compacts had operational disposal facilities. The following year, the 1980 Act would have given these three compacts the ability to exclude waste from nonmembers, and the remaining 31 States would have had no assured outlet for their low level radioactive waste. With this prospect looming, Congress passed the Low-Level Radioactive Waste Policy Amendments Act of 1985 which embodied a compromise. The sited States agreed to extend for seven years the period in which they would accept low level radioactive waste from other States. In exchange, the unsited States agreed to end their reliance on the sited States by 1992.

The Act directs: "Each State shall be responsible for providing, either by itself or in cooperation with other States, for the disposal of low-level radioactive waste generated within the State," with the exception of certain waste generated by the Federal Government. The Act authorizes States to "enter into such interstate compacts as may be necessary to provide for the establishment and operation of regional disposal facilities for low-level radioactive waste." For an additional seven years beyond the period contemplated by the 1980 Act, from the beginning of 1986 through the end of 1992, the three existing disposal sites "shall make disposal capacity available for low-level radioactive waste generated by any source," with certain exceptions not relevant here. But the three States in which the disposal sites are located are permitted to exact a graduated surcharge for waste arriving from outside the regional compact. After the 7-year transition period expires, approved regional compacts may exclude radioactive waste generated outside the region.

The Act provides three types of incentives to encourage the States to comply with their statutory obligation to provide for the disposal of waste generated within their borders.

1. *Monetary incentives.* One quarter of the surcharges collected by the sited States must be transferred to an escrow account held by the Secretary of Energy. The Secretary then makes payments from this account to each State that has complied with a series of deadlines. By July 1, 1986, each State was to have ratified legislation either joining a regional compact or indicating an intent to develop a disposal facility within the State. By January 1, 1988, each unsited compact was to have identified the State in which its facility would be located, and each compact or stand-alone State was to have developed a siting plan and taken other identified steps. By January 1, 1990, each State or compact was to have filed a complete application for a license to operate a disposal facility, or the Governor of any State that had not filed an application was to have certified that the State would be capable of disposing of all waste generated in the State after 1992. The rest of the account is to be paid out to those States or compacts able to dispose of all low level radioactive waste generated within their borders by January 1, 1993.

Each State that has not met the 1993 deadline must either take title to the waste generated within its borders or forfeit to the waste generators the incentive payments it has received.

2. *Access incentives.* The second type of incentive involves the denial of access to disposal sites. States that fail to meet the July 1986 deadline may be charged twice the ordinary surcharge for the remainder of 1986 and may be denied access to disposal facilities thereafter. States that fail to meet the 1988 deadline may be charged double surcharges for the first half of 1988 and quadruple surcharges for the second half of 1988, and may be denied access thereafter. States that fail to meet the 1990 deadline may be denied access. Finally, States that have not filed complete applications by January 1, 1992, for a license to operate a disposal facility, or States belonging to compacts that have not filed such applications, may be charged triple surcharges.

3. *The take title provision.* The third type of incentive is the most severe. The Act provides:

> If a State (or, where applicable, a compact region) in which low-level radioactive waste is generated is unable to provide for the disposal of all such waste generated within such State or compact region by January 1, 1996, each State in which such waste is generated, upon the request of the generator or owner of the waste, shall take title to the waste, be obligated to take possession of the waste, and shall be liable for all damages directly or indirectly incurred by such generator or owner as a consequence of the failure of the State to take possession of the waste as soon after January 1, 1996, as the generator or owner notifies the State that the waste is available for shipment.

In the seven years since the Act took effect, Congress has approved nine regional compacts, encompassing 42 of the States. New York, a State whose residents generate a relatively large share of the Nation's low level radioactive waste, did not join a regional compact. New York complied with the Act's requirements by enacting legislation providing for the siting and financing of a disposal facility in New York, and it identified five potential sites, but never developed them. Instead, the State of New York and the two counties filed this suit. Petitioners claim that the Act is inconsistent with the Tenth Amendment and the Guarantee Clause.

The constitutional line between federal and state power has given rise to many of the Court's most difficult cases. In some cases, the Court has inquired whether an Act of Congress is authorized by one of the powers delegated to Congress in Article I of the Constitution. In other cases, the Court has sought to determine whether an Act of Congress invades the province of state sovereignty reserved by the Tenth Amendment. In a case like these, the two inquiries are mirror images of each other. If a power is delegated to Congress in the Constitution, the Tenth Amendment expressly disclaims any reservation of that power to the States; if a power is an attribute of state sovereignty reserved by the Tenth Amendment, it is necessarily a power the Constitution has not conferred on Congress. It is in this sense that the Tenth Amendment "states but a truism that all is retained which has not been surrendered." *United States v. Darby*, 312 U.S. 100 (1941).

Petitioners do not contend that Congress lacks the power to regulate the disposal of low level radioactive waste. Space in radioactive waste disposal sites is frequently sold by residents of one State to residents of another. Regulation of the resulting interstate market in waste disposal is therefore well within Congress' authority under the Commerce Clause. *Cf. Philadelphia v. New Jersey*, 437 U.S. 617 (1978). Petitioners likewise do not dispute that under the Supremacy Clause Congress could, if it wished, pre-empt state radioactive waste regulation. Petitioners contend only that the Tenth Amendment limits the power of Congress to direct the States to regulate in this field.

Most of our recent cases interpreting the Tenth Amendment have concerned the authority of Congress to subject state governments to generally applicable laws. This litigation instead concerns whether Congress may direct or otherwise motivate the States to regulate in a particular field or a particular way. As an initial matter, Congress may not simply "commandeer the legislative processes of the States by directly compelling them to enact and enforce a federal regulatory program." *Hodel v. Virginia Surface Mining & Reclamation Assn., Inc.*, 452 U.S. 264 (1981). While Congress has substantial powers to govern the Nation directly, the Constitution has never been understood to confer upon Congress the ability to require the States to govern according to Congress's instructions. *Texas v. White*, 7 Wall. 700, 19 L.Ed. 227 (1869).

This is not to say that Congress lacks the ability to encourage a State to regulate in a particular way, or that Congress may not hold out incentives to the States as a method of influencing a State's policy choices. Our cases have identified a variety of methods, short of outright coercion, by which Congress may urge a State to adopt a legislative program consistent with federal interests. First, under Congress' spending power, "Congress may attach conditions on the receipt of federal funds." *South Dakota v. Dole*, 483 U.S., at 206. The conditions attached to the funds by Congress may influence a State's legislative choices. Second, where Congress has the authority to regulate private activity under the Commerce Clause, we have recognized Congress' power to offer States the choice of regulating that activity according to federal standards or having state law pre-empted by federal regulation. *Hodel v. Virginia Surface Mining & Reclamation Assn., Inc., supra.* This "program of cooperative federalism," is replicated in numerous federal statutory schemes including the Clean Water Act, and the Occupational Safety and Health Act of 1970.

Where Congress encourages state regulation rather than compelling it, state governments remain responsive to the local electorate's preferences; state officials remain accountable to the people. By contrast, where the Federal Government compels States to regulate, the accountability of both state and federal officials is diminished. If the citizens of New York, for example, do not consider that making provision for the disposal of radioactive waste is in their best interest, they may elect state officials who share their view. That view can always be pre-empted under the Supremacy Clause if it is contrary to the national view, but in such a case it is the Federal Government that makes the decision in full view of the public, and it will be federal officials that suffer the consequences if the decision turns out to be detrimental or unpopular.

We decline petitioners' invitation to construe §2021c(a)(1)(A), alone and in isolation, as a command to the States independent of the remainder of the Act. Construed as a whole, the Act comprises three sets of "incentives" for the States to provide for the disposal of low level radioactive waste generated within their borders. We consider each in turn.

The first set of incentives works in three steps. First, Congress has authorized States with disposal sites to impose a surcharge on radioactive waste received from other States. Second, the Secretary of Energy collects a portion of this surcharge and places the money in an escrow account. Third, States achieving a series of milestones receive portions of this fund. The first of these steps is an unexceptionable exercise of Congress' power to authorize the States to burden interstate commerce. While the Commerce Clause has long been understood to limit the States' ability to discriminate against interstate commerce, that limit may be lifted, as it has been here, by an expression of the "unambiguous intent" of Congress. The second step, the Secretary's collection of a percentage of the surcharge, is no more than a federal tax on interstate commerce, which petitioners do not claim to be an invalid exercise of either Congress' commerce or taxing power. *Cf. Steward Machine Co. v. Davis*, 301 U.S. 548 (1937). The third step is a conditional exercise of Congress' authority under the Spending Clause: Congress has placed conditions—the achievement of the milestones—on the receipt of federal funds. Petitioners do not contend that Congress has exceeded its authority in any of the four respects our cases have identified. *See generally South Dakota v. Dole*, 483 U.S., at 207-208.

In the second set of incentives, Congress has authorized States and regional compacts with disposal sites gradually to increase the cost of access to the sites, and then to deny access altogether, to radioactive waste generated in States that do not meet federal deadlines. This provision would be within the power of Congress to authorize the States to discriminate against interstate commerce. Where federal regulation of private activity is within the scope of the Commerce Clause, we have recognized the ability of Congress to offer States the choice of regulating that activity according to federal standards or having state law preempted by federal regulation. *See Hodel v. Virginia Surface Mining & Reclamation Assn., Inc.*, 452 U.S., at 288. The affected States are not compelled by Congress to regulate, because any burden caused by a State's refusal to regulate will fall on those who generate waste and find no outlet for its disposal, rather than on the State as a sovereign. As a result, the second set of incentives does not intrude on the sovereignty reserved to the States by the Tenth Amendment.

The take title provision is of a different character. In this provision, Congress has crossed the line distinguishing encouragement from coercion. The take title provision offers state governments a "choice" of either accepting ownership of waste or regulating according to the instructions of Congress. The Constitution would not permit Congress simply to transfer radioactive waste from generators to state governments. The same is true of the provision requiring the States to become liable for the generators' damages. Either type of federal action would "commandeer" state governments into the service of federal regulatory purposes, and would for this reason be inconsistent with the Constitution's division of authority between federal and state governments. On the other hand, the second alternative held out to state governments—regulating pursuant to Congress' direction—would, standing alone, present a simple command to state governments to implement legislation enacted by Congress. The Constitution does not empower Congress to subject state governments to this type of instruction. It follows that Congress lacks the power to offer the States a choice between the two. A choice between two unconstitutionally coercive regulatory techniques is no choice at all. Either way, "the Act commandeers the legislative processes of the States by directly compelling them to enact and enforce a federal regulatory program," an outcome that has never been understood to lie within the authority conferred upon Congress by the Constitution.

The United States argues that the Constitution envisions a role for Congress as an arbiter of interstate disputes. The Framers did *not* intend that Congress should exercise that power through the mechanism of mandating state regulation. When Congress exceeds its authority relative to the States, the departure from the constitutional plan cannot be ratified by the "consent" of state officials. Petitioners also contend that the Act is inconsistent with the Constitution's Guarantee Clause, which directs the United States to "guarantee to every State in this Union a Republican Form of Government." U.S. Const., Art. IV, §4. Because we have found the take title provision irreconcilable with the Tenth Amendment's reservation to the States of those powers not delegated to the Federal Government, we need only address the applicability of the Guarantee Clause to the Act's other two challenged provisions. Even if we assume that petitioners' claim is justiciable, neither the monetary incentives provided by the Act nor the possibility that a State's waste producers may find themselves excluded from the disposal sites of another State can reasonably be said to deny any State a republican form of government. Under each, Congress offers the States a legitimate choice rather than issuing an unavoidable command. The States thereby retain the ability to set their legislative agendas; state government officials remain accountable to the local electorate. The Court went on to hold that the take title provision could be severed from the remainder of the Act.

States are not mere political subdivisions of the United States. State governments are neither regional offices nor administrative agencies of the Federal Government. The Constitution instead "leaves to the several States a residuary and inviolable sovereignty," *The Federalist No. 39*, p. 245 (C. Rossiter ed., 1961), reserved explicitly to the States by the Tenth Amendment. Whatever the outer limits of that sovereignty may be, one thing is clear: The Federal Government may not compel the States to enact or administer a federal regulatory program.

The Constitution permits both the Federal Government and the States to enact legislation regarding the disposal of low level radioactive waste. The Constitution enables the Federal Government to pre-empt state regulation contrary to federal interests, and it permits the Federal Government to hold out incentives to the States as a means of encouraging them to adopt suggested regulatory schemes. It does not, however, authorize Congress simply to direct the States to provide for the disposal of the radioactive waste generated within their borders. While there may be many constitutional methods of achieving regional self-sufficiency in radioactive waste disposal, the method Congress has chosen is not one of them. The judgment of the Court of Appeals is accordingly

Affirmed in part and reversed in part.

Justice WHITE, with whom Justice BLACKMUN and Justice STEVENS join, *concurring in part* and *dissenting in part.*

Congress could have pre-empted the field by directly regulating the disposal of this waste, but the States wished to take the lead in achieving a solution to this problem and agreed among themselves to the various incentives and penalties implemented by Congress to ensure adherence to the various deadlines and goals. New York's actions subsequent to enactment of the 1980 and 1985 Acts fairly indicate its approval of the interstate agreement process embodied in those laws within the meaning of Art. I, §10, cl. 3, of the Constitution relating to agreements or compacts between states. First, the States—including New York—petitioned Congress for the 1980 and 1985 Acts. Second, New York acted in compliance with the requisites of both statutes in key respects by entering into compact negotiations with several other northeastern States before withdrawing to "go it alone." By 1988, New York had identified five potential sites, but public opposition caused the State to reconsider where to locate its waste disposal facility. New York continued to take full advantage of the import concession by exporting its low-level radioactive waste for the full 7-year extension period provided in the 1985 Act. By gaining these benefits and complying with the Act's deadlines, therefore, New York fairly evidenced its acceptance of the federal-state arrangement—including the take title provision. The State should be estopped from asserting the unconstitutionality of the provision. Seen as a term of an agreement entered into between the several States, this measure proves to be less constitutionally odious. The Court's refusal to force New York to accept responsibility for its own problem inevitably means that some other States' sovereignty will be impinged by it being forced, for public health reasons, to accept New York's low-level radioactive waste. I do not understand the principle of federalism to impede the National Government from acting as referee among the States to prohibit one from bullying another.

Our precedents leave open the possibility that Congress may create federal rights of action in the generators of low-level radioactive waste against persons acting under color of state law for their failure to meet certain functions designated in federal-state programs. In addition to compensating injured parties for the State's failure to act, the exposure to liability established by such suits also potentially serves as an inducement to compliance with the program mandate. The irony of the decision today is that in its formalistically rigid obeisance to "federalism," the Court gives Congress fewer incentives to defer to the wishes of state officials in achieving local solutions to local problems. This legislation was a classic example of Congress acting as arbiter among the States in their attempts to accept responsibility for managing a problem of grave import. By invalidating the measure, the Court upsets the delicate compromise achieved among the States and forces Congress to erect several additional formalistic hurdles to clear before achieving exactly the same objective.

Justice STEVENS, *concurring in part* and *dissenting in part.*

The notion that Congress does not have the power to issue "a simple command to state governments to implement legislation enacted by Congress," is incorrect and unsound. The Federal Government directs state governments in many realms. The Government regulates state-operated railroads, state school systems, state prisons, state elections, and a host of other state functions. Similarly, in time of war, Congress could either draft soldiers itself or command the States to supply their quotas of troops. I see no reason why Congress may not also command the States to enforce federal water and air quality standards or federal standards for the disposition of low-level radioactive wastes. If litigation should develop between States that have joined a compact, we would surely have the power to grant relief in the form of specific enforcement of the take title provision. Even if the statute had never been passed, if one State's radioactive waste created a nuisance that harmed its neighbors, it seems clear that we would have had the power to command the offending State to take remedial action. If this Court has such authority, surely Congress has similar authority. I respectfully *dissent.*

∾ PROBLEM: THE EDUCATION FOR A BETTER AMERICA ACT REPRISED—THERE'S GOT TO BE A BETTER WAY ∾

Suppose Congresswoman St. James concludes that federal resources are now so tight that the best way to improve education is for Congress to direct the states in doing so, and she would like you to advise her about what measures Congress might impose on the states. How would you advise her? In other words, what options are available after *New York v. United States?* How would you prioritize the options?

BACKGROUND
The "Brady Bill"

The "Brady Bill," more formally known as the Handgun Violence Prevention Act, took its name as a result of the handgun violence that occurred in Washington, D.C., on March 30, 1981. John Hinckley, a drifter who wanted to impress the actress Jodie Foster by assassinating President Ronald Reagan, shot Reagan and three others, including James Brady, President Reagan's press secretary. Brady was the most severely injured, paralyzed on his left side. He became an active gun control advocate. Hinckley was prosecuted in Washington, D.C., and the jury found him not guilty by reason of insanity. Hinckley was released from St. Elizabeth's Hospital in Washington in 2016.

Printz v. United States

521 U.S. 898 (1997)

Justice SCALIA delivered the opinion of the Court.

The question presented in these cases is whether certain interim provisions of the Brady Handgun Violence Prevention Act commanding state and local law enforcement officers to conduct background checks on prospective handgun purchasers and to perform certain related tasks, violate the Constitution.

The Gun Control Act of 1968 (GCA) establishes a detailed federal scheme governing the distribution of firearms. It prohibits firearms dealers from transferring handguns to any person under 21, not resident in the dealer's State, or prohibited by state or local law from purchasing or possessing firearms. It also forbids possession of a firearm by, and transfer of a firearm to, convicted felons, fugitives from justice, unlawful users of controlled substances, persons adjudicated as mentally defective or committed to mental institutions, aliens unlawfully present in the United States, persons dishonorably discharged from the Armed Forces, persons who have renounced their citizenship, and persons who have been subjected to certain restraining orders or been convicted of a misdemeanor offense involving domestic violence.

In 1993, Congress amended the GCA by enacting the Brady Act. The Act requires the Attorney General to establish a national instant background check system by November 30, 1998, and immediately puts in place certain interim provisions until that system becomes operative. Under the interim provisions, a firearms dealer who proposes to transfer a handgun must first: (1) receive from the transferee a statement (the Brady Form), containing the name, address and date of birth of the proposed transferee along with a sworn statement that the transferee is not among any of the classes of prohibited purchasers; (2) verify the identity of the transferee by examining an identification document; and (3) provide the "chief law enforcement officer" (CLEO) of the transferee's residence with notice of the contents (and a copy) of the Brady Form. With some exceptions, the dealer must then wait five business days before consummating the sale, unless the CLEO earlier notifies the dealer that he has no reason to believe the transfer would be illegal.

When a CLEO receives the required notice of a proposed transfer from the firearms dealer, the CLEO must "make a reasonable effort to ascertain within 5 business days whether receipt or possession would be in violation of the law, including research in whatever State and local recordkeeping systems are available and in a national system designated by the Attorney General." The Act does not require the CLEO to take any particular action if he determines that a pending transaction would be unlawful; he may notify the firearms dealer to that effect, but is not required to do so. If, however, the CLEO notifies a gun dealer that a prospective purchaser is ineligible to receive a handgun, he must, upon request, provide the would-be purchaser with a written statement of the reasons for that determination. Moreover, if the CLEO does not discover any basis for objecting to the sale, he must destroy any records in his possession relating to the transfer, including his copy of the Brady Form. Under a separate provision of the GCA, any person who "knowingly violates the section of the GCA amended by the Brady Act shall be fined under this title, imprisoned for no more than 1 year, or both."

Petitioners Jay Printz and Richard Mack, the CLEOs for Ravalli County, Montana, and Graham County, Arizona, respectively, filed separate actions challenging the constitutionality of the Brady Act's interim provisions. The Brady Act purports to direct state law enforcement officers to participate, albeit only temporarily, in the administration of a federally enacted regulatory scheme. Regulated firearms dealers are required to forward Brady Forms not to a federal officer or employee, but to the CLEOs, whose obligation to accept those forms is implicit in the duty imposed upon them to make "reasonable efforts" within five days to determine whether the sales reflected in the forms are lawful. While the CLEOs are subjected to no federal requirement that they prevent the sales determined to be unlawful (it is perhaps assumed that their state-law duties will require prevention or apprehension), they are empowered to grant, in effect, waivers of the federally prescribed 5-day waiting period for handgun purchases by notifying the gun dealers that they have no reason to believe the transactions would be illegal.

The petitioners here object to being pressed into federal service, and contend that congressional action compelling state officers to execute federal laws is unconstitutional. The Government observes that statutes enacted by the first Congresses required state courts to record applications for citizenship, to transmit abstracts of citizenship applications and other naturalization records to the Secretary of State, and to register aliens seeking naturalization and issue certificates of registry. It may well be that these requirements applied only in States that authorized their courts to conduct naturalization proceedings. We do not think the early statutes imply a power of Congress to impress the state executive into its service. Indeed, it can be argued that the numerousness of these statutes, contrasted with the utter lack of statutes imposing obligations on the States' executive (notwithstanding the attractiveness of that course to Congress), suggests an assumed absence of such power. The only early federal law the Government has brought to our attention that imposed duties on state executive officers is the Extradition Act of 1793, which required the "executive authority" of a State to cause the arrest and delivery of a fugitive from justice upon the request of the executive authority of the State from which the fugitive had fled. That was in direct implementation, however, of the Extradition Clause of the Constitution itself. To complete the historical record, there is not only an absence of executive-commandeering statutes in the early Congresses, but there is an absence of them in our later history as well, at least until very recent years.

We turn next to consideration of the structure of the Constitution, to see if we can discern among its "essential postulates" a principle that controls the present cases. The Constitution established a system of "dual sovereignty." Although the States surrendered many of their powers to the new Federal Government, they retained "a residuary and inviolable sovereignty." The Framers' experience under the Articles of Confederation persuaded them that using the States as the instruments of federal governance was both ineffectual and provocative of federal-state conflict. The Framers rejected the concept of a central government that would act upon and through the States, and instead designed a system in which the state and federal governments would exercise concurrent authority over the people—who were, in Hamilton's words, "the only proper objects of government." The Constitution thus contemplates that a State's government will represent and remain accountable to its own citizens. This separation of the two spheres is one of the Constitution's structural protections of liberty. The power of the Federal Government would be augmented immeasurably if it were able to impress into its service—and at no cost to itself—the police officers of the 50 States.

The Constitution does not leave to speculation who is to administer the laws enacted by Congress; the President, it says, "shall take Care that the Laws be faithfully executed," personally and through officers whom he appoints (save for such inferior officers as Congress may authorize to be appointed by the "Courts of Law" or by "the Heads of Departments" who are themselves presidential appointees). The Brady Act effectively transfers this responsibility to thousands of CLEOs in the 50 States, who are left to implement the program without meaningful Presidential control (if indeed meaningful Presidential control is possible without the power to appoint and remove). The insistence of the Framers upon unity in the Federal Executive—to insure both vigor and accountability—is well known. That unity would be shattered, and the power of the President would be subject to reduction, if Congress could act as effectively without the President as with him, by simply requiring state officers to execute its laws.

The dissent of course resorts to the last, best hope of those who defend ultra vires congressional action, the Necessary and Proper Clause. What destroys the dissent's Necessary and Proper Clause argument, however, is not the Tenth

Amendment but the Necessary and Proper Clause itself. When a "Law for carry-ing into Execution" the Commerce Clause violates the principle of state sover-eignty reflected in the various constitutional provisions we mentioned earlier, it is not a "Law proper for carrying into Execution the Commerce Clause," and is thus, in the words of *The Federalist,* "merely an act of usurpation" which "deserves to be treated as such."

Federal commandeering of state governments is such a novel phenomenon that this Court's first experience with it did not occur until the 1970's, when the Environmental Protection Agency promulgated regulations requiring States to prescribe auto emissions testing, monitoring and retrofit programs, and to desig-nate preferential bus and carpool lanes. After we granted certiorari to review the statutory and constitutional validity of the regulations, the Government declined even to defend them, and instead rescinded some and conceded the invalidity of those that remained. In *Hodel v. Virginia Surface Mining & Reclamation Assn., Inc.,* 452 U.S. 264 (1981), and *FERC v. Mississippi,* 456 U.S. 742 (1982), we sustained statutes against constitutional challenge only after assuring ourselves that they did not require the States to enforce federal law.

At issue in *New York v. United States,* 505 U.S. 144 (1992), were the so-called "take title" provisions of the Low-Level Radioactive Waste Policy Amendments Act of 1985, which required States either to enact legislation providing for the dis-posal of radioactive waste generated within their borders, or to take title to, and possession of the waste—effectively requiring the States either to legislate pursu-ant to Congress's directions, or to implement an administrative solution. We con-cluded that Congress could constitutionally require the States to do neither. "The Federal Government," we held, "may not compel the States to enact or admin-ister a federal regulatory program." The Government contends that *New York* is distinguishable in that the background-check provision of the Brady Act does not require state legislative or executive officials to make policy, but instead issues a final directive to state CLEOs. The Government's distinction between "making" law and merely "enforcing" it, between "policymaking" and mere "implemen-tation," is an interesting one. It is surely reminiscent of the line that separates proper congressional conferral of Executive power from unconstitutional delega-tion of legislative authority for federal separation-of-powers purposes. This Court has not been notably successful in describing the latter line; indeed, some think we have abandoned the effort to do so. We are doubtful that the new line the Government proposes would be any more distinct.

Even assuming that the Brady Act leaves no "policymaking" discretion with the States, we fail to see how that improves rather than worsens the intrusion upon state sovereignty. Preservation of the States as independent and autonomous political entities is arguably less undermined by requiring them to make policy in certain fields than by "reducing them to puppets of a ventriloquist Congress." It is an essential attribute of the States' retained sovereignty that they remain independent and autonomous within their proper sphere of authority. It is no more compatible with this independence and autonomy that their officers be "dragooned" into administering federal law, than it would be compatible with the independence and autonomy of the United States that its officers be impressed into service for the execution of state laws.

The Government also maintains that requiring state officers to perform discrete, ministerial tasks specified by Congress does not violate the principle of *New York* because it does not diminish the accountability of state or federal officials. This argument fails even on its own terms. By forcing state governments to absorb the financial burden of implementing a federal regulatory program, Members of Congress can take credit for "solving" problems without having to ask their constituents to pay for the solutions with higher federal taxes. Even when the States are not forced to absorb the costs of implementing a federal program, they are still put in the position of taking the blame for its burdensomeness and for its defects. Under the present law, for example, it will be the CLEO and not some federal official who stands between the gun purchaser and immediate possession of his gun. And it will likely be the CLEO, not some federal official, who will be blamed for any error (even one in the designated federal database) that causes a purchaser to be mistakenly rejected.

The Brady Act, the dissent asserts, is different from the "take title" provisions invalidated in *New York* because the former is addressed to individuals — namely CLEOs — while the latter were directed to the State itself. "A suit against a state official in his or her official capacity is not a suit against the official but rather is a suit against the official's office. As such, it is no different from a suit against the State itself." And the same must be said of a directive to an official in his or her official capacity. To say that the Federal Government cannot control the State, but can control all of its officers, is to say nothing of significance.

We held in *New York* that Congress cannot compel the States to enact or enforce a federal regulatory program. Today we hold that Congress cannot circumvent that prohibition by conscripting the States' officers directly. The Federal Government may neither issue directives requiring the States to address particular problems, nor command the States' officers, or those of their political subdivisions, to administer or enforce a federal regulatory program. It matters not whether policymaking is involved, and no case-by-case weighing of the burdens or benefits is necessary; such commands are fundamentally incompatible with our constitutional system of dual sovereignty. Accordingly, the judgment of the Court of Appeals for the Ninth Circuit is reversed.

It is so ordered.

Justice O'CONNOR, *concurring.*

Our holding does not spell the end of the Brady Act. States and chief law enforcement officers may voluntarily continue to participate in the federal program. Congress is also free to amend the interim program to provide for its continuance on a contractual basis with the States if it wishes, as it does with a number of other federal programs.

Justice THOMAS, *concurring.*

The Brady Act violates the Tenth Amendment in that it compels state law enforcement officers to "administer or enforce a federal regulatory program."

Justice STEVENS, with whom Justice SOUTER, Justice GINSBURG, and Justice BREYER join, *dissenting.*

Article I, §8 supports the regulation of commerce in handguns effected by the Brady Act. The Necessary and Proper Clause is surely adequate to support the temporary enlistment of local police officers in the process of identifying persons who should not be entrusted with the possession of handguns. The Tenth Amendment imposes no restriction on the exercise of delegated powers. Historical materials strongly suggest that the Founders intended to enhance the capacity of the federal government by empowering it—as a part of the new authority to make demands directly on individual citizens—to act through local officials. For example, statutes of the early Congresses required in mandatory terms that state judges and their clerks perform various executive duties with respect to applications for citizenship.

The majority expresses special concern that were its rule not adopted the Federal Government would be able to avail itself of the services of state government officials "at no cost to itself." The majority's rule seems more likely to damage than to preserve the safeguards against tyranny provided by the existence of vital state governments. By limiting the ability of the Federal Government to enlist state officials in the implementation of its programs, the Court creates incentives for the National Government to aggrandize itself. In the name of State's rights, the majority would have the Federal Government create vast national bureaucracies to implement its policies. This is exactly the sort of thing that the early Federalists promised would not occur, in part as a result of the National Government's ability to rely on the magistracy of the states.

New York v. United States squarely approved of cooperative federalism programs, designed at the national level but implemented principally by state governments. This case merely involves the imposition of modest duties on individual officers. The Court seems to accept the fact that Congress could require private persons, such as hospital executives or school administrators, to provide arms merchants with relevant information about a prospective purchaser's fitness to own a weapon; indeed, the Court does not disturb the conclusion that the burden on police officers would be permissible if a similar burden were also imposed on private parties with access to relevant data. The provision of the Brady Act that crosses the Court's newly defined constitutional threshold is more comparable to a statute requiring local police officers to report the identity of missing children to the Crime Control Center of the Department of Justice than to an offensive federal command to a sovereign state. If Congress believes that such a statute will benefit the people of the Nation, and serve the interests of cooperative federalism better than an enlarged federal bureaucracy, we should respect both its policy judgment and its appraisal of its constitutional power.

Justice SOUTER, *dissenting.*

In *The Federalist,* Hamilton says that the state governmental machinery "will be incorporated" into the Nation's operation. Their auxiliary functions will be the products of their obligations thus undertaken to support federal law, not of their own, or the States', unfettered choices.

Justice BREYER, with whom Justice STEVENS joins, *dissenting.*

There is no need to read the Brady Act as permitting the Federal Government to overwhelm a state civil service. The statute uses the words "reasonable effort"—words that easily can encompass the considerations of, say, time or cost, necessary to avoid any such result.

Note: Commandeering State Legislatures

In *Murphy v. National Collegiate Athletic Association,* 138 S. Ct. 1461 (2018), Congress passed the Professional and Amateur Sports Protection Act (PASPA), which made it a crime for a State or any of its subdivisions "to sponsor, operate, advertise, promote, license, or authorize by law or compact a lottery, sweepstakes, or other betting, gambling, or wagering scheme based on" competitive sporting events. The law did not make sports gambling a federal crime. Litigation arose after New Jersey voters approved an amendment to the State Constitution making it lawful for the legislature to authorize sports gambling, and in 2012 the legislature enacted a law doing just that. The 2012 Act quickly came under attack. The 2014 Act declares that it is not to be interpreted as causing the State to authorize, license, sponsor, operate, advertise, or promote sports gambling. Instead, it repeals the provisions of state law prohibiting sports gambling insofar as they concerned the "placement and acceptance of wagers" on sporting events by persons 21 years of age or older at a horseracing track or a casino or gambling house in Atlantic City. The new law also specified that the repeal was effective only as to wagers on sporting events not involving a New Jersey college team or a collegiate event taking place in the State. The Court struck PASPA down to the extent that it commandeered and controlled state legislative action:

> The Constitution limited but did not abolish the sovereign powers of the States, which retained "a residuary and inviolable sovereignty." The Federalist No. 39, p. 245. (Rossiter ed.1961). The Constitution limits state sovereignty in several ways. Some grants of power to the Federal Government have been held to impose implicit restrictions on the States. And the Constitution indirectly restricts the States by granting certain legislative powers to Congress, see Art. I, §8, while providing in the Supremacy Clause that federal law is the "supreme Law of the Land . . . ," Art. VI, cl. 2. The legislative powers granted to Congress are sizable, but they are not unlimited. The Constitution confers on Congress not plenary legislative power but only certain enumerated powers. All other legislative power is reserved for the States as the Tenth Amendment confirms. Conspicuously absent from the list of powers given to Congress is the power to issue direct orders to the governments of the States. The anticommandeering doctrine represents the recognition of this limit on congressional authority.

The PASPA provision at issue—prohibiting state authorization of sports gambling—violates the anticommandeering rule. That provision unequivocally dictates what a state legislature may and may not do. State legislatures are put under the direct control of Congress. It is as if federal officers were installed in state legislative chambers and were armed with the authority to stop legislators from voting on any offending proposals. A more direct affront to state sovereignty is not easy to imagine. Respondents and the United States defend the anti-authorization prohibition on the ground that it constitutes a valid preemption provision. It is clear that the PASPA provision prohibiting state authorization of sports gambling is not a preemption provision. It does not confer any federal rights on private actors interested in conducting sports gambling operations. Nor does it impose any federal restrictions on private actors. There is simply no way to understand the provision other than a direct command to the States. And that is exactly what the anticommandeering rule does not allow. Just as Congress lacks the power to order a state legislature not to enact a law authorizing sports gambling, it may not order a state legislature to refrain from enacting a law licensing sports gambling.

∼ PROBLEM: SCHOOL SAFETY AGENTS ∼

Suppose the President signs an Executive Order encouraging all states to "train and employ a person at every public school with a gun or similar weapon to provide safety as a surrogate law enforcement agent during and throughout the school day." Would such an Order be constitutional?

E. THE FEDERAL-STATE RELATIONSHIP IN THE AREA OF VOTING RIGHTS

In *Shelby County v. Holder,* 570 U.S. 529 (2013), the Court found Section 4 (b) of the Voting Rights Act unconstitutional. The Court held that the Act's coverage formula, which determined which jurisdictions would be required to preclear any changes in voting procedures with the Attorney General or D.C. District Court, was based on vastly outdated information. Writing for the majority, Chief Justice John Roberts Jr. found that, "It would have been irrational for Congress to distinguish between States in such a fundamental way based on 40-year-old data, when today's statistics tell an entirely different story." The Court left it to Congress to draft another formula, while leaving the actual preclearance requirement in Section 5 intact—although it will be without operative power until Congress revises Section 4's coverage formula. A core component of *Shelby County, Alabama* involved federalism. The case served to further delineate the long and winding dividing line between the federal and state governments on voting rights.

Shelby County v. Holder

570 U.S. 529 (2013)

Chief Justice ROBERTS delivered the opinion of the Court.

The Voting Rights Act of 1965 employed extraordinary measures to address an extraordinary problem. Section 5 of the Act required States to obtain federal permission before enacting any law related to voting—a drastic departure from basic principles of federalism. And §4 of the Act applied that requirement only to some States—an equally dramatic departure from the principle that all States enjoy equal sovereignty. This was strong medicine, but Congress determined it was needed to address entrenched racial discrimination in voting, "an insidious and pervasive evil which had been perpetuated in certain parts of our country through unremitting and ingenious defiance of the Constitution." *South Carolina v. Katzenbach*, 383 U.S. 301, 309 (1966). As we explained in upholding the law, "exceptional conditions can justify legislative measures not otherwise appropriate." Reflecting the unprecedented nature of these measures, they were scheduled to expire after five years. *See* Voting Rights Act of 1965, §4(a), 79 Stat. 438.

Nearly 50 years later, they are still in effect; indeed, they have been made more stringent, and are now scheduled to last until 2031. There is no denying, however, that the conditions that originally justified these measures no longer characterize voting in the covered jurisdictions. By 2009, "the racial gap in voter registration and turnout was lower in the States originally covered by §5 than it was nationwide." *Northwest Austin Municipal Util. Dist. No. One v. Holder*, 557 U.S. 193, 203–204 (2009). Since that time, Census Bureau data indicate that African American voter turnout has come to exceed white voter turnout in five of the six States originally covered by §5, with a gap in the sixth State of less than one half of one percent. *See* Dept. of Commerce, Census Bureau, Reported Voting and Registration, by Sex, Race and Hispanic Origin, for States (Nov. 2012) (Table 4b).

At the same time, voting discrimination still exists; no one doubts that. The question is whether the Act's extraordinary measures, including its disparate treatment of the States, continue to satisfy constitutional requirements. As we put it a short time ago, "the Act imposes current burdens and must be justified by current needs." *Northwest Austin*, 557 U.S., at 203. In *Northwest Austin*, we stated that "the Act imposes current burdens and must be justified by current needs." And we concluded that "a departure from the fundamental principle of equal sovereignty requires a showing that a statute's disparate geographic coverage is sufficiently related to the problem that it targets." These basic principles guide our review of the question before us.

The Constitution and laws of the United States are "the supreme Law of the Land." U.S. CONST., Art. VI, cl. 2. State legislation may not contravene federal law. The Federal Government does not, however, have a general right to review and veto state enactments before they go into effect. A proposal to grant such authority to "negative" state laws was considered at the Constitutional Convention, but rejected in favor of allowing state laws to take effect, subject to later challenge under the Supremacy Clause. *See* 1 Records of the Federal Convention of 1787, pp. 21, 164 (M. Farrand ed. 1911).

Outside the strictures of the Supremacy Clause, States retain broad autonomy in structuring their governments and pursuing legislative objectives. Indeed, the Constitution provides that all powers not specifically granted to the Federal Government are reserved to the States or citizens. Amdt. 10. This "allocation of powers in our federal system preserves the integrity, dignity, and residual sovereignty of the States." *Bond v. United States*, (2011) (slip op., at 9). But the federal balance "is not just an end in itself: Rather, federalism secures to citizens the liberties that derive from the diffusion of sovereign power." *Ibid.* More specifically, "the Framers of the Constitution intended the States to keep for themselves, as provided in the Tenth Amendment, the power to regulate elections." *Gregory v. Ashcroft*, 501 U.S. 452, 461 (1991). Drawing lines for congressional districts is likewise "primarily the duty and responsibility of the State." *Perry v. Perez*, 565 U.S. ___ (2012) (per curiam). Not only do States retain sovereignty under the Constitution, there is also a "fundamental principle of equal sovereignty" among the States. *Northwest Austin, supra*, at 203. Over a hundred years ago, this Court explained that our Nation "was and is a union of States, equal in power, dignity and authority." *Coyle v. Smith*, 221 U.S. 559, 567 (1911).

The Voting Rights Act sharply departs from these basic principles. It suspends "all changes to state election law— however innocuous—until they have been precleared by federal authorities in Washington, D.C." States must beseech the Federal Government for permission to implement laws that they would otherwise have the right to enact and execute on their own, subject of course to any injunction in a §2 action. The Attorney General has 60 days to object to a preclearance request, longer if he requests more information. If a State seeks preclearance from a three-judge court, the process can take years.

And despite the tradition of equal sovereignty, the Act applies to only nine States (and several additional counties). While one State waits months or years and expends funds to implement a validly enacted law, its neighbor can typically put the same law into effect immediately, through the normal legislative process. Even if a noncovered jurisdiction is sued, there are important differences between those proceedings and preclearance proceedings; the preclearance proceeding "not only switches the burden of proof to the supplicant jurisdiction, but also applies substantive standards quite different from those governing the rest of the nation."

All this explains why, when we first upheld the Act in 1966, we described it as "stringent" and "potent." *Katzenbach*, 383 U.S., at 308. We recognized that it "may have been an uncommon exercise of congressional power," but concluded that "legislative measures not otherwise appropriate" could be justified by "exceptional conditions." In 1966, we found these departures from the basic features of our system of government justified. The "blight of racial discrimination in voting" had "infected the electoral process in parts of our country for nearly a century." Several States had enacted a variety of requirements and tests "specifically designed to prevent" African Americans from voting. Case-by-case litigation had proved inadequate to prevent such racial discrimination, in part because States "merely switched to discriminatory devices not covered by the federal decrees," "enacted difficult new tests," or simply "defied and evaded court orders." Shortly before enactment of the Voting Rights Act, only 19.4 percent of African Americans of voting age were registered to vote in Alabama, only 31.8 percent in Louisiana, and only 6.4 percent in Mississippi. Those figures were roughly 50 percentage points or more below the figures for whites. In short, we concluded that "under the compulsion of these unique circumstances, Congress responded in a permissibly decisive manner." We also noted then and have emphasized since that this extraordinary legislation was intended to be temporary, set to expire after five years. At the time, the coverage formula—the means of linking the exercise of the unprecedented authority with the problem that warranted it made sense. "Congress chose to limit its attention to the geographic areas where immediate action seemed necessary." *Katzenbach*, 383 U.S., at 328. The areas where Congress found "evidence of actual voting discrimination" shared two characteristics: "the use of tests and devices for voter registration, and a voting rate in the 1964 presidential election at least 12 points below the national average."

Nearly 50 years later, things have changed dramatically. Shelby County contends that the preclearance requirement, even without regard to its disparate coverage, is now unconstitutional. Its arguments have a good deal of force. In the covered jurisdictions, "voter turnout and registration rates now approach parity. Blatantly discriminatory evasions of federal decrees are rare. And minority candidates hold office at unprecedented levels." *Northwest Austin*, 557 U.S., at 202. The tests and devices that blocked access to the ballot have been forbidden nationwide for over 40 years. See §6, 84 Stat. 315; §102, 89 Stat. 400. Those conclusions are not ours alone. Congress said the same when it reauthorized the Act in 2006, writing that "significant progress has been made in eliminating first generation barriers experienced by minority voters, including increased numbers of registered minority voters, minority voter turnout, and minority representation in Congress, State legislatures, and local elected offices."

More specifically, "the Framers of the Constitution intended the States to keep for themselves, as provided in the Tenth Amendment, the power to regulate elections." *Gregory v. Ashcroft*, 501 U.S. 452, 461 (1991). Of course, the Federal Government retains significant control over federal elections. For instance, the Constitution authorizes Congress to establish the time and manner for electing Senators and Representatives. But States have "broad powers to determine the conditions under which the right of suffrage may be exercised." *Carrington v. Rash*, 380 U.S. 89, 91 (1965). And "each State has the power to prescribe the qualifications of its officers and the manner in which they shall be chosen." *Boyd v. Nebraska ex rel. Thayer*, 143 U.S. 135, 161 (1892). Drawing lines for congressional districts is likewise "primarily the duty and responsibility of the State." *Perry v. Perez*, 565 U.S. ___, ___ (2012) (per curiam). Not only do States retain sovereignty under the Constitution, there is also a "fundamental principle of equal sovereignty" among the States. *Northwest Austin, supra*, at 203. Over a hundred years ago, this Court explained that our Nation "was and is a union of States, equal in power, dignity and authority." *Coyle v. Smith*, 221 U.S. 559, 567 (1911).

The Voting Rights Act sharply departs from these basic principles. It suspends "all changes to state election law—however innocuous—until they have been precleared by federal authorities in Washington, D.C." States must beseech the Federal Government for permission to implement laws that they would otherwise have the right to enact and execute on their own, subject of course to any injunction in a §2 action. The Attorney General has 60 days to object to a preclearance request, longer if he requests more information. See 28 CFR §§51.9, 51.37. If a State seeks preclearance from a three-judge court, the process can take years. And despite the tradition of equal sovereignty, the Act applies to only nine States (and several additional counties). While one State waits months or years and expends funds to implement a validly enacted law, its neighbor can typically put the same law into effect immediately, through the normal legislative process.

Striking down an Act of Congress "is the gravest and most delicate duty that this Court is called on to perform." *Blodgett v. Holden*, 275 U.S. 142, 148 (1927) (Holmes, J., concurring). We do not do so lightly. That is why, in 2009, we took care to avoid ruling on the constitutionality of the Voting Rights Act when asked to do so, and instead resolved the case then before us on statutory grounds. But in issuing that decision, we expressed our broader concerns about the constitutionality of the Act. Congress could have updated the coverage formula at that time, but did not do so. Its failure to act leaves us today with no choice but to declare §4(b) unconstitutional. The formula in that section can no longer be used as a basis for subjecting jurisdictions to preclearance.

Our decision in no way affects the permanent, nationwide ban on racial discrimination in voting found in §2. We issue no holding on §5 itself, only on the coverage formula. Congress may draft another formula based on current conditions. Such a formula is an initial prerequisite to a determination that exceptional conditions still exist justifying such an "extraordinary departure from the traditional course of relations between the States and the Federal Government." *Presley*, 502 U.S., at 500–501. Our country has changed, and while any racial discrimination in voting is too much, Congress must ensure that the legislation it passes to remedy that problem speaks to current conditions.

The judgment of the Court of Appeals is reversed.

It is so ordered.

F. OTHER FEDERALISM ISSUES

1. *The Federal Marijuana Policy*

The Obama administration walked a fine line of nonenforcement of its policy about marijuana as an illegal drug. It did so as more states de-criminalized marijuana, particularly when it is used for a medicinal purpose, and some legalized it, such as Colorado and Oregon. As one journalist noted, "Beginning in 2009, the Obama Justice Department advised selected U.S. Attorneys that while the prosecution of significant traffickers of illegal drugs would remain a priority, federal resources should not be focused on individuals who were in 'unambiguous compliance with existing state laws' and not involved in large-scale industrial marijuana cultivation centers." *See* Arlane de Vogue, "Obama Admin Weighs in on Legalized Marijuana at the Supreme Court," CNN On-Line (December 16, 2015). *http://www.cnn.com/2015/12/16/politics/supreme-court-marijuana-colorado-obama/.*

2. The Sovereignty of Puerto Rico

In the following case, the Court was presented with the question of whether Puerto Rico could charge a defendant with the same crime that the defendant had been charged with in federal court. Defendant was first charged with the illegal trafficking of weapons and ammunition in federal court and then, on essentially the same facts, with violating the Puerto Rico Weapons Act. The larger issue was whether Puerto Rico had any independent self-governing authority indicating it possessed a greater sovereignty than a territory. In Justice Kagan's opinion, the Court's answer to both the large and small questions was no.

Commonwealth of Puerto Rico v. Sanchez Valle et al.

136 S. Ct. 1863 (2016)

KAGAN, J.

The Double Jeopardy Clause of the Fifth Amendment prohibits more than one prosecution for the "same offence." But under what is known as the dual-sovereignty doctrine, a single act gives rise to distinct offenses—and thus may subject a person to successive prosecutions—if it violates the laws of separate sovereigns. To determine whether two prosecuting authorities are different sovereigns for double jeopardy purposes, this Court asks a narrow, historically focused question. The inquiry does not turn, as the term "sovereignty" sometimes suggests, on the degree to which the second entity is autonomous from the first or sets its own political course. Rather, the issue is only whether the prosecutorial powers of the two jurisdictions have independent origins—or, said conversely, whether those powers derive from the same "ultimate source." *United States* v. *Wheeler*, 435 U.S. 313, 320 (1978). In this case, we must decide if, under that test, Puerto Rico and the United States may successively prosecute a single defendant for the same criminal conduct. We hold they may not, because the oldest roots of Puerto Rico's power to prosecute lie in federal soil.

Puerto Rico became a territory of the United States in 1898, as a result of the Spanish-American War. The treaty concluding that conflict ceded the island, then a Spanish colony, to the United States, and tasked Congress with determining "the civil rights and political status" of its inhabitants. Treaty of Paris, Art.

9, Dec. 10, 1898, 30 Stat. 1759. In the ensuing hundred-plus years, the United States and Puerto Rico have forged a unique political relationship, built on the island's evolution into a constitutional democracy exercising local self-rule. The Puerto Rico Constitution created a new political entity, the Commonwealth of Puerto Rico—or, in Spanish, Estado Libre Asociado de Puerto Rico. See P. R. Const., Art. I, §1. Like the U.S. Constitution, it divides political power into three branches—the "legislative, judicial and executive." Art. I, §2. And again resonant of American founding principles, the Puerto Rico Constitution describes that tri-partite government as "republican in form" and "subordinate to the sovereignty of the people of Puerto Rico." The Commonwealth's power, the Constitution proclaims, "emanates from the people and shall be exercised in accordance with their will, within the terms of the compact agreed upon between the people of Puerto Rico and the United States." Art. I, §1.

This case involves the dual-sovereignty carve-out from the Double Jeopardy Clause. The ordinary rule under that Clause is that a person cannot be prose-cuted twice for the same offense. See U.S. Const., Amdt. 5 ("nor shall any person be subject for the same offence to be twice put in jeopardy of life or limb"). But two prosecutions, this Court has long held, are not for the same offense if brought by different sovereigns—even when those actions target the iden-tical criminal conduct through equivalent criminal laws. See, *e.g., United States v. Lanza,* 260 U.S. 377, 382 (1922). As we have put the point: "When the same act transgresses the laws of two sovereigns, it cannot be truly averred that the offender has been twice punished for the same offence; but only that by one act he has committed two offences." *Heath v. Alabama,* 474 U.S. 82, 88 (1985). The Double Jeopardy Clause thus drops out of the picture when the "entities that seek successively to prosecute a defendant for the same course of conduct are separate sovereigns." *Ibid.*

Truth be told, however, "sovereignty" in this context does not bear its ordinary meaning. For whatever reason, the test we have devised to decide whether two governments are distinct for double jeopardy purposes overtly disregards com-mon indicia of sovereignty. Under that standard, we do not examine the "extent of control" that "one prosecuting authority wields over the other." *Wheeler,* 435 U.S., at 320. The degree to which an entity exercises self-governance—whether autonomously managing its own affairs or continually submitting to outside direction—plays no role in the analysis. See *Shell Co.,* 302 U.S., at 261. Nor do we care about a government's more particular ability to enact and enforce its own criminal laws.

Rather, as Puerto Rico itself acknowledges, our test hinges on a single criterion: the "ultimate source" of the power undergirding the respective pros-ecutions. *Wheeler,* 435 U.S., at 320. Whether two prosecuting entities are dual sovereigns in the double jeopardy context, we have stated, depends on "whether they draw their authority to punish the offender from distinct sources of power." *Heath,* 474 U.S., at 88. The inquiry is thus historical, not functional—looking at the deepest wellsprings, not the current exercise, of prosecutorial authority. If two entities derive their power to punish from wholly independent sources (imagine here a pair of parallel lines), then they may bring successive prosecutions.

Under that approach, the States are separate sovereigns from the Federal Government (and from one another). See *Abbate v. United States*, 359 U.S. 187, 195 (1959). The States' "powers to undertake criminal prosecutions," we have explained, do not "derive from the Federal Government." *Id.*, at 89. Instead, the States rely on "authority originally belonging to them before admission to the Union and preserved to them by the Tenth Amendment;" see U.S. Const., Amdt. 10 ("The powers not delegated to the United States by the Constitution are reserved to the States"); *Blatchford v. Native Village of Noatak*, 501 U.S. 775, 779 (1991) (noting that the States "entered the Union with their sovereignty intact"). Said otherwise: Prior to forming the Union, the States possessed "separate and independent sources of power and authority," which they continue to draw upon in enacting and enforcing criminal laws. *Heath*, 474 U.S., at 89. State prosecutions therefore have their most ancient roots in an "inherent sovereignty" unconnected to, and indeed pre-existing, the U.S. Congress. *Ibid.* For similar reasons, Indian tribes also count as separate sovereigns under the Double Jeopardy Clause. Originally, this Court has noted, "the tribes were self-governing sovereign political communities," possessing (among other capacities) the "inherent power to prescribe laws for their members and to punish infractions of those laws." And most pertinent here, this Court concluded in the early decades of the last century that U.S. territories—including an earlier incarnation of Puerto Rico itself—are not sovereigns distinct from the United States.

On this settled approach, Puerto Rico cannot benefit from our dual-sovereignty doctrine. For starters, no one argues that when the United States gained possession of Puerto Rico, its people possessed independent prosecutorial power, in the way that the States or tribes did upon becoming part of this country. Puerto Rico was until then a colony "under Spanish sovereignty." Treaty of Paris, Art. 2, 30 Stat. 1755. And local prosecutors in the ensuing decades, as petitioner itself acknowledges, exercised only such power as was "delegated by Congress" through federal statutes. Their authority derived from, rather than pre-existed association with, the Federal Government.

Puerto Rico boasts "a relationship to the United States that has no parallel in our history." *Examining Bd.*, 426 U.S., at 596. And since the evens of the early 1950's, an integral aspect of that association has been the Commonwealth's wide-ranging self-rule, exercised under its own Constitution. As a result of that charter, Puerto Rico today can avail itself of a wide variety of futures. But for purposes of the Double Jeopardy Clause, the future is not what matters—and there is no getting away from the past. Because the ultimate source of Puerto Rico's prosecutorial power is the Federal Government—because when we trace that authority all the way back, we arrive at the doorstep of the U.S. Capitol—the Commonwealth and the United States are not separate sovereigns. That means the two governments cannot "twice put" respondents Sánchez Valle and Gómez Vázquez "in jeopardy" for the "same offence." U.S. Const., Amdt. 5. We accordingly *affirm* the judgment of the Supreme Court of Puerto Rico.

It is so ordered.

3. Sex Offenders' Registration

In *United States v. Felts*, 674 F.3d 599 (6th Cir. 2012), the Sixth Circuit considered whether a person could be convicted for failing to register under the federal Sex Offender Registration Notification Act (SORNA) in a state that had not yet fully adopted all of the requirements of the federal Act. Several aspects of federalism were considered in the case, including whether the federal government was commandeering state resources through the dictates of SORNA.

In this case, David Wayne Felts was convicted for failing to register as a sex offender under SORNA in Tennessee, a state that had not yet fully implemented the Act. Felts did not register as a sex offender despite a prior child rape conviction. Felts claimed that his conviction under SORNA for failing to register violated the Constitution, including a claim based on the Tenth Amendment. The Tenth Amendment claim was rebuffed by the Circuit Court, which upheld the conviction. Judge Boggs stated:

> Congress passed the Sex Offender Registration and Notification Act (SORNA),42 U.S.C. Section 16901 et seq., on July 27, 2006 for the purpose of "creating a national system for the registration of sex offenders." Rather than establishing a federal agency to implement SORNA, Congress, through its spending power, U.S. Const. Art. I, §8, directed all states and the District of Columbia to create local registries that comply with specific national standards. 42 U.S.C. Sections 16911(10), 16912(a).
>
> SORNA imposes an obligation on a sex offender to "register, and keep the registration current, in each jurisdiction where the offender resides, where the offender is an employee, and where the offender is a student." 42 U.S.C. Section 16913(a). Pursuant to SORNA, a sex offender is also required, "not later than 3 business days after each change of name, residence, employment, or student status, to appear in person" to update his or her registration information. 42 U.S.C. Section 16913(c). 18 U.S.C. Section 2250(a) mandates that whoever "is required to register under the Sex Offender Registration and Notification Act," is a "sex offender," and if he "knowingly fails to register or update a registration as required by the Sex Offender Registration and Notification Act," he "shall be fined under this title or imprisoned not more than 10 years, or both."
>
> The original deadline for states to implement SORNA was July 27, 2009. ("Each jurisdiction shall implement this title before the later of 3 years after the date of the enactment of this Act enacted July 27, 2006"). Currently, 15 states have "substantially implemented SORNA's requirements": Alabama, Delaware, Florida, Kansas, Louisiana, Maryland, Michigan, Mississippi, Missouri, Nevada, Ohio, South Carolina, South Dakota, Wyoming, and most saliently, *Tennessee*. U.S. Dep't of Justice, SMART Office "Newsroom," http://www.ojp.usdoj.gov/smart/newsroom.htm (last visited Mar. 8, 2012). As of the date of Felts's federal conviction for failure to register, however, Tennessee had not yet substantially implemented SORNA. *Appellant Br.* at 13 ("Though Tennessee's own sex registration form includes notification of the federal duty to register and alerts registrants to possible federal criminal penalties of 'up to 10 years imprisonment,' Tennessee has not yet taken the additional steps required to achieve substantial implementation.").

This appeal presents a case of first impression for this circuit—if Tennessee failed to implement SORNA, does Felts's failure to register in Tennessee's registry constitute a failure to register as required by SORNA?

The answer to that question—based on case law from all other circuits that have looked at this issue—is yes. The duty to register in a state registry is independent of a state's degree of implementation of SORNA.

The Court went on to analyze the workings of the federalism doctrine. The Court observed that even if states did not fully adopt the particular components of the federal law, potential registrants were not then free from federal compliance requirements. Instead, the federal law directed individuals to register under existing state laws:

Every state and the District of Columbia had a sex offender registration law prior to 2006. An individual may therefore comply with SORNA's registration requirements by registering through the state's sex offender registry, even if that jurisdiction has not implemented SORNA's administrative procedures.). "We conclude that the requirement imposed on individuals to register is independent of the requirement imposed on the States to implement the enhanced registration and notification standards of SORNA. Accordingly, SORNA's requirement that a sex offender register applies whether registration would be accomplished through preSORNA registration facilities or under SORNA-compliant programs."); *United States v. Hinckley*, 550 F.3d 926, 939 (10th Cir. 2008), *abrogated on other grounds by Reynolds v. United States*, ___U.S. ___ (2012) (finding that defendant had "knowledge of his duty to register under similar state and federal provisions"). Felts cites no contrary precedents.

Felts argues that "SORNA appears to require that persons register under its provisions only when States actually implement SORNA's regulatory scheme." From the context, it appears that by "actually implement," Felts means that a state "fully implements" SORNA. This cannot be correct, as at the time of SORNA's enactment in 2006, no state's registry was in compliance with SORNA. For Felts's argument to be true, Congress—which provided the states with three years to comply without penalty—would have effectively rendered SORNA nugatory in any non-compliant state until 2009.

Or, if a state chooses not to comply with SORNA—its sovereign prerogative, so long as it is willing to forego federal funding—a resident-sex offender would never have to register under federal law. *See Shenandoah*, 595 F.3d at 157. ("New York and Pennsylvania may never implement SORNA, choosing, for whatever reason, to forego a portion of their federal funding. This failure to implement a federal law, however, does not give sex offenders a reason to disregard their federal obligation to update their state registrations.")

The Court described one situation where a failure to utilize state registration requirements might not serve as the basis for a violation of SORNA:

The precedents from other circuits largely fail to address circumstances where an inconsistency between federal and non-complying state regimes would render it impractical, or even impossible, for an offender to register under federal law. The other courts that have addressed this issue have seemed to assume that the federal and state requirements in non-compliant jurisdictions are identical, or perhaps simply similar enough. This may not always be the case.

However, we need not reach this argument with respect to due process, as Felts's own conduct renders this defense unavailable. Under any *conceivable* definition of the word "register," Felts did not register.

The Respondent also claimed that SORNA violated the Tenth Amendment in that it commandeered the states to participate in the registration regime. The Court rejected this argument as well:

> Finally, Felts raises a commandeering argument—that is, that the enforcement of SORNA violates the Tenth Amendment because it "forces Tennessee officials to register sex offenders in compliance with SORNA's onerous requirements before the State of Tennessee has an opportunity to voluntarily comply with SORNA." The Tenth Amendment provides that "the powers not delegated to the United States by the Constitution, nor prohibited by it·to the States, are reserved to the States respectively, or to the people." U.S. Const. Amend X. Under the Tenth Amendment, federal officers are prohibited from conscripting, or commandeering, state officials to administer and enforce a federal regulatory program. *Printz v. United States*, 521 U.S. 898 (1997). Relying on *Printz*, Felts contends that Congress cannot "compel State officers to procure and accept registrations for a federally mandated sex offender program that the State has not voluntarily implemented."
>
> Nonetheless, Felts's constitutional claim fails. Under *Printz*, the "Federal Government may neither issue directives requiring the States to address particular problems, nor command the States' officers, or those of their political subdivisions, to administer or enforce a federal regulatory program." *Printz* at 935. However, SORNA does not fall under the rubric of *Printz*, but rather relies on Congress's spending power. Failure to implement SORNA results in a loss of 10% of federal funding under the Omnibus Crime Control and Safe Streets Act of 1968. Conditioning of funds in this manner is appropriate under *South Dakota v. Dole. See* 483 U.S. 203, 206 (1987) (stating that Congress's power to condition the receipt of federal funds under the spending power is valid so long as (1) the spending/withholding is in the pursuit of "the general welfare"; (2) the conditional nature is clear and unambiguous; (3) the condition is rationally related to the purpose of the federal interest, program, or funding; and (4) the conduct required to comply with the condition is not barred by the constitution itself).
>
> Unlike the situation with the Brady Handgun Violence Prevention Act in *Printz*, Congress through SORNA has not commandeered Tennessee, nor compelled the state to comply with its requirements. Congress has simply placed conditions on the receipt of federal funds. A state is free to keep its existing sex-offender registry system in place (and risk losing funding) or adhere to SORNA's requirements (and maintain funding). Since Felts's conviction, Tennessee has come into substantial compliance with SORNA. The choice is that of the state.
>
> SORNA does not violate the rights of Tennessee, or those of Felts as an individual, under the Tenth Amendment of the Constitution.

The judgment of the district court is *affirmed.*

4. Federal and State Prosecutions for the Same Conduct

In *Gamble v. United States*, 139 S. Ct. 1960 (2019), the Court considered whether to upend the well-established rule that because the federal and state governments are two different sovereigns, the Double Jeopardy Clause does not apply to successive prosecutions in state and federal courts for the same conduct. The Court decided to retain the established rule: "The language of the Clause protects individuals from being twice put in jeopardy 'for the same *offence,*' not for the same *conduct* or *actions*," *Grady v. Corbin*, 495 U.S. 508, 529 (1990), as Justice Scalia wrote in a soon-vindicated dissent. And the term "'offence' was commonly understood in 1791 to mean 'transgression,' that is, 'the Violation or Breaking of a Law.'" *Grady*, 495 U. S., at 529 (Scalia, J., dissenting). As originally understood, an "offence" is defined by a law, and each law is defined by a sovereign. So where there are two sovereigns, there are two laws, and two "offences." See *Grady*, 495 U. S., at 529 (Scalia, J., dissenting).

∼ PROBLEMS ∼

1. *Mandatory Continuing Teacher Education.* In considering whether to vote for the Education for a Better America Act, a Senator states, "I will vote for it only with this addition: 'States must provide a minimum of 12 hours of teaching training for the improvement of pedagogy, methodology, and student learning every year for all teachers.'" Would such an addition be constitutional under *Printz*?

2. *Civics.* Congresswoman St. James and others in Congress have become worried that the focus on math and science diminishes the attention paid to other subjects in American schools, particularly civics. She proposes a law requiring all public schools to teach a progression of three civics courses through sixth, seventh, and eighth grades. Would this law be constitutional under *Printz*?

3. *Driver's Privacy Protection Act.* The Driver's Privacy Protection Act of 1994 (DPPA) limits the ability of state departments of motor vehicles (DMVs) to disclose or resell personal information. The law was passed because state DMVs typically require drivers and automobile owners to provide personal information, including name, address, telephone number, vehicle description, Social Security number, medical information, and a photograph, as a condition of obtaining a driver's license or registering an automobile. Historically, many states have sold this personal information to individuals and businesses. Under the DPPA, the states may not disclose a driver's personal information without the driver's consent. The DPPA imposes civil and criminal penalties for violations. Contrary to the DPPA, Kentucky law provides that information contained in the state's DMV records is available to any person or entity that fills out a form listing the requester's name and address and stating that the information will not be used for telephone solicitation. State law allows the Kentucky DMV to charge a fee for releasing personal information, and it allows drivers to prohibit disclosure of their personal information by filling out a form. Does the DPPA violate the Tenth Amendment to the U.S. Constitution? In evaluating the constitutionality of the Act, which of the following arguments do you find more persuasive:

   a. The personal, identifying information that the DPPA regulates is an item of interstate commerce, and the sale or release of that information in interstate commerce is therefore a proper subject of congressional regulation;

b.   The DPPA violates the Tenth Amendment because it "thrusts upon the states all of the day-to-day responsibility for administering its complex provisions," and thereby makes "state officials the unwilling implementers of federal policy";

c.   The DPPA requires the state's employees to learn and apply the Act's substantive restrictions, and consumes the employees' time and thus the state's resources;

d.   The DPPA does not require the states in their sovereign capacity to regulate their own citizens; or

e.   The DPPA does not require the Kentucky legislature to enact any laws or regulations, and it does not require state officials to assist in the enforcement of federal statutes regulating private individuals, but simply regulates Kentucky's DMV.

See Reno v. Condon, 528 U.S. 141 (2000).

∿ REVIEW PROBLEMS ∿

1. *King of the World.* After *Garcia*, one member of Congress text messaged another: "Armed with the Commerce Clause, we are now unstoppable!" How would you reply? How does *United States v. Lopez*, 514 U.S. 549 (1995), a Commerce Clause decision, affect the Court's view of intergovernmental immunity issues?

2. *Prison or Jail—Take Your Pick.* Congress directs states to hold prisoners in jails, which usually hold persons awaiting trial, for no more than one year, unless documented "extraordinary circumstances" exist. Is this law constitutional?

3. *Tax Equity and Fiscal Responsibility Act.* In the past several years, Congress has become increasingly concerned about noncompliance with federal tax laws. Unreported income has grown from $31.1 billion in 1973 to $97 billion in 1981, and unregistered bonds were a factor in unreported income. Bonds can be issued as either registered bonds or bearer bonds; the two types of bonds differ in the way ownership and payments are made. Registered bonds are recorded on a central list, and a transfer of record ownership gets a notation on the list. The record owner is automatically sent interest payments. A bearer bond's ownership is presumed from possession, and transfer is made by physically delivering the bond. The bond owner presents the bond coupons to a bank, which presents the coupons to the issuer's paying agent. To address this problem, Congress passed Section 310(b)(1) of the Tax Equity and Fiscal Responsibility Act of 1982 (TEFRA), which denied federal tax-exempt status to interest earned on publicly offered long-term bonds issued by state and local governments unless they are issued in registered form. Kentucky challenges Section 310. Which of the following arguments for and against the law are the most persuasive regarding its constitutionality? a) Section 310 forces states to increase the interest paid on state bonds by 28 to 35 percent; b) Even though almost all state bonds were

issued in bearer form before Section 310 became effective, since then no state has issued a bearer bond; c) Because of its practical effects, for purposes of the Tenth Amendment, we must treat Section 310 as if it simply banned bearer bonds altogether without giving states the option to issue nonexempt bearer bonds; d) A blanket prohibition by Congress on the issuance of bearer bonds can apply to states without violating the Tenth Amendment; e) Kentucky has not alleged that it was deprived of any right to participate in the national political process or that it was singled out in a way that left it politically isolated and powerless; f) The political process failed here because Section 310(b)(1) was "imposed by the vote of an uninformed Congress relying upon incomplete information"; g) Section 310 is invalid because it commandeers the state legislative and administrative process by coercing states into enacting legislation authorizing bond registration and into administering the registration scheme; h) Section 310 does not abolish the tax exemption for state bond interest entirely but rather taxes the interest on state bonds only if the bonds are not issued in the form Congress requires. Should the law be upheld? *See South Carolina v. Baker*, 485 U.S. 505 (1988).

[Points to Remember for Chapter 4 is contained in online file.]

5

State Power to Regulate Commerce

U.S. CONSTITUTION, ARTICLE I

Section 8, Clause 3. The Congress shall have Power To regulate Commerce with foreign Nations, and among the several States, and with the Indian Tribes;

Section 10. No State shall enter into any Treaty, Alliance, or Confederation; grant Letters of Marque and Reprisal; coin Money; emit Bills of Credit; make any Thing but gold and silver Coin a Tender in Payment of Debts; pass any Bill of Attainder, ex post facto Law, or Law impairing the Obligation of Contracts, or grant any Title of Nobility.

No State shall, without the Consent of the Congress, lay any Imposts or Duties on Imports or Exports, except what may be absolutely necessary for executing its inspection Laws; and the net Produce of all Duties and Imposts, laid by any State on Imports or Exports, shall be for the Use of the Treasury of the United States; and all such Laws shall be subject to the Revision and Control of the Congress.

No State shall, without the Consent of Congress, lay any Duty of Tonnage, keep Troops, or Ships of War in time of Peace, enter into any Agreement or Compact with another State, or with a foreign Power, or engage in War, unless actually invaded, or in such imminent Danger as will not admit of delay.

U.S. CONSTITUTION, ARTICLE VI

Clause 3. This Constitution, and the laws of the United States which shall be made in Pursuance thereof; and all Treaties made, or which shall be made, under the Authority of the United States, shall be the supreme Law of the Land; and the Judges in every State shall be bound thereby, any Thing in the Constitution or Laws of any State to the contrary notwithstanding.

U.S. CONSTITUTION, ARTICLE IV

Section 2. The Citizens of each State shall be entitled to all Privileges and Immunities of Citizens in the several States.

U.S. CONSTITUTION, TENTH AMENDMENT

The powers not delegated to the United States by the Constitution, nor prohibited to it by the States, are reserved to the States respectively, or the people.

[Roadmap for Chapter 5 is contained in online file.]

∾ PROBLEM: KENTUCKY'S PROHIBITION AGAINST INTERNET GAMBLING ∾

The Commonwealth of Kentucky has a large horse racing industry that contributes much to the state's economy. In recent years, the racing industry has been in a state of decline due to a variety of factors. First, horse racing enthusiasts are rapidly growing older and dying, and are not being replaced by younger enthusiasts. Second, the neighboring State of Indiana has legalized casino gambling and has authorized the creation of several casinos near the Kentucky border, prompting Kentucky's gambling interests to call for government to find ways to place them on an equal footing with Indiana. Finally, the horse racing industry is facing competition from other entertainment industries (e.g., cable and satellite television and the Internet) that make horse racing and horse gambling less attractive to the population as a whole.

The decline of Kentucky's horse racing industry is amply illustrated in economic data. Betting "handles" and horse racing purses have declined. In addition, as other states have begun to provide incentives to their horse racing industries, Kentucky's breeders and trainers have moved their breeding and racing operations out of state. Kentucky's business and political leaders regard the situation as an "economic crisis."

Kentucky's governor, Wilbur Wonkley, was elected on a platform of legalizing additional gambling at Kentucky racetracks. Following his election, Wonkley floated proposals for video slots, as well as for casino-style gambling at racetracks. Despite Wonkley's persistent advocacy for the additional gambling, his proposals were never enacted because of strong legislative opposition.

Recently, Governor Wonkley became aware of Internet gambling in the state. These "internet casinos" are operated outside of the Commonwealth as well as outside the borders of the United States. Wonkley has expressed alarm about what he has termed this new "scourge." He fears that Kentuckians are being (and will be) lured into betting their "hard-earned money" at these new Internet casinos, and that online betting will have a devastating impact on Kentucky's families (who will be unable to buy bread and other necessities for their children because of gambling losses). As a result, Wonkley has urged the Kentucky legislature to immediately pass legislation protecting the state against what he has referred to as the "Internet casino menace."

Kentucky is a diverse state that includes some major cities (Louisville, Lexington, Covington, and Paducah), as well as a large rural population, and a large group of folks who live in the Appalachian Mountains on the eastern side of the state. In general, the population is fairly conservative (having voted decisively for Donald Trump over Hillary Clinton in the 2016 presidential election), and that is a significant part of the reason Wonkley's proposals for expanded gambling died in the state legislature. However, the evidence shows that Kentucky's horse racing interests enthusiastically support the Internet casino legislation. Some believe that they seek the new anti-Internet gambling legislation as a protectionist measure.

The Kentucky Legislature eventually passed anti-Internet casino gambling legislation (the Internet Casino Prohibition Act). It contained the following language:

> All Internet-based gambling (whether conducted by Kentuckians or by out-of-staters) is hereby prohibited within the borders of the Commonwealth. Any business or person that offers Internet gambling within the borders of the state is subject to imprisonment for up to 10 years, as well as fines of $10,000 per violation. The phrase "offers Internet gambling within the borders of the state" is defined to include a company or individual that makes its gambling service available to Kentuckians over the Internet. However, sanctions apply only when, and if, a Kentuckian actually accesses the website. Each access by a Kentuckian constitutes a violation under this law, and constitutes a separate violation of the Act. Kentucky's Attorney General is hereby authorized to seize the Internet domain names of any internet gambling site that operates within the Commonwealth.

In hearings leading to the Act's passage, evidence was adduced suggesting that Internet gambling is a greater threat, and poses greater social evils, than other types of gambling. In particular, the evidence shows that Internet gambling is more "available" to the average citizen than other forms of gambling because citizens can play at home at any time of the day or night. In other words, there are no "closing hours" for Internet casinos. In addition, because Internet gambling can be done in secret, it is more difficult for society to help protect citizens who have become addicted to gambling and who might be wreaking havoc on their families.

As you work your way through this chapter, consider whether the Internet Casino Prohibition Act is valid.

As we saw in Chapter 2, during the first third of the twentieth century, although Congress had the power to regulate commerce "among" the states, the Court construed the Tenth Amendment as giving the states a reserved power over "purely local" commerce. Thus, most Commerce Clause cases involved claims that the federal government was violating the states' reserved power, and many Commerce Clause cases focused on state power.

Following the constitutional crisis of the 1930s, the distinction between "local" commerce and commerce "among" the states began to disappear. Under decisions like *Wickard* and *Perez*, the federal government assumed much broader authority over both interstate and local commerce. Moreover, the Court began to treat the Tenth Amendment as a truism, thereby depriving states of their reserved power over commerce. Even though recent decisions (e.g., *Lopez* and *Morrison*) have pared back the scope of federal power, the federal commerce power remains broad.

Since the 1930s, the federal courts have faced quite different questions regarding the scope of state power. Some cases involve questions about whether federal law preempts state law. In other words, does the existence of federal regulation preclude state regulation? Most cases involve so-called "dormant" power situations—situations in which the federal government has the power to regulate a subject, but has not done so or has done so incompletely. In these dormant power situations, the question is whether the Commerce Clause contains negative implications that limit or preclude state regulation. In other words, is the federal commerce power "exclusive," so that the states are precluded from regulating an area within federal authority even in the absence of federal regulation? Or do the states have "concurrent" jurisdiction so that they are also free to regulate? If concurrent power exists, what limits apply to state power? A few cases focus on the Privileges and Immunities Clause, which protects citizens against discrimination in one state because of their status as citizens of another state.

The Constitution provides little guidance on these issues. Article I, Section 8 explicitly gives Congress the power to regulate commerce "among" the several states but does not say whether the states can also regulate commerce. That issue was left to the courts.

A. EARLY CASES

A number of early cases focused on whether the federal government's authority over commerce was exclusive, or whether the states also had concurrent power.

Gibbons v. Ogden

22 U.S. (9 Wheat.) 1 (1824)

Mr. Chief Justice MARSHALL delivered the opinion of the Court, and, after stating the case, proceeded as follows:

By the terms of a New York statute, Robert Livingston and Robert Fulton had the exclusive right to navigate steamboats in certain state waters. They assigned the route between New York and New Jersey to Aaron Ogden. When Thomas Gibbons sought to operate ships on the same route, under a license granted by an Act of Congress, Ogden sought injunctive relief on the basis that the federal license was invalid. After finding that the federal license was valid, the Court struck down New York's exclusive license on Supremacy Clause grounds. The Court did not resolve the question of whether, in the absence of a conflict between the state and federal license, the state was free to regulate and license navigation. The Court did make the following statements in dicta.

It has been urged with great earnestness, that, although the power of Congress to regulate commerce with foreign nations, and among the several States, be co-extensive with the subject itself, and have no other limits than are prescribed in the constitution, yet the States may severally exercise the same power, within their respective jurisdictions. In support of this argument, it is said, that they possessed it as an inseparable attribute of sovereignty, before the formation of the constitution, and still retain it, except so far as they have surrendered it by that instrument; that this principle results from the nature of the government, and is secured by the tenth amendment; that an affirmative grant of power is not exclusive, unless in its own nature it be such that the continued exercise of it by the former possessor is inconsistent with the grant, and that this is not of that description.

The grant of the power to lay and collect taxes is, like the power to regulate commerce, made in general terms, and has never been understood to interfere with the exercise of the same power by the State; and hence has been drawn an argument which has been applied to the question under consideration. But the two grants are not, it is conceived, similar in their terms or their nature. Although many of the powers formerly exercised by the States, are transferred to the government of the Union, yet the State governments remain, and constitute a most important part of our system. The power of taxation is indispensable to their existence, and is a power which, in its own nature, is capable of residing in, and being exercised by, different authorities at the same time.

Inspection laws are said to be regulations of commerce, and are certainly recognized in the constitution, as being passed in the exercise of a power remaining with the States. That inspection laws may have a remote and considerable influence on commerce, will not be denied; but that a power to regulate commerce is the source from which the right to pass them is derived, cannot be admitted. The object of inspection laws, is to improve the quality of articles produced by the labour of a country; to fit them for exportation; or, it may be, for domestic use. They act upon the subject before it becomes an article of foreign commerce, or of commerce among the States, and prepare it for that purpose. They form a portion of that immense mass of legislation, which embraces every thing within the territory of a State, not surrendered to the general government: all which can be most advantageously exercised by the States themselves. Inspection laws, quarantine laws, health laws of every description, as well as laws for regulating the internal commerce of a State, and those which respect turnpike roads, ferries, & c., are component parts of this mass.

No direct general power over these objects is granted to Congress; and, consequently, they remain subject to State legislation. If the legislative power of the Union can reach them, it must be for national purposes; it must be where the power is expressly given for a special purpose, or is clearly incidental to some power which is expressly given.

It has been contended by counsel for the appellant, that, as the word "to regulate" implies in its nature, full power over the thing to be regulated, it excludes, necessarily, the action of all others that would perform the same operation on the same thing. That regulation is designed for the entire result, applying to those parts which remain as they were, as well as to those which are altered. It produces a uniform whole, which is as much disturbed and deranged by changing what the regulating power designs to leave untouched, as that on which it has operated.

There is great force in this argument, and the Court is not satisfied that it has been refuted.

Notes and Questions

1. *Fraud and Deception. Plumley v. Commonwealth of Massachusetts*, 155 U.S. 461 (1894), reinforced the notion that the states retain control over certain internal matters. Plumley was convicted of violating a Massachusetts law prohibiting the sale of adulterated oleomargarine. Following his incarceration, Plumley sought a writ of habeas corpus, which was denied on the theory that the Massachusetts law did not violate Congress's power under the Commerce Clause: "If there be any subject over which it would seem the states ought to have plenary control, and the power to legislate in respect to which, it ought not to be supposed, was intended to be surrendered to the general government, it is the protection of the people against fraud and deception in the sale of food products."

2. *Chief Justice Marshall's Conception of Federal Power.* Note how broadly Chief Justice Marshall interprets the federal government's authority to regulate commerce in *Gibbons*: "the word 'to regulate' implies in its nature, full power over the thing to be regulated, it excludes, necessarily, the action of all others that would perform the same operation on the same thing." If the courts give this language full effect, following holdings like *Wickard* and *Perez* (which, of course, were restricted somewhat by later holdings like *Lopez*), how much power would the states have to regulate commerce today?

3. *Inspection Laws.* Justice Marshall characterizes inspection laws as acting "upon the subject before it becomes an article of foreign commerce, or of commerce among the States, and prepare it for that purpose." As a result, he deems "inspection laws, quarantine laws, health laws of every description, as well as laws for regulating the internal commerce of a State" to be within the scope of state

authority. "No direct general power over these objects is granted to Congress." In light of later commerce clause decisions, is this statement true? Do you agree that Congress lacks the power to enact inspection laws relating to interstate commerce?

∽ PROBLEM: MORE ON THE INTERNET CASINO PROHIBITION ACT ∽

Under Justice Marshall's conception of federal powers and state powers, would Kentucky have the power to enact its Internet Casino Prohibition Act?

Cooley v. Board of Wardens of the Port of Philadelphia

53 U.S. (12 How.) 299 (1851)

Mr. Justice CURTIS delivered the opinion of the court.

A Pennsylvania law required all ships either to use local pilots when they navigated in the Delaware River or to pay a penalty. The plaintiff paid the penalty and sued for restitution, claiming that the Pilot Law violated Congress's power to regulate commerce. Pennsylvania defended based on a 1789 federal law that gave states authority to enact local pilot laws.

We are brought directly and unavoidably to the question, whether the grant of the commercial power to Congress, did per se deprive the states of all power to regulate pilots. The grant of commercial power to Congress does not contain any terms which expressly exclude the states from exercising an authority over its subject-matter. If they are excluded it must be because the nature of the power, thus granted to Congress, requires that a similar authority should not exist in the states.

The power to regulate commerce, embraces a vast field, containing not only many, but exceedingly various subjects, quite unlike in their nature; some imperatively demanding a single uniform rule, operating equally on the commerce of the United States in every port; and some, like the subject now in question, as imperatively demanding that diversity, which alone can meet the local necessities of navigation.

Either absolutely to affirm, or deny that the nature of this power requires exclusive legislation by Congress, is to lose sight of the nature of the subjects of this power. Whatever subjects of this power are in their nature national, or admit only of one uniform system, or plan of regulation, may justly be said to be of such a nature as to require exclusive legislation by Congress. That this cannot be affirmed of laws for the regulation of pilots and pilotage is plain. The act of 1789 contains a clear and authoritative declaration by the first Congress, that the nature of this subject is such, that until Congress should find it necessary to exert its power, it should be left to the legislation of the states; that it is local and not national; that it is likely to be the best provided for, not by one system, or plan of regulations, but by as many as the legislative discretion of the several states should deem applicable to the local peculiarities of the ports within their limits.

Viewed in this light, so much of this act of 1789 as declares that pilots shall continue to be regulated "by such laws as the states may respectively hereafter enact for that purpose," instead of being held to be inoperative, as an attempt to confer on the states a power to legislate, of which the Constitution had deprived them, is allowed an appropriate and important signification. It manifests the understanding of Congress that the nature of this subject is not such as to require its exclusive legislation. The practice of the states, and of the national government, has been in conformity with this declaration, from the origin of the national government to this time; and the nature of the subject when examined, is such as to leave no doubt of the superior fitness and propriety, not to say the absolute necessity, of different systems of regulation, drawn from local knowledge and experience, and conformed to local wants. How then can we say, that by the mere grant of power to regulate commerce, the states are deprived of all the power to legislate on this subject, because from the nature of the power the legislation of Congress must be exclusive.

It is the opinion of a majority of the court that the mere grant to Congress of the power to regulate commerce, did not deprive the states of power to regulate pilots, and that although Congress has legislated on this subject, its legislation manifests an intention, with a single exception, not to regulate this subject, but to leave its regulation to the several states. This opinion does not extend to the question what other subjects, under the commercial power, are within the exclusive control of Congress, or may be regulated by the states in the absence of all congressional legislation; nor to the general question how far any regulation of a subject by Congress, may be deemed to operate as an exclusion of all legislation by the states upon the same subject.

For more than sixty years this subject has been acted on by the states, and the systems of some of them created and of others essentially modified during that period. To hold that pilotage fees and penalties demanded and received during that time, have been illegally exacted, under color of void laws, would work an amount of mischief which a clear conviction of constitutional duty, if entertained, must force us to occasion, but which could be viewed by no just mind without deep regret. Nor would the mischief be limited to the past. If Congress were now to pass a law adopting the existing state laws, if enacted without authority, and in violation of the Constitution, it would seem to us to be a new and questionable mode of legislation.

If the grant of commercial power in the Constitution has deprived the states of all power to legislate for the regulation of pilots, if their laws on this subject are mere usurpations upon the exclusive power of the general government, and utterly void, it may be doubted whether Congress could, with propriety, recognize them as laws, and adopt them as its own acts; and how are the legislatures of the states to proceed in future, to watch over and amend these laws, as the progressive wants of a growing commerce will require, when the members of those legislatures are made aware that they cannot legislate on this subject without violating the oaths they have taken to support the Constitution of the United States?

We are of opinion that this state law was enacted by virtue of a power, residing in the state to legislate; that it is not in conflict with any law of Congress; that it does not interfere with any system which Congress has established by making regulations, or by intentionally leaving individuals to their own unrestricted action; that this law is therefore valid, and the judgment of the Supreme Court of Pennsylvania in each case must be affirmed.

Mr. Justice McLEAN.

If the states had not the power to enact pilot laws, as connected with foreign commerce, in 1789, when did they get it? Congress may adopt the laws of a state, but it cannot enable a state to legislate. In other words, it cannot transfer to a state legislative powers. The majority concludes that state regulation is appropriate because the subject of this legislation is more appropriate for state than federal action; and consequently, it must be presumed the Constitution cannot have intended to inhibit state action. This is not a rule by which the Constitution is to be construed. It can receive but little support from the discussions which took place on the adoption of the Constitution, and none at all from the earlier decisions of this court.

Notes and Questions

1. Cooley *and* Gibbons. *Cooley* rejects the exclusivity approach articulated in *Gibbons*. Is *Cooley*'s approach better than *Gibbons*'s approach? How does a court know whether a matter is national or local?

2. *Congressional Authorization.* Can Congress authorize the states to exercise regulatory authority that they would not have had in the absence of congressional authorization? In *Leisy v. Hardin*, 135 U.S. 100 (1890), the Court held that "as the grant of the power to regulate commerce among the states, so far as one system is required, is exclusive, the states cannot exercise that power without the assent of congress." Likewise, in *Prudential Insurance Co. v. Benjamin*, 328 U.S. 408 (1946), the Court upheld a South Carolina tax imposed on foreign insurance companies as a condition of doing business in the state. The Court concluded that a federal law authorized the tax: "Congress has expressly stated its intent and policy in the Act. We think that the declaration's effect is clearly to sustain the exaction and that this can be done without violating any constitutional provision. Congress's purpose was to remove obstructions which might be thought to flow from its own power, whether dormant or exercised, except as otherwise expressly provided in the Act itself or in future legislation. The other was by declaring expressly and affirmatively that continued state regulation and taxation of this business is in the

public interest and that the business and all who engage in it 'shall be subject to' the laws of the several states in these respects." Should congressional authorization matter?

∽ PROBLEM: MORE ON THE INTERNET CASINO PROHIBITION ACT ∽

How would you assess the validity of the Internet Casino Prohibition Act under the *Cooley* approach to state power?

B. DISCRIMINATION AGAINST INTERSTATE COMMERCE

The Court has always scrutinized state and local legislation more closely when it involves discrimination against interstate commerce. Statutes that discriminate or directly regulate interstate commerce are presumptively unconstitutional and survive only if there are no less commerce-restrictive methods of achieving the statute's goals. This approach reflects the fact that the Framers gave Congress the power to regulate interstate commerce in order to prevent trade wars between the states. Thus, the Interstate Commerce Clause embodies a substantive policy of free trade among the states, a policy that a state can be countermand only for the most compelling reasons.

A number of questions are presented. First, why are discriminatory state statutes objectionable? Second, how does the Court go about determining whether a state law is discriminatory or non-discriminatory? Third, how does the Court apply these tests once it determines into which category the statute falls? Finally, does the doctrine make any sense? If it doesn't, what alternatives are available to guard against the Framers' fear of state-to-state trade wars? Consider the following cases.

1. *Facial Discrimination*

In some instances, state legislation explicitly and facially discriminates against out-of-state interests. The following cases illustrate the idea.

Granholm v. Heald

544 U.S. 460 (2005)

Justice KENNEDY delivered the opinion of the Court.

Like many other States, Michigan and New York regulate the sale and importation of alcoholic beverages, including wine, through a three-tier distribution system. Separate licenses are required for producers, wholesalers, and retailers. The three-tier scheme is preserved by a complex set of overlapping state and federal regulations. For example, both state and federal laws limit vertical integration between tiers. We have held previously that States can mandate a three-tier distribution scheme in the exercise of their authority under the Twenty-first Amendment. The three-tier system is, in broad terms and with refinements to be discussed, mandated by Michigan and New York only for sales from out-of-state wineries. In-state wineries, by contrast, can obtain a license for direct sales to consumers. The differential treatment between in-state and out-of-state wineries constitutes explicit discrimination against interstate commerce.

This discrimination substantially limits the direct sale of wine to consumers, an otherwise emerging and significant business. From 1994 to 1999, consumer spending on direct wine shipments doubled, reaching $500 million per year. The expansion has been influenced by several related trends. First, the number of small wineries in the United States has significantly increased. At the same time, the wholesale market has consolidated. Between 1984 and 2002, the number of licensed wholesalers dropped from 1,600 to 600. The increasing winery-to-wholesaler ratio means that many small wineries do not produce enough wine or have sufficient consumer demand for their wine to make it economical for wholesalers to carry their products. This has led many small wineries to rely on direct shipping to reach new markets. Technological improvements, in particular the ability of wineries to sell wine over the Internet, have helped make direct shipments an attractive sales channel.

Approximately 26 States allow some direct shipping of wine, with various restrictions. Thirteen of these States have reciprocity laws, which allow direct shipment from wineries outside the State, provided the State of origin affords similar nondiscriminatory treatment. In many parts of the country, however, state laws that prohibit or severely restrict direct shipments deprive consumers of access to the direct market.

The wine producers in the cases before us are small wineries that rely on direct consumer sales as an important part of their businesses. Domaine Alfred, a plaintiff in the Michigan suit, is a small winery located in San Luis Obispo, California. Domaine Alfred has received requests for its wine from Michigan consumers but cannot fill the orders because of the State's direct-shipment ban. Even if the winery could find a Michigan wholesaler to distribute its wine, the wholesaler's markup would render shipment through the three-tier system economically infeasible. Similarly, Juanita Swedenburg and David Lucas, two of the plaintiffs in the New York suit, operate small wineries in Virginia (the Swedenburg Estate Vineyard) and California (the Lucas Winery). Some of their customers are tourists, from other States, who purchase wine while visiting the wineries. If these customers wish to obtain Swedenburg or Lucas wines after they return home, they will be unable to do so if they reside in a State with restrictive direct-shipment laws. They are unable to fill orders from New York, the Nation's second-largest wine market, because of the limits that State imposes on direct wine shipments.

Most alcoholic beverages in Michigan are distributed through the State's three-tier system. Producers or distillers of alcoholic beverages, whether located in state or out of state, generally may sell only to licensed in-state wholesalers. Wholesalers, in turn, may sell only to in-state retailers. Licensed retailers are the final link in the chain, selling alcoholic beverages to consumers at retail locations and, subject to certain restrictions, through home delivery. There is, however, an exception for Michigan's approximately 40 in-state wineries, which are eligible for wine maker licenses that allow direct shipment to in-state consumers. For a small winery, the license is $25. Out-of-state wineries can apply for a $300 outside seller of wine license, but this license only allows them to sell to in-state wholesalers. The District Court sustained the Michigan scheme. The Court of Appeals for the Sixth Circuit reversed. Relying on *Bacchus Imports, Ltd. v. Dias*, 468 U.S. 263 (1984), the court rejected the argument that the Twenty-first Amendment immunizes all state liquor laws from the strictures of the Commerce Clause.

New York's licensing scheme channels most wine sales through the three-tier system, but it too makes exceptions for in-state wineries. The result is to allow local wineries to make direct sales to consumers in New York on terms not available to out-of-state wineries. Wineries that produce wine only from New York grapes can apply for a license that allows direct shipment to in-state consumers. These licensees are authorized to deliver the wines of other wineries as well, but only if the wine is made from grapes at least seventy-five percent the volume of which were grown in New York state. An out-of-state winery may ship directly to New York consumers only if it becomes a licensed New York winery, which requires the establishment of a branch factory, office or storeroom within the state of New York. The District Court granted summary judgment to the plaintiffs and the Court of Appeals for the Second Circuit reversed.

Time and again this Court has held that, in all but the narrowest circumstances, state laws violate the Commerce Clause if they mandate differential treatment of in-state and out-of-state economic interests that benefits the former and burdens the latter. *Oregon Waste Systems, Inc. v. Department of Environmental Quality of Ore.*, 511 U.S. 93, 99 (1994). This rule is essential to the foundations of the Union. The mere fact of nonresidence should not foreclose a producer in one State from access to markets in other States. *H.P. Hood & Sons, Inc. v. Du Mond*, 336 U.S. 525 (1949). States may not enact laws that burden out-of-state producers or shippers simply to give a competitive advantage to in-state businesses. This mandate reflects a central concern of the Framers that was an immediate reason for calling the Constitutional Convention: the conviction that in order to succeed, the new Union would have to avoid the tendencies toward economic Balkanization that had plagued relations among the Colonies and later among the States under the Articles of Confederation. *Hughes v. Oklahoma*, 441 U.S. 322, 325 (1979).

The rule prohibiting state discrimination against interstate commerce follows also from the principle that States should not be compelled to negotiate with each other regarding favored or disfavored status for their own citizens. States do not need, and may not attempt, to negotiate with other States regarding their mutual economic interests. *Cf.* U.S. Const., Art. I, §10, cl. 3. Rivalries among the States are thus kept to a minimum, and a proliferation of trade zones is prevented. *See C & A Carbone, Inc. v. Clarkstown,* 511 U.S. 383 (1994).

Laws of the type at issue in the instant cases contradict these principles. They deprive citizens of their right to have access to the markets of other States on equal terms. The perceived necessity for reciprocal sale privileges risks generating the trade rivalries and animosities, the alliances and exclusivity, that the Constitution and, in particular, the Commerce Clause were designed to avoid. State laws that protect local wineries have led to the enactment of statutes under which some States condition the right of out-of-state wineries to make direct wine sales to in-state consumers on a reciprocal right in the shipping State. California, for example, passed a reciprocity law in 1986, retreating from the State's previous regime that allowed unfettered direct shipments from out-of-state wineries. The obvious aim of the California statute was to open the interstate direct-shipping market for the State's many wineries. The current patchwork of laws—with some States banning direct shipments altogether, others doing so only for out-of-state wines, and still others requiring reciprocity—is essentially the product of an ongoing, low-level trade war. Allowing States to discriminate against out-of-state wine invites a multiplication of preferential trade areas destructive of the very purpose of the Commerce Clause. *Dean Milk Co. v. Madison,* 340 U.S. 349, 356 (1951).

The discriminatory character of the Michigan system is obvious. Michigan allows in-state wineries to ship directly to consumers, subject only to a licensing requirement. Out-of-state wineries, whether licensed or not, face a complete ban on direct shipment. The differential treatment requires all out-of-state wine, but not all in-state wine, to pass through an in-state wholesaler and retailer before reaching consumers. These two extra layers of overhead increase the cost of out-of-state wines to Michigan consumers. The cost differential, and in some cases the inability to secure a wholesaler for small shipments, can effectively bar small wineries from the Michigan market.

The New York regulatory scheme differs from Michigan's in that it does not ban direct shipments altogether. Out-of-state wineries are instead required to establish a distribution operation in New York in order to gain the privilege of direct shipment. The New York scheme grants in-state wineries access to the State's consumers on preferential terms. In-state producers, with the applicable licenses, can ship directly to consumers from their wineries. Out-of-state wineries must open a branch office and warehouse in New York. For most wineries, the expense of establishing a bricks-and-mortar distribution operation in 1 State, let alone all 50, is prohibitive. It comes as no surprise that not a single out-of-state winery has availed itself of New York's direct-shipping privilege. We have viewed with particular suspicion state statutes requiring business operations to be performed in the home State that could more efficiently be performed elsewhere. *Pike v. Bruce Church, Inc.,* 397 U.S. 137, 145 (1970). New York's in-state presence requirement runs contrary to our admonition that States cannot require an out-of-state firm to become a resident in order to compete on equal terms. *Halliburton Oil Well Cementing Co. v. Reily*, 373 U.S. 64, 72 (1963). New York discriminates against out-of-state wineries in other ways. Out-of-state wineries that establish the requisite branch office and warehouse in New York are still ineligible for a farm winery license, the license that provides the most direct means of shipping to New York consumers. Out-of-state wineries may apply only for a commercial winery license. Unlike farm wineries, however, commercial wineries must obtain a separate certificate from the state liquor authority authorizing direct shipments to consumers; and, of course, for out-of-state wineries there is the additional requirement of maintaining a distribution operation in New York. New York law also allows in-state wineries without direct-shipping licenses to distribute their wine through other wineries that have the applicable licenses. This is another privilege not afforded out-of-state wineries. We have no difficulty concluding that New York, like Michigan, discriminates against interstate commerce through its direct-shipping laws.

Michigan and New York contend their statutes are saved by §2 of the Twenty-first Amendment, which provides: "The transportation or importation into any State, Territory, or possession of the United States for delivery or use therein of intoxicating liquors, in violation of the laws thereof, is hereby prohibited." The aim of the Twenty-first Amendment was to allow States to maintain an effective and uniform system for controlling liquor by regulating its transportation, importation, and use. The Amendment did not give States the authority to pass nonuniform laws in order to discriminate against out-of-state goods, a privilege they had not enjoyed at any earlier time. The modern §2 cases fall into three categories. First, the Court has held that state laws that violate other provisions of the Constitution are not saved by the Twenty-first Amendment. The Court has applied this rule in the context of the First Amendment, the Establishment Clause, the Equal Protection Clause, and the Import-Export Clause. Second, the Court has held that §2 does not abrogate Congress' Commerce Clause powers with regard to liquor. Finally, and most relevant to the issue at hand, the Court has held that state regulation of alcohol is limited by the nondiscrimination principle of the Commerce Clause. *Bacchus*, 468 U.S. at 276; *Brown-Forman Distillers Corp. v. New York State Liquor Authority*, 476 U.S. 573 (1986). When a state statute directly regulates or discriminates against interstate commerce, or when its effect is to favor in-state economic interests over out-of-state interests, we have generally struck down the statute without further inquiry. *Brown-Forman, 476 U.S. at 579.*

A State which chooses to ban the sale and consumption of alcohol altogether could bar its importation. States may also assume direct control of liquor distribution through state-run outlets or funnel sales through the three-tier system. State policies are protected under the Twenty-first Amendment when they treat liquor produced out of state the same as its domestic equivalent. The instant cases, in contrast, involve straightforward attempts to discriminate in favor of local producers. The discrimination is contrary to the Commerce Clause and is not saved by the Twenty-first Amendment.

We still must consider whether either state regime advances a legitimate local purpose that cannot be adequately served by reasonable nondiscriminatory alternatives. *New Energy Co. of Ind.*, 486 U.S. at 278. The States claim that allowing direct shipment from out-of-state wineries undermines their ability to police underage drinking. Minors, the States argue, have easy access to credit cards and the Internet and are likely to take advantage of direct wine shipments as a means of obtaining alcohol illegally. A recent study found that the 26 States currently allowing direct shipments report no problems with minors' increased access to wine. FTC Report 34. This is not surprising. First, minors are less likely to consume wine, as opposed to beer, wine coolers, and hard liquor. Second, minors who decide to disobey the law have more direct means of doing so. Third, direct shipping is an imperfect avenue of obtaining alcohol for minors who want instant gratification. Our precedents require the clearest showing to justify discriminatory state regulation, *C & A Carbone, Inc.*, 511 U.S. at 393.

Even were we to credit the States' largely unsupported claim that direct shipping of wine increases the risk of underage drinking, this would not justify regulations limiting only out-of-state direct shipments. Minors are just as likely to order wine from in-state producers as from out-of-state ones. Michigan counters that it has greater regulatory control over in-state producers than over out-of-state wineries. This does not justify Michigan's discriminatory ban on direct shipping. Out-of-state wineries face the loss of state and federal licenses if they fail to comply with state law. This provides strong incentives not to sell alcohol to minors. In addition, the States can take less restrictive steps to minimize the risk that minors will order wine by mail. For example, the Model Direct Shipping Bill developed by the National Conference of State Legislatures requires an adult signature on delivery and a label so instructing on each package.

The States' tax-collection justification is also insufficient. Increased direct shipping, whether originating in state or out of state, brings with it the potential for tax evasion. Michigan, unlike many other States, does not rely on wholesalers to collect taxes on wines imported from out of state. Instead, Michigan collects taxes directly from out-of-state wineries on all wine shipped to in-state wholesalers. If licensing and self-reporting provide adequate safeguards for wine distributed through the three-tier system, there is no reason to believe they will not suffice for direct shipments. New York could protect itself against lost tax revenue by requiring a permit as a condition of direct shipping. This is the approach taken by New York for in-state wineries. The State offers no reason to believe the system would prove ineffective for out-of-state wineries. Licensees could be required to submit regular sales reports and to remit taxes. Indeed, various States use this approach for taxing direct interstate wine shipments, and report no problems with tax collection. *See* FTC Report 38-40. This is also the procedure sanctioned by the National Conference of State Legislatures in their Model Direct Shipping Bill.

Michigan and New York benefit, furthermore, from provisions of federal law that supply incentives for wineries to comply with state regulations. The Tax and Trade Bureau (formerly the Bureau of Alcohol, Tobacco and Firearms) has authority to revoke a winery's federal license if it violates state law. Without a federal license, a winery cannot operate in any State. *See* 27 U.S.C. §204. In addition the Twenty-first Amendment Enforcement Act gives state attorneys general the power to sue wineries in federal court to enjoin violations of state law. These federal remedies, when combined with state licensing regimes, adequately protect States from lost tax revenue. The States have not shown that tax evasion from out-of-state wineries poses such a unique threat that it justifies their discriminatory regimes.

Michigan and New York offer a handful of other rationales, such as facilitating orderly market conditions, protecting public health and safety, and ensuring regulatory accountability. These objectives can also be achieved through the alternative of an evenhanded licensing requirement. Finally, it should be noted that improvements in technology have eased the burden of monitoring out-of-state wineries. Background checks can be done electronically. Financial records and sales data can be mailed, faxed, or submitted via e-mail.

In summary, the States provide little concrete evidence for the sweeping assertion that they cannot police direct shipments by out-of-state wineries. Our Commerce Clause cases demand more than mere speculation to support discrimination against out-of-state goods. The burden is on the State to show that the *discrimination* is "demonstrably justified," *Chemical Waste Management, Inc. v. Hunt*, 504 U.S. 334, 344 (1992). The Court has upheld state regulations that discriminate against interstate commerce only after finding, based on concrete record evidence, that a State's nondiscriminatory alternatives will prove unworkable. *See, e.g., Maine v. Taylor*, 477 U.S. 131 (1986). Michigan and New York have not satisfied this exacting standard. If a State chooses to allow direct shipment of wine, it must do so on evenhanded terms. Without demonstrating the need for discrimination, New York and Michigan have enacted regulations that disadvantage out-of-state wine producers. Under our Commerce Clause jurisprudence, these regulations cannot stand.

We *affirm* the judgment of the Court of Appeals for the Sixth Circuit; and we *reverse* the judgment of the Court of Appeals for the Second Circuit and *remand* the case for further proceedings consistent with our opinion.

It is so ordered.

Justice STEVENS, with whom Justice O'CONNOR joins, *dissenting.*

Because the New York and Michigan laws regulate the transportation or importation of intoxicating liquors for delivery or use therein, they are exempt from dormant Commerce Clause scrutiny.

Justice THOMAS, with whom THE CHIEF JUSTICE, Justice STEVENS, and Justice O'CONNOR join, *dissenting.*

The Twenty-first Amendment freed the States from negative Commerce Clause restraints on discriminatory regulation.

Notes

1. *The* Baldwin *Decision.* One of the most famous discrimination decisions was rendered in *Baldwin v. G.A.F. Seelig, Inc.*, 294 U.S. 511 (1935). In that case, a milk dealer who purchased Vermont milk sought to challenge the New York Milk Control Act, which established "minimum prices" to be paid by dealers to milk producers. The producer was able to purchase the Vermont milk at prices below the minimum price, but New York refused to license his business unless he complied with the Act. In striking down the Act, the Court stated:

> New York has no power to project its legislation into Vermont by regulating the price to be paid in that state for milk acquired there. New York is equally without power to prohibit the introduction within her territory of milk of wholesome quality acquired in Vermont, whether at high prices or at low ones. New York asserts her power to outlaw milk so introduced by prohibiting its sale thereafter if the price that has been paid for it to the farmers of Vermont is less than would be owing in like circumstances to farmers in New York. The importer in that view may keep his milk or drink it, but sell it he may not. Such a power, if exerted, will set a barrier to traffic between one state and another as effective as if customs duties, equal to the price differential, had been laid upon the thing transported. Imposts or duties upon commerce with other countries are placed, by an express prohibition of the Constitution, beyond the power of a state, "except what may be absolutely necessary for executing its inspection Laws." U.S. Const., art. 1, §10, cl. 2. Imposts and duties upon interstate commerce are placed beyond the power of a state, without the mention of an exception, by the provision committing commerce of that order to the power of the Congress. U.S. Const., art. 1, §8, cl. 3. A chief occasion of the commerce clauses was "the mutual jealousies and aggressions of the States, taking form in customs barriers and other economic retaliation." Farrand, *Records of the Federal Convention*, vol. II, p. 308; vol. III, pp. 478, 547, 548; *The Federalist No. XLII*. If New York, in order to promote the economic welfare of her farmers, may guard them against competition with the cheaper prices of Vermont, the door has been opened to rivalries and reprisals that were meant to be averted by subjecting commerce between the states to the power of the nation.

The Court also rejected New York's argument that the law could be sustained on the basis that it was designed to ensure New Yorkers "a regular and adequate supply of pure and wholesome milk; the supply being put in jeopardy when the farmers of the state are unable to earn a living income." The Court disagreed: "Economic welfare is always related to health, for there can be no health if men are starving. Let such an exception be admitted, and all that a state will have to do in times of stress and strain is to say that its farmers and merchants and workmen must be protected against competition from without, lest they go upon the poor relief lists or perish altogether. To give entrance to that excuse would be to invite a speedy end of our national solidarity. The Constitution was framed under the dominion of a political philosophy that the peoples of the several states must sink or swim together, and that in the long run prosperity and salvation are in union and not division." The Court concluded that New York could deal with the problem of unsanitary milk in other, nonsanitary ways: "The evils springing from uncared for cattle must be remedied by measures of repression more direct and certain than the creation of a parity of prices between New York and other states. Appropriate certificates may be exacted from farmers in Vermont and elsewhere; milk may be excluded if necessary safeguards have been omitted; but commerce between the states is burdened unduly when one state regulates by indirection the prices to be paid to producers in another, in the faith that augmentation of prices will lift up the level of economic welfare, and that this will stimulate the observance of sanitary requirements in the preparation of the product. The next step would be to condition importation upon proof of a satisfactory wage scale in factory or shop, or even upon proof of the profits of the business." The Court nonetheless recognized that "a state may regulate the importation of unhealthy swine or cattle or decayed or noxious foods," but noted that there was no evidence of problems with Vermont milk. The Court concluded: "One state in its dealings with another may not place itself in a position of economic isolation. Formulas and catchwords are subordinate to this overmastering requirement. Neither the power to tax nor the police power may be used by the state of destination with the aim and effect of establishing an economic barrier against competition with the products of another state or the labor of its residents. Restrictions so contrived are an unreasonable clog upon the mobility of commerce. They set up what is equivalent to a rampart of customs duties designed to neutralize advantages belonging to the place of origin. They are thus hostile in conception as well as burdensome in result."

2. *Licensing Requirements.* May a state impose different licensing requirements on out-of-state individuals and businesses than it imposes on in-state individuals and businesses? *Welton v. Missouri*, 91 U.S. (1 Otto) 275 (1876), involved a Missouri law that provided that peddlers who sold products that were not the growth, produce, or manufacture of Missouri must first obtain a license, but those who sold products grown, produced, or manufactured in Missouri were not required to obtain one. The law was challenged by a sewing machine dealer who was convicted for selling sewing machines manufactured outside of Missouri without a license. The Court struck down the law: "The question is, whether legislation thus discriminating against the products of other States in the conditions of their sale by a certain class of dealers is valid under the Constitution of the United States. The Constitution protects property which is transported as an article of commerce from hostile or interfering legislation, until it has mingled with and become a part of the general property of the country, and subjected like it to similar protection, and to no greater burdens. It is sufficient to hold that the commercial power continues until the commodity has ceased to be the subject of discriminating legislation by reason of its foreign character. That power protects it, even after it has entered the State, from any burdens imposed by reason of its foreign origin. The act encroaches upon this power, and is therefore, in our judgment, unconstitutional and void."

3. *Protecting Local Needs and Interests.* Can a state prohibit exportation of products produced within the state? *Pennsylvania v. West Virginia*, 262 U.S. 553 (1923),

involved a West Virginia law that prohibited the interstate shipment of natural gas unless and until the state's own need for natural gas had been met. The law was passed following a winter in which gas supplies ran short and West Virginia consumer needs were unmet. The Court struck down the law as involving discrimination against interstate commerce: "In the matter of interstate commerce we are a single nation—one and the same people. All the states have assented to it, all are alike bound by it, and all are equally protected by it. Natural gas is a lawful article of commerce, and its transmission from one state to another for sale and consumption in the latter is interstate commerce. A state law, whether of the state where the gas is produced or that where it is to be sold, which by its necessary operation prevents, obstructs or burdens such transmission is a regulation of interstate commerce—a prohibited interference. West Virginia argued that the gas is a natural product of the state and has become a necessity therein, that the supply is waning and no longer sufficient to satisfy local needs and be used abroad, and that the act is therefore a legitimate measure of conservation in the interest of the people of the state. [This] situation affords no ground for assumption by the state of power to regulate interstate commerce. 'If the states have such power a singular situation might result. Pennsylvania might keep its coal, the Northwest its timber, the mining states their minerals. Embargo may be retaliated by embargo, and commerce will be halted at state lines. 'In matters of foreign and interstate commerce there are no state lines.'" Justice Holmes dissented: "The Constitution does not prohibit a State from securing a reasonable preference for its own inhabitants in the enjoyment of its products even when the effect of its law is to keep property within its boundaries that otherwise would have passed outside."

In *Hughes v. Oklahoma*, 441 U.S. 322 (1979), the Court rendered a similar decision striking down an Oklahoma law that provided that "no person may transport or ship minnows for sale outside the state which were seined or procured within the waters of this state." The Court held: "At a minimum such facial discrimination invokes the strictest scrutiny of any purported legitimate local purpose and of the absence of nondiscriminatory alternatives. The State's interest in maintaining the ecological balance in state waters by avoiding the removal of inordinate numbers of minnows may well qualify as a legitimate local purpose. But the fiction of state ownership may no longer be used to force those outside the State to bear the full costs of 'conserving' the wild animals within its borders when equally effective nondiscriminatory conservation measures are available. Far from choosing the least discriminatory alternative, Oklahoma has chosen to 'conserve' its minnows in the way that most overtly discriminates against interstate commerce. The State places no limits on the numbers of minnows that can be taken by licensed minnow dealers; nor does it limit in any way how these minnows may be disposed of within the State. Yet it forbids the transportation of any commercially significant number of natural minnows out of the State for sale." Justice Rehnquist, joined by Chief Justice Burger, dissented: "The Oklahoma law serves the special interest of the State, as representative of its citizens, in preserving and regulating exploitation of free-swimming minnows found within its waters. This is not a case where a State's regulation permits residents to export naturally seined minnows but prohibits nonresidents from so doing. No person is allowed to export natural minnows for sale outside of Oklahoma. The State has not used its power to protect its own citizens from outside competition. Appellant, or anyone else, may freely export as many minnows as he wishes, so long as the minnows so transported are hatchery minnows and not naturally seined minnows."

4. *Assessing Neutrality.* How does a court decide whether a seemingly neutral state law involves discrimination? *Kassel v. Consolidated Freightways Corp.*, 450 U.S. 662 (1981), involved an Iowa statute that prohibited most uses of 65-foot trucks on Iowa highways. In striking down the law, the Court found that it imposed a substantial burden on interstate commerce. Although the law generally banned large double trucks, it contained "several exemptions that secure to Iowans many of the benefits of large trucks while shunting to neighboring States many of the costs associated with their use. First, singles hauling livestock or farm vehicles were permitted to be as long as 60 feet. Second cities abutting other States were permitted to enact local ordinances adopting the larger length limitation of the neighboring State. The origin of the 'border cities exemption' also suggests that Iowa's statute may not have been designed to ban dangerous trucks, but rather to discourage interstate truck traffic. Iowa seems to have hoped to limit the use of its highways by deflecting some through traffic." Justice Rehnquist, joined by Chief Justice Burger and Justice Stewart, dissented, claiming that the law was reasonable: "Iowa adduced evidence supporting the relation between vehicle length and highway safety. Longer vehicles take greater time to be passed, thereby increasing the risks of accidents, particularly during the inclement weather not uncommon in Iowa. The 65-foot vehicle exposes a passing driver to visibility-impairing splash and spray during bad weather for a longer period than do the shorter trucks permitted in Iowa. Longer trucks are more likely to clog intersections. Trucks involved in accidents often must be unloaded at the scene, which would take longer the bigger the load. In sum, there was sufficient evidence to support the legislative determination that length is related to safety, and nothing in Consolidated's evidence undermines this conclusion." In addition, the dissenters rejected the idea that the legislation was protectionist.

PROBLEM: MORE ON THE INTERNET CASINO PROHIBITION ACT

Is Kentucky's Internet Casino Prohibition Act facially discriminatory against interstate commerce? Would a court be inclined, given the facts set forth in the problem described at the beginning of the chapter, to conclude that Kentucky intended to discriminate against interstate commerce? What weight do you attach to the fact that Governor Wonkley, ordinarily a strong supporter of gambling and gambling interests, strongly opposed internet gambling and decried the adverse effects of internet gambling on society and on Kentucky families? Was he concerned about those issues when he proposed expanded gambling at Kentucky's racetracks? Should that matter in assessing the validity of the Act? To what extent should the demographics of Kentucky and the defeat of expanded gambling at racetracks enter into your analysis?

City of Philadelphia v. New Jersey

437 U.S. 617 (1978)

Mr. Justice STEWART delivered the opinion of the Court.

A New Jersey law prohibits the importation of most "solid or liquid waste which originated or was collected outside the territorial limits of the State." In this case we are required to decide whether this statutory prohibition violates the Commerce Clause of the United States Constitution.

Immediately affected by this law were the operators of private landfills in New Jersey, and several cities in other States that had agreements with these operators for waste disposal. They brought suit against New Jersey and its Department of Environmental Protection in state court, attacking the statute and regulations on a number of state and federal grounds.

We reject the state court's suggestion that the banning of "valueless" out-of-state wastes by ch. 363 implicates no constitutional protection. Just as Congress has power to regulate the interstate movement of these wastes, States are not free from constitutional scrutiny when they restrict that movement. The crucial inquiry must be directed to determining whether ch. 363 is basically a protectionist measure, or whether it can fairly be viewed as a law directed to legitimate local concerns, with effects upon interstate commerce that are only incidental.

The purpose of ch. 363 is set out in the statute itself as follows: "The Legislature finds and determines that the volume of solid and liquid waste continues to rapidly increase, that the treatment and disposal of these wastes continues to pose an even greater threat to the quality of the environment of New Jersey, that the available and appropriate landfill sites within the State are being diminished, that the environment continues to be threatened by the treatment and disposal of waste which originated or was collected outside the State, and that the public health, safety and welfare require that the treatment and disposal within this State of all wastes generated outside of the State be prohibited."

The New Jersey Supreme Court accepted this statement of the state legislature's purpose. The state court additionally found that New Jersey's existing landfill sites will be exhausted within a few years; that to go on using these sites or to develop new ones will take a heavy environmental toll, both from pollution and from loss of scarce open lands; that new techniques to divert waste from landfills to other methods of disposal and resource recovery processes are under development, but that these changes will require time; and finally, that "the extension of the lifespan of existing landfills, resulting from the exclusion of out-of-state waste, may be of crucial importance in preventing further virgin wetlands or other undeveloped lands from being devoted to landfill purposes." Based on these findings, the court concluded that ch. 363 was designed to protect, not the State's economy, but its environment, and that its substantial benefits outweigh its "slight" burden on interstate commerce.

The appellants strenuously contend that ch. 363, "while outwardly cloaked 'in the currently fashionable garb of environmental protection,' is actually no more than a legislative effort to suppress competition and stabilize the cost of solid waste disposal for New Jersey residents." They cite passages of legislative history suggesting that the problem addressed by ch. 363 is primarily financial: Stemming the flow of out-of-state waste into certain landfill sites will extend their lives, thus delaying the day when New Jersey cities must transport their waste to more distant and expensive sites.

Appellees deny that ch. 363 was motivated by financial concerns or economic protectionism. In the words of their brief, "no New Jersey commercial interests stand to gain advantage over competitors from outside the state as a result of the ban on dumping out-of-state waste." Noting that New Jersey landfill operators are among the plaintiffs, the appellee's brief argues that "the complaint is not that New Jersey has forged an economic preference for its own commercial interests, but rather that it has denied a small group of its entrepreneurs an economic opportunity to traffic in waste in order to protect the health, safety and welfare of the citizenry at large."

This dispute about ultimate legislative purpose need not be resolved, because its resolution would not be relevant to the constitutional issue to be decided in this case. The evil of protectionism can reside in legislative means as well as legislative ends. Thus, it does not matter whether the ultimate aim of ch. 363 is to reduce the waste disposal costs of New Jersey residents or to save remaining open lands from pollution, for we assume New Jersey has every right to protect its residents' pocketbooks as well as their environment. And it may be assumed as well that New Jersey may pursue those ends by slowing the flow of all waste into the State's remaining landfills, even though interstate commerce may incidentally be affected. But whatever New Jersey's ultimate purpose, it may not be accomplished by discriminating against articles of commerce coming from outside the State unless there is some reason, apart from their origin, to treat them differently. Both on its face and in its plain effect, ch. 363 violates this principle of nondiscrimination.

The Court has consistently found parochial legislation of this kind to be constitutionally invalid, whether the ultimate aim of the legislation was to assure a steady supply of milk by erecting barriers to allegedly ruinous outside competition, or to create jobs by keeping industry within the State, or to preserve the State's financial resources from depletion by fencing out indigent immigrants. In each of these cases, a presumably legitimate goal was sought to be achieved by the illegitimate means of isolating the State from the national economy.

Also relevant here are the Court's decisions holding that a State may not accord its own inhabitants a preferred right of access over consumers in other States to natural resources located within its borders. *West, Attorney General of Oklahoma v. Kansas Natural Gas Co.*, 221 U.S. 229 (1911); *Pennsylvania v. West Virginia*, 262 U.S. 553 (1923). These cases stand for the basic principle that a "State is without power to prevent privately owned articles of trade from being shipped and sold in interstate commerce on the ground that they are required to satisfy local demands or because they are needed by the people of the State." *Foster-Fountain Packing Co. v. Haydel*, 278 U.S. 1, 10 (1928).

The New Jersey law at issue in this case falls squarely within the area that the Commerce Clause puts off limits to state regulation. On its face, it imposes on out-of-state commercial interests the full burden of conserving the State's remaining landfill space. It is true that in our previous cases the scarce natural resource was itself the article of commerce, whereas here the scarce resource and the article of commerce are distinct. But that difference is without consequence. In both instances, the State has overtly moved to slow or freeze the flow of commerce for protectionist reasons. It does not matter that the State has shut the article of commerce inside the State in one case and outside the State in the other. What is crucial is the attempt by one State to isolate itself from a problem common to many by erecting a barrier against the movement of interstate trade.

The appellees argue that not all laws which facially discriminate against out-of-state commerce are forbidden protectionist regulations. In particular, they point to quarantine laws, which this Court has repeatedly upheld even though they appear to single out interstate commerce for special treatment. In the appellees' view, ch. 363 is analogous to such health-protective measures, since it reduces the exposure of New Jersey residents to the allegedly harmful effects of landfill sites.

It is true that certain quarantine laws have not been considered forbidden protectionist measures, even though they were directed against out-of-state commerce. *See Asbell v. Kansas*, 209 U.S. 251. But those quarantine laws banned the importation of articles such as diseased livestock that required destruction as soon as possible because their very movement risked contagion and other evils. Those laws thus did not discriminate against interstate commerce as such, but simply prevented traffic in noxious articles, whatever their origin.

The New Jersey statute is not such a quarantine law. There has been no claim here that the very movement of waste into or through New Jersey endangers health, or that waste must be disposed of as soon and as close to its point of generation as possible. The harms caused by waste are said to arise after its disposal in landfill sites, and at that point there is no basis to distinguish out-of-state waste from domestic waste. If one is inherently harmful, so is the other. Yet New Jersey has banned the former while leaving its landfill sites open to the latter. The New Jersey law blocks the importation of waste in an obvious effort to saddle those outside the State with the entire burden of slowing the flow of refuse into New

Jersey's remaining landfill sites. That legislative effort is clearly impermissible under the Commerce Clause of the Constitution.

Today, cities in Pennsylvania and New York find it expedient or necessary to send their waste into New Jersey for disposal, and New Jersey claims the right to close its borders to such traffic. Tomorrow, cities in New Jersey may find it expedient or necessary to send their waste into Pennsylvania or New York for disposal, and those States might then claim the right to close their borders. The Commerce Clause will protect New Jersey in the future, just as it protects her neighbors now, from efforts by one State to isolate itself in the stream of interstate commerce from a problem shared by all. The judgment is

Reversed.

Mr. Justice REHNQUIST, with whom THE CHIEF JUSTICE joins, *dissenting.*

The Court recognizes that States can prohibit the importation of items "which, on account of their existing condition, would bring in and spread disease, pestilence, and death, such as rags or other substances infected with the germs of yellow fever or the virus of small-pox, or cattle or meat or other provisions that are diseased or decayed or otherwise, from their condition and quality, unfit for human use or consumption." As the Court points out, such "quarantine laws have not been considered forbidden protectionist measures, even though they were directed against out-of-state commerce."

In my opinion, these cases are dispositive of the present one. Under them, New Jersey may require germ-infected rags or diseased meat to be disposed of as best as possible within the State, but at the same time prohibit the importation of such items for disposal at the facilities that are set up within New Jersey for disposal of such material generated within the State. The physical fact of life that New Jersey must somehow dispose of its own noxious items does not mean that it must serve as a depository for those of every other State. Similarly, New Jersey should be free under our past precedents to prohibit the importation of solid waste because of the health and safety problems that such waste poses to its citizens. The fact that New Jersey continues to, and indeed must continue to, dispose of its own solid waste does not mean that New Jersey may not prohibit the importation of even more solid waste into the State. I simply see no way to distinguish solid waste, on the record of this case, from germ-infected rags, diseased meat, and other noxious items.

The Court's effort to distinguish these prior cases is unconvincing. It first asserts that the quarantine laws which have previously been upheld "banned the importation of articles such as diseased livestock that required destruction as soon as possible because their very movement risked contagion and other evils." Solid waste which is a health hazard when it reaches its destination may in all likelihood be an equally great health hazard in transit. The Court implies that the challenged laws must be invalidated because New Jersey has left its landfills open to domestic waste. But, as the Court notes, this Court has repeatedly upheld quarantine laws "even though they appear to single out interstate commerce for special treatment."

The Supreme Court of New Jersey expressly found that ch. 363 was passed "to preserve the health of New Jersey residents by keeping their exposure to solid waste and landfill areas to a minimum." The Court points to absolutely no evidence that would contradict this finding by the New Jersey Supreme Court.

Note: State Quarantine Laws

The Court has upheld state quarantine laws (e.g., laws prohibiting the importation of diseased livestock) despite the effect of those laws on interstate commerce. *See, e.g., Mintz v. Baldwin,* 289 U.S. 346 (1933); *Asbell v. Kansas,* 209 U.S. 251 (1908). In quarantine cases, the Court characterized the statutes as police measures designed to protect the citizenry's health and safety. By contrast, in *Railroad Co. v. Husen,* 95 U.S. 465 (1877), the Court struck down a Missouri statute banning the importation of Texas, Mexican, or Indian cattle between March 1 and November 1. The Court declined to characterize the law as a valid quarantine measure due to its categorical nature (i.e., banning the importation of not just diseased cattle, but of all cattle from a certain origin).

Food for Thought: Distinguishing Baldwin

Baldwin suggests that states may quarantine out-of-state diseased cattle in order to protect the health, welfare, and safety of their citizens. Does *Philadelphia* adequately distinguish *Baldwin*? Is it really true, as the Court claims, that there "has been no claim in the *Philadelphia* case that the very movement of waste into or through New Jersey endangers health, or that waste must be disposed of as soon and as close to its point of generation as possible"?

∾ PROBLEM: OTHER WAYS TO SKIN THE CAT? ∾

If New Jersey does not have the power to ban out-of-state waste, does that mean that New Jersey is powerless to protect its citizens? What regulatory restrictions might it impose? Could New Jersey impose the following regulatory requirements without discriminating against interstate commerce? a) A requirement that all New Jersey trash dumps be licensed; b) a requirement that all New Jersey trash dumps are subject to health and safety restrictions regarding the handling of certain types of toxic chemicals; c) a requirement that all New Jersey dumps be periodically inspected to make sure that they are being operated in compliance with local health and safety laws; d) a fee ($100) on each truckload of refuse deposited in a New Jersey dump; e) a limit on the total amount of refuse that can be deposited in a given dump; f) an "environmental fee" imposed on each truckload of refuse deposited in a New Jersey dump, designed to help New Jersey combat and clean up the ill effects of refuse in New Jersey dumps. Does the amount of the fee (e.g., $500 or $5,000) matter? As we shall see, such restrictions will also be subject to review under the Court's dormant Commerce Clause analysis.

2. *Facially Neutral Statutes with Discriminatory Purposes or Effects*

Rarely does a legislature announce its intention to discriminate against interstate commerce. In *Baldwin,* for example, the State of New York proclaimed an allegedly nondiscriminatory purpose: "The end to be served is the maintenance of a regular and adequate supply of pure and wholesome milk; the supply being put in jeopardy when the farmers of the state are unable to earn a living income." However, the Court pierced the state's analysis and concluded that its real goal was economic isolation. Suppose that a state has a valid nondiscriminatory purpose that cannot be served by other means. Can it still restrict interstate commerce? If the state has a bona fide alternative purpose, can the state argue that it has no intent to discriminate?

Dean Milk Co. v. City of Madison

340 U.S. 349 (1951)

Mr. Justice CLARK delivered the opinion of the Court.

This appeal challenges the constitutional validity of two sections of an ordinance of the City of Madison, Wisconsin, regulating the sale of milk and milk products within the municipality's jurisdiction. One section makes it unlawful to sell any milk as pasteurized unless it has been processed and bottled at an approved pasteurization plant within a radius of five miles from the central square of Madison. Another section, which prohibits the sale of milk, or the importation, receipt or storage of milk for sale, in Madison unless from a source of supply possessing a permit issued after inspection by Madison officials, is attacked insofar as it expressly relieves municipal authorities from any duty to inspect farms located beyond twenty-five miles from the center of the city.

Appellant is an Illinois corporation engaged in distributing milk and milk products in Illinois and Wisconsin. It contends that both the five-mile limit on pasteurization plants and the twenty-five-mile limit on sources of milk violate the Commerce Clause.

Appellant purchases and gathers milk from approximately 950 farms in northern Illinois and southern Wisconsin, none being within twenty-five miles of Madison. Its pasteurization plants are in Illinois, about 65 and 85 miles respectively from Madison. Appellant was denied a license to sell its products within Madison solely because its pasteurization plants were more than five miles away.

It is conceded that the milk which appellant seeks to sell in Madison is supplied from farms and processed in plants licensed and inspected by public health authorities of Chicago, and is labeled "Grade A" under the Chicago ordinance which adopts the rating standards recommended by the United States Public Health Service. Both the Chicago and Madison ordinances are largely patterned after the Model Milk Ordinance of the Public Health Service. However, Madison contends and we assume that in some particulars its ordinance is more rigorous than that of Chicago.

We agree with appellant that the ordinance imposes an undue burden on interstate commerce. In erecting an economic barrier protecting a major local industry against competition from without the State, Madison plainly discriminates against interstate commerce. This it cannot do, even in the exercise of its unquestioned power to protect the health and safety of its people, if reasonable nondiscriminatory alternatives, adequate to conserve legitimate local interests, are available. A different view, that the ordinance is valid simply because it professes to be a health measure, would mean that the Commerce Clause of itself imposes no limitations on state action other than those laid down by the Due Process Clause, save for the rare instance where a state artlessly discloses an avowed purpose to discriminate against interstate goods. Our issue then is whether the discrimination inherent in the Madison ordinance can be justified in view of the character of the local interests and the available methods of protecting them.

It appears that reasonable and adequate alternatives are available. If the City of Madison prefers to rely upon its own officials for inspection of distant milk sources, such inspection is readily open to it without hardship for it could charge the actual and reasonable cost of such inspection to the importing producers and processors. Moreover, appellee Health Commissioner of Madison testified that as proponent of the local milk ordinance he had submitted the provisions here in controversy and an alternative proposal based on §11 of the Model Milk Ordinance recommended by the United States Public Health Service. The Commissioner testified that Madison consumers "would be safeguarded adequately" under either proposal and that he had expressed no preference. The milk sanitarian of the Wisconsin State Board of Health testified that the State Health Department recommends the adoption of a provision based on the Model Ordinance. Both officials agreed that a local health officer would be justified in relying upon the evaluation by the Public Health Service of enforcement conditions in remote producing areas.

To permit Madison to adopt a regulation not essential for the protection of local health interests and placing a discriminatory burden on interstate commerce would invite a multiplication of preferential trade areas destructive of the very purpose of the Commerce Clause. Under the circumstances here presented, the regulation must yield to the principle that 'one state in its dealings with another may not place itself in a position of economic isolation.'

For these reasons we conclude that the judgment below sustaining the five-mile provision as to pasteurization must be reversed.

The Supreme Court of Wisconsin thought it unnecessary to pass upon the validity of the twenty-five-mile limitation, apparently in part for the reason that this issue was made academic by its decision upholding the five-mile section. In view of our conclusion as to the latter provision, a determination of appellant's contention as to the other section is now necessary. As to this issue, therefore, we vacate the judgment below and remand for further proceedings not inconsistent with the principles announced in this opinion. It is so ordered.

Judgment *vacated* and case *remanded.*

Note: Live Baitfish

In *Maine v. Taylor,* 477 U.S. 131 (1986), the Court upheld a Maine statute banning the importation of live baitfish. The statute discriminated against interstate commerce by imposing an embargo on baitfish imports. The Court held that the statute satisfied strict scrutiny because the state's purpose (protection of Maine's "unique and ecologically fragile" fisheries) could not be protected by a less burdensome method. The Court concluded that inspection methods, which test imported baitfish for parasites, could not reliably produce disease-free shipments.

∾ PROBLEM: MORE ON THE INTERNET CASINO PROHIBITION ACT ∾

Even if the Internet Casino Prohibition Act is facially neutral, can it be argued that the Act has a discriminatory purpose or effect? If so, how? How might the state show a non-discriminatory purpose or effect?

Exxon Corp. v. Maryland

437 U.S. 117 (1978)

Mr. Justice STEVENS delivered the opinion of the Court.

A Maryland statute provides that a producer or refiner of petroleum products may not operate any retail service station within the State. The questions presented are whether the statute violates the Commerce Clause of the Constitution of the United States.

The Maryland statute is an outgrowth of the 1973 shortage of petroleum. In response to complaints about inequitable distribution of gasoline among retail stations, the Governor of Maryland directed the State Comptroller to conduct a market survey. The results of that survey indicated that gasoline stations operated by producers or refiners had received preferential treatment during the period of short supply. The Comptroller therefore proposed legislation which was "designed to correct the inequities in the distribution and pricing of gasoline reflected by the survey." After legislative hearings and a "special veto hearing" before the Governor, the bill was enacted and signed into law. Shortly before the effective date of the Act, Exxon Corp. filed a declaratory judgment action challenging the statute. After trial, the Circuit Court held the entire statute invalid. The Maryland Court of Appeals reversed.

Appellants argue that the divestiture provisions of the Maryland statute violate the Commerce Clause in three ways: (1) by discriminating against interstate commerce; (2) by unduly burdening interstate commerce; and (3) by imposing controls on a commercial activity of such an essentially interstate character that it is not amenable to state regulation.

Plainly, the Maryland statute does not discriminate against interstate goods, nor does it favor local producers and refiners. Since Maryland's entire gasoline supply flows in interstate commerce and since there are no local producers or refiners, such claims of disparate treatment between interstate and local commerce would be meritless. Appellants, however, focus on the retail market arguing that the effect of the statute is to protect in-state independent dealers from out-of-state competition. They contend that the divestiture provisions "create a protected enclave for Maryland independent dealers." They rely on the fact that the burden of the divestiture requirements falls solely on interstate companies. But this fact does not lead, either logically or as a practical matter, to a conclusion that the State is discriminating against interstate commerce at the retail level.

As the record shows, there are several major interstate marketers of petroleum that own and operate their own retail gasoline stations. These interstate dealers, who compete directly with the Maryland independent dealers, are not affected by the Act because they do not refine or produce gasoline. In fact, the Act creates no barriers whatsoever against interstate independent dealers; it does not prohibit the flow of interstate goods, place added costs upon them, or distinguish between in-state and out-of-state companies in the retail market. The absence of any of these factors fully distinguishes this case from those in which a State has been found to have discriminated against interstate commerce. *See, e.g., Hunt v. Washington Apple Advertising Comm'n.*, 432 U.S. 333 (1977). These other cases involved statutes that raised the cost of doing business for out-of-state dealers, and, in various other ways, favored the in-state dealer in the local market. No comparable claim can be made here. While the refiners will no longer enjoy their same status in the Maryland market, in-state independent dealers will have no competitive advantage over out-of-state dealers. The fact that the burden of a state regulation falls on some interstate companies does not, by itself, establish a claim of discrimination against interstate commerce.

Appellants argue that this fact does show that the Maryland statute impermissibly burdens interstate commerce. They point to evidence which indicates that, because of the divestiture requirements, at least three refiners will stop selling in Maryland, and which also shows that the elimination of company-operated stations will deprive the consumer of certain special services. Neither assertion warrants a finding that the statute impermissibly burdens interstate commerce.

Some refiners may choose to withdraw entirely from the Maryland market, but there is no reason to assume that their share of the entire supply will not be promptly replaced by other interstate refiners. The source of the consumers' supply may switch from company-operated stations to independent dealers, but interstate commerce is not subjected to an impermissible burden simply because an otherwise valid regulation causes some business to shift from one interstate supplier to another.

Appellants claim that, regardless of whether the State has interfered with the movement of goods in interstate commerce, it has interfered "with the natural functioning of the interstate market either through prohibition or through burdensome regulation." Appellants then claim that the statute "will surely change the market structure by weakening the independent refiners." We cannot, however, accept appellants' notion that the Commerce Clause protects the particular structure or methods of operation in a retail market. The dormant Commerce Clause protects the interstate market, not particular interstate firms, from prohibitive or burdensome regulations. It may be true that the consuming public will be injured by the loss of the high-volume, low-priced stations operated by the independent refiners, but that argument relates to the wisdom of the statute, not to its burden on commerce.

We cannot adopt appellants' novel suggestion that because the economic market for petroleum products is nationwide, no State has the power to regulate the retail marketing of gas. Appellants point out that many state legislatures have either enacted or considered proposals similar to Maryland's, and that the cumulative effect of this sort of legislation may have serious implications for their national marketing operations. While this concern is a significant one, we do not find that the Commerce Clause, by its own force, pre-empts the field of retail gas marketing. This Court has only rarely held that the Commerce Clause pre-empts an entire field from state regulation, and then only when a lack of national uniformity would impede the flow of interstate goods. In the absence of a relevant congressional declaration of policy, or a showing of a specific discrimination against, or burdening of, interstate commerce, we cannot conclude that the States are without power to regulate in this area.

The judgment is *affirmed*.

So ordered.

Mr. Justice BLACKMUN, *concurring in part* and *dissenting in part*.

The divestiture provisions preclude out-of-state competitors from retailing gasoline within Maryland. The effect is to protect in-state retail service station dealers from the competition of the out-of-state businesses. This protectionist discrimination is not justified by any legitimate state interest that cannot be vindicated by more evenhanded regulation.

In 1974, of the 3,780 gasoline service stations in the State, 3,547 were operated by nonintegrated local retail dealers. Of the 233 company-operated stations, 197 belonged to out-of-state integrated producers or refiners. Thirty-four were operated by nonintegrated companies that would not have been affected immediately by the Maryland statute. The only in-state integrated petroleum firm, Crown Central Petroleum, Inc., operated just two service stations. Of the class of stations statutorily insulated from the competition of the out-of-state integrated firms, then, more than 99% were operated by local business interests. Of the class of enterprises excluded entirely from participation in the retail gasoline market, 95% were out-of-state firms, operating 98% of the stations in the class.

The discrimination suffered by the out-of-state integrated producers and refiners is significant. Five of the excluded enterprises, market nonbranded gasoline through price competition rather than through brand recognition. Of the 98 stations marketing gasoline in this manner, all but 6 are company operated. The company operations result from the dominant fact of price competition marketing. Such nonbranded stations can compete successfully only if they have day-to-day control of the retail price of their products, the hours of operation of their stations, and related business details. Only with such control can sufficient sales volume be achieved to produce satisfactory profits at prices two to three cents a gallon below those of the major branded stations. Therefore, because §§(b) and (c) forbid company operations, these out-of-state competitors will have to abandon the Maryland retail market altogether. For the same reason 32 other out-of-state national nonbranded integrated marketers, who operate their own stations without dealers, will be precluded from entering the Maryland retail gasoline market.

The discrimination will burden the operations of major branded companies, such as appellants Exxon, Phillips, Shell, and Gulf, all of which are out-of-state firms. The divestiture provisions, which will require the appellant majors to cease operation of property valued at more than $10 million, will inflict significant economic hardship on Maryland's major brand companies, all of which are out-of-state firms.

Similar hardship is not imposed upon the local service station dealers by the divestiture provisions. Indeed, rather than restricting their ability to compete, the Maryland Act effectively and perhaps intentionally improves their competitive position by insulating them from competition by out-of-state integrated producers and refiners. In its answers to the various complaints in this case, the State repeatedly conceded that the Act was intended to protect "the retail dealer as an independent businessman by reducing the control and dominance of the vertically integrated petroleum producer and refiner in the retail market." In short, the foundation of the discrimination in this case is that the local dealers may continue to enter retail transactions and to compete for retail profits while the statute will deny similar opportunities to the class composed almost entirely of out-of-state businesses.

The Court says that the discrimination against the class of out-of-state producers and refiners does not violate the Commerce Clause because the State
has not imposed similar discrimination against other out-of-state retailers. To
accept the argument of the Court, that is, that discrimination must be universal
to offend the Commerce Clause, naively will foster protectionist discrimination
against interstate commerce. In the future, States will be able to insulate in-state
interests from competition by identifying the most potent segments of out-of-
state business, banning them, and permitting less effective out-of-state actors to
remain.

The Court asserts that "the fact that the burden of a state regulation falls on
some interstate companies does not, by itself, establish a claim of discrimination
against interstate commerce." When the burden is significant, when it falls on the
most numerous and effective group of out-of-state competitors, when a similar
burden does not fall on the class of protected in-state businessmen, and when the
State cannot justify the resulting disparity by showing that its legislative interests
cannot be vindicated by more evenhanded regulation, unconstitutional discrimination exists. The facts of this litigation demonstrate such discrimination, and
the Court does not argue persuasively to the contrary.

The Court of Appeals reasoned that §§(b) and (c) did not discriminate
against the class of out-of-state refiners and producers because the wholesale flow
of petroleum products into the State was not restricted. This supposedly distinguished the present facts from those of *Dean Milk Co. v. Madison*, which involved
unconstitutional discrimination against interstate commerce. To begin with, however, the distinction drawn by the Court of Appeals is basically irrelevant. The
Maryland statute has not effected discrimination with regard to the wholesaling
or interstate transport of petroleum. The discrimination exists with regard to
retailing. The fact that gasoline will continue to flow into the State does not permit the State to deny out-of-state firms the opportunity to retail it once it arrives.

The State argues that discrimination against interstate commerce has not
occurred because "no nexus between interstate as opposed to local interests
inheres in the production or refining of petroleum." Although this statement
might be correct in the abstract, it is incorrect in reality, given the structure of
the Maryland petroleum market. Due to geological formation as so far known,
no petroleum is produced in Maryland; due to the economics of production and
refining, as well as to the geology, no petroleum is refined in Maryland. As a
matter of actual fact, then, an inherent nexus does exist between the out-of-state
status of producers and refiners and the distribution and retailing of gasoline in
Maryland. The Commerce Clause does not forbid only legislation that discriminates under all factual circumstances. It forbids discrimination in effect against
interstate commerce on the specific facts of each case. If production or refining
of gasoline occurred in Maryland, §§(b) and (c) might not be unconstitutional.
Under those different circumstances, however, the producers and refiners would
have a fair opportunity to influence their local legislators and thereby to prevent
the enactment of economically disruptive legislation. Under those circumstances,

the economic disruption would be felt directly in Maryland, which would tend to make the local political processes responsive to the problems thereby created. Under those circumstances, §§(b) and (c) might never have been passed. In this case however, the economic disruption of the sections is visited upon out-of-state economic interests and not upon in-state businesses. One of the basic assumptions of the Commerce Clause is that local political systems will tend to be unresponsive to problems not felt by local constituents; instead, local political units are expected to act in their constituents' interests. One of the basic purposes of the Clause, therefore, is to prevent the vindication of such self-interest from unfairly burdening out-of-state concerns and thereby disrupting the national economy.

I would *reverse* the judgment of the Maryland Court of Appeals.

Notes and Questions

1. *May a State Prohibit Particular Items?* In *Bowman v. Chicago & N.W. Railway Co.*, 125 U.S. 465 (1888), the Court struck down an Iowa statute prohibiting common carriers (i.e., railroads) from bringing alcohol into the state without a certificate stating that the recipient is licensed by the state. The Court suggested that it would strike down state laws banning all importation of particular (otherwise permissible) goods even if the laws are motivated by a state policy against the use of such a product.

2. *Fuel Sales-Tax Credits.* In *New Energy Co. of Indiana v. Limbach*, 486 U.S. 269 (1988), the Court struck down an Ohio law that awarded a tax credit against the Ohio motor vehicle fuel sales tax for each gallon of ethanol sold (as a component of gasohol) by fuel dealers, but only if the ethanol was produced in Ohio or in a state that granted similar tax advantages to those for ethanol produced in Ohio. Ethanol is made from corn and was originally promoted as a means of achieving energy independence while providing a market for surplus corn. Ethanol has environmental advantages as a replacement for lead in enhancing fuel octane, but it is more expensive than gasoline. The Court struck down the law: "The 'negative' aspect of the Commerce Clause prohibits economic protectionism—that is, regulatory measures designed to benefit in-state economic interests by burdening out-of-state competitors. The Ohio provision explicitly deprives certain products of generally available beneficial tax treatment because they are made in certain other States. The present law imposes an economic disadvantage upon out-of-state sellers; and the promise to remove that if reciprocity is accepted no more justifies disparity of treatment than it would justify categorical exclusion." The Court rejected the idea that the law could be justified under the "market-participant" doctrine: "The Ohio action is neither its purchase nor its sale of ethanol, but its assessment and computation of taxes—a primeval governmental activity. To be sure, the tax credit scheme has the purpose and effect of subsidizing a particular industry, as do many dispositions of the tax laws. That does not transform it into a form of state participation in the

free market." Finally, the Court rejected the argument that Ohio could validate the law "by showing that it advances a legitimate local purpose that cannot be adequately served by reasonable nondiscriminatory alternatives": "Appellees advance two justifications: health and commerce. As to the first, they argue that the provision encourages use of ethanol (in replacement of lead as a gasoline octane-enhancer) to reduce harmful exhaust emissions. Certainly the protection of health is a legitimate state goal, and we assume for purposes of this argument that use of ethanol generally furthers it. But there is no reason to suppose that ethanol produced in a State that does not offer tax advantages to ethanol produced in Ohio is less healthy, and thus should have its importation into Ohio suppressed by denial of the otherwise standard tax credit. The same reasoning also responds to the justification that the reciprocity requirement is designed to increase commerce in ethanol by encouraging other States to enact ethanol subsidies. What is encouraged is not ethanol subsidies in general, but only favorable treatment for Ohio-produced ethanol."

C. NONDISCRIMINATORY BURDENS ON INTERSTATE COMMERCE

Even when a state law does not discriminate against interstate commerce, the law may still affect interstate commerce and still be subject to judicial review. In general, when statutes regulate local and out-of-state interests evenhandedly and have only an indirect effect on interstate commerce, they are nonetheless examined to determine whether the burden on interstate commerce clearly exceeds the benefits. *See, e.g., Brown-Forman Distillers Corp. v. New York State Liquor Authority,* 476 U.S. 573, 578 (1986).

1. The Scope of Judicial Review

Some argue that the federal courts should be deferential to state legislation, recognizing that Congress is free to override state laws with which it disagrees. Others argue that courts should actively review state laws, and should strike down laws that burden interstate commerce. Which approach is preferable? Consider the following two cases, which reflect divergent approaches.

South Carolina State Highway Dept. v. Barnwell Bros.

303 U.S. 177 (1938)

Mr. Justice STONE delivered the opinion of the Court.

Act No. 259 of the General Assembly of South Carolina, of April 28, 1933, prohibits use on the state highways of motor trucks and "semi-trailer motor trucks" whose width exceeds 90 inches, and whose weight including load exceeds

20,000 pounds. The principal question for decision is whether these prohibitions impose an unconstitutional burden upon interstate commerce.

Congress has not undertaken to regulate the weight and size of motor vehicles in interstate motor traffic and has left undisturbed whatever authority in that regard the states have retained under the Constitution.

While the constitutional grant to Congress of power to regulate interstate commerce has been held to operate of its own force to curtail state power in some measure, there are matters of local concern, the regulation of which unavoidably involves some regulation of interstate commerce but which, because of their local character and their number and diversity, may never be fully dealt with by Congress. Notwithstanding the commerce clause, such regulation in the absence of congressional action has for the most part been left to the states by the decisions of this Court, subject to the other applicable constitutional restraints.

The present case affords no occasion for saying that the bare possession of power by Congress to regulate the interstate traffic forces the states to conform to standards which Congress might, but has not adopted, or curtails their power to take measures to insure the safety and conservation of their highways which may be applied to like traffic moving intrastate. Few subjects of state regulation are so peculiarly of local concern as is the use of state highways. There are few, local regulation of which is so inseparable from a substantial effect on interstate commerce. Unlike the railroads, local highways are built, owned, and maintained by the state or its municipal subdivisions. The state has a primary and immediate concern in their safe and economical administration. The present regulations, or any others of like purpose, if they are to accomplish their end, must be applied alike to interstate and intrastate traffic both moving in large volume over the highways. The fact that they affect alike shippers in interstate and intrastate commerce in large number within as well as without the state is a safeguard against their abuse.

The states may not, under the guise of regulation, discriminate against interstate commerce. But, "In the absence of national legislation especially covering the subject of interstate commerce, the state may rightly prescribe uniform regulations adapted to promote safety upon its highways and the conservation of their use, applicable alike to vehicles moving in interstate commerce and those of its own citizens." *Morris v. Duby*, 274 U.S. 135, 143 (1927). This Court has often sustained the exercise of that power, although it has burdened or impeded interstate commerce. It has upheld weight limitations lower than those presently imposed, applied alike to motor traffic moving interstate and intrastate. Restrictions favoring passenger traffic over the carriage of interstate merchandise by truck have been similarly sustained, as has the exaction of a reasonable fee for the use of the highways.

Congress, in the exercise of its plenary power to regulate interstate commerce, may determine whether the burdens imposed on it by state regulation, otherwise permissible, are too great, and may, by legislation designed to secure uniformity or in other respects to protect the national interest in the commerce, curtail to some extent the state's regulatory power. But that is a legislative, not a judicial, function, to be performed in the light of the congressional judgment of what is appropriate regulation of interstate commerce, and the extent to which, in that field, state power and local interests should be required to yield to the national authority and interest. In the absence of such legislation the judicial function, under the commerce clause, Const. art. 1, §8, cl. 3, as well as the Fourteenth Amendment, stops with the inquiry whether the state Legislature in adopting regulations such as the present has acted within its province, and whether the means of regulation chosen are reasonably adapted to the end sought.

Here the first inquiry has already been resolved by our decisions that a state may impose nondiscriminatory restrictions with respect to the character of motor vehicles moving in interstate commerce as a safety measure and as a means of securing the economical use of its highways. In resolving the second, courts do not sit as Legislatures, either state or national. They cannot act as Congress does when, after weighing all the conflicting interests, state and national, it determines when and how much the state regulatory power shall yield to the larger interests of a national commerce. And in reviewing a state highway regulation where Congress has not acted, a court is not called upon, as are state Legislatures, to determine what, in its judgment, is the most suitable restriction to be applied of those that are possible, or to choose that one which in its opinion is best adapted to all the diverse interests affected. When the action of a Legislature is within the scope of its power, fairly debatable questions as to its reasonableness, wisdom, and propriety are not for the determination of courts, but for the legislative body, on which rests the duty and responsibility of decision. This is equally the case when the legislative power is one which may legitimately place an incidental burden on interstate commerce. It is not any the less a legislative power committed to the states because it affects interstate commerce, and courts are not any the more entitled, because interstate commerce is affected, to substitute their own for the legislative judgment.

Since the adoption of one weight or width regulation, rather than another, is a legislative, not a judicial, choice, its constitutionality is not to be determined by weighing in the judicial scales the merits of the legislative choice and rejecting it if the weight of evidence presented in court appears to favor a different standard. Being a legislative judgment it is presumed to be supported by facts known to the Legislature unless facts judicially known or proved preclude that possibility. Hence, in reviewing the present determination, we examine the record, not to see whether the findings of the court below are supported by evidence, but to ascertain upon the whole record whether it is possible to say that the legislative choice is without rational basis. Not only does the record fail to exclude that possibility but it shows affirmatively that there is adequate support for the legislative judgment.

The regulatory measures taken by South Carolina are within its legislative power. They do not infringe the Fourteenth Amendment, and the resulting burden on interstate commerce is not forbidden.

Reversed.

∾ PROBLEM: MORE ON THE INTERNET
CASINO PROHIBITION ACT ∾

Under the *Barnwell* holding, is the Internet Casino Prohibition Act likely to pass constitutional muster? If so, why (or why not)?

Southern Pacific Co. v. Arizona

325 U.S. 761 (1945)

Mr. Chief Justice STONE delivered the opinion of the Court.

The Arizona Train Limit Law of May 16, 1912 makes it unlawful for any person or corporation to operate within the state a railroad train of more than fourteen passenger or seventy freight cars.

For a hundred years it has been accepted constitutional doctrine that the commerce clause, without the aid of Congressional legislation, thus affords some protection from state legislation inimical to the national commerce, and that where Congress has not acted, this Court, and not the state legislature, is under the commerce clause the final arbiter of the competing demands of state and national interests. *Cooley v. Board of Wardens, supra.*

There has thus been left to the states wide scope for the regulation of matters of local state concern, even though it in some measure affects the commerce, provided it does not materially restrict the free flow of commerce across state lines, or interfere with it in matters with respect to which uniformity of regulation is of predominant national concern.

Hence the matters for ultimate determination here are the nature and extent of the burden which the state regulation of interstate trains, adopted as a safety measure, imposes on interstate commerce, and whether the relative weights of the state and national interests involved are such as to make inapplicable the rule, generally observed, that the free flow of interstate commerce and its freedom from local restraints in matters requiring uniformity of regulation are interests safeguarded by the commerce clause from state interference.

The findings show that the operation of long trains, that is trains of more than fourteen passenger and more than seventy freight cars, is standard practice over the main lines of the railroads of the United States, and that, if the length of trains is to be regulated at all, national uniformity in the regulation adopted, such as only Congress can prescribe, is practically indispensable to the operation of an efficient and economical national railway system. On many railroads passenger trains of more than fourteen cars and freight trains of more than seventy cars are operated, and on some systems freight trains are run ranging from one hundred and twenty-five to one hundred and sixty cars in length. Outside of Arizona, where the length of trains is not restricted, appellant runs a substantial proportion of long trains. In 1939 on its comparable route for through traffic through Utah and Nevada from 66 to 85% of its freight trains were over 70 cars in length and over 43% of its passenger trains included more than fourteen passenger cars. In Arizona, approximately 93% of the freight traffic and 95% of the passenger traffic is interstate. Because of the Train Limit Law appellant is required to haul over 30% more trains in Arizona than would otherwise have been necessary.

The unchallenged findings leave no doubt that the Arizona Train Limit Law imposes a serious burden on interstate commerce. It materially impedes the movement of appellant's interstate trains through that state and interposes a substantial obstruction to the national policy proclaimed by Congress, to promote adequate, economical and efficient railway transportation service. Enforcement of the law in Arizona, while train lengths remain unregulated or are regulated by varying standards in other states, must inevitably result in an impairment of uniformity of efficient railroad operation because the railroads are subjected to regulation which is not uniform in its application. Compliance with a state statute limiting train lengths requires interstate trains of a length lawful in other states to be broken up and reconstituted as they enter each state according as it may impose varying limitations upon train lengths. The alternative is for the carrier to conform to the lowest train limit restriction of any of the states through which its trains pass, whose laws thus control the carriers' operations both within and without the regulating state.

At present the seventy freight car laws are enforced only in Arizona and Oklahoma, with a fourteen car passenger car limit in Arizona. The record shows that the Arizona statute results in freight trains being broken up and reformed at the California border and in New Mexico, some distance from the Arizona line. Frequently it is not feasible to operate a newly assembled train from the New Mexico yard nearest to Arizona, with the result that the Arizona limitation governs the flow of traffic as far east as El Paso, Texas. For similar reasons the Arizona law often controls the length of passenger trains all the way from Los Angeles to El Paso.

If one state may regulate train lengths, so may all the others, and they need not prescribe the same maximum limitation. The practical effect of such regulation is to control train operations beyond the boundaries of the state exacting it because of the necessity of breaking up and reassembling long trains at the nearest terminal points before entering and after leaving the regulating state. The serious impediment to the free flow of commerce by the local regulation of train lengths and the practical necessity that such regulation, if any, must be prescribed by a single body having a nation-wide authority are apparent.

The trial court found that the Arizona law had no reasonable relation to safety, and made train operation more dangerous. These facts which indicate that such increased danger of accident and personal injury as may result from the greater length of trains is more than offset by the increase in the number of accidents resulting from the larger number of trains when train lengths are reduced. In considering the effect of the statute as a safety measure, therefore, the factor of controlling significance for present purposes is not whether there is basis for the conclusion of the Arizona Supreme Court that the increase in length of trains beyond the statutory maximum has an adverse effect upon safety of operation. The decisive question is whether in the circumstances the total effect of the law as a safety measure in reducing accidents and casualties is so slight or problematical as not to outweigh the national interest in keeping interstate commerce free from interferences which seriously impede it and subject it to local regulation which does not have a uniform effect on the interstate train journey which it interrupts.

The principal source of danger of accident from increased length of trains is the resulting increase of "slack action" of the train. Slack action is the amount of free movement of one car before it transmits its motion to an adjoining coupled car. This free movement results from the fact that in railroad practice cars are loosely coupled, and the coupling is often combined with a stock-absorbing device, a "draft gear" which, under stress, substantially increases the free movement as the train is started or stopped. Loose coupling is necessary to enable the train to proceed freely around curves and is an aid in starting heavy trains, since the application of the locomotive power to the train operates on each car in the train successively, and the power is thus utilized to start only one car at a time.

The slack action between cars due to loose couplings varies from seven-eighths of an inch to one and one-eighth inches and, with the added free movement due to the use of draft gears, may be as high as six or seven inches between cars. The length of the train increases the slack since the slack action of a train is the total of the free movement between its several cars. The amount of slack action has some effect on the severity of the shock of train movements, and on freight trains sometimes results in injuries to operatives, which most frequently occur to occupants of the caboose. The amount and severity of slack action, however, are not wholly dependent upon the length of train, as they may be affected by the mode and conditions of operation as to grades, speed, and load. And accidents due to slack action also occur in the operation of short trains. On comparison of the number of slack action accidents in Arizona with those in Nevada, where the length of trains is now unregulated, the trial court found that with substantially the same amount of traffic in each state the number of accidents was relatively the same in long as in short train operations. While accidents from slack action do occur in the operation of passenger trains, it does not appear that they are more frequent or the resulting shocks more severe on long than on short passenger trains. Nor does it appear that slack action accidents occurring on passenger trains, whatever their length, are of sufficient severity to cause serious injury or damage.

Upon an examination of the whole case the trial court found that "if short-train operation may or should result in any decrease in the number or severity of the 'slack' or 'slack-surge' type of accidents or casualties, such decrease is substantially more than offset by the increased number of accidents and casualties from other causes that follow the arbitrary limitation of freight trains to 70 cars and passenger trains to 14 cars."

We think that the Arizona Train Limit Law, viewed as a safety measure, affords at most slight and dubious advantage, if any, over unregulated train lengths, because it results in an increase in the number of trains and train operations and the consequent increase in train accidents of a character generally more severe than those due to slack action. Its undoubted effect on the commerce is the regulation, without securing uniformity, of the length of trains operated in interstate commerce, which lack is itself a primary cause of preventing the free flow of commerce by delaying it and by substantially increasing its cost and impairing its efficiency. In these respects the case differs from those where a state, by regulatory measures affecting the commerce, has removed or reduced safety hazards without substantial interference with the interstate movement of trains.

Here we conclude that the state does go too far. Its regulation of train lengths, admittedly obstructive to interstate train operation, and having a seriously adverse effect on transportation efficiency and economy, passes beyond what is plainly essential for safety since it does not appear that it will lessen rather than increase the danger of accident. Its attempted regulation of the operation of interstate trains cannot establish nation-wide control such as is essential to the maintenance of an efficient transportation system, which Congress alone can prescribe. The state interest cannot be preserved at the expense of the national interest by an enactment which regulates interstate train lengths without securing such control, which is a matter of national concern. To this the interest of the state here asserted is subordinate.

Reversed.

Mr. Justice BLACK, *dissenting.*

The state trial judge heard evidence over a period of 5 months which appears in about 3000 pages of the printed record before us. It then adopted findings of fact which cover 148 printed pages, and conclusions of law which cover 5 pages. This new pattern of trial procedure makes it necessary for a judge to hear all the evidence offered as to why a legislature passed a law and to make findings of fact as to the validity of those reasons. If a court does make findings, as to a danger contrary to the findings of the legislature, and the evidence heard "lends support" to those findings, a court can then invalidate the law. In this respect, the Arizona County Court acted, and this Court today is acting, as a "super-legislature."

Even if this method of invalidating legislative acts is a correct one, I still think that the "findings" of the state court do not authorize today's decision. That court did not find that there is no unusual danger from slack movements in long trains. It did decide on disputed evidence that the long train "slack movement" dangers were more than offset by prospective dangers as a result of running a larger number of short trains, since many people might be hurt at grade crossings. There was undoubtedly some evidence before the state court from which it could have reached such a conclusion. There was undoubtedly as much evidence before it which would have justified a different conclusion.

Under those circumstances, the determination of whether it is in the interest of society for the length of trains to be governmentally regulated is a matter of public policy. Someone must fix that policy—either the Congress, or the state, or the courts. A century and a half of constitutional history and government admonishes this Court to leave that choice to the elected legislative representatives of the people themselves, where it properly belongs both on democratic principles and the requirements of efficient government.

There have been many sharp divisions of this Court concerning its authority, in the absence of congressional enactment, to invalidate state laws as violating the Commerce Clause. Even the broadest exponents of judicial power in this field have not heretofore expressed doubt as to a state's power, absent a paramount congressional declaration, to regulate interstate trains in the interest of safety.

When we finally get down to the gist of what the Court today actually decides, it is this: Even though more railroad employees will be injured by "slack action" movements on long trains than on short trains, there must be no regulation of this danger in the absence of "uniform regulations." That means that no one can legislate against this danger except the Congress; and even though the Congress is perfectly content to leave the matter to the different state legislatures, this Court, on the ground of "lack of uniformity," will require it to make an express avowal of that fact before it will permit a state to guard against that admitted danger.

Mr. Justice DOUGLAS, *dissenting.*

Courts should intervene only where the state legislation discriminated against interstate commerce or was out of harmony with laws which Congress had enacted.

Notes and Questions

1. *Distinguishing* Barnwell *and* Southern Pacific. Note how differently the Court perceives its role in the *Barnwell* and *Southern Pacific* cases. Which approach is better? In the absence of congressional action, should the courts be deferential to state legislation? After all, if the states decide to regulate and Congress does not like what the states have done, Congress can pass a law overriding those state laws. Moreover, if a state law unreasonably burdens commerce (e.g., the Arizona law), shouldn't we assume that those adversely affected by the law (in this case, the national railroad companies) will urge Congress to pass overriding legislation? If Congress decides not to pass such legislation, why should the courts intervene? On the other hand, is judicial intervention justified on the assumption that Congress does not have time to individually legislate on all of the burdens that states may place on commerce?

2. *The Black Dissent.* Justice Black's *Southern Pacific* dissent notes that the trial court heard five months of testimony and compiled a 3,000-page record before ruling on the validity of Arizona's law. Is it appropriate for a trial court to engage in such an intensive review process? If it does, is the trial court assuming more of a legislative role?

3. *Can a State Require Interstate Truckers to Install Contoured Mud Flaps? Bibb v. Navajo Freight Lines,* Inc., 359 U.S. 520 (1959), involved an Illinois statute that required the use of contoured rear fender mudguards on trucks and trailers. This mud flap differed from the conventional or straight mud flap permitted in 45 states and required in Arkansas. In *Bibb,* the Court struck the law down, emphasizing that contour mudguards have no advantages over conventional mudguards and indeed create safety hazards (they tend to cause heat to accumulate in the brake drum, thus decreasing effectiveness and potentially causing safety problems on the highway). The Court also found that the Illinois law "seriously interferes with the 'interline' operations of motor carriers—the interchanging of trailers between an originating carrier and another carrier. These 'interline' operations provide a speedy through-service for the shipper, but contemplates the physical transfer of the entire trailer with no unloading and reloading of the cargo. The interlining process is particularly vital in connection with shipment of perishables, or with the movement of explosives carried under seal. If an interchanged trailer of that carrier were hauled to or through Illinois, the statute would require that it contain contour guards. Since carriers which operate in and through Illinois cannot compel the originating carriers to equip their trailers with contour guards, they may be forced to cease interlining with those who do not meet the Illinois requirements. Over 60 percent of the business of 5 of the 6 plaintiffs is interline traffic." In addition, the Court found that it is extremely difficult to change mudguards at the state line, thereby "causing a significant delay [wben] prompt movement may be of the essence. From two to four hours of labor are required to install or remove a contour mudguard. Moreover, the contour guard is attached by welding and if the trailer is conveying a cargo of explosives it would be exceedingly dangerous to weld on a contour mudguard without unloading the trailer." As a result, the Court concluded that the case involved one of those instances "few in number—where local safety measures that are nondiscriminatory place an unconstitutional burden on interstate commerce."

4. *Regulating Truck Length.* There has been much litigation about the extent to which the states can regulate truck lengths. For example, in *Raymond Motor Transportation, Inc. v. Rice,* 434 U.S. 429 (1978), a Wisconsin statute prohibited trucks from pulling double trailers and also prohibited truck rigs longer than 55 feet in length, absent a special permit. Even though the Court emphasized its reluctance to invalidate "state legislation in the field of safety where the propriety of local regulation has long been recognized," and emphasized that it usually gives great deference to state safety regulations and applies a "strong presumption of their validity," the Court struck the Wisconsin law down, noting that the state's asserted safety justification (65-foot doubles take longer to pass or be passed than 55-foot singles) did not hold up as applied to trucks "on limited access, four-lane divided highways." In addition, the Court found that the law imposed a substantial burden on the interstate movement of goods: "The regulations substantially increase the cost of such movement and slow the movement of goods in interstate

commerce by forcing appellants to haul doubles across the State separately, to haul doubles around the State altogether, or to incur the delays caused by using singles instead of doubles to pick up and deliver goods. Finally, the regulations prevent appellants from accepting interline transfers of 65-foot doubles for movement through Wisconsin from carriers that operate only in the 33 States where the doubles are legal." Finally, when the Court analyzed the law's exceptions, it found that at "least one of these exceptions discriminates on its face in favor of Wisconsin industries and against the industries of other States, and there are indications in the record that a number of the other exceptions, although neutral on their face, were enacted at the instance of, and primarily benefit, important Wisconsin industries." As a result, the Court concluded that "the challenged regulations violate the Commerce Clause because they place a substantial burden on interstate commerce and they cannot be said to make more than the most speculative contribution to highway safety."

∼ PROBLEMS ∼

1. *State Regulation and New Technologies.* At this point, let's think a bit more about the *Bibb* decision, but let's alter the facts. In the actual case, the Court noted that Arkansas required a conventional mudguard and that the overwhelming majority of states permitted it. In addition, the Court found that the contoured mudguard possessed no safety advantages vis-à-vis the conventional mudguard and that it could even be dangerous. Suppose that a new type of mudguard is developed — the modified contoured mudguard ("modified mudguard") — and the scientific evidence demonstrates that this new mudguard possesses significant safety advantages over conventional mudguards. However, at this point, no other state has required the use of the modified mudguard, and three states require the use of the conventional mudguard. Could Illinois mandate use of the modified mudguard despite the possible impact on interline operations? Could Illinois argue that the contradictory state laws should, instead, be invalidated?

2. *More on the Internet Casino Prohibition Act.* Under the *Southern Pacific* balancing test, is the Internet Casino Prohibition Act likely to be upheld? If you are hired to represent the casinos, how might you argue that the Act places an undue burden on interstate commerce? Now, suppose that you represent the Commonwealth of Kentucky. How might you respond to those arguments?

2. Modern Applications of the Southern Pacific Test

Modern cases have used the *Southern Pacific* balancing test rather than the *Barnwell* test. The following cases illustrate modern applications of the test.

Minnesota v. Clover Leaf Creamery Co.

449 U.S. 456 (1981)

Justice BRENNAN delivered the opinion of the Court.

In 1977, the Minnesota Legislature enacted a statute banning the retail sale of milk in plastic nonreturnable, nonrefillable containers, but permitting such sale in other nonreturnable, nonrefillable containers, such as paperboard milk cartons. The purpose of the Minnesota statute is set out as §1:

> The legislature finds that the use of nonreturnable, nonrefillable containers for the packaging of milk and other milk products presents a solid waste management problem for the state, promotes energy waste, and depletes natural resources. The legislature therefore determines that the use of nonreturnable, nonrefillable containers for packaging milk and other milk products should be discouraged and that the use of returnable and reusable packaging for these products is preferred and should be encouraged.

Section 2 of the Act forbids the retail sale of milk and fluid milk products, other than sour cream, cottage cheese, and yogurt, in nonreturnable, nonrefillable rigid or semi-rigid containers composed at least 50% of plastic.

The Act was introduced with the support of the state Pollution Control Agency, Department of Natural Resources, Department of Agriculture, Consumer Services Division, and Energy Agency, and debated vigorously in the state legislature. Proponents of the legislation argued that it would promote resource conservation, ease solid waste disposal problems, and conserve energy. Relying on the results of studies, they stressed the need to stop introduction of the plastic nonreturnable container before it became entrenched in the market. Opponents of the Act, also presenting empirical evidence, argued that the Act would not promote the goals asserted by the proponents, but would merely increase costs of retail milk products and prolong the use of ecologically undesirable paperboard milk cartons.

After the Act was passed, respondents filed suit in state court to enjoin its enforcement. The trial court held the statute unconstitutional under the Commerce Clause because it imposes an unreasonable burden on interstate commerce. The Supreme Court of Minnesota affirmed. We conclude that the ban on plastic nonreturnable milk containers bears a rational relation to the State's objectives, and must be sustained.

If a state law purporting to promote environmental purposes is in reality "simple economic protectionism," we have applied a "virtually per se rule of invalidity." *Philadelphia v. New Jersey*, 437 U.S. 617 (1978). Even if a statute regulates "evenhandedly," and imposes only "incidental" burdens on interstate commerce, the courts must nevertheless strike it down if "the burden imposed on such commerce is clearly excessive in relation to the putative local benefits." Moreover, "the extent of the burden that will be tolerated will of course depend on the nature of the local interest involved, and on whether it could be promoted as well with a lesser impact on interstate activities."

Minnesota's statute does not effect "simple protectionism," but "regulates evenhandedly" by prohibiting all milk retailers from selling their products in plastic, nonreturnable milk containers, without regard to whether the milk, the containers, or the sellers are from outside the State. This statute is therefore unlike statutes discriminating against interstate commerce, which we have consistently struck down. *E.g., Philadelphia v. New Jersey, supra.* Since the statute does not discriminate between interstate and intrastate commerce, the controlling question is whether the incidental burden imposed on interstate commerce by the Minnesota Act is "clearly excessive in relation to the putative local benefits."

The burden imposed on interstate commerce by the statute is relatively minor. Milk products may continue to move freely across the Minnesota border, and since most dairies package their products in more than one type of containers, the inconvenience of having to conform to different packaging requirements in Minnesota and the surrounding States should be slight. Within Minnesota, business will presumably shift from manufacturers of plastic nonreturnable containers to producers of paperboard cartons, refillable bottles, and plastic pouches, but there is no reason to suspect that the gainers will be Minnesota firms, or the losers out-of-state firms. Indeed, two of the three dairies, the sole milk retailer, and the sole milk container producer challenging the statute in this litigation are Minnesota firms.

Pulpwood producers are the only Minnesota industry likely to benefit significantly from the Act at the expense of out-of-state firms. Plastic resin, the raw material used for making plastic nonreturnable milk jugs, is produced entirely by non-Minnesota firms, while pulpwood, used for making paperboard, is a major Minnesota product. Nevertheless, it is clear that respondents exaggerate the degree of burden on out-of-state interests, both because plastics will continue to be used in the production of plastic pouches, plastic returnable bottles, and paperboard itself, and because out-of-state pulpwood producers will presumably absorb some of the business generated by the Act.

Even granting that the out-of-state plastics industry is burdened relatively more heavily than the Minnesota pulpwood industry, we find that this burden is not "clearly excessive" in light of the substantial state interest in promoting conservation of energy and other natural resources and easing solid waste disposal problems. We find these local benefits ample to support Minnesota's decision under the Commerce Clause. Moreover, we find that no approach with "a lesser impact on interstate activities" is available. Suggested alternatives are either more burdensome on commerce than the Act (as, for example, banning all nonreturnables) or less likely to be effective (as, for example, providing incentives for recycling).

A nondiscriminatory regulation serving substantial state purposes is not invalid simply because it causes some business to shift from a predominantly out-of-state industry to a predominantly in-state industry. Only if the burden on interstate commerce clearly outweighs the State's legitimate purposes does such a regulation violate the Commerce Clause.

The judgment of the Minnesota Supreme Court is
Reversed.

West Lynn Creamery, Inc. v. Healy

512 U.S. 186 (1994)

Justice STEVENS delivered the opinion of the Court.

A Massachusetts pricing order imposes an assessment on all fluid milk sold by dealers to Massachusetts retailers. About two-thirds of that milk is produced out of State. The entire assessment, however, is distributed to Massachusetts dairy farmers. The question presented is whether the pricing order unconstitutionally discriminates against interstate commerce. We hold that it does.

Petitioner West Lynn Creamery, Inc., is a milk dealer licensed to do business in Massachusetts. It purchases raw milk, which it processes, packages, and sells to wholesalers, retailers, and other milk dealers. About 97% of the raw milk it purchases is produced by out-of-state farmers. Petitioner LeComte's Dairy, Inc., is also a licensed Massachusetts milk dealer. It purchases all of its milk from West Lynn and distributes it to retail outlets in Massachusetts.

In the 1980's and early 1990's, Massachusetts dairy farmers began to lose market share to lower cost producers in neighboring States. In response, the Governor of Massachusetts appointed a Special Commission to study the dairy industry. The Commission found that many producers had sold their dairy farms during the past decade and that if prices paid to farmers for their milk were not significantly increased, a majority of the remaining farmers in Massachusetts would be "forced out of business within the year." Relying on the Commission's Report, the Commissioner of the Massachusetts Department of Food and Agriculture (respondent) declared a State of Emergency. Promptly after his declaration of emergency, respondent issued the pricing order that is challenged in this proceeding.

The order requires every "dealer" in Massachusetts to make a monthly "premium payment" into the "Massachusetts Dairy Equalization Fund." The amount of those payments is computed in two steps. First, the monthly "order premium" is determined. Second, the premium is multiplied by the amount (in pounds) of the dealer's milk sales in Massachusetts. Each month the fund is distributed to Massachusetts producers. Each Massachusetts producer receives a share of the total fund equal to his proportionate contribution to the State's total production of raw milk.

Petitioners refused to make the premium payments, and respondent commenced license revocation proceedings. Petitioners then filed suit seeking an injunction against enforcement of the order on the ground that it violated the Commerce Clause of the Federal Constitution. The state court denied relief. We granted certiorari and now reverse.

The paradigmatic example of a law discriminating against interstate commerce is the protective tariff or customs duty, which taxes goods imported from other States, but does not tax similar products produced in State. A tariff is an attractive measure because it simultaneously raises revenue and benefits local producers by burdening their out-of-state competitors. Nevertheless, it violates the principle of the unitary national market by handicapping out-of-state competitors, thus artificially encouraging in-state production even when the same goods could be produced at lower cost in other States.

Because of their distorting effects on the geography of production, tariffs have long been recognized as violative of the Commerce Clause. *See Baldwin v. G.A.F. Seelig, Inc.,* 294 U.S. 511 (1935). Under these cases, Massachusetts' pricing order is clearly unconstitutional. Its avowed purpose and its undisputed effect are to enable higher cost Massachusetts dairy farmers to compete with lower cost dairy farmers in other States. The "premium payments" are effectively a tax which makes milk produced out of State more expensive. Although the tax also applies to milk produced in Massachusetts, its effect on Massachusetts producers is entirely (indeed more than) offset by the subsidy provided exclusively to Massachusetts dairy farmers. Like an ordinary tariff, the tax is thus effectively imposed only on out-of-state products. The pricing order thus allows Massachusetts dairy farmers who produce at higher cost to sell at or below the price charged by lower cost out-of-state producers.

Respondent argues that the payments to Massachusetts dairy farmers from the Dairy Equalization Fund are valid, because subsidies are constitutional exercises of state power, and that the order premium which provides money for the Fund is valid, because it is a nondiscriminatory tax. Therefore the pricing order is constitutional, because it is merely the combination of two independently lawful regulations. In effect, if the State may impose a valid tax on dealers, it is free to use the proceeds of the tax as it chooses; and if it may independently subsidize its farmers, it is free to finance the subsidy by means of any legitimate tax.

Even granting respondent's assertion that both components of the pricing order would be constitutional standing alone, the pricing order nevertheless must fall. A pure subsidy funded out of general revenue ordinarily imposes no burden on interstate commerce, but merely assists local business. The pricing order in this case is funded principally from taxes on the sale of milk produced in other States. By so funding the subsidy, respondent not only assists local farmers, but burdens interstate commerce. The pricing order thus violates the cardinal principle that a State may not "benefit in-state economic interests by burdening out-of-state competitors." *New Energy Co. of Indiana v. Limbach,* 486 U.S. 289 (1988).

More fundamentally, respondent errs in assuming that the constitutionality of the pricing order follows logically from the constitutionality of its component parts. By conjoining a tax and a subsidy, Massachusetts has created a program more dangerous to interstate commerce than either part alone. Nondiscriminatory measures, like the evenhanded tax at issue here, are generally upheld, in spite of any adverse effects on interstate commerce, in part because "the existence of major in-state interests adversely affected is a powerful safeguard against legislative abuse." *Minnesota v. Clover Leaf Creamery Co.,* 449 U.S. 456 (1981). However, when a nondiscriminatory tax is coupled with a subsidy to one of the groups hurt by the tax, a state's political processes can no longer be relied upon to prevent legislative abuse, because one of the in-state interests which would otherwise lobby against the tax has been mollified by the subsidy. One would ordinarily have expected at least three groups to lobby against the order premium, which, as a tax, raises the price (and hence lowers demand) for milk: dairy farmers, milk dealers, and consumers. But because the tax was coupled with a subsidy, one of the most powerful of these groups, Massachusetts dairy farmers, instead of exerting their influence against the tax, were in fact its primary supporters.

Respondent's argument would require us to analyze separately two parts of an integrated regulation, but we cannot divorce the premium payments from the use to which the payments are put. It is the entire program—not just the contributions to the fund or the distributions from that fund—that simultaneously burdens interstate commerce and discriminates in favor of local producers. The choice of constitutional means—nondiscriminatory tax and local subsidy—cannot guarantee the constitutionality of the program as a whole.

Respondent also argues that since the Massachusetts milk dealers who pay the order premiums are not competitors of the Massachusetts farmers, the pricing order imposes no discriminatory burden on commerce. This argument cannot withstand scrutiny. For over 150 years, our cases have rightly concluded that the imposition of a differential burden on any part of the stream of commerce—from wholesaler to retailer to consumer—is invalid, because a burden placed at any point will result in a disadvantage to the out-of-state producer.

Respondent also argues that "the operation of the Order disproves any claim of protectionism," because "only in-state consumers feel the effect of any retail price increase and the dealers themselves have a substantial in-state presence." This argument would undermine almost every discriminatory tax case. State taxes are ordinarily paid by in-state businesses and consumers, yet if they discriminate against out-of-state products, they are unconstitutional. The cost of a tariff is also borne primarily by local consumers, yet a tariff is the paradigmatic Commerce Clause violation.

Finally, respondent argues that any incidental burden on interstate commerce "is outweighed by the 'local benefits' of preserving the Massachusetts dairy industry." Respondent also urges that "the purpose of the order, to save an industry from collapse, is not protectionist." If we were to accept these arguments, we would make a virtue of the vice that the rule against discrimination condemns. Preservation of local industry by protecting it from the rigors of interstate competition is the hallmark of the economic protectionism that the Commerce Clause prohibits.

The judgment of the Supreme Judicial Court of Massachusetts is *reversed*.

It is so ordered.

Justice SCALIA, with whom Justice THOMAS joins, *concurring* in judgment.

In my view the challenged Massachusetts pricing order is invalid under our negative Commerce-Clause jurisprudence. I concur only in the judgment of the Court.

The purpose of the negative Commerce Clause is to create a national market. It does not follow from that, however, and we have never held, that every state law which obstructs a national market violates the Commerce Clause. Yet that is what the Court says today.

This expansive view of the Commerce Clause calls into question a wide variety of state laws that have hitherto been thought permissible. A State subsidy would clearly be invalid under any formulation of the Court's guiding principle identified above. The Court guardedly asserts that a "pure subsidy funded out of general revenue ordinarily imposes no burden on interstate commerce, but merely assists local business," but under its analysis that must be taken to be true only because most local businesses (e.g., the local hardware store) are not competing with businesses out of State. The Court notes that, in funding this subsidy, Massachusetts has taxed milk produced in other States, and thus "not only assists local farmers, but burdens interstate commerce." But the same could be said of almost all subsidies funded from general state revenues, which almost invariably include monies from use taxes on out-of-state products. And even where the funding does not come in any part from taxes on out-of-state goods, "merely assisting" in-state businesses, unquestionably neutralizes advantages possessed by out-of-state enterprises. Such subsidies, particularly where they are in the form of cash or (what comes to the same thing) tax forgiveness, are often admitted to have as their purpose—indeed, are nationally advertised as having as their purpose—making it more profitable to conduct business in-state than elsewhere, i.e., distorting normal market incentives.

The Court's guiding principle also appears to call into question many garden-variety state laws heretofore permissible under the negative Commerce Clause. A state law, for example, which requires, contrary to the industry practice, the use of recyclable packaging materials, favors local non-exporting producers, who do not have to establish an additional, separate packaging operation for in-state sales. If the Court's analysis is to be believed, such a law would be unconstitutional without regard to whether disruption of the "national market" is the real purpose of the restriction, and without the need to "balance" the importance of the state interests thereby pursued. These results would greatly extend the negative Commerce Clause beyond its current scope. If the Court does not intend these consequences, and does not want to foster needless litigation concerning them, it should not have adopted its expansive rationale. Another basis for deciding the case is available, which I proceed to discuss.

"The historical record provides no grounds for reading the Commerce Clause to be other than what it says—an authorization for Congress to regulate commerce." Nonetheless, we formally adopted the doctrine of the negative Commerce Clause 121 years ago, see Case of the State Freight Tax, 15 Wall. 232 (1873), and since then have decided a vast number of negative-Commerce-Clause cases, engendering considerable reliance interests. I will, on stare decisis grounds, enforce a self-executing "negative" Commerce Clause in two situations: (1) against a state law that facially discriminates against interstate commerce, and

(2) against a state law that is indistinguishable from a type of law previously held unconstitutional by this Court.

There are at least four possible devices that would enable a State to produce the economic effect that Massachusetts has produced here: (1) a discriminatory tax upon the industry, imposing a higher liability on out-of-state members than on their in-state competitors; (2) a tax upon the industry that is nondiscriminatory in its assessment, but that has an "exemption" or "credit" for in-state members; (3) a nondiscriminatory tax upon the industry, the revenues from which are placed into a segregated fund, which fund is disbursed as "rebates" or "subsidies" to in-state members of the industry (the situation at issue in this case); and (4) with or without nondiscriminatory taxation of the industry, a subsidy for the in-state members of the industry, funded from the State's general revenues. It is long settled that the first of these methodologies is unconstitutional under the negative Commerce Clause.

The issue before us in the present case is whether the third of these methodologies must fall. Although the question is close, I conclude it would not be a principled point at which to disembark from the negative-Commerce-Clause train. The only difference between methodology (2) (discriminatory "exemption" from nondiscriminatory tax) and methodology (3) (discriminatory refund of nondiscriminatory tax) is that the money is taken and returned rather than simply left with the favored in-state taxpayer in the first place. The difference between (3) and (4), on the other hand, is the difference between assisting in-state industry through discriminatory taxation, and assisting in-state industry by other means.

I would therefore allow a State to subsidize its domestic industry so long as it does so from nondiscriminatory taxes that go into the State's general revenue fund. Perhaps that line comports with an important economic reality: a State is less likely to maintain a subsidy when its citizens perceive that the money (in the general fund) is available for any number of competing, non-protectionist, purposes. That is not, however, the basis for my position, for as the Chief Justice explains, "analysis of interest group participation in the political process may serve many useful purposes, but serving as a basis for interpreting the dormant Commerce Clause is not one of them." Instead, I draw the line where I do because it is a clear, rational line at the limits of our extant negative-Commerce-Clause jurisprudence.

Chief Justice REHNQUIST, with whom Justice BLACKMUN joins, *dissenting*.

The Court strikes down this method of state subsidization because of its view that the method of imposing the tax and subsidy distorts the State's political process: the dairy farmers, who would otherwise lobby against the tax, have been mollified by the subsidy. But there are still at least two strong interest groups opposed to the milk order—consumers and milk dealers. Analysis of interest group participation in the political process may serve many useful purposes, but serving as a basis for interpreting the dormant Commerce Clause is not one of them. The wisdom of a messianic insistence on a grim sink-or-swim policy of laissez-faire economics would be debatable had Congress chosen to enact it; but Congress has done nothing of the kind. It is the Court which has imposed the policy under the dormant Commerce Clause, a policy which bodes ill for the values of federalism which have long animated our constitutional jurisprudence.

Note: Tolling Statutes

In *Bendix Autolite Corp. v. Midwesco Enterprises, Inc.*, 486 U.S. 888 (1998), the Court struck down an Ohio statute that tolled the four-year statute of limitations in actions for breach of contract or fraud for any period that a person or corporation was not "present" in the state. To be present in Ohio, a foreign corporation must appoint an agent for service of process, which operates as consent to the general jurisdiction of the Ohio courts. Although the Court could have struck the law down as involving discrimination against interstate commerce, the Court concluded that the law imposed an unreasonable burden on interstate commerce because it required foreign corporations to appoint an agent for service of process in all cases, and to defend themselves "with reference to all transactions, including those in which it did not have the minimum contacts necessary for supporting personal jurisdiction." The Court rejected Ohio's assertion that the law should be sustained as a means of protecting Ohio residents from corporations "who become liable for acts done within the State but later withdraw from the jurisdiction." The Court noted that Midwesco was subject to service under Ohio's long-arm statute throughout the limitations period. Justice Scalia concurred, arguing that he would "abandon the 'balancing' approach to these negative Commerce Clause cases, and hold that a state statute is invalid under the Commerce Clause if, and only if, it accords discriminatory treatment to interstate commerce in a respect not required to achieve a lawful state purpose. When such a validating purpose exists, it is for Congress and not us to determine it is not significant enough to justify the burden on commerce."

Questions

1. *Reconsidering* Bendix Autolite. Do you agree with Justice Scalia, dissenting in *Bendix Autolite,* that the Courts should abandon the balancing test and invalidate only legislation that involves discrimination against interstate commerce? Are courts competent to assess and evaluate claims relating to the burdensomeness of regulation?

2. *Subsidies to Dairy Farmers.* Could Massachusetts pass a law providing financial subsidies to its dairy farmers? Could it withhold the benefits of those subsidies from farmers in surrounding states? Could Massachusetts fund the subsidy by a retail tax on the price of milk? Would it matter whether the tax was directly linked

to the subsidy? What if the tax was passed a year later with no reference to the subsidy whatsoever?

American Trucking Associations, Inc. v. Michigan Public Service Commission

545 U.S. 429 (2005)

Justice BREYER delivered the opinion of the Court.

In this case, we consider whether a flat $100 fee that Michigan charges trucks engaging in intrastate commercial hauling violates the dormant Commerce Clause. We hold that it does not.

A subsection of Michigan's Motor Carrier Act imposes upon each motor carrier for the administration of this act, an annual fee of $100.00 for each self-propelled motor vehicle operated by or on behalf of the motor carrier. Mich. Comp. Laws Ann. §478.2 (1) (West 2002). The provision assesses the fee upon, and only upon, vehicles that engage in intrastate commercial operations—that is, on trucks that undertake point-to-point hauls between Michigan cities. Petitioners, USF Holland, Inc., a trucking company with trucks that engage in both interstate and intrastate hauling, and the American Trucking Associations, Inc. (ATA), asked the Michigan courts to invalidate the provision. Both petitioners told those courts that trucks that carry *both* interstate *and* intrastate loads engage in intrastate business less than trucks that confine their operations to the Great Lakes State. Hence, because Michigan's fee is flat, it discriminates against interstate carriers and imposes an unconstitutional burden upon interstate trade.

The Michigan Court of Claims rejected the carriers' claim and the Michigan Court of Appeals affirmed. The Michigan Supreme Court denied petitioners leave to appeal. We granted their petition for certiorari and consolidated the case with another case in which interstate truckers sought review of a separate state motor carrier fee. We now affirm the Michigan court's judgment sustaining §478.2 (1).

Our Constitution was framed upon the theory that the peoples of the several states must sink or swim together. *Baldwin v. G.A.F. Seelig, Inc.,* 294 U.S. 511, 523 (1935). Thus, this Court has consistently held that the Constitution's express grant to Congress of the power to regulate Commerce among the several States, Art. I, contains a further, negative command, known as the dormant Commerce Clause, that creates an area of trade free from interference by the States, *Boston Stock Exchange v. State Tax Comm'n.,* 429 U.S. 318 (1977). This negative command prevents a State from jeopardizing the welfare of the Nation as a whole by placing burdens on the flow of commerce across its borders that commerce wholly within those borders would not bear.

Thus, we have found unconstitutional state regulations that unjustifiably discriminate on their face against out-of-state entities, or that impose burdens on interstate trade that are clearly excessive in relation to the putative local benefits,

Pike v. Bruce Church, Inc., 397 U.S. 137, 142 (1970). We have held that States may not impose taxes that facially discriminate against interstate business and offer commercial advantage to local enterprises, that improperly apportion state assessments on transactions with out-of-state components, or that have the inevitable effect of threatening the free movement of commerce by placing a financial barrier around the State, *American Trucking Assns., Inc. v. Scheiner,* 483 U.S. 266, 284 (1987).

Applying these principles and precedents, we find nothing in §478.2 (1) that offends the Commerce Clause. To begin with, Michigan imposes the flat $100 fee only upon intrastate transactions—that is, upon activities taking place exclusively within the State's borders. Section 478.2 (1) does not facially discriminate against interstate or out-of-state activities or enterprises. The statute applies evenhandedly to all carriers that make domestic journeys. It does not reflect an effort to tax activity that takes place, in whole or in part, outside the State. Nothing in our case law suggests that such a neutral, locally focused fee or tax is inconsistent with the dormant Commerce Clause. States impose numerous flat fees upon local businesses and service providers, including, for example, upon insurers, auctioneers, ambulance operators, and hosts of others. Although we have long since rejected any suggestion that a state tax affecting interstate commerce is immune from Commerce Clause scrutiny because it attaches only to a local or intrastate activity, we have also made clear that the Constitution neither displaces States' authority to shelter their people from menaces to their health or safety, nor unduly curtails States' power to lay taxes for the support of state government, *McGoldrick v. Berwind-White Coal Mining Co.,* 309 U.S. 33, 48 (1940).

The record, moreover, shows no special circumstance suggesting that Michigan's fee operates in practice as anything other than an unobjectionable exercise of the State's police power. To the contrary, the record contains little, if any, evidence that the $100 fee imposes any significant practical burden upon interstate trade. The record does show, for example, that some interstate trucks top off some interstate hauls with intrastate pickups and deliveries. But it does not tell us the answers to such questions as: How often does topping off occur across the industry? Does the $100 charge make a difference by significantly discouraging interstate carriers from engaging in topping off? Does the possibility of obtaining a 72-hour intrastate permit for $10 alleviate the alleged problem? If the fees ($100 and $10) discourage topping off, does that *local* commercial effect make a significant *interstate* difference? Would a variable fee (of the kind the truckers advocate) eliminate such difference? The minimal facts in the record tell us little about these matters. And at oral argument, ATA conceded the absence of record facts that empirically could show that the $100 fee significantly deters interstate trade.

Neither does the record show that the flat assessment unfairly discriminates against interstate truckers. The fee seeks to defray costs such as those of regulating vehicular size and weight, of administering insurance requirements, and of applying safety standards. The bulk of such costs would seem more likely to vary per truck or per carrier than to vary per mile traveled. And that fact means that a per-truck, rather than a per-mile, assessment is likely fair.

Nor would an effort to switch the manner of fee assessment—from lump sum to, for example, miles traveled—be burden free. To obtain the same revenue (about $3.5 million) through a per-mile fee would require the State to create a data accumulation system capable of separating out intrastate hauls and determining their length, and to develop related liability, billing, and auditing mechanisms. The game is unlikely to be worth the candle. Petitioners do not provide the details of their preferred alternative administrative system nor point to record evidence showing its practicality.

Petitioners insist that they do not need empirically to demonstrate the existence of a burdensome or discriminatory impact upon interstate trucking, or (presumably) the unfairness of the assessment in relation to defrayed costs, or (presumably) the administrative practicality of the alternatives. They say that our earlier case, *American Trucking Assns., Inc. v. Scheiner*, 483 U.S. 266 (1987), requires invalidation of the $100 flat fee, even in the absence of such proof. We disagree.

Petitioners add that Michigan's fee fails the internal consistency test—a test that we have typically used where taxation of interstate transactions is at issue. Generally speaking, that test asks, What would happen if all States did the same? *See, e.g., Goldberg v. Sweet*, 488 U.S. 252, 261 (1989). If all States did the same, an interstate truck would have to pay fees totaling several hundred dollars, or even several thousand dollars, were it to top off its business by carrying local loads in many (or even all) other States. But it would have to do so only because it engages in *local* business in all those States. An interstate firm with local outlets normally expects to pay local fees that are uniformly assessed upon all those who engage in local business, interstate and domestic firms alike. A motor carrier is not special in this respect.

In sum, petitioners have failed to show that Michigan's fee, which does not seek to tax a share of interstate transactions, which focuses upon local activity, and which is assessed evenhandedly, either burdens or discriminates against interstate commerce, or violates the Commerce Clause in any other relevant way. *See Complete Auto Transit, Inc. v. Brady*, 430 U.S. 274 (1977).

For these reasons, the judgment of the Michigan Court of Appeals is *affirmed*. *It is so ordered.*

Justice SCALIA, *concurring* in the judgment.

I agree that this fee does not violate the negative Commerce Clause. Unlike the Court, I ask whether the fee facially discriminates against interstate commerce and whether it is indistinguishable from a type of law previously held unconstitutional by this Court. Michigan's fee does not facially discriminate against interstate commerce, and it is distinguishable from other cases.

Justice THOMAS, *concurring* in the judgment.

I would affirm because "'the negative Commerce Clause has no basis in the text of the Constitution, makes little sense, and has proved virtually unworkable in application,' and, consequently, cannot serve as a basis for striking down a state statute."

∼ PROBLEM: MORE ON THE INTERNET CASINO PROHIBITION ACT ∼

As you read the modern decisions, did your views regarding the possible validity or invalidity of the Internet Casino Prohibition Act change? If so, what factors led you to that conclusion? Do the more recent cases provide other ways to argue that the Act is valid (or, for that matter, invalid)?

D. THE STATE AS A MARKET PARTICIPANT

In some instances, instead of trying to regulate interstate commerce, the states intervene in commercial markets and become "market participants." Do different rules apply when a state acts as a market participant rather than as a market regulator?

Reeves, Inc. v. Stake

447 U.S. 429 (1980)

Mr. Justice BLACKMUN delivered the opinion of the Court.

The issue in this case is whether, consistent with the Commerce Clause, the State of South Dakota, in a time of shortage, may confine the sale of the cement it produces solely to its residents.

In 1919, South Dakota built a cement plant in response to recent regional cement shortages that "interfered with and delayed both public and private enterprises," and that were "threatening the people of this state." The plant soon produced more cement than South Dakotans could use. Over the years, buyers in no less than nine nearby States purchased cement from the State's plant. Between 1970 and 1977, some 40% of the plant's output went outside the State.

Reeves, Inc. is a ready-mix concrete distributor organized under Wyoming law. From the beginning of its operations and until 1978, Reeves purchased about 95% of its cement from the South Dakota plant. In 1977, its purchases were $1,172,000. In turn, Reeves has supplied three northwestern Wyoming counties with more than half their ready-mix concrete needs. For 20 years the relationship between Reeves and the South Dakota cement plant was amicable, uninterrupted, and mutually profitable.

As the 1978 construction season approached, difficulties at the plant slowed production. Meanwhile, a booming construction industry spurred demand for cement both regionally and nationally. The plant found itself unable to meet all orders. Faced with the same type of "serious cement shortage" that inspired the plant's construction, the Commission "reaffirmed its policy of supplying all South Dakota customers first and to honor all contract commitments, with the remaining volume allocated on a first come, first served basis." Reeves, which had no pre-existing long-term supply contract, was hit hard and quickly by this development. Unable to find another supplier, Reeves was forced to cut production by 76% in mid-July.

The Commerce Clause responds principally to state taxes and regulatory measures impeding free private trade in the national marketplace. There is no indication of a constitutional plan to limit the ability of the States themselves to operate freely in the free market.

Restraint in this area is also counseled by considerations of state sovereignty, the role of each State "'as guardian and trustee for its people,'" and "the long recognized right of trader or manufacturer, engaged in an entirely private business, freely to exercise his own independent discretion as to parties with whom he will deal." *United States v. Colgate & Co.,* 250 U.S. 300 (1919). Moreover, state proprietary activities may be, and often are, burdened with the same restrictions imposed on private market participants. Evenhandedness suggests that, when acting as proprietors, States should similarly share existing freedoms from federal constraints, including the inherent limits of the Commerce Clause. The competing considerations in cases involving state proprietary action often will be subtle, complex, politically charged, and difficult to assess under traditional Commerce Clause analysis. As a rule, the adjustment of interests in this context is a task better suited for Congress than this Court. South Dakota, as a seller of cement, unquestionably fits the "market participant" label. Thus, the general rule of *Hughes v. Alexandria Scrap Corp.,* 426 U.S. 794 (1976), plainly applies here.

In finding a Commerce Clause violation, the District Court found that, having long exploited the interstate market, South Dakota should not be permitted to withdraw from it when a shortage arises. It is somewhat self-serving to say that South Dakota has "exploited" the interstate market. An equally fair characterization is that neighboring States long have benefitted from South Dakota's foresight and industry.

Petitioner protests that South Dakota's preference for its residents responds solely to the "non-governmental objective" of protectionism. Therefore, petitioner argues, the policy is per se invalid. *See Philadelphia v. New Jersey,* 437 U.S. 617 (1978). We find the label "protectionism" of little help in this context. The State's refusal to sell to buyers other than South Dakotans is "protectionist" only in the sense that it limits benefits generated by a state program to those who fund the state treasury and whom the State was created to serve. Petitioner's argument apparently also would characterize as "protectionist" rules restricting to state residents the enjoyment of state educational institutions, energy generated by a state-run plant, police and fire protection, and agricultural improvement and business development programs. Such policies, while perhaps "protectionist" in a loose sense, reflect the essential and patently unobjectionable purpose of state government—to serve the citizens of the State.

Petitioner argues, "If a state in this union, were allowed to hoard its commodities or resources for the use of their own residents only, a drastic situation might evolve. For example, Pennsylvania or Wyoming might keep their coal, the northwest its timber, and the mining states their minerals. The result being that embargo may be retaliated by embargo and commerce would be halted at state lines." *See, e.g., Baldwin v. Montana Fish & Game Comm'n*, 436 U.S. 371 (1978). This argument, although rooted in the core purpose of the Commerce Clause, does not fit the present facts. Cement is not a natural resource, like coal, timber, wild game, or minerals. *Cf. Hughes v. Oklahoma*, 441 U.S. 322 (1979) (minnows); *Philadelphia v. New Jersey, supra* (landfill sites); *Pennsylvania v. West Virginia*, 262 U.S. 553 (1923) (natural gas). It is the end product of a complex process whereby a costly physical plant and human labor act on raw materials. South Dakota has not sought to limit access to the State's limestone or other materials used to make cement. Nor has it restricted the ability of private firms or sister States to set up plants within its borders. Moreover, petitioner has not suggested that South Dakota possesses unique access to the materials needed to produce cement. Whatever limits might exist on a State's ability to invoke the *Alexandria Scrap* exemption to hoard resources which by happenstance are found there, those limits do not apply here.

It is suggested that the South Dakota program is infirm because it places South Dakota suppliers of ready-mix concrete at a competitive advantage in the out-of-state market; Wyoming suppliers have little chance against South Dakota suppliers who can purchase cement from the State's plant and freely sell beyond South Dakota's borders. The force of this argument is seriously diminished, if not eliminated by several considerations. The argument necessarily implies that the South Dakota scheme would be unobjectionable if sales in other States were totally barred. It therefore proves too much, for it would tolerate even a greater measure of protectionism and stifling of interstate commerce than the challenge system allows. Nor is it to be forgotten that *Alexandria Scrap* approved a state program that "not only effectively protected scrap processors with existing plants in Maryland from the pressures of competitors with nearby out-of-state plants, but that implicitly offered to extend similar protection to any competitor willing to erect a scrap processing facility within Maryland's boundaries." Finally, the competitive plight of out-of-state ready-mix suppliers cannot be laid solely at the feet of South Dakota. It is attributable as well to their own States' not providing or attracting alternative sources of supply and to the suppliers' own failure to guard against shortages by executing long-term supply contracts with the South Dakota plant.

In its last argument, petitioner urges that, had South Dakota not acted, free market forces would have generated an appropriate level of supply at free market prices for all buyers in the region. Having replaced free market forces, South Dakota should be forced to replicate how the free market would have operated under prevailing conditions. This argument is simplistic and speculative. The very reason South Dakota built its plant was because the free market had failed adequately to supply the region with cement. It is quite possible that petitioner would never have existed—far less operated successfully for 20 years—had it not been for South Dakota cement.

We conclude, then, that the arguments for invalidating South Dakota's resident-preference program are weak at best. Reversal would discourage similar state projects, even though this project demonstrably has served the needs of state residents and has helped the entire region for more than a half century. Reversal also would rob South Dakota of the intended benefit of its foresight, risk, and industry. Under these circumstances, there is no reason to depart from the general rule of *Alexandria Scrap.*

The judgment of the United States Court of Appeals is *affirmed.*

It is so ordered.

Mr. Justice POWELL, with whom Mr. Justice BRENNAN, Mr. Justice WHITE, and Mr. Justice STEVENS join, *dissenting.*

South Dakota's policy represents precisely the kind of economic protectionism that the Commerce Clause was intended to prevent. I cannot agree that South Dakota may withhold its cement from interstate commerce in order to benefit private citizens and businesses within the State. The Commerce Clause has proved an effective weapon against protectionism. The Court has used it to strike down limitations on access to local goods, be they animal, vegetable, or mineral.

The application of the Commerce Clause should turn on the nature of the governmental activity involved. If a public enterprise undertakes an "integral operation in areas of traditional governmental functions," *National League of Cities v. Usery,* 426 U.S. 833 (1976), the Commerce Clause is not directly relevant. If, however, the State enters the private market and operates a commercial enterprise for the advantage of its private citizens, it may not evade the constitutional policy against economic Balkanization.

This distinction derives from the power of governments to supply their own needs, and from the purpose of the Commerce Clause itself, which is designed to protect "the natural functioning of the interstate market." In procuring goods and services for the operation of government, a State may act without regard to the private marketplace and remove itself from the reach of the Commerce Clause. But when a State itself becomes a participant in the private market for other purposes, the Constitution forbids actions that would impede the flow of interstate commerce. The threshold issue is whether South Dakota has undertaken integral government operations in an area of traditional governmental functions, or whether it has participated in the marketplace as a private firm. If the latter characterization applies, we also must determine whether the State Commission's marketing policy burdens the flow of interstate trade.

The marketing policy of the South Dakota Cement Commission has cut off interstate trade. The State can raise such a bar when it enters the market to supply its own needs. In order to ensure an adequate supply of cement for public uses, the State can withhold from interstate commerce the cement needed for public projects. The State, however, has no parallel justification for favoring private, in-state customers over out-of-state customers. In response to political concerns that likely would be inconsequential to a private cement producer, South Dakota has shut off its cement sales to customers beyond its borders. The effect on interstate trade is the same as if the state legislature had imposed the policy on private cement producers. The creation of a free national economy was a major goal of the States when they resolved to unite under the Federal Constitution. The decision today cannot be reconciled with that purpose.

Note: Fuel Taxes and Market Participation

Recall *New Energy Co. of Indiana v. Limbach*, 486 U.S. 269 (1988), mentioned earlier. That case involved an Ohio statute that awarded a tax credit against the Ohio motor vehicle fuel sales tax for each gallon of ethanol sold (as a component of gasohol) by fuel dealers, but only if the ethanol was produced in Ohio or in a state that grants similar tax advantages to ethanol produced in Ohio. In *Limbach*, the Court also rejected the idea that the law could be upheld on a market-participant theory:

> The market-participant doctrine has no application here. The Ohio action ultimately at issue is neither its purchase nor its sale of ethanol, but its assessment and computation of taxes—a primeval governmental activity. To be sure, the tax credit scheme has the purpose and effect of subsidizing a particular industry, as do many dispositions of the tax laws. That does not transform it into a form of state participation in the free market. Our opinion in *Hughes v. Alexandria Scrap Corp.*, 426 U.S. 794 (1976), does not remotely establish such a proposition. There we upheld against Commerce Clause attack on the basis of the market-participant doctrine, a Maryland cash subsidy program that discriminated in favor of in-state auto-hulk processors. The purpose of the program was to achieve the removal of unsightly abandoned autos from the State, and the Court characterized it as proprietary rather than regulatory activity, based on the analogy of the State to a private purchaser of the auto hulks. We have subsequently observed that subsidy programs unlike that of *Alexandria Scrap* might not be characterized as proprietary. *See Reeves, Inc., supra*, 447 U.S. at 440. We think it clear that Ohio's assessment and computation of its fuel sales tax, regardless of whether it produces a subsidy, cannot plausibly be analogized to the activity of a private purchaser.

South-Central Timber Development, Inc. v. Wunnicke

467 U.S. 82 (1984)

Justice WHITE delivered the opinion of the Court with respect to Parts I and II, and delivered an opinion with respect to Parts III and IV, in which Justice BRENNAN, Justice BLACKMUN, and Justice STEVENS joined.

We granted certiorari to review a decision of the Court of Appeals for the Ninth Circuit that held that Alaska's requirement that timber taken from state lands be processed within the State prior to export was "implicitly authorized" by Congress and therefore does not violate the Commerce Clause. We hold that it was not authorized and reverse the judgment of the Court of Appeals.

Our cases make clear that if a State is acting as a market participant, rather than as a market regulator, the dormant Commerce Clause places no limitation on its activities. The precise contours of the market-participant doctrine have yet to be established, however, the doctrine having been applied in only three cases of this Court to date.

The most recent of this Court's cases developing the market-participant doctrine is *White v. Massachusetts Council of Construction Employers, Inc.*, 460 U.S. 204 (1983), in which the Court sustained against a Commerce Clause challenge to an executive order of the Mayor of Boston that required all construction projects funded in whole or in part by city funds or city-administered funds to be performed by a work force of at least 50% city residents. The Court rejected the argument that the city was not entitled to the protection of the doctrine because the order had the effect of regulating employment contracts between public contractors and their employees. Recognizing that "there are some limits on a state or local government's ability to impose restrictions that reach beyond the immediate parties with which the government transacts business," the Court found it unnecessary to define those limits because "everyone affected by the order was, in a substantial if informal sense, 'working for the city.'" The fact that the employees were "working for the city" was "crucial" to the market-participant analysis in *White*.

The State of Alaska contends that its primary-manufacture requirement fits squarely within the market-participant doctrine, arguing that "Alaska's entry into the market may be viewed as precisely the same type of subsidy to local interests that the Court found unobjectionable in *Alexandria Scrap*." However, when Maryland became involved in the scrap market it was as a purchaser of scrap; Alaska, on the other hand, participates in the timber market, but imposes conditions downstream in the timber-processing market. Alaska is not merely subsidizing local timber processing in an amount "roughly equal to the difference between the price the timber would fetch in the absence of such a requirement and the amount the state actually receives." If the State directly subsidized the timber-processing industry by such an amount, the purchaser would retain the option of taking advantage of the subsidy by processing timber in the State or forgoing the benefits of the subsidy and exporting unprocessed timber. Under the Alaska requirement, however, the choice is made for him: if he buys timber from the State he is not free to take the timber out of state prior to processing.

The State also would have us find *Reeves* controlling. It states that "*Reeves* made it clear that the Commerce Clause imposes no limitation on Alaska's power to choose the terms on which it will sell its timber." Although *Reeves* did strongly endorse the right of a State to deal with whomever it chooses when it participates in the market, it did not sanction the imposition of any terms that the State might desire. The Court expressly noted in *Reeves* that "Commerce Clause scrutiny may well be more rigorous when a restraint on foreign commerce is alleged"; that a natural resource "like coal, timber, wild game, or minerals," was not involved, but instead the cement was "the end product of a complex process whereby a costly physical plant and human labor act on raw materials," and that South Dakota did not bar resale of South Dakota cement to out-of-state purchasers. In this case, all three of the elements that were not present in *Reeves*—foreign commerce, a natural resource, and restrictions on resale—are present.

Finally, Alaska argues that the primary-manufacture requirement is permissible, because the State is not regulating contracts for resale of timber or regulating the buying and selling of timber, but is instead "a seller of timber, pure and simple." Yet it is clear that the State is more than merely a seller of timber. In the commercial context, the seller usually has no say over, and no interest in, how the product is to be used after sale; in this case, however, payment for the timber does not end the obligations of the purchaser, for, despite the fact that the purchaser has taken delivery of the timber and has paid for it, he cannot do with it as he pleases. Instead, he is obligated to deal with a stranger to the contract after completion of the sale.

That privity of contract is not always the outer boundary of permissible state activity does not necessarily mean that the Commerce Clause has no application within the boundary of formal privity. The market-participant doctrine permits a State to influence "a discrete, identifiable class of economic activity in which it is a major participant." *White v. Massachusetts Council of Construction Inc.,* 460 U.S. 204, 211, n.7 (1983). Contrary to the State's contention, the doctrine is not carte blanche to impose any conditions that the State has the economic power to dictate, and does not validate any requirement merely because the State imposes it upon someone with whom it is in contractual privity.

The limit of the market-participant doctrine must be that it allows a State to impose burdens on commerce within the market in which it is a participant, but allows it to go no further. The State may not impose conditions, whether by statute, regulation, or contract, that have a substantial regulatory effect outside of that particular market. Unless the "market" is relatively narrowly defined, the doctrine has the potential of swallowing up the rule that States may not impose substantial burdens on interstate commerce even if they act with the permissible state purpose of fostering local industry.

There are sound reasons for distinguishing between a State's preferring its own residents in the initial disposition of goods when it is a market participant and a State's attachment of restrictions on dispositions subsequent to the goods coming to rest in private hands. First, a State market participant has a greater interest as a "private trader" in the immediate transaction than it has in what its purchaser does with the goods after the State no longer has an interest in them. The common law recognized such a notion in the doctrine of restraints on alienation. We reject the contention that a State's action as a market regulator may be upheld against Commerce Clause challenge on the ground that the State could achieve the same end as a market participant. We therefore find it unimportant for present purposes that the State could support its processing industry by sell-ing only to Alaska processors, by vertical integration, or by direct subsidy.

Second, downstream restrictions have a greater regulatory effect than do lim-itations on the immediate transaction. Instead of merely choosing its own trad-ing partners, the State is attempting to govern the private, separate economic relationships of its trading partners; that is, it restricts the post-purchase activity of the purchaser, rather than merely the purchasing activity. This restriction on private economic activity takes place after the completion of the parties' direct commercial obligations, rather than during the course of an ongoing commercial relationship in which the city retained a continuing proprietary interest in the sub-ject of the contract. In sum, the State may not avail itself of the market-participant doctrine to immunize its downstream regulation of the timber-processing market in which it is not a participant.

The judgment of the Court of Appeals is *reversed* and the case is *remanded* for proceedings consistent with the opinion of this Court.

It is so ordered.

Justice REHNQUIST, with whom Justice O'CONNOR joins, *dissenting.*

Alaska is merely paying the buyer of the timber indirectly, by means of a reduced price, to hire Alaska residents to process the timber. Under existing prec-edent, the State could accomplish that same result in any number of ways. For example, the State could choose to sell its timber only to those companies that maintain active primary-processing plants in *Alaska. Reeves, Inc. v. Stake*, 447 U.S. 429 (1980). Or the State could directly subsidize the primary-processing industry within the State. *Hughes v. Alexandria Scrap Corp.*, 426 U.S. 794 (1976). The State could even pay to have the logs processed and then enter the market only to sell processed logs. It seems to me unduly formalistic to conclude that the one path chosen by the State as best suited to promote its concerns is the path forbidden it by the Commerce Clause.

Note: Freedom of Information

In *McBurney v. Young*, 569 U.S. 221 (2013) (the privileges and immunities section of that opinion is set forth in the next section), the Court rejected a dor-mant Commerce Clause challenge to the Virginia Freedom of Information Act, Va. Code Ann. §§2.2-3700 *et seq.* That Act provided that "all public records shall be open to inspection and copying by any citizens of the Commonwealth," but it granted no rights to non-Virginians. In rejecting the Commerce Clause claim, the Court stated as follows:

> Hurlbert contends that Virginia's citizens-only FOIA provision violates the dormant Commerce Clause. Virginia's FOIA law neither "regulates" nor "burdens" interstate com-merce; it merely provides a service to local citizens that would not otherwise be available. The

"common thread" among cases in which the Court has found a dormant Commerce Clause violation is that "the State interfered with the natural functioning of the interstate market either through prohibition or through burdensome regulation." *Hughes v. Alexandria Scrap Corp.*, 426 U.S. 794, 806 (1976). Here Virginia neither prohibits access to an interstate market nor imposes burdensome regulation on that market. It merely creates and provides to its own citizens copies—which would not otherwise exist—of state records. The express purpose of Virginia's FOIA law is to "ensure the people of the Commonwealth ready access to public records in the custody of a public body or its officers and employees, and free entry to meetings of public bodies wherein the business of the people is being conducted." Va. Code Ann. §2.2-3700(B). Because it does not pose the question of the constitutionality of a state law that interferes with an interstate market through prohibition or burdensome regulations, this case is not governed by the dormant Commerce Clause. Even under our dormant Commerce Clause framework Hurlbert's claim would fail. Insofar as there is a "market" for public documents in Virginia, it is a market for a product that the Commonwealth has created and of which the Commonwealth is the sole manufacturer. A State does not violate the dormant Commerce Clause when, having created a market through a state program, it "limits benefits generated by that state program to those who fund the state treasury and whom the State was created to serve." *Reeves, Inc. v. Stake*, 447 U.S. 429, 442 (1980). "Such policies, while perhaps 'protectionist' in a loose sense, reflect the essential and patently unobjectionable purpose of state government—to serve the citizens of the State." *Ibid.* Virginia's citizens-only FOIA provision does not violate the dormant Commerce Clause.

Justice Thomas concurred: "The negative Commerce Clause has no basis in the text of the Constitution, makes little sense, and has proved virtually unworkable in application, and, consequently, cannot serve as a basis for striking down a state statute. *Hillside Dairy Inc. v. Lyons*, 539 U.S. 59, 68 (2003) (concurring in part and dissenting in part)."

∽ PROBLEM: MORE ON THE INTERNET CASINO PROHIBITION ACT ∽

Suppose that in addition to regulating gambling interests in the state, Kentucky owns and operates a state lottery. Funds from the lottery are used to pay education-related expenses. Could Kentucky justify the Internet Casino Prohibition Act under the "market participation" doctrine?

E. INTERSTATE PRIVILEGES AND IMMUNITIES CLAUSE

Article IV, Section 2 contains the Interstate Privileges and Immunities Clause: "The Citizens of each State shall be entitled to all Privileges and Immunities of Citizens in the several States." This clause was designed to ensure that states would not discriminate against the citizens of other states because of their citizenship in those states. Like most constitutional rights, the Privileges and Immunities Clause does not require states to treat nonresidents in exactly the same way that they treat their own citizens, and it does not impose an absolute ban on discrimination by one state against the citizens of another. States can treat the citizens of other states differently in some instances.

Baldwin v. Fish and Game Commission of Montana

436 U.S. 371 (1978)

Mr. Justice BLACKMUN delivered the opinion of the Court.

This case presents issues, under the Privileges and Immunities Clause of the Constitution's Art. IV, §2, and the Equal Protection Clause of the Fourteenth Amendment, as to the constitutional validity of disparities, as between residents and nonresidents, in a State's hunting license system.

Appellant Lester Baldwin is a Montana resident. He also is an outfitter holding a state license as a hunting guide. The majority of his customers are nonresidents who come to Montana to hunt elk and other big game. Appellants Carlson, Huseby, Lee and Moris are residents of Minnesota. They have hunted big game, particularly elk, in Montana in past years and wish to continue to do so.

For the 1975 hunting season, a Montana resident could purchase a license solely for elk for $4. The nonresident, however, in order to hunt elk, was required to purchase a combination license at a cost of $151; this entitled him to take one elk and two deer. For the 1976 season, the Montana resident could purchase a license solely for elk for $9. The nonresident, in order to hunt elk was required to purchase a combination license at a cost of $225; this entitled him to take one elk, one deer, one black bear, and game birds, and to fish with hook and line. A resident was not required to buy any combination of licenses, but if he did, the cost to him of all the privileges granted by the nonresident combination license was $30. The nonresident thus paid 7½ times as much as the resident, and if the nonresident wished to hunt only elk, he paid 25 times as much as the resident.

Montana maintains significant populations of big game, including elk, deer, and antelope. Its elk population is one of the largest in the United States. Elk are prized by big-game hunters who come from near and far to pursue the animals for sport. From 1960 to 1970 licenses issued by Montana increased by approximately 67% for residents and by approximately 530% for nonresidents. Owing to its successful management programs for elk, the State has not been compelled to limit the overall number of hunters by means of drawings or lotteries as have other States with harvestable elk populations. Elk are not hunted commercially in Montana. Nonresident hunters seek the animal for its trophy value; the trophy is the distinctive set of antlers. The interest of resident hunters more often may be in the meat. Elk are now found in the mountainous regions of western Montana. During the summer the animals move to higher elevations and lands that are largely federally owned. In the late fall they move down to lower privately owned lands that provide the winter habitat necessary to their survival. During the critical midwinter period elk are often supported by ranchers. Elk management is expensive. In regions of the State with significant elk population, more personnel time of the Fish and Game Commission is spent on elk than on any other species of big game.

Privileges and immunities. Appellants strongly urge here that the Montana licensing scheme for the hunting of elk violates the Privileges and Immunities Clause of Art. IV, §2, of our Constitution. The Privileges and Immunities Clause has been interpreted to prevent a State from imposing unreasonable burdens on citizens of other States in their pursuit of common callings within the State, *Ward v. Maryland*, 12 Wall. 418 (1871); in the ownership and disposition of privately held property within the State, *Blake v. McClung*, 172 U.S. 239 (1898); and in access to the courts of the State, *Canadian Northern Ry. Co. v. Eggen*, 252 U.S. 553 (1920).

It has not been suggested, however, that state citizenship or residency may never be used by a State to distinguish among persons. No one would suggest that the Privileges and Immunities Clause requires a State to open its polls to a person who declines to assert that the State is the only one where he claims a right to vote. The same is true as to qualification for an elective office of the State. *Kanapaux v. Ellisor*, 419 U.S. 891 (1974). Nor must a State always apply all its laws or all its services equally to anyone, resident or nonresident, who may request it so to do. Some distinctions between residents and nonresidents merely reflect the fact that this is a Nation composed of individual States, and are permitted; other distinctions are prohibited because they hinder the formation, the purpose, or the development of a single Union of those States. Only with respect to those "privileges" and "immunities" bearing upon the vitality of the Nation as a single entity must the State treat all citizens, resident and nonresident, equally. Here we must decide into which category falls a distinction with respect to access to recreational big-game hunting.

Many early cases embrace the concept that the States had complete ownership over wildlife within their boundaries, and the power to preserve this bounty for their citizens alone. Although the States were obligated to treat all those within their territory equally in most respects, they were not obliged to share those things they held in trust for their own people. In *Corfield v. Coryell*, 6 Fed. Cas. 546, although recognizing that the States may not interfere with the "right of a citizen of one state to pass through, or to reside in any other state, for purposes of trade, agriculture, professional pursuits, or otherwise; to claim the benefit of the writ of habeas corpus; to institute and maintain actions of any kind in the courts of the state; to take, hold and dispose of property, either real or personal," nonetheless concluded that access to oyster beds determined to be owned by New Jersey could be limited to New Jersey residents.

In more recent years, however, the Court has recognized that the States' interest in regulating and controlling those things they claim to "own," including wildlife, is by no means absolute. States may not compel the confinement of the benefits of their resources, even their wildlife, to their own people whenever such hoarding and confinement impedes interstate commerce. Nor does a

State's control over its resources preclude the proper exercise of federal power. And a State's interest in its wildlife and other resources must yield when, without reason, it interferes with a nonresident's right to pursue a livelihood in a State other than his own, a right that is protected by the Privileges and Immunities Clause. *Toomer v. Witsell*, 334 U.S. 385 (1948).

Does the distinction made by Montana between residents and nonresidents in establishing access to elk hunting threaten a basic right in a way that offends the Privileges and Immunities Clause? Elk hunting by nonresidents in Montana is a recreation and a sport. It is costly and obviously available only to the wealthy nonresident or to the one so taken with the sport that he sacrifices other values in order to indulge in it and to enjoy what it offers. It is not a means to the non-resident's livelihood. The mastery of the animal and the trophy are the ends that are sought; appellants are not totally excluded from these. The elk supply, which has been entrusted to the care of the State by the people of Montana, is finite and must be carefully tended in order to be preserved.

Appellants' interest in sharing this limited resource on more equal terms with Montana residents simply does not fall within the purview of the Privileges and Immunities Clause. Equality in access to Montana elk is not basic to the main-tenance or well-being of the Union. Appellants do not—and cannot—contend that they are deprived of a means of a livelihood by the system or of access to any part of the State to which they may seek to travel. Whatever rights or activities may be "fundamental" under the Privileges and Immunities Clause, we are persuaded, and hold, that elk hunting by nonresidents in Montana is not one of them.

The judgment of the District Court is *affirmed*.

It is so ordered.

Mr. Justice BRENNAN, with whom Mr. Justice WHITE and Mr. Justice MARSHALL join, dissenting.

An inquiry into whether a given right is "fundamental" has no place in our analysis of whether a State's discrimination against nonresidents—who "are not represented in the discriminating State's legislative halls"—violates the Clause. Our primary concern is the State's justification for its discrimination. A State's discrimination against nonresidents is permissible where (1) the presence or activity of nonresidents is the source or cause of the problem or effect with which the State seeks to deal, and (2) the discrimination practiced against nonresidents bears a substantial relation to the problem they present. A State's mere assertion that the discrimination practiced against nonresidents is justified by the pecu-liar problem nonresidents present will not prevail in the face of a prima facie showing that the discrimination is not supportable on the asserted grounds. This requirement that a State's unequal treatment of nonresidents be reasoned and suitably tailored furthers the federal interest in ensuring that "a norm of comity," prevails throughout the Nation while simultaneously guaranteeing to the States the needed leeway to draw viable distinctions between their citizens and those of other States.

It is clear that under a proper privileges and immunities analysis Montana's discriminatory treatment of nonresident big-game hunters in this case must fail. There are three possible justifications for charging nonresident elk hunters an amount at least 7.5 times the fee imposed on resident big-game hunters. The first is conservation. The State did not attempt to assert this as a justification for its discriminatory licensing scheme and it is difficult to see how it could do so. First, there is nothing in the record to indicate that the influx of nonresident hunters created a special danger to Montana's elk or to any of its other wildlife species. Nonresidents constituted only 13% of all hunters pursuing their sport in the State. Second, if Montana's discriminatorily high big-game license fee is an outgrowth of general conservation policy to discourage elk hunting, Montana makes no effort similarly to inhibit its own residents. As we said in *Douglas v. Seacoast Products, Inc.*, 431 U.S. 265 (1977), "a statute that leaves a State's residents free to destroy a natural resource while excluding aliens or nonresidents is not a conservation law at all." The second possible justification for the fee differential is a cost justification. The Clause allows additional charges to be made on nonresidents based on both the added enforcement costs the presence of nonresident hunters imposes on Montana and the State's conservation expenditures supported by resident-borne taxes. However, Montana's higher fee for nonresident elk hunters does not reflect an attempt to recoup state expenditures. Montana's attempt to cost-justify its discriminatory licensing practices thus fails under the second prong of a correct privileges and immunities analysis—that which requires the discrimination a State visits upon nonresidents to bear a substantial relation to the problem or burden they pose.

Note: **Toomer** *and Shrimp Fishing*

Toomer v. Witsell, 334 U.S. 385 (1948), involved a South Carolina law that regulated commercial shrimp fishing in the three-mile maritime belt off the coast of that state. Among other things, the law imposed a $2,500-per-boat fee on nonresidents while imposing a $25 fee on residents. Georgia shrimpers challenged the law as a violation of the Interstate Privileges and Immunities Clause. The Court struck down the law, noting that nothing "indicates that non-residents use larger boats or different fishing methods than residents, that the cost of enforcing the laws against them is appreciably greater, or that any substantial amount of the state's general funds is devoted to shrimp conservation." The Court did note that the state is not "without power to restrict the type of equipment used in its fisheries, to graduate license fees according to the size of the boats, or even to charge non-residents a differential which would merely compensate the State for any added enforcement burden they may impose or for any conservation expenditures from taxes which only residents pay." The Court specifically rejected the "whole ownership theory," which suggests that states have the "power to preserve and regulate the exploitation of an important resource."

Hicklin v. Orbeck

437 U.S. 518 (1978)

Mr. Justice BRENNAN delivered the opinion of the Court.

In 1972, professedly for the purpose of reducing unemployment in the State, the Alaska Legislature passed an Act entitled "Local Hire Under State Leases." Alaska Stat. Ann. §§38.40.010 to 38.40.090 (1977). The key provision of "Alaska Hire," as the Act has come to be known, is the requirement that "all oil and gas leases, easements or right-of-way permits for oil or gas pipeline purposes, unitization agreements, or any renegotiation of any of the preceding to which the state is a party" contain a provision "requiring the employment of qualified Alaska residents" in preference to nonresidents. This employment preference is administered by providing persons meeting the statutory requirements for Alaskan residency with certificates of residence — "resident cards" — that can be presented to an employer covered by the Act as proof of residency. Appellants were desirous of securing jobs covered by the Act but unable to qualify for the necessary resident cards.

Appellants' principal challenge to Alaska Hire is made under the Privileges and Immunities Clause of Art. IV, §2. Appellants' appeal to the protection of the Clause is strongly supported by this Court's decisions holding violative of the Clause state discrimination against nonresidents seeking to ply their trade, practice their occupation, or pursue a common calling within the State. For example, in *Ward v. Maryland*, 12 Wall. 418 (1871), a Maryland statute regulating the sale of most goods in the city of Baltimore fell to the privileges and immunities challenge of a New Jersey resident against whom the law discriminated. The statute discriminated against nonresidents of Maryland in several ways: It required nonresident merchants to obtain licenses in order to practice their trade without requiring the same of certain similarly situated Maryland merchants; it charged nonresidents a higher license fee than those Maryland residents who were required to secure licenses; and it prohibited both resident and nonresident merchants from using nonresident salesmen, other than their regular employees, to sell their goods in the city. In holding that the statute violated the Privileges and Immunities Clause, the Court observed that "the clause plainly and unmistakably secures and protects the right of a citizen of one State to pass into any other State of the Union for the purpose of engaging in lawful commerce, trade, or business without molestation." *Ward* thus recognized that a resident of one State is constitutionally entitled to travel to another State for purposes of employment free from discriminatory restrictions in favor of state residents imposed by the other State.

Even where the presence or activity of nonresidents causes or exacerbates the problem the State seeks to remedy, there must be a "reasonable relationship between the danger represented by non-citizens, as a class, and the discrimination practiced upon them." *Toomer*'s analytical framework was confirmed in *Mullaney v. Anderson*, 342 U.S. 415 (1952), where it was applied to invalidate a scheme used by the Territory of Alaska for the licensing of commercial fishermen in territorial waters; under that scheme residents paid a license fee of only $5 while nonresidents were charged $50.

Even assuming that a State may validly attempt to alleviate its unemployment problem by requiring private employers within the State to discriminate against nonresidents, it is clear that under the *Toomer* analysis reaffirmed in *Mullaney*, Alaska Hire's discrimination against nonresidents cannot withstand scrutiny under the Privileges and Immunities Clause. For although the statute may not violate the Clause if the State shows "something to indicate that noncitizens constitute a peculiar source of the evil at which the statute is aimed." And, beyond this, the State "has no burden to prove that its laws are not violative of the Clause," *Baldwin v. Montana Fish and Game Commn.*, 436 U.S. at 402 (Brennan, J., dissenting), certainly no showing was made on this record that nonresidents were "a peculiar source of the evil" Alaska Hire was enacted to remedy, namely, Alaska's "uniquely high unemployment." Alaska Stat. Ann. §38.40.020 (1977). The record indicates that the major cause of Alaska's high unemployment was not the influx of nonresidents seeking employment, but rather the fact that a substantial number of Alaska's jobless residents—especially the unemployed Eskimo and Indian residents—were unable to secure employment either because of their lack of education and job training or because of their geographical remoteness from job opportunities; and that the employment of nonresidents threatened to deny jobs to Alaska residents only to the extent that jobs for which untrained residents were being prepared might be filled by nonresidents before the residents' training was completed.

Even if the State's showing is accepted as sufficient to indicate that nonresidents were "a peculiar source of evil," *Toomer* and *Mullaney* compel the conclusion that Alaska Hire nevertheless fails to pass constitutional muster. For the discrimination the Act works against nonresidents does not bear a substantial relationship to the particular "evil" they are said to present. Alaska Hire simply grants all Alaskans, regardless of their employment status, education, or training, a flat employment preference for all jobs covered by the Act. A highly skilled and educated resident who has never been unemployed is entitled to precisely the same preferential treatment as the unskilled, habitually unemployed Arctic Eskimo enrolled in a job-training program. If Alaska is to attempt to ease its unemployment problem by forcing employers within the State to discriminate against nonresidents—again, a policy which may present serious constitutional questions—the means by which it does so must be more closely tailored to aid the unemployed the Act is intended to benefit.

Relying on *McCready v. Virginia*, 94 U.S. 391 (1877), Alaska contends that because the oil and gas that are the subject of Alaska Hire are owned by the State, this ownership, of itself, is sufficient justification for the Act's discrimination against nonresidents, and takes the Act totally without the scope of the Privileges and Immunities Clause. As the State sees it "the privileges and immunities clause does not apply to decisions by the states as to how they would permit the use and distribution of the natural resources which they own." We do not agree. "In more recent years, the Court has recognized that the States' interest in regulating and controlling those things they claim to 'own' is by no means absolute." *Baldwin v. Montana Fish and Game Comm'n.*, 436 U.S. at 385. A State's ownership of the property with which the statute is concerned is a factor—although often the crucial factor—to be considered in evaluating whether the statute's discrimination against noncitizens violates the Clause. Dispositive though this factor may be, it is not dispositive here.

But Alaska Hire extends to employers who have no connection whatsoever with the State's oil and gas, perform no work on state land, have no contractual relationship with the State, and receive no payment from the State. Moreover, the Act's coverage is not limited to activities connected with the extraction of Alaska's oil and gas. It encompasses "employment opportunities at refineries and in distribution systems utilizing oil and gas obtained under Alaska leases." In sum, the Act is an attempt to force virtually all businesses that benefit in some way from the economic ripple effect of Alaska's decision to develop its oil and gas resources to bias their employment practices in favor of the State's residents. We believe that Alaska's ownership of the oil and gas that is the subject matter of Alaska Hire simply constitutes insufficient justification for the pervasive discrimination against nonresidents that the Act mandates.

Prior precedent establishes that the Commerce Clause circumscribes a State's ability to prefer its own citizens in the utilization of natural resources found within its borders, but destined for interstate commerce. Alaska's oil and gas here are bound for out-of-state consumption. Although the fact that a state-owned resource is destined for interstate commerce does not, of itself, disable the State from preferring its own citizens in the utilization of that resource, it does inform analysis under the Privileges and Immunities Clause as to the permissibility of the discrimination the State visits upon nonresidents based on its ownership of the resource. Here, the oil and gas upon which Alaska hinges its discrimination against nonresidents are of profound national importance. The breadth of the discrimination mandated by Alaska Hire goes far beyond the degree of resident bias Alaska's ownership of the oil and gas can justifiably support. The confluence of these realities points to but one conclusion: Alaska Hire cannot withstand constitutional scrutiny. As Mr. Justice Cardozo observed in *Baldwin v. G.A.F. Seelig, Inc.*, 294 U.S. 511, 523 (1935), the Constitution "was framed upon the theory that the peoples of the several states must sink or swim together, and that in the long run prosperity and salvation are in union and not division."

Reversed.

Notes

1. *May a City Favor Its Residents on Public Works Contracts?* In *United Building and Construction Trades Council of Camden County v. City of Camden*, 465 U.S. 208 (1984),

the City of Camden, New Jersey, adopted an ordinance that required that at least 40 percent of the employees of contractors and subcontractors working on city construction projects be Camden residents. A resident was defined as anyone who lives in the City of Camden without regard to the length of residency. The Court concluded that the Privileges and Immunities Clause was applicable, and remanded for further hearings: "Given the Camden ordinance, an out-of-state citizen who ventures into New Jersey will not enjoy the same privileges as the New Jersey citizen residing in Camden. It is true that New Jersey citizens not residing in Camden will be affected by the ordinance as well as out-of-state citizens. And it is true that the disadvantaged New Jersey residents have no claim under the Privileges and Immunities Clause. But New Jersey residents at least have a chance to remedy at the polls any discrimination against them. We conclude that Camden's ordinance is not immune from constitutional review at the behest of out-of-state residents merely because some in-state residents are similarly disadvantaged." The Court went on to note that the "fact that Camden is expending its own funds or funds it administers in accordance with the terms of a grant is certainly a factor—perhaps the crucial factor—to be considered in evaluating whether the statute's discrimination violates the Privileges and Immunities Clause. But it does not remove the Camden ordinance completely from the purview of the Clause." Therefore, the Court remanded for consideration of whether Camden could offer a "substantial reason" for treating nonresidents differently as a remedy for the "peculiar source of the evil at which the statute is aimed." Justice Blackmun dissented, arguing that the Article VI Privileges and Immunities Clause was intended only to prohibit a state from discriminating between its own residents and residents of other states on the basis of state citizenship. In his view, it was not intended to prohibit discrimination "*among* state residents on the basis of *municipal* residence."

2. *The Practice of Law.* Does the Privileges and Immunities Clause protect the right to practice law in another state? *Supreme Court of New Hampshire v. Piper,* 470 U.S. 274 (1985), involved a New Hampshire law that allowed only New Hampshire residents to become attorneys as challenged by a Vermont resident who lived only 400 yards from the New Hampshire border. She had passed the New Hampshire bar examination, had been found to be of good moral character, and had met all other requirements for admission. In striking down the law, the Court emphasized that the clause was designed to ensure noncitizens the right to do business "on terms of substantial equality with the citizens" of the state. The Court concluded that this right extended to the practice of law because "out-of-state lawyers may—and often do—represent persons who raise unpopular federal claims. In some cases, representation by nonresident counsel may be the only means available for the vindication of federal rights." The Court rejected the idea that the clause should not apply because lawyers exercised "state power." The Court then evaluated and rejected the state's alleged justifications for the law, which included allegations that nonresident lawyers "would be less likely (i) to become, and remain, familiar with local rules and procedures; (ii) to behave ethically;

(iii) to be available for court proceedings; and (iv) to do *pro bono* and other volunteer work in the State." The Court concluded:

> We may not assume that a nonresident lawyer—any more than a resident—would disserve his clients by failing to familiarize himself with the rules. The nonresident lawyer's professional duty and interest in his reputation should provide the same incentive to maintain high ethical standards as they do for resident lawyers. One may assume that a high percentage of nonresident lawyers willing to take the state bar examination and pay the annual dues will reside in places reasonably convenient to New Hampshire. Furthermore, the State can protect its interests through less restrictive means by requiring any lawyer who resides at a great distance to retain a local attorney who will be available for unscheduled meetings and hearings. The final reason advanced by appellant is that nonresident members of the state bar would be disinclined to do their share of *pro bono* and volunteer work. It is reasonable to believe, however, that most lawyers who become members of a state bar will endeavor to perform their share of these services. Furthermore, a nonresident bar member, like the resident member, could be required to represent indigents and perhaps to participate in formal legal-aid work.

Justice Rehnquist dissented:

> The practice of law is—almost by definition—fundamentally different from other occupations that are practiced across state lines. The State has a substantial interest in creating its own set of laws responsive to its own local interests, and may decide that it has an interest in maximizing the number of resident lawyers, so as to increase the quality of the pool from which its lawmakers can be drawn. Each out-of-state lawyer who is allowed to practice necessarily takes legal work that could support an in-state lawyer. And the State likewise might conclude that those citizens trained in the law are likely to bring their useful expertise to other important functions that benefit from such expertise such as trusteeships, or directorships of corporations or charitable organizations, or school board positions, or merely the role of the interested citizen at a town meeting. The uncertainties of managing a trial docket are such that lawyers rarely are given a single date on which a trial will begin; they may be required to 'stand by' for days at a time, and then be expected to be ready in a matter of hours, with witnesses, when the case in front of them suddenly settles. A State reasonably can decide that a trial court should not have added to its present scheduling difficulties the uncertainties and added delays fostered by counsel who might reside 1,000 miles from New Hampshire. Surely the State has a substantial interest in taking steps to minimize this problem.

∾ PROBLEMS ∾

1. *More on the* Camden *Case.* In the *City of Camden* case, the city argued that it enacted the ordinance to counteract "grave economic and social ills," including "spiraling unemployment, a sharp decline in population, and a dramatic reduction in the number of businesses located in the city have eroded property values and depleted the city's tax base." The plan was designed "to increase the number of employed persons living in Camden and to arrest the 'middle class flight' currently plaguing the city." The city argues that all non-Camden residents employed on city public works projects essentially "live off" Camden without "living in" Camden. Finally, Camden argued that its municipal residency requirement was

"carefully tailored to alleviate this evil without unreasonably harming nonresidents, who still have access to 60% of the available positions." Under this analysis, can Camden justify discrimination against nonresidents notwithstanding the Privileges and Immunities Clause?

2. *More on the Internet Casino Prohibition Act.* If you were asked to represent companies that wish to challenge the Internet Casino Prohibition Act, how would you argue that it runs afoul of the Interstate Privileges and Immunities Clause? How might the state respond? Does the clause come into play at all in a situation like this?

McBurney v. Young

569 U.S. 201 (2013)

Justice ALITO delivered the opinion of the Court.

Petitioners Mark McBurney and Roger Hurlbert are citizens of Rhode Island and California respectively. McBurney and Hurlbert each requested documents under the Virginia FOIA, but their requests were denied because of their citizenship. McBurney is a former resident of Virginia whose ex-wife is a Virginia citizen. After his ex-wife defaulted on her child support obligations, McBurney asked the Commonwealth's Division of Child Support Enforcement to file a petition for child support on his behalf. The agency complied, but only after a 9-month delay. McBurney attributes that delay to agency error and says that it cost him nine months of child support. To ascertain the reason for the delay, McBurney filed a Virginia FOIA request seeking "all emails, notes, files, memos, reports, letters, policies, and opinions" pertaining to his family, along with all documents "regarding his application for child support" and all documents pertaining to the handling of child support claims like his. The agency denied McBurney's request on the ground that he was not a Virginia citizen. McBurney later requested the same documents under Virginia's Government Data Collection and Dissemination Practices Act, and through that request he received most of the information he had sought that pertained to his case. He did not, however, receive any general policy information about how the agency handled claims like his. Hurlbert is the sole proprietor of Sage Information Services, a business that requests real estate tax records on clients' behalf from state and local governments across the United States. In 2008, Hurlbert was hired by a land/title company to obtain real estate tax records for properties in Henrico County, Virginia. He filed a Virginia FOIA request for the documents with the Henrico County Real Estate Assessor's Office, but his request was denied because he was not a Virginia citizen.

Petitioners filed suit under 42 U.S.C. §1983, seeking declaratory and injunctive relief for violations of the Privileges and Immunities Clause and, in Hurlbert's case, the dormant Commerce Clause. The District Court granted Virginia's motion for summary judgment, and the Court of Appeals affirmed. We granted certiorari.

Under the Privileges and Immunities Clause, "the Citizens of each State are entitled to all Privileges and Immunities of Citizens in the several States." U.S.

528 5. State Power to Regulate Commerce

Const., Art. IV, §2, cl. 1. "The object of the Privileges and Immunities Clause is to 'strongly constitute the citizens of the United States as one people,' by 'placing the citizens of each State upon the same footing with citizens of other States, so far as the advantages resulting from citizenship in those States are concerned.'" *Lunding v. New York Tax Appeals Tribunal*, 522 U.S. 287, 296 (1998) (quoting *Paul v. Virginia*, 8 Wall. 168, 180, 19 L. Ed. 357 (1869)). This does not mean that "state citizenship or residency may never be used by a State to distinguish among persons." *Baldwin v. Fish and Game Comm'n of Mont.*, 436 U.S. 371, 383 (1978). "Nor must a State always apply all its laws or all its services equally to anyone, resident or nonresident, who may request it so to do." *Ibid.* We have held that the Privileges and Immunities Clause protects only those privileges and immunities that are "fundamental." Petitioners allege that Virginia's citizens-only FOIA provision violates four different "fundamental" privileges or immunities: the opportunity to pursue a common calling, the ability to own and transfer property, access to the Virginia courts, and access to public information. The first three items, however, are not abridged by the Virginia FOIA, and the fourth is not protected by the Privileges and Immunities Clause.

Hurlbert argues that Virginia's citizens-only FOIA provision abridges his ability to earn a living in his chosen profession, namely, obtaining property records from state and local governments on behalf of clients. He is correct that the Privileges and Immunities Clause protects the right of citizens to "ply their trade, practice their occupation, or pursue a common calling." *Hicklin v. Orbeck*, 437 U.S. 518, 524 (1978). But the Virginia FOIA does not abridge Hulbert's ability to engage in a common calling in the sense prohibited by the Privileges and Immunities Clause. The Court has struck laws down as violating the privilege of pursuing a common calling only when those laws were enacted for the protectionist purpose of burdening out-of-state citizens. See, *e.g.*, *Hicklin, supra*; *Toomer v. Witsell*, 334 U.S. 385 (1948); *United Building & Constr. Trades Council of Camden Cty. v. Mayor and Council of Camden*, 465 U.S. 208 (1984). In each case, the clear aim of the statute was to advantage in-state workers and commercial interests at the expense of their out-of-state counterparts. Virginia's FOIA differs sharply from those statutes. By its terms, Virginia's FOIA was enacted to "ensure the people of the Commonwealth ready access to public records in the custody of a public body or its officers and employees, and free entry to meetings of public bodies wherein the business of the people is being conducted." Va. Code Ann. §2.2-3700(B). Hurlbert does not allege that the challenged provision of the Virginia FOIA was enacted to provide a competitive economic advantage for Virginia citizens. Rather, the distinction that the statute makes between citizens and noncitizens has a distinctly nonprotectionist aim. The state FOIA essentially represents a mechanism by which those who ultimately hold sovereign power (citizens of the Commonwealth) may obtain an accounting from the public officials to whom they delegate the exercise of that power. See Va. Const., Art. I, §2; Va. Code Ann. §2.2-3700(B). In addition, the provision limiting the use of the state FOIA to Virginia citizens recognizes that Virginia taxpayers foot the bill for the fixed costs underlying recordkeeping in the Commonwealth. The challenged provision does not violate the Privileges and Immunities Clause simply because it has the incidental effect of preventing citizens of other States from making a profit by trading on information contained in state records. While the Clause forbids a State from intentionally giving its own citizens a competitive advantage in business or employment, the Clause does not require that a State tailor its every action to avoid any incidental effect on out-of-state tradesmen.

Hurlbert next alleges that the challenged provision abridges the right to own and transfer property in the Commonwealth. Like the right to pursue a common calling, the right to "take, hold and dispose of property, either real or personal," has long been seen as one of the privileges of citizenship. If a State prevented out-of-state citizens from accessing records—like title documents and mortgage records—that are necessary to the transfer of property, the State might well run afoul of the Privileges and Immunities Clause. Virginia, however, does not prevent citizens of other States from obtaining such documents. Under Virginia law, "any records and papers of every circuit court that are maintained by the clerk of the circuit court shall be open to inspection by any person and the clerk shall, when requested, furnish copies thereof." Va. Code Ann. §17.1-208.

A similar flaw undermines Hurlbert's claim that Virginia violates the Privileges and Immunities Clause by preventing citizens of other States from accessing real estate tax assessment records. Those records, while available to Virginia citizens under the state FOIA, are not required by statute to be made available to noncitizens. But Virginia and its subdivisions generally make these less essential records readily available to all. These records are considered non-confidential under Virginia law and may be posted online. Henrico County, from which Hurlbert sought real estate tax assessments, follows this practice, as does almost every other county in the Commonwealth. Requiring noncitizens to conduct Internet research in lieu of using a relatively cumbersome state FOIA process cannot be said to impose any significant burden on noncitizens' ability to own or transfer property in Virginia.

McBurney alleges that Virginia's citizens-only FOIA provision impermissibly burdens his "access to public proceedings." The Privileges and Immunities Clause "secures citizens of one State the right to resort to the courts of another, equally with the citizens of the latter State." *Missouri Pacific R. Co. v. Clarendon Boat Oar Co.*, 257 U.S. 533, 535 (1922). But petitioners do not suggest that the Virginia FOIA slams the courthouse door on noncitizens; the most they claim is that the law creates "an information asymmetry between adversaries based solely on state citizenship." The Privileges and Immunities Clause does not require States to erase any distinction between citizens and noncitizens that might conceivably give state citizens some detectable litigation advantage. Rather, the "constitutional requirement is satisfied if the non-resident is given access to the courts of the State upon terms which in themselves are reasonable and adequate for the enforcing of any rights he may have, even though they may not be technically and precisely the same in extent as those accorded to resident citizens." *Canadian*

Northern R. Co. v. Eggen, 252 U.S. 553, 562 (1920). The challenged provision of the Virginia FOIA does not deprive noncitizens of "reasonable and adequate" access to the Commonwealth's courts. Virginia's rules of civil procedure provide for both discovery, and subpoenas *duces tecum.* There is no reason to think that those mechanisms are insufficient to provide noncitizens with relevant, nonprivileged documents needed in litigation.

Moreover, Virginia law gives citizens and noncitizens alike access to judicial records. Va. Code Ann. §17.1-208. If Virginia has in its possession information about any person, whether a citizen of the Commonwealth or of another State, that person has the right under the Government Data Collection and Dissemination Practices Act to inspect that information. McBurney's case is illustrative. When his FOIA request was denied, McBurney was told that he should request the materials he sought pursuant to the Government Data Collection and Dissemination Practices Act. Under that Act, he ultimately received much of what he sought. Accordingly, Virginia's citizens-only FOIA provision does not impermissibly burden noncitizens' ability to access the Commonwealth's courts.

We reject petitioners' sweeping claim that the challenged provision of the Virginia FOIA violates the Privileges and Immunities Clause because it denies them the right to access public information on equal terms with citizens of the Commonwealth. We cannot agree that the Privileges and Immunities Clause covers this broad right. There is no constitutional right to obtain all the information provided by FOIA laws. See *Houchins v. KQED, Inc.*, 438 U.S. 1 (1978) (plurality opinion). It cannot be said that such a broad right has "at all times, been enjoyed by the citizens of the several states which compose this Union, from the time of their becoming free, independent, and sovereign." *Corfield*, 6 F. Cas., at 551. No such right was recognized at common law. Most founding-era English cases provided that only those persons who had a personal interest in non-judicial records were permitted to access them. See, *e.g., King v. Shelley*, 3 T.R. 141, 100 Eng. Rep. 498 (K.B. 1789).

Nineteenth-century American cases, while less uniform, do not support the proposition that a broad-based right to access public information was widely recognized in the early Republic. Nor is such a sweeping right "basic to the maintenance or well-being of the Union." *Baldwin*, 436 U.S., at 388. FOIA laws are of relatively recent vintage. The federal FOIA was enacted in 1966, Virginia's counterpart was adopted two years later. There is no contention that the Nation's unity foundered in their absence, or that it is suffering now because of the citizens-only FOIA provisions that several States have enacted.

The Court also rejected the plaintiff's Commerce Clause claim. Because Virginia's citizens-only FOIA provision neither abridges any of petitioners' fundamental privileges and immunities nor impermissibly regulates commerce, petitioners' constitutional claims fail. The judgment below is *affirmed.*

It is so ordered.

∽ PROBLEM: MEDICAL MARIJUANA LAWS ∽

Missouri adopts a new law authorizing the use of marijuana for medical purposes. However, Missouri provides that the law's benefits apply only to "Missouri residents" and specifically excludes anyone who claims resident privileges in any other state or country. Is the law consistent with the Privileges and Immunities Clause? What state interests might have prompted Missouri to limit the benefits of the law to residents? Are those justifications sufficient to sustain the law?

F. PREEMPTION

Preemption occurs when the federal government has exercised its power to regulate commerce and there is a conflict or a potential conflict between the federal law and a state law. *Gibbons* held that if the federal government has regulated a subject within the scope of its authority, and a state law conflicts, then the state law is invalid by virtue of the Supremacy Clause. In other words, the federal law preempts the state law.

Preemption can be either express or implied. In some instances, Congress makes a conscious decision to "preempt" a field and preclude state regulation. Assuming that the federal law is valid, state law must give way. *See Cipollone v. Liggett Group, Inc.,* 505 U.S. 504 (1992). In most instances, Congress does not clearly state its intention regarding preemption, and a reviewing court must decide whether Congress intended to preempt a field. The following cases focus on how the courts decide whether preemption exists.

Pacific Gas and Electric Co. v. State Energy Resources Conservation & Development Commission

461 U.S. 190 (1983)

Justice WHITE delivered the opinion of the Court.

The turning of swords into plowshares has symbolized the transformation of atomic power into a source of energy in American society. To facilitate this development the federal government relaxed its monopoly over fissionable materials and nuclear technology, and in its place, erected a complex scheme to promote the civilian development of nuclear energy, while seeking to safeguard the public and the environment from the unpredictable risks of a new technology. Early on, it was decided that the states would continue their traditional role in the regulation of electricity production. The interrelationship of federal and state authority in the nuclear energy field has not been simple; the federal regulatory structure has been frequently amended to optimize the partnership.

This case emerges from the intersection of the federal government's efforts to ensure that nuclear power is safe with the exercise of the historic state authority over the generation and sale of electricity. At issue is whether provisions in the 1976 amendments to California's Warren-Alquist Act, which condition the construction of nuclear plants on findings by the State Energy Resources Conservation and Development Commission that adequate storage facilities and means of disposal are available for nuclear waste, are preempted by the Atomic Energy Act of 1954.

A nuclear reactor must be periodically refueled and the "spent fuel" removed. This spent fuel is intensely radioactive and must be carefully stored. The general practice is to store the fuel in a water-filled pool at the reactor site. For many years, it was assumed that this fuel would be reprocessed; accordingly, the storage pools were designed as short-term holding facilities with limited storage capacities. As expectations for reprocessing remained unfulfilled, the spent fuel accumulated in the storage pools, creating the risk that nuclear reactors would have to be shut down. This could occur if there were insufficient room in the pool to store spent fuel and also if there were not enough space to hold the entire fuel core when certain inspections or emergencies required unloading of the reactor. In recent years, the problem has taken on special urgency. Some 8,000 metric tons of spent nuclear fuel have already accumulated, and it is projected that by the year 2000 there will be some 72,000 metric tons of spent fuel. Government studies indicate that a number of reactors could be forced to shut down in the near future due to the inability to store spent fuel.

There is a second dimension to the problem. Even with water-pools adequate to store safely all the spent fuel produced during the working lifetime of the reactor, permanent disposal is needed because the wastes will remain radioactive for thousands of years. A number of long-term nuclear waste management strategies have been extensively examined. These range from sinking the wastes in stable deep seabeds, to placing the wastes beneath ice sheets in Greenland and Antarctica, to ejecting the wastes into space by rocket. The greatest attention has been focused on disposing of the wastes in subsurface geologic repositories such as salt deposits. Problems of how and where to store nuclear wastes has engendered considerable scientific, political, and public debate. There are both safety and economic aspects to the nuclear waste issue: first, if not properly stored, nuclear wastes might leak and endanger both the environment and human health; second, the lack of a long-term disposal option increases the risk that the insufficiency of interim storage space for spent fuel will lead to reactor-shutdowns, rendering nuclear energy an unpredictable and uneconomical adventure.

The California laws at issue here are responses to these concerns. In 1974, California adopted the Warren-Alquist State Energy Resources Conservation and Development Act. The Act requires that a utility seeking to build in California any electric power generating plant, including a nuclear power plant, must apply for certification to the State Energy Resources and Conservation Commission

(Energy Commission). The Warren-Alquist Act was amended in 1976 to provide additional state regulation of new nuclear power plant construction.

Two sections of these amendments are before us. Section 25524.1(b) provides that before additional nuclear plants may be built, the Energy Commission must determine on a case-by-case basis that there will be "adequate capacity" for storage of a plant's spent fuel rods "at the time such nuclear facility requires such storage." The law also requires that each utility provide continuous, on-site, "full core reserve storage capacity" in order to permit storage of the entire reactor core if it must be removed to permit repairs of the reactor. In short, §25524.1(b) addresses the interim storage of spent fuel.

Section 25524.2 deals with the long-term solution to nuclear wastes. This section imposes a moratorium on the certification of new nuclear plants until the Energy Commission "finds that there has been developed and that the United States through its authorized agency has approved and there exists a demonstrated technology or means for the disposal of high-level nuclear waste." "Disposal" is defined as a "method for the permanent and terminal disposition of high-level nuclear waste." Cal. Pub. Res. Code §25524.2(a), (c). Such a finding must be reported to the state legislature, which may nullify it.

It is well-established that within Constitutional limits Congress may preempt state authority by so stating in express terms. Absent explicit preemptive language, Congress' intent to supersede state law altogether may be found from a "scheme of federal regulation so pervasive as to make reasonable the inference that Congress left no room to supplement it," "because the Act of Congress may touch a field in which the federal interest is so dominant that the federal system will be assumed to preclude enforcement of state laws on the same subject," or because "the object sought to be obtained by the federal law and the character of obligations imposed by it may reveal the same purpose." *Fidelity Federal Savings & Loan Assn. v. de la Cuesta*, 102 S.Ct. 3014 (1982). Even where Congress has not entirely displaced state regulation in a specific area, state law is preempted to the extent that it actually conflicts with federal law. Such a conflict arises when "compliance with both federal and state regulations is a physical impossibility," or where state law "stands as an obstacle to the accomplishment and execution of the full purposes and objectives of Congress." *Hines v. Davidowitz*, 312 U.S. 52, 67 (1941).

Even a brief perusal of the Atomic Energy Act reveals that, despite its comprehensiveness, it does not at any point expressly require the States to construct or authorize nuclear power plants or prohibit the States from deciding, as an absolute or conditional matter, not to permit the construction of any further reactors. Instead, petitioners argue that the Act is intended to preserve the federal government as the sole regulator of all matters nuclear, and that §25524.2 falls within the scope of this impliedly preempted field. But as we view the issue, Congress, in passing the 1954 Act and in subsequently amending it, intended that the federal government should regulate the radiological safety aspects involved in the construction and operation of a nuclear plant, but that the States retain their traditional responsibility in the field of regulating electrical utilities for determining questions of need, reliability, cost and other related state concerns.

Need for new power facilities, their economic feasibility, and rates and services, are areas that have been characteristically governed by the States. "Congress legislated here in a field which the States have traditionally occupied so we start with the assumption that the historic police powers of the States were not to be superseded by the Federal Act unless that was the clear and manifest purpose of Congress." *Rice v. Santa Fe Elevator Corp., 331 U.S. 218, 230 (1947).*

The Atomic Energy Act must be read, however, against another background. The Atomic Energy Act of 1954, 42 U.S.C. §§2011-2281 (1976), grew out of Congress' determination that the national interest would be best served if the Government encouraged the private sector to become involved in the development of atomic energy for peaceful purposes under a program of federal regulation and licensing. The Act implemented this policy decision by providing for licensing of private construction, ownership, and operation of commercial nuclear power reactors. *Duke Power Co. v. Carolina Environmental Study Group, Inc.,* 438 U.S. 59, 63 (1978). The AEC, however, was given exclusive jurisdiction to license the transfer, delivery, receipt, acquisition, possession and use of nuclear materials. 42 U.S.C. §§2014(e), (z), (aa), 2061-2064, 2071-2078, 2091-2099, 2111-2114 (1976 and Supp. IV 1980). Upon these subjects, no role was left for the states.

The Commission, however, was not given authority over the generation of electricity itself, or over the economic question whether a particular plant should be built. We observed in *Vermont Yankee,* 435 U.S. 519, 550 (1978) that "The Commission's prime area of concern in the licensing context, is national security, public health, and safety." The Nuclear Regulatory Commission (NRC), which now exercises the AEC's regulatory authority, does not purport to exercise its authority based on economic considerations, and has recently repealed its regulations concerning the financial qualifications and capabilities of a utility proposing to construct and operate a nuclear power plant. 47 Fed. Reg. 13751. In its notice of rule repeal, the NRC stated that utility financial qualifications are only of concern to the NRC if related to the public health and safety. It is almost inconceivable that Congress would have left a regulatory vacuum; the only reasonable inference is that Congress intended the states to continue to make these judgments. Any doubt that ratemaking and plant-need questions were to remain in state hands was removed by §271 which provided: "Nothing in this chapter shall be construed to affect the authority or regulations of any Federal, State or local agency with respect to the generation, sale, or transmission of electric power produced through the use of nuclear facilities licensed by the Commission."

This account indicates that from the passage of the Atomic Energy Act in 1954, through several revisions, and to the present day, Congress has preserved the dual regulation of nuclear-powered electricity generation: the federal government maintains complete control of the safety and "nuclear" aspects of energy generation; the states exercise their traditional authority over the need for additional generating capacity, the type of generating facilities to be licensed, land use, ratemaking, and the like.

The above is not particularly controversial. But deciding how §25524.2 is to be construed and classified is a more difficult proposition. The statute does not seek to regulate the construction or operation of a nuclear power plant. It would clearly be impermissible for California to attempt to do so, for such regulation, even if enacted out of non-safety concerns, would nevertheless directly conflict with the NRC's exclusive authority over plant construction and operation. Respondents appear to concede as much. Respondents do broadly argue, however, that although safety regulation of nuclear plants by states is forbidden, a state may completely prohibit new construction until its safety concerns are satisfied by the federal government. We reject this line of reasoning. State safety regulation is not preempted only when it conflicts with federal law. Rather, the federal government has occupied the entire field of nuclear safety concerns, except the limited powers expressly ceded to the states. When the federal government completely occupies a given field or an identifiable portion of it, as it has done here, the test of preemption is whether "the matter on which the state asserts the right to act is in any way regulated by the federal government." A state moratorium on nuclear construction grounded in safety concerns falls squarely within the prohibited field. Moreover, a state judgment that nuclear power is not safe enough to be further developed would conflict directly with the countervailing judgment of the NRC, that nuclear construction may proceed notwithstanding extant uncertainties as to waste disposal. A state prohibition on nuclear construction for safety reasons would also be in the teeth of the Atomic Energy Act's objective to insure that nuclear technology be safe enough for widespread development and use—and would be preempted for that reason.

That being the case, it is necessary to determine whether there is a non-safety rationale for §25524.2. California has maintained that §25524.2 was aimed at economic problems, not radiation hazards. The California Assembly Committee on Resources, Land Use, and Energy, which proposed a package of bills including §25524.2, reported that the waste disposal problem was "largely economic or the result of poor planning, not safety related." The Committee explained that the lack of a federally approved method of waste disposal created a "clog" in the nuclear fuel cycle. Storage space was limited while more nuclear wastes were continuously produced. Without a permanent means of disposal, the nuclear waste problem could become critical leading to unpredictably high costs to contain the problem or, worse, shutdowns in reactors. "Waste disposal safety," the Reassessment Report notes, "is not directly addressed by the bills, which ask only that a method of waste disposal be chosen and accepted by the federal government." We accept California's avowed economic purpose as the rationale for enacting §25524.2. Accordingly, the statute lies outside the occupied field of nuclear safety regulation.

Petitioners' second major argument concerns federal regulation aimed at the nuclear waste disposal problem itself. It is contended that §25524.2 conflicts with federal regulation of nuclear waste disposal, with the NRC's decision that it is permissible to continue to license reactors, notwithstanding uncertainty surrounding the waste disposal problem, and with Congress' recent passage of legislation directed at that problem.

The NRC's imprimatur, however, indicates only that it is safe to proceed with such plants, not that it is economically wise to do so. Because the NRC order does not and could not compel a utility to develop a nuclear plant, compliance with both it and §25524.2 are possible. Moreover, because the NRC's regulations are aimed at insuring that plants are safe, not necessarily that they are economical, §25524.2 does not interfere with the objective of the federal regulation.

Nor has California sought through §25524.2 to impose its own standards on nuclear waste disposal. The statute accepts that it is the federal responsibility to develop and license such technology. As there is no attempt on California's part to enter this field, one which is occupied by the federal government, we do not find §25524.2 preempted any more by the NRC's obligations in the waste disposal field than by its licensing power over the plants themselves.

Finally, it is strongly contended that §25524.2 frustrates the Atomic Energy Act's purpose to develop the commercial use of nuclear power. It is well established that state law is preempted if it "stands as an obstacle to the accomplishment of the full purposes and objectives of Congress." *Hines v. Davidowitz*, 312 U.S. 52, 67 (1941).

There is little doubt that a primary purpose of the Atomic Energy Act was, and continues to be, the promotion of nuclear power. The Act itself states that it is a program "to encourage widespread participation in the development and utilization of atomic energy for peaceful purposes to the maximum extent consistent with the common defense and security and with the health and safety of the public." 42 U.S.C. §2013(b).

The Court of Appeals is right, however, that the promotion of nuclear power is not to be accomplished "at all costs." The elaborate licensing and safety provisions and the continued preservation of state regulation in traditional areas belie that. Moreover, Congress has allowed the States to determine—as a matter of economics—whether a nuclear plant *vis-a-vis* a fossil fuel plant should be built. The decision of California to exercise that authority does not, in itself, constitute a basis for preemption.

The judgment of the Court of Appeals is
Affirmed.

Notes

1. *State Alien Registration Laws.* In *Hines v. Davidowitz*, 312 U.S. 52 (1941), Pennsylvania adopted a registration law that required all aliens 18 years of age or over to register with the state, pay a $1 annual registration fee, and carry an alien identification card. Subsequently, Congress enacted the federal Alien Registration

Act, which required a single registration of aliens 14 years of age and older and submission of detailed information, but which did not require aliens to carry a registration card and did not indicate whether the states could impose their own registration systems. The Court struck down the Pennsylvania law, stating:

> The supremacy of the national power in the general field of foreign affairs, including power over immigration, naturalization and deportation, is made clear by the Constitution and has been given continuous recognition by this Court. When the national government by treaty or statute has established rules and regulations touching the rights, privileges, obligations or burdens of aliens as such, the treaty or statute is the supreme law of the land. The power to restrict, limit, regulate, and register aliens as a distinct group is not an equal and continuously existing concurrent power of state and nation, but whatever power a state may have is subordinate to supreme national law. The legislative history of the Act indicates that Congress was trying to steer a middle path, realizing that any registration requirement was a departure from our traditional policy of not treating aliens as a thing apart, but also feeling that the Nation was in need of the type of information to be secured. Congress provided a standard for alien registration in a single integrated and all-embracing system. In doing so, Congress plainly manifested a purpose to protect the personal liberties of law-abiding aliens through one uniform national registration system, and to leave them free from the possibility of inquisitorial practices and police surveillance that might not only affect our international relations but might also generate the very disloyalty which the law has intended guarding against. Under these circumstances, the Pennsylvania Act cannot be enforced." Justice Stone dissented: "After entry, an alien resident within a state, like a citizen, is subject to the police powers of the state and, in the exercise of that power, state legislatures may pass laws applicable exclusively to aliens so long as the distinction taken between aliens and citizens is not shown to be without rational basis. Nothing indicates that Congress intended to withdraw from the state any part of their constitutional power over aliens within their borders. Congress was not unaware that some nineteen states have statutes or ordinances requiring some form of registration for aliens, seven of them dating from the last war. Here compliance with the state law does not preclude or even interfere with compliance with the act of Congress.

2. *Sedition Laws.* Congress passed the Smith Act, which prohibited the knowing advocacy of the overthrow of the government of the United States by force and violence. A few years later, Pennsylvania adopted a law that prohibited advocacy of either the overthrow of the U.S. government or the Commonwealth of Pennsylvania's government. In *Pennsylvania v. Nelson*, 350 U.S. 497 (1956), the Court held that the Smith Act preempted the Pennsylvania law:

> Looking at these laws in the aggregate, the conclusion is inescapable that Congress intended to occupy the field of sedition. Therefore, a state sedition statute is superseded regardless of whether it purports to supplement the federal law. The federal statutes 'touch a field in which the federal interest is so dominant that the federal system (must) be assumed to preclude enforcement of state laws on the same subject.' *Rice v. Santa Fe Elevator Corp.*, 331 U.S. 218, 230 (1947). Congress has devised an all-embracing program for resistance to the various forms of totalitarian aggression." Justice Reed, joined by two other Justices, dissented: "Congress has not specifically barred the exercise of state power to punish the same Acts. Absent federal legislation, there is no constitutional bar to punishment of sedition against the United States by both a State and the Nation. The federal sedition laws are distinct criminal statutes that punish willful advocacy of the use of force against 'the government of

the United States or the government of any State.' These criminal laws proscribe certain local activity without creating any statutory or administrative regulation. There is, consequently, no question as to whether some general congressional regulatory scheme might be upset by a coinciding state plan. In these circumstances the conflict should be clear and direct before this Court reads a congressional intent to void state legislation into the federal sedition acts. Since 1940 Congress has been keenly aware of the magnitude of existing state legislation proscribing sedition.

Gade v. National Solid Wastes Management Association

505 U.S. 88 (1992)

Justice O'CONNOR announced the judgment of the Court and delivered the opinion of the Court with respect to Parts I, III, and IV, and an opinion with respect to Part II in which THE CHIEF JUSTICE, Justice WHITE, and Justice SCALIA join.

In 1988, the Illinois General Assembly enacted the Hazardous Waste Crane and Hoisting Equipment Operators Licensing Act and the Hazardous Waste Laborers Licensing Act. The stated purpose of the licensing acts is both "to promote job safety" and "to protect life, limb and property." In this case, we consider whether these "dual impact" statutes, which protect both workers and the general public, are pre-empted by the federal Occupational Safety and Health Act of 1970, 29 U.S.C. §651 *et seq.* (OSH Act), and the standards promulgated thereunder by the Occupational Safety and Health Administration (OSHA).

The OSH Act authorizes the Secretary of Labor to promulgate federal occupational safety and health standards. In the Superfund Amendments and Reauthorization Act of 1986 (SARA), Congress directed the Secretary of Labor to "promulgate standards for the health and safety protection of employees engaged in hazardous waste operations" pursuant to her authority under the OSH Act. In response to this congressional directive, OSHA promulgated regulations on "Hazardous Waste Operations and Emergency Response," including detailed regulations on worker training requirements. While OSHA's interim hazardous waste regulations were in effect, the State of Illinois enacted the licensing acts at issue here. The laws are designated as acts "in relation to environmental protection," and their stated aim is to protect both employees and the general public by licensing hazardous waste equipment operators and laborers working at certain facilities.

Respondent National Solid Wastes Management Association (Association) brought a declaratory judgment action to enjoin the Illinois Environmental Protection Agency from enforcing the Illinois licensing acts. The District Court held that federal law did not preempt Illinois law. The United States Court of Appeals for the Seventh Circuit affirmed in part and reversed in part. We granted certiorari.

"The question whether a certain state action is pre-empted by federal law is one of congressional intent." In the OSH Act, Congress endeavored "to assure so far as possible every working man and woman in the Nation safe and healthful working conditions." To that end, Congress authorized the Secretary of Labor to set mandatory occupational safety and health standards applicable to all businesses affecting interstate commerce, and thereby brought the Federal Government into a field that traditionally had been occupied by the States. Federal regulation of the workplace was not intended to be all encompassing, however. First, Congress expressly saved two areas from federal pre-emption. Section 4(b)(4) of the OSH Act states that the Act does not "supersede or in any manner affect any workmen's compensation law or enlarge or diminish or affect in any other manner the common law or statutory rights, duties, or liabilities of employers and employees under any law with respect to injuries, diseases, or death of employees arising out of, or in the course of, employment." Second, Section 18(a) provides that the Act does not "prevent any State agency or court from asserting jurisdiction under State law over any occupational safety or health issue with respect to which no federal standard is in effect." 29 U.S.C. §667(a).

Congress not only reserved certain areas to state regulation, but it also, in §18(b) of the Act, gave the States the option of pre-empting federal regulation entirely. That section provides:

Submission of State plan for development and enforcement of State standards to preempt applicable Federal standards

Any State which, at any time, desires to assume responsibility for development and enforcement therein of occupational safety and health standards relating to any occupational safety or health issue with respect to which a Federal standard has been promulgated by the Secretary under the OSH Act shall submit a State plan for the development of such standards and their enforcement. 29 U.S.C. §667(b).

About half the States have received the Secretary's approval for their own state plans as described in this provision. Illinois is not among them.

Pre-emption may be either expressed or implied, and "is compelled whether Congress' command is explicitly stated in the statute's language or implicitly contained in its structure and purpose." Absent explicit pre-emptive language, we have recognized at least two types of implied pre-emption: field pre-emption, where the scheme of federal regulation is "so pervasive as to make reasonable the inference that Congress left no room for the States to supplement it," and conflict pre-emption, where "compliance with both federal and state regulations is a physical impossibility," or where state law "stands as an obstacle to the accomplishment and execution of the full purposes and objectives of Congress."

Our ultimate task in any pre-emption case is to determine whether state regulation is consistent with the structure and purpose of the statute as a whole. Looking to "the provisions of the whole law, and to its object and policy," we hold that nonapproved state regulation of occupational safety and health issues for which a federal standard is in effect is impliedly pre-empted as in conflict with the full purposes and objectives of the OSH Act. The design of the statute persuades us that Congress intended to subject employers and employees to only one set of regulations, be it federal or state, and that the only way a State may regulate an

OSHA-regulated occupational safety and health issue is pursuant to an approved state plan that displaces the federal standards.

The principal indication that Congress intended to pre-empt state law is §18(b)'s statement that a State "shall" submit a plan if it wishes to "assume responsibility" for "development and enforcement of occupational safety and health standards relating to any occupational safety or health issue with respect to which a Federal standard has been promulgated." The unavoidable implication of this provision is that a State may not enforce its own occupational safety and health standards without obtaining the Secretary's approval. Petitioner contends, however, that an approved plan is necessary only if the State wishes completely to replace the federal regulations, not merely to supplement them. The OSH Act as a whole evidences Congress' intent to avoid subjecting workers and employers to duplicative regulation; a State may develop an occupational safety and health program tailored to its own needs, but only if it is willing completely to displace the applicable federal regulations. Section 18(a) saves from pre-emption any state law regulating an occupational safety and health issue with respect to which no federal standard is in effect. Although this is a saving clause, not a pre-emption clause, the natural implication of this provision is that state laws regulating the same issue as federal laws are not saved, even if they merely supplement the federal standard.

Our understanding of the implications of §18(b) is bolstered by §18(c) of the Act. State standards that affect interstate commerce will be approved only if they "are required by compelling local conditions" and "do not unduly burden interstate commerce." If a State could supplement federal regulations without undergoing the §18(b) approval process, then the protections that §18(c) offers to interstate commerce would easily be undercut. It would make little sense to impose such a condition on state programs intended to supplant federal regulation and not those that merely supplement it.

Section 18(f) also confirms our view that States are not permitted to assume an enforcement role without the Secretary's approval, unless no federal standard is in effect. That provision gives the Secretary the authority to withdraw her approval of a state plan. §18(f) assumes that the State loses the power to enforce all of its occupational safety and health standards once approval is withdrawn.

Looking at the provisions of §18 as a whole, we conclude that the OSH Act precludes any state regulation of an occupational safety or health issue with respect to which a federal standard has been established, unless a state plan has been submitted and approved pursuant to §18(b). Congress sought to promote occupational safety and health while at the same time avoiding duplicative, and possibly counterproductive, regulation. It thus established a system of uniform federal occupational health and safety standards, but gave States the option of pre-empting federal regulations by developing their own occupational safety and health programs. In addition, Congress offered the States substantial federal grant moneys to assist them in developing their own programs. To allow a State selectively to "supplement" certain federal regulations with ostensibly nonconflicting standards would be inconsistent with this federal scheme of establishing uniform federal standards, on the one hand, and encouraging States to assume full responsibility for development and enforcement of their own OSH programs, on the other.

We cannot accept petitioner's argument that the OSH Act does not pre-empt nonconflicting state laws because those laws, like the Act, are designed to promote worker safety. In determining whether state law "stands as an obstacle" to the full implementation of a federal law "it is not enough to say that the ultimate goal of both federal and state law" is the same. "A state law also is pre-empted if it interferes with the methods by which the federal statute was designed to reach that goal."

Petitioner next argues that, even if Congress intended to pre-empt all non-approved state occupational safety and health regulations whenever a federal standard is in effect, the OSH Act's pre-emptive effect should not be extended to state laws that address public safety as well as occupational safety concerns. A dual impact state regulation cannot avoid OSH Act pre-emption simply because the regulation serves several objectives rather than one. Whatever the purpose or purposes of the state law, pre-emption analysis cannot ignore the effect of the challenged state action on the pre-empted field. The key question is thus at what point the state regulation sufficiently interferes with federal regulation that it should be deemed pre-empted under the Act. State laws of general applicability (such as laws regarding traffic safety or fire safety) that do not conflict with OSHA standards and that regulate the conduct of workers and nonworkers alike would generally not be pre-empted. Although some laws of general applicability may have a "direct and substantial" effect on worker safety, they cannot fairly be characterized as "occupational" standards, because they regulate workers simply as members of the general public. A law directed at workplace safety is not saved from pre-emption simply because the State can demonstrate some additional effect outside of the workplace. That such a law may also have a nonoccupational impact does not render it any less of an occupational standard for purposes of pre-emption analysis. If the State wishes to enact a dual impact law that regulates an occupational safety or health issue for which a federal standard is in effect, §18 of the Act requires that the State submit a plan for the approval of the Secretary.

The judgment of the Court of Appeals is hereby

Affirmed.

Justice SOUTER, with whom Justice BLACKMUN, Justice STEVENS, and Justice THOMAS join, *dissenting.*

"Where the field which Congress is said to have pre-empted has been traditionally occupied by the States, 'we start with the assumption that the historic police powers of the States were not to be superseded by the Federal Act unless that was the clear and manifest purpose of Congress.'" This assumption provides assurance that the 'federal-state balance' will not be disturbed unintentionally by Congress or unnecessarily by the courts. Subject to this principle, the enquiry into the possibly pre-emptive effect of federal legislation is an exercise of statutory construction. If the statute's terms can be read sensibly not to have a pre-emptive effect, the presumption controls and no pre-emption may be inferred.

Respondent argues that the only way that a state rule on a particular occupational safety and health issue may be enforced once a federal standard on the issue is also in place is by incorporating the state rule in a plan approved by the Secretary. That is not the necessary implication. Section 18(b) does not provide that absent such state pre-emption of federal rules, the State may not supplement the federal standards with consistent regulations of its own. The provision makes perfect sense if a dual regulatory scheme is permissible but subject to state pre-emption if the State wishes to shoulder enough of the federal mandate to gain approval of a plan. Nor does the provision setting out conditions for the Secretary's approval of a plan indicate that a state regulation on an issue federally addressed is never enforceable unless incorporated in a plan so approved.

In the absence of any clear expression of congressional intent to pre-empt, I can only conclude that, as long as compliance with federally promulgated standards does not render obedience to Illinois' regulations impossible, the enforcement of the state law is not prohibited by the Supremacy Clause. I respectfully *dissent.*

Notes

1. *The Scope of Federal Power and Preemption.* As we have seen, even after *Lopez,* the Commerce Clause provides Congress with a great deal of power to regulate economic activity. This power, when combined with the Supremacy Clause, means that if Congress decides to regulate in a given area, conflicting state regulations must give way. Preemption principles help courts determine whether there is a conflict.

2. *Strict Liability for Oil Spills.* In *Askew v. American Waterways Operators, Inc.,* 411 U.S. 325 (1973), the Court considered a Florida law that imposed strict liability for any damage incurred by the state or private persons as a result of an oil spill in a state's territorial waters. Liability was imposed on spills from any waterfront facility used for drilling for oil or handling the transfer or storage of oil (terminal facility) and from any ship destined for or leaving such a facility. Each owner or operator of a terminal facility or ship subject to the Act was required to show evidence of financial responsibility by insurance or a surety bond. The Act also required the state's Department of Natural Resources to regulate containment gear and other equipment that must be maintained by ships and terminal facilities for the prevention of oil spills. Several months prior to the enactment of the Act, Congress enacted the Water Quality Improvement Act of 1970, which subjected ship owners and terminal facilities to liability without fault up to $14,000,000 and $8,000,000, respectively, for cleanup costs incurred by the federal government as a result of oil spills. It also authorized the President

to promulgate regulations requiring ships and terminal facilities to maintain equipment for the prevention of oil spills. In upholding the Florida law against a preemption challenge, the Court stated: "We find no constitutional or statutory impediment to permitting Florida, in the present setting of this case, to establish any 'requirement or liability' concerning the impact of oil spillages on Florida's interests or concerns. It is clear at the outset that the Federal Act does not preclude, but in fact allows, state regulation. The reason for the provision in §1161(o)(2), stating that nothing in §1161 pre-empts any State 'from imposing any requirement or liability with respect to the discharge of oil into any waters within such State,' is that the scheme of the Act is one which allows—though it does not require—co-operation of the federal regime with a state regime."

∼ PROBLEMS ∼

1. *Local Noise Control.* A local ordinance makes it unlawful for aircraft to take off from the local airport during night hours (defined as between 11 p.m. and 7 a.m.). The ordinance is passed as a noise control measure. Two federal laws—the Federal Aviation Act of 1958 and the Noise Control Act of 1972—also pertain to aircrafts and aircraft noise. In deciding whether the federal law preempts the local ordinance, which of these factors are relevant? a) Noise control has traditionally been a matter reserved to the states; b) federal control over airplanes is relatively intensive in that planes move only by federal permission, subject to federal inspection, in the hands of federally certified personnel.

2. *More on the Internet Casino Prohibition Act.* Is the Internet Casino Prohibition Act preempted by federal law? Does it matter whether the U.S. Congress has, or has not, enacted legislation regulating (or, for that matter, outlawing) internet-based casino gambling? Should it matter that almost all internet casino gambling operations are located outside the United States?

Amidst a national dialogue on how to deal with persons crossing the borders into the United States unlawfully, Arizona's governor signed S.B. 1070, set to become effective 90 days following her signing, on July 29, 2010. These undocumented persons, called "aliens" in many statutes, often cross into the United States through the southern border with Mexico. Arizona's law was designed to prosecute and/or deport persons who are in the United States illegally. At least two of the law's components sparked controversy: the requirement that police check immigration status upon a reasonable suspicion for those persons who are arrested and those persons who are lawfully detained, and other regulation of the immigration of persons.

Arguments in favor of the law revolved around a need to take strong action to stem unlawful immigration. Arguments against the law focused on whether the law unconstitutionally exceeded federalism boundaries between federal and state laws and encouraged racial and ethnic profiling.

Shortly after it was signed into law, the United States challenged the law in federal court in Arizona, seeking an injunction. The federal district and circuit courts enjoined enforcement of the law, *inter alia*, on the ground that federal law preempted the Arizona law.

There was litigation in other states as well. In Nebraska, an ordinance required businesses to verify the legal status of their employees, and required an immigration status check on anyone seeking to rent a home or apartment in the city. An Alabama law required schools to verify that students are legally in the country.

Arizona v. United States

567 U.S. (2012)

Justice KENNEDY delivered the opinion of the Court.

To address pressing issues related to the large number of aliens within its borders who do not have a lawful right to be in this country, the State of Arizona in 2010 enacted a statute called the Support Our Law Enforcement and Safe Neighborhoods Act. S.B. 1070. Its stated purpose is to "discourage and deter the unlawful entry and presence of aliens and economic activity by persons unlawfully present in the United States." The law establishes an official state policy of "attrition through enforcement." The question is whether federal law preempts and renders invalid provisions of the state law.

The United States filed suit against Arizona, seeking to enjoin S.B. 1070 as preempted. Four provisions are at issue here. Two create new state offenses. Section 3 makes failure to comply with federal alien-registration requirements a state misdemeanor. Section 5, in relevant part, makes it a misdemeanor for an unauthorized alien to seek or engage in work in the State. Two provisions give specific arrest authority and investigative duties with respect to certain aliens to state and local law enforcement officers. Section 6 authorizes officers to arrest without a warrant a person "the officer has probable cause to believe has committed any public offense that makes the person removable from the United States." Section 2(B) provides that officers who conduct a stop, detention, or arrest must in some circumstances make efforts to verify the person's immigration status with the Federal Government. The United States District Court for the District of Arizona issued a preliminary injunction preventing the four provisions from taking effect. The Court of Appeals for the Ninth Circuit affirmed. This Court granted certiorari to resolve important questions concerning the interaction of state and federal power with respect to the law of immigration and alien status.

The United States has broad, undoubted power over the subject of immigration and the status of aliens. *See Toll v. Moreno*, 458 U.S. 1, 10 (1982). This authority rests, in part, on the National Government's constitutional power to "establish an uniform Rule of Naturalization," U.S. Const., Art. I, §8, cl. 4, and its inherent power as sovereign to control and conduct relations with foreign nations. The federal power to determine immigration policy is well settled. Immigration policy can affect trade, investment, tourism, and diplomatic relations for the entire Nation, as well as the perceptions and expectations of aliens in this country who seek the full protection of its laws. Perceived mistreatment of aliens in the United States may lead to harmful reciprocal treatment of American citizens abroad.

Foreign countries concerned about the status, safety, and security of their nationals in the United States must be able to confer and communicate on this subject with one national sovereign, not the 50 separate States. *See Chy Lung v. Freeman*, 92 U.S. 275 (1876). "One of the most important and delicate of all international relationships has to do with the protection of the just rights of a country's own nationals when those nationals are in another country." *Hines v. Davidowitz*, 312 U.S. 52, 64 (1941).

Federal governance of immigration and alien status is extensive and complex. Congress has specified categories of aliens who may not be admitted to the United States. *See* 8 U.S.C. §1182. Unlawful entry and unlawful reentry into the country are federal offenses. Once here, aliens are required to register with the Federal Government and to carry proof of status on their person. Failure to do so is a federal misdemeanor. Federal law also authorizes States to deny noncitizens a range of public benefits, and it imposes sanctions on employers who hire unauthorized workers. Congress has specified which aliens may be removed from the United States and the procedures for doing so. Aliens may be removed if they were inadmissible at the time of entry, have been convicted of certain crimes, or meet other criteria. Removal is a civil, not criminal, matter. A principal feature of the removal system is the broad discretion exercised by immigration officials. Federal officials must decide whether it makes sense to pursue removal at all. If removal proceedings commence, aliens may seek asylum and other discretionary relief allowing them to remain in the country or at least to leave without formal removal.

Discretion in the enforcement of immigration law embraces immediate human concerns. Unauthorized workers trying to support their families, for example, likely pose less danger than alien smugglers or aliens who commit a serious crime. The equities of an individual case may turn on many factors, including whether the alien has children born in the United States, long ties to the community, or a record of distinguished military service. Some discretionary decisions involve policy choices that bear on this Nation's international relations. Returning an alien to his own country may be deemed inappropriate even where he has committed a removable offense or fails to meet the criteria for admission. The foreign state may be mired in civil war, complicit in political persecution, or enduring conditions that create a real risk that the alien or his family will be harmed upon return. The dynamic nature of relations with other countries requires the Executive Branch to ensure that enforcement policies are consistent with this Nation's foreign policy with respect to these and other realities.

Agencies in the Department of Homeland Security play a major role in enforcing the country's immigration laws. United States Customs and Border Protection (CBP) is responsible for determining the admissibility of aliens and securing the country's borders. In 2010, CBP's Border Patrol apprehended almost half a million people. Immigration and Customs Enforcement (ICE), a second agency, "conducts criminal investigations involving the enforcement of immigration-related statutes." ICE also operates the Law Enforcement Support Center. LESC, as the Center is known, provides immigration status information to federal, state, and local officials around the clock. ICE officers are responsible "for the identification, apprehension, and removal of illegal aliens from the United States." Hundreds of thousands of aliens are removed by the Federal Government every year.

The pervasiveness of federal regulation does not diminish the importance of immigration policy to the States. Arizona bears many of the consequences of unlawful immigration. Hundreds of thousands of deportable aliens are apprehended in Arizona each year. Unauthorized aliens who remain in the State comprise almost six percent of the population. And in the State's most populous county, these aliens are responsible for a disproportionate share of serious crime. There is an "epidemic of crime, safety risks, serious property damage, and environmental problems" associated with the influx of illegal migration across private land near the Mexican border. Phoenix is a major city of the United States, yet signs along an interstate highway 30 miles to the south warn the public to stay away. One reads, "DANGER—PUBLIC WARNING—TRAVEL NOT RECOMMENDED / Active Drug and Human Smuggling Area / Visitors May Encounter Armed Criminals and Smuggling Vehicles Traveling at High Rates of Speed."

The issue is whether, under preemption principles, federal law permits Arizona to implement the state-law provisions in dispute. Federalism, central to the constitutional design, adopts the principle that both the National and State Governments have elements of sovereignty the other is bound to respect. *See Gregory v. Ashcroft*, 501 U.S. 452 (1991). From the existence of two sovereigns follows the possibility that laws can be in conflict or at cross-purposes. The Supremacy Clause provides that federal law "shall be the supreme Law of the Land; and the Judges in every State shall be bound thereby, any Thing in the Constitution or Laws of any State to the Contrary notwithstanding." Art. VI, cl. 2. There is no doubt that Congress may withdraw specified powers from the States by enacting a statute containing an express preemption provision. *See, e.g., Chamber of Commerce of United States of America v. Whiting*, 131 S.Ct. 1968, 1974-1975 (2011).

State law must also give way to federal law in at least two other circumstances. First, the States are precluded from regulating conduct in a field that Congress, acting within its proper authority, has determined must be regulated by its exclusive governance. *See Gade v. National Solid Wastes Management Assn.*, 505 U.S. 88 (1992). The intent to displace state law altogether can be inferred from a framework of regulation "so pervasive that Congress left no room for the States to supplement it" or where there is a "federal interest so dominant that the federal system will be assumed to preclude enforcement of state laws on the same subject." *Rice v. Santa Fe Elevator Corp.,* 331 U.S. 218, 230 (1947). Second, state laws are preempted when they conflict with federal law. This includes cases where "compliance with both federal and state regulations is a physical impossibility," and those instances where the challenged state law "stands as an obstacle to the accomplishment and execution of the full purposes and objectives of Congress," *Hines,* 312 U.S. at 67. In preemption analysis, courts should assume that "the historic police powers of the States" are not superseded "unless that was the clear and manifest purpose of Congress." *Rice,* at 230.

The four challenged provisions of the state law each must be examined under these preemption principles.

Section 3. Section 3 of S.B. 1070 creates a new state misdemeanor. It forbids the "willful failure to complete or carry an alien registration document in violation of 8 United States Code section 1304(e) or 1306(a)." In effect, §3 adds a state-law penalty for conduct proscribed by federal law. The United States contends that this state enforcement mechanism intrudes on the field of alien registration, a field in which Congress has left no room for States to regulate. The Court discussed federal alien-registration requirements in *Hines v. Davidowitz,* 312 U.S. 52. In 1940, as international conflict spread, Congress added a "complete system for alien registration." The new federal law struck a careful balance. It punished an alien's willful failure to register but did not require aliens to carry identification cards. There were also limits on the sharing of registration records and fingerprints. The Court found that Congress intended the federal plan for registration to be a "single integrated and all-embracing system." Because this "complete scheme for the registration of aliens" touched on foreign relations, it did not allow the States to "curtail or complement" federal law or to "enforce additional or auxiliary regulations." The Court ruled that Pennsylvania could not enforce its own alien-registration program.

The present regime of federal regulation is not identical to the framework considered in *Hines,* but it remains comprehensive. Federal law now includes a requirement that aliens carry proof of registration. Other aspects, however, have stayed the same. Aliens who remain in the country for more than 30 days must apply for registration and be fingerprinted. Detailed information is required, and any change of address has to be reported to the Federal Government. The statute continues to provide penalties for the willful failure to register.

The framework enacted by Congress leads to the conclusion here, as it did in *Hines,* that the Federal Government has occupied the field of alien registration. *See American Ins. Assn. v. Garamendi,* 539 U.S. 396 (2003); *Pennsylvania v. Nelson,* 350 U.S. 497 (1956). The federal statutory directives provide a full set of standards governing alien registration, including the punishment for noncompliance. It was designed as a "harmonious whole." *Hines, 312 U.S.* at 72. Where Congress occupies an entire field, as it has in the field of alien registration, even complementary state regulation is impermissible. Field preemption reflects a congressional decision to foreclose any state regulation in the area, even if it is parallel to federal standards. *See Silkwood v. Kerr-McGee Corp.*, 464 U.S. 238 (1984).

Federal law makes a single sovereign responsible for maintaining a comprehensive and unified system to keep track of aliens within the Nation's borders. If §3 of the Arizona statute were valid, every State could give itself independent authority to prosecute federal registration violations, "diminishing the Federal Government's control over enforcement" and "detracting from the 'integrated scheme of regulation' created by Congress." *Wisconsin Dept. of Industry v. Gould Inc.*, 475 U.S. 282, 288 (1986). Even if a State may make violation of federal law a crime in some instances, it cannot do so in a field (like the field of alien registration) that has been occupied by federal law.

Arizona contends that §3 survives preemption because it has the same aim as federal law and adopts its substantive standards. This argument ignores the basic premise of field preemption—that States may not enter, in any respect, an area the Federal Government has reserved for itself—but also is unpersuasive. Permitting the State to impose its own penalties for the federal offenses would conflict with the careful framework Congress adopted. The State would have the power to bring criminal charges against individuals for violating a federal law even in circumstances where federal officials in charge of the comprehensive scheme determine that prosecution would frustrate federal policies, and there is an inconsistency between §3 and federal law with respect to penalties. Under federal law, the failure to carry registration papers is a misdemeanor that may be punished by a fine, imprisonment, or a term of probation. State law rules out probation as a possible sentence (and also eliminates the possibility of a pardon). These specific conflicts underscore the reason for field preemption. With respect to the subject of alien registration, Congress intended to preclude States from "complementing the federal law, or enforcing additional or auxiliary regulations."

Section 5(c). Unlike §3, which replicates federal statutory requirements, §5(C) enacts a state criminal prohibition where no federal counterpart exists. The provision makes it a state misdemeanor for "an unauthorized alien to knowingly apply for work, solicit work in a public place or perform work as an employee or independent contractor" in Arizona. Violations can be punished by a $2,500 fine and incarceration for up to six months. The United States contends that the provision upsets the balance struck by the Immigration Reform and Control Act of 1986 (IRCA) and must be preempted as an obstacle to the federal plan of regulation and control. When there was no comprehensive federal program regulating the employment of unauthorized aliens, this Court found that a State had authority to pass its own laws on the subject. *De Canas v. Bica*, 424 U.S. 351 (1976). *De Canas* recognized that "States possess broad authority under their police powers to regulate the employment relationship to protect workers within the State." At that point, the Federal Government had expressed no more than "a peripheral concern with the employment of illegal entrants."

Current federal law is substantially different from the regime that prevailed when *De Canas* was decided. Congress enacted IRCA as a comprehensive framework for "combating the employment of illegal aliens." *Hoffman Plastic Compounds, Inc. v. NLRB*, 535 U.S. 137, 147 (2002). The law makes it illegal for employers to knowingly hire, recruit, refer, or continue to employ unauthorized workers. It also requires every employer to verify the employment authorization status of prospective employees. These requirements are enforced through criminal penalties and an escalating series of civil penalties tied to the number of times an employer has violated the provisions. This comprehensive framework does not impose federal criminal sanctions on the employee side (i.e., penalties on aliens who seek or engage in unauthorized work). Under federal law some civil penalties are imposed instead. With certain exceptions, aliens who accept unlawful employment are not eligible to have their status adjusted to that of a lawful permanent resident. Aliens also may be removed from the country for having engaged in unauthorized work. In addition to specifying these civil consequences, federal law makes it a crime for unauthorized workers to obtain employment through fraudulent means. Congress has made clear, however, that any information employees submit to indicate their work status "may not be used" for purposes other than prosecution under specified federal criminal statutes for fraud, perjury, and related conduct. *See* 8 U.S.C. §§1324a(b)(5), (d)(2)(F)-(G).

The legislative background of IRCA underscores the fact that Congress made a deliberate choice not to impose criminal penalties on aliens who seek, or engage in, unauthorized employment. A commission established by Congress to study immigration policy and to make recommendations concluded these penalties would be "unnecessary and unworkable." In the end, IRCA's framework reflects a considered judgment that making criminals out of aliens engaged in unauthorized work—aliens who already face the possibility of employer exploitation because of their removable status—would be inconsistent with federal policy and objectives.

IRCA's express preemption provision, which in most instances bars States from imposing penalties on employers of unauthorized aliens, is silent about whether additional penalties may be imposed against the employees themselves. But the existence of an "express pre-emption provision does *not* bar the ordinary working of conflict pre-emption principles" or impose a "special burden" that would make it more difficult to establish the preemption of laws falling outside the clause. *Geier v. American Honda Motor Co.,* 529 U.S. 861 (2000).

The ordinary principles of preemption include the well-settled proposition that a state law is preempted where it "stands as an obstacle to the accomplishment and execution of the full purposes and objectives of Congress." *Hines,* 312 U.S. at 67. Under §5(C) of S.B. 1070, Arizona law would interfere with the careful balance struck by Congress with respect to unauthorized employment of aliens. Although §5(C) attempts to achieve one of the same goals as federal law—the deterrence of unlawful employment—it involves a conflict in the method of enforcement. A "conflict in technique can be fully as disruptive to the system Congress enacted as conflict in overt policy." *Motor Coach Employees v. Lockridge,* 403 U.S. 274, 287 (1971). The text, structure, and history of IRCA show that

Congress decided it would be inappropriate to impose criminal penalties on aliens who seek or engage in unauthorized employment. A state law to the contrary is an obstacle to the regulatory system Congress chose. Section 5(C) is preempted by federal law.

Section 6. Section 6 of S.B. 1070 provides that a state officer, "without a warrant, may arrest a person if the officer has probable cause to believe the person has committed any public offense that makes him removable from the United States." As a general rule, it is not a crime for a removable alien to remain present in the United States. The Attorney General can issue a warrant for an alien's arrest and detention "pending a decision on whether the alien is to be removed from the United States." 8 U.S.C. §1226(a). And if an alien is ordered removed, the Attorney General will issue a warrant. The warrants are executed by federal officers who have received training in the enforcement of immigration law. Section 6 provides state officers even greater authority to arrest aliens on the basis of possible removability than Congress has given to trained federal immigration officers. Under state law, officers who believe an alien is removable by reason of some "public offense" would have the power to arrest regardless of whether a federal warrant has issued or the alien is likely to escape. This state authority could be exercised without any input from the Federal Government about whether an arrest is warranted in a particular case. This would allow the State to achieve its own immigration policy. The result could be unnecessary harassment of some aliens (for instance, a veteran, college student, or someone assisting with a criminal investigation) whom federal officials determine should not be removed. By authorizing state officers to decide whether an alien should be detained for being removable, §6 violates the principle that the removal process is entrusted to the discretion of the Federal Government. A decision on removability requires a determination whether it is appropriate to allow a foreign national to continue living in the United States. Decisions of this nature touch on foreign relations and must be made with one voice. *See Jama v. Immigration and Customs Enforcement,* 543 U.S. 335, 348 (2005).

In defense of §6, a federal statute permits state officers to "cooperate with the Attorney General in the identification, apprehension, detention, or removal of aliens not lawfully present in the United States." 8 U.S.C. §1357(g)(10)(B). There may be some ambiguity as to what constitutes cooperation, but no coherent understanding of the term would incorporate the unilateral decision of state officers to arrest an alien for being removable absent any request, approval, or other instruction from the Federal Government. Section 6 is preempted by federal law.

Section 2(B). Section 2(B) of S.B. 1070 requires state officers to make a "reasonable attempt to determine the immigration status" of any person they stop, detain, or arrest on some other legitimate basis if "reasonable suspicion exists that the person is an alien and is unlawfully present in the United States." The law also provides that "any person who is arrested shall have the person's immigration status determined before the person is released." The accepted way to perform these status checks is to contact ICE, which maintains a database of immigration records. Three limits are built into the state provision. First, a detainee is presumed not to be an alien unlawfully present in the United States if he or she provides a valid Arizona driver's license or similar identification. Second, officers "may not consider race, color or national origin except to the extent permitted by the United States and Arizona constitutions." Third, the provisions must be "implemented in a manner consistent with federal law regulating immigration, protecting the civil rights of all persons and respecting the privileges and immunities of United States citizens." The United States and *amici* contend that, even with these limits, the State's verification requirements pose an obstacle to the framework Congress put in place.

Consultation between federal and state officials is an important feature of the immigration system. No formal agreement or special training needs to be in place for state officers to "communicate with the Federal Government regarding the immigration status of any individual, including reporting knowledge that a particular alien is not lawfully present in the United States." 8 U.S.C. §1357(g)(10)(A). Congress requires ICE to respond to any request made by state officials for verification of a person's citizenship or immigration status. ICE's Law Enforcement Support Center operates "24 hours a day, seven days a week, 365 days a year" and provides "immigration status, identity information and real-time assistance to local, state and federal law enforcement agencies." LESC responded to more than one million requests for information in 2009 alone. The United States argues that making status verification mandatory interferes with the federal immigration scheme. It is true that §2(B) does not allow state officers to consider federal enforcement priorities in deciding whether to contact ICE about someone they have detained. In other words, the officers must make an inquiry even in cases where it seems unlikely that the Attorney General would have the alien removed. This might be the case, for example, when an alien is an elderly veteran with significant and longstanding ties to the community.

Congress has done nothing to suggest it is inappropriate to communicate with ICE in these situations, however. Indeed, it has encouraged the sharing of information about possible immigration violations. A federal statute regulating the public benefits provided to qualified aliens in fact instructs that "no State or local government entity may be prohibited, or in any way restricted, from sending to or receiving from ICE information regarding the immigration status, lawful or unlawful, of an alien in the United States." §1644. The federal scheme thus leaves room for a policy requiring state officials to contact ICE as a routine matter. *Cf. Whiting*, 131 S.Ct. at 1985-1986.

Some argue that, in practice, state officers will be required to delay the release of some detainees for no reason other than to verify their immigration status. Detaining individuals solely to verify their immigration status would raise constitutional concerns. *See, e.g., Arizona v. Johnson*, 555 U.S. 323, 333 (2009); *Illinois v. Caballes*, 543 U.S. 405, 407 (2005). And it would disrupt the federal framework to put state officers in the position of holding aliens in custody for possible unlawful presence without federal direction and supervision. The program put in place by Congress does not allow state or local officers to adopt this enforcement mechanism. But §2(B) could be read to avoid these concerns. For example, a person might be stopped for jaywalking in Tucson and be unable to produce identification. The first sentence of §2(B) instructs officers to make a "reasonable" attempt to verify his immigration status with ICE if there is reasonable suspicion that his presence in the United States is unlawful. The state courts may conclude that, unless the person continues to be suspected of some crime for which he may be detained by state officers, it would not be reasonable to prolong the stop for the immigration inquiry. *Cf. Muehler v. Mena*, 544 U.S. 93, 101 (2005). To take another example, a person might be held pending release on a charge of driving under the influence of alcohol. As this goes beyond a mere stop, the arrestee (unlike the jaywalker) would appear to be subject to the categorical requirement in the second sentence of §2(B) that "any person who is arrested shall have the person's immigration status determined before he is released." State courts may read this as an instruction to initiate a status check every time someone is arrested, or a command to hold the person until the check is complete no matter the circumstances. Even if the law is read as an instruction to complete a check while the person is in custody, it is not clear on this record that the verification process would result in prolonged detention. There is no need to address whether reasonable suspicion of illegal entry or another immigration crime would be a legitimate basis for prolonging a detention, or whether this too would be preempted by federal law. *See, e.g., United States v. Di Re*, 332 U.S. 581, 589 (1948).

The Federal Government has brought suit against a sovereign State to challenge the provision before the law has gone into effect. There is uncertainty about what the law means and how it will be enforced. Without the benefit of a definitive interpretation from the state courts, it would be inappropriate to assume §2(B) will be construed in a way that creates a conflict with federal law. This opinion does not foreclose other preemption and constitutional challenges after the law goes into effect.

Immigration policy shapes the destiny of the Nation. The history of the United States is in part made of the stories, talents, and lasting contributions of those who crossed oceans and deserts to come here. The National Government has significant power to regulate immigration. With power comes responsibility, and the sound exercise of national power over immigration depends on the Nation's meeting its responsibility to base its laws on a political will informed by searching, thoughtful, rational civic discourse. Arizona may have understandable frustrations with the problems caused by illegal immigration, but the State may not pursue policies that undermine federal law.

The judgment of the Court of Appeals for the Ninth Circuit is *affirmed in part* and *reversed in part*. The case is *remanded* for further proceedings consistent with this opinion.

It is so ordered.

Justice SCALIA, *concurring in part* and *dissenting in part.*

Today's opinion deprives States of what most would consider the defining characteristic of sovereignty: the power to exclude from the sovereign's territory people who have no right to be there. *See* I R. PHILLIMORE, COMMENTARIES UPON INTERNATIONAL LAW, pt. III, ch. X, p. 233 (1854). There is no federal law prohibiting the States' sovereign power to exclude. What this case comes down to, then, is whether the Arizona law conflicts with federal immigration law. §2(B). This conflict-pre-emption claim calls on us "to determine whether, *under the circumstances of this particular case,* the State's law stands as an obstacle to the accomplishment and execution of the full purposes and objectives of Congress." *Hines,* 312 U.S. at 67. It is impossible to make such a finding without a factual record concerning the manner in which Arizona is implementing these provisions. §6. It is consistent with the "cooperative" system that Congress has created, for state officials to arrest a removable alien, contact federal immigration authorities, and follow their lead on what to do next §3. A State may make violation of federal law a violation of state law as well. *Hines* did not establish a "field preemption" that implicitly eliminates the States' sovereign power to exclude those whom federal law excludes. It held that the States are not permitted to establish "additional or auxiliary" registration requirements for aliens. §5(C). Common sense suggests that the specification of pre-emption for laws punishing "those who employ" implies the lack of pre-emption for other laws, including laws punishing "those who seek or accept employment." Arizona has moved to protect its sovereignty—not in contradiction of federal law, but in complete compliance with it. The laws under challenge here do not extend or revise federal immigration restrictions, but merely enforce those restrictions more effectively.

Justice THOMAS, *concurring in part* and *dissenting in part.*

Federal immigration law does not pre-empt any of the challenged provisions of S.B. 1070. There is no conflict between the "ordinary meaning" of the relevant federal laws and that of the four provisions of Arizona law at issue here. Nothing in the text of Section 2(B) prohibits Arizona from directing its officers to make immigration-related inquiries. States, as sovereigns, have inherent authority to conduct arrests for violations of federal law, unless and until Congress removes that authority. Here, no federal statute purports to withdraw that authority. Nothing in the text of the relevant federal statutes indicates that Congress intended enforcement of its registration requirements to be exclusively the province of the Federal Government. Section 5(C) operates only on individuals whom Congress has already declared ineligible to work in the United States. Nothing in the text of the federal immigration laws prohibits States from imposing their own criminal penalties on such individuals. The "purposes and objectives" theory of implied pre-emption is inconsistent with the Constitution because it invites courts to engage in freewheeling speculation about congressional purpose that roams well beyond statutory text. Even assuming the existence of some tension between Arizona's law and the supposed "purposes and objectives" of Congress, I would not hold that any of the provisions of the Arizona law at issue here are pre-empted on that basis.

Justice Alito, *concurring in part* and *dissenting in part.*

§2(B): The United States suggests that a state law may be pre-empted because it is inconsistent with a federal agency's current enforcement priorities. Those priorities, however, are not law. It has been suggested that §2(B) will cause some persons who are lawfully stopped to be detained in violation of their constitutional rights while a prolonged investigation of their immigration status is undertaken. But nothing on the face of the law suggests that it will be enforced in a way that violates the Fourth Amendment or any other provision of the Constitution. Section 3 is pre-empted because *Hines* requires that result. If we credit our holding in *Hines* that Congress has enacted "a single integrated and all-embracing system" of alien registration and that States cannot "complement" that system or "enforce additional or auxiliary regulations," then Arizona's attempt to impose additional, state-law penalties for violations of federal registration requirements must be invalidated. *Section 5(C):* Congress chose not to impose *federal* criminal penalties on aliens who seek or obtain unauthorized work. But that does not mean that Congress also chose to pre-empt *state* criminal penalties. Given that Congress expressly pre-empted certain state and local laws pertaining to employers but remained silent about laws pertaining to employees, one could infer that Congress intended to preserve state and local authority to regulate the employee side of the equation. *Section 6:* Our cases establish that state and local officers may make warrantless arrests for violations of federal law. *Di Re,* 332 U.S. at 589. State and local officers do not frustrate the removal process by arresting criminal aliens. The Executive retains complete discretion over whether those aliens are ultimately removed. The trouble with this premature, facial challenge is that it affords Arizona no opportunity to implement its law in a way that would avoid any potential conflicts with federal law.

Notes: Federal Immigration & Licensing Schemes

In *Chamber of Commerce of the United States v. Whiting,* 563 U.S. 582 (2011), the Court upheld the Legal Arizona Workers Act, which provided that the licenses of state employers that knowingly or intentionally employ unauthorized aliens may be, and in certain circumstances must be, suspended or revoked. The Court held that the law was not preempted, either expressly or impliedly, by federal law. The Court noted that the relevant law expressly preempts States from imposing "civil or criminal sanctions" on those who employ unauthorized aliens, "other than through licensing and similar laws." 8 U.S.C. §1324a(h)(2). The Court noted, among other things, that the Arizona law purports to impose sanctions through licensing laws. The Court also upheld that portion of the law that required employers to use the federal E-Verify system to determine whether an employee is authorized to work. The Court also held that this provision was not preempted.

∼ PROBLEMS ∼

1. *The Napolitano Memo.* Shortly before the decision was handed down in the *Arizona* case, Janet Napolitano, Secretary of Homeland Security, issued a memo indicating that she would exempt from immigration enforcement approximately 1.4 million illegal immigrants provided that they could satisfy the following requirements: a) they came to the United States under the age of 16; b) they had continuously resided in the United States for at least five years; c) they are currently in school, have graduated from high school, have obtained a general education development certificate, or are an honorably discharged veteran; d) they have not been convicted of a serious crime; and e) they are not above the age of 30. How should that memo have affected the outcome of the case, if at all?

2. *More on the* Arizona *Case.* The Court upheld Section 2(c) against a facial challenge. When the case goes back to the lower court, what types of evidence must the plaintiffs produce in order to accomplish a successful "as applied" challenge?

3. *The Alabama Case.* Assume that Alabama law requires school districts to verify the immigration status of students. After the *Arizona* decision, is such a law valid?

[Points to Remember for Chapter 5 is contained in online file.]

6

State Action

[Roadmap for Chapter 6 is contained in online file.]

∾ PROBLEM: THE TOWN, THE PRIVATE UTILITY, AND THE CLUB ∾

The City of Orange, which has 35,000 residents, is located in the sunny state of Florida. The community holds concerts and other public events in the Downtown District, where many popular restaurants are located as well as the town's only movie theater and park. The district covers almost the entire downtown and accounts for a third of the town's land area.

Power House, Inc., is a private utility corporation that provides electric and water services for the town. Power House is certified by the state and bound by state regulatory requirements. Power House owns the Downtown District. When citizens of Orange wish to hold events on the park, sidewalks, or streets of the Downtown District, they are required to submit a permit application to Power House. Under Orange's rules and regulations, Power House "has sole discretion to approve events it considers appropriate."

Power House recently purchased land and the larger of the two public swimming pools from Orange in order to develop an exclusive country club, Palm Valley Country Club. One day Mr. and Mrs. Johnson, two well-off African American citizens who reside on the west side of Orange, attended the club's cocktail hour and applied for membership. Their experience was not pleasant, however, as the club's management refused to believe the 50-year-old citizens were over 21, the minimum age to legally drink alcohol. Furthermore, three days later the Johnsons received a letter from the club stating that their membership application was denied because the club does not admit "African Americans, Hispanics, Asians, Jews, Muslims, women, and homosexuals" as members.

Because of membership restrictions at the new country club, there has been a large influx of citizens wanting to use the only remaining Orange community pool. However, after several members of the community filed complaints with the town about "overcrowding, noise, and undesirable elements" at the community pool, Orange decided to close the pool. Five members of the community applied to Power House for a permit to hold a rally in the Downtown District's park to protest the town's recent decisions. Power House denied their permit application, stating "this type of protest is inappropriate." Then, without prior notice, Power House shut off power and water to the homes of those five members of the community who had applied for the permit because they were late with their utility payments.

As we go through this chapter, we will ask you to place yourself in the role of attorneys representing the various parties in the dispute. You will need to argue on behalf of those parties as to whether Power House's actions constitute state action.

———

Most provisions of the Bill of Rights, as well as the Fourteenth and Fifteenth Amendments, were designed to protect individuals against action by federal, state, or local governments, but not action by private persons or entities. They protect only against "state action," with the word *state* meaning *governmental*. An exception to this state action requirement is the Thirteenth Amendment's prohibition of slavery, which applies to private persons as well as the state. Although private conduct may be actionable under civil law (e.g., tort or contract law) or criminal law, the general rule is that only state actors can violate your constitutional rights because it is only against the state that one has constitutional rights.

A. REQUIRING STATE ACTION

The Thirteenth Amendment ("Neither slavery nor involuntary servitude shall exist within the United States") applies to both the state and private individuals. It was coauthored and sponsored by Representatives James Mitchell Ashley (Republican, Ohio) and James F. Wilson (Republican, Iowa) and Senator John B. Henderson (Democrat, Missouri). President Abraham Lincoln took an active role in pushing its passage through the House by ensuring that the amendment was added to the Republican Party platform for the upcoming presidential election. Adopted in 1865, the Thirteenth Amendment formally abolished slavery, thus fulfilling the Emancipation Proclamation issued by President Lincoln in 1863.

State action became an issue after the Civil War Amendments were enacted under the authority of the Thirteenth, Fourteenth, and Fifteenth Amendments, which grant Congress the power to protect civil rights and to enforce them "by appropriate legislation." Pursuant to those Amendments, Congress adopted the Civil Rights Acts of 1866, 1870, 1871, and 1875 to address pervasive racial discrimination in the public and private sectors. In *The Civil Rights Cases,* indictments were brought against individuals and railroads that had excluded Black persons from railroads, hotels, and theaters because of race in contravention of the Acts. The defendants appealed, arguing that Congress exceeded its constitutional authority in enacting the Acts because it attempted to regulate private action. The decision in those cases established the state action requirement.

The Civil Rights Cases

109 U.S. 3 (1883)

BRADLEY, J.

The Civil Rights Act of 1875 declares that, in the enjoyment of the accommodations and privileges of inns, public conveyances, theaters, and other places of public amusement, no distinction shall be made between citizens of different race or color, or between those who have, and those who have not, been slaves. Its effect is to declare that colored citizens shall have the same accommodations and privileges as are enjoyed by white citizens; and vice versa.

Has congress constitutional power to make such a law? It is state action that is prohibited. Individual invasion of individual rights is not the subject-matter of the fourteenth amendment. It nullifies and makes void all state legislation, and state action of every kind, which impairs the privileges and immunities of citizens of the United States, or which injures them in life, liberty, or property without due process of law, or which denies to any of them the equal protection of the laws. The last section of the amendment invests congress with power to enforce it by appropriate legislation. To enforce what? To adopt appropriate legislation for correcting the effects of such prohibited state law and state acts, and thus to render them effectually null, void, and innocuous. It does not authorize congress to create a code of municipal law for the regulation of private rights.

The Civil Rights Act makes no reference whatever to any supposed or apprehended violation of the fourteenth amendment on the part of the states. It declares that certain acts committed by individuals shall be deemed offenses, and shall be prosecuted and punished by proceedings in the courts of the United States. It applies equally to cases arising in states which have the justest laws respecting the personal rights of citizens, and whose authorities are ever ready to enforce such laws as to those which arise in states that may have violated the prohibition of the amendment. In other words, it lays down rules for the conduct of individuals in society towards each other, and imposes sanctions for the enforcement of those rules, without referring in any manner to any supposed action of the state or its authorities.

If this legislation is appropriate for enforcing the prohibitions of the amendment, it is difficult to see where it is to stop. Why may not congress, with equal show of authority, enact a code of laws for the enforcement and vindication of all rights of life, liberty, and property? The assumption is made that if the states are forbidden to legislate or act in a particular way on a particular subject, and power is conferred upon congress to enforce the prohibition, this gives congress power to legislate generally upon that subject, and not merely power to provide modes of redress against such state legislation or action. The assumption is repugnant to the tenth amendment of the constitution, which declares that powers not delegated to the United States by the constitution, nor prohibited by it to the states, are reserved to the states respectively or to the people.

Civil rights, such as are guaranteed by the constitution against state aggression, cannot be impaired by the wrongful acts of individuals, unsupported by state authority in the shape of laws, customs, or judicial or executive proceedings. The wrongful act of an individual, unsupported by any such authority, is simply a private wrong, or a crime of that individual; an invasion of the rights of the injured party, it is true, whether they affect his person, his property, or his reputation; but if not sanctioned in some way by the state, or not done under state authority, his rights remain in full force, and may presumably be vindicated by resort to the laws of the state for redress.

Of course, these remarks do not apply when congress is clothed with direct and plenary powers of legislation over the whole subject, accompanied with an express or implied denial of such power to the states, as in the regulation of commerce with foreign nations, among the several states, and with the Indian tribes, the coining of money, the establishment of post-offices and post-roads, the declaring of war, etc. In these cases congress has power to pass laws for regulating the subjects specified, and the conduct and transactions of individuals respect thereof. But where a subject is not submitted to the general legislative power of congress, but is only submitted for the purpose of rendering effective some prohibition against particular state legislation or state action in reference to that subject, the power given is limited by its object, and any legislation by congress in the matter must necessarily be corrective in its character, adapted to counteract and redress the operation of such prohibited state laws or proceedings of state officers. If the principles of interpretation which we have laid down are correct, the law in question cannot be sustained by any grant of legislative power made to congress by the fourteenth amendment.

The power of congress to adopt direct and primary, as distinguished from corrective, legislation on the subject is sought, in the second place, from the thirteenth amendment, which abolishes slavery. It is assumed that the power vested in congress to enforce the Thirteenth Amendment by appropriate legislation, clothes congress with power to pass all laws necessary and proper for abolishing all badges and incidents of slavery in the United States; and upon this assumption it is claimed that this is sufficient authority for declaring by law that all persons shall have equal accommodations and privileges in all inns, public conveyances, and places of public amusement; the argument being that the denial of such equal accommodations and privileges is in itself a subjection to a species of servitude within the meaning of the amendment. An act of refusal has nothing to do with slavery or involuntary servitude. If it is violative of any right of the party, his redress is under the laws of the state; or, if those laws are adverse to his rights and do not protect him, his remedy will be found in the corrective legislation which congress has adopted, or may adopt, for counteracting the effect of state laws, or state action, prohibited by the fourteenth amendment. It would be running the slavery argument into the ground to make it apply to every act of discrimination.

The law in question must necessarily be declared void, at least so far as its operation in the several states is concerned.

So ordered.

HARLAN, J., *dissenting.*

If any right was created by the Fourteenth Amendment, the grant of power, through appropriate legislation, to enforce its provisions authorizes congress, by means of legislation operating throughout the entire Union, to guard, secure, and protect that right.

This restrictive reading of the state action requirement in *The Civil Rights Cases* permitted racial discrimination to flourish in the South. For example, the Court upheld the "white primary," a device used to circumvent the Fifteenth Amendment, in *Grovey v. Townsend*, 295 U.S. 45 1292 (1935). The Court reasoned that because political parties were private organizations, their primary elections did not constitute state action. The Court began to move away from a strict state action requirement in the 1940s. In *Smith v. Allwright*, 321 U.S. 649 (1944), the Court struck down the white primary as violating the Fifteenth Amendment, thus

overruling *Grovey.* The Court now found that primary elections played an important part in the democratic process and must be considered as officially sanctioned by the state.

Notes and Questions

1. *Sufficient Governmental Involvement?* In most instances, when plaintiffs assert
a violation of the Bill of Rights or the Fourteenth Amendment, state involvement
will be obvious. In other words, Congress or a state legislature will have passed
a law, or a governmental agency or government official will have taken action
against the citizen. More difficult questions arise when the violation seems to be
the result of private action but the government is involved or implicated in the
private action in some way. As we shall see, government is involved in virtually
all private conduct in one way or another (for example, because it either passed
a law authorizing the conduct or failed to pass a law prohibiting the conduct).
Thus, the real question is whether the government is sufficiently involved so that
ostensibly private action effectively becomes "state action." Questions about state
action present difficult issues for the courts.

2. *Modern Civil Rights Statutes.* Many modern civil rights statutes are based on
Congress's Commerce Clause power rather than on the Fourteenth Amendment.
Of course, as we saw in Chapter 2, in order for such legislation to be sustained,
there must be a sufficient relationship between the prohibited activity and interstate commerce.

∾ PROBLEM: REWRITING THE CIVIL RIGHTS ACT ∾

In *The Civil Rights Cases,* the Court found that Congress was trying to
limit and control private action. However, the Court suggests that there are
circumstances in which the actions of private individuals might be attributed
to the state. What governmental actions might make state and local governments responsible for private discrimination? Would it have been possible to
rewrite the Civil Rights Act so that it is constitutional and encompasses only
such actions?

B. GOVERNMENT FUNCTION

One situation in which the Court has found state action is when a private entity
performs a traditional governmental function. There are a number of "governmental function" cases.

1. Company Towns

So-called "company towns," as found to exist in the following case, provide a classic example of state action.

Marsh v. Alabama

326 U.S. 501 (1946)

Mr. Justice BLACK delivered the opinion of the Court.

We are asked to decide whether a State, consistently with the First and Fourteenth Amendments, can impose criminal punishment on a person who undertakes to distribute religious literature on the premises of a company-owned town contrary to the wishes of the town's management. The town, a suburb of Mobile, Alabama, known as Chickasaw, is owned by the Gulf Shipbuilding Corporation. It has all the characteristics of any other American town. The property consists of residential buildings, streets, a system of sewers, a sewage disposal plant and a "business block" on which business places are situated. A deputy of the Mobile County Sheriff, paid by the company, serves as the town's policeman. Merchants and service establishments have rented the stores and business places on the business block and the United States uses one of the places as a post office from which six carriers deliver mail to the town and the adjacent area. The town cannot be distinguished from the surrounding neighborhood by anyone not familiar with the property lines, and the residents use the business block as their regular shopping center. To do so, they make use of a company-owned paved street and sidewalk in order to enter and leave the stores and the post office. Intersecting company-owned roads at each end of the business block lead into a four-lane public highway which runs parallel to the business block at a distance of thirty feet. There is nothing to stop highway traffic from coming onto the business block and upon arrival a traveler may make free use of the facilities available there. In short the town and its shopping district are accessible to and freely used by the public in general and there is nothing to distinguish them from any other town and shopping center except the fact that the title to the property belongs to a private corporation.

Appellant, a Jehovah's Witness, came onto the sidewalk and undertook to distribute religious literature. The corporation had posted a notice which read as follows: "This Is Private Property, and Without Written Permission, No Street, or House Vendor, Agent or Solicitation of Any Kind Will Be Permitted." Appellant was warned that she could not distribute the literature without a permit and told that no permit would be issued to her. She was asked to leave, but refused. The deputy sheriff arrested her and she was charged with remaining on the premises of another after having been warned not to do so. Appellant argued that the statute abridged her First and Fourteenth Amendment rights to freedom of the press and freedom of religion. She was convicted.

Had the title to Chickasaw belonged not to a private but to a municipal corporation, it would have been clear that appellant's conviction must be reversed. Under *Lovell v. Griffin*, 303 U.S. 444, neither a state nor a municipality can completely bar the distribution of literature containing religious or political ideas on its streets, sidewalks and public places or make the right to distribute dependent on a flat license tax or permit to be issued by an official who could deny it at will. The State argues that the corporation's right to control the inhabitants of Chickasaw is coextensive with the right of a homeowner to regulate the conduct of his guests. We can not accept that contention. The more an owner, for his advantage, opens up his property for use by the public, the more his rights become circumscribed by the statutory and constitutional rights of those who use it.

It makes no significant constitutional difference as to the relationship between the rights of the owner and those of the public that the State allowed the corporation to use its property as a town. Whether a corporation or a municipality owns or possesses the town the public has an interest that the channels of communication remain free. The town of Chickasaw does not function differently from any other town. The "business block" serves as the community shopping center and is freely accessible and open to the people in the area and those passing through. The managers of the corporation cannot curtail the liberty of press and religion in violation of the Constitutional guarantees, and a state statute which criminally punishes those who attempt to distribute religious literature violates the First and Fourteenth Amendments to the Constitution.

When we balance the Constitutional rights of owners of property against those of the people to enjoy freedom of press and religion, the latter occupy a preferred position. The right to exercise the liberties safeguarded by the First Amendment "lies at the foundation of free government by free men." *Schneider v. State*, 308 U.S. 147. The circumstance that the property rights to the premises where the deprivation of liberty took place, were held by others than the public, is not sufficient to justify the State's permitting a corporation to govern a community of citizens so as to restrict their fundamental liberties and the enforcement of such restraint by the application of a State statute. Insofar as the State has attempted to impose criminal punishment on appellant for undertaking to distribute religious literature in a company town, its action cannot stand.

Reversed and remanded.

Mr. Justice REED, *dissenting.*

This is the first case to extend by law the privilege of religious exercises beyond public places or to private places without the assent of the owner. We find nothing in the principles of the First Amendment, adopted now into the Fourteenth, which justifies their application to the facts of this case.

Notes and Questions

1. *Are Shopping Malls the Modern Equivalent of "Company Towns"?* As city life has gravitated from downtown to the suburbs, have suburban shopping malls become the functional equivalent of company towns? If so, should individuals have the right to engage in First Amendment activities (e.g., give speeches and distribute fliers and circulars) on shopping mall premises? In *Amalgamated Food Employees Union v. Logan Valley Plaza, Inc.*, 391 U.S. 308 (1968), union members peacefully picketed a business located in a private shopping center. When the owners of the center sought to enjoin the picketing as a trespass, the Court held that the shopping center's actions constituted state action so that the First Amendment applied: "The similarities between the business block in *Marsh* and the shopping center in the present case are striking. The perimeter of Logan Valley Mall is a little less than 1.1 miles. Inside the mall were two substantial commercial enterprises. Immediately adjacent to the mall are two roads, one of which is a heavily traveled state highway and from both of which lead entrances directly into the mall. Adjoining the buildings in the middle of the mall are sidewalks for the use of pedestrians going to and from their cars and from building to building. In the parking areas are roadways for the use of vehicular traffic entering and leaving the mall. The general public has unrestricted access to the mall property. The shopping center here is clearly the functional equivalent of the business district of Chickasaw involved in *Marsh*."

However, in subsequent decisions, the Court overruled *Logan Valley*. *Lloyd Corp., Ltd. v. Tanner*, 407 U.S. 551 (1972), involved a large shopping center, covering nearly 50 acres of ground, with all stores located within a single multilevel building complex that contained interior promenades with large sidewalks. The center was generally open to the public, and various civic groups were allowed to hold events on the premises, but it was "policed" by private security guards hired by the center. The case arose when the center's security guards told several individuals, who were distributing handbills in the shopping center, to leave or they would be arrested. The handbills stated opposition to the Vietnam War and the draft. The individuals left, but then sought declaratory relief and injunctive relief on First Amendment grounds. The Court held that the center's conduct constituted private action, distinguishing *Marsh* and *Logan Valley*: "*Logan Valley* was carefully phrased to limit its holding to the picketing involved, where the picketing was 'directly related in its purpose to the use to which the shopping center property was being put,' and where the store was located in the center of a large private enclave with the consequence that no other reasonable opportunities for the pickets to convey their message to their intended audience were available. Neither of these elements is present in the case now before the Court." In *Hudgens v. NLRB*, 424 U.S. 507 (1976), the Court flatly overruled *Logan Valley*. *Hudgens* involved union members who engaged in peaceful protesting inside a privately owned shopping center. When the protesters were threatened with arrest by an agent of the owner, they sought declaratory and injunctive relief. The question was whether the threat constituted an unfair labor practice within the meaning of the National Labor Relations Act. The National Labor Relations Board (NLRB) issued a cease-and-desist order concluding that the picketers had a First Amendment right to picket Hudgens's mall. The Court disagreed: "the constitutional guarantee of free expression has no part to play in a case such as this."

2. *Private Military Contractors:* Since 9/11 the U.S. Government has increasingly outsourced functions previously carried out by members of the military or other government employees to corporations. The contracted services range from personal security for American, Iraqi, or Afghan officials, to protection of oil facilities from attacks, to conducting interrogations and other intelligence work. In *Estate of Manook v. Research Triangle Institute,* 759 F. Supp. 674 (2010) the district court found no state action when the government subcontractor hired another company whose employees shot and killed Iraqi citizens while providing security services. In the case of *In re: XE Services Alien Tort Litigation,* 665 F.Supp.2d 569 (2009), 64 plaintiffs sought damages for the deaths or serious injuries caused by employees of XE Services (formerly known as Blackwater), a defense contractor. XE Services sought to substitute the U.S. Government in its place arguing that XE Services was an "employee of the government." Although XE Services's motion was denied, should the perception of a private actor that it is performing a traditional government function and is a government employee factor into a court's decision of whether the company is performing a traditional government function?

∾ PROBLEM: MORE ON THE TOWN, THE PRIVATE UTILITY, AND THE CLUB ∾

Let's return to the problem at the beginning of the chapter. Based on your reading of *Marsh* and the cases mentioned in this section, does Power House's control over the Downtown District in Orange amount to the performance of a traditional government function? How would you argue the case for the plaintiffs? How might the utility respond? In formulating your arguments, consider whether you can draw an analogy between the Downtown District and a company town or a shopping mall. Does it matter that the Downtown District includes streets, sidewalks, and the only park in Orange? Is the size of the Downtown District relevant?

2. *Party Primaries*

The party primaries cases arose from the Texas Democratic Party's efforts to preclude Blacks from participating in party primaries. Since political parties are generally treated as voluntary associations of private individuals, defendants argued that their conduct should be treated as private action. However, in a series of cases decided between 1927 and 1953, the Court concluded otherwise.

Nixon v. Herndon, 273 U.S. 536 (1927), involved a Texas statute that explicitly prohibited Blacks from voting in the Democratic primary. The Court struck down the law, concluding that its mandated discrimination constituted state action. Following *Nixon,* after the Texas legislature passed a new law giving the Democratic Party's executive committee the right to decide who could vote in its party primaries, the party passed a resolution providing that only white Democrats would be allowed to vote. In *Nixon v. Condon,* 286 U.S. 73 (1932), the Court struck this law down, too. The Court found "state action" on the basis that the "Committee operated as representative of the State in the discharge of the State's authority."

Condon left open the question of a party's inherent power "to determine its own membership." That issue was presented in *Smith v. Allwright,* 321 U.S. 649 (1944). After the prior laws were struck down, the Texas Democratic Party passed a resolution limiting party membership to white citizens of the State of Texas. Because only party members could vote in the Democratic primary, this resolution effectively precluded Blacks from participating. The resolution was adopted by the party on its own without statutory authorization. Although the Court had previously upheld a similar restriction, the Court reversed in *Smith* and held that state action existed: The "statutory system for the selection of party nominees for inclusion on the general election ballot makes the party which is required to follow these legislative directions an agency of the state in so far as it determines the participants in a primary election. The privilege of membership in a party may be no concern of a state. But when, as here, that privilege is also the essential qualification for voting in a primary to select nominees for a general election, the state makes the action of the party the action of the state."

Terry v. Adams

345 U.S. 461 (1953)

Mr. Justice BLACK announced the judgment of the Court and an opinion in which Mr. Justice DOUGLAS and Mr. Justice BURTON join.

This case raises questions concerning the constitutional power of a Texas county political organization called the Jaybird Democratic Association or Jaybird Party to exclude Negroes from its primaries on racial grounds. The Jaybirds deny that their racial exclusions violate the Fifteenth Amendment. They contend that the Amendment applies only to elections or primaries held under state regulation, that their association is not regulated by the state at all, and that it is not a political party but a self-governing voluntary club.

The Jaybird Association or Party was organized in 1889. Its membership has always been limited to white people; they are automatically members if their names appear on the official list of county voters. It is run like other political parties with an executive committee. Expenses of the party are paid by the assessment of candidates for office in its primaries. Candidates for county offices submit their names to the Jaybird Committee. Advertisements and posters proclaim that these candidates are running subject to the action of the Jaybird primary. While there is no legal compulsion on successful Jaybird candidates to enter Democratic primaries they have nearly always done so and with few exceptions have won without opposition in the primaries and the general elections. Thus the party has been the dominant political group in the county since organization, having endorsed every county-wide official elected since 1889.

Precisely the same qualifications to vote at county-operated primaries are adopted as the sole qualifications entitling electors to vote at the county-wide Jaybird primaries with a single proviso—Negroes are excluded. Everyone concedes that such a proviso in the county-operated primaries would be unconstitutional. The Jaybird Party thus brings into being and holds precisely the kind of election that the Fifteenth Amendment seeks to prevent. When it produces the equivalent of the prohibited election, the damage has been done.

The use of the county-operated primary to ratify the result of the prohibited election merely compounds the offense. It violates the Fifteenth Amendment for a state, by such circumvention, to permit within its borders the use of any device that produces an equivalent of the prohibited election. The only election that has counted in this Texas county for more than fifty years has been that held by the Jaybirds from which Negroes were excluded. It is immaterial that the state does not control that part of this elective process which it leaves for the Jaybirds to manage. The Jaybird primary has become an integral part, indeed the only effective part, of the elective process that determines who shall rule and govern in the county. The effect of the whole procedure, Jaybird primary plus Democratic primary plus general election, is to do precisely that which the Fifteenth Amendment forbids—strip Negroes of every vestige of influence in selecting the officials who control the local county matters that intimately touch the daily lives of citizens. The combined Jaybird-Democratic-general election machinery has deprived these petitioners of their right to vote on account of their race and color.

Reversed and remanded.

Mr. Justice FRANKFURTER.

Those charged by State law with the duty of assuring all eligible voters an opportunity to participate in the selection of candidates participate in the Jaybird primary. They join the white voting community in a wholly successful effort to withdraw significance from the State-prescribed primary, to subvert the operation of what is formally the law of the State for primaries in this county.

Mr. Justice CLARK, with whom THE CHIEF JUSTICE, Mr. Justice REED, and Mr. Justice JACKSON join, *concurring.*

Because the Jaybird-indorsed nominee meets no opposition in the Democratic primary, the Negro minority's vote is nullified at the sole stage of the local political process where the bargaining and interplay of rival political forces would make it count.

Mr. Justice MINTON, *dissenting.*

I am not concerned in the least as to what happens to the Jaybirds or their unworthy scheme. This Court has power to redress a wrong under that Fifteenth Amendment only if the wrong is done by the State. That Amendment erects no shield against merely private conduct, however discriminatory or wrongful. Mr. Justice Frankfurter thinks it is enough to constitute state action if a state official participates in the Jaybird primary. Everything done by a person who is an official is not done officially and as a representative of the State. I find nothing that shows the state or county officials participating in the Jaybird primary.

There is not one iota of state action sufficient to support an inference that the Jaybird Association is associated with or cooperates in any manner with the Democratic Party or with the State. It calls itself the Jaybird Democratic Association because its interest is only in the candidates of the Democratic Party in the county. Even if it be said to be a political organization, the Jaybird Association avails itself of no state law open to political organizations.

The Association's activities are not forbidden by the law of the State of Texas. Does such failure of the State to act to prevent individuals from doing what they have the right as individuals to do amount to state action? It does not. Surely white or colored members of any political faith or economic belief may hold caucuses. It is only when the State by action of its legislative bodies or action of some of its officials in their official capacity cooperates with such political party or gives it direction in its activities that the Federal Constitution may come into play. A political organization not using state machinery or depending upon state law to authorize what it does could not be within the ban of the Fifteenth Amendment. The Jaybird Association did not attempt to conform or in any way comply with the statutes of Texas covering primaries. No action of any legislative or quasi-legislative body or of any state official or agency ever denied the vote to Negroes, even in the Jaybird primaries. So there is no state action, and the Jaybird Democratic Association is in no sense a part of the Democratic Party.

I do not understand that concerted action of individuals which is successful somehow becomes state action. The candidates endorsed by the Jaybird Association have several times been defeated in primaries and elections and the Jaybird Association's activities are confined to one County where a group of citizens have appointed themselves the censors of those who would run for public offices. Apparently so far they have succeeded in convincing the voters of this County in most instances that their supported candidates should win. In other localities, candidates are carefully selected to give proper weight to Jew, Protestant and Catholic, and certain posts are considered the sole possession of certain ethnic groups. The propriety of these practices is something the courts sensibly have left to the good or bad judgment of the electorate. It must be recognized that elections and other public business are influenced by all sorts of pressures including pressure from labor unions, from the National Association of Manufacturers, from the National Association for the Advancement of Colored People, from the Ku Klux Klan and others. The courts do not normally pass upon these pressure groups, whether their causes are good or bad, highly successful or unsuccessful. It is difficult to see how this Jaybird Association is anything but such a pressure group.

Food for Thought

1. *"Careful Selection" of Candidates.* Justice Minton refers to places where candidates are "carefully selected" to give proper weight to Jewish, Protestant, or Catholic interests. After this decision, does such selection constitute private action or state action? Does it matter who does the selection?

2. *Committee for a Feminist Majority.* The Committee for a Feminist Majority (COFM) was organized to help elect women to public office in Louisville, Kentucky. In addition to encouraging and recruiting female candidates, COFM holds a pre-primary designed to pick a "preferred" candidate behind whom COFM members can unite. Since women comprise a majority of the Louisville population, and women (and some men) tend to rally behind COFM-endorsed candidates, COFM candidates almost always win. COFM precludes men from membership as well as from voting in its pre-primary. Under *Terry*, does COFM's pre-primary constitute state action?

3. *African American Jaybirds?* Would there be state action if Blacks organized a pre-primary in a city that has a majority Black population? Would your analysis be affected by the fact that the Black candidate always wins?

3. Utility Service

Marsh, Herndon, and *Condon* were decided during the first half of the twentieth century. During the latter part of the century, the Court's analysis of state action cases began to change. The following case illustrates the Court's modern precedent.

Jackson v. Metropolitan Edison Company

419 U.S. 345 (1974)

Mr. Justice REHNQUIST delivered the opinion of the Court.

Respondent Metropolitan Edison Co. is a privately owned and operated Pennsylvania corporation which holds a certificate of public convenience issued by the Pennsylvania Public Utility Commission empowering it to deliver electricity to an area which includes the city of York, Pa. As a condition of holding its certificate, it is subject to extensive regulation by the Commission. Under a provision of its general tariff filed with the Commission, it has the right to discontinue service to any customer on reasonable notice of nonpayment of bills. Petitioner Catherine Jackson is a resident of York. When petitioner failed to pay her bills, Metropolitan terminated her service. Petitioner filed suit against Metropolitan under the Civil Rights Act of 1871, 42 U.S.C. §1983, seeking damages for the termination and an injunction requiring continued service to her residence. She urged that under state law she had an entitlement to reasonably continuous electrical service and that Metropolitan's termination of her service for alleged nonpayment, action allowed by a provision of its general tariff filed with the Commission, constituted "state action" depriving her of property in violation of the Fourteenth Amendment's guarantee of due process of law.

While the principle that private action is immune from the restrictions of the Fourteenth Amendment is well established and easily stated, the question whether particular conduct is "private," on the one hand, or "state action," frequently admits of no easy answer. Here the action complained of was taken by a utility company which is privately owned and operated, but which in many particulars of its business is subject to extensive state regulation. The mere fact that a business is subject to state regulation does not by itself convert its action into that of the State for purposes of the Fourteenth Amendment. Nor does the fact that the regulation is extensive and detailed. It may well be that acts of a heavily regulated utility with at least something of a governmentally protected monopoly will more readily be found to be "state" acts than will the acts of an entity lacking these characteristics. But there must be a sufficiently close nexus between the State and the challenged action of the regulated entity so that the action of the latter may be fairly treated as that of the State itself.

Petitioner argues that "state action" is present because of the monopoly status allegedly conferred upon Metropolitan by the State of Pennsylvania. Assuming that Metropolitan had been granted a monopoly, this fact is not determinative.

Petitioner next urges that state action is present because respondent provides an essential public service required to be supplied on a reasonably continuous basis by Pa. Stat. Ann., Tit. 66, §1171 (1959), and hence performs a "public function." We have found state action present in the exercise by a private entity of powers traditionally exclusively reserved to the State. If we were dealing with the exercise by Metropolitan of some power delegated to it by the State which is traditionally associated with sovereignty, such as eminent domain, the case would be quite different. But while the Pennsylvania statute imposes an obligation to furnish service on regulated utilities, it imposes no such obligation on the State. Pennsylvania courts have rejected the contention that the furnishing of utility services is either a state function or a municipal duty.

Petitioner invites adoption of a broad principle that all businesses "affected with the public interest" are state actors in all their actions. We decline the invitation for reasons stated long ago in *Nebbia v. New York*, 291 U.S. 502 (1934). "It is clear that there is no closed class or category of businesses affected with a public interest." Doctors, optometrists, lawyers, Metropolitan, and Nebbia's milk sales are all in regulated businesses, providing arguably essential goods and services, "affected with a public interest." We do not believe that such a status converts their every action, absent more, into that of the State.

We also reject the notion that Metropolitan's termination is state action because the State "has specifically authorized and approved" the termination practice. Metropolitan filed with the Public Utility Commission a general tariff — a provision of which states the right to terminate service for nonpayment. This provision has appeared in Metropolitan's previously filed tariffs for many years and has never been the subject of scrutiny by the Commission. Although the Commission did hold hearings on Metropolitan's rate increase, it never considered this provision. The provision became effective when not disapproved.

Metropolitan is a privately owned corporation, and it does not lease its facilities from the state. It alone is responsible for the provision of power to its customers. In common with all corporations of the State it pays taxes to the State, and it is subject to a form of extensive regulation by the State in a way that most other business enterprises are not. But this was likewise true of the appellant club in *Moose Lodge No. 107 v. Irvis*, where we said: "However detailed this type of regulation may be in some particulars, it cannot be said to make the State in any realistic sense a partner or even a joint venturer in the club's enterprise."

All of petitioner's arguments taken together show no more than that Metropolitan was a heavily regulated, privately owned utility, enjoying at least a partial monopoly in the providing of electrical service within its territory, and that it elected to terminate service to petitioner in a manner which the Pennsylvania Public Utility Commission found permissible under state law. This is not sufficient to connect the State of Pennsylvania with respondent's action so as to make the latter's conduct attributable to the State for purposes of the Fourteenth Amendment. The judgment of the Court of Appeals for the Third Circuit is therefore

Affirmed.

Mr. Justice Douglas, *dissenting.*

This case depicts a monopolist providing essential public services as a licensee of the State within a framework of extensive state supervision and control. The particular regulations, promulgated by the monopolist, were authorized by state law and were enforceable by the weight and authority of the State. The State retains the power of oversight to review and amend the regulations if the public interest so requires. Respondent's actions are sufficiently intertwined with those of the State, and its termination-of-service provisions are sufficiently buttressed by state law to warrant a holding that respondent's actions in terminating this householder's service were "state action" for the purpose of giving federal jurisdiction over respondent under 42 U.S.C. §1983.

Mr. Justice MARSHALL, *dissenting*.

Metropolitan Edison Co. provides an essential public service and is the only entity public or private, that is authorized to do so in most of the community. The State imposes extensive regulations and cooperates with the company in myriad ways. The State has granted its approval to the company's mode of service termination. I have no difficulty finding state action. The State has sufficiently "insinuated itself into a position of interdependence with (the company) that it must be recognized as a joint participant in the challenged activity."

PROBLEM: MORE ON THE TOWN, THE PRIVATE UTILITY, AND THE CLUB

Returning to the problem at the beginning of the chapter, suppose that you are hired to represent the five members of the community whose permit applications were denied. How would you argue that Power House's status as a public utility implicates state action? Now, assuming that you are hired instead to represent Power House, how would you respond to these arguments? Has the Court's attitude regarding state action and the governmental function exception changed since *Marsh*?

4. Schools and School Associations

When, and under what circumstances, may the actions of private schools and private school associations be regarded as performing a government function? Consider the following cases.

Rendell-Baker v. Kohn

457 U.S. 830 (1982)

Chief Justice BURGER delivered the opinion of the Court.

We granted certiorari to decide whether a private school, whose income is derived primarily from public sources and which is regulated by public authorities, acted under color of state law when it discharged certain employees.

Respondent Kohn is the director of the New Perspectives School, a nonprofit institution located on privately owned property in Brookline, Massachusetts. The school was founded as a private institution and is operated by a board of directors, none of whom are public officials or are chosen by public officials. The school specializes in dealing with students who have experienced difficulty completing public high schools; many have drug, alcohol, or behavioral problems, or other special needs. In recent years, nearly all of the students at the school have been referred to it by the Brookline or Boston School Committees, or by the Drug Rehabilitation Division of the Massachusetts Department of Mental Health. The school issues high school diplomas certified by the Brookline School Committee. When students are referred to the school by Brookline or Boston under Chapter 766 of the Massachusetts Acts of 1972, the School Committees in those cities pay for the students' education. The school also receives funds from a number of other state and federal agencies. In recent years, public funds have accounted for at least 90%, and in one year 99%, of respondent school's operating budget. There were approximately 50 students at the school in those years and none paid tuition.

To be eligible for tuition funding under Chapter 766, the school must comply with a variety of regulations, many of which are common to all schools. The State has issued detailed regulations concerning matters ranging from recordkeeping to student-teacher ratios. Concerning personnel policies, the Chapter 766 regulations require the school to maintain written job descriptions and written statements describing personnel standards and procedures, but they impose few specific requirements. The school is also regulated by Boston and Brookline as a result of its Chapter 766 funding. By its contract with the Boston School Committee, which refers to the school as a "contractor," the school must agree to carry out the individualized plan developed for each student referred to the school by the Committee. The contract specifies that school employees are not city employees. The school also has a contract with the State Drug Rehabilitation Division. Like the contract with the Boston School Committee, that agreement refers to the school as a "contractor." It provides for reimbursement for services provided for students referred to the school by the Drug Rehabilitation Division, and includes requirements concerning the services to be provided. Except for general requirements, such as an equal employment opportunity requirement, the agreement does not cover personnel policies.

Petitioner Rendell-Baker was a vocational counselor hired under a grant from the federal Law Enforcement Assistance Administration, whose funds are distributed in Massachusetts through the State Committee on Criminal Justice. As a condition of the grant, the Committee on Criminal Justice must approve the school's initial hiring decisions. The purpose of this requirement is to insure that the school hires vocational counselors who meet the qualifications described in the school's grant proposal to the Committee; the Committee does not interview applicants for counselor positions. Rendell-Baker was discharged by the school in January 1977, and the five other petitioners were discharged in June 1978. A dispute arose when some students presented a petition to the school's board of directors seeking greater responsibilities for the student-staff council. Director Kohn opposed the proposal, but Rendell-Baker supported it and so advised the board. On December 13, Kohn notified the State Committee on Criminal Justice, which funded Rendell-Baker's position, that she intended to dismiss Rendell-Baker and employ someone else. Rendell-Baker then filed this suit under 42 U.S.C. §1983, alleging that she had been discharged in violation of her rights under the First,

Fifth, and Fourteenth Amendments. When other teachers protested the dismissal and indicated that they were going to form a union, Kohn discharged the teachers. They sued seeking relief under §1983, alleging that their rights under the First, Fifth, and Fourteenth Amendments had been violated.

The issue is whether the school's action in discharging petitioners can fairly be seen as state action. In *Blum v. Yaretsky*, 457 U.S. 991, the Court considered whether certain nursing homes were state actors for the purpose of determining whether decisions regarding transfers of patients could be fairly attributed to the State, and hence be subjected to Fourteenth Amendment due process requirements. The challenged transfers primarily involved decisions, made by physicians and nursing home administrators, to move patients from "skilled nursing facilities" to less expensive "health related facilities." Like the New Perspectives School, the nursing homes were privately owned and operated. This Court held that, "a State normally can be held responsible for a private decision only when it has exercised coercive power or has provided such significant encouragement, either overt or covert, that the choice must in law be deemed to be that of the State." In determining that the transfer decisions were not actions of the State, the Court considered each of the factors alleged by petitioners here to make the discharge decisions of the New Perspectives School fairly attributable to the State.

First, the nursing homes, like the school, depended on the State for funds; the State subsidized the operating and capital costs of the nursing homes, and paid the medical expenses of more than 90% of the patients. We held that the dependence of the nursing homes did not make the acts of the physicians and nursing home administrators acts of the State, and we conclude that the school's receipt of public funds does not make the discharge decisions acts of the State. Acts of such private contractors do not become acts of the government by reason of their significant or even total engagement in performing public contracts.

A second factor considered in *Blum* was the extensive regulation of the nursing homes by the State. There the State was indirectly involved in the transfer decisions because a primary goal of the State in regulating nursing homes was to keep costs down by transferring patients from intensive treatment centers to less expensive facilities when possible. Both state and federal regulations encouraged the nursing homes to transfer patients to less expensive facilities when appropriate. The Court relied on *Jackson*, where we held that state regulation, even if "extensive and detailed" did not make a utility's actions state action. Here the decisions to discharge the petitioners were not compelled or even influenced by any state regulation. Indeed, the various regulators showed relatively little interest in the school's personnel matters. The Committee on Criminal Justice had the power to approve persons hired as vocational counselors. Such a regulation is not sufficient to make a decision to discharge, made by private management, state action.

The third factor asserted to show that the school is a state actor is that it performs a "public function." The question is whether the function performed has been "traditionally the exclusive prerogative of the State." There can be no doubt that the education of maladjusted high school students is a public function. Chapter 766 of the Massachusetts Acts of 1972 demonstrates that the State intends to provide services for such students at public expense. That legislative policy choice in no way makes these services the exclusive province of the State. Indeed, until recently the State had not undertaken to provide education for students who could not be served by traditional public schools. That a private entity performs a function which serves the public does not make its acts state action.

Fourth, petitioners argue that there is a "symbiotic relationship" between the school and the State similar to the relationship involved in *Burton v. Wilmington Parking Authority*, 365 U.S. 715 (1961). The school's fiscal relationship with the State is not different from that of many contractors performing services for the government. No symbiotic relationship such as existed in *Burton* exists here.

We hold that petitioners have not stated a claim for relief under 42 U.S.C. §1983; accordingly, the judgment of the Court of Appeals for the First Circuit is
Affirmed.

Justice WHITE, *concurring* in the judgments.

The critical factor is the absence of any allegation that the employment decision was itself based upon some rule of conduct or policy put forth by the State. The employment decision remains a private decision not fairly attributable to the State.

Justice MARSHALL, with whom Justice BRENNAN joins, *dissenting.*

Where there is a symbiotic relationship between the State and a privately owned enterprise, so that they are participants in a joint venture, the actions of the private enterprise may be attributable to the State. Here, the facts and circumstances leads inexorably to the conclusion that the actions of the New Perspectives School should be attributed to the State; it is difficult to imagine a closer relationship between a government and a private enterprise. The New Perspectives School receives virtually all of its funds from state sources. The school's very survival depends on the State. If the State chooses, it may exercise complete control over the school's operations simply by threatening to withdraw financial support if the school takes action that it considers objectionable. The school is heavily regulated and closely supervised by the State. Almost every decision the school makes is substantially affected in some way by the State's regulations. The fact that the school is providing a substitute for public education is also an important indicium of state action. The provision of education is one of the most important tasks performed by government: it ranks at the very apex of the function of a State. The fact that a private entity is performing a vital public function, when coupled with other factors demonstrating a close connection with the State, may justify a finding of state action. Clearly, if the State had decided to provide the service itself, its conduct would be measured against constitutional standards. The State should not be permitted to avoid constitutional requirements simply by delegating its statutory duty to a private entity.

Brentwood Academy v. Tennessee Secondary School Athletic Association

531 U.S. 288 (2001)

Justice SOUTER delivered the opinion of the Court.

The issue is whether a statewide association incorporated to regulate inter-scholastic athletic competition among public and private secondary schools may be regarded as engaging in state action when it enforces a rule against a member school. We hold that the association's regulatory activity should be treated as state action owing to the pervasive entwinement of state school officials in the structure of the association, there being no offsetting reason to see the association's acts in any other way.

Respondent Tennessee Secondary School Athletic Association is a not-for-profit membership corporation organized to regulate interscholastic sport among the public and private high schools in Tennessee. No school is forced to join, but TSSAA enjoys the memberships of almost all the State's public high schools (290 or 84% of the Association's voting membership), far outnumbering the 55 private schools that belong. A member school's team may play or scrimmage only against the team of another member, absent a dispensation. The Association's rulemaking arm is its legislative council, while its board of control tends to administration. The voting membership of each of these nine-person committees is limited under the Association's bylaws to high school principals, assistant principals, and superintendents elected by the member schools. Although the Association's staff members are not paid by the State, they are eligible to join the State's public retirement system for its employees. Member schools pay dues to the Association, though the bulk of its revenue is gate receipts at member teams' football and basketball tournaments, many of them held in public arenas rented by the Association.

The constitution, bylaws, and rules of the Association set standards of school membership and the eligibility of students to play in interscholastic games. Each school is regulated in awarding financial aid, most coaches must have a Tennessee state teaching license, and players must meet minimum academic standards and hew to limits on student employment. Under the bylaws, "in all matters pertaining to the athletic relations of his school," the principal is responsible to the Association, which has the power "to suspend, to fine, or otherwise penalize any member school for the violation of any of the rules of the Association or for other just cause."

Since the Association was incorporated in 1925, Tennessee's State Board of Education (State Board) has acknowledged the corporation's functions "in providing standards, rules and regulations for interscholastic competition in the public schools of Tennessee." In 1972, it went so far as to adopt a rule expressly "designating" the Association as "the organization to supervise and regulate the athletic activities in which the public junior and senior high schools in Tennessee participate on an interscholastic basis." The Rule instructed the State Board's

chairman to "designate a person or persons to serve in an ex-officio capacity
on the Association's governing bodies." That same year, the State Board specifically approved the Association's rules and regulations, while reserving the right
to review future changes. On several occasions over the next 20 years, the State
Board reviewed, approved, or reaffirmed its approval of the recruiting Rule at
issue in this case. In 1996, the State Board dropped the original rule expressly
designating the Association as regulator and substituted a statement "recognizing the value of participation in interscholastic athletics and the role of the
Association in coordinating interscholastic athletic competition," while "authorizing the public schools of the state to voluntarily maintain membership in the
Association."

This action involves a regulatory enforcement proceeding brought against
petitioner, Brentwood Academy, a private parochial high school member of the
Association. The board of control found that Brentwood violated a rule prohibiting "undue influence" in recruiting athletes, when it wrote to incoming students and their parents about spring football practice. The Association placed
Brentwood's athletic program on probation for four years, declared its football
and boys' basketball teams ineligible to compete in playoffs for two years, and
imposed a $3,000 fine. When these penalties were imposed, all the voting mem-
bers of the board of control and legislative council were public school administrators. Brentwood sued the Association and its executive director under 42 U.S.C.
§1983, claiming that enforcement of the Rule was state action and a violation of
the First and Fourteenth Amendments. The District Court found the Association
to be a state actor. The United States Court of Appeals for the Sixth Circuit
reversed applying criteria derived from *Blum v. Yaretsky*, 457 U.S. 991 (1982),
Lugar v. Edmondson Oil Co., 457 U.S. 922 (1982), and *Rendell-Baker v. Kohn*, 457
U.S. 830 (1982). We granted certiorari and now reverse.

Our cases try to plot a line between state action subject to Fourteenth
Amendment scrutiny and private conduct that is not. The judicial obligation is
not only to "'preserve an area of individual freedom by limiting the reach of federal law' and avoid the imposition of responsibility on a State for conduct it could
not control," but also to assure that constitutional standards are invoked "when it
can be said that the State is *responsible* for the specific conduct of which the plaintiff complains." If the Fourteenth Amendment is not to be displaced, the deed of
an ostensibly private organization or individual is to be treated sometimes as if a
State had caused it to be performed. State action may be found if, though only
if, there is such a "close nexus between the State and the challenged action" that
seemingly private behavior "may be fairly treated as that of the State itself." What
is fairly attributable is a matter of normative judgment, and the criteria lack rigid
simplicity.

No one fact can function as a necessary condition across the board for finding state action; nor is any set of circumstances absolutely sufficient, for there
may be some countervailing reason against attributing activity to the government. Our cases have identified a host of facts that can bear on the fairness of

such an attribution. We have held that a challenged activity may be state action when it results from the State's exercise of "coercive power," when the State provides "significant encouragement, either overt or covert," or when a private actor operates as a "willful participant in joint activity with the State or its agents." We have treated a nominally private entity as a state actor when it is controlled by an "agency of the State," when it has been delegated a public function by the State, when it is "entwined with governmental policies," or when government is "entwined in its management or control," *Evans v. Newton*, 382 U.S. 296 (1966).

The character of a legal entity is determined neither by its expressly private characterization in statutory law, nor by the failure of the law to acknowledge the entity's inseparability from recognized government officials or agencies. *Lebron v. National Railroad Passenger Corporation*, 513 U.S. 374 (1995), held that Amtrak was the Government for constitutional purposes, regardless of its congressional designation as private; it was organized under federal law to attain governmental objectives and was directed and controlled by federal appointees. *Pennsylvania v. Board of Directors of City Trusts of Philadelphia* held the privately endowed Girard College to be a state actor and enforcement of its private founder's limitation of admission to whites attributable to the State, because the college's board of directors was a state agency established by state law. The converse occurred in *Evans v. Newton* which held that private trustees to whom a city had transferred a park were nonetheless state actors since the park served the public purpose and "the municipality remained entwined in its management and control."

The nominally private character of the Association is overborne by the pervasive entwinement of public institutions and public officials in its composition and workings, and there is no substantial reason to claim unfairness in applying constitutional standards to it. The Association is not an organization of natural persons acting on their own, but of schools, and of public schools to the extent of 84% of the total. Under the Association's bylaws, each member school is represented by its principal or a faculty member, who has a vote in selecting members of the governing legislative council and board of control from eligible principals, assistant principals, and superintendents.

Public school officials act within the scope of their duties when they represent their institutions. Interscholastic athletics obviously play an integral part in the public education of Tennessee, where nearly every public high school spends money on competitions among schools. These public teams need some mechanism to produce rules and regulate competition. The mechanism is an organization overwhelmingly composed of public school officials who select representatives (all of them public officials at the time in question here), who in turn adopt and enforce the rules that make the system work. By giving these jobs to the Association, the 290 public schools of Tennessee can sensibly be seen as exercising their own authority to meet their own responsibilities. Half the council or board meetings were held during official school hours, and public schools have largely provided for the Association's financial support. A small portion of the Association's revenue comes from membership dues paid by the schools, and the principal part from gate receipts at tournaments among the member schools. The schools here obtain membership in the service organization and give up sources of their own income to their collective association. The Association thus exercises the authority of the predominantly public schools to charge for admission to their games and enjoys the schools' moneymaking capacity as its own.

In sum, to the extent of 84% of its membership, the Association is an organization of public schools represented by their officials acting in their official capacity to provide an integral element of secondary public schooling. There would be no recognizable Association, legal or tangible, without the public school officials, who do not merely control but overwhelmingly perform all but the purely ministerial acts by which the Association exists and functions in practical terms. Only the 16% minority of private school memberships prevents this entwinement of the Association and the public school system from being total and their identities totally indistinguishable. State Board members are assigned *ex officio* to serve as members of the board of control and legislative council, and the Association's ministerial employees are treated as state employees to the extent of being eligible for membership in the state retirement system.

The terms of the State Board's Rule expressly designating the Association as regulator of interscholastic athletics in public schools were deleted in 1996, the year after a court held that the Association was a state actor. But the removal of the designation language affected nothing but words. Today the State Board's member-designees continue to sit on the Association's committees as nonvoting members, and the State continues to welcome Association employees in its retirement scheme. The close relationship is confirmed by the Association's enforcement of the same preamendment rules and regulations reviewed and approved by the State Board and by the State Board's continued willingness to allow students to satisfy its physical education requirement by taking part in interscholastic athletics sponsored by the Association. The State Board once freely acknowledged the Association's official character but now does it by winks and nods.

Entwinement will support a conclusion that an ostensibly private organization ought to be charged with a public character and judged by constitutional standards; entwinement to the degree shown here requires it. It avails the Association nothing to stress that the State neither coerced nor encouraged the actions complained of. "Coercion" and "encouragement" are like "entwinement" in referring to kinds of facts that can justify characterizing an ostensibly private action as public. Facts that address any of these criteria are significant, but no one criterion must necessarily be applied. When the relevant facts show pervasive entwinement to the point of largely overlapping identity, the implication of state action is not affected by pointing out that the facts might not loom large under a different test.

Even facts that suffice to show public action may be outweighed in the name of some value at odds with finding public accountability in the circumstances. In *Polk County,* 454 U.S., at 322, a defense lawyer's actions were deemed private even though she was employed by the county and was acting within the scope of her duty as a public defender. Full-time public employment would be conclusive of state action for some purposes, but not when the employee is doing a defense lawyer's primary job; then, the public defender does "not act on behalf of the State; he is the State's adversary." The state-action doctrine does not convert opponents into virtual agents.

Every other Court of Appeals to consider a statewide athletic association has found it a state actor. No one, however, has pointed to any explosion of §1983 cases against interscholastic athletic associations in the affected jurisdictions. The judgment of the Court of Appeals for the Sixth Circuit is reversed, and the case is remanded for further proceedings consistent with this opinion.

It is so ordered.

Justice THOMAS, with whom THE CHIEF JUSTICE, Justice SCALIA, and Justice KENNEDY join, *dissenting.*

We have never found state action based upon mere "entwinement." Until today, we have found a private organization's acts to constitute state action only when the organization performed a public function; was created, coerced, or encouraged by the government; or acted in a symbiotic relationship with the government. The majority's holding not only extends state-action doctrine beyond its permissible limits but also encroaches upon the realm of individual freedom that the doctrine was meant to protect.

Common sense dictates that the TSSAA's actions cannot constitute state action. The State of Tennessee did not create the TSSAA. The State does not fund the TSSAA and does not pay its employees. In fact, only 4% of the TSSAA's revenue comes from dues paid by member schools; the bulk of its operating budget is derived from gate receipts at tournaments it sponsors. The State does not permit the TSSAA to use state-owned facilities for a discounted fee, and it does not exempt the TSSAA from state taxation. No Tennessee law authorizes the State to coordinate interscholastic athletics or empowers another entity to organize interscholastic athletics on behalf of the State. The only state pronouncement acknowledging the TSSAA's existence is a rule providing that the State Board of Education permits public schools to maintain membership in the TSSAA. Moreover, the State of Tennessee has never had any involvement in the particular action taken by the TSSAA in this case. The TSSAA's authority to enforce its recruiting rule arises solely from the voluntary membership contract that each member school signs, agreeing to conduct its athletics in accordance with the rules and decisions of the TSSAA.

The TSSAA has not performed a function that has been "traditionally exclusively reserved to the State." The organization of interscholastic sports is neither a traditional nor an exclusive public function of the States. In Tennessee, the State did not show an interest in interscholastic athletics until 47 years after the TSSAA had been in existence. Even then, the State Board of Education merely acquiesced in the TSSAA's actions and did not assume the role of regulating interscholastic athletics. The TSSAA no doubt serves the public, particularly the public schools, but the mere provision of a service to the public does not render such provision a traditional and exclusive public function. It is also obvious that the TSSAA is not an entity created and controlled by the government for the purpose of fulfilling a government objective. The State of Tennessee played no role in the creation of the TSSAA as a private corporation. Although the board of control currently is composed of public school officials, and public schools currently account for the majority of the TSSAA's membership, this is not required by the TSSAA's constitution.

In addition, the State of Tennessee has not "exercised coercive power or provided such significant encouragement to the TSSAA, either overt or covert," that the TSSAA's regulatory activities must in law be deemed to be those of the State. The State has not promulgated any regulations of interscholastic sports, and has not encouraged or coerced the TSSAA in enforcing its recruiting rule. Public schools do provide a small portion of the TSSAA's funding through their membership dues, but no one argues that these dues are somehow conditioned on the TSSAA's enactment and enforcement of recruiting rules. Even if the TSSAA were dependent on state funding, mere financial dependence on the State does not convert the TSSAA's actions into acts of the State. There is no evidence of "joint participation" between the State and the TSSAA in the TSSAA's enforcement of its recruiting rule. The TSSAA's board of control enforces its recruiting rule solely in accordance with the authority granted to it under the contract that each member signs.

There is no "symbiotic relationship" between the State and the TSSAA. The TSSAA's "fiscal relationship with the State is not different from that of many contractors performing services for the government." The TSSAA provides a service—the organization of athletic tournaments—in exchange for membership dues and gate fees, just as a vendor could contract with public schools to sell refreshments at school events.

The majority holds that the combination of factors it identifies evidences "entwinement" of the State with the TSSAA, and that such entwinement converts private action into state action. This new "entwinement" theory lacks any support in our state-action jurisprudence. The majority's new entwinement test could affect many organizations that foster activities, enforce rules, and sponsor extracurricular competition among high schools—not just in athletics, but in such diverse areas as agriculture, mathematics, music, marching bands, forensics, and cheerleading. The state-action doctrine was developed to reach only those actions that are truly attributable to the State, not to subject private citizens to the control of federal courts hearing §1983 actions. I respectfully dissent.

Notes and Questions

1. *Private Prisons.* The Commonwealth of Kentucky contracts with a private corrections corporation (Ajax Prison Corporation) to house and rehabilitate

prison inmates. An Ajax employee subjects a state prisoner to cruel and inhumane treatment (the employee beat the inmate and led him around on a dog leash). Under such circumstances, does Ajax qualify as a state actor? Does the decision hinge on whether the housing of prisoners is regarded as a traditional governmental function?

2. *Is the National Collegiate Athletic Association a "State Actor"?* Jerry Tarkanian, the former head basketball coach at the University of Nevada-Las Vegas was the "winningest active basketball coach" based on his team's incredible streak of wins. He became a national celebrity when he transformed a mediocre team to a third-place finisher in the National Collegiate Athletic Association (NCAA) final basketball tournament, sometimes referred to as March Madness. After the tournament, the NCAA put Tarkanian's team on probation and threatened additional penalties unless the university severed its ties with the coach. The university informed Tarkanian that he was fired based on 38 alleged violations — 10 of which involved him directly. The NCAA is a 960-member unincorporated association, which includes private and state colleges. The coach filed suit against the NCAA, claiming that UNLV delegated its functions to the NCAA, clothing the association with authority both to adopt rules governing UNLV's athletic programs and to enforce those rules on behalf of UNLV. Is the NCAA a state actor? In *National Collegiate Athletic Assn. v. Tarkanian*, 488 U.S. 170 (1988), the majority relied on the fact that the NCAA did not have any power to take action directly against Tarkanian as indicating that the NCAA was not a state actor.

5. *Public Access Cable Channels*

Manhattan Community Access Corp. v. Halleck

139 S. Ct. 1921 (2019)

Justice KAVANAUGH delivered the opinion of the Court.

The Free Speech Clause of the First Amendment constrains governmental actors and protects private actors. To draw the line between governmental and private, this Court applies what is known as the state-action doctrine. Under that doctrine, a private entity may be considered a state actor when it exercises a function "traditionally exclusively reserved to the State." *Jackson v. Metropolitan Edison Co.*, 419 U.S. 345, 352 (1974).

This case concerns the public access channels on Time Warner's cable system in Manhattan. Public access channels are available for private citizens to use. The public access channels on Time Warner's cable system in Manhattan are operated by a private nonprofit corporation known as MNN. The question is whether operation of public access channels on a cable system is a traditional, exclusive public function? If so, then the First Amendment would restrict MNN's exercise of editorial discretion over the speech and speakers on the public access channels.

Since the 1970s, public access channels have been a regular feature on cable television systems throughout the United States. Congress passed the Cable Communications Policy Act of 1984. The Act authorized state and local governments to require cable operators to set aside channels on their cable systems for public access. The New York State Public Service Commission regulates cable franchising in New York State and requires cable operators in the State to set aside channels on their cable systems for public access. State law requires that use of the public access channels be free of charge and first-come, first-served. Under state law, the cable operator operates the public access channels unless the local government chooses to itself operate the channels or designates a private entity to operate the channels. Time Warner operates a cable system in Manhattan. Under state law, Time Warner must set aside some channels on its cable system for public access. New York City has designated a private nonprofit corporation named Manhattan Neighborhood Network (MNN) to operate Time Warner's public access channels.

Dee Dee Halleck and Jesus Papoleto Melendez produced public access programming in Manhattan. They made a film about MNN's alleged neglect of the East Harlem community. Halleck submitted the film to MNN for airing on MNN's public access channels, and MNN later televised the film. Afterwards, MNN fielded multiple complaints about the film's content. In response, MNN temporarily suspended Halleck from using the public access channels. Halleck and Melendez soon became embroiled in a dispute with MNN staff. In the wake of that dispute, MNN suspended Halleck and Melendez from all MNN services and facilities. Halleck and Melendez then sued MNN. The two claimed that MNN violated their First Amendment free-speech rights when MNN restricted their access to the public access channels because of the content of their film. MNN moved to dismiss on the ground that MNN is not a state actor and therefore is not subject to First Amendment restrictions on its editorial discretion. The District Court agreed and dismissed the producers' First Amendment claim. The Second Circuit reversed. We granted certiorari.

Ratified in 1868, the Fourteenth Amendment makes the First Amendment's Free Speech Clause applicable against the States: "No State shall make or enforce any law which shall abridge the privileges or immunities of citizens of the United States; nor shall any State deprive any person of life, liberty, or property, without due process of law." The text and original meaning of those Amendments, as well as precedent, establish that the Free Speech Clause prohibits only governmental abridgment of speech. The Free Speech Clause does not prohibit private abridgment of speech. *See, e.g., Hudgens v. NLRB*, 424 U.S. 507 (1976). This Court's state-action doctrine distinguishes the government from individuals and private entities. By enforcing that constitutional boundary between the governmental and the private, the state-action doctrine protects a robust sphere of individual liberty.

A private entity may qualify as a state actor when it exercises "powers traditionally exclusively reserved to the State." *Jackson*, 419 U.S. at 352. It is not enough that the federal, state, or local government exercised the function in the past, or still does. And it is not enough that the function serves the public good or the public interest. Rather, to qualify as a traditional, exclusive public function within the meaning of our state-action precedents, the government must have traditionally and exclusively performed the function. *See Rendell-Baker v. Kohn*, 457 U.S. 830, 842 (1982); *Jackson*, 419 U.S. at 352. "Very few" functions fall into that category. Those functions include running elections and operating a company town. *See Terry v. Adams*, 345 U.S. 461 (1953); *Marsh v. Alabama*, 326 U.S. 501 (1946). A variety of functions do not fall into that category, including running sports associations and leagues, administering insurance payments, operating nursing homes, providing special education, representing indigent criminal defendants, resolving private disputes, and supplying electricity. *See American Mfrs. Mut. Ins. Co. v. Sullivan*, 526 U.S. 40 (1999); *National Collegiate Athletic Assn. v. Tarkanian*, 488 U.S. 179 (1988). The relevant function in this case is operation of public access channels on a cable system. That function has not traditionally and exclusively been performed by government.

Since the 1970s, when public access channels became a regular feature on cable systems, a variety of private and public actors have operated public access channels, including: private cable operators; private nonprofit organizations; municipalities; and other public and private community organizations such as churches, schools, and libraries. The history of public access channels in Manhattan further illustrates the point. In 1971, public access channels first started operating in Manhattan. Those early Manhattan public access channels were operated in large part by private cable operators, with some help from private nonprofit organizations. In the early 1990s, MNN (also a private entity) began to operate the public access channels. In short, operating public access channels on a cable system is not a traditional, exclusive public function.

The producers contend that the relevant function here is not the operation of public access channels on a cable system, but rather the operation of a public forum for speech. According to the producers, operation of a public forum for speech is a traditional, exclusive public function. When the government provides a forum for speech, the government may be constrained by the First Amendment, meaning that the government ordinarily may not exclude speech or speakers from the forum on the basis of viewpoint, or sometimes even on the basis of content. *See, e.g., Police Dept. of Chicago v. Mosley*, 408 U.S. 92 (1972). By contrast, when a private entity provides a forum for speech, the private entity is not ordinarily constrained by the First Amendment. The private entity may thus exercise editorial discretion over the speech and speakers in the forum. A private entity who provides a forum for speech is not transformed by that fact alone into a state actor. Private property owners and private lessees often open their property for speech. Grocery stores put up community bulletin boards. Comedy clubs host open mic nights.

Merely hosting speech by others is not a traditional, exclusive public function and does not alone transform private entities into state actors subject to First

Amendment constraints. If the rule were otherwise, all private property owners and private lessees who open their property for speech would be subject to First Amendment constraints and would lose the ability to exercise appropriate editorial discretion within that open forum. Private property owners and private lessees would face the unappetizing choice of allowing all comers or closing the platform altogether. "The Constitution by no means requires such an attenuated doctrine of dedication of private property to public use." *Hudgens*, 424 U.S. at 519. Benjamin Franklin did not have to operate his newspaper as "a stagecoach, with seats for everyone." That principle still holds true. To hold that private property owners providing a forum for speech are constrained by the First Amendment would be "to create a court-made law wholly disregarding the constitutional basis on which private ownership of property rests in this country." The Constitution does not disable private property owners and private lessees from exercising editorial discretion over speech and speakers on their property. The producers here are seeking to circumvent case law.

The producers retort that this case differs from *Hudgens* because New York City has designated MNN to operate the public access channels on Time Warner's cable system, and because New York State heavily regulates MNN with respect to the public access channels. However, New York City's designation of MNN to operate the public access channels is analogous to a government license, a government contract, or a government-granted monopoly. The fact that the government licenses, contracts with, or grants a monopoly to a private entity does not convert the private entity into a state actor—unless the private entity is performing a traditional, exclusive public function. *See, e.g., Blum*, 457 U.S. at 1011. The same principle applies if the government funds or subsidizes a private entity. *See Rendell-Baker*, 457 U.S. at 840. Numerous private entities obtain government licenses, government contracts, or government-granted monopolies. If those facts sufficed to transform a private entity into a state actor, a large swath of private entities would suddenly be turned into state actors and be subject to a variety of constitutional constraints on their activities. That is not the law. The City's designation of MNN to operate the public access channels on Time Warner's cable system does not make MNN a state actor. So, too, New York State's regulation of MNN's operation of the public access channels does not make MNN a state actor. Under the regulations, air time on the public access channels must be free, and programming must be aired on a first-come, first-served basis. Those regulations restrict MNN's editorial discretion and in effect require MNN to operate almost like a common carrier. But those restrictions do not render MNN a state actor. In *Jackson v. Metropolitan Edison Co.*, the Court stated that the "fact that a business is subject to state regulation does not by itself convert its action into that of the State." The Court held that "a heavily regulated, privately owned utility, enjoying at least a partial monopoly in the providing of electrical service within its territory," was not a state actor. Nor did it matter whether the State had authorized the utility to provide electric service to the community, or whether the utility was the only entity providing electric service to much of that community.

This case closely parallels Jackson. MNN is "a heavily regulated, privately owned" entity. As in *Jackson*, the regulations do not transform the regulated private entity into a state actor. Put simply, being regulated by the State does not make one a state actor. The "being heavily regulated makes you a state actor" theory of state action is circular and would significantly endanger individual liberty and private enterprise. The theory would be especially problematic in the speech context, because it could eviscerate private entities' rights to exercise editorial control over speech and speakers on their properties or platforms. We conclude that MNN is not subject to First Amendment constraints on how it exercises its editorial discretion with respect to the public access channels. To be sure, MNN is subject to state-law constraints on its editorial discretion (assuming those state laws do not violate a federal statute or the Constitution). If MNN violates those state laws, or violates applicable contracts, MNN could perhaps face state-law sanctions or liability of some kind. We take no position on any potential state-law questions. We simply conclude that MNN, as a private actor, is not subject to First Amendment constraints on how it exercises editorial discretion over the speech and speakers on its public access channels.

The producers alternatively contend that the public access channels are actually the property of New York City, not the property of Time Warner or MNN. On this theory, the producers say that MNN is in essence simply managing government property on behalf of New York City. The short answer is that public access channels are not the property of New York City. Nothing suggests that a government owns or leases either the cable system or the public access channels at issue here. Both Time Warner and MNN are private entities. Time Warner is the cable operator, and it owns its cable network, which contains the public access channels. MNN operates those public access channels with its own facilities and equipment. The City does not own or lease the public access channels, and the City does not possess a formal easement or other property interest in those channels. The franchise agreements between the City and Time Warner do not say that the City has any property interest in the public access channels. On the contrary, the franchise agreements expressly place the public access channels "under the jurisdiction" of MNN. Moreover, the producers did not allege that the City has a property interest in the channels. And the producers have not cited any basis in state law for such a conclusion. Put simply, the City does not have "any formal easement or other property interest in those channels." *Denver Area*, 518 U.S. at 828 (Thomas, J.). It does not matter that a provision in the franchise agreements allowed the City to designate a private entity to operate the public access channels on Time Warner's cable system. Time Warner still owns the cable system. And MNN still operates the public access channels.

It is true that the City has allowed the cable operator, Time Warner, to lay cable along public rights-of-way in the City. But Time Warner's access to public rights-of-way does not alter the state-action analysis. For Time Warner, as for other cable operators, access to public rights-of-way is essential to lay cable and construct a physical cable infrastructure. *See Turner Broadcasting System, Inc. v. FCC,*

512 U.S. 622 (1994). But the same is true for utility providers, such as the electric utility in *Jackson*. Put simply, a private entity's permission from government to use public rights-of-way does not render that private entity a state actor.

Under the laws in certain States, including New York, a local government may decide to itself operate the public access channels on a local cable system (as many local governments do), or could take appropriate steps to obtain a property interest in the public access channels. Depending on the circumstances, the First Amendment might then constrain the local government's operation of the public access channels. We decide only the case before us in light of the record before us.

It is sometimes said that the bigger the government, the smaller the individual. Consistent with the text of the Constitution, the state-action doctrine enforces a critical boundary between the government and the individual, and thereby protects a robust sphere of individual liberty. Expanding the state-action doctrine beyond its traditional boundaries would expand governmental control while restricting individual liberty and private enterprise. We decline to do so. MNN is a private entity that operates public access channels on a cable system. Operating public access channels on a cable system is not a traditional, exclusive public function. A private entity such as MNN who opens its property for speech by others is not transformed by that fact alone into a state actor. Under the text of the Constitution and our precedents, MNN is not a state actor subject to the First Amendment. We reverse and remand for further proceedings consistent with this opinion.

It is so ordered.

Justice SOTOMAYOR, with whom Justice GINSBURG, Justice BREYER, and Justice KAGAN join, dissenting.

This is a case about an organization appointed by the government to administer a constitutional public forum. New York City secured a property interest in public-access television channels when it granted a cable franchise to a cable company. State regulations require those public-access channels to be open to the public on terms that render them a public forum. The City contracted out the administration of that forum to a private organization, Manhattan Community Access Corporation (MNN). By accepting that agency relationship, MNN stepped into the City's shoes and thus qualifies as a state actor, subject to the First Amendment.

C. STATE INVOLVEMENT OR ENCOURAGEMENT

State action may also be found to exist when the government is involved with, or encourages, private action. But what level of government support or encouragement is sufficient? Consider the following cases.

1. Government Regulation

Burton v. Wilmington Parking Authority

365 U.S. 715 (1961)

Mr. Justice CLARK delivered the opinion of the Court.

The Eagle Coffee Shoppe, Inc., a restaurant located within an off-street automobile parking building in Wilmington, Delaware, refused to serve appellant food or drink solely because he is a Negro. The parking building is owned and operated by the Wilmington Parking Authority, an agency of the State of Delaware, and the restaurant is the Authority's lessee. Appellant claims that such refusal abridges his rights under the Equal Protection Clause of the Fourteenth Amendment to the United States Constitution. The Supreme Court of Delaware held that Eagle was acting in "a purely private capacity" under its lease; that its action was not that of the Authority and was not, therefore, state action within the contemplation of the prohibitions contained in that Amendment. We conclude that the exclusion of appellant under the circumstances present here was discriminatory state action in violation of the Equal Protection Clause of the Fourteenth Amendment.

The Authority was created by the City of Wilmington pursuant to 22 Del. Code, §§501-515. It is "a public body exercising public powers of the State as an agency thereof." Its statutory purpose is to provide adequate parking facilities for the convenience of the public. To secure additional capital, and thereby to make bond financing practicable, the Authority decided to enter long-term leases for commercial use of some of the space available in the projected "garage building." A lease was made with Eagle Coffee Shoppe, Inc., for operation of a "restaurant, dining room, banquet hall, cocktail lounge and bar." Eagle's space, although "within the exterior walls of the structure, has no marked public entrance leading from the parking facility into the restaurant." The Authority agreed to complete "the decorative finishing of the leased premises and utilities without cost to Eagle." Eagle then spent $220,000 to make the space suitable for its operation. The Authority retained the right to place directional signs on the exterior to the let space which would not interfere with or obscure Eagle's display signs. At an annual rental of $28,700, Eagle covenanted to "occupy and use the leased premises in accordance with all applicable laws, statutes, ordinances and rules and regulations of any federal, state or municipal authority." Its lease, however, contains no requirement that its restaurant services be made available to the general public on a nondiscriminatory basis, in spite of the fact that the Authority has power to adopt rules and regulations respecting the use of its facilities except any as would impair the security of its bondholders. The Authority placed signs on the building indicating the public character of the building, and flew state and national flags on the roof.

Only by sifting facts and weighing circumstances can the involvement of the State in private conduct be attributed its true significance. The land and building were publicly owned. As an entity, the building was dedicated to "public uses" in performance of the Authority's "essential governmental functions." The costs of land acquisition, construction, and maintenance are defrayed entirely from donations by the City of Wilmington, from loans and revenue bonds and from the proceeds of rentals and parking services out of which the loans and bonds were payable. The commercially leased areas were not surplus state property, but constituted a physically and financially integral and, indeed, indispensable part of the State's plan to operate its project as a self-sustaining unit. Upkeep and maintenance of the building, including necessary repairs, were responsibilities of the Authority and were payable out of public funds. It cannot be doubted that the peculiar relationship of the restaurant to the parking facility in which it is located confers on each an incidental variety of mutual benefits. Guests of the restaurant are afforded a convenient place to park their automobiles, even if they cannot enter the restaurant directly from the parking area. Similarly, its convenience for diners may well provide additional demand for the Authority's parking facilities. Should any improvements effected in the leasehold by Eagle become part of the realty, there is no possibility of increased taxes being passed on to it since the fee is held by a tax-exempt government agency. Neither can it be ignored, especially in view of Eagle's affirmative allegation that for it to serve Negroes would injure its business, that profits earned by discrimination not only contribute to, but also are indispensable elements in, the financial success of a governmental agency.

Addition of all these activities, obligations and responsibilities of the Authority, the benefits mutually conferred, together with the obvious fact that the restaurant is operated as an integral part of a public building devoted to a public parking service, indicates that degree of state participation and involvement in discriminatory action which it was the design of the Fourteenth Amendment to condemn. It is irony amounting to grave injustice that in one part of a single building, erected and maintained with public funds by an agency of the State to serve a public purpose, all persons have equal rights, while in another portion, also serving the public, a Negro is a second-class citizen, offensive because of his race, without rights and unentitled to service. The Authority could have affirmatively required Eagle to discharge the responsibilities under the Fourteenth Amendment imposed upon the private enterprise as a consequence of state participation. But no State may effectively abdicate its responsibilities by either ignoring them or by merely failing to discharge them whatever the motive may be. It is of no consolation to an individual denied the equal protection of the laws that it was done in good faith. By its inaction, the Authority, and through it the State, has not only made itself a party to the refusal of service, but has elected to place its power, property and prestige behind the admitted discrimination. The State has so far insinuated itself into a position of interdependence with Eagle that it must be recognized as a joint participant in the challenged activity, which, on that account, cannot be considered to have been so "purely private" as to fall without the scope of the Fourteenth Amendment.

We hold today that when a State leases public property in the manner and for the purpose shown to have been the case here, the proscriptions of the Fourteenth Amendment must be complied with by the lessee as certainly as though they were binding covenants written into the agreement itself. The judgment of the Supreme Court of Delaware is reversed and the cause remanded for further proceedings consistent with this opinion.

Reversed and remanded.

Mr. Justice STEWART, *concurring.*

The highest court of Delaware has construed this legislative enactment as authorizing discriminatory classification based exclusively on color. Such a law seems to me clearly violative of the Fourteenth Amendment.

Notes and Questions

1. *Racially Segregated Parks. Gilmore v. City of Montgomery,* 417 U.S. 556 (1974), involved the City of Montgomery, Alabama's decision to allow racially segregated schools, and other nonschool groups that allegedly discriminated on the basis of race, to use public park recreational facilities. Petitioners claimed that Montgomery officials were under an affirmative duty to bring about and maintain a desegregated public school system, and argued that the City's decision to allow the schools and groups to use the parks involved the state in the private discrimination. The Court concluded that, while private schools could use the park, they could not be given exclusive use. Justice Frankfurter dissented: "The city's actions significantly enhanced the attractiveness of segregated private schools, formed in reaction against the federal court school order, by enabling them to offer complete athletic programs. This assistance significantly tended to undermine the federal court order mandating the establishment and maintenance of a unitary school system in Montgomery. It therefore was wholly proper for the city to be enjoined from permitting exclusive access to public recreational facilities by segregated private schools and by groups affiliated with such schools." Justice White concurred: "I would also bar the use of city-owned recreation facilities by students from segregated schools for events or occasions that are part of the school curriculum or organized and arranged by the school as part of its own program. I see no difference between this type of use and the exclusive use that the majority agrees may not be permitted consistent with the Equal Protection Clause."

2. *The Segregation Ordinance.* In *Peterson v. City of Greenville,* 373 U.S. 244 (1963), petitioners were convicted of trespassing for refusing to leave a lunch counter when asked to do so "because integrated service was 'contrary to local customs of segregation at lunch counters' as well as in violation of a Greenville City ordinance requiring separation of the races in restaurants." Petitioners argued that South Carolina had deprived them of equal protection under the Fourteenth Amendment. The Court agreed, finding that the restaurant's action constituted

state action: "These convictions cannot stand, even assuming that the manager would have acted as he did independently of the existence of the ordinance. When a state agency passes a law compelling persons to discriminate against other persons because of race, and the State's criminal processes are employed in a way which enforces the discrimination mandated by that law, such a palpable violation of the Fourteenth Amendment cannot be saved by attempting to separate the mental urges of the discriminators."

3. *The Textbook Loans.* In *Norwood v. Harrison*, 413 U.S. 455 (1973), the State of Mississippi provided textbooks to private schools that discriminated on the basis of race. The Court held that the state thereby implicated itself in the private discrimination: "An inescapable educational cost is the expense of providing all necessary learning materials. When, as here, that necessary expense is borne by the State, the economic consequence is to give aid to the enterprise; if the school engages in discriminatory practices the State by tangible aid in the form of textbooks thereby gives support to such discrimination. Racial discrimination in state-operated schools is barred by the Constitution and it is also axiomatic that a state may not induce, encourage or promote private persons to accomplish what it is constitutionally forbidden to accomplish."

Moose Lodge v. Irvis

407 U.S. 163 (1972)

Mr. Justice REHNQUIST delivered the opinion of the Court.

Appellee Irvis, a Negro, was refused service by appellant Moose Lodge, a local branch of the national fraternal organization located in Harrisburg, Pennsylvania, and then brought this action under 42 U.S.C. §1983. While conceding the right of private clubs to choose members upon a discriminatory basis, appellee asserts that the licensing of Moose Lodge to serve liquor by the Pennsylvania Liquor Control Board amounts to such state involvement with the club's activities as to make its discriminatory practices forbidden by the Equal Protection Clause of the Fourteenth Amendment. The relief sought was an injunction forbidding the licensing by the liquor authority of Moose Lodge until it ceased its discriminatory practices. We conclude that Moose Lodge's refusal to serve food and beverages to a guest by reason of the fact that he was a Negro does not, under the circumstances here presented, violate the Fourteenth Amendment.

The Court has never held that discrimination by an otherwise private entity would be violative of the Equal Protection Clause if the private entity receives any sort of benefit or service at all from the State, or if it is subject to state regulation in any degree whatever. Since state-furnished services include such necessities of life as electricity, water, and police and fire protection, such a holding would utterly emasculate the distinction between private as distinguished from state conduct set forth in *The Civil Rights Cases.* Our holdings indicate that where the impetus for the discrimination is private, the State must have "significantly involved itself with invidious discriminations," *Reitman v. Mulkey*, 387 U.S. 369, 380 (1967), in order for the discriminatory action to fall within the ambit of the constitutional prohibition.

Our prior decisions dealing with discriminatory refusal of service in public eating places are significantly different factually from the case now before us. *Peterson v. City of Greenville*, 373 U.S. 244 (1963), dealt with the trespass prosecution of persons who "sat in" at a restaurant to protest its refusal of service to Negroes. There the Court held that although the ostensible initiative for the trespass prosecution came from the proprietor, the existence of a local ordinance requiring segregation of races in such places was tantamount to the State having "commanded a particular result." There is no suggestion in this record that the Pennsylvania statutes and regulations governing the sale of liquor are intended either overtly or covertly to encourage discrimination.

Here there is nothing approaching the symbiotic relationship between lessor and lessee that was present in *Burton*. The Moose Lodge is on land owned by it, not by any public authority. Far from holding itself out as a place of public accommodation, Moose Lodge ostentatiously proclaims the fact that it is not open to the public. Nor is it located and operated in surroundings that although private in name, it discharges a function or performs a service that would otherwise be performed by the State. While Eagle was a public restaurant in a public building, Moose Lodge is a private social club in a private building.

The Pennsylvania Liquor Control Board plays absolutely no part in establishing or enforcing the membership or guest policies of the club that it licenses to serve liquor. There is no suggestion that Pennsylvania law, either as written or as applied, discriminates against minority groups in their right to apply for club licenses or in their right to purchase and be served liquor in places of public accommodation. The only effect that the state license to serve liquor can be said to have on the right of any other Pennsylvanian to buy or be served liquor is that club licenses are counted in the maximum number of licenses that may be issued in a given municipality.

The District Court pointed out what it considered to be the "pervasive" nature of the regulation of private clubs by the Pennsylvania Liquor Control Board. An applicant for a club license must make such physical alterations in its premises as the board may require, must file a list of the names and addresses of its members and employees, and must keep extensive financial records. The board is granted the right to inspect the licensed premises at any time when patrons, guests, or members are present.

However detailed this type of regulation may be in some particulars, it cannot be said to foster or encourage racial discrimination. Nor can it be said to make the State a partner or even a joint venturer in the club's enterprise. The limited effect of the prohibition against obtaining additional club licenses when the maximum number of retail licenses allotted to a municipality has been issued, when considered together with the availability of liquor from hotel, restaurant, and retail licensees, falls far short of conferring upon club licensees a monopoly in the dispensing of liquor in any given municipality or in the State as a whole.

We therefore hold that, with the exception hereafter noted, the operation of
the regulatory scheme enforced by the Pennsylvania Liquor Control Board does
not sufficiently implicate the State in the discriminatory guest policies of Moose
Lodge to make the latter "state action" within the ambit of the Equal Protection
Clause of the Fourteenth Amendment.

   The regulations of the Liquor Control Board adopted pursuant to statute
affirmatively require that "every club licensee shall adhere to all of the provisions
of its Constitution and By-Laws." Even though the Liquor Control Board regulation in question is neutral in its terms, the result of its application in a case where
the constitution and bylaws of a club required racial discrimination would be to
invoke the sanctions of the State to enforce a concededly discriminatory private
rule. *Shelley v. Kraemer,* 334 U.S. 1 (1948), makes it clear that the application of
state sanctions to enforce such a rule would violate the Fourteenth Amendment.
Appellee was entitled to a decree enjoining the enforcement of §113.09 of the
regulations promulgated insofar as that regulation requires compliance by Moose
Lodge with provisions of its constitution and bylaws containing racially discriminatory provisions. The judgment of the District Court is reversed, and the cause
remanded with instructions to enter a decree in conformity with this opinion.

   Reversed and remanded.

Mr. Justice DOUGLAS, with whom Mr. Justice MARSHALL joins, *dissenting.*

   Liquor licenses in Pennsylvania, unlike driver's licenses, or marriage licenses,
are not freely available to those who meet racially neutral qualifications. There
is a complex quota system and the quota for Harrisburg has been full for many
years. This state-enforced scarcity of licenses restricts the ability of blacks to obtain
liquor, for liquor is commercially available only at private clubs for a significant
portion of each week. Without a liquor license a fraternal organization would be
hard pressed to survive. Thus, the State of Pennsylvania is putting the weight of
its liquor license, concededly a valued and important adjunct to a private club,
behind racial discrimination.

Mr. Justice BRENNAN, with whom Mr. Justice MARSHALL joins, *dissenting.*

   When Moose Lodge obtained its liquor license, the State of Pennsylvania
became an active participant in the operation of the Lodge bar. Liquor licensing
laws are primarily pervasive regulatory schemes under which the State dictates
and continually supervises virtually every detail of the operation of the licensee's
business.

Note and Question

   Broadcasters and Advertising. In *CBS, Inc. v. Democratic National Committee,* 412
U.S. 94 (1973), the Democratic National Committee (DNC) and the Business
Executives' Move for Vietnam Peace (BEM), a national organization of business-
men opposed to U.S. involvement in the Vietnam conflict, filed a complaint with

the Federal Communications Commission (FCC) against radio station WTOP in Washington, D.C. BEM charged that WTOP refused to sell it time to broadcast a series of one-minute spot announcements expressing BEM views on Vietnam. WTOP, in common with many, but not all, broadcasters, followed a policy of refusing to sell time for spot announcements to individuals and groups who wished to expound their views on controversial issues. WTOP took the position that since it presented full and fair coverage of important public questions, including the Vietnam conflict, it was justified in refusing to accept editorial advertisements. WTOP submitted evidence showing that the station had aired the views of critics of the Vietnam policy on numerous occasions. BEM challenged the fairness of WTOP's coverage. BEM challenged WTOP's action on First Amendment grounds. Is WTOP a "state actor"?

CBS argued that because the nation has a limited number of broadcast frequencies, and the government chooses those on whom licenses are bestowed, state action is implicated. FCC rules and regulations do not require, or prohibit, licensees from broadcasting ads like BEM's. The FCC does regard licensees as "public trustees" who are obligated to broadcast with fairness, balance, and objectivity, but otherwise it grants licensees discretion about what to air. The Court held that a broadcast licensee's refusal to accept a paid editorial advertisement does not constitute "governmental action" for First Amendment purposes. The Court explained that the Government is neither a "partner" to the action complained of nor engaged in a "symbiotic relationship" with the licensee. Under the Communications Act a broadcast licensee is vested with substantial journalistic discretion in deciding how to meet its statutory obligations as a "public trustee." The licensee's policy against accepting editorial advertising is compatible with the Communications Act and with the broadcaster's obligation to provide a balanced treatment of controversial questions. It was a matter within the area of journalistic discretion.

∽ PROBLEM: MORE ON THE TOWN, THE PRIVATE UTILITY, AND THE CLUB ∽

Suppose that Mr. and Mrs. Johnson come to you for legal advice. They would like to bring an equal protection claim against Palm Valley Country Club. How would you advise them? Can they establish state action based on the close relationships between the club, Power House, and the City of Orange? Does the club's legal requirement to comply with state liquor license regulations help them?

Reitman v. Mulkey

387 U.S. 369 (1967)

Mr. Justice WHITE delivered the opinion of the Court.

The question here is whether Art. I, §26, of the California Constitution denies "to any person the equal protection of the laws" within the meaning of the Fourteenth Amendment of the Constitution of the United States. Section 26 of Art. I, an initiated measure submitted to the people as Proposition 14 in a statewide ballot in 1964, provides in part as follows: "Neither the State nor any subdivision or agency thereof shall deny, limit or abridge, directly or indirectly, the right of any person, who is willing or desires to sell, lease or rent any part or all of his real property, to decline to sell, lease or rent such property to such person or persons as he, in his absolute discretion, chooses." The real property covered by §26 is limited to residential property and contains an exception for state-owned real estate.

In *Reitman*, the Mulkeys who are husband and wife, sued under §51 and §52 of the California Civil Code alleging that petitioners had refused to rent them an apartment solely on account of their race. Petitioners moved for summary judgment on the ground that §§51 and 52 had been rendered null and void by Proposition 14. In *Prendergast*, respondents filed suit to enjoin eviction from their apartment alleging that the eviction was motivated by racial prejudice. Petitioner sought a declaration that he was entitled to terminate the month-to-month tenancy even if his action was based on racial considerations. The California Supreme Court held in both cases that Art. I, §26, was invalid as denying the equal protection of the laws guaranteed by the Fourteenth Amendment. We granted certiorari and affirm.

The California Legislature has attempted to prohibit discrimination in various contexts. It was against this background that Proposition 14 was enacted. Its immediate design and intent were "to overturn state laws that bore on the right of private sellers and lessors to discriminate," and "to forestall future state action that might circumscribe this right." This aim was successfully achieved: the adoption of Proposition 14 "generally nullifies both the Acts as they apply to the housing market," and establishes "a purported constitutional right to privately discriminate on grounds which admittedly would be unavailable under the Fourteenth Amendment should state action be involved."

Petitioners contend that the California court misconstrued the Fourteenth Amendment in holding that the repeal of a statute prohibiting racial discrimination, which is constitutionally permissible, may be said to "authorize" and "encourage" discrimination because it makes legally permissible that which was formerly proscribed. As we understand the California court, it did not posit a constitutional violation on the mere repeal of the California Acts. What the court did was to reject the notion that the State was required to have a statute prohibiting racial discriminations in housing. Second, it held the intent of §26 was to authorize private racial discriminations in the housing market, to repeal existing Acts and to create a constitutional right to discriminate on racial grounds in the sale and leasing of real property. Hence, the court dealt with §26 as though it expressly authorized and constitutionalized the private right to discriminate. Third, the court concluded that the section would encourage and significantly involve the State in private racial discrimination contrary to the Fourteenth Amendment.

The California court could very reasonably conclude that §26 would and did have wider impact than a mere repeal of existing statutes. Section 26 mentioned no statute in so many words. Instead, it announced the constitutional right of any person to decline to sell or lease his real property to anyone to whom he did not desire to sell or lease. Existing statutes were thereby *pro tanto* repealed. But the section struck more deeply and more widely. Private discriminations in housing were now not only free from existing statutes but they also enjoyed a far different status than was true before the passage of those statutes. The right to discriminate, including the right to discriminate on racial grounds, was now embodied in the State's basic charter, immune from legislative, executive, or judicial regulation at any level of the state government. Those practicing racial discriminations need no longer rely solely on their personal choice. They could now invoke express constitutional authority, free from censure or interference of any kind from official sources. All individuals, partnerships, corporations and other legal entities, as well as their agents and representatives, could now discriminate with respect to their residential real property, which is defined as any interest in real property of any kind or quality, "irrespective of how obtained or financed," and seemingly irrespective of the relationship of the State to such interests in real property. Only the State is excluded with respect to property owned by it.

This Court has never attempted the "impossible task" of formulating an infallible test for determining whether the State "in any of its manifestations" has become significantly involved in private discriminations. Here the California court, armed as it was with the knowledge of the facts and circumstances concerning the passage and potential impact of §26, and familiar with the milieu in which that provision would operate, has determined that the provision would involve the State in private racial discriminations to an unconstitutional degree. We accept this holding.

The assessment of §26 by the California court is similar to what this Court has done in appraising state statutes or other official actions in other contexts. In *McCabe v. Atchison, Topeka & Santa Fe Ry. Co.*, 235 U.S. 151, the Court dealt with a statute which authorized carriers to provide cars for white persons but not for Negroes. The Court held that the statute was invalid under the Fourteenth Amendment because a carrier refusing equal service to Negroes would be "acting in the matter under the authority of a state law." *Nixon v. Condon*, 286 U.S. 73, involved a statute empowering the executive committee of a political party to prescribe the qualifications of its members for voting or for other participation, but containing no directions with respect to the exercise of that power. Reposing this power in the executive committee was said to insinuate the State into the self-regulatory, decision-making scheme of the voluntary association; the exercise of the power was viewed as an expression of state authority contrary to the Fourteenth Amendment.

None of these cases squarely controls the case we now have before us. But they do illustrate the range of situations in which discriminatory state action has been identified. They do exemplify the necessity for a court to assess the potential impact of official action in determining whether the State has significantly involved itself with invidious discriminations. Here we are dealing with a provision which does not just repeal an existing law forbidding private racial discriminations. Section 26 was intended to authorize, and does authorize, racial discrimination in the housing market. The right to discriminate is now one of the basic policies of the State. The California Supreme Court believes that the section will significantly encourage and involve the State in private discriminations. We have been presented with no persuasive considerations indicating that these judgments should be overturned.

Affirmed.

Mr. Justice DOUGLAS, *concurring.*

Proposition 14 is a form of sophisticated discrimination whereby the people of California harness the energies of private groups to do indirectly what they cannot under our decisions allow their government to do.

Mr. Justice HARLAN, whom Mr. Justice BLACK, Mr. Justice CLARK, and Mr. Justice STEWART join, *dissenting.*

California, acting through the initiative and referendum, has decided to remain "neutral" in the realm of private discrimination affecting the sale or rental of private residential property; in such transactions private owners are now free to act in a discriminatory manner previously forbidden to them. All that has happened is that California has effected a *pro tanto* repeal of its prior statutes forbidding private discrimination. This runs no more afoul of the Fourteenth Amendment than would have California's failure to pass any such antidiscrimination statutes in the first instance. The fact that such repeal was also accompanied by a constitutional prohibition against future enactment of such laws by the California Legislature cannot well be thought to affect the validity of what California has done. The Fourteenth Amendment does not reach such state constitutional action any more than it does a simple legislative repeal of legislation forbidding private discrimination.

～ PROBLEM: CONSTITUTIONAL AMENDMENTS PERMITTING DISCRIMINATION ～

After *Reitman,* would it have been possible for California citizens to pass a constitutional amendment permitting private discrimination? If so, how should the amendment have been phrased?

2. *Judicial Involvement*

May the courts enforce private rights without transforming private discrimination into state action? Or does judicial involvement necessarily implicate state action?

Shelley v. Kreamer

334 U.S. 1 (1948)

Mr. Chief Justice VINSON delivered the opinion of the Court.

These cases present questions relating to the validity of court enforcement of private agreements, generally described as restrictive covenants, which have as their purpose the exclusion of persons of designated race or color.

On February 16, 1911, thirty of thirty-nine property owners signed an agreement, which was subsequently recorded, providing in part: "the said property is hereby restricted to the use and occupancy for the term of Fifty (50) years from this date, so that it shall be a condition whether recited and referred to as (sic) not in subsequent conveyances and shall attach to the land, as a condition precedent to the sale of the same, that no part of said property or any portion thereof shall be occupied by any person not of the Caucasian race, it being intended hereby to restrict the use of said property against the occupancy as owners or tenants of any portion of said property for resident or other purpose by people of the Negro or Mongolian Race." The agreement included fifty-seven parcels of land including the parcel involved in this case. Five of the parcels in the district were owned by Negroes.

On August 11, 1945, pursuant to contract, petitioners Shelley, who are Negroes, for valuable consideration received from one Fitzgerald a warranty deed to the parcel in question. The trial court found that petitioners had no actual knowledge of the restrictive agreement at the time of the purchase. Respondents, as owners of other property subject to the terms of the restrictive covenant, brought suit in state court praying that petitioners Shelley be restrained from taking possession of the property and that judgment be entered divesting title out of petitioners Shelley and reverting title in the immediate grantor or in such other person as the court should direct. The trial court denied the requested relief.

Petitioners argue that judicial enforcement of the restrictive agreements in these cases has violated rights guaranteed to petitioners by the Fourteenth Amendment of the Federal Constitution. Specifically, petitioners urge that they have been denied the equal protection of the laws, deprived of property without due process of law, and have been denied privileges and immunities of citizens of the United States. Not only does the restriction seek to proscribe use and occupancy of the affected properties by members of the excluded class, but the agreement requires that title of any person who uses his property in violation of the restriction shall be divested. The excluded class is defined wholly in terms of race or color.

Here the particular patterns of discrimination are determined by the terms of agreements among private individuals. We conclude that the restrictive agreements standing alone cannot be regarded as a violation of any rights guaranteed to petitioners by the Fourteenth Amendment. So long as the purposes of those agreements are effectuated by voluntary adherence to their terms, it would appear clear that there has been no action by the State and the provisions of the Amendment have not been violated.

But these are cases in which the purposes of the agreements were secured only by judicial enforcement by state courts of the restrictive terms of the agreements. Respondents urge that judicial enforcement of private agreements does not amount to state action; or, in any event, the participation of the State is so attenuated in character as not to amount to state action within the meaning of the Fourteenth Amendment. That the action of state courts and of judicial officers in their official capacities is to be regarded as action of the State within the meaning of the Fourteenth Amendment, is a proposition which has long been established by decisions of this Court. *Ex parte Commonwealth of Virginia*, 1880, 100 U.S. 339. In *Strauder v. West Virginia*, 1880, 100 U.S. 303, this Court declared invalid a state statute restricting jury service to white persons as amounting to a denial of the equal protection of the laws to the colored defendant in that case. The action of state courts in imposing penalties or depriving parties of other substantive rights without providing adequate notice and opportunity to defend, has, of course, long been regarded as a denial of the due process of law guaranteed by the Fourteenth Amendment. *Moore v. Dempsey*, 1923, 261 U.S. 86.

But the examples of state judicial action which have been held by this Court to violate the Amendment's commands are not restricted to situations in which the judicial proceedings were found in some manner to be procedurally unfair. It has been recognized that the action of state courts in enforcing a substantive common-law rule formulated by those courts, may result in the denial of rights guaranteed by the Fourteenth Amendment, even though the judicial proceedings in such cases may have been in accord with procedural due process. In *Cantwell v. Connecticut*, 1940, 310 U.S. 296, a conviction in a state court of the common-law crime of breach of the peace was found to be a violation of the Amendment's commands relating to freedom of religion. From the time of the adoption of the Fourteenth Amendment until the present, it has been the consistent ruling of this Court that the action of the States to which the Amendment has reference, includes action of state courts and state judicial officials.

Against this background of judicial construction, extending over a period of some three-quarters of a century, we are called upon to consider whether enforcement by state courts of the restrictive agreements in these cases may be deemed to be the acts of those States; and, if so, whether that action has denied these petitioners the equal protection of the laws which the Amendment was intended to insure. We have no doubt that there has been state action in these cases in the full and complete sense of the phrase. The undisputed facts disclose that petitioners were willing purchasers of properties upon which they desired to establish homes. The owners of the properties were willing sellers; and contracts of sale were accordingly consummated. It is clear that but for the active intervention of the state courts, supported by the full panoply of state power, petitioners would have been free to occupy the properties in question without restraint.

These are not cases in which the States have merely abstained from action, leaving private individuals free to impose such discriminations as they see fit. Rather, these are cases in which the States have made available to such individuals the full coercive power of government to deny to petitioners, on the grounds of race or color, the enjoyment of property rights in premises which petitioners are willing and financially able to acquire and which the grantors are willing to sell. The difference between judicial enforcement and nonenforcement of the restrictive covenants is the difference to petitioners between being denied rights of property available to other members of the community and being accorded full enjoyment of those rights on an equal footing.

The enforcement of the restrictive agreements by the state courts in these cases was directed pursuant to the common-law policy of the states as formulated by those courts in earlier decisions. In the Missouri case, enforcement of the covenant was directed by the highest court of the State after the trial court had determined the agreement to be invalid for want of the requisite number of signatures. The judicial action in each case bears the clear and unmistakable imprimatur of the State. Previous decisions of this Court have established the proposition that judicial action is not immunized from the operation of the Fourteenth Amendment simply because it is taken pursuant to the state's common-law policy. Nor is the Amendment ineffective simply because the particular pattern of discrimination, which the State has enforced, was defined initially by the terms of a private agreement. State action refers to exertions of state power in all forms. And when the effect of that action is to deny rights subject to the protection of the Fourteenth Amendment, it is the obligation of this Court to enforce the constitutional commands.

We hold that in granting judicial enforcement of the restrictive agreements in these cases, the States have denied petitioners the equal protection of the laws and that, therefore, the action of the state courts cannot stand. The judgment of the Supreme Court of Missouri and the judgment of the Supreme Court of Michigan must be reversed.

Reversed.

Notes and Questions

1. *The Segregated Park.* In *Evans v. Newton*, 382 U.S. 296 (1966), a U.S. Senator devised land in his will to the City of Macon on condition that the land be reserved as a park for Caucasians. The will stated that, while the Senator had only the kindest feeling for Blacks, he believed that the two races should be kept separate. The city kept the park segregated for years, but then began to integrate the park, contending that it was constitutionally impermissible to segregate a public facility. At that point, the trustees of the will sued to remove the city as trustee and to appoint private trustees. The Court concluded that the park could not be segregated whether or not it was in private hands: "Where the tradition of municipal control had become firmly established, we cannot take judicial notice that the mere substitution of trustees instantly transferred this park from the public to the private sector. The predominant character and purpose of this

park are municipal and requires that it be treated as a public institution subject to the command of the Fourteenth Amendment, regardless of who now has title under state law." Justice Harlan, joined by Justice Stewart, dissented: "I do not think that the Fourteenth Amendment permits this Court to frustrate the terms of the will, now that the city is no longer connected with the administration of the park. The Equal Protection Clause reaches only discriminations that are the product of capricious state action; it does not touch discriminations whose origins and effectuation arise solely out of individual predilections, prejudices, and acts."

2. *Reclaiming the Park.* Following the decision in *Newton*, suppose that the Senator's heirs sue to reclaim the park. They claim that, since the Senator's intention to provide a park for whites only cannot be fulfilled, the trust fails and the park reverts by law to the heirs. The petitioners challenge the termination as a violation of equal protection. Does judicial enforcement of the reversion provision constitute discriminatory state action? *See Evans v. Abney*, 396 U.S. 435 (1970).

3. *Damages for Covenant Violations.* Despite *Shelley*'s holding, would it be possible to seek damages for violation of a racially restrictive covenant without there being state action? *See Barrows v. Jackson*, 346 U.S. 249 (1953).

4. *Examining Shelley.* Do you agree with the holding in *Shelley*? Indisputably, the actions of judicial officials in their official capacities constitute governmental action. But, if judicial enforcement of private rights constitutes state action, is it possible to maintain a meaningful distinction between private action and state action? After all, private rights come from the state in the sense that the law (be it constitutional, statutory, or common law) either grants the right or fails to forbid it. Moreover, the essence of a "right" is enforceability in state courts; otherwise, a "right" is not a "right." So, if private individuals have the right to discriminate, should they also have the power to enforce that right in court?

5. Shelley*'s Limits.* How far can *Shelley*'s reasoning be pushed? Suppose that a racist couple issues invitations to a dinner party on a racially discriminatory basis. Someone of a different race, who was not invited to the dinner party, decides to crash it. The racists call the police and seek to press charges against the trespassers. Does judicial enforcement of state trespass laws, which under *Shelley* is viewed as involving state support for the discrimination, transform the private discrimination into state-sanctioned discrimination?

∾ PROBLEM: MORE ON THE TOWN, THE PRIVATE UTILITY, AND THE CLUB ∾

If a citizen of the City of Orange believes that the town's decision to turn one community pool into a private club and close the other pool involved illegal racial discrimination, would the state action doctrine bar the citizen from suing Orange or Power House, Inc.?

Flagg Brothers, Inc. v. Brooks

436 U.S. 149 (1978)

Mr. Justice REHNQUIST delivered the opinion of the Court.

The question presented by this litigation is whether a warehouseman's proposed sale of goods entrusted to him for storage, as permitted by New York Uniform Commercial Code §7-210 (McKinney 1964), is an action properly attributable to the State of New York.

Respondent Shirley Brooks and her family were evicted from their apartment in Mount Vernon, N.Y. The city marshal arranged for Brooks' possessions to be stored by petitioner Flagg Brothers, Inc., in its warehouse. Brooks was informed of the cost of moving and storage, and she instructed the workmen to proceed, although she found the price too high. After a series of disputes over the validity of the charges being claimed, Brooks received a letter demanding that her account be brought up to date within 10 days "or your furniture will be sold." When Brooks was unable to resolve the dispute, she initiated this class action under 42 U.S.C. §1983, seeking damages, an injunction against the threatened sale of her belongings, and the declaration that a sale pursuant to §7-210 would violate the Due Process and Equal Protection Clauses of the Fourteenth Amendment. We granted certiorari to decide the meaning of "state action" as that term is associated with the Fourteenth Amendment.

Some rights established by the Constitution or by federal law are protected from both governmental and private deprivation. Although a private person may cause a deprivation of such a right, he may be subjected to liability under §1983 only when he does so under color of law. Most rights secured by the Constitution are protected only against infringement by governments. Respondents allege that Flagg Brothers has deprived them of their Fourteenth Amendment right to be free from state deprivations of property without due process of law. They must establish not only that Flagg Brothers acted under color of the challenged statute, but also that its actions are properly attributable to the State of New York.

Respondents have named no public officials in this action. The City Marshal, who supervised their evictions, was dismissed from the case by the consent of all the parties. This total absence of overt official involvement plainly distinguishes this case from earlier decisions imposing procedural restrictions on creditors' remedies such as *North Georgia Finishing, Inc. v. Di-Chem, Inc.,* 419 U.S. 601 (1975); *Fuentes v. Shevin,* 407 U.S. 67 (1972); *Sniadach v. Family Finance Corp.,* 395 U.S. 337 (1969). In those cases, the Court was careful to point out that the dictates of the Due Process Clause "attach only to the deprivation of an interest encompassed within the Fourteenth Amendment's protection." The only issue presented by this case is whether Flagg Brothers' action may fairly be attributed to the State of New York. We conclude that it may not.

Respondents' primary contention is that New York has delegated to Flagg Brothers a power "traditionally exclusively reserved to the State." They argue that the resolution of private disputes is a traditional function of civil government, and that the State in §7-210 has delegated this function to Flagg Brothers. Respondents read too much into our previous cases. While many functions have been traditionally performed by governments, very few have been "exclusively reserved to the State."

One such area has been elections. A second line of cases under the public-function doctrine originated with *Marsh v. Alabama*, 326 U.S. 501 (1946) involving company towns. These two branches of the public-function doctrine have in common the feature of exclusivity. Although the elections held by the Democratic Party and its affiliates were the only meaningful elections in Texas, and the streets owned by the Gulf Shipbuilding Corp. were the only streets in Chickasaw, the proposed sale by Flagg Brothers under §7-210 is not the only means of resolving this purely private dispute. Respondent Brooks has never alleged that state law barred her from seeking a waiver of Flagg Brothers' right to sell her goods at the time she authorized their storage. The challenged statute itself provides a damages remedy against the warehouseman for violations of its provisions. This system of rights and remedies, recognizing the traditional place of private arrangements in ordering relationships in the commercial world, can hardly be said to have delegated to Flagg Brothers an exclusive prerogative of the sovereign.

Whatever the particular remedies available under New York law, we do not consider a more detailed description of them necessary to our conclusion that the settlement of disputes between debtors and creditors is not traditionally an exclusive public function. Creditors and debtors have had available to them historically a far wider number of choices than has one who would be an elected public official, or a member of Jehovah's Witnesses who wished to distribute literature in *Marsh*. This entire field of activity is outside the scope of *Terry* and *Marsh*. This is true whether these commercial rights and remedies are created by statute or decisional law.

Respondents further urge that Flagg Brothers' proposed action is properly attributable to the State because the State has authorized and encouraged it in enacting §7-210. This Court has never held that a State's mere acquiescence in a private action converts that action into that of the State. It is quite immaterial that the State has embodied its decision not to act in statutory form. If New York had no commercial statutes at all, its courts would still be faced with the decision whether to prohibit or to permit the sort of sale threatened here the first time an aggrieved bailor came before them for relief. A judicial decision to deny relief would be no less an "authorization" or "encouragement" of that sale than the legislature's decision embodied in this statute. If the mere denial of judicial relief is considered sufficient encouragement to make the State responsible for those private acts, all private deprivations of property would be converted into public acts whenever the State denies relief sought by the putative property owner. The State of New York is in no way responsible for Flagg Brothers' decision, a decision which the State in §7-210 permits but does not compel, to threaten to sell these respondents' belongings.

We conclude that the allegations of these complaints do not establish a violation of these respondents' Fourteenth Amendment rights by either petitioner Flagg Brothers or the State of New York. The District Court properly concluded that their complaints failed to state a claim for relief under 42 U.S.C. §1983. The judgment of the Court of Appeals holding otherwise is
Reversed.

Mr. Justice MARSHALL, *dissenting.*
The Court approaches the question before us as if it can be decided without reference to the role that the State has always played in lien execution by forced sale. In so doing, the Court treats the State as if it were "a monolithic, abstract concept hovering in the legal stratosphere."

Mr. Justice STEVENS, with whom Mr. Justice WHITE and Mr. Justice MARSHALL join, *dissenting.*
Whatever power of sale the warehouseman has derives solely from the State, and specifically from §7-210 of the New York Uniform Commercial Code. The Court reasons that the warehouseman's proposed sale is solely private action because the state statute "permits but does not compel" the sale, and because the warehouseman has not been delegated a power "exclusively reserved to the State." Under this approach a State could enact laws authorizing private citizens to use self-help in countless situations. A state statute could authorize finance companies to enter private homes to repossess merchandise; or could authorize "any person with sufficient physical power," to acquire and sell the property of his weaker neighbor. The Court's rationale would characterize action pursuant to such a statute as purely private action, which the State permits but does not compel, in an area not exclusively reserved to the State.

The distinctions between "permission" and "compulsion" on the one hand, and "exclusive" and "nonexclusive," on the other, cannot be determinative factors in state-action analysis. The State of New York, by enacting §7-210 of the Uniform Commercial Code, has acted in the most effective and unambiguous way a State can act. This section specifically authorizes petitioner Flagg Brothers to sell respondents' possessions; it details the procedures that petitioner must follow; and it grants petitioner the power to convey good title to goods that are now owned by respondents to a third party.

New York has authorized the warehouseman to perform what is clearly a state function. The test of what is a state function is most frequently presented in terms of whether the State has delegated a function traditionally and historically associated with sovereignty. The Court reasons that state action cannot be found because the State has not delegated to the warehouseman an exclusive sovereign function. This distinction, however, is not consistent with our prior decisions on state action and is inconsistent with the line of cases beginning with *Sniadach v. Family Finance Corp.,* 395 U.S. 337.

Since *Sniadach* this Court has scrutinized various state statutes regulating the debtor-creditor relationship for compliance with the Due Process Clause. *See also North Georgia Finishing, Mitchell v. W. T. Grant Co.,* and *Shevin.* The Court today seeks to explain these findings on the ground that there was some element of "overt official involvement." This explanation is baffling. In *North Georgia Finishing,* the official involvement consisted of a court clerk who issued a writ of garnishment based solely on the affidavit of the creditor. The clerk's actions were purely ministerial. *North Georgia Finishing* must be viewed as reflecting the significance of the State's role in defining and controlling the debtor-creditor relationship. In *Shevin* the Court stressed that the statutes in question "abdicated effective state control over state power." Of concern was the private use of state power to achieve a nonconsensual resolution of a commercial dispute. This same point was made in *Mitchell* and *North Georgia Finishing.* Yet the very defect that made the statutes in *Shevin* and *North Georgia Finishing* unconstitutional — lack of state control — is, under today's decision, the factor that precludes constitutional review. If it is unconstitutional for a State to allow a private party to exercise a traditional state power because the state supervision of that power is purely mechanical, the State surely cannot immunize its actions from constitutional scrutiny by removing even the mechanical supervision.

Not only has the State removed nominal supervision, it has authorized a private party to exercise a governmental power that is equally, if not more, significant than the power exercised in *Shevin* or *North Georgia Finishing.* In *Shevin,* the Florida statute allowed the debtor's property to be seized and held pending the outcome of the creditor's action for repossession. In *North Georgia Finishing,* the state statute provided for a garnishment procedure which deprived the debtor of the use of property in the garnishee's hands pending the outcome of litigation. The warehouseman's power under §7-210 is far broader. The warehouseman, unquestionably an interested party, is authorized by law to resolve any disputes over storage charges finally and unilaterally. Whether termed "traditional," "exclusive," or "significant," the state power to order binding, nonconsensual resolution of a conflict between debtor and creditor is exactly the sort of power with which the Due Process Clause is concerned. The State's delegation of that power to a private party is, accordingly, subject to due process scrutiny. This conclusion does not even remotely suggest that "all private deprivations of property will be converted into public acts." The focus is not on the private deprivation but on the state authorization. The State's conduct in this case takes the concrete form of a statutory enactment, and it is that statute that may be challenged.

The overwhelming majority of disputes in our society are resolved in the private sphere. But it is no longer possible, if it ever was, to believe that a sharp line can be drawn between private and public actions. We expect government "to provide a reasonable and fair framework of rules which facilitate commercial transactions." The power to order legally binding surrenders of property and the constitutional restrictions on that power are necessary correlatives in our system. Today's decision allows the State to divorce these two elements by the simple expedient of transferring the implementation of its policy to private parties. I respectfully dissent.

Lugar v. Edmondson Oil Co.

457 U.S. 922 (1982)

Justice WHITE delivered the opinion of the Court.

In 1977, petitioner, a lessee-operator of a truckstop in Virginia, was indebted to his supplier, Edmondson Oil Co., Inc. Edmondson sued on the debt in Virginia state court. Ancillary to that action and pursuant to state law, Edmondson sought prejudgment attachment of certain of petitioner's property. The prejudgment attachment procedure required only that Edmondson allege, in an *ex parte* petition, a belief that petitioner was disposing of or might dispose of his property in order to defeat his creditors. Acting upon that petition, a Clerk of the state court issued a writ of attachment, which was then executed by the County Sheriff. This effectively sequestered petitioner's property, although it was left in his possession. Pursuant to the statute, a hearing on the propriety of the attachment and levy was later conducted. Thirty-four days after the levy, a state trial judge ordered the attachment dismissed because Edmondson had failed to establish the statutory grounds for attachment alleged in the petition.

Petitioner subsequently brought this action under against Edmondson and its president. His complaint alleged that in attaching his property respondents had acted jointly with the State to deprive him of his property without due process of law.

Although the Court of Appeals correctly perceived the importance of *Flagg Brothers* to a proper resolution of this case, it misread that case. It also failed to give sufficient weight to that line of cases, beginning with *Sniadach v. Family Finance Corp.*, 395 U.S. 337 (1969), in which the Court considered constitutional due process requirements in the context of garnishment actions and prejudgment attachments. *See North Georgia Finishing, Inc. v. Di-Chem, Inc.*, 419 U.S. 601 (1975); *Mitchell v. W. T. Grant Co.*, 416 U.S. 600 (1974); *Fuentes v. Shevin*, 407 U.S. 67 (1972). Each of these cases involved a finding of state action as an implicit predicate of the application of due process standards. *Flagg Brothers* distinguished them on the ground that in each there was overt, official involvement in the property deprivation; there was no such overt action by a state officer in *Flagg Brothers*.

As a matter of substantive constitutional law the state-action requirement reflects judicial recognition of the fact that "most rights secured by the Constitution are protected only against infringement by governments." Careful adherence to the "state action" requirement preserves an area of individual freedom by limiting the reach of federal law and federal judicial power. It also avoids imposing on the State, its agencies or officials, responsibility for conduct for which they cannot fairly be blamed. A major consequence is to require the courts to respect the limits of their own power as directed against state governments and private interests. Whether this is good or bad policy, it is a fundamental fact of our political order.

Our cases have accordingly insisted that the conduct allegedly causing the deprivation of a federal right be fairly attributable to the State. These cases reflect a two-part approach to this question of "fair attribution." First, the deprivation must be caused by the exercise of some right or privilege created by the State or by a rule of conduct imposed by the state or by a person for whom the State is responsible. In *Sniadach, Fuentes, W. T. Grant*, and *North Georgia*, for example, a state statute provided the right to garnish or to obtain prejudgment attachment, as well as the procedure by which the rights could be exercised. Second, the party charged with the deprivation must be a person who may fairly be said to be a state actor. This may be because he is a state official, because he has acted together with or has obtained significant aid from state officials, or because his conduct is otherwise chargeable to the State. Without a limit such as this, private parties could face constitutional litigation whenever they seek to rely on some state rule governing their interactions with the community surrounding them.

Turning to this case, the first question is whether the claimed deprivation has resulted from the exercise of a right or privilege having its source in state authority. The second question is whether, under the facts of this case, respondents, who are private parties, may be appropriately characterized as "state actors." While private misuse of a state statute does not describe conduct that can be attributed to the State, the procedural scheme created by the statute obviously is the product of state action. This is subject to constitutional restraints and properly may be addressed in a §1983 action, if the second element of the state-action requirement is met as well. We have consistently held that a private party's joint participation with state officials in the seizure of disputed property is sufficient to characterize that party as a "state actor" for purposes of the Fourteenth Amendment.

The Court of Appeals erred in holding that in this context "joint participation" required something more than invoking the aid of state officials to take advantage of state-created attachment procedures. That holding is contrary to the conclusions we have reached as to the applicability of due process standards to such procedures. Whatever may be true in other contexts, this is sufficient when the State has created a system whereby state officials will attach property on the *ex parte* application of one party to a private dispute.

Chief Justice BURGER, *dissenting.*

Whether we are dealing with suits under §1983 or suits brought pursuant to the Fourteenth Amendment, in my view the inquiry is the same: is the claimed infringement of a federal right fairly attributable to the State. Applying this standard, it cannot be said that the actions of the named respondents are fairly attributable to the State. Respondents did no more than invoke a presumptively valid state prejudgment attachment procedure available to all. Relying on a dubious "but for" analysis, the Court erroneously concludes that the subsequent procedural steps taken by the State in attaching a putative debtor's property in some way transforms respondents' acts into actions of the State. This case is no different from the situation in which a private party commences a lawsuit and secures injunctive relief which, even if temporary, may cause significant injury to the defendant. Invoking a judicial process, of course, implicates the State and its officers but does not transform essentially private conduct into actions of the State.

Notes and Questions

1. *Distinguishing* Lugar *from* Flagg Brothers. Is the primary difference between *Lugar* and *Flagg Brothers* the direct involvement of the sheriff in *Lugar* whereas *Flagg Brothers* involved self-help?

2. *State Workers' Compensation Schemes.* In *American Manufacturers Mutual Insurance Company v. Sullivan*, 526 U.S. 40 (1999), the Court considered whether the decisions of private insurers to defer workers' compensation payments as well as its review process, constituted state action. Prior to the enactment of workers' compensation laws, employees who suffered work-related injuries or occupational disease could recover compensation from their employers only through common-law tort remedies. Recovery was often difficult because employees were forced to prove negligence and damages. In the early twentieth century, most states created compulsory insurance systems that required employers to compensate employees for work-related injuries without regard to fault. Pennsylvania's Workers' Compensation Act (PWCA) created such a system by forcing employers to obtain insurance or to request permission to self-insure. In an attempt to control costs, the PWCA created a "utilization review" procedure under which the reasonableness and necessity of an employee's past, ongoing, or prospective medical treatment could be reviewed before a medical bill must be paid. If an insurer "disputes the reasonableness or necessity of the treatment provided," it may request a utilization review and withhold the payment. A "utilization review organization" (URO), a private organization consisting of health care providers who are "licensed in the same profession and having the same or similar specialty," then reviews the care and decides whether treatment was reasonable or necessary.

Do the decisions of private insurers to defer payment, and the URO review process, constitute state action? Consider the following arguments: 1) action taken by private entities with the mere approval or acquiescence of the state is not state action; 2) the state authorizes, but does not require, insurers to withhold payments for disputed medical treatment; 3) while the decision of a URO, like that of any judicial official, may properly be considered state action, a private party's mere use of the state's dispute resolution machinery, without the "overt, significant assistance of state officials," cannot; 4) the state has delegated to insurers the traditionally exclusive governmental function of deciding whether to suspend payment for disputed medical treatment; 5) the PWCA "inextricably entangles the insurance companies in a partnership with the Commonwealth such that they become an integral part of the state in administering the statutory scheme"; 6) the relevant state actors, rather than the particular parties to the payment disputes, are the state-appointed decision makers who implement the exclusive procedure that the state has created to protect respondents' rights. The court concluded that an insurer's decision to withhold payment and seek utilization review of the reasonableness and necessity of particular medical treatment was not fairly attributable to the state.

3. *The Welfare Agency and the Abused Boy.* A boy who was being beaten by his father was removed from the home by state-employed social workers but was later returned to the father's care. Subsequently, the boy was beaten again by his father and suffered permanent injuries, including retardation. The petitioner sued the social workers and other local officials, claiming that their failure to remove the boy from a dangerous situation deprived him of his liberty in violation of the Due Process Clause of the Fourteenth Amendment to the U.S. Constitution. Was there sufficient state action to hold the government accountable for the injuries caused by the father? In *DeShaney v. Winnebago County*, 489 U.S. 189 (1989), the Court found no state action, holding that "nothing in the language of the Due Process Clause itself requires the State to protect the life, liberty, and property of its citizens against invasion by private actors."

4. *Disguised Merits Decisions.* Doctrines like standing and ripeness (and other justiciability doctrines) have frequently been regarded as "disguised decisions on the merits." In other words, if the Court is disinclined to rule in favor of the plaintiff on the merits, the Court rejects the case on threshold grounds (e.g., standing or ripeness). Does the state action doctrine serve that same function?

Edmonson v. Leesville Concrete Company, Inc.

500 U.S. 614 (1991)

Justice KENNEDY delivered the opinion of the Court.

Thaddeus Edmonson, a construction worker, was injured and sued Leesville Concrete Company for negligence. During *voir dire*, Leesville used two peremptory challenges to remove black persons from the prospective jury. Relying on *Batson v. Kentucky*, 476 U.S. 79 (1986), Edmonson, who is black, requested that the court require Leesville to articulate a race-neutral explanation for striking the jurors. The trial court denied the request on the ground that *Batson* does not apply in civil proceedings. A divided court of appeals affirmed. We granted certiorari and now reverse.

In *Powers v. Ohio*, 499 U.S. 400 (1991), we held that a criminal defendant, regardless of his or her race, may object to a prosecutor's race-based exclusion of persons from the petit jury. Discrimination on the basis of race in selecting a jury in a civil proceeding harms the excluded juror no less than discrimination in a criminal trial. In either case, race is the sole reason for denying the excluded venireperson the privilege of participating in our system of justice.

The Constitution's protections of individual liberty and equal protection apply in general only to action by the government. Racial discrimination, though invidious, violates the Constitution only when it may be attributed to state action. Thus, the legality of the exclusion here turns on the extent to which a litigant in a civil case may be subject to the Constitution's restrictions. In prior cases, we asked first whether the claimed constitutional deprivation resulted from the exercise of a right or privilege having its source in state authority, and second, whether the private party charged with the deprivation could be described in all fairness as a state actor. The first part of the test is satisfied here. By their very nature, peremptory challenges have no significance outside a court of law. Their sole purpose is to permit litigants to assist the government in the selection of an impartial trier of fact. There is no constitutional obligation to allow peremptory challenges which are permitted when the government, by statute or decisional law, decides to allow parties to exclude a given number of persons who otherwise would satisfy the requirements for jury service. In the case before us, the challenges were exercised under a federal statute. Without this authorization, granted by an Act of Congress, Leesville would not have been able to engage in the alleged discriminatory acts.

The second part of the test focuses on whether a private litigant in all fairness must be deemed a government actor in the use of peremptory challenges. In determining whether a particular action is governmental in character, it is relevant to examine the extent to which the actor relies on governmental assistance and benefits, whether the actor is performing a traditional governmental function, and whether the injury caused is aggravated in a unique way by the incidents of governmental authority. Based on these principles, we hold that the exercise of peremptory challenges involves state action.

Our cases have found state action when private parties make extensive use of state procedures with "the overt, significant assistance of state officials." Without such participation, the peremptory challenge system could not exist. In the federal system, Congress has established the qualifications for jury service, and has outlined the procedures by which jurors are selected including policies of random juror selection from a fair cross section of the community, and non-exclusion on account of race, color, religion, sex, national origin, or economic status. Statutes prescribe many of the details of the jury plan, defining the jury wheel, voter lists, and jury commissions. A statute also authorizes procedures for assignment to grand and petit juries, and for lawful excuse from jury service.

At the outset of the selection process, prospective jurors must complete jury qualification forms. Counsel rely on these forms when exercising their peremptory strikes. The clerk of the court, a federal official, summons potential jurors who are required to travel to a United States courthouse, where they must report at the direction of the court and its officers. Summoned jurors receive a per diem for their service. The trial judge exercises substantial control over *voir dire* in the federal system. The judge determines the range of information that may be discovered about a prospective juror. Judges may even conduct the *voir dire* themselves and they oversee the exclusion of jurors for cause. In cases involving multiple parties, the trial judge decides how peremptory challenges shall be allocated.

When a lawyer exercises a peremptory challenge, the judge advises the juror he or she has been excused.

A private party could not exercise its peremptory challenges absent the overt, significant assistance of the court. The government summons jurors, constrains their freedom of movement, and subjects them to public scrutiny and examination. The party who exercises a challenge invokes the formal authority of the court, which must discharge the prospective juror, thus effecting the "final and practical denial" of the excluded individual's opportunity to serve on the petit jury. Without the direct and indispensable participation of the judge, who beyond all question is a state actor, the peremptory challenge system would serve no purpose. By enforcing a discriminatory peremptory challenge, the court "has not only made itself a party to the biased act, but has elected to place its power, property and prestige behind the alleged discrimination." In so doing, the government has "created the legal framework governing the challenged conduct," and in a significant way has involved itself with invidious discrimination.

A traditional function of government is evident here. The jury exercises the power of the court and of the government. The jury performs the critical governmental functions of guarding the rights of litigants and "ensuring continued acceptance of the laws by all of the people." In the federal system, the Constitution commits the trial of facts in a civil cause to the jury which becomes the principal factfinder, charged with weighing the evidence, judging the credibility of witnesses, and reaching a verdict. The jury's factual determinations as a general rule are final. In all jurisdictions a true verdict will be incorporated in a judgment enforceable by the court. These are traditional functions of government, not of a select, private group beyond the reach of the Constitution.

If a government confers on a private body the power to choose the government's employees or officials, the private body will be bound by the constitutional mandate of race neutrality. *Terry v. Adams*, 345 U.S. 461 (1953). This applies with even greater force in the context of jury selection through the use of peremptory challenges. The fact that the government delegates some portion of this power to private litigants does not change the governmental character of the power exercised. The delegation of authority occurs here through explicit statutory authorization. The selection of jurors represents a unique governmental function delegated to private litigants by the government and attributable to the government for purposes of invoking constitutional protections against discrimination.

In most civil cases, the initial decision whether to sue at all, the selection of counsel, and any number of ensuing tactical choices in the course of discovery and trial may be without the requisite governmental character to be deemed state action. That cannot be said of the exercise of peremptory challenges, however; when private litigants participate in the selection of jurors, they serve an important function within the government and act with its substantial assistance. If peremptory challenges based on race were permitted, persons could be required by summons to be put at risk of open and public discrimination as a condition of their participation in the justice system. The injury to excluded jurors would be the direct result of governmental delegation and participation. The injury caused by the discrimination is made more severe because the government permits it to occur within the courthouse itself. Within the courtroom, the government invokes its laws to determine the rights of those who stand before it. Race discrimination within the courtroom raises serious questions as to the fairness of the proceedings conducted there. Racial bias mars the integrity of the judicial system and prevents the idea of democratic government from becoming a reality. To permit racial exclusion in this official forum compounds the racial insult inherent in judging a citizen by the color of his or her skin.

The judgment is reversed, and the case is remanded for further proceedings consistent with our opinion.

It is so ordered.

Justice O'CONNOR, with whom THE CHIEF JUSTICE and Justice SCALIA join, *dissenting.*

A civil trial is by design largely a stage on which private parties may act; it is a forum through which they can resolve their disputes in a peaceful and ordered manner. The government erects the platform; it does not thereby become responsible for all that occurs upon it. As much as we would like to eliminate from the courtroom the specter of racial discrimination, the Constitution does not sweep that broadly.

The peremptory challenge allows *private* parties, to exclude potential jurors and is left wholly within the discretion of the litigant. The peremptory is, by design, an enclave of private action in a government-managed proceeding. This evidence is irrelevant. The bulk of the practices the Court describes—the establishment of qualifications for jury service, the location and summoning of prospective jurors, the jury wheel, the voter lists, the jury qualification forms, the per diem for jury service—are independent of the statutory entitlement to peremptory strikes. The Government would do these things even if there were no peremptory challenges. The judge does not "encourage" the use of a peremptory challenge at all. The decision to strike a juror is entirely up to the litigant, and the reasons for doing so are of no consequence to the judge. The judge does little more than acquiesce in this decision by excusing the juror. The action here is a far cry from *Shelley v. Kraemer,* 334 U.S. 1 (1948). The state courts in *Shelley* used coercive force to impose conformance on parties who did not wish to discriminate. "Enforcement" of peremptory challenges does not compel anyone to discriminate; the discrimination is wholly a matter of private choice. Judicial acquiescence does not convert private choice into that of the State.

In *Polk County v. Dodson,* 454 U.S. 312 (1981), we held that a public defender does not act under color of state law when representing a defendant in a criminal trial. Government employment is not sufficient to create state action. Attorneys for private litigants do not act on behalf of the government, or even the public as a whole; attorneys represent their clients. A peremptory strike is a traditional adversarial act; parties use these strikes to further their own perceived interests, not as an aid to the government's process of jury selection. The government does not encourage or approve these strikes, or direct that they be used in any particular way, or even that they be used at all. The government is simply not "responsible" for the use of peremptory strikes by private litigants. Racism is a terrible thing, particularly in a courtroom. But the Fifth Amendment's Due Process Clause prohibits only actions for which the Government can be held responsible. The Government is not responsible for a peremptory challenge by a private litigant.

Justice SCALIA, *dissenting.*

The Court's newly discovered constitutional rule will not necessarily help minority litigants obtain racially diverse juries. A minority defendant can no longer seek to prevent an all-white jury, or to seat as many jurors of his own race as possible. Peremptory challenges are sometimes used to *assure* rather than to *prevent* a racially diverse jury.

Note and Question: Physician Contracted to Provide Care for Prison Inmates

A private physician contracts with a state prison to provide medical care for inmates. The physician is not on the state payroll, but is paid on a contract basis. However, inmates are allowed to use only this physician. Does the doctor's care constitute "state action" if he exhibits "deliberate indifference" to the medical needs of inmates? In *West v. Atkins,* 487 U.S. 42 (1988), the court held that "the dispositive issue concerns the relationship among the State, the physician, and the prisoner. Contracting out prison medical care does not relieve the State of its constitutional duty to provide adequate medical treatment to those in its custody, and it does not deprive the State's prisoners of the means to vindicate their Eighth Amendment rights. The State bore an affirmative obligation to provide adequate medical care to West; the State delegated that function to respondent Atkins; and respondent voluntarily assumed that obligation by contract. Doctor Atkins must be considered to be a state actor."

3. Government Funding

Blum v. Yaretsky

457 U.S. 991 (1982)

Justice REHNQUIST delivered the opinion of the Court.

Respondents represent a class of Medicaid patients challenging decisions by the nursing homes in which they reside to discharge or transfer patients without notice or an opportunity for a hearing. The question is whether the State may be held responsible for those decisions so as to subject them to the strictures of the Fourteenth Amendment. Congress established the Medicaid program in 1965 as

Title XIX of the Social Security Act, 42 U.S.C. §1396, to provide federal financial assistance to states that choose to reimburse certain medical costs incurred by the poor. As a participating state, New York provides Medicaid assistance to eligible persons who receive care in private nursing homes, which are designated as either "skilled nursing facilities" (SNF's) or "health related facilities" (HRF's). The latter provide less extensive, and generally less expensive, medical care than the former. Nursing homes chosen by Medicaid patients are directly reimbursed by the State for the reasonable cost of health care services.

An individual must meet two conditions to obtain Medicaid assistance. He must satisfy eligibility standards defined in terms of income or resources and he must seek medically necessary services. To assure that the latter condition is satisfied, federal regulations require each nursing home to establish a utilization review committee (URC) of physicians whose functions include periodically assessing whether each patient is receiving the appropriate level of care, and thus whether the patient's continued stay in the facility is justified. If the URC determines that the patient should be discharged or transferred to a different level of care, either more or less intensive, it must notify the state agency responsible for administering Medicaid assistance.

Respondents were Medicaid patients in the American Nursing Home, an SNF located in New York City. The nursing home's URC decided that respondents did not need the care they were receiving and should be transferred to a lower level of care in an HRF. New York City officials, responsible for administering the Medicaid program, were notified of this decision and prepared to reduce or terminate payments to the nursing home for respondents' care. Following administrative hearings, state social service officials affirmed the decision. Respondents then commenced this suit, individually and as a class, alleging that the defendants had not afforded them adequate notice either of URC decisions and the reasons supporting them or of their right to an administrative hearing to challenge those decisions. Respondents alleged a violation of the Due Process Clause of the Fourteenth Amendment and sought injunctive relief and damages. The District Court issued various orders and court of appeals affirmed. We granted certiorari to consider the Court of Appeals' conclusions about the nature of state action.

Respondents are not challenging particular state regulations or procedures, and their arguments concede that the decision to discharge or transfer a patient originates not with state officials, but with nursing homes that are privately owned and operated. Their lawsuit, therefore, seeks to hold state officials liable for the actions of private parties, and the injunctive relief they have obtained requires the State to adopt regulations that will prohibit the private conduct of which they complain.

This case is obviously different from those cases in which the defendant is a private party and the question is whether his conduct has sufficiently received the imprimatur of the State so as to make it "state" action for purposes of the Fourteenth Amendment. It also differs from other "state action" cases in which the challenged conduct consists of enforcement of state laws or regulations by state officials who are themselves parties in the lawsuit; in such cases the question typically is whether the private motives which triggered the enforcement of those laws can fairly be attributed to the State.

"The mere fact that a business is subject to state regulation does not by itself convert its action into that of the State for purposes of the Fourteenth Amendment." *Jackson v. Metropolitan Edison Co.*, 419 U.S., at 350. The complaining party must also show that "there is a sufficiently close nexus between the State and the challenged action of the regulated entity so that the action of the latter may be fairly treated as that of the State itself." The purpose of this requirement is to assure that constitutional standards are invoked only when it can be said that the State is *responsible* for the specific conduct of which the plaintiff complains. A State normally can be held responsible for a private decision only when it has exercised coercive power or has provided such significant encouragement, either overt or covert, that the choice must in law be deemed to be that of the State. Mere approval of or acquiescence in the initiatives of a private party is not sufficient to justify holding the State responsible for those initiatives under the terms of the Fourteenth Amendment. The required nexus may be present if the private entity has exercised powers that are "traditionally the exclusive prerogative of the State."

The finding of state action cannot stand. The court reasoned that state action was present in the discharge or transfer decisions because the State responded to those decisions by adjusting the patient's Medicaid benefits. Respondents, however, do not challenge the adjustment of benefits, but the discharge or transfer of patients to lower levels of care without adequate notice or hearings. That the State responds to such actions by adjusting benefits does not render it *responsible* for those actions. The decisions are made by physicians and nursing home administrators, all of whom are concededly private parties. There is no suggestion that those decisions were influenced in any degree by the State's obligation to adjust benefits in conformity with changes in the cost of medically necessary care.

Respondents argue that the State "affirmatively commands" the summary discharge or transfer of Medicaid patients who are thought to be inappropriately placed in their nursing facilities. The regulations require SNF's and HRF's "to make all efforts possible to transfer patients to the appropriate level of care or home as indicated by the patient's medical condition or needs." The nursing homes are required to complete patient care assessment forms designed by the State and "provide the receiving facility or provider with a current copy of same at the time of discharge to an alternate level of care facility or home." The regulations do not require the nursing homes to rely on the forms in making discharge or transfer decisions, nor do they demonstrate that the State is responsible for the decision to discharge or transfer particular patients. Those decisions ultimately turn on medical judgments made by private parties according to professional standards that are not established by the State.

Respondents point to regulations which, they say, impose a range of penalties on nursing homes that fail to discharge or transfer patients whose continued stay is inappropriate. Those regulations themselves do not dictate the decision to discharge or transfer in a particular case. Consequently, penalties imposed for violating the regulations add nothing to respondents' claim of state action.

Respondents argue that even if the State does not command the transfers at issue, it reviews and either approves or rejects them on the merits. Nothing in the regulations authorizes the officials to approve or disapprove decisions either to retain or discharge particular patients, and petitioners specifically disclaim any such responsibility.

Finally, respondents argue that such a relationship exists between the State and the nursing homes it regulates that the State may be considered a joint participant in the homes' discharge and transfer of Medicaid patients. Respondents argue that state subsidization of the operating and capital costs of the facilities, payment of the medical expenses of more than 90% of the patients in the facilities, and the licensing of the facilities by the State, taken together convert the action of the homes into "state" action. We are unable to agree. Privately owned enterprises providing services that the State would not necessarily provide, even though they are extensively regulated, do not fall within the ambit of *Burton*. That programs undertaken by the State result in substantial funding of the activities of a private entity is no more persuasive than the fact of regulation of such an entity in demonstrating that the State is responsible for decisions made by the entity in the course of its business.

We are also unable to conclude that the nursing homes perform a function that has been "traditionally the exclusive prerogative of the State." Respondents argue that both the Medicaid statute and the New York Constitution make the State responsible for providing every Medicaid patient with nursing home services. Even if respondents' characterization of the State's duties were correct, it would not follow that decisions made in the day-to-day administration of a nursing home are the kind of decisions traditionally and exclusively made by the sovereign for and on behalf of the public.

We conclude that respondents have failed to establish "state action" in the nursing homes' decisions to discharge or transfer Medicaid patients to lower levels of care. The contrary judgment of the Court of Appeals is accordingly

Reversed.

Justice BRENNAN, with whom Justice MARSHALL joins, *dissenting.*

The level-of-care decisions, even when characterized as the "independent" decision of the nursing home, have far less to do with the exercise of independent professional judgment than they do with the *State's* desire to save money. To be sure, standards for implementing the level-of-care scheme established by the Medicaid program are framed with reference to the underlying purpose of that program—to provide needed medical services. Not surprisingly, the State relies on doctors to implement this aspect of its Medicaid program. But the two levels of long-term institutionalized care enshrined in the Medicaid scheme are legislative constructs, designed to serve governmental cost-containment policies. The vigor with which these reviews are performed in the nursing home context is extraordinarily *un* medical in character. From a purely medical standpoint, the idea of shifting nursing home residents from a "higher level of care" to a "lower level of care," which almost invariably involves transfer from one facility to another, rarely makes sense. The proportion of SNF and ICF beds varied enormously from State to State. The answer to this disparity lies not in medical considerations or judgments, but rather in the varying fiscal policies, and the vigor of enforcement, in the participating States.

The State established the system of treatment levels and utilization review in order to further its own fiscal goals, but the state (and Federal Government) have created, and administer, the level system as a cost-saving tool of the Medicaid program. The impetus for this active program of review imposed upon the nursing home operator is primarily this fiscal concern. The State has set forth precisely the standards upon which the level-of-care determinations are to be made, and has delegated administration of the program to the nursing home operators, rather than assume the burden of administering the program itself. "These requirements make the State responsible for actual decisions to discharge or transfer particular patients." Where a private party acts on behalf of the State to implement state policy, his action is state action.

The private nursing homes of the Nation exist, and profit, at the sufferance of state and federal Medicaid and Medicare agencies. The State subsidizes practically all of the operating and capital costs of the facility, and pays the medical expenses of more than 90% of its residents. And, in setting reimbursement rates, the State generally affords the nursing homes a profit as well. The residents of those homes are utterly dependent on the State for their support and their placement. For many, the totality of their social network is the nursing home community. Within that environment, the nursing home operator is the immediate authority, the provider of food, clothing, shelter, and health care, and, in every significant respect, the functional equivalent of a State. We must be especially alert to those situations in which the State "has elected to place its power, property and prestige behind" the actions of the nursing home owner.

The State has not simply left nursing home patients to the care of nursing home operators. Nursing homes are "pervasively regulated" by State and Federal Governments; virtually every action by the operator is subject to state oversight. We are confronted with the question *preliminary* to any Fourteenth Amendment challenge: whether the State has brought its force to bear against the plaintiffs through the office of private parties. When the State chooses to perform governmental undertakings through private institutions, and with the aid of private parties, not every action of those private parties is state action. When the State directs, supports, and encourages those private parties to take specific action, that is state action.

∾ PROBLEM: SOLDIER FIELD ∾

The Chicago Bears Football Club plays its home games at Soldier Field in Chicago. Soldier Field is publicly funded, and its operating agreement provides that the Chicago Park District has the authority to approve any special events held there. Beckman, a season ticket holder to Bears football games, is a Green Bay Packers fan. When the Bears decided to hold a pre-season event at Soldier Field, they announce that no one will be allowed into the stadium wearing the gear of opposing teams. As a result, Beckman is denied entry into the event. Was there sufficient state action so that Beckman can claim that the denial implicated his free speech rights? *See Beckman v. Chicago Bears Football Club*, 2018 WL 1561719 (N.D. Ill. 2018).

4. *Quasi-Governmental Corporations*

Should the actions of a quasi-governmental corporation be regarded as the actions of the government (e.g., state action) or the actions of a private corporation? Consider the following case.

Lebron v. National Railroad Passenger Corporation

513 U.S. 374 (1995)

Justice SCALIA delivered the opinion of the Court.

In this case we consider whether actions of the National Railroad Passenger Corporation, commonly known as Amtrak, are subject to the constraints of the Constitution.

Petitioner, Michael A. Lebron, creates billboard displays that involve commentary on public issues. In 1991, he contacted Transportation Displays, Incorporated (TDI), which manages the leasing of the billboards in Amtrak's Pennsylvania Station in New York City, seeking to display an advertisement on a billboard of colossal proportions, known to New Yorkers as "the Spectacular." The Spectacular is a curved, illuminated billboard, approximately 103 feet long and 10 feet high, which dominates the main entrance to Penn Station's waiting room and ticket area.

Lebron signed a contract with TDI to display an advertisement on the Spectacular for two months beginning in January 1993. The contract provided that "all advertising copy is subject to approval of TDI and Amtrak as to character, text, illustration, design and operation." Lebron declined to disclose the specific content of his advertisement throughout his negotiations with TDI, although he did explain to TDI that it was generally political. He submitted to TDI (and TDI later forwarded to Amtrak) the following advertisement: "The work is a photomontage, accompanied by text. Taking off on a widely circulated Coors beer advertisement which proclaims Coors to be the 'Right Beer,' Lebron's piece is captioned 'Is it the Right's Beer Now?' It includes photographic images of convivial drinkers of Coors beer, juxtaposed with a Nicaraguan village scene in which peasants are menaced by a can of Coors that hurtles towards them, leaving behind a trail of fire, as if it were a missile. The text, appearing on either end of the montage, criticizes the Coors family for its support of right-wing causes, particularly the contras in Nicaragua. Again taking off on Coors' advertising which uses the slogan of 'Silver Bullet' for its beer cans, the text proclaims that Coors is 'The Silver Bullet that aims The Far Right's political agenda at the heart of America.' " Amtrak's vice president disapproved the advertisement, invoking Amtrak's policy, inherited from its predecessor as landlord of Penn Station, the Pennsylvania Railroad Company, "that it will not allow political advertising on the Spectacular advertising sign." Lebron then filed suit against Amtrak and TDI, claiming, *inter alia,* that the refusal to place his advertisement on the Spectacular had violated his First and Fifth Amendment rights.

Actions of private entities can sometimes be regarded as governmental action for constitutional purposes. Congress established Amtrak in order to avert the threatened extinction of passenger trains in the United States. The statute that created it begins with the congressional finding that "the public convenience and necessity require the continuance and improvement" of railroad passenger service. Rail Passenger Service Act of 1970 (RPSA). Amtrak is incorporated under the District of Columbia Business Corporation Act, but is subject to the provisions of that Act only insofar as the RPSA does not provide to the contrary. It does provide to the contrary with respect to many matters of structure and power, including the manner of selecting the company's board of directors. The RPSA provides for a board of nine members, six of whom are appointed directly by the President of the United States. The Secretary of Transportation, or his designee, sits *ex officio.* The President appoints three more directors with the advice and consent of the Senate, selecting one from a list of individuals recommended by the Railway Labor Executives Association, one "from among the Governors of States with an interest in rail transportation," and one as a "representative of business with an interest in rail transportation." The President appoints two additional directors without the involvement of the Senate, choosing them from a list of names submitted by various commuter rail authorities. The holders of Amtrak's preferred stock select two more directors. Since the United States presently holds all of Amtrak's preferred stock, which it received in exchange for its subsidization of Amtrak's perennial losses, the Secretary of Transportation selects these two directors. The ninth member of the board is Amtrak's president, who serves as the chairman of the board, is selected by the other eight directors, and serves at their pleasure. Amtrak's four private shareholders have not been entitled to vote in selecting the board of directors since 1981. Amtrak is required to submit three different annual reports to the President and Congress. One of these, a "report on the effectiveness of this chapter in meeting the requirements for a balanced national transportation system, together with any legislative recommendations," is made part of the Department of Transportation's annual report to Congress.

Amtrak claims that, whatever its relationship with the Federal Government, its charter's disclaimer of agency status prevents it from being considered a Government entity. Section 541 is assuredly dispositive of Amtrak's status as a Government entity for purposes of matters within Congress' control—for example, whether it is subject to statutes that impose obligations or confer powers upon Government entities, such as the Administrative Procedure Act, the Federal Advisory Committee Act, and the laws governing Government procurement. Even beyond that, the statutory disavowal of Amtrak's agency status deprives Amtrak of sovereign immunity from suit, and of the ordinarily presumed power of Government agencies authorized to incur obligations to pledge the credit of the United States. But it is not for Congress to make the final determination of Amtrak's status as a government entity for purposes of determining the constitutional rights of citizens affected by its actions. We conclude that it is an agency or instrumentality of the United States for the purpose of individual rights guaranteed against the Government by the Constitution.

This conclusion seems to us in accord with public and judicial understanding of the nature of Government-created and -controlled corporations over the years. A remarkable feature of the heyday of those corporations, in the 1930's and 1940's, was that, even while they were praised for their status "as agencies separate and distinct, administratively and financially and legally, from the government itself, which has facilitated their adoption of commercial methods of accounting and financing, avoidance of political controls, and utilization of regular procedures of business management," it was fully acknowledged that they were a "device" of "government," and constituted "federal corporate agencies" apart from "regular government departments." This Court has shared that view. For example, in *Reconstruction Finance Corp. v. J.G. Menihan Corp.*, 312 U.S. 81 (1941), Chief Justice Hughes, writing for the Court, described the RFC, whose organic statute did not state it to be a Government instrumentality, as, nonetheless, "a corporate agency of the government," and said that "it acts as a governmental agency in performing its functions." Even Congress itself appeared to acknowledge that Government-created and -controlled corporations were part of the Government. From the 1930's onward, many of the statutes creating Government-controlled corporations said explicitly that they were agencies or instrumentalities of the United States. That Government-created and -controlled corporations are (for many purposes at least) part of the Government itself has a strong basis, not merely in past practice and understanding, but in reason itself. It surely cannot be that government, state or federal, is able to evade the most solemn obligations imposed in the Constitution by simply resorting to the corporate form. On that thesis, *Plessy v. Ferguson*, 163 U.S. 537 (1896), can be resurrected by the simple device of having the State of Louisiana operate segregated trains through a state-owned Amtrak.

Amtrak was created by a special statute, explicitly for the furtherance of federal governmental goals. Six of the corporation's eight externally named directors (the ninth is named by a majority of the board itself) are appointed directly by the President of the United States—four of them (including the Secretary of Transportation) with the advice and consent of the Senate. Although the statute restricts most of the President's choices to persons suggested by certain organizations or persons having certain qualifications, those restrictions have been tailor-made by Congress for this entity alone. They do not in our view establish an absence of control by the Government as a whole, but rather constitute a restriction imposed by one of the political branches upon the other. Moreover, Amtrak is not merely in the temporary control of the Government (as a private corporation whose stock comes into federal ownership might be); it is established and organized under federal law for the very purpose of pursuing federal governmental objectives, under the direction and control of federal governmental appointees. It is in that respect no different from the so-called independent regulatory agencies such as the Federal Communications Commission or the Securities Exchange Commission, which are run by Presidential appointees with fixed terms. It is true that the directors of Amtrak, unlike commissioners of independent regulatory agencies, are not, by the explicit terms of the statute, removable by the President for cause, and are not impeachable by Congress. But any reduction in the immediacy of accountability for Amtrak directors vis-a-vis regulatory commissioners seems to us of minor consequence for present purposes — especially since, by the very terms of the chartering Act, Congress's "right to repeal, alter, or amend this chapter at any time is expressly reserved."

Where, as here, the Government creates a corporation by special law, for the furtherance of governmental objectives, and retains for itself permanent authority to appoint a majority of the directors of that corporation, the corporation is part of the Government for purposes of the First Amendment. We express no opinion as to whether Amtrak's refusal to display Lebron's advertisement violated that Amendment. The judgment of the Court of Appeals is reversed, and the case is remanded for further proceedings consistent with this opinion.

It is so ordered.

Justice O'CONNOR, *dissenting.*

I see no basis to impute to the Government Amtrak's decision to disapprove Lebron's advertisement. Although a number of factors indicate the Government's pervasive influence in Amtrak's management and operation, none suggest that the Government had any effect on Amtrak's decision to turn down Lebron's proposal. The advertising policy that allegedly violates the First Amendment originated with a predecessor to Amtrak, the wholly private Pennsylvania Railroad Company. Amtrak simply continued this policy after it took over. The specific decision to disapprove Lebron's advertising was made by Amtrak's Vice President of Real Estate and Operations Development, who, as a corporate officer, was neither appointed by the President nor directed by the President-appointed board to disapprove Lebron's proposal. The particular lease which permitted Amtrak to disallow Lebron's billboard was neither reviewed nor approved directly by the board. In short, nothing in this case suggests that the Government controlled, coerced, or even influenced Amtrak's decision, made pursuant to corporate policy and private business judgment, to disapprove the advertisement proposed by Lebron. The Court of Appeals properly did not impute Amtrak's decision to the Government.

Notes and Questions

1. *U.S. Olympic Committee.* Should the U.S. Olympic Committee (USOC), another quasi-governmental corporation, be regarded as a "state actor" when it engages in discrimination on the basis of sexual orientation? The facts reveal that Congress has authorized the USOC to assume responsibility for coordinating amateur athletics (something not previously coordinated by the government), granted the USOC a corporate charter, and provided for some USOC funding through exclusive use of the Olympic words and symbols, and through direct grants. However, the USOC functions independently of the government, which played no role in the decision to discriminate (other than acquiescence). In evaluating the USOC's status, should it matter that the USOC is the nation's "exclusive representative to the International Olympic Committee (IOC)," that membership in the IOC is "structured according to nations," that athletes are viewed as representing their nations (e.g., athletes never say that they want to win "for the USOC" but instead say that they want to win "for the United States"), or that "Olympic participation is inescapably nationalist"? Also, should it matter that the Olympic pageant is nation focused, with athletes wearing national costumes, the raising of national flags and the playing of national anthems at the medal ceremony, and an official tally of medals won by each national team reinforcing the national significance of Olympic participation? Is the USOC acting "privately," or is it more like the company town in *Marsh*? Or is it more like the NCAA in *NCAA v. Tarkanian*?

In *San Francisco Arts & Athletics, Inc. v. United States Olympic Committee*, 483 U.S. 522 (1987), the Court found that the USOC was not a state actor. The Court stated that government "normally can be held responsible for a private decision only when it has exercised coercive power or has provided such significant encouragement, either overt or covert, that the choice must in law be deemed to be that of the government." The Court reasoned that the "USOC's choice of how to enforce its exclusive right to use the word 'Olympic' simply is not a governmental decision. There is no evidence that the Federal Government coerced or encouraged the USOC in the exercise of its right. At most, the Federal Government, by failing to supervise the USOC's use of its rights, can be said to exercise 'mere approval of or acquiescence in the initiatives' of the USOC. This is not enough to make the USOC's actions those of the Government."

2. *Reconsidering Prior Decisions After* Brentwood. Would the Court's "entwinement" test in *Brentwood* require a different result in previously decided cases? Consider the following cases: a) *Moose Lodge v. Irvis*, in which the state granted a liquor license to a racially exclusive club. The evidence revealed that only a limited number of licenses were available, and the allotment had been exhausted. Moose Lodge conceded that it would be extremely difficult for a club to survive without a liquor license. b) *Jackson*, in which a utility service terminated service to a delinquent customer. c) *Rendall-Kohn*, in which a teacher was fired from a private school. The overwhelming majority of the school's students were referred

to the school, and their tuition was paid for, by the government. In addition, the teacher was hired using government funds. d) *Blum v. Yaretsky*, in which a nursing home patient was reclassified and reassigned to a different facility.

3. *Restructuring Amtrak?* Could the government have structured Amtrak in such a way as to prevent its actions from being labeled as "state action"? If so, how?

∾ PROBLEM: MORE ON THE TOWN, THE PRIVATE UTILITY, AND THE CLUB ∾

Based on your reading of *Blum* and *Lebron,* if Orange initiated the creation of Power House and holds a 50% interest in the company, is Power House now a state actor? What if Orange appoints a percentage of the board of directors?

[Points to Remember for Chapter 6 is contained in online file.]

7

Procedural Due Process

[Roadmap for Chapter 7 is contained in online file.]

∽ PROBLEM: THE PROFESSOR AND THE AMSTERDAM TRIP ∽

A sociology professor routinely teaches a course about public mores and social attitudes toward sex. As part of the course, he takes a group of students to Amsterdam, in the Netherlands, so that they can view the red-light district and observe the free use of marijuana. While in Amsterdam, the professor holds discussions with his students about what they have seen. Following the most recent trip, one student, on condition of anonymity, reported to the university that the professor made sexually suggestive comments to her.

The university's Office of Discrimination investigated the complaint and decided that there was no sexual harassment in the strict sense. However, the investigating official concluded (based on discussions with the complaining student) that the professor really should have been a bit more discreet in how he talked with students about the controversial issues raised in his course. The investigating official did not discuss the student's allegations with the professor. No other student made a similar complaint.

The dean of the college has indicated his intention to remove the professor from the class and to prohibit the professor from going on overnight trips with his students. From the professor's perspective, these proposed actions would have substantial professional repercussions. In addition to being precluded from taking students on the Amsterdam trip, the professor will not be allowed to take research trips with his students or go with them to academic conferences (to support them when they make presentations). Because of the potential impact on his career, the professor demands a full-scale adversary hearing at which he would be entitled to "confront the witnesses against him." The university is reluctant to provide the professor with such a hearing because of doubts about whether the complaining student would be willing to testify.

As you work your way through this chapter, consider whether the professor is entitled to a due process hearing. If you decide that he is, think about the type of hearing to which he might be entitled.

A. LEGISLATIVE DETERMINATIONS

For procedural due process purposes, a distinction is made between so-called "legislative" determinations and "adjudicative" determinations. Consider the following two cases.

Bi-Metallic Investment Co. v. State Board of Equalization

239 U.S. 441 (1915)

Mr. Justice HOLMES delivered the opinion of the Court.

This is a suit to enjoin the State Board of Equalization and the Colorado Tax Commission from putting in force and the defendant Pitcher, as assessor of Denver, from obeying, an order of the boards, increasing the valuation of all taxable property in Denver 40 per cent. The order was sustained and the suit directed to be dismissed by the supreme court of the state. The plaintiff is the owner of real estate in Denver and contends that it was given no opportunity to be heard, and that therefore its property will be taken without due process of law, contrary to the 14th Amendment of the Constitution of the United States.

We assume that the constitutional question is presented in the baldest way,—that neither the plaintiff nor the assessor of Denver, nor any representative of the city and county, was given an opportunity to be heard, other than such as they may have had by reason of the fact that the time of meeting of the boards is fixed by law. On this assumption it is obvious that injustice may be suffered if some property in the county already has been valued at its full worth. But if certain property has been valued at a rate different from that generally prevailing in the county, the owner has had his opportunity to protest and appeal as usual in our system of taxation, so that it must be assumed that the property owners in the county all stand alike. The question, then, is whether all individuals have a constitutional right to be heard before a matter can be decided in which all are equally concerned,—here, for instance, before a superior board decides that the local taxing officers have adopted a system of undervaluation throughout a county, as notoriously often has been the case. The answer of this court in the *State R. Tax Cases*, 92 U.S. 575, (1875) at least, as to any further notice, was that it was hard to believe that the proposition was seriously made.

Where a rule of conduct applies to more than a few people, it is impracticable that everyone should have a direct voice in its adoption. The Constitution does not require all public acts to be done in town meeting or an assembly of the whole. General statutes within the state power are passed that affect the person or property of individuals, sometimes to the point of ruin, without giving them a chance to be heard. Their rights are protected in the only way that they can be in a complex society, by their power, immediate or remote, over those who make the rule. If the result in this case had been reached, as it might have been by the state's doubling the rate of taxation, no one would suggest that the 14th Amendment was violated unless every person affected had been allowed an opportunity to raise his voice against it before the body intrusted by the state Constitution with the power. In considering this case in this court we must assume that the proper state machinery has been used, and the question is whether, if the state Constitution had declared that Denver had been undervalued as compared with the rest of the state, and had decreed that for the current year the valuation should be 40 per cent higher, the objection now urged could prevail. It appears to us that to put the question is to answer it. There must be a limit to individual argument in such matters if government is to go on. *See Londoner v. Denver*, 210 U.S. 373 (1908).

Judgment affirmed.

Londoner v. City and County of Denver

210 U.S. 373 (1908)

Mr. Justice MOODY delivered the opinion of the Court.

The plaintiffs in error challenge a tax assessment for the cost of paving a street upon which the lands abutted. The Colorado Supreme Court held that the tax was assessed in conformity with the Constitution and laws of the state, and its decision of that question is conclusive.

The tax was assessed under the charter of the city of Denver, which confers upon the city the power to make local improvements and to assess the cost upon property specially benefitted. The board of public works, upon the petition of a majority of the owners of the frontage to be assessed, may order the paving of a street. The board must recommend to the city council a form of ordinance authorizing it, and establishing an assessment district, which is not amendable by the council. The council may then, in its discretion, pass or refuse to pass the ordinance. If the ordinance is passed, the contract for the work is made by the mayor. The Board then assesses the cost upon the landowners after due notice and opportunity for hearing.

The board took the first step by transmitting to the council the resolution to do the work in the form of an ordinance authorizing it. That ordinance, after reciting a compliance by the board with the charter in other respects, and that "certain petitions for said improvements were first presented to the said board, subscribed by the owners of a majority of the frontage to be assessed for said improvements, as by the city charter required," enacted "That, upon consideration of the premises, by city council doth find that, in their action and proceedings in relation to said Eighth avenue paving district Number 1, the said board of public works has fully complied with the requirements of the city charter relating thereto." The state supreme court held that the determination of the city council was conclusive that a proper petition was filed, and that decision must be accepted by us as the law of the state. The only question for this court is whether the charter provision authorizing such a finding, without notice to the landowners, denies to them due process of law. We think it does not. The proceedings, from the beginning up to and including the passage of the ordinance authorizing the work, did not include any assessment or necessitate any assessment, although they laid the foundation for an assessment, which might or might not subsequently be made. All this might validly be done without hearing to the landowners, provided a hearing upon the assessment itself is afforded. *Voigt v. Detroit*, 184 U.S. 115 (1902). The legislature might have authorized the making of improvements by the city council without any petition.

The fifth assignment raises the question whether the assessment was made without notice and opportunity for hearing to those affected by it, thereby denying to them due process of law. After the improvement was completed, the board of public works, in compliance with §29 of the charter, certified to the city clerk a statement of the cost, and an apportionment of it to the lots of land to be assessed. Thereupon the city clerk published a notice, stating, *inter alia*, that the written complaints or objections of the owners, if filed within thirty days, would be "heard and determined by the city council before the passage of any ordinance assessing the cost." Those interested, therefore, were informed that if they reduced their complaints and objections to writing, and filed them within thirty days, those complaints and objections would be heard, and would be heard before any assessment was made. The notice purported only to fix the time for filing the complaints and objections, and to inform those who should file them that they would be heard before action.

In the assessment, apportionment, and collection of taxes upon property within their jurisdiction, the Constitution of the United States imposes few restrictions upon the states. In the enforcement of such restrictions as the

Constitution does impose, this court has regarded substance, and not form. Where the legislature of a state, instead of fixing the tax itself, commits to some subordinate body the duty of determining whether, in what amount, and upon whom it shall be levied, and of making its assessment and apportionment, due process of law requires that, at some stage of the proceedings, before the tax becomes irrevocably fixed, the taxpayer shall have an opportunity to be heard, of which he must have notice, either personal, by publication, or by a law fixing the time and place of the hearing. *Hagar v. Reclamation Dist. No. 108*, 111 U.S. 701 (1884).

If it is enough that, under such circumstances, an opportunity is given to submit in writing all objections to and complaints of the tax to the board, then there was a hearing afforded in the case at bar. But we think that something more than that, even in proceedings for taxation, is required by due process of law. Many requirements essential in strictly judicial proceedings may be dispensed with in proceedings of this nature. But even here a hearing, in its very essence, demands that he who is entitled to it shall have the right to support his allegations by argument, however brief: and, if need be, by proof, however informal. *Pittsburgh, C.C. & St. L. R. Co. v. Backus*, 154 U.S. 421 (1884).

It is apparent that such a hearing was denied to the plaintiffs in error. The denial was by the city council, which, while acting as a board of equalization, represents the state. The assessment was therefore void, and the plaintiffs in error were entitled to a decree discharging their lands from a lien on account of it. It is not now necessary to consider the tenth assignment of error.

Judgment reversed.

∾ PROBLEMS ∾

1. *The State Income Tax.* Suppose that your state legislature decides to enact a statute providing for a state income tax (or, if your state already has a state income tax, suppose it decides to increase the tax by 1%). Taxpayers claim a due process right to a hearing before the legislature to express their concerns regarding the wisdom and desirability of enacting the tax (or the tax increase, as the case may be). Under *Londoner* and *Bi-Metallic*, do taxpayers have a right to notice and an opportunity to be heard before the tax is imposed?

2. *An Individual Taxpayer's Bill.* In the preceding problem, after the tax (or tax increase) is adopted and goes into effect, the state assesses a taxpayer $10,000 for taxes. Does the individual taxpayer have the right to notice and an opportunity to be heard regarding the amount of his taxes?

3. Londoner *Assessments.* In *Londoner*, once the assessments are made, does the taxpayer have a due process right to challenge the amount of tax levied on his property?

B. ADJUDICATIVE DETERMINATIONS

Londoner and *Bi-Metallic* suggest that legislative determinations are generally not subject to due process protections. What about individual adjudicative-type determinations? Are they subject to procedural due process protections?

1. *Foundational Principles*

BACKGROUND
Privilege Cases?

Under the Court's pre-*Goldberg* jurisprudence, a distinction was made between the deprivation of so-called "privileges" and the deprivation of life, liberty, or property. As a general rule, there was no right to a hearing when the deprivation of a privilege was involved.

Under both the Fifth Amendment and the Fourteenth Amendment, however, there is a constitutional right to be heard prior to the deprivation of "life, liberty, or property." This right applies when the state seeks to deprive someone of liberty (e.g., through imprisonment), property (e.g., through fines), or life (e.g., through capital punishment). The difficulty is that, in the modern welfare society, many "benefits" that citizens possess do not necessarily qualify as "property." The question is whether individuals have the right to a hearing before being deprived of these benefits.

Goldberg v. Kelly

397 U.S. 254 (1970)

Mr. Justice BRENNAN delivered the opinion of the Court.

This action was brought by residents of New York City receiving financial aid under the federally assisted program of Aid to Families with Dependent Children (AFDC) or under New York State's general Home Relief program. Their complaint alleged that the New York State and New York City officials administering these programs terminated, or were about to terminate, such aid without prior notice and hearing, thereby denying them due process of law. At the time the suits were filed there was no requirement of prior notice or hearing of any kind before termination of financial aid. However, the State and city adopted procedures for notice and hearing after the suits were brought, and the appellees challenged the constitutional adequacy of those procedures.

The State Commissioner of Social Services amended the State Department of Social Services' Official Regulations to require that local social services officials proposing to discontinue or suspend a recipient's financial aid do so according to a procedure that conforms to either subdivision (a) or subdivision (b) of §351.26 of the regulations as amended. The City of New York elected to promulgate a local procedure according to subdivision (b).

Pursuant to subdivision (b), the New York City Department of Social Services promulgated Procedure No. 68-18. A caseworker who has doubts about the recipient's continued eligibility must first discuss them with the recipient. If the caseworker concludes that the recipient is no longer eligible, he recommends termination of aid to a unit supervisor. If the latter concurs, he sends the recipient a letter stating the reasons for proposing to terminate aid and notifying him that within seven days he may request that a higher official review the record, and may support the request with a written statement prepared personally or with the aid of an attorney or other person. If the reviewing official affirms the determination of ineligibility, aid is stopped immediately and the recipient is informed by letter of the reasons for the action. Appellees' challenge to this procedure emphasizes the absence of any provisions for the personal appearance of the recipient before the reviewing official, for oral presentation of evidence, and for confrontation and cross-examination of adverse witnesses. The letter does inform the recipient that he may request a post-termination "fair hearing." This is a proceeding before an independent state hearing officer at which the recipient may appear personally, offer oral evidence, confront and cross-examine the witnesses against him, and have a record made of the hearing. If the recipient prevails at the "fair hearing" he is paid all funds erroneously withheld. A recipient whose aid is not restored by a "fair hearing" decision may have judicial review. The recipient is so notified.

The constitutional issue to be decided is the narrow one whether the Due Process Clause requires that the recipient be afforded an evidentiary hearing before the termination of benefits. The District Court held that only a pretermination evidentiary hearing would satisfy the Constitution, and rejected the argument that the combination of the post-termination "fair hearing" with the informal pre-termination review disposed of all due process claims.

Appellant does not contend that procedural due process is not applicable to the termination of welfare benefits. Such benefits are a matter of statutory entitlement for persons qualified to receive them.[1] Their termination involves state

---

1. "It may be realistic today to regard welfare entitlements as more like 'property' than a 'gratuity.' Much of the existing wealth in this country takes the form of rights that do not fall within traditional common-law concepts of property. Many of the most important of these entitlements now flow from government: subsidies to farmers and businessmen, routes for airlines and channels for television stations; long term contracts for defense, space, and education; social security pensions for individuals. Such sources of security, whether private or public, are no longer regarded as luxuries or gratuities; to the recipients they are essentials, fully deserved, and in no sense a form of charity. It is only the poor whose entitlements, although recognized by public policy, have not been effectively enforced." Reich, *Individual Rights and Social Welfare: The Emerging Legal Issues,* 74 Yale L.J. 1245, 1225 (1965).

action that adjudicates important rights. The constitutional challenge cannot be answered by an argument that public assistance benefits are "a 'privilege' and not a 'right.'" Relevant constitutional restraints apply as much to the withdrawal of public assistance benefits as to disqualification for unemployment compensation, or to denial of a tax exemption, or to discharge from public employment. The extent to which procedural due process must be afforded the recipient is influenced by the extent to which he may be "condemned to suffer grievous loss," and depends upon whether the recipient's interest in avoiding that loss outweighs the governmental interest in summary adjudication. Accordingly, as we said in *Cafeteria & Restaurant Workers Union v. McElroy*, 367 U.S. 886 (1961), "consideration of what procedures due process may require under any given set of circumstances must begin with a determination of the precise nature of the government function involved as well as of the private interest that has been affected by governmental action."

It is true, of course, that some governmental benefits may be administratively terminated without affording the recipient a pre-termination evidentiary hearing. But when welfare is discontinued, only a pre-termination evidentiary hearing provides the recipient with procedural due process. For qualified recipients, welfare provides the means to obtain essential food, clothing, housing, and medical care. Thus the crucial factor in this context—a factor not present in the case of the blacklisted government contractor, the discharged government employee, the taxpayer denied a tax exemption, or virtually anyone else whose governmental entitlements are ended—is that termination of aid pending resolution of a controversy over eligibility may deprive an eligible recipient of the very means by which to live while he waits. Since he lacks independent resources, his situation becomes immediately desperate. His need to concentrate upon finding the means for daily subsistence, in turn, adversely affects his ability to seek redress from the welfare bureaucracy.

Moreover, important governmental interests are promoted by affording recipients a pre-termination evidentiary hearing. From its founding the Nation's basic commitment has been to foster the dignity and well-being of all persons within its borders. We have come to recognize that forces not within the control of the poor contribute to their poverty. This perception, against the background of our traditions, has significantly influenced the development of the contemporary public assistance system. Welfare, by meeting the basic demands of subsistence, can help bring within the reach of the poor the same opportunities that are available to others to participate meaningfully in the life of the community. At the same time, welfare guards against the societal malaise that may flow from a widespread sense of unjustified frustration and insecurity. Public assistance, then, is not mere charity, but a means to "promote the general Welfare, and secure the Blessings of Liberty to ourselves and our Posterity." The same governmental interests that counsel the provision of welfare, counsel as well its uninterrupted provision to those eligible to receive it; pre-termination evidentiary hearings are indispensable to that end.

Appellant does not challenge the force of these considerations but argues that they are outweighed by countervailing governmental interests in conserving fiscal and administrative resources. These interests, the argument goes, justify the delay of any evidentiary hearing until after discontinuance of the grants. Summary adjudication protects the public fisc by stopping payments promptly upon discovery of reason to believe that a recipient is no longer eligible. Since most terminations are accepted without challenge, summary adjudication also conserves both the fisc and administrative time and energy by reducing the number of evidentiary hearings actually held.

These governmental interests are not overriding in the welfare context. The requirement of a prior hearing doubtless involves some greater expense, and the benefits paid to ineligible recipients pending decision at the hearing probably cannot be recouped, since these recipients are likely to be judgment-proof. But the State is not without weapons to minimize these increased costs. Much of the drain on fiscal and administrative resources can be reduced by developing procedures for prompt pre-termination hearings and by skillful use of personnel and facilities. Indeed, the very provision for a post-termination evidentiary hearing in New York's Home Relief program is itself cogent evidence that the State recognizes the primacy of the public interest in correct eligibility determinations and therefore in the provision of procedural safeguards. Thus, the interest of the eligible recipient in uninterrupted receipt of public assistance, coupled with the State's interest that his payments not be erroneously terminated, clearly outweighs the State's competing concern to prevent any increase in its fiscal and administrative burdens. As the District Court correctly concluded, "the stakes are simply too high for the welfare recipient, and the possibility for honest error or irritable misjudgment too great, to allow termination of aid without giving the recipient a chance, if he so desires, to be fully informed of the case against him so that he may contest its basis and produce evidence in rebuttal."

Affirmed.

Mr. Justice BLACK, *dissenting.*

In the last half century the United States, along with many other nations of the world, has moved far toward becoming a welfare state, that is, a nation that for one reason or another taxes its most affluent people to help support, feed, clothe, and shelter its less fortunate citizens. The result is that today more than nine million men, women, and children in the United States receive some kind of state or federally financed public assistance in the form of allowances or gratuities, generally paid them periodically, usually by the week, month, or quarter. Since these gratuities are paid on the basis of need, the list of recipients is not static, and some people go off the lists and others are added from time to time. These ever-changing lists put a constant administrative burden on government and it certainly could not have reasonably anticipated that this burden would include the additional procedural expense imposed by the Court today.

The more than a million names on the relief rolls in New York, and the more than nine million names on the rolls of all the 50 States were not put there at random. The names are there because state welfare officials believed that those people were eligible for assistance. Probably, many names were put there erroneously in order to alleviate immediate suffering, and undoubtedly some people are drawing relief who are not entitled under the law to do so. Doubtless some draw relief checks from time to time who know they are not eligible. Many of those who thus draw undeserved gratuities are without sufficient property to enable the government to collect back from them any money they wrongfully receive. But the Court today holds that it would violate the Due Process Clause of the Fourteenth Amendment to stop paying those people weekly or monthly allowances unless the government first affords them a full "evidentiary hearing" even though welfare officials are persuaded that the recipients are not rightfully entitled to receive a penny under the law. Although some recipients might be on the lists because of deliberate fraud on their part, the government is helpless and must continue, until after an evidentiary hearing, to pay money that it does not owe, never has owed, and never could owe. I do not believe there is any provision in our Constitution that should thus paralyze the government's efforts to protect itself against making payments to people who are not entitled to them.

The Court relies upon the Fourteenth Amendment and in effect says that failure of the government to pay a promised charitable installment to an individual deprives that individual of his own property, in violation of the Due Process Clause of the Fourteenth Amendment. It somewhat strains credulity to say that the government's promise of charity to an individual is property belonging to that individual when the government denies that the individual is honestly entitled to receive such a payment. Today's result doesn't depend on the language of the Constitution itself or the principles of other decisions, but solely on the collective judgment of the majority as to what would be a fair and humane procedure in this case.

I know of no situation in our legal system in which the person alleged to owe money to another is required by law to continue making payments to a judgment-proof claimant without the benefit of any security or bond to insure that these payments can be recovered if he wins his legal argument.

Notes

1. *Due Process for Contract Professors. Goldberg* dramatically expanded the potential application of the Due Process Clause, and subsequent cases were required to determine the scope of the due process guarantee. In *Board of Regents v. Roth*, 408 U.S. 564 (1972), an assistant professor was hired by state university for a fixed term of one academic year. When he was informed that he would not be rehired for the next academic year, the Court held that he was not entitled to a hearing before the decision not to renew was made:

To determine whether due process requirements apply in the first place, we look not to the 'weight' but to the nature of the interest at stake. We must look to see if the interest is within the Fourteenth Amendment's protection of liberty and property. The Court has fully and finally rejected the wooden distinction between 'rights' and 'privileges' that once seemed to govern the applicability of procedural due process rights. The Court has also made clear that the property interests protected by procedural due process extend well beyond actual ownership of real estate, chattels, or money. 'While this court has not attempted to define with exactness the liberty guaranteed (by the Fourteenth Amendment), the term denotes not merely freedom from bodily restraint but also the right of the individual to contract, to engage in any of the common occupations of life, to acquire useful knowledge, to marry, establish a home and bring up children, to worship God according to the dictates of his own conscience, and generally to enjoy those privileges long recognized as essential to the orderly pursuit of happiness by free men.' In a Constitution for a free people, there can be no doubt that the meaning of 'liberty' must be broad indeed. There might be cases in which a State refused to re-employ a person under such circumstances that interests in liberty would be implicated. But this is not such a case. The State, in declining to rehire the respondent, did not make any charge against him that might seriously damage his standing and associations in his community. Similarly, there is no suggestion that the State imposed on him a stigma or other disability that foreclosed his freedom to take advantage of other employment opportunities. To be sure, respondent has alleged that the nonrenewal of his contract was based on his exercise of his right to freedom of speech. But this allegation is not now before us. On the record, all that clearly appears is that the respondent was not rehired for one year at one university. It stretches the concept too far to suggest that a person is deprived of 'liberty' when he simply is not rehired in one job but remains as free as before to seek another. The Fourteenth Amendment's procedural protection of property is a safeguard of the security of interests that a person has already acquired in specific benefits. To have a property interest in a benefit, a person clearly must have more than an abstract need or desire for it. He must have more than a unilateral expectation of it. He must, instead, have a legitimate claim of entitlement to it. Just as the welfare recipients' 'property' interest in welfare payments was created and defined by statutory terms, so the respondent's 'property' interest in employment at Wisconsin State University—Oshkosh was created and defined by the terms of his appointment. Those terms specifically provided that the respondent's employment was to terminate on June 30. They did not provide for contract renewal absent 'sufficient cause.' Indeed, they made no provision for renewal whatsoever. Thus, the terms of the respondent's appointment secured absolutely no interest in re-employment for the next year. In these circumstances, the respondent surely had an abstract concern in being rehired, but he did not have a property interest sufficient to require the University authorities to give him a hearing when they declined to renew his contract of employment."

Justice Douglas dissented, arguing that Roth was entitled to a hearing because of a suspected infringement of his First Amendment rights.

2. *The Bitter with the Sweet? Roth* seemed to suggest that an individual's right to a hearing should be determined by the law creating that right. In *Arnett v. Kennedy*, 416 U.S. 134 (1974), a plurality of the Court affirmed that idea when it suggested that the legislature could limit and condition an individual's right to a hearing: "Where the grant of a substantive right is inextricably intertwined with the limitations on the procedures which are to be employed in determining that right, a litigant in the position of appellee must take the bitter with the sweet." However, in *Cleveland Board of Education v. Loudermill*, 470 U.S. 532 (1985), the

Court reversed itself and rejected the "bitter with the sweet" approach because it "misconceives the constitutional guarantee. The Due Process Clause provides that certain substantive rights—life, liberty, and property—cannot be deprived except pursuant to constitutionally adequate procedures. The right to due process 'is conferred, not by legislative grace, but by constitutional guarantee. While the legislature may elect not to confer a property interest in public employment, it may not constitutionally authorize the deprivation of such an interest, once conferred, without appropriate procedural safeguards.' *Arnett v. Kennedy*, 416 U.S. 134, 167 (1974) (Powell, J., concurring). In short, once it is determined that the Due Process Clause applies, 'the question remains what process is due.' The answer to that question is not to be found in the Ohio statute." Justice Rehnquist dissented: "The Court ignores our duty under *Roth* to rely on state law as the source of property interests for purposes of applying the Due Process Clause of the Fourteenth Amendment."

Paul v. Davis

424 U.S. 693 (1976)

Mr. Justice REHNQUIST delivered the opinion of the Court.

Petitioner Edgar Paul is the Chief of Police of the Louisville, Ky., Division of Police, while petitioner McDaniel occupies the same position in the Jefferson County, Ky., Division of Police. In late 1972 they agreed to combine their efforts for the purpose of alerting local area merchants to possible shoplifters who might be operating during the Christmas season. In early December petitioners distributed to approximately 800 merchants in the Louisville metropolitan area a "flyer," which began as follows: "TO: BUSINESS MEN IN THE METROPOLITAN AREA The Chiefs of The Jefferson County and City of Louisville Police Departments, in an effort to keep their officers advised on shoplifting activity, have approved the attached alphabetically arranged flyer of subjects known to be active in this criminal field. This flyer is being distributed to you, the business man, so that you may inform your security personnel to watch for these subjects. These persons have been arrested during 1971 and 1972 or have been active in various criminal fields in high density shopping areas. Only the photograph and name of the subject is shown on this flyer, if additional information is desired, please forward a request in writing." The flyer consisted of five pages of "mug shot" photos, arranged alphabetically. In approximately the center of page 2 there appeared photos and the name of the respondent, Edward Charles Davis III.

Respondent appeared on the flyer because on June 14, 1971, he had been arrested in Louisville on a charge of shoplifting. He had been arraigned on this charge in September 1971, and, upon his plea of not guilty, the charge had been "filed away with leave (to reinstate)," a disposition which left the charge outstanding. Thus, at the time petitioners caused the flyer to be prepared and circulated respondent had been charged with shoplifting but his guilt or innocence of that offense had never been resolved. Shortly after circulation of the flyer the charge against respondent was finally dismissed by a judge of the Louisville Police Court.

At the time the flyer was circulated respondent was employed as a photographer by the Louisville Courier-Journal and Times. The flyer, and respondent's inclusion therein, soon came to the attention of respondent's supervisor, the executive director of photography for the two newspapers. This individual called respondent in to hear his version of the events leading to his appearing in the flyer. Following this discussion, the supervisor informed respondent that although he would not be fired, he "had best not find himself in a similar situation" in the future.

Respondent thereupon brought this §1983 action in the District Court for the Western District of Kentucky, seeking redress for the alleged violation of rights guaranteed to him by the Constitution of the United States.

Respondent's due process claim is grounded upon his assertion that the flyer, and in particular the phrase "Active Shoplifters" appearing at the head of the page upon which his name and photograph appear, impermissibly deprived him of some "liberty" protected by the Fourteenth Amendment. His complaint asserted that the "active shoplifter" designation would inhibit him from entering business establishments for fear of being suspected of shoplifting and possibly apprehended, and would seriously impair his future employment opportunities.

The words "liberty" and "property" as used in the Fourteenth Amendment do not in terms single out reputation as a candidate for special protection over and above other interests that may be protected by state law. While we have in a number of our prior cases pointed out the frequently drastic effect of the "stigma" which may result from defamation by the government in a variety of contexts, this line of cases does not establish the proposition that reputation alone, apart from some more tangible interests such as employment, is either "liberty" or "property" by itself sufficient to invoke the procedural protection of the Due Process Clause. While not uniform in their treatment of the subject, we think that the weight of our decisions establishes no constitutional doctrine converting every defamation by a public official into a deprivation of liberty within the meaning of the Due Process Clause of the Fifth or Fourteenth Amendment.

It is apparent from our decisions that there exists a variety of interests which are difficult of definition but are nevertheless comprehended within the meaning of either "liberty" or "property" as meant in the Due Process Clause. These interests attain this constitutional status by virtue of the fact that they have been initially recognized and protected by state law, and we have repeatedly ruled that the procedural guarantees of the Fourteenth Amendment apply whenever the State seeks to remove or significantly alter that protected status. In *Bell v. Burson*, 402 U.S. 535 (1971), for example, the State by issuing drivers' licenses recognized in its citizens a right to operate a vehicle on the highways of the State. The Court held that the State could not withdraw this right without giving petitioner due process. In *Morrissey v. Brewer*, 408 U.S. 471 (1972), the State afforded parolees the right to remain at liberty as long as the conditions of their parole were not violated. Before the State could alter the status of a parolee because of alleged violations of these conditions, we held that the Fourteenth Amendment's guarantee of due process of law required certain procedural safeguards.

The interest in reputation alone which respondent seeks to vindicate in this action in federal court is quite different from the "liberty" or "property" recognized in those decisions. Kentucky law does not extend to respondent any legal guarantee of present enjoyment of reputation which has been altered as a result of petitioners' actions. Rather his interest in reputation is simply one of a number which the State may protect against injury by virtue of its tort law, providing a forum for vindication of those interests by means of damages actions. And any harm or injury to that interest, even where as here inflicted by an officer of the State, does not result in a deprivation of any "liberty" or "property" recognized by state or federal law, nor has it worked any change of respondent's status as theretofore recognized under the State's laws. For these reasons we hold that the interest in reputation asserted in this case is neither "liberty" nor "property" guaranteed against state deprivation without due process of law.

Respondent in this case cannot assert denial of any right vouchsafed to him by the State and thereby protected under the Fourteenth Amendment. That being the case, petitioners' defamatory publications, however seriously they may have harmed respondent's reputation, did not deprive him of any "liberty" or "property" interests protected by the Due Process Clause.

Reversed.

Mr. Justice BRENNAN, with whom Mr. Justice MARSHALL *concurs* and Mr. Justice WHITE *concurs in part, dissenting.*

The stark fact is that the police here have officially imposed on respondent the stigmatizing label "criminal" without the salutary and constitutionally mandated safeguards of a criminal trial. Our prior decisions are cogent authority that a person's interest in his good name and reputation falls within the broad term "liberty" and clearly require that the government afford procedural protections before infringing that name and reputation by branding a person as a criminal. The Court is reduced to discrediting the clear thrust of these decisions by excluding the interest in reputation from all constitutional protection "if there is any other possible interpretation" by which to deny their force as precedent according constitutional protection for the interest in reputation.

Moreover, the analysis has a hollow ring in light of the Court's acceptance of the truth of the allegation that the "active shoplifter" label would "seriously impair (respondent's) future employment opportunities." This is clear recognition that an official "badge of infamy" affects tangible interests of the defamed individual and not merely an abstract interest in how people view him; for the "badge of infamy" has serious consequences in its impact on no less than the opportunities open to him to enjoy life, liberty, and the pursuit of happiness. It is inexplicable how the Court can say that a person's status is "altered" when the State suspends him from school, revokes his driver's license, fires him from a job, or denies him the right to purchase a drink of alcohol, but is in no way "altered" when it officially pins upon him the brand of a criminal, particularly since the Court recognizes how deleterious will be the consequences that inevitably flow from its official act. Our precedents clearly mandate that a person's interest in his good name and reputation is cognizable as a "liberty" interest within the meaning of the Due Process Clause, and the Court has simply failed to distinguish those precedents in any rational manner in holding that no invasion of a "liberty" interest was effected in the official stigmatizing of respondent as a criminal without any "process" whatsoever.

I have always thought that one of this Court's most important roles is to provide a formidable bulwark against governmental violation of the constitutional safeguards securing in our free society the legitimate expectations of every person to innate human dignity and sense of worth. It is a regrettable abdication of that role and a saddening denigration of our majestic Bill of Rights when the Court tolerates arbitrary and capricious official conduct branding an individual as a criminal without compliance with constitutional procedures designed to ensure the fair and impartial ascertainment of criminal culpability. Today's decision must surely be a short-lived aberration.

Note: Procedural Due Process and Parole

In *Swarthout v. Cooke*, 562 U.S. 216 (2011), an individual who had been given a sentence of seven years to life was denied parole by the State of California, and he filed a habeas corpus challenging the denial. Although the Court recognized that there is no federal right to conditional release (parole), California was free to transform that interest into a protected liberty interest. Finding that it did, the Court stated that when "a State creates a liberty interest, the Due Process Clause requires fair procedures for its vindication—and federal courts will review the application of those constitutionally required procedures."

∾ PROBLEMS ∾

1. *More on the Contract Professor.* Let's think about the *Roth* case a bit more. Would the result have been different (in the sense that Roth would have been entitled to a due process hearing) if Roth: a) was fired for "moral turpitude" prior to the expiration of his contract; or b) did not have his contract renewed because the university concluded (and stated) that he was incompetent and dishonest? Do *Roth* and *Paul* suggest that Roth would be entitled to a hearing regarding his renewal under those two circumstances?

2. *The Tenured Professor.* The terms of tenure at a state university provide for continued employment absent "incompetence" or "immoral" behavior. The university wants to fire a tenured professor for incompetence. You are the university counsel. Does the professor have a constitutional right to a hearing prior to dismissal? What kind of hearing?

3. *The Psychiatric Commitment.* Eddie was found not guilty of murder by reason of insanity under Alabama law and was committed indefinitely to a psychiatric hospital even though he was admittedly no longer mentally ill (the insanity was caused by a tumor on his brain, which was subsequently removed). Under state law, the hospital is allowed to release Eddie only if he "is no longer dangerous to himself or others." Eddie, who desperately wants to be released, claims that he is entitled to a hearing on whether he is dangerous. Does procedural due process apply? Explain.

4. *More on the Professor and the Amsterdam Trip.* Consider the problem at the beginning of the chapter. You represent the dean of the college, who is deciding how to proceed (if at all) against the professor. Based on your reading of *Goldberg* and *Paul,* and the other cases mentioned in this section, is the professor entitled to a due process hearing? Why, or why not?

2. *Procedural Requirements*

Goldberg v. Kelly opened a Pandora's box for the Court. If due process requires notice and an opportunity to be heard, what type of hearing is required? Does the hearing requirement vary from one type of case to another? In *Goldberg,* the Court concluded that welfare recipients were not entitled to a formal proceeding, in the sense of a "complete record and a comprehensive opinion," but rather were entitled to only a "fair hearing." In reaching this conclusion, the Court emphasized that both the state and the recipients have an "interest in relatively speedy resolution of questions of eligibility," both are "used to dealing with one another informally," and "some welfare departments have very burdensome caseloads." As a result, the Court required only "minimum procedural safeguards, adapted to the particular characteristics of welfare recipients, and to the limited nature of the controversies to be resolved." In the Court's view, welfare recipients were entitled to an "opportunity to be heard" at a "meaningful time and in a meaningful manner." This would include a requirement that the agency provide the recipient with "timely and adequate notice detailing the reasons for a proposed termination, and an effective opportunity to defend by confronting any adverse witnesses and by presenting his own arguments and evidence orally." Absent extraordinary circumstances, the agency need not provide the recipient with the opportunity to file a written brief, especially given that many welfare recipients may "lack the educational attainment necessary to write effectively and cannot obtain professional assistance." However, welfare recipients must be allowed to state their positions orally using informal procedures, and recipients must be allowed "to confront and cross-examine adverse witnesses." In addition, to the extent that the agency engages in fact finding, "the evidence used to prove the government's case must be disclosed to the individual so that he has an opportunity to show that it is untrue." Although the agency need not provide a recipient with an attorney, "the recipient must be allowed to retain an attorney if he so desires." "Finally, the decisionmaker's conclusion as to a recipient's eligibility must rest solely on the legal rules and evidence adduced at the hearing and the decision maker should state the reasons for his determination and indicate the evidence he relied on, though his statement need not amount to a full opinion or even formal findings of fact and conclusions of law. And, of course, an impartial decision maker is essential."

After *Goldberg*, questions arose about whether a "fair hearing" would be required in other contexts, and whether this hearing must be provided before a termination of rights. The following cases address that issue.

Mathews v. Eldridge

424 U.S. 319 (1976)

Mr. Justice Powell delivered the opinion of the Court.

Cash benefits are provided to workers during periods in which they are completely disabled under the disability insurance benefits program created by the 1956 amendments to Title II of the Social Security Act. Respondent Eldridge was first awarded benefits in 1968. In 1972, he received a questionnaire from the state agency charged with monitoring his medical condition. Eldridge completed the questionnaire, indicating that his condition had not improved and identifying the medical sources, including physicians, from whom he had received treatment recently. The state agency then obtained reports from his physician and a psychiatric consultant. After considering these reports and other information in his file the agency informed Eldridge by letter that it had made a tentative determination that his disability had ceased in May 1972. The letter included a statement of reasons for the proposed termination of benefits, and advised Eldridge that he might request reasonable time in which to obtain and submit additional information pertaining to his condition.

In his written response, Eldridge disputed one characterization of his medical condition and indicated that the agency already had enough evidence to establish his disability. The state agency then made its final determination that he had ceased to be disabled in May 1972. This determination was accepted by the Social Security Administration (SSA), which notified Eldridge in July that his benefits would terminate after that month. The notification also advised him of his right to seek reconsideration by the state agency of this initial determination within six months.

Instead of requesting reconsideration Eldridge commenced this action challenging the constitutional validity of the administrative procedures established by the Secretary of Health, Education, and Welfare for assessing whether there exists a continuing disability. He sought an immediate reinstatement of benefits pending a hearing on the issue of his disability. The Secretary moved to dismiss on the grounds that Eldridge's benefits had been terminated in accordance with valid administrative regulations and procedures and that he had failed to exhaust available remedies. In support of his contention that due process requires a pre-termination hearing, Eldridge relied exclusively upon this Court's decision in *Goldberg v. Kelly* which established a right to an "evidentiary hearing" prior to termination of welfare benefits.

This Court consistently has held that some form of hearing is required before an individual is finally deprived of a property interest. The "right to be heard before being condemned to suffer grievous loss of any kind, even though it may not involve the stigma and hardships of a criminal conviction, is a principle basic to our society." The fundamental requirement of due process is the opportunity to be heard "at a meaningful time and in a meaningful manner." Eldridge agrees that the review procedures available to a claimant before the initial determina-tion of ineligibility becomes final would be adequate if disability benefits were not terminated until after the evidentiary hearing stage of the administrative process. The dispute centers upon what process is due prior to the initial termination of benefits, pending review.

In recent years this Court increasingly has had occasion to consider the extent to which due process requires an evidentiary hearing prior to the depri-vation of some type of property interest even if such a hearing is provided there-after. In only one case, *Goldberg v. Kelly*, has the Court held that a hearing closely approximating a judicial trial is necessary. In other cases requiring some type of pretermination hearing as a matter of constitutional right the Court has spoken sparingly about the requisite procedures.

These decisions underscore the truism that "'due process,' unlike some legal rules, is not a technical conception with a fixed content unrelated to time, place and circumstances." "Due process is flexible and calls for such procedural protections as the particular situation demands." Accordingly, resolution of the issue whether the administrative procedures provided here are constitutionally sufficient requires analysis of the governmental and private interests that are affected. More precisely, our prior decisions indicate that identification of the specific dictates of due process generally requires consideration of three distinct factors: First, the private interest that will be affected by the official action; sec-ond, the risk of an erroneous deprivation of such interest through the procedures used, and the probable value, if any, of additional or substitute procedural safe-guards; and finally, the Government's interest, including the function involved and the fiscal and administrative burdens that the additional or substitute proce-dural requirement would entail.

We turn first to a description of the procedures for the termination of Social Security disability benefits and thereafter consider the factors bearing upon the constitutional adequacy of these procedures. The disability insurance program is administered jointly by state and federal agencies. State agencies make the initial determination whether a disability exists, when it began, and when it ceased. The standards applied and the procedures followed are prescribed by the Secretary who has delegated his responsibilities and powers under the Act to the SSA. The principal reasons for benefits terminations are that the worker is no longer disabled or has returned to work. As Eldridge's benefits were terminated because he was determined to be no longer disabled, we consider only the sufficiency of the procedures involved in such cases.

The continuing-eligibility investigation is made by a state agency acting through a "team" consisting of a physician and a nonmedical person trained in disability evaluation. The agency periodically communicates with the disabled worker, usually by mail, in which case he is sent a detailed questionnaire or by telephone, and requests information concerning his present condition, including current medical restrictions and sources of treatment, and any additional information that he considers relevant to his continued entitlement to benefits.

Information regarding the recipient's current condition is also obtained from his sources of medical treatment. If there is a conflict between the information provided by the beneficiary and that obtained from medical sources such as his physician, or between two sources of treatment, the agency may arrange for an examination by an independent consulting physician. Whenever the agency's tentative assessment of the beneficiary's condition differs from his own assessment, the beneficiary is informed that benefits may be terminated, provided a summary of the evidence upon which the proposed determination to terminate is based, and afforded an opportunity to review the medical reports and other evidence in his case file. He also may respond in writing and submit additional evidence.

The state agency then makes its final determination, which is reviewed by an examiner in the SSA Bureau of Disability Insurance. If the SSA accepts the agency determination it notifies the recipient in writing, informing him of the reasons for the decision, and of his right to seek de novo reconsideration by the state agency. Upon acceptance by the SSA, benefits are terminated effective two months after the month in which medical recovery is found to have occurred.

If the recipient seeks reconsideration by the state agency and the determination is adverse, the SSA reviews the reconsideration determination and notifies the recipient of the decision. He then has a right to an evidentiary hearing before an SSA administrative law judge. The hearing is nonadversary, and the SSA is not represented by counsel. As at all prior and subsequent stages of the administrative process, however, the claimant may be represented by counsel or other spokesmen. If this hearing results in an adverse decision, the claimant is entitled to request discretionary review by the SSA Appeals Council.

Should it be determined at any point after termination of benefits, that the claimant's disability extended beyond the date of cessation initially established, the worker is entitled to retroactive payments. If, on the other hand, a beneficiary receives any payments to which he is later determined not to be entitled, the statute authorizes the Secretary to attempt to recoup these funds in specified circumstances.

Despite the elaborate character of the administrative procedures provided by the Secretary, the courts below held them to be constitutionally inadequate, concluding that due process requires an evidentiary hearing prior to termination. In light of the private and governmental interests at stake here and the nature of the existing procedures, we think this was error. Since a recipient whose benefits are terminated is awarded full retroactive relief if he ultimately prevails, his sole interest is in the uninterrupted receipt of this source of income pending final administrative decision on his claim. His potential injury is thus similar in nature to that of the welfare recipient in *Goldberg.*

Only in *Goldberg* has the Court held that due process requires an evidentiary hearing prior to a temporary deprivation. It was emphasized there that welfare assistance is given to persons on the very margin of subsistence: "The crucial factor in this context a factor not present in the case of virtually anyone else whose governmental entitlements are ended is that termination of aid pending resolution of a controversy over eligibility may deprive an eligible recipient of the very means by which to live while he waits." Eligibility for disability benefits, in contrast, is not based upon financial need. Indeed, it is wholly unrelated to the worker's income or support from many other sources, such as earnings of other family members, workmen's compensation awards, tort claims awards, savings, private insurance, public or private pensions, veterans' benefits, food stamps, public assistance, or the "many other important programs, both public and private, which contain provisions for disability payments affecting a substantial portion of the work force." *Richardson v. Belcher,* 404 U.S. 78, 85-87 (1971) (Douglas, J., *dissenting*).

As *Goldberg* illustrates, the degree of potential deprivation that may be created by a particular decision is a factor to be considered in assessing the validity of any administrative decisionmaking process. The potential deprivation here is generally likely to be less than in *Goldberg,* although the degree of difference can be overstated. To remain eligible for benefits a recipient must be "unable to engage in substantial gainful activity." Thus, in contrast to the discharged federal employee in *Arnett,* there is little possibility that the terminated recipient will be able to find even temporary employment to ameliorate the interim loss.

The Secretary concedes that the delay between a request for a hearing before an administrative law judge and a decision on the claim is currently between 10 and 11 months. Since a terminated recipient must first obtain a reconsideration decision as a prerequisite to invoking his right to an evidentiary hearing, the delay between the actual cutoff of benefits and final decision after a hearing exceeds one year.

In view of the torpidity of this administrative review process, and the typically modest resources of the family unit of the physically disabled worker, the hardship imposed upon the erroneously terminated disability recipient may be significant. Still, the disabled worker's need is likely to be less than that of a welfare recipient. In addition to the possibility of access to private resources, other forms of government assistance will become available where the termination of disability benefits places a worker or his family below the subsistence level. In view of these potential sources of temporary income, there is less reason here than in *Goldberg* to depart from the ordinary principle, established by our decisions, that something less than an evidentiary hearing is sufficient prior to adverse administrative action.

An additional factor to be considered here is the fairness and reliability of the existing pretermination procedures, and the probable value, if any, of additional procedural safeguards. Central to the evaluation of any administrative process is the nature of the relevant inquiry. In order to remain eligible for benefits the disabled worker must demonstrate by means of "medically acceptable clinical and laboratory diagnostic techniques," that he is unable "to engage in any substantial gainful activity by reason of any medically determinable physical or mental impairment." In short, a medical assessment of the worker's physical or mental condition is required. This is a more sharply focused and easily documented decision than the typical determination of welfare entitlement. In the latter case, a wide variety of information may be deemed relevant, and issues of witness credibility and veracity often are critical to the decisionmaking process. *Goldberg* noted that in such circumstances "written submissions are a wholly unsatisfactory basis for decision."

By contrast, the decision whether to discontinue disability benefits will turn, in most cases, upon "routine, standard, and unbiased medical reports by physician specialists," concerning a subject whom they have personally examined. In *Richardson* the Court recognized the "reliability and probative worth of written medical reports," emphasizing that while there may be "professional disagreement with the medical conclusions" the "specter of questionable credibility and veracity is not present." To be sure, credibility and veracity may be a factor in the ultimate disability assessment in some cases. But procedural due process rules are shaped by the risk of error inherent in the truthfinding process as applied to the generality of cases, not the rare exceptions. The potential value of an evidentiary hearing, or even oral presentation to the decisionmaker, is substantially less in this context than in *Goldberg*.

The decision in *Goldberg* also was based on the Court's conclusion that written submissions were an inadequate substitute for oral presentation because they did not provide an effective means for the recipient to communicate his case to the decisionmaker. Written submissions were viewed as an unrealistic option, for most recipients lacked the "educational attainment necessary to write effectively" and could not afford professional assistance. In addition, such submissions would not provide the "flexibility of oral presentations" or "permit the recipient to mold his argument to the issues the decision maker appears to regard as important." In the context of the disability-benefits-entitlement assessment the administrative procedures under review here fully answer these objections.

The detailed questionnaire which the state agency periodically sends the recipient identifies with particularity the information relevant to the entitlement decision, and the recipient is invited to obtain assistance from the local SSA office in completing the questionnaire. More important, the information critical to the entitlement decision usually is derived from medical sources, such as the treating physician. Such sources are likely to be able to communicate more effectively through written documents than are welfare recipients or the lay witnesses supporting their cause. The conclusions of physicians often are supported by X-rays and the results of clinical or laboratory tests, information typically more amenable to written than to oral presentation.

A further safeguard against mistake is the policy of allowing the disability recipient's representative full access to all information relied upon by the state agency. In addition, prior to the cutoff of benefits the agency informs the recipient of its tentative assessment, the reasons therefor, and provides a summary of the evidence that it considers most relevant. Opportunity is then afforded the recipient to submit additional evidence or arguments, enabling him to challenge directly the accuracy of information in his file as well as the correctness of the agency's tentative conclusions. These procedures, again as contrasted with those before the Court in *Goldberg*, enable the recipient to "mold" his argument to respond to the precise issues which the decisionmaker regards as crucial.

Amici point to the significant reversal rate for appealed cases as clear evidence that the current process is inadequate. Depending upon the base selected and the line of analysis followed, the relevant reversal rates urged by the contending parties vary from a high of 58.6% for appealed reconsideration decisions to an overall reversal rate of only 3.3%. Bare statistics rarely provide a satisfactory measure of the fairness of a decisionmaking process. Their adequacy is especially suspect here since the administrative review system is operated on an open-file basis.

In striking the appropriate due process balance the final factor to be assessed is the public interest. This includes the administrative burden and other societal costs that would be associated with requiring, as a matter of constitutional right, an evidentiary hearing upon demand in all cases prior to the termination of disability benefits. The most visible burden would be the incremental cost resulting from the increased number of hearings and the expense of providing benefits to ineligible recipients pending decision. No one can predict the extent of the increase, but the fact that full benefits would continue until after such hearings would assure the exhaustion in most cases of this attractive option. Nor would the theoretical right of the Secretary to recover undeserved benefits result, as a practical matter, in any substantial offset to the added outlay of public funds. The parties submit widely varying estimates of the probable additional financial cost. We only need say that experience with the constitutionalizing of government procedures suggests that the ultimate additional cost in terms of money and administrative burden would not be insubstantial.

Financial cost alone is not a controlling weight in determining whether due process requires a particular procedural safeguard prior to some administrative decision. But the Government's interest, and hence that of the public, in conserving scarce fiscal and administrative resources is a factor that must be weighed. At some point the benefit of an additional safeguard to the individual affected by the administrative action and to society in terms of increased assurance that the action is just, may be outweighed by the cost. Significantly, the cost of protecting those whom the preliminary administrative process has identified as likely to be found undeserving may in the end come out of the pockets of the deserving since resources available for any particular program of social welfare are not unlimited.

But more is implicated in cases of this type than *ad hoc* weighing of fiscal and administrative burdens against the interests of a particular category of claimants. The ultimate balance involves a determination as to when, under our constitutional system, judicial-type procedures must be imposed upon administrative action to assure fairness. The judicial model of an evidentiary hearing is neither a required, nor even the most effective, method of decisionmaking in all circumstances. The essence of due process is the requirement that "a person in jeopardy of serious loss be given notice of the case against him and opportunity to meet it." All that is necessary is that the procedures be tailored, in light of the decision to be made, to "the capacities and circumstances of those who are to be heard," *Goldberg v. Kelly*, 397 U.S. 254, 268-269 (1970), to insure that they are given a meaningful opportunity to present their case. In assessing what process is due in this case, substantial weight must be given to the good-faith judgments of the individuals charged by Congress with the administration of social welfare programs that the procedures they have provided assure fair consideration of the entitlement claims of individuals. This is especially so where, as here, the prescribed procedures not only provide the claimant with an effective process for asserting his claim prior to any administrative action, but also assure a right to an evidentiary hearing, as well as to subsequent judicial review, before the denial of his claim becomes final.

We conclude that an evidentiary hearing is not required prior to the termination of disability benefits and that the present administrative procedures fully comport with due process.

The judgment of the Court of Appeals is
Reversed.

Notes: Adequacy of Procedures

1. *Fast-Track Deportations.* In *Department of Homeland Security v. Thuraissigiam*, 140 S. Ct. 1959 (2020), the Court upheld the Trump Administration's right to quickly deport illegal immigrants who fail their initial asylum screening and thereby become eligible for fast-track deportation. The Court held that the immigrant was not entitled to remain in the country and pursue additional administrative review of the denial.

2. *Parole Procedures in California.* In *Swarthout v. Cooke*, 562 U.S. 216 (2011), referred to earlier in this chapter, the Court held that an individual who has been sentenced to seven years to life had a protected liberty interest under state law in

the possibility of conditional release (parole). California law provided that officials could deny a request for parole whenever there is "some evidence" supporting the conclusion that the inmate "is unsuitable for parole because he or she currently is dangerous." The Court upheld the California law: "In the context of parole, we have held that the procedures required are minimal. In *Greenholtz*, we found that a prisoner subject to a parole statute similar to California's received adequate process when he was allowed an opportunity to be heard and was provided a statement of the reasons why parole was denied. 'The Constitution,' we held, 'does not require more.' Cooke and Clay received at least this amount of process: They were allowed to speak at their parole hearings and to contest the evidence against them, were afforded access to their records in advance, and were notified as to the reasons why parole was denied."

2. *The Requirement of Appointed Counsel.* In *Turner v. Rogers*, 564 U.S. 431 (2011), South Carolina enforced its child support orders by threatening those who are subject to child support orders with civil contempt if they are able to comply with that order, but fail to do so. The Court held that the Fourteenth Amendment's Due Process Clause did not require the State to provide counsel (at a civil contempt hearing) to an *indigent* person potentially faced with incarceration when the custodial parent is not represented by counsel, provided that the states uses processes "that assure a fundamentally fair determination of the critical incarceration-related question, whether the supporting parent is able to comply with the support order." The Court applied the balancing test articulated in *Mathews v. Eldridge*, 424 U.S. 319, 335 (1976), in reaching its decision.

∾ PROBLEMS ∾

1. *The Tenured Professor.* Recall the tenured professor at a state university who was fired for incompetence. What, if any, procedural protections apply to a hearing regarding the professor's dismissal? *See Greene v. Greenwood Public School District*, 890 F.3d 240 (5th Cir. 2018).

2. *The Grievance Against the Tenured Professor.* Suppose that a grievance is brought against a tenured professor, claiming that he intentionally and willfully misrepresented an applicant's employment history (the applicant was a visiting faculty member at the professor's university when his application was rejected). The university's grievance procedures do not provide for (or, for that matter, prohibit) discovery by participants in grievance proceedings. However, since the professor is being charged with moral turpitude, and because the grievant is seeking severe sanctions (up to and including dismissal), the professor seeks discovery from the applicant. The professor believes that the applicant misrepresented his employment history during the employment process, believes that he will continue to do so during the grievance process, and the professor claims that

he cannot fairly and adequately defend himself without discovery. Does the Due Process Clause require the grievance committee to provide the professor with discovery regarding the grievant's employment history?

Goss v. Lopez

419 U.S. 565 (1975)

Mr. Justice WHITE delivered the opinion of the Court.

Ohio law empowers the principal of an Ohio public school to suspend a pupil for misconduct for up to 10 days or to expel him. In either case, he must notify the student's parents within 24 hours and state the reasons for his action. A pupil who is expelled, or his parents, may appeal the decision to the Board of Education and in connection therewith shall be permitted to be heard at the board meeting. The Board may reinstate the pupil following the hearing. No similar procedure is provided in §3313.66 or any other provision of state law for a suspended student. Aside from a regulation tracking the statute, at the time of the imposition of the suspensions in this case the CPSS Cleveland Public School System itself had not issued any written procedure applicable to suspensions. Nor, so far as the record reflects, had any of the individual high schools involved in this case. Each, however, had formally or informally described the conduct for which suspension could be imposed.

The nine named appellees, each of whom had been suspended from public high school in Columbus for up to 10 days without a hearing pursuant to §3313.66, filed an action under 42 U.S.C. §1983 against the Columbus Board of Education and various administrators of the CPSS. The complaint sought a declaration that §3313.66 was unconstitutional in that it permitted public school administrators to deprive plaintiffs of their rights to an education without a hearing of any kind, in violation of the procedural due process component of the Fourteenth Amendment. It also sought to enjoin the public school officials from issuing future suspensions pursuant to §3313.66 and to require them to remove references to the past suspensions from the records of the students in question.

The suspensions arose out of a period of widespread student unrest in the CPSS during February and March 1971. Six of the named plaintiffs were students at the Marion-Franklin High School and were each suspended for 10 days on account of disruptive or disobedient conduct committed in the presence of the school administrator who ordered the suspension. One of these, Tyrone Washington, was among a group of students demonstrating in the school auditorium while a class was being conducted there. He was ordered by the school principal to leave, refused to do so, and was suspended. Rudolph Sutton, in the presence of the principal, physically attacked a police officer who was attempting to remove Tyrone Washington from the auditorium. He was immediately suspended. The other four students were suspended for similar conduct. None was given a hearing to determine the operative facts underlying the suspension, but each, together with his or her parents, was offered the opportunity to attend a conference, subsequent to the effective date of the suspension, to discuss the student's future.

Two named plaintiffs were students at the Central High School and McGuffey Junior High School, respectively. One was suspended in connection with a disturbance in the lunchroom which involved some physical damage to school property. Lopez another of the students testified that at least 75 other students were suspended from his school on the same day. He also testified that he was not a party to the destructive conduct but was instead an innocent bystander. Because no one from the school testified with regard to this incident, there is no evidence in the record indicating the official basis for concluding otherwise. Lopez never had a hearing. Betty Crome a third student was present at a demonstration at a high school other than the one she was attending. There she was arrested together with others, taken to the police station, and released without being formally charged. Before she went to school on the following day, she was notified that she had been suspended for a 10-day period. Because no one from the school testified with respect to this incident, the record does not disclose how the McGuffey Junior High School principal went about making the decision to suspend Crome, nor does it disclose on what information the decision was based. It is clear from the record that no hearing was ever held. There was no testimony with respect to the suspension of the ninth named plaintiff, Carl Smith. The school files were also silent as to his suspension, although as to some, but not all, of the other named plaintiffs the files contained either direct references to their suspensions or copies of letters sent to their parents advising them of the suspension.

Appellants contend that because there is no constitutional right to an education at public expense, the Due Process Clause does not protect against expulsions from the public school system. The Fourteenth Amendment forbids the State to deprive any person of life, liberty, or property without due process of law. Protected interests in property are normally "not created by the Constitution. Rather, they are created and their dimensions are defined" by an independent source such as state statutes or rules entitling the citizen to certain benefits. Appellees plainly had legitimate claims of entitlement to a public education. Ohio Rev. Code Ann. §§3313.48 and 3313.64 direct local authorities to provide a free education to all residents between five and 21 years of age, and a compulsory-attendance law requires attendance for a school year of not less than 32 weeks. Having chosen to extend the right to an education to people of appellees' class generally, Ohio may not withdraw that right on grounds of misconduct absent, fundamentally fair procedures to determine whether the misconduct has occurred. The authority possessed by the State to prescribe and enforce standards of conduct in its schools, although concededly very broad, must be exercised consistently with constitutional safeguards. Among other things, the State is constrained to recognize a student's legitimate entitlement to a public education as a property interest which is protected by the Due Process Clause and which may not be taken away for misconduct without adherence to the minimum procedures required by that Clause.

Appellants argue that the loss of 10 days is neither severe nor grievous and the Due Process Clause is therefore of no relevance. In determining "whether due process requirements apply in the first place, we must look not to the 'weight' but to the nature of the interest at stake." Appellees were excluded from school only temporarily, it is true, but the length and consequent severity of a deprivation, while another factor to weigh in determining the appropriate form of hearing, "is not decisive of the basic right" to a hearing of some kind. The Court's view has been that as long as a property deprivation is not *de minimis,* its gravity is irrelevant to the question whether account must be taken of the Due Process Clause. A 10-day suspension from school is not *de minimis* in our view and may not be imposed in complete disregard of the Due Process Clause.

A short suspension is, of course, a far milder deprivation than expulsion. But, "education is perhaps the most important function of state and local governments," and the total exclusion from the educational process for more than a trivial period, and certainly if the suspension is for 10 days, is a serious event in the life of the suspended child. Neither the property interest in educational benefits temporarily denied nor the liberty interest in reputation, which is also implicated, is so insubstantial that suspensions may constitutionally be imposed by any procedure the school chooses, no matter how arbitrary.

"Once it is determined that due process applies, the question remains what process is due." We turn to that question, fully realizing as our cases regularly do that the interpretation and application of the Due Process Clause are intensely practical matters and that "the very nature of due process negates any concept of inflexible procedures universally applicable to every imaginable situation." At the very minimum, therefore, students facing suspension and the consequent interference with a protected property interest must be given some kind of notice and afforded some kind of hearing.

It also appears from our cases that the timing and content of the notice and the nature of the hearing will depend on appropriate accommodation of the competing interests involved. The student's interest is to avoid unfair or mistaken exclusion from the educational process, with all of its unfortunate consequences. The Due Process Clause will not shield him from suspensions properly imposed, but it disserves both his interest and the interest of the State if his suspension is in fact unwarranted. The concern would be mostly academic if the disciplinary process were a totally accurate, unerring process, never mistaken and never unfair. Unfortunately, that is not the case, and no one suggests that it is. Disciplinarians, although proceeding in utmost good faith, frequently act on the reports and advice of others; and the controlling facts and the nature of the conduct under challenge are often disputed. The risk of error is not at all trivial, and it should be guarded against if that may be done without prohibitive cost or interference with the educational process.

The difficulty is that our schools are vast and complex. Some modicum of discipline and order is essential if the educational function is to be performed. Events calling for discipline are frequent occurrences and sometimes require immediate, effective action. Suspension is considered not only to be a necessary tool to maintain order but a valuable educational device. The prospect of imposing elaborate hearing requirements in every suspension case is viewed with great concern, and many school authorities may well prefer the untrammeled power to act unilaterally, unhampered by rules about notice and hearing. But it would be a strange disciplinary system in an educational institution if no communication was sought by the disciplinarian with the student in an effort to inform him of his dereliction and to let him tell his side of the story in order to make sure that an injustice is not done.

We do not believe that school authorities must be totally free from notice and hearing requirements if their schools are to operate with acceptable efficiency. Students facing temporary suspension have interests qualifying for protection of the Due Process Clause, and due process requires, in connection with a suspension of 10 days or less, that the student be given oral or written notice of the charges against him and, if he denies them, an explanation of the evidence the authorities have and an opportunity to present his side of the story. The Clause requires at least these rudimentary precautions against unfair or mistaken findings of misconduct and arbitrary exclusion from school.

There need be no delay between the time "notice" is given and the time of the hearing. In the great majority of cases the disciplinarian may informally discuss the alleged misconduct with the student minutes after it has occurred. We hold only that, in being given an opportunity to explain his version of the facts at this discussion, the student first be told what he is accused of doing and what the basis of the accusation is. Since the hearing may occur almost immediately following the misconduct, it follows that as a general rule notice and hearing should precede removal of the student from school. There are recurring situations in which prior notice and hearing cannot be insisted upon. Students whose presence poses a continuing danger to persons or property or an ongoing threat of disrupting the academic process may be immediately removed from school. In such cases, the necessary notice and rudimentary hearing should follow as soon as practicable.

We do not believe that we have imposed procedures on school disciplinarians which are inappropriate in a classroom setting. Instead we have imposed requirements which are, if anything, less than a fair-minded school principal would impose upon himself in order to avoid unfair suspensions. We stop short of construing the Due Process Clause to require, countrywide, that hearings in connection with short suspensions must afford the student the opportunity to secure counsel, to confront and cross-examine witnesses supporting the charge, or to call his own witnesses to verify his version of the incident. Brief disciplinary suspensions are almost countless. To impose in each such case even truncated trial-type procedures might well overwhelm administrative facilities in many places and, by diverting resources, cost more than it would save in educational effectiveness. Moreover, further formalizing the suspension process and escalating its formality and adversary nature may not only make it too costly as a regular disciplinary tool but also destroy its effectiveness as part of the teaching process.

On the other hand, requiring effective notice and informal hearing permitting the student to give his version of the events will provide a meaningful hedge against erroneous action. At least the disciplinarian will be alerted to the existence of disputes about facts and arguments about cause and effect. He may then determine himself to summon the accuser, permit cross-examination, and allow the student to present his own witnesses. In more difficult cases, he may permit counsel. In any event, his discretion will be more informed and we think the risk of error substantially reduced.

Requiring that there be at least an informal give-and-take between student and disciplinarian, preferably prior to the suspension, will add little to the fact-finding function where the disciplinarian himself has witnessed the conduct forming the basis for the charge. But things are not always as they seem to be, and the student will at least have the opportunity to characterize his conduct and put it in what he deems the proper context.

We have addressed ourselves solely to the short suspension, not exceeding 10 days. Longer suspensions or expulsions for the remainder of the school term, or permanently, may require more formal procedures. Nor do we put aside the possibility that in unusual situations, although involving only a short suspension, something more than the rudimentary procedures will be required. The District Court found each of the suspensions involved here to have occurred without a hearing, either before or after the suspension, and that each suspension was therefore invalid and the statute unconstitutional insofar as it permits such suspensions without notice or hearing. Accordingly, the judgment is

Affirmed.

Mr. Justice POWELL, with whom THE CHIEF JUSTICE, Mr. Justice BLACKMUN, and Mr. Justice REHNQUIST join, *dissenting.*

I would conclude that a deprivation of not more than 10 days' suspension from school, imposed as a routine disciplinary measure, does not assume constitutional dimensions. Absences of such limited duration will rarely affect a pupil's opportunity to learn or his scholastic performance. Indeed, the record in this case reflects no educational injury to appellees. Each completed the semester in which the suspension occurred and performed at least as well as he or she had in previous years. This Court has explicitly recognized that school authorities must have broad discretionary authority in the daily operation of public schools. This includes wide latitude with respect to maintaining discipline and good order. Such an approach properly recognizes the unique nature of public education and the correspondingly limited role of the judiciary in its supervision.

The State's generalized interest in maintaining an orderly school system is not incompatible with the individual interest of the student. Education in any meaningful sense includes the inculcation of an understanding in each pupil of the necessity of rules and obedience thereto. In assessing in constitutional terms the need to protect pupils from unfair minor discipline by school authorities, the Court ignores the commonality of interest of the State and pupils in the public school system. Rather, it thinks in traditional judicial terms of an adversary situation. To be sure, there will be the occasional pupil innocent of any rule infringement who is mistakenly suspended or whose infraction is too minor to justify suspension. But, while there is no evidence indicating the frequency of unjust suspensions, common sense suggests that they will not be numerous in relation to the total number, and that mistakes or injustices will usually be righted by informal means.

One of the more disturbing aspects of today's decision is its indiscriminate reliance upon the judiciary, and the adversary process, as the means of resolving many of the most routine problems arising in the classroom. In mandating due process procedures the Court misapprehends the reality of the normal teacher-pupil relationship. There is an ongoing relationship, one in which the teacher must occupy many roles—educator, adviser, friend, and, at times, parent-substitute. It is rarely adversary in nature except with respect to the chronically disruptive or insubordinate pupil whom the teacher must be free to discipline without frustrating formalities. If, as seems apparent, the Court will now require due process procedures whenever such routine school decisions are challenged, the impact upon public education will be serious indeed. The discretion and judgment of federal courts will be substituted for that of the 50-state legislatures, the 14,000 school boards, and the 2,000,000 teachers who heretofore have been responsible for the administration of the American public school system.

∾ PROBLEMS ∾

1. *Suspended.* Pursuant to Arizona law, "All suspensions from public schools of ten days or longer require the provision of oral or written notice after the suspension has commenced." Chante is suspended for smoking cigarettes on the grounds of her public high school in Phoenix. Because she feels that there is a stigma attached to a suspension, and because she believes that her absence from school will adversely affect her grades and class rank, Chante demands a pre-suspension hearing. Is she entitled to one? Why, or why not?

2. *The Lawyer's Basketball League.* The City of Louisville maintains a variety of basketball leagues, including the "Lawyer's Basketball League," in which all participants must be licensed lawyers or work for a local law firm. One team, upset by a referee's call that cost it a game, demands the right to "file briefs and have oral argument" regarding the validity of the call. The team is seeking to have the call invalidated and the game replayed (the complaining team lost by a point). You

are the city's lawyer. Must you grant the request for a hearing, or can you treat the referee's call as "final"?

3. *Due Process in Sexual Assault Cases.* In recent years, there has been considerable controversy regarding the level of process that universities must provide faculty and students who are charged with sexual harassment. The Obama administration urged colleges and universities to decide such cases more informally with a university official conducting an investigation and issuing a decision. Those charged with sexual assault complained, alleging that they have a constitutional right to "confront" their accusers and to subject the accusers to cross-examination. After *Goss*, can it be said that the consequences of a sexual assault determination are severe enough to require an adversarial hearing, including the right to cross-examination? *See Doe v. University of Cincinnati*, 872 F.3d 393 (6th Cir. 2017).

4. *The TSA "No Fly" List.* The Transportation Safety Administration (TSA) has established a "no fly" list. People can be placed on that list by the Terrorist Screening Center (TSC), and inclusion on the list precludes them from boarding commercial air flights. In general, TSC treats the criteria for placing individuals on the list as "secret," fearing that disclosure will compromise aviation safety by alerting terrorists to the considerations deemed relevant by the TSC. Does an individual have the right to due process before inclusion on the "no fly" list? Once placed on that list, and denied the right to fly, what procedural rights should the individual have in terms of obtaining removal from the list? *See Mokdad v. Lynch*, 876 F.3d 167 (6th Cir. 2017).

5. *The "Blighted" Property.* Suppose that, as part of an urban renewal project, a property owner receives a notice regarding the "condition" of its property. Unsure regarding the nature of the hearing, the owner calls the city and is told "not to worry" about the hearing. At that hearing, the city finds that the property is "blighted" and therefore subject to condemnation for urban renewal purposes. Although the property owner had 30 days to challenge the finding, he was not notified of the finding until after the 30 day period had run. Was the city required to notify the property owner of the "blighted" finding? *See M.A.K. Investment Group, LLC v. City of Glendale*, 889 F.3d 1173 (10th Cir. 2018).

Board of Curators of the University of Missouri v. Horowitz

435 U.S. 78 (1978)

Mr. Justice REHNQUIST delivered the opinion of the Court.

Respondent, a student at the University of Missouri—Kansas City Medical School, was dismissed by petitioner officials of the school during her final year of study for failure to meet academic standards. Respondent sued alleging that petitioners had not accorded her procedural due process prior to her dismissal. We granted certiorari to consider what procedures must be accorded to a student at a state educational institution whose dismissal may constitute a deprivation of "liberty" or "property" within the meaning of the Fourteenth Amendment.

Respondent was admitted with advanced standing to the Medical School in the fall of 1971. During the final years of a student's education at the school, the student is required to pursue in "rotational units" academic and clinical studies pertaining to various medical disciplines such as obstetrics-gynecology, pediatrics, and surgery. Each student's academic performance at the school is evaluated on a periodic basis by the Council on Evaluation, a body composed of both faculty and students, which can recommend various actions including probation and dismissal. The recommendations of the Council are reviewed by the Coordinating Committee, a body composed solely of faculty members, and must ultimately be approved by the Dean. Students are not typically allowed to appear before either the Council or the Coordinating Committee on the occasion of their review of the student's academic performance.

In the spring of respondent's first year of study, several faculty members expressed dissatisfaction with her clinical performance during a pediatrics rotation. The faculty members noted that respondent's "performance was below that of her peers in all clinical patient-oriented settings," that she was erratic in her attendance at clinical sessions, and that she lacked a critical concern for personal hygiene. Upon the recommendation of the Council on Evaluation, respondent was advanced to her second and final year on a probationary basis.

Faculty dissatisfaction with respondent's clinical performance continued during the following year. For example, respondent's docent, or faculty adviser, rated her clinical skills as "unsatisfactory." In the middle of the year, the Council again reviewed respondent's academic progress and concluded that respondent should not be considered for graduation in June of that year; the Council recommended that, absent "radical improvement," respondent be dropped from the school.

Respondent was permitted to take a set of oral and practical examinations as an "appeal" of the decision not to permit her to graduate. Pursuant to this "appeal," respondent spent a substantial portion of time with seven practicing physicians in the area who enjoyed a good reputation among their peers. The physicians were asked to recommend whether respondent should be allowed to graduate on schedule and, if not, whether she should be dropped immediately or allowed to remain on probation. Only two of the doctors recommended that respondent be graduated on schedule. Of the other five, two recommended that she be immediately dropped from the school. The remaining three recommended that she not be allowed to graduate in June and be continued on probation pending further reports on her clinical progress. Upon receipt of these recommendations, the Council on Evaluation reaffirmed its prior position.

The Council met again in mid-May to consider whether respondent should be allowed to remain in school beyond June of that year. Noting that the report on respondent's recent surgery rotation rated her performance as "low-satisfactory," the Council unanimously recommended that "barring receipt of any reports that Miss Horowitz has improved radically, she not be allowed to re-enroll in the School of Medicine." The Council delayed making its recommendation official until receiving reports on other rotations; when a report on respondent's emergency rotation also turned out to be negative, the Council unanimously reaffirmed its recommendation that respondent be dropped from the school. The Coordinating Committee and the Dean approved the recommendation and notified respondent, who appealed the decision in writing to the University's Provost for Health Sciences. The Provost sustained the school's actions after reviewing the record compiled during the earlier proceedings.

To be entitled to the procedural protections of the Fourteenth Amendment, respondent must in a case such as this demonstrate that her dismissal from the school deprived her of either a "liberty" or a "property" interest. Respondent has never alleged that she was deprived of a property interest recognized by Missouri state law. Instead, respondent argued that her dismissal deprived her of "liberty" by substantially impairing her opportunities to continue her medical education or to return to employment in a medically related field.

We have recently had an opportunity to elaborate upon the circumstances under which an employment termination might infringe a protected liberty interest. In *Bishop v. Wood*, 426 U.S. 341 (1976), we upheld the dismissal of a policeman without a hearing; we rejected the theory that the mere fact of dismissal, absent some publicizing of the reasons for the action, could amount to a stigma infringing one's liberty: In *Board of Regents v. Roth*, 408 U.S. 564, we recognized that the nonretention of an untenured college teacher might make him somewhat less attractive to other employers, but nevertheless concluded that it would stretch the concept too far "to suggest that a person is deprived of 'liberty' when he simply is not rehired in one position but remains as free as before to seek another." This same conclusion applies to the discharge of a public employee whose position is terminable at the will of the employer when there is no public disclosure of the reasons for the discharge.

We need not decide whether respondent's dismissal deprived her of a liberty interest in pursuing a medical career. Nor need we decide whether respondent's dismissal infringed any other interest constitutionally protected against deprivation without procedural due process. Assuming the existence of a liberty or property interest, respondent has been awarded at least as much due process as the Fourteenth Amendment requires. The school fully informed respondent of the faculty's dissatisfaction with her clinical progress and the danger that this posed to timely graduation and continued enrollment. The ultimate decision to dismiss respondent was careful and deliberate. These procedures were sufficient under the Due Process Clause of the Fourteenth Amendment. Respondent "was afforded full procedural due process by the school." In fact, "the school went beyond constitutionally required procedural due process by affording respondent the opportunity to be examined by seven independent physicians in order to be absolutely certain that their grading of the respondent in her medical skills was correct."

In *Goss v. Lopez*, 419 U.S. 565 (1975), we held that due process requires, in connection with the suspension of a student from public school for disciplinary reasons, "that the student be given oral or written notice of the charges against him and, if he denies them, an explanation of the evidence the authorities have and an opportunity to present his side of the story." The Court of Appeals apparently read *Goss* as requiring some type of formal hearing at which respondent could defend her academic ability and performance. All that *Goss* required was an "informal give-and-take" between the student and the administrative body dismissing him that would, at least, give the student "the opportunity to characterize his conduct and put it in what he deems the proper context." But we have frequently emphasized that "the very nature of due process negates any concept of inflexible procedures universally applicable to every imaginable situation." The need for flexibility is well illustrated by the significant difference between the failure of a student to meet academic standards and the violation by a student of valid rules of conduct. This difference calls for far less stringent procedural requirements in the case of an academic dismissal.

Since the issue first arose 50 years ago, state and lower federal courts have recognized that there are distinct differences between decisions to suspend or dismiss a student for disciplinary purposes and similar actions taken for academic reasons which may call for hearings in connection with the former but not the latter. Reason clearly supports the perception of these decisions. A school is an academic institution, not a courtroom or administrative hearing room. In *Goss,* this Court felt that suspensions of students for disciplinary reasons have a sufficient resemblance to traditional judicial and administrative factfinding to call for a "hearing" before the relevant school authority. While recognizing that school authorities must be afforded the necessary tools to maintain discipline, the Court concluded: "It would be a strange disciplinary system in an educational institution if no communication was sought by the disciplinarian with the student in an effort to inform him of his dereliction and to let him tell his side of the story in order to make sure that an injustice is not done."

"Requiring effective notice and informal hearing permitting the student to give his version of the events will provide a meaningful hedge against erroneous action. At least the disciplinarian will be alerted to the existence of disputes about facts and arguments about cause and effect." Even in the context of a school disciplinary proceeding, however, the Court stopped short of requiring a formal hearing since "further formalizing the suspension process and escalating its formality and adversary nature may not only make it too costly as a regular disciplinary tool but also destroy its effectiveness as a part of the teaching process."

Academic evaluations of a student, in contrast to disciplinary determinations, bear little resemblance to the judicial and administrative fact-finding proceedings to which we have traditionally attached a full-hearing requirement. In *Goss,* the school's decision to suspend the students rested on factual conclusions that the individual students had participated in demonstrations that had disrupted classes, attacked a police officer, or caused physical damage to school property. The requirement of a hearing, where the student could present his side of the factual issue, could under such circumstances "provide a meaningful hedge against erroneous action." The decision to dismiss respondent, by comparison, rested on the academic judgment of school officials that she did not have the necessary clinical ability to perform adequately as a medical doctor and was making insufficient progress toward that goal. Such a judgment is by its nature more subjective and evaluative than the typical factual questions presented in the average disciplinary decision. Like the decision of an individual professor as to the proper grade for a student in his course, the determination whether to dismiss a student for academic reasons requires an expert evaluation of cumulative information and is not readily adapted to the procedural tools of judicial or administrative decisionmaking.

Under such circumstances, we decline to ignore the historic judgment of educators and thereby formalize the academic dismissal process by requiring a hearing. The educational process is not by nature adversary; instead it centers around a continuing relationship between faculty and students, "one in which the teacher must occupy many roles—educator, adviser, friend, and, at times, parent-substitute." *Goss v. Lopez*, 419 U.S. at 594 (Powell, J., dissenting). This is especially true as one advances through the varying regimes of the educational system, and the instruction becomes both more individualized and more specialized. In *Goss*, this Court concluded that the value of some form of hearing in a disciplinary context outweighs any resulting harm to the academic environment. Influencing this conclusion was clearly the belief that disciplinary proceedings, in which the teacher must decide whether to punish a student for disruptive or insubordinate behavior, may automatically bring an adversary flavor to the normal student-teacher relationship. The same conclusion does not follow in the academic context. We decline to further enlarge the judicial presence in the academic community and thereby risk deterioration of many beneficial aspects of the faculty-student relationship. We recognize, as did the Massachusetts Supreme Judicial Court over 60 years ago, that a hearing may be "useless or harmful in finding out the truth as to scholarship." "Judicial interposition in the operation of the public school system of the Nation raises problems requiring care and restraint."

We agree with the District Court that no showing of arbitrariness or capriciousness has been made in this case. Courts are particularly ill-equipped to evaluate academic performance. The factors discussed in Part II with respect to procedural due process speak a fortiori here and warn against any such judicial intrusion into academic decisionmaking.

The judgment of the Court of Appeals is therefore

Reversed.

Mr. Justice MARSHALL, *concurring in part* and *dissenting in part.*

Resolution of this case under our traditional approach does not turn on whether the dismissal of respondent is characterized as one for "academic" or "disciplinary" reasons. A talismanic reliance on labels should not be a substitute for sensitive consideration of the procedures required by due process. When the facts disputed are of a type susceptible of determination by third parties, as the allegations about respondent plainly were, there is no more reason to deny all procedural protection to one who will suffer a serious loss than there was in *Goss,* and indeed there may be good reason to provide even more protection. A court's characterization of the reasons for a student's dismissal adds nothing to the effort to find procedures that are fair to the student and the school, and that promote the elusive goal of determining the truth in a manner consistent with both individual dignity and society's limited resources.

∾ PROBLEMS ∾

1. *More on the Professor and the Amsterdam Trip.* Let's return to the problem at the beginning of the chapter. Assume that you represent the dean who must decide what action to take against the professor (if any). Is the professor entitled to a hearing before you impose the contemplated sanctions (e.g., barring him from taking the Amsterdam trip as well as from going on overnight trips with students, because of his prior inappropriate behavior)? If so, how must the hearing be structured, and what rights does the professor have (right to counsel, right to cross-examination, etc.)? If you were asked to represent the professor, what arguments would you make on his behalf for expanded hearing rights?

2. *The Plagiarizing Student.* Professor Royster, who teaches at a state law school, believes that a student (John O'Reilly) engaged in plagiarism on a take-home writing project. The professor reached his conclusion based on statements made by other students (who purportedly overheard O'Reilly bragging that he plagiarized) as well as on an internet search through law-school-papers.com (a website that provides research papers for law students). The internet search revealed that the identical paper was available for purchase online. Royster took the information about O'Reilly to the law school dean. You are the university counsel, and the dean has come to you for advice about how to proceed. You have checked the law school's rules and regulations and found that the university does not have an established disciplinary procedure for students. The dean has asked you for advice about what procedures must be accorded to O'Reilly as a necessary predicate to disciplinary action. What advice would you give him about how to proceed?

3. *The Failing Grade.* A student receives a failing grade. The student has met with the professor who adamantly defends the grade. In his view, the student was "off track" and missed the critical issue. Just as adamantly, the student disagrees and believes that the grade was unfair. He believes that the professor undervalued the issue that the student actually discussed. Does the student have a due process right to a review of the professor's grade? If so, what must the student allege? If a hearing is granted, what procedures must be accorded to the student?

4. *Student Due Process Rights.* The U.S. Department of Education's Office for Civil Rights (OCR) has issued guidelines interpreting Title IX. Under those guidelines, some universities have adopted new procedures for investigating claims of sexual assault. At one university, for example, a university administrator conducted an investigation which involved interviewing witnesses and participants, the making of a decision about whether a sexual assault occurred, and the imposition of punishment (which involved expulsion from the university). Under *Goss*, is such a procedure constitutionally valid? Can a student be expelled without being given a formal hearing, including the right to confront his/her accusers? In another case, which also resulted in expulsion, the judge allowed the accused to cross-examine his accuser, but required that he be separated from the accuser by a screen which blocked him from seeing her. Also, the judge controlled the cross-examination and disallowed 23 of the accuser's 32 questions. Is such a hearing permissible?

[Points to Remember for Chapter 7 is contained in online file.]

8

Substantive Protection of Economic Rights

U.S. CONSTITUTION, FIFTH AMENDMENT

Due Process Clause. No person shall be deprived of life, liberty, or property, without due process of law.

U.S. CONSTITUTION, FIFTH AMENDMENT

Takings Clause. nor shall private property be taken for public use, without just compensation.

U.S. CONSTITUTION, FOURTEENTH AMENDMENT

Due Process Clause. nor shall any State deprive any person of life, liberty, or property, without due process of law.

U.S. CONSTITUTION, ARTICLE I

Contract Clause. No State shall pass any Law impairing the Obligation of Contracts.

[Roadmap for Chapter 8 is contained in online file.]

∾ PROBLEM: SAVE THE BEACH ∾

The City of Pensacola, Florida, has become increasingly concerned about issues involving beach erosion, storms, and especially oil spills, given the relatively close Deepwater Horizon oil leak in 2010. That leak occurred after an April 20, 2010, explosion on the rig, killing 11 people. The oil spilled out at a rate of up to several hundred thousand barrels a day, meaning that it equaled the horrific Exxon Valdez spill in Alaska in a little over a week.

Pensacola decided it needs to make significant changes in its current relaxed approach to property preservation. The basis for its concern derived from studies that show some beach areas on the Gulf of Mexico are eroding at a rate of 5 to 10 feet per year. Other studies show that the force of hurricanes is greater without the coastal wetlands to act as buffers.

Since Pensacola does not have the resources to finance environmentally sound development, it is determined to find inexpensive ways to implement its preservation proposals. The city council is considering adopting a variety of different proposals. One proposal is tentatively titled "Save Our Beaches." After asserting that each of the provisions is severable upon a finding of invalidity, the law states in part:

(a) *Seawalls.* All private property owners whose property is located directly on the beach must build seawalls or implement acceptable alternative wave dispersal technology, such as breakwaters, or dredge sand off the beach.

(b) *Accretions and Avulsions.* Accretions are sand, sediment, and other similar deposits that create additional dry land. Accretions usually occur slowly over time. Unlike the common law and prior Florida law, in Pensacola the city shall from this day forward have title to any accretions that occur. Avulsions are areas of dry land created from land once covered by water and are usually uncovered based on sudden events. Regardless of how they are uncovered, the state shall continue to hold title to such land in trust for the people. Thus, while the technical property boundary of littoral land owners might change, the right to access to the water shall be preserved as will other common law riparian rights, unless changed by valid state law.

(c) *Contracts.* Any contractual agreements changed by this law shall be based only on substantial justification of preserving the beach and its central role in Pensacola culture.

(d) *Natural State.* All property owners within one-half mile of the beach must leave at least 50% of that property in its natural state or with some form of wetland vegetation, if feasible, after neutral study. (This section applies prospectively only, with no change to existing structures.)

(e) *Clean-up.* All beach-front landowners must cleanup any oil, oil products, or related waste on their property within seven (7) days of its deposit on the property.

(f) *Building Moratorium.* There shall be no more building on beach-front property for a minimum of six months to assess and determine the impact of the Deepwater Horizon oil leak.

(g) *Colors.* To promote Pensacola, all buildings within a mile of the beach must comply with the city color scheme, with yellow and blue predominating, unless a variance is permitted.

The city council is thinking about imposing fines of up to $10,000 a month for each violation and seeking injunctive relief and possibly criminal penalties.

As you work your way through this chapter, you will be asked to play various roles—for example, an attorney who is advising the city council or an attorney who represents affected landowners—and to consider the validity of this legislation under various factual scenarios.

Economic rights have assumed increasing significance in recent years, especially in light of the serious financial difficulties experienced by the United States. Terms such as *collateralized debt obligations* and *credit swap derivatives* have surfaced in the American vernacular, and the consequences of those financial instruments have led to a call for greater regulation of financial markets. Some politicians and observers have framed the issue as a clash between the interests of Wall Street and Main Street.

The question whether economic interests warrant protection, as a matter of constitutional right or liberty, highlights a long-persisting controversy over the role of the judiciary and its relationship to the elected branches of government. Early interpretations of the Contract Clause reflected a judicial interest in prohibiting state laws that retroactively impaired private contractual rights and expectations. Indeed, until the late nineteenth century, the Contract Clause represented the primary constitutional basis for protecting private property interests against government action.

By contrast, judicial interpretations of the Takings Clause suggest that it applies when government acquires private property through eminent domain or regulates land in a manner that impairs its use. However, over the years, the Takings Clause has tended to be an inconsistent and uncertain source of protection for private property rights. The Commerce Clause, sometimes in conjunction with preemption principles, has been another significant tool for managing the boundaries of economic freedom. Interpretation of the Commerce Clause, depending upon prevailing doctrine, has expanded or restricted a state's power to regulate economic activity.

Although largely consigned to history, utilization of the substantive Due Process Clauses to define and protect economic rights and liberties has been a focal point of the debate over constitutional interpretation and the role of the judiciary. The emergence of substantive due process, to develop and account for economic rights and liberties, was previewed in *Dred Scott v. Sandford*, 60 U.S. 393 (1857), when the Court attempted to resolve the slavery issue on constitutional grounds. As Chief Justice Roger B. Taney put it, "the right of property in a slave is distinctly and expressly affirmed in the Constitution." And, federal legislation depriving a citizen of "his property in a particular Territory could hardly be dignified with the name due process of law."

Notwithstanding the eventual repudiation of *Dred Scott* by war, constitutional amendment, and later judicial review, economic rights theory gained increasing currency as the latter half of the nineteenth century progressed. In *The Slaughterhouse Cases*, 83 U.S. 36 (1872), the Court's seminal interpretation of the Fourteenth Amendment, Justice Stephen Field urged an understanding that would include "the right to acquire and possess property of every kind" as a matter that "of right belongs to the citizens of all free governments." *Id.* at 76. Justice Field's argument, echoed by three other dissenting justices, pertained to the Privileges and Immunities Clause of the Fourteenth Amendment. His broad interpretation of the incidents of federal citizenship did not command a majority of the *Slaughterhouse* Court, and the Privileges and Immunities Clause largely has been of limited consequence since.

Economic rights theory, which the Court repudiated in the privileges and immunities context, broke through slightly as an animating source for the Due

Process Clause more than two decades later. In *Allgeyer v. Louisiana*, 165 U.S. 578 (1897), the Court embraced the Due Process Clause as the basis for

> the right of the citizen to be free in the enjoyment of all his faculties; to be free to use them in all lawful ways; to live and work where he will; to earn his livelihood by any lawful calling; to pursue any livelihood or avocation; and for that purpose to enter into all contracts which may be proper, necessary and essential to his carrying out to a successful conclusion the purposes above mentioned.

Id. at 589.

The *Allgeyer* decision heralded an era of judicially identified and developed rights and liberties that engendered controversy with respect to not only the Court's outputs but also to its standards of review and role in the context of representative governance. Debate over the Court's performance and function has persisted long after the economic rights doctrine was abandoned in the late 1930s. Among other things, it is a reference point for modern dialogue regarding the Due Process Clause as a source of fundamental albeit unenumerated rights and liberties.

This chapter focuses on the substantive Due Process Clauses of the Fifth and Fourteenth Amendments, the Takings Clause, and the Contracts Clause as constitutional means of accounting for economic rights and liberties.

A. SUBSTANTIVE DUE PROCESS: FROM *ALLGEYER* TO *LOCHNER* TO *NEBBIA*

The concept of "substantive due process" has emerged as a limit on government powers. The idea of a "substantive" limit distinguishes the "process" orientation of the Due Process Clause and protects particular values, such as economic freedom or personal privacy.

The need for substantive due process presupposes an otherwise valid exercise of government power. It is well established that states possess "police powers" that predated the Constitution and were acknowledged in it. The federal government also may enact laws that indirectly provide for the health, welfare, safety, and morals of society through the Commerce Clause and other powers. These "police power" regulations (also known as "health and welfare regulations") can take many different forms. For example, a legislature might limit the number of hours that employees can work or mandate minimum compensation. Alternatively, a legislature might place conditions on the ability of out-of-state companies to do business within the state, or choose to prohibit certain types of businesses (e.g., brothels).

Health, welfare, and safety regulations might be challenged and curtailed on any number of constitutional grounds, including the Contract Clause, the protection of "liberty" contained in the Fourteenth Amendment, the Equal Protection Clause, and sometimes the Privileges and Immunities Clause. The conceptualization of economic substantive due process emerged from the interpretation of the word *liberty* in the Fourteenth Amendment. For example, in *Allgeyer v. Louisiana,* 165 U.S. 578 (1897), a state law prohibited foreign insurance companies from doing business within the state without a license and an agent authorized to conduct business on its behalf. The Court struck down the law:

> We think the statute is a violation of the fourteenth amendment of the federal constitution, in that it deprives the defendants of their liberty without due process of law. The 'liberty' mentioned in that amendment means, not only the right of the citizen to be free from the mere physical restraint of his person, as by incarceration, but the term is deemed to embrace the right of the citizen to be free in the enjoyment of all his faculties; to be free to use them in all lawful ways; to live and work where he will; to earn his livelihood by any lawful calling; to pursue any livelihood or avocation; and for that purpose to enter into all contracts which may be proper, necessary, and essential to his carrying out to a successful conclusion the purposes above mentioned.

See also Holden v. Hardy, 169 U.S. 366 (1898) (the Court sustained a Utah law regulating the hours of employment in underground mines and in smelters and ore reduction works).

Resolution of these controversies implicates competing theories of judicial review, and judicial outcomes hinge in large part on whether the Court embraces a model that defers to or independently evaluates legislative outputs and premises. Early substantive due process review, which focused largely on economic rights and liberties, proceeded on the premise that the judiciary should evaluate both legislative means and ends. This practice was challenged by critics then and now who viewed it as "antidemocratic" in the sense that it transformed the Court into a super-legislature. The following case illuminates the methodology of constitutionally managed economic rights through the Due Process Clause. It also is the source of shorthand terminology (*Lochnerism*) that detractors use in criticizing the judiciary's development of rights that the Constitution does not specifically enumerate.

1912 Vegetable Cannery – Wisconsin

Lochner v. New York

198 U.S. 45 (1905)

Mr. Justice PECKHAM delivered the opinion of the Court.

Joseph Lochner was indicted on a charge that he "wrongfully and unlawfully required and permitted an employee working for him in his biscuit, bread, and cake bakery and confectionery establishment, at the city of Utica, to work more than sixty hours in one week." The plaintiff was convicted and ordered to pay a fine of $50.

There is no pretense that the statute was intended to meet a case of involuntary labor in any form. The mandate of the statute provides that 'no employee shall contract or agree to work,' more than ten hours per day. The employee may desire to earn the extra money which would arise from his working more than the prescribed time, but this statute forbids the employer from permitting the employee to earn it.

The statute necessarily interferes with the right of contract between the employer and employees. The general right to make a contract in relation to his business is part of the liberty of the individual protected by the 14th Amendment of the Federal Constitution. *Allgeyer v. Louisiana*, 165 U.S. 578. No state can deprive any person of life, liberty, or property without due process of law. The right to purchase or to sell labor is part of the liberty protected by this amendment, unless there are circumstances which exclude the right. There are, however, powers existing in the sovereignty of each state in the Union, somewhat vaguely termed police powers that relate to the safety, health, morals, and general welfare of the public. Both property and liberty are held on such reasonable conditions as may be imposed by the governing power of the state in the exercise of those powers, and with such conditions the 14th Amendment was not designed to interfere.

The state has power to prevent the individual from making certain kinds of contracts. When the state, by its legislature, in the assumed exercise of its police powers, has passed an act which seriously limits the right to labor or the right of contract in regard to their means of livelihood between employer and employee, it becomes of great importance to determine which shall prevail,—the right of the individual to labor for such time as he may choose, or the right of the state to prevent the individual from laboring, or from entering into any contract to labor, beyond a certain time prescribed by the state.

It must, of course, be conceded that there is a limit to the valid exercise of the police power by the state. Otherwise the 14th Amendment would have no efficacy and the legislatures of the states would have unbounded power, and it would be enough to say that any piece of legislation was enacted to conserve the morals, the health, or the safety of the people. In every case where legislation of this character is concerned, the question necessarily arises: Is this a fair, reasonable, and appropriate exercise of the police power of the state, or is it an unreasonable, unnecessary, and arbitrary interference with the right of the individual to his personal liberty, or to enter into those contracts in relation to labor which may seem to him appropriate or necessary for the support of himself and his family? Of course the liberty of contract relating to labor includes both parties. The one has as much right to purchase as the other to sell labor.

This is not a question of substituting the judgment of the court for that of the legislature. If the act be within the power of the state it is valid, although the judgment of the court might be totally opposed to the enactment of such a law. But the question would still remain: Is it within the police power of the state? and that question must be answered by the court.

The question whether this act is valid as a labor law, pure and simple, may be dismissed in a few words. There is no reasonable ground for interfering with the liberty of person or the right of free contract, by determining the hours of labor, in the occupation of a baker. There is no contention that bakers as a class are not equal in intelligence and capacity to men in other trades or manual occupations, or that they are not able to assert their rights and care for themselves without the protecting arm of the state, interfering with their independence of judgment and of action. They are in no sense wards of the state. This law involves neither the safety, the morals, nor the welfare, of the public, and that the interest of the public is not in the slightest degree affected by such an act. The law must be upheld, if at all, as a law pertaining to the health of the individual engaged in the occupation of a baker. It does not affect any other portion of the public. Clean and wholesome bread does not depend upon whether the baker works but ten hours per day or only sixty hours a week.

The mere assertion that the subject relates, though but in a remote degree, to the public health, does not necessarily render the enactment valid. The act must have a more direct relation, as a means to an end, and the end itself must be appropriate and legitimate, before an act can be held to be valid which interferes with the general right of an individual to be free in his person and in his power to contract in relation to his own labor.

We think the limit of the police power has been reached and passed in this case. There is, in our judgment, no reasonable foundation for holding this to be necessary or appropriate as a health law to safeguard the public health, or the health of the individuals who are following the trade of a baker. If this statute be valid, and if a proper case is made out in which to deny the right of an individual, as employer or employee, to make contracts for the labor of the latter under the protection of the provisions of the Federal Constitution, there would seem to be no length to which legislation of this nature might not go.

There can be no fair doubt that the trade of a baker, in and of itself, is not an unhealthy one to that degree which would authorize the legislature to interfere with the right to labor, and with the right of free contract on the part of the individual, either as employer or employee. There must be more than the mere fact of the possible existence of some small amount of unhealthiness to warrant legislative interference with liberty. Labor, in any department, may possibly carry with it the seeds of unhealthiness. But are we all, on that account, at the mercy of legislative majorities? A printer, a tinsmith, a locksmith, a carpenter, a cabinetmaker, a dry goods clerk, a bank's, a lawyer's, or a physician's clerk, or a clerk in almost any kind of business, would all come under the power of the legislature, on this assumption. No trade, no occupation, no mode of earning one's living, could escape this all-pervading power, and the acts of the legislature in limiting the hours of labor in all employments would be valid, although such limitation might seriously cripple the ability of the laborer to support himself and his family.

It is urged that it is to the interest of the state that its population should be strong and robust, and therefore any legislation which may be said to tend to make people healthy must be valid as health laws, enacted under the police power. Any law might find shelter under such assumptions, and conduct as well as contract, would come under the restrictive sway of the legislature. Not only the hours of employees, but the hours of employers, could be regulated, and doctors, lawyers, scientists, all professional men, as well as athletes and artisans, could be forbidden to fatigue their brains and bodies by prolonged hours of exercise, lest the fighting strength of the state be impaired. We think that such a law as this, although passed in the assumed exercise of the police power, and as relating to the public health, or the health of the employees named, is not within that power, and is invalid. The act is not, within any fair meaning of the term, a health law, but is an illegal interference with the rights of individuals, both employers and employees, to make contracts regarding labor upon such terms as they may think best, or which they may agree upon with the other parties to such contracts. Statutes of this nature, limiting the hours in which grown and intelligent men may labor to earn their living, are mere meddlesome interferences with the rights of the individual, and they are not saved from condemnation by the claim that they are passed in the exercise of the police power and upon the subject of the health of the individual whose rights are interfered with, unless there be some fair ground, reasonable in and of itself, to say that there is material danger to the public health, or to the health of the employees, if the hours of labor are not curtailed. A prohibition to enter into any contract of labor in a bakery for more than a certain number of hours a week is, in our judgment, so wholly beside the matter of a proper, reasonable, and fair provision as to run counter to that liberty of person and of free contract provided for in the Federal Constitution.

It was further urged on the argument that restricting the hours of labor in the case of bakers was valid because it tended to cleanliness on the part of the workers, as a man was more apt to be cleanly when not overworked, and if cleanly then his 'output' was also more likely to be so. What has already been said applies with equal force to this contention.

From the character of the law and the subject upon which it legislates, it is apparent that the public health or welfare bears but the most remote relation to the law. It seems to us that the real object and purpose were simply to regulate the hours of labor between the master and his employees in a private business, not dangerous in any degree to morals, or in any real and substantial degree to the health of the employees.

The judgment must be reversed and the case remanded to the County Court for further proceedings not inconsistent with this opinion.

Reversed.

Mr. Justice HOLMES *dissenting*:

If it were a question whether I agreed with the legislature's economic theory, I should desire to study it further before making up my mind. But I do not conceive that to be my duty, because my agreement or disagreement has nothing to do with the right of a majority to embody their opinions in law. It is settled by various decisions of this court that state constitutions and state laws may regulate life in many ways which we might think as injudicious, or tyrannical, and which interfere with the liberty to contract. Some of these laws embody convictions or prejudices which judges are likely to share. Some may not. But a Constitution is not intended to embody a particular economic theory. The word 'liberty,' in the 14th Amendment, is perverted when it is held to prevent the natural outcome of a dominant opinion, unless it can be said that a rational and fair man necessarily would admit that the statute proposed would infringe fundamental principles as they have been understood by the traditions of our people and our law. No such sweeping condemnation can be passed upon the statute before us. A reasonable man might think it a proper measure on the score of health.

Mr. Justice HARLAN (with whom Mr. Justice WHITE and Mr. Justice DAY *concurred*) *dissenting*:

The police power extends at least to the protection of the lives, the health, and the safety of the public against the injurious exercise by any citizen of his own rights. The state, in the exercise of its powers, may not unduly interfere with the right of the citizen to enter into contracts that may be necessary and essential in the enjoyment of the inherent rights belonging to everyone, among which rights is the right "to be free in the enjoyment of all his faculties, to be free to use them in all lawful ways, to live and work where he will, to earn his livelihood by any lawful calling, to pursue any livelihood or avocation." *See Allgeyer v. Louisiana*, 165 U.S. 578. "But the liberty of contract may, within certain limits, be subjected to regulations designed and calculated to promote the general welfare, or to guard the public health, the public morals, or the public safety." *Jacobson v. Massachusetts*, 197 U.S. 11.

A legislative enactment, Federal or state, is never to be disregarded or held invalid unless it be plainly and palpably in excess of legislative power. If there be doubt, that doubt must be resolved in favor of its validity, and the courts must keep their hands off, leaving the legislature to meet the responsibility for unwise legislation. If the end which the legislature seeks to accomplish be one to which its power extends, and if the means employed to that end, although not the wisest or best, are yet not plainly and palpably unauthorized by law, then the court cannot interfere. The burden of proof, so to speak, is upon those who assert it to be unconstitutional.

It is plain that this statute was enacted in order to protect the physical well-being of those who work in bakery and confectionery establishments. It may be that the statute had its origin in the belief that employers and employees in such establishments were not upon an equal footing, and that the necessities of the latter often compelled them to submit to such exactions as unduly taxed their strength. Be this as it may, the statute must be taken as expressing the belief of the people of New York that, in the case of the average man, labor in excess of sixty hours during a week in such establishments may endanger the health of those who thus labor. Whether or not this be wise legislation it is not the province of the court to inquire. Under our systems of government the courts are not concerned with the wisdom or policy of legislation. In determining the question of power to interfere with liberty of contract, the court may inquire whether the means devised by the state are germane to an end which may be lawfully accomplished and have a real or substantial relation to the protection of health, as involved in the daily work of the persons, male and female, engaged in bakery and confectionery establishments. I find it impossible, in view of common experience, to say that there is here no real or substantial relation between the means employed by the state and the end sought to be accomplished by its legislation. Nor can I say that the statute has no appropriate or direct connection with that protection to health which each state owes to her citizens or that it is not promotive of the health of the employees in question or that the regulation prescribed by the state is utterly unreasonable and extravagant or wholly arbitrary. Still less can I say that the statute is, beyond question, a plain, palpable invasion of rights secured by the fundamental law. Therefore I submit that this court will transcend its functions if it assumes to annul the statute of New York. It must be remembered that this statute does not apply to all kinds of business. It applies only to work in bakery and confectionery establishments, in which, as all know, the air constantly breathed by workmen is not as pure and healthful as that to be found in some other establishments or out of doors.

We know that the question of the number of hours during which a workman should continuously labor has been, for a long period, and is yet, a subject of serious consideration among civilized peoples, and by those having special knowledge of the laws of health. Suppose the statute prohibited labor in bakery and confectionery establishments in excess of eighteen hours each day. No one, I take it, could dispute the power of the state to enact such a statute. The statute before us does not embrace extreme or exceptional cases. The number of hours that should constitute a day's labor in particular occupations involving the physical strength and safety of workmen has been the subject of enactments by Congress and by nearly all of the states. Many, if not most, of those enactments fix eight hours as the proper basis of a day's labor.

I do not stop to consider whether any particular view of this economic question presents the sounder theory. It is enough for the determination of this case that there is room for debate and for an honest difference of opinion. There are many reasons of a weighty, substantial character, based upon the experience of mankind, in support of the theory that, all things considered, more than ten hours' steady work each day, from week to week, in a bakery or confectionery establishment, may endanger the health and shorten the lives of the workmen, thereby diminishing their physical and mental capacity to serve the state and to provide for those dependent upon them.

If such reasons exist that ought to be the end of this case, for the state is not amenable to the judiciary, in respect of its legislative enactments, unless such enactments are plainly, palpably, beyond all question, inconsistent with the Constitution of the United States. Our duty is to sustain the statute as not being in conflict with the Federal Constitution, it is not shown to be plainly and palpably inconsistent with that instrument. Let the state alone in the management of its purely domestic affairs, so long as it does not appear beyond all question that it has violated the Federal Constitution. This view necessarily results from the principle that the health and safety of the people of a state are primarily for the state to guard and protect.

The judgment, in my opinion, should be affirmed.

Notes

1. *Lochner's Aftermath.* The Court used the *Lochner* decision to strike down state legislation in several other cases. *See, e.g., Coppage v. Kansas*, 236 U.S. 1 (1915) (striking down state law that made it illegal for an employer to require employees not to join a union); *Adair v. United States*, 208 U.S. 161 (1908).

2. *Means-Ends Analysis.* Note how both the majority and dissenting opinions invoke "means-ends" analysis. Under such analysis, a reviewing court examines the "end" that the legislature is seeking to accomplish as well as the "means" by which the legislature seeks to accomplish it. Means-ends analysis remains important today, and its application is examined in various contexts in this and succeeding chapters.

∼ PROBLEMS ∼

1. *Save the Beach, Continued.* Do the private property owners' "liberty interests" in the City of Pensacola preclude the city from imposing significant restrictions on the private ownership rights to deter waterfront erosion and deterioration? Would *Lochner* provide the property owners with a winning argument in the early 1900s? Justice Scalia, in *Stop the Beach Renourishment v. Florida Dept. of Environmental Protection*, 560 U.S. 702 (2010), *infra*, criticized Justice Kennedy for using substantive due process relating to a matter involving economic rights: "The second problem is that we have held for many years (logically or not) that the 'liberties' protected by Substantive Due Process do not include economic liberties. *See, e.g., Lincoln Fed. Labor Union v. Northwestern Iron & Metal Co.*, 335 U.S. 525 (1949).

674 8. Substantive Protection of Economic Rights

Justice Kennedy's language ('If a judicial decision eliminates an established property right, the judgment could be set aside as a deprivation of property without due process of law') propels us back to what is referred to (usually deprecatingly) as 'the *Lochner* era.' *See Lochner v. New York*, 198 U.S. 45 (1905)." Would Justice Scalia have endorsed a constrained return to a *Lochner*-type analysis?

2. *Cigarettes and Twinkies.* Suppose that a New York Columbia Hospital study conclusively demonstrates that cigarette smoking in the workplace is unhealthy for the workers. It also proves that it is unhealthy for workers to eat foods such as Twinkies. In response, New York enacts a new law prohibiting both of these activities in the workplace. Suppose you are a federal judge assigned to hear the case. Using the majority opinion in *Lochner*, should you uphold the law? What if you rely on the reasoning in Justice Holmes's dissent? Which result is preferable? Why?

3. *Cigarettes and Twinkies II.* Suppose the court agrees with the study with respect to cigarettes but not Twinkies. Will the outcome of the two opinions be affected by whether the court agrees or disagrees with the legislature? What is the appropriate judicial role?

4. *Supersize My Soda.* Suppose the City of New York, through the Mayor of New York and a vote of the Board of Health, bans large sugary drinks in restaurants, movie theaters, street carts, and several other venues to combat a growing problem with obesity. The state legislature then decides that the ban is a good idea and votes to ban the sale of all sodas and other soft drinks with high-fructose corn syrup larger than 16 ounces within the state. Opponents of the ban say that people should be able to make their own beverage choices. Is this ban constitutional?

Nebbia v. New York

291 U.S. 502 (1934)

Mr. Justice ROBERTS delivered the opinion of the Court.

In 1932, New York milk prices were below the cost of production. The plight of dairy producers became so desperate that the New York legislature appointed a committee to study the causes of the decline and the effect of low prices on the dairy industry. Based on the study, the legislature established a Milk Control Board with power, among other things to "fix minimum and maximum retail prices to be charged by stores to consumers for consumption off the premises where sold." The board fixed nine cents as the price to be charged by a store for a quart of milk. Nebbia, the proprietor of a grocery store in Rochester, sold two quarts and a 5-cent loaf of bread for 18 cents; and was convicted for violating the board's order. The question is whether the Federal Constitution prohibits a state from so fixing the selling price of milk.

Under our form of government the use of property and the making of contracts are normally matters of private and not of public concern. The general rule is that both shall be free of governmental interference. But neither property rights nor contract rights are absolute; for government cannot exist if the citizen may at will use his property to the detriment of his fellows, or exercise his free-dom of contract to work them harm. Equally fundamental with the private right is that of the public to regulate it in the common interest. The Fifth Amendment and the Fourteenth do not prohibit governmental regulation for the public wel-fare. They merely condition the exertion of the admitted power, by securing that the end shall be accomplished by methods consistent with due process. And the guaranty of due process demands only that the law shall not be unreasonable, arbitrary, or capricious, and that the means selected shall have a real and substan-tial relation to the object sought to be attained. It results that a regulation valid for one sort of business, or in given circumstances, may be invalid for another sort, or for the same business under other circumstances, because the reasonable-ness of each regulation depends upon the relevant facts.

The court has repeatedly sustained curtailment of enjoyment of private property in the public interest. Laws passed for the suppression of immorality, in the interest of health, to secure fair trade practices, and to safeguard the interests of depositors in banks, have been found consistent with due process. These mea-sures not only affected the use of private property, but also interfered with the right of private contract. Other instances are numerous where valid regulation has restricted the right of contract, while less directly affecting property rights. The Constitution does not guarantee the unrestricted privilege to engage in a business or to conduct it as one pleases.

The milk industry in New York has been the subject of long-standing and dras-tic regulation in the public interest. The legislative investigation of 1932 showed that unrestricted competition aggravated existing evils and that the normal law of supply and demand was insufficient to correct maladjustments detrimental to the community. The inquiry disclosed destructive and demoralizing competitive conditions and unfair trade practices which resulted in retail price cutting and reduced the income of the farmer below the cost of production. The legislature believed conditions could be improved by preventing destructive price-cutting by stores which, due to the flood of surplus milk, were able to buy at much lower prices than the larger distributors and to sell without incurring the delivery costs of the latter. The Milk Control Board fixed a price of 10 cents per quart for sales by a distributor to a consumer, and 9 cents by a store to a consumer, thus recog-nizing the lower costs of the store, and endeavoring to establish a differential which would be just to both. In the light of the facts the order appears not to be unreasonable or arbitrary, or without relation to the purpose to prevent ruthless competition from destroying the wholesale price structure on which the farmer depends for his livelihood, and the community for an assured supply of milk.

Appellant urges that direct fixation of prices is a type of regulation absolutely forbidden. The argument runs that the public control of rates or prices is per se unreasonable and unconstitutional, save as applied to businesses affected with a public interest such as a public utility. If the dairy industry is subject to regulation in the public interest, what constitutional principle bars the state from correcting existing maladjustments by legislation touching prices? We think there is no such principle. The due process clause makes no mention of sales or of prices any more than it speaks of business or contracts or buildings or other incidents of property. It is clear that there is no closed class or category of businesses affected with a public interest, and the function of courts in the application of the Fifth and Fourteenth Amendments is to determine in each case whether circumstances vindicate the challenged regulation as a reasonable exertion of governmental authority or condemn it as arbitrary or discriminatory. The phrase "affected with a public interest" can mean no more than that an industry, for adequate reason, is subject to control for the public good. There can be no doubt that upon proper occasion and by appropriate measures the state may regulate a business in any of its aspects, including the prices to be charged for the products or commodities it sells.

So far as the requirement of due process is concerned, and in the absence of other constitutional restriction, a state is free to adopt whatever economic policy may reasonably be deemed to promote public welfare, and to enforce that policy by legislation adapted to its purpose. The courts are without authority either to declare such policy, or, when it is declared by the legislature, to override it. If the laws passed are seen to have a reasonable relation to a proper legislative purpose, and are neither arbitrary nor discriminatory, the requirements of due process are satisfied. If the legislative policy be to curb unrestrained and harmful competition by measures which are not arbitrary or discriminatory it does not lie with the courts to determine that the rule is unwise. With the wisdom of the policy adopted, with the adequacy or practicability of the law enacted to forward it, the courts are both incompetent and unauthorized to deal. The course of decision in this court exhibits a firm adherence to these principles. The Legislature is primarily the judge of the necessity of such an enactment, every possible presumption is in favor of its validity, and though the court may hold views inconsistent with the wisdom of the law, it may not be annulled unless palpably in excess of legislative power.

Tested by these considerations we find no basis in the due process clause of the Fourteenth Amendment for condemning the provisions of the Agriculture and Markets Law here drawn into question.

The judgment is affirmed.

Mr. Justice McREYNOLDS, joined by Justices BUTLER, SUTHERLAND, and VAN DEVANTER, *dissented.*

This Court must have regard to the wisdom of the enactment. At least, we must inquire concerning its purpose and decide whether the means proposed have reasonable relation to something within legislative power — whether the end is legitimate, and the means appropriate. If a statute to prevent conflagrations, should require householders to pour oil on their roofs as a means of curbing the spread of fire when discovered in the neighborhood, we could hardly uphold it. Here, we find direct interference with guaranteed rights defended upon the ground that the purpose was to promote the public welfare by increasing milk prices at the farm. Unless we can affirm that the end proposed is proper and the means adopted have reasonable relation to it, this action is unjustifiable.

The court below has not indicated how higher charges at stores to impoverished customers can possibly increase receipts at the farm. The Legislative Committee pointed out as the obvious cause of decreased consumption, notwithstanding low prices, the consumers' reduced buying power. Higher store prices will not enlarge this power; nor will they decrease production. Not only does the statute interfere arbitrarily with the rights of the little grocer to conduct his business but it takes away the liberty of 12,000,000 consumers to buy a necessity of life in an open market. To those with less than 9 cents it says: You cannot procure a quart of milk from the grocer although he is anxious to accept what you can pay and the demands of your household are urgent! A superabundance; but no child can purchase from a willing storekeeper below the figure appointed by three men at headquarters! And this is true although the storekeeper himself may have bought from a willing producer at half that rate and must sell quickly or lose his stock through deterioration.

The Legislature cannot lawfully destroy guaranteed rights of one man with the prime purpose of enriching another, even if for the moment, this may seem advantageous to the public. Grave concern for embarrassed farmers is everywhere; but this should neither obscure the rights of others nor obstruct judicial appraisement of measures proposed for relief. The ultimate welfare of the producer, like that of every other class, requires dominance of the Constitution. Zealously to uphold this in all its parts is the highest duty entrusted to the courts.

Notes and Questions

1. *Aftermath.* By the 1930s, following the constitutional crisis (see the discussion of President Roosevelt's so-called Court Packing Plan in Chapter 2, *supra*), *Lochnerian* approaches to economic rights disappeared along with the Court's more restrictive interpretation of the Commerce Clause. In addition to *Nebbia*, the Court decided *West Coast Hotel Co. v. Parrish*, 300 U.S. 379 (1937), which involved a constitutional challenge to a State of Washington law stipulating minimum wages for women and minors. In an opinion by Justice Hughes, the Court upheld the law:

> The constitutional provision invoked is the due process clause of the Fourteenth Amendment. In each case the violation alleged by those attacking minimum wage regulations for women is deprivation of freedom of contract. What is this freedom? The Constitution does not speak of freedom of contract. It speaks of liberty and prohibits the deprivation of liberty without due process of law. In prohibiting that deprivation, the Constitution does not recognize an absolute and uncontrollable liberty. Liberty under the Constitution is thus necessarily subject to the restraints of due process, and regulation which is reasonable in relation to its subject and is adopted in the interests of the community is due process. The point that has been strongly stressed that adult employees should be deemed competent to make their own contracts was decisively met nearly forty years ago. The exploitation of a class of workers who are in an

unequal position with respect to bargaining power and are thus relatively defenseless against the denial of a living wage is not only detrimental to their health and well being, but casts a direct burden for their support upon the community. What these workers lose in wages the taxpayers are called upon to pay. The bare cost of living must be met. We may take judicial notice of the unparalleled demands for relief which arose during the recent period of depression and still continue to an alarming extent despite the degree of economic recovery which has been achieved. It is unnecessary to cite official statistics to establish what is of common knowledge through the length and breadth of the land.

2. *More on* Lochner*'s Aftermath.* In *Williamson v. Lee Optical,* 348 U.S. 483 (1955), an Oklahoma law made it illegal for anyone except a licensed optometrist or ophthalmologist to fit lenses to a face or to duplicate or replace into frames lenses or other optical appliances, except upon written prescriptive authority of an Oklahoma-licensed ophthalmologist or optometrist. Effectively, the law precluded an optician from fitting old glasses into new frames or supplying a lens, whether it was a new lens or one to duplicate a lost or broken lens, without a prescription. In an opinion by Justice Douglas, the Court upheld the law: "The Oklahoma law may exact a needless, wasteful requirement in many cases. But it is for the legislature, not the courts, to balance the advantages and disadvantages of the new requirement. The day is gone when this Court uses the Due Process Clause of the Fourteenth Amendment to strike down state laws, regulatory of business and industrial conditions, because they may be unwise, improvident, or out of harmony with a particular school of thought. We emphasize again what Chief Justice Waite said in *Munn v. State of Illinois,* 94 U.S. 113, 'For protection against abuses by legislatures the people must resort to the polls, not to the courts.'"

3. Carolene Products *Footnote 4.* The now-famous footnote 4 from the *Carolene Products* case offered a new approach to constitutional analysis:

There may be narrower scope for operation of the presumption of constitutionality when legislation appears on its face to be within a specific prohibition of the Constitution, such as those of the first ten Amendments, which are deemed equally specific when held to be embraced within the Fourteenth. *See Stromberg v. California,* 283 U.S. 359; *Lovell v. Griffin,* 303 U.S. 444. It is unnecessary to consider now whether legislation which restricts those political processes which can ordinarily be expected to bring about repeal of undesirable legislation, is to be subjected to more exacting judicial scrutiny under the general prohibitions of the Fourteenth Amendment than are most other types of legislation. On restrictions upon the right to vote, *see Nixon v. Herndon,* 273 U.S. 536; on restraints upon the dissemination of information, *see Near v. Minnesota,* 283 U.S. 697; *Lovell v. Griffin, supra;* on interferences with political organizations, *see Stromberg v. California, supra,* 283 U.S. 359; as to prohibition of peaceable assembly, *see De Jonge v. Oregon,* 299 U.S. 353. Nor need we enquire whether similar considerations enter into the review of statutes directed at particular religious, *Pierce v. Society of Sisters,* 268 U.S. 510, or national, *Meyer v. Nebraska,* 262 U.S. 390, or racial minorities. *Nixon v. Herndon, supra; Nixon v. Condon, supra;* whether prejudice against discrete and insular minorities may be a special condition, which tends seriously to curtail the operation of those political processes ordinarily to be relied upon to protect minorities, and which may call for a correspondingly more searching judicial inquiry. *Compare McCulloch v. Maryland,* 4 Wheat. 316, 428, 4 L.Ed. 579.

United States v. Carolene Prod. Co., 304 U.S. 144

∾ PROBLEMS ∾

1. Lochner's *Reprise.* After *Nebbia* was decided, suppose that the New York legislature immediately reimposes the law that was struck down in *Lochner.* After *Nebbia,* would the Court uphold the law or would it still strike it down? Explain.

2. *Legal Grounds.* Wilkes-Barre, Pennsylvania, enacts a statute "protecting the right to contract and to sell one's economic labor as a fundamental right of individuals in society." The statute is premised on the proposition that "economic interests go to the heart of an individual's ability to support him or herself and are essential to the individual's well-being." It goes on to state: "Under the Contract Clause, the Takings Clause, and the original constitutional imperative of forming a viable economic union, economic freedom should be viewed as an implied fundamental right, no different than voting or travel." a) Do you agree with the premise of the statute? Do constitutional rights have to be enumerated? Why or why not? Are there logical indications of a union or constitutional governance, such as a right to travel or the right to vote, that do not require enumeration? Answers to questions like these are critical to the ability to frame and develop a theory of judicial review. b) Would such a statute be upheld after *Nebbia*?

B. THE TAKINGS CLAUSE

The Fifth Amendment Takings Clause, sometimes referred to as the "Eminent Domain" Clause, prohibits the government from taking private property for public purpose without providing "just compensation." A taking for purposes of this clause either involves an actual taking (in the sense that government assumes title to the property) or results from the government's regulation of land that significantly restricts its use. Two major issues arise under this clause. First, some litigants question whether their property is being taken for a "public purpose" (as opposed to a private purpose) and therefore argue that the taking is impermissible. Second, at times, there are disputes about whether there is a "taking" at all.

As the following case illustrates, the first issue, whether a taking is for a public purpose, has generally been resolved in favor of the government.

Kelo v. City of New London

545 U.S. 469 (2005)

Justice STEVENS delivered the opinion of the Court.

The city of New London approved a development plan that, in the words of the Supreme Court of Connecticut, was "projected to create in excess of 1,000 jobs, to increase tax and other revenues, and to revitalize an economically

distressed city, including its downtown and waterfront areas." The city's development agent seeks to use the power of eminent domain to acquire property from
those unwilling to sell. The question presented is whether the city's proposed
disposition of this property qualifies as a "public use" within the meaning of the
Takings Clause of the Fifth Amendment to the Constitution.[1]

Decades of economic decline led a state agency in 1990 to designate the City
of New London a "distressed municipality." In 1996, the Federal Government
closed the Naval Undersea Warfare Center, which had employed over 1,500
people. In 1998, the City's unemployment rate was nearly double that of the
State. These conditions prompted state and local officials to target New London,
and particularly its Fort Trumbull area, for economic revitalization. To this end,
respondent New London Development Corporation (NLDC), a private nonprofit
entity established some years earlier to assist the City in planning economic development, was reactivated. In January 1998, the State authorized a $5.35 million
bond issue to support the NLDC's planning activities and a $10 million bond
issue toward the creation of a Fort Trumbull State Park. In February, the pharmaceutical company Pfizer Inc. announced that it would build a $300 million
research facility on a site immediately adjacent to Fort Trumbull; local planners
hoped that Pfizer would draw new business to the area, thereby serving as a catalyst to the area's rejuvenation. After a series of neighborhood meetings, the city
council authorized the NLDC to formally submit its plans to the relevant state
agencies for review. Upon obtaining state-level approval, the NLDC finalized an
integrated development plan focused on 90 acres of the Fort Trumbull area.

The Fort Trumbull area is situated on a peninsula that juts into the Thames
River. The area comprises approximately 115 privately owned properties, as well
as the 32 acres of land formerly occupied by the naval facility (Trumbull State
Park now occupies 18 of those 32 acres). The development plan encompasses
seven parcels. Parcel 1 is designated for a waterfront conference hotel at the
center of a "small urban village" that will include restaurants and shopping. This
parcel will also have marinas for both recreational and commercial uses. A pedestrian "riverwalk" will originate here and continue down the coast, connecting the
waterfront areas of the development. Parcel 2 will be the site of approximately
80 new residences organized into an urban neighborhood and linked by public
walkway to the remainder of the development, including the state park. This
parcel also includes space reserved for a new U.S. Coast Guard Museum. Parcel
3, which is located immediately north of the Pfizer facility, will contain at least
90,000 square feet of research and development office space. Parcel 4A is a 2.4-
acre site that will be used either to support the adjacent state park, by providing
parking or retail services for visitors, or to support the nearby marina. Parcel
4B will include a renovated marina, as well as the final stretch of the riverwalk.

---

1. "Nor shall private property be taken for public use, without just compensation." U.S. Const., Amdt.
5. That Clause is made applicable to the States by the Fourteenth Amendment.

Parcels 5, 6, and 7 will provide land for office and retail space, parking, and water-dependent commercial uses.

The NLDC intended the development plan to capitalize on the arrival of the Pfizer facility and the new commerce it was expected to attract. In addition to creating jobs, generating tax revenue, and helping to "build momentum for the revitalization of downtown New London," the plan was also designed to make the City more attractive and to create leisure and recreational opportunities on the waterfront and in the park.

The city council approved the plan in January 2000, and designated the NLDC as its development agent in charge of implementation. The city council also authorized the NLDC to purchase property or to acquire property by exercising eminent domain in the City's name. The NLDC successfully negotiated the purchase of most of the real estate in the 90-acre area, but its negotiations with petitioners failed. As a consequence, the NLDC initiated the condemnation proceedings that gave rise to this case.

Petitioner Susette Kelo has lived in the Fort Trumbull area since 1997. She has made extensive improvements to her house, which she prizes for its water view. Petitioner Wilhelmina Dery was born in her Fort Trumbull house in 1918 and has lived there her entire life. Her husband Charles (also a petitioner) has lived in the house since they married some 60 years ago. In all, the nine petitioners own 15 properties in Fort Trumbull — 4 in parcel 3 and 11 in parcel 4A. Ten of the parcels are occupied by the owner or a family member; the other five are held as investment properties. There is no allegation that any of these properties is blighted or otherwise in poor condition; they were condemned only because they happen to be located in the development area.

In December 2000, petitioners brought this action in the New London Superior Court. They claimed, among other things, that the taking of their properties would violate the "public use" restriction in the Fifth Amendment. The Superior Court granted a permanent restraining order prohibiting the taking of the properties located in parcel 4A (park or marina support). It, however, denied petitioners relief as to the properties located in parcel 3 (office space). The Supreme Court of Connecticut held that all of the City's proposed takings were valid. Relying on cases such as *Hawaii Housing Authority v. Midkiff*, 467 U.S. 229 (1984), and *Berman v. Parker*, 348 U.S. 26 (1954), the court held that such economic development qualified as a valid public use under both the Federal and State Constitutions. We granted certiorari to determine whether a city's decision to take property for the purpose of economic development satisfies the "public use" requirement of the Fifth Amendment.

It has long been accepted that the sovereign may not take the property of *A* for the sole purpose of transferring it to another private party *B*, even though *A* is paid just compensation. On the other hand, it is equally clear that a State may transfer property from one private party to another if future "use by the public" is the purpose of the taking; the condemnation of land for a railroad with common-carrier duties is a familiar example.

The City would no doubt be forbidden from taking petitioners' land for the purpose of conferring a private benefit on a particular private party. See *Midkiff,* 467 U.S., at 245. Nor would the City be allowed to take property under the mere pretext of a public purpose, when its actual purpose was to bestow a private benefit. The takings before us, however, would be executed pursuant to a "carefully considered" development plan. The trial judge and the Supreme Court of Connecticut agreed that there was no evidence of an illegitimate purpose. Therefore, as was true in *Midkiff,* the City's development plan was not adopted "to benefit a particular class of identifiable individuals."

On the other hand, this is not a case in which the City is planning to open the condemned land—at least not in its entirety—to use by the general public. Nor will the private lessees of the land in any sense be required to operate like common carriers, making their services available to all comers. While many state courts in the mid-19th century endorsed "use by the public" as the proper definition of public use, that narrow view steadily eroded over time. Not only was the "use by the public" test difficult to administer (e.g., what proportion of the public need have access to the property? at what price?), but it proved to be impractical given the diverse and always evolving needs of society. Accordingly, when this Court began applying the Fifth Amendment to the States at the close of the 19th century, it embraced the broader and more natural interpretation of public use as "public purpose." *See, e.g., Fallbrook Irrigation Dist. v. Bradley,* 164 U.S. 112 (1896).

The disposition of this case therefore turns on the question whether the City's development plan serves a "public purpose." Our cases have defined that concept broadly, reflecting our longstanding policy of deference to legislative judgments in this field. In *Berman,* this Court upheld a redevelopment plan targeting a blighted area of Washington, D.C., in which most of the housing for the area's 5,000 inhabitants was beyond repair. Under the plan, the area would be condemned and part of it utilized for the construction of streets, schools, and other public facilities. The remainder of the land would be leased or sold to private parties for the purpose of redevelopment, including the construction of low-cost housing. The owner of a department store located in the area challenged the condemnation. Writing for a unanimous Court, Justice Douglas refused to evaluate this claim in isolation, deferring instead to the legislative and agency judgment that the area "must be planned as a whole" for the plan to be successful. The Court explained that "community redevelopment programs need not, by force of the Constitution, be on a piecemeal basis—lot by lot, building by building." The public use underlying the taking was unequivocally affirmed: "We do not sit to determine whether a particular housing project is or is not desirable. The concept of the public welfare is broad and inclusive. The values it represents are spiritual as well as physical, aesthetic as well as monetary. It is within the power of the legislature to determine that the community should be beautiful as well as healthy, spacious as well as clean, well-balanced as well as carefully patrolled. In the present case, the Congress and its authorized agencies have made determinations that take into account a wide variety of values. It is not for us to reappraise them. If those who govern the District of Columbia decide that the Nation's Capital should be beautiful as well as sanitary, there is nothing in the Fifth Amendment that stands in the way."

In *Hawaii Housing Authority* the Court considered a Hawaii statute whereby fee title was taken from lessors and transferred to lessees (for just compensation) in order to reduce the concentration of land ownership. We unanimously upheld the statute and rejected the Ninth Circuit's view that it was "a naked attempt on the part of the state of Hawaii to take the property of *A* and transfer it to *B* solely for *B*'s private use and benefit." Reaffirming *Berman*'s deferential approach to legislative judgments in this field, we concluded that the State's purpose of eliminating the "social and economic evils of a land oligopoly" qualified as a valid public use. Our opinion also rejected the contention that the mere fact that the State immediately transferred the properties to private individuals upon condemnation somehow diminished the public character of the taking. "It is only the taking's purpose, and not its mechanics," we explained, that matters in determining public use.

To effectuate this plan, the City has invoked a state statute that specifically authorizes the use of eminent domain to promote economic development. Given the comprehensive character of the plan, the thorough deliberation that preceded its adoption, and the limited scope of our review, it is appropriate for us, as it was in *Berman*, to resolve the challenges of the individual owners, not on a piecemeal basis, but rather in light of the entire plan. Because that plan unquestionably serves a public purpose, the takings challenged here satisfy the public use requirement of the Fifth Amendment.

Petitioners urge us to adopt a new bright-line rule that economic development does not qualify as a public use. Promoting economic development is a traditional and long accepted function of government. There is, moreover, no principled way of distinguishing economic development from the other public purposes that we have recognized. In our cases upholding takings that facilitated agriculture and mining, for example, we emphasized the importance of those industries to the welfare of the States in question; in *Berman*, we endorsed the purpose of transforming a blighted area into a "well-balanced" community through redevelopment,[13] in *Midkiff*, we upheld the interest in breaking up a land oligopoly that "created artificial deterrents to the normal functioning of the State's residential land market," and in *Monsanto*, we accepted Congress' purpose of eliminating a "significant barrier to entry in the pesticide market." It would be incongruous to hold that the City's interest in the economic benefits to be derived from the development of the Fort

---

13. It is a misreading of *Berman* to suggest that the only public use upheld in that case was the initial removal of blight. The public use in *Berman* extended beyond that to encompass the purpose of *developing* that area to create conditions that would prevent a reversion to blight in the future. Had the public use in *Berman* been defined more narrowly, it would have been difficult to justify the taking of the plaintiff's nonblighted department store.

Trumbull area has less of a public character than any of those other interests. There is no basis for exempting economic development from our tradition-ally broad understanding of public purpose.

The government's pursuit of a public purpose will often benefit individual private parties. In *Midkiff,* the forced transfer of property conferred a direct and significant benefit on those lessees who were previously unable to purchase their homes. In *Monsanto,* the "most direct beneficiaries" of the data-sharing provisions were the subsequent pesticide applicants, but benefiting them was necessary to promoting competition in the pesticide market.

It is further argued that without a bright-line rule nothing would stop a city from transferring citizen *A*'s property to citizen *B* for the sole reason that citizen *B* will put the property to a more productive use and thus pay more taxes. The hypothetical cases posited by petitioners can be confronted if and when they arise.

Petitioners maintain that for takings of this kind we should require a "rea-sonable certainty" that the expected public benefits will actually accrue. "When the legislature's purpose is legitimate and its means are not irrational, our cases make clear that empirical debates over the wisdom of takings are not to be car-ried out in the federal courts." *Midkiff,* 467 U.S., at 242. A constitutional rule that required postponement of the judicial approval of every condemnation until the likelihood of success of the plan had been assured would unquestionably impose a significant impediment to the successful consummation of many such plans.

We also decline to second-guess the City's determinations as to what lands it needs to acquire in order to effectuate the project. "Once the question of the public purpose has been decided, the amount and character of land to be taken for the project and the need for a particular tract to complete the integrated plan rests in the discretion of the legislative branch." *Berman,* 348 U.S., at 35-36.

We do not minimize the hardship that condemnations may entail, notwith-standing the payment of just compensation. Nothing precludes any State from placing further restrictions on its exercise of the takings power. Indeed, many States already impose "public use" requirements that are stricter than the federal baseline. Some of these requirements have been established as a matter of state constitutional law. The necessity and wisdom of using eminent domain to pro-mote economic development are certainly matters of legitimate public debate. This Court's authority, however, extends only to determining whether the City's proposed condemnations are for a "public use" within the meaning of the Fifth Amendment to the Federal Constitution. Because over a century of our case law interpreting that provision dictates an affirmative answer to that question, we may not grant petitioners the relief that they seek.

The judgment of the Supreme Court of Connecticut is *affirmed.*

It is so ordered.

Justice KENNEDY, *concurring.*

Even the dissenting justices on the Connecticut Supreme Court agreed that respondents' development plan was intended to revitalize the local economy, not to serve the interests of Pfizer, Corcoran Jennison, or any other private party.

This case, then, survives the meaningful rational basis review that in my view is required under the Public Use Clause. My agreement with the Court does not foreclose the possibility that there may be private transfers in which the risk of undetected impermissible favoritism of private parties is so acute that a presumption (rebuttable or otherwise) of invalidity is warranted under the Public Use Clause.

This taking occurred in the context of a comprehensive development plan meant to address a serious city-wide depression, and the projected economic benefits of the project cannot be characterized as *de minimus*. The identity of most of the private beneficiaries were unknown at the time the city formulated its plans. In sum, while there may be categories of cases in which the transfers are so suspicious, or the procedures employed so prone to abuse, or the purported benefits are so trivial or implausible, that courts should presume an impermissible private purpose, no such circumstances are present in this case.

See e.g., Benjamin Weingarten, *10 years later, here's what happened to the land seized and sold to developers in a controversial Supreme Court case,* THE BLAZE (Jun. 23, 2015, 11:18AM), http://www.theblaze.com/blog/2015/06/23/10-years-later-heres-what-happened-to-the-land-seized-and-sold-to-developers-in-a-controversial-supreme-court-case/.

Justice O'CONNOR, with whom THE CHIEF JUSTICE, Justice SCALIA, and Justice THOMAS join, *dissenting.*

In *Berman* and *Midkiff,* precondemnation use of the targeted property inflicted affirmative harm on society—in *Berman* through blight resulting from extreme poverty and in *Midkiff* through oligopoly resulting from extreme wealth. And in both cases, the relevant legislative body had found that eliminating the existing property use was necessary to remedy the harm. Thus a public purpose was realized when the harmful use was eliminated. Because each taking *directly* achieved a public benefit, it did not matter that the property was turned over to private use. Here, in contrast, New London does not claim that Susette Kelo's and Wilhelmina Dery's well-maintained homes are the source of any social harm. In moving away from our decisions sanctioning the condemnation of harmful property use, the Court today significantly expands the meaning of public use. It holds that the sovereign may take private property currently put to ordinary private use, and give it over for new, ordinary private use, so long as the new use is predicted to generate some secondary benefit for the public—such as increased tax revenue, more jobs, maybe even aesthetic pleasure. But nearly any lawful use of real private property can be said to generate some incidental benefit to the public. Thus, if predicted positive side-effects are enough to render transfer from one private party to another constitutional, then the words "for public use" do not realistically exclude *any* takings, and thus do not exert any constraint on the eminent domain power. The beneficiaries are likely to be those citizens with disproportionate influence and power in the political process, including large corporations and development firms. The Founders cannot have intended this perverse result. I would hold that the takings in both Parcel 3 and Parcel 4A are unconstitutional.

Justice THOMAS, *dissenting.*

When the government takes property and gives it to a private individual, and the public has no right to use the property, it strains language to say that the public is "employing" the property, regardless of the incidental benefits that might accrue to the public from the private use. It is implausible that the Framers intended to defer to legislatures as to what satisfies the Public Use Clause. Yet today the Court tells us that we are not to "second-guess the City's considered judgments," when the issue is whether the government may take the infinitely more intrusive step of tearing down petitioners' homes. Though citizens are safe from the government in their homes, the homes themselves are not.

I would return to the original meaning of the Public Use Clause: that the government may take property only if it actually uses or gives the public a legal right to use the property. So-called "urban renewal" programs provide some compensation for the properties they take, but no compensation is possible for the subjective value of these lands to the individuals displaced and the indignity inflicted by uprooting them from their homes. Extending the concept of public purpose to encompass any economically beneficial goal guarantees that these losses will fall disproportionately on poor communities. Those communities are not only systematically less likely to put their lands to the highest and best social use, but are also the least politically powerful. The deferential standard this Court has adopted encourages "those citizens with disproportionate influence and power in the political process, including large corporations and development firms" to victimize the weak.

Note: The Kelo Property

The City of New London condemned Susette Kelo's home and the homes of her neighbors. The city and state then spent millions of dollars to get the property ready for luxury condominiums. Pfizer, Inc., instead of pursuing further development, stated that it would close its headquarters in New London.

BACKGROUND
The Kelo Backlash

After *Kelo*, many citizens, members of the media, businesspersons, and politicians decried the result. In the backlash that followed, state legislatures enacted laws limiting the purposes for which land could be taken. Some businesses announced they would not lend money to developers who planned to build on condemned land. George Will, the columnist, wrote in *Newsweek* that the *Kelo* decision was "the best thing that has happened since the New Deal to the movement to strengthen property rights." ("Legal Theft In Norwood," April 24, 2006.) Many states enacted laws limiting their own use of the eminent domain power. One example was Ohio, which made eminent domain much more challenging for public entities with respect to any property not within a blighted area if the primary purpose of the condemnation was to transfer the property to another private party. Congress also included language in the Federal Appropriations Act of 2006 prohibiting the use of funds for eminent domain outside of traditional governmental purposes.

∾ PROBLEMS ∾

1. *Berwick.* You are the Mayor of Berwick, a small town in Pennsylvania. You are asked to propose legislation to placate angry landowners about the possibility of condemning their land for use by corporate and other private entities. What legislation would you propose?

2. *Berwick II.* Before you can propose legislation, a Dell computer company representative approaches you with a proposition. The representative informs you that if a large house and its 20 acres on the edge of town are taken by eminent domain and given to a subsidiary of Dell, then a Dell equipment quality control operation will operate out of the house, creating seven new jobs. The house and surrounding land are worth $250,000. The jobs are worth $150,000 in salaries. Having Dell present in the community is worth at least $50,000. Could the property be properly taken under *Kelo*?

BACKGROUND
Remaining Takings Issues

In addition to the question whether a taking is for a public purpose, the second dominant issue in the field relates to whether government action in the form of land use regulation constitutes a taking. This issue has generated the highest volume of litigation under the Takings Clause and yielded disparate outcomes. These results are consistent with persisting differences in perspective on the Takings Clause's meaning. It is a provision that clearly applies when government condemns a person's property and assumes title to it. Government may acquire private property, but it must pay "just compensation." Many Takings Clause cases do not involve a literal "taking" in the sense of an acquisition, however, but instead concern land use control for an articulated public good. Such regulation can assume many different forms, including zoning restrictions. In these cases, the question is whether government may regulate without paying the property owner for the diminished value of the property.

Penn Central Transportation Company v. City of New York

438 U.S. 104 (1978)

Mr. Justice BRENNAN delivered the opinion of the Court.

New York City adopted its Landmarks Preservation Law in 1965 because "the standing of New York City as a world-wide tourist center and world capital of business, culture and government" would be threatened if legislation were not enacted to protect historic landmarks and neighborhoods from precipitate decisions to destroy or fundamentally alter their character. The city believed that comprehensive measures to safeguard desirable features of the existing urban fabric would benefit its citizens in a variety of ways: e.g., fostering "civic pride in the beauty and noble accomplishments of the past"; protecting and enhancing "the city's attractions to tourists and visitors"; "supporting and stimulating business and industry"; "strengthening the economy of the city"; and promoting "the use of historic districts, landmarks, interior landmarks and scenic landmarks for the education, pleasure and welfare of the people of the city."

The New York City law is typical of many urban landmark laws in that its primary method of achieving its goals is not by acquisitions of historic properties, but rather by involving public entities in land-use decisions affecting these properties and providing services, standards, controls, and incentives that will encourage preservation by private owners and users. While the law does place special restrictions on landmark properties as a necessary feature to the attainment of its larger objectives, the major theme of the law is to ensure the owners of any such properties both a "reasonable return" on their investments and maximum latitude to use their parcels for purposes not inconsistent with the preservation goals.

Final designation as a landmark results in restrictions upon the property owner's options concerning use of the landmark site. The law imposes a duty upon the owner to keep the exterior features of the building "in good repair" to assure that the law's objectives not be defeated by the landmark's falling into a state of irremediable disrepair. The Commission must approve in advance any proposal to alter the exterior architectural features of the landmark or to construct any exterior improvement on the landmark site, thus ensuring that decisions concerning construction on the landmark site are made with due consideration of both the public interest in the maintenance of the structure and the landowner's interest in use of the property.

Although the designation of a landmark and landmark site restricts the owner's control over the parcel, designation also enhances the economic position of the landmark owner in one significant respect. Under New York City's zoning laws, owners of real property who have not developed their property to the full extent permitted by the applicable zoning laws are allowed to transfer development rights to contiguous parcels on the same city block. A 1968 ordinance gave the owners of landmark sites additional opportunities to transfer development rights to other parcels. A 1969 amendment permits, in highly commercialized areas like midtown Manhattan, the transfer of all unused development rights to a single parcel.

Grand Central Terminal (Terminal) is owned by the Penn Central Transportation Co. and is one of New York City's most famous buildings. Opened in 1913, it is regarded not only as providing an ingenious engineering solution to the problems presented by urban railroad stations, but also as a magnificent example of the French beaux-arts style. The Terminal is located in midtown Manhattan near 42d Street and Park Avenue. The Terminal itself is an eight-story structure which Penn Central uses as a railroad station and in which it rents space not needed for railroad purposes. Penn Central entered into a 50-year lease with appellant UGP Properties, Inc. (UGP). UGP was to construct a multistory office building above the Terminal and to pay Penn Central $1 million annually during construction and at least $3 million annually thereafter. UGP and Penn Central then applied to the Commission for permission to construct an office building atop the Terminal. The Commission denied the application. Appellants filed suit claiming that application of the Landmarks Preservation Law had "taken" their property without just compensation in violation of the Fifth and Fourteenth Amendments. We noted probable jurisdiction. We affirm lower court decisions rejecting this contention.

While this Court has recognized that the "Fifth Amendment's guarantee is designed to bar Government from forcing some people alone to bear public burdens which, in all fairness and justice, should be borne by the public as a whole," this Court has been unable to develop any "set formula" for determining when "justice and fairness" require that economic injuries caused by public action be compensated by the government, rather than remain disproportionately concentrated on a few persons. This Court's decisions identify several factors that have particular significance. The economic impact of the regulation on the claimant and, particularly, the extent to which the regulation has interfered with distinct investment-backed expectations are relevant considerations. *See Goldblatt v. Hempstead* 369 U.S. 590 (1962). So, too, is the character of the governmental action. A "taking" may more readily be found when the interference with property can be characterized as a physical invasion by government, than when interference arises from some public program adjusting the benefits and burdens of economic life to promote the common good. "Government hardly could go on if to some extent values incident to property could not be diminished without paying for every such change in the general law," *Pennsylvania Coal Co. v. Mahon*, 260 U.S. 393 (1922), and this Court has recognized, in a wide variety of contexts, that government may execute laws or programs that adversely affect recognized economic values. This Court has dismissed "taking" challenges on the ground that, while the challenged government action caused economic harm, it did not interfere with interests that were sufficiently bound up with the reasonable expectations of the claimant to constitute "property" for Fifth Amendment purposes. *See, e.g., United States v. Willow River Power Co.*, 324 U.S. 499 (1945).

In instances in which a state tribunal reasonably concluded that "the health, safety, morals, or general welfare" would be promoted by prohibiting particular contemplated uses of land, this Court has upheld land-use regulations that destroyed or adversely affected recognized real property interests. Zoning laws are, of course, the classic example which has been viewed as permissible governmental action even when prohibiting the most beneficial use of the property. *See Goldblatt v. Hempstead, supra,* 369 U.S., at 592-593.

Zoning laws generally do not affect existing uses of real property, but "taking" challenges have also been held to be without merit in a wide variety of situations when the challenged governmental actions prohibited a beneficial use to which individual parcels had previously been devoted and thus caused substantial individualized harm. *Goldblatt v. Hempstead* involved a city safety ordinance that banned any excavations below the water table and effectively prohibited the claimant from continuing a sand and gravel mining business that had been in operation since 1927. The ordinance did not prevent the owner's reasonable use of the property since the owner made no showing of an adverse effect on the value of the land. Because the restriction served a substantial public purpose, the Court held no taking had occurred. It is, of course, implicit in *Goldblatt* that a use restriction on real property may constitute a "taking" if not reasonably necessary to the effectuation of a substantial public purpose or perhaps if it has an unduly harsh impact upon the owner's use of the property.

Pennsylvania Coal Co. v. Mahon, 260 U.S. 393 (1922), is the leading case for the proposition that a state statute that substantially furthers important public policies may so frustrate distinct investment-backed expectations as to amount to a "taking." There the claimant had sold the surface rights to particular parcels of property, but expressly reserved the right to remove the coal thereunder. A Pennsylvania statute, enacted after the transactions, forbade any mining of coal that caused the subsidence of any house, unless the house was the property of the owner of the underlying coal and was more than 150 feet from the improved property of another. Because the statute made it commercially impracticable to mine the coal, and thus had nearly the same effect as the complete destruction of rights claimant had reserved from the owners of the surface land, the Court held that the statute was invalid as effecting a "taking" without just compensation.

Finally, government actions that may be characterized as acquisitions of resources to permit or facilitate uniquely public functions have often been held to constitute "takings." *United States v. Causby,* 328 U.S. 256 (1946), is illustrative. In holding that direct overflights above the claimant's land, that destroyed the present use of the land as a chicken farm, constituted a "taking," *Causby* emphasized that Government had not "merely destroyed property but was using a part of it for the flight of its planes."

In contending that the New York City law has "taken" their property in violation of the Fifth and Fourteenth Amendments, appellants urge that the Landmarks Law has deprived them of any gainful use of their "air rights" above the Terminal and that, irrespective of the value of the remainder of their parcel, the city has "taken" their right to this superadjacent airspace, thus entitling them to "just compensation." The argument that appellants may establish a "taking" simply by showing that they have been denied the ability to exploit a property interest that they heretofore had believed was available for development is untenable. "Taking" jurisprudence does not divide a single parcel into discrete segments and attempt to determine whether rights in a particular segment have been entirely abrogated. In deciding whether a particular governmental action has effected a taking, this Court focuses rather both on the character of the action and on the nature and extent of the interference with rights in the parcel as a whole—here, the city tax block designated as the "landmark site."

Appellants, focusing on the character and impact of the law, argue that it effects a "taking" because its operation has significantly diminished the value of the Terminal site. Appellants concede that the decisions sustaining other land-use regulations uniformly reject the proposition that diminution in property value, standing alone, can establish a "taking," *see Euclid v. Ambler Realty Co.*, 272 U.S. 365 (1926) (75% diminution in value caused by zoning law), and that the "taking" issue in these contexts is resolved by focusing on the uses the regulations permit.

Appellants' position appears to be that the only means of ensuring that selected owners are not singled out to endure financial hardship for no reason is to hold that any restriction imposed on individual landmarks pursuant to the New York City scheme is a "taking" requiring the payment of "just compensation." Agreement with this argument would, of course, invalidate all comparable landmark legislation in the Nation. We find no merit in it.

It is true that both historic-district legislation and zoning laws regulate all properties within given physical communities whereas landmark laws apply only to selected parcels. But, landmark laws are not like discriminatory, or "reverse spot," zoning: that is, a land-use decision which arbitrarily singles out a particular parcel for different, less favorable treatment than the neighboring ones. In contrast to discriminatory zoning, the New York City law embodies a comprehensive plan to preserve structures of historic or aesthetic interest wherever they might be found in the city, and over 400 landmarks and 31 historic districts have been designated pursuant to this plan.

Equally without merit is the argument that the decision to designate a structure as a landmark "is inevitably arbitrary or at least subjective, because it is basically a matter of taste," thus unavoidably singling out individual landowners for disparate and unfair treatment. The argument has a hollow ring. Appellants not only did not seek judicial review of either the designation, but do not even now suggest that the Commission's decisions concerning the Terminal were in any sense arbitrary or unprincipled.

It is true that the Landmarks Law has a more severe impact on some landowners than on others, but that in itself does not mean that the law affects a "taking." Legislation designed to promote the general welfare commonly burdens some more than others. The owners of the brickyard in *Hadacheck*, of the cedar trees in *Miller v. Schoene*, and of the gravel and sand mine in *Goldblatt*, were uniquely burdened by the legislation sustained in those cases. Similarly, zoning laws often affect some property owners more severely than others but have not been held to be invalid on that account. For example, the property owner in *Euclid* who wished to use its property for industrial purposes was affected far more severely by the ordinance than its neighbors who wished to use their land for residences.

In any event, appellants' repeated suggestions that they are solely burdened and unbenefited are factually inaccurate. This contention overlooks the fact that the New York City law applies to vast numbers of structures in the city in addition to the Terminal—all the structures contained in the 31 historic districts and over 400 individual landmarks, many of which are close to the Terminal. Unless we are to reject the judgment of the New York City Council that the preservation of landmarks benefits all New York citizens and all structures, both economically and by improving the quality of life in the city as a whole—which we are unwilling to do—we cannot conclude that the owners of the Terminal have in no sense been benefited by the Landmarks Law.

We still must consider whether the interference with appellants' property is of such a magnitude that "there must be an exercise of eminent domain and compensation to sustain it." *Pennsylvania Coal Co. v. Mahon*, 260 U.S., at 413. That inquiry may be narrowed to the question of the severity of the impact of the law on appellants' parcel, and its resolution in turn requires a careful assessment of the impact of the regulation on the Terminal site.

Unlike the governmental acts in *Goldblatt, Miller, Causby, Griggs,* and *Hadacheck,* the New York City law does not interfere in any way with the present uses of the Terminal. Its designation as a landmark not only permits but contemplates that appellants may continue to use the property precisely as it has been used for the past 65 years: as a railroad terminal containing office space and concessions. So the law does not interfere with what must be regarded as Penn Central's primary expectation concerning the use of the parcel. More importantly, we regard the New York City law as permitting Penn Central not only to profit from the Terminal but also to obtain a "reasonable return" on its investment.

Appellants exaggerate the effect of the law on their ability to make use of the air rights above the Terminal in two respects. First, it simply cannot be maintained that appellants have been prohibited from occupying *any* portion of the airspace above the Terminal. The Commission's report emphasized that whether any construction would be allowed depended upon whether the proposed addition "would harmonize in scale, material and character with the Terminal." Since appellants have not sought approval for the construction of a smaller structure, we do not know that appellants will be denied any use of any portion of the airspace above the Terminal.

Second, to the extent appellants have been denied the right to build above the Terminal, it is not literally accurate to say that they have been denied *all* use of even those pre-existing air rights. Their ability to use these rights has not been abrogated; they are made transferable to at least eight parcels in the vicinity of the Terminal, one or two of which have been found suitable for the construction of new office buildings. While these rights may well not have constituted "just compensation" if a "taking" had occurred, the rights nevertheless undoubtedly mitigate whatever financial burdens the law has imposed on appellants and are to be taken into account in considering the impact of regulation.

We conclude that the application of New York City's Landmarks Law has not affected a "taking" of appellants' property. The restrictions imposed are substantially related to the promotion of the general welfare and not only permit reasonable beneficial use of the landmark site but also afford appellants opportunities further to enhance not only the Terminal site proper but also other properties.

Affirmed.

Mr. Justice REHNQUIST, with whom THE CHIEF JUSTICE and Mr. Justice STEVENS join, *dissenting.*

Typical zoning restrictions may so limit the prospective uses of a piece of property as to diminish the value of that property in the abstract because it may not be used for the forbidden purposes. But any such abstract decrease in value will more than likely be at least partially offset by an increase in value which flows from similar restrictions as to use on neighboring properties. Where a relatively few individual buildings, all separated from one another, are singled out and treated differently from surrounding buildings, no such reciprocity exists. The cost to the property owner which results from the imposition of restrictions applicable only to his property and not that of his neighbors may be substantial—in this case, several million dollars—with no comparable reciprocal benefits. And the cost associated with landmark legislation is likely to be of a completely different order of magnitude than that which results from the imposition of normal zoning restrictions. Under the historic-landmark preservation scheme adopted by New York, the property owner is under an affirmative duty to *preserve* his property *as a landmark* at his own expense.

Before the city of New York declared Grand Central Terminal to be a landmark, Penn Central could have used its "air rights" over the Terminal to build a multistory office building, at an apparent value of several million dollars per year. Today, the Terminal cannot be modified in *any* form, including the erection of additional stories, without the permission of the Landmark Preservation Commission, a permission which appellants, despite good-faith attempts, have so far been unable to obtain. While neighboring landowners are free to use their land and "air rights" in any way consistent with the broad boundaries of New York zoning, Penn Central, absent the permission of appellees, must forever maintain its property in its present state. The property has been thus subjected to a nonconsensual servitude not borne by any neighboring or similar properties. Appellees have thus destroyed—in a literal sense, "taken"—substantial property rights of Penn Central.

Appellees' actions do not merely *prohibit* Penn Central from using its property in a narrow set of noxious ways. Instead, appellees have placed an *affirmative* duty on Penn Central to maintain the Terminal in its present state and in "good repair." While Penn Central may continue to use the Terminal as it is presently designed, appellees otherwise "exercise complete dominion and control over the surface of the land," and must compensate the owner for his loss. Property is taken in the constitutional sense when inroads are made upon an owner's use of it to an extent that, as between private parties, a servitude has been acquired." *United States v. Dickinson*, 331 U.S. 745 (1947).

The benefits that appellees believe will flow from preservation of the Grand Central Terminal will accrue to all the citizens of New York City. There is no reason to believe that appellants will enjoy a substantially greater share of these benefits. If the cost of preserving Grand Central Terminal were spread evenly across the entire population of the city of New York, the burden per person would be in cents per year. However, appellees impose the entire cost of several million dollars per year on Penn Central. It is precisely this sort of discrimination that the Fifth Amendment prohibits.

Appellees argue that a taking only occurs where a property owner is denied *all* reasonable value of his property. The Court has frequently held that, even where a destruction of property rights would not *otherwise* constitute a taking, the inability of the owner to make a reasonable return on his property requires compensation under the Fifth Amendment. But the converse is not true. A taking does not become a noncompensable exercise of police power simply because the government in its grace allows the owner to make some "reasonable" use of his property. "It is the character of the invasion, not the amount of damage resulting from it, so long as the damage is substantial, that determines the question whether it is a taking." *United States v. Cress*, 243 U.S. 316 (1917); *United States v. Causby*, 328 U.S., at 266.

Appellees allow a property owner to "transfer" his previous right to develop the landmark property to adjacent properties under his control. Appellees call this system "Transfer Development Rights," or TDR's. The Fifth Amendment does not allow approximate compensation but requires "a full and perfect equivalent for the property taken." *Monongahela Navigation Co. v. United States*, 148 U.S., at 326. I would remand for a determination of whether TDR's constitute a "full and perfect equivalent for the property taken."

Notes

1. *What Constitutes Property?* In *United States v. General Motors Corp.*, 323 U.S. 373 (1945), the Court held that the concept of "property" should be broadly defined: Property refers to the entire "group of rights inhering in the citizen's relation to the physical thing, as the right to possess, use and dispose of it. The constitutional provision is addressed to every sort of interest the citizen may possess." *Id.* at 378.

2. *Lawyers Trust Accounts.* In *Phillips v. Washington Legal Foundation*, 524 U.S. 156 (1998), the Court was confronted by a challenge to the District of Columbia's

Interest on Lawyers Trust Account (IOLTA) program. Under this program, the interest generated on client funds held by attorneys in connection with their practices are paid into foundations that finance legal services for low-income individuals. The Court held that the interest was the client's.

3. *Mandatory Easements.* In *Nollan v. California Coastal Commission,* 483 U.S. 825 (1987), the Nollans applied for permission to demolish a small old ocean-front home and build a new one in its place. The California Coastal Commission approved the project on condition that the Nollans create a public easement across their oceanfront property. The commission found that the new home would block the ocean views, thus contributing to the development of "a 'wall' of residential structures" that would prevent the public "psychologically from realizing a stretch of coastline exists nearby that they have every right to visit." *Id.* at 828-829. The new house would also increase private use of the shorefront. These effects of the new construction, along with other area development, would cumulatively "burden the public's ability to traverse to and along the shorefront." *Id.* at 829. Therefore the commission concluded that it could properly require the Nollans to offset that burden by providing additional lateral access to the public beaches in the form of an easement across their property. The Court concluded that the easement requirement constituted a taking without just compensation:

> Had California simply required the Nollans to make an easement across their beach-front available to the public on a permanent basis in order to increase public access to the beach, rather than conditioning their permit to rebuild their house on their agreeing to do so, we have no doubt there would have been a taking. The question becomes whether requiring it to be conveyed as a condition for issuing a land-use permit alters the outcome. We have long recognized that land-use regulation does not affect a taking if it "substantially advances legitimate state interests" and does not "deny an owner economically viable use of his land," *Agins v. Tiburon,* 447 U.S. 255 (1980). The Commission argues that among these permissible purposes are protecting the public's ability to see the beach, assisting the public in overcoming the "psychological barrier" to using the beach created by a developed shorefront, and preventing congestion on the public beaches. We assume, without deciding, that this is so—in which case the Commission unquestionably would be able to deny the Nollans their permit outright if their new house (alone, or by reason of the cumulative impact produced in conjunction with other construction) would substantially impede these purposes.
>
> The Commission argues that a permit condition that serves the same legitimate police-power purpose as a refusal to issue the permit should not be found to be a taking if the refusal to issue the permit would not constitute a taking. We agree. Thus, if the Commission attached to the permit some condition that would have protected the public's ability to see the beach notwithstanding construction of the new house—for example, a height limitation, a width restriction, or a ban on fences—so long as the Commission could have exercised its police power (as we have assumed it could) to forbid construction of the house altogether, imposition of the condition would also be constitutional. Moreover (and here we come closer to the facts of the present case), the condition would be constitutional even if it consisted of the requirement that the Nollans provide a viewing spot on their property for passersby with whose sighting of the ocean their new house would interfere. The Commission's assumed power to forbid construction of the house in order to protect the public's view of the beach must surely include the power to condition construction upon some concession by the owner, even a concession of property rights, that serves the same end.

The evident constitutional propriety disappears, however, if the condition substituted for the prohibition utterly fails to further the end advanced as the justification for the prohibition. Here, the lack of nexus between the condition and the original purpose of the building restriction converts that purpose to something other than what it was. The purpose then becomes, quite simply, the obtaining of an easement to serve some valid governmental purpose, but without payment of compensation. Whatever may be the outer limits of "legitimate state interests" in the takings and land-use context, this is not one of them. In short, unless the permit condition serves the same governmental purpose as the development ban, the building restriction is not a valid regulation of land use but "an out-and-out plan of extortion."

It is quite impossible to understand how a requirement that people already on the public beaches be able to walk across the Nollans' property reduces any obstacles to viewing the beach created by the new house. It is also impossible to understand how it lowers any "psychological barrier" to using the public beaches, or how it helps to remedy any additional congestion on them "caused by construction of the Nollans" new house. We therefore find that the Commission's imposition of the permit condition cannot be treated as an exercise of its land-use power for any of these purposes.

Id. at 831-839. (Justices Brennan, Marshall, Blackburn, and Stevens dissented.)

4. *Unconstitutional Conditions.* In *Dolan v. City of Tigard*, 512 U.S. 374 (1994), Dolan sought a permit allowing her to double the size of her store and pave her gravel parking lot. Under the city's land development plan, property that bordered Fanno Creek was to be used only as "greenways" to minimize flooding. The city granted Dolan's request on condition that she dedicate portions of her property for a public greenway. Dolan claimed that conditioning the permit in exchange for the dedication was an unconstitutional condition. Dolan claimed the condition was unconstitutional because it did not have the required "essential nexus" between the state's interest and the permit condition as required in *Nollan, supra.* The Court found that the city did not meet the nexus requirement here, without some quantification of some of its findings about how a greenway would offset traffic congestion.

∽ PROBLEMS ∽

1. *Setback Requirements.* The City of Glenview Hills, worried about crowding, establishes setback requirements that prohibit the building of homes within five (5) feet of a property line. The city first imposes the requirement on all property within the city, even in the northeast section called Virginia-Lowlands, which has many houses comfortably located within five (5) feet of the property boundaries. Two years later, the city council, led by Dana, modifies the law to permit a street-by-street vote of the property owners. A nonconsenting property owner, Dana's brother Damon, who lives on a fiercely divided street, claims a taking. Should he win? *See Eubank v. Richmond*, 226 U.S. 137 (1912).

2. *Save the Beach, Continued.* Did Pensacola's law, which changed existing statutory and common law property rights, constitute a taking? Does it matter if the

rights were changed minimally? If the law changed one of the rights, accretion of land,, and all of the other "bundle of rights" were left in place, would it be a taking? Explain.

3. *Rent Control.* Congress passed a law in 1919 establishing a commission in the District of Columbia to ensure that rents are "fair and reasonable," after many complaints in the growing federal enclave, and allowing tenants to hold over after the expiration of their lease in many circumstances. The law was enacted due to deplorable conditions in rental properties as an outgrowth of World War I and the need to maintain standards in the nation's capitol. Is the rent control law constitutional? *See Block v. Hirsh,* 256 U.S. 135 (1921) (Holmes, J.). Does the rent control law also raise an impairment of contracts issue under the Contract Clause?

4. *The Public Park.* Greensboro, North Carolina, eyed a portion of town it wanted to turn into a public park. It bought some of the land in question, but realized it did not have the money to buy all of it without straining its finances. Rather than giving up on its goal, Greensboro devised a plan to secure the park. It passed a law stating that for the transfer of parcels privately owned in that part of town, any conveyance, *inter vivos* or by will, requires the city of Greensboro to have the right of first refusal. Is this law constitutional? *See Hodel v. Irving,* 481 U.S. 704 (1987).

5. *The Novel Coronavirus and the Moratorium on Evictions.* With the stay-at-home orders imposed to combat the novel coronavirus spread in many states, the unemployment rates rose to unprecedented levels. To combat a chain reaction from the suddenly stilled economy, many governors imposed a moratorium on evictions of tenants. Were these moratoriums takings? How does *Sierra-Tahoe* apply, if at all? Is *Block v. Hirsh,* 256 U.S. 135 (1921), controlling?

6. *The Novel Coronavirus and Wedding/Event Deposits.* For many people planning a wedding or other significant event, this meant securing an event space and other items required for that event—flowers, food, chairs, a band, and more. The planning mostly culminated in contracts in which a deposit was placed to hold the space, flowers, etc. With government orders against more than ten people congregating together and unessential businesses forced to close, many people sought the return of their deposits. When the businesses refused to return the deposits, the party-hosts were faced with a dilemma—postpone their event indefinitely, or hope there was a *force majeure* clause in the agreement covering the return of deposits. Could an alternate analysis here be one of takings? Does *Lucas* apply? If so, how?

Lucas v. South Carolina Coastal Council

505 U.S. 1003 (1992)

Justice SCALIA delivered the opinion of the Court.

In 1986, petitioner David H. Lucas paid $975,000 for two residential lots on the Isle of Palms in Charleston County, South Carolina, on which he intended to build single-family homes. In 1988, however, the South Carolina Legislature enacted the Beachfront Management Act, S.C. Code Ann. §48-39-250 *et seq.*, which had the direct effect of barring petitioner from erecting any permanent habitable structures on his two parcels. A state trial court found that this prohibition rendered Lucas's parcels "valueless." This case requires us to decide whether the Act's dramatic effect on the economic value of Lucas's lots accomplished a taking of private property under the Fifth and Fourteenth Amendments requiring the payment of "just compensation." U.S. Const., Amdt. 5.

In the aftermath of Congress's passage of the federal Coastal Zone Management Act of 1972, the South Carolina legislature enacted its own law. The South Carolina Act required owners of coastal zone land that qualified as a "critical area" (defined in the legislation to include beaches and immediately adjacent sand dunes) to obtain a permit from the newly created South Carolina Coastal Council (Council) prior to committing the land to a "use other than the use the critical area was devoted to on September 28, 1977."

In the late 1970's, Lucas and others began extensive residential development of the Isle of Palms, a barrier island situated eastward of the city of Charleston. In 1986, Lucas purchased the two lots at issue in this litigation. No portion of the lots, which were located approximately 300 feet from the beach, qualified as a "critical area" under the 1977 Act; accordingly, at the time Lucas acquired these parcels, he was not legally obliged to obtain a permit from the Council in advance of any development activity. His intention with respect to the lots was to do what the owners of the immediately adjacent parcels had already done: erect single-family residences. He commissioned architectural drawings for this purpose.

The Beachfront Management Act brought Lucas's plans to an abrupt end. Under that 1988 legislation, the Council was directed to establish a "baseline" connecting the landward-most "points of erosion during the past forty years" in the region of the Isle of Palms. The Council fixed this baseline landward of Lucas's parcels. Under the Act construction of occupiable improvements was flatly prohibited seaward of a line drawn 20 feet landward of, and parallel to, the baseline. The Act provided no exceptions.

Lucas promptly filed suit contending that the Beachfront Management Act's construction bar effected a taking of his property without just compensation. The trial court agreed concluding Lucas's properties had been "taken" and it ordered respondent to pay "just compensation" in the amount of $1,232,387.50. The Supreme Court of South Carolina reversed holding that when a regulation respecting the use of property is designed "to prevent serious public harm," no compensation is owing under the Takings Clause regardless of the regulation's effect on the property's value. We granted certiorari.

Prior to Justice Holmes's exposition in *Pennsylvania Coal Co. v. Mahon*, 260 U.S. 393 (1922), it was generally thought that the Takings Clause reached only a "direct appropriation" of property, or the functional equivalent of a "practical ouster of the owner's possession," *Transportation Co. v. Chicago*, 99 U.S. 635 (1879). Justice Holmes recognized in *Mahon* that if the protection against physical appropriations of private property was to be meaningfully enforced, the government's power to redefine the range of interests included in the ownership of property was necessarily constrained by constitutional limits. If, instead, the uses of private property were subject to unbridled, uncompensated qualification under the police power, "the natural tendency of human nature would be to extend the qualification more and more until at last private property disappeared." These considerations gave birth in that case to the oft-cited maxim that, "while property may be regulated to a certain extent, if regulation goes too far it will be recognized as a taking."

Mahon offered little insight into when, and under what circumstances, a given regulation would be seen as going "too far" for purposes of the Fifth Amendment. We have generally eschewed any "'set formula'" for determining how far is too far, preferring to "engage in essentially ad hoc, factual inquiries." *Penn Central Transportation Co. v. New York City*, 438 U.S. 104 (1978). We have, however, described at least two discrete categories of regulatory action as compensable without case-specific inquiry into the public interest advanced in support of the restraint. The first encompasses regulations that compel the property owner to suffer a physical "invasion" of his property. In general (at least with regard to permanent invasions), no matter how minute the intrusion, and no matter how weighty the public purpose behind it, we have required compensation. For example, we determined that New York's law requiring landlords to allow television cable companies to emplace cable facilities in their apartment buildings constituted a taking even though the facilities occupied at most only 1 cubic feet of the landlords' property.

The second situation in which we have found categorical treatment appropriate is where regulation denies all economically beneficial or productive use of land. We have never set forth the justification for this rule. Perhaps it is simply, as Justice Brennan suggested, that total deprivation of beneficial use is, from the landowner's point of view, the equivalent of a physical appropriation. *See San Diego Gas & Electric Co. v. San Diego*, 450 U.S., at 652 (dissenting opinion). In the extraordinary circumstance when *no* productive or economically beneficial use of land is permitted, it is less realistic to indulge our usual assumption that the legislature is simply "adjusting the benefits and burdens of economic life," in a manner that secures an "average reciprocity of advantage" to everyone concerned. And the *functional* basis for permitting the government, by regulation, to affect property values without compensation — that "Government hardly could go on if to some extent values incident to property could not be diminished without paying for every such change in the general law," — does not apply to the relatively rare situations where the government has deprived a landowner of all economically beneficial uses.

Regulations that leave the owner of land without economically beneficial or productive options for its use carry with them a heightened risk that private property is being pressed into some form of public service under the guise of mitigating serious public harm. The many statutes on the books that provide for the use of eminent domain to impose servitudes on private scenic lands preventing developmental uses, or to acquire such lands altogether, suggest the practical equivalence in this setting of negative regulation and appropriation. In short, that there are good reasons for our frequently expressed belief that when the owner of real property has been called upon to sacrifice *all* economically beneficial uses in the name of the common good, that is, to leave his property economically idle, he has suffered a taking.

The trial court found Lucas's two beachfront lots to have been rendered valueless by respondent's enforcement of the coastal-zone construction ban. Petitioner "conceded that the beach/dune area of South Carolina's shores is an extremely valuable public resource; that the erection of new construction, *inter alia,* contributes to the erosion and destruction of this public resource; and that discouraging new construction in close proximity to the beach/dune area is necessary to prevent a great public harm." In the trial court's view, these concessions brought petitioner's challenge within a long line of this Court's cases sustaining against Due Process and Takings Clause challenges the State's use of its "police powers" to enjoin a property owner from activities akin to public nuisances. *See Mugler v. Kansas*, 123 U.S. 623 (1887) (law prohibiting manufacture of alcoholic beverages). It is correct that many of our prior opinions have suggested that "harmful or noxious uses" of property may be proscribed by government regulation without the requirement of compensation. However, we think the South Carolina Supreme Court was too quick to conclude that that principle decides the present case. The "harmful or noxious uses" principle was the Court's early attempt to describe in theoretical terms why government may, consistent with the Takings Clause, affect property values by regulation without incurring an obligation to compensate — a reality we nowadays acknowledge explicitly with respect to the full scope of the State's police power. *See, e.g., Penn Central Transportation Co.,* 438 U.S., at 125. "Harmful or noxious use" analysis was, in other words, simply the progenitor of our more contemporary statements that "land-use regulation does not effect a taking if it 'substantially advances legitimate state interests.'"

The transition from our early focus on control of "noxious" uses to our contemporary understanding of the broad realm within which government may regulate without compensation was an easy one, since the distinction between "harm-preventing" and "benefit-conferring" regulation is often in the eye of the beholder. It is quite possible, for example, to describe in *either* fashion the ecological, economic, and esthetic concerns that inspired the South Carolina Legislature in the present case. One could say that imposing a servitude on Lucas's land is necessary in order to prevent his use of it from "harming" South Carolina's ecological resources; or, instead, in order to achieve the "benefits" of an ecological preserve. Whether Lucas's construction of single-family residences on his parcels should be described as bringing "harm" to South Carolina's adjacent ecological resources thus depends principally upon whether the describer believes that the State's use interest in nurturing those resources is so important that *any* competing adjacent use must yield. *A fortiori* the legislature's recitation of a noxious-use justification cannot be the basis for departing from our categorical rule that total regulatory takings must be compensated. If it were, departure would virtually always be allowed.

Where the State seeks to sustain regulation that deprives land of all economically beneficial use, we think it may resist compensation only if the logically antecedent inquiry into the nature of the owner's estate shows that the proscribed use interests were not part of his title to begin with. This accords, we think, with our "takings" jurisprudence, which has traditionally been guided by the understandings of our citizens regarding the content of, and the State's power over, the "bundle of rights" that they acquire when they obtain title to property. It seems to us that the property owner necessarily expects the uses of his property to be restricted, from time to time, by various measures newly enacted by the State in legitimate exercise of its police powers. And in the case of personal property, by reason of the State's traditionally high degree of control over commercial dealings, he ought to be aware of the possibility that new regulation might even render his property economically worthless (at least if the property's only economically productive use is sale or manufacture for sale). The notion that title is somehow held subject to the "implied limitation" that the State may subsequently eliminate all economically valuable use is inconsistent with the historical compact recorded in the Takings Clause that has become part of our constitutional culture.

Where "permanent physical occupation" of land is concerned, we have refused to allow the government to decree it anew (without compensation), no matter how weighty the asserted "public interests" involved—though we assuredly *would* permit the government to assert a permanent easement that was a pre-existing limitation upon the landowner's title. We believe similar treatment must be accorded confiscatory regulations, i.e., regulations that prohibit all economically beneficial use of land: Any limitation so severe cannot be newly legislated or decreed (without compensation), but must inhere in the title itself, in the restrictions that background principles of the State's law of property and nuisance already place upon land ownership.

On this analysis, the owner of a lake-bed, for example, would not be entitled to compensation when he is denied the requisite permit to engage in a landfilling operation that would have the effect of flooding others' land. Nor the corporate owner of a nuclear generating plant, when it is directed to remove all improvements from its land upon discovery that the plant sits astride an earthquake fault. Such regulatory action may well have the effect of eliminating the land's only economically productive use, but it does not proscribe a productive use that was previously permissible under relevant property and nuisance principles. This recognition that the Takings Clause does not require compensation when an owner is barred from putting land to a use that is proscribed by those "existing rules or understandings" is surely unexceptional. When, however, a regulation that declares "off-limits" all economically productive or beneficial uses of land goes beyond what the relevant background principles would dictate, compensation must be paid to sustain it.[17]

The "total taking" inquiry we require today will ordinarily entail analysis of, among other things, the degree of harm to public lands and resources, or adjacent private property, posed by the claimant's proposed activities, the social value of the claimant's activities and their suitability to the locality in question, and the relative ease with which the alleged harm can be avoided through measures taken by the claimant and the government (or adjacent private landowners) alike. The fact that a particular use has long been engaged in by similarly situated owners ordinarily imports a lack of any common-law prohibition (though changed circumstances or new knowledge may make what was previously permissible no longer so). So also does the fact that other landowners, similarly situated, are permitted to continue the use denied to the claimant.

It seems unlikely that common-law principles would have prevented the erection of any habitable or productive improvements on petitioner's land; they rarely support prohibition of the "essential use" of land. The question, however, is one of state law to be dealt with on remand. To win its case South Carolina must do more than proffer the legislature's declaration that the uses Lucas desires are inconsistent with the public interest, or the conclusory assertion that they violate a common-law maxim. Instead, as it would be required to do if it sought to restrain Lucas in a common-law action for public nuisance, South Carolina must identify background principles of nuisance and property law that prohibit the uses he now intends in the circumstances in which the property is presently found. Only on this showing can the State fairly claim that, in proscribing all such beneficial uses, the Beachfront Management Act is taking nothing.

The judgment is reversed, and the case is remanded for proceedings not inconsistent with this opinion.

So ordered.

Justice KENNEDY, *concurring* in the judgment.

The finding of no value must be considered under the Takings Clause by reference to the owner's reasonable, investment-backed expectations. The Takings Clause, while conferring substantial protection on property owners, does not eliminate the police power of the State to enact limitations on the use of their property. *Mugler v. Kansas*, 123 U.S. 623 (1887). The rights conferred by the Takings Clause and the police power of the State may coexist without conflict. Property is bought and sold, investments are made, subject to the State's power to regulate. Where a taking is alleged from regulations which deprive the property

---

17. Of course, the State may elect to rescind its regulation and thereby avoid having to pay compensation for a permanent deprivation. But "where the regulation has already worked a taking of all use of property, no subsequent action by the government can relieve it of the duty to provide compensation for the period during which the taking was effective."

of all value, the test must be whether the deprivation is contrary to reasonable, investment-backed expectations.

In my view, reasonable expectations must be understood in light of the whole of our legal tradition. The common law of nuisance is too narrow a confine for the exercise of regulatory power in a complex and interdependent society. *Goldblatt v. Hempstead*, 369 U.S. 590 (1962). The State should not be prevented from enacting new regulatory initiatives in response to changing conditions, and courts must consider all reasonable expectations whatever their source. The Takings Clause does not require a static body of state property law; it protects private expectations to ensure private investment. The promotion of tourism, for instance, ought not to suffice to deprive specific property of all value without a corresponding duty to compensate. Furthermore, the means, as well as the ends, of regulation must accord with the owner's reasonable expectations. Here, the State did not act until after the property had been zoned for individual lot development and most other parcels had been improved, throwing the whole burden of the regulation on the remaining lots. This too must be measured in the balance.

Justice BLACKMUN, *dissenting*.

Today the Court launches a missile to kill a mouse. Petitioner Lucas is a contractor, manager, and part owner of the Wild Dune development on the Isle of Palms. He has lived there since 1978. In December 1986, he purchased two of the last four pieces of vacant property in the development. The area is notoriously unstable. In roughly half of the last 40 years, all or part of petitioner's property was part of the beach or flooded twice daily by the ebb and flow of the tide. Between 1963 and 1973 the shoreline was 100 to 150 feet onto petitioner's property. The first line of stable vegetation was about halfway through the property. Between 1981 and 1983, the Isle of Palms issued 12 emergency orders for sandbagging to protect property in the Wild Dune development. Determining that local habitable structures were in imminent danger of collapse, the Council issued permits for two rock revetments to protect condominium developments near petitioner's property from erosion; one of the revetments extends more than halfway onto one of his lots.

The South Carolina Supreme Court found that the Beachfront Management Act did not take petitioner's property without compensation. The decision rested on two premises that until today were unassailable — that the State has the power to prevent any use of property it finds to be harmful to its citizens, and that a state statute is entitled to a presumption of constitutionality.

The Beachfront Management Act includes a finding by the South Carolina General Assembly that the beach/dune system serves the purpose of "protecting life and property by serving as a storm barrier which dissipates wave energy and contributes to shoreline stability in an economical and effective manner." The General Assembly also found that "development unwisely has been sited too close to the beach/dune system. This type of development has jeopardized the stability of the beach/dune system, accelerated erosion, and endangered adjacent property."

If the state legislature is correct that the prohibition on building in front of the setback line prevents serious harm, then, under this Court's prior cases, the Act is constitutional. "Long ago it was recognized that all property in this country is held under the implied obligation that the owner's use of it shall not be injurious to the community." *Keystone Bituminous Coal Assn. v. DeBenedictis,* 480 U.S. 470 (1987). The Court consistently has upheld regulations imposed to arrest a significant threat to the common welfare, whatever their economic effect on the owner. *See, e.g., Goldblatt v. Hempstead,* 369 U.S. 590 (1962).

"The existence of facts supporting the legislative judgment is to be presumed." *United States v. Carolene Products Co.,* 304 U.S. 144 (1938). This Court always has required plaintiffs challenging the constitutionality of an ordinance to provide "some factual foundation of record" that contravenes the legislative findings. *O'Gorman & Young,* 282 U.S., at 258. In the absence of such proof, "the presumption of constitutionality must prevail." Rather than invoking these traditional rules, the Court decides the State has the burden to convince the courts that its legislative judgments are correct.

The Court takes the opportunity to create a new scheme for regulations that eliminate all economic value. From now on, there is a categorical rule finding these regulations to be a taking unless the use they prohibit is a background common-law nuisance or property principle.

I first question the Court's rationale in creating a category that obviates a "case-specific inquiry into the public interest advanced," if all economic value has been lost. When the government regulation prevents the owner from any economically valuable use of his property, the private interest is unquestionably substantial, but we have never before held that no public interest can outweigh it. The Court's prior decisions "uniformly reject the proposition that diminution in property value, standing alone, can establish a 'taking.'" *Penn Central Transp. Co. v. New York City,* 438 U.S. 104 (1978).

This Court repeatedly has recognized the ability of government, in certain circumstances, to regulate property without compensation no matter how adverse the financial effect on the owner may be. In none of the cases did the Court suggest that the right of a State to prohibit certain activities without paying compensation turned on the availability of some residual valuable use. Instead, the cases depended on whether the government interest was sufficient to prohibit the activity, given the significant private cost. The State has full power to prohibit an owner's use of property if it is harmful to the public.

The Court decides that it will permit a State to regulate all economic value only if the State prohibits uses that would not be permitted under "background principles of nuisance and property law." Until today, the Court explicitly had rejected the contention that the government's power to act without paying compensation turns on whether the prohibited activity is a common-law nuisance. The threshold inquiry for imposition of the Court's new rule, "deprivation of all economically valuable use," itself cannot be determined objectively. As the

Court admits, whether the owner has been deprived of all economic value of his property will depend on how "property" is defined. There is no "objective" way to define what that denominator should be.

Even more perplexing, however, is the Court's reliance on common-law principles of nuisance in its quest for a value-free takings jurisprudence. In determining what is a nuisance at common law, state courts make exactly the decision that the Court finds so troubling when made by the South Carolina General Assembly today: They determine whether the use is harmful. Common-law public and private nuisance law is simply a determination whether a particular use causes harm. There simply is no reason to believe that new interpretations of the hoary common-law nuisance doctrine will be particularly "objective" or "value free." One searches in vain, I think, for anything resembling a principle in the common law of nuisance.

Nor does history indicate any common-law limit on the State's power to regulate harmful uses even to the point of destroying all economic value. Nothing in the discussions in Congress concerning the Takings Clause indicates that the Clause was limited by the common-law nuisance doctrine. Common-law courts themselves rejected such an understanding. In short, I find no clear and accepted "historical compact" or "understanding of our citizens" justifying the Court's new takings doctrine.

The Court makes sweeping and, in my view, misguided and unsupported changes in our takings doctrine. While it limits these changes to the most narrow subset of government regulation — those that eliminate all economic value from land — these changes go far beyond what is necessary to secure petitioner Lucas' private benefit. I dissent.

Justice STEVENS, *dissenting.*

Although in dicta we have sometimes recited that a law "effects a taking if it denies an owner economically viable use of his land," our *rulings* have rejected such an absolute position. *See, e.g., First English Evangelical Lutheran Church of Glendale v. County of Los Angeles,* 482 U.S. 304 (1987), "'Although a comparison of values before and after' a regulatory action 'is relevant, it is by no means conclusive.'"

In addition to lacking support in past decisions, the Court's new rule is wholly arbitrary. A landowner whose property is diminished in value 95% recovers nothing, while an owner whose property is diminished 100% recovers the land's full value.

The Court's holding today effectively freezes the State's common law, denying the legislature much of its traditional power to revise the law governing the rights and uses of property. New appreciation of the significance of endangered species, the importance of wetlands, and the vulnerability of coastal lands, shapes our evolving understandings of property rights. The Court's categorical approach rule will, I fear, greatly hamper the efforts of local officials and planners who must deal with increasingly complex problems in land-use and environmental regulation.

The Just Compensation Clause "was designed to bar Government from forcing some people alone to bear public burdens which, in all fairness and justice, should be borne by the public as a whole." A diminution in value caused by a zoning regulation is far less likely to constitute a taking if it is part of a general and comprehensive land-use plan.

In view of all of these factors, even assuming that petitioner's property was rendered valueless, the risk inherent in investments of the sort made by petitioner, the generality of the Act, and the compelling purpose motivating the South Carolina Legislature persuade me that the Act did not effect a taking of petitioner's property. I respectfully dissent.

∼ PROBLEMS ∼

1. *The Woodpecker.* Oklahoma City enacts an ordinance related to undeveloped land after recent sightings of the red-cockaded woodpecker. While this bird is considered to be somewhat of a pest because it pokes small holes in cavities in the bark of pine trees in order to create its home, the city wants to save the bird's habitat. The ordinance permits "recreational use of the properties, such as hunting, fishing and camping, but no development." Is this ordinance constitutional after *Lucas*?

2. *Louisville Lights Out.* The City of Louisville believes that the Shelbyville Road corridor (on the east side of Louisville) is becoming too commercial. Accordingly, the city bans all further commercial development in that corridor, the dimensions of which are specified in the law. For an owner of undeveloped property who would like to develop it, does the ban constitute a taking under *Lucas*?

3. *Required Maintenance.* Suppose that, after *Lucas* is decided, the State of South Carolina decides not to pay him, but instead to let Lucas build on the property. However, the State imposes building conditions requiring owners who wish to erect new structures to take steps to prevent beach erosion. a) South Carolina restricts the costs of the erosion-prevention structures to 1% of the cost of the property, with the State paying the rest. Is this provision constitutional? b) What if the costs are not restricted and vary from year to year? For example, during especially windy and stormy years, the costs of sand replenishment, maintenance of sea walls, and more could triple, all to be paid by the landowner. Is this provision constitutional?

Tahoe-Sierra Preservation Council v. Tahoe Regional Planning Agency

535 U.S. 302 (2002)

Justice STEVENS delivered the opinion of the Court.

Lake Tahoe is "uniquely beautiful." Mark Twain aptly described the clarity of its waters as "'not *merely* transparent, but dazzlingly, brilliantly so.'" Lake Tahoe's exceptional clarity is attributed to the absence of algae that obscures the waters of most other lakes. Historically, the lack of nitrogen and phosphorous, which nourish the growth of algae, has ensured the transparency of its waters. Unfortunately, the lake's pristine state has deteriorated rapidly over the past 40 years; increased land development in the Lake Tahoe Basin (Basin) has threatened the "'noble sheet of blue water'" beloved by Twain and countless others. "Dramatic decreases in clarity first began to be noted in the late 1950's/early 1960's, shortly after development at the lake began in earnest." The lake's unsurpassed beauty, it seems, is the wellspring of its undoing. The upsurge of development in the area has caused "increased nutrient loading of the lake largely because of the increase in impervious coverage of land in the Basin resulting from that development." "Impervious coverage—such as asphalt, concrete, buildings, and even packed dirt—prevents precipitation from being absorbed by the soil. Instead, the water is gathered and concentrated by such coverage. Larger amounts of water flowing off a driveway or a roof have more erosive force than scattered raindrops falling over a dispersed area—especially one covered with indigenous vegetation, which softens the impact of the raindrops themselves." The District Court predicted that "unless the process is stopped, the lake will lose its clarity and its trademark blue color, becoming green and opaque for eternity."

In the 1960's, when the problems associated with the burgeoning development began to receive significant attention, jurisdiction over the Basin, which occupies 501 square miles, was shared by the States of California and Nevada, five counties, several municipalities, and the Forest Service of the Federal Government. In 1968, the legislatures of the two States adopted the Tahoe Regional Planning Compact. The compact set goals for the protection and preservation of the lake and created TRPA as the agency assigned "to coordinate and regulate development in the Basin and to conserve its natural resources." In order to give itself time to develop an adequate plan, TRPA imposed an eight month moratorium on development and followed it with a 32 month moratorium. It is argued that moratoria constitute a taking.

Petitioners contend that the mere enactment of a temporary regulation that, while in effect, denies a property owner all viable economic use of her property gives rise to an unqualified constitutional obligation to compensate her for the value of its use during that period. Under their proposed rule, there is no need to evaluate the landowners' investment-backed expectations, the actual impact of the regulation on any individual, the importance of the public interest served by the regulation, or the reasons for imposing the temporary restriction. For petitioners, it is enough that a regulation imposes a temporary deprivation—no matter how brief—of all economically viable use to trigger a *per se* rule that a taking has occurred. In our view the answer to the abstract question whether a temporary moratorium effects a taking is neither "yes, always" nor "no, never"; the answer depends upon the particular circumstances of the case. The circumstances in this case are best analyzed within the *Penn Central* framework.

The text of the Fifth Amendment itself provides a basis for drawing a distinction between physical takings and regulatory takings. Its plain language requires the payment of compensation whenever the government acquires private property for a public purpose, whether the acquisition is the result of a condemnation proceeding or a physical appropriation. But the Constitution contains no comparable reference to regulations that prohibit a property owner from making certain uses of her private property.

When the government physically takes possession of an interest in property for some public purpose, it has a categorical duty to compensate the former owner regardless of whether the interest that is taken constitutes an entire parcel or merely a part thereof. Thus, compensation is mandated when a leasehold is taken and the government occupies the property for its own purposes, even though that use is temporary. *United States v. General Motors Corp.*, 323 U.S. 373 (1945). Similarly, when the government appropriates part of a rooftop in order to provide cable TV access for apartment tenants, or when its planes use private airspace to approach a government airport, it is required to pay for that share no matter how small. But a government regulation that merely prohibits landlords from evicting tenants unwilling to pay a higher rent, *Block v. Hirsh*, 256 U.S. 135 (1921); that bans certain private uses of a portion of an owner's property, or that forbids the private use of certain airspace, does not constitute a categorical taking. "The first category of cases requires courts to apply a clear rule; the second necessarily entails complex factual assessments of the purposes and economic effects of government actions." *Yee v. Escondido*, 503 U.S. 519 (1992).

This longstanding distinction between acquisitions of property for public use, on the one hand, and regulations prohibiting private uses, on the other, makes it inappropriate to treat cases involving physical takings as controlling precedents for the evaluation of a claim that there has been a "regulatory taking," and vice versa. For the same reason that we do not ask whether a physical appropriation advances a substantial government interest or whether it deprives the owner of all economically valuable use, we do not apply our precedent from the physical takings context to regulatory takings claims. Land-use regulations are ubiquitous and most of them impact property values in some tangential way—often in completely unanticipated ways. Treating them all as *per se* takings would transform government regulation into a luxury few governments could afford. By contrast, physical appropriations are relatively rare, easily identified, and usually represent a greater affront to individual property rights.

Petitioners rely principally on our decision in *Lucas v. South Carolina Coastal Council*, 505 U.S. 1003 (1992)—a regulatory takings case that, nevertheless, applied a categorical rule—to argue that the *Penn Central* framework is inapplicable here. *Pennsylvania Coal Co. v. Mahon*, 260 U.S. 393 (1922), gave birth to our regulatory takings jurisprudence. In subsequent opinions we have repeatedly and consistently endorsed Holmes' observation that "if regulation goes too far it will be recognized as a taking." After *Mahon*, neither a physical appropriation nor a public use has ever been a necessary component of a "regulatory taking."

In the decades following that decision, we have "generally eschewed" any set formula for determining how far is too far, choosing instead to engage in "'essentially ad hoc, factual inquiries.'" Indeed, we still resist the temptation to adopt *per se* rules in cases involving partial regulatory takings, preferring to examine "a number of factors" rather than a simple "mathematically precise" formula. Even though multiple factors are relevant in the analysis of regulatory takings claims, in such cases we must focus on "the parcel as a whole" including the character of the action and the nature and extent of the interference with rights in the parcel as a whole—here, the city tax block designated as the "landmark site."

This requirement that "the aggregate must be viewed in its entirety" explains why restrictions on the use of only limited portions of the parcel, such as setback ordinances, or a requirement that coal pillars be left in place to prevent mine subsidence, were not considered regulatory takings. In each of these cases, we affirmed that "where an owner possesses a full 'bundle' of property rights, the destruction of one 'strand' of the bundle is not a taking."

First English, 482 U.S., at 315, identified two reasons why a regulation temporarily denying an owner all use of her property might not constitute a taking. First, we recognized that "the county might avoid the conclusion that a compensable taking had occurred by establishing that the denial of all use was insulated as a part of the State's authority to enact safety regulations." Second, we limited our holding "to the facts presented" and recognized "the quite different questions that would arise in the case of normal delays in obtaining building permits, changes in zoning ordinances, variances, and the like which were not before us." Thus, our decision in *First English* surely did not approve, and implicitly rejected, the categorical submission that petitioners are now advocating.

Similarly, our decision in *Lucas* is not dispositive. The categorical rule that we applied in *Lucas* states that compensation is required when a regulation deprives an owner of "*all* economically beneficial uses" of his land. But our holding was limited to "the extraordinary circumstance when *no* productive or economically beneficial use of land is permitted." The emphasis on the word "no" in the text of the opinion was, in effect, reiterated in a footnote explaining that the categorical rule would not apply if the diminution in value were 95% instead of 100%. Anything less than a "complete elimination of value," or a "total loss," the Court acknowledged, would require the kind of analysis applied in *Penn Central.*

Certainly, our holding that the permanent "obliteration of the value" of a fee simple estate constitutes a categorical taking does not answer the question whether a regulation prohibiting any economic use of land for a 32-month period has the same legal effect. Petitioners seek to bring this case under the rule announced in *Lucas* by arguing that we can effectively sever a 32-month segment from the remainder of each landowner's fee simple estate, and then ask whether that segment has been taken in its entirety by the moratoria. Of course, defining the property interest taken in terms of the very regulation being challenged is circular. With property so divided, every delay would become a total ban; the moratorium and the normal permit process alike would constitute categorical takings. Petitioners' "conceptual severance" argument is unavailing because it ignores *Penn Central*'s admonition that in regulatory takings cases we must focus on "the parcel as a whole." The starting point for the court's analysis should have been to ask whether there was a total taking of the entire parcel; if not, then *Penn Central* was the proper framework.

An interest in real property is defined by the metes and bounds that describe its geographic dimensions and the term of years that describes the temporal aspect of the owner's interest. Both dimensions must be considered if the interest is to be viewed in its entirety. Hence, a permanent deprivation of the owner's use of the entire area is a taking of "the parcel as a whole," whereas a temporary restriction that merely causes a diminution in value is not. Logically, a fee simple estate cannot be rendered valueless by a temporary prohibition on economic use, because the property will recover value as soon as the prohibition is lifted.

Neither *Lucas,* nor *First English,* nor any of our other regulatory takings cases compels us to accept petitioners' categorical submission. In fact, these cases make clear that the categorical rule in *Lucas* was carved out for the "extraordinary case" in which a regulation permanently deprives property of all value; the default rule remains that, in the regulatory taking context, we require a more fact specific inquiry.

Petitioners' argument would apply to numerous "normal delays in obtaining building permits, changes in zoning ordinances, variances, and the like," as well as to orders temporarily prohibiting access to crime scenes, businesses that violate health codes, fire-damaged buildings, or other areas that we cannot now foresee. Such a rule would undoubtedly require changes in numerous practices that have long been considered permissible exercises of the police power. A rule that required compensation for every delay in the use of property would render routine government processes prohibitively expensive or encourage hasty decision-making. Such an important change in the law should be the product of legislative rulemaking rather than adjudication.

We are persuaded that the better approach to claims that a regulation has effected a temporary taking requires careful examination and weighing of all the relevant circumstances. The concepts of 'fairness and justice' that underlie the Takings Clause, of course, are less than fully determinate. Accordingly, we have eschewed "any 'set formula' for determining when 'justice and fairness' require that economic injuries caused by public action be compensated by the government, rather than remain disproportionately concentrated on a few persons. The outcome instead depends largely upon the particular circumstances in that case."

In rejecting petitioners' *per se* rule, we do not hold that the temporary nature of a land-use restriction precludes finding that it effects a taking; we simply recognize that it should not be given exclusive significance one way or the other. A narrower rule that excluded the normal delays associated with processing permits, or that covered only delays of more than a year, would certainly have a less severe impact on prevailing practices, but it would still impose serious financial constraints on the planning process. Unlike the "extraordinary circumstance" in which the government deprives a property owner of all economic use, moratoria like Ordinance 81-5 and Resolution 83-21 are used widely among land-use planners to preserve the status quo while formulating a more permanent development strategy. In fact, the consensus in the planning community appears to be that moratoria, or "interim development controls" as they are often called, are an essential tool of successful development. Yet even the weak version of petitioners' categorical rule would treat these interim measures as takings regardless of the good faith of the planners, the reasonable expectations of the landowners, or the actual impact of the moratorium on property values.

The interest in facilitating informed decision-making by regulatory agencies counsels against adopting a *per se* rule that would impose such severe costs on their deliberations. Otherwise, the financial constraints of compensating property owners during a moratorium may force officials to rush through the planning process or to abandon the practice altogether. To the extent that communities are forced to abandon using moratoria, landowners will have incentives to develop their property quickly before a comprehensive plan can be enacted, thereby fostering inefficient and ill-conceived growth. Indeed, the interest in protecting the decisional process is even stronger when an agency is developing a regional plan than when it is considering a permit for a single parcel. In the proceedings involving the Lake Tahoe Basin, for example, the moratoria enabled TRPA to obtain the benefit of comments and criticisms from interested parties during its deliberations. Moreover, with a temporary ban on development there is a lesser risk that individual landowners will be "singled out" to bear a special burden that should be shared by the public as a whole. At least with a moratorium there is a clear "reciprocity of advantage," because it protects the interests of all affected landowners against immediate construction that might be inconsistent with the provisions of the plan that is ultimately adopted. "While each of us is burdened somewhat by such restrictions, we, in turn, benefit greatly from the restrictions that are placed on others." In fact, there is reason to believe property values often will continue to increase despite a moratorium. Such an increase makes sense in this context because property values throughout the Basin can be expected to reflect the added assurance that Lake Tahoe will remain in its pristine state. Since in some cases a 1-year moratorium may not impose a burden at all, we should not adopt a rule that assumes moratoria always force individuals to bear a special burden that should be shared by the public as a whole.

It may well be true that any moratorium that lasts for more than one year should be viewed with special skepticism. But given the fact that the District Court found that the 32 months required by TRPA to formulate the 1984 Regional Plan was not unreasonable, we could not conclude that every delay of over one year is constitutionally unacceptable. The duration of the restriction is one of the important factors that a court must consider in the appraisal of a regulatory takings claim, but the "temptation to adopt what amount to *per se* rules in either direction must be resisted." Petitioners' proposed rule is simply "too blunt an instrument" for identifying those cases. We conclude, therefore, that the interest in "fairness and justice" will be best served by relying on the familiar *Penn Central* approach when deciding cases like this, rather than by attempting to craft a new categorical rule.

Accordingly, the judgment of the Court of Appeals is *affirmed*.

It is so ordered.

Chief Justice REHNQUIST, with whom Justice SCALIA and Justice THOMAS join, *dissenting.*

For over half a decade petitioners were prohibited from building homes, or any other structures, on their land. Because the Takings Clause requires the government to pay compensation when it deprives owners of all economically viable use of their land and because a ban on all development lasting almost six years does not resemble any traditional land-use planning device, I dissent.

A distinction between "temporary" and "permanent" prohibitions is tenuous. The "temporary" prohibition in this case that the Court finds is not a taking lasted almost six years. The "permanent" prohibition that the Court held to be a taking in *Lucas* lasted less than two years because the law, as it often does, changed. The South Carolina Legislature in 1990 decided to amend the 1988 Beachfront Management Act to allow the issuance of " 'special permits' for the construction or reconstruction of habitable structures seaward of the baseline." Land-use regulations are not irrevocable. And the government can even abandon condemned land. Under the Court's decision today, the takings question turns entirely on the initial label given a regulation, a label that is often without much meaning.

Even if a practical distinction between temporary and permanent deprivations were plausible, to treat the two differently in terms of takings law would be at odds with the justification for the *Lucas* rule. The *Lucas* rule is derived from the fact that a "total deprivation of beneficial use is, from the landowner's point of view, the equivalent of a physical appropriation." The regulation in *Lucas* was the "practical equivalence" of a long-term physical appropriation, i.e., a condemnation, so the Fifth Amendment required compensation. The "practical equivalence," from the landowner's point of view, of a "temporary" ban on all economic use is a forced leasehold.

The Court analogizes to other areas of takings law in which we have distinguished between regulations and physical appropriations. But whatever basis there is for such distinctions in those contexts does not apply when a regulation deprives a landowner of all economically beneficial use of his land. In "the extraordinary circumstance when *no* productive or economically beneficial use of land is permitted," it is less likely that "the legislature is simply 'adjusting the benefits and burdens of economic life' in a manner that secures an 'average reciprocity of advantage' to everyone concerned," and more likely that the property "is being pressed into some form of public service under the guise of mitigating serious public harm."

The Court worries that applying *Lucas* here compels finding that an array of traditional, short-term, land-use planning devices are takings. When a regulation merely delays a final land-use decision, we have recognized that there are other background principles of state property law that prevent the delay from being deemed a taking. We thus noted in *First English* that our discussion of temporary takings did not apply "in the case of normal delays in obtaining building permits, changes in zoning ordinances, variances, and the like." The short-term delays attendant to zoning and permit regimes are a longstanding feature of state property law and part of a landowner's reasonable investment-backed expectations.

But a moratorium prohibiting all economic use for a period of six years is not one of the longstanding, implied limitations of state property law. Typical moratoria thus prohibit only certain categories of development, such as fast-food restaurants, or adult businesses, or all commercial development. Such moratoria do not implicate *Lucas* because they do not deprive landowners of all economically beneficial use of their land. As for moratoria that prohibit all development, these do not have the lineage of permit and zoning requirements and thus it is less certain that property is acquired under the "implied limitation" of a moratorium prohibiting all development. Moreover, unlike a permit system in which it is expected that a project will be approved so long as certain conditions are satisfied, a moratorium that prohibits all uses is by definition contemplating a new land-use plan that would prohibit all uses.

The duration of this "moratorium" far exceeds that of ordinary moratoria. California, where much of the land at issue in this case is located, provides that a moratorium "shall be of no further force and effect 45 days from its date of adoption," and caps extension of the moratorium so that the total duration cannot exceed two years. Others limit moratoria to six months without any possibility of an extension. Resolution 83-21 reflected this understanding of the limited duration of moratoria in initially limiting the moratorium in this case to 90 days. But what resulted—a "moratorium" lasting nearly six years—bears no resemblance to the short-term nature of traditional moratoria as understood from these background examples of state property law. Because the prohibition on development of nearly six years in this case cannot be said to resemble any "implied limitation" of state property law, it is a taking that requires compensation.

Justice THOMAS, with whom Justice SCALIA joins, *dissenting*.

I would hold that regulations prohibiting all productive uses of property are subject to *Lucas' per se* rule, regardless of whether the property so burdened retains theoretical useful life and value if, and when, the "temporary" moratorium is lifted. Such potential future value bears on the amount of compensation due and has nothing to do with whether there was a taking in the first place.

∼ PROBLEMS ∼

1. *Remodeling TBA.* Suppose a federal financial reform law places a number of limitations on firms receiving federal T.A.R.P. money. The law contains a provision that prohibited remodeling or upgrading of property owned by persons subject to bonus restrictions for eight months from the date of the law's enactment.

Would this provision be constitutional? *See First English Evangelical Lutheran Church v. County of Los Angeles*, 482 U.S. 304 (1987).

2. *Jackpot.* Suppose in Reno, Nevada, the city council imposed a six-month moratorium on development in the most congested area of town. A local casino, Calico Jack's, which did not intend to expand and actually had no resources with which to do so, brought suit, challenging the constitutionality of the law because it "took a valued and essential right of property ownership, that of developing property." Should Calico Jack's prevail? Suppose Reno condemns land owned by Calico Jack's that lies in a sump-hole and has been used for garbage dumping for many years. Calico Jack's had tried to sell the land, but it was unsuitable for any development. If fixed up at a cost of $1 million, the land would be worth $50,000. (Reno wanted to fix up the property because it bordered a beautiful public recreational area, the value of which was reduced by estimates of up to $2 million since it was next to such a messy piece of property.) What should Reno pay Calico Jack's for the land, if anything? *See Brown v. Legal Foundation of Washington*, 538 U.S. 216 (2003).

3. *Save the Beach, Continued.* Was the moratorium on beach development in the Pensacola law presented in the introductory problem at the beginning of the chapter justified after *Tahoe-Sierra Preservation Council*? How would you argue both sides of the issue?

Notes

1. *Judicial Takings.* If state law generally defines property interests, shaping the contours of takings analysis, can a judicial decision about state law constitute a taking under the federal Constitution? Florida viewed ownership of beach-front

property as follows: "In Florida, as at common law, the littoral owner automatically takes title to dry land added to his property by accretion; but formerly submerged land that has become dry land by avulsion continues to belong to the owner of the seabed (usually the State)." *Stop the Beach Renourishment, Inc. v. Florida Department of Environmental Protection,* 506 U.S. 702 (2010). Now suppose in 2003, a Florida city, Destin, and a county, Walton, applied for permits to restore almost 7 miles of beach that was eroded by various hurricanes. The restoration would involve depositing sand to create approximately 75 feet of additional beach—pushing out the high-water line seaward. That beach under the existing law would be ostensibly owned by the State. Does that creation of state-owned beach between the private landowners and the ocean create a taking? If the Florida Supreme Court in litigation declares that not to be a taking, could that in itself be a taking?

Justice Scalia, in *Stop the Beach Renourishment, Inc., supra,* said: "If a legislature *or a court* declares that what was once an established right of private property no longer exists, it has taken that property, no less than if the State had physically appropriated it or destroyed its value by regulation. 'A State, by *ipse dixit,* may not transform private property into public property without compensation.'"

The majority of the Court did not agree with Justice Scalia about the concept of judicial takings. Several subsequent cases involving eminent domain litigation generally circumvented the judicial taking analysis by noting that the judicial taking mechanism was recognized only by a plurality of the Court. For example, in *Sagarin v. City of Bloomington,* 932 N.E. 2d 739 (Ind. Ct. App. 2010), the Court considered the types of compensation that were appropriate pursuant to a taking. The petitioner cited *Stop the Beach Renourishment, Inc.,* and in footnote 2, the Court responded: "Sagarin and Jablonski submitted Notice of Additional Authority, citing *Stop the Beach Renourishment, Inc. v. Florida Department of Environmental Protection,* 130 S.Ct. 2592 (2010), to support the idea that monetary compensation is not the sole remedy for inverse condemnation. However, the citations refer only to the plurality portions of the opinion. Therefore, those sections are without precedential authority."

2. *Conditional Rezoning.* In *Bettendorf v. St. Croix County of Wisconsin,* 631 F.3rd 421 (7th Cir. 2011), the Court considered a landowner's claim that conditional rezoning of his property from commercial to agricultural and residential uses constituted a constructive taking requiring just compensation. The Seventh Circuit Court of Appeals noted the *Stop the Beach Renourishment* decision, stating:

Lurking in this case are two issues that sharply divided the Supreme Court of the United States without producing a majority opinion in *Stop the Beach Renourishment, Inc. v. Florida Department of Environmental Protection,* 130 S.Ct. 2592 (2010). The issues are first, whether a court decision can effect a compensable taking of property, and second, if so, what role federal courts might play in reviewing those decisions. Justice Scalia's plurality opinion for four Justices concluded that a state court decision could effect a compensable taking by reversing well-established property law, and that such issues could be brought to the Supreme Court but probably not to lower federal courts. Four other Justices declined to reach the first issue and pointed out the potential for significant change in the roles of federal courts in deciding state property law. I do not think we need to reach these issues in this case because I do not think the state court decision itself effected any taking of Bettendorf's property. It is the county's threats to enforce the revised zoning law that may have already effected a temporary taking of his property and the county's efforts to enforce the court decision that could effect a permanent taking.

3. *More* Nollan *and* Dolan *and Conditioning of Land-Use Permits.* In *Koontz v. St. Johns River Water Management District,* 570 U.S. 595 (2013), the Court considered whether a denial of a permit could fall within the prescription of conditioning permits on the relinquishment of an interest in land. The Court stated:

> In those cases, we held that a unit of government may not condition the approval of a land-use permit on the owner's relinquishment of a portion of his property unless there is a "nexus" and "rough proportionality" between the government's demand and the effects of the proposed land use. In this case, the St. Johns River Water Management District (District) believes that it circumvented *Nollan* and *Dolan* because of the way in which it structured its handling of a permit application submitted by Coy Koontz, Sr., whose estate is represented in this Court by Coy Koontz, Jr. The District did not approve his application on the condition that he surrender an interest in his land. Instead, the District, after suggesting that he could obtain approval by signing over such an interest, denied his application because he refused to yield. The Florida Supreme Court blessed this maneuver and thus effectively interred those important decisions. Because we conclude that *Nollan* and *Dolan* cannot be evaded in this way, the Florida Supreme Court's decision must be reversed.

Calculating Regulatory Takings

The multiple-factor test for regulatory takings received another framing in 2017 by the Supreme Court in a new context—whether a state law limiting the sale or improvement of a "substandard" sized lot—and effectively merging two lots into one—constitutes a regulatory taking. The Court focused on what constituted the proper "denominator," meaning the land serving as the basis for comparison against what was alleged to have been taken by the government.

Murr v. Wisconsin

137 S. Ct. 1933 (2017)

Justice KENNEDY delivered the opinion of the Court.

The classic example of a property taking by the government is when the property has been occupied or otherwise seized. In the case now before the Court, petitioners contend that governmental entities took their real property—an undeveloped residential lot—not by some physical occupation but instead by enacting burdensome regulations that forbid its improvement or separate sale because it is classified as substandard in size. The relevant governmental entities are the respondents.

Against the background justifications for the challenged restrictions, respondents contend there is no regulatory taking because petitioners own an adjacent lot. The regulations, in effecting a merger of the property, permit the continued residential use of the property including for a single improvement to extend over both lots. This retained right of the landowner, respondents urge, is of sufficient offsetting value that the regulation is not severe enough to be a regulatory taking.

Petitioners are two sisters and two brothers in the Murr family. Petitioners' parents arranged for them to receive ownership of two lots the family used for recreation along the Lower St. Croix River in the town of Troy, Wisconsin. The lots are adjacent, but the parents purchased them separately, put the title of one in the name of the family business, and later arranged for transfer of the two lots, on different dates, to petitioners. The lots are referred to in this litigation as Lots E and F.

For the area where petitioners' property is located, the Wisconsin rules prevent the use of lots as separate building sites unless they have at least one acre of land suitable for development. A grandfather clause relaxes this restriction for substandard lots which were "in separate ownership from abutting lands" on January 1, 1976, the effective date of the regulation § NR 118.08(4)(a)(1). The clause permits the use of qualifying lots as separate building sites. The rules also include a merger provision, however, which provides that adjacent lots under common ownership may not be "sold or developed as separate lots" if they do not meet the size requirement. § NR 118.08(4)(a)(2). The Wisconsin rules require localities to adopt parallel provisions so the St. Croix County zoning ordinance contains identical restrictions. The Wisconsin rules also authorize the local zoning authority to grant variances from the regulations where enforcement would create "unnecessary hardship." § NR 118.09(4)(b).

Petitioners' parents purchased Lot F in 1960 and built a small recreational cabin on it. In 1961, they transferred title to Lot F to the family plumbing company. In 1963, they purchased neighboring Lot E, which they held in their own names. The lots have the same topography. A steep bluff cuts through the middle of each, with level land suitable for development above the bluff and next to the water below it. The line dividing Lot E from Lot F runs from the river front to the far end of the property, crossing the blufftop along the way. Lot E has approximately 60 feet of river frontage, and Lot F has approximately 100 feet. Though each lot is approximately 1.25 acres in size, because of the waterline and the steep bank they each have less than one acre of land suitable for development. Even when combined, the lots' buildable land area is only 0.98 acres due to the steep terrain.

The lots remained under separate ownership, with Lot F owned by the plumbing company and Lot E owned by petitioners' parents, until transfers to petitioners. Lot F was conveyed to them in 1994, and Lot E was conveyed to them in 1995. A decade later, petitioners became interested in moving the cabin on Lot F to a different portion of the lot and selling Lot E to fund the project. The unification of the lots under common ownership, however, had implicated the state and local rules barring their separate sale or development. Petitioners then sought variances from the St. Croix County Board of Adjustment to enable their building and improvement plan, including a variance to allow the separate sale or use of the lots. The Board denied the requests, and the state courts affirmed. Petitioners filed the present action in state court, alleging that the state and county regulations worked a regulatory taking by depriving them of "all, or practically all, of the use of Lot E because the lot cannot be sold or developed as a separate lot." Respondents' appraisal included values of $698,300 for the lots together as regulated; $771,000 for the lots as two distinct buildable properties; and $373,000 for Lot F as a single lot with improvements. Petitioners' appraisal included an unrebutted, estimated value of $40,000 for Lot E as an undevelopable lot, based on the counterfactual assumption that it could be sold as a separate property.

The Takings Clause of the Fifth Amendment provides that private property shall not "be taken for public use, without just compensation." The Clause is applicable to the States through the Fourteenth Amendment. *Chicago, B. & Q. R. Co. v. Chicago*, 166 U. S. 226 (1897). The plain language of the Takings Clause "requires the payment of compensation whenever the government acquires private property for a public purpose," *Tahoe-Sierra Preservation Council, Inc. v. Tahoe Regional Planning Agency*, 535 U. S. 302, 321 (2002), but does not address in specific terms the imposition of regulatory burdens on private property. "Prior to Justice Holmes's exposition in *Pennsylvania Coal Co. v. Mahon*, 260 U. S. 393 (1922), it was generally thought that the Takings Clause reached only a direct appropriation of property, or the functional equivalent of a practical ouster of the owner's possession," like the permanent flooding of property. *Lucas v. South Carolina Coastal Council*, 505 U. S. 1003 (1992). *Mahon* initiated this Court's regulatory takings jurisprudence, declaring that "while property may be regulated to a certain extent, if regulation goes too far it will be recognized as a taking." A regulation can be so burdensome as to become a taking, yet the *Mahon* Court did not formulate more detailed guidance for determining when this limit is reached.

In the near century since *Mahon*, the Court for the most part has refrained from elaborating this principle through definitive rules. This area of the law has been characterized by "ad hoc, factual inquiries, designed to allow careful examination and weighing of all the relevant circumstances." *Tahoe-Sierra, supra,* at 322. The Court has, however, stated two guidelines relevant here for determining when government regulation is so onerous that it constitutes a taking. First, "with certain qualifications a regulation which 'denies all economically beneficial or productive use of land' will require compensation under the Takings Clause." *Palazzolo v. Rhode Island*, 533 U. S. 606, 617 (2001) (*quoting Lucas, supra,* at 1015). Second, when a regulation impedes the use of property without depriving the owner of all economically beneficial use, a taking still may be found based on "a complex of factors," including (1) the economic impact of the regulation on the claimant; (2) the extent to which the regulation has interfered with distinct investment-backed expectations; and (3) the character of the governmental action. *Palazzolo, supra,* at 617.

By declaring that the denial of all economically beneficial use of land constitutes a regulatory taking, *Lucas* stated what it called a "categorical" rule. In *Lucas*, the Court included a caveat recognizing the relevance of state law and land-use customs: The complete deprivation of use will not require compensation if the challenged limitations "inhere in the restrictions that background principles of the State's law of property and nuisance already placed upon land ownership." A central dynamic of the Court's regulatory takings jurisprudence, then, is its flexibility. This has been and remains a means to reconcile two competing objectives central to regulatory takings doctrine. One is the individual's right to retain the interests and exercise the freedoms at the core of private property ownership. The other persisting interest is the government's well-established power to "adjust rights for the public good." *Andrus v. Allard*, 444 U. S. 51 (1979). As Justice Holmes declared, "Government hardly could go on if to some extent values incident to property could not be diminished without paying for every such change in the general law." *Mahon, supra*, at 413. In all instances, the analysis must be driven "by the purpose of the Takings Clause, which is to prevent the government from 'forcing some people alone to bear public burdens which, in all fairness and justice, should be borne by the public as a whole.'" *Palazzolo, supra*, at 617 *(quoting Armstrong v. United States*, 364 U. S. 40, 49 (1960)).

This case presents a question that is linked to the ultimate determination whether a regulatory taking has occurred: What is the proper unit of property against which to assess the effect of the challenged governmental action? Put another way, "one of the critical questions is determining how to define the unit of property 'whose value is to furnish the denominator of the fraction.'" *Keystone Bituminous Coal Assn. v. DeBenedictis*, 480 U. S. 470, 497 (1987) (*quoting* Michelman, *Property, Utility, and Fairness*, 80 HARV. L. REV. 1165, 1992 (1967)). This Court has explained that the question is important to the regulatory takings inquiry. "To the extent that any portion of property is taken, that portion is always taken in its entirety; the relevant question, however, is whether the property taken is all, or only a portion of, the parcel in question." *Concrete Pipe & Products of Cal., Inc. v. Construction Laborers Pension Trust for Southern Cal.*, 508 U. S. 602, 644 (1993).

Defining the property at the outset should not necessarily preordain the outcome in every case. In some, though not all, cases the effect of the challenged regulation must be assessed and understood by the effect on the entire property held by the owner, rather than just some part of the property that, considered just on its own, has been diminished in value. This demonstrates the contrast between regulatory takings, where the goal is usually to determine how the challenged regulation affects the property's value to the owner, and physical takings, where the impact of physical appropriation or occupation of the property will be evident.

While the Court has not set forth specific guidance on how to identify the relevant parcel for the regulatory taking inquiry, there are two concepts which the Court has indicated can be unduly narrow. First, the Court has declined to limit the parcel in an artificial manner to the portion of property targeted by the challenged regulation. In *Penn Central,* for example, the Court rejected a challenge to the denial of a permit to build an office tower above Grand Central Terminal. The Court refused to measure the effect of the denial only against the "air rights" above the terminal, cautioning that "'taking' jurisprudence does not divide a single parcel into discrete segments and attempt to determine whether rights in a particular segment have been entirely abrogated." The second concept about which the Court has expressed caution is the view that property rights under the Takings Clause should be coextensive with those under state law. Although property interests have their foundations in state law, the *Palazzolo* Court reversed a state-court decision that rejected a takings challenge to regulations that pre-dated the landowner's acquisition of title. The Court explained that States do not have the unfettered authority to "shape and define property rights and rea-sonable investment-backed expectations," leaving landowners without recourse against unreasonable regulations.

By the same measure, defining the parcel by reference to state law could defeat a challenge even to a state enactment that alters permitted uses of prop-erty in ways inconsistent with reasonable investment-backed expectations. For example, a State might enact a law that consolidates nonadjacent property owned by a single person or entity in different parts of the State and then imposes devel-opment limits on the aggregate set. If a court defined the parcel according to the state law requiring consolidation, this improperly would fortify the state law against a takings claim, because the court would look to the retained value in the property as a whole rather than considering whether individual holdings had lost all value.

As the foregoing discussion makes clear, no single consideration can sup-ply the exclusive test for determining the denominator. Instead, courts must consider a number of factors. These include the treatment of the land under state and local law; the physical characteristics of the land; and the prospective value of the regulated land. The endeavor should determine whether reasonable expectations about property ownership would lead a landowner to anticipate that his holdings would be treated as one parcel, or, instead, as separate tracts. The inquiry is objective, and the reasonable expectations at issue derive from back-ground customs and the whole of our legal tradition.

The State of Wisconsin and petitioners each ask this Court to adopt a for-malistic rule to guide the parcel inquiry. Neither proposal suffices to capture the central legal and factual principles that inform reasonable expectations about property interests. Wisconsin would tie the definition of the parcel to state law, considering the two lots here as a single whole due to their merger under the challenged regulations. That approach simply assumes the answer to the ques-tion: May the State define the relevant parcel in a way that permits it to escape its responsibility to justify regulation in light of legitimate property expectations? It is, of course, unquestionable that the law must recognize those legitimate expec-tations in order to give proper weight to the rights of owners and the right of the State to pass reasonable laws and regulations. Petitioners propose a different test that is also flawed. They urge the Court to adopt a presumption that lot lines define the relevant parcel in every instance, making Lot E the necessary denominator. Petitioners' argument ignores the fact that lot lines are themselves creatures of state law, which can be overridden by the State in the reasonable exercise of its power. In effect, petitioners ask this Court to credit the aspect of state law that favors their preferred result (lot lines) and ignore that which does not (merger provision).

The merger provision here is likewise a legitimate exercise of government power, as reflected by its consistency with a long history of state and local merger regulations that originated nearly a century ago. Merger provisions often form part of a regulatory scheme that establishes a minimum lot size in order to preserve open space while still allowing orderly development. When States or localities first set a minimum lot size, there often are existing lots that do not meet the new requirements, and so local governments will strive to reduce substandard lots in a gradual manner. The regulations here represent a classic way of doing this: by implementing a merger provision, which combines contiguous substandard lots under common ownership, alongside a grandfather clause, which preserves adjacent substandard lots that are in separate ownership. The harshness of a merger provision may be ameliorated by the availability of a variance from the local zoning authority for landowners in special circumstances. Petitioners' insistence that lot lines define the relevant parcel ignores the well-settled reliance on the merger provision as a common means of balancing the legitimate goals of regulation with the reasonable expectations of landowners. Petitioners' reliance on lot lines also is problematic for another reason. Lot lines have varying degrees of formality across the States, so it is difficult to make them a standard measure of the reasonable expectations of property owners. Indeed, in some jurisdictions, lot lines may be subject to informal adjustment by property owners, with minimal government oversight. The ease of modifying lot lines also creates the risk of gamesmanship by landowners, who might seek to alter the lines in anticipation of regulation that seems likely to affect only part of their property.

Under the appropriate multifactor standard, it follows that for purposes of determining whether a regulatory taking has occurred here, petitioners' property should be evaluated as a single parcel consisting of Lots E and F together. First, the treatment of the property under state and local law indicates petitioners' property should be treated as one when considering the effects of the restrictions. As the Wisconsin courts held, the state and local regulations merged Lots E and F. The decision to adopt the merger provision was for a specific and legitimate purpose, consistent with the widespread understanding that lot lines are not dominant or controlling in every case. Petitioners' land was subject to this regulatory burden only because of voluntary conduct in bringing the lots under common ownership after the regulations were enacted. As a result, the valid merger of the lots under state law informs the reasonable expectation they will be treated as a single property. Second, the physical characteristics of the property support its treatment as a unified parcel. The lots are contiguous along their longest edge. Their rough terrain and narrow shape make it reasonable to expect their range of potential uses might be limited. ("[Petitioners] asserted Lot E could not be put to alternative uses like agriculture or commerce due to its size, location and steep terrain"). The land's location along the river is also significant. Petitioners could have anticipated public regulation might affect their enjoyment of their property, as the Lower St. Croix was a regulated area under federal, state, and local law long before petitioners possessed the land. Third, the prospective value that Lot E brings to Lot F supports considering the two as one parcel for purposes of determining if there is a regulatory taking. Petitioners are prohibited from selling Lots E and F separately or from building separate residential structures on each. Yet this restriction is mitigated by the benefits of using the property as an integrated whole, allowing increased privacy and recreational space, plus the optimal location of any improvements. ("They have an elevated level of privacy because they do not have close neighbors and are able to swim and play volleyball at the property").

The special relationship of the lots is further shown by their combined valuation. Were Lot E separately saleable but still subject to the development restriction, petitioners' appraiser would value the property at only $40,000. We express no opinion on the validity of this figure. The number is not particularly helpful for under standing petitioners' retained value in the properties because Lot E, under the regulations, cannot be sold without Lot F. The point that is useful for these purposes is that the combined lots are valued at $698,300, which is far greater than the summed value of the separate regulated lots (Lot F with its cabin at $373,000, according to respondents' appraiser, and Lot E as an undevelopable plot at $40,000, according to petitioners' appraiser). The value added by the lots' combination shows their complementarity and supports their treatment as one parcel.

Petitioners have not suffered a taking under *Lucas*, as they have not been deprived of all economically beneficial use of their property. They can use the property for residential purposes, including an enhanced, larger residential improvement. Petitioners furthermore have not suffered a taking under the more general test of *Penn Central*. The expert appraisal relied upon by the state courts refutes any claim that the economic impact of the regulation is severe. Petitioners cannot claim that they reasonably expected to sell or develop their lots separately given the regulations which predated their acquisition of both lots. Finally, the governmental action was a reasonable land-use regulation, enacted as part of a coordinated federal, state, and local effort to preserve the river and surrounding land.

The judgment of the Wisconsin Court of Appeals is affirmed.

It is so ordered.

Chief Justice ROBERTS, with whom Justice THOMAS and Justice ALITO join, dissenting.

The Court today holds that the regulation does not effect a taking that requires just compensation. This bottom-line conclusion does not trouble me; the majority presents a fair case that the Murrs can still make good use of both lots, and that the ordinance is a commonplace tool to preserve scenic areas, such as the Lower St. Croix River, for the benefit of landowners and the public alike. Where the majority goes astray, however, is in concluding that the definition of the "private property" at issue in a case such as this turns on an elaborate test looking not only to state and local law, but also to (1) "the physical characteristics of the land," (2) "the prospective value of the regulated land," (3) the "reasonable expectations" of the owner, and (4) "background customs and the whole of our legal tradition." The majority's new, malleable definition of "private property"—adopted solely "for purposes of the takings inquiry,"—undermines that protection.

I would stick with our traditional approach: State law defines the boundaries of distinct parcels of land, and those boundaries should determine the "private property" at issue in regulatory takings cases. Whether a regulation effects a taking of that property is a separate question, one in which common ownership of adjacent property may be taken into account.

The question presented in today's case concerns the "parcel as a whole" language from *Penn Central.* This enigmatic phrase has created confusion about how to identify the relevant property in a regulatory takings case when the claimant owns more than one plot of land. Should the impact of the regulation be evaluated with respect to each individual plot, or with respect to adjacent plots grouped together as one unit? According to the majority, a court should answer this question by considering a number of facts about the land and the regulation at issue. The end result turns on whether those factors "would lead a landowner to anticipate that his holdings would be treated as one parcel, or, instead, as separate tracts." The answer is far more straightforward: State laws define the boundaries of distinct units of land, and those boundaries should, in all but the most exceptional circumstances, determine the parcel at issue. Even in regulatory takings cases, the first step of the Takings Clause analysis is still to identify the relevant "private property." States create property rights with respect to particular "things." And in the context of real property, those "things" are horizontally bounded plots of land. *Tahoe-Sierra,* 535 U. S. at 331. States may define those plots differently—some using metes and bounds, others using government surveys, recorded plats, or subdivision maps. But the definition of property draws the basic line between, as P. G. Wodehouse would put it, meum and tuum. The rules must provide a readily ascertainable definition of the land to which a particular bundle of rights attaches that does not vary depending upon the purpose at issue. See, e.g., Wis. Stat. §236.28 (2016).

Following state property lines is entirely consistent with *Penn Central.* Requiring consideration of the "parcel as a whole" is a response to the risk that owners will strategically pluck one strand from their bundle of property rights—such as the air rights at issue in *Penn Central*—and claim a complete taking based on that strand alone. That risk of strategic unbundling is not present when a legally distinct parcel is the basis of the regulatory takings claim. State law defines all of the interests that come along with owning a particular parcel, and both property owners and the government must take those rights as they find them.

The Takings Clause was adopted to ensure such security by protecting property rights as they exist under state law. Deciding whether a regulation has gone so far as to constitute a "taking" of one of those property rights is, properly enough, a fact-intensive task that relies "as much on the exercise of judgment as on the application of logic." *MacDonald, Sommer & Frates v. Yolo County*, 477 U. S. 340, 349 (1986) (alterations and internal quotation marks omitted). But basing the definition of "property" on a judgment call, too, allows the government's interests to warp the private rights that the Takings Clause is supposed to secure. I respectfully dissent.

JUSTICE THOMAS, dissenting.

I join the Chief Justice's dissent because it correctly applies this Court's regulatory takings precedents. The Court, however, has never purported to ground those precedents in the Constitution as it was originally understood. In *Pennsylvania Coal Co. v. Mahon*, 260 U. S. 393, 415 (1922), the Court announced a "general rule" that "if regulation goes too far it will be recognized as a taking." But we have since observed that, prior to *Mahon*, "it was generally thought that the Takings Clause reached only a 'direct appropriation' of property, or the functional equivalent of a 'practical ouster of the owner's possession,' *Transportation Co. v. Chicago*, 99 U. S. 635, 642 (1879)." *Lucas v. South Carolina Coastal Council*, 505 U. S. 1003, 1014 (1992). In my view, it would be desirable for us to take a fresh look at our regulatory takings jurisprudence, to see whether it can be grounded in the original public meaning of the Takings Clause of the Fifth Amendment or the Privileges or Immunities Clause of the Fourteenth Amendment.

∾ PROBLEM: SAVE THE BEACH, CONTINUED ∾

Assume the Pensacola law in the introductory problem, which changed existing statutory and common law property rights, was challenged in the Florida courts. Assume the trial court found that no taking occurred, and on appeal the First District Court of Appeals affirmed, as did the Florida Supreme Court. More than two years after the litigation was initiated, the case was reviewed by the U.S. Supreme Court on a writ of certiorari, and the decision was reversed. Should the Court find that a judicial taking has occurred? If so, what should be the "just compensation"

Notes

1. *The Timing of Takings.* When does a taking actually occur? Does it occur when the government appropriates the private property or when the claimant pursues compensation in state court and is denied that compensation? What are the best arguments using a literal interpretation of the Takings Clause? Or a more dynamic, contextual interpretation of the purpose of the Clause? In *Knick v. Township of Scott*, 587 U. S.__ (2019), the Court overruled existing precedent to

allow for more takings suits in federal court. It also concluded that a constitutional violation when the taking occurred, even if compensation was subsequently paid.

The question before the Court was whether a property owner must meet a state-litigation requirement before bringing a Fifth Amendment Takings claim in Federal Court under 42 U.S.C. §1983. The divided Court answered by saying that a litigation requirement is not a prerequisite to a finding that a taking occurred. In overruling *Williamson County Regional Planning Comm'n v. Hamilton Bank of Johnson City*, 473 U.S. 172 (1985), the Court raised questions of when overruling established Supreme Court precedent is appropriate.

The case was brought by Petitioner Rose Mary Knick, who owned 90 acres of land in Scott Township, Pennsylvania. She had a home on the property, as well as a small graveyard where some of her neighbors' ancestors were buried. These family cemeteries were common and lawful. In 2012, however, the Township enacted a law requiring all cemeteries to be open to the public "during daylight hours" and allowed Township employees to enter private property to determine if any landowners were violating the law. Petitioner claimed this was a taking.

The Court found that the state-litigation prerequisite watered-down the potency of the Takings Clause:

> The state-litigation requirement relegates the Takings Clause "to the status of a poor relation" among the provisions of the Bill of Rights. *Dolan v. City of Tigard*, 512 U.S. 374, 392 (1994). Plaintiffs asserting any other constitutional claim are guaranteed a federal forum under §1983, but the state-litigation requirement "hand[s] authority over federal takings claims to state courts." *San Remo*, 545 U. S., at 350 (Rehnquist, C. J., concurring in judgment). Fidelity to the Takings Clause and our cases construing it requires overruling *Williamson County* and restoring takings claims to the full-fledged constitutional status the Framers envisioned when they included the Clause among the other protections in the Bill of Rights.

The Court cast *Williamson* in a critical light, and overruled it, allowing plaintiffs to proceed directly to federal court, instead of having to litigate first in state court:

> The *Williamson County* Court anticipated that if the property owner failed to secure just compensation under state law in state court, he would be able to bring a "ripe" federal takings claim in federal court. But as we later held in *San Remo Hotel, L. P. v. City and County of San Francisco*, 545 U.S. 323 (2005), a state court's resolution of a claim for just compensation under state law generally has preclusive effect in any subsequent federal suit. The takings plaintiff thus finds himself in a Catch-22: He cannot go to federal court without going to state court first; but if he goes to state court and loses, his claim will be barred in federal court. The federal claim dies aborning.

C. THE CONTRACT CLAUSE

As noted at the beginning of this chapter, contractual interests and expectations inform more than one constitutional provision. The emergence of liberty of contract, as a fundamental right driven by judicial construction rather than textual specificity, was a defining aspect of the *Lochner* era's substantive due process review. Prior to this controversial and eventually abandoned application of the Fourteenth Amendment, constitutional protection of contractual interests was grounded in the Contract Clause. As set forth by Article I, Section 10, this clause prohibits the state from enacting any "Law impairing the Obligation of Contracts." This provision specifically applies to existing contracts.

Early use of the Contract Clause yielded results that were consistent with the Marshall Court's vision and the facilitation of nation building. In *Fletcher v. Peck*, 10 U.S. (6 Cranch) 87 (1810), the Court reviewed the Georgia legislature's rescission of a land grant that had been tainted by bribery and fraud. The law was challenged by persons who acquired land in the aftermarket and claimed they were purchasers in due course. The Court, in an ambiguous decision referencing the Contract Clause and principles of natural law, overturned the rescission. *See also Dartmouth College v. Woodward*, 17 U.S. (4 Wheat.) 518 (1819) (striking down New Hampshire's attempt to alter the college's charter, in an effort to change the composition of the board, violating the existing charter, which gave the board the right to fill vacancies). Modern interpretation of the Contract Clause is less expansive and ambitious, but not without potential force particularly with respect to a state's power to modify public contracts and private expectations.

Home Building & Loan Assn. v. Blaisdell

290 U.S. 398 (1934)

Mr. Chief Justice HUGHES delivered the opinion of the Court.

Appellant contests the validity of the Minnesota Mortgage Moratorium Law as being repugnant to the contract clause (Art. 1, §10). The act provides that, during the emergency declared to exist, relief may be had through authorized judicial proceedings with respect to foreclosures of mortgages, and execution sales, of real estate; that sales may be postponed and periods of redemption may be extended. The act is to remain in effect 'only during the continuance of the emergency and in no event beyond May 1, 1935.' No extension of the period for redemption and no postponement of sale is to be allowed which would have the effect of extending the period of redemption beyond that date.

This case concerns the provisions of part 1, §4, authorizing the district court of the county to extend the period of redemption from foreclosure sales 'for such additional time as the court may deem just and equitable,' subject to the above-described limitation. The extension is to be made upon application to the court, on notice, for an order determining the reasonable value of the income on the property involved in the sale, or, if it has no income, then the reasonable rental value of the property, and directing the mortgagor 'to pay all or a reasonable part of such income or rental value, in or toward the payment of taxes, insurance, interest, mortgage indebtedness at such times and in such manner' as shall be determined by the court. The time for redemption from foreclosure sales, which otherwise would expire less than thirty days after the approval of the act, shall be extended to a date thirty days after its approval, and application may be made to the court within that time for a further extension as provided in the section. No action, prior to May 1, 1935, may be maintained for a deficiency judgment until the period of redemption as allowed by existing law or as extended under the provisions of the act has expired. Prior to the expiration of the extended period of redemption, the court may revise or alter the terms of the extension as changed circumstances may require.

Invoking the statute, appellees applied for an order extending the period of redemption from a foreclosure sale. Their petition stated that they owned a lot in Minneapolis which they had mortgaged to appellant; that the mortgage contained a valid power of sale by advertisement, and that by reason of their default the mortgage had been foreclosed and sold to appellant; that appellant was the holder of the sheriff's certificate of sale; that, because of the economic depression, appellees had been unable to obtain a new loan or to redeem, and that, unless the period of redemption were extended, the property would be irretrievably lost; and that the reasonable value of the property greatly exceeded the amount due on the mortgage, including all liens, costs, and expenses. Appellant objected that the statute was invalid under the federal and state Constitutions. The motion was granted. The Supreme Court of the state reversed the decision of the district court.

We assume that the mortgage contained a valid power of sale to be exercised in case of default; that this power was validly exercised; that under the law then applicable the period of redemption from the sale was one year, and that it has been extended by the judgment of the court over the opposition of the mortgagee-purchaser; and that, during the period thus extended, and unless the order for extension is modified, the mortgagee-purchaser will be unable to obtain possession, or to obtain or convey title in fee, as he would have been able to do had the statute not been enacted. The statute does not impair the integrity of the mortgage indebtedness. The obligation for interest remains. The statute does not affect the validity of the sale or the right of a mortgagee-purchaser to title in fee, or his right to obtain a deficiency judgment, if the mortgagor fails to redeem within the prescribed period. Aside from the extension of time, the other conditions of redemption are unaltered. While the mortgagor remains in possession, he must pay the rental value as that value has been determined, upon notice and hearing, by the court. The rental value so paid is devoted to the carrying of the property by the application of the required payments to taxes, insurance, and interest on the mortgage indebtedness. While the mortgagee-purchaser is debarred from actual possession, he has, so far as rental value is concerned, the equivalent of possession during the extended period.

While emergency does not create power, emergency may furnish the occasion for the exercise of power. The reasons which led to the adoption of that clause, and of the other prohibitions of section 10 of article 1, are not left in doubt. The widespread distress following the revolutionary period and the plight of debtors had called forth in the States an ignoble array of legislative schemes for the defeat of creditors and the invasion of contractual obligations. Legislative interferences had been so numerous and extreme that the confidence essential to prosperous trade had been undermined and the utter destruction of credit was threatened. 'The sober people of America' were convinced that some 'thorough reform' was needed which would 'inspire a general prudence and industry, and give a regular course to the business of society.' *The Federalist No. 44.*

The contract clause is not an absolute and is not to be read with literal exactness like a mathematical formula. This Court has said that 'the laws which subsist at the time and place of the making of a contract, and where it is to be performed, enter into and form a part of it, as if they were expressly referred to or incorporated in its terms. Nothing can be more material to the obligation than the means of enforcement. But without impairing the obligation of the contract, the remedy may certainly be modified as the wisdom of the nation shall direct.' The policy of protecting contracts against impairment presupposes the maintenance of a government by virtue of which contractual relations are worthwhile, — a government which retains adequate authority to secure the peace and good order of society. This principle of harmonizing the constitutional prohibition with the necessary residuum of state power has had progressive recognition in the decisions of this Court.

The economic interests of the state may justify the exercise of its continuing and dominant protective power notwithstanding interference with contracts. The question is not whether the legislative action affects contracts incidentally, or directly or indirectly, but whether the legislation is addressed to a legitimate end and the measures taken are reasonable and appropriate to that end. The state power may be addressed directly to the prevention of the enforcement of contracts only when these are of a sort which the Legislature in its discretion may denounce as being in themselves hostile to public morals, or public health, safety, or welfare, or where the prohibition is merely of injurious practices; that interference with the enforcement of other and valid contracts according to appropriate legal procedure, although the interference is temporary and for a public purpose, is not permissible. This is but to contend that in the latter case the end is not legitimate in the view that it cannot be reconciled with a fair interpretation of the constitutional provision.

Undoubtedly, whatever is reserved of state power must be consistent with the fair intent of the constitutional limitation of that power. This principle precludes a construction which would permit the state to adopt as its policy the repudiation of debts or the destruction of contracts or the denial of means to enforce them. But it does not follow that conditions may not arise in which a temporary restraint of enforcement may be consistent with the spirit and purpose of the constitutional provision and thus be found to be within the range of the reserved power of the state to protect the vital interests of the community. If state power exists to give temporary relief from the enforcement of contracts in the presence of disasters due to physical causes such as fire, flood, or earthquake, that power cannot be said to be nonexistent when the urgent public need demanding such relief is produced by other and economic causes.

There has been a growing appreciation of public needs and of the necessity of finding ground for a rational compromise between individual rights and public welfare. It is no answer to say that this public need was not apprehended a century ago, or to insist that what the provision of the Constitution meant to the vision of that day it must mean to the vision of our time. If by the statement that what the Constitution meant at the time of its adoption it means to-day, it is intended to say that the great clauses of the Constitution must be confined to the interpretation which the framers, with the conditions and outlook of their time, would have placed upon them, the statement carries its own refutation. Chief Justice Marshall uttered the memorable warning: 'We must never forget, that it is a constitution we are expounding' (*McCulloch v. Maryland*, 4 Wheat. 316, 407, 4 L.Ed. 579); 'a constitution intended to endure for ages to come, and, consequently, to be adapted to the various crises of human affairs.' When we are dealing with the words of the Constitution, said this Court in *Missouri v. Holland*, 252 U.S. 416, 'we must realize that they have called into life a being the development of which could not have been foreseen completely by the most gifted of its begetters. The case before us must be considered in the light of our whole experience and not merely in that of what was said a hundred years ago.'

Nor is it helpful to attempt to draw a fine distinction between the intended meaning of the words of the Constitution and their intended application. With a growing recognition of public needs and the relation of individual right to public security, the court has sought to prevent the perversion of the clause through its use as an instrument to throttle the capacity of the states to protect their fundamental interests. Applying the criteria established by our decisions, we conclude:

1. An emergency existed in Minnesota which furnished a proper occasion for the exercise of the reserved power of the state to protect the vital interests of the community.

2. The legislation was addressed to a legitimate end; that is, the legislation was not for the mere advantage of particular individuals but for the protection of a basic interest of society.

3. In view of the nature of the contracts in question—mortgages of unquestionable validity—the relief afforded and justified by the emergency, in order not to contravene the constitutional provision, could only be of a character appropriate to that emergency, and could be granted only upon reasonable conditions.

4. The conditions upon which the period of redemption is extended do not appear to be unreasonable. The initial extension of the time of redemption for thirty days from the approval of the act was obviously to give a reasonable opportunity for the authorized application to the court. The integrity of the mortgage indebtedness is not impaired; interest continues to run; the validity of the sale and the right of a mortgagee-purchaser to title or to obtain a deficiency judgment, if the mortgagor fails to redeem within the extended period, are maintained; and the conditions of redemption, if redemption there be, stand

as they were under the prior law. The mortgagor during the extended period is not ousted from possession, but he must pay the rental value of the premises as ascertained in judicial proceedings and this amount is applied to the carrying of the property and to interest upon the indebtedness. The mortgagee-purchaser during the time that he cannot obtain possession thus is not left without compensation for the withholding of possession. Also important is the fact that mortgagees, as is shown by official reports of which we may take notice, are predominantly corporations, such as insurance companies, banks, and investment and mortgage companies. These, and such individual mortgagees as are small investors, are not seeking homes or the opportunity to engage in farming. Their chief concern is the reasonable protection of their investment security. It does not matter that there are, or may be, individual cases of another aspect. The Legislature was entitled to deal with the general or typical situation. The relief afforded by the statute has regard to the interest of mortgagees as well as to the interest of mortgagors. The legislation seeks to prevent the impending ruin of both by a considerate measure of relief.

In the absence of legislation, courts of equity have exercised jurisdiction in suits for the foreclosure of mortgages to fix the time and terms of sale and to refuse to confirm sales upon equitable grounds where they were found to be unfair or inadequacy of price was so gross as to shock the conscience. Although the courts would have no authority to alter a statutory period of redemption, the legislation in question permits the courts to extend that period, within limits and upon equitable terms, thus providing a procedure and relief which are cognate to the historic exercise of the equitable jurisdiction. If it be determined, as it must be, that the contract clause is not an absolute and utterly unqualified restriction of the state's protective power, this legislation is clearly so reasonable as to be within the legislative competency.

5. The legislation is temporary in operation. It is limited to the exigency which called it forth. While the postponement of the period of redemption from the foreclosure sale is to May 1, 1935, that period may be reduced by the order of the court under the statute, in case of a change in circumstances, and the operation of the statute itself could not validly outlast the emergency or be so extended as virtually to destroy the contracts.

We are of the opinion that the Minnesota statute as here applied does not violate the contract clause of the Federal Constitution. Whether the legislation is wise or unwise as a matter of policy is a question with which we are not concerned.

The judgment of the Supreme Court of Minnesota is *affirmed*.

Judgment *affirmed*.

Mr. Justice SUTHERLAND, *dissenting*.

"The Constitution of the United States is a law for rulers and people, equally in war and in peace, and covers with the shield of its protection all classes of men, at all times, and under all circumstances. No doctrine, involving more pernicious consequences, was ever invented by the wit of man than that any of its provisions can be suspended during any of the great exigencies of government. Such a doctrine leads directly to anarchy or despotism." The contract impairment clause denies to the several states the power to mitigate hard consequences resulting to debtors from financial or economic exigencies by an impairment of the obligation of contracts of indebtedness. The present exigency is nothing new. From the beginning of our existence as a nation, periods of depression, of industrial failure, of financial distress, of unpaid and unpayable indebtedness, have alternated with years of plenty. The defense of the Minnesota law is made upon grounds which were discountenanced by the makers of the Constitution and have many times been rejected by this Court. A statute which materially delays enforcement of the mortgagee's contractual right of ownership and possession does not modify the remedy merely; it destroys, for the period of delay, all remedy so far as the enforcement of that right is concerned.

∾ PROBLEMS ∾

1. Blaisdell *Revisited.* Arizona enacts a new law, the Mortgage Modification Act of 2009, requiring lenders and borrowers of problem loans, as defined in the statute, to go to mediation to come up with an alternative payment plan, if feasible, prior to pursuing foreclosure proceedings. Would this law violate the Contract Clause under *Blaisdell*?

2. *Tolls.* In order to ensure that toll revenue would be available to pay bondholders, New Jersey and New York passed laws providing that toll revenue from the Port Authority of New Jersey and New York could not be used to subsidize railroad passenger service (but instead would be devoted to bond payments). The statutory provisions were incorporated into the bonds. In the early 1970s, during an energy crisis, both states passed laws authorizing the use of toll revenues to subsidize railroad passenger service.

a) Does the statutory repeal impair the obligation of contracts under *Blaisdell*?

b) What if the Court adopts rules that treat the impairment of government contracts—in which the government is a party—differently than the impairment of contracts between private parties? Should the courts be more deferential to state impairment of private contracts or contracts in which the government is a party? *See United States Trust Co. v. New Jersey,* 431 U.S. 1 (1997).

3. *The New York Financial Reform Law.* After the collapse of the mortgage market and the failure of many banks, which caused a severe recession, the State of New York is considering the possibility of enacting a law prohibiting "excessive bonuses in the finance industry." "Excessive" would be defined as any bonus that exceeds 10% of the employee's ordinary salary, adjusted by the percentage of profit of the company over the preceding five years. Under the proposed law, excessive bonuses would be considered unlawful, would subject the company that gives the bonus to a $500,000 fine, and would subject the receiver of the bonus to a fine

of up to $100,000 and imprisonment for a period of up to one year, if the excess bonus is not returned within one month. You are counsel to the legislative committee that is considering the law. If it is enacted, would the law be constitutional?

4. *Save the Beach, Continued.* Suppose Pensacola in the introductory problem contemplated modifying its contractual obligations through the enactment of the Pensacola "save our beaches" law for the specific purpose of saving its beaches from oil spills, hurricanes, and general erosion. Would such modifications run afoul of the Contract Clause? Why or why not?

Allied Structural Steel Company v. Spannaus

438 U.S. 234 (1978)

Mr. Justice STEWART delivered the opinion of the Court.

The issue in this case is whether the application of Minnesota's Private Pension Benefits Protection Act to the appellant violates the Contract Clause of the United States Constitution.

In 1963, Allied Structural Steel Co. (company) adopted a single-employer pension plan under the Internal Revenue Code, 26 U.S.C. §401 (1976 ed.), for salaried employees. The company was the sole contributor to the pension trust fund, and each year it made contributions to the fund. Although those contributions were irrevocable, the plan neither required the company to make specific contributions nor imposed any sanction on it for failing to contribute adequately to the fund. The company not only retained a virtually unrestricted right to amend the plan, but was also free to terminate the plan and distribute the trust assets at any time and for any reason. In sum, an employee who did not die, did not quit, and was not discharged before meeting the requirements of the plan would receive a fixed pension at age 65 if the company remained in business and elected to continue the pension plan in essentially its existing form.

In 1974, Minnesota enacted the Private Pension Benefits Protection Act which provided that a private employer of 100 employees or more—at least one of whom was a Minnesota resident—who provided pension benefits under a plan meeting the qualifications of §401 of the Internal Revenue Code, was subject to a "pension funding charge" if he either terminated the plan or closed a Minnesota office. The charge was assessed if the pension funds were not sufficient to cover full pensions for all employees who had worked at least 10 years. The Act required the employer to satisfy the deficiency by purchasing deferred annuities, payable to the employees at their normal retirement age. When the company began closing its Minnesota office in 1974, it discharged 11 of its 30 Minnesota employees. Nine of the discharged employees did not have any vested pension rights under the company's plan, but had worked for the company for 10 years or more and thus qualified as pension obligees under Minnesota law. The State notified the company that it owed a pension funding charge of $185,000 under the Act. The company brought suit claiming that the Act unconstitutionally impaired its contractual obligations to its employees under its pension agreement. We noted probable jurisdiction.

Although the contract clause was perhaps the strongest single constitutional check on state legislation during our early years as a Nation, the Contract Clause receded into comparative desuetude with the adoption of the Fourteenth Amendment, and particularly with the development of the large body of jurisprudence under the Due Process Clause of that Amendment. Nonetheless, the Contract Clause is not a dead letter.

The Contract Clause does not obliterate the police power of the States. This power, which is an exercise of the sovereign right of the Government to protect the lives, health, morals, comfort and general welfare of the people, and is paramount to any rights under contracts between individuals." *Manigault v. Springs*, 199 U.S. 473. If the Contract Clause is to retain any meaning at all, however, it must be understood to impose *some* limits upon the power of a State to abridge existing contractual relationships, even in the exercise of its otherwise legitimate police power. The existence and nature of those limits were clearly indicated in a series of cases in this Court arising from the efforts of the States to deal with the unprecedented emergencies brought on by the severe economic depression of the early 1930's. In *Home Building & Loan Assn. v. Blaisdell*, 290 U.S. 398, the Court upheld against a Contract Clause attack a mortgage moratorium law that Minnesota had enacted to provide relief for homeowners threatened with foreclosure. Although the legislation conflicted directly with lenders' contractual foreclosure rights, the Court acknowledged that, despite the Contract Clause, the States retain residual authority to enact laws "to safeguard the vital interests of their people." In upholding the state mortgage moratorium law, the Court found five factors significant. First, the state legislature had declared in the Act itself that an emergency need for the protection of homeowners existed. Second, the state law was enacted to protect a basic societal interest, not a favored group. Third, the relief was appropriately tailored to the emergency that it was designed to meet. Fourth, the imposed conditions were reasonable. And, finally, the legislation was limited to the duration of the emergency.

The most recent Contract Clause case in this Court was *United States Trust Co. v. New Jersey*, 431 U.S. 1. In that case the Court again recognized that the absolute language of the Clause must leave room for "the 'essential attributes of sovereign power,' necessarily reserved by the States to safeguard the welfare of their citizens," that power has limits when its exercise effects substantial modifications of private contracts. Despite the customary deference courts give to state laws directed to social and economic problems, "legislation adjusting the rights and responsibilities of contracting parties must be upon reasonable conditions and of a character appropriate to the public purpose justifying its adoption." Evaluating with particular scrutiny a modification of a contract to which the State itself was a party, the Court held that legislative alteration of the rights and remedies of Port Authority bondholders violated the Contract Clause because the legislation was neither necessary nor reasonable.

In applying these principles to the present case, the first inquiry must be whether the state law has operated as a substantial impairment of a contractual relationship. The severity of the impairment measures the height of the hurdle the state legislation must clear. Minimal alteration of contractual obligations may end the inquiry at its first stage. Severe impairment, on the other hand, will push the inquiry to a careful examination of the nature and purpose of the state legislation. The severity of an impairment of contractual obligations can be measured by the factors that reflect the high value the Framers placed on the protection of private contracts. Contracts enable individuals to order their personal and business affairs according to their particular needs and interests. Once arranged, those rights and obligations are binding under the law, and the parties are entitled to rely on them.

Here, the company's contracts of employment with its employees included as a fringe benefit or additional form of compensation, the pension plan. The company's maximum obligation was to set aside each year an amount based on the plan's requirements for vesting. The plan satisfied the current federal income tax code and was subject to no other legislative requirements. And, of course, the company was free to amend or terminate the pension plan at any time. The company thus had no reason to anticipate that its employees' pension rights could become vested except in accordance with the terms of the plan. It relied heavily, and reasonably, on this legitimate contractual expectation in calculating its annual contributions to the pension fund.

The effect of Minnesota's Private Pension Benefits Protection Act on this contractual obligation was severe. The company was required in 1974 to have made its contributions throughout the pre-1974 life of its plan as if employees' pension rights had vested after 10 years, instead of vesting in accord with the terms of the plan. Thus a basic term of the pension contract—one on which the company had relied for 10 years—was substantially modified. The result was that, although the company's past contributions were adequate when made, they were not adequate when computed under the 10-year statutory vesting requirement. The Act thus forced a current recalculation of the past 10 years' contributions based on the new, unanticipated 10-year vesting requirement.

Not only did the state law thus retroactively modify the compensation that the company had agreed to pay its employees from 1963 to 1974, but also it did so by changing the company's obligations in an area where the element of reliance was vital—the funding of a pension plan. Moreover, the retroactive state-imposed vesting requirement was applied only to those employers who terminated their pension plans or who closed their Minnesota offices. The company was thus forced to make all the retroactive changes in its contractual obligations at one time. By simply proceeding to close its office in Minnesota, a move that had been planned before the passage of the Act, the company was assessed an immediate pension funding charge of approximately $185,000.

Thus, the statute in question here nullifies express terms of the company's contractual obligations and imposes a completely unexpected liability in potentially disabling amounts. There is not even any provision for gradual applicability or grace periods. Yet there is no showing in the record before us that this severe disruption of contractual expectations was necessary to meet an important general social problem. The presumption favoring "legislative judgment as to the necessity and reasonableness of a particular measure," simply cannot stand in this case. "It seems clear that the problem of plant closure and pension plan termination was brought to the attention of the Minnesota legislature when the Minneapolis-Moline Division of White Motor Corporation closed one of its Minnesota plants and attempted to terminate its pension plan." Whether or not the legislation was aimed largely at a single employer, it clearly has an extremely narrow focus. It applies only to private employers who have at least 100 employees, at least one of whom works in Minnesota, and who have established voluntary private pension plans, qualified under §401 of the Internal Revenue Code. And it applies only when such an employer closes his Minnesota office or terminates his pension plan. Thus, this law can hardly be characterized, like the law at issue in the *Blaisdell* case, as one enacted to protect a broad societal interest rather than a narrow class.

Moreover, in at least one other important respect the Act does not resemble the mortgage moratorium legislation whose constitutionality was upheld in the *Blaisdell* case. This legislation, imposing a sudden, totally unanticipated, and substantial retroactive obligation upon the company to its employees, was not enacted to deal with a situation remotely approaching the broad and desperate emergency economic conditions of the early 1930's.

Entering a field it had never before sought to regulate, the Minnesota Legislature grossly distorted the company's existing contractual relationships with its employees by superimposing retroactive obligations upon the company substantially beyond the terms of its employment contracts. And that burden was imposed upon the company only because it closed its office in the State.

This Minnesota law simply does not possess the attributes of those state laws that in the past have survived challenge under the Contract Clause of the Constitution. The law was not even purportedly enacted to deal with a broad, generalized economic or social problem. It did not operate in an area already subject to state regulation at the time the company's contractual obligations were originally undertaken, but invaded an area never before subject to regulation by the State. It did not effect simply a temporary alteration of the contractual relationships of those within its coverage, but worked a severe, permanent, and immediate change in those relationships—irrevocably and retroactively. And its narrow aim was leveled, not at every Minnesota employer, not even at every Minnesota employer who left the State, but only at those who had in the past been sufficiently enlightened as voluntarily to agree to establish pension plans for their employees.

If the Contract Clause means anything at all, it means that Minnesota could not constitutionally do what it tried to do to the company in this case.

The judgment of the District Court is *reversed.*

It is so ordered.

Mr. Justice BRENNAN, with whom Mr. Justice WHITE and Mr. Justice MARSHALL join, *dissenting.*

Today's decision greatly expands the reach of the Contract Clause. The Minnesota Private Pension Benefits Protection Act (Act) does not abrogate or dilute any obligation due a party to a private contract; rather, like all positive social legislation, the Act imposes new, additional obligations on a particular class of persons. In my view, any constitutional infirmity in the law must therefore derive, not from the Contract Clause, but from the Due Process Clause of the Fourteenth Amendment. I perceive nothing in the Act that works a denial of due process and therefore I dissent.

Minnesota adopted the Act to remedy, *inter alia,* what was viewed as a related serious social problem: the frustration of expectation interests that can occur when an employer closes a single plant and terminates the employees who work there. Here and as will generally be true, the possibility of a plant's closing was not relied upon by actuaries in calculating the amount of the employer's contributions to the plan, an adequate pension plan fund would include contributions on behalf of terminated employees of 10 or more years' service whose rights had not vested. Indeed, without the Act, the closing of the plant would create a windfall for the employer, because, due to the resulting surplus in the fund, his future contributions would be reduced. In denying the windfall, the Act requires that the employer use the money he will save in the future to purchase annuities for the terminated employees. Of course, the consequence for the employer may be a slightly higher pension expense because the past contributions to the plan would have reflected the actuarial possibility that some of the employees who had served 10 years might not ultimately satisfy the plan's vesting requirement.

It is an abuse to interpret the term "impairing" as including laws which create new duties. While such laws may be conceptualized as "enlarging" the obligation of a contract when they add to the burdens that had previously been imposed by a private agreement, such laws cannot be prohibited by the Clause because they do not dilute or nullify a duty a person had previously obligated himself to perform.

More fundamentally, the Court's distortion of the meaning of the Contract Clause creates anomalies of its own and threatens to undermine the jurisprudence of property rights developed over the last 40 years. The Contract Clause is but one of several clauses in the Constitution that protect existing economic values from governmental interference. Decisions over the past 50 years have developed a coherent, unified interpretation of all the constitutional provisions that may protect economic expectations and these decisions have recognized a broad latitude in States to effect even severe interference with existing economic values when reasonably necessary to promote the general welfare. *See Penn Central Transp. Co. v. New York City,* 438 U.S. 104. The prohibition of the Contract Clause, consistently with its wording and historic purposes, has been limited in application to state laws that diluted, with utter indifference to the legitimate interests of the beneficiary of a contract duty, the existing contract obligation.

Today's conversion of the Contract Clause into a limitation on the power of States to enact laws that impose duties additional to obligations assumed under private contracts must inevitably produce results difficult to square with any rational conception of a constitutional order. To permit this level of scrutiny of laws that interfere with contract-based expectations is an anomaly. Laws that interfere with settled expectations created by state property law (and which impose severe economic burdens) are uniformly held constitutional where reasonably related to the promotion of the general welfare.

∾ PROBLEMS ∾

1. *Severance Tax Passthroughs.* Oil and gas producers entered into contracts for the sale of their products. The contracts allowed them to pass along any severance taxes paid on the products. A subsequent Alabama law increased the severance tax and made it illegal for oil and gas producers to pass the tax on (directly or indirectly) to consumers. Does the Alabama law violate the Contract Clause? Should it matter that the new law was broadly applicable to all producers and was not aimed at the appellant producers? *See Exxon Corp. v. Eagerton*, 462 U.S. 176 (1983).

2. *Increased Exemptions.* A debtor entered into an agreement with a creditor in North Carolina. During a period of economic distress, the State of North Carolina increased the number of exemptions available to a debtor in bankruptcy, although it did not remove the creditor's right to sue on the debt. Does an increase in bankruptcy exemptions amount to an impairment of the obligation of contract under the Contract Clause? *See Edwards v. Kearzey*, 96 U.S. 595 (1877).

3. *Moratorium on Rental Contracts.* A landlord entered into a number of rental contracts that provided for the surrender of possession of the property in the event of default. The contracts were all valid under the New York law in existence at the time of contracting. Subsequently, during a period of economic distress, New York placed a temporary moratorium on forced surrenders. However, tenants remaining on the premises were required to pay a reasonable rent for their use and occupation. Does the New York law impair the obligation of contract under the Contract Clause? *See Block v. Hirsh*, 256 U.S. 135 (1921).

The Contract Clause represented a seminal constitutional restraint on state police power. Although states may not bargain away their police power, the Contract Clause has imposed a reasonableness requirement on its exercise. Case law has varied with respect to the intensity of reasonableness as a standard of review. With the Fourteenth Amendment as a primary incident of Reconstruction, the growing significance of the Commerce Clause power over the course of the twentieth century, and preemption principles under the Supremacy Clause, the Court acquired more powerful tools for evaluating the constitutionality of action pursuant to state police power. Varied as these constitutional reference points may be, each in its own way implicates and engenders an ongoing debate over whether the judiciary should play a larger or smaller role in reviewing outputs of the political branches of government.

[Note: The Points to Remember for Chapter 8 is contained in an online file.]

9

Substantive Due Process: Modern Fundamental Rights

U.S. CONSTITUTION, FIFTH AMENDMENT

No person shall be deprived of life, liberty, or property, without due process of law.

U.S. CONSTITUTION, NINTH AMENDMENT

The enumeration in the Constitution, of certain rights, shall not be construed to deny or disparage others retained by the people.

U.S. CONSTITUTION, FOURTEENTH AMENDMENT

Section 1. Nor shall any State deprive any person of life, liberty, or property, without due process of law.

[Roadmap for Chapter 9 is contained in online file.]

∾ PROBLEM: CHILD CUSTODY, TRANSGENDER, AND SAME-SEX RELATIONSHIPS ∾

In a state that has amended its state constitution to allow it to discriminate against gays and lesbians in child custody and adoption disputes, the following proposed statute is introduced in the legislature:

In any custody dispute between a heterosexual individual and a homosexual individual, the Family Courts of this state shall presume that the heterosexual individual is the more

739

fit and appropriate parent to assume custody, and that awarding custody to the heterosexual parent is in the child's best interest. Custody may not be awarded to the homosexual parent unless the Court finds, as a matter of law, that the heterosexual parent is "unfit."

The proposed statute would also contain a presumption that transgender individuals are unfit parents.

Suppose that you are working as a legal advisor to a legislative committee that is about to hold hearings on this bill. The committee has asked you for your opinion about whether the proposed law is constitutional. As you work your way through this chapter, you will be asked to give your thoughts on that issue. You can ignore the equal protection issues (which will be examined in the next chapter) and focus on issues related to privacy and liberty.

———————————

Modern substantive due process review generates much the same debate that was triggered by the judiciary's identification, development, and protection of economic rights during the first third of the twentieth century. Critics of this judicial function view it essentially as neo-*Lochnerian* and antidemocratic. Exponents maintain that there are fundamental values that are not textually expressed as rights and liberties, but are no less basic. From their perspective, it is better to have those rights and liberties defined by an institution that is buffered from rather than driven by political pressures.

The generally discredited legacy of economic rights jurisprudence has left a significant mark on the Court's approach to substantive due process review. Cases establishing or expanding the right to privacy, for instance, include disclaimers to the effect that the Court is not replicating its stigmatized past. Consistent with this interest in separating modern substantive due process review from its relatively standardless antecedent, the Court has introduced criteria to guide its discernment of fundamental rights that are not explicated by the Constitution itself. The primary focal points for this purpose are whether an interest is "implicit in the concept of ordered liberty," is "rooted in the Nation's traditions and history," or is "fundamental to the American scheme of justice." To the extent the Court finds that an interest can be so described, the Court is prepared to recognize it as fundamental and thus of constitutional stature. Debate persists as to whether these imprecise standards sufficiently cabin the judiciary in its relationship to the political process.

The Due Process clauses of the Fifth and Fourteenth Amendments are multidimensional with respect to their function. They are a source of procedural fairness, when state deprivation of life, liberty, and property is a possibility. The liberty component of the Due Process clauses also has emerged, through the process of judicial review, as a platform for establishing fundamental rights that operate against the state and federal governments. It also has served as the vehicle through which provisions of the Bill of Rights have been applied to the states.

A. INCORPORATION

The Bill of Rights, as originally framed and ratified, charted basic rights and liberties for individuals only in their relationship with the federal government. The push to extend the scope of operation of the Bill of Rights was initially prevented by the Court in *Barron v. City Council of Baltimore*, 32 U.S. 243 (1833). In that case, it was argued that the Fifth Amendment prohibition against taking property without just compensation applied not only to the federal government but also to state governments. In an opinion by Chief Justice Marshall, the Court found that the question was "of great importance," but not "much difficulty," and that the proposition should be rejected: "The Constitution was ordained and established by the people of the United States for their own government, and not for the government of the individual states. Each state established a constitution for itself, and in that constitution, provided such limitations and restrictions on the powers of its particular government, as its judgment dictated. The Fifth Amendment to the Constitution, declaring that private property shall not be taken for public use, without just compensation, is intended solely as a limitation on the exercise of the power by the government of the United States, and is not applicable to the legislation of the states."

Reconstruction of the Union following the Civil War reordered the relationship between national citizenship and state citizenship, insofar as it made the latter a derivative of the former, and established the incidents of federal citizenship. Although it did not represent a consensual point of view, significant sentiment supported the notion that these incidents included the Bill of Rights. The original vessel touted for their incorporation was the Privileges and Immunities Clause. This proposed structure crashed, however, when the *Slaughterhouse Cases*, 83 U.S. 36 (1873), defined the privileges and immunities of national citizenship in narrow terms that pointedly excluded the Bill of Rights. This ruling reverted the Privileges and Immunities Clause to a functionally dormant status.

With the Privileges and Immunities Clause foreclosed as a predicate, the incorporation agenda pushed toward other platforms. Early incorporations of provisions of the Bill of Rights were brought about through substantive due process review. By amplifying the meaning of *liberty* as set forth in the Due Process Clause, the Court developed a set of fundamental rights applicable to the states. Some of these guarantees paralleled those set forth in the Bill of Rights, and others, like liberty of contract, were judicially constructed. The liberty provision of the Due Process Clause itself, rather than the Bill of Rights, was the springboard for rights implementation. Although the effect may have been the same, the process at this stage involved direct application rather than incorporation.

With the foreclosure of the *Lochner* model of substantive due process, the Court announced in *United States v. Carolene Products Co.*, 304 U.S. 144, 154 n.4

(1938), that it would reserve heightened review for instances "when legislation appears to be within a specific provision of the Constitution, such as the first ten amendments, which are deemed equally specific when held to be embraced within the Fourteenth." The Court thus held that the Fourteenth Amendment was not an incubator of rights independently, but a structure through which provisions of the Bill of Rights itself would be incorporated. This understanding, however, prefaced a significant debate that shaped the incorporation process. The issue, which generated sharp debate within the Court over the subsequent decades, was whether provisions of the Bill of Rights should be incorporated on a selective or wholesale basis. In *Palko v. Connecticut*, the Court considered arguments that the Double Jeopardy Clause was incorporated through the Due Process Clause of the Fourteenth Amendment. Justice Cardozo authored an opinion for the Court that rejected this proposition and subscribed to the theory of selective incorporation.

Palko v. Connecticut

302 U.S. 319 (1937)

Mr. Justice CARDOZO delivered the opinion of the Court.

Appellant was indicted in Fairfield County, Conn., for the crime of murder in the first degree. A jury found him guilty of murder in the second degree, and he was sentenced to confinement in the state prison for life. Thereafter the State of Connecticut, with the permission of the judge presiding at the trial, gave notice of appeal to the Supreme Court of Errors.

Pursuant to the mandate of the Supreme Court of Errors, defendant was brought to trial again. Before a jury was impaneled, and also at later stages of the case, he made the objection that the effect of the new trial was to place him twice in jeopardy for the same offense, and in so doing to violate the Fourteenth Amendment of the Constitution of the United States. Upon the overruling of the objection the trial proceeded. The jury returned a verdict of murder in the first degree, and the court sentenced the defendant to the punishment of death. The Supreme Court of Errors affirmed the judgment of conviction.

The argument for appellant is that whatever is forbidden by the Fifth Amendment is forbidden by the Fourteenth also. The Fifth Amendment, which is not directed to the States, but solely to the federal government, creates immunity from double jeopardy. No person shall be "subject for the same offense to be twice put in jeopardy of life or limb." The Fourteenth Amendment ordains, "nor shall any State deprive any person of life, liberty, or property, without due process of law." To retry a defendant, though under one indictment and only one, subjects him, it is said, to double jeopardy in violation of the Fifth Amendment, if the prosecution is one on behalf of the United States. From this the consequence is said to follow that there is a denial of life or liberty without due process of law, if the prosecution is one on behalf of the people of a state.

Appellant's thesis is that whatever would be a violation of the original bill of rights (Amendments 1 to 8) if done by the federal government is now equally unlawful by force of the Fourteenth Amendment if done by a state. There is no such general rule.

The Fifth Amendment provides, among other things, that no person shall be held to answer for a capital or otherwise infamous crime unless on presentment or indictment of a grand jury. This court has held that, in prosecutions by a state, presentment or indictment by a grand jury may give way to informations at the instance of a public officer. The Fifth Amendment provides also that no person shall be compelled in any criminal case to be a witness against himself. This court has said that, in prosecutions by a state, the exemption will fail if the state elects to end it. On the other hand, the due process clause of the Fourteenth Amendment may make it unlawful for a state to abridge by its statutes the freedom of speech which the First Amendment safeguards against encroachment by the Congress, or the like freedom of the press, or the free exercise of religion (or the right of peaceable assembly, without which speech would be unduly trammeled), or the right of one accused of crime to the benefit of counsel. In these and other situations immunities that are valid as against the federal government by force of the specific pledges of particular amendments have been found to be implicit in the concept of ordered liberty, and thus, through the Fourteenth Amendment, become valid as against the states.

The line of division may seem to be wavering and broken if there is a hasty catalogue of the cases on the one side and the other. Reflection and analysis will induce a different view. There emerges the perception of a rationalizing principle which gives to discrete instances a proper order and coherence. The right to trial by jury and the immunity from prosecution except as the result of an indictment may have value and importance. Even so, they are not of the very essence of a scheme of ordered liberty. To abolish them is not to violate a "principle of justice so rooted in the traditions and conscience of our people as to be ranked as fundamental." Few would be so narrow or provincial as to maintain that a fair and enlightened system of justice would be impossible without them. What is true of jury trials and indictments is true also of the immunity from compulsory self-incrimination. This too might be lost, and justice still be done. No doubt there would remain the need to give protection against torture, physical or mental. Justice, however, would not perish if the accused were subject to a duty to respond to orderly inquiry. The exclusion of these immunities and privileges from the privileges and immunities protected against the action of the States has not been arbitrary or casual. It has been dictated by a study and appreciation of the meaning, the essential implications, of liberty itself.

We reach a different plane of social and moral values when we pass to the privileges and immunities that have been taken over from the earlier articles of the Federal Bill of Rights and brought within the Fourteenth Amendment by a process of absorption. These in their origin were effective against the federal government alone. If the Fourteenth Amendment has absorbed them, the process of absorption has had its source in the belief that neither liberty nor justice would exist if they were sacrificed. This is true, for illustration, of freedom of thought and speech. Of that freedom one may say that it is the matrix, the indispensable condition, of nearly every other form of freedom. With rare aberrations a pervasive recognition of that truth can be traced in our history, political and legal. So it has come about that the domain of liberty, withdrawn by the Fourteenth Amendment from encroachment by the states, has been enlarged by latter-day judgments to include liberty of the mind as well as liberty of action. The extension became, indeed, a logical imperative when once it was recognized, as long ago it was, that liberty is something more than exemption from physical restraint, and that even in the field of substantive rights and duties the legislative judgment, if oppressive and arbitrary, may be overridden by the courts.

Our survey of the cases serves, we think, to justify the statement that the dividing line between them, if not unfaltering throughout its course, has been true for the most part to a unifying principle. On which side of the line the case made out by the appellant has appropriate location must be the next inquiry and the final one. Is that kind of double jeopardy to which the statute has subjected him a hardship so acute and shocking that our policy will not endure it? Does it violate those "fundamental principles of liberty and justice which lie at the base of all our civil and political institutions"? The answer surely must be "no." What the answer would have to be if the state were permitted after a trial free from error to try the accused over again or to bring another case against him, we have no occasion to consider. We deal with the statute before us and no other. The state is not attempting to wear the accused out by a multitude of cases with accumulated trials. It asks no more than this, that the case against him shall go on until there shall be a trial free from the corrosion of substantial legal error. This is not cruelty at all, nor even vexation in any immoderate degree. If the trial had been infected with error adverse to the accused, there might have been review at his instance, and as often as necessary to purge the vicious taint. A reciprocal privilege, subject at all times to the discretion of the presiding judge has now been granted to the state. There is here no seismic innovation. The edifice of justice stands, its symmetry, to many, greater than before.

Notes and Questions

1. *Total Versus Selective Incorporation.* The Court eventually incorporated the Double Jeopardy Clause into the Fourteenth Amendment, but not without significant debate concerning the method for achieving this result. *Benton v. Maryland,* 395 U.S. 784 (1969). The absorption of federal rights and liberties was possible on either a wholesale or discrete basis. The theory of total incorporation advocated applying the entire Bill of Rights to the states. Selective incorporation proposed that each guarantee should be assessed for purposes of determining whether it was essential to liberty and justice. In *Adamson v. California,* the

competing viewpoints on selective and total incorporation were illuminated by Justice Frankfurter and Justice Black, respectively.

2. *Is It Appropriate to Construe the Fourteenth Amendment as Containing Substantive Protections?* The Fourteenth Amendment, Section 1 (the Fourteenth Amendment Due Process Clause) seems to be phrased in procedural terms ("Nor shall any State deprive any person of life, liberty, or property, without due process of law"). How can the clause construed as containing substantive protections for "liberty"?

3. *Necessity of Substantive Protections?* Are substantive protections both inevitable and necessary in a free society?

∾ PROBLEMS ∾

1. *Life Shall End at Age 75.* Suppose that, as the baby boom generation moves into its retirement years, the Social Security system falls into bankruptcy. As the crisis worsens, Congress passes a law decreeing, "Life shall end at age 75." Under this law, no one shall be allowed to draw Social Security benefits, or for that matter to live, beyond the age of 75. We all know that it is extremely unlikely that Congress would pass such a law. After all, many members of Congress are of advanced age (or will be someday), and many more have senior parents and other older relatives. In addition, it is extremely unlikely that the people would accept such a law. But, if the Fourteenth Amendment is not construed as containing a substantive component, is there any other constitutional provision that would render the law unconstitutional? If the courts apply the Due Process Clause literally, does that mean that the courts are allowed to inquire only whether Congress duly passed the law and whether it provided affected citizens with a "full and fair hearing" on the issue of whether they have reached age 75? If they answer those questions in the affirmative, are they required to uphold the law?

2. *One Child Per Family.* Suppose that, as the U.S. population continues to grow, Congress decides to take measures to limit the rate of future growth. To this end, Congress passes a law providing that no family can have more than one child and mandating sterilization of all persons who have a living child. Is there any provision in the Constitution that specifically prohibits Congress from enacting such a law?

3. *Bans on Interracial Marriage.* At one point in history, various states prohibited interracial marriage. Is there any constitutional provision that guarantees people the right to marry? Is there any provision that protects interracial marriage? Can the Fourteenth Amendment be construed as including a prohibition that relates to racial discrimination?

4. *Stay-at-Home Orders.* During the 2020 Covid-19 pandemic, a number of state governors issued "stay-at-home" orders, and also issued orders requiring all non-essential businesses to close. Many citizens complained about these orders, viewing them as "unconstitutional" intrusions into their lives. This was especially true for business owners who were required to shut down. Is there a constitutional

right to operate one's otherwise lawful business or to go out in public? If so, where does that right come from?

5. *The Ninth Amendment.* As you think about the preceding problems, consider the text of the Ninth Amendment: "The enumeration in the Constitution, of certain rights, shall not be construed to deny or disparage others retained by the people." If "other" rights exist, how does the judiciary find or declare them without simply imposing its own wishes and desires?

Adamson v. California

332 U.S. 46 (1947)

Mr. Justice REED delivered the opinion of the Court.

Appellant contends that if the privilege against self-incrimination is not a right protected by the Privileges and Immunities Clause of the Fourteenth Amendment against state action, this privilege, to its full scope under the Fifth Amendment, inheres in the right to a fair trial. A right to a fair trial is a right admittedly protected by the due process clause of the Fourteenth Amendment. Therefore, appellant argues, the due process clause of the Fourteenth Amendment protects his privilege against self-incrimination. The due process clause of the Fourteenth Amendment, however, does not draw all the rights of the federal Bill of Rights under its protection. That contention was made and rejected in *Palko v. Connecticut.* It was rejected with citation of the cases excluding several of the rights, protected by the Bill of Rights, against infringement by the National Government. Nothing has been called to our attention that either the framers of the Fourteenth Amendment or the states that adopted intended its due process clause to draw within its scope the earlier amendments to the Constitution. *Palko* held that such provisions of the Bill of Rights as were "implicit in the concept of ordered liberty," became secure from state interference by the clause. But it held nothing more.

Mr. Justice FRANKFURTER, *concurring.*

Between the incorporation of the Fourteenth Amendment into the Constitution and the beginning of the present membership of the Court—a period of 70 years—the scope of that Amendment was passed upon by 43 judges. Of all these judges, only one, who may respectfully be called an eccentric exception, ever indicated that due process incorporated those eight Amendments as restrictions upon the powers of the States. They were judges mindful of the relation of our federal system to a progressively democratic society and therefore duly regardful of the scope of authority that was left to the States even after the Civil War. And so they did not find that the Fourteenth Amendment, concerned as it was with matters fundamental to the pursuit of justice, fastened upon the States procedural arrangements which, in the language of Mr. Justice Cardozo, only those who are "narrow or provincial" would deem essential to "a fair and enlightened system of justice."

The short answer to the suggestion that the provision of the Fourteenth Amendment, which ordains "nor shall any State deprive any person of life, liberty, or property, without due process of law," was a way of saying that every State must thereafter initiate prosecutions through indictment by a grand jury, must have a trial by a jury of 12 in criminal cases, and must have trial by such a jury in common law suits where the amount in controversy exceeds $20, is that it is a strange way of saying it. It would be extraordinarily strange for a Constitution to convey such specific commands in such a roundabout and inexplicit way. At the time of the ratification of the Fourteenth Amendment the constitutions of nearly half of the ratifying States did not have the rigorous requirements of the Fifth Amendment for instituting criminal proceedings through a grand jury. It could hardly have occurred to these States that by ratifying the Amendment they uprooted their established methods for prosecuting crime and fastened upon themselves a new prosecutorial system.

A construction which gives to due process no independent function but turns it into a summary of the specific provisions of the Bill of Rights would tear up by the roots much of the fabric of law in the several States, and would deprive the States of opportunity for reforms in legal process designed for extending the area of freedom. It would assume that no other abuses would reveal themselves in the course of time than those which had become manifest in 1791. Such a view not only disregards the historic meaning of "due process." It leads inevitably to a warped construction of specific provisions of the Bill of Rights to bring within their scope conduct clearly condemned by due process but not easily fitting into the pigeon-holes of the specific provisions.

When a conviction in a State court is here for review under a claim that a right protected by the Due Process Clause of the Fourteenth Amendment has been denied, the relevant question is whether the criminal proceedings which resulted in conviction deprived the accused of the due process of law to which the United States Constitution entitled him. Judicial review of that guaranty of the Fourteenth Amendment inescapably imposes upon this Court an exercise of judgment upon the whole course of the proceedings in order to ascertain whether they offend those canons of decency and fairness which express the notions of justice of English-speaking peoples even toward those charged with the most heinous offenses. These standards of justice are not authoritatively formulated anywhere as though they were prescriptions in a pharmacopoeia. But neither does the application of the Due Process Clause imply that judges are wholly at large. The judicial judgment in applying the Due Process Clause must move within the limits of accepted notions of justice and is not to be based upon the idiosyncrasies of a merely personal judgment. The fact that judges among themselves may differ whether in a particular case a trial offends accepted notions of justice is not disproof that general rather than idiosyncratic standards are applied. An important safeguard against such merely individual judgment is an alert deference to the judgment of the State court under review.

Mr. Justice BLACK, *dissenting.*

Prior decisions have suggested that the Court is endowed by the Constitution with boundless power under "natural law" periodically to expand and contract constitutional standards to conform to the Court's conception of what at a particular time constitutes "civilized decency" and "fundamental principles of liberty and justice." I think that the "natural law" theory of the Constitution degrades the constitutional safeguards of the Bill of Rights and simultaneously appropriates for this Court a broad power which we are not authorized by the Constitution to exercise.

The first 10 amendments were proposed and adopted largely because of fear that Government might unduly interfere with prized individual liberties. My study of the historical events that culminated in the Fourteenth Amendment, and the expressions of those who sponsored and favored, as well as those who opposed its submission and passage, persuades me that one of the chief objects that the provisions of the Amendment's first section, separately, and as a whole, were intended to accomplish was to make the Bill of Rights, applicable to the states. This historical purpose has never received full consideration or exposition in any opinion of this Court interpreting the Amendment.

I fear the consequences of the Court's practice of substituting its own concepts of decency and fundamental justice for the language of the Bill of Rights as its point of departure in interpreting and enforcing that Bill of Rights. If the choice must be between the selective process of the *Palko* decision applying some of the Bill of Rights to the States, or the *Twining* rule applying none of them, I would choose the *Palko* selective process. But rather than accept either of these choices. I would follow what I believe was the original purpose of the Fourteenth Amendment—to extend to all the people of the nation the complete protection of the Bill of Rights. I would therefore hold in this case that the full protection of the Fifth Amendment's proscription against compelled testimony must be afforded by California.

It is an illusory apprehension that literal application of some or all of the provisions of the Bill of Rights to the States would unwisely increase the sum total of the powers of this Court to invalidate state legislation. Since *Marbury v. Madison* was decided, the practice has been firmly established for better or worse, that courts can strike down legislative enactments which violate the Constitution. This process, of course, involves interpretation, and since words can have many meanings, interpretation obviously may result in contraction or extension of the original purpose of a constitutional provision thereby affecting policy. But to pass upon the constitutionality of statutes by looking to the particular standards enumerated in the Bill of Rights and other parts of the Constitution is one thing; to invalidate statutes because of application of "natural law" deemed to be above and undefined by the Constitution is another. "In the one instance, courts proceeding within clearly marked constitutional boundaries seek to execute policies written into the Constitution; in the other they roam at will in the limitless area of their own beliefs as to reasonableness and actually select policies, a responsibility which the Constitution entrusts to the legislative representatives of the people."

Mr. Justice DOUGLAS joins in this opinion.

Note: More on Incorporation

The primary formulas for selective incorporation have focused on whether a provision of the Bill of Rights is so fundamental as to be "implicit in the concept of ordered liberty" or "so rooted in the traditions and conscience of our people as to be fundamental." *Palko v. Connecticut*, 302 U.S. 319, 325 (1937). In the context of reviewing constitutional guarantees relating to the criminal justice process, the Court has pondered which procedures are "necessary to an Anglo-American regime of ordered liberty." *Duncan v. Louisiana*, 391 U.S. 145, 148-149 (1968). The incorporation process for practical purposes has achieved over the course of time what total incorporation would have achieved in a single exercise. The only provisions of the Bill of Rights that have failed the incorporation test are the grand jury clause of the Fifth Amendment and the Seventh Amendment guarantee of a jury trial in civil cases.

Although the incorporation process largely has become a historical concern, there is a corollary debate that survived the incorporation controversy. The issue is whether incorporation passed through both a given right or liberty and the case law associated with it. In *Malloy v. Hogan*, 378 U.S. 1 (1964), the second Justice Harlan argued that failure to factor the entire body of law was unsettling to principles of federalism. As he put it, in *Malloy:*

> The argument is made that continuing reexamination of the constitutional conception of Fourteenth Amendment "due process" of law is required, and that development of the community's sense of justice may in time lead to expansion of the protection, which due process affords. I do not understand, however, how this process of re-examination, which must refer always to the guiding standard of due process of law, including, of course, reference to the particular guarantees of the Bill of Rights, can be short-circuited by the simple device of incorporating into due process, without critical examination, the whole body of law which surrounds a specific prohibition directed against the Federal Government. The consequence of such an approach to due process as it pertains to the States is inevitably disregard of all relevant differences which may exist between state and federal criminal law and its enforcement. The ultimate result is compelled uniformity, which is inconsistent with the purpose of our federal system and which is achieved either by encroachment of the States' sovereign powers or by dilution in federal law enforcement of specific protections found in the Bill of Rights. It is apparent that Mr. Justice Cardozo's metaphor of "absorption" was not intended to suggest the transplantation of case law surrounding the specifics of the first eight Amendments to the very different soil of the Fourteenth Amendment's Due Process Clause. As he made perfectly plain, what the Fourteenth Amendment requires

of the States does not basically depend on what the first eight Amendments require of the Federal Government.

Justice Harlan's perspective correlates to earlier usage of the Due Process Clause as the actual platform for rights and liberties applicable to the states rather than an incorporating device for prohibitions set forth in the Bill of Rights. Writing for the majority in *Malloy v. Hogan*, Justice Brennan maintained that incorporation transplanted not only the basic principle but also its interpretive incidents. As he put it, incorporated rights and liberties were to be "enforced against the States under the Fourteenth Amendment according to the same standards that protect those personal rights against federal encroachment. The Court thus has rejected the notion that the Fourteenth Amendment applies to the States only a 'watered-down, subjective version of the individual guarantees of the Bill of Rights.'"

The debate with respect to the details of incorporation resurfaced in the context of the right to a jury trial. In *Duncan v. Louisiana*, 391 U.S. 145 (1968), Justice Fortas advanced the notion that jury trials concerned not just a right but systems of administration such as jury size and the nature of a verdict. He thus argued that these aspects or traditions, such as a 12-person jury or unanimous verdict, might not be fundamental and thus apt for incorporation. In *Williams v. Florida*, 399 U.S. 78 (1970), the Court upheld a state's provision for six-person juries. This determination reflected the Court's sense that the traditional 12-person jury was a historical accident and not specifically mandated by the Sixth Amendment. Justice Harlan, in a concurring opinion, expressed concern that the space being afforded to the states had the potential for reverse incorporation and a consequent dilution of federal guarantees. In *Apodaca v. Oregon*, 406 U.S. 404 (1972), the Court split on whether the requirement of a unanimous verdict was implicit in the right to a jury trial. In a separate opinion, which determined the result, Justice Powell maintained that the Sixth Amendment required unanimity in the federal system but that this incident did not carry through to the states through the Fourteenth Amendment. Despite the outcome, and the difference over whether a unanimous verdict was required at the federal level, near unanimity was reached on the proposition that the rights and liberties incorporated through the Fourteenth Amendment apply with equal force to both federal and state governments. However, the Court reversed itself and required unanimity in its later decision in *Ramos v. Louisiana*, 140 S. Ct. 1390 (2020).

Question: Privileges and Immunities

The Fourteenth Amendment contains several key clauses that were significant in the reconstruction of the Union after the Civil War. The citizenship clause inverted prior understandings by making state citizenship derivative of federal citizenship. The Due Process Clause replicated a similar Fifth Amendment provision that operates against the federal government and traditionally had accounted for procedural fairness. The Equal Protection Clause accounted for inequalities under the law that postdated slavery. The Privileges and Immunities Clause was rejected by the Court as an agent for extending the Bill of Rights to the states. Based on the arguments presented in *Adamson*, and historical experience with the Due Process Clause, would the Privileges and Immunities Clause be a more logical and less distorting basis for incorporation and for generating rights that are not constitutionally enumerated?

B. THE RIGHT OF PRIVACY

Does the concept of ordered liberty include a right of privacy against governmental intrusion?

1. Seminal Developments

The Constitution speaks to privacy interests in discrete contexts such as the First, Third, and Fourth Amendments. A general right of privacy in the constitutional sense, however, is a function of judicial construction. The origin of this guarantee was recognized in late-nineteenth-century legal scholarship. Samuel D. Warren and Louis D. Brandeis, in a pioneering law review article, described the interest as "the right to be let alone." Samuel D. Warren & Louis D. Brandeis, *The Right to Privacy*, 4 HARV. L. REV. 193 (1890). This concept initially was introduced as, and became the basis for, tort-based laws that developed protection against various types of invasion of privacy. Over the course of the twentieth century, it acquired dimension.

The first significant constitutional statement on privacy was made during a period of peak activity in the Court's development of liberty as a substantive incident of due process. In *Meyer v. Nebraska*, 262 U.S. 390 (1923), the Court invalidated a state law that prohibited teaching in any language other than English in public and private schools. The Court concluded that the liberty protected by the Due Process Clause included "not merely freedom from bodily restraint but also the right of the individual to contract, to engage in any of the common occupations of life, to acquire useful knowledge, to marry, establish a home and bring up children, to worship God according to the dictates of his own conscience, and generally to enjoy those privileges long recognized at common law as essential to the orderly pursuit of happiness by free men."

Meyer was reinforced by the Court's ruling in *Pierce v. Society of Sisters*, 268 U.S. 510 (1925), which struck down a state law requiring parents to send their children to public schools. Taken together, these decisions established a predicate for expanding privacy beyond notions of place and experience to concepts of personal and family autonomy. These understandings survived the Court's abandonment of economic due process in *United States v. Carolene Products Co.*, 304 U.S. 144 (1938). Although the Court indicated in *Carolene Products* that searching review would be reserved for instances when enumerated rights and liberties or discrete and insular minorities were burdened, it became apparent a few years later that this characterization was an overstatement. In *Skinner v. Oklahoma*, 316 U.S. 535 (1942), the Court reviewed a state law that mandated sterilization for habitual felons. Although it had determined in *Buck v. Bell*, 274 U.S. 200 (1927), that compulsory sterilization was not a constitutional concern, the Court invalidated the measure on the grounds that it implicated fundamental interests in marriage and procreation.

Skinner v. Oklahoma

316 U.S. 535 (1942)

Mr. Justice Douglas delivered the opinion of the Court.

This case touches a sensitive and important area of human rights. Oklahoma deprives certain individuals of a right which is basic to the perpetuation of a race—the right to have offspring. Oklahoma has decreed the enforcement of its law against petitioner, overruling his claim that it violated the Fourteenth Amendment. Because that decision raised grave and substantial constitutional questions, we granted the petition for certiorari.

The statute involved is Oklahoma's Habitual Criminal Sterilization Act. That Act defines an "habitual criminal" as a person who, having been convicted two or more times for crimes "amounting to felonies involving moral turpitude" either in an Oklahoma court or in a court of any other State, is thereafter convicted of such a felony in Oklahoma and is sentenced to a term of imprisonment in an Oklahoma penal institution. Machinery is provided for the institution by the Attorney General of a proceeding against such a person in the Oklahoma courts for a judgment that such person shall be rendered sexually sterile.

There is a feature of the Act which clearly condemns it. That is its failure to meet the requirements of the equal protection clause of the Fourteenth Amendment. We do not stop to point out all of the inequalities in this Act. A few examples will suffice. A person who enters a chicken coop and steals chickens commits a felony; and he may be sterilized if he is thrice convicted. If, however, he is a bailee of the property and fraudulently appropriates it, he is an embezzler. Hence no matter how habitual his proclivities for embezzlement are and no matter how often his conviction, he may not be sterilized. Thus the nature of the two crimes is intrinsically the same and they are punishable in the same manner.

It was stated in *Buck v. Bell* that the claim that state legislation violates the equal protection clause of the Fourteenth Amendment is "the usual last resort of constitutional arguments." But the instant legislation runs afoul of the equal protection clause, though we give Oklahoma that large deference which the rule of the foregoing cases requires. We are dealing here with legislation which involves one of the basic civil rights of man. Marriage and procreation are fundamental to the very existence and survival of the race. The power to sterilize, if exercised, may have subtle, far-reaching and devastating effects. In evil or reckless hands it can cause races or types which are inimical to the dominant group to wither and disappear. There is no redemption for the individual whom the law touches. Any experiment which the State conducts is to his irreparable injury. He is forever deprived of a basic liberty. We mention these matters not to reexamine the scope of the police power of the States. We advert to them merely in emphasis of our view that strict scrutiny of the classification which a State makes in a sterilization law is essential, lest unwittingly or otherwise invidious discriminations are made against groups or types of individuals in violation of the constitutional guaranty of just and equal laws. The guaranty of "equal protection of the laws is a pledge of the protection of equal laws." When the law lays an unequal hand on those who have committed intrinsically the same quality of offense and sterilizes one and not the other, it has made as an invidious a discrimination as if it had selected a particular race or nationality for oppressive treatment. Sterilization of those who have thrice committed grand larceny with immunity for those who are embezzlers is a clear, pointed, unmistakable discrimination.

Mr. Chief Justice STONE, *concurring.*

I concur in the result, but I am not persuaded that we are aided in reaching it by recourse to the equal protection clause. If Oklahoma may resort generally to the sterilization of criminals on the assumption that their propensities are transmissible to future generations by inheritance, I seriously doubt that the equal protection clause requires it to apply the measure to all criminals in the first instance, or to none.

There are limits to the extent to which the presumption of constitutionality can be pressed, especially where the liberty of the person is concerned and where the presumption is resorted to only to dispense with a procedure which the ordinary dictates of prudence would seem to demand for the protection of the individual from arbitrary action. Although petitioner here was given a hearing to ascertain whether sterilization would be detrimental to his health, he was given none to discover whether his criminal tendencies are of an inheritable type. Undoubtedly a state may, after appropriate inquiry, constitutionally interfere with the personal liberty of the individual to prevent the transmission by inheritance of his socially injurious tendencies. But until now we have not been called upon to say that it may do so without giving him a hearing and opportunity to challenge the existence as to him of the only facts which could justify so drastic a measure.

A law which condemns, without hearing, all the individuals of a class to so harsh a measure as the present because some or even many merit condemnation, is lacking in the first principles of due process.

Mr. Justice JACKSON, *concurring.*

I join the Chief Justice in holding that the hearings provided are too limited to afford due process of law. I also agree with Justice Douglas that the scheme of classification set forth in the Act denies equal protection of the law. I disagree with each opinion insofar as it rejects or minimizes the grounds taken by the other. I also think the present plan presents other constitutional questions of gravity. There are limits to the extent to which a legislatively represented majority may conduct biological experiments at the expense of the dignity and personality and natural powers of a minority—even those who have been guilty of what the majority define as crimes.

Note: "Fundamental" Rights

The *Skinner* Court, sensitive to the recently disavowed legacy of *Lochner*-style review, grounded its decision in the Equal Protection Clause and avoided any reference to due process. Identification of rights as fundamental, when not enumerated by the Constitution, required a theory of review that was demonstrably and understandably principled. Toward this end, and mindful still of the discredited nature of substantive due process review, the Court explored other possibilities for anchorage. These alternatives included penumbras, which had a mixed history. In *Dred Scott v. Sandford,* 60 U.S. 393 (1857), the Court referenced several constitutional provisions relating to slavery as an indication of a general right to own slaves. A century later, in *NAACP v. Alabama ex rel. Patterson,* 357 U.S. 449 (1958), the Court constructed the right of association as an implication of freedom of speech. Drawing upon this model, the Court in *Griswold v. Connecticut* announced a right to privacy and used it as the basis for striking down a state law prohibiting the distribution and use of contraceptives.

Question: Alternative Theories

Skinner was announced five years after the Court abandoned substantive due process review in *United States v. Carolene Products Co.* Establishing marriage and procreation as fundamental rights and protecting them through the Equal Protection Clause do not avoid the controversy triggered by the judiciary's identification and development of rights that are not constitutionally enumerated. Is there a principled way of recognizing and accounting for these interests through privileges and immunities or due process review? Is there an advantage to using the Equal Protection Clause in this context?

Griswold v. Connecticut

381 U.S. 479 (1965)

Mr. Justice Douglas delivered the opinion of the Court.

The executive director of the Planned Parenthood League of Connecticut and the medical director for the league at its New Haven Center were arrested and convicted for giving information, instruction, and medical advice on birth control to married persons. State law prohibited the use of anticonception devices and imposed liability upon anyone who assisted, abetted, or counseled a violation.

Coming to the merits, we are met with a wide range of questions that implicate the Due Process Clause of the Fourteenth Amendment. Overtones of some arguments suggest that *Lochner v. New York* should be our guide. We decline that invitation. We do not sit as a super-legislature to determine the wisdom, need, and propriety of laws that touch economic problems, business affairs, or social conditions. This law, however, operates directly on an intimate relation of husband and wife and their physician's role in one aspect of that relation.

The association of people is not mentioned in the Constitution nor in the Bill of Rights. The right to educate a child in a school of the parents' choice—whether public or private or parochial—is also not mentioned. Nor is the right to study any particular subject or any foreign language. Yet the First Amendment has been construed to include certain of those rights.

By *Pierce v. Society of Sisters*, the right to educate one's children as one chooses is made applicable to the States by the force of the First and Fourteenth Amendments. By *Meyer v. State of Nebraska*, the same dignity is given the right to study the German language in a private school. In other words, the State may not, consistently with the spirit of the First Amendment, contract the spectrum of available knowledge. The right of freedom of speech and press includes not only the right to utter or to print, but the right to distribute, the right to receive, the right to read and freedom of inquiry, freedom of thought, and freedom to teach—indeed the freedom of the entire university community. Without those peripheral rights the specific rights would be less secure. And so we reaffirm the principle of the *Pierce* and the *Meyer* cases.

In *NAACP v. Alabama*, we protected the "freedom to associate and privacy in one's associations," noting that freedom of association was a peripheral First Amendment right. Disclosure of membership lists of a constitutionally valid association, we held, was invalid "as entailing the likelihood of a substantial restraint upon the exercise by petitioner's members of their right to freedom of association." In other words, the First Amendment has a penumbra where privacy is protected from governmental intrusion. In like context, we have protected forms of "association" that are not political in the customary sense but pertain to the social, legal, and economic benefit of the members. Those cases involved more than the "right of assembly"—a right that extends to all irrespective of their race or ideology. The right of "association," like the right of belief is more than the right to attend a meeting; it includes the right to express one's attitudes or philosophies by membership in a group or by affiliation with it or by other lawful means. Association in that context is a form of expression of opinion; and while it is not expressly included in the First Amendment its existence is necessary in making the express guarantees fully meaningful.

The foregoing cases suggest that specific guarantees in the Bill of Rights have penumbras, formed by emanations from those guarantees that help give them life and substance. Various guarantees create zones of privacy. The right of association contained in the penumbra of the First Amendment is one. The Third Amendment in its prohibition against the quartering of soldiers "in any house" in time of peace without the consent of the owner is another facet of that privacy. The Fourth Amendment explicitly affirms the "right of the people to be secure in their persons, houses, papers, and effects, against unreasonable searches and seizures." The Fifth Amendment in its Self-Incrimination Clause enables the citizen to create a zone of privacy which government may not force him to surrender to his detriment. The Ninth Amendment provides: "The enumeration in the Constitution, of certain rights, shall not be construed to deny or disparage others retained by the people."

The Fourth and Fifth Amendments have been described as protection against all governmental invasions "of the sanctity of a man's home and the privacies of life." We recently referred to the Fourth Amendment as creating a "right to privacy, no less important than any other right carefully and particularly reserved to the people."

We have had many controversies over these penumbral rights of "privacy and repose." These cases bear witness that the right of privacy which presses for recognition here is a legitimate one.

The present case, then, concerns a relationship lying within the zone of privacy created by several fundamental constitutional guarantees. And it concerns a law which, in forbidding the use of contraceptives rather than regulating their manufacture or sale, seeks to achieve its goals by means having a maximum destructive impact upon that relationship. Such a law cannot stand in light of the familiar principle, so often applied by this Court, that a "governmental purpose to control or prevent activities constitutionally subject to state regulation may not be achieved by means which sweep unnecessarily broadly and thereby invade the area of protected freedoms." Would we allow the police to search the sacred precincts of marital bedrooms for telltale signs of the use of contraceptives? The very idea is repulsive to the notions of privacy surrounding the marriage relationship.

We deal with a right of privacy older than the Bill of Rights—older than our political parties, older than our school system. Marriage is a coming together for better or for worse, hopefully enduring, and intimate to the degree of being sacred. It is an association that promotes a way of life, not causes; a harmony in living, not political faiths; a bilateral loyalty, not commercial or social projects. Yet it is an association for as noble a purpose as any involved in our prior decisions.
Reversed.

Mr. Justice GOLDBERG, whom THE CHIEF JUSTICE and Mr. Justice BRENNAN join, *concurring*.

I agree with the Court that Connecticut's birth-control law unconstitutionally intrudes upon the right of marital privacy. Although I have not accepted the view that "due process" as used in the Fourteenth Amendment includes all of the first eight Amendments, I do agree that the concept of liberty protects those personal rights that are fundamental, and is not confined to the specific terms of the Bill of Rights. The concept of liberty embraces the right of marital privacy though that right is not mentioned explicitly in the Constitution is supported both by numerous decisions of this Court, referred to in the Court's opinion, and by the language and history of the Ninth Amendment.

The Court stated many years ago that the Due Process Clause protects those liberties that are "so rooted in the traditions and conscience of our people as to be ranked as fundamental." This Court has held that the Fourteenth Amendment absorbs and applies to the States those specifics of the first eight amendments which express fundamental personal rights. The language and history of the Ninth Amendment reveal that the Framers of the Constitution believed that there are additional fundamental rights, protected from governmental infringement, which exist alongside those fundamental rights specifically mentioned in the first eight constitutional amendments.

The Ninth Amendment reads, "The enumeration in the Constitution, of certain rights, shall not be construed to deny or disparage others retained by the people." The Amendment was proffered to quiet expressed fears that a bill of specifically enumerated rights could not be sufficiently broad to cover all essential rights and that the specific mention of certain rights would be interpreted as a denial that others were protected.

In determining which rights are fundamental, judges are not left at large to decide cases in light of their personal and private notions. Rather, they must look to the "traditions and (collective) conscience of our people" to determine whether a principle is "so rooted there as to be ranked as fundamental." The inquiry is whether a right involved is of such a character that it cannot be denied without violating those "fundamental principles of liberty and justice which lie at the base of all our civil and political institutions." "Liberty" also "gains content from the emanations of specific constitutional guarantees" and "from experience with the requirements of a free society."

The entire fabric of the Constitution and the purposes that clearly underlie its specific guarantees demonstrate that the rights to marital privacy and to marry and raise a family are of similar order and magnitude as the fundamental rights specifically protected. The fact that no particular provision of the Constitution explicitly forbids the State from disrupting the traditional relation of the family—a relation as old and as fundamental as our entire civilization—surely does not show that the Government was meant to have the power to do so. Rather, as the Ninth Amendment expressly recognizes, there are fundamental personal rights such as this one, which are protected from abridgment by the Government though not specifically mentioned in the Constitution.

The logic of the dissents would sanction federal or state legislation that seems to me even more plainly unconstitutional than the statute before us. Surely the Government, absent a showing of a compelling subordinating state interest, could not decree that all husbands and wives must be sterilized after two children have been born to them. Yet by their reasoning such an invasion of marital privacy would not be subject to constitutional challenge because, while it might be "silly," no provision of the Constitution specifically prevents the Government from curtailing the marital right to bear children and raise a family. While it may shock some of my Brethren that the Court today holds that the Constitution protects the right of marital privacy, in my view it is far more shocking to believe that the personal liberty guaranteed by the Constitution does not include protection against such totalitarian limitation of family size, which is at complete variance with our constitutional concepts. Yet, if upon a showing of a slender basis of rationality, a law outlawing voluntary birth control by married persons is valid, then, by the same reasoning, a law requiring compulsory birth control also would seem to be valid. In my view, however, both types of law would unjustifiably intrude upon rights of marital privacy which are constitutionally protected.

I believe that the right of privacy in the marital relation is fundamental and basic — a personal right "retained by the people" within the meaning of the Ninth Amendment. Connecticut cannot constitutionally abridge this fundamental right, which is protected by the Fourteenth Amendment from infringement by the States.

Mr. Justice HARLAN, *concurring in the judgment.*

The proper constitutional inquiry is whether this Connecticut statute infringes the Due Process Clause of the Fourteenth Amendment because the enactment violates basic values "implicit in the concept of ordered liberty." I believe that it does. While the inquiry may be aided by resort to one or more of the provisions of the Bill of Rights, it is not dependent on them or any of their radiations. The Due Process Clause of the Fourteenth Amendment stands on its own bottom.

Mr. Justice WHITE, *concurring in the judgment.*

This Connecticut law as applied to married couples deprives them of "liberty" without due process of law, as that concept is used in the Fourteenth Amendment. This is not the first time this Court has had occasion to articulate that the liberty entitled to protection under the Fourteenth Amendment includes the right "to marry, establish a home and bring up children." Our decisions affirm that there is a "realm of family life which the state cannot enter" without substantial justification. Surely the right invoked in this case, to be free of regulation of the intimacies of the marriage relationship, "comes to this Court with a momentum for respect lacking when appeal is made to liberties which derive merely from shifting economic arrangements."

Mr. Justice BLACK, with whom Mr. Justice STEWART joins, *dissenting*.

The Court talks about a constitutional "right of privacy" as though there is some constitutional provision or provisions forbidding any law ever to be passed which might abridge the "privacy" of individuals. But there is not. There are, of course, guarantees in certain specific constitutional provisions which are designed in part to protect privacy at certain times and places with respect to certain activities. Such, for example, is the Fourth Amendment's guarantee against "unreasonable searches and seizures." But I think it belittles that Amendment to talk about it as though it protects nothing but "privacy."

The due process argument which my Brothers Harlan and White adopt here is based on the premise that this Court is vested with power to invalidate all state laws that it consider to be arbitrary, capricious, unreasonable, or oppressive, or this Court's belief that a particular state law under scrutiny has no "rational or justifying" purpose, or is offensive to a "sense of fairness and justice." If these formulas based on "natural justice," or others which mean the same thing, are to prevail, they require judges to determine what is or is not constitutional on the basis of their own appraisal of what laws are unwise or unnecessary. The power to make such decisions is of course that of a legislative body. Surely it has to be admitted that no provision of the Constitution specifically gives such blanket power to courts to exercise such a supervisory veto over the wisdom and value of legislative policies and to hold unconstitutional those laws which they believe unwise or dangerous. I readily admit that no legislative body, state or national, should pass laws that can justly be given any of the invidious labels invoked as constitutional excuses to strike down state laws. But perhaps it is not too much to say that no legislative body ever does pass laws without believing that they will accomplish a sane, rational, wise and justifiable purpose. While I completely subscribe to the holding of *Marbury,* I do not believe that we are granted power by the Due Process Clause or any other constitutional provision to measure constitutionality by our belief that legislation is arbitrary, capricious or unreasonable, or accomplishes no justifiable purpose, or is offensive to our own notions of "civilized standards of conduct." Such an appraisal of the wisdom of legislation is an attribute of the power to make laws, not of the power to interpret them. The use by federal courts of such a formula or doctrine to veto federal or state laws simply takes away from Congress and States the power to make laws based on their own judgment of fairness and wisdom and transfers that power to this Court for ultimate determination—a power which was specifically denied to federal courts by the convention that framed the Constitution.

Of the cases on which my Brothers White and Goldberg rely so heavily, undoubtedly the reasoning of two of them supports their result here—as would that of a number of others which they do not bother to name, e.g., *Lochner v. State of New York.*

My Brother Goldberg suggests that the Ninth Amendment as well as the Due Process Clause can be used by this Court as authority to strike down all state legislation which this Court thinks violates "fundamental principles of liberty and justice," or is contrary to the "traditions and (collective) conscience of our people." He also states that in making decisions on this basis judges will not consider "their personal and private notions." One may ask how they can avoid considering them. Our Court certainly has no machinery with which to take a Gallup Poll. And the scientific miracles of this age have not yet produced a gadget which the Court can use to determine what traditions are rooted in the "collective conscience of our people." Moreover, one would certainly have to look far beyond the language of the Ninth Amendment to find that the Framers vested in this Court any such awesome veto powers over lawmaking. Nor does anything in the history of the Amendment offer any support for such a shocking doctrine. The whole history of the adoption of the Constitution and Bill of Rights points the other way, and the very material quoted by my Brother Goldberg shows that the Ninth Amendment was passed, not to broaden the powers of this Court or any other department of "the General Government," but to assure the people that the Constitution in all its provisions was intended to limit the Federal Government to the powers granted expressly or by necessary implication. If any broad, unlimited power to hold laws unconstitutional because they offend what this Court conceives to be the "collective conscience of our people" is vested in this Court by the Ninth Amendment, the Fourteenth Amendment, or any other provision of the Constitution, it was not given by the Framers, but rather has been bestowed on the Court by the Court. This fact is perhaps responsible for the peculiar phenomenon that for a period of a century and a half no serious suggestion was ever made that the Ninth Amendment, enacted to protect state powers against federal invasion, could be used as a weapon of federal power to prevent state legislatures from passing laws they consider appropriate to govern local affairs. Use of any such broad, unbounded judicial authority would make of this Court's members a day-to-day constitutional convention.

This Court does have power, which it should exercise, to hold laws unconstitutional where they are forbidden by the Federal Constitution. My point is that there is no provision of the Constitution which either expressly or impliedly vests power in this Court to sit as a supervisory agency over acts of duly constituted legislative bodies and set aside their laws because of the Court's belief that the legislative policies adopted are unreasonable, unwise, arbitrary, capricious or irrational. The adoption of such a loose, flexible, uncontrolled standard for holding laws unconstitutional, if ever it is finally achieved, will amount to a great unconstitutional shift of power to the courts which will be bad for the courts and worse for the country. Subjecting federal and state laws to such an unrestrained and unrestrainable judicial control as to the wisdom of legislative enactments would, I fear, jeopardize the separation of governmental powers that the Framers set up and at the same time threaten to take away much of the power of States to govern themselves which the Constitution plainly intended them to have.

I realize that many good and able men have eloquently spoken and written, sometimes in rhapsodical strains, about the duty of this Court to keep the

Constitution in tune with the times. The idea is that the Constitution must be changed from time to time and that this Court is charged with a duty to make those changes. I must with all deference reject that philosophy. The Constitution makers knew the need for change and provided for it. Amendments suggested by the people's elected representatives can be submitted to the people or their selected agents for ratification. The Due Process Clause with an "arbitrary and capricious" or "shocking to the conscience" formula was liberally used by this Court to strike down economic legislation in the early decades of this century, threatening, many people thought, the tranquility and stability of the Nation. That formula, based on subjective considerations of "natural justice," is no less dangerous when used to enforce this Court's views about personal rights than those about economic rights. I had thought that we had laid that formula, as a means for striking down state legislation, to rest once and for all.

So far as I am concerned, Connecticut's law as applied here is not forbidden by any provision of the Federal Constitution as that Constitution was written, and I would therefore affirm.

Mr. Justice STEWART, whom Mr. Justice BLACK joins, *dissenting.*

Since 1879 Connecticut has had on its books a law which forbids the use of contraceptives by anyone. I think this is an uncommonly silly law. I believe the use of contraceptives in the relationship of marriage should be left to personal and private choice, based upon each individual's moral, ethical, and religious beliefs. As a matter of social policy, I think professional counsel about methods of birth control should be available to all, so that each individual's choice can be meaningfully made. But we are not asked in this case to say whether we think this law is unwise, or even asinine. We are asked to hold that it violates the United States Constitution. And that I cannot do.

In the course of its opinion the Court refers to no less than six Amendments to the Constitution: the First, the Third, the Fourth, the Fifth, the Ninth, and the Fourteenth. But the Court does not say which of these Amendments, if any, it thinks is infringed by this Connecticut law.

There is no claim that this law, duly enacted by the Connecticut Legislature, is unconstitutionally vague. There is no claim that the appellants were denied any of the elements of procedural due process at their trial, so as to make their convictions constitutionally invalid. And, as the Court says, the day has long passed since the Due Process Clause was regarded as a proper instrument for determining 'the wisdom, need, and propriety' of state laws.

As to the First, Third, Fourth, and Fifth Amendments, I can find nothing in any of them to invalidate this Connecticut law, even assuming that all those Amendments are fully applicable against the States. The Court also quotes the Ninth Amendment. But to say that the Ninth Amendment has anything to do with this case is to turn somersaults with history. The Ninth Amendment, like its companion the Tenth, which this Court held "states but a truism that all is retained which has not been surrendered," was framed by James Madison and adopted by the States simply to make clear that the adoption of the Bill of Rights did not alter the plan that the Federal Government was to be a government of express and limited powers, and that all rights and powers not delegated to it were retained by the people and the individual States. Until today no member of this Court has ever suggested that the Ninth Amendment meant anything else, and the idea that a federal court could ever use the Ninth Amendment to annul a law passed by the elected representatives of the people of the State of Connecticut would have caused James Madison no little wonder.

What provision of the Constitution, then, does make this state law invalid? The Court says it is the right of privacy "created by several fundamental constitutional guarantees." With all deference, I can find no such general right of privacy in the Bill of Rights, in any other part of the Constitution, or in any case ever before decided by this Court.

We are here to decide cases "agreeably to the Constitution and laws of the United States." It is the essence of judicial duty to subordinate our own personal views, our own ideas of what legislation is wise and what is not. If the law before us does not reflect the standards of the people of Connecticut, the people of Connecticut can freely exercise their true Ninth and Tenth Amendment rights to persuade their elected representatives to repeal it. That is the constitutional way to take this law off the books.

Notes and Questions

1. *Griswold's Logic.* Does *Griswold's* logic hold together? Consider the following: Justice Douglas's argument seems to go something like this: Since the Constitution, in various "specifics of the Bill of Rights and in their penumbra, protects rights which partake of privacy, it protects other aspects of privacy as well, indeed it recognizes a general, complete right of privacy. And since the right emanates from specific fundamental rights, it too is 'fundamental,' its infringement is suspect and calls for strict scrutiny, and it can be justified only by a high level of public good. A logician, I suppose, might have trouble with that argument. A legal draftsman, indeed, might suggest the opposite: when the Constitution sought to protect private rights it specified them; that it explicitly protects some elements of privacy, but not others, suggests that it did not mean to protect those not mentioned." *See* Louis Henkin, *Privacy and Autonomy,* 74 COLUM. L. REV. 1410, 1421-1422 (1974).

2. *The Ninth Amendment.* Does the Ninth Amendment (which provides that "the enumeration in the Constitution, of certain rights, shall not be construed to deny or disparage others retained by the people") provide a basis for disagreeing with the views expressed in the prior paragraph? But, if other rights are to be found under the Ninth Amendment, where are they to come from? Are there neutral principles for ascertaining and articulating them?

✥ PROBLEMS ✥

1. *Are There Limits to the Individual Interest in Liberty and Privacy?* As we see in *Griswold,* the Fourteenth Amendment has been interpreted as protecting the individual interest in "liberty" and "privacy." But is that individual interest absolute? During a time of war, may the government draft young men and women and force them to serve in the armed forces? As part of this armed service, may the government send draftees (against their will) into harm's way and force them to risk life and limb? If the individual interest must give way to the societal interest in some cases, where is the dividing line?

2. *More on the Proposed Child Custody Statute.* Consider the problem that introduces this chapter. Does the proposed statute implicate privacy interests? Does it also implicate interests protected by the Ninth Amendment or by "liberty" interests?

In *Poe v. Ullman,* 367 U.S. 497 (1961), the Court dismissed a challenge to a Connecticut contraception law on grounds that a real threat of enforcement was lacking and thus no case or controversy existed. In a dissenting opinion, Justice Harlan laid significant groundwork for further development of the right of privacy.

Poe v. Ullman

367 U.S. 497 (1961)

Mr. Justice HARLAN, *dissenting.*

I consider that this Connecticut legislation, as construed to apply to these appellants, violates the Fourteenth Amendment. I believe that a statute making it a criminal offense for married couples to use contraceptives is an intolerable and unjustifiable invasion of privacy in the conduct of the most intimate concerns of an individual's personal life. Since the contention draws its basis from no explicit language of the Constitution, and has yet to find expression in any decision of this Court, I feel it desirable at the outset to state the framework of Constitutional principles in which I think the issue must be judged.

Were due process merely a procedural safeguard it would fail to reach those situations where the deprivation of life, liberty or property was accomplished by legislation which by operating in the future could, given even the fairest possible procedure in application to individuals, nevertheless destroy the enjoyment of all three. Thus the guaranties of due process, though having their roots in Magna Carta's *"per legem terrae"* and considered as procedural safeguards "against executive usurpation and tyranny," have in this country "become bulwarks also against arbitrary legislation."

However it is not the particular enumeration of rights in the first eight Amendments which spells out the reach of Fourteenth Amendment due process, but rather, as was suggested in another context long before the adoption of that Amendment, those concepts which are considered to embrace those rights which are fundamental; *which belong to the citizens of all free governments, for "the purposes of securing which men enter into society."* Again and again this Court has resisted the notion that the Fourteenth Amendment is no more than a shorthand reference to what is explicitly set out elsewhere in the Bill of Rights. Indeed the fact that an identical provision limiting federal action is found among the first eight Amendments, applying to the Federal Government, suggests that due process is a discrete concept which subsists as an independent guaranty of liberty and procedural fairness, more general and inclusive than the specific prohibitions.

Due process has not been reduced to any formula; its content cannot be determined by reference to any code. The best that can be said is that through the course of this Court's decisions it has represented the balance which our Nation, built upon postulates of respect for the liberty of the individual, has struck between that liberty and the demands of organized society. If the supplying of content to this Constitutional concept has of necessity been a rational process, it certainly has not been one where judges have felt free to roam where unguided speculation might take them. The balance of which I speak is the balance struck by this country, having regard to what history teaches are the traditions from which it developed as well as the traditions from which it broke. That tradition is a living thing. A decision of this Court which radically departs from it could not long survive, while a decision which builds on what has survived is likely to be sound. No formula could serve as a substitute, in this area, for judgment and restraint.

It is this outlook which has led the Court continuingly to perceive distinctions in the imperative character of Constitutional provisions, since that character must be discerned from a particular provision's larger context. And inasmuch as this context is one not of words, but of history and purposes, the full scope of the liberty guaranteed by the Due Process Clause cannot be found in or limited by the precise terms of the specific guarantees elsewhere provided in the Constitution. This "liberty" is not a series of isolated points pricked out in terms of the taking of property; the freedom of speech, press, and religion; the right to keep and bear arms; the freedom from unreasonable searches and seizures; and so on. It is a rational continuum which, broadly speaking, includes a freedom from all substantial arbitrary impositions and purposeless restraints, and which also recognizes, what a reasonable and sensitive judgment must, that certain interests require particularly careful scrutiny of the state needs asserted to justify their abridgment.

Each new claim to Constitutional protection must be considered against a background of Constitutional purposes, as they have been rationally perceived and historically developed. Though we exercise limited and sharply restrained judgment, yet there is no "mechanical yardstick," no "mechanical answer." The decision of an apparently novel claim must depend on grounds which follow closely on well-accepted principles and criteria. The new decision must take "its place in relation to what went before and further cut a channel for what is to come." The matter was well put in *Rochin v. California*:

> The vague contours of the Due Process Clause do not leave judges at large. We may not draw on our merely personal and private notions and disregard the limits that bind judges in their judicial function. Even though the concept of due process of law is not final and fixed, these limits are derived from considerations that are fused in the whole nature of our judicial process. These are considerations deeply rooted in reason and in the compelling traditions of the legal profession.

Notes and Questions

1. *Post-*Griswold *Decisions.* The *Griswold* decision established the right of privacy, albeit not without significant dissent and uncertainty with respect to its anchorage. The right was expanded in *Eisenstadt v. Baird*, 405 U.S. 438 (1972), when the Court struck down a state law restricting the availability of contraceptives to unmarried persons. Relying upon equal protection principles, the Court determined that "if the right of privacy means anything, it is the right of the individual, married or single, to be free from unwanted intrusion into matters so fundamentally affecting a person as the decision whether to bear or beget a child." In *Carey v. Population Services International*, 431 U.S. 678 (1977), the Court struck down a state law authorizing only pharmacists to sell nonprescription contraceptives and prohibiting their sale to persons under the age of 16. The Court referenced *Eisenstadt* for the proposition that "the teaching of *Griswold* is that the Constitution protects individual decisions in matters of childbearing from unjustified intrusion by the State." This observation reflects privacy's passage from a concept that protected choice with respect to contraceptive usage to one that secured reproductive autonomy.

2. *Thinking About Penumbras.* How apt or unprincipled is the penumbral model as a basis for identifying and developing fundamental rights? Does it avoid the concerns of *Lochnerian* substantive due process review? Does it follow logically that freedom of association is an extension of and thus within the penumbra of freedom of speech? Does it follow logically that a right to own slaves is an extension of and thus within the various constitutional provisions that accounted for or accommodated slavery?

∾ PROBLEM: *BUCK* AND PRIVACY ∾

Justice Black expressed an appreciation of privacy but no tolerance for it as a constitutional right. In *Buck v. Bell*, 274 U.S. 200 (1927), the Court upheld a state law that mandated sterilization of "mentally defective" or "feebleminded" persons. This decision is memorable, among other things, for Justice Holmes's seemingly gratuitous observation that "three generations of imbeciles is enough." How would Justice Black respond to this enactment? If he was unwilling to budge, how would this hard line affect your assessment of his position? Would it make any difference that the criteria for mental deficiency under the law were calibrated so that half of the nation's adult male population might be candidates for surgery? *See* Laurence H. Tribe, God Save This Honorable Court (Random House 1988).

2. Abortion

Clarity with respect to the basis of the right of privacy was provided in *Roe v. Wade*, when the Court established that a woman's liberty to elect an abortion was grounded in the Due Process Clause of the Fourteenth Amendment.

Roe v. Wade

410 U.S. 113 (1973)

Mr. Justice Blackmun delivered the opinion of the Court.

This Texas federal appeal and its Georgia companion present constitutional challenges to state criminal abortion legislation.

We acknowledge the sensitive and emotional nature of the abortion controversy, of the vigorous opposing views, even among physicians, and of the deep and seemingly absolute convictions that the subject inspires. One's philosophy, one's experiences, one's exposure to the raw edges of human existence, one's religious training, one's attitudes toward life and family and their values, and the moral standards one establishes and seeks to observe, are all likely to influence and to color one's thinking and conclusions about abortion. In addition, population growth, pollution, poverty, and racial overtones tend to complicate and not to simplify the problem.

Our task, of course, is to resolve the issue by constitutional measurement, free of emotion and of predilection. We seek earnestly to do this, and, because we do, we have inquired into, and in this opinion place some emphasis upon, medical and medical-legal history and what that history reveals about man's attitudes toward the abortion procedure over the centuries. We bear in mind, too, Mr. Justice Holmes' admonition in his now-vindicated dissent in *Lochner v. New York*:

> The Constitution is made for people of fundamentally differing views, and the accident of our finding certain opinions natural and familiar, or novel, and even shocking, ought not to conclude our judgment upon the question whether statutes embodying them conflict with the Constitution of the United States.

The Texas statutes that concern us here make it a crime to "procure an abortion," as therein defined, or to attempt one, except with respect to "an abortion procured or attempted by medical advice for the purpose of saving the life of the mother." Similar statutes are in existence in a majority of the States.

Jane Roe, a single woman residing in Texas, instituted this federal action seeking a declaratory judgment that the Texas criminal abortion statutes were unconstitutional on their face, and an injunction restraining the defendant from enforcing the statutes.

Roe alleged that she was unmarried and pregnant; that she wished to terminate her pregnancy by an abortion "performed by a competent, licensed physician, under safe, clinical conditions"; that she was unable to get a "legal" abortion in Texas because her life did not appear to be threatened by the continuation of her pregnancy; and that she could not afford to travel to another jurisdiction in order to secure a legal abortion under safe conditions. She claimed that the Texas statutes were unconstitutionally vague and that they abridged her right of personal privacy, protected by the First, Fourth, Fifth, Ninth, and Fourteenth Amendments. By an amendment to her complaint Roe purported to sue "on behalf of herself and all other women" similarly situated.

The principal thrust of appellant's attack on the Texas statutes is that they improperly invade a right, said to be possessed by the pregnant woman, to choose to terminate her pregnancy. Appellant would discover this right in the concept of personal "liberty" embodied in the Fourteenth Amendment's Due Process Clause; or in personal marital, familial, and sexual privacy said to be protected by the Bill of Rights or its penumbras.

The American law. In this country, the law in effect in all but a few States until mid-19th century was the pre-existing English common law. Connecticut, the first State to enact abortion legislation, adopted in 1821 that part of Lord Ellenborough's Act that related to a woman "quick with child." The death penalty was not imposed. Abortion before quickening was made a crime in that State only in 1860. In 1828, New York enacted legislation that was to serve as a model for early anti-abortion statutes. First, while barring destruction of an unquickened fetus as well as a quick fetus, it made the former only a misdemeanor, but the latter second-degree manslaughter. Second, it incorporated a concept of therapeutic abortion by providing that an abortion was excused if it "shall have been necessary to preserve the life of such mother, or shall have been advised by two physicians to be necessary for such purpose." By 1840, when Texas received the common law, only eight American States had statutes dealing with abortion. It was not until after the War Between the States that legislation began generally to replace the common law. Most of these initial statutes dealt severely with abortion after quickening but were lenient with it before quickening. Most punished attempts equally with completed abortions. While many statutes included an exception for an abortion thought by one or more physicians to be necessary to save the mother's life, that provision soon disappeared and the typical law required that the procedure actually be necessary for that purpose.

Gradually, in the middle and late 19th century the quickening distinction disappeared from the statutory law of most States and the degree of the offense and the penalties were increased. By the end of the 1950s a large majority of the jurisdictions banned abortion, however and whenever performed, unless done to save or preserve the life of the mother. The exceptions, Alabama and the District of Columbia, permitted abortion to preserve the mother's health. Three States permitted abortions that were not "unlawfully" performed or that were not "without lawful justification," leaving interpretation of those standards to the courts. In the past several years, however, a trend toward liberalization of abortion statutes has resulted in adoption, by about one-third of the States, of less stringent laws, most of them patterned after the ALI Model Penal Code.

It is thus apparent that at common law, at the time of the adoption of our Constitution, and throughout the major portion of the 19th century, abortion was viewed with less disfavor than under most American statutes currently in effect. Phrasing it another way, a woman enjoyed a substantially broader right to terminate a pregnancy than she does in most States today. At least with respect to the early stage of pregnancy, and very possibly without such a limitation, the opportunity to make this choice was present in this country well into the 19th century. Even later, the law continued for some time to treat less punitively an abortion procured in early pregnancy.

Three reasons have been advanced to explain historically the enactment of criminal abortion laws in the 19th century and to justify their continued existence.

It has been argued occasionally that these laws were the product of a Victorian social concern to discourage illicit sexual conduct. Texas, however, does not advance this justification in the present case, and it appears that no court or commentator has taken the argument seriously. A second reason is concerned with abortion as a medical procedure. When most criminal abortion laws were first enacted, the procedure was a hazardous one for the woman. Abortion mortality was high. Even after 1900, and perhaps until as late as the development of antibiotics in the 1940s, standard modern techniques such as dilation and curettage were not nearly so safe as they are today. Thus, it has been argued that a State's real concern in enacting a criminal abortion law was to protect the pregnant woman, that is, to restrain her from submitting to a procedure that placed her life in serious jeopardy.

Modern medical techniques have altered this situation. Appellants refer to medical data indicating that abortion in early pregnancy, that is, prior to the end of the first trimester, although not without its risk, is now relatively safe. Mortality rates for women undergoing early abortions, where the procedure is legal, appear to be as low as or lower than the rates for normal childbirth. Consequently, any interest of the State in protecting the woman from an inherently hazardous procedure, except when it would be equally dangerous for her to forgo it, has largely disappeared. Of course, important state interests in the areas of health and medical standards do remain.

The third reason is the State's interest—some phrase it in terms of duty—in protecting prenatal life. Some of the argument for this justification rests on the theory that a new human life is present from the moment of conception. The

State's interest and general obligation to protect life then extends, it is argued, to prenatal life. Only when the life of the pregnant mother herself is at stake, balanced against the life she carries within her, should the interest of the embryo or fetus not prevail. Logically, of course, a legitimate state interest in this area need not stand or fall on acceptance of the belief that life begins at conception or at some other point prior to life birth. In assessing the State's interest, recognition may be given to the less rigid claim that as long as at least potential life is involved, the State may assert interests beyond the protection of the pregnant woman alone. Parties challenging state abortion laws have sharply disputed that a purpose of these laws was to protect prenatal life. They claim that most state laws were designed solely to protect the woman. Because medical advances have lessened this concern, at least with respect to abortion in early pregnancy, they argue that with respect to such abortions the laws can no longer be justified by any state interest.

The Constitution does not explicitly mention any right of privacy. The Court has recognized that a right of personal privacy, or a guarantee of certain areas or zones of privacy, does exist under the Constitution. These decisions make it clear that only personal rights that can be deemed "fundamental" or "implicit in the concept of ordered liberty," are included in this guarantee of personal privacy. They also make it clear that the right has some extension to activities relating to marriage; procreation; contraception; family relationships; and child rearing and education.

This right of privacy, whether it be founded in the Fourteenth Amendment's concept of personal liberty and restrictions upon state action, as we feel it is, or, in the Ninth Amendment's reservation of rights to the people, is broad enough to encompass a woman's decision whether or not to terminate her pregnancy. The detriment that the State would impose upon the pregnant woman by denying this choice altogether is apparent. Specific and direct harm medically diagnosable even in early pregnancy may be involved. Maternity, or additional offspring, may force upon the woman a distressful life and future. Psychological harm may be imminent. Mental and physical health may be taxed by child care. There is also the distress, for all concerned, associated with the unwanted child, and there is the problem of bringing a child into a family already unable, psychologically and otherwise, to care for it. In other cases, as in this one, the additional difficulties and continuing stigma of unwed motherhood may be involved. All these are factors the woman and her responsible physician necessarily will consider in consultation.

On the basis of elements such as these, appellant and some amici argue that the woman's right is absolute and that she is entitled to terminate her pregnancy at whatever time, in whatever way, and for whatever reason she alone chooses. With this we do not agree. Appellant's arguments that Texas either has no valid interest at all in regulating the abortion decision, or no interest strong enough to support any limitation upon the woman's sole determination, are unpersuasive. The Court's decisions recognizing a right of privacy also acknowledge that some state regulation in areas protected by that right is appropriate. A State may properly assert important interests in safeguarding health, in maintaining medical standards, and in protecting potential life. At some point in pregnancy, these respective interests become sufficiently compelling to sustain regulation of the factors that govern the abortion decision. The privacy right involved, therefore, cannot be said to be absolute. In fact, it is not clear to us that the claim asserted by some amici that one has an unlimited right to do with one's body as one pleases bears a close relationship to the right of privacy previously articulated in the Court's decisions. The Court has refused to recognize an unlimited right of this kind in the past.

We, therefore, conclude that the right of personal privacy includes the abortion decision, but that this right is not unqualified and must be considered against important state interests in regulation. Where certain "fundamental rights" are involved, the Court has held that regulation limiting these rights may be justified only by a "compelling state interest." The District Court held that the appellee failed to meet his burden of demonstrating that the Texas statute's infringement upon Roe's rights was necessary to support a compelling state interest, and that, although the appellee presented "several compelling justifications for state presence in the area of abortions," the statutes outstripped these justifications and swept "far beyond any areas of compelling state interest."

The appellee and certain amici argue that the fetus is a "person" within the language and meaning of the Fourteenth Amendment. In support of this, they outline at length and in detail the well-known facts of fetal development. If this suggestion of personhood is established, the appellant's case collapses for the fetus' right to life would then be guaranteed specifically by the Amendment. On the other hand, no case could be cited that holds that a fetus is a person within the meaning of the Fourteenth Amendment. The Constitution does not define "person" in so many words. Although the term is used throughout the document, in nearly all these instances, the use of the word is such that it has application only postnatally. None indicates, with any assurance, that it has any possible prenatal application. All this, together with our observation, that throughout the major portion of the 19th century prevailing legal abortion practices were far freer than they are today, persuades us that the word "person," as used in the Fourteenth Amendment, does not include the unborn. This is in accord with the results reached in those few cases where the issue has been squarely presented.

The pregnant woman carries an embryo and, later, a fetus, if one accepts the medical definitions of the developing young in the human uterus. The situation therefore is inherently different from marital intimacy, or bedroom possession of obscene material, or marriage, or procreation, or education, with which prior cases were concerned. It is reasonable and appropriate for a State to decide that at some point in time another interest, that of health of the mother or that of potential human life, becomes significantly involved. The woman's privacy is no longer sole and any right of privacy she possesses must be measured accordingly.

Texas urges that, apart from the Fourteenth Amendment, life begins at conception and is present throughout pregnancy, and that, therefore, the State has a compelling interest in protecting that life from and after conception. We need not resolve the difficult question of when life begins. When those trained in the respective disciplines of medicine, philosophy, and theology are unable to arrive at any consensus, the judiciary, at this point in the development of man's knowledge, is not in a position to speculate as to the answer.

It should be sufficient to note briefly the wide divergence of thinking on this most sensitive and difficult question. There has always been strong support for the view that life does not begin until live birth. It appears to be the predominant attitude of the Jewish faith. A large segment of the Protestant community has generally regarded abortion as a matter for the conscience of the individual and her family. Physicians and their scientific colleagues have tended to focus either upon conception, upon live birth, or upon the interim point at which the fetus becomes "viable," that is, potentially able to live outside the mother's womb, albeit with artificial aid. Viability is usually placed at about seven months (28 weeks) but may occur earlier, even at 24 weeks. The Aristotelian theory of "mediate animation," that held sway throughout the Middle Ages and the Renaissance in Europe, continued to be official Roman Catholic dogma until the 19th century, despite opposition to this "ensoulment" theory from those in the Church who would recognize the existence of life from the moment of conception. The latter is now, of course, the official belief of the Catholic Church. This is a view strongly held by many non-Catholics as well, and by many physicians. Substantial problems for precise definition of this view are posed, however, by new embryological data that purport to indicate that conception is a "process" over time, rather than an event, and by new medical techniques such as menstrual extraction, the "morning-after" pill, implantation of embryos, artificial insemination, and even artificial wombs. In areas other than criminal abortion, the law has been reluctant to endorse any theory that life, as we recognize it, begins before life birth or to accord legal rights to the unborn except in narrowly defined situations and except when the rights are contingent upon life birth.

In view of all this, we do not agree that, by adopting one theory of life, Texas may override the rights of the pregnant woman that are at stake. The State does have an important and legitimate interest in preserving and protecting the health of the pregnant woman, whether she be a resident of the State or a nonresident who seeks medical consultation and treatment there, and that it has still another important and legitimate interest in protecting the potentiality of human life. These interests are separate and distinct. Each grows in substantiality as the woman approaches term and, at a point during pregnancy, each becomes "compelling."

With respect to the State's important and legitimate interest in the health of the mother, the "compelling" point, in the light of present medical knowledge, is at approximately the end of the first trimester. This is so because of the now-established medical fact that until the end of the first trimester mortality in abortion may be less than mortality in normal childbirth. It follows that, from and after this point, a State may regulate the abortion procedure to the extent that the regulation reasonably relates to the preservation and protection of maternal health. Examples of permissible state regulation in this area are requirements as to the qualifications of the person who is to perform the abortion; as to the licensure of that person; as to the facility in which the procedure is to be performed, that is, whether it must be a hospital or may be a clinic or some other place of less-than-hospital status; as to the licensing of the facility; and the like.

This means that, for the period of pregnancy prior to this "compelling" point, the attending physician, in consultation with his patient, is free to determine, without regulation by the State, that, in his medical judgment, the patient's pregnancy should be terminated. If that decision is reached, the judgment may be effectuated by an abortion free of interference by the State.

With respect to the State's important and legitimate interest in potential life, the "compelling" point is at viability. This is so because the fetus then presumably has the capability of meaningful life outside the mother's womb. State regulation protective of fetal life after viability thus has both logical and biological justifications. If the State is interested in protecting fetal life after viability, it may go so far as to proscribe abortion during that period, except when it is necessary to preserve the life or health of the mother.

Measured against these standards, the Texas law, in restricting legal abortions to those "procured or attempted by medical advice for the purpose of saving the life of the mother," sweeps too broadly. The statute makes no distinction between abortions performed early in pregnancy and those performed later, and it limits to a single reason, "saving" the mother's life, the legal justification for the procedure. The statute, therefore, cannot survive the constitutional attack made upon it here.

To summarize and to repeat: A state criminal abortion statute of the current Texas type, that excepts from criminality only a life-saving procedure on behalf of the mother, without regard to pregnancy stage and without recognition of the other interests involved, is violative of the Due Process Clause of the Fourteenth Amendment.

(a) For the stage prior to approximately the end of the first trimester, the abortion decision and its effectuation must be left to the medical judgment of the pregnant woman's attending physician.

(b) For the stage subsequent to approximately the end of the first trimester, the State, in promoting its interest in the health of the mother, may, if it chooses, regulate the abortion procedure in ways that are reasonably related to maternal health.

(c) For the stage subsequent to viability, the State in promoting its interest in the potentiality of human life may, if it chooses, regulate, and even proscribe, abortion except where it is necessary, in appropriate medical judgment, for the preservation of the life or health of the mother.

This holding is consistent with the relative weights of the respective interests involved, with the lessons and examples of medical and legal history, with the lenity of the common law, and with the demands of the profound problems of the present day. The decision leaves the State free to place increasing restrictions on abortion as the period of pregnancy lengthens, so long as those restrictions are tailored to the recognized state interests. The decision vindicates the right of the physician to administer medical treatment according to his professional judgment up to the points where important state interests provide compelling justifications for intervention. Up to those points, the abortion decision in all its aspects is inherently, and primarily, a medical decision, and basic responsibility for it must rest with the physician. If an individual practitioner abuses the privilege of exercising proper medical judgment, the usual remedies, judicial and intra-professional, are available.

Affirmed in part and reversed in part.

Mr. Justice STEWART, *concurring.*

Several decisions of this Court make clear that freedom of personal choice in matters of marriage and family life is one of the liberties protected by the Due Process Clause of the Fourteenth Amendment. That right necessarily includes the right of a woman to decide whether or not to terminate her pregnancy. Certainly the interests of a woman in giving of her physical and emotional self during pregnancy and the interests that will be affected throughout her life by the birth and raising of a child are of a far greater degree of significance and personal intimacy than the right to send a child to private school or the right to teach a foreign language. Clearly, therefore, the Court today is correct in holding that the right asserted by Jane Roe is embraced within the personal liberty protected by the Due Process Clause of the Fourteenth Amendment.

Mr. Justice REHNQUIST, *dissenting.*

While the Court's opinion quotes from the dissent of Mr. Justice Holmes in *Lochner v. New York*, the result it reaches is more closely attuned to the majority opinion in that case. As in *Lochner* and similar cases applying substantive due process standards to economic and social welfare legislation, the adoption of the compelling state interest standard will inevitably require this Court to examine the legislative policies and pass on the wisdom of these policies in the very process of deciding whether a particular state interest put forward may or may not be "compelling." The decision here to break pregnancy into three distinct terms and to outline the permissible restrictions the State may impose in each one, for example, partakes more of judicial legislation than it does of a determination of the intent of the drafters of the Fourteenth Amendment.

The fact that a majority of the States reflecting have had restrictions on abortions for at least a century is a strong indication that the asserted right to an abortion is not "so rooted in the traditions and conscience of our people as to be ranked as fundamental." When society's views on abortion are changing, the very existence of the debate is evidence that the "right" to an abortion is not universally accepted.

To reach its result, the Court necessarily has had to find within the Scope of the Fourteenth Amendment a right that was apparently completely unknown to the drafters of the Amendment. As early as 1821, the first state law dealing directly with abortion was enacted by the Connecticut Legislature. By the time of the adoption of the Fourteenth Amendment in 1868, there were at least 36 laws enacted by state or territorial legislatures limiting abortion. While many States have amended or updated their laws, 21 of the laws on the books in 1868 remain in effect today. Indeed, the Texas statute struck down today was, as the majority notes, first enacted in 1857 and "has remained substantially unchanged to the present time." There apparently was no question concerning the validity of this provision or of any of the other state statutes when the Fourteenth Amendment was adopted. The only conclusion possible from this history is that the drafters did not intend to have the Fourteenth Amendment withdraw from the States the power to legislate with respect to this matter.

BACKGROUND
Roe's *Impact*

The *Roe* decision undid abortion laws in nearly half of the union. Two decades earlier, when the Court struck down segregation in the South, resistance to the Court in most affected states was intense. A similar response was engendered by the abortion decision. Unlike the united front that the Court presented throughout the 1960s on the desegregation front, it was divided on abortion from the outset. Despite these internal divisions and an abundance of challenges, the Court was generally consistent through the late 1980s in striking down laws perceived as a significant burden upon a woman's liberty to elect an abortion.

Notes

1. *Criticism of* Roe. *Roe* was a lightning rod for criticism that the Court had overreached its function and reverted to the antidemocratic model of the *Lochner* era. A particularly strong critic of the decision, Judge Robert Bork, characterized it as "an exercise in moral and political philosophy" and an "assumption of illegitimate power and a usurpation of the democratic authority of the American people." ROBERT BORK, THE TEMPTING OF AMERICA (Touchstone 1990). Exponents of modern substantive due process review distinguish outputs like *Roe* on grounds that the Court's review is not unbounded. Consistent with Justice Harlan's concurrence in *Griswold,* the Court, pursuant to self-imposed standards, must probe whether an interest is "implicit in the concept of ordered liberty" or "rooted in

the Nation's history and tradition." Interpretivists are not impressed with what some have dismissed as "pretty vaporous stuff" and what they contrast with the greater clarity and framing of a textually enumerated right or liberty.

2. *Restrictions on Abortion.* In *Doe v. Bolton,* 410 U.S. 179 (1973), the Court invalidated provisions of a state law that required abortions to be performed in a hospital approved by a specific accrediting agency, to be authorized by a hospital committee, and to be done only after examination by two other physicians. Critical to the Court's analysis was the fact that these restrictions applied to no other surgical procedure but abortion. In *Planned Parenthood v. Danforth,* 428 U.S. 52 (1976), the Court struck down state provisions for spousal and parental consent for unmarried women under the age of 18. The basis for this holding was that the state could not delegate to a person power it did not have during the first trimester. The Court emphasized that the woman, as the child bearer, "is the more directly and immediately affected by the pregnancy, the balance weighs in her favor." Because of age and maturity factors, it also noted that some minor children might not be able to provide effective consent. Following up on this point, the Court in *Planned Parenthood v. Ashcroft,* 462 U.S. 476 (1983), upheld a parental consent or notification requirement provided that the minor could bypass it through a judicial procedure. The responsibility of the court, in this circumstance, is to find either that the minor was sufficiently mature to make the decision herself or that an abortion was in her best interest.

3. *Further Abortion Issues.* The Court continued to strike down regulations that constituted significant roadblocks to a woman's ability to exercise her liberty. In *City of Akron v. Akron Center for Reproductive Health,* 462 U.S. 416 (1983), it struck down a state law requiring physicians to provide specific information concerning the medical risks and morality of abortion, impose a 24-hour waiting period, and require all post–first-trimester abortions to be performed in hospitals. The Court found that these restrictions constituted "a heavy and unnecessary burden" upon a woman's liberty interest. Another set of restrictions, requiring disclosure of the names of referring and performing physicians and the woman seeking an abortion, and mandating that post-viability abortions be conducted in a way that maximizes the chances for fetal survival, was struck down in *Thornburgh v. American College of Obstetricians and Gynecologists,* 476 U.S. 747 (1986). These restrictions were perceived as imposing too high a risk of deterring the exercise of the liberty. Through the *Thornburgh* decision, the Court rather consistently had struck down laws that limited a woman's freedom to choose an abortion. It also had etched a line between burdens that restricted the liberty and public funding decisions that imposed no obligation upon government to subsidize the right.

Questions

1. *Are There Significant Differences Between* Lochner *and* Roe? *Lochner* is now widely repudiated on the basis that the federal courts should not sit as

"super-legislatures" that pass on the wisdom of legislation. How does *Griswold* review differ from *Lochner* review? Are the values, the results, or the model of review more principled in *Griswold?* How helpful is it to focus on the "implications of ordered liberty" or "the nation's traditions and history" as a basis for separating the two models of substantive due process review? Does it matter that a majority of the states at the time of *Roe* had imposed restrictions on abortion for more than a century? Is the better analogy for *Roe* not *Lochner* but *Brown v. Board of Education*, the decision that struck down official segregation in public schools? If *Brown* is the better reference point, does this relationship cut in favor of *Roe* or against *Brown?*

2. Roe *and Judicial Legitimacy.* Justice Rehnquist, in his dissent, notes that "a majority of the States have had restrictions on abortions for at least a century." If Justice Rehnquist is correct, how does that fact affect (if at all) *Roe*'s legitimacy? Do you agree with Justice Rehnquist that this fact shows "the asserted right to an abortion is not 'so rooted in the traditions and conscience of our people as to be ranked as fundamental' "?

3. *Defining Privacy Rights. Roe* makes clear that the right to an abortion constitutes a "fundamental" right that is "implicit in the concept of ordered liberty." In earlier cases, the Court had indicated that it is not "at large" in defining the Fourteenth Amendment, and that it is not free to substitute its own views for that of the legislature. But are there neutral principles that dictate recognition of a right to privacy that includes the right to have an abortion? How might the State of Texas argue that abortion falls outside the right?

4. *Status of the Fetus.* In *Roe,* the Court refused to decide whether a fetus is a "person" within the meaning of the Constitution. Some churches (e.g., the Catholic Church) and others believe that life begins at conception. Had the Court accepted that view, how would it have affected the outcome of the case? If life prior to viability is a potentiality, does subordination of a fetus to actual personhood and the real life incident to it become sensible? *See* Catherine MacKinnon, *Reflections on Sex Equality Under Law,* 100 Yale L.J. 1281, 1315 (1991); John Noonan, *The Root and Branch of Roe v. Wade,* 63 Neb. L. Rev. 668 (1984).

5. *Establishment Clause Concerns.* Does the argument that life, real or potential, is valuable to the point that it overrides a right to obtain an abortion represent an essentially religious viewpoint? Are restrictions on abortion thus susceptible to review on grounds that they violate the Establishment Clause? *See Harris v. McRae,* 448 U.S. 297 (1980); Ronald Dworkin, *Unenumerated Rights: Whether and How* Roe *Should Be Overruled,* 59 U. Chi. L. Rev. 381 (1992).

6. *More on* Griswold*'s Limits.* The *Griswold* decision established a right of privacy that accounts for personal choice that was denied by prohibitions on using birth control devices. Under the right of privacy, is there a logical connection between protecting choice in the context of contraception and accounting for it in the purview of child bearing? *See* Charles Fried, Order and Law 77 (Simon & Schuster 1991).

∼ PROBLEMS ∼

1. Roe *and the Shifting State of Medical Technology.* When *Roe* was decided, a fetus was not sustainable outside the womb until the third trimester. As medical technology advances, suppose that it becomes possible to sustain a fetus outside the womb as early as the tenth week of pregnancy, and that medical procedures advance to the point that it is possible to remove the fetus (without aborting) with no greater risk to the mother than an abortion. a) Under such circumstances, would the pregnant woman still have an absolute right to abort the fetus? b) Under the *Roe* line of cases, the Court has held that the woman may choose to abort notwithstanding the objections of the father. Under the circumstances listed above, would the father's wishes assume greater significance? Why or why not? c) Does the Court have to periodically update the *Roe* decision in light of current technology? If so, how? Does the idea of "periodic updating" in light of technology suggest that the judiciary has exceeded its function?

2. *The Divorcing Couple and the Embryos.* A married couple is having difficulty conceiving and resorts to in-vitro fertilization. As a result of this process, eight eggs are fertilized and three are implanted in the wife. The pregnancy does not take. Following the unsuccessful implantation, the couple divorce. In the divorce proceeding, the mother seeks "custody" of the eggs on the theory that she is (otherwise) unlikely to be able to conceive. She claims a "liberty" and "privacy" interest in being able to choose whether to have children. The father opposes the mother's request because he does not wish to be a father, especially with his soon-to-be ex-wife, and he bases his argument on "liberty" and "privacy" concerns. Does the wife have a constitutional liberty or privacy right that entitles her to the eggs?

Webster and Doctrinal Turmoil

In *Webster v. Reproductive Health Systems, Inc.*, 492 U.S. 490 (1989), the Court signaled that it might be backing away from *Roe* in some respects. The Missouri statute in question contained a preamble that stated that "the life of each human being begins at conception," and that "unborn children have protectable interests in life, health, and well-being." It also mandated that state laws be interpreted to provide unborn children with "all the rights, privileges, and immunities available to other persons, citizens, and residents of this state," subject to the Constitution and prior precedent. A plurality of the Court upheld the preamble, noting that it "does not by its terms regulate abortion or any other aspect of appellees' medical practice" and can be regarded as nothing more than the state's value judgment.

The statute also provided that "it shall be unlawful for any public employee within the scope of his employment to perform or assist an abortion, not necessary to save the life of the mother," and also made it "unlawful for any public

facility to be used for the purpose of performing or assisting an abortion not necessary to save the life of the mother." The plurality also upheld these provisions.
"Our cases have recognized that the Due Process Clauses generally confer no
affirmative right to governmental aid, even where such aid may be necessary to
secure life, liberty, or property interests of which the government itself may not
deprive the individual."

Finally, the Missouri statute imposed a viability testing requirement that
applied when a physician has reason to believe that a woman is "carrying an
unborn child of twenty or more weeks of gestational age." The Court explained
that the statute creates what is essentially a presumption of viability at 20 weeks,
which the physician must rebut with tests indicating that the fetus is not viable
prior to performing an abortion. It also directs the physician's determination as
to viability by specifying consideration, if feasible, of gestational age, fetal weight,
and lung capacity. The plurality upheld the provision: "The Missouri testing
requirement here is reasonably designed to ensure that abortions are not performed where the fetus is viable—an end which all concede is legitimate—and
that is sufficient to sustain its constitutionality."

While *Webster's* holding on the merits was significant, the decision was doc-
trinally important because it signaled that a number of Justices had reservations
about *Roe* and its trimester analysis. The plurality stated:

> We think that the doubt cast upon the Missouri statute by these cases is not so much a
> flaw in the statute as it is a reflection of the fact that the rigid trimester analysis of the course
> of a pregnancy enunciated in *Roe* has made this area a virtual Procrustean bed. *Stare decisis*
> is a cornerstone of our legal system, but it has less power in constitutional cases, where, save
> for constitutional amendments, this Court is the only body able to make needed changes.
> We have not refrained from reconsideration of a prior construction of the Constitution that
> has proved "unsound in principle and unworkable in practice." We think the *Roe* trimester
> framework falls into that category.
>
> In the first place, the rigid *Roe* framework is hardly consistent with the notion of a
> Constitution cast in general terms, as ours is, and usually speaking in general principles, as ours
> does. The key elements of the *Roe* framework—trimesters and viability—are not found in the
> text of the Constitution or in any place else one would expect to find a constitutional principle.
> Since the bounds of the inquiry are essentially indeterminate, the result has been a web of legal
> rules that have become increasingly intricate, resembling a code of regulations rather than a
> body of constitutional doctrine. As Justice White has put it, the trimester framework has left this
> Court to serve as the country's "ex officio medical board with powers to approve or disapprove
> medical and operative practices and standards throughout the United States."
>
> In the second place, we do not see why the State's interest in protecting potential
> human life should come into existence only at the point of viability, and that there should
> therefore be a rigid line allowing state regulation after viability but prohibiting it before
> viability. The dissenters in *Thornburgh* would have recognized this fact by positing against the
> "fundamental right" recognized in *Roe* the State's "compelling interest" in protecting poten-
> tial human life throughout pregnancy. "The State's interest, if compelling after viability, is
> equally compelling before viability."

Nevertheless, the plurality rejected the request of some appellants and amici to
flatly overrule *Roe*. Justice Scalia, concurring, suggested outright that he "would

overrule *Roe v. Wade.*" Justice Blackmun, who also concurred, suggested that "Today, *Roe v. Wade,* and the fundamental constitutional right of women to decide whether to terminate a pregnancy, survive but are not secure."

Webster was widely cited as an indication that the *Roe* ruling was in terminal condition. Doctrinal turmoil was evidenced further in *Hodgson v. Minnesota,* 497 U.S. 417 (1990), when the Court invalidated a two-parent notice requirement for minors 48 hours prior to undergoing an abortion but upheld it when coupled with a judicial bypass requirement. These outcomes were reached pursuant to five-to-four votes, with Justice O'Connor being the pivotal figure with respect to both outcome and rationale. From her perspective, the two-parent constitutional requirement imposed an "undue burden" particularly to the extent that only half of the state's minors lived with both biological parents. For a majority of the judges, the question was whether the notification requirement "reasonably" promoted a legitimate state interest. This terminology, reminiscent of rational basis analysis, compounded the uncertainty with respect to the standard of review governing abortion regulations. In *Planned Parenthood of Southeastern Pennsylvania v. Casey,* the Court reviewed statutory provisions for informed consent, a 24-hour waiting period, parental consent with a judicial bypass option, spousal notification, and reporting requirements for abortion providers. Although affirming that a woman's liberty to elect an abortion is fundamental, the Court effectively previewed the dismantling of *Roe*'s trimester regime.

∾ PROBLEMS ∾

1. *Must the State Pay for Abortions for Indigent Women? Roe* makes clear that the "right of personal privacy includes the abortion decision" and that such "fundamental rights" can only be overridden by a "compelling state interest." If a woman is too poor to pay for her own abortion, does her "fundamental right" include the right to state funding for an abortion? Should it matter that the state discriminates between abortion and childbirth by paying for the costs of childbirth but not the costs of abortion? Consider the following arguments regarding the validity of the state denial:

A. The stark reality for too many indigent pregnant women is that indigency makes access to competent licensed physicians not merely "difficult" but "impossible." The State's denial of funding, therefore, operates to coerce indigent pregnant women to bear children they would not otherwise choose to have, and this coercion can only operate upon the poor, who are uniquely the victims of this form of financial pressure.

B. *Roe v. Wade* and cases following it hold that an area of privacy invulnerable to the State's intrusion surrounds the decision of a pregnant woman whether or not to carry her pregnancy to term. The Connecticut scheme clearly infringes upon that area of privacy by bringing financial pressures on indigent women that force them to bear children they would not otherwise have.

C. An indigent woman who desires an abortion suffers no disadvantage as a consequence of Connecticut's decision to fund childbirth; she continues as before to be dependent on private sources for the service she desires. The State may have made childbirth a more attractive alternative, thereby influencing the woman's decision, but it has imposed no restriction on access to abortions that was not already there. The indigency that may make it difficult and in some cases, perhaps, impossible for some women to have abortions is neither created nor in any way affected by the Connecticut regulation.

D. There is a basic difference between direct state interference with a protected activity and state encouragement of an alternative activity consonant with legislative policy. Constitutional concerns are greatest when the State attempts to impose its will by force of law; the State's power to encourage actions deemed to be in the public interest is necessarily far broader.

E. The State unquestionably has a "strong and legitimate interest in encouraging normal childbirth," an interest honored over the centuries. Nor can there be any question that the Connecticut regulation rationally furthers that interest. The medical costs associated with childbirth are substantial, and have increased significantly in recent years. Such costs are significantly greater than those normally associated with elective abortions during the first trimester. The subsidizing of costs incident to childbirth is a rational means of encouraging childbirth.

F. We certainly are not unsympathetic to the plight of an indigent woman who desires an abortion, but "the Constitution does not provide judicial remedies for every social and economic ill." Our cases uniformly have accorded the States a wider latitude in choosing among competing demands for limited public funds.

Which arguments are more persuasive? *See Maher v. Roe*, 432 U.S. 464 (1977).

2. *Denying Abortion Funding.* Instead of a state law that denies funding for abortions, suppose that a federal statute precludes the medical program for indigents (Medicaid) from providing coverage for abortions. Is it permissible for the federal government to provide a general program of medical care for indigents, but to deny coverage even for medically necessary abortions? Does protection of the woman's health, coupled with the woman's constitutional right to have an abortion, justify forcing the state to pay for a medically necessary abortion? Is it enough to say that the denial of Medicaid coverage leaves an indigent woman with at least the same range of choice in deciding whether to obtain a medically necessary abortion as she would have had if Congress had chosen to subsidize no health care costs at all? Which arguments hold greater sway? *See Harris v. McRae*, 448 U.S. 297 (1980).

3. *Moral Objections.* In evaluating the preceding problem, what weight (if any) would you attach to the fact that the chief sponsor of the federal legislation flatly stated that a motivating consideration behind the law was the fact that he regarded abortion as a means for killing innocent pre-born children. Is moral objectionability a basis for restricting abortion funding? How should the government lawyer respond to arguments that the amendment is fatally flawed?

Planned Parenthood of Southeastern Pennsylvania v. Casey

410 U.S. 113 (1993)

Justice O'CONNOR, Justice KENNEDY, and Justice SOUTER announced the judgment of the Court and delivered the opinion of the Court with respect to Parts I, II,

III, V-A, V-C, and VI, an opinion with respect to Part V-E, in which Justice Stevens joins, and an opinion with respect to Parts IV, V-B, and V-D.

I

Nineteen years after our holding that the Constitution protects a woman's right to terminate her pregnancy in its early stages, *Roe v. Wade*, that definition of liberty is still questioned. The United States, as it has done in five other cases in the last decade, again asks us to overrule *Roe*.

At issue in these cases are five provisions of the Pennsylvania Abortion Control Act of 1982, as amended in 1988 and 1989. We acknowledge that our decisions after *Roe* cast doubt upon the meaning and reach of its holding. Further, the Chief Justice admits that he would overrule the central holding of *Roe* and adopt the rational relationship test as the sole criterion of constitutionality. State and federal courts as well as legislatures throughout the Union must have guidance as they seek to address this subject in conformance with the Constitution. Given these premises, we find it imperative to review once more the principles that define the rights of the woman and the legitimate authority of the State respecting the termination of pregnancies by abortion procedures.

After considering the fundamental constitutional questions resolved by *Roe*, principles of institutional integrity, and the rule of *stare decisis*, we are led to conclude this: the essential holding of *Roe v. Wade* should be retained and once again reaffirmed. *Roe*'s essential holding has three parts. First is a recognition of the right of the woman to choose to have an abortion before viability and to obtain it without undue interference from the State. Before viability, the State's interests are not strong enough to support a prohibition of abortion or the imposition of a substantial obstacle to the woman's effective right to elect the procedure. Second is a confirmation of the State's power to restrict abortions after fetal viability, if the law contains exceptions for pregnancies which endanger the woman's life or health. And third is the principle that the State has legitimate interests from the outset of the pregnancy in protecting the health of the woman and the life of the fetus that may become a child. These principles do not contradict one another; and we adhere to each.

II

Constitutional protection of the woman's decision to terminate her pregnancy derives from the Due Process Clause of the Fourteenth Amendment. It declares that no State shall "deprive any person of life, liberty, or property, without due process of law." The controlling word in the cases before us is "liberty." Although a literal reading of the Clause might suggest that it governs only the procedures by which a State may deprive persons of liberty, for at least 105 years, the Clause has been understood to contain a substantive component as well, one "barring certain government actions regardless of the fairness of the procedures used to implement them." "Thus all fundamental rights comprised within the term liberty are protected by the Federal Constitution from invasion by the States."

The most familiar of the substantive liberties protected by the Fourteenth Amendment are those recognized by the Bill of Rights. We have held that the Due Process Clause of the Fourteenth Amendment incorporates most of the Bill of Rights against the States. It is tempting, as a means of curbing the discretion of federal judges, to suppose that liberty encompasses no more than those rights already guaranteed to the individual against federal interference by the express provisions of the first eight Amendments to the Constitution. But of course this Court has never accepted that view.

It is also tempting to suppose that the Due Process Clause protects only those practices, defined at the most specific level, that were protected against government interference by other rules of law when the Fourteenth Amendment was ratified. But such a view would be inconsistent with our law. It is a promise of the Constitution that there is a realm of personal liberty which the government may not enter. Neither the Bill of Rights nor the specific practices of States at the time of the adoption of the Fourteenth Amendment marks the outer limits of the substantive sphere of liberty which the Fourteenth Amendment protects.

The inescapable fact is that adjudication of substantive due process claims may call upon the Court in interpreting the Constitution to exercise that same capacity which by tradition courts always have exercised: reasoned judgment. Its boundaries are not susceptible of expression as a simple rule. That does not mean we are free to invalidate state policy choices with which we disagree; yet neither does it permit us to shrink from the duties of our office.

Men and women of good conscience can disagree, and we suppose some always shall disagree, about the profound moral and spiritual implications of terminating a pregnancy, even in its earliest stage. Some of us as individuals find abortion offensive to our most basic principles of morality, but that cannot control our decision. Our obligation is to define the liberty of all, not to mandate our own moral code. The underlying constitutional issue is whether the State can resolve these philosophic questions in such a definitive way that a woman lacks all choice in the matter, except perhaps in those rare circumstances in which the pregnancy is itself a danger to her own life or health, or is the result of rape or incest.

Our law affords constitutional protection to personal decisions relating to marriage, procreation, contraception, family relationships, child rearing, and education. These matters, involving the most intimate and personal choices a person may make in a lifetime, choices central to personal dignity and autonomy, are central to the liberty protected by the Fourteenth Amendment. At the heart of liberty is the right to define one's own concept of existence, of meaning, of the universe, and of the mystery of human life. Beliefs about these matters could not define the attributes of personhood were they formed under compulsion of the State.

These considerations begin our analysis of the woman's interest in terminating her pregnancy but cannot end it, for this reason: though the abortion decision may originate within the zone of conscience and belief, it is more than a philosophic exercise. Abortion is a unique act. It is an act fraught with consequences for others: for the woman who must live with the implications of her decision; for the persons who perform and assist in the procedure; for the spouse, family, and society which must confront the knowledge that these procedures exist, procedures some deem nothing short of an act of violence against innocent human life; and, depending on one's beliefs, for the life or potential life that is aborted. Though abortion is conduct, it does not follow that the State is entitled to proscribe it in all instances. That is because the liberty of the woman is at stake in a sense unique to the human condition and so unique to the law. The mother who carries a child to full term is subject to anxieties, to physical constraints, to pain that only she must bear. That these sacrifices have from the beginning of the human race been endured by woman with a pride that ennobles her in the eyes of others and gives to the infant a bond of love cannot alone be grounds for the State to insist she make the sacrifice. Her suffering is too intimate and personal for the State to insist, without more, upon its own vision of the woman's role, however dominant that vision has been in the course of our history and our culture. The destiny of the woman must be shaped to a large extent on her own conception of her spiritual imperatives and her place in society.

The reservations any of us may have in reaffirming the central holding of *Roe* are outweighed by the explication of individual liberty combined with *stare decisis*.

III

For two decades of economic and social developments, people have organized intimate relationships and made choices that define their views of themselves and their places in society, in reliance on the availability of abortion in the event that contraception should fail. The ability of women to participate equally in the economic and social life of the Nation has been facilitated by their ability to control their reproductive lives. The Constitution serves human values, and while the effect of reliance on *Roe* cannot be exactly measured, neither can the certain cost of overruling *Roe* for people who have ordered their thinking and living around that case be dismissed.

We have seen how time has overtaken some of *Roe*'s factual assumptions: advances in maternal health care allow for abortions safe to the mother later in pregnancy than was true in 1973, and advances in neonatal care have advanced viability to a point somewhat earlier. But these facts have no bearing on the validity of *Roe*'s central holding, that viability marks the earliest point at which the State's interest in fetal life is constitutionally adequate to justify a legislative ban on nontherapeutic abortions. The soundness or unsoundness of that constitutional judgment in no sense turns on whether viability occurs at approximately 28 weeks, as was usual at the time of *Roe*, at 23 to 24 weeks, as it sometimes does today, or at some moment even slightly earlier in pregnancy, as it may if fetal respiratory capacity can somehow be enhanced in the future. Whenever it may occur, the attainment of viability may continue to serve as the critical fact, just as it has done since *Roe* was decided; which is to say that no change in *Roe*'s factual underpinning has left its central holding obsolete, and none supports an argument for overruling it.

An entire generation has come of age free to assume *Roe*'s concept of liberty in defining the capacity of women to act in society, and to make reproductive decisions; no erosion of principle going to liberty or personal autonomy has left *Roe*'s central holding a doctrinal remnant. The stronger argument is for affirming *Roe*'s central holding, not for overruling it.

The Court's power lies in its legitimacy, a product of substance and perception that shows itself in the people's acceptance of the Judiciary as fit to determine what the Nation's law means and to declare what it demands. The underlying substance of this legitimacy is of course the warrant for the Court's decisions in the Constitution and the lesser sources of legal principle on which the Court draws. A decision without principled justification would be no judicial act at all. Even when justification is furnished, something more is required. The Court must take care to speak and act in ways that allow people to accept its decisions on the terms the Court claims for them, as grounded truly in principle, not as compromises with social and political pressures having, as such, no bearing on the principled choices that the Court is obliged to make. Thus, the Court's legitimacy depends on making legally principled decisions under circumstances in which their principled character is sufficiently plausible to be accepted by the Nation.

Where, in the performance of its judicial duties, the Court decides a case in such a way as to resolve the sort of intensely divisive controversy reflected in *Roe*, only the most convincing justification under accepted standards of precedent could suffice to demonstrate that a later decision overruling the first was anything but a surrender to political pressure, and an unjustified repudiation of the principle on which the Court staked its authority in the first instance. Pressure to overrule *Roe*, like pressure to retain it, has grown more intense. A decision to overrule *Roe*'s essential holding under the existing circumstances would address error, if error there was, at the cost of both profound and unnecessary damage to the Court's legitimacy, and to the Nation's commitment to the rule of law. It is therefore imperative to adhere to the essence of *Roe*'s original decision, and we do so today.

IV

Much criticism has been directed at *Roe,* a criticism that always inheres when the Court draws a specific rule from what in the Constitution is but a general standard. We conclude, however, that the urgent claims of the woman to retain the ultimate control over her destiny and her body, claims implicit in the meaning of liberty, require us to perform that function. Liberty must not be extinguished for want of a line that is clear. And it falls to us to give some real substance to the woman's liberty to determine whether to carry her pregnancy to full term.

We conclude the line should be drawn at viability, so that before that time the woman has a right to choose to terminate her pregnancy. We adhere to this principle for two reasons. First, as we have said, is the doctrine of *stare decisis.* Any judicial act of line-drawing may seem somewhat arbitrary, but *Roe* was a reasoned statement, elaborated with great care. The second reason is that the concept of viability, as we noted in *Roe*, is the time at which there is a realistic possibility of maintaining and nourishing a life outside the womb, so that the independent existence of the second life can in reason and all fairness be the object of state protection that now overrides the rights of the woman. The woman's right to terminate her pregnancy before viability is the most central principle of *Roe*. It is a rule of law and a component of liberty we cannot renounce.

On the other side of the equation is the interest of the State in the protection of potential life. *Roe* recognized the State's "important and legitimate interest in protecting the potentiality of human life." Subsequent cases decided that any regulation touching upon the abortion decision must survive strict scrutiny, to be sustained only if drawn in narrow terms to further a compelling state interest. Not all of these cases can be reconciled with the holding in *Roe* itself. In resolving this tension, we choose to rely upon *Roe*, as against the later cases.

We reject the trimester framework, which we do not consider to be part of the essential holding of *Roe*. Measures aimed at ensuring that a woman's choice contemplates the consequences for the fetus do not necessarily interfere with the right recognized in *Roe*, although those measures have been found to be inconsistent with the rigid trimester framework announced in that case. A logical reading of the central holding in *Roe* itself, and a necessary reconciliation of the liberty of the woman and the interest of the State in promoting prenatal life, require that we abandon the trimester framework as a rigid prohibition on all previability regulation aimed at the protection of fetal life. The trimester framework suffers from these basic flaws: in its formulation it misconceives the nature of the pregnant woman's interest; and in practice it undervalues the State's interest in potential life, as recognized in *Roe*.

Not every law which makes a right more difficult to exercise is, *ipso facto*, an infringement of that right. Numerous forms of state regulation might have the incidental effect of increasing the cost or decreasing the availability of medical care, whether for abortion or any other medical procedure. Only where state regulation imposes an undue burden on a woman's ability to make this decision does the power of the State reach into the heart of the liberty protected by the Due Process Clause.

Not all governmental intrusion is of necessity unwarranted; and that brings us to the other basic flaw in the trimester framework: even in *Roe*'s terms, in practice it undervalues the State's interest in the potential life within the woman. *Roe* was express in its recognition of the State's "important and legitimate interests in preserving and protecting the health of the pregnant woman and in protecting the potentiality of human life." The trimester framework, however, does not fulfill *Roe*'s own promise that the State has an interest in protecting fetal life or potential life. The undue burden standard is the appropriate means of reconciling the State's interest with the woman's constitutionally protected liberty. A statute which, while furthering the interest in potential life or some other valid state interest, has the effect of placing a substantial obstacle in the path of a woman's choice cannot be considered a permissible means of serving its legitimate ends. In our considered judgment, an undue burden is an unconstitutional burden.

We give this summary:

(a) To protect the central right recognized by *Roe v. Wade* while at the same time accommodating the State's profound interest in potential life, we will employ the undue burden analysis. An undue burden exists, and therefore a provision of law is invalid, if its purpose or effect is to place a substantial obstacle in the path of a woman seeking an abortion before the fetus attains viability.

(b) We reject the rigid trimester framework of *Roe*. To promote the State's profound interest in potential life, throughout pregnancy the State may take measures to ensure that the woman's choice is informed, and measures designed to advance this interest will not be invalidated as long as their purpose is to persuade the woman to choose childbirth over abortion. These measures must not be an undue burden on the right.

(c) As with any medical procedure, the State may enact regulations to further the health or safety of a woman seeking an abortion. Unnecessary health regulations that have the purpose or effect of presenting a substantial obstacle to a woman seeking an abortion impose an undue burden on the right.

(d) The undue burden analysis does not disturb the central holding of *Roe*, and we reaffirm that holding. A State may not prohibit any woman from making the ultimate decision to terminate her pregnancy before viability.

(e) We also reaffirm *Roe*'s holding that "subsequent to viability, the State in promoting its interest in the potentiality of human life may, if it chooses, regulate, and even proscribe, abortion except where it is necessary, in appropriate medical judgment, for the preservation of the life or health of the mother."

These principles control our assessment of the Pennsylvania statute.

V

A

We begin with the statute's definition of medical emergency. A medical emergency is that condition which, on the basis of the physician's good faith clinical judgment, so complicates the medical condition of a pregnant woman as to necessitate the immediate abortion of her pregnancy to avert her death or for which a delay will create serious risk of substantial and irreversible impairment of a major bodily function.

Petitioners argue that the definition forecloses the possibility of an immediate abortion despite some significant health risks. While the definition could be interpreted in an unconstitutional manner, the Court of Appeals construed the phrase "serious risk" to assure that compliance with its abortion regulations would not in any way "pose a significant threat to the life or health of a woman." We conclude that, as construed, the medical emergency definition imposes no undue burden on a woman's abortion right.

B

We next consider the informed consent requirement. Except in a medical emergency, the statute requires that at least 24 hours before performing an abortion a physician inform the woman of the nature of the procedure, the health risks of the abortion and of childbirth, and the "probable gestational age of the unborn child." The physician or a qualified nonphysician must inform the woman of the availability of printed materials published by the State describing the fetus and providing information about medical assistance for childbirth, information about child support from the father, and a list of agencies which provide adoption and other services as alternatives to abortion. An abortion may not be performed unless the woman certifies in writing that she has been informed of the availability of these printed materials and has been provided them if she chooses to view them.

The idea that important decisions will be more informed and deliberate if they follow some period of reflection does not strike us as unreasonable, particularly where the statute directs that important information become part of the background of the decision. The statute permits avoidance of the waiting period in the event of a medical emergency and the record shows that in the vast majority of cases, a 24-hour delay does not create any appreciable health risk. In theory, at least, the waiting period is a reasonable measure to implement the State's interest in protecting the life of the unborn, a measure that does not amount to an undue burden.

Whether the mandatory 24-hour waiting period is nonetheless invalid because it is a substantial obstacle to a woman's choice to terminate her pregnancy is a closer question. The District Court found that because of the distances many women must travel to reach an abortion provider, the practical effect will often be a delay of much more than a day because the waiting period requires that a woman seeking an abortion make at least two visits to the doctor. The District Court also found that in many instances this will increase the exposure of women seeking abortions to "the harassment and hostility of antiabortion protestors demonstrating outside a clinic." As a result, the District Court found that for those women who have the fewest financial resources, those who must travel long distances, and those who have difficulty explaining their whereabouts to husbands, employers, or others, the 24-hour waiting period will be "particularly burdensome." These findings are troubling, but they do not demonstrate that the waiting period constitutes an undue burden. We do not doubt that the waiting period has the effect of "increasing the cost and risk of delay of abortions," but the District Court did not conclude that the increased costs and potential delays amount to substantial obstacles.

C

The state abortion law provides, except in cases of medical emergency, that no physician shall perform an abortion on a married woman without receiving a signed statement from the woman that she has notified her spouse that she is about to undergo an abortion. The woman has the option of providing an alternative signed statement certifying that her husband is not the man who impregnated her; that her husband could not be located; that the pregnancy is the result of spousal sexual assault which she has reported; or that the woman believes that notifying her husband will cause him or someone else to inflict bodily injury upon her. A physician who performs an abortion on a married woman without receiving the appropriate signed statement will have his or her license revoked, and is liable to the husband for damages.

In well-functioning marriages, spouses discuss important intimate decisions such as whether to bear a child. But there are millions of women in this country who are the victims of regular physical and psychological abuse at the hands of their husbands. Should these women become pregnant, they are not exempt from the notification requirement. Many may fear devastating forms of psychological abuse from their husbands, including verbal harassment, threats of future violence, the destruction of possessions, physical confinement to the home, the withdrawal of financial support, or the disclosure of the abortion to family and friends. These methods of psychological abuse may act as even more of a deterrent to notification than the possibility of physical violence, but women who are the victims of the abuse are not exempt from the notification requirement. And many women who are pregnant as a result of sexual assaults by their husbands will be unable to avail themselves of the exception for spousal sexual assault, because the exception requires that the woman have notified law enforcement authorities within 90 days of the assault, and her husband will be notified of her report once an investigation begins. The spousal notification requirement is thus likely to prevent a significant number of women from obtaining an abortion. It is an undue burden, and therefore invalid. Whether the prospect of notification itself deters such women from seeking abortions, or whether the husband, through physical force or psychological pressure or economic coercion, prevents his wife from obtaining an abortion until it is too late, the notice requirement will often be tantamount to the veto found unconstitutional in *Danforth.*

D

We next consider the parental consent provision. Except in a medical emergency, an unemancipated young woman under 18 may not obtain an abortion unless she and one of her parents (or guardian) provides informed consent as defined above. If neither a parent nor a guardian provides consent, a court may authorize the performance of an abortion upon a determination that the young woman is mature and capable of giving informed consent and has in fact given her informed consent, or that an abortion would be in her best interests. Our cases establish, and we reaffirm today, that a State may require a minor seeking an abortion to obtain the consent of a parent or guardian, provided that there is an adequate judicial bypass procedure.

E

Under the recordkeeping and reporting requirements of the statute, every facility which performs abortions is required to file a report stating its name and address as well as the name and address of any related entity, such as a controlling or subsidiary organization. In the case of state-funded institutions, the information becomes public.

For each abortion performed, a report must be filed identifying: the physician (and the second physician where required); the facility; the referring physician or agency; the woman's age; the number of prior pregnancies and prior abortions she has had; gestational age; the type of abortion procedure; the date of the abortion; whether there were any pre-existing medical conditions which would complicate pregnancy; medical complications with the abortion; where applicable, the basis for the determination that the abortion was medically necessary; the weight of the aborted fetus; and whether the woman was married, and if so, whether notice was provided or the basis for the failure to give notice. Every abortion facility must also file quarterly reports showing the number of abortions performed broken down by trimester. In all events, the identity of each woman who has had an abortion remains confidential.

We have held that record keeping and reporting provisions "that are reasonably directed to the preservation of maternal health and that properly respect a patient's confidentiality and privacy are permissible." All the provisions at issue here, except that relating to spousal notice, are constitutional. The collection of information with respect to actual patients is a vital element of medical research. Nor do we find that the requirements impose a substantial obstacle to a woman's choice. At most they might increase the cost of some abortions by a slight amount. There is no showing that the increased cost has become a substantial obstacle.

VI

Our Constitution is a covenant running from the first generation of Americans to us and then to future generations. We accept our responsibility not to retreat from interpreting the full meaning of the covenant in light of all of our precedents. We invoke it once again to define the freedom guaranteed by the Constitution's own promise, the promise of liberty.

Affirmed in part and reversed in part.

Justice STEVENS, *concurring in part* and *dissenting in part.*

Roe has been a "part of our law" for almost two decades. The societal costs of overruling *Roe* at this late date would be enormous. *Roe* is an integral part of a correct understanding of both the concept of liberty and the basic equality of men and women.

The statute includes sections requiring a physician or counselor to provide the woman with a range of materials clearly designed to persuade her to choose not to undergo the abortion. While the Commonwealth is free to produce and disseminate such material, the Commonwealth may not inject such information into the woman's deliberations just as she is weighing such an important choice.

Provisions which require the physician to inform a woman of the nature and risks of the abortion procedure and the medical risks of carrying to term, are neutral requirements comparable to those imposed in other medical procedures. Those sections indicate no effort by the Commonwealth to influence the woman's choice in any way. If anything, such requirements enhance, rather than skew, the woman's decision-making.

The 24-hour waiting period raises serious concerns. Such a requirement arguably furthers the Commonwealth's interests in two ways, neither of which is constitutionally permissible. First, it may be argued that the 24-hour delay is likely to reduce the number of abortions, thus furthering the Commonwealth's interest in potential life. The Commonwealth cannot further its interests by simply wearing down the ability of the pregnant woman to exercise her constitutional right. Second, the 24-hour delay furthers the Commonwealth's interest in ensuring that the woman's decision is informed and thoughtful. But there is no evidence that the mandated delay benefits women or that it is necessary to enable the physician to convey any relevant information to the patient. The mandatory delay thus appears to rest on outmoded and unacceptable assumptions about the decision-making capacity of women.

The delay requirement may be premised on the belief that the decision to terminate a pregnancy is presumptively wrong. A woman who has, in the privacy of her thoughts and conscience, weighed the options and made her decision cannot be forced to reconsider all, simply because the State believes she has come to the wrong conclusion. A woman who decides to terminate her pregnancy is entitled to the same respect as a woman who decides to carry the fetus to term. The mandatory waiting period denies women that equal respect.

A correct application of the "undue burden" standard leads to the same conclusion concerning the constitutionality of these requirements. The 24-hour delay requirement fails both parts of this test. The 24-hour delay requirement imposes a severe burden on many pregnant women and there is no evidence that such a delay serves a useful and legitimate purpose. The counseling provisions are similarly infirm. Whenever government commands private citizens to speak or to listen, careful review of the justification for that command is particularly appropriate. In these cases, the Pennsylvania statute directs that counselors provide women seeking abortions with information concerning alternatives to abortion, the availability of medical assistance benefits, and the possibility of child-support payments. I conclude that the information requirements do not serve a useful purpose and thus constitute an unnecessary—and therefore undue—burden on the woman's constitutional liberty to decide to terminate her pregnancy.

Justice BLACKMUN, *concurring in part, concurring in the judgment in part,* and *dissenting in part.*

I join Parts I, II, III, V-A, V-C, and VI of the joint opinion of Justices O'CONNOR, KENNEDY, and SOUTER.

Three years ago, in *Webster,* four Members of this Court appeared poised to "cast into darkness the hopes and visions of every woman in this country" who had come to believe that the Constitution guaranteed her the right to reproductive choice. But now, just when so many expected the darkness to fall, the flame has grown bright. I remain steadfast in my belief that the right to reproductive choice is entitled to the full protection afforded by this Court before *Webster.* And I fear for the darkness as four Justices anxiously await the single vote necessary to extinguish the light.

The Constitution and decisions of this Court require that a State's abortion restrictions be subjected to the strictest judicial scrutiny. Under this standard, the Pennsylvania statute's provisions requiring content-based counseling, a 24-hour delay, informed parental consent, and reporting of abortion-related information must be invalidated. While a State has "legitimate interests from the outset of the pregnancy in protecting the health of the woman and the life of the fetus that may become a child," legitimate interests are not enough. The interests must be compelling. *Roe's* requirement of strict scrutiny as implemented through a trimester framework should not be disturbed.

The 24-hour waiting period could lead to delays in excess of 24 hours, thus increasing health risks and would require two visits to the abortion provider, thereby increasing travel time, exposure to further harassment, and financial cost. The mandatory delay rests either on outmoded or unacceptable assumptions about the decision-making capacity of women or the belief that the decision to terminate the pregnancy is presumptively wrong.

While the State has an interest in encouraging parental involvement in the minor's abortion decision, the state law is not narrowly drawn to serve that interest.

The Pennsylvania statute requires every facility performing abortions to report its activities to the Commonwealth including the identities and medical judgment of physicians involved in abortions. Many physicians, particularly those who have previously discontinued performing abortions because of harassment, would refuse to refer patients to abortion clinics if their names were to appear on these reports. The confidential reporting requirements are unconstitutional insofar as they require the name of the referring physician.

The Chief Justice's criticism of *Roe* follows from his stunted conception of individual liberty. In the Chief Justice's world, a woman considering whether to terminate a pregnancy is entitled to no more protection than adulterers, murderers, and so-called sexual deviates. Given The Chief Justice's exclusive reliance on tradition, people using contraceptives seem the next likely candidate for his list of outcasts.

Even more shocking than The Chief Justice's cramped notion of individual liberty is his complete omission of any discussion of the effects that compelled childbirth and motherhood have on women's lives. The Chief Justice's view of the State's compelling interest in maternal health has less to do with health than it does with compelling women to be maternal.

The Chief Justice's narrow conception of individual liberty and *stare decisis* leads him to propose the same standard of review proposed by the plurality in *Webster*. "States may regulate abortion procedures in ways rationally related to a legitimate state interest." The Chief Justice then further weakens the test by providing an insurmountable requirement for facial challenges: Petitioners must "show that no set of circumstances exists under which the provision would be valid." We are reassured there is always the protection of the democratic process. While there is much to be praised about our democracy, our country since its founding has recognized that there are certain fundamental liberties that are not to be left to the whims of an election. A woman's right to reproductive choice is one of those fundamental liberties. That liberty need not seek refuge at the ballot box.

I am 83 years old. I cannot remain on this Court forever, and when I do step down, the confirmation process for my successor well may focus on the issue before us today. That, I regret, may be exactly where the choice between the two worlds will be made.

Chief Justice REHNQUIST, with whom Justice WHITE, Justice SCALIA, and Justice THOMAS join, *concurring in the judgment in part* and *dissenting in part*.

We believe that *Roe* was wrongly decided, and that it can and should be overruled. Although they reject the trimester framework that formed the underpinning of *Roe,* the joint opinion adopts a revised undue burden standard to analyze the challenged regulations. Such an outcome is an unjustified constitutional compromise.

Unlike marriage, procreation, and contraception, abortion "involves the purposeful termination of a potential life." The abortion decision must therefore "be recognized as *sui generis,* different in kind from the others that the Court has protected under the rubric of personal or family privacy and autonomy." The decision to abort necessarily involves the destruction of a fetus.

Nor do the historical traditions of the American people support the view that the right to terminate one's pregnancy is "fundamental." The common law which we inherited from England made abortion after "quickening" an offense. At the time of the adoption of the Fourteenth Amendment, statutory prohibitions or restrictions on abortion were commonplace; in 1868, at least 28 of the then-37 States and 8 Territories had statutes banning or limiting abortion. By the turn of the century virtually every State had a law prohibiting or restricting abortion on its books. By the middle of the present century, a liberalization trend had set in. But 21 of the restrictive abortion laws in effect in 1868 were still in effect in 1973 when *Roe* was decided, and an overwhelming majority of the States prohibited abortion unless necessary to preserve the life or health of the mother. On this record, it can scarcely be said that any deeply rooted tradition of relatively unrestricted abortion in our history supported the classification of the right to abortion as "fundamental" under the Due Process Clause of the Fourteenth Amendment.

Both in view of this history and of our decided cases dealing with substantive liberty under the Due Process Clause, the Court was mistaken in *Roe* when it classified a woman's decision to terminate her pregnancy as a "fundamental right" that could be abridged only in a manner which withstood "strict scrutiny." The Court in *Roe* reached too far when it analogized the right to abort a fetus to the rights involved in *Pierce, Meyer, Loving,* and *Griswold,* and thereby deemed the right to abortion fundamental.

Instead of claiming that *Roe* was correct as a matter of original constitutional interpretation, the joint opinion contains an elaborate discussion of *stare decisis*. *Roe* decided that a woman had a fundamental right to an abortion. The joint opinion rejects that view. *Roe* decided that abortion regulations were to be subjected to "strict scrutiny" and could be justified only in the light of "compelling state interests." The joint opinion rejects that view. *Roe* analyzed abortion regulation under a rigid trimester framework, a framework which has guided this Court's decisionmaking for 19 years. The joint opinion rejects that framework. While purporting to adhere to precedent, the joint opinion instead revises it. *Roe* continues to exist, but only in the way a storefront on a western movie set exists: a mere facade to give the illusion of reality.

Authentic principles of *stare decisis* do not require that any portion of the reasoning in *Roe* be kept intact. It is our duty to reconsider constitutional interpretations that "depart from a proper understanding" of the Constitution. The correct analysis is that set forth by the plurality opinion in *Webster*. A woman's interest in having an abortion is a form of liberty protected by the Due Process Clause, but States may regulate abortion procedures in ways rationally related to a legitimate state interest. Each provision of the state law was found to be rationally related to a legitimate state interest.

Justice SCALIA, with whom THE CHIEF JUSTICE, Justice WHITE, and Justice THOMAS join, *concurring in the judgment in part* and *dissenting in part*.

My views on this matter are unchanged from those I set forth in *Webster*. The permissibility of abortion, and the limitations upon it, are to be resolved like most important questions in our democracy: by citizens trying to persuade one another and then voting. A State's choice between two positions on which reasonable people can disagree is constitutional even when it intrudes upon a "liberty" in the absolute sense. The issue is not whether it is a liberty of great importance to many women. The issue is whether it is a liberty protected by the Constitution of the United States. I am sure it is not.

The ultimately standardless nature of the "undue burden" inquiry is a reflection of the underlying fact that the concept has no principled or coherent legal basis.

Roe's mandate for abortion on demand destroyed the compromises of the past, rendered compromise impossible for the future, and required the entire issue to be resolved uniformly, at the national level. *Roe* fanned into life an issue that has inflamed our national politics in general, and has obscured with its smoke the selection of Justices to this Court in particular, ever since. And by keeping us in the abortion-umpiring business, it is the perpetuation of that disruption, rather than of any *Pax Roeana,* that the Court's new majority decrees.

It is particularly difficult to sit still for the Court's lengthy lecture upon the virtues of "constancy," of "remaining steadfast," and adhering to "principle." Among the five Justices who purportedly adhere to *Roe,* at most three agree upon the principle that constitutes adherence (the joint opinion's "undue burden" standard)—and that principle is inconsistent with *Roe.* To make matters worse, two of the three, in order thus to remain steadfast, had to abandon previously stated positions. It is beyond me how the Court expects these accommodations to be accepted "as grounded truly in principle, not as compromises with social and political pressures having, as such, no bearing on the principled choices that the Court is obliged to make." The only principle the Court "adheres" to, it seems to me, is the principle that the Court must be seen as standing by *Roe.* That is not a principle of law (which is what I thought the Court was talking about), but a principle of Realpolitik—and a wrong one at that.

Whether it would "subvert the Court's legitimacy" or not, the notion that we would decide a case differently from the way we otherwise would have in order to show that we can stand firm against public disapproval is frightening. It is a bad enough idea, even in the head of someone like me, who believes that the text of the Constitution, and our traditions, say what they say and there is no fiddling with them. But when it is in the mind of a Court that believes the Constitution has an evolving meaning, that the Ninth Amendment's reference to "other" rights is not a disclaimer, but a charter for action, and that the function of this Court is to "speak before all others for the people's constitutional ideals" unrestrained by meaningful text or tradition—then the notion that the Court must adhere to a decision for as long as the decision faces "great opposition" and the Court is "under fire" acquires a character of almost czarist arrogance. We are offended by these marchers who descend upon us, every year on the anniversary of *Roe,* to protest our saying that the Constitution requires what our society has never thought the Constitution requires. These people who refuse to be "tested by following" must be taught a lesson. We have no Cossacks, but at least we can stubbornly refuse to abandon an erroneous opinion that we might otherwise change—to show how little they intimidate us.

I am as distressed as the Court is about the "political pressure" directed to the Court: the marches, the mail, the protests aimed at inducing us to change our opinions. How upsetting it is, that so many of our citizens (good people, not lawless ones, on both sides of this abortion issue, and on various sides of other issues as well) think that we Justices should properly take into account their views, as though we were engaged not in ascertaining an objective law but in determining some kind of social consensus. The Court would profit, I think, from giving less attention to the fact of this distressing phenomenon, and more attention to the cause of it. That cause permeates today's opinion: a new mode of constitutional adjudication that relies not upon text and traditional practice to determine the law, but upon what the Court calls "reasoned judgment," which turns out to be nothing but philosophical predilection and moral intuition. All manner of "liberties," the Court tells us, inhere in the Constitution and are enforceable by this Court—not just those mentioned in the text or established in the traditions of our society. Why even the Ninth Amendment—which says only that "the enumeration in the Constitution, of certain rights, shall not be construed to deny or disparage others retained by the people"—is, despite our contrary understanding for almost 200 years, a literally boundless source of additional, unnamed, unhinted-at "rights," definable and enforceable by us, through "reasoned judgment."

As long as this Court thought (and the people thought) that we Justices were doing essentially lawyers' work up here—reading text and discerning our society's traditional understanding of that text—the public pretty much left us alone. Texts and traditions are facts to study, not convictions to demonstrate about. But if our pronouncement of constitutional law rests primarily on value judgments, then a free and intelligent people's attitude towards us can be expected to be (ought to be) quite different. The people know that their value judgments are quite as good as those taught in any law school—maybe better. If, indeed, the "liberties" protected by the Constitution are, as the Court says, undefined and unbounded, then the people should demonstrate, to protest that we do not implement their values instead of ours. Not only that, but confirmation hearings for new Justices should deteriorate into question-and-answer sessions in which Senators go through a list of their constituents' most favored and most disfavored alleged constitutional rights, and seek the nominee's commitment to support or oppose them. Value judgments, after all, should be voted on, not dictated; and if our Constitution has somehow accidently committed them to the Supreme Court, at least we can have a sort of plebiscite each time a new nominee to that body is put forward. Justice Blackmun not only regards this prospect with equanimity, he solicits it.

By foreclosing all democratic outlet for the deep passions this issue arouses, by banishing the issue from the political forum that gives all participants, even the losers, the satisfaction of a fair hearing and an honest fight, by continuing the imposition of a rigid national rule instead of allowing for regional differences, the Court merely prolongs and intensifies the anguish. We should get out of this area, where we have no right to be, and where we do neither ourselves nor the country any good by remaining.

Note: Undue Burdens

Although propounded by three justices in *Casey*, the undue burden test has gained traction with a majority of the Court. In *Mazurek v. Armstrong*, 520 U.S. 968 (1997), the Court reviewed a state law limiting the performance of abortions to licensed physicians. The law was upheld on grounds that it did not impose a substantial obstacle to obtaining an abortion. Criticism of the undue burden standard focuses largely on its ad hoc nature, which critics believe reduces it to an exercise in value selection and judgment. From their perspective, the undue burden test replicates the evils of *Lochnerism* and correlates outputs to the unpredictable perspectives of individual justices. Although differences were evident with respect to what constituted an undue burden, a majority of the Court in *Stenberg v. Carhart* determined that a state law prohibiting partial birth abortions created substantial obstacles to a woman's freedom to obtain an abortion.

∾ PROBLEM: THE ABORTION FORM ∾

Congress passed a law, 21 U.S.C. §1802, that states: "(A) all individuals obtaining an abortion must sign a form indicating they 1) recognize the importance of such a decision and 2) are having the abortion only because it is reasonably necessary and beyond mere convenience." Is this law constitutional?

Stenberg v. Carhart

530 U.S. 914 (2000)

Justice BREYER delivered the opinion of the Court.

We again consider the right to an abortion. We understand the controversial nature of the problem. Millions of Americans believe that life begins at conception and consequently that an abortion is akin to causing the death of an innocent child; they recoil at the thought of a law that would permit it. Other millions fear that a law that forbids abortion would condemn many American women to lives that lack dignity, depriving them of equal liberty and leading those with least resources to undergo illegal abortions with the attendant risks of death and suffering. Taking account of these virtually irreconcilable points of view, aware that constitutional law must govern a society whose different members sincerely hold directly opposing views, and considering the matter in light of the Constitution's guarantees of fundamental individual liberty, this Court, in the course of a generation, has determined and then redetermined that the Constitution offers basic protection to the woman's right to choose. We shall not revisit those legal principles. Rather, we apply them to the circumstances of this case.

Three established principles determine the issue before us. First, before "viability the woman has a right to choose to terminate her pregnancy." Second, "a law designed to further the State's interest in fetal life which imposes an undue burden on the woman's decision before fetal viability" is unconstitutional. An "undue burden is shorthand for the conclusion that a state regulation has the purpose or effect of placing a substantial obstacle in the path of a woman seeking an abortion of a nonviable fetus." Third, "subsequent to viability, the State in promoting its interest in the potentiality of human life may, if it chooses, regulate, and even proscribe, abortion except where it is necessary, in appropriate medical judgment, for the preservation of the life or health of the mother."

We apply these principles to a Nebraska law banning "partial birth abortion." The statute reads as follows:

> No partial birth abortion shall be performed in this state, unless such procedure is necessary to save the life of the mother whose life is endangered by a physical disorder, physical illness, or physical injury, including a life-endangering physical condition caused by or arising from the pregnancy itself.

The statute defines "partial birth abortion" as "an abortion procedure in which the person performing the abortion partially delivers vaginally a living unborn child before killing the unborn child and completing the delivery."

The Nebraska statute, making criminal the performance of a "partial birth abortion," violates the Federal Constitution for at least two independent reasons. First, the law lacks any exception "for the preservation of the health of the mother." Second, it "imposes an undue burden on a woman's ability" to choose a D&E abortion, thereby unduly burdening the right to choose abortion itself.

The *Casey* joint opinion reiterated what the Court held in *Roe;* that "subsequent to viability, the State in promoting its interest in the potentiality of human life may, if it chooses, regulate, and even proscribe, abortion except where it is necessary, in appropriate medical judgment, for the preservation of the life or health of the mother."

The fact that Nebraska's law applies both pre- and postviability aggravates the constitutional problem presented. The State's interest in regulating abortion previability is considerably weaker than postviability. Since the law requires a health exception in order to validate even a postviability abortion regulation, it at a minimum requires the same in respect to previability regulation.

The quoted standard also depends on the state regulations "promoting the State's interest in the potentiality of human life." The Nebraska law, of course, does not directly further an interest "in the potentiality of human life" by saving the fetus in question from destruction, as it regulates only a method of performing abortion. Nebraska describes its interests differently. It says the law "shows concern for the life of the unborn," "prevents cruelty to partially born children," and "preserves the integrity of the medical profession." But we cannot see how the interest-related differences could make any difference to the question at hand, namely, the application of the "health" requirement.

Consequently, the governing standard requires an exception "where it is necessary, in appropriate medical judgment for the preservation of the life or health of the mother," for this Court has made clear that a State may promote but not endanger a woman's health when it regulates the methods of abortion.

Justice Thomas says that the cases just cited limit this principle to situations where the pregnancy itself creates a threat to health. He is wrong. The cited cases, reaffirmed in *Casey,* recognize that a State cannot subject women's health to significant risks both in that context, and also where state regulations force women to use riskier methods of abortion. Our cases have repeatedly invalidated statutes that in the process of regulating the methods of abortion, imposed significant health risks. They make clear that a risk to a women's health is the same whether it happens to arise from regulating a particular method of abortion, or from barring abortion entirely. Our holding does not go beyond those cases, as ratified in *Casey.*

Our earlier discussion of the D&E procedure shows that it falls within the statutory prohibition. The statute forbids "deliberately and intentionally delivering into the vagina a living unborn child, or a substantial portion thereof, for the purpose of performing a procedure that the person performing such procedure knows will kill the unborn child." We do not understand how one could distinguish, using this language, between D&E (where a foot or arm is drawn through the cervix) and D&X (where the body up to the head is drawn through the cervix). Evidence before the trial court makes clear that D&E will often involve a physician pulling a "substantial portion" of a still living fetus, say, an arm or leg, into the vagina prior to the death of the fetus. Indeed D&E involves dismemberment that commonly occurs only when the fetus meets resistance that restricts the motion of the fetus: "The dismemberment occurs between the traction of the instrument and the counter-traction of the internal os of the cervix." And these events often do not occur until after a portion of a living fetus has been pulled into the vagina.

Even if the statute's basic aim is to ban D&X, its language makes clear that it also covers a much broader category of procedures. The language does not track the medical differences between D&E and D&X — though it would have been a simple matter, for example, to provide an exception for the performance of D&E and other abortion procedures. Nor does the statute anywhere suggest that its application turns on whether a portion of the fetus' body is drawn into the vagina as part of a process to extract an intact fetus after collapsing the head as opposed to a process that would dismember the fetus. Thus, the dissenters' argument that the law was generally intended to bar D&X can be both correct and irrelevant. The relevant question is not whether the legislature wanted to ban D&X; it is whether the law was intended to apply only to D&X. The plain language covers both procedures.

The Nebraska State Attorney General argues that the statute does differentiate between the two procedures. He says that the statutory words "substantial portion" mean "the child up to the head." He consequently denies the statute's application where the physician introduces into the birth canal a fetal arm or leg or anything less than the entire fetal body. Our precedent warns against accepting as "authoritative" an Attorney General's interpretation of state law when "the

Attorney General does not bind the state courts or local law enforcement authorities." Some present prosecutors and future Attorneys General may choose to pursue physicians who use D&E procedures, the most commonly used method for performing previability second trimester abortions. All those who perform abortion procedures using that method must fear prosecution, conviction, and imprisonment. The result is an undue burden upon a woman's right to make an abortion decision. We must consequently find the statute unconstitutional.

Justice STEVENS, with whom Justice GINSBURG joins, *concurring*.

Although much ink is spilled today describing the gruesome nature of late-term abortion procedures, that rhetoric does not provide me a reason to believe that the procedure Nebraska here claims it seeks to ban is more brutal, more gruesome, or less respectful of "potential life" than the equally gruesome procedure Nebraska claims it still allows. The notion that either of these two equally gruesome procedures performed at this late stage of gestation is more akin to infanticide than the other, or that the State furthers any legitimate interest by banning one but not the other, is simply irrational.

Justice O'CONNOR, *concurring*.

I agree that Nebraska's statute cannot be reconciled with our decision in *Casey*, and is therefore unconstitutional. The Nebraska statute lacks an exception for those instances when the banned procedure is necessary to preserve the health of the mother and imposes an undue burden on a woman's right to choose to terminate her pregnancy before viability. Nebraska's ban also covers the dilation and evacuation (D&E) procedure. A ban on partial-birth abortion that only proscribed the D&X method of abortion and that included an exception to preserve the life and health of the mother would be constitutional in my view.

Justice GINSBURG, with whom Justice STEVENS joins, *concurring*.

A state regulation that "has the purpose or effect of placing a substantial obstacle in the path of a woman seeking an abortion of a nonviable fetus" violates the Constitution. Such an obstacle exists if the State stops a woman from choosing the procedure her doctor "reasonably believes will best protect the woman in the exercise of her constitutional liberty."

Chief Justice REHNQUIST, *dissenting*.

I did not join the joint opinion in *Casey* and continue to believe that case is wrongly decided. Despite my disagreement with the opinion, I believe Justice Kennedy and Justice Thomas have correctly applied *Casey*'s principles and join their dissenting opinions.

Justice SCALIA, *dissenting*.

I am optimistic enough to believe that, one day, *Stenberg v. Carhart* will be assigned its rightful place in the history of this Court's jurisprudence beside

Korematsu and *Dred Scott.* The method of killing a human child — one cannot even accurately say an entirely unborn human child — proscribed by this statute is so horrible that the most clinical description of it evokes a shudder of revulsion. And the Court must know (as most state legislatures banning this procedure have concluded) that demanding a "health exception" — which requires the abortionist to assure himself that, in his expert medical judgment, this method is, in the case at hand, marginally safer than others (how can one prove the contrary beyond a reasonable doubt?) — is to give live-birth abortion free rein. The notion that the Constitution of the United States, designed, among other things, "to establish Justice, insure domestic Tranquility, and secure the Blessings of Liberty to ourselves and our Posterity," prohibits the States from simply banning this visibly brutal means of eliminating our half-born posterity is quite simply absurd.

The Court invalidates this humane law because it fails to allow an exception for the situation in which the abortionist believes that this live-birth method of destroying the child might be safer for the woman. Today's decision is an "unprecedented expansion" of our prior cases, "is not mandated" by *Casey*'s "undue burden" test, and can even be called (though this pushes me to the limit of my belief) "obviously irreconcilable with *Casey*'s explication of what its undue-burden standard requires." But I never put much stock in *Casey*'s explication of the inexplicable. In the last analysis, my judgment that *Casey* does not support today's tragic result can be traced to the fact that what I consider to be an "undue burden" is different from what the majority considers to be an "undue burden" — a conclusion that can not be demonstrated true or false by factual inquiry or legal reasoning. It is a value judgment, dependent upon how much one respects (or believes society ought to respect) the life of a partially delivered fetus, and how much one respects (or believes society ought to respect) the freedom of the woman who gave it life to kill it. Evidently, the five Justices in today's majority value the former less, or the latter more, (or both), than the four of us in dissent. Case closed. There is no cause for anyone who believes in *Casey* to feel betrayed by this outcome. It has been arrived at by precisely the process *Casey* promised — a democratic vote by nine lawyers, not on the question whether the text of the Constitution has anything to say about this subject (it obviously does not); nor even on the question (also appropriate for lawyers) whether the legal traditions of the American people would have sustained such a limitation upon abortion (they obviously would); but upon the pure policy question whether this limitation upon abortion is "undue" — i.e., goes too far.

The "undue burden" test created a standard that was "as doubtful in application as it is unprincipled in origin," "hopelessly unworkable in practice," and "ultimately standardless." Today's decision is the proof. It is really quite impossible for us dissenters to contend that the majority is wrong on the law. The most that we can honestly say is that we disagree with the majority on their policy-judgment-couched-as-law. And those who believe that a 5-to-4 vote on a policy matter by unelected lawyers should not overcome the judgment of 30 state legislatures have a problem, not with the application of *Casey*, but with its existence. *Casey* must be overruled.

Today's decision, that the Constitution of the United States prevents the prohibition of a horrible mode of abortion, will be greeted by a firestorm of criticism—as well it should. I cannot understand why those who acknowledge that, in the opening words of Justice O'Connor's concurrence, "the issue of abortion is one of the most contentious and controversial in contemporary American society," persist in the belief that this Court, armed with neither constitutional text nor accepted tradition, can resolve that contention and controversy rather than be consumed by it. If only for the sake of its own preservation, the Court should return this matter to the people—where the Constitution, by its silence on the subject, left it—and let them decide, State by State, whether this practice should be allowed. *Casey* must be overruled.

Justice KENNEDY, with whom THE CHIEF JUSTICE joins, *dissenting.*

When the Court reaffirmed the essential holding of *Roe*, a central premise was that the States retain a critical and legitimate role in legislating on the subject of abortion, as limited by the woman's right the Court restated and again guaranteed. The political processes of the State are not to be foreclosed from enacting laws to promote the life of the unborn and to ensure respect for all human life and its potential. The State's constitutional authority is a vital means for citizens to address these grave and serious issues, as they must if we are to progress in knowledge and understanding and in the attainment of some degree of consensus.

The Court's decision today, in my submission, repudiates this understanding by invalidating a statute advancing critical state interests, even though the law denies no woman the right to choose an abortion and places no undue burden upon the right. The legislation is well within the State's competence to enact. States may take sides in the abortion debate and come down on the side of life, even life in the unborn. States also have an interest in forbidding medical procedures which, in the State's reasonable determination, might cause the medical profession or society as a whole to become insensitive, even disdainful, to life, including life in the human fetus. A State may take measures to ensure the medical profession and its members are viewed as healers, sustained by a compassionate and rigorous ethic and cognizant of the dignity and value of human life, even life which cannot survive without the assistance of others.

Some argue that the D&E method, which Nebraska claims to be beyond its intent to regulate, can still be used to abort a fetus and is no less dehumanizing than the D&X method. The issue is not whether members of the judiciary can see a difference between the two procedures. It is whether Nebraska can. The Court's refusal to recognize Nebraska's right to declare a moral difference between the procedure is a dispiriting disclosure of the illogic and illegitimacy of the Court's approach to the entire case.

Nebraska was entitled to find the existence of a consequential moral difference between the procedures. The Court is without authority to second-guess this conclusion. It ill-serves the Court, its institutional position, and the constitutional sources it seeks to invoke to refuse to issue a forthright affirmation of Nebraska's right to declare that critical moral differences exist between the two procedures.

Demonstrating a further and basic misunderstanding of *Casey*, the Court holds the ban on the D&X procedure fails because it does not include an exception permitting an abortionist to perform a D&X whenever he believes it will best preserve the health of the woman. Casting aside the views of distinguished physicians and the statements of leading medical organizations, the Court awards each physician a veto power over the State's judgment that the procedures should not be performed. No studies support the contention that the D&X abortion method is safer than other abortion methods. *Casey* recognized that the physician's ability to practice medicine was "subject to reasonable regulation by the State" and would receive the "same solicitude it receives in other contexts." In other contexts, the State is entitled to make judgments where high medical authority is in disagreement.

Ignoring substantial medical and ethical opinion, the Court substitutes its own judgment for the judgment of Nebraska and some 30 other States and sweeps the law away. The decision nullifies a law expressing the will of the people of Nebraska that medical procedures must be governed by moral principles having their foundation in the intrinsic value of human life, including life of the unborn.

From the decision, the reasoning, and the judgment, I dissent.

Justice THOMAS, with whom THE CHIEF JUSTICE and Justice SCALIA join, *dissenting*.

The *Roe* decision was grievously wrong. Nothing in our Federal Constitution deprives the people of this country of the right to determine whether the consequences of abortion to the fetus and to society outweigh the burden of an unwanted pregnancy on the mother. Although a State may permit abortion, nothing in the Constitution dictates that a State must do so.

So long as state regulation of abortion furthers legitimate interests—that is, interests not designed to strike at the right itself—the regulation is invalid only if it imposes an undue burden on a woman's ability to obtain an abortion, meaning that it places a substantial obstacle in the woman's path. Today's decision is so obviously irreconcilable with *Casey*'s explication of what its undue-burden standard requires, let alone the Constitution, that it should be seen for what it is, a reinstitution of the pre-*Webster* abortion-on-demand era in which the mere invocation of "abortion rights" trumps any contrary societal interest.

From reading the majority's sanitized description, one would think that this case involves state regulation of a widely accepted routine medical procedure. Nothing could be further from the truth. The most widely used method of abortion during this stage of pregnancy is so gruesome that its use can be traumatic even for the physicians and medical staff who perform it. The particular procedure at issue in this case, "partial birth abortion," so closely borders on infanticide that 30 States have attempted to ban it.

Nebraska, along with 29 other States, has attempted to ban the partial birth abortion procedure. Although the Nebraska statute purports to prohibit only "partial birth abortion," a phrase which is commonly used to refer to the breech extraction version of intact D&E, the majority concludes that this statute could also be read in some future case to prohibit ordinary D&E. According to the majority, such an application would pose a substantial obstacle to some women seeking abortions and, therefore, the statute is unconstitutional. The majority errs with its very first step. The Nebraska statute does not prohibit the D&E procedure. The Nebraska statute, by its own terms, applies only to "partial birth abortion."

There is no question that the State of Nebraska has a valid interest—one not designed to strike at the right itself—in prohibiting partial birth abortion. *Casey* itself noted that States may "express profound respect for the life of the unborn." States may, without a doubt, express this profound respect by prohibiting a procedure that approaches infanticide, and thereby dehumanizes the fetus and trivializes human life. The "partial birth" gives the fetus an autonomy which separates it from the right of the woman to choose treatments for her own body. Thirty States have concurred with this view.

We were reassured repeatedly in *Casey* that not all regulations of abortion are unwarranted and that the States may express profound respect for fetal life. Under *Casey*, the regulation before us today should easily pass constitutional muster. But the Court's abortion jurisprudence is a particularly virulent strain of constitutional exegesis. And so today we are told that 30 States are prohibited from banning one rarely used form of abortion that they believe to border on infanticide. It is clear that the Constitution does not compel this result.

Note: New Abortion Laws

Requiring Admitting Privileges. In *June Medical Services L.L.C. v. Russo*, 140 S. Ct. 2103 (2020), a plurality of the Court reaffirmed *Whole Woman's Health* in striking down a Louisiana statute that also required abortion providers to hold "active admitting privileges at a hospital that is located not further than thirty miles from the location at which the abortion is performed or induced and that provides obstetrical or gynecological health care services." La. Rev. Stat. Ann. §40:1061.10(A)(2)(a). The statute defined "active admitting privileges" to mean that the doctor must be "a member in good standing" of the hospital's "medical staff . . . with the ability to admit a patient and to provide diagnostic and surgical services to such patient." Failure to comply could lead to fines of up to $4,000 per violation, license revocation, and civil liability.

Humane and Dignified Disposal. In *Box v. Planned Parenthood of Indiana and Kentucky, Inc.*, 139 S. Ct. 1780 (2019), the Court upheld an Indiana law that excluded fetal remains from the definition of "infectious and pathological waste," thereby preventing incineration of fetal remains as surgical byproducts, and requiring "humane and dignified disposal." Since there was no claim that the law implicated a fundamental right, the Court applied a rational basis standard, and concluded that Indiana had a "legitimate interest in the proper disposal of fetal remains."

However, a number of other cases, raising a variety of issues, are percolating through the lower federal courts, including the following:

1. *Abortions During the Pandemic.* In response to the Covid-19 pandemic, Alabama issued an order postponing "all dental, medical, or surgical procedures," with two exceptions: (a) those "necessary to treat an emergency medical condition" and (b) those "necessary to avoid serious harm from an underlying condition or disease, or necessary as part of a patient's ongoing and active treatment." The goal was to promote social distancing and preserve medical supplies during the pandemic. Alabama officials indicated that abortions are exempt from the order only when necessary to preserve the life and health of the mother. While the court rejected the idea that women had an unqualified right to have an abortion during the pandemic, the court did indicate that medical providers should consider a variety of factors in deciding whether to go forward with an abortion (e.g., whether a woman might lose her right to have an abortion if a procedure is delayed). *See Robinson v. Marshall,* __ F.Supp.3d ___ 2020 WL 1847128 (M.D. Ala. 2020); *see also South Wind Women's Center, LLC v. Stitt,* __ F.Supp.3d ___ 2020 WL 1932900 (10th Cir. 2020).

2. *Ultrasound and Informed Consent.* In *EMW Women's Surgical Center, P.S.C. v. Beshear,* 920 F. 3d 421 (6th Cir.), *cert. denied sub nom., EMW Women's Surgical Center, P.S.C. v. Meier,* 140 S. Ct. 655 (2019), the court upheld a Kentucky law that requires physicians to perform ultrasound examinations before performing an abortion. The physician is required to make any heart sounds audible, place the images where the woman can see them, and describe the images to the patient. The court held that the process did not involve a compelled disclosure and only incidentally burdens speech. Likewise, in *Box v. Planned Parenthood of Indiana and Kentucky, Inc., 139 S. Ct. 1780 (2019),* the Court overturned a lower ruling enjoining an Indiana law that required an ultrasound at least 18 hours before an abortion.

3. *Dismemberment Abortions.* Indiana sought to prohibit D & E (dilation and extraction) abortions of "living fetuses." Opponents refer to D & E as "dismemberment abortions" because pieces of the fetus are extracted one piece at a time. In striking down the law, the court concluded that it imposed an "undue burden" on a woman's right to have an abortion because D & E is the most common, safest, often most cost effective, and best understood method of second trimester abortion, and noting that other alternatives are medically riskier, more costly, less reliable, and in some instances simply unavailable. *See Bernard v. Individual Members of Indiana Licensing Board,* 392 F. Supp.3d 935 (S.D. In. 2019); *see also EMW Women's Surgical Center, P.S.C. v. Friedlander,* 960 F.3d 785 (6th Cir. 2020); *Whole Woman's Health v. Paxton,* 280 F. Supp.3d 938 (W.D. Tex. 2017).

4. *Banning Abortions After 15 Weeks.* The court struck down Mississippi's ban on abortions after the 15th week of pregnancy. *Jackson Women's Health Organization v. Currier,* 945 F.3d 265 (5th Cir. 2018).

5. *Medicines and Admitting Privileges.* In *Planned Parenthood of Arkansas & Eastern Oklahoma v. Jegley,* 2018 WL 3029104 (E.D. Ark. 2018), a trial court temporarily enjoined an Arkansas law that required health care providers that prescribe abortion-inducing medications to also have a contract with a physician with admitting privileges at a local hospital.

6. *Prohibiting Discriminatory Abortions.* An Indiana law prohibited abortions that are based on the sex, race or disability. In *Planned Parenthood of Indiana and Kentucky, Inc. v. Commissioner,* 888 F.3d 300 (7th Cir. 2018), the Court struck down the prohibition as an improper restriction on a woman's right to have an abortion.

7. *72 Hour Waiting Period.* In *Planned Parenthood of Heartland, Inc. v. Reynolds,* __ F. Supp.3d ___, 2019 WL 312072 (D. Iowa 2020), the court struck down a 72 hour waiting period.

8. *Parental Notification.* In *Box v. Planned Parenthood of Indiana & Kentucky,* 139 S. Ct. 1780 (2019), the Court set aside a lower court ruling that prohibited Indiana from enforcing a law requiring a pregnant minor's parents be informed prior to a court-authorized abortion.

∾ PROBLEMS ∾

1. *Spousal Notification.* Consider a state law that gives a woman the final decision about terminating her pregnancy but requires her to notify her spouse and give him an opportunity, when there is no risk of abuse, to negotiate on behalf of the child's birth. Would it be permissible to mandate an accelerated mediation process, subsidized by the state, provided that the woman's ultimate autonomy is preserved?

2. *Prohibiting Abortions After 20 Weeks.* Six states (Idaho, Indiana, Kansas, Oklahoma, Alabama, and Nebraska) have banned abortions after 20 weeks of gestation on the theory that the fetus can feel pain at that point. Studies show that only 1.5% of all abortions take place after the twentieth week. There is no exception in the laws for fetuses that are physically impaired. Since a fetus is not "viable" outside of the womb until the twenty-fourth week of pregnancy, are the new laws invalid? *See Isaacson v. Horne,* 716 F.3d 1213 (9th Cir. 2013).

3. *Abortion Questionnaires.* An Oklahoma law requires a woman seeking an abortion to fill out a lengthy questionnaire that asks, *inter alia,* about her race, her level of education, and her reason for seeking an abortion (e.g., is the motivation financial, a result of relationship problems, or due to a fear that having a baby would dramatically change her life?). The law, which would keep women's identities private, was justified on the basis that information obtained from the questionnaire would help legislators understand why women seek abortions. Opponents claim that the law is offensive because no woman makes the decision to abort lightly, and it makes a "difficult decision more painful." Is the law constitutionally permissible?

4. *Regulating the Abortion Procedure.* Kansas enacts a new statute that imposes a number of requirements on abortion providers, covering such items as the size of the operating room where the procedure is performed; the stocking of equipment, medication, and blood supplies; and ties to nearby hospitals. The supporting legislators claims that the "government has a right to demand a certain amount of protection for patients." Opponents claim that the requirements were onerous and could be satisfied by only one of the three existing Kansas abortion clinics. Is the regulation valid? *See Planned Parenthood of Kansas* and *Mid-Missouri v. Brownback*, 799 F. Supp. 2d 1218 (D. Kan. 2011).

5. *Disclosure Regarding Suicide.* South Dakota's legislature is considering enacting a statute that requires physicians to disclose to women seeking abortions that they are at an increased risk of suicide. Suppose that you are legal counsel to the legislature. Would you advise it that this law would unduly burden a woman's right to have an abortion? Suppose that there is evidence showing that women who have had abortions are, in fact, more likely to commit suicide. However, the evidence fails to show a causal link between the abortions and the suicides. Is the law valid? *See Planned Parenthood v. Rounds*, 686 F.3d 889 (8th Cir. 2012).

6. *Sonograms, Waiting Periods, and Informed Consent.* Texas has enacted a new statute entitled the Woman's Right to Know Act (WRKA). The Act requires the physician "who is to perform an abortion" to perform and display a sonogram of the fetus, make audible the heart auscultation of the fetus for the woman to hear, and explain to her the results of each procedure and to wait 24 hours, in most cases, between the disclosures and performing the abortion. A woman may decline to view the images or hear the heartbeat, but she may decline to receive an explanation of the sonogram images only on certification that her pregnancy falls into one of the statutory exceptions (e.g., for rape and incest). Suppose that the law is challenged by abortion providers. How might they argue that the law constitutes an undue burden on a woman's right to have an abortion? How might Texas defend the law? Is the law valid? *See Texas Medical Providers Performing Abortion Services v. Lakey*, 667 F.3d 570 (5th Cir. 2012).

7. *Prohibiting Off-Medication Abortions.* North Dakota has adopted a law that prohibits the use of medications to cause abortions unless those medications are approved for that usage by the Food and Drug Administration. Is such a restriction permissible even though doctors sometimes prescribe drugs for uses that are not approved by the FDA? *See MKB Management Corp. v. Burdick*, 855 N.W.2d 31 (N.D. 2014).

3. Family Liberty

Well-established case law suggests that there is a constitutional right to personal choice with respect to family life. In *Meyer v. Nebraska*, 262 U.S. 390 (1923), the Court referenced a liberty interest in "establishing a home and bringing up children." This characterization preceded the formal recognition of privacy as a fundamental right several decades later. In *Village of Belle Terre v. Boraas*, 416 U.S. 1 (1974), the Court marked an outer limit of this liberty when it upheld a local ordinance restricting occupancy in single-family dwellings to persons related by blood. A few years later, in *Moore v. City of East Cleveland*, a plurality of the Court struck down a law that prohibited extended families from living together in the same home.

Moore v. City of East Cleveland

431 U.S. 494 (1977)

Mr. Justice POWELL announced the judgment of the Court, and delivered an opinion in which Mr. Justice BRENNAN, Mr. Justice MARSHALL, and Mr. Justice BLACKMUN joined.

East Cleveland's housing ordinance, like many throughout the country, limits occupancy of a dwelling unit to members of a single family. But the ordinance contains an unusual and complicated definitional section that recognizes as a "family" only a few categories of related individuals. Because her family, living together in her home, fits none of those categories, appellant stands convicted of a criminal offense. The question in this case is whether the ordinance violates the Due Process Clause of the Fourteenth Amendment.

The city argues that our decision in *Village of Belle Terre v. Boraas* requires us to sustain the ordinance attacked here. But one overriding factor sets this case apart from *Belle Terre*. The ordinance there affected only unrelated individuals. It expressly allowed all who were related by "blood, adoption, or marriage" to live together, and in sustaining the ordinance we were careful to note that it promoted "family needs" and "family values." East Cleveland, in contrast, has chosen to regulate the occupancy of its housing by slicing deeply into the family itself. This is no mere incidental result of the ordinance. On its face it selects certain categories of relatives who may live together and declares that others may not. In particular, it makes a crime of a grandmother's choice to live with her grandson in circumstances like those presented here.

When a city undertakes such intrusive regulation of the family, *Belle Terre* does not govern; the usual judicial deference to the legislature is inappropriate. "This Court has long recognized that freedom of personal choice in matters of marriage and family life is one of the liberties protected by the Due Process Clause of the Fourteenth Amendment." A host of cases, tracing their lineage to *Meyer v. Nebraska* and *Pierce v. Society of Sisters*, have consistently acknowledged a "private realm of family life which the state cannot enter." Of course, the family is not beyond regulation. But when the government intrudes on choices concerning family living arrangements, this Court must examine carefully the importance of the governmental interests advanced and the extent to which they are served by the challenged regulation.

When thus examined, this ordinance cannot survive. The city seeks to justify it as a means of preventing overcrowding, minimizing traffic and parking congestion, and avoiding an undue financial burden on East Cleveland's school system. Although these are legitimate goals, the ordinance before us serves them marginally, at best. For example, the ordinance permits any family consisting only of husband, wife, and unmarried children to live together, even if the family contains a half dozen licensed drivers, each with his or her own car. At the same time it forbids an adult brother and sister to share a household, even if both faithfully use public transportation. The ordinance would permit a grandmother to live with a single dependent son and children, even if his school-age children number a dozen, yet it forces Mrs. Moore to find another dwelling for her grandson John, simply because of the presence of his uncle and cousin in the same household. We need not labor the point. The ordinance has but a tenuous relation to alleviation of the conditions mentioned by the city.

The city would distinguish the cases based on *Meyer* and *Pierce.* It points out that none of them "gives grandmothers any fundamental rights with respect to grandsons," and suggests that any constitutional right to live together as a family extends only to the nuclear family essentially a couple and their dependent children. To be sure, these cases did not expressly consider the family relationship presented here. But unless we close our eyes to the basic reasons why certain rights associated with the family have been accorded shelter under the Fourteenth Amendment's Due Process Clause, we cannot avoid applying the force and rationale of these precedents to the family choice involved in this case.

Substantive due process has at times been a treacherous field for this Court. There are risks when the judicial branch gives enhanced protection to certain substantive liberties without the guidance of the more specific provisions of the Bill of Rights. As the history of the *Lochner* era demonstrates, there is reason for concern lest the only limits to such judicial intervention become the predilections of those who happen at the time to be Members of this Court. That history counsels caution and restraint. But it does not counsel abandonment, nor does it require what the city urges here: cutting off any protection of family rights at the first convenient, if arbitrary boundary the boundary of the nuclear family.

Appropriate limits on substantive due process come not from drawing arbitrary lines but rather from careful "respect for the teachings of history (and), solid recognition of the basic values that underlie our society." Our decisions establish that the Constitution protects the sanctity of the family precisely because the institution of the family is deeply rooted in this Nation's history and tradition. It is through the family that we inculcate and pass down many of our most cherished values, moral and cultural.

Ours is by no means a tradition limited to respect for the bonds uniting the members of the nuclear family. The tradition of uncles, aunts, cousins, and especially grandparents sharing a household along with parents and children has roots equally venerable and equally deserving of constitutional recognition. Over the years millions of our citizens have grown up in just such an environment, and most, surely, have profited from it. Even if conditions of modern society have brought about a decline in extended family households, they have not erased the accumulated wisdom of civilization, gained over the centuries and honored throughout our history, that supports a larger conception of the family. Out of choice, necessity, or a sense of family responsibility, it has been common for close relatives to draw together and participate in the duties and the satisfactions of a common home. Decisions concerning child rearing long have been shared with grandparents or other relatives who occupy the same household indeed who may take on major responsibility for the rearing of the children. Especially in times of adversity, such as the death of a spouse or economic need, the broader family has tended to come together for mutual sustenance and to maintain or rebuild a secure home life. This is apparently what happened here.

Whether or not such a household is established because of personal tragedy, the choice of relatives in this degree of kinship to live together may not lightly be denied by the State. The Constitution prevents East Cleveland from standardizing its children and its adults by forcing all to live in certain narrowly defined family patterns.

Reversed.

Mr. Justice BRENNAN, with whom Mr. Justice MARSHALL joins, *concurring.*

The "extended family" that provided generations of early Americans with social services and economic and emotional support in times of hardship, and was the beachhead for successive waves of immigrants who populated our cities, remains not merely still a pervasive living pattern, but under the goad of brutal economic necessity, a prominent pattern virtually a means of survival for large numbers of the poor and deprived minorities of our society. The "extended" form is especially familiar among black families. I do not wish to be understood as implying that East Cleveland's enforcement of its ordinance is motivated by a racially discriminatory purpose. It suffices that in prohibiting this pattern of family living as a means of achieving its objectives, appellee city has chosen a device that deeply intrudes into family associational rights that historically have been central, and today remain central, to a large proportion of our population.

Mr. Justice STEVENS, *concurring in the judgment.*

There appears to be no precedent for an ordinance which excludes any of an owner's relatives from the group of persons who may occupy his residence on a permanent basis. Nor does there appear to be any justification for such a restriction on an owner's use of his property. Since this ordinance has not been shown to have any "substantial relation to the public health, safety, morals, or general welfare" of the city of East Cleveland, and since it cuts so deeply into a fundamental right normally associated with the ownership of residential property that of an owner to decide who may reside on his or her property it must fall. East Cleveland's unprecedented ordinance constitutes a taking of property without due process and without just compensation.

Mr. Chief Justice BURGER, *dissenting.*

It is unnecessary for me to reach the difficult constitutional issue this case presents. Appellant's deliberate refusal to use a plainly adequate administrative remedy a variance proceeding provided by the city should foreclose her from pressing in this Court any constitutional objections to the city's zoning ordinance.

Mr. Justice STEWART, with whom Mr. Justice REHNQUIST joins, *dissenting.*

When the Court has found that the Fourteenth Amendment placed a substantive limitation on a State's power to regulate, it has been in those rare cases in which the personal interests at issue have been deemed "implicit in the concept of ordered liberty." The interest that the appellant may have in permanently sharing a single kitchen and a suite of contiguous rooms with some of her relatives simply does not rise to that level. To equate this interest with the fundamental decisions to marry and to bear and raise children is to extend the limited substantive contours of the Due Process Clause beyond recognition.

Mr. Justice WHITE, *dissenting.*

I would underline Mr. Justice Black's constant reminder to his colleagues that the Court has no license to invalidate legislation which it thinks merely arbitrary or unreasonable. And no one was more sensitive than Mr. Justice Harlan to any suggestion that his approach to the Due Process Clause would lead to judges "roaming at large in the constitutional field."

That the Court has ample precedent for the creation of new constitutional rights should not lead it to repeat the process at will. The Judiciary, including this Court is the most vulnerable and comes nearest to illegitimacy when it deals with judge-made constitutional law having little or no cognizable roots in the language or even the design of the Constitution. The Court should be extremely reluctant to breathe still further substantive content into the Due Process Clause so as to strike down legislation adopted by a State or city to promote its welfare. Whenever the Judiciary does so, it unavoidably pre-empts for itself another part of the governance of the country without express constitutional authority.

There are various "liberties" which require that infringing legislation be given closer judicial scrutiny, not only with respect to existence of a purpose and the means employed, but also with respect to the importance of the purpose itself relative to the invaded interest. Some interest would appear almost impregnable to invasion, such as the freedoms of speech, press, and religion, and the freedom from cruel and unusual punishments. Other interests, for example, the right of association, the right to vote, and various claims sometimes referred to under the general rubric of the right to privacy, also weigh very heavily against state claims of authority to regulate. It is this category of interests which, as I understand it, Mr. Justice Stewart refers to as "implicit in the concept of ordered liberty."

Given his premise, he is surely correct. Under our cases, the Due Process Clause extends substantial protection to various phases of family life, but none requires that the claim made here be sustained. I cannot believe that the interest in residing with more than one set of grandchildren is one that calls for any kind of heightened protection under the Due Process Clause. To say that one has a personal right to live with all, rather than some, of one's grandchildren and that this right is implicit in ordered liberty is, as my Brother Stewart says, "to extend the limited substantive contours of the Due Process Clause beyond recognition." The present claim is hardly one of which it could be said that "neither liberty nor justice would exist if (it) were sacrificed."

Mr. Justice Powell would apparently construe the Due Process Clause to protect from all but quite important state regulatory interests any right or privilege that in his estimate is deeply rooted in the country's traditions. For me, this suggests a far too expansive charter for this Court. What the deeply rooted traditions of the country are is arguable; which of them deserve the protection of the Due Process Clause is even more debatable. The suggested view would have the courts substantively weighing and very likely invalidating a wide range of measures that Congress and state legislatures think appropriate to respond to a changing economic and social order.

Notes and Questions

1. *The* Moore *Standard.* The family living restrictions struck down in *Moore* implicated a concern that, at least from the Powell plurality's perspective, was fundamental. The Court's factoring of whether the state had an "important" interest indicated a standard of review that was heightened but not strict. The elevated standard of review nonetheless was triggered by a sense that the interest was grounded in the nation's history and traditions. Critics have noted that this criterion, which is supposed to be a limiting principle for otherwise unbounded judicial review, has rather limitless potential for purposes of developing fundamental rights and liberties. This concern was manifest in the dissenting opinions in *Moore*, which indicate a growing interest in how precisely the tradition should be defined.

2. *Cultural Myopia?* Justices Brennan and Marshall expressed concern that the East Cleveland ordinance reflects a sense of "cultural myopia" by prioritizing the nuclear family model "found in much of white suburbia" over the extended family structure that they characterized as a "means of survival" for many poor African-American families. To what extent should it matter that the burden in this instance was imposed in a community that was predominantly African American and where the political leadership reflected this makeup?

∽ PROBLEMS ∽

1. *Defining "Family."* Suppose a community enacts an ordinance that restricts housing occupancy to single families, but defines a family unit in a way that excludes cousins beyond the first order. Would this restriction be analyzed more appropriately pursuant to *Boraas* or *Moore?*

2. *Natural Fathers.* Consider a state law providing that a mother's consent is sufficient for adoption if the natural but unwed father has not legitimized the child. Would the natural father have a right to protest and preclude the adoption? *See Quilloin v. Walcott,* 434 U.S. 246 (1978). Would it make any difference whether the adoption was by the mother's husband or into an entirely different family unit?

3. *More on the Proposed Child Custody Statute.* If the proposed statute described in the introductory problem is enacted, what standard of review should apply? What would you guess is the state's asserted interest in passing such a law? Is it legitimate? Is the interest sufficient to overcome the parents' privacy interests in being involved in the raising of their children?

4. The Right to Marry

Marriage is a relationship with a well-established tradition and history that the Court has protected through due process review. In *Meyer v. Nebraska,* 262 U.S. 290 (1923), the right was referenced explicitly as a constitutionally protected liberty interest. In *Loving v. Virginia,* 388 U.S. 1 (1967), the right to marry also was identified as a basis for striking down antimiscegenation laws. In the following case, the Court reviewed a state law that prohibited marriage by residents who were in arrears in their child support obligations and could not demonstrate that their offspring were unlikely to become "public charges."

Zablocki v. Redhail

434 U.S. 374 (1978)

Mr. Justice MARSHALL delivered the opinion of the Court.

At issue in this case is the constitutionality of a Wisconsin statute restricting marriage by a "resident having minor children not in his custody and which he is under obligation to support by any court order or judgment." For such individuals a marriage license may be granted only upon proof of compliance with the child support obligation and that the children "are not then and are not likely thereafter to become public charges."

The leading decision of this Court on the right to marry is *Loving v. Virginia.* In that case, an interracial couple who had been convicted of violating Virginia's miscegenation laws challenged the statutory scheme on both equal protection and due process grounds. The Court's opinion could have rested solely on the ground that the statutes discriminated on the basis of race in violation of the Equal Protection Clause. But the Court went on to hold that the laws arbitrarily deprived the couple of a fundamental liberty protected by the Due Process Clause, the freedom to marry. The Court's language on the latter point bears repeating:

> The freedom to marry has long been recognized as one of the vital personal rights essential to the orderly pursuit of happiness by free men.

Marriage is one of the "basic civil rights of man," fundamental to our very existence and survival.

Although *Loving* arose in the context of racial discrimination, prior and subsequent decisions of this Court confirm that the right to marry is of fundamental importance for all individuals. Long ago, the Court characterized marriage as "the most important relation in life," and as "the foundation of the family and of society, without which there would be neither civilization nor progress."

More recent decisions have established that the right to marry is part of the fundamental "right of privacy" implicit in the Fourteenth Amendment's Due Process Clause. It is not surprising that the decision to marry has been placed on the same level of importance as decisions relating to procreation, childbirth, child rearing, and family relationships. As the facts of this case illustrate, it would make little sense to recognize a right of privacy with respect to other matters of family life and not with respect to the decision to enter the relationship that is the foundation of the family in our society.

By reaffirming the fundamental character of the right to marry, we do not mean to suggest that every state regulation which relates in any way to the incidents of or prerequisites for marriage must be subjected to rigorous scrutiny. To the contrary, reasonable regulations that do not significantly interfere with decisions to enter into the marital relationship may legitimately be imposed. The statutory classification at issue here, however, clearly does interfere directly and substantially with the right to marry.

Under the challenged statute, no Wisconsin resident in the affected class may marry in Wisconsin or elsewhere without a court order, and marriages contracted in violation of the statute are both void and punishable as criminal offenses. Some of those in the affected class, like appellee, will never be able to obtain the necessary court order, because they either lack the financial means to meet their support obligations or cannot prove that their children will not become public charges. These persons are absolutely prevented from getting married. Many others, able in theory to satisfy the statute's requirements, will be sufficiently burdened by having to do so that they will in effect be coerced into forgoing their right to marry. And even those who can be persuaded to meet the statute's requirements suffer a serious intrusion into their freedom of choice in an area in which we have held such freedom to be fundamental.

When a statutory classification significantly interferes with the exercise of a fundamental right, it cannot be upheld unless it is supported by sufficiently important state interests and is closely tailored to effectuate only those interests. Appellant asserts that two interests are served by the challenged statute: the permission-to-marry proceeding furnishes an opportunity to counsel the applicant as to the necessity of fulfilling his prior support obligations; and the welfare of the out-of-custody children is protected. We may accept for present purposes that these are legitimate and substantial interests, but, since the means selected by the State for achieving these interests unnecessarily impinge on the right to marry, the statute cannot be sustained.

With regard to safeguarding the welfare of the out-of-custody children, appellant's brief does not make clear the connection between the State's interest and the statute's requirements. At argument, appellant's counsel suggested that, since permission to marry cannot be granted unless the applicant shows that he has satisfied his court-determined support obligations to the prior children and that those children will not become public charges, the statute provides incentive for the applicant to make support payments to his children. This "collection device" rationale cannot justify the statute's broad infringement on the right to marry.

First, with respect to individuals who are unable to meet the statutory requirements, the statute merely prevents the applicant from getting married, without delivering any money at all into the hands of the applicant's prior children. More importantly, regardless of the applicant's ability or willingness to meet the statutory requirements, the State already has numerous other means for exacting compliance with support obligations, means that are at least as effective as the instant statute's and yet do not impinge upon the right to marry. Under Wisconsin law, whether the children are from a prior marriage or were born out of wedlock, court-determined support obligations may be enforced directly via wage assignments, civil contempt proceedings, and criminal penalties. And, if the State believes that parents of children out of their custody should be responsible for ensuring that those children do not become public charges, this interest can be achieved by adjusting the criteria used for determining the amounts to be paid under their support orders.

There is also some suggestion that the law protects the ability of marriage applicants to meet support obligations to prior children by preventing the applicants from incurring new support obligations. But the challenged provisions are grossly underinclusive with respect to this purpose, since they do not limit in any way new financial commitments by the applicant other than those arising out of the contemplated marriage. The statutory classification is substantially overinclusive as well: Given the possibility that the new spouse will actually better the applicant's financial situation, by contributing income from a job or otherwise, the statute in many cases may prevent affected individuals from improving their ability to satisfy their prior support obligations. And, although it is true that the applicant will incur support obligations to any children born during the contemplated marriage, preventing the marriage may only result in the children being born out of wedlock, as in fact occurred in appellee's case. Since the support obligation is the same whether the child is born in or out of wedlock, the net result of preventing the marriage is simply more illegitimate children.

The statutory classification created by this law thus cannot be justified by the interests advanced in support of it.

Mr. Justice STEWART, *concurring in the judgment.*

The Constitution does not specifically mention freedom to marry, but it is settled that the "liberty" protected by the Due Process Clause of the Fourteenth

Amendment embraces more than those freedoms expressly enumerated in the Bill of Rights. And the decisions of this Court have made clear that freedom of personal choice in matters of marriage and family life is one of the liberties so protected.

Mr. Justice REHNQUIST, *dissenting*.

I would view this legislative judgment in the light of the traditional presumption of validity. I think that under the Equal Protection Clause the statute need pass only the "rational basis test," and that under the Due Process Clause it need only be shown that it bears a rational relation to a constitutionally permissible objective. The statute so viewed is a permissible exercise of the State's power to regulate family life and to assure the support of minor children, despite its possible imprecision in the extreme cases envisioned in the concurring opinions.

Notes

1. Zablocki *and Substantive Due Process Review.* The *Zablocki* decision reaffirmed an established principle, but recast it to the extent that the right to marry was brought within the right of privacy. Utilization of the Equal Protection Clause may have reflected the Court's general uneasiness with substantive due process review and the discredited legacy of which it evoked memories. As with the use of penumbras in *Griswold,* reliance on the Equal Protection Clause did not obscure a model of review that fundamentally is indistinguishable from substantive due process review.

2. *Same-Sex Marriage and Substantive Due Process.* A number of state supreme courts, applying state constitutional provisions, invalidated state laws that do not permit same-sex couples to marry. These decisions were followed by the *Obergefell* decision, *infra,* which held that there is a constitutional right to same-sex marriage.

∽ PROBLEMS ∽

1. *Remarriage and Support Orders.* What if the state adopts a law that presumes that remarriage will have a detrimental effect on children of a previous marriage who are the subject of a support order? So long as there is an opportunity to rebut this presumption, or demonstrate good reason for not being able to comply with the support order, would there be a due process problem?

2. *Polygamy.* Some religions believe in polygamy. Does the fundamental right to marry include the right to engage in polygamy? *See Reynolds v. United States,* 98 U.S. (8 Otto) 145 (1878) (upholding a federal law prohibiting polygamy, as applied to a Mormon whose religion required him to engage in that practice, drawing a distinction between "belief" and "conduct," and concluding that the

government has broad authority to prohibit religious conduct); *Davis v. Beason*, 133 U.S. 333 (1890) (reaffirming *Reynolds*).

5. Parental Rights

The nature and scope of parental liberty have been factored in a series of contexts. In *Wisconsin v. Yoder*, 406 U.S. 205 (1972), the Court found that a mandatory school attendance law was at odds with the free exercise of religion when applied to members of the Amish religion. It also noted that compulsory education in this circumstance implicated "traditional concepts of parental control over the religious upbringing and education of their minor children." Parental rights have been balanced against a minor child's liberty to obtain an abortion, insofar as the Court has upheld parental consent requirements but insisted on a judicial bypass option. *E.g., Hodgson v. Minnesota*, 497 U.S. 417 (1990).

The relationship between parent and child, though implicating fundamental interests, is not constitutionally sacrosanct. In *Quilloin v. Walcott*, the Court upheld a state law that allowed the mother to adopt her child in a new family unit if the natural father did not object. As the Court saw it, a contrary outcome would have undermined a result sought by everyone except the natural father, who was not himself seeking custody. In *Michael H. v. Gerald D.*, the Court reviewed a natural father's claim of a filial relationship and visitation rights with his daughter. The child's birth as a result of an extramarital affair led a plurality of the Court to conclude that the father had no liberty interest protected under the Fourteenth Amendment.

Michael H. v. Gerald D.

491 U.S. 110 (1989)

Justice SCALIA announced the judgment of the Court and delivered an opinion, in which THE CHIEF JUSTICE joins, and in all but footnote 6 of which Justice O'CONNOR and Justice KENNEDY join.

Under California law, a child born to a married woman living with her husband is presumed to be a child of the marriage. The presumption of legitimacy may be rebutted only by the husband or wife, and then only in limited circumstances. The instant appeal presents the claim that this presumption infringes upon the due process rights of a man who wishes to establish his paternity of a child born to the wife of another man, and the claim that it infringes upon the constitutional right of the child to maintain a relationship with her natural father.

The facts of this case are, we must hope, extraordinary. In 1976, Carole D., an international model, and Gerald D., a top executive in a French oil company, were married. The couple established a home in California in which they resided as husband and wife when one or the other was not out of the country on business.

In 1978, Carole became involved in an adulterous affair with a neighbor, Michael H. In September 1980, she conceived a child, Victoria D., who was born in 1981. Gerald was listed as father on the birth certificate and has always held Victoria out to the world as his daughter. Soon after delivery of the child, however, Carole informed Michael that she believed he might be the father. For her first three years, the child and mother lived at times with Michael, who held out that the child was his. The mother and child also resided at times with Gerald and another man. Gerald was listed on the birth certificate as the father and has claimed her accordingly, but blood tests showed a 98.07 percent probability that the child is Michael's. California law presumes that a child born to a mother living with her husband is of the marriage. Pursuant to this presumption, the state courts denied Michael paternity and visitation rights.

Michael contends as a matter of substantive due process that, because he has established a parental relationship with Victoria, protection of Gerald's and Carole's marital union is an insufficient state interest to support termination of that relationship. This argument is predicated on the assertion that Michael has a constitutionally protected liberty interest in his relationship with Victoria.

In an attempt to limit and guide interpretation of the Clause, we have insisted not merely that the interest denominated as a "liberty" be "fundamental" (a concept that, in isolation, is hard to objectify), but also that it be an interest traditionally protected by our society. As we have put it, the Due Process Clause affords only those protections "so rooted in the traditions and conscience of our people as to be ranked as fundamental."

This insistence that the asserted liberty interest be rooted in history and tradition is evident, as elsewhere, in our cases according constitutional protection to certain parental rights. Michael maintains that a liberty interest is created by biological fatherhood plus an established parental relationship—factors that exist in the present case. We think that distorts the rationale of prior cases. As we view them, they rest not upon such isolated factors but upon the historic respect—indeed, sanctity would not be too strong a term—traditionally accorded to the relationships that develop within the unitary family.

The legal issue in the present case reduces to whether the relationship between persons in the situation of Michael and Victoria has been treated as a protected family unit under the historic practices of our society, or whether on any other basis it has been accorded special protection. We think it impossible to find that it has. In fact, quite to the contrary, our traditions have protected the marital family (Gerald, Carole, and the child they acknowledge to be theirs) against the sort of claim Michael asserts.

We have found nothing in the older sources, nor in the older cases, addressing specifically the power of the natural father to assert parental rights over a child born into a woman's existing marriage with another man. Since it is Michael's burden to establish that such a power (at least where the natural father has established a relationship with the child) is so deeply embedded within our traditions as to be a fundamental right, the lack of evidence alone might defeat his case.

But the evidence shows that even in modern times—when, as we have noted, the rigid protection of the marital family has in other respects been relaxed—the ability of a person in Michael's position to claim paternity has not been generally acknowledged.

Moreover, even if it were clear that one in Michael's position generally possesses, and has generally always possessed, standing to challenge the marital child's legitimacy, that would still not establish Michael's case. As noted earlier, what is at issue here is not entitlement to a state pronouncement that Victoria was begotten by Michael. It is no conceivable denial of constitutional right for a State to decline to declare facts unless some legal consequence hinges upon the requested declaration. What Michael asserts here is a right to have himself declared the natural father and thereby to obtain parental prerogatives. What he must establish, therefore, is not that our society has traditionally allowed a natural father in his circumstances to establish paternity, but that it has traditionally accorded such a father parental rights, or at least has not traditionally denied them. Even if the law in all States had always been that the entire world could challenge the marital presumption and obtain a declaration as to who was the natural father, that would not advance Michael's claim.

Thus, it is ultimately irrelevant, even for purposes of determining current social attitudes towards the alleged substantive right Michael asserts, that the present law in a number of States appears to allow the natural father—including the natural father who has not established a relationship with the child—the theoretical power to rebut the marital presumption. What counts is whether the States in fact award substantive parental rights to the natural father of a child conceived within, and born into, an extant marital union that wishes to embrace the child. We are not aware of a single case, old or new, that has done so. This is not the stuff of which fundamental rights qualifying as liberty interests are made.[6]

We do not accept Justice Brennan's criticism that this result "squashes" the liberty that consists of "the freedom not to conform." It seems to us that reflects the erroneous view that there is only one side to this controversy—that one disposition can expand a "liberty" of sorts without contracting an equivalent "liberty" on the other side. Here, to provide protection to an adulterous natural father is to deny protection to a marital father, and vice versa. If Michael has a "freedom not to conform" (whatever that means), Gerald must equivalently have a "freedom to conform." One of them will pay a price for asserting that "freedom"—Michael by being unable to act as father of the child he has

---

6. Justice Brennan criticizes our methodology in using historical traditions specifically relating to the rights of an adulterous natural father, rather than inquiring more generally "whether parenthood is an interest that historically has received our attention and protection." There seems to us no basis for the contention that this methodology is "novel." We refer to the most specific level at which a relevant tradition protecting, or denying protection to, the asserted right can be identified. If, for example, there were no societal tradition, either way, regarding the rights of the natural father of a child adulterously conceived, we would have to consult, and (if possible) reason from, the traditions regarding natural fathers in general. But there is such a more specific tradition, and it unqualifiedly denies protection to such a parent.

adulterously begotten, or Gerald by being unable to preserve the integrity of the traditional family unit he and Victoria have established. Our disposition does not choose between these two "freedoms," but leaves that to the people of California. Justice Brennan's approach chooses one of them as the constitutional imperative, on no apparent basis except that the unconventional is to be preferred.

The judgment of the California Court of Appeal is
Affirmed.

Justice O'CONNNOR, with whom Justice KENNEDY joins, *concurring in part.*

I concur in all but footnote 6 of Justice Scalia's opinion. This footnote sketches a mode of historical analysis to be used when identifying liberty interests protected by the Due Process Clause of the Fourteenth Amendment that may be somewhat inconsistent with our past decisions in this area. On occasion the Court has characterized relevant traditions protecting asserted rights at levels of generality that might not be "the most specific level" available. I would not foreclose the unanticipated by the prior imposition of a single mode of historical analysis.

Justice STEVENS, *concurring in the judgment.*

Justice Scalia seems to reject the possibility that a natural father might ever have a constitutionally protected interest in his relationship with a child whose mother was married to, and cohabiting with, another man at the time of the child's conception and birth. Prior cases demonstrate that enduring "family" relationships may develop in unconventional settings. I therefore would not foreclose the possibility that a constitutionally protected relationship between a natural father and his child might exist in a case like this. Indeed, I am willing to assume for the purpose of deciding this case that Michael's relationship with Victoria is strong enough to give him a constitutional right to try to convince a trial judge that Victoria's best interest would be served by granting him visitation rights. I am satisfied, however, that the California statute, as applied in this case, gave him that opportunity.

Justice BRENNAN, with whom Justice MARSHALL and Justice BLACKMUN join, *dissenting.*

It is ironic that an approach so utterly dependent on tradition is so indifferent to our precedents. The plurality acts as though English legal treatises and the American Law Reports always have provided the sole source for our constitutional principles. They have not. " 'Liberty' and 'property' are broad and majestic terms. They are among the 'great constitutional concepts purposely left to gather meaning from experience. They relate to the whole domain of social and economic fact, and the statesmen who founded this Nation knew too well that only a stagnant society remains unchanged.' "

The plurality does not ask whether parenthood is an interest that historically has received our attention and protection; the answer to that question is too clear for dispute. Instead, the plurality asks whether the specific variety of parenthood under consideration — a natural father's relationship with a child whose mother is married to another man—has enjoyed such protection. If we had looked to tradition with such specificity in past cases, many a decision would have reached a different result. Surely the use of contraceptives by unmarried couples, or even by married couples, were not "interests traditionally protected by our society," at the time of their consideration by this Court. That we did not ask this question in those cases highlights the novelty of the interpretive method that the plurality opinion employs today.

In the plurality's constitutional universe, we may not take notice of the fact that the original reasons for the conclusive presumption of paternity are out of place in a world in which blood tests can prove virtually beyond a shadow of a doubt who sired a particular child and in which the fact of illegitimacy no longer plays the burdensome and stigmatizing role it once did. By describing the decisive question as whether Michael's and Victoria's interest is one that has been "traditionally protected by our society," rather than one that society traditionally has thought important (with or without protecting it), and by suggesting that our sole function is to "discern the society's views," the plurality acts as if the only purpose of the Due Process Clause is to confirm the importance of interests already protected by a majority of the States.

The document that the plurality construes today is unfamiliar to me. It is not the living charter that I have taken to be our Constitution; it is instead a stagnant, archaic, hidebound document steeped in the prejudices and superstitions of a time long past. This Constitution does not recognize that times change, does not see that sometimes a practice or rule outlives its foundations. I cannot accept an interpretive method that does such violence to the charter that I am bound by oath to uphold.

Justice WHITE, with whom Justice BRENNAN joins, *dissenting.*

Prior cases have recognized the liberty interest of a father in his relationship with his child. In none of these cases did we indicate that the father's rights were dependent on the marital status of the mother or biological father. The basic principle enunciated in the Court's unwed father cases is that an unwed father who has demonstrated a sufficient commitment to his paternity by way of personal, financial, or custodial responsibilities has a protected liberty interest in a relationship with his child.

"The emphasis of the Due Process Clause is on 'process.'" I fail to see how Michael was granted any meaningful opportunity to be heard when he was precluded at the very outset from introducing evidence which would support his assertion of paternity. Michael has never been afforded an opportunity to present his case in any meaningful manner.

As the Court has said: "The significance of the biological connection is that it offers the natural father an opportunity that no other male possesses to develop a relationship with his offspring. If he grasps that opportunity and accepts some measure of responsibility for the child's future, he may enjoy the blessings of the parent-child relationship and make uniquely valuable contributions to the child's development." Michael eagerly grasped the opportunity to have a relationship with his daughter (he lived with her; he declared her to be his child; he provided financial support for her) and still, with today's opinion, his opportunity has vanished. He has been rendered a stranger to his child.

Because the state law as applied, should be held unconstitutional under the Due Process Clause of the Fourteenth Amendment, I respectfully dissent.

Note: Defining "Liberty"

A particularly notable aspect of Justice Scalia's opinion was his argument (in footnote 6) that the inquiry into whether a right or liberty is fundamental should "refer to the most specific level at which a relevant tradition can be identified." Defining the liberty interest at a high level of specificity correspondingly diminishes the likelihood that the interest will be denominated fundamental. Although the general concept of parental rights thus might be understood as rooted in the nation's traditions, societal support predictably would diminish for this proposition when extended to parents of children who were conceived in an adulterous relationship. Definition of the liberty interest with specificity thus represents a method of review that limits the judiciary's role in identifying and developing rights and liberties that are not enumerated by the Constitution.

∾ PROBLEMS ∾

1. *Reference Points.* Consider the implications of tradition depending on whether the concept is defined with specificity or as an abstraction. Would specificity or abstraction be a friendlier inquiry for purposes of determining whether, prior to Reconstruction, there was a fundamental right to own slaves? Which of these reference points would be more supportive of segregation as a system that reflects the different property interest of racial identity? Since traditions evolve, at what point would concepts like desegregation become a factor in defining racial liberties and equalities?

2. *More on the Proposed Child Custody Statute.* Let's go back to the problem at the beginning of the chapter. In light of the Court's decisions on parental rights, what standard of review would you expect courts to apply to the proposed statute if it is enacted? What result? Why?

6. Sexual Orientation

The understanding of the liberty interest at stake and thus how it is defined can have an outcome-determinative bearing on fundamental rights analysis. This predictability factor was evidenced in *Bowers v. Hardwick*, 478 U.S. 186 (1986), when the Court examined a law that made sodomy a crime. The law was applied to an individual who was found engaged in homosexual conduct in the privacy of his home. In upholding the law, the Court concluded that the U.S. Constitution does not confer a fundamental right on homosexuals to engage in sodomy. The Court distinguished sodomy from other privacy cases such as *Meyer v. Nebraska* (dealing with child rearing and education), *Prince v. Massachusetts* (family relationships), *Skinner v. Oklahoma* (procreation), *Loving v. Virginia* (marriage), *Griswold v. Connecticut* and *Eisenstadt v. Baird* (contraception), and *Roe v. Wade* (abortion), on the following basis:

> None of the rights announced in those cases bears any resemblance to the claimed constitutional right of homosexuals to engage in acts of sodomy that is asserted in this case. No connection between family, marriage, or procreation on the one hand and homosexual activity on the other has been demonstrated. Moreover, any claim that these cases nevertheless stand for the proposition that any kind of private sexual conduct between consenting adults is constitutionally insulated from state proscription is unsupportable. Indeed, the Court's opinion in *Carey* twice asserted that the privacy right, which the *Griswold* line of cases found to be one of the protections provided by the Due Process Clause, did not reach so far.
>
> It is obvious to us that neither of these formulations would extend a fundamental right to homosexuals to engage in acts of consensual sodomy. Proscriptions against that conduct have ancient roots. Sodomy was a criminal offense at common law and was forbidden by the laws of the original thirteen States when they ratified the Bill of Rights. In 1868, when the Fourteenth Amendment was ratified, all but 5 of the 37 States in the Union had criminal sodomy laws. In fact, until 1961, all 50 States outlawed sodomy, and today, 24 States and the District of Columbia continue to provide criminal penalties for sodomy performed in private and between consenting adults. Against this background, to claim that a right to engage in such conduct is "deeply rooted in this Nation's history and tradition" or "implicit in the concept of ordered liberty" is, at best, facetious.
>
> Nor are we inclined to take a more expansive view of our authority to discover new fundamental rights imbedded in the Due Process Clause. The Court is most vulnerable and comes nearest to illegitimacy when it deals with judge-made constitutional law having little or no cognizable roots in the language or design of the Constitution. That this is so was painfully demonstrated by the face-off between the Executive and the Court in the 1930's, which resulted in the repudiation of much of the substantive gloss that the Court had placed on the Due Process Clauses of the Fifth and Fourteenth Amendments. There should be, therefore, great resistance to expand the substantive reach of those Clauses, particularly if it requires redefining the category of rights deemed to be fundamental. Otherwise, the Judiciary necessarily takes to itself further authority to govern the country without express constitutional authority. The claimed right pressed on us today falls far short of overcoming this resistance.

Although the Court repudiated any basis for sexual orientation being a concern of the Due Process Clause, it has been responsive to government action that singles out homosexuals for disadvantaged treatment under the law. In *Roemer v. Evans*, the Court invalidated a state constitutional amendment that prohibited government action that would protect homosexuals from discrimination. This result was achieved without reference to a fundamental right, and thus the Court's orientation in *Hardwick* was unaltered. It is noteworthy, moreover, that the result was based on the Equal Protection Clause pursuant to a rational basis standard of review. In a dissenting opinion, Justice Scalia found no basis for distinguishing the power to criminalize homosexuality from the restrictions reviewed in *Evans*. In both instances, homosexuality was targeted. In neither instance was sexual orientation identified as a fundamental liberty interest.

Lawrence v. Texas

539 U.S. 558 (2003)

Justice KENNEDY delivered the opinion of the Court.

Liberty protects the person from unwarranted government intrusions into a dwelling or other private places. In our tradition the State is not omnipresent in the home. And there are other spheres of our lives and existence, outside the home, where the State should not be a dominant presence. Freedom extends beyond spatial bounds. Liberty presumes an autonomy of self that includes freedom of thought, belief, expression, and certain intimate conduct. The instant case involves liberty of the person both in its spatial and more transcendent dimensions.

The question before the Court is the validity of a Texas statute making it a crime for two persons of the same sex to engage in certain intimate sexual conduct.

In Houston, Texas, officers of the Harris County Police Department were dispatched to a private residence in response to a reported weapons disturbance. They entered an apartment where one of the petitioners, John Geddes Lawrence, resided. The right of the police to enter does not seem to have been questioned. The officers observed Lawrence and another man, Tyron Garner, engaging in a sexual act. The two petitioners were arrested, held in custody over night, and charged and convicted before a Justice of the Peace. The complaints described their crime as "deviate sexual intercourse, namely anal sex, with a member of the same sex (man)."

We granted certiorari to consider three questions:

"1. Whether Petitioners' criminal convictions under the Texas "Homosexual Conduct" law—which criminalizes sexual intimacy by same-sex couples, but not identical behavior by different-sex couples—violate the Fourteenth Amendment guarantee of equal protection of laws?

"2. Whether Petitioners' criminal convictions for adult consensual sexual intimacy in the home violate their vital interests in liberty and privacy protected by the Due Process Clause of the Fourteenth Amendment?

"3. Whether *Bowers v. Hardwick* should be overruled?"

The petitioners were adults at the time of the alleged offense. Their conduct was in private and consensual.

We conclude the case should be resolved by determining whether the petitioners were free as adults to engage in the private conduct in the exercise of their liberty under the Due Process Clause of the Fourteenth Amendment to the Constitution. For this inquiry we deem it necessary to reconsider the Court's holding in *Bowers.*

There are broad statements of the substantive reach of liberty under the Due Process Clause in earlier cases, including *Pierce v. Society of Sisters* and *Meyer v. Nebraska*; but the most pertinent beginning point is our decision in *Griswold v. Connecticut. Griswold* invalidated a state law prohibiting the use of drugs or devices of contraception and counseling or aiding and abetting the use of contraceptives. The Court described the protected interest as a right to privacy and placed emphasis on the marriage relation and the protected space of the marital bedroom.

The opinions in *Griswold* and *Eisenstadt* were part of the background for the decision in *Roe v. Wade. Roe* recognized the right of a woman to make certain fundamental decisions affecting her destiny and confirmed once more that the protection of liberty under the Due Process Clause has a substantive dimension of fundamental significance in defining the rights of the person.

The Court began its substantive discussion in *Bowers* as follows: "The issue presented is whether the Federal Constitution confers a fundamental right upon homosexuals to engage in sodomy and hence invalidates the laws of the many States that still make such conduct illegal and have done so for a very long time." That statement, we now conclude, discloses the Court's own failure to appreciate the extent of the liberty at stake. To say that the issue in *Bowers* was simply the right to engage in certain sexual conduct demeans the claim the individual put forward, just as it would demean a married couple were it to be said marriage is simply about the right to have sexual intercourse. The laws involved in *Bowers* and here are, to be sure, statutes that purport to do no more than prohibit a particular sexual act. Their penalties and purposes, though, have more far-reaching consequences, touching upon the most private human conduct, sexual behavior, and in the most private of places, the home. The statutes do seek to control a personal relationship that, whether or not entitled to formal recognition in the law, is within the liberty of persons to choose without being punished as criminals.

This, as a general rule, should counsel against attempts by the State, or a court, to define the meaning of the relationship or to set its boundaries absent injury to a person or abuse of an institution the law protects. It suffices for us to acknowledge that adults may choose to enter upon this relationship in the confines of their homes and their own private lives and still retain their dignity as free persons. When sexuality finds overt expression in intimate conduct with another person, the conduct can be but one element in a personal bond that is more enduring. The liberty protected by the Constitution allows homosexual persons the right to make this choice.

Having misapprehended the claim of liberty there presented to it, and thus stating the claim to be whether there is a fundamental right to engage in consensual sodomy, the *Bowers* Court said: "Proscriptions against that conduct have ancient roots." It should be noted that there is no longstanding history in this country of laws directed at homosexual conduct as a distinct matter. It was not until the 1970's that any State singled out same-sex relations for criminal prosecution, and only nine States have done so. Post-*Bowers* even some of these States did not adhere to the policy of suppressing homosexual conduct. Over the course of the last decades, States with same-sex prohibitions have moved toward abolishing them. In summary, the historical grounds relied upon in *Bowers* are more complex than the majority opinion and the concurring opinion by Chief Justice Burger indicate. Their historical premises are not without doubt and, at the very least, are overstated.

It must be acknowledged, of course, that the Court in *Bowers* was making the broader point that for centuries there have been powerful voices to condemn homosexual conduct as immoral. The condemnation has been shaped by religious beliefs, conceptions of right and acceptable behavior, and respect for the traditional family. For many persons these are not trivial concerns but profound and deep convictions accepted as ethical and moral principles to which they aspire and which thus determine the course of their lives. These considerations do not answer the question before us, however. The issue is whether the majority may use the power of the State to enforce these views on the whole society through operation of the criminal law.

Chief Justice Burger joined the opinion for the Court in *Bowers* and further explained his views as follows: "Decisions of individuals relating to homosexual conduct have been subject to state intervention throughout the history of Western civilization. Condemnation of those practices is firmly rooted in Judeo-Christian moral and ethical standards." As with Justice White's assumptions about history, scholarship casts some doubt on the sweeping nature of the statement by Chief Justice Burger as it pertains to private homosexual conduct between consenting adults. In all events we think that our laws and traditions in the past half century are of most relevance here. These references show an emerging awareness that liberty gives substantial protection to adult persons in deciding how to conduct their private lives in matters pertaining to sex. "History and tradition are the starting point but not in all cases the ending point of the substantive due process inquiry."

This emerging recognition should have been apparent when *Bowers* was decided. In 1955 the American Law Institute promulgated the Model Penal Code and made clear that it did not recommend or provide for "criminal penalties for consensual sexual relations conducted in private." It justified its decision on three grounds: (1) The prohibitions undermined respect for the law by penalizing conduct many people engaged in; (2) the statutes regulated private conduct not harmful to others; and (3) the laws were arbitrarily enforced and thus invited the danger of blackmail.

In *Bowers* the Court referred to the fact that before 1961 all 50 States had outlawed sodomy, and that at the time of the Court's decision 24 States and the District of Columbia had sodomy laws. Justice Powell pointed out that these prohibitions often were being ignored, however. Georgia, for instance, had not sought to enforce its law for decades. The sweeping references by Chief Justice Burger to the history of Western civilization and to Judeo-Christian moral and ethical standards did not take account of other authorities pointing in an opposite direction. A committee advising the British Parliament recommended in 1957 repeal of laws punishing homosexual conduct. Of even more importance, almost five years before *Bowers* was decided the European Court of Human Rights considered a case with parallels to *Bowers* and to today's case. The court held that the laws proscribing the conduct were invalid under the European Convention on Human Rights. Authoritative in all countries that are members of the Council of Europe (21 nations then, 45 nations now), the decision is at odds with the premise in *Bowers* that the claim put forward was insubstantial in our Western civilization.

In our own constitutional system the deficiencies in Bowers became even more apparent in the years following its announcement. The 25 States with laws prohibiting the relevant conduct referenced in the *Bowers* decision are reduced now to 13, of which 4 enforce their laws only against homosexual conduct. In those States where sodomy is still proscribed, whether for same-sex or heterosexual conduct, there is a pattern of nonenforcement with respect to consenting adults acting in private. The State of Texas admitted in 1994 that as of that date it had not prosecuted anyone under those circumstances.

Two principal cases decided after *Bowers* cast its holding into even more doubt. In *Planned Parenthood of Southeastern Pa. v. Casey*, the Court reaffirmed the substantive force of the liberty protected by the Due Process Clause. The *Casey* decision again confirmed that our laws and tradition afford constitutional protection to personal decisions relating to marriage, procreation, contraception, family relationships, child rearing, and education. In explaining the respect the Constitution demands for the autonomy of the person in making these choices, we stated as follows:

> These matters, involving the most intimate and personal choices a person may make in a lifetime, choices central to personal dignity and autonomy, are central to the liberty protected by the Fourteenth Amendment. At the heart of liberty is the right to define one's own concept of existence, of meaning, of the universe, and of the mystery of human life. Beliefs about these matters could not define the attributes of personhood were they formed under compulsion of the State.

Persons in a homosexual relationship may seek autonomy for these purposes, just as heterosexual persons do. The decision in *Bowers* would deny them this right.

The second post-*Bowers* case of principal relevance is *Romer v. Evans*. There the Court struck down class-based legislation directed at homosexuals as a violation of the Equal Protection Clause. *Romer* invalidated an amendment to Colorado's constitution which named as a solitary class persons who were homosexuals, lesbians, or bisexual either by "orientation, conduct, practices or relationships," and deprived them of protection under state antidiscrimination laws. We concluded that the provision was "born of animosity toward the class of persons affected" and further that it had no rational relation to a legitimate governmental purpose.

As an alternative argument in this case, counsel for the petitioners and some amici contend that *Romer* provides the basis for declaring the Texas statute invalid under the Equal Protection Clause. That is a tenable argument, but we conclude the instant case requires us to address whether *Bowers* itself has continuing validity. Were we to hold the statute invalid under the Equal Protection Clause some might question whether a prohibition would be valid if drawn differently, say, to prohibit the conduct both between same-sex and different-sex participants.

Equality of treatment and the due process right to demand respect for conduct protected by the substantive guarantee of liberty are linked in important respects, and a decision on the latter point advances both interests. If protected conduct is made criminal and the law which does so remains unexamined for its substantive validity, its stigma might remain even if it were not enforceable as drawn for equal protection reasons. When homosexual conduct is made criminal by the law of the State, that declaration in and of itself is an invitation to subject homosexual persons to discrimination both in the public and in the private spheres. The central holding of *Bowers* has been brought in question by this case, and it should be addressed. Its continuance as precedent demeans the lives of homosexual persons.

The stigma this criminal statute imposes, moreover, is not trivial. The offense, to be sure, is but a minor offense in the Texas legal system. Still, it remains a criminal offense with all that imports for the dignity of the persons charged. The petitioners will bear on their record the history of their criminal convictions. We are advised that if Texas convicted an adult for private, consensual homosexual conduct under the statute here in question the convicted person would come within the registration laws of at least four States were he or she to be subject to their jurisdiction. This underscores the consequential nature of the punishment and the state-sponsored condemnation attendant to the criminal prohibition. Furthermore, the Texas criminal conviction carries with it the other collateral consequences always following a conviction, such as notations on job application forms, to mention but one example.

The foundations of *Bowers* have sustained serious erosion from our recent decisions in *Casey* and *Romer*. When our precedent has been thus weakened, criticism from other sources is of greater significance. In the United States criticism of *Bowers* has been substantial and continuing, disapproving of its reasoning in all respects, not just as to its historical assumptions. The courts of five different States have declined to follow it in interpreting provisions in their own state constitutions parallel to the Due Process Clause of the Fourteenth Amendment.

To the extent *Bowers* relied on values we share with a wider civilization, it should be noted that the reasoning and holding in *Bowers* have been rejected elsewhere. The European Court of Human Rights has followed not *Bowers* but its own decision in *Dudgeon v. United Kingdom*. Other nations, too, have taken action consistent with an affirmation of the protected right of homosexual adults to engage in intimate, consensual conduct. The right the petitioners seek in this case has been accepted as an integral part of human freedom in many other countries. There has been no showing that in this country the governmental interest in circumscribing personal choice is somehow more legitimate or urgent. *Bowers* itself causes uncertainty, for the precedents before and after its issuance contradict its central holding.

The rationale of *Bowers* does not withstand careful analysis. In his dissenting opinion in *Bowers* Justice Stevens came to these conclusions:

> Our prior cases make two propositions abundantly clear. First, the fact that the governing majority in a State has traditionally viewed a particular practice as immoral is not a sufficient reason for upholding a law prohibiting the practice; neither history nor tradition could save a law prohibiting miscegenation from constitutional attack. Second, individual decisions by married persons, concerning the intimacies of their physical relationship, even when not intended to produce offspring, are a form of "liberty" protected by the Due Process Clause of the Fourteenth Amendment. Moreover, this protection extends to intimate choices by unmarried as well as married persons.

Justice Stevens' analysis, in our view, should have been controlling in *Bowers* and should control here.

Bowers was not correct when it was decided, and it is not correct today. It ought not to remain binding precedent. *Bowers v. Hardwick* should be and now is overruled.

The present case does not involve minors. It does not involve persons who might be injured or coerced or who are situated in relationships where consent might not easily be refused. It does not involve public conduct or prostitution. It does not involve whether the government must give formal recognition to any relationship that homosexual persons seek to enter. The case does involve two adults who, with full and mutual consent from each other, engaged in sexual practices common to a homosexual lifestyle. The petitioners are entitled to respect for their private lives.

The State cannot demean their existence or control their destiny by making their private sexual conduct a crime. Their right to liberty under the Due Process Clause gives them the full right to engage in their conduct without intervention of the government. "It is a promise of the Constitution that there is a realm of personal liberty which the government may not enter."

The Texas statute furthers no legitimate state interest which can justify its intrusion into the personal and private life of the individual.

Had those who drew and ratified the Due Process Clauses of the Fifth Amendment or the Fourteenth Amendment known the components of liberty in its manifold possibilities, they might have been more specific. They did not presume to have this insight. They knew times can blind us to certain truths and later generations can see that laws once thought necessary and proper in fact serve only to oppress. As the Constitution endures, persons in every generation can invoke its principles in their own search for greater freedom.

The judgment of the Court of Appeals for the Texas Fourteenth District is reversed, and the case is remanded for further proceedings not inconsistent with this opinion.

It is so ordered.

Justice O'CONNOR, *concurring in the judgment.*

The Court today overrules *Bowers v. Hardwick.* I joined *Bowers,* and do not join the Court in overruling it. Nevertheless, I agree with the Court that Texas' statute banning same-sex sodomy is unconstitutional. Rather than relying on the substantive component of the Fourteenth Amendment's Due Process Clause, as the Court does, I base my conclusion on the Fourteenth Amendment's Equal Protection Clause.

The statute at issue here makes sodomy a crime only if a person "engages in deviate sexual intercourse with another individual of the same sex." Sodomy between opposite-sex partners, however, is not a crime in Texas. That is, Texas treats the same conduct differently based solely on the participants. Those harmed by this law are people who have a same-sex sexual orientation and thus are more likely to engage in behavior prohibited by the state law.

The Texas statute makes homosexuals unequal in the eyes of the law by making particular conduct—and only that conduct—subject to criminal sanction. It appears that prosecutions under Texas' sodomy law are rare. This case shows, however, that prosecutions under the state law do occur. And while the penalty imposed on petitioners in this case was relatively minor, the consequences of conviction are not.

Texas attempts to justify its law, and the effects of the law, by arguing that the statute satisfies rational basis review because it furthers the legitimate governmental interest of the promotion of morality. We have never held that moral disapproval, without any other asserted state interest, is a sufficient rationale under the Equal Protection Clause to justify a law that discriminates among groups of persons.

That this law as applied to private, consensual conduct is unconstitutional under the Equal Protection Clause does not mean that other laws distinguishing between heterosexuals and homosexuals would similarly fail under rational basis review. Unlike the moral disapproval of same-sex relations—the asserted state interest in this case—other reasons exist to promote the institution of marriage beyond mere moral disapproval of an excluded group.

Justice SCALIA, with whom THE CHIEF JUSTICE and Justice THOMAS join, *dissenting.*

Though there is discussion of "fundamental propositions" and "fundamental decisions," nowhere does the Court's opinion declare that homosexual sodomy is a "fundamental right" under the Due Process Clause; nor does it subject the Texas law to the standard of review that would be appropriate (strict scrutiny) if homosexual sodomy were a "fundamental right."

The Texas statute undoubtedly imposes constraints on liberty. So do laws prohibiting prostitution, recreational use of heroin, and, for that matter, working more than 60 hours per week in a bakery. Our opinions applying the doctrine known as "substantive due process" hold that the Due Process Clause prohibits States from infringing fundamental liberty interests, unless the infringement is narrowly tailored to serve a compelling state interest. We have held repeatedly, in cases the Court today does not overrule, that only fundamental rights qualify for this so-called "heightened scrutiny" protection — that is, rights which are "deeply rooted in this Nation's history and tradition." All other liberty interests may be abridged or abrogated pursuant to a validly enacted state law if that law is rationally related to a legitimate state interest.

Bowers held, first, that criminal prohibitions of homosexual sodomy are not subject to heightened scrutiny because they do not implicate a "fundamental right" under the Due Process Clause. Noting that "proscriptions against that conduct have ancient roots," that "sodomy was a criminal offense at common law and was forbidden by the laws of the original 13 States when they ratified the Bill of Rights," and that many States had retained their bans on sodomy, *Bowers* concluded that a right to engage in homosexual sodomy was not "deeply rooted in this Nation's history and tradition."

The Court today does not overrule this holding. Not once does it describe homosexual sodomy as a "fundamental right" or a "fundamental liberty interest," nor does it subject the Texas statute to strict scrutiny. Instead, having failed to establish that the right to homosexual sodomy is "deeply rooted in this Nation's history and tradition," the Court concludes that the application of Texas's statute to petitioners' conduct fails the rational-basis test, and overrules *Bowers*' holding to the contrary. "The Texas statute furthers no legitimate state interest which can justify its intrusion into the personal and private life of the individual."

The Court makes the claim that "laws prohibiting sodomy do not seem to have been enforced against consenting adults acting in private." The key qualifier here is "acting in private" — since the Court admits that sodomy laws were enforced against consenting adults (although the Court contends that prosecutions were "infrequent"). Surely that lack of evidence would not sustain the proposition that consensual sodomy on private premises with the doors closed and windows covered was regarded as a "fundamental right," even though all other consensual sodomy was criminalized. Realizing that fact, the Court instead says: "We think that our laws and traditions in the past half century are of most relevance here. These references show an emerging awareness that liberty gives substantial protection to adult persons in deciding how to conduct their private lives in matters pertaining to sex." Apart from the fact that such an "emerging awareness" does not establish a "fundamental right," the statement is factually false. States continue to prosecute all sorts of crimes by adults "in matters pertaining to sex."

I turn now to the ground on which the Court squarely rests its holding: the contention that there is no rational basis for the law here under attack. This

proposition is so out of accord with our jurisprudence—indeed, with the jurisprudence of any society we know—that it requires little discussion. The Texas
statute undeniably seeks to further the belief of its citizens that certain forms of
sexual behavior are "immoral and unacceptable," the same interest furthered by
criminal laws against fornication, bigamy, adultery, adult incest, bestiality, and
obscenity. *Bowers* held that this was a legitimate state interest. The Court today
reaches the opposite conclusion. The Texas statute, it says, "furthers no legitimate state interest which can justify its intrusion into the personal and private
life of the individual." The Court embraces instead Justice Stevens' declaration
in his *Bowers* dissent, that "the fact that the governing majority in a State has traditionally viewed a particular practice as immoral is not a sufficient reason for
upholding a law prohibiting the practice." This effectively decrees the end of all
morals legislation. If, as the Court asserts, the promotion of majoritarian sexual
morality is not even a legitimate state interest, none of the above-mentioned laws
can survive rational-basis review.

Today's opinion is the product of a Court, which is the product of a law-
profession culture, that has largely signed on to the so-called homosexual agenda,
by which I mean the agenda promoted by some homosexual activists directed at
eliminating the moral opprobrium that has traditionally attached to homosexual
conduct. I noted in an earlier opinion the fact that the American Association of
Law Schools (to which any reputable law school must seek to belong) excludes
from membership any school that refuses to ban from its job-interview facilities a
law firm (no matter how small) that does not wish to hire as a prospective partner
a person who openly engages in homosexual conduct.

One of the most revealing statements in today's opinion is the Court's grim
warning that the criminalization of homosexual conduct is "an invitation to subject homosexual persons to discrimination both in the public and in the private
spheres." It is clear from this that the Court has taken sides in the culture war,
departing from its role of assuring, as neutral observer, that the democratic rules
of engagement are observed. Many Americans do not want persons who openly
engage in homosexual conduct as partners in their business, as scoutmasters for
their children, as teachers in their children's schools, or as boarders in their
home. They view this as protecting themselves and their families from a lifestyle
that they believe to be immoral and destructive. The Court views it as "discrimination" which it is the function of our judgments to deter. So imbued is the
Court with the law profession's anti-anti-homosexual culture, that it is seemingly
unaware that the attitudes of that culture are not obviously "mainstream"; that
in most States what the Court calls "discrimination" against those who engage in
homosexual acts is perfectly legal; that proposals to ban such "discrimination"
under Title VII have repeatedly been rejected by Congress; that in some cases
such "discrimination" is mandated by federal statute; and that in some cases such
"discrimination" is a constitutional right.

Let me be clear that I have nothing against homosexuals, or any other group,
promoting their agenda through normal democratic means. Social perceptions

of sexual and other morality change over time, and every group has the right to persuade its fellow citizens that its view of such matters is the best. That homosexuals have achieved some success in that enterprise is attested to by the fact that Texas is one of the few remaining States that criminalize private, consensual homosexual acts. But persuading one's fellow citizens is one thing, and imposing one's views in absence of democratic majority will is something else. I would no more require a State to criminalize homosexual acts — or, for that matter, display any moral disapprobation of them — than I would forbid it to do so. What Texas has chosen to do is well within the range of traditional democratic action, and its hand should not be stayed through the invention of a brand-new "constitutional right" by a Court that is impatient of democratic change. It is indeed true that "later generations can see that laws once thought necessary and proper in fact serve only to oppress," and when that happens, later generations can repeal those laws. But it is the premise of our system that those judgments are to be made by the people, and not imposed by a governing caste that knows best.

One of the benefits of leaving regulation of this matter to the people rather than to the courts is that the people, unlike judges, need not carry things to their logical conclusion. The people may feel that their disapprobation of homosexual conduct is strong enough to disallow homosexual marriage, but not strong enough to criminalize private homosexual acts — and may legislate accordingly. The Court today pretends that it possesses a similar freedom of action, so that that we need not fear judicial imposition of homosexual marriage, as has recently occurred in Canada (in a decision that the Canadian Government has chosen not to appeal). At the end of its opinion — after having laid waste the foundations of our rational-basis jurisprudence — the Court says that the present case "does not involve whether the government must give formal recognition to any relationship that homosexual persons seek to enter." Do not believe it. More illuminating than this bald, unreasoned disclaimer is the progression of thought displayed by an earlier passage in the Court's opinion, which notes the constitutional protections afforded to "personal decisions relating to marriage, procreation, contraception, family relationships, child rearing, and education," and then declares that "persons in a homosexual relationship may seek autonomy for these purposes, just as heterosexual persons do." Today's opinion dismantles the structure of constitutional law that has permitted a distinction to be made between heterosexual and homosexual unions, insofar as formal recognition in marriage is concerned. If moral disapprobation of homosexual conduct is "no legitimate state interest" for purposes of proscribing that conduct, and if, as the Court coos (casting aside all pretense of neutrality), "when sexuality finds overt expression in intimate conduct with another person, the conduct can be but one element in a personal bond that is more enduring;" what justification could there possibly be for denying the benefits of marriage to homosexual couples exercising "the liberty protected by the Constitution"? Surely not the encouragement of procreation, since the sterile and the elderly are allowed to marry. This case "does not involve" the issue of homosexual marriage only if one entertains the belief that principle and logic have nothing to do with the decisions of this Court. Many will hope that, as the Court comfortingly assures us, this is so.

Justice THOMAS, *dissenting*.

As a member of this Court I am not empowered to help petitioners and others similarly situated. My duty, rather, is to "decide cases 'agreeably to the Constitution and laws of the United States.'" And, just like Justice Stewart, I "can find neither in the Bill of Rights nor any other part of the Constitution a general right of privacy," or as the Court terms it today, the "liberty of the person both in its spatial and more transcendent dimensions."

◆ PROBLEMS: GROOMING RESTRICTIONS ◆

Consider a police department regulation that imposes grooming restrictions on officers. Does this restriction implicate a constitutionally protected privacy interest? *See Kelley v. Johnson*, 425 U.S. 238 (1976).

Consistent with Justice Scalia's prediction, the issue of same-sex marriage came before the Court in a number of cases in recent years, and the issue has now been resolved. In 2013, in *United States v. Windsor*, 570 U.S. 693 (2013), the Court struck down Section 3 of the Defense of Marriage Act (DOMA), 110 Stat. 2419. That section provided a federal definition of "marriage" and "spouse": "In determining the meaning of any Act of Congress, or of any ruling, regulation, or interpretation of the various administrative bureaus and agencies of the United States, the word 'marriage' means only a legal union between one man and one woman as husband and wife, and the word 'spouse' refers only to a person of the opposite sex who is a husband or a wife." Recognizing that "the definition and regulation of marriage has been treated as being within the authority and realm of the separate States," the Court noted that the federal government has historically "deferred to state-law policy decisions with respect to domestic relations," and that "DOMA rejects the long-established precept that the incidents, benefits, and obligations of marriage are uniform for all married couples within each State." The Court noted that the individual state's decision to give a given class of citizens the right to marry confers "upon them a dignity and status of immense import." In striking down the law, the Court noted that DOMA departs from the "history and tradition of reliance on state law to define marriage." Noting that "DOMA seeks to injure the very class New York seeks to protect," the Court concluded that "it violates basic due process and equal protection principles applicable to the Federal Government."

At the same time, the Court decided *Hollingsworth v. Perry*, 570 U.S. 693 (2013), in which the Court refused to decide the question of whether the Equal Protection Clause "prohibits the State of California from defining marriage as the union of a man and a woman." The Court held that a challenge by same-sex couples was not justiciable. The case arose in 2008 after the California Supreme Court held that limiting the official designation of marriage to opposite-sex couples violated the equal protection clause of the California Constitution. *In re Marriage Cases*, 43 Cal. 4th 757, 183 P.3d 384. California voters responded by passing a ballot initiative (Proposition 8) that amended California's Constitution to provide that "only marriage between a man and a woman is valid or recognized in California." Cal. Const., Art. I, §7.5. Respondents, two same-sex couples who wished to marry, filed suit in federal court challenging Proposition 8 under the Due Process and Equal Protection Clauses of the Fourteenth Amendment to the Federal Constitution. The District Court declared Proposition 8 unconstitutional, permanently enjoining the California officials named as defendants from enforcing the law, and "directing the official defendants that all persons under their control or supervision" shall not enforce it. *Perry v. Schwarzenegger*, 704 F. Supp. 2d 921, 1004 (N.D. Cal. 2010). When those officials elected not to appeal the order, the proponents of the ballot initiative attempted to do so. The Court concluded that they lacked standing. Following these decisions, lower courts around the country began recognizing a constitutional right to same-sex marriage. However, one circuit concluded that there was no constitutional right. The Court then decided the following case.

Obergefell v. Hodges

135 S. Ct. 2584 (2015)

Justice KENNEDY delivered the opinion of the Court.

These cases come from Michigan, Kentucky, Ohio, and Tennessee, States that define marriage as a union between one man and one woman. Petitioners are 14 same-sex couples and two men whose same-sex partners are deceased. Respondents are state officials. Petitioners claim the respondents violate the Fourteenth Amendment by denying them the right to marry or to have their marriages, lawfully performed in another State, given full recognition. Petitioners filed these suits in United States District Courts in their home States. Each District Court ruled in their favor. Respondents appealed. The Court of Appeals held that a State has no constitutional obligation to license same-sex marriages or to recognize same-sex marriages performed out of State. Petitioners sought certiorari.

The annals of human history reveal the transcendent importance of marriage. The lifelong union of a man and a woman always has promised nobility and dignity to all persons, without regard to their station in life. The centrality of marriage to the human condition makes it unsurprising that the institution has existed for millennia and across civilizations. Marriage has transformed strangers into relatives, binding families and societies together. These references were based on the understanding that marriage is a union between two persons of the opposite sex. To Respondents, it would demean a timeless institution if the concept and lawful status of marriage were extended to two persons of the same sex. Marriage, in their view, is by its nature a gender-differentiated union of man and woman. This view long has been held in good faith by reasonable and sincere people here and throughout the world. Far from seeking to devalue marriage, petitioners seek it for themselves because of their respect—and need—for its privileges and responsibilities. Their immutable nature dictates that same-sex marriage is their only real path to this profound commitment.

The history of marriage is one of continuity and change. Marriage was once an arrangement by the parents based on political, religious, and financial concerns; by the time of the Nation's founding it was a voluntary contract between a man and a woman. Under the centuries-old doctrine of coverture, a married man and woman were treated by the State as a single, male-dominated legal entity. *See* 1 W. BLACKSTONE, COMMENTARIES ON THE LAWS OF ENGLAND 430 (1765). As women gained legal, political, and property rights, and as society began to understand that women have equal dignity, the law of coverture was abandoned. These and other developments in the institution of marriage worked deep transformations, affecting aspects of marriage long viewed by many as essential.

Changed understandings of marriage are characteristic of a Nation where new dimensions of freedom become apparent to new generations, often through pleas or protests and then in the political sphere and the judicial process. This dynamic can be seen in the Nation's experiences with the rights of gays and lesbians. Until the mid-20th century, same-sex intimacy had been condemned as immoral in most Western nations. Many persons did not deem homosexuals to have dignity in their own identity. Even when a greater awareness of the humanity and integrity of homosexual persons came after World War II, the argument that gays and lesbians had a just claim to dignity was in conflict with both law and widespread social conventions. Same-sex intimacy remained a crime in many States. Gays and lesbians were prohibited from most government employment, barred from military service, excluded under immigration laws, targeted by police, and burdened in their rights to associate. For much of the 20th century, homosexuality was treated as an illness. Only in recent years have psychiatrists and others recognized that sexual orientation is a normal expression of human sexuality and immutable. In the late 20th century, following substantial cultural and political developments, same-sex couples began to lead more open and public lives and to establish families. This development was followed by a discussion of the issue in both governmental and private sectors and by a shift in public attitudes toward greater tolerance.

This Court first gave detailed consideration to the legal status of homosexuals in *Bowers v. Hardwick*, 478 U.S. 186 (1986). There it upheld the constitutionality of a Georgia law deemed to criminalize certain homosexual acts. Ten years later, in *Romer v. Evans*, 517 U.S. 620 (1996), the Court invalidated an amendment to Colorado's Constitution that sought to foreclose any branch or political subdivision of the State from protecting persons against discrimination based on sexual orientation. In 2003, the Court overruled *Bowers*, holding that laws making same-sex intimacy a crime "demean the lives of homosexual persons." *Lawrence v. Texas*, 539 U.S. 558, 575.

In 1993, the Hawaii Supreme Court held Hawaii's law restricting marriage to opposite-sex couples constituted a classification on the basis of sex and was therefore subject to strict scrutiny under the Hawaii Constitution. Although this decision did not mandate that same-sex marriage be allowed, some States were concerned by its implications and reaffirmed in their laws that marriage is defined as a union between opposite-sex partners. In 1996, Congress passed the Defense of Marriage Act (DOMA), defining marriage for all federal-law purposes as "only a legal union between one man and one woman as husband and wife." 1 U.S.C. §7. The discussion led other States to a different conclusion. In 2003, the Supreme Judicial Court of Massachusetts held the State's Constitution guaranteed same-sex couples the right to marry. After that ruling, some additional States granted marriage rights to same-sex couples, either through judicial or legislative processes. Two Terms ago, in *United States v. Windsor*, 570 U.S. ___ (2013), this Court invalidated DOMA to the extent it barred the Federal Government from treating same-sex marriages as valid even when they were lawful in the State where they were licensed. DOMA, the Court held, impermissibly disparaged those same-sex couples "who wanted to affirm their commitment to one another before their children, their family, their friends, and their community."

Numerous cases about same-sex marriage have reached the United States Courts of Appeals in recent years. Courts have written a substantial body of law considering these issues. There also have been many thoughtful District Court decisions addressing same-sex marriage—and most have concluded same-sex couples must be allowed to marry. In addition the highest courts of many States have contributed decisions interpreting their own State Constitutions. The States are now divided on the issue of same-sex marriage.

Under the Due Process Clause of the Fourteenth Amendment, no State shall "deprive any person of life, liberty, or property, without due process of law." The fundamental liberties protected by this Clause include most of the rights enumerated in the Bill of Rights. See *Duncan v. Louisiana*, 391 U.S. 145 (1968). In addition these liberties extend to certain personal choices central to individual dignity and autonomy, including intimate choices that define personal identity and beliefs. See, *e.g., Eisenstadt v. Baird*, 405 U.S. 438 (1972); *Griswold v. Connecticut*, 381 U.S. 479 (1965). The identification and protection of fundamental rights is an enduring part of the judicial duty to interpret the Constitution. That responsibility, however, "has not been reduced to any formula." *Poe v. Ullman*, 367 U.S. 497 (1961) (Harlan, J., dissenting). Rather, it requires courts to exercise reasoned judgment in identifying interests of the person so fundamental that the State must accord them its respect. That process is guided by many of the same considerations relevant to analysis of other constitutional provisions that set forth broad principles rather than specific requirements. History and tradition guide and discipline this inquiry but do not set its outer boundaries. See *Lawrence, supra*, at 572. That method respects our history and learns from it without allowing the past alone to rule the present. The nature of injustice is that we may not always see it in our own times. The generations that wrote and ratified the Bill of Rights and the Fourteenth Amendment did not presume to know the extent of freedom in all of its dimensions, and so they entrusted to future generations a charter protecting the right of all persons to enjoy liberty as we learn its meaning. When new insight reveals discord between the Constitution's central protections and a received legal stricture, a claim to liberty must be addressed.

The Court has long held the right to marry is protected by the Constitution. In *Loving v. Virginia*, 388 U.S. 1 (1967), which invalidated bans on interracial unions, a unanimous Court held marriage is "one of the vital personal rights essential to the orderly pursuit of happiness by free men." The Court reaffirmed that holding in *Zablocki v. Redhail*, 434 U.S. 374 (1978), which held the right to marry was burdened by a law prohibiting fathers who were behind on child support from marrying. The Court again applied this principle in *Turner v. Safley*, 482 U.S. 78 (1987), which held the right to marry was abridged by regulations limiting the privilege of prison inmates to marry. In other contexts, the Court has reiterated that the right to marry is fundamental under the Due Process Clause. See, *e.g.*, *M.L.B. v. S.L.J.*, 519 U.S. 102 (1996); *Cleveland Bd. of Ed. v. LaFleur*, 414 U.S. 632 (1974); *Griswold, supra*, at 486; *Skinner v. Oklahoma ex rel. Williamson*, 316 U.S. 535 (1942); *Meyer v. Nebraska*, 262 U.S. 390 (1923).

This Court's cases describing the right to marry presumed a relationship involving opposite-sex partners. This was evident in *Baker v. Nelson*, 409 U.S. 810, a summary decision issued in 1972, holding the exclusion of same-sex couples from marriage did not present a federal question. There are other, more instructive precedents. In defining the right to marry these cases have identified essential attributes of that right based in history, tradition, and other constitutional liberties inherent in this intimate bond. See, *e.g.*, *Zablocki, supra*, at 384; *Loving, supra*, at 12. In assessing whether the force and rationale of its cases apply to same-sex couples, the Court must respect the basic reasons why the right to marry has been long protected.

This analysis compels the conclusion that same-sex couples may exercise the right to marry. The four principles and traditions to be discussed demonstrate that the reasons marriage is fundamental under the Constitution apply with equal force to same-sex couples.

A first premise is that the right to personal choice regarding marriage is inherent in the concept of individual autonomy. Like choices concerning contraception, family relationships, procreation, and childrearing, all of which are protected by the Constitution, decisions concerning marriage are among the most intimate that an individual can make. The nature of marriage is that, through its enduring bond, two persons together can find other freedoms, such as expression, intimacy, and spirituality. This is true for all persons, whatever their sexual orientation.

A second principle is that the right to marry is fundamental because it supports a two-person union unlike any other in its importance to the committed individuals. Marriage offers the hope of companionship and understanding and assurance that while both still live there will be someone to care for the other.

Same-sex couples have the same right as opposite-sex couples to enjoy intimate association. *Lawrence* invalidated laws that made same-sex intimacy a criminal act. It acknowledged that "when sexuality finds overt expression in intimate conduct with another person, the conduct can be but one element in a personal bond that is more enduring." While *Lawrence* confirmed a dimension of freedom that allows individuals to engage in intimate association without criminal liability, it does not follow that freedom stops there. Outlaw to outcast may be a step forward, but it does not achieve the full promise of liberty.

A third basis for protecting the right to marry is that it safeguards children and families. Marriage affords the permanency and stability important to children's best interests. Many same-sex couples provide loving and nurturing homes to their children, whether biological or adopted. Without the recognition, stability, and predictability marriage offers, their children suffer the stigma of knowing their families are somehow lesser. The marriage laws at issue here thus harm and humiliate the children of same-sex couples.

Fourth, this Court's cases and the Nation's traditions make clear that marriage is a keystone of our social order. In *Maynard v. Hill*, 125 U.S. 190, 211 (1888), the Court echoed de Tocqueville, explaining that marriage is "the foundation of the family and of society, without which there would be neither civilization nor progress." Just as a couple vows to support each other, so does society pledge to support the couple, offering symbolic recognition and material benefits to protect and nourish the union. While the States are free to vary the benefits they confer on all married couples, they have throughout our history made marriage the basis for an expanding list of governmental rights, benefits, and responsibilities. These aspects of marital status include: taxation; inheritance and property rights; rules of intestate succession; spousal privilege in the law of evidence; hospital access; medical decisionmaking authority; adoption rights; the rights and benefits of survivors; birth and death certificates; professional ethics rules; campaign finance restrictions; workers' compensation benefits; health insurance; and child custody, support, and visitation rules. Valid marriage under state law is also a significant status for over a thousand provisions of federal law.

By virtue of their exclusion, same-sex couples are denied the constellation of benefits that the States have linked to marriage. This harm results in more than just material burdens. Exclusion has the effect of teaching that gays and lesbians are unequal in important respects. It demeans gays and lesbians for the State to lock them out of a central institution of the Nation's society. Same-sex couples may aspire to the transcendent purposes of marriage and seek fulfillment in its highest meaning. The limitation of marriage to opposite-sex couples may long have seemed natural and just, but its inconsistency with the fundamental right to marry is now manifest. Laws excluding same-sex couples from the marriage right impose stigma and injury of the kind prohibited by our basic charter.

Respondents refer to *Washington v. Glucksberg*, 521 U.S. 702 (1997), which called for a "careful description" of fundamental rights. They assert petitioners do not seek to exercise the right to marry but rather a new and nonexistent "right to same-sex marriage." *Glucksberg* did insist that liberty under the Due Process Clause must be defined in a circumscribed manner, with central reference to specific historical practices. While that approach may have been appropriate for the right there involved (physician-assisted suicide), it is inconsistent with the approach this Court has used in discussing other fundamental rights, including marriage and intimacy. *Loving, Turner* and *Zablocki* inquired about the right to marry in its comprehensive sense, asking if there was a sufficient justification for excluding the relevant class from the right. That principle applies here. If rights were defined by who exercised them in the past, then received practices serve as their own continued justification and new groups could not invoke rights once denied. This Court has rejected that approach.

The right to marry is fundamental as a matter of history and tradition, but rights come not from ancient sources alone. They rise, too, from a better informed understanding of how constitutional imperatives define a liberty that remains urgent in our own era. Many who deem same-sex marriage to be wrong reach that conclusion based on decent and honorable religious or philosophical premises, and neither they nor their beliefs are disparaged here. But when that sincere, personal opposition becomes enacted law and public policy, the necessary consequence is to put the imprimatur of the State itself on an exclusion that demeans or stigmatizes those whose own liberty is then denied. Under the Constitution, same-sex couples seek in marriage the same legal treatment as opposite-sex couples, and it would disparage their choices and diminish their personhood to deny them this right.

The right of same-sex couples to marry is part of the liberty promised by the Fourteenth Amendment is derived, too, from that Amendment's guarantee of the equal protection of the laws. Rights implicit in liberty and rights secured by equal protection rest on different precepts and are not always co-extensive, yet each may be instructive as to the meaning and reach of the other. The Court's cases touching upon the right to marry reflect this dynamic. In *Loving* the Court invalidated a prohibition on interracial marriage under both the Equal Protection Clause and the Due Process Clause. The Court declared the prohibition invalid because of its unequal treatment of interracial couples. With this link to equal protection the Court proceeded to hold that "to deny this fundamental freedom on racial classifications is to deprive all the State's citizens of liberty without due process of law." In *Zablocki*, the Court invoked the Equal Protection Clause as its basis for invalidating the challenged law, which barred fathers who were behind on child-support payments from marrying without judicial approval. Each concept — liberty and equal protection — leads to a stronger understanding of the other.

In interpreting the Equal Protection Clause, the Court has recognized that new insights and societal understandings can reveal unjustified inequality within our most fundamental institutions that once passed unnoticed and unchallenged. Notwithstanding the gradual erosion of the doctrine of coverture, invidious sex-based classifications in marriage remained common through the mid-20th century. Responding to a new awareness, the Court invoked equal protection principles to invalidate laws imposing sex-based inequality on marriage. See *Kirchberg v. Feenstra*, 450 U.S. 455 (1981). These precedents show the Equal Protection Clause can help to identify and correct inequalities in the institution of marriage, vindicating precepts of liberty and equality under the Constitution. In *M.L.B. v. S.L.J.*, the Court invalidated under due process and equal protection principles a statute requiring indigent mothers to pay a fee in order to appeal the termination of their parental rights. In *Eisenstadt v. Baird*, the Court invoked both principles to invalidate a prohibition on the distribution of contraceptives to unmarried persons but not married persons. And in *Skinner v. Oklahoma ex rel. Williamson*, the Court invalidated under both principles a law that allowed sterilization of habitual criminals. In *Lawrence* the Court acknowledged the interlocking nature of these constitutional safeguards in the legal treatment of gays and lesbians.

This dynamic applies to same-sex marriage. The challenged laws burden the liberty of same-sex couples, and they abridge central precepts of equality. Here the marriage laws are in essence unequal: same-sex couples are denied all the benefits afforded to opposite-sex couples and are barred from exercising a fundamental right. Against a long history of disapproval of their relationships, this denial of the right to marry works a grave and continuing harm. The imposition of this disability on gays and lesbians serves to disrespect and subordinate them. The Equal Protection Clause, like the Due Process Clause, prohibits this unjustified infringement of the fundamental right to marry. See, *e.g., Zablocki, supra,* at 383-388; *Skinner*, 316 U.S., at 541.

These considerations lead to the conclusion that the right to marry is a fundamental right inherent in the liberty of the person, and under the Due Process and Equal Protection Clauses of the Fourteenth Amendment couples of the same-sex may not be deprived of that right and that liberty. The Court now holds that same-sex couples may exercise the fundamental right to marry. No longer may this liberty be denied to them. *Baker v. Nelson* is overruled, and the State laws challenged in these cases are invalid to the extent they exclude same-sex couples from civil marriage on the same terms and conditions as opposite-sex couples.

There may be an initial inclination to proceed with caution—to await further legislation, litigation, and debate. Respondents warn there has been insufficient democratic discourse before deciding an issue so basic as the definition of marriage. Yet there have been referenda, legislative debates, and grassroots campaigns, as well as countless studies, papers, books, and other popular and scholarly writings. There has been extensive litigation in state and federal courts. Judicial opinions addressing the issue have been informed by the contentions of parties and counsel, which, in turn, reflect the more general, societal discussion of same-sex marriage and its meaning that has occurred over the past decades. Many of the central institutions in American life—state and local governments, the military, large and small businesses, labor unions, religious organizations, law enforcement, civic groups, professional organizations, and universities—have devoted substantial attention to the question. This has led to an enhanced understanding of the issue—an understanding reflected in the arguments now presented for resolution as a matter of constitutional law.

The Constitution contemplates that democracy is the appropriate process for change, so long as that process does not abridge fundamental rights. It is most often through democracy that liberty is preserved and protected in our lives. But when the rights of persons are violated, "the Constitution requires redress by the courts," notwithstanding the more general value of democratic decisionmaking. Individuals need not await legislative action before asserting a fundamental right. The idea of the Constitution "was to withdraw certain subjects from the vicissitudes of political controversy, to place them beyond the reach of majorities and officials and to establish them as legal principles to be applied by the courts." *West Virginia Bd. of Ed. v. Barnette*, 319 U.S. 624, 638 (1943). "Fundamental rights may not be submitted to a vote; they depend on the outcome of no elections." *Ibid.* The issue is the legal question whether the Constitution protects the right of same-sex couples to marry.

This is not the first time the Court has been asked to adopt a cautious approach to recognizing and protecting fundamental rights. Although *Bowers* was repudiated in *Lawrence*, men and women were harmed in the interim, and the substantial effects of these injuries no doubt lingered. Dignitary wounds cannot always be healed with the stroke of a pen. A ruling against same-sex couples would be unjustified under the Fourteenth Amendment. Petitioners' stories make clear the urgency of the issue. James Obergefell asks whether Ohio can erase his marriage to John Arthur for all time. April DeBoer and Jayne Rowse ask whether Michigan may continue to deny them the certainty and stability all mothers desire to protect their children. Ijpe DeKoe and Thomas Kostura ask whether Tennessee can deny to one who has served this Nation the basic dignity of recognizing his New York marriage. Properly presented with petitioners' cases, the Court has a duty to address these claims and answer these questions. Were the Court to uphold the challenged laws as constitutional, it would teach the Nation that these laws are in accord with our society's most basic compact. Were the Court to stay its hand to allow slower, case-by-case determination, it still would deny gays and lesbians many rights and responsibilities intertwined with marriage.

Respondents argue allowing same-sex couples to wed will harm marriage as an institution. This may occur, respondents contend, because licensing same-sex marriage severs the connection between natural procreation and marriage. Decisions about whether to marry and raise children are based on many personal, romantic, and practical considerations; and it is unrealistic to conclude that an opposite-sex couple would choose not to marry simply because same-sex couples may do so. Respondents have not shown that allowing same-sex marriage will cause harmful outcomes. These cases involve the rights of two consenting adults whose marriages would pose no risk of harm to themselves or third parties.

It must be emphasized that religions, and those who adhere to religious doctrines, may continue to advocate with utmost, sincere conviction that, by divine precepts, same-sex marriage should not be condoned. The First Amendment ensures that religious organizations and persons are given proper protection as they seek to teach the principles that are fulfilling and central to their lives and faiths, and to their own deep aspirations to continue the family structure they have long revered. The same is true of those who oppose same-sex marriage for other reasons. In turn, those who believe allowing same-sex marriage is proper or indeed essential, whether as a matter of religious conviction or secular belief, may engage those who disagree with their view in an open and searching debate.

These cases also present the question whether the Constitution requires States to recognize same-sex marriages validly performed out of State. Being married in one State but having that marriage denied in another is one of "the most perplexing and distressing complications" in the law of domestic relations. For some couples, even an ordinary drive into a neighboring State to visit family or friends risks causing severe hardship in the event of a spouse's hospitalization while across state lines. In light of the fact that many States already allow same-sex marriage, the disruption caused by the recognition bans is significant and ever-growing. If States are required by the Constitution to issue marriage licenses to same-sex couples, the justifications for refusing to recognize those marriages performed elsewhere are undermined. There is no lawful basis for a State to refuse to recognize a lawful same-sex marriage performed in another State on the ground of its same-sex character.

No union is more profound than marriage, for it embodies the highest ideals of love, fidelity, devotion, sacrifice, and family. In forming a marital union, two people become something greater than once they were. Marriage embodies a love that may endure even past death. It would misunderstand these men and women to say they disrespect the idea of marriage. Their plea is that they respect it so deeply that they seek to find its fulfillment for themselves. Their hope is not to be condemned to live in loneliness, excluded from one of civilization's oldest institutions. They ask for equal dignity in the eyes of the law. The Constitution grants them that right.

The judgment of the Court of Appeals for the Sixth Circuit is *reversed*.

It is so ordered.

Chief Justice ROBERTS, with whom Justice SCALIA and Justice THOMAS join, *dissenting*.

This Court is not a legislature. Under the Constitution, judges have power to say what the law is, not what it should be. Although the policy arguments for extending marriage to same-sex couples may be compelling, the legal arguments for requiring such an extension are not. The fundamental right to marry does not include a right to make a State change its definition of marriage. A State's decision to maintain the meaning of marriage that has persisted in every culture throughout human history can hardly be called irrational. Our Constitution does not enact any one theory of marriage. The people of a State are free to expand marriage to include same-sex couples, or to retain the historic definition.

Many people will rejoice at this decision, and I begrudge none their celebration. But for those who believe in a government of laws, not of men, the majority's approach is deeply disheartening. Supporters of same-sex marriage have achieved considerable success persuading their fellow citizens—through the democratic process—to adopt their view. Five lawyers have closed the debate and enacted their own vision of marriage as a matter of constitutional law. Stealing this issue from the people will cast a cloud over same-sex marriage, making a dramatic social change that much more difficult to accept.

The majority's decision is an act of will, not legal judgment. The right it announces has no basis in the Constitution or this Court's precedent. The majority expressly disclaims judicial "caution" and omits even a pretense of humility, openly relying on its desire to remake society according to its own "new insight" into the "nature of injustice." As a result, the Court invalidates the marriage laws of more than half the States and orders the transformation of a social institution that has formed the basis of human society for millennia, for the Kalahari Bushmen and the Han Chinese, the Carthaginians and the Aztecs. Just who do we think we are?

It can be tempting for judges to confuse our own preferences with the requirements of the law. The majority seizes for itself a question the Constitution leaves to the people, at a time when the people are engaged in a vibrant debate on that question. It answers that question based not on neutral principles of constitutional law, but on its own "understanding of what freedom is and must become." This dissent is not about whether the institution of marriage should be changed to include same-sex couples. It is instead about whether, in our democratic republic, that decision should rest with the people acting through their elected representatives, or with five lawyers who happen to hold commissions authorizing them to resolve legal disputes according to law.

The Constitution protects a right to marry and requires States to apply their marriage laws equally. The real question is what constitutes "marriage," or—more precisely—*who decides* what constitutes "marriage"? Marriage "has existed for millennia and across civilizations." For all those millennia, across all those civilizations, "marriage" referred to only the union of a man and a woman. Marriage arose in the nature of things to meet a vital need: ensuring that children are conceived by a mother and father committed to raising them in the stable conditions of a lifelong relationship. The premises supporting this concept of marriage are fundamental. The human race must procreate to survive. Procreation occurs through sexual relations between a man and a woman. When sexual relations result in the conception of a child, that child's prospects are generally better if the mother and father stay together rather than going their separate ways. Therefore, for the good of children and society, sexual relations that can lead to procreation should occur only between a man and a woman committed to a lasting bond. Society has recognized that bond as marriage. By bestowing a respected status and material benefits on married couples, society encourages men and women to conduct sexual relations within marriage rather than without. This singular understanding of marriage has prevailed in the United States through-out our history. To those who drafted and ratified the Constitution, this con-ception of marriage and family "was a given: its structure, its stability, roles, and values accepted by all." Forte, The Framers' Idea of Marriage and Family, in The Meaning of Marriage 100, 102 (R. George & J. Elshtain eds. 2006).

The Constitution itself says nothing about marriage, and the Framers entrusted the States with "the whole subject of the domestic relations of hus-band and wife." *Windsor*, 570 U.S., at ___ (slip op., at 17). Every State at the founding—and every State throughout our history until a dozen years ago—defined marriage in the traditional, biologically rooted way. This Court's precedents have repeatedly described marriage in ways that are consistent only with its traditional meaning. Early cases on the subject referred to marriage as "the union for life of one man and one woman," *Murphy v. Ramsey*, 114 U.S. 15 (1885), which forms "the foundation of the family and of society, without which there would be neither civili-zation nor progress," *Maynard v. Hill*, 125 U.S. 190, 211 (1888). We later described marriage as "fundamental to our very existence and survival," an understanding that necessarily implies a procreative component. *Loving v. Virginia*, 388 U.S. 1, 12 (1967). More recent cases have directly connected the right to marry with the "right to procreate." *Zablocki v. Redhail*, 434 U.S. 374 (1978).

Some aspects of marriage have changed over time. Arranged marriages have largely given way to pairings based on romantic love. States have replaced cover-ture with laws that respect each participant's separate status. Racial restrictions on marriage, which "arose as an incident to slavery" to promote "White Supremacy," were repealed by many States and ultimately struck down by this Court. These developments did not work any transformation in the core structure of marriage as the union between a man and a woman. The core meaning of marriage has endured. Shortly after this Court struck down racial restrictions on marriage in *Loving*, a gay couple in Minnesota sought a marriage license. They argued that the Constitution required States to allow marriage between people of the same sex for the same reasons that it requires States to allow marriage between people of different races. The Minnesota Supreme Court rejected their analogy, and this Court summarily dismissed an appeal. *Baker v. Nelson*, 409 U.S. 810 (1972).

In the decades after *Baker*, greater numbers of gays and lesbians began living openly, and many expressed a desire to have their relationships recognized as marriages. Over time, more people came to see marriage in a way that could be extended to such couples. Until recently, this new view of marriage remained a minority position. In all, voters and legislators in eleven States and the District of Columbia have changed their definitions of marriage to include same-sex cou-ples. The highest courts of five States have decreed that same result under their own Constitutions. The remainder of the States retain the traditional definition of marriage.

The majority purports to identify four "principles and traditions" in this Court's due process precedents that support a fundamental right for same-sex couples to marry. In reality, however, the majority's approach has no basis in principle or tradition, except for the unprincipled tradition of judicial policy-making that characterized discredited decisions such as *Lochner v. New York*, 198 U.S. 45. Stripped of its shiny rhetorical gloss, the majority's argument is that the Due Process Clause gives same-sex couples a fundamental right to marry because it will be good for them and for society. If I were a legislator, I would certainly consider that view as a matter of social policy. But as a judge, I find the majority's position indefensible as a matter of constitutional law.

Petitioners' "fundamental right" claim falls into the most sensitive category of constitutional adjudication. Petitioners do not contend that their States' marriage laws violate an *enumerated* constitutional right. They argue instead that the laws violate a right *implied* by the Fourteenth Amendment's requirement that "liberty" may not be deprived without "due process of law." This Court has interpreted the Due Process Clause to include a "substantive" component that protects certain liberty interests against state deprivation "no matter what process is provided." *Reno v. Flores*, 507 U.S. 292 (1993). The theory is that some liberties are "so rooted in the traditions and conscience of our people as to be ranked as fundamental," and therefore cannot be deprived without compelling justification. *Snyder v. Massachusetts*, 291 U.S. 97 (1934).

Allowing unelected federal judges to select which unenumerated rights rank as "fundamental"—and to strike down state laws on the basis of that determination—raises obvious concerns about the judicial role. Our precedents have insisted that judges "exercise the utmost care" in identifying implied fundamental rights, "lest the liberty protected by the Due Process Clause be subtly transformed into the policy preferences of the Members of this Court." *Washington v. Glucksberg*, 521 U.S. 702, 720 (1997). The need for restraint in administering the strong medicine of substantive due process is a lesson this Court learned the hard way. By empowering judges to elevate their own policy judgments to the status of constitutionally protected "liberty," the *Lochner* line of cases left "no alternative to regarding the court as a legislative chamber." L. HAND, THE BILL OF RIGHTS 42 (1958). Eventually, the Court recognized its error and vowed not to repeat it. We have returned to the original constitutional proposition that courts do not substitute their social and economic beliefs for the judgment of legislative bodies, who are elected to pass laws." *Ferguson v. Skrupa*, 372 U.S. 726 (1963); see *Day-Brite Lighting, Inc. v. Missouri*, 342 U.S. 421 (1952) ("we do not sit as a super-legislature to weigh the wisdom of legislation").

To avoid repeating *Lochner*'s error of converting personal preferences into constitutional mandates, our modern substantive due process cases have stressed the need for "judicial self-restraint." Our precedents have required that implied fundamental rights be "objectively, deeply rooted in this Nation's history and tradition," and "implicit in the concept of ordered liberty, such that neither liberty nor justice would exist if they were sacrificed." *Glucksberg*, 521 U.S., at 720-721. Although the Court articulated the importance of history and tradition to the fundamental rights inquiry most precisely in *Glucksberg*, many other cases both before and after have adopted the same approach.

Proper reliance on history and tradition of course requires looking beyond the individual law being challenged, so that every restriction on liberty does not supply its own constitutional justification. Given the few "guideposts for responsible decisionmaking in this unchartered area," "an approach grounded in history imposes limits on the judiciary that are more meaningful than any based on an abstract formula," *Moore*, 431 U.S., at 504, n.12 (plurality opinion). Expanding a right suddenly and dramatically is likely to require tearing it from its roots. The only way to ensure restraint in this delicate enterprise is "continual insistence upon respect for the teachings of history, solid recognition of the basic values that underlie our society, and wise appreciation of the great roles of the doctrines of federalism and separation of powers." *Griswold v. Connecticut*, 381 U.S. 479, 501 (1965) (Harlan, J., concurring).

The majority's aggressive application of substantive due process breaks sharply with decades of precedent and returns to the unprincipled approach of *Lochner*. The majority's driving themes are that marriage is desirable and petitioners desire it. The opinion repeatedly insists that petitioners do not seek to "demean," "devalue," "denigrate," or "disrespect" the institution. Nobody disputes those points. When the majority turns to the law, it relies primarily on precedents discussing the fundamental "right to marry." *Turner v. Safley*, 482 U.S. 78 (1987); *Zablocki*, 434 U.S., at 383; *Loving*, 388 U.S., at 12. None of the laws at issue in those cases purported to change the core definition of marriage as the union of a man and a woman. These precedents say nothing at all about a right to make a State change its definition of marriage. Neither petitioners nor the majority cites a single case or other legal source providing any basis for such a constitutional right. None exists, and that is enough to foreclose their claim.

The majority suggests that "there are other, more instructive precedents" informing the right to marry. This reference seems to be to a line of cases discussing an implied fundamental "right of privacy." *Griswold*, 381 U.S., at 486. In the first of those cases, the Court invalidated a criminal law that banned the use of contraceptives. In the Court's view, such laws infringed the right to privacy in its most basic sense: the "right to be let alone." *Eisenstadt v. Baird*, 405 U.S. 438, 453 (1972). The Court also invoked the right to privacy in *Lawrence v. Texas*, 539 U.S. 558 (2003), which struck down a Texas statute criminalizing homosexual sodomy. Neither *Lawrence* nor any other precedent supports the right that petitioners assert here. Unlike criminal laws banning contraceptives and sodomy, marriage laws involve no government intrusion. They create no crime and impose no punishment. Same-sex couples remain free to live together, to engage in intimate conduct, and to raise their families as they see fit. The laws in no way interfere with the "right to be let alone." The majority also relies on Justice Harlan's influential dissenting opinion in *Poe v. Ullman*, 367 U.S. 497 (1961). Justice Harlan's opinion makes clear that courts implying fundamental rights are not "free to roam where unguided speculation might take them." They must instead have "regard to what history teaches" and exercise not only "judgment" but "restraint." The privacy cases provide no support for the majority's position, because petitioners do not seek privacy. Quite the opposite, they seek public recognition of their relationships, along with corresponding government benefits. Our cases have consistently refused to allow litigants to convert the shield provided by constitutional liberties into a sword to demand positive entitlements from the State. The right to privacy provides no affirmative right to redefine marriage and no basis for striking down the laws at issue here.

Perhaps recognizing how little support it can derive from precedent, the majority goes out of its way to jettison the "careful" approach to implied fundamental rights taken in *Glucksberg*. The majority opens its opinion by announcing petitioners' right to "define and express their identity." The majority later explains that "the right to personal choice regarding marriage is inherent in the concept of individual autonomy." This freewheeling notion of individual autonomy echoes "the general right of an individual to be *free in his person* and in his power to contract in relation to his own labor." *Lochner*, 198 U.S., at 58. The majority does not suggest that its individual autonomy right is entirely unconstrained. The constraints it sets are precisely those that accord with its own "reasoned judgment," informed by its "new insight" into the "nature of injustice," which was invisible to all who came before but has become clear "as we learn the meaning" of liberty. The truth is that today's decision rests on nothing more than the majority's own conviction that same-sex couples should be allowed to marry because they want to, and that "it would disparage their choices and diminish their personhood to deny them this right." Whatever force that belief may have as a matter of moral philosophy, it has no more basis in the Constitution than did the naked policy preferences adopted in *Lochner*.

One immediate question invited by the majority's position is whether States may retain the definition of marriage as a union of two people. Although the majority randomly inserts the adjective "two" in various places, it offers no reason why the two-person element of the core definition of marriage may be preserved while the man-woman element may not. From the standpoint of history and tradition, a leap from opposite-sex marriage to same-sex marriage is much greater than one from a two-person union to plural unions, which have deep roots in some cultures around the world. If the majority is willing to take the big leap, it is hard to see how it can say no to the shorter one. It is striking how much of the majority's reasoning would apply with equal force to the claim of a fundamental right to plural marriage. If "there is dignity in the bond between two men or two women who seek to marry and in their autonomy to make such profound choices," why would there be any less dignity in the bond between three people who, in exercising their autonomy, seek to make the profound choice to marry? If a same-sex couple has the constitutional right to marry because their children would otherwise "suffer the stigma of knowing their families are somehow lesser," why wouldn't the same reasoning apply to a family of three or more persons raising children? If not having the opportunity to marry "serves to disrespect and subordinate" gay and lesbian couples, why wouldn't the same "imposition of this disability," serve to disrespect and subordinate people who find fulfillment in polyamorous relationships?

Expanding marriage to include same-sex couples, the majority insists, would "pose no risk of harm to themselves or third parties." This argument echoes *Lochner*, which relied on its assessment that "we think that a law like the one before us involves neither the safety, the morals nor the welfare of the public, and that the interest of the public is not in the slightest degree affected by such an act." Assertion of the "harm principle" sounds more in philosophy than law. The elevation of the fullest individual self-realization over the constraints that society has expressed in law may or may not be attractive moral philosophy. But a Justice's commission does not confer any special moral, philosophical, or social insight sufficient to justify imposing those perceptions on fellow citizens under the pretense of "due process." There is indeed a process due the people on issues of this sort—the democratic process. Respecting that understanding requires the Court to be guided by law, not any particular school of social thought.

The majority's understanding of due process lays out a tantalizing vision of the future: If an unvarying social institution enduring over all of recorded history cannot inhibit judicial policymaking, what can? The purpose of insisting that implied fundamental rights have roots in the history and tradition of our people is to ensure that when unelected judges strike down democratically enacted laws, they do so based on something more than their own beliefs. The Court today not only overlooks our country's entire history and tradition but actively repudiates it, preferring to live only in the heady days of the here and now.

Petitioners contend that the Equal Protection Clause requires their States to license and recognize same-sex marriages. The "modern Supreme Court's treatment of equal protection claims has used a means-ends methodology in which judges ask whether the classification the government is using is sufficiently related to the goals it is pursuing." Yet the majority fails to provide even a single sentence explaining how the Equal Protection Clause supplies independent weight for its position, nor does it attempt to justify its gratuitous violation of the canon against unnecessarily resolving constitutional questions. In any event, the marriage laws at issue here do not violate the Equal Protection Clause, because distinguishing between opposite-sex and same-sex couples is rationally related to the States' "legitimate state interest" in "preserving the traditional institution of marriage." *Lawrence*, 539 U.S., at 585 (O'Connor, J., concurring).

It is important to note with precision which laws petitioners have challenged. Although they discuss some of the ancillary legal benefits that accompany marriage, such as hospital visitation rights and recognition of spousal status on official documents, petitioners' lawsuits target the laws defining marriage generally rather than those allocating benefits specifically. The equal protection analysis might be different if we were confronted with a more focused challenge to the denial of certain tangible benefits. Those more selective claims will not arise now that the Court has taken the drastic step of requiring every State to license and recognize marriages between same-sex couples.

The legitimacy of this Court ultimately rests "upon the respect accorded to its judgments." That respect flows from the perception—and reality—that we exercise humility and restraint in deciding cases according to the Constitution and law. The role of the Court envisioned by the majority is anything but humble or restrained. Over and over, the majority exalts the role of the judiciary in delivering social change. In the majority's telling, it is the courts, not the people, who are responsible for making "new dimensions of freedom apparent to new generations," for providing "formal discourse" on social issues, and for ensuring "neutral discussions, without scornful or disparaging commentary." Nowhere is the majority's extravagant conception of judicial supremacy more evident than in its description—and dismissal—of the public debate regarding same-sex marriage. The majority concedes, on one side are thousands of years of human history in every society known to have populated the planet. But on the other side, there has been "extensive litigation," "many thoughtful District Court decisions," "countless studies, papers, books, and other popular and scholarly writings," and "more than 100" *amicus* briefs. What would be the point of allowing the democratic process to go on? It is high time for the Court to decide the meaning of marriage, based on five lawyers' "better informed understanding" of "a liberty that remains urgent in our own era."

Those who founded our country would not recognize the majority's conception of the judicial role. They risked their lives and fortunes for the precious right to govern themselves. They would never have imagined yielding that right on a question of social policy to unaccountable and unelected judges. They certainly would not have been satisfied by a system empowering judges to override policy judgments so long as they do so after "a quite extensive discussion." The Court's accumulation of power does not occur in a vacuum. It comes at the expense of the people. Here and abroad, people are in the midst of a serious and thoughtful public debate on the issue of same-sex marriage. They see voters carefully considering same-sex marriage, casting ballots in favor or opposed, and sometimes changing their minds. They see political leaders similarly reexamining their positions, and either reversing course or explaining adherence to old convictions confirmed anew. They see governments and businesses modifying policies and practices with respect to same-sex couples, and participating actively in the civic discourse. This deliberative process is making people take seriously questions that they may not have even regarded as questions before. When decisions are reached through democratic means, some people will inevitably be disappointed with the results. But those whose views do not prevail at least know that they have had their say, and accordingly are—in the tradition of our political culture—reconciled to the result of a fair and honest debate. In addition, they can gear up to raise the issue later, hoping to persuade enough on the winning side to think again. That is exactly how our system of government is supposed to work. Today the Court puts a stop to all that. By deciding this question under the Constitution, the Court removes it from the realm of democratic decision. Closing debate tends to close minds. People denied a voice are less likely to accept the ruling of a court on an issue that does not seem to be the sort of thing courts usually decide.

Today's decision creates serious questions about religious liberty. Many good and decent people oppose same-sex marriage as a tenet of faith, and their freedom to exercise religion is—unlike the right imagined by the majority—actually spelled out in the Constitution. Respect for sincere religious conviction has led voters and legislators in every State that has adopted same-sex marriage democratically to include accommodations for religious practice. The majority graciously suggests that religious believers may continue to "advocate" and "teach" their views of marriage. The First Amendment guarantees, however, the freedom to "*exercise*" religion. Ominously, that is not a word the majority uses. Hard questions arise when people of faith exercise religion in ways that may be seen to conflict with the new right to same-sex marriage—when, for example, a religious college provides married student housing only to opposite-sex married couples, or a religious adoption agency declines to place children with same-sex married couples. The Solicitor General acknowledged that the tax exemptions of some religious institutions would be in question if they opposed same-sex marriage. There is little doubt that these and similar questions will soon be before this Court. People of faith can take no comfort in the treatment they receive from the majority today.

Perhaps the most discouraging aspect of today's decision is the extent to which the majority feels compelled to sully those on the other side of the debate. The majority explains that "the necessary consequence" of laws codifying the traditional definition of marriage is to "demean or stigmatize" same-sex couples. Americans who did nothing more than follow the understanding of marriage that has existed for our entire history—in particular, the tens of millions of people who voted to reaffirm their States' enduring definition of marriage—have acted to "disparage," "disrespect and subordinate," and inflict "dignitary wounds" upon their gay and lesbian neighbors. These assaults on the character of fairminded people will have an effect, in society and in court. Moreover, they are entirely gratuitous. It is one thing for the majority to conclude that the Constitution protects a right to same-sex marriage; it is something else to portray everyone who does not share the majority's "better informed understanding" as bigoted.

A much different view of the Court's role is possible. That view is more modest and restrained. It is more skeptical that the legal abilities of judges also reflect insight into moral and philosophical issues. It is more sensitive to the fact that judges are unelected and unaccountable, and that the legitimacy of their power depends on confining it to the exercise of legal judgment. It is more attuned to the lessons of history, and what it has meant for the country and Court when Justices have exceeded their proper bounds. And it is less pretentious than to suppose that while people around the world have viewed an institution in a particular way for thousands of years, the present generation and the present Court are the ones chosen to burst the bonds of that history and tradition.

If you are among the many Americans—of whatever sexual orientation—who favor expanding same-sex marriage, by all means celebrate today's
decision. Celebrate the achievement of a desired goal. Celebrate the opportunity
for a new expression of commitment to a partner. Celebrate the availability of
new benefits. But do not celebrate the Constitution. It had nothing to do with it.

Justice SCALIA, with whom Justice THOMAS joins, *dissenting.*

I join The Chief Justice's opinion in full. The substance of today's decree is
not of immense personal importance to me. The law can recognize as marriage
whatever sexual attachments and living arrangements it wishes, and can accord
them favorable civil consequences, from tax treatment to rights of inheritance. It
is of overwhelming importance, however, who it is that rules me. Today's decree
says that my Ruler, and the Ruler of 320 million Americans coast-to-coast, is a
majority of the nine lawyers on the Supreme Court. The opinion in these cases is
the furthest extension of the Court's claimed power to create "liberties" that the
Constitution and its Amendments neglect to mention. This practice of constitutional revision by an unelected committee of nine, always accompanied (as it is
today) by extravagant praise of liberty, robs the People of the most important liberty they asserted in the Declaration of Independence and won in the Revolution
of 1776: the freedom to govern themselves.

Until the courts put a stop to it, public debate over same-sex marriage displayed American democracy at its best. Individuals on both sides of the issue
passionately, but respectfully, attempted to persuade their fellow citizens to
accept their views. Americans considered the arguments and put the question
to a vote. The electorates of 11 States, either directly or through their representatives, chose to expand the traditional definition of marriage. Many more
decided not to. Win or lose, advocates for both sides continued pressing their
cases, secure in the knowledge that an electoral loss can be negated by a later
electoral win. That is exactly how our system of government is supposed to work.

The Constitution places some constraints on self-rule—constraints adopted
by the People themselves when they ratified the Constitution and its Amendments.
Forbidden are laws "impairing the Obligation of Contracts," denying "Full Faith
and Credit" to the "public Acts" of other States, prohibiting the free exercise
of religion, abridging the freedom of speech, infringing the right to keep and
bear arms, authorizing unreasonable searches and seizures, and so forth. These
cases ask us to decide whether the Fourteenth Amendment contains a limitation
that requires the States to license and recognize marriages between two people
of the same sex. Does it remove *that* issue from the political process? Of course
not. It would be surprising to find a prescription regarding marriage in the
Federal Constitution since "regulation of domestic relations is an area that has
long been regarded as a virtually exclusive province of the States." "The Federal
Government, through our history, has deferred to state-law policy decisions with
respect to domestic relations."

When the Fourteenth Amendment was ratified in 1868, every State limited marriage to one man and one woman, and no one doubted the constitutionality of doing so. That resolves these cases. When it comes to determining the meaning of a vague constitutional provision — such as "due process of law" or "equal protection of the laws" — it is unquestionable that the People who ratified that provision did not understand it to prohibit a practice that remained both universal and uncontroversial in the years after ratification. We have no basis for striking down a practice that is not expressly prohibited by the Fourteenth Amendment's text, and that bears the endorsement of a long tradition of open, widespread, and unchallenged use dating back to the Amendment's ratification.

But the Court ends this debate, in an opinion lacking even a thin veneer of law. Buried beneath the passages is a candid and startling assertion: No matter *what* it was the People ratified, the Fourteenth Amendment protects those rights that the Judiciary, in its "reasoned judgment," thinks the Fourteenth Amendment ought to protect. That is so because "the generations that wrote and ratified the Bill of Rights and the Fourteenth Amendment did not presume to know the extent of freedom in all of its dimensions." What logically follows, in the majority's judge-empowering estimation, is: "and so they entrusted to future generations a charter protecting the right of all persons to enjoy liberty as we learn its meaning." The "we," needless to say, is the nine of us. Rather than focusing on *the People's* understanding of "liberty" — at the time of ratification or even today — the majority focuses on four "principles and traditions" that, *in the majority's view*, prohibit States from defining marriage as an institution consisting of one man and one woman. This is a naked judicial claim to legislative — indeed, *super*–legislative — power; a claim fundamentally at odds with our system of government. A system of government that makes the People subordinate to a committee of nine unelected lawyers does not deserve to be called a democracy.

Judges are selected precisely for their skill as lawyers; whether they reflect the policy views of a particular constituency is not (or should not be) relevant. The Federal Judiciary is hardly a cross-section of America. This Court consists of nine men and women, all of them successful lawyers who studied at Harvard or Yale Law School. Four are natives of New York City. Eight grew up in east- and west-coast States. Only one hails from the vast expanse in-between. Not a single Southwesterner or even, to tell the truth, a genuine Westerner (California does not count). Not a single evangelical Christian (a group that comprises one quarter of Americans), or even a Protestant of any denomination. The strikingly unrepresentative character of the body voting on today's social upheaval would be irrelevant if they were functioning as *judges*, answering the legal question whether the American people had ever ratified a constitutional provision that was understood to proscribe the traditional definition of marriage. But of course the Justices are not voting on that basis. To allow the policy question of same-sex marriage to be considered and resolved by a select, patrician, highly unrepresentative panel of nine is to violate a principle even more fundamental than no taxation without representation: no social transformation without representation.

But what really astounds is the hubris reflected in today's judicial Putsch. The five Justices who compose today's majority have discovered in the Fourteenth Amendment a "fundamental right" overlooked by every person alive at the time of ratification, and almost everyone else since. They see what lesser legal minds—minds like Thomas Cooley, John Marshall Harlan, Oliver Wendell Holmes, Jr., Learned Hand, Louis Brandeis, Benjamin Cardozo, Hugo Black, Felix Frankfurter, and Henry Friendly—could not. They are certain that the People ratified the Fourteenth Amendment to bestow on them the power to remove questions from the democratic process when that is called for by their "reasoned judgment." These Justices *know* that limiting marriage to one man and one woman is contrary to reason; they *know* that an institution as old as government itself, and accepted by every nation in history until 15 years ago, cannot possibly be supported by anything other than ignorance or bigotry. Any citizen who does not agree with that, who adheres to what was, until 15 years ago, the unanimous judgment of all generations and societies, stands against the Constitution.

The opinion is as pretentious as its content is egotistic. It is one thing for concurring or dissenting opinions to contain extravagances; it is something else for the opinion of the Court to do so. Rights, we are told, can "rise from a better informed understanding of how constitutional imperatives define a liberty that remains urgent in our own era." The stuff contained in today's opinion has to diminish this Court's reputation for clear thinking and sober analysis.

Justice THOMAS, with whom Justice SCALIA joins, *dissenting.*

The Framers created our Constitution to preserve liberty. The majority invokes our Constitution in the name of a "liberty" that the Framers would not have recognized, to the detriment of the liberty they sought to protect. It rejects the idea—captured in our Declaration of Independence—that human dignity is innate and suggests that it comes from Government. This distortion of our Constitution not only ignores the text, it inverts the relationship between the individual and the state in our Republic. I cannot agree.

I have explained the dangerous fiction of treating the Due Process Clause as a font of substantive rights. It distorts the constitutional text, which guarantees only whatever "process" is "due" before a person is deprived of life, liberty, and property. U.S. Const., Amdt. 14, §1. Worse, it invites judges to do exactly what the majority has done here—" 'roam at large in the constitutional field' guided only by their personal views" as to the "fundamental rights" protected by that document. *Planned Parenthood of Southeastern Pa. v. Casey*, 505 U.S. 833 (1992) (Rehnquist, C.J., concurring in part and dissenting in part). By straying from the text of the Constitution, substantive due process exalts judges at the expense of the People from whom they derive their authority. Petitioners argue that by enshrining the traditional definition of marriage in their State Constitutions through voter-approved amendments, the States have put the issue "beyond the reach of the normal democratic process." The result petitioners seek is less democratic. They ask nine judges to enshrine their definition of marriage in the

Constitution and put it beyond the reach of the normal democratic process for the Nation.

To invoke the protection of the Due Process Clause at all—whether under a theory of "substantive" or "procedural" due process—a party must first identify a deprivation of "life, liberty, or property." The majority claims these state laws deprive petitioners of "liberty," but the concept of "liberty" it conjures up bears no resemblance to any plausible meaning of that word as it is used in the Due Process Clauses. In enacting the Fifth Amendment's Due Process Clause, the Framers chose to employ the "life, liberty, or property" formulation. When read in light of the history of that formulation, it is hard to see how the "liberty" protected by the Clause could be interpreted to include anything broader than freedom from physical restraint. That was the consistent usage of the time when "liberty" was paired with "life" and "property." And that usage avoids rendering superfluous those protections for "life" and "property."

Petitioners cannot claim, under the most plausible definition of "liberty," that they have been imprisoned or physically restrained by the States for participating in same-sex relationships. They have been able to cohabitate and raise their children in peace. They have been able to hold civil marriage ceremonies in States that recognize same-sex marriages and private religious ceremonies in all States. They have been able to travel freely, making their homes where they please. Far from being incarcerated or physically restrained, petitioners have been left alone to order their lives as they see fit. Nor, can they claim that the States have restricted their ability to go about their daily lives as they would be able to absent governmental restrictions. Petitioners do not ask this Court to order the States to stop restricting their ability to enter same-sex relationships, to engage in intimate behavior, to make vows to their partners in public ceremonies, to engage in religious wedding ceremonies, to hold themselves out as married, or to raise children. Nor have the States prevented petitioners from approximating a number of incidents of marriage through private legal means, such as wills, trusts, and powers of attorney. Instead, the States have refused to grant them governmental entitlements. Petitioners claim that as a matter of "liberty," they are entitled to access privileges and benefits that exist solely *because of* the government. They want, for example, to receive the State's *imprimatur* on their marriages—on state issued marriage licenses, death certificates, or other official forms. They want to receive various monetary benefits, including reduced inheritance taxes upon the death of a spouse, compensation if a spouse dies as a result of a work-related injury, or loss of consortium damages in tort suits. But receiving governmental recognition and benefits has nothing to do with any understanding of "liberty" that the Framers would have recognized.

To the extent that the Framers would have recognized a natural right to marriage that fell within the broader definition of liberty, it would not have included a right to governmental recognition and benefits. Instead, it would have included a right to engage in the very same activities that petitioners have been left free to engage in—making vows, holding religious ceremonies celebrating those vows, raising children, and otherwise enjoying the society of one's spouse—without governmental interference. Petitioners misunderstand the institution of marriage when they say that it would "mean little" absent governmental recognition.

Petitioners' misconception of liberty carries over to their discussion of our precedents identifying a right to marry, not one of which has expanded the concept of "liberty" beyond the concept of negative liberty. Those precedents all involved absolute prohibitions on private actions associated with marriage. In a concession to petitioners' misconception of liberty, the majority characterizes petitioners' suit as a quest to "find liberty by marrying someone of the same sex and having their marriages deemed lawful on the same terms and conditions as marriages between persons of the opposite sex." As a philosophical matter, liberty is only freedom from governmental action, not an entitlement to governmental benefits. As a constitutional matter, it is likely even narrower than that, encompassing only freedom from physical restraint and imprisonment. The majority's "better informed understanding of how constitutional imperatives define liberty,"—better informed, we must assume, than that of the people who ratified the Fourteenth Amendment—runs headlong into the reality that our Constitution is a "collection of 'Thou shalt nots,'" *Reid v. Covert*, 354 U.S. 1 (1957) (plurality opinion), not "Thou shalt provides." The majority's inversion of the original meaning of liberty will cause collateral damage to other aspects of our constitutional order that protect liberty.

The majority disregards the political process as a protection for liberty. Although men, in forming a civil society, "give up all the power necessary to the ends for which they unite into society, to the majority of the community," Locke §99, at 49, they reserve the authority to exercise natural liberty within the bounds of laws established by that society. To protect that liberty from arbitrary interference, they establish a process by which society can adopt and enforce its laws. In our country, that process is primarily representative government at the state level, with the Federal Constitution serving as a backstop for that process. When the States act through their representative governments or by popular vote, the liberty of their residents is fully vindicated. This is no less true when some residents disagree with the result; indeed, it seems difficult to imagine *any* law on which all residents of a State would agree. What matters is that the process established by those who created the society has been honored. The definition of marriage has been the subject of heated debate in the States. 35 States have put the question to the People themselves. In 32 of those 35 States, the People have opted to retain the traditional definition of marriage. That petitioners disagree with the result of that process does not make it any less legitimate. Their civil liberty has been vindicated.

The majority's decision threatens the religious liberty our Nation has long sought to protect. Many of the earliest immigrants to America came seeking freedom to practice their religion without restraint. Every State save Connecticut adopted protections for religious freedom in their State Constitutions by 1789, and, of course, the First Amendment enshrined protection for the free exercise of religion in the U.S. Constitution. The Federal Government and the States have reaffirmed their commitment to religious liberty by codifying protections for religious practice. In our society, marriage is not simply a governmental institution; it is a religious institution. It appears all but inevitable that the two will come into conflict, particularly as individuals and churches are confronted with demands to participate in and endorse civil marriages between same-sex couples. Religious liberty is about more than just the protection for "religious organizations and persons as they seek to teach the principles that are so fulfilling and so central to their lives and faiths." Religious liberty is about freedom of action in matters of religion generally, and the scope of that liberty is directly correlated to the civil restraints placed upon religious practice. Had the majority allowed the definition of marriage to be left to the political process—as the Constitution requires—the People could have considered the religious liberty implications of deviating from the traditional definition as part of their deliberative process. Instead, the majority's decision short-circuits that process, with potentially ruinous consequences for religious liberty.

Perhaps recognizing that these cases do not actually involve liberty as it has been understood, the majority goes to great lengths to assert that its decision will advance the "dignity" of same-sex couples. The Constitution contains no "dignity" Clause, and even if it did, the government would be incapable of bestowing dignity. Human dignity has long been understood in this country to be innate. When the Framers proclaimed in the Declaration of Independence that "all men are created equal" and "endowed by their Creator with certain unalienable Rights," they referred to a vision of mankind in which all humans are created in the image of God and therefore of inherent worth. That vision is the foundation upon which this Nation was built. The corollary of that principle is that human dignity cannot be taken away by the government. Slaves did not lose their dignity (any more than they lost their humanity) because the government allowed them to be enslaved. Those held in internment camps did not lose their dignity because the government confined them. Those denied governmental benefits do not lose their dignity because the government denies them those benefits. The government cannot bestow dignity, and it cannot take it away. The majority's rejection of laws preserving the traditional definition of marriage can have no effect on the dignity of the people who voted for them. Its disdain for the understandings of liberty and dignity upon which this Nation was founded can have no effect on the dignity of Americans who continue to believe in them. Our Constitution—like the Declaration of Independence before it—was predicated on a simple truth: One's liberty, not to mention one's dignity, was something to be shielded from—not provided by—the State. Today's decision casts that truth aside. In its haste to reach a desired result, the majority misapplies a clause focused on "due process" to afford substantive rights, disregards the most plausible understanding of the "liberty" protected by that clause, and distorts the principles on which this Nation was founded.

Justice ALITO, with whom Justice SCALIA and Justice THOMAS join, *dissenting.*

Until the courts intervened, the American people were engaged in a debate about whether their States should recognize same-sex marriage. The question in these cases is not what States *should* do about same-sex marriage but whether the Constitution answers that question for them. It does not. The Constitution leaves that question to be decided by the people of each State.

Our Nation was founded upon the principle that every person has the unalienable right to liberty, but liberty is a term of many meanings. To prevent five unelected Justices from imposing their personal vision of liberty upon the American people, the Court has held that "liberty" under the Due Process Clause should be understood to protect only those rights that are "deeply rooted in this Nation's history and tradition." *Washington v. Glucksberg*, 521 U.S. 701 (1997). It is beyond dispute that the right to same-sex marriage is not among those rights. No State permitted same-sex marriage until the Massachusetts Supreme Judicial Court held in 2003 that limiting marriage to opposite-sex couples violated the State Constitution. Nor is the right to same-sex marriage deeply rooted in the traditions of other nations. No country allowed same-sex couples to marry until the Netherlands did so in 2000.

"What those arguing in favor of a constitutional right to same sex marriage seek, therefore, is not the protection of a deeply rooted right but the recognition of a very new right, and they seek this innovation not from a legislative body elected by the people, but from unelected judges. Faced with such a request, judges have cause for both caution and humility." *Id.*, at ___ (slip op., at 7-8).

For today's majority, it does not matter that the right to same-sex marriage lacks deep roots or even that it is contrary to long-established tradition. The Justices in the majority claim the authority to confer constitutional protection upon that right simply because they believe that it is fundamental. Attempting to circumvent the problem presented by the newness of the right found in these cases, the majority claims that the issue is the right to equal treatment. Noting that marriage is a fundamental right, the majority argues that a State has no valid reason for denying that right to same-sex couples. This reasoning is dependent upon a particular understanding of the purpose of civil marriage. Although the Court expresses the point in loftier terms, its argument is that the fundamental purpose of marriage is to promote the well-being of those who choose to marry. By benefiting persons who choose to wed, marriage indirectly benefits society because persons who live in stable, fulfilling, and supportive relationships make better citizens. It is for these reasons, the argument goes, that States encourage and formalize marriage, confer special benefits on married persons, and also impose some special obligations. This understanding of the States' reasons for recognizing marriage enables the majority to argue that same-sex marriage serves the States' objectives in the same way as opposite-sex marriage.

This understanding of marriage, which focuses almost entirely on the happiness of persons who choose to marry, is shared by many people today, but it is not the traditional one. For millennia, marriage was inextricably linked to the one thing that only an opposite-sex couple can do: procreate. Adherents to different schools of philosophy use different terms to explain why society should formalize marriage and attach special benefits and obligations to persons who marry. Here, the States defending their adherence to the traditional understanding of marriage have explained their position using the pragmatic vocabulary that characterizes most American political discourse. Their basic argument is that States formalize and promote marriage, unlike other fulfilling human relationships, in order to encourage potentially procreative conduct to take place within a lasting unit that has long been thought to provide the best atmosphere for raising children. They thus argue that there are reasonable secular grounds for restricting marriage to opposite-sex couples.

If this traditional understanding of the purpose of marriage does not ring true to all ears today, that is probably because the tie between marriage and procreation has frayed. Today, for instance, more than 40% of all children in this country are born to unmarried women. This development undoubtedly is both a cause and a result of changes in our society's understanding of marriage. While, for many, the attributes of marriage in 21st-century America have changed, those States that do not want to recognize same-sex marriage have not yet given up on the traditional understanding. They worry that by officially abandoning the older understanding, they may contribute to marriage's further decay. It is far beyond the outer reaches of this Court's authority to say that a State may not adhere to the understanding of marriage that has long prevailed, not just in this country and others with similar cultural roots, but also in a great variety of countries and cultures all around the globe.

Today's decision usurps the constitutional right of the people to decide whether to keep or alter the traditional understanding of marriage. The decision will be used to vilify Americans who are unwilling to assent to the new orthodoxy. The majority compares traditional marriage laws to laws that denied equal treatment for African-Americans and women. The implications of this analogy will be exploited by those who are determined to stamp out every vestige of dissent. The majority attempts to reassure those who oppose same-sex marriage that their rights of conscience will be protected. We will see whether this proves to be true. I assume that those who cling to old beliefs will be able to whisper their thoughts in the recesses of their homes, but if they repeat those views in public, they will risk being labeled as bigots and treated as such by governments, employers, and schools.

If the issue of same-sex marriage had been left to the people of the States, it is likely that some States would recognize same-sex marriage and others would not. It is also possible that some States would tie recognition to protection for conscience rights. The majority makes that impossible. By imposing its own views on the entire country, the majority facilitates the marginalization of the many Americans who have traditional ideas. If a bare majority of Justices can invent a new right and impose that right on the rest of the country, the only real limit on what future majorities will be able to do is their own sense of what those with political power and cultural influence are willing to tolerate. Even enthusiastic supporters of same-sex marriage should worry about the scope of the power that today's majority claims.

Decades of attempts to restrain this Court's abuse of its authority have failed. A lesson that some will take from today's decision is that preaching about the proper method of interpreting the Constitution or the virtues of judicial self-restraint and humility cannot compete with the temptation to achieve what is viewed as a noble end by any practicable means. I do not doubt that the majority sincerely see in the Constitution a vision of liberty that happens to coincide with their own. But this sincerity is cause for concern, not comfort. What it evidences is the deep and perhaps irremediable corruption of our legal culture's conception of constitutional interpretation.

Most Americans—understandably—will cheer or lament today's decision because of their views on the issue of same-sex marriage. But all Americans, whatever their thinking on that issue, should worry about what the majority's claim of power portends.

Notes

1. *Emerging Issues.* As lesbians and gays have gained increased rights, including and in particular the right to marry, other issues have come to the forefront. For example, in *Campaign for Southern Equality v. Mississippi Department of Human Services*, 175 F. Supp. 3d 691 (S.D. Miss. 2016), the court struck down a state law prohibiting same-sex couples from adopting children. In *V.L. v. E.L.*, 136 S. Ct. 1017 (2016), the Court stayed an Alabama court order that prohibited a lesbian from having contact with the three children that she adopted in a neighboring state.

2. *Employment Protections.* In *Bostock v. Clayton County, Georgia*, 140 S. Ct. 1731 (2020), the Court extended the protection of the 1964 Civil Rights Act to gay, lesbian, and transgender persons. That Act protects individuals against discrimination in employment.

∼ PROBLEMS ∼

1. *The Standard of Review?* After reading the *Obergefell* case, are you clear regarding the standard of review that the Court applies to governmental discrimination based on sexual orientation? Is the Court effectively applying strict scrutiny? On the other hand, is it applying only "rational basis," but simply concluding that discrimination on the basis of sexual orientation is not "reasonable" in the context of marriage? Is the Court clear on this issue?

2. *Explicit v. Unenumerated Rights.* The Constitution and the Bill of Rights explicitly protect certain rights, including the right to free speech, the right to be

free from unreasonable searches and seizures, and the right to be free from self-incrimination. Of course, the Ninth Amendment explicitly contemplates the existence of other "unenumerated" rights: "The enumeration in the Constitution, of certain rights, shall not be construed to deny or disparage others retained by the people." But, if "other rights" exist, how does the Court find them? Historically, the Court has looked to the history and traditions of the nation. Using that standard, would same-sex marriages be entitled to protection?

3. *Polygamous Marriage.* After *Obergefell*, do those who wish to enter into polygamous marriages have a constitutional basis for claiming a right to do so? What about polyandry (when a wife has more than one husband)? Note Chief Justice Roberts's dissent in which he suggests that polygamous marriage is a smaller leap (constitutionally) than same-sex marriage. If we have moved to a "consent-based" view of marriage, should polygamy be constitutionally protected if it is consensual? *See Brown v. Buhman*, 822 F.3d 1151 (10th Cir. 2016).

4. *Child Adoption and Child Custody.* After *Obergefell*, could a state decline to allow same-sex couples to adopt children, and could it discriminate against gays and lesbians in child custody cases? What standard of review should apply? *See Stewart v. Heineman*, 296 Neb. 262, 892 N.W.2d 542 (Neb. 2017).

5. *The Potential Collision Between Gay Rights and Religious Beliefs.* Does *Obergefell* create a possible clash between gay/lesbian rights and religious beliefs? A number of state and local laws prohibit businesses from discriminating based on an individual's sexual preferences. Suppose that a woman who runs a small photography business objects on religious grounds to homosexuality. When a gay couple asks her to take pictures at their wedding, the woman refuses. She tells the gay couple that she is religiously opposed to homosexuality, would not feel comfortable taking pictures at a gay wedding, and is concerned that her work product would be of poor quality. The gay couple files a discrimination complaint against the photographer. Is the photographer entitled to a religious exemption from the discrimination law? *See Elaine Photography LLC v. Willock*, 309 P.3d 53 (N.M. 2013). Would you view the situation differently as applied to a religious official or a religious organization? In light of a local or state law prohibiting discrimination based on sexual preferences, could a minister who holds a religiously based belief that marriage can only be between a man and a woman refuse to perform marriages for same-sex couples? Could a religious college whose underlying doctrine provides that marriage can only be between a man and a woman treat same-sex couples differently than opposite-sex married couples regarding housing and other benefits? Of course, many religiously-based colleges receive federal funding of various sorts for the construction of buildings, student financial aid, etc. If the state otherwise respects a college's decision to deny benefits to same-sex couples, can it withhold financial aid from colleges that do so? Must it?

6. *Religious Exemptions.* Could a state create an exemption from its antidiscrimination law for "sincerely held religious beliefs"? Should it create such an exemption? In Indiana, there was considerable controversy after the state passed a religious freedom law that some believed would have authorized discrimination

against gays and lesbians. *See* Cara Anthony, *Thousands Protest "Religious Freedom" Law,* Louisville Courier-J., Mar. 29, 2015, at 2B. In response to the controversy, Indiana amended the law. However, comparable legislation has been introduced into Congress.

7. Transgender Status

Notes

1. *Employment Protections.* In *Bostock v. Clayton County, Georgia,* 140 S. Ct. 1731 (2020), the Court extended the protection of the 1964 Civil Rights Act to gay, lesbian, and transgender persons. That Act protects individuals against discrimination in employment.

2. *Bathroom Access.* In recent years, there has been considerable controversy regarding the rights of transgender individuals to use the bathroom that corresponds to their gender identity rather than the one that corresponds to their biological sex. The Obama administration issued guidance documents that took the position that transgender individuals had a statutory right to use the bathroom that corresponds to their gender identity, and threatened schools with the loss of federal funds for noncompliance. However, in the Trump administration, Attorney General Sessions reversed that determination. President Trump also limited the ability of transgendered individuals to serve in the military. That limitation was partially enjoined by a federal district court. The issue continues to percolate in the courts.

3. *Transgender Soldiers.* Under Directive-type Memorandum-19-004 that took effect in 2019, transgender personnel are not allowed to serve or enlist in the United States military, except if they serve in their original sex assignment, had been grandfathered in prior to April 12, 2019, or were given a waiver. Cases challenging that waiver are pending in various federal courts. *See Stone v. Trump,* 400 F. Supp.3d 317 (D. Md. 2019). The outcome of those cases could be affected by the holding in *Bostock, supra,* which extended the protection of the 1964 Civil Rights Act to transgendered individuals.

PROBLEMS

1. *Reviewing Transgender Classifications.* What standard of review should apply to transgender classifications? Should they be subjected to rational basis? Strict scrutiny? Intermediate scrutiny?

2. *Right to Marry.* Presumably, *Obergefell* gives transgender individuals an equal right to marry. May legislatures legitimately impose any special restrictions on transgender marriages (e.g., disclosure of transgender status to a potential spouse)?

3. *Transgender Bathrooms.* May states constitutionally require individuals to use only the bathroom that corresponds to their biological sex? What considerations militate in favor of, or against, the constitutionality of such a law? *See Doe v. Boyertown Area School District,* 2018 WL 3016864 (3rd Cir. 2018); *Grimm v. Gloucester County School Board,* 2018 WL 2328233 (E.D. Va. 2018).

4. *Transgender Individuals and Sports.* Suppose that transgender individuals want to compete in sports as females. Some women and girls, who believe that transgender women have an unfair advantage over them in sports like track and wrestling, object. Should transgender individuals have a right to compete in sports based on their chosen gender identity? Does that involve discrimination against genetic females? Should it matter whether they are on female hormones? Have had gender confirmation surgery? Does the holding in *Bostock* affect the analysis?

8. Right to Die

Termination of life other than by natural causes presents questions of a profound moral nature. Issues of this type have intersected with the debate over capital punishment and abortion, insofar as fundamental values have vied to shape the law and the judiciary's role in developing principles that affect the understanding, potential, and duration of life. Case law concerning the right to die reflects a cautious attitude toward this liberty interest. In the following case, the Court announced the right's existence but found that it does not trump a state's interest in determining by clear and convincing evidence a person's desire to discontinue medical treatment.

Cruzan v. Director, Missouri Dept. of Health

497 U.S. 261 (1990)

Chief Justice REHNQUIST delivered the opinion of the Court.

Petitioner Nancy Beth Cruzan was rendered incompetent as a result of severe injuries sustained during an automobile accident. Co-petitioners Lester and Joyce Cruzan, Nancy's parents and coguardians, sought a court order directing the withdrawal of their daughter's artificial feeding and hydration equipment after it became apparent that she had virtually no chance of recovering her cognitive faculties. The Supreme Court of Missouri held that because there was no clear and convincing evidence of Nancy's desire to have life-sustaining treatment withdrawn under such circumstances, her parents lacked authority to effectuate such a request. We granted certiorari and now affirm.

The Fourteenth Amendment provides that no State shall "deprive any person of life, liberty, or property, without due process of law." The principle that a competent person has a constitutionally protected liberty interest in refusing unwanted medical treatment may be inferred from our prior decisions.

But determining that a person has a "liberty interest" under the Due Process Clause does not end the inquiry; "whether respondent's constitutional rights have been violated must be determined by balancing his liberty interests against the relevant state interests."

Petitioners insist that under the general holdings of our cases, the forced administration of life-sustaining medical treatment, and even of artificially delivered food and water essential to life, would implicate a competent person's liberty interest. Although we think the logic of the cases would embrace such a liberty interest, the dramatic consequences involved in refusal of such treatment would inform the inquiry as to whether the deprivation of that interest is constitutionally permissible. But for purposes of this case, we assume that the United States Constitution would grant a competent person a constitutionally protected right to refuse lifesaving hydration and nutrition.

Petitioners go on to assert that an incompetent person should possess the same right in this respect as is possessed by a competent person. The difficulty with petitioners' claim is that in a sense it begs the question: An incompetent person is not able to make an informed and voluntary choice to exercise a hypothetical right to refuse treatment or any other right. Such a "right" must be exercised for her, if at all, by some sort of surrogate. Here, Missouri has in effect recognized that under certain circumstances a surrogate may act for the patient in electing to have hydration and nutrition withdrawn in such a way as to cause death, but it has established a procedural safeguard to assure that the action of the surrogate conforms as best it may to the wishes expressed by the patient while competent. Missouri requires that evidence of the incompetent's wishes as to the withdrawal of treatment be proved by clear and convincing evidence. The question, then, is whether the United States Constitution forbids the establishment of this procedural requirement by the State. We hold that it does not.

Whether or not Missouri's clear and convincing evidence requirement comports with the United States Constitution depends in part on what interests the State may properly seek to protect in this situation. Missouri relies on its interest in the protection and preservation of human life, and there can be no gainsaying this interest. As a general matter, the States—indeed, all civilized nations—demonstrate their commitment to life by treating homicide as a serious crime. Moreover, the majority of States in this country have laws imposing criminal penalties on one who assists another to commit suicide. We do not think a State is required to remain neutral in the face of an informed and voluntary decision by a physically able adult to starve to death.

But in the context presented here, a State has more particular interests at stake. The choice between life and death is a deeply personal decision of obvious and overwhelming finality. We believe Missouri may legitimately seek to safeguard the personal element of this choice through the imposition of heightened evidentiary requirements. It cannot be disputed that the Due Process Clause protects an interest in life as well as an interest in refusing life-sustaining medical treatment. Not all incompetent patients will have loved ones available to serve as surrogate decision-makers. And even where family members are present, "there will, of course, be some unfortunate situations in which family members will not act to protect a patient." A State is entitled to guard against potential abuses in such situations. Similarly, a State is entitled to consider that a judicial proceeding to make a determination regarding an incompetent's wishes may very well not be an adversarial one, with the added guarantee of accurate factfinding that the adversary process brings with it. Finally, we think a State may properly decline to make judgments about the "quality" of life that a particular individual may enjoy, and simply assert an unqualified interest in the preservation of human life to be weighed against the constitutionally protected interests of the individual.

Missouri has permissibly sought to advance these interests through the adoption of a "clear and convincing" standard of proof to govern such proceedings. "The function of a standard of proof, as that concept is embodied in the Due Process Clause and in the realm of factfinding, is to 'instruct the factfinder concerning the degree of confidence our society thinks he should have in the correctness of factual conclusions for a particular type of adjudication.'"

The interests at stake in the instant proceedings are more substantial, both on an individual and societal level, than those involved in a run-of-the-mill civil dispute. But not only does the standard of proof reflect the importance of a particular adjudication, it also serves as "a societal judgment about how the risk of error should be distributed between the litigants." The more stringent the burden of proof a party must bear, the more that party bears the risk of an erroneous decision. We believe that Missouri may permissibly place an increased risk of an erroneous decision on those seeking to terminate an incompetent individual's life-sustaining treatment. An erroneous decision not to terminate results in a maintenance of the status quo; the possibility of subsequent developments such as advancements in medical science, the discovery of new evidence regarding the patient's intent, changes in the law, or simply the unexpected death of the patient despite the administration of life-sustaining treatment at least create the potential that a wrong decision will eventually be corrected or its impact mitigated. An erroneous decision to withdraw life-sustaining treatment, however, is not susceptible of correction.

In sum, we conclude that a State may apply a clear and convincing evidence standard in proceedings where a guardian seeks to discontinue nutrition and hydration of a person diagnosed to be in a persistent vegetative state. We note that many courts which have adopted some sort of substituted judgment procedure in situations like this, whether they limit consideration of evidence to the prior expressed wishes of the incompetent individual, or whether they allow more general proof of what the individual's decision would have been, require a clear and convincing standard of proof for such evidence.

Petitioners alternatively contend that Missouri must accept the "substituted judgment" of close family members even in the absence of substantial proof that their views reflect the views of the patient. But we do not think these cases support their claim. Here again petitioners would seek to turn a decision which allowed a State to rely on family decisionmaking into a constitutional requirement that the State recognize such decisionmaking. But constitutional law does not work that way.

Nancy Cruzan's mother and father are loving and caring parents. If the State were required by the United States Constitution to repose a right of "substituted judgment" with anyone, the Cruzans would surely qualify. But we do not think the Due Process Clause requires the State to repose judgment on these matters with anyone but the patient herself. Close family members may have a strong feeling—a feeling not at all ignoble or unworthy, but not entirely disinterested, either—that they do not wish to witness the continuation of the life of a loved one which they regard as hopeless, meaningless, and even degrading. But there is no automatic assurance that the view of close family members will necessarily be the same as the patient's would have been had she been confronted with the prospect of her situation while competent. All of the reasons previously discussed for allowing Missouri to require clear and convincing evidence of the patient's wishes lead us to conclude that the State may choose to defer only to those wishes, rather than confide the decision to close family members.

The judgment of the Supreme Court of Missouri is

Affirmed.

Justice O'CONNOR, *concurring.*

I agree that a protected liberty interest in refusing unwanted medical treatment may be inferred from our prior decisions, and that the refusal of artificially delivered food and water is encompassed within that liberty interest. I write separately to clarify why I believe this to be so.

The liberty interest in refusing medical treatment flows from decisions involving the State's invasions into the body. Because our notions of liberty are inextricably entwined with our idea of physical freedom and self-determination, the Court has often deemed state incursions into the body repugnant to the interests protected by the Due Process Clause. Our Fourth Amendment jurisprudence has echoed this same concern. The State's imposition of medical treatment on an unwilling competent adult necessarily involves some form of restraint and intrusion. A seriously ill or dying patient whose wishes are not honored may feel a captive of the machinery required for life-sustaining measures or other medical interventions. Such forced treatment may burden that individual's liberty interests as much as any state coercion.

The State's artificial provision of nutrition and hydration implicates identical concerns. Artificial feeding cannot readily be distinguished from other forms of medical treatment. Whether or not the techniques used to pass food and water into the patient's alimentary tract are termed "medical treatment," it is clear they all involve some degree of intrusion and restraint. Feeding a patient by means of a nasogastric tube requires a physician to pass a long flexible tube through the patient's nose, throat, and esophagus and into the stomach. Because of the discomfort such a tube causes, "many patients need to be restrained forcibly and

their hands put into large mittens to prevent them from removing the tube."
A gastrostomy tube (as was used to provide food and water to Nancy Cruzan) or
jejunostomy tube must be surgically implanted into the stomach or small intes-
tine. Requiring a competent adult to endure such procedures against her will
burdens the patient's liberty, dignity, and freedom to determine the course of her
own treatment. Accordingly, the liberty guaranteed by the Due Process Clause
must protect, if it protects anything, an individual's deeply personal decision to
reject medical treatment, including the artificial delivery of food and water.

The Court does not decide the issue whether a State must also give effect to
the decisions of a surrogate decision-maker. In my view, such a duty may be constitutionally required to protect the patient's liberty interest in refusing medical
treatment. Few individuals provide explicit oral or written instructions regarding
their intent to refuse medical treatment should they become incompetent. States
which decline to consider any evidence other than such instructions may frequently fail to honor a patient's intent. Such failures might be avoided if the State
considered an equally probative source of evidence: the patient's appointment of
a proxy to make health care decisions on her behalf. These procedures for surrogate decisionmaking, which appear to be rapidly gaining in acceptance, may be
a valuable additional safeguard of the patient's interest in directing his medical
care. Moreover, as patients are likely to select a family member as a surrogate giving effect to a proxy's decisions may also protect the "freedom of personal choice
in matters of family life."

Today's decision, holding only that the Constitution permits a State to
require clear and convincing evidence of Nancy Cruzan's desire to have artificial hydration and nutrition withdrawn, does not preclude a future determination that the Constitution requires the States to implement the decisions of a
patient's duly appointed surrogate. Nor does it prevent States from developing
other approaches for protecting an incompetent individual's liberty interest in
refusing medical treatment. As is evident from the Court's survey of state court
decisions, no national consensus has yet emerged on the best solution for this
difficult and sensitive problem. Today we decide only that one State's practice
does not violate the Constitution.

Justice SCALIA, *concurring.*

The various opinions in this case portray quite clearly the difficult, indeed
agonizing, questions that are presented by the constantly increasing power of science to keep the human body alive for longer than any reasonable person would
want to inhabit it. While I agree with the Court's analysis today, I would have preferred that we announce that the federal courts have no business in this field, and
hence, that even when it is demonstrated by clear and convincing evidence that a
patient no longer wishes certain measures to be taken to preserve his or her life,
it is up to the citizens of Missouri to decide, through their elected representatives,
whether that wish will be honored.

The text of the Due Process Clause does not protect individuals against deprivations of liberty simpliciter. It protects them against deprivations of liberty "without due process of law." To determine that such a deprivation would not occur if Nancy Cruzan were forced to take nourishment against her will, it is unnecessary to reopen the historically recurrent debate over whether "due process" includes substantive restrictions. It is at least true that no "substantive due process" claim can be maintained unless the claimant demonstrates that the State has deprived him of a right historically and traditionally protected against state interference. That cannot possibly be established here.

The dissents of Justices Brennan and Stevens make a plausible case for our intervention here only by embracing a political principle that the States are free to adopt, but that is demonstrably not imposed by the Constitution. "The State," says Justice Brennan, "has no legitimate general interest in someone's life, completely abstracted from the interest of the person living that life, that could outweigh the person's choice to avoid medical treatment." Justice Brennan's position ultimately rests upon the proposition that it is none of the State's business if a person wants to commit suicide. Justice Stevens is explicit on the point: "Choices about death touch the core of liberty. Not much may be said with confidence about death unless it is said from faith, and that alone is reason enough to protect the freedom to conform choices about death to individual conscience." This is a view that some societies have held, and that our States are free to adopt if they wish. But it is not a view imposed by our constitutional traditions, in which the power of the State to prohibit suicide is unquestionable.

Our salvation is the Equal Protection Clause, which requires the democratic majority to accept for themselves and their loved ones what they impose on you and me. This Court need not, and has no authority to, inject itself into every field of human activity where irrationality and oppression may theoretically occur, and if it tries to do so it will destroy itself.

Justice BRENNAN, with whom Justice MARSHALL and Justice BLACKMUN join, *dissenting*.

Because I believe that Nancy Cruzan has a fundamental right to be free of unwanted artificial nutrition and hydration, which right is not outweighed by any interests of the State, and because I find that the improperly biased procedural obstacles imposed by the Missouri Supreme Court impermissibly burden that right, I respectfully dissent. Nancy Cruzan is entitled to choose to die with dignity.

The question before this Court is a relatively narrow one: whether the Due Process Clause allows Missouri to require a now-incompetent patient in an irreversible persistent vegetative state to remain on life support absent rigorously clear and convincing evidence that avoiding the treatment represents the patient's prior, express choice.

The Court concedes that our prior decisions "support the recognition of a general liberty interest in refusing medical treatment." But if a competent person has a liberty interest to be free of unwanted medical treatment, it must be fundamental. "We are dealing here with a decision which involves one of the basic civil rights of man." Whatever other liberties protected by the Due Process Clause are fundamental, "those liberties that are 'deeply rooted in this Nation's history and tradition'" are among them. "Such a tradition commands respect in part because the Constitution carries the gloss of history." No material distinction can be drawn between the treatment to which Nancy Cruzan continues to be subject—artificial nutrition and hydration—and any other medical treatment. The artificial delivery of nutrition and hydration is undoubtedly medical treatment.

Nor does the fact that Nancy Cruzan is now incompetent deprive her of her fundamental rights. The question is not whether an incompetent has constitutional rights, but how such rights may be exercised. There are affirmative reasons why someone like Nancy might choose to forgo artificial nutrition and hydration under these circumstances. Dying is personal. It is profound. For many, the thought of an ignoble end, steeped in decay, is abhorrent. A quiet, proud death, bodily integrity intact, is a matter of extreme consequence.

Although the right to be free of unwanted medical intervention, like other constitutionally protected interests, may not be absolute, no state interest could outweigh the rights of an individual in Nancy Cruzan's position. Whatever a State's possible interests in mandating life-support treatment under other circumstances, there is no good to be obtained here by Missouri's insistence that Nancy Cruzan remain on life-support systems if it is indeed her wish not to do so. Missouri does not claim, nor could it, that society as a whole will be benefited by Nancy's receiving medical treatment. No third party's situation will be improved and no harm to others will be averted.

The only state interest asserted here is a general interest in the preservation of life. But the State has no legitimate general interest in someone's life, completely abstracted from the interest of the person living that life, that could outweigh the person's choice to avoid medical treatment. This is not to say that the State has no legitimate interests to assert here. As the majority recognizes, Missouri has a *parens patriae* interest in providing Nancy Cruzan, now incompetent, with as accurate as possible a determination of how she would exercise her rights under these circumstances. Second, if and when it is determined that Nancy Cruzan would want to continue treatment, the State may legitimately assert an interest in providing that treatment. But until Nancy's wishes have been determined, the only state interest that may be asserted is an interest in safe-guarding the accuracy of that determination.

The majority claims that the allocation of the risk of error is justified because it is more important not to terminate life support for someone who would wish it continued than to honor the wishes of someone who would not. An erroneous decision to terminate life support is irrevocable, says the majority, while an erroneous decision not to terminate "results in a maintenance of the status quo." But, from the point of view of the patient, an erroneous decision in either direction is irrevocable. An erroneous decision to terminate artificial nutrition and hydration, to be sure, will lead to failure of that last remnant of physiological life, the brain stem, and result in complete brain death. An erroneous decision not to terminate life support, however, robs a patient of the very qualities protected by the right to avoid unwanted medical treatment. His own degraded existence is perpetuated; his family's suffering is protracted; the memory he leaves behind becomes more and more distorted.

Finally, I cannot agree with the majority that where it is not possible to determine what choice an incompetent patient would make, a State's role as *parens patriae* permits the State automatically to make that choice itself. A State may ensure that the person who makes the decision on the patient's behalf is the one whom the patient himself would have selected to make that choice for him. And a State may exclude from consideration anyone having improper motives. But a State generally must either repose the choice with the person whom the patient himself would most likely have chosen as proxy or leave the decision to the patient's family.

Justice STEVENS, *dissenting.*

The Constitution requires the State to care for Nancy Cruzan's life in a way that gives appropriate respect to her own best interests. Medical advances have altered the physiological conditions of death in ways that may be alarming: Highly invasive treatment may perpetuate human existence through a merger of body and machine that some might reasonably regard as an insult to life rather than as its continuation. But those same advances, and the reorganization of medical care accompanying the new science and technology, have also transformed the political and social conditions of death: People are less likely to die at home, and more likely to die in relatively public places, such as hospitals or nursing homes.

Ultimate questions that might once have been dealt with in intimacy by a family and its physician have now become the concern of institutions. When the institution is a state hospital, as it is in this case, the government itself becomes involved. Dying nonetheless remains a part of "the life which characteristically has its place in the home." The "integrity of that life is something so fundamental that it has been found to draw to its protection the principles of more than one explicitly granted Constitutional right," and our decisions have demarcated a "private realm of family life which the state cannot enter." The physical boundaries of the home, of course, remain crucial guarantors of the life within it. Nevertheless, this Court has long recognized that the liberty to make the decisions and choices constitutive of private life is so fundamental to our "concept of ordered liberty," that those choices must occasionally be afforded more direct protection.

It is against this background of decisional law, and the constitutional tradition which it illuminates, that the right to be free from unwanted life-sustaining medical treatment must be understood. Choices about death touch the core of liberty. Our duty, and the concomitant freedom, to come to terms with the conditions of our own mortality are undoubtedly "so rooted in the traditions and conscience of our people as to be ranked as fundamental," and indeed are essential incidents of the unalienable rights to life and liberty endowed us by our Creator.

To be constitutionally permissible, Missouri's intrusion upon these fundamental liberties must, at a minimum, bear a reasonable relationship to a legitimate state end. Missouri asserts that its policy is related to a state interest in the protection of life. In my view, however, it is an effort to define life, rather than to protect it, that is the heart of Missouri's policy. Missouri insists, without regard to Nancy Cruzan's own interests, upon equating her life with the biological persistence of her bodily functions. Nancy Cruzan, it must be remembered, is not now simply incompetent. She is in a persistent vegetative state and has been so for seven years. The trial court found, and no party contested, that Nancy has no possibility of recovery and no consciousness.

My disagreement with the Court is thus unrelated to its endorsement of the clear and convincing standard of proof for cases of this kind. Indeed, I agree that the controlling facts must be established with unmistakable clarity. The failure of Missouri's policy to heed the interests of a dying individual with respect to matters so private is ample evidence of the policy's illegitimacy. A State that seeks to demonstrate its commitment to life may do so by aiding those who are actively struggling for life and health. In this endeavor, unfortunately, no State can lack for opportunities: There can be no need to make an example of tragic cases like that of Nancy Cruzan.

Notes and Questions

1. Cruzan's *Underpinnings*. *Cruzan* grounded the right to refuse medical treatment in the Due Process Clause. The majority opinion by Chief Justice Rehnquist was noteworthy insofar as he generally had been a forceful exponent of the notion that modern substantive due process review essentially constituted a neo-*Lochnerian* exercise. In *Washington v. Glucksberg*, the Court considered a due process challenge to a state law making it a felony knowingly to assist in an individual's suicide. Referencing traditional prohibitions against suicide, and pursuant to a careful description of the proposed liberty interest, the Court found no protected right.

2. *More on Defining "Liberty."* Is the liberty interest at stake in *Cruzan* defined with a high level of specificity, or a high level of abstraction? How could it be drafted with greater specificity? What difference would that make?

⮑ PROBLEMS ⮑

1. *The Schiavo Case.* In 2005, right-to-die issues resurfaced in the Terri Schiavo case. Schiavo, who was in a persistent vegetative state, was the subject of a bitter dispute between her husband (who claimed that she had expressed a desire not to remain alive in a vegetative state) and her parents (who wanted to keep her alive). After lengthy judicial proceedings, and an attempt by Congress to

intervene, the husband was allowed to exercise a decision to let Terri die. How should the courts resolve such disputes between spouses and parents?

2. *Terminally Ill Patients and Refusal of Treatment.* Consider Justice Scalia's arguments against recognizing the right to refuse unwanted medical treatment as fundamental. Minus that right, would a terminal cancer patient be compelled to take drugs that prolong life even though they diminish the quality of life?

3. *Required Immunizations.* Consider state laws or school district rules that require children to be immunized against certain diseases. May a child, or parent or guardian, refuse immunization on the grounds that it constitutes unwanted medical treatment?

Washington v. Glucksberg

521 U.S. 702 (1997)

Chief Justice REHNQUIST delivered the opinion of the Court.

The question presented in this case is whether Washington's prohibition against "causing" or "aiding" a suicide offends the Fourteenth Amendment to the United States Constitution. We hold that it does not.

It has always been a crime to assist a suicide in the State of Washington. At the same time, Washington's Natural Death Act, enacted in 1979, states that the "withholding or withdrawal of life-sustaining treatment" at a patient's direction "shall not, for any purpose, constitute a suicide."

Respondents are physicians who practice in Washington. These doctors occasionally treat terminally ill, suffering patients, and declare that they would assist these patients in ending their lives if not for Washington's assisted-suicide ban. They are seeking a declaration that is, on its face, unconstitutional.

We begin by examining our Nation's history, legal traditions, and practices. In almost every State—indeed, in almost every western democracy—it is a crime to assist a suicide. The States' assisted-suicide bans are not innovations. Rather, they are longstanding expressions of the States' commitment to the protection and preservation of all human life. Indeed, opposition to and condemnation of suicide—and, therefore, of assisting suicide—are consistent and enduring themes of our philosophical, legal, and cultural heritages. More specifically, for over 700 years, the Anglo-American common-law tradition has punished or otherwise disapproved of both suicide and assisting suicide.

The Due Process Clause guarantees more than fair process, and the "liberty" it protects includes more than the absence of physical restraint. The Clause also provides heightened protection against government interference with certain fundamental rights and liberty interests. In a long line of cases, we have held that, in addition to the specific freedoms protected by the Bill of Rights, the "liberty" specially protected by the Due Process Clause includes the rights to marry; to have children; to direct the education and upbringing of one's children; to marital privacy; to use contraception; to bodily integrity; and to abortion. We have also assumed, and strongly suggested, that the Due Process Clause protects the traditional right to refuse unwanted lifesaving medical treatment.

But we "have always been reluctant to expand the concept of substantive due process because guideposts for responsible decision-making in this unchartered area are scarce and open-ended." By extending constitutional protection to an asserted right or liberty interest, we, to a great extent, place the matter outside the arena of public debate and legislative action. We must therefore "exercise the utmost care whenever we are asked to break new ground in this field," lest the liberty protected by the Due Process Clause be subtly transformed into the policy preferences of the Members of this Court.

Our established method of substantive-due-process analysis has two primary features: First, we have regularly observed that the Due Process Clause specially protects those fundamental rights and liberties which are, objectively, "deeply rooted in this Nation's history and tradition," and "implicit in the concept of ordered liberty," such that "neither liberty nor justice would exist if they were sacrificed." Second, we have required in substantive-due-process cases a "careful description" of the asserted fundamental liberty interest. Our Nation's history, legal traditions, and practices thus provide the crucial "guideposts for responsible decision-making, that direct and restrain our exposition of the Due Process Clause."

As we stated recently in *Flores*, the Fourteenth Amendment "forbids the government to infringe 'fundamental' liberty interests at all, no matter what process is provided, unless the infringement is narrowly tailored to serve a compelling state interest."

Justice Souter, relying on Justice Harlan's dissenting opinion in *Poe v. Ullman*, would largely abandon this restrained methodology, and instead ask "whether Washington's statute sets up one of those 'arbitrary impositions' or 'purposeless restraints' at odds with the Due Process Clause of the Fourteenth Amendment." In our view, however, the development of this Court's substantive-due-process jurisprudence has been a process whereby the outlines of the "liberty" specially protected by the Fourteenth Amendment—never fully clarified, to be sure, and perhaps not capable of being fully clarified—have at least been carefully refined by concrete examples involving fundamental rights found to be deeply rooted in our legal tradition. This approach tends to rein in the subjective elements that are necessarily present in due-process judicial review. By establishing a threshold requirement—that a challenged state action implicate a fundamental right—before requiring more than a reasonable relation to a legitimate state interest to justify the action, it avoids the need for complex balancing of competing interests in every case.

We have a tradition of carefully formulating the interest at stake in substantive-due-process cases. For example, although *Cruzan* is often described as a "right to die" case, we were more precise: We assumed that the Constitution granted competent persons a "constitutionally protected right to refuse lifesaving hydration and nutrition." The Washington statute at issue prohibits "aiding another person to attempt suicide," and, thus, the question is whether the "liberty" specially protected by the Due Process Clause includes a right to commit suicide which itself includes a right to assistance.

We now inquire whether this asserted right has any place in our Nation's traditions. Here, we are confronted with a consistent and almost universal tradition that has long rejected the asserted right, and continues explicitly to reject it today, even for terminally ill, mentally competent adults. To hold for respondents, we would have to reverse centuries of legal doctrine and practice, and strike down the considered policy choice of almost every State.

The right assumed in *Cruzan* was not simply deduced from abstract concepts of personal autonomy. Given the common-law rule that forced medication was a battery, and the long legal tradition protecting the decision to refuse unwanted medical treatment, our assumption was entirely consistent with this Nation's history and constitutional traditions. The decision to commit suicide with the assistance of another may be just as personal and profound as the decision to refuse unwanted medical treatment, but it has never enjoyed similar legal protection. Indeed, the two acts are widely and reasonably regarded as quite distinct. In *Cruzan* itself, we recognized that most States outlawed assisted suicide — and even more do today — and we certainly gave no intimation that the right to refuse unwanted medical treatment could be somehow transmuted into a right to assistance in committing suicide.

The history of the law's treatment of assisted suicide in this country has been and continues to be one of the rejection of nearly all efforts to permit it. That being the case, our decisions lead us to conclude that the asserted "right" to assistance in committing suicide is not a fundamental liberty interest protected by the Due Process Clause. The Constitution also requires, however, that Washington's assisted-suicide ban be rationally related to legitimate government interests. This requirement is unquestionably met here.

First, Washington has an "unqualified interest in the preservation of human life." The State's prohibition on assisted suicide, like all homicide laws, both reflects and advances its commitment to this interest. This interest is symbolic and aspirational as well as practical.

Washington has rejected this sliding-scale approach and, through its assisted-suicide ban, insists that all persons' lives, from beginning to end, regardless of physical or mental condition, are under the full protection of the law. As we have previously affirmed, the States "may properly decline to make judgments about the 'quality' of life that a particular individual may enjoy." This remains true, as *Cruzan* makes clear, even for those who are near death.

Relatedly, all admit that suicide is a serious public-health problem, especially among persons in otherwise vulnerable groups. The State has an interest in preventing suicide, and in studying, identifying, and treating its causes.

Those who attempt suicide — terminally ill or not — often suffer from depression or other mental disorders. Research indicates, however, that many people who request physician-assisted suicide withdraw that request if their depression and pain are treated. Thus, legal physician-assisted suicide could make it more difficult for the State to protect depressed or mentally ill persons, or those who are suffering from untreated pain, from suicidal impulses.

The State also has an interest in protecting the integrity and ethics of the medical profession. The American Medical Association, like many other medical and physicians' groups, has concluded that "physician-assisted suicide is fundamentally incompatible with the physician's role as healer."

Next, the State has an interest in protecting vulnerable groups — including the poor, the elderly, and disabled persons — from abuse, neglect, and mistakes. If physician-assisted suicide were permitted, many might resort to it to spare their families the substantial financial burden of end-of-life health-care costs.

The State's interest here goes beyond protecting the vulnerable from coercion; it extends to protecting disabled and terminally ill people from prejudice, negative and inaccurate stereotypes, and "societal indifference." The State's assisted-suicide ban reflects and reinforces its policy that the lives of terminally ill, disabled, and elderly people must be no less valued than the lives of the young and healthy, and that a seriously disabled person's suicidal impulses should be interpreted and treated the same way as anyone else's.

Finally, the State may fear that permitting assisted suicide will start it down the path to voluntary and perhaps even involuntary euthanasia. If suicide is protected as a matter of constitutional right, it is argued, "every man and woman in the United States must enjoy it." Thus, it turns out that what is couched as a limited right to "physician-assisted suicide" is likely, in effect, a much broader license, which could prove extremely difficult to police and contain. Washington's ban on assisting suicide prevents such erosion.

We need not weigh exactly the relative strengths of these various interests. They are unquestionably important and legitimate, and Washington's ban on assisted suicide is at least reasonably related to their promotion and protection. We therefore hold that the state law does not violate the Fourteenth Amendment, either on its face or "as applied to competent, terminally ill adults who wish to hasten their deaths by obtaining medication prescribed by their doctors."

Throughout the Nation, Americans are engaged in an earnest and profound debate about the morality, legality, and practicality of physician-assisted suicide. Our holding permits this debate to continue, as it should in a democratic society. The decision of the en banc Court of Appeals is reversed, and the case is remanded for further proceedings consistent with this opinion.

Justice SOUTER, *concurring in the judgment.*

We are dealing with a claim to rights sometimes described as rights of substantive due process and sometimes as unenumerated rights, in view of the breadth and indeterminacy of the "due process" serving as the claim's textual basis. The doctors accordingly arouse the skepticism of those who find the Due Process Clause an unduly vague or oxymoronic warrant for judicial review of substantive state law, just as they also invoke two centuries of American constitutional practice in recognizing unenumerated, substantive limits on governmental action. Although this practice has neither rested on any single textual basis nor expressed a consistent theory (or, before *Poe v. Ullman*, a much articulated one), a brief overview of its history is instructive on two counts. The persistence of substantive due process in our cases points to the legitimacy of the modern justification for such judicial review found in Justice Harlan's dissent in *Poe*, on which I will dwell further on, while the acknowledged failures of some of these cases point with caution to the difficulty raised by the present claim.

The *Poe* dissent is important for three things that point to our responsibilities today. The first is Justice Harlan's respect for the tradition of substantive due process review itself, and his acknowledgment of the Judiciary's obligation to carry it on. For two centuries American courts, and for much of that time this Court, have thought it necessary to provide some degree of review over the substantive content of legislation under constitutional standards of textual breadth. This enduring tradition of American constitutional practice is, in Justice Harlan's view, nothing more than what is required by the judicial authority and obligation to construe constitutional text and review legislation for conformity to that text. Like many judges who preceded him and many who followed, he found it impossible to construe the text of due process without recognizing substantive, and not merely procedural, limitations. "Were due process merely a procedural safeguard it would fail to reach those situations where the deprivation of life, liberty or property was accomplished by legislation which by operating in the future could, given even the fairest possible procedure in application to individuals, nevertheless destroy the enjoyment of all three." The text of the Due Process Clause thus imposes nothing less than an obligation to give substantive content to the words "liberty" and "due process of law."

Following the first point of the *Poe* dissent, on the necessity to engage in the sort of examination we conduct today, the dissent's second and third implicitly address those cases, already noted, that are now condemned with virtual unanimity as disastrous mistakes of substantive due process review. The second of the dissent's lessons is a reminder that the business of such review is not the identification of extratextual absolutes but scrutiny of a legislative resolution (perhaps unconscious) of clashing principles, each quite possibly worthy in and of itself, but each to be weighed within the history of our values as a people. It is a comparison of the relative strengths of opposing claims that informs the judicial task, not a deduction from some first premise. Thus informed, judicial review still has no warrant to substitute one reasonable resolution of the contending positions for another, but authority to supplant the balance already struck between the contenders only when it falls outside the realm of the reasonable. Part III, below, deals with this second point, and also with the dissent's third, which takes the form of an object lesson in the explicit attention to detail that is no less essential to the intellectual discipline of substantive due process review than an understanding of the basic need to account for the two sides in the controversy and to respect legislation within the zone of reasonableness.

My understanding of unenumerated rights in the wake of the *Poe* dissent and subsequent cases avoids the absolutist failing of many older cases without embracing the opposite pole of equating reasonableness with past practice described at a very specific level.

"Due Process has not been reduced to any formula; its content cannot be determined by reference to any code. The best that can be said is that through the course of this Court's decisions it has represented the balance which our Nation, built upon postulates of respect for the liberty of the individual, has struck between that liberty and the demands of organized society. If the supplying of content to this Constitutional concept has of necessity been a rational process, it certainly has not been one where judges have felt free to roam where unguided speculation might take them. The balance of which I speak is the balance struck by this country, having regard to what history teaches are the traditions from which it developed as well as the traditions from which it broke. That tradition is a living thing. A decision of this Court which radically departs from it could not long survive, while a decision which builds on what has survived is likely to be sound. No formula could serve as a substitute, in this area, for judgment and restraint."

After the *Poe* dissent, as before it, this enforceable concept of liberty would bar statutory impositions even at relatively trivial levels when governmental restraints are undeniably irrational as unsupported by any imaginable rationale.

This approach calls for a court to assess the relative "weights" or dignities of the contending interests, and to this extent the judicial method is familiar to the common law. Common-law method is subject to two important constraints in the hands of a court engaged in substantive due process review. First, such a court is bound to confine the values that it recognizes to those truly deserving constitutional stature, either to those expressed in constitutional text, or those exemplified by "the traditions from which the Nation developed," or revealed by contrast with "the traditions from which it broke." "We may not draw on our personal and private notions and disregard the limits derived from considerations that are fused in the whole nature of our judicial process 'considerations deeply rooted in reason and in the compelling traditions of the legal profession.'"

The second constraint, again, simply reflects the fact that constitutional review, not judicial lawmaking, is a court's business here. The weighing or valuing of contending interests in this sphere is only the first step, forming the basis for determining whether the statute in question falls inside or outside the zone of what is reasonable in the way it resolves the conflict between the interests of state and individual. It is no justification for judicial intervention merely to identify a reasonable resolution of contending values that differs from the terms of the legislation under review. It is only when the legislation's justifying principle, critically valued, is so far from being commensurate with the individual interest as to be arbitrarily or pointlessly applied that the statute must give way. Only if this standard points against the statute can the individual claimant be said to have a constitutional right. Precision in terminology, however, favors reserving the label "right" for instances in which the individual's liberty interest actually trumps the government's countervailing interests; only then does the individual have anything legally enforceable as against the state's attempt at regulation.

The *Poe* dissent thus reminds us of the nature of review for reasonableness or arbitrariness and the limitations entailed by it. But the opinion cautions against the repetition of past error in another way as well, more by its example than by any particular statement of constitutional method: it reminds us that the process of substantive review by reasoned judgment is one of close criticism going to the details of the opposing interests and to their relationships with the historically recognized principles that lend them weight or value.

The *Poe* dissent disclaims the possibility of a general formula for due process analysis (beyond the basic analytic structure just described). When identifying and assessing the competing interests of liberty and authority, for example, the breadth of expression that a litigant or a judge selects in stating the competing principles will have much to do with the outcome and may be dispositive. As in any process of rational argumentation, we recognize that when a generally accepted principle is challenged, the broader the attack the less likely it is to succeed. The principle's defenders will, indeed, often try to characterize any challenge as just such a broadside, perhaps by couching the defense as if a broadside attack had occurred. So the Court in *Dred Scott* treated prohibition of slavery in the Territories as nothing less than a general assault on the concept of property.

Just as results in substantive due process cases are tied to the selections of statements of the competing interests, the acceptability of the results is a function of the good reasons for the selections made. It is here that the value of common-law method becomes apparent, for the usual thinking of the common law is suspicious of the all-or-nothing analysis that tends to produce legal petrification instead of an evolving boundary between the domains of old principles. Common-law method tends to pay respect instead to detail, seeking to understand old principles afresh by new examples and new counterexamples. The "tradition is a living thing," albeit one that moves by moderate steps carefully taken. "The decision of an apparently novel claim must depend on grounds which follow closely on well-accepted principles and criteria. The new decision must take its place in relation to what went before and further cut a channel for what is to come." Exact analysis and characterization of any due process claim are critical to the method and to the result.

The argument supporting respondents' position thus progresses through three steps of increasing forcefulness. First, it emphasizes the decriminalization of suicide. Reliance on this fact is sanctioned under the standard that looks not only to the tradition retained, but to society's occasional choices to reject traditions of the legal past. While the common law prohibited both suicide and aiding a suicide, with the prohibition on aiding largely justified by the primary prohibition on self-inflicted death itself, the State's rejection of the traditional treatment of the one leaves the criminality of the other open to questioning that previously would not have been appropriate. The second step in the argument is to emphasize that the State's own act of decriminalization gives a freedom of choice much like the individual's option in recognized instances of bodily autonomy. One of these, abortion, is a legal right to choose in spite of the interest a State may legitimately invoke in discouraging the practice, just as suicide is now subject to choice, despite a state interest in discouraging it. The third step is to emphasize that respondents claim a right to assistance not on the basis of some broad principle that would be subject to exceptions if that continuing interest of the State's in discouraging suicide were to be recognized at all. Respondents base their claim on the traditional right to medical care and counsel, subject to the limiting conditions of informed, responsible choice when death is imminent, conditions that support a strong analogy to rights of care in other situations in which medical counsel and assistance have been available as a matter of course. There can be no stronger claim to a physician's assistance than at the time when death is imminent, a moral judgment implied by the State's own recognition of the legitimacy of medical procedures necessarily hastening the moment of impending death.

In my judgment, the importance of the individual interest here, as within that class of "certain interests" demanding careful scrutiny of the State's contrary claim, cannot be gainsaid. Whether that interest might in some circumstances, or at some time, be seen as "fundamental" to the degree entitled to prevail is not, however, a conclusion that I need draw here, for I am satisfied that the State's interests described in the following section are sufficiently serious to defeat the present claim that its law is arbitrary or purposeless.

The State has put forward several interests to justify the Washington law as applied to physicians treating terminally ill patients, even those competent to make responsible choices: protecting life generally, and protecting terminally ill patients from involuntary suicide and euthanasia, both voluntary and nonvoluntary.

It is not necessary to discuss the exact strengths of the first two claims of justification in the present circumstances, for the third is dispositive for me. That third justification is different from the first two, for it addresses specific features of respondents' claim, and it opposes that claim not with a moral judgment contrary to respondents', but with a recognized state interest in the protection of nonresponsible individuals and those who do not stand in relation either to death or to their physicians as do the patients whom respondents describe. The State claims interests in protecting patients from mistakenly and involuntarily deciding to end their lives, and in guarding against both voluntary and involuntary euthanasia. Leaving aside any difficulties in coming to a clear concept of imminent death, mistaken decisions may result from inadequate palliative care or a terminal prognosis that turns out to be error; coercion and abuse may stem from the large medical bills that family members cannot bear or unreimbursed hospitals decline to shoulder. Voluntary and involuntary euthanasia may result once doctors are authorized to prescribe lethal medication in the first instance, for they might find it pointless to distinguish between patients who administer their own fatal drugs and those who wish not to, and their compassion for those who suffer may obscure the distinction between those who ask for death and those who may be unable to request it. The argument is that a progression would occur, obscuring the line between the ill and the dying, and between the responsible and the unduly influenced, until ultimately doctors and perhaps others would abuse a limited freedom to aid suicides by yielding to the impulse to end another's suffering under conditions going beyond the narrow limits the respondents propose. The State thus argues, essentially, that respondents' claim is not as narrow as it sounds, simply because no recognition of the interest they assert could be limited to vindicating those interests and affecting no others. The State says that the claim, in practical effect, would entail consequences that the State could, without doubt, legitimately act to prevent.

Respondents propose an answer to all this, the answer of state regulation with teeth. Legislation proposed in several States, for example, would authorize physician-assisted suicide but require two qualified physicians to confirm the patient's diagnosis, prognosis, and competence; and would mandate that the patient make repeated requests witnessed by at least two others over a specified timespan; and would impose reporting requirements and criminal penalties for various acts of coercion.

At this moment there are reasons for caution in predicting the effectiveness of the teeth proposed. Respondents' proposals, as it turns out, sound much like the guidelines now in place in the Netherlands, the only place where experience with physician-assisted suicide and euthanasia has yielded empirical evidence about how such regulations might affect actual practice. Dutch physicians must engage in consultation before proceeding, and must decide whether the patient's decision is voluntary, well considered, and stable, whether the request to die is enduring and made more than once, and whether the patient's future will involve unacceptable suffering. There is, however, a substantial dispute today about what the Dutch experience shows. Some commentators marshall evidence that the Dutch guidelines have in practice failed to protect patients from involuntary euthanasia and have been violated with impunity. This evidence is contested. The day may come when we can say with some assurance which side is right, but for now it is the substantiality of the factual disagreement, and the alternatives for resolving it, that matter. They are, for me, dispositive of the due process claim at this time.

I take it that the basic concept of judicial review with its possible displacement of legislative judgment bars any finding that a legislature has acted arbitrarily when the following conditions are met: there is a serious factual controversy over the feasibility of recognizing the claimed right without at the same time making it impossible for the State to engage in an undoubtedly legitimate exercise of power; facts necessary to resolve the controversy are not readily ascertainable through the judicial process; but they are more readily subject to discovery through legislative factfinding and experimentation. It is assumed in this case, and must be, that a State's interest in protecting those unable to make responsible decisions and those who make no decisions at all entitles the State to bar aid to any but a knowing and responsible person intending suicide, and to prohibit euthanasia. How, and how far, a State should act in that interest are judgments for the State, but the legitimacy of its action to deny a physician the option to aid any but the knowing and responsible is beyond question.

Legislatures have superior opportunities to obtain the facts necessary for a judgment about the present controversy. Not only do they have more flexible mechanisms for factfinding than the Judiciary, but their mechanisms include the power to experiment, moving forward and pulling back as facts emerge within their own jurisdictions. There is, indeed, good reason to suppose that in the absence of a judgment for respondents here, just such experimentation will be attempted in some of the States.

Sometimes a court may be bound to act regardless of the institutional preferability of the political branches as forums for addressing constitutional claims. It is enough to say that our examination of legislative reasonableness should consider the fact that the Legislature of the State of Washington is no more obviously at fault than this Court is in being uncertain about what would happen if respondents prevailed today. We therefore have a clear question about which institution, a legislature or a court, is relatively more competent to deal with an emerging issue as to which facts currently unknown could be dispositive. The answer has to be, for the reasons already stated, that the legislative process is to be preferred. There is a closely related further reason as well.

One must bear in mind that the nature of the right claimed, if recognized as one constitutionally required, would differ in no essential way from other constitutional rights guaranteed by enumeration or derived from some more definite textual source than "due process." An unenumerated right should not therefore be recognized, with the effect of displacing the legislative ordering of things, without the assurance that its recognition would prove as durable as the recognition of those other rights differently derived. To recognize a right of lesser promise would simply create a constitutional regime too uncertain to bring with it the expectation of finality that is one of this Court's central obligations in making constitutional decisions.

Legislatures, however, are not so constrained. The experimentation that should be out of the question in constitutional adjudication displacing legislative judgments is entirely proper, as well as highly desirable, when the legislative power addresses an emerging issue like assisted suicide. The Court should accordingly stay its hand to allow reasonable legislative consideration. While I do not decide for all time that respondents' claim should not be recognized, I acknowledge the legislative institutional competence as the better one to deal with that claim at this time.

Note

1. *Equal Protection and Physician Assistance.* In *Vacco v. Quill,* 521 U.S. 793 (1997), the Court rejected an equal protection challenge to a state law prohibiting

physician-assisted suicide. However, in *Myers v. Schneiderman*, 28 N.Y.3d 1131 46 N.Y.S.3d 835, 69 N.E.3d 623 (N.Y. 2017), the court held that New York law does not create a constitutional right to assisted suicide.

2. *The Right to Assistance.* In recent years, several states have recognized a right to obtain aid to die. Included are New Mexico (judicial decision), Oregon (statute), and Washington (statute). Nearly half the states are considering whether to adopt such legislation. *See* Malak Monir, *Half of States Plus D.C. Look at Right-to-Die Legislation*, USA Today, Apr. 20, 2015, at 2A.

∾ PROBLEMS ∾

1. *Constructing Arguments.* In constructing an argument for physician-assisted suicide as a fundamental liberty interest, how would counsel best use *Roe v. Wade* in support of that position? What case law would provide the best counterpoint?

2. *Describing the Right of Privacy.* Based on how the right of privacy has evolved over the past several decades, how might counsel describe it in a way that makes sense to a client?

9. A Constitutional Right to Sexual Gratification?

∾ PROBLEMS ∾

1. *A Constitutional Right to Purchase Sex Toys?* Is there a constitutional right on the part of consenting adults to engage in sexual intimacy? Does that right include the ability to use "sex toys" and sex enhancements? How would those seeking the right to use sex toys argue their case? How might the state respond? *See Flanigan's Enterprises, Inc. v. City of Sandy Springs*, 831 F.3d 1342 (11th Cir. 2016).

2. *A Constitutional Right to Access Prostitutes?* Does the proposed right of sexual intimacy include the right to access prostitutes? How would you argue the case for those seeking access? How might the state respond? *See Erotic Service Provides Legal Education & Research Project v. Gascon*, 880 F.3d 450 (9th Cir. 2018).

10. A Constitutional Right to Clean Water?

∾ PROBLEM: *THE FLINT MICHIGAN CASE* ∾

The City of Flint, Michigan, suffered a severe water quality problem that exposed residents to a high level of lead contamination, and potential exposure to Legionnaires' disease. Residents of Flint sued, claiming a constitutional right to clean drinking water. Is there such a right? Does it matter that state officials knew that their actions (in switching Flint from Detroit water to Flint River water) would expose residents to health risks, and that officials tried to cover up the health risks? *See Boler v. Earley*, 865 F.3d 391 (6th Cir., en banc, 2017).

[Points to Remember for Chapter 9 is contained in online file.]

10

Equal Protection

U.S. CONSTITUTION, FOURTEENTH AMENDMENT

Section 1. All persons born or naturalized in the United States, and subject to the jurisdiction thereof, are citizens of the United States and of the State wherein they reside. No State shall make or enforce any law which shall abridge the privileges or immunities of citizens of the United States; nor shall any State deprive any person of life, liberty, or property, without due process of law; nor deny to any person within its jurisdiction equal protection of the laws.

Section 5. The Congress shall have power to enforce, by appropriate legislation, the provisions of this article.

[Roadmap for Chapter 10 is contained in online file.]

∼ PROBLEM: THE DIVERSITY INITIATIVE ∼

New World University (NWU) is a state institution that seeks to prepare its students to thrive in an increasingly diverse, twenty-first-century world. To that end, NWU is considering the adoption of a new mission statement that will help it better educate and prepare its students. In particular, NWU is thinking about a statement that adopts the goal of "preparing students to work and thrive in a multicultural and diverse world, while ensuring that they do not lose pride in their racial or ethnic identity." NWU is also thinking about revising its admissions and financial aid policies to help it secure a more diverse student body. NWU thinks that broad educational diversity is attainable when students come from different backgrounds, including differences based on race, gender, socioeconomic class, sexual orientation, nationality, geography, and other factors. You have recently been appointed university counsel at NWU, and its board of regents has asked for your advice about whether it can adopt the proposed mission statement, as well as whether it can adjust its admissions and financial aid policies to take various diversity factors into account in hiring and admissions. If you believe such changes are possible, the Board would like your advice about how to frame the mission statement and the diversity plans. As we progress through this chapter, we will examine these issues, and we will ask you to advise NWU's board of regents.

—————————

Equality under the law was not a significant factor or concern in the original constitutional framing process. Although the Declaration of Independence flatly declares that "all men are created equal," the idea of equality did not animate the new Union. Indeed, at the time of the Republic's founding, slavery was well established and many states, in both the North and South, denied persons of African descent the right to sue in court, contract, or acquire, own, or sell property. *See* Don E. FEHRENBACHER, THE DRED SCOTT CASE 349-350 (Oxford 1978).

The Fourteenth Amendment's provision that no state shall "deny to any person within its jurisdiction the equal protection of the laws" is a constitutional guarantee of mixed signals. In its initial reading of the Fourteenth Amendment, the Court observed in the *Slaughterhouse Cases,* 83 U.S. 36, 81 (1873), that "the existence of laws in the States where the newly emancipated negroes resided, which discriminated with gross injustice and hardship against them as a class, was the evil to be remedied by" the Equal Protection Clause.

The laws the Court referenced were the Black Codes that many former Confederate states adopted in response to the Thirteenth Amendment (which abolished slavery). These codes defined racial status, prohibited intermarriage, established dual systems of criminal justice, and imposed restrictions on employment, travel, residence, and assembly. The codes diminished the force of the Thirteenth Amendment's abolishment of badges and incidents of slavery, and consequently inspired the Reconstruction Congress to pass the Civil Rights Act of 1866. As the nation's first civil rights law, the 1866 Act prohibited "discrimination in civil rights or immunities" and extended to persons of every race "the same rights to make and enforce contracts, to sue, be parties, and give evidence, to inherit, purchase, lease, sell, hold and convey real and personal property, and to full and equal benefit of all laws and proceedings for the security of persons and property, and be subject to like punishment." *Cong. Globe,* 39th Cong., 1st Sess. 474 (1866).

Although members of the Reconstruction Congress varied in their sense of the Fourteenth Amendment's scope, it was generally agreed that it at least was "designed to embody or incorporate the Civil Rights Act." HOWARD J. GRAHAM, EVERYMAN'S CONSTITUTION 291 n.73 (State Historical Society of Wisconsin 1968). The equal protection guarantee in particular responded to the "gross injustice and hardship" of the Black Codes, which were the Civil Rights Act of 1866's primary concern. CHARLES FAIRMAN, VII HISTORY OF THE SUPREME COURT OF THE UNITED STATES, RECONSTRUCTION AND REUNION, pt. 1, at 134 (Macmillan 1987). Consistent with this understanding, the *Slaughterhouse* Court doubted whether "any action of a State not directed by way of discrimination against the negroes as a class, or on account of their race, will ever be held to come within the purview of this provision." *Slaughterhouse Cases,* 83 U.S. at 81.

This race-specific vision of equal protection was reaffirmed in *Bradwell v. Illinois,* 83 U.S. 130 (1873), when the Court upheld a state law that denied women the opportunity to practice law. Hesitation to expand the contours of equal protection set a pattern that has persisted for much of the provision's history. Restrained use of the guarantee initially reflected resistance toward or caution with respect to the implications of Reconstruction. Even as the Due Process Clause became a basis for expansive judicial review during the early twentieth century, equal protection's currency remained limited. Justice Holmes thus dismissed the provision as "the usual last resort of constitutional arguments." *Buck v. Bell,* 274 U.S. 200, 208 (1927).

The equal protection guarantee eventually emerged as a powerful tool for undoing official segregation. Outside a few well-defined contexts, however, the Court has used the Equal Protection Clause sparingly and with deference to the legislative process. As the Court stated in *Lindsley v. Natural Carbonic Gas Co.,* 220 U.S. 61, 78 (1911), "if any state of facts reasonably can be conceived that would sustain the classification, the existence of that state of facts at the time the law was enacted must be assumed." The Court went on to hold that classifications that have a reasonable basis do not violate equal protection "merely because they are not made with mathematical nicety or because in practice they result in some inequality." This deference to the legislative process reflects the judicial concern that, because laws by their nature classify, an untethered equal protection guarantee might "invalidate, a whole range of tax, welfare, public service, regulatory, and licensing statutes." *Washington v. Davis,* 426 U.S. 229, 248 (1976).

From the beginning, the Court has struggled to define the exact contours of the Equal Protection Clause of the Fourteenth Amendment. Initially, the Court announced the doctrine of reasonable government classifications, applying rational basis scrutiny to government policies. By the mid-twentieth century, the Court had established strict scrutiny for government classifications based on race, national origin, and alienage. The Court also applied intermediate scrutiny to gender and illegitimacy classifications. As you read the following cases, try to identify and master the level of scrutiny applied by the Court to different types of equal protection classifications.

An equality principle once established is difficult to confine and has a tendency to spread and eventually "to lift all to the level of the most favored." FAIRMAN, RECONSTRUCTION AND REUNION, at 134. Indeed, once the Court used the equal protection guarantee to undo racial segregation, it was predictable that other groups would seek to invoke it to advance their causes. For purposes of judicial review, the challenge has been to determine which classifications or discriminations merit close scrutiny. Historically, factors such as historical disadvantage, exclusion from the political process, and immutable physical characteristics have been regarded by the courts as relevant considerations. *See United States v. Carolene Products Co.*, 304 U.S. 144, n.4 (1938). Indeed, the Court has identified four types of classification—race, gender, alienage, and illegitimacy—that warrant a heightened level of review. It also has determined that selective denial of a fundamental right or liberty, regardless of the group affected, merits a more robust standard of review.

For purposes of equal protection, the standards of review are strict scrutiny, intermediate scrutiny, and rational basis. Rational basis scrutiny applies to most legislative classifications. Strict scrutiny is used for all racial and most alienage classifications, as well as selective denials of or burdens on fundamental rights. Intermediate scrutiny governs gender and illegitimacy classifications. The elements of these tests are set forth in ascending order in the following table.

Standard of review	*Quality of government interest*	*Relationship between classification and goal*
Rational basis scrutiny	Rational basis	Reasonably related
Intermediate scrutiny	Important	Substantially related
Strict scrutiny	Compelling	Narrowly tailored

The goals of this chapter are to provide an understanding of 1) the history and evolution of the Equal Protection Clause, 2) the practical usage and application of the Equal Protection Clause, and 3) competing theories with respect to the scope and intensity of judicial review.

As we proceed, we will examine three recurring questions. First, *does the law classify?* After reading a few cases, you should recognize that many laws create classifications. Legislatures "classify" in tax codes, welfare guidelines, and many other laws. For equal protection purposes, the terms *classification* and *discrimination* are interchangeable. Second, *what is the nature of the classification?* The starting point for equal protection review is to determine the nature of the classification. Most classifications are not constitutionally significant and do not invoke heightened judicial scrutiny. To the extent that classifications are based on race, gender, alienage, or illegitimacy, or they burden or deny someone's "fundamental right," courts are more likely to apply a heightened standard of review. Third, when a classification is challenged, *which standard of review should a court apply?* In general, courts apply rational basis scrutiny to economic and social classifications. All classifications based on race and, in some instances, alienage are subject to strict scrutiny. Gender classifications are subject to intermediate scrutiny. As you read the cases, try to identify the standard of review applied by the Court.

A. STATE ECONOMIC REGULATIONS (AND OTHER CLASSIFICATIONS OF MINIMAL CONSTITUTIONAL CONCERN)

For most government classifications, the Court applies rational basis review. The government policy is presumed to be valid, and the person challenging the policy must allege and prove that it is arbitrary or irrational. Under rational basis scrutiny, the government almost always prevails.

Equal protection standards of review are informed by many of the same concerns that operate in the due process context. In *United States v. Carolene Products Co.*, 304 U.S. 144, n.4 (1938), the Court announced that it would reserve searching review for instances when a specific provision of the Bill of Rights is implicated or a burden is imposed on a group that is formally excluded from the political process. Rational basis review thus became the primary model for evaluating economic or social legislation, whether the challenged involves due process or equal protection. The rational basis test typically reflects a high level of judicial deference. Its accommodating nature is reflected in the following case, which is widely regarded as a benchmark for the review of general economic or social classifications.

Railway Express Agency v. New York

336 U.S. 106 (1949)

Mr. Justice DOUGLAS delivered the opinion of the Court.

A city ordinance provides that no person may operate a vehicle that displays advertising, except for business delivery vehicles engaged in their usual business or the owner's regular work.

The question of equal protection of the laws is pressed more strenuously on us. It is pointed out that the regulation draws the line between advertisements of products sold by the owner of the truck and general advertisements. It is argued that unequal treatment on the basis of such a distinction is not justified by the aim and purpose of the regulation. It is said, for example, that one of appellant's trucks carrying the advertisement of a commercial house would not cause any greater distraction of pedestrians and vehicle drivers than if the commercial house carried the same advertisement on its own truck. Yet the regulation allows the latter to do what the former is forbidden from doing. It is therefore contended that the classification which the regulation makes has no relation to the traffic problem since a violation turns not on what kind of advertisements are carried on trucks but on whose trucks they are carried.

That, however, is a superficial way of analyzing the problem, even if we assume that it is premised on the correct construction of the regulation. The local authorities may well have concluded that those who advertised their own wares on their trucks do not present the same traffic problem in view of the nature or extent of the advertising which they use. It would take a degree of omniscience which we lack to say that such is not the case. If that judgment is correct, the advertising displays that are exempt have less impact on traffic than those of appellants.

We cannot say that that judgment is not an allowable one. Yet if it is, the classification has relation to the purpose for which it is made and does not contain the kind of discrimination against which the Equal Protection Clause affords protection. It is by such practical considerations based on experience rather than by theoretical inconsistencies that the question of equal protection is to be answered. And the fact that New York City sees fit to eliminate from traffic this kind of distraction but does not touch what may be even greater ones in a different category, such as the vivid displays on Times Square, is immaterial. It is no requirement of equal protection that all evils of the same genus be eradicated or none at all.

Mr. Justice JACKSON, *concurring.*

Invocation of the equal protection clause, as opposed to the Due Process Clause, does not disable any governmental body from dealing with the subject at hand. It merely means that the prohibition or regulation must have a broader impact. I regard it as a salutary doctrine that cities, states and the Federal Government must exercise their powers so as not to discriminate between their inhabitants except upon some reasonable differentiation fairly related to the object of regulation. This equality is not merely abstract justice. The framers of the Constitution knew, and we should not forget today, that there is no more effective practical guaranty against arbitrary and unreasonable government than to require that the principles of law which officials would impose upon a minority must be imposed generally. Conversely, nothing opens the door to arbitrary action so effectively as to allow those officials to pick and choose only a few to whom they will apply legislation and thus to escape the political retribution that might be visited upon them if larger numbers were affected. Courts can take no better measure to assure that laws will be just than to require that laws be equal in operation.

Notes and Questions

1. *Standards of Review.* One of the key questions in equal protection cases is the appropriate standard of review to be applied. In general, as noted, economic classifications are subject to a low standard of review (typically, rational basis scrutiny). Why is that so?

2. *"Rigorous" Rational Basis Review.* The rational basis test generally is renowned for its deference to the political process. There are instances, however, when the Court employs a higher intensity version of rational basis review. Although a

classification may not be "facially invidious," it nonetheless may reflect a "recurring constitutional difficulty." The Court thus may insist that the "classification reflects a reasoned judgment" and advance substantial state interests. *Plyler v. Doe*, 457 U.S. 202 (1982). This enhanced version of rational basis review has been evidenced in decisions invalidating laws that discriminated against persons on the basis of mental retardation, *City of Cleburne v. Cleburne Living Center*, 473 U.S. 432 (1985); sexual orientation, *Romer v. Evans*, 517 U.S. 620 (1996); and children of undocumented aliens, *Plyler v. Doe*. *See* Kenji Yoshino, *The New Equal Protection*, 124 Harv. L. Rev. 747 (2011) (discussing three standards of review and the competing forms of rationality review appearing in equal protection cases).

3. *First Amendment Considerations.* The outcome in *Railway Express Agency* was achieved before the Court determined, nearly 30 years later, that the First Amendment protected commercial speech. Fundamental rights, whether denied selectively or on a wholesale basis, are usually subject to more rigorous scrutiny. The advertising regulation, if challenged today, thus would likely be subjected to a higher level of review.

4. *Under-inclusiveness.* The *Railway Express Agency.* The Court's allowance of piecemeal legislative efforts (a partial ban on display advertising) to respond to a larger problem (distractions to motorists) illustrates the concept of under-inclusiveness. A particularly good example of under-inclusiveness (and over-inclusiveness) is a statute that the Court invalidated a quarter of a century later as an impermissible gender classification. That statute, reviewed in *Craig v. Boren*, 429 U.S. 190 (1976), prohibited the sale of 3.2% beer to males under the age of 21 and females under the age of 18. The law's burden was under-inclusive (and the law's benefit over-inclusive) to the extent that it did not reach women who would be a source of such risk. The burden was over-inclusive (and the benefit under-inclusive) insofar as many between the ages of 18 and 21 would not present the risk of an alcohol-related driving offense. The tolerance level for over-inclusiveness and under-inclusiveness depends on the standard of review, which is a function of whether the classification counts for equal protection purposes.

∾ PROBLEMS ∾

1. *Is Discrimination Necessarily "Bad"?* Many assume that the term *"discrimination"* has only negative connotations, and to say that someone is a *"discriminator"* is usually regarded as a pejorative statement. But does the word *"discrimination"* also have positive connotations? For example, a person might be described as a "discriminating shopper"—meaning, of course, that he or she exercises good judgment. Of course, the astute student may suggest that there is a substantial difference between governmental discrimination and shopper discrimination. But is there really a difference? Suppose that a city decides to provide reduced bus fares to senior citizens and to students. Such a scheme necessarily involves

discrimination (between seniors and students on the one hand, and everyone else), but is the discrimination necessarily bad or constitutionally impermissible? In fact, are there sound and desirable reasons for providing seniors and students with reduced fares? Should government have discretion to provide seniors and students with that benefit?

2. *Are There Sound Reasons for Providing Less Protection to Economic Classifications Than to Racial Classifications?* If some discrimination is desirable, and other discrimination is objectionable, how do courts distinguish between permissible and impermissible discrimination? That issue is the overriding concern of this chapter. As the preceding problem reveals, one role of government is to make decisions, and those decisions frequently involve classifications that discriminate. In some cases (e.g., reduced bus fares for senior citizens and students), those classifications may be permissible. In other instances (e.g., invidious race discrimination), those classifications are impermissible. How and why do courts decide which classifications are permissible and which are impermissible?

**Federal Communications Commission v.
Beach Communications, Inc.**

508 U.S. 307 (1993)

Justice THOMAS delivered the opinion of the Court.

This case arises out of an FCC proceeding clarifying the agency's interpretation of the term cable system as it is used in the Cable Act. In this proceeding, the Commission addressed the application of the exemption codified in §602(7)(B) to satellite master antenna television (SMATV) facilities. Unlike a traditional cable television system, which delivers video programming to a large community of subscribers through coaxial cables laid under city streets or along utility lines, an SMATV system typically receives a signal from a satellite through a small satellite dish located on a rooftop and then retransmits the signal by wire to units within a building or complex of buildings. The Commission ruled that an SMATV system that serves multiple buildings via a network of interconnected physical transmission lines is a cable system, unless it falls within the §602(7)(B) exemption. Consistent with the plain terms of the statutory exemption, the Commission concluded that such an SMATV system is subject to the franchise requirement if its transmission lines interconnect separately owned and managed buildings or if its lines use or cross any public right of way.

Respondents Beach Communications, Inc., et al.,—SMATV operators that would be subject to franchising under the Cable Act as construed by the Commission—petitioned the Court of Appeals for review. The Court of Appeals rejected respondents' statutory challenge to the Commission's interpretation, but a majority of the court found merit in the claim that §602(7) violates the implied equal protection guarantee of the Due Process Clause. In the absence of what it termed the predominant rationale for local franchising (use of public rights of way), the court saw no rational basis on the record, and was unable to imagine any conceivable basis, for distinguishing between those facilities exempted by the statute and those SMATV cable systems that link separately owned and managed buildings. The court remanded the record and directed the FCC to provide additional legislative facts to justify the distinction.

A report subsequently filed by the Commission failed to satisfy the Court of Appeals. Because the Court of Appeals held an Act of Congress unconstitutional, we granted certiorari. We now reverse.

Whether embodied in the Fourteenth Amendment or inferred from the Fifth, equal protection is not a license for courts to judge the wisdom, fairness, or logic of legislative choices. In areas of social and economic policy, a statutory classification that neither proceeds along suspect lines nor infringes fundamental constitutional rights must be upheld against equal protection challenge if there is any reasonably conceivable state of facts that could provide a rational basis for the classification. Where there are plausible reasons for Congress' action, our inquiry is at an end. This standard of review is a paradigm of judicial restraint. The Constitution presumes that, absent some reason to infer antipathy, even improvident decisions will eventually be rectified by the democratic process and that judicial intervention is generally unwarranted no matter how unwisely we may think a political branch has acted.

On rational basis review, a classification in a statute such as the Cable Act comes to us bearing a strong presumption of validity, and those attacking the rationality of the legislative classification have the burden to negative every conceivable basis which might support it. Moreover, because we never require a legislature to articulate its reasons for enacting a statute, it is entirely irrelevant for constitutional purposes whether the conceived reason for the challenged distinction actually motivated the legislature.

Applying these principles, we conclude that the common ownership distinction is constitutional. There are at least two possible bases for the distinction; either one suffices. First, Congress borrowed §602(7)(B) from pre–Cable Act regulations, and although the existence of a prior administrative scheme is certainly not necessary to the rationality of the statute, it is plausible that Congress also adopted the FCC's earlier rationale. Under that rationale, common ownership was thought to be indicative of those systems for which the costs of regulation would outweigh the benefits to consumers. Because the number of subscribers was a similar indicator, the Commission also exempted cable facilities that served fewer than 50 subscribers. *See* 47 C.F.R. §76.5(a) (1984). There is a second conceivable basis for the statutory distinction. Suppose competing SMATV operators wish to sell video programming to subscribers in a group of contiguous buildings, such as a single city block, which can be interconnected by wire without crossing a public right of way. If all the buildings belong to one owner or are commonly managed, that owner or manager could freely negotiate a deal for all subscribers on a competitive basis. But if the buildings are separately owned and managed, the first SMATV operator who gains a foothold by signing a contract and installing a satellite dish and associated transmission equipment on one of the buildings would enjoy a powerful cost advantage in competing for the remaining subscribers: he could connect additional buildings for the cost of a few feet of cable, whereas any competitor would have to recover the cost of his own satellite headend facility. Thus, the first operator could charge rates well above his cost and still undercut the competition. This potential for effective monopoly power might theoretically justify regulating the latter class of SMATV systems and not the former.

The Court of Appeals quite evidently believed that the crossing or use of a public right of way is the only conceivable basis upon which Congress could rationally require local franchising of SMATV systems. As we have indicated, however, there are plausible rationales unrelated to the use of public rights of way for regulating cable facilities serving separately owned and managed buildings. The assumptions underlying these rationales may be erroneous, but the very fact that they are arguable is sufficient, on rational basis review, to immunize the congressional choice from constitutional challenge.

The judgment of the Court of Appeals is *reversed*, and the case is *remanded* for further proceedings consistent with this opinion.

∾ PROBLEMS ∾

1. *More on the Diversity Initiative.* Suppose that the board of regents in the introductory problem is thinking about basing all scholarships at NWU on student need, and wants your advice about whether it would be permissible to do so. What standard of review would apply?

2. *The Diversity Initiative and Preferential Admissions.* Suppose that the board of regents is also thinking about giving preferential admission (especially to the law and medical schools) based on economic need. In other words, the university will preferentially admit students who come from poor backgrounds. Is such an admissions policy permissible? What standard of review should be applied?

3. *Age and Driving Restrictions.* The City of Restraint enacts an ordinance prohibiting persons under the age of 21 and over the age of 70 from driving on public highways. In enacting the ordinance, the city states that younger persons have a tendency to drive recklessly and that older drivers have poorer vision because of their age. Suppose that Barb (an 18-year-old college freshman and campus president of Mothers Against Drunk Driving) and Homer (a 71-year-old CEO of a Fortune 500 company who pilots his own plane) seek your counsel on whether to file discrimination lawsuits against the ordinance. What would your advice be with respect to whether they could bring viable equal protection claims? In equal protection cases, rationality review is the default standard that will apply unless a policy or rule employs a classification that is inherently suspect or invidious or that burdens a fundamental right. *Schweiker v. Wilson*, 450 U.S. 221, 230 (1981).

See Massachusetts Board of Retirement v. Murgia, 427 U.S. 307 (1976). Would your counsel be influenced by the fact that neither Bart nor Homer is as reckless as many drivers in the licensed driver group?

B. RACIAL CLASSIFICATIONS

The Constitutional Convention was inspired largely by the political and economic dysfunction experienced under the Articles of Confederation. Trade wars among the new states resulted in a nation whose sum was less than its parts. Despite a common objective of creating a viable political and economic union, some significant divisions among the Framers had to be overcome. Political representation in the national government, for instance, pitted larger states against smaller states. This dispute was resolved by the creation of a bicameral legislature.

One of the most problematic issues confronting the Framers was slavery. James Madison observed that "sectional friction was attributable partly to climate but principally to the effects of states having or not having slaves. These two causes concur in forming the great division of interests in the United States. It did not lie between the large and small states; it lay, between the Northern and Southern states." 1 M. FARRAND, THE RECORDS OF THE FEDERAL CONVENTION OF 1787 486 (Yale 1937). The premise that slave and non-slave states could coexist within a single union ultimately foundered upon the realities of territorial expansion and fugitive slave controversies. With the creation of each new territory and state, the question of slavery's expansion was renewed. Congress attempted to resolve the problem through compromise. Lasting solutions broke down as westward expansion increased and each side feared that the other would gain the upper hand and define the Union according to its will. The abolitionist movement in the 1830s campaigned for revising the Constitution, through either interpretation or amendment, to eliminate slavery. This development reflected an intensifying constitutional competition. The southern counterpoint was that slave owner rights were protected by the Due Process Clause of the Fifth Amendment. The federal government was an agent of the states, and thus was obligated to support their policies.

As slave owners traveled to and from non-slave states and territories, questions arose regarding the legal status of the slaves. The southern position was the dominant influence on case law concerning sojourning or fugitive status. Northern case law with respect to sojourning slaves generally applied the law of the relevant slave state to questions of whether their presence in a free jurisdiction was sufficient grounds for emancipating them. Many northern states, however, adopted laws that prevented slave owners from recapturing a runaway slave without judicial process. In *Prigg v. Pennsylvania*, 41 U.S. 539 (1842), the Court invalidated an anti-kidnapping law on grounds it conflicted with federal law allowing slave owners to recapture runaway slaves. This outcome had significant consequences for both the North and the South. While northerners were sensitized to their complicity in slavery, southerners became aware that the federal interest that cut in its favor eventually could turn the other way. By the 1850s, the political process had become gridlocked on the various issues relating to slavery. Within this context, the political branches themselves welcomed the Supreme Court's engagement. As the Court soon discovered, it could choose sides but ultimately not impose its will.

Dred Scott v. Sandford

60 U.S. 393 (1857)

Mr. Chief Justice Taney delivered the opinion of the Court.

The question is simply this: Can a negro, whose ancestors were imported into this country, and sold as slaves, become a member of the political community formed and brought into existence by the Constitution of the United States, and as such become entitled to all the rights, and privileges, and immunities, guarantied by that instrument to the citizen? One of which rights is the privilege of suing in a court of the United States in the cases specified in the Constitution.

The words "people of the United States" and "citizens" are synonymous terms. They both describe the political body who, according to our republican institutions, form the sovereignty, and who hold the power and conduct the Government through their representatives. They are what we familiarly call the "sovereign people," and every citizen is one of this people, and a constituent member of this sovereignty. The question before us is, whether the class of persons described in the plea compose a portion of this people, and are constituent members of this sovereignty? We think they are not, and that they are not included, and were not intended to be included, under the word "citizens" in the Constitution, and can therefore claim none of the rights and privileges which that instrument provides for and secures to citizens of the United States. On the contrary, they were at that time considered as a subordinate and inferior class of beings, who had been subjugated by the dominant race, and, whether emancipated or not, yet remained subject to their authority, and had no rights or privileges but such as those who held the power and the Government might choose to grant them.

The question arises whether the provisions of the Constitution, in relation to the personal rights and privileges to which the citizen of a State should be entitled, embraced the negro African race, at that time in this country, or who might afterwards be imported, who had then or should afterwards be made free in any State; and to put it in the power of a single State to make him a citizen of the United States, and endue him with the full rights of citizenship in every other State without their consent? Does the Constitution of the United States act upon him whenever he shall be made free under the laws of a State, and raised there to the rank of a citizen, and immediately clothe him with all the privileges of a citizen in every other State, and in its own courts?

The court thinks the affirmative of these propositions cannot be maintained. And if it cannot, the plaintiff in error could not be a citizen of the State of Missouri, within the meaning of the Constitution of the United States, and, consequently, was not entitled to sue in its courts.

It is true, every person, and every class and description of persons, who were at the time of the adoption of the Constitution recognized as citizens in the several States, became also citizens of this new political body; but none other; it was formed by them, and for them and their posterity, but for no one else. And the personal rights and privileges guarantied to citizens of this new sovereignty were intended to embrace those only who were then members of the several State communities, or who should afterwards by birthright or otherwise become members, according to the provisions of the Constitution and the principles on which it was founded.

It becomes necessary, therefore, to determine who were citizens of the several States when the Constitution was adopted. We must inquire who, at that time, were recognized as the people or citizens of a State, whose rights and liberties had been outraged by the English Government; and who declared their independence, and assumed the powers of Government to defend their rights by force of arms. The legislation and histories of the times, and the language used in the Declaration of Independence, show, that neither the class of persons who had been imported as slaves, nor their descendants, whether they had become free or not, were then acknowledged as a part of the people, nor intended to be included in the general words used in that memorable instrument. They had for more than a century before been regarded as beings of an inferior order, and altogether unfit to associate with the white race, either in social or political relations; and so far inferior, that they had no rights which the white man was bound to respect; and that the negro might justly and lawfully be reduced to slavery for his benefit. He was bought and sold, and treated as an ordinary article of merchandise and traffic, whenever a profit could be made by it. This opinion was at that time fixed and universal in the civilized portion of the white race.

The rights of property are united with the rights of person, and placed on the same ground by the fifth amendment to the Constitution, which provides that no person shall be deprived of life, liberty, and property, without due process of law. And an act of Congress which deprives a citizen of the United States of his liberty or property, merely because he came himself or brought his property into a particular Territory of the United States, and who had committed no offence against the laws, could hardly be dignified with the name of due process of law.

The right of property in a slave is distinctly and expressly affirmed in the Constitution. The right to traffic in it, like an ordinary article of merchandise and property, was guarantied to the citizens of the United States, in every State that might desire it, for twenty years. And the Government in express terms is pledged to protect it in all future time, if the slave escapes from his owner. This is done in

896   10. Equal Protection

plain words. And no word can be found in the Constitution which gives Congress a greater power over slave property, or which entitles property of that kind to less protection than property of any other description. The only power conferred is the power coupled with the duty of guarding and protecting the owner in his rights.

Upon these considerations, it is the opinion of the court that the act of Congress which prohibited a citizen from holding and owning property of this kind in the territory of the United States north of the line therein mentioned, is not warranted by the Constitution, and is therefore void; and that neither Dred Scott himself, nor any of his family, were made free by being carried into this territory; even if they had been carried there by the owner, with the intention of becoming a permanent resident. Although there were many separate opinions, only two justices dissented from the holding.

Notes

1. *The Black Codes.* The constitutional end of slavery gave rise to a new model of racial control in the form of the Black Codes. These enactments, adopted by former slave states, "forbade blacks from pursuing certain occupations or professions, forbade owning firearms or weapons; controlled the movement of blacks by systems of passes; required proof of residence; prohibited the congregation of groups of blacks; restricted blacks from residing in certain areas; specified an etiquette of deference to whites, forbade racial intermarriage and provided the death penalty for blacks raping white women and excluded blacks from jury duty, public office, and voting." HAROLD HYMAN & WILLIAM WIECEK, EQUAL JUSTICE UNDER LAW 319 (Harper & Row 1982).

2. *The Civil Rights Act of 1866.* Congress responded to the Black Codes by enacting the Civil Rights Act of 1866, which prohibited discrimination on the basis of race with respect to civil rights and immunities and provided that the "inhabitants of every race shall have the same rights to make and enforce contracts, to sue, be parties, and give evidence, to inherit, purchase, lease, sell, hold and convey real and personal property, and to full and equal benefit of all laws and proceedings for the security of persons and property, and shall be subject to like punishment." *Cong. Globe,* 39th Cong., 1st Sess. 474 (1866).

3. *The Fourteenth Amendment.* There is a general consensus among historians that the Fourteenth Amendment was fashioned to incorporate and fortify the Civil Rights Act of 1866. If correct, the guarantee as it has evolved is much more and much less. The amendment has become the basis for prohibiting classifications on the basis of not only race but also on other grounds such as gender, alienage, and illegitimacy. It also has become a predicate for securing fundamental rights, such as privacy, travel, and voting, that are not textually enumerated. Although the Fourteenth Amendment has expanded into contexts beyond what

the Framers anticipated, as a function of judicial review, for most of its history it has been interpreted in ways that have accommodated rather than prohibited racial discrimination.

Notably missing from the Fourteenth Amendment's ambit of concern, as initially framed, was the right to vote. This omission reflected the reality that the constitutional impact would touch not only the South, but also the North. Reluctance to protect this political right broke down, however, as the nation factored in southern intransigence and the burdens and costs of reconstruction. As the right to vote became viewed as a means of speeding reconstruction toward its end, the Fifteenth Amendment was framed and ratified. Its exponents anticipated that the right to vote would provide the ultimate protection against hostile legislation.

4. *The* Slaughterhouse Cases. The Court's first exposure to the Fourteenth Amendment arose in a context unrelated to race. In the *Slaughterhouse Cases*, 83 U.S. 36 (1873), the Court spurned arguments that the Fourteenth Amendment represented a redistribution of authority over civil rights from states to the federal government. It thus defined the incidents of national citizenship, under the Privileges and Immunities Clause, in profoundly narrow terms. At the same time, the Court stressed that the equal protection guarantee was concerned exclusively with racial discrimination. It observed that

> in the light of the history of these amendments, and the pervading purpose of them, which we have already discussed, it is not difficult to give a meaning to this clause. The existence of laws in the States where the newly emancipated negroes resided, which discriminated with gross injustice and hardship against them as a class, was the evil to be remedied by this clause, and by it such laws are forbidden.
>
> If, however, the States did not conform their laws to its requirements, then by the fifth section of the article of amendment Congress was authorized to enforce it by suitable legislation. We doubt very much whether any action of a State not directed by way of discrimination against the negroes as a class, or on account of their race, will ever be held to come within the purview of this provision. It is so clearly a provision for that race and that emergency, that a strong case would be necessary for its application to any other. But as it is a State that is to be dealt with, and not alone the validity of its laws, we may safely leave that matter until Congress shall have exercised its power, or some case of State oppression, by denial of equal justice in its courts, shall have claimed a decision at our hands. We find no such case in the one before us, and do not deem it necessary to go over the argument again, as it may have relation to this particular clause of the amendment. 83 U.S. at 81.

5. *Discrimination Implying Inferiority.* In striking down the Civil Rights Act of 1875, which prohibited discrimination in public accommodations, *The Civil Rights Cases*, 109 U.S. 3, 24-25 (1883), indicated that these "mere discriminations" were constitutionally insignificant. It also noted that "when a man has emerged from slavery, and by the aid of beneficent legislation has shaken off the inseparable concomitants of that state, there must be some stage in the progress of his elevation when he takes the rank of mere citizen, and ceases to be the special favorite of the laws."

1. Separate but Equal

The letter and spirit of *The Civil Rights Cases* heralded an accommodating constitutional environment for the ideology of racial supremacy. Beginning in the late 1880s, southern states implemented laws designed to maintain racial separation, protect racial integrity, preserve white supremacy, and minimize cross-racial mingling. This system of racial management actually had its prototype in the North, where public education was often segregated and economic opportunity was racially determined. *E.g., State v. McCann*, 21 Ohio St. 198 (1872); *Roberts v. City of Boston*, 59 Mass. 198 (1850). The Court referenced this history when, in *Plessy v. Ferguson*, it determined that official segregation was the extension of a natural societal order.

Plessy v. Ferguson

163 U.S. 537 (1896)

Mr. Justice BROWN delivered the opinion of the Court.

This case turns upon the constitutionality of an act of the general assembly of the state of Louisiana, passed in 1890, providing for separate railway carriages for the white and colored races.

The constitutionality of this act is attacked upon the ground that it conflicts both with the thirteenth amendment of the constitution, abolishing slavery, and the fourteenth amendment, which prohibits certain restrictive legislation on the part of the states. The object of the Fourteenth amendment was undoubtedly to enforce the absolute equality of the two races before the law, but, in the nature of things, it could not have been intended to abolish distinctions based upon color, or to enforce social, as distinguished from political, equality, or a commingling of the two races upon terms unsatisfactory to either. Laws permitting, and even requiring, their separation, in places where they are liable to be brought into contact, do not necessarily imply the inferiority of either race to the other, and have been generally, if not universally, recognized as within the competency of the state legislatures in the exercise of their police power. The most common instance of this is connected with the establishment of separate schools for white and colored children, which have been held to be a valid exercise of the legislative power even by courts of states where the political rights of the colored race have been longest and most earnestly enforced. Laws forbidding the intermarriage of the two races may be said in a technical sense to interfere with the freedom of contract, and yet have been universally recognized as within the police power of the state. The distinction between laws interfering with the political equality of the negro and those requiring the separation of the two races in schools, theaters, and railway carriages has been frequently drawn by this court.

It is claimed by the plaintiff in error that, in any mixed community, the reputation of belonging to the dominant race, in this instance the white race, is "property," in the same sense that a right of action or of inheritance is property.

We are unable to see how this statute deprives him of, or in any way affects his right to, such property. If he be a white man, and assigned to a colored coach, he may have his action for damages against the company for being deprived of his so-called "property." Upon the other hand, if he be a colored man, and be so assigned, he has been deprived of no property, since he is not lawfully entitled to the reputation of being a white man.

So far, then, as a conflict with the fourteenth amendment is concerned, the case reduces itself to the question whether the statute of Louisiana is a reasonable regulation, and with respect to this there must necessarily be a large discretion on the part of the legislature. In determining the question of reasonableness, it is at liberty to act with reference to the established usages, customs, and traditions of the people, and with a view to the promotion of their comfort, and the preservation of the public peace and good order. Gauged by this standard, we cannot say that a law which authorizes or even requires the separation of the two races in public conveyances is unreasonable, or more obnoxious to the fourteenth amendment than the acts of congress requiring separate schools for colored children in the District of Columbia, the constitutionality of which does not seem to have been questioned, or the corresponding acts of state legislatures.

We consider the underlying fallacy of the plaintiff's argument to consist in the assumption that the enforced separation of the two races stamps the colored race with a badge of inferiority. If this be so, it is not by reason of anything found in the act, but solely because the colored race chooses to put that construction upon it. The argument necessarily assumes that if, the colored race should become the dominant power in the state legislature, and should enact a law in precisely similar terms, it would thereby relegate the white race to an inferior position. We imagine that the white race, at least, would not acquiesce in this assumption. The argument also assumes that social prejudices may be overcome by legislation, and that equal rights cannot be secured to the negro except by an enforced commingling of the two races. If the two races are to meet upon terms of social equality, it must be the result of natural affinities, a mutual appreciation of each other's merits, and a voluntary consent of individuals. When the government, therefore, has secured to each of its citizens equal rights before the law, and equal opportunities for improvement and progress, it "has accomplished the end for which it was organized, and performed all of the functions respecting social advantages with which it is endowed." Legislation is powerless to eradicate racial instincts, or to abolish distinctions based upon physical differences, and the attempt to do so can only result in accentuating the difficulties of the present situation. If the civil and political rights of both races be equal, one cannot be inferior to the other civilly or politically. If one race be inferior to the other socially, the constitution of the United States cannot put them upon the same plane.

The judgment of the court below is therefore *affirmed*.

Mr. Justice HARLAN *dissenting*.

It was said in argument that the statute of Louisiana does not discriminate against either race, but prescribes a rule applicable alike to white and colored citizens. Everyone knows that the statute in question had its origin in the purpose to exclude colored people from coaches occupied by or assigned to white persons. The thing to accomplish was, under the guise of giving equal accommodation for whites and blacks, to compel the latter to keep to themselves while traveling in railroad passenger coaches. The fundamental objection, therefore, to the statute, is that it interferes with the personal freedom of citizens. If a white man and a black man choose to occupy the same public conveyance on a public highway, it is their right to do so; and no government, proceeding alone on grounds of race, can prevent it without infringing the personal liberty of each.

The white race deems itself to be the dominant race in this country. And so it is, in prestige, in achievements, in education, in wealth, and in power. But in view of the constitution, in the eye of the law, there is in this country no superior, dominant, ruling class of citizens. Our constitution is color-blind, and neither knows nor tolerates classes among citizens. All citizens are equal before the law. It is therefore to be regretted that this high tribunal, the final expositor of the fundamental law of the land, has reached the conclusion that it is competent for a state to regulate the enjoyment by citizens of their civil rights solely upon the basis of race.

The judgment this day rendered will, in time, prove to be quite as pernicious as the decision made by this tribunal in the *Dred Scott* case. The recent amendments of the constitution, it was supposed, had eradicated that decision and its principles from our institutions. But it seems that we have yet, in some of the states, a dominant race,—a superior class of citizens,—which assumes to regulate the enjoyment of civil rights, common to all citizens, upon the basis of race. The present decision will encourage the belief that it is possible to defeat the beneficent purposes of the recent amendments of the constitution, by one of which the blacks of this country were made citizens of the United States and of the states in which they respectively reside, and whose privileges and immunities, as citizens, the states are forbidden to abridge. What can more certainly arouse race hate, what more certainly create and perpetuate a feeling of distrust between these races, than state enactments which, in fact, proceed on the ground that colored citizens are so inferior and degraded that they cannot be allowed to sit in public coaches occupied by white citizens? That is the real meaning of such legislation as was enacted in Louisiana. For the reasons stated, I am constrained to withhold my assent from the opinion and judgment of the majority.

Notes

1. *"Equality" Under "Separate but Equal."* Notwithstanding its facial symmetry, the separate but equal doctrine provided much more "separateness" than "equality." In *Cumming v. Richmond County Board of Education*, 175 U.S. 528 (1899), the Court upheld the closure of an all-Black high school. The school board justified

the closure on grounds that its financial resources were limited. The Court refused to order the closure of the all-white school, noting that it would burden one set of students without benefiting the other. This outcome evidenced that equality was a secondary concern. Segregation in public schools was revisited in *Gong Lum v. Rice*, 275 U.S. 78, 86 (1927). The plaintiff was the father of a nine-year-old girl who argued that she had been misclassified as "colored" and thus denied the opportunity to attend a public school reserved for whites. The Court concluded that the same claim had been rejected numerous times in cases brought by Black children who were excluded from attending schools for whites. The Court found no basis for differentiating the outcome where the issue is between white pupils and pupils of Asian races.

BACKGROUND

For race and most alienage classifications, the Court applies strict scrutiny to government actions. In other words, the government action is presumed invalid and the government must justify its classification by showing that there is a compelling government interest and that the classification is narrowly tailored to achieve the compelling interest. Under strict scrutiny, the government action usually is invalidated, either because the government interest is not sufficiently compelling or, most often, because the regulation is not narrowly tailored.

---

2. *The NAACP's Role.* A key factor in the eventual dismantling of official segregation was the National Association for the Advancement of Colored People's (NAACP) emergence as a litigation force. The NAACP, in the 1930s, launched a desegregation strategy that successfully attacked the overt inequalities in education. Its early successes included a ruling, in *Missouri ex rel. Gaines v. Canada*, 305 U.S. 337 (1938), that a state must create a law school for nonwhites or else admit them to its only public law school.

3. *The* Carolene *Decision.* Another significant step toward segregation's deconstruction was the Court's indication, in *United States v. Carolene Products Co.*, 304 U.S. 144, 154 n.4 (1938), that "prejudice against discrete and insular minorities may be a special condition, which tends seriously to curtail the operation of the political processes ordinarily relied upon to protect minorities, and which may call for a correspondingly more searching inquiry." The Court thus indicated that it might use a higher standard of review when a group was excluded from and could not represent itself in the political process. In *Korematsu v. United States*, 323 U.S. 214 (1944), the Court introduced "strict scrutiny" as the standard of review for racial classifications.

Korematsu v. United States

323 U.S. 214 (1944)

Mr. Justice BLACK delivered the opinion of the Court.

The petitioner, an American citizen of Japanese descent, was convicted in a federal district court for remaining in San Leandro, California, a 'Military Area', contrary to Civilian Exclusion Order No. 34 of the Commanding General of the Western Command, U.S. Army, which directed that after May 9, 1942, all persons of Japanese ancestry should be excluded from that area. No question was raised as to petitioner's loyalty to the United States.

All legal restrictions which curtail the civil rights of a single racial group are immediately suspect. That is not to say that all such restrictions are unconstitutional. It is to say that courts must subject them to the most rigid scrutiny. Pressing public necessity may sometimes justify the existence of such restrictions; racial antagonism never can.

It is said that we are dealing here with the case of imprisonment of a citizen in a concentration camp solely because of his ancestry, without evidence or inquiry concerning his loyalty and good disposition towards the United States. Our task would be simple, our duty clear, were this a case involving the imprisonment of a loyal citizen in a concentration camp because of racial prejudice. Regardless of the true nature of the assembly and relocation centers—and we deem it unjustifiable to call them concentration camps with all the ugly connotations that term implies—we are dealing specifically with nothing but an exclusion order. To cast this case into outlines of racial prejudice, without reference to the real military dangers which were presented, merely confuses the issue. Korematsu was not excluded from the Military Area because of hostility to him or his race. He was excluded because we are at war with the Japanese Empire, because the properly constituted military authorities feared an invasion of our West Coast and felt constrained to take proper security measures, because they decided that the military urgency of the situation demanded that all citizens of Japanese ancestry be segregated from the West Coast temporarily, and finally, because Congress, reposing its confidence in this time of war in our military leaders—as inevitably it must—determined that they should have the power to do just this. There was evidence of disloyalty on the part of some, the military authorities considered that the need for action was great, and time was short. We cannot—by availing ourselves of the calm perspective of hindsight—now say that at that time these actions were unjustified.

Affirmed.

Mr. Justice MURPHY, *dissenting.*

This exclusion of 'all persons of Japanese ancestry, both alien and non-alien,' from the Pacific Coast area on a plea of military necessity in the absence of martial law ought not to be approved. Such exclusion goes over 'the very brink of constitutional power' and falls into the ugly abyss of racism.

Justification for the exclusion is sought mainly upon questionable racial and sociological grounds not ordinarily within the realm of expert military judgment, supplemented by certain semi-military conclusions drawn from an unwarranted use of circumstantial evidence. Individuals of Japanese ancestry are condemned because they are said to be 'a large, unassimilated, tightly knit racial group, bound to an enemy nation by strong ties of race, culture, custom and religion.' They are claimed to be given to 'emperor worshipping ceremonies' and to 'dual citizenship.' Japanese language schools and allegedly pro-Japanese organizations are cited as evidence of possible group disloyalty, together with facts as to certain persons being educated and residing at length in Japan. It is intimated that many of these individuals deliberately resided 'adjacent to strategic points,' thus enabling them 'to carry into execution a tremendous program of sabotage on a mass scale should any considerable number of them have been inclined to do so.' The need for protective custody is also asserted. The report refers without identity to 'numerous incidents of violence' as well as to other admittedly unverified or cumulative incidents. From this, plus certain other events not shown to have been connected with the Japanese Americans, it is concluded that the 'situation was fraught with danger to the Japanese population itself' and that the general public 'was ready to take matters into its own hands.' Finally, it is intimated, though not directly charged or proved, that persons of Japanese ancestry were responsible for three minor isolated shellings and bombings of the Pacific Coast area, as well as for unidentified radio transmissions and night signaling.

The main reasons relied upon by those responsible for the forced evacuation, therefore, do not prove a reasonable relation between the group characteristics of Japanese Americans and the dangers of invasion, sabotage and espionage. The reasons appear, instead, to be largely an accumulation of much of the misinformation, half-truths and insinuations that for years have been directed against Japanese Americans by people with racial and economic prejudices—the same people who have been among the foremost advocates of the evacuation. A military judgment based upon such racial and sociological considerations is not entitled to the great weight ordinarily given the judgments based upon strictly military considerations. Especially is this so when every charge relative to race, religion, culture, geographical location, and legal and economic status has been substantially discredited by independent studies made by experts in these matters.

I dissent, therefore, from this legalization of racism. Racial discrimination in any form and in any degree has no justifiable part whatever in our democratic way of life. It is unattractive in any setting but it is utterly revolting among a free people who have embraced the principles set forth in the Constitution of the United States. All residents of this nation are kin in some way by blood or culture to a foreign land. Yet they are primarily and necessarily a part of the new and distinct civilization of the United States. They must accordingly be treated at all times as the heirs of the American experiment and as entitled to all the rights and freedoms guaranteed by the Constitution.

Mr. Justice JACKSON, *dissenting*.

Korematsu was born on our soil, of parents born in Japan. The Constitution makes him a citizen of the United States by nativity and a citizen of California by residence. No claim is made that he is not loyal to this country. There is no suggestion that apart from the matter involved here he is not law-abiding and well disposed. Korematsu, however, has been convicted of an act not commonly a crime. It consists merely of being present in the state whereof he is a citizen, near the place where he was born, and where all his life he has lived.

Much is said of the danger to liberty from the Army program for deporting and detaining these citizens of Japanese extraction. But a judicial construction of the due process clause that will sustain this order is a far more subtle blow to liberty than the promulgation of the order itself. A military order, however unconstitutional, is not apt to last longer than the military emergency. But once a judicial opinion rationalizes such an order to show that it conforms to the Constitution, or rather rationalizes the Constitution to show that the Constitution sanctions such an order, the Court for all time has validated the principle of racial discrimination in criminal procedure and of transplanting American citizens. The principle then lies about like a loaded weapon ready for the hand of any authority that can bring forward a plausible claim of an urgent need. Nothing better illustrates this danger than does the Court's opinion in this case.

Notes

1. *Applying Strict Scrutiny.* The strict scrutiny standard of review eventually became a key tool for dismantling official segregation. Another decade would pass, however, before the separate but equal doctrine was laid to rest. During this time, the NAACP shifted its strategy from a focus on funding equality to the premise that segregation inherently was unequal. Its initial efforts in this regard were unproductive. Upon being ordered to desegregate its public law school or create a parallel institution for nonwhites, Oklahoma cordoned off a section of the state capitol building and declared it a separate but equal facility. The difficulty of maintaining a system of segregation increased when the Court determined that equalization of professional education was not reducible to tangible factors alone. In *Sweatt v. Painter*, 339 U.S. 629 (1950), it noted that factors such as faculty reputation, alumni influence, institutional prestige, and networking potential could not be equalized by dollars. The Court in *McLaurin v. Oklahoma State Board of Regents*, 339 U.S. 637 (1950), found that racially based restrictions on classroom seating and access to the library and cafeteria undermined an effective education. It thus ordered the university to desegregate its program.

2. *The* Brown *Decision.* The outcomes described in the preceding note did not eliminate the separate but equal doctrine, but significantly weakened its foundation. Movement beyond this increment of change was dependent on a change in the Court's leadership. A new Chief Justice, Earl Warren, was appointed to the

Court one year after *Brown v. Board of Education* (*Brown I*) first was argued. *Brown* was the lead case in a group of five lower court decisions in Kansas, Delaware, Virginia, South Carolina, and the District of Columbia that addressed the separate but equal doctrine's continuing vitality.

2. Desegregation

Brown v. Board of Education

347 U.S. 483 (1954)

Mr. Chief Justice WARREN delivered the opinion of the Court.

These cases come to us from the States of Kansas, South Carolina, Virginia, and Delaware. They are premised on different facts and different local conditions, but a common legal question justifies their consideration together in this consolidated opinion.

In each of the cases, minors of the Negro race, through their legal representatives, seek the aid of the courts in obtaining admission to the public schools of their community on a nonsegregated basis. In each instance, they have been denied admission to schools attended by white children under laws requiring or permitting segregation according to race. This segregation was alleged to deprive the plaintiffs of the equal protection of the laws under the Fourteenth Amendment.

The plaintiffs contend that segregated public schools are not 'equal' and cannot be made 'equal,' and that hence they are deprived of the equal protection of the laws. Because of the obvious importance of the question presented, the Court took jurisdiction. Argument was heard in the 1952 Term, and reargument was heard this Term on certain questions propounded by the Court.

Reargument was largely devoted to the circumstances surrounding the adoption of the Fourteenth Amendment in 1868. It covered exhaustively consideration of the Amendment in Congress, ratification by the states, then existing practices in racial segregation, and the views of proponents and opponents of the Amendment. This discussion and our own investigation convince us that, although these sources cast some light, it is not enough to resolve the problem with which we are faced. At best, they are inconclusive.

An additional reason for the inconclusive nature of the Amendment's history, with respect to segregated schools, is the status of public education at that time. In the South, the movement toward free common schools, supported by general taxation, had not yet taken hold. Education of white children was largely in the hands of private groups. Education of Negroes was almost nonexistent, and practically all of the race were illiterate. In fact, any education of Negroes was forbidden by law in some states. Today, in contrast, many Negroes have achieved outstanding success in the arts and sciences as well as in the business and professional world. It is true that public school education at the time of the Amendment had advanced further in the North, but the effect of the Amendment on Northern States was generally ignored in the congressional debates. Even in the North, the conditions of public education did not approximate those existing today. The curriculum was usually rudimentary; ungraded schools were common in rural areas; the school term was but three months a year in many states; and compulsory school attendance was virtually unknown. As a consequence, it is not surprising that there should be so little in the history of the Fourteenth Amendment relating to its intended effect on public education.

In approaching this problem, we cannot turn the clock back to 1868 when the Amendment was adopted, or even to 1896 when *Plessy v. Ferguson* was written. We must consider public education in the light of its full development and its present place in American life throughout the Nation. Only in this way can it be determined if segregation in public schools deprives these plaintiffs of the equal protection of the laws.

Today, education is perhaps the most important function of state and local governments. Compulsory school attendance laws and the great expenditures for education both demonstrate our recognition of the importance of education to our democratic society. It is required in the performance of our most basic public responsibilities, even service in the armed forces. It is the very foundation of good citizenship. Today it is a principal instrument in awakening the child to cultural values, in preparing him for later professional training, and in helping him to adjust normally to his environment. In these days, it is doubtful that any child may reasonably be expected to succeed in life if he is denied the opportunity of an education. Such an opportunity, where the state has undertaken to provide it, is a right which must be made available to all on equal terms.

We come then to the question presented: Does segregation of children in public schools solely on the basis of race, even though the physical facilities and other 'tangible' factors may be equal, deprive the children of the minority group of equal educational opportunities? We believe that it does. Such considerations apply with added force to children in grade and high schools. To separate them from others of similar age and qualifications solely because of their race generates a feeling of inferiority as to their status in the community that may affect their hearts and minds in a way unlikely ever to be undone.

Whatever may have been the extent of psychological knowledge at the time of *Plessy v. Ferguson*, this finding is amply supported by modern authority. Any language in *Plessy* contrary to this finding is rejected.

We conclude that in the field of public education the doctrine of 'separate but equal' has no place. Separate educational facilities are inherently unequal. Therefore, we hold that the plaintiffs and others similarly situated for whom the actions have been brought are, by reason of the segregation complained of, deprived of the equal protection of the laws guaranteed by the Fourteenth Amendment. This disposition makes unnecessary any discussion whether such segregation also violates the Due Process Clause of the Fourteenth Amendment.

Because these are class actions, because of the wide applicability of this decision, and because of the great variety of local conditions, the formulation of decrees in these cases presents problems of considerable complexity. On reargument, the consideration of appropriate relief was necessarily subordinated to the primary question—the constitutionality of segregation in public education. We have now announced that such segregation is a denial of the equal protection of the laws. In order that we may have the full assistance of the parties in formulating decrees, the cases will be restored to the docket, and the parties are requested to present further argument pertaining to remediation.

It is so ordered.

Notes and Questions

1. *Scrutiny of Racial Classifications.* Earlier, we saw that economic classifications are subject to a lower level of scrutiny, typically rational basis review. After *Brown*, is it apparent that racial classifications should be subject to heightened scrutiny? Does the *Brown* decision explain clearly why that should be the case? What factors might lead you to conclude that racial classifications should be treated differently than, say, economic classifications, and that they should be subject to a higher standard of review?

2. *Desegregation.* As the NAACP continued to chip away at the foundation of the separate but equal doctrine, states began to pay more attention to the second half of the doctrine. Dramatic increases in funding of minority schools were a hallmark of segregation's final years. Last-minute efforts to shore up the separate but equal doctrine failed, however, when the Court heard re-arguments in *Brown*. The Vinson Court had asked lawyers for both sides to research the history of the Fourteenth Amendment and present their findings. Under the leadership of Chief Justice Warren, the Court determined that it could "not turn the clock back to 1868 when the Fourteenth Amendment was adopted, or even to 1896 when *Plessy v. Ferguson* was written." It thus abandoned the separate but equal doctrine altogether in the field of public education.

3. *District of Columbia Segregation.* Segregation in the District of Columbia presented a technical challenge, insofar as the Fifth Amendment does not include an Equal Protection Clause. The Court, in *Bolling v. Sharpe*, 347 U.S. 497 (1954), found that the narrower guarantee of equal protection is implicit in the more generalized Fifth Amendment Due Process Clause.

∾ PROBLEMS ∾

1. *A Competing African American Perspective.* Desegregation of public education was challenged within the African American community by those who believed it would cause more harm than good. Among its detractors was W.E.B. DuBois, who cofounded the NAACP but split from the organization once it embarked upon its desegregation strategy. DuBois maintained that "other things being equal, the racially mixed school is the broader, more natural basis for the education of all

youth, but things seldom are equal, and in that case sympathy, knowledge, and the truth outweigh all the mixed school can offer." As an attorney making the state's case for segregation, and in particular having to dispute evidence of psychological damage to minority children, how might DuBois's premise help support the state's case?

2. *The Historical Record.* After the initial hearing in *Brown v. Board of Education* (*Brown II*), the Court asked each side to examine the original purpose of the Fourteenth Amendment. Both sides conducted extensive historical research. Assume that you are a historian who has been retained by the NAACP. What evidence might you muster in support of desegregation? How would you respond to the reality that, at the time the Fourteenth Amendment was framed and ratified, Congress provided for segregation of public schools in the District of Columbia and some northern states did likewise?

Viewed as an abstraction, the desegregation principle had the potential for societal restructuring that ranged from formalistic to profound. The mildest action might have been for the Court to declare segregation unconstitutional but require no affirmative action to undo it. Under this option, segregation probably would have persisted in function following tradition and personal choice (at least unless and until the political process insisted otherwise). The Court chose a remedial course that required the actual dismantling of official segregation in public schools and the creation of racially unitary schools. The remedial process was set forth in *Brown v. Board of Education II*, which set out the standard of desegregation "with all deliberate speed." In framing this process, the Court referenced traditional equitable powers and the need for flexibility in reckoning with problems that might vary from one school district to another.

Brown v. Board of Education

349 U.S. 294 (1955)

Mr. Chief Justice WARREN delivered the opinion of the Court.

Because these cases arose under different local conditions and their disposition will involve a variety of local problems, we requested further argument on the question of relief. In view of the nationwide importance of the decision, we invited the Attorney General of the United States and the Attorneys General of all states requiring or permitting racial discrimination in public education to present their views on that question.

Full implementation of these constitutional principles may require solution of varied local school problems. School authorities have the primary responsibility for elucidating, assessing, and solving these problems; courts will have to consider whether the action of school authorities constitutes good faith implementation of the governing constitutional principles. Because of their proximity to local conditions and the possible need for further hearings, the courts which originally heard these cases can best perform this judicial appraisal. Accordingly, we believe it appropriate to remand the cases to those courts. In fashioning and effectuating the decrees, the courts will be guided by equitable principles. Traditionally, equity has been characterized by a practical flexibility in shaping its remedies and by a facility for adjusting and reconciling public and private needs. These cases call for the exercise of these traditional attributes of equity power. At stake is the personal interest of the plaintiffs in admission to public schools as soon as practicable on a nondiscriminatory basis. To effectuate this interest may call for elimination of a variety of obstacles in making the transition to school systems operated in accordance with the constitutional principles set forth in our May 17, 1954, decision. Courts of equity may properly take into account the public interest in the elimination of such obstacles in a systematic and effective manner. But it should go without saying that the vitality of these constitutional principles cannot be allowed to yield simply because of disagreement with them.

While giving weight to these public and private considerations, the courts will require that the defendants make a prompt and reasonable start toward full compliance with our ruling. Once such a start has been made, the courts may find that additional time is necessary to carry out the ruling in an effective manner. The burden rests upon the defendants to establish that such time is necessary in the public interest and is consistent with good faith compliance at the earliest practicable date. To that end, the courts may consider problems related to administration, arising from the physical condition of the school plant, the school transportation system, personnel, revision of school districts and attendance areas into compact units to achieve a system of determining admission to the public schools on a nonracial basis, and revision of local laws and regulations which may be necessary in solving the foregoing problems. They will also consider the adequacy of any plans the defendants may propose to meet these problems and to effectuate a transition to a racially nondiscriminatory school system. During this period of transition, the courts will retain jurisdiction of these cases.

Notes

1. *"All Deliberate Speed" and Resistance.* The "all deliberate speed" standard was framed pursuant to input that the Court had invited from the parties and those states that would be most affected by the desegregation mandate. This engagement, however, did not defuse resistance to effective implementation. Lower courts generally interpreted *Brown* in undemanding ways. Typifying this performance was the district court's opinion in the South Carolina case. In *Briggs v. Elliott,* 132 F. Supp. 776, 77 (E.D.S.C. 1955), the district court in a *per curiam* opinion concluded that "the Constitution does not require integration. It merely forbids discrimination. It does not forbid such segregation as occurs as the result of voluntary action. It merely forbids the use of governmental power to enforce segregation." As the South Carolina court saw it, constitutional requirements were satisfied merely by dispelling the legal force of segregation.

2. *Hostility to the NAACP.* Official reaction to the desegregation mandate, in those states ordered to comply with it, was characterized by efforts to avoid or delay its impact. In some instances, the response was more belligerent. The Arkansas legislature denounced the desegregation decision as unconstitutional and maintained that no remedy could be imposed without its approval. Some states resorted to preemptive tactics in an effort to deter litigation aimed at compelling desegregation. As the primary organizer of desegregation lawsuits in the decade after the *Brown* ruling, the NAACP was a target of legislation aimed at disabling its viability. The Alabama legislature, for instance, passed a law requiring the organization to make its membership list public. *NAACP ex. rel. Alabama v. Patterson,* 357 U.S. 449 (1958). Virginia used an antisolicitation rule against the NAACP to deter its litigative activities. *NAACP v. Button,* 371 U.S. 415 (1963). Although the Court struck down both laws, the states' actions reflected the generally hostile environment in which the desegregation mandate operated.

Donald E. Lively, *The Constitution and Race*

114-117 (Praeger 1992)

Reaction to the desegregation mandate was electric and decidedly negative. Typical desegregation plans were shams, subterfuges, or inactions that effectively maintained segregation as a function of custom rather than official dictate. Some states passed laws intended to preclude actual desegregation or at least ripple the process. Deferring to local idiosyncrasies, sensing the need for grass-roots support, and aiming to minimize the divisive potential of its decision, the Court originally structured desegregation with an eye to enhancing its accountability. Reality, however, quickly defeated anticipation.

The first major test of the *Brown* principle presented itself in Little Rock, Arkansas. Although local authorities had devised a desegregation plan, the state legislature enacted a law purporting to relieve students from compulsory attendance at racially mixed schools. When the governor summoned the National Guard to prevent black students from entering the city's all-white high school, President Eisenhower responded by dispatching federal troops to enforce desegregation. The intensity of public reaction to the events prompted the school board to move for a delay in the implementation of its plan. In support of postponement, the board cited impairment of the educational process attributable to demonstrable tension and conflict. Although acknowledging that the educational process might suffer, and without doubting the board's good faith, the Court in *Cooper v. Aaron* denied the requested delay.

The *Cooper* case was an extension of the persisting debate over federal and state interests reckoned with in *Brown* but for practical purposes still unresolved. Commencing with the premise that the Constitution is supreme and the judiciary has the power to "say what the law is," the Court characterized the desegregation mandate as "the supreme law of the land and binding on the states." The decision in *Cooper* was prompted by the sense that "the constitutional rights of respondents are not to be sacrificed or yielded to the violence and disorder which have followed upon the actions of the Governor and Legislature." Given the linkage between official action and public antagonism in Little Rock, the Court determined that "law and order are not here to be preserved by depriving the Negro children of their constitutional rights." It also warned that the desegregation mandate was not to be compromised either directly by legislative, executive, or judicial officers or indirectly by official evasion.

BACKGROUND

De jure segregation in public schools is unconstitutional. School districts operating *de jure* segregated schools have an affirmative duty to establish unitary school systems in which students are not segregated by race. *De facto* segregation in public schools is not unconstitutional unless it is the result of intentional segregative acts by school officials. Where *de facto* segregation results from private economic choices or changing demographics, school officials have no duty to maintain racial balance.

By the end of the 1960s, the changes contemplated by *Brown* had bypassed an entire generation of public school students. Conditions in the region most affected by the desegregation principle for practical purposes had remained largely unchanged. One of the districts subject to the original desegregation order in *Brown* remained "totally segregated" a decade later. Given the circumstances, the Court in *Green v. County School Board of New Kent County, Virginia* asserted that "the time for mere 'deliberate speed' has run out." It accordingly demanded that school boards come forward with a desegregation "plan that promises realistically to work, and promises realistically to work *now*." The *Green* Court also announced "an affirmative duty to take whatever steps might be necessary to convert to a unitary system in which racial discrimination would be eliminated root and branch." 391 U.S. 430, 437 (1968).

Movement from a standard of "all deliberate speed" to one of immediate relief fortified the Court's role in the desegregation process. The *Griffin v. County School Board* decision had suggested that equitable powers might be used prohibitively and affirmatively to halt public funding of private schools and to reopen and operate public schools. In *Swann v. Charlotte-Mecklenburg Board of Education*, the Court elaborated on the subject of remedial authority and defined the possibilities for relief expansively.

Swann v. Charlotte-Mecklenburg Board of Education

402 U.S. 1 (1971)

Mr. Chief Justice Burger delivered the opinion of the Court.

These cases present us with the problem of defining in more precise terms than heretofore the scope of the duty of school authorities and district courts in implementing *Brown I* and the mandate to eliminate dual systems and establish unitary systems at once.

If school authorities fail in their affirmative obligations under these holdings, judicial authority may be invoked. Once a right and a violation have been shown, the scope of a district court's equitable powers to remedy past wrongs is broad, for breadth and flexibility are inherent in equitable remedies.

In seeking to define even in broad and general terms how far this remedial power extends it is important to remember that judicial powers may be exercised only on the basis of a constitutional violation. Remedial judicial authority does not put judges automatically in the shoes of school authorities whose powers are plenary. Judicial authority enters only when local authority defaults.

School authorities are traditionally charged with broad power to formulate and implement educational policy and might well conclude, for example, that in order to prepare students to live in a pluralistic society each school should have a prescribed ratio of Negro to white students reflecting the proportion for the district as a whole. To do this as an educational policy is within the broad discretionary powers of school authorities; absent a finding of a constitutional violation, however, that would not be within the authority of a federal court. As with any equity case, the nature of the violation determines the scope of the remedy. In default by the school authorities of their obligation to proffer acceptable remedies, a district court has broad power to fashion a remedy that will assure a unitary school system.

The central issue in this case is that of student assignment, and there are essentially four problem areas: (1) to what extent racial balance or racial quotas may be used as an implement in a remedial order to correct a previously segregated system; (2) whether every all-Negro and all-white school must be eliminated as an indispensable part of a remedial process of desegregation; (3) what the limits are, if any, on the rearrangement of school districts and attendance zones, as a remedial measure; and (4) what the limits are, if any, on the use of transportation facilities to correct state-enforced racial school segregation.

(1) Racial Balances or Racial Quotas. The constant theme and thrust of every holding from *Brown I* to date is that state-enforced separation of races in public schools is discrimination that violates the Equal Protection Clause. The remedy commanded was to dismantle dual school systems.

Our objective in dealing with the issues presented by these cases is to see that school authorities exclude no pupil of a racial minority from any school, directly or indirectly, on account of race. In this case it is urged that the District Court has imposed a racial balance requirement of 71%-29% on individual schools. The constitutional command to desegregate schools does not mean that every school in every community must always reflect the racial composition of the school system as a whole.

The use made of mathematical ratios was no more than a starting point in the process of shaping a remedy, rather than an inflexible requirement. From that starting point the District Court proceeded to frame a decree that was within its discretionary powers, as an equitable remedy for the particular circumstances. A school authority's remedial plan or a district court's remedial decree is to be judged by its effectiveness. Awareness of the racial composition of the whole school system is likely to be a useful starting point in shaping a remedy to correct past constitutional violations. In sum, the very limited use made of mathematical ratios was within the equitable remedial discretion of the District Court.

(2) One-Race Schools. The existence of some small number of one-race, or virtually one-race, schools within a district is not in and of itself the mark of a system that still practices segregation by law. The district judge or school authorities should make every effort to achieve the greatest possible degree of actual desegregation and will thus necessarily be concerned with the elimination of one-race schools. No *per se* rule can adequately embrace all the difficulties of reconciling the competing interests involved; but in a system with a history of segregation the need for remedial criteria of sufficient specificity to assure a school authority's compliance with its constitutional duty warrants a presumption against schools that are substantially disproportionate in their racial composition.

(3) Remedial Altering of Attendance Zones. Absent a constitutional violation there would be no basis for judicially ordering assignment of students on a racial basis. All things being equal, with no history of discrimination, it might well be desirable to assign pupils to schools nearest their homes. But all things are not equal in a system that has been deliberately constructed and maintained to enforce racial segregation. The remedy for such segregation may be administratively awkward, inconvenient, and even bizarre in some situations and may impose burdens on some; but all awkwardness and inconvenience cannot be avoided in the interim period when remedial adjustments are being made to eliminate the dual school systems.

(4) Transportation of Students. The scope of permissible transportation of students as an implement of a remedial decree has never been defined by this Court. No rigid guidelines as to student transportation can be given for application to the infinite variety of problems presented in thousands of situations. Bus transportation has been an integral part of the public education system for years, and was perhaps the single most important factor in the transition from the one-room schoolhouse to the consolidated school. Eighteen million of the Nation's public school children, approximately 39%, were transported to their schools by bus in 1969-1970 in all parts of the country.

The importance of bus transportation as a normal and accepted tool of educational policy is readily discernible. The decree provided that the buses used to implement the plan would operate on direct routes. Students would be picked up at schools near their homes and transported to the schools they were to attend. The trips for elementary school pupils average about seven miles and the District

Court found that they would take 'not over 35 minutes at the most.' This system compares favorably with the transportation plan previously operated in Charlotte under which each day 26,600 students on all grade levels were transported an average of 15 miles one way for an average trip requiring over an hour. In these circumstances, we find no basis for holding that the local school authorities may not be required to employ bus transportation as one tool of school desegregation. Desegregation plans cannot be limited to the walk-in school.

An objection to transportation of students may have validity when the time or distance of travel is so great as to either risk the health of the children or significantly impinge on the educational process.

At some point, these school authorities and others like them should have achieved full compliance with this Court's decision in *Brown I*. The systems would then be 'unitary.'

It does not follow that the communities served by such systems will remain demographically stable, for in a growing, mobile society, few will do so. Neither school authorities nor district courts are constitutionally required to make year-by-year adjustments of the racial composition of student bodies once the affirmative duty to desegregate has been accomplished and racial discrimination through official action is eliminated from the system. This does not mean that federal courts are without power to deal with future problems; but in the absence of a showing that either the school authorities or some other agency of the State has deliberately attempted to fix or alter demographic patterns to affect the racial composition of the schools, further intervention by a district court should not be necessary.

Note: Political Realities and Desegregation

Case law of the late 1960s and early 1970s represented the high-water mark of the desegregation mandate. The overarching remedial benchmark, as stated by the Court in *Green v. County School Board*, was elimination of "the vestiges of racial discrimination root and branch." Achievement of this goal, however, required change that extended beyond those places where segregation was formal and highly visible. Particularly as busing came to be understood as the primary methodology for effecting unitary schools, the political process began to hedge its support for the desegregation process. Personnel turnover on the Court was a critical factor in making the *Brown* decision possible. The same phenomenon influenced the desegregation mandate's eventual reach.

∾ PROBLEMS ∾

1. *Segregative Intent.* Assume that the school board decides to locate a high school in a neighborhood that is 95% African American. Because students attend neighborhood schools, it can be anticipated that enrollments will reflect residential demographics. You have been retained as counsel for a parents' group that

opposes the school board's decision. Would the foreseeability of the outcome give you a basis for establishing segregative intent? *See Columbus Board of Education v. Penick*, 443 U.S. 449 (1979).

2. *Passage of Time.* Assume that you are counsel for a school board in a midwestern community where a *de jure* system of segregation was maintained. No action ever was taken after *Brown v. Board of Education* was decided to dismantle the dual school system. Your advice to the school board, 25 years later, was that there was no constitutional obligation to desegregate the school system. How would that advice stand up in litigation? *See Dayton Board of Education v. Brinkman*, 443 U.S. 406 (1977).

3. *White Flight.* Assume that you represent a parents' group in a community that, to avoid the possibility of having to desegregate, white families have exited. If you were to prove *de jure* segregation, and absent any responsibility on the part of other communities, what remedy would be available? Is there a difference between desegregation and integration? If so, does it reduce desegregation to formalism? If so, would desegregation differ from what was achievable under the separate but equal doctrine? *See Milliken v. Bradley (II)*, 433 U.S. 267 (1977).

4. *"Normal Pattern of Human Migration."* Assume that you are a legal historian who is researching the history of segregation. Would you equate or differentiate Justice Rehnquist's reference to a "quite normal pattern of human migration" and the characterization of racial segregation (in *Plessy v. Ferguson*) as "in the nature of things"?

Case law in the 1970s increasingly accommodated circumstances that made desegregation in many metropolitan settings an exercise in form rather than function. Insistence on effective remedies became displaced by concern that the courts were not the appropriate authority for achieving durable results. Second thoughts about the judiciary's role were expressed by Justice Powell, who noted that "in city after city" desegregation merely was a prelude to "resegregation, stimulated by resentment against judicial coercion." *Columbus Board of Education v. Penick*, 443 U.S. 449, 483 (1979) (Powell, J., dissenting). He also adverted to "familiar segregated housing patterns caused by social, economic, and demographic forces for which no school board is responsible." Consistent with this spirit, Justice Rehnquist observed that "even if the Constitution required it, and it were possible for federal courts to do it, no equitable decree can fashion an 'Emerald City' where all races, ethnic groups, and persons of various income levels live side by side." *Cleveland Board of Education v. Reed*, 445 U.S. 935, 938 (1980) (Rehnquist, J., dissenting from denial of certiorari). These sentiments reflected a growing sense of judicial restraint coupled with an interest in restoring full control over education to school boards. By the 1990s, the desegregation mandate had been recalibrated accordingly. Insistence upon erasing the vestiges of segregation "root and branch" thus was reduced, in *Board of Education of Oklahoma City Schools v. Dowell*, to a requirement that they be eliminated "to the extent practicable."

Board of Education of Oklahoma City Schools v. Dowell

498 U.S. 237 (1991)

Chief Justice REHNQUIST delivered the opinion of the Court.

This school desegregation litigation began almost 30 years ago. In 1961, respondents, black students and their parents, sued petitioners, the Board of Education of Oklahoma City (Board), to end *de jure* segregation in the public schools. In 1963, the District Court found that Oklahoma City had intentionally segregated both schools and housing in the past, and that Oklahoma City was operating a "dual" school system—one that was intentionally segregated by race. In 1965, the District Court found that the School Board's attempt to desegregate by using neighborhood zoning failed to remedy past segregation because residential segregation resulted in one-race schools. Residential segregation had once been state imposed, and it lingered due to discrimination by some realtors and financial institutions. The District Court found that school segregation had caused some housing segregation. In 1972, finding that previous efforts had not been successful at eliminating state imposed segregation, the District Court ordered the Board to adopt the "Finger Plan," under which kindergartners would be assigned to neighborhood schools unless their parents opted otherwise; children in grades 1-4 would attend formerly all white schools, and thus black children would be bused to those schools; children in grade five would attend formerly all black schools, and thus white children would be bused to those schools; students in the upper grades would be bused to various areas in order to maintain integrated schools; and in integrated neighborhoods there would be stand-alone schools for all grades.

In 1977, after complying with the desegregation decree for five years, the Board made a "Motion to Close Case." The District Court held in its "Order Terminating Case": "The Court has concluded that the Finger Plan worked and that substantial compliance with the constitutional requirements has been achieved.

In 1984, the School Board faced demographic changes that led to greater burdens on young black children. As more and more neighborhoods became integrated, more stand-alone schools were established, and young black students had to be bused further from their inner-city homes to outlying white areas. In an effort to alleviate this burden and to increase parental involvement, the Board adopted the Student Reassignment Plan (SRP), which relied on neighborhood assignments for students in grades K-4 beginning in the 1985-1986 school year. Busing continued for students in grades 5-12. Any student could transfer from a school where he or she was in the majority to a school where he or she would be in the minority. Faculty and staff integration was retained, and an "equity officer" was appointed.

In 1985, respondents filed a "Motion to Reopen the Case," contending that the School District had not achieved "unitary" status and that the SRP was a return to segregation. Under the SRP, 11 of 64 elementary schools would be greater than

90% black, 22 would be greater than 90% white plus other minorities, and 31 would be racially mixed.

The District Court found that demographic changes made the Finger Plan unworkable, that the Board had done nothing for 25 years to promote residential segregation, and that the school district had bused students for more than a decade in good-faith compliance with the court's orders. The District Court found that present residential segregation was the result of private decisionmaking and economics, and that it was too attenuated to be a vestige of former school segregation. It also found that the district had maintained its unitary status, and that the neighborhood assignment plan was not designed with discriminatory intent. The court concluded that the previous injunctive decree should be vacated and the school district returned to local control. The Court of Appeals reversed.

In *Milliken v. Bradley* (*Milliken II*), 433 U.S. 267 (1977), we said: "Federal-court decrees must directly address and relate to the constitutional violation itself. Because of this inherent limitation upon federal judicial authority, federal-court decrees exceed appropriate limits if they are aimed at eliminating a condition that does not violate the Constitution or does not flow from such a violation." From the very first, federal supervision of local school systems was intended as a temporary measure to remedy past discrimination. *Brown* considered the "complexities arising from the transition to a system of public education freed of racial discrimination" in holding that the implementation of desegregation was to proceed "with all deliberate speed." *Green* also spoke of the "transition to a unitary, nonracial system of public education."

Local control over the education of children allows citizens to participate in decision-making, and allows innovation so that school programs can fit local needs. The legal justification for displacement of local authority by an injunctive decree in a school desegregation case is a violation of the Constitution by the local authorities. Dissolving a desegregation decree after the local authorities have operated in compliance with it for a reasonable period of time properly recognizes that "necessary concern for the important values of local control of public school systems dictates that a federal court's regulatory control of such systems not extend beyond the time required to remedy the effects of past intentional discrimination."

A district court need not accept at face value the profession of a school board which has intentionally discriminated that it will cease to do so in the future. But in deciding whether to modify or dissolve a desegregation decree, a school board's compliance with previous court orders is obviously relevant. In this case the original finding of de jure segregation was entered in 1961, the injunctive decree from which the Board seeks relief was entered in 1972, and the Board complied with the decree in good faith until 1985.

Justice MARSHALL, with whom Justice BLACKMUN and Justice STEVENS join, *dissenting*.

The practical question now before us is whether, 13 years after the injunction was imposed, the same School Board should have been allowed to return many of its elementary schools to their former one-race status. The majority today suggests that 13 years of desegregation was enough. The Court remands the case for further evaluation of whether the purposes of the injunctive decree were achieved sufficient to justify the decree's dissolution. However, the inquiry it commends to the District Court fails to recognize explicitly the threatened reemergence of one-race schools as a relevant "vestige" of *de jure* segregation.

In my view, the standard for dissolution of a school desegregation decree must reflect the central aim of our school desegregation precedents. In *Brown v. Board of Education*, a unanimous Court declared that racially "separate educational facilities are inherently unequal." This holding rested on the Court's recognition that state-sponsored segregation conveys a message of "inferiority as to the status of Afro-American school children in the community that may affect their hearts and minds in a way unlikely ever to be undone." Remedying this evil and preventing its recurrence were the motivations animating our requirement that formerly de jure segregated school districts take all feasible steps to eliminate racially identifiable schools.

I believe a desegregation decree cannot be lifted so long as conditions likely to inflict the stigmatic injury condemned in *Brown I* persist and there remain feasible methods of eliminating such conditions. Because the record here shows, and the Court of Appeals found, that feasible steps could be taken to avoid one-race schools, it is clear that the purposes of the decree have not yet been achieved and the Court of Appeals' reinstatement of the decree should be affirmed. I therefore dissent.

Notes

1. *Partial Relinquishment of Control.* Insofar as local authorities comply with particular aspects of a desegregation order, a court may downsize its supervision incrementally. This proposition was set forth in *Freeman v. Pitts*, 503 U.S. 467, 489-490 (1992). The case concerned the DeKalb County School System (DCCS) in Georgia, which, until placed under judicial supervision in 1969, had maintained a racially segregated school system. On determining that the DCCS had achieved unitary status in some but not in all categories, the district court relinquished control over those elements but retained supervision in those areas where full compliance had not been achieved. The Court determined that partial withdrawal of judicial supervision was permissible and desirable. It thus noted:

> Partial relinquishment of judicial control, where justified by the facts of the case, can be an important and significant step in fulfilling the district court's duty to return the operations and control of schools to local authorities. In *Dowell*, we emphasized that federal judicial supervision of local school systems was intended as a "temporary measure." Although this temporary measure has lasted decades, the ultimate objective has not changed—to return school districts to the control of local authorities.

> Just as a court has the obligation at the outset of a desegregation decree to structure a plan so that all available resources of the court are directed to comprehensive supervision of its decree, so too must a court provide an orderly means for withdrawing from control when it is shown that the school district has attained the requisite degree of compliance. A transition phase in which control is relinquished in a gradual way is an appropriate means to this end.

2. *Resegregation and Contemporary Constitutional Realities.* Although courts have a broad arsenal of devices for remedying segregation, these tools are usable only in instances of *de jure* segregation and may not exceed the scope of the violation. Modern segregation is attributable primarily to demographic realignments, as findings of intentional segregation have become increasingly rare. The reemergence of racially identifiable schools, that are constitutionally inconsequential, has prompted efforts through judicial and political processes to increase or maintain diversity. Although diversity has been recognized as a compelling interest in higher education (as discussed later), the Court has rejected diversity initiatives in primary and secondary public school settings.

Missouri v. Jenkins

515 U.S. 70 (1995)

Chief Justice REHNQUIST delivered the opinion of the Court.

In 1977, the KCMSD, the school board, and the children of two school board members brought suit against the State and other defendants. Plaintiffs alleged that the State, the surrounding suburban school districts (SSD's), and various federal agencies had caused and perpetuated a system of racial segregation in the schools of the Kansas City metropolitan area. The District Court dismissed the case against the federal defendants and the SSD's, but determined that the State and the KCMSD were liable for an intradistrict violation, i.e., they had operated a segregated school system within the KCMSD. The District Court determined that prior to 1954 "Missouri mandated segregated schools for black and white children." Furthermore, the KCMSD and the State had failed in their affirmative obligations to eliminate the vestiges of the State's dual school system within the KCMSD.

The District Court, pursuant to plans submitted by the KCMSD and the State, ordered a wide range of quality education programs for all students attending the KCMSD. The total cost for these quality education programs has exceeded $220 million.

The District Court also set out to desegregate the KCMSD but believed that "to accomplish desegregation within the boundary lines of a school district whose enrollment remains 68.3% black is a difficult task." Because it had found no interdistrict violation, the District Court could not order mandatory interdistrict redistribution of students between the KCMSD and the surrounding SSD's.

In November 1986, the District Court approved a comprehensive magnet school and capital improvements plan and held the State and the KCMSD jointly and severally liable for its funding. Under the District Court's plan, every senior high school, every middle school, and one-half of the elementary schools were converted into magnet schools. The District Court adopted the magnet-school program to "provide a greater educational opportunity to all KCMSD students," and because it believed "that the proposed magnet plan was so attractive that it would draw non-minority students from the private schools who have abandoned or avoided the KCMSD, and draw in additional non-minority students from the suburbs." The District Court felt that "the long-term benefit of all KCMSD students of a greater educational opportunity in an integrated environment is worthy of such an investment." Since its inception, the magnet school program has operated at a cost, including magnet transportation, in excess of $448 million. The District Court also adopted a long-range capital improvement plan costing more than $187 million and teacher salary increases exceeding $200 million.

The District Court's desegregation plan has been described as the most ambitious and expensive remedial program in the history of school desegregation. The annual cost per pupil at the KCMSD far exceeds that of the neighboring SSD's or of any school district in Missouri. Nevertheless, the KCMSD, which has pursued a "friendly adversary" relationship with the plaintiffs, has continued to propose ever more expensive programs. As a result, the desegregation costs have escalated and now are approaching an annual cost of $200 million. These massive expenditures have financed

> high schools in which every classroom will have air conditioning, an alarm system, and 15 microcomputers; a 2,000-square-foot planetarium; green houses and vivariums; a 25-acre farm with an air-conditioned meeting room for 104 people; a Model United Nations wired for language translation; broadcast capable radio and television studios with an editing and animation lab; a temperature controlled art gallery; movie editing and screening rooms; a 3,500-square-foot dust-free diesel mechanics room; 1,875-square-foot elementary school animal rooms for use in a zoo project; swimming pools; and numerous other facilities.

Not surprisingly, the cost of this remedial plan has "far exceeded KCMSD's budget, or for that matter, its authority to tax." The State, through the operation of joint-and-several liability, has borne the brunt of these costs.

The proper response by the District Court should have been to eliminate to the extent practicable the vestiges of prior *de jure* segregation within the KCMSD: a system-wide reduction in student achievement and the existence of 25 racially identifiable schools with a population of over 90% black students. The District Court and Court of Appeals, however, have felt that because the KCMSD's enrollment remained 68.3% black, a purely intradistrict remedy would be insufficient. Instead of seeking to remove the racial identity of the various schools within the KCMSD, the District Court has set out on a program to create a school district that was equal to or superior to the surrounding SSD's. Its remedy has focused on "desegregative attractiveness," coupled with "suburban comparability."

The purpose of desegregative attractiveness has been not only to remedy the system-wide reduction in student achievement, but also to attract nonminority students not presently enrolled in the KCMSD. This remedy has included an elaborate program of capital improvements, course enrichment, and extracurricular enhancement not simply in the formerly identifiable black schools, but in schools throughout the district. The District Court's remedial orders have converted every senior high school, every middle school, and one-half of the elementary schools in the KCMSD into "magnet" schools. The District Court's remedial order has all but made the KCMSD itself into a magnet district.

We previously have approved of intradistrict desegregation remedies involving magnet schools. Magnet schools have the advantage of encouraging voluntary movement of students within a school district in a pattern that aids desegregation on a voluntary basis, without requiring extensive busing and redrawing of district boundary lines. The District Court's remedial plan in this case, however, is not designed solely to redistribute the students within the KCMSD in order to eliminate racially identifiable schools within the KCMSD. Instead, its purpose is to attract nonminority students from outside the KCMSD schools. But this interdistrict goal is beyond the scope of the intradistrict violation identified by the District Court. In effect, the District Court has devised a remedy to accomplish indirectly what it admittedly lacks the remedial authority to mandate directly: the interdistrict transfer of students.

Respondents argue that the District Court's reliance upon desegregative attractiveness is justified in light of the District Court's statement that segregation has "led to white flight from the KCMSD to suburban districts." In *Freeman*, we stated that "the vestiges of segregation that are the concern of the law in a school case may be subtle and intangible but nonetheless they must be so real that they have a causal link to the de jure violation being remedied." The record here does not support the District Court's reliance on "white flight" as a justification for a permissible expansion of its intradistrict remedial authority through its pursuit of desegregative attractiveness.

Nor are there limits to the duration of the District Court's involvement. The expenditures per pupil in the KCMSD currently far exceed those in the neighboring SSD's. Sixteen years after this litigation began, the District Court recognized that the KCMSD has yet to offer a viable method of financing the "wonderful school system being built." But our cases recognize that local autonomy of school districts is a vital national tradition, and that a district court must strive to restore state and local authorities to the control of a school system operating in compliance with the Constitution.

The District Court's order requiring the State to continue to fund the quality education programs because student achievement levels were still "at or below national norms at many grade levels" cannot be sustained. The State challenges the requirement of indefinite funding of a quality education program until national norms are met, based on the assumption that while a mandate for significant educational improvement, both in teaching and in facilities, may have been justified originally, its indefinite extension is not.

The basic task of the District Court is to decide whether the reduction in achievement by minority students attributable to prior *de jure* segregation has been remedied to the extent practicable. The District Court never has identified the incremental effect that segregation has had on minority student achievement or the specific goals of the quality education programs. In reconsidering this order, the District Court should apply our three-part test from *Freeman v. Pitts.*

On remand, the District Court must bear in mind that its end purpose is not only "to remedy the violation" to the extent practicable, but also "to restore state and local authorities to the control of a school system that is operating in compliance with the Constitution." The judgment of the Court of Appeals is *reversed.*

Justice O'CONNOR, *concurring.*

Remedying desegregative attractiveness is within the District Court's authority only if it is "directly caused by the constitutional violation." The District Court admitted that the segregative effects of KCMSD's constitutional violation did not transcend its geographical boundaries. In light of that finding, the District Court cannot order remedies seeking to rectify regional demographic trends that go beyond the nature and scope of the constitutional violation. The necessary restrictions on our jurisdiction and authority contained in Article III of the Constitution limit the judiciary's institutional capacity to prescribe palliatives for societal ills. The unfortunate fact of racial imbalance and bias in our society, however pervasive or invidious, does not admit of judicial intervention absent a constitutional violation.

Justice THOMAS, *concurring.*

The District Court here sought to convert the KCMSD into a "magnet district" that would reverse the "white flight" caused by desegregation. Courts must not confuse the consequences of *de jure* segregation with the results of larger social forces or of private decisions. When a district court holds the State liable for discrimination almost 30 years after the last official state action, it must do more than show that there are schools with high black populations or low test scores. Without a basis in any real finding of intentional government action, the District Court's imposition of liability upon the State of Missouri improperly rests upon a theory that racial imbalances are unconstitutional. This position appears to rest upon the idea that any school that is black is inferior, and that blacks cannot succeed without the benefit of the company of whites.

Justice SOUTER, with whom Justice STEVENS, Justice GINSBURG, and Justice BREYER join, *dissenting.*

In 1984, 30 years after *Brown*, the State of Missouri had failed to reform the segregated scheme of public school education in the KCMSD, previously mandated by the State. Before a district court may grant a school district partial release from a desegregation decree, it must first consider "whether there has been full and satisfactory compliance with the decree in those aspects of the system where supervision is to be withdrawn." Before the District Court's remedial plan was placed into effect the schools in the unreformed segregated system were physically a shambles. The cost of turning this shambles into habitable schools was enormous. Property tax–paying parents of white children, seeing the handwriting on the wall in 1985, could well have decided that the inevitable cost of clean-up would produce an intolerable tax rate and could have moved to escape it. Was the white flight caused by segregation or desegregation? The distinction has no significance.

3. Discriminatory Purpose Requirement

The desegregation principle, as announced in *Brown*, was quickly extended to public contexts beyond education. To the extent that laws were a function of segregative or discriminatory intent, they consistently were invalidated. This result was achieved even when racial sensitivity and selectivity arguably were factors that connected with other legitimate purposes. The use of peremptory challenges of prospective jurors, for instance, traditionally has included an appreciation that racial bias may be a factor in how evidence is processed. In a series of cases beginning with *Batson v. Kentucky*, 476 U.S. 79 (1986), the Court determined that peremptory challenges could not be correlated to race. Given the demands of the discriminatory purpose standard, and human ability to cover actual motive, proving wrongful intent has remained a challenge.

The reconstruction of constitutional principle to defeat prescriptive segregation nonetheless recaptured the promise of *Strauder v. West Virginia*, 100 U.S. 303 (1879), which had interpreted the Fourteenth Amendment as a barrier to legislation reflecting racial animus. In *Loving v. Virginia*, the Court examined an antimiscegenation law that the state justified on grounds it applied evenhandedly. Despite this neutrality argument, the Court concluded that the enactment was an extension of racist ideology and thus invidious.

∿ PROBLEM: RACE IN PRISONS ∿

The separate but equal doctrine was grounded, at least in part, on the need to preserve "public peace and good order." Assume that you have been asked to provide counsel to a state prison warden who is concerned with racial tensions among inmates and the potential for violence. Would you recommend racial segregation of the prison population as a policy option? *See Johnson v. California*, 543 U.S. 499 (2005).

Loving v. Virginia

388 U.S. 1 (1967)

Mr. Chief Justice WARREN delivered the opinion of the Court.

This case presents a constitutional question never addressed by this Court: whether a statutory scheme adopted by the State of Virginia to prevent marriages between persons solely on the basis of racial classifications violates the Equal Protection and Due Process Clauses of the Fourteenth Amendment.

In June 1958, two residents of Virginia, Mildred Jeter, a Negro woman, and Richard Loving, a white man, were married in the District of Columbia pursuant to its laws. Shortly after their marriage, the Lovings returned to Virginia and established their marital abode in Caroline County. A grand jury issued an indictment charging the Lovings with violating Virginia's ban on interracial marriages. The Lovings pleaded guilty to the charge and were sentenced to one year in jail; however, the trial judge suspended the sentence for a period of 25 years on the condition that the Lovings leave the State and not return. He stated in an opinion that: 'Almighty God created the races white, black, yellow, malay and red, and he placed them on separate continents. And but for the interference with his arrangement there would be no cause for such marriages. The fact that he separated the races shows that he did not intend for the races to mix.' The Supreme Court of Appeals of Virginia upheld the constitutionality of the anti-miscegenation statutes and, after modifying the sentence, affirmed the convictions.

Virginia is now one of 16 States which prohibit and punish marriages on the basis of racial classifications. Penalties for miscegenation arose as an incident to slavery and have been common in Virginia since the colonial period. The present statutory scheme dates from the adoption of the Racial Integrity Act of 1924, passed during the period of extreme nativism which followed the end of the First World War. The central features of this Act are the absolute prohibition of a 'white person' marrying other than another 'white person,' a prohibition against issuing marriage licenses until the issuing official is satisfied that the applicants' statements as to their race are correct, certificates of 'racial composition' to be kept by both local and state registrars, and the carrying forward of earlier prohibitions against racial intermarriage.

The State contends that, because its miscegenation statutes punish equally both the white and the Negro participants in an interracial marriage, these statutes, despite their reliance on racial classifications do not constitute an invidious discrimination based upon race. Because we reject the notion that the mere 'equal application' of a statute containing racial classifications is enough to remove the classifications from the Fourteenth Amendment's proscription of all invidious racial discriminations, we do not accept the State's contention that these statutes should be upheld if there is any possible basis for concluding that they serve a rational purpose. We deal with statutes containing racial classifications, and the fact of equal application does not immunize the statute from the very heavy burden of justification which the Fourteenth Amendment has traditionally required of state statutes drawn according to race.

There can be no question but that Virginia's miscegenation statutes rest solely upon distinctions drawn according to race. The statutes proscribe generally accepted conduct if engaged in by members of different races. This Court has consistently repudiated 'distinctions between citizens solely because of their ancestry' as being 'odious to a free people whose institutions are founded upon the doctrine of equality.' At the very least, the Equal Protection Clause demands that racial classifications, especially suspect in criminal statutes, be subjected to the 'most rigid scrutiny,' and, if they are ever to be upheld, they must be shown to be necessary to the accomplishment of some permissible state objective, independent of the racial discrimination which it was the object of the Fourteenth Amendment to eliminate.

There is patently no legitimate overriding purpose independent of invidious racial discrimination which justifies this classification. The fact that Virginia prohibits only interracial marriages involving white persons demonstrates that the racial classifications must stand on their own justification, as measures designed to maintain White Supremacy. We have consistently denied the constitutionality of measures which restrict the rights of citizens on account of race. There can be no doubt that restricting the freedom to marry solely because of racial classifications violates the central meaning of the Equal Protection Clause.

These statutes also deprive the Lovings of liberty without due process of law in violation of the Due Process Clause of the Fourteenth Amendment. The freedom to marry has long been recognized as one of the vital personal rights essential to the orderly pursuit of happiness by free men. The Fourteenth Amendment requires that the freedom of choice to marry not be restricted by invidious racial discriminations. These convictions must be reversed.

Mr. Justice STEWART, *concurring.*

'It is simply not possible for a state law to be valid under our Constitution which makes the criminality of an act depend upon the race of the actor.' I concur.

Note: Discriminatory Purpose and Disproportionate Impact

The *Loving* decision reflected an instance in which discriminatory purpose was overt. Once declared illegal, discrimination increasingly morphed from visible and easily discernible to subtle and difficult to detect. Given the nation's well-documented history of racial discrimination, one school of thought argued that showings of disproportionate impact should be sufficient to establish an equal protection claim. In *Palmer v. Thompson*, 403 U.S. 217 (1971), the Court declined to review legislative motive as a basis for determining whether closure of city pools constituted an equal protection violation. Because the ruling was premised on the ground that the city had no obligation to operate public pools, it did not help either the discriminatory purpose requirement or the discriminatory effect standard to gain traction.

The Court's decision in *Keyes v. School District No. 1*, 413 U.S. 189 (1973), established intentional segregation as the basis for relief in the public school context. In the following case, the Court confirmed that purposeful discrimination was a threshold requirement for a viable equal protection claim. Richard A. Primus, *Equal Protection and Disparate Impact: Round Three*, 117 HARV. L. REV. 493

(2003) (examining the tensions between disproportionate impact standards and the equal protection requirement of discriminatory purpose).

Washington v. Davis

426 U.S. 229 (1976)

Mr. Justice WHITE delivered the opinion of the Court.

This case involves the validity of a qualifying test administered to applicants for positions as police officers in the District of Columbia Metropolitan Police Department. To be accepted by the Department and to enter an intensive 17-week training program, the police recruit was required to satisfy certain physical and character standards, to be a high school graduate or its equivalent, and to receive a grade of at least 40 out of 80 on "Test 21," which is "an examination that is used generally throughout the federal service," which "was developed by the Civil Service Commission, not the Police Department," and which was "designed to test verbal ability, vocabulary, reading and comprehension."

The validity of Test 21 was the sole issue before the court on the motions for summary judgment. The District Court denied the motion for summary judgment, but the Court of Appeals reversed, holding that Test 21 invidiously discriminated against Negroes and hence denied them due process of law contrary to the commands of the Fifth Amendment. We reverse its judgment in respondents' favor.

The central purpose of the Equal Protection Clause of the Fourteenth Amendment is the prevention of official conduct discriminating on the basis of race. It is also true that the Due Process Clause of the Fifth Amendment contains an equal protection component prohibiting the United States from invidiously discriminating between individuals or groups. But our cases have not embraced the proposition that a law or other official act, without regard to whether it reflects a racially discriminatory purpose, is unconstitutional solely because it has a racially disproportionate impact.

Almost 100 years ago, *Strauder v. West Virginia*, 100 U.S. 303 (1879), established that the exclusion of Negroes from grand and petit juries in criminal proceedings violated the Equal Protection Clause, but the fact that a particular jury or a series of juries does not statistically reflect the racial composition of the community does not in itself make out an invidious discrimination forbidden by the Clause. "A purpose to discriminate must be present which may be proven by systematic exclusion of eligible jurymen of the proscribed race or by unequal application of the law to such an extent as to show intentional discrimination."

The school desegregation cases have also adhered to the basic equal protection principle that the invidious quality of a law claimed to be racially discriminatory must ultimately be traced to a racially discriminatory purpose. That there are both predominantly black and predominantly white schools in a community is not alone violative of the Equal Protection Clause. The essential element of de jure segregation is "a current condition of segregation resulting from intentional state action. The differentiating factor between de jure segregation and so-called de facto segregation is the purpose or intent to segregate."

This is not to say that the necessary discriminatory racial purpose must be express or appear on the face of the statute, or that a law's disproportionate impact is irrelevant in cases involving Constitution-based claims of racial discrimination. A statute, otherwise neutral on its face, must not be applied so as invidiously to discriminate on the basis of race. When a *prima facie* case made out, the burden of proof shifts to the State to rebut the presumption of unconstitutional action by showing that permissible racially neutral selection criteria and procedures have produced the monochromatic result.

An invidious discriminatory purpose may often be inferred from the totality of the relevant facts, including the fact, if it is true, that the law bears more heavily on one race than another. This may be true where there is the total or seriously disproportionate exclusion of Negroes that is very difficult to explain on nonracial grounds. Nevertheless, we have not held that a law, neutral on its face and serving ends otherwise within the power of government to pursue, is invalid under the Equal Protection Clause simply because it may affect a greater proportion of one race than of another. Disproportionate impact is not irrelevant, but it is not the sole touchstone of an invidious racial discrimination forbidden by the Constitution. Standing alone, it does not trigger the rule, that racial classifications are to be subjected to the strictest scrutiny and are justifiable only by the weightiest of considerations.

Test 21, which is administered generally to prospective Government employees, concededly seeks to ascertain whether those who take it have acquired a particular level of verbal skill; and it is untenable that the Constitution prevents the Government from seeking modestly to upgrade the communicative abilities of its employees rather than to be satisfied with some lower level of competence, particularly where the job requires special ability to communicate orally and in writing. Respondents, as Negroes, could no more successfully claim that the test denied them equal protection than could white applicants who also failed. The conclusion would not be different in the face of proof that more Negroes than whites had been disqualified by Test 21. That other Negroes also failed to score well would, alone, not demonstrate that respondents individually were being denied equal protection of the laws by the application of an otherwise valid qualifying test being administered to prospective police recruits.

Nor on the facts of the case before us would the disproportionate impact of Test 21 warrant the conclusion that it is a purposeful device to discriminate against Negroes and hence an infringement of the constitutional rights of respondents as well as other black applicants. The test is neutral on its face and rationally may be said to serve a purpose the Government is constitutionally empowered to pursue. The affirmative efforts of the Metropolitan Police Department to recruit black officers, the changing racial composition of the recruit classes and of the force in general, and the relationship of the test to the training program negated any inference that the Department discriminated on the basis of race or that "a police officer qualifies on the color of his skin rather than ability."

A rule that a statute designed to serve neutral ends is nevertheless invalid, absent compelling justification, if in practice it benefits or burdens one race more than another would be far-reaching and would raise serious questions about, and perhaps invalidate, a whole range of tax, welfare, public service, regulatory, and licensing statutes that may be more burdensome to the poor and to the average black than to the more affluent white. In our view, extension of the rule beyond those areas where it is already applicable by reason of statute, such as in the field of public employment, should await legislative prescription.

The judgment of the Court of Appeals accordingly is *reversed.*

Mr. Justice STEVENS, *concurring.*

Frequently the most probative evidence of intent will be objective evidence of what actually happened rather than evidence describing the subjective state of mind of the actor. For normally the actor is presumed to have intended the natural consequences of his deeds. This is particularly true in the case of governmental action which is frequently the product of compromise, of collective decision-making, and of mixed motivation. It is unrealistic, on the one hand, to require the victim of alleged discrimination to uncover the actual subjective intent of the decision-maker or, conversely, to invalidate otherwise legitimate action simply because an improper motive affected the deliberation of a participant in the decisional process. A law conscripting clerics should not be invalidated because an atheist voted for it.

My point in making this observation is to suggest that the line between discriminatory purpose and discriminatory impact is not nearly as bright, and perhaps not quite as critical, as the reader of the Court's opinion might assume. I agree, of course, that a constitutional issue does not arise every time some disproportionate impact is shown. On the other hand, when the disproportion is as dramatic, it really does not matter whether the standard is phrased in terms of purpose or effect.

Mr. Justice BRENNAN, with whom Mr. Justice MARSHALL joins, *dissenting.*

The Court holds that the job qualification examination (Test 21) given by the District of Columbia Metropolitan Police Department does not unlawfully discriminate on the basis of race under either constitutional or statutory standards.

Initially, it seems to me that the Court should not pass on the statutory questions, because they are not presented by this case. The Court says that respondents' summary judgment motion "rested on purely constitutional grounds," and that "the Court of Appeals erroneously applied the legal standards applicable to Title VII cases in resolving the constitutional issue before it." There is a suggestion, however, that petitioners are entitled to prevail because they met the burden of proof imposed by 5 U.S.C. §3304. As I understand the opinion, the Court therefore holds that Test 21 is job related under §3304, but not necessarily under Title VII. But that provision, by the Court's own analysis, is no more in the case than Title VII; respondents' "complaint asserted no claim under §3304." If it was "plain error" for the Court of Appeals to apply a statutory standard to this case, as the Court asserts, then it is unfortunate that the Court does not recognize that it is also plain error to address the statutory issues in Part III of its opinion.

Nevertheless, although it appears unnecessary to reach the statutory questions, I will accept the Court's conclusion that respondents were entitled to summary judgment if they were correct in their statutory arguments, and I would affirm the Court of Appeals because petitioners have failed to prove that Test 21 satisfies the applicable statutory standards. All parties' arguments and both lower court decisions were based on Title VII standards. In this context, I think it wrong to focus on §3304 to the exclusion of the Title VII standards, particularly because the Civil Service Commission views the job-relatedness standards of Title VII and §3304 as identical.

In applying a Title VII test, both the District Court and the Court of Appeals held that respondents had offered sufficient evidence of discriminatory impact to shift to petitioners the burden of proving job-relatedness. The Court does not question these rulings, and the only issue before us is what petitioners were required to show and whether they carried their burden. The Court agrees with the District Court's conclusion that Test 21 was validated by a positive relationship between Test 21 scores and performance in police training courses. This result is based upon the Court's reading of the record, its interpretation of instructions governing testing practices issued by the Civil Service Commission (CSC), and "the current views of the Civil Service Commissioners who were parties to the case." We are also assured that today's result is not foreclosed by *Griggs v. Duke Power Co.*, 401 U.S. 424 (1971), and *Albemarle Paper Co. v. Moody*, 422 U.S. 405 (1975). Finally, the Court asserts that its conclusion is "the much more sensible construction of the job-relatedness requirement."

But the CSC instructions cited by the Court do not support the District Court's conclusion. More importantly, the brief filed in this Court by the CSC takes the position that petitioners did not satisfy the burden of proof imposed by the CSC guidelines. It also appears that longstanding regulations of the Equal Employment Opportunity Commission (EEOC) — previously endorsed by this Court — require a result contrary to that reached by the Court. Furthermore, the Court's conclusion is inconsistent with my understanding of the interpretation of Title VII in *Griggs* and *Albemarle*. I do not find this conclusion "much more sensible," and with all respect I suggest that today's decision has the potential of significantly weakening statutory safeguards against discrimination in employment.

Village of Arlington Heights v. Metropolitan Housing Development Corp.

429 U.S. 252 (1977)

Mr. Justice POWELL delivered the opinion of the Court.

This case concerns a village's refusal to rezone land from single-family usage to accommodate multiple-family dwellings and thus enable the respondent to construct racially integrated housing.

Our decision last Term in *Washington v. Davis* made it clear that official action will not be held unconstitutional solely because it results in a "racially disproportionate impact." Disproportionate impact is not irrelevant, but it is not the sole touchstone of an invidious racial discrimination. Proof of racially discriminatory intent or purpose is required to show a violation of the Equal Protection Clause. Although some contrary indications may be drawn from some of our cases, the holding in *Davis* reaffirmed a principle well established in a variety of contexts.

Davis does not require a plaintiff to prove that the challenged action rested solely on racially discriminatory purposes. Rarely can it be said that a legislature or administrative body operating under a broad mandate made a decision motivated solely by a single concern, or even that a particular purpose was the "dominant" or "primary" one. In fact, it is because legislators and administrators are properly concerned with balancing numerous competing considerations that courts refrain from reviewing the merits of their decisions, absent a showing of arbitrariness or irrationality. But racial discrimination is not just another competing consideration. When there is a proof that a discriminatory purpose has been a motivating factor in the decision, this judicial deference is no longer justified.

Determining whether invidious discriminatory purpose was a motivating factor demands a sensitive inquiry into such circumstantial and direct evidence of intent as may be available. The impact of the official action whether it "bears more heavily on one race than another," may provide an important starting point. Sometimes a clear pattern, unexplainable on grounds other than race, emerges from the effect of the state action even when the governing legislation appears neutral on its face. The evidentiary inquiry is then relatively easy. But such cases are rare. Absent a pattern as stark as that in *Gomillion* or *Yick Wo*, impact alone is not determinative, and the Court must look to other evidence.

The historical background of the decision is one evidentiary source, particularly if it reveals a series of official actions taken for invidious purposes. The specific sequence of events leading up the challenged decision also may shed some light on the decision-maker's purposes. For example, if the property involved here always had been zoned R-5 but suddenly was changed to R-3 when the town learned of MHDC's plans to erect integrated housing, we would have a far different case. Departures from the normal procedural sequence also might afford evidence that improper purposes are playing a role. Substantive departures too may be relevant, particularly if the factors usually considered important by the decision-maker strongly favor a decision contrary to the one reached. The legislative or administrative history may be highly relevant, especially where there are contemporary statements by members of the decision-making body, minutes of its meetings, or reports.

The foregoing summary identifies, without purporting to be exhaustive, subjects of proper inquiry in determining whether racially discriminatory intent existed. With these in mind, we now address the case before us.

We have reviewed the evidence. The impact of the Village's decision does arguably bear more heavily on racial minorities. Minorities constitute 18% of the Chicago area population, and 40% of the income groups said to be eligible for Lincoln Green. But there is little about the sequence of events leading up to the decision that would spark suspicion. The area around the Victorian property has been zoned R-3 since 1959, the year when Arlington Heights first adopted a zoning map. Single-family homes surround the 80-acre site, and the Village is undeniably committed to single-family homes as its dominant residential land use. The rezoning request progressed according to the usual procedures. The Planning Commission even scheduled two additional hearings, at least in part to accommodate MHDC and permit it to supplement its presentation with answers to questions generated at the first hearing.

The statements by the Plan Commission and Village Board members, as reflected in the official minutes, focused almost exclusively on the zoning aspects of the MHDC petition, and the zoning factors on which they relied are not novel criteria in the Village's rezoning decisions. There is no reason to doubt that there has been reliance by some neighboring property owners on the maintenance of single-family zoning in the vicinity. The Village originally adopted its buffer policy long before MHDC entered the picture and has applied the policy too consistently for us to infer discriminatory purpose from its application in this case. Finally, MHDC called one member of the Village Board to the stand at trial. Nothing in her testimony supports an inference of invidious purpose.

In sum, the evidence does not warrant overturning the concurrent findings of both courts below. Respondents simply failed to carry their burden of proving that discriminatory purpose was a motivating factor in the Village's decision.

Note: Applying the Discriminatory Motive Requirement

The discriminatory motive requirement represented a critical milestone in the evolution of equal protection jurisprudence. Review hinged on judicial discernment of official intent as involving discrimination only if it is prescriptive or overt. In this vein, the Court in *Hunter v. Underwood*, 471 U.S. 222 (1981), struck down a law that denied voting rights to persons who had been convicted of a crime involving "moral turpitude." Tracing the law to its early-twentieth-century origin, the Court was able to glean "beyond peradventure" an intent to discriminate. Case law demonstrates that the Court will strike down laws that it finds, through a process of elimination, have no basis for existence other than a purpose to discriminate. Legislative redistricting that attempted to increase minority representation, by configuring districts with highly irregular contours, exemplifies this type of outcome. In *Shaw v. Reno*, 509 U.S. 630, 642 (1993), the Court held that a North Carolina congressional redistricting plan constituted one of "those 'rare' statutes that, although race neutral, are, on their face unexplainable on grounds other than race." The Court, in *Miller v. Johnson*, 515 U.S. 900 (1995), noted that that a plaintiff must "show, either through circumstantial evidence or a district's shape and demographics or more direct evidence going to legislative

purpose, that race was the predominant factor motivating the legislature's decision to place a significant number of voters within or without a particular district."
Strict scrutiny, which was fatal to the districting plan in *Miller v. Johnson*, thus may
be triggered when race is the "predominant factor" in decision making. Despite
the identification of some racially neutral considerations in North Carolina, the
Court in *Shaw v. Hunt*, 517 U.S. 899 (1996), found that the irregularly shaped
congressional district was predominantly a function of race. The predominant
factor test also was used, in *Bush v. Vera*, 517 U.S. 952 (1996), to strike down a
majority-minority redistricting plan.

In *Ashcroft v. Iqbal*, 556 U.S. 662 (2009), a case concerning claims of discrimination against a detained Pakistani Muslim, the Court determined that government officials were not liable for the alleged wrongful acts of prison officials.
Plaintiff, who had been charged with fraud in the use of a social security card,
claimed federal officials (including the director of the FBI and the attorney general) condoned the discrimination. He maintained that his race, religion, and
national origin were the basis for characterizing him as a person "of high interest" in the wake of terrorist attacks in New York on September 11, 2001. Plaintiff
maintained that, while in detention, prison guards physically attacked him,
impeded his right to pray, and committed other violations. A Justice Department
investigation confirmed that he had been abused by prison guards. The Court
held that government officials could not be held liable for their subordinates'
alleged unconstitutional conduct. In order to prevail on a discrimination claim
under either the First or Fifth Amendment, the plaintiff must plead and prove
discriminatory purpose. Minus a facially adequate basis for inferring liability, the
Court concluded that the claim could not survive a motion to dismiss. It observed
that, to the extent terrorist attacks had been perpetrated by Arab Muslims, it was
not unexpected that there would be a disparate impact on this group. From the
Court's perspective there were no facts stated from which discrimination reasonably could be inferred. It thus remanded the case for a determination of whether
the plaintiff should be allowed to amend his claim. Four justices dissented.

∾ PROBLEM: MORE ON THE DIVERSITY INITIATIVE ∾

Let's return to the problem described at the beginning of the chapter.
Suppose that NWU is thinking about giving preferential admission to law and
medical school applicants who come from economically disadvantaged backgrounds. The board of regents does not appear to have any intent to discriminate
in favor of any particular racial or ethnic group. However, the evidence shows that
a disproportionate number of poor and economically disadvantaged students in
the applicant pool are of African American or Hispanic heritage. As a result,
while the policy of favoring economically disadvantaged applicants will benefit
students of all races who come from economically disadvantaged backgrounds, it

will disproportionately benefit African American and Hispanic applicants. Under these circumstances, what would you tell the board about whether the proposed admissions policy creates a racial classification? If the policy is challenged in court, what standard of review would you expect a reviewing court to apply?

4. Affirmative Action

The desegregation experience established a model of remediation that aimed to redress the wrongs committed by official discrimination. In the context of public education, not only did official segregation have to be undone, but also schools that were racially identifiable had to become racially unitary. This result was achieved by a process of affirmative action that included racial quotas and goals.

The term *affirmative action* typically refers to programs or policies that establish preferences on the basis of group status. The separate but equal doctrine, upheld in *Plessy v. Ferguson*, exemplified an affirmative action model that allocated burdens and benefits consistent with the interests of the dominant racial group. Affirmative action for contemporary purposes initially was designed to help minorities who had been the victims of racial discrimination. The Court has restricted remedial classifications to discrete instances where intentional discrimination has been established. It also has recognized diversity in postsecondary education as a compelling justification for taking race into account on a limited basis.

Much of the constitutional debate over affirmative action has focused on whether it can be used to remedy the consequences of racial discrimination. The Court has acknowledged the "nation's sorry legacy of private and public discrimination." *City of Richmond v. J.A. Croson Co.*, 488 U.S. 469 (1989). This understanding, however, did not lead to a conclusion that remedial classifications are permissible. Whether racial classifications designed to remedy the vestiges of discrimination should be strictly scrutinized (like those that burdened minorities) was the subject of extended and intense debate.

Over the course of the 1980s, the Court's decisions yielded mixed and uncertain results. In *Fullilove v. Klutznick*, 448 U.S. 448 (1980), it upheld a federal setaside program for minority contractors in public works projects. A three-justice plurality, in an opinion authored by Chief Justice Burger, referenced Congress's power to enforce the Fourteenth Amendment as a determinative factor. Three justices, maintaining that remedial classifications that benefited minorities were less objectionable than classifications that burdened them, advocated for an intermediate standard of review that required careful but not strict scrutiny. Two justices expressed opposition to any racial classifications, and another objected to them under most circumstances.

Movement toward a majority position was evident in *Wygant v. Jackson Board of Education*, 476 U.S. 267 (1986). That case concerned a collectively bargained layoff plan that protected more recently hired minorities in the event of job cutbacks. *Wygant* focused on whether remediation of societal discrimination was an adequate basis for race-conscious remedies. Justice Powell, writing for a plurality of four justices, maintained that societal discrimination by itself was "too amorphous a basis for imposing a racially classified remedy." From the plurality's perspective, a racially based remedy was permissible only upon "some showing of prior discrimination by the governmental unit involved." The plurality dismissed the interest in minority role models as an adequate basis for remedial classifications. It also identified strict scrutiny as the appropriate standard of review. Justice Stevens dissented and proposed a forward-looking perspective that stressed the value of diversity as it relates to the educational process.

Consistent with the plurality's premise in *Wygant,* the Court in *United States v. Paradise,* 480 U.S. 149 (1987), provided race-conscious relief that addressed an identifiable instance of discrimination by a government unit. At issue was a court-ordered plan that set aside, for qualified Black state troopers in Alabama, at least 50% of the promotions to the rank of corporal. This order was made pursuant to well-documented findings of discrimination and a record of remedial inaction. Justice Brennan, in a plurality opinion, maintained that the plan would survive even strict scrutiny. Agreeing with the result in a separate opinion, Justice Powell referenced a persistent violation of constitutional rights and disregard of court orders. In an opinion joined by Justices Rehnquist and Scalia, Justice O'Connor maintained that the remedial classifications were not narrowly tailored and thus did not survive strict scrutiny. She noted the availability of alternative remedies, such as appointment of a trustee to establish promotion procedures and penalties for violation of court orders.

Adarand Constructors, Inc. v. Pena

515 U.S. 200 (1995)

Justice O'CONNOR announced the judgment of the Court and delivered an opinion with respect to Parts I, II, III-A, III-B, III-D, and IV, which is for the Court except insofar as it might be inconsistent with the views expressed in Justice SCALIA's concurrence, and an opinion with respect to Part III-C in which Justice KENNEDY joins.

Petitioner Adarand Constructors, Inc., claims that the Federal Government's practice of giving general contractors on Government projects a financial incentive to hire subcontractors controlled by "socially and economically disadvantaged individuals," and the Government's use of race-based presumptions in identifying such individuals, violates the equal protection component of the Fifth Amendment's Due Process Clause. The Court of Appeals rejected Adarand's claim. We vacate and remand the case for further proceedings.

III

A

Through the 1940's, this Court had routinely taken the view in non-race-related cases that, "unlike the Fourteenth Amendment, the Fifth contains no equal protection clause and it provides no guaranty against discriminatory legislation by Congress." In *Bolling v. Sharpe*, 347 U.S. 497 (1954), the Court explicitly questioned the existence of any difference between the obligations of the Federal Government and the States to avoid racial classifications. The Court's observations that "distinctions between citizens solely because of their ancestry are by their very nature odious," and that "all legal restrictions which curtail the civil rights of a single racial group are immediately suspect," carry no less force in the context of federal action than in the context of action by the States.

B

In *City of Richmond v. J.A. Croson Co.*, 488 U.S. 469 (1989), the Court finally agreed that the Fourteenth Amendment requires strict scrutiny of all race-based action by state and local governments. But *Croson* of course had no occasion to declare what standard of review the Fifth Amendment requires for such action taken by the Federal Government.

A year later, the Court took a surprising turn. *Metro Broadcasting, Inc. v. FCC*, 497 U.S. 547 (1990), involved a Fifth Amendment challenge to two race-based policies of the Federal Communications Commission (FCC). In *Metro Broadcasting*, the Court repudiated the long-held notion that "it would be unthinkable that the same Constitution would impose a lesser duty on the Federal Government" than it does on a State to afford equal protection of the laws.

We adhere to *Croson*'s view today, despite the surface appeal of holding "benign" racial classifications to a lower standard, because "it may not always be clear that a so-called preference is in fact benign." "More than good motives should be required when government seeks to allocate its resources by way of an explicit racial classification system."

The Fifth and Fourteenth Amendments to the Constitution protect *persons,* not *groups.* It follows from that principle that all governmental action based on race—a *group* classification long recognized as "in most circumstances irrelevant and therefore prohibited"—should be subjected to detailed judicial inquiry to ensure that the *personal* right to equal protection of the laws has not been infringed. These ideas have long been central to this Court's understanding of equal protection, and holding "benign" state and federal racial classifications to different standards does not square with them. "A free people whose institutions are founded upon the doctrine of equality," should tolerate no retreat from the principle that government may treat people differently because of their race only for the most compelling reasons. Accordingly, we hold today that all racial classifications, imposed by whatever federal, state, or local governmental actor, must be analyzed by a reviewing court under strict scrutiny. Such classifications are constitutional only if they are narrowly tailored measures that further compelling governmental interests. To the extent that *Metro Broadcasting* is inconsistent with that holding, it is overruled.

Justice Stevens chides us for our "supposed inability to differentiate between 'invidious' and 'benign' discrimination," because it is in his view sufficient that "people understand the difference between good intentions and bad." But the point of strict scrutiny is to "differentiate between" permissible and impermissible governmental use of race. And Justice Stevens himself has already explained in his dissent in *Fullilove* why "good intentions" alone are not enough to sustain a supposedly "benign" racial classification: "A statute of this kind inevitably is perceived by many as resting on an assumption that those who are granted this special preference are less qualified in some respect that is identified purely by their race. Because that perception—*especially when fostered by the Congress of the United States*—can only exacerbate rather than reduce racial prejudice, it will delay the time when race will become a truly irrelevant, or at least insignificant, factor." The application of strict scrutiny determines whether a compelling governmental interest justifies the infliction of that injury.

D

Federal racial classifications, like those of a State, must serve a compelling governmental interest, and must be narrowly tailored to further that interest. To the extent that *Fullilove* held federal racial classifications to be subject to a less rigorous standard, it is no longer controlling. We agree with Justice Stevens that, "because racial characteristics so seldom provide a relevant basis for disparate treatment, and because classifications based on race are potentially so harmful to the entire body politic, it is especially important that the reasons for any such classification be clearly identified and unquestionably legitimate," and that "racial classifications are simply too pernicious to permit any but the most exact connection between justification and classification." Requiring strict scrutiny is the best way to ensure that courts will consistently give racial classifications that kind of detailed examination, both as to ends and as to means.

Finally, we wish to dispel the notion that strict scrutiny is "strict in theory, but fatal in fact." The unhappy persistence of both the practice and the lingering effects of racial discrimination against minority groups in this country is an unfortunate reality, and government is not disqualified from acting in response to it. As recently as 1987, for example, every Justice of this Court agreed that the Alabama Department of Public Safety's "pervasive, systematic, and obstinate discriminatory conduct" justified a narrowly tailored race-based remedy. *United States v. Paradise.* When race-based action is necessary to further a compelling interest, such action is within constitutional constraints if it satisfies the "narrow tailoring" test this Court has set out in previous cases.

IV

The question whether any of the ways in which the Government uses subcontractor compensation clauses can survive strict scrutiny, and any relevance distinctions such as these may have to that question, should be addressed in the first instance by the lower courts.

Accordingly, the judgment of the Court of Appeals is vacated, and the case is remanded for further proceedings consistent with this opinion.

Justice SCALIA, *concurring in part* and *concurring in the judgment.*

Government can never have a "compelling interest" in discriminating on the basis of race in order to "make up" for past racial discrimination in the opposite direction. Individuals who have been wronged by unlawful racial discrimination should be made whole; but under our Constitution there can be no such thing as either a creditor or a debtor race. That concept is alien to the Constitution's focus upon the individual, and its rejection of dispositions based on race, or based on blood. To pursue the concept of racial entitlement—even for the most admirable and benign of purposes—is to reinforce and preserve for future mischief the way of thinking that produced race slavery, race privilege and race hatred. In the eyes of government, we are just one race here. It is American. It is unlikely, if not impossible, that the challenged program would survive under this understanding of strict scrutiny.

Justice THOMAS, *concurring in part* and *concurring in the judgment.*

Strict scrutiny applies to *all* government classifications based on race. There is a "moral and constitutional equivalence," between laws designed to subjugate a race and those that distribute benefits on the basis of race in order to foster some current notion of equality. Government cannot make us equal; it can only recognize, respect, and protect us as equal before the law. That these programs may have been motivated, in part, by good intentions cannot provide refuge from the principle that under our Constitution, the government may not make distinctions on the basis of race. The paternalism that appears to lie at the heart of this program is at war with the principle of inherent equality that underlies and infuses our Constitution.

These programs undermine the moral basis of the equal protection principle. Such classifications ultimately have a destructive impact on the individual and our society. Racial paternalism and its unintended consequences can be as poisonous and pernicious as any other form of discrimination. So-called "benign" discrimination teaches many that minorities cannot compete with them without their patronizing indulgence. Inevitably, such programs engender attitudes of superiority or, alternatively, provoke resentment among those who believe that they have been wronged by the government's use of race. These programs stamp minorities with a badge of inferiority and may cause them to develop dependencies or to adopt an attitude that they are "entitled" to preferences. Government-sponsored racial discrimination based on benign prejudice is just as noxious as discrimination inspired by malicious prejudice. In each instance, it is racial discrimination, plain and simple.

Justice STEVENS, with whom Justice GINSBURG joins, *dissenting*.

A court should be wary of a governmental decision that relies upon a racial classification. "Because racial characteristics so seldom provide a relevant basis for disparate treatment, and because classifications based on race are potentially so harmful to the entire body politic," a reviewing court must satisfy itself that the reasons for any such classification are "clearly identified and unquestionably legitimate."

There is no moral or constitutional equivalence between a policy that is designed to perpetuate a caste system and one that seeks to eradicate racial subordination. Invidious discrimination is an engine of oppression, subjugating a disfavored group to enhance or maintain the power of the majority. Remedial race-based preferences reflect the opposite impulse: a desire to foster equality in society. People understand the difference between good intentions and bad. Nothing is inherently wrong with applying a single standard to fundamentally different situations, as long as that standard takes relevant differences into account. But a single standard that purports to equate remedial preferences with invidious discrimination cannot be defended in the name of "equal protection." As a matter of constitutional and democratic principle, a decision by representatives of the majority to discriminate against the members of a minority race is fundamentally different from those same representatives' decision to impose incidental costs on the majority of their constituents in order to provide a benefit to a disadvantaged minority. The former is virtually always repugnant to the principles of a free and democratic society, whereas the latter is, in some circumstances, entirely consistent with the ideal of equality.

The Court's concept of "congruence" assumes that there is no significant difference between a decision by the Congress of the United States to adopt an affirmative-action program and such a decision by a State or a municipality. In my opinion that assumption is untenable. I would affirm the judgment of the Court of Appeals.

Justice SOUTER, with whom Justice GINSBURG and Justice BREYER join, *dissenting*.

The Court's recognition today that strict scrutiny can be compatible with the survival of a classification demonstrates that our concepts of equal protection enjoy a greater elasticity than the standard categories might suggest.

Justice GINSBURG, with whom Justice BREYER joins, *dissenting*.

The divisions in this difficult case should not obscure the Court's recognition of the persistence of racial inequality and a majority's acknowledgment of Congress' authority to act affirmatively, not only to end discrimination, but also to counteract discrimination's lingering effects. Those effects, reflective of a system of racial caste only recently ended, are evident in our workplaces, markets, and neighborhoods. Job applicants with identical resumes, qualifications, and interview styles still experience different receptions, depending on their race. White and African-American consumers still encounter different deals. People of color looking for housing still face discriminatory treatment by landlords, real estate agents, and mortgage lenders. Minority entrepreneurs sometimes fail to gain contracts though they are the low bidders, and they are sometimes refused work even after winning contracts. Given this history and its practical consequences, Congress surely can conclude that a carefully designed affirmative action program may help to realize, finally, the "equal protection of the laws."

The strict standard announced is indeed "fatal" for classifications burdening groups that have suffered discrimination in our society. For a classification made to hasten the day when "we are just one race," however, the lead opinion has dispelled the notion that "strict scrutiny" is "fatal in fact." Properly, a majority of the Court calls for review that is searching, in order to ferret out classifications in reality malign, but masquerading as benign.

∾ PROBLEM: THE DIVERSITY INITIATIVE AND RACE-BASED ADMISSIONS POLICIES ∾

In the introductory problem, suppose that NWU is also thinking about giving preferential admission to members of certain specified minority groups (e.g., African Americans, Hispanics, and Asian-Americans). NWU's board of regents has asked you for advice about whether it may do so. Based on what you have read to this point, how would you advise the board? What must the university show in order to adopt such a policy? Can it adopt the policy for all "minority" racial groups? Continue to think about these issues as you review the following cases and notes.

The Court's initial exposure to affirmative action was in *DeFunis v. Odegaard*, 416 U.S. 312 (1974). That case concerned a state university's admission policy that gave preference to members of groups that traditionally had experienced discrimination. Because the plaintiff student was nearing graduation, the Court determined that the parties would be unaffected by any relief and thus dismissed the case as moot.

Four years later, in *Regents of the University of California v. Bakke*, 438 U.S. 265 (1978), the Court examined a preferential admissions program at a state university medical school. The policy was challenged by a white male who maintained that he had been denied admission on the basis of his race. In striking down the admissions program, the Court treated the race-based program as a suspect classification. The opinion noted that if "petitioner's purpose is to assure within its student body some specified percentage of a particular group merely because of its race or ethnic origin, such a preferential purpose must be rejected not as insubstantial but as facially invalid. Preferring members of any one group for no reason other than race or ethnic origin is discrimination for its own sake. This the Constitution forbids." The Court acknowledged that the State "certainly has a legitimate and substantial interest in ameliorating, or eliminating where feasible, the disabling effects of identified discrimination." Nevertheless, the Court noted that it had "never approved a classification that aids persons perceived as members of relatively victimized groups at the expense of other innocent individuals in the absence of judicial, legislative, or administrative findings of constitutional or statutory violations. After such findings have been made, the governmental interest in preferring members of the injured groups at the expense of others is substantial, since the legal rights of the victims must be vindicated."

The Court also addressed the medical school's assertion that it had a legitimate interest in attaining a "diverse student body." It noted:

> Ethnic diversity, however, is only one element in a range of factors a university properly may consider in attaining the goal of a heterogeneous student body. Although a university must have wide discretion in making the sensitive judgments as to who should be admitted, constitutional limitations protecting individual rights may not be disregarded. It may be assumed that the reservation of a specified number of seats in each class for individuals from the preferred ethnic groups would contribute to the attainment of considerable ethnic diversity in the student body. But petitioner's argument that this is the only effective means of serving the interest of diversity is seriously flawed. In a most fundamental sense the argument misconceives the nature of the state interest that would justify consideration of race or ethnic background. It is not an interest in simple ethnic diversity, in which a specified percentage of the student body is in effect guaranteed to be members of selected ethnic groups, with the remaining percentage an undifferentiated aggregation of students. The diversity that furthers a compelling state interest encompasses a far broader array of qualifications and characteristics of which racial or ethnic origin is but a single though important element. Petitioner's special admissions program, focused *solely* on ethnic diversity, would hinder rather than further attainment of genuine diversity.
>
> Nor would the state interest in genuine diversity be served by expanding petitioner's two-track system into a multitrack program with a prescribed number of seats set aside for each identifiable category of applicants. The experience of other university admissions programs, which take race into account in achieving the educational diversity valued by the First Amendment, demonstrates that the assignment of a fixed number of places to a minority group is not a necessary means toward that end.
>
> Race or ethnic background may be deemed a "plus" in a particular applicant's file, yet it does not insulate the individual from comparison with all other candidates for the available seats. The file of a particular black applicant may be examined for his potential contribution to diversity without the factor of race being decisive when compared, for example, with that of an applicant identified as an Italian-American if the latter is thought to exhibit qualities more likely to promote beneficial educational pluralism. Such qualities could include exceptional personal talents, unique work or service experience, leadership potential, maturity, demonstrated compassion, a history of overcoming disadvantage, ability to communicate with the poor, or other qualifications deemed important. In short, an admissions program operated in this way is flexible enough to consider all pertinent elements of diversity in light of the particular qualifications of each applicant, and to place them on the same footing for consideration, although not necessarily according them the same weight. Indeed, the weight attributed to a particular quality may vary from year to year depending upon the "mix" both of the student body and the applicants for the incoming class.

Justice Powell's opinion, though standing alone, was a strong influence on the Court's eventual adoption of a strict scrutiny standard and determination that race could be a nonexclusive factor in the university admission process.

Grutter v. Bollinger

539 U.S. 306 (2003)

Justice O'Connor delivered the opinion of the Court.

This case requires us to decide whether the use of race as a factor in student admissions by the University of Michigan Law School (Law School) is unlawful.

The Law School ranks among the Nation's top law schools. It receives more than 3,500 applications each year for a class of around 350 students. Seeking to "admit a group of students who individually and collectively are among the most capable," the Law School looks for individuals with "substantial promise for success in law school" and "a strong likelihood of succeeding in the practice of law and contributing in diverse ways to the well-being of others." More broadly, the Law School seeks "a mix of students with varying backgrounds and experiences who will respect and learn from each other."

The hallmark of the school's admissions policy is its focus on academic ability coupled with a flexible assessment of applicants' talents, experiences, and potential "to contribute to the learning of those around them." The policy requires admissions officials to evaluate each applicant based on all the information available in the file, including a personal statement, letters of recommendation, and an essay describing the ways in which the applicant will contribute to the life and diversity of the Law School. In reviewing an applicant's file, admissions officials must consider the applicant's undergraduate grade point average (GPA) and Law School Admissions Test (LSAT) score because they are important (if imperfect) predictors of academic success in law school. The policy stresses that "no applicant should be admitted unless we expect that applicant to do well enough to graduate with no serious academic problems." The policy makes clear, however, that even the highest possible score does not guarantee admission to the Law School. Nor does a low score automatically disqualify an applicant. Rather, the policy requires admissions officials to look beyond grades and test scores to other criteria that are important to the Law School's educational objectives. So-called "'soft' variables" such as "the enthusiasm of recommenders, the quality of the undergraduate institution, the quality of the applicant's essay, and the areas and difficulty of undergraduate course selection" are all brought to bear in assessing an "applicant's likely contributions to the intellectual and social life of the institution."

The policy aspires to "achieve that diversity which has the potential to enrich everyone's education and thus make a law school class stronger than the sum of its parts." The policy does not restrict the types of diversity contributions eligible for "substantial weight" in the admissions process, but instead recognizes "many possible bases for diversity admissions." The policy does, however, reaffirm the Law School's longstanding commitment to "one particular type of diversity," that is, "racial and ethnic diversity with special reference to the inclusion of students from groups which have been historically discriminated against, like African-Americans, Hispanics and Native Americans, who without this commitment might not be represented in our student body in meaningful numbers." By enrolling a "'critical mass' of underrepresented minority students," the Law School seeks to "ensure their ability to make unique contributions to the character of the Law School."

The policy does not define diversity "solely in terms of racial and ethnic status." Nor is the policy "insensitive to the competition among all students for admission to the Law School." Rather, the policy seeks to guide admissions officers in "producing classes both diverse and academically outstanding, classes made up of students who promise to continue the tradition of outstanding contribution by Michigan Graduates to the legal profession."

Petitioner Barbara Grutter is a white Michigan resident who applied to the Law School in 1996 with a 3.8 grade point average and 161 LSAT score. The Law School initially placed petitioner on a waiting list, but subsequently rejected her application. She sued, alleging that respondents discriminated against her on the basis of race in violation of the Fourteenth Amendment. Petitioner also alleged that respondents "had no compelling interest to justify their use of race in the admissions process."

Since *Bakke,* Justice Powell's opinion has served as the touchstone for constitutional analysis of race-conscious admissions policies. Public and private universities across the Nation have modeled their own admissions programs on Justice Powell's views on permissible race-conscious policies. We endorse Justice Powell's view that student body diversity is a compelling state interest that can justify the use of race in university admissions.

We apply strict scrutiny to all racial classifications to "'smoke out' illegitimate uses of race by assuring that the government is pursuing a goal important enough to warrant use of a highly suspect tool." Strict scrutiny is not "strict in theory, but fatal in fact." Not all governmental uses of race are invalidated by it. When race-based action is necessary to further a compelling governmental interest, such action does not violate the constitutional guarantee of equal protection so long as the narrow-tailoring requirement is also satisfied.

Respondents assert only one justification for their use of race in the admissions process: obtaining "the educational benefits that flow from a diverse student body." The Law School asks us to recognize, in the context of higher education, a compelling state interest in student body diversity. We have never held that the only governmental use of race that can survive strict scrutiny is remedying past discrimination. Today, we hold that the Law School has a compelling interest in attaining a diverse student body. The Law School's educational judgment that such diversity is essential to its educational mission is one to which we defer. Our holding today is in keeping with our tradition of giving a degree of deference to a university's academic decisions, within constitutionally prescribed limits.

Given the important purpose of public education and the expansive freedoms of speech and thought associated with the university environment, universities occupy a special niche in our constitutional tradition. In announcing the principle of student body diversity as a compelling state interest, Justice Powell invoked our cases recognizing a constitutional dimension, grounded in the First Amendment, of educational autonomy: "The freedom of a university to make its own judgments as to education includes the selection of its student body." By claiming "the right to select those students who will contribute the most to the 'robust exchange of ideas,'" a university "seeks to achieve a goal that is of paramount importance in the fulfillment of its mission." Our conclusion that the Law School has a compelling interest in a diverse student body is informed by our view that attaining a diverse student body is at the heart of the Law School's proper institutional mission, and that "good faith" on the part of a university is "presumed" absent "a showing to the contrary."

As part of its goal of "assembling a class that is both exceptionally academically qualified and broadly diverse," the Law School seeks to "enroll a 'critical mass' of minority students." The Law School's interest is not simply "to assure within its student body some specified percentage of a particular group merely because of its race or ethnic origin." That would amount to outright racial balancing, which is patently unconstitutional. Rather, the Law School's concept of critical mass is defined by reference to the educational benefits that diversity is designed to produce. These benefits are substantial. The Law School's admissions policy promotes "cross-racial understanding," helps to break down racial stereotypes, and "enables students to better understand persons of different races." These benefits are "important and laudable," because "classroom discussion is livelier, more spirited, and simply more enlightening and interesting" when the students have "the greatest possible variety of backgrounds."

These benefits are not theoretical but real, as major American businesses have made clear that the skills needed in today's increasingly global marketplace can only be developed through exposure to widely diverse people, cultures, ideas, and viewpoints. High-ranking retired officers and civilian leaders of the United States military assert that a "highly qualified, racially diverse officer corps is essential to the military's ability to fulfill its principle mission to provide national security." "The military cannot achieve an officer corps that is both highly qualified and racially diverse without using limited race-conscious recruiting and admissions policies."

We have repeatedly acknowledged the overriding importance of preparing students for work and citizenship, describing education as pivotal to "sustaining our political and cultural heritage" with a fundamental role in maintaining the fabric of society. The diffusion of knowledge and opportunity through public institutions of higher education must be accessible to all individuals regardless of race or ethnicity. The United States affirms that "ensuring that public institutions are open and available to all segments of American society, including people of all races and ethnicities, represents a paramount government objective." "Nowhere is the importance of such openness more acute than in the context of higher education." Effective participation by members of all racial and ethnic groups in the civic life of our Nation is essential if the dream of one Nation, indivisible, is to be realized.

Even in the limited circumstance when drawing racial distinctions is permissible to further a compelling state interest, the means chosen to accomplish the government's asserted purpose must be specifically and narrowly framed to accomplish that purpose.

We find that the Law School's admissions program bears the hallmarks of a narrowly tailored plan. Universities cannot establish quotas for members of certain racial groups or put members of those groups on separate admissions tracks. Nor can universities insulate applicants who belong to certain racial or ethnic groups from the competition for admission. Universities can, however, consider race or ethnicity more flexibly as a "plus" factor in the context of individualized consideration of each and every applicant. The Law School's goal of attaining a critical mass of underrepresented minority students does not transform its program into a quota. Here, the Law School engages in a highly individualized, holistic review of each applicant's file, giving serious consideration to all the ways an applicant might contribute to a diverse educational environment. The Law School affords this individualized consideration to applicants of all races. There is no policy, either de jure or de facto, of automatic acceptance or rejection based on any single "soft" variable.

Petitioner and the United States argue that the Law School's plan is not narrowly tailored because race-neutral means exist to obtain the educational benefits of student body diversity that the Law School seeks. We disagree. Narrow tailoring does not require exhaustion of every conceivable race-neutral alternative. Nor does it require a university to choose between maintaining a reputation for excellence or fulfilling a commitment to provide educational opportunities to members of all racial groups.

We acknowledge that "there are serious problems of justice connected with the idea of preference itself." Narrow tailoring, therefore, requires that a race-conscious admissions program not unduly harm members of any racial group. We are satisfied that the Law School's admissions program does not. Because the Law School considers "all pertinent elements of diversity," it can (and does) select nonminority applicants who have greater potential to enhance student body diversity over underrepresented minority applicants. As Justice Powell recognized in *Bakke*, so long as a race-conscious admissions program uses race as a "plus" factor in the context of individualized consideration, a rejected applicant will not have been foreclosed from all consideration for that seat simply because he was not the right color or had the wrong surname.

The Law School concedes that all "race-conscious programs must have reasonable durational limits." It has been 25 years since Justice Powell first approved the use of race to further an interest in student body diversity in the context of public higher education, and the number of minority applicants with high grades and test scores has indeed increased. We expect that 25 years from now, the use of racial preferences will no longer be necessary to further the interest approved today.

In summary, the Equal Protection Clause does not prohibit the Law School's narrowly tailored use of race in admissions decisions to further a compelling interest in obtaining the educational benefits that flow from a diverse student body.

Justice GINSBURG, with whom Justice BREYER joins, *concurring.*

Conscious and unconscious race bias, even rank discrimination based on race, remain alive in our land, impeding realization of our highest values and ideals. Many minority students encounter markedly inadequate and unequal educational opportunities. One may hope, but not firmly forecast, that over the next generation's span, progress toward nondiscrimination and genuinely equal opportunity will make it safe to sunset affirmative action.

Chief Justice REHNQUIST, with whom Justice SCALIA, Justice KENNEDY, and Justice THOMAS join, *dissenting.*

Stripped of its "critical mass" veil, the Law School's program is revealed as a naked effort to achieve racial balancing. Before today's decision, we consistently applied the same strict scrutiny analysis regardless of the government's purported reason for using race and regardless of the setting in which race was being used. Although the Court recites the language of our strict scrutiny analysis, its application of that review is unprecedented in its deference.

Only when the "critical mass" label is discarded does a likely explanation for these numbers emerge. From 1995 through 2000 the percentage of admitted applicants who were members of these minority groups closely tracked the percentage of individuals in the school's applicant pool who were from the same groups. The Law School has managed its admissions program, not to achieve a "critical mass," but to extend offers of admission to members of selected minority groups in proportion to their statistical representation in the applicant pool. This is precisely the type of racial balancing that the Court itself calls "patently unconstitutional."

The Law School's program fails strict scrutiny because it is devoid of any reasonably precise time limit on the Law School's use of race in admissions. The Court suggests a possible 25-year limitation. In truth, they permit the Law School's use of racial preferences on a seemingly permanent basis. Thus, an important component of strict scrutiny—that a program be limited in time—is casually subverted.

Notes

1. *The* Gratz *Decision. Gratz v. Bollinger,* 539 U.S. 244 (2003), was decided on the same day as *Grutter,* but it struck down an undergraduate affirmative action plan at the University of Michigan. In that case, the plaintiffs filed a class action lawsuit challenging the undergraduate admission policy, which gave an undergraduate applicant 20 points based solely on his or her membership in an underrepresented racial or ethnic group. An applicant needed approximately 100 points for presumptive admission. Plaintiffs alleged that the allocation of a fixed number of points based on race violated their constitutional and statutory rights.

The Court agreed, holding that the manner in which Michigan considered the race of the applicant in undergraduate admissions was not narrowly tailored to achieve a compelling state interest and therefore violated the equal protection guarantee of the Fourteenth Amendment as well as Title VI of the 1964 Civil Rights Act. Three justices filed dissenting opinions.

2. *Michigan and* Grutter. Following the decision in *Grutter*, Michigan voters adopted Proposal 2, which amended Michigan's Constitution to prohibit Michigan's public colleges and universities from granting "preferential treatment to any individual or group on the basis of sex, color, ethnicity, or national origin." The proposal was upheld in *Schuette v. Coalition to Defend Affirmative Action*, 572 U.S. 291 (2014).

∽ PROBLEM: MORE ON THE DIVERSITY INITIATIVE ∽

Think back to the introductory problem. Suppose that NWU's board of regents is thinking about adopting a policy designed to bring greater diversity to NWU's faculty and student body. The evidence shows that both the faculty and students are overwhelmingly white, and overwhelmingly from middle- and upper-class backgrounds. The board wants you to advise it about how to construct a constitutionally permissible policy. What advice would you give? Try to construct an appropriate plan.

5. *Diversity*

BACKGROUND

School officials cannot assign students to schools based on crude racial categories to maintain racial balance. School officials may consider the racial makeup of schools and adopt general policies to encourage a diverse student body. They are also free to devise race-conscious measures to advance the goal of equal opportunity, so long as school officials do not treat each student differently solely on the basis of a systematic, individual typing by race. School boards may seek diverse educational environments by employing strategic site selection, drawing attendance zones, using targeted recruitment of students and faculty, and tracking enrollments, performance, and other statistics by race.

---

* * *

As demographic trends continued to erode many of the diversity gains incident to desegregation, and consistent with a sense that student diversity has inherent value, some school systems adopted plans to achieve or maintain racially balanced student bodies. The Court, in the following case, assessed two of these plans (in Seattle and Louisville, respectively). The result was a decision that narrowly circumscribed the use of race as a factor in determining where students attend school. The case split the Court into two factions (four justices each): one that advocated absolute color-blindness and a second that viewed this position as compromising the "promise" of *Brown*.

Parents Involved in Community Schools v. Seattle School District No. 1

551 U.S. 701 (2007)

Chief Justice ROBERTS announced the judgment of the Court, and delivered the opinion of the Court with respect to Parts I, II, III-A, and III-C, and an opinion with respect to Parts III-B and IV, in which Justices SCALIA, THOMAS, and ALITO join.

The school districts in these cases voluntarily adopted student assignment plans that rely upon race to determine which public schools certain children may attend. The Seattle school district classifies children as white or nonwhite; the Jefferson County school district as black or "other." In Seattle, this racial classification is used to allocate slots in oversubscribed high schools. In Jefferson County, it is used to make certain elementary school assignments and to rule on transfer requests. In each case, the school district relies upon an individual student's race in assigning that student to a particular school, so that the racial balance at the school falls within a predetermined range based on the racial composition of the school district as a whole. Parents of students denied assignment to particular schools under these plans solely because of their race brought suit, contending that allocating children to different public schools on the basis of race violated the Fourteenth Amendment guarantee of equal protection. The Courts of Appeals below upheld the plans. We granted certiorari, and now reverse.

I

Both cases present the same underlying legal question—whether a public school that had not operated legally segregated schools or has been found to be unitary may choose to classify students by race and rely upon that classification in making school assignments. Although we examine the plans under the same legal framework, the specifics of the two plans, and the circumstances surrounding their adoption, are in some respects quite different.

III

A

It is well established that when the government distributes burdens or benefits on the basis of individual racial classifications, that action is reviewed under strict scrutiny. As the Court recently reaffirmed, "racial classifications are simply too pernicious to permit any but the most exact connection between justification and classification." *Gratz v. Bollinger*, 539 U.S. 244, 270 (2003). In order to satisfy this searching standard of review, the school districts must demonstrate that the use of individual racial classifications in the assignment plans here under review is "narrowly tailored" to achieve a "compelling" government interest.

Without attempting in these cases to set forth all the interests a school district might assert, it suffices to note that our prior cases, in evaluating the use of racial classifications in the school context, have recognized two interests that qualify as compelling. The first is the compelling interest of remedying the effects of past intentional discrimination. *See Freeman v. Pitts*, 503 U.S. 467, 494 (1992). Yet the Seattle public schools have not shown that they were ever segregated by law, and were not subject to court-ordered desegregation decrees. The Jefferson County public schools were previously segregated by law and were subject to a desegregation decree entered in 1975. In 2000, the District Court that entered that decree dissolved it, finding that Jefferson County had "eliminated the vestiges associated with the former policy of segregation and its pernicious effects," and thus had achieved "unitary" status. *Hampton*, 102 F. Supp. 2d, at 360. Jefferson County accordingly does not rely upon an interest in remedying the effects of past intentional discrimination in defending its present use of race in assigning students. Nor could it. We have emphasized that the harm being remedied by mandatory desegregation plans is the harm that is traceable to segregation, and that "the Constitution is not violated by racial imbalance in the schools, without more." *Milliken v. Bradley*, 433 U.S. 267, 280, n.14 (1977). Once Jefferson County achieved unitary status, it had remedied the constitutional wrong that allowed race-based assignments. Any continued use of race must be justified on some other basis.

The second government interest we have recognized as compelling for purposes of strict scrutiny is the interest in diversity in higher education upheld in *Grutter*, 539 U.S. at 328. The specific interest found compelling in *Grutter* was student body diversity "in the context of higher education." The diversity interest was not focused on race alone but encompassed "all factors that may contribute to student body diversity." We described the various types of diversity that the law school sought:

> The law school's policy makes clear there are many possible bases for diversity admissions, and provides examples of admittees who have lived or traveled widely abroad, are fluent in several languages, have overcome personal adversity and family hardship, have

exceptional records of extensive community service, and have had successful careers in other fields.

The Court quoted the articulation of diversity from Justice Powell's opinion in *Regents of the University of California v. Bakke*, 438 U.S. 265 (1978), noting that "it is not an interest in simple ethnic diversity, in which a specified percentage of the student body is in effect guaranteed to be members of selected ethnic groups, that can justify the use of race." Instead, what was upheld in *Grutter* was consideration of "a far broader array of qualifications and characteristics of which racial or ethnic origin is but a single though important element."

The entire gist of the analysis in *Grutter* was that the admissions program at issue there focused on each applicant as an individual, and not simply as a member of a particular racial group. The classification of applicants by race upheld in *Grutter* was only as part of a "highly individualized, holistic review," As the Court explained, "the importance of this individualized consideration in the context of a race-conscious admissions program is paramount." The point of the narrow tailoring analysis in which the *Grutter* Court engaged was to ensure that the use of racial classifications was indeed part of a broader assessment of diversity, and not simply an effort to achieve racial balance, which the Court explained would be "patently unconstitutional."

In the present cases, by contrast, race is not considered as part of a broader effort to achieve "exposure to widely diverse people, cultures, ideas, and viewpoints," race, for some students, is determinative standing alone. The districts argue that other factors, such as student preferences, affect assignment decisions under their plans, but under each plan when race comes into play, it is decisive by itself. It is not simply one factor weighed with others in reaching a decision, as in *Grutter*; it is *the* factor. Like the University of Michigan undergraduate plan struck down in *Gratz*, 539 U.S. at 275, the plans here "do not provide for a meaningful individualized review of applicants" but instead rely on racial classifications in a "nonindividualized, mechanical" way.

Even when it comes to race, the plans here employ only a limited notion of diversity, viewing race exclusively in white/nonwhite terms in Seattle and black/ "other" terms in Jefferson County.

In upholding the admissions plan in *Grutter*, though, this Court relied upon considerations unique to institutions of higher education, noting that in light of "the expansive freedoms of speech and thought associated with the university environment, universities occupy a special niche in our constitutional tradition." The Court explained that "context matters" in applying strict scrutiny, and repeatedly noted that it was addressing the use of race "in the context of higher education." The Court in *Grutter* expressly articulated key limitations on its holding—defining a specific type of broad-based diversity and noting the unique context of higher education—but these limitations were largely disregarded by the lower courts in extending *Grutter* to uphold race-based assignments in elementary and secondary schools. The present cases are not governed by *Grutter*.

B

Perhaps recognizing that reliance on *Grutter* cannot sustain their plans, both school districts assert additional interests, distinct from the interest upheld in *Grutter*, to justify their race-based assignments. In briefing and argument before this Court, Seattle contends that its use of race helps to reduce racial concentration in schools and to ensure that racially concentrated housing patterns do not prevent nonwhite students from having access to the most desirable schools. Jefferson County has articulated a similar goal, phrasing its interest in terms of educating its students "in a racially integrated environment." Each school district argues that educational and broader socialization benefits flow from a racially diverse learning environment, and each contends that because the diversity they seek is racial diversity—not the broader diversity at issue in *Grutter*—it makes sense to promote that interest directly by relying on race alone.

The parties and their *amici* dispute whether racial diversity in schools in fact has a marked impact on test scores and other objective yardsticks or achieves intangible socialization benefits. The debate is not one we need to resolve, however, because it is clear that the racial classifications employed by the districts are not narrowly tailored to the goal of achieving the educational and social benefits asserted to flow from racial diversity. In design and operation, the plans are directed only to racial balance, pure and simple, an objective this Court has repeatedly condemned as illegitimate.

In *Grutter*, the number of minority students the school sought to admit was an undefined "meaningful number" necessary to achieve a genuinely diverse student body. Although the matter was the subject of disagreement on the Court, the majority concluded that the law school did not count back from its applicant pool to arrive at the "meaningful number" it regarded as necessary to diversify its student body. Here the racial balance the districts seek is a defined range set solely by reference to the demographics of the respective school districts.

This working backward to achieve a particular type of racial balance, rather than working forward from some demonstration of the level of diversity that provides the purported benefits, is a fatal flaw under our existing precedent. We have many times over reaffirmed that "racial balance is not to be achieved for its own sake." *Grutter* itself reiterated that "outright racial balancing" is "patently unconstitutional."

Accepting racial balancing as a compelling state interest would justify the imposition of racial proportionality throughout American society, contrary to our repeated recognition that "at the heart of the Constitution's guarantee of equal protection lies the simple command that the Government must treat citizens as individuals, not as simply components of a racial, religious, sexual or national class." Allowing racial balancing as a compelling end in itself would "effectively assure that race will always be relevant in American life, and that the 'ultimate goal' of 'eliminating entirely from governmental decisionmaking such irrelevant factors as a human being's race' will never be achieved." An interest "linked to nothing other than proportional representation of various races would support indefinite use of racial classifications, employed first to obtain the appropriate mixture of racial views and then to ensure that the program continues to reflect that mixture."

The principle that racial balancing is not permitted is one of substance, not semantics. Racial balancing is not transformed from "patently unconstitutional" to a compelling state interest simply by relabeling it "racial diversity." While the school districts use various verbal formulations to describe the interest they seek to promote—racial diversity, avoidance of racial isolation, racial integration—they offer no definition of the interest that suggests it differs from racial balance.

Jefferson County phrases its interest as "racial integration," but integration certainly does not require the sort of racial proportionality reflected in its plan. Even in the context of mandatory desegregation, we have stressed that racial proportionality is not required, *Swann v. Charlotte-Mecklenburg Bd. of Ed.*, 402 U.S. 1, 24 (1971) ("The constitutional command to desegregate schools does not mean that every school in every community must always reflect the racial composition of the school system as a whole"), and here Jefferson County has already been found to have eliminated the vestiges of its prior segregated school system.

The en banc Ninth Circuit declared that "when a racially diverse school system is the goal (or racial concentration or isolation is the problem), there is no more effective means than a consideration of race to achieve the solution." For the foregoing reasons, this conclusory argument cannot sustain the plans. However closely related race-based assignments may be to achieving racial balance, that itself cannot be the goal, whether labeled "racial diversity" or anything else. To the extent the objective is sufficient diversity so that students see fellow students as individuals rather than solely as members of a racial group, using means that treat students solely as members of a racial group is fundamentally at cross-purposes with that end.

The districts have also failed to show that they considered methods other than explicit racial classifications to achieve their stated goals. Narrow tailoring requires "serious, good faith consideration of workable race-neutral alternatives," *Grutter, supra,* at 339, and yet in Seattle several alternative assignment plans—many of which would not have used express racial classifications—were rejected with little or no consideration. Jefferson County has failed to present any evidence that it considered alternatives, even though the district already claims that its goals are achieved primarily through means other than the racial classifications.

IV

Justice Breyer's dissent takes a different approach to these cases, one that fails to ground the result it would reach in law. Instead, it selectively relies on inapplicable precedent and even dicta while dismissing contrary holdings, alters and misapplies our well-established legal framework for assessing equal protection challenges to express racial classifications, and greatly exaggerates the consequences of today's decision.

If the need for the racial classifications embraced by the school districts is unclear, even on the districts' own terms, the costs are undeniable. "Distinctions between citizens solely because of their ancestry are by their very nature odious to a free people whose institutions are founded upon the doctrine of equality." Government action dividing us by race is inherently suspect because such classifications promote "notions of racial inferiority and lead to a politics of racial hostility, reinforce the belief, held by too many for too much of our history, that individuals should be judged by the color of their skin," and "endorse race-based reasoning and the conception of a Nation divided into racial blocs, thus contributing to an escalation of racial hostility and conflict." As the Court explained in *Rice v. Cayetano*, 528 U.S. 495, 517 (2000), "one of the principal reasons race is treated as a forbidden classification is that it demeans the dignity and worth of a person to be judged by ancestry instead of by his or her own merit and essential qualities."

All this is true enough in the contexts in which these statements were made—government contracting, voting districts, allocation of broadcast licenses, and electing state officers—but when it comes to using race to assign children to schools, history will be heard. In *Brown v. Board of Education*, 347 U.S. 483 (1954) (*Brown I*), we held that segregation deprived black children of equal educational opportunities regardless of whether school facilities and other tangible factors were equal, because government classification and separation on grounds of race themselves denoted inferiority. It was not the inequality of the facilities but the fact of legally separating children on the basis of race on which the Court relied to find a constitutional violation in 1954. The next Term, we accordingly stated that "full compliance" with *Brown I* required school districts "to achieve a system of determining admission to the public schools *on a nonracial basis.*"

The parties and their *amici* debate which side is more faithful to the heritage of *Brown*, but the position of the plaintiffs in *Brown* was spelled out in their brief and could not have been clearer: "The Fourteenth Amendment prevents states from according differential treatment to American children on the basis of their color or race." What do the racial classifications at issue here do, if not accord differential treatment on the basis of race? As counsel who appeared before this Court for the plaintiffs in *Brown* put it: "We have one fundamental contention which we will seek to develop in the course of this argument, and that contention is that no State has any authority under the equal-protection clause of the Fourteenth Amendment to use race as a factor in affording educational opportunities among its citizens." There is no ambiguity in that statement. And it was that position that prevailed in this Court, which emphasized in its remedial opinion that what was "at stake is the personal interest of the plaintiffs in admission to public schools as soon as practicable *on a nondiscriminatory basis,*" and what was required was "determining admission to the public schools *on a nonracial basis.*" What do the racial classifications do in these cases, if not determine admission to a public school on a racial basis? Before *Brown*, schoolchildren were told where they could and could not go to school based on the color of their skin. The school districts in these cases have not carried the heavy burden of demonstrating that we should allow this once again—even for very different reasons. For schools that never segregated on the basis of race, such as Seattle, or that have removed the vestiges of past segregation, such as Jefferson County, the way "to achieve a system of determining admission to the public schools on a nonracial basis," is to stop assigning students on a racial basis. The way to stop discrimination on the basis of race is to stop discriminating on the basis of race.

The judgments of the Courts of Appeals for the Sixth and Ninth Circuits are reversed, and the cases are remanded for further proceedings. It is so ordered.

Justice KENNEDY, *concurring in part* and *concurring in the judgment.*

The Nation's schools strive to teach that our strength comes from people of different races, creeds, and cultures uniting in commitment to the freedom of all. In these cases two school districts in different parts of the country seek to teach that principle by having classrooms that reflect the racial makeup of the surrounding community. That the school districts consider these plans to be necessary should remind us our highest aspirations are yet unfulfilled. But the solutions mandated by these school districts must themselves be lawful. To make race matter now so that it might not matter later may entrench the very prejudices we seek to overcome. In my view the state-mandated racial classifications at issue, official labels proclaiming the race of all persons in a broad class of citizens—elementary school students in one case, high school students in another—are unconstitutional as the cases now come to us.

I agree with the Chief Justice that we have jurisdiction to decide the cases before us and join Parts I and II of the Court's opinion. I also join Parts III-A and III-C for reasons provided below. My views do not allow me to join the balance of the opinion by the Chief Justice, which seems to me to be inconsistent in both its approach and its implications with the history, meaning, and reach of the Equal Protection Clause. Justice Breyer's dissenting opinion, on the other hand, rests on what in my respectful submission is a misuse and mistaken interpretation of our precedents. This leads it to advance propositions that, in my view, are both erroneous and in fundamental conflict with basic equal protection principles. As a consequence, this separate opinion is necessary to set forth my conclusions in the two cases before the Court.

The opinion of the Court and Justice Breyer's dissenting opinion (hereinafter dissent) describe in detail the history of integration efforts in Louisville and Seattle. These plans classify individuals by race and allocate benefits and burdens on that basis; and as a result, they are to be subjected to strict scrutiny. The dissent finds that the school districts have identified a compelling interest in increasing diversity, including for the purpose of avoiding racial isolation. The plurality, by contrast, does not acknowledge that the school districts have identified a compelling interest here. For this reason, among others, I do not join Parts III-B and IV.

Diversity, depending on its meaning and definition, is a compelling educational goal a school district may pursue.

It is well established that when a governmental policy is subjected to strict scrutiny, "the government has the burden of proving that racial classifications 'are narrowly tailored measures that further compelling governmental interests.'" "Absent searching judicial inquiry into the justification for such race-based measures, there is simply no way of determining what classifications are 'benign' or 'remedial' and what classifications are in fact motivated by illegitimate notions of racial inferiority or simple racial politics." And the inquiry into less restrictive alternatives demanded by the narrow tailoring analysis requires in many cases a thorough understanding of how a plan works. The government bears the burden of justifying its use of individual racial classifications. As part of that burden it must establish, in detail, how decisions based on an individual student's race are made in a challenged governmental program.

II

Our Nation from the inception has sought to preserve and expand the promise of liberty and equality on which it was founded. Today we enjoy a society that is remarkable in its openness and opportunity. Yet our tradition is to go beyond present achievements, however significant, and to recognize and confront the flaws and injustices that remain. This is especially true when we seek assurance that opportunity is not denied on account of race. The enduring hope is that race should not matter; the reality is that too often it does.

This is by way of preface to my respectful submission that parts of the opinion by the Chief Justice imply an all-too-unyielding insistence that race cannot be a factor in instances when, in my view, it may be taken into account. The plurality opinion is too dismissive of the legitimate interest government has in ensuring all people have equal opportunity regardless of their race. The plurality's postulate that "the way to stop discrimination on the basis of race is to stop discriminating on the basis of race," is not sufficient to decide these cases. Fifty years of experience since *Brown v. Board of Education* should teach us that the problem before us defies so easy a solution. School districts can seek to reach *Brown*'s objective of equal educational opportunity. The plurality opinion is at least open to the interpretation that the Constitution requires school districts to ignore the problem of *de facto* resegregation in schooling. I cannot endorse that conclusion. To the extent the plurality opinion suggests the Constitution mandates that state and local school authorities must accept the status quo of racial isolation in schools, it is, in my view, profoundly mistaken.

The statement by Justice Harlan that "our Constitution is color-blind" was most certainly justified in the context of his dissent in *Plessy v. Ferguson*. The Court's decision in that case was a grievous error it took far too long to overrule. *Plessy*, of course, concerned official classification by race applicable to all persons who sought to use railway carriages. And, as an aspiration, Justice Harlan's axiom must command our assent. In the real world, it is regrettable to say, it cannot be a universal constitutional principle.

In the administration of public schools by the state and local authorities it is permissible to consider the racial makeup of schools and to adopt general policies to encourage a diverse student body, one aspect of which is its racial composition. If school authorities are concerned that the student-body compositions of certain schools interfere with the objective of offering an equal educational opportunity to all of their students, they are free to devise race-conscious measures to address the problem in a general way and without treating each student in different fashion solely on the basis of a systematic, individual typing by race.

School boards may pursue the goal of bringing together students of diverse backgrounds and races through other means, including strategic site selection of new schools; drawing attendance zones with general recognition of the demographics of neighborhoods; allocating resources for special programs; recruiting students and faculty in a targeted fashion; and tracking enrollments, performance, and other statistics by race. These mechanisms are race conscious but do not lead to different treatment based on a classification that tells each student he or she is to be defined by race, so it is unlikely any of them would demand strict scrutiny to be found permissible.

C

The idea that if race is the problem, race is the instrument with which to solve it cannot be accepted as an analytical leap forward. And if this is a frustrating duality of the Equal Protection Clause it simply reflects the duality of our history and our attempts to promote freedom in a world that sometimes seems set against it. Under our Constitution the individual, child or adult, can find his own identity, can define her own persona, without state intervention that classifies on the basis of his race or the color of her skin.

This Nation has a moral and ethical obligation to fulfill its historic commitment to creating an integrated society that ensures equal opportunity for all of its children. A compelling interest exists in avoiding racial isolation, an interest that a school district, in its discretion and expertise, may choose to pursue. Likewise, a district may consider it a compelling interest to achieve a diverse student population. Race may be one component of that diversity, but other demographic factors, plus special talents and needs, should also be considered. What the government is not permitted to do, absent a showing of necessity not made here, is to classify every student on the basis of race and to assign each of them to schools based on that classification. Crude measures of this sort threaten to reduce children to racial chits valued and traded according to one school's supply and another's demand.

That statement, to be sure, invites this response: A sense of stigma may already become the fate of those separated out by circumstances beyond their immediate control. But to this the replication must be: Even so, measures other than differential treatment based on racial typing of individuals first must be exhausted.

The decision today should not prevent school districts from continuing the important work of bringing together students of different racial, ethnic, and economic backgrounds. Due to a variety of factors—some influenced by government, some not—neighborhoods in our communities do not reflect the diversity of our Nation as a whole. Those entrusted with directing our public schools can bring to bear the creativity of experts, parents, administrators, and other concerned citizens to find a way to achieve the compelling interests they face without resorting to widespread governmental allocation of benefits and burdens on the basis of racial classifications.

With this explanation I concur in the judgment of the Court.

Justice BREYER, with whom Justice STEVENS, Justice SOUTER, and Justice GINSBURG join, *dissenting.*

These cases consider the longstanding efforts of two local school boards to integrate their public schools. The school board plans before us resemble many others adopted in the last 50 years by primary and secondary schools throughout the Nation. All of those plans represent local efforts to bring about the kind of racially integrated education that *Brown v. Board of Education,* long ago promised— efforts that this Court has repeatedly required, permitted, and encouraged local authorities to undertake. This Court has recognized that the public interests at stake in such cases are "compelling." We have approved of "narrowly tailored" plans that are no less race-conscious than the plans before us. And we have understood that the Constitution *permits* local communities to adopt desegregation plans even where it does not *require* them to do so.

The plans in both Louisville and Seattle grow out of these earlier remedial efforts. Both districts faced problems that reflected initial periods of severe racial segregation, followed by such remedial efforts as busing, followed by evidence of resegregation, followed by a need to end busing and encourage the return of suburban students through increased student choice. When formulating the plans under review, both districts drew upon their considerable experience with earlier plans, having revised their policies periodically in light of that experience. Both districts rethought their methods over time and explored a wide range of other means, including non-race-conscious policies. Both districts also considered elaborate studies and consulted widely within their communities.

II

The Legal Standard. A longstanding and unbroken line of legal authority tells us that the Equal Protection Clause permits local school boards to use race-conscious criteria to achieve positive race-related goals, even when the Constitution does not compel it. Because of its importance, I shall repeat what this Court said about the matter in *Swann*. Chief Justice Burger, on behalf of a unanimous Court in a case of exceptional importance, wrote:

> School authorities are traditionally charged with broad power to formulate and implement educational policy and might well conclude, for example, that in order to prepare students to live in a pluralistic society each school should have a prescribed ratio of Negro to white students reflecting the proportion for the district as a whole. To do this as an educational policy is within the broad discretionary powers of school authorities.

The statement was not a technical holding in the case. But the Court set forth in *Swann* a basic principle of constitutional law — a principle of law that has found "wide acceptance in the legal culture."

Thus, in *North Carolina Bd. of Ed. v. Swann*, 402 U.S. 43, 45 (1971), this Court, citing *Swann*, restated the point. "School authorities," the Court said, "have wide discretion in formulating school policy, and as a matter of educational policy school authorities may well conclude that some kind of racial balance in the schools is desirable quite apart from any constitutional requirements." Then-Justice Rehnquist echoed this view in *Bustop, Inc. v. Los Angeles Bd. of Ed.*, 439 U.S. 1380, 1383 (1978), making clear that he too believed that *Swann*'s statement reflected settled law: "While I have the gravest doubts that a state supreme court was *required* by the United States Constitution to take the desegregation action that it has taken in this case, I have very little doubt that it was *permitted* by that Constitution to take such action."

These statements nowhere suggest that this freedom is limited to school districts where court-ordered desegregation measures are also in effect. Indeed, in *McDaniel*, a case decided the same day as *Swann*, a group of parents challenged a race-conscious student assignment plan that the Clarke County School Board had *voluntarily* adopted as a remedy without a court order (though under federal agency pressure — pressure Seattle also encountered). The plan required that each elementary school in the district maintain 20% to 40% enrollment of African-American students, corresponding to the racial composition of the district. This Court upheld the plan, rejecting the parents' argument that "a person may not be *included* or *excluded* solely because he is a Negro or because he is white."

This Court has also held that school districts may be required by federal statute to undertake race-conscious desegregation efforts even when there is no likelihood that *de jure* segregation can be shown. In *Board of Ed. of City School Dist. of New York v. Harris*, 444 U.S. 130, 148-149 (1979), the Court concluded that a federal statute required school districts receiving certain federal funds to remedy faculty segregation, even though in this Court's view the racial disparities in the affected schools were purely *de facto* and would not have been actionable under the Equal Protection Clause. Not even the dissenters thought the race-conscious remedial program posed a *constitutional* problem. Lower state and federal courts had considered the matter settled and uncontroversial even before this Court decided *Swann*. Indeed, in 1968, the Illinois Supreme Court rejected an equal protection challenge to a race-conscious state law seeking to undo *de facto* segregation:

> To support their claim, the defendants heavily rely on three Federal cases, each of which held, no State law being involved, that a local school board does not have an affirmative constitutional duty to act to alleviate racial imbalance in the schools that it did not cause." However, the question as to whether the constitution requires a local school board, or a State, to act to undo *de facto* school segregation is simply not here concerned. The issue here is whether the constitution permits, rather than prohibits, voluntary State action aimed toward reducing and eventually eliminating *de facto* school segregation.
>
> "State laws or administrative policies, directed toward the reduction and eventual elimination of *de facto* segregation of children in the schools and racial imbalance, have been approved by every high State court which has considered the issue. Similarly, the Federal courts which have considered the issue have recognized that voluntary programs of local school authorities designed to alleviate *de facto* segregation and racial imbalance in the schools are not constitutionally forbidden.

That *Swann*'s legal statement should find such broad acceptance is not surprising. For *Swann* is predicated upon a well-established legal view of the Fourteenth Amendment. That view understands the basic objective of those who wrote the Equal Protection Clause as forbidding practices that lead to racial exclusion. The Amendment sought to bring into American society as full members those whom the Nation had previously held in slavery.

There is reason to believe that those who drafted an Amendment with this basic purpose in mind would have understood the legal and practical difference between the use of race-conscious criteria in defiance of that purpose, namely to keep the races apart, and the use of race-conscious criteria to further that purpose, namely to bring the races together.

Several of these cases were significantly more restrictive than *Swann* in respect to the degree of leniency the Fourteenth Amendment grants to programs designed to *include* people of all races. *See, e.g., Adarand, supra; Gratz, supra; Grutter, supra.* But that legal circumstance cannot make a critical difference here for two separate reasons.

First, no case—not *Adarand, Gratz, Grutter,* or any other—has ever held that the test of "strict scrutiny" means that all racial classifications—no matter whether they seek to include or exclude—must in practice be treated the same. The Court did not say in *Adarand* or in *Johnson* or in *Grutter* that it was overturning *Swann* or its central constitutional principle.

Indeed, in its more recent opinions, the Court recognized that the "fundamental purpose" of strict scrutiny review is to "take relevant differences" between "fundamentally different situations into account." The Court made clear that "strict scrutiny does not treat dissimilar race-based decisions as though they were equally objectionable." It added that the fact that a law "treats a person unequally because of his or her race says nothing about the ultimate validity of any particular law." And the Court, using the very phrase that Justice Marshall had used to describe strict scrutiny's application to any *exclusionary* use of racial criteria, sought to "*dispel the notion* that strict scrutiny" is as likely to condemn *inclusive* uses of "race-conscious" criteria as it is to invalidate *exclusionary* uses. That is, it is *not* in all circumstances "strict in theory, but fatal in fact."

The Court in *Grutter* elaborated: "Strict scrutiny is not 'strict in theory, but fatal in fact.' Although all governmental uses of race are subject to strict scrutiny, not all are invalidated by it." "Context matters when reviewing race-based governmental action under the Equal Protection Clause. Not every decision influenced by race is equally objectionable, and strict scrutiny is designed to provide a framework for carefully examining the importance and the sincerity of the reasons advanced by the governmental decisionmaker for the use of race in that particular context." The Court's holding in *Grutter* demonstrates that the Court meant what it said, for the Court upheld an elite law school's race-conscious admissions program.

The cases to which the plurality refers, though all applying strict scrutiny, do not treat exclusive and inclusive uses the same. Rather, they apply the strict scrutiny test in a manner that is "fatal in fact" only to racial classifications that harmfully *exclude;* they apply the test in a manner that is *not* fatal in fact to racial classifications that seek to *include.*

The plurality cannot avoid this simple fact. Today's opinion reveals that the plurality would rewrite this Court's prior jurisprudence, at least in practical application, transforming the "strict scrutiny" test into a rule that is fatal in fact across the board. In doing so, the plurality parts company from this Court's prior cases, and it takes from local government the longstanding legal right to use race-conscious criteria for inclusive purposes in limited ways.

Second, as *Grutter* specified, "context matters when reviewing race-based governmental action under the Equal Protection Clause." And contexts differ dramatically one from the other. Governmental use of race-based criteria can arise in the context of, for example, census forms, research expenditures for diseases, assignments of police officers patrolling predominantly minority-race neighborhoods, efforts to desegregate racially segregated schools, policies that favor minorities when distributing goods or services in short supply, actions that create majority-minority electoral districts, peremptory strikes that remove potential jurors on the basis of race, and others. Given the significant differences among these contexts, it would be surprising if the law required an identically strict legal test for evaluating the constitutionality of race-based criteria as to each of them.

Here, the context is one in which school districts seek to advance or to maintain racial integration in primary and secondary schools. It is a context, as *Swann* makes clear, where history has required special administrative remedies. And it is a context in which the school boards' plans simply set race-conscious limits at the outer boundaries of a broad range.

This context is *not* a context that involves the use of race to decide who will receive goods or services that are normally distributed on the basis of merit and which are in short supply. It is not one in which race-conscious limits stigmatize or exclude; the limits at issue do not pit the races against each other or otherwise significantly exacerbate racial tensions. They do not impose burdens unfairly upon members of one race alone but instead seek benefits for members of all races alike. The context here is one of racial limits that seek, not to keep the races apart, but to bring them together.

If one examines the context more specifically, one finds that the districts' plans reflect efforts to overcome a history of segregation, embody the results of broad experience and community consultation, seek to expand student choice while reducing the need for mandatory busing, and use race-conscious criteria in highly limited ways that diminish the use of race compared to preceding integration efforts. They do not seek to award a scarce commodity on the basis of merit, for they are not magnet schools; rather, by design and in practice, they offer substantially equivalent academic programs and electives. Although some parents or children prefer some schools over others, school popularity has varied significantly over the years. In a word, the school plans under review do not involve the kind of race-based harm that has led this Court, in other contexts, to find the use of race-conscious criteria unconstitutional.

In my view, this contextual approach to scrutiny is altogether fitting. I believe that the law requires application here of a standard of review that is not "strict" in the traditional sense of that word, although it does require the careful review I have just described. Apparently Justice Kennedy also agrees that strict scrutiny would not apply in respect to certain "race-conscious" school board policies.

Nonetheless, in light of *Grutter* and other precedents, I shall adopt the first alternative. I shall apply the version of strict scrutiny that those cases embody. I shall consequently ask whether the school boards in Seattle and Louisville adopted these plans to serve a "compelling governmental interest" and, if so, whether the plans are "narrowly tailored" to achieve that interest. If the plans survive this strict review, they would survive less exacting review *a fortiori*. Hence, I conclude that the plans before us pass both parts of the strict scrutiny test. Consequently I must conclude that the plans here are permitted under the Constitution.

Until today, this Court understood the Constitution as affording the people, acting through their elected representatives, freedom to select the use of "race-conscious" criteria from among their available options. Today, however, the Court restricts (and some Members would eliminate) that leeway. I fear the consequences of doing so for the law, for the schools, for the democratic process, and for America's efforts to create, out of its diversity, one Nation.

VI

To show that the school assignment plans here meet the requirements of the Constitution, I have written at exceptional length. But that length is necessary. I cannot refer to the history of the plans in these cases to justify the use of race-conscious criteria without describing that history in full. I cannot rely upon *Swann*'s statement that the use of race-conscious limits is permissible without showing, rather than simply asserting, that the statement represents a constitutional principle firmly rooted in federal and state law. Nor can I explain my disagreement with the Court's holding and the plurality's opinion, without offering a detailed account of the arguments they propound and the consequences they risk.

Thus, the opinion's reasoning is long. But its conclusion is short: The plans before us satisfy the requirements of the Equal Protection Clause. And it is the plurality's opinion, not this dissent that "fails to ground the result it would reach in law."

Finally, what of the hope and promise of *Brown*? For much of this Nation's history, the races remained divided. It was not long ago that people of different races drank from separate fountains, rode on separate buses, and studied in separate schools. In this Court's finest hour, *Brown v. Board of Education* challenged this history and helped to change it. For *Brown* held out a promise. It was a promise embodied in three Amendments designed to make citizens of slaves. It was the promise of true racial equality—not as a matter of fine words on paper, but as a matter of everyday life in the Nation's cities and schools. It was about the nature of a democracy that must work for all Americans. It sought one law, one Nation, one people, not simply as a matter of legal principle but in terms of how we actually live.

The last half-century has witnessed great strides toward racial equality, but we have not yet realized the promise of *Brown*. To invalidate the plans under review is to threaten the promise of *Brown*. The plurality's position, I fear, would break that promise. This is a decision that the Court and the Nation will come to regret.

I must dissent.

Note and Question

1. Grutter *'s Vitality.* Does the *Parents Involved* decision affect *Grutter*'s continuing vitality? Based on *Grutter*, would you have expected the *Parents Involved* case to have been decided differently? If so, how do you explain the result in *Parents Involved*?

2. *The* Fisher *Case.* In *Fisher v. University of Texas at Austin*, 570 U.S. 297 (2013) (*Fisher I*), the Court, in a 7-1 decision written by Justice Kennedy, affirmed the central precepts of *Bakke*, *Gratz*, and *Grutter*, holding that institutions of higher education could seek to achieve the educational benefits of diversity, so long as their policies meet judicial standards under strict scrutiny. The Court vacated the decision and remanded the case to the Court of Appeals to determine if the University had met its heavy evidentiary burden under strict scrutiny. Justice Ginsburg dissented, finding that the Court of Appeals had applied the proper analysis. Going forward, it appears a majority of the Court will reject the use of

race in higher education admissions policies, unless the government can meet rigorous narrow-tailoring analysis, including proof that the government could not achieve its compelling purpose using race-neutral alternatives. The majority wrote: "The reviewing court must ultimately be satisfied that no workable race-neutral alternatives would produce the educational benefits of diversity."

Fisher v. University of Texas at Austin

579 U.S. _ (2016)

Justice KENNEDY delivered the opinion of the Court.

The Court is asked once again to consider whether the race-conscious admissions program at the University of Texas is lawful under the Equal Protection Clause. The University of Texas at Austin (or University) relies upon a complex system of admissions that has undergone significant evolution over the past two decades. Until 1996, the University made its admissions decisions primarily based on a measure called "Academic Index" (or AI), which it calculated by combining an applicant's SAT score and academic performance in high school. In assessing applicants, preference was given to racial minorities.

In 1996, the Court of Appeals for the Fifth Circuit invalidated this admissions system, holding that any consideration of race in college admissions violates the Equal Protection Clause. One year later the University adopted a new admissions policy. Instead of considering race, the University began making admissions decisions based on an applicant's AI and his or her "Personal Achievement Index" (PAI). The PAI was a numerical score based on a holistic review of an application. Included in the number were the applicant's essays, leadership and work experience, extracurricular activities, community service, and other "special characteristics" that might give the admissions committee insight into a student's background. Consistent with *Hopwood*, race was not a consideration in calculating an applicant's AI or PAI.

The Texas Legislature responded to Hopwood as well. It enacted H. B. 588, commonly known as the Top Ten Percent Law. As its name suggests, the Top Ten Percent Law guarantees college admission to students who graduate from a Texas high school in the top 10 percent of their class. Those students may choose to attend any of the public universities in the State. The University implemented the Top Ten Percent Law in 1998. After first admitting any student who qualified for admission under that law, the University filled the remainder of its incoming freshman class using a combination of an applicant's AI and PAI scores—again, without considering race.

The University used this admissions system until 2003, when this Court decided the companion cases of *Grutter v. Bollinger*, 539 U. S. 306, and *Gratz v. Bollinger*, 539 U. S. 244. In *Gratz*, this Court struck down the University of Michigan's undergraduate system of admissions, which at the time allocated predetermined points to racial minority candidates. In *Grutter*, however, the Court upheld the University of Michigan Law School's system of holistic review—a system that did not mechanically assign points but rather treated race as a relevant feature within the broader context of a candidate's application. In upholding this nuanced use of race, *Grutter* implicitly overruled *Hopwood*'s categorical prohibition.

In the wake of *Grutter*, the University embarked upon a year-long study seeking to ascertain whether its admissions policy was allowing it to provide "the educational benefits of a diverse student body to all of the University's undergraduate students." The University concluded that its admissions policy was not providing these benefits.

To change its system, the University submitted a proposal to the Board of Regents that requested permission to begin taking race into consideration as one of "the many ways in which an academically qualified individual might contribute to, and benefit from, the rich, diverse, and challenging educational environment of the University." After the board approved the proposal, the University adopted a new admissions policy to implement it. The University has continued to use that admissions policy to this day.

Although the University's new admissions policy was a direct result of *Grutter*, it is not identical to the policy this Court approved in that case. Instead, consistent with the State's legislative directive, the University continues to fill a significant majority of its class through the Top Ten Percent Plan (or Plan). Today, up to 75 percent of the places in the freshman class are filled through the Plan. As a practical matter, this 75 percent cap, which has now been fixed by statute, means that, while the Plan continues to be referenced as a "Top Ten Percent Plan," a student actually needs to finish in the top seven or eight percent of his or her class in order to be admitted under this category.

The University did adopt an approach similar to the one in *Grutter* for the remaining 25 percent or so of the incoming class. This portion of the class continues to be admitted based on a combination of their AI and PAI scores. Now, however, race is given weight as a sub-factor within the PAI. The PAI is a number from 1 to 6 (6 is the best) that is based on two primary components. The first component is the average score a reader gives the applicant on two required essays. The second component is a full-file review that results in another 1-to-6 score, the "Personal Achievement Score" or PAS. The PAS is determined by a separate reader, who (1) rereads the applicant's required essays, (2) reviews any supplemental information the applicant submits (letters of recommendation, resumes, an additional optional essay, writing samples, artwork, etc.), and (3) evaluates the applicant's potential contributions to the University's student body based on the applicant's leadership experience, extracurricular activities, awards/honors, community service, and other "special circumstances." "Special circumstances" include the socioeconomic status of the applicant's family, the socioeconomic status of the applicant's school, the applicant's family responsibilities, whether the applicant lives in a single-parent home, the applicant's SAT score in relation to the average SAT score at the applicant's school, the language spoken at the applicant's home, and, finally, the applicant's race. Both the essay readers and the full-file readers who assign applicants their PAI undergo extensive training to ensure that they are scoring applicants consistently. The Admissions Office undertakes regular "reliability analyses" to "measure the frequency of readers scoring within one point of each other." Both the intensive training and the reliability analyses aim to ensure that similarly situated applicants are being treated identically regardless of which admissions officer reads the file.

Once the essay and full-file readers have calculated each applicant's AI and PAI scores, admissions officers from each school within the University set a cutoff PAI/AI score combination for admission, and then admit all of the applicants who are above that cutoff point. In setting the cutoff, those admissions officers only know how many applicants received a given PAI/AI score combination. They do not know what factors went into calculating those applicants' scores. The admissions officers who make the final decision as to whether a particular applicant will be admitted make that decision without knowing the applicant's race. Race enters the admissions process, then, at one stage and one stage only—the calculation of the PAS.

Therefore, although admissions officers can consider race as a positive feature of a minority student's application, there is no dispute that race is but a "factor of a factor of a factor" in the holistic-review calculus. Furthermore, consideration of race is contextual and does not operate as a mechanical plus factor for underrepresented minorities. There is also no dispute that race, when considered in conjunction with other aspects of an applicant's background, can alter an applicant's PAS score. Thus, race, in this indirect fashion, considered with all of the other factors that make up an applicant's AI and PAI scores, can make a difference to whether an application is accepted or rejected.

Petitioner Abigail Fisher applied for admission to the University's 2008 freshman class. She was not in the top 10 percent of her high school class, so she was evaluated for admission through holistic, full-file review. Petitioner's application was rejected. Petitioner then filed suit alleging that the University's consideration of race as part of its holistic-review process disadvantaged her and other Caucasian applicants, in violation of the Equal Protection Clause.

Fisher I set forth three controlling principles relevant to assessing the constitutionality of a public university's affirmative-action program. First, "because racial characteristics seldom provide a relevant basis for disparate treatment," *Richmond v. J. A. Croson Co.*, 488 U. S. 469, 505 (1989), "race may not be considered by a university unless the admissions process can withstand strict scrutiny." Strict scrutiny requires the university to demonstrate with clarity that its "purpose or interest is both constitutionally permissible and substantial, and that its use of the classification is necessary to the accomplishment of its purpose." Second, *Fisher I* confirmed that "the decision to pursue 'the educational benefits that flow from student body diversity' is, in substantial measure, an academic judgment to which some, but not complete, judicial deference is proper." A university cannot impose a fixed quota or otherwise "define diversity as 'some specified percentage of a particular group merely because of its race or ethnic origin.'" Once, however, a university gives "a reasoned, principled explanation" for its decision, deference must be given "to the University's conclusion, based on its experience and expertise, that a diverse student body would serve its educational goals." Third, *Fisher I* clarified that no deference is owed when determining whether the use of race is narrowly tailored to achieve the university's permissible goals. A university bears the burden of proving a "nonracial approach" would not promote its interest in the educational benefits of diversity "about as well and at tolerable administrative expense." Though "narrow tailoring does not require exhaustion of every conceivable race-neutral alternative" or "require a university to choose between maintaining a reputation for excellence and fulfilling a commitment to provide educational opportunities to members of all racial groups," it does impose "on the university the ultimate burden of demonstrating" that "race-neutral alternatives" that are both "available" and "workable" "do not suffice."

Fisher I held only that the District Court and the Court of Appeals had "confined the strict scrutiny inquiry in too narrow a way by deferring to the University's good faith in its use of racial classifications." The Court remanded the case, with instructions to evaluate the record under the correct standard and to determine whether the University had made "a showing that its plan is narrowly tailored to achieve" the educational benefits that flow from diversity. On remand, the Court of Appeals determined that the program conformed with the strict scrutiny mandated by *Fisher I*.

In seeking to reverse the judgment, petitioner makes four arguments. First, she argues that the University has not articulated its compelling interest with sufficient clarity. According to petitioner, the University must set forth more precisely the level of minority enrollment that would constitute a "critical mass." Without a clearer sense of what the University's ultimate goal is, petitioner argues, a reviewing court cannot assess whether the University's admissions program is narrowly tailored to that goal. As this Court's cases have made clear, the compelling interest that justifies consideration of race in college admissions is not an interest in enrolling a certain number of minority students. Rather, a university may institute a race-conscious admissions program as a means of obtaining "the educational benefits that flow from student body diversity." Enrolling a diverse student body "promotes cross-racial understanding, helps to break down racial stereotypes, and enables students to better understand persons of different races." Equally important, "student body diversity promotes learning outcomes, and better prepares students for an increasingly diverse workforce and society." Increasing minority enrollment may be instrumental to these educational benefits, but it is not, as petitioner seems to suggest, a goal that can or should be reduced to pure numbers. Indeed, since the University is prohibited from seeking a particular number or quota of minority students, it cannot be faulted for failing to specify the particular level of minority enrollment at which it believes the educational benefits of diversity will be obtained.

On the other hand, asserting an interest in the educational benefits of diversity writ large is insufficient. A university's goals cannot be elusory or amorphous—they must be sufficiently measurable to permit judicial scrutiny of the policies adopted to reach them. In setting forth its current admissions policy, the University articulated concrete and precise goals. On the first page of its 2004 "Proposal to Consider Race and Ethnicity in Admissions," the University identifies the educational values it seeks to realize through its admissions process: the destruction of stereotypes, the "promotion of cross-racial understanding," the preparation of a student body "for an increasingly diverse workforce and society," and the "cultivation of a set of leaders with legitimacy in the eyes of the citizenry." Later, the University explains that it strives to provide an "academic environment" that offers a "robust exchange of ideas, exposure to differing cultures, preparation for the challenges of an increasingly diverse workforce, and acquisition of competencies required of future leaders." All of these objectives, as a general matter, mirror the "compelling interest" this Court has approved in its prior cases.

The University has provided in addition a "reasoned, principled explanation" for its decision to pursue these goals. The University's 39-page proposal was written following a year-long study, which concluded that "the use of race-neutral policies and programs had not been successful" in "providing an educational setting that fosters cross-racial understanding, providing enlightened discussion and learning, or preparing students to function in an increasingly diverse workforce and society." Further support for the University's conclusion can be found in the depositions and affidavits from various admissions officers, all of whom articulate the same, consistent "reasoned, principled explanation." Petitioner's contention that the University's goal was insufficiently concrete is rebutted by the record.

Second, petitioner argues that the University has no need to consider race because it had already "achieved critical mass" by 2003 using the Top Ten Percent Plan and race-neutral holistic review. A university bears a heavy burden in showing that it had not obtained the educational benefits of diversity before it turned to a race-conscious plan. The record reveals, however, that, at the time of petitioner's application, the University could not be faulted on this score. Before changing its policy the University conducted "months of study and deliberation, including retreats, interviews, and review of data," and concluded that "the use of race-neutral policies and programs had not been successful in achieving" sufficient racial diversity at the University. At no stage in this litigation has petitioner challenged the University's good faith in conducting its studies, and the Court properly declines to consider the extra record materials the dissent relies upon, many of which are tangential to this case at best and none of which the University has had a full opportunity to respond to.

The record contains significant evidence, both statistical and anecdotal, in support of the University's position. The demographic data the University has submitted show consistent stagnation in terms of the percentage of minority students enrolling at the University from 1996 to 2002. In 1996, 266 African-American freshmen enrolled, 4.1 percent of the incoming class. In 2003, the year *Grutter* was decided, 267 African-American students enrolled—again, 4.1 percent of the incoming class. The numbers for Hispanic and Asian-American students tell a similar story. Although demographics alone are by no means dispositive, they do have some value as a gauge of the University's ability to enroll students who can offer underrepresented perspectives.

In addition to this broad demographic data, the University put forward evidence that minority students admitted under the Hopwood regime experienced feelings of loneliness and isolation. This evidence is bolstered by further, more nuanced quantitative data. In 2002, 52 percent of undergraduate classes with at least five students had no African-American students enrolled in them, and 27 percent had only one African-American student. In other words, only 21 percent of undergraduate classes with five or more students in them had more than one African-American student enrolled. Twelve percent of these classes had no Hispanic students, as compared to 10 percent in 1996. Though a college must continually reassess its need for race-conscious review, here that assessment appears to have been done with care, and a reasonable determination was made that the University had not yet attained its goals.

Third, petitioner argues that considering race was not necessary because such consideration has had only a "'minimal impact' in advancing the University's compelling interest." The record does not support this assertion. In 2003, 11 percent of the Texas residents enrolled through holistic review were Hispanic and 3.5 percent were African-American. In 2007, by contrast, 16.9 percent of the Texas holistic-review freshmen were Hispanic and 6.8 percent were African-American. Those increases—of 54 percent and 94 percent, respectively—show that consideration of race has had a meaningful, if still limited, effect on the diversity of the University's freshman class. In any event, it is not a failure of narrow tailoring for the impact of racial consideration to be minor. The fact that race consciousness played a role in only a small portion of admissions decisions should be a hallmark of narrow tailoring, not evidence of unconstitutionality.

Petitioner's final argument is that "there are numerous other available race-neutral means of achieving" the University's compelling interest. A review of the record reveals, however, that, at the time of petitioner's application, none of her proposed alternatives was a workable means for the University to attain the benefits of diversity it sought. For example, petitioner suggests that the University could intensify its outreach efforts to African-American and Hispanic applicants. But the University submitted extensive evidence of the many ways in which it already had intensified its outreach efforts to those students. The University has created three new scholarship programs, opened new regional admissions centers, increased its recruitment budget by half-a-million dollars, and organized over 1,000 recruitment events. Perhaps more significantly, in the wake of *Hopwood*, the University spent seven years attempting to achieve its compelling interest using race-neutral holistic review. None of these efforts succeeded, and petitioner fails to offer any meaningful way in which the University could have improved upon them at the time of her application.

Petitioner also suggests altering the weight given to academic and socioeconomic factors in the University's admissions calculus. The University tried, and failed, to increase diversity through enhanced consideration of socioeconomic and other factors. This Court's precedent makes clear that the Equal Protection Clause does not force universities to choose between a diverse student body and a reputation for academic excellence.

Petitioner's final suggestion is to uncap the Top Ten Percent Plan, and admit more—if not all—the University's students through a percentage plan. Petitioner overlooks the fact that the Top Ten Percent Plan, though facially neutral, cannot be understood apart from its basic purpose, which is to boost minority enrollment. Percentage plans are "adopted with racially segregated neighborhoods and schools front and center stage." "It is race consciousness, not blindness to race, that drives such plans." Consequently, petitioner cannot assert simply that increasing the University's reliance on a percentage plan would make its admissions policy more race neutral.

Even if, as a matter of raw numbers, minority enrollment would increase under such a regime, petitioner would be hard-pressed to find convincing support for the proposition that college admissions would be improved if they were a function of class rank alone. That approach would sacrifice all other aspects of diversity in pursuit of enrolling a higher number of minority students. A system that selected every student through class rank alone would exclude the star athlete or musician whose grades suffered because of daily practices and training. It would exclude a talented young biologist who struggled to maintain above-average grades in humanities classes. And it would exclude a student whose freshman-year grades were poor because of a family crisis but who got herself back on track in her last three years of school, only to find herself just outside of the top decile of her class.

These are but examples of the general problem. Class rank is a single metric, and like any single metric, it will capture certain types of people and miss others. This does not imply that students admitted through holistic review are necessarily more capable or more desirable than those admitted through the Top Ten Percent Plan. It merely reflects the fact that privileging one characteristic above all others does not lead to a diverse student body. Indeed, to compel universities to admit students based on class rank alone is in deep tension with the goal of educational diversity as this Court's cases have defined it. At its center, the Top Ten Percent Plan is a blunt instrument that may well compromise the University's own definition of the diversity it seeks.

In addition to these fundamental problems, an admissions policy that relies exclusively on class rank creates perverse incentives for applicants. Percentage plans "encourage parents to keep their children in low-performing segregated schools, and discourage students from taking challenging classes that might lower their grade point averages." For all these reasons, although it may be true that the Top Ten Percent Plan in some instances may provide a path out of poverty for those who excel at schools lacking in resources, the Plan cannot serve as the admissions solution that petitioner suggests. Wherever the balance between percentage plans and holistic review should rest, an effective admissions policy cannot prescribe, realistically, the exclusive use of a percentage plan.

In short, none of petitioner's suggested alternatives—nor other proposals considered or discussed in the course of this litigation—have been shown to be "available" and "workable" means through which the University could have met its educational goals, as it understood and defined them in 2008. The University has thus met its burden of showing that the admissions policy it used at the time it rejected petitioner's application was narrowly tailored.

A university is in large part defined by those intangible "qualities which are incapable of objective measurement but which make for greatness." Considerable deference is owed to a university in defining those intangible characteristics, like student body diversity, that are central to its identity and educational mission. But still, it remains an enduring challenge to our Nation's education system to reconcile the pursuit of diversity with the constitutional promise of equal treatment and dignity.

In short, none of petitioner's suggested alternatives—nor other proposals considered or discussed in the course of this litigation—have been shown to be "available" and "workable" means through which the University could have met its educational goals, as it understood and defined them in 2008. The University has thus met its burden of showing that the admissions policy it used at the time it rejected petitioner's application was narrowly tailored.

A university is in large part defined by those intangible "qualities which are incapable of objective measurement but which make for greatness." Considerable deference is owed to a university in defining those intangible characteristics, like student body diversity, that are central to its identity and educational mission. But still, it remains an enduring challenge to our Nation's education system to reconcile the pursuit of diversity with the constitutional promise of equal treatment and dignity.

In striking this sensitive balance, public universities, like the States themselves, can serve as "laboratories for experimentation." The University of Texas at Austin has a special opportunity to learn and to teach. The University now has at its disposal valuable data about the manner in which different approaches to admissions may foster diversity or instead dilute it. The University must continue to use this data to scrutinize the fairness of its admissions program; to assess whether changing demographics have undermined the need for a race-conscious policy; and to identify the effects, both positive and negative, of the affirmative-action measures it deems necessary.

The Court's affirmance of the University's admissions policy today does not necessarily mean the University may rely on that same policy without refinement. It is the University's ongoing obligation to engage in constant deliberation and continued reflection regarding its admissions policies. The judgment of the Court of Appeals is *affirmed.*

Justice ALITO, with whom THE CHIEF JUSTICE and Justice THOMAS join, *dissenting*.

Something strange has happened since our prior decision in this case. In *Fisher I*, we held that strict scrutiny requires the University of Texas to show that its use of race and ethnicity in making admissions decisions serves compelling interests and that its plan is narrowly tailored to achieve those ends. Rejecting the argument that we should defer to UT's judgment on those matters, we made it clear that UT was obligated (1) to identify the interests justifying its plan with enough specificity to permit a reviewing court to determine whether the requirements of strict scrutiny were met, and (2) to show that those requirements were in fact satisfied. On remand, UT failed to do what our prior decision demanded. The University has still not identified with any degree of specificity the interests that its use of race and ethnicity is supposed to serve. Its primary argument is that merely invoking "the educational benefits of diversity" is sufficient and that it need not identify any metric that would allow a court to determine whether its plan is needed to serve, or is actually serving, those interests. This is nothing less than the plea for deference that we emphatically rejected in our prior decision. Today, the Court inexplicably grants that request.

What is not at stake is whether UT or any other university may adopt an admissions plan that results in a student body with a broad representation of students from all racial and ethnic groups. UT previously had a race-neutral plan that it claimed had "effectively compensated for the loss of affirmative action and UT could have taken other steps that would have increased the diversity of its admitted students without taking race or ethnic background into account.

What is at stake is whether university administrators may justify systematic racial discrimination simply by asserting that such discrimination is necessary to achieve "the educational benefits of diversity," without explaining—much less proving—why the discrimination is needed or how the discriminatory plan is well crafted to serve its objectives. Even though UT has never provided any coherent explanation for its asserted need to discriminate on the basis of race, and even though UT's position relies on a series of unsupported and noxious racial assumptions, the majority concludes that UT has met its heavy burden. This conclusion is remarkable—and remarkably wrong.

Note: The Validity of Constitutional Amendments Prohibiting Affirmative Action

In *Schuette v. Coalition to Defend Affirmative Action, Integration, Immigrant Rights and Fight for Equality by any Means Necessary*, 572 U.S. 291 (2014), the Court was confronted by a state constitutional amendment that banned affirmative action. The amendment was offered following the Court's decision in the University of Michigan's undergraduate affirmative action plan in *Gratz v. Bollinger*, 539 U.S. 244, upholding a law school admission plan was addressed in *Grutter v. Bollinger*, 539 U.S. 306. Although both admissions plans permitted the explicit consideration of an applicant's race, *Gratz* invalidated the undergraduate plan, and *Grutter* upheld the law school admission plan's more limited use of race-based preferences. In response to *Gratz*, the university revised its undergraduate admissions process, but the revision still allowed limited use of race-based preferences. Thereafter, Michigan voters adopted the constitutional amendment which prohibited state and other governmental entities in Michigan from granting certain preferences, including race-based preferences, in a wide range of actions and decisions. Noting that the case was not about the permissibility of race-conscious admissions policies in higher education, the Court upheld the constitutional amendment. "The question here is whether, and in what manner, voters in the States may choose to prohibit the consideration of racial preferences in governmental decisions, in particular with respect to school admissions." Noting that the Amendment "reflects in part the national dialogue regarding the wisdom and practicality of race-conscious admissions policies in higher education," the Court upheld the Amendment: "there was no infliction of a specific injury of the kind at issue in *Mulkey* and Hunter," the Court refused to restrict "the right of Michigan voters to determine that race-based preferences granted by Michigan governmental entities should be ended." "Here Michigan voters acted in concert and statewide to seek consensus and adopt a policy on a difficult subject against a historical background of race in America that has been a source of tragedy and persisting injustice. Were the Court to rule that the question addressed by Michigan voters is too sensitive or complex to be within the grasp of the electorate; or that the policies at issue remain too delicate to be resolved save by university officials or faculties, acting at some remove from immediate public scrutiny and control; or that these matters are so arcane that the electorate's power must be limited because the people cannot prudently exercise that power even after a full debate, that holding would be an unprecedented restriction on the exercise of a fundamental right held not just by one person but by all in common. It is the right to speak and debate and learn and then, as a matter of political will, to act through a lawful electoral process."

Note: The Trump Guidance

In 2018, the Trump administration revoked Obama administration guidance which encouraged universities to pursue affirmative action program to promote diverse faculties and student bodies. The Trump administration's guidance urges universities to move to race-neutral policies. Universities who do not are potentially subject to a U.S. Department of Justice investigation or law suit and potentially to the loss of federal funding.

∾ PROBLEMS ∾

1. *Discrimination Against Asian-Americans.* One of the potential consequences of affirmative action is that some ethnic groups may be adversely and disproportionately affected. For example, in 2015, a coalition of Asian-American organizations filed a complaint asking the U.S. Department of Education to

investigate possible racial bias in undergraduate admissions at elite universities. The complaint alleged that, while Asians often present some of the highest academic credentials to college admissions committees, they have lower acceptance rates at the nation's best schools. In particular, the complaint alleged that "Asian-Americans have the lowest acceptance rate for each SAT test score bracket, having to score on average approximately 140 points higher than a white student, 270 points higher than a Hispanic student and 450 points higher than a black student on the SAT to be on equal footing." Jason L. Riley, *The New Jews of Harvard Admissions*, Wall St. J., May 20, 2015, at A-11. Suppose that you are the general counsel for a large public university. How, if at all, would the complaint affect your analysis of how to implement affirmative action at your university?

2. *Harvard's Assessment of Candidates.* In the law suit by Asian-Americans against Harvard University, there is evidence suggesting that Asian-Americans scored higher than any other racial group on measures such as test scores, grades and extracurricular activities. However, Harvard evaluators consistently gave Asian-Americans lower evaluations on criteria such as "personality ratings." If judged solely based on academic merit, Asian-Americans would have been admitted to Harvard at a 43% rate (rather than a 19% rate). At your university, is it appropriate to consider such "personality ratings?"

C. GENDER CLASSIFICATIONS

Does the Constitution require that gender classifications receive heightened review like classifications that involve race? Among gender classifications, should it matter whether a classification disadvantages women as opposed to men? As we shall see, the Court's approach to gender-based classifications has changed considerably over the years.

1. Early Gender Jurisprudence

For more than a century, until the 1970s, the Court applied minimal scrutiny to gender classifications. In the process, the Court routinely upheld sex-based stereotypes that were used to justify treating women differently than men (and, in some instances, to disadvantage men). In many instances, these stereotypes resulted in protective legislation that hampered women's ability to work or manage their affairs, and conversely gave men much greater control over their affairs.

Bradwell v. Illinois, 83 U.S. 130 (1873), reflects the early stereotype-based jurisprudence. That decision held that the federal Privileges and Immunities

Clause did not apply to women. Rejecting a woman's claimed right to practice law, the Court used the woman-as-homemaker stereotype to justify the exclusion of women from the workplace and from full participation in civil society. In a concurring opinion, Justice Bradley explained why women had no claim to the privileges and immunities of men "to engage in any lawful employment" under either common law or the Constitution:

> It certainly cannot be affirmed, as an historical fact, that the right of females to pursue any lawful employment has ever been established as one of the fundamental privileges and immunities of the sex. On the contrary, the civil law, as well as nature herself, has always recognized a wide difference in the respective spheres and destinies of man and woman. Man is, or should be, woman's protector and defender. The natural and proper timidity and delicacy which belongs to the female sex evidently unfits it for many of the occupations of civil life. The constitution of the family organization, which is founded in the divine ordinance, as well as in the nature of things, indicates the domestic sphere as that which properly belongs to the domain and functions of womanhood. The harmony, not to say identity, of interest and views which belong, or should belong, to the family institution is repugnant to the idea of a woman adopting a distinct and independent career from that of her husband. So firmly fixed was this sentiment in the founders of the common law that it became a maxim of that system of jurisprudence that a woman had no legal existence separate from her husband, who was regarded as her head and representative in the social state; and, notwithstanding some recent modifications of this civil status, many of the special rules of law flowing from and dependent upon this cardinal principle still exist in full force in most States. It is true that many women are unmarried and not affected by any of the duties, complications, and incapacities arising out of the married state, but these are exceptions to the general rule. The paramount destiny and mission of woman are to fulfill the noble and benign offices of wife and mother. This is the law of the Creator. And the rules of civil society must be adapted to the general constitution of things, and cannot be based upon exceptional cases. The humane movements of modern society, which have for their object the multiplication of avenues for woman's advancement, and of occupations adapted to her condition and sex, have my heartiest concurrence. But I am not prepared to say that it is one of her fundamental rights and privileges to be admitted into every office and position, including those which require highly special qualifications and demanding special responsibilities.

Two terms later, in *Minor v. Happersett*, 88 U.S. 162 (1875), the Court upheld a state law denying women the right to vote.

Despite the Court-imposed limits on women's federal constitutional rights under the Privileges and Immunities Clause, the statutory law of some states began to recognize men and women as equal even in the institution of marriage. Lawyers seeking equality for women relied on the developing substantive due process analysis associated with *Lochner*. Recognizing this trend, the Court, in *Muller v. Oregon*, 208 U.S. 41 (1908), stated: "The current runs steadily and strongly in the direction of the emancipation of the wife, and the policy in this state is to place her upon the same footing as if she were a femme sole, not only with respect to her separate property, but as it affects her right to make binding contracts; and the remedies for the enforcement of liabilities." In *Muller*, an employer was convicted for violating a state statute that prohibited women from working more than 10 hours per day in laundry facilities. The law was challenged on the ground that it abridged women's individual liberty right of contract under *Lochner*. Social progressives were fighting for more state and federal legislative protection of workers and the eventual reversal of *Lochner*. Ironically, *Lochner* provided the primary basis for gaining protective legislation for women in the workplace.

Yet even cases like *Muller*, brought to protect women from harsh working conditions, employed the weaker-sex paradigm to justify excluding women from more lucrative employment in the same workplace. The Court cited extensively from the legal realist "Brandeis' brief," progressive in its day, but based on the prevailing natural law view of women as married, child-bearing, and in the home. The Court noted that the brief contained extracts from more than 90 government reports from this country and Europe to the effect that "long hours of labor are dangerous for women, primarily because of their special physical organization, their maternal functions, the rearing and education of the children, the maintenance of the home—all so important and so far reaching that the need for such reduction need hardly be discussed." The Court took "judicial cognizance of all matters of general knowledge," noting:

> That woman's physical structure and the performance of maternal functions place her at a disadvantage in the struggle for subsistence is obvious. This is especially true when the burdens of motherhood are upon her. Even when they are not, healthy mothers are essential to vigorous offspring and the physical well-being of woman becomes an object of public interest and care in order to preserve the strength and vigor of the race. History discloses that woman has always been dependent upon man. While now the doors of the school room are opened and her opportunities for acquiring knowledge are great, it is still true that in the struggle for subsistence she is not an equal competitor with her brother. Though limitations upon personal and contractual rights may be removed by legislation, there is that in her disposition and habits of life which will operate against a full assertion of those rights. She will still be where some legislation to protect her seems necessary to secure a real equality of right. The limitations which this statute places upon her contractual powers, upon her right to agree with her employer as to the time she shall labor, are not imposed solely for her benefit, but also largely for the benefit of all. The two sexes differ and this difference justifies a difference in legislation and upholds that which is designed to compensate for some of the burdens which rest upon her.

The Court also rejected women's claims under the Equal Protection Clause. *Quong Wing v. Kirkendall*, 223 U.S. 59 (1912), dealt with a Montana statute that imposed a higher tax on hand laundry shops than on steam laundry shops. The statute was challenged on the grounds that it discriminated against men in favor of women (Chinese men operated the majority of hand laundries). Justice Holmes, writing for the majority, said, "The Fourteenth Amendment does not create a fictitious equality where there is real difference." The "real difference" according to Justice Holmes was between men and women, and these differences justified the different tax scheme.

BACKGROUND
Older Gender Cases

In *Dominion Hotel v. Arizona*, 249 U.S. 265 (1919), Justice Holmes upheld a law restricting the number of hours women could work. Likewise, in *Hoyt v. Florida*, 368 U.S. 57 (1961), the Court upheld a state statute that exempted women from jury duty. The Court characterized women as the "center of home and family life" and reasoned that women should be allowed to decide whether their "special responsibilities" were consistent with such duty.

∼ PROBLEM: PRECIPITATING SOCIAL CHANGE ∼

During the *Bradwell, Muller,* and *Holt* era, suppose that you were working with a group (composed of both men and women) that wanted to bring about social change, in particular to establish and recognize women as equal citizens with equal rights in the workplace. Given the prevailing judicial climate, how would you have gone about achieving your objectives? Would you have been better off proceeding through the judicial arena, the legislative arena, or some other arena?

2. Doctrinal Turmoil and Evolution

In the 1960s and 1970s, attitudes and approaches toward gender issues began to change. As the historical stereotypes started to break down, they gave way to remedial legislation such as the Equal Pay Act and Title VII and Title IX of the Civil Rights Act. In the 1970s, Congress passed the Equal Rights Amendment (ERA), which provided that "equality of rights under the law shall not be denied or abridged by the United States or by any State on account of sex" and authorized Congress to enact implementing legislation. Although the deadline for ratification was extended to 1982, and although 35 states ultimately ratified the Amendment, the ERA failed to gain ratification from the 38 states needed for it to become law. Beginning in the 1970s, while the ERA was pending, the Court's gender-based equal protection analysis began to undergo a significant shift toward what has come to be called "gender-neutral equality."

Reed v. Reed

404 U.S. 71 (1971)

Mr. Chief Justice BURGER delivered the opinion of the Court.

A separated husband and wife each seek to be appointed as administrator of their deceased son's estate. By law, when competing applications for letters of administration have been filed by both male and female members of the same entitlement class, the male must be chosen. The state justified the presumption in favor of males on the basis that it would reduce the court's workload.

§15-314 provides that different treatment be accorded to the applicants on the basis of their sex; it thus establishes a classification subject to scrutiny under the Equal Protection Clause. In applying that clause, this Court has consistently recognized that the Fourteenth Amendment does not deny to States the power to treat different classes of persons in different ways. *Railway Express Agency v. New York*, 336 U.S. 106 (1949). A classification 'must be reasonable, not arbitrary, and must rest upon some ground of difference having a fair and substantial relation to the object of the legislation, so that all persons similarly circumstanced shall be treated alike.' The question presented by this case is whether a difference in the sex of competing applicants for letters of administration bears a rational relationship to a state objective that is sought to be advanced. The objective of reducing the workload on probate courts by eliminating one class of contests is not without some legitimacy. To give a mandatory preference to members of either sex over members of the other, merely to accomplish the elimination of hearings on the merits, is to make the very kind of arbitrary legislative choice forbidden by the Equal Protection Clause of the Fourteenth Amendment; and whatever may be said as to the positive values of avoiding intrafamily controversy, the choice in this context may not lawfully be mandated solely on the basis of sex. By providing dissimilar treatment for men and women who are thus similarly situated, the challenged section violates the Equal Protection Clause.

The judgment of the Idaho Supreme Court is *reversed* and the case *remanded* for further proceedings not inconsistent with this opinion.

Frontiero v. Richardson

411 U.S. 677 (1973)

Mr. Justice BRENNAN announced the judgment of the Court in an opinion in which Mr. Justice DOUGLAS, Mr. Justice WHITE, and Mr. Justice MARSHALL join.

Appellant Sharon Frontiero, a lieutenant in the United States Air Force, sought increased quarters allowances, and housing and medical benefits for her husband on the ground that he was her 'dependent.' Although such benefits would automatically have been granted with respect to the wife of a male member of the uniformed services, appellant's application was denied because she failed to demonstrate that her husband was dependent on her for more than one-half of his support. In essence, appellants asserted that the discriminatory impact of the statutes is twofold: first, as a procedural matter, a female member is required to demonstrate her spouse's dependency, while no such burden is imposed upon male members; and, second, as a substantive matter, a male member who does not provide more than one-half of his wife's support receives benefits, while a similarly situated female member is denied such benefits.

   The District Court surmised that Congress might reasonably have concluded that, since the husband in our society is generally the 'breadwinner' in
the family—and the wife typically the 'dependent' partner—it would be more
economical to require married female members claiming husbands to prove
actual dependency than to extend the presumption of dependency to such
members. Indeed, given the fact that approximately 99% of all members of the
uniformed services are male, the District Court speculated that such differential treatment might conceivably lead to a 'considerable saving of administrative
expense and manpower.'

   Appellants contend that classifications based upon sex, like classifications
based upon race, alienage, and national origin, are inherently suspect and must
therefore be subjected to close judicial scrutiny. We agree and, indeed, find at
least implicit support for such an approach in our unanimous decision only last
Term in *Reed v. Reed.* 'There can be no doubt that our Nation has had a long and
unfortunate history of sex discrimination,' *Bradwell v. State of Illinois,* 16 Wall. 130
(1873) (Bradley, J., concurring). It is true that the position of women in America
has improved markedly in recent decades. Nevertheless, it can hardly be doubted
that women still face pervasive, although more subtle, discrimination in our educational institutions, in the job market and, perhaps most conspicuously, in the
political arena. It is true, of course, that when viewed in the abstract, women do
not constitute a small and powerless minority. Nevertheless, in part because of
past discrimination, women are vastly underrepresented in this Nation's decision-
making councils.

   Moreover, since sex, like race and national origin, is an immutable characteristic determined solely by the accident of birth, the imposition of special disabilities
upon the members of a particular sex because of their sex would seem to violate
'the basic concept of our system that legal burdens should bear some relationship
to individual responsibility.' And what differentiates sex from such non-suspect sta-
tuses as intelligence or physical disability, and aligns it with the recognized suspect
criteria, is that the sex characteristic frequently bears no relation to ability to perform or contribute to society. As a result, statutory distinctions between the sexes
often have the effect of invidiously relegating the entire class of females to inferior
legal status without regard to the actual capabilities of its individual members.

   With these considerations in mind, we can only conclude that classifications
based upon sex, like classifications based upon race, alienage, or national origin,
are inherently suspect, and must therefore be subjected to strict judicial scrutiny.
Applying the analysis mandated by that stricter standard of review, it is clear that
the statutory scheme now before us is constitutionally invalid.

   Reversed.

Mr. Justice POWELL, with whom THE CHIEF JUSTICE and Mr. Justice BLACKMUN join,
concurring in the judgment.

   The challenged statutes constitute an unconstitutional discrimination against
servicewomen in violation of the Due Process Clause of the Fifth Amendment,

but I cannot agree that classifications based upon sex, 'like classifications based upon race, alienage, and national origin,' are 'inherently suspect and must therefore be subjected to close judicial scrutiny.' We should decide this case on the authority of *Reed* and reserve for the future any expansion of its rationale.

Note and Questions

1. *Charting a New Course.* Following *Reed* and *Frontiero,* it was clear that the Court was prepared to chart a new course with regard to gender classifications, but the new course was far from clear. Obviously, *Reed*'s approach differed significantly from the approach applied by the *Frontiero* plurality. In some instances, the Court invoked non-equal protection principles to invalidate gender classifications. *See, e.g., Stanley v. Illinois,* 405 U.S. 645 (1972) (holding that a gender classification that created a "conclusive presumption" violated due process).

2. *Gender Scrutiny.* Do you agree with the *Frontiero* plurality that classifications based on gender should be subject to strict scrutiny? In concluding that race is a suspect class, what criteria did the Court rely on? Does it make sense to apply strict scrutiny to gender classifications? Have women suffered from a history of discrimination? But do women constitute a discrete and insular minority? Is the characteristic immutable? What significance do you attach to the fact that women constitute a majority, rather than a minority, in this country?

Craig v. Boren

429 U.S. 190 (1976)

Mr. Justice BRENNAN delivered the opinion of the Court.

The interaction of two sections of an Oklahoma statute prohibits the sale of "nonintoxicating" 3.2% beer to males under the age of 21 and to females under the age of 18. The question to be decided is whether such a gender-based differential constitutes a denial to males 18–20 years of age of the equal protection of the laws in violation of the Fourteenth Amendment. To withstand constitutional challenge, previous cases establish that classifications by gender must serve important governmental objectives and must be substantially related to achievement of those objectives. We turn then to the question whether, under *Reed,* the difference between males and females with respect to the purchase of 3.2% beer warrants the differential in age drawn by the Oklahoma statute. We conclude that it does not.

Statutes justified on grounds of administrative convenience, the use of gender as an inaccurate proxy for "archaic and overbroad generalizations" about the financial position of women, and increasingly outdated misconceptions concerning the role of females in the home rather than in the "marketplace and world of ideas" have been rejected as loose-fitting characterizations incapable of supporting state statutory schemes that were premised upon their accuracy.

We accept for purposes of discussion the District Court's identification of the legislative objective as the enhancement of traffic safety. Clearly, the protection of public health and safety represents an important function of state and local governments. However, appellees' statistics cannot support the conclusion that the gender-based distinction closely serves to achieve that objective and therefore the distinction cannot under *Reed* withstand equal protection challenge.

Even were statistical evidence accepted as accurate, it nevertheless offers only a weak answer to the equal protection question presented here. If maleness is to serve as a proxy for drinking and driving, a correlation of 2% must be considered an unduly tenuous "fit." Prior cases have consistently rejected the use of sex as a decisionmaking factor even when the statutes in question rested on far more predictive empirical relationships than this. Many of the studies, while graphically documenting the unfortunate increase in driving while under the influence of alcohol, make no effort to relate their findings to age-sex differentials. The only survey that explicitly centered its attention upon young drivers and their use of beer albeit apparently not of the diluted 3.2% variety reached results that hardly can be viewed as impressive in justifying either a gender or age classification. The showing offered by appellees does not satisfy us that sex represents a legitimate, accurate proxy for the regulation of drinking and driving. In fact, when it is further recognized that Oklahoma's statute prohibits only the selling of 3.2% beer to young males and not their drinking the beverage once acquired (even after purchase by their 18–20-year-old female companions), the relationship between gender and traffic safety becomes far too tenuous to satisfy *Reed*'s requirement that the gender-based difference be substantially related to achievement of the statutory objective.

We hold that Oklahoma's 3.2% beer statute invidiously discriminates against males 18–20 years of age. The statute constitutes a denial of the equal protection of the laws to males aged 18–20. Judgement *reversed*.

Mr. Justice POWELL, *concurring*.

I find it unnecessary to read *Reed* as broadly as some of the Court's language may imply. The Court has had difficulty in agreeing upon a standard of equal protection analysis that can be applied consistently to the wide variety of legislative classifications. There are valid reasons for dissatisfaction with the "two-tier" approach that has been prominent in the Court's decisions in the past decade. Although viewed by many as a result-oriented substitute for more critical analysis, that approach with its narrowly limited "upper-tier" now has substantial precedential support. Our decision today will be viewed by some as a "middle-tier" approach. While I would not endorse that characterization and would not welcome a further subdividing of equal protection analysis, candor compels the recognition that the relatively deferential "rational basis" standard of review normally applied takes on a sharper focus when we address a gender-based classification. So much is clear from our recent cases.

Mr. Justice STEVENS, *concurring.*

There is only one Equal Protection Clause. It requires every State to govern impartially. It does not direct the courts to apply one standard of review in some cases and a different standard in other cases. What has become known as the two-tiered analysis of equal protection claims does not describe a completely logical method of deciding cases, but rather is a method the Court has employed to explain decisions that actually apply a single standard in a reasonably consistent fashion. A careful explanation of the reasons motivating particular decisions may contribute more to an identification of that standard than an attempt to articulate it in all-encompassing terms.

Mr. Justice REHNQUIST, *dissenting.*

The Court's disposition of this case is objectionable on two grounds. First is its conclusion that men challenging a gender-based statute which treats them less favorably than women may invoke a more stringent standard of judicial review than pertains to most other types of classifications. Second is the Court's enunciation of this standard as being that "classifications by gender must serve important governmental objectives and must be substantially related to achievement of those objectives." The only redeeming feature of the Court's opinion is that it apparently signals a retreat from *Frontiero*'s view that sex is a "suspect" classification for purposes of equal protection analysis. The Oklahoma statute challenged here need pass only the "rational basis" equal protection analysis and is constitutional under that analysis.

Before today, no decision of this Court has applied an elevated level of scrutiny to invalidate a statutory discrimination harmful to males, except where the statute impaired an important personal interest protected by the Constitution. There being no such interest here, and there being no plausible argument that this is a discrimination against females, the Court's reliance on our previous sex-discrimination cases is ill-founded. The Court's conclusion that a law which treats males less favorably than females "must serve important governmental objectives and must be substantially related to achievement of those objectives" apparently comes out of thin air. The Equal Protection Clause contains no such language. How is this Court to divine what objectives are important? How is it to determine whether a particular law is "substantially" related to the achievement of such objective, rather than related in some other way to its achievement? Both of the phrases used are so diaphanous and elastic as to invite subjective judicial preferences.

This is not a case where the classification can only be justified on grounds of administrative convenience. Since males drink and drive at a higher rate than the age group as a whole, I fail to see how a statutory bar with regard only to them can create any due process problem. There being no violation of either equal protection or due process, the statute should accordingly be upheld.

Note and Questions

1. *Administrative Convenience.* In *Reed, Frontiero,* and *Craig,* the Court rejected the government's claim of "administrative convenience" to justify the differential treatment accorded men and women. In *Frontiero,* there was no concrete evidence to establish that the government saved money by requiring women, but not men, to prove that their spouse was a dependent. The Court in *Craig* noted that "decisions following *Reed* rejected administrative ease and convenience as sufficiently important objectives to justify gender-based classifications."

2. *Analyzing Craig.* Do you agree with the *Craig* majority that gender classifications should be subjected to intermediate scrutiny rather than strict scrutiny? Why, or why not?

3. Recognition of Differences

In recent years, the Court has moved away from the doctrine of gender equality toward a recognition that there are legitimate biological differences between males and females. In such cases, the task for the courts is to differentiate legitimate gender differences from unjustified stereotypes. Consider the following case.

United States v. Virginia

518 U.S. 515 (1996)

Justice GINSBURG delivered the opinion of the Court.

Virginia's public institutions of higher learning include an incomparable military college, Virginia Military Institute (VMI). The United States maintains that the Constitution's equal protection guarantee precludes Virginia from reserving exclusively to men the unique educational opportunities VMI affords. We agree.

Founded in 1839, VMI is today the sole single-sex school among Virginia's 15 public institutions of higher learning. VMI's distinctive mission is to produce "citizen-soldiers," men prepared for leadership in civilian life and in military service. Assigning prime place to character development, VMI uses an "adversative method" modeled on English public schools and once characteristic of military instruction. VMI constantly endeavors to instill physical and mental discipline in its cadets and impart to them a strong moral code. The school's graduates leave VMI with heightened comprehension of their capacity to deal with duress and stress, and a large sense of accomplishment for completing the hazardous course. VMI has notably succeeded in its mission to produce leaders; among its alumni are military generals, Members of Congress, and business executives. The school's alumni overwhelmingly perceive that their VMI training helped them to realize their personal goals. VMI's endowment reflects the loyalty of its graduates. The school's impressive record in producing leaders has made admission desirable to some women. Nevertheless, Virginia has elected to preserve exclusively for men the advantages and opportunities a VMI education affords.

VMI is financially supported by Virginia and "subject to the control of the Virginia General Assembly." In contrast to the federal service academies, institutions maintained "to prepare cadets for career service in the armed forces," VMI's program "is directed at preparation for both military and civilian life"; "only about 15% of VMI cadets enter career military service."

VMI produces its "citizen-soldiers" through "an adversative, or doubting, model of education" which features "physical rigor, mental stress, absolute equality of treatment, absence of privacy, minute regulation of behavior, and indoctrination in desirable values." The adversative method "dissects the young student," and makes him aware of his "limits and capabilities,'" so that he knows "'how far he can go with his anger, how much he can take under stress, exactly what he can do when he is physically exhausted."

VMI cadets live in spartan barracks where surveillance is constant and privacy nonexistent; they wear uniforms, eat together in the mess hall, and regularly participate in drills. Entering students are incessantly exposed to the rat line, "an extreme form of the adversative model," comparable in intensity to Marine Corps boot camp. Tormenting and punishing, the rat line bonds new cadets to their fellow sufferers and, when they have completed the 7-month experience, to their former tormentors. "Women have no opportunity anywhere to gain the benefits of the system of education at VMI."

In 1990, the United States sued the Commonwealth of Virginia and VMI, alleging that VMI's exclusively male admission policy violated the Equal Protection Clause of the Fourteenth Amendment. The District Court ruled in favor of VMI. The Court of Appeals for the Fourth Circuit vacated the District Court's judgment. In response to the Fourth Circuit's ruling, Virginia proposed a parallel program for women: Virginia Women's Institute for Leadership (VWIL). The 4-year, state-sponsored undergraduate program would be located at Mary Baldwin College, a private liberal arts school for women, and would be open, initially, to about 25 to 30 students. Although VWIL would share VMI's mission — to produce "citizen-soldiers" — the VWIL program would differ from VMI in academic offerings, methods of education, and financial resources. The average combined SAT score of entrants at Mary Baldwin is about 100 points lower than the score for VMI freshmen. Mary Baldwin's faculty holds "significantly fewer Ph.D.'s than the faculty at VMI," and receives significantly lower salaries. While VMI offers degrees in liberal arts, the sciences, and engineering, Mary Baldwin, at the time of trial, offered only bachelor of arts degrees. A VWIL student seeking to earn an engineering degree could gain one, without public support, by attending Washington University in St. Louis, Missouri, for two years, paying the required private tuition.

Experts in educating women at the college level composed the Task Force charged with designing the VWIL program. VWIL students would participate in ROTC programs and a newly established, "largely ceremonial" Virginia Corps of Cadets, but the VWIL House would not have a military format, and VWIL would not require its students to eat meals together or to wear uniforms during the schoolday. The VWIL Task Force favored "a cooperative method which reinforces self-esteem." In addition to the standard bachelor of arts program, VWIL students would take courses in leadership, complete an off-campus leadership externship, participate in community service projects, and assist in arranging a speaker series.

Virginia represented that it will provide equal financial support for in-state VWIL students and VMI cadets, and the VMI Foundation agreed to supply a $5.4625 million endowment for the VWIL program. The VMI Alumni Association has developed a network of employers interested in hiring VMI graduates. The Association has agreed to open its network to VWIL graduates.

Virginia returned to the District Court seeking approval of its proposed remedial plan, and the court decided the plan met the requirements of the Equal Protection Clause. A divided Court of Appeals affirmed.

The suit presents two ultimate issues. First, does Virginia's exclusion of women from the educational opportunities provided by VMI deny to women "capable of all of the individual activities required of VMI cadets," the equal protection of the laws guaranteed by the Fourteenth Amendment? Second, if VMI's "unique" situation offends the Constitution's equal protection principle, what is the remedial requirement?

Under *J.E.B. v. Alabama ex rel. T. B.*, 511 U.S. 127 (1994), and *Mississippi Univ. for Women*, 458 U.S. at 724, parties who seek to defend gender-based government action must demonstrate an "exceedingly persuasive justification" for that action. Without equating gender classifications to classifications based on race or national origin, the Court, in post-*Reed* decisions, has carefully inspected official action that closes a door or denies opportunity to women (or to men). The reviewing court must determine whether the proffered justification is "exceedingly persuasive." The State must show "at least that the challenged classification serves 'important governmental objectives and that the discriminatory means employed' are 'substantially related to the achievement of those objectives.'" The justification must be genuine, not hypothesized or invented *post hoc* in response to litigation. And it must not rely on overbroad generalizations about the different talents, capacities, or preferences of males and females.

The heightened review standard our precedent establishes does not make sex a proscribed classification. Supposed "inherent differences" are no longer accepted as a ground for race or national origin classifications. "Inherent differences" between men and women remain cause for celebration, but not for denigration of the members of either sex or for artificial constraints on an individual's opportunity. Sex classifications may be used to compensate women "for particular economic disabilities they have suffered," to "promote equal employment opportunity," to advance full development of the talent and capacities of our Nation's people. But such classifications may not be used, as they once were, to create or perpetuate the legal, social, and economic inferiority of women.

We conclude that Virginia has shown no "exceedingly persuasive justification" for excluding all women from the citizen-soldier training afforded by VMI. Because the remedy proffered by Virginia—the Mary Baldwin VWIL program—does not cure the constitutional violation, i.e., it does not provide equal opportunity, we reverse the Fourth Circuit's final judgment in this case.

Virginia asserts two justifications in defense of VMI's exclusion of women. First, the Commonwealth contends, "single-sex education provides important educational benefits," and the option of single-sex education contributes to "diversity in educational approaches." Second, the "unique VMI method of character development and leadership training," the school's adversative approach, would have to be modified were VMI to admit women.

Single-sex education affords pedagogical benefits to at least some students and it is not disputed that diversity among public educational institutions can serve the public good. But Virginia has not shown that VMI was established, or has been maintained, with a view to diversifying, by its categorical exclusion of women, educational opportunities within the Commonwealth. No such policy can be discerned from the movement of all other public colleges and universities in Virginia away from single-sex education. A purpose genuinely to advance an array of educational options is not served by VMI's historic and constant plan to "afford a unique educational benefit only to males." However "liberally" this plan serves the Commonwealth's sons, it makes no provision whatever for her daughters. That is not *equal* protection.

Virginia next argues that VMI's adversative method of training provides educational benefits that cannot be made available to women. Alterations to accommodate women would necessarily be "radical," so "drastic," Virginia asserts, as to transform, indeed "destroy," VMI's program. Men would be deprived of the unique opportunity currently available to them; women would not gain that opportunity because their participation would "eliminate the very aspects of the program that distinguish VMI from other institutions of higher education in Virginia." The District Court forecast that coeducation would materially affect "at least these three aspects of VMI's program—physical training, the absence of privacy, and the adversative approach."

It is uncontested that women's admission would require accommodations, primarily in arranging housing assignments and physical training programs for female cadets. It is also undisputed that "the VMI methodology could be used to educate women" and that some women may prefer it to the methodology a women's college might pursue. The parties agree that "*some* women can meet the physical standards." In sum, "neither the goal of producing citizen soldiers," VMI's *raison d'etre,* "nor VMI's implementing methodology is inherently unsuitable to women."

The District Court made "findings" on "gender-based developmental differences." These "findings" restate the opinions of Virginia's expert witnesses about typically male or typically female "tendencies." For example, "males tend to need an atmosphere of adversativeness," while "females tend to thrive in a cooperative atmosphere." State actors controlling gates to opportunity may not exclude qualified individuals based on "fixed notions concerning the roles and abilities of males and females." *Mississippi Univ. for Women,* 458 U.S. at 725. It may be assumed that most women would not choose VMI's adversative method. The issue is whether the Commonwealth can constitutionally deny to women who have the will and capacity, the training and attendant opportunities that VMI uniquely affords.

The notion that admission of women would downgrade VMI's stature, destroy the adversative system and, with it, even the school, is a judgment hardly different from other "self-fulfilling prophecies," once routinely used to deny rights or opportunities. Women's successful entry into the federal military academies, and their participation in the Nation's military forces, indicate that Virginia's fears for the future of VMI may not be solidly grounded. The Commonwealth's justification for excluding all women from "citizen-soldier" training for which some are qualified cannot rank as "exceedingly persuasive." VMI's mission is to produce "citizen-soldiers," individuals. Surely that goal is great enough to accommodate women. Just as surely, the Commonwealth's great goal is not substantially advanced by women's categorical exclusion, in total disregard of their individual merit, from the Commonwealth's premier "citizen-soldier" corps. Virginia, in sum, "has fallen far short of establishing the 'exceedingly persuasive justification'" that must be the solid base for any gender-defined classification.

A remedial decree must closely fit the constitutional violation; it must be shaped to place persons unconstitutionally denied an opportunity or advantage in "the position they would have occupied in the absence of discrimination." *See Milliken v. Bradley,* 433 U.S. 267 (1977). Virginia chose not to eliminate, but to leave untouched, VMI's exclusionary policy and proposed a separate program, different in kind from VMI and unequal in tangible and intangible facilities. Virginia was obliged to show that its remedial proposal "directly addressed and related to" the violation, the equal protection denied to women ready, willing, and able to benefit from educational opportunities of the kind VMI offers.

VWIL affords women no opportunity to experience the rigorous military training for which VMI is famed. Instead, the VWIL program "deemphasizes" military education, and uses a "cooperative method" of education "which reinforces self-esteem." Virginia maintains that these methodological differences are "justified pedagogically," based on "important differences between men and women in learning and developmental needs," "psychological and sociological differences" Virginia describes as "real" and "not stereotypes." Generalizations about "the way women are," estimates of what is appropriate for *most women,* no longer justify denying opportunity to women whose talent and capacity place them outside the average description. VMI offers an educational opportunity no other Virginia institution provides, and the school's "prestige"—associated with its success in developing "citizen-soldiers"—is unequaled. Virginia has closed this facility to its daughters and, instead, has devised for them a "parallel program," with a faculty less impressively credentialed and less well paid, more limited course offerings, fewer opportunities for military training and for scientific specialization. VMI, beyond question, "possesses to a far greater degree" than the VWIL program "those qualities which are incapable of objective measurement but which make for greatness in a school," including "position and influence of the alumni, standing in the community, traditions and prestige." Women seeking and fit for a VMI-quality education cannot be offered anything less, under the Commonwealth's obligation to afford them genuinely equal protection. A prime part of the history of our Constitution is the story of the extension of constitutional rights and protections to people once ignored or excluded.

For the reasons stated, the initial judgment of the Court of Appeals is *affirmed,* the final judgment of the Court of Appeals is *reversed,* and the case is *remanded* for further proceedings consistent with this opinion.

It is so ordered.

Chief Justice REHNQUIST, *concurring in the judgment.*

In *Craig v. Boren,* 429 U.S. 190 (1976), we announced that "to withstand constitutional challenge, classifications by gender must serve important governmental objectives and must be substantially related to achievement of those objectives." The majority says that the Commonwealth must demonstrate an "exceedingly persuasive justification" to support a gender-based classification. It is unfortunate that the Court thereby introduces an element of uncertainty respecting the appropriate test.

Had Virginia made a genuine effort to devote comparable public resources to a facility for women, and followed through on such a plan, it might well have avoided an equal protection violation. But neither the governing board of VMI nor the Commonwealth took any action after 1982. If diversity in the form of single-sex, as well as coeducational, institutions of higher learning were to be available to Virginians, that diversity had to be available to women as well as to men.

A State does not have substantial interest in the adversative methodology unless it is pedagogically beneficial. There is no evidence that an adversative method is pedagogically beneficial or is any more likely to produce character traits than other methodologies. In the end, the women's institution Virginia proposes, VWIL, fails as a remedy, because it is distinctly inferior to the existing men's institution and will continue to be for the foreseeable future. I therefore ultimately agree with the Court that Virginia has not provided an adequate remedy.

Justice SCALIA, *dissenting.*

The Court explicitly rejects the finding that there exist "gender-based developmental differences" supporting Virginia's restriction of the "adversative" method to only a men's institution, and the finding that the all-male composition of the Virginia Military Institute (VMI) is essential to that institution's character. "When a practice not expressly prohibited by the text of the Bill of Rights bears the endorsement of a long tradition of open, widespread, and unchallenged use that dates back to the beginning of the Republic, we have no proper basis for striking it down." *Rutan v. Republican Party of Ill.*, 497 U.S. 62 (1990) (Scalia, J., dissenting). The same applies, more broadly, to single-sex education in general. Government-run *non*military educational institutions for the two sexes have until very recently also been part of our national tradition.

We evaluate a statutory classification based on gender using "intermediate scrutiny" and under it have inquired whether the statutory classification is "substantially related to an important governmental objective." *Heckler v. Mathews*, 465 U.S. 728 (1984). The Court instead prefers the phrase "exceedingly persuasive justification" from *Hogan*. Only the amorphous "exceedingly persuasive justification" phrase, and not the standard elaboration of intermediate scrutiny, can be made to yield this conclusion that VMI's single-sex composition is unconstitutional because there exist several women (or, one would have to conclude under the Court's reasoning, a single woman) willing and able to undertake VMI's program. Intermediate scrutiny has never required a least-restrictive-means analysis, but only a "substantial relation" between the classification and the state interests that it serves. If the question of the applicable standard of review for sex-based classifications were to be regarded as an appropriate subject for reconsideration, the stronger argument would be not for elevating the standard to strict scrutiny, but for reducing it to rational-basis review. The latter certainly has a firmer foundation in our past jurisprudence. It is hard to consider women a "discrete and insular minority" unable to employ the "political processes ordinarily to be relied upon," when they constitute a majority of the electorate. And the suggestion that they are incapable of exerting that political power smacks of the same paternalism that the Court so roundly condemns. Moreover, a long list of legislation proves the proposition false. *See, e.g.,* Equal Pay Act of 1963, 29 U.S.C. §206(d); Title VII of the Civil Rights Act of 1964, 42 U.S.C. §2000e-2; Title IX of the Education Amendments of 1972, 20 U.S.C. §1681; Women's Business Ownership Act of 1988, 102 Stat. 2689; Violence Against Women Act of 1994, 108 Stat. 1902.

Virginia has an important state interest in providing effective college education for its citizens. That single-sex instruction is an approach substantially related to that interest should be evident from the long and continuing history in this country of men's and women's colleges. Virginia demonstrated at trial that "a substantial body of contemporary scholarship and research supports the proposition that, although males and females have significant areas of developmental overlap, they also have differing developmental needs that are deep-seated."

VMI employs a "distinctive educational method," sometimes referred to as the "adversative, or doubting, model of education." A State's decision to maintain one school that provides the adversative method is "substantially related" to its goal of good education. It was uncontested that "if the state were to establish a women's VMI-type i.e., adversative program, the program would attract an insufficient number of participants to make the program work," and if Virginia were to include women in VMI, the school "would find it necessary to drop the adversative system altogether." Thus, Virginia's options were an adversative method that excludes women or no adversative method at all. There can be no serious dispute that single-sex education and a distinctive educational method "represent legitimate contributions to diversity in the Virginia higher education system."

The Court argues that VMI would not have to change very much if it were to admit women. Changes that the District Court's detailed analysis found would be required include new allowances for personal privacy in the barracks, such as locked doors and coverings on windows, which would detract from VMI's approach of regulating minute details of student behavior, "contradict the principle that everyone is constantly subject to scrutiny by everyone else," and impair VMI's "total egalitarian approach" under which every student must be "treated alike"; changes in the physical training program, which would reduce "the intensity and aggressiveness of the current program"; and various modifications in other respects of the adversative training program that permeates student life.

VWIL is, under our established test, irrelevant, so long as VMI's all-male character is "substantially related" to an important state goal. VWIL was carefully designed by professional educators who have long experience in educating young women. The Court simply declares, with no basis in the evidence, that these professionals acted on "'overbroad' generalizations."

Notes

1. *Jurisprudence of Difference.* The Court has rejected the original jurisprudence of difference, but it has yet to fully embrace the modern view. Commentators question both the original equality of difference represented in *Mueller v. Oregon* and the modern liberal neutrality principle governing gender claims of inequality since *Craig v. Boren*, the ultimate statement of gender-neutral equality. In cases rejecting single-sex schools and upholding sex-based affirmative action plans, the "similarly situated" concept employed under gender-neutral interpretations of the Fourteenth Amendment Equal Protection Clause is reconceived as a barrier to equality for women. Moreover, although the terms *sex* and *gender* were used interchangeably in earlier eras, courts and academics question not only the distinction between but also the meaning of gender and sex equality. *See* Katherine Franke, *The Central Mistake of Sex Discrimination Law: The Disaggregation of Sex from Gender,* 144 U. PA. L. REV. 1 (1995). Finally, just as the levels of heightened scrutiny appear to shift in racial equality cases, the meaning of intermediate scrutiny has also shifted from its first iteration in *Frontiero* to more recent pronouncements in *Casey* and *United States v. Virginia.*

2. *The Formal Equality Model. Geduldig v. Aiello,* 417 U.S. 484 (1974), triggered a rethinking of the formal equality model, which had succeeded in getting the courts and lawmakers to identify where men and women are similarly situated.

The issue was whether women were entitled to disability benefits for pregnancy and delivery:

We cannot agree that the exclusion of this disability from coverage amounts to invidious discrimination under the Equal Protection Clause. The classification challenged relates to the asserted underinclusiveness of the set of risks that the State has selected to insure. Although California has created a program to insure most risks of employment disability, it has not chosen to insure all such risks, and this decision is reflected in the level of annual contributions exacted from participating employees. This Court has held that, consistently with the Equal Protection Clause, a State may take one step at a time, addressing itself to the phase of the problem which seems most acute to the legislative mind. The legislature may select one phase of one field and apply a remedy there, neglecting the others. Particularly with respect to social welfare programs, so long as the line drawn by the State is rationally supportable, the courts will not interpose their judgment as to the appropriate stopping point. The District Court suggested that moderate alterations in what it regarded as 'variables' of the disability insurance program could be made to accommodate the substantial expense required to include normal pregnancy within the program's protection. The same can be said, however, with respect to the other expensive class of disabilities that are excluded from coverage—short-term disabilities. If the Equal Protection Clause were thought to compel disability payments for normal pregnancy, it is hard to perceive why it would not also compel payments for short-term disabilities suffered by participating employees.

Justice Brennan, joined by two other justices, dissented:

Because I believe that *Reed* and *Frontiero* mandate a stricter standard of scrutiny which the State's classification fails to satisfy, I respectfully dissent. The essence of the State's justification for excluding disabilities caused by a normal pregnancy from its disability compensation scheme is that covering such disabilities would be too costly. To be sure, the present level of benefits for insured disabilities could not be maintained without increasing the employee contribution rate, raising or lifting the yearly contribution ceiling, or securing state subsidies. But whatever role such monetary considerations may play in traditional equal protection analysis, the State's interest in preserving the fiscal integrity of its disability insurance program simply cannot render the State's use of a suspect classification constitutional. While "a State has a valid interest in preserving the fiscal integrity of its programs, a State may not accomplish such a purpose by invidious distinctions between classes of its citizens." When a statutory classification is subject to strict judicial scrutiny, the State "must do more than show that denying (benefits to the excluded class) saves money."

3. *Gender, Statutory Actions, and Class Actions.* In *Wal-Mart Stores, Inc. v. Dukes,* 564 U.S. 338 (2011), a case that arose under the Civil Rights Act of 1964, the Court overturned a lower court decision allowing a class action that would have included some 1.5 million plaintiffs.

PROBLEMS

1. *Analyzing* Virginia*'s Holding.* Does the *Virginia* holding make sense? The Court requires VMI to admit women but allows it to hold them to the male-based system used at VMI. While that approach might give some women (those who

are interested in, and capable of, performing in VMI's system) what they desire, where does that leave women who might prefer a cooperative approach to education? Would women, as a group, have been better off if the Court had required the Commonwealth of Virginia to devote more resources to VWIL rather than requiring it to integrate VMI?

2. *"Real" Versus "Stereotypical" Gender Differences.* The Court seems to suggest that there are "real" as opposed to "stereotypical" differences between men and women. Obviously, there are physical and chemical differences between the sexes. There are also perceived behavioral differences. However, for years a debate has raged about whether these behavioral differences are rooted in "nature" or "nurture." In other words, are behavioral differences attributable to socialization, or are they attributable to real differences between the sexes? How does a court determine whether differences are based on stereotypes or on actual physical differences?

3. *Formal Equality or Relevant Differences?* Consider the following excerpts from *United States v. Virginia* in regard to the question of whether social and biological differences have relevance for Fourteenth Amendment equal protection jurisprudence: a) "Physical differences between men and women, however, are enduring: 'The two sexes are not fungible; a community made up exclusively of one sex is different from a community composed of both.' *Ballard v. United States*, 329 U.S. 187 (1946)." b) " 'Inherent differences' between men and women, we have come to appreciate, remain cause for celebration, but not for denigration of the members of either sex or for artificial constraints on an individual's opportunity. Sex classifications may be used to compensate women 'for particular economic disabilities they have suffered,' *Califano v. Webster*, 430 U.S. 313 (1977) (per curiam); to 'promote equal employment opportunity,' *see California Federal Savings & Loan Assn. v. Guerra*, 479 U.S. 272 (1987); or to advance full development of the talents and capacities of our Nation's people. But such classifications may not be used, as they once were, *see Goesaert*, 335 U.S. at 467, to create or perpetuate the legal, social, and economic inferiority of women." c) "Single-sex education affords pedagogical benefits to at least some students, Virginia emphasizes, and that reality is uncontested in this litigation. Similarly, it is not disputed that diversity among public educational institutions can serve the public good. In cases of this genre, our precedent instructs that 'benign' justifications proffered in defense of categorical exclusions will not be accepted automatically; a tenable justification must describe actual state purposes, not rationalizations for actions in fact differently grounded."

4. *Hockey Scholarships.* The State of Maine enacts a law providing for ice hockey scholarships for special ice hockey camps that will convene every December. The scholarships, a $700 value, were given to 21 males and 2 females in 2002. Nine out of every ten ice hockey players in Maine are male. The bill's sponsor stated in arguing for its passage: "Our young lads need the extra work if they are to compete against the neighboring states. The boys are losing out to the big-spending ways of Massachusetts and New Hampshire." If this law is challenged, what level of scrutiny will apply?

6. *More on the Diversity Initiative.* Consider again the problem described at the beginning of the chapter. Suppose that NWU decides to include women as part of its diversity initiative. As a result, NWU is considering giving women preferences in admissions and financial aid as well as in faculty hiring. NWU is contemplating this approach on the theory that women have suffered from discrimination and stereotypes, and therefore deserve a "boost" in terms of admissions and aid. Under the gender precedent that you have examined thus far, would it be permissible to provide such preferences? How would you advise NWU? What would the university have to show in order to justify the preferences?

4. Discrimination Against Men

The theory of formal equality rejects gender-based classifications. Justice Brennan was the major proponent of this view in gender discrimination cases, although he advocated against the application of formal equality in race discrimination cases. According to Justice Brennan and others on the Court, men are as entitled as women to challenge gender-based classifications. Pay close attention to Justice Rehnquist's critique of this logic.

Michael M. v. Superior Court of Sonoma County

450 U.S. 464 (1981)

Justice REHNQUIST announced the judgment of the Court and delivered an opinion, in which THE CHIEF JUSTICE, Justice STEWART, and Justice POWELL joined.

The question presented in this case is whether California's "statutory rape" law violates the Equal Protection Clause of the Fourteenth Amendment. The statute makes men alone criminally liable for the act of sexual intercourse.

The Court has had some difficulty in agreeing upon the proper approach and analysis in cases involving challenges to gender-based classifications. We have not held that gender-based classifications are "inherently suspect" and thus we do not apply so-called "strict scrutiny" to those classifications. Our cases have held, however, that the traditional minimum rationality test takes on a somewhat "sharper focus" when gender-based classifications are challenged.

Underlying our decisions is the principle that a legislature may not "make overbroad generalizations based on sex which are entirely unrelated to any differences between men and women or which demean the ability or social status of the affected class." But because the Equal Protection Clause does not "demand that a statute necessarily apply equally to all persons" or require "things which are different in fact to be treated in law as though they were the same," this Court has consistently upheld statutes where the gender classification is not invidious, but rather realistically reflects the fact that the sexes are not similarly situated in certain circumstances. As the Court has stated, a legislature may "provide for the special problems of women." *Weinberger v. Wiesenfeld,* 420 U.S. 636 (1975).

The justification for the statute offered by the State is that the legislature sought to prevent illegitimate teenage pregnancies. That finding, of course, is entitled to great deference. We are satisfied not only that the prevention of illegitimate pregnancy is at least one of the "purposes" of the statute, but also that the State has a strong interest in preventing such pregnancy. Teenage pregnancies, which have increased dramatically over the last two decades, have significant social, medical, and economic consequences for both the mother and her child, and the State. Half of all teenage pregnancies end in abortion. And of those children who are born, their illegitimacy makes them likely candidates to become wards of the State. We need not be medical doctors to discern that young men and young women are not similarly situated with respect to the problems and the risks of sexual intercourse. Only women may become pregnant, and they suffer disproportionately the profound physical, emotional and psychological consequences of sexual activity. The statute at issue here protects women from sexual intercourse at an age when those consequences are particularly severe.

The question thus boils down to whether a State may attack the problem of sexual intercourse and teenage pregnancy directly by prohibiting a male from having sexual intercourse with a minor female. We hold that such a statute is sufficiently related to the State's objectives to pass constitutional muster. Because virtually all of the significant harmful and inescapably identifiable consequences of teenage pregnancy fall on the young female, a legislature acts well within its authority when it elects to punish only the participant who, by nature, suffers few of the consequences of his conduct. It is hardly unreasonable for a legislature acting to protect minor females to exclude them from punishment. Moreover, the risk of pregnancy itself constitutes a substantial deterrence to young females. No similar natural sanctions deter males. A criminal sanction imposed solely on males thus serves to roughly "equalize" the deterrents on the sexes.

This is not a case where a statute is being challenged on the grounds that it "invidiously discriminates" against females. To the contrary, the statute places a burden on males which is not shared by females. But we find nothing to suggest that men, because of past discrimination or peculiar disadvantages, are in need of the special solicitude of the courts. Nor is this a case where the gender classification is made "solely for administrative convenience," as in or rests on "the baggage of sexual stereotypes." The statute instead reasonably reflects the fact that the consequences of sexual intercourse and pregnancy fall more heavily on the female than on the male. Accordingly, the judgment of the California Supreme Court is

Affirmed.

Justice STEWART, *concurring.*

The Constitution is violated when government, state or federal, invidiously classifies similarly situated people on the basis of the immutable characteristics with which they were born. Detrimental racial classifications by government always violate the Constitution, for the simple reason that, so far as the Constitution is concerned, people of different races are always similarly situated. While detrimental gender classifications by government often violate the Constitution, they do not always do so, for the reason that there are differences between males and females that the Constitution necessarily recognizes. In this case we deal with the most basic of these differences: females can become pregnant as the result of sexual intercourse; males cannot. The Equal Protection Clause does not mean that the physiological differences between men and women must be disregarded. While those differences must never be permitted to become a pretext for invidious discrimination, no such discrimination is presented by this case. The Constitution surely does not require a State to pretend that demonstrable differences between men and women do not really exist.

Justice BRENNAN, with whom Justices WHITE and MARSHALL join, *dissenting*.

Whether the admittedly gender-based classification in the statutory rape law bears a sufficient relationship to the State's asserted goal of preventing teenage pregnancies to survive the "mid-level" constitutional scrutiny mandated by *Craig v. Boren*. Applying the analytical framework provided by our precedents, the classification must be declared unconstitutional. The plurality opinion places too much emphasis on the desirability of achieving the State's asserted statutory goal—prevention of teenage pregnancy—and not enough emphasis on the fundamental question of whether the sex-based discrimination in the California statute is *substantially* related to the achievement of that goal. The State has not shown that this statute is any more effective than a gender-neutral law would be in deterring minor females from engaging in sexual intercourse. It has therefore not met its burden of proving that the statutory classification is substantially related to the achievement of its asserted goal.

Justice STEVENS, *dissenting*.

The only acceptable justification for a general rule requiring disparate treatment of the two participants in a joint act must be a legislative judgment that one is more guilty than the other. The risk-creating conduct that this statute is designed to prevent requires the participation of two persons—one male and one female. In many situations it is probably true that one is the aggressor and the other is either an unwilling, or at least a less willing, participant in the joint act. If a statute authorized punishment of only one participant and required the prosecutor to prove that that participant had been the aggressor, the discrimination would be valid. I also assume that it would be permissible to punish only the male participant, if one element of the offense were proof that he had been the aggressor, or at least in some respects the more responsible participant in the joint act. The statute at issue in this case, however, requires no such proof.

Notes

1. *Parental Rights of Unmarried Fathers.* In a series of family law cases, the Court extended protection to the parental rights of unmarried fathers. In *Stanley v. Illinois*, 405 U.S. 645 (1972), the Court held that a father of illegitimate children was entitled to a hearing on his fitness as a parent before the children could be taken from him by the State of Illinois. The interests that the Court found controlling in *Stanley* were the integrity of the family against state interference and the freedom of a father to raise his own children. *Quilloin v. Walcott*, 434 U.S. 246 (1978), involved the constitutionality of a Georgia statute that authorized the adoption, over the objection of the natural father, of a child born out of wedlock. The father in that case had never legitimated the child. It was only after the mother had remarried and her new husband had filed an adoption petition that the natural father sought visitation rights and filed a petition for legitimation. The trial court found adoption by the new husband to be in the child's best interests and consistent with the Due Process Clause.

2. *Property Tax Exemptions.* In *Kahn v. Shevin*, 415 U.S. 351 (1974), the Court upheld a Florida law that provided a $500-per-year property tax exemption for widows but not for widowers. The Court held that the legislation involved an effort to reduce "the disparity between the economic capabilities of men and women," noting that there could "be no dispute that the financial difficulties confronting the lone woman in Florida or in any other State exceed those facing the man. Whether from overt discrimination or from the socialization process of a male-dominated culture, the job market is inhospitable to the woman seeking any but the lowest paid jobs."

3. *Peremptory Challenges.* In *J.E.B. v. Alabama*, 511 U.S. 127 (1994), the State of Alabama filed a complaint seeking to establish paternity and imposing child support obligations against a man. The trial involved a panel of 36 potential jurors, 12 males and 24 females, of which the judge excused three jurors for cause. Only 10 of the remaining 33 jurors were male. The State then used nine of its ten peremptory strikes to remove male jurors, and the petitioner used all but one of his strikes to remove female jurors. As a result, all the selected jurors were female. The jury found that the petitioner was the father of the child, and entered an order directing him to pay child support. Relying on *Batson v. Kentucky*, 476 U.S. 79 (1986), in which the Court held that peremptory challenges could not be used to exclude Blacks from a jury, the Court held that the state's gender-based peremptory strikes violated equal protection. The State had argued that its decision "may reasonably have been based upon the perception, supported by history, that men otherwise totally qualified to serve upon a jury in any case might be more sympathetic and receptive to the arguments of a man alleged in a paternity action to be the father of an out-of-wedlock child, while women equally qualified to serve upon a jury might be more sympathetic and receptive to the arguments of the complaining witness who bore the child." The Court found a violation of equal protection: "Respondent offers virtually no

support for the conclusion that gender alone is an accurate predictor of juror's attitudes; yet it urges this Court to condone the same stereotypes that justified the wholesale exclusion of women from juries and the ballot box. Respondent seems to assume that gross generalizations that would be deemed impermissible if made on the basis of race are somehow permissible when made on the basis of gender. Discrimination in jury selection, whether based on race or on gender, causes harm to the litigants, the community, and the individual jurors who are wrongfully excluded from participation in the judicial process. The litigants are harmed by the risk that the prejudice that motivated the discriminatory selection of the jury will infect the entire proceedings. The community is harmed by the State's participation in the perpetuation of invidious group stereotypes and the inevitable loss of confidence in our judicial system that state-sanctioned discrimination in the courtroom engenders."

4. *Adoption and Parental Rights.* In *Caban v. Mohammed*, 441 U.S. 380 (1979), the Court considered a case involving a man and woman who produced two illegitimate children together and maintained joint custody of the children from the time of their birth until the children were two and four years old. After the mother left the father and remarried, the father maintained close contact with the children. Nevertheless, the mother sought to have her new husband adopt the children. Under New York's Domestic Relations Law, an unwed mother can block the adoption of her children simply by withholding consent, but an unwed father has far fewer rights. The Court struck down the law: "Gender-based distinctions 'must serve important governmental objectives and must be substantially related to achievement of those objectives' in order to withstand judicial scrutiny under the Equal Protection Clause." Although the state argued that it had an important interest in making sure that illegitimate children obtained fathers, the Court concluded that this interest was insufficient, stating that the law "is another example of 'overbroad generalizations' in gender-based classifications. The effect of New York's classification is to discriminate against unwed fathers even when their identity is known and they have manifested a significant paternal interest in the child. Section 111 both excludes some loving fathers from full participation in the decision whether their children will be adopted and, at the same time, enables some alienated mothers arbitrarily to cut off the paternal rights of fathers. We conclude that this undifferentiated distinction between unwed mothers and unwed fathers, does not bear a substantial relationship to the State's asserted interests." By contrast, the Court upheld a state law cutting off a father's rights in *Lehr v. Robertson*, 463 U.S. 248 (1983). In that case, the Court emphasized that the father had never established a substantial relationship with his child, and therefore that the failure to give him notice of pending adoption proceedings did not deprive him of equal protection. The Court noted that the father could have protected his rights by sending a postcard to the putative father registry.

5. *Wrongful Death Actions.* In *Parham v. Hughes*, 441 U.S. 347 (1979), the Court dealt with a Georgia law that allowed the mother of an illegitimate child to sue

for the wrongful death of that child, but precluded a father from doing so unless he has previously legitimated the child. In upholding the law, the Court stated:

> The Georgia statute does not invidiously discriminate against the appellant simply because he is of the male sex. The fact is that mothers and fathers of illegitimate children are not similarly situated. Under Georgia law, only a father can by voluntary unilateral action make an illegitimate child legitimate. Unlike the mother of an illegitimate child whose identity will rarely be in doubt, the identity of the father will frequently be unknown. By coming forward, a father can both establish his identity and make his illegitimate child legitimate. Thus, the conferral of the right of a natural father to sue for the wrongful death of his child only if he has previously acted to identify himself, undertake his paternal responsibilities, and make his child legitimate, does not reflect any overbroad generalizations about men as a class, but rather the reality that in Georgia only a father can by unilateral action legitimate an illegitimate child. Since fathers who do legitimate their children can sue for wrongful death in precisely the same circumstances as married fathers whose children were legitimate *ab initio*, the statutory classification does not discriminate against fathers as a class but instead distinguishes between fathers who have legitimated their children and those who have not.

∽ PROBLEMS ∽

1. *Is It Appropriate to Apply the Same Standard of Review to Classifications Involving Men?* Do decisions like *Bradwell* suggest that men have historically held a privileged position, indeed a dominant position, vis-à-vis women? If so, should they receive less protection under the Equal Protection Clause? Consider Leo Kanowitz, *"Benign" Sex Discrimination: Its Troubles and Their Cure,* 31 HASTINGS L.J. 1379, 1394 (1980):

> A casual glance at the treatment males have received at the hands of the law solely because they are males suggests that they have paid an awesome price for other advantages they have presumably enjoyed over females in our society. Whether one talks of the male's unique obligation of compulsory military service, his primary duty for spousal and child support, his lack of the same kinds of protective labor legislation that have traditionally been enjoyed by women, or the statutory or judicial preference in child custody disputes that has long been accorded to mothers vis-à-vis fathers of minor children, sex discrimination against males in statutes and judicial decisions has been widespread and severe."

Do you agree?

2. *Alimony Discrimination.* A state statute provides that husbands may be required to pay alimony to their ex-wives, but it contains no comparable provision for women. Jane James, a high-level corporate official in a Fortune 500 company, files for divorce against her husband, John James, an unemployed construction worker. John's request for post-divorce alimony is rejected on the basis that state law does not provide for an alimony award in favor of a man. The state seeks to justify the law on grounds of administrative convenience. In the state's view, few men need alimony compared to women. Does this state law violate the Equal Protection Clause? Why, or why not? *See Orr v. Orr,* 440 U.S. 268 (1979).

3. *Even More on the Diversity Initiative.* In regard to the introductory problem, suppose that, instead of adopting a preference in favor of women, NWU decides that women and men should be represented equally in the student body and on the faculty in proportion to their percentages in the overall population. In other words, in a given year, if women are underrepresented in the student body or on the faculty, then preferences in terms of hiring, admissions, and financial aid will be extended to women. By contrast, if men are underrepresented, then they will receive preferences. Under the gender precedent that you have examined thus far, would these proposals be constitutional? How would you advise NWU? What would the university have to show to justify such policies?

Nguyen v. Immigration and Naturalization Service

533 U.S. 53 (2001)

Justice KENNEDY delivered the opinion of the Court.

This case presents a question not resolved by a majority of the Court in a case before us three Terms ago in *Miller v. Albright.* Title 8 U.S.C. §1409 governs the acquisition of United States citizenship by persons born to one United States citizen parent and one noncitizen parent when the parents are unmarried and the child is born outside of the United States or its possessions. The statute imposes different requirements for the child's acquisition of citizenship depending upon whether the citizen parent is the mother or the father. The question before us is whether the statutory distinction is consistent with the equal protection guarantee embedded in the Due Process Clause of the Fifth Amendment.

Petitioner Tuan Anh Nguyen was born in Saigon, Vietnam, in 1969, to copetitioner Joseph Boulais and a Vietnamese citizen. Boulais and Nguyen's mother were not married. In June 1975, Nguyen, then almost six years of age, came to the United States. He became a lawful permanent resident and was raised in Texas by Boulais. In 1992, Nguyen pleaded guilty in a Texas state court to two counts of sexual assault on a child. He was sentenced to eight years in prison on each count. Three years later, the United States Immigration and Naturalization Service (INS) initiated deportation proceedings against Nguyen as a convicted alien. Though later he would change his position and argue he was a United States citizen, Nguyen testified at his deportation hearing that he was a citizen of Vietnam. The Immigration Judge found him deportable.

The constitutionality of the distinction between unwed fathers and mothers was argued in *Miller,* but a majority of the Court did not resolve the issue. Since *Miller,* the Courts of Appeal have divided over the constitutionality of §1409. The father is before the Court in this case; and we now resolve it. We hold that §1409(a) is consistent with the constitutional guarantee of equal protection.

For a gender-based classification to withstand equal protection scrutiny, it must be established "at least that the challenged classification serves 'important governmental objectives and that the discriminatory means employed' are 'substantially related to the achievement of those objectives.'" We conclude the statute satisfies this standard.

The first governmental interest to be served is the importance of assuring that a biological parent-child relationship exists. In the case of the mother, the relation is verifiable from the birth itself. The mother's status is documented in most instances by the birth certificate or hospital records and the witnesses who attest to her having given birth. Given the proof of motherhood that is inherent in birth itself, it is unremarkable that Congress did not require the same affirmative steps of mothers.

To require Congress to speak without reference to the gender of the parent with regard to its objective of ensuring a blood tie between parent and child would be to insist on a hollow neutrality. Congress could have required both mothers and fathers to prove parenthood within 30 days or, for that matter, 18 years, of the child's birth. Given that the mother is always present at birth, but that the father need not be, the facially neutral rule would sometimes require fathers to take additional affirmative steps which would not be required of mothers, whose names will appear on the birth certificate as a result of their presence at the birth, and who will have the benefit of witnesses to the birth to call upon. The issue is not the use of gender specific terms instead of neutral ones. Just as neutral terms can mask discrimination that is unlawful, gender specific terms can mark a permissible distinction. The equal protection question is whether the distinction is lawful. Here, the use of gender specific terms takes into account a biological difference between the parents. The differential treatment is inherent in a sensible statutory scheme, given the unique relationship of the mother to the event of birth.

Having concluded that facilitation of a relationship between parent and child is an important governmental interest, the question remains whether the means Congress chose to further its objective—the imposition of certain additional requirements upon an unwed father—substantially relate to that end. Under this test, the means Congress adopted must be sustained. In this difficult context of conferring citizenship on vast numbers of persons, the means adopted by Congress are in substantial furtherance of important governmental objectives. The fit between the means and the important end is "exceedingly persuasive." *See Virginia, supra.* The statutory scheme's satisfaction of the equal protection scrutiny we apply to gender-based classifications constitutes a sufficient basis for upholding it.

To fail to acknowledge even our most basic biological differences—such as the fact that a mother must be present at birth but the father need not be—risks making the guarantee of equal protection superficial, and so disserving it. Mechanistic classification of all our differences as stereotypes would operate to obscure those misconceptions and prejudices that are real. The distinction embodied in the statutory scheme here at issue is not marked by misconception and prejudice, nor does it show disrespect for either class. The difference between

men and women in relation to the birth process is a real one, and the principle of equal protection does not forbid Congress to address the problem at hand in a manner specific to each gender. The judgment of the Court of Appeals is
>   *Affirmed.*

Justice O'CONNOR, with whom Justice SOUTER, Justice GINSBURG, and Justice BREYER join, *dissenting.*

In a long line of cases spanning nearly three decades, this Court has applied heightened scrutiny to legislative classifications based on sex. The Court today confronts another statute that classifies individuals on the basis of their sex. While the Court invokes heightened scrutiny, the manner in which it explains and applies this standard is a stranger to our precedents. Because the Immigration and Naturalization Service (INS) has not shown an exceedingly persuasive justification for the sex-based classification embodied in 8 U.S.C. §1409(a)(4)—i.e., because it has failed to establish at least that the classification substantially relates to the achievement of important governmental objectives—I would reverse the judgment of the Court of Appeals.

Note

In *Sessions v. Morales-Santana*, 137 S. Ct. 1678 (2017), six members of the Court held that a gender-based classification in the federal immigration laws governing the acquisition of citizenship by a child born abroad to an unwed citizen father is incompatible with the Equal Protection guarantee of the Fifth Amendment. Under the relevant statutes, an unwed US-citizen mother could transmit citizenship to her child if she had lived in the US for just one year prior to the child's birth. Unwed US-citizen fathers had to live in the US for five years prior to their child's birth to transmit citizenship. Writing for the majority, Justice Ginsburg explained that under the Court's exceedingly persuasive justification standard:

> The defender of legislation that differentiates on the basis of gender must show "at least that the challenged classification serves important governmental objectives and that the discriminatory means employed are substantially related to the achievement of those objectives." *Virginia*, 518 U.S., at 533 (quoting *Mississippi Univ. for Women v. Hogan*, 458 U.S. 718, 724 (1982). Moreover, the classification must substantially serve an important governmental interest today, for "in interpreting the equal protection guarantee, we have recognized that new insights and societal understandings can reveal unjustified inequality that once passed unnoticed and unchallenged." *Obergefell v. Hodges*, 35 S. Ct. 2584 (2015). Here, the Government has supplied no "exceedingly persuasive justification," *Virginia*, 518 U. S., at 531, for §1409(a) and (c)'s "gender-based" and "gender-biased" disparity, *Westcott*, 443 U. S. at 84.

The Court rejected both the Government's strong connection to the US and its risk of statelessness justifications for the gender discrimination against unwed

US-citizen fathers. Justices Thomas and Alito concurred in part, but would not have reached the merits. Justice Gorsuch took no part in the decision.

∾ PROBLEMS ∾

1. *The Self-Defense Course.* Jacksonville State University (JSU), a public university with approximately 5,000 undergraduate and 1,000 graduate students, decides to boost safety on its Jacksonville, Florida, campus. With a budget of more than $1 million, the school adds security personnel, closed-circuit cameras, and an advertising campaign to promote public safety awareness. In addition, the school creates a noncredit self-defense course, paid for entirely by the school, taught in a side room in the school gym. The course is designed to teach women the art of self-defense and consequently is restricted to women only. The course is taught by renowned judo and karate experts for both beginners and advanced students and consists of one class per week for nine weeks of intensive training, including discussions about sexual assault and how to fight off an attacker. A psychologist also lectures on the psychology of female protection and instructs students in the art of psychological self-defense. The course is filled to capacity—25 students—and a second section is added with the same number of students. The second section also is filled to capacity, with at least 20 women turned away from the program. Chad Bailey, a 5-foot 8-inch, 140-pound male sophomore engineering student at JSU, is very interested in self-defense classes but cannot find any corresponding class for males on campus. He can find several self-defense courses just off campus, at a fee of $20 per course. These courses are comparable to the JSU course in content, and are co-ed. The instructors are just as renowned as those who teach the JSU classes. There is no psychology component to the off-campus courses, however. In addition, Chad has to walk ten minutes to reach the off-campus courses, whereas the on-campus JSU course requires only a five-minute walk. Chad brings suit against JSU, seeking to attend the self-defense class offered by the university. Assume that the Supreme Court grants Chad's certiorari petition. What is the most likely ruling by the current Court? Why?

2. *Field Hockey.* Mark loves to play field hockey. At his public high school, he states his desire to play. Unfortunately, there is no boys' field hockey team, only a girls' team. Mark files suit, claiming that his equal protection rights have been violated. How would you argue the case for Mark? How might the school respond?

5. Gender Classifications in Context

Over the last 30-plus years, the Court has applied gender review standards in a variety of contexts.

a. Single-Sex Schools

One issue that has generated much litigation is the fact that some states provide single-sex schools. As *United States v. Virginia* illustrates, the courts have generally focused on whether such discrimination is based on stereotypes or on real differences in ability. For example, in *Mississippi University for Women v. Hogan*, 458 U.S. 718 (1982), men sought admission to an all-women's nursing school. The state-asserted justification for excluding men was that it was engaging in "educational affirmative action" by "compensating for discrimination against women." Undertaking a "searching analysis," the Court found no close resemblance between "the alleged objective" and "the actual purpose underlying the discriminatory classification."

∾ PROBLEMS ∾

1. *Does United States v. Virginia Doom the Possibility of Single-Sex Schools?* Suppose that you are the attorney for a school district that is thinking about establishing single-sex schools for girls. The school points to sociological studies demonstrating that many girls thrive in such schools because they can more readily free themselves from sexual stereotypes and feel less pressure about their clothes and looks. The school has asked you to advise them regarding this decision. What would the district need to show to justify the schools? What does *United States v. Virginia* require? What weight, if any, would you give to Justice Scalia's dissent in *United States v. Virginia*, which states that "educational experts in recent years have increasingly come to 'support the view that substantial educational benefits flow from a single-gender environment, be it male or female, *that cannot be replicated in a coeducational setting*' "?

2. *More on Single-Sex Schools.* In the preceding problem, assume that the district decides to establish single-sex schools. After the schools have been in operation for several years, the evidence reveals that girls are performing far better than they performed in co-ed schools. They are also performing better than boys. As a result, most girls opt to attend all-girl schools. At that point, a boy, claiming that he is being deprived of an equal education, seeks to challenge the single-sex school system. Is it a defense to argue that the co-ed schools are "separate but equal"? How else might the all-girl, single-sex schools be defended?

3. *Single-Sex Schools for Boys.* Suppose that sociological studies also demonstrate that African American (and other minority) boys thrive better in single-sex schools. Would it be permissible for a state to establish single-sex schools either for boys or for African American boys? Do the same rules apply to single-sex schools for boys that would apply to single-sex schools for girls? Would *United States v. Virginia* allow local school districts to establish boys-only schools?

4. *Single-Sex Bathrooms.* Are there ways in which society should or must distinguish between men and women? For example, is it necessary or desirable to

maintain single-sex bathrooms? In some countries (e.g., Belgium) unisex bathrooms have been established (although they have individual stalls so that persons have some privacy when performing excretory functions). Suppose that women in Louisville, Kentucky, seek to challenge a local ordinance mandating single-sex bathrooms. They claim that the law is discriminatory because, for some unknown reason (biology?), there are always long lines at the women's bathroom at public events (e.g., at the Kentucky Center for the Arts or at University of Louisville football and basketball games). One woman, frustrated with the long lines, decides to use the male bathroom (where there is no line) and is charged under the ordinance. Should the ordinance be struck down?

5. *More on the Diversity Initiative.* In the introductory problem, suppose that NWU believes that single-sex classes would be beneficial for both men and women. May it create segregated classes in traditional subjects (e.g., English literature) on the theory that women will learn better in such classes? May it create such classes if it thinks that *both* men and women will learn better under such conditions?

b. Public Benefits

In the 1970s, the Court reviewed a series of cases brought by both men and women challenging the differential treatment of men and women in establishing eligibility for public benefits under Social Security and in the military. In general, these laws favored women. One issue raised in these cases was whether laws favoring women disfavored men and, if so, whether the continued favored treatment of women was necessary to compensate for societal and workplace discrimination. Another issue was whether the different treatment of women was based on "archaic and overbroad generalizations."

In *Weinberger v. Wiesenfeld*, 420 U.S. 636 (1975), a man who had been left to care for his infant son upon the death of his wife applied for Social Security Act survivors' benefits for himself and his son. His wife had been a teacher whose earnings had been the couple's principal source of support during their marriage and from whose earnings social security contributions had been deducted. Although he obtained benefits for the son, the widower was denied benefits for himself on the ground that survivors' benefits were allowable only to women. The Court held that the statute's sex-based distinction, which meant that the efforts of women workers required to make Social Security contributions produced less protection for their families than was produced by the efforts of men, violated the right to equal protection under the Due Process Clause of the Fifth Amendment. The Court found that the distinction could not be justified on the basis of the "noncontractual" character of Social Security benefits, or the ground that the sex-based classification was one really designed to compensate women beneficiaries as a group for the economic difficulties confronting women who sought to support themselves and their families. A series of cases challenging the gender-based distinctions in the Social Security statutes followed.

Califano v. Goldfarb

430 U.S. 199 (1977)

Mr. Justice BRENNAN announced the judgment of the Court and delivered an opinion in which Mr. Justice WHITE, Mr. Justice MARSHALL, and Mr. Justice POWELL joined.

Leon Goldfarb, a widower, applied for Social Security survivors' benefits upon the death of his wife, Hannah. During the 25 years of her employment in the New York City public school system, she paid all required Social Security taxes in full. The application was denied.

Under the Federal Old-Age, Survivors, and Disability Insurance Benefits (OASDI) program, survivors' benefits based on the earnings of a deceased husband covered by the Act are payable to his widow. Such benefits on the basis of the earnings of a deceased wife covered by the Act are payable to the widower, however, only if he 'was receiving at least one-half of his support' from his deceased wife. The question in this case is whether this gender-based distinction violates the Due Process Clause of the Fifth Amendment.

A three-judge court held that the different treatment of men and women mandated by the statute constituted invidious discrimination against female wage earners by affording them less protection for their surviving spouses than is provided to male employees. We affirm.

The gender-based distinction drawn by the statute burdening a widower but not a widow with the task of proving dependency upon the deceased spouse presents an equal protection question indistinguishable from that decided in *Weinberger v. Wiesenfeld, supra*. That decision and the decision in *Frontiero* plainly require affirmance of the judgment. *Wiesenfeld* inescapably compels the conclusion that the gender-based differentiation that results in the efforts of female workers required to pay social-security taxes producing less protection for their spouses than is produced by the efforts of men is forbidden by the Constitution, at least when supported by no more substantial justification than "archaic and overbroad" generalizations such as "assumptions as to dependency." These generalizations are more consistent with "the role-typing society has long imposed," than with contemporary reality. By providing dissimilar treatment for men and women who are similarly situated, the statute violates the (Fifth Amendment).

Appellant would focus equal protection analysis, not upon the discrimination against the covered wage earning female, but rather upon whether her surviving widower was unconstitutionally discriminated against by burdening him but not a surviving widow with proof of dependency. The gist of the argument is that "the denial of benefits reflected the congressional judgment that aged widowers as a class were sufficiently likely not to be dependent upon their wives that it was appropriate to deny them benefits unless they were in fact dependent."

But *Wiesenfeld* rejected the virtually identical argument when appellant's predecessor argued that the statutory classification there attacked should be regarded from the perspective of the prospective beneficiary and not from that of the covered wage earner. The disadvantage to the woman wage earner is even more pronounced in the case of old-age benefits, to which a similarly unequal dependency requirement applies. Where the insured herself is still living, she is denied not only "the dignity of knowing (during her working career) that her social security tax would contribute to their joint welfare when the couple or one of them retired and to her husband's welfare should she predecease him," but also the more tangible benefit of an increase in the income of the family unit of which she remains a part.

Finally, the legislative history of the Act refutes appellant's contention. There is every indication that "the framers of the Act legislated on the 'then generally accepted presumption that a man is responsible for the support of his wife and children.'"

We conclude, therefore, that the differential treatment of nondependent widows and widowers results not from a deliberate congressional intention to remedy the arguably greater needs of the former, but rather from an intention to aid the dependent spouses of deceased wage earners, coupled with a presumption that wives are usually dependent. This presents precisely the situation faced in *Frontiero* and *Wiesenfeld*. The only conceivable justification for writing the presumption of wives' dependency into the statute is the assumption, not verified by the Government in *Frontiero*, or here, but based simply on "archaic and overbroad" generalizations that it would save the Government time, money, and effort simply to pay benefits to all widows, rather than to require proof of dependency of both sexes. Such assumptions do not suffice to justify a gender-based discrimination in the distribution of employment-related benefits.

Affirmed.

Mr. Justice REHNQUIST, with whom THE CHIEF JUSTICE, Mr. Justice STEWART, and Mr. Justice BLACKMUN join, *dissenting*.

The effect of the statutory scheme is to make it easier for widows to obtain benefits than it is for widowers, since the former qualify automatically while the latter must show proof of need. Such a requirement in no way perpetuates or exacerbates the economic disadvantage which has led the Court to conclude that gender-based discrimination must meet a different test from other types of classifications. It is, like the property tax exemption to widows in *Kahn*, a differing treatment which "rest(s) upon some ground of difference having a fair and substantial relation to the object of the legislation."

The very most that can be squeezed out of the facts of this case in the way of cognizable 'discrimination' is a classification which favors aged widows. This is scarcely an invidious discrimination. A waiver of the dependency prerequisite for benefits, in the case of this same class of aged widows, under a program explicitly aimed at the assistance of needy groups, appears to be well within the holding of the *Kahn* case, which upheld a flat $500 exemption to widows, without any consideration of need.

Note: Review Standards in Benefits Cases

In the benefits cases, the Court split on several issues: the applicable level of scrutiny; when administrative convenience was a legitimate reason for gender-based classification; and who was actually being discriminated against, women or men. Who is actually being discriminated against?

∽ PROBLEMS ∽

1. *Workers' Compensation.* Missouri's workers' compensation law provides that, when a man dies, his widow is automatically entitled to benefits. By contrast, when a woman dies, benefits are payable to her spouse only if he is mentally or physically incapacitated or was to some extent dependent upon her. In evaluating the law, is it appropriate to view the law as involving a classification affecting only men (the widower), only women (the deceased female's spouse), or both?

2. *More on Workers' Compensation.* Under the statute referred to in the preceding problem, suppose that, when a man's wife dies, he challenges the law as discrimination against her (her work is devalued because her surviving husband must prove incapacity or dependency in order to recover). Does the law involve invalid gender discrimination? Consider the following arguments: a) The substantive difference in the economic standing of working men and women justifies the advantage that the statute administratively gives to a widow. b) Surely the needs of surviving widows and widowers would be completely served either by paying benefits to all members of both classes or by paying benefits only to those members of either class who can demonstrate their need. c) The substantive difference in the economic standing of working men and women justifies the advantage that the law administratively gives to a widow. d) Why pay all surviving widows without requiring proof of dependency? e) It is more efficient to presume dependency in the case of women than to engage in case-to-case determination, because individualized inquiries in the postulated few cases in which men might be dependent are not prohibitively costly. *See Wengler v. Druggists Mutual Insurance Co.*, 446 U.S. 142 (1980).

c. The Military

Historically, women were restricted from certain jobs in the U.S. military. Are sexual classifications relating to military service now subject to heightened review?

Rostker v. Goldberg

453 U.S. 57 (1981)

REHNQUIST, J., delivered the opinion of the Court.

The question presented is whether the Military Selective Service Act violates the Fifth Amendment to the United States Constitution in authorizing the President to require the registration of males and not females.

Congress is given the power under the Constitution "To raise and support Armies," "To provide and maintain a Navy," and "To make Rules for the Government and Regulation of the land and naval Forces." Art. I, §8, cls. 12-14. Congress is a coequal branch of government whose Members take the same oath we do to uphold the Constitution of the United States. We must have "due regard to the fact that this Court is not exercising a primary judgment but is sitting in judgment upon those who also have taken the oath to observe the Constitution and who have the responsibility for carrying on government." The customary deference accorded the judgments of Congress is certainly appropriate when, as here, Congress specifically considered the question of the Act's constitutionality. This is not, however, merely a case involving the customary deference accorded congressional decisions. The case arises in the context of Congress' authority over national defense and military affairs, and perhaps in no other area has the Court accorded Congress greater deference. In rejecting the registration of women, Congress explicitly relied upon its constitutional powers under Art. I, §8, cls. 12-14. This Court has consistently recognized Congress' "broad constitutional power" to raise and regulate armies and navies.

Not only is the scope of Congress' constitutional power in this area broad, but the lack of competence on the part of the courts is marked. "It is difficult to conceive of an area of governmental activity in which the courts have less competence." The operation of a healthy deference to legislative and executive judgments in the area of military affairs is evident in several recent decisions of this Court. None of this is to say that Congress is free to disregard the Constitution when it acts in the area of military affairs. Congress remains subject to the limitations of the Due Process Clause but the tests and limitations to be applied may differ because of the military context. We do not abdicate our responsibility to decide the constitutional question, but simply recognize that the Constitution itself requires deference to congressional choice. We must be particularly careful not to substitute our judgment of what is desirable for that of Congress, or our own evaluation of evidence for a reasonable evaluation by the Legislative Branch.

This case is quite different from several of the gender-based discrimination cases we have considered in that Congress did not act "unthinkingly" or "reflexively and not for any considered reason." The principle that women should not intentionally and routinely engage in combat is fundamental, and enjoys wide support among our people. It is universally supported by military leaders who have testified before the Committee. Current law and policy exclude women from being assigned to combat in our military forces, and the Committee reaffirms this policy. The existence of the combat restrictions clearly indicates the basis for Congress' decision to exempt women from registration. The purpose of registration was to prepare for a draft of combat troops. Since women are excluded from combat, Congress concluded that they would not be needed in the event of a draft, and therefore decided not to register them.

Congress' decision to authorize the registration of only men does not violate the Due Process Clause. The exemption of women from registration is not only sufficiently but also closely related to Congress' purpose in authorizing registration. The Constitution requires that Congress treat similarly situated persons similarly, not that it engage in gestures of superficial equality. In light of the foregoing, we conclude that Congress acted well within its constitutional authority when it authorized the registration of men, and not women, under the Military Selective Service Act. The decision of the District Court holding otherwise is accordingly,

Reversed.

Justice WHITE, with whom Justice BRENNAN joins, *dissenting.*

I assume what has not been challenged in this case—that excluding women from combat positions does not offend the Constitution. If during mobilization for war, all noncombat military positions must be filled by combat-qualified personnel available to be moved into combat positions, there would be no occasion whatsoever to have any women in the Army, whether as volunteers or inductees. The Court appears to say, that Congress concluded as much and that we should accept that judgment. The Court's position in this regard is most unpersuasive. There is little indication that Congress itself concluded that every position in the military, no matter how far removed from combat, must be filled with combat-ready men. Common sense and experience in recent wars, where women volunteers were employed in substantial numbers, belie this view. I discern no adequate justification for this kind of discrimination between men and women. I dissent.

Justice MARSHALL, with whom Justice BRENNAN joins, *dissenting.*

The Court today places its imprimatur on one of the most potent remaining public expressions of "ancient canards about the proper role of women." It upholds a statute that requires males but not females to register for the draft, and which thereby categorically excludes women from a fundamental civic obligation. Because I believe the Court's decision is inconsistent with the Constitution's guarantee of equal protection of the laws, I dissent.

Statutes which discriminate on the basis of gender, must be examined under "heightened" scrutiny. The Government does not defend the exclusion of women from registration on the ground that preventing women from serving in the military is substantially related to the effectiveness of the Armed Forces. "Legislative classifications which distribute benefits and burdens on the basis of gender *carry the inherent risk of reinforcing sexual stereotypes about the 'proper place' of women and their need for special protection.*" Neither the Senate Report itself nor the testimony presented at the congressional hearings provides any support for the conclusion that drafting a limited number of women would burden training and administrative facilities. In concluding that the Government has carried its burden in this case, the Court adopts "an appropriately deferential examination of *Congress'* evaluation of the evidence" (emphasis in original). Congressional enactments in the area of military affairs must, like all other laws, be *judged* by the standards of the Constitution. "When it appears that an Act of Congress conflicts with a constitutional provision, we have no choice but to enforce the paramount commands of the Constitution." I would *affirm the judgment.*

Notes: Gender Ambiguity

1. *Gender Ambiguity.* The discussion about sex discrimination assumes that the sex of a human can be easily determined. Yet, the more research that is done, the less this assumption holds up. The old chromosome tests, in which scientists looked at whether the individual had XX or XY chromosomes, do not suffice. Some people are intersex, meaning they have characteristics of both sexes: "The problem, said Dr. Joe Leigh Simpson, a pediatric geneticist at Florida International University, is that genetic or hormonal abnormalities can affect any organ system, including the gonads and external genitalia. When such anomalies occur, 'it can produce confusion' because hormone levels and other aspects of physiology may not match appearance. Moreover, there is 'no single process' for determining sex because every case is different, he said." Thomas Maugh II, *Row over South African Athlete Highlights Ambiguities of Gender,* L.A. Times, Sports, Aug. 21, 2009.

2. *Sports, Gender, and an Equal Playing Field.* Sports is one area of particular concern involving the equal protection notion of an even playing field. This issue becomes readily evident in the Olympics, when gender testing occurs with publicized frequency. A particularly notable case was the controversy surrounding the South African 800-meter runner, Caster Semenya, who won the 2009 World Championship. The problems for the testers are considerable.

> Genes are only a blueprint, and sometimes nature doesn't follow the blueprint precisely. Take the examples of XY athletes who appear to be women. At least five enzymes are required to synthesize testosterone, the hormone that produces most male characteristics. Occasionally one of those enzymes is defective. When that happens, the genitals are typically male, but tiny, the person doesn't have much body hair and is generally feminized. Such people are normally eligible to compete as women. In other genetic males, the receptor that the testosterone binds to is defective and it doesn't matter how much testosterone is present. That male is classified as androgen insensitive, but the results are the same: feminization. Genitalia are typically female. Often, such people grow up as females and don't find out they have male genes until they don't get menstrual periods. They are often tall, slender and attractive. Neither anomaly gives the person strength or endurance beyond that of a normal woman and subjects are allowed to compete as women. The condition of being genetically female, or XX, but appearing male can often be traced to congenital adrenal hyperplasia, in which the adrenal glands produce excess testosterone. The woman may look like a boy with tiny male genitals, but once a month will pass blood. If the condition is caught early in life, doctors

usually recommend surgery to create female genitalia. But many persons with the condition live normal lives as men.

Thomas Maugh II, *Row over South African Athlete Highlights Ambiguities of Gender,* L.A. Times, Sports, Aug. 21, 2009. One expert further highlighted why rigid sex categories do not work: "Eric Vilain, a professor of human genetics and pediatrics at U.C.L.A., specializes in sex development, so he knows that looking at genes will not tell you simply how a body is functioning. And what we care about is function. 'The best biological marker, if you want a level playing field, would probably be functional testosterone,' Vilain said. 'There is a good correlation between functional testosterone and muscle mass.'" Alice Dreger, *The Sex of Athletes: One Issue, Many Variables,* N.Y. Times, New York ed. SP 8, Oct. 24, 2009.

◇ PROBLEMS ◇

1. Rostker *Today.* If *Rostker* arose today, would it be decided the same way? During the past 25 years, women have assumed a much larger role in the military and have even been assigned to combat roles (from which they were previously excluded). Do these facts require a difference in result? How does the holding in *United States v. Virginia* affect the analysis?

2. *The Draft.* You are a law clerk to a federal judge who is hearing the case of *United States v. Sprague.* In this case, a law enacted by Congress is at the heart of the dispute. It provides: "There shall be a special draft for combat purposes of both men and women between the ages of eighteen and twenty. Those persons from this special draft who can demonstrate (a) a certain level of physical fitness, to be measured by cardiovascular, endurance and strength tests such as running, jumping and the lifting of weights, and (b) psychological suitability, shall be considered for elite combat units. The men and women chosen for these units shall be strictly separated based on gender—one unit of twenty spots shall be reserved for women and one unit of twenty spots will be reserved for men. If more men and women qualify, additional separate units shall be created. This separation is justified by gender differences in biology and physiology as well as affirmative action goals." Advise the judge. Is the law constitutional?

3. *Armed Services Tenure.* Congress has placed a limit on the navy's enlisted personnel and a correlative limit on the number of active line officers as a percentage of the personnel figure. Congress has also established a ratio for the distribution of line officers in the several grades above lieutenant in fixed proportions to the total number of line officers. Because the navy has a pyramidal organizational structure, fewer officers are needed at each higher rank than are needed in the rank below. In the absence of some mandatory attrition of naval officers, the result would be stagnation of promotion of younger officers and disincentive to naval service. Accordingly, Congress has provided that male lieutenants who have been twice passed over for promotion will be mandatorily discharged.

Women are entitled to a 13-year tenure of commissioned service before they face mandatory discharge regardless of whether they have been passed over twice. Consider the following arguments in favor of and against the statute: a) Male and female line officers in the navy are not similarly situated with respect to opportunities for professional service because of restrictions on women officers' participation in combat and in most sea duty. Congress may thus quite rationally have believed that women line officers had less opportunity for promotion than did their male counterparts, and that a longer period of tenure for women officers would, therefore, be consistent with the goal to provide women officers with "fair and equitable career advancement programs." b) A legislative classification that is premised solely on gender must be subjected to close judicial scrutiny, and the State's asserted interest is insufficient to satisfy that standard. *Schlesinger v. Ballard*, 419 U.S. 498 (1975).

D. THE RIGHTS OF ALIENS

Are aliens deserving of special protection, or should classifications involving them be subjected to rational basis review? The Court has used different standards of scrutiny for governmental classifications that affect legal resident aliens. In its early decisions, the Court gave little protection to persons in this class. Even though aliens were held to be "persons" entitled to the protection of the Equal Protection Clause, *see Yick Wo v. Hopkins*, 118 U.S. 356 (1886), this protection was limited for more than 60 years. The Court permitted discrimination against aliens when the governmental action was justified by a "special public interest," and the Court upheld statutes prohibiting aliens from using natural resources, entering various occupations, and owning land. The Court's precedents upholding laws limiting the rights of aliens served as *de facto* recognition of racial classifications, since Chinese and Japanese persons were not eligible for citizenship during the era when their "alienage" was a permanent status.

    The turning point for the Court's modern approach came in *Takahashi v. Fish & Game Commission*, 334 U.S. 410 (1948), when the Court rejected the idea that a "special public interest" is a justification for denying a resident Japanese alien the right to make a living in commercial fishing activity in state coastal waters. The law prohibiting Japanese fisherman had existed for decades without alienage restrictions, but was amended after persons of Japanese ancestry in California were sent to internment camps following the attack on Pearl Harbor. The amended law prohibited the issuance of licenses to anyone "ineligible for citizenship" under federal law, thereby preventing persons of Japanese or Chinese ancestry from obtaining licenses because they were ineligible for naturalization. The State defended the law based on its "special public interest" in preserving the stocks of coastal fish, and argued that the excluded aliens lacked the "community" interest possessed by citizens in that state resource. But the Court held that the

Equal Protection Clause protected the right of all aliens residing lawfully in the United States to "abide in any State" and to enjoy "an equality of legal privileges" possessed by citizens. Therefore, the State's interest in coastal fish did not justify the establishment of a monopoly for citizens to engage in commercial fishing without competition from aliens who were denied access to the same livelihood.

Notably, the Court also rejected the State's claim of authority to limit the state-law rights of aliens within its borders using the classifications in the federal naturalization laws. After observing that Congress has the exclusive authority under the Constitution to regulate immigration, the Court noted that state alienage classifications should be invalidated under the Supremacy Clause when they conflict with federal law or policy. The California law conflicted with federal law by imposing "discriminatory burdens upon the entrance or residence of aliens lawfully within the United States." By contrast, Congress recognized the right of aliens to "entrance and abode" in any State, which right necessarily required the protection of their "opportunity of earning a livelihood" in their State of abode. The California licensing law imposed a discriminatory burden because of its impairment of that opportunity.

By the early 1970s, equal protection doctrine had evolved dramatically since the *Takahashi* decision, and a majority of the Court was prepared to apply that doctrine to alienage classifications. As revealed in the next case, the Court established strict scrutiny as the standard of review for state-law alienage classifications. But the Court held that only rational basis scrutiny would apply to state laws that restricted certain government jobs to citizens, and the "political function" exception was created to define those jobs. The Court continued to enforce the Supremacy Clause by invalidating state alienage laws that conflicted with federal immigration policy, and in deference to the broad authority of Congress regarding that policy, the Court also endorsed a form of "relaxed scrutiny" resembling the rational basis standard of review for alienage classifications in federal laws.

∾ PROBLEM: STANDARDS OF REVIEW ∾

What standard of review should be applied to classifications that affect aliens? Are aliens a "distinct and insular" minority? In terms of political clout, aliens are definitely minorities since they do not have the right to vote. Historically, have aliens been subject to discrimination? Is the status of alienage immutable? If not, does that fact alone justify treating aliens differently compared with classifications involving race?

1. State Laws Regulating Aliens

In the decades following *Takahashi*, the States continued to defend statutory restrictions of the rights of aliens on the basis of a "special public interest" in preserving resources and other benefits for state citizens. The next case marked the clear ending of that era and the establishment of meaningful constitutional requirements for the equal treatment of aliens and citizens.

Graham v. Richardson

403 U.S. 365 (1971)

Mr. Justice BLACKMUN delivered the opinion of the Court.

The issue here is whether the Equal Protection Clause of the Fourteenth Amendment prevents a State from conditioning welfare benefits either (a) upon the beneficiary's possession of United States citizenship under the Pennsylvania statute, or (b) if the beneficiary is an alien, upon his having resided in this country for a specified number of years under the Arizona statute requiring 15 years of residency. In each case, after years of residency, the alien plaintiffs became disabled and could no longer work, which loss of employment caused their indigency. They sought welfare benefits in order to obtain funds for food, clothing, and shelter.

It has long been settled that the term "person" in the Fourteenth Amendment encompasses lawfully admitted resident aliens as well as citizens and entitles both citizens and aliens to the equal protection of the laws of the State in which they reside. *Yick Wo v. Hopkins*, 118 U.S. 356 (1886). Nor is it disputed that the Arizona and Pennsylvania statutes create two classes of needy persons, indistinguishable except with respect to whether they are or are not citizens. Classifications based on alienage, like those based on nationality or race, are inherently suspect and subject to close judicial scrutiny. Aliens as a class are a prime example of a "discrete and insular" minority for whom such heightened judicial solicitude is appropriate.

Arizona and Pennsylvania seek to justify their restrictions on the eligibility of aliens for public assistance solely on the basis of a State's "special public interest" in favoring its own citizens over aliens in the distribution of limited resources such as welfare benefits. *Takahashi v. Fish & Game Comm'n*, 334 U.S. 410 (1948), however, cast doubt on the continuing validity of the special public-interest doctrine in all contexts. We conclude that a State's desire to preserve limited welfare benefits for its own citizens is inadequate to justify the alien exclusions here. "A State has a valid interest in preserving the fiscal integrity of its programs but may not accomplish such a purpose by invidious distinctions between classes of its citizens. The saving of welfare costs cannot justify an otherwise invidious classification." *Shapiro v. Thompson*, 394 U.S. 618, 633 (1969). Here the concern for fiscal integrity is not compelling.

The "justification of limiting expenses is particularly inappropriate and unreasonable when the discriminated class consists of aliens. Aliens like citizens pay taxes and may be called into the armed forces. They may live within a state for many years, work in the state and contribute to the economic growth of the state." *Leger v. Sailer*, 321 F. Supp. 250, 253 (E.D. Pa. 1970). There can be no "special public interest" in tax revenues to which aliens have contributed on an equal basis with the residents of the State. Accordingly, we hold that the statutes violate the Equal Protection Clause.

An additional reason why the statutes do not withstand constitutional scrutiny is that Congress has not seen fit to impose any burden or restriction on aliens who become indigent after their entry into the United States. Aliens lawfully within this country have a right to enter and abide in any State in the Union "on an equality of legal privileges with all citizens under non-discrimination laws." *Takahashi*, 334 U.S. at 420. State laws that restrict the eligibility of aliens for welfare benefits merely because of their alienage conflict with these overriding national policies in an area constitutionally entrusted to the Federal Government. The statutes here impose auxiliary burdens upon the entrance or residence of aliens who suffer the distress, after entry, of economic dependency on public assistance. Alien residency requirements for welfare benefits necessarily operate to discourage entry into or continued residency in the State. Since such laws encroach upon exclusive federal power, they are constitutionally impermissible.

Notes

1. *Categories of Aliens.* Although the Court seeks to identify the immigration status of aliens in equal protection cases, it may be difficult to discern whether that status is an important factor in the Court's holding. Most alienage cases involve litigation by noncitizen plaintiffs who are "immigrant aliens" (also known as "resident aliens," "lawful resident aliens," "lawful permanent residents," or "permanent resident aliens"). These aliens possess a "green card," are eligible for naturalization, and obtained admission to the United States based on their relationship to a family member who is a citizen. Typically, an immigrant alien must reside in this country for five years before applying for naturalization. Although they may choose to reside in the country indefinitely without becoming a citizen, most immigrant aliens become citizens. By contrast, the category of "nonimmigrant aliens" includes noncitizens who have qualified for a visa in one of 24 categories established by federal statute. Their admission to the United States is temporary, and its specified duration and purpose is prescribed by their visa category. Once they are admitted, nonimmigrant aliens may be eligible to obtain a visa in a different category, and thereby remain in the United States. They may also be eligible to apply for permanent residency status and thereby become immigrant aliens with a path to citizenship. The terms "undocumented aliens" or "undocumented immigrants" refers to persons who have no lawful immigration status or persons who do not possess valid immigration documentation. It is useful to consider whether and how the Court's reasoning in a given case may be applicable in a case that involves discrimination against a different "class" of aliens.

2. *Strict Scrutiny Formula.* By the mid-1980s, the Supreme Court's equal protection opinions on alienage classifications reflected the modern definition of

strict scrutiny: "In order to withstand strict scrutiny, the law must advance a compelling state interest by the least restrictive means available." *Bernal v. Fainter*, 467 U.S. 216, 219 (1984). In the 1970s, however, the Court sometimes used the terms "substantial," "overriding," or "important," as synonyms for "compelling." *See In re Griffiths*, 413 U.S. 717, 722 & n.9 (1973). The earlier opinions also referred to the state's burden of proof as requiring a showing that its "purpose or interest" is "constitutionally permissible" (not invidious discrimination) and "that its use of the classification is necessary to the accomplishment of its purpose of the safeguarding of its interest." *Id.* at 722. This focus on "necessity" may be compared to the modern requirement that a statute must be so "narrowly tailored" as to be the "least restrictive means available."

3. *Exclusion from Law Practice.* The Court applied strict scrutiny to invalidate a state rule requiring bar applicants to be citizens of the United States in *In re Griffiths*, 413 U.S. 719 (1973). Plaintiff was an alien who came to the United States on a tourist visa, but who became a "resident alien" when she married a citizen, but chose not to apply for U.S. citizenship. Her application to take the Connecticut bar exam was denied solely because she did not meet the citizenship requirement imposed by local rules. The state sought to justify the requirement on the basis of the state's interest in ensuring that bar applicants will dutifully fulfill their responsibilities to courts and faithfully protect the interests of their clients. Although the Court found this to be a "constitutionally permissible and substantial interest," it held that the state could not show that the exclusion of aliens was necessary to promote or safeguard that interest. The state argued that a citizen may have an "undivided allegiance to this country," whereas a resident alien may have a "possible conflict of loyalties," which "might" lead the alien to "ignore his responsibilities to the courts or even his clients in favor of the interest of a foreign power." The Court rejected these arguments, concluding that the state failed to show "the relevance of citizenship to any likelihood that a lawyer will fail to protect faithfully the interest of clients" or that aliens would act "adversely to the interest of the United States." The Court reasoned that the state's interest was safeguarded sufficiently by the bar disciplinary system, and that the mere "possibility" that some aliens "might be unsuited to the practice of law" did not justify a "wholesale ban." The Court also rejected the argument that lawyers are "officers of the court," who act "with the authority of the State," and are "entrusted" with the "exercise of actual government power" like government officials, and therefore must be citizens because they are "office holders" who "participate in the government structure." The Court held that lawyers "are not officials of government," but instead are "engaged in a private profession." Thus, the rules failed strict scrutiny.

4. *Eligibility for Civil Service Employment.* In *Sugarman v. Dougall*, 413 U.S. 634 (1973), the Court used strict scrutiny to invalidate a "statutory prohibition on the employment of aliens in the competitive classified civil service" in New York. The prohibition extended to a range of positions, covering an array of work tasks, from "the menial to the policy making." By contrast, the state imposed no citizenship

requirement on four other classes of public employees, including "higher offices" in state executive departments, "unskilled laborers," positions "for which a non-competitive examination would be practicable," and the "unclassified service," which included all elective offices as well as teachers. As in *Griffiths*, the Court recognized the "substantial" state interest in having employees of "undivided loyalty," especially when they participate in the "formulation and execution of government," and who are "free of competing obligations" "attendant upon foreign citizenship," which might "jeopardize public confidence" in the "employee's objectivity." However, the Court found that "the means" employed by the state to achieve this end were not "precisely drawn in light of the acknowledged purpose." The alien prohibition swept "indiscriminately" to cover "the sanitation man," "the typist," and "the office worker," as well as people who formulated important state policy. The state's interest had little relationship to many of the covered positions. Paradoxically, aliens were not barred from positions in the other four employee classes which arguably had a stronger relationship to the state's interest. Thus, the state failed to satisfy the demand of the strict scrutiny standard because it was "neither narrowly confined nor precise in its application." The Court also rejected an array of other proffered state interests, including the argument that the state had a "special public interest" in reserving "public employment" for state citizens. The Court further noted that *Graham* had repudiated the "special public interest" doctrine, and the Court rejected the idea that the alien exclusion provision could be defended on the theory that "career civil service is intended for the long-term employee," and an alien "is likely to remain only temporarily in a civil service position." The Court doubted that long-term permanent resident aliens in New York "would be a poorer risk for a career position" than American citizens. Finally, the state argued that "aliens are more likely to leave their work than citizens," and, therefore, the exclusion saves the state "the expense of hiring and training replacements." The Court concluded that the state "justification of limiting expenses is particularly inappropriate and unreasonable when the discriminated class consists of aliens," who share the obligations of citizens to pay taxes and serve in the armed forces.

5. *The Supremacy Clause and the Benefits of "In-State" Status.* In *Toll v. Moreno*, 458 U.S. 1 (1982), the Court considered a constitutional challenge to a Maryland law that allowed "immigrant alien" students but not "nonimmigrant alien" students to qualify for "in-state" status that would entitle them to reduced tuition fees and advantageous admission standards. The excluded plaintiffs were dependents of nonimmigrant aliens holding G-4 visas which are issued to officers or employees of certain international organizations and members of their immediate families. The Court found that the state law violated the Supremacy Clause because the law imposed additional burdens not contemplated by Congress upon aliens who had been lawfully admitted to the country. When enacting the Immigration and Nationality Act, Congress made the decision to allow G-4 aliens to acquire domicile in the United States. The state's decision to deny "in-state" status to such aliens resulted in the imposition of higher tuition and fees on them compared to

other domiciliaries. In addition, the policy of the state law conflicted with federal policies expressed in federal statutes, treaties, and international agreements that provide tax exemptions for G-4 aliens. The Court did not address the equal protection claim based on the different treatment of alien classes, and relied instead on the Supremacy Clause to invalidate the state law.

∾ PROBLEMS ∾

1. *Debate over Strict Scrutiny.* The Court was not unanimous in *Graham, Griffiths,* or *Sugarman* because the dissenting Justices objected to the use of strict scrutiny for alienage classifications. Consider the Court's declaration in *Graham* that aliens constitute a suspect class. What arguments could be made by the Court regarding the history of discrimination against aliens, their political powerlessness as a group, and the immutability of their alien status? What counterarguments could be made by the dissenting Justices who oppose the use of strict scrutiny? *See Nyquist v. Mauclet,* 432 U.S. 1 (1977).

2. *Practice of Engineering.* A state statute prohibits anyone other than U.S. citizens from practicing privately as a civil engineer in a state that shares a border with Mexico. The state offers two justifications for the statute. First, it is necessary to prevent the "uncontrolled" immigration of Spanish-speaking aliens in the engineering field. Second, it is necessary to provide civil engineering clients with the assurance that if the engineer's work is flawed, it will be easier for the clients to demand financial accountability from the engineer. Is the statute constitutional? *See Examining Board v. Flores de Otero,* 426 U.S. 572 (1976) (Puerto Rico statute prohibiting anyone other than U.S. citizens from "private practice of engineering").

3. *Access to Financial Aid.* Assume that a state statute provides three types of financial assistance to students who wish to enroll in a college or university. One type of assistance is a scholarship based upon performance in a competitive examination. A second type is tuition assistance which depends on a student's income. The third type is a student loan that also depends upon income. All applicants, however, must have been a resident of New York for six months, and also 1) must be U.S. citizens; or 2) must have filed an application for U.S. citizenship; or 3) must have filed a statement affirming his or her intent to apply for U.S. citizenship as soon as he or she is eligible. The impact of the statute is to bar many aliens from applying for state financial aid, such as those who have student visas and are not eligible for the permanent resident status needed to apply for U.S. citizenship. Is the statute constitutional? *See Nyquist v. Mauclet,* 432 U.S. 1 (1977).

4. *Nonimmigrant Alien Attorneys.* Assume that a state statute prohibits a nonimmigrant alien who has graduated from a foreign law school from taking the state bar exam, and thereby prohibits such an alien from obtaining a state license to practice law. Only a U.S. citizen or a lawful resident alien may take the state bar

exam, namely those aliens who have qualified for permanent resident status. By contrast, a nonimmigrant alien is a person who is lawfully admitted to the United States temporarily but is not entitled to live and work in the United States permanently. Is this statute constitutional? How can the reasoning of *In re Griffiths* be distinguished? *See LeClerc v. Webb*, 419 F.3d 405 (5th Cir. 2005); *Dandamundi v. Tisch*, 686 F.3d 66 (2d Cir. 2012).

5. *More on the Diversity Initiative.* Consider the problem described at the beginning of this chapter. Suppose that NWU decides to include immigrants in its diversity initiative on the theory that they bring unique socioeconomic perspectives, and other cultural and life perspectives, to the educational process. As a result, NWU has decided to give immigrants preferences in admissions and financial aid. What standard of review would apply to such a program? Is it constitutional to include immigrants in the initiative? Would the Court review the program any differently if it applied to illegal immigrants as well as legal immigrants and is challenged by a U.S. citizen who was denied similar assistance and similar financial aid?

2. Political Function Exception

In *Sugarman v. Dougall*, 413 U.S. 634 (1973), the Court observed in dicta that demanding scrutiny should not be applied to state laws that require citizenship as a qualification for the employment of "persons holding state elective or important nonelective executive, legislative, and judicial positions," if those persons "participate directly in the formulation, execution or review of broad public policy." The Court gives states more deference in recognition of a state's "historical power to exclude aliens from participation in its democratic political institutions," and its "constitutional responsibility for the establishment and operation of its own government." A state's restriction "on the employment of noncitizens, narrowly confined," may be justified in some circumstances as an exercise of the state's responsibility to "preserve the basic conception of a political community." This dicta became the blueprint for the "political function" exception to strict scrutiny that is illustrated in the next case.

Bernal v. Fainter

467 U.S. 216 (1984)

Justice MARSHALL delivered the opinion of the Court.

The question is whether a Texas statute violates the Equal Protection Clause by denying aliens the opportunity to become notaries public. Bernal is a Mexican citizen who has lived in Texas as a resident alien for more than 20 years. As a paralegal for Texas Rural Legal Aid, he helps migrant farm workers on employment and civil rights matters, and he wishes to administer oaths to these workers and notarize their statements for use in civil litigation. Under Texas law, notaries public authenticate written instruments, administer oaths, and take out-of-court depositions. The Texas Secretary of State denied Bernal's application because he was not a citizen of the United States.

We have developed a narrow exception to the rule that discrimination based on alienage triggers strict scrutiny. This exception has been labeled the "political function" exception and applies to laws that exclude aliens from positions intimately related to the process of democratic self-government. In *Foley v. Connellie*, 435 U.S. 291 (1978), we held that a State may require police to be citizens because, in performing a fundamental obligation of government, police "are clothed with authority to exercise an almost infinite variety of discretionary powers" often involving the most sensitive areas of daily life. In *Cabell v. Chavez-Salido*, 454 U.S. 432 (1982), we held that a State may bar aliens from positions as probation officers because they routinely exercise discretionary power, involving a basic governmental function, that places them in a position of direct authority over other individuals.

The rationale behind the political-function exception is that within broad boundaries a State may establish its own form of government and limit the right to govern to those who are full-fledged members of the political community. Some public positions are so closely bound up with the formulation and implementation of self-government that the State is permitted to exclude from those positions persons outside the political community, hence persons who have not become part of the process of democratic self-determination.

We have therefore lowered our standard of review when evaluating the validity of exclusions that entrust only to citizens important elective and nonelective positions whose operations "go to the heart of representative government." *Sugarman v. Dougall*, 413 U.S. 634 (1973). To determine whether a restriction based on alienage fits within the narrow political-function exception, we devised in *Cabell* a two-part test.

> First, the specificity of the classification will be examined: a classification that is substantially overinclusive or underinclusive tends to undercut the governmental claim that the classification serves legitimate political ends. Second, even if the classification is sufficiently tailored, it may be applied in the particular case only to "persons holding state elective or important nonelective executive, legislative, and judicial positions," those officers who "participate directly in the formulation, execution, or review of broad public policy" and hence "perform functions that go to the heart of representative government."

Unlike the statute invalidated in *Sugarman*, the Texas statute does not indiscriminately sweep within its ambit a wide range of offices and occupations but specifies only one particular post with respect to which the State has a right to exclude aliens. Clearly, the statute is not overinclusive; it applies narrowly to only one category of persons: those wishing to obtain appointments as notaries. Less clear is whether the statute is underinclusive. Texas does not require court reporters to be United States citizens even though they perform some of the same services as notaries. Nor does Texas require that its Secretary of State be a citizen, even though he holds the highest appointive position in the State and performs many important functions, including supervision of the licensing of all notaries public. We need not decide this issue, however, because of our decision with respect to the second prong of the *Cabell* test.

Texas maintains that the designation of notaries as public officers by the Texas Constitution indicates that the State views notaries as important officials occupying posts central to the State's definition of itself as a political community. This Court, however, has never deemed the source of a position as the dispositive factor in determining whether a State may entrust the position only to citizens. Rather, this Court has always looked to the actual function of the position as the dispositive factor.

The State maintains that the duties of Texas notaries entail the performance of functions sufficiently consequential to be deemed "political." We recognize the critical need for a notary's duties to be carried out correctly and with integrity. But a notary's duties, important as they are, are essentially clerical and ministerial. To be sure, considerable damage could result from the negligent or dishonest performance of a notary's duties. But the same could be said for the duties performed by cashiers, building inspectors, the janitors who clean up the offices of public officials, and numerous other categories of personnel. What distinguishes such personnel from those to whom the political-function exception is properly applied is that the latter are invested either with policymaking responsibility or broad discretion in the execution of public policy that requires the routine exercise of authority over individuals. Neither of these characteristics pertains to the functions performed by Texas notaries.

The inappropriateness of applying the political-function exception to Texas notaries is further underlined by our decision in *In re Griffiths,* 413 U.S. 634 (1973), in which we subjected to strict scrutiny a Connecticut statute that prohibited noncitizens from becoming members of the State Bar. Along with the usual powers and privileges accorded to members of the bar, Connecticut gave them additional authority that encompasses the very duties performed by Texas notaries. If it is improper to apply the political-function exception to a citizenship requirement governing eligibility for membership in a state bar, it would be anomalous to apply the exception to the citizenship requirement that governs eligibility to become a Texas notary. We conclude, then, that the "political function" exception is inapplicable to the Texas statute and that the statute is therefore subject to strict judicial scrutiny.

To satisfy strict scrutiny, the State must show that the statute furthers a compelling state interest by the least restrictive means practically available. The State maintains that the statute serves its "legitimate concern that notaries be reasonably familiar with state law and institutions" and "that notaries may be called upon years later to testify to acts they have performed." However, both of these asserted justifications utterly fail to meet the stringent requirements of strict scrutiny. There is nothing in the record that indicates that resident aliens, as a class, are so incapable of familiarizing themselves with Texas law as to justify the State's absolute and classwide exclusion. The possibility that some resident aliens are unsuitable for the position cannot justify a wholesale ban against all resident aliens. Furthermore, if the State's concern with ensuring a notary's familiarity with state law were truly "compelling," one would expect the State to give some sort of test actually measuring a person's familiarity with the law. The State, however, administers no such test. If the State's concern were truly "compelling," one would expect the State to give some sort of test actually measuring a person's familiarity with the law. But there is no such test. Similarly inadequate is the State's purported interest in insuring the later availability of notaries' testimony. The State fails to advance a factual showing that the unavailability of notaries' testimony presents a real, as opposed to a merely speculative, problem to the State. Without a factual underpinning, the State's asserted interest lacks the weight we have required of interests properly denominated as compelling.

We conclude that the Texas statute violates the Fourteenth Amendment of the United States Constitution. Accordingly the judgment of the Court of Appeals is *reversed*, and the case is *remanded*.

It is so ordered.

∼ PROBLEMS ∼

1. *Aliens and In-State Tuition at Public Universities.* May a state deny lawful resident aliens and their dependents eligibility for in-state status relating to admission to the state university and tuition fees? Does a state have valid reasons for denying preferential admission and in-state tuition to aliens? Should it matter whether the aliens are long-time residents who pay taxes in the state? Does Congress's power over immigration, and the special status accorded to diplomats, affect the analysis? Suppose that the plaintiffs are dependents of "nonimmigrant aliens" holding a "G-4" visa, issued to officers and employees of certain international organizations and members of their immediate families. Because of the University of Maryland's proximity to Washington, D.C., significant numbers of such dependents sought to enroll in the university. Should it matter that, under the federal Immigration and Nationality Act of 1952, "G-4 aliens" are not barred from acquiring domicile in the United States? Can it be argued that Maryland's law creates a burden on such aliens that conflicts with the federal policies exemplified in various federal tax statutes, treaties, and international agreements? *See Toll v. Moreno,* 458 U.S. 1 (1982).

2. *The Teaching Certificate.* Norwick is a lawful resident alien who is married to a U.S. citizen. She meets all of New York's requirements for certification as a public school teacher, but her application for a teaching certificate covering nursery school through sixth grade was denied because she is not a U.S. citizen. Norwick is eligible to become a citizen but does not wish to do so.

The state argues that its exclusion of aliens is justified under a rational basis standard according to the "political function" exception of *Foley* and *Sugarman v. Dougall*. What arguments may be made on both sides of this argument? *See Ambach v. Norwick*, 441 U.S. 68 (1979).

3. Federal Laws Regulating Aliens

The Court has described the standard of review for federal classifications of aliens as "relaxed scrutiny," which in practice resembles the rational basis standard. In *Mathews v. Diaz*, 426 U.S. 67 (1976), the Court upheld a Social Security Act provision limiting the eligibility of aliens for supplemental medical insurance that could be obtained by citizens over age 65. Specifically, the Act made insurance available only to permanent resident aliens over age 65 who had resided continuously for five years in the U.S. The Court declined to follow *Graham*'s strict scrutiny analysis because the law involved the relationship "between aliens and the Federal Government." The challenge to the Act was based on the theory that "statutory discrimination within the class of aliens allowing benefits to some aliens but not to others" was a violation of equal protection. The Court accepted plaintiff's premises that "the five-year line drawn by Congress is longer than necessary to protect the fiscal integrity of the program," and that the line caused "unnecessary hardship" to aliens who were excluded from eligibility for medical insurance. Even so, the Court reasoned that "Congress has no constitutional duty to provide aliens with welfare benefits provided to citizens," and that the millions of aliens in the U.S. have a wide range of ties to this country. Therefore, it was "reasonable for Congress to make an alien's eligibility depend on both the character and the duration of his residence," and to conclude that the five-year line defined an eligible class of aliens who "have a greater affinity with the U.S."

In *Hampton v. Mow Sun Wong*, 426 U.S. 116 (1976), the Court considered but found it unnecessary to decide the equal protection claim of aliens who challenged a federal agency regulation adopted by the U.S. Civil Service Commission that excluded virtually all noncitizens from most federal civil service jobs. The Court recognized that *Sugarman*'s strict scrutiny analysis regarding state civil service exclusions did not control because "overriding national interests may provide a justification for a citizenship requirement for the federal service." However, the Court pointed out that the Civil Service Commission has no responsibility for alien-related governmental functions, such as those related to foreign affairs, treaty negotiations, immigration quotas or conditions of entry, naturalization policies, or the employment of aliens in the national labor market, and instead performs "a limited and specific function" with its only concern being "the promotion of an efficient federal service." The only relevant government interest proffered by the Commission in support of its alien exclusion rule was "administrative convenience," which the Court deemed to be a "hypothetical justification," because there was no evidence that the Commission had "made any considered evaluation" of the rule. On the record, the Court held that the Commission's rule violated due process because it deprived aliens of their liberty interest by "broadly denying them substantial opportunities for employment." In dicta, the Court noted its assumption that under equal protection doctrine, national policy interests could be identified to support "an explicit determination by Congress or the President to exclude all noncitizens from the federal service." A few years after *Hampton*, the validity of this assumption was expressed in federal court decisions rejecting equal protection challenges to President Reagan's executive order excluding aliens from federal civil service jobs. These decisions reasoned that his order was supported by the national interest in creating an incentive for aliens to become naturalized citizens.

∾ PROBLEMS ∾

1. *Termination of Medicaid Benefits.* Plaintiffs suffer from potentially life-threatening illnesses, and are "permanently residing in the United States under color of law" (PRUCOLs), but are not lawfully admitted permanent residents (green card holders). The PRUCOL designation applies to aliens of whom the INS is aware but has no plans to deport. But for their exclusion under state law, they would qualify for state Medicaid benefits. They seek a declaratory judgment that the exclusion violates Equal Protection. Until 1996, New York law did not distinguish between aliens and citizens regarding Medicaid. This changed after Congress enacted the Personal Responsibility and Work Opportunity Reconciliation Act of 1996 (PRWORA). The Act was designed to "discourage aliens from immigrating here just to avail themselves of welfare or other public resources." The Act distinguishes between aliens who are green card holders, or who have been granted asylum, designated refugees, Cuban and Haitian entrants, or victims of battering by a spouse or family member, and (on the other hand) other aliens, including PRUCOLs like the plaintiffs who are "not qualified." The Act makes PRUCOLs ineligible for State Medicaid (a shared program between state and federal governments) but authorizes states to provide State Medicaid to PRUCOLs (even to illegal aliens). In response to PRWORA, New York terminated Medicaid for PRUCOLs and other "non-qualified" aliens. Plaintiffs argue that strict scrutiny should apply. Explain how this debate should be resolved in light of relevant precedents. *See Lewis v. Thompson*, 252 F.2d 567 (2d Cir. 2001); *In re Aliessa v. Novello*, 754 N.E.2d 1085 (N.Y. 2001).

2. *State Retraction of Health Care Coverage.* Assume that a federal law authorizes the states to provide health care coverage for aliens, but does not require coverage. Initially, the Maine legislature enacted a provision that extends coverage to aliens under its state health care law. When faced with a budget crisis the next year, the legislature amended the law and retracted the health care coverage for aliens. If this statutory retraction is challenged on equal protection grounds, how should the Court rule? *See Bruns v. Mayhew*, 750 F.3d 61 (1st Cir. 2014).

4. *State Laws Regulating Undocumented Aliens*

When does the Equal Protection Clause protect undocumented aliens who are not lawful residents of the United States? In *Plyler v. Doe*, 457 U.S. 202 (1982), the Court invalidated a state law that did not authorize the use of state funds for the public school education of undocumented children and allowed such children to be excluded from school. According to the Court, the statute did not advance a substantial state objective. Moreover, since the children had been brought to the United States illegally by adults, the Court reasoned that it was unfair to exclude the children from school because of the illegal conduct of their parents. However, the federal government retained the right to deport the children.

∾ PROBLEMS ∾

1. *Supremacy Clause and Undocumented Aliens.* Under a California statute, an employer is prohibited from knowingly employing an alien who is not entitled to lawful residence in the U.S. if such employment would have an adverse effect on lawful resident workers. Is the statute unconstitutional as a regulation of immigration, or preempted by the Immigration and Nationality Act under the Supremacy Clause? *See De Canas v. Bica*, 424 U.S. 351 (1976).

2. *Diversity Initiative and Aliens.* Assume that in the problem at the beginning of the chapter, NWU decides to include "immigrant aliens" (permanent resident aliens) in its diversity initiative on the theory that they bring unique perspectives to the educational process, including socioeconomic, cultural, and life experience perspectives. Specifically, NWU decides to give immigrant aliens preferences in admissions and financial aid. What standard of review should apply to such a program? Can this NWU initiative satisfy that standard? Now assume that NWU expands its initiative to include both "immigrant aliens" and undocumented aliens (who are not lawfully admitted to the United States) in the group that is eligible for preferences. The constitutionality of this expanded initiative is challenged by a U.S. citizen who applies to NWU but does not receive the same preferences in admissions and financial aid that are reserved for the two categories of aliens. What standard of review will apply to the expanded NWU initiative? Can it satisfy that standard?

E. THE RIGHTS OF UNMARRIED PARENTS AND THEIR CHILDREN

Are the children of unmarried parents entitled to heightened review in regard to classifications that discriminate against them? During the 1960s, the evolution of equal protection doctrine led to the invalidation of arbitrary legislative classifications based on the "illegitimate" status of children born out of wedlock and their parents. Modern judicial review of such classifications may be characterized as intermediate scrutiny, which falls between rational basis and strict scrutiny standards. Intermediate scrutiny requires that the classification must be substantially related to an important governmental interest. Most of the Court's holdings between 1968 and 1988 are consistent with this standard, and in the post-1988 era, the Court has explicitly embraced this standard of review. In the fields of inheritance rights and the rights to sue for wrongful death benefits and parental support, the Court has invalidated government regulations in most of its decisions. The Court has also invalidated regulations in the fields of welfare and workers' compensation benefits. Although the Court has strongly supported parents' rights to notice and consent in the context of adoption of their children, federal immigration preferences that exclude some children of unmarried U.S. citizens have been held to be constitutional.

1. Inheritance Rights

Trimble v. Gordon

430 U.S. 762 (1977)

Mr. Justice POWELL delivered the opinion of the Court.

At issue in this case is the constitutionality of §12 of the Illinois Probate Act, which allows illegitimate children to inherit by intestate succession only from their mothers. Under Illinois law, legitimate children are allowed to inherit by intestate succession from both their mothers and their fathers. Jessie Trimble and Sherman Gordon lived with their illegitimate daughter for four years until Gordon died intestate. The father openly acknowledged his daughter as his child and supported her under a paternity order. When the child's mother filed a petition for a determination of heirship in probate court, the child was excluded as an heir because of her illegitimate status; if she had been a legitimate child, she would have inherited her father's entire estate, which consisted of an automobile worth $2,500. The Illinois statute required not only the father's acknowledgment of the paternity of an illegitimate child, but also the legitimation of a child through the "intermarriage" of his or her parents after the child's birth, as absolute preconditions to inheritance through intestate succession from the child's father. We conclude that the statutory discrimination against illegitimate children is unconstitutional.

In upholding Section 3, the Illinois Supreme Court relied on the State's purported interest in "the promotion of (legitimate) family relationships." Section 12 bears only the most attenuated relationship to the asserted goal. The Equal Protection Clause requires more than the mere incantation of a proper state purpose. In our precedents, we have expressly considered and rejected the argument that a State may attempt to influence the actions of men and women by imposing sanctions on the children born of their illegitimate relationships. While parents have the ability to conform their conduct to societal norms, their illegitimate children can affect neither their parents' conduct nor their own status.

The Illinois Supreme Court relied on a more substantial justification: the State's interest in "establish(ing) a method of property disposition." Focusing on the difficulty of proving paternity and the related danger of spurious claims, the court concluded that this interest explained and justified the asymmetrical statutory discrimination against the illegitimate children of intestate men. The more favorable treatment of illegitimate children claiming from their mothers' estates was justified because "proof of a lineal relationship is more readily ascertainable when dealing with maternal ancestors." Alluding to the possibilities of abuse, the court rejected a case-by-case approach to claims based on alleged paternity.

We think that the state court failed to consider the possibility of a middle ground between the extremes of complete exclusion and case-by-case determination of paternity. For at least some significant categories of illegitimate children of intestate men, inheritance rights can be recognized without jeopardizing the orderly settlement of estates or the dependability of titles to property passing under intestacy laws. Because it excludes those categories of illegitimate children unnecessarily, §12 is constitutionally flawed. We conclude that §12 is not "carefully tuned to alternative considerations." Difficulties of proving paternity in some situations do not justify the total statutory disinheritance of illegitimate children whose fathers die intestate. The facts of this case graphically illustrate the constitutional defect of §12. The state court's finding of paternity and support order should be equally sufficient to establish Gordon's daughter's right to claim a child's share of Gordon's estate, for the State's interest in the accurate and efficient disposition of property at death would not be compromised in any way by allowing her claim in these circumstances. The reach of the statute extends well beyond the asserted purposes.

We conclude that §12 of the Illinois Probate Act cannot be squared with the command of the Equal Protection Clause of the Fourteenth Amendment.

Accordingly, we *reverse* the judgment of the Illinois Supreme Court and *remand* the case for further proceedings not inconsistent with this opinion.

Notes

1. *Pre-*Trimble *Precedent.* The Illinois Supreme Court had upheld the succession statute in *Trimble* on the authority of *Labine v. Vincent,* 401 U.S. 532 (1971). The child in *Labine* had been formally "acknowledged" as the "natural child" of her father in a notarized document signed by both parents, which served as a recognition of "paternity." But the father had not taken the extra step of "legitimating" his daughter by "stating his desire to legitimate" her in the acknowledgment document. A Louisiana statute barred such a child from receiving a share of the father's intestate succession in the same way as children born to married

parents. The *Labine* Court affirmed the constitutional validity of this statute, and *Trimble* did not overrule this holding. Instead, the Court distinguished *Labine*, by emphasizing that the *Labine* statute allowed a child of unmarried parents to inherit either through a simple "legitimation" document or through post-birth marriage to the child's mother, whereas the *Trimble* statute completely barred a child of unmarried parents from inheriting from her father in the absence of such a marriage. Justice Rehnquist wrote for the four dissenters in *Trimble* who would have upheld the Illinois statute, reasoning that the *Trimble* majority's decision "requires a conscious second-guessing of legislative judgment in an area where this Court has no special expertise."

2. *Post-*Trimble *Developments.* In *Reed v. Campbell*, 476 U.S. 852 (1986), the Court held that the *Trimble* doctrine applied to a child of unmarried parents in Texas whose father died before *Trimble* was decided, but whose estate was in progress on the date of that decision. The Court noted that "after an estate has been finally distributed, the interest in finality may provide a valid justification for barring the belated assertion of claims, even though they may be meritorious"; however, in *Reed,* the post-*Trimble* assertion of the *Trimble* equal protection right by a child of unmarried parents "should have been given controlling effect." *Reed* did not hold that *Trimble* should be retroactively applied in all cases, however.

∼ PROBLEMS ∼

1. *Suspect Classification?* Given the other equal protection categories that have been held to be "suspect" classifications, are there reasons for treating classifications relating to "nonmarital" children as suspect as well? Is the condition immutable? Have those in this classification historically been subject to discrimination? Are there valid reasons, related to the status, for treating them differently?

2. *Intestate Succession.* A New York statute requires children of unmarried parents to provide a particular form of proof of paternity (an "order of filiation") in order to inherit from their fathers by intestate succession. Children born to married parents are not subject to the same requirement. Robert claims to be the son of Mario, who died intestate. Robert's mother, Rosa, died five years before his father's death and never was married to his father. Neither of Robert's parents obtained for him a court "order of filiation," declaring the paternity of Mario either during Rosa's pregnancy or within two years from the date of Robert's birth. Yet the New York statute provides that such an order is required for a child of unmarried parents to inherit from a father by intestate succession, and that "the existence of an agreement obligating the father to support the child does not qualify such child to inherit from the father in the absence of an order of filiation." Robert challenges the New York law as a violation of the Equal Protection Clause. How would you argue the case on Robert's behalf? How might the state respond? Who should win? *See Lalli v. Lalli*, 439 U.S. 259 (1978).

2. Rights to Sue and to Receive Government Benefits

a. Suits for Wrongful Death or Parental Support

In two of the Supreme Court's earliest decisions involving the rights of non-marital children and their parents, statutory bars to tort suits for wrongful death were invalidated in cases where such persons were prohibited from exercising the right to bring such suits. These decisions were followed by others that invalidated time limits on suits by non-marital children who sought to establish the right to parental support through paternity actions.

Levy v. Louisiana

391 U.S. 68 (1968)

Mr. Justice Douglas delivered the opinion of the Court.

Five children sought to recover wrongful-death damages for the loss of their mother as well as damages based on a cause of action for pain and suffering that their mother had at the time of her death. The defendants were the doctor who treated their mother and an insurance company. The children lived with their mother, who worked as a domestic servant to support them and to pay for their education. The tort action was dismissed, and the state courts ruled that the right to bring such a suit was limited to children born to married parents, "based on morals and the general welfare because it discourages bringing children into the world out of wedlock." By contrast, state law allowed a dependent child of unmarried parents to recover worker's compensation benefits for the death of a parent; state law also imposed a duty on parents to support all their children, including those born when the parents are not married.

The rights asserted here involve the intimate, familial relationship between a child and his own mother. When the child's claim of damage for loss of his mother is in issue, why, in terms of "equal protection," should the tortfeasors go free merely because the child is illegitimate? Why should the illegitimate child be denied rights merely because of his birth out of wedlock? He certainly is subject to all the responsibilities of a citizen, including the payment of taxes and conscription under the Selective Service Act. How under our constitutional regime can he be denied correlative rights which other citizens enjoy?

Legitimacy or illegitimacy of birth has no relation to the nature of the wrong allegedly inflicted on the mother. These children, though illegitimate, were dependent on her; she cared for them and nurtured them; they were indeed hers in the biological and in the spiritual sense; in her death they suffered wrong in the sense that any dependent would.

We conclude that it is invidious to discriminate against them when no action, conduct, or demeanor of theirs is possibly relevant to the harm that was done the mother.

Reversed.

Note: Wrongful Death Actions

In *Glona v. American Guarantee & Liability Insurance Co.*, 391 U.S. 73 (1968), a case decided the same day as *Levy,* the Court upheld the right of a mother to bring suit for the wrongful death of her child, who had been killed in a car accident. The mother was not married to the father of the child. The Louisiana courts interpreted the state wrongful death statute to require that a decedent must be "legitimate" in order for a parent or sibling to bring an action. The *Glona* Court invalidated this interpretation, holding that the mother's right to equal protection was violated by the bar to her wrongful death suit, reasoning as follows:

> We see no possible rational basis for assuming that if the natural mother is allowed recovery for the wrongful death of her illegitimate child, the cause of illegitimacy will be served. It would, indeed, be farfetched to assume that women have illegitimate children so that they can be compensated in damages for their death. A law which creates an open season on illegitimates in the area of automobile accidents gives a windfall to tortfeasors. But it hardly has a causal connection with the "sin," which is, we are told, the historic reason for the creation of the disability. To say that the test of equal protection should be the "legal" rather than the biological relationship is to avoid the issue. For the Equal Protection Clause necessarily limits the authority of a State to draw such 'legal' lines as it chooses. Opening the courts to suits of this kind may conceivably be a temptation to some to assert motherhood fraudulently. That problem, however, concerns burden of proof. Where the claimant is plainly the mother, the State denies equal protection of the laws to withhold relief merely because the child, wrongfully killed, was born to her out of wedlock.

∼ PROBLEMS ∼

1. Formalization? Justice Harlan wrote for three justices who dissented in *Levy* and *Glona,* arguing that when a state bases the right to recover for wrongful death strictly on family relationships, the state should be able to demand "that those relationships be formalized." Justice Harlan reasoned:

> One important reason why recovery for wrongful death had everywhere to await statutory delineation is that the interest one person has in the life of another is inherently intractable. Rather than hear offers of proof of love and affection and economic dependence from every person who might think or claim that the bell had tolled for him, the courts stayed their hands pending legislative action. Legislatures, responding to the same diffuseness of interests, generally defined classes of proper plaintiffs by highly arbitrary lines based on family relationships, excluding issues concerning the actual effect of the death on the plaintiff. Louisiana has chosen to define these classes of proper plaintiffs in terms of their legal rather than their biological relation to the deceased. The majority rules that the State must base its arbitrary definition of the plaintiff class on biological rather than legal relationships. Exactly how this makes the Louisiana scheme even marginally more "rational" is not clear, for neither a biological relationship nor legal acknowledgment is indicative of the love or economic dependence that may exist between two persons. If the State has power to provide

that people who choose to live together should go through the formalities of marriage and, in default, that people who bear children should acknowledge them, it is logical to enforce these requirements by declaring that the general class of rights that are dependent upon family relationships shall be accorded only when the formalities as well as the biology of those relationships are present. Moreover, a State may choose to simplify a particular proceeding by reliance on formal papers rather than a contest of proof. That suits for wrongful death must as a constitutional matter deal with every claim of biological paternity or maternity on its merits is an exceedingly odd proposition.

Do you agree with the majority or with Justice Harlan?

2. *Wrongful Death.* Curtis is the biological father of Lemuel. Lemuel and his mother are killed in an auto accident. Curtis and Lemuel's mother were never married, and Curtis never "legitimated" Lemuel under Georgia law by court order. Curtis did sign Lemuel's birth certificate and contribute to his support. Lemuel took Curtis's name and Curtis visited him regularly. However, when Curtis sought to file a wrongful death action against the driver of the car that caused Lemuel's death, his suit was dismissed because a Georgia statute prohibits a father who has not "legitimated" a child by court order from pursuing a wrongful death action. By contrast, an unmarried mother of a child can sue for the wrongful death of that child, and a father who has legitimated a child by court order can sue for the wrongful death of the child if "there is no mother." When Curtis challenges the dismissal of his action on equal protection grounds, the challenge is rejected by the trial and appellate courts, which find that three state interests justify the statutory bar to suit: a) the interest in avoiding difficult problems of proving paternity in wrongful death actions, b) the interest in promoting a "legitimate" family unit, and c) the interest in setting a standard of morality by not according to the father of a nonmarital child the statutory right to sue for the child's death. What arguments will Curtis make to attack the statute in the Supreme Court? What counter-arguments may be made to justify the statutory bar to Curtis's suit? *See Parham v. Hughes*, 441 U.S. 347 (1979).

Clark v. Jeter

486 U.S. 456 (1988)

Justice O'CONNOR delivered the opinion of the Court.

Under Pennsylvania law, an illegitimate child must prove paternity before seeking support from his or her father, and a suit to establish paternity ordinarily must be brought within six years of an illegitimate child's birth. By contrast, a legitimate child may seek support from his or her parents at any time. Ten years after the birth out of wedlock of her daughter, the mother, Cherlyn Clark, filed a support complaint on behalf of her child, naming Gene Jeter as the father. The court ordered blood tests, which showed a 99.3% probability that Jeter was the father. Jeter moved to dismiss on the ground that the suit on behalf of his daughter was barred by the six-year statute of limitations for paternity actions. Clark's response challenged this statute on equal protection grounds.

This Court has developed a particular framework for evaluating equal protection challenges to statutes of limitations that apply to suits to establish paternity, and thereby limit the ability of illegitimate children to obtain support.

> First, the period for obtaining support must be sufficiently long in duration to present a reasonable opportunity for those with an interest in such children to assert claims on their behalf. Second, any time limitations placed on that opportunity must be substantially related to the State's interest in avoiding the litigation of stale or fraudulent claims.

Mills v. Habluetzel, 456 U.S. 91 (1982) holding that the Texas one-year statute of limitations failed both criteria.

We conclude that Pennsylvania's (six)-year statute of limitations violates the Equal Protection Clause. Even six years does not necessarily provide a reasonable opportunity to assert a claim on behalf of an illegitimate child. "The unwillingness of the mother to file a paternity action on behalf of her child, which could stem from her relationship with the natural father or from the emotional strain of having an illegitimate child, or even from the desire to avoid community and family disapproval, may continue years after the child is born. *Mills, supra,* at 105, n.4 (O'Connor, J., concurring). Not all of these difficulties are likely to abate in six years. A mother might realize only belatedly "a loss of income attributable to the need to care for the child." *Pickett v. Brown*, 462 U.S. 1, 12 (1983) (holding that the two-year Tennessee statute of limitations failed both *Mills* criteria). Furthermore, financial difficulties are likely to increase as the child matures and incurs expenses for clothing, school, and medical care. Thus, it is questionable whether a State acts reasonably when it requires most paternity and support actions to be brought within six years of an illegitimate child's birth.

Moreover, we are confident that the six-year statute of limitations is not substantially related to Pennsylvania's interest in avoiding the litigation of stale or fraudulent claims. In a number of circumstances, Pennsylvania permits the issue of paternity to be litigated more than six years after the birth of an illegitimate child. The statute itself permits a suit to be brought more than six years after the child's birth if it is brought within two years of a support payment made by the father. And in other types of suits, Pennsylvania places no limits on when the issue of paternity may be litigated.

A more recent indication that Pennsylvania does not consider proof problems insurmountable is the enactment by the Pennsylvania Legislature in 1985 of an 18-year statute of limitations for paternity and support actions. To be sure the legislature did not act spontaneously, but rather under the threat of losing some federal funds. The federal Child Support Enforcement Amendments of 1984 required all States participating in the federal child support program to have procedures to establish the paternity of a child who is less than 18 years old. Nevertheless, the new statute is a tacit concession that proof problems are not overwhelming. The legislative history of the Amendments explains why Congress thought such statutes of limitations are reasonable. Congress adverted to the problem of stale and fraudulent claims, but recognized that increasingly sophisticated tests for genetic markers permit the exclusion of over 99% of those who might be accused of paternity, regardless of the age of the child. This scientific evidence is available throughout the child's minority, and it is an additional reason to doubt that Pennsylvania had a substantial reason for limiting the time within which paternity and support actions could be brought.

We conclude that the Pennsylvania statute does not withstand heightened scrutiny under the Equal Protection Clause. The judgment of the Superior Court is reversed, and the case is remanded for further proceedings not inconsistent with this opinion.

Note: Judicially Enforceable Rights and Unmarried Parents

In *Gomez v. Perez*, 409 U.S. 535 (1973), the Court established the foundation for the decisions in *Mills, Pickett,* and *Clark,* by holding that a state cannot create a judicially enforceable right for children of married parents to seek needed support from their natural fathers and then deny this right to the children of unmarried parents. After a hearing on a child's petition for support from Perez, a court found that Perez was the biological father of the child (whose mother was Gomez) and that the child needed the support and maintenance of her father. However, the court dismissed the child's petition because she was born to unmarried parents. The Court held that this dismissal violated equal protection, relying on *Levy*'s holding that "a State may not create a right of action in favor of children for the wrongful death of a parent and exclude illegitimate children from the benefit of such a right." The more general principle endorsed by *Gomez* was that "a State may not invidiously discriminate against illegitimate children by denying them substantial benefits accorded children generally." *Gomez* acknowledged that it was important to "recognize the lurking problems with respect to proof of paternity" in the context of claims for support by children of unmarried parents. Yet it concluded that while "those problems are not to be lightly brushed aside, neither can they be made into an impenetrable barrier that works to shield otherwise invidious discrimination."

∼ PROBLEMS ∼

1. *Advising on Legislation.* Assume that after the *Clark* decision is announced, you are asked to provide a legal opinion concerning the constitutionality of new Pennsylvania legislation that creates a time limit for suits like the one in *Clark.* What time limit do you think is likely to pass constitutional muster? Why?

2. *Filing Suit in Time.* Assume that the Texas legislature enacts a statute establishing the procedural requirements for filing a paternity suit for the purpose of identifying the biological father of a non-marital child. Should a court uphold the statute if the time limit for filing the suit expires when the child is one-year old? Or two-years old? *See Mills v. Habluetzel,* 456 U.S. 91 (1982); *Pickett v. Brown,* 462 U.S. 1 (1983).

b. Workers' Compensation, Welfare, and Social Security Survivors' Benefits

Weber v. Aetna Casualty & Surety Co.

406 U.S. 164 (1972)

Mr. Justice POWELL delivered the opinion of the Court.

The question before us concerns the right of dependent unacknowledged, illegitimate children to recover under Louisiana workmen's compensation laws benefits for the death of their natural father on an equal footing with his dependent legitimate children. We hold that Louisiana's denial of equal recovery rights to dependent unacknowledged illegitimates violates the Equal Protection Clause of the Fourteenth Amendment. Two children sought to recover compensation benefits when their father, Stokes, died of injuries received during the course of his employment. Stokes and Weber (the mother) had never married. They lived with their children and with four other children born of a marriage between Stokes and another woman who was committed to a mental hospital. Stokes never divorced his wife. The Louisiana workmen's compensation statute defined children to include "only legitimate children, stepchildren, posthumous children, adopted children, and illegitimate children acknowledged under civil code requirements." Unacknowledged children of unmarried parents were relegated to the lesser status of "other dependents" who could recover benefits only if the benefits were not exhausted by the surviving dependents in the classification of "children." The children of Stokes and Weber were not eligible for legal "acknowledgement" as their parents "were incapable of contract marriage at the time of conception" because Stokes was already married.

Both the statute in *Levy v. Louisiana,* 391 U.S. 68 (1968), and the present case involve state-created compensation schemes, designed to provide close relatives and dependents of a deceased a means of recovery for his often abrupt and accidental death. Both wrongful-death statutes and workmen's compensation codes represent outgrowths and modifications of our basic tort law. The former alleviated the harsh common-law rule under which 'no person could inherit the personal right of another to recover for tortuous injuries to his body'; the latter removed difficult obstacles to recovery in work-related injuries by offering a more certain, though generally less remunerative, compensation. In the instant case, the recovery sought under the workmen's compensation statute was in lieu of an action under the identical death statute which was at issue in *Levy.* Given the similarities in the origins and purposes of these two statutes, and the similarity of Louisiana's pattern of discrimination in recovery rights, it would require a disregard of precedent and the principles of *stare decisis* to hold that *Levy* did not control the facts of the case before us. It makes no difference that illegitimates are not so absolutely or broadly barred here as in *Levy;* the discrimination remains apparent.

The Louisiana Supreme Court emphasized strongly the State's interest in protecting "legitimate family relationships," and the regulation and protection of the family unit have indeed been a venerable state concern. We do not question the importance of that interest; what we do question is how the challenged statute will promote it. It cannot be thought here that persons will shun illicit relations because the offspring may not one day reap the benefits of workmen's compensation.

It may perhaps be said that statutory distinctions between the legitimate and illegitimate reflect closer family relationships in that the illegitimate is more often not under care in the home of the father nor even supported by him. The illegitimate, so this argument runs, may thus be made less eligible for the statutory recoveries and inheritances reserved for those more likely to be within the ambit of familial care and affection. This contention is not compelling in a statutory compensation scheme where dependency on the deceased is a prerequisite to anyone's recovery, and where the acknowledgment so necessary to equal recovery rights may be unlikely to occur or legally impossible to effectuate even where the illegitimate child may be nourished and loved.

By limiting recovery to dependents of the deceased, Louisiana substantially lessens the possible problems of locating illegitimate children and of determining uncertain claims of parenthood. Our decision will not expand claimants for workmen's compensation beyond those in a direct blood and dependency relationship with the deceased. The state interest in legitimate family relationships is not served by the statute; the state interest in minimizing problems of proof is not significantly disturbed by our decision. The inferior classification of dependent unacknowledged illegitimates bears, in this instance, no significant relationship to those recognized purposes of recovery which workmen's compensation statutes commendably serve.

Reversed and remanded.

Notes

1. *The Rehnquist Dissent.* Justice Rehnquist dissented in *Weber,* noting his support for Justice Harlan's objections to the results in *Levy* and *Glona:*

> In this case I cannot condemn as irrational Louisiana's distinction between legitimate and illegitimate children. In a statutory compensation scheme such as this, the State must inevitably draw rather fine and arbitrary lines. For example, Louisiana declares that parents will have priority in this scheme over first cousins, regardless of the degree of dependency

or affection in any given case. Surely, no one would condemn this classification as violative of the Fourteenth Amendment, since it is likely to reflect fairly the unarticulated intent of the decedent. Similarly, the State might rationally presume that the decedent would have preferred the compensation to go to his legitimate children, rather than those illegitimates whom he has not acknowledged.

2. *Welfare Benefits.* In *New Jersey Welfare Rights Organization v. Cahill,* 411 U.S. 619 (1973), the Court invalidated a state welfare program rule that limited benefits to families of married adults who have at least one child of both parents, or the "natural" child of one adopted by the other, or a child adopted by both. The trial court recognized that the classification "operates almost invariably to deny benefits to illegitimate children while granting benefits to those children who are legitimate," but upheld the rule on the ground that its purpose was "to preserve and strengthen traditional family life." The Court rejected this justification, relying on the holdings and rationales of *Levy, Weber,* and *Gomez* to conclude that welfare benefits "are as indispensable to the health and well-being of illegitimate children as to those who are legitimate." The state interest was viewed as identical to the interest rejected in prior precedents—namely, the condemnation of extramarital relations through the imposition of disabilities on children of unmarried parents. Justice Rehnquist dissented on the grounds that a rational basis for the law could be found, based on the idea that the state was trying to protect certain family units "from dissolution due to the economic vicissitudes of modern life." Justice Rehnquist would have upheld the limit on welfare benefits.

3. *Disability Benefits.* In *Jiminez v. Weinberger,* 417 U.S. 628 (1974), the Court invalidated a statutory classification relating to the eligibility of children of unmarried parents for disability benefits under the Social Security Act. One group of children was eligible for benefits, even if they were born after the onset of the parent's disability; this group included these subgroups: a) "legitimate" children, b) children capable of inheriting personal property under state intestacy law, and c) children who were "illegitimate" solely because of a "nonobvious defect" in their parents' marriage. Another group of "after-born" children were not eligible for benefits—namely, all other children of unmarried parents. They were denied benefits, regardless of any showing of dependency. The finding of a violation of the Equal Protection Clause because of the discrimination against the "after-born" children of unmarried parents was based on the Court's rejection of the government's claim that the classification system was based on the need for trustworthy proof of dependency.

∾ PROBLEM: SURVIVORSHIP BENEFITS ∾

Robert lived with Belmira for 18 years; they had two children but never married. Then they separated and Robert died two years later. Robert never acknowledged in writing his paternity of either child, and his paternity was never determined in a judicial proceeding during his lifetime. Belmira filed an application for "surviving children's benefits" under the federal Social Security Act, on behalf of the two children. Robert did die "insured" under the Act. The Act requires that a survivor's benefit will be provided to a child who is under 18 and "dependent" on an insured parent at the time of the parent's death. A child qualifies as "dependent," in fact, if the child can prove that the insured father was living with or contributing to the child's support at the time of death. Some children are entitled to a presumption of dependency, including the following groups: a) "legitimate" children; b) children who would be entitled to inherit personal property from the insured parent's estate under state intestacy law; and c) children whose decedent parent (i) went through a marriage ceremony with the other parent that would have been valid, or (ii) in writing acknowledged the child to be his child, or (iii) had been decreed by a court to be the child's father, or (iv) had been ordered by a court to support the child because the child was his. After a hearing on Belmira's application, the Social Security examiner found that Robert was the children's father but that the children were unable to prove that they were "dependents" under the statute. Robert was not living with the children or contributing to their support at the time of his death, and the children did not fit any of the six statutory classifications that created a presumption of dependency. The denial of "surviving children's benefits" was challenged as a violation of equal protection because other children, including all "legitimate" children, are statutorily entitled to survivorship benefits regardless of actual dependency, whereas the children of Robert were not. What arguments can be made on both sides of the constitutional issue? *See Mathews v. Lucas,* 427 U.S. 495 (1976).

∾ PROBLEMS ∾

1. *Right to Veto Adoption.* Assume that the mother of a non-marital child wants her new husband (not the father) to adopt her child. Does the biological father of the child have the right to veto that adoption? *See Quilloin v. Wolcott,* 434 U.S. 246 (1978).

2. *Putative Father Registry.* Assume that the biological father of a two-year-old non-marital child initially neither sought to establish a relationship with the child nor accepted responsibility for her. Now the father wishes to make a claim that he is the father of the child. Under state law, such a father may file a statement in which he makes that claim, which statement will be placed in the "putative father registry." This registration means that the father will be notified of any adoption proceedings. Is the father entitled to additional rights under due process or equal protection? *See Lehr v. Robertson,* 463 U.S. 248 (1983).

3. *Presumption That Husband Is Father.* Assume that a state statute establishes a presumption that when a woman is lawfully married to a man, a legal presumption exists that any child born to the woman is also the child of her husband. Does

this presumption violate either equal protection or due process? *See Michael H. v. Gerald D.*, 491 U.S. 110 (1989).

3. *Rights of Unmarried Parents to Retain Custody of Their Children*

In *Stanley v. Illinois*, 405 U.S. 645 (1972), the Court struck down a law that caused the children of unwed fathers to be declared wards of the state upon the death of their mother. This declaration did not require a hearing on the parental fitness of the father or proof of any neglect by the father. The effect of the declaration was to place the children with court-appointed guardians, and thus to cause the father to lose custody of the children. By contrast, the children of married parents, divorced parents, and unmarried mothers could not legally be separated from their parents or mothers without a hearing on parental fitness and proof of neglect. *Stanley* held that the denial of a "fitness" hearing to an unmarried father was a form of discrimination that violated equal protection. Chief Justice Burger authored a dissent for two justices, arguing that the state could distinguish constitutionally between unwed fathers and mothers because unwed mothers are more readily identifiable and locatable, and because a mother is a more dependable protector.

In a decision that is consistent with *Stanley*'s concern with the rights of unwed fathers, the Court invalidated a New York law that treated unwed mothers and unwed fathers differently with respect to the right to block an adoption of their children in *Caban v. Mohammed*, 441 U.S. 380 (1979). The law allowed an unwed mother to block the adoption of her child simply by withholding consent, but gave an unwed father no such right; instead, an unwed father was required to show that the adoption of his child was not in the child's best interest. In *Caban*, a mother succeeded in gaining the adoption of her child (whose father she had not married) by her husband (whom she married after the breakup of her relationship with the child's father), over the father's objection. The *Caban* Court invalidated the law because the classification that discriminated against unwed fathers "does not bear a substantial relation" to the state's interest in providing adoptive homes for children of unmarried parents. Four justices dissented, arguing that the different treatment of the unwed father in *Caban* was not as harsh as the law in *Stanley* that treated unwed fathers as unfit parents as a matter of law. Because the dissenters endorsed the assumption that the mother "will be the more, and often the only, responsible parent" in the context of adoption proceedings for children of unmarried parents, a state should be allowed to reject a paternal consent requirement in order to facilitate that process.

4. *Immigration Preferences*

In *Fiallo v. Bell*, 430 U.S. 787 (1977), the Court upheld provisions of the federal Immigration and Nationality Act that distinguished between children of married parents and children of unmarried parents for purposes of the immigration status of "aliens." Under the Act, one group of children (or parents of such children) is allowed entry into the United States without regard to numerical quotas or labor certification requirements, while another group is not. The favored group includes these subgroups: 1) "legitimate" or "legitimated" children, 2) stepchildren, 3) adopted children, and 4) children of unmarried parents who seek an immigration preference by virtue of their relationship with their natural mothers. The disfavored group includes illegitimate children seeking preference by virtue of their relationship with their natural fathers. *Fiallo* emphasized the "limited scope of judicial inquiry into immigration legislation," and noted that Congress presumably had determined that "preferential status is not warranted" for the disfavored group "because of a perceived absence in most cases of close family ties as well as a concern with the serious problems of proof that usually lurk in paternity determinations." *See Nguyen v. Immigration and Naturalization Service*, 533 U.S. 53 (2001).

F. THE RIGHTS OF PERSONS WITH MENTAL DISABILITIES

Should people with mental disabilities be treated differently, for equal protection purposes, than people without disabilities? The Court considered a government classification relating to mentally ill persons in *Schweiker v. Wilson*, 450 U.S. 221 (1981), which involved the question of whether Congress had the power to deny small monthly cash stipends to "inmates" in public mental institutions, while providing such stipends to inmates of institutions that received Medicaid funds (including public medical hospitals and private mental institutions). The stipends were Supplementary Security Income (SSI) benefits, called a "comfort allowance," and were provided for the purpose of meeting personal needs other than maintenance or medical care. The *Schweiker* plaintiffs argued that a classification based on mental illness required "special justification" because mental illness "greatly resembles other characteristics found to be inherently suspect as a means of legislative classification." The Court declined to address that argument, finding that the statute did not "classify directly on the basis of mental health" because some mentally ill individuals received benefits along with non–mentally ill individuals. The Court applied the rational basis standard of equal protection analysis, and upheld the classification. The Court recognized the validity of the asserted government purpose "to avoid spending federal resources on behalf of individuals whose care and treatment" are deemed to be a state responsibility.

The *Schweiker* Court expressly reserved the question as to "what standard of review applies to legislation expressly classifying the mentally ill as a discrete group." Only a few years later, the Court decided to resolve that issue and to retain the rational basis standard for such classifications.

City of Cleburne v. Cleburne Living Center

473 U.S. 432 (1985)

Justice WHITE delivered the opinion of the Court.

A Texas city denied a special use permit for the operation of a group home for the mentally retarded, acting pursuant to a municipal zoning ordinance requiring permits for such homes. The Court of Appeals for the Fifth Circuit held that mental retardation is a "quasi-suspect" classification and that the ordinance violated the Equal Protection Clause because it did not substantially further an important governmental purpose. We hold that a lesser standard of scrutiny is appropriate, but conclude that the ordinance is invalid as applied.

The Equal Protection Clause of the Fourteenth Amendment commands that no State shall "deny to any person within its jurisdiction the equal protection of the laws," which is essentially a direction that all persons similarly situated should be treated alike. Legislation is presumed to be valid and will be sustained if the classification drawn by the statute is rationally related to a legitimate state interest. When social or economic legislation is at issue, the Equal Protection Clause allows the States wide latitude, and the Constitution presumes that even improvident decisions will eventually be rectified by the democratic processes.

The general rule gives way, however, when a statute classifies by race, alienage, or national origin. These factors are so seldom relevant to the achievement of any legitimate state interest that laws grounded in such considerations are deemed to reflect prejudice and antipathy—a view that those in the burdened class are not as worthy or deserving as others. These laws are subjected to strict scrutiny and will be sustained only if they are suitably tailored to serve a compelling state interest.

Where individuals in the group affected by a law have distinguishing characteristics relevant to interests the State has the authority to implement, the courts have been very reluctant, as they should be in our federal system and with our respect for the separation of powers, to closely scrutinize legislative choices as to whether, how, and to what extent those interests should be pursued. In such cases, the Equal Protection Clause requires only a rational means to serve a legitimate end.

The Court of Appeals erred in holding mental retardation a quasi-suspect classification calling for a more exacting standard of judicial review than is normally accorded economic and social legislation. First, it is undeniable that those who are mentally retarded have a reduced ability to cope with and function in the everyday world. They range from those whose disability is not immediately evident to those who must be constantly cared for. They are thus different, immutably so, in relevant respects, and the States' interest in dealing with and providing for them is plainly a legitimate one. How this large and diversified group is to be treated is very much a task for legislators guided by qualified professionals and not by the perhaps ill-informed opinions of the judiciary. Heightened scrutiny inevitably involves substantive judgments about legislative decisions, and we doubt that the predicate for such judicial oversight is present where the classification deals with mental retardation. Second, the distinctive legislative response, both national and state, to the plight of those who are mentally retarded demonstrates not only that they have unique problems, but also that lawmakers have addressed their difficulties in a manner that belies a continuing antipathy or prejudice. The Federal Government has not only outlawed discrimination against the mentally retarded in federally funded programs, but it has also provided the retarded with the right to receive "appropriate treatment, services, and habilitation" in a setting that is "least restrictive of their personal liberty." In addition, the Government has conditioned federal education funds on a State's assurance that retarded children will enjoy an education that, "to the maximum extent appropriate," is integrated with that of non–mentally retarded children. The Government has also facilitated the hiring of the mentally retarded into the federal civil service by exempting them from the requirement of competitive examination. The State of Texas has similarly enacted legislation that acknowledges the special status of the mentally retarded by conferring certain rights upon them, such as "the right to live in the least restrictive setting appropriate to their individual needs and abilities," including "the right to live in a group home." Such legislation thus singling out the retarded for special treatment reflects the real and undeniable differences between the retarded and others. It may be that legislation designed to benefit, rather than disadvantage, the retarded would generally withstand examination under a test of heightened scrutiny. Third, the legislative response, which could hardly have occurred and survived without public support, negates any claim that the mentally retarded are politically powerless in the sense that they have no ability to attract the attention of the lawmakers. Fourth, if the large and amorphous class of the mentally retarded were deemed quasi-suspect, it would be difficult to find a principled way to distinguish a variety of other groups who have perhaps immutable disabilities setting them off from others. One need mention in this respect only the aging, the disabled, the mentally ill, and the infirm. We are reluctant to set out on that course, and we decline to do so.

Doubtless, there have been and there will continue to be instances of discrimination against the retarded that are in fact invidious, and that are properly subject to judicial correction under constitutional norms. But the appropriate method of reaching such instances is not to create a new quasi-suspect classification and subject all governmental action based on that classification to more searching evaluation. Rather, we should look to the likelihood that governmental action premised on a particular classification is valid as a general matter, not merely to the specifics of the case before us. Because mental retardation is a characteristic that the government may legitimately take into account in a wide range of decisions, and because both State and Federal Governments have recently committed themselves to assisting the retarded, we will not presume that any given legislative action, even one that disadvantages retarded individuals, is rooted in considerations that the Constitution will not tolerate.

Our refusal to recognize the retarded as a quasi-suspect class does not leave them entirely unprotected from invidious discrimination. To withstand equal protection review, legislation that distinguishes between the mentally retarded and others must be rationally related to a legitimate governmental purpose. This standard affords government the latitude necessary both to pursue policies designed to assist the retarded in realizing their full potential, and to freely and efficiently engage in activities that burden the retarded in what is essentially an incidental manner. The State may not rely on a classification whose relationship to an asserted goal is so attenuated as to render the distinction arbitrary or irrational. Furthermore, some objectives such as "a bare desire to harm a politically unpopular group," are not legitimate state interests. Beyond that, the mentally retarded, like others, have and retain their substantive constitutional rights in addition to the right to be treated equally by the law.

The city does not require a special use permit in an R-3 zone for apartment houses, multiple-dwellings, boarding and lodging houses, fraternity or sorority houses, dormitories, apartment hotels, hospitals, sanitariums, nursing homes for convalescents or the aged (other than for the insane or feebleminded or alcoholics or drug addicts), private clubs or fraternal orders, and other specified uses. It does, however, insist on a special permit for a facility for the mentally retarded. May the city require the permit for this facility when other care and multiple-dwelling facilities are freely permitted? The record does not reveal any rational basis for believing that the home would pose any special threat to the city's legitimate interests. We affirm the judgment below insofar as it holds the ordinance invalid as applied in this case.

The City Council's insistence on the permit rested on several factors. First, the Council was concerned with the negative attitude of the majority of property owners as well as with the fears of elderly residents. But mere negative attitudes, or fear, unsubstantiated by factors which are properly cognizable in a zoning proceeding, are not permissible bases for treating a home for the mentally retarded differently from apartment houses, multiple dwellings, and the like. The electorate as a whole, whether by referendum or otherwise, could not order city action violative of the Equal Protection Clause, and the city may not avoid the strictures of that Clause by deferring to the wishes or objections of some fraction of the body politic. "Private biases may be outside the reach of the law, but the law cannot, directly or indirectly, give them effect."

Second, the Council had two objections to the location of the facility. It was concerned that the facility was across the street from a junior high school, and it feared that the students might harass the occupants of the home. But the school itself is attended by about 30 mentally retarded students, and denying a permit based on such vague, undifferentiated fears is again permitting some portion of the community to validate what would otherwise be an equal protection violation.

The other objection to the home's location was that it was located on "a five hundred year flood plain." This concern with the possibility of a flood, however, can hardly be based on a distinction between this home and, for example, nursing homes, homes for convalescents or the aged, or sanitariums or hospitals, any of which could be located on the site without obtaining a special use permit. The same may be said of another concern of the Council—doubts about the legal responsibility for actions which the mentally retarded might take. If there is no concern about legal responsibility with respect to other uses that would be permitted in the area, such as boarding and fraternity houses, it is difficult to believe that the groups of mildly or moderately mentally retarded individuals would present any different or special hazard.

Fourth, the Council was concerned with the size of the home and the number of people that would occupy it. But there would be no restrictions on the number of people who could occupy this home as a boarding house, nursing home, family dwelling, fraternity house, or dormitory. Requiring the permit in this case appears to us to rest on an irrational prejudice against the mentally retarded, including those who would occupy the facility and who would live under the closely supervised and highly regulated conditions expressly provided for by state and federal law.

The judgment of the Court of Appeals is affirmed insofar as it invalidates the zoning ordinance as applied to the Featherston home. The judgment is otherwise vacated, and the case is remanded.

It is so ordered.

Justice STEVENS, with whom THE CHIEF JUSTICE joins, *concurring.*

Our cases reflect a continuum of judgmental responses to differing classifications ranging from "strict scrutiny" at one extreme to "rational basis" at the other. I have never been persuaded that these so-called "standards" adequately explain the decisional process. The term "rational," of course, includes a requirement that an impartial lawmaker could logically believe that the classification would serve a legitimate public purpose that transcends the harm to the members of the disadvantaged class. The rational-basis test adequately explains why a law that deprives a person of the right to vote because his skin has a different pigmentation than that of other voters violates the Equal Protection Clause. None of these attributes has any bearing at all on the citizen's willingness or ability to exercise that civil right. We do not need to apply a special standard, or to apply "strict scrutiny," or even "heightened scrutiny," to decide such cases.

Every law that places the mentally retarded in a special class is not presumptively irrational. The differences between mentally retarded persons and those with greater mental capacity are obviously relevant to certain legislative decisions. An impartial lawmaker could rationally vote in favor of a law providing funds for special education and special treatment for the mentally retarded. A mentally retarded person could also recognize that he is a member of a class that might need special supervision in some situations, both to protect himself and to protect others. Restrictions on his right to drive cars or to operate hazardous equipment might well seem rational even though they deprived him of employment opportunities and the kind of freedom of travel enjoyed by other citizens.

Justice MARSHALL, with whom Justice BRENNAN and Justice BLACKMUN join, *concurring in the judgment in part* and *dissenting in part.*

Mental retardation *per se* cannot be a proxy for depriving retarded people of their rights and interests without regard to variations in individual ability. The Equal Protection Clause requires attention to the capacities and needs of retarded people as individuals. The Court holds the ordinance invalid on rational-basis grounds and disclaims that anything special, in the form of heightened scrutiny, is taking place. Yet Cleburne's ordinance surely would be valid under the traditional rational-basis test applicable to economic and commercial regulation. I dissent from the Court's disclaimer that no "more exacting standard" than ordinary rational-basis review is being applied.

The level of scrutiny employed in an equal protection case should vary with "the constitutional and societal importance of the interest adversely affected and the recognized invidiousness of the basis upon which the particular classification is drawn." When a zoning ordinance works to exclude the retarded from all residential districts in a community, these two considerations require that the ordinance be convincingly justified as substantially furthering legitimate and important purposes. First, the interest of the retarded in establishing group homes is substantial. Excluding group homes deprives the retarded of much of what makes for human freedom and fulfillment—the ability to form bonds and take part in the life of a community. Second, the mentally retarded have been subject to a "lengthy and tragic history" of segregation and discrimination that can only be called grotesque.

In light of the importance of the interest at stake and the history of discrimination the retarded have suffered, the Equal Protection Clause requires us to do more than review the distinctions drawn by Cleburne's zoning ordinance as if they appeared in a taxing statute or in economic or commercial legislation. For the retarded, much has changed in recent years, but much remains the same; outdated statutes are still on the books, and irrational fears or ignorance, traceable to the prolonged social and cultural isolation of the retarded, continue to stymie recognition of the dignity and individuality of retarded people. Heightened judicial scrutiny of action appearing to impose unnecessary barriers to the retarded is required in light of increasing recognition that such barriers are inconsistent with evolving principles of equality embedded in the Fourteenth Amendment.

Notes

1. *The Classification of Mentally Retarded Persons.* As the *City of Cleburne* Court noted, mentally retarded individuals fall into four "distinct" categories. Eighty-nine percent are "mildly" retarded, with IQs between 50 and 70; 6% are "moderately" retarded, with IQs between 35 and 50; and 5% are either severely or profoundly retarded, with IQs between 20 and 35 or below 20. However, as *Cleburne* noted, "Mental retardation is not defined by reference to intelligence or

IQ alone. The American Association on Mental Deficiency (AAMD) has defined mental retardation as 'significantly subaverage general intellectual functioning existing concurrently with deficits in adaptive behavior and manifested during the developmental period.' Mental retardation is caused by a variety of factors, some genetic, some environmental, and some unknown."

2. *The Rehabilitation Act.* In recent years, legislation has been passed that shows sensitivity to the needs of mentally retarded persons, including the Rehabilitation Act of 1973 (outlawing discrimination against the mentally retarded in federally funded programs); the Developmental Disabilities Assistance and Bill of Rights Act (guaranteeing "treatment, services and habilitation" in a setting that is "least restrictive of their personal liberty"); the Education of the Handicapped Act (states receive federal education funds on the condition that retarded children enjoy an education that is integrated with that of non–mentally retarded children "to the maximum extent appropriate"); and legislation that facilitates "the hiring of the mentally retarded into the federal civil service by exempting them from the requirement of competitive examination."

3. *The As-Applied Remedy in City of Cleburne.* Justice Marshall's dissent in *City of Cleburne* objected to the Court's use of a "novel and truncated" remedy of invalidating the ordinance only as it applied to the plaintiff group home, instead of invalidating the ordinance on its face. By contrast, the *City of Cleburne* majority preferred an as-applied inquiry that required a constitutional invalidation of the statute. The Court described this approach as "the preferred course of adjudication since it enables courts to avoid making unnecessarily broad constitutional judgments."

∽ PROBLEMS ∽

1. *Should Mental Disability Classifications Be Regarded as Suspect?* When we examined racial classifications, we saw that the Court has historically treated them as suspect for a variety of reasons, including the fact that race is immutable, it generally bears no rational relationship to one's ability (or lack of ability), and there has been a long history of discrimination (both *de jure* and *de facto*) on the basis of race. Do these factors provide insight into the question of whether classifications based on mental disability should be subjected to strict scrutiny? Are there other factors that should be considered? Do these factors suggest that classifications based on mental disability should be subjected to rational basis review or to a higher standard? If a higher standard, which one? Why?

2. *Advising the City.* You have been asked by the city council of Cleburne for advice on the types of future applications of the zoning ordinance that might be upheld under the Equal Protection Clause. Do any examples come to mind? If so, describe them. What are the benefits of redrafting the ordinance to achieve narrower objectives instead of leaving the ordinance on the books and applying it to future applicants?

3. *Commitment to Mental Institutions.* A state law provides that mentally ill persons may be involuntarily committed to an institution based on a higher burden of proof than applies to mentally retarded persons. Mentally ill persons may be institutionalized against their will under a beyond a reasonable doubt standard. The standard that governs involuntary commitment of mentally retarded persons is clear and convincing evidence. What version of rational basis review should govern an equal protection challenge to the criteria governing involuntary commitment of mentally ill persons? How should this issue be resolved? *See Heller v. Doe*, 509 U.S. 312 (1993).

G. SEXUAL ORIENTATION

What standard of review should apply to distinctions based on sexual orientation? For some time, the most contentious issues in sexual orientation cases have involved the protection of sexual intimacy against criminal sodomy laws and same-sex marriage. *Bowers v. Hardwick*, 476 U.S. 186 (1986), upheld criminal sodomy laws and rejected claims of due process violations based on sexual orientation. However, *Bowers* did not close the door to constitutional challenges to classifications intended to require different treatment based on sexual orientation. In *Romer v. Evans*, 517 U.S. 620 (1996), the majority of the Court, applying rational basis scrutiny, held that legislation discriminating against homosexuals violates the Equal Protection Clause. Finally, in *Lawrence v. Texas*, 539 U.S. 558 (2003), the Court overturned *Bowers* and extended constitutional protections to homosexual activities.

Reread the same-sex marriage cases from Chapter 9 before you attempt to answer the following problems.

∽ PROBLEMS ∽

1. *Higher Review for Gay and Lesbian Classifications?* Throughout this chapter, we have focused on factors that suggest that a particular equal protection classification should be subject to a higher level of scrutiny. What factors suggest that classifications affecting gays and lesbians should be subjected to a higher level of review? For example, is homosexual behavior immutable? Have gays been subject to a history of discrimination? Does homosexual behavior have any correlation with ability or performance? How might you argue that classifications affecting homosexuals should not be subject to heightened scrutiny? How would you argue for the contrary proposition?

2. *More on the Diversity Initiative.* Let's return to the problem described at the beginning of the chapter. Suppose that NWU decides to offer preferential admissions and financial aid to gay, lesbian, and transgender students. NWU

believes that such students bring diverse perspectives to the classroom, that such students have suffered from social disadvantage and stigma, and that therefore they deserve preferences. What standard of review would the courts apply to such preferences? Are the preferences likely to be upheld, or struck down?

H. THE FUNDAMENTAL RIGHTS STRAND OF EQUAL PROTECTION

Equal protection interests are implicated when government classifies for purposes of distributing burdens or benefits. A heightened standard of review may be triggered when discrimination is a function of group status. It also may be generated when a fundamental right has been denied on a selective basis. In this instance, the nature of the group is irrelevant. What counts, for purposes of elevating the standard of review, is the discriminatory deprivation of a fundamental right.

Fundamental rights analysis in the equal protection context parallels the standards of review and controversies that arise in the due process context. Insofar as a textually enumerated right or liberty is selectively denied, such as freedom of speech, the standard of review for the alleged equal protection and First Amendment violation will be coextensive. Protection of rights and liberties not set forth by the Constitution itself engenders the same debate encountered in the due process setting. In either instance, the judiciary's power to identify and develop fundamental rights minus textual enumeration is a central issue. Competing perspectives have vied in the context of economic liberty and its contours in the early twentieth century and the right of privacy and its incidents over the past several decades. The debate generally has not extended to the right to vote and the right to travel. The right to vote, though not specifically provided by the Constitution, generally is understood to be implicit in a system of representative governance. Likewise, the right to travel can be viewed as a logical extension of a viable union. The Privileges and Immunities Clause of Article IV, Section II provides an additional predicate for this guarantee.

In determining whether due process or equal protection analysis governs the deprivation of a fundamental right or liberty, it is important to focus on the impact of the violation. Government action that operates in a broad-spectrum manner and thus denies a right or liberty to all persons is reviewable under the Due Process Clause. Equal protection interests are implicated only when the deprivation is directed at a particular subset of persons. The right of privacy, which includes the choice to have an abortion, the right to marry and procreate, the right to structure one's family, and the right to refuse unwanted medical treatment, is discussed from a due process perspective in Chapter 7. The equal protection dimensions are not discussed in this chapter, which focuses on actual and proposed rights and liberties that are not grounded in the Due Process Clause itself.

1. Freedom of Speech

Equal protection interests intersect First Amendment concerns when government discriminates on the basis of content or viewpoint. The significance of this convergence was noted in *Police Department of City of Chicago v. Mosley*, 408 U.S. 92, 95 (1972), where the Court observed that "under the Equal Protection Clause, not to mention the First Amendment itself, government may not grant the use of a forum to people whose views it finds acceptable, but deny use to those wishing to express less favored or more controversial views. And it may not select which issues are worth discussing or debating in public facilities. There is an 'equality of status in the field of ideas,' and government must afford all points of view an equal opportunity to be heard." This sense of an equal opportunity to promote one's ideas is a fundamental predicate for First Amendment jurisprudence relating to public forum management. The basic principle is that when a forum is opened to assembly or speaking, individuals may not be excluded on the basis of content or viewpoint.

2. Access to the Justice System: The Right to Counsel

Case law relating to an individual's access to the justice system, or the rights therein, implicates both equal protection and procedural due process issues. It also comprehends specific constitutional guarantees and other incidents of fairness. The Sixth Amendment gives the accused "in all criminal prosecutions the Assistance of Counsel for his defense." U.S. Const., Amend. VI. In *Gideon v. Wainwright*, 372 U.S. 335 (1963), the Court determined that this guarantee was incorporated through the Fourteenth Amendment. Indigent defendants thus were entitled to state-appointed counsel in the event they could not afford their representation.

The equal protection guarantee has been the basis for extending the right to counsel to the appellate process. In *Douglas v. California*, 368 U.S. 815 (1963), the Court determined that the state must appoint counsel to indigent appellants when pursuing a first appeal as a matter of right. Consistent with this marking, the Court declined to extend the right to discretionary appeals. *Ross v. Moffitt*, 417 U.S. 600 (1974). As the *Douglas* Court saw it, the state had etched "an unconstitutional line between rich and poor" that it was obligated to erase. This result cuts against the general current of constitutional law insofar as government typically is not required to subsidize the exercise of a right or liberty. *E.g., Harris v. McRae*, 448 U.S. 297 (1980) (no government duty to subsidize a woman's abortion).

Case law concerning subsidized access to counsel and other support systems in the criminal justice process has referenced both equal protection and due process concerns. As the Court noted in *Bearden v. Georgia*, different inquiries are required pursuant to each guarantee. Due process analysis focuses on the fairness of the relationship between the defendant and the criminal justice process, whereas equal protection inquiry centers on whether the defendant invidiously has been denied an important benefit afforded other classes of defendants.

Bearden v. Georgia

461 U.S. 660 (1983)

Justice O'CONNOR delivered the opinion of the Court.

This Court has long been sensitive to the treatment of indigents in our criminal justice system. Over a quarter-century ago, Justice Black declared that "there can be no equal justice where the kind of trial a man gets depends on the amount of money he has." *Griffin v. Illinois*, 351 U.S. 12 (1956). *Griffin*'s principle of "equal justice," which the Court applied in that case to strike down a state practice of granting appellate review only to persons able to afford a trial transcript, has been applied in numerous other contexts. *See, e.g., Douglas v. California* (indigent entitled to counsel on first direct appeal); *Roberts v. LaVallee* (indigent entitled to free transcript of preliminary hearing for use at trial); *Mayer v. Chicago*, 404 U.S. 189 (1971) (indigent cannot be denied an adequate record to appeal a conviction under a fine-only statute). Most relevant to the issue here is the holding in *Williams v. Illinois*, 339 U.S. 235 (1970), that a State cannot subject a class of convicted defendants to a period of imprisonment beyond the statutory maximum solely because they are too poor to pay the fine. *Williams* was followed and extended in *Tate v. Short*, 401 U.S. 395 (1971), which held that a State cannot convert a fine imposed under a fine-only statute into a jail term solely because the defendant is indigent and cannot immediately pay the fine in full. But the Court has also recognized limits on the principle of protecting indigents in the criminal justice system. For example, in *Ross v. Moffitt*, 417 U.S. 600 (1974), we held that indigents had no constitutional right to appointed counsel for a discretionary appeal. In *United States v. MacCollum*, 426 U.S. 317 (1976), we rejected an equal protection challenge to a federal statute which permits a district court to provide an indigent with a free trial transcript only if the court certifies that the challenge to his conviction is not frivolous and the transcript is necessary to prepare his petition.

Due process and equal protection principles converge in these cases. We generally analyze the fairness of relations between the criminal defendant and the State under the Due Process Clause, while we approach the question whether the State has invidiously denied one class of defendants a substantial benefit available to another class of defendants under the Equal Protection Clause.

The question presented here is whether a sentencing court can revoke a defendant's probation for failure to pay the imposed fine and restitution, absent evidence and findings that the defendant was somehow responsible for the failure or that alternative forms of punishment were inadequate. There is no doubt that the State has treated the petitioner differently from a person who did not fail to pay the imposed fine and therefore did not violate probation. To determine whether this differential treatment violates the Equal Protection Clause, one must determine whether, and under what circumstances, a defendant's indigent status may be considered in the decision whether to revoke probation. This is substantially similar to asking directly the due process question of whether and when it is fundamentally unfair or arbitrary for the State to revoke probation when an indigent is unable to pay the fine. Whether analyzed in terms of equal protection or due process, the issue requires a careful inquiry into such factors as "the nature of the individual interest affected, the extent to which it is affected, the rationality of the connection between legislative means and purpose, and the existence of alternative means for effectuating the purpose."

The rule of *Williams* and *Tate* is that the State cannot "impose a fine as a sentence and then automatically convert it into a jail term solely because the defendant is indigent and cannot forthwith pay the fine in full." A distinction, based on the reasons for nonpayment, is of critical importance here. If the probationer has willfully refused to pay the fine or restitution when he has the means to pay, the State is perfectly justified in using imprisonment as a sanction to enforce collection. Similarly, a probationer's failure to make sufficient bona fide efforts to seek employment or borrow money in order to pay the fine or restitution may reflect an insufficient concern for paying the debt he owes to society for his crime. In such a situation, the State is likewise justified in revoking probation and using imprisonment as an appropriate penalty for the offense. But if the probationer has made all reasonable efforts to pay the fine or restitution, and yet cannot do so through no fault of his own, it is fundamentally unfair to revoke probation automatically without considering whether adequate alternative methods of punishing the defendant are available. This lack of fault provides a "substantial reason which justifies or mitigates the violation and makes revocation inappropriate." The State, of course, has a fundamental interest in appropriately punishing persons — rich and poor — who violate its criminal laws. A defendant's poverty in no way immunizes him from punishment. Thus, when determining initially whether the State's penological interests require imposition of a term of imprisonment, the sentencing court can consider the entire background of the defendant, including his employment history and financial resources.

The decision to place the defendant on probation, however, reflects a determination by the sentencing court that the State's penological interests do not require imprisonment. A probationer's failure to make reasonable efforts to repay his debt to society may indicate that this original determination needs reevaluation, and imprisonment may now be required to satisfy the State's interests. But a probationer who has made sufficient bona fide efforts to pay his fine and restitution, and who has complied with the other conditions of probation, has demonstrated a willingness to pay his debt to society and an ability to conform his conduct to social norms. The State nevertheless asserts three reasons why imprisonment is required to further its penal goals.

We hold, therefore, that in revocation proceedings for failure to pay a fine or restitution, a sentencing court must inquire into the reasons for the failure to pay. If the probationer willfully refused to pay or failed to make sufficient bona fide efforts legally to acquire the resources to pay, the court may revoke probation and sentence the defendant to imprisonment within the authorized range of its sentencing authority. If the probationer could not pay despite sufficient bona fide efforts to acquire the resources to do so, the court must consider alternative measures of punishment other than imprisonment. Only if alternative measures are not adequate to meet the State's interests in punishment and deterrence may the court imprison a probationer who has made sufficient bona fide efforts to pay. To do otherwise would deprive the probationer of his conditional freedom simply because, through no fault of his own, he cannot pay the fine. Such a deprivation would be contrary to the fundamental fairness required by the Fourteenth Amendment.

At the probation revocation hearing, the petitioner and his wife testified about their lack of income and assets and of his repeated efforts to obtain work. The sentencing court made no finding that the petitioner had not made sufficient bona fide efforts to find work, and the record as it presently stands would not justify such a finding. The focus of the court's concern, then, was that the petitioner had disobeyed a prior court order to pay the fine, and for that reason must be imprisoned. By sentencing petitioner to imprisonment simply because he could not pay the fine, without considering the reasons for the inability to pay or the propriety of reducing the fine or extending the time for payments or making alternative orders, the court automatically turned a fine into a prison sentence.

If, upon remand, the Georgia courts determine that petitioner did not make sufficient bona fide efforts to pay his fine, or determine that alternative punishment is not adequate to meet the State's interests in punishment and deterrence, imprisonment would be a permissible sentence. Unless such determinations are made, however, fundamental fairness requires that the petitioner remain on probation.

The judgment is reversed, and the case remanded for further proceedings not inconsistent with this opinion.

It is so ordered.

Justice WHITE, with whom THE CHIEF JUSTICE, Justice POWELL, and Justice REHNQUIST join, *concurring in the judgment.*

When probation is revoked for failure to pay a fine, I find nothing in the Constitution to prevent the trial court from revoking probation and imposing a term of imprisonment if revocation does not automatically result in the imposition of a long jail term and if the sentencing court makes a good-faith effort to impose a jail sentence that in terms of the State's sentencing objectives will be roughly equivalent to the fine and restitution that the defendant failed to pay.

Note

Although similar results are achievable pursuant to both due process and equal protection review, the focal points of these analytical models are different. Justice Harlan, in *Douglas v. California*, criticized the Court's "blend of the Equal Protection and Due Process Clauses." He noted that the equal protection guarantee prohibits states from formally discriminating between rich and poor in developing and applying the law. He maintained, however, that the guarantee did not bar states from enacting laws of general applicability that disproportionately affect the poor more severely. As he put it:

> every financial exaction which the State imposes on a uniform basis is more easily satisfied by the well-to-do than by the indigent. Yet I take it that no one would dispute the constitutional power of the State to levy a uniform sales tax, to charge tuition at a state university, to fix rates for the purchase of water from a municipal corporation, to impose a standard fine for criminal violations, or to establish minimum bail for certain categories of offenses. Nor could it be contended that the State may not classify as crimes acts which the poor are more likely to commit than are the rich. And surely, there would be no basis for attacking a state law which provided benefits for the needy simply because those benefits fell short of the goods or services that others could purchase for themselves. Laws such as these do not deny equal protection to the less fortunate for one essential reason: the Equal Protection Clause does not impose on the States 'an affirmative duty to lift the handicaps flowing from differences in economic circumstances.' To so construe it would read into the Constitution a philosophy of leveling that would be foreign to many of our basic concepts of the proper relations between government and society.

Douglas v. California, 372 U.S. 353 (1963) (Harlan, J., dissenting).

∾ PROBLEMS ∾

1. *Imprisoning for Failure to Pay.* A statute converts fines into prison terms for persons unable to make payment. The statute was applied to all offenses, including traffic violations and even offenses that were punishable only by fine in the absence of inability to pay. Does the statute violate the Equal Protection Clause? *See Tate v. Short*, 401 U.S. 395 (1971).

2. *Counsel in Post-Conviction Proceedings.* Based on the factors that are balanced and accounted for in *Griffin* and its progeny, should counsel be provided to indigent parties in the context of post-conviction proceedings? What about claims that the death penalty violates the Eighth Amendment prohibition against cruel and unusual punishment? *See Murray v. Giarratano*, 492 U.S. 1 (1989). What about garden-variety *habeas corpus* claims?

3. *Bankruptcy Filing Fee.* A majority of the Court in *Boddie* determined that a $60 filing fee denied due process, although two justices would have found an equal protection violation. The Court, in *United States v. Kras*, 409 U.S. 434 (1973),

concluded that a $50 filing fee for voluntary bankruptcy contravened neither the due process nor the equal protection guarantee. With respect to the equal protection claim in particular, the Court determined that bankruptcy is not as fundamental a concern as marriage. In reviewing whether an indigent plaintiff had to pay a $25 court filing fee to contest the reduction of his welfare benefits, should a court be guided by *Boddie*, or *Kras*? *See Ortwein v. Schwab*, 410 U.S. 656 (1973).

4. *Explaining the Vacillation.* Why has the Court vacillated between reference to the due process and the equal protection guarantees in these cases? What, if any, difference does the choice of provision make?

3. The Right to Travel

The Constitution, as previously noted, does not indicate specifically a right to interstate travel. Discerning its fundamental nature may be facilitated by attempting to comprehend a viable political and economic union without a right to travel freely across state lines. Consistent with this reality, the Court evolved the right to travel initially without any grounding in a particular constitutional provision. It thus has been regarded historically as a logical incident of the nation's structure.

As the Court recognized in *Saenz v. Roe*, 526 U.S. 489 (1999), the right to travel has three separate and distinct components: "It protects the right of a citizen of one State to enter and to leave another State, the right to be treated as a welcome visitor rather than an unfriendly alien when temporarily present in the second State, and for those travelers who elect to become permanent residents, the right to be treated like other citizens of that State."

For equal protection purposes, the right to travel has been examined most often in connection with residence-based eligibility requirements for public benefits. These cases do not turn upon the state's legitimate interest in establishing bona fide residence. A state law conditioning free education on a student's attendance in the relevant school district, *Martinez v. Bynum*, 461 U.S. 321 (1983), for instance, reflects this type of law. Although it classifies on the basis of in-state and out-of-state residence, the Court reviews such differentiations pursuant to a rational basis standard. Equal protection issues may rise to a higher level, however, when eligibility for a benefit or right hinges on residence for a designated length of time. Depending on the nature of the benefit, a prolonged delay in qualifying for it may be construed as a burden on the right to interstate travel.

Shapiro v. Thompson

394 U.S. 618 (1969)

Mr. Justice BRENNAN delivered the opinion of the Court.

This case concerns a challenge to state laws that condition eligibility for welfare benefits on a one-year residence requirement. The effect of the waiting-period requirement in each case is to create two classes of needy resident families indistinguishable from each other except that one is composed of residents who have resided a year or more, and the second of residents who have resided less than a year, in the jurisdiction. On the basis of this sole difference the first class is granted and the second class is denied welfare aid upon which may depend the ability of the families to obtain the very means to subsist—food, shelter, and other necessities of life. Appellees met the test for residence in their jurisdictions, as well as all other eligibility requirements except the requirement of residence for a full year prior to their applications. Appellees' central contention is that the statutory prohibition of benefits to residents of less than a year creates a classification which constitutes an invidious discrimination denying them equal protection of the laws. We agree.

Appellants justify the waiting-period requirement as a protective device to preserve the fiscal integrity of state public assistance programs. It is asserted that people who require welfare assistance during their first year of residence in a State are likely to become continuing burdens on state welfare programs. Therefore, the argument runs, if such people can be deterred from entering the jurisdiction by denying them welfare benefits during the first year, state programs to assist long-time residents will not be impaired by a substantial influx of indigent newcomers. We do not doubt that the one-year waiting period device is well suited to discourage the influx of poor families in need of assistance. An indigent who desires to migrate, resettle, find a new job, and start a new life will doubtless hesitate if he knows that he must risk making the move without the possibility of falling back on state welfare assistance during his first year of residence, when his need may be most acute. But the purpose of inhibiting migration by needy persons into the State is constitutionally impermissible.

This Court long ago recognized that the nature of our Federal Union and our constitutional concepts of personal liberty unite to require that all citizens be free to travel throughout the length and breadth of our land uninhibited by statutes, rules, or regulations which unreasonably burden or restrict this movement. The right finds no explicit mention in the Constitution. The reason, it has been suggested, is that a right so elementary was conceived from the beginning to be a necessary concomitant of the stronger Union the Constitution created. In any event, freedom to travel throughout the United States has long been recognized as a basic right under the Constitution. Thus, the purpose of deterring the in-migration of indigents cannot serve as justification for the classification created by the one-year waiting period, since that purpose is constitutionally impermissible. "If a law has no other purpose than to chill the assertion of constitutional rights by penalizing those who choose to exercise them, then it is patently unconstitutional."

Appellants argue that even if it is impermissible for a State to attempt to deter the entry of all indigents, the challenged classification may be justified as a permissible state attempt to discourage those indigents who would enter the

State solely to obtain larger benefits. None of the statutes before us is tailored to serve that objective. Rather, the class of barred newcomers is all-inclusive, lumping the great majority who come to the State for other purposes with those who come for the sole purpose of collecting higher benefits. More fundamentally, a State may no more try to fence out those indigents who seek higher welfare benefits than it may try to fence out indigents generally. Implicit in any such distinction is the notion that indigents who enter a State with the hope of securing higher welfare benefits are somehow less deserving than indigents who do not take this consideration into account. But we do not perceive why a mother who is seeking to make a new life for herself and her children should be regarded as less deserving because she considers, among others factors, the level of a State's public assistance.

Appellants argue that the challenged classification may be sustained as an attempt to distinguish between new and old residents on the basis of the contribution they have made to the community through the payment of taxes. We have difficulty seeing how long-term residents who qualify for welfare are making a greater present contribution to the State in taxes than indigent residents who have recently arrived. Appellants' reasoning would logically permit the State to bar new residents from schools, parks, and libraries or deprive them of police and fire protection. Indeed it would permit the State to apportion all benefits and services according to the past tax contributions of its citizens. The Equal Protection Clause prohibits such an apportionment of state services.

We recognize that a State has a valid interest in preserving the fiscal integrity of its programs. It may legitimately attempt to limit its expenditures, whether for public assistance, public education, or any other program. But a State may not accomplish such a purpose by invidious distinctions between classes of its citizens. It could not, for example, reduce expenditures for education by barring indigent children from its schools. In the cases before us, appellants must do more than show that denying welfare benefits to new residents saves money. The saving of welfare costs cannot justify an otherwise invidious classification.

In sum, neither deterrence of indigents from migrating to the State nor limitation of welfare benefits to those regarded as contributing to the State is a constitutionally permissible state objective.

Appellants next advance as justification certain administrative and related governmental objectives allegedly served by the waiting-period requirement. They argue that the requirement (1) facilitates the planning of the welfare budget; (2) provides an objective test of residency; (3) minimizes the opportunity for recipients fraudulently to receive payments from more than one jurisdiction; and (4) encourages early entry of new residents into the labor force. We reject appellants' argument. In moving from State to State or to the District of Columbia appellees were exercising a constitutional right, and any classification which serves to penalize the exercise of that right, unless shown to be necessary to promote a compelling governmental interest, is unconstitutional. Under this standard, the waiting-period requirement clearly violates the Equal Protection Clause.

Mr. Justice STEWART, *concurring.*

The constitutional right to travel is a virtually unconditional personal right, guaranteed by the Constitution to us all.

Mr. Justice HARLAN, *dissenting.*

I disagree both with the Court's result and with its reasoning. A legislature might rationally find that the imposition of a welfare residence requirement would aid in the accomplishment of at least four valid governmental objectives. It might also find that residence requirements have advantages not shared by other methods of achieving the same goals. In light of this undeniable relation of residence requirements to valid legislative aims, it cannot be said that the requirements are "arbitrary" or "lacking in rational justification." I can find no objection to these residence requirements under the Equal Protection Clause of the Fourteenth Amendment or under the analogous standard embodied in the Due Process Clause of the Fifth Amendment.

The issue is whether a one-year welfare residence requirement amounts to an undue burden upon the right of interstate travel. In my view, a number of considerations militate in favor of constitutionality. The requirements upon the freedom of individuals to travel interstate is indirect and insubstantial. These are not cases in which a State or States, acting alone, have attempted to interfere with the right of citizens to travel. The governmental purposes served by the requirements are legitimate and real, and the residence requirements are clearly suited to their accomplishment. Residence requirements have advantages, such as administrative simplicity and relative certainty, which are not shared by the alternative solutions proposed by the appellees. I cannot find that the burden imposed by residence requirements upon ability to travel outweighs the governmental interests in their continued employment. Nor do I believe that the period of residence required to these cases — one year — is so excessively long as to justify a finding of unconstitutionality on that score. For anyone who, like myself, believes that it is an essential function of this Court to maintain the constitutional divisions between state and federal authority and among the three branches of the Federal Government, today's decision is a step in the wrong direction.

Notes

1. *Welfare Benefits and Waiting Periods.* In *Saenz v. Roe*, 526 U.S. 489 (1999), the Court struck down a California law that limited welfare benefits under the state's Temporary Assistance for Needy Families (TANF) program during an individual's first year of residence in the state. Such individuals could not receive more

than the amount they received in their prior state of residence, even if California pays higher benefits to its own residents. The Court held that an individual's right to travel is explicitly protected under the Constitution, and guarantees individuals who elect to become a citizen of another state "the right to be treated like other citizens of that State." The Court concluded that the California law burdened that right, noting that California's asserted interest (saving money) "would logically permit the State to bar new residents from schools, parks, and libraries or deprive them of police and fire protection. Indeed, it would permit the State to apportion all benefits and services according to the past tax contributions of its citizens." In short, the Court held that the state's interest in saving money provides "no justification for its decision to discriminate among equally eligible citizens."

2. *Medical Care.* In *Memorial Hospital v. Maricopa County*, 415 U.S. 250 (1974), the Court struck down a state law that limited subsidized nonemergency medical care to individuals who had lived in the state for one year. Once again, because the law interfered with the right to travel, the Court applied strict scrutiny. The Court held that it is "clear that medical care is as much 'a basic necessity of life' to an indigent as welfare assistance. And, governmental privileges or benefits necessary to basic sustenance have often been viewed as being of greater constitutional significance than less essential forms of governmental entitlements of residence." The Court rejected the state's claim that the limitation was needed to preserve the public fisc, noting that "a State may not protect the public fisc by drawing an invidious distinction between classes of its citizens."

3. *The Right to Divorce.* In *Sosna v. Iowa*, 419 U.S. 393 (1975), the Court upheld an Iowa law that imposed a one-year residency requirement on the right to obtain a divorce. The Court held that the restriction was justified by the state's interest in requiring those seeking a divorce from its courts to be genuinely attached to the state, as well as by the state's desire to insulate its divorce decrees from the likelihood of successful collateral attack.

4. *Interstate Travel and the Right to Vote. Dunn v. Blumstein*, 405 U.S. 330 (1972), struck down Tennessee's requirement of one year of residency in the state and one year of residency in the county as conditions for voting in state elections. Tennessee had asserted that the requirements were needed to "insure the purity of the ballot box" against fraud (and to insure that those who attempted to vote were actually entitled to do so), as well as by the state interest in having "knowledgeable voters." The Court concluded that the interests were not compelling and could be adequately protected by other means: "Durational residence laws penalize those persons who have traveled from one place to another to establish a new residence during the qualifying period. By denying some citizens the right to vote, such laws deprive them of 'a fundamental political right, preservative of all rights.' *Reynolds v. Sims*, 377 U.S. 533, 562 (1964)." The Court noted that the state's interest could be adequately protected by voter registration schemes as well as by "a variety of criminal laws that are more than adequate to detect and deter whatever fraud may be feared."

Food for Thought

Can a state enhance the penalty for abandonment of a child if the parent leaves the state? Does this constitute disparate treatment of the type encountered in *Shapiro* and its progeny? *See Jones v. Helms*, 452 U.S. 412 (1981).

∾ PROBLEMS ∾

1. *More on Limiting Welfare Benefits.* After *Shapiro*, we know that a state may not limit welfare benefits to those who have lived in the state for at least a year. Suppose that the State of California passes a law that omits the one-year residency requirement, but instead provides that the amount of welfare benefits new residents may receive is limited to the amount they would have received in the state of their prior residence. Would such a limitation violate the fundamental right to travel? Does it matter that the state sought to justify the limitation as a financial measure that would save it more than $10 million per year? *See Saenz v. Roe*, 526 U.S. 489 (1999).

2. *Residency Requirement for City Employees.* The City of Louisville adopts a law requiring all municipal employees to be residents of the city. The city believes that taxpayer resources should be expended only on residents and not on non-residents. Would this condition be a bona fide residency requirement or an equal protection problem? *See McCarthy v. Philadelphia Civil Service Commission*, 424 U.S. 645 (1976).

3. *The Right to Travel During a Pandemic.* In 2020, during the Covid-19 pandemic, some governors sought to limit the flow of interstate travel. For example, Kentucky's Governor prohibited Kentuckians from leaving the state, and required anyone who entered Kentucky from out-of-state to quarantine for fourteen days. Should such measures be regarded as reasonable and permissible responses to the pandemic? Can they be applied to someone who lives in Louisville but who works in Indiana (on the other side of the Ohio River), or to an Indiana resident who works in Louisville? Could Florida restrict travel from New York when the latter was the epicenter of the pandemic?

Zobel v. Williams

457 U.S. 55 (1982)

Chief Justice BURGER delivered the opinion of the Court.

The question presented on this appeal is whether a statutory scheme by which a State distributes income derived from its natural resources to the adult citizens of the State in varying amounts, based on the length of each citizen's residence, violates the equal protection rights of newer state citizens.

The 1967 discovery of large oil reserves on state-owned land in the Prudhoe Bay area of Alaska resulted in a windfall to the State. The State, which had a total budget of $124 million in 1969, before the oil revenues began to flow into the state coffers, received $3.7 billion in petroleum revenues during the 1981 fiscal year. This income will continue, and most likely grow for some years in the future. Recognizing that its mineral reserves, although large, are finite and that the resulting income will not continue in perpetuity, the State took steps to assure that its current good fortune will bring long-range benefits. To accomplish this, Alaska in 1976 adopted a constitutional amendment establishing the Permanent Fund into which the State must deposit at least 25% of its mineral income each year. The amendment prohibits the legislature from appropriating any of the principal of the Fund but permits use of the Fund's earnings for general governmental purposes.

In 1980, the legislature enacted a dividend program to distribute annually a portion of the Fund's earnings directly to the State's adult residents. Under the plan, each citizen 18 years of age or older receives one dividend unit for each year of residency subsequent to 1959, the first year of statehood. The statute fixed the value of each dividend unit at $50 for the 1979 fiscal year; a one-year resident thus would receive one unit, or $50, while a resident of Alaska since it became a State in 1959 would receive 21 units, or $1,050. The value of a dividend unit will vary each year depending on the income of the Permanent Fund and the amount of that income the State allocates for other purposes. The State now estimates that the 1985 fiscal year dividend will be nearly four times as large as that for 1979.

The Alaska dividend distribution law is quite unlike the durational residency requirements we examined in *Shapiro v. Thompson,* which required new residents to reside in the State a fixed minimum period to be eligible for welfare benefits available on an equal basis to all other residents. The Alaska statute does not impose any threshold waiting period on those seeking dividend benefits; persons with less than a full year of residency are entitled to share in the distribution. Nor does the statute purport to establish a test of the bona fides of state residence. Instead, the dividend statute creates fixed, permanent distinctions between an ever-increasing number of perpetual classes of concededly bona fide residents, based on how long they have been in the State.

Appellants established residence in Alaska two years before the dividend law was passed. The distinction they complain of is not one which the State makes between those who arrived in Alaska after the enactment of the dividend distribution law and those who were residents prior to its enactment. Appellants instead challenge the distinctions made within the class of persons who were residents when the dividend scheme was enacted in 1980. The distinctions appellants attack include the preference given to persons who were residents when Alaska became a State in 1959 over all those who have arrived since then, as well as the distinctions made between all bona fide residents who settled in Alaska at different times during the 1959 to 1980 period.

The Alaska statute does not simply make distinctions between native-born Alaskans and those who migrate to Alaska from other states; it does not discriminate only against those who have recently exercised the right to travel, as did the statute involved in *Shapiro*. The Alaska statute also discriminates among long-time residents and even native-born residents. For example, a person born in Alaska in 1962 would have received $100 less than someone who was born in the State in 1960. Of course the native Alaskan born in 1962 would also receive $100 less than the person who moved to the State in 1960. The statute does not involve the kind of discrimination which the Privileges and Immunities Clause of Art. IV was designed to prevent. That Clause "was designed to insure to a citizen of State A who ventures into State B the same privileges which the citizens of State B enjoy." The Clause is thus not applicable to this case.

When a state distributes benefits unequally, the distinctions it makes are subject to scrutiny under the Equal Protection Clause of the Fourteenth Amendment. Generally, a law will survive that scrutiny if the distinction it makes rationally furthers a legitimate state purpose. Some particularly invidious distinctions are subject to more rigorous scrutiny.

The State advanced and the Alaska Supreme Court accepted three purposes justifying the distinctions made by the dividend program: (a) creation of a financial incentive for individuals to establish and maintain residence in Alaska; (b) encouragement of prudent management of the Permanent Fund; and (c) apportionment of benefits in recognition of undefined "contributions of various kinds, both tangible and intangible, which residents have made during their years of residency."

The first two state objectives—creating a financial incentive for individuals to establish and maintain Alaska residence, and assuring prudent management of the Permanent Fund and the State's natural and mineral resources—are not rationally related to the distinctions Alaska seeks to distinctions make between newer residents and those who have been in the State since 1959. Assuming, *arguendo*, that granting increased dividend benefits for each year of continued Alaska residence might give some residents an incentive to stay in the State in order to reap increased dividend benefits in the future, the State's interest is not in any way served by granting greater dividends to persons for their residency during the 21 years prior to the enactment. Nor does the State's purpose of furthering the prudent management of the Permanent Fund and the State's resources support retrospective application of its plan to the date of statehood. On this score the State's contention is straightforward.

The State similarly argues that equal per capita distribution would encourage rapacious development of natural resources. Even if we assume that the state interest is served by increasing the dividend for each year of residency beginning with the date of enactment, is it rationally served by granting greater dividends in varying amounts to those who resided in Alaska during the 21 years prior to enactment? We think not.

The last of the State's objectives—to reward citizens for past contributions—alone was relied upon by the Alaska Supreme Court to support the retrospective application of the law to 1959. However, that objective is not a legitimate state purpose. If the states can make the amount of a cash dividend depend on length of residence, what would preclude varying university tuition on a sliding scale based on years of residence—or even limiting access to finite public facilities, eligibility for student loans, for civil service jobs, or for government contracts by length of domicile? Could states impose different taxes based on length of residence? Alaska's reasoning could open the door to state apportionment of other rights, benefits, and services according to length of residency. It would permit the states to divide citizens into expanding numbers of permanent classes. Such a result would be clearly impermissible.

The only apparent justification for the retrospective aspect of the program, "favoring established residents over new residents," is constitutionally unacceptable. In our view Alaska has shown no valid state interests which are rationally served by the distinction it makes between citizens who established residence before 1959 and those who have become residents since then.

We hold that the Alaska dividend distribution plan violates the guarantees of the Equal Protection Clause of the Fourteenth Amendment. Accordingly, the judgment of the Alaska Supreme Court is reversed, and the case is remanded for further proceedings not inconsistent with this opinion.

Justice BRENNAN with whom Justice MARSHALL, Justice BLACKMUN, and Justice POWELL join, *concurring.*

The retrospective aspects of Alaska's dividend-distribution law are not rationally related to a legitimate state purpose. The Fourteenth Amendment guarantees the equal protection of the law to anyone who may be within the territorial jurisdiction of a State. That Amendment does not suggest that equal treatment might be denied a person depending upon how long that person *has been* within the jurisdiction of the State. Equality of citizenship is of the essence in our Republic. States may not "divide citizens into expanding numbers of permanent classes."

The Constitution does not bar the States from making reasoned distinctions between citizens if those distinctions are rationally related to legitimate ends. But we have never suggested that duration of residence *vel non* provides a valid justification for discrimination. To be sure, allegiance and attachment may be rationally measured by length of residence. But those instances in which length of residence could provide a legitimate basis for distinguishing one citizen from another are rare. To a limited extent, recognition and reward of past public service have independent utility for the State, for such recognition may encourage other people to engage in comparably meritorious service. But even the idea of rewarding past public service offers scarce support for the durational-residence classifications since length of residence has only the most tenuous relation to the *actual* service of individuals to the State. It is difficult to escape from the recognition that underlying any scheme of classification on the basis of duration of residence, we shall almost invariably find the unstated premise that "some citizens are more equal than others." We rejected that premise and, I believe, implicitly rejected most forms of discrimination based upon length of residence, when we adopted the Equal Protection Clause.

Justice O'CONNOR, *concurring in the judgment.*

Alaska's desire "to reward citizens for past contributions" is neither inherently invidious nor irrational. Even a generalized desire to reward citizens for past endurance, particularly in a State where years of hardship only recently have produced prosperity, is not innately improper. The difficulty is that plans enacted to further this objective necessarily treat new residents of a State less favorably than the longer term residents who have past contributions to "reward." This inequality conflicts with the constitutional purpose of maintaining a Union rather than a mere "league of States." The right infringed in this case is "fundamental." Alaska has not shown that its new residents are the "peculiar source" of any evil addressed by its disbursement scheme and has not chosen a cure that bears a "substantial relationship" to the malady. The dividends awarded to new residents may be too small to encourage them to stay in Alaska and gives them only a weak interest in prudent management of the State's resources. As a reward for prior contributions, Alaska's scheme is quite ill-suited. Persons who have migrated to Alaska may have contributed significantly more to the State, both before and after their arrival, than have some natives. Alaska's disbursement scheme violates Art. IV's Privileges and Immunities Clause.

Justice REHNQUIST, *dissenting.*

Alaska's dividend distribution scheme represents one State's effort to apportion unique economic benefits among its citizens. The distribution scheme being in the nature of economic regulation, I am at a loss to see the rationality behind the Court's invalidation of it as a denial of equal protection. This Court has long held that state economic regulations are presumptively valid, and violate the Fourteenth Amendment only in the rarest of circumstances. The distribution scheme at issue in this case impedes no person's right to travel to and settle in Alaska; if anything, the prospect of receiving annual cash dividends would encourage immigration to Alaska. The state legislature acted rationally when it concluded that dividends retroactive to the year of statehood would "recognize the 'contributions of various kinds, both tangible and intangible,' which residents have made during their years of state residency." Alaska, perhaps more than any other State in the Union, has good reason for recognizing such contributions.

Note

Zobel was notable for disclosing a compounding lack of consensus on a theory for the right to travel. In his concurring opinion, Justice Brennan cited the

Citizenship Clause of the Fourteenth Amendment as a basis for limiting state power to discriminate on the basis of length of residence. Justice O'Connor, in her concurrence, advocated reinvigoration of the Article IV, Section II Privileges and Immunities Clause as the predicate for the right to travel. The influence of her thinking in this regard was evidenced in *Saenz v. Roe*, which, as previously noted, cited this Privileges and Immunities Clause as a basis for the right to travel. Justice Rehnquist argued in dissent that, because no Alaska citizen was denied benefits under the plan, the right to travel was not burdened.

∾ PROBLEMS ∾

1. *Shifting the Focus?* The Court has evaluated burdens on the right to travel in terms of whether they penalize interstate travel. Should the focus instead be on whether residence requirements deter interstate travel? Would it make a difference with respect to the outcomes in *Shapiro* and *Memorial Hospital,* cases in which no proof was presented of any person actually being deterred?

2. *College Education as a Basic Necessity.* Public universities typically establish separate tuition schedules for in-state and out-of-state residents. Does a university or college education represent a basic necessity, particularly in an increasingly competitive environment? Are these differentials at odds with the equal protection guarantee? *See Vlandis v. Kline,* 412 U.S. 441 (1973).

3. *Preferential Hiring for Kentucky Veterans.* The Commonwealth of Kentucky creates a preferential hiring policy that favors veterans who were residents when they entered military service. The Commonwealth justifies the preference on the basis that resident veterans who take time away from their careers to serve their country are entitled to help as they try to restart or develop their civilian careers. Kentucky does not prefer out-of-state veterans because it believes that they should receive help from their home states. Is the preference constitutional? *See Attorney General v. Soto-Lopez,* 476 U.S. 898 (1986).

4. Voting

The Constitution does not establish a general right to vote. Consistent with this premise, the Court has found that "the right to vote in federal elections is conferred by Art. I, §2, of the Constitution, but the right to vote in state elections is nowhere expressly mentioned." *Harper v. Virginia State Board of Elections*, 383 U.S. 663, 665 (1966). Notwithstanding this differentiation in grounding, and within the context of state political processes, the franchise has been described as "a fundamental matter in a free and democratic society, especially since the right to exercise the franchise in a free and unimpaired manner is preservative of other basic civil and political rights." The importance of the franchise is further evidenced by the volume of constitutional amendments concerned with protecting it. The Fifteenth Amendment prohibits denial of the right to vote "on account of race, color, or previous condition of servitude." U.S. CONST., AMEND. XV. The Nineteenth Amendment prohibits abridgment of the right to vote "on account of sex." *Id.*, AMEND. XIX. The Twenty-fourth Amendment prohibits poll taxes. *Id.*, Amend. XXIV. The Twenty-sixth Amendment extends the right to vote to citizens who are 18 or older. *Id.*, AMEND. XXVI.

The concept of voting as a fundamental right was introduced in the context of equal protection review. In *Baker v. Carr*, 369 U.S. 186 (1962), the Court struck down a state's legislative apportionment scheme on grounds it violated the premise of "one man, one vote." An equality principle thus was established as a primary basis for challenging laws that deny or dilute the right to vote.

In *Husted v. A. Philip Randolph Institute*, 138 S. Ct. 1883 (2018), the Court upheld an Ohio law that allowed the removal of voters from the voting rolls. Basically, if a voter failed to vote in two straight elections, Ohio would send a preaddressed, postage prepaid card to the individual. Only if the individual did not return the card, or otherwise notify the state that he had not moved, could the voter be removed from the voting rolls. The case involved an interpretation of the National Voter Registration Act, and the Court held that the Ohio law was consistent with that Act.

a. Denial of the Right to Vote

Although the states have authority to establish the basic terms of voting, conditions that burden the franchise through qualifications unrelated to age, citizenship, or residence typically will "be carefully and meticulously scrutinized." *Harper v. Virginia State Board of Elections*, 383 U.S. 663 (1966). This higher level of review may extend to residence requirements, as evidenced by the Court's invalidation of a one-year state and three-month county waiting period for local, state, and congressional elections. *Dunn v. Blumstein*, 405 U.S. 330 (1972).

Equal protection activity with respect to denial of the right to vote has centered primarily on poll taxes and voter eligibility requirements for special-purpose government districts. Poll taxes historically were part of the system of racial management that denied meaningful participation in the political process. They were prohibited by the Twenty-fourth Amendment. The Court's outputs with respect to voter requirements for special-purpose district elections has been mixed with respect to both standards of review and results.

(1) *Poll Taxes*

A classic example of an impermissible denial of the right to vote is a poll tax. In *Harper v. Virginia State Board of Elections*, 383 U.S. 663 (1966), the Court found no basis for making wealth a qualification for voting. As Justice Douglas put it: "Wealth, like race, creed, or color, is not germane to the power to participate intelligently in the electoral process. Lines drawn on the basis of wealth or property, like those of race, are traditionally disfavored. To introduce wealth or payment of a fee as a measure of a voter's qualifications is to introduce a capricious or irrelevant factor. The degree of the discrimination is irrelevant. In this context—that is, as a condition of obtaining a ballot—the requirement of fee paying causes an 'invidious' discrimination."

∾ PROBLEM: ENSURING AN INFORMED AND LITERATE ELECTORATE ∾

Like poll taxes, literacy tests have a history of being used to discriminate against persons on the basis of race. Assume that a state wants to ensure that its voters can read, and are conversant with candidates and issues, before they cast their ballot. Assume further that it can be demonstrated that the state's only concern is that voting reflect the informed judgment of the electorate. Is a test designed to ensure competency in this regard inappropriate as a means for establishing voter qualifications?

(2) *Land Ownership*

Special restrictions on eligibility for school board elections also have been the basis for "a close and exacting examination." In *Kramer v. Union Free School District*, 395 U.S. 621 (1969), the Court reviewed a state law that narrowed eligibility for voting in school board elections to otherwise qualified voters who owned or leased property in the district or whose children were enrolled in the district's schools. The eligibility requirements were designed to limit electoral participation to resident citizens " 'primarily interested' in school affairs." The Court determined that this objective was not promoted with "satisfactory precision." To the contrary, it excluded some who had a distinct and direct interest in school affairs and included others who had a remote and indirect concern with them.

For districts that have a special purpose, eligibility requirements may be a function of the narrowness of the scope of governmental authority. Case law suggests that districts with a narrower purpose may have the ability to establish more detailed voter eligibility standards. In *Salyer Land Co. v. Tulare Lake Basin Water Storage District*, 410 U.S. 719 (1973), the Court upheld a law limiting participation in water storage district elections to landowners. Absentee landowners thus could vote, but district residents who did not own land were excluded. The result reflected the Court's sense that the water storage district was not a " 'normal government' authority" and "its actions disproportionately affect landowners." It also was achieved pursuant to rational basis review rather than the strict scrutiny standard used in *Kramer*. The different standards of review appear to correlate with a sense that, as a district's ambit of concern narrows, more room is needed to establish requirements that ensure an "interested" electorate. Barring a special-interest election, as the Court noted in *Hill v. Stone*, 421 U.S. 289 (1975), classifications restricting the right to vote "cannot stand unless the district or State can demonstrate that the classification serves a compelling state interest."

∼ PROBLEMS ∼

1. *Landownership Requirements.* Would landownership be a valid requirement for voting in an election to select members of a board of freeholders? Would this condition be justified by the need for an informed electorate? *See Quinn v. Millsap*, 491 U.S. 95 (1989). Would a system that correlated voting strength with the amount of land owned, in a district that managed water and sold electricity, violate the equal protection guarantee? *See Ball v. James*, 451 U.S. 355 (1981).

2. *Bonds and Property Interests.* Consider a city bond issue that limited the right to vote based on whether property owners had listed or rendered their property for taxation in the election district. This requirement varied from state law, which established listing alone as the basis for eligibility. Is the election one of general or special interest? Does the provision for rendering constitute an equal protection problem? *See Hill v. Stone*, 421 U.S. 289 (1975).

(3) *Other Restrictions on the Right to Vote*

In recent years, a number of states have enacted voter identification laws. Basically, these laws provide that voters must produce a valid photo identification in order to vote in state and federal elections. States usually attempt to justify these laws on the basis that they help prevent voter fraud by ensuring that only eligible individuals vote in elections. Representatives of minority groups claim that African Americans and Hispanics are disproportionately unable to obtain valid photo identifications. Is the state interest in preventing voter fraud sufficient to sustain voter ID laws? How does a court determine whether a law suffers from discriminatory animus? *See Veasey v. Abbott*, 888 F.3d 792 (5th Cir. 2018) (upholding Texas law); *Lee v. Virginia State Board of Elections*, 2016 WL 6921611 (E.D. Va. 2016); *Greater Birmingham Ministries v. Merrill*, 284 F. Supp. 3rd 1253 (N.D. Ala. 2018) (upholding Alabama law); *Gentges v. Oklahoma State Election Board*, 419 P.3d 224 (Okla. 2018) (upholding Oklahoma's voter ID law). A Kansas law requiring a voter to provide proof of citizenship was struck down in *Fish v. Schwab*, 957 F.3d 1105 (10th Cir. 2020). Among other things, the court held that the Kansas law was preempted by the National Voting Rights Act.

∼ PROBLEM: REDUCING EARLY VOTING PERIODS ∼

Until this year, Ohio had a 35-day early voting period (allowing voters to vote prior to election day). In a recent law, Ohio reduced the early voting period from 35 days to 29 days. In the process, it also eliminated the "Golden Week" (the early voting days that were eliminated) during which voters could both register and vote at the same time. The law is challenged on the basis that it imposes an undue burden on the voting rights of African Americans. The state defends the law on the basis that there is no constitutional right to an early voting period, and (in any event) a 29-day early voting period is ample. Does the reduction constitute an unconstitutional restriction on the right to vote? *See Ohio Democratic Party v. Husted*, 834 F.3d 620 (6th Cir. 2016).

b. Dilution of the Right to Vote

The right to vote may also be abridged by dilution. Methodologies of dilution include apportionment schemes that weight votes differently, restrictions on ballot access that narrow the range of voter options, and processes for recording and counting votes. Districting processes for political representation generally are governed by the principle of one person, one vote. Allowable deviations from the norm and standards of review vary depending on whether federal, state, or local representation is implicated. With respect to ballot access, the focus is on the degree of burden imposed by the restriction.

(1) *Apportionment*

The basis for determining representation in the political process has been a source of contention since the nation's founding. Next to slavery, the determining factors for representation in the national government probably were the most divisive issue at the Constitutional Convention. The compromise effected by the founders was a bicameral legislature that correlated representation in the House with state population and gave every state the same number of senators. Most states also have adopted a bicameral model. The dual sovereign relationship between the federal and state governments, however, is not replicated at the state level. Counties and districts are subsets or units of state government, rather than independent sovereigns. Lacking a true parallel to the federal system, the Court has concluded that representation in state legislatures must follow a rule of proportionality that translates generally into one person, one vote.

Reynolds v. Sims

377 U.S. 533 (1964)

Mr. Chief Justice WARREN delivered the opinion of the Court.

The Alabama legislature failed to reapportion legislative districts after 1901. By 1960, the state's legislative districts were lopsided so that 25% of the population was able to elect a majority of the state Senate, and 25% could elect a majority of the House of Representatives. Lower courts struck down the existing districts under the Equal Protection Clause of the Federal Constitution, and also struck down two proposed apportionment plans. In addition, they put into effect a temporary reapportionment plan comprised of parts of the proposed but judicially disapproved measures.

The Constitution of the United States protects the right of all qualified citizens to vote, in state as well as in federal elections, and to have their votes counted. *See United States v. Mosley,* 238 U.S. 383 (1915). Racially based gerrymandering and the conducting of white primaries, both of which result in denying to some citizens their right to vote, have been held to be constitutionally impermissible. And history has seen a continuing expansion of the scope of the right of suffrage in this country. The right to vote freely for the candidate of one's choice is of the essence of a democratic society, and any restrictions on that right strike at the heart of representative government.

A predominant consideration in determining whether a State's legislative apportionment scheme constitutes an invidious discrimination violative of rights asserted under the Equal Protection Clause is that the rights allegedly impaired are individual and personal in nature. While a court decision in a state legislative apportionment controversy restructured the geographical distribution of seats in a state legislature, the judicial focus must be concentrated upon ascertaining whether there has been discrimination against citizens which constitutes an impermissible impairment of their constitutionally protected right to vote. The right of suffrage is a fundamental matter in a free and democratic society. Especially since the right to exercise the franchise in a free and unimpaired manner is preservative of other basic civil and political rights, any alleged infringement of the right of citizens to vote must be carefully and meticulously scrutinized.

Legislators represent people, not trees or acres. Legislators are elected by voters, not farms or cities or economic interests. As long as ours is a representative form of government, and our legislatures are those instruments of government elected directly by and directly representative of the people, the right to elect legislators in a free and unimpaired fashion is a bedrock of our political system. It could hardly be gainsaid that a constitutional claim had been asserted by an allegation that certain otherwise qualified voters had been entirely prohibited from voting for members of their state legislature. And, if a State should provide that the votes of citizens in one part of the State should be given two times, or five times, or 10 times the weight of votes of citizens in another part of the State, it could hardly be contended that the right to vote of those residing in the disfavored areas had not been effectively diluted. The effect of state legislative districting schemes which give the same number of representatives to unequal numbers of constituents is identical.

We are told that the matter of apportioning representation in a state legislature is a complex and many-faceted one and that States can rationally consider factors other than population in apportioning legislative representation. We are admonished not to restrict the power of the States to impose differing views as to political philosophy on their citizens. We are cautioned about the dangers of entering into political thickets and mathematical quagmires. Our answer is this: a denial of constitutionally protected rights demands judicial protection; our oath and our office require no less of us. The basic principle of representative government remains, and must remain, unchanged—the weight of a citizen's vote cannot be made to depend on where he lives. Population is, of necessity, the starting point for consideration and the controlling criterion for judgment in legislative apportionment controversies. A citizen, a qualified voter, is no more nor no less so because he lives in the city or on the farm. This is an essential part of the concept of a government of laws and not men. The Equal Protection Clause demands no less than substantially equal state legislative representation for all citizens, of all places as well as of all races. Since, under neither the existing apportionment provisions nor either of the proposed plans was either of the houses of the Alabama Legislature apportioned on a population basis, all three of these schemes were constitutionally invalid.

The system of representation in the two Houses of the Federal Congress is one ingrained in our Constitution. Arising from unique historical circumstances, it is based on the consideration that in establishing our type of federalism a group of formerly independent States bound themselves together under one national government. At the time of the inception of the system of representation in the Federal Congress, a compromise between the larger and smaller States on this matter averted a deadlock in the Constitutional Convention which had threatened to abort the birth of our Nation. Political subdivisions of States—counties, cities, or whatever—never were and never have been considered as sovereign entities. Rather, they have been traditionally regarded as subordinate governmental instrumentalities created by the State to assist in the carrying out of state governmental functions. The relationship of the States to the Federal Government could hardly be less analogous.

We hold that the Equal Protection Clause requires both houses of a state legislature to be apportioned on a population basis. The right of a citizen to equal representation and to have his vote weighted equally with those of all other citizens in the election of members of one house of a bicameral state legislature would amount to little if States could effectively submerge the equal-population principle in the apportionment of seats in the other house. If such a scheme were permissible, an individual citizen's ability to exercise an effective voice in the only instrument of state government directly representative of the people might be almost as effectively thwarted as if neither house were apportioned on a population basis. Deadlock between the two bodies might result in compromise and concession on some issues. In all too many cases the more probable result would be frustration of the majority will through minority veto in the house not apportioned on a population basis, stemming directly from the failure to accord adequate overall legislative representation to all of the State's citizens on a nondiscriminatory basis. We can perceive no constitutional difference, with respect to the geographical distribution of state legislative representation, between the two houses of a bicameral state legislature.

We do not believe that the concept of bicameralism is rendered anachronistic and meaningless when the predominant basis of representation in the two state legislative bodies is required to be the same—population. A prime reason for bicameralism, modernly considered, is to insure mature and deliberate consideration of, and to prevent precipitate action on, proposed legislative measures. Simply because the controlling criterion for apportioning representation is required to be the same in both houses does not mean that there will be no differences in the composition and complexion of the two bodies. One body could be composed of single-member districts while the other could have at least some multimember districts. The length of terms of the legislators in the separate bodies could differ. The numerical size of the two bodies could be made to differ, even significantly, and the geographical size of districts from which legislators are elected could also be made to differ. And apportionment in one house could be arranged so as to balance off minor inequities in the representation of certain areas in the other house. These and other factors could be, and are presently in many States, utilized to engender differing complexions and collective attitudes in the two bodies of a state legislature, although both are apportioned substantially on a population basis.

The Equal Protection Clause requires that a State make an honest and good faith effort to construct districts, in both houses of its legislature, as nearly of equal population as is practicable. We realize that it is a practical impossibility to arrange legislative districts so that each one has an identical number of residents, or citizens, or voters. Some distinctions may well be made between congressional and state legislative representation. Since, almost invariably, there is a significantly larger number of seats in state legislative bodies to be distributed within a State than congressional seats, it may be feasible to use political subdivision lines to a greater extent in establishing state legislative districts than in congressional districting while still affording adequate representation to all parts of the State. To do so would be constitutionally valid, so long as the resulting apportionment was one based substantially on population and the equal-population principle was not diluted in any significant way. We deem it expedient not to attempt to spell out any precise constitutional tests. What is marginally permissible in one State may be unsatisfactory in another, depending on the particular circumstances of the case.

History indicates, however, that many States have deviated, to a greater or lesser degree, from the equal-population principle in the apportionment of seats in at least one house of their legislatures. So long as the divergences from a strict population standard are based on legitimate considerations incident to the effectuation of a rational state policy, some deviations from the equal-population principle are constitutionally permissible with respect to the apportionment of seats in either or both of the two houses of a bicameral state legislature. But neither history alone, nor economic or other sorts of group interests, are permissible factors in attempting to justify disparities from population-based representation. Citizens cast votes. Considerations of area alone provide an insufficient justification for deviations from the equal-population principle. Modern developments and improvements in transportation and communications make rather hollow, in the mid-1960's, most claims that deviations from population-based representation can validly be based solely on geographical considerations. Arguments for allowing such deviations in order to insure effective representation for sparsely settled areas and to prevent legislative districts from becoming so large that the availability of access of citizens to their representatives is impaired are today, for the most part, unconvincing.

A consideration that appears to be of more substance in justifying some deviations from population-based representation in state legislatures is that of insuring some voice to political subdivisions, as political subdivisions. A State can rationally consider according political subdivisions some independent representation in at least one body of the state legislature, as long as the basic standard of equality of population among districts is maintained. Local governmental entities are frequently charged with various responsibilities incident to the operation of state government. In many States much of the legislature's activity involves the enactment of so-called local legislation, directed only to the concerns of particular political subdivisions. And a State may legitimately desire to construct districts along political subdivision lines to deter the possibilities of gerrymandering. However, permitting deviations from population-based representation does not mean that each local governmental unit or political subdivision can be given separate representation, regardless of population. But if, even as a result of a clearly rational state policy of according some legislative representation to political subdivisions, population is submerged as the controlling consideration in the apportionment of seats in the particular legislative body, then the right of all of the State's citizens to cast an effective and adequately weighted vote would be unconstitutionally impaired.

That the Equal Protection Clause requires that both houses of a state legislature be apportioned on a population basis does not mean that States cannot adopt some reasonable plan for periodic revision of their apportionment schemes. Limitations on the frequency of reapportionment are justified by the need for stability and continuity in the organization of the legislative system, although undoubtedly reapportioning no more frequently than every 10 years leads to some imbalance in the population of districts toward the end of the decennial period and also to the development of resistance to change on the part of some incumbent legislators. We do not regard the Equal Protection Clause as requiring daily, monthly, annual or biennial reapportionment, so long as a State has a reasonably conceived plan for periodic readjustment of legislative representation. Decennial reapportionment would clearly meet the minimal requirements for maintaining a reasonably current scheme of legislative representation. But if reapportionment were accomplished with less frequency, it would assuredly be constitutionally suspect.

We find, therefore, that the action taken by the District Court in this case, in ordering into effect a reapportionment of both houses of the Alabama Legislature for purposes of the 1962 primary and general elections, by using the best parts of the two proposed plans which it had found, as a whole, to be invalid, was an appropriate and well-considered exercise of judicial power.

Affirmed and remanded.

Mr. Justice CLARK, *concurring in the affirmance.*

The Court goes much beyond the necessities of this case in laying down a new 'equal population' principle for state legislative apportionment. All that the Court need say is that each plan considered by the trial court is 'a crazy quilt,' clearly revealing invidious discrimination in each house of the Legislature and therefore violative of the Equal Protection Clause.

Mr. Justice HARLAN, *dissenting.*

The Equal Protection Clause was never intended to inhibit the States in choosing any democratic method they pleased for the apportionment of their legislatures. The consequence of today's decision is that the local courts are given blanket authority and the constitutional duty to supervise apportionment of the State Legislatures. It is difficult to imagine a more intolerable and inappropriate interference by the judiciary with the independent legislatures of the States. No set of standards can guide a court which has to decide how many legislative districts a State shall have, or what the shape of the districts shall be, or where to draw a particular district line. No judicially manageable standard can determine whether a State should have single-member districts or multimember districts or some combination of both. No such standard can control the balance between keeping up with population shifts and having stable districts. In all these respects, the courts will be called upon to make particular decisions with respect to which a principle of equally populated districts will be of no assistance whatsoever. There are limitless possibilities for districting consistent with such a principle. The Court's opinion nevertheless fully demonstrates how far removed these problems are from fields of judicial competence.

I know of no principle of logic or practical or theoretical politics, still less any constitutional principle, which supports this decision. The Court says only that 'legislators represent people, not trees or acres,' that 'citizens, not history or economic interests, cast votes,' that 'people, not land or trees or pastures, vote.' It is surely equally obvious, and, in the context of elections, more meaningful to note that people are not ciphers and that legislators can represent their electors only by speaking for their interests—economic, social, political—many of which do reflect the place where the electors live. The Court does not establish that conflicting interests within a State can only be adjusted by disregarding them when voters are grouped for purposes of representation.

Judicial entry into this realm is profoundly ill-advised and constitutionally impermissible. The vitality of our political system, on which in the last analysis all else depends, is weakened by reliance on the judiciary for political reform; in time a complacent body politic may result. These decisions also cut deeply into the fabric of our federalism. The aftermath of these cases will have been achieved at the cost of a radical alteration in the relationship between the States and the Federal Government, more particularly the Federal Judiciary. These decisions give support to a current mistaken view that every major social ill in this country can find its cure in some constitutional "principle," and that this Court should "take the lead" in promoting reform when other branches of government fail to act. The Constitution is an instrument of government, fundamental to which is the premise that in a diffusion of governmental authority lies the greatest promise that this Nation will realize liberty for all its citizens. This Court does not serve its high purpose when it exceeds its authority, even to satisfy justified impatience with the slow workings of the political process. When, in the name of constitutional interpretation, the Court adds something to the Constitution that was deliberately excluded from it, the Court in reality substitutes its view of what should be so for the amending process.

Notes

1. *Local Elections.* In *Hadley v. Junior College District of Metropolitan Kansas City*, 397 U.S. 50 (1970), the Court extended *Reynolds* to local government elections and the election of non-legislative officials: "Whenever a state or local government decides to select persons by popular election to perform governmental functions, the Equal Protection Clause of the Fourteenth Amendment requires that each qualified voter must be given an equal opportunity to participate in that election, and when members of an elected body are chosen from separate districts, each district must be established on a basis that will insure, as far as is practicable, that equal numbers of voters can vote for proportionally equal numbers of officials."

2. *Permissible Deviations.* In *Harris v. Arizona Independent Redistricting Commission*, 136 S. Ct. 1301 (2016), the Court rejected a challenge to a state legislature redistricting plan despite a claim that the districts were insufficiently equal in population. The Court held that, because the maximum population deviation between the largest and the smallest district is less than 10%, appellants cannot simply rely upon the numbers to show that the plan violates the Constitution. The Court went on to hold that appellants provided insufficient other evidence of disparity.

∾ PROBLEMS ∾

1. *Fashioning Court Orders.* A court concludes that the State of Alabama's congressional districts are malapportioned. How should the court reapportion? Should the court undertake the reapportionment itself? Or should it "remand" the matter to the state legislature, ordering it to constitutionally apportion districts? What is the proper relationship between the courts and the state legislature?

2. *Advising the Legislature.* Suppose that you are the counsel to a state legislative committee, and the committee is thinking about amending the state constitution. The amendment would provide for a bicameral legislature with the house apportioned on the basis of population, but the senate apportioned by taking into account various factors, including population. However, population would not be regarded as "controlling." Other relevant factors are "geography, compactness and contiguity of territory, accessibility, observance of natural boundaries, and conformity to historical divisions such as county lines and prior representation districts." After *Reynolds,* how would you advise the committee regarding the constitutionality of this proposed provision? *See Lucas v. Forty-fourth General Assembly of Colorado,* 377 U.S. 713 (1964).

3. *At-Large Representation.* A county government's charter provides that county commissioners must live in specified districts, but that commissioners are elected by the population of the entire county and are expected to represent the entire county. Under such circumstances, must legislative districts be equal? *See Dallas County v. Reese,* 421 U.S. 477 (1975).

4. *Permissible/Impermissible Deviations.* How much deviation from "one person, one vote" is permissible? Again, suppose that you are the counsel to a legislative committee that is undertaking redistricting. The committee proposes a redistricting plan that contemplates 46,685 persons per delegate. However, the district population totals vary from 6.8% above the 46,685 figure to 9.6% below the figure. How would you advise the committee? Is the proposed plan constitutional? Can the deviation be justified by the committee's desire to maintain district lines consistent with county and city boundaries? *See Mahan v. Howell,* 410 U.S. 315 (1973).

5. *"One Person, One Vote" and Supermajorities.* Suppose that a state apportions its legislative districts in accordance with *Reynolds.* However, the state constitution prohibits the state from increasing taxes without the vote of a supermajority of legislators. Is the supermajority requirement constitutional under *Reynolds* given that a minority can thwart the majority's will? *See Gordon v. Lance,* 403 U.S. 1 (1971); *Town of Lockport v. Citizens for Community Action, Inc.,* 430 U.S. 259 (1977).

6. *Proportional Representation.* Is there a constitutional right to proportional representation? Although a city is divided into legislative districts, and commissioners must reside in the districts they represent, all commissioners are elected on an "at large" basis. In other words, the entire county is allowed to vote in each commissioner's election. Minority voters challenge the at-large elections on the basis that the county has a Caucasian majority and the system helps ensure that all elected representatives are Caucasian. Do minority voters (who make up 20% of the population) have the right to proportional representation? Do they have a "right" to have only voters from their own district (which is dominated by minorities) vote for their commissioner? *See City of Mobile v. Bolden,* 446 U.S. 55 (1980).

7. *More on Proportional Representation.* In the preceding problem, suppose that minority voters file suit alleging that the at-large system is designed to prevent them from electing a minority commissioner. What must the minority voters show

to establish the at-large system as a racial classification that is subject to strict scrutiny?

(2) *Political Gerrymandering*

The principle of one person, one vote has had a significant impact on how state legislative districts are drawn. The *Reynolds* decision itself responded to apportionment models that largely had become outdated, but entrenched, as a function of demographic evolution from rural to urban. Equal weighting of votes may be difficult to achieve with mathematical precision. The one person, one vote principle also operates in conjunction with other legitimate apportionment factors, including, as the Court noted in *Karcher v. Daggett*, "making districts compact, respecting municipal boundaries, preserving the cores of private districts, and avoiding contests between incumbent Representatives." *Karcher v. Daggett*, 462 U.S. 725 (1983). Against this backdrop, greater deviation is permitted in legislative districting for state purposes. State apportionment may factor in traditional political boundaries, but it must reflect a good-faith effort to achieve equality of representation. Because congressional districts do not correlate with traditional state subdivisions, deviation from the equality principle is minimal. A 0.7% deviation thus was found impermissible in *Karcher*.

For state legislative districting processes, which may consider traditional political boundaries, there is more tolerance for deviation. A 16.4% deviation thus was allowed in Virginia and an 89% underrepresentation factor was permitted in Wyoming. *See Mahan v. Howell*, 410 U.S. 315 (1973). The allowable deviation in the first instance was coupled with the observation that there are no "specialized calipers" that enable courts or legislatures to determine "what range of percentage deviations are permissible, and what are not." In the Wyoming scenario, deviation largely was a function of a legislative seat being assigned to the state's least-populated county. It is unlikely that such an extreme departure would be justified on a broader-spectrum basis.

Multimember districts may represent a subtle mechanism for diluting the right to vote. Systems of at-large representation on city councils, for instance, historically have operated to diminish the influence of minority voters. At-large voting schemes that discriminate on the basis of race, as noted in *Rogers v. Lodge*, 458 U.S. 613 (1982), violate the equal protection guarantee. To establish a classification on the basis of race, as with any other equal protection claim correlated with group status, it is necessary to prove discriminatory purpose. City of *Mobile v. Bolden*, 446 U.S. 55 (1980).

Inherent in a political process driven by competing self-interests is the motivation to tilt the playing field for partisan purposes. The opportunity to achieve this result is presented by processes of reapportionment based on population changes reflected in decennial census reports. The mere lack of proportional representation owing to gerrymandering, as the Court notes in the following case, does not violate the equal protection guarantee.

Over the last couple of years, increasing numbers of partisan gerrymandering claims have been filed, including in Maryland, Wisconsin and North Carolina. The Court dealt with one of these suits (the Wisconsin plan) in *Gill v. Whitford*, 138 S. Ct. 1916 (2018), a case in which the Court concluded that the case was not justiciable because plaintiffs lacked standing, but the Court remanded the case to the lower courts to give plaintiffs a chance to formulate their standing allegations differently. In *Gil*, plaintiffs claimed that Wisconsin had "packed" and "cracked" voters in an effort to give Republicans an electoral advantage. Cracking involves dividing a party's supporters among multiple districts so that they lack a majority in each one, and packing involves concentrating one party's backers in a few districts that they win by overwhelming margins. As a result, even if Republicans received less than a majority of the votes, their chances of controlling the state legislature were high. The Court held that plaintiffs lacked standing to bring the suit. The Court reiterated that standing in partisan gerrymandering cases requires plaintiffs to satisfy the traditional three part test for standing. In other words, they must show that they have: (1) suffered an injury in fact, (2) that is fairly traceable to the challenged conduct of the defendant, and (3) that is likely to be redressed by a favorable judicial decision." *Spokeo, Inc. v. Robins*, 578 U.S. __, __ (2016) (slip op., at 6). Foremost among these requirements is injury in fact—a plaintiff's pleading and proof must show that he has suffered the "invasion of a legally protected interest" that is "concrete and particularized," i.e., which "affects the plaintiff in a personal and individual way." *Lujan v. Defenders of Wildlife*, 504 U.S. 555, 560 (1992).

The Court concluded that voters must make district specific allegations of injury, and the remedy lies in revising the boundaries of the district to eliminate the injury. Plaintiffs who complain of racial gerrymandering in their State cannot sue to invalidate the State's entire legislative districting map; such complaints must proceed "district-by-district." The Court rejected plaintiff's argument that their injury extends to the statewide harm to their interest "in their collective representation in the legislature," and in influencing the legislature's overall "composition and policymaking." The Court concluded that this did not establish an individual and personal injury of the kind required for Article III standing. Justice Kagen filed a lengthy dissent offering suggestions about how plaintiffs might be able to establish standing for a state-wide claim.

Rucho v. Common Cause

139 S. Ct. 2484 (2019)

Chief Justice ROBERTS delivered the opinion of the Court.

Plaintiffs challenged their States' congressional districting maps as unconstitutional partisan gerrymanders. The North Carolina plaintiffs complained that the State's districting plan discriminated against Democrats; the Maryland plaintiffs complained that their State's plan discriminated against Republicans. These cases require us to consider again whether claims of excessive partisanship in districting are "justiciable."

The first case involves a challenge to the congressional redistricting plan enacted by the Republican-controlled North Carolina General Assembly in 2016. Republican legislators instructed their mapmaker to use political data to draw a map that would produce a congressional delegation of ten Republicans and three Democrats. One Democratic state senator objected because, as recently as 2012, "Democratic congressional candidates had received more votes on a statewide basis than Republican candidates." The General Assembly approved the 2016 Plan by a party-line vote. In 2016, North Carolina conducted congressional elections using the Plan, and Republican candidates won 10 of the 13 congressional districts. Plaintiffs challenged the Plan on multiple constitutional grounds. A three-judge District Court unanimously concluded that the 2016 Plan violated the Equal Protection Clause and Article I of the Constitution [and] the First Amendment. Defendants appealed. While that appeal was pending, we decided *Gill v. Whitford*, 138 S.Ct. 1916 (2018). In that case, we held that a plaintiff asserting a partisan gerrymandering claim based on a theory of vote dilution must establish standing by showing he lives in an allegedly "cracked" or "packed" district. A "cracked" district is one in which a party's supporters are divided among multiple districts, so that they fall short of a majority in each; a "packed" district is one in which a party's supporters are highly concentrated, so they win that district by a large margin, "wasting" many votes that would improve their chances in others. After deciding *Gill*, we remanded. On remand, the District Court again struck down the 2016 Plan.

The second case is *Lamone v. Benisek*. In 2011, the Maryland Legislature—dominated by Democrats—undertook to redraw the lines of that State's eight congressional districts. The Governor, Democrat Martin O'Malley, appointed a redistricting committee to redraw the map. The Governor's aim was to "use redistricting to change the overall composition of Maryland's congressional delegation to 7 Democrats and 1 Republican by flipping" one district. The Plan reduced the number of registered Republicans in the Sixth District by about 66,000 and increased the number of registered Democrats by about 24,000. The map was adopted by a party-line vote. It was used in the 2012 election and succeeded in flipping the Sixth District. A Democrat has held the seat ever since. Three Maryland voters filed this lawsuit. The District Court entered summary judgment for plaintiffs. Defendants appealed directly to this Court under 28 U.S.C. §1253.

Article III of the Constitution limits federal courts to deciding "Cases" and "Controversies." Federal courts can address only questions "historically viewed as capable of resolution through the judicial process." *Flast v. Cohen*, 392 U.S. 83, 95 (1968). Chief Justice Marshall famously wrote that it is "the province and duty of the judicial department to say what the law is." *Marbury v. Madison*, 5 U.S. 137 (1803). Sometimes, "the judicial department has no business entertaining the claim of unlawfulness—because the question is entrusted to one of the political branches or involves no judicially enforceable rights." *Vieth v. Jubelirer*, 541 U.S.

267, 277 (2004) (plurality opinion). In such a case the claim is said to present a "political question" and to be nonjusticiable—outside the courts' competence and therefore beyond the courts' jurisdiction. *Baker v. Carr*, 369 U.S. 186 (1962). Among the political question cases are those that lack "judicially discoverable and manageable standards for resolving them." The question is whether there is an "appropriate role for the Federal Judiciary" in remedying the problem of partisan gerrymandering—whether such claims are claims of *legal* right, resolvable according to *legal* principles, or political questions that must find their resolution elsewhere.

Partisan gerrymandering is nothing new. Nor is frustration with it. The practice was known in the Colonies prior to Independence, and the Framers were familiar with it at the time of the drafting and ratification of the Constitution. The Framers addressed the election of Representatives to Congress in the Elections Clause. Art. I, §4, cl. 1. That provision assigns to state legislatures the power to prescribe the "Times, Places and Manner of holding Elections" for Members of Congress, while giving Congress the power to "make or alter" any such regulations. Congress has regularly exercised its Elections Clause power, including to address partisan gerrymandering. The Apportionment Act of 1842, which required single-member districts for the first time, specified that those districts be "composed of contiguous territory" in "an attempt to forbid the practice of the gerrymander." Later statutes added requirements of compactness and equality of population. Congress also used its Elections Clause power in 1870, enacting the first comprehensive federal statute dealing with elections as a way to enforce the Fifteenth Amendment. In the 1950s, Congress enacted a series of laws to protect the right to vote through measures such as the suspension of literacy tests and the prohibition of English-only elections.

In two areas—one-person, one-vote and racial gerrymandering—there is a role for the courts with respect to at least some issues that could arise from a State's drawing of congressional districts. But the Framers were aware of electoral districting problems. They settled on a characteristic approach, assigning the issue to the state legislatures, expressly checked and balanced by the Federal Congress. At no point was there a suggestion that the federal courts had a role to play. Nor was there any indication that the Framers had heard of courts doing such a thing. Courts have been called upon to resolve a variety of questions surrounding districting. *See Wood v. Broom*, 287 U.S. 1 (1932); *Colegrove v. Green*, 328 U.S. 549 (1946). In *Baker v. Carr*, voters in Tennessee complained that the State's districting plan for state representatives "debased" their votes, because the plan was predicated on a 60-year-old census that no longer reflected the distribution of population in the State. Plaintiffs argued that votes of people in overpopulated districts held less value than those of people in less-populated districts, and that this inequality violated the Equal Protection Clause of the Fourteenth Amendment. The District Court dismissed on the ground that the claim was not justiciable. This Court reversed. It identified various considerations relevant to determining whether a claim is a nonjusticiable political question, including whether there is "a lack of judicially discoverable and manageable standards for resolving it." The claim of population inequality among districts did not fall into that category, because such a claim could be decided under basic equal protection principles. In *Wesberry v. Sanders*, the Court extended its ruling to malapportionment of congressional districts, holding that Article I, §2, required that "one man's vote in a congressional election be worth as much as another's." Another line of challenges to districting plans has focused on race. Laws that explicitly discriminate on the basis of race, as well as those that are race neutral on their face but are unexplainable on grounds other than race, are presumptively invalid. The Court applied those principles to electoral boundaries in *Gomillion v. Lightfoot*, concluding that a challenge to an "uncouth twenty-eight sided" municipal boundary line that excluded black voters from city elections stated a constitutional claim. In *Wright v. Rockefeller*, 376 U.S. 52 (1964), the Court extended the reasoning of *Gomillion* to congressional districting.

Partisan gerrymandering claims have proved far more difficult to adjudicate. While it is illegal for a jurisdiction to depart from the one-person, one-vote rule, or to engage in racial discrimination in districting, "a jurisdiction may engage in constitutional political gerrymandering." *Hunt v. Cromartie*, 526 U.S. 541, 551 (1999); *Shaw v. Hunt*, 517 U.S. 899 (1996). To hold that legislators cannot take partisan interests into account when drawing district lines would essentially countermand the Framers' decision to entrust districting to political entities. The "central problem" is not determining whether a jurisdiction has engaged in partisan gerrymandering. It is "determining when political gerrymandering has gone too far." *Vieth*, 541 U.S. at 296 (plurality opinion).

We first considered a partisan gerrymandering claim in *Gaffney v. Cummings* in 1973. There we rejected an equal protection challenge to Connecticut's redistricting plan, which "aimed at a rough scheme of proportional representation of the two major political parties" by "wiggling and joggling boundary lines" to create the appropriate number of safe seats for each party. In upholding the plan, we reasoned that districting "inevitably has and is intended to have substantial political consequences." Thirteen years later, in *Davis v. Bandemer*, we addressed a claim that Indiana Republicans had cracked and packed Democrats in violation of the Equal Protection Clause. 478 U.S. 109 (1986) (plurality opinion). A majority agreed that the case was justiciable, but the Court splintered over the proper standard to apply. The Court held that plaintiffs failed to show that the plan violated the Constitution. Eighteen years later, in *Vieth*, the plaintiffs complained that Pennsylvania's legislature "ignored all traditional redistricting criteria, including the preservation of local government boundaries," in order to benefit Republican congressional candidates. Once again a majority could not find a justiciable standard for resolving the plaintiffs' partisan gerrymandering claims.

Any standard for resolving such claims must be grounded in a "limited and precise rationale" and be "clear, manageable, and politically neutral." An expansive standard requiring "the correction of all election district lines drawn for partisan reasons would commit federal and state courts to unprecedented intervention in the American political process," *Vieth*, 541 U.S. at 306 (Kennedy, J.). If federal courts are to "inject themselves into the most heated partisan issues" by adjudicating partisan gerrymandering claims, they must be armed with a standard that can reliably differentiate unconstitutional from "constitutional political gerrymandering." *Cromartie*, 526 U.S. at 551.

Partisan gerrymandering claims rest on an instinct that groups with a certain level of political support should enjoy a commensurate level of political power and influence. A districting map is alleged to be unconstitutional because it makes it too difficult for one party to translate statewide support into seats in the legislature. Partisan gerrymandering claims invariably sound in a desire for proportional representation. The Founders certainly did not think proportional representation was required. For more than 50 years after ratification of the Constitution, many States elected their congressional representatives through at-large or "general ticket" elections. Such States typically sent single-party delegations to Congress. That meant that a party could garner nearly half of the vote statewide and wind up without any seats in the congressional delegation. The Whigs in Alabama suffered that fate in 1840. Unable to claim that the Constitution requires proportional representation, plaintiffs ask the courts to make their own political judgment about how much representation particular political parties *deserve*—based on the votes of their supporters—and to rearrange the challenged districts to achieve that end. But federal courts are not equipped to apportion political power as a matter of fairness, nor is there any basis for concluding that they were authorized to do so.

The difficulty in settling on a "clear, manageable and politically neutral" test for fairness is that it is not clear what fairness looks like. There is "unfairness" in any winner-take-all system. Fairness may mean a greater number of competitive districts. Such a claim seeks to undo packing and cracking so that supporters of the disadvantaged party have a better shot at electing their preferred candidates. But making as many districts as possible competitive could be a disaster for the disadvantaged party. "A narrow statewide preference for either party would produce an overwhelming majority for the winning party in the state legislature." *Bandemer*, 478 U.S. at 130 (plurality). Perhaps the ultimate objective of a "fairer" share of seats in the congressional delegation is most readily achieved by yielding to the gravitational pull of proportionality and engaging in cracking and packing, to ensure each party its "appropriate" share of "safe" seats. Such an approach comes at the expense of competitive districts and of individuals in districts allocated to the opposing party. Or perhaps fairness should be measured by adherence to "traditional" districting criteria, such as maintaining political subdivisions, keeping communities of interest together, and protecting incumbents. But protecting incumbents enshrines a particular partisan distribution. And the "natural political geography" of a State—such as the fact that urban electoral districts are often dominated by one political party—can itself lead to inherently packed districts. Traditional criteria such as compactness and contiguity "cannot promise political neutrality. A decision under these standards would unavoidably have significant political effect, whether intended or not." *Vieth*, 541 U.S. at 308 (Kennedy concurring). There are no legal standards discernible in the Constitution for making such judgments, let alone limited and precise standards that are clear, manageable, and politically neutral. Any judicial decision on what is "fair" in this context would be an "unmoored determination" of the sort characteristic of a political question beyond the competence of the federal courts.

Only after determining how to define fairness can [one] begin to answer the determinative question: "How much is too much?" If compliance with traditional districting criteria is the touchstone, how much deviation from those criteria is constitutionally acceptable and how should mapdrawers prioritize competing criteria? Should a court "reverse gerrymander" other parts of a State to counteract "natural" gerrymandering caused by the urban concentration of one party? If a districting plan protected half of the incumbents but redistricted the rest into head to head races, would that be constitutional? A court would have to rank the relative importance of traditional criteria and weigh how much deviation to allow. If a court focused on the respective number of seats in the legislature, it would have to decide the ideal number of seats for each party and determine at what point deviation from that balance went too far. If a 5–3 allocation corresponds most closely to statewide vote totals, is a 6–2 allocation permissible, given that legislatures have the authority to engage in a degree of partisan gerrymandering? Which seats should be packed and which cracked? Or if the goal is as many competitive districts as possible, how close does the split need to be for the district to be considered competitive? Even assuming the court knew which version of fairness to be looking for, there are no discernible and manageable standards for deciding whether there has been a violation. The questions are "unguided and ill suited to the development of judicial standards," *Vieth*, 541 U.S. at 296 (plurality opinion), and "results from one gerrymandering case to the next would likely be disparate and inconsistent."

Appellees contend that if we can adjudicate one-person, one-vote claims, we can also assess partisan gerrymandering claims. But the one-person, one-vote rule is relatively easy to administer as a matter of math. The same cannot be said of partisan gerrymandering claims, because the Constitution supplies no objective measure for assessing whether a districting map treats a political party fairly. "The Court's constitutionally prescribed role is to vindicate the individual rights of the people appearing before it." Nor do our racial gerrymandering cases provide an appropriate standard for assessing partisan gerrymandering. A racial gerrymandering claim does not ask for a fair share of political power and influence, with all the justiciability conundrums that entails. It asks for the elimination of a racial classification. A partisan gerrymandering claim cannot ask for the elimination of partisanship.

Appellees and the dissent propose a number of "tests" for evaluating partisan gerrymandering claims, but none meets the need for a limited and precise standard that is judicially discernible and manageable. And none provides a solid grounding for judges to take the extraordinary step of reallocating power and influence between political parties. The *Common Cause* District Court required plaintiffs to prove "that a legislative mapdrawer's predominant purpose in drawing the lines of a particular district was to 'subordinate adherents of one political party and entrench a rival party in power.'" The District Court next required a showing "that the dilution of the votes of supporters of a disfavored party in a particular district—by virtue of cracking or packing—is likely to persist in subsequent elections such that an elected representative from the favored party in the district will not feel a need to be responsive to constituents who support the disfavored party." Finally, after a prima facie showing of partisan vote dilution, the District Court shifted the burden to defendants to prove that the discriminatory effects are "attributable to a legitimate state interest or other neutral explanation." In racial gerrymandering cases, we rely on a "predominant intent" inquiry to determine whether race was, in fact, the reason particular district boundaries were drawn the way they were. If district lines were drawn for the purpose of separating racial groups, then they are subject to strict scrutiny because "race-based decisionmaking is inherently suspect." *Miller*, 515 U.S. at 915. But determining that lines were drawn on the basis of partisanship does not indicate that the districting was improper. A permissible intent—securing partisan advantage—does not become constitutionally impermissible, like racial discrimination, when that permissible intent "predominates." Appellees assure us that "the persistence of a party's advantage may be shown through probing how a plan would perform under other plausible electoral conditions." Experience proves that accurately predicting electoral outcomes is not so simple, either because the plans are based on flawed assumptions about voter preferences and behavior or because demographics and priorities change over time. In our two leading partisan gerrymandering cases, the predictions of durability proved to be dramatically wrong. In 1981, Republicans controlled both houses of the Indiana Legislature as well as the governorship. Democrats challenged the state legislature districting map enacted by the Republicans. *Bandemer* rejected that challenge, and just months later the Democrats increased their share of House seats in the 1986 elections. Two years later the House was split 50–50 between Democrats and Republicans, and the Democrats took control of the chamber in 1990. Democrats also challenged the Pennsylvania congressional districting plan at issue in *Vieth*. Two years after that challenge failed, they gained four seats in the delegation, going from a 12–7 minority to an 11–8 majority. At the next election, they flipped another Republican seat. Even the most sophisticated districting maps cannot reliably account for some of the reasons voters prefer one candidate over another, or why their preferences may change. Voters elect individual candidates in individual districts, and their selections depend on the issues that matter to them, the quality of the candidates, the tone of the candidates' campaigns, the performance of an incumbent, national events or local issues that drive voter turnout, and other considerations. Many voters split their tickets. Others never register with a political party, and vote for candidates from both major parties at different points.

Asking judges to predict how a particular districting map will perform in future elections risks basing constitutional holdings on unstable ground outside judicial expertise. It is hard to see what the District Court's third prong—providing the defendant an opportunity to show that the discriminatory effects were due to a "legitimate redistricting objective"—adds to the inquiry. The first prong already requires the plaintiff to prove that partisan advantage predominates.

The District Courts also found partisan gerrymandering claims justiciable [focusing on] proof of intent to burden individuals based on their voting history or party affiliation; an actual burden on political speech or associational rights; and a causal link between the invidious intent and actual burden. Both District Courts concluded that the districting plans at issue violated the plaintiffs' First Amendment right to association. The District Court in North Carolina relied on testimony that, after the 2016 Plan, the plaintiffs faced "difficulty raising money, attracting candidates, and mobilizing voters to support the political causes and issues such Plaintiffs sought to advance." Similarly, the District Court in Maryland examined testimony that "revealed a lack of enthusiasm, indifference to voting, a sense of disenfranchisement, a sense of disconnection, and confusion," and concluded that Republicans "were burdened in fundraising, attracting volunteers, campaigning, and generating interest in voting." There are no restrictions on speech, association, or any other First Amendment activities in the districting plans at issue. Plaintiffs are free to engage in those activities no matter what the effect of a plan may be on their district. Plaintiffs' argument is that partisanship in districting should be regarded as discrimination against supporters of the opposing party on the basis of political viewpoint. Under that theory, any level of partisanship in districting would constitute an infringement of First Amendment rights. But the First Amendment test simply describes the act of districting for partisan advantage. It provides no standard for determining when partisan activity goes too far. How much of a decline in voter engagement is enough to constitute a First Amendment burden? How many petitions unsigned? How many calls for volunteers unheeded? The *Common Cause* District Court held that a partisan gerrymander places an unconstitutional burden on speech if it has more than a "*de minimis*" "chilling effect or adverse impact" on First Amendment activity. But the First Amendment analysis offers no "clear" and "manageable" way of distinguishing permissible from impermissible partisan motivation. The *Common Cause* court [concluded] that "a judicially manageable framework for evaluating partisan gerrymandering claims need not distinguish an 'acceptable' level of partisan gerrymandering from 'excessive' partisan gerrymandering" because "the Constitution does not authorize state redistricting bodies to engage in such partisan gerrymandering." The decisions prove the prediction of the *Vieth* plurality that "a First Amendment claim, if sustained, would render unlawful *all* consideration of political affiliation in districting" contrary to our established precedent.

The dissent proposes using a State's own districting criteria as a neutral baseline from which to measure a partisan gerrymander. The dissent would have us line up all the possible maps drawn using those criteria according to the partisan distribution they would produce. Distance from the "median" map would indicate whether a particular districting plan harms supporters of one party to an unconstitutional extent. As an initial matter, it does not make sense to use criteria that will vary from State to State and year to year as the baseline for determining whether a gerrymander violates the Federal Constitution. The degree of partisan advantage that the Constitution tolerates should not turn on criteria offered by the gerrymanderers themselves. The same map could be constitutional or not depending solely on what the mapmakers said they set out to do. Even if we were to accept the dissent's baseline, it would return us to "the original unanswerable question (How much political motivation and effect is too much?)." *Vieth*, 541 U.S. at 296 (plurality opinion). Would twenty percent from the median map be okay? Forty percent? Sixty percent? The dissent argues that there are other instances in law where matters of degree are left to the courts. True enough. But those instances typically involve constitutional or statutory provisions or common law confining and guiding the exercise of judicial discretion. Here, the Constitution provides no basis to guide the exercise of judicial discretion. Common experience gives content to terms such as "substantial risk" or "substantial harm," but the same cannot be said of substantial deviation from a median map. There is no way to tell whether the prohibited deviation from that map should kick in at 25 percent or 75 percent or some other point. The only provision in the Constitution that specifically addresses the matter assigns it to the political branches. See Art. I, §4, cl. 1.

The North Carolina District Court concluded that the 2016 Plan exceeded the North Carolina General Assembly's Elections Clause authority because, among other reasons, "the Elections Clause did not empower State legislatures to disfavor the interests of supporters of a particular candidate or party in drawing congressional districts." The court further held that partisan gerrymandering infringes the right of "the People" to select their representatives. The plurality in *Vieth* concluded that neither §2 nor §4 of Article I "provides a judicially enforceable limit on the political considerations that the States and Congress may take into account when districting." The District Court nevertheless asserted that partisan gerrymanders violate "the core principle of our republican government" preserved in Art. I, §2, "namely, that the voters should choose their representatives, not the other way around." That seems like an objection more properly grounded in the Guarantee Clause of Article IV, §4, which "guarantees to every State in the Union a Republican Form of Government." This Court has several times concluded that the Guarantee Clause does not provide the basis for a justiciable claim. See, *e.g., Pacific States Telephone & Telegraph Co. v. Oregon*, 223 U.S. 118 (1912).

Excessive partisanship in districting leads to results that reasonably seem unjust. But the fact that gerrymandering is "incompatible with democratic principles," does not mean that the solution lies with the federal judiciary. Partisan gerrymandering claims present political questions beyond the reach of the federal courts. Federal judges have no license to reallocate political power between the two major political parties, with no plausible grant of authority in the Constitution, and no legal standards to limit and direct their decisions. "Judicial action must be governed by *standard*, by *rule*," and must be "principled, rational, and based upon reasoned distinctions" found in the Constitution or laws. *Vieth*, 541 U.S. at 278 (plurality opinion). Judicial review of partisan gerrymandering does not meet those basic requirements. The dissent essentially embraces the argument that "this Court *can* address the problem of partisan gerrymandering because it *must*." That is not the test of our authority under the Constitution; that document "confines the federal courts to a properly judicial role." *Town of Chester v. Laroe Estates, Inc.*, 137 S. Ct. 1645, 1650 (2017). Appellees and dissent seek an unprecedented expansion of judicial power. We have never struck down a partisan gerrymander as unconstitutional. The expansion of judicial authority would be into one of the most intensely partisan aspects of American political life. That intervention would be unlimited in scope and duration—it would recur over and over around the country with each new round of districting, for state as well as federal representatives. Consideration of the impact of today's ruling on democratic principles cannot ignore the effect of the unelected and politically unaccountable branch of the Federal Government assuming such an extraordinary and unprecedented role.

Our conclusion does not condone excessive partisan gerrymandering. The States are actively addressing the issue on a number of fronts. In 2015, the Supreme Court of Florida struck down that State's congressional districting plan as a violation of the Fair Districts Amendment to the Florida Constitution. The dissent wonders why we can't do the same. The answer is that there is no "Fair Districts Amendment" to the Federal Constitution. Numerous other States are restricting partisan considerations in districting through legislation. Voters in Colorado and Michigan approved constitutional amendments creating multi-member commissions that will be responsible in whole or in part for creating and approving district maps for congressional and state legislative districts. [In] Missouri, voters overwhelmingly approved the creation of a state demographer to draw state legislative district lines. Other States have mandated some of the traditional districting criteria for their mapmakers. Some have outright prohibited partisan favoritism in redistricting.

The Framers gave Congress the power to do something about partisan gerrymandering in the Elections Clause. The first bill introduced in the 116th Congress would require States to create 15-member independent commissions to draw congressional districts and would establish certain redistricting criteria, including protection for communities of interest, and ban partisan gerrymandering. Dozens of other bills have been introduced to limit reliance on political considerations in redistricting. In 2010, H. R. 6250 would have required States to follow standards of compactness, contiguity, and respect for political subdivisions in redistricting. It also would have prohibited the establishment of congressional districts "with the major purpose of diluting the voting strength of any person, or group, including any political party," except when necessary to comply with the Voting Rights Act of 1965. We express no view on any of these proposals. We simply note that the avenue for reform established by the Framers, and used by Congress in the past, remains open.

We have no commission to allocate political power and influence in the absence of a constitutional directive or legal standards to guide us in the exercise of such authority. "It is emphatically the province and duty of the judicial department to say what the law is." *Marbury v. Madison*, 1 Cranch at 177. In this rare circumstance, that means our duty is to say "this is not law."

The judgments of the United States District Court for the Middle District of North Carolina and the United States District Court for the District of Maryland are vacated, and the cases are remanded with instructions to dismiss for lack of jurisdiction.

It is so ordered.

Justice KAGAN, with whom Justice GINSBURG, Justice BREYER, and Justice SOTOMAYOR join, dissenting.

The partisan gerrymanders in these cases deprived citizens of the most fundamental of their constitutional rights: the rights to participate equally in the political process, to join with others to advance political beliefs, and to choose their political representatives. In so doing, the gerrymanders debased and dishonored our democracy, turning upside-down the core American idea that all governmental power derives from the people. These gerrymanders enabled politicians to entrench themselves in office against voters' preferences. They promoted partisanship. They encouraged a politics of polarization and dysfunction. If left unchecked, gerrymanders irreparably damage our system of government. Courts across the country have coalesced around manageable judicial standards to resolve partisan gerrymandering claims. The standards allow judicial intervention in the worst-of-the-worst cases of democratic subversion, causing blatant constitutional harms. In giving such gerrymanders a pass from judicial review, the majority goes tragically wrong. By drawing districts to maximize the power of some voters and minimize the power of others, a party in office can entrench itself for a decade or more, no matter what the voters would prefer. Partisan gerrymandering turns it around. Politicians can cherry-pick voters to ensure their reelection.

Big data and modern technology—of the kind that the mapmakers in North Carolina and Maryland used—make today's gerrymandering altogether different from the crude linedrawing of the past. County-level voting data has given way to precinct-level or city-block-level data; and mapmakers avail themselves of data sets providing wide-ranging information about even individual voters. While bygone mapmakers may have drafted three or four districting plans, today's mapmakers can generate thousands of possibilities at the touch of a key—and then choose the one giving their party maximum advantage (while still meeting traditional districting requirements). The 2010 redistricting cycle produced some of the most extreme partisan gerrymanders in this country's history. Someplace along this road, "we the people" become sovereign no longer. The Fourteenth Amendment "guarantees the opportunity for equal participation by all voters in the election" of legislators. *Reynolds v. Sims,* 377 U.S. 533, 566 (1964). That opportunity "can be denied by a debasement or dilution of the weight of a citizen's vote just as effectively as by wholly prohibiting the free exercise of the franchise." *Id.,* at 555. Partisan gerrymandering implicates the First Amendment too. That Amendment gives its greatest protection to political beliefs, speech, and association. Yet partisan gerrymanders subject certain voters to "disfavored treatment"—counting their votes for less—precisely because of "their voting history and their expression of political views." *Vieth,* 541 U.S. at 314 (Kennedy, J.). Representative democracy is "unimaginable without the ability of citizens to band together in support of candidates who espouse their political views." *California Democratic Party v. Jones,* 530 U.S. 567, 574 (2000).

The majority declines to provide any remedy. Federal courts across the country have converged on a standard for adjudicating partisan gerrymandering claims. The standard does not use any judge-made conception of electoral fairness—either proportional representation or any other; instead, it takes as its baseline a State's *own* criteria of fairness, apart from partisan gain. The standard invalidates the most extreme partisan gerrymanders. Gerrymandering is anti-democratic in the most profound sense. In our government, "all political power flows from the people." That means, as Alexander Hamilton said, "that the people should choose whom they please to govern them." 2 Debates on the Constitution 257 (J. Elliot ed. 1891). In Maryland and North Carolina they cannot. The practices challenged in these cases imperil our system of government. Part of the Court's role in that system is to defend its foundations. None is more important than free and fair elections. With respect but deep sadness, I dissent.

(3) *Racial Gerrymandering*

The political gerrymandering cases establish that a mere failure of proportionality in representation does not establish an equal protection violation. Rather, there must be purposeful discrimination and a demonstrable discriminatory effect on the targeted group. Considerations such as compactness, contiguity, and respect for political subdivisions and communities with common interests have been recognized bases for deviation from otherwise strict proportionality. Bloc voting on the basis of race is a common phenomenon in elections that reflects a perceived shared interest on the basis of group identity. Districting plans that overtly accounted for this factor presented an analytical choice for the Court. They could be assessed pursuant to the political gerrymandering decisions, in which race would be simply another factor among many competing interests, or race-conscious policies could be analyzed as a form of affirmative action that merited strict scrutiny.

Beginning with *Shaw v. Reno,* 509 U.S. 630 (1993), the Court opted to apply strict scrutiny. Following the 1990 census, North Carolina became entitled to a

12th seat in the United States House of Representatives, and the General Assembly created two majority-Black districts of dramatically irregular shape. One state legislator remarked that "if you drove down the interstate with both car doors open, you'd kill most of the people in the district." The Court held that appellants (who challenged the districts) stated a claim upon which relief could be granted under the Equal Protection Clause. The Court began by noting that no "inquiry into legislative purpose is necessary when the racial classification appears on the face of the statute," because explicit racial classifications are immediately suspect since, "absent searching judicial inquiry, there is simply no way of determining what classifications are 'benign' or 'remedial' and what classifications are in fact motivated by illegitimate notions of racial inferiority or simple racial politics." The Court suggested that it would assume racial motivation when a district was so bizarrely shaped that it is "unexplainable on grounds other than race." Of course, when "members of a racial group live together in one community, a reapportionment plan that concentrates members of the group in one district and excludes them from others may reflect wholly legitimate purposes. The district lines may be drawn, for example, to provide for compact districts of contiguous territory, or to maintain the integrity of political subdivisions." However, when a plan places members of the same race in a single district "who are otherwise widely separated by geographical and political boundaries," the Court regarded it as similar to "political apartheid." The Court went on to note that such districting:

> reinforces the perception that members of the same racial group—regardless of their age, education, economic status, or the community in which they live—think alike, share the same political interests, and will prefer the same candidates at the polls. We have rejected such perceptions elsewhere as impermissible racial stereotypes. By perpetuating such notions, a racial gerrymander may exacerbate the very patterns of racial bloc voting that majority-minority districting is sometimes said to counteract. The message that such districting sends to elected representatives is equally pernicious. When a district obviously is created solely to effectuate the perceived common interests of one racial group, elected officials are more likely to believe that their primary obligation is to represent only the members of that group, rather than their constituency as a whole. This is altogether antithetical to our system of representative democracy.

As a result, a plaintiff challenging a reapportionment statute under the Equal Protection Clause may state a claim by alleging that the legislation, although race neutral on its face, rationally cannot be understood as anything other than an effort to separate voters into different districts on the basis of race, and that the separation lacks sufficient justification. The Court went on to note that:

> Racial classifications of any sort pose the risk of lasting harm to our society. They reinforce the belief, held by too many for too much of our history, that individuals should be judged by the color of their skin. Racial classifications with respect to voting carry particular dangers. Racial gerrymandering, even for remedial purposes, may balkanize us into competing racial factions; it threatens to carry us further from the goal of a political system in which race no longer matters—a goal that the Fourteenth and Fifteenth Amendments embody,

and to which the Nation continues to aspire. It is for these reasons that race-based districting by our state legislatures demands close judicial scrutiny.

Justice White dissented: "It strains credulity to suggest that North Carolina's purpose in creating a second majority-minority district was to discriminate against members of the majority group by 'impairing or burdening their opportunity to participate in the political process.'" He went on to argue that the State's interest was simply in "improving the minority group's prospects of electing a candidate of its choice" and he argued that whites could not complain of "discriminatory treatment." In any event, he argued that "a State's compliance with the Voting Rights Act clearly constitutes a compelling interest." Justice Stevens, who also dissented, argued that there is "no independent constitutional requirement of compactness or contiguity." He contended that the "Equal Protection Clause is violated when the State creates the kind of uncouth district boundaries seen in this case, for the sole purpose of making it more difficult for members of a minority group to win an election. That duty, however, is not violated when the majority acts to facilitate the election of a member of a group that lacks such power because it remains underrepresented in the state legislature." Justice Souter, who also dissented, argued that the Voting Rights Act sometimes requires and certainly allows consideration of race in apportioning districts. In his view, in "order to obtain relief under the Fourteenth Amendment, the purpose and effect of the districting must be to devalue the effectiveness of a voter compared to what, as a group member, he would otherwise be able to enjoy."

Ultimately, in *Shaw v. Hunt*, 517 U.S. 899 (1996), the Court determined that race was the predominant factor in configuring the congressional district and that the plan could not withstand strict scrutiny. Because the plan was not designed to remedy past discrimination, it was not supported by a compelling state interest. Although compliance with the Voting Rights Act might rise to the level of a compelling state interest, the plan exceeded that enactment's mandate and thus was not narrowly tailored.

In *Hunt v. Cromartie*, 526 U.S. 541 (1999), a follow-up case, the Court reversed a summary judgment award on a claim alleging that subsequent drawing of the congressional district still was motivated by racial factors. Noting competing evidence of political motivations, the Court concluded that summary judgment was inappropriate. It also stressed "the sensitive nature of redistricting" and the need to presume that legislation is enacted in "good faith."

The *Hunt* ruling tracked the Court's thinking a year earlier in a Georgia case concerning three majority-minority congressional districts. In *Miller v. Johnson*, 515 U.S. 900 (1995), the Court correlated its decision more closely with the premises underlying its affirmative action jurisprudence. When race is a predominant factor in districting, it is necessary to show a compelling interest in remedying past discrimination. Although compliance with the Voting Rights Act may be an imperative, the Court will strike down plans that reflect or facilitate racial stereotyping. *Miller* involved a congressional district that extended from Atlanta to the

Atlantic Ocean, covering 6,784.2 square miles, splitting eight counties and five municipalities along the way, but creating three majority-Black districts. In deciding the case, the Court began by reinforcing the idea that racial classifications "carry particular dangers," and emphasized that the shape of a district "is relevant not because bizarreness is a necessary element of the constitutional wrong or a threshold requirement of proof, but because it may be persuasive circumstantial evidence that race for its own sake, and not other districting principles, was the legislature's dominant and controlling rationale in drawing its district lines." Of course, plaintiffs can "rely on evidence other than bizarreness to establish race-based districting." However, plaintiffs are required to show "that race was the predominant factor motivating the legislature's decision to place a significant number of voters within or without a particular district. To make this showing, a plaintiff must prove that the legislature subordinated traditional race-neutral districting principles, including but not limited to compactness, contiguity, respect for political subdivisions or communities defined by actual shared interests, to racial considerations. Where these or other race-neutral considerations are the basis for redistricting legislation, and are not subordinated to race, a state can 'defeat a claim that a district has been gerrymandered on racial lines.'"

In *Miller*, the State did not argue that it had created the district to remedy past discrimination, but rather that it had done so to satisfy the Justice Department's preclearance demand that it maximize majority-Black districts. The Court concluded that this interest was not compelling and that the State must show the harm that is being remedied. Moreover, the Court doubted that the misconfigured district was required by the Voting Rights Act. As a result, the Court held that "Congress' exercise of its Fifteenth Amendment authority even when otherwise proper still must 'consist with the letter and spirit of the constitution'": "It takes a shortsighted and unauthorized view of the Voting Rights Act to invoke that statute, which has played a decisive role in redressing some of our worst forms of discrimination, to demand the very racial stereotyping the Fourteenth Amendment forbids."

Justice Stevens dissented, arguing that he does not see how "a districting plan that favors a politically weak group can violate equal protection." Justice Ginsburg, joined by two other justices, also dissented. She argued that the Court has generally respected state decisions when they reflect consideration of "traditional districting factors (such as keeping political subdivisions intact) and the usual political process of compromise and trades for a variety of nonracial reasons." "Until now, no constitutional infirmity has been seen in districting Irish or Italian voters together, for example, so long as the delineation does not abandon familiar apportionment practices." "Special circumstances justify vigilant judicial inspection to protect minority voters—circumstances that do not apply to majority voters. A history of exclusion from state politics left racial minorities without clout to extract provisions for fair representation in the lawmaking forum."

In *Bethune-Hill v. Virginia State Board of Elections*, 137 S. Ct. 788 (2017), the Court considered challenges to the State of Virginia's reapportionment, and provided further guidance regarding how to resolve claims of racial gerrymandering. The case arose after the Court had held that §4(b) of the Voting Rights Act could no longer be used to require preclearance under §5 of the Voting Rights Act. *See Shelby County v. Holder*, 570 U.S. 529 (2013). Because many of the minority-majority districts were underpopulated, the legislature was required to move non-minority voters into some of those districts. Nevertheless, the legislature sought to achieve a 55% majority-minority balance in certain districts. The Court offered additional insights into how a plaintiff might establish that race played a predominant role in redistricting:

> This Court has held that a plaintiff alleging racial gerrymandering bears the burden "to show, either through circumstantial evidence of a district's shape and demographics or more direct evidence going to legislative purpose, that race was the predominant factor motivating the legislature's decision to place a significant number of voters within or without a particular district." *Miller*, 515 U.S. at 916. To satisfy this burden, the plaintiff "must prove that the legislature subordinated traditional race-neutral districting principles to racial considerations."
>
> The State contends that race does not have a prohibited effect on a district's lines if the legislature could have drawn the same lines in accordance with traditional criteria. That argument parallels the District Court's reasoning that a reapportionment plan is not an express racial classification unless a racial purpose is apparent from the face of the plan based on the irregular nature of the lines themselves. This is incorrect. The racial predominance inquiry concerns the actual considerations that provided the essential basis for the lines drawn, not *post hoc* justifications the legislature in theory could have used but in reality did not. Traditional redistricting principles are numerous and malleable. The District Court here identified no fewer than 11 race-neutral redistricting factors a legislature could consider. By deploying those factors in various combinations and permutations, a State could construct a plethora of potential maps that look consistent with traditional, race-neutral principles. But if race for its own sake is the overriding reason for choosing one map over others, race still may predominate. For these reasons, a conflict or inconsistency between the enacted plan and traditional redistricting criteria is not a threshold requirement or a mandatory precondition in order for a challenger to establish a claim of racial gerrymandering. Of course, a conflict or inconsistency may be persuasive circumstantial evidence tending to show racial predomination, but there is no rule requiring challengers to present this kind of evidence in every case.
>
> In many cases, perhaps most cases, challengers will be unable to prove an unconstitutional racial gerrymander without evidence that the enacted plan conflicts with traditional redistricting criteria. In general, legislatures that engage in impermissible race-based redistricting will find it necessary to depart from traditional principles in order to do so. And, in the absence of a conflict with traditional principles, it may be difficult for challengers to find other evidence sufficient to show that race was the overriding factor causing neutral considerations to be cast aside. This Court to date has not affirmed a predominance finding, or remanded a case for a determination of predominance, without evidence that some district lines deviated from traditional principles. Yet the law responds to proper evidence and valid inferences in ever-changing circumstances, as it learns more about ways in which its commands are circumvented. So there may be cases where challengers will be able to establish racial predominance in the absence of an actual conflict by presenting direct evidence of the legislative purpose and intent or other compelling circumstantial evidence.
>
> This is not to suggest that courts evaluating racial gerrymandering claims may not consider evidence pertaining to an area that is larger or smaller than the district at issue. The Court has recognized that "voters, of course, can present statewide evidence in order to prove racial gerrymandering in a particular district." *Alabama*, 135 S. Ct.at 1265. Districts share

borders, and a legislature may pursue a common redistricting policy toward multiple districts. Likewise, a legislature's race-based decisionmaking may be evident in a notable way in
a particular part of a district. It follows that a court may consider evidence regarding certain
portions of a district's lines, including portions that conflict with traditional redistricting
principles.

      The ultimate object of the inquiry is the legislature's predominant motive for the design
of the district as a whole. A court faced with a racial gerrymandering claim therefore must
consider all of the lines of the district at issue; any explanation for a particular portion of the
lines must take account of the district wide context. Concentrating on particular portions in
isolation may obscure the significance of relevant district wide evidence, such as stark splits in
the racial composition of populations moved into and out of disparate parts of the district, or
the use of an express racial target. A holistic analysis is necessary to give that kind of evidence
its proper weight.

Nevertheless, the Court assumed that compliance with the Voting Rights Act
constituted a compelling state interest. "Narrow tailoring" exists when the legislature has "good reasons to believe" it must use race in order to satisfy the Voting
Rights Act, "even if a court does not find that the actions were necessary for statutory compliance." The Court concluded that the "State had sufficient grounds
to determine that the race-based calculus it employed in District 75 was necessary
to avoid violating §5." "Redrawing this district presented a difficult task, and the
result reflected the good-faith efforts of Delegate Jones and his colleagues to
achieve an informed bipartisan consensus."

Cooper v. Harris

137 S. Ct. 1455 (2017)

Justice KAGAN delivered the opinion of the Court.

      The Constitution entrusts States with the job of designing congressional dis-
tricts. But a State may not use race as the predominant factor in drawing district
lines unless it has a compelling reason. In this case, a three-judge District Court
ruled that North Carolina officials violated that bar when they created two districts whose voting-age populations were majority black. Applying a deferential
standard of review to the factual findings underlying that decision, we affirm.

      The Equal Protection Clause of the Fourteenth Amendment limits racial
gerrymanders in legislative districting plans. It prevents a State, in the absence
of "sufficient justification," from "separating its citizens into different voting districts on the basis of race." *Bethune–Hill v. Virginia State Bd. of Elections*, 137 S. Ct.
788, ___ (2017). When a voter sues state officials for drawing such race-based
lines, our decisions call for a two-step analysis. First, plaintiff must prove that "race
was the predominant factor motivating the legislature's decision to place a significant number of voters within or without a particular district." *Miller v. Johnson*,
515 U.S. 900, 916 (1995). That entails demonstrating that the legislature "subordinated" other factors—compactness, respect for political subdivisions, partisan
advantage—to "racial considerations." Plaintiff may make the required showing

through "direct evidence" of legislative intent, "circumstantial evidence of a district's shape and demographics," or a mix of both. Second, if racial considerations predominated, the design of the district must withstand strict scrutiny. The burden thus shifts to the State to prove that its race-based sorting of voters serves a "compelling interest" and is "narrowly tailored" to that end. This Court has long assumed that one compelling interest is complying with operative provisions of the Voting Rights Act of 1965 (VRA or Act), 79 Stat. 437, as amended, 52 U.S.C. §10301 et seq. *See, e.g., Shaw v. Hunt,* 517 U.S. 899 (1996) (*Shaw II*).

Two provisions of the VRA—§2 and §5—are involved in this case. Section 2 prohibits any "standard, practice, or procedure" that "results in a denial or abridgement of the right to vote on account of race." §10301(a). We have construed that ban to extend to "vote dilution"—brought about by the "dispersal of a group's members into districts in which they constitute an ineffective minority of voters." *Thornburg v. Gingles,* 478 U.S. 30, 46 (1986). Section 5, at the time, worked through a different mechanism. Before this Court invalidated its coverage formula, that section required certain jurisdictions (including various North Carolina counties) to pre-clear voting changes with the Department of Justice, so as to forestall "retrogression" in the ability of racial minorities to elect their preferred candidates. When a State invokes the VRA to justify race-based districting, it must show (to meet the "narrow tailoring" requirement) that it had "a strong basis in evidence" for concluding that the statute required its action. *Alabama Legislative Black Caucus v. Alabama,* 135 S. Ct. 1257 (2015). The State must establish that it had "good reasons" to think that it would transgress the Act if it did not draw race-based district lines. That "strong basis" (or "good reasons") standard gives States "breathing room" to adopt reasonable compliance measures that may prove, in perfect hindsight, not to have been needed.

A district court's assessment of a districting plan, in accordance with the two-step inquiry warrants significant deference. We retain full power to correct a court's errors of law, at either stage of the analysis. But the court's findings of fact—whether racial considerations predominated in drawing district lines—are subject to review only for clear error. *See* Fed. Rule Civ. Proc. 52(a)(6); *Easley v. Cromartie,* 532 U.S. 234 (2001) (*Cromartie II*). We may not reverse just because we "would have decided the matter differently." *Anderson v. Bessemer City,* 470 U.S. 564, 573 (1985). A finding that is "plausible" in light of the full record—even if another is equally or more so—must govern.

This case concerns North Carolina's redrawing of two congressional districts, both of which have long included substantial populations of black voters. District 1 is anchored in the northeastern part of the State, with appendages stretching south and west. District 12 begins in the south-central part of the State and then travels northeast, zig-zagging to the State's northern border. In *Shaw v. Reno,* 509 U.S. 630 (1993), we held that voters stated an equal protection claim by alleging that Districts 1 and 12 were unwarranted racial gerrymanders. After remand, the case arrived back at our door. That time, we dismissed the challenge to District 1 for lack of standing, but struck down District 12. The design of that "serpentine" district was race-centric, and could not be justified as a reasonable attempt to comply with the VRA. The next year, the State responded with a new districting plan, including a new District 12—and residents brought another lawsuit alleging an impermissible racial gerrymander. A District Court sustained the claim twice, but both times this Court reversed. Racial considerations did not predominate in designing the revised District 12. Rather, that district was the result of a political gerrymander—an effort to engineer, mostly "without regard to race," a safe Democratic seat. The State redrew its congressional districts in 2001, to account for population changes revealed in the prior year's census. Under the 2001 map, which went unchallenged, neither District 1 nor District 12 had a black voting-age population (a "BVAP") that was a majority of the whole: The former had a BVAP of around 48%, the latter a BVAP of around 43%. Nonetheless, in five successive general elections conducted in those reconfigured districts, all the candidates preferred by most African-American voters won their contests—and by some handy margins. In District 1, black voters' candidates of choice garnered as much as 70% of the total vote, and never less than 59%. In District 12, those candidates won with 72% of the vote at the high end and 64% at the low.

Another census, in 2010, necessitated yet another congressional map—the one at issue in this case. State Senator Robert Rucho and State Representative David Lewis, both Republicans, chaired the two committees responsible for preparing the revamped plan. They hired Dr. Thomas Hofeller, a veteran political mapmaker, to assist them in redrawing district lines. The new map significantly altered both District 1 and District 12. The 2010 census revealed District 1 to be substantially underpopulated: To comply with the Constitution's one-person-one-vote principle, the State needed to place almost 100,000 new people within the district's boundaries. Rucho, Lewis, and Hofeller chose to take most of those people from heavily black areas of Durham, requiring a finger-like extension of the district. With that addition, District 1's BVAP rose from 48.6% to 52.7%. District 12 had no need for significant total-population changes: It was overpopulated by fewer than 3,000 people out of over 730,000. Still, Rucho, Lewis, and Hofeller decided to reconfigure the district, further narrowing its already snakelike body while adding areas at either end. Those changes shifted the racial composition of District 12: As the district gained some 35,000 African-Americans of voting age and lost some 50,000 whites of that age, its BVAP increased from 43.8% to 50.7%.

Registered voters in the two districts (plaintiffs) brought this suit against North Carolina officials, complaining of impermissible racial gerrymanders. A three-judge District Court held both districts unconstitutional. The North Carolina NAACP and several other civil rights groups challenged Districts 1 and 12 in state court immediately after their enactment, charging that they were unlawful racial gerrymanders. By the time plaintiffs filed this action, the state trial court had rejected those claims. The North Carolina Supreme Court affirmed that decision.

We turn to the merits, beginning with District 1. The court below found that race furnished the predominant rationale for that district's redesign. It held that the State's interest in complying with the VRA could not justify that consideration of race. We uphold both conclusions. Uncontested evidence shows that the State's mapmakers, in considering District 1, purposefully established a racial target: African-Americans should make up no less than a majority of the voting-age population. The 50%-plus racial target "had a direct and significant impact" on District 1's configuration. Hofeller moved the district's borders to encompass the heavily black parts of Durham (and only those parts), thus taking in tens of thousands of additional African-American voters. That change and similar ones deviated from the districting practices he otherwise would have followed. The result is a district with stark racial borders: Within the same counties, the portions that fall inside District 1 have black populations two to three times larger than the portions placed in neighboring districts. Faced with this evidence — showing an announced racial target that subordinated other districting criteria and produced boundaries amplifying divisions between blacks and whites — the District Court did not clearly err in finding that race predominated in drawing District 1.

The more substantial question is whether District 1 can survive the strict scrutiny applied to racial gerrymanders. We have long assumed that complying with the VRA is a compelling interest. We have held that race-based districting is narrowly tailored to that objective if a State had "good reasons" for thinking that the Act demanded such steps. North Carolina argues that District 1 passes muster under that standard: The General Assembly (says the State) had "good reasons to believe it needed to draw District 1 as a majority-minority district to avoid Section 2 liability" for vote dilution.

This Court identified, in *Thornburg v. Gingles*, three conditions for proving vote dilution under §2 of the VRA. First, a "minority group" must be "sufficiently large and geographically compact to constitute a majority" in some reasonably configured legislative district. Second, the minority group must be "politically cohesive." Third, a district's white majority must "vote sufficiently as a bloc" to usually "defeat the minority's preferred candidate." Those three showings are needed to establish that "the minority group has the potential to elect a representative of its own choice" in a possible district, but that racially polarized voting prevents it from doing so in the district because it is "submerged in a larger white voting population." *Growe v. Emison*, 507 U.S. 25, 40 (1993). If a State has good reason to think that all the "preconditions" are met, then it has reason to believe that §2 requires drawing a majority-minority district. *See Bush v. Vera*, 517 U.S. 952 (1996) (plurality opinion). But if not, then not.

Here, electoral history provided no evidence that a §2 plaintiff could demonstrate the third *Gingles* prerequisite — effective white bloc-voting. For most of the twenty years prior to the new plan's adoption, African-Americans had made up less than a majority of District 1's voters; usually between 46% and 48%. Yet, District 1 was "an extraordinarily safe district for African-American preferred candidates." In the closest election during that period, African-Americans' candidate of choice received 59% of the total vote; in other years, the share of the vote garnered by those candidates rose to as much as 70%. Those victories occurred because the district's white population did not "vote sufficiently as a bloc" to thwart black voters' preference; rather, a meaningful number of white voters joined a politically cohesive black community to elect that group's favored candidate. District 1 functioned, year in and year out, as a "crossover" district, in which members of the majority help a "large enough" minority to elect its candidate of choice. When voters act in that way, "it is difficult to see how the majority-bloc-voting requirement could be met"—and hence how §2 liability could be established. Experience gave the State no reason to think that the VRA required it to ramp up District 1's BVAP.

The State had to redraw its whole congressional map following the 2010 census to add nearly 100,000 new people to District 1 to meet the one-person-one-vote standard. 13% of the voters in the new district would never have voted there before. A legislature undertaking a redistricting must assess whether the new districts it contemplates conform to the VRA's requirements. An inescapable influx of additional voters into a district may suggest the possibility that its former track record of compliance can continue only if the legislature intentionally adjusts its racial composition. North Carolina can point to no meaningful legislative inquiry into what it now rightly identifies: whether a new, enlarged District 1, created without a focus on race but however else the State would choose, could lead to §2 liability. The prospect of a significant population increase in a district only raises the question whether §2 requires deliberate measures to augment the district's BVAP. To have a strong basis to conclude that §2 demands race-based steps, the State must carefully evaluate whether a plaintiff could establish the Gingles preconditions—including effective white bloc-voting—in a new district created without those measures. We see nothing that fits that description.

That absence is no accident: Rucho and Lewis proceeded under a wholly different theory—arising from *Bartlett v. Strickland*—of what §2 demanded in drawing District 1. *Strickland* involved a geographic area in which African-Americans could not form a majority of a reasonably compact district. The African–American community was sizable enough to enable the formation of a crossover district, in which a substantial bloc of black voters, receiving help from some white ones, could elect the candidates of their choice. A plurality, invoking the first *Gingles* precondition, held that §2 did not require creating that district. When a minority group is not sufficiently large to make up a majority in a reasonably shaped district, §2 simply does not apply. Rucho and Lewis reasoned that, if §2 does not require crossover districts (for groups insufficiently large under *Gingles*), then §2 also cannot be satisfied by crossover districts (for groups in fact meeting *Gingles'* size condition). *Strickland*, far from supporting North Carolina's view, underscored the necessity of demonstrating effective white bloc-voting to prevail in a §2 vote-dilution suit. "In areas with substantial crossover voting," §2 plaintiffs would not "be able to establish the third *Gingles* precondition" and so "majority-minority districts would not be required." Thus, North Carolina's belief that it was compelled to redraw District 1 as a majority-minority district rested on a pure error of law. Accordingly, North Carolina's use of race as the predominant factor in designing District 1 does not withstand strict scrutiny.

We now look to District 12. This time, the district's legality turns solely on which of two possible reasons predominantly explains its most recent reconfiguration. Plaintiffs contended that the General Assembly chose voters for District 12, as for District 1, because of their race; more particularly, they urged that the Assembly intentionally increased District 12's BVAP in the name of ensuring preclearance under the VRA's §5. But North Carolina declined to mount any defense that §5's requirements in fact justified race-based changes to District 12. Instead, the State denied that racial considerations accounted for District 12's redesign. According to the State, Rucho, Lewis, and Dr. Hofeller moved voters in and out of the district as part of a "strictly" political gerrymander, without regard to race. The mapmakers drew their lines to "pack" District 12 with Democrats, not African-Americans. In the more usual case alleging a racial gerrymander—where no one has raised a partisanship defense—the court can make real headway by exploring the challenged district's conformity to traditional districting principles, such as compactness and respect for county lines. In *Shaw II*, this Court emphasized the "highly irregular" shape of then-District 12 in concluding that race predominated in its design. But such evidence loses much of its value when the State asserts partisanship as a defense, because a bizarre shape can arise from a "political motivation" as well as a racial one. *Cromartie I*, 526 U.S. at 547. That is because "racial identification is highly correlated with political affiliation." *Cromartie II*, 532 U.S. at 243. As a result of those realities, a trial court must make "a sensitive inquiry" into all "circumstantial and direct evidence of intent" to assess whether the plaintiffs have managed to disentangle race from politics and prove that the former drove a district's lines. *Cromartie I*, 526 U.S. at 546. Our job is different. We review a district court's finding as to racial predominance only for clear error, except when the court made a legal mistake. Under that standard of review, we affirm the court's finding so long as it is "plausible"; we reverse only when "left with the definite and firm conviction that a mistake has been committed." *Anderson*, 470 U.S. at 573. We give singular deference to a trial court's judgments about the credibility of witnesses because the various cues that "bear so heavily on the listener's understanding of and belief in what is said" are lost on an appellate court later sifting through a paper record. *Anderson*, 470 U.S. at 575.

In light of those principles, we uphold the District Court's finding of racial predominance respecting District 12. The evidence offered at trial adequately supports the conclusion that race, not politics, accounted for the district's reconfiguration. District 12 was approximately the right size as it was: North Carolina did not—could not—much change its total population. But by slimming the district and adding a couple of knobs to its snakelike body, the General Assembly incorporated tens of thousands of new voters and pushed out tens of thousands of old ones. The new District 12 had 35,000 more African-Americans of voting age and 50,000 fewer whites of that age. (The difference was made up of voters from other racial categories.) Those voter exchanges produced a sizable jump in the district's BVAP, from 43.8% to 50.7%. The Assembly thus turned District 12 (as it did District 1) into a majority-minority district.

Rucho and Lewis publicly stated that racial considerations lay behind District 12's augmented BVAP. In a release issued with their draft districting plan, the two legislators ascribed that change to the need to achieve preclearance of the plan under §5 of the VRA. At that time, §5 covered Guilford County and thus prohibited any "retrogression in the electoral position of racial minorities" there. Part of Guilford County lay within District 12, which meant that the Department of Justice would closely scrutinize that district's new lines. In light of those facts, Rucho and Lewis wrote: "Because of the presence of Guilford County, we have drawn our proposed Twelfth District at a BVAP level that is above the percentage of BVAP found in the current Twelfth District." According to the two legislators, that race-based "measure would ensure preclearance of the plan." Thus, Rucho's and Lewis's own account "evinced intentionality" as to District 12's racial composition. Hofeller confirmed that intent in deposition testimony and an expert report. Before the redistricting, Hofeller testified, the legislators "decided to reunite the black community in Guilford County into the Twelfth." Why? Hofeller responded, "In order to be cautious and draw a plan that would pass muster under the Voting Rights Act." "Mindful that Guilford County was covered" by §5, Hofeller explained, the legislature "determined that it was prudent to reunify the county's African-American community" into District 12. That change caused the district's compactness to decrease, but that would "avoid the possibility of a VRA charge" that would "inhibit preclearance." The State's preclearance submission to the Justice Department indicated a similar determination to concentrate black voters in District 12. "One of the concerns of the Redistricting Chairs," North Carolina noted, had to do with the Justice Department's years-old objection to "a failure by the State to create a second majority minority district." The submission went on to explain that after considering alternatives, the redistricters had designed a version of District 12 that would raise its BVAP to 50.7%. Thus, concluded the State, the new District 12 "increases the African-American community's ability to elect their candidate of choice."

Perhaps the most dramatic testimony came when Congressman Mel Watt (who represented District 12 for 20 years) recounted a conversation he had with Rucho in 2011 about the district's future make-up. According to Watt, Rucho said that "his leadership had told him that he had to ramp the minority percentage in District 12 to over 50 percent to comply with the Voting Rights Law." It would then be Rucho's "job to convince the African-American community" that such a racial target "made sense." Watt's account was of a piece with the other evidence—including the redistricters' on-the-nose attainment of a 50% BVAP—indicating that the General Assembly, in the name of VRA compliance, deliberately redrew District 12 as a majority-minority district.

The State's story—that politics alone drove decisionmaking—came in mostly through Hofeller's testimony. Hofeller explained that Rucho and Lewis instructed him to make the map "more favorable to Republican candidates."

One stratagem was to pack the historically Democratic District 12 with even more Democratic voters, thus leaving surrounding districts more reliably Republican. Hofeller recounted, he drew District 12's new boundaries based on political data—the voting behavior of precincts in the 2008 Presidential election between Barack Obama and John McCain. He claimed he displayed only this data, and no racial data, on his computer screen while mapping the district. Hofeller further stated that the Obama–McCain data explained his incorporation of the black, but not the white, parts of Guilford County then located in District 13. Only after he drew a politics-based line between those adjacent areas, Hofeller testified, did he "find out" that District 12 "did not have a §5 issue." The District Court disbelieved Hofeller's asserted indifference to the new district's racial composition. The court recalled Hofeller's contrary deposition testimony—that Rucho and Lewis "decided" to shift African-American voters into District 12 "in order to" ensure preclearance under §5. At trial, Hofeller had given testimony that undermined his "blame it on politics" claim. Right after asserting that Rucho and Lewis told him "not to use race" in designing District 12, Hofeller added a qualification: "except perhaps with regard to Guilford County." That is the kind of "exception" that goes pretty far toward swallowing the rule. District 12 saw a net increase of more than 25,000 black voters in Guilford County, relative to a net gain of fewer than 35,000 across the district: So the newly added parts of that county played a major role in pushing the district's BVAP over 50%. The District Court came away unpersuaded that this decisive influx of black voters was an accident. Hofeller's denial of race-based districting "rang hollow."

Finally, an expert report by Dr. Stephen Ansolabehere lent circumstantial support to the plaintiffs' race-not-politics case. Ansolabehere looked at the six counties overlapping with District 12. The question he asked was: Who from those counties actually ended up in District 12? The answer: Only 16% of the region's white registered voters, but 64% of the black ones. Ansolabehere next controlled for party registration, but discovered that doing so made no difference: Only 18% of the region's white Democrats wound up in District 12, whereas 65% of the black Democrats did. The upshot was that, regardless of party, a black voter was three to four times more likely than a white voter to cast his ballot within District 12's borders. Those stark disparities led Ansolabehere to conclude that "race, and not party," was "the dominant factor" in District 12's design.

The District Court's assessment that this evidence proved racial predominance clears clear error review. The districting plan's architects had repeatedly described the influx of African–Americans into District 12 as a §5 compliance measure, not a side-effect of political gerrymandering. Those contemporaneous descriptions comported with the court's credibility determinations about the trial testimony. We cannot disrespect such credibility judgments. Generally, we will not take it upon ourselves to weigh the trial evidence as if we were the first to hear it. Other interpretations of that evidence were permissible. Maybe we would have evaluated the testimony differently had we presided over the trial; or maybe we would not have. Either way, we are far from having a "definite and firm conviction" that the District Court made a mistake in concluding from the record before it that racial considerations predominated in District 12's design.

When race and politics are competing explanations of a district's lines, argues North Carolina, the party challenging the district must introduce "an alternative map that achieves the legislature's political objectives while improving racial balance." Because plaintiffs did not present a counter-map, North Carolina concludes that they cannot prevail. The dissent echoes that argument. An alternative districting plan can serve as key evidence in a race-versus-politics dispute. One, often highly persuasive way to disprove a State's contention that politics drove a district's lines is to show that the legislature had the capacity to accomplish its partisan goals without moving so many members of a minority group into the district. But they are hardly the only means. A plaintiff's task is simply to persuade the trial court that race (not politics) was the "predominant consideration in deciding to place a significant number of voters within or without a particular district." *Alabama Legislative Black Caucus*, 135 S. Ct. at ___. Plaintiff will sometimes need an alternative map to make his case. But in no area of our equal protection law have we forced plaintiffs to submit one particular form of proof to prevail. This case turned on direct evidence of the General Assembly's intent in creating the actual District 12.

Applying a clear error standard, we uphold the District Court's conclusions that racial considerations predominated in designing District 1 and District 12. For District 12, that is all we must do, because North Carolina made no attempt to justify race-based districting there. For District 1, we uphold the District Court's decision that §2 of the VRA gave North Carolina no good reason to reshuffle voters because of their race. We affirm the judgment of the District Court.

It is so ordered.

JUSTICE ALITO, with whom THE CHIEF JUSTICE and JUSTICE KENNEDY join, concurring in the judgment in part and dissenting in part.

Recognizing "the intrusive potential of judicial intervention into the legislative realm," courts must be very cautious about imputing a racial motive to a State's redistricting plan. That caution "is especially appropriate where the State has articulated a legitimate political explanation for its districting decision, and the voting population is one in which race and political affiliation are highly correlated." *Cromartie II*, 532 U.S. at 242. We have repeatedly acknowledged the problem of distinguishing between racial and political motivations in the redistricting context. The problem arises from the confluence of two factors. The first is the status under the Constitution of partisan gerrymandering. Partisan gerrymandering dates back to the founding, and while some might find it distasteful, "our prior decisions have made clear that a jurisdiction may engage in constitutional political gerrymandering, even if it happens that the most loyal Democrats happen to be black Democrats and even if the State were conscious of that fact." *Cromartie I, supra*, at 551. The second factor is that "racial identification is highly correlated with political affiliation" in many jurisdictions. *Cromartie II*, 532 U.S. at

243. This phenomenon makes it difficult to distinguish between political and race-based decisionmaking. The party attacking the legislatively drawn boundaries must show at the least that the legislature could have achieved its legitimate political objectives in alternative ways that are comparably consistent with traditional districting principles. That party must also show that those districting alternatives would have brought about significantly greater racial balance."

When a federal court says that race was a legislature's predominant purpose in drawing a district, it accuses the legislature of "offensive and demeaning" conduct. But if a court mistakes a political gerrymander for a racial gerrymander, it illegitimately invades a traditional domain of state authority, usurping the role of a State's elected representatives. This does violence to both the proper role of the Judiciary and the powers reserved to the States under the Constitution. Unless courts "exercise extraordinary caution" in distinguishing race-based redistricting from politics-based redistricting, they will invite the losers in the redistricting process to seek to obtain in court what they could not achieve in the political arena.

The District Court's finding that race predominated in the drawing of District 12 is clearly erroneous. The State offered strong and coherent evidence that politics, not race, was the legislature's predominant aim, and the evidence supporting the District Court's contrary finding is weak and manifestly inadequate in light of the high evidentiary standard that our cases require challengers to meet in order to prove racial predominance. When a new census requires redistricting, it is a common practice to start with the plan used in the prior map and to change the boundaries of the prior districts only as needed to comply with the one-person, one-vote mandate and to achieve other desired ends. This approach honors settled expectations and, if the prior plan survived legal challenge, minimizes the risk that the new plan will be overturned. That is the approach taken by the veteran mapmaker in the present case. Using the prior design as his starting point, Dr. Hofeller assumed that District 12 would remain a "strong Democratic district." He drew "the overall redistricting plan to have an increased number of competitive districts for GOP candidates," and he therefore moved more Democratic voters into District 12 in order to "increase Republican opportunities in the surrounding districts." To do this, Dr. Hofeller set out in search of pockets of Democratic voters that could be moved into District 12 from areas adjoining or very close to District 12's prior boundaries. As a measure of voting preferences, Dr. Hofeller used the results of the then-most recent Presidential election, i.e., the election of 2008. In that election, three counties voted strongly for the Democratic candidate while the other three counties all voted for the Republican candidate. Two of the three Democratic counties are located at the northern end of District 12, while the other Democratic county is on the southern end. The middle of the district passes through the three more Republican-friendly counties. Thus, if a mapmaker sat down to increase the proportion of Democrats in District 12 and to reduce the proportion in neighboring districts, the most obvious way to do that was to pull additional Democrats into the district from the north and south (the most populous and heavily Democratic counties) while shifting Republican voters out of the corridor. That, in essence, is what Dr. Hofeller did.

Our cases say that we must "exercise extraordinary caution" "where the State has articulated a legitimate political explanation for its districting decision," *Cromartie II, supra,* at 242; the majority ignores that political explanation. Our cases say that "the good faith of a state legislature must be presumed," *Miller,* 515 U.S. at 915; the majority presumes the opposite. And *Cromartie II* held that plaintiffs in a case like this are obligated to produce a map showing that the legislature could have achieved its political objectives without the racial effect seen in the challenged plan; here, the majority junks that rule and says that the plaintiffs' failure to produce such a map simply "does not matter." I dissent.

Note: Burden of Proof Issues

In *Abbott v. Perez,* 138 S. Ct. 2305 (2018), the Court offered insights into the burden of proof in racial gerrymandering cases. Following the 2010 census, Texas added four congressional seats, and in 2011 developed a redistricting plan for use in the 2012 elections. The redistricting plan was challenged under the equal protection clause as well as under the Voting Rights Act. While the redistricting plan was tied up in litigation, a federal district court undertook to create its own redistricting plan, and Texas decided in 2013 to adopt the court-drawn plan as its own. However, the lower court concluded that the 2013 plan was deficient because the legislature failed to "cure" the "taint" attached to the 2011 plan. The Court reversed, concluding that the legislature was not obligated to show that it had "cured" the unlawful intent attributed to the 2011 Legislature. On the contrary, the "good faith of the state legislature must be presumed," and the allocation of the burden of proof and the presumption of legislative good faith are not changed by a finding of past discrimination. The "ultimate question remains whether a discriminatory intent has been proved." The "historical background" of a legislative enactment is simply "one evidentiary source" relevant to the question of intent. In upholding the Texas plan, the Court emphasized that the Texas Legislature did not re-enact the plan previously passed by its 2011 predecessor. Instead, it enacted, with only small changes, plans that had been developed by the Texas court pursuant to instructions from this Court. Under these circumstances, the Court concluded that plaintiffs bore the burden of overcoming the presumption of legislative good faith and of proving that the legislature acted with invidious intent. The Court rejected the lower court's conclusion that the legislature was required to prove that it had experienced a true "change of heart" and had "engaged in a deliberative process to ensure that the 2013 plans cured any taint from the 2011 plans." Of course, legislative intent "must be weighed together with any other direct and circumstantial evidence of that Legislature's intent." The Court held that there was insufficient evidence of the fact that the legislature had "acted in bad faith and engaged in intentional discrimination."

∾ PROBLEMS ∾

1. *Relevant Factors.* What factors should a court consider in determining whether a district has been racially gerrymandered in violation of the Equal Protection Clause? What factors were important in *Shaw* and *Miller*?

2. *Advising the Legislature.* Following the decisions in *Shaw* and *Miller,* and after the 2020 census, the Commonwealth of Kentucky decides to redraw its congressional district lines. The legislature is approached by the U.S. Department of Justice (DOJ), which expresses concern about the fact that although Kentucky has large African American populations in some cities, it has no African American representatives in Congress. Relying on the Voting Rights Act, DOJ demands that Kentucky draw its district lines to create a majority African American district. You serve as counsel to the legislative committee that is drawing the redistricting plan. Although it is possible to create a majority African American district, it will be extremely difficult to do so without creating a very strangely configured district. How would you advise the legislature to respond to DOJ?

(4) *Vote Recording and Counting*

Voter understanding of equipment operation is a factor that typically is accounted for by officials who provide instructions for recording preferences on the ballot. The quality of this education may vary from one district or state to another. Variances also exist with respect to processes for counting votes, which may affect their relative weighting.

Bush v. Gore

531 U.S. 98 (2000)

PER CURIAM

On December 8, 2000, the Supreme Court of Florida ordered that the Circuit Court of Leon County tabulate by hand 9,000 ballots in Miami-Dade County. It also ordered the inclusion in the certified vote totals of 215 votes identified in Palm Beach County and 168 votes identified in Miami-Dade County for Vice President Albert Gore, Jr., and Senator Joseph Lieberman, Democratic candidates for President and Vice President. The State Supreme Court noted that petitioner, George W. Bush, asserted that the net gain for Vice President Gore in Palm Beach County was 176 votes, and directed the Circuit Court to resolve that dispute on remand. The court further held that relief would require manual recounts in all Florida counties where so-called "undervotes" had not been subject to manual tabulation. The court ordered all manual recounts to begin at once. Governor Bush and Richard Cheney, Republican candidates for President and Vice President, filed an emergency application for a stay of this mandate.

The day following the Presidential election, the Florida Division of Elections reported that petitioner Bush had received 2,909,135 votes, and respondent Gore had received 2,907,351 votes, a margin of 1,784 for Governor Bush. Because Governor Bush's margin of victory was less than "one-half of a percent of the votes cast," an automatic machine recount was conducted, the results of which showed Governor Bush still winning the race but by a diminished margin. Vice President Gore then sought manual recounts in several counties, pursuant to Florida's election protest provisions. A dispute arose concerning the deadline for local county canvassing boards to submit their returns to the Secretary of State (Secretary). The Secretary declined to waive the deadline imposed by statute. The Florida Supreme Court, however, set a new deadline. We granted certiorari and vacated the Florida Supreme Court's decision, finding considerable uncertainty as to the grounds on which it was based. The Florida Supreme Court then issued a decision on remand reinstating that date.

On November 26, the Florida Elections Canvassing Commission certified the results of the election and declared Governor Bush the winner of Florida's 25 electoral votes. Vice President Gore, pursuant to Florida's contest provisions, filed a complaint in Leon County Circuit Court contesting the certification. The Circuit Court denied relief, stating that Vice President Gore failed to meet his burden of proof.

The Supreme Court held that Vice President Gore had satisfied his burden of proof with respect to his challenge to Miami-Dade County's failure to tabulate, by manual count, 9,000 ballots on which the machines had failed to detect a vote for President ("undervotes"). Noting the closeness of the election, the court explained that "on this record, there can be no question that there are legal votes within the 9,000 uncounted votes sufficient to place the results of this election in doubt." A "legal vote," as determined by the Supreme Court, is "one in which there is a 'clear indication of the intent of the voter.'" The court therefore ordered a hand recount of the 9,000 ballots in Miami-Dade County. Observing that the contest provisions vest broad discretion in the circuit judge to "provide any relief appropriate under such circumstances," the Supreme Court further held that the Circuit Court could order "the Supervisor of Elections and the Canvassing Boards, as well as the necessary public officials, in all counties that have not conducted a manual recount or tabulation of the undervotes to do so forthwith, said tabulation to take place in the individual counties where the ballots are located."

The Supreme Court explained that the recount deadline was not intended to exclude votes identified after that date through ongoing manual recounts. As to Miami-Dade County, the court concluded that although the 168 votes identified were the result of a partial recount, they were "legal votes that could change the outcome of the election." The Supreme Court therefore directed the Circuit Court to include those totals in the certified results, subject to resolution of the actual vote total from the Miami-Dade partial recount.

The petition presents the following question: whether the use of standardless manual recounts violates the Equal Protection and Due Process Clauses. With respect to the equal protection question, we find a violation of the Equal Protection Clause.

The closeness of this election, and the multitude of legal challenges which have followed in its wake, have brought into sharp focus a common, if heretofore unnoticed, phenomenon. Nationwide statistics reveal that an estimated 2% of ballots cast do not register a vote for President for whatever reason, including deliberately choosing no candidate at all or some voter error, such as voting for two candidates or insufficiently marking a ballot. This case has shown that punch-card balloting machines can produce an unfortunate number of ballots which are not punched in a clean, complete way by the voter.

The individual citizen has no federal constitutional right to vote for electors for the President of the United States unless and until the state legislature chooses a statewide election as the means to implement its power to appoint members of the Electoral College. U.S. Const., Art. II, §1. When the state legislature vests the right to vote for President in its people, the right to vote as the legislature has prescribed is fundamental; and one source of its fundamental nature lies in the equal weight accorded to each vote and the equal dignity owed to each voter. The right to vote is protected in more than the initial allocation of the franchise. Equal protection applies as well to the manner of its exercise. Having once granted the right to vote on equal terms, the State may not, by later arbitrary and disparate treatment, value one person's vote over that of another. "The right of suffrage can be denied by a debasement or dilution of the weight of a citizen's vote just as effectively as by wholly prohibiting the free exercise of the franchise."

The question before us is whether the recount procedures the Florida Supreme Court has adopted are consistent with its obligation to avoid arbitrary and disparate treatment of the members of its electorate. Much of the controversy seems to revolve around ballot cards designed to be perforated by a stylus but which, either through error or deliberate omission, have not been perforated with sufficient precision for a machine to register the perforations. In some cases a piece of the card—a chad—is hanging, say, by two corners. In other cases there is no separation at all, just an indentation.

The Florida Supreme Court has ordered that the intent of the voter be discerned from such ballots. It is not necessary to decide whether the Florida Supreme Court had the authority under the legislative scheme for resolving election disputes to define what a legal vote is and to mandate a manual recount implementing that definition. The recount mechanisms implemented in response to the decisions of the Florida Supreme Court do not satisfy the minimum requirement for nonarbitrary treatment of voters necessary to secure the fundamental right. Florida's basic command for the count of legally cast votes is to consider the "intent of the voter." This is unobjectionable as an abstract proposition and a starting principle. The problem inheres in the absence of specific standards to ensure its equal application. The formulation of uniform rules to determine intent based on these recurring circumstances is practicable and, we conclude, necessary.

The law does not refrain from searching for the intent of the actor in a multitude of circumstances; and in some cases the general command to ascertain intent is not susceptible to much further refinement. In this instance, however, the question is not whether to believe a witness but how to interpret the marks or holes or scratches on an inanimate object, a piece of cardboard or paper which, it is said, might not have registered as a vote during the machine count. The fact-finder confronts a thing, not a person. The search for intent can be confined by specific rules designed to ensure uniform treatment.

The want of those rules here has led to unequal evaluation of ballots in various respects. The standards for accepting or rejecting contested ballots might vary not only from county to county but indeed within a single county from one recount team to another.

An early case in our one-person, one-vote jurisprudence arose when a State accorded arbitrary and disparate treatment to voters in its different counties. The Court found a constitutional violation. "The idea that one group can be granted greater voting strength than another is hostile to the one man, one vote basis of our representative government."

The State Supreme Court ratified this uneven treatment. It mandated that the recount totals from two counties, Miami-Dade and Palm Beach, be included in the certified total. The court also appeared to hold *sub silentio* that the recount totals from Broward County, which were not completed until after the original certification by the Secretary, were to be considered part of the new certified vote totals even though the county certification was not contested by Vice President Gore. Yet each of the counties used varying standards to determine what was a legal vote. Broward County used a more forgiving standard than Palm Beach County, and uncovered almost three times as many new votes, a result markedly disproportionate to the difference in population between the counties.

In addition, the recounts in these three counties were not limited to so-called undervotes but extended to all of the ballots. The distinction has real consequences. A manual recount of all ballots identifies not only those ballots which show no vote but also those which contain more than one, the so-called overvotes. Neither category will be counted by the machine. This is not a trivial concern. Respondents estimated there are as many as 110,000 overvotes statewide.

As a result, the citizen whose ballot was not read by a machine because he failed to vote for a candidate in a way readable by a machine may still have his vote counted in a manual recount; on the other hand, the citizen who marks two candidates in a way discernible by the machine will not have the same opportunity to have his vote count, even if a manual examination of the ballot would reveal the requisite indicia of intent. Furthermore, the citizen who marks two candidates, only one of which is discernible by the machine, will have his vote counted even though it should have been read as an invalid ballot. The State Supreme Court's inclusion of vote counts based on these variant standards exemplifies concerns with the remedial processes that were under way.

That brings the analysis to yet a further equal protection problem. The votes certified by the court included a partial total from one county. The Florida Supreme Court's decision thus gives no assurance that the recounts included in a final certification must be complete. Indeed, respondents contend that it would be consistent with the rules of the recount procedures to include whatever partial counts are done by the time of final certification, and we interpret the Florida Supreme Court's decision to permit this. The press of time does not diminish the constitutional concern. A desire for speed is not a general excuse for ignoring equal protection guarantees.

The question before the Court is not whether local entities, in the exercise of their expertise, may develop different systems for implementing elections. Instead, we are presented with a situation where a state court with the power to assure uniformity has ordered a statewide recount with minimal procedural safeguards. When a court orders a statewide remedy, there must be at least some assurance that the rudimentary requirements of equal treatment and fundamental fairness are satisfied.

Upon due consideration of the difficulties identified to this point, it is obvious that the recount cannot be conducted in compliance with the requirements of equal protection and due process without substantial additional work. It would require not only the adoption (after opportunity for argument) of adequate statewide standards for determining what is a legal vote, and practicable procedures to implement them, but also orderly judicial review of any disputed matters that might arise. In addition, the Secretary has advised that the recount of only a portion of the ballots requires that the vote tabulation equipment be used to screen out undervotes, a function for which the machines were not designed. If a recount of overvotes were also required, perhaps even a second screening would be necessary. Use of the equipment for this purpose, and any new software developed for it, would have to be evaluated for accuracy by the Secretary, as required by state law.

The Supreme Court of Florida has said that the legislature intended the State's electors to "participate fully in the federal electoral process." That statute, in turn, requires that any controversy or contest that is designed to lead to a conclusive selection of electors be completed by December 12. That date is upon us, and there is no recount procedure in place under the State Supreme Court's order that comports with minimal constitutional standards. Because it is evident that any recount seeking to meet the December 12 date will be unconstitutional for the reasons we have discussed, we reverse the judgment of the Supreme Court of Florida ordering a recount to proceed.

None are more conscious of the vital limits on judicial authority than are the Members of this Court, and none stand more in admiration of the Constitution's design to leave the selection of the President to the people, through their legislatures, and to the political sphere. When contending parties invoke the process of the courts, however, it becomes our unsought responsibility to resolve the federal and constitutional issues the judicial system has been forced to confront.

The judgment of the Supreme Court of Florida is reversed, and the case is remanded for further proceedings not inconsistent with this opinion.

Chief Justice Rehnquist, with whom Justice Scalia and Justice Thomas join, *concurring.*

We join the *per curiam* opinion. We write separately because we believe there are additional grounds that require us to reverse the Florida Supreme Court's decision. In most cases, comity and respect for federalism compel us to defer to the decisions of state courts on issues of state law. That practice reflects our understanding that the decisions of state courts are definitive pronouncements of the will of the States as sovereigns. Of course, in ordinary cases, the distribution of powers among the branches of a State's government raises no questions of federal constitutional law, subject to the requirement that the government be republican in character. But Article II, §1, cl. 2, provides that "each State shall appoint, in such Manner as the *Legislature* thereof may direct," electors for President and Vice President. Thus, the text of the election law itself, and not just its interpretation by the courts of the States, takes on independent significance. With respect to a Presidential election, the court must be both mindful of the legislature's role under Article II in choosing the manner of appointing electors and deferential to those bodies expressly empowered by the legislature to carry out its constitutional mandate.

In order to determine whether a state court has infringed upon the legislature's authority, we necessarily must examine the law of the State as it existed prior to the action of the court. Though we generally defer to state courts on the interpretation of state law, there are of course areas in which the Constitution requires this Court to undertake an independent, if still deferential, analysis of state law. This inquiry does not imply a disrespect for state *courts* but rather a respect for the constitutionally prescribed role of state *legislatures.*

Justice Stevens, with whom Justice Ginsburg and Justice Breyer join, *dissenting.*

The Constitution assigns to the States the primary responsibility for determining the manner of selecting the Presidential electors. *See* Art. II, §1, cl. 2. When questions arise about the meaning of state laws, including election laws, it is our settled practice to accept the opinions of the highest courts of the States as providing the final answers. On rare occasions, however, either federal statutes or the Federal Constitution may require federal judicial intervention in state elections. This is not such an occasion. Admittedly, the use of differing standards for determining voter intent in different counties employing similar voting systems may raise serious concerns. Those concerns are alleviated—if not eliminated—by the fact that a single impartial magistrate will ultimately adjudicate all objections arising from the recount process.

Even assuming that aspects of the remedial scheme might ultimately be found to violate the Equal Protection Clause, I could not subscribe to the majority's disposition of the case. Once a state legislature determines to select electors through a popular vote, the right to have one's vote counted is of constitutional stature. Florida law holds that all ballots that reveal the intent of the voter constitute valid votes. Recognizing these principles, the majority nonetheless orders the termination of the contest proceeding before all such votes have been tabulated.

Under their own reasoning, the appropriate course of action would be to remand to allow more specific procedures for implementing the legislature's uniform general standard to be established.

In the interest of finality, however, the majority effectively orders the disenfranchisement of an unknown number of voters whose ballots reveal their intent—and are therefore legal votes under state law—but were for some reason rejected by ballot-counting machines. It does so on the basis of the deadlines set forth in Title 3 of the United States Code. Those provisions merely provide rules of decision for Congress to follow when selecting among conflicting slates of electors. They do not prohibit a State from counting what the majority concedes to be legal votes until a bona fide winner is determined. As the majority notes, "a desire for speed is not a general excuse for ignoring equal protection guarantees."

The Florida Supreme Court's decisions were rooted in long-established precedent and were consistent with the relevant statutory provisions, taken as a whole. It did what courts do—it decided the case before it in light of the legislature's intent to leave no legally cast vote uncounted. In so doing, it relied on the sufficiency of the general "intent of the voter" standard articulated by the state legislature, coupled with a procedure for ultimate review by an impartial judge, to resolve the concern about disparate evaluations of contested ballots. If we assume—as I do—that the members of that court and the judges who would have carried out its mandate are impartial, its decision does not even raise a colorable federal question.

Justice SOUTER, with whom Justice BREYER joins, and with whom Justice STEVENS and Justice GINSBURG join as to all but Part III, *dissenting*.

The Court should not have reviewed this case, and should not have stopped Florida's attempt to recount all undervote ballots by issuing a stay of the Florida Supreme Court's orders during the period of this review. The interpretations by the Florida court raise no substantial question under Article II. That court engaged in permissible construction in determining that Gore had instituted a contest authorized by the state statute, and it proceeded to direct the trial judge to deal with that contest in the exercise of the discretionary powers generously conferred by state law. Our customary respect for state interpretations of state law counsels against rejection of the Florida court's determinations in this case.

Petitioners have raised an equal protection claim (or, alternatively, a due process claim) in the charge that unjustifiably disparate standards are applied in different electoral jurisdictions to otherwise identical facts. It is true that the Equal Protection Clause does not forbid the use of a variety of voting mechanisms within a jurisdiction, even though different mechanisms will have different levels of effectiveness in recording voters' intentions; local variety can be justified by concerns about cost, the potential value of innovation, and so on. But evidence in the record here suggests that a different order of disparity obtains under rules for determining a voter's intent that have been applied (and could continue to be applied) to identical types of ballots used in identical brands of machines and exhibiting identical physical characteristics (such as "hanging" or "dimpled" chads). I can conceive of no legitimate state interest served by these differing treatments of the expressions of voters' fundamental rights. The differences appear wholly arbitrary.

In deciding what to do about this, we should take account of the fact that electoral votes are due to be cast in six days. I would therefore remand the case to the courts of Florida with instructions to establish uniform standards for evaluating the several types of ballots that have prompted differing treatments, to be applied within and among counties when passing on such identical ballots in any further recounting (or successive recounting) that the courts might order. I see no warrant for this Court to assume that Florida could not possibly comply with this requirement before the date set for the meeting of electors, December 18. Although one of the dissenting justices of the State Supreme Court estimated that disparate standards potentially affected 170,000 votes, the number at issue is significantly smaller. To recount these manually would be a tall order, but before this Court stayed the effort to do that the courts of Florida were ready to do their best to get that job done. There is no justification for denying the State the opportunity to try to count all disputed ballots now.

Justice GINSBURG, with whom Justice STEVENS joins, and with whom Justice SOUTER and Justice BREYER join as to Part I, *dissenting*.

The extraordinary setting of this case has obscured the ordinary principle that dictates its proper resolution: Federal courts defer to state high courts' interpretations of their state's own law. This principle reflects the core of federalism, on which all agree. Were the other Members of this Court as mindful as they generally are of our system of dual sovereignty, they would affirm the judgment of the Florida Supreme Court.

I agree with Justice Stevens that petitioners have not presented a substantial equal protection claim. Ideally, perfection would be the appropriate standard for judging the recount. But we live in an imperfect world, one in which thousands of votes have not been counted. I cannot agree that the recount adopted by the Florida court, flawed as it may be, would yield a result any less fair or precise than the certification that preceded that recount.

The Court assumes that time will not permit "orderly judicial review of any disputed matters that might arise." But no one has doubted the good faith and diligence with which Florida election officials, attorneys for all sides of this controversy, and the courts of law have performed their duties. Notably, the Florida Supreme Court has produced two substantial opinions within 29 hours of oral argument. In sum, the Court's conclusion that a constitutionally adequate recount is impractical is a prophecy the Court's own judgment will not allow to be tested. Such an untested prophecy should not decide the Presidency of the United States.

Justice BREYER, with whom Justice STEVENS and Justice GINSBURG join except as to Part I-A-1, and with whom Justice SOUTER joins as to Part I, *dissenting*.

The Court was wrong to take this case. It was wrong to grant a stay. It should now vacate that stay and permit the Florida Supreme Court to decide whether the recount should resume. The political implications of this case for the country are momentous. But the federal legal questions presented, with one exception, are insubstantial. The majority raises three equal protection problems with the Florida Supreme Court's recount order: first, the failure to include overvotes in the manual recount; second, the fact that *all* ballots, rather than simply the undervotes, were recounted in some, but not all, counties; and third, the absence of a uniform, specific standard to guide the recounts. As far as the first issue is concerned, petitioners presented no evidence, to this Court or to any Florida court, that a manual recount of overvotes would identify additional legal votes. The same is true of the second, and, in addition, the majority's reasoning would seem to invalidate any state provision for a manual recount of individual counties in a statewide election.

There is no justification for the majority's remedy, which is simply to reverse the lower court and halt the recount entirely. An appropriate remedy would be, instead, to remand this case with instructions that, even at this late date, would permit the Florida Supreme Court to require recounting *all* undercounted votes in Florida, whether or not previously recounted prior to the end of the protest period, and to do so in accordance with a single uniform standard. By halting the manual recount, and thus ensuring that the uncounted legal votes will not be counted under any standard, this Court crafts a remedy out of proportion to the asserted harm. And that remedy harms the very fairness interests the Court is attempting to protect. The manual recount would itself redress a problem of unequal treatment of ballots. Nor do I understand why the Florida Supreme Court's recount order, which helps to redress this inequity, must be entirely prohibited based on a deficiency that could easily be remedied.

∾ PROBLEMS ∾

1. *Tolerance Levels.* States and jurisdictions within states use varying technologies to record and count votes. Implicit in these differences are variances with respect to reliability. What tolerance level should there be for deviations not just in the recounting process but in the counting process itself?

2. *Standing and Political Question Issues.* Should *Bush v. Gore* have been dismissed on standing or political question grounds? Did then-Governor Bush have standing to challenge the recount methods in Florida? Third-party standing?

3. *Halting the Recount.* Do you agree with the Court's conclusion that the recount should have been halted? What about the argument, in more than one dissent, that the case should have been remanded to the Florida Supreme Court for the development of standards that would satisfy the Equal Protection Clause?

c. Access to the Ballot

Standards of review for determining access to the ballot depend on the degree of burden. Regulations that seriously impede access to the ballot will be evaluated more carefully than those perceived as imposing minimal burdens. In *American Party of Texas v. White*, 415 U.S. 767 (1974), the Court upheld a provision requiring parties that received less than 2% of the gubernatorial vote in the prior election to obtain signatures of at least 1% of those who voted. This prescription, from the Court's perspective, was not excessively burdensome. A law that requires candidates to pay a filing fee, totaling 2% of the annual salary of the office sought, was found to violate the Equal Protection Clause. In *Lubin v. Panish*, 415 U.S. 709 (1974), the Court found that the regulation unduly burdened the ability of indigent candidates to secure a position on the ballot. In addition to being a method of diluting the right to vote, restrictions on access to the ballot may implicate the right of association.

d. Voting Rights During a Pandemic

During the Covid-19 pandemic, there has been much litigation regarding the right to vote. In *Texas Democratic Party v. Abbott*, 961 F.3d 389 (5th Cir. 2020), the court stayed a trial court order ordering Texas to allow mail-in voting because of the pandemic. In *Thomas v. Andino*, __ F.Supp.3d __ 2020 WL 2617329 (D.S.C. 2020), the court stayed a requirement that an absentee ballot contain a witness' signature. At the same time, the South Carolina Supreme Court was asked to require the state to expand the use of absentee ballots. *See Bailey v. South Carolina State Election Commission*, 844 S.E.2d 390 (S.C. 2020). In *Gottlieb v. Lamont*, __ F.Supp.3d __ 2020 WL 3046205 (D. Conn. 2020), plaintiffs sought unsuccessfully to have Connecticut's petition signature requirements relaxed because of the pandemic. A similar decision was rendered in *Second Chances v. Hobbs*, __ F.Supp.3d __ 2020 WL 1905747 (Ariz. 2020). In *Gottlieb v. Lamont*, __ F.Supp.3d __ 2020 WL 3046205 (D. Conn. 2020), the court held that Connecticut's ballot access rules (which required independent candidates to obtain signatures from 5% of the population of the district) were unconstitutional given the pandemic. In *People First of Alabama v. Merrill*, __ F.Supp.3d __ 2020 WL 3207824 (N.D. Ala. 2020), two individuals who were at higher risk from Covid-19 challenged Alabama's absentee process which required proof of identity plus a witness signature, and obtained a preliminary injunction against enforcement. However, the U.S. Supreme Court, in *Merrill v. People First of Alabama*, __ S. Ct. __ 2020 WL 3604049 (2020), stayed the order.

5. Education

An understanding that education is a fundamental right goes back to the early twentieth century. In *Pierce v. Society of Sisters*, 268 U.S. 510 (1925), the Court struck down a state law requiring parents to send their children to public schools. The holding was accompanied by the observation that the statute "unreasonably interferes with the liberty of parents and guardians to direct the upbringing and education of their children." The importance of education, from both individual and societal perspectives, was noted in case law that undid official segregation. In *Brown v. Board of Education*, 347 U.S. 483 (1954), the Court described education as "perhaps the most important function of state and local government, the very foundation of good citizenship, and a principal instrument in awakening the child to cultural values, in preparing him for later professional training, and in helping him to adjust normally to his environment." The *Brown* Court further observed that when the state provides for public education, it is "a right that must be made available to all on equal terms." In *Bolling v. Sharpe*, 347 U.S. 497 (1954), the Court found that segregated public education effected a "deprivation of liberty under the Due Process Clause." Equalization of educational opportunity implicates not only desegregation but also social, philosophical, and economic policy.

San Antonio Independent School District v. Rodriguez

411 U.S. 1 (1973)

Mr. Justice POWELL delivered the opinion of the Court.

This suit attacking the Texas system of financing public education was initiated by Mexican-American parents whose children attend the elementary and secondary schools in the Edgewood Independent School District, an urban school district in San Antonio, Texas. They brought a class action on behalf of schoolchildren throughout the State who are members of minority groups or who are poor and reside in school districts having a low property tax base.

Texas was a predominantly rural State and its population and property wealth were spread relatively evenly across the State. Sizable differences in the value of assessable property between local school districts became increasingly evident as the State became more industrialized and as rural-to-urban population shifts became more pronounced. These growing disparities in population and taxable property between districts were responsible in part for increasingly notable differences in levels of local expenditure for education.

Recognizing the need for increased state funding to help offset disparities in local spending and to meet Texas' changing educational requirements, the state legislature in the late 1940's undertook a thorough evaluation of public education with an eye toward major reform. It enacted the "Foundation Program," which provided for state and local contributions to a fund earmarked specifically for teacher salaries, operating expenses, and transportation costs. The State, supplying funds from its general revenues, finances approximately 80% of the Program, and the school districts are responsible—as a unit—for providing the remaining 20%. The districts' share, known as the Local Fund Assignment, is apportioned among the school districts under a formula designed to reflect each district's relative taxpaying ability. The district finances its share of the Assignment out of revenues from local property taxation.

The design of this complex system was twofold. First, it was an attempt to assure that the Foundation Program would have an equalizing influence on expenditure levels between school districts by placing the heaviest burden on the school districts most capable of paying. Second, the Program's architects sought to establish a Local Fund Assignment that would force every school district to contribute to the education of its children but that would not by itself exhaust any district's resources. Today every school district does impose a property tax from which it derives locally expendable funds in excess of the amount necessary to satisfy its Local Fund Assignment under the Foundation Program.

The school district in which appellees reside, the Edgewood Independent School District, has been compared throughout this litigation with the Alamo Heights Independent School District. This comparison between the least and most affluent districts in the San Antonio area serves to illustrate the manner in which the dual system of finance operates and to indicate the extent to which substantial disparities exist despite the State's impressive progress in recent years. Edgewood is one of seven public school districts in the metropolitan area. The district has 25 elementary schools situated in the core-city sector of San Antonio in a residential neighborhood that has little commercial or industrial property. The residents are predominantly of Mexican-American descent: approximately 90% of the student population is Mexican-American and over 6% is Negro. The average assessed property value per pupil is $5,960—the lowest in the metropolitan area—and the median family income ($4,686) is also the lowest. At an equalized tax rate of $1.05 per $100 of assessed property—the highest in the metropolitan area—the district contributed $26 to the education of each child for the 1967–1968 school year above its Local Fund Assignment for the Minimum Foundation Program. The Foundation Program contributed $222 per pupil for a state-local total of $248. Federal funds added another $108 for a total of $356 per pupil.

Alamo Heights is the most affluent school district in San Antonio. Its six schools house approximately 5,000 students. The school population is predominantly 'Anglo,' having only 18% Mexican-Americans and less than 1% Negroes. The assessed property value per pupil exceeds $49,000, and the median family income is $8,001. In 1967–1968 the local tax rate of $.85 per $100 of valuation yielded $333 per pupil over and above its contribution to the Foundation Program. Coupled with the $225 provided from that Program, the district was able to supply $558 per student. Supplemented by a $36 per-pupil grant from federal sources, Alamo Heights spent $594 per pupil.

It was these disparities, largely attributable to differences in the amounts of money collected through local property taxation, that led the District Court to conclude that Texas' dual system of public school financing violated the Equal Protection Clause. The District Court held that the Texas system discriminates on the basis of wealth in the manner in which education is provided for its people. Finding that wealth is a 'suspect' classification and that education is a 'fundamental' interest, the District Court held that the Texas system could be sustained only if the State could show that it was premised upon some compelling state interest. The court found no compelling or even reasonable basis for the classifications.

Texas virtually concedes that its historically rooted dual system of financing education could not withstand the strict judicial scrutiny that this Court has found appropriate in reviewing legislative judgments that interfere with fundamental constitutional rights or that involve suspect classifications.

We must decide, first, whether the Texas system of financing public education operates to the disadvantage of some suspect class or impinges upon a fundamental right explicitly or implicitly protected by the Constitution, thereby requiring strict judicial scrutiny. If so, the judgment of the District Court should be affirmed. If not, the Texas scheme must still be examined to determine whether it rationally furthers some legitimate, articulated state purpose and therefore does not constitute an invidious discrimination in violation of the Equal Protection Clause of the Fourteenth Amendment.

In concluding that strict judicial scrutiny was required, the District Court relied on decisions dealing with the rights of indigents to equal treatment in the criminal trial and appellate processes, and on cases disapproving wealth restrictions on the right to vote. It then reasoned that there is a fundamental right to education and that, absent some compelling state justification, the Texas system could not stand. We find neither the suspect-classification nor the fundamental-interest analysis persuasive.

The wealth discrimination is quite unlike any of the forms of wealth discrimination heretofore reviewed by this Court. The courts assumed that since, under the traditional systems of financing public schools, some poorer people receive less expensive educations than other more affluent people, these systems discriminate on the basis of wealth. However described, appellees' suit asks this Court to extend its most exacting scrutiny to review a system that allegedly discriminates against a large, diverse, and amorphous class, unified only by the common factor of residence in districts that happen to have less taxable wealth than other districts. The system of alleged discrimination and the class it defines have none of the traditional indicia of suspectness: the class is not saddled with such disabilities, or subjected to such a history of purposeful unequal treatment, or relegated to such a position of political powerlessness as to command extraordinary protection from the majoritarian political process. We thus conclude that the Texas system does not operate to the peculiar disadvantage of any suspect class. This Court has never heretofore held that wealth discrimination alone provides an adequate basis for invoking strict scrutiny.

Appellees also assert that the State's system impermissibly interferes with the exercise of a 'fundamental' right. It is this question—whether education is a fundamental right, in the sense that it is among the rights and liberties protected by the Constitution—which has so consumed the attention of courts and commentators in recent years. In *Brown v. Board of Education*, a unanimous Court recognized that 'education is perhaps the most important function of state and local governments.' What was said there in the context of racial discrimination has lost none of its vitality with the passage of time:

> Compulsory school attendance laws and the great expenditures for education both demonstrate our recognition of the importance of education to our democratic society. It is required in the performance of our most basic public responsibilities, even service in the armed forces. It is the very foundation of good citizenship. Today it is a principal instrument in awakening the child to cultural values, in preparing him for later professional training, and in helping him to adjust normally to his environment. In these days, it is doubtful that any child may reasonably be expected to succeed in life if he is denied the opportunity of an education. Such an opportunity, where the state has undertaken to provide it, is a right which must be made available to all on equal terms.

This theme, expressing an abiding respect for the vital role of education in a free society, may be found in numerous opinions of Justices of this Court writing both before and after *Brown* was decided. We are in complete agreement that 'the grave significance of education both to the individual and to our society' cannot be doubted.

But the importance of a service performed by the State does not determine whether it must be regarded as fundamental for purposes of examination under the Equal Protection Clause. In *Dandridge v. Williams*, the Court's explicit recognition of the fact that the 'administration of public welfare assistance involves the most basic economic needs of impoverished human beings,' provided no basis for departing from the settled mode of constitutional analysis of legislative classifications involving questions of economic and social policy. As in the case of housing, the central importance of welfare benefits to the poor was not an adequate foundation for requiring the State to justify its law by showing some compelling state interest. The lesson of these cases is plain. It is not the province of this Court to create substantive constitutional rights in the name of guaranteeing equal protection of the laws. The key to discovering whether education is 'fundamental' is not to be found in comparisons of the relative societal significance of education as opposed to subsistence or housing. Nor is it to be found by weighing whether education is as important as the right to travel. Rather, the answer lies in assessing whether there is a right to education explicitly or implicitly guaranteed by the Constitution.

Education, of course, is not among the rights afforded explicit protection under our Federal Constitution. Nor do we find any basis for saying it is implicitly so protected. Appellees contend, however, that education is distinguishable from other services and benefits provided by the State because it bears a peculiarly close relationship to other rights and liberties accorded protection under the Constitution. Specifically, they insist that education is itself a fundamental personal right because it is essential to the effective exercise of First Amendment freedoms and to intelligent utilization of the right to vote. In asserting a nexus between speech and education, appellees urge that the right to speak is meaningless unless the speaker is capable of articulating his thoughts intelligently and persuasively. The 'marketplace of ideas' is an empty forum for those lacking basic communicative tools. Likewise, they argue that the corollary right to receive information becomes little more than a hollow privilege when the recipient has not been taught to read, assimilate, and utilize available knowledge.

A similar line of reasoning is pursued with respect to the right to vote. Exercise of the franchise, it is contended, cannot be divorced from the educational foundation of the voter. The electoral process, if reality is to conform to the democratic ideal, depends on an informed electorate: a voter cannot cast his ballot intelligently unless his reading skills and thought processes have been adequately developed.

We need not dispute any of these propositions. The Court has long afforded zealous protection against unjustifiable governmental interference with the individual's rights to speak and to vote. Yet we have never presumed to possess either the ability or the authority to guarantee to the citizenry the most effective speech or the most informed electoral choice. Even if it were conceded that some identifiable quantum of education is a constitutionally protected prerequisite to the meaningful exercise of either right, we have no indication that the present levels of educational expenditures in Texas provide an education that falls short. Furthermore, the logical limitations on appellees' nexus theory are difficult to perceive. How, for instance, is education to be distinguished from the significant personal interests in the basics of decent food and shelter? The ill-fed, ill-clothed, and ill-housed are among the most ineffective participants in the political process, and they derive the least enjoyment from the benefits of the First Amendment.

We have carefully considered each of the arguments supportive of the District Court's finding that education is a fundamental right or liberty and have found those arguments unpersuasive. The present case, in another basic sense, is significantly different from any of the cases in which the Court has applied strict scrutiny to state or federal legislation touching upon constitutionally protected rights. Each of our prior cases involved legislation which 'deprived,' 'infringed,' or 'interfered' with the free exercise of some such fundamental personal right or liberty.

It should be clear that this is not a case in which the challenged state action must be subjected to the searching judicial scrutiny reserved for laws that create suspect classifications or impinge upon constitutionally protected rights. Application of the traditional standard of review requires only that the State's system be shown to bear some rational relationship to legitimate state purposes. We have here nothing less than a direct attack on the way in which Texas has chosen to raise and disburse state and local tax revenues. We are asked to condemn the State's judgment in conferring on political subdivisions the power to tax local property to supply revenues for local interests. In so doing, appellees would have the Court intrude in an area in which it has traditionally deferred to state legislatures. This Court has often admonished against such interferences with the State's fiscal policies under the Equal Protection Clause.

We stand on familiar grounds when we continue to acknowledge that the Justices of this Court lack both the expertise and the familiarity with local problems so necessary to the making of wise decisions with respect to the raising and disposition of public revenues. Yet, we are urged to direct the States either to alter drastically the present system or to throw out the property tax altogether in favor of some other form of taxation. No scheme of taxation, whether the tax is imposed on property, income, or purchases of goods and services, has yet been devised which is free of all discriminatory impact. In such a complex arena in which no perfect alternatives exist, the Court does well not to impose too rigorous a standard of scrutiny lest all local fiscal schemes become subjects of criticism under the Equal Protection Clause.

In addition to matters of fiscal policy, this case also involves the most persistent and difficult questions of educational policy, another area in which this Court's lack of specialized knowledge and experience counsels against premature interference with the informed judgments made at the state and local levels. The very complexity of the problems of financing and managing a statewide public school system suggests that 'there will be more than one constitutionally permissible method of solving them,' and that, within the limits of rationality, 'the legislature's efforts to tackle the problems' should be entitled to respect. The judiciary is well advised to refrain from imposing on the States inflexible constitutional restraints that could circumscribe or handicap the continued research and experimentation so vital to finding even partial solutions to educational problems and to keeping abreast of ever-changing conditions.

It must be remembered, also, that every claim arising under the Equal Protection Clause has implications for the relationship between national and state power under our federal system. It would be difficult to imagine a case having a greater potential impact on our federal system than the one now before us, in which we are urged to abrogate systems of financing public education presently in existence in virtually every State.

The foregoing considerations buttress our conclusion that Texas' system of public school finance is an inappropriate candidate for strict judicial scrutiny. These same considerations are relevant to the determination whether that system, with its conceded imperfections, nevertheless bears some rational relationship to a legitimate state purpose. It is to this question that we next turn our attention.

To the extent that the Texas system of school financing results in unequal expenditures between children who happen to reside in different districts, we cannot say that such disparities are the product of a system that is so irrational as to be invidiously discriminatory. The Texas plan is not the product of purposeful discrimination against any group or class. It is rooted in decades of experience in Texas and elsewhere, and in major part is the product of responsible studies by qualified people. The system here challenged is not peculiar to Texas or to any other State. In its essential characteristics, the Texas plan for financing public education reflects what many educators for a half century have thought was an enlightened approach to a problem for which there is no perfect solution. We are unwilling to assume for ourselves a level of wisdom superior to that of legislators, scholars, and educational authorities in 50 States, especially where the alternatives proposed are only recently conceived and nowhere yet tested. The constitutional standard under the Equal Protection Clause is whether the challenged state action rationally furthers a legitimate state purpose or interest. We hold that the Texas plan abundantly satisfies this standard. The ultimate solutions must come from the lawmakers and from the democratic pressures of those who elect them.

Mr. Justice STEWART, *concurring.*

I am convinced that any other course would mark an extraordinary departure from principled adjudication under the Equal Protection Clause of the Fourteenth Amendment. Unlike other provisions of the Constitution, the Equal Protection Clause confers no substantive rights and creates no substantive liberties. The function of the Equal Protection Clause is simply to measure the validity of classifications created by state laws. There is hardly a law on the books that does not affect some people differently from others. It has long been settled that the Equal Protection Clause is offended only by laws that are invidiously discriminatory—only by classifications that are wholly arbitrary or capricious. The Texas system has hardly created the kind of objectively identifiable classes that are cognizable under the Equal Protection Clause. Even assuming the existence of such discernible categories, the classifications are in no sense based upon constitutionally 'suspect' criteria. The Texas system does not rest 'on grounds wholly irrelevant to the achievement of the State's objective.' Finally, the Texas system impinges upon no substantive constitutional rights or liberties.

Mr. Justice BRENNAN, *dissenting.*

I disagree with the Court's rather distressing assertion that a right may be deemed 'fundamental' for the purposes of equal protection analysis only if it is 'explicitly or implicitly guaranteed by the Constitution.' Our prior cases stand for the proposition that 'fundamentality' is, in large measure, a function of the right's importance in terms of the effectuation of those rights which are in fact constitutionally guaranteed. There can be no doubt that education is inextricably linked to the right to participate in the electoral process and to the rights of free speech and association guaranteed by the First Amendment. This being so, any classification affecting education must be subjected to strict judicial scrutiny, and since even the State concedes that the statutory scheme now before us cannot pass constitutional muster under this stricter standard of review, I can only conclude that the Texas school-financing scheme is constitutionally invalid.

Mr. Justice WHITE, with whom Mr. Justice DOUGLAS and Mr. Justice BRENNAN join, *dissenting.*

The Equal Protection Clause permits discriminations between classes but requires that the classification bear some rational relationship to a permissible object sought to be attained by the statute and that the means chosen by the State must also be rationally related to the end sought to be achieved. If the State aims at maximizing local initiative and local choice, by permitting school districts to resort to the real property tax if they choose to do so, it utterly fails in achieving its purpose in districts with property tax bases so low that there is little if any opportunity for interested parents, rich or poor, to augment school district revenues. Requiring the State to establish only that unequal treatment is in furtherance of a permissible goal, without also requiring the State to show that the means chosen to effectuate that goal are rationally related to its achievement, makes equal protection analysis no more than an empty gesture. The parents and children in Edgewood, and in like districts, suffer from an invidious discrimination violative of the Equal Protection Clause.

Mr. Justice MARSHALL, with whom Mr. Justice DOUGLAS *concurs, dissenting.*

The right of every American to an equal start in life, so far as the provision of a state service as important as education is concerned, is far too vital to permit state discrimination on grounds as tenuous as those presented by this record. Nor can I accept the notion that it is sufficient to remit these appellees to the vagaries of the political process.

Even before this Court recognized its duty to tear down the barriers of state-enforced racial segregation in public education, it acknowledged that inequality in the educational facilities provided to students may be discriminatory state action as contemplated by the Equal Protection Clause. A difference in the funds available to districts results in a difference in educational inputs available for a child's public education in Texas. This situation, which is directly attributable to the Texas financing scheme, raises a grave question of state-created discrimination in the provision of public education. The burden of proving that these disparities do not in fact affect the quality of children's education must fall upon the appellants. Yet appellants made no effort to demonstrate that educational quality is not affected by variations in funding and in resulting inputs.

It is inequality—not some notion of gross inadequacy—of educational opportunity that raises a question of denial of equal protection of the laws. Appellees have made a substantial showing of wide variations in educational funding and the resulting educational opportunity afforded to the schoolchildren of Texas. This discrimination is, in large measure, attributable to significant disparities in the taxable wealth of local Texas school districts. This is a sufficient showing to raise a substantial question of discriminatory state action in violation of the Equal Protection Clause.

This Court has repeatedly held that state discrimination which either adversely affects a 'fundamental interest' or is based on a distinction of a suspect character must be carefully scrutinized to ensure that the scheme is necessary to promote a substantial, legitimate state interest. I cannot accept the majority's labored efforts to demonstrate that fundamental interests, which call for strict scrutiny of the challenged classification, encompass only established rights which we are somehow bound to recognize from the text of the Constitution itself. The fundamental importance of education is amply indicated by the prior decisions of this Court, by the unique status accorded public education by our society, and by the close relationship between education and some of our most basic constitutional values.

Discrimination on the basis of group wealth in this case likewise calls for careful judicial scrutiny. Local district wealth bears no relationship whatsoever to the interest of Texas schoolchildren in the educational opportunity afforded them by the State of Texas. Insofar as group wealth discrimination involves wealth over which the disadvantaged individual has no significant control, it represents in fact a more serious basis of discrimination than does personal wealth. Such discrimination is no reflection of the individual's characteristics or his abilities. And thus—particularly in the context of a disadvantaged class composed of children—we have previously treated discrimination on a basis which the individual cannot control as constitutionally disfavored.

Nor can we ignore the extent to which the State is responsible for the wealth discrimination in this instance. The means for financing public education in Texas are selected and specified by the State. The invidious characteristics of the group wealth classification present in this case merely serve to emphasize the need for careful judicial scrutiny of the State's justifications for the resulting interdistrict discrimination in the educational opportunity afforded to the schoolchildren of Texas.

Note

The *Rodriguez* decision illuminated the Court's general reticence to use the Equal Protection Clause as a means for redistributing wealth. The majority opinion, authored by Justice Powell, nonetheless left open the possibility of a different result in the event that the state "occasioned an absolute denial of educational opportunities." This reservation prefaced the Court's determination, in *Plyler v. Doe*, that denial of public education to the children of illegal aliens violated the Equal Protection Clause.

∼ PROBLEMS ∼

1. *"Rooted in the Nation's Traditions"?* The Court in *Brown v. Board of Education* characterized education as "perhaps the most important function of state and local governments" and as "the very foundation of good citizenship." Given the significance of education for purposes of developing individual opportunity and an informed electorate, has it become "rooted in the nation's traditions"?

2. *Judicial Review.* How should a state law distributing monies unevenly among state school districts be reviewed when there is no local real estate tax factored into the equation?

3. *Challenging Teacher Tenure Rules.* In California, a judge struck down the state's teacher tenure system. *See Vergara v. California,* 2014 WL 2598719 (L.A. Sup.). In the suit, plaintiffs had argued that state statutes governing teacher tenure, teacher dismissals, and layoffs ("last in, first out") have a negative impact on poor students' ability to obtain a quality education. They argued that the more qualified teachers tend to shy away from troubled schools, which are populated by the worst teachers. Under *Rodriguez,* if the plaintiffs can show a "cause" and "effect" from the policies, should the tenure rules be struck down? What do they need to show in order to prevail?

Plyler v. Doe

457 U.S. 202 (1982)

Justice BRENNAN delivered the opinion of the Court.

The question presented by these cases is whether, consistent with the Equal Protection Clause of the Fourteenth Amendment, Texas may deny to undocumented school-age children the free public education that it provides to children who are citizens of the United States or legally admitted aliens.

Since the late 19th century, the United States has restricted immigration into this country. Despite legal restrictions, a substantial number of persons have succeeded in unlawfully entering the United States, and now live within various States. In 1975, the Texas Legislature revised its education laws to withhold from local school districts any state funds for the education of children who were not "legally admitted" into the United States. The law also authorized local school districts to deny enrollment to children not "legally admitted" to the country.

Appellants argue that undocumented aliens, because of their immigration status, are not "persons within the jurisdiction" of the State of Texas, and that they therefore have no right to the equal protection of Texas law. We reject this argument. Whatever his status under the immigration laws, an alien is surely a "person" in any ordinary sense of that term. The Equal Protection Clause was intended to work nothing less than the abolition of all caste-based and invidious class-based legislation. That objective is fundamentally at odds with the power the State asserts here to classify persons subject to its laws as nonetheless excepted from its protection.

The more difficult question is whether the Equal Protection Clause has been violated by the refusal of the State of Texas to reimburse local school boards for the education of children who cannot demonstrate that their presence within the United States is lawful, or by the imposition by those school boards of the burden of tuition on those children. The Equal Protection Clause directs that "all persons similarly circumstanced shall be treated alike." But so too, "the Constitution does not require things which are different in fact or opinion to be treated in law as though they were the same." The initial discretion to determine what is "different" and what is "the same" resides in the legislatures of the States. A legislature must have substantial latitude to establish classifications that roughly approximate the nature of the problem perceived, that accommodate competing concerns both public and private, and that account for limitations on the practical ability of the State to remedy every ill. In applying the Equal Protection Clause to most forms of state action, we thus seek only the assurance that the classification at issue bears some fair relationship to a legitimate public purpose.

But we would not be faithful to our obligations under the Fourteenth Amendment if we applied so deferential a standard to every classification. The Equal Protection Clause was intended as a restriction on state legislative action inconsistent with elemental constitutional premises. Thus we have treated as presumptively invidious those classifications that disadvantage a "suspect class," or that impinge upon the exercise of a "fundamental right." With respect to such classifications, it is appropriate to enforce the mandate of equal protection by requiring the State to demonstrate that its classification has been precisely tailored to serve a compelling governmental interest. In addition, we have recognized that certain forms of legislative classification, while not facially invidious, nonetheless give rise to recurring constitutional difficulties; in these limited circumstances we have sought the assurance that the classification reflects a reasoned judgment consistent with the ideal of equal protection by inquiring whether it may fairly be viewed as furthering a substantial interest of the State.

Sheer incapability or lax enforcement of the laws barring entry into this country, coupled with the failure to establish an effective bar to the employment of undocumented aliens, has resulted in the creation of a substantial "shadow population" of illegal migrants—numbering in the millions—within our borders. This situation raises the specter of a permanent caste of undocumented resident aliens, encouraged by some to remain here as a source of cheap labor, but nevertheless denied the benefits that our society makes available to citizens and lawful residents. The existence of such an underclass presents most difficult problems for a Nation that prides itself on adherence to principles of equality under law.

The children who are plaintiffs in these cases are special members of this underclass. A State may withhold its beneficence from those whose very presence within the United States is the product of their own unlawful conduct. But the children of those illegal entrants are not comparably situated and "can affect neither their parents' conduct nor their own status." Of course, undocumented status is not irrelevant to any proper legislative goal. Nor is undocumented status an absolutely immutable characteristic since it is the product of conscious, indeed unlawful, action. But the state law is directed against children, and imposes its discriminatory burden on the basis of a legal characteristic over which children can have little control. It is difficult to conceive of a rational justification for penalizing these children for their presence within the United States.

Public education is not a "right" granted to individuals by the Constitution. But neither is it merely some governmental "benefit" indistinguishable from other forms of social welfare legislation. Both the importance of education in maintaining our basic institutions, and the lasting impact of its deprivation on the life of the child, mark the distinction. Education has a fundamental role in maintaining the fabric of our society. We cannot ignore the significant social costs borne by our Nation when select groups are denied the means to absorb the values and skills upon which our social order rests.

In addition to the pivotal role of education in sustaining our political and cultural heritage, denial of education to some isolated group of children poses an affront to one of the goals of the Equal Protection Clause: the abolition of governmental barriers presenting unreasonable obstacles to advancement on the basis of individual merit. By depriving the children of any disfavored group of an education, we foreclose the means by which that group might raise the level of esteem in which it is held by the majority. But more directly, "education prepares individuals to be self-reliant and self-sufficient participants in society." Illiteracy is an enduring disability. The inestimable toll of that deprivation on the social, economic, intellectual, and psychological well-being of the individual, and the obstacle it poses to individual achievement, make it most difficult to reconcile the cost or the principle of a status-based denial of basic education with the framework of equality embodied in the Equal Protection Clause.

These well-settled principles allow us to determine the proper level of deference to be afforded the state law. Undocumented aliens cannot be treated as a suspect class because their presence in this country in violation of federal law is not a "constitutional irrelevancy." Nor is education a fundamental right; a State need not justify by compelling necessity every variation in the manner in which education is provided to its population. But the state law imposes a lifetime hardship on a discrete class of children not accountable for their disabling status. The stigma of illiteracy will mark them for the rest of their lives. By denying these children a basic education, we deny them the ability to live within the structure of our civic institutions, and foreclose any realistic possibility that they will contribute in even the smallest way to the progress of our Nation. In determining the state law's rationality, we may appropriately take into account its costs to the Nation and to the innocent children who are its victims. In light of these countervailing costs, the discrimination contained in the state law can hardly be considered rational unless it furthers some substantial goal of the State.

The State argues that the undocumented status of these children *vel non* establishes a sufficient rational basis for denying them benefits that a State might choose to afford other residents. The State notes that while other aliens are admitted "on an equality of legal privileges with all citizens under non-discriminatory laws," the asserted right of these children to an education can claim no implicit congressional imprimatur. In the State's view, Congress' apparent disapproval of the presence of these children within the United States, and the evasion of the federal regulatory program that is the mark of undocumented status, provides authority for its decision to impose upon them special disabilities. But we are unable to find in the congressional immigration scheme any statement of policy that might weigh significantly in arriving at an equal protection balance concerning the State's authority to deprive these children of an education. Like all persons who have entered the United States unlawfully, these children are subject to deportation. But there is no assurance that a child subject to deportation will ever be deported. We are reluctant to impute to Congress the intention to withhold from these children, for so long as they are present in this country through no fault of their own, access to a basic education.

Appellants argue that the classification at issue furthers an interest in the "preservation of the state's limited resources for the education of its lawful residents." Of course, a concern for the preservation of resources standing alone can hardly justify the classification used in allocating those resources. The State must do more than justify its classification with a concise expression of an intention to discriminate.

We discern three colorable state interests that might support the law. First, appellants suggest that the State may seek to protect itself from an influx of illegal immigrants. Few if any illegal immigrants come to this country in order to avail themselves of a free education. "Charging tuition to undocumented children constitutes a ludicrously ineffectual attempt to stem the tide of illegal immigration," at least when compared with the alternative of prohibiting the employment of illegal aliens. Second, appellants suggest that undocumented children are appropriately singled out for exclusion because of the special burdens they impose on the State's ability to provide high-quality public education. In terms of educational cost and need, undocumented children are "basically indistinguishable" from legally resident alien children. Finally, appellants suggest that undocumented children are appropriately singled out because their unlawful presence within the United States renders them less likely than other children to remain within the boundaries of the State, and to put their education to productive social or political use within the State. The record is clear that many of the undocumented children disabled by this classification will remain in this country indefinitely, and that some will become lawful residents or citizens of the United States. It is difficult to understand precisely what the State hopes to achieve by promoting the creation and perpetuation of a subclass of illiterates within our boundaries, surely adding to the problems and costs of unemployment, welfare, and crime. Whatever savings might be achieved by denying these children an education, they are wholly insubstantial in light of the costs involved to these children, the State, and the Nation.

If the State is to deny a discrete group of innocent children the free public education that it offers to other children residing within its borders, that denial must be justified by a showing that it furthers some substantial state interest. No such showing was made here. Accordingly, the judgment of the Court of Appeals in each of these cases is affirmed.

Justice MARSHALL, *concurring.*

An individual's interest in education is fundamental. A class-based denial of public education is utterly incompatible with the Equal Protection Clause of the Fourteenth Amendment.

Justice BLACKMUN, *concurring.*

The children involved in this litigation "should not be left on the streets uneducated." When the State provides an education to some and denies it to others, it immediately and inevitably creates class distinctions of a type fundamentally inconsistent with the purposes of the Equal Protection Clause. Children denied an education are placed at a permanent and insurmountable competitive disadvantage and will have been converted into a discrete underclass.

Justice POWELL, *concurring.*

The State's denial of education to these children bears no substantial relation to any substantial state interest. An uncertain but significant percentage of illegal alien children will remain in Texas as residents and many eventually will become citizens. The exclusion of appellees' class of children from state-provided education is a type of punitive discrimination based on status that is impermissible under the Equal Protection Clause.

Chief Justice BURGER, with whom Justice WHITE, Justice REHNQUIST, and Justice O'CONNOR join, *dissenting.*

Were it our business to set the Nation's social policy, I would agree without hesitation that it is senseless for an enlightened society to deprive any children—including illegal aliens—of an elementary education. However, the Constitution does not vest in this Court the authority to strike down laws because they do not meet our standards of desirable social policy, "wisdom," or "common sense." The Court employs, and in my view abuses, the Fourteenth Amendment in an effort to become an omnipotent and omniscient problem solver. That the motives for doing so are noble and compassionate does not alter the fact that the Court distorts our constitutional function.

Once it is conceded—as the Court does—that illegal aliens are not a suspect class, and that education is not a fundamental right, our inquiry should focus on and be limited to whether the legislative classification at issue bears a rational relationship to a legitimate state purpose. The State contends that the state law prevents undue depletion of its limited revenues available for education, and preserves the fiscal integrity of the State's school-financing system against an ever-increasing flood of illegal aliens. Of course such fiscal concerns alone could not justify discrimination against a suspect class or an arbitrary and irrational denial of benefits to a particular group of persons. Yet I assume no Member of this Court would argue that prudent conservation of finite state revenues is *per se* an illegitimate goal.

It simply is not "irrational" for a state to conclude that it does not have the same responsibility to provide benefits for persons whose very presence in the state and this country is illegal as it does to provide for persons lawfully present. Illegal aliens have no right whatever to be here, and the state may reasonably, and constitutionally, elect not to provide them with governmental services at the expense of those who are lawfully in the state. The fact that there are sound *policy* arguments against the Texas Legislature's choice does not render that choice an unconstitutional one. Today's cases present yet another example of unwarranted judicial action which in the long run tends to contribute to the weakening of our political processes.

Note

The *Plyler* decision was an anomaly in two regards. First, it departed from the Court's reluctance to use the Equal Protection Clause to effect redistribution of wealth or opportunity. Second, though applying rational basis scrutiny in form, the Court independently reviewed the logic and utility of the state's methods. This functional application of heightened scrutiny was consistent with the Court's sense that education, while not a fundamental right, is not "merely some governmental 'benefit' indistinguishable from other forms of social welfare legislation."

The possibility that the *Plyler* decision might elevate the importance of education for equal protection purposes, or establish the basis for more analytical flexibility, was diminished by subsequent case law. In *Kadrmas v. Dickinson Public Schools*, 487 U.S. 450 (1988), the Court upheld a state law that allowed school districts to charge a school bus transportation fee. Although indigent children could not afford the cost, the Court restated that education is not a fundamental right and employed the traditionally deferential rational basis standard of review. For practical purposes the *Plyler* decision was limited to its facts.

∼ PROBLEMS ∼

1. *Denial of Public Education.* Consider a state law that denies free public education to a student who lives in a district, apart from his or her parent or guardian, for the primary purpose of attending on a tuition-free basis. This law is applied to an eight-year-old child who is a citizen of the United States, but whose parents live in Mexico, where they are citizens. Should this provision be analyzed pursuant to *Rodriguez* or *Plyler*? Does it burden the right to travel?

2. *A Constitutional Right to Food?* In discussions of matters fundamental to personhood and livelihood, food is almost always taken for granted. In light of the current recession and the growing number of Americans receiving food stamps

and other assistance for necessities, should there be a constitutional right to food? This question is being addressed in other countries. India, which has some supportive aspirational language in its constitution, was considering this question in July 2010. The party in power, the Indian National Congress Party, has been divided over whether to support such a right. *See* Jim Yardley, *India Asks, Should Food Be a Right for the Poor?*, N.Y. Times, Asia Pacific, Aug. 8, 2010. Would it be appropriate for the U.S. Supreme Court to hold that people have a constitutional right to food?

[Points to Remember for Chapter 10 is contained in online file.]

11

Freedom of Speech

U.S. CONSTITUTION, FIRST AMENDMENT

Congress shall make no law respecting an establishment of religion, or prohibiting the free exercise thereof; or abridging the freedom of speech, or of the press, or the right of the people peaceably to assemble, and to petition the Government for a redress of grievances.

[Roadmap for Chapter 11 is contained in online file.]

∽ PROBLEM: AN INTERNATIONAL TREATY REGULATING THE INTERNET ∽

During the last 30 years, the internet has developed into a major method of communication. It is an inherently democratic medium in the sense that anyone can easily and readily gain access, and therefore internet communication is accessible by virtually everyone. As a result, many have hailed the internet as a way to enhance knowledge, improve political processes, and generally facilitate communication. However, the internet also has a dark underside. Unscrupulous individuals have tried to use the internet to perpetrate financial scams and swindles, and the internet is routinely used by purveyors of hate as well as peddlers of pornography, including child pornography.

Because of concerns about harmful material on the internet, a conference has been called to develop an international treaty regulating the internet. Representatives from various nations will attend the conference, and they all have very different concerns about the types of speech that should be regulated and how they should be regulated. Governments in some countries (e.g., China and Iran) think that any treaty that results from the talks should address issues related to defamatory political speech and sedition, and should also promote intergovernmental cooperation to curb "subversive" speech. Governments in other countries (e.g., Germany and France) believe that the treaty should prohibit such things as Holocaust denial, race-based speech, and other types of speech that degrade human dignity. Some countries believe that all pornography should be prohibited both because of its adverse effects on society and because it is degrading to women. Most societies agree that child pornography should be prohibited in order to protect children.

Suppose that you have been designated the U.S. representative to the talks. As your work your way through this chapter, think about the type of treaty that the United States might be able to enter into (or, for that matter, might be precluded from entering into). As you do, recall the discussion of treaties in Chapters 2 and 3.

A. HISTORICAL INTENTIONS AND UNDERLYING VALUES

The First Amendment is phrased in broad and unqualified terms: "Congress shall make no law abridging the freedom of speech, or of the press." Justice Black once argued that the language should be taken literally: "The unequivocal command that there shall be no abridgment of the rights of free speech and assembly shows that those who drafted our Bill of Rights did all the 'balancing' that was to be done in this field. The very object of adopting the First Amendment was to put the freedoms protected there completely out of the area of any congressional control that may be attempted through the exercise of precisely those powers that are now being used to 'balance' the Bill of Rights out of existence." *Konigsberg v. State Bar of California*, 366 U.S. 36, 60-61 (1961). But the Court ultimately rejected Justice Black's position in favor of a less "absolutist" view of the First Amendment. As Justice Holmes argued, "the most stringent protection of free speech would not protect a man in falsely shouting fire in a theatre and causing a panic." *Schenck v. United States*, 249 U.S. 47 (1919). But if First Amendment protections are not absolute and must give way at times to "other interests," what are those "other interests"?

1. Framers' Intent

The Framers of the U.S. Constitution omitted speech protections from the original Constitution because they believed that such protections were unnecessary. They viewed the federal government's powers as limited and enumerated, and argued that there was no need to explicitly protect specific rights. Indeed, some

Framers believed that it would be undesirable to list specific rights because the mere fact of enumeration might imply that other rights were not constitutionally protected. However, when the Constitution was sent to the states for ratification, it became clear that the Constitution would not be ratified without some protection for speech. Because this sentiment was so pronounced, there was little debate in Congress or the states about why the First Amendment was needed or how it should be applied.

We do know something about historical conditions in the colonies that might have led the colonists to demand speech protections. In addition to licensing restrictions (which required a publisher to have approval from English authorities in the form of a license to publish), the colonists were subjected to seditious libel prosecutions. "Seditious libel" developed in England in the case of *de Libellis Famosis*, 77 Eng. Rep. 250 (Star Chamber 1606), involving defendants who had ridiculed clergy of high station. Over time, government officials used the crime to stifle criticism. *See* William T. Mayton, *Seditious Libel and the Lost Guarantee of a Freedom of Expression*, 84 COLUM. L. REV. 91 (1984). The crime was particularly objectionable because truth was no defense: "Since maintaining a proper regard for government was the goal, it followed that truth was just as reprehensible as falsehood and was eliminated as a defense." *Id.* Seditious libel also existed in the colonies. *See* Lawrence W. Crispo, Jill M. Slansky & Geanene M. Yriarte, *Jury Nullification: Law Versus Anarchy*, 31 LOY. L.A. L. REV. 1, 7 (1997). As in England, truth was not a defense.

Zechariah Chafee has argued that the Framers intended to "wipe out the common law of sedition and make further prosecutions for criticism of the government, without any incitement to law-breaking, forever impossible." ZECHARIAH CHAFEE, FREE SPEECH IN THE UNITED STATES (Harvard 1941). However, others have disagreed. *See, e.g.*, Leonard W. Levy, *The Legacy Reexamined*, 37 STAN. L. REV. 767 (1985). Notwithstanding the existence of the First Amendment, Congress enacted the Alien and Sedition Act of 1798, which made it illegal to publish "false, scandalous, and malicious writing against the Government of the United States with intent to defame, or to bring them into contempt or disrepute, or to excite against them hatred of the good people of the United States, or to stir up sedition within the United States." In addition, just prior to the Civil War, some states enacted laws prohibiting speech that advocated the abolition of slavery.

2. Underlying Values

Given that the drafters and ratifiers of the First Amendment did not leave clear evidence regarding their intent, the meaning of the First Amendment has been a subject of debate. As part of that debate, various scholars have offered theories about the function of the First Amendment and its application.

Thomas I. Emerson, *Toward a General Theory of the First Amendment*

72 Yale L.J. 877 (1963)[1]

The right of the individual to freedom of expression is an integral part of the great intellectual and social movement beginning with the Renaissance which transformed the Western world from a feudal and authoritarian society to one whose faith rested upon the dignity, the reason and the freedom of the individual. The values sought by society in protecting the right to freedom of expression may be grouped into four broad categories.

A. Individual Self-Fulfillment

The right to freedom of expression is justified first of all from the widely accepted premise of Western thought that the proper end of man is the realization of his character and potentialities as a human being. The achievement of self-realization commences with development of the mind. But the process of conscious thought can have no limits. It is an individual process. Every person—in the development of his or her own personality—has the right to form his own beliefs and opinions and the right to express these beliefs and opinions. For expression is an integral part of the development of ideas, of mental exploration and of the affirmation of self. There follows the right of the individual to access to knowledge; to shape his own views; to communicate his needs, preferences and judgments; in short, to participate in formulating the aims and achievements of his society and his state. To cut off his search for truth, or his expression of it, is thus to elevate society and the state to a despotic command and to reduce the individual to the arbitrary control of others. Freedom of expression, while not the sole or sufficient end of society, is a good in itself, or at least an essential element in a good society. A society or the state is entitled to exercise control over action—whether by prohibiting or compelling it—on an entirely different and vastly more extensive basis. But expression occupies a specially protected position.

B. Attainment of Truth

Freedom of expression is not only an individual but also a social good. It is, to begin with, the best process for advancing knowledge and discovering truth. The soundest and most rational judgment is arrived at by considering all facts and arguments, which can be put forth on behalf of or against any proposition. Suppression of information, discussion, or the clash of opinion prevents one from reaching the most rational judgment, blocks the generation of new ideas, and tends to perpetuate error. The theory demands that discussion must be kept open no matter how certainly true an accepted opinion may seem to be. Many

---

1. Reprinted by permission of The Yale Law Journal Company and William S. Hein Company from The Yale Law Journal, Vol. 72, pp. 877-956.

of the most widely acknowledged truths have turned out to be erroneous. Many of the most significant advances in human knowledge—from Copernicus to Einstein—have resulted from challenging hitherto unquestioned assumptions. The process also applies regardless of how false or pernicious the new opinion appears to be. For there is no way of suppressing the false without suppressing the true. Furthermore, even if the new opinion is wholly false, its presentation and open discussion serves a vital social purpose. It compels a rethinking and retesting of the accepted opinion. It results in a deeper understanding of the reasons for holding the opinion and a fuller appreciation of its meaning. The only justification for suppressing an opinion is that those who seek to suppress it are infallible in their judgment of the truth. But no individual or group can be infallible, particularly in a constantly changing world. Through the acquisition of new knowledge, the toleration of new ideas, the testing of opinion in open competition, the discipline of rethinking its assumptions, a society will be better able to reach common decisions that will meet the needs and aspirations of its members.

C. Participation in Decisionmaking

Every government must have some process for feeding back to it information concerning the attitudes, needs and wishes of its citizens. The crucial point is not that freedom of expression is politically useful, but that it is indispensable to the operation of a democratic form of government. Once one accepts the premise of the Declaration of Independence—that governments derive "their just powers from the consent of the governed"—it follows that the governed must, in order to exercise their right of consent, have full freedom of expression both in forming individual judgments and in forming the common judgment. Once a society was committed to democratic procedures, or rather in the process of committing itself, it necessarily embraced the principle of open political discussion.

D. Balance Between Stability and Change

Suppression of discussion makes a rational judgment impossible. In effect it substitutes force for logic. Moreover, coercion of expression is likely to be ineffective. While it may prevent social change, at least for a time, it cannot eradicate thought or belief; nor can it promote loyalty or unity. Suppression of expression conceals the real problems confronting a society and diverts public attention from the critical issues. It is likely to result in neglect of the grievances which are the actual basis of the unrest, and thus prevent their correction. Further, suppression drives opposition underground, leaving those suppressed either apathetic or desperate. It thus saps the vitality of the society or makes resort to force more likely. And finally it weakens and debilitates the majority whose support for the common decision is necessary. For it hinders an intelligent understanding of the reasons for adopting the decision. In short, suppression of opposition may well mean that when change is finally forced on the community it will come in more violent and radical form. Allowing dissidents to expound their views enables them "to let off steam." This results in a release of energy, a lessening of frustration, and a channeling of resistance into courses consistent with law and order. It operates, in short, as a catharsis throughout the body politic. The principle of political legitimation asserts that persons who have had full freedom to state their position and to persuade others to adopt it will, when the decision goes against them, be more ready to accept the common judgment. They will recognize that they have been treated fairly, in accordance with rational rules for social living. Only a government which consistently fails to relieve valid grievances need fear the outbreak of violent opposition.

C. Edwin Baker, *Scope of the First Amendment Freedom of Speech*

25 UCLA L. Rev. 964 (1978)[2]

The classic marketplace of ideas model argues that truth (or the best perspectives or solutions) can be discovered through robust debate, free from governmental interference. Defending this theory in *On Liberty,* John Stuart Mill argued that three situations are possible: 1) if heretical opinion contains the truth, and if we silence it, we lose the chance of exchanging truth for error; 2) if received and contesting opinions each hold part of the truth, their clash in open discussion provides the best means to discover the truth in each; 3) even if the heretical view is wholly false and the orthodoxy contains the whole truth, the received truth, unless debated and challenged, will be held in the manner of prejudice or dead dogma, its meaning may be forgotten or enfeebled, and it will be inefficacious for good. Moreover, without free speech, totally false heretical opinions which could not survive open discussion will not disappear; instead, driven underground, these opinions will smolder, their fallacies protected from exposure and opposition. In this model, the value of free speech lies not in the liberty interests of individual speakers but in the societal benefits derived from unimpeded discussion. This social gain is so great, and any loss from allowing speech is so small, that society should tolerate no restraint on the verbal search for truth.

The assumptions on which the classic marketplace of ideas theory rests are almost universally rejected today. The hope that the marketplace leads to truth, or even to the best or most desirable decision, becomes implausible. First, truth is not objective. Knowledge depends on how people's interests, needs, and experiences lead them to slice and categorize an expanding mass of sense data. And even if "rational" debate can play some role in advancing understanding within a given paradigm, discussion appears insufficient by itself to evaluate different paradigms. Protecting free speech insures that the individual will have more information and, thus, be able to make a more informed choice. The problem

2. Originally published in 25 UCLA L. Rev. 964. Copyright © 1978. The Regents of the University of California. All Rights Reserved.

with this defense is that the individual is as likely to find needed information in experiences as in free speech.

If truth or understanding are created or chosen, an evaluation of the marketplace must consider whether the values of different people or groups are furthered by the choice or creation of the same truth or understanding. If groups have divergent interests concerning the choice of perspectives, one can presume that the marketplace of ideas (and other activities which might be protected) leads to the "best" or "proper" or "progressive" understanding only if the marketplace favors those groups who should be favored or "properly" distributes influence among various people or groups such that optimal compromises are reached. For example, Herbert Marcuse concluded that in the present historical circumstances the marketplace of ideas would work properly only if the rich and powerful were completely excluded and access were limited to progressive, leftist elements; others argue for more or less equal access for all groups in the market place.

The classic model also requires that people be able to use their rational capacities to eliminate distortion caused by the form and frequency of message presentation and to find the core of relevant information or argument. Emotional or "irrational" appeals have great impact; "subconscious" repressions, phobias, or desires influence people's assimilation of messages; and, most obviously, stimulus-response mechanisms and selective attention and retention processes influence understanding or perspectives. Since interests vary with social position, the perspectives that are reinforced will also vary. People maintain perspectives which promote one's interest even when presented with contrary information or alterative perspectives. These psychological insights, extensively relied upon in practice by advertisers and propagandists, eviscerate the faith in the ability of the marketplace of ideas to lead to the "best" truths or understandings. Even if one assumes that some understandings are best, one has no reason to expect these to be discovered in the marketplace of ideas. Furthermore, the theory cannot be defended on the grounds that it provides a "fair" or otherwise justifiable process for regulating the struggle between opposing groups. The incredible inequalities of opportunity to use the marketplace cause a fairness defense to fail.

My thesis is that the first amendment protects a broad realm of nonviolent, noncoercive activity. Professor Emerson finds first amendment freedom essential for four values. However, it is informative to see that the first value, self-fulfillment, and the third, participation in change, are key values. To justify legal obligation, the community must respect individuals as equal, rational and autonomous moral beings. Respecting people's autonomy as well as people's equal worth requires that people be allowed an equal right to participate in the process of group decision making—which is precisely Emerson's other key value, participation in collective decision making. Either all people have a right to participate in the individual and social processes of *self*-determination or a "better" individual and collective expression of humanity results from this social process because of the increased opportunity of each to freely participate. Either ground justifies protecting people's liberty to engage in substantively valued conduct.

Robert H. Bork, *Neutral Principles and Some First Amendment Problems*

47 Ind. L.J. 1 (1971)[3]

Constitutional protection should be accorded only to speech that is explicitly political. There is no basis for judicial intervention to protect any other form of expression, be it scientific, literary or that variety of expression we call obscene or pornographic. Moreover, within that category of speech we ordinarily call political, there should be no constitutional obstruction to laws making criminal any speech that advocates forcible overthrow of the government or the violation of any law. The men who adopted the first amendment did not display a strong libertarian stance with respect to speech. In colonial times and during and after the Revolution they displayed a determination to punish speech thought dangerous to government, much of it expression that we should think harmless and well within the bounds of legitimate discourse.

The first amendment indicates that there is something special about speech. The entire structure of the Constitution creates a representative democracy, a form of government that would be meaningless without freedom to discuss government and its policies. Freedom for political speech could and should be inferred even if there were no first amendment.

The first two proffered benefits of speech—development of individual faculties and the achievement of pleasure—are found, for both speaker and hearer, in all varieties of speech, from political discourse to shop talk or salacious literature. These benefits do not distinguish speech from any other human activity. An individual may develop his or her faculties or derive pleasure from trading on the stock market, working as a barmaid, engaging in sexual activity, playing tennis, or in any of thousands of endeavors. Speech with only the first two benefits can be preferred to other activities only by ranking forms of personal gratification. These functions or benefits of speech are, therefore, to the principled judge, indistinguishable from the functions or benefits of all other human activity. A judge cannot, on neutral grounds, choose to protect speech that has only these functions more than he or she protects any other claimed freedom. The third benefit of speech the safety valve function raises only issues of expediency or prudence, and, therefore, raises issues to be determined solely by the legislature or, in some cases, by the executive. The legislature may decide not to repress speech advocating the forcible overthrow of the government because it thinks repression would cause more trouble than it would prevent. The category of protected speech should consist of speech concerned with governmental behavior, policy or personnel, whether the government unit involved is executive, legislative, judicial or administrative. The line drawn must lie between the explicitly political and all else.

Alexander Meiklejohn, *The First Amendment as an Absolute*

1961 Sup. Ct. Rev. 245[4]

The First Amendment does not protect a "freedom to speak." It protects the freedom of these activities of thought and communication by which we "govern." It is concerned, not with a private right, but with a public power, a governmental responsibility. But voting is merely the external expression of a wide and diverse number of activities by means of which citizens attempt to meet the responsibilities of making judgments, which that freedom to govern lays upon them. That freedom implies and requires what we call "the dignity of the individual." Self-government can exist only insofar as the voters acquire the intelligence, integrity, sensitivity, and generous devotion to the general welfare that, in theory, casting a ballot is assumed to express.

There are many forms of thought and expression within the range of human communications from which the voter derives the knowledge, intelligence, sensitivity to human values; the capacity for sane and objective judgment which, so far as possible, a ballot should express. I list four of them below.

1. Education is the attempt to so inform and cultivate the mind and will of a citizen that each person shall have the wisdom, the independence, and, therefore, the dignity of a governing citizen. Freedom of education is, thus, as we all recognize, a basic postulate in the planning of a free society.
2. The achievements of philosophy and the sciences in creating knowledge and understanding of ourselves and our world must be made available, without abridgement, to every citizen.
3. Literature and the arts must be protected by the First Amendment. They lead the way toward sensitive and informed appreciation and response to the values out of which the riches of the general welfare are created.
4. Public discussions of public issues, together with the spreading of information and opinion bearing on those issues, must have a freedom unabridged by our agents. Over our governing, they have no power. Over their governing we have sovereign power.

Literature and the arts are protected because they have a "social importance" which I have called a "governing" importance. The novel is a powerful determinative of our views of what human beings are, how they can be influenced, in which directions they should be influenced by many forces, including, especially,

4. Reprinted by permission.

their own judgments and appreciations. Shall the government establish a censorship to distinguish between "good" novels and "bad" ones? The First Amendment seems to answer that question with an unequivocal "no." The authority of citizens to decide what they shall write, and, more fundamental, what they shall read and see, has not been delegated to any of the subordinate branches of government. It is "reserved to the people," each deciding to whom each will listen, whom each will read, what portrayal of the human scene each finds worthy of his attention.

Questions

1. *Evaluating the Justifications for Protecting Speech.* Do you accept the four justifications for protecting speech (marketplace of ideas, safety valve, self-fulfillment, and democratic process)? If one accepts the idea of self-fulfillment as a justification for protecting speech, is there *any* speech that does not deserve protection? Under that justification, does speech protection become subjective and individualistic in that any speech that an individual deems to be "self-fulfilling" is necessarily worthy of protection?

2. *Weighing and Balancing the Justifications.* Are some of the justifications for protecting speech more compelling than others? For example, should we ascribe more importance to speech related to the democratic process than to speech that promotes self-fulfillment?

3. *Artificial Intelligence, Robotic Speech, and the First Amendment.* With the rise of so-called "bots," which are controlled by artificial intelligence rather than by humans, questions have arisen regarding whether robotic speech should be protected under the First Amendment. Some note that there are now 100 million online bots which can produce messages that recipients perceive as human generated. Can bots be viewed as simply a free speech outlet for their human creators? Should it matter whether the speech is a direct reflection of the human's thoughts or has been altered by the bot? Should a bot be required to disclose that it is not human?

❧ PROBLEMS: MORE ON THE INTERNATIONAL TREATY REGULATING THE INTERNET ❧

1. *Can There Be Agreement Regarding the Justifications for Protecting Speech?* Should the new treaty reflect one of the justifications for protecting speech presented in the articles above? A multitude of countries will be in attendance at the conference, and it is likely that they will have very different governmental systems (e.g., some democratic, some not). In addition, they are likely to hold very different views regarding the value of speech and its place in society. Are there certain fundamental ideas about the importance of speech, and the justifications

for protecting speech, that all countries might be able to agree on? If so, what are they?

2. *The Justifications for and Shape of the Treaty.* As you prepare to attend the convention, think about which underlying values help shape your views regarding whether particular types of speech should (or should not) be protected. For example, with regard to sexual speech (some of which may be obscene and some not obscene), which justifications make you more or less likely to argue that it deserves protection (e.g., self-fulfillment, safety valve, marketplace of ideas, or democratic process theory)? Could hardcore sexual speech contain political ideas?

B. CATEGORIES OF SPEECH

The Court has never regarded the right to freedom of expression as absolute. In *Chaplinsky v. New Hampshire*, 315 U.S. 568 (1942), a unanimous Court flatly stated that there are "certain well-defined and narrowly limited *classes* of speech, the prevention and punishment of which have never been thought to raise any Constitutional problem." *Chaplinsky* included within these classes "the lewd and obscene, the profane, the libelous, and the insulting or 'fighting' words." In this section, we examine the Court's handling of various "excluded" categories of speech.

1. Advocacy of Illegal Action

In applying the First Amendment, there has been much debate about whether the First Amendment protects those who advocate illegal action. Undoubtedly, certain types of speech (e.g., solicitation to commit murder) can and should be criminalized. However, in many instances, advocacy of illegal action involves nothing more than criticism of government, and therefore criminalization raises the specter of seditious libel.

a. Early Cases

Early seditious libel cases arose during World War I. There was significant opposition to U.S. entry into the war, including calls to resist or obstruct recruitment and enlistment in the U.S. armed forces. The situation was aggravated by the collapse of the Russian monarchy and the emergence of the Bolshevik regime. These events led to a "Red Scare"—a fear that Communism would sweep the world.

Schenck v. United States

249 U.S. 47 (1919)

Mr. Justice HOLMES delivered the opinion of the Court.

This is an indictment in three counts. The first charges a conspiracy to violate the Espionage Act of June 15, 1917, §3, by causing and attempting to cause insubordination, &c., in the military and naval forces of the United States, and to obstruct the recruiting and enlistment service of the United States, when the United States was at war with the German Empire, to-wit, that the defendant wilfully conspired to have printed and circulated to men who had been called and accepted for military service under the Act of May 18, 1917, a document set forth and alleged to be calculated to cause such insubordination and obstruction. The count alleges overt acts in pursuance of the conspiracy, ending in the distribution of the document. Defendants were also charged with using the U.S. mail to transmit the documents. The defendants were found guilty on all the counts. They set up the First Amendment to the Constitution forbidding Congress to make any law abridging the freedom of speech, or of the press as a defense.

The document in question recited the first section of the Thirteenth Amendment, said that the idea embodied in it was violated by the Conscription Act and that a conscript is little better than a convict. In impassioned language it intimated that conscription was despotism in its worst form and a monstrous wrong against humanity in the interest of Wall Street's chosen few. It said, "Do not submit to intimidation," but in form at least confined itself to peaceful measures such as a petition for the repeal of the act. The other side of the sheet was headed "Assert Your Rights." It stated reasons for alleging that any one violated the Constitution when he refused to recognize "your right to assert your opposition to the draft," and went on "If you do not assert and support your rights, you are helping to deny or disparage rights which it is the solemn duty of all citizens and residents of the United States to retain." It described the arguments on the other side as coming from cunning politicians and a mercenary capitalist press, and even silent consent to the conscription law as helping to support an infamous conspiracy. It denied the power to send our citizens away to foreign shores to shoot up the people of other lands, and added that words could not express the condemnation such cold-blooded ruthlessness deserves, and winding up, "You must do your share to maintain, support and uphold the rights of the people of this country." Of course the document would not have been sent unless it had been intended to have some effect, and we do not see what effect it could be expected to have upon persons subject to the draft except to influence them to obstruct the carrying of it out. The defendants do not deny that the jury might find against them on this point.

But it is said that the circular is protected by the First Amendment to the Constitution. In many places and in ordinary times the defendants in saying all that was said in the circular would have been within their constitutional rights. But the character of every act depends upon the circumstances in which it is done. The most stringent protection of free speech would not protect a man in falsely shouting fire in a theatre and causing a panic. The question is whether the words used are used in such circumstances and are of such a nature as to create a clear and present danger that they will bring about the substantive evils that Congress has a right to prevent. It is a question of proximity and degree. When a nation is at war many things that might be said in time of peace are such a hindrance to its effort that their utterance will not be endured so long as men fight and that no Court could regard them as protected by any constitutional right. If an actual obstruction of the recruiting service were proved, liability for words that produced that effect might be enforced. The statute of 1917 punishes conspiracies to obstruct as well as actual obstruction. If the act, (speaking, or circulating a paper,) its tendency and the intent with which it is done are the same, we perceive no ground for saying that success alone warrants making the act a crime.

Judgments affirmed.

Notes: *Early Subversive Advocacy Prosecutions*

1. *Pro-Germany Editorials. Frohwerk v. United States*, 249 U.S. 204 (1919), involved a charge of conspiracy to obstruct the draft under the Espionage Act. Defendants, Frohwerk and his employer, Gleeser, who "prepared and published the *Missouri Staats Zeitung*," were convicted and sentenced to prison. The conviction was based on articles condemning the illegal use of troops in support of Britain, praising the "unconquerable spirit and undiminished strength of the German nation," blaming the war on Wall Street, and giving "a picture of the sufferings of a drafted man, of his then recognizing that his country is not in danger and that he is being sent to a foreign land to fight in a cause that neither he nor anyone else knows anything of, and reaching the conviction that this is but a war to protect some rich men's money." The article argued that "we are led and ruled by England, that our sons, our taxes and our sacrifices are only in the interest of England," and that "the Central powers are carrying on a defensive war." Justice Holmes reasoned as follows in affirming the conviction:

> The First Amendment while prohibiting legislation against free speech cannot have been, and obviously was not, intended to give immunity for every possible use of language. Neither Hamilton nor Madison ever supposed that to make criminal the counseling of a murder within the jurisdiction of Congress would be an unconstitutional interference with free speech. We do not lose our right to condemn either measures or men because the country is at war. It does not appear that there was any special effort to reach men who were subject to the draft; and if the evidence should show that the defendant was a poor man, turning out copy for Gleeser, his employer, at less than a day laborer's pay, for Gleeser to use or reject as he saw fit, in a newspaper of small circulation, there would be a natural inclination to test every question of law very thoroughly before upholding the very severe penalty imposed. But, on the record, it is impossible to say that it might not have been found that the circulation of the paper was in quarters where a little breath would be enough to kindle a flame and that the fact was known and relied upon by those who sent the paper out. Small compensation would not exonerate the defendant if it were found that he expected the result, even if pay were his chief desire.

2. *The Presidential Campaign Speech. Debs v. United States,* 249 U.S. 211 (1919), involved a U.S. presidential candidate, Eugene Debs, who was charged with violating the Espionage Act by attempting to obstruct the draft and incite insubordination in the military forces. The charges were based on a speech that Debs gave in Canton, Ohio, in 1918 (during World War I), as part of his campaign for the presidency as the Socialist Party candidate. The speech discussed Socialism, its growth, and a prophecy of its ultimate success. During the speech, Debs claimed that he had visited "loyal comrades" who had been convicted of aiding and abetting another person in failing to register for the draft, that the men were "paying the penalty for standing erect and for seeking to pave the way to better conditions for all mankind," and that the master class "has always declared the war and the subject class has always fought the battles—that the subject class has had nothing to gain and all to lose, including their lives; that the working class, who furnish the corpses, have never yet had a voice in declaring war and never yet had a voice in declaring peace." He also referred to the conviction of a woman for attempting to cause insubordination and refusal of duty in the military forces, and stated that "she went out to render her service to the cause in this day of crises, and they sent her to the penitentiary for ten years." He then forecast the success of the international Socialist crusade and stated, "You need to know that you are fit for something better than slavery and cannon fodder," and "Don't worry about the charge of treason to your masters; but be concerned about the treason that involves yourselves." In reference to a charge that he had obstructed the war, he said, "I have been accused of obstructing the war. I admit it. Gentlemen, I abhor war. I would oppose the war if I stood alone." Justice Holmes noted that about an hour before his speech, Debs had stated that he approved "in spirit and substance" of the Socialist Party platform (entitled the "Anti-War Proclamation and Program"), which declared: "We brand the declaration of war by our Governments as a crime against the people of the United States and against the nations of the world. In all modern history there has been no war more unjustifiable than the war in which we are about to engage." Its first recommendation was "continuous, active, and public opposition to the war, through demonstrations, mass petitions, and all other means within our power." In upholding Debs's conviction, Justice Holmes writing for the Court stated:

The jury was warranted in finding that one purpose of the campaign speech, whether incidental or not, was to oppose not only war in general but this war, and that the opposition was so expressed that its natural and intended effect would be to obstruct recruiting. If that was intended and if that would be its probable effect, it would not be protected by reason of its being part of a general program and expressions of a general and conscientious belief. Evidence that the defendant accepted the view expressed in the Party platform at the time that he made his speech is evidence that if in that speech he used words tending to obstruct the recruiting service he meant that they should have that effect. The jury were most carefully instructed that they could not find the defendant guilty for advocacy unless the words used had as their natural tendency and reasonably probable effect to obstruct the recruiting service, and unless the defendant had the specific intent to do so in his mind.

Holmes derived the "tendency and intent" test set forth in *Schenck* from criminal law conspiracy concepts in a traditional criminal law context removed from factual situations involving the expression of political protest.

∾ PROBLEMS ∾

1. *The Justifications for Protecting Speech.* Now consider the *Schenck* and *Debs* decisions in light of the justifications for according special status to speech. Which, if any, of the four justifications (self-fulfillment, safety valve, democratic process, marketplace of ideas) did their speech serve? Can you make an argument that their speech deserves constitutional protection?

2. *Incitement to Illegal Action.* How would *Schenck* apply to the examples below if defendant is charged with conspiracy to obstruct the draft or of advocating "the violent overthrow of government"? A) A group of college students opposed to World War I holds a "peace vigil" at which they "rally for peace" as well as against the war and the draft; B) A professor discusses the "moral imperative" that requires every "good and moral citizen" to oppose the war and the draft. Would it matter whether students actually resisted the draft? C) A student wears a jacket bearing the message "Fuck the Draft" to express his opposition to the war; D) On a remote piece of property, Ku Klux Klan members hold a rally at which they burn a cross, denounce public officials, and discuss the need to take "revenge" against members of certain minority groups and government officials; E) The *Courier-Journal,* a large daily newspaper in Louisville, Kentucky, publishes editorials and articles that are critical of the war and the draft and that discuss the "moral imperative" of all citizens to resist the draft.

3. *Expressing Opposition.* Under *Schenck, Frohwerk,* and *Debs,* how could a newspaper publisher, journalist, or politician have expressed opposition to the participation of the United States in World War I without risking conviction under the Espionage Act for conspiracy to obstruct the draft? What language would have been safe to use, expressed in what manner, and under what circumstances?

4. *More on the International Treaty Regulating the Internet.* Suppose that the European delegates to the convention would like to add language to the treaty that tracks the European Convention on Human Rights, and in particular Article 10, Section 2, of that convention, provides: "The exercise of these freedoms, since it carries with it duties and responsibilities, may be subject to such formalities, conditions, restrictions or penalties as are prescribed by law and are necessary in a democratic society, in the interests of national security, territorial integrity or public safety, for the prevention of disorder or crime, for the protection of health or morals, for the protection of the reputation or the rights of others, for preventing the disclosure of information received in confidence, or for maintaining the authority and impartiality of the judiciary." In light of the cases that you have

read thus far, and consistently with the First Amendment, can you agree to add such language to the treaty?

b. Justice Holmes's *Abrams* Dissent

Justice Holmes challenged the Court's approach to subversive advocacy in *Abrams v. United States*, 250 U.S. 616 (1919), when he dissented from the Court's affirmance of convictions of self-described Russian-born "anarchists" and "socialists" who distributed 5,000 circulars. Some of the circulars were thrown from the window of a building while others were distributed secretly in New York. The Espionage Act amendments of 1918 made it a crime to conspire, during the war with Germany, to publish "disloyal, scurrilous and abusive language about the form of government," or language "intended to bring the form of government" into "contempt, scorn, contumely and disrepute," or language "intended to incite, provoke and encourage resistance" to the United States in the war. The fourth crime encompassed those who would "urge, incite and advocate curtailment of production of things," like ordnance and ammunition, "necessary and essential to the prosecution of the war."

Defendants were charged with all four crimes based on two circulars. The first circular was entitled "The Hypocrisy of the United States and Her Allies." After denouncing President Wilson as "a hypocrite and a coward," it went on to state: "the President's shameful, cowardly silence about the intervention in Russia reveals the hypocrisy of the plutocratic gang in Washington and vicinity. He the President is too much of a coward to come out openly and say: We capitalistic nations cannot afford to have a proletarian republic in Russia. The Russian Revolution cries: Workers of the World!; Awake!; Rise!; Put down your enemy and mine!; Yes friends, there is only one enemy of the workers of the world and that is CAPITALISM." The circular concluded, "Awake!; Awake, you Workers of the World!; REVOLUTIONISTS."

The second circular was entitled "Workers—Wake Up." After referring to "his Majesty, Mr. Wilson, and the rest of the gang, dogs of all colors!"; it continued: "Workers, Russian emigrants, you who had the least belief in the honesty of *our* government must now throw away all confidence, must spit in the face of the false, hypocritic, military propaganda which has fooled you so relentlessly, calling forth your sympathy, your help, to the prosecution of the war. With the money which you have loaned, or are going to loan them, they will make bullets not only for the Germans, but also for the Workers Soviets of Russia. *Workers in the ammunition factories, you are producing bullets, bayonets, cannon, to murder not only the Germans, but also your dearest, best, who are in Russia and are fighting for freedom.* America and her Allies have betrayed the Workers. Their robberish aims are clear to all men. The destruction of the Russian Revolution, that is the politics of the march to Russia. *Workers, our reply to the barbaric intervention has to be a general strike!; An open challenge* only will let the government know that not only the Russian Worker fights for freedom, but also *here in America lives the spirit of Revolution.* Do not let the government scare you with their wild punishment in prisons, hanging and shooting. We must not and will not betray the splendid fighters of Russia. *Workers, up to fight.* Woe unto those who will be in the way of progress. Let solidarity live!" It was signed "The Rebels."

The majority opinion interpreted the language of the circular as appealing to workers to topple the U.S. government by force, and as seeking to persuade readers "to cease to render assistance to the government" in the war effort. "Even if their primary purpose was to aid the cause of the Russian Revolution, their plan of action necessarily involved defeat of the war program of the United States." The "obvious effect" of this appeal would be to persuade people "not to aid government loans and not to work in ammunition factories." Furthermore, the purpose was to defeat the war plans "by bringing upon the country the paralysis of a general strike," "to throw the country into a state of revolution, and to thereby frustrate" the war effort. Justice Holmes responded with the following dissent.

Abrams v. United States

250 U.S. 616 (1919)

Mr. Justice HOLMES, *dissenting.*

This indictment is founded upon the publication of two leaflets. The third count alleges a conspiracy to encourage resistance to the United States in the war against Germany and to attempt to effectuate the purpose by publishing the same leaflets. The fourth count lays a conspiracy to incite curtailment of production of things necessary to the prosecution of the war and to attempt to accomplish it by publishing the second leaflet.

Focusing on the fourth count, it seems too plain to be denied that the suggestion to workers in the ammunition factories that they are producing bullets to murder their dearest, and the further advocacy of a general strike, both in the second leaflet, do urge curtailment of production of things necessary to the prosecution of the war within the meaning of the Act. But to make the conduct criminal that statute requires that it should be "with intent by such curtailment to cripple or hinder the United States in the prosecution of the war." It seems to me that no such intent is proved. A deed is not done with intent to produce a consequence unless that consequence is the aim of the deed.

This statute must be taken to use its words in a strict and accurate sense. A patriot might think that we were wasting money on aeroplanes, or making more cannon of a certain kind than we needed, and might advocate curtailment with success, yet even if it turned out that the curtailment hindered and was thought by other minds to have been obviously likely to hinder the United States in the prosecution of the war, no one would hold such conduct a crime.

I never have seen any reason to doubt that *Schenck, Frohwerk,* and *Debs,* were rightly decided. The United States constitutionally may punish speech that produces or is intended to produce a clear and imminent danger that it will bring about forthwith certain substantive evils that the United States constitutionally may seek to prevent. The power undoubtedly is greater in time of war than in time of peace because war opens dangers that do not exist at other times.

As against dangers peculiar to war, it is only the present danger of immediate evil or an intent to bring it about that warrants Congress in setting a limit to the expression of opinion where private rights are not concerned. Congress certainly cannot forbid all effort to change the mind of the country. Nobody can suppose that the surreptitious publishing of a silly leaflet by an unknown man, without more, would present any immediate danger that its opinions would hinder the success of the government arms or have any appreciable tendency to do so. Publishing those opinions for the very purpose of obstructing, however, might indicate a greater danger and at any rate would have the quality of an attempt. So I assume that the second leaflet if published for the purposes alleged in the fourth count might be punishable.

I do not see how anyone can find the intent required by the statute in any of the defendant's words. The second leaflet is the only one that affords even a foundation for the charge. Without invoking the hatred of German militarism expressed in the former one, it is evident that the only object of the paper is to help Russia and stop American intervention there—not to impede the United States in the war that it was carrying on.

Sentences of twenty years imprisonment have been imposed for the publishing of two leaflets that defendants had as much right to publish as the Government has to publish the Constitution of the United States now vainly invoked by them. Even if I am wrong, the most nominal punishment seems to me all that possibly could be inflicted, unless defendants are to be made to suffer for the creed that they avow.

Persecution for the expression of opinions seems to me perfectly logical. If you have no doubt of your premises or your power and want a certain result with all your heart you naturally express your wishes in law and sweep away all opposition. To allow opposition by speech seems to indicate that you think the speech impotent, as when a man says that he has squared the circle, or that you do not care whole-heartedly for the result, or that you doubt either your power or your premises. But when men have realized that time has upset many fighting faiths, they may come to believe even more than they believe the very foundations of their own conduct that the ultimate good desired is better reached by free trade in ideas—that the best test of truth is the power of the thought to get itself accepted in the competition of the market, and that truth is the only ground upon which their wishes safely can be carried out. That at any rate is the theory of our Constitution. It is an experiment, as all life is an experiment. Every year if not every day we wager our salvation upon some prophecy based upon imperfect knowledge. We should be eternally vigilant against attempts to check the expression of opinions that we loathe unless they so imminently threaten immediate interference with the lawful and pressing purposes of the law that an immediate check is required to save the country. I wholly disagree with the argument that the First Amendment left the common law as to seditious libel in force. History seems to me against the notion. Only the emergency that makes it immediately dangerous to leave the correction of evil counsels to time warrants making any exception to the sweeping command, "Congress shall make no law abridging the freedom of speech." I am speaking only of expressions of opinion and exhortations, which were all that were uttered here, but in their conviction upon this indictment the defendants were deprived of their rights under the Constitution of the United States.

Notes and Questions

1. *"Acts" Versus "Utterances."* The Espionage Act of 1917 punished only "acts" such as "obstruction" or "insubordination," rather than the advocacy of ideas. However, amendments to the Act created various "speech" crimes for which the *Abrams* defendants were convicted. In the *Schenck* era, the "clear and present danger" test was applied to both conduct crimes and speech crimes, and was used to express the legislature's inherent power to punish speech that caused harm. In cases involving the First Amendment, Justice Holmes assumed that the judiciary should engage in its traditional oversight function, examining the record to detrermine whether it contained sufficient evidence of the elements of the crime. Courts created "sufficiency of the evidence" formulas that could be either demanding or deferential, depending on the crime and on the court's judgment regarding the need to control prosecutorial discretion and provide guidance to juries. The "clear and present danger" test began as such a formula, and it possessed the inherent flexibility to be used for either affirming convictions based on ready assumptions about an antiwar speaker's dangerousness or for creating safeguards for speakers in the form of stringent proof requirements concerning the "clarity" (or likelihood) and "imminence" of a dangerous act of lawlessness. The Court relied on the test in the Espionage Act cases, involving state criminal syndicalism statutes and federal Smith Act prosecutions, both of which primarily involved criminalization of Communist or Socialist Party advocacy. After *Abrams*, Justices Holmes and Brandeis continued to dissent from the Court's application of the "clear and present danger" test, and to articulate the policy reasons for creating broad First Amendment defenses to criminal prosecutions of antigovernment speakers and writers.

2. *The Holmes Dissent and Prior Precedent.* Can you reconcile Justice Holmes's *Abrams* dissent with his willingness to uphold convictions in *Schenck, Frohwerk,* and *Debs?*

3. *Incitement Reprise.* How would Justice Holmes's *Abrams* dissent apply to the scenarios in Problem 2 following the *Schenck* opinion?

∾ PROBLEMS ∾

1. *Newspaper Reprise.* How could a newspaper publisher, journalist, or politician have expressed opposition to U.S. participation in World War I without risking conviction under the Espionage Act for conspiracy to obstruct the draft under Justice Holmes's *Abrams* dissent? During war time, what language would have been safe to use, expressed in what manner, and under what circumstances?

2. *More on the International Treaty Regulating the Internet.* If Justice Holmes's *Abrams* dissent were treated as "law" (in the sense that the Court adopted it as the prevailing test), what would be your position on whether the United States can accept the European request to include the proposed language from the European Convention on Human Rights in the treaty on the internet?

c. The Criminal Syndicalism Cases of the 1920s

Gitlow and *Whitney* are the most famous decisions from the "Red Scare" era, and *Gitlow* is especially noteworthy because the Court announced that "we may and do assume that freedom of speech and of the press—which are protected by the First Amendment from abridgment by Congress—are among the fundamental personal rights and 'liberties' protected by the due process clause of the Fourteenth Amendment from impairment by the States."

Gitlow v. New York

268 U.S. 652 (1925)

Mr. Justice SANFORD delivered the opinion of the Court.

Benjamin Gitlow was convicted of criminal anarchy. The contention is that the statute is repugnant to the due process clause of the Fourteenth Amendment. Its material provisions are:

> §160. *Criminal anarchy defined.* Criminal anarchy is the doctrine that organized government should be overthrown by force or violence, or by assassination of the executive head or of any of the executive officials of government, or by any unlawful means. The advocacy of such doctrine either by word of mouth or writing is a felony.
>
> §161. *Advocacy of criminal anarchy.* Any person who:
>
> 1. By word of mouth or writing advocates, advises or teaches the duty, necessity or propriety of overthrowing or overturning organized government by force or violence, or by assassination of the executive head or of any of the executive officials of government, or by any unlawful means; or,
>
> 2. Prints, publishes, edits, issues or knowingly circulates, sells, distributes or publicly displays any book, paper, document, or written or printed matter in any form, containing or advocating, advising or teaching the doctrine that organized government should be overthrown by force, violence or any unlawful means 'Is guilty of a felony and punishable' by imprisonment or fine, or both.

The indictment was in two counts. The first charged that the defendant had advocated, advised and taught the duty, necessity and propriety of overthrowing and overturning organized government by force, violence and unlawful means, by certain writings therein set forth entitled "The Left Wing Manifesto"; the second that he had printed, published and knowingly circulated and distributed a certain paper called "The Revolutionary Age," containing the writings set forth in the first count.

The statute does not penalize the utterance or publication of abstract "doctrine" or academic discussion having no quality of incitement to any concrete action. It is not aimed against mere historical or philosophical essays. It does not restrain the advocacy of changes in the form of government by constitutional and lawful means. What it prohibits is language advocating, advising or teaching the overthrow of organized government by unlawful means. These words imply urging to action. It is not the abstract "doctrine" of overthrowing organized government by unlawful means which is denounced by the statute, but the advocacy of action for the accomplishment of that purpose.

The Manifesto is neither the statement of abstract doctrine nor mere prediction that industrial disturbances and revolutionary mass strikes will result spontaneously in an inevitable process of evolution in the economic system. It advocates and urges in fervent language mass action which shall progressively foment industrial disturbances and through political mass strikes and revolutionary mass action overthrow and destroy organized parliamentary government. It concludes with a call to action: "The proletariat revolution and the Communist reconstruction of society—*the struggle for these*—is now indispensable. The Communist International calls the proletariat of the world to the final struggle!" This is not the expression of philosophical abstraction, the mere prediction of future events; it is the language of direct incitement.

The means advocated for bringing about the destruction of organized parliamentary government, namely, mass industrial revolts usurping the functions of municipal government, political mass strikes directed against the parliamentary state, and revolutionary mass action for its final destruction, necessarily imply the use of force and violence, and in their essential nature are inherently unlawful in a constitutional government of law and order. That the jury were warranted in finding that the Manifesto advocated not merely the abstract doctrine of overthrowing organized government by force, violence and unlawful means, but action to that end, is clear.

We assume that freedom of speech and of the press—which are protected by the First Amendment from abridgment by Congress—are among the fundamental personal rights and "liberties" protected by the due process clause of the Fourteenth Amendment from impairment by the States. By enacting the present statute the State has determined, through its legislative body, that utterances advocating the overthrow of organized government by force, violence and unlawful means, are so inimical to the general welfare and involve such danger of substantive evil that they may be penalized in the exercise of its police power. That determination must be given great weight. Such utterances, by their very nature, involve danger to the public peace and to the security of the State. They threaten breaches of the peace and ultimate revolution. The immediate danger is none the less real and substantial, because the effect of a given utterance cannot be accurately foreseen. A single revolutionary spark may kindle a fire that, smouldering for a time, may burst into a sweeping and destructive conflagration. The State cannot reasonably be required to defer the adoption of measures for its own peace and safety until the revolutionary utterances lead to actual disturbances of the public peace or imminent and immediate danger of its own destruction; but it may, in the exercise of its judgment, suppress the threatened danger in its incipiency.

We cannot hold that the present statute is an arbitrary or unreasonable exercise of the police power of the State unwarrantably infringing the freedom of speech or press. This being so it may be applied to every utterance—not too trivial to be beneath the notice of the law—which is of such a character and used with such intent and purpose as to bring it within the prohibition of the statute. When the legislative body has determined generally, in the constitutional exercise of its discretion, that utterances of a certain kind involve such danger of substantive evil that they may be punished, the question whether any specific utterance coming within the prohibited class is likely, in and of itself, to bring about the substantive evil, is not open to consideration. It is sufficient that the statute itself be constitutional and that the use of the language comes within its prohibition.

The provisions of the statute may be constitutionally applied to the specific utterance of the defendant if its natural tendency and probable effect was to bring about the substantive evil which the legislative body might prevent. The general statement in *Schenck* that the "question in every case is whether the words used are used in such circumstances and are of such a nature as to create a clear and present danger that they will bring about the substantive evils"—upon which great reliance is placed in the defendant's argument—was manifestly intended, as shown by the context, to apply only in cases of this class, and has no application to those like the present, where the legislative body itself has previously determined the danger of substantive evil arising from utterances of a specified character.

None of these convictions involved any invasion of the constitutional rights of the defendant. It was not necessary, within the meaning of the statute, that the defendant should have advocated "some definite or immediate act or acts" of force, violence or unlawfulness. It was sufficient if such acts were advocated in general terms; and it was not essential that their immediate execution should have been advocated. Nor was it necessary that the language should have been "reasonably and ordinarily calculated to incite certain persons" to acts of force, violence or unlawfulness. The advocacy need not be addressed to specific persons.

Affirmed.

Mr. Justice HOLMES, *dissenting.*

Mr. Justice Brandeis and I are of opinion that this judgment should be reversed. The principle of free speech is included in the Fourteenth Amendment.

It is said that this manifesto was more than a theory, that it was an incitement. Every idea is an incitement. It offers itself for belief and if believed it is acted on unless some other belief outweighs it or some failure of energy stifles the movement at its birth. The only difference between the expression of an opinion and an incitement in the narrower sense is the speaker's enthusiasm for the result. Eloquence may set fire to reason. Whatever may be thought of the redundant discourse before us it had no chance of starting a present conflagration. If in the long run the beliefs expressed in proletarian dictatorship are destined to be accepted by the dominant forces of the community, the only meaning of free speech is that they should be given their chance. If this document had been an attempt to induce an uprising against government at once and not at some indefinite time in the future it would have presented a different question. The object would have been one with which the law might deal, subject to the doubt whether there was any danger that the publication could produce any result, or in other words, whether it was not futile and too remote from possible consequences. But the indictment alleges the publication and nothing more.

Whitney v. California

274 U.S. 357 (1927)

Mr. Justice SANFORD delivered the opinion of the Court.

California law defined *criminal syndicalism* as "any doctrine or precept advocating, teaching or aiding and abetting the commission of crime, sabotage (defined as willful and malicious physical damage or injury to physical property), or unlawful acts of force and violence or unlawful methods of terrorism as a means of accomplishing a change in industrial ownership or control or effecting any political change." Anita Whitney was convicted based on proof that she "did organize and assist in organizing, and was, is, and knowingly became a member of an organization, society, group and assemblage of persons organized and assembled to advocate, teach, aid and abet criminal syndicalism."

Defendant had been a member of the Oakland branch of the Socialist Party. This Local sent delegates to the national convention of the Socialist Party in Chicago in 1919, which resulted in a split between the "radical" group and the old-wing Socialists. The "radicals" — to whom the Oakland delegates adhered — being ejected, went to another hall, and formed the Communist Labor Party of America. In its "Platform and Program" the Party declared that its purpose was "to create a unified revolutionary working class movement in America," organizing the workers as a class, in a revolutionary class struggle to conquer the capitalist state, for the overthrow of capitalist rule, the conquest of political power and the establishment of a working class government, the Dictatorship of the Proletariat. Shortly thereafter the Local Oakland withdrew from the Socialist Party, and sent accredited delegates, including the defendant, to a convention held in Oakland in November 1919, for the purpose of organizing a California branch of the Communist Labor Party. Defendant, after taking a temporary membership in the Communist

Labor Party, attended this convention as a delegate and took an active part in its proceedings.

While it is not denied that defendant became a member of and assisted in organizing the Communist Labor Party of California, and that this was organized to advocate, teach, aid or abet criminal syndicalism as defined by the Act, it is urged that the Act, as construed and applied, deprived defendant of her liberty without due process of law in that it has made her action in attending the Oakland convention unlawful by reason of "a subsequent event brought about against her will, by the agency of others," with no showing of a specific intent on her part to join in the forbidden purpose of the association, and merely because, by reason of a lack of "prophetic" understanding, she failed to foresee the quality that others would give to the convention. This contention is nothing more than an effort to review the weight of the evidence. This question is foreclosed by the verdict of the jury, involving as it does no constitutional question whatever.

Nor is the Syndicalism Act as applied in this case repugnant to the due process clause as a restraint of the rights of free speech, assembly, and association. By enacting the Syndicalism Act the State has declared, through its legislative body, that to knowingly be or become a member of or assist in organizing an association to advocate, teach or aid and abet the commission of crimes or unlawful acts of force, violence or terrorism as a means of accomplishing industrial or political changes, involves such danger to the public peace and the security of the State, that these acts should be penalized in the exercise of its police power. That determination must be given great weight. The statute may not be declared unconstitutional unless it is an arbitrary or unreasonable attempt to exercise the authority vested in the State in the public interest.

The essence of the offense denounced by the Act is the combining with others in an association for the accomplishment of the desired ends through the advocacy and use of criminal and unlawful methods. It partakes of the nature of a criminal conspiracy. That such united and joint action involves even greater danger to the public peace and security than the isolated utterances and acts of individuals, is clear. We cannot hold that the Act is an unreasonable or arbitrary exercise of the police power of the State, unwarrantably infringing any right of free speech, assembly or association, or that those persons are protected from punishment by the due process clause who abuse such rights by joining and furthering an organization thus menacing the peace and welfare of the State.

Affirmed.

Mr. Justice BRANDEIS, *concurring.*

Although the rights of free speech and assembly are fundamental, they are not absolute. Their exercise is subject to restriction, if the particular restriction is required in order to protect the state from destruction or from serious injury, political, economic or moral. That the necessity which is essential to a valid restriction does not exist unless speech would produce, or is intended to produce, a clear and imminent danger of some substantive evil which the State constitutionally may seek to prevent has been settled.

Those who won our independence believed that in its government the deliberative forces should prevail over the arbitrary. Believing in the power of reason as applied through public discussion, they eschewed silence coerced by law—the argument of force in its worst form. Recognizing the occasional tyrannies of governing majorities, they amended the Constitution so that free speech and assembly should be guaranteed.

Fear of serious injury cannot alone justify suppression of free speech and assembly. It is the function of speech to free men from the bondage of irrational fears. To justify suppression of free speech there must be reasonable ground to fear that serious evil will result if free speech is practiced. There must be reasonable ground to believe that the danger apprehended is imminent. There must be reasonable ground to believe that the evil to be prevented is a serious one. Every denunciation of existing law tends in some measure to increase the probability that there will be violation of it. Propagation of the criminal state of mind by teaching syndicalism increases it. Advocacy of law-breaking heightens it still further. But even advocacy of violation, however reprehensible morally, is not a justification for denying free speech where the advocacy falls short of incitement and there is nothing to indicate that the advocacy would be immediately acted on.

Those who won our independence by revolution did not fear political change. They did not exalt order at the cost of liberty. Even imminent danger cannot justify resort to prohibition of these functions essential to effective democracy, unless the evil apprehended is relatively serious. Prohibition of free speech and assembly is a measure so stringent that it would be inappropriate as the means for averting a relatively trivial harm to society. The fact that speech is likely to result in some violence or in destruction of property is not enough to justify its suppression. There must be the probability of serious injury to the State. Among free men, the deterrents ordinarily to be applied to prevent crime are education and punishment for violations of the law, not abridgment of the rights of free speech and assembly.

The Syndicalism Act satisfies the requirement of the constitution of the State concerning emergency legislation. But it must remain open to defendant to present the issue whether there actually did exist at the time a clear danger; whether the danger, if any, was imminent; and whether the evil apprehended was one so substantial as to justify the stringent restriction interposed by the legislature. The legislative declaration creates merely a rebuttable presumption that these conditions have been satisfied. I am unable to assent to the suggestion of the Court that assembling with a political party, formed to advocate the desirability of a proletarian revolution by mass action at some date necessarily far in the future, is not a right within the protection of the Fourteenth Amendment. In the present case, there was other testimony which tended to establish the existence of a conspiracy, on the part of members of the International Workers of the World, to commit present serious crimes; and that such a conspiracy would be furthered by the activity of the society of which Miss Whitney was a member. Under these circumstances the judgment of the state court cannot be disturbed.

∼ PROBLEMS ∼

1. *Applying* Whitney *and* Gitlow. How would *Whitney* and *Gitlow* apply to the following situations if the crime charged is advocacy of criminal syndicalism? A) A group of Marxist college students holds a rally on campus calling for a radical restructuring of the government and economy of the United States; B) In a philosophy class, a professor discusses Marxist theory, presents criticisms of the U.S. system, and concludes that the U.S. governmental and economic system is immoral; C) A student wears a jacket with the message "Communism Now" that contains Communist symbols, including an upraised fist, as a way of expressing his concerns about the U.S. governmental and economic system; D) On a remote piece of property, Ku Klux Klan members hold a rally at which they burn a cross, denounce public officials, and discuss the need to take "revenge" against members of certain minority groups; E) The *Glenview-Journal*, a large daily newspaper in Glenview Hills, Kentucky, publishes editorials and articles that are critical of the U.S. governmental and economic system and suggest a "moral imperative" to move toward a Marxist system.

2. *Applying* Whitney *and* Gitlow *to the International Treaty Regulating the Internet.* Do *Whitney* and *Gitlow* affect your conclusions about whether you can accept European demands to include language from the European Convention on Human Rights in the treaty regulating the internet?

d. "Clear and Present Danger" Cases from the McCarthy Era

Subversive advocacy cases reappeared before the Court in the 1950s in the so-called "Smith Act prosecutions."

Dennis v. United States

341 U.S. 494 (1951)

Mr. Chief Justice VINSON announced the judgment of the Court and an opinion in which Mr. Justice REED, Mr. Justice BURTON, and Mr. Justice MINTON join.

Petitioners were indicted in July, 1948, for violation of the conspiracy provisions of the Smith Act, during the period of April, 1945, to July, 1948 and found guilty. The Court of Appeals affirmed the convictions. We granted certiorari.

Sections 2 and 3 of the Smith Act provide as follows:

> Sec. 2. (a) It shall be unlawful for any person—
> (1) to knowingly or willfully advocate, abet, advise, or teach the duty, necessity, desirability, or propriety of overthrowing or destroying any government in the United States by force or violence, or by the assassination of any officer of any such government;
> (2) with intent to cause the overthrow or destruction of any government in the United States, to print, publish, edit, issue, circulate, sell, distribute, or publicly display any

written or printed matter advocating, advising, or teaching the duty, necessity, desirability, or propriety of overthrowing or destroying any government in the United States by force or violence;

(3) to organize or help to organize any society, group, or assembly of persons who teach, advocate, or encourage the overthrow or destruction of any government in the United States by force or violence; or to be or become a member of, or affiliate with, any such society, group, or assembly of persons, knowing the purposes thereof.

Sec. 3. It shall be unlawful for any person to attempt to commit, or to conspire to commit, any of the acts prohibited by the provisions of this title.

The indictment charged the petitioners with wilfully and knowingly conspiring (1) to organize as the Communist Party of the United States of America a society, group and assembly of persons who teach and advocate the overthrow and destruction of the Government of the United States by force and violence, and (2) knowingly and wilfully to advocate and teach the duty and necessity of overthrowing and destroying the Government of the United States by force and violence. The indictment further alleged that §2 of the Smith Act proscribes these acts and that any conspiracy to take such action is a violation of §3 of the Act.

The trial extended over nine months, six of which were devoted to the taking of evidence, resulting in a record of 16,000 pages. The Court of Appeals found that the Communist Party is a highly disciplined organization, adept at infiltration into strategic positions, use of aliases, and double-meaning language; that the Party is rigidly controlled; that Communists, unlike other political parties, tolerate no dissension from the policy laid down by the guiding forces, but that the approved program is slavishly followed by the members of the Party; that the literature of the Party and the statements and activities of its leaders, petitioners here, advocate, and the general goal of the Party was, to achieve a successful overthrow of the existing order by force and violence.

The purpose of the Smith Act is to protect Government, not from change by peaceable, lawful and constitutional means, but from change by violence, revolution and terrorism. That it is within the *power* of the Congress to protect the Government of the United States from armed rebellion is a proposition which requires little discussion. The question with which we are concerned is whether the *means* which it has employed conflict with the First and Fifth Amendments to the Constitution.

Gitlow made no distinction between a federal statute which made certain acts unlawful, the evidence to support the conviction being speech, and a statute which made speech itself the crime. *Whitney* repeated that even though the legislature had designated certain speech as criminal, this could not prevent the defendant from showing that there was no danger that the substantive evil would be brought about. Although no case subsequent to *Whitney* and *Gitlow* has expressly overruled the opinions in those cases, there is little doubt that subsequent opinions have inclined toward the Holmes-Brandeis rationale.

In this case we are squarely presented with the application of the "clear and present danger" test, and must decide what that phrase imports. Many cases in which this Court has reversed convictions have been based on the fact that the interest which the State was attempting to protect was too insubstantial to warrant restriction of speech. Overthrow of the Government by force and violence is certainly a substantial enough interest for the Government to limit speech. If, then, this interest may be protected, the literal problem which is presented is what has been meant by the use of the phrase "clear and present danger" of the utterances bringing about the evil within the power of Congress to punish.

The words cannot mean that before the Government may act, it must wait until the *putsch* is about to be executed, the plans have been laid and the signal is awaited. If Government is aware that a group aiming at its overthrow is attempting to indoctrinate its members and to commit them to a course whereby they will strike when the leaders feel the circumstances permit, action by the Government is required. An attempt to overthrow the Government by force, even though doomed from the outset because of inadequate numbers or power of the revolutionists, is a sufficient evil for Congress to prevent. The damage which such attempts create both physically and politically to a nation makes it impossible to measure the validity in terms of the probability of success, or the immediacy of a successful attempt. The trial judge charged the jury that they could not convict unless they found that petitioners intended to overthrow the Government "as speedily as circumstances would permit." This does not mean that they would not strike until there was certainty of success. What was meant was that the revolutionists would strike when they thought the time was ripe. We must therefore reject the contention that success or probability of success is the criterion.

The situation with which Justices Holmes and Brandeis were concerned in *Gitlow* was a comparatively isolated event, bearing little relation in their minds to any substantial threat to the safety of the community. The Court was not confronted with a situation comparable to the instant one—the development of an apparatus designed and dedicated to the overthrow of the Government, in the context of world crisis after crisis.

Chief Judge Learned Hand, writing for the majority below, interpreted the phrase as follows: "In each case courts must ask whether the gravity of the 'evil,' discounted by its improbability, justifies such invasion of free speech as is necessary to avoid the danger." We adopt this statement of the rule. It takes into consideration those factors which we deem relevant.

The requisite danger existed. The fact that from the period 1945 to 1948 petitioners' activities did not result in an attempt to overthrow the Government by force and violence is no answer to the fact that there was a group that was ready to make the attempt. The formation by petitioners of such a highly organized conspiracy, with rigidly disciplined members subject to call when the leaders felt that the time had come for action, coupled with the inflammable nature of world conditions, similar uprisings in other countries, and the touch-and-go nature of our relations with countries with whom petitioners were ideologically attuned, convince us that their convictions were justified. This analysis disposes of the contention that a conspiracy to advocate, as distinguished from the advocacy itself, cannot be constitutionally restrained, because it comprises only the preparation. It is the existence of the conspiracy which creates the danger. If the ingredients of the reaction are present, we cannot bind the Government to wait until the catalyst is added.

Defendants argue that a jury must decide a question of the application of the First Amendment. We do not agree. The doctrine that there must be a clear and present danger of a substantive evil that Congress has a right to prevent is a judicial rule to be applied as a matter of law by the courts.

We hold that §§2(a)(1), 2(a)(3) and 3 of the Smith Act do not inherently, or as construed or applied, violate the First Amendment and other provisions of the Bill of Rights. Petitioners intended to overthrow the Government of the United States as speedily as the circumstances would permit. Their conspiracy to organize the Communist Party and to teach and advocate the overthrow of the Government of the United States by force and violence created a "clear and present danger" of an attempt to overthrow the Government by force and violence. They were properly and constitutionally convicted for violation of the Smith Act.

The judgments of conviction are *affirmed.*

Mr. Justice FRANKFURTER, *concurring in affirmance of the judgment.*

Free-speech cases are not an exception to the principle that we are not legislators. Defendants have been convicted of conspiring to organize a party of persons who advocate the overthrow of the Government by force and violence. The jury found that the object of the conspiracy is advocacy as "a rule or principle of action," "by language reasonably and ordinarily calculated to incite persons to such action," and with the intent to cause the overthrow "as speedily as circumstances would permit." On any scale of values, speech of this sort ranks low.

Throughout our decisions there has recurred a distinction between the statement of an idea which may prompt its hearers to take unlawful action, and advocacy that such action be taken. Exposition of ideas readily merges into advocacy. That such a distinction could be used unreasonably by those in power against hostile or unorthodox views does not negate the fact that it may be used reasonably against an organization wielding the power of the centrally controlled international Communist movement. The object of the conspiracy before us is so clear that the chance of error in saying that the defendants conspired to advocate rather than to express ideas is slight. The conspiracy before us is not a conspiracy to overthrow the Government. But it would be equally wrong to treat it as a seminar in political theory.

On the one hand is the interest in security. The Communist Party rejects the basic premise of our political system — that change is to be brought about by nonviolent constitutional process. The evidence would justify a legislature in concluding that recruitment of additional members for the Party would create a substantial danger to national security. On the other hand is the interest in free speech. The right to exert all governmental powers in aid of maintaining our institutions and resisting their physical overthrow does not include intolerance of opinions and speech that cannot do harm although opposed and perhaps alien to dominant, traditional opinion. It is better for those who have almost unlimited power in their hands to err on the side of freedom. We have enjoyed so much freedom for so long that we are perhaps in danger of forgetting how much blood it cost to establish the Bill of Rights.

A public interest is not wanting in granting freedom to speak their minds even to those who advocate the overthrow of the Government by force. Coupled with such advocacy is criticism of defects in our society. No matter how clear that defendants are preparing to overthrow our Government at the propitious moment, it is self-delusion to think that we can punish them for their advocacy without adding to the risks run by loyal citizens who honestly believe in some of the reforms these defendants advance.

Congress has determined that the danger created by advocacy of overthrow justifies the ensuing restriction on freedom of speech. The determination was made after due deliberation. To make validity of legislation depend on judicial reading of events still in the womb of time—a forecast, that is, of the outcome of forces at best appreciated only with knowledge of the topmost secrets of nations—is to charge the judiciary with duties beyond its equipment. In finding that Congress has acted within its power, a judge does not remotely imply that he favors the implications that lie beneath the legal issues.

Mr. Justice JACKSON, *concurring.*

The Communist Party is a relatively small party whose strength is in selected, dedicated, indoctrinated, and rigidly disciplined members. It seeks members that are, or may be, secreted in strategic posts in transportation, communications, industry and government. Through these placements in positions of power it seeks a leverage over society that will make up in power of coercion what it lacks in power of persuasion. Communist technique in the overturn of a free government was disclosed by the *coup d'etat* in which they seized power in Czechoslovakia. A virtually bloodless abdication whereupon they instituted a reign of oppression and terror, and ruthlessly denied to all others the freedoms which had sheltered their conspiracy.

When the issue is criminality of hot-headed speech on a street corner, or circulation of a few incendiary pamphlets, or parading by zealots behind a red flag, or refusal of a handful of school children to salute our flag, it is not beyond the capacity of the judicial process to gather, comprehend, and weigh the necessary materials for decision whether it is a clear and present danger of substantive evil or a harmless letting off of steam. But if we must decide that this Act and its application are constitutional only if we are convinced that petitioner's conduct creates a "clear and present danger" of violent overthrow, we would have to foresee and predict the effectiveness of Communist propaganda, opportunities for infiltration, whether, and when, a time will come that they consider propitious for action, and whether and how fast our existing government will deteriorate. The authors of the clear and present danger test never applied it to a case like this. It means that Communist plotting is protected during its period of incubation; its preliminary stages of organization and preparation are immune from the law; the Government can move only after imminent action is manifest, when it would, of course, be too late. Direct incitement to violent overthrow by speech or writing can be made a crime, and I think there can be a conviction without proving that the odds favored its success by 99 to 1. If it is not forbidden to put down force or violence, it is not forbidden to punish its teaching or advocacy, and the end being punishable, there is no doubt of the power to punish conspiracy for the purpose.

Mr. Justice BLACK, *dissenting.*

The only way to affirm these convictions is to repudiate directly or indirectly the established "clear and present danger" rule. I cannot agree that the First Amendment permits us to sustain laws suppressing freedom of speech and press on the basis of Congress' or our own notions of mere "reasonableness."

Mr. Justice DOUGLAS, *dissenting.*

If this were a case where those who claimed protection under the First Amendment were teaching the techniques of sabotage, the assassination of the President, the filching of documents from public files, the planting of bombs, the art of street warfare, and the like, I would have no doubts. But no such evidence was introduced. What petitioners did was to organize people to teach and themselves teach the Marxist-Leninist doctrine contained chiefly in four books: Stalin, *Foundations of Leninism* (1924); Marx and Engels, *The Communist Manifesto* (1848); Lenin, *The State and Revolution* (1917) (1939). The Court does not outlaw these texts nor condemn them to the fire, as the Communists do literature offensive to their creed. But if the books themselves are not outlawed, if they can lawfully remain on library shelves, by what reasoning does their use in a classroom become a crime? The Act, as construed, requires the element of intent—that those who teach the creed believe in it. The crime then depends not on what is taught but on who the teacher is. That is to make freedom of speech turn not on *what is said*, but on the *intent* with which it is said.

There comes a time when even speech loses its constitutional immunity. When conditions are so critical that there will be no time to avoid the evil that the speech threatens, it is time to call a halt. This record, however, contains no evidence showing that the acts charged *viz.*, the teaching of the Soviet theory of revolution with the hope that it will be realized, have created any clear and present danger to the Nation. As a political party they are of little consequence. Communism has been so thoroughly exposed in this country that it has been crippled as a political force. Free speech has destroyed it as an effective political party. How it can be said that there is a clear and present danger that this advocacy will succeed is, therefore, a mystery. Some nations less resilient than the United States, where illiteracy is high and where democratic traditions are only budding, might have to take drastic steps and jail these men for merely speaking their creed. But in America they are miserable merchants of unwanted ideas; their wares remain unsold.

The political impotence of the Communists in this country does not, of course, dispose of the problem. Their numbers; their positions in industry and government; the extent to which they have in fact infiltrated the police, the armed services, transportation, stevedoring, power plants, munitions works, and other critical places — these facts all bear on the likelihood that their advocacy of the Soviet theory of revolution will endanger the Republic. But the record is silent on these facts. On this record no one can say that petitioners and their converts have even the slightest chance of achieving their aims.

Notes

1. *An "Advocacy of Action" Requirement.* In *Yates v. United States*, 354 U.S. 298 (1957), the Court interpreted *Dennis* to require the "advocacy to action" requirement that Justices Douglas and Black had urged upon the Court in their dissenting opinions in *Dennis*. Fourteen Communist Party leaders were charged with conspiracy and sentenced to 5 years in prison. Based on defects in the trial court proceedings, the Court reversed defendants' convictions, acquitted five of them, and remanded the nine remaining defendants for retrial. The Court explained that the legislative history of the Smith Act revealed that it was aimed at the "advocacy and teaching of concrete action for the forcible overthrow of the Government, and not of principles divorced from action." Importantly, he took pains to elaborate on the meaning of *Dennis*:

> The essence of *Dennis* was that indoctrination of a group in preparation for future violent action, as well as exhortation to immediate action, by advocacy directed to "action for the accomplishment" of forcible overthrow, to violence as "a rule or principle of action," and employing "language of incitement," is not constitutionally protected when the group is of sufficient size and cohesiveness, is sufficiently oriented towards action, and other circumstances are such as reasonably to justify apprehension that action will occur. This is a different thing from the view that mere doctrinal justification of forcible overthrow, if engaged in with the intent to accomplish overthrow, is punishable per se under the Smith Act. That sort of advocacy, even though uttered with the hope that it may ultimately lead to violent revolution, is too remote from concrete action to be regarded as the kind of indoctrination preparatory to action which was condemned in *Dennis*. *Dennis* was concerned with a conspiracy to advocate presently the taking of forcible action in the future. It was action, not advocacy, that was to be postponed until "circumstances" would "permit."

Justice Clark dissented, as he would have affirmed all the convictions, while Justices Black and Douglas would have reversed all the convictions.

2. *Membership Convictions Under the Smith Act.* Four years after *Yates*, in two companion cases, the Court applied the *Yates* standard reinterpreting *Dennis* to the "membership" provision of the Smith Act. In *Noto v. United States*, 367 U.S. 203 (1961), Justice Harlan explained that the evidence was insufficient to show "some substantial direct or circumstantial evidence of a call to violence now or in the

future which is both sufficiently strong and sufficiently pervasive to lend color to the otherwise ambiguous theoretical material regarding Communist Party teaching, and to justify the inference that such a call to violence may fairly be imputed to the Party as a whole, and not merely to some narrow segment of it." When "there is no evidence that acts of sabotage were presently advocated," there is insufficient evidence of "present advocacy" of "action," which is a required element of the crime under the membership clause. A second element requires "clear proof that defendant 'specifically intends to accomplish (the aims of the organization by resort to violence.'" In *Scales v. United States*, 367 U.S. 203 (1961), the Court approved a jury instruction that required proof that defendant was "an 'active' member of the Party, and not merely 'a nominal, passive, inactive or purely technical' member, with knowledge of the Party's illegal advocacy and a specific intent to bring about violent overthrow 'as speedily as circumstances would permit.'" The Court summarized the types of evidence that could be used to prove "present advocacy" of "action": "(a) the teaching of forceful overthrow, accompanied by directions as to the type of illegal action which must be taken when the time for the revolution is reached; and (b) the teaching of forceful overthrow, accompanied by a contemporary, though legal, course of conduct clearly undertaken for the specific purpose of rendering effective the later illegal activity which is advocated."

3. *Parallel Developments.* The Court's movement away from *Dennis* can be seen in other Smith Act cases, as well as in a variety of precedents in fields outside of "subversive advocacy" speech laws. One dramatic doctrinal evolution during the civil rights era occurred in the field of "hostile audience" law, where the Court expanded the rights of anti-segregation protestors to march and demonstrate without being convicted of "disorderly conduct" even though crowds of onlookers threatened violence. In the "fighting words" area, the Court narrowed the definition of unprotected speech and expanded speech protections for soapbox orators whose commentary offended their audiences and possessed the potential to provoke disorder. The definition of "unprotected speech" shrank as obscenity definitions narrowed, and as greater protections were afforded to critics of government officials through new tort law immunities from libel suits. The Court also protected antiwar speech on some occasions during the Vietnam War under circumstances that would have led to convictions under the Espionage Act of 1917. This protection of Vietnam War protestors signaled another step in the Court's readiness to reverse speech convictions when the record lacked concrete proof of imminent harm—and another step toward *Brandenburg* and away from all the old "clear and present danger" formulas.

～ PROBLEM: APPLYING *DENNIS* ～

How would *Dennis* apply to the five scenarios in Problem 1 following the *Gitlow* and *Whitney* opinions, if the defendant is charged with conspiracy to advocate criminal syndicalism?

e. Modern Cases

Brandenburg v. Ohio

395 U.S. 444 (1969)

PER CURIAM.

Appellant, a leader of a Ku Klux Klan group, was convicted under the Ohio Criminal Syndicalism statute for "advocating the duty, necessity, or propriety of crime, sabotage, violence, or unlawful methods of terrorism as a means of accomplishing industrial or political reform" and for "voluntarily assembling with any society, group, or assemblage of persons formed to teach or advocate the doctrines of criminal syndicalism." Ohio Rev. Code Ann. §2923.13. He was fined $1,000 and sentenced to one to 10 years' imprisonment. The appellant challenged the constitutionality of the criminal syndicalism statute under the First and Fourteenth Amendments to the United States Constitution, but the Ohio court of appeals and supreme court affirmed. We reverse.

Appellant telephoned an announcer-reporter on the staff of a Cincinnati television station and invited him to come to a Ku Klux Klan "rally" to be held at a farm in Hamilton County. The reporter and a cameraman attended the meeting and filmed the events. Portions of the films were later broadcast on the local station and on a national network.

The prosecution's case rested on the films and on testimony identifying appellant as the person who communicated with the reporter and who spoke at the rally. The State also introduced into evidence several articles appearing in the film, including a pistol, a rifle, a shotgun, ammunition, a Bible, and a red hood worn by the speaker in the films. One film showed 12 hooded figures, some of whom carried firearms. They were gathered around a large wooden cross, which they burned. No one was present other than the participants and the newsmen who made the film. Most of the words uttered during the scene were incomprehensible when the film was projected, but scattered phrases could be understood that were derogatory of Negroes and, in one instance, Jews. Another scene showed appellant, in Klan regalia, making a speech. The speech, in full, was as follows:

> This is an organizers' meeting. We have had quite a few members here today which are—we have hundreds, hundreds of members throughout the State of Ohio. I can quote from a newspaper clipping from the Columbus, Ohio Dispatch, five weeks ago Sunday morning. The Klan has more members in the State of Ohio than does any other organization. We're not a revengeant organization, but if our President, our Congress, our Supreme Court, continues to suppress the white, Caucasian race, it's possible that there might have to be some revengeance taken.
>
> We are marching on Congress July the Fourth, four hundred thousand strong. From there we are dividing into two groups, one group to march on St. Augustine, Florida, the other group to march into Mississippi. Thank you.

The second film showed six hooded figures one of whom, later identified as appellant, repeated a speech very similar to that recorded on the first film. The reference to the possibility of "revengeance" was omitted, and one sentence was added: "Personally, I believe the nigger should be returned to Africa, the Jew returned to Israel." Though some of the figures in the films carried weapons, the speaker did not.

The Ohio Criminal Syndicalism Statute was enacted in 1919. From 1917 to 1920, identical or quite similar laws were adopted by 20 States and two territories. E. Dowell, *A History of Criminal Syndicalism Legislation in the United States* 21 (Johns Hopkins University 1939). In 1927, this Court sustained the constitutionality of California's Criminal Syndicalism Act, the text of which is quite similar to that of the laws of Ohio. *Whitney v. California*, 274 U.S. 37 (1927). The Court upheld the statute on the ground that, without more, "advocating" violent means to effect political and economic change involves such danger to the security of the State that the State may outlaw it. But *Whitney* has been thoroughly discredited. *See Dennis v. United States*, 341 U.S. 494 (1951). These later decisions fashioned the principle that the constitutional guarantees of free speech and free press do not permit a State to forbid or proscribe advocacy of the use of force or of law violation except where such advocacy is directed to inciting or producing imminent lawless action and is likely to incite or produce such action. As we said in *Noto v. United States*, 367 U.S. 290 (1961), "the mere abstract teaching of the moral propriety or even moral necessity for a resort to force and violence, is not the same as preparing a group for violent action and steeling it to such action." A statute which fails to draw this distinction impermissibly intrudes upon the freedoms guaranteed by the First and Fourteenth Amendments. It sweeps within its condemnation speech which our Constitution has immunized from governmental control. *Cf. Yates v. United States*, 354 U.S. 298 (1957).

Ohio's Criminal Syndicalism Act cannot be sustained. The Act punishes persons who "advocate or teach the duty, necessity, or propriety" of violence "as a means of accomplishing industrial or political reform"; or who publish or circulate or display any book or paper containing such advocacy; or who "justify" the commission of violent acts "with intent to exemplify, spread or advocate the propriety of the doctrines of criminal syndicalism"; or who "voluntarily assemble" with a group formed "to teach or advocate the doctrines of criminal syndicalism." Neither the indictment nor the trial judge's instructions to the jury refined the statute's bald definition of the crime in terms of mere advocacy not distinguished from incitement to imminent lawless action.

Accordingly, we are here confronted with a statute which, by its own words and as applied, purports to punish mere advocacy and to forbid, on pain of criminal punishment, assembly with others merely to advocate the described type of action. Such a statute falls within the condemnation of the First and Fourteenth Amendments. The contrary teaching of *Whitney v. California* cannot be supported, and that decision is therefore overruled.

Mr. Justice BLACK, *concurring.*

I agree with Mr. Justice Douglas that the "clear and present danger" doctrine should have no place in the interpretation of the First Amendment.

Mr. Justice DOUGLAS, *concurring.*

While I join the opinion of the Court, I enter a caveat. The dissents in *Abrams, Schaefer,* and *Pierce* show how easily "clear and present danger" is manipulated to crush what Brandeis called "the fundamental right of free men to strive for better conditions through new legislation and new institutions" by argument and discourse even in time of war. Though I doubt if the "clear and present danger" test is congenial to the First Amendment in time of a declared war, I am certain it is not reconcilable with the First Amendment in days of peace. The Court quite properly overrules *Whitney v. California,* 274 U.S. 357, which involved advocacy of ideas which the majority of the Court deemed unsound and dangerous.

Mr. Justice Holmes, though never formally abandoning the "clear and present danger" test, moved closer to the First Amendment ideal when he said in dissent in *Gitlow*:

> Every idea is an incitement. It offers itself for belief and if believed it is acted on unless some other belief outweighs it or some failure of energy stifles the movement at its birth. The only difference between the expression of an opinion and an incitement in the narrower sense is the speaker's enthusiasm for the result. Eloquence may set fire to reason. But whatever may be thought of the redundant discourse before us it had no chance of starting a present conflagration. If in the long run the beliefs expressed in proletarian dictatorship are destined to be accepted by the dominant forces of the community, the only meaning of free speech is that they should be given their chance and have their way.

We have never been faithful to the philosophy of that dissent.

The Court in *Herndon v. Lowry,* 301 U.S. 242, overturned a conviction for exercising First Amendment rights to incite insurrection because of lack of evidence of incitement. In *Dennis v. United States,* 341 U.S. 494, we opened wide the door, distorting the 'clear and present danger' test beyond recognition. In that case the prosecution dubbed an agreement to teach the Marxist creed a "conspiracy." The Court sustained convictions under the charge, construing it to mean a determination of "whether the gravity of the 'evil,' discounted by its improbability, justifies such invasion of free speech as is necessary to avoid the danger."

Out of the "clear and present danger" test came other offspring. Advocacy and teaching of forcible overthrow of government as an abstract principle is immune from prosecution. *Yates v. United States,* 354 U.S. 298. But an "active" member, who has a guilty knowledge and intent of the aim to overthrow the Government by violence, may be prosecuted. *Scales v. United States,* 367 U.S. 203. Judge Learned Hand, who wrote for the Court of Appeals in affirming the judgment in *Dennis,* coined the "not improbable" test which Judge Hand preferred over the "clear and present danger" test.

I see no place in the regime of the First Amendment for any "clear and present danger" test. When one reads the opinions closely and sees when and how the "clear and present danger" test has been applied, great misgivings are aroused. First, the threats were often loud but always puny and made serious only by judges so wedded to the status quo that critical analysis made them nervous. Second, the test was so twisted and perverted in *Dennis* as to make the trial of those teachers of Marxism a political trial which was part and parcel of the cold war that has eroded substantial parts of the First Amendment.

Action is often a method of expression and within the protection of the First Amendment. One's beliefs have long been thought to be sanctuaries which government could not invade. The lines drawn by the Court between the criminal act of being an "active" Communist and the innocent act of being a nominal or inactive Communist mark the difference only between deep and abiding belief and casual or uncertain belief. I think that all matters of belief are beyond the reach of subpoenas or the probings of investigators. That is why the invasions of privacy made by investigating committees were notoriously unconstitutional. That is the deep-seated fault in the infamous loyalty-security hearings which, since 1947 when President Truman launched them, have processed 20,000,000 men and women. Those hearings were primarily concerned with one's thoughts, ideas, beliefs, and convictions. They were the most blatant violations of the First Amendment we have ever known.

The line between what is permissible and not subject to control and what may be made impermissible and subject to regulation is the line between ideas and overt acts. The example given by those who would punish speech is the case of one who falsely shouts fire in a crowded theatre. This is a classic case where speech is brigaded with action. They are indeed inseparable and a prosecution can be launched for the overt acts actually caused. Apart from rare instances of that kind, speech is, I think, immune from prosecution. There is no constitutional line between advocacy of abstract ideas as in *Yates* and advocacy of political action as in *Scales*. The quality of advocacy turns on the depth of the conviction; and government has no power to invade that sanctuary of belief and conscience.

Notes and Questions

1. *Brandenburg's Ambiguities. Brandenburg* clearly repudiates *Whitney*, but it is silent concerning the earlier decisions of the World War I era (*Schenck, Frohwerk, Debs*) while citing the decisions of the McCarthy era cases with approval (*Dennis, Yates, Noto*). Justice Douglas provides a brief overview of these decisions, and argues that *Brandenburg* should have repudiated explicitly both the "clear and present danger" test and the *Dennis* decision's reliance upon it. Thus, several mysteries are presented by the different portraits of the past provided by the *Brandenburg* opinions. First, why is the "clear and present danger" test so controversial? The *per curiam* opinion scrupulously avoids any reference to that test,

and instead endorses the formula for which *Brandenburg* is now famous. A second mystery concerns the effect of *Brandenburg* on precedents from the three earlier doctrinal eras. Besides *Whitney*, it is unclear which opinions are "dead letter" and which remain operative. The third mystery concerns whether a narrowly drafted indictment and jury instruction incorporating the new "imminent lawless action" test would permit a conviction on the *Brandenburg* facts.

2. *Take the Street Later. Hess v. Indiana*, 414 U.S. 105 (1973), involved an antiwar demonstration at Indiana University at which 100 to 150 demonstrators blocked a public street. When the demonstrators refused directions to "clear the street," the police began forcibly moving demonstrators to the curb. After being moved to the side of the road, Gregory Hess yelled, "We'll take the fucking street later," or "We'll take the fucking street again." Hess did not appear to be exhorting the crowd to return to the streets. Even though he was facing the crowd when he made the statement, he did not appear to address any particular person or group, and his tone, though loud, was no louder than that of other people in the area. In overturning Hess's conviction, the Court concluded that his statements did not satisfy the *Brandenburg* requirements: "At best, the statement could be taken as counsel for present moderation; at worst, it amounted to nothing more than advocacy of illegal action at some indefinite future time." The Court noted that since "Hess's statement was not directed to, any person or group of persons," the Court held that "it cannot be said that he was advocating in the normal sense, any action." The "import of the language" used by defendant provided neither "evidence" nor a "rational inference" that his words "were intended to produce, and likely to produce, imminent disorder." The *Hess* dissenters argued that defendant's statement could be characterized "as an exhortation, particularly when uttered in a loud voice while facing a crowd." The dissenters disagreed with the Court's emphasis on the word *later* in defendant's statement, and found that "there are possible constructions of the statement which would encompass more or less immediate and continuing action against the harassed police."

3. *Schenck and* Brandenburg. How would *Schenck* be decided under the *Brandenburg* test?

4. *Return to the Justifications for Protecting Speech*. At the beginning of this chapter, we noted four justifications for protecting free speech: the marketplace of ideas, self-fulfillment, safety valve, and democratic process. Which decision, *Schenck* or *Brandenburg*, better serves these justifications?

5. *Protected Advocacy Versus Illegal Conspiracy*. A distinction has always been made between crimes like conspiracy and solicitation, on the one hand, and protected speech on the other. For example, if A solicits B to rob a bank, and offers B $100,000 for committing the crime, A can be convicted of solicitation. Likewise, if A and B conspire to rob a bank, they can be convicted of conspiracy to rob the bank. By contrast, if A makes a public speech calling on "every moral human being to resist the draft," the speech is protected unless the *Brandenburg* test is satisfied. While the distinction between the two types of situations is clear, the dividing line between the two cannot always be precisely ascertained. In *United States v.*

Hassan, 742 F.3d 104 (4th Cir. 2014), three men plotted to attack a Marine Corps base in Virginia and to attack various sites overseas. In the prosecution, the government sought to introduce e-mails, Facebook postings, and YouTube links in which defendants expressed their desire to engage in violent jihad and the need to raise money to support jihadist efforts to undercover government agents. The court upheld the admission of those statements.

∾ PROBLEMS ∾

1. *The New Ohio Statute.* The Ohio legislature enacts a statute that incorporates the *Brandenburg* definition of criminal syndicalism. Following passage, if the *Brandenburg* defendant commits the same acts, is there sufficient evidence to convict? How will the state argue that sufficient evidence exists?

2. *Reconsideration of Problems.* How would *Brandenberg* apply to the situations listed earlier in the chapter? A) A group of college students opposed to World War I holds a "peace vigil" at which they "rally for peace" as well as against the war and the draft; B) A professor discusses the "moral imperative" that requires every "good and moral citizen" to oppose the war and the draft. Would it matter whether students actually resisted the draft? C) A student wears a jacket with the message "Fuck the Draft" to express his opposition to the war; D) On a remote piece of property, Ku Klux Klan members hold a rally at which they burn a cross, denounce public officials, and discuss the need to take "revenge" against members of certain minority groups as well as against governmental officials; E) *The Courier-Journal*, a large daily newspaper in Louisville, Kentucky, publishes editorials and articles that are critical of the war and the draft and that discuss the "moral imperative" of all citizens to resist the draft.

3. *More on Newspapers and Expressing Opposition.* Recall the earlier problem that dealt with a newspaper publisher, journalist, or politician who wanted to express opposition to U.S. participation in a war without risking conviction under the Espionage Act for conspiracy to obstruct the draft. Suppose that you were asked to give legal advice on how to construct an article so as to avoid conviction under *Brandenburg*'s standards. What would you advise?

4. *The Sociology Professor's Comments.* During a sociology class discussion of President George W. Bush, a sociology professor at the University of Louisville purportedly referred to "religious zealots who say they are voting on morals" and stated "I think we should all buy AK-47s and shoot them all! That's what I would suggest, if it were allowed." The professor is subsequently charged with incitement to murder. Can he be convicted consistently with the First Amendment? Suppose that the professor claims that the statement was made sarcastically and that the students understood it that way. Even if the professor cannot be criminally prosecuted for his comments, might the university take disciplinary action against the professor for his comments?

5. *The Abdel Rahman Case.* A federal statute, 18 U.S.C. §2384, punishes the crime of "seditious conspiracy." It provides: "If two or more persons in any State or Territory, or in any place subject to the jurisdiction of the United States, conspire to overthrow, put down, or destroy by force the Government of the United States, or to levy war against them, or to oppose by force the authority thereof they shall be imprisoned not more than twenty years." Abdel Rahman, a scholar and cleric, was alleged to be the leader of a seditious conspiracy. The government claims that, by urging his coconspirators to "do jihad with the sword, with the cannon, with grenades and with missiles against God's enemies," and by advising the conspirators concerning the best strategies for violent attacks on persons and property, Rahman supported defendants' violent conduct which included the bombing of the World Trade Center and attempts to bomb the United Nations and the Lincoln and Holland Tunnels in New York. Rahman told his followers that the formation of a jihad army was necessary in order to defeat the oppressors of Islam, including the U.S. In effect, a conspiracy to wage a war of urban terrorism against the U.S. and forcibly oppose its authority. The government contends that speech is punished only when it constitutes a "conspiracy"—that is, an agreement to use force against the U.S. On appeal Rahman's counsel argues that §2384 is facially invalid because it criminalizes protected expression. You are a law clerk to the judge who has been assigned to write the opinion in Rahman's appeal. The judge tells you that the panel has voted unanimously to reject the First Amendment attack on the statute. Draft the opinion. *See United States v. Rahman,* 189 F.3d 88 (2d Cir. 1994).

6. Brandenburg *in the Cyber Village.* How would *Brandenburg* apply to internet communications? Suppose that a blogger repeatedly and consistently urges people to "resist the draft by all means, including force," during war time. The *Brandenburg* test seems to contemplate a situation in which an individual tries to whip a mob into immediate violence. Can the imminence requirement be satisfied by an internet communication? On the other hand, is the internet a potentially more dangerous method of communication? In recent years, individuals have been able to organize so-called flash mobs using social networking and text messaging. Often, these flash mobs are for benign purposes (e.g., snowball fights or pillow fights). Suppose that these flash mobs are designed for more nefarious purposes: to stimulate assaults or brawls. At what point may the police intervene?

7. *More on the Cyber-Village.* An American who has converted to Islam maintains an online blog that repeatedly urges individuals to make off-hour attacks on KFC restaurants, banks, mobile phone stores, and other corporate outposts. His reason for promoting "off-hour" attacks is to ensure that people are not hurt, and he claims that he has never advocated the use of explosives. In the posts, he argues that nonviolent protests are "futile" and constitute simply an opportunity to "get arrested or shot by the police." His posts have led individuals to bomb places of business, and they sometimes claim responsibility using his hashtags. In addition, his blog posts are widely circulated among activists. Under the *Brandenburg* test, can the blog poster be criminally prosecuted for these posts?

See David D. Kirkpatrick, *American Agitator Helps Fuel Attacks in Egypt,* N.Y. Times, Feb. 28, 2015, at A-1.

8. *Online Radicalization.* Governmental officials have become concerned about "online radicalization" of young people. Although this type of radicalization is often associated with Muslim organizations like ISIS, and other violent jihadists, it is also associated with white supremacist groups. Prior to the internet, groups like the KKK grew through personal connections and word of mouth. Now, they do so through online messaging, recruitment and organization. Does the government have the power to prohibit all speech by such groups? Can it prohibit, in particular, all white-supremacist speech—even speech that does not advocate illegal action or violence? Can it prohibit such speech when it makes vague and indefinite calls for future violence?

9. *More on the International Treaty Regulating the Internet.* In light of the *Brandenburg* decision, what would be your position at the convention on whether the United States can accept the European request to include the following language from the European Convention on Human Rights in the treaty regulating the internet? "The exercise of these freedoms, since it carries with it duties and responsibilities, may be subject to such formalities, conditions, restrictions or penalties as are prescribed by law and are necessary in a democratic society, in the interests of national security, territorial integrity or public safety, for the prevention of disorder or crime, for the protection of health or morals, for the protection of the reputation or the rights of others, for preventing the disclosure of information received in confidence, or for maintaining the authority and impartiality of the judiciary." What language might you be able to propose to the other delegates? Do you anticipate that your alternative language will be acceptable to them?

f. Speech and Terrorism After 9/11

Within two months after the terrorist attacks of September 11, 2001, Congress enacted the USA PATRIOT Act, which included a variety of provisions that expanded government surveillance powers, and created an array of crimes related to terrorist activity. In the following case, the Court rejects plaintiffs' First Amendment arguments and establishes new law concerning the government's interest in combating terrorism.

Holder v. Humanitarian Law Project

561 U.S. 1 (2010)

Chief Justice ROBERTS delivered the opinion of the Court.

The following conduct is prohibited under 18 U.S.C. §2339B(a): "Whoever provides material support or resources to a foreign terrorist organization, or attempts or conspires to do so, shall be fined or imprisoned not more than 15 years, or both, and if the death of any person results, shall be imprisoned for any term of years or for life. To violate this provision, a person must have knowledge that the organization is a designated terrorist organization under federal law, or that the organization has engaged or engages in terrorist activity or terrorism as defined under federal law." The key term "material support or resources" is defined under 18 U.S.C. §2339A(b)(1)-(3) as including: "any property, tangible or intangible, or service, including currency or monetary instruments or financial securities, financial services, lodging, *training, expert advice or assistance,* safehouses, false documentation or identification, communications equipment, facilities, weapons, lethal substances, explosives, *personnel* (one or more individuals who may be or include oneself), and transportation, except medicine or religious materials." The term "*training*" means "instruction or teaching designed to impart a specific skill, as opposed to general knowledge." The term "*expert advice or assistance*" means "advice or assistance derived from scientific, technical or other specialized knowledge."

A key limitation is defined in 18 U.S.C. §2339B(h): "No person may be prosecuted in connection with the term '*personnel*' unless that person has knowingly provided, attempted to provide, or conspired to provide a foreign terrorist organization with one or more individuals (who may be or include himself) to work under that terrorist organization's direction or control or to organize, manage, supervise, or otherwise direct the operation of that organization. Individuals who act entirely independently of the foreign terrorist organization to advance its goals or objectives shall not be considered to be working under the foreign terrorist organization's direction and control."

The plaintiffs included the Humanitarian Law Project (HLP) "(a human rights organization with consultative status to the United Nations)"; the HLP President, a Tamil physician "(born in Sri Lanka and a naturalized U.S. citizen)"; and "five nonprofit groups dedicated to the interests of persons of Tamil descent." The two relevant foreign terrorist organizations were designated as such in 1997: the Kurdistan Workers' Party (PKK) and the Liberation Tigers of Tamil Eelam (LTTE). The plaintiffs claimed "that they wished to provide support for the humanitarian and political activities of the PKK and the LTTE in the form of monetary contributions, other tangible aid, legal training, and political advocacy, but that they could not do so for fear of prosecution under §2339B."

We consider whether the material-support statute, as applied to plaintiffs, violates the freedom of speech guaranteed by the First Amendment. Under the material-support statute, plaintiffs may say anything they wish on any topic. They may advocate before the United Nations. Section 2339B also "does not prevent plaintiffs from becoming members of the PKK Kurdistan Workers' Party and LTTE Liberation Tigers of Tamil Eelam or impose any sanction on them for doing so." Congress has not, therefore, sought to suppress ideas or opinions in the form of "pure political speech." Rather, Congress has prohibited "material support," which most often does not take the form of speech at all. And when it does, the statute is carefully drawn to cover only a narrow category of speech to, under the direction of, or in coordination with foreign groups that the speaker knows to be foreign terrorist organizations.

The Government claims that the only thing truly at issue in this litigation is conduct, not speech, and that the law only incidentally burdens the plaintiffs' expression. The Government argues that the proper standard of review is set out in *United States v. O'Brien*, 391 U.S. 367 (1968). But *O'Brien* does not provide the applicable standard for reviewing a content-based regulation of speech, and §2339B regulates speech on the basis of its content. Plaintiffs want to speak to the PKK and the LTTE, and whether they may do so under §2339B depends on what they say. If plaintiffs' speech to those groups imparts a "specific skill" or communicates advice derived from "specialized knowledge"—for example, training on the use of international law or advice on petitioning the United Nations—then it is barred. On the other hand, plaintiffs' speech is not barred if it imparts only general or unspecialized knowledge.

The Government argues that §2339B should nonetheless receive intermediate scrutiny because it functions as a regulation of conduct. That argument runs headlong into a number of precedents, most prominently *Cohen v. California*, 403 U.S. 15 (1971). As we explained in *Texas v. Johnson*: "If the Government's regulation is not related to expression, then the less stringent standard we announced in *O'Brien* for regulations of noncommunicative conduct controls. If it is, then we are outside of *O'Brien*'s test, and we must apply a more demanding standard." 491 U.S. at 403.

The First Amendment issue before us is whether the Government may prohibit what plaintiffs want to do—provide material support to the PKK and LTTE in the form of speech. Everyone agrees that the Government's interest in combating terrorism is an urgent objective of the highest order. Plaintiffs' complaint is that the ban on material support, applied to what they wish to do, is not "necessary to further that interest" because their support will advance only the legitimate activities of the designated terrorist organizations, not their terrorism.

When it enacted §2339B in 1976, Congress made specific findings regarding the serious threat posed by international terrorism. "Foreign organizations that engage in terrorist activity are so tainted by their criminal conduct that *any contribution to such an organization* facilitates that conduct." Material support meant to "promote peaceable, lawful conduct" can further terrorism by foreign groups in multiple ways. "Material support" is a valuable resource by definition. Such support frees up other resources within the organization that may be put to violent ends. It also importantly helps lend legitimacy to foreign terrorist groups—legitimacy that makes it easier for those groups to persist, to recruit members, and to raise funds—all of which facilitate more terrorist attacks. The dissent argues that there is "no natural stopping place" for the proposition that aiding a foreign terrorist organization's lawful activity promotes the terrorist organization as a whole. But Congress has settled on just such a natural stopping place: The statute reaches only material support coordinated with or under the direction of a designated foreign terrorist organization. Independent advocacy that might be viewed as promoting the group's legitimacy is not covered.

Providing foreign terrorist groups with material support in any form also furthers terrorism by straining the United States' relationships with its allies and undermining cooperative efforts between nations to prevent terrorist attacks. We see no reason to question Congress's finding that "international cooperation is required for an effective response to terrorism." The material-support statute furthers this international effort by prohibiting aid for foreign terrorist groups that harm the United States' partners abroad.

In analyzing whether it is possible in practice to distinguish material support for a foreign terrorist group's violent activities and its nonviolent activities, we do not rely exclusively on our own inferences drawn from the record evidence. We have an affidavit stating the Executive Branch's conclusion on that question from the State Department. That evaluation of the facts by the Executive, like Congress's assessment, is entitled to deference.

Our precedents make clear that concerns of national security and foreign relations do not warrant abdication of the judicial role. We do not defer to the Government's reading of the First Amendment, even when such interests are at stake. But when it comes to collecting evidence and drawing factual inferences in this area, "the lack of competence on the part of the courts is marked," and respect for the Government's conclusions is appropriate. *Rostker v. Goldberg*, 453 U.S. 57, 65 (1981).

One reason for that respect is that national security and foreign policy concerns arise in connection with efforts to confront evolving threats in an area where information can be difficult to obtain and the impact of certain conduct difficult to assess. The statute criminalizes not terrorist attacks themselves, but aid that makes the attacks more likely to occur. The Government, when seeking to prevent imminent harms in the context of international affairs and national security, is not required to conclusively link all the pieces in the puzzle before we grant weight to its empirical conclusions.

Plaintiffs disagree with the considered judgment of Congress and the Executive that providing material support to a designated foreign terrorist organization—even seemingly benign support—bolsters the terrorist activities of that organization. That judgment, however, is entitled to significant weight, and we have persuasive evidence to sustain it. Given the sensitive interests in national security and foreign affairs at stake, the political branches have adequately substantiated their determination that, to serve the Government's interest in preventing terrorism, it was necessary to prohibit providing material support in the form of training, expert advice, personnel, and services to foreign terrorist groups, even if the supporters meant to promote only the groups' nonviolent ends.

We turn to the particular speech plaintiffs propose to undertake. First, plaintiffs propose to "train members of the PKK on how to use humanitarian and international law to peacefully resolve disputes." Congress can, consistent with the First Amendment, prohibit this direct training. It is wholly foreseeable that the PKK could use the "specific skills" that plaintiffs propose to impart as a part of a broader strategy to promote terrorism. The PKK could, for example, pursue peaceful negotiation as a means of buying time to recover from short-term setbacks, lulling opponents into complacency, and ultimately preparing for renewed attacks. A foreign terrorist organization introduced to the structures of the international legal system might use the information to threaten, manipulate, and disrupt. This possibility is real, not remote.

Second, plaintiffs propose to "teach PKK members how to petition various representative bodies such as the United Nations for relief." The Government acts within First Amendment strictures in banning this proposed speech because it teaches the organization how to acquire "relief," which could readily include monetary aid. Money is fungible, and Congress logically concluded that money a terrorist group such as the PKK obtains using the techniques plaintiffs propose to teach could be redirected to funding the group's violent activities.

Finally, plaintiffs propose to "engage in political advocacy" on behalf of Kurds who live in Turkey and Tamils who live in Sri Lanka. Plaintiffs do not specify their expected level of coordination with the PKK or LTTE or suggest what exactly their "advocacy" would consist of. Plaintiffs' proposals are phrased at such a high level of generality that they cannot prevail in this preenforcement challenge.

All this is not to say that any future applications of the material-support statute to speech or advocacy will survive First Amendment scrutiny, or that any other statute relating to speech and terrorism would satisfy the First Amendment. In particular, we in no way suggest that a regulation of independent speech would pass constitutional muster, even if the Government were to show that such speech benefits foreign terrorist organizations. We also do not suggest that Congress could extend the same prohibition on material support at issue here to domestic organizations. We simply hold that, in prohibiting the particular forms of support that plaintiffs seek to provide to foreign terrorist groups, §2339B does not violate the freedom of speech.

The judgment of the Court of Appeals is affirmed in part and reversed in part, and the cases are remanded for further proceedings consistent with this opinion.

It is so ordered.

Justice BREYER, with whom Justices GINSBURG and SOTOMAYOR join, *dissenting.*

I cannot agree with the conclusion that the Constitution permits the Government to prosecute the plaintiffs criminally for engaging in coordinated teaching and advocacy furthering the designated organizations' lawful political objectives. In my view, the Government has not met its burden of showing that an interpretation of the statute that would prohibit this speech-and-association-related activity serves the Government's compelling interest in combating terrorism. The First Amendment protects advocacy even of unlawful action so long as that advocacy is not "directed to inciting or producing *imminent lawless action* and *likely to incite or produce* such action." *Brandenburg v. Ohio,* 395 U.S. 444, 447 (1969) (emphasis added). Here the plaintiffs seek to advocate peaceful, lawful action to secure political ends; and they seek to teach others how to do the same.

Not even the "serious and deadly problem" of international terrorism can require automatic forfeiture of First Amendment rights. *United States v. Robel,* 389 U.S. 258, 264 (1967). Where a statute applies criminal penalties and arguably does so on the basis of content-based distinctions, we would scrutinize the statute and justifications "strictly" to determine whether the prohibition is justified by a "compelling" need that cannot be "less restrictively" accommodated. Even if "strict scrutiny" does not apply, we must at the very least "measure the validity of the means adopted by Congress against both the goal it has sought to achieve and the specific prohibitions of the First Amendment." I doubt that the statute can survive any reasonably applicable First Amendment standard.

The Government does identify a compelling interest in protecting the security of the United States and its nationals from the threats that foreign terrorist organizations pose by denying those organizations financial and other fungible resources. I dispute whether the interest can justify the statute's criminal prohibition. How does application of the statute to the protected activities before us *help achieve* that important security-related end? The Government says that the plaintiffs' support for these organizations is "fungible" in that plaintiffs' support could free up other resources, which the organization might put to terrorist ends. It is far from obvious that advocacy activities can themselves be redirected, or will free other resources that can be directed, towards terrorist ends. The Government says that the plaintiffs' proposed activities will "bolster a terrorist organization's efficacy and strength in a community" and "undermine this nation's efforts to *delegitimize and weaken* those groups." Speech, association, and related activities will often help to legitimate a group. Regardless, the "legitimacy" justification is inconsistent with critically important First Amendment case law. Consider the cases involving the protection the First Amendment offered those who joined the Communist Party intending only to further its peaceful activities. The Court held that the First Amendment protected an American's right to belong to that party—despite whatever "legitimating" effect membership might have had—as long as the person did not share the party's unlawful purposes. Nor can the Government overcome these considerations simply by narrowing the covered activities to those that involve *coordinated,* rather than *independent,* advocacy. I am not aware of any words that might be used to describe "coordination" that would not, at a minimum, seriously chill not only the kind of activities the plaintiffs raise before us, but also the "independent advocacy" the Government purports to permit. I am not aware of any case—not *Gitlow v. New York,* 268 U.S. 652 (1925), not *Schenck v. United States,* 249 U.S. 47 (1919), not the later Communist Party cases decided during the heat of the Cold War—in which the Court accepted anything like a claim that speech or teaching might be criminalized lest it buy negotiating time for an opponent who would put that time to bad use.

Notes

1. *Florida Imams.* In 2011, Hafiz Kahn and his son Izhar Kahn, imams of mosques in Miami and Margate, Florida, respectively, were arrested and charged with providing material support to the Pakistani Taliban, together with other indicted family members in Pakistan. The indictment stated that they sent more than $50,000 to the Taliban that was used to buy guns and support Taliban fighters and their families. The money was also used to start a school in Pakistan, but the men denied a link to the Taliban and denied that the school was used for terrorist training. The men pleaded not guilty and were denied bail. *See* Evan Perez, *U.S. Charges Six with Terror Support in Pakistan,* Wall St. J., May 14, 2011, http://online.wsj.com/article/SB10001424052748703730804576323190890136916.html.

2. *Anti-War Protestors.* Members of the Anti-War Committee, residents of Chicago, organized demonstrations against the Afghanistan War, the Iraq War, and the provision of aid to Colombia. One anti-war demonstration at the Republican National Convention in 2008 drew thousands of people. After the *Holder* decision, the FBI obtained warrants to search the homes of eight people for evidence related to the crime of conspiracy for providing "material support" to terrorist organizations. The agents seized electronics, photographs, address books, and letters. No arrests were made, and attorney for the suspects dismissed the investigation as "political." In response, protestors in Chicago planned to demonstrate. One attorney, who represented a Chicago resident whose home was searched, opined that the *Holder* opinion "had opened the door to such raids." *See* Colin Moynihan, *FBI Searches Antiwar Activists' Homes,* N.Y. Times, Sept. 24, 2010, http://www.nytimes.com/2010/09/25/us/politics/25search.html?_r=1; Associated Press, *Activists to Protest Recent FBI Raids on Anti-War Members,* FoxNews.com, Sept. 26, 2010, http://www.foxnews.com/us/2010/09/26/activists-protest-recent-fbi-raids-anti-war-members/.

3. *Jihadist Material Online.* In discussing the federal prosecution of Tarek Mehanna under the material support statute in 2009, one reporter noted that under *Holder,* even protected speech can be criminalized if it occurs at the direction of a terrorist organization. So is it possible for a person to be convicted of materially supporting terrorism "for translating a document or putting an extremist video online"? In the view of David Cole, the attorney who argued *Humanitarian Law Project,* the Court held that if a person "is doing it on behalf of a designated group, he is providing a service and that's the crime and it doesn't matter if the speech itself is violent or non-violent." *See* Adam Serwer, *Does Posting Jihadist Material Make Terek Mehanna a Terrorist?,* Mother Jones, Dec. 16, 2011, http://www.motherjones.com/politics/2011/12/ tarek-mehanna-terrorist; Carol Rose, *It's Official. There Is a Muslim Exception to the First Amendment,* On Liberty, BostonGlobe.com, April 12, 2012, http://boston.com/community/blogs/on_liberty/2012/04/its_official_there_is_a_muslim.html.

4. *NSA Surveillance of Telephone and Internet Users.* Reports published by *The Guardian* and the *Washington Post* in 2013 revealed that the National Security

Agency "is currently collecting the telephone records of millions of US customers of Verizon," under "a secret court order" of the Foreign Intelligence
Surveillance Court (FISC). The order applies to calls "both within the US and
between the US and other countries," and requires information that includes
"the numbers of both parties on a call," as well as "location data, call duration,
unique identifiers, and the time and duration of all calls." *See* Glenn Greenwald,
NSA Collecting Phone Records of Millions of Verizon Customers Daily, The Guardian
(Manchester), June 5, 2013, http://www.guardian.co.uk/world/2013/jun/
06/nsa-phone-records-verizon-court-order. The day after the revelations about
the Verizon order, other reports revealed the existence of the NSA program
called PRISM, operated since 2007, which gathers information about internet
user data by means of orders from FISC that direct material to be supplied
by companies that currently include Yahoo!, Microsoft, Google, Facebook,
Skype, YouTube, and AOL. *See* Glenn Greenwald & Ewen MacAskill, *NSA
PRISM Program Taps in to User Data of Apple, Google and Others*, The Guardian
(Manchester), June 6, 2013, http://www.guardian.co.uk/world/2013/jun/
06/us-tech-giants-nsa-data.

   5. *ACLU Lawsuit Regarding NSA Surveillance.* On June 10, 2013, the American
Civil Liberties Union filed a motion with the FISC "seeking release of secret court
opinions that permit the government to acquire Americans' phone records,"
relying, in part, on media reports after June 6 that "have made it clear that
the Verizon order belongs to a much larger surveillance program — covering all
the major telephone companies — that has been in existence for the past seven
years." Patrick C. Toomey, *ACLU Seeks Secret Court Opinions Authorizing NSA's
Mass Acquisition of Americans' Phone Records*, June 10, 2013, http://www.aclu.org/
blog/national-security-technology-and-liberty/aclu-seeks-secret-court-opinions-
authorizing-nsas-mass. Then, the ACLU filed a complaint challenging the NSA's
collection of telephone records as a violation of the organization's First and
Fourth Amendment rights. The ACLU's standing was based on its status as a
customer of Verizon Business Network, and it argued "that the government's
blanket seizure of and ability to search the ACLU's phone records compromises
sensitive information about its work, undermining the organization's ability to
engage in legitimate communications with clients, journalists, advocacy partners, and others." Only a few months earlier, a suit by the ACLU and other
plaintiffs challenging a warrantless wiretapping program was dismissed for lack
of standing in *Clapper v. Amnesty International USA*, 568 U.S. 398 (2013), because
the plaintiffs "could not prove that they had been monitored" under the FISA
Amendments Act.

   6. *Violent Jihad.* In May 2014, Mostafa Kamel Mostafa, a British cleric, was convicted on terrorism-related charges. Mostafa, also known as Abu Hamza al-Masri,
was convicted of having helped orchestrate the kidnappings of Americans and of
an attempt to create a terrorist training camp. The question was whether he was
being prosecuted for his fiery statements (e.g., about devoting his life to violent
jihad) or for specific acts of terrorism.

2. *Fighting Words and Hostile Audiences*

During World War II, the Court created two new First Amendment doctrines designed to balance the needs of the police to maintain public order against the rights of individuals to exercise their freedom of speech in public appearances, whether in demonstrations or in a variety of "street corner" activities related to speech rights. The "fighting words" doctrine gave police the power to arrest an individual for using insulting speech that might provoke a reasonable person to fight. Although a person who actually fights might be arrested for assault or battery, the Court recognized the police could treat the provoking speaker as a guilty participant in the ensuing or potentially ensuing "breach of the peace." However, judicial recognition of the criminality of "fighting words" created a new imperative to define such words (and the circumstances in which their utterance could lead to prosecution) in a sufficiently narrow way to protect the exercise of First Amendment "dissenters" whose provocatively unpopular ideas could not be punished. The "hostile audience" doctrine does not describe a category of "unprotected speech" like fighting words, but rather identifies a situation where an individual is using "protected speech" that provokes his or her audience to violent action or that may provoke such action. The question is how the police should respond to that speech.

Cantwell v. Connecticut

310 U.S. 296 (1940)

Mr. Justice ROBERTS, delivered the opinion of the Court.

Newton Cantwell and his two sons, Jesse and Russell, members of the Jehovah's witnesses, and claiming to be ordained ministers, were going singly from house to house in New Haven in April 1938, equipped with books and pamphlets on religious subjects, a portable phonograph and a set of records. Cassius Street is in a thickly populated neighborhood, where about ninety per cent of the residents are Roman Catholics. Jesse Cantwell stopped two men in the street, asked, and received, permission to play a phonograph record, and played the record "Enemies," which attacked the religion and church of the two men, who were Catholics. Both were incensed by the contents of the record and were tempted to strike Cantwell unless he went away. On being told to be on his way he left their presence. There was no evidence that he was personally offensive or entered into any argument with those he interviewed. The record played by Cantwell "singled out the Roman Catholic Church for strictures couched in terms which naturally would offend not only persons of that persuasion, but all others who respect the honestly held religious faith of their fellows. The hearers were in fact highly offended. One of them said he felt like hitting Cantwell and the other that he was tempted to throw Cantwell off the street." The lower court held that the charge was not assault or breach of the peace or threats on Cantwell's part, but the common law offense of invoking or inciting others to breach of the peace, and that the facts supported the conviction of that offense.

The conviction of Jesse Cantwell must be set aside. The state of Connecticut has an obvious interest in the preservation and protection of peace and good order within her borders. But Cantwell's conviction was not pursuant to a statute evincing a legislative judgment that the playing of a phonograph on the streets should in the interest of comfort or privacy be limited or prevented. The judgment is based on a common law concept of the most general and undefined nature. The offense known as breach of the peace embraces a great variety of conduct destroying or menacing public order and tranquility. It includes not only violent acts but acts and words likely to produce violence in others. No one would suggest that the principle of freedom of speech sanctions incitement to riot or that religious liberty connotes the privilege to exhort others to physical attack upon those belonging to another sect. When clear and present danger of riot, disorder, interference with traffic upon the public streets, or other immediate threat to public safety, peace, or order, appears, the power of the state to prevent or punish is obvious. Equally obvious is that a state may not unduly suppress free communication of views, religious or other, under the guise of conserving desirable conditions. Here we have a situation analogous to a conviction under a statute sweeping in a great variety of conduct under a general and indefinite characterization, and leaving to the executive and judicial branches too wide a discretion in its application.

One may be guilty of the offense if he commit acts or make statements likely to provoke violence and disturbance of good order, even though no such eventuality be intended. In practically all decisions, the provocative language which was held to amount to a breach of the peace consisted of profane, indecent, or abusive remarks directed to the person of the hearer. Resort to epithets or personal abuse is not in any proper sense communication of information or opinion safeguarded by the Constitution, and its punishment as a criminal act would raise no question under that instrument.

We find in the instant case no assault or threatening of bodily harm, no truculent bearing, no intentional discourtesy, no personal abuse. On the contrary, we find only an effort to persuade a willing listener to buy a book or to contribute money in the interest of what Cantwell, however misguided others may think him, conceived to be true religion. In the realm of religious faith, and in that of political belief, sharp differences arise. In both fields the tenets of one man may seem the rankest error to his neighbor. To persuade others to his own point of view, the pleader, at times, resorts to exaggeration, to vilification of men who have been, or are, prominent in church or state, and even to false statement. But the people of this nation have ordained in the light of history, that, in spite of the probability of excesses and abuses, these liberties are, in the long view, essential to enlightened opinion and right conduct on the part of the citizens of a democracy.

The essential characteristic of these liberties is, that under their shield many types of life, character, opinion and belief can develop unmolested and unobstructed. Nowhere is this shield more necessary than in our own country for a people composed of many races and of many creeds. There are limits to the exercise of these liberties. The danger in these times from the coercive activities of those who in the delusion of racial or religious conceit would incite violence and breaches of the peace in order to deprive others of their equal right to the exercise of their liberties, is emphasized by events familiar to all. These and other transgressions of those limits the states appropriately may punish.

Although the contents of the record not unnaturally aroused animosity, we think that, in the absence of a statute narrowly drawn to define and punish specific conduct as constituting a clear and present danger to a substantial interest of the State, Cantwell's communication, considered in the light of the constitutional guarantees, raised no such clear and present menace to public peace and order as to render him liable to conviction of the common law offense in question.

The judgment affirming the conviction is reversed and the cause is remanded for further proceedings not inconsistent with this opinion. So ordered.

⮀ PROBLEM: THE ANTIABORTION CAMPAIGN ⮀

The Center for Bio-Ethical Reform (CBEF) promotes "prenatal justice" through a variety of means, including graphic displays of aborted first-term fetuses on the sides of trucks. The center targets middle and high school students in an effort to discourage abortions, and a CBEF member frequently drives one of the center's trucks around the perimeters of school grounds. A local ordinance makes it illegal to enter school grounds, or to drive on adjacent streets, without lawful business, when "one's presence or acts interfere with the peaceful conduct of school activities or disrupts the school or its pupils or school activities." The center is asked to remove its truck from the school's vicinity after several female students cried when they saw the truck, some boys threw rocks, and some teachers objected to the antiabortion message. Can the center be forced to discontinue its speech and be successfully prosecuted if it fails to do so? How does the presence of the school affect the analysis? *See* Center for *Bio-Ethical Reform Inc. v. Los Angeles County Sheriff Department*, 533 F.3d 780 (9th Cir. 2008), *cert. denied*, 553 U.S. 1098 (2009).

Chaplinsky v. New Hampshire

315 U.S. 568 (1942)

Mr. Justice MURPHY delivered the opinion of the Court.

Walter Chaplinsky, a member of the sect known as Jehovah's Witnesses, was convicted for violating the following New Hampshire statute: "No person shall address any offensive, derisive or annoying word to any other person who is lawfully in any street or other public place, nor call him by any offensive or derisive

1178 11. Freedom of Speech

name, nor make any noise or exclamation in his presence and hearing with intent to deride, offend or annoy him, or to prevent him from pursuing his lawful business or occupation." Chaplinsky was charged only with addressing "offensive, derisive and annoying words and names" to another.

Chaplinsky was distributing the literature of his sect on the streets of Rochester on a busy Saturday afternoon. Members of the local citizenry complained to the City Marshal, Bowering, that Chaplinsky was denouncing all religion as a "racket." Bowering told them that Chaplinsky was lawfully engaged, and then warned Chaplinsky that the crowd was getting restless. Some time later a disturbance occurred and the traffic officer on duty at the busy intersection started with Chaplinsky for the police station, but did not inform him that he was under arrest or that he was going to be arrested. On the way they encountered Marshal Bowering who had been advised that a riot was under way and was therefore hurrying to the scene. Bowering repeated his earlier warning to Chaplinsky who then addressed to Bowering these words: "You are a God damned racketeer" and "a damned Fascist and the whole government of Rochester are Fascists or agents of Fascists". Chaplinsky testified that when he met Bowering, he asked him to arrest the ones responsible for the disturbance. In reply Bowering cursed him. Chaplinsky admitted that he said the words charged in the complaint with the exception of the name of the Deity.

Over Chaplinsky's objection the trial court excluded as immaterial testimony relating to his treatment at the hands of the crowd, and the alleged neglect of duty on the part of the police. The court below held that neither provocation nor the truth of the utterance would constitute a defense to the charge. Chaplinsky argues that the statute violated the Fourteenth Amendment in that it placed an unreasonable restraint on freedom of speech, and because it was vague and indefinite.

Allowing the broadest scope to the language and purpose of the Fourteenth Amendment, it is well understood that the right of free speech is not absolute at all times and under all circumstances. There are certain well-defined and narrowly limited classes of speech, the prevention and punishment of which has never been thought to raise any Constitutional problem. These include the lewd and obscene, the profane, the libelous, and the insulting or "fighting" words—those which by their very utterance inflict injury or tend to incite an immediate breach of the peace. Chafee, *Free Speech in the United States* 149 (1941). It has been well observed that such utterances are no essential part of any exposition of ideas, and are of such slight social value as a step to truth that any benefit that may be derived from them is clearly outweighed by the social interest in order and morality. "Resort to epithets or personal abuse is not in any proper sense communication of information or opinion safeguarded by the Constitution, and its punishment as a criminal act would raise no question under that instrument." *Cantwell v. Connecticut*, 310 U.S. 296 (1940).

The state statute comes to us authoritatively construed by the highest court of New Hampshire. The state court declared that the statute's purpose was to preserve the public peace, no words being "forbidden except such as have a direct tendency to cause acts of violence by the person to whom, individually, the remark is addressed." It was further said by that court:

> The word "offensive" is not to be defined in terms of what a particular addressee thinks. The test is what men of common intelligence would understand would be words likely to cause an average addressee to fight. The English language has a number of words that are expressions which by general consent are "fighting words" when said without a disarming smile. Such words, as ordinary men know, are likely to cause a fight. So are threatening, profane or obscene revilings. Derisive and annoying words can be taken as coming within the purview of the statute as heretofore interpreted only when they have this characteristic of plainly tending to excite the addressee to a breach of the peace. The statute, as construed, does no more than prohibit face-to-face words plainly likely to cause a breach of the peace by the addressee, words whose speaking constitute a breach of the peace by the speaker—including "classical fighting words," words in current use less "classical" but equally likely to cause violence, and other disorderly words, including profanity, obscenity and threats.

We are unable to say that the limited scope of the statute as thus construed contravenes the constitutional right of free expression. It is a statute narrowly drawn and limited to define and punish specific conduct lying within the domain of state power, the use in a public place of words likely to cause a breach of the peace. Thus the statute is not so vague and indefinite as to render a conviction a violation of due process.

Nor can application of the statute to the facts disclosed by the record substantially or unreasonably impinges upon the privilege of free speech. The appellations 'damn racketeer' and 'damn Fascist' are epithets likely to provoke the average person to retaliation, and thereby cause a breach of the peace. Refusal of the state court to admit evidence of provocation and evidence bearing on the truth or falsity of the utterances is open to no Constitutional objection. Whether the facts sought to be proved by such evidence constitute a defense to the charge or may be shown in mitigation are questions for the state court to determine. Our function is fulfilled by a determination that the challenged statute, on its face and as applied, does not contravene the Fourteenth Amendment.

Affirmed.

Notes and Questions

1. *The Justifications for Protecting Speech.* Do "fighting words," as reflected in *Chaplinsky* and *Cantwell*, satisfy the justifications for protecting speech presented at the beginning of this chapter? Do they provide a safety valve, do they promote self-fulfillment or the marketplace of ideas, or are they related to the democratic process? If so, what type of showing should be required to allow the prosecution of statements like those made in *Chaplinsky* and *Cantwell?* Was *Cantwell* correctly decided?

2. *Early Perspective on "Incitement."* *Cantwell's* reliance on the "clear and present danger" standard reflects the pre-*Brandenburg* approach to assessing the likelihood of violence or lawless action in response to an "incitement." At the time, the deferential approach of *Gitlow v. New York* was still good law, and precedents permitted the Court to hold that convictions may be based on proof that acts or statements are "likely to provoke violence and disturbance of good order, even though no such eventuality be intended."

3. *Overbreadth and Vagueness.* The *Cantwell* Court's concern with "overbreadth" foreshadows a speech-protective doctrine that was to arrive with even greater force two decades later. In later years, the Court's scrutiny of potentially vague language in fighting words statutes would become more rigorous.

4. *The Narrow Scope of the "Fighting Words" Doctrine.* In the decades that followed, the Court relied on specific language to emphasize that the "fighting words" doctrine is limited to "face-to-face words," "directed to the person of the hearer," and with an inflammatory content that was likely to provoke "the average person to retaliation, and thereby cause a breach of the peace." *See Street v. New York*, 394 U.S. 576 (1969).

∿ PROBLEMS ∿

1. *Unprotected Words?* Under the *Chaplinsky* "fighting words" doctrine, which of the following statements would qualify as unprotected "fighting words"? A) A man, upset by a second man's religious and political views, approaches him on the street and loudly and angrily denounces the man's views; B) In the preceding situation, the man prefaces his statements by referring to the other man as a "dirty, rotten SOB"; C) At a protest against the Iraq War, observed by both supporters and opponents of the war, a man burns an American flag while stating, "We don't need no damned flag"; D) During the Vietnam War, when the government is drafting young men to serve in the Army, a man wears a jacket emblazoned with a profane expression ("Fuck the Draft") into a courthouse; E) At a protest demonstration, a man burns an American flag; F) A speaker delivers an anti-Semitic speech to a crowd of 800 people while 1,000 people gather outside in a hostile audience. The crowd gets increasingly restless and upset.

2. *Fighting Words Directed at Public Officials.* Should it matter whether fighting words are directed at public officials rather than at private individuals? *Chaplinsky* did not deem it relevant that the defendant's "fighting words" were uttered in the context of criticism of public officials, and were explicitly directed at the city marshal. But consider the comments of Justice Powell in another fighting words case: "If these words had been addressed by one citizen to another, face to face and in a hostile manner, they would be 'fighting words.' But the situation may be different where such words are addressed to a police officer trained to exercise a higher degree of restraint than the average citizen." *Lewis v. City of New Orleans,*

408 U.S. 913 (1972) (Powell, J., concurring). *See also New York Times v. Sullivan Co.*, 376 U.S. 254 (1964). Which approach is preferable?

3. *The Pastor and the Koran.* Terry Jones, a pastor in Gainesville, Florida, threatened to burn a copy of the Koran in 2010, as a protest against the possible development of an Islamic Center near Ground Zero in Manhattan. The pastor was dissuaded from doing so by the pleas of government officials and religious leaders, who feared that the burning of the Koran would spark an anti-U.S. backlash around the world. However, Jones later declared that he would "put the Koran on trial," and he burned a copy of the Koran in a ceremony at his church in 2011. This event triggered violent mob action that resulted in the deaths of more than 20 UN employees and others in Afghanistan, and injury to scores of others. Jones then announced plans for a Koran-burning rally on Good Friday outside the largest mosque in the United States together with a group of armed protestors (with concealed-weapons permits). Can the City of Dearborn stop the rally from taking place on the ground that the act will incite violence from a hostile audience? *See* Bernie Woodall, *Michigan Prosecutor Files to Stop Koran-Burning Pastor*, Reuters: U.S. ed., Apr. 19, 2011, http://www.reuters.com/article/2011/04/19/us-pastor-koran-idUSTRE73I5WW20110419.

4. *More on the International Treaty Regulating the Internet.* Does the *Chaplinsky* decision alter your position on whether the United States can accept the European request to include language from the European Convention on Human Rights (in particular the language authorizing government to limit speech as necessary to the "public safety" as well as for "the prevention of disorder or crime") as part of the treaty regulating the internet? If you cannot accept the convention's language, what language might you be able to accept? What language would you propose to the other delegates?

Gooding v. Wilson

405 U.S. 518 (1972)

Mr. Justice BRENNAN delivered the opinion of the Court.

Johnny Wilson was convicted on two counts of using opprobrious words and abusive language in violation of the Georgia Code which provides: "Any person who shall, without provocation, use to or of another, and in his presence opprobrious words or abusive language, tending to cause a breach of the peace shall be guilty of a misdemeanor." The Supreme Court of Georgia rejected his contention that the statute was vague and overbroad. The Georgia Supreme Court sustained the conviction. Wilson then sought and obtained federal habeas corpus relief. The Court of Appeals affirmed. We affirm.

With others, Wilson picketed the building in which the 12th Corps Headquarters of the United States Army was located, carrying signs opposing the war in Viet Nam. When the inductees arrived at the building, these persons began to block the door so that the inductees could not enter. They were requested by police officers to move from the door, but refused to do so. The officers attempted to remove them from the door, and a scuffle ensued. Wilson also committed assault and battery on the two police officers named in the indictment. The indictment alleged that Wilson "did use to M. G. Redding the following language: 'White son of a bitch, I'll kill you.' 'You son of a bitch, I'll choke you to death,' and that Gooding did use to and of T. L. Raborn the following language: 'You son of a bitch, if you ever put your hands on me again, I'll cut you all to pieces.'"

The state argues that the Georgia appellate courts have by construction limited the proscription of opprobrious words or abusive language, tending to cause a breach of the peace to "fighting" words as defined in *Chaplinsky*. Our examination brings us to the conclusion that the Georgia appellate decisions have not construed the statute to be limited, as in *Chaplinsky*, to words that "have a direct tendency to cause acts of violence by the person to whom, individually, the remark is addressed."

The dictionary definitions of "opprobrious" and "abusive" give them greater reach than "fighting" words. Webster's *Third New International Dictionary* (1961) defined "opprobrious" as "conveying or intended to convey disgrace," and "abusive" as including "harsh insulting language." Georgia appellate decisions have construed the statute to apply to utterances that, although within these definitions, are not "fighting" words as *Chaplinsky* defines them. The statute is not limited to words that "naturally tend to provoke violent resentment." We conclude that "the separation of legitimate from illegitimate speech calls for more sensitive tools than (Georgia) has supplied." *Speiser v. Randall*, 357 U.S. 513 (1958). Because earlier appellate decisions applied the statute to utterances where there was no likelihood that the person addressed would make an immediate violent response, it is clear that the standard allowing juries to determine guilt "measured by common understanding and practice" does not limit the application of the statute to "fighting" words defined by *Chaplinsky*. Rather, that broad standard effectively "licenses the jury to create its own standard in each case."

Accordingly, we agree with the conclusion of the District Court, "the fault of the statute is that it leaves wide open the standard of responsibility, so that it is easily susceptible to improper application." Unlike the construction of the New Hampshire statute by the New Hampshire Supreme Court in *Chaplinsky*, the Georgia appellate courts have not construed the statute "so as to avoid all constitutional difficulties."

Affirmed.

Note: The *Gooding* Dissents

Chief Justice Burger dissented in *Gooding*, arguing that the Georgia precedents "do nothing to demonstrate that the narrow language of the Georgia statute has any significant potential for sweeping application to suppress or deter important protected speech." Justice Blackmun also dissented and argued that "the words of the Georgia Code statute are clear. They are also concise. They are not, in my view, overbroad or incapable of being understood. Except perhaps for the 'big' word 'opprobrious,' any Georgia schoolboy would expect that this defendant's fighting and provocative words to the officers were covered by the statute."

∽ PROBLEMS ∽

1. *Fighting Words in Context.* After *Chaplinsky* and *Gooding*, which of the following statements constitute prohibitable fighting words? A) A mother, upset about her son's arrest, referred to police officers as "you G—d—m—f—police," and is prosecuted under a statute that provides that "it shall be unlawful and a breach of the peace for any person wantonly to curse or revile or to use obscene or opprobrious language toward or with reference to any member of the city police while in the actual performance of his duty." *See Lewis v. New Orleans*, 408 U.S. 913 (1972); B) In *Lyons v. State*, 94 Ga. App. 570, 95 S.E.2d 478 (1956), a man was charged for awakening ten women scout leaders on a campout by shouting, "Boys, this is where we are going to spend the night." "Get the G—d—bed rolls out let's see how close we can come to the G—d—tents."; C) In *Fish v. State*, 124 Ga. 416, 52 S.E. 737 (1905), a man was charged for stating to another man: "You swore a lie."; D) In *Jackson v. State*, 14 Ga. App. 19, 80 S.E. 20 (1913), a motorist was charged for saying to another motorist: "God damn you, why don't you get out of the road?"

2. *Conviction Today?* Consider how *Chaplinsky* should be decided in the post-*Gooding* era. Identify the arguments that the defendant would make relying on *Gooding*, and explain how the government lawyer would attempt to distinguish the *Chaplinsky* facts, statutory language, and state court interpretation of that language from the same elements of *Gooding*, and thereby defend against a modern vagueness challenge in *Chaplinsky*.

3. *Remarks to Police Officers.* Police officers, believing that two teenage girls have stolen some bicycles, question the girls. When the questioning is over, as the girls are walking away, they turn and yell in unison, "Fuck you, pigs." The officers pursue the girls down an alley and arrest them for disorderly conduct under a statute that reads: "Whoever in a public or private place, having reasonable grounds to know that the conduct of engaging in offensive, obscene or abusive language will tend to alarm, anger or disturb others or provoke an assault or breach of peace, is guilty of disorderly conduct." One of the officers testified at trial: "I was mad. I was upset. They didn't have a right to say that to me." The officer admitted during cross-examination that he had received some sensitivity training on how to respond to name calling, and that he did not react violently or have fear because of the speakers' age, sex, and size. The girls are convicted and appeal in state court alleging overbreadth and vagueness. How must the

state supreme court construe the disorderly conduct statute in order to satisfy *Gooding* and uphold the statute against the overbreadth and vagueness challenge? Assuming that the statute is construed narrowly in compliance with *Gooding*, is there sufficient evidence to uphold the conviction? *See* Matter of Welfare of S.L.J., 263 N.W.2d 412 (Minn. 1978).

4. *The Danish Cartoons as "Fighting Words"?* A Danish newspaper published caricatures of the Prophet Mohammed to criticize Muslim violence and suicide bombing. Many Muslims were furious about the publication because Muslim law prohibits the publication of pictures of the Prophet and because the Prophet was portrayed as a terrorist. The publication produced widespread protests, some peaceful, but others very violent with property damage and deaths. Does the "fighting words" doctrine apply to the cartoons so that the government may prohibit them or prosecute their publication under an appropriately worded law? Does the doctrine apply to publication as opposed to spoken words?

The "hostile audience" doctrine is traditionally traced to *Feiner v. New York*, which was decided in 1951, the same year as *Dennis v. United States*.

Feiner v. New York

340 U.S. 315 (1951)

Mr. Chief Justice Vinson delivered the opinion of the Court.

On March 8, 1949, petitioner Irving Feiner was addressing an open-air meeting in the City of Syracuse. The police received a telephone complaint concerning the meeting, and two officers were detailed to investigate. They found a crowd of about seventy-five or eighty people, both Negro and white, filling the sidewalk and spreading out into the street. Feiner, standing on a large wooden box on the sidewalk, was addressing the crowd through a loud-speaker system attached to an automobile. Although the purpose of his speech was to urge his listeners to attend a meeting to be held that night in the Syracuse Hotel, in its course he was making derogatory remarks concerning President Truman, the American Legion, the Mayor of Syracuse, and other local political officials.

The police made no effort to interfere with petitioner's speech, but were concerned with the effect of the crowd on both pedestrian and vehicular traffic. Some pedestrians were forced to walk in the street to avoid the crowd. Since traffic was passing, the officers attempted to get the people back on the sidewalk. The crowd was restless and there was some pushing, shoving and milling around. One officer telephoned the police station. At this time, Feiner was speaking in a "loud, high-pitched voice." He gave the impression that he was endeavoring to arouse the Negro people against the whites, urging that they rise up in arms and fight for equal rights. The statements before such a mixed audience "stirred up a little excitement." Some of the onlookers made remarks to the police about their inability to handle the crowd and at least one threatened violence if the police did not act. There were others who appeared to be favoring Feiner's arguments. Because of the feeling that existed in the crowd both for and against the speaker, the officers finally "stepped in to prevent it from resulting in a fight." One of the officers approached Feiner, not for the purpose of arresting him, but to get him to break up the crowd. He asked Feiner to get down off the box, but Feiner refused to accede to his request and continued talking. The officer waited for a minute and then demanded that he cease talking. Although the officer twice requested Feiner to stop over the course of several minutes, Feiner continued talking. During all this time, the crowd was pressing closer. Finally, the officer told Feiner he was under arrest and ordered him to get down from the box, reaching up to grab him. Feiner stepped down, announcing over the microphone that "the law has arrived, and I suppose they will take over now." In all, the officer had asked petitioner to get down off the box three times over a space of four or five minutes. Feiner had been speaking for over a half hour.

Feiner was charged with "ignoring and refusing to heed and obey reasonable police orders issued at the time and place mentioned in the Information to regulate and control said crowd and to prevent a breach or breaches of the peace and to prevent injury to pedestrians attempting to use said walk, and being forced into the highway adjacent to the place in question, and prevent injury to the public generally." The statute defined disorderly conduct as follows: "Any person who with intent to provoke a breach of the peace, or whereby a breach of the peace may be occasioned, commits any of the following acts shall be deemed to have committed the offense of disorderly conduct: '1. Uses offensive, disorderly, threatening, abusive or insulting language, conduct or behavior; 2. Acts in such a manner as to annoy, disturb, interfere with, obstruct, or be offensive to others; 3. Congregates with others on a public street and refuses to move on when ordered by the police.'" Feiner was convicted of the offense of disorderly conduct, and was sentenced to thirty days in the county penitentiary. The conviction was affirmed by the state courts.

The language of *Cantwell v. State of Connecticut*, 310 U.S. 296 (1940), is appropriate here. "The offense known as breach of the peace embraces a great variety of conduct destroying or menacing public order and tranquility. It includes not only violent acts but acts and words likely to produce violence in others. When clear and present danger of riot, disorder, interference with traffic upon the public streets, or other immediate threat to public safety, peace, or order, appears, the power of the State to prevent or punish is obvious." The findings of the New York courts as to the condition of the crowd and Feiner's refusal to obey the police requests are persuasive that Feiner's conviction for violation of public peace, order and authority does not exceed the bounds of proper state police action. This Court respects, as it must, the interest of the community in maintaining peace and order on its streets.

We are well aware that the ordinary murmurings and objections of a hostile audience cannot be allowed to silence a speaker, and are also mindful of the danger of giving overzealous police officials complete discretion to break up oth-erwise lawful public meetings. As *Cantwell* determined, "a State may not unduly suppress free communication of views, religious or other, under the guise of con-serving desirable conditions." But it is one thing to say that the police cannot be used as an instrument for suppression of unpopular views, and another to say that, when the speaker passes the bounds of argument or persuasion and under-takes incitement to riot, they are powerless to prevent a breach of the peace. The findings of state courts as to the existing situation and the imminence of greater disorder coupled with Feiner's deliberate defiance of the police officers convince us that we should not reverse this conviction in the name of free speech.

Affirmed.

Mr. Justice BLACK, *dissenting.*

Feiner, a college student, has been sentenced to the penitentiary for the unpopular views he expressed on matters of public interest while lawfully making a street-corner speech. The end result approves a simple and readily available technique by which cities and states can subject speeches to the supervision and censorship of the local police. This is a long step toward totalitarian authority.

It seems farfetched to suggest that the "facts" show any imminent threat of riot or uncontrollable disorder. It is neither unusual nor unexpected that some people at public street meetings mutter, mill about, push, shove, or disagree, even violently, with the speaker. Indeed, it is rare where controversial topics are discussed that an outdoor crowd does not do some or all of these things. Nor does one isolated threat to assault the speaker forebode disorder. Especially should the danger be discounted where, as here, the person threatening was a man whose wife and two small children accompanied him and who was never close enough to petitioner to carry out the threat. Assuming that the "facts" did indicate a criti-cal situation, I reject the implication that the police had no obligation to protect Feiner's constitutional right to talk. If, in the name of preserving order, they ever can interfere with a lawful public speaker, they first must make all reasonable efforts to protect him. Here the police did not even try to protect petitioner or arrest the man who threatened to interfere. Instead, they acted only to suppress the right to speak.

I cannot agree that Feiner's disregard of the policeman's unexplained request amounted to such "deliberate defiance" as would justify an arrest or con-viction for disorderly conduct. The policeman's action was a 'deliberate defiance' of ordinary official duty as well as of the constitutional right of free speech. Feiner was 'asked' then 'told' then 'commanded' to stop speaking, but a man making a lawful address is not required to be silent merely because an officer directs it. Feiner was entitled to know why he should cease doing a lawful act. People in authoritarian countries must obey arbitrary orders. I had hoped that there was no such duty in the United States. Today's holding means that minority speakers can be silenced in any city. Despite the First and Fourteenth Amendments, the policeman's club can take heavy toll of a current administration's public critics.

Criticism of public officials will be too dangerous for all but the most courageous. I would *reverse* the conviction.

Notes and Questions

1. *The Trial Record.* Justice Douglas dissented in *Feiner*, noting that the record revealed only six "excerpts" of Feiner's speech: "Mayor Costello (of Syracuse) is a champagne-sipping bum; he does not speak for the negro people; The 15th Ward is run by corrupt politicians, and there are horse rooms operating there; President Truman is a bum; Mayor O'Dwyer is a bum; The American Legion is a Nazi Gestapo; The negroes don't have equal rights; they should rise up in arms and fight for their rights."

2. *The Heckler's Veto.* In the "hostile audience" situation, the police order the speaker to cease talking and may eventually arrest if there is noncompliance. The arrest usually is for the offense of disobeying a police order, disorderly conduct, or breach of the peace. The constitutional imperative in this scenario is to create a doctrine that will protect the provocatively unpopular speaker from "the heckler's veto." As one scholar explained the "hostile audience" problem, "by giving the police wide discretion to stop the speaker because of audience hostility, the state in effect transfers the power of censorship to the crowd. Moreover, the police are likely to share the views of the angry audience; hence, their perception of the unrest may be colored by their assessment of the speaker's message. The end result is the censorship of wholly permissible content." HARRY KALVEN, JR., A WORTHY TRADITION: FREEDOM OF SPEECH IN AMERICA 90 (Harper & Row 1988). Kalven's insight may be applicable to the "fighting words" doctrine as well, because that concept reflects an assumption that police have discretion to make judgments about whether a "provoking" speaker should be arrested, and thereby to act as censors of a message that police view as inimical to public order. The censorship power is masked in both the "fighting words" and "hostile audience" contexts by the neutral nature of the conduct crimes for which the speaker typically is arrested.

3. *The Level of Danger.* The Court notes in *Feiner* that "when clear and present danger of riot, disorder, interference with traffic upon the public streets, or other immediate threat to public safety, peace, or order, appears, the power of the State to prevent or punish is obvious." Although the "clear and present danger" test is largely of historical significance today, do the facts reveal a clear and present danger of riot, disorder, and interference with traffic in this case, or were the police trying to repress Feiner's ideas?

4. *The Nazi March.* In *Village of Skokie v. National Socialist Party of America*, 69 Ill. 2d 605, 373 N.E.2d 21 (Ill. 1978), members of the National Socialist Party of America wanted to march in Skokie, Illinois, a predominantly Jewish village with a significant number of Holocaust survivors, and the marchers planned to wear Nazi uniforms and swastikas. Jewish groups threatened a violent response to the

march. The Illinois Supreme Court held that the Nazis had a right to march, noting that "the heavy presumption against the constitutional validity of a prior restraint" could not be overcome. The court cited 1960s precedents like *Gregory* for the proposition that "a hostile audience is not a basis for restraining otherwise legal First Amendment activity," and noted that "courts have consistently refused to ban speech because of the possibility of unlawful conduct by those opposed to the speaker's philosophy." In a different phase of the Skokie litigation, the village conceded that it did not rely on a fear of responsive violence as an argument for stopping the Nazi march, and promised to "make every effort to protect the demonstrators" from "responsive violence" if required by a court order to permit the march to take place. Ultimately, the Nazis decided to hold the march elsewhere.

5. *Anti-Islamic Video Protests.* In July 2012, a 14-minute video was uploaded to YouTube, and was represented as a trailer for a film. The video appeared under two titles, "The Real Life of Muhammad" and the "Muhammad Movie Video," and anti-Islamic content had been added to the video by "overdubbing." The video was later dubbed in Arabic, received notice from a blogger, and broadcast on an Egyptian television station. The video produced worldwide protests. About 3,000 demonstrators protested the YouTube video outside the Cairo Embassy, demanding that the film be taken out of circulation. The United States Embassy in Cairo issued a statement rejecting the use of free speech to insult the religion of others. Nevertheless, protestors scaled the embassy walls and destroyed a U.S. flag. An attack on the U.S. Embassy in Benghazi killed the U.S. ambassador to Libya, and three other embassy staffers. While initial reports suggested that the Benghazi attack was a protest against the film, it was later determined that the attacks were planned in advance by Al Qaeda.

These attacks were followed by a wave of attacks against other U.S. interests, and ultimately some 75 people were killed in attacks on installations at the U.S. embassy in Sana'a, Yemen; the Multinational Force and Observers in the Sinai Peninsula; the U.S. Embassy and the American Cooperative School in Tunis; and the U.S. Consulate in Chennai, India. Protestors in Islamabad demonstrated outside the U.S. Embassy, called for execution of the filmmaker, and urged that the U.S. Embassy be closed. There were Taliban attacks on Camp Bastion in the Helmand province of Afghanistan; two American Marines were killed. Although YouTube and Google (the owner of YouTube) refused to remove the video, they did block its dissemination in Egypt, Libya, Indonesia, Saudi Arabia, Malaysia, India, Singapore, Pakistan, and Jordan. Other countries blocked the YouTube website for its failure to block the video.

On September 17, up to 500 protestors attacked the U.S. embassy in Jakarta, Indonesia. In September, an Egyptian militant group attacked Israeli soldiers near the Israel-Egypt border; the group claimed the film motivated their attack. On September 23, Greek Muslims protested in Athens, calling on the United States to "hang" the filmmaker. There were additional protests in many other countries. After a week of protests in Pakistan, a cabinet minister, Ghulam Ahmed Bilour, announced a $100,000 bounty for the killing of the video's producer. The producer was later identified as a 55-year-old Coptic Christian from Egypt, and he was arrested by federal authorities in Los Angeles for violating the terms of his probation, which included the making of false statements regarding his role in the film's production.

∽ PROBLEMS ∽

1. *The Police Duty.* In *Feiner*, the Court concludes that the police may stop Feiner's speech in order to protect the public against riot or disorder. Suppose that Feiner is allowed to continue to speak and others begin to threaten him unless he stops. What is the proper police response? Should the police be required to protect Feiner against the hostile crowd and to arrest those who threaten a breach of the peace? Assume that the police try to protect Feiner and that the crowd becomes increasingly disorderly. Is there a point at which First Amendment rights should give way to the public interest in maintaining the peace? With regard to Feiner's speech, when would he reach that point?

2. *Future Similar Speeches.* Assume that you have been asked to advise Feiner after he lost his case. He would like to avoid arrest for disorderly conduct, but he would like to make a similar sort of speech on the same street corner. Describe the specific advice that you would provide. How could Feiner preserve his ability to make First Amendment arguments at trial, assuming that he is arrested?

3. *Proselytizing at the Festival.* The Arab Festival is an annual event in Dearborn, Michigan, that is open to the public and attracts 250,000 people. A Christian evangelical group targets the event as a way to convert non-believers. Members of the group attend the festival wearing T-shirts with printed slogans: "Jesus is the Way, All Others are Thieves and Robbers," "Be Converted That Your Sins May Be Blotted Out," and "Islam is a Religion of Blood and Murder." Some festival attendees react to the T-shirts by throwing water and garbage at the wearers. Police are summoned by bystanders to the scene of the altercation. The officers warn the t-shirt wearers that they will receive citations for the crime of disorderly conduct if they do not leave the festival immediately. Under the circumstances, is the police order consistent with the First Amendment? *Compare Bible Believers v. Wayne County*, 765 F.3d 578 (6th Cir. 2014).

4. *The Charlottesville Protests.* One of the most dramatic examples of violence in the context of hostile audiences occurred in Charlottesville, Virginia, in August 2017, when a group of white supremacists decided to hold a rally. Some of the protesters openly carried weapons and one of the counter-protesters was killed. Others were injured. Suppose that members of a white supremacist group plan to hold a rally in Toledo, Ohio. Prior to the rally, police receive reports indicating that counter-protesters are going to "turn out in force." According to police intelligence, some of these groups have a history of engaging in violent acts at protests. May the police prohibit the rally? If the police allow the rally to go ahead, but then there are violent acts committed by some protesters and counter-protesters

(throwing rocks, engaging in vandalism and looting, and setting fires), at what point may the police shut down the rally for the safety of the community? See FINAL REPORT: INDEPENDENT REVIEW OF THE 2017 PROTEST EVENTS IN CHARLOTTESVILLE, VIRGINIA, Hunton & Williams, LLP, December 1, 2017.

3. Offensive Speech

Is "offensive speech" entitled to special constitutional protection? Prior decisions, like *Chaplinsky* and *Cantwell*, pointed in different directions. *Chaplinsky* seemed to allow punishment for uttering "offensive words," and his conviction was upheld because the crime was construed as requiring the use of fighting words that had a "direct tendency to cause acts of violence" by the person to whom they were addressed. Yet *Cantwell* established that "offensive words" involving criticism of the religion of the listener were protected speech. As a result, "offensive words" did not fall into the fighting words category when the "offensive words" were not "epithets" or "abuse" directed at the listener. Even if the listener was offended by criticism, and even if any reasonable listener would be similarly offended, the critical speech did not lose its protection. In the absence of evidence of an intent to incite, the religious criticism could not be punished by the common law crime of "inciting" the listener to a breach of the peace. In 1971, the Court used the following case to construct an edifice of policy judgments about the governmental interests in regulating offensive speech.

Cohen v. California

403 U.S. 15 (1971)

Mr. Justice HARLAN delivered the opinion of the Court.

Defendant was observed in the Los Angeles County Courthouse in the corridor outside of division 20 of the municipal court wearing a jacket bearing the words "Fuck the Draft" which were plainly visible. There were women and children present in the corridor. Defendant testified that he wore the jacket knowing that the words were on the jacket as a means of informing the public of the depth of his feelings against the Vietnam War and the draft. Defendant did not engage in, nor threaten to engage in, nor did anyone as the result of his conduct in fact commit or threaten to commit any act of violence. Defendant did not make any loud or unusual noise, nor was there any evidence that he uttered any sound prior to his arrest. When Cohen entered a courtroom in the building, "he removed his jacket and stood with it folded over his arm"; then "a policeman sent the presiding judge a note suggesting that Cohen be held in contempt of court," but "the judge declined to do so and Cohen was arrested by the officer after he emerged from the courtroom." Cohen was convicted and given 30 days in prison for the crime of "maliciously and willfully disturbing the peace or quiet of any neighborhood or person by offensive conduct." The California Supreme Court declined review. We now reverse.

The conviction rests upon the asserted offensiveness of the words Cohen used to convey his message to the public. The only "conduct" which the State sought to punish is the fact of communication. Thus, we deal with a conviction resting solely upon "speech," not upon any separately identifiable conduct which was intended by Cohen to be perceived by others as expressive of particular views but which, on its face, does not necessarily convey any message and arguably could be regulated without effectively repressing Cohen's ability to express himself. *Cf. United States v. O'Brien*, 391 U.S. 367 (1968). The State certainly lacks power to punish Cohen for the underlying content of the message. So long as there is no showing of an intent to incite disobedience to or disruption of the draft, Cohen could not, consistently with the First and Fourteenth Amendments, be punished for asserting the evident position on the inutility or immorality of the draft his jacket reflected. *Yates v. United States*, 354 U.S. 298 (1957).

Cohen's conviction rests squarely upon his exercise of the "freedom of speech" protected from arbitrary governmental interference by the Constitution and can be justified, if at all, only as a valid regulation of the manner in which he exercised that freedom, not as a permissible prohibition on the substantive message it conveys. The First and Fourteenth Amendments have never been thought to give absolute protection to every individual to speak whenever or wherever he pleases or to use any form of address in any circumstances that he chooses.

Any attempt to support this conviction on the ground that the statute seeks to preserve an appropriately decorous atmosphere in the courthouse where Cohen was arrested must fail in the absence of any language in the statute that would have put appellant on notice that otherwise permissible speech or conduct would nevertheless, under California law, not be tolerated in certain places. No fair reading of the phrase "offensive conduct" can sufficiently to inform the ordinary person that distinctions between certain locations are thereby created.

This case cannot fall within those relatively few categories of instances where prior decisions have established the power of government to deal with certain forms of individual expression simply upon a showing that such a form was employed. This is not, for example, an obscenity case. Such expression must be, in some significant way, erotic. *Roth v. United States*, 354 U.S. 476 (1957). It cannot be maintained that this vulgar allusion to the Selective Service System would conjure up such psychic stimulation in anyone likely to be confronted with Cohen's crudely defaced jacket. The States are free to ban the simple use, without a demonstration of additional justifying circumstances, of so-called "fighting words." *Chaplinsky v. New Hampshire*, 315 U.S. 568 (1942). While the four-letter word displayed by Cohen is not uncommonly employed in a personally provocative fashion, in this instance it was clearly not "directed to the person of the hearer." No individual actually or likely to be present could reasonably have regarded the words as a direct personal insult. Nor do we have here an instance of the exercise of the State's police power to prevent a speaker from intentionally provoking a given group to hostile reaction. *Cf. Feiner v. New York*, 340 U.S. 315 (1951). There is no showing that anyone who saw Cohen was in fact violently aroused or that appellant intended such a result.

Much has been made of the claim that Cohen's distasteful mode of expression was thrust upon unwilling or unsuspecting viewers, and that the State might therefore legitimately act to protect the sensitive from unavoidable exposure to appellant's crude form of protest. Of course, the mere presumed presence of unwitting listeners or viewers does not serve automatically to justify curtailing all speech capable of giving offense. While government may properly act in many situations to prohibit intrusion into the privacy of the home of unwelcome views and ideas which cannot be totally banned from the public dialogue, we have stressed that "we are often 'captives' outside the sanctuary of the home and subject to objectionable speech." *Rowan v. United States Post Office Dept.*, 397 U.S. 728 (1970). The ability of government, consonant with the Constitution, to shut off discourse solely to protect others from hearing it is dependent upon a showing that substantial privacy interests are being invaded in an essentially intolerable manner. Any broader view of this authority would effectively empower a majority to silence dissidents simply as a matter of personal predilections.

Persons confronted with Cohen's jacket were in a quite different posture than, say, those subjected to the raucous emissions of sound trucks blaring outside their residences. Those in the Los Angeles courthouse could effectively avoid further bombardment of their sensibilities simply by averting their eyes. While it may be that one has a more substantial claim to a recognizable privacy interest when walking through a courthouse corridor than strolling through Central Park, surely it is nothing like the interest in being free from unwanted expression in the confines of one's own home. Given the subtlety and complexity of the factors involved, if Cohen's "speech" was entitled to constitutional protection, we do not think the fact that some unwilling "listeners" in a public building may have been briefly exposed to it can justify this breach of the peace conviction where, as here, there was no evidence that persons powerless to avoid appellant's conduct did in fact object to it, and where that portion of the statute upon which Cohen's conviction rests evinces no concern, either on its face or as construed by the California courts, with the special plight of the captive auditor, but, instead, indiscriminately sweeps within its prohibitions all "offensive conduct" that disturbs "any neighborhood or person."

Against this background, the issue is whether California can excise, as "offensive conduct," one particular scurrilous epithet from the public discourse, either upon the theory of the court below that its use is inherently likely to cause violent reaction or upon a more general assertion that the States, acting as guardians of public morality, may properly remove this offensive word from the public vocabulary.

The rationale of the California court is untenable. At most it reflects an "undifferentiated fear or apprehension of disturbance which is not enough to overcome the right to freedom of expression." We have been shown no evidence that substantial numbers of citizens are standing ready to strike out physically at whoever may assault their sensibilities with execrations like that uttered by Cohen. There may be some persons with such lawless and violent proclivities, but that is an insufficient base upon which to erect, consistently with constitutional values, a governmental power to force persons who wish to ventilate their dissident views into avoiding particular forms of expression. The argument amounts to little more than the self-defeating proposition that to avoid physical censorship of one who has not sought to provoke such a response by a hypothetical coterie of the violent and lawless, States may more effectuate that censorship themselves.

It is not obvious that the First and Fourteenth Amendments disable the States from punishing public utterance of this unseemly expletive in order to maintain a suitable level of discourse within the body politic. We think, however, that examination and reflection reveal the shortcomings of a contrary viewpoint. Most situations where the State has a justifiable interest in regulating speech will fall within one or more of the various established exceptions to the usual rule that governmental bodies may not prescribe the form or content of individual expression. The constitutional right of free expression is powerful medicine in a society as diverse and populous as ours. It is designed and intended to remove governmental restraints from the arena of public discussion, putting the decision as to what views shall be voiced largely into the hands of each of us, in the hope that use of such freedom will ultimately produce a more capable citizenry and more perfect polity and in the belief that no other approach would comport with the premise of individual dignity and choice upon which our political system rests. To many, the consequence of this freedom may often appear to be only verbal tumult, discord, and even offensive utterance. These are, within established limits, in truth necessary side effects of the broader enduring values which the process of open debate permits us to achieve. That the air may at times seem filled with verbal cacophony is not a sign of weakness but of strength. We cannot lose sight of the fact that, in what otherwise might seem a trifling and annoying instance of individual distasteful abuse of a privilege, these fundamental societal values are truly implicated.

Against the constitutional policies involved, we discern more particularized considerations that call for reversal of this conviction. First, the principle contended for by the State seems inherently boundless. How is one to distinguish this from any other offensive word? Surely the State has no right to cleanse public debate to the point where it is grammatically palatable to the most squeamish. Yet no readily ascertainable general principle exists for stopping short of that result were we to affirm the judgment below. While the particular four-letter word here is perhaps more distasteful than most others of its genre, it is nevertheless often true that one man's vulgarity is another's lyric. Indeed, it is largely because governmental officials cannot make principled distinctions in this area that the Constitution leaves matters of taste and style so largely to the individual.

Much linguistic expression serves a dual communicative function: it conveys not only ideas capable of relatively precise, detached explication, but otherwise inexpressible emotions as well. In fact, words are often chosen as much for their emotive as their cognitive force. We cannot sanction the view that the Constitution, while solicitous of the cognitive content of individual speech has little or no regard for that emotive function which practically speaking, may often be the more important element of the overall message sought to be communicated.

In the same vein, we cannot indulge the facile assumption that one can forbid particular words without also running a substantial risk of suppressing ideas. Indeed, governments might soon seize upon the censorship of particular words as a convenient guise for banning the expression of unpopular views. We have been able to discern little social benefit that might result from running the risk of opening the door to such grave results. It is our judgment that, absent a more particularized and compelling reason for its actions, the State may not, consistently with the First and Fourteenth Amendments, make the simple public display here involved of this single four-letter expletive a criminal offense.

Reversed.

Mr. Justice BLACKMUN, with whom THE CHIEF JUSTICE and Mr. Justice BLACK join, *concurring.*

Cohen's absurd and immature antic was mainly conduct and little speech. The case appears to be within the sphere of *Chaplinsky.* This Court's agonizing over First Amendment values seems misplaced and unnecessary.

Food for Thought: The Justifications for Protecting Speech.

Did Cohen's speech satisfy any of the justifications for protecting speech presented at the beginning of this chapter? In other words, did it provide a safety valve, did it promote self-fulfillment or the marketplace of ideas, or was it related to the democratic process? If so, what type of showing should be required to allow the prosecution of statements like those made by Cohen?

Notes and Questions

1. *Catalogue of "Inapplicable Theories" and Broad First Amendment Values.* Once the *Cohen* majority endorses a narrow definition of "fighting words," its rejection of that theory (arguing that Cohen's message might cause others to "rise up to commit a violent act") seems foreordained. The staying power of *Cohen's* narrow definition of fighting words is illustrated in *Texas v. Johnson,* 491 U.S. 397 (1989) (striking down a statute that punished flag desecration). *Cohen's* rejection of the idea that the "state should be the moral guardian of speech" led to a discussion of First Amendment values that has been influential in subsequent case law, especially the notion of the "emotive value of speech" and the reminder about the difficulty of making "principled distinctions" in a field of offensive speech when one person's "vulgarity" is another's "lyric."

2. *Slight Social Value. Cohen* contradicts the "slight social value" rationale for the unprotected status of "fighting words" endorsed in *Chaplinsky*, emphasizing that "fundamental societal values are truly implicated" even in the "trifling and annoying instance of individual distasteful abuse of a privilege" represented by Cohen's message on his jacket. However, *Cohen* ignored rather than repudiated the "slight social value" theory.

3. *Disparaging Trademarks. Matal v. Tam,* 137 S. Ct. 1744 (2017), was a trademark case in which petitioner tried to trademark his band's name, "The Slants." The Patent and Trademark Office (PTO) declined to register the name, relying on a provision of federal law that allowed the PTO to reject a trademark that might "disparage or bring into contempt or disrepute" any "persons living or dead." The Court struck down the law as a violation of free speech because it offended a "bedrock First Amendment principle": "The government may not prohibit the expression of an idea simply because society finds the idea itself offensive or disagreeable." *Texas v. Johnson,* 491 U. S. 397, 414 (1989). The Court explained: "We have said time and again that 'the public expression of ideas may not be prohibited merely because the ideas are themselves offensive to some of their hearers.'" *Street v. New York,* 394 U. S. 576, 592 (1969). Justice Kennedy, joined by three other justices, authored a concurring opinion: "The viewpoint discrimination rationale renders unnecessary any extended treatment of other questions raised by the parties. It is a fundamental principle of the First Amendment that the government may not punish or suppress speech based on disapproval of the ideas or perspectives the speech conveys. An applicant may register a positive or benign mark but not a derogatory one. The law thus reflects the Government's disapproval of a subset of messages it finds offensive. This is the essence of viewpoint discrimination."

4. *Little Eichmanns.* In 2009, a jury held that Professor Ward Churchill was wrongfully dismissed from his post at the University of Colorado. Churchill was a tenured ethnic studies professor who referred to victims of the 9/11 terrorist attacks as "little Eichmanns." The jury concluded that Churchill's views were a substantial or motivating factor in his dismissal, and that he otherwise would not have been dismissed (despite claims of plagiarism and falsification of research). The jury awarded Churchill $1 in damages (because damages were not requested), and the judge refused to order reinstatement. *See* Kirk Johnson & Katharine Q. Seelye, *Jury Says Professor Was Wrongly Fired,* N.Y. Times, Apr. 2, 2009; *see also* http://www.nytimes.com/2009/04/03/us/03churchill.html?_r=1&scp=3&sq=ward%20churchill&st=cse.

5. *The Confederate Battle Flag.* Although individuals have a constitutional right to display the Confederate battle flag, there have been public and private movements against this flag. Following the murders of nine church attendees in Charleston, the South Carolina legislature voted to remove the flag from a Confederate monument on the state house grounds. Also, a number of large merchants (e.g., Walmart) decided that they would no longer sell the flag and some manufacturers decided to stop producing it.

5. *Private Policing of Speech.* Because of the internet, much speech is disseminated over private platforms (e.g., Twitter). Although the First Amendment limits

the ability of the government to restrict offensive speech, private entities usually function outside its restrictions. These private entities sometimes censor or control speech on their platforms. For example, following the beheading of a journalist by ISIS, Twitter decided to remove grisly images of the beheading from its platform. *See* Yoree Koh & Reed Albergotti, *Twitter Faces Free-Speech Dilemma*, Wall St. J., (Aug. 22, 2014), at B-1.

Iancu v. Brunetti

139 S. Ct. 2294 (2019)

Justice KAGAN delivered the opinion of the Court.

Brunetti is an artist and entrepreneur who founded a clothing line that uses the trademark FUCT. According to Brunetti, the mark (which functions as the clothing's brand name) is pronounced as four letters, one after the other: F-U-C-T. But you might read it differently and, if so, you would hardly be alone. That common perception caused difficulties for Brunetti when he tried to register his mark with the U. S. Patent and Trademark Office (PTO).

Under the Lanham Act, the PTO administers a federal registration system for trademarks. Registration of a mark is not mandatory. The owner of an unregistered mark may still use it in commerce and enforce it against infringers. But registration gives trademark owners valuable benefits. Registration constitutes "prima facie evidence" of the mark's validity. And registration serves as "constructive notice of the registrant's claim of ownership," which forecloses some defenses in infringement actions. Generally, a trademark is eligible for registration, and receipt of such benefits, if it is "used in commerce." But the Act directs the PTO to "refuse registration" of certain marks. The PTO cannot register a mark that "so resembles" another mark as to create a likelihood of confusion. It cannot register a mark that is "merely descriptive" of the goods on which it is used. It cannot register a mark containing the flag or insignia of any nation or State. There are five or ten more. Until we invalidated the criterion, the PTO could not register a mark that "disparaged" a "person, living or dead."

This case involves the Lanham Act's prohibitions on marks that "consist of or comprise immoral or scandalous matter." The PTO applies that bar as a "unitary provision," rather than treating the two adjectives in it separately. To determine whether a mark fits in the category, the PTO asks whether a "substantial composite of the general public" would find the mark "shocking to the sense of truth, decency, or propriety"; "giving offense to the conscience or moral feelings"; "calling out for condemnation"; "disgraceful"; "offensive"; "disreputable"; or "vulgar." Both a PTO examining attorney and the PTO's Trademark Trial and Appeal Board decided that Brunetti's mark flunked that test. Brunetti brought a facial challenge to the "immoral or scandalous" bar. The Court of Appeals for the Federal Circuit found the prohibition to violate the First Amendment. We granted certiorari.

This Court first considered a First Amendment challenge to a trademark registration restriction in *Tam* [which] declared unconstitutional the Lanham Act's ban on registering marks that "disparage" any "person, living or dead." §1052(a). The Court could not agree on the overall framework for deciding the case. But all Justices agreed on two propositions. First, if a trademark registration bar is viewpoint-based, it is unconstitutional. And second, the disparagement bar was viewpoint-based. If the "immoral or scandalous" bar similarly discriminates on the basis of viewpoint, it must also collide with our First Amendment doctrine. Is the "immoral or scandalous" criterion in the Lanham Act viewpoint-neutral or viewpoint-based? It is viewpoint-based. The meanings of "immoral" and "scandalous" are not mysterious. The Lanham Act permits registration of marks that champion society's sense of rectitude and morality, but not marks that denigrate those concepts. When is such material "scandalous"? When it "gives offense to the conscience or moral feelings"; "excites reprobation"; or "calls out condemnation." Or when it is "shocking to the sense of truth, decency, or propriety"; "disgraceful"; "offensive"; or "disreputable." So the Lanham Act allows registration of marks when their messages accord with, but not when their messages defy, society's sense of decency or propriety. The facial viewpoint bias in the law results in viewpoint-discriminatory application.

The Government that the provision is salvageable by virtue of its constitutionally permissible applications (in the Government's view, its applications to lewd, sexually explicit, or profane marks). Once we have found that a law "aims at the suppression of" views, why would it matter that Congress could have captured some of the same speech through a viewpoint-neutral statute? In any event, the "immoral or scandalous" bar is substantially overbroad. There are a great many immoral and scandalous ideas in the world (even more than swearwords), and the Lanham Act covers them all. It therefore violates the First Amendment.

We accordingly affirm the judgment of the Court of Appeals.

It is so ordered.

Justice ALITO, concurring.

Viewpoint discrimination is poison to a free society. At a time when free speech is under attack, it is especially important for this Court to remain firm on the principle that the First Amendment does not tolerate viewpoint discrimination. Our decision does not prevent Congress from adopting a more carefully focused statute that precludes the registration of marks containing vulgar terms that play no real part in the expression of ideas. The particular mark in question could be denied registration under such a statute.

Chief Justice ROBERTS, concurring in part and dissenting in part.

I agree that the "immoral" portion of the provision is not susceptible of a narrowing construction that would eliminate its viewpoint bias. The term "scandalous" can be read narrowly to bar only marks that offend because of their mode of expression — marks that are obscene, vulgar, or profane. Refusing registration to obscene, vulgar, or profane marks does not offend the First Amendment. The First Amendment protects freedom of speech; it does not require the Government to give aid and comfort to those using obscene, vulgar, and profane modes of expression.

Justice BREYER, concurring in part and dissenting in part.

Regulations governing trademark registration "inevitably involve content discrimination." The statute leaves businesses free to use highly vulgar or obscene words on their products, and even to use such words directly next to other registered marks. Indeed, a business owner might even use a vulgar word as a trademark, provided that he or she is willing to forgo the benefits of registration. An applicant who seeks to register a mark should not expect complete freedom to say what she wishes, but should instead expect linguistic regulation. The Government has at least a reasonable interest in ensuring that it is not involved in promoting highly vulgar or obscene speech, and that it will not be associated with such speech. These attention-grabbing words, though financially valuable to businesses that seek to attract interest in their products, may lead to the creation of public spaces that many will find repellant, perhaps on occasion creating the risk of verbal altercations or even physical confrontations. (Think how you might react if you saw someone wearing a t-shirt or product emblazoned with an odious racial epithet.) The Government has an interest in seeking to disincentivize the use of such words in commerce by denying the benefit of trademark registration. The prohibition on registering "scandalous" marks does not "work harm to First Amendment interests that is disproportionate in light of the relevant regulatory objectives." The bar on registering "immoral" marks violates the First Amendment.

Justice SOTOMAYOR, with whom Justice BREYER joins, concurring in part and dissenting in part.

With the Lanham Act's scandalous-marks provision struck down as unconstitutional viewpoint discrimination, the Government will have no statutory basis to refuse registering marks containing the most vulgar, profane, or obscene words and images imaginable. It is possible to read that provision's bar on the registration of "scandalous" marks to address only obscenity, vulgarity, and profanity.

∾ PROBLEMS ∾

1. *Protecting Offensive Speech.* Under *Cohen*, which of these situations can be prohibited consistently with the First Amendment? A) At a public school board meeting, the defendant "used the adjective 'm—f—' on four different occasions" with nouns that included "teachers, the community, the school system, the school board, the country, the county, and the town," and he is prosecuted under

a statute that provides that "any person who utters loud and offensive or profane or indecent language in any public street or other public place, public conveyance, or place to which the public is invited is a disorderly person." *See Rosenfeld v. New Jersey*, 408 U.S. 901 (1972); B) At a political meeting at which the defendant was invited to present the "Black Panther viewpoint," he refers to police officers as "m—f—fascist pig cops." He is prosecuted under a statute that prohibits "any obscene or lascivious language or word in any public place, or in the presence of females." *See Brown v. Oklahoma*, 408 U.S. 914 (1972).

2. *The Nursing Student's MySpace Comments.* A nursing student at the University of Louisville, whose overall performance has consistently been rated satisfactory, was expelled after posting offensive comments on her MySpace page. In those comments, she defended the right to bear arms and made profane observations regarding race, sex, and religion, including statements about Christians and Blacks. In dismissing the student, the university claimed that she had violated the School of Nursing's Honor Code, which provides as follows: "As a representative of the School of Nursing, I pledge to adhere to the highest standards of honesty, integrity, accountability, confidentiality, and professionalism, in all my written work, spoken words, actions and interactions with patients, families, peers and faculty." Although the student did not reveal any confidential information about her patients, the MySpace posting did state that the area surrounding the School of Nursing is "inhabited by humanoids who have an IQ of 10 and whose needs and actions are basically instinctive. As in, all they do is eat and kill each other." In another entry, she refers to the birth of a child (she does not name the patient), stating: "Out came a wrinkly bluish creature, all Picasso-like and weird, ugly as hell screeching and waving its tentacles in the air. Fifteen minutes later, it turned into a pink, itty bitty baby girl." Did the university violate the First Amendment in expelling the student? *See* Andrew Wolfson, *U of L Dismisses Student Over Blog Posts: Woman Files Lawsuit to Gain Restatement*, Louisville Courier-Journal, B-1, c. 1-5, Mar. 14, 2009.

3. *The Skokie Ordinance.* In response to the American Nazi Party's decision to hold a march in Skokie, Illinois, suppose that the Skokie Village Council drafts an ordinance that provides as follows: "The dissemination of any materials within the Village of Skokie which promotes and incites hatred against persons by reason of their race, national origin, or religion, and is intended to do so, is prohibited. Dissemination of materials includes publication or display or distribution of posters, signs, handbills, or writings and public display of markings and clothing of symbolic significance. Public demonstrations by members of political parties while wearing 'military-style' uniforms is also prohibited. The penalty is a fine of up to $500 and imprisonment up to six months." If you represent the Nazi Party, how do you argue that the law is unconstitutional? If you represent the Village Council, how would you argue that the ordinance is constitutional?

4. *More on "Civility."* The Kentucky Bar Association (KBA) adopts a rule entitled "Social Media Concerns." Among other things, the rule tells prospective applicants to the KBA: "Be conscious of the dangers of social media, and be sure

that photographs and commentary are both professional and polite." Can the KBA, as a condition of admission to the bar, require potential applicants to be "professional" and "polite"?

5. *Profanity Near Houses of Worship.* A Missouri law makes it a crime to engage in "profane," "rude," or "indecent" behavior outside of a house of worship. The law is challenged by individuals who advocate for greater inclusion of women and gay men in the Catholic Church and who are vocal regarding clergy child abuse. Is the law likely to survive First Amendment scrutiny? *See Survivors Network of Those Abused by Priests, Inc. v. Joyce*, No. 13-3036 (8th Cir. 2015).

6. *More on the International Treaty Regulating the Internet.* At the convention, a number of European representatives are keen to ban both Nazi symbols as well as denials that the Holocaust actually occurred, and they think that it is very important for the United States to support them in this effort. Under the First Amendment, can you agree to a treaty that allows governments to ban all Nazi symbols from the internet, or that includes a prohibition against Holocaust denial?

4. Defamatory Statements

The Court's attitude toward defamation has shifted over time. The *Chaplinsky* Court noted that defamatory statements were not protected under the First Amendment. In *Beauharnais v. Illinois*, 343 U.S. 250 (1952), the Court rejected a due process challenge to a criminal law prohibiting libels based on race, color, creed, or religion. The Court emphasized that such utterances are unprotected speech, and that courts need not evaluate the efficacy of such laws." As a result, the states were free to define the tort of defamation and to determine the scope of the remedy. Most states readily imposed liability for defamatory statements. However, the law changed in 1964 in the following case.

a. The Constitutionalization of Defamation

New York Times Co. v. Sullivan

376 U.S. 254 (1964)

Mr. Justice BRENNAN delivered the opinion of the Court.

We are required in this case to determine the extent to which the constitutional protections for speech and press limit a State's power to award damages in a libel action brought by a public official against critics of his official conduct.

Respondent Sullivan is one of three elected Commissioners of the City of Montgomery, Alabama. His duties involve "supervision of the Police Department, Fire Department, Department of Cemetery and Department of Scales." He brought this civil libel action against petitioners, who are Negroes and Alabama clergymen, and the New York Times Company, a corporation which publishes the New York Times, a daily newspaper. An Alabama jury awarded him $500,000 and the Supreme Court of Alabama affirmed.

Respondent alleges that he was libeled by statements in a full-page advertisement in the New York Times. Entitled "Heed Their Rising Voices," the advertisement began by stating that "As the whole world knows, thousands of Southern Negro students are engaged in widespread non-violent demonstrations in positive affirmation of the right to live in human dignity as guaranteed by the U.S. Constitution and the Bill of Rights." It went on to charge that "in their efforts to uphold these guarantees, they are being met by an unprecedented wave of terror by those who would deny and negate that document which the whole world looks upon as setting the pattern for modern freedom." Succeeding paragraphs illustrate the "wave of terror" by describing alleged events. The text concluded with an appeal for funds for three purposes: support of the student movement, "the struggle for the right-to-vote," and the legal defense of Dr. Martin Luther King, Jr., leader of the movement, against a perjury indictment. The text appeared over the names of 64 persons, many widely known for their activities in public affairs, religion, trade unions, and the performing arts. Below these names, and under a line reading "We in the south who are struggling daily for dignity and freedom warmly endorse this appeal," appeared the names of the four individual petitioners and of 16 other persons, all but two of whom were identified as clergymen in various Southern cities. The advertisement was signed at the bottom of the page by the "Committee to Defend Martin Luther King and the Struggle for Freedom in the South," and the officers of the Committee were listed.

The third paragraph and the sixth were the basis of respondent's claim of libel. They read as follows: Third paragraph: "In Montgomery, Alabama, after students sang 'My Country, 'Tis of Thee' on the State Capitol steps, their leaders were expelled from school, and truckloads of police armed with shotguns and tear-gas ringed the Alabama State College Campus. When the entire student body protested to state authorities by refusing to re-register, their dining hall was padlocked in an attempt to starve them into submission." Sixth paragraph: "Again and again the Southern violators have answered Dr. King's peaceful protests with intimidation and violence. They have bombed his home almost killing his wife and child. They have assaulted his person. They have arrested him seven times—for 'speeding,' 'loitering' and similar 'offenses.' Now they have charged him with 'perjury'—a felony under which they could imprison him for ten years."

Although neither of these statements mentions respondent by name, he contended that the word "police" referred to him as the Montgomery Commissioner who supervised the Police Department, so that he was accused of "ringing" the campus with police. He claimed that the paragraph would be read as imputing to the police, and hence to him, the padlocking of the dining hall in order to starve the students into submission. As to the sixth paragraph, he contended that since arrests are ordinarily made by the police, the statement "They have arrested Dr. King seven times" would be read as referring to him; he further contended that the "They" who did the arresting would be equated with the "They" who committed the other described acts and with the "Southern violators." Thus, he argued, the paragraph would be read as accusing the Montgomery police, and hence him, of answering Dr. King's protests with "intimidation and violence," bombing his home, assaulting his person, and charging him with perjury. Respondent and six other Montgomery residents testified that they read some or all of the statements as referring to him in his capacity as Commissioner.

It is uncontroverted that some of the statements contained in the two paragraphs were not accurate descriptions of events which occurred in Montgomery. Although Negro students staged a demonstration on the State Capital steps, they sang the National Anthem and not "My Country, 'Tis of Thee." Although nine students were expelled, this was not for leading the demonstration at the Capitol, but for demanding service at a lunch counter in the Montgomery County Courthouse on another day. Not the entire student body, but most of it, had protested the expulsion, not by refusing to register, but by boycotting classes on a single day; virtually all the students did register for the ensuing semester. The campus dining hall was not padlocked on any occasion, and the only students who may have been barred from eating there were the few who had neither signed a preregistration application nor requested temporary meal tickets. Although the police were deployed near the campus in large numbers on three occasions, they did not "ring" the campus, and they were not called to the campus in connection with the demonstration on the State Capitol steps. Dr. King had not been arrested seven times, but only four; and although he claimed to have been assaulted some years earlier in connection with his arrest for loitering outside a courtroom, one of the officers who made the arrest denied that there was such an assault.

On the premise that the charges in the sixth paragraph could be read as referring to him, respondent was allowed to prove that he had not participated in the events described. Although Dr. King's home had in fact been bombed twice when his wife and child were there, both of these occasions antedated respondent's tenure as Commissioner, and the police were not only not implicated in the bombings, but had made every effort to apprehend those who were. Three of Dr. King's four arrests took place before respondent became Commissioner. Although Dr. King had in fact been indicted (he was subsequently acquitted) on two counts of perjury, each of which carried a possible five-year sentence, respondent had nothing to do with procuring the indictment.

Respondent made no effort to prove that he suffered actual pecuniary loss as a result of the alleged libel.[3] One of his witnesses, a former employer, testified that if he had believed the statements, he doubted whether he "would want to be associated with anybody who would be a party to such things that are stated

---

3. Approximately 394 copies of the edition of the *Times* containing the advertisement were circulated in Alabama. Of these, about 35 copies were distributed in Montgomery County. The total circulation of the *Times* for that day was approximately 650,000 copies.

in that ad," and that he would not re-employ respondent if he believed "that he allowed the Police Department to do the things that the paper say he did." But neither this witness nor any other testified that he actually believed the statements in their supposed reference to respondent.

The cost of the advertisement was approximately $4800, and it was published by the Times upon an order from a New York advertising agency acting for the signatory Committee. The agency submitted the advertisement with a letter certifying that the persons whose names appeared on the advertisement had given their permission. The manager of the Advertising Department testified that he had approved the advertisement because he knew nothing to cause him to believe that anything in it was false, and because it bore the endorsement of "a number of people who are well known and whose reputation" he "had no reason to question." Neither he nor anyone else at the Times made an effort to confirm the accuracy of the advertisement, either by checking it against recent Times news stories or by any other means.

Because of the importance of the constitutional issues involved, we granted certiorari. We reverse the judgment.

Under Alabama law, once "libel per se" has been established, the defendant has no defense as to stated facts unless he can persuade the jury that they were true in all their particulars. His privilege of "fair comment" for expressions of opinion depends on the truth of the facts upon which the comment is based. Unless he can discharge the burden of proving truth, general damages are presumed, and may be awarded without proof of pecuniary injury. A showing of actual malice is apparently a prerequisite to recovery of punitive damages, and defendant may forestall a punitive award by a retraction meeting the statutory requirements. Good motives and belief in truth do not negate an inference of malice, but are relevant only in mitigation of punitive damages.

The question is whether this rule of liability, as applied to an action brought by a public official against critics of his official conduct, abridges the freedom of speech and of the press that is guaranteed by the First and Fourteenth Amendments. Respondent relies heavily on statements of this Court to the effect that the Constitution does not protect libelous publications. Those statements do not foreclose our inquiry here. The general proposition that freedom of expression upon public questions is secured by the First Amendment has long been settled by our decisions. The constitutional safeguard "was fashioned to assure unfettered interchange of ideas for the bringing about of political and social changes desired by the people." "The maintenance of the opportunity for free political discussion to the end that government may be responsive to the will of the people and that changes may be obtained by lawful means, an opportunity essential to the security of the Republic, is a fundamental principle of our constitutional system." *Stromberg v. California*, 283 U.S. 359.

Thus we consider this case against the background of a profound national commitment to the principle that debate on public issues should be uninhibited, robust, and wide-open, and that it may well include vehement, caustic, and sometimes unpleasantly sharp attacks on government and public officials. The present advertisement, as an expression of grievance and protest on one of the major public issues of our time, would seem clearly to qualify for the constitutional protection. The question is whether it forfeits that protection by the falsity of some of its factual statements and by its alleged defamation of respondent.

Authoritative interpretations of the First Amendment guarantees have consistently refused to recognize an exception for any test of truth—whether administered by judges, juries, or administrative officials—and especially one that puts the burden of proving truth on the speaker. The constitutional protection does not turn upon "the truth, popularity, or social utility of the ideas and beliefs which are offered." Erroneous statement is inevitable in free debate, and it must be protected if the freedoms of expression are to have the "breathing space" that they "need to survive." *N.A.A.C.P. v. Button*, 371 U.S. 415.

Injury to official reputation affords no more warrant for repressing speech that would otherwise be free than does factual error. Where judicial officers are involved, this Court has held that concern for the dignity and reputation of the courts does not justify the punishment as criminal contempt of criticism of the judge or his decision. This is true even though the utterance contains "half-truths" and "misinformation." Such repression can be justified, if at all, only by a clear and present danger of the obstruction of justice. If judges are to be treated as "men of fortitude, able to thrive in a hardy climate," surely the same must be true of other government officials, such as elected city commissioners. Criticism of their official conduct does not lose its constitutional protection merely because it is effective criticism and hence diminishes their official reputations.

If neither factual error nor defamatory content suffices to remove the constitutional shield from criticism of official conduct, the combination of the two elements is no less inadequate. What a State may not constitutionally bring about by means of a criminal statute is likewise beyond the reach of its civil law of libel. The fear of damage awards under a rule such as that invoked by the Alabama courts here may be markedly more inhibiting than the fear of prosecution under a criminal statute. The judgment awarded in this case—without the need for any proof of actual pecuniary loss—was one thousand times greater than the maximum fine provided by the Alabama criminal libel statute, and one hundred times greater than that provided by the Sedition Act. And since there is no double-jeopardy limitation applicable to civil lawsuits, this is not the only judgment that may be awarded against petitioners for the same publication.[18] Whether or not a newspaper can survive a succession of such judgments, the pall of fear and timidity imposed upon those who would give voice to public criticism is an atmosphere in which the First Amendment freedoms cannot survive. Plainly the Alabama law

18. The *Times* states that four other libel suits based on the advertisement have been filed against it by others who have served as Montgomery City Commissioners and by the Governor of Alabama; that another $500,000 verdict has been awarded in the only one of these cases that has yet gone to trial; and that the damages sought in the other three total $2,000,000.

of civil libel is "a form of regulation that creates hazards to protected freedoms markedly greater than those that attend reliance upon the criminal law."

The state rule of law is not saved by its allowance of the defense of truth. A rule compelling the critic of official conduct to guarantee the truth of all his factual assertions—and to do so on pain of libel judgments virtually unlimited in amount—leads to a comparable "self-censorship." Allowance of the defense of truth, with the burden of proving it on the defendant, does not mean that only false speech will be deterred. Even courts accepting this defense as an adequate safeguard have recognized the difficulties of adducing legal proofs that the alleged libel was true in all its factual particulars. Under such a rule, would-be critics of official conduct may be deterred from voicing their criticism, even though it is believed to be true and even though it is in fact true, because of doubt whether it can be proved in court or fear of the expense of having to do so. They tend to make only statements which "steer far wider of the unlawful zone." The rule thus dampens the vigor and limits the variety of public debate. It is inconsistent with the First and Fourteenth Amendments.

The constitutional guarantees require, we think, a federal rule that prohibits a public official from recovering damages for a defamatory falsehood relating to his official conduct unless he proves that the statement was made with "actual malice"—that is, with knowledge that it was false or with reckless disregard of whether it was false or not.

Such a privilege for criticism of official conduct is appropriately analogous to the protection accorded a public official when he is sued for libel by a private citizen. In *Barr v. Matteo*, 360 U.S. 564 (1959), this Court held the utterance of a federal official to be absolutely privileged if made "within the outer perimeter" of his duties. The threat of damage suits would otherwise "inhibit the fearless, vigorous, and effective administration of policies of government" and "dampen the ardor of all but the most resolute, or the most irresponsible, in the unflinching discharge of their duties." Analogous considerations support the privilege for the citizen-critic of government. It would give public servants an unjustified preference over the public they serve, if critics of official conduct did not have a fair equivalent of the immunity granted to the officials themselves. We conclude that such a privilege is required by the First and Fourteenth Amendments. While Alabama law apparently requires proof of actual malice for an award of punitive damages, where general damages are concerned malice is "presumed." Such a presumption is inconsistent with the federal rule.

Since respondent may seek a new trial, considerations of effective judicial administration require us to review the evidence in the present record to determine whether it could constitutionally support a judgment for respondent. We must "make an independent examination of the whole record," so as to assure ourselves that the judgment does not constitute a forbidden intrusion on the field of free expression. We consider that the proof presented to show actual malice lacks the convincing clarity which the constitutional standard demands, and hence would not constitutionally sustain the judgment for respondent under the proper rule of law. Even assuming that the individual respondents authorized the use of their names on the advertisement, there was no evidence that they were aware of any erroneous statements or were in any way reckless in that regard. The judgment against them is thus without constitutional support.

As to the Times, we similarly conclude that the facts do not support a finding of actual malice. The statement by the Times' Secretary that he thought the advertisement was "substantially correct," affords no warrant for the Alabama Supreme Court's conclusion "of bad faith and maliciousness." The statement does not indicate malice at the time of the publication and there was no evidence to impeach the witness' good faith in holding it. The Times' failure to retract upon respondent's demand is likewise not adequate evidence of malice. Whether or not a failure to retract may ever constitute such evidence, there are two reasons why it does not here. First, the letter written by the Times reflected a reasonable doubt on its part as to whether the advertisement could reasonably be taken to refer to respondent at all. Second, it was not a final refusal, since it asked for an explanation—a request that respondent chose to ignore.

There is evidence that the Times published the advertisement without checking its accuracy against the news stories in the Times' own files. The mere presence of the stories in the files does not, of course, establish that the Times "knew" the advertisement was false, since the state of mind required for actual malice involves the persons having responsibility for publication of the advertisement. With respect to the failure of those persons to make the check, the record shows that they relied upon their knowledge of the good reputation of many of those whose names were listed as sponsors of the advertisement, and upon the letter from A. Philip Randolph, known to them as a responsible individual, certifying that the use of the names was authorized. There was testimony that the persons handling the advertisement saw nothing in it that would render it unacceptable under the Times' policy of rejecting advertisements containing "attacks of a personal character"; their failure to reject it on this ground was not unreasonable. We think the evidence against the Times supports at most a finding of negligence in failing to discover the misstatements, and is constitutionally insufficient to show the recklessness that is required for a finding of actual malice.

The judgment of the Supreme Court of Alabama is reversed and the case is remanded to that court for further proceedings not inconsistent with this opinion.

Reversed and remanded.

Mr. Justice BLACK, with whom Mr. Justice DOUGLAS joins, *concurring.*

The Federal Constitution has dealt with this deadly danger to the press in the only way possible without leaving the free press open to destruction—by granting the press absolute immunity for criticism of the way public officials do their public duty. Stopgap measures like those the Court adopts are not enough. Since the adoption of the Fourteenth Amendment a State has no more power than the Federal Government to use a civil libel law or any other law to impose damages for merely discussing public affairs and criticizing public officials. The power of the United States to do that is precisely nil.

Elected officials are responsible to the people for the way they perform their duties. To punish the exercise of this right to discuss public affairs or to penalize it through libel judgments is to abridge or shut off discussion of the very kind most needed. This Nation, I suspect, can live in peace without libel suits based on public discussions of public affairs and public officials. But I doubt that a country can live in freedom where its people can be made to suffer physically or financially for criticizing their government, its actions, or its officials. An unconditional right to say what one pleases about public affairs is what I consider to be the minimum guarantee of the First Amendment. I regret that the Court has stopped short of this holding indispensable to preserve our free press from destruction.

Mr. Justice GOLDBERG, with whom Mr. Justice DOUGLAS joins, *concurring in the result*.

In a democratic society, one who assumes to act for the citizens in an executive, legislative, or judicial capacity must expect that his official acts will be commented upon and criticized. Such criticism cannot, in my opinion, be muzzled or deterred by the courts at the instance of public officials under the label of libel. It may be urged that deliberately and maliciously false statements have no conceivable value as free speech. That argument, however, is not responsive to the issue of whether that freedom of speech which all agree is constitutionally protected can be effectively safeguarded by a rule allowing the imposition of liability upon a jury's evaluation of the speaker's state of mind. If individual citizens may be held liable in damages for strong words, which a jury finds false and maliciously motivated, there can be little doubt that public debate and advocacy will be constrained. And if newspapers, publishing advertisements dealing with public issues, thereby risk liability, there can also be little doubt that the ability of minority groups to secure publication of their views on public affairs and to seek support for their causes will be greatly diminished. The conclusion that the Constitution affords the citizen and the press an absolute privilege for criticism of official conduct does not leave the public official without defenses against unsubstantiated opinions or deliberate misstatements. "Under our system of government, counterargument and education are the weapons available to expose these matters, not abridgment of free speech." *Wood v. Georgia*, 370 U.S. 375, 389.

Notes and Questions

1. Sullivan *and the Justifications for Protecting Speech.* Did the speech involved in *Sullivan* meet any of the justifications for protecting speech discussed at the beginning of this chapter? In other words, did the ad provide a safety valve, did it promote self-fulfillment or the marketplace of ideas, or was it related to the democratic process?

2. *Public Figures.* A few years after the Court decided *Sullivan*, it extended the actual malice standard to defamatory statements made about public figures. *Curtis Publishing Co. v. Butts*, 388 U.S. 130 (1967), involved a *Saturday Evening Post* article which alleged that Wallace Butts, the former football coach and then-athletic director at the University of Georgia, had conspired to fix a football game. The jury returned a verdict for $60,000 in general damages and $3 million in punitive damages which was reduced to $460,000 on appeal. *Associated Press v. Walker*, 388 U.S. 130 (1967), involved a press release stating that Edwin Walker, a retired major general and candidate for Texas governor, led a violent crowd against federal marshals during a riot in response to James Meredith's enrollment at Ole Miss. The Court concluded that Butts and Walker were public figures, and Justice Harlan's plurality advocated a gross negligence standard for their cases:

> The public interest in the circulation of the materials here involved, and the publisher's interest in circulating them, is not less than that involved in *New York Times*. Both Butts and Walker commanded a substantial amount of independent public interest at the time of the publications; both, in our opinion, would have been labeled "public figures" under ordinary tort rules. Butts may have attained that status by position alone and Walker by his purposeful activity amounting to a thrusting of his personality into the "vortex" of an important public controversy, but both commanded sufficient continuing public interest and had sufficient access to the means of counterargument to be able "to expose through discussion the falsehood and fallacies" of the defamatory statements. These similarities and differences between libel actions involving persons who are public officials and libel actions involving those circumstanced as were Butts and Walker, viewed in light of the principles of liability which are of general applicability in our society, lead us to the conclusion that libel actions of the present kind cannot be left entirely to state libel laws, unlimited by any overriding constitutional safeguard, but that the rigorous federal requirements of *New York Times* are not the only appropriate accommodation of the conflicting interests at stake. We hold that a "public figure" who is not a public official may also recover damages for a defamatory falsehood whose substance makes substantial danger to reputation apparent, on a showing of highly unreasonable conduct constituting an extreme departure from the standards of investigation and reporting ordinarily adhered to by responsible publishers.

But the *Sullivan* rule prevailed and Chief Justice Warren's plurality opinion reasoned:

> Although they are not subject to the restraints of the political process, "public figures," like "public officials," often play an influential role in ordering society. And surely as a class these "public figures" have as ready access as "public officials" to mass media of communication, both to influence policy and to counter criticism of their views and activities. Our citizenry has a legitimate and substantial interest in the conduct of such persons, and freedom of the press to engage in uninhibited debate about their involvement in public issues and events is as crucial as it is in the case of "public officials." The fact that they are not amenable to the restraints of the political process only underscores the legitimate and substantial nature of the interest, since it means that public opinion may be the only instrument by which society can attempt to influence their conduct.

3. *Injunctive Relief and Prior Restraints.* Prior to the *Sullivan* decision, the Court applied its general prohibition against prior restraints to defamatory statements.

In *Near v. Minnesota*, 283 U.S. 697 (1931), public officials sought and obtained an injunction against what they described as a "malicious, scandalous and defamatory newspaper." The Court reversed, establishing a broad rule against prior restraints: "Public officers, whose character and conduct remain open to debate and free discussion in the press, find their remedies for false accusations in actions under libel laws providing for redress and punishment, and not in proceedings to restrain the publication of newspapers and periodicals."

4. *Confidentiality of Sources.* In *Sullivan*'s aftermath, one issue that arose was whether a journalist could protect his or her sources against disclosure. In *Desai v. Hersh*, 954 F.2d 1408 (7th Cir. 1992), the court rejected a journalist's attempt to protect the confidentiality of his sources in a defamation action: "In defamation actions in which a plaintiff must establish 'malice' on the part of a defendant, the reporters privilege must give way to disclosure."

5. *Does the "Actual Malice" Standard Provide Too Little Protection to the Media?* In *Herbert v. Lando*, 441 U.S. 153 (1979), in an effort to prove that an article was published with "actual malice," plaintiff sought extensive discovery regarding the editorial processes that led to publication of an article. In *Lando*, the deposition continued for more than a year and involved 3,000 pages and 240 exhibits. In *Dun & Bradstreet, infra,* Justice White offered these thoughts about *Lando*: "The burden that plaintiffs must meet invites long and complicated discovery involving detailed investigation of the workings of the press, how a news story is developed, and the state of mind of the reporter and publisher. That kind of litigation is very expensive. I suspect that the press would be no worse off financially if the common-law rules were to apply and if the judiciary was careful to insist that damages awards be kept within bounds." Similarly, in the 1980s, a Libel Defense Resource Center Press Release showed "a dramatic increase in the already-high average of damage awards against media defendants in libel (and related) cases. Compared to the prior two-year period, the average award increased ten-fold, from almost half-a-million in 1987-88 to just under $4.5 million in 1989-90." These statistics prompted one scholar to observe that "the onslaught of defamation actions is greater in number and severity than it was in the 'bad old days' of common law libel notwithstanding *New York Times*." Richard A. Epstein, *Was New York Times v. Sullivan Wrong?*, 53 U. Chi. L. Rev. 782, 783 (1986). Do these facts suggest that the Court should provide even greater protection to newspapers and broadcasters including, possibly, a ban on libel suits by public officials? *See* Martin Garbus, *25 Years After "Times v. Sullivan": What Remains to Be Done*, 201 N.Y. L.J. 2-3 (1989).

6. *Empirical Evidence.* The Libel Resource Defense Center's data is contradicted by empirical research conducted by Professors Russell L. Weaver and Geoffrey J.G. Bennett during the 1990s. Weaver and Bennett found that the U.S. media is generally unconcerned about the threat of defamation liability:

The reason U.S. newspapers and broadcasters are less concerned about defamation is because they are threatened with suit, and actually sued, far less frequently than their British counterparts. Editors and producers in the United States are not so relaxed that they ignore the possibility of defamation liability. But, because the threat of suit is much lower, they often tend to be more worried about other matters (e.g., journalistic accuracy and integrity) than they are about the threat of liability. These attitudes are reflected in the day-to-day functioning of U.S. newspapers and broadcasters. Unlike the British, U.S. newspapers and broadcasters do not have teams of lawyers that comb through copy searching for material that may be defamatory. Most papers and broadcasters allow editors and producers to decide for themselves whether material is potentially defamatory and whether to involve counsel. If an editor or producer feels comfortable with a piece, he may publish or air it without any input from counsel. Thus, the possibility of defamation suits has some impact on reporting. But most interviewees indicated that the impact was minimal. Few editors or producers reported that they had ever killed a story for fear of defamation liability. Moreover, few indicated that they were unable to make a statement for fear of liability. They were often reluctant to rely entirely on confidential sources. In addition, if they had inadequate support for a piece, they might seek additional support. Alternatively, they might soften a statement or attempt to present it in a more balanced way. But there was a very good chance that the allegation would still be made.

Russell L. Weaver & Geoffrey J.G. Bennett, *Is the* New York Times *"Actual Malice" Standard Really Necessary? A Comparative Perspective,* 53 La. L. Rev. 1153 (1993).

7. *Is a "Public Interest" Standard Preferable to a "Public Figure" Standard?* Sullivan focused not on whether the communication involved a matter of "public interest" (although notions of public interest seemed to impact the analysis), but on the plaintiff's status as a public official. In *Rosenbloom v. Metromedia, Inc.*, 403 U.S. 29 (1971), a plurality suggested that the *Sullivan* standard derives "from the question whether the allegedly defamatory publication concerns a matter of public or general interest." But, in the Court's later decision in *Gertz v. Robert Welch, Inc., infra,* the Court rejected a "public interest" standard. Should the focus be on the status of the individual or on the public interest? England has adopted press protections based on a public interest standard. *See Reynolds v. Times Newspapers,* 2001 2 AC 127 (HL).

8. *Alternate Approaches.* By and large, courts and legislatures in other countries have chosen not to adopt the *N.Y. Times* actual malice standard. For example, both Australia and England opted instead for an extension of common law qualified privilege as a way of providing greater protection to defamation defendants. *See Jameel v. Wall Street Journal Europe,* 2006 U.K.H.L. 44; *Reynolds v. Times Newspapers* 2001 2 A.C. 127 (HL); *Lange v. Australian Broadcasting Corp.* (1997) 189 C.L.R. 520, 521 (Austl.). The evidence suggests that this approach did not satisfactorily strike a balance between the interest in free expression, and the individual interest in reputation. *See* Russell L. Weaver, Andrew T. Kenyon, David F. Partlett & Clive P. Walker, *The Right to Speak Ill: Defamation, Free Speech and Reputation* (2006). On the contrary, because the Australian decision focused on the lower standard of "reasonableness," and because the English decision provided a list of factors to be considered, it is not clear that either approach provided sufficient "breathing space" for free expression. *See id.* Britain recently replaced its judicial decision with statutory protections, but the statute also contains a list of factors. *See* Defamation Act, 2013, c. 26 (U.K.).

9. *Declarations of Truth and Falsity.* In *Dun & Bradstreet, infra,* Justice White, concurring, suggested that even if damages are not permitted, juries should be able to declare whether statements are true or false: "I can discern nothing in the Constitution which forbids a plaintiff to obtain a judicial decree that a statement is false—a decree he can then use in the community to clear his name and to prevent further damage from a defamation already published." Would it be desirable to allow officials to obtain a declaration of truth or falsity?

10. *Enforcement of Foreign Speech Judgments.* Foreign judgments awarding damages that implicate speech interests are not enforceable in U.S. courts unless they were rendered under standards consistent with the First Amendment to the U.S. Constitution. *See Sarl Louis Feraud International v. Viewfinder, Inc.,* 406 F. Supp. 2d 274 (S.D.N.Y. 2005). United States courts also have refused to enforce Canadian defamation judgments. *See Investorshub.com v. Mina Mar Group Inc.,* 39 Media L. Rptr. 2078 (N.D. Fla. 2011).

11. *Legislative Abolition.* The United Kingdom abolished the crimes of criminal libel and seditious libel when Section 73 of the Coroners and Justice Act of 2009 eliminated "the old common law offenses of sedition, seditious libel, obscene libel, and defamatory libel." According to Justice Minister Claire Ward, "Abolishing these offenses will allow the UK to take a lead in challenging similar laws in other countries, where they are used to suppress free speech." *Criminal libel and sedition offenses abolished,* Press Gazette (UK), January 13, 2010, http://www.pressgazette.co.uk/story.asp?storycode=44884.

12. *Justice Thomas and the* New York Times *Decision.* In *McKee v. Cosby,* 139 S. Ct. 675 (2019) (Thomas, J., concurring), Justice Thomas critiqued the constitutionality of the *Sullivan* decision. The case involved a woman's defamation suit against former actor and comedian Bill Cosby, and the trial court's conclusion that she became a "limited-purpose public figure" by voluntarily disclosing her accusations against Cosby to a reporter, thereby thrusting herself to the forefront of the sexual allegations against Cosby. Thomas decried *Sullivan* and its progeny as "policy-driven decisions masquerading as constitutional law" and argued that the Court "should not continue to reflexively apply this policy-driven approach to the Constitution." He emphasized that,

From the founding of the Nation until 1964, the law of defamation was almost exclusively the business of state courts and legislatures. *New York Times* was "the first major step in what proved to be a seemingly irreversible process of constitutionalizing the entire law of libel and slander." *Dun & Bradstreet,* 472 U.S., at 766 (White, J., concurring). The Court expanded the actual-malice rule to all defamed "public figures," which it defined to include private persons who "thrust themselves to the forefront of particular public controversies in order to influence the resolution of the issues involved," *Gertz, supra,* at 345. The Court also extended the actual-malice rule to criminal libel prosecutions, *Garrison v. Louisiana,* 379 U.S. 64 (1964), and even restricted the situations in which private figures could recover for defamation against media defendants. None of these decisions made a sustained effort to ground their holdings in the Constitution's original meaning. The constitutional libel rules adopted by this Court broke sharply from the common law of libel. Common-law protections for the "core private right" of a person's "uninterrupted enjoyment of his reputation" formed the backdrop against which the First and Fourteenth Amendments were ratified. We consistently recognized that the First Amendment did not displace the common law of libel. There are sound reasons to question whether either the First or Fourteenth Amendment, as originally understood, encompasses an actual-malice standard for public figures or otherwise displaces vast swaths of state defamation law. Historical practice further suggests that protections for free speech and a free press—whether embodied in state constitutions, the First Amendment, or the Fourteenth Amendment—did not abrogate the common law of libel. We should reconsider our jurisprudence in this area.

Do you agree with Justice Thomas that the *Sullivan* decision should be overruled?

∾ PROBLEMS ∾

1. *The Offended Mayor.* The *Louisville Times* publishes an exposé about corruption in city government that makes extensive allegations regarding mayoral corruption. The mayor, incensed by the allegations, which he regards as viciously untrue, comes to you for legal advice. The mayor seeks a remedy against the *Times.* How would you advise the mayor to proceed? Would it be advisable for the mayor to a) seek injunctive relief against the *Times* to prevent publication of further articles on the subject, or b) bring a damage action against the *Times* to recover for defamatory injury? If you are unwilling to recommend either action, how would you advise the mayor to proceed? What remedies are open to him? Is there any remedy that will be effective?

2. *Proving "Actual Malice."* Assume that the mayor in the preceding problem decides to bring a damage action against the *Times.* Under the *Sullivan* decision, you know that the mayor will be required to prove that the *Times* acted with "actual malice" in publishing the stories. As an attorney, how will you go about satisfying that standard? In discovery, whom might you depose? What types of questions will you ask in the deposition?

3. *Defamation on Contingency?* Many U.S. lawyers take various types of tort cases (e.g., personal injury cases) on a contingency fee basis. Given the requirements of the actual malice standard and the nature of appellate review in defamation cases, would you be inclined to take the mayor's case on a contingency fee basis? Or would you insist on an hourly rate?

4. *More on the International Treaty Regulating the Internet.* The German Basic Law (effectively, the German Constitution) provides specific protections for "human dignity." Accordingly, the German delegates to the convention demand that the treaty contain specific protections against defamatory speech. What kind of language regarding human dignity can you agree to in the treaty that is consistent with the U.S. Constitution? Is such language likely to satisfy the German delegates?

b. Application of the "Actual Malice" Standard

Post-*Sullivan* decisions reveal how the actual malice standard has been applied.

St. Amant v. Thompson

390 U.S. 727 (1968)

Mr. Justice WHITE delivered the opinion of the Court.

Petitioner St. Amant, a candidate for public office, made a televised speech in Baton Rouge, Louisiana. In the course of this speech, St. Amant read a series of questions which he had put to J.D. Albin, a member of a Teamsters Union local, and Albin's answers to those questions. The exchange concerned the allegedly nefarious activities of E.G. Partin, the president of the local, and the alleged relationship between Partin and St. Amant's political opponent. One of Albin's answers concerned his efforts to prevent Partin from secreting union records; in this answer Albin referred to Herman A. Thompson, an East Baton Rouge Parish deputy sheriff and respondent here:

> Now, we knew that this safe was gonna be moved that night, but imagine our predicament, knowing of Ed's connections with the Sheriff's office through Herman Thompson, who made recent visits to the Hall to see Ed. We also knew of money that had passed hands between Ed and Herman Thompson. We also knew of his connections with State Trooper Lieutenant Joe Green. We knew we couldn't get any help from there and we didn't know how far that he was involved in the Sheriff's office or the State Police office through that, and it was out of the jurisdiction of the City Police.

Thompson promptly brought suit for defamation, claiming that the publication had "imputed gross misconduct" and "inferred conduct of the most nefarious nature." The case was tried prior to the decision in *New York Times*. The trial judge ruled in Thompson's favor and awarded $5,000 in damages.

We accept the determinations of the Louisiana courts that the material published by St. Amant charged Thompson with criminal conduct, that the charge was false, and that Thompson was a public official and so had the burden of proving that the false statements about Thompson were made with actual malice. We cannot, however, agree that Thompson sustained this burden.

The Louisiana Supreme Court ruled that St. Amant had broadcast false information about Thompson recklessly, though not knowingly. Several reasons were given for this conclusion. St. Amant had no personal knowledge of Thompson's activities; he relied solely on Albin's affidavit although the record was silent as to Albin's reputation for veracity; he failed to verify the information with those in the union office who might have known the facts; he gave no consideration to whether or not the statements defamed Thompson and went ahead heedless of the consequences; and he mistakenly believed he had no responsibility for the broadcast because he was merely quoting Albin's words.

These considerations fall short of proving St. Amant's reckless disregard for the accuracy of his statements about Thompson. "Reckless disregard" cannot be fully encompassed in one infallible definition. Inevitably its outer limits will be marked through case-by-case adjudication. Our cases, however, have furnished meaningful guidance for the further definition of a reckless publication. In *New York Times*, the plaintiff did not satisfy his burden because the record failed to show that the publisher was aware of the likelihood that he was circulating false information. In *Garrison v. State of Louisiana*, 379 U.S. 64 (1964), the opinion emphasized the necessity for a showing that a false publication was made with a "high degree of awareness of probable falsity." Mr. Justice Harlan's opinion in *Curtis Publishing Co. v. Butts*, 388 U.S. 130 (1967), stated that evidence of either deliberate falsification or reckless publication "despite the publisher's awareness of probable falsity" was essential to recovery by public officials in defamation actions. These cases are clear that reckless conduct is not measured by whether a reasonably prudent man would have published, or would have investigated before publishing. There must be sufficient evidence to permit the conclusion that the defendant in fact entertained serious doubts as to the truth of his publication. Publishing with such doubts shows reckless disregard for truth or falsity and demonstrates actual malice.

It may be said that such a test puts a premium on ignorance, encourages the irresponsible publisher not to inquire, and permits the issue to be determined by the defendant's testimony that he published the statement in good faith and unaware of its probable falsity. Concededly the reckless disregard standard may permit recovery in fewer situations than would a rule that publishers must satisfy the standard of the reasonable man or the prudent publisher. But *New York Times* emphasized that the stake of the people in public business and the conduct of public officials is so great that neither the defense of truth nor the standard of ordinary care would protect against self-censorship and thus adequately implement First Amendment policies. Neither lies nor false communications serve the ends of the First Amendment, and no one suggests their desirability or further proliferation. But to insure the ascertainment and publication of the truth about public affairs, it is essential that the First Amendment protect some erroneous publications as well as true ones.

The defendant in a defamation action brought by a public official cannot, however, automatically insure a favorable verdict by testifying that he published with a belief that the statements were true. The finder of fact must determine whether the publication was indeed made in good faith. Professions of good faith will be unlikely to prove persuasive, for example, where a story is fabricated by the defendant, is the product of his imagination, or is based wholly on an unverified anonymous telephone call. Nor will they be likely to prevail when the publisher's allegations are so inherently improbable that only a reckless man would have put them in circulation. Likewise, recklessness may be found where there are obvious reasons to doubt the veracity of the informant or the accuracy of his reports.

By no proper test of reckless disregard was St. Amant's broadcast a reckless publication about a public officer. Nothing indicates an awareness by St. Amant of the probable falsity of Albin's statement about Thompson. Failure to investigate does not in itself establish bad faith. St. Amant's mistake about his probable legal liability does not evidence a doubtful mind on his part. That he failed to realize the import of what he broadcast—and was thus "heedless" of the consequences for Thompson—is similarly colorless. Closer to the mark are considerations of

Albin's reliability. However, the most the state court could say was that there was no evidence in the record of Albin's reputation for veracity, and this fact merely underlines the failure of Thompson's evidence to demonstrate a low community assessment of Albin's trustworthiness or unsatisfactory experience with him by St. Amant.

Other facts support our view. St. Amant made his broadcast in June 1962. He had known Albin since October 1961, when he first met with members of the dissident Teamsters faction. St. Amant testified that he had verified other aspects of Albin's information and that he had affidavits from others. Moreover Albin swore to his answers, first in writing and later in the presence of newsmen. According to Albin, he was prepared to substantiate his charges. St. Amant knew that Albin was engaged in an internal struggle in the union; Albin seemed to St. Amant to be placing himself in personal danger by publicly airing the details of the dispute.

Because the state court misunderstood and misapplied the actual malice standard which must be observed in a public official's defamation action, the judgment is reversed and the case remanded for further proceedings not inconsistent with this opinion.

Reversed and remanded.

Mr. Justice Fortas, *dissenting.*

I do not believe that petitioner satisfied the minimal standards of care specified by *New York Times*. The affidavit that petitioner broadcast contained a seriously libelous statement directed against respondent. Petitioner's casual, careless, callous use of the libel cannot be rationalized as resulting from the heat of a campaign. Under *New York Times*, this libel was broadcast by petitioner with "actual malice." The First Amendment is not a shelter for the character assassinator, whether his action is heedless and reckless or deliberate. The occupation of public officeholder does not forfeit one's membership in the human race. The public official should be subject to severe scrutiny and to free and open criticism. But if he is needlessly, heedlessly, falsely accused of crime, he should have a remedy in law. *New York Times* does not preclude this minimal standard of civilized living. Petitioner had a duty here to check the reliability of the libelous statement about respondent. If he had made a good-faith check, he should be protected even if the statement were false, because the interest of public officials in their reputation must endure this degree of assault. But since he made no check, *New York Times* does not prohibit recovery. I would affirm.

Notes and Questions

1. *Irresponsible Journalism?* Does the actual malice standard encourage irresponsible journalism? Does it provide too little protection to public officials and thereby discourage quality individuals from running for office? Consider the remarks of Honorable Abner J. Mikva, *In My Opinion, Those Are Not Facts*, 11 GA. ST.

U. L. Rev. 291 (1995): "a feeling is abroad among some judges that the Supreme Court has gone too far in protecting the media from defamation actions resulting from irresponsible journalism."

2. *Should the "Actual Malice" Standard Apply to Low-Level Officials?* Does *New York Times* justify subjecting low-level governmental officials (an assistant deputy sheriff or a desk worker in the department of motor vehicles) to the "actual malice" standard? Prominent public officials can easily attract media coverage and can therefore respond to allegations against them. Do low-level official have the same opportunity? Does it matter whether the allegations relate to a matter of "public interest"? *See Coughlin v. Westinghouse Broadcasting and Cable, Inc.*, 780 F.2d 340 (3d Cir. 1985).

3. *Officials Who Have Left Office.* After the mayor of a large city leaves public office, suppose that the local newspaper continues to report incessantly regarding her activities. After leaving office, is the mayor still subject to the actual malice standard? Should it matter whether the reporting relates to the mayor's administration or to her private life? Is she forever a "public figure?" *See Zerangue v. TSP Newspapers, Inc.*, 814 F.2d 1066 (5th Cir. 1987).

4. *Actual Malice and Quotations. Masson v. New Yorker Magazine, Inc.*, 501 U.S. 496 (1991), involved a reporter for the *New Yorker* magazine who published an interview with a prominent individual that contained a number of statements in quotation marks. The interviewee sued, claiming that he did not make some of the statements, and alleging that the reporter falsely placed them in quotation marks to suggest that they were the interviewee's remarks. The Court concluded that the mere fact that a reporter fabricated a quotation was not sufficient to satisfy the actual malice standard. Indeed, the Court indicated that it might be permissible for a reporter who is interviewing a prominent athlete to change statements to make them grammatical. The Court ultimately concluded that liability should turn on whether the alteration results in a material change in the meaning conveyed by the statement or is merely a trivial change.

5. *Immunity from Defamation Suit.* The Communications Decency Act of 1996, 47 U.S.C. §230, gives internet service providers immunity from defamation liability: "No provider or user of an interactive computer service shall be treated as the publisher or speaker of any information provided by another information content provider." As explained in *Zeran v. America Online, Inc.*, 129 F.3d 327 (4th Cir. 1997), this provision allows an internet service to exercise "a publisher's traditional editorial functions," such as "whether to publish, withdraw, postpone or alter content," without fear of tort liability. Congress enacted §230 with the purposes of preserving "the robust nature of internet communications," protecting freedom of speech in such communications, and encouraging "the development of technologies, procedures and techniques by which objectionable material could be blocked or deleted." Congress feared that the "specter of tort liability" would produce two kinds of "chilling effects." Given the fact that it "would be impossible for service providers to screen" millions of postings, they "might severely restrict the number and type of messages posted." Also, tort liability

would create a "disincentive" for the development of filtering technologies, such as those that allow parents to "restrict their children's access" to particular types of online content.

∿ PROBLEMS ∿

1. *Proving Actual Malice.* Previously, we focused on the mayor of a city who was allegedly defamed by the local newspaper, which alleged corruption and extramarital affairs. Notwithstanding the fact that the mayor will have to satisfy the "actual malice" standard, the mayor has decided to sue the newspaper. You know that the allegations are untrue. How will you go about proving that the newspaper acted with "actual malice"? Would you be willing to take the case on a contingency fee basis?

2. *Disappearance in Aruba.* A woman, Natalee Holloway, disappeared in Aruba in 2005 after leaving a bar with Deepak Kalpoe and his brother. The disappearance generated substantial controversy and lots of news coverage. Assume that Deepak is interviewed by the police about the disappearance, speaks to the media about it several times, and tries to obtain a book contract regarding the story of the disappearance. Based on criticism of Deepak's conduct by Holloway's mother and Aruban government officials, Deepak files a defamation suit against them in the U.S. Is Deepak a public figure? Why? Assume that the same criticisms are made about Deepak's brother. However, he never spoke to the media and never sought a book contract. Is the brother a public figure? *See McGraw v. Superior Court,* 42 Cal. Rptr. 1481 (Ct. App. 2014).

3. *The "Birther" Parody.* One day after the release of a book questioning whether President Barack Obama is a U.S. citizen, and therefore is eligible for the U.S. presidency, a magazine publishes a satirical article about the book. The article suggests that the publisher is in the process of withdrawing the book from distribution, and will provide refunds to all who have purchased the book. In response to the article, bookstores began pulling the book from their shelves, and purchasers began demanding refunds. If the magazine intended for the article to be satirical, would it matter whether some readers perceived it as fact rather than satire? In other words, for First Amendment purposes, could the article be regarded as a false assertion of fact? How does a reviewing court go about deciding whether to treat the article as an assertion of fact or as satire? *See Farah v. Esquire Magazine,* 736 F.3d 528 (D.C. Cir. 2013).

c. Private Plaintiffs

After the Court rendered the *Sullivan* and *Butts* decisions, it struggled to determine whether a different and lesser liability standard should be applied when the plaintiff is a private individual rather than a public figure.

Gertz v. Robert Welch, Inc.

418 U.S. 323 (1974)

Mr. Justice POWELL delivered the opinion of the Court.

In 1968 a Chicago policeman named Nuccio shot and killed a youth named Nelson. State authorities prosecuted Nuccio for the homicide and ultimately obtained a conviction for murder in the second degree. The Nelson family retained petitioner Elmer Gertz, a reputable attorney, to represent them in civil litigation against Nuccio.

Respondent publishes *American Opinion,* a monthly outlet for the views of the John Birch Society. In the 1960's the magazine began to warn of a nation-wide conspiracy to discredit local law enforcement agencies and create a national police force capable of supporting a Communist dictatorship. In an effort to alert the public to this assumed danger, the *American Opinion* commissioned an article on the murder trial of Officer Nuccio. In 1969 respondent published the result-ing article under the title "FRAME-UP: Richard Nuccio And The War On Police." The article purports to demonstrate that the testimony against Nuccio at his crim-inal trial was false and that his prosecution was part of the Communist campaign against the police.

As counsel for the Nelson family in the civil litigation, petitioner attended the coroner's inquest into the boy's death and initiated actions for damages, but he neither discussed Officer Nuccio with the press nor played any part in the crim-inal proceeding. Notwithstanding petitioner's remote connection with the pros-ecution of Nuccio, respondent's magazine portrayed him as an architect of the "frame-up." According to the article, the police file on petitioner took "a big, Irish cop to lift." The article stated that petitioner had been an official of the "Marxist League for Industrial Democracy, originally known as the Intercollegiate Socialist Society, which has advocated the violent seizure of our government." It labeled Gertz a "Leninist" and a "Communist-fronter." It also stated that Gertz had been an officer of the National Lawyers Guild, described as a Communist organization that "probably did more than any other outfit to plan the Communist attack on the Chicago police during the 1968 Democratic Convention."

The article contained serious inaccuracies. The implication that petitioner had a criminal record was false. Petitioner had been a member and officer of the National Lawyers Guild some 15 years earlier, but there was no evidence that he or that organization had taken any part in planning the 1968 demonstrations in Chicago. There was also no basis for the charge that petitioner was a "Leninist" or a "Communist-fronter." And he had never been a member of the "Marxist League for Industrial Democracy" or the "Intercollegiate Socialist Society."

The managing editor of *American Opinion* made no effort to verify or sub-stantiate the charges against petitioner. Instead, he appended an introduction stating that the author had "conducted extensive research into the Nuccio Case." And he included in the article a photograph of petitioner and wrote the caption that appeared under it: "Elmer Gertz of Red Guild harasses Nuccio." Respondent placed the issue containing the article on sale at newsstands throughout the country and distributed reprints of the article on the streets of Chicago. The District Court entered judgment for respondent.

The principal issue is whether a newspaper or broadcaster that publishes defamatory falsehoods about an individual who is neither a public official nor a public figure may claim a constitutional privilege against liability for the injury inflicted by those statements. The Court considered this question on the rather different set of facts presented in *Rosenbloom v. Metromedia, Inc.*, 403 U.S. 29 (1971). Rosenbloom, a distributor of nudist magazines, was arrested for selling allegedly obscene material while making a delivery to a retail dealer. Afterward, he sued a radio station for defamation related to its report on the arrest and obtained a judgment. In *Rosenbloom*, this Court affirmed the decision below, but no majority could agree on a controlling rationale. The eight Justices announced their views in five separate opinions. The several statements reflect divergent traditions of thought about the general problem of reconciling the law of defamation with the First Amendment. One approach has been to extend the *New York Times* test to an expanding variety of situations. Another has been to vary the level of constitutional privilege for defamatory falsehood with the status of the person defamed. And a third view would grant to the press and broadcast media absolute immunity from liability for defamation. In his opinion for the plurality, Mr. Justice Brennan concluded that the actual malice standard should extend to defamatory falsehoods relating to private persons if the statements concerned matters of general or public interest.

Our decisions recognize that a rule of strict liability that compels a publisher or broadcaster to guarantee the accuracy of his factual assertions may lead to intolerable self-censorship. The need to avoid self-censorship by the news media is, however, not the only societal value at issue. If it were, this Court would have embraced the view that publishers and broadcasters enjoy an unconditional and indefeasible immunity from liability for defamation. The legitimate state interest underlying the law of libel is the compensation of individuals for the harm inflicted on them by defamatory falsehood. We would not lightly require the State to abandon this purpose, for, as Mr. Justice Stewart has reminded us, the individual's right to the protection of his own good name "reflects no more than our basic concept of the essential dignity and worth of every human being—a concept at the root of any decent system of ordered liberty." *Rosenblatt v. Baer*, 383 U.S. 75 (1966) (concurring opinion).

Some tension necessarily exists between the need for a vigorous and uninhibited press and the legitimate interest in redressing wrongful injury. In our continuing effort to define the proper accommodation between these competing concerns, we have been especially anxious to assure to the freedoms of speech and press that "breathing space" essential to their fruitful exercise. To that end this Court has extended a measure of strategic protection to defamatory falsehood.

The *New York Times* standard defines the level of constitutional protection appropriate to the context of defamation of a public person. Those who, by reason of the notoriety of their achievements or the vigor and success with which they seek the public's attention, are properly classed as public figures and those who hold governmental office. This standard exacts a high price from the victims of defamatory falsehood. Many deserving plaintiffs, including some intentionally subjected to injury, will be unable to surmount the barrier of the *New York Times* test. We think that these decisions are correct, but we believe that the *New York Times* rule states an accommodation between this concern and the limited state interest present in the context of libel actions brought by public persons. The state interest in compensating injury to the reputation of private individuals requires that a different rule should obtain with respect to them.

We have no difficulty in distinguishing among defamation plaintiffs. The first remedy of any victim of defamation is self-help—using available opportunities to contradict the lie or correct the error and thereby to minimize its adverse impact on reputation. Public officials and public figures usually enjoy significantly greater access to the channels of effective communication and hence have a more realistic opportunity to counteract false statements then private individuals normally enjoy.[9] Private individuals are therefore more vulnerable to injury, and the state interest in protecting them is correspondingly greater.

More important, there is a compelling normative consideration underlying the distinction between public and private defamation plaintiffs. An individual who decides to seek governmental office must accept certain necessary consequences of that involvement in public affairs. He runs the risk of closer public scrutiny than might otherwise be the case. And society's interest in the officers of government is not strictly limited to the formal discharge of official duties. The public's interest extends to "anything which might touch on an official's fitness for office. Few personal attributes are more germane to fitness for office than dishonesty, malfeasance, or improper motivation, even though these characteristics may also affect the official's private character." Those classed as public figures stand in a similar position. Hypothetically, it may be possible for someone to become a public figure through no purposeful action of his own, but the instances of truly involuntary public figures must be exceedingly rare. For the most part those who attain this status have assumed roles of especial prominence in the affairs of society. Some occupy positions of such persuasive power and influence that they are deemed public figures for all purposes. More commonly, those classed as public figures have thrust themselves to the forefront of particular public controversies in order to influence the resolution of the issues involved. In either event, they invite attention and comment.

Even if the foregoing generalities do not obtain in every instance, the communications media are entitled to act on the assumption that public officials

9. Of course, an opportunity for rebuttal seldom suffices to undo harm of defamatory falsehood. Indeed, the law of defamation is rooted in our experience that the truth rarely catches up with a lie. But the fact that the self-help remedy of rebuttal, standing alone, is inadequate to its task does not mean that it is irrelevant to our inquiry.

and public figures have voluntarily exposed themselves to increased risk of injury from defamatory falsehood concerning them. No such assumption is justified with respect to a private individual. He has not accepted public office or assumed an "influential role in ordering society." He has relinquished no part of his interest in the protection of his own good name, and consequently he has a more compelling call on the courts for redress of injury inflicted by defamatory falsehood. Thus, private individuals are not only more vulnerable to injury than public officials and public figures; they are also more deserving of recovery.

For these reasons we conclude that the States should retain substantial latitude in their efforts to enforce a legal remedy for defamatory falsehood injurious to the reputation of a private individual. The extension of the *New York Times* test proposed by the *Rosenbloom* plurality would abridge this legitimate state interest to a degree that we find unacceptable. And it would occasion the difficulty of forcing judges to decide which publications address issues of "general or public interest" and which do not. We doubt the wisdom of committing this task to the conscience of judges. The "public or general interest" test for determining the applicability of the *New York Times* standard to private defamation actions inadequately serves both of the competing values at stake.

We hold that, so long as they do not impose liability without fault, the States may define for themselves the appropriate standard of liability for a publisher or broadcaster of defamatory falsehood injurious to a private individual. This approach provides a more equitable boundary between the competing concerns involved here. It recognizes the strength of the legitimate state interest in compensating private individuals for wrongful injury to reputation, yet shields the press and broadcast media from the rigors of strict liability for defamation. The strong and legitimate state interest in compensating private individuals for injury to reputation extends no further than compensation for actual injury. We hold that the States may not permit recovery of presumed or punitive damages, at least when liability is not based on a showing of knowledge of falsity or reckless disregard for the truth.

The common law of defamation is an oddity of tort law, for it allows recovery of purportedly compensatory damages without evidence of actual loss. Under the traditional rules pertaining to actions for libel, the existence of injury is presumed from the fact of publication. Juries may award substantial sums as compensation for supposed damage to reputation without any proof that such harm actually occurred. The largely uncontrolled discretion of juries to award damages where there is no loss unnecessarily compounds the potential of any system of liability for defamatory falsehood to inhibit the vigorous exercise of First Amendment freedoms. Additionally, the doctrine of presumed damages invites juries to punish unpopular opinion rather than to compensate individuals for injury sustained by the publication of a false fact. The States have no substantial interest in securing for plaintiffs such as this petitioner gratuitous awards of money damages far in excess of any actual injury.

Here we are attempting to reconcile state law with a competing interest grounded in the constitutional command of the First Amendment. It is therefore appropriate to require that state remedies for defamatory falsehood reach no farther than is necessary to protect the legitimate interest involved. It is necessary to restrict defamation plaintiffs who do not prove knowledge of falsity or reckless disregard for the truth to compensation for actual injury which is not limited to out-of-pocket loss. The more customary types of actual harm inflicted by defamatory falsehood include impairment of reputation and standing in the community, personal humiliation, and mental anguish and suffering. Of course, juries must be limited by appropriate instructions, and all awards must be supported by competent evidence concerning the injury, although there need be no evidence which assigns an actual dollar value to the injury.

We also find no justification for allowing awards of punitive damages against publishers and broadcasters. Juries assess punitive damages in wholly unpredictable amounts bearing no necessary relation to the actual harm caused. And they remain free to use their discretion selectively to punish expressions of unpopular views. Like the doctrine of presumed damages, jury discretion to award punitive damages exacerbates the danger of media self-censorship, but punitive damages are wholly irrelevant to the state interest that justifies a negligence standard for private defamation actions. They are not compensation for injury. Instead, they are private fines levied by civil juries to punish reprehensible conduct and to deter its future occurrence. In short, the private defamation plaintiff who establishes liability under a less demanding standard than that stated by *New York Times* may recover only such damages as are sufficient to compensate him for actual injury.

Respondent contends that we should affirm on the ground that petitioner is either a public official or a public figure. There is little basis for the former assertion. Several years prior to the present incident, petitioner served briefly on housing committees appointed by the mayor of Chicago, but he never held any remunerative governmental position. Respondent argues that petitioner's appearance at the coroner's inquest rendered him a "de facto public official." Our cases recognized no such concept. Respondent's suggestion would sweep all lawyers under the *New York Times* rule as officers of the court and distort the plain meaning of the "public official" category beyond all recognition. We decline to follow it.

Respondent's characterization of petitioner as a public figure raises a different question. That designation may rest on either of two alternative bases. In some instances an individual may achieve such pervasive fame or notoriety that he becomes a public figure for all purposes and in all contexts. More commonly, an individual voluntarily injects himself or is drawn into a particular public controversy and thereby becomes a public figure for a limited range of issues. In either case such persons assume special prominence in the resolution of public questions.

Petitioner has long been active in community and professional affairs. He has served as an officer of local civic groups and of various professional organizations, and he has published several books and articles on legal subjects. Although petitioner was consequently well known in some circles, he had achieved no general fame or notoriety in the community. We would not lightly assume that a citizen's participation in community and professional affairs rendered him a public figure for all purposes. Absent clear evidence of general fame or notoriety in the community, and pervasive involvement in the affairs of society, an individual should not be deemed a public personality for all aspects of his life. In this context it is plain that petitioner was not a public figure. He played a minimal role at the coroner's inquest, and his participation related solely to his representation of a private client. He took no part in the criminal prosecution of Officer Nuccio. Moreover, he never discussed either the criminal or civil litigation with the press and was never quoted as having done so. He plainly did not thrust himself into the vortex of this public issue, nor did he engage the public's attention in an attempt to influence its outcome. We are persuaded that the trial court did not err in refusing to characterize petitioner as a public figure for the purpose of this litigation.

We therefore conclude that the *New York Times* standard is inapplicable to this case and that the trial court erred in entering judgment for respondent. Because the jury was allowed to impose liability without fault and was permitted to presume damages without proof of injury, a new trial is necessary. We reverse and remand for further proceedings in accord with this opinion.

It is ordered.

Reversed and remanded.

Mr. Chief Justice BURGER, *dissenting.*

The important public policy which underlies the right to counsel would be gravely jeopardized if every lawyer who takes an "unpopular" case, civil or criminal, would automatically become fair game for irresponsible reporters and editors who might, for example, describe the lawyer as a "mob mouthpiece" for representing a client with a serious prior criminal record.

Mr. Justice DOUGLAS, *dissenting.*

The vehicle for publication in this case was the *American Opinion,* a most controversial periodical which disseminates the views of the John Birch Society, an organization which many deem to be quite offensive. The subject matter involved "Communist plots," "conspiracies against law enforcement agencies," and the killing of a private citizen by the police. With any such amalgam of controversial elements, a jury determination, unpredictable in the most neutral circumstances, becomes a virtual roll of the dice separating them from liability for often massive claims of damage. It is only the hardy publisher who will engage in discussion in the face of such risk, and the Court's preoccupation with proliferating standards increases the risks. The First and Fourteenth Amendments prohibit the imposition of damages for this discussion of public affairs.

Mr. Justice BRENNAN, *dissenting.*

Matters of public or general interest do not "suddenly become less so merely because a private individual is involved, or because in some sense the individual did not 'voluntarily' choose to become involved." The Court's broad-ranging examples of "actual injury," including impairment of reputation and standing in the community, as well as personal humiliation, and mental anguish and suffering, inevitably allow a jury bent on punishing expression of unpopular views a formidable weapon for doing so. Finally, even a limitation of recovery to "actual injury" will not provide the necessary elbowroom for First Amendment expression. "The very possibility of having to engage in litigation, an expensive and protracted process, is threat enough to cause discussion and debate to 'steer far wider of the unlawful zone' thereby keeping protected discussion from public cognizance."

Notes and Questions

1. *Private Individuals and Matters of Purely Private Concern.* In *Dun & Bradstreet, Inc. v. Greenmoss Builders, Inc.*, 472 U.S. 749 (1985), the Court confronted the question whether a lower liability standard should apply in defamation cases involving "private plaintiffs" involved in matters of "purely private concern." The case involved a credit reporting agency that inaccurately reported that plaintiff's business was in bankruptcy:

> It is speech on "matters of public concern" that is "at the heart of the First Amendment's protection." Speech on matters of purely private concern is of less First Amendment concern. The role of the Constitution in regulating state libel law is far more limited when the concerns that activated *New York Times* and *Gertz* are absent. In such a case, "there is no threat to the free and robust debate of public issues; there is no potential interference with a meaningful dialogue of ideas concerning self-government; and there is no threat of liability causing a reaction of self-censorship by the press. Courts for centuries have allowed juries to presume that some damage occurred from many defamatory utterances and publications. This rule furthers the state interest in providing remedies for defamation by ensuring that those remedies are effective. In light of the reduced constitutional value of speech involving no matters of public concern, we hold that the state interest adequately supports awards of presumed and punitive damages—even absent a showing of 'actual malice.'"
>
> "Whether speech addresses a matter of public concern must be determined by the expression's content, form, and context as revealed by the whole record." These factors indicate that petitioner's credit report concerns no public issue. It was speech solely in the individual interest of the speaker and its specific business audience. Since the credit report was made available to only five subscribers, who could not disseminate it further, it cannot be said that the report involves any "strong interest in the free flow of commercial information." There is simply no credible argument that this type of credit reporting requires special protection to ensure that "debate on public issues will be uninhibited, robust, and wide-open."

We conclude that permitting recovery of presumed and punitive damages in defamation cases absent a showing of "actual malice" does not violate the First Amendment when the defamatory statements do not involve matters of public concern.

Justice Brennan dissented: "Speech about commercial or economic matters is an important part of public discourse. It is difficult to suggest that a bankruptcy is not a subject matter of public concern when federal law requires invocation of judicial mechanisms to effectuate it and makes the fact of the bankruptcy a matter of public record."

2. *Burden of Proof.* At common law, in a defamation case, the defendant bore the burden of proving that the allegedly defamatory statements were true. In *Philadelphia Newspapers, Inc. v. Hepps*, 475 U.S. 767 (1986), the Court reversed that presumption and held that, when a newspaper publishes matters of public concern, a private-figure plaintiff cannot recover damages without proving that the statements are false. Justice Stevens dissented: "The overriding concern for reliable protection of truthful statements must make room for 'the legitimate state interest in compensating individuals for the harm inflicted on them by defamatory falsehood.'"

Food for Thought

Given that Gertz was a lawyer, had served on various community committees, and was involved (albeit peripherally) in a case of great public interest, should the court have treated him as a public figure?

More Notes and Questions

1. *The* Firestone *Case.* In *Time, Inc. v. Firestone*, 424 U.S. 448 (1976), the Court rejected public-figure status for a petitioner in a divorce proceeding:

> Dissolution of a marriage through judicial proceedings is not the sort of "public controversy" referred to in *Gertz*, even though the marital difficulties of extremely wealthy individuals may be of interest to some portion of the reading public. Nor did respondent freely choose to publicize issues as to the propriety of her married life. She was compelled to go to court by the State in order to obtain legal release from the bonds of matrimony. Her actions, both in instituting the litigation and in its conduct, were quite different from those of General Walker in *Curtis Publishing Co.* She assumed no "special prominence in the resolution of public questions." We hold respondent was not a "public figure."

Consider Justice Marshall's dissent in *Firestone*:

> Mrs. Firestone was "prominent among the '400' of Palm Beach society," and an "active (member) of the sporting set," whose activities predictably attracted the attention of a sizable portion of the public. Mrs. Firestone's appearances in the press were frequent enough to warrant her subscribing to a press-clipping service. Mr. and Mrs. Firestone's "marital difficulties were well-known," and the lawsuit became "a veritable cause celebre

in social circles across the country." The 17-month trial and related events attracted national news coverage, and elicited no fewer than 88 articles in three local newspapers. Far from shunning the publicity, Mrs. Firestone held several press conferences in the course of the proceedings. These facts warrant the conclusion that Mary Alice Firestone was a "public figure" for purposes of reports on the judicial proceedings she initiated. If these actions fail to establish that she "voluntarily exposed (herself) to increased risk of injury from defamatory falsehood," surely they are sufficient to entitle the press to act on the assumption that she did.

Do you agree with the majority or with Justice Marshall?

5. *Public Figures, Private Lives.* There has been much debate about whether a different, lower standard should apply to allegations regarding the private life of a public official or public figure. Suppose, for example, a newspaper alleges that a politician has engaged in an adulterous affair. Should the *Sullivan* actual malice standard apply to the allegation, or should some lower standard (the *Gertz* or *Dun & Bradstreet* standard) apply? *See Monitor Patriot Co. v. Roy*, 401 U.S. 265 (1971).

6. *The Internet and Defamatory Speech.* As the internet spawns new forms of communication, defamation principles are being applied in new contexts involving non-media professionals. For example, in a number of instances, individual bloggers have been sued for defamation. *See* Caryn Rousseau, *Bloggers Learn to Deal with Media Pitfalls: Citizen Journalists Get Training*, Louisville Courier-Journal, A-6, c. 1-3, June 15, 2008. While some bloggers are journalists who work for traditional newspapers, others are individuals who choose to comment on social, political, or economic issues. *See id.* Similar issues have arisen regarding websites. *See* David L. Hudson, Jr., *Taming the Gossip Mongers: Websites That Dish Dirt May Soon Get Their Publishers' Hands Muddy*, A.B.A. J. 19 (July 2008).

7. *A Cosby Accuser.* In *McKee v. Cosby*, 874 F.3d 54 (1st Cir. 2017), a defamation suit involved the plaintiff Katherine McKee's media allegation that the actor Bill Cosby had sexually assaulted her. McKee filed suit after the publication of a letter from Cosby's lawyer, attacking her credibility and suggesting that she was not believable. Since McKee had voluntarily chosen to make her public allegation against Cosby, the court concluded that she was a "limited purpose public figure" and therefore required McKee to satisfy the actual malice standard in order to prevail. Ultimately, she failed to meet that burden of proof and her suit was dismissed. Later, after a mistrial on the charge of sexually assaulting Andrea Costand, Cosby was convicted at a second trial in 2018 at which five other women testified that he had sexually assaulted them also. Roughly 60 women have accused Cosby of sexual assault. *See* Jen Kirby, *Bill Cosby convicted of sexual assault*, Vox, April 26, 2018, https://www.vox.com/2018/4/26/17272470/bill-cosby-trial-verdict-guilty-sexual-assault-Andrea-Costand.

8. *The Section 230 Shield.* Under Section 230 of the Communications Decency Act, online publishers are generally shielded from liability against defamation liability: "No provider . . . of an interactive computer service shall be treated as the publisher or speaker of any information provided by another information content provider." 47 U.S.C. § 230(c). However, the shield applies only if the

computer service provider is not also an "information content provider," which the law defines as someone who is "responsible, in whole or in part, for the creation or development of" the offending content. Recently, Congress overwhelmingly supported an amendment to Section 230 and President Trump signed the new legislation known as the Allow States and Victims to Fight Online Sex Trafficking Act (FOSTA). The statute creates an exception to Section 230 so that its shield "does not apply to criminal or civil charges of sex trafficking or to conduct that 'promotes or facilitates prostitution.'" Adi Robertson, *Trump signs anti-trafficking law that weakens online free speech protections*, The Verge, April 11, 2018, https://www.the verge.com.

9. *Remove the Section 230 Shield?* President Trump, upset that certain social media companies have flagged some of his tweets for "fact checking," has questioned whether they should retain their Section 230 exemption from liability. As a result, President Trump issued an Executive Order designed to prompt reconsideration of the defense. Executive Order on Preventing Online Censorship (May 28, 2020). That order does several things: 1) it directs the Secretary of Commerce to file a petition with the FCC asking the FCC to more clearly define the limits of Section 230; 2) it directs the head of each executive agency to review any advertising and marketing funds spent with online firms and assess whether those online firms are "problematic vehicles for government speech due to viewpoint discrimination, deception to consumers, or other bad practices; 3) directs the Federal Trade Commission to investigate practices of online platforms that "restrict speech in ways that do not align with those entities' public representations about those practices"; 4) envisions the creation of a working group of state attorneys general with respect to the enforcement of state laws prohibiting deceptive practices. Is the Executive Order sound?

∽ PROBLEMS ∽

1. *The False Rolling Stone Article.* Rolling Stone magazine published an article entitled "A Rape on Campus: A Brutal Assault and a Struggle for Justice" which described a brutal gang rape of a first-year female student at an on-campus fraternity house. The story was later found to have been fabricated and the magazine withdrew the story. Can members of the fraternity recover for defamation, even if they were not named in the story, as long as they appear to have been referenced in the story? Assuming that it is necessary under state defamation law for a plaintiff to show that false statements were "of and concerning" the plaintiff as an individual, what standard should be used by the court to determine whether each of the unnamed fraternity members can satisfy that requirement? In the alternative, assume that it may be possible for all the members of the fraternity—both named and unnamed—to recover under a different theory. Ordinarily, a statement about an organization is not understood to refer to any of its individual

members. But state defamation law allows a "small group defamation claim" to be brought in a suit for individual injuries by each plaintiff that result from a defamatory comment about the group to which all the plaintiffs belong. Under this theory, what requirements should the court use to determine whether the fraternity members should qualify for a small group defamation claim as a policy matter? *See Elias v. Rolling Stone LLC*, 872 F.3d 97 (2d Cir. 2017).

2. *Ag-Gag Laws.* Activists have attempted to enter agricultural facilities to document the alleged mistreatment of animals. Since truth is a complete defense in a defamation action, the owners of those facilities cannot sue the activists for defamation or disparagement if the allegations are true. As a result, some states have enacted laws limiting the ability of individuals to enter and report on what happens in non-public areas. For example, North Carolina's so-called "Ag-Gag Law" prohibits individuals from entering private property ("non-public areas") to investigate the alleged mistreatment of animals. Of course, one of the concerns is that activists will apply for jobs at facilities in order to gain entry and to do "economic or other injury to an agricultural production facility." Idaho and Iowa laws make it a crime to make misrepresentations to gain entry to an agricultural production facility, and also to make recordings of the operations. Are such laws valid? *See People for the Ethical Treatment of Animals v. Stein*, 737 Fed. Appx. 122 (4th Cir. 2018); *Animal Legal Defense Fund v. Wasden*, 312 F. Supp.3d 929 (D. Idaho 2018); *Animal Legal Defense Fund v. Reynolds*, 353 F.Supp.3d 812 (S.D. Iowa 2019).

3. *Planned Parenthood Videos.* Suppose that defendants, activists who are opposed to abortion, create fake corporations and fake identifications in order to gain access to a Planned Parenthood convention. Once inside the convention, they produce videos which Planned Parenthood regards as "false" and "misleading." In particular, although the videos purport to show Planned Parenthood employees discussing violations of federal law related to fetal tissue donations, Planned Parenthood claims that the videos were altered to distort the actual conversations. Can the activists be held liable consistently with the First Amendment? On what grounds? *See Planned Parenthood Federation of America, Inc. v. Center for Medical Progress*, 890 F.3d 828 (9th Cir. 2018).

4. *Bloggers and the International Treaty Regulating the Internet.* Should bloggers, as the new "press," receive special protections under the treaty that you are negotiating? Indeed, in light of the *New York Times* "actual malice" standard, would U.S. courts draw a distinction between traditional media (e.g., newspapers, radio, and television) and internet publications (e.g., blogs)?

5. *More on the International Treaty Regulating the Internet.* Let's think a bit more about the German delegates' demands that the treaty provide specific protections for "human dignity." Do the holdings in *Gertz* and *Dun & Bradstreet* give you more freedom to craft language that, while not totally acceptable to the German delegates, at least gives a nod toward their concerns? Can you agree to include language in the treaty that would leave the German government free to handle defamatory speech in a manner consistent with the German Constitution?

d. Fact Versus Opinion

Should a distinction be made between statements of "fact" and statements of "opinion"? Consider the next case.

Milkovich v. Lorain Journal Co.

497 U.S. 1 (1990)

Chief Justice REHNQUIST delivered the opinion of the Court.

Respondent J. Theodore Diadiun authored a newspaper article that implied that petitioner Michael Milkovich, a high school wrestling coach, lied under oath in a judicial proceeding about an incident involving his team which occurred at a wrestling match. Petitioner sued Diadiun and the newspaper for libel.

Respondents would have us recognize First Amendment protection for defamatory statements which are categorized as "opinion" as opposed to "fact." For this proposition they rely principally on the following dictum from our opinion in *Gertz*: "Under the First Amendment there is no such thing as a false idea. However pernicious an opinion may seem, we depend for its correction not on the conscience of judges and juries but on the competition of other ideas. But there is no constitutional value in false statements of fact."

We do not think this passage was intended to create a wholesale exemption for anything that might be labeled "opinion." Not only would such an interpretation be contrary to the tenor and context of the passage, but it would also ignore the fact that expressions of "opinion" may often imply an assertion of objective fact. If a speaker says, "In my opinion John Jones is a liar," he implies a knowledge of facts which lead to the conclusion that Jones told an untruth.

We think the " 'breathing space' " which " 'freedoms of expression require in order to survive' " is adequately secured by existing constitutional doctrine without the creation of an artificial dichotomy between "opinion" and fact. A statement on matters of public concern must be provable as false before there can be liability under state defamation law, at least where a media defendant is involved. Next, our cases provide protection for statements that cannot "reasonably be interpreted as stating actual facts" about an individual. This provides assurance that public debate will not suffer for lack of "imaginative expression" or the "rhetorical hyperbole" which has traditionally added much to the discourse of our Nation.

Where a statement of "opinion" on a matter of public concern reasonably implies false and defamatory facts regarding public figures or officials, those individuals must show that such statements were made with knowledge of their false implications or with reckless disregard of their truth. Similarly, where a statement involves a private figure on a matter of public concern, a plaintiff must show that the false connotations were made with some level of fault as required by *Gertz*. Enhanced appellate review provides assurance that the foregoing determinations will be made so as not to "constitute a forbidden intrusion into free expression."

The connotation that petitioner committed perjury is sufficiently factual to be susceptible of being proved true or false. A determination whether petitioner lied can be made on a core of objective evidence by comparing, inter alia, petitioner's testimony before the OHSAA board with his subsequent testimony before the trial court.

The judgment of the Ohio Court of Appeals is reversed, and the case is remanded for further proceedings not inconsistent with this opinion.

Reversed.

Justice BRENNAN, with whom Justice MARSHALL joins, *dissenting.*

No reasonable reader could understand Diadiun to be impliedly asserting—as fact—that Milkovich had perjured himself. Nor could such a reader infer that Diadiun had further information about Milkovich's court testimony on which his belief was based. It is plain from the column that Diadiun did not attend the court hearing. Diadiun also clearly had no detailed second-hand information about what Milkovich had said in court. Instead, what suffices for "detail" and "color" are quotations from the OHSAA hearing—old news compared to the court decision which prompted the column—and a vague quotation from an OHSAA commissioner. Readers could see that Diadiun was focused on the court's reversal of the OHSAA's decision and was angrily supposing what must have led to it.

Even the insinuation that Milkovich had repeated, in court, a more plausible version of the misrepresentations he had made at the OHSAA hearing is preceded by the cautionary term "apparently"—an unmistakable sign that Diadiun did not know what Milkovich had actually said in court. "Cautionary language or interrogatories of this type put the reader on notice that what is being read is opinion and thus weaken any inference that the author possesses knowledge of damaging, undisclosed facts. In a word, when the reasonable reader encounters cautionary language, he tends to 'discount that which follows.'"

Furthermore, the tone and format of the piece notify readers to expect speculation and personal judgment. The tone is pointed, exaggerated, and heavily laden with emotional rhetoric and moral outrage. Diadiun never says that Milkovich committed perjury. He says that "anyone who attended the meet knows in his heart" that Milkovich lied—obvious hyperbole as Diadiun does not purport to have researched what everyone who attended the meet knows in his heart. Punishing such conjecture protects reputation only at the cost of expunging a genuinely useful mechanism for public debate. "In a society which takes seriously the principle that government rests upon the consent of the governed, freedom of the press must be the most cherished tenet."

Notes

1. *"Statements of Fact" and "Hyperbole."* Within the defamation continuum, there has been considerable litigation regarding whether certain labels can be

regarded as defamatory, in the sense that they involve false assertions of fact, or whether (perhaps) they involve just "hyperbole." In *Buckley v. Littell*, 539 F.2d 882, 895 (2d Cir. 1976), *cert. denied*, 429 U.S. 1062 (1977), the court held that the use of the term *fascist* could not "be regarded as a statement of fact because of the tremendous imprecision of the meaning and usage of this term." In *Henderson v. Times Mirror Co.*, 669 F. Supp. 356 (D. Colo. 1987), in a statement to newspaper reporters, the defendant referred to the plaintiff as a "sleaze-bag agent" who "slimed up from the bayou." The plaintiff, an agent for professional football players, sued, naming as defendants a news editor and two newspaper companies whose papers published the defendant's remarks. The Court held that the statements constituted just hyperbole.

2. *No Longer Defamatory Per Se.* In *Stern v. Cosby*, 645 F. Supp. 2d 258 (S.D.N.Y. 2009), the federal district court judge concluded that if the issue were to come before it, the New York Court of Appeals would decide that a statement falsely implying that a person is a gay man or a lesbian would not be defamatory *per se*. However, in *Yonaty v. Mincolla*, 2011 N.Y. slip op. 51037(U) (Supreme Court, Broome Cty., June 8, 2011), a state trial judge concluded that he could not ignore the contrary precedent suggesting that a plaintiff could proceed with a defamation action in which he claimed that he was falsely alleged to be gay or bisexual. Subsequently, the state appellate court ruled that it is not inherently defamatory to falsely impute homosexuality to another person. Under New York law, only a "handful" of statements remain defamatory *per se*, including "falsely charging someone with a serious crime, making statements that damage a person in his or her profession, suggesting that an individual has a loathsome disease or accusing a woman of unchastity." John Caher, *Panel Finds False "Gay" Label Is No Longer Per Se Defamation.* N.Y. Bar J. (June 1, 2012), http://www.newyorklawjournal.com/PubArticleNY.jsp?id=1202556645479&slreturn=1.

∾ PROBLEMS ∾

1. *Libel-Proof?* Howard K. Stern brought a libel action against the author and publisher of *Blonde Ambition: The Untold Story Behind Anna Nicole Smith's Death*. In *Stern v. Cosby*, 645 F. Supp. 2d 258 (S.D.N.Y. 2009), Stern was described by the federal district court as "the former lawyer for and companion of the late Anna Nicole Smith." Defendants argued that Stern is "libel-proof" because "his reputation is already so bad that it cannot be further damaged." They based this claim on the fact that he had been the subject of critical discussion on tabloid television and in celebrity gossip magazines. Can a plaintiff be libel proof?

2. *The Porn Star.* In 2018, "Stormy Daniels," a porn star who allegedly had a sexual affair with President Donald Trump, burst onto the public scene after she challenged a nondisclosure agreement that she made with Trump. Later, she filed a defamation action against Trump after he made statements on Twitter questioning her credibility. Daniels had released a sketch of a man who allegedly

threatened her in order to encourage her to remain silent about the affair. Trump's tweet referred to Daniels' allegations as a "total con job." Since Daniels is a public figure, is she likely to prevail in a defamation action against Trump? What would she be required to show in order to satisfy the actual malice standard?

3. *More on the International Treaty on the Internet.* Suppose that the delegates to the convention wish to discuss the standards that apply to defamation actions. As we have seen, the standards vary dramatically from nation to nation. What treaty provisions can you agree to?

5. Privacy

The tort of invasion of privacy was influenced by the landmark article *The Right of Privacy*, 4 Harv. L. Rev. 193 (1890). In that article, future Supreme Court Justice Louis Brandeis and Samuel Warren described the right of "privacy," which they also referred to as "the right to be let alone" and "the right most valued by civilized men." The common law tort of privacy included four separate and distinct actions: 1) appropriation of the plaintiff's name or likeness in commercial advertising, 2) intrusion on the plaintiff's solitude or seclusion or on the plaintiff's private affairs in a way that would be highly offensive to a reasonable person, 3) publication of private facts about the plaintiff's life when disclosure would be highly offensive to a reasonable person and is not a matter of public concern, and 4) a showing of the plaintiff in a false light.

In some instances, the tort action directly conflicts with the right of free speech. For example, *Florida Star v. B.J.F.*, 491 U.S. 524 (1989), involved a Florida statute that made it unlawful to "print, publish, or broadcast in any instrument of mass communication" the name of the victim of a sexual offense. Under the statute, the *Florida Star* was held civilly liable for publishing the name of a rape victim, which it had obtained from a publicly released police report. The Court struck down the law as unconstitutional: "If a newspaper lawfully obtains truthful information about a matter of public significance then state officials may not constitutionally punish publication of the information, absent a need to further a state interest of the highest order." The Court concluded that the interest in shielding the rape victim (which the Court suggested might be an interest of the "highest order") was insufficient given that the name was already in the public domain.

Time, Inc. v. Hill

385 U.S. 374 (1967)

Mr. Justice BRENNAN delivered the opinion of the Court.

The question is whether appellant, publisher of *Life* magazine, was denied constitutional protections of speech and press by an award of damages on allegations that *Life* falsely reported that a new play portrayed an experience suffered by appellee and his family.

The article appeared in *Life* in February 1955. It was entitled "'True Crime Inspires Tense Play,' with the subtitle, 'The ordeal of a family trapped by convicts gives Broadway a new thriller, *The Desperate Hours*.'" The text of the article reads as follows:

> Three years ago Americans all over the country read about the desperate ordeal of the James Hill family, who were held prisoners in their home outside Philadelphia by three escaped convicts. Later they read about it in Joseph Hayes's novel, *The Desperate Hours*, inspired by the family's experience. Now they can see the story re-enacted in Hayes's Broadway play based on the book, and next year will see it in his movie, which has been filmed but is being held up until the play has a chance to pay off.
>
> The play, directed by Robert Montgomery and expertly acted, is a heart-stopping account of how a family rose to heroism in a crisis. LIFE photographed the play during its Philadelphia tryout, and transported some of the actors to the actual house where the Hills were besieged. On the next page scenes from the play are re-enacted on the site of the crime.

The pictures on the ensuing two pages included an enactment of the son being "roughed up" by one of the convicts, entitled "brutish convict," a picture of the daughter biting the hand of a convict to make him drop a gun, entitled "daring daughter," and one of the father throwing his gun through the door after a "brave try" to save his family is foiled.

The James Hill referred to in the article is appellee. He and his wife and five children involuntarily became the subjects of a front-page news story after being held hostage by three escaped convicts in their suburban Pennsylvania, home for 19 hours. The family was released unharmed. In an interview with newsmen after the convicts departed, appellee stressed that the convicts had treated the family courteously, had not molested them, and had not been at all violent. The convicts were thereafter apprehended in a widely publicized encounter with the police which resulted in the killing of two of the convicts. Shortly thereafter the family moved to Connecticut. Appellee discouraged all efforts to keep them in the public spotlight through magazine articles or appearances on television.

A year later, Joseph Hayes' novel, *The Desperate Hours*, was published. The story depicted the experience of a family of four held hostage by three escaped convicts in the family's suburban home. But, unlike Hill's experience, the family of the story suffer violence at the hands of the convicts; the father and son are beaten and the daughter subjected to a verbal sexual insult. The book was made into a play and it is *Life*'s article about the play which is the subject of appellee's action. The complaint sought damages under state law on allegations that the *Life* article was intended to, and did, give the impression that the play mirrored the Hill family's experience, which, to the knowledge of defendant, "was false and untrue." Appellant's defense was that the article was "a subject of legitimate news interest," "a subject of general interest and of value and concern to the public" at the time of publication, and that it was "published in good faith without any malice whatsoever."

The jury awarded appellee $50,000 compensatory and $25,000 punitive damages. On appeal the Appellate Division of the Supreme Court ordered a new trial as to damages but sustained the verdict of liability. "Although the play was fictionalized, *Life*'s article portrayed it as a reenactment of the Hills' experience. This was done to advertise and attract further attention to the play, and to increase present and future magazine circulationl. The article cannot be characterized as a mere dissemination of news, nor even an effort to supply legitimate newsworthy information in which the public had, or might have a proper interest." At the new trial on damages, the court awarded $30,000 compensatory damages without punitive damages.

The guarantees for speech and press are not the preserve of political expression or comment upon public affairs, essential as those are to healthy government. One need only pick up any newspaper or magazine to comprehend the vast range of published matter which exposes persons to public view, both private citizens and public officials. Exposure of the self to others in varying degrees is a concomitant of life in a civilized community. The risk of this exposure is an essential incident of life in a society which places a primary value on freedom of speech and of press. "Freedom of discussion, if it would fulfill its historic function in this nation, must embrace all issues about which information is needed or appropriate to enable the members of society to cope with the exigencies of their period." We have no doubt that the subject of the *Life* article, the opening of a new play linked to an actual incident, is a matter of public interest. Erroneous statement is no less inevitable in such a case than in the case of comment upon public affairs, and in both, if innocent or merely negligent, it must be protected if the "freedoms of expression are to have the 'breathing space' that they 'need to survive.'" We create a grave risk of serious impairment of the indispensable service of a free press in a free society if we saddle the press with the impossible burden of verifying to a certainty the facts associated in news articles with a person's name, picture or portrait, particularly as related to nondefamatory matter. Even negligence would be a most elusive standard, especially when the content of the speech itself affords no warning of prospective harm to another through falsity. A negligence test would place on the press the intolerable burden of guessing how a jury might assess the reasonableness of steps taken by it to verify the accuracy of every reference to a name, picture or portrait.

In this context, sanctions against either innocent or negligent misstatement would present a grave hazard of discouraging the press from exercising the constitutional guarantees. Those guarantees are not for the benefit of the press so much as for the benefit of all of us. A broadly defined freedom of the press assures the maintenance of our political system and an open society. Fear of large verdicts in damage suits for innocent or merely negligent misstatement, even fear of the expense involved in their defense, must inevitably cause publishers to "steer wider of the unlawful zone," and thus "create the danger that the legitimate utterance will be penalized." But the constitutional guarantees can tolerate sanctions against calculated falsehood without significant impairment of their essential function. We held in *New York Times* that calculated falsehood enjoyed no immunity in the case of alleged defamation of a public official concerning his official conduct. Similarly, calculated falsehood should enjoy no immunity in the situation here presented us.

We find applicable here the standard of knowing or reckless falsehood. This is neither a libel action by a private individual nor a statutory action by a public official. Therefore, although the First Amendment principles pronounced in *New York Times* guide our conclusion, we reach that conclusion only by applying these principles in this discrete context. Were this a libel action, the distinction which has been suggested between the relative opportunities of the public official and the private individual to rebut defamatory charges might be germane. And the additional state interest in the protection of the individual against damage to his reputation would be involved. Moreover, a different test might be required in a statutory action by a public official, as opposed to a libel action by a public official or a statutory action by a private individual. Different considerations might arise concerning the degree of "waiver" of the protection the State might afford. But the question whether the same standard should be applicable both to persons voluntarily and involuntarily thrust into the public limelight is not here before us.

Turning to the facts of the present case, the proofs reasonably would support either a jury finding of innocent or merely negligent misstatement by *Life,* or a finding that *Life* portrayed the play as a reenactment of the Hill family's experience reckless of the truth or with actual knowledge that the portrayal was false. We do not think, however, that the instructions confined the jury to a verdict of liability based on a finding that the statements in the article were made with knowledge of their falsity or in reckless disregard of the truth.

The judgment of the Court of Appeals is set aside and the case is remanded for further proceedings not inconsistent with this opinion.

It is so ordered.

Notes and Questions

1. *Other Privacy Torts. Time, Inc. v. Hill* dealt with the "false light" form of the tort of privacy, and the Court held that an individual involved in a matter of public interest must satisfy the actual malice standard in order to recover. Of course, there are three other possible bases of liability in privacy actions: (1) intrusion on the plaintiff's seclusion or solitude; (2) public disclosure of private embarrassing facts about the plaintiff; and (3) appropriation for the defendant's advantage of plaintiff's name or likeness. *See* Prosser, *Privacy*, 48 CAL. L. REV. 383 (1960). Courts are much more likely to award damages or injunctive relief when the defendant has intruded on plaintiff's seclusion or solitude (e.g., breaking into plaintiff's house in order to gather information or associating plaintiff's name or likeness with defendant's business).

2. *Appropriation and Intrusion on Seclusion.* Courts are much more likely to grant relief when one of these other torts is involved. In *In re Weingand*, 41 Cal. Rptr. 778 (Ct. App. 1964), the Court held that defendant had inappropriately utilized plaintiff's name and likeness in his business. Similarly, in *Galella v. Onassis*, 353 F. Supp. 196 (S.D.N.Y. 1972), a self-styled "paparazzi" photographer (Galella) was sued by former First Lady Jacqueline (Kennedy) Onassis for invasion of privacy. In an effort to produce interesting and saleable pictures of Mrs. Onassis and her children, Galella maintained constant surveillance of them, and he used "secret agent" tactics such as hiding behind restaurant coat racks, sneaking into beauty parlors, donning disguises, hiding in theater boxes, intruding into school buildings, bribing doormen, and romancing maids. In an effort to catch them in interesting poses, he tried to frighten them by jumping, lunging, leaping, rushing out, bumping, blocking, or scuffling with them, and he would make "offensive" noises near them, including grunting, yelling, and making "strange sounds." In addition, Galella contrived to have himself photographed with Mrs. Onassis and thereafter would claim to have an intimate knowledge of her every move. The Court held that injunctive relief for invasion of privacy was warranted.

3. *The Rape Victim.* In *Cox Broadcasting Corp. v. Cohn*, 420 U.S. 469 (1975), plaintiff sought damages on privacy grounds for a broadcast that revealed the name of his daughter (identifying her as a dead rape victim) during the news coverage of the trial of the alleged perpetrators of the crime. The television reporter obtained the daughter's name from official court documents which were open to public inspection. The Court held that the First Amendment barred recovery against the broadcaster under such circumstances, but left open the question whether tort liability could be allowed if a name were obtained from unofficial sources.

4. *Private Individuals.* In *Gertz v. Robert Welch, Inc.*, 418 U.S. 323 (1974), the Court distinguished between public officials and public figures, on the one hand, and private individuals, on the other, and held that lesser liability standards should apply in *defamation* cases involving private individuals. Does *Gertz* affect *Hill*'s holding so that a lower standard (than the actual malice standard) applies in privacy cases involving private individuals? If a distinction is made between private individuals and public officials or public figures, how should the Hills be treated? Did they become "involuntary public figures" by the extensive news reporting about their ordeal?

5. *Stealing the Show.* A performer's act involved him serving as a "human cannonball." Although plaintiff conceded that the press could report his appearance at the fair where he was performing his act, and could both describe his act and comment on it, he sued when a television station filmed his entire act in a 15-second film clip and displayed it on the nightly news. He claimed that this involved an "appropriation of his professional property," which was protected by the state tort law right of publicity, and he sought compensatory damages. In *Zacchini v. Scripps-Howard Broadcasting Co.*, 433 U.S. 562 (1977), the Court sided with the entertainer. The Court emphasized that the state interest in creating a publicity action for a performer like Zacchini is to "protect the proprietary

interest of an individual in his art," in order to encourage the production of entertainment. The Court noted that performers who bring publicity suits usually have no objection to publicity as long as they receive commercial benefit from their performances. The Court held that the First Amendment did not permit the broadcast without compensation of "a performer's entire act without his consent," because such publicity is no different from the impermissible broadcast of "a copyrighted dramatic work without liability to the copyright owner."

6. *Privacy in Europe.* In general, European nations have been much more privacy protective than the United States. Perhaps this difference is attributable to the fact that the United States places greater importance on freedom of expression, and (as in *Time, Inc. v. Hill*) is inclined to subordinate privacy interests to free speech interests. Recently, the European Court of Justice declared a "right to be forgotten" and ordered Google to expunge records in appropriate cases. *See* David Streitfeld, *European Court Lets Users Erase Records on Web,* N.Y. Times, May 13, 2014. Not long afterward, a U.S. court refused to enter a similar order. *See Google, Inc. v. Expunction Order,* 441 S.W.3d 644 (Tex. App. 2014).

7. *The Constitutionality of Revenge Porn Laws.* In *Ex Parte Jones,* 2018 WL 1835925 (Tex. Ct. App. April 18, 2018), the court struck down a Texas revenge porn law. That law made it a crime to intentionally disclose, without consent, pictures of another person with their "intimate parts exposed." The court held that the law was a content-based restriction on speech. Although the court held that the state has a compelling interest in protecting privacy, it struck down the statute because it was not narrowly drawn. Under the law, a third party, who had no knowledge regarding the circumstances under which a picture was created, could be subject to prosecution for disclosing it.

8. *Narrower Revenge Porn Law.* Missouri was the 39th state to enact a revenge porn statute, which includes two crimes. Both use narrow definitions of "private sexual images" and their *mens rea* requirements are more demanding than the that of the invalidated Texas law described in the prior note. The first crime of "nonconsensual dissemination" occurs when a person intentionally disseminates a private sexual image of the victim, having obtained the image under circumstances "in which a reasonable person would know or understand" that the person in the image has not consented to the dissemination. The second crime of "threatening nonconsensual dissemination" occurs when a person gains or attempts to gain anything of value, or coerces or attempts to coerce another person to act or refrain from acting, by threatening to disseminate a private sexual image of the other person. The Missouri Governor signed the revenge porn legislation only hours before he resigned after "scandals grew" around him, including the allegation that he took "a nonconsensual photo of a partially nude woman with whom he had an affair" and warned her "that he would distribute it if she ever spoke of their encounter." *See* David A. Lieb, *Missouri governor quits in scandal, signs 'revenge porn' law,* The Washington Post, June 1, 2018, https.//www.washingtonpost.com/national/missouri-to-get-new-leader-as-scandal-plagued-governor-quits/2018/06/01/e0abee48-6551-11e8-81ca-bb14593acaab_story.html?noredirect=on&utmm_term=.479fc9f2f989

9. *The ALI Approach.* A draft ALI statute gives an individual a cause of action against a person who discloses an "intimate image" of an individual, without the individual's consent, if the image was created or obtained in circumstances under which the individual had a reasonable expectation of privacy and the disclosure harmed the individual. The Act provides remedies, including actual damages, automatic civil damages of up to $10,000, disgorgement of profit made by the disclosure, punitive damages, attorney's fees and additional relief including injunctive relief. Is the law constitutional? *See* Vincent Cardi, *Uniform Act Creating Civil Remedies for Unauthorized Disclosure of Intimate Images: A Discussion Paper* (unpublished, copy on file with author).

∾ PROBLEMS ∾

1. *The Disc Jockey and the Anchor.* A radio talk show host dates a female anchor of a morning television show. After the two break up, the talk show host talks about the female anchor on his show. In particular, he mentions that the anchor has had breast implants and he gives some really personal details about her (e.g., how she grooms her pubic hair). Because the allegations are true, the anchor cannot recover for defamation. Does she have a claim for invasion of privacy? Of the common law theories, which apply? How does the First Amendment affect the analysis?

2. *Framing the Injunction.* After the court concluded that Onassis was entitled to injunctive relief against Galella, how should the injunction have been framed? For example, would it have been appropriate for the judge to prohibit Galella from reporting on Onassis as well as from taking her picture? Or was a more limited injunction more appropriate?

3. *Dealing with Aggressive Paparazzi.* Suppose that you are the legal adviser to the Los Angeles City Council. In recent years, there have been a number of incidents between famous personalities and aggressive paparazzi (journalists who follow personalities around hoping to snap interesting pictures). Concerns have been raised regarding the fact that paparazzi travel in packs, run red lights, and make unsafe U-turns. In addition, because of their aggressiveness and their willingness to place themselves in the way of personalities who are trying to avoid them, paparazzi have sometimes suffered broken toes when cars run over them. A good deal of police work is devoted to dealing with the paparazzi. *See* Jennifer Steinhauer, *Los Angeles Proposes Restraints on Paparazzi*, N.Y. Times, A-12, c. 1-6, Aug. 1, 2008. The city counsel has asked you for advice about how it might limit or control paparazzi. Some have proposed that the paparazzi be licensed. Others have suggested the creation of "comfort zones" around personalities in which paparazzi may not intrude. Is either of these suggestions constitutional? What other steps might the city take?

4. The *O'Bannon* Case. The National Collegiate Athletic Association (NCAA) regulates college sports, and it considers players to be "student athletes" rather

than professionals. Although players can receive tuition and fees, as well as room, board, and required course-related books, they cannot be paid. The NCAA, by contrast, produces video games that use the players' likenesses. Some of these games are very lifelike in the sense that they depict players who have all of the attributes of players on particular teams. In other words, the players in the games wear the same numbers as the actual team players, have the same height and weight, and often exhibit the same tendencies (e.g., dribbling with the left hand). Can the players recover for the use of their names and likenesses in the video games? How much?

5. *"Lamarvelous."* Lamar Jackson is a quarterback for the Baltimore Ravens football team in the National Football League (NFL). Jackson won the Heisman Trophy as a college football player, and the NFL's Most Valuable Player award in 2019. Several names and phrases are associated with Jackson, including "Action Jackson," "Lamarvelous" and "Not Bad For A Running Back." Suppose that items are selling on Amazon with these phrases. Can Lamar recover for misappropriation of his personality?

6. *The Clash Between Trademark Protection & Expressive Freedom.* Jack Daniels obtained a trademark for the bottle design on its Black Label Tennessee Whiskey. Jack Daniels regards its trademark as an "idealized image" of its brand as a representation of product excellence. VIP Products has decided to produce a rubber dog toy that resembles the appearance of the Jack Daniels bottle. The toy is called the "Bad Spaniels Silly Squeaker" and claims to be "43% poo by volume." Since the toy is a parody of the Jack Daniels bottle, is it protected expression? Should Jack Daniels be able to obtain an injunction against production of the toy on trademark infringement grounds?

7. *"Catch and Kill" Agreements.* In some instances, news outlets have purchased the exclusive rights to news stories which include an agreement by the source not to disclose the information to anyone else. In some instances, these agreements are legitimate in that a media outlet is paying for the exclusive right to a story. In other instances, the purchaser is trying to kill the story by purchasing the exclusive rights with no intention of ever airing the story. Should these so-called "catch and kill" agreements be enforceable? Do they violate public policy because they keep legitimate information from the public? Are there situations when catch and kill agreements might have legitimate purposes?

8. *Privacy Interests and the International Treaty Regulating the Internet.* Many European governments provide a much higher level of protection for privacy interests and are willing to proscribe speech (to a greater or lesser extent) in pursuit of those interests. In some instances, they impose privacy protections under their general protections for "human dignity." Suppose that some European delegates push for the treaty to contain very specific protections designed to protect individual privacy as part of human dignity. Can you agree to such provisions? What language might you be able to agree to in the proposed treaty?

9. *Copyright Interests and the International Treaty Regulating the Internet.* Suppose that artists and performers are clamoring for protections against what they regard as "internet piracy" (the practice of some individuals to steal the art and performances of others). They are seeking protections under the new treaty regulating the internet. Although these copyright protections can be easily enforced in the U.S., there are many countries where copyright enforcement is lax. You have been asked whether it is possible to incorporate language in the treaty protecting copyright interests on the internet and giving copyright holders the ability to enforce those interests in foreign countries. Can you accommodate their interests? What language would you use?

10. *Paparazzi and the International Treaty Regulating the Internet.* A number of famous people have approached you about whether it might be possible to use the treaty to constrain the actions of paparazzi by prohibiting or limiting (in some fashion) their publication of pictures or information on the internet. European delegates, who are concerned about the more aggressive paparazzi found in Europe, are particularly desirous of including a provision of this type. Various suggestions have been made to you about how this might be done. For example, some have suggested that (as a condition of using the internet) paparazzi should be forced to "register" and to "certify" that they are using "nonaggressive methods" and that they are giving due deference to "privacy interests." In addition, a proposal has been made to allow governments to ban extremely aggressive paparazzi from publishing on the internet. Can you agree to either of these proposals? If not, what other language might be acceptable?

6. Emotional Distress

Should the tort of intentional infliction of mental and emotional distress be treated differently, from a constitutional free speech perspective, than the torts of defamation or privacy? Consider the following case.

Hustler Magazine, Inc. v. Falwell

485 U.S. 46 (1988)

Chief Justice REHNQUIST delivered the opinion of the Court.

Respondent Jerry Falwell is a nationally known minister who has been active as a commentator on politics and public affairs. The inside front cover of the November 1983 issue of *Hustler* magazine featured a "parody" of an advertisement for Campari Liqueur that contained the name and picture of respondent and was entitled "Jerry Falwell talks about his first time." This parody was modeled after actual Campari ads that included interviews with various celebrities about their "first times." Although it was apparent by the end of each interview that this meant the first time they sampled Campari, the ads clearly played on the sexual double entendre of the general subject of "first times." Copying the form

and layout of these Campari ads, *Hustler*'s editors chose respondent as the featured celebrity and drafted an alleged "interview" with him in which he states that
his "first time" was during a drunken incestuous rendezvous with his mother in an
outhouse. The *Hustler* parody portrays respondent and his mother as drunk and
immoral, and suggests that respondent is a hypocrite who preaches only when he
is drunk. In small print at the bottom of the page, the ad contains the disclaimer,
"ad parody—not to be taken seriously." The magazine's table of contents also
lists the ad as "Fiction; Ad and Personality Parody."

Falwell brought suit for intentional infliction of mental distress, and a jury
awarded him $100,000 in compensatory damages, as well as $50,000 each in punitive damages from petitioners. The verdict was affirmed on appeal. We granted
certiorari.

We must decide whether a public figure may recover damages for emotional
harm caused by the publication of an ad parody offensive to him, and doubtless
gross and repugnant in the eyes of most. Respondent would have us find that a
State's interest in protecting public figures from emotional distress is sufficient
to deny First Amendment protection to speech that is patently offensive and is
intended to inflict emotional injury, even when that speech could not reasonably
have been interpreted as stating actual facts about the public figure involved.
This we decline to do.

At the heart of the First Amendment is the recognition of the fundamental
importance of the free flow of ideas and opinions on matters of public interest and concern. The sort of robust political debate encouraged by the First
Amendment is bound to produce speech that is critical of those who hold public
office or those public figures who are "intimately involved in the resolution of
important public questions or, by reason of their fame, shape events in areas of
concern to society at large."

Of course, this does not mean that any speech about a public figure is immune
from sanction in the form of damages. Since *New York Times Co. v. Sullivan*, 376
U.S. 254 (1964), we have consistently ruled that a public figure may hold a speaker
liable for a defamatory falsehood if the statement was made "with knowledge that
it was false or with reckless disregard of whether it was false or not." Respondent
argues that a different standard should apply in this case because here the State
seeks to prevent the severe emotional distress suffered by the person who is the subject of an offensive publication. In respondent's view, so long as the utterance was
intended to inflict emotional distress, was outrageous, and did in fact inflict serious
emotional distress, it is of no constitutional import whether the statement was a fact
or an opinion, or whether it was true or false. It is the intent to cause injury that
is the gravamen of the tort, and the State's interest in preventing emotional harm
simply outweighs whatever interest a speaker may have in speech of this type.

Generally speaking the law does not regard the intent to inflict emotional
distress as one which should receive much solicitude, and most if not all jurisdictions have chosen to make it civilly culpable where the conduct in question is
sufficiently "outrageous." But in the world of debate about public affairs, many

things done with motives that are less than admirable are protected by the First Amendment. In *Garrison v. Louisiana*, 379 U.S. 64 (1964), we held that even when a speaker or writer is motivated by hatred or ill-will his expression was protected by the First Amendment: "Debate on public issues will not be uninhibited if the speaker must run the risk that it will be proved in court that he spoke out of hatred; even if he did speak out of hatred, utterances honestly believed contribute to the free interchange of ideas and the ascertainment of truth." Thus while such a bad motive may be deemed controlling for purposes of tort liability in other areas of the law, we think the First Amendment prohibits such a result in the area of public debate about public figures.

Were we to hold otherwise, there can be little doubt that political cartoonists and satirists would be subjected to damages awards without any showing that their work falsely defamed its subject. The appeal of the political cartoon or caricature is often based on exploitation of unfortunate physical traits or politically embarrassing events—an exploitation often calculated to injure the feelings of the subject of the portrayal. The art of the cartoonist is often not reasoned or evenhanded, but slashing and one-sided. One cartoonist expressed the nature of the art in these words: "The political cartoon is a weapon of attack, of scorn and ridicule and satire; it is least effective when it tries to pat some politician on the back. It is usually as welcome as a bee sting and is always controversial in some quarters." Long, "The Political Cartoon: Journalism's Strongest Weapon," *The Quill* 56, 57 (Nov. 1962). Several famous examples of this type of intentionally injurious speech were drawn by Thomas Nast, probably the greatest American cartoonist to date, who was associated for many years during the post–Civil War era with *Harper's Weekly*. In the pages of that publication Nast conducted a graphic vendetta against William M. "Boss" Tweed and his corrupt associates in New York City's "Tweed Ring." It has been described by one historian of the subject as "a sustained attack which in its passion and effectiveness stands alone in the history of American graphic art." Morton Keller, *The Art and Politics of Thomas Nast* 177 (Oxford 1968).

Despite their sometimes caustic nature, from the early cartoon portraying George Washington as an ass down to the present day, graphic depictions and satirical cartoons have played a prominent role in public and political debate. Nast's castigation of the Tweed Ring, Walt McDougall's characterization of Presidential candidate James G. Blaine's banquet with the millionaires at Delmonico's as "The Royal Feast of Belshazzar," and numerous other efforts have undoubtedly had an effect on the course and outcome of contemporaneous debate. Our political discourse would have been considerably poorer without them.

Respondent contends that the caricature was so "outrageous" as to distinguish it from more traditional political cartoons. There is no doubt that the caricature of respondent and his mother published in *Hustler* is at best a distant cousin of the political cartoons described above, and a rather poor relation at that. If it were possible by laying down a principled standard to separate the one from the other, public discourse would probably suffer little or no harm. But we doubt that there is any such standard, and we are quite sure that the pejorative description "outrageous" does not supply one. "Outrageousness" in the area of political and social discourse has an inherent subjectiveness about it which would allow a jury to impose liability on the basis of the jurors' tastes or views, or perhaps on the basis of their dislike of a particular expression. An "outrageousness" standard thus runs afoul of our longstanding refusal to allow damages to be awarded because the speech in question may have an adverse emotional impact on the audience.

Admittedly, these oft-repeated First Amendment principles, like other principles, are subject to limitations. We recognized in *FCC v. Pacifica Foundation*, 438 U.S. 726 (1978), that speech that is vulgar, offensive, and shocking is not entitled to absolute constitutional protection under all circumstances. In *Chaplinsky*, we held that a State could lawfully punish an individual for the use of insulting fighting words—those which by their very utterance inflict injury or tend to incite an immediate breach of the peace. These limitations are but recognition that this Court has long recognized that not all speech is of equal First Amendment importance. But the sort of expression involved in this case does not seem to us to be governed by any exception to the general First Amendment principles stated above.

We conclude that public figures and public officials may not recover for the tort of intentional infliction of emotional distress by reason of publications without showing that the publication contains a false statement of fact which was made with "actual malice," i.e., with knowledge that the statement was false or with reckless disregard as to whether or not it was true. This is not merely a "blind application" of the *New York Times* standard, it reflects our considered judgment that such a standard is necessary to give adequate "breathing space" to the freedoms protected by the First Amendment.

It is clear that Falwell is a "public figure."[5] The jury found against respondent on his libel claim because the ad parody could not "reasonably be understood as describing actual facts." For reasons heretofore stated this claim cannot, consistently with the First Amendment, form a basis for the award of damages when the conduct in question is the publication of a caricature such as the ad parody involved here. The judgment of the Court of Appeals is accordingly

Reversed.

∿ PROBLEMS ∿

1. *The Justifications for Protecting Speech.* Did the speech involved in *Falwell* meet any of the justifications for protecting speech presented earlier in the chapter?

---

5. He is the host of a nationally syndicated television show and was the founder and president of a political organization formerly known as the Moral Majority. He is also the founder of Liberty University in Lynchburg, Virginia, and is the author of several books and publications.

In other words, did it provide a safety valve, did it promote self-fulfillment or the marketplace of ideas, or was it related to the democratic process?

2. *Public Figures Versus Private Individuals.* In the Court's defamation decisions, particularly *Gertz* and *Dun & Bradstreet,* the Court has distinguished between public officials and public figures, on the one hand, and private individuals, on the other. The states are free to provide fewer protections to those who defame private individuals. Should a similar distinction apply to the tort of intentional infliction of mental and emotional distress? If such a distinction is to be made, how would it apply? In the *Falwell* case, suppose that the suit had been brought by Falwell's mother rather than Falwell, and also suppose that she is very private and shuns the spotlight. Should she be able to recover?

3. *Should First Amendment Protections Apply Only to "High-Minded Discourse"?* Suppose that *Falwell* had asserted a dividing line between constitutionally protected and unprotected speech that focuses on whether the defendant's action involves "high-minded" discourse. Do you agree? Should it matter that *Hustler* parodies Falwell in a lewd and disgusting manner as opposed to a "high-minded" manner? *See Dworkin v. Hustler Magazine, Inc.,* 867 F.2d 1188 (9th Cir. 1988).

Snyder v. Phelps

562 U.S. 433 (2011)

Chief Justice ROBERTS delivered the opinion of the Court.

Fred Phelps founded the Westboro Baptist Church whose congregation believes that God hates and punishes the United States for its tolerance of homosexuality, particularly in America's military. The church frequently communicates its views by picketing, often at military funerals. In the more than 20 years that the members of Westboro Baptist have publicized their message, they have picketed nearly 600 funerals. Marine Lance Corporal Matthew Snyder was killed in Iraq in the line of duty. Lance Corporal Snyder's father selected the Catholic church in the Snyders' hometown of Westminster, Maryland, as the site for his son's funeral. Local newspapers provided notice of the time and location of the service.

Phelps decided to travel to Maryland with six other Westboro Baptist parishioners (two of his daughters and four of his grandchildren) to picket. On the day of the memorial service, the Westboro congregation members picketed on public land adjacent to public streets near the Maryland State House, the United States Naval Academy, and Matthew Snyder's funeral. The Westboro picketers carried signs that stated, for instance: "God Hates the USA/Thank God for 9/11," "America is Doomed," "Don't Pray for the USA," "Thank God for IEDs," "Thank God for Dead Soldiers," "Pope in Hell," "Priests Rape Boys," "God Hates Fags," "You're Going to Hell," and "God Hates You."

The church had notified the authorities in advance of its intent to picket at the time of the funeral, and the picketers complied with police instructions in staging their demonstration. The picketing took place within a 10- by 25-foot plot of public land adjacent to a public street, behind a temporary fence. That plot was approximately 1,000 feet from the church where the funeral was held. Several buildings separated the picket site from the church. The Westboro picketers displayed their signs for about 30 minutes before the funeral began and sang hymns and recited Bible verses. None of the picketers entered church property or went to the cemetery. They did not yell or use profanity, and there was no violence associated with the picketing.

The funeral procession passed within 200 to 300 feet of the picket site. Although Snyder testified that he could see the tops of the picket signs as he drove to the funeral, he did not see what was written on the signs until later that night, while watching a news broadcast covering the event.[2]

Snyder filed suit against Phelps, Phelps's daughters, and the Westboro Baptist Church in the United States District Court for the District of Maryland. Snyder alleged five state tort law claims: defamation, publicity given to private life, intentional infliction of emotional distress, intrusion upon seclusion, and civil conspiracy. The District Court awarded Westboro summary judgment on Snyder's claims for defamation and publicity given to private life. A trial was held on the remaining claims during which Snyder described the severity of his emotional injuries. He testified that he is unable to separate the thought of his dead son from his thoughts of Westboro's picketing, and that he often becomes tearful, angry, and physically ill when he thinks about it. Expert witnesses testified that Snyder's emotional anguish had resulted in severe depression and had exacerbated pre-existing health conditions. A jury found for Snyder on the intentional infliction of emotional distress, intrusion upon seclusion, and civil conspiracy claims, and held Westboro liable for $2.9 million in compensatory damages and $8 million in punitive damages. The District Court remitted the punitive damages award to $2.1 million, but left the jury verdict otherwise intact. The Court of Appeals concluded that Westboro's statements were entitled to First Amendment protection. We granted certiorari.

To succeed on a claim for intentional infliction of emotional distress in Maryland, a plaintiff must demonstrate that the defendant intentionally or recklessly engaged in extreme and outrageous conduct that caused the plaintiff to suffer severe emotional distress. The Free Speech Clause of the First Amendment—"Congress shall make no law abridging the freedom of speech"—can serve as a defense in state tort suits, including suits for intentional infliction of emotional distress. *See, e.g., Hustler Magazine, Inc. v. Falwell*, 485 U.S.

---

2. A few weeks after the funeral, one of the picketers posted a message on Westboro's Web site discussing the picketing and containing religiously oriented denunciations of the Snyders, interspersed among lengthy Bible quotations. Snyder discovered the posting, referred to by the parties as the "epic," during an Internet search for his son's name. The epic is not properly before us. Snyder never mentioned it in his petition for certiorari. Given the foregoing and the fact that an Internet posting may raise distinct issues in this context, we decline to consider the epic in deciding this case.

46 (1988).[3] Whether the First Amendment prohibits holding Westboro liable for its speech in this case turns largely on whether that speech is of public or private concern, as determined by all the circumstances of the case. "Speech on 'matters of public concern' is 'at the heart of the First Amendment's protection.'" *Dun & Bradstreet, Inc. v. Greenmoss Builders, Inc.*, 472 U.S. 749, 758-759 (1985) (opinion of Powell, J.) (quoting *First Nat. Bank of Boston v. Bellotti*, 435 U.S. 765, 776 (1978)). The First Amendment reflects "a profound national commitment to the principle that debate on public issues should be uninhibited, robust, and wide-open." *New York Times Co. v. Sullivan*, 376 U.S. 254, 270 (1964). That is because "speech concerning public affairs is more than self-expression; it is the essence of self-government." *Garrison v. Louisiana*, 379 U.S. 64, 74-75 (1964). Accordingly, "speech on public issues occupies the highest rung of the hierarchy of First Amendment values, and is entitled to special protection." *Connick v. Myers*, 461 U.S. 138, 145 (1983).

"'Not all speech is of equal First Amendment importance,'" however, and where matters of purely private significance are at issue, First Amendment protections are often less rigorous. That is because restricting speech on purely private matters does not implicate the same constitutional concerns as limiting speech on matters of public interest: "There is no threat to the free and robust debate of public issues; there is no potential interference with a meaningful dialogue of ideas"; and the "threat of liability" does not pose the risk of "a reaction of self-censorship" on matters of public import. *Dun & Bradstreet, supra,* at 760.

We noted a short time ago, in considering whether public employee speech addressed a matter of public concern, that "the boundaries of the public concern test are not well defined." *San Diego v. Roe*, 543 U.S. 77, 83 (2004) (*per curiam*). Although that remains true today, we have articulated some guiding principles, principles that accord broad protection to speech to ensure that courts themselves do not become inadvertent censors. Speech deals with matters of public concern when it can "be fairly considered as relating to any matter of political, social, or other concern to the community," or when it "is a subject of legitimate news interest; that is, a subject of general interest and of value and concern to the public," *San Diego, supra,* at 83-84. The arguably "inappropriate or controversial character of a statement is irrelevant to the question whether it deals with a matter of public concern." *Rankin v. McPherson*, 483 U.S. 378, 387 (1987).

Our opinion in *Dun & Bradstreet* held that information about a particular individual's credit report "concerns no public issue." The content of the report, "was speech solely in the individual interest of the speaker and its specific business audience." The particular report was sent to only five subscribers to the reporting service, who were bound not to disseminate it further. We concluded in *San Diego* v. *Roe* that videos of an employee engaging in sexually explicit acts did not address

---

3. The dissent attempts to draw parallels between this case and hypothetical cases involving defamation or fighting words. But there is "no suggestion that the speech at issue falls within one of the categorical exclusions from First Amendment protection, such as those for obscenity or 'fighting words.'"

a public concern; the videos "did nothing to inform the public about any aspect of the employing agency's functioning or operation."

Deciding whether speech is of public or private concern requires us to examine the "content, form, and context" of that speech, "as revealed by the whole record." *Dun & Bradstreet, supra,* at 761. As in other First Amendment cases, the court is obligated "to 'make an independent examination of the whole record' in order to make sure that 'the judgment does not constitute a forbidden intrusion on the field of free expression.'" *Bose Corp. v. Consumers Union of United States, Inc.,* 466 U.S. 485, 499 (1984) (quoting *New York Times, supra,* at 284-286). In considering content, form, and context, no factor is dispositive, and it is necessary to evaluate all the circumstances of the speech, including what was said, where it was said, and how it was said.

The "content" of Westboro's signs plainly relates to broad issues of interest to society at large, rather than matters of "purely private concern." *Dun & Bradstreet, supra,* at 759. The placards read "God Hates the USA/Thank God for 9/11," "America is Doomed," "Don't Pray for the USA," "Thank God for IEDs," "Fag Troops," "Semper Fi Fags," "God Hates Fags," "Maryland Taliban," "Fags Doom Nations," "Not Blessed Just Cursed," "Thank God for Dead Soldiers," "Pope in Hell," "Priests Rape Boys," "You're Going to Hell," and "God Hates You." While these messages may fall short of refined social or political commentary, the issues they highlight—the political and moral conduct of the United States and its citizens, the fate of our Nation, homosexuality in the military, and scandals involving the Catholic clergy—are matters of public import. The signs certainly convey Westboro's position on those issues, in a manner designed, unlike the private speech in *Dun & Bradstreet,* to reach as broad a public audience as possible. And even if a few of the signs—such as "You're Going to Hell" and "God Hates You"—were viewed as containing messages related to Matthew Snyder or the Snyders specifically, that would not change the fact that the overall thrust and dominant theme of Westboro's demonstration spoke to broader public issues.

Snyder contends that the "context" of the speech—its connection with his son's funeral—makes the speech a matter of private rather than public concern. Westboro's signs, displayed on public land next to a public street, reflect the fact that the church finds much to condemn in modern society. Its speech is "fairly characterized as constituting speech on a matter of public concern," *Connick,* 461 U.S. at 146, and the funeral setting does not alter that conclusion.

Snyder argues that the church members mounted a personal attack on Snyder and his family, and then attempted to "immunize their conduct by claiming that they were actually protesting the United States' tolerance of homosexuality or the supposed evils of the Catholic Church." We are not concerned that Westboro's speech on public matters was in any way contrived to insulate speech on a private matter from liability. Westboro had been actively engaged in speaking on the subjects addressed in its picketing long before it became aware of Matthew Snyder, and there can be no serious claim that Westboro's picketing did not represent its "honestly believed" views on public issues. There was no pre-existing relationship or conflict between Westboro and Snyder that might suggest Westboro's speech on public matters was intended to mask an attack on Snyder over a private matter.

Westboro's choice to convey its views in conjunction with Matthew Snyder's funeral made the expression of those views particularly hurtful to many, especially to Matthew's father. The applicable legal term—"emotional distress"—fails to capture fully the anguish Westboro's choice added to Mr. Snyder's already incalculable grief. But Westboro conducted its picketing peacefully on matters of public concern at a public place adjacent to a public street. Such space occupies a "special position in terms of First Amendment protection." *United States v. Grace*, 461 U.S. 171, 180 (1983). "We have repeatedly referred to public streets as the archetype of a traditional public forum," noting that "'time out of mind' public streets and sidewalks have been used for public assembly and debate." *Frisby v. Schultz*, 487 U.S. 474, 480 (1988). Westboro's choice of where and when to conduct its picketing is not beyond the Government's regulatory reach—it is "subject to reasonable time, place, or manner restrictions" that are consistent with the standards announced in this Court's precedents. *Clark v. Community for Creative Non-Violence*, 468 U.S. 288, 293 (1984). Maryland now has a law imposing restrictions on funeral picketing as do 43 other States and the Federal Government. To the extent these laws are content neutral, they raise very different questions from the tort verdict at issue in this case. Maryland's law, however, was not in effect at the time of the events at issue here, so we have no occasion to consider how it might apply to facts such as those before us, or whether it or other similar regulations are constitutional.

We have identified a few limited situations where the location of targeted picketing can be regulated under provisions that the Court has determined to be content neutral. In *Frisby*, for example, we upheld a ban on such picketing "before or about" a particular residence. In *Madsen v. Women's Health Center, Inc.*, we approved an injunction requiring a buffer zone between protesters and an abortion clinic entrance. 512 U.S. 753, 768 (1994). The facts here are obviously quite different, both with respect to the activity being regulated and the means of restricting those activities.

Simply put, the church members had the right to be where they were. Westboro alerted local authorities to its funeral protest and fully complied with police guidance on where the picketing could be staged. The picketing was conducted under police supervision some 1,000 feet from the church, out of the sight of those at the church. The protest was not unruly; there was no shouting, profanity, or violence. Any distress occasioned by Westboro's picketing turned on the content and viewpoint of the message conveyed, rather than any interference with the funeral itself. A group of parishioners standing at the very spot where Westboro stood, holding signs that said "God Bless America" and "God Loves You," would not have been subjected to liability. It was what Westboro said that exposed it to tort damages.

Given that Westboro's speech was at a public place on a matter of public concern, that speech is entitled to "special protection" under the First Amendment.

Such speech cannot be restricted simply because it is upsetting or arouses contempt. "If there is a bedrock principle underlying the First Amendment, it is that the government may not prohibit the expression of an idea simply because society finds the idea itself offensive or disagreeable." *Texas v. Johnson*, 491 U.S. 397, 414 (1989). Indeed, "the point of all speech protection is to shield just those choices of content that in someone's eyes are misguided, or even hurtful." *Hurley v. Irish-American Gay, Lesbian and Bisexual Group of Boston, Inc.*, 515 U.S. 557, 574 (1995).

The jury was instructed that it could hold Westboro liable for intentional infliction of emotional distress based on a finding that Westboro's picketing was "outrageous." "Outrageousness," however, is a highly malleable standard with "an inherent subjectiveness about it which would allow a jury to impose liability on the basis of the jurors' tastes or views, or perhaps on the basis of their dislike of a particular expression." *Hustler*, 485 U.S. at 55. In a case such as this, a jury is "unlikely to be neutral with respect to the content of the speech," posing "a real danger of becoming an instrument for the suppression of 'vehement, caustic, and sometimes unpleasant'" expression. *Bose Corp.*, 466 U.S. at 510 (quoting *New York Times*, 376 U.S. at 270). Such a risk is unacceptable; "in public debate we must tolerate insulting, and even outrageous, speech in order to provide adequate 'breathing space' to the freedoms protected by the First Amendment." *Boos v. Barry*, 485 U.S. 312, 322 (1988). What Westboro said, in the whole context of how and where it chose to say it, is entitled to "special protection" under the First Amendment, and that protection cannot be overcome by a jury finding that the picketing was outrageous. For all these reasons, the jury verdict imposing tort liability on Westboro for intentional infliction of emotional distress must be set aside.

Snyder argues that the church is not immunized from liability for intrusion upon seclusion because Snyder was a member of a captive audience at his son's funeral. We do not agree. In most circumstances, "the Constitution does not permit the government to decide which types of otherwise protected speech are sufficiently offensive to require protection for the unwilling listener or viewer. Rather, the burden normally falls upon the viewer to avoid further bombardment of his sensibilities simply by averting his eyes." *Erznoznik v. Jacksonville*, 422 U.S. 205, 210 (1975). As a result, "the ability of government, consonant with the Constitution, to shut off discourse solely to protect others from hearing it is dependent upon a showing that substantial privacy interests are being invaded in an essentially intolerable manner." *Cohen v. California*, 403 U.S. 15, 21 (1971). We have applied the captive audience doctrine only sparingly to protect unwilling listeners from protected speech. For example, we have upheld a statute allowing a homeowner to restrict the delivery of offensive mail to his home, *see Rowan v. Post Office Dept.*, 397 U.S. 728, 736 (1970), and an ordinance prohibiting picketing "before or about" any individual's residence, *Frisby*. Westboro stayed well away from the memorial service. Snyder could see no more than the tops of the signs when driving to the funeral. There is no indication that the picketing in any way interfered with the funeral service itself. We decline to expand the captive audience doctrine to the circumstances presented here.

Because we find that the First Amendment bars Snyder from recovery for intentional infliction of emotional distress or intrusion upon seclusion, we must likewise hold that Snyder cannot recover for civil conspiracy based on those torts. Our holding today is narrow. Westboro believes that America is morally flawed; many Americans might feel the same about Westboro. Westboro's funeral picketing is certainly hurtful and its contribution to public discourse may be negligible. But Westboro addressed matters of public import on public property, in a peaceful manner, in full compliance with the guidance of local officials. The speech was indeed planned to coincide with Matthew Snyder's funeral, but did not itself disrupt that funeral, and Westboro's choice to conduct its picketing at that time and place did not alter the nature of its speech.

Speech is powerful. It can stir people to action, move them to tears of both joy and sorrow, and — as it did here — inflict great pain. We cannot react to that pain by punishing the speaker. As a Nation we have chosen a different course — to protect even hurtful speech on public issues to ensure that we do not stifle public debate. That choice requires that we shield Westboro from tort liability for its picketing in this case.

The judgment of the United States Court of Appeals for the Fourth Circuit is affirmed.

It is so ordered.

Justice BREYER, *concurring.*

The Court does not say anything about Internet postings. The Court does not hold or imply that the State is always powerless to provide private individuals with necessary protection. Westboro's means of communicating its views consisted of picketing in a place where picketing was lawful and in compliance with all police directions. The picketing could not be seen or heard from the funeral ceremony itself. Snyder testified that he saw no more than the tops of the picketers' signs as he drove to the funeral. To uphold the application of state law in these circumstances would punish Westboro for seeking to communicate its views on matters of public concern without proportionately advancing the State's interest in protecting its citizens against severe emotional harm.

Justice ALITO, *dissenting.*

Our profound national commitment to free and open debate is not a license for the vicious verbal assault that occurred in this case. Petitioner is not a public figure. He is simply a parent whose son was killed in Iraq. Mr. Snyder wanted what is surely the right of any parent who experiences such an incalculable loss: to bury his son in peace. Respondents deprived him of that right by launching a malevolent verbal attack on Matthew and his family at a time of acute emotional vulnerability. The Court now holds that the First Amendment protected respondents' right to brutalize Mr. Snyder. I cannot agree.

Respondents have strong opinions on certain moral, religious, and political issues, and the First Amendment ensures that they have almost limitless opportunities to express their views. They may write and distribute books, articles, and other texts; they may create and disseminate video and audio recordings; they may circulate petitions; they may speak to individuals and groups in public forums and in any private venue that wishes to accommodate them; they may picket peacefully in countless locations; they may appear on television and speak on the radio; they may post messages on the Internet and send out e-mails. They may express their views in terms that are "uninhibited," "vehement," and "caustic." *New York Times Co. v. Sullivan*, 376 U.S. 254, 270 (1964). It does not follow that they may intentionally inflict severe emotional injury on private persons at a time of intense emotional sensitivity by launching vicious verbal attacks that make no contribution to public debate.

To recover, a plaintiff must show that the conduct at issue caused harm that was truly severe. Plaintiff must also establish that the defendant's conduct was "so outrageous in character, and so extreme in degree, as to go beyond all possible bounds of decency, and to be regarded as atrocious, and utterly intolerable in a civilized community." Although the elements of the IIED tort are difficult to meet, respondents did not dispute that Snyder suffered "wounds that are truly severe and incapable of healing themselves." Nor did they dispute that their speech was "so outrageous in character, and so extreme in degree, as to go beyond all possible bounds of decency, and to be regarded as atrocious, and utterly intolerable in a civilized community." Instead, they maintained that the First Amendment gave them a license to engage in such conduct. They are wrong.

The First Amendment does not entirely preclude liability for the intentional infliction of emotional distress by means of speech. This Court has recognized that words may "by their very utterance inflict injury" and the First Amendment does not shield utterances that form "no essential part of any exposition of ideas, and are of such slight social value as a step to truth that any benefit that may be derived from them is clearly outweighed by the social interest in order and morality." *Chaplinsky v. New Hampshire*, 315 U.S. 568, 572 (1942). When grave injury is intentionally inflicted by means of an attack like the one at issue here, the First Amendment should not interfere with recovery. Respondents brutally attacked Matthew Snyder, and this attack, which was almost certain to inflict injury, was central to respondents' strategy for attracting public attention. On the morning of Matthew Snyder's funeral, respondents could have chosen to stage their protest at countless locations. They could have picketed the United States Capitol, the White House, the Supreme Court, the Pentagon, or any of more than 5,600 military recruiting stations in this country. They could have returned to the Maryland State House or the United States Naval Academy, where they had been the day before. They could have selected any public road where pedestrians are allowed. They could have staged their protest in a public park. They could have chosen any Catholic church where no funeral was taking place. But of course, a small group picketing at any of these locations would have probably gone unnoticed.

The Westboro Baptist Church, however, has devised a strategy that remedies this problem. Church members have protested at nearly 600 military funerals. They have also picketed the funerals of police officers, firefighters, and the victims of natural disasters, accidents, and shocking crimes. In advance of these protests, they issue press releases to ensure that their protests will attract public attention.

This strategy works because it is expected that respondents' verbal assaults will wound the family and friends of the deceased and because the media is irresistibly drawn to the sight of persons who are visibly in grief. The more outrageous the funeral protest, the more publicity the Westboro Baptist Church is able to obtain. When the church recently announced its intention to picket the funeral of a 9-year-old girl killed in the shooting spree in Tucson—proclaiming that she was "better off dead"—their announcement was national news, and the church was able to obtain free air time on the radio in exchange for canceling its protest. In 2006, the church got air time on a talk radio show in exchange for canceling its threatened protest at the funeral of five Amish girls killed by a crazed gunman.

In this case, respondents implemented the publicity-seeking strategy. Their press release stated that they were going "to picket the funeral of Lance Cpl. Matthew A. Snyder" because "God Almighty killed Lance Cpl. Snyder. He died in shame, not honor—for a fag nation cursed by God. Now in Hell—sine die." This announcement guaranteed that Matthew's funeral would be transformed into a raucous media event and began the wounding process. It is well known that anticipation may heighten the effect of a painful event. On the day of the funeral, respondents displayed placards that conveyed the message promised in their press release. Signs stating "God Hates You" and "Thank God for Dead Soldiers" reiterated the message that God had caused Matthew's death in retribution for his sins. Others, stating "You're Going to Hell" and "Not Blessed Just Cursed," conveyed the message that Matthew was "in Hell—sine die."

The meaning of these signs would not have been missed. Since respondents chose to stage their protest at Matthew Snyder's funeral and not at any of the other countless available venues, a reasonable person would have assumed that there was a connection between the messages and the deceased. Moreover, since a church funeral is an event that naturally brings to mind thoughts about the afterlife, some of respondents' signs—e.g., "God Hates You," "Not Blessed Just Cursed," and "You're Going to Hell"—would have likely been interpreted as referring to God's judgment of the deceased. Other signs would most naturally have been understood as suggesting—falsely—that Matthew was gay. Homosexuality was the theme of many of the signs. There were signs reading "God Hates Fags," "Semper Fi Fags," "Fags Doom Nations," and "Fag Troops." Another placard depicted two men engaging in anal intercourse. A reasonable bystander seeing those signs would have likely concluded that they were meant to suggest that the deceased was a homosexual. After the funeral, the Westboro picketers reaffirmed the meaning of their protest. They posted an online account entitled "The Burden of Marine Lance Cpl. Matthew A. Snyder. The Visit of Westboro Baptist Church to Help the Inhabitants of Maryland Connect the Dots!" Belying any suggestion that they had simply made general comments about homosexuality, the Catholic Church, and the United States military, the "epic" addressed the Snyder family directly:

> "God blessed you, Mr. and Mrs. Snyder, with a resource and his name was Matthew. He was an arrow in your quiver! In thanks to God for the comfort the child could bring you, you had a DUTY to prepare that child to serve the LORD his GOD—PERIOD! You did JUST THE OPPOSITE—you raised him for the devil. "Albert and Julie RIPPED that body apart and taught Matthew to defy his Creator, to divorce, and to commit adultery. They taught him how to support the largest pedophile machine in the history of the entire world, the Roman Catholic monstrosity. Every dime they gave the Roman Catholic monster they condemned their own souls. They also, in supporting satanic Catholicism, taught Matthew to be an idolater. "Then after all that they sent him to fight for the United States of Sodom, a filthy country that is in lock step with his evil, wicked, and sinful manner of life, putting him in the cross hairs of a God that is so mad He has smoke coming from his nostrils and fire from his mouth! How dumb was that?"

Respondents, going far beyond commentary on matters of public concern, specifically attacked Matthew Snyder because (1) he was a Catholic and (2) he was a member of the United States military. Both Matthew and petitioner were private figures, and this attack was not speech on a matter of public concern. While commentary on the Catholic Church or the United States military constitutes speech on matters of public concern, speech regarding Matthew Snyder's purely private conduct does not. Justice Breyer provides an apt analogy to a case in which the First Amendment would permit recovery in tort for a verbal attack. This captures what respondents did in this case. Indeed, this is the strategy that they have routinely employed—and that they will now continue to employ—inflicting severe and lasting emotional injury on an ever growing list of innocent victims.

The Court finds that "the overall thrust and dominant theme of the demonstration spoke to" broad public issues. This portrayal is inaccurate. In any event, I fail to see why actionable speech should be immunized simply because it is interspersed with speech that is protected. The First Amendment allows recovery for defamatory statements that are interspersed with nondefamatory statements on matters of public concern. Respondents' motivation—"to increase publicity for its views,"—did not transform their statements attacking the character of a private figure into statements that made a contribution to debate on matters of public concern. Nor did their publicity-seeking motivation soften the sting of their attack. There is no reason why a public street in close proximity to the scene of a funeral should be regarded as a free-fire zone in which otherwise actionable verbal attacks are shielded from liability. If the First Amendment permits the States to protect their residents from the harm inflicted by such attacks, then the location of the tort should not be dispositive. Neither "fighting words" nor defamatory statements are immunized when they occur in a public place, and there is no reason to treat a verbal assault based on the conduct or character of a private figure like Matthew Snyder any differently.

The Court suggests that the wounds inflicted by vicious verbal assaults at funerals will be prevented or at least mitigated in the future by new laws that restrict picketing within a specified distance of a funeral. The enactment of these laws is no substitute for the protection provided by the IIED tort. Funerals are unique events at which special protection against emotional assaults is in order. At funerals, the emotional well-being of bereaved relatives is particularly vulnerable. Exploitation of a funeral for the purpose of attracting public attention "intrudes upon their grief," and may permanently stain their memories of the final moments before a loved one is laid to rest. Allowing family members to have a few hours of peace without harassment does not undermine public debate.

Hustler did involve an IIED claim, but the plaintiff there was a public figure, and the Court did not suggest that its holding would also apply in a case involving a private figure. Nor did the Court suggest that its holding applied to all types of IIED claims. Instead, the holding was limited to "publications such as the one here at issue," namely, a caricature in a magazine. Unless a caricature of a public figure can reasonably be interpreted as stating facts that may be proved to be wrong, the caricature does not have the same potential to wound as a personal verbal assault on a vulnerable private figure.

Respondents' outrageous conduct caused petitioner great injury, and the Court now compounds that injury by depriving petitioner of a judgment that acknowledges the wrong he suffered. In order to have a society in which public issues can be openly and vigorously debated, it is not necessary to allow the brutalization of innocent victims like petitioner. I respectfully dissent.

∾ PROBLEMS ∾

1. *Choice of Site and Method.* Justice Alito suggests that the Westboro protestors were free to hold their protests at lots of other sites. They could have, for example, called a "news conference" and stated their views in front of the Wesboro Baptist Church. Why do you think that they choose to protest at funerals as opposed to giving speeches in front of their own church? Can you reconcile Justice Alito's position with other First Amendment precedent? *See Cohen v. California*, 403 U.S. 15 (1971).

2. *The Epic.* The Court did not deal with the material that Westboro Baptist Church posted on the internet related to Matthew Snyder. Would it be appropriate to impose liability on respondents for the online posting? Is it more outrageous? More deserving of liability? Does it also relate to matters of public interest?

3. *Emotional Distress and Twitter.* Eve leads a small Buddhist sect and runs a spiritual retreat center. Eve is reputed to be a reincarnate tulku, or high-ranking lama. Jon became a member of Eve's inner circle after persuading Eve that he was also a tulku. Eve forced Jon to leave the center after learning that Jon was only pretending to be a tulku. Jon then sent hundreds of "tweet" messages making negative references to Eve and members of her inner circle. A few illustrations

reveal two typical themes: 1) "Eve is a false guide and she corrupts Buddhism" and 2) "Eve makes her living off suckers who need to believe in fairy tales." The second theme also involved derogatory personal comments about Eve: 3) "Eve is so nasty her mama took her out in the stroller so she wouldn't have to kiss her goodbye," 4) "Eve is a reputed ex-prostitute," and 5) "Eve is like a waterfront whore: her price goes down as the night wears on." Jon used an alias for his Twitter account so that his tweets were anonymous. Eve received Jon's tweets only because she signed up to be Jon's "follower." Moreover, Eve sends out her own tweets from her Twitter account, and she has 17,000 Twitter followers. Assume that the federal interstate stalking statute includes the following expanded provisions: "It is a crime to use the mail or any interactive computer service to engage in a course of conduct that causes *substantial emotional distress* to a person in another State, with the *intent to harass or cause substantial emotional distress* to that person." Suppose that Jon is indicted on the basis of Eve's claim that she suffers substantial emotional distress because of Jon's critical and derogatory tweets, and that she has been so upset that she has not left her house for several months, except to see her psychiatrist to obtain treatment for her emotional distress. Can Jon be convicted consistently with the First Amendment? *See United States v. Cassidy*, 814 F. Supp. 2d 574 (D. Md. 2011).

4. *Revenge Porn*. A spurned boyfriend posts pornographic pictures of his former girlfriend on a website along with her actual name, Facebook page, and other personal information. The pictures were taken by the boyfriend with the woman's consent while they were in an intimate relationship. What avenues of redress are available to the woman? Would the answer be different if the pictures were taken surreptitiously rather than with her consent? What if the boyfriend promised not to reveal the photos to anyone else in order to encourage the woman to let him take them? What if the photos were selfies, taken by the woman to track her weight loss, that were stolen from her computer by a hacker who posted them? In any of these examples, would it matter if the photos were taken before the woman turned 18 years of age? Can the woman seek a remedy against the website hosts, assuming that they know that the posted photos were taken without the consent of the subject, and that they fail to take action to remove them when the woman demands that they do so?

5. *Legislative Responses?* Suppose that you are a legislator who is concerned about the growing availability of revenge porn sites, and you wish to take legislative action designed to curtail the practice. What alternatives are available to you? Can you criminalize such conduct? Can you provide tort remedies? Is injunctive relief possible? What about copyright remedies? Consider the fact scenarios described in the prior problem and decide which remedies should be available in each situation. Would the following revenge porn law be valid: "An actor may not knowingly disclose an image of another, identifiable, person, whose intimate parts are exposed or who is engaged in a sexual act, when the actor knows or should have known that the depicted person has not consented to such disclosure." *See* Mary Anne Franks, *Drafting an Effective "Revenge Porn" Law: A Guide for*

Legislators (2015), *available at* http://ssrn.com/abstract=2468823. What about the following law: "It is a criminal offense for any person, in the absence of a purpose to convey or disseminate information or ideas, to do any act intended to cause or otherwise attempt to cause extreme emotional distress to another person." *See* John A. Humbach, *How to Write a Constitutional "Revenge Porn" Law* (draft 2014). Should there be an exception for revenge porn that involves politicians or matters of public interest (e.g., photos of a politician involved in an extramarital affair)? If so, how would you define the "public interest"? *See Bollea v. Gawker Media LLC,* 913 F. Supp. 2d 1325 (M.D. Fla. 2012).

6. *Drafting a Valid Cyberbullying Law.* In addition to revenge porn, emotional distress can also be caused by so-called cyberbullying. Legislators have tried to draft valid laws to protect individuals against such bullying. Which of the following laws are valid under the First Amendment? Consider the following Acts that prohibit: 1) "any act of communicating or causing a communication to be sent by mechanical or electronic means, posting on the internet or through a computer or e-mail network; disseminating embarrassing or sexually explicit photographs; disseminating private, personal, false or sexual information; or sending hate mail, with no legitimate private, personal, or public purpose and with the intent to harass, annoy, threaten, abuse, taunt, intimidate, torment, humiliate or otherwise inflict significant emotional harm on another person." Would the law withstand a First Amendment challenge as applied to a high school student who posted sexual information regarding his or her classmates? *See People v. Marquan M.,* 24 N.Y.3d 1, 19 N.E.3d 480, 994 N.Y.S.2d 554 (N.Y. App. 2014). 2) "any act that involves a knowing pattern of conduct that seriously alarms the target and would cause a reasonable person to suffer substantial emotional distress." Will the law hold up under the First Amendment as applied to the prosecution of a couple who e-mails threats against their neighbors (referring to personal information, and inciting a confederate to file a child abuse claim against them), and lures others into unwittingly joining the harassment by posting false Craigslist advertisements that prompted lots of phone calls? *See Commonwealth v. Johnson,* 470 Mass. 300, 21 N.E.3d 937 (Mass. 2014).

7. *The Disputed Call.* After the University of Kentucky lost a game in the NCAA Basketball Tournament, Kentucky fans blamed the officiating of a referee who they then targeted for abuse. As a result of the abuse, the referee closed his Facebook page, his voicemail system was overwhelmed, his business ratings collapsed, his family was threatened, and his business received over 800 threatening calls. The referee sued a radio station, alleging that it's post-game coverage, including the speech of a talk show host and a website writer, incited the harassment by fans that caused his business losses. The complaint alleged intentional infliction of emotional distress. Was the radio station's coverage protected by the First Amendment? *See Higgins v. Kentucky Sports Radio, LLC,* 951 F.3d 728 (6th Cir. 2020).

8. *More on the International Treaty Regulating the Internet.* The German Basic Law provides very specific protections for "personal dignity," and French law

provides very specific prohibitions against "degrading human dignity." Suppose
that the German and French delegates to the convention push hard for language
that bans "outrageous speech" designed to damage personal dignity or degrade
human dignity. Can you accept such language? Is there language that you might
be able to accept that would be agreetable to both the German and French
delegates?

7. Obscenity

Chaplinsky named "obscenity" as one of those categories of speech the prohibition of which had "never been thought to raise any Constitutional problem."
Although later cases affirmed the "unprotected" status of "obscene" speech, the
Court struggled to define the term *obscenity* and to distinguish it from other sex-
related speech.

a. Defining Obscenity

Roth v. United States

354 U.S. 476 (1957)

Mr. Justice BRENNAN delivered the opinion of the Court.

Samuel Roth, a publisher of books, photographs and magazines was convicted of mailing obscene circulars and advertising, and an obscene book. David
Alberts conducted a mail-order business and was convicted of keeping for sale
obscene and indecent books, and with writing, composing and publishing an
obscene advertisement of them.

Obscenity is not protected by the freedoms of speech and press. Ten of the
14 States which by 1792 had ratified the Constitution gave no absolute protection
for every utterance. As early as 1712, Massachusetts made it criminal to publish
"any filthy, obscene, or profane song, pamphlet, libel or mock sermon" in imita-
tion or mimicking of religious services. In light of this history, it is apparent that
the unconditional phrasing of the First Amendment was not intended to protect
every utterance. The protection given speech and press was fashioned to assure
unfettered interchange of ideas for the bringing about of political and social
changes desired by the people. All ideas having even the slightest redeeming
social importance—unorthodox ideas, controversial ideas, even ideas hateful to
the prevailing climate of opinion—have the full protection of the guaranties,
unless excludable because they encroach upon the limited area of more important interests. But implicit in the history of the First Amendment is the rejection
of obscenity as utterly without redeeming social importance. This rejection is
mirrored in the universal judgment that obscenity should be restrained, reflected
in the international agreement of over 50 nations, in the obscenity laws of all of

the 48 States, and in the 20 obscenity laws enacted by the Congress from 1842 to 1956. In *Chaplinsky v. New Hampshire*, 315 U.S. 568, we recognized that obscene speech is "no essential part of any exposition of ideas, and are of such slight social value as a step to truth that any benefit that may be derived from them is clearly outweighed by the social interest in order and morality." We hold that obscenity is not within the area of constitutionally protected speech or press.

It is insisted that the constitutional guaranties are violated because convictions may be had without proof either that obscene material will perceptibly create a clear and present danger of antisocial conduct, or will probably induce its recipients to such conduct. In light of our holding that obscenity is not protected speech, it is unnecessary to consider the issues behind the phrase "clear and present danger."

However, sex and obscenity are not synonymous. Obscene material is material which deals with sex in a manner appealing to prurient interest. The A.L.I. *Model Penal Code* §207.10(2) (Tent. Draft No. 6, 1957) defines obscenity in the following way: "A thing is obscene if, considered as a whole, its predominant appeal is to prurient interest, i.e., a shameful or morbid interest in nudity, sex or excretion, and if it goes substantially beyond customary limits of candor in description or representation of such matters." The portrayal of sex, e.g., in art, literature and scientific works, is not itself sufficient reason to deny material the constitutional protection of freedom of speech and press. Sex, a great and mysterious motive force in human life, has indisputably been a subject of absorbing interest to mankind through the ages; it is one of the vital problems of human interest and public concern.

The fundamental freedoms of speech and press have contributed greatly to the development and well-being of our free society and are indispensable to its continued growth. Ceaseless vigilance is the watchword to prevent their erosion by Congress or by the States. It is therefore vital that the standards for judging obscenity safeguard the protection of freedom of speech and press for material which does not treat sex in a manner appealing to prurient interest.

The early leading standard of obscenity allowed material to be judged merely by the effect of an isolated excerpt upon particularly susceptible persons. *Regina v. Hicklin*, (1868) L.R. 3 Q.B. 360. Some American courts adopted this standard but later decisions rejected it and asked whether to the average person, applying contemporary community standards, the dominant theme of the material taken as a whole appeals to prurient interest. The *Hicklin* test, judging obscenity by the effect of isolated passages upon the most susceptible persons, might well encompass material legitimately treating with sex, and so it must be rejected as unconstitutionally restrictive of the freedoms of speech and press. The substituted standard provides safeguards adequate to withstand the charge of constitutional infirmity.

It is argued that the statutes do not provide reasonably ascertainable standards of guilt and therefore violate the constitutional requirements of due process. The federal obscenity statute makes punishable the mailing of material that is "obscene, lewd, lascivious, or filthy or other publication of an indecent character." The California statute makes punishable, *inter alia*, the keeping for sale or advertising material that is "obscene or indecent." Many decisions have recognized that these terms are not precise. This Court, however, has consistently held that lack of precision is not itself offensive to the requirements of due process. The Constitution does not require impossible standards; all that is required is that the language "conveys sufficiently definite warning as to the proscribed conduct when measured by common understanding and practices." *United States v. Petrillo*, 332 U.S. 1. These words give adequate warning of the conduct proscribed and mark "boundaries sufficiently distinct for judges and juries fairly to administer the law. That there may be marginal cases in which it is difficult to determine the side of the line on which a particular fact situation falls is no sufficient reason to hold the language too ambiguous to define a criminal offense."

In summary, we hold that these statutes, applied according to the proper standard for judging obscenity, do not offend constitutional safeguards against convictions based upon protected material, or fail to give mean in acting adequate notice of what is prohibited.

The judgments are *affirmed*.

Mr. Chief Justice WARREN, *concurring in the result*.

The line dividing the salacious or pornographic from literature or science is not straight and unwavering. The same object may have a different impact, varying according to the part of the community it reached. The conduct of the defendant is the central issue. The nature of the materials is, of course, relevant as an attribute of the defendant's conduct, but the materials are thus placed in context from which they draw color and character. A wholly different result might be reached in a different setting.

Under the California law, the prohibited activity must be done "wilfully and lewdly." The federal statute limits the crime to acts done "knowingly." The district judge stated that the matter must be "calculated" to corrupt or debauch. The defendants in both these cases were engaged in the business of purveying textual or graphic matter openly advertised to appeal to the erotic interest of their customers. They were plainly engaged in the commercial exploitation of the morbid and shameful craving for materials with prurient effect. The State and Federal Governments can constitutionally punish such conduct.

Mr. Justice HARLAN, *concurring in the result* in *Alberts*, and *dissenting* in *Roth*.

Many juries might find that Joyce's "Ulysses" or Bocaccio's "Decameron" was obscene, and yet the conviction of a defendant for selling either book would raise the gravest constitutional problems, for no such verdict could convince me, without more, that these books are "utterly without redeeming social importance."

I concur in *Alberts*. We can inquire only whether the state action so subverts the fundamental liberties implicit in the Due Process Clause that it cannot be sustained as a rational exercise of power. The state legislature has made the judgment that printed words can "deprave or corrupt" the reader—that words can incite to anti-social or immoral action. There is a school of thought, particularly in the scientific community, which denies any causal connection between the reading of pornography and immorality, crime, or delinquency. It is not our function to decide this question. That function belongs to the state legislature. The State can reasonably draw the inference that over a long period of time the indiscriminate dissemination of materials, the essential character of which is to degrade sex, will have an eroding effect on moral standards. The State has a legitimate interest in protecting the privacy of the home against invasion of unsolicited obscenity. This Court should be slow to interfere with state legislation calculated to protect that morality. Appellant's conviction must be affirmed.

I dissent in *Roth*. The same book which is freely read in one State might be classed as obscene in another. Edmund Wilson's "Memoirs of Hecate County" was found obscene in New York, *see Doubleday v. New York,* 354 U.S. 476 (1957); but a bookseller indicted for selling the same book was acquitted in California. "God's Little Acre" was held to be obscene in Massachusetts, not obscene in New York and Pennsylvania. No overwhelming danger to our freedom to experiment and to gratify our tastes in literature is likely to result from the suppression of a borderline book in one of the States, so long as other States are free to experiment with the same or bolder books. Quite a different situation is presented where the Federal Government imposes the ban. The fact that no person in the United States should be allowed to do so seems to me to be intolerable, and violative of both the letter and spirit of the First Amendment.

Roth was convicted under a statute which makes it criminal to sell books which "tend to stir sexual impulses and lead to sexually impure thoughts." Much of the great literature of the world could lead to conviction under such a statute. The Federal Government has no business to bar the sale of books because they might lead to any kind of "thoughts." It is no answer to say that obscenity is not protected speech. This statute defines obscenity so widely that it encompasses matters which might very well be protected speech. I do not think that the federal statute can be constitutionally construed to reach other than "hard-core" pornography. Nor do I think the statute can be read as directed only at persons engaged in the business of catering to the prurient minded, even though their wares fall short of hard-core pornography. Since the material involved cannot be said to be hard-core pornography, I would reverse with instructions to dismiss the indictment.

Mr. Justice DOUGLAS, with whom Mr. Justice BLACK *concurs, dissenting.*

Even the ill-starred *Dennis* case conceded that speech to be punishable must have some relation to action which could be penalized by government. This issue cannot be avoided by saying that obscenity is not protected by the First Amendment. The question remains, what is the constitutional test of obscenity? The tests by which these convictions were obtained require only the arousing of sexual thoughts. Yet the arousing of sexual thoughts and desires happens every day in normal life in dozens of ways. To allow the State to step in and punish mere speech or publication that the judge or the jury thinks has an undesirable impact on thoughts but that is not shown to be a part of unlawful action is drastically to curtail the First Amendment. If we were certain that impurity of sexual thoughts impelled to action, we would be on less dangerous ground in punishing the distributors of this sex literature. But it is by no means clear that obscene literature is a significant factor in influencing substantial deviations from the community standards. The absence of dependable information should put us on the side of protecting society's interest in literature, except and unless it can be said that the particular publication has an impact on action that the government can control. I have the same confidence in the ability of our people to reject noxious literature as I have in their capacity to sort out the true from the false in theology, economics, politics, or any other field.

Notes and Questions

1. *"Patently Offensive" and "Redeeming Social Value."* In the post-*Roth* era, the Court added two new elements to the "prurient interest" test for obscenity: the requirements of "patent offensiveness" and being "utterly without redeeming social importance." *Jacobellis v. Ohio*, 378 U.S. 184 (1964). The latter element was restated as "utterly without redeeming social value" in the famous three-part *Memoirs* test, which captured the votes of only a plurality of the Court: "(a) the dominant theme of the material taken as a whole appeals to a prurient interest in sex; (b) the material is patently offensive because it affronts contemporary community standards relating to the description or representation of sexual matters; and (c) the material is utterly without redeeming social value." *See Memoirs v. Massachusetts*, 383 U.S. 413 (1966). "In the absence of a majority view, the Court was compelled to embark on the practice of summarily reversing convictions for the dissemination of materials that at least five members of the Court, applying their separate tests, found to be protected by the First Amendment. *Redrup v. New York*, 386 U.S. 767 (1967). The *Redrup* procedure cast us in the role of an unreviewable board of censorship for the 50 States, subjectively judging each piece of material brought before us." *Miller v. California*, 413 U.S. 15, 23 (1973). During the post-*Memoirs* era, justices Black and Douglas remained committed to their positions in *Roth* and *Alberts* that obscenity is not unprotected. Justices White and Clark objected to the third element of *Memoirs*, concerning the utter lack of redeeming social value. Justice Stewart maintained his view that "hard-core pornography" should be unprotected, but he could not define it: "I shall not attempt further to describe the kinds of material included within that shorthand description. But I know it when I see it." *Jacobellis v. Ohio*, 378 U.S. 184, 197 (1964) (Stewart, J., concurring).

2. *Obscenity and the Justifications for Protecting Speech.* Does obscene speech meet any of the justifications for protecting speech presented earlier in this chapter? In other words, does it provide a safety valve, does it promote self-fulfillment or the marketplace of ideas, or is it related to the democratic process? Does the answer to this question depend on the content and purpose of the obscene speech?

3. *More on Defining Obscenity.* After reading *Roth* and the above note discussing *Memoirs*, are you clear about what constitutes "obscenity"? For example, do magazines like *Playboy* and *Penthouse* (which display nude pictures but also include articles about art, literature, and famous people) qualify as "obscene"? If not, what must be shown to establish obscenity?

4. *National or Local Standards?* In *Roth* and *Alberts*, the Court did not explicitly address the issue of whether a national or a state-by-state standard (or other "local" standard) should be used in applying the prurient interest test. Justice Harlan argued for a state-by-state standard, but in *Jacobellis v. Ohio*, 378 U.S. 184 (1964), the Court endorsed a national standard, declaring that such a standard was implicit in *Roth*, and also endorsed the principle that de novo review of the fact-finding on the legal issue of obscenity would be available in reviewing courts. Does it make sense to use a national versus a local standard? How will the use of one of these standards, as opposed to the other, affect the outcome of a case?

5. *Fanny Hill.* In 1967, a state trial court found that John Cleland's book, *Memoirs*, written around 1750, was obscene. The evidence at trial consisted solely of expert evidence from literature professors and book reviews. One expert concluded that "the book is without literary merit and is obscene, impure, hard core pornography, and is patently offensive." Other critical commentary on the book provided the following observations:

> Fanny Hill is nothing but a harlot—a sensualist—exploiting her sexual attractions which she sold for fun, for money, for lodging and keep, for an inheritance, and finally for a husband. If she was curious about life, her curiosity extended only to the pursuit of sexual delight. The book describes nothing in the 'external world' except bawdy houses and debaucheries. Fanny confines her observations and 'experiments' to sex, with primary attention to depraved, lewd, and deviant practices. However, several experts testify that the book has merit. For example, one expert testifies that the book represents "social history of interest to anyone who is interested in fiction as a way of understanding the past." Another expert's testimony is summarized as follows: "Although many scenes, if translated into the present day language of 'the realistic, naturalistic novel, could be quite offensive,' these scenes are not described in such language. The book contains no dirty words and its language 'functions to create a distance, even when the sexual experiences are portrayed.' The response, therefore, is a literary response. The descriptions of depravity are not obscene because 'they are subordinate to an interest which is primarily literary'; Fanny's reaction to the scenes of depravity was 'anger,' 'disgust, horror, (and) indignation.' The book 'belongs to the history of English literature rather than the history of smut.'"

The conviction was affirmed. What arguments will each side make before the Court about whether the judgment as to obscenity should be affirmed?

Miller v. United States

413 U.S. 15 (1973)

Mr. Chief Justice BURGER delivered the opinion of the Court.

Marvin Miller conducted a mass mailing campaign to advertise the sale of illustrated books, euphemistically called "adult" material. Appellant's conviction was specifically based on his conduct in causing five unsolicited advertising brochures to be sent through the mail to California. The envelope was opened by the addressee and his mother. They had not requested the brochures; they complained to the police. The Court described the brochures as advertisements for four books "entitled 'Intercourse,' 'Man-Woman,' 'Sex Orgies Illustrated,' and 'An Illustrated History of Pornography'" and a film "entitled 'Marital Intercourse.'" The brochures "primarily consist of pictures and drawings very explicitly depicting men and women in groups of two or more engaging in a variety of sexual activities, with genitals often prominently displayed."

This case involves the application of a State's criminal obscenity statute to a situation in which sexually explicit materials have been thrust by aggressive sales action upon unwilling recipients who had in no way indicated any desire to receive such materials. We are called on to define the standards which must be used to identify obscene material that a State may regulate without infringing on the First Amendment as applicable to the States through the Fourteenth Amendment. The Court noted that "the material in this case is more accurately defined in lay terms as 'pornography' or 'pornographic material,'" and that "pornographic material which is obscene forms a subgroup of all 'obscene' expression," which has "a specific judicial meaning which derives from the *Roth* case." The California statute was amended after *Alberts* to incorporate the MPC definition of prurient interest and the three-part *Memoirs* test; it covered a long list of written materials, and punished the acts of knowingly sending or bringing obscene material into the state for sale or distribution, or knowingly preparing, publishing, printing, exhibiting, or distributing such material.

We acknowledge the inherent dangers of undertaking to regulate any form of expression. State statutes designed to regulate obscene materials must be carefully limited. As a result, we confine the permissible scope of such regulation to works which depict or describe sexual conduct. That conduct must be specifically defined by the applicable state law, as written or authoritatively construed. A state offense must also be limited to works which, taken as a whole, appeal to the prurient interest in sex, which portray sexual conduct in a patently offensive way, and which, taken as a whole, do not have serious literary, artistic, political, or scientific value.

The basic guidelines for the trier of fact must be: (a) whether "the average person, applying contemporary community standards" would find that the work, taken as a whole, appeals to the prurient interest; (b) whether the work depicts or describes, in a patently offensive way, sexual conduct specifically defined by the applicable state law; and (c) whether the work, taken as a whole, lacks serious literary, artistic, political, or scientific value. We do not adopt as a constitutional standard the "utterly without redeeming social value" test of *Memoirs*; that concept has never commanded the adherence of more than three Justices at one time. If a state law that regulates obscene material is thus limited, as written or construed, the First Amendment values applicable to the States through the Fourteenth Amendment are adequately protected by the ultimate power of appellate courts to conduct an independent review of constitutional claims when necessary.

We emphasize that it is not our function to propose regulatory schemes for the States. That must await their concrete legislative efforts. It is possible, however, to give a few plain examples of what a state statute could define for regulation under part (b) of the standard announced in this opinion that is, sexual conduct specifically defined.

(a) Patently offensive representations or descriptions of ultimate sexual acts, normal or perverted, actual or simulated.

(b) Patently offensive representation or descriptions of masturbation, excretory functions, and lewd exhibition of the genitals.

Sex and nudity may not be exploited without limit by films or pictures exhibited or sold in places of public accommodation any more than live sex and nudity can be exhibited or sold without limit in such public places. At a minimum, prurient, patently offensive depiction or description of sexual conduct must have serious literary, artistic, political, or scientific value to merit First Amendment protection. For example, medical books for the education of physicians and related personnel necessarily use graphic illustrations and descriptions of human anatomy. In resolving the inevitably sensitive questions of fact and law, we must continue to rely on the jury system, accompanied by the safeguards that judges, rules of evidence, presumption of innocence, and other protective features provide, as we do with rape, murder, and a host of other offenses against society and its individual members.

Under the holdings announced today, no one will be subject to prosecution for the sale or exposure of obscene materials unless these materials depict or describe patently offensive "hard core" sexual conduct specifically defined by the regulating state law, as written or construed. These specific prerequisites will provide fair notice to a dealer in such materials that his public and commercial activities may bring prosecution. If the inability to define regulated materials with ultimate, god-like precision altogether removes the power of the States or the Congress to regulate, then "hard core" pornography may be exposed without limit to the juvenile, the passerby, and the consenting adult alike. Today, for the first time since *Roth* was decided in 1957, a majority of this Court has agreed on concrete guidelines to isolate "hard core" pornography from expression protected by the First Amendment. Now we may attempt to provide positive guidance to federal and state courts alike.

Under a National Constitution, fundamental First Amendment limitations on the powers of the States do not vary from community to community, but this does not mean that there are, or should or can be, fixed, uniform national standards of precisely what appeals to the "prurient interest" or is "patently offensive." These are essentially questions of fact, and our Nation is simply too big and too diverse for this Court to reasonably expect that such standards could be articulated for all 50 States in a single formulation, even assuming the prerequisite consensus exists. When triers of fact are asked to decide whether "the average person, applying contemporary community standards" would consider certain materials "prurient," it would be unrealistic to require that the answer be based on some abstract formulation. The adversary system, with lay jurors as the usual ultimate factfinders in criminal prosecutions, has historically permitted triers of fact to draw on the standards of their community, guided always by limiting instructions on the law. To require a State to structure obscenity proceedings around evidence of a national "community standard" would be an exercise in futility.

During the trial, both the prosecution and the defense assumed that the relevant "community standards" in making the factual determination of obscenity were those of the State of California, not some hypothetical standard of the entire United States of America. Defense counsel at trial never objected to the testimony of the State's expert on community standards or to the instructions of the trial judge on "statewide" standards. On appeal to the state appellate court appellant for the first time contended that application of state, rather than national, standards violated the First and Fourteenth Amendments.

Neither the State's alleged failure to offer evidence of "national standards," nor the trial court's charge that the jury consider state community standards, were constitutional errors. Nothing in the First Amendment requires that a jury must consider hypothetical and unascertainable "national standards" when attempting to determine whether certain materials are obscene as a matter of fact. It is neither realistic nor constitutionally sound to read the First Amendment as requiring that the people of Maine or Mississippi accept public depiction of conduct found tolerable in Las Vegas, or New York City. People in different States vary in their tastes and attitudes, and this diversity is not to be strangled by the absolutism of imposed uniformity. As the Court has made clear, the primary concern with requiring a jury to apply the standard of "the average person, applying contemporary community standards" is to be certain that, so far as material is not aimed at a deviant group, it will be judged by its impact on an average person, rather than a particularly susceptible or sensitive person—or indeed a totally insensitive one. The requirement that the jury evaluate the materials with reference to "contemporary standards of the State of California" serves this protective purpose and is constitutionally adequate.

To equate the free and robust exchange of ideas and political debate with commercial exploitation of obscene material demeans the grand conception of the First Amendment and its high purposes in the historic struggle for freedom. The First Amendment protects works which, taken as a whole, have serious literary, artistic, political, or scientific value, regardless of whether the government or a majority of the people approve of the ideas these works represent. "The protection given speech and press was fashioned to assure unfettered interchange of ideas for the bringing about of political and social changes desired by the people." But the public portrayal of hard-core sexual conduct for its own sake, and for the ensuing commercial gain, is a different matter.

There is no evidence, empirical or historical, that the stern 19th century American censorship of public distribution and display of material relating to sex in any way limited or affected expression of serious literary, artistic, political, or scientific ideas. On the contrary, it is beyond question that the era following Thomas Jefferson to Theodore Roosevelt was an "extraordinarily vigorous period," not just in economics and politics, but in belles lettres and in "the outlying fields of social and political philosophies." We do not see the harsh hand of censorship of ideas—good or bad, sound or unsound—and "repression" of political liberty lurking in every state regulation of commercial exploitation of human interest in sex.

We (a) reaffirm the *Roth* holding that obscene material is not protected by the First Amendment; (b) hold that such material can be regulated by the States, subject to the specific safeguards enunciated above, without a showing that the material is "utterly without redeeming social value"; and (c) hold that obscenity is to be determined by applying "contemporary community standards," not "national standards." The judgment is vacated and the case remanded to that court for further proceedings not inconsistent with the First Amendment standards established by this opinion.

Vacated and remanded.

Mr. Justice Douglas, *dissenting.*

The Court retreats from the earlier formulations of the constitutional test and undertakes to make new definitions. This effort, like the earlier ones, is earnest and well intentioned. The difficulty is that we do not deal with constitutional terms, since "obscenity" is not mentioned in the Constitution or Bill of Rights. There are no constitutional guidelines for deciding what is and what is not "obscene." The Court is at large because we deal with tastes and standards of literature. What shocks me may be sustenance for my neighbor. What causes one person to boil up in rage over one pamphlet or movie may reflect only his neurosis, not shared by others. We deal here with a regime of censorship which, if adopted, should be done by constitutional amendment after full debate by the people.

We deal with highly emotional, not rational, questions. To many the Song of Solomon is obscene. I do not think we, the judges, were ever given the constitutional power to make definitions of obscenity. If it is to be defined, let the people debate and decide by a constitutional amendment what they want to ban as obscene and what standards they want the legislatures and the courts to apply. Perhaps the people will decide that the path towards a mature, integrated society requires that all ideas competing for acceptance must have no censor. Perhaps they will decide otherwise. Whatever the choice, the courts will have some guidelines. Now we have none except our own predilections.

Mr. Justice BRENNAN, with whom Mr. Justice STEWART and Mr. Justice MARSHALL join, *dissenting.*

Appellant was convicted of distributing obscene matter in violation of state law on the basis of evidence that he had caused to be mailed unsolicited brochures advertising various books and a movie. I need not now decide whether a statute might be drawn to impose, within the requirements of the First Amendment, criminal penalties for the precise conduct at issue here. For the statute under which the prosecution was brought is unconstitutionally overbroad, and therefore invalid on its face. "The transcendent value to all society of constitutionally protected expression is deemed to justify allowing 'attacks on overly broad statutes with no requirement that the person making the attack demonstrate that his own conduct could not be regulated by a statute drawn with the requisite narrow specificity.'" *Gooding v. Wilson*, 405 U.S. 518 (1972). Justice Brennan would reverse the judgment and remand the case for proceedings not inconsistent with his dissent in *Paris Adult Theatre I v. Slaton*, 413 U.S. 49 (1973), *infra.*

Notes

1. *Serious Value and National Standards.* In *Pope v. Illinois*, 481 U.S. 497 (1987), the Court decided that *Miller* implicitly required that the element of "lack of serious literary, artistic, political, or scientific value" should be judged by national standards, reasoning as follows: "Just as the ideas a work represents need not obtain majority approval to merit protection, neither, insofar as the First Amendment is concerned, does the value of the work vary from community to community based on the degree of local acceptance it has won. The proper inquiry is not whether an ordinary member of any given community would find serious literary, artistic, political, or scientific value in allegedly obscene material, but whether a reasonable person would find such value in the material, taken as a whole."

2. *Jury Instructions.* In decisions after *Miller*, the Court took a flexible approach to resolving specific challenges to jury instructions that defined the key elements of *Miller*'s obscenity definitions. *See, e.g., Hamling v. United States*, 418 U.S. 87 (1974) ("a juror is entitled to draw on his own knowledge of the views of the average person in the community or vicinage from which he comes for making the required determination," and a precise "statewide standard" is not required in instructions); *Jenkins v. Georgia*, 418 U.S. 153 (1974) (approving instructions to "apply community standards" without specifying what "community").

∼ PROBLEMS ∼

1. *More on Defining Obscenity.* After *Miller* and *Pope*, are you more clear about what constitutes "obscenity" and whether (or why) magazines like *Playboy* and

Penthouse fit within the definition? If they do not fit, what more is required to render a publication "obscene"?

2. *Ultimate Sex Acts.* Now consider the movie *Carnal Knowledge.* The plot involves two college-age men, roommates and lifelong friends, who are obsessed with sex. While the two first met as virgins, one is more attractive and is described as a "burgeoning bastard." The other man is a nice but troubled guy who falls in love with the lovely Susan and unknowingly shares her with his college buddy. Since the other character is the "safer" one of the two, Susan selects him for marriage. Later scenes show the two men, now in their 30s, pursuing successful careers in New York. The first dates about a dozen women a year but has never managed to meet the "right one" (defined as a woman with a full bosom, good legs, and a properly rounded bottom) until he comes across Ann-Margret, an aging bachelorette with substantial cleavage and something of a past. She accepts his invitation to "shack up," and a "horrendous relationship ensues" complicated "by her paranoidal desire to marry." By this time, the thrill has gone out of the other marriage. The movie contains occasional scenes of nudity and scenes in which sexual conduct, including "ultimate sexual acts," is understood to be taking place, even though the camera does not focus on the bodies or genitals of the actors at such times. Is the movie "obscene" under *Miller? See Jenkins v. Georgia,* 436 U.S. 293 (1978).

3. *Nasty as We Wanna Be.* A county sheriff seizes copies of the music CD by 2 Live Crew entitled *Nasty as We Wanna Be* (*Nasty*). The band has made another version of *Nasty* with the same music but different lyrics (without the use of profanities), entitled *Clean as We Wanna Be.* The sheriff commences an obscenity prosecution against the music CD *Nasty,* seeking an injunction to ban its distribution in the county. At the obscenity trial, one of the members of 2 Live Crew testifies that no social message of any importance was intended by the band when they created the CD as their musical work. One expert testifies that the work has value because the music and lyrics represent a variety of musical traditions. How will the lawyer for the band argue that the music CD is not obscene under *Miller?*

4. *More on the International Treaty Regulating the Internet.* At the convention, a number of European representatives are keen to ban both Nazi symbols and denial that the Holocaust actually occurred, and they think that it is very important for the United States to support them in this effort. Under the First Amendment, can you agree to a treaty that allows governments to ban all Nazi symbols from the internet, or that allows a prohibition against Holocaust denial?

5. *More on the International Treaty Regulating the Internet.* Some delegates to the convention believe that the treaty should contain tight restrictions on sexually oriented material on the internet. They view such speech as "damaging to society" and believe that it should be prohibited. Others, particularly the Danish, Swedish, and French delegates, believe that the American attitude toward sexual speech is a bit "prudish." They argue that the sexual urge is one of the most basic and instinctual urges, and contend that the right to distribute and view sexual materials should be regarded as a "fundamental right in a free society." As a result,

the Danish, Swedish, and French delegates believe that sexual speech should be limited and controlled only to the extent that it protects children from exposure to the material or protects children from exploitation. What kind of language should you agree to in the treaty regarding the regulation of sexual material? Can you strike a balance between these very different perspectives on sexual speech? What type of language do you think the final treaty should contain?

b. "Consenting Adults" and "Adult Possession"

Do adults have special rights to purchase, view, or possess obscenity? Consider the following cases.

Paris Adult Theatre I v. Slaton

413 U.S. 49 (1973)

Mr. Chief Justice BURGER delivered the opinion of the Court.

Petitioners are two Atlanta, Georgia, movie theaters and their owners and managers, operating in the style of "adult" theaters. Civil complaints were filed against the petitioners alleging that they were exhibiting two obscene films, and an injunction was sought against the exhibition of the films. The two films in question, "Magic Mirror" and "It All Comes Out in the End," depict sexual conduct characterized by the Georgia Supreme Court as "hard core pornography" leaving "little to the imagination."

The two films were exhibited at trial along with pictures of the theater entrance, which showed a conventional, inoffensive theater entrance, without any pictures, but with signs indicating that the theaters exhibit "Atlanta's Finest Mature Feature Films." On the door itself is a sign saying: "Adult Theatre—You must be 21 and able to prove it. If viewing the nude body offends you, Please Do Not Enter." Criminal investigators testified that they saw nothing on the outside of the theater which indicated that the films depicted—as they did—scenes of simulated fellatio, cunnilingus, and group sex intercourse. There was no evidence that minors had ever entered the theater. Nor was there evidence presented that petitioners had a systematic policy of barring minors, apart from posting signs at the entrance. The trial judge dismissed the complaints, assuming "that obscenity is established," but holding "that the display of these films in a commercial theatre, when surrounded by requisite notice to the public of their nature and by reasonable protection against the exposure of these films to minors, is constitutionally permissible." The Georgia Supreme Court reversed.

We disapprove the theory that obscene, pornographic films acquire constitutional immunity from state regulation simply because they are exhibited for consenting adults only. Although we have recognized the high importance of the state interest in regulating the exposure of obscene materials to juveniles and unconsenting adults, this Court has never declared these to be the only legitimate state interests permitting regulation of obscene material. States have a long-recognized legitimate interest in regulating the use of obscene material in local commerce and in all places of public accommodation. These include the interest of the public in the quality of life and the total community environment, the tone of commerce in city centers, and, possibly, the public safety itself. The Hill-Link Minority Report of the Commission on Obscenity and Pornography indicates that there is at least an arguable correlation between obscene material and crime. Quite apart from sex crimes, there remains one problem of large proportions aptly described by Professor Bickel: "It concerns the tone of the society, the mode, or to use terms that have perhaps greater currency, the style and quality of life, now and in the future. A man may be entitled to read an obscene book in his room, or expose himself indecently there. We should protect his privacy. But if he demands a right to obtain the books and pictures he wants in the market, and to foregather in public places—discreet, if you will, but accessible to all—with others who share his tastes, then to grant him his right is to affect the world about the rest of us, and to impinge on other privacies. What is commonly read and seen and heard and done intrudes upon us all, want it or not." 22 *The Public Interest* 25-26 (Winter 1971).

Although there is no conclusive proof of a connection between antisocial behavior and obscene material, the legislature of Georgia could quite reasonably determine that such a connection does or might exist. In *Roth*, this Court implicitly accepted that a legislature could legitimately act on such a conclusion to protect "the social interest in order and morality." If we accept the unprovable assumption that a complete education requires the reading of certain books, and the well nigh universal belief that good books, plays, and art lift the spirit, improve the mind, enrich the human personality, and develop character, can we then say that a state legislature may not act on the corollary assumption that commerce in obscene books, or public exhibitions focused on obscene conduct, have a tendency to exert a corrupting and debasing impact leading to antisocial behavior? The sum of experience affords an ample basis for legislatures to conclude that a sensitive, key relationship of human existence, central to family life, community welfare, and the development of human personality, can be debased and distorted by crass commercial exploitation of sex. Nothing in the Constitution prohibits a State from reaching such a conclusion and acting on it legislatively simply because there is no conclusive evidence or empirical data.

Our prior decisions recognizing a right to privacy guaranteed by the Fourteenth Amendment included only personal rights that can be deemed "fundamental" or "implicit in the concept of ordered liberty." *Roe v. Wade*, 410 U.S. 113 (1973). This privacy right encompasses and protects the personal intimacies of the home, the family, marriage, motherhood, procreation, and child rearing. Nothing in this Court's decisions intimates that there is any "fundamental" privacy right "implicit in the concept of ordered liberty" to watch obscene movies in places of public accommodation. For us to say that our Constitution incorporates the proposition that conduct involving consenting adults only is always beyond state regulation, is a step we are unable to take. The States have a legitimate interest in regulating commerce in obscene material and in regulating exhibition of obscene material in places of public accommodation, including so-called "adult" theaters from which minors are excluded. Nothing precludes the State of Georgia from the regulation of the allegedly obscene material exhibited in Paris Adult Theatre I or II, provided that the applicable Georgia law, as written or authoritatively interpreted by the Georgia courts, meets the First Amendment standards set forth in *Miller v. California.* The judgment is vacated and the case remanded to the Georgia Supreme Court for further proceedings not inconsistent with this opinion.

Vacated and remanded.

Mr. Justice BRENNAN, with whom Mr. Justice STEWART and Mr. Justice MARSHALL join, *dissenting.*

After 16 years of experimentation and debate I am reluctantly forced to the conclusion that none of the available formulas can reduce the vagueness to a tolerable level while at the same time striking an acceptable balance between the protections of the First and Fourteenth Amendments and the asserted state interest in regulating the dissemination of certain sexually oriented materials. Any effort to draw a constitutionally acceptable boundary on state power must resort to such indefinite concepts as "prurient interest," "patent offensiveness," "serious literary value," and the like. The meaning of these concepts necessarily varies with the experience, outlook, and even idiosyncrasies of the person defining them. Although we have assumed that obscenity does exist and that we "know it when (we) see it," we are manifestly unable to describe it in advance except by reference to concepts so elusive that they fail to distinguish clearly between protected and unprotected speech.

The vagueness of the standards in the obscenity area produces a number of separate problems. First, a vague statute fails to provide adequate notice to persons who are engaged in the type of conduct that the statute could be thought to proscribe. Even the most painstaking efforts to determine in advance whether certain sexually oriented expression is obscene must inevitably prove unavailing. The insufficiency of the notice compels persons to guess not only whether their conduct is covered by a criminal statute, but also whether their conduct falls within the constitutionally permissible reach of the statute. As a result, one cannot say with certainty that material is obscene until at least five members of this Court, applying inevitably obscure standards, have pronounced it so.

Our experience since *Roth* requires us not only to abandon the effort to pick out obscene material on a case-by-case basis, but also to reconsider a fundamental postulate of *Roth*: that there exists a definable class of sexually oriented expression that may be suppressed by the Federal and State Governments. "Obscenity" cannot be defined with sufficient specificity and clarity to provide fair notice to persons who create and distribute sexually oriented materials, to prevent substantial erosion of protected speech as a byproduct of the attempt to suppress unprotected speech, and to avoid costly institutional harms. If, as the Court today assumes, "a state legislature may act on the assumption that commerce in obscene books, or public exhibitions focused on obscene conduct, have a tendency to exert a corrupting and debasing impact leading to antisocial behavior," then it is hard to see how state-ordered regimentation of our minds can ever be forestalled.

While I cannot say that the interests of the State—apart from the question of juveniles and unconsenting adults—are trivial or nonexistent, I conclude that these interests cannot justify the substantial damage to constitutional rights that inevitably results from state efforts to bar the distribution even of unprotected material to consenting adults. I would hold, therefore, that at least in the absence of distribution to juveniles or obtrusive exposure to unconsenting adults, the First and Fourteenth Amendments prohibit the State and Federal Governments from attempting wholly to suppress sexually oriented materials on the basis of their allegedly "obscene" contents. Nothing in this approach precludes those governments from taking action to serve what may be strong and legitimate interests through regulation of the manner of distribution of sexually oriented material.

Stanley v. Georgia

394 U.S. 557 (1969)

Mr. Justice MARSHALL delivered the opinion of the Court.

While executing a search warrant for Robert Stanley's home to look for evidence of bookmaking, officers found three reels of eight-millimeter film in a bedroom, and viewed them by using a projector found in the living room. The officers seized the reels after concluding that the films were obscene. Stanley was convicted under a statute that prohibited "knowingly" having possession of any obscene matter. Stanley argues that the Georgia statute, insofar as it punishes private possession of obscene matter, violates the First Amendment, and we agree. The Court assumed that the films were obscene.

Georgia concedes that the present case appears to be one of "first impression" but contends that since "obscenity is not within the area of constitutionally protected speech or press" under *Roth v. United States*, the States are free, subject to the limits of other provisions of the Constitution, to deal with it any way deemed necessary, just as they may deal with possession of other things thought to be detrimental to the welfare of their citizens. If the State can protect the body of a citizen, may it not, argues Georgia, protect his mind?

Roth and the cases following it discerned such an "important interest" in the regulation of commercial distribution of obscene material. That holding cannot foreclose an examination of the constitutional implications of a statute forbidding mere private possession of such material. It is now well established that the Constitution protects the right to receive information and ideas. "This freedom (of speech and press) necessarily protects the right to receive." *Martin v. City of Struthers*, 319 U.S. 141 (1943). This right to receive information and ideas, regardless of their social worth, is fundamental to our free society. Moreover, in this case—a prosecution for mere possession of printed or filmed matter in the privacy of a person's own home—that right takes on an added dimension. Also fundamental is the right to be free, except in very limited circumstances, from unwanted governmental intrusions into one's privacy.

Appellant asserts the right to read or observe what he pleases—the right to satisfy his intellectual and emotional needs in the privacy of his own home. He asserts the right to be free from state inquiry into the contents of his library. Georgia contends that there are certain types of materials that the individual may not read or even possess. Georgia justifies this assertion by arguing that the films in the present case are obscene. But mere categorization of these films as "obscene" is insufficient justification for such a drastic invasion of personal liberties guaranteed by the First and Fourteenth Amendments. Whatever may be the justifications for statutes regulating obscenity, we do not think they reach into the privacy of one's own home. If the First Amendment means anything, it means that a State has no business telling a man, sitting alone in his own house, what books he may read or what films he may watch. Our constitutional heritage rebels at the thought of giving government the power to control men's minds.

In the face of these traditional notions of individual liberty, Georgia asserts the right to protect the individual's mind from the effects of obscenity. We are not certain that this argument amounts to anything more than the assertion that the State has the right to control the moral content of a person's thoughts. To some, this may be a noble purpose, but it is inconsistent with the philosophy of the First Amendment. As the Court said in *Kingsley International Pictures Corp. v. Regents*, 360 U.S. 684 (1959), "the Constitution's guarantee is not confined to the expression of ideas that are conventional or shared by a majority. In the realm of ideas it protects expression which is eloquent no less than that which is unconvincing." Nor is it relevant that obscene materials in general, or the particular films before the Court, are arguably devoid of any ideological content. The line between the transmission of ideas and mere entertainment is much too elusive for this Court to draw, if indeed such a line can be drawn at all. Whatever the power of the state to control public dissemination of ideas inimical to the public morality, it cannot constitutionally premise legislation on the desirability of controlling a person's private thoughts.

Perhaps recognizing this, Georgia asserts that exposure to obscene materials may lead to deviant sexual behavior or crimes of sexual violence. There appears to be little empirical basis for that assertion. More important, if the State is only concerned about printed or filmed materials inducing antisocial conduct, in the context of private consumption of ideas and information we should adhere to the view that "among free men, the deterrents ordinarily to be applied to prevent crime are education and punishment for violations of the law." *Whitney v. California*, 274 U.S. 357 (1927) (Brandeis, J., concurring). Given the present state of knowledge, the State may no more prohibit mere possession of obscene matter on the ground that it may lead to antisocial conduct than it may prohibit possession of chemistry books on the ground that they may lead to the manufacture of homemade spirits.

In *Roth* this Court rejected the necessity of proving that exposure to obscene material would create a clear and present danger of antisocial conduct or would probably induce its recipients to such conduct. But that case dealt with public distribution of obscene materials and such distribution is subject to different objections. There is always the danger that obscene material might fall into the hands of children, or that it might intrude upon the sensibilities or privacy of the general public. No such dangers are present in this case. The Court also noted that "the Model Penal Code provisions dealing with obscene materials are limited to cases of commercial dissemination."

Finally, we are faced with the argument that prohibition of possession of obscene materials is a necessary incident to statutory schemes prohibiting distribution. That argument is based on alleged difficulties of proving an intent to distribute or in producing evidence of actual distribution. We are not convinced that such difficulties exist, but even if they did we do not think that they would justify infringement of the individual's right to read or observe what he pleases. Because that right is so fundamental to our scheme of individual liberty, its restriction may not be justified by the need to ease the administration of otherwise valid criminal laws. We hold that the First and Fourteenth Amendments prohibit making mere private possession of obscene material a crime. *Roth* and the cases following that decision are not impaired by today's holding. As we have said, the States retain broad power to regulate obscenity; that power simply does not extend to mere possession by the individual in the privacy of his own home. Accordingly, the judgment of the court below is reversed and the case is remanded for proceedings not inconsistent with this opinion.

It is so ordered.

Judgment reversed and case remanded.

Note: Stanley's Limits and Impact

Although *Stanley* was a unanimous judgment, three Justices concurred on Fourth Amendment grounds. The reluctance of some members of the Court to endorse *Stanley*'s First Amendment holding was later reflected in a pre-*Miller* case that limited *Stanley*'s impact. In *United States v. Reidel,* 402 U.S. 351 (1971), the Court held that even though a person has the right to possess obscene material under *Stanley,* no one has the right to sell or deliver it to that person. As a result, the Court upheld a federal statute that prohibited the knowing use of the mails for the delivery of obscene matter, and held that *Roth* precluded invalidation of the statute as applied to willing adult recipients of such matter. In *Osborne v. Ohio,* 495 U.S. 103 (1990), the Court distinguished *Stanley* in holding that possession of child pornography could be prohibited.

c. Special Rules for Minors?

Are their special rules for sexual material that is obscene or harmful for minors?

Ginsberg v. New York

390 U.S. 629 (1968)

Mr. Justice BRENNAN delivered the opinion of the Court.

Ginsberg and his wife operate "Sam's Stationery and Luncheonette" in Bellmore, Long Island. They have a lunch counter, and also sell magazines including some so-called "girlie" magazines. Ginsberg was charged with and convicted of selling a 16-year-old boy two "girlie" magazines. The statute made it a crime knowingly to sell to a minor under 17 (a) any picture which depicts nudity and which is harmful to minors, and (b) any magazine which contains such pictures and which, taken as a whole, is harmful to minors. The judge found (1) that the magazines contained pictures which depicted female "nudity" in a manner defined in the statute, that is, "the showing of female buttocks with less than a full opaque covering, or the showing of the female breast with less than a fully opaque covering of any portion thereof below the top of the nipple"; and also found (2) that the pictures were "harmful to minors" in that they had that "quality of representation of nudity which (i) predominantly appeals to the prurient, shameful or morbid interest of minors, and (ii) is patently offensive to prevailing standards in the adult community as a whole with respect to what is suitable material for minors, and (iii) is utterly without redeeming social importance for minors." We affirm.

The "girlie" picture magazines involved here are not obscene for adults, and the statute does not bar appellant from stocking the magazines and selling them to persons 17 years of age or older. Ginsberg's attack is leveled at the power of the State to adapt the *Memoirs* formulation to define the material's obscenity on the basis of its appeal to minors, and thus exclude material so defined from the area of protected expression. He makes no argument that the magazines are not "harmful to minors." Ginsberg's contention is that the constitutional freedom of expression secured to a citizen to read or see material concerned with sex cannot be made to depend upon whether the citizen is an adult or a minor. He insists that the denial to minors under 17 of access to material condemned by the statute, insofar as that material is not obscene for persons 17 years of age or older, constitutes an unconstitutional deprivation of protected liberty.

We do not regard New York's regulation in defining obscenity on the basis of its appeal to minors under 17 as involving an invasion of such minors' constitutionally protected freedoms. Rather the statute simply adjusts the definition of obscenity "to social realities by permitting the appeal of this type of material to be assessed in term of the sexual interests" of such minors. That the State has power to make that adjustment seems clear, for we have recognized that even where there is an invasion of protected freedoms "the power of the state to control the conduct of children reaches beyond the scope of its authority over adults." *Prince v. Commonwealth of Massachusetts*, 321 U.S. 158.

The well-being of children is a subject within the State's constitutional power to regulate, and two interests justify limitations upon the availability of sex material to minors under 17, at least if it was rational for the legislature to find that the minors' exposure to such material might be harmful. First, constitutional interpretation has consistently recognized that the parents' claim to authority in their own household to direct the rearing of their children is basic in the structure of our society. The legislature could properly conclude that parents and teachers who have this primary responsibility for children's well-being are entitled to the support of laws designed to aid discharge of that responsibility. Indeed, the statute expressly recognizes the parental role in assessing sex-related material harmful to minors according "to prevailing standards in the adult community as a whole with respect to what is suitable material for minors." Moreover, the prohibition against sales to minors does not bar parents who so desire from purchasing the magazines for their children. The State also has an independent interest in the well-being of its youth.

To sustain state power to exclude material defined as obscenity by the statute requires only that we be able to say that it was not irrational for the legislature to find that exposure to material condemned by the statute is harmful to minors. To be sure, there is no lack of "studies" which purport to demonstrate that obscenity is or is not "a basic factor in impairing the ethical and moral development of youth and a clear and present danger to the people of the state." But the growing consensus is that "a causal link has not been disproved either." We cannot say that the statute, in defining the obscenity of material on the basis of its appeal to minors under 17, has no rational relation to the objective of safeguarding such minors from harm.

Ginsberg argues that the definition of obscenity "harmful to minors" is so vague that an honest distributor of publications cannot know when he might be held to have violated the statute. But the New York Court of Appeals construed this definition to be "virtually identical to the Supreme Court's most recent statement of the elements of obscenity." The definition gives "men adequate notice of what is prohibited" and does not offend the requirements of due process.

Affirmed.

Mr. Justice FORTAS, *dissenting.*

The Court cannot properly avoid its fundamental duty to define "obscenity" for purposes of censorship of material sold to youths. The Court cannot mean that the States and cities and counties and villages have unlimited power to withhold anything and everything that is written or pictorial from younger people. But it justifies the conviction of Ginsberg because the impact of the Constitution, it says, is variable, and what is not obscene for an adult may be obscene for a child. To assess the principle—certainly to apply it—the Court must define it. We must know the extent to which literature or pictures may be less offensive than *Roth* requires in order to be "obscene" for purposes of a statute confined to youth. This decision does not merely protect children from activities which all sensible parents would condemn. Rather, its undefined and unlimited approval of state censorship denies to children free access to books and works of art to which many parents may wish their children to have uninhibited access. Denial of access to these magazines, without any standard or definition of their allegedly distinguishing characteristics, is also denial of access to great works of art and literature. If this statute were confined to the punishment of pushers or panderers of vulgar literature I would not be so concerned by the Court's failure to circumscribe state power by defining its limits in terms of the meaning of "obscenity" in this field. I would therefore reverse the conviction.

Notes

1. *Software Filters in Libraries to Prevent Juvenile Access to Pornography.* In *United States v. American Library Association, Inc.*, 539 U.S. 194 (2003), the Court upheld the constitutionality of the Children's Internet Protection Act provision that conditioned federal funds for internet services at public libraries on the installation of software to block minors from obtaining access to "obscenity," "child pornography," and "visual depictions" that are "harmful to minors." The Court relied on the fact that library staff have the ability to unblock any erroneously blocked site, and that a "legislature's decision not to subsidize the exercise of a fundamental right does not infringe that right." *Rust v. Sullivan*, 500 U.S. 173 (1991).

2. *Transmitting, Sending, or Displaying Indecent Messages to Juveniles.* In 1996, Congress enacted the Communications Decency Act (CDA) to regulate the internet transmission of "indecent," "patently offensive," or "obscene" messages to juveniles. The obscenity ban was not challenged, but the other provisions were held to be overbroad and vague in *Reno v. American Civil Liberties Union*, 521 U.S. 844 (1997). After *Reno*, Congress enacted the Child Online Protection Act (COPA) in 1998, in an effort to respond to the *Reno* Court's criticisms of the CDA and to come closer to the standards of *Ginsberg v. New York* and *Miller v. California*. In *Ashcroft v. American Civil Liberties Union (Ashcroft I)*, 535 U.S. 564 (2002), the courts partially upheld COPA. However, the Court later struck COPA down. *See American Civil Liberties Union v. Mukasey*, 534 F.3d 181 (3d Cir. 2008), *cert. denied*, 555 U.S. 1137 (2009). These cases are discussed more fully later in this chapter.

∼ PROBLEMS ∼

1. *Appeal to "Lust."* What arguments could be made after *Ginsberg* to challenge a statute that prohibits the sale to minors "of any magazine" that "would appeal to the lust of persons under the age of eighteen years or to their curiosity

as to sex or anatomical differences between the sexes"? *See Rabeck v. New York,* 391 U.S. 462 (1968).

2. *Movie Classifications.* What arguments could be made after *Ginsberg* to challenge a statute that classifies movies as either suitable or unsuitable for minors, and makes it a crime to admit a minor to a movie classified as unsuitable, when one definition of *unsuitable* is: the portrayal "of sexual promiscuity or extramarital sexual relations in such a manner as to encourage sexual promiscuity on the part of young persons"? *See Interstate Circuit, Inc. v. City of Dallas,* 390 U.S. 676 (1968).

3. *"Harmful Matter" in Vending Machines.* Assume that a California statute bans the sale of "harmful matter" in unsupervised sidewalk vending machines. Harmful matter is defined as "matter, taken as a whole, which to the average person, applying contemporary community standards, appeals to the prurient interest, and which, taken as a whole, depicts or describes in a patently offensive way sexual conduct, and which, taken as a whole, lacks literary, artistic, political or scientific value for minors." The California legislature did not make any specific findings concerning the purpose of the statute. Publishers and vendors of adult-oriented publications sue to enjoin enforcement of the statute on First Amendment grounds. You represent the State of California. What arguments can be made for attacking the statute on First Amendment grounds (aside from overbreadth and vagueness)? What arguments will you make in defense of the statute?

4. *More on the International Treaty Regulating the Internet.* At the convention, there is much discussion about the extent to which the treaty should protect minors against sexually explicit material. In light of *Ginsburg* and other U.S. precedents, what type of restrictions can you agree to in the treaty? How would you frame those restrictions?

8. Child Pornography

Between the 1950s and the 1970s, *Chaplinsky*'s catalogue of unprotected speech categories continued to shrink. By the 1980s, the Court had adopted a new starting point for analysis of speech regulations that are "content-based," while allowing the various doctrines created for speech in the *Chaplinsky* catalogue to retain validity as *sui generis,* historic exceptions to the new "content-based" model. For content regulations of speech in other contexts, government litigants faced the burden of satisfying the Court's "strict scrutiny" and of demonstrating that regulations were narrowly tailored and necessary to achieve a compelling governmental interest. This burden also might include the need to prove that the regulation was the least restrictive alternative in terms of its impact on protected speech. Not surprisingly, some government litigants sought to expand the *Chaplinsky* catalogue in order to escape the burden of strict scrutiny. Yet the doctrinal demands required for creation of a new unprotected speech category were necessarily different in the 1980s. In the 1940s, *Chaplinsky* simply announced the catalogue as reflecting the consensus of history, according to the Court's own jurisprudence and the views of state courts. By the 1980s, the overbreadth and vagueness doctrines had become significant limitations on content-based regulations of speech. Moreover, the speech-protective values of the strict scrutiny model implicitly required that a category of unprotected speech be created in a way that satisfied those values. Ultimately, the most notable such category created during this era was "child pornography."

Ferber v. New York

458 U.S. 747 (1982)

Justice WHITE delivered the opinion of the Court.

At issue in this case is the constitutionality of a New York criminal statute which prohibits persons from knowingly promoting sexual performances by children under the age of 16 by distributing material which depicts such performances.

The exploitive use of children in the production of pornography has become a serious national problem. The Federal Government and 47 States have sought to combat the problem with statutes specifically directed at the production of child pornography. At least half of such statutes do not require that the materials produced be legally obscene. Thirty-five States and the United States Congress have passed legislation prohibiting the distribution of such materials; 20 States prohibit the distribution of material depicting children engaged in sexual conduct without requiring that the material be legally obscene.

New York is one of the 20. In 1977, the New York Legislature enacted a child pornography statute, which provides: "A person is guilty of promoting a sexual performance by a child when, knowing the character and content thereof, he produces, directs or promotes any performance which includes sexual conduct by a child less than sixteen years of age." To "promote" is also defined: " 'Promote' means to procure, manufacture, issue, sell, give, provide, lend, mail, deliver, transfer, transmute, publish, distribute, circulate, disseminate, present, exhibit or advertise, or to offer or agree to do the same." A "sexual performance" is defined as "any performance or part thereof which includes sexual conduct by a child less than sixteen years of age." "Sexual conduct" is in turn defined as "actual or simulated sexual intercourse, deviant sexual intercourse, sexual bestiality, masturbation, sado-masochistic abuse, or lewd exhibition of the genitals." A "performance" is defined as "any play, motion picture, photograph or dance" or "any other visual representation exhibited before an audience."

This case arose when Paul Ferber, proprietor of a Manhattan bookstore specializing in sexually oriented products, sold two films to an undercover police officer. The films are devoted almost exclusively to depicting young boys masturbating. Ferber was charged with violating the child pornography statute and convicted, but his convictions were reversed. We granted the State's petition for certiorari.

This case constitutes our first examination of a statute directed at and limited to depictions of sexual activity involving children. We believe our inquiry should begin with the question of whether a State has somewhat more freedom in proscribing works which portray sexual acts or lewd exhibitions of genitalia by children.

In *Miller v. California*, 413 U.S. 15 (1973), the Court agreed that a "state offense must also be limited to works which, taken as a whole, appeal to the prurient interest in sex, which portray sexual conduct in a patently offensive way, and which, taken as a whole, do not have serious literary, artistic, political, or scientific value." Over the past decade, we have adhered to the guidelines expressed in *Miller* which was an accommodation between the State's interests in protecting the "sensibilities of unwilling recipients" from exposure to pornographic material and the dangers of censorship inherent in unabashedly content-based laws. Like obscenity statutes, laws directed at the dissemination of child pornography run the risk of suppressing protected expression by allowing the hand of the censor to become unduly heavy. However, we are persuaded that the States are entitled to greater leeway in the regulation of pornographic depictions of children.

First. A State's interest in "safeguarding the physical and psychological well-being of a minor" is "compelling." *Globe Newspaper Co. v. Superior Court*, 457 U.S. 596 (1982). "A democratic society rests, for its continuance, upon the healthy, well-rounded growth of young people into full maturity as citizens." *Prince v. Massachusetts*, 321 U.S. 158 (1944). Accordingly, we have sustained legislation aimed at protecting the physical and emotional well-being of youth even when the laws have operated in the sensitive area of constitutionally protected rights. In *Ginsberg v. New York*, 390 U.S. 629 (1968), we sustained a New York law protecting children from exposure to nonobscene literature. Most recently, we held that the Government's interest in the "well-being of its youth" justified special treatment of indecent broadcasting received by adults as well as children. *FCC v. Pacifica Foundation*, 438 U.S. 726 (1978).

Prevention of sexual exploitation and abuse of children constitutes a government objective of surpassing importance. The legislative findings accompanying passage of the New York laws reflect this concern: "There has been a proliferation of exploitation of children as subjects in sexual performances. The care of children is a sacred trust and should not be abused by those who seek to profit through a commercial network based upon the exploitation of children. The public policy of the state demands the protection of children from exploitation through sexual performances. 1977 N.Y. Laws, ch. 910, §1." We shall not second-guess this legislative judgment. Virtually all States and the United States have passed legislation proscribing the production of or otherwise combating "child pornography." The legislative judgment, as well as the judgment in the relevant literature, is that the use of children as subjects of pornographic materials is harmful to the physiological, emotional, and mental health of the child. That judgment easily passes muster under the First Amendment. Research shows "that sexually exploited children are unable to develop healthy affectionate relationships in later life, have sexual dysfunctions, and have a tendency to become sexual abusers as adults," that "sexually exploited children predisposed to self-destructive behavior such as drug and alcohol abuse or prostitution," and that "sexual molestation by adults is often involved in the production of child sexual performances."

Second. The distribution of photographs and films depicting sexual activity by juveniles is intrinsically related to the sexual abuse of children in at least two ways. First, the materials produced are a permanent record of the children's participation and the harm to the child is exacerbated by their circulation. Second, the distribution network for child pornography must be closed if the production of material which requires the sexual exploitation of children is to be effectively controlled. Indeed, there is no serious contention that the legislature was unjustified in believing that it is difficult, if not impossible, to halt the exploitation of children by pursuing only those who produce the photographs and movies. While the production of pornographic materials is a clandestine industry, the need to market the resulting products requires a visible apparatus of distribution. The most expeditious if not the only practical method of law enforcement may be to dry up the market for this material by imposing severe criminal penalties on persons selling, advertising, or otherwise promoting the product. Thirty-five States and Congress have concluded that restraints on the distribution of pornographic materials are required in order to effectively combat the problem, and there is a body of literature and testimony to support these legislative conclusions.

Ferber does not contend that the State is unjustified in pursuing those who distribute child pornography. Rather, he argues that it is enough for the State to prohibit the distribution of materials that are legally obscene under the *Miller* test. The *Miller* standard, like all general definitions of what may be banned as obscene, does not reflect the State's particular and more compelling interest in prosecuting those who promote the sexual exploitation of children. The question under *Miller* of whether a work, taken as a whole, appeals to the prurient interest of the average person bears no connection to the issue of whether a child has been physically or psychologically harmed in the production of the work. Similarly, a sexually explicit depiction need not be "patently offensive" in order to have required the sexual exploitation of a child for its production. In addition, a work which, taken on the whole, contains serious literary, artistic, political, or scientific value may nevertheless embody the hardest core of child pornography. "It is irrelevant to the child who has been abused whether or not the material has a literary, artistic, political or social value." Memorandum of Assemblyman Lasher. We therefore cannot conclude that the *Miller* standard is a satisfactory solution to the child pornography problem. Legal obscenity under *Miller* is a function of "contemporary community standards," and "it would be unrealistic to equate a community's toleration for sexually oriented material with the permissible scope of legislation aimed at protecting children from sexual exploitation."

Third. The advertising and selling of child pornography provide an economic motive for and are thus an integral part of the production of such materials, an activity illegal throughout the Nation.

Fourth. The value of permitting live performances and photographic reproductions of children engaged in lewd sexual conduct is exceedingly modest, if not *de minimis.* We consider it unlikely that visual depictions of children performing sexual acts or lewdly exhibiting their genitals would often constitute an important and necessary part of a literary performance or scientific or educational work. If it were necessary for literary or artistic value, a person over the statutory age who perhaps looked younger could be utilized. Simulation outside of the prohibition of the statute could provide another alternative. Nor is there any question here of censoring a particular literary theme or portrayal of sexual activity. The First Amendment interest is limited to rendering the portrayal somewhat more "realistic" by utilizing or photographing children.

Fifth. Recognizing and classifying child pornography as a category of material outside the protection of the First Amendment is not incompatible with our earlier decisions. It is not rare that a content-based classification of speech has been accepted because it may be appropriately generalized that within the confines of the given classification, the evil to be restricted so overwhelmingly outweighs the expressive interests, if any, at stake, that no process of case-by-case adjudication is required. When a definable class of material bears so heavily and pervasively on the welfare of children engaged in its production, the balance of competing interests is struck and it is permissible to consider these materials as without the protection of the First Amendment.

There are, of course, limits on the category of child pornography which, like obscenity, is unprotected by the First Amendment. As with all legislation in this sensitive area, the conduct to be prohibited must be adequately defined by the applicable state law, as written or authoritatively construed. The nature of the harm to be combated requires that the state offense be limited to works that *visually* depict sexual conduct by children below a specified age. The category of "sexual conduct" proscribed must also be suitably limited and described.

The test for child pornography is separate from the obscenity standard enunciated in *Miller,* but may be compared to it for the purpose of clarity. The *Miller* formulation is adjusted in the following respects: A trier of fact need not find that the material appeals to the prurient interest of the average person; it is not required that sexual conduct portrayed be done so in a patently offensive manner; and the material at issue need not be considered as a whole. We note that the distribution of descriptions or other depictions of sexual conduct, not otherwise obscene, which do not involve live performance or photographic or other visual reproduction of live performances, retains First Amendment protection. As with obscenity laws, criminal responsibility may not be imposed without some element of scienter on the part of the defendant.

The New York statute's prohibition incorporates a definition of sexual conduct that comports with the above-stated principles. The forbidden acts to be depicted are listed with sufficient precision and represent the kind of conduct that, if it were the theme of a work, could render it legally obscene: "actual or simulated sexual intercourse, deviate sexual intercourse, sexual bestiality, masturbation, sado-masochistic abuse, or lewd exhibition of the genitals." The term "lewd exhibition of the genitals" is not unknown in this area and, indeed, was given in *Miller* as an example of a permissible regulation. A performance is defined only to include live or visual depictions: "any play, motion picture, photograph or dance or other visual representation exhibited before an audience." §263.00(4). The statute expressly includes a scienter requirement.

We hold that the statute sufficiently describes a category of material the production and distribution of which is not entitled to First Amendment protection. There is nothing unconstitutionally "underinclusive" about a statute that singles out this category of material for proscription. It also follows that the State is not barred by the First Amendment from prohibiting the distribution of unprotected materials produced outside the State.

It remains to address the claim that the New York statute is unconstitutionally overbroad because it would forbid the distribution of material with serious literary, scientific, or educational value or material which does not threaten the harms sought to be combated by the State. We consider this the paradigmatic case of a statute whose legitimate reach dwarfs its arguably impermissible applications. New York may constitutionally prohibit dissemination of material specified in the statute. While the reach of the statute is directed at the hard core of child pornography, the Court of Appeals was concerned that some protected expression, ranging from medical textbooks to pictorials in the *National Geographic* would fall prey to the statute. How often, if ever, it may be necessary to employ children to engage in conduct clearly within the reach of the statute in order to produce educational, medical, or artistic works cannot be known with certainty. We seriously doubt that these arguably impermissible applications of the statute amount to more than a tiny fraction of the materials within the statute's reach. Nor will we assume that the New York courts will widen the possibly invalid reach of the statute by giving an expansive construction to the proscription on "lewd exhibitions of the genitals." Under these circumstances, the statute is "not substantially overbroad and whatever overbreadth may exist should be cured through case-by-case analysis of the fact situations to which its sanctions, assertedly, may not be applied." *Broadrick v. Oklahoma*, 413 U.S. at 615-616.

Because the statute is not substantially overbroad, it is unnecessary to consider its application to material that does not depict sexual conduct of a type that New York may restrict consistent with the First Amendment. As applied to Paul Ferber and to others who distribute similar material, the statute does not violate the First Amendment as applied to the States through the Fourteenth. The judgment of the New York Court of Appeals is reversed, and the case is remanded to that court for further proceedings not inconsistent with this opinion.

So ordered.

Justice O'CONNOR, *concurring.*

The Court does not hold that New York must except "material with serious literary, scientific, or educational value," from its statute. The Court merely holds that, even if the First Amendment shelters such material, New York's current statute is not sufficiently overbroad to support respondent's facial attack. The compelling interests suggest that the Constitution might in fact permit New York to ban knowing distribution of works depicting minors engaged in explicit sexual conduct, regardless of the social value. Or it is quite possible that New York's statute is overbroad because it bans depictions that do not actually threaten the harms identified by the Court. For example, clinical pictures of adolescent sexuality, such as those that might appear in medical textbooks, might not involve the type of sexual exploitation and abuse targeted by New York's statute. Nor might such depictions feed the poisonous "kiddie porn" market that New York and other States have attempted to regulate. Similarly, pictures of children engaged in rites widely approved by their cultures, such as those that might appear in issues of the *National Geographic,* might not trigger the compelling interests identified by the Court. It is not necessary to address these possibilities today because this potential overbreadth is not sufficiently substantial to warrant facial invalidation of New York's statute.

Justice BRENNAN, with whom Justice MARSHALL joins, *concurring in the judgment.*

The special and compelling interest, and the particular vulnerability of children, afford the State the leeway to regulate pornographic material, the promotion of which is harmful to children, even though the State does not have such leeway when it seeks only to protect consenting adults from exposure to such material. I also agree with the Court that the "tiny fraction," of material of serious artistic, scientific, or educational value that could conceivably fall within the reach of the statute is insufficient to justify striking the statute on the grounds of overbreadth. In my view application of the statute or any similar statute to depictions of children that in themselves do have serious literary, artistic, scientific, or medical value, would violate the First Amendment. The limited classes of speech, the suppression of which does not raise serious First Amendment concerns, have two attributes. They are of exceedingly "slight social value," and the State has a compelling interest in their regulation. The First Amendment value of depictions of children that are in themselves serious contributions to art, literature, or science, is, by definition, simply not "*de minimis.*" At the same time, the State's interest in suppression of such materials is likely to be far less compelling. The production of materials of serious value is not the "low-profile, clandestine industry" that according to the Court produces purely pornographic materials. In short, it is inconceivable how a depiction of a child that is itself a serious contribution to the world of art or literature or science can be deemed "material outside the protection of the First Amendment." With this understanding, I *concur.*

Notes and Questions

1. *Scope of Opinion.* The *Ferber* opinion could be read narrowly as defining the speech category of child pornography under the parameters of the New York

statute, and as requiring sexual performance, sexual conduct, and visual images of real minors under 16. But the opinion could also be read more broadly, so that not all of these elements would have to be satisfied in order to uphold a more broadly phrased child pornography statute. The Court's assessment of this speech as having "*de minimis*" value, as well as its refusal to impose a requirement that material of "literary, artistic, political and social value" should be exempted from the *Ferber* ban, implied that the Court might find other types of bans to be constitutional. Once the Court broke from the *Miller* model in *Ferber* because of *Miller*'s inapposite policy goals, it was evident that the Court might similarly break from the *Miller* commitment to requiring a single "approved" statutory definition of obscenity, and approve instead a variety of statutory definitions of child pornography. Finally, the role of the overbreadth and vagueness doctrines in the context of a *Ferber* type of speech regulation remained unclear after *Ferber*. Initially, the Court continued to interpret *Ferber* as involving a distinctly different category of speech from *Miller*, and validated the consensus judgment of the lower courts that rejected the *Stanley* doctrine as applied to possession prosecutions for child pornography. Later, as we shall see, as legislatures enacted a wide range of "juvenile protection" statutes involving speech on the internet, the Court retreated from an expansive interpretation of *Ferber*.

2. *Child Pornography and the Justifications for Protecting Speech.* Does "child pornography" meet any of the justifications for protecting speech discussed at the beginning of this chapter? In other words, does it provide a safety valve, does it promote self-fulfillment or the marketplace of ideas, or is it related to the democratic process? Does the answer to this question depend on the content of the pornography?

3. *Blocking Child Pornography.* In July 2008, the largest cable operators in the United States agreed to block child pornography websites identified by the National Center for Missing and Exploited Children. Since most cable operators also provide broadband service, the agreement provides some protection against child pornography sites.

4. *Sexting.* In recent years, some prosecutors have charged teens who send text messages that show nude photos of themselves or other minors with child pornography. *See* Chana Joffe-Walt, *"Sexting": A Disturbing New Teen Trend?*, National Public Radio (Mar. 12, 2009). Prosecutors have also charged minors who received text message photos and did not delete them from their phones. Students have a variety of motivations for sending these text images. In some instances, when they send text message photos of themselves, they are engaging in a high-tech method of flirting. In other instances, students send text message photos of others to harass or embarrass them (e.g., after a high school boy and girl break up, one sends nude pictures of the other to friends out of spite). Under these circumstances, are child pornography charges permissible under an appropriately drafted statute? Can or should the problem be dealt with through charges or in other ways?

5. *Possession of Child Pornography. Osborne v. Ohio*, 495 U.S. 103 (1990), involved an Ohio law that made it illegal to possess child pornography, and the Court

was forced to determine whether the holding in *Stanley v. Georgia*, 394 U.S. 557 (1969) (individuals have a right to possess obscenity in the privacy of their own homes), extended to and protected the possession of child pornography in one's own home. In *Osborne*, the Court held that a criminal statute that prohibited the possession of child pornography in one's home did not violate the Constitution. In reaching that conclusion, the Court observed that the value of unprotected *Ferber* materials is *de minimis*, and that the compelling government interests in restricting child pornography "far exceed the interests" that justified the *Stanley* statute. The Court viewed the *Stanley* statute as a "paternalistic" attempt to exercise thought control over people, whereas the Ohio law was designed to protect victims of child sexual abuse who have been used as models for pornography. The Court also found that the criminalization of possession of child pornography would likely decrease its production, and that the criminalization of possession was even more important since the child pornography industry had been "driven underground" by the *Ferber* decision, causing 17 states to enact possession statutes in an attempt to "dry up the market." In addition, the Court found that the law might encourage consumers to destroy child pornography, "which might not only dry up the market but also remove materials from the hands of pedophiles who might use it for luring children into sexual activity."

6. *Civil Remedy for Victims of Child Pornography Crimes.* In 2003, Congress enacted 18 U.S.C §2252B, as a companion statute to the criminal prohibition in §2252A, which defines the federal version of the *Ferber* crime. The civil remedy provision in §2252B provides as follows: "Any person who, while a minor, was a victim of a violation of §2252A, and who suffers personal injury as a result of such violation, regardless of whether the injury occurred while such person was a minor, may sue in any appropriate U.S. District Court and shall recover the actual damages such person sustains and the cost of the suit, including a reasonable attorney's fee. Any person as described in the preceding sentence shall be deemed to have sustained damages of no less than $150,000 in value." Under this statute, parents may bring suits on behalf of their minor children against those who engage in conduct such as possession of images of these children in violation of the child pornography statute, §2252A.

Ashcroft v. Free Speech Coalition

525 U.S. 234 (2002)

Justice KENNEDY delivered the opinion of the Court.

We consider in this case whether the Child Pornography Prevention Act of 1996 (CPPA) abridges the freedom of speech. The CPPA extends the federal prohibition against child pornography to sexually explicit images that appear to depict minors but were produced without using any real children. The statute prohibits, in specific circumstances, possessing or distributing these images, which may be created by using adults who look like minors or by using computer imaging. The new technology makes it possible to create realistic images of children who do not exist. By prohibiting child pornography that does not depict an actual child, the statute goes beyond *New York v. Ferber*, 458 U.S. 747 (1982), which distinguished child pornography from other sexually explicit speech because of the State's interest in protecting the children exploited by the production process. As a general rule, pornography can be banned only if obscene, but under *Ferber*, pornography showing minors can be proscribed whether or not the images are obscene under the definition set forth in *Miller v. California*, 413 U.S. 15 (1973). *Ferber* recognized that "the *Miller* standard, like all general definitions of what may be banned as obscene, does not reflect the State's particular and more compelling interest in prosecuting those who promote the sexual exploitation of children."

The apparent age of persons engaged in sexual conduct is relevant to whether a depiction offends community standards. Pictures of young children engaged in certain acts might be obscene where similar depictions of adults, or perhaps even older adolescents, would not. The CPPA, however, is not directed at speech that is obscene. The CPPA seeks to reach beyond obscenity, and it makes no attempt to conform to the *Miller* standard. For instance, the statute would reach visual depictions, such as movies, even if they have redeeming social value.

Before 1996, Congress defined child pornography as the type of depictions at issue in *Ferber*, images made using actual minors. The CPPA retains that prohibition and adds three other prohibited categories of speech. Section 2256(8)(B) prohibits "any visual depiction, including any photograph, film, video, picture, or computer or computer-generated image or picture," that "is, or appears to be, of a minor engaging in sexually explicit conduct." The prohibition on "any visual depiction" does not depend at all on how the image is produced. The section captures a range of depictions, sometimes called "virtual child pornography," which include computer-generated images, as well as images produced by more traditional means. For instance, the literal terms of the statute embrace a Renaissance painting depicting a scene from classical mythology, a "picture" that "appears to be, of a minor engaging in sexually explicit conduct." The statute also prohibits Hollywood movies, filmed without any child actors, if a jury believes an actor "appears to be" a minor engaging in "actual or simulated sexual intercourse." §2256(2).

These images do not involve, let alone harm, any children in the production process; but Congress decided the materials threaten children in other, less direct, ways. Pedophiles might use the materials to encourage children to participate in sexual activity. Congressional Finding (3). Furthermore, pedophiles might "whet their own sexual appetites" with the pornographic images, "thereby increasing the creation and distribution of child pornography and the sexual abuse and exploitation of actual children." Finding (4). Under these rationales, harm flows from the content of the images, not from the means of their production. In addition, Congress identified another problem created by computer-generated images: Their existence can make it harder to prosecute pornographers who do use real minors. Finding (6)(A). As imaging technology improves, Congress found, it becomes more difficult to prove that a particular picture was produced using actual children. To ensure that defendants possessing child pornography using real minors cannot evade prosecution, Congress extended the ban to virtual child pornography.

Section 2256(8)(C) prohibits a more common and lower tech means of creating virtual images, known as computer morphing. Rather than creating original images, pornographers can alter innocent pictures of real children so that the children appear to be engaged in sexual activity. Although morphed images may fall within the definition of virtual child pornography, they implicate the interests of real children and are in that sense closer to the images in *Ferber*. Respondents do not challenge this provision, and we do not consider it.

Respondents do challenge §2256(8)(D). Section 2256(8)(D) defines child pornography to include any sexually explicit image that was "advertised, promoted, presented, described, or distributed in such a manner that conveys the impression" it depicts "a minor engaging in sexually explicit conduct." One Committee Report identified the provision as directed at sexually explicit images pandered as child pornography. The statute is not so limited in its reach as it punishes even those possessors who took no part in pandering. Once a work has been described as child pornography, the taint remains on the speech in the hands of subsequent possessors, making possession unlawful even though the content otherwise would not be objectionable.

Respondent Free Speech Coalition and others challenged the statute in federal court. The Coalition, a California trade association for the adult-entertainment industry, alleged that its members did not use minors in their sexually explicit works, but they believed some of these materials might fall within the CPPA's expanded definition of child pornography. Other respondents are Bold Type, Inc., publisher of a book advocating the nudist lifestyle; Jim Gingerich, a painter of nudes; and Ron Raffaelli, a photographer specializing in erotic images. Respondents alleged that the "appears to be" and "conveys the impression" provisions are overbroad and vague, chilling them from producing works protected by the First Amendment. The District Court disagreed and granted summary judgment to the Government. The Court of Appeals for the Ninth Circuit reversed. Four other Courts of Appeals sustained the CPPA.

A law imposing criminal penalties on protected speech is a stark example of speech suppression. The CPPA's penalties are indeed severe. A first offender may be imprisoned for 15 years. A repeat offender faces a prison sentence of not less than 5 years and not more than 30 years in prison. With these severe penalties in force, few legitimate movie producers or book publishers, or few other speakers in any capacity, would risk distributing images in or near the uncertain reach of this law. The Constitution gives significant protection from overbroad laws that chill speech within the First Amendment's vast and privileged sphere. Under this principle, the CPPA is unconstitutional on its face if it prohibits a substantial amount of protected expression. *See Broadrick v. Oklahoma*, 413 U.S. 601 (1973).

The sexual abuse of a child is a most serious crime and an act repugnant to the moral instincts of a decent people. In its legislative findings, Congress recognized that there are subcultures of persons who harbor illicit desires for children and commit criminal acts to gratify the impulses. Congress also found that surrounding the serious offenders are those who flirt with these impulses and trade pictures and written accounts of sexual activity with young children.

Congress may pass valid laws to protect children from abuse, and it has. The prospect of crime, however, by itself does not justify laws suppressing protected speech. It is well established that speech may not be prohibited because it concerns subjects offending our sensibilities. *See FCC v. Pacifica Foundation,* 438 U.S. 726 (1978). As a general principle, the First Amendment bars the government from dictating what we see or read or speak or hear. The freedom of speech has its limits; it does not embrace certain categories of speech, including defamation, incitement, obscenity, and pornography produced with real children. While these categories may be prohibited without violating the First Amendment, none of them includes the speech prohibited by the CPPA.

The CPPA is much more than a supplement to the existing federal prohibition on obscenity. The CPPA extends to images that appear to depict a minor engaging in sexually explicit activity without regard to the *Miller* requirements. The materials need not appeal to the prurient interest. Any depiction of sexually explicit activity, no matter how it is presented, is proscribed. The CPPA applies to a picture in a psychology manual, as well as a movie depicting the horrors of sexual abuse. It is not necessary that the image be patently offensive. Pictures of what appear to be 17-year-olds engaging in sexually explicit activity do not in every case contravene community standards. The CPPA prohibits speech despite its serious literary, artistic, political, or scientific value. The statute proscribes the visual depiction of an idea—that of teenagers engaging in sexual activity—that is a fact of modern society and has been a theme in art and literature throughout the ages. Under the CPPA, images are prohibited so long as the persons appear to be under 18 years of age. This is higher than the legal age for marriage in many States, as well as the age at which persons may consent to sexual relations. It is, of course, undeniable that some youths engage in sexual activity before the legal age, either on their own inclination or because they are victims of sexual abuse.

Both themes—teenage sexual activity and the sexual abuse of children— have inspired countless literary works. William Shakespeare created the most famous pair of teenage lovers, one of whom is just 13 years of age. *See Romeo and Juliet,* act I, sc. 2, l. 9. In the drama, Shakespeare portrays the relationship as something splendid and innocent, but not juvenile. The work has inspired no less than 40 motion pictures, some of which suggest that the teenagers consummated their relationship. Shakespeare may not have written sexually explicit scenes for the Elizabethan audience, but were modern directors to adopt a less conventional approach, that fact alone would not compel the conclusion that the work was obscene. Contemporary movies pursue similar themes. Last year's Academy Awards featured the movie, *Traffic,* which was nominated for Best Picture. The film portrays a teenager, identified as a 16-year-old, who becomes addicted to drugs. The viewer sees the degradation of her addiction, which in the end leads her to a filthy room to trade sex for drugs. The year before, *American Beauty* won the Academy Award for Best Picture. In the course of the movie, a teenage girl engages in sexual relations with her teenage boyfriend, and another yields herself to the gratification of a middle-aged man. The film also contains a scene where, although the audience understands the act is not taking place, one character believes he is watching a teenage boy performing a sexual act on an older man.

Our society, like other cultures, has empathy and enduring fascination with the lives and destinies of the young. Art and literature express the vital interest we all have in the formative years we ourselves once knew, when wounds can be so grievous, disappointment so profound, and mistaken choices so tragic, but when moral acts and self-fulfillment are still in reach. Whether or not the films we mention violate the CPPA, they explore themes within the wide sweep of the statute's prohibitions. If these films, or hundreds of others that explore those subjects, contain a single graphic depiction of sexual activity within the statutory definition, the possessor of the film would be subject to severe punishment without inquiry into the work's redeeming value. This is inconsistent with an essential First Amendment rule: The artistic merit of a work does not depend on the presence of a single explicit scene. Under *Miller,* the First Amendment requires that redeeming value be judged by considering the work as a whole. Where the scene is part of the narrative, the work itself does not for this reason become obscene, even though the scene in isolation might be offensive. For this reason, the CPPA cannot be read to prohibit obscenity, because it lacks the required link between its prohibitions and the affront to community standards prohibited by the definition of obscenity.

Ferber upheld a prohibition on the distribution and sale of child pornography, as well as its production, because these acts were "intrinsically related" to the sexual abuse of children in two ways. First, as a permanent record of a child's abuse, the continued circulation itself would harm the child who had participated. Each new publication of the speech would cause new injury to the child's reputation and emotional well-being. Second, because the traffic in child pornography was an economic motive for its production, the State had an interest in closing the distribution network. "The most expeditious if not the only practical method of law enforcement may be to dry up the market for this material by imposing severe criminal penalties on persons selling, advertising, or otherwise promoting the product." Under either rationale, the speech had what the Court in effect held was a proximate link to the crime from which it came. Later, in *Osborne v. Ohio,* 495 U.S. 103 (1990), the Court ruled that these same interests justified a ban on the possession of pornography produced by using children.

In contrast to the speech in *Ferber,* speech that itself is the record of sexual abuse, the CPPA prohibits speech that records no crime and creates no victims by its production. Virtual child pornography is not "intrinsically related" to the sexual abuse of children. While the Government asserts that the images can lead to actual instances of child abuse, the causal link is contingent and indirect. The harm does not necessarily follow from the speech, but depends upon some unquantified potential for subsequent criminal acts. The Government says these indirect harms are sufficient because child pornography rarely can be valuable speech. This argument suffers from two flaws. First, *Ferber*'s judgment about child pornography was based upon how it was made, not on what it communicated. The case reaffirmed that where the speech is neither obscene nor the product of sexual abuse, it does not fall outside the protection of the First Amendment. The second flaw in the Government's position is that *Ferber* did not hold that child pornography is by definition without value. The Court recognized some works in this category might have significant value, but relied on virtual images—the very images prohibited by the CPPA—as an alternative and permissible means of expression.

The Government argues that the CPPA is necessary because pedophiles may use virtual child pornography to seduce children. There are many things innocent in themselves, however, such as cartoons, video games, and candy, that might be used for immoral purposes, yet we would not expect those to be prohibited because they can be misused. The Government, of course, may punish adults who provide unsuitable materials to children, *see Ginsberg v. New York*, 390 U.S. 629 (1968), and it may enforce criminal penalties for unlawful solicitation. The precedents establish that speech within the rights of adults to hear may not be silenced completely in an attempt to shield children from it. In *Butler v. Michigan*, 352 U.S. 380 (1957), the Court invalidated a statute prohibiting distribution of an indecent publication because of its tendency to " 'incite minors to violent or depraved or immoral acts.' " A unanimous Court agreed that the State could not "reduce the adult population to reading only what is fit for children."

Here, the Government wants to keep speech from children not to protect them from its content but to protect them from those who would commit other crimes. However, the Government cannot ban speech fit for adults simply because it may fall into the hands of children. The evil depends upon the actor's unlawful conduct, conduct defined as criminal quite apart from any link to the speech in question. This establishes that the speech ban is not narrowly drawn. The objective is to prohibit illegal conduct, but this restriction goes well beyond that interest by restricting the speech available to law-abiding adults.

The Government submits that virtual child pornography whets the appetites of pedophiles and encourages them to engage in illegal conduct. The mere tendency of speech to encourage unlawful acts is not a sufficient reason for banning it. The government "cannot constitutionally premise legislation on the desirability of controlling a person's private thoughts." *Stanley v. Georgia*, 394 U.S. 557 (1969). First Amendment freedoms are most in danger when the government seeks to control thought or to justify its laws for that impermissible end. The right to think is the beginning of freedom, and speech must be protected from the government because speech is the beginning of thought.

The Court's First Amendment cases draw vital distinctions between words and deeds, between ideas and conduct. The government may not prohibit speech because it increases the chance an unlawful act will be committed "at some indefinite future time." The government may suppress speech for advocating the use of force or a violation of law only if "such advocacy is directed to inciting or producing imminent lawless action and is likely to incite or produce such action." *Brandenburg v. Ohio*, 395 U.S. 444 (1969) (per curiam). There is here no attempt, incitement, solicitation, or conspiracy. The Government has shown no more than a remote connection between speech that might encourage thoughts or impulses and any resulting child abuse. Without a significantly stronger, more direct connection, the Government may not prohibit speech on the ground that it may encourage pedophiles to engage in illegal conduct.

The Government next argues that its objective of eliminating the market for pornography produced using real children necessitates a prohibition on virtual images as well. Virtual images, the Government contends, are indistinguishable from real ones; they are part of the same market and are often exchanged. In this way, it is said, virtual images promote the trafficking in works produced through the exploitation of real children. The hypothesis is somewhat implausible. If virtual images were identical to illegal child pornography, the illegal images would be driven from the market by the indistinguishable substitutes. Few pornographers would risk prosecution by abusing real children if fictional, computerized images would suffice.

In the case of the material covered by *Ferber*, the creation of the speech is itself the crime of child abuse; the prohibition deters the crime by removing the profit motive. Even where there is an underlying crime, however, the Court has not allowed the suppression of speech in all cases. We need not consider where to strike the balance in this case, because here, there is no underlying crime at all. Even if the Government's market deterrence theory were persuasive in some contexts, it would not justify this statute.

Finally, the Government says that the possibility of producing images by using computer imaging makes it very difficult for it to prosecute those who produce pornography by using real children. Experts, we are told, may have difficulty in saying whether the pictures were made by using real children or by using computer imaging. The necessary solution, the argument runs, is to prohibit both kinds of images. The Government may not suppress lawful speech as the means to suppress unlawful speech. The overbreadth doctrine prohibits the Government from banning unprotected speech if a substantial amount of protected speech is prohibited or chilled in the process.

The Government would have us read the CPPA not as a measure suppressing speech but as a law shifting the burden to the accused to prove the speech is lawful. The Government relies on an affirmative defense which allows a defendant to avoid conviction for nonpossession offenses by showing that the materials were produced using only adults and were not otherwise distributed in a manner conveying the impression that they depicted real children. *See* 18 U.S.C. §2252A(C). The Government raises serious constitutional difficulties by seeking to impose on defendant the burden of proving his speech is not unlawful. An affirmative defense applies only after prosecution has begun, and the speaker must himself prove, on pain of a felony conviction, that his conduct falls within the affirmative defense. Where the defendant is not the producer of the work, he may have no way of establishing the identity, or even the existence, of the actors. The statute, moreover, applies to work created before 1996, and the producers themselves may not have preserved the records necessary to meet the burden of proof. Failure to establish the defense can lead to a felony conviction.

We need not decide whether the Government could impose this burden on a speaker. The defense is incomplete and insufficient. It allows persons to be convicted in some instances where they can prove children were not exploited in the production. A defendant charged with possessing, as opposed to distributing, proscribed works may not defend on the ground that the film depicts only adult actors. So while the affirmative defense may protect a movie producer from prosecution for the act of distribution, that same producer, and all other persons in the subsequent distribution chain, could be liable for possessing the prohibited work. Furthermore, the affirmative defense provides no protection to persons who produce speech by using computer imaging, or through other means that do not involve the use of adult actors who appear to be minors. In these cases, the defendant can demonstrate no children were harmed in producing the images, yet the affirmative defense would not bar the prosecution. The affirmative defense cannot save the statute, for it leaves unprotected a substantial amount of speech not tied to the Government's interest in distinguishing images produced using real children from virtual ones.

In sum, §2256(8)(B) covers materials beyond the categories recognized in *Ferber* and *Miller*, and the reasons the Government offers in support of limiting the freedom of speech have no justification in our precedents or in the law of the First Amendment. The provision abridges the freedom to engage in a substantial amount of lawful speech. For this reason, it is overbroad and unconstitutional.

Respondents challenge §2256(8)(D) as well. This provision bans depictions of sexually explicit conduct that are "advertised, promoted, presented, described, or distributed in such a manner that conveys the impression that the material is or contains a visual depiction of a minor engaging in sexually explicit conduct." The parties treat the section as nearly identical to the provision prohibiting materials that appear to be child pornography. In the Government's view, the difference between the two is that "the 'conveys the impression' provision requires the jury to assess the material at issue in light of the manner in which it is promoted." The Government's assumption, however, is that the determination would still depend principally upon the content of the prohibited work.

We disagree. The CPPA prohibits sexually explicit materials that "convey the impression" they depict minors. While that phrase may sound like the "appears to be" prohibition, it requires little judgment about the content of the image. Even if a film contains no sexually explicit scenes involving minors, it could be treated as child pornography if the title and trailers convey the impression that the scenes would be found in the movie. The determination turns on how the speech is presented, not on what is depicted. While the legislative findings address the problems posed by materials that look like child pornography, they are silent on the evils posed by images simply pandered that way.

The Government does not offer a serious defense of this provision. The Court has recognized that pandering may be relevant, as an evidentiary matter, to the question whether particular materials are obscene. *See Ginzburg v. United States*, 383 U.S. 463 (1966). Section 2256(8)(D), however, prohibits a substantial amount of speech that falls outside *Ginzburg*'s rationale. Materials falling within the proscription are tainted and unlawful in the hands of all who receive it, though they bear no responsibility for how it was marketed, sold, or described. The statute does not require that the context be part of an effort at "commercial exploitation." As a consequence, the CPPA does more than prohibit pandering. It prohibits possession of material described, or pandered, as child pornography by someone earlier in the distribution chain. The provision prohibits a sexually explicit film containing no youthful actors, just because it is placed in a box suggesting a prohibited movie. Possession is a crime even when the possessor knows the movie was mislabeled. The First Amendment requires a more precise restriction. §2256(8)(D) is substantially overbroad and in violation of the First Amendment.

For the reasons we have set forth, the prohibitions of §§2256(8)(B) and 2256(8)(D) are overbroad and unconstitutional. We need not address respondents' further contention that the provisions are unconstitutional because of vague statutory language.

The judgment of the Court of Appeals is *affirmed.*

It is so ordered.

Justice O'CONNOR, with whom THE CHIEF JUSTICE and Justice SCALIA join as to Part II, *concurring in the judgment in part* and *dissenting in part.*

The Court has long recognized that the Government has a compelling interest in protecting our Nation's children. These efforts are supported by the CPPA's ban on virtual child pornography. Such images whet the appetites of child molesters who may use the images to seduce young children. Of more serious concern is the prospect that defendants indicted for the production, distribution, or possession of actual child pornography may evade liability by claiming that the images attributed to them are computer-generated. Given the rapid pace of advances in computer-graphics technology, the Government's concern is reasonable. Our cases do not require Congress to wait for harm to occur before it can legislate against it.

The Court concludes that the CPPA's ban on virtual child pornography is overbroad. Overbreadth litigants bear the heavy burden of demonstrating that the regulation forbids a substantial amount of valuable or harmless speech. Respondents have not made such a demonstration. Respondents provide no examples of films or other materials that are wholly computer generated and contain images that "appear to be of minors" engaging in indecent conduct, but that have serious value or do not facilitate child abuse. Their overbreadth challenge therefore fails. I would strike down the CPPA's ban on material that "conveys the impression" that it contains actual child pornography, but uphold the ban on pornographic depictions that "appear to be" of minors so long as it is not applied to youthful adult pornography.

Chief Justice REHNQUIST, with whom Justice SCALIA joins in part, *dissenting.*

Congress has a compelling interest in ensuring the ability to enforce prohibitions of actual child pornography, and we should defer to its findings that rapidly advancing technology soon will make it all but impossible to do so. I agree with Justice O'Connor that serious First Amendment concerns would arise were the Government ever to prosecute someone for simple distribution or possession of a film with literary or artistic value, such as *Traffic* or *American Beauty.* The CPPA need not be construed to reach such materials. Read as a whole, the Act reaches only the sort of "hard core of child pornography" that we found without protection in *Ferber.* So construed, the CPPA bans visual depictions of youthful looking adult actors engaged in *actual* sexual activity; mere *suggestions* of sexual activity, such as youthful looking adult actors squirming under a blanket, are more akin to written descriptions than visual depictions, and thus fall outside the purview of the statute. The inclusion of "simulated" conduct, alongside "actual" conduct, does not change the "hard core" nature of the image banned. Neither actual conduct nor simulated conduct, however, is properly construed to reach depictions such as those in a film portrayal of *Romeo and Juliet.* Indeed, we should be loath to construe a statute as banning film portrayals of Shakespearian tragedies, without some indication—from text or legislative history—that such a result was intended. In fact, Congress explicitly instructed that such a reading of the CPPA would be wholly unwarranted.

Had "sexually explicit conduct" been thought to reach the sort of material the Court says it does, films such as *Traffic* and *American Beauty* would not have been made the way they were. To the extent the CPPA prohibits possession or distribution of materials that "convey the impression" of a child engaged in sexually explicit conduct, that prohibition can and should be limited to reach "the sordid business of pandering" which lies outside the bounds of First Amendment protection. *Ginzburg v. United States,* 383 U.S. 463 (1966). The First Amendment may protect the video shopowner or film distributor who promotes material as "entertaining" or "acclaimed" regardless of whether the material contains depictions of youthful looking adult actors engaged in nonobscene but sexually suggestive conduct. The First Amendment does not, however, protect the panderer. The Court says that "conveys the impression" goes well beyond *Ginzburg* to "prohibit the possession of material described, or pandered, as child pornography by someone earlier in the distribution chain." Consistent with the narrow class of images the CPPA is intended to prohibit, the CPPA can be construed to prohibit only the knowing possession of such materials. The mere possession of materials containing only suggestive depictions of youthful looking adult actors need not be so included.

The aim of ensuring the enforceability of our Nation's child pornography laws is a compelling one. The CPPA is targeted to this aim by extending the definition of child pornography to reach computer-generated images that are virtually indistinguishable from real children engaged in sexually explicit conduct. The statute need not be read to do any more than precisely this, which is not offensive to the First Amendment. I would construe the CPPA in a manner consistent with the First Amendment, reverse the Court of Appeals' judgment, and uphold the statute in its entirety.

Notes

1. Ginsburg *and* Ashcroft. Like the 1968 *Ginsburg* decision regarding the governmental interest in the protection of minors from non-obscene sex-related materials, the 1966 *Ginzburg* decision involving "pandering" as a basis for an obscenity prosecution has retained vitality in the modern era, providing a source of government arguments for regulating speech outside the obscenity context. For a view favoring further expansion of the scope of unprotected speech in the context of sex-related materials, *see Ashcroft v. American Civil Liberties Union* (*Ashcroft II*), 542 U.S. 656 (2004) (Scalia, J., dissenting) ("commercial entities which engage in 'the sordid business of pandering' by 'deliberately emphasizing the sexually provocative aspects of their non-obscene products, in order to catch the salaciously disposed,' engage in constitutionally unprotected behavior").

2. *Website Access.* In *Packingham v. North Carolina*, 137 S. Ct. 1730 (2017), the Court struck down a state law that prohibited registered sex offenders from accessing a number of websites, including commonplace social media websites like Facebook and Twitter. The opinion is set forth later in this chapter.

∼ PROBLEMS ∼

1. *Advancing Technology.* Suppose that computer technology advances to the point that it becomes virtually (no pun intended) impossible to distinguish between actual child pornography and virtual child pornography. Would or should the Court shift its position on Congress's ability to prohibit virtual child pornography? Would it matter whether there was proof that pornographers continued to use actual children in the production of their images?

2. *Pandering Material as Child Pornography.* After *Ashcroft v. Free Speech Coalition*, 535 U.S. 234 (2002), invalidated the "pandering" provision of the Child Pornography Prevention Act, Congress enacted a "pandering" provision in the 2003 Prosecutorial Remedies and Other Tools to End the Exploitation of Children Today Act (PROTECT Act). That Act made it a crime to "knowingly advertise or promote in interstate or foreign commerce any material in a

manner that reflects the belief, or that is intended to cause another to believe, that the material is or contains either a) an obscene visual depiction of a minor engaging in sexually explicit conduct, or b) a visual depiction of an actual minor engaging in sexually explicit conduct." The term *sexually explicit conduct* is defined to include "the lascivious exhibition of the genitals or pubic area of any person." There was no community standard required for determining whether an image of a nude child is "lascivious." In defense of the statute, the government relies on *Ginzburg v. United States*, 383 U.S. 463 (1966). When the statute is challenged on the grounds that it cannot survive strict scrutiny, how should the court rule? Explain. *See United States v. Williams*, 444 F.3d 1286 (11th Cir. 2006) 553 U.S. 285 (2008).

3. *More on the International Treaty Regulating the Internet.* Most countries agree that child pornography should be prohibited. Of course, part of the problem is that some web posters use so-called "anonymous re-mailers" to distribute child pornography. The re-mailer receives child pornography from one source, strips all identifying information from the e-mail message (thereby rendering it anonymous), and then e-mails the child pornography to others. When such re-mailers are used, it can be very difficult to determine the original source of the child pornography. For example, in one case, when governmental officials seized the computers of an anonymous re-mailer in Europe (in an attempt to determine the source of child pornography), the government learned that the child pornography had been sent by another anonymous re-mailer in Asia. In an effort to stop child pornography, what language might you be able to agree to for inclusion in the treaty that would help control the spread of child pornography on the internet? Would you suggest any special provisions that would assist governments in tracking down the source of these anonymous postings?

9. Pornography That Degrades Women

After *Ferber* revealed that the Court was willing to expand the definition of unprotected speech, a movement began to enact ordinances that would define pornography as being harmful to women, and to impose civil penalties on specific types of such pornography, including violent pornography. When these ordinances were adopted by some cities, they were challenged on First Amendment grounds.

American Booksellers Association, Inc. v. Hudnut

771 F.2d 323 (7th Cir. 1985)

EASTERBROOK, Circuit Judge

Indianapolis enacted an ordinance defining "pornography" as a practice that discriminates against women. "Pornography" is to be redressed through the administrative and judicial methods used for other discrimination. The City's definition of "pornography" is considerably different from "obscenity," which the Supreme Court has held is not protected by the First Amendment.

To be "obscene" under *Miller v. California*, 413 U.S. 15 (1973), "a publication must, taken as a whole, appeal to the prurient interest, must contain patently offensive depictions or descriptions of specified sexual conduct, and on the whole have no serious literary, artistic, political, or scientific value." Offensiveness must be assessed under the standards of the community. Both offensiveness and an appeal to something other than "normal, healthy sexual desires" are essential elements of "obscenity."

"Pornography" under the ordinance is "the graphic sexually explicit subordination of women, whether in pictures or in words, that also includes one or more of the following: (1) Women are presented as sexual objects who enjoy pain or humiliation; or (2) Women are presented as sexual objects who experience sexual pleasure in being raped; or (3) Women are presented as sexual objects tied up or cut up or mutilated or bruised or physically hurt, or as dismembered or truncated or fragmented or severed into body parts; or (4) Women are presented as being penetrated by objects or animals; or (5) Women are presented in scenarios of degradation, injury, abasement, torture, shown as filthy or inferior, bleeding, bruised, or hurt in a context that makes these conditions sexual; or (6) Women are presented as sexual objects for domination, conquest, violation, exploitation, possession, or use, or through postures or positions of servility or submission or display." Indianapolis Code §16-3(q). The statute provides that the "use of men, children, or transsexuals in the place of women in paragraphs (1) through (6) above shall also constitute pornography under this section."

The Indianapolis ordinance does not refer to the prurient interest, to offensiveness, or to the standards of the community. It demands attention to particular depictions, not to the work judged as a whole. It is irrelevant under the ordinance whether the work has literary, artistic, political, or scientific value. The City and many amici point to these omissions as virtues. They maintain that pornography influences attitudes, and the statute is a way to alter the socialization of men and women rather than to vindicate community standards of offensiveness. And as one of the principal drafters of the ordinance has asserted, "if a woman is subjected, why should it matter that the work has other value?" Catharine A. MacKinnon, *Pornography, Civil Rights, and Speech*, 20 Harv. C.R.-C.L. L. Rev. 1, 21 (1985).

Those supporting the ordinance say that it will play a role in reducing the tendency of men to view women as sexual objects, a tendency that leads to both unacceptable attitudes and discrimination in the workplace and violence away from it. Those opposing the ordinance point out that much radical feminist literature is explicit and depicts women in ways forbidden by the ordinance. It is unclear how Indianapolis would treat works from James Joyce's *Ulysses* to Homer's *Iliad*; both depict women as submissive objects for conquest and domination.

We do not try to balance the arguments for and against an ordinance such as this. The ordinance discriminates on the ground of the content of the speech. Speech treating women in the approved way—in sexual encounters "premised on equality"—is lawful no matter how sexually explicit. Speech treating women in the disapproved way—as submissive in matters sexual or as enjoying humiliation—is unlawful no matter how significant the literary, artistic, or political qualities of the work taken as a whole. The state may not ordain preferred viewpoints in this way. The Constitution forbids the state to declare one perspective right and silence opponents.

The ordinance contains four prohibitions. People may not "traffic" in pornography, "coerce" others into performing in pornographic works, or "force" pornography on anyone. Anyone injured by someone who has seen or read pornography has a right of action against the maker or seller. Trafficking is defined in §16-3(g)(4) as the "production, sale, exhibition, or distribution of pornography." The offense excludes exhibition in a public or educational library, but a "special display" in a library may be sex discrimination. Section 16-3(g)(4)(C) provides that the trafficking paragraph "shall not be construed to make isolated passages or isolated parts actionable."

"Coercion into pornographic performance" is defined in §16-3(g)(5) as "coercing, intimidating or fraudulently inducing any person into performing for pornography." The ordinance specifies that proof of any of the following "shall not constitute a defense: I. That the person is a woman; VI. That the person has previously posed for sexually explicit pictures with anyone; VIII. That the person actually consented to a use of the performance that is changed into pornography; IX. That the person knew that the purpose of the acts or events in question was to make pornography; XI. That the person signed a contract, or made statements affirming a willingness to cooperate in the production of pornography; XII. That no physical force, threats, or weapons were used in the making of the pornography; or XIII. That the person was paid or otherwise compensated."

"Forcing pornography on a person," according to §16-3(g)(5), is the "forcing of pornography on any woman, man, child, or transsexual in any place of employment, in education, in a home, or in any public place." The statute does not define forcing, but one of its authors states that the definition reaches pornography shown to medical students as part of their education or given to language students for translation. *MacKinnon, supra,* at 40-41.

Section 16-3(g)(7) defines as a prohibited practice the "assault, physical attack, or injury of any woman, man, child, or transsexual in a way that is directly caused by specific pornography."

For purposes of all four offenses, it is generally "not a defense that the respondent did not know or intend that the materials were pornography." Section 16-3(g)(8). But the ordinance provides that damages are unavailable in trafficking cases unless the complainant proves "that the respondent knew or had reason to know that the materials were pornography." It is a complete defense to a trafficking case that all of the materials in question were pornography only by virtue of category (6) of the definition of pornography. In cases of assault caused by pornography, those who seek damages from "a seller, exhibitor or distributor" must show that the defendant knew or had reason to know of the material's status as pornography. By implication, those who seek damages from an author need not show this.

A woman aggrieved by trafficking in pornography may file a complaint "as a woman acting against the subordination of women" with the office of equal opportunity. A man, child, or transsexual also may protest trafficking "but must prove injury in the same way that a woman is injured." Subsection (a) also provides, however, that "any person claiming to be aggrieved" by trafficking, coercion, forcing, or assault may complain against the "perpetrators." The office may make findings and enter orders, including both orders to cease and desist and orders to take further affirmative action including but not limited to the power to restore complainant's losses. The district court held the ordinance unconstitutional.

"If there is any fixed star in our constitutional constellation, it is that no official, high or petty, can prescribe what shall be orthodox in politics, nationalism, religion, or other matters of opinion or force citizens to confess by word or act their faith therein." *West Virginia State Board of Education v. Barnette*, 319 U.S. 624 (1943). Under the First Amendment the government must leave to the people the evaluation of ideas. Bald or subtle, an idea is as powerful as the audience allows it to be. A belief may be pernicious—the beliefs of Nazis led to the death of millions, those of the Klan to the repression of millions. A pernicious belief may prevail. Totalitarian governments today rule much of the planet, practicing suppression of billions and spreading dogma that may enslave others. One of the things that separates our society from theirs is our absolute right to propagate opinions that the government finds wrong or even hateful.

Under the ordinance graphic sexually explicit speech is "pornography" or not depending on the perspective the author adopts. Speech that "subordinates" women and also, for example, presents women as enjoying pain, humiliation, or rape, or even simply presents women in "positions of servility or submission or display" is forbidden, no matter how great the literary or political value of the work taken as a whole. Speech that portrays women in positions of equality is lawful, no matter how graphic the sexual content. This is thought control. It establishes an "approved" view of women, of how they may react to sexual encounters, of how the sexes may relate to each other. Those who espouse the approved view may use sexual images; those who do not, may not.

Indianapolis justifies the ordinance on the ground that pornography affects thoughts. Men who see women depicted as subordinate are more likely to treat them so. Pornography is an aspect of dominance. It does not persuade people so much as change them. It works by socializing, by establishing the expected and the permissible. In this view pornography is not an idea; pornography is the injury.

There is much to this perspective. Beliefs are also facts. People often act in accordance with the images and patterns they find around them. People raised in a religion tend to accept the tenets of that religion, often without independent examination. People taught from birth that black people are fit only for slavery rarely rebelled against that creed; beliefs coupled with the self-interest of the masters established a social structure that inflicted great harm while enduring for centuries. Words and images act at the level of the subconscious before they persuade at the level of the conscious. Even the truth has little chance unless a statement fits within the framework of beliefs that may never have been subjected to rational study.

Therefore we accept the premises of this legislation. Depictions of subordination tend to perpetuate subordination. The subordinate status of women in turn leads to affront and lower pay at work, insult and injury at home, battery and rape on the streets. In the language of the legislature, "pornography is central in creating and maintaining sex as a basis of discrimination. Pornography is a systematic practice of exploitation and subordination based on sex which differentially harms women. The bigotry and contempt it produces, with the acts of aggression it fosters, harm women's opportunities for equality and rights of all kinds." Indianapolis Code §16-1(a)(2).

Yet this simply demonstrates the power of pornography as speech. All of these unhappy effects depend on mental intermediation. Pornography affects how people see the world, their fellows, and social relations. If pornography is what pornography does, so is other speech. Racial bigotry, anti-semitism, violence on television, reporters' biases—these and many more influence the culture and shape our socialization. None is directly answerable by more speech, unless that speech too finds its place in the popular culture. Yet all is protected as speech, however insidious. Any other answer leaves the government in control of all of the institutions of culture, the great censor and director of which thoughts are good for us.

Sexual responses often are unthinking responses, and the association of sexual arousal with the subordination of women therefore may have a substantial effect. But almost all cultural stimuli provoke unconscious responses. Religious ceremonies condition their participants. Television scripts contain unarticulated assumptions. People may be conditioned in subtle ways. If the fact that speech plays a role in a process of conditioning were enough to permit governmental regulation, that would be the end of freedom of speech.

Indianapolis emphasizes the injury that models in pornographic films and pictures may suffer. The record contains materials depicting sexual torture, penetration of women by red-hot irons and the like. The image of pain is not necessarily pain. In *Body Double,* a woman who has disrobed and presented a sexually explicit display is murdered by an intruder with a drill. The film is sexually explicit and a murder occurs—yet no one believes that the actress suffered pain or died. In *Carnal Knowledge* a woman grovels to please the sexual whims of a character played by Jack Nicholson; no one believes that there was a real sexual submission. Depictions may affect slavery, war, or sexual roles, but a book about slavery is not itself slavery, or a book about death by poison a murder.

Much of Indianapolis's argument rests on the belief that when speech is "unanswerable," and the metaphor that there is a "marketplace of ideas" does not apply, the First Amendment does not apply either. The metaphor is honored on the ground that the truth will prevail. The Framers undoubtedly believed it. As a general matter it is true. But the Constitution does not make the dominance of truth a necessary condition of freedom of speech. To say that it does would be to confuse an outcome of free speech with a necessary condition for the application of the amendment.

A power to limit speech on the ground that truth has not yet prevailed and is not likely to prevail implies the power to declare truth. Under the First Amendment, however, there is no such thing as a false idea so the government may not restrict speech on the ground that in a free exchange truth is not yet dominant. Supporters of minority candidates may be forever "excluded" from the political process because their candidates never win, because few people believe their positions. This does not mean that freedom of speech has failed.

We come, finally, to the argument that pornography is "low value" speech, that it is enough like obscenity that Indianapolis may prohibit it. Some cases hold that speech far removed from politics and other subjects at the core of the Framers' concerns may be subjected to special regulation. *E.g., FCC v. Pacifica Foundation*, 438 U.S. 726 (1978). These cases do not sustain statutes that select among viewpoints. At all events, "pornography" is not low value speech within the meaning of these cases. Indianapolis seeks to prohibit certain speech because it believes this speech influences social relations and politics on a grand scale, that it controls attitudes at home and in the legislature. This precludes a characterization of the speech as low value. True, pornography and obscenity have sex in common. But Indianapolis left out of its definition any reference to literary, artistic, political, or scientific value. The ordinance applies to graphic sexually explicit subordination in works great and small. The Court sometimes balances the value of speech against the costs of its restriction, but it does this by category of speech and not by the content of particular works. Indianapolis has created an approved point of view and so loses the support of these cases.

Any rationale we could imagine in support of this ordinance could not be limited to sex discrimination. Free speech has been on balance an ally of those seeking change. Governments that want stasis start by restricting speech. Culture is a powerful force of continuity; Indianapolis paints pornography as part of the culture of power. Change in any complex system ultimately depends on the ability of outsiders to challenge accepted views and the reigning institutions. Without a strong guarantee of freedom of speech, there is no effective right to challenge what is.

The definition of "pornography" is unconstitutional. No construction or excision of particular terms could save it. Without question a state may prohibit fraud, trickery, or the use of force to induce people to perform—in pornographic films or in any other films. Such a statute may be written without regard to the viewpoint depicted in the work. But the Indianapolis ordinance is not neutral with respect to viewpoint. The ban on distribution of works containing coerced performances is limited to pornography; coercion is irrelevant if the work is not "pornography," and we have held the definition of "pornography" to be defective root and branch.

The offense of forcing pornography on unwilling recipients is harder to assess. Many kinds of forcing may themselves be protected speech. *Rowan v. Post Office*, 397 U.S. 728 (1970), shows that a state may permit people to insulate themselves from categories of speech—in *Rowan* sexual mail—but that the government must leave the decision about what items are forbidden in the hands of the potentially offended recipients. Exposure to sex is not something the government may prevent. We therefore could not save the offense of "forcing" by redefining "pornography" as all sexually-offensive speech or some related category. The statute needs a definition of "forcing" that removes the government from the role of censor.

The section creating remedies for injuries and assaults attributable to pornography also is salvageable in principle. The First Amendment does not prohibit redress of all injuries caused by speech. Cases such as *Brandenburg v. Ohio* and *NAACP v. Claiborne Hardware* hold that a state may not penalize speech that does not cause immediate injury. But we do not doubt that if, immediately after the Klan's rally in *Brandenburg,* a mob had burned to the ground the house of a nearby black person, that person could have recovered damages from the speaker who whipped the crowd into a frenzy. Certainly no damages could be awarded unless the harm flowed directly from the speech and there was an element of intent on the part of the speaker.

Much speech is dangerous. Chemists whose work might help someone build a bomb, political theorists whose papers might start political movements that lead to riots, speakers whose ideas attract violent protesters, all these and more leave loss in their wake. Unless the remedy is very closely confined, it could be more dangerous to speech than all the libel judgments in history. The constitutional requirements for a valid recovery for assault caused by speech might turn out to be too rigorous for any plaintiff to meet. But the Indianapolis ordinance requires the complainant to show that the attack was "directly caused by specific pornography," and it is not beyond the realm of possibility that a state court could construe this limitation in a way that would make the statute constitutional. We are not authorized to prevent the state from trying.

No amount of struggle with particular words and phrases in this ordinance can leave anything in effect. The district court came to the same conclusion. Its judgment is therefore
Affirmed.

Note and Question: A "Feminist Critique"

In evaluating the Indianapolis ordinance, consider Nadine Strossen, *A Feminist Critique of "the" Feminist Critique of Pornography,* 79 Va. L. Rev. 1099 (1993). Strossen argues that, given "the pervasive presence of sexist, violent imagery in mainstream American culture, most such imagery would remain intact, even if 'pornography' could be effectively suppressed." Moreover, she questions the assumptions on which the ordinance is based: The "conclusion that the costs of 'pornography' censorship outweigh its putative benefits, in terms of women's rights, is reinforced by the lack of evidence to substantiate the alleged casual link between exposure to 'pornography' and misogynistic discrimination or violence." Finally, she argues that the "speculative, attenuated benefits of censoring 'pornography,' in terms of reducing violence and discrimination against women, are far outweighed by the substantial, demonstrable costs of such a censorship regime in terms of women's rights." She notes that "throughout history, censorial power has consistently been used to stifle women's sexuality, women's expression, and women's full and equal participation in our society." As a result, she concludes that "as is true for all relatively disempowered groups, women have a special stake in preserving our system of free expression. For those women who find certain 'pornographic' imagery troubling, their most effective weapon is to raise their voices and say so." Do you agree?

∾ PROBLEMS ∾

1. *Redrafting the Ordinance.* Assume that the Indianapolis City Council wants to redraft the ordinance in a way that may survive constitutional challenge. You are the city attorney. How would you redraft the ordinance?

2. *More on the International Treaty Regulating the Internet.* Again, as part of their general effort to protect individuals against degradation of their human dignity, European delegates demand that the treaty contain explicit language prohibiting the "degradation of women." In light of the First Amendment, can you agree to such language? What language might you agree to that could (potentially) be acceptable to (or, at least, would make a good-faith effort to satisfy) the European delegates?

10. Near Obscene

After the boundaries of "obscene" speech were settled in *Miller,* the question remained whether content regulations of non-obscene materials related to sex should be treated in the same manner as other content regulations. Varying answers to this question have been given, and although all non-obscene sex-related speech is theoretically treated as "protected speech," there are contexts in which the "low value" of that speech may be used to justify deviation from the strict scrutiny model. For example, some regulations of non-obscene speech that is close to the obscenity boundary, and hence "near obscene," have provoked controversial uses of a variety of "content-neutral" doctrines, including the "time, place, manner" test, the "secondary effects" analysis, and the *O'Brien* test. Sharp divisions on the Court have produced opinions where only a plurality consensus can be reached, sometimes to yield to a majority produced after years of debate. However, some "near-obscene" speech regulations remain subject to strict scrutiny analysis. The "near-obscene" category of speech, not envisioned before *Miller,* is not a category that is characterized by uniform standards of review, and since the 1980s it has become one of the most rapidly evolving fields of speech doctrine.

Erznoznik v. City of Jacksonville

422 U.S. 205 (1975)

Mr. Justice POWELL delivered the opinion of the Court.

This case presents a challenge to the facial validity of a Jacksonville, Fla., ordinance that prohibits showing films containing nudity by a drive-in movie theater when its screen is visible from a public street or place.

Appellant, Richard Erznoznik, is the manager of the University Drive-In Theatre in Jacksonville. When the theatre was showing *Class of '74,* a movie rated R, he was charged with the crime of exhibiting a motion picture, visible from public streets, in which "female buttocks and bare breasts were shown." The ordinance provides: "It shall be unlawful and it is hereby declared a public nuisance for any ticket seller, ticket taker, usher, motion picture projection machine operator, manager, owner, or any other person connected with or employed by any drive-in theater in the City to exhibit, or aid or assist in exhibiting, any motion picture, slide, or other exhibit in which the human male or female bare buttocks, human female bare breasts, or human bare pubic areas are shown, if such motion picture, slide, or other exhibit is visible from any public street or public place." Appellant successfully stayed the prosecution so that the validity of the ordinance could be tested. The city introduced evidence showing that appellant's screen is visible from two adjacent public streets and a nearby church parking lot and people had been observed watching films while sitting outside the theater in parked cars and in the grass.

The City concedes that its ordinance sweeps beyond the permissible restraints on obscenity, and applies to films that are protected by the First Amendment. Nevertheless, it maintains that any movie containing nudity which is visible from a public place may be suppressed as a nuisance and that it may protect its citizens against unwilling exposure to materials that may be offensive. Jacksonville's ordinance, however, does not protect citizens from all movies that might offend; rather it singles out films containing nudity, presumably because lawmakers considered them especially offensive to passersby.

This Court has considered analogous issues—pitting the First Amendment rights of speakers against the privacy rights of those who may be unwilling viewers or auditors—in a variety of contexts. Some general principles have emerged. A State or municipality may protect individual privacy by enacting reasonable time, place, and manner regulations applicable to all speech irrespective of content. But when the government, acting as censor, undertakes selectively to shield the public from some kinds of speech on the ground that they are more offensive than others, the First Amendment strictly limits its power. Such selective restrictions have been upheld only when the speaker intrudes on the privacy of the home, or the degree of captivity makes it impractical for the unwilling viewer or auditor to avoid exposure. As Mr. Justice Harlan cautioned: "The ability of government, consonant with the Constitution, to shut off discourse solely to protect others from hearing it is dependent upon a showing that substantial privacy interests are being invaded in an essentially intolerable manner. Any broader view of this authority would effectively empower a majority to silence dissidents simply as a matter of personal predilections." *Cohen v. California*, 403 U.S. at 21.

The plain, if at times disquieting, truth is that in our pluralistic society, constantly proliferating new and ingenious forms of expression, "we are inescapably captive audiences for many purposes." Much that we encounter offends our esthetic, if not our political and moral, sensibilities. Nevertheless, the Constitution does not permit government to decide which types of otherwise protected speech are sufficiently offensive to require protection for the unwilling listener or viewer. Absent narrow circumstances, the burden normally falls upon the viewer to "avoid further bombardment of (his) sensibilities simply by averting (his) eyes." *Cohen v. California, supra*, 403 U.S. at 21.

The Jacksonville ordinance discriminates among movies solely on the basis of content. Its effect is to deter drive-in theaters from showing movies containing any nudity, however innocent or even educational. This discrimination cannot be justified as a means of preventing significant intrusions on privacy. The ordinance seeks only to keep these films from being seen from public streets and places where the offended viewer readily can avert his eyes. In short, the screen of a drive-in theater is not "so obtrusive as to make it impossible for an unwilling individual to avoid exposure to it." Thus, we conclude that the limited privacy interest of persons on the public streets cannot justify this censorship of otherwise protected speech on the basis of its content.

The City maintains that even though it cannot prohibit the display of films containing nudity to adults, the ordinance is a reasonable means of protecting minors from this type of visual influence. It is well settled that a State or municipality can adopt more stringent controls on communicative materials available to youths than on those available to adults. *See, e.g., Ginsberg v. New York*, 390 U.S. 629 (1968). Nevertheless, minors are entitled to a significant measure of First Amendment protection, and only in relatively narrow and well-defined circumstances may government bar public dissemination of protected materials to them. Assuming the ordinance is aimed at prohibiting youths from viewing the films, the restriction is broader than permissible. The ordinance is not directed against sexually explicit nudity, nor is it otherwise limited. Rather, it sweepingly forbids display of all films containing any uncovered buttocks or breasts, irrespective of context or pervasiveness. Thus it would bar a film containing a picture of a baby's buttocks, the nude body of a war victim, or scenes from a culture in which nudity is indigenous. The ordinance also might prohibit newsreel scenes of the opening of an art exhibit as well as shots of bathers on a beach. Clearly all nudity cannot be deemed obscene even as to minors. Nor can such a broad restriction be justified by any other governmental interest pertaining to minors. Speech that is neither obscene as to youths nor subject to some other legitimate proscription cannot be suppressed solely to protect the young from ideas or images that a legislative body thinks unsuitable for them. In most circumstances, the values protected by the First Amendment are no less applicable when government seeks to control the flow of information to minors. Thus, if Jacksonville's ordinance is intended to regulate expression accessible to minors it is overbroad in its proscription.

At oral argument the City sought to justify its ordinance as a traffic regulation. It claimed that nudity on a drive-in movie screen distracts passing motorists, thus slowing the flow of traffic and increasing the likelihood of accidents. Nothing in the record or in the ordinance suggests that it is aimed at traffic regulation. But even if this were the purpose of the ordinance, it nonetheless would be invalid. By singling out movies containing even the most fleeting and innocent glimpses of nudity the legislative classification is strikingly underinclusive. There is no reason to think that a wide variety of other scenes in the customary screen diet, ranging from soap opera to violence, would be any less distracting to the passing motorist. This Court frequently has upheld underinclusive classifications on the sound theory that a legislature may deal with one part of a problem without addressing all of it. This presumption of statutory validity, however, has less force when a classification turns on the subject matter of expression. Even a traffic regulation cannot discriminate on the basis of content unless there are clear reasons for the distinctions.

The Court has held that a state statute should not be deemed facially invalid unless it is not readily subject to a narrowing construction by the state courts, and its deterrent effect on legitimate expression is both real and substantial. *See Broadrick v. Oklahoma*, 413 U.S. 601 (1973). The ordinance by its plain terms is not easily susceptible of a narrowing construction. Moreover, the deterrent effect of this ordinance is both real and substantial. Since it applies specifically to all persons employed by or connected with drive-in theaters, the owners and operators of these theaters are faced with an unwelcome choice: to avoid prosecution of themselves and their employees they must either restrict their movie offerings or construct adequate protective fencing which may be extremely expensive or even physically impracticable.

Where First Amendment freedoms are at stake we have repeatedly emphasized that precision of drafting and clarity of purpose are essential. These prerequisites are absent here. Accordingly the judgment below is reversed.

Reversed.

Mr. Chief Justice BURGER, with whom Mr. Justice REHNQUIST joins, *dissenting.*

Whatever validity the notion that passersby may protect their sensibilities by averting their eyes may have when applied to words printed on an individual's jacket, it distorts reality to apply that notion to the outsize screen of a drive-in movie theater that is a unique type of eye-catching display that can be highly intrusive and distracting. Public authorities have a legitimate interest in regulating such displays under the police power. I think it not unreasonable for lawmakers to believe that public nudity on a giant screen, visible at night to hundreds of drivers of automobiles, may have a tendency to divert attention from their task and cause accidents.

The owner of a drive-in movie theater is not prevented from exhibiting non-obscene films involving nudity so long as he effectively shields the screen from public view. Thus, the ordinance is not a restriction of any "message." The First Amendment interests involved in this case are trivial at best. Assuming that there could be a play performed in a theater by nude actors involving genuine communication of ideas, the same conduct in a public park or street could be prosecuted under an ordinance prohibiting indecent exposure. This is so because the police power has long been interpreted to authorize the regulation of nudity in areas to which all members of the public have access, regardless of any incidental effect upon communication. Whether such regulation is justified as necessary to protect public mores or simply to insure the undistracted enjoyment of open areas by the greatest number of people—or for traffic safety—its rationale applies a fortiori to giant displays which through technology are capable of revealing and emphasizing the most intimate details of human anatomy.

∼ PROBLEMS: ORDINANCE DRAFTING ∼

Assume that you are asked to help the city council draft an ordinance regulating drive-in movie theaters that is addressed to the government interest in traffic safety. Can such an ordinance be drafted without overbreadth problems? In order to avoid strict scrutiny of content-based regulations of drive-in movie theaters as exemplified in *Erznoznik*, the city council asks you to draft an ordinance that may be deemed to be "content-neutral" and that will also solve a variety of problems the city has with drive-in movie theaters. First, think of all the possible problems that the city may have with such theaters. Then explain what sorts of suggested ordinances you can offer.

Young v. American Mini Theatres, Inc.

427 U.S. 50 (1976)

Mr. Justice STEVENS delivered the opinion of the Court. Part III of this opinion is joined by only THE CHIEF JUSTICE, Mr. Justice WHITE, and Mr. Justice REHNQUIST.

Detroit adopted ordinances requiring that "adult" theaters be dispersed. Specifically, an adult theater may not be located within 1,000 feet of any two other "regulated uses" or within 500 feet of a residential area. The term "regulated uses" includes 10 different kinds of establishments in addition to adult theaters including adult bookstores; cabarets; establishments for the sale of beer or intoxicating liquor for consumption on the premises; hotels or motels; pawnshops; pool or billiard halls; public lodging houses; secondhand stores; shoeshine parlors; and taxi dance halls.

The classification of a theater as "adult" is expressly predicated on the character of the motion pictures which it exhibits. If the theater is used to present "material distinguished or characterized by an emphasis on matter depicting, describing or relating to 'Specified Sexual Activities' or 'Specified Anatomical Areas,'" it is an adult establishment. "Specified Sexual Activities" is defined as: 1) Human genitals in a state of sexual stimulation or arousal; 2) Acts of human masturbation, sexual intercourse, or sodomy; 3) Fondling or other erotic touching of human genitals, pubic region, buttock, or female breast. And "Specified Anatomical Areas" is defined as: 1) Less than completely and opaquely covered: a) human genitals, pubic region, b) buttock, and c) female breast below a point immediately above the top of the areola; and 2) Human male genitals in a discernibly turgid state, even if completely and opaquely covered.

The ordinance involved amendments to an "Anti–Skid Row Ordinance" adopted 10 years earlier. At that time the Detroit Common Council made a finding that some uses of property are especially injurious to a neighborhood when they are concentrated in limited areas. The decision to add adult motion picture theaters and adult book stores to the list was, in part, a response to the significant growth in the number of such establishments. In the opinion of urban planners and real estate experts, the location of several such businesses in the same neighborhood tends to attract an undesirable quantity and quality of transients, adversely affects property values, causes an increase in crime, especially prostitution, and encourages residents and businesses to move elsewhere.

I

We find it unnecessary to consider the validity of the vagueness arguments. If the statute's deterrent effect on legitimate expression is not "both real and substantial," and if the statute is "readily subject to a narrowing construction by the state courts," *see Erznoznik v. City of Jacksonville,* 422 U.S. 205, the litigant is not permitted to assert the rights of third parties. We are not persuaded that the Detroit zoning ordinances will have a significant deterrent effect on the exhibition of films protected by the First Amendment. Since there is surely a less vital interest in the uninhibited exhibition of material that is on the borderline between pornography and artistic expression than in the free dissemination of ideas of social and political significance, and since the limited amount of uncertainty in the ordinances is easily susceptible of a narrowing construction, this is an inappropriate case in which to adjudicate the hypothetical claims of persons not before the Court.

II

Respondents argue that the ordinances are invalid prior restraints on free speech. The ordinances do not impose a limit on the total number of adult theaters which may operate in the city of Detroit. There is no claim that distributors or exhibitors of adult films are denied access to the market or, conversely, that the viewing public is unable to satisfy its appetite for sexually explicit fare. We have no doubt that the municipality may control the location of theaters as well as the location of other commercial establishments, either by confining them to certain specified commercial zones or by requiring that they be dispersed throughout the city. We are persuaded that the 1,000-foot restriction does not, in itself, create an impermissible restraint on protected communication. The city's interest in planning and regulating the use of property for commercial purposes is clearly adequate to support that kind of restriction applicable to all theaters within the city limits.

III

As we said in *Mosley:* "Above all else, the First Amendment means that government has no power to restrict expression because of its message, its ideas, its subject matter, or its content." *Police Dept. of Chicago v. Mosley,* 408 U.S. 92 (1972). But the question whether speech is, or is not, protected by the First Amendment often depends on the content of the speech. Even though we recognize that the First Amendment will not tolerate the total suppression of erotic materials that have some arguably artistic value, it is manifest that society's interest in protecting this type of expression is of a wholly different, and lesser, magnitude than the interest in untrammeled political debate. The State may legitimately use the content of these materials as the basis for placing them in a different classification from other motion pictures.

The remaining question is whether the line drawn by these ordinances is justified by the city's interest in preserving the character of its neighborhoods. It is not our function to appraise the wisdom of its decision to require adult theaters to be separated rather than concentrated in the same areas. In either event, the city's interest in attempting to preserve the quality of urban life is one that must be accorded high respect. Moreover, the city must be allowed a reasonable opportunity to experiment with solutions to admittedly serious problems.

Since what is ultimately at stake is nothing more than a limitation on the place where adult films may be exhibited, even though the determination of whether a particular film fits that characterization turns on the nature of its content, we conclude that the city's interest in the present and future character of its neighborhoods adequately supports its classification of motion pictures. We hold that the zoning ordinances requiring that adult motion picture theaters not be located within 1,000 feet of two other regulated uses does not violate the constitution.

The judgment of the Court of Appeals is
Reversed.

Mr. Justice POWELL, *concurring in the judgment and portions of the opinion.*

There is no indication that the application of the Anti–Skid Row Ordinance to adult theaters has the effect of suppressing production of or, to any significant degree, restricting access to adult movies. At most the impact of the ordinance on First Amendment interests is incidental and minimal. Detroit has silenced no message, has invoked no censorship, and has imposed no limitation upon those who wish to view them. The ordinance is addressed only to the places at which this type of expression may be presented, a restriction that does not interfere with content. Nor is there any significant overall curtailment of adult movie presentations, or the opportunity for a message to reach an audience. In these circumstances, it is appropriate to analyze the permissibility of Detroit's action under the four-part test of *United States v. O'Brien*, 391 U.S. 367 (1968). Under that test, a governmental regulation is sufficiently justified, despite its incidental impact upon First Amendment interests, "if it is within the constitutional power of the Government; if it furthers an important or substantial governmental interest; if the governmental interest is unrelated to the suppression of free expression; and if the incidental restriction on First Amendment freedoms is no greater than is essential to the furtherance of that interest." Under the *O'Brien* analysis, Justice Powell would uphold the ordinance.

Mr. Justice STEWART, with whom Mr. Justice BRENNAN, Mr. Justice MARSHALL, and Mr. Justice BLACKMUN join, *dissenting.*

This case involves the constitutional permissibility of selective interference with protected speech whose content is thought to produce distasteful effects. The Court has not shied from its responsibility to protect "offensive" speech from governmental interference. *Erznoznik v. City of Jacksonville* is almost on "all fours" with this case. Much speech that seems to be of little or no value will enter the market place of ideas, threatening the quality of our social discourse and, more generally, the serenity of our lives. But that is the price to be paid for constitutional freedom.

Question: Time, Place, and Manner Analysis

Does the *Young* case pose a public forum issue in the same way that *Erznoznik* does? If not, then why and how is the "time, place, manner" doctrine being used in the *Young* plurality opinion?

∾ PROBLEMS ∾

1. *More on Zoning.* A city adopts a zoning ordinance that prohibits adult motion picture theaters from locating within 1,000 feet of any residential zone, single- or multiple-family dwelling, church, park, or school. The term *adult motion picture theater* was defined as "an enclosed building used for presenting motion picture films, video cassettes, cable television, or any other such visual media, distinguished or characterized by an emphasis on matter depicting, describing or relating to 'specified sexual activities' or 'specified anatomical areas' for

observation by patrons therein." Under the precedent established in *Young*, is this ordinance valid? Suppose that the city argues that the ordinance is directed at the "secondary effects" of adult theaters, including crime prevention, protection of the city's retail trade, the maintenance of property values, and a general desire to "protect and preserve the quality of the city's neighborhoods, commercial districts, and the quality of urban life." Is there a "substantial government interest" that supports the regulation? Does the city leave open "reasonable alternative avenues of communication"? *See City of Renton v. Playtime Theatres, Inc.*, 475 U.S. 41 (1986).

2. *Requiring Adult Bookstores to Close at Night.* A city enacts an ordinance requiring all adult bookstores to close between the hours of midnight and 10:00 A.M. The asserted justification for the ordinance is that there will be fewer armed robberies. The ordinance allows other commercial establishments to remain open, including liquor stores, pharmacies, and convenience stores, on the theory that the patrons of adult bookstores would be more likely to be carrying cash than the patrons of other establishments, and therefore are more attractive targets for potential robbers. Is the ordinance constitutional? Would it matter that total crime increased following enactment of the ordinance? *See Annex Books, Inc. v. City of Indianapolis*, 740 F.3d 1136 (7th Cir. 2014).

Schad v. Borough of Mount Ephraim

452 U.S. 61 (1981)

Justice WHITE delivered the opinion of the Court.

Appellants, who operate an adult bookstore, were convicted of offering coin-operated live dancing that could be viewed behind a glass panel. As the Mount Ephraim Code has been construed, "live entertainment," including nude dancing, is "not a permitted use in any establishment" in the Borough of Mount Ephraim. By excluding live entertainment throughout the Borough, the ordinance prohibits a wide range of expression that has long been held to be within the protections of the First and Fourteenth Amendments. Entertainment, as well as political and ideological speech, falls within the First Amendment guarantee. Nor may an entertainment program be prohibited solely because it displays the nude human figure. "Nudity alone" does not place otherwise protected material outside the mantle of the First Amendment.

The Mount Ephraim ordinance prohibits all live entertainment in the Borough: no property in the Borough may be principally used for the commercial production of plays, concerts, musicals, dance, or any other form of live entertainment. Borough counsel conceded that noncommercial live entertainment such as a high school play would be allowed if the school did not charge admission. "Because overbroad laws, like vague ones, deter privileged activities, our cases firmly establish appellant's standing to raise an overbreadth challenge." *Grayned v. City of Rockford*, 408 U.S. 104 (1972).

This case is not controlled by *Young v. American Mini Theatres, Inc.*, 427 U.S. 50 (1976). Although the Court there stated that a zoning ordinance is not invalid merely because it regulates activity protected under the First Amendment, it emphasized that the challenged restriction on the location of adult movie theaters imposed a minimal burden on protected speech. The restriction did not affect the number of adult movie theaters that could operate in the city; it merely dispersed them. The Court did not imply that a municipality could ban all adult theaters—much less all live entertainment or all nude dancing—from its commercial districts citywide. The evidence indicated that the concentration of adult movie theaters in limited areas led to deterioration of surrounding neighborhoods, and it was concluded that the city had justified the incidental burden on First Amendment interests resulting from merely dispersing, but not excluding, adult theaters.

Mount Ephraim has not adequately justified its substantial restriction of protected activity. First, the Borough contends that permitting live entertainment would conflict with its plan to create a commercial area that caters only to the "immediate needs" of its residents and that would enable them to purchase at local stores the few items they occasionally forgot to buy outside the Borough. But the Borough permits motels, hardware stores, lumber stores, banks, offices, and car showrooms in its commercial zones. Virtually the only item or service that may not be sold in a commercial zone is live entertainment. The Borough's first justification is patently insufficient. Second, Mount Ephraim contends that it may selectively exclude commercial live entertainment from the broad range of commercial uses permitted in the Borough to avoid the problems that may be associated with live entertainment, such as parking, trash, police protection, and medical facilities. It may be that some forms of live entertainment would create problems that are not associated with the commercial uses presently permitted in Mount Ephraim. Yet this ordinance is not narrowly drawn to respond to what might be the distinctive problems arising from certain types of live entertainment. The Borough has not established that its interests could not be met by restrictions that are less intrusive on protected forms of expression.

The Borough also suggests that the zoning ordinance is a reasonable "time, place, and manner" restriction. To be reasonable, time, place, and manner restrictions not only must serve significant state interests but also must leave open adequate alternative channels of communication. Here, the Borough totally excludes all live entertainment, including nonobscene nude dancing that is otherwise protected by the First Amendment. The Borough contends that live entertainment in general and nude dancing in particular are amply available in close-by areas outside the limits of the Borough. "One is not to have the exercise of his liberty of expression in appropriate places abridged on the plea that it may be exercised in some other place." *Schneider v. State*, 308 U.S. 147 (1939).

Accordingly, the convictions of these appellants are infirm, and the judgment of the Appellate Division of the Superior Court of New Jersey is reversed and the case is remanded for further proceedings not inconsistent with this opinion.

So ordered.

Justice STEVENS, *concurring in the judgment.*

The Borough must shoulder the burden of demonstrating that appellants' introduction of live entertainment had an identifiable adverse impact on the neighborhood or on the Borough as a whole. It might be appropriate to presume that such an adverse impact would occur if the zoning plan itself were narrowly drawn to create categories of commercial uses that unambiguously differentiated this entertainment from permitted uses. However, this open-ended ordinance affords no basis for any such presumption.

Chief Justice BURGER, with whom Justice REHNQUIST joins, *dissenting.*

Even assuming that the "expression" manifested in the nude dancing is somehow protected speech under the First Amendment, the Borough of Mount Ephraim is entitled to regulate it. Here, as in *Young*, the zoning ordinance imposes a minimal intrusion on genuine rights of expression. Mount Ephraim is a small community on the periphery of two major urban centers where this kind of entertainment may be found acceptable. The fact that nude dancing has been totally banned in this community is irrelevant. Citizens should be free to choose to shape their community so that it embodies their conception of the "decent life." This will sometimes mean deciding that certain forms of activity—factories, gas stations, sports stadia, bookstores, and surely live nude shows—will not be allowed. That a community is willing to tolerate such a commercial use as a convenience store, a gas station, a pharmacy, or a delicatessen does not compel it also to tolerate every other "commercial use," including pornography peddlers and live nude shows.

∽ PROBLEMS ∽

1. *Additional Facts.* If you were the attorney for the Borough of Mount Ephraim, what other kinds of evidence might you have submitted in defense of the ordinance? Consider whether these additional facts are relevant (as set forth in the *Schad* dissent): Mount Ephraim is a small borough in Camden County, N.J., which is located on the main artery connecting Atlantic City with Camden and Philadelphia. Mount Ephraim is about 17 miles from Camden and about the same distance from the river that separates New Jersey from Pennsylvania. For 250 feet on either side of the turnpike, the borough maintains a commercial zone. The rest of the community is zoned for residential use, single- and multiple-family units of the inhabitants of Mount Ephraim who commute to either Camden or Philadelphia for work, but live in this placid, "bedroom" community of a few thousand people.

2. *Ordinance Drafting.* Assume that you are the attorney for the Borough of Mount Ephraim, assigned to redraft the ordinance to limit "live nude dancing" as much as possible. What changes would you propose to make in the ordinance to avoid the problems of the *Schad* ordinance and take advantage of *Young*?

3. *Couch Dancing.* A Nashville ordinance provides: "No entertainer, employee or customer, in any adult cabaret providing live entertainment involving any nudity, shall be permitted to have any physical contact with any other entertainer, employee or customer on the premises during any live performance, and all live performances shall only occur upon a stage removed at least six feet from the nearest entertainer, employee or customer." Zoom Lens (ZL), a nightclub with erotic topless dancing, presents "couch dancing" between entertainers and customers in an area separated from the main stage. This activity involves an entertainer sitting on the lap of a clothed customer and "dancing." ZL also offers "interactive" dances during which customers take spoons and scrape various substances (e.g., Cool Whip) off the bodies of dancers. The local prosecutor sues, seeking to close down ZL because of these violations. What arguments do you expect the club's lawyer to make to attack the ordinance on First Amendment grounds? What arguments will Nashville offer in response? How are *Erznoznik*, *Young*, and *Schad* relevant?

City of Erie v. Pap's A. M.

529 U.S. 277 (2000)

Justice O'CONNOR announced the judgment of the Court and delivered the opinion of the Court with respect to Parts I and II, and an opinion with respect to Parts III and IV, in which THE CHIEF JUSTICE, Justice KENNEDY, and Justice BREYER join.

The city council for Erie, Pennsylvania, enacted a public indecency ordinance that makes it a summary offense to knowingly or intentionally appear in public in a "state of nudity." *Nudity* means "the showing of the human male or female genital *sic*, pubic area or buttocks with less than a fully opaque covering; the showing of the female breast with less than a fully opaque covering of any part of the nipple; the exposure of any device, costume, or covering which gives the appearance of or simulates the genitals, pubic hair, natal cleft, perineum anal region or pubic hair region; or the exposure of any device worn as a cover over the nipples and/or areola of the female breast, which device simulates and gives the realistic appearance of nipples and/or areola." The ordinance defines *public place* as including "all outdoor places owned by or open to the general public, and all buildings and enclosed places owned by or open to the general public, including places of entertainment, taverns, restaurants, clubs, theaters, dance halls, banquet halls, party rooms or halls limited to specific members, restricted to adults or to patrons invited to attend, whether or not an admission charge is levied." Respondent Pap's operated an establishment known as "Kandyland" that featured totally nude erotic dancing performed by women. To comply with the ordinance, these dancers must wear, at a minimum, "pasties" and a "G-string." Pap's filed a suit seeking declaratory relief and a permanent injunction against the enforcement of the ordinance.

III

In *Barnes v. Glen Theater, Inc.*, 501 U.S. 560 (1991), we analyzed an almost identical statute, holding that Indiana's public nudity ban did not violate the First Amendment, although no five Members of the Court agreed on a single rationale for that conclusion. We now clarify that government restrictions on public nudity such as the ordinance at issue here should be evaluated under the framework set forth in *O'Brien* for content-neutral restrictions on symbolic speech.

The city of Erie argues that the ordinance is a content-neutral restriction reviewable under *United States v. O'Brien*, 391 U.S. 367 (1968), because the ordinance bans conduct, not speech; specifically, public nudity. Respondent counters that the ordinance targets nude dancing and is aimed specifically at suppressing expression, making the ordinance a content-based restriction that must be subjected to strict scrutiny. The ordinance here, like the statute in *Barnes,* is on its face a general prohibition on public nudity. By its terms, the ordinance regulates conduct alone. It does not target nudity that contains an erotic message; rather, it bans all public nudity, regardless of whether that nudity is accompanied by expressive activity. Like the statute in *Barnes* the Erie ordinance replaces and updates an "Indecency and Immorality" ordinance that has been on the books since 1866, predating the prevalence of nude dancing establishments such as Kandyland.

Respondent contends that the ordinance is related to the suppression of expression because the ordinance's preamble suggests that its purpose is to prohibit erotic dancing of the type performed at Kandyland. In the preamble, the city council stated that it was adopting the regulation "'for the purpose of limiting a recent increase in nude live entertainment within the City, which activity adversely impacts and threatens to impact on the public health, safety and welfare by providing an atmosphere conducive to violence, sexual harassment, public intoxication, prostitution, the spread of sexually transmitted diseases and other deleterious effects.'" The Pennsylvania Supreme Court construed this language to mean that one purpose was "to combat negative secondary effects."

As Justice Souter noted in *Barnes*, "on its face, the governmental interest in combating prostitution and other criminal activity is not at all inherently related to expression." In that sense, this case is similar to *O'Brien*. In that case, the Government regulation prohibiting the destruction of draft cards was aimed at maintaining the integrity of the Selective Service System and not at suppressing the message of draft resistance that O'Brien sought to convey by burning his draft card. Here, the ordinance prohibiting public nudity is aimed at combating crime and other negative secondary effects caused by the presence of adult entertainment establishments like Kandyland and not at suppressing the erotic message conveyed by this type of nude dancing. The ordinance does not attempt to regulate the primary effects of expression, i.e., the effect on the audience of watching nude erotic dancing, but rather the secondary effects, such as the impacts on public health, safety, and welfare, which we have previously recognized are "caused by the presence of even one such" establishment. *Renton v. Playtime Theatres, Inc.*, 475 U.S. 41 (1986).

Respondent's argument that the ordinance is "aimed" at suppressing expression through a ban on nude dancing is really an argument that the city council had an illicit motive in enacting the ordinance. This Court will not strike down an otherwise constitutional statute on the basis of an alleged illicit motive. *O'Brien, supra*, at 382-383. In light of the Pennsylvania court's determination that one purpose of the ordinance is to combat harmful secondary effects, the ban on public nudity here is no different from the ban on burning draft registration cards in *O'Brien*. The State's interest in preventing harmful secondary effects is not related to the suppression of expression. In trying to control the secondary effects of nude dancing, the ordinance seeks to deter crime and the other deleterious effects caused by the presence of such an establishment in the neighborhood. Even if Erie's public nudity ban has some minimal effect on the erotic message by muting that portion of the expression that occurs when the last stitch is dropped, the dancers at Kandyland and other such establishments are free to perform wearing pasties and G-strings. Any effect on overall expression is *de minimis*. If States are to be able to regulate secondary effects, then *de minimis* intrusions on expression such as those at issue here cannot be sufficient to render the ordinance content based.

While the doctrinal theories behind "incidental burdens" and "secondary effects" are, of course, not identical, there is nothing objectionable about a city passing a general ordinance to ban public nudity (even though such a ban may place incidental burdens on some protected speech) and at the same time recognizing that one specific occurrence of public nudity — nude erotic dancing — is particularly problematic because it produces harmful secondary effects.

We conclude that Erie's asserted interest in combating the negative secondary effects associated with adult entertainment establishments like Kandyland is unrelated to the suppression of the erotic message conveyed by nude dancing. The ordinance prohibiting public nudity is therefore valid if it satisfies the four-factor test from *O'Brien* for evaluating restrictions on symbolic speech.

IV

Erie's ordinance is justified under *O'Brien*. The first factor of the *O'Brien* test is whether the government regulation is within the constitutional power of the government. Here, Erie's efforts to protect public health and safety are clearly within the city's police powers. The second factor is whether the regulation furthers an important or substantial government interest. The asserted interests of regulating conduct through a public nudity ban and of combating the harmful secondary effects associated with nude dancing are undeniably important. In demonstrating that such secondary effects pose a threat, the city need not "conduct new studies or produce evidence independent of that already generated by other cities" to demonstrate the problem of secondary effects, "so long as whatever evidence is reasonably believed to be relevant to the problem that the city addresses." Because the nude dancing at Kandyland is of the same character as the adult entertainment at issue in *Renton,* it was reasonable for Erie to conclude that such nude dancing was likely to produce the same secondary effects. And Erie could reasonably rely on the evidentiary foundation set forth in *Renton* and *American Mini Theatres* to the effect that secondary effects are caused by the presence of even one adult entertainment establishment in a given neighborhood. In fact, Erie expressly relied on *Barnes* and its discussion of secondary effects, including its reference to *Renton* and *American Mini Theatres.* The evidentiary standard described in *Renton* controls here, and Erie meets that standard. The ordinance also satisfies *O'Brien's* third factor, that the government interest is unrelated to the suppression of free expression. The fourth and final *O'Brien* factor — that the restriction is no greater than is essential to the furtherance of the government interest — is satisfied as well. The ordinance regulates conduct, and any incidental impact on the expressive element of nude dancing is *de minimis.* The requirement that dancers wear pasties and G-strings is a minimal restriction in furtherance of the asserted government interests, and the restriction leaves ample capacity to convey the dancer's erotic message.

   We hold, therefore, that Erie's ordinance is a content-neutral regulation that is valid under *O'Brien.* Accordingly, the judgment of the Pennsylvania Supreme Court is reversed, and the case is remanded for further proceedings.

   It is so ordered.

Justice SCALIA, with whom Justice THOMAS joins, *concurring in the judgment.*

   Even if one hypothesizes that the city's object was to suppress nude dancing, that would not establish an intent to suppress what (if anything) nude dancing communicates. I do not feel the need to identify some "secondary effects" associated with nude dancing that the city could properly seek to eliminate. (I am skeptical that the addition of pasties and G-strings will at all reduce the tendency of establishments such as Kandyland to attract crime and prostitution, and foster sexually transmitted disease.) The traditional power of government to foster good morals, and the traditional judgment that nude public dancing *itself* is immoral, have not been repealed by the First Amendment.

Justice SOUTER, *concurring in part* and *dissenting in part.*

   Erie's stated interest in combating the secondary effects associated with nude dancing establishments is an interest unrelated to the suppression of expression under *O'Brien.* I do not believe that the city has made a sufficient evidentiary showing to sustain its regulation. The record before us today is deficient in its failure to reveal any evidence on which Erie may have relied, either for the seriousness of the threatened harm or for the efficacy of its chosen remedy.

Justice STEVENS, with whom Justice GINSBURG joins, *dissenting.*

In both *Renton* and *American Mini Theatres*, the zoning ordinances were analyzed as mere "time, place, and manner" regulations. Because time, place, and manner regulations must "leave open ample alternative channels for communication of the information," a total ban would necessarily fail that test. We so held in *Schad v. Mount Ephraim*, 452 U.S. 61 (1981). The Court's use of the secondary effects rationale to permit a total ban has grave implications for basic free speech principles. Under today's opinion, a State may totally ban speech based on its secondary effects—which are defined as those effects that "happen to be associated" with speech; yet the regulation is not presumptively invalid. Today's holding has the effect of swallowing whole a most fundamental principle of First Amendment jurisprudence.

The plurality concedes that "requiring dancers to wear pasties and G-strings may not greatly reduce these secondary effects." To believe that the mandatory addition of pasties and a G-string will have *any* kind of noticeable impact on secondary effects requires nothing short of a titanic surrender to the implausible. There is no reason to believe that such a requirement "will at all reduce the tendency of establishments such as Kandyland to attract crime and prostitution, and hence to foster sexually transmitted disease."

The plurality is mistaken in equating our secondary effects cases with the "incidental burdens" doctrine applied in cases such as *O'Brien*. The incidental burdens doctrine applies when "'speech' and 'nonspeech' elements are combined in the same course of conduct," and the government's interest in regulating the latter justifies incidental burdens on the former. Secondary effects, on the other hand, are indirect consequences of protected speech and may justify regulation of the places where that speech may occur. When a State enacts a regulation, it might focus on the secondary effects of speech as its aim, or it might concentrate on nonspeech related concerns, having no thoughts at all with respect to how its regulation will affect speech—and only later, when the regulation is found to burden speech, justify the imposition as an unintended incidental consequence. But those interests are not the same, and the plurality cannot ignore their differences and insist that both aims are equally unrelated to speech simply because Erie might have "recognized" that it could possibly have had either aim in mind. If Erie's concern with the effects of the message were unrelated to the message itself, it is strange that the only means used to combat those effects is the suppression of the message.

Question: Reappraisal of the Justifications for Protecting Speech

Does *Erie* speech satisfy any of the justifications for protecting speech presented at the beginning of this chapter? In other words, does it provide a safety valve, promote self-fulfillment or the marketplace of ideas, or is it related to the democratic process?

∾ PROBLEMS ∾

1. *Drafting Issues.* Now that city attorneys, city council members, and prosecutors know what evidence is required to obtain a majority vote for a "secondary-effects-*O'Brien*" analysis (at least, they did while Justice Souter was still on the Court), how will such evidence be obtained? As the city attorney for Erie, what advice would you give regarding the legislative history that must be created to support a "secondary effects" government interest in a future case, in order to obtain Justice Souter's vote?

2. *The Full Monty.* Suppose that a city prosecutor wants to enforce the Erie ordinance against a theater that is planning to produce a musical in which nudity occurs, such as *The Full Monty.* What arguments will the prosecutor and the theater owner make about the constitutionality of this action under the "near-obscene" precedents?

3. *Cocoa Beach Ordinance.* The City of Cocoa Beach, Fla., passes an ordinance regulating adult entertainment establishments. The city is 6 miles long and 1 mile wide, with 2,000 acres, of which 150 are zoned for commercial use. The ordinance defines an adult entertainment establishment as one in which the dancers dance for tips or in close proximity to the patrons (no matter how much skin the dancers expose). The ordinance also contains a total ban on nudity by employees of such establishments, defining *nudity* as the exposure of specified anatomical areas including genitalia, buttocks, and female breasts, so that G-strings and pasties are sufficient to avoid violation of the ordinance. However, the ordinance does not prohibit nudity anywhere else in the city of Cocoa Beach. Sass, an adult night club, attacks the ordinance on First Amendment grounds, arguing that the ordinance should be struck down so that Sass dancers can dance nude. Should Sass prevail?

4. *Second Cocoa Beach Ordinance.* Suppose that Cocoa Beach also adopts an ordinance regulating the location of adult entertainment establishments. The ordinance sets aside only three sites for such businesses, which happen to correspond exactly to the sites of three adult businesses that have been open for 30 years. Sass, which has not yet opened, argues that its proposed site is excluded and that there is no site at which it can locate under this zoning ordinance. As a result, Sass claims a violation of the First Amendment. Should Sass prevail?

11. *"Hate" Speech*

The term *hate speech* is difficult to define, but is often used to refer to expression that targets individuals or groups by reason of their race, ethnicity, sex, or sexual preference. In an early decision, *Beauharnais v. Illinois*, 343 U.S. 250 (1952), the Court upheld a conviction under an Illinois statute that made it unlawful to portray "depravity, criminality, unchastity, or lack of virtue of a class of citizens, of any race, color, creed or religion which said publication or exhibition exposes the citizens of any race, color, creed or religion to contempt, derision, or obloquy or which is productive of breach of the peace or riots." The Court stated that the "precise question before us is whether the protection of 'liberty' in the Due Process Clause of the Fourteenth Amendment prevents a State from punishing such libels — as criminal libel has been defined, limited and constitutionally recognized time out of mind — directed at designated collectivities and flagrantly disseminated." The Court concluded that it could not "deny to a State power to punish the same utterance directed at a defined group." However, in subsequent decisions, the Court cast doubt on *Beauharnais*'s validity, as well as on the power of the state to impose punishment for criminal libel.

R.A.V. v. City of St. Paul

505 U.S. 377 (1992)

Justice SCALIA delivered the opinion of the Court.

In the predawn hours of June 21, 1990, petitioner and several other teenagers allegedly assembled a crudely made cross by taping together broken chair legs. They then allegedly burned the cross inside the fenced yard of a black family that lived across the street from the house where petitioner was staying. Although this conduct could have been punished under any of a number of laws,[1] one of the two provisions under which respondent city of St. Paul chose to charge petitioner (then a juvenile) was the St. Paul Bias-Motivated Crime Ordinance, which provides:

> Whoever places on public or private property a symbol, object, appellation, characterization or graffiti, including, but not limited to, a burning cross or Nazi swastika, which one knows or has reasonable grounds to know arouses anger, alarm or resentment in others on the basis of race, color, creed, religion or gender commits disorderly conduct and shall be guilty of a misdemeanor.

Petitioner moved to dismiss this count on First Amendment grounds. The trial court granted this motion, but the Minnesota Supreme Court reversed.

We accept the Minnesota Supreme Court's authoritative statement that the ordinance reaches only those expressions that constitute "fighting words" within the meaning of *Chaplinsky v. New Hampshire*, 315 U.S. 568 (1942). Assuming that all of the expression reached by the ordinance is proscribable under the "fighting words" doctrine, we nonetheless conclude that the ordinance is facially unconstitutional in that it prohibits otherwise permitted speech solely on the basis of the subjects the speech addresses.

---

1. *See, e.g.,* Minn. Stat. §609.713(1) (1987) (providing for up to five years in prison for terroristic threats); §609.563 (arson) (providing for up to five years and a $10,000 fine, depending on the value of the property intended to be damaged); §609.595 (Supp. 1992) (criminal damage to property) (providing for up to one year and a $3,000 fine, depending upon the extent of damage.

The First Amendment generally prevents government from proscribing speech, or even expressive conduct, because of disapproval of the ideas expressed. Content-based regulations are presumptively invalid. From 1791 to the present, our society has permitted restrictions upon the content of speech in a few limited areas, which are "of such slight social value as a step to truth that any benefit that may be derived from them is clearly outweighed by the social interest in order and morality." *Chaplinsky,* 315 U.S. at 572. Our decisions since the 1960's have narrowed the scope of the traditional categorical exceptions for defamation, and for obscenity, but a limited categorical approach has remained an important part of our First Amendment jurisprudence.

We have sometimes said that these categories of expression are "not within the area of constitutionally protected speech," or that the "protection of the First Amendment does not extend" to them. Such statements must be taken in context, however, and are no more literally true than is the occasionally repeated short-hand characterizing obscenity "as not being speech at all." What they mean is that these areas of speech can, consistently with the First Amendment, be regulated *because of their constitutionally proscribable content* (obscenity, defamation, etc.) — not that they are categories of speech entirely invisible to the Constitution, so that they may be made the vehicles for content discrimination unrelated to their distinctively proscribable content. Thus, the government may proscribe libel; but it may not make the further content discrimination of proscribing *only* libel critical of the government.

Our cases do not establish the proposition that the First Amendment imposes no obstacle whatsoever to regulation of particular instances of such proscribable expression, so that the government "may regulate them freely." That would mean that a city council could enact an ordinance prohibiting only those legally obscene works that contain criticism of the city government or, indeed, that do not include endorsement of the city government. Such a simplistic, all-or-nothing-at-all approach to First Amendment protection is at odds with common sense and with our jurisprudence as well. It is not true that "fighting words" have at most a "*de minimis*" expressive content, or that their content is *in all respects* "worthless and undeserving of constitutional protection"; sometimes they are quite expressive indeed. We have not said that they constitute "*no* part of the expression of ideas," but only that they constitute "no *essential* part of any exposition of ideas."

The proposition that a particular instance of speech can be proscribable on the basis of one feature (e.g., obscenity) but not on the basis of another (e.g., opposition to the city government) has found application in many contexts. We have long held that nonverbal expressive activity can be banned because of the action it entails, but not because of the ideas it expresses — so that burning a flag in violation of an ordinance against outdoor fires could be punishable, whereas burning a flag in violation of an ordinance against dishonoring the flag is not. We have upheld reasonable "time, place, or manner" restrictions, but only if they are "*justified* without reference to the content of the regulated speech." Just as the power to proscribe particular speech on the basis of a noncontent element (e.g., noise) does not entail the power to proscribe the same speech on the basis of a content element; so also, the power to proscribe it on the basis of *one* content element (e.g., obscenity) does not entail the power to proscribe it on the basis of *other* content elements.

The exclusion of "fighting words" from the scope of the First Amendment simply means that, for purposes of that Amendment, the unprotected features of the words are, despite their verbal character, essentially a "nonspeech" element of communication. Fighting words are thus analogous to a noisy sound truck: Each is, as Justice Frankfurter recognized, a "mode of speech"; both can be used to convey an idea; but neither has, in and of itself, a claim upon the First Amendment. As with the sound truck, however, so also with fighting words: The government may not regulate use based on hostility—or favoritism—towards the underlying message expressed.

The concurrences describe us as setting forth a new First Amendment principle that prohibition of constitutionally proscribable speech cannot be "underinclusive"—a First Amendment "absolutism" whereby "within a particular 'proscribable' category of expression, a government must either proscribe *all* speech or no speech at all." In our view, the First Amendment imposes not an "underinclusiveness" limitation but a "content discrimination" limitation upon a State's prohibition of proscribable speech. There is no problem whatever, for example, with a State's prohibiting obscenity (and other forms of proscribable expression) only in certain media or markets, for although that prohibition would be "underinclusive," it would not discriminate on the basis of content.

Even the prohibition against content discrimination is not absolute. It applies differently in the context of proscribable speech than in the area of fully protected speech. The rationale of the general prohibition is that content discrimination "raises the specter that the Government may effectively drive certain ideas or viewpoints from the marketplace." But content discrimination among various instances of a class of proscribable speech often does not pose this threat. When the basis for the content discrimination consists entirely of the very reason the entire class of speech at issue is proscribable, no significant danger of idea or viewpoint discrimination exists. Such a reason, having been adjudged neutral enough to support exclusion of the entire class of speech from First Amendment protection, is neutral enough to form the basis of distinction within the class. A State might choose to prohibit only that obscenity which is the most patently offensive *in its prurience*—i.e., that which involves the most lascivious displays of sexual activity. But it may not prohibit only that obscenity which includes offensive *political* messages.

Another valid basis for according differential treatment to even a content-defined subclass of proscribable speech is that the subclass happens to be associated with particular "secondary effects" of the speech, so that the regulation is "*justified* without reference to the content of the speech." A State could permit all obscene live performances except those involving minors. Moreover, since words can in some circumstances violate laws directed not against speech but against conduct (a law against treason, for example, is violated by telling the enemy the Nation's defense secrets), a particular content-based subcategory of a proscribable class of speech can be swept up incidentally within the reach of a statute directed at conduct rather than speech. Thus, for example, sexually derogatory "fighting words," among other words, may produce a violation of Title VII's general prohibition against sexual discrimination in employment practices. Where the government does not target conduct on the basis of its expressive content, acts are not shielded from regulation merely because they express a discriminatory idea or philosophy.

These bases for distinction refute the proposition that the selectivity of the restriction is "even arguably 'conditioned upon the sovereign's agreement with what a speaker may intend to say.'" There may be other such bases as well. Indeed, to validate such selectivity (where totally proscribable speech is at issue) it may not even be necessary to identify any particular "neutral" basis, so long as the nature of the content discrimination is such that there is no realistic possibility that official suppression of ideas is afoot. (We cannot think of any First Amendment interest that would stand in the way of a State's prohibiting only those obscene motion pictures with blue-eyed actresses.) Save for that limitation, the regulation of "fighting words," like the regulation of noisy speech, may address some offensive instances and leave other, equally offensive, instances alone.

Applying these principles to the St. Paul ordinance, we conclude that, even as narrowly construed by the Minnesota Supreme Court, the ordinance is facially unconstitutional. Although the phrase in the ordinance, "arouses anger, alarm or resentment in others," has been limited by the Minnesota Supreme Court's construction to reach only those symbols or displays that amount to "fighting words," the ordinance applies only to "fighting words" that insult, or provoke violence, "on the basis of race, color, creed, religion or gender." Displays containing abusive invective, no matter how vicious or severe, are permissible unless they are addressed to one of the specified disfavored topics. Those who wish to use "fighting words" in connection with other ideas—to express hostility, for example, on the basis of political affiliation, union membership, or homosexuality—are not covered. The First Amendment does not permit St. Paul to impose special prohibitions on those speakers who express views on disfavored subjects.

In its practical operation, moreover, the ordinance goes even beyond mere content discrimination, to actual viewpoint discrimination. Displays containing some words—odious racial epithets, for example—would be prohibited to proponents of all views. But "fighting words" that do not themselves invoke race, color, creed, religion, or gender—aspersions upon a person's mother, for example—would seemingly be usable *ad libitum* in the placards of those arguing *in favor* of racial, color, etc., tolerance and equality, but could not be used by those speakers' opponents. One could hold up a sign saying, for example, that all "anti-Catholic bigots" are misbegotten; but not that all "papists" are, for that would insult and provoke violence "on the basis of religion." St. Paul has no such authority to license one side of a debate to fight freestyle, while requiring the other to follow Marquis of Queensberry rules.

What we have here is not a prohibition of fighting words that are directed at certain persons or groups (which would be *facially* valid if it met the requirements of the Equal Protection Clause); but rather, a prohibition of fighting words that contain messages of "bias-motivated" hatred and in particular, as applied to this case, messages "based on virulent notions of racial supremacy." One must agree with the Minnesota Supreme Court that "it is the responsibility, even the obligation, of diverse communities to confront such notions in whatever form they appear," but the manner of that confrontation cannot consist of selective limitations upon speech. St. Paul asserts that a general "fighting words" law would not meet the city's needs because only a content-specific measure can communicate to minority groups that the "group hatred" aspect of such speech "is not condoned by the majority." The point of the First Amendment is that majority preferences must be expressed in some fashion other than silencing speech on the basis of its content.

Despite the fact that the Minnesota Supreme Court and St. Paul acknowledge that the ordinance is directed at expression of group hatred, Justice Stevens suggests that it is directed not to speech of a particular content, but to particular "injuries" that are "qualitatively different" from other injuries. This is wordplay. What makes the anger, fear, sense of dishonor, etc., produced by violation of this ordinance distinct from the anger, fear, sense of dishonor, etc., produced by other fighting words is nothing other than the fact that it is caused by a distinctive idea, conveyed by a distinctive message. The First Amendment cannot be evaded that easily. Symbols which will arouse "anger, alarm or resentment in others on the basis of race, color, creed, religion or gender" are symbols that communicate a message of hostility based on one of these characteristics. St. Paul concedes that the ordinance applies only to "racial, religious, or gender-specific symbols" such as "a burning cross, Nazi swastika or other instrumentality of like import." Indeed, St. Paul argued that "the burning of a cross does express a message and it is the content of that message which the St. Paul Ordinance attempts to legislate."

The content-based discrimination reflected in the St. Paul ordinance does not fall within the exception for content discrimination based on the very reasons why the particular class of speech at issue (here, fighting words) is proscribable. The reason why fighting words are categorically excluded from the protection of the First Amendment is not that their content communicates any particular idea, but that their content embodies a particularly intolerable (and socially unnecessary) *mode* of expressing *whatever* idea the speaker wishes to convey. St. Paul has not singled out an especially offensive mode of expression — it has not, for example, selected for prohibition only those fighting words that communicate ideas in a threatening (as opposed to a merely obnoxious) manner. Rather, it has proscribed fighting words of whatever manner that communicate messages of racial, gender, or religious intolerance. Selectivity of this sort creates the possibility that the city is seeking to handicap the expression of particular ideas. That possibility would alone be enough to render the ordinance presumptively invalid, but St. Paul's comments and concessions in this case elevate the possibility to a certainty.

St. Paul argues that the ordinance comes within another of the specific exceptions we mentioned, the one that allows content discrimination aimed only at the "secondary effects" of the speech. According to St. Paul, the ordinance is intended, "not to impact on *sic* the right of free expression of the accused," but rather to "protect against the victimization of a person or persons who are particularly vulnerable because of their membership in a group that historically has been discriminated against." The St. Paul ordinance is not directed to secondary effects within the meaning of *Renton.* As we said in *Boos v. Barry,* 485 U.S. 312 (1988), "Listeners' reactions to speech are not the type of 'secondary effects' we referred to in *Renton.*" "The emotive impact of speech on its audience is not a 'secondary effect.'"[7]

It hardly needs discussion that the ordinance does not fall within some more general exception permitting all selectivity that for any reason is beyond the suspicion of official suppression of ideas. The statements of St. Paul in this very case afford ample basis for, if not full confirmation of, that suspicion.

Finally, St. Paul argues that, even if the ordinance regulates expression based on hostility towards its protected ideological content, this discrimination is nonetheless justified because it is narrowly tailored to serve compelling state interests. Specifically, they assert that the ordinance helps to ensure the basic human rights of members of groups that have historically been subjected to discrimination, including the right of such group members to live in peace where they wish. We do not doubt that these interests are compelling, and that the ordinance can be said to promote them. But the "danger of censorship" presented by a facially content-based statute requires that that weapon be employed only where it is "*necessary* to serve the asserted compelling interest." The dispositive question in this case is whether content discrimination is reasonably necessary to achieve St. Paul's compelling interests; it plainly is not. An ordinance not limited to the favored topics would have precisely the same beneficial effect. In fact the only interest distinctively served by the content limitation is that of displaying the city council's special hostility towards the particular biases thus singled out. That is precisely what the First Amendment forbids. The politicians of St. Paul are entitled to express that hostility—but not through the means of imposing unique limitations upon speakers who disagree.

Let there be no mistake about our belief that burning a cross in someone's front yard is reprehensible. But St. Paul has sufficient means at its disposal to prevent such behavior without adding the First Amendment to the fire.

---

7. St. Paul has not argued in this case that the ordinance merely regulates that subclass of fighting words which is most likely to provoke a violent response. But even if one assumes that the categories selected may be so described, that would not justify selective regulation under a "secondary effects" theory. It is clear that the St. Paul ordinance regulates on the basis of the "primary" effect of the speech—i.e., its persuasive (or repellant) force.

The judgment of the Minnesota Supreme Court is reversed, and the case is remanded for proceedings not inconsistent with this opinion.

It is so ordered.

Justice WHITE, with whom Justice BLACKMUN and Justice O'CONNOR join, and with whom Justice STEVENS joins except as to Part I-A, *concurring in the judgment.*

This Court's decisions have plainly stated that expression falling within certain limited categories so lacks the values the First Amendment was designed to protect that the Constitution affords no protection to that expression. The present Court submits that such clear statements "must be taken in context" and are not "literally true." This categorical approach is a firmly entrenched part of our First Amendment jurisprudence.

Fighting words are not a means of exchanging views, rallying supporters, or registering a protest; they are directed against individuals to provoke violence or to inflict injury. Therefore, a ban on all fighting words or on a subset of the fighting words category would restrict only the social evil of hate speech, without creating the danger of driving viewpoints from the marketplace.

Any contribution of this holding to First Amendment jurisprudence is surely a negative one, since it signals that expressions of violence, such as the message of intimidation and racial hatred conveyed by burning a cross on someone's lawn, are of sufficient value to outweigh the social interest in order and morality that has traditionally placed such fighting words outside the First Amendment.[11] By characterizing fighting words as a form of "debate," the majority legitimates hate speech as a form of public discussion.

Furthermore, the Court obscures the line between speech that could be regulated freely on the basis of content (i.e., the narrow categories of expression falling outside the First Amendment) and that which could be regulated on the basis of content only upon a showing of a compelling state interest (i.e., all remaining expression). By placing fighting words, which the Court has long held to be valueless, on at least equal constitutional footing with political discourse and other forms of speech that we have deemed to have the greatest social value, the majority devalues the latter category.

Assuming that the St. Paul ordinance is a content-based regulation of protected expression, it nevertheless would pass First Amendment review under settled law upon a showing that the regulation "'is necessary to serve a compelling state interest and is narrowly drawn to achieve that end.'" St. Paul has urged that its ordinance, in the words of the majority, "helps to ensure the basic human rights of members of groups that have historically been subjected to discrimination." The majority has engrafted the following exception onto its newly

---

11. This does not suggest, of course, that cross burning is always unprotected. Burning a cross at a political rally would almost certainly be protected expression. But in such a context, the cross burning could not be characterized as a "direct personal insult or an invitation to exchange fisticuffs," to which the fighting words doctrine applies.

announced First Amendment rule: Content-based distinctions may be drawn within an unprotected category of speech if the basis for the distinctions is "the very reason the entire class of speech at issue is proscribable." The exception swallows the rule. Certainly, it should apply to the St. Paul ordinance, since "the reasons why fighting words are outside the First Amendment have special force when applied to groups that have historically been subjected to discrimination."

The Court suggests that fighting words are simply a mode of communication, rather than a content-based category, and that the St. Paul ordinance has not singled out a particularly objectionable mode of communication. A prohibition on fighting words is not a time, place, or manner restriction; it is a ban on a class of speech that conveys an overriding message of personal injury and imminent violence, a message that is at its ugliest when directed against groups that have long been the targets of discrimination. Accordingly, the ordinance falls within the first exception to the majority's theory.

The St. Paul ordinance is unconstitutional. I would decide the case on overbreadth grounds. The Minnesota court has ruled that St. Paul may constitutionally prohibit expression that "by its very utterance" causes "anger, alarm or resentment." Our fighting words cases have made clear that such generalized reactions are not sufficient to strip expression of its constitutional protection. The mere fact that expressive activity causes hurt feelings, offense, or resentment does not render the expression unprotected.

Justice BLACKMUN, *concurring in the judgment.*

I see no First Amendment values that are compromised by a law that prohibits hoodlums from driving minorities out of their homes by burning crosses on their lawns, but I see great harm in preventing the people of Saint Paul from specifically punishing the race-based fighting words that so prejudice their community. I concur because this ordinance reaches beyond fighting words to speech protected by the First Amendment.

Justice STEVENS, with whom Justice WHITE and Justice BLACKMUN join as to Part I, *concurring in the judgment.*

The St. Paul ordinance is unconstitutionally overbroad. I am troubled by the Court's suggestion that content based distinctions are not permissible. Our entire First Amendment jurisprudence creates a regime based on the content of speech. Whether a magazine is obscene, a gesture a fighting word, or a photograph child pornography is determined, in part, by its content.

A selective, subject-matter regulation on proscribable speech is constitutional. By hypothesis the ordinance bars only low-value speech, namely, fighting words. The ordinance regulates "expressive conduct rather than the written or spoken word." It is significant that the ordinance (by hypothesis) regulates *only* fighting words. The St. Paul ordinance restricts speech in confrontational and potentially violent situations. The case at hand is illustrative. The cross burning in this case—directed as it was to a single African-American family trapped in their home—was nothing more than a crude form of physical intimidation. That this cross burning sends a message of racial hostility does not automatically endow it with complete constitutional protection.

Significantly, the St. Paul ordinance regulates speech not on the basis of its subject matter or the viewpoint expressed, but rather on the basis of the *harm* the speech causes. The ordinance regulates only a subcategory of expression that causes *injuries based on* "race, color, creed, religion or gender," not a subcategory that involves *discussions* that concern those characteristics. The ordinance criminalizes expression that "one knows by its very utterance inflicts injury on others on the basis of race, color, creed, religion or gender." In this regard, the ordinance resembles the child pornography law at issue in *Ferber*, which in effect singled out child pornography because those publications caused far greater harms than pornography involving adults.

The St. Paul ordinance is evenhanded. In a battle between advocates of tolerance and advocates of intolerance, the ordinance does not prevent either side from hurling fighting words at the other on the basis of their conflicting ideas, but it does bar both sides from hurling such words on the basis of the target's "race, color, creed, religion or gender." To extend the Court's pugilistic metaphor, the St. Paul ordinance simply bans punches "below the belt"—by either party. It does not, therefore, favor one side of any debate.

Finally, it is noteworthy that the St. Paul ordinance is quite narrow. The St. Paul ordinance does not ban all "hate speech," nor does it ban, say, all cross burnings or all swastika displays. Rather it only bans a subcategory of the already narrow category of fighting words. Such a limited ordinance leaves open and protected a vast range of expression on the subjects of racial, religious, and gender equality. The ordinance certainly does not "'raise the specter that the Government may effectively drive certain ideas or viewpoints from the marketplace.'" Petitioner is free to burn a cross to announce a rally or to express his views about racial supremacy, he may do so on private property or public land, at day or at night, so long as the burning is not so threatening and so directed at an individual as to "by its very execution inflict injury." Such a limited proscription scarcely offends the First Amendment.

In sum, the St. Paul ordinance regulates expressive activity that is wholly proscribable and does so not on the basis of viewpoint, but rather in recognition of the different harms caused by such activity.

Notes and Questions

1. *Sentencing and Associational Evidence. Dawson v. Delaware*, 503 U.S. 159 (1992), involved testimony in a capital sentencing proceeding to the effect that the defendant was a member of the Aryan Brotherhood, a white supremacist group. The trial court admitted the evidence, and the jury concluded that the aggravating evidence outweighed the mitigating evidence and recommended

that Dawson be sentenced to death. The trial court imposed the death penalty. The Court reversed:

> The First Amendment protects an individual's right to join groups and associate with others holding similar beliefs. Even if the Delaware group to which Dawson allegedly belongs is racist, those beliefs had no relevance to the sentencing proceeding in this case. The murder victim was white, as is Dawson; elements of racial hatred were therefore not involved in the killing. Associational evidence might serve a legitimate purpose in showing that a defendant represents a future danger to society. Other evidence concerning a defendant's associations might be relevant in proving other aggravating circumstances. One is left with the feeling that the Aryan Brotherhood evidence was employed simply because the jury would find these beliefs morally reprehensible. Because Delaware failed to do more, we cannot find the evidence was properly admitted as relevant character evidence."

Justice Thomas dissented: "Under Delaware law, after a jury finds a statutory aggravating factor, it may consider 'all relevant evidence in aggravation or mitigation' relating to either the crime or the 'character and propensities' of the defendant. Under this provision, Dawson's character became an issue in determining whether he should receive the death penalty. A jury reasonably could infer that its members in one way or another act upon their racial prejudice. The Aryan Brotherhood does not exist merely to facilitate formulation of abstract racist thoughts, but to 'respond' to gangs of racial minorities. The evidence thus tends to establish that Dawson has not been 'a well-behaved and well-adjusted prisoner' which itself is an indication of future dangerousness."

2. *Defining "Hate Speech."* Of course, one of the problems with "hate speech" is how to define it. Does the definition depend on who is doing the defining? In the 1830s, a number of Southern states enacted law suppressing abolitionist speech. Senator John C. Calhoun denounced abolitionists on the basis that those who criticized slavery "libeled the South and inflicted emotional injury." Of course, the right to free expression was of essential importance to the modern civil rights movement. As Congressman John Lewis stated, "Without freedom of speech and the right to dissent, the Civil Rights movement would have been a bird without wings." But should government have the right to choose which speech should be allowed and which speech should be prohibited? In modern times, is there a risk that the definition of "hate speech" may reflect nothing more than the decisionmaker's own perspective on what constitutes "hate?" For example, some would condemn as "hate speech" those who advocate that marriage should involve only relationships between a man and a woman, and should not include same-sex relationships. In a free society, should those who hold this more restrictive view of marriage be prohibited from expressing it?

3. *Sentence Enhancement.* In *Wisconsin v. Mitchell*, 508 U.S. 476 (1993), Mitchell's sentence for aggravated battery was enhanced because he intentionally selected his victim on account of the victim's race. The Court upheld the enhancement, rejecting arguments that "the only reason for the enhancement is the defendant's discriminatory motive for selecting his victim" and therefore

the Court concluded that "the statute violates the First Amendment by punishing offenders' bigoted beliefs." The Court noted:

> Traditionally, sentencing judges have considered a wide variety of factors in addition to evidence bearing on guilt in determining what sentence to impose on a convicted defendant. The defendant's motive for committing the offense is one important factor. Thus, in many States the commission of a murder, or other capital offense, for pecuniary gain is a separate aggravating circumstance under the capital sentencing statute. But a defendant's abstract beliefs, however obnoxious to most people, may not be taken into consideration by a sentencing judge. But motive plays the same role under the Wisconsin statute as it does under federal and state antidiscrimination laws, which we have previously upheld against constitutional challenge. Nothing in *R.A.V.* compels a different result. Whereas the ordinance struck down in *R.A.V.* was explicitly directed at expression (i.e., "speech" or "messages"), the statute in this case is aimed at conduct unprotected by the First Amendment. Moreover, the Wisconsin statute singles out for enhancement bias-inspired conduct because this conduct is thought to inflict greater individual and societal harm. Bias-motivated crimes are more likely to provoke retaliatory crimes, inflict distinct emotional harms on their victims, and incite community unrest. The State's desire to redress these perceived harms provides an adequate explanation for its penalty-enhancement provision over and above mere disagreement with offenders' beliefs or biases.

4. *Campus Speech Codes.* In recent years, many colleges and universities have enacted speech codes designed to prohibit so-called "hate speech." In general, these codes have been struck down on vagueness or overbreadth grounds. *See UMW Post, Inc. v. Board of Regents of University of Wisconsin,* 774 F. Supp. 1162 (E.D. Wis. 1991) (striking down the University of Wisconsin's prohibition against discriminatory epithets); *Doe v. University of Michigan,* 721 F. Supp. 852 (E.D. Mich. 1989) (striking down the University of Michigan's antiharassment code as vague and overbroad). Might they also be content-based and viewpoint-based restrictions on speech?

5. *Hate Speech and the Justifications for Protecting Speech.* Did the speech involved in *R.A.V.* meet any of the justifications for protecting speech presented at the beginning of this chapter? In other words, did it provide a safety valve, did it promote self-fulfillment or the marketplace of ideas, or was it related to the democratic process?

6. *The Lawrence Argument.* Professor Charles R. Lawrence III, in *If He Hollers Let Him Go: Regulating Racist Speech on Campus,* 1990 Duke L.J. 431 (1990), contends that minorities and women often find "themselves speechless in the face of discriminatory verbal attacks." Why? In his view, the words "denote one's subhuman status and untouchability," and "there is little (if anything) that can be said to redress either the emotional or reputational injury." He questions whether minorities and women should be required to bear this "burden for the good of society—to pay the price for the societal benefit of creating more room for speech." He goes on to note that "we assign this burden to them without seeking their advice, or consent. This amounts to white domination, pure and simple. It is taxation without representation." Is Lawrence right? Should the right of free speech give way in this context?

7. *The Continued Existence of Hate Speech.* In a particularly dramatic illustration of the presence of racism in our society, President Obama's launch of a new

Twitter account was met with an outpouring of profanity-laced racist posts. In addition to hurling racial epithets at Obama, responders also referred to him as a "monkey." *See* Julie Hirschfeld Davis, *Slurs Hurled at President Via Twitter*, N.Y. Times, May 22, 2015, at A-15.

8. *Increasing Intolerance for Free Speech?* Some question whether U.S. society has become increasingly intolerant of speech, especially on college campuses. For example, at the University of Michigan, a showing of the film "American Sniper" was cancelled because of objections to the way that it depicted certain racial groups. *See* Ronald K.L. Collins, *"American Sniper" Cancelled at U. Michigan—Part of "Speech Destroying Storm" Says Floyd Abrams*, First Amendment News (Apr. 8, 2015). Following a panel discussion at Smith College on the subject of free speech and civil discourse, a speaker was labeled as "racist" because of her defense of free speech. She criticized campus speech codes, and urged the audience to defend free speech over parochial notions of "civility." In addition, she questioned the desirability of replacing offensive words (*e.g.*, the N-word) with initials. *See, e.g.*, Harvey Silverglate, *Liberals Are Killing the Liberal Arts*, Wall St. J., Nov. 10, 2014, at A17. At the University of Iowa College of Law, a candidate for a faculty position sued claiming that she had been discriminated against because of her conservative views. *See Wagner v. Jones*, 758 F.3d 1030 (8th Cir. 2014).

9. *The Amy Wax/Larry Alexander Controversy.* Amy Wax, a law professor at the University of Pennsylvania, and Larry Alexander, a law professor at the University of San Diego, jointly published an op-ed article which called for a renewal of the "cultural script" that prevailed in the 1950s and (as they claimed) still prevails among affluent Americans." In particular, they suggested that people should get married before they have children and "strive to stay married for the children's sake." They also advocated that people should get the education they need for gainful employment, and that people should work hard, avoid idleness, and avoid substance abuse and crime. The Dean of the Penn Law School denounced the op-ed as "divisive, even noxious," and a number of Wax's Penn colleagues issued a letter denouncing her views. The Dean of the USD Law School also condemned the op-ed and announced new efforts to compensate "vulnerable, marginalized" students for the "racial discrimination and subordination they experience." *See* Amy Wax and Larry Alexander, *Paying the Price for Breakdown of Country's Bourgeois Culture, The Inquirer*, Aug. 9, 2017, http://www.philly.com/philly/opinion/commentary/paying-the-price-for-breakdown-of-country's-bourgeois-culture-20170809.html; *see generally* Prof. Wax op-ed on "bourgeois culture" stirs intense debate, strong reactions, Sept. 5, 2017.

∾ PROBLEMS ∾

1. *Ordinance Drafting.* After *R.A.V.*, is it possible for the City of St. Paul to draft a valid ordinance designed to deal with the problem of "hate speech"? Can the ordinance avoid the problems of content-based and viewpoint-based

discrimination against speech as well as vagueness and overbreadth? If so, how should the ordinance be drafted?

2. *Messages of Inferiority.* The University of Louisville promulgates a regulation that prohibits any student from engaging in speech that conveys a "message of inferiority" to any racial group, or makes that group feel "excluded." In promulgating the regulation, the university emphasizes that Louisville (and Kentucky) have a history of slavery and segregation, and that Black students have historically felt "excluded" at the university. Is the regulation valid?

3. *Regulatory Applications.* Suppose that, after the regulation referred to in the preceding problem is promulgated, the following events occur. Which of these events are proscribable? A) At a Halloween party, a number of students perform skits. One student dresses up in Ku Klux Klan robes and poses as a Klansman. At the end of the skit, he pulls off his Klan robes (thereby revealing his identity) and burns them; B) In the prior example, suppose that the student is African American (as was true in an actual case at the University of Louisville). Does that change the result? C) At the same Halloween party, a white student wears "black face" and imitates a Black rapper. The lyrics used are not racist, but instead come directly from one of the rapper's songs. After *R.A.V.* and *Black,* can these student be punished by the university under the regulation?

4. *The KKK and the Adopt-a-Highway Program.* Suppose that the Commonwealth of Kentucky creates an "adopt-a-highway" program. Under this program, groups can agree to "adopt" highway sections if they agree to regularly pick up litter in those sections. Suppose that you work for the Kentucky Department of Transportation office when the Ku Klux Klan applies to adopt a section of a state highway. Can you reject the application on the theory that the KKK is an extremist group and its participation in the program would be morally offensive to many Kentuckians? Suppose that the state decides to grant the application. Is there anything that prevents the state from granting the KKK's request, but then renaming that section of the highway "The Martin Luther King, Jr., Highway"?

5. *Hostile Work Environments.* Even though the state generally may be precluded from engaging in content-based or viewpoint-based discrimination against speech, can it prohibit employers and employees from creating "hostile working environments"? Suppose that a supervisor at a government agency routinely refers to Black subordinates using the "N-word" or as "boy." Under the First Amendment, can the local equal rights commission sanction the supervisor for creating a "hostile work environment"? Could a university prohibit professors from using the N-word or from making derogatory references to women in class? Likewise, could the university sanction a professor who uses the N-word in a discussion of a self-defense case because one of the parties to that case used it, and the professor is trying to emphasize the impact of the word on one of the parties to the case? Should similar rules apply to students?

6. *Striking a Balance Between Free Expression and the Creation of Less Hostile Work Environments.* Even if it is permissible for an employer to prohibit supervisors and employees from creating hostile work environments, or for a university to prohibit

racist or sexist speech, what is the scope of the employer/university's authority? Suppose, for example, that a university decides to prohibit "micro-aggressions" based on race or sex. It defines the following statements as constituting "micro-aggressions": "America is a land of opportunity"; "America is a 'melting pot'"; "I believe the most qualified person should get the job"; "Affirmative action is racist." Can the university prohibit these statements on the basis that they create a "hostile" work or academic environment, or that they involve "slights, snubs, or insults, whether intentional or unintentional, that communicate hostile, deroga-tory, or negative messages to target persons based solely upon their marginal-ized group membership"? *See* Eugene Volokh, *Op-Ed: U.C.'s PC Police*, L.A. Times, June 23, 2015, http://www.latimes.com/opinion/op-ed/la-oe-0623-volokh-uc-microaggressions-20150623-story.html.

7. *More on Striking the Balance.* There has been considerable controversy regard-ing the case of Professor Laura Kipnis of Northwestern University, described as a "feminist film professor," who wrote an article about sexual mores on campus and university attempts to regulate romantic relationships. Two students filed Title IX charges against Kipnis on the grounds that her article might chill the reporting of sexual harassment claims. *See* Rachel Martin, *Laura Kipnis: The Boundaries of Sexual Assault Have Stretched*, National Public Radio, Weekend Edition Sunday, June 7, 2015; David Brooks, *The Campus Crusaders*, N.Y. Times, June 2, 2015. Even if a uni-versity has the right to prevent faculty or staff from creating a "hostile work envi-ronment," or from unduly inhibiting the reporting of sexual harassment claims, how far does that authority extend? Should it preclude professors like Kipnis from writing articles expressing their views?

8. *Student Speech.* Suppose that, in a discussion of gender equality during a class, a conservative fundamentalist student states that "a woman's place is in the home." Can the university sanction professors and students for making such statements? Does context matter? Suppose that college students derogatorily use the N-word outside of class through postings on their Facebook pages. Could the college expel them for creating a "hostile learning environment" based on their social media statements? *See* Manny Fernandez & Erik Eckholm, *Expulsion of Two Oklahoma Students over Video Leads to Free Speech Debate*, N.Y. Times, Mar. 12, 2015, at A-14.

9. *More on Sexual Harassment.* Some civil rights groups (e.g., FIRE, the Foundation for Individual Rights in Education), complained about what they regarded as Obama administration "overreaching" in areas involving free expres-sion. In particular, concerns were raised regarding an expansion of "sexual harassment" to include "cruel jokes" rather than focusing on the more limited definition articulated by the Court in *Davis v. Monroe County Board of Education*, 526 U.S. 629 (1999) (in order to qualify as "harassment," conduct must be "so severe, pervasive and objectively offensive, that the victim-students are effectively denied access to an institution's resources and opportunities"). Should it be per-missible under the First Amendment to define sexual harassment broadly enough to include a joke?

10. *"All Lives Matter."* Suppose that, in response to a "Black Lives Matter" protest, some students at the University of Louisville hold up "All Lives Matter" signs. Others hold up "White Lives Matter, Too" signs. Or, suppose that conservative students display signs promoting heterosexual values, and suggesting that homosexual sex is immoral. Assume that the University's Vice President for Diversity is outraged by the "All Lives Matter" and "White Lives Matter, Too" signs, and the signs regarding homosexual sex. Can she impose discipline on the students who held up those signs? Can she require those students to go through "extensive training for racial and cultural competency"?

11. *Loss of Federal Funds.* When Milo Yiannopoulos, an editor for Breitbart News, was scheduled to speak at U.C. Berkeley in 2017, a crowd of 1,500 protesters gathered and engaged in violent acts that included throwing smoke bombs and setting fires. Police locked down the campus and the speech was cancelled. In response, President Trump tweeted as follows: "If U.C. Berkeley does not allow free speech and practices violence on innocent people with a different point of view—NO FEDERAL FUNDS?" Would Congress violate the First Amendment by enacting a federal statute that provides for the withdrawal of federal funds from universities that allow faculty and students to stifle free expression? In 2019, President Trump translated his threats into an executive order which directed 12 federal agencies, including the Departments of Education and Defense and the National Science Foundation, that fund college and university research and education to add the following language to the agreements institutions sign to receive the money: "The heads of covered agencies shall, in coordination with the Director of the Office of Management and Budget, take appropriate steps, in a manner consistent with applicable law, including the First Amendment, to ensure institutions that receive Federal research or education grants promote free inquiry, including through compliance with all applicable Federal laws, regulations, and policies." While the order refers to "education grants," that would not include federal student aid that goes directly to students to pay college expenses. The types of "education grants" seemingly referred to in the order include institutional capacity-building grants such as those made to minority-serving institutions. Is the EO constitutionally valid?

12. *Facebook Posts and Criminal Convictions.* Defendant is charged with illegal firearm possession as well as possession of crack cocaine with intent to distribute. At his trial, the prosecution seeks to introduce a Facebook video that defendant posted which contained the following lyrics: "Real thugz 'bout dat, get at me. Bang, bang!!!!!!!!!!" The gun that was found in defendant's vehicle (on which the firearms charge was based) had a fingerprint which corresponded to the way defendant held the gun in the video, and the prosecution felt that it helped show "knowing possession." Would it violate defendant's First Amendment rights to admit the video against him? *See United States v. Rembert,* 851 F.3d 836 (8th Cir. 2017).

13. *The U. Chicago Policy on Free Expression.* The University of Chicago in its Report on the Committee on Freedom of Expression, explicitly affirmed its

commitment "to the principle that debate or deliberation may not be suppressed because the ideas put forth are thought by some or even by most members of the University community to be offensive, unwise, immoral, or wrong-headed. It is for the individual members of the University community, not for the University as an institution, to make those judgments for themselves, and to act on those judgments not by seeking to suppress speech, but by openly and vigorously contesting the ideas they oppose." One of the authors of the report stated that "College is a time to learn to deal with challenging, unsettling, and even offensive and hateful ideas. In the real world, we are inevitably confronted with these ideas, and college should prepare our graduates to know how to respond to such ideas courageously, effectively and persuasively." Are "trigger warnings" and the concept of "micro-aggressions" consistent with the University of Chicago policy? Does the policy make sense?

14. *More on the International Treaty Regulating the Internet.* At the convention, suppose that the German and French delegates demand protections against hate speech on the grounds that it "degrades human dignity" and that it is likely to cause breaches of the peace. In light of the holding in *R.A.V.*, what restrictions can you agree to impose on hate speech?

12. True Threats

Virginia v. Black

538 U.S. 343 (2003)

Justice O'CONNOR announced the judgment of the Court and delivered the opinion of the Court with respect to Parts I, II, and III, and an opinion with respect to Parts IV and V, in which THE CHIEF JUSTICE, Justice STEVENS, and Justice BREYER join.

In this case we consider whether the Commonwealth of Virginia's statute banning cross burning with "an intent to intimidate a person or group of persons" violates the First Amendment. We conclude that while a State, consistent with the First Amendment, may ban cross burning carried out with the intent to intimidate, the provision in the Virginia statute treating any cross burning as prima facie evidence of intent to intimidate renders the statute unconstitutional in its current form.

I

Respondents Barry Black, Richard Elliott, and Jonathan O'Mara were convicted separately of violating Virginia's cross-burning statute, §18.2-423. That statute provides: "It shall be unlawful for any person or persons, with the intent of intimidating any person or group of persons, to burn, or cause to be burned, a cross on the property of another, a highway or other public place. Any person who shall violate any provision of this section shall be guilty of a Class 6 felony." Any such burning of a cross shall be prima facie evidence of an intent to intimidate a person or group of persons.

On August 22, 1998, Barry Black led a Ku Klux Klan rally in Virginia. Twenty-five to thirty people attended this gathering, which occurred on private property with the permission of the owner. The property was located on an open field just off a state highway. When the sheriff learned that a Klan rally was occurring in his county, he went to observe it from the side of the road. During the approximately one hour that the sheriff was present, about 40 to 50 cars passed the site, a "few" of which stopped to ask what was happening. Eight to ten houses were located in the vicinity of the rally. Rebecca Sechrist "sat and watched to see what was going on" from the lawn of her in-laws' house. During the rally, Sechrist heard Klan members speak about "what they were" and "what they believed in." The speakers "talked real bad about the blacks and the Mexicans." One speaker told the assembled gathering that "he would love to take a .30/.30 and just randomly shoot the blacks." The speakers also talked about "President Clinton and Hillary Clinton," and about how their tax money "goes to the black people." Sechrist testified that this language made her "very scared." At the conclusion, the crowd circled around a 25- to 30-foot cross. The cross was between 300 and 350 yards away from the road. The cross "then all of a sudden went up in a flame." As the cross burned, the Klan played *Amazing Grace* over the loudspeakers. Sechrist stated that the cross burning made her feel "awful" and "terrible." The sheriff arrested Black for burning a cross with the intent of intimidating a person or group of persons, in violation of §18.2-423. At trial, the jury was instructed that "intent to intimidate means the motivation to intentionally put a person or a group of persons in fear of bodily harm. Such fear must arise from the willful conduct of the accused rather than from some mere temperamental timidity of the victim." The trial court also instructed the jury that "the burning of a cross by itself is sufficient evidence from which you may infer the required intent." The jury found Black guilty, and fined him $2,500. The Court of Appeals of Virginia affirmed.

On May 2, 1998, respondents Richard Elliott and Jonathan O'Mara, as well as a third individual, attempted to burn a cross on the yard of James Jubilee. Jubilee, an African-American, was Elliott's next-door neighbor in Virginia. Before the burning, Jubilee spoke to Elliott's mother to inquire about shots being fired from behind the Elliott home. The next morning, as Jubilee was pulling his car out of the driveway, he noticed the partially burned cross approximately 20 feet from his house. After seeing the cross, Jubilee was "very nervous" because he "didn't know what would be the next phase," and because "a cross burned in your yard tells you that it's just the first round." Elliott and O'Mara were charged with attempted cross burning and conspiracy to commit cross burning. O'Mara pleaded guilty to both counts and was sentenced to 90 days in jail and fined $2,500, but the judge suspended 45 days of the sentence and $1,000 of the fine. At Elliott's trial, the jury found Elliott guilty of attempted cross burning and acquitted him of conspiracy to commit cross burning. It sentenced Elliott to 90 days in jail and a

$2,500 fine. The Court of Appeals of Virginia affirmed. But the Supreme Court of Virginia struck the law down, relying on *R.A.V. v. St. Paul*, 505 U.S. 377 (1992).

II

Cross burning originated in the 14th century as a means for Scottish tribes to signal each other. Sir Walter Scott used cross burnings for dramatic effect in *The Lady of the Lake*, where the burning cross signified both a summons and a call to arms. *See* W. Scott, *The Lady of the Lake*, canto third. Cross burning in this country, however, long ago became unmoored from its Scottish ancestry. Burning a cross in the United States is inextricably intertwined with the history of the Ku Klux Klan.

The first Ku Klux Klan began in 1866. The Klan fought Reconstruction and the drive to allow freed blacks to participate in the political process. The Klan imposed "a veritable reign of terror" throughout the South. The Klan employed tactics such as whipping, threatening to burn people at the stake, and murder. The Klan's victims included blacks, southern whites who disagreed with the Klan, and "carpetbagger" northern whites. In response, Congress passed what is now known as the Ku Klux Klan Act. 42 U.S.C. §§1983, 1985, and 1986. President Grant used these new powers to suppress the Klan. By the end of Reconstruction in 1877, the first Klan no longer existed.

The genesis of the second Klan began in 1905, with the publication of Thomas Dixon's *The Clansmen: An Historical Romance of the Ku Klux Klan*. Dixon's book was a sympathetic portrait of the first Klan, depicting the Klan as a group of heroes "saving" the South from blacks and the "horrors" of Reconstruction. Although the first Klan never actually practiced cross burning, Dixon's book depicted the Klan burning crosses to celebrate the execution of former slaves. When D.W. Griffith turned Dixon's book into the movie *The Birth of a Nation* in 1915, the association between cross burning and the Klan became indelible. In addition to the cross burnings in the movie, a poster advertising the film displayed a hooded Klansman riding a hooded horse, with his left hand holding the reins of the horse and his right hand holding a burning cross above his head.

From the inception of the second Klan, cross burnings have been used to communicate both threats of violence and messages of shared ideology. The new Klan's ideology did not differ much from that of the first Klan. As one Klan publication emphasized, "We avow the distinction between the races, and we shall ever be true to the faithful maintenance of White Supremacy and will strenuously oppose any compromise." Violence was an elemental part of this new Klan. By September 1921, the *New York World* newspaper documented 152 acts of Klan violence, including 4 murders, 41 floggings, and 27 tar-and-featherings. Often, the Klan used cross burnings as a tool of intimidation and a threat of impending violence. After one cross burning at a synagogue, a Klan member noted that if the cross burning did not "shut the Jews up, we'll cut a few throats and see what happens." In Miami in 1941, the Klan burned four crosses in front of a proposed housing project, declaring, "We are here to keep niggers out of your town. When the law fails you, call on us." These cross burnings embodied threats to people whom the Klan deemed antithetical to its goals. These threats had special force given the long history of Klan violence. The Klan continued to use cross burnings to intimidate after World War II. In one incident, an African-American "school teacher who recently moved his family into a block formerly occupied only by whites asked the protection of city police after the burning of a cross in his front yard." These incidents of cross burning, among others, helped prompt Virginia to enact its first version of the cross-burning statute in 1950.

The decision in *Brown v. Board of Education*, 347 U.S. 483 (1954), along with the civil rights movement of the 1950's and 1960's, sparked another outbreak of Klan violence. These acts of violence included bombings, beatings, shootings, stabbings, and mutilations. Members of the Klan burned crosses on the lawns of those associated with the civil rights movement, assaulted the Freedom Riders, bombed churches, and murdered blacks as well as whites viewed as sympathetic toward the civil rights movement.

Throughout the history of the Klan, cross burnings have remained potent symbols of shared group identity and ideology. The burning cross became a symbol of the Klan itself and a central feature of Klan gatherings. According to the Klan constitution (the kloran), the "fiery cross" was the "emblem of that sincere, unselfish devotedness of all klansmen to the sacred purpose and principles we have espoused." The Klan has published its newsletters and magazines under the name The Fiery Cross. At Klan gatherings, cross burning became the climax of the rally or the initiation. Posters advertising an upcoming Klan rally often featured a Klan member holding a cross. Throughout the Klan's history, the Klan continued to use the burning cross in ritual ceremonies. In 1960, the Klan engaged in rallies and cross burnings throughout the South in an attempt to recruit 10 million members. Cross burnings featured prominently in Klan rallies when the Klan moved toward more nonviolent tactics to stop integration. In short, a burning cross has remained a symbol of Klan ideology and of Klan unity.

Regardless of whether the message is a political one or whether the message is also meant to intimidate, the burning of a cross is a "symbol of hate." And while cross burning sometimes carries no intimidating message, at other times the intimidating message is the *only* message conveyed. When a cross burning is directed at a particular person not affiliated with the Klan, the burning cross often serves as a message of intimidation, designed to inspire in the victim a fear of bodily harm. Moreover, the history of violence associated with the Klan shows that the possibility of injury or death is not just hypothetical. The person who burns a cross directed at a particular person often is making a serious threat, meant to coerce the victim to comply with the Klan's wishes unless the victim is willing to risk the wrath of the Klan. As the cases of respondents Elliott and O'Mara indicate, individuals without Klan affiliation who wish to threaten or menace another person sometimes use cross burning because of this association between a burning cross and violence. In sum, while a burning cross does not inevitably convey a message of intimidation, often the cross burner intends that the recipients of the message fear for their lives. And when a cross burning is used to intimidate, few if any messages are more powerful.

III

The First Amendment, applicable to the States through the Fourteenth Amendment, provides that "Congress shall make no law abridging the freedom of speech." The hallmark of the protection of free speech is to allow "free trade in ideas"—even ideas that the overwhelming majority of people might find distasteful or discomforting. The First Amendment affords protection to symbolic or expressive conduct as well as to actual speech.

The protections afforded by the First Amendment, however, are not absolute, and we have long recognized that the government may regulate certain categories of expression consistent with the Constitution. Thus, for example, a State may punish those words "which by their very utterance inflict injury or tend to incite an immediate breach of the peace." We have consequently held that fighting words—"those personally abusive epithets which, when addressed to the ordinary citizen, are, as a matter of common knowledge, inherently likely to provoke violent reaction"—are generally proscribable under the First Amendment. Furthermore, "the constitutional guarantees of free speech and free press do not permit a State to forbid or proscribe advocacy of the use of force or of law violation except where such advocacy is directed to inciting or producing imminent lawless action and is likely to incite or produce such action." *Brandenburg v. Ohio*, 395 U.S. 444 (1969) (per curiam). The First Amendment also permits a State to ban a "true threat." *Watts v. United States*, 394 U.S. 705 (1969) (per curiam).

"True threats" encompass those statements where the speaker means to communicate a serious expression of an intent to commit an act of unlawful violence to a particular individual or group of individuals. The speaker need not actually intend to carry out the threat. Rather, a prohibition on true threats "protects individuals from the fear of violence" and "from the disruption that fear engenders," in addition to protecting people "from the possibility that the threatened violence will occur." Intimidation in the constitutionally proscribable sense of the word is a type of true threat, where a speaker directs a threat to a person or group of persons with the intent of placing the victim in fear of bodily harm or death. Respondents do not contest that some cross burnings fit within this meaning of intimidating speech, and rightly so. The history of cross burning in this country shows that cross burning is often intimidating, intended to create a pervasive fear in victims that they are a target of violence.

The Supreme Court of Virginia ruled that in light of *R.A.V.*, even if it is constitutional to ban cross burning in a content-neutral manner, the Virginia cross-burning statute is unconstitutional because it discriminates on the basis of content and viewpoint. It is true that the burning of a cross is symbolic expression. The reason why the Klan burns a cross at its rallies, or individuals place a burning cross on someone else's lawn, is that the burning cross represents the message that the speaker wishes to communicate. Individuals burn crosses as opposed to other means of communication because cross burning carries a message in an effective and dramatic manner. The fact that cross burning is symbolic expression, however, does not resolve the constitutional question.

In *R.A.V.*, we held that a local ordinance that banned certain symbolic conduct, including cross burning, was unconstitutional. We held that the ordinance did not pass constitutional muster because it discriminated on the basis of content by targeting only those individuals who "provoke violence" on a basis specified in the law. This content-based discrimination was unconstitutional because it allowed the city "to impose special prohibitions on those speakers who express views on disfavored subjects." We did not hold in *R.A.V.* that the First Amendment prohibits *all* forms of content-based discrimination within a proscribable area of speech. Rather, we specifically stated that some types of content discrimination did not violate the First Amendment:

> When the basis for the content discrimination consists entirely of the very reason the entire class of speech at issue is proscribable, no significant danger of idea or viewpoint discrimination exists. Such a reason, having been adjudged neutral enough to support exclusion of the entire class of speech from First Amendment protection, is also neutral enough to form the basis of distinction within the class.

Indeed, we noted that it would be constitutional to ban only a particular type of threat: "The Federal Government can criminalize only those threats of violence that are directed against the President since the reasons why threats of violence are outside the First Amendment have special force when applied to the person of the President." A State may "choose to prohibit only that obscenity which is the most patently offensive *in its prurience*—i.e., that which involves the most lascivious displays of sexual activity." Consequently, while *R.A.V.* does not permit a State to ban only obscenity based on "offensive *political* messages," or "only those threats against the President that mention his policy on aid to inner cities," the First Amendment permits content discrimination "based on the very reasons why the particular class of speech at issue is proscribable."

Similarly, Virginia's statute does not run afoul of the First Amendment insofar as it bans cross burning with intent to intimidate. The Virginia statute does not single out for opprobrium only that speech directed toward "one of the specified disfavored topics." It does not matter whether an individual burns a cross with intent to intimidate because of the victim's race, gender, or religion, or because of the victim's "political affiliation, union membership, or homosexuality." It is not true that cross burners direct their intimidating conduct solely to racial or religious minorities. Indeed, in the case of Elliott and O'Mara, it is at least unclear whether the respondents burned a cross due to racial animus.

The First Amendment permits Virginia to outlaw cross burnings done with the intent to intimidate because burning a cross is a particularly virulent form of intimidation. Instead of prohibiting all intimidating messages, Virginia may choose to regulate this subset of intimidating messages in light of cross burning's long and pernicious history as a signal of impending violence. Thus, just as a State may regulate only that obscenity which is the most obscene due to its prurient content, so too may a State choose to prohibit only those forms of intimidation that are most likely to inspire fear of bodily harm. A ban on cross burning carried out with the intent to intimidate is fully consistent with our holding in *R.A.V.* and is proscribable under the First Amendment.

IV

The Supreme Court of Virginia ruled that Virginia's cross-burning statute was unconstitutionally overbroad due to its provision stating that "any such burning of a cross shall be prima facie evidence of an intent to intimidate a person or group of persons." Va. Code Ann. §18.2-423 (1996). The prima facie provision strips away the very reason why a State may ban cross burning with the intent to intimidate. The prima facie evidence provision permits a jury to convict in every cross-burning case in which defendants exercise their constitutional right not to put on a defense. And even where a defendant like Black presents a defense, the prima facie evidence provision makes it more likely that the jury will find an intent to intimidate regardless of the particular facts of the case. The provision permits the Commonwealth to arrest, prosecute, and convict a person based solely on the fact of cross burning itself.

The provision as so interpreted "would create an unacceptable risk of the suppression of ideas." The act of burning a cross may mean that a person is engaging in constitutionally proscribable intimidation. But that same act may mean only that the person is engaged in core political speech. The prima facie evidence chills constitutionally protected political speech because of the possibility that a State will prosecute—and potentially convict—somebody engaging only in lawful political speech at the core of what the First Amendment is designed to protect.

A burning cross is not always intended to intimidate. Sometimes cross burning is a statement of ideology, a symbol of group solidarity. It is a ritual used at Klan gatherings, and is used to represent the Klan itself. "Burning a cross at a political rally would almost certainly be protected expression." Occasionally a person who burns a cross does not intend to express either a statement of ideology or intimidation. Cross burnings have appeared in movies such as *Mississippi Burning,* and in plays such as Sir Walter Scott's *The Lady of the Lake.*

The prima facie provision makes no effort to distinguish among these different types of cross burnings. It does not distinguish between a cross burning done with the purpose of creating anger or resentment and a cross burning done with the purpose of threatening or intimidating a victim. It does not distinguish between a cross burning at a public rally or a cross burning on a neighbor's lawn. It does not treat the cross burning directed at an individual differently from the cross burning directed at a group of like-minded believers. It allows a jury to treat a cross burning on the property of another with the owner's acquiescence in the same manner as a cross burning on the property of another without the owner's permission. The prima facie evidence provision can "skew jury deliberations toward conviction in cases where the evidence of intent to intimidate is relatively weak and arguably consistent with a solely ideological reason for burning."

It may be true that a cross burning, even at a political rally, arouses a sense of anger or hatred among the vast majority of citizens who see a burning cross. But this sense of anger or hatred is not sufficient to ban all cross burnings. The prima facie evidence provision in this case ignores the contextual factors that are necessary to decide whether a particular cross burning is intended to intimidate. The First Amendment does not permit such a shortcut.

For these reasons, the prima facie evidence provision, as interpreted through the jury instruction and as applied in Barry Black's case, is unconstitutional on its face. We refuse to speculate on whether *any* interpretation of the prima facie evidence provision would satisfy the First Amendment. We recognize the theoretical possibility that the court, on remand, could interpret the provision in a manner different from that so far set forth in order to avoid the constitutional objections we have described. We also leave open the possibility that the provision is severable.

V

With respect to Barry Black, we agree with the Supreme Court of Virginia that his conviction cannot stand, and we affirm the judgment of the Supreme Court of Virginia. With respect to Elliott and O'Mara, we vacate the judgment of the Supreme Court of Virginia, and remand the case for further proceedings.

It is so ordered.

Justice STEVENS, *concurring.*

Cross burning with "an intent to intimidate" unquestionably qualifies as the kind of threat that is unprotected by the First Amendment.

Justice SCALIA, with whom Justice THOMAS joins as to Parts I and II, *concurring in part, concurring in the judgment in part,* and *dissenting in part.*

Under *R.A.V.,* a State may, without infringing the First Amendment, prohibit cross burning carried out with the intent to intimidate. Accordingly, I join Parts I-III of the Court's opinion. I also agree that we should vacate and remand the judgment of the Virginia Supreme Court so that that Court can have an opportunity authoritatively to construe the prima-facie-evidence provision. The Virginia Supreme Court did not suggest that a jury may ignore any rebuttal evidence that has been presented and, solely on the basis of a showing that the defendant burned a cross, find that he intended to intimidate. The effect of the prima-facie-evidence provision is far more limited. It suffices to "insulate the Commonwealth from a motion to strike the evidence *at the end of its case-in-chief,*" but it does nothing more. Our overbreadth jurisprudence has consistently focused on whether *the prohibitory terms* of a particular statute extend to protected conduct; that is, we have inquired whether individuals who engage in protected conduct can be *convicted* under a statute, not whether they might be subject to arrest and prosecution. *E.g., Houston v. Hill,* 482 U.S. 451 (1987).

Justice SOUTER, with whom Justice KENNEDY and Justice GINSBURG join, *concurring in the judgment in part* and *dissenting in part.*

I agree that the Virginia statute makes a content-based distinction within the category of punishable intimidating or threatening expression, the very type of distinction we considered in *R.A.V.* I disagree that any exception should save Virginia's law from unconstitutionality under the holding in *R.A.V.* or any acceptable variation of it.

The prohibition of cross burning with intent to intimidate selects a symbol with particular content from the field of all proscribable expression meant to intimidate. Even when the symbolic act is meant to terrify, a burning cross may carry a further, ideological message of white Protestant supremacy. The ideological message not only accompanies many threatening uses of the symbol, but is also expressed when a burning cross is not used to threaten but merely to symbolize the supremacist ideology and the solidarity of those who espouse it. The burning cross can broadcast threat and ideology together, ideology alone, or threat alone, as was the choice of respondents Elliott and O'Mara.

Because of the burning cross's extraordinary force as a method of intimidation, the *R.A.V.* exception most likely to cover the statute is an exception for content discrimination on a basis that "consists entirely of the very reason the entire class of speech at issue is proscribable." I do not think that the Virginia statute qualifies for this virulence exception. The first example of permissible distinction is for a prohibition of obscenity unusually offensive "in its prurience." Distinguishing obscene publications on this basis does not suggest discrimination on the basis of the message conveyed. The opposite is true, however, when a general prohibition of intimidation is rejected in favor of a distinct proscription of intimidation by cross burning. The cross may have been selected because of its special power to threaten, but it may also have been singled out because of disapproval of its message of white supremacy, either because a legislature thought white supremacy was a pernicious doctrine or because it found that dramatic, public espousal of it was a civic embarrassment. Nor does this case present any analogy to the statute prohibiting threats against the President. Threats against the President are not generally identified by reference to the content of any message that may accompany the threat, let alone any viewpoint, and there is no obvious correlation in fact between victim and message.

R.A.V.'s third exception allows content-based discrimination within a proscribable category when its "nature" is such "that there is no realistic possibility that official suppression of ideas is afoot." I believe the prima facie evidence provision stands in the way of any such finding. To the extent the prima facie evidence provision skews prosecutions, then, it skews the statute toward suppressing ideas.

I would therefore affirm the judgment of the Supreme Court of Virginia vacating the respondents' convictions and dismissing the indictments.

Justice THOMAS, *dissenting.*

Although it is constitutionally permissible to "ban cross burning carried out with intent to intimidate," the majority errs in imputing an expressive component to this activity. The Klan is a terrorist organization, which, in its endeavor to intimidate, or even eliminate those it dislikes, uses the most brutal of methods. For those not easily frightened, cross burning has been followed by more extreme measures, such as beatings and murder. In our culture, cross burning has almost invariably meant lawlessness and understandably instills in its victims well-grounded fear of physical violence. It is simply beyond belief that the Virginia legislature was concerned with anything but penalizing conduct it must have viewed as particularly vicious. Just as one cannot burn down someone's house to make a political point and then seek refuge in the First Amendment, those who hate cannot terrorize and intimidate to make their point. Since the statute addresses only conduct, there is no need to analyze it under our First Amendment tests. The fact that the statute permits a jury to draw an inference of intent to intimidate from the cross burning itself presents no constitutional problems. Virginia law still requires the jury to find the existence of each element, including intent to intimidate, beyond a reasonable doubt.

Notes and Questions

1. *Definition of "True Threat."* In *Watts v. United States*, 394 U.S. 705 (1969), the Court held that a federal statute prohibiting the act of "knowingly and willfully making any threat" to "inflict bodily harm upon the President" was constitutional on its face, but concluded that "a threat must be distinguished from constitutionally protected speech." *Watts* reversed the defendant's conviction because the government did not prove a "true threat" based on the defendant's utterance of "political hyperbole," which was merely a "very crude offensive method of stating a political opposition to the President." The Court's interpretation of defendant's speech as not being a "true threat" was based on context, the reaction of the listeners, and its expressly conditional nature.

2. *Mental State for "True Threat."* In *United States v. Elonis*, 575 U.S. 723 (2015), the Court refused to definitively define the mental state required for a "true threat" under the First Amendment. 18 U.S.C. §875(c), prohibits "any communication containing any threat to injure the person of another." The defendant posted rap lyrics on Facebook that contained violent language and imagery, along with disclaimers that his lyrics depicted real persons, and claims that he was simply exercising his First Amendment rights. However, the lyrics were viewed as threatening by his estranged wife, his co-workers, and the FBI agents who arrested him. At trial, although the defense sought a jury instruction that required proof of

an "intent to communicate a true threat," the trial judge gave the jury the following instruction: "A statement is a true threat when a defendant intentionally makes a statement in a context or under such circumstances wherein a reasonable person would foresee that the statement would be interpreted by those to whom the maker communicates the statement as a serious expression of an intention to inflict bodily injury or take the life of an individual." The Court reversed, holding that as a matter of statutory interpretation, when a statute is silent regarding the required mental state, a court must imply a mental state that "is necessary to separate wrongful conduct from otherwise innocent conduct." With regard to the threat statute, the Court believed that " 'the crucial element separating legal innocence from wrongful conduct' is the threatening nature of the communication," which is why "the mental state requirement must apply to the fact that the communication contains a threat." Thus, the Court regarded the "reasonable person" or negligence standard argued for by the government as "inconsistent with 'the conventional requirement for criminal conduct—*awareness* of some wrongdoing.' " "If the defendant transmits a communication for the purpose of issuing a threat, or with knowledge that the communication will be viewed as a threat," then "the mental state requirement of §875(c) is satisfied." The Court refused to decide whether recklessness would be sufficient under the statute because that issue was not briefed or argued by either party. On remand, Elonis' conviction was reinstated. *See United States v. Elonis*, 841 F.3d 589 (3rd Cir. 2016). The court held that, if "a defendant transmits a communication for the purpose of issuing a threat or with knowledge that the recipient will view it as a threat, and a jury determines that the communication is objectively threatening, then the defendant has violated Section 875(c) whether or not he agrees the communication was objectively threatening." Given the overwhelming evidence that this standard was satisfied, the Third Circuit concluded that the error in the original jury instruction was "harmless." The Supreme Court refused to hear the case a second time.

3. *Comparing Scenarios.* Does *Virginia v. Black* cast doubt on the continuing validity of the holding in *Brandenburg v. Ohio*? Note that the Court quotes *Brandenburg* with approval. If *Brandenburg* arose today, would the result be different? Does the fact that *Brandenburg* invited a reporter to the rally and allowed him to film the proceedings affect the analysis?

4. *California Cross-Burning Statute.* Would a California cross-burning statute be treated (for constitutional purposes) like the Virginia statute? Does California have the same history of cross burning as Virginia does? Is a Los Angeles resident as likely to perceive a burning cross as a "true threat" and as "intimidation" as a Virginia resident is? In other words, do cultural and historical context affect the Court's view of cross burning?

5. *The Abortion "Wanted" Posters.* In *Planned Parenthood of Columbia/Willamette, Inc. v. American Coalition of Life Activists*, 422 F.3d 949 (9th Cir. 2005), the Court applied the "true threat" doctrine to abortion protestors who sought to intimidate abortion providers. The case involved a civil suit by four physicians and

two health clinics that provided abortions against the American Coalition of Life Activists (ACLA), which produced posters that made threats, including the Deadly Dozen "GUILTY" poster (which set forth the names of various abortion providers), the Crist "GUILTY" poster (which contained a physician's name, address, and photograph), and the "Nuremberg Files" (which involved a list of names of abortion providers who the ACLA believed or hoped might be put on trial for crimes against humanity one day). The posters were regarded as "true threats" because they were circulated following the circulation of other, similar posters that had identified abortion providers who were subsequently murdered. The suit was brought under the Freedom of Access to Clinic Entrances (FACE) Act and the Racketeer Influenced and Corrupt Organizations (RICO) Act, 18 U.S.C. §§1961-1968. The plaintiffs were awarded both compensatory damages and punitive damages. However, the initial award of $108.5 million in punitive damages was remitted to $45,000 to $75,000 per defendant.

6. *Dieudonné M'bala M'bala and Charlie Hebdo.* Other nations can be much more aggressive about banning so-called "hate speech" even when it does not rise to the level of a "true threat." For example, Dieudonné M'bala M'bala, a French comedian, performs a routine in which he mocks the Holocaust and makes anti-Semitic remarks. The routine has been banned in France, and Dieudonné has been convicted and fined "dozens of times" for anti-Semitic slander. Most recently, he was convicted of publicly condoning terrorism, a crime punishable by five years in prison, or seven years when it occurs in the media or social media. Dieudonné received a two-month jail sentence for posting these words on his Facebook page: "Tonight, as far as I'm concerned, I feel like Charlie Coulibaly." This posting occurred after the killing of four people at a kosher supermarket in Paris by Amedy Coulibaly, who described his acts as an expression of solidarity with the terrorist killings by the Kouachi brothers of 12 Charlie Hebdo journalists and one police officer. The latter terrorist attack inspired the slogan, *I am Charlie (Je suis Charlie)*, which was reflected in the Facebook reference to "*Charlie Coulibaly.*" Dieudonné's defense counsel planned an appeal, and emphasized that the comedian's posting should be interpreted "in the context of all the other messages he published on Facebook," in which "he paid tribute to all the victims of the attacks and clearly condemned the acts." *See* Aurelien Breeden, *Dieudonné M'bala M'bala, French Comedian, Convicted of Condoning Terrorism*, N.Y. Times, Mar. 18, 2015, http://www.nytimes.com/2015/03/19/world/europe/dieudonne-mbala-mbala-french-comedian-convicted-of-condoning-terrorism.html?_r=0. In the week following the Charlie Hebdo and kosher supermarket killings, 54 people were detained in France and some were jailed "for a variety of remarks shouted in the street or posted on social media." So-called fast-track custodial sentences were "handed down in cities across France for expressions of support for the gunmen in the two terrorist attacks." For example, one man received a one-year prison sentence "for posting a video on Facebook that mocked policeman Ahmed, who was shot at point-blank range by one of the Kouachis." Another was jailed for shouting obscenities at police and saying "the Kouachi brothers were

'just the start.'" The fast-track sentences were "condemned" by France's League of Human Rights (LDH). *See* Paul Kirby, Inside Europe Blog, *Paris Attacks: France Grapples with Freedom of Speech*, BBC News, Jan. 15, 2015, http://www.bbc.com/news/blogs-eu-30829005.

Food for Thought

Are there any other symbols that carry the message of intimidation conveyed by a burning cross, or is the cross *sui generis*? Suppose that a Los Angeles gang has a symbol (a coiled snake) that it marks on the doors of those whom it intends to hurt, maim, or kill. Might this symbol be treated like the burning cross for constitutional purposes?

∽ PROBLEMS ∽

1. *Kentucky Cross Burning.* Assume that Kentucky has a cross-burning statute that is identical to the Virginia statute. On Halloween night, a student at the University of Louisville dresses up like a Klansman and burns a cross as part of a skit. When the police charge the student under the statute, he defends on the basis that it was Halloween night and he was just "having fun." In other words, there was no intent to intimidate. At the student's trial, Black students testify that they were "intimidated" by the cross burning, which they viewed as racist and as designed to place them in a subservient status. The jury convicts the defendant. After *Black*, can the conviction stand? Suppose that the burning takes place on the oval in front of the University of Louisville's administration building. The university has a regulation that prohibits "open fires" on campus. The student is charged with violating the regulation. After *Black*, is it permissible to punish the student for violating the open fires regulation? Would it matter why the regulation was promulgated? Suppose that the university adopted the rule to limit the potential for fire hazards on campus. On the other hand, suppose that the university adopted the policy to prevent the KKK from burning crosses on campus.

2. *More on True Threats Against the President.* Suppose that a member of a white supremacist group writes a poem about the murder of a Black President and posts it on the internet. The poem, which describes in graphic detail how the murder is committed, has been posted on the internet for some time when federal agents arrest the author (and poster) for making a threat against the life of then President Obama. The poem read as follows:

> THE SNIPER: As the tyrant enters his cross hairs the breath he takes is deep; His focus is square on the target as he begins to release; A patriot for his people he knows this shot will cost his life; But for his race and their existence it is a small sacrifice; The bullet that he has chambered is one of the purest pride; And the inspiration on the casing reads DIE negro

DIE; He breathes out as he pulls the trigger releasing all his hate; And a smile appears upon his face as he seals that monkey's fate; The bullet screams toward its mark bringing with it death; And where there was once a face there is nothing left; Two blood covered agents star *sic* in horror and dismay; Looking down toward the ground where their president now lay; Now the screams of one old negro broad pierces through the air; Setting off panic from every eyewitness that was there; And among all the confusion the hero calmly slips away; Laughing for he knows there will be another negro holiday.

Is the speech protected under the precedent established in *Brandenburg, Black,* and *Watts?*

3. *Hanging Barack Obama in Effigy.* Before the 2008 presidential election, a number of incidents occurred during which then-candidate Barack Obama was hung in effigy. For example, in Clarksville, Indiana, a man hung an effigy of Obama from a tree in his front yard. *See* Harold J. Adams, *Indiana Man Hung Obama Doll from Tree,* Louisville Courier-Journal, B. 3, c. 2-4, Oct. 30, 2008. The man explained that he was opposed to having Obama become President because he would then become the Commander-in-Chief, and the man was fearful because he has relatives fighting in the Middle East. *Id.* In a like incident, a student hung an Obama effigy from a tree on the University of Kentucky campus. *See* Nancy S. Rodriguez, *Obama Effigy Sparks Anger: Dummy Was Hung from Tree at UK,* Louisville Courier-Journal, B-1, c. 2-5, Oct. 30, 2008. Can the two men be prosecuted for threatening then-candidate Obama? Does the fact that Obama is Black make a difference? Does the history of violence against Blacks in the South by the KKK make a difference?

4. *The University of Louisville Response.* In response to the Obama incident at the University of Kentucky (referred to in the prior problem), the University of Louisville issued this statement:

> The University of Louisville strives to foster and sustain an environment of inclusiveness that empowers us all to achieve our highest potential without fear of prejudice or bias. We commit ourselves to building an exemplary educational community that offers a nurturing and challenging intellectual climate, a respect for the spectrum of human diversity, and a genuine understanding of the many differences—including race, ethnicity, gender identity/expression, sexual orientation, age, socioeconomic status, disability, religion, national origin or military status—that enrich a vibrant metropolitan research university. We expect every member of our academic family to embrace the underlying values of this vision and to demonstrate a strong commitment to attracting, retaining and supporting students, faculty and staff who reflect the diversity of our larger society.

Should the university's policy be regarded as mandatory or as aspirational? If mandatory, in the sense that those who do not join or comply can be sanctioned, is it constitutionally valid?

5. *The Sexual Harassment Policy.* Glenview Hills University adopts a sexual harassment policy that prohibits "expressive, visual or physical conduct of a sexual or gender-motivated nature that has the purpose or effect of unreasonably interfering with another individual's work, educational performance or status, or that has the effect of creating a hostile, intimidating or offensive environment."

The university seeks to justify the policy as necessary to create a welcoming and tolerant environment for women, as well as a way to implement federal antidiscrimination laws. The policy is challenged by a graduate history student who claims that the policy inhibits him from expressing his opinions in class regarding women in combat and women in the military, as well as from expressing his broader social, cultural, religious, and political views. Is the policy constitutional? How might the student argue that the policy is unconstitutional? *See DeJohn v. Temple University*, 537 F.3d 301 (3d Cir. 2008).

6. *More on the Danish Cartoons.* In the "Fighting Words" section earlier in this chapter, there is a discussion of the controversial Danish cartoons. You should re-read it. Under *Black,* or the Court's other hate speech precedent, may the government prohibit publication of the cartoons?

7. *MySpace Page and Written Threats.* Holcomb, who is in the middle of a custody battle with the mother of his daughter, is charged with violating the following Virginia statute for postings that he made on his MySpace page: "Anyone who knowingly communicates in writing (including an electronic message) a threat to kill or do bodily injury to a person, regarding that person or any member of his family, and the threat places such person in reasonable apprehension of death or bodily injury to himself or his family member, is guilty of a Class 6 felony." One post read as follows: "Unfinished Bizness God, I Give You the Woodroll family. Woodroll was the mother's maiden name. Tell them to F the F Off and Get Off Me." Holcomb's second post consisted of the following "rap lyrics": "Poof! Make ya daughter disappear like 2pac! He knew now what he do like 2 cops. With no vest, off'd with 2 shots. Thru the chest from 2 blocks!" A third post read as follows: "Custody battles, restraining orders. Bitch made me go mad I just had to stab her. Blind now I see her true colors. On the front cover of The World's Most Murdered Mothers. By Americas Most Wanted Fathers." When Holcomb was charged with violating the statute, he offered a First Amendment defense, arguing that: 1) the MySpace profile never mentioned the mother by name; 2) Holcomb never invited the mother or her family to visit the website; and 3) Holcomb is a rap artist, and his lyrics reflect nothing more than his chosen means of artistic expression. However, Holcomb made no effort to hide his posts from others. Should the appellate court uphold his conviction under the First Amendment? *See Holcomb v. Commonwealth,* 709 S.E.2d 711 (Va. App. 2011).

8. *More Online (and Other) Threats Against President Obama.* When then-President Obama was going to give a speech in the city where he lives, a man posted on Facebook that he intends to kill the President and he makes similar statements to a number of people. When charged, he claims that his threat could not have been taken as a "true threat" because he did not have a ticket to the Obama event, had no weapon other than a slingshot, and freely discussed his plan with others who had the power to stop him. Is there a "true threat" against the President so that conviction is appropriate? *See United States v. Dutcher,* 851 F. 3d 757 (7th Cir. 2017).

9. *The Rap Song.* A rap artist, whose work is described as "controversial," argues that he is simply "putting on an image" or trying to "sell records." He has a rap group called "Ghetto Superstar Committee." After the artist is arrested and charged with possession of controlled substances, he writes a song entitled "F**k the Police" which contains violent rhetoric regarding the police, including the two officers who arrested him. The song contains lyrics which state that "I'ma jam this rusty knife all in his guts and chop his feet," "shift over at three and I'm gonna f**k up where you sleep" and "kill him wit a Glock." Has the rap artist made a "true threat" against the police? Alternatively, should the song be regarded as nothing more than "art?" *See Commonwealth v. Knox,* 190 A.3d 1146 (Penn. 2017), *cert. denied,* 139 S.Ct. 1547 (2019).

10. *More on the International Treaty Regulating the Internet.* At the convention, suppose that the German and French delegates again demand that all Nazi symbols be banned from the internet. Based on the holding in *Black,* can you agree to their demands? Would *Black* allow you to ban any other symbols (besides swastikas and other Nazi symbols) from the internet?

13. Possible Additional Categories for Exclusion of Speech Protection

Should the Court find that other categories of speech do not deserve constitutional protection? In the following case, the Court considered whether to except so-called "crush videos" from First Amendment protection.

United States v. Stevens

559 U.S. 460 (2010)

Chief Justice ROBERTS delivered the opinion of the Court.

Section 48 establishes a criminal penalty of up to five years in prison for anyone who knowingly "creates, sells, or possesses a depiction of animal cruelty," if done "for commercial gain" in interstate or foreign commerce. 18 U.S.C. §48(a). A depiction of "animal cruelty" is defined as one "in which a living animal is intentionally maimed, mutilated, tortured, wounded, or killed," if that conduct violates federal or state law where "the creation, sale, or possession takes place." §48(c)(1). In what is referred to as the "exceptions clause," the law exempts from prohibition any depiction "that has serious religious, political, scientific, educational, journalistic, historical, or artistic value." §48(b).

The legislative background of §48 focused primarily on the interstate market for "crush videos." According to the House Committee Report on the bill, such videos feature the intentional torture and killing of helpless animals, including cats, dogs, monkeys, mice, and hamsters. Crush videos often depict women slowly crushing animals to death "with their bare feet or while wearing high heeled shoes," sometimes while "talking to the animals in a kind of dominatrix patter" over "the cries and squeals of the animals, obviously in great pain." Apparently these depictions "appeal to persons with a very specific sexual fetish who find them sexually arousing or otherwise exciting." The acts depicted in crush videos are typically prohibited by the animal cruelty laws enacted by all 50 States and the District of Columbia. But crush videos rarely disclose the participants' identities, inhibiting prosecution of the underlying conduct.

This case, however, involves an application of §48 to depictions of animal fighting. Dogfighting, for example, is unlawful in all 50 States and the District of Columbia, and has been restricted by federal law since 1976. Respondent Robert J. Stevens ran a business, "Dogs of Velvet and Steel," and an associated Web site, through which he sold videos of pit bulls engaging in dogfights and attacking other animals. Among these videos were Japan Pit Fights and Pick-A-Winna: A Pit Bull Documentary, which include contemporary footage of dogfights in Japan (where such conduct is allegedly legal) as well as footage of American dogfights from the 1960's and 1970's. A third video, Catch Dogs and Country Living, depicts the use of pit bulls to hunt wild boar, as well as a "gruesome" scene of a pit bull attacking a domestic farm pig. On the basis of these videos, Stevens was indicted on three counts of violating §48.

Stevens moved to dismiss the indictment, arguing that §48 is facially invalid under the First Amendment. The District Court held that the depictions subject to §48, like obscenity or child pornography, are categorically unprotected by the First Amendment. The en banc Third Circuit declared §48 facially unconstitutional. We granted certiorari.

The Government's primary submission is that §48 necessarily complies with the Constitution because the banned depictions of animal cruelty, as a class, are categorically unprotected by the First Amendment. We disagree.

The First Amendment provides that "Congress shall make no law abridging the freedom of speech." "As a general matter, the First Amendment means that government has no power to restrict expression because of its message, its ideas, its subject matter, or its content." *Ashcroft v. American Civil Liberties Union*, 535 U.S. 564, 573 (2002). Section 48 explicitly regulates expression based on content: The statute restricts "visual and auditory depictions," such as photographs, videos, or sound recordings, depending on whether they depict conduct in which a living animal is intentionally harmed. As such, §48 is "'presumptively invalid,' and the Government bears the burden to rebut that presumption." *United States v. Playboy Entertainment Group, Inc.*, 529 U.S. 803, 817 (2000) (quoting *R.A.V. v. St. Paul*, 505 U.S. 377, 382 (1992)).

"From 1791 to the present," however, the First Amendment has "permitted restrictions upon the content of speech in a few limited areas," and has never "included a freedom to disregard these traditional limitations." *Id.* at 382-383. These "historic and traditional categories long familiar to the bar," including obscenity, defamation, fraud, incitement, and speech integral to criminal conduct—are "well-defined and narrowly limited classes of speech, the prevention and punishment of which have never been thought to raise any Constitutional problem." *Chaplinsky v. New Hampshire*, 315 U.S. 568, 571-572 (1942).

The Government argues that "depictions of animal cruelty" should be added to the list. It contends that depictions of "illegal acts of animal cruelty" that are "made, sold, or possessed for commercial gain" necessarily "lack expressive value," and may accordingly "be regulated as *unprotected* speech." The claim is not just that Congress may regulate depictions of animal cruelty subject to the First Amendment, but that these depictions are outside the reach of that Amendment altogether—that they fall into a "First Amendment Free Zone." *Board of Airport Commrs. of Los Angeles v. Jews for Jesus, Inc.*, 482 U.S. 569 (1987).

Prohibition of animal cruelty itself has a long history in American law, starting with the early settlement of the Colonies. But we are unaware of any similar tradition excluding *depictions* of animal cruelty from "the freedom of speech" codified in the First Amendment, and the Government points to none. The Government contends that "historical evidence" about the reach of the First Amendment is not "a necessary prerequisite for regulation today," and that categories of speech may be exempted from the First Amendment's protection without any long-settled tradition of subjecting that speech to regulation. Instead, the Government points to Congress's "legislative judgment that depictions of animals being intentionally tortured and killed are of such minimal redeeming value as to render them unworthy of First Amendment protection," and asks the Court to uphold the ban on the same basis. The Government thus proposes that a claim of categorical exclusion should be considered under a simple balancing test: "Whether a given category of speech enjoys First Amendment protection depends upon a categorical balancing of the value of the speech against its societal costs."

As a free-floating test for First Amendment coverage, that sentence is startling and dangerous. The First Amendment's guarantee of free speech does not extend only to categories of speech that survive an ad hoc balancing of relative social costs and benefits. The First Amendment itself reflects a judgment by the American people that the benefits of its restrictions on the Government outweigh the costs. Our Constitution forecloses any attempt to revise that judgment simply on the basis that some speech is not worth it. The Constitution is not a document "prescribing limits, and declaring that those limits may be passed at pleasure." *Marbury v. Madison*, 1 Cranch 137, 178, 2 L.Ed. 60 (1803).

To be fair to the Government, its view did not emerge from a vacuum. As the Government correctly notes, this Court has often *described* historically unprotected categories of speech as being " 'of such slight social value as a step to truth that any benefit that may be derived from them is clearly outweighed by the social interest in order and morality.' " *R.A.V., supra*, at 383 (quoting *Chaplinsky, supra*, at 572). In *New York v. Ferber*, 458 U.S. 747 (1982), we noted that within these categories of unprotected speech, "the evil to be restricted so overwhelmingly outweighs the expressive interests, if any, at stake, that no process of case-by-case adjudication is required," because "the balance of competing interests is clearly struck." The Government derives its proposed test from these descriptions in our precedents.

But such descriptions are just that—descriptive. They do not set forth a test that may be applied as a general matter to permit the Government to imprison any speaker so long as his speech is deemed valueless or unnecessary, or so long as an ad hoc calculus of costs and benefits tilts in a statute's favor.

When we have identified categories of speech as fully outside the protection of the First Amendment, it has not been on the basis of a simple cost-benefit analysis. In *Ferber,* for example, we classified child pornography as such a category. We noted that the State of New York had a compelling interest in protecting children from abuse, and that the value of using children in these works (as opposed to simulated conduct or adult actors) was *de minimis.* But our decision did not rest on this "balance of competing interests" alone. We made clear that *Ferber* presented a special case: The market for child pornography was "intrinsically related" to the underlying abuse, and was therefore "an integral part of the production of such materials, an activity illegal throughout the Nation." As we noted, " 'it rarely has been suggested that the constitutional freedom for speech and press extends its immunity to speech or writing used as an integral part of conduct in violation of a valid criminal statute.' " *Ferber* thus grounded its analysis in a previously recognized, long-established category of unprotected speech, and our subsequent decisions have shared this understanding. *See Osborne v. Ohio,* 495 U.S. 103, 110 (1990); *Ashcroft v. Free Speech Coalition,* 535 U.S. 234, 249-250 (2002).

Our decisions in *Ferber* and other cases cannot be taken as establishing a freewheeling authority to declare new categories of speech outside the scope of the First Amendment. Maybe there are some categories of speech that have been historically unprotected, but have not yet been specifically identified or discussed as such in our case law. But if so, there is no evidence that "depictions of animal cruelty" is among them. We need not foreclose the future recognition of such additional categories to reject the Government's highly manipulable balancing test as a means of identifying them.

In addition, the law suffers from overbreadth. However "growing" and "lucrative" the markets for crush videos and dogfighting depictions might be, they are dwarfed by the market for other depictions, such as hunting magazines and videos, that we have determined to be within the scope of §48. We therefore need not and do not decide whether a statute limited to crush videos or other depictions of extreme animal cruelty would be constitutional. We hold only that §48 is not so limited but is instead substantially overbroad, and therefore invalid under the First Amendment.

The judgment of the United States Court of Appeals for the Third Circuit is affirmed.

It is so ordered.

Justice ALITO, *dissenting.*

The Court strikes down a valuable statute that was enacted not to suppress speech, but to prevent horrific acts of animal cruelty—in particular, the creation and commercial exploitation of "crush videos," a form of depraved entertainment that has no social value. The Court's approach, which has the practical effect of legalizing the sale of such videos and is thus likely to spur a resumption of their production, is unwarranted.

As the Court of Appeals recognized, "the primary conduct that Congress sought to address through its passage of §48 was the creation, sale, or possession of 'crush videos.'" It is undisputed that the *conduct* depicted in crush videos may constitutionally be prohibited. All 50 States and the District of Columbia have enacted statutes prohibiting animal cruelty. But before the enactment of §48, the underlying conduct depicted in crush videos was nearly impossible to prosecute. These videos, which "often appeal to persons with a very specific sexual fetish," were made in secret, generally without a live audience, and "the faces of the women inflicting the torture in the material often were not shown, nor could the location of the place where the cruelty was being inflicted or the date of the activity be ascertained from the depiction." Thus, law enforcement authorities often were not able to identify the parties responsible for the torture. In the rare instances in which it was possible to identify and find the perpetrators, they "often were able to successfully assert as a defense that the State could not prove its jurisdiction over the place where the act occurred or that the actions depicted took place within the time specified in the State statute of limitations." H.R. Rep., at 3.

In light of the practical problems thwarting the prosecution of the creators of crush videos under state animal cruelty laws, Congress concluded that the only effective way of stopping the underlying criminal conduct was to prohibit the commercial exploitation of the videos of that conduct. And Congress' strategy appears to have been vindicated. We are told that "by 2007, sponsors of §48 declared the crush video industry dead. Even overseas Websites shut down in the wake of §48. Now, after the Third Circuit's decision facially invalidating the statute, crush videos are already back online."

The First Amendment protects freedom of speech, but it does not protect violent criminal conduct, even if engaged in for expressive purposes. Crush videos present a highly unusual free speech issue because they are closely linked with violent criminal conduct. The videos record the commission of violent criminal acts, and that these crimes are committed for the sole purpose of creating the videos. Congress was presented with compelling evidence that the only way of preventing these crimes was to target the sale of the videos. Under these circumstances, I cannot believe that the First Amendment commands Congress to step aside and allow the underlying crimes to continue.

The most relevant of our prior decisions is *Ferber*. The Court there held that child pornography is not protected speech, and *Ferber*'s reasoning dictates a similar conclusion here. In *Ferber*, an important factor—the most important f actor—was that child pornography involves the commission of a crime that inflicts severe personal injury to the "children who are made to engage in sexual conduct for commercial purposes." Second, *Ferber* emphasized the fact that these underlying crimes could not be effectively combated without targeting the distribution of child pornography. Third, the *Ferber* Court noted that the value of child pornography "is exceedingly modest, if not *de minimis*," and that any such value was "overwhelmingly outweighed" by "the evil to be restricted."

All these characteristics are shared by §48, as applied to crush videos. First, the conduct depicted in crush videos is criminal in every State and the District of

Columbia. Any crush video made in this country records the actual commission of a criminal act that inflicts severe physical injury and excruciating pain and ultimately results in death. Those who record the underlying criminal acts are likely to be criminally culpable, either as aiders and abettors or conspirators. In the tight and secretive market for these videos, some who sell the videos or possess them with the intent to make a profit may be similarly culpable. (For example, in some cases, crush videos were commissioned by purchasers who specified the details of the acts that they wanted to see performed.) To the extent that §48 reaches such persons, it surely does not violate the First Amendment. Second, the criminal acts shown in crush videos cannot be prevented without targeting the conduct prohibited by §48—the creation, sale, and possession for sale of depictions of animal torture with the intention of realizing a commercial profit. Finally, the harm caused by the underlying crimes vastly outweighs any minimal value that the depictions might conceivably be thought to possess. Unlike the child pornography statute in *Ferber*, 18 U.S.C. §2252, §48(b) provides an exception for depictions having any "serious religious, political, scientific, educational, journalistic, historical, or artistic value."

Section 48 differs from a child pornography law in an important respect: preventing the abuse of children is certainly much more important than preventing the torture of the animals used in crush videos. The animals used in crush videos are living creatures that experience excruciating pain. Our society has long banned such cruelty, which is illegal throughout the country. Section 48's ban on trafficking in crush videos also helps to enforce the criminal laws and to ensure that criminals do not profit from their crimes. We have already judged that taking the profit out of crime is a compelling interest. *See Simon & Schuster, Inc. v. Members of N.Y. State Crime Victims Bd.*, 502 U.S. 105 (1991). Applying the principles set forth in *Ferber*, I would hold that crush videos are not protected by the First Amendment.

Application of the *Ferber* framework supports the constitutionality of §48 as applied to depictions of brutal animal fights. (For convenience, I will focus on dogfights which appear to be the most common type of animal fight videos.) First, such depictions, like crush videos, record the actual commission of a crime involving deadly violence. Dogfights are illegal in every State and the District of Columbia, and under federal law constitute a felony punishable by imprisonment for up to five years. Second, Congress had an ample basis for concluding that the crimes depicted in these videos cannot be effectively controlled without targeting the videos. The commercial trade in videos of dogfights is "an integral part of the production of such materials." Some dogfighting videos are made "solely for the purpose of selling the video (and not for a live audience)." In short, because videos depicting live dogfights are essential to the success of the criminal dogfighting subculture, the commercial sale of such videos helps to fuel the market for, and thus to perpetuate the perpetration of, the criminal conduct depicted in them.

Third, depictions of dogfights that fall within §48's reach have by definition no appreciable social value. Finally, the harm caused by the underlying criminal acts greatly outweighs any trifling value that the depictions might be thought to possess. As the Humane Society explains: "The abused dogs used in fights endure physical torture and emotional manipulation throughout their lives to predispose them to violence; common tactics include feeding the animals hot peppers and gunpowder, prodding them with sticks, and electrocution. Dogs are conditioned never to give up a fight, even if they will be gravely hurt or killed. As a result, dogfights inflict horrific injuries on the participating animals, including lacerations, ripped ears, puncture wounds and broken bones. Losing dogs are routinely refused treatment, beaten further as "punishment" for the loss, and executed by drowning, hanging, or incineration." For these dogs, unlike the animals killed in crush videos, the suffering lasts for years rather than minutes. As with crush videos, the statutory ban on commerce in dogfighting videos is supported by compelling governmental interests in effectively enforcing the Nation's criminal laws and preventing criminals from profiting from their illegal activities.

Notes and Questions: Rewriting the Crush Video Statute

After *Stevens*, Congress revised §48 to make it a crime to knowingly create, sell, market, advertise, exchange, or distribute an "animal crush video" that (1) depicts actual conduct in which one or more non-human animals is intentionally crushed, burned, drowned, suffocated, impaled, or otherwise subjected to serious bodily injury; and (2) is obscene. 18 U.S.C. §48 (2010). Does the revised law pass muster under the First Amendment? *See United States v. Richards*, 755 F.3d 269 (5th Cir. 2014), *cert. denied*, 575 U.S. 915 (2015).

Note: Violent Video Games

In *Brown v. Entertainment Merchants Association*, 564 U.S. 786 (2011), the Court invalidated a California statute that prohibited the sale or rental of "violent video games" to minors. The Court characterized the law as "a State's attempt to shoehorn speech about violence into obscenity," and held that the case was controlled by *Stevens*. The law provided for a civil fine of up to $1,000 and applied to video games in which the range of options available to a player includes killing, maiming, dismembering, or sexually assaulting an image of a human being, if those acts are depicted in a manner: (A) that a reasonable person, considering the game as a whole would find appeals to a deviant or morbid interest of minors; (B) that is patently offensive to prevailing standards in the community as to what is suitable for minors; and (C) that causes the game, as a whole, to lack serious literary, artistic, political, or scientific value for minors.

Brown observed that the statute's mimicry of *Ginsberg's* "obscenity for minors" statute was irrelevant because the State did not seek to "adjust the boundaries of an existing category of unprotected speech to ensure that a definition designed for adults does not apply to children" as in *Ginsberg*. Instead, the State sought "to create a wholly new category of content-based regulation that is permissible only for speech directed at children." This goal conflicted with the principle that the State has no "free-floating power to restrict the ideas to which children may be exposed." The Court noted that minors are exposed to depictions of violence through books, movies, radio, comic books, television, music lyrics, and now video games. Like these other protected speech forms, video games "communicate ideas—and even social messages—through many familiar literary devices (such as characters, dialogue, plot, and music)."

The Court held that the state was required to satisfy strict scrutiny in *Brown*, and could not do so. A compelling governmental interest was lacking because of the State's failure to "show a direct causal link between violent video games and harm to minors." California was only able to submit the findings of a "few" research psychologists which showed that such games only have "some" effect on children's feelings of aggression that are "indistinguishable from effects produced by other media," including "cartoons starring Bugs Bunny or the Road Runner." The Court found the statute to be "wildly underinclusive" for that reason, as well as because any parent, aunt, or uncle could "veto" the statute by renting or purchasing the prohibited games for a minor. Finally, the Court judged the statute to be "vastly overinclusive" because the law's "entire effect is only in support of what the State thinks parents ought to want." Nor did the Court agree that the State had an alternative compelling interest in serving the need of those parents who "wish to restrict their children's access" to the games but cannot do so." The Court noted that parents are served already by the age-specific voluntary rating system of the video game industry.

Justice Alito and Chief Justice Roberts concurred, agreeing that the California law "cannot be sustained," but preferring to invalidate it on vagueness grounds. They pointed to the terms *deviant* and *morbid* as failing to provide fair notice as to the law's meaning, and they faulted the legislature's "decision to lump all minors together." They disagreed with the Court's holding because they did not think that *Stevens* should control the case, and they did not want to "squelch legislative efforts" "prematurely" or suggest that no regulation of minors' access to violent video games is allowed. Justice Breyer dissented and would have upheld the law on the theory that the State could satisfy strict scrutiny; he argued that the Court should have deferred to the legislature's judgment regarding "legislative facts" beyond the competence of the Court. Justice Thomas dissented and would have upheld the law on the theory that the First Amendment does not protect either a right of minors to "access speech" "without going through their parents," or a right to speak to minors without doing so.

United States v. Alvarez

567 U.S. 709 (2012)

Justice KENNEDY announced the judgment of the Court and delivered an opinion, in which THE CHIEF JUSTICE, Justice GINSBURG, and Justice SOTOMAYOR join.

Lying was his habit. Xavier Alvarez, respondent lied when he said that he played hockey for the Detroit Red Wings and that he once married a starlet from Mexico. But when he lied in announcing he held the Congressional Medal of Honor, respondent violated a federal criminal statute, the Stolen Valor Act of 2005. 18 U.S.C. §704. In 2007, respondent attended his first public meeting as a board member of the Three Valley Water District Board. The board is a governmental entity with headquarters in Claremont, California. He introduced himself as follows: "I'm a retired marine of 25 years. I retired in the year 2001. Back in 1987, I was awarded the Congressional Medal of Honor. I got wounded many times by the same guy." None of this was true. Respondent's statements were a pathetic attempt to gain respect that eluded him. The statements do not seem to have been made to secure employment or financial benefits or admission to privileges reserved for those who had earned the Medal.

Respondent was indicted under the Stolen Valor Act for lying about the Congressional Medal of Honor at the meeting. The District Court rejected his claim that the statute is invalid under the First Amendment. Respondent pleaded guilty to one count, reserving the right to appeal. The Ninth Circuit held the Act invalid under the First Amendment and reversed the conviction. This Court granted certiorari.

It is right and proper that Congress, over a century ago, established an award so the Nation can hold in its highest respect and esteem those who, in the course of carrying out the "supreme and noble duty of contributing to the defense of the rights and honor of the nation," Selective Draft Law Cases, 245 U.S. 366, 390 (1918), have acted with extraordinary honor. And it should be uncontested that this is a legitimate Government objective, indeed a most valued national aspiration and purpose. This does not end the inquiry, however. Fundamental constitutional principles require that laws enacted to honor the brave must be consistent with the precepts of the Constitution for which they fought.

The Government contends the criminal prohibition is a proper means to further its purpose in creating and awarding the Medal. When content-based speech regulation is in question, exacting scrutiny is required. Statutes suppressing or restricting speech must be judged by the principles of the First Amendment. By this measure, the statutory provisions under which respondent was convicted must be held invalid, and his conviction must be set aside.

Respondent's claim to hold the Congressional Medal of Honor was false. There is no room to argue about interpretation or shades of meaning. On this premise, respondent violated §704(b); and, because the lie concerned the Congressional Medal of Honor, he was subject to an enhanced penalty under subsection (c). Those statutory provisions are as follows:

"(b) FALSE CLAIMS ABOUT RECEIPT OF MILITARY DECORATIONS OR MEDALS. — Whoever falsely represents himself or herself, verbally or in writing, to have been awarded any decoration or medal authorized by Congress for the Armed Forces of the United States shall be fined under this title, imprisoned not more than six months, or both.

"(c) ENHANCED PENALTY FOR OFFENSES INVOLVING CONGRESSIONAL MEDAL OF HONOR. —

"(1) IN GENERAL.—If a decoration or medal involved in an offense under subsection (a) or (b) is a Congressional Medal of Honor, in lieu of the punishment provided in that subsection, the offender shall be fined under this title, imprisoned not more than 1 year, or both."

Respondent challenges the statute as a content-based suppression of pure speech, speech not falling within any of the few categories of expression where content-based regulation is permissible. The Government defends the statute as necessary to preserve the integrity and purpose of the Medal, an integrity and purpose it contends are compromised and frustrated by the false statements the statute prohibits. It argues that false statements "have no First Amendment value in themselves," and thus "are protected only to the extent needed to avoid chilling fully protected speech." Although the statute covers respondent's speech, the Government argues that it leaves breathing room for protected speech, for example speech which might criticize the idea of the Medal or the importance of the military. The Government's arguments cannot suffice to save the statute.

"As a general matter, the First Amendment means that government has no power to restrict expression because of its message, its ideas, its subject matter, or its content." *Ashcroft v. American Civil Liberties Union*, 535 U.S. 564, 573 (2002). As a result, the Constitution "demands that content-based restrictions on speech be presumed invalid and that the Government bear the burden of showing their constitutionality." *Ashcroft v. American Civil Liberties Union*, 542 U.S. 656, 660 (2004).

In light of the substantial and expansive threats to free expression posed by content-based restrictions, this Court has rejected as "startling and dangerous" a "free-floating test for First Amendment coverage based on an ad hoc balancing of relative social costs and benefits." *United States v. Stevens*, 130 S.Ct. 1577, 1585 (2010). Instead, content-based restrictions on speech have been permitted, as a general matter, only when confined to the few "'historic and traditional categories of expression long familiar to the bar.'" *Id.* at 1584 (quoting *Simon & Schuster, Inc. v. Members of N.Y. State Crime Victims Bd.*, 502 U.S. 105, 127 (1991) (Kennedy, J., concurring in judgment)). Among these categories are advocacy intended, and likely, to incite imminent lawless action, defamation, speech integral to criminal conduct, so-called "fighting words," child pornography, fraud, true threats, and speech presenting some grave and imminent threat the government has the power to prevent, although a restriction under the last category is most difficult to sustain, *see New York Times Co. v. United States*, 403 U.S. 713 (1971) (*per curiam*). These categories have a historical foundation in the Court's free speech tradition. The vast realm of free speech and thought always protected in our tradition can still thrive, and even be furthered, by adherence to those categories and rules.

Absent from those few categories where the law allows content-based regulation of speech is any general exception to the First Amendment for false statements. This comports with the common understanding that some false statements are inevitable if there is to be an open and vigorous expression of views in public and private conversation, expression the First Amendment seeks to guarantee. *See Sullivan, supra,* at 271.

The Government cites language from this Court's precedents to support its contention that false statements have no value and hence no First Amendment protection. For instance, the Court has stated, "false statements of fact are particularly valueless because they interfere with the truth-seeking function of the marketplace of ideas," *Hustler Magazine, Inc. v. Falwell,* 485 U.S. 46, 52 (1988), and that false statements "are not protected by the First Amendment in the same manner as truthful statements," *Brown v. Hartlage,* 456 U.S. 45, 60-61 (1982). These quotations all derive from cases discussing defamation, fraud, or some other legally cognizable harm associated with a false statement, such as an invasion of privacy or the costs of vexatious litigation. In those decisions the falsity of the speech at issue was not irrelevant to our analysis, but neither was it determinative. The Court has never endorsed the categorical rule the Government advances: that false statements receive no First Amendment protection. Our prior decisions have not confronted a measure, like the Stolen Valor Act, that targets falsity and nothing more. Even when considering some instances of defamation and fraud, moreover, the Court has been careful to instruct that falsity alone may not suffice to bring the speech outside the First Amendment. The statement must be a knowing or reckless falsehood. *See Sullivan, supra,* at 280; *see also Garrison, supra,* at 73.

The Government thus seeks to use this principle for a new purpose. It seeks to convert a rule that limits liability even in defamation cases where the law permits recovery for tortious wrongs into a rule that expands liability in a different, far greater realm of discourse and expression. That inverts the rationale for the exception. The requirement of a knowing falsehood or reckless disregard for the truth as the condition for recovery in certain defamation cases exists to allow more speech, not less. A rule designed to tolerate certain speech ought not blossom to become a rationale for a rule restricting it.

The Government then gives three examples of regulations on false speech that courts generally have found permissible: first, the criminal prohibition of a false statement made to a Government official, 18 U.S.C. §1001; second, laws punishing perjury; and third, prohibitions on the false representation that one is speaking as a Government official or on behalf of the Government, *see, e.g.,* §912; §709. These restrictions, however, do not establish a principle that all proscriptions of false statements are exempt from exacting First Amendment scrutiny.

The federal statute prohibiting false statements to Government officials punishes "whoever, in any matter within the jurisdiction of the executive, legislative, or judicial branch of the Government, makes any materially false, fictitious, or fraudulent statement or representation." §1001. Section 1001's prohibition on false statements made to Government officials, in communications concerning official matters, does not lead to the broader proposition that false statements are unprotected when made to any person, at any time, in any context.

The same point can be made about what the Court has confirmed is the "unquestioned constitutionality of perjury statutes," both the federal statute and its state-law equivalents. *United States v. Grayson,* 438 U.S. 41, 54 (1978). It is not simply because perjured statements are false that they lack First Amendment protection. Perjured testimony "is at war with justice" because it can cause a court to render a "judgment not resting on truth." *In re Michael*, 326 U.S. 224, 227 (1945). Perjury undermines the function and province of the law and threatens the integrity of judgments that are the basis of the legal system. Unlike speech in other contexts, testimony under oath has the formality and gravity necessary to remind the witness that his or her statements will be the basis for official governmental action, action that often affects the rights and liberties of others. Sworn testimony is quite distinct from lies not spoken under oath and simply intended to puff up oneself.

Statutes that prohibit falsely representing that one is speaking on behalf of the Government, or that prohibit impersonating a Government officer, also protect the integrity of Government processes, quite apart from merely restricting false speech. Title 18 U.S.C. §912, for example, prohibits impersonating an officer or employee of the United States. Even if that statute may not require proving an "actual financial or property loss" resulting from the deception, the statute is itself confined to "maintaining the general good repute and dignity of government service itself." *United States v. Lepowitch*, 318 U.S. 702, 704 (1943). The same can be said for prohibitions on the unauthorized use of the names of federal agencies such as the Federal Bureau of Investigation in a manner calculated to convey that the communication is approved, or using words such as "Federal" or "United States" in the collection of private debts in order to convey that the communication has official authorization. These examples, to the extent that they implicate fraud or speech integral to criminal conduct, are inapplicable here.

As our law and tradition show, then, there are instances in which the falsity of speech bears upon whether it is protected. Some false speech may be prohibited even if analogous true speech could not be. This opinion does not imply that any of these targeted prohibitions are somehow vulnerable. But it also rejects the notion that false speech should be in a general category that is presumptively unprotected.

Although the First Amendment stands against any "freewheeling authority to declare new categories of speech outside the scope of the First Amendment," *Stevens*, 130 S.Ct. at 1586, the Court has acknowledged that perhaps there exist "some categories of speech that have been historically unprotected but have not yet been specifically identified or discussed in our case law." *Ibid.* Before exempting a category of speech from the normal prohibition on content-based restrictions, however, the Court must be presented with "persuasive evidence that a novel restriction on content is part of a long (if heretofore unrecognized) tradition of proscription," *Brown v. Entertainment Merchants Assn.*, 131 S.Ct. 2729, 2734 (2011). The Government has not demonstrated that false statements generally should constitute a new category of unprotected speech on this basis.

The probable, and adverse, effect of the Act on freedom of expression illustrates, in a fundamental way, the reasons for the Law's distrust of content-based speech prohibitions. The Act by its plain terms applies to a false statement made at any time, in any place, to any person. It can be assumed that it would not apply to, say, a theatrical performance. Still, the sweeping, quite unprecedented reach of the statute puts it in conflict with the First Amendment. Here the lie was made in a public meeting, but the statute would apply with equal force to personal, whispered conversations within a home. The statute seeks to control and suppress all false statements on this one subject in almost limitless times and settings. And it does so entirely without regard to whether the lie was made for the purpose of material gain.

Permitting the government to decree this speech to be a criminal offense, whether shouted from the rooftops or made in a barely audible whisper, would endorse government authority to compile a list of subjects about which false statements are punishable. That governmental power has no clear limiting principle. Our constitutional tradition stands against the idea that we need Oceania's Ministry of Truth. *See* G. Orwell, *Nineteen Eighty-Four* (1949) (Centennial ed. 2003). Were this law to be sustained, there could be an endless list of subjects the National Government or the States could single out. Where false claims are made to effect a fraud or secure moneys or other valuable considerations, say offers of employment, it is well established that the Government may restrict speech without affronting the First Amendment. *See, e.g., Virginia Bd. of Pharmacy*, 425 U.S. at 771. But the Stolen Valor Act is not so limited in its reach. Were the Court to hold that the interest in truthful discourse alone is sufficient to sustain a ban on speech, absent any evidence that the speech was used to gain a material advantage, it would give government a broad censorial power unprecedented in this Court's cases or in our constitutional tradition. The mere potential for the exercise of that power casts a chill, a chill the First Amendment cannot permit if free speech, thought, and discourse are to remain a foundation of our freedom.

The previous discussion shows that the Act conflicts with free speech principles. But even when examined within its own narrow sphere of operation, the Act cannot survive. In assessing content-based restrictions on protected speech, the Court has not adopted a free-wheeling approach, but rather has applied the "most exacting scrutiny." *Turner Broadcasting System, Inc. v. FCC*, 512 U.S. 622 (1994). Although the objectives the Government seeks to further by the statute are not without significance, the Court must, and now does, find the Act does not satisfy exacting scrutiny.

The Government is correct when it states military medals "serve the important public function of recognizing and expressing gratitude for acts of heroism and sacrifice in military service," and also "'foster morale, mission accomplishment and esprit de corps' among service members." General George Washington observed that an award for valor would "cherish a virtuous ambition in soldiers, as well as foster and encourage every species of military merit." *General Orders of George Washington Issued at Newburgh on the Hudson, 1782-1783* (Aug. 7, 1782), p. 30 (E. Boynton ed. 1883). Time has not diminished this idea. In periods of war and peace alike public recognition of valor and noble sacrifice by men and women in uniform reinforces the pride and national resolve that the military relies upon to fulfill its mission.

These interests are related to the integrity of the military honors system in general, and the Congressional Medal of Honor in particular. Although millions have served with brave resolve, the Medal, which is the highest military award for valor against an enemy force, has been given just 3,476 times. Established in 1861, the Medal is reserved for those who have distinguished themselves "conspicuously by gallantry and intrepidity at the risk of his life above and beyond the call of duty." 10 U.S.C. §§3741 (Army), 6241 (Navy and Marine Corps), 8741 (Air Force), 14 U.S.C. §491 (Coast Guard). The stories of those who earned the Medal inspire and fascinate, from Dakota Meyer, who in 2009 drove five times into the midst of a Taliban ambush to save 36 lives, to Desmond Doss, who served as an army medic on Okinawa in 1945, rescued 75 fellow soldiers, and who, after being wounded, gave up his own place on a stretcher so others could be taken to safety. The rare acts of courage the Medal celebrates led President Truman to say he would "rather have that medal round my neck than be president of the United States." The Government's interest in protecting the integrity of the Medal of Honor is beyond question.

But to recite the Government's compelling interests is not to end the matter. The First Amendment requires that the Government's chosen restriction on the speech at issue be "actually necessary" to achieve its interest. *Entertainment Merchants Assn.*, 131 S.Ct. at 2378. There must be a direct causal link between the restriction imposed and the injury to be prevented. The link between the Government's interest in protecting the integrity of the military honors system and the Act's restriction on the false claims of liars like respondent has not been shown. Although appearing to concede that "an isolated misrepresentation by itself would not tarnish the meaning of military honors," the Government asserts it is "common sense that false representations have the tendency to dilute the value and meaning of military awards." When a pretender claims the Medal to be his own, the lie might harm the Government by demeaning the high purpose of the award, diminishing the honor it confirms, and creating the appearance that the Medal is awarded more often than is true. Furthermore, the lie may offend the true holders of the Medal. From one perspective it insults their bravery and high principles when falsehood puts them in the unworthy company of a pretender.

Yet these interests do not satisfy the Government's heavy burden when it seeks to regulate protected speech. The Government points to no evidence showing that the public's general perception of military awards is diluted by false claims such as those made by Alvarez. As one of the Government's *amici* notes, "there is nothing that charlatans such as Xavier Alvarez can do to stain the Medal winners' honor." This general proposition is sound, even if true holders of the Medal might experience anger and frustration.

The lack of a causal link between the Government's stated interest and the Act is not the only way in which the Act is not actually necessary to achieve the Government's stated interest. The Government has not shown, and cannot show, why counterspeech would not suffice to achieve its interest. The facts of this case indicate that the dynamics of free speech, of counterspeech, of refutation, can overcome the lie. Respondent lied at a public meeting. Even before the FBI began investigating him for his false statements "Alvarez was perceived as a phony." Once the lie was made public, he was ridiculed online, his actions were reported in the press, and a fellow board member called for his resignation. There is good reason to believe that a similar fate would befall other false claimants. Indeed, the outrage and contempt expressed for respondent's lies can serve to reawaken and reinforce the public's respect for the Medal, its recipients, and its high purpose. The acclaim that recipients of the Congressional Medal of Honor receive also casts doubt on the proposition that the public will be misled by the claims of charlatans or become cynical of those whose heroic deeds earned them the Medal by right.

The remedy for speech that is false is speech that is true. This is the ordinary course in a free society. The response to the unreasoned is the rational; to the uninformed, the enlightened; to the straight-out lie, the simple truth. *See Whitney v. California*, 274 U.S. 357 (1927) (Brandeis, J., concurring). The theory of our Constitution is "that the best test of truth is the power of the thought to get itself accepted in the competition of the market," *Abrams v. United States*, 250 U.S. 616, 630 (1919) (Holmes, J., dissenting). The First Amendment ensures the right to respond to speech we do not like, and for good reason. Freedom of speech and thought flows not from the beneficence of the state but from the inalienable rights of the person. Suppression of speech by the government can make exposure of falsity more difficult, not less so. Society has the right and civic duty to engage in open, dynamic, rational discourse. These ends are not well served when the government seeks to orchestrate public discussion through content-based mandates.

Expressing its concern that counterspeech is insufficient, the Government responds that because "some military records have been lost some claims are unverifiable." This proves little, however; for without verifiable records, successful criminal prosecution under the Act would be more difficult in any event. So, in cases where public refutation will not serve the Government's interest, the Act will not either. In addition, the Government claims that "many false claims will remain unchallenged." The Government provides no support for the contention. In order to show that public refutation is not an adequate alternative, the Government must demonstrate that unchallenged claims undermine the public's perception of the military and the integrity of its awards system. This showing has not been made.

Any true holders of the Medal who had heard of Alvarez's false claims would have been fully vindicated by the community's expression of outrage, showing as it did the Nation's high regard for the Medal. The same can be said for the Government's interest. The American people do not need the assistance of a government prosecution to express their high regard for the special place that military heroes hold in our tradition. Only a weak society needs government protection or intervention before it pursues its resolve to preserve the truth. Truth needs neither handcuffs nor a badge for its vindication.

When the Government seeks to regulate protected speech, the restriction must be the "least restrictive means among available, effective alternatives." *Ashcroft*, 542 U.S. at 666. There is, however, at least one less speech-restrictive means by which the Government could likely protect the integrity of the military awards system. A Government-created database could list Congressional Medal of Honor winners. Were a database accessible through the internet, it would be easy to verify and expose false claims. It appears some private individuals have already created databases similar to this, and at least one database of past winners is online and fully searchable, see Congressional Medal of Honor Society, Full Archive, http://www.cmohs.org/recipient-archive.php. The Solicitor General responds that although Congress and the Department of Defense investigated the feasibility of establishing a database in 2008, the Government "concluded that such a database would be impracticable and insufficiently comprehensive." Without more explanation, it is difficult to assess the Government's claim, especially when at least one database of Congressional Medal of Honor winners already exists.

The Government may have responses to some of these criticisms, but there has been no clear showing of the necessity of the statute, the necessity required by exacting scrutiny.

The Nation well knows that one of the costs of the First Amendment is that it protects the speech we detest as well as the speech we embrace. Though few might find respondent's statements anything but contemptible, his right to make those statements is protected by the Constitution's guarantee of freedom of speech and expression. The Stolen Valor Act infringes upon speech protected by the First Amendment.

The judgment of the Court of Appeals is affirmed.

It is so ordered.

Justice BREYER, with whom Justice KAGAN joins, *concurring in the judgment.*

The Stolen Valor Act of 2005 violates the First Amendment. In this case, the Court's term "intermediate scrutiny" describes what I think we should do. As the dissent points out, "there are broad areas in which any attempt by the state to penalize purportedly false speech would present a grave and unacceptable danger of suppressing truthful speech." Laws restricting false statements about philosophy, religion, history, the social sciences, the arts, and the like raise such concerns, and in many contexts have called for strict scrutiny. But the dangers of suppressing valuable ideas are lower where the regulations concern false statements about easily verifiable facts that do not concern such subject matter. Such false factual statements are less likely than are true factual statements to make a valuable contribution to the marketplace of ideas. The government often has good reasons to prohibit such false speech. But its regulation can nonetheless threaten speech-related harms.

I would read the statute favorably to the Government as criminalizing only false factual statements made with knowledge of their falsity and with the intent that they be taken as true. As so interpreted the statute covers only lies. But although this interpretation diminishes the extent to which the statute endangers First Amendment values, it does not eliminate the threat. This Court has frequently said or implied that false factual statements enjoy little First Amendment protection. *See, e.g., Hustler Magazine, Inc. v. Falwell,* 485 U.S. 46 (1988). But these judicial statements cannot be read to mean "no protection at all." False factual statements can serve useful human objectives, for example: in social contexts, where they may prevent embarrassment, protect privacy, shield a person from prejudice, provide the sick with comfort, or preserve a child's innocence; in public contexts, where they may stop a panic or otherwise preserve calm in the face of danger; and even in technical, philosophical, and scientific contexts, where (as Socrates' methods suggest) examination of a false statement (even if made deliberately to mislead) can promote a form of thought that ultimately helps realize the truth. *See, e.g.,* S. Bok, *Lying: Moral Choice in Public and Private Life* (1999); J. Mill, *On Liberty* 15 (Blackwell ed. 1947).

The threat of criminal prosecution for making a false statement can inhibit the speaker from making true statements, thereby "chilling" a kind of speech that lies at the First Amendment's heart. *See, e.g., Gertz, supra,* at 340-341. Hence, the Court emphasizes *mens rea* requirements that provide "breathing room" for more valuable speech by reducing an honest speaker's fear that he may accidentally incur liability for speaking. The pervasiveness of false statements, made for better or for worse motives, made thoughtlessly or deliberately, made with or without accompanying harm, provides a weapon to a government broadly empowered to prosecute falsity without more. And those who are unpopular may fear that the government will use that weapon selectively, say by prosecuting a pacifist who supports his cause by (falsely) claiming to have been a war hero, while ignoring members of other political groups who might make similar false claims.

Many statutes and common-law doctrines make the utterance of certain kinds of false statements unlawful. Those prohibitions tend to be narrower than the statute before us, in that they limit the scope of their application, sometimes by requiring proof of specific harm to identifiable victims; sometimes by specifying that the lies be made in contexts in which a tangible harm to others is especially likely to occur; and sometimes by limiting the prohibited lies to those that are particularly likely to produce harm. Fraud statutes, for example, require proof of a misrepresentation that is material, upon which the victim relied, and which caused actual injury. *See* Restatement (Second) of Torts §525 (1976). Defamation statutes focus upon statements of a kind that harm the reputation of another or deter third parties from association or dealing with the victim. *See id.* §§558, 559. Torts involving the intentional infliction of emotional distress (like torts involving placing a victim in a false light) concern falsehoods that tend to cause harm to a specific victim of an emotional-, dignitary-, or privacy-related kind. *See id.* §652E. Perjury statutes prohibit a particular set of false statements—those made under oath—while requiring a showing of materiality. *See, e.g.,* 18 U.S.C. §1621. Statutes forbidding lying to a government official (not under oath) are typically limited to circumstances where a lie is likely to work particular and specific harm by interfering with the functioning of a government department, and those statutes also require a showing of materiality. See, *e.g.,* §1001. Statutes prohibiting false claims of terrorist attacks, or other lies about the commission of crimes or catastrophes, require proof that substantial public harm be directly foreseeable, or, if not, involve false statements that are very likely to bring about that harm. *See, e.g.,* 47 CFR §73.1217 (2011); 18 U.S.C. §1038(a)(1). Statutes forbidding impersonation of a public official typically focus on *acts* of impersonation, not mere speech, and may require a showing that, for example, someone was deceived into following a "course of action he would not have pursued but for the deceitful conduct." *United States v. Lepowitch,* 318 U.S. 702, 704 (1943).

Statutes prohibiting trademark infringement present, perhaps, the closest analogy to the present statute. Trademarks identify the source of a good; and infringement causes harm by causing confusion among potential customers (about the source) and thereby diluting the value of the mark to its owner, to consumers, and to the economy. Similarly, a false claim of possession of a medal or other honor creates confusion about who is entitled to wear it, thus diluting its value to those who have earned it, to their families, and to their country. But trademark statutes are focused upon commercial and promotional activities that are likely to dilute the value of a mark. Indeed, they typically require a showing of likely confusion, a showing that tends to assure that the feared harm will in fact take place. *See* 15 U.S.C. §1114(1)(a); *KP Permanent Make-Up, Inc. v. Lasting Impression I, Inc.,* 543 U.S. 111, 117 (2004).

In virtually all these instances limitations of context, requirements of proof of injury, and the like, narrow the statute to a subset of lies where specific harm is more likely to occur. The limitations help to make certain that the statute does not allow its threat of liability or criminal punishment to roam at large, discouraging or forbidding the telling of the lie in contexts where harm is unlikely or the need for the prohibition is small.

The statute before us may be construed to prohibit only knowing and intentional acts of deception about readily verifiable facts within the personal knowledge of the speaker, thus reducing the risk that valuable speech is chilled. But it still ranges very broadly. And that breadth means that it creates a significant risk of First Amendment harm. As written, it applies in family, social, or other private contexts, where lies will often cause little harm. It also applies in political contexts, where although such lies are more likely to cause harm, the risk of censorious selectivity by prosecutors is also high. Further, given the potential haziness of individual memory along with the large number of military awards covered, there remains a risk of chilling that is not completely eliminated by *mens rea* requirements; a speaker might still be worried about being *prosecuted* for a careless false statement, even if he does not have the intent required to render him liable. And so the prohibition may be applied where it should not be applied, for example, to bar stool braggadocio or, in the political arena, subtly but selectively to speakers that the Government does not like. These considerations lead me to believe that the statute as written risks significant First Amendment harm.

We must ask whether it is possible substantially to achieve the Government's objective in less burdensome ways. It should be possible significantly to diminish or eliminate these remaining risks by enacting a similar but more finely tailored statute that insists upon a showing that the false statement caused specific harm or at least was material, or focus its coverage on lies most likely to be harmful or on contexts where such lies are most likely to cause harm. In some contexts, particularly political contexts, such a narrowing will not always be easy to achieve. In the political arena a false statement is more likely to make a behavioral difference (say, by leading the listeners to vote for the speaker) but at the same time criminal prosecution is particularly dangerous (say, by radically changing a potential election result) and consequently can more easily result in censorship of speakers and their ideas. Thus, the statute may have to be significantly narrowed in its applications. Accurate information will normally counteract the lie. An accurate, publicly available register of military awards, easily obtainable by political opponents, may well adequately protect the integrity of an award against those who would falsely claim to have earned it. The statute as presently drafted works disproportionate constitutional harm. It consequently fails intermediate scrutiny, and violates the First Amendment.

Justice ALITO, with whom Justice SCALIA and Justice THOMAS join, *dissenting.*

Only the bravest of the brave are awarded the Congressional Medal of Honor, but the Court holds that every American has a constitutional right to claim to have received this award. This Act applies to only a narrow category of false representations about objective facts that can almost always be proved or disproved with near certainty; facts that are squarely within the speaker's personal knowledge; requires proof beyond a reasonable doubt that the speaker actually knew that the representation was false; applies only to statements that could reasonably be interpreted as communicating actual facts; does not reach dramatic performances, satire, parody, hyperbole, or the like; and is viewpoint neutral and highly unlikely to be tied to any particular political or ideological message.

Congress passed the Stolen Valor Act in response to a proliferation of false claims concerning the receipt of military awards. As Congress recognized, the lies proscribed by the Stolen Valor Act inflict substantial harm. Individuals often falsely represent themselves as award recipients in order to obtain financial or other material rewards, such as lucrative contracts and government benefits. Twelve men defrauded the Department of Veterans Affairs out of more than $1.4 million in veteran's benefits. The lies proscribed by the Stolen Valor Act tend to debase the distinctive honor of military awards.

The chief alternative recommended is the compilation and release of a comprehensive list or database of actual medal recipients. This remedy will not work. The Department of Defense has explained that the most that it can do is to create a database of recipients of certain top military honors awarded since 2001. Because a sufficiently comprehensive database is not practicable, lies about military awards cannot be remedied by what the plurality calls "counterspeech."

A steady stream of stories in the media about the exposure of imposters would increase skepticism among the public about the entire awards system.

The plurality recommends a law that would apply only to lies that are intended to "secure moneys or other valuable considerations." The concurrence comments that "a more finely tailored statute might insist upon a showing that the false statement caused specific harm." But much damage is caused, both to real award recipients and to the system of military honors, by false statements that are not linked to any financial or other tangible reward.

False factual statements possess no intrinsic First Amendment value. *See Illinois ex rel. Madigan v. Telemarketing Associates, Inc.*, 538 U.S. 600, 612 (2003); *Gertz, supra,* at 340 ("Erroneous statement of fact is not worthy of constitutional protection."). Laws prohibiting fraud, perjury, and defamation, for example, were in existence when the First Amendment was adopted, and their constitutionality is now beyond question. The right to freedom of speech has been held to permit recovery for the intentional infliction of emotional distress by means of a false statement, See *Falwell, supra,* at 56. And in *Hill,* the Court concluded that the free speech right allows recovery for the even more modern tort of false-light invasion of privacy, *see* PROSSER AND KEETON §117, at 863.

The First Amendment is not offended by certain prominent criminal statutes. Section 18 U.S.C. §1001 makes it a crime to "knowingly and willfully" make any "materially false, fictitious, or fraudulent statement or representation" in "any matter within the jurisdiction of the executive, legislative, or judicial branch of the Government of the United States." Unlike perjury, §1001 is not limited to statements made under oath or before an official government tribunal. Nor does it require any showing of "pecuniary or property loss to the government." *United States v. Gilliland*, 312 U.S. 86, 93 (1941). Instead, the statute is based on the need to protect "agencies from the perversion which *might* result from the deceptive practices described." Still other statutes make it a crime to falsely represent that one is speaking on behalf of, or with the approval of, the Federal Government. *See, e.g.,* 18 U.S.C. §912 (making it a crime to falsely impersonate a federal officer); §709 (making it a crime to knowingly use, without authorization, the names of enumerated federal agencies, such as "Federal Bureau of Investigation," in a manner reasonably calculated to convey the impression that a communication is approved or authorized by the agency). We have recognized that §912, like §1001, does not require a showing of pecuniary or property loss and that its purpose is to "'maintain the general good repute and dignity'" of Government service. *United States v. Lepowitch*, 318 U.S. 702 (1943). All told there are more than 100 federal criminal statutes that punish false statements made in connection with areas of federal agency concern.

These examples amply demonstrate that false statements of fact merit no First Amendment protection in their own right. Many in our society either approve or condone certain discrete categories of false statements, including false statements made to prevent harm to innocent victims and so-called "white lies." Respondent's false claim to have received the Medal of Honor did not fall into any of these categories. His lie did not "prevent embarrassment, protect privacy, shield a person from prejudice, provide the sick with comfort, or preserve a child's innocence." Nor did his lie "stop a panic or otherwise preserve calm in the face of danger" or further philosophical or scientific debate. Respondent's claim served no valid purpose. The lies covered by the Stolen Valor Act have no intrinsic value and thus merit no First Amendment protection unless their prohibition would chill other expression that falls within the Amendment's scope.

While false statements of fact do not merit First Amendment protection for their own sake, it is sometimes necessary to "extend a measure of strategic protection" to these statements in order to ensure sufficient "'breathing space'" for protected speech. *Gertz,* 418 U.S. at 342. In order to prevent the chilling of truthful speech on matters of public concern, we have held that liability for the defamation of a public official or figure requires proof that defamatory statements were made with knowledge or reckless disregard of their falsity. *See New York Times Co. v. Sullivan,* 376 U.S. 254 (1964). This same requirement applies when public officials and figures seek to recover for the tort of intentional infliction of emotional distress. *See Falwell,* 485 U.S. at 55-56. These proof requirements have the effect of bringing some false factual statements within the protection of the First Amendment, but this is justified in order to prevent the chilling of other, valuable speech. There are broad areas in which any attempt by the state to penalize purportedly false speech would present a grave and unacceptable danger of suppressing truthful speech. Laws restricting false statements about philosophy, religion, history, the social sciences, the arts, and other matters of public concern would present such a threat. The point is not that there is no such thing as truth or falsity or that the truth is always impossible to ascertain, but rather that it is perilous to permit the state to be the arbiter of truth.

Even where there is a scholarly consensus concerning a particular matter, truth is served by allowing that consensus to be challenged without fear of reprisal. Today's accepted wisdom sometimes turns out to be mistaken. "Even a false statement may be deemed to make a valuable contribution to public debate, since it brings about 'the clearer perception and livelier impression of truth, produced by its collision with error.'" *Sullivan, supra,* at 279, n. 19 (quoting J. Mill, *On Liberty* 15 (R. McCallum ed. 1947)). Allowing the state to proscribe false statements in these areas also opens the door for the state to use its power for political ends. Statements about history illustrate this point. If some false statements about historical events may be banned, how certain must it be that a statement is false before the ban may be upheld? And who should make that calculation? While our cases prohibiting viewpoint discrimination would fetter the state's power to some degree, the potential for abuse of power in these areas is simply too great.

The Stolen Valor Act presents no risk at all that valuable speech will be suppressed. Speech punished by the Act is not only verifiably false and entirely lacking in intrinsic value, but it fails to serve any instrumental purpose that the First Amendment might protect. Neither of the opinions endorsed by Justices in the majority claims that the false statements covered by the Stolen Valor Act possess intrinsic or instrumental value. Instead, those opinions appear to be based on the distinct concern that the Act suffers from overbreadth. But to strike down a statute on the basis that it is overbroad, it is necessary to show that the statute's "overbreadth is *substantial,* not only in an absolute sense, but also relative to its plainly legitimate sweep." *United States v. Williams,* 553 U.S. 285, 292 (2008). The plurality and the concurrence do not even attempt to make this showing.

Note: Truth, Lies & History

A law passed by the French Senate would have made it a crime to deny that the Ottoman Empire had committed genocide against the Armenians, with the law was enforced by penalties that included fines up to €45,000 and up to a year in prison. Some believe that 1.5 million Armenians were killed in the genocide. Turkey argues that no more than 500,000 people died, and that many of these individuals died from starvation or exposure rather than as a result of deliberate killings. The law created a potential conflict with a Turkish law that makes it a crime to insult Turkishness. Then French President Nicholas Sarkozy was prohibited from signing the law until the French Constitutional Court could rule on its constitutionality. On February 28, 2012, the Constitutional Court struck the law down. *See* Scott Sayare, *French Council Strikes Down Bill on Armenian Genocide Law,* Int'l Herald Trib., Feb. 29, 2012, A6. By contrast, the French courts upheld the French Gayssot Law, which makes it illegal to deny that the Holocaust occurred and also prohibits individuals from contesting the rulings of the Nuremburg War Crimes Tribunal. *See* Russell L. Weaver, Nicolas Delpierre & Laurence Boissier, *Holocaust Denial and Governmentally Declared "Truth": French and American Perspectives,* 41 Texas Tech L. Rev. 495 (2009).

Food for Thought: Prohibitions Against False Campaign Speech

Susan B. Anthony List v. Driehaus, 573 U.S. 149 (2014), involved an Ohio statute that prohibited "false statements" that are made "during the course of any campaign for nomination or election to public office or office of a political party." The statute prohibited false statements regarding the "voting record of a candidate or public official," and applied to anyone who had posted, published, circulated, distributed, or otherwise disseminated a false statement regarding a candidate "either knowing the same to be false or with reckless disregard of whether it was false or not." When Susan B. Anthony List ("List") stated that a congressman effectively voted for taxpayer-funded abortions when he voted for the Affordable Care Act. The congressman believed that the statement was demonstrably false, and brought charges against Susan B. Anthony List before the Ohio Elections Commission (OEC). When the congressman lost the election, he dropped the charges. Nevertheless, the List sought to challenge the law, claiming that it intended to make similar allegations in future elections. The Court concluded that the List had standing to challenge the law, that a case or controversy existed, and remanded the case. Suppose that you are the judge assigned to hear the case on remand. Can Ohio prohibit false statements during an election?

∾ PROBLEMS ∾

1. *Amending the Stolen Valor Act.* Following the *Alvarez* decision, suppose that Congress amends the Stolen Valor Act (now the "Fraudulent Valor Act") to make it illegal for an individual to "defraud" another person for material gain. Would the amended Act be constitutional? Could it be challenged on vagueness or overbreadth grounds? Following enactment of the Fraudulent Valor Act (referred to in the prior problem), suppose that Alvarez applies for a job, falsely listing on his resume that he had won the Congressional Medal of Honor. A prospective employer questions Alvarez extensively about the "facts" related to his winning the honor, is duly impressed with Alvarez's response, and gives him the job. In a bleak economy, Alvarez beats out hundreds of other applicants for the job, and does so based on his false claim. Can Alvarez be criminally prosecuted for his fraudulent statements? Are there less intrusive alternatives?

2. *More on Applying the Fraudulent Valor Act.* Suppose that, instead of seeking employment, Alvarez is "down on his luck." In addition to being broke and out of work, Alvarez needs a kidney transplant and lacks the money to pay for it. Passing himself off as a Congressional Medal of Honor winner, Alvarez talks the local newspaper into running an article about his plight, and the article plays up the angle that a Medal of Honor winner has been "abandoned" by his country in a time of need. At the end of the article, there is a plea for contributions. Alvarez manages to raise $200,000 in contributions based on the article. Can Alvarez be prosecuted under the FVA? Would it matter whether Alvarez also misrepresented his need for a kidney transplant?

3. *The Fraudulent Valor Act and the Candidate.* Suppose that after Congress passes the FVA, Alvarez, now a candidate for the U.S. House of Representatives, falsely represents that he won the Congressional Medal of Honor. If he made the representation with an intent to obtain votes, can he validly be prosecuted under the FVA? Are there less restrictive alternatives?

4. *The Ag-Gag Law.* The State of Iowa has enacted a law that makes it illegal for individuals to misrepresent themselves in order to gain access to a farm. The law was enacted in response to animal rights activists who went undercover and applied for jobs on farms, in order to obtain video surveillance of what they regard as animal abuse and mistreatment. The goal of the activists is "to alert the public about how animals are mistreated." The law is enforceable by a fine of up to $1,500 and up to one year in prison. Can the State of Iowa prohibit these types of misrepresentations?

5. *False Information about the Pandemic.* In a Fox News program on March 9, 2020, Sean Hannity and Trish Regan made statements on the air regarding the pandemic. Hannity opined, for example, that, "I didn't like how we're scaring people unnecessarily [about the virus]." "I see it, again, as like, let's bludgeon Trump with this new hoax." Based on those comments, the Washington League for Increased Transparency and Ethics, a nonprofit entity, filed suit against Fox News, arguing that Hannity had "deceived people about the pandemic" and claiming that his statements violated a state consumer protection law in Washington. Fox News files a motion to dismiss the suit on First Amendment grounds. Should misrepresentations be handled differently during a pandemic? *See Washington League for Increased Transparency and Ethics v. Fox Corporation,* 2020 WL 2759011 (Wash. Super.) (Trial Order), May 27, 2020; Wendy Davis, *Fox News Defeats Lawsuit Over COVID-19 Comments,* MEDIA DAILY NEWS, May 27, 2020, https://www.media-post.com/publications/article/351870/fox-news-defeats-lawsuit-over-covid-19-comments.html?edition=118551

6. *The Sandy Hook Tragedy.* In 2012, children were murdered at school in Newton, Connecticut. Afterwards, Alex Jones used his Infowars website speculated that the attack had been staged, and that crisis actors had been used to make it appear real. Plaintiff, a father of one of the murdered children, was alleged to have lied about the death of his son in order to promote stronger gun laws. Can plaintiff recover for defamation against Jones and Infowars? *See Jones v. Heslin,* 2020 WL 1452025 (Tex.App. 2020).

7. *The Boris Johnson Affair.* During the Brexit campaign in 2016, which led to Britain's decision to leave the European Union, then British House of Commons member, Boris Johnson, alleged that the UK was sending 350 million British pounds to the EU every week. Because the allegation was regarded as false, Johnson was criminally charged with deliberately lying to the public. Is it appropriate/permissible for a politician to be criminally charged for making allegedly false statements during a political campaign?

14. Commercial Speech

In *Virginia State Board of Pharmacy v. Virginia Citizens Consumer Council,* 425 U.S. 748 (1976), the Court held that commercial speech is protected under the First Amendment. The Court defined commercial speech as speech that does "no more than propose a commercial transaction." However, the Court noted that some advertisements might qualify as traditional noncommercial "political speech." *See New York Times v. Sullivan,* 376 U.S. 254 (1964). In addition, the reference to a specific product or the economic motivation of the speaker does not automatically demonstrate that speech qualifies as "commercial speech." *See Bolger v. Youngs Drug Products Corp.,* 463 U.S. 60 (1963). In *Bolger,* a drug company mailed informational brochures about birth control devices; these advertisements were held to be commercial speech, and the Court declared that the fact that advertising of a product is linked "to a current public debate" is not sufficient *per se* to qualify the advertising as political speech. Even though commercial speech may not be accorded the same status as political speech, *Virginia State Board of Pharmacy* recognized that society (advertisers, consumers, and society at large) needs commercial speech information, including information from advertisements (in that case, advertising about prescription drug prices):

> We may assume that the advertiser's interest is a purely economic one. That hardly disqualifies him from protection under the First Amendment. As to the consumer's interest in the free flow of commercial information, that interest may be as keen, if not keener by far, than his interest in the day's most urgent political debate. Those whom the suppression of prescription drug price information hits the hardest are the poor, the sick, and particularly the aged. A disproportionate amount of their income tends to be spent on prescription drugs; yet they are the least able to learn, by shopping from pharmacist to pharmacist, where their scarce dollars are best spent. When drug prices vary strikingly do, information as to who is charging what becomes more than a convenience. It could mean the alleviation of physical pain or the enjoyment of basic necessities.
>
> Society may have a strong interest in the free flow of commercial information. Even an individual advertisement, though entirely "commercial," may be of general public interest. Decided cases furnish illustrations: advertisements stating that referral services for legal abortions are available, that a manufacturer of artificial furs promotes his product as an alternative to the extinction by his competitors of fur-bearing mammals, and that a domestic producer advertises his product as an alternative to imports that tend to deprive American residents of their jobs. Obviously, not all commercial messages contain the same or even a very great public interest element. There are few to which such an element, however, could not be added. Our pharmacist could cast himself as a commentator on store-to-store disparities in drug prices, giving his own and those of a competitor as proof. We see little point in requiring him to do so, and little difference if he does not.
>
> There is another consideration that suggests that no line between publicly "interesting" or "important" commercial advertising and the opposite kind could ever be drawn. Advertising, however tasteless and excessive it may seem, is nonetheless dissemination of information as to who is producing and selling what product, for what reason, and at what price. So long as we preserve a predominantly free enterprise economy, the allocation of our resources in large measure will be made through numerous private economic decisions. It is a matter of public interest that those decisions, in the aggregate, be intelligent and well informed. To this end, the free flow of commercial information is indispensable. If it is indispensable to the proper allocation of resources in a free enterprise system, it is also indispensable to the formation of intelligent opinions as to how that system ought to be regulated or altered. Even if the First Amendment were thought to be primarily an instrument to enlighten public decisionmaking in a democracy, we could not say that the free flow of information does not serve that goal.

Lorillard Tobacco Co. v. Reilly

533 U.S. 525 (2001)

Justice O'CONNOR delivered the opinion of the Court.

In January 1999, Massachusetts promulgated comprehensive regulations governing the advertising and sale of cigarettes, smokeless tobacco, and cigars.

Petitioners, a group of cigarette, smokeless tobacco, and cigar manufacturers and retailers, sued, claiming that the regulations violate the United States
Constitution.

The purpose of the cigarette and smokeless tobacco regulations is "to eliminate deception and unfairness in the way cigarettes and smokeless tobacco products are marketed, sold and distributed in Massachusetts in order to address the
incidence of cigarette smoking and smokeless tobacco use by children under legal
age and in order to prevent access to such products by underage consumers."
The purpose of the cigar regulations is "to eliminate deception and unfairness
in the way cigars and little cigars are packaged, marketed, sold and distributed in
Massachusetts so that consumers may be adequately informed about the health
risks associated with cigar smoking, its addictive properties, and the false perception that cigars are a safe alternative to cigarettes and so that the incidence of
cigar use by children under legal age is addressed in order to prevent access to
such products by underage consumers." The regulations place a variety of restrictions on outdoor advertising, point-of-sale advertising, retail sales transactions,
transactions by mail, promotions, sampling of products, and labels for cigars.

The cigarette and smokeless tobacco regulations being challenged before
this Court provide:

> (2) Retail Outlet Sales Practices. Except as otherwise provided, it shall be an unfair
> or deceptive act or practice for any person who sells or distributes cigarettes or smokeless
> tobacco products through a retail outlet located within Massachusetts to engage in any of the
> following retail outlet sales practices:
>> (c) Using self-service displays of cigarettes or smokeless tobacco products;
>> (d) Failing to place cigarettes and smokeless tobacco products out of the reach of all
> consumers, and in a location accessible only to outlet personnel.
> (5) Advertising Restrictions. Except as otherwise provided, it shall be an unfair or
> deceptive act or practice for any manufacturer, distributor or retailer to engage in any of the
> following practices:
>> (a) Outdoor advertising, including advertising in enclosed stadiums and advertising
> from within a retail establishment that is directed toward or visible from the outside of the
> establishment, in any location that is within a 1,000 foot radius of any public playground,
> playground area in a public park, elementary school or secondary school;
>> (b) Point-of-sale advertising of cigarettes or smokeless tobacco products any portion
> of which is placed lower than five feet from the floor of any retail establishment which is
> located within a one thousand foot radius of any public playground, playground area in a
> public park, elementary school or secondary school, and which is not an adult-only retail
> establishment.

The cigar regulations that are still at issue provide:

> (1) Retail Sales Practices. Except as otherwise provided, it shall be an unfair or decep-
> tive act or practice for any person who sells or distributes cigars or little cigars directly to
> consumers within Massachusetts to engage in any of the following practices:
>> (a) Sampling of cigars or little cigars or promotional give-aways of cigars or little cigars.
> (2) Retail Outlet Sales Practices. Parallel provisions to those relating to cigarettes
> were cited.

We must analyze the cigarette as well as the smokeless tobacco and cigar petitioners' claim that certain sales practices regulations for tobacco products violate
the First Amendment.

For over 25 years, the Court has recognized that commercial speech does not
fall outside the purview of the First Amendment. In recognition of the "distinction between speech proposing a commercial transaction, which occurs in an area
traditionally subject to government regulation, and other varieties of speech," we
developed a framework for analyzing regulations of commercial speech that is
"substantially similar" to the test for time, place, and manner restrictions. The
analysis contains four elements:

> At the outset, we must determine whether the expression is protected by the First Amendment.
> For commercial speech to come within that provision, it at least must concern lawful activ-
> ity and not be misleading. Next, we ask whether the asserted governmental interest is sub-
> stantial. If both inquiries yield positive answers, we must determine whether the regulation
> directly advances the governmental interest asserted, and whether it is not more extensive
> than is necessary to serve that interest. *Central Hudson Gas & Electric Corp. v. Public Service
> Commission of New York*, 447 U.S. 557 (1980).

Petitioners urge us to reject the *Central Hudson* analysis and apply strict scrutiny. But we see no need to break new ground. *Central Hudson,* as applied in our
more recent commercial speech cases, provides an adequate basis for decision.

Only the last two steps of *Central Hudson*'s four-part analysis are at issue here.
The Attorney General has assumed for purposes of summary judgment that petitioners' speech is entitled to First Amendment protection. With respect to the
second step, none of the petitioners contests the importance of the State's interest in preventing the use of tobacco products by minors.

The third step of *Central Hudson* concerns the relationship between the
harm that underlies the State's interest and the means identified by the State to
advance that interest. It requires that

> the speech restriction directly and materially advances the asserted governmental interest.
> "This burden is not satisfied by mere speculation or conjecture; rather, a governmental body
> seeking to sustain a restriction on commercial speech must demonstrate that the harms it
> recites are real and that its restriction will in fact alleviate them to a material degree."

Greater New Orleans Broadcasting Assn., Inc. v. United States, 527 U.S. 173 (1999).
We do not require that "empirical data come accompanied by a surfeit of background information and we have permitted litigants to justify speech restrictions
by reference to studies and anecdotes pertaining to different locales altogether,
or even, in a case applying strict scrutiny, to justify restrictions based solely on
history, consensus, and 'simple common sense.'"

The last step of the *Central Hudson* analysis "complements" the third step,
"asking whether the speech restriction is not more extensive than necessary to
serve the interests that support it." *Greater New Orleans, supra,* at 188. We have
made it clear that "the least restrictive means" is not the standard; instead,

the case law requires a reasonable "'fit between the legislature's ends and the means chosen to accomplish those ends, a means narrowly tailored to achieve the desired objective.'" *Board of Trustees of State Univ. of N.Y. v. Fox*, 492 U.S. 469 (1989). Focusing on the third and fourth steps of the *Central Hudson* analysis, we first address the outdoor advertising and point-of-sale advertising regulations for smokeless tobacco and cigars. We then address the sales practices regulations for all tobacco products.

The outdoor advertising regulations prohibit smokeless tobacco or cigar advertising within a 1,000-foot radius of a school or playground. The smokeless tobacco and cigar petitioners contend that the Attorney General's regulations do not satisfy *Central Hudson*'s third step. They maintain that although the Attorney General may have identified a problem with underage cigarette smoking, he has not identified an equally severe problem with respect to underage use of smokeless tobacco or cigars. The smokeless tobacco petitioner emphasizes the "lack of parity" between cigarettes and smokeless tobacco. The cigar petitioners catalog a list of differences between cigars and other tobacco products, including the characteristics of the products and marketing strategies. The petitioners finally contend that the Attorney General cannot prove that advertising has a causal link to tobacco use such that limiting advertising will materially alleviate any problem of underage use of their products.

In previous cases, we have acknowledged the theory that product advertising stimulates demand for products, while suppressed advertising may have the opposite effect. *See United States v. Edge Broadcasting Co.*, 509 U.S. 418 (1993). The Attorney General cites numerous studies to support this theory in the case of tobacco products.

Our review reveals that the Attorney General has provided ample documentation of the problem with underage use of smokeless tobacco and cigars. In addition, we disagree with petitioners' claim that there is no evidence that preventing targeted campaigns and limiting youth exposure to advertising will decrease underage use of smokeless tobacco and cigars. On this record and in the posture of summary judgment, we are unable to conclude that the Attorney General's decision to regulate advertising of smokeless tobacco and cigars in an effort to combat the use of tobacco products by minors was based on mere "speculation and conjecture." *Edenfield v. Fane*, 507 U.S. 761 (1993).

The regulations do not satisfy the fourth step of the *Central Hudson* analysis. The final step of the *Central Hudson* analysis, the "critical inquiry in this case," requires a reasonable fit between the means and ends of the regulatory scheme. The Attorney General's regulations do not meet this standard. The broad sweep of the regulations indicates that the Attorney General did not "carefully calculate the costs and benefits associated with the burden on speech imposed" by the regulations. The outdoor advertising regulations prohibit any smokeless tobacco or cigar advertising within 1,000 feet of schools or playgrounds. In the District Court, petitioners maintained that this prohibition would prevent advertising in 87% to 91% of Boston, Worcester, and Springfield, Massachusetts. The 87% to

91% figure appears to include not only the effect of the regulations, but also the limitations imposed by other generally applicable zoning restrictions. The substantial geographical reach of the Attorney General's outdoor advertising regulations is compounded by other factors. "Outdoor" advertising includes not only advertising located outside an establishment, but also advertising inside a store if that advertising is visible from outside the store. The regulations restrict advertisements of any size and the term advertisement also includes oral statements.

In some geographical areas, these regulations would constitute nearly a complete ban on the communication of truthful information about smokeless tobacco and cigars to adult consumers. The breadth and scope of the regulations, and the process by which the Attorney General adopted the regulations, do not demonstrate a careful calculation of the speech interests involved.

First, the Attorney General did not seem to consider the impact of the 1,000-foot restriction on commercial speech in major metropolitan areas. The Attorney General apparently selected the 1,000-foot distance based on the FDA's decision to impose an identical 1,000-foot restriction when it attempted to regulate cigarette and smokeless tobacco advertising. But the FDA's 1,000-foot regulation was not an adequate basis for the Attorney General to tailor the Massachusetts regulations. The degree to which speech is suppressed—or alternative avenues for speech remain available—under a particular regulatory scheme tends to be case specific. The FDA's regulations would have had widely disparate effects nationwide. Even in Massachusetts, the effect of the Attorney General's speech regulations will vary based on whether a locale is rural, suburban, or urban. The uniformly broad sweep of the geographical limitation demonstrates a lack of tailoring.

The range of communications restricted seems unduly broad. For instance, it is not clear from the regulatory scheme why a ban on oral communications is necessary to further the State's interest. Apparently that restriction means that a retailer is unable to answer inquiries about its tobacco products if that communication occurs outdoors. To the extent that studies have identified particular advertising and promotion practices that appeal to youth, tailoring would involve targeting those practices while permitting others. As crafted, the regulations make no distinction among practices on this basis.

The State's interest in preventing underage tobacco use is substantial, and even compelling, but it is no less true that the sale and use of tobacco products by adults is a legal activity. We must consider that tobacco retailers and manufacturers have an interest in conveying truthful information about their products to adults, and adults have a corresponding interest in receiving truthful information about tobacco products. As the State protects children from tobacco advertisements, tobacco manufacturers and retailers and their adult consumers still have a protected interest in communication.

In some instances, Massachusetts' outdoor advertising regulations would impose particularly onerous burdens on speech. For example, we disagree with the Court of Appeals' conclusion that because cigar manufacturers and retailers conduct a limited amount of advertising in comparison to other tobacco products, "the relative lack of cigar advertising also means that the burden imposed on cigar advertisers is correspondingly small." If some retailers have relatively small advertising budgets, and use few avenues of communication, then the Attorney General's outdoor advertising regulations potentially place a greater, not lesser, burden on those retailers' speech. Furthermore, to the extent that cigar products and cigar advertising differ from that of other tobacco products, that difference should inform the inquiry into what speech restrictions are necessary.

A retailer in Massachusetts may have no means of communicating to passersby on the street that it sells tobacco products because alternative forms of advertisement, like newspapers, do not allow that retailer to propose an instant transaction in the way that onsite advertising does. The ban on indoor advertising that is visible from the outside also presents problems in establishments like convenience stores, which have unique security concerns that counsel in favor of full visibility of the store from the outside. It is these sorts of considerations that the Attorney General failed to incorporate into the regulatory scheme.

A careful calculation of the costs of a speech regulation does not mean that a State must demonstrate that there is no incursion on legitimate speech interests, but a speech regulation cannot unduly impinge on the speaker's ability to propose a commercial transaction and the adult listener's opportunity to obtain information about products. After reviewing the outdoor advertising regulations, we find the calculation in these cases insufficient for purposes of the First Amendment.

Massachusetts has also restricted indoor, point-of-sale advertising for smokeless tobacco and cigars. Advertising cannot be "placed lower than five feet from the floor of any retail establishment which is located within a one thousand foot radius of" any school or playground. The District Court invalidated these provisions, concluding that the Attorney General had not provided a sufficient basis for regulating indoor advertising. We conclude that the point-of-sale advertising regulations fail both the third and fourth steps of the *Central Hudson* analysis. A regulation cannot be sustained if it " 'provides only ineffective or remote support for the government's purpose,' " or if there is "little chance" that the restriction will advance the State's goal, *Greater New Orleans, supra,* at 193. As outlined above, the State's goal is to prevent minors from using tobacco products and to curb demand for that activity by limiting youth exposure to advertising. The 5-foot rule does not seem to advance that goal. Not all children are less than 5 feet tall, and those who are certainly have the ability to look up and take in their surroundings. Massachusetts may wish to target tobacco advertisements and displays that entice children, much like floor-level candy displays in a convenience store, but the blanket height restriction does not constitute a reasonable fit with that goal. We conclude that the restriction on the height of indoor advertising is invalid under *Central Hudson*'s third and fourth prongs.

The Attorney General promulgated a number of regulations that restrict sales practices by cigarette, smokeless tobacco, and cigar manufacturers and retailers. The regulations require tobacco retailers to place tobacco products behind counters and require customers to have contact with a salesperson before they are able to handle a tobacco product. Assuming that petitioners have a cognizable speech interest in a particular means of displaying their products, these regulations withstand First Amendment scrutiny. The State has demonstrated a substantial interest in preventing access to tobacco products by minors and has adopted an appropriately narrow means of advancing that interest.

Unattended displays of tobacco products present an opportunity for access without the proper age verification required by law. Thus, the State prohibits self-service and other displays that would allow an individual to obtain tobacco products without direct contact with a salesperson. It is clear that the regulations leave open ample channels of communication. The regulations do not significantly impede adult access to tobacco products. Moreover, retailers have other means of exercising any cognizable speech interest in the presentation of their products. We presume that vendors may place empty tobacco packaging on open display, and display actual tobacco products so long as that display is only accessible to sales personnel. As for cigars, there is no indication in the regulations that a customer is unable to examine a cigar prior to purchase, so long as that examination takes place through a salesperson.

The sales practices regulations withstand First Amendment scrutiny. The means chosen by the State are narrowly tailored to prevent access to tobacco products by minors, are unrelated to expression, and leave open alternative avenues for vendors to convey information about products and for would-be customers to inspect products before purchase.

We have observed that "tobacco use, particularly among children and adolescents, poses perhaps the single most significant threat to public health in the United States." From a policy perspective, it is understandable for the States to attempt to prevent minors from using tobacco products before they reach an age where they are capable of weighing for themselves the risks and potential benefits of tobacco use, and other adult activities. The First Amendment, however, constrains state efforts to limit advertising of tobacco products, because so long as the sale and use of tobacco is lawful for adults, the tobacco industry has a protected interest in communicating information about its products and adult customers have an interest in receiving that information.

To the extent that federal law and the First Amendment do not prohibit state action, States and localities remain free to combat the problem of underage tobacco use by appropriate means. The judgment of the United States Court of Appeals for the First Circuit is therefore affirmed in part and reversed in part, and the cases are remanded for further proceedings consistent with this opinion.

It is so ordered.

Justice THOMAS, *concurring in part* and *concurring in the judgment.*

When the government seeks to restrict truthful speech in order to suppress the ideas it conveys, strict scrutiny is appropriate, whether or not the speech in question may be characterized as "commercial." The advertising restrictions violate the First Amendment. Underlying many of the arguments of respondents and their *amici* is the idea that tobacco is in some sense *sui generis* and that application of normal First Amendment principles should be suspended. Smoking poses serious health risks, and advertising may induce children (who lack the judgment to make an intelligent decision about whether to smoke) to begin smoking, which can lead to addiction. The State's assessment of the urgency of the problem posed by tobacco is a policy judgment, and it is not this Court's place to second-guess it. Nevertheless, to uphold the tobacco regulations would be to accept a line of reasoning that would permit restrictions on advertising for a host of other products.

Although every State prohibits the sale of alcohol to those under age 21, much alcohol advertising is viewed by children. There is considerable evidence that exposure to alcohol advertising is associated with underage drinking. Like underage tobacco use, underage drinking has effects that cannot be undone later in life. Those who begin drinking early are much more likely to become dependent on alcohol. Respondents have identified no principle of law or logic that would preclude the imposition of restrictions on fast food and alcohol advertising similar to those they seek to impose on tobacco advertising. In effect, they seek a "vice" exception to the First Amendment. No such exception exists. If it did, it would have almost no limit, for "any product that poses some threat to public health or public morals might reasonably be characterized by a state legislature as relating to 'vice activity.'"

No legislature has ever sought to restrict speech about an activity it regarded as harmless and inoffensive. Calls for limits on expression always are made when the specter of some threatened harm is looming. It is therefore no answer for the State to say that the makers of cigarettes are doing harm: perhaps they are. But in that respect they are no different from the purveyors of other harmful products, or the advocates of harmful ideas. When the State seeks to silence them, they are all entitled to the protection of the First Amendment.

Notes

1. *The* Lorillard *Consensus.* In *44 Liquormart, Inc. v. Rhode Island*, 517 U.S. 484 (1996), a plurality, led by Justice O'Connor, advocated reliance on *Central Hudson* for all commercial speech problems; another plurality, led by Justice Stevens, advocated a two-track system of scrutiny. Specifically, the *Central Hudson* test, applied a lesser standard than strict scrutiny, applies when a regulation seeks to protect consumers from misleading, deceptive, or aggressive sales practices or requires the disclosure of beneficial consumer information. However, a tougher form of scrutiny, labeled "special care" review, applies when a state entirely prohibits the dissemination of truthful, non-misleading commercial messages for reasons unrelated to the preservation of a fair bargaining process.

In *Lorillard,* the debate between these two pluralities dropped from sight. However, four Justices dissented "in part" and would have remanded for trial regarding the validity of the "1,000-foot rule," on the grounds that the record did not contain enough information to evaluate the existence of "alternate avenues of communication." Justice Stevens led a plurality in arguing that the sales practices and indoor advertising restrictions should be upheld as conduct regulations under *O'Brien.*

2. *Disparaging Trademarks and Commercial Speech. Matal v. Tam,* 137 S. Ct. 1744 (2017), was a trademark case in which petitioner tried to trademark his band's name, "The Slants." The Patent and Trademark Office (PTO) declined to register the name, relying on a provision of federal law that allowed the PTO to reject a trademark that might "disparage or bring into contempt or disrepute" any "persons living or dead." The Court struck down the law on the basis that it violated the Free Speech Clause of the First Amendment. The Court rejected the idea that the law could be upheld as a legitimate restriction on commercial speech:

> We confront a dispute between the parties on the question whether trademarks are commercial speech and are thus subject to the relaxed scrutiny outlined in *Central Hudson Gas & Elec. Corp. v. Public Serv. Comm'n of N. Y.,* 447 U. S. 557 (1980). We need not resolve this debate between the parties because the disparagement clause cannot withstand even *Central Hudson* review. Under *Central Hudson,* a restriction of speech must serve "a substantial interest," and it must be "narrowly drawn." This means, among other things, that "the regulatory technique may extend only as far as the interest it serves." The disparagement clause fails this requirement. It is claimed that the disparagement clause serves two interests. The first is "encouraging racial tolerance and protecting the privacy and welfare of individuals." The unmistakable thrust is this: The Government has an interest in preventing speech expressing ideas that offend. As we have explained, that idea strikes at the heart of the First Amendment. Speech that demeans on the basis of race, ethnicity, gender, religion, age, disability, or any other similar ground is hateful; but the proudest boast of our free speech jurisprudence is that we protect the freedom to express "the thought that we hate." *United States v. Schwimmer,* 279 U. S. 644 (1929) (Holmes, J., dissenting). The second interest asserted is protecting the orderly flow of commerce. Commerce, we are told, is disrupted by trademarks that "involve disparagement of race, gender, ethnicity, national origin, religion, sexual orientation, and similar demographic classification." A simple answer to this argument is that the disparagement clause is not "narrowly drawn" to drive out trademarks that support invidious discrimination. The clause reaches any trademark that disparages any person, group, or institution. It applies to trademarks like the following: "Down with racists," "Down with sexists," "Down with homophobes." It is not an anti-discrimination clause; it is a happy-talk clause. There is a deeper problem with the argument that commercial speech may be cleansed of any expression likely to cause offense. The commercial market is well stocked with merchandise that disparages prominent figures and groups, and the line between commercial and non-commercial speech is not always clear. If affixing the commercial label permits the suppression of any speech that may lead to political or social "volatility," free speech would be endangered.

3. *The Regulation of Professionals.* The Court's decisions relating to advertisements by lawyers, accountants, and other professionals recognize the right to advertise and the state's interest in regulation. *See, e.g., Florida Bar v. Went For It,*

Inc., 515 U.S. 618 (1995) (personal injury attorneys may not use targeted direct-mail solicitations for 30 days after an accident); *Ibanez v. Florida Department of Business and Professional Regulation, Board of Accountancy*, 512 U.S. 136 (1994) (lawyer may refer to CPA and certification as financial planner in stationery, business cards, and advertising); *Edenfield v. Fane*, 507 U.S. 761 (1993) (accountants may solicit business clients in person); *Peel v. Attorney Registration and Disciplinary Commission of Illinois*, 496 U.S. 91 (1990) (lawyer may advertise certification as trial specialist); *Shapero v. Kentucky Bar Association*, 486 U.S. 466 (1988) (lawyer may solicit legal business by sending letters to potential clients known to face particular legal problems); *In re R.M.J.*, 455 U.S. 191 (1982) (lawyer may not be disciplined for identifying jurisdiction where he is licensed to practice, or for mailing cards to friends, relatives, and clients about opening a new office); *In re Primus*, 436 U.S. 412 (1978) (ACLU "cooperating lawyer" may not be disciplined for soliciting a prospective litigant by mail after meeting litigant at a gathering related to the relevant issue); *Ohralik v. Ohio State Bar Association*, 436 U.S. 447 (1978) (lawyer may be disciplined for contacting accident victims in hospital room); *Bates v. State Bar of Arizona*, 433 U.S. 350 (1977) (lawyers may advertise legal services and fees in newspaper).

4. *Geographic Limitations on Commercial Speech.* Some of the Court's commercial speech cases have established limits on the power of the state to regulate particular locations, including public fora. *See, e.g., City of Cincinnati v. Discovery Network, Inc.*, 507 U.S. 410 (1993) (city may not refuse to allow commercial speech advertisements to be placed in news racks on sidewalks throughout the city when noncommercial speech is allowed in news racks); *Metromedia, Inc. v. San Diego*, 453 U.S. 490 (1981) (allowing city to ban outdoor advertising billboards when "offsite" but not to ban "onsite" advertising signs); *Linmark Associates, Inc. v. Township of Willingboro*, 431 U.S. 85 (1977) (town may not ban "For Sale" and "Sold" signs from residential property).

5. *Broadcasting and Commercial Speech.* The Court's decisions involving advertising bans on broadcasting have relied on *Central Hudson* and have reached different results in different contexts. *Compare Greater New Orleans Broadcasting Association v. United States*, 527 U.S. 173 (1999) (federal ban on broadcasting advertisements of private casino gambling information violated the right of radio and television stations in a state where gambling is legal to broadcast such advertisements), *with United States v. Edge Broadcasting Co.*, 509 U.S. 418 (1993) (same federal ban is constitutional as applied to broadcast advertising by radio station in a state where such gambling is not authorized).

6. *Liquor Advertising.* A Rhode Island law prohibited liquor vendors licensed in the state (as well as out-of-state manufacturers, wholesalers, and shippers) from "advertising in any manner whatsoever" the price of any alcoholic beverage offered for sale in the state. The only exception was for price tags or signs displayed with the merchandise inside licensed premises and not visible from the street. The law also prohibited the news media from publishing or broadcasting any advertisements, even those referring to liquor being sold in other states, that

"make reference to the price of any alcoholic beverage." In *44 Liquormart, Inc. v. Rhode Island*, 517 U.S. 484 (1996), a plurality concluded that the law was unconstitutional: "It is perfectly obvious that alternative forms of regulation that would not involve any restriction on speech would be more likely to achieve the State's goal of promoting temperance. As the State's own expert conceded, higher prices can be maintained either by direct regulation or by increased taxation. Per capita purchases could be limited as is the case with prescription drugs. Even educational campaigns focused on the problems of excessive, or even moderate, drinking might prove to be more effective. The alcohol ad ban statutes are even more extensive than the tobacco regulations that were invalidated in *Lorillard*, including the outdoor 1,000 foot regulation and indoor five-feet-from-the-floor regulation. So the alcohol ad ban statutes must be invalidated under *Central Hudson*."

7. *Regulation of Drug Prescription Information.* In *Sorrell v. IMS Health, Inc.*, 564 U.S. 522 (2011), the Court invalidated a state law that prohibited: 1) the sale of "prescriber-identifying information" by pharmacies; 2) the disclosure by pharmacies of such information for marketing purposes; and 3) the use of such information by pharmaceutical manufacturers. Before the law was enacted, a pharmacy could sell such information to "data miners" who would produce reports about prescriber behavior that would be leased to drug companies, which would, in turn, employ "detailers," who would seek to improve marketing strategies and increase sales of the companies' brand-name drugs to doctors. The Court held that the law was not narrowly drawn to advance the State's governmental interest in protecting the confidentiality of prescriber information. Such an interest might have been used to justify a law that provided only limited disclosure exceptions, but here the law disallowed only disclosure for marketing purposes, and therefore limited speech "for a narrow class of disfavored speakers" while allowing the information to be made widely available otherwise. Second, the Court found that the law did not advance the interests of lowering medical costs and promoting public health "in a permissible way." Instead, the law relied on "the indirect means of restraining speech by certain speakers" in order to diminish the influence of the detailers to promote brand-name drugs. The Court noted that the State may not create burdens for protected speech "in order to tilt public debate in a preferred direction." In response to the State's claim that the law protected doctors from "harassing sales behaviors," the Court noted that doctors "can simply decline to meet with detailers," and the State provided no explanation why similar remedies other than the content-based law were not adequate. As for the State's argument that the detailers' use of prescriber information "undermines the doctor-patient relationship," the Court noted that if the detailers' "marketing affects treatment decisions," then "it does so because doctors find it persuasive," and "the fear that speech might persuade provides no lawful basis for quieting it."

8. In *Expressions Hair Design v. Schneiderman*, 137 S. Ct. 1144 (2017), the merchants wanted to implement a "single sticker regime" in which they post a cash price with an additional credit card surcharge. The Court held that the New York statute that prohibited this regime was a regulation of "speech" because it

regulated the communication of prices, although not the prices themselves. The Court also held that the statute was not void for vagueness and remanded the case for a determination whether the statute violates the First Amendment.

9. *National Institute of Family and Life Advocates v. Becerra*, 138 S. Ct. 2361 (2018), involved California's FACT Act which required crisis pregnancy centers to inform women that "California has public programs that provide immediate free or low-cost access to comprehensive family planning services (including all FDA-approved methods of contraception), prenatal care, and abortion for eligible women. To determine whether you qualify, contact the county social services office at [insert telephone number]." The centers, which were generally pro-life, objected to the idea of being required to inform women about abortion options. The Court struck the law down viewing the notice as a content-based restriction on speech which was subject to strict scrutiny because it altered the content of the centers' speech. The Court refused to regulate the speech as "professional speech":

> Speech is not unprotected merely because it is uttered by "professionals." This Court has afforded less protection for professional speech in two circumstances—neither of which turned on the fact that professionals were speaking. First, our precedents have applied more deferential review to laws that require professionals to disclose factual, noncontroversial information in their "commercial speech." *See, e.g., Zauderer v. Office of Disciplinary Counsel of Supreme Court of Ohio*, 471 U. S. 626 (1985). Second, States may regulate professional conduct even though that conduct incidentally involves speech. *See Planned Parenthood of Southeastern Pa. v. Casey*, 505 U. S. 833 (1992) (opinion of O'Connor). Neither line of precedents is implicated here.
>
> This Court's precedents have applied a lower level of scrutiny to laws that compel disclosures in certain contexts. In *Zauderer*, this Court upheld a rule requiring lawyers who advertised their services on a contingency-fee basis to disclose that clients might be required to pay some fees and costs. Noting that the disclosure requirement governed only "commercial advertising" and required the disclosure of "purely factual and uncontroversial information about the terms under which services will be available," the Court explained that such requirements should be upheld unless they are "unjustified or unduly burdensome." *Zauderer* does not apply here. The licensed notice is not limited to "purely factual and uncontroversial information about the terms under which services will be available." The notice in no way relates to the services that licensed clinics provide. Instead, it requires these clinics to disclose information about state-sponsored services—including abortion, anything but an "uncontroversial" topic.
>
> This Court has upheld regulations of professional conduct that incidentally burden speech. *Sorrell v. IMS Health Inc.*, 564 U. S. 552, 567 (2011). In *Planned Parenthood of Southeastern Pa. v. Casey*, this Court upheld a law requiring physicians to obtain informed consent before they could perform an abortion. 505 U. S., at 884. Pennsylvania law required physicians to inform their patients of "the nature of the procedure, the health risks of the abortion and childbirth, and the 'probable gestational age of the unborn child.'" The law also required physicians to inform patients of the availability of printed materials from the State, which provided information about the child and various forms of assistance. The licensed notice at issue is not an informed-consent requirement or any other regulation of professional conduct. The notice does not facilitate informed consent to a medical procedure. In fact, it is not tied to a procedure at all. It applies to all interactions between a covered facility and its clients, regardless of whether a medical procedure is sought, offered, or performed. Tellingly,

many facilities that provide the exact same services as covered facilities—such as general practice clinics, are not required to provide the licensed notice. The licensed notice regulates speech as speech.

Outside of the contexts discussed, this Court's precedents have long protected the First Amendment rights of professionals. This Court has applied strict scrutiny to content-based laws that regulate the noncommercial speech of lawyers, *Reed*, 576 U. S., at ___ (slip op., at 10); professional fundraisers, *Riley*, 487 U. S., at 798; and organizations that provided specialized advice about international law, *Holder v. Humanitarian Law Project*, 561 U. S. 1 (2010). And the lawyer's statements in *Zauderer* would have been "fully protected" if they were made in a context other than advertising. Moreover, this Court has stressed the danger of content-based regulations "in the fields of medicine and public health, where information can save lives." *Sorrell, supra*, at 566. Regulating the content of professionals' speech "poses the inherent risk that the Government seeks not to advance a legitimate regulatory goal, but to suppress unpopular ideas or information." *Turner Broadcasting*, 512 U. S., at 641.

When government polices the content of professional speech, it can fail to "preserve an uninhibited marketplace of ideas in which truth will ultimately prevail." *McCullen v. Coakley*, 573 U. S. ___, ___ (2014) (slip op., at 8–9). "The best test of truth is the power of the thought to get itself accepted in the competition of the market," *Abrams v. United States*, 250 U. S. 616, 630 (1919) (Holmes, J., dissenting), and the people lose when the government is the one deciding which ideas should prevail. "Professional speech" is also a difficult category to define with precision. As defined by the courts of appeals, the professional-speech doctrine would cover a wide array of individuals—doctors, lawyers, nurses, physical therapists, truck drivers, bartenders, barbers, and many others. All that is required to make something a "profession" is that it involves personalized services and requires a professional license from the State. But that gives the States unfettered power to reduce a group's First Amendment rights by simply imposing a licensing requirement. States cannot choose the protection that speech receives under the First Amendment, as that would give them a powerful tool to impose "invidious discrimination of disfavored subjects." *Cincinnati v. Discovery Network, Inc.*, 507 U. S. 410, 423 (1993).

The Court concluded that the "licensed notice could not survive even intermediate scrutiny," stating that:

> California asserts a single interest: providing low-income women with information about state-sponsored services. If California's goal is to educate low-income women about the services it provides, the licensed notice is "wildly underinclusive." The notice applies only to clinics that have a "primary purpose" of "providing family planning or pregnancy-related services" and that provide two of six categories of specific services. California has "nearly 1,000 community clinics"—including "federally designated community health centers, migrant health centers, rural health centers, and frontier health centers"—that "serve more than 5.6 million patients annually through over 17 million patient encounters." But most of those clinics are excluded from the licensed notice requirement. Such "underinclusiveness raises serious doubts about whether the government is in fact pursuing the interest it invokes, rather than disfavoring a particular speaker or viewpoint." *Entertainment Merchants Assn.*, 564 U. S., at 802. The FACT Act also excludes federal clinics and Family PACT providers from the licensed-notice requirement. If the goal is to maximize women's awareness of these programs, then it would seem that California would ensure that the places that can immediately enroll women also provide this information. The FACT Act's exemption for these clinics, which serve many women who are pregnant or could become pregnant, demonstrates the disconnect between its stated purpose and its actual scope. "Precision must be the touchstone" when it comes to regulations of speech, which "so closely touch our most precious freedoms." *Button*, 371

U. S., at 438. Further, California could inform low-income women about its services "without burdening a speaker with unwanted speech." It could inform the women itself with a public-information campaign. California could even post the information on public property near crisis pregnancy centers.

As to unlicensed facilities, the Court rejected the idea that *Zauderer* applied to them either:

> Under *Zauderer*, a disclosure requirement cannot be "unjustified or unduly burden-some." The only justification that the California Legislature put forward was ensuring that "pregnant women in California know when they are getting medical care from licensed pro-fessionals." California points to nothing suggesting that pregnant women do not already know that the covered facilities are staffed by unlicensed medical professionals. And California already makes it a crime for individuals without a medical license to practice medicine. The FACT Act unduly burdens protected speech. The unlicensed notice imposes a government-scripted, speaker-based disclosure requirement that is wholly disconnected from California's informational interest. The unlicensed notice applies only to facilities that primarily provide "pregnancy-related" services. Thus, a facility that advertises and provides pregnancy tests is covered by the unlicensed notice, but a facility that advertises and provides nonprescription contraceptives is excluded—even though the latter is no less likely to make women think it is licensed. This Court's precedents are deeply skeptical of laws that "distinguish among different speakers, allowing speech by some but not others." *Citizens United v. Federal Election Comm'n*, 558 U. S. 310, 340 (2010). The application of the unlicensed notice to advertise-ments demonstrates just how burdensome it is. The notice applies to all "print and digi-tal advertising materials" by an unlicensed covered facility. These materials must include a government-drafted statement that "this facility is not licensed as a medical facility by the State of California and has no licensed medical provider who provides or directly supervises the provision of services." An unlicensed facility must call attention to the notice, instead of its own message, by some method such as larger text or contrasting type or color. This scripted language must be posted in English and as many other languages as California chooses to require. A billboard for an unlicensed facility that says "Choose Life" would have to surround that two-word statement with a 29-word statement from the government, in as many as 13 different languages. In this way, the unlicensed notice drowns out the facility's own message. The "detail required" by the unlicensed notice "effectively rules out" the possibility of having such a billboard. The notice targets speakers, not speech, and imposes an unduly burden-some disclosure requirement that will chill their protected speech.

Barr v. American Association of Political Consultants, Inc.

140 S.Ct. 2335 (2020)

Justice KAVANAUGH announced the judgment of the Court and delivered an opin-ion, in which THE CHIEF JUSTICE and Justice ALITO join, and in which Justice THOMAS joins as to Parts I and II.

Americans are largely united in their disdain for robocalls. The Federal Government receives a staggering number of complaints about robocalls—3.7 million complaints in 2019. The States likewise field a constant barrage of complaints. For nearly 30 years, the people's representatives in Congress have been fighting back. As relevant here, the Telephone Consumer Protection Act of

1991, known as the TCPA, generally prohibits robocalls to cell phones and home phones. But a 2015 amendment to the TCPA allows robocalls that are made to collect debts owed to or guaranteed by the Federal Government, including robocalls made to collect many student loan and mortgage debts. This case concerns robocalls to cell phones. Plaintiffs are political and nonprofit organizations that want to make political robocalls to cell phones. Invoking the First Amendment, they argue that the 2015 government-debt exception unconstitutionally favors debt-collection speech over political and other speech. They urge us to invalidate the entire 1991 robocall restriction. The judgment of the U. S. Court of Appeals for the Fourth Circuit is affirmed.

I

In 1991, Congress passed and President George H. W. Bush signed the Telephone Consumer Protection Act. The Act responded to a torrent of vociferous consumer complaints about intrusive robocalls. A growing number of telemarketers were using equipment that could automatically dial a telephone number and deliver an artificial or prerecorded voice message. At the time, more than 300,000 solicitors called more than 18 million Americans every day. Consumers were "outraged" and considered robocalls an invasion of privacy "regardless of the content or the initiator of the message." In enacting the TCPA, Congress found that banning robocalls was "the only effective means of protecting telephone consumers from this nuisance and privacy invasion." The TCPA imposed various restrictions on the use of automated telephone equipment. One restriction prohibited "any call (other than a call made for emergency purposes or with the prior express consent of the called party) using any automatic telephone dialing system or an artificial or prerecorded voice" to "any telephone number assigned to a paging service, *cellular telephone service*, specialized mobile radio service, or other radio common carrier service, or any service for which the called party is charged for the call." The TCPA prohibited almost all robocalls to cell phones. In 2015, Congress passed and President Obama signed the Bipartisan Budget Act. In addition to making other changes, that Act amended the TCPA's restriction on robocalls to cell phones. It stated: "(a) In General. — Section 227(b) of the Communications Act of 1934 is amended — (1) in paragraph (1) — (A) in subparagraph (A)(iii), by inserting 'unless such call is made solely to collect a debt owed to or guaranteed by the United States' after 'charged for the call.'" In other words, Congress carved out a new government-debt exception to the general robocall restriction. The TCPA imposes tough penalties for violating the robocall restriction. Private parties can sue to recover up to $1,500 per violation or three times their actual monetary losses, which can add up quickly in a class action. States may bring civil actions against robocallers on behalf of their citizens. And the Federal Communications Commission can seek forfeiture penalties for willful or repeated violations of the statute.

Plaintiffs are the American Association of Political Consultants and three other organizations that participate in the political system. Plaintiffs and their members make calls to citizens to discuss candidates and issues, solicit donations, conduct polls, and get out the vote. Plaintiffs believe that their political outreach would be more effective and efficient if they could make robocalls to cell phones. But because plaintiffs are not in the business of collecting government debt, §227(b)(1)(A)(iii) prohibits them from making those robocalls. The U. S. District Court for the Eastern District of North Carolina determined that the robocall restriction with the government-debt exception was a content-based speech regulation, thereby triggering strict scrutiny. But the court concluded that the law survived strict scrutiny. The U. S. Court of Appeals for the Fourth Circuit vacated the judgment. We granted certiorari.

II

The First Amendment provides that Congress shall make no law "abridging the freedom of speech." Above "all else, the First Amendment means that government" generally "has no power to restrict expression because of its message, its ideas, its subject matter, or its content." *Police Dept. of Chicago v. Mosley*, 408 U. S. 92, 95 (1972). The Court's precedents restrict the government from discriminating "in the regulation of expression on the basis of the content of that expression." *Hudgens v. NLRB*, 424 U. S. 507, 520 (1976). Content-based laws are subject to strict scrutiny. See *Reed v. Town of Gilbert*, 576 U. S. 155 (2015). A law is content-based if "a regulation of speech 'on its face' draws distinctions based on the message a speaker conveys." *Reed*, 576 U. S., at 163. That description applies to a law that "singles out specific subject matter for differential treatment." *Id.*, at 169. For example, "a law banning the use of sound trucks for political speech—and only political speech—would be a content-based regulation, even if it imposed no limits on the political viewpoints that could be expressed." *Ibid.* Under §227(b)(1)(A)(iii), the legality of a robocall turns on whether it is "made solely to collect a debt owed to or guaranteed by the United States." A robocall that says, "Please pay your government debt" is legal. A robocall that says, "Please donate to our political campaign" is illegal. Because the law favors speech made for collecting government debt over political and other speech, the law is a content-based restriction on speech.

The Government advances three main arguments for deeming the statute content-neutral, but none is persuasive. *First*, the Government suggests that §227(b)(1)(A)(iii) draws distinctions based on speakers (authorized debt collectors), not based on content. But this statute singles out calls "made solely to collect a debt owed to or guaranteed by the United States," not all calls from authorized debt collectors. Indeed, the Court has held that "laws favoring some speakers over others demand strict scrutiny when the legislature's speaker preference reflects a content preference." *Reed*, 576 U. S., at 170. *Second*, the Government argues that the legality of a robocall under the statute depends simply on whether the caller is engaged in a particular economic activity, not on the content of speech. We disagree. The law here focuses on whether the caller is *speaking* about a particular topic. *Third*, according to the Government, if this statute is content-based because it singles out debt-collection speech, then so are statutes that *regulate* debt collection, like the Fair Debt Collection Practices Act. That argument is unpersuasive. As we explained in *Sorrell*, "the First Amendment does not prevent restrictions directed at commerce or conduct from imposing incidental burdens on speech." The courts have generally been able to distinguish impermissible content-based speech restrictions from traditional or ordinary economic regulation of commercial activity that imposes incidental burdens on speech. The issue before us concerns only robocalls to cell phones. Our decision is not intended to expand existing First Amendment doctrine or to otherwise affect traditional or ordinary economic regulation of commercial activity.

In short, the robocall restriction with the government-debt exception is content-based. Under the Court's precedents, a "law that is content based" is "subject to strict scrutiny." *Reed*, 576 U. S., at 165. The Government concedes that it cannot satisfy strict scrutiny to justify the government-debt exception. Although collecting government debt is a worthy goal, the Government concedes that it has not sufficiently justified the differentiation between government-debt collection speech and other important categories of robocall speech, such as political speech, charitable fundraising, issue advocacy, commercial advertising, and the like.

III

Having concluded that the 2015 government-debt exception created an unconstitutional exception to the 1991 robocall restriction, we must decide whether to invalidate the entire 1991 robocall restriction, or instead to invalidate and sever the 2015 government-debt exception. The correct result in this case is to sever the 2015 government-debt exception and leave in place the longstanding robocall restriction.[12]

It is so ordered.

Justice SOTOMAYOR, concurring in the judgment.

The government-debt exception in 47 U. S. C. §227(b) fails intermediate scrutiny because it is not "narrowly tailored to serve a significant governmental interest." *Ward v. Rock Against Racism*, 491 U. S. 781, 791 (1989). The Government has not explained how a debt-collection robocall about a government-backed debt is any less intrusive or could be any less harassing than a debt-collection robocall about a privately backed debt. The Government could have employed far less restrictive means to further its interest in collecting debt, such as "securing consent from the debtors to make debt-collection calls" or "placing the calls itself." Nor has the Government "sufficiently justified the differentiation between government-debt collection speech and other important categories of robocall speech, such as political speech, charitable fundraising, issue advocacy, commercial advertising, and the like." I agree that the offending provision is severable.

Justice BREYER, with whom Justice GINSBURG and Justice KAGAN join, concurring in the judgment with respect to severability and dissenting in part.

There is no basis here to apply "strict scrutiny" based on "content-discrimination." "The First Amendment was fashioned to assure unfettered inter-change of ideas for the bringing about of political and social changes desired by the people." *Meyer v. Grant*, 486 U. S. 414, 421 (1988). The free marketplace of ideas is not simply a debating society for expressing thought. It is in significant part an instrument for "bringing about political and social change." *Meyer*, 486 U. S., at 421. Our First Amendment jurisprudence has long reflected these core values. This Court's cases have provided heightened judicial protection for political speech, public forums, and the expression of all viewpoints on any given issue. "Governments must not be allowed to choose which issues are worth discussing or debating." *Reed*, 576 U. S., at 182 (Kagan, J., concurring).

From a democratic perspective, it is equally important that courts not use the First Amendment in a way that would threaten the workings of ordinary regulatory programs posing little threat to the free marketplace of ideas enacted as result of that public discourse. The strictest scrutiny should not apply indiscriminately to the very "political and social changes desired by the people." *Meyer*, 486 U. S., at 421. Otherwise, our democratic system would fail, not through the inability of the people to speak or to transmit their views to government, but because of an elected government's inability to translate those views into action. Thus, it is not surprising that this Court has applied less strict standards when reviewing speech restrictions embodied in government regulatory programs. This Court, for example, has applied a "rational basis" standard for reviewing those restrictions when they have only indirect impacts on speech. And it has applied a mid-level standard of review—often termed "intermediate scrutiny"—when the government directly restricts protected commercial speech. See *Central Hudson Gas & Elec. Corp. v. Public Serv. Comm'n of N. Y.*, 447 U. S. 557 (1980).

To reflexively treat all content-based distinctions as subject to strict scrutiny regardless of context or practical effect is to engage in an analysis untethered from the First Amendment's objectives. In this case, strict scrutiny is inappropriate. Regulation of debt collection does not fall on the first side of the democratic equation. It has next to nothing to do with the free marketplace of ideas or the transmission of the people's thoughts and will to the government. It has everything to do with the government response to the public will through ordinary commercial regulation. To apply the strictest level of scrutiny to the economically based exemption here is remarkable. Much of human life involves activity that takes place through speech. And much regulatory activity turns upon speech content. Treating all content-based distinctions on speech as presumptively unconstitutional is unworkable and would obstruct the ordinary workings of democratic governance.

The Court has held that entire categories of speech—for example, obscenity, fraud, and speech integral to criminal conduct—are generally unprotected by the First Amendment entirely because of their content. See *Miller v. California*, 413

U. S. 15, 23 (1973). As Justice Stevens pointed out, "our entire First Amendment jurisprudence creates a regime based on the content of speech." *R. A. V. v. St. Paul*, 505 U. S. 377, 420 (1992) (concurring). Given that this Court looks to the nature and content of speech to determine whether, or to what extent, the First Amendment protects it, it makes little sense to treat *every* content-based distinction Congress has made as presumptively unconstitutional. Our First Amendment jurisprudence has always been contextual and has defied straightforward reduction to unyielding categorical rules. That said, I am not arguing for the abolition of the concept of "content discrimination." There are times when using content discrimination to trigger scrutiny is eminently reasonable. Specifically, when content-based distinctions are used as a method for suppressing particular viewpoints or threatening the neutrality of a traditional public forum, content discrimination triggering strict scrutiny is generally appropriate. Neither of those situations is present here. Outside of these circumstances, content discrimination can at times help determine the strength of a government justification or identify a potential interference with the free marketplace of ideas.

Given that the government-debt exception does directly impact a means of communication, a proper inquiry should examine the seriousness of the speech-related harm, the importance of countervailing objectives, the likelihood that the restriction will achieve those objectives, and whether there are other, less restrictive ways of doing so. Narrow tailoring in this context does not necessarily require the use of the least-restrictive means of furthering those objectives. We have called this approach "intermediate scrutiny." As Justice Kavanaugh notes, the government-debt exception provides no basis for undermining the general cell phone robocall restriction. Indeed, looking at the government-debt exception in context, we see that the practical effect of the exception, taken together with the rest of the statute, is to put *non*-government debt collectors at a disadvantage. Their speech operates in the same sphere as government-debt collection speech, communicates comparable messages, and yet does not have the benefit of a particular instrument of communication (robocalls). While this is a speech-related harm, debt-collection speech is both commercial and highly regulated. The speech-related harm at issue here—and any related effect on the marketplace of ideas—is modest. The purpose of the exception is to further the protection of the public fisc. That protection is an important governmental interest. Private debt typically involves private funds; public debt typically involves funds that, in principle, belong to all of us, and help to implement numerous governmental policies that the people support. Congress has minimized any speech-related harm by tying the exception directly to the Government's interest in preserving the public fisc. Calls will only fall within the bounds of that exception if they are "made *solely* to collect" Government debt. Thus, the exception cannot be used to permit communications unrelated or less directly related to that public fiscal interest.

Justice GORSUCH, with whom Justice THOMAS joins as to Part II, concurring in the judgment in part and dissenting in part.

II

The TCPA's rule against cellphone robocalls is a content-based restriction that fails strict scrutiny. [I am unable] to support the remedy the Court endorses today. Respectfully, if this is what modern "severability doctrine" has become, it seems to me all the more reason to reconsider our course.

∾ PROBLEMS ∾

1. *Gun Sale Advertising.* San Mateo County, California has a fairgrounds that is leased for various events throughout the year. Between 1990 and 1997, gun shows were held at the fairgrounds. In 1998, a new clause was added to the lease which stated that any tenant "shall not permit any gun shows" at the fairgrounds. The San Mateo County Board of Supervisors offered three purposes for the ban: "to avoid sending the wrong message to the community relative to support of gun usage, to improve the Fairgrounds' image, and to reduce the fiscal impact of criminal justice activities in response to gun-related violence." GunsAmerica (GA) has previously conducted gun shows at the fairgrounds, and GA tries to negotiate with the county in order to remove the new clause from the lease for an upcoming event. During negotiations, the county sends a letter informing GA that the new clause is "intended to prohibit gun sales or offers to sell guns later, but not to prohibit the exchange of information or ideas about guns, gun safety, or the display of guns for historical or educational purposes." After receiving the letter, GA files suit seeking a declaratory judgment that the new clause violates the First Amendment. What arguments will you make to persuade the court to invalidate the clause? What counterarguments do you expect the county's lawyer to make in response? (Do not argue vagueness or overbreadth.)

2. *Calorie Posting.* New York City's health code requires all chain restaurants that have 15 or more establishments nationally to reveal the calorie counts of their food. The information must be displayed on menus and menu boards in a specific formulation that is clear and conspicuous and that is adjacent or close to each menu item. A restaurant association challenges the code provisions, claiming an infringement of its members' right to free speech. Consistent with the First Amendment, can New York impose the calorie count requirement? *See New York State Restaurant Assn. v. New York City Board of Health,* 556 F.3d 114 (2d Cir. 2009).

3. *Regulating Bulk E-Mail (Spam) Transmissions.* In an effort to control the dissemination of "spam" (unsolicited bulk e-mail messages), the Virginia Computer Crimes Act (VCCA) makes it illegal to use a computer or computer network with the intent to falsify or forge electronic mail transmission information or other routing information in any manner in connection with the transmission of unsolicited bulk electronic mail through or into the computer network of an electronic mail service provider or its subscribers. However, unlike some other statutes that prohibit only commercial e-mail messages, the VCCA applies to all e-mail messages, including those that contain religious or political messages.

The VCCA makes it a felony to transmit more than 10,000 e-mail messages to attempted recipients in any 24-hour time period, to 100,000 attempted recipients in any 30-day time period, or to 1 million attempted recipients in any 1-year time period. The defendant sent 10,000 messages to subscribers of America Online (AOL). Although the defendant tried to hide his identity, investigators were able to track him down. Would the VCCA be valid as applied to e-mail messages proposing a commercial transaction? Does the state have an interest in controlling unsolicited bulk commercial e-mail messages (based either on the annoyance to e-mail recipients or on the increased costs to internet service providers)? Does the state also have an interest in ensuring that the senders of such e-mail messages identify themselves? *See Jaynes v. Commonwealth*, 666 S.E.2d 303 (Va. 2008).

4. *More on Spam E-Mail Transmissions.* Would the VCCA be valid as applied to all e-mail messages, including those with religious or political subjects? Could Virginia also prohibit anonymous e-mail messages? What standard of review should apply? What result? *See McIntyre v. Ohio Elections Commission*, 514 U.S. 334, 342 (1995).

5. *The Parenting Advice Columnist.* A licensed psychologist has been dispensing parenting advice in a newspaper column for the last 20 years. The column is distributed through more than 200 newspapers nationwide. However, the columnist is licensed in North Carolina, and some Kentucky psychologists seek to prohibit him from referring to himself as a "psychologist" on the basis that he is not licensed in Kentucky. The Kentucky psychologists view the column as involving the illegal practice of psychology. Suppose that you are hired to advise the Commonwealth of Kentucky. Can Kentucky prohibit the columnist from referring to himself as a "psychologist"? *See* Matthew Barakat, *Parenting Columnist Targeted by Ky. Sues*, Louisville Courier-J., July 18, 2013, at B-3.

6. *Meat Labeling Requirements.* Under prior labeling rules, meat producers were allowed to label meat as the "product" of countries where any production steps had taken place. Under a revised rule, subject to some minor exceptions, they are required to indicate each country where any of the following happened: the animal was born, raised, or slaughtered. Is the government entitled to impose such labeling requirements on meat producers? What is the state interest in imposing such a regulation? *See American Meat Institute v. USDA*, 746 F.3d 1065 (D.C. Cir. 2014).

7. *More on the International Treaty Regulating the Internet.* Various delegates to the convention want to place restrictions on commercial speech. Some want to ban commercial speech that is "fraudulent." Others want to ban speech that infringes on commercial interests in their own countries. For example, in France, it is impermissible to use the word *champagne* to refer to "sparkling wine" unless the grapes were grown in the Champagne region of France. France would like to see similar restrictions placed on internet advertising of sparkling wine. What restrictions on commercial speech can you agree to? Can you accede to the French demands? American sparkling wine producers prefer to use the label *champagne* for their product (rather than the term *sparkling wine*) because they believe that it has greater commercial appeal.

C. SYMBOLIC SPEECH

The civil rights era required the Court to confront First Amendment issues arising in the context of public demonstrations, and initially the Court was divided
as to how to distinguish "speech" from "conduct." Ultimately, however, the Court
developed a consensus that "conduct" may be "sufficiently imbued with elements
of communication" to deserve constitutional protection, as long as the speaker
has "an intent to convey a particularized message" under circumstances where
"the likelihood was great that the message would be understood by those who
viewed it." *Spence v. Washington*, 418 U.S. 405, 409 (1974). In 1989, the Court enumerated the cases in which "communicative conduct" or "symbolic speech" was
protected:

> We have recognized the expressive nature of students' wearing of black armbands to protest
> American military involvement in Vietnam, *Tinker v. Des Moines Independent Community School
> Dist.*, 393 U.S. 503 (1969); of a sit-in by blacks in a "whites only" area to protest segregation,
> *Brown v. Louisiana*, 383 U.S. 131 (1966); of the wearing of American military uniforms in
> a dramatic presentation criticizing *American involvement in Vietnam*, *Schacht v. United States*,
> 398 U.S. 58 (1970); and of picketing about a wide variety of causes, *see, e.g., United States
> v. Grace*, 461 U.S. 171 (1983) picketing on the sidewalk across from the Court. Attaching a
> peace sign to the flag, *Spence v. Washington*, 418 U.S. 405 (1974); refusing to salute the flag,
> *West Virginia Board of Education v. Barnette*, 319 U.S. 624 (1943); and displaying a red flag,
> *Stromberg v. California*, 283 U.S. 359 (1931), we have held, all may find shelter under the First
> Amendment.

Texas v. Johnson, 491 U.S. 397, 404-405 (1989) (holding that burning a flag during
a public demonstration was protected speech).

The more difficult issue in "symbolic speech" cases is how to treat the government interest. During the almost 50 years between the *Barnette* flag salute
case and the *Johnson* flag-burning case, the Court evolved a strict scrutiny test for
content-based regulations of speech. Yet in a "symbolic speech" case, the government interest expressed a statutory regulation of "conduct" that might not
resemble the typical censorship-oriented interest advanced to support a "content" regulation of a particular kind of speech. Therefore, the question arising
in many "symbolic speech" regulation cases is whether the government's interest
might be characterized as "content-neutral," and if so, what sort of scrutiny might
be appropriate for such a non-censorship-oriented interest and what sort of government burden of "tailoring" the regulation might require.

United States v. O'Brien

391 U.S. 367 (1968)

Mr. Chief Justice WARREN delivered the opinion of the Court.

David Paul O'Brien and three companions burned their Selective Service
registration certificates on the steps of the South Boston Courthouse. A sizable

crowd, including several agents of the Federal Bureau of Investigation, witnessed the event. Immediately after the burning, members of the crowd began attacking O'Brien and his companions. For this act, O'Brien was indicted, tried, convicted, and sentenced under a federal law prohibiting the destruction of draft cards. O'Brien did not contest the fact that he had burned the certificate. He stated that he burned the certificate publicly to influence others to adopt his antiwar beliefs, "so that other people would reevaluate their positions with Selective Service, with the armed forces, and reevaluate their place in the culture of today."

When a male reaches the age of 18, he is required by the Universal Military Training and Service Act to register with a local draft board. He is assigned a Selective Service number, and he is issued a registration certificate. Subsequently, and based on a questionnaire completed by the registrant, he is assigned a classification denoting his eligibility for induction, and 'as soon as practicable' thereafter he is issued a Notice of Classification. This initial classification is not permanent, and if in the interim before induction the registrant's status changes in some relevant way, he may be reclassified. After a reclassification, the local board issues to the registrant a new Notice of Classification.

The registration certificate is a small white card, approximately 2 by 3 inches. The registration certificate specifies the name of the registrant, the date of registration, and the number and address of the local board with which he is registered. Also inscribed are the date and place of the registrant's birth, his residence at registration, his physical description, his signature, and his Selective Service number. The Selective Service number itself indicates his State of registration, his local board, his year of birth, and his chronological position in the local board's classification record. The registration certificate bears notices that the registrant must notify his local board in writing of every change in address, physical condition, and occupational, marital, family, dependency, and military status, and of any other fact which might change his classification. It also contains a notice that the registrant's Selective Service number should appear on all communications to his local board.

Congress demonstrated its concern that certificates issued by the Selective Service System might be abused well before the 1965 Amendment here challenged. The 1948 Act prohibited many different abuses including alteration or forgery. In addition, regulations of the Selective Service System required registrants to keep both their registration and classification certificates in their personal possession at all times. The Act made knowing violation of any provision of the Act or rules and regulations a felony.

By the 1965 Amendment, Congress added the provision here at issue, subjecting to criminal liability not only one who "forges, alters, or in any manner changes" but also one who "knowingly destroys (or) knowingly mutilates" a certificate. The 1965 Amendment does not abridge free speech on its face. The amendment deals with conduct having no connection with speech. It prohibits the knowing destruction of certificates issued by the Selective Service System. The Amendment does not distinguish between public and private destruction, and does not punish only destruction engaged in for the purpose of expressing views.

O'Brien argues that the 1965 Amendment is unconstitutional as applied to him because his act of burning his registration certificate was protected "symbolic speech" within the First Amendment. His argument is that freedom of expression includes all modes of "communication of ideas by conduct," and that his conduct is within this definition because he did it in "demonstration against the war and against the draft." On the assumption that O'Brien's conduct is sufficient to bring into play the First Amendment, it does not necessarily follow that the destruction of a registration certificate is constitutionally protected activity. When "speech" and "nonspeech" elements are combined in the same course of conduct, a sufficiently important governmental interest in regulating the nonspeech element can justify incidental limitations on First Amendment freedoms. A government regulation is sufficiently justified if it is within the constitutional power of the Government; if it furthers an important or substantial governmental interest; if the governmental interest is unrelated to the suppression of free expression; and if the incidental restriction on alleged First Amendment freedoms is no greater than is essential to the furtherance of that interest. The 1965 Amendment meets all of these requirements, and O'Brien can be constitutionally convicted for violating it.

The constitutional power of Congress to raise and support armies and to make all laws necessary and proper to that end is broad and sweeping. The power of Congress to classify and conscript manpower for military service is "beyond question." Congress may establish a system of registration for individuals liable for training and service, and may require such individuals within reason to cooperate in the registration system. The issuance of certificates indicating the registration and eligibility classification of individuals is a legitimate and substantial administrative aid in the functioning of this system. And legislation to insure the continuing availability of issued certificates serves a legitimate and substantial purpose in the system's administration.

O'Brien essentially adopts the position that such certificates are so many pieces of paper designed to notify registrants of their registration or classification, to be retained or tossed in the wastebasket according to the convenience or taste of the registrant. Once the registrant has received notification, according to this view, there is no reason for him to retain the certificates. O'Brien notes that most of the information on a registration certificate serves no notification purpose at all; the registrant hardly needs to be told his address and physical characteristics. We agree that the registration certificate contains much information of which the registrant needs no notification. This circumstance, however, does not lead to the conclusion that the certificate serves no purpose, but that, like the classification certificate, it serves purposes in addition to initial notification. Many of these purposes would be defeated by the certificates' destruction or mutilation. Among these are:

1. The registration certificate serves as proof that the individual described thereon has registered for the draft. Voluntarily displaying the two

certificates is an easy and painless way for a young man to dispel a question as to whether he might be delinquent in his Selective Service obligations. Correspondingly, the availability of the certificates for such display relieves the Selective Service System of the administrative burden it would otherwise have in verifying the registration and classification of all suspected delinquents. It is in the interest of the just and efficient administration of the system that they be continually available. In a time of national crisis, reasonable availability to each registrant of the two small cards assures a rapid and uncomplicated means for determining his fitness for immediate induction, no matter how distant in our mobile society he may be from his local board.

2. Information supplied on the certificates facilitates communication between registrants and local boards, simplifying the system and benefiting all concerned. Each certificate bears the address of the registrant's local board. Further, each card bears the registrant's Selective Service number, and a registrant can make simpler the board's task in locating his file. Finally, a registrant's inquiry concerning his eligibility status is frequently answerable simply on the basis of his classification certificate.

3. Certificates carry continual reminders that the registrant must notify his local board of any change of address, and other specified changes in his status. The destruction of certificates deprives the system of a potentially useful notice device.

4. The regulatory scheme involving Selective Service certificates includes clearly valid prohibitions against the alteration, forgery, or similar deceptive misuse of certificates. The destruction or mutilation of certificates obviously increases the difficulty of detecting and tracing abuses. Further, a mutilated certificate might itself be used for deceptive purposes.

The many functions performed by Selective Service certificates establish beyond doubt that Congress has a legitimate and substantial interest in preventing their wanton and unrestrained destruction and assuring their continuing availability by punishing people who knowingly and wilfully destroy or mutilate them. And we are unpersuaded that the pre-existence of the nonpossession regulations in any way negates this interest.

A comparison of the regulations with the 1965 Amendment indicates that they protect overlapping but not identical governmental interests, and that they reach somewhat different classes of wrongdoers. The gravamen of the offense is the deliberate rendering of certificates unavailable for the various purposes which they may serve. Whether registrants keep their certificates in their personal possession at all times, as required by the regulations, is of no particular concern under the 1965 Amendment, as long as they do not mutilate or destroy the certificates so as to render them unavailable. Finally, the 1965 Amendment, like the statutory provision it amended, is concerned with abuses involving any issued Selective Service certificates, not only with the registrant's own certificates. The knowing destruction or mutilation of someone else's certificates would therefore violate the statute but not the nonpossession regulations.

The continuing availability to each registrant of his Selective Service certificates substantially furthers the smooth and proper functioning of the system that Congress has established to raise armies. The Nation has a vital interest in having a system for raising armies that functions with maximum efficiency and is capable of easily and quickly responding to continually changing circumstances. For these reasons, the Government has a substantial interest in assuring the continuing availability of issued Selective Service certificates.

The 1965 Amendment specifically protects this substantial governmental interest. We perceive no alternative means that would more precisely and narrowly assure the continuing availability of issued Selective Service certificates than a law which prohibits their wilful mutilation or destruction. The 1965 Amendment prohibits such conduct and nothing more. Both the governmental interest and the operation of the 1965 Amendment are limited to the noncommunicative aspect of O'Brien's conduct. The governmental interest and the scope of the 1965 Amendment are limited to preventing harm to the smooth and efficient functioning of the Selective Service System. When O'Brien deliberately rendered unavailable his registration certificate, he wilfully frustrated this governmental interest. For this noncommunicative impact of his conduct, and for nothing else, he was convicted. The case at bar is therefore unlike one where the alleged governmental interest in regulating conduct arises in some measure because the communication allegedly integral to the conduct is itself thought to be harmful.

Because of the Government's substantial interest in assuring the continuing availability of issued Selective Service certificates, because amended §462(b) is an appropriately narrow means of protecting this interest and condemns only the independent noncommunicative impact of conduct within its reach, and because the noncommunicative impact of O'Brien's act of burning his registration certificate frustrated the Government's interest, a sufficient governmental interest has been shown to justify O'Brien's conviction.

O'Brien finally argues that the 1965 Amendment is unconstitutional as enacted because what he calls the "purpose" of Congress was "to suppress freedom of speech." The purpose of Congress, as O'Brien uses that term, is not a basis for declaring this legislation unconstitutional. Inquiries into congressional motives or purposes are a hazardous matter. When the issue is simply the interpretation of legislation, the Court will look to statements by legislators for guidance as to the purpose of the legislature, because the benefit to sound decision-making in this circumstance is thought sufficient to risk the possibility of misreading Congress' purpose. It is entirely a different matter when we are asked to void a statute that is, under well-settled criteria, constitutional on its face, on the basis of what a handful of Congressmen said about it. What motivates one legislator to make a speech about a statute is not necessarily what motivates scores of others to enact it, and the stakes are sufficiently high for us to eschew guesswork. We decline to void legislation which Congress had the undoubted power to enact and which could be reenacted in its exact form if the same or another legislator made a "wiser" speech about it.

We think it not amiss to comment upon O'Brien's legislative-purpose argument. There was little floor debate on this legislation in either House. Only Senator Thurmond commented on its substantive features. After his brief statement, and without any additional substantive comments, the bill passed the Senate. In the House debate only two Congressmen addressed the Amendment. The bill was passed without any further debate by a vote of 393 to 1. It is on the basis of the statements by three Congressmen that O'Brien makes his congressional-"purpose" argument. If we were to examine legislative purpose in the instant case, we would be obliged to consider not only these statements but also the more authoritative reports of the Senate and House Armed Services Committees. While both reports make clear a concern with the "defiant" destruction of so-called "draft cards" and with "open" encouragement to others to destroy their cards, both reports indicate that this concern stemmed from an apprehension that unrestrained destruction of cards would disrupt the smooth functioning of the Selective Service System.

Since the 1965 Amendment is constitutional as enacted and as applied, the Court of Appeals should have affirmed the judgment of conviction entered by the District Court. Accordingly, we vacate the judgment of the Court of Appeals, and reinstate the judgment and sentence of the District Court.

It is so ordered.

Note: The O'Brien *Test*

The *O'Brien* four-part test has been applied to a range of First Amendment problems. Typically, the triggers for use of the test are the existence of a regulation that might be a labeled a "conduct" regulation, a government interest that might be labeled as being "unrelated to the suppression of expression," the existence of a claim for the protection of "symbolic speech" or "communicative conduct," or some combination of these elements. The *O'Brien* opinion did not describe the analysis that might be appropriate when a government regulation is aimed at conduct that occurs in a public forum, thus implicating both the four-part *O'Brien* test and the "time, place, manner" test of the "public forum" doctrine. When the occasion arose for the Court to deal with such a two-dimensional problem, its solution was to require the government to satisfy the requirements of each test separately. The apparent similarity of the two tests was revealed by their simultaneous use in *Clark v. Community for Creative Non-Violence* in 1984. Yet despite the similarities, each test is used most commonly in its own doctrinal sphere. The *O'Brien* test's usage in the context of symbolic speech has taken on particular importance in the field of "near obscene" speech regulation. Further examination of the "time, place, manner" test for the "public forum" doctrine is provided in the section below on "Access to Government Property." The *Clark* opinion that follows provides further insight into the application of *O'Brien,* and also serves as an introduction to the elements of "time, place, manner" analysis.

∾ PROBLEMS ∾

1. *The Hypothetical Dissent.* You are the law clerk for one of the Justices in *O'Brien* who wants to file a dissent on the merits. What arguments can be made to rebut the *O'Brien* Court's arguments on each of the elements of the four-part test?

2. *More on the International Treaty Regulating the Internet.* At the convention, suppose that the German and French delegates again demand a prohibition against Nazi symbols. Does the *O'Brien* decision alter (or cause you to rethink) your position regarding those demands?

Clark v. Community for Creative Non-Violence

468 U.S. 288 (1984)

Justice WHITE delivered the opinion of the Court.

The issue in this case is whether a National Park Service regulation prohibiting camping in certain parks violates the First Amendment when applied to prohibit demonstrators from sleeping in Lafayette Park and the Mall in connection with a demonstration intended to call attention to the plight of the homeless. We hold that it does not.

The Interior Department, through the National Park Service, is charged with responsibility for the management and maintenance of the National Parks and is authorized to promulgate rules and regulations for the use of the parks in accordance with the purposes for which they were established. The network of National Parks includes the National Memorial–core parks, Lafayette Park and the Mall, which are set in the heart of Washington, D.C. Lafayette Park is a roughly 7-acre square located across Pennsylvania Avenue from the White House. Although originally part of the White House grounds, President Jefferson set it aside as a park for the use of residents and visitors. It is a "garden park with a formal landscaping of flowers and trees, with fountains, walks and benches." The Mall is a stretch of land running westward from the Capitol to the Lincoln Memorial some two miles away. It includes the Washington Monument, a series of reflecting pools, trees, lawns, and other greenery. It is bordered by, *inter alia,* the Smithsonian Institution and the National Gallery of Art. Both the Park and the Mall were included in Major Pierre L'Enfant's original plan for the Capital. Both are visited by vast numbers of visitors.

Under the regulations, camping in National Parks is permitted only in campgrounds designated for that purpose. No such campgrounds have ever been designated in Lafayette Park or the Mall. Demonstrations for the airing of views or grievances are permitted in the Memorial-core parks, but for the most part only

C. Symbolic Speech   1403

by Park Service permits. Temporary structures may be erected for demonstration purposes but may not be used for camping. In 1982, the Park Service issued a renewable permit to respondent Community for Creative Non-Violence (CCNV) to conduct a wintertime demonstration in Lafayette Park and the Mall for the purpose of demonstrating the plight of the homeless. The permit authorized the erection of two symbolic tent cities: 20 tents in Lafayette Park that would accommodate 50 people and 40 tents in the Mall with a capacity of up to 100. The Park Service, however, relying on the above regulations, specifically denied CCNV's request that demonstrators be permitted to sleep in the symbolic tents. CCNV and several individuals then filed an action to prevent the application of the no-camping regulations to the proposed demonstration. The District Court granted summary judgment in favor of the Park Service. The Court of Appeals reversed. We reverse.

We assume that overnight sleeping in connection with the demonstration is expressive conduct protected to some extent by the First Amendment. But this assumption only begins the inquiry. Expression, whether oral or written or symbolized by conduct, is subject to reasonable time, place, or manner restrictions. We have often noted that restrictions of this kind are valid provided that they are justified without reference to the content of the regulated speech, that they are narrowly tailored to serve a significant governmental interest, and that they leave open ample alternative channels for communication of the information.

It is also true that a message may be delivered by conduct that is intended to be communicative and that, in context, would reasonably be understood by the viewer to be communicative. Symbolic expression of this kind may be forbidden or regulated if the conduct itself may constitutionally be regulated, if the regulation is narrowly drawn to further a substantial governmental interest, and if the interest is unrelated to the suppression of free speech.

Petitioners submit that the regulation forbidding sleeping is defensible either as a time, place, or manner restriction or as a regulation of symbolic conduct. We agree with that assessment. The permit that was issued authorized the demonstration but required compliance with the regulation which prohibits "camping" on park lands, that is, the use of park lands for living accommodations, such as sleeping, storing personal belongings, making fires, digging, or cooking. These provisions, including the ban on sleeping, are clearly limitations on the manner in which the demonstration could be carried out. That sleeping, like the symbolic tents themselves, may be expressive and part of the message delivered by the demonstration does not make the ban any less a limitation on the manner of demonstrating, for reasonable time, place, or manner regulations normally have the purpose and direct effect of limiting expression but are nevertheless valid. Neither does the fact that sleeping, *arguendo*, may be expressive conduct, rather than oral or written expression, render the sleeping prohibition any less a time, place, or manner regulation. To the contrary, the Park Service neither attempts to ban sleeping generally nor to ban it everywhere in the parks. It has established areas for camping and forbids it elsewhere, including Lafayette Park and the

Mall. We have very little trouble concluding that the Park Service may prohibit overnight sleeping in the parks involved here.

The requirement that the regulation be content-neutral is clearly satisfied. It is not disputed that the prohibition on camping, and on sleeping specifically, is content-neutral and is not being applied because of disagreement with the message presented. Neither was the regulation faulted on the ground that without overnight sleeping the plight of the homeless could not be communicated in other ways. The regulation otherwise left the demonstration intact, with its symbolic city, signs, and the presence of those who were willing to take their turns in a day-and-night vigil. Respondents do not suggest that there was, or is, any barrier to delivering to the media, or to the public by other means, the intended message concerning the plight of the homeless.

The regulation narrowly focuses on the Government's substantial interest in maintaining the parks in the heart of our Capital in an attractive and intact condition, readily available to the millions of people who wish to see and enjoy them by their presence. To permit camping—using these areas as living accommodations—would be totally inimical to these purposes, as would be readily understood by those who have frequented the National Parks across the country and observed the unfortunate consequences of the activities of those who refuse to confine their camping to designated areas.

Respondents argue that if the symbolic city of tents was to be permitted and if the demonstrators did not intend to cook, dig, or engage in aspects of camping other than sleeping, the incremental benefit to the parks could not justify the ban on sleeping, which was here an expressive activity said to enhance the message concerning the plight of the poor and homeless. We cannot agree. In the first place, we seriously doubt that the First Amendment requires the Park Service to permit a demonstration in Lafayette Park and the Mall involving a 24-hour vigil and the erection of tents to accommodate 150 people. Furthermore, although we have assumed for present purposes that the sleeping banned in this case would have an expressive element, it is evident that its major value to this demonstration would be facilitative. Without a permit to sleep, it would be difficult to get the poor and homeless to participate or to be present at all. The sleeping ban, if enforced, would thus effectively limit the nature, extent, and duration of the demonstration and to that extent ease the pressure on the parks.

Beyond this, however, it is evident from our cases that the validity of this regulation need not be judged solely by reference to the demonstration at hand. Absent the prohibition on sleeping, there would be other groups who would demand permission to deliver an asserted message by camping in Lafayette Park. Some of them would surely have as credible a claim as does CCNV, and the denial of permits to still others would present difficult problems for the Park Service. With the prohibition, however, at least some around-the-clock demonstrations lasting for days on end will not materialize, others will be limited in size and duration, and the purposes of the regulation will thus be materially served. Perhaps these purposes would be more effectively and not so clumsily achieved by preventing tents and 24-hour vigils entirely in the core areas. But the Park Service's decision to permit nonsleeping demonstrations does not, in our view, impugn the camping prohibition as a valuable, but perhaps imperfect, protection to the parks. If the Government has a legitimate interest in ensuring that the National Parks are adequately protected, and if the parks would be more exposed to harm without the sleeping prohibition than with it, the ban is safe from invalidation under the First Amendment as a reasonable regulation of the manner in which a demonstration may be carried out.

We have difficulty, therefore, in understanding why the prohibition against camping, with its ban on sleeping overnight, is not a reasonable time, place, or manner regulation that withstands constitutional scrutiny. None of its provisions appears unrelated to the ends that it was designed to serve. Nor is it any less valid when applied to prevent camping in Memorial-core parks by those who wish to demonstrate and deliver a message to the public and the central Government. Damage to the parks as well as their partial inaccessibility to other members of the public can as easily result from camping by demonstrators as by nondemonstrators. In neither case must the Government tolerate it. All those who would resort to the parks must abide by otherwise valid rules for their use, just as they must observe the traffic laws, sanitation regulations, and laws to preserve the public peace. This is no more than a reaffirmation that reasonable time, place, or manner restrictions on expression are constitutionally acceptable.

The foregoing analysis demonstrates that the Park Service regulation is sustainable under the four-factor standard of *United States v. O'Brien*, 391 U.S. 367 (1968), for validating a regulation of expressive conduct, which is little, if any, different from the standard applied to time, place, or manner restrictions. No one contends that aside from its impact on speech a rule against camping or overnight sleeping in public parks is beyond the constitutional power of the Government to enforce. There is a substantial Government interest in conserving park property, an interest that is plainly served by, and requires for its implementation, measures such as the proscription of sleeping that are designed to limit the wear and tear on park properties. That interest is unrelated to suppression of expression.

We are unmoved by the view that the challenged regulation is unnecessary, and hence invalid, because there are less speech-restrictive alternatives that could have satisfied the Government interest in preserving park lands. The suggestions that the Park Service minimize the possible injury by reducing the size, duration, or frequency of demonstrations would still curtail the total allowable expression in which demonstrators could engage and these suggestions represent no more than a disagreement with the Park Service over how much protection the core parks require or how an acceptable level of preservation is to be attained. We do not believe that either *O'Brien* or the time, place, or manner decisions assign to the judiciary the authority to replace the Park Service as the manager of the Nation's parks or endow the judiciary with the competence to judge how much protection of park lands is wise and how that level of conservation is to be attained.

Accordingly, the judgment of the Court of Appeals is
Reversed.

Justice MARSHALL, with whom Justice BRENNAN joins, *dissenting*.

The activity in which respondents seek to engage — sleeping in a highly pub-lic place, outside, in the winter for the purpose of protesting homelessness — is symbolic speech protected by the First Amendment. Missing from the majority's description is any inkling that Lafayette Park and the Mall have served as the sites for some of the most rousing political demonstrations in the Nation's history. "On any given day there will be an average of three or so demonstrations going on" in the Mall–Lafayette Park area.

In a long line of cases, this Court has afforded First Amendment protection to symbolic speech. Here respondents intended to protest the reality of home-lessness by sleeping outdoors in the winter in the near vicinity of the magisterial residence of the President of the United States. In the circumstances the likeli-hood was great that the political significance of sleeping in the parks would be understood by those who viewed it. Certainly the news media understood the sig-nificance of respondents' proposed activity. Ordinary citizens, too, would likely understand the political message intended by respondents. This likelihood stems from the remarkably apt fit between the activity in which respondents seek to engage and the social problem they seek to highlight.

The Government contends that a forseeable difficulty of administration counsels against recognizing sleep as a mode of expression protected by the First Amendment. The predicament the Government envisions can be termed "the imposter problem": the problem of distinguishing bona fide protesters from imposters whose requests for permission to sleep in Lafayette Park or the Mall on First Amendment grounds would mask ulterior designs — the simple desire to avoid the expense of hotel lodgings. The administrative difficulty the Government envisions is now nothing more than a vague apprehension.

I agree with the standard enunciated by the majority. I conclude, however, that the regulations at issue in this case, as applied to respondents, fail to sat-isfy this standard. The significant Government interest advanced is the inter-est in "maintaining the parks in the heart of our capital in an attractive and intact condition, readily available to the millions of people who wish to see and enjoy them by their presence." That interest is significant. However, neither the Government nor the majority adequately explains how prohibiting respondents' planned activity will substantially further that interest. The majority fails to offer evidence indicating that the absence of an absolute ban on sleeping would pres-ent administrative problems to the Park Service that are substantially more dif-ficult than those it ordinarily confronts. Moreover, if the Government's interest in avoiding administrative difficulties were truly "substantial," one would expect the agency most involved in administering the parks at least to allude to such an interest. The perceived difficulty of administering requests from other dem-onstrators seeking to convey messages through sleeping was not among the rea-sons underlying the Park Service regulations. Nor was it mentioned by the Park Service in its rejection of respondents' particular request. The majority cites no evidence indicating that sleeping as symbolic speech will cause substantial wear and tear on park property. The Government offers no justification for applying its absolute ban on sleeping yet is willing to allow respondents to engage in activities—such as feigned sleeping—that is no less burdensome. In short, there are no substantial Government interests advanced by the Government's regulations as applied to respondents. What the Court fails to recognize is that public officials have strong incentives to overregulate even in the absence of an intent to censor particular views. The evidence in this case should have impelled the Court to subject the Government's restrictive policy to something more than minimal scrutiny. I respectfully dissent.

Note: The "Gateway" Element

In later years, the third part of the *O'Brien* test emerged as the "gateway" element. That is, once the government litigant persuades a court that "the governmental interest is unrelated to the suppression of free expression," the remaining parts of the four-part test control the analysis. Thus, a vital element for a court's use of the *O'Brien* test is the identification of a government interest that can be labeled as "unrelated" to the suppression of speech. In subsequent cases, the Court established a dichotomy between a government interest that may be characterized as being related only to the "secondary effects" of speech and an interest that is related to the effect that speech may have on an audience. The former type of interest typically qualifies as being "unrelated" to the suppression of speech, whereas the latter type of interest is usually treated as being aimed at the suppression of speech. Thus, the failure of the government litigant to satisfy the third part of the *O'Brien* test must lead to a determination that a government interest is related to the suppression of expression, which in turn may lead to the requirement that the strict scrutiny test must be satisfied.

∼ PROBLEM: SYMBOLIC SPEECH ANALYSIS ∼

Consider how the analysis or result in *Clark* might have been different if "symbolic speech" had not been involved in the case, so that *O'Brien* would have been irrelevant to the decision. For example, suppose that the regulation at issue in *Clark* was a speech regulation that limited the use of the park, for example, to small groups of demonstrators (no more than ten people in a group and only one demonstration a day) in order to protect the park grounds. How would the "time, place, manner" arguments by the demonstrators and the Park Service in that hypothetical case differ from the arguments made in *Clark* on the "time, place, manner" issue?

Texas v. Johnson

491 U.S. 397 (1989)

Justice BRENNAN delivered the opinion of the Court.

After publicly burning an American flag as a means of political protest, Gregory Lee Johnson was convicted of desecrating a flag in violation of Texas law. This case presents the question whether his conviction is consistent with the First Amendment. We hold that it is not.

While the Republican National Convention was taking place in Dallas in 1984, respondent Johnson participated in a political demonstration dubbed the "Republican War Chest Tour." As explained in literature distributed by the demonstrators and in speeches, the purpose of this event was to protest policies of the Reagan administration and of certain Dallas-based corporations. The demonstrators marched through Dallas streets, chanting political slogans and stopping at several corporate locations to stage "die-ins" intended to dramatize the consequences of nuclear war. On several occasions they spray-painted the walls of buildings and overturned potted plants, but Johnson himself took no part in such activities. He did accept an American flag handed to him by a fellow protestor who had taken it from a flagpole outside one of the targeted buildings. The demonstration ended in front of Dallas City Hall, where Johnson unfurled the American flag, doused it with kerosene, and set it on fire. While the flag burned, the protestors chanted: "America, the red, white, and blue, we spit on you." No one was physically injured or threatened with injury, though several were seriously offended by the flag burning. Johnson was charged with violation of a state statute that provides: A person commits an offense if he intentionally or knowingly desecrates a state or national flag; "desecrate" means deface, damage, or otherwise physically mistreat in a way that the actor knows will seriously offend one or more persons likely to observe or discover his action. He was convicted, sentenced to one year in prison, and fined $2,000.

We must determine whether Johnson's burning of the flag constituted expressive conduct, permitting him to invoke the First Amendment in challenging his conviction. *See, e.g., Spence v. Washington,* 418 U.S. 405 (1974). If his conduct was expressive, we next decide whether the State's regulation is related to the suppression of free expression. *See, e.g., United States v. O'Brien,* 391 U.S. 367 (1968). If the State's regulation is not related to expression, then the less stringent standard we announced in *O'Brien* for regulations of noncommunicative conduct controls. If it is, then we are outside of *O'Brien*'s test, and we must ask whether this interest justifies Johnson's conviction under a more demanding standard. A third possibility is that the State's asserted interest is simply not implicated on these facts, and in that event the interest drops out of the picture.

The First Amendment literally forbids the abridgment only of "speech," but we have long recognized that its protection does not end at the spoken or written word. While we have rejected "the view that an apparently limitless variety of conduct can be labeled 'speech' whenever the person engaging in the conduct intends thereby to express an idea," we have acknowledged that conduct may be "sufficiently imbued with elements of communication to fall within the scope of the First and Fourteenth Amendments." In deciding whether particular conduct possesses sufficient communicative elements to bring the First Amendment into play, we have asked whether "an intent to convey a particularized message was present, and whether the likelihood was great that the message would be understood by those who viewed it." *Spence, supra,* at 409.

We have not automatically concluded that any action taken with respect to our flag is expressive. In *Spence,* we emphasized that Spence's taping of a peace sign to his flag was "roughly simultaneous with and concededly triggered by the Cambodian incursion and the Kent State tragedy." Spence's conduct was a form of communication. The State of Texas conceded that Johnson's conduct was expressive conduct. Johnson burned an American flag as part—indeed, the culmination—of a political demonstration that coincided with the convening of the Republican Party and its renomination of Ronald Reagan for President. The expressive, overtly political nature of this conduct was both intentional and apparent. In these circumstances, Johnson's burning of the flag was conduct "sufficiently imbued with elements of communication," to implicate the First Amendment.

The government generally has a freer hand in restricting expressive conduct than it has in restricting the written or spoken word. It may not, however, proscribe particular conduct *because* it has expressive elements. It is, in short, not simply the verbal or nonverbal nature of the expression, but the governmental interest at stake, that helps to determine whether a restriction on that expression is valid.

Although we have recognized that where "'speech' and 'nonspeech' elements are combined in the same course of conduct, a sufficiently important governmental interest in regulating the non-speech element can justify incidental limitations on First Amendment freedoms," we have limited the applicability of *O'Brien*'s lenient standard to those cases in which "the governmental interest is unrelated to the suppression of free expression."

In order to decide whether *O'Brien*'s test applies here, therefore, we must decide whether Texas has asserted an interest in support of Johnson's conviction that is unrelated to the suppression of expression. The State offers two separate interests to justify this conviction: preventing breaches of the peace and preserving the flag as a symbol of nationhood and national unity. We hold that the first interest is not implicated on this record and that the second is related to the suppression of expression.

Texas claims that its interest in preventing breaches of the peace justifies Johnson's conviction for flag desecration. However, no disturbance of the peace actually occurred or threatened to occur because of Johnson's burning of the flag. The only evidence offered by the State was the testimony of several persons who had been seriously offended by the flag burning. The State's position, therefore, amounts to a claim that an audience that takes serious offense at particular expression is necessarily likely to disturb the peace and that the expression may be prohibited on this basis. Our precedents recognize that a principal "function of free speech under our system of government is to invite dispute. It may indeed best serve its high purpose when it induces a condition of unrest, creates dissatisfaction with conditions as they are, or even stirs people to anger." We have not permitted the government to assume that every expression of a provocative idea will incite a riot, but have instead required careful consideration of the actual circumstances surrounding such expression, asking whether the expression "is directed to inciting or producing imminent lawless action and is likely to incite or produce such action." *Brandenburg v. Ohio*, 395 U.S. 444 (1969). To accept Texas' arguments that it need only demonstrate "the potential for a breach of the peace," and that every flag burning necessarily possesses that potential, would be to eviscerate our holding in *Brandenburg*. Nor does Johnson's expressive conduct fall within that small class of "fighting words" that are "likely to provoke the average person to retaliation, and thereby cause a breach of the peace." *Chaplinsky v. New Hampshire*, 315 U.S. 568 (1942). No reasonable onlooker would have regarded Johnson's generalized expression of dissatisfaction with the policies of the Federal Government as a direct personal insult or an invitation to exchange fisticuffs. We conclude that the State's interest in maintaining order is not implicated on these facts. Texas already has a statute specifically prohibiting breaches of the peace, which tends to confirm that Texas need not punish this flag desecration in order to keep the peace.

The State asserts an interest in preserving the flag as a symbol of nationhood and national unity. In *Spence*, we acknowledged that the government's interest in preserving the flag's special symbolic value "is directly related to expression in the context of activity" such as affixing a peace symbol to a flag. We are equally persuaded that this interest is related to expression in the case of Johnson's burning of the flag. The State, apparently, is concerned that such conduct will lead people to believe either that the flag does not stand for nationhood and national unity, but instead reflects other, less positive concepts, or that the concepts reflected in the flag do not in fact exist, that is, that we do not enjoy unity as a Nation. These concerns blossom only when a person's treatment of the flag communicates some message, and thus are related "to the suppression of free expression" within the meaning of *O'Brien*. We are thus outside of *O'Brien*'s test altogether.

It remains to consider whether the State's interest in preserving the flag as a symbol of nationhood and national unity justifies Johnson's conviction. Johnson was not prosecuted for the expression of just any idea; he was prosecuted for his expression of dissatisfaction with the policies of this country, expression situated at the core of our First Amendment values. Moreover, Johnson was prosecuted because he knew that his politically charged expression would cause "serious offense." If he had burned the flag as a means of disposing of it because it was dirty or torn, he would not have been convicted of flag desecration under this Texas law. The Texas law is designed to protect it only against impairments that would cause serious offense to others.

Whether Johnson's treatment of the flag violated Texas law thus depended on the likely communicative impact of his expressive conduct. Our decision in *Boos v. Barry*, 485 U.S. 312 (1988) tells us that "the emotive impact of speech on its audience is not a 'secondary effect'" unrelated to the content of the expression itself. According to the principles announced in *Boos*, Johnson's political expression was restricted because of the content of the message he conveyed. We must therefore subject the State's asserted interest in preserving the special symbolic character of the flag to "the most exacting scrutiny." Texas argues that its interest in preserving the flag as a symbol of nationhood and national unity survives this close analysis. Quoting extensively from the writings of this Court chronicling the flag's historic and symbolic role in our society, the State emphasizes the "special place" reserved for the flag in our Nation. The State's argument is that it has an interest in preserving the flag as a symbol of *nationhood* and *national unity*, a symbol with a determinate range of meanings. According to Texas, if one physically treats the flag in a way that would tend to cast doubt on either the idea that nationhood and national unity are the flag's referents or that national unity actually exists, the message conveyed thereby is a harmful one and therefore may be prohibited.

If there is a bedrock principle underlying the First Amendment, it is that the government may not prohibit the expression of an idea simply because society finds the idea itself offensive or disagreeable. We have not recognized an exception to this principle even where our flag has been involved. In *Street v. New York*, 394 U.S. 576 (1969), we held that a State may not criminally punish a person for uttering words critical of the flag. Nor may the government, we have held in *West Virginia Board of Education v. Barnette*, 319 U.S. 624 (1943), compel conduct that would evince respect for the flag. In *Spence,* we held that the same interest asserted by Texas here was insufficient to support a criminal conviction under a flag-misuse statute for the taping of a peace sign to an American flag. We never held that the Government may ensure that a symbol be used to express only one view of that symbol or its referents. Could the government prohibit the burning of state flags? Of copies of the Presidential seal? Of the Constitution? In evaluating these choices under the First Amendment, how would we decide which symbols were sufficiently special to warrant this unique status? To do so, we would be forced to consult our own political preferences, and impose them on the citizenry, in the very way that the First Amendment forbids us to do.

There is no indication—either in the text of the Constitution or in our cases interpreting it—that a separate juridical category exists for the American flag alone. The First Amendment does not guarantee that other concepts virtually sacred to our Nation as a whole—such as the principle that discrimination on the basis of race is odious and destructive—will go unquestioned in the marketplace of ideas. We decline to create for the flag an exception to the joust of principles protected by the First Amendment.

It is not the State's ends, but its means, to which we object. There is a special place reserved for the flag in this Nation, and thus we do not doubt that the government has a legitimate interest in making efforts to "preserve the national flag as an unalloyed symbol of our country." *Spence,* 418 U.S. at 412. To say that the government has an interest in encouraging proper treatment of the flag, however, is not to say that it may criminally punish a person for burning a flag as a means of political protest. We are tempted to say that the flag's deservedly cherished place in our community will be strengthened, not weakened, by our holding today. Our decision is a reaffirmation of the principles of freedom and inclusiveness that the flag best reflects, and of the conviction that our toleration of criticism such as Johnson's is a sign and source of our strength. Indeed, one of the proudest images of our flag, the one immortalized in our own national anthem, is of the bombardment it survived at Fort McHenry. It is the Nation's resilience, not its rigidity, that Texas sees reflected in the flag—and it is that resilience that we reassert today.

The way to preserve the flag's special role is not to punish those who feel differently about these matters. It is to persuade them that they are wrong. Precisely because it is our flag that is involved, one's response to the flag burner may exploit the uniquely persuasive power of the flag itself. We can imagine no more appropriate response to burning a flag than waving one's own, no better way to counter a flag burner's message than by saluting the flag that burns, no surer means of preserving the dignity even of the flag that burned than by—as one witness here did—according its remains a respectful burial. We do not consecrate the flag by punishing its desecration, for in doing so we dilute the freedom that this cherished emblem represents.

Johnson was convicted for engaging in expressive conduct. The State's interest in preventing breaches of the peace does not support his conviction because Johnson's conduct did not threaten to disturb the peace. Nor does the State's interest in preserving the flag as a symbol of nationhood and national unity justify his criminal conviction for engaging in political expression. The judgment of the Texas Court of Criminal Appeals is therefore

Affirmed.

Justice KENNEDY, *concurring.*

I agree that the flag holds a lonely place of honor in an age when absolutes are distrusted and simple truths are burdened by unneeded apologetics. It is poignant but fundamental that the flag protects those who hold it in contempt. The fact remains that Johnson's acts were speech. So I agree with the Court that he must go free.

Chief Justice REHNQUIST, with whom Justice WHITE and Justice O'CONNOR join, *dissenting.*

For more than 200 years, the American flag has occupied a unique position as the symbol of our Nation, a uniqueness that justifies a governmental prohibition against flag burning. The flag symbolizes the Nation in peace as well as in war. It signifies our national presence on battleships, airplanes, military installations, and public buildings from the United States Capitol to the thousands of county courthouses and city halls throughout the country. Two flags are prominently placed in our courtroom. Countless flags are placed by the graves of loved ones each year on what was first called Decoration Day, and is now called Memorial Day. The flag is traditionally placed on the casket of deceased members of the Armed Forces, and it is later given to the deceased's family. Congress has provided that the flag be flown at half-staff upon the death of the President, Vice President, and other government officials "as a mark of respect to their memory." No other American symbol has been as universally honored as the flag. In 1931, Congress declared "The Star-Spangled Banner" to be our national anthem. In 1949, Congress declared June 14th to be Flag Day. In 1987, John Philip Sousa's "The Stars and Stripes Forever" was designated as the national march. Congress has also established "The Pledge of Allegiance to the Flag" and the manner of its deliverance. The flag has appeared as the principal symbol on approximately 33 United States postal stamps and in the design of at least 43 more.

Both Congress and the States have enacted numerous laws regulating misuse of the American flag. Until 1967, Congress left the regulation of misuse of the flag up to the States. Now, however, 18 U.S.C. §700(a) provides that: "Whoever knowingly casts contempt upon any flag of the United States by publicly mutilating, defacing, defiling, burning, or trampling upon it shall be fined not more than $1,000 or imprisoned for not more than one year, or both." With the exception of Alaska and Wyoming, all of the States now have statutes prohibiting the burning of the flag. Most were passed by the States at about the time of World War I.

The American flag, then, throughout more than 200 years of our history, has come to be the visible symbol embodying our Nation. The flag is not simply another "idea" or "point of view" competing for recognition in the marketplace of ideas. Millions and millions of Americans regard it with an almost mystical reverence regardless of what sort of social, political, or philosophical beliefs they may have. I cannot agree that the First Amendment invalidates the Act of Congress, and the laws of 48 of the 50 States, which make criminal the public burning of the flag.

Freedom of expression is not absolute. As with "fighting words," so with flag burning, for purposes of the First Amendment: It is "no essential part of any exposition of ideas, and is of such slight social value as a step to truth that any benefit that may be derived from it is clearly outweighed" by the public interest in avoiding a probable breach of the peace. The highest courts of several States have upheld state statutes prohibiting the public burning of the flag on the grounds that it is so inherently inflammatory that it may cause a breach of public order.

Flag burning is the equivalent of an inarticulate grunt or roar that, it seems fair to say, is most likely to be indulged in not to express any particular idea, but to antagonize others. The Texas statute deprived Johnson of one rather inarticulate symbolic form of protest—a form of protest that was profoundly offensive to many—and left him with a full panoply of other symbols and every conceivable form of verbal expression to express his deep disapproval of national policy. In no way can it be said that Texas is punishing him because his hearers — or any other group of people — were profoundly opposed to the message that he sought to convey. It was Johnson's use of this particular symbol, and not the idea that he sought to convey, for which he was punished. Surely one of the high purposes of a democratic society is to legislate against conduct that is regarded as evil and profoundly offensive to the majority of people — whether it be murder, embezzlement, pollution, or flag burning. I would uphold the Texas statute.

Justice STEVENS, *dissenting.*

A country's flag is a symbol of more than "nationhood and national unity." It also signifies the ideas that characterize the society that has chosen that emblem as well as the special history that has animated the growth and power of those ideas. It is more than a proud symbol of the courage, the determination, and the gifts of nature that transformed 13 fledgling Colonies into a world power. It is a symbol of freedom, of equal opportunity, of religious tolerance, and of good will for other peoples who share our aspirations. The symbol carries its message to dissidents both at home and abroad who may have no interest at all in our national unity or survival.

The value of the flag as a symbol cannot be measured. The interest in preserving that value for the future is both significant and legitimate. Conceivably that value will be enhanced by the Court's conclusion that our national commitment to free expression is so strong that even the United States as ultimate guarantor of that freedom is without power to prohibit the desecration of its unique symbol. In my considered judgment, sanctioning the public desecration of the flag will tarnish its value. That tarnish is not justified by the trivial burden on free expression occasioned by requiring that an available, alternative mode of expression — including uttering words critical of the flag.

The Court is quite wrong in blandly asserting that respondent "was prosecuted for his expression of dissatisfaction with the policies of this country, expression situated at the core of our First Amendment values." Respondent was prosecuted because of the method he chose to express his dissatisfaction with those policies. Had he chosen to spray-paint his message of dissatisfaction on the facade of the Lincoln Memorial, there would be no question about the power of the Government to prohibit his means of expression. The prohibition would be supported by the legitimate interest in preserving the quality of an important national asset. Though the asset at stake in this case is intangible, given its unique value, the same interest supports a prohibition on the desecration of the American flag. I respectfully dissent.

Notes

1. *Flag Desecration.* In *United States v. Eichman,* 496 U.S. 310 (1990), the Court invalidated a federal statute that was enacted by Congress as a response to the

decision in *Texas v. Johnson.* The relevant provision of the Flag Protection Act of 1989 punished the knowing mutilation, defacement, burning, maintaining on the floor or ground, or trampling upon any flag of the United States. The government interest was the protection of the physical flag, including privately owned flags. The Court found this interest to be related to the suppression of free expression: "The Government's desire to preserve the flag as a symbol for certain national ideals is implicated 'only when a person's treatment of the flag communicates a message' to others that is inconsistent with those ideals." The dissenters argued that the government's interest in protecting the flag's symbolic value outweighed the interest of speakers in expressing messages through flag burning.

2. *A Constitutional Amendment?* Following the decisions in *Johnson* and *Eichman,* there have been numerous attempts to amend the Constitution to permit punishment of flag desecration. All of these attempts have failed.

∾ PROBLEMS ∾

1. *More on Flag Burning.* A constitutional amendment to ban flag burning is close to passage in the House of Representatives. Jane and friends, upset by the proposed amendment, protest by marching to the town center. Jane takes her U.S. flag with her. No one notices. Eventually, one of Jane's fellow marchers says, "Maybe we should burn the flag. People aren't paying attention." Jane borrows some matches and sets the flag on fire. The flag doesn't burn, but the event begins to attract attention. "Hey," someone shouts, "they're burning a flag!" The crowd quickly swells to 40, and a police officer says, "Put out the fire and go home, or we'll take you in." At that moment, a man yells: "This is disgusting! You don't belong in America!" He throws a punch at Jane but misses. The police blow their whistles and order Jane's group to disperse. When they do not leave, Jane is arrested. You are Jane's lawyer. Consider what arguments you will make when Jane is charged with each of these five state crimes: a) arson, which involves the creation or maintenance of an open fire in public; b) burning the U.S. flag; c) using fighting words ("it is a crime to cause a breach of the peace by the use of words that are, or actions that constitute, personally abusive epithets which are inherently likely to provoke a violent reaction when directed to the person of an ordinary citizen"); d) disorderly conduct ("it is a crime to engage in conduct which causes an imminent, unlawful threat of public riot or breach of the peace"); and e) unlawful burning ("it is a crime to burn any material in a public place without a permit"). What counterarguments do you expect the prosecutor to make in reply?

2. *Save Our Wildlife.* Harry is a member of Save Our Wildlife, an organization devoted to publicizing the plight of hunted animals and advocating government bans on hunting. Sally is a hunter who travels to Indiana to hunt deer. Harry approaches Sally as she stands on public land with her rifle aimed at a deer. Harry takes Sally's photograph and puts a leaflet with anti-hunting messages at her

feet. Sally reports Harry to the police, and he is arrested and charged under the Indiana Hunter Interference Prohibition Act, which makes it a crime to "disturb another person who is engaged in the lawful taking of a wild animal, with intent to dissuade or otherwise prevent the taking." On appeal, Harry's lawyer concedes that the elements of the crime were proved by the facts introduced at trial, but maintains that the statute violates the First Amendment. What arguments do you expect Harry to make? What can be argued in response?

3. *The Sagging Pants Ordinance.* Holly Beach, Florida, enacted the following "Sagging Pants" (SP) ordinance: It is a crime to knowingly wear pants below the waistline, in a public place, in a manner that exposes the person's underwear or bare buttocks. Underwear is any clothing worn between the skin and outer layer of clothing, including but not limited to boxer shorts and thongs. The ordinance is punishable by a $150 fine. The ordinance was enacted with support from more than 75% of the voters. During the hearings leading to passage, the mayor stated, "Cities should have the right to maintain social standards of decency." Since its enactment, two dozen young men have been charged with violating the ordinance, most of them African Americans. Several of them seek to challenge the ordinance. Plaintiffs presented an expert witness, a former New York fashion designer, who testified that the "low slung pants look" started off "as an expressive concept" and has "gone mainstream" in recent years. When plaintiffs asked arresting officers why they were being singled out for arrest, one replied, "Weapons can be hidden in overly large pants, and your sagging pants could be hiding one." Another officer responded, "I just enforce the law. When I can see the waistband of your underwear, and that waistband is below your belly button, then that's against the law." You are the judge's law clerk, and she asks for your help in evaluating the ordinance and in deciding whether it should be upheld or invalidated. How would you advise her? What arguments would you give?

4. *More on the International Treaty Regulating the Internet.* At the convention, a number of countries wish to include language that precludes depictions of their flags that involve desecration. What, if anything, can you agree to regarding the content of such a prohibition?

D. OVERBREADTH AND VAGUENESS

The vagueness doctrine ensures that a statute's meaning is clear enough to provide fair notice of its prohibitions to people who wish to engage in protected speech activities, and to ensure that the statute will not be subject to arbitrary enforcement. By contrast, the overbreadth doctrine is designed to ensure that a statute sweeps in only speech that the government has the power to regulate (either a core of unprotected speech or a core of speech subject to legitimate regulation) and does not sweep in activities that the government does not have the power to regulate. A statute that sweeps in both is "overbroad." Both the vagueness and overbreadth doctrines reflect a concern that statutes "chill" individuals in their exercise of First Amendment rights.

Board of Airport Commissioners of the City of Los Angeles v. Jews for Jesus, Inc.

482 U.S. 569 (1987)

Justice O'CONNOR delivered the opinion of the Court.

The issue presented in this case is whether a resolution banning all "First Amendment activities" at Los Angeles International Airport (LAX) violates the First Amendment. On July 13, 1983, the Board of Airport Commissioners (Board) adopted Resolution No. 13787, which provides in pertinent part:

> NOW, THEREFORE, BE IT RESOLVED by the Board of Airport Commissioners that the Central Terminal Area at Los Angeles International Airport is not open for First Amendment activities by any individual and/or entity; and
>
> BE IT FURTHER RESOLVED that after the effective date of this Resolution, if any individual and/or entity seeks to engage in First Amendment activities within the Central Terminal Area at Los Angeles International Airport, said individual and/or entity shall be deemed to be acting in contravention of the stated policy of the Board of Airport Commissioners in reference to the uses permitted within the Central Terminal Area at Los Angeles International Airport; and
>
> BE IT FURTHER RESOLVED that if any individual or entity engages in First Amendment activities within the Central Terminal Area at Los Angeles International Airport, the City Attorney of the City of Los Angeles is directed to institute appropriate litigation against such individual and/or entity to ensure compliance with this Policy statement of the Board of Airport Commissioners.

Respondent Jews for Jesus, Inc., is a nonprofit religious corporation. Alan Snyder, a minister of the Gospel for Jews for Jesus, was stopped by a Department of Airports peace officer while distributing free religious literature on a pedestrian walkway in the Central Terminal Area at LAX. The officer showed Snyder a copy of the resolution, explained that Snyder's activities violated the resolution, and requested that Snyder leave LAX. The officer warned Snyder that the city would take legal action against him if he refused to leave as requested. Snyder stopped distributing the leaflets and left the airport terminal. Jews for Jesus and Snyder then filed this action challenging the constitutionality of the resolution. Both the federal district court and the Ninth Circuit Court of Appeals held that the resolution is facially unconstitutional. We granted certiorari and affirm.

Under the First Amendment overbreadth doctrine, an individual whose own speech or conduct may be prohibited is permitted to challenge a statute on its face "because it also threatens others not before the court—those who desire to engage in legally protected expression but who may refrain from doing so rather than risk prosecution or undertake to have the law declared partially invalid." *Brockett v. Spokane Arcades, Inc.*, 472 U.S. 491 (1985). A statute may be invalidated on its face only if the overbreadth is "substantial." *Broadrick v. Oklahoma*, 413 U.S. 601 (1973). The requirement that the overbreadth be substantial arose from our recognition that application of the overbreadth doctrine is "manifestly, strong medicine," and that "there must be a realistic danger that the statute itself will significantly compromise recognized First Amendment protections of parties not before the Court for it to be facially challenged on overbreadth grounds." *City Council of Los Angeles v. Taxpayers for Vincent*, 466 U.S. 789 (1984).

On its face, the resolution in this case reaches the universe of expressive activity, and, by prohibiting *all* protected expression, purports to create a virtual "First Amendment Free Zone" at LAX. The resolution does not merely regulate expressive activity in the Central Terminal Area that might create problems such as congestion or the disruption of the activities of those who use LAX. Instead, the resolution expansively states that LAX "is not open for First Amendment activities by any individual and/or entity," and that "any individual and/or entity who seeks to engage in First Amendment activities within the Central Terminal Area shall be deemed to be acting in contravention of the stated policy of the Board of Airport Commissioners." The resolution therefore does not merely reach the activity of respondents at LAX; it prohibits even talking and reading, or the wearing of campaign buttons or symbolic clothing. Under such a sweeping ban, virtually every individual who enters LAX may be found to violate the resolution by engaging in some "First Amendment activity." We think it obvious that such a ban cannot be justified even if LAX were a nonpublic forum because no conceivable governmental interest would justify such an absolute prohibition of speech.

We find no saving construction of the resolution. The resolution expressly applies to all "First Amendment activities," and the words of the resolution simply leave no room for a narrowing construction. The Court sometimes has used either abstention or certification when the state courts have not had the opportunity to give the statute under challenge a definite construction. Neither option is appropriate in this case because California has no certification procedure, and the resolution is not "fairly subject to an interpretation which will render unnecessary or substantially modify the federal constitutional question." This Court has invalidated a law on overbreadth grounds when it was not "open to one or a few interpretations, but to an indefinite number," and concluded that "it is fictional to believe that anything less than extensive adjudications, under the impact of a variety of factual situations, would bring the law within the bounds of permissible constitutional certainty." *Baggett v. Bullitt*, 377 U.S. 360 (1964). Here, it is difficult to imagine that the resolution could be limited by anything less than a series of adjudications, and the chilling effect of the resolution on protected speech in the meantime would make such a case-by-case adjudication intolerable.

The petitioners suggest that the resolution is not substantially overbroad because it is intended to reach only expressive activity unrelated to airport-related purposes. Such a limiting construction, however, is of little assistance in substantially reducing the overbreadth of the resolution. Much nondisruptive speech — such as the wearing of a T-shirt or button that contains a political message — may not be "airport related," but is still protected speech even in a nonpublic forum. Moreover, the vagueness of this suggested construction itself presents serious constitutional difficulty. The line between airport-related speech and nonairport-related speech is, at best, murky. The petitioners suggest that an individual who reads a newspaper or converses with a neighbor at LAX is engaged in permitted "airport-related" activity because reading or conversing permits the traveling public to "pass the time." We presume, however, that petitioners would not so categorize the activities of a member of a religious or political organization who decides to "pass the time" by distributing leaflets to fellow travelers. In essence, the result of this vague limiting construction would be to give LAX officials alone the power to decide in the first instance whether a given activity is airport related. Such a law that "confers on police a virtually unrestrained power to arrest and charge persons with a violation" of the resolution is unconstitutional because "the opportunity for abuse, especially where a statute has received a virtually open-ended interpretation, is self-evident." *Lewis v. City of New Orleans*, 425 U.S. 130 (1974) (Powell, J., concurring).

We conclude that the resolution is substantially overbroad, and is not fairly subject to a limiting construction. Accordingly, we hold that the resolution violates the First Amendment. The judgment of the Court of Appeals is

Affirmed.

Note: Distinguishing Vagueness and Overbreadth

The plaintiff in *Board of Airport Commissioners* argued that the resolution was "vague" as well as "overbroad," arguments commonly made together in First Amendment litigation. Laws are sometimes characterized as vague when no reasonable person can ascertain the meaning of their language. In *Papachristou v. City of Jacksonville*, 405 U.S. 156 (1972), the Court stated: "This ordinance is void for vagueness, both in the sense that it fails to give a person of ordinary intelligence fair notice that his contemplated conduct is forbidden by the statute, and because it encourages arbitrary and erratic arrests and convictions. Living under a rule of law entails various suppositions, one of which is that (all persons) are entitled to be informed as to what the State commands or forbids." It is possible that a statute may be vague but not substantially overbroad, or arguably overbroad but not particularly vague. However, it is also true that a high degree of vagueness in a statute is likely to create a potential overbreadth problem, and that an extremely overbroad statute may be vague in its contours. Thus, the two statutory "vices" may coexist in a statute.

∾ PROBLEMS ∾

1. *Tools for Analyzing Vagueness.* Any law may have a degree of overbreadth, and the Court's task in an overbreadth case is to perform the difficult subjective assessment of determining whether that overbreadth is "substantial" or in effect "too overbroad." What analytical tools does Justice O'Connor use in the reasoning of *Board of Airport Commissioners* to perform this measurement?

2. *The Identification Statute.* A California criminal statute provides: "Every person who commits any of the following acts is guilty of disorderly conduct, a misdemeanor: (e) Who loiters or wanders upon the streets or from place to place without apparent reason or business and who refuses to identify himself and to account for his presence when requested by any peace officer to do so, if the surrounding circumstances are such as to indicate to a reasonable man that the public safety demands such identification." A state court has interpreted the identification requirement as necessitating the production of "credible and reliable" identification, meaning that the identification "carries a reasonable assurance that the identification is authentic and providing means for later getting in touch with the person who has identified himself." Is the statute unduly vague because it fails to define the term *identification* (e.g., does it vest arbitrary and potentially discriminatory power in the police to arrest)? Does the clarification of *credible and reliable* provide adequate qualification? Could the California statute constitutionally be applied to 1) a man who is caught jogging on a city street late at night; 2) a homeless person found "loitering" on city streets? *See Kolender v. Lawson,* 461 U.S. 352 (1983).

3. *The Student Demonstration.* Suppose that an ordinance makes it a crime "for three or more persons to assemble, except at a public meeting of citizens, on any of the sidewalks, street corners, vacant lots, or mouths of alleys, and there conduct themselves in a manner annoying to persons passing by, or occupants of adjacent buildings." Assume that a student, involved in a political street demonstration, is arrested and convicted under this ordinance. As the lawyer for the student, how will you argue that the ordinance is overbroad and vague, and how will your overbreadth and vagueness arguments differ? *See Coates v. City of Cincinnati,* 402 U.S. 611 (1971).

4. *Rogues and Vagabonds.* Suppose that you are hired to challenge the following ordinance: "Rogues and vagabonds, or dissolute persons who go about begging, common gamblers, persons who use juggling or unlawful games or plays, common drunkards, common night walkers, thieves, pilferers or pickpockets, traders in stolen property, lewd and lascivious persons, keepers of gambling places, common brawlers, persons wandering or strolling around from place to place without any lawful purpose or object, habitual loafers, disorderly persons, persons neglecting all lawful business and habitually spending their time by frequenting houses of ill fame, gaming houses, or places where alcoholic beverages are served, persons able to work but habitually living upon the earnings of their

wives or minor children, shall be deemed vagrants and, upon conviction, shall be punished with up to 90 days imprisonment, up to a $500 fine, or both." How would you challenge the ordinance? *See Papachristou v. City of Jacksonville*, 405 U.S. 156 (1972).

5. *Flag Desecration.* Assume that a man wears a small cloth version of the U.S. flag sewn to the seat of his pants. The flag is approximately 4 by 6 inches and is displayed on the left rear pocket of his jeans. A police officer sees the man and arrests him under the following statute: "Whoever publicly mutilates, tramples upon, defaces or treats contemptuously the flag of the United States, whether such flag is public or private property, shall be punished by a fine of not less than ten nor more than one hundred dollars or by imprisonment for not more than one year or both." Construct arguments to challenge the ordinance on the grounds of vagueness. How might the state respond? *See Smith v. Goguen*, 415 U.S. 566 (1974).

6. *The Noise Ordinance.* The following statute is challenged on vagueness and overbreadth grounds: "No person, while on public or private grounds adjacent to any building in which a school or any class thereof is in session, shall willfully make or assist in the making of any noise or diversion which disturbs or tends to disturb the peace or good order of such school session or class thereof." Explain how the defense to the vagueness challenge differs from the defense to the overbreadth challenge. *See Grayned v. Rockford*, 408 U.S. 104 (1972).

City of Houston v. Hill

482 U.S. 451 (1987)

Justice BRENNAN delivered the opinion of the Court.

Appellee Raymond Wayne Hill is a lifelong resident of Houston, Texas, who worked as a paralegal and as executive director of the Houston Human Rights League. On February 14, 1982, Hill observed a friend, Charles Hill, intentionally stopping traffic on a busy street, evidently to enable a vehicle to enter traffic. Two Houston police officers, one of whom was named Kelley, approached Charles and began speaking with him. "Shortly thereafter" Hill began shouting at the officers "in an admitted attempt to divert Kelley's attention from Charles Hill." Hill testified that his "motivation was to stop the officers from hitting Charles." He also explained: "I would rather that I get arrested than those whose careers can be damaged or whose families wouldn't understand or couldn't spend a long time in jail. I am prepared to respond in any legal, nonaggressive or nonviolent way, to any illegal police activity, at any time, under any circumstances." Hill first shouted: "Why don't you pick on somebody your own size?" After Officer Kelley responded: "Are you interrupting me in my official capacity as a Houston police officer?" Hill then shouted: "Yes, why don't you pick on somebody my size?" Hill was arrested under Houston Code of Ordinances §34-11(a), for "wilfully or intentionally interrupting a city policeman by verbal challenge during an investigation." Charles Hill was not arrested. Hill was then acquitted after a nonjury trial in Municipal Court.

Code of Ordinances, City of Houston, Texas, §34-11(a) (1984), reads:

> Sec. 34-11. Assaulting or interfering with policemen.
>
> (a) It shall be unlawful for any person to assault, strike or in any manner oppose, molest, abuse or interrupt any policeman in the execution of his duty, or any person summoned to aid in making an arrest.

A conviction is punishable by a fine of not more than $200. Following his acquittal, Hill brought suit seeking declaratory and injunctive relief, as well as damages and attorney's fees under 42 U.S.C. §§1983 and 1988 arguing that the ordinance violated the First Amendment and that it was both vague and overbroad. The District Court rejected Hill's contention that the ordinance was unconstitutionally vague or overbroad on its face. The Court of Appeals reversed. We affirm.

The elements of First Amendment overbreadth analysis are familiar. Only a statute that is substantially overbroad may be invalidated on its face. "In a facial challenge to the overbreadth and vagueness of a law, a court's first task is to determine whether the enactment reaches a substantial amount of constitutionally protected conduct." *Kolender v. Lawson*, 461 U.S. 352 (1983). Criminal statutes must be scrutinized with particular care and those that make unlawful a substantial amount of constitutionally protected conduct may be held facially invalid even if they also have legitimate application.

The city argues that the ordinance does not inhibit the exposition of ideas, and that it bans "core criminal conduct" not protected by the First Amendment. We disagree. First, the ordinance deals not with core criminal conduct, but with speech. The language in the ordinance making it unlawful for any person to "assault" or "strike" a police officer is pre-empted by the Texas Penal Code. The enforceable portion ordinance makes it "unlawful for any person to in any manner oppose, molest, abuse or interrupt any policeman in the execution of his duty," and thereby prohibits verbal interruptions of police officers. Second, the First Amendment protects a significant amount of verbal criticism and challenge directed at police officers. "Speech is often provocative and challenging. But it is nevertheless protected against censorship or punishment, unless shown likely to produce a clear and present danger of a serious substantive evil that rises far above public inconvenience, annoyance, or unrest." *Terminiello v. Chicago*, 337 U.S. 1 (1949). In *Lewis v. City of New Orleans*, 415 U.S. 130 (1974), appellant yelled obscenities and threats at an officer who had asked appellant's husband to produce his driver's license. We vacated the conviction and invalidated the ordinance as facially overbroad because the ordinance "punished only spoken words" and was not limited in scope to fighting words that "by their very utterance inflict injury or tend to incite an immediate breach of the peace."

The Houston ordinance is more sweeping than the municipal ordinance struck down in *Lewis*. It is not limited to fighting words nor even to obscene or opprobrious language, but prohibits speech that "in any manner interrupts" an officer. The Constitution does not allow such speech to be made a crime. The freedom of individuals verbally to oppose or challenge police action without risking arrest is one of the principal characteristics by which we distinguish a free nation from a police state. The city argues that the ordinance's sweeping nature is both inevitable and essential to maintain public order. Although we appreciate the difficulties of drafting precise laws, we have repeatedly invalidated laws that provide the police with unfettered discretion to arrest individuals for words or conduct that annoy or offend them. It is unlikely that limiting the ordinance's application to genuine "fighting words" would be incompatible with the full and adequate performance of an officer's duties. The present ordinance tends to be invoked only where there is no other valid basis for arresting an objectionable or suspicious person. The opportunity for abuse, especially where a statute has received a virtually open-ended interpretation, is self-evident.

Houston's ordinance criminalizes a substantial amount of constitutionally protected speech, and accords the police unconstitutional discretion in enforcement. The ordinance's plain language is admittedly violated scores of times daily, yet only some individuals — those chosen by the police in their unguided discretion — are arrested. Far from providing the "breathing space" that "First Amendment freedoms need to survive," the ordinance is susceptible of regular application to protected expression. We conclude that the ordinance is substantially overbroad.

The city has urged us not to reach the merits of Hill's constitutional challenge, but rather to require plaintiff to file the same suit in state court because there are limiting constructions readily available to the state courts that would eliminate the ordinance's overbreadth. Even if this case did not involve a facial challenge under the First Amendment, we would find abstention inappropriate. This ordinance is not susceptible to a limiting construction because its language is plain and its meaning unambiguous. Nor can the ordinance be limited by severing discrete unconstitutional subsections from the rest. For example, it cannot be limited to "core criminal conduct" such as physical assaults or fighting words because those applications are pre-empted by state law. The enforceable portion of this ordinance is a general prohibition of speech that "simply has no core" of constitutionally unprotected expression to which it might be limited. When a statute is not ambiguous, there is no need to abstain even if state courts have never interpreted the statute. Houston's Municipal Courts have had numerous opportunities to narrow the scope of the ordinance. There is no evidence that they have done so.

In the face of verbal challenges to police action, officers and municipalities must respond with restraint. Preservation of liberty depends in part upon maintenance of social order. But the First Amendment recognizes, wisely we think, that a certain amount of expressive disorder not only is inevitable in a society committed to individual freedom, but must itself be protected if that freedom would survive. We affirm the judgment of the Court of Appeals.

It is so ordered.

Justice POWELL, with whom Justice O'CONNOR joins, and with whom THE CHIEF JUSTICE joins as to Parts I and II, and Justice SCALIA joins as to Parts II and III, *concurring in the judgment in part* and *dissenting in part.*

The terms of the ordinance—"oppose, molest, abuse or interrupt any policeman in the execution of his duty"—include general words that can apply as fully to conduct as to speech. The ordinance evidently would punish individuals who—without saying a single word—obstructed an officer's access to the scene of an ongoing public disturbance, or indeed the scene of a crime. I agree that the ordinance can be applied to speech in some cases. I also agree that the First Amendment protects a good deal of speech that may be directed at police officers. But I question the implication that the First Amendment generally protects verbal "challenges directed at police officers." A "challenge" often takes the form of opposition or interruption of performance of duty. In many situations, speech directed at police officers will be functionally indistinguishable from conduct that the First Amendment clearly does not protect. For example, a municipality constitutionally may punish an individual who chooses to stand near a police officer and persistently attempt to engage the officer in conversation while the officer is directing traffic at a busy intersection. Similarly, an individual, by contentious and abusive speech, could interrupt an officer's investigation of possible criminal conduct. A person observing an officer pursuing a person suspected of a felony could run beside him in a public street shouting at the officer. Similar tactics could interrupt a policeman lawfully attempting to interrogate persons believed to be witnesses to a crime.

This ordinance is intended primarily to further the public's interest in law enforcement. I agree that the ambiguous terms of this ordinance "confer on police a virtually unrestrained power to arrest and charge persons with a violation. The opportunity for abuse, especially where a statute has received a virtually open-ended interpretation, is evident." People have been charged with such crimes as "Remaining," "Refusing to remain silent," and "Talking." When government protects society's interests in a manner that restricts some speech the law must be framed more precisely than the ordinance before us. In view of the difficulty of drafting precise language that never restrains speech and yet serves the public interest, the attempts of States and municipalities to draft laws should be accorded some leeway. I am convinced that the Houston ordinance is too vague to comport with the First and Fourteenth Amendments. It should be possible for the present ordinance to be reframed in a way that would limit the broad discretion of officers and at the same time protect the city's legitimate interests. For example, the ordinance could make clear that it applies to speech only if the purpose of the speech were to interfere with the performance by a police officer of his lawful duties.

Chief Justice REHNQUIST, *dissenting.*

I do not agree that the Houston ordinance, in the absence of an authoritative construction by the Texas courts, is unconstitutional.

Notes and Questions: Merits Versus Overbreadth Challenges

From Hill's point of view, what were the benefits of bringing an overbreadth challenge against the Houston ordinance as opposed to challenging the ordinance "on the merits"? From the Court's point of view, describe the costs and benefits of grounding a First Amendment holding in the overbreadth doctrine instead of ruling on the merits of a First Amendment claim.

∼ PROBLEMS ∼

1. *The Beggar's Signs.* An Arizona criminal statute provides six months' imprisonment for "persons wandering abroad and begging, or for going about in public or private ways or other places for the purpose of begging or receiving alms." Bounds challenges the statute on First Amendment grounds, claiming that she is homeless and subsists on the money she receives from begging. During the day, she sits in various parks holding signs that request help and refer to love, peace, and food, holding a cup into which people may deposit money. Sometimes, if a passerby is willing, Sara talks about the messages on her signs and about homelessness. Sara does not approach anyone and does not block any sidewalk or store entrance. Sara has been arrested several times for violating the anti-begging statute. What arguments can be made regarding whether the Arizona statute suffers from overbreadth or vagueness?

2. *"Adversely Affecting" a Funeral.* Michigan enacts a statute in response to the military funeral protests carried out by Fred Phelps and the Westboro church which reads as follows: "A person shall not do any of the following within 500 feet of a building or other location where a funeral, memorial service, or viewing of a deceased person is being conducted, or within 500 feet of a funeral procession or burial: a) Make loud and raucous noise and continue to do so after being asked to stop; or b) Engage in any other conduct that the person knows or should reasonably know will disturb, disrupt, or *adversely affect* the funeral, memorial service, viewing of the deceased person, funeral procession, or burial." Is the statute unduly vague? Suppose that Phelps and the Westboro protesters do *not* make an appearance in a Michigan town at a military funeral, but that the Motts (friends of the deceased) do appear to support the deceased's family. However,

the Motts have a bumper sticker on their car that says "Get Our Troops Out of Afghanistan Now!" Suppose that the Motts are prosecuted under the law, on the theory that the bumper sticker may have an adverse effect on the funeral service, and they challenge the statute on vagueness and overbreadth grounds. Is the statute unduly vague or overbroad? *See Lowden v. Clare County,* 2011 WL 3958488 (E.D. Mich. Sept. 8, 2011).

United States v. Stevens

559 U.S. 460 (2010)

Chief Justice ROBERTS delivered the opinion of the Court.

Section 48 establishes a criminal penalty of up to five years in prison for anyone who knowingly "creates, sells, or possesses a depiction of animal cruelty," if done "for commercial gain" in interstate or foreign commerce. 18 U.S.C. §48(a). A depiction of "animal cruelty" is defined as one "in which a living animal is intentionally maimed, mutilated, tortured, wounded, or killed," if that conduct violates federal or state law where "the creation, sale, or possession takes place." §48(c)(1). In what is referred to as the "exceptions clause," the law exempts from prohibition any depiction "that has serious religious, political, scientific, educational, journalistic, historical, or artistic value." §48(b).

The legislative background of §48 focused primarily on the interstate market for "crush videos." According to the House Committee Report, such videos feature the intentional torture and killing of helpless animals, including cats, dogs, monkeys, mice, and hamsters. Crush videos often depict women slowly crushing animals to death "with their bare feet or while wearing high heeled shoes," sometimes while "talking to the animals in a kind of dominatrix patter" over "the cries and squeals of the animals, obviously in great pain." These depictions "appeal to persons with a very specific sexual fetish who find them sexually arousing or otherwise exciting." The acts depicted in crush videos are typically prohibited by the animal cruelty laws enacted by all 50 States and the District of Columbia. But crush videos rarely disclose the participants' identities, inhibiting prosecution of the underlying conduct.

This case, however, involves an application of §48 to depictions of animal fighting. Dogfighting, for example, is unlawful in all 50 States and the District of Columbia, and has been restricted by federal law since 1976. Respondent Robert J. Stevens ran a business, "Dogs of Velvet and Steel," and an associated Web site, through which he sold videos of pit bulls engaging in dogfights and attacking other animals. Among these videos were Japan Pit Fights and Pick-A-Winna: A Pit Bull Documentary, which include contemporary footage of dogfights in Japan (where such conduct is allegedly legal) as well as footage of American dogfights from the 1960's and 1970's. A third video, Catch Dogs and Country Living, depicts the use of pit bulls to hunt wild boar, as well as a "gruesome" scene of a pit bull attacking a domestic farm pig. On the basis of these videos, Stevens was indicted on three counts of violating §48.

Stevens moved to dismiss the indictment, arguing that §48 is facially invalid under the First Amendment. The District Court held that the depictions, like obscenity or child pornography, are categorically unprotected by the First Amendment. The en banc Third Circuit declared §48 facially unconstitutional and declined to recognize a new category of unprotected speech for depictions of animal cruelty. We granted certiorari.

The Government's primary submission is that §48 necessarily complies with the Constitution because the banned depictions of animal cruelty, as a class, are categorically unprotected by the First Amendment. We disagree. Because we decline to carve out from the First Amendment any novel exception for §48, we review Stevens's First Amendment challenge under our existing doctrine.

Stevens challenged §48 on its face, arguing that any conviction under the statute would be unconstitutional. To succeed in a facial attack, Stevens would have to establish "that no set of circumstances exists under which §48 would be valid," or that the statute lacks any "plainly legitimate sweep," *Washington v. Glucksberg*, 521 U.S. 702, 740 (1997) (Stevens, J., concurring in judgments). Here the Government asserts that Stevens cannot prevail because §48 is plainly legitimate as applied to crush videos and animal fighting depictions. Deciding this case through a traditional facial analysis would require us to resolve whether these applications of §48 are in fact consistent with the Constitution.

In the First Amendment context, this Court recognizes "a second type of facial challenge," whereby a law may be invalidated as overbroad if "a substantial number of its applications are unconstitutional, judged in relation to the statute's plainly legitimate sweep." *Washington State Grange v. Washington State Republican Party*, 552 U.S. 442, 449 (2008). Stevens argues that §48 applies to common depictions of ordinary and lawful activities, and that these depictions constitute the vast majority of materials subject to the statute. The Government makes no effort to defend such a broad ban as constitutional. Instead, the Government's defense of §48 rests on interpreting the statute as narrowly limited to specific types of "extreme" material. Therefore, the constitutionality of §48 hinges on how broadly it is construed.

"The first step in overbreadth analysis is to construe the challenged statute; it is impossible to determine whether a statute reaches too far without first knowing what the statute covers." *United States v. Williams*, 553 U.S. 285, 293 (2008). We read §48 to create a criminal prohibition of alarming breadth. The text of the ban on a "depiction of animal cruelty" nowhere requires that the depicted conduct be cruel. That text applies to "any depiction" in which "a living animal is intentionally maimed, mutilated, tortured, wounded, or killed." §48(c)(1). "Maimed, mutilated, and tortured" convey cruelty, but "wounded" or "killed" does not suggest any such limitation. The Government contends that the terms in the definition should be read to require the additional element of "accompanying acts of cruelty." (The dissent hinges on the same assumption.) The Government bases this argument on the definiendum, "depiction of animal cruelty," and on "'the commonsense canon of *noscitur a sociis*.'" As that canon recognizes, an ambiguous term may be "given more precise content by the neighboring words with which it is associated." Likewise, an unclear definitional phrase may take meaning from the term to be defined. But the phrase "wounded or killed" at issue here contains little ambiguity. "Wounded" and "killed" should be read according to their ordinary meaning. Nothing about that meaning requires cruelty.

While not requiring cruelty, §48 does require that the depicted conduct be "illegal." But this requirement does not limit §48. There are myriad federal and state laws concerning the proper treatment of animals, but many are not designed to guard against animal cruelty. Protections of endangered species, for example, restrict even the humane "wounding or killing" of "living animals." §48(c)(1). Livestock regulations are often designed to protect the health of human beings, and hunting and fishing rules (seasons, licensure, bag limits, weight requirements) can be designed to raise revenue, preserve animal populations, or prevent accidents. The text of §48(c) draws no distinction based on the reason the intentional killing of an animal is made illegal, and includes, for example, the humane slaughter of a stolen cow.

Application of §48 to depictions of illegal conduct extends to conduct that is illegal in only a single jurisdiction. Under subsection (c)(1), the depicted conduct need only be illegal in "the State in which the creation, sale, or possession takes place, regardless of whether the wounding or killing took place in that State." A depiction of lawful conduct runs afoul of the ban if that depiction later finds its way into another State where the same conduct is unlawful. This provision greatly expands the scope of §48, because although there may be "a broad societal consensus" against cruelty to animals, there is substantial disagreement on what types of conduct are properly regarded as cruel. Both views about cruelty to animals and regulations having no connection to cruelty vary widely from place to place. In the District of Columbia, for example, all hunting is unlawful. Other jurisdictions permit or encourage hunting, and there is an enormous national market for hunting-related depictions in which a living animal is intentionally killed. Hunting periodicals have circulations in the hundreds of thousands or millions, and hunting television programs, videos, and Web sites are equally popular. The demand for hunting depictions exceeds the estimated demand for crush videos or animal fighting depictions by several orders of magnitude. Nonetheless, because the statute allows each jurisdiction to export its laws to the rest of the country, §48(a) extends to *any* magazine or video depicting lawful hunting, so long as that depiction is sold within the Nation's Capital. Those seeking to comply with the law thus face a bewildering maze of regulations from at least 56 separate jurisdictions. Some States permit hunting with crossbows, while others forbid it, or restrict it only to the disabled. Missouri allows the "canned" hunting of ungulates held in captivity, but Montana restricts such hunting to certain bird species. The sharp-tailed grouse may be hunted in Idaho, but not in Washington.

The disagreements among the States—and the "commonwealths, territories, or possessions of the United States," 18 U.S.C. §48(c)(2)—extend well beyond hunting. State agricultural regulations permit different methods of livestock slaughter in different places or as applied to different animals. California has recently banned cutting or "docking" the tails of dairy cattle, which other States permit. Even cockfighting, long considered immoral in much of America, is legal in Puerto Rico, and was legal in Louisiana until 2008. An otherwise-lawful image of any of these practices, if sold or possessed for commercial gain within a State that happens to forbid the practice, falls within the prohibition of §48(a).

The only thing standing between defendants who sell such depictions and five years in federal prison—other than the mercy of a prosecutor—is the statute's exceptions clause. Subsection (b) exempts from prohibition "any depiction that has serious religious, political, scientific, educational, journalistic, historical, or artistic value." The Government argues that this clause substantially narrows the statute's reach: News reports about animal cruelty have "journalistic" value; pictures of bullfights in Spain have "historical" value; and instructional hunting videos have "educational" value. Thus, the Government argues, §48 reaches only crush videos, depictions of animal fighting (other than Spanish bullfighting), and perhaps other depictions of "extreme acts of animal cruelty." The Government's attempt to narrow the statutory ban, however, requires an unrealistically broad reading of the exceptions clause. As the Government reads the clause, any material with "redeeming societal value," "at least some minimal value," or anything more than "scant social value," is excluded under §48(b). But the text says "serious" value. The District Court's jury instructions required value that is "significant and of great import," and the Government defended these instructions as properly relying on "a commonly accepted meaning of the word 'serious.'"

The excepted speech must also fall within one of the enumerated categories. Much speech does not. Most hunting videos, for example, are not obviously instructional in nature. According to Safari Club International and the Congressional Sportsmen's Foundation, many popular videos "have primarily entertainment value" and are designed to "entertain the viewer, market hunting equipment, or increase the hunting community." The National Rifle Association agrees that "much of the content of hunting media is merely *recreational* in nature." The Government offers no principled explanation why these depictions of hunting or depictions of Spanish bullfights would be *inherently* valuable while those of Japanese dogfights are not. The dissent contends that hunting depictions must have serious value because hunting has serious value, in a way that dogfights presumably do not. But §48(b) addresses the value of the *depictions*, not of the underlying activity. There is simply no adequate reading of the exceptions clause that results in the statute's banning only the depictions the Government would like to ban.

The Government explains that the language of §48(b) was largely drawn from our opinion in *Miller v. California*, 413 U.S. 15 (1973), which excepted from its definition of obscenity any material with "serious literary, artistic, political, or scientific value." According to the Government, this incorporation of the *Miller* standard into §48 is therefore surely enough to answer any First Amendment objection. In *Miller* we held that "serious" value shields depictions of sex from regulation as obscenity. Limiting *Miller*'s exception to "serious" value ensured that "'a quotation from Voltaire in the flyleaf of a book would not constitutionally redeem an otherwise obscene publication.'" We did not, however, determine that serious value could be used as a general precondition to protecting *other* types of speech in the first place. *Most* of what we say to one another lacks "religious, political, scientific, educational, journalistic, historical, or artistic value" (let alone serious value), but it is still sheltered from government regulation. Even "'wholly neutral futilities come under the protection of free speech as fully as do Keats' poems or Donne's sermons.'" *Cohen v. California*, 403 U.S. 15, 25 (1971) (quoting *Winters v. New York*, 333 U.S. 507, 528 (1948) (Frankfurter, J., dissenting)). Thus, the protection of the First Amendment presumptively extends to many forms of speech that do not qualify for the serious-value exception of §48(b), but nonetheless fall within the broad reach of §48(C).

Not to worry, the Government says: The Executive Branch construes §48 to reach only "extreme" cruelty, and it "neither has brought nor will bring a prosecution for anything less." The Government; invokes its prosecutorial discretion several times. But the First Amendment does not leave us at the mercy of *noblesse oblige*. We would not uphold an unconstitutional statute merely because the Government promised to use it responsibly. This prosecution is itself evidence of the danger in putting faith in government representations of prosecutorial restraint. When this legislation was enacted, the Executive Branch announced that it would interpret §48 as covering only depictions "of wanton cruelty to animals designed to appeal to a prurient interest in sex." *See* Statement by President William J. Clinton upon Signing H.R. 1887, 34 Weekly Comp. Pres. Doc. 2557 (Dec. 9, 1999). No one suggests that the videos in this case fit that description.

Nor can we rely upon the canon of construction that "ambiguous statutory language should be construed to avoid serious constitutional doubts." *FCC v. Fox Television Stations, Inc.*, 129 S.Ct. 1800, 1811 (2009). "This Court may impose a limiting construction on a statute only if it is 'readily susceptible' to such a construction." *Reno v. American Civil Liberties Union*, 521 U.S. 844, 884 (1997). We "'will not rewrite a law to conform it to constitutional requirements,'" for doing so would constitute a "serious invasion of the legislative domain," and sharply diminish Congress's "incentive to draft a narrowly tailored law in the first place," *Osborne*, 495 U.S. at 121. To read §48 as the Government desires requires rewriting, not just reinterpretation.

The Government makes no effort to defend the constitutionality of §48 as applied beyond crush videos and depictions of animal fighting. It argues that those particular depictions are intrinsically related to criminal conduct or are analogous to obscenity (if not themselves obscene), and that the ban on such speech is narrowly tailored to reinforce restrictions on the underlying conduct, prevent additional crime arising from the depictions, or safeguard public mores. But the Government nowhere attempts to extend these arguments to depictions of any other activities—depictions that are presumptively protected by the First Amendment but that remain subject to the criminal sanctions of §48. Nor does the Government seriously contest that the presumptively impermissible applications of §48 (properly construed) far outnumber any permissible ones. However "growing" and "lucrative" the markets for crush videos and dogfighting depictions might be, they are dwarfed by the market for other depictions, such as hunting magazines and videos, that we have determined to be within the scope of §48. We therefore need not and do not decide whether a statute limited to crush videos or other depictions of extreme animal cruelty would be constitutional. We hold only that §48 is not so limited but is instead substantially overbroad, and therefore invalid under the First Amendment.

The judgment of the United States Court of Appeals for the Third Circuit is affirmed.

It is so ordered.

Justice ALITO, *dissenting.*

Today's decision strikes down §48 using the "strong medicine" of the overbreadth doctrine, *United States v. Williams,* 553 U.S. 285 (2008), a potion that generally should be administered only as "a last resort." A party seeking to challenge the constitutionality of a statute generally must show that the statute violates the party's own rights. *New York v. Ferber,* 458 U.S. 747 (1982). The First Amendment overbreadth doctrine carves out a narrow exception to that general rule. Because an overly broad law may deter constitutionally protected speech, the overbreadth doctrine allows a party to whom the law may constitutionally be applied to challenge the statute on the ground that it violates the First Amendment rights of others. *See, e.g., Board of Trustees of State Univ. of N.Y. v. Fox,* 492 U.S. 469, 483 (1989).

The "strong medicine" of overbreadth invalidation need not and generally should not be administered when the statute under attack is unconstitutional as applied to the challenger before the court. I see no reason to depart here from the generally preferred procedure of considering the question of overbreadth only as a last resort. Because the Court has addressed the overbreadth question, I will explain why I do not think that the record supports the conclusion that §48, when properly interpreted, is overly broad.

The overbreadth doctrine "strikes a balance between competing social costs." The doctrine seeks to balance the "harmful effects" of "invalidating a law that in some of its applications is perfectly constitutional" against the possibility that "the threat of enforcement of an overbroad law will deter people from engaging in constitutionally protected speech." "In order to maintain an appropriate balance, we have vigorously enforced the requirement that a statute's overbreadth be *substantial,* not only in an absolute sense, but also relative to the statute's plainly legitimate sweep." In determining whether a statute's overbreadth is substantial, we consider a statute's application to real-world conduct, not fanciful hypotheticals. We have repeatedly emphasized that an overbreadth claimant bears the burden of demonstrating, "from the text of the law *and from actual fact,*" that substantial overbreadth exists. Similarly, "there must be a *realistic danger* that the statute itself will significantly compromise recognized First Amendment protections of parties not before the Court for it to be facially challenged on overbreadth grounds." *Members of City Council of Los Angeles v. Taxpayers for Vincent*, 466 U.S. 789, 801 (1984).

In holding that §48 violates the overbreadth rule, the Court declines to decide whether, as the Government maintains, §48 is constitutional as applied to two broad categories of depictions that exist in the real world: crush videos and depictions of deadly animal fights. Instead, the Court tacitly assumes for the sake of argument that §48 is valid as applied to these depictions, but the Court concludes that §48 reaches too much protected speech to survive. The Court relies primarily on depictions of hunters killing or wounding game and depictions of animals being slaughtered for food.

I turn first to depictions of hunting. As the Court notes, photographs and videos of hunters shooting game are common. But hunting is legal in all 50 States, and §48 applies only to a depiction of conduct that is illegal in the jurisdiction in which the depiction is created, sold, or possessed. Therefore, in all 50 States, the creation, sale, or possession for sale of the vast majority of hunting depictions indisputably falls outside §48's reach. Straining to find overbreadth, the Court suggests that §48 prohibits the sale or possession in the District of Columbia of any depiction of hunting because the District—undoubtedly because of its urban character—does not permit hunting within its boundaries. The Court also suggests that, because some States prohibit a particular type of hunting (e.g., hunting with a crossbow or "canned" hunting) or the hunting of a particular animal (e.g., the "sharp-tailed grouse"), §48 makes it illegal for persons in such States to sell or possess for sale a depiction of hunting that was perfectly legal in the State in which the hunting took place.

The Court's interpretation is seriously flawed. "When a federal court is dealing with a federal statute challenged as overbroad, it should construe the statute to avoid constitutional problems, if the statute is subject to such a limiting construction." *Ferber*, 458 U.S. at 769, n.24. Applying this canon, I would hold that §48 does not apply to depictions of hunting. First, because §48 targets depictions of "animal cruelty," I would interpret that term to apply only to depictions involving acts of animal cruelty as defined by applicable state or federal law, not to depictions of acts that happen to be illegal for reasons having nothing to do with the prevention of animal cruelty. Virtually all state laws prohibiting animal cruelty either expressly define the term "animal" to exclude wildlife or else specifically exempt lawful hunting activities, so the statutory prohibition set forth in §48(a) may reasonably be interpreted not to reach most if not all hunting depictions. Second, even if the hunting of wild animals were otherwise covered by §48(a), I would hold that hunting depictions fall within the exception in §48(b) for depictions that have "serious" (i.e., not "trifling") "scientific," "educational," or "historical" value. The predominant view in this country has long been that hunting serves many important values, and it is clear that Congress shares that view. It is widely thought that hunting has "scientific" value in that it promotes conservation, "historical" value in that it provides a link to past times when hunting played a critical role in daily life, and "educational" value in that it furthers the understanding and appreciation of nature and our country's past and instills valuable character traits. If hunting itself is widely thought to serve these values, then it takes but a small step to conclude that depictions of hunting make a non-trivial contribution to the exchange of ideas. Hunting depictions fall comfortably within the exception set out in §48(b).

I do not have the slightest doubt that Congress, in enacting §48, had no intention of restricting the creation, sale, or possession of depictions of hunting. But even if §48 did impermissibly reach the sale or possession of depictions of hunting in a few unusual situations, those isolated applications would hardly show that §48 bans a substantial amount of protected speech.

Although the Court's overbreadth analysis rests primarily on the proposition that §48 substantially restricts the sale and possession of hunting depictions, the Court cites a few additional examples, including depictions of methods of slaughter and the docking of the tails of dairy cows. Such examples do not show that the statute is substantially overbroad, for two reasons. First, §48 can reasonably be construed to apply only to depictions involving acts of animal cruelty as defined by applicable state or federal law, and anti-cruelty laws do not ban the sorts of acts depicted in the Court's hypotheticals. Second, depictions created to show proper methods of slaughter or tail-docking would presumably have serious "educational" value, and depictions created to focus attention on methods thought to be inhumane or otherwise objectionable would presumably have either serious "educational" or "journalistic" value or both. The Court notes, finally, that cock-fighting, which is illegal in all States, is still legal in Puerto Rico, and it would be impermissible to ban the creation, sale, or possession in Puerto Rico of a depiction of a cockfight that was legally staged in Puerto Rico. But assuming for the sake of argument that this is correct, this sliver of unconstitutionality would not justify striking down §48 *in toto*.

In sum, we have a duty to interpret §48 so as to avoid serious constitutional concerns, and §48 may reasonably be construed not to reach almost all, if not all, of the depictions that the Court finds constitutionally protected. Thus, §48 does not appear to have a large number of unconstitutional applications. Invalidation for overbreadth is appropriate only if the challenged statute suffers from *substantial* overbreadth—judged not just in absolute terms, but in relation to the statute's "plainly legitimate sweep." As I explain in the following Part, §48 has a substantial core of constitutionally permissible applications. It is undisputed that the *conduct* depicted in crush videos may constitutionally be prohibited. All 50 States and the District of Columbia have enacted statutes prohibiting animal cruelty. But before the enactment of §48, the underlying conduct depicted in crush videos was nearly impossible to prosecute. These videos were made in secret, generally without a live audience, and "the faces of the women inflicting the torture in the material often were not shown, nor could the location of the place where the cruelty was being inflicted or the date of the activity be ascertained from the depiction." Thus, law enforcement authorities often were not able to identify the parties responsible for the torture. In the rare instances in which it was possible to identify and find the perpetrators, they "often were able to successfully assert as a defense that the State could not prove its jurisdiction over the place where the act occurred or that the actions depicted took place within the time specified in the State statute of limitations." H.R. Rep., at 3.

The First Amendment protects freedom of speech, but it does not protect violent criminal conduct, even if engaged in for expressive purposes. Crush videos present a highly unusual free speech issue because they are so closely linked with violent criminal conduct. The videos record the commission of violent criminal acts, and it appears that these crimes are committed for the sole purpose of creating the videos. In addition, Congress was presented with compelling evidence that the only way of preventing these crimes was to target the sale of the videos. I cannot believe that the First Amendment commands Congress to step aside and allow the underlying crimes to continue.

In sum, §48 may validly be applied to at least two broad real-world categories of expression covered by the statute: crush videos and dogfighting videos. Thus, the statute has a substantial core of constitutionally permissible applications. Moreover, the record does not show that §48, properly interpreted, bans a substantial amount of protected speech in absolute terms. *A fortiori*, respondent has not met his burden of demonstrating that any impermissible applications of the statute are "substantial" in relation to its "plainly legitimate sweep." I would reject respondent's claim that §48 is facially unconstitutional under the overbreadth doctrine.

E. PRIOR RESTRAINTS

A "prior restraint" is a restriction on speech that is imposed prior to publication or dissemination. In common law England, prior restraints were common and took many different forms. In this country, there has been a general presumption against the validity of prior restraints. As the Court stated in *Bantam Books, Inc. v. Sullivan*, 372 U.S. 58, 70 (1962): "Any system of prior restraints of expression comes to this Court bearing a heavy presumption against its constitutional validity." Prior restraints are undesirable because they prevent ideas from reaching the public.

1. Licensing

The invention of the printing press brought about a major technological shift that made it possible for people to communicate among themselves much more easily and effectively. Prior to that invention, people were forced to communicate orally or by handwritten documents, methods that were slow and inefficient. Because the printing press enabled mass communication, many governments regarded it as dangerous. The English Crown responded by imposed licensing restrictions that required the press to obtain the approval of censors prior to publication. If governmental ministers found that the proposed publication contained objectionable ideas, they could deny the license or grant it on condition that objectionable information be modified or deleted.

Lovell v. City of Griffin

303 U.S. 444 (1938)

Mr. Chief Justice HUGHES delivered the opinion of the Court.

Appellant, Alma Lovell, was convicted in the recorder's court of the City of Griffin, Ga., of the violation of a city ordinance and was sentenced to imprisonment for fifty days in default of the payment of a fine of $50. The ordinance in question is as follows:

> Section 1. That the practice of distributing, either by hand or otherwise, circulars, hand-books, advertising, or literature of any kind, whether said articles are being delivered free, or whether same are being sold, within the limits of the City of Griffin, without first obtaining written permission from the City Manager of the City of Griffin, such practice shall be deemed a nuisance, and punishable as an offense against the City of Griffin.

The violation, which is not denied, consisted of the distribution without the required permission of a pamphlet and magazine in the nature of religious tracts, setting forth the gospel of the "Kingdom of Jehovah." Appellant did not apply for a permit, as she regarded herself as sent "by Jehovah to do His work" and that such an application would have been "an act of disobedience to His commandment."

The ordinance in its broad sweep prohibits the distribution of "circulars, handbooks, advertising, or literature of any kind." It manifestly applies to pamphlets, magazines, and periodicals. The evidence against appellant was that she distributed a certain pamphlet and a magazine called the "Golden Age." Whether in actual administration the ordinance is applied, as apparently it could be, to newspapers does not appear. The ordinance is not limited to "literature" that is obscene or offensive to public morals or that advocates unlawful conduct. There is no suggestion that the pamphlet and magazine distributed in the instant case were of that character. The ordinance embraces "literature" in the widest sense.

The ordinance is comprehensive with respect to the method of distribution. It covers every sort of circulation "either by hand or otherwise." There is thus no restriction in its application with respect to time or place. It is not limited to ways which might be regarded as inconsistent with the maintenance of public order, or as involving disorderly conduct, the molestation of the inhabitants, or the misuse or littering of the streets. The ordinance prohibits the distribution of literature of any kind at any time, at any place, and in any manner without a permit from the city manager.

1436   11. Freedom of Speech

We think that the ordinance is invalid on its face. Whatever the motive which induced its adoption, its character is such that it strikes at the very foundation of the freedom of the press by subjecting it to license and censorship. The struggle for the freedom of the press was primarily directed against the power of the licensor. It was against that power that John Milton directed his assault by his "Appeal for the Liberty of Unlicensed Printing." And the liberty of the press became initially a right to publish "without a license what formerly could be published only with one." While this freedom from previous restraint upon publication cannot be regarded as exhausting the guaranty of liberty, the prevention of that restraint was a leading purpose in the adoption of the constitutional provision. Legislation of the type of the ordinance in question would restore the system of license and censorship in its baldest form.

The liberty of the press is not confined to newspapers and periodicals. It necessarily embraces pamphlets and leaflets. These indeed have been historic weapons in the defense of liberty, as the pamphlets of Thomas Paine and others in our own history abundantly attest. The press in its connotation comprehends every sort of publication which affords a vehicle of information and opinion. What we have had recent occasion to say with respect to the vital importance of protecting this essential liberty from every sort of infringement need not be repeated.

The ordinance cannot be saved because it relates to distribution and not to publication. "Liberty of circulating is as essential to that freedom as liberty of publishing; indeed, without the circulation, the publication would be of little value." Ex parte Jackson, 96 U.S. 727. As the ordinance is void on its face, it was not necessary for appellant to seek a permit under it. She was entitled to contest its validity in answer to the charge against her.

The judgment is reversed and the cause is remanded for further proceedings not inconsistent with this opinion.

It is so ordered.

Notes

1. *Content-Neutral Time, Place, and Manner Restrictions.* Even though the Court routinely strikes down prior restraints, it has upheld content-neutral time, place, and manner restrictions (including permit requirements) on events like public parades. *See Cox v. New Hampshire*, 312 U.S. 569 (1941). Permit requirements are regarded as essential in this context because they "prevent confusion by overlapping parades or processions, to secure convenient use of the streets by other travelers, and to minimize the risk of disorder."

2. *Licenses for Professional Fundraisers. Riley v. National Federation of the Blind,* 487 U.S. 781 (1988), involved a North Carolina act that required licenses for professional fundraisers. In striking down the law, the Court stated that "a speaker is no less a speaker because he or she is paid to speak. Generally, speakers need not obtain a license to speak." Chief Justice Rehnquist, joined by Justice O'Connor,

dissented: "The requirement does not put any burden on the charities' ability to speak. The effect is to require only that the charity hires is a fundraiser who has been licensed by the State."

∽ PROBLEMS ∽

1. Obama and Abortion Protestors. A District of Columbia law makes it illegal to "write, mark, draw, or paint on any word, sign, or figure on public property." A group of antiabortion protestors, distressed by President Obama's position on abortion rights, writes chalk messages on Pennsylvania Avenue in front of the White House. Can the law be used to prosecute the protestors? Is the law content-neutral? Does it matter that the chalk is of a type that would disappear with the next rain? *See Mahoney v. Doe*, 642 F.3d 1112 (D.C. Cir. 2011).

2. Murals. Atlanta has enacted an ordinance which precludes murals on private property absent the approval of the mayor, the city council and the Urban Design Commission. The ordinance provides that approval can be denied for murals that "constitute a traffic hazard or undue or dangerous distraction to motorists or pedestrians," or that is inconsistent with the city's public art program. Under *Lovell*, is the ordinance valid? If the second justification (consistency with the city's public art program) were dropped, and the city focuses only on whether a proposed mural creates a traffic hazard, would the ordinance be more likely to be upheld? *See Complaint in Williams v. City of Atlanta*, Georgia, Docket No. 1:17-cv-01943, N.D. Ga., May 30, 2017, https://www.courtlistener.com/docket/6158329/williams-v-city-of-atlanta-georgia/

3. International Treaty on the Internet. At the convention, China and other countries argue that "seditious" and "subversive" speech, as well as "defamatory" speech, has been posted on the internet, and they suggest the creation of an international licensing board for internet communications. Under the proposed scheme, before any information can be posted on the internet, it must be submitted to the review board and must be licensed. Can you agree to such a proposal in any form?

Freedman v. Maryland

380 U.S. 51 (1965)

Mr. Justice BRENNAN delivered the opinion of the Court.

Appellant sought to challenge the constitutionality of the Maryland motion picture censorship statute, Md. Ann. Code, 1957, Art. 66A, and exhibited the film "Revenge at Daybreak" at his Baltimore theatre without first submitting the picture to the State Board of Censors as required by §2 thereof. The State concedes that the picture does not violate the statutory standards and would have received a license if properly submitted, but the appellant was convicted of a §2 violation despite his contention that the statute in its entirety unconstitutionally impaired freedom of expression. The Court of Appeals of Maryland affirmed, and we noted probable jurisdiction. We reverse.

In *Times Film Corp. v. City of Chicago*, 365 U.S. 43 (1961), we considered and upheld a requirement of submission of motion pictures in advance of exhibition. The question in that case was "whether a prior restraint was necessarily unconstitutional *under all circumstances.*" The exhibitor contended that the "constitutional protection includes complete and absolute freedom to exhibit, at least once, any and every kind of motion picture even if this film contains the basest type of pornography, or incitement to riot, or forceful overthrow of orderly government." The Court held that the argument stated the principle against prior restraints too broadly.

Appellant does not argue that §2 is unconstitutional simply because it may prevent even the first showing of a film whose exhibiting may legitimately be the subject of an obscenity prosecution. He argues that §2 constitutes an invalid prior restraint because it presents a danger of unduly suppressing protected expression. He focuses on the procedure for an initial decision by the censorship board, which, without judicial participation, bars exhibition of any disapproved film, unless and until the exhibitor undertakes a time-consuming appeal to the courts and succeeds in having the Board's decision reversed. Under the statute, the exhibitor is required to submit the film to the Board for examination, but no time limit is imposed for completion of Board action. Thus there is no statutory provision for judicial participation in the procedure which bars a film, nor even assurance of prompt judicial review. Risk of delay is built into the Maryland procedure, as is borne out by experience; in the only reported case the initial judicial determination has taken four months and final vindication of the film on appellate review, six months.

In the area of freedom of expression it is well established that one has standing to challenge a statute on the ground that it delegates overly broad licensing discretion to an administrative office, whether or not his conduct could be proscribed by a properly drawn statute, and whether or not he applied for a license. Standing is recognized in such cases because of the "danger of tolerating, in the area of First Amendment freedoms, the existence of a penal statute susceptible of sweeping and improper application." *NAACP v. Button*, 371 U.S. 145, 433. Appellant's assertion of a similar danger in the Maryland apparatus of censorship—one always fraught with danger and viewed with suspicion—gives him standing to make that challenge. His argument is that, because the apparatus operates in a statutory context in which judicial review may be too little and too late, the statute lacks sufficient safeguards for confining the censor's action to judicially determined constitutional limits, and therefore contains the same vice as a statute delegating excessive administrative discretion.

Although motion pictures are not "necessarily subject to the precise rules governing any other particular method of expression," "any system of prior restraints of expression comes to this Court bearing a heavy presumption against its constitutional validity." *Bantam Books.* The administration of a censorship system for motion pictures presents peculiar dangers to constitutionally protected speech. Unlike a prosecution for obscenity, a censorship proceeding puts the initial burden on the exhibitor or distributor. Because the censor's business is to censor, he may well be less responsive than a court—part of an independent branch of government—to the constitutionally protected interests in free expression. If it is made unduly onerous, by reason of delay or otherwise, to seek judicial review, the censor's determination may in practice be final.

A noncriminal process which requires the prior submission of a film to a censor avoids constitutional infirmity only if it takes place under procedural safeguards designed to obviate the dangers of a censorship system. First, the burden of proving that the film is unprotected expression must rest on the censor. Second, while the State may require advance submission of all films, in order to proceed effectively to bar all showings of unprotected films, the requirement cannot be administered in a manner which would lend an effect of finality to the censor's determination whether a film constitutes protected expression. Because only a judicial determination in an adversary proceeding ensures the necessary sensitivity to freedom of expression, only a procedure requiring a judicial determination suffices to impose a valid final restraint. The exhibitor must be assured, by statute or authoritative judicial construction, that the censor will, within a specified brief period, either issue a license or go to court to restrain showing the film. Any restraint imposed in advance of a final judicial determination on the merits must be limited to preservation of the status quo for the shortest fixed period compatible with sound judicial resolution. We are well aware that, even after expiration of a temporary restraint, an administrative refusal to license, signifying the censor's view that the film is unprotected, may have a discouraging effect on the exhibitor. Therefore, the procedure must also assure a prompt final judicial decision, to minimize the deterrent effect of an interim and possibly erroneous denial of a license.

Without these safeguards, it may prove too burdensome to seek review of the censor's determination. Particularly in the case of motion pictures, it may take very little to deter exhibition in a given locality. The exhibitor's stake in any one picture may be insufficient to warrant a protracted and onerous course of litigation. The distributor, on the other hand, may be equally unwilling to accept the burdens and delays of litigation in a particular area when, without such difficulties, he can freely exhibit his film in most of the rest of the country; for we are told that only four States and a handful of municipalities have active censorship laws.

The Maryland procedural scheme does not satisfy these criteria. First, once the censor disapproves the film, the exhibitor must assume the burden of instituting judicial proceedings and of persuading the courts that the film is protected expression. Second, once the Board has acted against a film, exhibition is prohibited pending judicial review, however protracted. Under the statute, appellant could have been convicted if he had shown the film after unsuccessfully seeking a license, even though no court had ever ruled on the obscenity of the film.

Third, the Maryland statute provides no assurance of prompt judicial determination. We hold, therefore, that appellant's conviction must be reversed. The Maryland scheme fails to provide adequate safeguards against undue inhibition of protected expression, and this renders the §2 requirement of prior submission of films to the Board an invalid previous restraint.

How or whether Maryland is to incorporate the required procedural safeguards in the statutory scheme is for the State to decide. But a model is not lacking: In *Kingsley Books, Inc. v. Brown*, 354 U.S. 436 (1957), we upheld a New York injunctive procedure designed to prevent the sale of obscene books. That procedure postpones any restraint against sale until a judicial determination of obscenity following notice and an adversary hearing. The statute provides for a hearing one day after joinder of issue; the judge must hand down his decision within two days after termination of the hearing. The New York procedure operates without prior submission to a censor, but the chilling effect of a censorship order, even one which requires judicial action for its enforcement, suggests all the more reason for expeditious determination of the question whether a particular film is constitutionally protected.

The requirement of prior submission to a censor sustained in *Times Film* is consistent with our recognition that films differ from other forms of expression. Similarly, we think that the nature of the motion picture industry may suggest different time limits for a judicial determination. It is common knowledge that films are scheduled well before actual exhibition, and the requirement of advance submission in §2 recognizes this. We do not mean to lay down rigid time limits or procedures, but to suggest considerations in drafting legislation to accord with local exhibition practices, and in doing so to avoid the potentially chilling effect of the Maryland statute on protected expression.

Reversed.

Notes and Questions

1. *Film Licensing. Kingsley International Pictures Corp. v. Regents*, 354 U.S. 436 (1957), involved a New York statute that allowed censors to refuse to license any film containing material that was "obscene, indecent, immoral, inhuman, sacrilegious, or was of such a character that its exhibition would tend to corrupt morals or incite to crime." Appellant's application for a license to distribute *Lady Chatterley's Lover* was denied on the basis that the film was immoral because it presented "adultery as a desirable, acceptable and proper pattern of behavior." The Court held that the licensing authority had acted improperly: "What New York has done is to prevent the exhibition of a motion picture because that picture advocates an idea—that adultery under certain circumstances may be proper behavior. The First Amendment's basic guarantee is of freedom to advocate ideas." Justice Douglas concurred: I can find in the First Amendment no room for

any censor whether he is scanning an editorial, reading a news broadcast, editing a novel or a play, or previewing a movie.

2. *Licensing of Sexually Oriented Businesses.* In *FW/PBS, Inc. v. City of Dallas*, 493 U.S. 215 (1990), the Court applied the *Freedman* standards to a municipal ordinance requiring a license for the operation of a sexually oriented business. The Court held that the Dallas licensing scheme did not provide sufficient procedural safeguards. Although there was no majority opinion, a majority agreed that "the first two *Freedman* safeguards are essential: the licensor must make the decision whether to issue the license within a specified and reasonable time period during which the status quo is maintained, and there must be the possibility of prompt judicial review in the event that the license is erroneously denied."

3. *Prompt Judicial Review.* Does the term *prompt judicial review* mean that the unsuccessful applicant for an adult business license must be assured a prompt judicial *determination* on the merits of the permit denial, or does it mean only that prompt *access* to judicial review is required? If a statute provides for "prompt review" but the court fails to promptly review, is that sufficient? In *City News & Novelty, Inc. v. City of Waukesha*, 531 U.S. 278 (2001), although the Court failed to reach the issue on mootness grounds, it suggested that a defendant could not suffer adverse action until judicial action was complete.

4. *Commission to Encourage Morality.* Rhode Island created the Rhode Island Commission to Encourage Morality in Youth and charged it with "the duty to educate the public concerning any book, picture, pamphlet, ballad, printed paper or other thing containing obscene, indecent or impure language, or manifestly tending to the corruption of the youth, and to investigate and recommend the prosecution of all violations of said sections." The commission issued notices to distributors on official commission stationery, stating that certain designated books or magazines distributed by them had been reviewed by the commission and had been declared by a majority of its members to be objectionable for sale, distribution, or display to youths under 18 years of age. The notice reminded distributors of the commission's obligation to recommend to the attorney general the prosecution of purveyors of obscenity. In *Bantam Books, Inc. v. Sullivan*, 372 U.S. 58 (1963), the Court held that the commission's actions were unconstitutional and that a system of informal censorship of this nature was not permitted under the First Amendment.

5. *Newspaper Racks.* A city ordinance permitted newspapers to place coin-operated newspaper-dispensing devices on city sidewalks, but only with the consent of the mayor, who was given broad discretion to deny applications on any "terms and conditions deemed reasonable and necessary by the mayor," but the mayor was required to "state the reasons for such denial." Dispensing licenses had to be renewed every year. In *City of Lakewood v. Plain Dealer Publishing Co.*, 486 U.S. 750 (1988), the Court struck down the ordinance because it vested too much discretionary licensing authority in governmental officials.

∽ PROBLEM: MORE ON THE INTERNATIONAL
TREATY REGULATING THE INTERNET ∽

Do *Freedman,* and the other precedent cited above change your thoughts about whether the treaty can provide for a review board and licensing restrictions on speech? As presently constituted, the internet contains movies and other videos (on YouTube, for example). Some of these movies and videos are arguably "indecent" (e.g., George Carlin's monologue "The Seven Filthy Words") or blasphemous (e.g., George Carlin's monologue "Religion Is Bullshit"). In light of *Freedman,* and other precedent interpreting and applying the First Amendment, can you agree to create such a licensing board? If you can, what kind of content may the board license, and what type of content must be free of licensorial control? Can you accede to Chinese demands regarding the scope of the board's authority? Could you, perhaps, agree that each country (to the extent that its law permits) can establish its own licensing board and apply whatever rules its domestic law permits? Should you agree to such a provision?

2. Injunctions

We have examined prior restraints imposed by statute (or ordinance) and administered by Executive Branch bureaucrats. Prior restraints can also take the form of injunctions. Are injunctions, which are imposed by courts rather than by administrative officials, less objectionable (or more objectionable)?

Near v. Minnesota

283 U.S. 697 (1931)

Mr. Chief Justice HUGHES delivered the opinion of the Court.

Chapter 285 of the Session Laws of Minnesota for the year 1925 provides for the abatement, as a public nuisance, of a "malicious, scandalous and defamatory newspaper, magazine or other periodical."

Under this statute (section 1, clause (b)), the county attorney of Hennepin County brought this action to enjoin the publication of what was described as a "malicious, scandalous and defamatory newspaper, magazine or other periodical," known as *The Saturday Press,* published by the defendants in the city of Minneapolis. The complaint alleged that the defendants, on September 24, 1927, and on eight subsequent dates in October and November, 1927, published and circulated editions of that periodical which were "largely devoted to malicious, scandalous and defamatory articles."

The articles charged, in substance, that a Jewish gangster was in control of gambling, bootlegging, and racketeering in Minneapolis, and that law enforcing officers and agencies were not energetically performing their duties. Most of the charges were directed against the chief of police; he was charged with gross neglect of duty, illicit relations with gangsters, and participation in graft. The county attorney was charged with knowing the conditions and with failure to take adequate measures to remedy them. The mayor was accused of inefficiency and dereliction. One member of the grand jury was stated to be in sympathy with the gangsters. A special grand jury and a special prosecutor were demanded to deal with the situation, and, in particular, to investigate an attempt to assassinate one Guilford, one of the original defendants, who, it appears from the articles, was shot by gangsters after the first issue of the periodical had been published. There is no question but that the articles made serious accusations against the public officers and others in connection with the prevalence of crimes and the failure to expose and punish them. The trial court continued the injunction, and the Minnesota courts affirmed.

The operation and effect of the statute is that public authorities may bring the owner or publisher of a newspaper or periodical before a judge upon a charge of conducting a business of publishing scandalous and defamatory matter—in particular that the matter consists of charges against public officers of official dereliction—and, unless the owner or publisher is able and disposed to bring competent evidence to satisfy the judge that the charges are true and are published with good motives and for justifiable ends, his newspaper or periodical is suppressed and further publication is made punishable as a contempt. This is of the essence of censorship.

The question is whether a statute authorizing such proceedings in restraint of publication is consistent with the conception of the liberty of the press as historically conceived and guaranteed. It has been generally, if not universally, considered that it is the chief purpose of the guaranty to prevent previous restraints upon publication. The struggle in England, directed against the legislative power of the licenser, resulted in renunciation of the censorship of the press. The liberty deemed to be established was thus described by Blackstone: "The liberty of the press is indeed essential to the nature of a free state; but this consists in laying no previous restraints upon publications, and not in freedom from censure for criminal matter when published. Every freeman has an undoubted right to lay what sentiments he pleases before the public; to forbid this, is to destroy the freedom of the press; but if he publishes what is improper, mischievous or illegal, he must take the consequence of his own temerity." 4 William Blackstone, Commentaries 151, 152. As Madison said, "security of the freedom of the press requires that it should be exempt not only from previous restraint by the Executive, as in Great Britain, but from legislative restraint also." Report on the Virginia Resolutions, *Madison's Works*, vol. IV, p. 543. For whatever wrong the appellant has committed or may commit, by his publications, the state appropriately affords both public and private redress by its libel laws. The statute does not deal with punishments, except in case of contempt for violation of the court's order, but for suppression and injunction—that is, for restraint upon publication.

The protection as to previous restraint is not absolutely unlimited. But the limitation has been recognized only in exceptional cases. "When a nation is at war many things that might be said in time of peace are such a hindrance to its effort that their utterance will not be endured so long as men fight and that no Court could regard them as protected by any constitutional right." *Schenck v. United States*, 249 U.S. 47, 52. No one would question that a government might prevent actual obstruction to its recruiting service or the publication of the sailing dates of transports or the number and location of troops. On similar grounds, the primary requirements of decency may be enforced against obscene publications. The security of community life may be protected against incitements to acts of violence and the overthrow by force of orderly government. The constitutional guaranty of free speech does not "protect a man from an injunction against uttering words that may have all the effect of force." *Schenck v. United States*. These limitations are not applicable here. Nor are we concerned with questions as to the extent of authority to prevent publications in order to protect private rights according to the principles governing the exercise of the jurisdiction of courts of equity.

The exceptional nature of its limitations places in a strong light the general conception that liberty of the press, historically considered and taken up by the Federal Constitution, has meant, principally although not exclusively, immunity from previous restraints or censorship. The conception of liberty of the press in this country had broadened with the exigencies of the colonial period and with the efforts to secure freedom from oppressive administration. That liberty was especially cherished for the immunity it afforded from previous restraint of the publication of censure of public officers and charges of official misconduct.

"Some degree of abuse is inseparable from the proper use of everything, and in no instance is this more true than in that of the press. It has accordingly been decided by the practice of the States, that it is better to leave a few of its noxious branches to their luxuriant growth, than, by pruning them away, to injure the vigour of those yielding the proper fruits. Can the wisdom of this policy be doubted by any who reflect that to the press alone, chequered as it is with abuses, the world is indebted for all the triumphs which have been gained by reason and humanity over error and oppression; who reflect that to the same beneficent source the United States owe much of the lights which conducted them to the ranks of a free and independent nation, and which have improved their political system into a shape so auspicious to their happiness? Had 'Sedition Acts,' forbidding every publication that might bring the constituted agents into contempt or disrepute, or that might excite the hatred of the people against the authors of unjust or pernicious measures, been uniformly enforced against the press, might not the United States have been languishing at this day under the infirmities of a sickly Confederation? Might they not, possibly, be miserable colonies, groaning under a foreign yoke?"

The fact that for approximately one hundred and fifty years there has been almost an entire absence of attempts to impose previous restraints upon publications relating to the malfeasance of public officers is significant of the deep-seated conviction that such restraints would violate constitutional right. Public officers, whose character and conduct remain open to debate and free discussion in the press, find their remedies for false accusations in actions under libel laws providing for redress and punishment, and not in proceedings to restrain the publication of newspapers and periodicals. The general principle that the constitutional guaranty of the liberty of the press gives immunity from previous restraints has been approved in many decisions under state constitutions.

The importance of this immunity has not lessened. While reckless assaults upon public men, and efforts to bring obloquy upon those whom are endeavoring faithfully to discharge official duties, exert a baleful influence and deserve the severest condemnation in public opinion, it cannot be said that this abuse is greater, and it is believed to be less, than that which characterized the period in which our institutions took shape. Meanwhile, the administration of government has become more complex, the opportunities for malfeasance and corruption have multiplied, crime has grown to most serious proportions, and the danger of its protection by unfaithful officials and of the impairment of the fundamental security of life and property by criminal alliances and official neglect, emphasizes the primary need of a vigilant and courageous press, especially in great cities. The fact that the liberty of the press may be abused by miscreant purveyors of scandal does not make any the less necessary the immunity of the press from previous restraint in dealing with official misconduct. Subsequent punishment for such abuses as may exist is the appropriate remedy, consistent with constitutional privilege.

In attempted justification of the statute, it is said that it deals not with publication per se, but with the "business" of publishing defamation. If, however, the publisher has a constitutional right to publish, without previous restraint, an edition of his newspaper charging official derelictions, it cannot be denied that he may publish subsequent editions for the same purpose. He does not lose his right by exercising it. If his right exists, it may be exercised in publishing nine editions as well as in one edition. If previous restraint is permissible, it may be imposed at once; indeed, the wrong may be as serious in one publication as in several. Characterizing the publication as a business, and the business as a nuisance, does not permit an invasion of the constitutional immunity against restraint. It does not matter that the newspaper or periodical is found to be "largely" or "chiefly" devoted to the publication of such derelictions. If the publisher has a right, without previous restraint, to publish them, his right cannot be deemed to be dependent upon his publishing something else, more or less, with the matter to which objection is made.

Nor can it be said that the constitutional freedom from previous restraint is lost because charges are made of derelictions which constitute crimes. With the multiplying provisions of penal codes, and of municipal charters and ordinances carrying penal sanctions, the conduct of public officers is very largely within the purview of criminal statutes. Freedom of the press from previous restraint has never been regarded as outside the range of these enactments.

The statute in question cannot be justified by reason of the fact that the publisher is permitted to show, before injunction issues, that the matter published is true and is published with good motives and for justifiable ends. If a statute, authorizing suppression and injunction on such a basis, is constitutionally valid, it would be permissible for the Legislature to provide that at any time the publisher of any newspaper could be brought before a court, or even an administrative officer (as the constitutional protection may not be regarded as resting on mere procedural details), and required to produce proof of the truth of his publication, or of what he intended to publish and of his motives, or stand enjoined. If this can be done, the Legislature may provide machinery for determining in the exercise of its discretion what are justifiable ends and restrain publication accordingly. It would be but a step to a complete system of censorship. The recognition of authority to impose previous restraint upon publication in order to protect the community against the circulation of charges of misconduct, and especially of official misconduct, necessarily would carry with it the admission of the authority of the censor against which the constitutional barrier was erected. The preliminary freedom, by virtue of the very reason for its existence, does not depend, as this court has said, on proof of truth.

Equally unavailing is the insistence that the statute is designed to prevent the circulation of scandal which tends to disturb the public peace and to provoke assaults and the commission of crime. Charges of reprehensible conduct, and in particular of official malfeasance, unquestionably create a public scandal, but the theory of the constitutional guaranty is that even a more serious public evil would be caused by authority to prevent publication. "To prohibit the intent to excite those unfavorable sentiments against those who administer the Government, is equivalent to a prohibition of the actual excitement of them; and to prohibit the actual excitement of them is equivalent to a prohibition of discussions having that tendency and effect; which, again, is equivalent to a protection of those who administer the Government, if they should at any time deserve the contempt or hatred of the people, against being exposed to it by free animadversions on their characters and conduct." Charges of reprehensible conduct may create resentment and the disposition to resort to violent means of redress, but this tendency did not alter the determination to protect the press against censorship and restraint upon publication. As was said in *New Yorker Staats-Zeitung v. Nolan*, 89 N.J. Eq. 387, 388, 105 A. 72: "If the township may prevent the circulation of a newspaper for no reason other than that some of its inhabitants may violently disagree with it, and" prevents its "circulation by resorting to physical violence, there is no limit to what may be prohibited." The danger of violent reactions becomes greater with effective organization of defiant groups resenting exposure, and, if this consideration warranted legislative interference with freedom of publication, the constitutional protection would be reduced to a mere form of words.

For these reasons we hold the statute, so far as it authorized the proceedings in this action under clause (b) of section 1, to be an infringement of the liberty of the press guaranteed by the Fourteenth Amendment. This decision rests upon the operation and effect of the statute, without regard to the question of the truth of the charges contained in the particular periodical. The fact that the public officers, and those associated with the charges of official dereliction, may be deemed to be impeccable, cannot affect the conclusion that the statute imposes an unconstitutional restraint upon publication.

Judgment reversed.

Mr. Justice BUTLER, *dissenting.*

Defendants' regular business was the publication of malicious, scandalous, and defamatory articles concerning the principal public officers, leading newspapers of the city, many private persons, and the Jewish race. It was their intent to continue to carry on the business. In every edition slanderous and defamatory matter predominates to the practical exclusion of all else. Many of the statements are so highly improbable as to compel a finding that they are false. The articles themselves show malice.

It is of the greatest importance that the states shall be untrammeled and free to employ all just and appropriate measures to prevent abuses of the liberty of the press. "The language of the First amendment imports no more than that every man shall have a right to speak, write, and print his opinions upon any subject whatsoever, without any prior restraint, so always that he does not injure any other person in his rights, person, property, or reputation; and so always that he does not thereby disturb the public peace, or attempt to subvert the government. It is neither more nor less than an expansion of the great doctrine recently brought into operation in the law of libel, that every man shall be at liberty to publish what is true, with good motives and for justifiable ends. With this reasonable limitation it is not only right in itself, but it is an inestimable privilege in a free government. Without such a limitation, it might become the scourge of the republic, denouncing the principles of liberty, and then, by rendering the most virtuous patriots odious through the terrors of the press, introducing despotism in its worst form."

The Minnesota statute does not operate as a previous restraint on publication within the proper meaning of that phrase. It does not authorize administrative control in advance such as was formerly exercised by licensers and censors, but prescribes a remedy to be enforced by a suit in equity. In this case there was previous publication made in the course of the business of regularly producing malicious, scandalous, and defamatory periodicals. The business and publications unquestionably constitute an abuse of the right of free press. The statute denounces the things done as a nuisance on the ground that they threaten morals, peace, and good order. There is no question of the power of the state to denounce such transgressions. The restraint is only in respect of continuing to do what has been duly adjudged to constitute a nuisance.

It is well known that existing libel laws are inadequate effectively to suppress evils resulting from the kind of business and publications that are shown in this case. The doctrine that measures such as the one before us are invalid because

they operate as previous restraints to infringe freedom of press exposes the peace
and good order of every community and the business and private affairs of every
individual to the constant and protracted false and malicious assaults of any insol-
vent publisher who may have purpose and sufficient capacity to contrive and
put into effect a scheme or program for oppression, blackmail or extortion. The
judgment should be affirmed.

Notes and Questions

1. *Help Wanted Advertising.* In *Pittsburgh Press Co. v. Pittsburgh Commission on
Human Relations*, 413 U.S. 376 (1973), the Court upheld an ordinance that prohibited newspapers from carrying "help wanted" advertisements in sex-designated
columns except when the employer or advertiser is free to make hiring or employment referral decisions on the basis of sex. The Court concluded that the ads
constituted commercial speech and upheld the ordinance.

2. *Remedies for Public Officials?* What remedies (if any) are available to plaintiffs like those in *Near?* How do defamed public officials vindicate their reputations? What happened to the notion that equity will act when a plaintiff's legal
remedies are inadequate?

3. *Defamation of Public Figures.* In *Tory v. Cochran,* 544 U.S. 734 (2005), a former
client, Ulysses Tory, made numerous allegations of dishonesty and lack of professionalism against famous lawyer (now deceased) Johnnie Cochran. Cochran
gained notoriety as one of O.J. Simpson's defense attorneys in his murder trial. At
trial, the evidence shows that Tory claims that Cochran owes him money, has written Cochran threatening letters demanding $10 million, has picketed Cochran's
office with signs containing insults and obscenities, and has pursued Cochran
while chanting similar threats and insults. If the trial court concludes that Tory's
claims are without basis (as it did), may it enjoin Tory from engaging in further
such conduct? Is injunctive relief consistent with the holding in *Near?* Is your
analysis affected by the news of Cochran's death (which, of course, means that
Cochran is no longer practicing law)?

4. *National Security and Intelligence Agency Pre-Publication Review.* The federal
government requires pre-publication review of books or articles that national
security or intelligence officials wish to publish. As part of that process, the government reserves the right to require redaction or modification of information
that might damage national security or intelligence interests. Despite the general
prohibition against pre-publication review systems, courts have upheld restrictions in these areas provided that they are reasonable. *See Edgar v. Coates,* 454
F. Supp.3d 502.

5. *Bolton Memoir.* The Department of Justice sought, but failed to obtain,
an injunction blocking publication of John Bolton's memoir regarding his
work with the Trump Administration entitled *The Room Where It Happened.* The
Department claimed that the book contained classified information, harmful to

national security, and that Bolton violated non-disclosure agreements by failing to obtain approval from the National Security Counsel prior to publication. The judge noted that the book had been printed and shipped, with advance copies in the possession of reviewers, so an injunction would be ineffectual. Could the Justice Department seek recovery of the royalties given that the book was improperly published? *See* Harper Neidig & Jesse Byrnes, *Judge Denies Request to Block Bolton Book*, THE HILL, June 20, 2010, https://thehill.com/regulation/court-battles/503695-judge-denies-request-to-block-bolton-book

∾ PROBLEM: MORE ON THE INTERNATIONAL TREATY REGULATING THE INTERNET ∾

At the convention, some countries (e.g., China) demand the right to seek injunctive relief against "defamatory," "seditious," and "subversive" speech, and they wish to include provisions authorizing the courts of each country to grant injunctive relief and providing that the courts of other countries shall give "full faith and credit" to such injunctions. You are concerned because you know that a number of Chinese dissidents live in the United States, and you know that they use the internet to air their criticisms of the Chinese government (as ex-patriots from other countries air their critiques of their own countries). In addition, you are aware that Google and other U.S. companies do business in China, and therefore are subject to the jurisdiction of Chinese courts. In light of *Near*, what treaty provisions can or should you agree to regarding injunctive relief and the enforceability of injunctions in the United States?

New York Times Co. v. United States

403 U.S. 713 (1971)

(THE "PENTAGON PAPERS" CASE)

PER CURIAM.

The *Pentagon Papers* case consolidated two separate proceedings in which the United States sought to enjoin newspapers from publishing classified documents regarding U.S. participation in the Vietnam War. In both cases the district courts refused to issue injunctions. On appeal, the government prevailed in the Court of Appeals for the Second Circuit (the *New York Times* case) but lost in the District of Columbia (the *Washington Post* case). The cases then went to the U.S. Supreme Court. In his dissent, *infra*, Justice Harlan describes the "frenzied train of events" leading to the Court's decision.

We granted certiorari in these cases in which the United States seeks to enjoin the *New York Times* and the *Washington Post* from publishing the contents of a classified study entitled "History of U.S. Decision-Making Process on Viet Nam Policy."

"Any system of prior restraints of expression comes to this Court bearing a heavy presumption against its constitutional validity." *Bantam Books, Inc. v. Sullivan*, 372 U.S. 58, 70 (1963). The Government "thus carries a heavy burden of showing justification for the imposition of such a restraint." The District Court for the Southern District of New York in the *New York Times* case, and the District Court for the District of Columbia and the Court of Appeals for the District of Columbia Circuit in the *Washington Post* case held that the Government had not met that burden. We agree.

The judgment of the Court of Appeals for the District of Columbia Circuit is therefore affirmed. The order of the Court of Appeals for the Second Circuit is reversed, and the case is remanded with directions to enter a judgment affirming the judgment of the District Court for the Southern District of New York. The stays entered June 25, 1971, by the Court are vacated. The judgments shall issue forthwith.

So ordered.

Mr. Justice BLACK, with whom Mr. Justice DOUGLAS joins, *concurring.*

The Government's case against the *Washington Post* should have been dismissed and the injunction vacated without oral argument. Every moment's continuance of the injunctions against these newspapers amounts to a flagrant, indefensible, and continuing violation of the First Amendment. It is unfortunate that some of my Brethren are willing to hold that the publication of news may sometimes be enjoined. Both the history and language of the First Amendment support the view that the press must be left free to publish news, whatever the source, without censorship, injunctions, or prior restraints. Paramount among the responsibilities of a free press is the duty to prevent any part of the government from deceiving the people and sending them off to distant lands to die of foreign fevers and foreign shot and shell. Far from deserving condemnation for their courageous reporting, the *New York Times,* the *Washington Post,* and other newspapers should be commended for serving the purpose that the Founding Fathers saw so clearly. In revealing the workings of government that led to the Vietnam war, the newspapers nobly did precisely that which the Founders hoped and trusted they would do.

We are asked to hold that despite the First Amendment's emphatic command, the Executive Branch, the Congress, and the Judiciary can make laws enjoining publication of current news and abridging freedom of the press in the name of "national security." The word "security" is a broad, vague generality whose contours should not be invoked to abrogate the fundamental law embodied in the First Amendment. The guarding of military and diplomatic secrets at the expense of informed representative government provides no real security for our Republic.

Mr. Justice DOUGLAS, with whom Mr. Justice BLACK joins, *concurring.*

The First Amendment leaves no room for governmental restraint on the press. These disclosures may have a serious impact. But that is no basis for sanctioning a previous restraint on the press. The Government says that it has inherent powers to go to court and obtain an injunction to protect the national interest, which in this case is alleged to be national security. *Near v. Minnesota* repudiated that expansive doctrine in no uncertain terms. The First Amendment was adopted against the widespread use of the common law of seditious libel to punish the dissemination of material that is embarrassing to the powers-that-be. A debate of large proportions goes on in the Nation over our posture in Vietnam. That debate antedated the disclosure of the present documents. The latter are highly relevant to the debate in progress. Secrecy in government is fundamentally anti-democratic, perpetuating bureaucratic errors. Open debate and discussion of public issues are vital to our national health. On public questions there should be "uninhibited, robust, and wide-open" debate. *New York Times Co. v. Sullivan*, 376 U.S. 254.

I would affirm the judgment of the Court of Appeals in the *Post* case, vacate the stay of the Court of Appeals in the *Times* case and direct that it affirm the District Court. The stays in these cases that have been in effect for more than a week constitute a flouting of the principles of the First Amendment as interpreted in *Near*.

Mr. Justice BRENNAN, *concurring*.

The First Amendment stands as an absolute bar to the imposition of judicial restraints in circumstances of the kind presented by these cases. The error that has pervaded these cases from the outset was the granting of any injunctive relief whatsoever. The entire thrust of the Government's claim has been that publication of the material sought to be enjoined "could," or "might," or "may" prejudice the national interest in various ways. But the First Amendment tolerates absolutely no prior judicial restraints of the press predicated upon surmise or conjecture that untoward consequences may result. There is a single, extremely narrow class of cases in which the First Amendment's ban on prior judicial restraint may be overridden. Such cases arise only when the Nation "is at war," during which times "no one would question but that a government might prevent actual obstruction to its recruiting service or the publication of the sailing dates of transports or the number and location of troops." Even if the present world situation were tantamount to a time of war, or if the power of presently available armaments would justify even in peacetime the suppression of information that would set in motion a nuclear holocaust, in neither of these actions has the Government presented or even alleged that publication of items from or based upon the material at issue would cause the happening of an event of that nature. Only governmental allegation and proof that publication must inevitably, directly, and immediately cause the occurrence of an event kindred to imperiling the safety of a transport already at sea can support even the issuance of an interim restraining order. Unless and until the Government has clearly made out its case, the First Amendment commands that no injunction may issue.

Mr. Justice STEWART, with whom Mr. Justice WHITE joins, *concurring.*

The only effective restraint upon executive policy and power in the areas of national defense and international affairs may lie in an enlightened citizenry—in an informed and critical public opinion which alone can here protect the values of democratic government. It is perhaps here that a press that is alert, aware, and free most vitally serves the basic purpose of the First Amendment. Yet it is elementary that the successful conduct of international diplomacy and the maintenance of an effective national defense require both confidentiality and secrecy. Other nations can hardly deal with this Nation in an atmosphere of mutual trust unless they can be assured that their confidences will be kept. Within our own executive departments, the development of considered and intelligent international policies would be impossible if those charged with their formulation could not communicate with each other freely, frankly, and in confidence.

If the Constitution gives the Executive a large degree of unshared power in the conduct of foreign affairs and the maintenance of our national defense, then under the Constitution the Executive must have the largely unshared duty to determine and preserve the degree of internal security necessary to exercise that power successfully. This is not to say that Congress and the courts have no role to play. Undoubtedly Congress has the power to enact specific and appropriate criminal laws to protect government property and preserve government secrets. Congress has passed such laws. If a criminal prosecution is instituted, it will be the responsibility of the courts to decide the applicability of the criminal law under which the charge is brought.

But in the cases before us we are asked neither to construe specific regulations nor to apply specific laws. We are asked, instead, to perform a function that the Constitution gave to the Executive, not the Judiciary. We are asked to prevent the publication by two newspapers of material that the Executive Branch insists should not, in the national interest, be published. I am convinced that the Executive is correct with respect to some of the documents involved. But I cannot say that disclosure of any of them will surely result in direct, immediate, and irreparable damage to our Nation or its people. That being so, there can under the First Amendment be but one judicial resolution of the issues before us. I join the judgments of the Court.

Mr. Justice WHITE, with whom Mr. Justice STEWART joins, *concurring.*

I concur only because of the concededly extraordinary protection against prior restraints enjoyed by the press under our constitutional system. The United States has not satisfied the very heavy burden that it must meet to warrant an injunction against publication, at least in the absence of express and appropriately limited congressional authorization for prior restraints in circumstances such as these. In the absence of legislation by Congress, I am unable to agree that the inherent powers of the Executive and the courts authorize remedies having such sweeping potential for inhibiting publications by the press. Much of the difficulty inheres in the "grave and irreparable danger" standards. If the

United States were to have judgment under such a standard, our decision would be of little guidance to courts in other cases, for the material at issue here would not be available from the Court's opinion or from public records, nor would it be published by the press. Congress has addressed itself to the problems of protecting the security of the country and the national defense from unauthorized disclosure of potentially damaging information. I am not saying that either of these newspapers has yet committed a crime or that either would commit a crime if it published all the material now in its possession. That matter must await resolution in the context of a criminal proceeding if one is instituted.

Mr. Justice MARSHALL, *concurring.*

It is a traditional axiom that a court of equity will not do a useless thing just as it is a traditional axiom that equity will not enjoin the commission of a crime. The Solicitor General does not even mention in his brief whether the Government considers that there is probable cause to believe a crime has been committed or whether there is a conspiracy to commit future crimes.

Mr. Chief Justice BURGER, *dissenting.*

The Times has had unauthorized possession of the documents for months, during which it has had its expert analysts studying them, digesting them and preparing the material for publication. During this time, the *Times,* presumably in its capacity as trustee of the public's "right to know," has held up publication for purposes it considered proper and thus public knowledge was delayed. After these months of deferral, the alleged "right to know" has somehow become a right that must be vindicated instanter. The consequence of this melancholy series of events is that we literally do not know what we are acting on. We have been forced to deal with litigation concerning rights of great magnitude without an adequate record, and without time for adequate treatment. I am not prepared to reach the merits. We all crave speedier judicial processes but when judges are pressured as in these cases the result is a parody of the judicial function.

Mr. Justice HARLAN, with whom THE CHIEF JUSTICE and Mr. Justice BLACKMUN join, *dissenting.*

Both the Court of Appeals for the Second Circuit and the Court of Appeals for the District of Columbia Circuit rendered judgment on June 23. *The New York Times'* petition for certiorari, its motion for accelerated consideration thereof, and its application for interim relief were filed in this Court on June 24 at about 11 a.m. The application of the United States for interim relief in the *Post* case was also filed here on June 24 at about 7:15 p.m. This Court's order setting a hearing before us on June 26 at 11 a.m., a course which I joined only to avoid the possibility of even more peremptory action by the Court, was issued less than 24 hours before. The record in the *Post* case was filed with the Clerk shortly before 1 p.m. on June 25; the record in the *Times* case did not arrive until 7 or 8 o'clock that same night. The briefs of the parties were received less than two hours before argument on June 26. This frenzied train of events took place in the name of the presumption against prior restraints created by the First Amendment. Due regard for the extraordinarily important and difficult questions involved in these litigations should have led the Court to shun such a precipitate timetable.

Forced as I am to reach the merits of these cases, I dissent. I agree that, in performance of its duty to protect the values of the First Amendment against political pressures, the judiciary must review the initial Executive determination to the point of satisfying itself that the subject matter of the dispute does lie within the proper compass of the President's foreign relations power. Moreover, the judiciary may properly insist that the determination that disclosure of the subject matter would irreparably impair the national security be made by the head of the Executive Department concerned after actual personal consideration by that officer. But in my judgment the judiciary may not properly go beyond these two inquiries and redetermine for itself the probable impact of disclosure on the national security. Accordingly, I would vacate the judgment of the Court of Appeals for the District of Columbia Circuit on this ground and remand the case for further proceedings in the District Court.

Mr. Justice BLACKMUN, *dissenting.*

The First Amendment is only one part of an entire Constitution. Article II of the great document vests in the Executive Branch primary power over the conduct of foreign affairs and places in that branch the responsibility for the Nation's safety. Each provision of the Constitution is important, and I cannot subscribe to a doctrine of unlimited absolutism for the First Amendment at the cost of downgrading other provisions. What is needed here is a weighing, upon properly developed standards, of the broad right of the press to print and of the very narrow right of the Government to prevent. Such standards are not yet developed. Even the newspapers concede that there are situations where restraint is in order and is constitutional. Mr. Justice Holmes gave us a suggestion when he said in *Schenck,* "It is a question of proximity and degree. When a nation is at war many things that might be said in time of peace are such a hindrance to its effort that their utterance will not be endured so long as men fight and that no Court could regard them as protected by any constitutional right." I would remand these cases to be developed expeditiously, but on a schedule permitting the orderly presentation of evidence from both sides, with the use of discovery, if necessary, and with the preparation of briefs, oral argument, and court opinions. These cases and the issues involved and the courts, including this one, deserve better than has been produced thus far.

Notes

1. *The Progressive and the H-Bomb Secret. United States v. The Progressive, Inc.,* 467 F. Supp. 990 (W.D. Wis. 1979), involved a federal law, 42 U.S.C. §§2274(b)

and 2280, that authorized the government to seek relief against anyone who attempted to disclose restricted data "with reason to believe such data will be utilized to injure the United States or to secure an advantage to any foreign nation." *The Progressive* magazine wanted to publish an article on how to build an H-bomb. When the U.S. government sought injunctive relief to prevent publication, the magazine defended on the basis that its goal was to demonstrate laxness in the government's security system. It would do so by showing that it compiled the article based on publicly available information. The government nonetheless sought to prevent disclosure, asserting that the public would be harmed because others (including medium-sized nations) might not have the capability to build thermonuclear weapons without reading the article. In the case, although the trial court initially entered the injunction, it lifted the injunction when it became clear that another magazine had published similar information.

2. *The WikiLeaks Controversy.* Following the WikiLeaks controversy, in which thousands of secret documents were stolen from the U.S. government and published by WikiLeaks and in various newspapers, U.S. Army Pfc. Bradley Manning (now Chelsea Manning) was convicted of multiple counts of violating the Espionage Act for stealing the documents. The government aggressively sought to determine whether WikiLeaks had collaborated with Manning in stealing the documents, and eventually brought criminal charges against WikiLeaks' founder, Julian Assange.

3. *The Snowden Affair.* In June 2013, Edward Snowden, a contractor at the National Security Agency (NSA), leaked documents to the media showing that the government was collecting extensive amounts of data from phone and internet companies. The collection was done completely in secret, and everyone (including contractors like Snowden, as well as the phone and internet companies subject to the collection process) was ordered to be secret about the program. Although President Obama claimed that the program did not target the communications of U.S. citizens, he admitted that it could target U.S. citizens who were communicating with foreigners. Snowden felt that the U.S. people had the right to be informed regarding the existence of the program, and disclosed secret NSA documents revealing the substance of the collection program. The government disagreed, claiming that national security had been compromised, and indicated its intent to prosecute Snowden under the Espionage Act for revealing the existence of the NSA program.

∾ PROBLEMS ∾

1. *Proper Injunction?* As noted, in *United States v. The Progressive*, the trial court lifted its injunction when another magazine published similar information. Did the court act properly in issuing the injunction in the first place? Are the facts of this case sufficiently distinguishable from the "Pentagon Papers" case as to make injunctive relief appropriate? Why or why not?

2. *NSL Gag Orders.* Under federal law, the Federal Bureau of Investigation (FBI) can issue "national security letters" (NSLs) to internet service providers (ISPs) seeking information about customers' internet usage. *See* 18 U.S.C. §§2709 and 3511. The law also contains a provision allowing the government to impose a "gag order" that prohibits the ISP from disclosing the existence of the NSL. Such gag orders can be imposed only when a senior FBI official certifies that, absent the gag order, "there may result a danger to the national security of the United States, interference with a criminal, counterterrorism, or counterintelligence investigation, interference with diplomatic relations, or danger to the physical safety of any person." An ISP, against which a gag order has been obtained, wishes to disclose to its customers the fact that the FBI has obtained access to customer information. Are the gag orders permissible prior restraints? Should any sort of judicial review or intervention be mandated as a condition for sustaining a gag order? *See John Doe, Inc. v. Mukasey,* 549 F.3d 861 (2d Cir. 2008).

3. *Misrepresentations and Injunctions.* Suppose that representatives of an anti-abortion group, which is dedicated among other things to ending governmental funding for Planned Parenthood, gain a admittance to a National Abortion Federation convention (NAF is a pro-choice group) by misrepresenting themselves as "journalists." Once inside, they make several undercover films which they allege show "shady practices" by abortion providers. They make the films even though they signed an entrance contract that prohibited the film. The NAF seeks an injunction prohibiting distribution of the videotape, including on YouTube. Is an injunction appropriate in this context? *See National Abortion Federation v. Center for Medical Progress,* 685 Fed. Appx. 623 (9th Cir. 2018).

4. *3-D Printed Guns.* A non-profit organization, which designs firearms that can be downloaded from the internet and printed with a 3-D printer seeks to challenge a U.S. Department of State's pre-publication approval requirement for technical data published on the internet. Using 3-D printers, individuals can create fully functional, unserialized, and untraceable metal AR–15 lower receivers in a largely automated fashion. The regulation applies even though it is legal for U.S. citizens to own the weapons that would be created with the printer. The U.S. government claims that publication of the directions is prohibited under the International Traffic in Arms Regulation which seeks to prohibit the export of certain types of weapons. The government claims a vital interest in preventing foreign nationals—including all manner of enemies of this country—from obtaining technical data on how to produce weapons and weapon parts. Suppose that the non-profit seeks an injunction allowing it to publish the 3-D instructions. Should the injunction be granted? How would you weigh the governmental interest in national defense and national security against the organization's free speech rights in this context? *See Defense Distributed v. U.S. Department of State,* 838 F.3d 451 (5th Cir. 2016).

5. *Suppression Order in Comic-Con Litigation.* Plaintiff SDCC sponsors a "Comic-Con convention" in San Diego that is dedicated to comics and other popular arts and Defendant Dan Farr Productions (DFP) produces the "Salt Lake Comic Con" in Salt Lake City for the same purposes. When plaintiff SDCC filed a trademark

action against DFP, claiming that DFP's use of the term "Comic Con" infringed on SDCC's rights, DFP defended on the basis that this term is generic and descriptive. During the first three years of the litigation, DFP posted news articles and case documents on its website and on social media platforms, seeking "moral and material support from comic fans everywhere who use the term 'comic con.'" As the trial date approached, Plaintiff sought a protective order to stop DFP from making public statements about the merits of the case, arguing that the purpose of DFP's postings was to taint the jury pool. The district court granted a suppression order that prohibited DFP from posting any information or opinions about the Comic-Con litigation, including publicly available case filings. The order also required DFP to post a disclaimer "on its website, on social media sites, and in any print or broadcast advertisement or press release" describing the terms of the suppression order. What arguments can be made by DFP's attorney that the suppression order violates the First Amendment as an unconstitutional prior restraint? *See In re Dan Farr Productions*, 874 F.3d 590 (9th Cir. 2017).

6. *More on the International Treaty Regulating the Internet.* After reading the "Pentagon Papers" case, have your views on the inclusion of language regarding injunctions, and the enforceability of foreign injunctions, changed? What language would you be inclined to agree to regarding those issues?

Madsen v. Women's Health Center, Inc.

512 U.S. 753 (1994)

Chief Justice REHNQUIST delivered the opinion of the Court.

Petitioners challenge the constitutionality of an injunction entered by a Florida state court which prohibits antiabortion protestors from demonstrating in certain places and in various ways outside of a health clinic that performs abortions. We hold that the establishment of a 36-foot buffer zone on a public street from which demonstrators are excluded passes muster under the First Amendment, but that several other provisions of the injunction do not.

Respondents operate abortion clinics throughout central Florida. Petitioners and other groups and individuals are engaged in activities near the site of one such clinic in Melbourne, Florida. They picketed and demonstrated where the public street gives access to the clinic. In September 1992, a Florida state court permanently enjoined petitioners from blocking or interfering with public access to the clinic, and from physically abusing persons entering or leaving the clinic. Six months later, respondents sought to broaden the injunction, complaining that access to the clinic was still impeded by petitioners' activities and that such activities had also discouraged some potential patients from entering the clinic, and had deleterious physical effects on others. The trial court thereupon issued a broader injunction, which is challenged here.

We begin by addressing petitioners' contention that the state court's order, because it is an injunction that restricts only the speech of antiabortion protesters, is necessarily content or viewpoint based. Accordingly, they argue, we should examine the entire injunction under the strictest standard of scrutiny. We disagree. To accept petitioners' claim would be to classify virtually every injunction as content or viewpoint based. An injunction, by its very nature, applies only to a particular group (or individuals) and regulates the activities, and perhaps the speech, of that group. It does so, however, because of the group's past actions in the context of a specific dispute between real parties. The parties seeking the injunction assert a violation of their rights; the court hearing the action is charged with fashioning a remedy for a specific deprivation, not with the drafting of a statute addressed to the general public. The fact that the injunction in the present case did not prohibit activities of those demonstrating in favor of abortion is justly attributable to the lack of any similar demonstrations by those in favor of abortion, and of any consequent request that their demonstrations be regulated by injunction. There is no suggestion that Florida law would not equally restrain similar conduct directed at a target having nothing to do with abortion; none of the restrictions imposed by the court were directed at the contents of petitioner's message.

Our principal inquiry in determining content neutrality is whether the government has adopted a regulation of speech "without reference to the content of the regulated speech." *Ward v. Rock Against Racism*, 491 U.S. 781, 791 (1989); *R.A.V. v. St. Paul*, 505 U.S. 377, 386 (1992) ("The government may not regulate speech based on hostility—or favoritism—towards the underlying message expressed."). We look to the government's purpose as the threshold consideration. Here, the state court imposed restrictions on petitioners incidental to their antiabortion message because they repeatedly violated the court's original order. That petitioners all share the same viewpoint regarding abortion does not in itself demonstrate that some invidious content- or viewpoint-based purpose motivated the issuance of the order. It suggests only that those in the group whose conduct violated the court's order happen to share the same opinion regarding abortions being performed at the clinic. In short, the fact that the injunction covered people with a particular viewpoint does not itself render the injunction content or viewpoint based. Accordingly, the injunction issued in this case does not demand a level of heightened scrutiny.

If this were a content-neutral, generally applicable statute, instead of an injunctive order, its constitutionality would be assessed under the standard set forth in *Ward v. Rock Against Racism, supra*, 491 U.S. at 791. Given that the forum around the clinic is a traditional public forum, we would determine whether the time, place, and manner regulations were "narrowly tailored to serve a significant governmental interest." *Ward, supra*, 491 U.S. at 791. There are obvious differences, however, between an injunction and a generally applicable ordinance. Ordinances represent a legislative choice regarding the promotion of particular societal interests. Injunctions are remedies imposed for violations (or threatened violations) of a legislative or judicial decree. Injunctions also carry greater risks of censorship and discriminatory application than do general ordinances.

We believe that these differences require a somewhat more stringent application of general First Amendment principles in this context. In past cases evaluating injunctions restricting speech, we have relied upon such general principles while seeking to ensure that the injunction was no broader than necessary to achieve its desired goals. Our close attention to the fit between the objectives of an injunction and the restrictions it imposes on speech is consistent with the general rule, quite apart from First Amendment considerations, "that injunctive relief should be no more burdensome to the defendants than necessary to provide complete relief to the plaintiffs." *Califano v. Yamasaki,* 442 U.S. 682 (1979). When evaluating a content-neutral injunction, we think that our standard time, place, and manner analysis is not sufficiently rigorous. We must ask instead whether the challenged provisions of the injunction burden no more speech than necessary to serve a significant government interest.

We begin with the 36-foot buffer zone. The state court prohibited petitioners from "congregating, picketing, patrolling, demonstrating or entering" any portion of the public right-of-way or private property within 36 feet of the property line of the clinic as a way of ensuring access to the clinic. This speech-free buffer zone requires that petitioners move to the other side of Dixie Way and away from the driveway of the clinic, where the state court found that they repeatedly had interfered with the free access of patients and staff. The buffer zone also applies to private property to the north and west of the clinic property. We examine each portion of the buffer zone separately.

We have noted a distinction between the type of focused picketing banned from the buffer zone and the type of generally disseminated communication that cannot be completely banned in public places, such as handbilling and solicitation. Here the picketing is directed primarily at patients and staff of the clinic. The 36-foot buffer zone protecting the entrances to the clinic and the parking lot is a means of protecting unfettered ingress to and egress from the clinic, and ensuring that petitioners do not block traffic on Dixie Way. The state court seems to have had few other options to protect access given the narrow confines around the clinic. Dixie Way is only 21 feet wide in the area of the clinic. Allowing the petitioners to remain on the clinic's sidewalk and driveway was not a viable option in view of the failure of the first injunction to protect access. And allowing the petitioners to stand in the middle of Dixie Way would obviously block vehicular traffic.

The need for a complete buffer zone near the clinic entrances and driveway may be debatable, but some deference must be given to the state court's familiarity with the facts and the background of the dispute between the parties even under our heightened review. Moreover, one of petitioners' witnesses during the evidentiary hearing before the state court conceded that the buffer zone was narrow enough to place petitioners at a distance of no greater than 10 to 12 feet from cars approaching and leaving the clinic. Protesters standing across the narrow street from the clinic can still be seen and heard from the clinic parking lots. We also bear in mind the fact that the state court originally issued a much narrower injunction, providing no buffer zone, and that this order did not succeed in protecting access to the clinic. The failure of the first order to accomplish its purpose may be taken into consideration in evaluating the constitutionality of the broader order. On balance, we hold that the 36-foot buffer zone around the clinic entrances and driveway burdens no more speech than necessary to accomplish the governmental interest at stake.

The inclusion of private property on the back and side of the clinic in the 36-foot buffer zone raises different concerns. The accepted purpose of the buffer zone is to protect access to the clinic and to facilitate the orderly flow of traffic on Dixie Way. Patients and staff wishing to reach the clinic do not have to cross the private property abutting the clinic property on the north and west, and nothing indicates that petitioners' activities on the private property have obstructed access to the clinic. Nor was evidence presented that protestors located on the private property blocked vehicular traffic on Dixie Way. Absent evidence that petitioners standing on the private property have obstructed access to the clinic, blocked vehicular traffic, or otherwise unlawfully interfered with the clinic's operation, this portion of the buffer zone fails to serve the significant government interests. We hold that the 36-foot buffer zone as applied to the private property to the north and west of the clinic burdens more speech than necessary to protect access to the clinic.

In response to high noise levels outside the clinic, the state court restrained the petitioners from "singing, chanting, whistling, shouting, yelling, use of bullhorns, auto horns, sound amplification equipment or other sounds or images observable to or within earshot of the patients inside the clinic" during the hours of 7:30 a.m. through noon on Mondays through Saturdays. We must take account of the place to which the regulations apply in determining whether these restrictions burden more speech than necessary. We have upheld similar noise restrictions in the past, and as we noted in upholding a local noise ordinance around public schools, "the nature of a place, 'the pattern of its normal activities, dictate the kinds of regulations that are reasonable.'" *Grayned v. City of Rockford*, 408 U.S. 104, 116 (1972). Noise control is particularly important around hospitals and medical facilities during surgery and recovery periods. We hold that the limited noise restrictions imposed by the state court order burden no more speech than necessary to ensure the health and well-being of the patients at the clinic. The First Amendment does not demand that patients at a medical facility undertake Herculean efforts to escape the cacophony of political protests.

The same, cannot be said for the "images observable" provision of the state court's order. Clearly, threats to patients or their families, however communicated, are proscribable under the First Amendment. Rather than prohibiting the display of signs that could be interpreted as threats or veiled threats, the state court issued a blanket ban on all "images observable." This broad prohibition on all "images observable" burdens more speech than necessary to achieve the purpose of limiting threats to clinic patients or their families. If the blanket ban on "images observable" was intended to reduce the level of anxiety and hypertension suffered by the patients inside the clinic, it would still fail. The only plausible reason a patient would be bothered by "images observable" inside the clinic would be if the patient found the expression contained in such images disagreeable. But it is much easier for the clinic to pull its curtains than for a patient to stop up her ears, and no more is required to avoid seeing placards through the windows of the clinic. This provision of the injunction violates the First Amendment.

The state court ordered that petitioners refrain from physically approaching any person seeking services of the clinic "unless such person indicates a desire to communicate" in an area within 300 feet of the clinic. The state court was attempting to prevent clinic patients and staff from being "stalked" or "shadowed" by the petitioners as they approached the clinic. But it is difficult to justify a prohibition on all uninvited approaches of persons seeking the services of the clinic, regardless of how peaceful the contact may be, without burdening more speech than necessary to prevent intimidation and to ensure access to the clinic. Absent evidence that the protesters' speech is independently proscribable (i.e., "fighting words" or threats), or so infused with violence as to be indistinguishable from a threat of physical harm, this provision cannot stand. "As a general matter, in public debate our own citizens must tolerate insulting, and even outrageous, speech in order to provide adequate breathing space to the freedoms protected by the First Amendment." *Boos v. Barry*, 485 U.S. at 322. The "consent" requirement alone invalidates this provision; it burdens more speech than is necessary to prevent intimidation and to ensure access to the clinic.

The final substantive regulation relates to a prohibition against picketing, demonstrating, or using sound amplification equipment within 300 feet of the residences of clinic staff. The prohibition also covers impeding access to streets that provide the sole access to streets on which those residences are located. The same analysis applies to the use of sound amplification equipment: the government may simply demand that petitioners turn down the volume if the protests overwhelm the neighborhood.

As for the picketing, our prior decision upholding a law banning targeted residential picketing remarked on the unique nature of the home, as " 'the last citadel of the tired, the weary, and the sick.' " *Frisby*, 487 U.S. at 484. " 'The State's interest in protecting the well-being, tranquility, and privacy of the home is certainly of the highest order in a free and civilized society.' " But the 300-foot zone around the residences in this case is much larger than the zone provided for in the ordinance which we approved in *Frisby*. The ordinance there made it "unlawful for any person to engage in picketing before or about the residence or dwelling of any individual." The prohibition was limited to "focused picketing taking place solely in front of a particular residence." By contrast, the 300-foot zone would ban "general marching through residential neighborhoods, or even walking a route in front of an entire block of houses." The record does not contain sufficient justification for this broad a ban on picketing; a limitation on the time, duration of picketing, and number of pickets outside a smaller zone could have accomplished the desired result.

In sum, we uphold the noise restrictions and the 36-foot buffer zone around the clinic entrances and driveway because they burden no more speech than necessary to eliminate the unlawful conduct targeted by the state court's injunction. We strike down as unconstitutional the 36-foot buffer zone as applied to the private property to the north and west of the clinic, the "images observable" provision, the 300-foot no-approach zone around the clinic, and the 300-foot buffer zone around the residences, because these provisions sweep more broadly than necessary to accomplish the permissible goals of the injunction. Accordingly, the judgment of the Florida Supreme Court is

Affirmed in part, and reversed in part.

Justice STEVENS, *concurring in part* and *dissenting in part.*

Injunctive relief should be judged by a more lenient standard than legislation. Legislation is imposed on an entire community, regardless of individual culpability. By contrast, injunctions apply solely to an individual or a limited group of individuals who, by engaging in illegal conduct, have been judicially deprived of some liberty—the normal consequence of illegal activity. Given this distinction, a statute prohibiting demonstrations within 36 feet of an abortion clinic would probably violate the First Amendment, but an injunction directed at a limited group of persons who have engaged in unlawful conduct in a similar zone might well be constitutional.

The standard governing injunctions has two obvious dimensions. The injunction should be no more burdensome than necessary to provide complete relief. In a First Amendment context, the propriety of the remedy depends almost entirely on the character of the violation and the likelihood of its recurrence. On the other hand, even when an injunction impinges on constitutional rights, more than "a simple proscription against the precise conduct previously pursued" may be required; the remedy must include appropriate restraints on "future activities both to avoid a recurrence of the violation and to eliminate its consequences." "The judicial remedy for a proven violation of law will often include commands that the law does not impose on the community at large." *Teachers v. Hudson,* 475 U.S. 292, 309 (1986). Repeated violations may justify sanctions that might be invalid if applied to a first offender or if enacted by the legislature. In this case, the trial judge found that petitioners not only had engaged in tortious conduct, but also had repeatedly violated an earlier injunction. The injunction is thus twice removed from a legislative proscription applicable to the general public and should be judged by a standard that gives appropriate deference to the judge's unique familiarity with the facts.

Justice SCALIA, with whom Justice KENNEDY and Justice THOMAS join, *concurring in the judgment in part* and *dissenting in part.*

A restriction upon speech imposed by injunction (whether nominally content based or nominally content neutral) is at least as deserving of strict scrutiny as a statutory, content-based restriction for several reasons: The danger of content-based statutory restrictions upon speech is that they may be designed and used precisely to suppress the ideas in question rather than to achieve any other proper governmental aim. But that same danger exists with injunctions. A speech-restricting injunction lends itself to the targeted suppression of particular ideas. Targeting of one or the other side of an ideological dispute cannot readily be achieved in speech-restricting general legislation except by making content the basis of the restriction; it is achieved in speech-restricting injunctions almost invariably. The injunction in this case was sought against a single-issue advocacy group by persons and organizations with a business or social interest in suppressing that group's point of view. The second reason speech-restricting injunctions are deserving of strict scrutiny is obvious enough: they are the product of individual judges rather than of legislatures—and often of judges who have been chagrined by prior disobedience of their orders. The right to free speech should not lightly be placed within the control of a single man or woman. The third reason is that the injunction is a much more powerful weapon than a statute, and should be subjected to greater safeguards. When injunctions are enforced through contempt proceedings, only the defense of factual innocence is available. The collateral bar rule eliminates the defense that the injunction itself was unconstitutional. Persons subject to a speech-restricting injunction who have not the money or not the time to lodge an immediate appeal face a Hobson's choice: they must remain silent, since if they speak their First Amendment rights are no defense in subsequent contempt proceedings. This is good reason to require the strictest standard for issuance of such orders. Finally, the injunction in the present case was content based (indeed, viewpoint based) to boot. The Court claims that it was directed, not at those who spoke certain things (anti-abortion sentiments), but at those who did certain things (violated the earlier injunction). If that were true, then the injunction's residual coverage of "all persons acting in concert or participation with the named individuals and organizations, or on their behalf" would not include those who merely entertained the same beliefs and wished to express the same views as the named defendants. All those who wish to express the same views as the named defendants are deemed to be "acting in concert or participation." An injunction against speech is the very prototype of the greatest threat to First Amendment values, the prior restraint. We have said that a "prior restraint on expression comes to this Court with a 'heavy presumption' against its constitutional validity," and have repeatedly struck down speech-restricting injunctions.

∾ PROBLEM: PROTESTS AT MILITARY FUNERALS ∾

Would it make a difference if the *Madsen* ban had been imposed by statute rather than by injunction? The Reverend Fred Phelps and members of the Westboro Baptist Church of Topeka, Kansas, believe that the deaths of military soldiers in Iraq are a "sign" of God's wrath for America's tolerance of homosexuality. As a result, Phelps and members of his church have been traveling around the country protesting at military funerals. In response to protests in the state, the Kentucky legislature enacts the following statute on interference with funerals:

> A person is guilty of interference with a funeral when he or she at any time on any day:
>
> 1. Blocks, impedes, inhibits, or in any other manner obstructs or interferes with access into or from any building or parking lot of a building in which a funeral, wake, memorial service, or burial is being conducted, or any burial plot or the parking lot of the cemetery in which a funeral, wake, memorial service, or burial is being conducted;
>
> 2. Congregates, pickets, patrols, demonstrates, or enters on that portion of a public right-of-way or private property that is within three hundred (300) feet of an event specified in paragraph (1 of this subsection); or
>
> 3. Without authorization from the family of the deceased or person conducting the service, during a funeral, wake, memorial service, or burial: A. Sings, chants, whistles, shouts, yells, or uses a bullhorn, auto horn, sound amplification equipment, or other sounds or images observable to or within earshot of participants in the funeral, wake, memorial service, or burial; or B. Distributes literature or any other item.
>
> Interference with a funeral is a Class B misdemeanor.

In support of the legislation, Kentucky legislators made statements to the effect that "people should be allowed to attend funerals without outside stress from protesters" and "virtually every civilized society today holds sacred the right to peacefully bury their dead." Is this statute (or parts thereof) any more constitutional than the injunctive ban imposed in *Madsen*?

F. THE PRESS

In England before the modern era, the government tried to control the press by imposing licensing restrictions and by using seditious libel to criminally prosecute those who criticized the government. In the American colonies, although licensing schemes were rare, there were prosecutions for seditious libel. *See* LEONARD W. LEVY, LEGACY OF SUPPRESSION 8-17 (1960). The Framers were aware of this history when they included press protections in the First Amendment.

Despite the First Amendment, press suppression was commonplace in the postcolonial era. Early in the twentieth century, those who expressed opposition to American participation in World War I or advocated Communism were routinely prosecuted under federal espionage and state sedition laws. This was possible because the press clause was not incorporated into the Fourteenth Amendment and imposed on the states until 1931.

1. Does the Constitution Grant the Press a Privileged Position?

Some have argued that the press clause provides the press with special privileges different from those granted to the general public under the free speech clause. Justice Powell stated in a concurring opinion in *Branzburg v. Hayes*, 408 U.S. 665 (1972): "The press has a preferred position in our constitutional scheme, not to enable it to make money, not to set newsmen apart as a favored class, but to bring fulfillment to the public's right to know. The right to know is crucial to the governing powers of the people. Knowledge is essential to informed decisions." Justice Stewart agreed: "The Free Press Clause extends protection to an institution. The publishing business is, in short, the only organized private business that is given explicit constitutional protection. If the Free Press guarantee meant no more than freedom of expression, it would be a constitutional redundancy." Potter Stewart, *Or of the Press,* 26 Hastings L.J. 631 (1975).

Others believe that the press receives no special protection under the press clause. In *First National Bank of Boston v. Bellotti,* 435 U.S. 765 (1978), Chief Justice Burger stated: "The history of the Press Clause does not suggest that the authors contemplated a 'special' or 'institutional' privilege. The Speech Clause standing alone makes no fundamental distinction between expression and dissemination. The liberty encompassed by the Press Clause, although complementary to and a natural extension of Speech Clause liberty, merited special mention simply because it had been more often the object of official restraints. Soon after the invention of the printing press, English and continental monarchs, fearful of the power implicit in its use and the threat to Establishment thought and order—political and religious—devised restraints, such as licensing, censors, lists of prohibited books, and prosecutions for seditious libel, which generally were unknown in the pre–printing press era."

Note and Question: Is It Possible to Define "the Press"?

In recent years, new types of media have emerged, including (but not limited to) blogs and listservs. In addition, entirely online newspapers have emerged in certain locales. Indeed, because of economic challenges, some traditional newspapers (e.g., the *Seattle Post-Intelligencer*) have shifted from being produced as print media to being produced as digital media. Do these new forms of publication require us to alter our definition of "the press"? For example, should someone who publishes a blog on political and social issues be regarded as a member of the press? For that matter, should online newspapers be treated similarly to newspapers that are published in print form?

2. Does the Press Have Special Immunities?

Some have argued that the press is entitled to special immunities, including the right to shield their sources and their notes from disclosure in criminal proceedings.

Branzburg v. Hayes

408 U.S. 665 (1972)

Opinion of the Court by Mr. Justice WHITE, announced by THE CHIEF JUSTICE.

The issue is the obligation of reporters to respond to grand jury subpoenas as other citizens do and to answer questions relevant to an investigation into the commission of crime. Citizens generally are not constitutionally immune from grand jury subpoenas; and neither the First Amendment nor any other constitutional provision protects the average citizen from disclosing to a grand jury information that he has received in confidence. The claim is, however, that reporters are exempt from these obligations because if forced to respond to subpoenas and identify their sources or disclose other confidences, their informants will refuse to be reluctant to furnish newsworthy information in the future. This asserted burden on news gathering is said to make compelled testimony from newsmen constitutionally suspect and to require a privileged position for them.

Until now the only testimonial privilege for unofficial witnesses that is rooted in the Federal Constitution is the Fifth Amendment privilege against compelled self-incrimination. We are asked to create another by interpreting the First Amendment to grant newsmen a testimonial privilege that other citizens do not enjoy. This we decline to do. Fair and effective law enforcement aimed at providing security for the person and property of the individual is a fundamental function of government, and the grand jury plays an important, constitutionally mandated role in this process. We perceive no basis for holding that the public interest in law enforcement and in ensuring effective grand jury proceedings is insufficient to override the consequential, but uncertain, burden on news gathering said to result from insisting that reporters, like other citizens, respond to questions put to them in the course of a valid grand jury investigation or criminal trial.

This conclusion involves no restraint on what newspapers may publish or on the type or quality of information reporters may seek to acquire, nor does it threaten the vast bulk of confidential relationships between reporters and their sources. Only where news sources themselves are implicated in crime or possess information relevant to the grand jury's task need they or the reporter be concerned about grand jury subpoenas. Nothing indicates that a large percentage of *all* confidential news sources falls into either category and would in any way be deterred by our holding that the Constitution does not exempt the newsman from performing the citizen's normal duty of appearing and furnishing information relevant to the grand jury's task.

We cannot seriously entertain the notion that the First Amendment protects a newsman's agreement to conceal the criminal conduct of his source, or evidence thereof, on the theory that it is better to write about crime than to do something about it. The crimes of news sources are no less reprehensible and threatening to the public interest when witnessed by a reporter than when they are not. There remain those situations where a source is not engaged in criminal conduct but has information suggesting illegal conduct by others. Newsmen frequently receive information from such sources pursuant to a tacit or express agreement to withhold the source's name and suppress any information that the source wishes not published. Such informants presumably desire anonymity in order to avoid being entangled as a witness in a criminal trial or grand jury investigation. They may fear that disclosure will threaten their job security or personal safety or that it will simply result in dishonor or embarrassment.

The argument that the flow of news will be diminished by compelling reporters to aid the grand jury in a criminal investigation is not irrational. We remain unclear how often and to what extent informers are actually deterred from furnishing information when newsmen are forced to testify before a grand jury. The available data indicate that some newsmen rely a great deal on confidential sources and that some informants are particularly sensitive to the threat of exposure and may be silenced if it is held by this Court that, ordinarily, newsmen must testify pursuant to subpoenas, but the evidence fails to demonstrate that there would be a significant constriction of the flow of news to the public if this Court reaffirms the prior common-law and constitutional rule regarding the testimonial obligations of newsmen. Reliance by the press on confidential informants does not mean that all such sources will in fact dry up because of the later possible appearance of the newsman before a grand jury. The reporter may never be called and if he objects to testifying, the prosecution may not insist. Also, the relationship of many informants to the press is a symbiotic one which is unlikely to be greatly inhibited by the threat of subpoena: quite often, such informants are members of a minority political or cultural group that relies heavily on the media to propagate its views, publicize its aims, and magnify its exposure to the public. Moreover, grand juries characteristically conduct secret proceedings, and law enforcement officers are themselves experienced in dealing with informers, and have their own methods for protecting them without interference with the effective administration of justice. There is little before us indicating that informants whose interest in avoiding exposure is that it may threaten job security, personal safety, or peace of mind, would in fact be in a worse position, or would think they would be, if they risked placing their trust in public officials as well as reporters. We doubt if the informer who prefers anonymity but is sincerely interested in furnishing evidence of crime will always or very often be deterred by the prospect of dealing with these public authorities characteristically charged with the duty to protect the public interest as well as his.

Accepting the fact that an undetermined number of informants not themselves implicated in crime will nevertheless, for whatever reason, refuse to talk to newsmen if they fear identification by a reporter in an official investigation, we cannot accept the argument that the public interest in possible future news about crime from undisclosed, unverified sources must take precedence over the public interest in pursuing and prosecuting those crimes reported to the press by informants and in thus deterring the commission of such crimes in the future. We are admonished that refusal to provide a First Amendment reporter's privilege will undermine the freedom of the press to collect and disseminate news. But this is not the lesson history teaches us. From the beginning of our country the press has operated without constitutional protection for press informants, and the press has flourished. The existing constitutional rules have not been a serious obstacle to either the development or retention of confidential news sources by the press.

Congress and the states have freedom to determine whether a statutory newsman's privilege is necessary and desirable and to fashion standards and rules as narrow or broad as deemed necessary to deal with the evil discerned and to refashion those rules as experience from time to time may dictate. Furthermore, if what the newsmen urged in these cases is true—that law enforcement cannot hope to gain and may suffer from subpoenaing newsmen before grand juries—prosecutors will be loath to risk so much for so little. Official harassment of the press undertaken not for purposes of law enforcement but to disrupt a reporter's relationship with his news sources would have no justification. Grand juries are subject to judicial control and subpoenas to motions to quash.

Mr. Justice POWELL, *concurring*.

The Court does not hold that newsmen, subpoenaed to testify before a grand jury, are without constitutional rights with respect to the gathering of news or in safeguarding their sources. If the newsman is called upon to give information bearing only a remote and tenuous relationship to the subject of the investigation, or if he has some other reason to believe that his testimony implicates confidential source relationship without a legitimate need of law enforcement, he will have access to a motion to quash and an appropriate protective order may be entered. The asserted claim to privilege should be judged on its facts by the striking of a proper balance between freedom of the press and the obligation of all citizens to give relevant testimony with respect to criminal conduct. The courts will be available to newsmen under circumstances where legitimate First Amendment interests require protection.

Mr. Justice DOUGLAS, *dissenting*.

Today's decision will impede the wide-open and robust dissemination of ideas and counter-thought which a free press both fosters and protects and which is essential to the success of intelligent self-government. Forcing a reporter before a grand jury will have two retarding effects upon the ear and the pen of the press. Fear of exposure will cause dissidents to communicate less openly to trusted reporters. Fear of accountability will cause editors and critics to write with more restrained pens. The press has a preferred position in our constitutional scheme. A reporter is not better than his source of information. If he can be summoned to testify in secret before a grand jury, his sources will dry up and the attempted exposure, the effort to enlighten the public, will be ended. If what the Court sanctions today becomes settled law, then the reporter's main function in American society will be to pass on to the public the press releases which the departments of government issue.

Mr. Justice STEWART, with whom Mr. Justice BRENNAN and Mr. Justice MARSHALL join, *dissenting*.

The Court's crabbed view of the First Amendment reflects a disturbing insensitivity to the critical role of an independent press in our society. A corollary to the right to publish must be the right to gather news. The right to gather news implies a right to a confidential relationship between a reporter and his source. This proposition follows as a matter of simple logic once three factual predicates are recognized: (1) newsmen require informants to gather news; (2) confidentiality is essential to the creation and maintenance of a news-gathering relationship with informants; and (3) an unbridled subpoena power—the absence of a constitutional right protecting a confidential relationship from compulsory process—will either deter sources from divulging information or deter reporters from gathering and publishing information.

Notes

1. *Subpoenas and Sources.* *Branzburg* was followed by a case that arose out of the Court of Appeals for the District of Columbia. *See In Re Grand Jury Subpoena, Judith Miller,* 397 F.3d 964 (D.C. Cir. 2005). That case involved a special counsel investigation relating to leaks that outed a CIA operative. Grand jury subpoenas were issued to the *New York Times* and two of its reporters, Matthew Cooper and Judith Miller, requiring them to divulge their sources. Both refused to comply with the subpoenas. Miller was ultimately sent to jail for her refusal. Cooper escaped imprisonment when, at the eleventh hour, his source authorized disclosure.

2. *Reporter Protections.* Despite *Branzburg,* some courts have used the First Amendment to protect reporters from compelled disclosure of sources. *See, e.g., Silkwood v. Kerr-McGee Corp.,* 563 F.2d 433, 437 (10th Cir. 1977). In addition, federal and some state laws protect reporters legislatively. *See* 42 U.S.C. §2000aa:

§2000aa. Searches and Seizures by Government Officers and Employees in Connection with Investigation or Prosecution of Criminal Offenses

(a) Work product materials

Notwithstanding any other law, it shall be unlawful for a government officer or employee, in connection with the investigation or prosecution of a criminal offense, to search for or seize any work product materials possessed by a person reasonably believed to have a purpose to disseminate to the public a newspaper, book, broadcast, or other similar form of public communication, in or affecting interstate or foreign commerce; but this provision shall not impair or affect the ability of any government officer or employee, pursuant to otherwise applicable law, to search for or seize such materials, if (1) there is probable cause to believe that the person possessing such materials has committed or is committing the criminal offense to which the materials relate; or (2) there is reason to believe that the immediate seizure of such materials is necessary to prevent the death of, or serious bodily injury to, a human being.

The Act contains another provision regarding "documentary materials, other than work product materials, possessed by a person in connection with a purpose to disseminate to the public a newspaper, book, broadcast, or other similar form of public communication, in or affecting interstate or foreign commerce." The Act also creates a civil action on behalf of those whose rights under the Act are violated.

3. *Search Warrants.* In *Zurcher v. Stanford Daily*, 436 U.S. 547 (1978), after a demonstration at Stanford University during which police officers were attacked, the *Stanford Daily* published articles and photographs about the incident. Afterward, the police sought and obtained a warrant authorizing them to search the *Daily*'s offices for negatives, film, and pictures showing the events and occurrences. The ensuring search extended to the *Daily*'s photographic laboratories, filing cabinets, desks, and wastepaper baskets. The officers read notes and correspondence during the search. The *Daily*, and various members of its staff, sought declaratory and injunctive relief against further such invasions. The Court held that injunctive relief was inappropriate:

> The Framers took the enormously important step of subjecting searches to the test of reasonableness and to the general rule requiring search warrants issued by neutral magistrates. They did not forbid warrants where the press was involved, did not require special showings that subpoenas would be impractical, and did not insist that the owner of the place to be searched, if connected with the press, must be shown to be implicated in the offense being investigated. Our cases do no more than insist that the courts apply the warrant requirements with particular exactitude when First Amendment interests would be endangered by the search. Properly administered, the preconditions for a warrant—probable cause, specificity with respect to the place to be searched and the things to be seized, and overall reasonableness—should afford sufficient protection against the harms that are assertedly threatened by warrants for searching newspaper offices.

Justice Stewart dissented: "Police searches of newspaper offices burden the freedom of the press. The most immediate and obvious First Amendment injury caused by such a visitation by the police is physical disruption of the operation of the newspaper. But there is another and more serious burden on a free press imposed by an unannounced police search of a newspaper office: the possibility of disclosure of information received from confidential sources, or of the identity of the sources themselves. A search warrant allows police officers to ransack the files of a newspaper, reading each and every document until they have found the one named in the warrant. The knowledge that police officers can make an unannounced raid on a newsroom is thus bound to have a deterrent effect on the availability of confidential news sources. The end result will be a diminishing flow of potentially important information to the public."

The Ninth Circuit Court of Appeals, in *Lacey v. Maricopa County*, 649 F.3d 1118 (9th Cir. 2011), considered whether the late-night arrest of two newspaper executives was substantially designed to deter the exercise of their First Amendment rights. The arrests took place following publication of an article highly critical of county officials, including the county attorney, sheriff, and special prosecutor (each of whom allegedly had a role in the arrests). Although many of the alleged actions were protected by absolute or qualified immunity, the court of appeals allowed claims to proceed against the special prosecutor. It noted that "to demonstrate a First Amendment violation, Plaintiffs must provide evidence showing that by his actions the special prosecutor deterred or chilled Plaintiffs' political speech and such deterrence was a substantial or motivating factor in the special prosecutor's conduct." In making this proof, the Court of Appeals indicated that the plaintiffs need not show their "speech was actually inhibited or suppressed." Instead, it was necessary to demonstrate only "that defendants intended to interfere with Plaintiffs' First Amendment rights." The court of appeals further observed, citing *Branzburg v. Hayes*, that "this chilling effect is especially apparent when investigative activities are alleged to have been carried out in bad faith leading to the arrest and detention of the targets, as is alleged here."

4. *Disseminating Discovery. Seattle Times Co. v. Rhinehart*, 467 U.S. 20 (1984), involved the question of whether the parties to civil litigation have a First Amendment right to disseminate information gained through the pretrial discovery process. The Court answered the question in the negative even though the information pertained to a public figure: "A litigant has no First Amendment right of access to information made available only for purposes of trying his suit. Continued court control over the discovered information does not raise the same specter of government censorship that such control might suggest in other situations. Restraints placed on discovered, but not yet admitted, information are not a restriction on a traditionally public source of information. Rule 26(c) furthers a substantial governmental interest unrelated to the suppression of expression."

5. *Breach of Confidentiality Suits.* In *Cohen v. Cowles Media Co.,* 501 U.S. 663 (1991), a newspaper reporter promised a source confidentiality in exchange for information, but subsequently breached that promise and revealed the name of the source. When the source sued, seeking damages for promissory estoppel, the reporter asserted the First Amendment as a shield against liability (on the theory that he had truthfully reported on matters of public interest). In *Cohen,* the Court held that the reporter could be held liable, noting that the action for promissory estoppel is applicable to all of society, and there is no exemption for reporters.

∾ PROBLEM: MORE ON THE INTERNATIONAL TREATY REGULATING THE INTERNET ∾

At the convention, questions arise regarding whether reporters should be allowed to shield their sources from disclosure. Under the First Amendment, can you agree to shield them from disclosure? Should you? What impact would a treaty provision (shielding reporters' sources from disclosure) have on state or federal court criminal proceedings where disclosure of sources is sought?

3. Press Access

The Court has rendered a number of decisions on press access. In *Gannett, Inc. v. DePasquale*, 443 U.S. 363 (1979), the Court upheld a district court order closing pretrial proceedings on the basis that the Sixth Amendment right to a public trial is personal to the defendant and may not be asserted by anyone else. In *Richmond Newspapers, Inc. v. Virginia*, 448 U.S. 555 (1980), the Court held that open trials provide an important check on official misconduct, and access to the judicial process is necessary if the public is to be informed and educated. Finally, in *Waller v. Georgia*, 467 U.S. 39 (1984), the Court held that a trial court could not close a hearing over the defendant's objections. On the contrary, closure is appropriate only when there is an overriding interest, a narrowly tailored order, and an exhaustion of less burdensome alternatives.

Globe Newspaper Co. v. Superior Court

457 U.S. 596 (1982)

Justice BRENNAN delivered the opinion of the Court.

Section 16A of Chapter 278 of the Massachusetts General Laws, as construed by the Massachusetts Supreme Judicial Court, requires trial judges, at trials for specific sexual offenses involving a victim under the age of 18, to exclude the press and general public from the courtroom during the testimony of that victim. The question presented is whether the statute thus construed violates the First Amendment as applied to the States through the Fourteenth Amendment.

The Court's recent decision in *Richmond Newspapers, Inc. v. Virginia*, 448 U.S. 555 (1980), firmly established for the first time that the press and general public have a constitutional right of access to criminal trials. This right of access is not explicitly mentioned in terms in the First Amendment. But we have long eschewed any "narrow, literal conception" of the Amendment's terms, for the Framers were concerned with broad principles, and wrote against a background of shared values and practices. The First Amendment is thus broad enough to encompass those rights that, while not unambiguously enumerated in the very terms of the Amendment, are nonetheless necessary to the enjoyment of other First Amendment rights. To the extent that the First Amendment embraces a right of access to criminal trials, it is to ensure that this constitutionally protected "discussion of governmental affairs" is an informed one.

Two features of the criminal justice system, emphasized in the various opinions in *Richmond Newspapers*, together serve to explain why a right of access is properly afforded protection by the First Amendment. First, the criminal trial historically has been open to the press and general public. "At the time when our organic laws were adopted, criminal trials both here and in England had long been presumptively open." *Richmond Newspapers, Inc. v. Virginia*, 448 U.S. 555 (1980) (plurality opinion). And since that time, the presumption of openness has remained secure. Indeed, at the time of this Court's decision *In re Oliver*, 333 U.S.

257 (1948), the presumption was so solidly grounded that the Court was "unable to find a single instance of a criminal trial conducted in camera in any federal, state, or municipal court during the history of this country." This uniform rule of openness has been viewed as significant in constitutional terms not only "because the Constitution carries the gloss of history," but also because "a tradition of accessibility implies the favorable judgment of experience."

Second, the right of access to criminal trials plays a particularly significant role in the functioning of the judicial process and the government as a whole. Public scrutiny of a criminal trial enhances the quality and safeguards the integrity of the factfinding process, with benefits to both the defendant and to society as a whole. Moreover, public access to the criminal trial fosters an appearance of fairness, thereby heightening public respect for the judicial process. And in the broadest terms, public access to criminal trials permits the public to participate in and serve as a check upon the judicial process — an essential component in our structure of self-government. In sum, the institutional value of the open criminal trial is recognized in both logic and experience.

Although the right of access to criminal trials is of constitutional stature, it is not absolute. But the circumstances under which the press and public can be barred from a criminal trail are limited; the State's justification in denying access must be a weighty one. Where the State attempts to deny the right of access in order to inhibit the disclosure of sensitive information, it must be shown that the denial is necessitated by a compelling governmental interest, and is narrowly tailored to serve that interest.

The state interests asserted to support §16A, though articulated in various ways, are reducible to two: the protection of minor victims of sex crimes from further trauma and embarrassment; and the encouragement of such victims to come forward and testify in a truthful and credible manner. We consider these interests in turn.

We agree with appellee that the first interest — safeguarding the physical and psychological well-being of a minor — is a compelling one. But as compelling as that interest is, it does not justify a mandatory closure rule, for it is clear that the circumstances of the particular case may affect the significance of the interest. A trial court can determine on a case-by-case basis whether closure is necessary to protect the welfare of a minor victim. Among the factors to be weighed are the minor victim's age, psychological maturity and understanding, the nature of the crime, the desires of the victim, and the interests of parents and relatives. Section 16A, in contrast, requires closure even if the victim does not seek the exclusion of the press and general public and would not suffer injury by their presence.

Nor can §16A be justified on the basis of the Commonwealth's second asserted interest — the encouragement of minor victims of sex crimes to come forward and provide accurate testimony. The Commonwealth has offered no empirical support for the claim that the rule of automatic closure contained in §16A bars the press and general public from the courtroom during the testimony of minor sex victims, the press is not denied access to the transcript, court personnel, or another possible source that could provide an account of the minor victim's testimony. Thus §16A cannot prevent the press from publicizing the substance of a minor victim's testimony, as well as his or her identity. If the commonwealth's interest in encouraging minor victims to come forward depends on keeping such matters secret, §16A hardly advances that interest in an effective manner. And even if §16A effectively advanced the State's interest, it is doubtful that the interest would be sufficient to overcome the constitutional attack, for that same interest could be relied on to support an array of mandatory closure rules designed to encourage victims to come forward: Surely it cannot be suggested that minor victims of sex crimes are the only crime victims who, because of publicity attendant to criminal trials, are reluctant to come forward and testify. The State's argument based on this interest therefore proves too much, and runs contrary to the very foundation of the right of access recognized in *Richmond Newspapers*: namely, "that a presumption of openness inheres in the very nature of a criminal trial under our system of justice" (plurality opinion).

For the foregoing reasons, we hold that §16A, as construed by the Massachusetts Supreme Judicial Court, violates the First Amendment to the Constitution. Accordingly, the judgment of the Massachusetts Supreme Judicial Court is

Reversed.

Chief Justice BURGER, with whom Justice REHNQUIST joins, *dissenting.*

Historically our society has gone to great lengths to protect minors charged with crime, particularly by prohibiting the release of the names of offenders, barring the press and public from juvenile proceedings, and sealing the records of those proceedings. Yet today the Court holds unconstitutional a state statute designed to protect not the accused, but the minor victims of sex crimes. The Court has tried to make its holding a narrow one by not disturbing the authority of state legislatures to enact more narrowly drawn statutes giving trial judges the discretion to exclude the public and the press from the courtroom during the minor victim's testimony.

I do not read the Court's opinion as foreclosing a state statute which mandates closure except in cases where the victim agrees to testify in open court. But the Court's decision is nevertheless a gross invasion of state authority and a state's duty to protect its citizens—in this case minor victims of crime. A First Amendment right of access to proceedings other than trials hinges upon considerations of tradition and exigencies. Determinative factors are whether a given jurisdiction's proceedings historically have been open or closed, particularized findings have been made that the defendant's right to a fair trial would be prejudiced and reasonable alternatives exist to closure.

Notes and Questions

1. *Defendant's Motion to Exclude the Press.* In *Press-Enterprise Co. v. Superior Court,* 478 U.S. 1 (1986), a preliminary hearing was held at which Robert Diaz, a nurse,

was charged with murdering 12 patients. Diaz moved to exclude the public from the proceedings in order to protect his "right to a fair and impartial trial." The court granted the motion, finding that closure was necessary because the case had attracted national publicity and "only one side may get reported in the media." At the conclusion of the hearing, petitioner Press-Enterprise Company asked that the transcript of the proceedings be released. The magistrate refused and sealed the record, noting "a reasonable likelihood that release of all or any part of the transcripts might prejudice defendant's right to a fair and impartial trial." The Court disagreed, holding that even though "the defendant has a right to a fair trial," "one of the important means of assuring a fair trial is that the process be open to neutral observers." The Court went on to note that the "right to an open public trial is a shared right of the accused and the public, the common concern being the assurance of fairness." The Court extended this right to preliminary hearings.

2. *Cameras in the Courtroom.* As of the mid-1990s, 47 states allowed cameras in their courtrooms. Increased use of technology is driven by technological advances that diminish the intrusiveness of cameras and other recording devices.

3. *Telephone Live Streaming.* Because of the coronavirus pandemic, which required closure of the Supreme Court building, for the first time, the Court heard oral arguments by telephone and allowed the audio to be streamed online and on C-Span. Nina Totenberg, *Supreme Court Arguments Resume, But with a Twist*, NPR, May 4, 2020, https://www.npr.org/2020/05/04/847785015/supreme-court-arguments-resume-but-with-a-twist

4. *Overcoming the Right to Press Access.* In numerous cases, although the Court has recognized that the press has a right of access to trials and preliminary hearings, the Court has held that the right of access is not absolute. What circumstances might encourage a court to close a proceeding? Should it matter that both the prosecution and the defense prefer that a proceeding be closed?

5. *Televising Trials.* Over the defendant's objection, a trial court decided to permit radio, television, and still photographic coverage of a criminal trial for public broadcast. Before the Court, the defendant argued that "the televising of criminal trials is inherently a denial of due process" because there is a risk that television coverage will "adversely affect the conduct of the participants and the fairness of the trial." In *Chandler v. Florida*, 449 U.S. 560 (1981), the Court held that the burden is on the defendant to demonstrate that the presence of cameras actually prejudiced a jury's ability to perform its function fairly and effectively.

6. *Press Access to News Conferences.* In recent years, there has been much controversy about the fact that politicians have refused to admit certain reporters to their news conferences. President Trump, for one, has excluded reporters from news organizations which have been critical of him (e.g., The New York Times, BuzzFeed News, CNN, The Los Angeles Times, Politico, the BBC and the Huffington Post). However, other politicians have engaged in similar conduct. For example, a Democratic candidate excluded a reporter from the conservative publication, the Washington Free Beacon, and a Republican candidate excluded a reporter from the liberal website, ThinkProgress. Should there be a right of

access to press briefings? Can politicians limit such events to "invitees only?" More to the point, may public officials discriminate on the basis of viewpoint in terms of the reporters to whom they give access? *See* Luke M. Milligan, *Rethinking Press Rights of Equal Access*, 65 WASH. & LEE L. REV. 1103 (2008). Is it permissible for the President to give an "exclusive interview" to a favorable news outlet? Would the selective exclusion of reporters from news briefings be permissible when only a limited number of spaces are available, and when the politician (in particular, the President) is simply trying to open up such events to news organizations that have historically been excluded from such press conferences, and is willing to include all news organization on a rotating basis? *See Sherrill v. Knight*, 569 F.2d 124 (D.C. Cir. 1977).

∾ PROBLEMS: PROTECTING JURORS ∾

1. *Prohibiting Juror Interviews.* A judge enters an order prohibiting the media from interviewing jurors about their deliberations. The order is to be effective even after the jury is released, but the press is allowed to interview jurors about their votes as well as about other matters. The court justifies the order on the following grounds: "This is a long contentious high-profile criminal case involving well-known defendants of power and influence. Indeed, the witnesses include an archbishop and a former governor. Cases like this do not even remotely resemble the everyday civil or criminal trial in terms of the stress and anxiety inflicted upon those asked to serve as jurors. In such cases, it is particularly important for jurors to be secure in the knowledge that the play-by-play of their thought processes during deliberations will not be in the newspaper once the trial is over, in order for them to deliberate frankly and honestly, without fear of later public embarrassment, harassment or retaliation." If a newspaper challenges the order as an infringement of its First Amendment rights, claiming that the public is entitled to understand the basis for the jury's decision, and that it is inappropriate to protect jury deliberations after the trial has ended, is the gag order valid?

2. *Anonymous Juror Pools.* Regardless of what you decided in the preceding problem, suppose that, in a case of great local public interest—involving criminal allegations that a former county coroner used his office for private gain—the judge orders that the jury be anonymously seated. In other words, jury selection will be conducted by written questionnaires that do not contain the juror's names or identifying information. Is the press entitled to discover the names of jurors seated for a criminal trial? What justifications might be offered in support of the judge's decision to seat an anonymous jury? What counterarguments would you make if you were asked to represent a local newspaper that sought to obtain the jurors' names? *See United States v. Wecht*, 537 F.3d 222 (3d Cir. 2007).

4. Access to Prisons

The press has also sought access to prisons in an effort to report on prison conditions. *Pell v. Procunier*, 417 U.S. 817 (1974), involved a California prison regulation providing that "press and other media interviews with specific individual inmates will not be permitted." The regulation was challenged by members of the media who had requested permission to speak with specific inmates and been denied permission. They claimed that the regulation infringed the freedom of the press guaranteed by the First and Fourteenth Amendments. The Court upheld the regulation:

> "Lawful incarceration brings about the necessary withdrawal or limitation of many privileges and rights, a retraction justified by the considerations underlying our penal system." In the First Amendment context a corollary of this principle is that a prison inmate retains those First Amendment rights that are not inconsistent with his status as a prisoner or with the legitimate penological objectives of the corrections system. An important function of the corrections system is the deterrence of crime. The premise is that by confining criminal offenders in a facility where they are isolated from the rest of society, a condition that most people presumably find undesirable, they and others will be deterred from committing additional criminal offenses. Since most offenders will eventually return to society, another paramount objective of the corrections system is the rehabilitation of those committed to its custody. Finally, central to all other corrections goals is the institutional consideration of internal security within the corrections facilities themselves.
>
> We think that the regulation cannot be considered in isolation but must be viewed in the light of the alternative means of communication permitted under the regulations with persons outside the prison. One such alternative available to California prison inmates is communication by mail. In *Procunier v. Martinez*, 416 U.S. 396, 416 (1974), we held that "the interests of prisoners and their correspondents in uncensored communication by letter, grounded as it is in the First Amendment, is plainly a 'liberty' interest within the meaning of the Fourteenth Amendment even though qualified of necessity by the circumstance of imprisonment." Moreover, inmates are permitted to receive limited visits from members of their families, the clergy, their attorneys, and friends of prior acquaintance. More importantly, however, inmates have an unrestricted opportunity to communicate with the press or any other member of the public through their families, friends, clergy, or attorneys who are permitted to visit them at the prison. This provides another alternative avenue of communication.

The Court also rejected arguments that the regulation violated the freedom of the press, noting that the regulation is "not part of an attempt by the State to conceal the conditions in its prisons or to frustrate the press' investigation and reporting of those conditions." On the contrary, "both the press and the general public are accorded full opportunities to observe prison conditions" and to stop and speak with inmates. The Court also cited other means of access. "The sole limitation on newsgathering in California prisons is the prohibition in §415.071 of interviews with individual inmates specifically designated by representatives of the press." The Court expressed concern that the prior practice of designating specific inmates "had resulted in press attention being concentrated on a relatively small number of inmates who, as a result, became virtual 'public figures' within the prison society and gained a disproportionate degree of notoriety and influence among their fellow inmates. Because of this notoriety and influence, these inmates often became the source of severe disciplinary problems."

Justice Douglas dissented, arguing that "the State's interest in order and prison discipline cannot justify its total ban on all media interviews with any individually designated inmate on any matter whatsoever. Prisons, like all other public institutions, are ultimately the responsibility of the populace. The public's interest in being informed about prisons is thus paramount. As with the prisoners' free speech claim, no one asserts that the free press right is such that the authorities are powerless to impose reasonable regulations as to the time, place, and manner of interviews to effectuate prison discipline and order. The only issue here is whether the complete ban on interviews with inmates selected by the press goes beyond what is necessary for the protection of these interests and infringes upon our cherished right of a free press."

Pell was reinforced by the holding in *Houchins v. KQED, Inc.*, 438 U.S. 1 (1978). In *Houchins*, a radio and television broadcasting company sought access to a county jail to interview inmates and make sound recordings, films, and photographs for publication and broadcasting by newspapers, radio, and television. The request came following the suicide of a prisoner in the Greystone section of the Santa Rita jail. The report included a statement by a psychiatrist that the conditions at the Greystone facility were responsible for the illnesses of his patient-prisoners there, and a statement from the director denying that prison conditions were responsible for the prisoners' illnesses. After the company filed suit, the prison announced a program of regular public tours in which the press was allowed to participate. One of the respondent's reporters participated in the first tour, but the tour did not include the disciplinary cells or the portions of the jail known as "Little Greystone," the scene of alleged rapes, beatings, and adverse physical conditions. Photographs of some parts of the jail were made available, but no cameras or tape recorders were allowed on the tours. Those on the tours were not permitted to interview inmates, and inmates were generally removed from view.

Notwithstanding the holding in *Pell*, respondents asserted that they had a constitutionally guaranteed right to gather news, which included an implied special right of access to government-controlled sources of information. The respondents contended that public access to penal institutions was necessary to prevent officials from concealing prison conditions from the voters and impairing the public's right to discuss and criticize the prison system and its administration. In a plurality opinion, with two justices not participating in the case at all, the Court rejected these arguments:

> Conditions in jails and prisons are matters "of great public importance." The role of the media is important; acting as the "eyes and ears" of the public, they can be a powerful and constructive force, contributing to remedial action in the conduct of public business. But like all other components of our society media representatives are subject to limits. The issue is a claimed special privilege of access which the Court rejected in *Pell* and *Saxbe*, a right which is

not essential to guarantee the freedom to communicate or publish. A number of alternatives are available to prevent problems in penal facilities from escaping public attention. Citizen task forces and prison visitation committees play an important role in keeping the public informed on deficiencies of prison systems and need for reforms. Grand juries, with the potent subpoena power—not available to the media—traditionally concern themselves with conditions in public institutions; a prosecutor or judge may initiate similar inquiries, and the legislative power embraces an arsenal of weapons for inquiry relating to tax-supported institutions. These public bodies are generally compelled to publish their findings and, if they default, the power of the media is always available to generate public pressure for disclosure. But the choice as to the most effective and appropriate method is a policy decision to be resolved by legislative decision.

Petitioner cannot prevent respondents from learning about jail conditions in a variety of ways, albeit not as conveniently as they might prefer. Respondents have a First Amendment right to receive letters from inmates criticizing jail officials and reporting on conditions. Respondents are free to interview those who render the legal assistance to which inmates are entitled. They are also free to seek out former inmates, visitors to the prison, public officials, and institutional personnel, as they sought out the complaining psychiatrist here. Moreover, California statutes provide for a prison Board of Corrections that has the authority to inspect jails and prisons and must provide a public report at regular intervals. Health inspectors are required to inspect prisons and provide reports to a number of officials, including the State Attorney General and the Board of Corrections. Fire officials are also required to inspect prisons. Following the reports of the suicide at the jail involved here, the County Board of Supervisors called for a report from the County Administrator; held a public hearing on the report, which was open to the media; and called for further reports when the initial report failed to describe the conditions in the cells in the Greystone portion of the jail.

Justice Stewart *concurred:*

That the First Amendment speaks separately of freedom of speech and freedom of the press is no constitutional accident, but an acknowledgment of the critical role played by the press in American society. The Constitution requires sensitivity to that role, and to the special needs of the press in performing it effectively. Terms of access that are reasonably imposed on individual members of the public may, if they impede effective reporting without sufficient justification, be unreasonable as applied to journalists who are there to convey to the general public what the visitors see. Under these principles, KQED was clearly entitled to some form of preliminary injunctive relief.

Justice Stevens, joined by Justices Brennan and Powell, *dissented:*

The First Amendment serves an essential societal function. Our system of self-government assumes the existence of an informed citizenry. Without some protection for the acquisition of information about the operation of public institutions such as prisons by the public at large, the process of self-governance contemplated by the Framers would be stripped of its substance. While prison officials have an interest in the time and manner of public acquisition of information about the institutions they administer, there is no legitimate penological justification for concealing from citizens the conditions in which their fellow citizens are being confined.

The reasons which militate in favor of providing special protection to the flow of information to the public about prisons relate to the unique function they perform in a democratic society. Not only are they public institutions, financed with public funds and administered by public servants, they are an integral component of the criminal justice system. The public interest survives the judgment of conviction and appropriately carries over to an interest in how the convicted person is treated during his period of punishment and hoped-for rehabilitation. Some inmates are pretrial detainees. Society has a special interest in ensuring that unconvicted citizens are treated in accord with their status. Both the public and the press had been consistently denied any access to the inner portions of the Santa Rita jail, and there had been excessive censorship of inmate correspondence. An official prison policy of concealing such knowledge from the public by arbitrarily cutting off the flow of information at its source abridges the freedom of speech and of the press protected by the First and Fourteenth Amendments to the Constitution.

In *Beard v. Banks*, 548 U.S. 521 (2006), the Court upheld a prison policy that denied newspapers, magazines, and photographs to a group of especially dangerous and recalcitrant inmates. Relying on *Overton v. Bazzetta*, 539 U. S. 126 (2003), which held that the courts must show deference to prison officials, the Court upheld the restriction as applied to inmates who "exhibit behavior that is continually disruptive, violent, dangerous or a threat to the orderly operation of their assigned facility."

5. The Press and Due Process

As the foregoing discussion reveals, the courts have usually given the press easy access to judicial proceedings. But press access does not come without cost, and there is always the risk that a criminal defendant's right to a fair trial will be endangered by excessive press coverage. When a trial has a sensational element, the press is likely to provide significant and at times excessive coverage.

Sheppard v. Maxwell

384 U.S. 333 (1966)

Mr. Justice CLARK delivered the opinion of the Court.

Petitioner's pregnant wife was bludgeoned to death in the upstairs bedroom of their lakeshore home in Bay Village, Ohio, a suburb of Cleveland. On the day of the tragedy, Sheppard pieced together for several local officials the following story: after dinner Sheppard became drowsy and dozed off to sleep on a couch. The next thing he remembered was hearing his wife cry out in the early morning hours. He hurried upstairs and in the dim light from the hall saw a "form" standing next to his wife's bed. As he struggled with the "form" he was struck on the back of the neck and rendered unconscious.

From the outset officials focused suspicion on Sheppard. After a search of the house and premises on the morning of the tragedy, the Coroner is reported to have told his men, "Well, it is evident the doctor did this, so let's go get the confession out of him." The press opened fire with a front-page charge that some-body is "getting away with murder." The newspapers emphasized evidence that tended to incriminate Sheppard and pointed out discrepancies in his statements to authorities. At the same time, Sheppard made many public statements to the press and wrote feature articles asserting his innocence.

The case came on for trial two weeks before the November general election at which the chief prosecutor was a candidate for common pleas judge and the trial judge was a candidate to succeed himself. Twenty-five days before the case was set, 75 veniremen were called as prospective jurors. All three Cleveland news-papers published the names and addresses of the veniremen. Anonymous letters and telephone calls, as well as calls from friends, regarding the impending pros-ecution were received by all of the prospective jurors. The selection of the jury began on October 18, 1954.

The courtroom in which the trial was held measured 26 by 48 feet. A long temporary table was set up inside the bar, in back of the single counsel table. It ran the width of the courtroom, parallel to the bar railing, with one end less than three feet from the jury box. Approximately 20 representatives of newspapers and wire services were assigned seats at this table by the court. Behind the bar railing there were four rows of benches. These seats were likewise assigned by the court for the entire trial. The first row was occupied by representatives of television and radio stations, and the second and third rows by reporters from out-of-town newspapers and magazines. One side of the last row, which accommodated 14 people, was assigned to Sheppard's family and the other to Marilyn's. The public was permitted to fill vacancies in this row on special passes only. Representatives of the news media also used all the rooms on the courtroom floor, including the room where cases were ordinarily called and assigned for trial. Private telephone lines and telegraphic equipment were installed in these rooms so that reports from the trial could be speeded to the papers. Station WSRS was permitted to set up broadcasting facilities on the third floor of the courthouse next door to the jury room, where the jury rested during recesses in the trial and deliberated. Newscasts were made from this room throughout the trial, and while the jury reached its verdict.

On the sidewalk and steps in front of the courthouse, television and news-reel cameras were occasionally used to take motion pictures of the participants in the trial, including the jury and the judge. Indeed, one television broadcast carried a staged interview of the judge as he entered the courthouse. In the cor-ridors outside the courtroom there was a host of photographers and television personnel with flash cameras, portable lights and motion picture cameras. This group photographed the prospective jurors during selection of the jury. After the trial opened, the witnesses, counsel, and jurors were photographed and televised whenever they entered or left the courtroom. Sheppard was brought to the court-room about 10 minutes before each session began; he was surrounded by report-ers and extensively photographed for the newspapers and television. A rule of court prohibited picture-taking in the courtroom during the actual sessions of the court, but no restraints were put on photographers during recesses, which were taken once each morning and afternoon, with a longer period for lunch.

All of these arrangements with the news media and their massive coverage of the trial continued during the entire nine weeks of the trial. The courtroom remained crowded to capacity with representatives of news media. Their movement in and out of the courtroom often caused so much confusion that, despite the loud-speaker system installed in the courtroom, it was difficult for the witnesses and counsel to be heard. Furthermore, the reporters clustered within the bar of the small courtroom made confidential talk among Sheppard and his counsel almost impossible during the proceedings. They frequently had to leave the courtroom to obtain privacy. And many times when counsel wished to raise a point with the judge out of the hearing of the jury it was necessary to move to the judge's chambers. Even then, news media representatives so packed the judge's anteroom that counsel could hardly return from the chambers to the courtroom. The reporters vied with each other to find out what counsel and the judge had discussed, and often these matters later appeared in newspapers accessible to the jury.

The daily record of the proceedings was made available to the newspapers and the testimony of each witness was printed verbatim in the local editions, along with objections of counsel, and rulings by the judge. Pictures of Sheppard, the judge, counsel, pertinent witnesses, and the jury often accompanied the daily newspaper and television accounts. At times the newspapers published photographs of exhibits introduced at the trial, and the rooms of Sheppard's house were featured along with relevant testimony.

The jurors themselves were constantly exposed to the news media. Every juror, except one, testified at *voir dire* to reading about the case in the Cleveland papers or to having heard broadcasts about it. Seven of the 12 jurors who rendered the verdict had one or more Cleveland papers delivered in their home; the remaining jurors were not interrogated on the point. Nor were there questions as to radios or television sets in the jurors' homes, but we must assume that most of them owned such conveniences. As the selection of the jury progressed, individual pictures of prospective members appeared daily. During the trial, pictures of the jury appeared over 40 times in the Cleveland papers alone. The court permitted photographers to take pictures of the jury in the box, and individual pictures of the members in the jury room. One newspaper ran pictures of the jurors at the Sheppard home when they went there to view the scene of the murder. Another paper featured the home life of an alternate juror. The day before the verdict was rendered—while the jurors were at lunch and sequestered by two bailiffs—the jury was separated into two groups to pose for photographs which appeared in the newspapers.

The principle that justice cannot survive behind walls of silence has long been reflected in the "Anglo-American distrust for secret trials." A responsible press has always been regarded as the handmaiden of effective judicial administration, especially in the criminal field. Its function in this regard is documented by an impressive record of service over several centuries. The press does not simply publish information about trials but guards against the miscarriage of justice by subjecting the police, prosecutors, and judicial processes to extensive public scrutiny and criticism. This Court has, therefore, been unwilling to place any direct limitations on the freedom traditionally exercised by the news media for "what transpires in the court room is public property." The "unqualified prohibitions laid down by the framers were intended to give to liberty of the press the broadest scope that could be countenanced in an orderly society." And where there was "no threat or menace to the integrity of the trial," we have consistently required that the press have a free hand, even though we sometimes deplored its sensationalism.

But the Court has also pointed out that "legal trials are not like elections, to be won through the use of the meeting-hall, the radio, and the newspaper." And the Court has insisted that no one be punished for a crime without "a charge fairly made and fairly tried in a public tribunal free of prejudice, passion, excitement, and tyrannical power." "Freedom of discussion should be given the widest range compatible with the essential requirement of the fair and orderly administration of justice." But it must not be allowed to divert the trial from the "very purpose of a court system to adjudicate controversies, both criminal and civil, in the calmness and solemnity of the courtroom according to legal procedures." Among these "legal procedures" is the requirement that the jury's verdict be based on evidence received in open court, not from outside sources.

Sheppard was not granted a change of venue to a locale away from where the publicity originated; nor was his jury sequestered. On the contrary, the Sheppard jurors were subjected to newspaper, radio and television coverage of the trial while not taking part in the proceedings. They were allowed to go their separate ways outside of the courtroom, without adequate directions not to read or listen to anything concerning the case. The judge's "admonitions" at the beginning of the trial are representative: "I would suggest to you and caution you that you do not read any newspapers during the progress of this trial, that you do not listen to radio comments nor watch or listen to television comments, insofar as this case is concerned. You will feel very much better as the trial proceeds. I am sure that we shall all feel very much better if we do not indulge in any newspaper reading or listening to any comments whatever about the matter while the case is in progress. After it is all over, you can read it all to your heart's content." At intervals during the trial, the judge simply repeated his "suggestions" and "requests" that the jurors not expose themselves to comment upon the case. Moreover, the jurors were thrust into the role of celebrities by the judge's failure to insulate them from reporters and photographers. The numerous pictures of the jurors, with their addresses, which appeared in the newspapers before and during the trial exposed them to expressions of opinion from both cranks and friends. The fact that anonymous letters had been received by prospective jurors should have made the judge aware that this publicity seriously threatened the jurors' privacy.

Sheppard stood indicted for the murder of his wife; the State was demanding the death penalty. For months the virulent publicity about Sheppard and the murder had made the case notorious. Charges and countercharges were aired in the news media besides those for which Sheppard was called to trial.

While we cannot say that Sheppard was denied due process by the judge's refusal to take precautions against the influence of pretrial publicity alone, the court's later rulings must be considered against the setting in which the trial was held. In light of this background, we believe that the arrangements made by the judge with the news media caused Sheppard to be deprived of that "judicial serenity and calm to which he was entitled." The fact is that bedlam reigned at the courthouse during the trial and newsmen took over practically the entire courtroom, hounding most of the participants in the trial, especially Sheppard. At a temporary table within a few feet of the jury box and counsel table sat some 20 reporters staring at Sheppard and taking notes. The erection of a press table for reporters inside the bar is unprecedented. The bar of the court is reserved for counsel, providing them a safe place in which to keep papers and exhibits, and to confer privately with client and co-counsel. It is designed to protect the witness and the jury from any distractions, intrusions or influences, and to permit bench discussions of the judge's rulings away from the hearing of the public and the jury. Having assigned almost all of the available seats in the courtroom to the news media the judge lost his ability to supervise that environment. The movement of the reporters in and out of the courtroom caused frequent confusion and disruption of the trial. And the record reveals constant commotion within the bar. Moreover, the judge gave the throng of newsmen gathered in the corridors of the courthouse absolute free rein. Participants in the trial, including the jury, were forced to run a gauntlet of reporters and photographers each time they entered or left the courtroom. The total lack of consideration for the privacy of the jury was demonstrated by the assignment to a broadcasting station of space next to the jury room on the floor above the courtroom, as well as the fact that jurors were allowed to make telephone calls during their five-day deliberation.

There can be no question about the nature of the publicity which surrounded Sheppard's trial. We agree with the findings in Judge Bell's opinion for the Ohio Supreme Court: "Murder and mystery, society, sex and suspense were combined in this case in such a manner as to intrigue and captivate the public fancy to a degree perhaps unparalleled in recent annals. Throughout the preindictment investigation, the subsequent legal skirmishes and the nine-week trial, circulation-conscious editors catered to the insatiable interest of the American public in the bizarre. In this atmosphere of a 'Roman holiday' for the news media, Sam Sheppard stood trial for his life." Every court that has considered this case, save the court that tried it, has deplored the manner in which the news media inflamed and prejudiced the public.

Much of the material printed or broadcast during the trial was never heard from the witness stand, such as the charges that Sheppard had purposely impeded the murder investigation and must be guilty since he had hired a prominent criminal lawyer; that Sheppard was a perjurer; that he had sexual relations with numerous women; that his slain wife had characterized him as a "Jekyll-Hyde"; that he was "a bare-faced liar" because of his testimony as to police treatment; and finally, that a woman convict claimed Sheppard to be the father of her illegitimate child. As the trial progressed, the newspapers summarized and interpreted the evidence, devoting particular attention to the material that incriminated Sheppard, and often drew unwarranted inferences from testimony. At one point, a front-page picture of Mrs. Sheppard's blood-stained pillow was published after being "doctored" to show more clearly an alleged imprint of a surgical instrument.

Nor is there doubt that this deluge of publicity reached at least some of the jury. On the only occasion that the jury was queried, two jurors admitted in open court to hearing the highly inflammatory charge that a prison inmate claimed Sheppard as the father of her illegitimate child. Despite the extent and nature of the publicity to which the jury was exposed during trial, the judge refused defense counsel's other requests that the jurors be asked whether they had read or heard specific prejudicial comment about the case, including the incidents we have previously summarized. In these circumstances, we can assume that some of this material reached members of the jury.

Since the state trial judge did not fulfill his duty to protect Sheppard from the inherently prejudicial publicity which saturated the community and to control disruptive influences in the courtroom, we must reverse the denial of the habeas petition. The case is remanded to the District Court with instructions to issue the writ and order that Sheppard be released from custody unless the State puts him to its charges again within a reasonable time.

It is so ordered.

Notes

1. *Change of Venue.* One remedy for excessive press coverage is provided by Fed. R. Crim. P. 21(a), which permits a change of venue when the trial judge is "satisfied that there exists in the district where the prosecution is pending so great a prejudice that he cannot obtain a fair and impartial trial." In *Irwin v. Dowd*, 366 U.S. 717 (1961), the petitioner was denied a second change of venue despite extensive press coverage that aroused "great excitement and indignation." The Court reversed: "Here the 'pattern of deep and bitter prejudice' shown to be present throughout the community was clearly reflected in the sum total of the *voir dire* examination of a majority of the jurors finally placed in the jury box."

2. *An Ignorant Jury?* The Constitution does not require that a jury be ignorant of all publicity. In *Murphy v. Florida*, 421 U.S. 794 (1975), the defendant was charged with breaking and entering a home, while armed, with intent to commit robbery and with assault with intent to commit robbery. The case received extensive press coverage because the petitioner was notorious (he had participated in the 1964 theft of the Star of India sapphire from a museum in New York) and

lived a flamboyant lifestyle. The media referred to him as "Murph the Surf" and wrote scores of articles about him. The Court upheld the conviction: "The constitutional standard of fairness requires that a defendant have a 'panel of impartial, indifferent' jurors. Qualified jurors need not, however, be totally ignorant of the facts and issues involved. It is sufficient if the juror can lay aside his impression or opinion and render a verdict based on the evidence presented in court." *See also Patton v. Yount*, 467 U.S. 1025 (1984).

∾ PROBLEMS ∾

1. *Finding a Fair and Unbiased Jury.* Is it possible to seat a fair and unbiased jury in a case that generates extensive publicity (e.g., the O.J. Simpson murder case, of which news organizations gave incessant coverage suggestive of Simpson's guilt)? Does the fact that the O.J. Simpson case resulted in a not guilty verdict suggest that jurors may not be biased by extensive (and, at times, obsessive) press coverage?

2. *The Internet and Prejudicial Publicity. Nebraska Press Association* (see below) suggests that one remedy for potentially prejudicial pretrial publicity is a change of venue. Does the internet undermine the effectiveness of that remedy? For example, when Karen Cunagin Sypher was charged in Louisville, Kentucky, with trying to extort money from then-University of Louisville basketball coach Rick Pitino, she moved for a change of venue. The prosecution opposed the request because Pitino is famous throughout the commonwealth (in addition to coaching at Louisville, he was the coach at the University of Kentucky), and the internet made the information equally accessible to individuals throughout the commonwealth. Is this an adequate basis for denying the request for a change of venue? If change of venue is now a less effective remedy for prejudicial pretrial publicity, does that fact make a gag order less objectionable?

3. *More on the International Treaty Regulating the Internet.* At the convention, a number of delegates push for restrictions on the ability of individuals, corporations, and media outlets to publish information regarding pending criminal proceedings. Britain, Canada, and Australia, in particular, seek such restrictions, arguing that their domestic law makes it illegal for newspapers and other media outlets to publish such information on the theory that it can undermine the fairness and integrity of criminal proceedings. Canadians, in particular, are worried that internet bloggers and others, many located in the United States, will make information regarding pending Canadian criminal proceedings readily available to Canadians. As a result, the effectiveness of Canada's anti-publication laws will be undercut. Can you agree to the proposed restrictions? Might it be permissible to agree to such restrictions insofar as they relate to criminal proceedings taking place outside of the United States?

6. Due Process and Prior Restraints

Following the *Sheppard* decision, courts struggled to find ways to protect a defendant's right to due process. Consider the following case.

Nebraska Press Association v. Stuart

427 U.S. 539 (1976)

Mr. Chief Justice BURGER delivered the opinion of the Court.

The respondent State District Judge entered an order restraining the petitioners from publishing or broadcasting accounts of confessions or admission made by the accused or facts "strongly implicative" of the accused in a widely reported murder of six persons. We granted certiorari to decide whether the entry of such an order on the showing made before the state court violated the constitutional guarantee of freedom of the press.

On the evening of October 18, 1975, local police found the six members of the Henry Kellie family murdered in their home in Sutherland, Neb., a town of about 850 people. Police released the description of a suspect, Erwin Charles Simants, to the reporters who had hastened to the scene of the crime. Simants was arrested and arraigned in Lincoln County Court the following morning, ending a tense night for this small rural community.

The crime immediately attracted widespread news coverage, by local, regional, and national newspapers, radio and television stations. Three days after the crime, the County Attorney and Simants' attorney joined in asking the County Court to enter a restrictive order relating to "matters that may or may not be publicly reported or disclosed to the public," because of the "mass coverage by news media" and the "reasonable likelihood of prejudicial news which would make difficult, if not impossible, the impaneling of an impartial jury and tend to prevent a fair trial." The County Court heard oral argument but took no evidence; no attorney for members of the press appeared at this stage. The County Court granted the prosecutor's motion for a restrictive order and entered it the next day, October 22. The order prohibited everyone in attendance from "releasing or authorizing the release for public dissemination in any form or manner whatsoever any testimony given or evidence adduced"; the order also required members of the press to observe the Nebraska Bar-Press Guidelines.

Simants' preliminary hearing was held the same day, open to the public but subject to the order. The County Court bound over the defendant for trial to the State District Court. The charges, as amended to reflect the autopsy findings, were that Simants had committed the murders in the course of a sexual assault.

Petitioners—several press and broadcast associations, publishers, and individual reporters—moved on October 23 for leave to intervene in the District Court, asking that the restrictive order imposed by the County Court be vacated. The court conducted a hearing, at which the County Judge testified and newspaper articles about the *Simants* case were admitted in evidence. The judge granted petitioners' motion to intervene and entered his own restrictive order. The judge found "because of the nature of the crimes charged in the complaint that there is a clear and present danger that pre-trial publicity could impinge upon the defendant's right to a fair trial." The order applied only until the jury was impaneled, and specifically prohibited petitioners from reporting five subjects: (1) the existence or contents of a confession Simants had made to law enforcement officers, which had been introduced in open court at arraignment; (2) the fact or nature of statements Simants had made to other persons; (3) the contents of a note he had written the night of the crime; (4) certain aspects of the medical testimony at the preliminary hearing; and (5) the identity of the victims of the alleged sexual assault and the nature of the assault. It also prohibited reporting the exact nature of the restrictive order itself. Like the County Court's order, this order incorporated the Nebraska Bar-Press Guidelines. Finally, the order set out a plan for attendance, seating, and courthouse traffic control during the trial.

The problems presented by this case are almost as old as the Republic. Neither in the Constitution nor in contemporaneous writings do we find that the conflict between these two important rights was anticipated, yet it is inconceivable that the authors of the Constitution were unaware of the potential conflicts between the right to an unbiased jury and the guarantee of freedom of the press.

The thread running through earlier cases is that prior restraints on speech and publication are the most serious and the least tolerable infringement on First Amendment rights. A criminal penalty or a judgment in a defamation case is subject to the whole panoply of protections afforded by deferring the impact of the judgment until all avenues of appellate review have been exhausted. Only after judgment has become final, correct or otherwise, does the law's sanction become fully operative.

A prior restraint, by contrast and by definition, has an immediate and irreversible sanction. If it can be said that a threat of criminal or civil sanctions after publication "chills" speech, prior restraint "freezes" it at least for the time.

The damage can be particularly great when the prior restraint falls upon the communication of news and commentary on current events. Truthful reports of public judicial proceedings have been afforded special protection against subsequent punishment. For the same reasons the protection against prior restraint should have particular force as applied to reporting of criminal proceedings, whether the crime in question is a single isolated act or a pattern of criminal conduct.

A responsible press has always been regarded as the handmaiden of effective judicial administration, especially in the criminal field. Its function in this regard is documented by an impressive record of service over several centuries. The press does not simply publish information about trials but guards against the miscarriage of justice by subjecting the police, prosecutors, and judicial processes to extensive public scrutiny and criticism.

The extraordinary protections afforded by the First Amendment carry with them something in the nature of a fiduciary duty to exercise the protected rights responsibly—a duty widely acknowledged but not always observed by editors and publishers. It is not asking too much to suggest that those who exercise First Amendment rights in newspapers or broadcasting enterprises direct some effort to protect the rights of an accused to a fair trial by unbiased jurors.

Of course, the order at issue—like the order requested in *New York Times*—does not prohibit but only postpones publication. Some news can be delayed and most commentary can even more readily be delayed without serious injury, and there often is a self-imposed delay when responsible editors call for verification of information. But such delays are normally slight and they are self-imposed. Delays imposed by governmental authority are a different matter.

We have learned, and continue to learn, from what we view as the unhappy experiences of other nations where government has been allowed to meddle in the internal editorial affairs of newspapers. Regardless of how beneficent-sounding the purposes of controlling the press might be, we "remain intensely skeptical about those measures that would allow government to insinuate itself into the editorial rooms of this Nation's press." *Miami Herald Publishing Co. v. Tornillo*, 418 U.S. 241, 259 (1974) (White, J., concurring).

As a practical matter, the element of time is not unimportant if press coverage is to fulfill its traditional function of bringing news to the public promptly.

We turn now to the record in this case to determine whether, as Learned Hand put it, "the gravity of the 'evil,' discounted by its improbability, justifies such invasion of free speech as is necessary to avoid the danger." To do so, we must examine the evidence before the trial judge when the order was entered to determine (a) the nature and extent of pretrial news coverage; (b) whether other measures would be likely to mitigate the effects of unrestrained pretrial publicity; and (c) how effectively a restraining order would operate to prevent the threatened danger. The precise terms of the restraining order are also important. We must then consider whether the record supports the entry of a prior restraint on publication, one of the most extraordinary remedies known to our jurisprudence.

Our review of the pretrial record persuades us that the trial judge was justified in concluding that there would be intense and pervasive pretrial publicity concerning this case. He could also reasonably conclude, based on common human experience, that publicity might impair the defendant's right to a fair trial. He did not purport to say more, for he found only "a clear and present danger that pre-trial publicity *could* impinge upon the defendant's right to a fair trial." His conclusion as to the impact of such publicity on prospective jurors was of necessity speculative, dealing as he was with factors unknown and unknowable.

We find little in the record that goes to another aspect of our task, determining whether measures short of an order restraining all publication would have insured the defendant a fair trial. Although the entry of the order might be read as a judicial determination that other measures would not suffice, the trial court made no express findings to that effect; the Nebraska Supreme Court referred to the issue only by implication.

Most of the alternatives to prior restraint of publication in these circumstances were discussed with obvious approval in *Sheppard v. Maxwell*: (a) change of trial venue to a place less exposed to the intense publicity that seemed imminent in Lincoln County; (b) postponement of the trial to allow public attention to subside; (c) searching questioning of prospective jurors, as Mr. Chief Justice Marshall used in the *Burr* Case, to screen out those with fixed opinions as to guilt or innocence; (d) the use of emphatic and clear instructions on the sworn duty of each juror to decide the issues only on evidence presented in open court. Sequestration of jurors is, of course, always available. Although that measure insulates jurors only after they are sworn, it also enhances the likelihood of dissipating the impact of pretrial publicity and emphasizes the elements of the jurors' oaths.

We must also assess the probable efficacy of prior restraint on publication as a workable method of protecting Simants' right to a fair trial, and we cannot ignore the reality of the problems of managing and enforcing pretrial restraining orders. The territorial jurisdiction of the issuing court is limited by concepts of sovereignty. The need for *in personam* jurisdiction also presents an obstacle to a restraining order that applies to publication at large as distinguished from restraining publication within a given jurisdiction.

Finally, we note that the events disclosed by the record took place in a community of 850 people. It is reasonable to assume that, without any news accounts being printed or broadcast, rumors would travel swiftly by word of mouth. One can only speculate on the accuracy of such reports, given the generative propensities of rumors; they could well be more damaging than reasonably accurate news accounts. But plainly a whole community cannot be restrained from discussing a subject intimately affecting life within it.

Given these practical problems, it is far from clear that prior restraint on publication would have protected Simants' rights.

Mr. Justice BRENNAN, with whom Mr. Justice STEWART and Mr. Justice MARSHALL join, *concurring in the judgment.*

The right to a fair trial by a jury of one's peers is unquestionably one of the most precious and sacred safeguards enshrined in the Bill of Rights. Resort to prior restraints on the freedom of the press is a constitutionally impermissible method for enforcing that right; judges have at their disposal a broad spectrum of devices for ensuring that fundamental fairness is accorded the accused without necessitating so drastic an incursion on the equally fundamental and salutary constitutional mandate that discussion of public affairs in a free society cannot depend on the preliminary grace of judicial censors.

I would reject the contention that speculative deprivation of an accused's Sixth Amendment right to an impartial jury is comparable to the damage to the Nation or its people that *Near* and *New York Times* would have found sufficient to justify a prior restraint on reporting. Damage to that Sixth Amendment right could never be considered so direct, immediate and irreparable, and based on such proof rather than speculation, that prior restraints on the press could be justified on this basis.

Notes and Questions

1. *The Press Conference.* In *Gentile v. State Bar of Nevada,* 501 U.S. 1030 (1991), the Court struck down n reprimand for an attorney who held a press conference following the indictment of his client. The Court noted that the case involved "classic political speech" because petitioner was asserting that his client was a "scapegoat" and that "crooked cops" had not "been honest enough to indict the people who did it." The Court concluded: "Public awareness and criticism have greater importance where, as here, they concern allegations of police corruption, or where the criticism questions the judgment of an elected public prosecutor." The Court noted that the "record does not support the conclusion that petitioner knew or reasonably should have known his remarks created a substantial likelihood of material prejudice, if the Rule's terms are given any meaningful content." Five Justices suggested that attorney comments could be limited in appropriate cases. Justice Rehnquist, joined by three other Justices, argued that because "lawyers have special access to information through discovery and client communications, their extrajudicial statements pose a threat to the fairness of a pending proceeding since lawyers' statements are likely to be received as especially authoritative." Like the majority, he would have applied a "substantial likelihood of material prejudice" standard. Applying that standard, he would have reached a different result: "The restraint on speech is narrowly tailored to achieve those objectives."

2. *Protecting a Defendant's Right to a Fair Trial.* In light of decisions such as *Nebraska Press Association,* that limited the right to restrict press access to or coverage of a trial, how can courts protect a defendant's right to a fair trial? In a well-publicized case (e.g., the recent highly publicized trial about the 1964 killings of civil rights workers in Mississippi), what can the judge do to ensure a fair trial?

3. *The Roger Stone Gag Order.* In 2019, Roger Stone, a special adviser to President Trump, was indicted for lying to Congress regarding his communications with WikiLeaks and its founder, Julian Assange, as well as for witness tampering and obstruction of an investigation. The judge entered an order prohibiting Stone, his attorneys, and attorneys working for Special Counsel Robert Mueller, from making public statements that could bias any jurors who might be selected to hear the case. The judge tightened the gag order after Stone published a picture of her in the sights of a rifle. She prohibited from all media interviews and social media posts related to his case. She did allow him to claim his innocence in emails seeking contributions for his defense fund.

∽ PROBLEM: MORE ON THE INTERNATIONAL TREATY REGULATING THE INTERNET ∽

Having read *Nebraska Press Association,* do you think that you have any more "wiggle room" to agree to provisions restricting internet communications regarding pending criminal proceedings (in the United States or abroad)? If so, what language might you be able to agree to include in the treaty?

G. ACCESS TO GOVERNMENT PROPERTY

The trace elements of modern public forum law can be traced to the 1930s where the Court invalidated total bans on certain types of communications in public streets. In *Schneider v. New Jersey,* 308 U.S. 147 (1939), the Court invalidated a ban on leafleting in public streets and other public places. In *Lovell v. City of Griffin,* 303 U.S. 444 (1938), the Court struck down a ban on the distribution of literature within a city. By the 1980s, this area was being referred to as the "public forum" doctrine. *See* Harry Kalven, *The Concept of the Public Forum: Cox v. Louisiana,* 1965 Sup. Ct. Rev. 1. The label is a shorthand reference to cases involving government regulation of government-owned property. This property includes the most ancient Greek-like fora of streets and parks where citizens gather to discuss the issues of the day, as well as newer fora that have been "opened" by the government and "dedicated" to speech in some way.

One explanation for the First Amendment right of access to what we would now call "the public forum," given in *Hague v. CIO,* 307 U.S. 496 (1939), goes as follows:

> Wherever the title of streets and parks may rest, they have immemorially been held in trust for the use of the public and, time out of mind, have been used for purposes of assembly, communicating thoughts between citizens, and discussing public questions. Such use of the streets and public places, has, from ancient times, been a part of the privileges, immunities, rights, and liberties of citizens. It is not absolute, but relative, and must be exercised in subordination to the general comfort and convenience, and in consonance with peace and good order; but it must not, in the guise of regulation, be abridged or denied.

By the 1980s, the Court had identified four forum types. Included were the categories of "traditional public fora" (e.g., sidewalks, streets, and parks), "designated public fora" (government property that has been intentionally opened up for the purpose of serving the function of a traditional public forum), "limited public fora" (in which the government has "reserved" a forum "for certain groups or for the discussion of certain topics"), and "nonpublic fora" (in which the government is "acting as a proprietor" and "managing its internal operations"). *See Walker v. Texas Division, Sons of Confederate Veterans, Inc.,* 576 U.S. 200 (2015). As we shall see, the Court has applied different standards of review to different types of fora.

In this section, we focus on how to distinguish between the different types of fora, and the rules and standards applicable to each type of forum.

International Society for Krishna Consciousness, Inc. v. Lee

505 U.S. 672 (1992)

Chief Justice REHNQUIST delivered the opinion of the Court.

In this case we consider whether an airport terminal operated by a public authority is a public forum and whether a regulation prohibiting solicitation in the interior of an airport terminal violates the First Amendment.

Petitioner International Society for Krishna Consciousness, Inc. (ISKCON), is a not-for-profit religious corporation whose members perform a ritual known as *sankirtan*. The ritual consists of "going into public places, disseminating religious literature and soliciting funds to support the religion." The primary purpose of this ritual is raising funds for the movement. Respondent Walter Lee is the police superintendent of the Port Authority of New York and New Jersey and was charged with enforcing the regulation at issue. The Port Authority owns and operates three major airports in the greater New York City area: John F. Kennedy International Airport (Kennedy), La Guardia Airport (La Guardia), and Newark International Airport (Newark). The three airports collectively form one of the world's busiest metropolitan airport complexes. They serve approximately 8% of this country's domestic airline market and more than 50% of the trans-Atlantic market.

The airports are funded by user fees and operated to make a regulated profit. Most space at the three airports is leased to commercial airlines, which bear primary responsibility for the leasehold. The Port Authority retains control over unleased portions, including La Guardia's Central Terminal Building, portions of Kennedy's International Arrivals Building, and Newark's North Terminal Building. The terminals are generally accessible to the general public and contain various commercial establishments such as restaurants, snack stands, bars, newsstands, and stores of various types. Virtually all who visit the terminals do so for purposes related to air travel. These visitors principally include passengers, those meeting or seeing off passengers, flight crews, and terminal employees.

The Port Authority adopted a regulation forbidding within the terminals the repetitive solicitation of money or distribution of literature. The regulation states: "1. The following conduct is prohibited within the interior areas of buildings or structures at an air terminal if conducted by a person to or with passers-by in a continuous or repetitive manner: (a) The sale or distribution of any merchandise, including but not limited to jewelry, food stuffs, candles, flowers, badges and clothing. (b) The sale or distribution of flyers, brochures, pamphlets, books or any other printed or written material; (c) The solicitation and receipt of funds." The regulation governs only the terminals; the Port Authority permits solicitation and distribution on the sidewalks outside the buildings. The regulation effectively prohibits ISKCON from performing *sankirtan* in the terminals. ISKCON brought suit seeking declaratory and injunctive relief under 42 U.S.C. §1983, alleging that the regulation deprived its members of rights guaranteed under the First Amendment.

It is uncontested that solicitation is a form of speech protected under the First Amendment. But it is also well settled that the government need not permit all forms of speech on property that it owns and controls. Where the government is acting as a proprietor, managing its internal operations, rather than acting as lawmaker with the power to regulate or license, its action will not be subjected to the heightened review to which its actions as a lawmaker may be subject. Thus, we have upheld a ban on political advertisements in city-operated transit vehicles, even though the city permitted other types of advertising on those vehicles. Similarly, we have permitted a school district to limit access to an internal mail system used to communicate with teachers employed by the district. *Perry Ed. Assn. v. Perry Local Educators' Assn.*, 460 U.S. 37 (1983).

These cases reflect, either implicitly or explicitly, a "forum based" approach for assessing restrictions that the government seeks to place on the use of its property. *Cornelius v. NAACP Legal Defense & Ed. Fund, Inc.*, 473 U.S. 788 (1985). Under this approach, regulation of speech on government property that has traditionally been available for public expression is subject to the highest scrutiny. Such regulations survive only if they are narrowly drawn to achieve a compelling state interest. The second category of public property is the designated public forum, whether of a limited or unlimited character—property that the State has opened for expressive activity by part or all of the public. Regulation of such property is subject to the same limitations as that governing a traditional public forum. Finally, there is all remaining public property. Limitations on expressive activity conducted on this last category of property must survive only a much more limited review. The challenged regulation need only be reasonable, as long as the regulation is not an effort to suppress the speaker's activity due to disagreement with the speaker's view.

The parties do not disagree that this is the proper framework. Rather, they disagree whether airport terminals are public fora or nonpublic fora. They also disagree whether the regulation survives the "reasonableness" review governing nonpublic fora, should that prove the appropriate category. We conclude that the terminals are nonpublic fora and that the regulation reasonably limits solicitation.

The suggestion that the government has a high burden in justifying speech restrictions relating to traditional public fora made its first appearance in *Hague v. Committee for Industrial Organization*, 307 U.S. 496 (1939). Justice Roberts, concluding that individuals have a right to use "streets and parks for communication of views," reasoned that such a right flowed from the fact that "streets and parks have immemorially been held in trust for the use of the public and, time out of mind, have been used for purposes of assembly, communicating thoughts between citizens, and discussing public questions." We confirmed this observation in *Frisby v. Schultz*, 487 U.S. 474 (1988), where we held that a residential street was a public forum.

Our recent cases provide additional guidance on the characteristics of a public forum. In *Cornelius* we noted that a traditional public forum is property that has as "a principal purpose the free exchange of ideas." Consistent with the notion that the government—like other property owners—"has power to preserve the property under its control for the use to which it is lawfully dedicated," the government does not create a public forum by inaction. Nor is a public forum created "whenever members of the public are permitted freely to visit a place owned or operated by the Government." The decision to create a public forum must be made "by intentionally opening a nontraditional forum for public discourse." The location of property also has bearing because separation from acknowledged public areas may indicate that the separated property is a special enclave, subject to greater restriction. *United States v. Grace*, 461 U.S. 171 (1983).

These precedents foreclose the conclusion that airport terminals are public fora. Reflecting the general growth of the air travel industry, airport terminals have only recently achieved their contemporary size and character. But given the lateness with which the modern air terminal has made its appearance, it hardly qualifies for the description of having "immemorially time out of mind" been held in the public trust and used for purposes of expressive activity. Within the rather short history of air transport, it is only "in recent years that it has become a common practice for various religious and non-profit organizations to use commercial airports as a forum for the distribution of literature, the solicitation of funds, the proselytizing of new members, and other similar activities." 45 Fed. Reg. 35314 (1980). Thus, the tradition of airport activity does not demonstrate that airports have historically been made available for speech activity. Nor can we say that these particular terminals, or airport terminals generally, have been intentionally opened by their operators to such activity; the frequent and continuing litigation evidencing the operators' objections belies any such claim. In short, there can be no argument that society's time-tested judgment, expressed through acquiescence in a continuing practice, has resolved the issue in petitioners' favor.

Petitioners attempt to circumvent the history and practice governing airport activity by pointing to the variety of speech activity that they claim historically occurred at various "transportation nodes" such as rail stations, bus stations, wharves, and Ellis Island. Such evidence is of little import for two reasons. First, much of the evidence is irrelevant to *public* fora analysis, because bus and rail terminals traditionally have had *private* ownership. The practices of privately held transportation centers do not bear on the government's regulatory authority over a publicly owned airport. Second, the relevant unit for our inquiry is an airport, not "transportation nodes" generally. When new methods of transportation develop, it will be a new inquiry whether transportation necessities are compatible with various kinds of expressive activity. The "security magnet," for example, is an airport commonplace that lacks a counterpart in bus terminals and train stations.

Public access to air terminals is also not infrequently restricted. To blithely equate airports with other transportation centers, therefore, would be a mistake.

The differences among such facilities are unsurprising since airports are commercial establishments funded by users fees and designed to make a regulated profit, and where nearly all who visit do so for some travel related purpose. It cannot fairly be said that an airport terminal has as a principal purpose promoting "the free exchange of ideas." *Cornelius v. NAACP Legal Defense & Ed. Fund, Inc.,* 473 U.S. 788 (1985). Port Authority management considers the purpose of the terminals to be the facilitation of passenger air travel, not the promotion of expression. The terminals have never been dedicated (except under threat of court order) to expression in the form sought to be exercised here: i.e., the solicitation of contributions and the distribution of literature.

The terminals here are far from atypical. Airport builders and managers focus their efforts on providing terminals that will contribute to efficient air travel. Although many airports have expanded their function beyond merely contributing to efficient air travel, few have included among their purposes the designation of a forum for solicitation and distribution activities. Neither by tradition nor purpose can the terminals be described as satisfying the standards we have previously set out for identifying a public forum. The restrictions here challenged, therefore, need only satisfy a requirement of reasonableness. We reiterate what we stated in *Kokinda*: The restriction "need only be *reasonable*; it need not be the most reasonable or the only reasonable limitation." We have no doubt that under this standard the prohibition on solicitation passes muster.

We have on many prior occasions noted the disruptive effect that solicitation may have on business. "Solicitation requires action by those who would respond: The individual solicited must decide whether or not to contribute (which might involve reading the solicitor's literature or hearing his pitch), and then, having decided to do so, reach for a wallet, search it for money, write a check, or produce a credit card." Passengers who wish to avoid the solicitor may have to alter their paths, slowing both themselves and those around them. The result is that the normal flow of traffic is impeded. This is especially so in an airport, where "air travelers, who are often weighted down by cumbersome baggage may be hurrying to catch a plane or to arrange ground transportation." Delays may be costly in this setting, as a flight missed by only a few minutes can result in hours worth of subsequent inconvenience.

Face-to-face solicitation presents risks of duress that are an appropriate target of regulation. The skillful, and unprincipled, solicitor can target the most vulnerable, including those accompanying children or those suffering physical impairment and who cannot easily avoid the solicitation. The unsavory solicitor can also commit fraud through concealment of his affiliation or through deliberate efforts to shortchange those who agree to purchase. Compounding this problem is the fact that, in an airport, the targets of such activity frequently are on tight schedules. This in turn makes such visitors unlikely to stop and formally complain to airport authorities. As a result, the airport faces considerable difficulty in achieving its legitimate interest in monitoring solicitation activity to assure that travelers are not interfered with unduly.

The Port Authority has concluded that its interest in monitoring the activities can best be accomplished by limiting solicitation and distribution to the sidewalk areas outside the terminals. This sidewalk area is frequented by an overwhelming percentage of airport users. Thus the access of those who would solicit the general public is quite complete. In turn we think it would be odd to conclude that the Port Authority's terminal regulation is unreasonable despite the Port Authority having otherwise assured access to an area universally traveled.

The inconveniences to passengers and the burdens on Port Authority officials flowing from solicitation activity may seem small, but viewed against the fact that "pedestrian congestion is one of the greatest problems facing terminals," the Port Authority could reasonably worry that even incremental effects would prove disruptive. Moreover, "the justification for the Rule should not be measured by the disorder that would result from granting an exemption solely to ISKCON." For if ISKCON is given access, so too must other groups. "Obviously, there would be a much larger threat to the State's interest in crowd control if all other religious, nonreligious, and noncommercial organizations could likewise move freely." As a result, we conclude that the solicitation ban is reasonable.

For the foregoing reasons, the judgment of the Court of Appeals sustaining the ban on solicitation in Port Authority terminals is

Affirmed.

Justice KENNEDY, with whom Justice BLACKMUN, Justice STEVENS, and Justice SOUTER join as to Part I, *concurring in the judgment.*

While I concur in the judgment affirming this case which upholds a ban on solicitation of funds at the airport terminals, in my view, the airport corridors and shopping areas outside of the passenger security zones are public forums, and speech in those places is entitled to protection against all government regulation inconsistent with public forum principles.

I

The Court's error lies in its conclusion that the public forum status of the property depends on the government's defined purpose of the property, or on an explicit decision by the government to dedicate the property to expressive activity. In my view, the inquiry must be an objective one, based on the actual, physical characteristics and uses of the property. The Court's approach is contrary to the underlying purposes of the public forum doctrine. The liberties protected by our doctrine derive from the Assembly, as well as the Speech and Press Clauses of the First Amendment and are essential to a functioning democracy. *See* Kalven, *The Concept of a Public Forum: Cox v. Louisiana,* 1965 S.CT. REV. 1. Public places are of necessity the locus for discussion of public issues, as well as protest against arbitrary government action. In a free nation citizens must have the right to gather and speak with other persons in public places. The recognition that certain government-owned property is a public forum provides open notice to citizens that their freedoms may be exercised there without fear of a censorial government, adding tangible reinforcement to the idea that we are a free people.

The notion that traditional public forums are property which have public discourse as their principal purpose is a most doubtful fiction. The types of property recognized as the quintessential public forums are streets, parks, and sidewalks. The principal purpose of streets and sidewalks, like airports, is to facilitate transportation, not public discourse. The purpose for the creation of public parks may be as much for beauty and open space as for discourse. Thus under the Court's analysis, even the quintessential public forums would lack the necessary elements of what the Court defines as a public forum. Under the Court's analysis today few if any types of property other than those already recognized as public forums will be accorded that status. If the objective physical characteristics of the property at issue and the actual public access and uses which have been permitted by the government indicate that expressive activity would be appropriate and compatible with those uses, the property is a public forum. The possibility of some theoretical inconsistency between expressive activities and the property's uses should not bar a finding of a public forum. When a property is a protected public forum the state may not by fiat assert broad control over speech or expressive activities; it must alter the objective physical character or uses of the property, and bear the attendant costs, to change the property's forum status.

Under this analysis it is evident that the public spaces of the Port Authority's airports are public forums. First, there are physical similarities between airports and public streets. The public spaces in airports are broad, public thoroughfares full of people and lined with stores and other commercial activities. An airport corridor is not a street, but that is not the proper inquiry. The question is one of physical similarities, sufficient to suggest that the airport corridor should be a public forum for the same reasons that streets and sidewalks have been treated as public forums. Second, airport areas are open to the public without restriction. Plaintiffs do not seek access to the secured areas of the airports. While most people who come to the Port Authority's airports do so for a reason related to air travel, either because they are passengers or because they are picking up or dropping off passengers, this does not distinguish an airport from streets or sidewalks, which most people use for travel. Third, and perhaps most important, when adequate time, place, and manner regulations are in place, expressive activity is quite compatible with the uses of major airports. The Port Authority argues that congestion in its airports' corridors makes expressive activity inconsistent with the airports' primary purpose, which is to facilitate air travel. The First Amendment is often inconvenient. But inconvenience does not absolve the government of its obligation to tolerate speech.

The danger of allowing the government to suppress speech is shown in the case before us. A grant of plenary power allows the government to tilt the dialogue heard by the public, to exclude many, more marginal voices. The right to distribute flyers and literature lies at the heart of the liberties guaranteed by the

Speech and Press Clauses of the First Amendment. The Port Authority's rule, which prohibits almost all such activity, is among the most restrictive possible. I have no difficulty deciding the regulation cannot survive the far more stringent rules applicable to regulations in public forums. The regulation is not drawn in narrow terms, and it does not leave open ample alternative channels for communication. The Port Authority's concerns with the problem of congestion can be addressed through narrow restrictions on the time and place of expressive activity.

II

It is my view that the Port Authority's ban on the "solicitation and receipt of funds" within its airport terminals should be upheld under the standards applicable to speech regulations in public forums. The regulation may be upheld as either a reasonable time, place, and manner restriction, or as a regulation directed at the nonspeech element of expressive conduct. The two standards have considerable overlap in a case like this one. "Even in a public forum the government may impose reasonable restrictions on the time, place, or manner of protected speech, provided the restrictions 'are justified without reference to the content of the regulated speech, that they are narrowly tailored to serve a significant governmental interest, and that they leave open ample alternative channels for communication of the information.'" *Ward, supra,* at 791 (quoting *Clark v. Community for Creative Non-Violence,* 468 U.S. 288 (1984)). The government in appropriate circumstances may regulate conduct, even if the conduct has an expressive component. *United States v. O'Brien,* 391 U.S. 367 (1968). The standards for assessing time, place, and manner restrictions are little different from the standards applicable to regulations of conduct with an expressive component. *Clark, supra,* 468 U.S. at 298. The confluence of the two tests is demonstrated by a case like this, where the government regulation at issue can be described with equal accuracy as a regulation of the manner of expression, or as a regulation of conduct with an expressive component.

Solicitation is a form of protected speech. If the Port Authority's solicitation regulation prohibited all speech that requested the contribution of funds, I would conclude that it was a direct, content-based restriction of speech in clear violation of the First Amendment. This regulation reaches only personal solicitations for immediate payment of money. The regulation does not cover the distribution of preaddressed envelopes along with a plea to contribute money to the distributor or his organization. So viewed, I believe the Port Authority's rule survives our test for speech restrictions in the public forum. In-person solicitation of funds, when combined with immediate receipt, creates a risk of fraud and duress that is well recognized, and that is different in kind from other forms of expression or conduct. Questionable practices associated with solicitation can include the targeting of vulnerable and easily coerced persons, misrepresentation of the solicitor's cause, and outright theft. Because the Port Authority's solicitation ban is directed at these abusive practices and not at any particular message, idea, or form of speech, the regulation is a content-neutral rule serving a significant government interest. I have little difficulty deciding that the Port Authority has left open ample alternative channels for the communication of the message which is an aspect of solicitation.

Notes

1. *Definitional Debates.* In *Cornelius v. NAACP Legal Defense and Educational Fund, Inc.,* 473 U.S. 788 (1985), Justice O'Connor wrote for a plurality in holding that a fundraising drive for charitable purposes in the federal workplace should be treated as a nonpublic forum. She focused on the significance of examining the policy and practice of the government, the nature of the property, and its "compatibility" with expressive activity. But she also observed that "government does not create a public forum by inaction or by permitting limited discourse, but only by intentionally opening a non-traditional forum for public discourse." The Court "will not find that a public forum has been created in the face of clear evidence of a contrary intent," nor will the Court "infer that the Government intended to create a public forum when the nature of the property is inconsistent with expressive activity."

2. *The Unique Character of Particular Fora.* The *ISKCON* majority provides examples of notable pre-*ISKCON* holdings on the issue of a forum's status. In *Lehman v. City of Shaker Heights,* 418 U.S. 298 (1974), the Court concluded that the "car card space" on a bus was a nonpublic forum: "The city is engaged in commerce. It must provide rapid, convenient, pleasant, and inexpensive service. The car card space, although incidental to the provision of public transportation, is a part of the commercial venture. In much the same way that a newspaper or periodical, or even a radio or television station, need not accept every proffer of advertising from the general public, a city transit system has discretion to develop and make reasonable choices concerning the type of advertising that may be displayed in its vehicles." Likewise, in *Greer v. Spock,* 424 U.S. 828 (1976), a military base was held to be a nonpublic forum: "It is 'the primary business of armies and navies to fight or be ready to fight wars should the occasion arise.' It is the business of a military installation like Fort Dix to train soldiers, not to provide a public forum. The notion that federal military reservations, like municipal streets and parks, have traditionally served as a place for free public assembly and communication of thoughts by private citizens is historically and constitutionally false." As *Lehman* and *Greer* suggest, decisions regarding the status of fora reflect consideration of a totality of circumstances on a case-by-case basis and depend on certain *sui generis* aspects of those fora.

3. *"Selective Access" as Evidence of Nonpublic Forum Status.* The Court observed famously in *Arkansas Educational Television Commission v. Forbes,* 523 U.S. 666, 677 (1998), that aside from traditional public fora and designated public fora, "other government properties are either nonpublic fora or not fora at all." Since the

traditional public forum category is limited to its "historic confines" of the streets, parks and sidewalks, many cases pose the question whether a forum falls into the "designated public forum" or the "nonpublic forum" category. Starting in the 1980s, the Court adopted the position that in order to qualify as a "designated public forum," the government must intend to make the property "generally available" with "general access" provided for a class of speakers. In *Widmar v. Vincent*, 454 U.S. 263 (1982), a state university policy allowed all registered student groups to use the university's meeting facilities, and the Court characterized those facilities as a designated public forum because they had been made generally available to the class of speakers comprising the registered student groups. As a result, when a student religious group was later denied access to the university's facilities, that exclusion was invalidated as an impermissibly content-based regulation of a designated public forum. But *Widmar* was the rare case in which the Court recognized that the excluded speakers could point to evidence of a right of "general access" for the class to which they belonged. More often, the Court decided that the government did not intend to create a designated public forum because the government allowed only "selective access" to a forum by "reserving eligibility" for forum use to "a particular class of speakers, whose members must then, as individuals, obtain permission" from government officials to use it. The "selective access" type of forum is a nonpublic forum.

4. *The Limits of a "Limited" Public Forum.* Also beginning in the 1980s, the Court began to examine the claims of speakers who argued that even when a forum was not "generally available" to a broad class of speakers, the government had established a "limited" public forum by granting access to particular speakers in a class to which the plaintiff belonged. But in most of the Court's precedents in which the plaintiffs have made this argument, it has not been successful. An early example is *Perry Education Association v. Perry Local Educators' Association*, 460 U.S. 37 (1983), where the forum at issue was the interschool mail system that could be used to deliver messages to teacher mailboxes in roughly a dozen public schools. Initially, the mail system was open to school employees and to the two unions that represented the district's teachers. But when one union became the exclusive representative for the teachers, it obtained exclusive access to the interschool mail system from the school district. In challenging its own loss of access, the rival union relied on evidence that some speakers in "outside groups" had been granted access to the mail system, including YMCA and Cub Scout groups, as well as other civic and religious organizations. Since the government had opened a "limited" public forum for these "non-school-connected groups," the plaintiff union urged the Court to invalidate the exclusion of the union, given its identity as another such group.

However, the *Perry* Court rejected this argument and its analysis reflected two key limitations on the potential use of the "limited" public forum concept. First, the Court concluded that the outside organizations only had "selective access" and not "general access" to the mail system forum, since "permission to use the system to communicate with teachers must be secured from the individual building principal." Such "selective access" is the sign of a nonpublic forum. Second, the Court held that even assuming that the government had created a "limited public forum" with "general access" allowed for some outside groups, the "resulting constitutional right of access" would extend "only to other entities of similar character." Then the Court chose to define the "character" of the outside groups in *Perry* as "organizations that engage in activities of interest and educational relevance to students." This narrow definition meant that the plaintiff union could not qualify as an entity of similar character, as in the Court's eyes, the union's interest was limited to "the terms and conditions of teacher employment." Thus, the plaintiff union could claim no right of "general access" to the hypothetical "limited public forum" in *Perry*.

5. *Forum Analysis Inapplicable to Government Speech.* Since forum analysis is designed to evaluate "government restrictions on purely private speech that occurs on government property," such analysis does not govern "government speech" cases in which "the State is speaking on its own behalf." In these cases, the government "is not barred by the Free Speech Clause from determining the content of what it says." In *Walker v. Sons of Confederate Veterans, Inc.*, 135 S. Ct. 2239, 2250 (2015), the Court held that specialty license plates should be characterized as government speech, given the history of license plate designs in communicating messages from the States, the close identification of those designs with the States in the public mind, and the existence of State control over the messages conveyed in license plate designs. Since the plate designs are government speech and not purely private speech, the *Walker* Court found that they license plates did not constitute a forum of any kind. The topic of government speech will be studied in Part C of Chapter 8.

6. *Licensing Requirements.* When a group wishes to use a traditional public forum, such as a sidewalk or a park, for a parade or other demonstration, or for an event involving the distribution of literature or solicitation of funds, a permit may be required. Such a regulation will be subjected to scrutiny as a regulation of the time, place, and manner of speech in the public forum. Also, the regulation will need to satisfy the Court's doctrines concerning the "prior restraint" of a licensing scheme. For example, in *Cox v. State of New Hampshire*, 312 U.S. 569 (1941), a state statute prohibited a "parade or procession" upon a public street without a "special license" to be obtained from municipal officials. The government interests included these goals: 1) to give "the public authorities notice in advance so as to afford opportunity for proper policing"; 2) to "prevent confusion by overlapping parades or processions"; 3) to "secure convenient use of the streets by other travelers"; and 4) to "minimize the risk of disorder." The Court upheld this statutory permit requirement, reasoning that the statute required officials to issue licenses with "uniformity of method of treatment upon the facts of each application, free from improper or inappropriate considerations and from unfair discrimination." A group had the right to receive "a license to march" at a particular time and place, assuming that "after a required investigation it was found that the convenience of the public in the use of the streets would not

thereby be unduly disturbed, upon such conditions or changes in time, place and manner as would avoid disturbance." The state court construed the statute as requiring "a reasonable fixing of the amount of the fee" for the license, which could be imposed "to meet the expense incident to the administration of the law and to the maintenance of public order." The Supreme Court rejected the argument that a flat fee should be required, finding instead that local governments could "frame a fair fee schedule to meet all circumstances," depending on the "greater public expense of policing" some events.

Although the Court has not addressed the question of whether a single speaker or small group in a public forum may be required to obtain a permit, the consensus of the federal courts is that such a requirement would violate the First Amendment. *See Berger v. City of Seattle,* 569 F.3d 1029 (9th Cir. 2009). As a prior restraint on speech, a permit requirement bears a heavy presumption of unconstitutionality according to Court precedent, at least outside the context of large groups of people traveling together on streets and sidewalks. This principle is illustrated by precedents invalidating permit requirements for "door-to-door canvassing" by individuals. These cases involved speakers who come upon private property when they approach houses and ring doorbells and otherwise use the public forum territory of sidewalks when traveling from house to house.

7. *More on Licensing.* In *Watchtower Bible and Tract Society of New York v. Village of Stratton,* 536 U.S. 150 (2002), the Court invalidated a permit requirement that was challenged by Jehovah's Witnesses whose members wished to engage in door-to-door canvassing to distribute free religious literature. The ordinance prohibited the "practice of going in and upon private property and/or the private residence of Village residents in the Village by canvassers, solicitors, peddlers, hawkers, itinerant merchants or transient vendors of merchandise or services, not having been invited to do so by the owners or occupants of such private property or residences, and not having first obtained a permit, for the purpose of advertising, *promoting,* selling and/or explaining *any* product, service, organization or *cause,* or for the purpose of soliciting orders for the sale of goods, wares, merchandise or services without first registering and obtaining a Solicitation Permit." Once the permit was obtained, the canvasser was required to carry the permit and show it to any police officer or resident who asked to see it. Even though the permit was issued routinely and without charge, the registration form required an applicant to provide the following information in order to obtain the permit: 1) The registrant's name and home address; 2) A brief description of the nature and purpose of the business, promotion, solicitation, organization, cause, and/or the goods or services offered; 3) The name and address of the employer or affiliated organization; 4) The length of time for which the privilege to canvass or solicit is desired; and 5) The address of each private residence at which the registrant intends to engage in the conduct. The Village argued that the ordinance served three governmental interests: the prevention of fraud; the prevention of crime; and protection of the privacy of residents. The ordinance also authorized residents to prohibit such canvassers from coming to their doors by posting "No Solicitation"

signs. The Court invalidated the ordinance, emphasizing the historical importance of distributing leaflets door-to-door as a way of disseminating speech and ideas, especially for proselytizing groups like the Witnesses who seek to use inexpensive methods of communication. The Court reasoned that it is offensive "to the very notion of a free society" that "a citizen must first inform the government of her desire to speak to her neighbors and then obtain a permit to do so." Also, the permit scheme constituted "a dramatic departure from our national heritage and constitutional tradition.." Even assuming that the governmental interest in preventing fraud "could adequately support the ordinance, that interest provided "no support for its application to petitioners, to political campaigns, or to enlisting support for unpopular causes." Finally, there was no evidence "of a special crime problem related to door-to-door solicIt seemed unlikely "that the absence of a permit would preclude criminals from knocking on doors and engaging in conversations not covered by the ordinance."

8. *Level of Scrutiny.* *Watchtower* expressly noted that it was not necessary to use the "intermediate scrutiny" standard of review in assessing whether a permit ordinance advanced important interests by a narrowly tailored means—two aspects of the familiar standard for assessing content-neutral regulations of speech in the public forum. Instead, the Court articulated a balancing approach in describing the need for courts to "appraise the substantiality" of the government interests and to "examine the effect of the challenged legislation" on First Amendment rights. Given the Court's analysis, it seems likely that the permit ordinance in *Watchtower* would not have satisfied the intermediate scrutiny standard. *Cox* implicitly reflected the same balancing of concerns that was explicitly described in *Watchtower.* As the *Cox* opinion noted, the parade permit scheme had many "obvious advantages" as a means for achieving all of the government interests it was designed to serve, and the scheme's "interference with liberty of speech and writing seemed slight." The statute only provided for limitations on the time, place, and manner of parades and placed no restrictions on the distribution of literature by individuals or groups "traveling in unorganized fashion." By contrast, the Court was presented with a more burdensome permit scheme in *Watchtower,* whose burdens would create predictably "pernicious" effects on speakers and their speech. Unlike the government interests in *Cox,* the interests in *Watchtower* could be achieved more readily with "less intrusive and more effective" methods to protect privacy and deter crime.

Minnesota Voters Alliance v. Mansky

136 S. Ct. 1876 (2018)

Chief Justice ROBERTS delivered the opinion of the Court.
   Americans going to their polling places on Election Day expect to wait in line, briefly interact with an election official, enter a private voting booth, and cast an anonymous ballot. Little about this ritual would have been familiar to a

voter in the mid-to-late nineteenth century. Voters typically deposited privately prepared ballots at the polls instead of completing official ballots on-site. These pre-made ballots often took the form of "party tickets"—printed slates of candidate selections, often distinctive in appearance, that political parties distributed to their supporters and pressed upon others around the polls. See R. BENSEL, THE AMERICAN BALLOT BOX IN THE MID-NINETEENTH CENTURY 14–15 (2004). The polling place often consisted simply of a "voting window" through which the voter would hand his ballot to an election official situated in a separate room with the ballot box. As a result of this arrangement, "the actual act of voting was usually performed in the open," frequently within view of interested onlookers. Rusk, *The Effect of the Australian Ballot Reform on Split Ticket Voting: 1876–1908*, AM. POL. SCI. REV. 1220, 1221 (1970). As documented in *Burson v. Freeman*, 504 U. S. 191 (1992), "approaching the polling place under this system was akin to entering an open auction place." *Id.*, at 202. The room containing the ballot boxes was "usually quiet and orderly," but "the public space outside the window was chaotic." BENSEL 13. Electioneering of all kinds was permitted. Crowds would gather to heckle and harass voters who appeared to be supporting the other side. "In short, these early elections were not a very pleasant spectacle for those who believed in democratic government." *Burson*, 504 U. S., at 202 (plurality opinion).

By the nineteenth century, States began implementing reforms to address these vulnerabilities and improve the reliability of elections. Between 1888 and 1896, nearly every State adopted the secret ballot. Because voters now needed to mark their state-printed ballots on-site and in secret, voting moved into a sequestered space where the voters could "deliberate and make a decision in privacy." In addition, States enacted "viewpoint-neutral restrictions on election-day speech" in the immediate vicinity of the polls. Today, all 50 States and the District of Columbia have laws curbing various forms of speech in and around polling places on Election Day. Minnesota's law contains three prohibitions, only one of which is challenged here. *See* Minn. Stat. §211B.11(1) (Supp. 2017). The first sentence of §211B.11(1) forbids any person to "display campaign material, post signs, ask, solicit, or in any manner try to induce or persuade a voter within a polling place or within 100 feet of the building in which a polling place is situated" to "vote for or refrain from voting for a candidate or ballot question." The second sentence prohibits the distribution of "political badges, political buttons, or other political insignia to be worn at or about the polling place." The third sentence—the "political apparel ban"—states that a "political badge, political button, or other political insignia may not be worn at or about the polling place." Versions of all three prohibitions have been on the books in Minnesota for over a century. There is no dispute that the political apparel ban applies only within the polling place, and covers articles of clothing and accessories with "political insignia" upon them. Minnesota election judges—temporary government employees working the polls on Election Day—have the authority to decide whether a particular item falls within the ban. If a voter shows up wearing a prohibited item, the election judge is to ask the individual to conceal or remove it. If the individual refuses, the election judge must allow him to vote, while making clear that the incident "will be recorded and referred to appropriate authorities." Violators are subject to an administrative process before the Minnesota Office of Administrative Hearings, which may issue a reprimand or impose a civil penalty. That administrative body may also refer the complaint to the county attorney for prosecution as a petty misdemeanor; the maximum penalty is a $300 fine.

Petitioner Minnesota Voters Alliance (MVA) is a nonprofit organization that "seeks better government through election reforms." Petitioner Andrew Cilek is a registered voter and the executive director of MVA; petitioner Susan Jeffers served in 2010 as a Ramsey County election judge. Five days before the 2010 election, MVA, Jeffers, and other likeminded groups and individuals filed a lawsuit challenging the political apparel ban on First Amendment grounds. The District Court denied the request for a temporary restraining order and preliminary injunction and allowed the apparel ban to remain in effect for the election. In response, officials distributed to election judges an "Election Day Policy," providing guidance on enforcement of the political apparel ban. The Policy specified that examples of apparel falling within the ban "include, but are not limited to": "Any item including the name of a political party in Minnesota, such as the Republican, Democratic-Farmer-Labor, Independence, Green or Libertarian parties. Any item including the name of a candidate at any election. Any item in support of or opposition to a ballot question at any election. Issue oriented material designed to influence or impact voting (including specifically the 'Please I.D. Me' buttons). Material promoting a group with recognizable political views (such as the Tea Party, MoveOn.org, and so on)." Some voters associated with EIW ran into trouble with the ban on Election Day. One individual was asked to cover up his Tea Party shirt. Another refused to conceal his "Please I.D. Me" button, and an election judge recorded his name and address for possible referral. Petitioner Cilek—who was wearing the same button and a T-shirt with the words "Don't Tread on Me" and the Tea Party Patriots logo—was twice turned away from the polls, then finally permitted to vote after an election judge recorded his information. The District Court granted the State's motions to dismiss, and the Court of Appeals for the Eighth Circuit affirmed in part and reversed in part. We granted certiorari.

The First Amendment prohibits laws "abridging the freedom of speech." Minnesota's ban on wearing any "political badge, political button, or other political insignia" plainly restricts a form of expression within the protection of the First Amendment. But the ban applies only in a specific location: the interior of a polling place. It therefore implicates our "'forum based' approach for assessing restrictions that the government seeks to place on the use of its property." *International Soc. for Krishna Consciousness, Inc. v. Lee*, 505 U. S. 672, 678 (1992) (ISKCON). Generally, our cases recognize three types of government-controlled spaces: traditional public forums, designated public forums, and nonpublic forums. In a traditional public forum—parks, streets, sidewalks, and the like—the government may impose reasonable time, place, and manner restrictions on private speech, but restrictions based on content must satisfy strict scrutiny, and those based on viewpoint are prohibited. The same standards apply in designated public forums—spaces that have "not traditionally been regarded as a public forum" but which the government has "intentionally opened up for that purpose." In a nonpublic forum, on the other hand—a space that "is not by tradition or designation a forum for public communication"—the government has more flexibility to craft rules limiting speech. *Perry Ed. Assn. v. Perry Local Educators' Assn.*, 460 U. S. 37 (1983). The government may reserve such a forum "for its intended purposes, communicative or otherwise, as long as the regulation on speech is reasonable and not an effort to suppress expression merely because public officials oppose the speaker's view." *Ibid.* This Court employs a distinct standard of review to assess speech restrictions in nonpublic forums because the government, "no less than a private owner of property," retains the "power to preserve the property under its control for the use to which it is lawfully dedicated." *Adderley v. Florida*, 385 U. S. 39, 47 (1966). "Nothing in the Constitution requires the Government freely to grant access to all who wish to exercise their right to free speech on every type of Government property without regard to the nature of the property or to the disruption that might be caused by the speaker's activities." *Cornelius v. NAACP Legal Defense & Ed. Fund, Inc.*, 473 U. S. 788, 799 (1985). Accordingly, our decisions have long recognized that the government may impose some content-based restrictions on speech in nonpublic forums, including restrictions that exclude political advocates and forms of political advocacy.

A polling place in Minnesota qualifies as a nonpublic forum. It is, on Election Day, government-controlled property set aside for the sole purpose of voting. Rules strictly govern who may be present, for what purpose, and for how long. While the four-Justice plurality in *Burson* and Justice Scalia's concurrence parted ways over whether the public sidewalks and streets surrounding a polling place qualify as a nonpublic forum, neither suggested that the interior of the building was anything but. We therefore evaluate MVA's First Amendment challenge under the nonpublic forum standard. The text of the apparel ban makes no distinction based on the speaker's political persuasion, so MVA does not claim that the ban discriminates on the basis of viewpoint. The question is whether Minnesota's ban on political apparel is "reasonable in light of the purpose served by the forum": voting. *Cornelius*, 473 U. S., at 806.

We first consider whether Minnesota is pursuing a permissible objective in prohibiting voters from wearing particular kinds of expressive apparel or accessories while inside the polling place. The natural starting point for evaluating a First Amendment challenge to such a restriction is *Burson* which upheld a Tennessee law imposing a 100-foot campaign-free zone around polling place entrances. Under the Tennessee law—much like Minnesota's buffer-zone provision—no person could solicit votes for or against a candidate, party, or ballot measure, distribute campaign materials, or "display campaign posters, signs or other campaign materials" within the restricted zone. The plurality found that the law withstood even the strict scrutiny applicable to speech restrictions in traditional public forums. In concurring, Justice Scalia argued that the less rigorous "reasonable-ness" standard of review should apply, and found the law "at least reasonable." That analysis emphasized the problems of fraud, voter intimidation, confusion, and general disorder that had plagued polling places in the past. The plurality and Justice Scalia upheld Tennessee's determination, supported by overwhelm-ing consensus among the States and "common sense," that a campaign-free zone outside the polls was "necessary" to secure the advantages of the secret ballot and protect the right to vote. "The State of Tennessee has decided that the last 15 sec-onds before its citizens enter the polling place should be their own, as free from interference as possible." That was not "an unconstitutional choice." Campaign buttons and apparel did come up in *Burson*, but neither the plurality nor Justice Scalia addressed such applications of the law. Nor did either opinion specifically consider the interior of the polling place.

We see no basis for rejecting Minnesota's determination that some forms of advocacy should be excluded from the polling place, to set it aside as "an island of calm in which voters can peacefully contemplate their choices." Casting a vote is a weighty civic act, akin to a jury's return of a verdict, or a representa-tive's vote on a piece of legislation. It is a time for choosing, not campaigning. The State may reasonably decide that the interior of the polling place should reflect that distinction. To be sure, our decisions have noted the "nondisruptive" nature of expressive apparel in more mundane settings. *Board of Airport Comm'rs of Los Angeles v. Jews for Jesus, Inc.*, 482 U. S. 569, 576 (1987) (airport); *Tinker v. Des Moines Independent Community School Dist.*, 393 U. S. 503, 508 (1969) (stu-dents wearing black armbands to protest the Vietnam War engaged in "silent, passive expression of opinion, unaccompanied by any disorder or disturbance"). But those observations do not speak to the unique context of a polling place on Election Day. Members of the public are brought together at that place, at the end of what may have been a divisive election season, to reach considered decisions about their government and laws. The State may reasonably take steps to ensure that partisan discord not follow the voter up to the voting booth, and distract from a sense of shared civic obligation at the moment it counts the most. That interest may be thwarted by displays that do not raise significant concerns in other situations. Other States can see the matter differently, and some do. The majority agree with Minnesota that at least some kinds of campaign-related cloth-ing and accessories should stay outside. That broadly shared judgment is entitled to respect. In light of the special purpose of the polling place, Minnesota may choose to prohibit certain apparel because of the message it conveys, so that vot-ers may focus on the important decisions immediately at hand. But the State must draw a reasonable line. Although there is no requirement of narrow tailoring in a nonpublic forum, the State must be able to articulate some sensible basis for distinguishing what may come in from what must stay out. Here, the unmoored use of the term "political" in the Minnesota law, combined with haphazard inter-pretations the State has provided in official guidance and representations to this Court, cause Minnesota's restriction to fail even this forgiving test. The statute prohibits wearing a "political badge, political button, or other political insignia." It does not define the term "political." And the word can encompass anything "of or relating to government, a government, or the conduct of governmental affairs," Webster's Third New International Dictionary 1755 (2002), or anything "of, relating to, or dealing with the structure or affairs of government, politics, or the state," AMERICAN HERITAGE DICTIONARY 1401 (3d ed. 1996). Under a literal reading, a button or T-shirt merely imploring others to "Vote!" could qualify.

According to the State, the statute does not prohibit "any conceivably 'political' message" or cover "all 'political' speech, broadly construed." Instead, the State interprets the ban to proscribe "only words and symbols that an objectively reasonable observer would perceive as conveying a message about the electoral choices at issue in the polling place." At the same time, the State argues that the category of "political" apparel is not limited to campaign apparel. After all, the reference to "campaign material" in the first sentence of the statute—describing what one may not "display" in the buffer zone as well as inside the polling place—implies that the distinct term "political" should be understood to cover a broader class of items. As the State's counsel explained, Minnesota's law "expands the scope of what is prohibited from campaign speech to additional political speech." Far from clarifying the scope of the political apparel provision, the State's "electoral choices" construction introduces confusing problems. The State points to the 2010 Election Day Policy—which it continues to hold out as authoritative guidance regarding the statute. The first three examples in the Policy are clear enough: items displaying the name of a political party, items displaying the name of a candidate, and items demonstrating "support of or opposition to a ballot question." But the next example—"issue oriented material designed to influence or impact voting,"—raises more questions than it answers. What qualifies as an "issue"? The answer, as far as we can tell is any subject on which a political candidate or party has taken a stance. For instance, the Election Day Policy notes that the "Please I.D. Me" buttons are prohibited. But a voter identification requirement was not on the ballot in 2010, so a Minnesotan would have had no explicit "electoral choice" to make in that respect. The buttons were nonetheless covered because the Republican candidates for Governor and Secretary of State had staked out positions on whether photo identification should be required. A rule whose fair enforcement requires an election judge to maintain a mental index of the platforms and positions of every candidate and party on the ballot is not reasonable. Candidates for statewide and federal office and major political parties can take positions on a wide array of subjects of local and national import. Would a "Support Our Troops" shirt be banned, if one of the candidates or parties had expressed a view on military funding or aid for veterans? What about a "#MeToo" shirt, referencing the movement to increase awareness of sexual harassment and assault? The State indicated that the ban would cover such an item if a candidate had "brought up" the topic.

The next broad category in the Election Day Policy—any item "promoting a group with recognizable political views,"—makes matters worse. The State construes the category as limited to groups with "views" about "the issues confronting voters in a given election." The State does not confine that category to groups that have endorsed a candidate or taken a position on a ballot question. Any number of associations, educational institutions, businesses, and religious organizations could have an opinion on an "issue confronting voters in a given election." For instance, the American Civil Liberties Union, the AARP, the World Wildlife Fund, and Ben & Jerry's all have stated positions on matters of public concern. If the views of those groups align or conflict with the position of a candidate or party on the ballot, does that mean that their insignia are banned? In the run-up to the 2012 election, Presidential candidates of both major parties issued public statements regarding the then-existing policy of the Boy Scouts of America to exclude members on the basis of sexual orientation. Should a Scout leader in 2012 stopping to vote on his way to a troop meeting have been asked to cover up his uniform? The State emphasizes that the ban covers only apparel promoting groups whose political positions are sufficiently "well-known." But that requirement, if anything, only increases the potential for erratic application. Well known by whom? The State tells us the lodestar is the "typical observer" of the item. But that measure may turn in significant part on the background knowledge and media consumption of the particular election judge applying it. The State's "electoral choices" standard, considered together with the nonexclusive examples in the Election Day Policy, poses riddles that even the State's top lawyers struggle to solve. A shirt declaring "All Lives Matter" could be "perceived" as political. How about a shirt bearing the name of the National Rifle Association? Definitely out. That said, a shirt displaying a rainbow flag could be worn "unless there was an issue on the ballot" that "related somehow to gay rights." A shirt simply displaying the text of the Second Amendment? Prohibited. But a shirt with the text of the First Amendment? "It would be allowed."

"Perfect clarity and precise guidance have never been required even of regulations that restrict expressive activity." *Ward v. Rock Against Racism*, 491 U. S. 781, 794 (1989). But the State's difficulties with its restriction go beyond close calls on borderline or fanciful cases. That is a serious matter when the whole point of the exercise is to prohibit the expression of political views. An indeterminate prohibition carries with it "the opportunity for abuse, especially where it has received a virtually open-ended interpretation." *Jews for Jesus*, 482 U. S., at 576. Election judges "have the authority to decide what is political" when screening individuals at the entrance to the polls. We do not doubt that the vast majority of election judges strive to enforce the statute in an evenhanded manner, nor that some degree of discretion in this setting is necessary. But that discretion must be guided by objective, workable standards. Without them, an election judge's own politics may shape his views on what counts as "political." If voters experience or witness episodes of unfair or inconsistent enforcement of the ban, the State's interest in maintaining a polling place free of distraction and disruption would be undermined by the very measure intended to further it. That is not to say that Minnesota has set upon an impossible task. Other States have laws proscribing displays (including apparel) in more lucid terms. We do not suggest that such provisions set the outer limit of what a State may proscribe. But we do hold that if a State wishes to set its polling places apart as areas free of partisan discord, it must employ a more discernible approach than the one Minnesota has offered here.

Cases like this "present us with a particularly difficult reconciliation: the accommodation of the right to engage in political discourse with the right to vote." *Burson*, 504 U. S., at 198 (plurality opinion). Minnesota, like other States, has sought to strike the balance in a way that affords the voter the opportunity to exercise his civic duty in a setting removed from the clamor and din of electioneering. While that choice is generally worthy of our respect, Minnesota has not supported its good intentions with a law capable of reasoned application.

The judgment of the Court of Appeals is reversed, and the case is remanded for further proceedings consistent with this opinion.

It is so ordered.

Justice SOTOMAYOR, with whom Justice BREYER joins, dissenting.

In holding that a polling place constitutes a nonpublic forum and that a State must establish only that its limitations on speech inside the polling place are reasonable, the Court goes a long way in preserving States' discretion to determine what measures are appropriate to further important interests in maintaining order and decorum, preventing confusion and intimidation, and protecting the integrity of the voting process. The Court errs in declaring Minnesota's political apparel ban unconstitutional under that standard, without any guidance from the State's highest court on the proper interpretation of that state law.

∾ PROBLEMS ∾

1. *No-Demonstration Zones.* A regulation restricts "demonstration activity" near the U.S. Capitol, including "parading, picketing, leafleting, holding vigils, sit-ins, or other expressive conduct or speechmaking that conveys a message supporting or opposing a point of view and has the intent, effect or propensity to attract a crowd of onlookers, but does not include merely wearing T-shirts, buttons, or other similar articles of apparel that convey a message." The regulation creates a zone in which "demonstration activity" is entirely barred. The zone includes the sidewalk at the foot of the Senate steps on the Capitol's East Front. The Capitol police arrest an artist participating in the annual Arts Advocacy Day because he distributed leaflets publicizing a lawsuit regarding artist rights on that sidewalk. Before they arrested the artist, the police told him that he could pass out his leaflets 150 feet away from the Capitol on the lawn on the far side of the East Front plaza. But the artist believed that he could not reach his intended audience from the lawn, insisted on his right to leaflet on the sidewalk, and was arrested. The sidewalk is part of the Capitol Grounds, a 60-acre area designed by Frederick Law

Olmstead in the late 1870s. Although barricades prevent vehicles from entering this area except through designated gatehouses, no barriers impede pedestrian access. Members of the public use the area extensively, commuting to work, sight-seeing, posing for pictures, jogging, and walking dogs. The East Front sidewalk is continuously open, often uncongested, and a place where people may enjoy the open air. Is the sidewalk at the foot of the Senate steps a "public forum"? Assume that a court determines that the sidewalk is a "public forum" or a "nontraditional public forum" and not a nonpublic forum. Assume that any regulation in this forum must be content-neutral, justified by a significant government interest, and narrowly tailored, and also must allow for ample alternative channels of communication. Explain the arguments that will be made by the speech litigant who seeks to have the regulation invalidated under this "time, place, manner" test.

2. *The Democratic National Convention.* In 2008, the Democratic Party held its national convention in Denver, Colorado. Citing security concerns, Denver police sought to keep protestors away from the convention. In one instance, although Denver granted a parade permit to protestors, it required the parade to end approximately one third of a mile away from the convention center. *See* Kirk Johnson, *Judge to Rule on Limits at Denver Convention,* N.Y. Times, A-15, c. 1-6, Aug. 1, 2008. Is Denver required to allow the protestors to get close enough to the center that convention-goers can see and hear them? Are protestors entitled to be close enough that they can use the center as a media backdrop?

3. *Art or Vandalism?* An artist is known for his "street art"—art painted on public buildings or structures—especially his portraits of Barack Obama. When he painted a portrait on a railroad trestle, he was charged with vandalism. *See* Abby Goodnough, *Boston Vandalism Charges Stir Debate on Art's Place,* N.Y. Times, A-14, c. 1-5, Mar. 12, 2009. Do artists have a constitutional right to appropriate public spaces for their art?

4. *Begging on Public Streets.* A city passes an ordinance prohibiting begging on public streets. The city argues that begging is not "protected speech," that the ordinance limits "conduct" rather than "speech," that some begging is fraudulent (in that the solicitors are not really "homeless"), and that passers-by feel threatened when beggars solicit money from them. Plaintiffs contend that begging is no different than charitable solicitation, which the Court upheld as constitutionally protected in *Village of Schaumburg v. Citizens for a Better Environment,* 444 U.S. 620 (1980). Is begging "communicative activity," and should it be regarded as protected under the First Amendment? *See Speet v. Schuette,* 726 F.3d 867 (6th Cir. 2013).

5. *Homeless Newspaper Sales.* A group of homeless individuals in the City of Brentwood, California, produce and sell a newspaper. A city ordinance prohibits the sale of newspapers "on any portion of any street within the city." Thus, newspapers can be sold only door to door, or on park property, or on sidewalks. In addition, motorists can buy newspapers provided that the vendor remains on the sidewalk. The city justifies the prohibition of sales "on the streets" on safety grounds. Does the ordinance constitute a permissible time, place, and

manner restriction? *Compare The Contributor v. City of Brentwood,* 726 F.3d 861 (6th Cir. 2013).

6. *The President's Twitter Account.* President Donald Trump used a personal Twitter account, @realDonaldTrump, extensively in his bid for the Presidency, and he has continued to use the account since his election. The account is "generally accessible to the public at large" and the White House Social Media Director assists in the operation of the account. However, President Trump has chosen to block individuals whose replies to his tweets have been critical of him or his policies. Assume that several blocked individuals file suit, arguing that one aspect of the Twitter account is subject to public forum analysis—specifically, the interactive space for replies and retweets created by each tweet that is sent from the account by the President. Should a court find that this space is a designated public forum or a non-public forum? Does the President's blocking of the plaintiffs violate the First Amendment in either case? Does it matter whether President Trump uses the account occasionally "to communicate about other issues not directly related to official government business"? President Trump has argued that critics have plenty of other avenues for responding to his Tweets. What impact should this fact have on the court's analysis of the public forum issue? Should it matter whether the Twitter account is a "personal" account as opposed to an "official" Twitter account (the "POTUS Account") in which the President is blocking people whose replies are critical of his policies? *See Knight First Amendment Institute at Columbia University v. Trump,* 928 F.3d 226 (2d Cir. 2019).

Christian Legal Society Chapter of the University of California v. Martinez

561 U.S. 661 (2010)

Justice GINSBURG delivered the opinion of the Court.

Like many institutions of higher education, Hastings encourages students to form extracurricular associations that "contribute to the Hastings community and experience." These groups offer students "opportunities to pursue academic and social interests outside of the classroom to further their education" and to help them "develop leadership skills." Through its "Registered Student Organization" (RSO) program, Hastings extends official recognition to student groups. Several benefits attend this school-approved status. RSOs are eligible to seek financial assistance from the Law School, which subsidizes their events using funds from a mandatory student-activity fee imposed on all students. RSOs may also use Law-School channels to communicate with students: They may place announcements in a weekly Office-of-Student-Services newsletter; advertise events on designated bulletin boards; send e-mails using a Hastings-organization address; participate in an annual Student Organizations Fair designed to advance recruitment efforts; apply for permission to use the Law School's facilities for meetings and office space; and use the Hastings name and logo. In exchange for these benefits, RSOs must abide by certain conditions. Only a "non-commercial organization whose membership is limited to Hastings students may become an RSO." A prospective RSO must submit its bylaws to Hastings for approval, and if it intends to use the Law School's name or logo, it must sign a license agreement. All RSOs must comply with Hastings' "Policies and Regulations Applying to College Activities, Organizations and Students."

The Law School's Policy on Nondiscrimination, which binds RSOs, states: "Hastings is committed to a policy against legally impermissible, arbitrary or unreasonable discriminatory practices. All groups, including administration, faculty, student governments, Hastings-owned student residence facilities and programs sponsored by Hastings, are governed by this policy of nondiscrimination. Hasting's policy on nondiscrimination is to comply fully with applicable law. Hastings shall not discriminate unlawfully on the basis of race, color, religion, national origin, ancestry, disability, age, sex or sexual orientation. This nondiscrimination policy covers admission, access and treatment in Hastings-sponsored programs and activities." Hastings interprets the Nondiscrimination Policy, as it relates to the RSO program, to mandate acceptance of all comers: School-approved groups must "allow any student to participate, become a member, or seek leadership positions in the organization, regardless of her status or beliefs."[2]

Christian Legal Society (CLS) sought an exemption from the policy. Christian Legal Society (CLS-National), an association of Christian lawyers and law students, charters student chapters at law schools throughout the country. CLS chapters must adopt bylaws that, *inter alia,* require members and officers to sign a "Statement of Faith" and to conduct their lives in accord with prescribed principles. Among those tenets is the belief that sexual activity should not occur outside of marriage between a man and a woman; CLS thus interprets its bylaws to exclude from affiliation anyone who engages in "unrepentant homosexual conduct." CLS also excludes students who hold religious convictions different from those in the Statement of Faith. CLS submitted to Hastings an application for RSO status. The Law School rejected the application; CLS's bylaws, Hastings explained, did not comply with the Nondiscrimination Policy because CLS barred students based on religion and sexual orientation. CLS formally requested an exemption from the Nondiscrimination Policy, but Hastings declined to grant one. If CLS chose to operate outside the RSO program, the school "would be pleased to provide CLS the use of Hastings facilities for its meetings and activities." CLS would also have access to chalkboards and generally available campus bulletin boards to announce its events. Hastings would do nothing to suppress CLS's endeavors, but neither would it lend RSO-level support for them. Refusing to alter its bylaws, CLS did not obtain RSO status. It did, however, operate during the 2004-2005 academic year. CLS held weekly Bible-study meetings and invited

2. "This policy does not foreclose neutral and generally applicable membership requirements unrelated to 'status or beliefs.'" So long as all students have the *opportunity* to participate on equal terms, RSOs may require them to pay dues, maintain good attendance, refrain from gross misconduct, or pass a skill-based test, such as the writing competitions administered by law journals.

Hastings students to Good Friday and Easter Sunday church services. It also hosted a beach barbeque, Thanksgiving dinner, campus lecture on the Christian faith and the legal practice, fellowship dinners, an end-of-year banquet, and other informal social activities. CLS filed suit against various Hastings officers and administrators under 42 U.S.C. §1983. Its complaint alleged that Hastings' refusal to grant the organization RSO status violated CLS's First and Fourteenth Amendment rights to free speech, expressive association, and free exercise of religion. The suit sought injunctive and declaratory relief. On cross-motions for summary judgment, the U.S. District Court ruled in favor of Hastings and the Ninth Circuit affirmed. We affirm.

CLS draws on two lines of decisions. First, this Court has employed forum analysis to determine when a governmental entity, in regulating property in its charge, may place limitations on speech. The Court has permitted restrictions on access to a limited public forum, like the RSO program here, with this key caveat: Any barrier must be reasonable and viewpoint neutral, *e.g., Rosenberger v. Rector and Visitors of Univ. of Va.*, 515 U.S. 819 (1995). Second, this Court has rigorously reviewed laws and regulations that constrain associational freedom. In the context of public accommodations, we have subjected restrictions to close scrutiny; such restrictions are permitted only if they serve "compelling state interests" that are "unrelated to the suppression of ideas"—interests that cannot be advanced "through significantly less restrictive means." *Roberts v. United States Jaycees*, 468 U.S. 609, 623 (1984). "Freedom of association," we have recognized, "plainly presupposes a freedom not to associate." *Roberts*, 468 U.S. at 623. Insisting that an organization embrace unwelcome members "directly and immediately affects associational rights." *Boy Scouts of America v. Dale*, 530 U.S. 640, 659 (2000).

Three observations lead us to conclude that our limited-public-forum precedents supply the appropriate framework for assessing both CLS's speech and association rights. First, the same considerations that led us to apply a less restrictive level of scrutiny to speech in limited public forums as compared to other environments, apply with equal force to expressive association occurring in limited public forums. Speech and expressive-association rights are closely linked. Second, the strict scrutiny we have applied in some settings to laws that burden expressive association would, in practical effect, invalidate a defining characteristic of limited public forums—the State may "reserve them for certain groups." *Rosenberger*, 515 U.S. at 829. Schools, including Hastings, ordinarily, and without controversy, limit official student-group recognition to organizations comprising only students—even if those groups wish to associate with nonstudents. The same ground rules must govern both speech and association challenges in the limited-public-forum context, lest strict scrutiny trump a public university's ability to "confine a speech forum to the limited and legitimate purposes for which it was created." *Rosenberger*, 515 U.S. at 829. Third, this case fits comfortably within the limited-public-forum category, for CLS, in seeking what is effectively a state subsidy, faces only indirect pressure to modify its membership policies; CLS may exclude any person for any reason if it forgoes the benefits of official recognition.

The expressive-association precedents on which CLS relies, in contrast, involved regulations that *compelled* a group to include unwanted members, with no choice to opt out. Our decisions have distinguished between policies that require action and those that withhold benefits. Application of the less-restrictive limited-public-forum analysis better accounts for the fact that Hastings, through its RSO program, is dangling the carrot of subsidy, not wielding the stick of prohibition. We are persuaded that our limited-public-forum precedents adequately respect both CLS's speech and expressive-association rights, and fairly balance those rights against Hastings' interests as property owner and educational institution.

We have three times before considered clashes between public universities and student groups seeking official recognition or its attendant benefits. In *Healy v. James*, 408 U.S. 169, 170 (1972), a state college denied school affiliation to a student group that wished to form a local chapter of Students for a Democratic Society (SDS). A public educational institution exceeds constitutional bounds, we held, when it "restricts speech or association simply because it finds the views expressed by a group to be abhorrent." In *Widmar v. Vincent*, 454 U.S. 263, 270 (1981), a public university had closed its facilities to a registered student group that sought to use university space for religious worship and discussion. Because the university singled out religious organizations for disadvantageous treatment, we found that the school's interest "in maintaining strict separation of church and State was not sufficiently compelling to justify viewpoint discrimination against religious speech." In *Rosenberger*, we reiterated that by "selecting for disfavored treatment those student journalistic efforts with religious editorial viewpoints," the university had engaged in "viewpoint discrimination, which is presumed impermissible when directed against speech otherwise within the forum's limitations." In all three cases, we ruled that student groups had been unconstitutionally singled out because of their points of view. "Once it has opened a limited public forum," we emphasized, "the State must respect the lawful boundaries it has set, and may not exclude speech where its distinction is not reasonable in light of the purpose served by the forum, nor may it discriminate against speech on the basis of viewpoint."

We first consider whether Hastings' policy is reasonable taking into account the RSO forum's function and "all the surrounding circumstances." Our inquiry is shaped by the educational context in which it arises. This Court is the final arbiter of the question whether a public university has exceeded constitutional constraints, and we owe no deference to universities when we consider that question. Cognizant that judges lack the expertise and experience of school administrators, however, we have cautioned courts to resist "substituting their own notions of sound educational policy for those of the school authorities which they review." *Board of Ed. of Hendrick Hudson Central School Dist., Westchester Cty. v. Rowley*, 458 U.S. 176, 206 (1982). A college's commission—and its concomitant license to choose among pedagogical approaches—is not confined to the classroom, for extracurricular programs are, today, essential parts of the educational process. Schools enjoy "a significant measure of authority over the type of officially recognized activities in which their students participate." *Board of Ed. of Westside Community Schools (Dist. 66) v. Mergens*, 496 U.S. 226, 240 (1990). We "approach our task with special caution," mindful that Hastings' decisions about the character of its student-group program are due decent respect.

Hastings offers several justifications in defense of its all-comers requirement. First, the open-access policy "ensures that the leadership, educational, and social opportunities afforded by RSOs are available to all students." Just as "Hastings does not allow its professors to host classes open only to those students with a certain status or belief," so the Law School may decide "that the educational experience is best promoted when all participants provide equal access to all students." RSOs are eligible for financial assistance drawn from mandatory student-activity fees; the all-comers policy ensures that no Hastings student is forced to fund a group that would reject her as a member. The all-comers requirement helps Hastings police the written terms of its Nondiscrimination Policy without inquiring into an RSO's motivation for membership restrictions.

The Law School reasonably adheres to the view that an all-comers policy, to the extent it brings together individuals with diverse backgrounds and beliefs, "encourages tolerance, cooperation, and learning among students." So long as a public university does not contravene constitutional limits, its choice to advance state-law goals through the school's educational endeavors stands on firm footing. In sum, the several justifications Hastings asserts in support of its all-comers requirement are surely reasonable in light of the RSO forum's purposes.

The Law School's policy is all the more creditworthy in view of the "substantial alternative channels that remain open for CLS-student communication to take place." *Perry Ed. Assn.*, 460 U.S. at 53. When access barriers are viewpoint neutral, our decisions have counted it significant that other available avenues for the group to exercise its First Amendment rights lessen the burden created by those barriers. In this case, Hastings offered CLS access to school facilities to conduct meetings and the use of chalkboards and generally available bulletin boards to advertise events. Although CLS could not take advantage of RSO-specific methods of communication, the advent of electronic media and social-networking sites reduces the importance of those channels. CLS hosted a variety of activities the year after Hastings denied it recognition, and the number of students attending those meetings and events doubled. Nonrecognition of a student organization is not equivalent to prohibiting its members from speaking.

CLS nevertheless deems Hastings' all-comers policy "frankly absurd." "There can be no diversity of viewpoints in a forum," it asserts, "if groups are not permitted to form around viewpoints." We have repeatedly stressed that a State's restriction on access to a limited public forum "need not be the most reasonable or the only reasonable limitation." *Cornelius*, 473 U.S. at 808. CLS assails the reasonableness of the all-comers policy in light of the RSO forum's function by forecasting that the policy will facilitate hostile takeovers; saboteurs will infiltrate groups to subvert their mission and message. This supposition strikes us as more hypothetical than real. CLS points to no history or prospect of RSO-hijackings at Hastings. Students tend to self-sort and presumably will not endeavor en masse to join — let alone seek leadership positions in — groups pursuing missions wholly at odds with their personal beliefs. If a rogue student intent on sabotaging an organization's objectives nevertheless attempted a take-over, the members of that group would not likely elect her as an officer. RSOs, moreover, in harmony with the all-comers policy, may condition eligibility for membership and leadership on attendance, the payment of dues, or other neutral requirements designed to ensure that students join because of their commitment to a group's vitality, not its demise. Several RSOs at Hastings limit their membership rolls and officer slates in just this way. A reasonable policy need not anticipate and preemptively close off every opportunity for avoidance or manipulation. If students exploit an all-comers policy by hijacking organizations to distort or destroy their missions, Hastings presumably would revisit and revise its policy. Hastings, caught in the crossfire between a group's desire to exclude and students' demand for equal access, may reasonably draw a line in the sand permitting *all* organizations to express what they wish but *no* group to discriminate in membership.

In contrast to *Healy, Widmar,* and *Rosenberger,* in which universities singled out organizations for disfavored treatment because of their points of view, Hastings' all-comers requirement draws no distinction between groups based on their message or perspective. An all-comers condition on access to RSO status, in short, is textbook viewpoint neutral. CLS attacks the regulation as vulnerable to constitutional assault because "it systematically and predictably burdens most heavily those groups whose viewpoints are out of favor with the campus mainstream." "A regulation that serves purposes unrelated to the content of expression is deemed neutral, even if it has an incidental effect on some speakers or messages but not others." *Ward v. Rock Against Racism,* 491 U.S. 781, 791 (1989). Even if a regulation has a differential impact on groups wishing to enforce exclusionary membership policies, "where the State does not target conduct on the basis of expressive content, acts are not shielded from regulation merely because they express a discriminatory idea or philosophy." *R.A.V. v. St. Paul,* 505 U.S. 377, 390 (1992).

Hastings' requirement that student groups accept all comers "is justified without reference to the content or viewpoint of the regulated speech." *Ward,* 491 U.S. at 791. The Law School's policy aims at the *act* of rejecting would-be group members without reference to the reasons motivating that behavior: Hastings' "desire to redress the perceived harms" of exclusionary membership policies "provides an adequate explanation for its all-comers condition over and above mere disagreement with any student group's beliefs or biases." *Wisconsin v. Mitchell,* 508 U.S. 476, 488 (1993). As Hastings observes, "CLS is simply confusing its *own* viewpoint-based objections to nondiscrimination laws (which it is entitled to have and to voice) with viewpoint *discrimination.*" Finding Hastings' open-access condition on RSO status reasonable and viewpoint neutral, we reject CLS' free-speech and expressive-association claims.

For the foregoing reasons, we affirm the Court of Appeals' ruling that the all-comers policy is constitutional and remand the case for further proceedings consistent with this opinion.

It is so ordered.

Justice STEVENS, *concurring.*

The Nondiscrimination Policy is content and viewpoint neutral. It does not reflect a judgment by school officials about the substance of any student group's speech. Nor does it exclude any would-be groups on the basis of their convictions. Indeed, it does not regulate expression or belief at all. The policy is "directed at the organization's activities rather than its philosophy," *Healy v. James,* 408 U.S. 169 (1972). Regardless of whether they are the product of secular or spiritual feeling, hateful or benign motives, all acts of religious discrimination are equally covered. There is, moreover, no evidence that the policy was adopted because of any reason related to the particular views that religious individuals or groups might have, much less because of a desire to suppress or distort those views. The policy's religion clause was plainly meant to promote, not to undermine, religious freedom.

An RSO program is a *limited* forum — the boundaries of which may be *delimited* by the proprietor. When a religious association, or a secular association, operates in a wholly public setting, it must be allowed broad freedom to control its membership and its message, even if its decisions cause offense to outsiders. But CLS aspires to be an RSO. As a general matter, courts should respect universities' judgments and let them manage their own affairs. The RSO forum is not an open commons that Hastings happens to maintain. It is a mechanism through which Hastings confers certain benefits and pursues certain aspects of its educational mission. Having exercised its discretion to establish an RSO program, a university must treat all participants evenhandedly. But the university need not remain neutral in determining which goals the program will serve and which rules are best suited to facilitate those goals. These are not legal questions but policy questions; they are not for the Court but for the university to make. When any group refuses to comply with the rules, the RSO sponsor need not admit that group at the cost of undermining the program and the values reflected therein. Petitioner excludes students who will not sign its Statement of Faith or who engage in "unrepentant homosexual conduct." Other groups may exclude or mistreat Jews, blacks, and women — or those who do not share their contempt for Jews, blacks, and women. A free society must tolerate such groups. It need not subsidize them, give them its official imprimatur, or grant them equal access to law school facilities.

Justice KENNEDY, *concurring.*

The policy in question is not content based either in its formulation or evident purpose. The policy applies equally to all groups and views. An objection might be that the all-comers policy, even if not so designed or intended, makes it difficult for certain groups to express their views in a manner essential to their message. Petitioner would have a substantial case if it were shown that the all-comers policy was designed or used to infiltrate the group or challenge its leadership in order to stifle its views. But that has not been shown to be likely or self-evident as a matter of group dynamics in this setting.

Justice ALITO, with whom THE CHIEF JUSTICE, Justice SCALIA, and Justice THOMAS join, *dissenting*.

Once a public university opens a limited public forum, it must maintain strict viewpoint neutrality. When Hastings refused to register CLS, it claimed that the CLS bylaws impermissibly discriminated on the basis of religion and sexual orientation. Both grounds constituted impermissible viewpoint discrimination. The policy singled out one category of expressive associations for disfavored treatment: groups formed to express a religious message. Only religious groups were required to admit students who did not share their views. An environmentalist group was not required to admit students who rejected global warming. An animal rights group was not obligated to accept students who supported the use of animals to test cosmetics. But CLS was required to admit avowed atheists. This was patent viewpoint discrimination. Hastings' sudden adoption and selective application of its accept-all-comers policy was a pretext for the law school's unlawful denial of CLS's registration application under the Nondiscrimination Policy. During a recent year, CLS had seven members. Suppose that 10 students who are members of denominations that disagree with CLS decided that CLS was misrepresenting true Christian doctrine. Suppose that these students joined CLS, elected officers who shared their views, ended the group's affiliation with the national organization, and changed the group's message. A true accept-all-comers policy permits small unpopular groups to be taken over by students who wish to change the views that the group expresses.

Lee v. International Society for Krishna Consciousness, Inc.

505 U.S. 830 (1992)

PER CURIAM.

For the reasons expressed in the opinions of Justice O'Connor, Justice Kennedy, and Justice Souter in *International Society for Krishna Consciousness v. Lee*, the judgment of the Court of Appeals holding that the ban on distribution of literature in the Port Authority airport terminals is invalid under the First Amendment is
   Affirmed.

Chief Justice REHNQUIST, with whom Justice WHITE, Justice SCALIA, and Justice THOMAS, join, *dissenting*.

Leafleting presents risks of congestion similar to those posed by solicitation. It presents, in addition, some risks unique to leafleting. And, of course, as with solicitation, these risks must be evaluated against a backdrop of the substantial congestion problem facing the Port Authority and with an eye to the cumulative impact that will result if all groups are permitted terminal access. Viewed in this light, I conclude that the distribution ban, no less than the solicitation ban, is reasonable.

The risks and burdens posed by leafleting are quite similar to those posed by solicitation. The weary, harried, or hurried traveler may have no less desire and need to avoid the delays generated by having literature foisted upon him than he does to avoid delays from a financial solicitation. And while a busy passenger may succeed in fending off a leafletter with minimal disruption to himself by agreeing simply to take the proffered material, this does not completely ameliorate the dangers of congestion flowing from such leafleting. Others may choose not simply to accept the material but also to stop and engage the leafletter in debate, obstructing those who follow. Moreover, those who accept material may often simply drop it on the floor once out of the leafletter's range, creating an eyesore, a safety hazard, and additional cleanup work for the airport staff.

In addition, a differential ban that permits leafleting but prohibits solicitation, while giving the impression of permitting the Port Authority at least half of what it seeks, may in fact prove for the Port Authority to be a much more Pyrrhic victory. Under the regime that is today sustained, the Port Authority is obliged to permit leafleting. But monitoring leafleting activity in order to ensure that it is only leafleting that occurs, and not also soliciting, may prove little less burdensome than the monitoring that would be required if solicitation were permitted. At a minimum, therefore, I think it remains open whether at some future date the Port Authority may be able to reimpose a complete ban, having developed evidence that enforcement of a differential ban is overly burdensome. Until now it has had no reason or means to do this, since it is only today that such a requirement has been announced.

Note: Justice O'Connor and ISKCON

Justice O'Connor provided the fifth vote to invalidate the ban on the distribution of literature. The other votes came from Justices Kennedy and Souter, whose separate opinions (joined by Justices Blackmun and Stevens) supported Justice Kennedy's views. Justice O'Connor found that the ban was an unreasonable regulation of a nonpublic forum:

> "The reasonableness of the Government's restriction must be assessed in light of the purpose of the forum and all the surrounding circumstances." "Consideration of a forum's special attributes is relevant to the constitutionality of a regulation since the significance of the governmental interest must be assessed in light of the characteristic nature and function of the particular forum involved." In this case, the "special attributes" and "surrounding circumstances" of airports operated by the Port Authority are determinative. Not only has the Port Authority chosen not to limit access to the airports, it has created a huge complex open to

traveler and nontravelers alike. The airports house restaurants, cafeterias, snack bars, coffee shops, drug stores, food stores, nurseries, barber shops, currency exchanges, art exhibits, commercial advertising displays, bookstores, newsstands, dental offices and private clubs. The International Arrivals Building at JFK Airport even has two branches of Bloomingdale's.

A restriction on speech in a nonpublic forum is "reasonable" when it is "consistent with the government's legitimate interest in preserving the property for the use to which it is lawfully dedicated." The Port Authority is operating a shopping mall as well as an airport. The reasonableness inquiry, therefore, is not whether the restrictions on speech are "consistent with preserving the property" for air travel, but whether they are reasonably related to maintaining the multi-purpose environment that the Port Authority has created. The regulation banning leafleting cannot be reasonable. Leafleting does not entail the same kind of problems presented by face-to-face solicitation. With the possible exception of avoiding litter, it is difficult to point to any problems intrinsic to the act of leafleting that would make it naturally incompatible with a large, multipurpose forum such as airport terminals. Of course, it is still open for the Port Authority to promulgate regulations of the time, place, and manner of leafleting which are "content-neutral, narrowly tailored to serve a significant government interest, and leave open ample alternative channels of communication." During the many years that this litigation has been in progress, the Port Authority has not banned sankirtan completely from JFK International Airport, but has restricted it to a relatively uncongested part of the airport terminals, the same part that houses the chapel. That regulation meets the standards applied to time, place, and manner restrictions of protected expression.

Note: Public Access Channels

Manhattan Community Access Corp. v. Halleck, 139 S. Ct. 1921 (2019), involved a New York cable operator that was required by its contract (and by government regulation) to create public access channels. The operator decided to ban two producers from those channels because of their viewpoint (they were critical of the operator). Applying the state action doctrine, the Court held that the cable operator was a private actor, rather than a state actor, because it did not perform a function "traditionally exclusively reserved to the State": "A private entity who opens its property for speech by others is not transformed by that fact alone into a state actor. In operating the public access channels, MNN is a private actor, not a state actor, and MNN therefore is not subject to First Amendment constraints on its editorial discretion." The Court rejected the idea that the public access channels involved a public forum for speech: "The Constitution does not disable private property owners and private lessees from exercising editorial discretion over speech and speakers on their property." Justice Sotomayor, joined by three other justices, dissented: "This is a case about an organization appointed by the government to administer a constitutional public forum. New York City secured a property interest in public-access television channels when it granted a cable franchise to a cable company. State regulations require those public-access channels to be open to the public on terms that render them a public forum. The City contracted out the administration of that forum to a private organization, Manhattan Community Access Corporation (MNN). By accepting that agency relationship, MNN stepped into the City's shoes and thus qualifies as a state actor, subject to the First Amendment."

∾ PROBLEMS ∾

1. *The Port Authority's Ban on Literature.* Suppose that after September 11, 2001, the Port Authority of New York decides to reinstate a total ban on the distribution of literature in airport terminals, arguing that conditions have changed and that the *Lee* Court's decision to invalidate the ban must be reconsidered in light of airport security issues. (Assume that the bans on literature sales and solicitation of funds are still in place, after being upheld in *ISKCON.*) If you are the lawyer for the Port Authority, what arguments will you make to support the reinstatement of the ban on the distribution of literature? If the airport is still considered to be a nonpublic forum, so that the "reasonableness" test applies, what arguments will you make? Then, if you assume that you must prepare for the possibility that the Court will reverse its earlier finding in *ISKCON* and declare the airport to be a public forum, so that the "time, place, manner" test applies, will your arguments be different?

2. *Campus Free Speech Zone.* Suppose that a public college decides to establish a "free speech zone" and prohibits all free speech activities outside that zone. However, the zone comprises only .003% of the college's 426 acre campus, and the zone can be used only from 9:00 a.m. to 7:00 p.m., Monday through Friday. In order to use the free speech zone, a student must apply for a permit at least three days in advance, and the application must submit his or her name and the name of the organization with which he or she is affiliated. A Hispanic student at the college wishes to distribute Spanish-language versions of the U.S. Constitution to all students on campus. He objects to the free speech zone because he believes that it is enforced in a selective and discriminatory way. Consistently with the First Amendment, can the college limit all free speech activities on campus to a small "free speech zone?" Can it require applicants to provide a copy of all information and materials that they wish to distribute as part of the permit process? *See Shaw v. Burke,* 2018 WL 459661 (C.D. Cal. Jan. 17, 2018).

1. Content-Based Restrictions

As the next case reveals, the use of strict scrutiny emerged in First Amendment doctrine as a borrowing from equal protection doctrine. The requirements imposed by strict scrutiny in modern cases, however, depend on the status of the forum in which the content-based regulation operates.

Police Department of City of Chicago v. Mosley

408 U.S. 92 (1972)

Mr. Justice MARSHALL delivered the opinion of the Court.

At issue in this case is the constitutionality of the following Chicago ordinance: "A person commits disorderly conduct when he knowingly: (i) Pickets or demonstrates on a public way within 150 feet of any primary or secondary school building while the school is in session and one-half hour before the school is in session and one-half hour after the school session has been concluded, provided, that this subsection does not prohibit the peaceful picketing of any school involved in a labor dispute."

The suit was brought by Earl Mosley, a federal postal employee, who for seven months prior to the enactment of the ordinance had frequently picketed Jones Commercial High School in Chicago. During school hours and usually by himself, Mosley would walk the public sidewalk adjoining the school, carrying a sign that read: "Jones High School practices black discrimination. Jones High School has a black quota." His lonely crusade was always peaceful, orderly, and quiet, and was conceded to be so by the city of Chicago.

On March 26, 1968, Chapter 1931 (i) was passed, to become effective on April 5. Seeing a newspaper announcement of the new ordinance, Mosley contacted the Chicago Police Department to find out how the ordinance would affect him; he was told that, if his picketing continued, he would be arrested. On April 4, the day before the ordinance became effective, Mosley ended his picketing next to the school. Thereafter, he brought this federal suit seeking declaratory and injunctive relief on constitutional grounds.

The city of Chicago exempts peaceful labor picketing from its general prohibition on picketing next to a school. The question we consider here is whether this selective exclusion from a public place is permitted. Our answer is "No."

We apply "strict scrutiny," requiring the government to have a compelling interest to justify the regulation, and requiring that the regulation must be narrowly tailored that interest. The central problem with Chicago's ordinance is that it describes permissible picketing in terms of its subject matter. Peaceful picketing on the subject of a school's labor-management dispute is permitted, but all other peaceful picketing is prohibited. The operative distinction is the message on a picket sign. But, above all else, the First Amendment means that government has no power to restrict expression because of its message, its ideas, its subject matter, or its content. *Cohen v. California*, 403 U.S. 15 (1971). To permit the continued building of our politics and culture, and to assure self-fulfillment for each individual, our people are guaranteed the right to express any thought, free from government censorship. The essence of this forbidden censorship is content control. Any restriction on expressive activity because of its content would completely undercut the "profound national commitment to the principle that debate on public issues should be uninhibited, robust, and wide-open."

Necessarily, under the First Amendment, government may not grant the use of a forum to people whose views it finds acceptable, but deny use to those wishing to express less favored or more controversial views. And it may not select which issues are worth discussing or debating in public facilities. There is an "equality of status in the field of ideas," and government must afford all points of view an equal opportunity to be heard. Once a forum is opened up to assembly or speaking by some groups, government may not prohibit others from assembling or speaking on the basis of what they intend to say. Selective exclusions from a public forum may not be based on content alone, and may not be justified by reference to content alone.

Guided by these principles, we have frequently condemned such discrimination among different users of the same medium for expression. In *Niemotko v. Maryland*, 340 U.S. 268 (1951), a group of Jehovah's Witnesses were denied a permit to use a city park for Bible talks, although other political and religious groups had been allowed to put the park to analogous uses. Concluding that the permit was denied because of the city's "dislike for or disagreement with the Witnesses or their views," this Court held that the permit refusal violated "the right to equal protection of the laws, in the exercise of those freedoms of speech and religion protected by the First Amendment." *See also Cox v. Louisiana*, 379 U.S. 536 (1965).

This is not to say that all picketing must always be allowed. We have continually recognized that reasonable "time, place and manner" regulations of picketing may be necessary to further significant governmental interests. There may be sufficient regulatory interests justifying selective exclusions or distinctions among pickets. Conflicting demands on the same place may compel the State to make choices among potential users and uses. And the State may have a legitimate interest in prohibiting some picketing to protect public order. But these justifications for selective exclusions from a public forum must be carefully scrutinized. Because picketing plainly involves expressive conduct within the protection of the First Amendment, discriminations among pickets must be tailored to serve a significant later Court would say "compelling" governmental interest.

In this case, the ordinance itself describes impermissible picketing not in terms of time, place, and manner, but in terms of subject matter. The regulation "thus slips from the neutrality of time, place, and circumstance into a concern about content." This is never permitted. In spite of this, Chicago urges that the ordinance is not improper content censorship, but rather a device for preventing disruption of the school. Cities certainly have a substantial interest in stopping picketing which disrupts a school. Although preventing school disruption is a city's legitimate concern, Chicago itself has determined that peaceful labor picketing during school hours is not an undue interference with school. Under the Equal Protection Clause, Chicago may not maintain that other picketing disrupts the school unless that picketing is clearly more disruptive than the picketing Chicago already permits.

Similarly, we reject the city's argument that, although it permits peaceful labor picketing, it may prohibit all nonlabor picketing because, as a class, nonlabor picketing is more prone to produce violence than labor picketing. Predictions about imminent disruption from picketing involve judgments appropriately made on an individualized basis, not by means of broad classifications, especially those based on subject matter. Freedom of expression, and its intersection with the guarantee of equal protection, would rest on a soft foundation indeed if government could distinguish among picketers on such a wholesale and categorical basis. "In our system, undifferentiated fear or apprehension of disturbance is not enough to overcome the right to freedom of expression." Some labor picketing is peaceful, some disorderly; the same is true of picketing on other themes. No labor picketing could be more peaceful or less prone to violence than Mosley's solitary vigil. In seeking to restrict nonlabor picketing that is clearly more disruptive than peaceful labor picketing, Chicago may not prohibit all nonlabor picketing at the school forum.

Chicago may not vindicate its interest in preventing disruption by the wholesale exclusion of picketing on all but one preferred subject. Given what Chicago tolerates from labor picketing, the excesses of some nonlabor picketing may not be controlled by a broad ordinance prohibiting both peaceful and violent picketing. Such excesses "can be controlled by narrowly drawn statutes," focusing on the abuses and dealing evenhandedly with picketing regardless of subject matter. Far from being tailored to a substantial later Courts would say "compelling" governmental interest, the discrimination among pickets is based on the content of their expression. Therefore, it may not stand.

The judgment is affirmed.

Notes

1. Selective Exclusions. In post-*Mosley* cases, the Court held that the strict scrutiny standard for selective exclusions of speech or speakers from public fora should not be used in nonpublic forum cases. Instead, selective exclusion regulations may be upheld as long as they are "viewpoint-neutral," even though they are not "content-neutral" but rather "content-based" regulations. *See Cornelius v. NAACP Legal Defense and Educational Fund, Inc.,* 473 U.S. 788 (1985) (holding that the exclusion of legal defense and political advocacy groups from the nonpublic forum of a workplace fundraising drive was "viewpoint neutral"); *Perry Education Association v. Perry Local Educators' Association,* 460 U.S. 37 (1983) (holding that teacher mailboxes were nonpublic forums, and that the restriction of the mailboxes to the elected teachers' union, as well as a variety of other organizations, and the exclusion of a competing union from access to the mailboxes were "viewpoint-neutral" regulations).

2. More on Time, Place, and Manner Restrictions. In *Heffron v. International Society for Krishna Consciousness, Inc.,* 452 U.S. 640 (1981), the Court upheld a regulation

requiring a religious organization desiring to distribute and sell religious literature and to solicit donations at a state fair to conduct those activities only at an
assigned location within the fairgrounds even though the rule limited the religious practices of the organization. Minnesota State Fair Rule 6.05 provided in
relevant part that "sale or distribution of any merchandise, including printed or
written material except under license issued by the Society and/or from a duly-
licensed location shall be a misdemeanor." As Rule 6.05 is construed, "all persons, groups or firms which desire to sell, exhibit or distribute materials during
the annual State Fair must do so only from fixed locations on the fairgrounds."
Although the Rule does not prevent organizational representatives from walking about the fairgrounds and communicating the organization's views with fair
patrons in face-to-face discussions, it does require that any exhibitor conduct its
sales, distribution, and fund solicitation operations from a booth rented from the
Society. Space in the fairgrounds is rented to all comers in a nondiscriminatory
fashion on a first-come, first-served basis. The Rule applies to nonprofit, charitable, and commercial enterprises.

In upholding the regulation, the Court noted that, although ISKCON's
activities were protected by the First Amendment, they were subject to reasonable time, place, and manner restrictions, and the Court held that Rule 6.05 was
a permissible restriction on the place and manner of practicing Sankirtan which
involved the solicitation of donations. The Court noted that the Rule applied
evenhandedly to all who wished to distribute and sell written materials or to
solicit funds so that nobody was required to do so from a booth. The Court held
that the Rule served "significant governmental interests": the need to maintain
the orderly movement of the crowd given the large number of exhibitors and
persons attending the fair; an interest in protecting fairgoers from "fraudulent
solicitations, deceptive or false speech, and undue annoyance"; and the interest in protecting them "from being harassed or otherwise being bothered" as
a captive audience. The Court emphasized that a State's interest in protecting
the "safety and convenience" of persons using a public forum was a valid governmental objective because a "fair is a temporary event attracting great numbers of
visitors" and the "flow of the crowd and demands of safety are more pressing." If
an exception were granted to ISKCON, others would also demand exceptions,
including perhaps commercial organizations, and disorder would result.

3. *More on* Heffron. *Heffron* illustrates the substantive application of the
"time, place, manner" formula used for "content-neutral" regulations in a "public forum." The *Heffron* regulation was "content-neutral" because it was not based
on the substance of the speaker's message, and the state fair was assumed to be a
public forum either because it is like streets and parks, which "have immemorially been held in trust for the use of the public" and "for purposes of assembly,"
or because it is a newer forum that has been "opened" by the government for
such purposes. If the regulation in *Heffron* had been "content-based" in a "public
forum," then the strict scrutiny test would have been applied, and a compelling
governmental interest would have been required. *See Police Department of City of*

Chicago v. Mosley, 408 U.S. 92 (1972). By contrast, if the *Heffron* regulation had related to a "nonpublic forum," then if the regulation were "content-neutral," it would be required only to be "reasonable." If it were "content-based" in a "non-public forum," it would be acceptable as long as it is "not an effort to suppress the speaker's activity due to disagreement with the speaker's view" — that is to say, not "viewpoint-neutral." *See Perry Education Association v. Perry Local Educators' Assn.*, 460 U.S. 37 (1983).

∾ PROBLEMS ∾

1. *Sidewalks Near Embassies.* A provision of the D.C. Code makes it unlawful "to display any flag, banner, placard, or device designed or adapted to intimidate, coerce, or bring into public odium any foreign government, party, or organization, or any officers thereof, or to bring into public disrepute [the] political social or economic acts, views or purposes of any foreign government, party or organization within 500 feet of any building or premises within the District of Columbia used or occupied by any foreign government or its representatives as an embassy, legation, consulate, or for other official purposes." Plaintiffs file suit, challenging this provision because they wish to carry signs critical of the Russian Federation on the public sidewalk within 500 feet of the government's embassy on Wisconsin Avenue in Washington, D.C. How will the court analyze the constitutionality of the D.C. code provision under *Mosley*? *See Boos v. Barry*, 485 U.S. 312 (1988).

2. *Hyperlinks to a City's Web Site.* Suppose that a city government maintains a Web site on which it provides a hyperlink to state- and town-sponsored nonpartisan outside events (e.g., a day-long discussion at a middle school designed to promote community spirit, civic discourse, and the organization of community-defined projects and action groups), but the city rejects a hyperlink for a partisan political group that is critical of the government. The city draws a distinction between providing hyperlinks to partisan and nonpartisan events, and indicates that it will allows links for the latter events but not the former. In providing hyperlinks, did the city create a public forum? Did the city engage in viewpoint discrimination? Would it matter that the city demanded information from the partisan group regarding its mission, members, and finances? *See Sutliffe v. Epping School District*, 584 F.3d 314 (1st Cir. 2009).

3. *The Warning Brochures.* A private group (the Illinois Dunes Preservation Society) believes that the Illinois Beach State Park is contaminated by asbestos, and asks the State of Illinois to install racks for the group to display brochures warning visitors about the dangers. The state refuses the request even though it permits other brochure racks in the park. However, all of the other brochures are placed there by the state and are designed to encourage people to frequent the parks. Does the Society have a First Amendment right to display the warning brochures at the park? *See Illinois Dunesland Preservation Society v. Illinois Department of Natural Resources*, 584 F.3d 719 (7th Cir. 2009).

4. *Election Speech.* In *Burson v. Freeman*, 504 U.S. 191 (1992), the Court used the *Mosley* analysis to upheld a ban on election speech (not including exit polling) within 100 feet of the entrance to a polling place. Four Justices found the 100-foot zone to be a public forum and held that strict scrutiny was satisfied, noting that there was sufficient evidence in the record that political candidates had used campaign workers to commit voter intimidation or electoral fraud at polling places, but had not used other forms of solicitation or exit polling to commit "electoral abuses." "The State, as recognized administrator of elections, has asserted that the exercise of free speech rights conflicts with another fundamental right, the right to cast a ballot in an election free from the taint of intimidation and fraud. A long history, a substantial consensus, and simple common sense shows that some restricted zone around polling places is necessary to protect that fundamental right." Two Justices voted with the plurality to uphold the regulation on the merits, but they would have found the entrance to the polling place to be a nonpublic forum. Three Justices would have invalidated the statute on the grounds that the *Mosley* test could not be satisfied, assuming without deciding that the 100-foot zone was a public forum.

5. *Speech on Private Property.* The Court has used different doctrines for evaluating challenges brought by speech litigants to regulations involving protected speech on private property. In *Marsh v. Alabama*, 326 U.S. 501 (1946), the Court held that a "company town" could not require written permission for speech activities on the street, including solicitation of funds, without First Amendment scrutiny, and the company's attempt to enforce this requirement through soliciting a criminal prosecution for trespass was held to be unconstitutional. The fact that a corporation-employer owned all the property of the town did not exempt the owner from the necessity of recognizing First Amendment rights, and "the more an owner, for his advantage opens up his property for use by the public in general, the more do his rights become circumscribed by the constitutional rights of those who use it." In *Amalgamated Food Employees Union v. Logan Valley Plaza, Inc.*, 391 U.S. 308 (1968), the Court held that a state court could not enjoin peaceful picketing of a store in a mall shopping center because the shopping center was the "functional equivalent" of the public business district in *Marsh* where trespass laws could not be enforced at the will of the owner. However, in *Lloyd Corp. Ltd. v. Tanner*, 407 U.S. 551 (1972), the Court refused to uphold an injunction to prevent the arrest of peaceful leafletters at a shopping mall, because the message of those leafletters was addressed to the general public and not, as in *Logan Valley Plaza*, solely to the members of the public who patronized a particular store in the mall. Finally, in *Hudgens v. NLRB*, 424 U.S. 507 (1976), the Court overruled *Logan Valley Plaza* while affirming *Marsh*, and held that a shopping mall does not compare to a municipality, and the owner may regulate expression on the basis of the content of the expression.

6. *Nationwide Protests by the Occupy Movement.* The Occupy Wall Street movement, which began in New York in 2011, taking up residence in Zuccotti Park raised public forum issues. The Occupy movement consisted of a diverse group

of individuals, many from the left side of the political spectrum and unemployed. The movement purported to represent what they claimed was the 99% of the population who were disadvantaged by the current political and economic system. Occupy Wall Street did not have an organized plan of action or a set of demands. Indeed, given its anarchic roots, the Occupy movement may have simply been reluctant to embrace leaders or specific policy positions. The Occupy movement had an aversion to hierarchy and to formal leaders, but a strong commitment to democratic principles. Participants in the movement seemed to share an elevated level of anger regarding wealth disparities, special interests, and the prevailing political system. Separate issues bubbled to the surface in other protests, including unemployment and the high levels of student debt. Occupy protestors took over certain public places such as public squares, parks, and city property. In some cases, Occupy protestors literally lived at these sites, bringing in camping gear, tents, and cook stoves. Protests spread quickly to foreign countries and around the United States with protests involving thousands of people.

7. *Attorneys' Fees for Plaintiffs Who Obtain Injunctions.* In *Lefemine v. Wideman,* 568 U.S. 1 (2012), the Court held that the plaintiff was entitled to attorneys' fees under 42 U.S.C. §1988 as the "prevailing party" in a §1983 suit that led to an injunction on First Amendment grounds. Plaintiff abandoned his first sidewalk demonstration protesting the availability of abortions when police officers told him that he would be cited for disorderly conduct if he did not discard the graphic "pictures of aborted fetuses" that he was using in his protest. Later, when plaintiff informed the sheriff that he planned to conduct another demonstration using the same images, he was again threatened with citation. The trial court granted summary judgment for plaintiff on First Amendment grounds, and permanently enjoyed defendants "from engaging in content-based discrimination regarding plaintiff's display of graphic signs under similar circumstances." The Court held that plaintiffs were entitled to receive attorneys' fees as a "prevailing party" since they obtained "actual relief on the merits" of a claim that "materially alters the legal relationship between the parties by modifying the defendant's behavior in a way that directly benefits the plaintiff." The Court noted that it had "repeatedly held that an injunction or declaratory judgment, like a damages award, will usually satisfy that test."

∽ PROBLEMS ∽

1. *Access to Health Care Statute.* A Colorado statute makes it illegal to come within 8 feet of another person, without that person's consent, within 100 feet of the entrance to any health care facility, "for the purpose of passing a leaflet or handbill to, displaying a sign to, or engaging in oral protest, education, or counseling with such other person." The legislative history of the statute reveals that it was enacted to provide unimpeded access to health care facilities, promote

the avoidance of potential trauma to patients associated with confrontational protests, and protect unwilling listeners from unwanted communications. The statute covers three types of communications: the display of signs, leafleting, and oral speech. Assume that a lawsuit is brought challenging the statute on First Amendment grounds. What arguments might be made by the government in support of the statute, and by speech litigants to invalidate the statute? *See Hill v. Colorado*, 530 U.S. 703 (2000).

2. *Government Center Complex.* A Mount Vernon, Maryland, ordinance limits protests to the grassy median at the entrance to the Government Center Complex. The Complex is located in a largely wooded area that is removed from residential, commercial, and office areas, and is accessed from a horseshoe-shaped driveway that leads from the parkway to the front door of the building and back to the parkway. By the driveway is a median consisting of grass, trees, brick, and concrete, which is referred to as the Center Island and is about 30 yards wide and 200 yards long. Sidewalks circumnavigate the island. The area is not enclosed, but rather is open to the public. May Mount Vernon limit displays and protests to the Center Island?

3. *Peace, Hope, and Love.* In the preceding problem, assume that the ordinance further provides: "The use of the common areas is limited to individual residents or employees of the county, and permits may be obtained for displays on the Center Island. Each display is limited to one week per year, and it must clearly state that it is a private display." Rita Wax applies to Mount Vernon for a permit to display a message of "peace, hope, and love" on a grassy median near the Complex. The county denies the permit because the median is designated for displays only by county residents and employees, and Rita is neither (she lives in another county). After Rita's application is denied, she files suit in federal court challenging the county's decision on First Amendment grounds. What First Amendment arguments can you make on her behalf? What counterarguments do you expect the county to make in response? (Do not argue vagueness or overbreadth.)

McCullen v. Coakley

573 U.S. 464 (2014)

Chief Justice ROBERTS delivered the opinion of the Court.

In 2000, the Massachusetts Legislature enacted the Massachusetts Reproductive Health Care Facilities Act, Mass. Gen. Laws, ch. 266, §120E (West 2000). The law was designed to address clashes between abortion opponents and advocates of abortion rights that were occurring outside clinics where abortions were performed. The Act established a defined area with an 18-foot radius around the entrances and driveways of such facilities. Anyone could enter that area, but once within it, no one (other than certain exempt individuals) could knowingly approach within six feet of another person—unless that person consented — "for the purpose of passing a leaflet or handbill to, displaying a sign to, or engaging in oral protest, education, or counseling with such other person." A separate provision subjected to criminal punishment anyone who "knowingly obstructs, detains, hinders, impedes or blocks another person's entry to or exit from a reproductive health care facility." The statute was modeled on a similar Colorado law that this Court upheld in *Hill v. Colorado,* 530 U. S. 703 (2000). The United States Court of Appeals for the First Circuit sustained the statute against a First Amendment challenge.

By 2007, some Massachusetts legislators and law enforcement officials had come to regard the 2000 statute as inadequate. At legislative hearings, multiple witnesses recounted violations of the law. Massachusetts Attorney General Martha Coakley played a video depicting protestors approaching patients and clinic staff within the buffer zones, ostensibly without consent. Clinic employees and volunteers testified that protestors congregated near the doors and driveways of the clinics, with the result that prospective patients occasionally retreated from the clinics rather than try to make their way to the clinic entrances or parking lots. Captain Evans of the Boston Police Department testified that his officers had made "no more than five or so arrests" at the Planned Parenthood clinic in Boston and that what few prosecutions had been brought were unsuccessful. Captain Evans testified that the 18-foot zones were so crowded with protestors that it was hard to determine whether a protestor had deliberately approached a patient or whether the patient had consented. Coakley concluded that the six-foot no-approach zones were "unenforceable." What the police needed, she said, was a fixed buffer zone around clinics that protestors could not enter. Evans agreed. To address these concerns, the Massachusetts Legislature amended the statute, replacing the six-foot no-approach zones (within the 18-foot area) with a 35-foot fixed buffer zone from which individuals are categorically excluded: "No person shall knowingly enter or remain on a public way or sidewalk adjacent to a reproductive health care facility within a radius of 35 feet of any portion of an entrance, exit or driveway of a reproductive health care facility or within the area within a rectangle created by extending the outside boundaries of any entrance, exit or driveway of a reproductive health care facility in straight lines to the point where such lines intersect the sideline of the street in front of such entrance, exit or driveway." A "reproductive health care facility" is defined as "a place, other than within or upon the grounds of a hospital, where abortions are offered or performed."

The 35-foot buffer zone applies only "during a facility's business hours," and the area must be "clearly marked and posted." Facilities mark the zones with painted arcs and posted signs on sidewalks and streets. A first violation of the statute is punishable by a fine of up to $500, up to three months in prison, or both, while a subsequent offense is punishable by a fine of between $500 and $5,000, up to two and a half years in prison, or both. The Act exempts four classes of individuals: (1) "persons entering or leaving such facility"; (2) "employees or agents of such facility acting within the scope of their employment"; (3) "law enforcement, ambulance, firefighting, construction, utilities, public works and other municipal agents acting within the scope of their employment"; and (4) "persons using the public sidewalk or street right-of-way adjacent to such facility solely for the purpose of reaching a destination other than such facility." One provision proscribes the knowing obstruction of access to a facility.

Some of the individuals who stand outside Massachusetts abortion clinics are protestors who express their moral or religious opposition to abortion through signs and chants or more aggressive methods such as face-to-face confrontation. Petitioners attempt to engage women approaching the clinics in what they call "sidewalk counseling," which involves offering information about alternatives to abortion and help pursuing those options. Eleanor McCullen, for instance, will typically initiate a conversation this way: "Good morning, may I give you my literature? Is there anything I can do for you? I'm available if you have any questions." If the woman seems receptive, McCullen will provide additional information. Petitioners consider it essential to maintain a caring demeanor, a calm tone of voice, and direct eye contact during these exchanges. Such interactions, petitioners believe, are a much more effective means of dissuading women from having abortions than confrontational methods such as shouting or brandishing signs, which tend only to antagonize their intended audience. Petitioners say they have collectively persuaded hundreds of women to forgo abortions. The buffer zones have displaced petitioners from their previous positions outside the clinics. McCullen offers counseling outside a Planned Parenthood clinic in Boston, as do petitioners Zarrella and Cadin. Petitioner Smith prays the rosary there. The clinic occupies its own building on a street corner. Its main door is recessed into an open foyer, approximately 12 feet back from the public sidewalk. Before the Act was amended to create buffer zones, petitioners stood near the entryway to the foyer. Now a buffer zone—marked by a painted arc and a sign—surrounds the entrance. This zone extends 23 feet down the sidewalk in one direction, 26 feet in the other, and outward just one foot short of the curb. The clinic's entrance adds another seven feet to the width of the zone. Petitioners are effectively excluded from a 56-foot-wide expanse of the public sidewalk in front of the clinic.

Petitioners Bashour and Clark offer counseling and information outside a Planned Parenthood clinic in Worcester. The Worcester clinic sits well back from the public street and sidewalks. Patients enter the clinic in one of two ways. Those arriving on foot turn off the public sidewalk and walk down a nearly 54-foot-long private walkway to the main entrance. More than 85% of patients arrive by car, turning onto the clinic's driveway from the street, parking in a private lot, and walking to the main entrance on a private walkway. Bashour and Clark would like to stand where the private walkway or driveway intersects the sidewalk and offer leaflets to patients as they walk or drive by. But a painted arc extends 35 feet down the sidewalk in either direction and outward nearly to the curb on the opposite side of the street. Another arc surrounds the driveway's entrance, covering more than 93 feet of the sidewalk (including the width of the driveway) and extending across the street and nearly six feet onto the sidewalk on the opposite side.

Bashour and Clark must now stand either some distance down the sidewalk from the private walkway and driveway or across the street.

Petitioner Cyril Shea stands outside a Planned Parenthood clinic in Springfield, which, like the Worcester clinic, is set back from the public streets. 90% of patients arrive by car and park in private lots surrounding the clinic. Shea used to position himself at an entrance to one of the driveways leading to the parking lots. Painted arcs now surround the entrances, each spanning approximately 100 feet of the sidewalk parallel to the street (again, including the width of the driveways) and extending outward well into the street. Shea now stands far down the sidewalk from the driveway entrances. Petitioners claim that the buffer zones have considerably hampered their counseling efforts. Although they have managed to conduct some counseling and distribute some literature outside the buffer zones—particularly at the Boston clinic—they have had many fewer conversations and distributed many fewer leaflets since the zones went into effect.

The second statutory exemption allows clinic employees and agents acting within the scope of their employment to enter the buffer zones. Relying on this exemption, the Boston clinic uses "escorts" to greet women as they approach the clinic, accompanying them through the zones to the clinic entrance. Petitioners claim that the escorts sometimes thwart petitioners' attempts to communicate with patients by blocking petitioners from handing literature to patients, telling patients not to "pay any attention" or "listen to" petitioners, and disparaging petitioners as "crazy."

Petitioners sued Coakley and other Commonwealth officials. They sought to enjoin enforcement of the Act, alleging that it violates the First and Fourteenth Amendments, both on its face and as applied to them. The District Court denied petitioners' facial challenge. The Court of Appeals for the First Circuit affirmed. The case then returned to the District Court. After another bench trial, it denied the remaining as-applied challenge, finding that the Act left petitioners ample alternative channels of communication. The Court of Appeals once again affirmed. We granted certiorari.

The Massachusetts Act regulates access to "public ways" and "sidewalks." Such areas occupy a "special position in terms of First Amendment protection" because of their historic role as sites for discussion and debate. *United States v. Grace*, 461 U.S. 171 (1983). These places—labeled "traditional public fora"—"have immemorially been held in trust for the use of the public and, time out of mind, have been used for purposes of assembly, communicating thoughts between citizens, and discussing public questions." *Pleasant Grove City v. Summum*, 555 U.S. 460 (2009). It is no accident that public streets and sidewalks have developed as venues for the exchange of ideas. Even today, they remain one of the few places where a speaker can be confident that he is not simply preaching to the choir. With respect to other means of communication, an individual confronted with an uncomfortable message can always turn the page, change the channel, or leave the Web site. Not so on public streets and sidewalks. There, a listener often encounters speech he might otherwise tune out. In light of the

First Amendment's purpose "to preserve an uninhibited marketplace of ideas in which truth will ultimately prevail," *FCC v. League of Women Voters of Cal.*, 468 U. S. 364 (1984), this aspect of traditional public fora is a virtue, not a vice. In short, traditional public fora are areas that have historically been open to the public for speech activities. Thus, even though the Act says nothing about speech on its face, there is no doubt that it restricts access to traditional public fora and is therefore subject to First Amendment scrutiny.

Consistent with the traditionally open character of public streets and sidewalks, the government's ability to restrict speech in such locations is "very limited." *Grace, supra,* at 177. The guiding First Amendment principle that the "government has no power to restrict expression because of its message, its ideas, its subject matter, or its content" applies with full force in a traditional public forum. *Police Dept. of Chicago v. Mosley,* 408 U. S. 92 (1972). In such a forum the government may not "selectively shield the public from some kinds of speech on the ground that they are more offensive than others." *Erznoznik v. Jacksonville,* 422 U. S. 205 (1975). "Even in a public forum the government may impose reasonable restrictions on the time, place, or manner of protected speech, provided the restrictions 'are justified without reference to the content of the regulated speech, that they are narrowly tailored to serve a significant governmental interest, and that they leave open ample alternative channels for communication of the information.'" *Ward,* 491 U. S. at 791 (quoting *Clark v. Community for Creative Non-Violence,* 468 U. S. 288 (1984)).

Petitioners contend that the Act is not content neutral for two reasons: First, they argue that it discriminates against abortion-related speech because it establishes buffer zones only at clinics that perform abortions. Second, petitioners contend that the Act, by exempting clinic employees and agents, favors one viewpoint about abortion over the other. If either of these arguments is correct, then the Act must satisfy strict scrutiny—that is, it must be the least restrictive means of achieving a compelling state interest. See *United States v. Playboy Entertainment Group, Inc.,* 529 U. S. 803 (2000).

The Act applies only at a "reproductive health care facility," defined as "a place, other than within or upon the grounds of a hospital, where abortions are offered or performed." Given this definition, petitioners argue, "virtually all speech affected by the Act is speech concerning abortion," thus rendering the Act content based. We disagree. The Act does not draw content-based distinctions on its face. Contrast *Boos v. Barry,* 485 U. S. 312 (1988); *Carey v. Brown,* 447 U. S. 455 (1980). The Act would be content based if it required "enforcement authorities" to "examine the content of the message that is conveyed to determine whether" a violation has occurred. It does not. Whether petitioners violate the Act "depends" not "on what they say," but simply on where they say it. Petitioners can violate the Act merely by standing in a buffer zone, without displaying a sign or uttering a word.

By limiting the buffer zones to abortion clinics, the Act has the "inevitable effect" of restricting abortion-related speech more than speech on other subjects.

But a facially neutral law does not become content based simply because it may disproportionately affect speech on certain topics. On the contrary, "a regulation that serves purposes unrelated to the content of expression is deemed neutral, even if it has an incidental effect on some speakers or messages but not others." *Ward, supra,* at 791. The question is whether the law is "justified without reference to the content of the regulated speech." *Renton v. Playtime Theatres, Inc.,* 475 U. S. 41 (1986). The stated purpose is to "increase forthwith public safety at reproductive health care facilities." Respondents have articulated similar purposes namely, "public safety, patient access to healthcare, and the unobstructed use of public sidewalks and roadways." We have previously deemed the foregoing concerns to be content neutral. See *Boos,* 485 U. S. at 321. Obstructed access and congested sidewalks are problems no matter what caused them. A group of individuals can obstruct clinic access and clog sidewalks just as much when they loiter as when they protest abortion or counsel patients.

The Act would not be content neutral if it were concerned with undesirable effects that arise from "the direct impact of speech on its audience" or "listeners' reactions to speech." If the speech outside Massachusetts abortion clinics caused offense or made listeners uncomfortable, such offense or discomfort would not give the Commonwealth a content-neutral justification to restrict the speech. All of the problems identified by the Commonwealth arise irrespective of any listener's reactions. Whether or not a single person reacts to abortion protestors' chants or petitioners' counseling, large crowds outside abortion clinics can compromise public safety, impede access, and obstruct sidewalks.

Petitioners do not dispute that the Commonwealth's interests in ensuring safety and preventing obstruction are content neutral. But petitioners note that these interests "apply outside every building in the State that hosts any activity that might occasion protest or comment," not just abortion clinics. By choosing to pursue these interests only at abortion clinics, petitioners argue, the Massachusetts Legislature evinced a purpose to "single out for regulation speech about one particular topic: abortion." We cannot infer such a purpose from the Act's limited scope. The broad reach of a statute can help confirm that it was not enacted to burden a narrower category of disfavored speech. At the same time, "States adopt laws to address the problems that confront them. The First Amendment does not require States to regulate for problems that do not exist." *Burson v. Freeman,* 504 U. S. 191 (1992) (plurality opinion). The Massachusetts Legislature amended the Act in 2007 in response to a problem that was, in its experience, limited to abortion clinics. There was a record of crowding, obstruction, and even violence outside such clinics. There were apparently no similar recurring problems associated with other kinds of healthcare facilities, let alone with "every building in the State that hosts any activity that might occasion protest or comment." In light of the limited nature of the problem, it was reasonable for the Massachusetts Legislature to enact a limited solution. When selecting among various options for combating a particular problem, legislatures should be encouraged to choose the one that restricts less speech, not more.

Justice Scalia objects that the statute does restrict more speech than necessary, because "only one Massachusetts abortion clinic is known to have been beset by the problems that the statute supposedly addresses." But there are no grounds for inferring content-based discrimination simply because the legislature acted with respect to abortion facilities generally rather than proceeding on a facility-by-facility basis. The poor fit goes to the question of narrow tailoring, which we consider below.

Petitioners argue that the Act is content based because it exempts four classes of individuals, one of which comprises "employees or agents of a reproductive healthcare facility acting within the scope of their employment." This exemption, petitioners say, favors one side in the abortion debate and thus constitutes viewpoint discrimination—an "egregious form of content discrimination," *Rosenberger v. Rector and Visitors of Univ. of Va.*, 515 U. S. 819, 829 (1995). Petitioners argue that the exemption allows clinic employees and agents—including the volunteers who "escort" patients arriving at the Boston clinic—to speak inside the buffer zones. Of course, "an exemption from an otherwise permissible regulation of speech may represent a governmental 'attempt to give one side of a debatable public question an advantage in expressing its views to the people.'" *City of Ladue v. Gilleo*, 512 U. S. 43, 51 (1994) (quoting *First Nat. Bank of Boston v. Bellotti*, 435 U. S. 765, 785–786 (1978)). The statutory exemption for clinic employees and agents acting within the scope of their employment does not appear to be such an attempt. There is nothing inherently suspect about providing some kind of exemption to allow individuals who work at the clinics to enter or remain within the buffer zones. The exemption cannot be regarded as simply a carve-out for the clinic escorts; it also covers employees such as the maintenance worker shoveling a snowy sidewalk or the security guard patrolling a clinic entrance. Given the need for an exemption for clinic employees, the "scope of their employment" qualification simply ensures that the exemption is limited to its purpose of allowing the employees to do their jobs. It performs the same function as the identical "scope of their employment" restriction on the exemption for "law enforcement, ambulance, fire-fighting, construction, utilities, public works and other municipal agents." The limitation makes clear—with respect to both clinic employees and municipal agents—that exempted individuals are allowed inside the zones only to perform those acts authorized by their employers.

There is no suggestion that any of the clinics authorize their employees to speak about abortion in the buffer zones. Petitioners did testify about instances in which escorts at the Boston clinic had expressed views about abortion to the women they were accompanying, thwarted petitioners' attempts to speak and hand literature to the women, and disparaged petitioners in various ways. It is unclear whether these alleged incidents occurred within the buffer zones. There is no viewpoint discrimination if the incidents occurred outside the zones because petitioners are equally free to say whatever they would like in that area. Even assuming the incidents occurred inside the zones, the record does not suggest that they involved speech within the scope of the escorts' employment. If the speech was beyond the scope of their employment, then each of the alleged incidents would violate the Act's express terms. Petitioners' complaint would then be that the police were failing to *enforce* the Act equally against clinic escorts. While such allegations might state a claim of official viewpoint discrimination, that would not go to the validity of the Act. In any event, petitioners nowhere allege selective enforcement.

It would be a very different question if a clinic authorized escorts to speak about abortion inside the buffer zones. The Act's exemption for clinic employees would then facilitate speech on only one side of the abortion debate—a clear form of viewpoint discrimination that would support an as-applied challenge to the buffer zone at that clinic. The record contains insufficient evidence to show that the exemption operates in this way at any of the clinics, perhaps because the clinics do not want to doom the Act by allowing their employees to speak about abortion within the buffer zones.

Even though the Act is content neutral, it must be "narrowly tailored to serve a significant governmental interest." *Ward*, 491 U. S. at 796. The tailoring requirement does not simply guard against an impermissible desire to censor. The government may attempt to suppress speech not only because it disagrees with the message being expressed, but also for mere convenience. Where speech is associated with particular problems, silencing the speech is sometimes the path of least resistance. By demanding a close fit between ends and means, the tailoring requirement prevents the government from too readily "sacrificing speech for efficiency." *Riley v. National Federation of Blind of N. C., Inc.*, 487 U. S. 781 (1988). For a content-neutral time, place, or manner regulation to be narrowly tailored, it must not "burden substantially more speech than is necessary to further the government's legitimate interests." *Ward*, 491 U. S. at 799. Such a regulation "need not be the least restrictive or least intrusive means of" serving the government's interests. But the government "may not regulate expression in such a manner that a substantial portion of the burden on speech does not serve to advance its goals."

Respondents claim that the Act promotes "public safety, patient access to healthcare, and the unobstructed use of public sidewalks and roadways." We have recognized the legitimacy of the government's interests in "ensuring public safety and order, promoting the free flow of traffic on streets and sidewalks, protecting property rights, and protecting a woman's freedom to seek pregnancy-related services." *Schenck v. Pro-Choice Network of Western N. Y.*, 519 U. S. 357, 376 (1997). The buffer zones serve these interests. At the same time, the buffer zones impose serious burdens on petitioners' speech. At each of the three Planned Parenthood clinics where petitioners attempt to counsel patients, the zones carve out a significant portion of the adjacent public sidewalks, pushing petitioners well back from the clinics' entrances and driveways. The zones compromise petitioners' ability to initiate the close, personal conversations that they view as essential to "sidewalk counseling." McCullen explained that she often cannot distinguish patients from passers by in time to initiate a conversation before they enter the buffer zone.

Even when she does manage to begin a discussion outside the zone, she must stop abruptly at its border, which causes her to appear "untrustworthy" or "suspicious." McCullen is often reduced to raising her voice at patients from outside the zone—a mode of communication sharply at odds with the compassionate message she wishes to convey. Clark gave similar testimony about her experience at the Worcester clinic.

These burdens have clearly taken their toll. Although McCullen claims that she has persuaded about 80 women not to terminate their pregnancies since the 2007 amendment, she reaches "far fewer people" than she did before the amendment. Zarrella estimated having about 100 successful interactions over the years before the 2007 amendment, but not a single one since. At the Worcester clinic, Clark testified that "only one woman out of 100 will make the effort to walk across the street to speak with her."

The buffer zones have also made it substantially more difficult for petitioners to distribute literature to arriving patients. Because petitioners in Boston cannot readily identify patients before they enter the zone, they often cannot approach them in time to place literature near their hands—the most effective means of getting the patients to accept it. In Worcester and Springfield, the zones have pushed petitioners so far back from the clinics' driveways that they can no longer even attempt to offer literature as drivers turn into the parking lots. In short, the Act operates to deprive petitioners of their two primary methods of communicating with patients. While the First Amendment does not guarantee a speaker the right to any particular form of expression, some forms—such as normal conversation and leafletting on a public sidewalk—have historically been more closely associated with the transmission of ideas than others.

In the context of petition campaigns, "one-on-one communication" is "the most effective, fundamental, and perhaps economical avenue of political discourse." *Meyer v. Grant*, 486 U. S. 414, 424 (1988). "Handing out leaflets in the advocacy of a politically controversial viewpoint is the essence of First Amendment expression"; "no form of speech is entitled to greater constitutional protection." *McIntyre v. Ohio Elections Comm'n*, 514 U. S. 334, 347 (1995). When the government makes it more difficult to engage in these modes of communication, it imposes an especially significant First Amendment burden.

Respondents emphasize that the Act does not prevent petitioners from engaging in various forms of "protest"—such as chanting slogans and displaying signs—outside the buffer zones. That misses the point. Petitioners are not protestors. They seek not merely to express their opposition to abortion, but to inform women of various alternatives and to provide help in pursuing them. Petitioners believe that they can accomplish this objective only through personal, caring, consensual conversations. It is easier to ignore a strained voice or a waving hand than a direct greeting or an outstretched arm. While petitioners have been able to have a number of quiet conversations outside the buffer zones, the conversations have been far less frequent and far less successful since the buffer zones were instituted. It is no answer to say that petitioners can still be "seen and heard" by women within the buffer zones. If all that the women can see and hear are vociferous opponents of abortion, then the buffer zones have effectively stifled petitioners' message.

Respondents suggest that, at Worcester and Springfield, petitioners are prevented from communicating with patients not by the buffer zones but by the fact that most patients arrive by car and park in the clinics' private lots. The layout of the two clinics would prevent petitioners from approaching the clinics' *doorways*, even without the buffer zones. But petitioners do not claim a right to trespass. They instead claim a right to stand on the sidewalks by the driveway as cars turn into the parking lot. Before the buffer zones, they could do so. Now they must stand a substantial distance away. The Act is responsible for that restriction on their ability to convey their message.

The buffer zones burden substantially more speech than necessary to achieve the Commonwealth's asserted interests. Respondents identify no other State with a law that creates fixed buffer zones around abortion clinics. That of course does not mean that the law is invalid. It does raise concern that the Commonwealth has too readily forgone options that could serve its interests just as well, without substantially burdening the kind of speech in which petitioners wish to engage. The Commonwealth's interests include ensuring public safety outside abortion clinics, preventing harassment and intimidation of patients and clinic staff, and combating deliberate obstruction of clinic entrances. The Act itself contains a separate provision that subjects to criminal punishment "any person who knowingly obstructs, detains, hinders, impedes or blocks another person's entry to or exit from a reproductive health care facility." If Massachusetts determines that broader prohibitions along the same lines are necessary, it could enact legislation similar to the federal Freedom of Access to Clinic Entrances Act of 1994 (FACE Act), 18 U. S. C. §248(a)(1), which subjects to both criminal and civil penalties anyone who "by force or threat of force or by physical obstruction, intentionally injures, intimidates or interferes with or attempts to injure, intimidate or interfere with any person because that person is or has been, or in order to intimidate such person or any other person or any class of persons from, obtaining or providing reproductive health services." Some dozen other States have done so. If the Commonwealth is particularly concerned about harassment, it could also consider an ordinance such as the one adopted in New York City that not only prohibits obstructing access to a clinic, but also makes it a crime "to follow and harass another person within 15 feet of the premises of a reproductive health care facility." N. Y. C. Admin. Code §8–803(a)(3) (2014).[5]

The Commonwealth points to a substantial public safety risk created when protestors obstruct driveways leading to the clinics. That is an example of

5. We do not "give our approval" to this or any of the other alternatives we discuss. We merely suggest that a law like the New York City ordinance could constitute a permissible alternative. Whether such a law would pass constitutional muster would depend on a number of other factors, such as whether the term "harassment" had been authoritatively construed to avoid vagueness and overbreadth problems.

its failure to look to less intrusive means of addressing its concerns. Any such obstruction can readily be addressed through existing local ordinances. See, *e.g.*, Boston, Mass., Municipal Code, ch. 16–41.2(d) (2013) ("No person shall solicit while walking on, standing on or going into any street or highway used for motor vehicle travel, or any area appurtenant thereto (including medians, shoulder areas, bicycle lanes, ramps and exit ramps)"). All of the foregoing measures are, in addition to available generic criminal statutes forbidding assault, breach of the peace, trespass, vandalism, and the like. Subsection (e) of the Act, the FACE Act, and the New York City anti-harassment ordinance are all enforceable not only through criminal prosecutions but also through public and private civil actions for injunctions and other equitable relief. We have noted the First Amendment virtues of targeted injunctions as alternatives to broad, prophylactic measures. Such an injunction "regulates the activities, and perhaps the speech, of a group," but only "because of the group's past *actions* in the context of a specific dispute between real parties." *Madsen*, 512 U. S. at 762. Moreover, given the equitable nature of injunctive relief, courts can tailor a remedy to ensure that it restricts no more speech than necessary. In short, injunctive relief focuses on the precise individuals and the precise conduct causing a particular problem. The Act, by contrast, categorically excludes non-exempt individuals from the buffer zones, unnecessarily sweeping in innocent individuals and their speech.

The Commonwealth also asserts an interest in preventing congestion in front of abortion clinics. Even when individuals do not deliberately obstruct access to clinics, they can inadvertently do so simply by gathering in large numbers. But the Commonwealth could address that problem through more targeted means. Some localities have ordinances that require crowds blocking a clinic entrance to disperse when ordered to do so by the police, and that forbid individuals to reassemble within a certain distance of the clinic for a certain period. We upheld a similar law forbidding three or more people "to congregate within 500 feet of a foreign embassy, and refuse to disperse after having been ordered so to do by the police," *Boos*, 485 U. S. at 316 — an order the police could give only when they "reasonably believed that a threat to the security or peace of the embassy was present." To the extent the Commonwealth argues that even these types of laws are ineffective, it has another problem. The portions of the record that respondents cite to support the anticongestion interest pertain mainly to one place at one time: the Boston Planned Parenthood clinic on Saturday mornings. Respondents point to no evidence that individuals regularly gather at other clinics, or at other times in Boston, in sufficiently large groups to obstruct access. For a problem shown to arise only once a week in one city at one clinic, creating 35-foot buffer zones at every clinic across the Commonwealth is hardly a narrowly tailored solution.

The Commonwealth has available to it a variety of approaches that appear capable of serving its interests, without excluding individuals from areas historically open for speech and debate. Respondents emphasize the history in Massachusetts of obstruction at abortion clinics, and the Commonwealth's allegedly failed attempts to combat such obstruction with injunctions and individual prosecutions. They also point to the Commonwealth's experience under the 2000 Act, during which the police found it difficult to enforce the six-foot no-approach zones given the "frenetic" activity in front of clinic entrances. Respondents identify not a single prosecution brought under those laws within at least the last 17 years. While they claim that the Commonwealth "tried injunctions," the last injunctions they cite date to the 1990s. In short, the Commonwealth has not shown that it seriously undertook to address the problem with less intrusive tools readily available to it. Nor has it shown that it considered different methods that other jurisdictions have found effective.

Respondents contend that the alternatives suffer from two defects: First, given the "widespread" nature of the problem, it is simply not "practicable" to rely on individual prosecutions and injunctions. But the problem appears to be limited principally to the Boston clinic on Saturday mornings. By their own account, the police appear perfectly capable of singling out lawbreakers. The legislative testimony revealed substantial police and video monitoring at the clinics, especially when large gatherings were anticipated. Officers are so familiar with the scene outside the Boston clinic that they "know all the players down there." If Commonwealth officials can compile an extensive record of obstruction and harassment to support legislation, we do not see why they cannot do the same to support injunctions and prosecutions against those who might deliberately flout the law.

The second supposed defect is that laws like subsection (e) of the Act and the federal FACE Act require a showing of intentional or deliberate obstruction, intimidation, or harassment, which is often difficult to prove. As Captain Evans predicted, fixed buffer zones "make our job so much easier." Of course they would. But that is not enough to satisfy the First Amendment. To meet the requirement of narrow tailoring, the government must demonstrate that alternative measures that burden substantially less speech would fail to achieve the government's interests, not simply that the chosen route is easier. A painted line on the sidewalk is easy to enforce, but the prime objective of the First Amendment is not efficiency. We do not think that showing intentional obstruction is nearly so difficult in this context as respondents suggest. To determine whether a protestor intends to block access to a clinic, a police officer need only order him to move. If he refuses, then his continued conduct is knowing or intentional.

Respondents' reliance on our decision in *Burson v. Freeman* is misplaced. There, we upheld a state statute that established 100-foot buffer zones outside polling places on election day within which no one could display or distribute campaign materials or solicit votes. We approved the buffer zones as a valid prophylactic measure, noting that existing "intimidation and interference laws fall short of serving a State's compelling interests because they 'deal with only the most blatant and specific attempts' to impede elections." Such laws were insufficient because "voter intimidation and election fraud are difficult to detect." Obstruction of abortion clinics and harassment of patients, by contrast, are anything but subtle. We noted in *Burson* that under state law, "law enforcement officers generally are barred from the vicinity of the polls to avoid any appearance of coercion in the electoral process," with the result that "many acts of interference would go undetected." Not so here. The police maintain a significant presence outside Massachusetts abortion clinics.

Petitioners wish to converse with their fellow citizens about an important subject on the public streets and sidewalks—sites that have hosted discussions about the issues of the day throughout history. Respondents assert undeniably significant interests in maintaining public safety on those same streets and sidewalks, as well as in preserving access to adjacent healthcare facilities. But the Commonwealth has pursued those interests by the extreme step of closing a substantial portion of a traditional public forum to all speakers. It has done so without seriously addressing the problem through alternatives that leave the forum open for its time-honored purposes. The Commonwealth may not do that consistent with the First Amendment. The judgment of the Court of Appeals for the First Circuit is reversed, and the case is remanded for further proceedings consistent with this opinion.

It is so ordered.

Justice SCALIA, with whom Justice KENNEDY and Justice THOMAS join, *concurring in the judgment.*

Today's opinion carries forward this Court's practice of giving abortion-rights advocates a pass when it comes to suppressing the free-speech rights of their opponents. It blinks reality to say, as the majority does, that a blanket prohibition on the use of streets and sidewalks where speech on only one politically controversial topic is likely to occur—and where that speech can most effectively be communicated—is not content based. The structure of the Act indicates that it rests on content-based concerns. The goals of "public safety, patient access to healthcare, and the unobstructed use of public sidewalks and roadways," are achieved by an earlier-enacted subsection of the statute, which provides criminal penalties for "any person who knowingly obstructs, detains, hinders, impedes or blocks another person's entry to or exit from a reproductive health care facility." That provision is easy to enforce. The speech-free zones carved out by subsection (b) add nothing to safety and access; what they achieve, and what they were obviously designed to achieve, is the suppression of speech opposing abortion. Protecting people from speech they do not want to hear is not a function that the First Amendment allows the government to undertake in the public streets and sidewalks.

Petitioners contend that the Act targets speech opposing abortion (and thus constitutes a presumptively invalid viewpoint-discriminatory restriction). It exempts "employees or agents" of an abortion clinic acting within the scope of their employment. There is not a shadow of a doubt that the assigned or foreseeable conduct of a clinic employee or agent can include both speaking in favor of abortion rights and countering the speech of people like petitioners. Indeed, the trial record includes testimony that escorts at the Boston clinic "expressed views about abortion to the women they were accompanying, thwarted petitioners' attempts to speak and hand literature to the women, and disparaged petitioners in various ways," including by calling them "crazy." In sum, the Act should be reviewed under the strict-scrutiny standard applicable to content-based legislation. Having determined that the Act is content based and does not withstand strict scrutiny, I need not pursue the inquiry whether the statute is "narrowly tailored to serve a significant governmental interest."

Justice ALITO, *concurring in the judgment.*

The Massachusetts statute at issue in this case violates the First Amendment. It is clear on the face of the law that it discriminates based on viewpoint. Speech in favor of the clinic and its work by employees and agents is permitted; speech criticizing the clinic and its work is a crime. If the law were truly content neutral, the law would still be unconstitutional on the ground that it burdens more speech than is necessary to serve the Commonwealth's asserted interests.

Note: "As Applied" Challenges

McCullen noted that it was applying "an uncontroversial principle of constitutional adjudication: that a plaintiff generally cannot prevail on an *as-applied* challenge without showing that the law has in fact been (or is sufficiently likely to be) unconstitutionally *applied* to him. When someone challenges a law as viewpoint discriminatory but it is not clear from the face of the law which speakers will be allowed to speak, he must show that he was prevented from speaking while someone espousing another viewpoint was permitted to do so." The Court emphasized that "we do not hold that speech restrictions favoring one viewpoint over another are not content based unless it can be shown that the favored viewpoint has actually been expressed."

∼ PROBLEMS ∼

1. *Buffer Zone for Parking Enforcement Officers.* A city employs parking enforcement officers (PEOs) to make daily rounds of the parking meters downtown in order to issue tickets for cars parked at expired meters. Protestors follow the PEOs, looking for expired meters, inserting coins before a ticket can issue. They leave a card on the car windshield that reads: "Your meter expired! However, we saved you from the king's tariff!" The protestors also talk to the PEOs, criticize them for attempting to issue tickets, and encourage them to quit their jobs. The city seeks to enjoin the protesters from "communicating with any PEO" or coming within "a safety zone of 30 feet" of any on-duty PEO, and prohibiting protestors from "touching, taunting, obstructing, detaining, hindering, impeding, blocking,

intimidating, or harassing" conduct within that safety zone. At trial, several PEOs testify that the protestors made them feel anxious and harassed, and that they considered quitting their jobs. The attorney for the protestors argues that the suit should be dismissed because the requested injunction would violate the First Amendment, citing *McCullen v. Coakley* and *Snyder v. Phelps.* How should the court rule? *See City of Keene v. Cleaveland,* 2015 LEXIS 53 (N.H.) (June 9, 2015).

2. *Roadway Medians.* A county ordinance prohibits the conduct of "distributing handbills, soliciting contributions, or selling merchandise to car drivers or passengers while standing in county roadways, including median areas." Following passage of the law, homeless persons continue to solicit financial donations in the medians, but they did so while sitting down. The police chief then proposes that the ordinance be amended to prohibit sitting, as well, on the basis that it would make the roads safer. His testimony is based on his personal opinion, rather than on consultations with traffic-safety experts, and he cannot give any examples of accidents caused by people in the median areas who were engaged in acts prohibited by the ordinance. However, the county attorney's office reported an "increased number of complaints from county motorists concerning panhandling in the medians" of particular roadways. Based on the chief's testimony and the report, the board amends the ordinance to prohibit the distribution of handbills, the solicitation of contributions, or the selling of merchandise to car drivers or passengers, "*while in the highway,*" defined as "the entire width of a road or street that is improved, designed, or ordinarily used for vehicular travel and the shoulder, *the median,* and the area between the travel lane and the back of the curb." The amended ordinance was challenged on First Amendment grounds by a group that included homeless persons (who wanted to solicit donations) and by people who wanted to distribute campaign literature. Under *McCullen,* is the law valid? *See Reynolds v. Middleton,* 779 F.3d 222 (4th Cir. 2015).

3. *Homeless Newspaper Sales.* A group of homeless individuals in the City of Brentwood, California, produce and sell a newspaper. A city ordinance prohibits the sale of newspapers "on any portion of any street within the city." Thus, newspapers can be sold only door to door, or on park property, or on sidewalks. In addition, motorists can buy newspapers provided that the vendor remains on the sidewalk. The city justifies the prohibition on safety grounds. Does the ordinance constitute a permissible time, place, and manner restriction? *See The Contributor v. City of Brentwood,* 726 F.3d 861 (6th Cir. 2013).

4. *Restrictions on Park Vendors.* City officials in New York City are concerned about the aesthetics and congestion in the city's public parks, and so they enact regulations that impose restrictions on the size and placement of vendor tables, and the places where tables can be placed. The restrictions only apply in parks that are determined to be suffering from serious congestion issues. Under the regulations, "expressive-matter" vendors are allowed to sell their materials without obtaining the permit required for other types of vendors. But "expressive-matter" vendors are subject to the size and location restrictions applicable to all

other vendors. Are these restrictions constitutional? *See Ledgeman v. N.Y.C. Dep't of Parks & Recreation*, 731 F.3d 199 (2d Cir. 2013).

Reed v. Town of Gilbert

576 U.S. 155 (2015)

Justice THOMAS delivered the opinion of the Court.

Gilbert, Arizona adopted a code governing the manner in which people may display outdoor signs. The Sign Code identifies categories of signs based on the type of information they convey, then subjects each category to different restrictions. One category is "Temporary Directional Signs Relating to a Qualifying Event," loosely defined as signs directing the public to a meeting of a nonprofit group. The Code imposes more stringent restrictions on these signs than it does on signs conveying other messages. These provisions are content-based regulations of speech that cannot survive strict scrutiny.

The Sign Code prohibits the display of outdoor signs anywhere without a permit, but exempts 23 categories of signs from that requirement. These exemptions include everything from bazaar signs to flying banners. Three categories of exempt signs are particularly relevant here. The first is "Ideological Signs." This category includes any "sign communicating a message or ideas for noncommercial purposes that is not a Construction Sign, Directional Sign, Temporary Directional Sign Relating to a Qualifying Event, Political Sign, Garage Sale Sign, or a sign owned or required by a governmental agency." The Code treats ideological signs most favourably, allowing them to be up to 20 square feet in area and to be placed in all "zoning districts" without time limits. The second category is "Political Signs." This includes any "temporary sign designed to influence the outcome of an election called by a public body." The Code treats these signs less favourably than ideological signs. The Code allows the placement of political signs up to 16 square feet on residential property and up to 32 square feet on nonresidential property, undeveloped municipal property, and "rights-of-way." These signs may be displayed up to 60 days before a primary election and up to 15 days following a general election. The third category is "Temporary Directional Signs Relating to a Qualifying Event." A temporary sign is defined as a "sign not permanently attached to the ground, a wall or a building, and not designed or intended for permanent display." This includes any "Temporary Sign intended to direct pedestrians, motorists, and other passers by to a 'qualifying event.'" A "qualifying event" is any "assembly, gathering, activity, or meeting sponsored, arranged, or promoted by a religious, charitable, community service, educational, or other similar non-profit organization." The Code treats temporary directional signs even less favourably than political signs. Temporary directional signs may be no larger than six square feet. They may be placed on private property or on a public right-of-way. But no more than four signs may be placed on a single property at any time. They may be displayed no more than 12 hours before the "qualifying event" and no more than 1 hour afterward.

Petitioners Good News Community Church and its pastor, Clyde Reed, wish to advertise the time and location of their Sunday church services. The Church is a small, cash-strapped entity that owns no building, so it holds its services at elementary schools or other locations. To inform the public about its services, which are held in a variety of locations, the Church began placing 15 to 20 temporary signs around the Town, frequently in the public right-of-way abutting the street. The signs displayed the Church's name, along with the time and location of the upcoming service. Church members would post the signs early on Saturday and then remove them around midday on Sunday. The display requires little money and manpower, and thus has proved to be an economical and effective way for the Church to let the community know where its services are being held. The Town's Sign Code compliance manager twice cited the Church for violating the Code. The first citation noted that the Church exceeded the time limits for displaying its temporary directional signs. The second citation referred to the same problem, along with the Church's failure to include the date of the event on the signs. Town officials even confiscated one of the Church's signs. Reed contacted the Sign Code Compliance Department in an attempt to reach an accommodation. His efforts proved unsuccessful. The Town's Code compliance manager informed the Church that there would be "no leniency under the Code" and promised to punish any future violations.

Thereafter, petitioners filed a complaint in the United States District Court for the District of Arizona. The District Court denied the petitioners' motion for a preliminary injunction. The Court of Appeals for the Ninth Circuit affirmed. On remand, the District Court granted summary judgment in favour of the Town. The Court of Appeals again affirmed. We granted certiorari and now reverse.

Under the First Amendment, a government, including a municipal government vested with state authority, "has no power to restrict expression because of its message, its ideas, its subject matter, or its content." *Police Dept. of Chicago v. Mosley*, 408 U.S. 92, 95 (1972). Content-based laws—those that target speech based on its communicative content—are presumptively unconstitutional and may be justified only if the government proves that they are narrowly tailored to serve compelling state interests. Government regulation of speech is content based if a law applies to particular speech because of the topic discussed or the idea or message expressed. "Content based" requires a court to consider whether a regulation of speech "on its face" draws distinctions based on the message a speaker conveys. Some facial distinctions based on a message are obvious, defining regulated speech by particular subject matter, and others are more subtle, defining regulated speech by its function or purpose. Both are distinctions based on the message a speaker conveys, and, therefore, are subject to strict scrutiny. Our precedents have recognized a separate and additional category of laws that, though facially content neutral, will be considered content-based regulations of speech: laws that cannot be "'justified without reference to the content of the regulated speech,'" or that were adopted by the government "because of disagreement with the message the speech conveys," *Ward v. Rock Against Racism*, 491 U.S. 781, 791 (1989). Those laws, like those that are content based on their face, must also satisfy strict scrutiny.

The Town's Sign Code is content based on its face. It defines "Temporary Directional Signs" on the basis of whether a sign conveys the message of directing the public to church or some other "qualifying event." It defines "Political Signs" on the basis of whether a sign's message is "designed to influence the outcome of an election." And it defines "Ideological Signs" on the basis of whether a sign "communicates a message or ideas" that do not fit within the Code's other categories. It then subjects each of these categories to different restrictions. The restrictions that apply to any given sign depend entirely on the communicative content of the sign. If a sign informs its reader of the time and place a book club will discuss John Locke's Two Treatises of Government, that sign will be treated differently from a sign expressing the view that one should vote for one of Locke's followers in an upcoming election, and both signs will be treated differently from a sign expressing an ideological view rooted in Locke's theory of government. The Church's signs inviting people to attend its worship services are treated differently from signs conveying other types of ideas. On its face, the Sign Code is a content-based regulation of speech. We thus have no need to consider the government's justifications or purposes for enacting the Code to determine whether it is subject to strict scrutiny.

The Court of Appeals determined that the Sign Code was content neutral because the Town "did not adopt its regulation of speech based on disagreement with the message conveyed," and its justifications for regulating temporary directional signs were "unrelated to the content of the sign." The United States contends that a sign regulation is content neutral—even if it draws distinctions based on the sign's communicative content—if those distinctions can be "'justified without reference to the content of the regulated speech.'" This analysis skips the crucial first step in content-neutrality analysis: determining whether the law is content neutral on its face. A law that is content based on its face is subject to strict scrutiny regardless of the government's benign motive, content-neutral justification, or lack of "animus toward the ideas contained" in the regulated speech. An innocuous justification cannot transform a facially content-based law into one that is content neutral. That is why we have repeatedly considered whether a law is content neutral on its face *before* turning to the law's justification or purpose. *See United States v. Eichman*, 496 U. S. 310 (1990); *United States v. O'Brien*, 391 U.S. 367 (1968). Because strict scrutiny applies either when a law is content based on its face or when the purpose and justification for the law are content based, a court must evaluate each question before it concludes that the law is content neutral and thus subject to a lower level of scrutiny.

Innocent motives do not eliminate the danger of censorship presented by a facially content-based statute, as future government officials may one day wield such statutes to suppress disfavoured speech. That is why the First Amendment targets the operation of laws—*i.e.,* the "abridgement of speech"—rather than merely the motives of those who enacted them. "The vice of content-based legislation is not that it is always used for invidious, thought-control purposes, but that it lends itself to use for those purposes." *Hill, supra,* at 743 (Scalia, J., dissenting). For instance, in *NAACP v. Button,* 371 U.S. 415 (1963), the Court encountered a State's attempt to use a statute prohibiting " 'improper solicitation' " by attorneys to outlaw litigation-related speech of the National Association for the Advancement of Colored People. Although *Button* predated our recent formulations of strict scrutiny, the Court rightly rejected the State's claim that its interest in the "regulation of professional conduct" rendered the statute consistent with the First Amendment. One could easily imagine a Sign Code compliance manager who disliked the Church's substantive teachings deploying the Sign Code to make it more difficult for the Church to inform the public of the location of its services. We have "rejected the argument that 'discriminatory treatment is suspect under the First Amendment only when the legislature intends to suppress certain ideas.' " *Discovery Network,* 507 U.S. at 429.

In the Town's view, a sign regulation that "does not censor or favour particular viewpoints or ideas" cannot be content based. But "the First Amendment's hostility to content-based regulation extends not only to restrictions on particular viewpoints, but also to prohibition of public discussion of an entire topic." *Consolidated Edison Co. of N.Y. v. Public Serv. Comm'n of N.Y.,* 447 U.S. 530 (1980). The Town's Sign Code singles out specific subject matter for differential treatment, even if it does not target viewpoints within that subject matter. Ideological messages are given more favorable treatment than messages concerning a political candidate, which are themselves given more favorable treatment than messages announcing an assembly of like-minded individuals. That is a paradigmatic example of content-based discrimination.

Finally, the Court of Appeals characterized the Sign Code's distinctions as turning on "the content-neutral elements of who is speaking through the sign and whether and when an event is occurring." That analysis is mistaken. The Sign Code's distinctions are not speaker based. The restrictions for political, ideological, and temporary event signs apply no matter who sponsors them. If Reed had decided to display signs in support of a particular candidate, he could have made those signs far larger—and kept them up for far longer—than signs inviting people to attend his church services. If the Code's distinctions were truly speaker based, both types of signs would receive the same treatment.

The fact that a distinction is speaker based does not, as the Court of Appeals seemed to believe, automatically render the distinction content neutral. Because "speech restrictions based on the identity of the speaker are all too often a means to control content," we have insisted that "laws favoring some speakers over others demand strict scrutiny when the legislature's speaker preference reflects a content preference," *Turner,* 512 U.S. at 658. Thus, a law limiting the content of newspapers, but only newspapers, could not evade strict scrutiny simply because it could be characterized as speaker based. Likewise, a content-based law that restricted the political speech of all corporations would not become content neutral just because it singled out corporations as a class of speakers. Characterizing a distinction as speaker based is only the beginning of the inquiry.

Nor do the Sign Code's distinctions hinge on "whether and when an event is occurring." The Code does not permit citizens to post signs on any topic whatsoever within a set period leading up to an election. Come election time, it requires Town officials to determine whether a sign is "designed to influence the outcome of an election" (and thus "political") or merely "communicating a message or ideas for noncommercial purposes" (and thus "ideological"). That obvious content-based inquiry does not evade strict scrutiny review simply because an event (*i.e.*, an election) is involved. The fact that a distinction is event based does not render it content neutral. A speech regulation is content based if the law applies to particular speech because of the topic discussed or the idea or message expressed. A regulation that targets a sign because it conveys an idea about a specific event is no less content based than a regulation that targets a sign because it conveys some other idea. Here, the Code singles out signs bearing a particular message: the time and location of a specific event. This type of ordinance may seem like a perfectly rational way to regulate signs, but a clear and firm rule governing content neutrality is an essential means of protecting the freedom of speech, even if laws that might seem "entirely reasonable" will sometimes be "struck down because of their content-based nature." *City of Ladue v. Gilleo*, 512 U.S. 43 (1994) (O'Connor, J., concurring).

Because the Town's Sign Code imposes content-based restrictions on speech, those provisions can stand only if they survive strict scrutiny. It is the Town's burden to demonstrate that the Code's differentiation between temporary directional signs and other types of signs, such as political signs and ideological signs, furthers a compelling governmental interest and is narrowly tailored to that end. The Town cannot do so. It has offered only two governmental interests in support of the distinctions the Sign Code draws: preserving the Town's aesthetic appeal and traffic safety. Assuming for the sake of argument that those are compelling governmental interests, the Code's distinctions are hopelessly underinclusive. Starting with aesthetics, temporary directional signs are "no greater an eyesore," *Discovery Network*, 507 U.S. at 425, than ideological or political ones. Yet the Code allows unlimited proliferation of larger ideological signs while strictly limiting the number, size, and duration of smaller directional ones. The Town cannot claim that placing strict limits on temporary directional signs is necessary to beautify the Town while at the same time allowing unlimited numbers of other types of signs that create the same problem. The Town similarly has not shown that limiting temporary directional signs is necessary to eliminate threats to traffic safety. The Town has offered no reason to believe that directional signs pose a greater threat to safety than do ideological or political signs. If anything, a sharply worded ideological sign seems more likely to distract a driver than a sign directing the public to a meeting. In light of this underinclusiveness, the Town has not met its burden to prove that its Sign Code is narrowly tailored to further a compelling government interest. Because a " 'law cannot be regarded as protecting an interest of the highest order, and thus as justifying a restriction on truthful speech, when it leaves appreciable damage to that supposedly vital interest unprohibited,' " *Republican Party of Minn. v. White*, 536 U.S. 765, 780 (2002), the Sign Code fails strict scrutiny.

Our decision will not prevent governments from enacting effective sign laws. The Town asserts that an " 'absolutist' " content-neutrality rule would render "virtually all distinctions in sign laws subject to strict scrutiny." Not "all distinctions" are subject to strict scrutiny, only *content-based* ones. Laws that are *content neutral* are subject to lesser scrutiny. The Town has ample content-neutral options available to resolve problems with safety and aesthetics. For example, its current Code regulates many aspects of signs that have nothing to do with a sign's message: size, building materials, lighting, moving parts, and portability. On public property, the Town may go a long way toward entirely forbidding the posting of signs, so long as it does so in an evenhanded, content-neutral manner. See *Taxpayers for Vincent*, 466 U.S. at 817.

A city might reasonably view the general regulation of signs as necessary because signs "take up space and may obstruct views, distract motorists, displace alternative uses for land, and pose other problems that legitimately call for regulation." *City of Ladue*, 512 U.S. at 48. At the same time, the presence of certain signs may be essential, both for vehicles and pedestrians, to guide traffic or to identify hazards and ensure safety. A sign ordinance narrowly tailored to the challenges of protecting the safety of pedestrians, drivers, and passengers—such as warning signs marking hazards on private property, signs directing traffic, or street numbers associated with private houses—well might survive strict scrutiny. The signs at issue, including political and ideological signs and signs for events, are far removed from those purposes. They are facially content based and are neither justified by traditional safety concerns nor narrowly tailored.

We reverse the judgment of the Court of Appeals and remand the case for proceedings consistent with this opinion.

It is so ordered.

Justice ALITO, with whom Justice KENNEDY and Justice SOTOMAYOR join, *concurring.*

Here are some rules that would not be content based: 1. Rules regulating the size of signs. 2. Rules regulating the locations in which signs may be placed. 3. Rules distinguishing between lighted and unlighted signs. 4. Rules distinguishing between signs with fixed messages and electronic signs with messages that change. 5. Rules that distinguish between the placement of signs on private and public property. 6. Rules distinguishing between the placement of signs on commercial and residential property. 7. Rules distinguishing between on-premises and off-premises signs. 8. Rules restricting the total number of signs allowed per mile of roadway. 9. Rules imposing time restrictions on signs advertising a one-time event. Rules of this nature do not discriminate based on topic or subject and are akin to rules restricting the times within which oral speech or music is allowed. Properly understood, today's decision will not prevent cities from regulating signs in a way that fully protects public safety and serves legitimate esthetic objectives.

Justice KAGAN, with whom Justice GINSBURG and Justice BREYER join, *concurring in the judgment.*

Countless cities and towns across America have adopted ordinances regulating the posting of signs, while exempting certain categories of signs based on their subject matter. For example, some municipalities generally prohibit illuminated signs in residential neighborhoods, but lift that ban for signs that identify the address of a home or the name of its owner or occupant. In other municipalities, safety signs such as "Blind Pedestrian Crossing" and "Hidden Driveway" can be posted without a permit, even as other permanent signs require one. Elsewhere, historic site markers—for example, "George Washington Slept Here"—are also exempt from general regulations. Similarly, the federal Highway Beautification Act limits signs along interstate highways unless, for instance, they direct travelers to "scenic and historical attractions" or advertise free coffee.

Many sign ordinances are now in jeopardy. Says the majority: When laws "single out specific subject matter," they are "facially content based"; and when they are facially content based, they are automatically subject to strict scrutiny. The government must show that a content-based distinction "is necessary to serve a compelling state interest and is narrowly drawn to achieve that end." *Arkansas Writers' Project, Inc. v. Ragland,* 481 U.S. 221 (1987). Courts would have to find that a town has no other way to prevent hidden-driveway mishaps than by specially treating hidden-driveway signs. The consequence is that our communities will find themselves in an unenviable bind: They will have to repeal the exemptions that allow for helpful signs on streets and sidewalks, or else lift their sign restrictions altogether and resign themselves to the resulting clutter.

This Court's decisions articulate two important and related reasons for subjecting content-based speech regulations to the most exacting standard of review. The first is "to preserve an uninhibited marketplace of ideas in which truth will ultimately prevail." *McCullen v. Coakley,* 134 S.Ct. 2518, ___ (2014). The second is to ensure that the government has not regulated speech "based on hostility—or favoritism—towards the underlying message expressed." *R.A.V. v. St. Paul,* 505 U.S. 377, 386 (1992). The subject-matter exemptions included in many sign ordinances do not implicate those concerns. Allowing residents to install a light bulb over "name and address" signs but no others does not distort the marketplace of ideas. Nor does that different treatment give rise to an inference of impermissible government motive.

We apply strict scrutiny to facially content-based regulations of speech when there is a "realistic possibility that official suppression of ideas is afoot." *Davenport v. Washington Ed. Assn.,* 551 U.S. 177 (2007). That is always the case when the regulation facially differentiates on the basis of viewpoint. It is also the case (except in non-public or limited public forums) when a law restricts "discussion of an entire topic" in public debate. "If the marketplace of ideas is to remain free and open, governments must not be allowed to choose 'which issues are worth discussing or debating.'" *Consolidated Edison Co. of N.Y. v. Public Serv. Comm'n of N.Y.*, 447 U.S. 530 (1980). Such subject-matter restrictions, even though viewpoint-neutral on their face, may "suggest an attempt to give one side of a debatable public question an advantage in expressing its views to the people." *First Nat. Bank of Boston v. Bellotti*, 435 U.S. 765 (1978). Subject-matter regulation may have the intent or effect of favoring some ideas over others. When that is realistically possible—when the restriction "raises the specter that the Government may effectively drive certain ideas or viewpoints from the marketplace"—we insist that the law pass the most demanding constitutional test. *R.A.V. v. St. Paul*, 505 U.S. 377 (1992).

We may do well to relax our guard so that "entirely reasonable" laws imperiled by strict scrutiny can survive. Our concern with content-based regulation arises from the fear that the government will skew the public's debate of ideas—so when "that risk is inconsequential, strict scrutiny is unwarranted." *Davenport v. Washington Ed. Assn*, 551 U.S. 177, 188 (2007). To do its intended work the category of content-based regulation triggering strict scrutiny must sweep more broadly than the actual harm; that category exists to create a buffer zone guaranteeing that the government cannot favor or disfavor certain viewpoints. But we can administer our content-regulation doctrine with a dose of common sense, so as to leave standing laws that in no way implicate its intended function.

Our cases have been far less rigid than the majority admits in applying strict scrutiny to facially content-based laws. In *Members of City Council of Los Angeles v. Taxpayers for Vincent*, 466 U.S. 789 (1984), the Court declined to apply strict scrutiny to a municipal ordinance that exempted address numbers and markers commemorating "historical, cultural, or artistic events" from a generally applicable limit on sidewalk signs. We explained, the law's enactment and enforcement revealed "not even a hint of bias or censorship." In *City of Ladue v. Gilleo*, 512 U. S. 43 (1994), the Court assumed *arguendo* that a sign ordinance's exceptions for address signs, safety signs, and for-sale signs in residential areas did not trigger strict scrutiny. The Town of Gilbert's defense of its sign ordinance—the law's distinctions between directional signs and others—does not pass strict scrutiny, or intermediate scrutiny, or even the laugh test. The Town provides no reason at all for prohibiting more than four directional signs on a property while placing no limits on the number of other types of signs. Similarly, the Town offers no coherent justification for restricting the size of directional signs to 6 square feet while allowing other signs to reach 20 square feet. Why a smaller sign better helps travelers get to where they are going is left a mystery. The absence of any sensible basis for these and other distinctions dooms the Town's ordinance under even the intermediate scrutiny that the Court typically applies to "time, place, or manner" speech regulations. There is no need to decide whether strict scrutiny applies to every sign ordinance in every town across this country containing a subject-matter exemption.

Thousands of towns have ordinances, many "entirely reasonable." As the challenges mount, courts will have to invalidate one after the other. Courts will strike down those democratically enacted local laws even though no one has ever explained why the vindication of First Amendment values requires that result. I concur only in the judgment.

Justice BREYER, *concurring in the judgment.*

I join Justice Kagan's opinion. To use content discrimination to trigger strict scrutiny sometimes makes perfect sense. There are cases in which the Court has found content discrimination an unconstitutional method for suppressing a viewpoint. There are cases where the Court has found content discrimination to reveal that rules governing a traditional public forum are not a neutral way of fairly managing the forum in the interest of all speakers. In these cases, strict scrutiny is often appropriate, and content discrimination has served a useful purpose. But content discrimination, while helping courts identify unconstitutional suppression of expression, cannot and should not *always* trigger strict scrutiny. Content discrimination, as a conceptual tool, can sometimes reveal weaknesses in the government's rationale for a rule that limits speech. If a city looks to litter prevention as the rationale for a prohibition against placing newsracks dispensing free advertisements on public property, why does it exempt other newsracks causing similar litter? Whenever government disfavors one kind of speech, it places that speech at a disadvantage, potentially interfering with the free marketplace of ideas and with an individual's ability to express thoughts and ideas that can help that individual determine the kind of society in which he wishes to live, help shape that society, and help define his place within it.

To hold that content discrimination triggers strict scrutiny is to write a recipe for judicial management of ordinary government regulatory activity. Consider governmental regulation of securities (requirements for content that must be included in a registration statement); of energy conservation labeling-practices (requirements for content that must be included on labels of certain consumer electronics); of prescription drugs (requiring a prescription drug label to bear the symbol "Rx only"); of doctor-patient confidentiality (requiring confidentiality of certain medical records, but allowing a physician to disclose that the patient has HIV to the patient's spouse or sexual partner); of income tax statements (requiring taxpayers to furnish information about foreign gifts received if the aggregate amount exceeds $10,000); of commercial airplane briefings (requiring pilots to ensure that each passenger has been briefed on flight procedures, such as seatbelt fastening); of signs at petting zoos (requiring petting zoos to post a sign at every exit " 'strongly recommending that persons wash their hands upon exiting the petting zoo area' "). Nor can the majority avoid application of strict scrutiny to all sorts of justifiable governmental regulations by relying on this Court's many subcategories and exceptions to the rule.

The better approach is to treat content discrimination as a strong reason weighing against the constitutionality of a rule where a traditional public forum, or where viewpoint discrimination, is threatened, but elsewhere treat it as a rule of thumb, finding it a helpful, but not determinative legal tool, in an appropriate case, to determine the strength of a justification. I would use content discrimination as a supplement to a more basic analysis, which, tracking most of our First Amendment cases, asks whether the regulation at issue works harm to First Amendment interests that is disproportionate in light of the relevant regulatory objectives. Answering this question requires examining the seriousness of the harm to speech, the importance of the countervailing objectives, the extent to which the law will achieve those objectives, and whether there are other, less restrictive ways of doing so. Admittedly, this approach does not have the simplicity of a mechanical use of categories. But it does permit the government to regulate speech in numerous instances where the voters have authorized the government to regulate and where courts should hesitate to substitute judicial judgment for that of administrators. Here, regulation of signage along the roadside, for purposes of safety and beautification is at issue. There is no traditional public forum nor do I find any general effort to censor a particular viewpoint. Consequently, the specific regulation at issue does not warrant "strict scrutiny." Nonetheless, I believe that the Town of Gilbert's regulatory rules violate the First Amendment. I consequently concur in the Court's judgment only.

∽ PROBLEMS ∽

1. *Liberal Attacks on Conservative Speakers.* In recent years, liberal activists have aggressively moved to stop conservative speakers from giving speeches on university campuses. For example, University of California at Berkeley administrators cancelled a planned speech by conservative provocateur Milo Yiannopoulous after riots broke out in advance of the speech. Afterwards, one alumnus of the school said that he was glad that the school had denied "that fascist" the right to speak, but felt that it should have intervened sooner. When conservative talk show host Ann Coulter was invited to campus, University administrators changed the date of the speech, noting an obligation to ensure that First Amendment rights can be successfully exercised, and that the public is protected against violence. Is it permissible for university officials to treat conservative speakers differently than liberal speakers? What if there is a threat of violence against the conservative speakers, but not against the liberal speakers? How specific and imminent must a threat of violence be in order to curb freedom of expression? How should officials respond to that threat?

2. *A Legislative Response to Repression.* The Heritage Foundation has proposed the that universities adopt the following rules regarding outside speakers: 1) an official policy that strongly affirms the importance of free expression and the nullification of restrictive speech codes; 2) a declaration that the campus is open to anyone invited by members of the campus community which includes a bar against university administrators from excluding invited speakers, no matter how

controversial; 3) the imposition of disciplinary sanctions on anyone who inter-feres with the free speech rights of others; & 4) the creation of a right to sue, by anyone whose free speech rights have been infringed, which includes the right to recover courts costs and attorneys fees. Should universities adopt such a policy?

3. *Prohibitions on Spoken Panhandling.* Suppose that a city adopts an ordinance prohibiting spoken requests for donations of money, but does allow panhandlers to use signs. The city attempts to justify the ban on the basis that spoken requests might be regarded as more threatening to the recipient than written requests. Can the restriction be justified as a content-neutral time, place, and manner restriction? *See Norton v. City of Springfield,* 768 F.3d 713 (7th Cir. 2014).

4. *The Billboard Permit System.* A state law prohibits the placement of outdoor advertising without a license. However, the ordinance provides that the issuance of a permit rests in the "sole discretion" of the responsible administrator based on his assessment of its harmony with the surrounding area. In addition, the ordinance provides that a license can be revoked at any time "without limita-tion." Is the ordinance valid? *See Van Wagner Boston, LLC v. Davey,* 770 F.3d 33 (1st Cir. 2014).

H. FIRST AMENDMENT RIGHTS OF PUBLIC EMPLOYEES

In a number of cases, the Court has struggled to decide whether government employees have fewer speech rights than other citizens.

1. *Prohibiting Electioneering*

Public employees might engage in a variety of First Amendment activities, includ-ing participation in partisan political practices.

United Public Workers of America (C.I.O.) v. Mitchell

330 U.S. 75 (1947)

Mr. Justice REED delivered the opinion of the Court.

The Hatch Act, enacted in 1940, declares unlawful certain political activities of federal employees. Appellants sought an injunction prohibiting members of the United States Civil Service Commission from enforcing §9(a) of the Hatch Act, which reads, "No officer or employee in the Executive Branch of the Federal Government shall take any active part in political management or in political campaigns." Various employees of the federal executive civil service allege that they desire to engage in acts of political management and in political campaigns outside of the hours of employment. The District Court upheld the Act.

The issue is whether a breach of the Hatch Act and Rule 1 of the Commission can, without violating the Constitution, be made the basis for disciplinary action. The right claimed is the right of a citizen to act as a party official or worker to further his own political views. The influence of political activity by government employees, if evil in its effects on the service, the employees or people dealing with them, is hardly less so because that activity takes place after hours. The question of the need for this regulation is for other branches of government. Our duty ends if the Hatch Act provision is constitutional. This Court must balance the extent of the guarantees of freedom against a congressional enactment to protect a democratic society against the supposed evil of political partisanship by classified employees of government.

The practice of excluding classified employees from party offices and personal political activity at the polls has been in effect for several decades. In *Ex parte Curtis*, 106 U.S. 371 (1882), we recognized the power of Congress, within reasonable limits, to regulate, so far as it might deem necessary, the political conduct of its employees. The conviction that an actively partisan governmental personnel threatens good administration has deepened since *Curtis*. Congress recognizes danger to the service in that political rather than official effort may earn advancement and to the public in that governmental favor may be channeled through political connections.

The provisions of §9 of the Hatch Act and the Civil Service Rule 1 are not dissimilar in purpose from the statutes against political contributions of money. The prohibitions are directed at political contributions of energy by Government employees. Congress and the President are responsible for an efficient public service. If, in their judgment, efficiency may be best obtained by prohibiting active participation by classified employees in politics as party officers or workers, we see no constitutional objection. Congress leaves untouched full participation by employees in political decisions at the ballot box and forbids only the partisan activity of federal personnel deemed offensive to efficiency. With that limitation only, employees may make their contributions to public affairs or protect their own interests, as before the passage of the act.

The argument that political neutrality is not indispensable to a merit system for federal employees may be accepted. But because it is not indispensable does not mean that it is not desirable or permissible. Congress may have considered that parties would be more truly devoted to the public welfare if public servants were not over active politically.

Appellants urge that federal employees are protected by the Bill of Rights. None would deny such limitations on Congressional power but because there are some limitations it does not follow that a prohibition against acting as ward leader or worker at the polls is invalid. It is only partisan political activity that is interdicted. It is active participation in political management and political campaigns. Expressions, public or private, on public affairs, personalities and matters of public interest, not an objective of party action, are unrestricted by law so long as the Government employee does not direct his activities toward party success.

It is urged that Congress has gone further than necessary in prohibiting political activity to all types of classified employees. Appellant Poole is a roller in the Mint. This job calls for the qualities of a skilled mechanic and does not involve contact with the public. If in free time he is engaged in political activity, Congress may have concluded that the activity may promote or retard his advancement. Congress may have thought that Government employees are handy elements for leaders in political policy to use in building a political machine. It is not necessary that the act regulated be anything more than an act reasonably deemed by Congress to interfere with the efficiency of the public service. There are hundreds of thousands of United States employees with positions no more influential upon policy determination. Evidently what Congress feared was the cumulative effect on employee morale of political activity by all employees who could be induced to participate actively. It does not seem to us an unconstitutional basis for legislation.

We have said that Congress may regulate the political conduct of Government employees "within reasonable limits." The determination of the extent to which political activities of governmental employees shall be regulated lies primarily with Congress. Courts will interfere only when such regulation passes beyond the general existing conception of governmental power. When actions of civil servants in the judgment of Congress menace the integrity and the competency of the service, legislation to forestall such danger and adequate to maintain its usefulness is required. The Hatch Act is the answer of Congress to this need. We cannot say with such a background that these restrictions are unconstitutional.

The activities of Mr. Poole, as ward executive committeeman and a worker at the polls, obviously fall within the prohibitions of §9 of the Hatch Act against taking an active part in political management and political campaigns.

The judgment of the District Court is accordingly affirmed.

Affirmed.

Mr. Justice BLACK, *dissenting.*

The Commission prohibited the following activities: serving as an election officer; publicly expressing political views at a party caucus or political gathering for or against any candidate or cause identified with a party; soliciting votes for a party or candidate; participating in a political parade; writing for publication or publishing any letter or article, signed or unsigned, in favor of or against any political party, candidate, or faction; initiating, or canvassing for signatures on, community petitions or petitions to Congress.

It is little consolation to employees that the Act contradictorily says that they may "express their opinions on all political subjects and candidates." Whatever opinions employees may dare to express, even secretly, must be at their peril. They cannot know what particular expressions may be reported to the Commission and held by it to be a sufficient political activity to cost them their jobs. Their peril is all the greater because "Employees are accountable for political activity by persons other than themselves, including wives or husbands, if, in fact, the employees are thus accomplishing by collusion and indirection what they may not lawfully do directly and openly." Thus are the families of public employees stripped of their freedom of political action. The result is that the sum of political privilege left to government and state employees, and their families: They may vote in silence; they may carefully and quietly express a political view at their peril; and they may become "spectators" at campaign gatherings, though it may be highly dangerous for them to "second a motion" or let it be known that they agree or disagree with a speaker.

Had this measure deprived five million farmers, or a million businessmen of all right to participate in elections, because Congress thought that federal farm or business subsidies might prompt some of them to be susceptible to a corrupting influence on politics or government, I would not sustain such an Act. Laws which restrict First Amendment liberties should be narrowly drawn to meet the evil and affect only the minimum number of people necessary to prevent a grave and imminent danger to the public. It is hardly imperative to muzzle millions of citizens because some of them might corrupt the political process. It may be true that some higher employees, unless restrained, might coerce their subordinates or that Government employees might use their official position to coerce other citizens. The same argument would support a law to suppress the political freedom of all employees of employers who borrow money or draw subsidies from the Government. If the practice of making discharges, promotions or recommendations for promotions on a political basis is so great an evil as to require legislation, the law could punish those public officials who engage in the practice. To punish millions of employees and to deprive the nation of their contribution to public affairs, in order to remove temptation from a proportionately small number of public officials, seems at the least to be a novel method of suppressing what is thought to be an evil practice.

Our political system rests on the foundation of a belief in rule by the people. In a country whose people elect their leaders and decide great public issues, the voice of none should be suppressed.

Mr. Justice DOUGLAS, *dissenting in part.*

The political regimentation of industrial workers produces its own crop of abuses. Those in top policy posts or other supervisors might seek to knit the industrial workers in civil service into a political machine by making the advancement of industrial workers dependent on political loyalty, on financial contributions, or on other partisan efforts. Offset against that public concern are the interests of the employees in the exercise of cherished constitutional rights. If those rights are to be qualified by the larger requirements of modern democratic government, the restrictions should be narrowly and selectively drawn to define and punish the specific conduct which constitutes a clear and present danger to the operations of government. Those rights are too basic and fundamental in our democratic political society to be sacrificed or qualified for anything short of a clear and present danger to the civil service system. No such showing has been made.

Note: Other Justifications

In *United States Civil Service Commission v. National Association of Letter Carriers, AFL-CIO*, 413 U.S. 548 (1973), the Court reaffirmed the holding in *Mitchell.* In doing so, the Court noted that "forbidding partisan political activities will reduce the hazards to fair and effective government." It also noted that another "major concern was that the rapidly expanding Government work force should not be employed to build a powerful, invincible, and perhaps corrupt political machine. A related concern was the goal that employment and advancement in the Government service not depend on political performance, and that Government employees should be free from pressure and from express or tacit invitation to vote in a certain way or perform political chores in order to curry favor with their superiors rather than to act out their own beliefs. It is not enough merely to forbid one employee to attempt to influence or coerce another."

∾ PROBLEM: MORE ON THE INTERNATIONAL TREATY REGULATING THE INTERNET ∾

Under the *United Public Workers* decision and its progeny, could you agree to any special restrictions on the internet speech of government employees? If so, what type of language would be permissible?

2. Other Employee Speech

Do government employees have limited rights to speak because of their employment?

Connick v. Myers

461 U.S. 138 (1983)

Justice WHITE delivered the opinion of the Court.

In *Pickering v. Board of Education*, 391 U.S. 563 (1968), we stated that a public employee does not relinquish First Amendment rights to comment on matters of public interest by virtue of government employment. We also recognized that the State's interests as an employer in regulating the speech of its employees "differ significantly from those it possesses in connection with regulation of the speech of the citizenry in general." The problem was arriving "at a balance between the interests of the employee, as a citizen, in commenting upon matters of public concern and the interest of the State, as an employer, in promoting the efficiency of the public services it performs through its employees." We return to this problem today and consider whether the First and Fourteenth Amendments prevent the discharge of a state employee for circulating a questionnaire concerning internal office affairs.

Respondent, Sheila Myers, was employed as an Assistant District Attorney in New Orleans for five and a half years. She served at the pleasure of petitioner Harry Connick, the District Attorney for Orleans Parish. During this period Myers competently performed her responsibilities of trying criminal cases. In 1980, Myers was informed that she would be transferred to prosecute cases in a different section of the criminal court. Myers was strongly opposed to the proposed transfer and expressed her view to several of her supervisors. Despite her objections, Myers was notified that she was being transferred. Myers expressed her reluctance to accept the transfer. That night Myers prepared a questionnaire soliciting the views of her fellow staff members concerning office transfer policy, office morale, the need for a grievance committee, the level of confidence in supervisors, and whether employees felt pressured to work in political campaigns. Early the following morning, Myers typed and copied the questionnaire. She also met with Connick who urged her to accept the transfer. Myers then distributed the questionnaire to 15 assistant district attorneys. Shortly after noon, when Connick learned that Myers was distributing the survey and was creating a "mini-insurrection" in the office, Connick terminated Myers for her refusal to accept the transfer and for "insubordination" for distributing the questionnaire. Connick particularly objected to the question which inquired whether employees "had confidence in and would rely on the word" of various superiors in the office, and to a question concerning pressure to work in political campaigns which he felt would be damaging if discovered by the press. Myers filed suit claiming that she was terminated for exercising her constitutionally-protected right of free speech. The District Court agreed and the court of appeals affirmed. We granted certiorari.

The repeated emphasis in *Pickering* on the right of a public employee "as a citizen, in commenting upon matters of public concern," was not accidental. This language reflects both the historical evolvement of the rights of public employees, and the common sense realization that government offices could not function if every employment decision became a constitutional matter. For most of this century, the unchallenged dogma was that a public employee had no right to object to conditions placed upon the terms of employment—including those which restricted the exercise of constitutional rights. The Court cast new light on the matter in a series of cases arising from the widespread efforts in the 1950s and early 1960s to require public employees, particularly teachers, to swear oaths of loyalty to the state and reveal the groups with which they associated. The explanation is no mystery. The First Amendment "was fashioned to assure unfettered interchange of ideas for the bringing about of political and social changes desired by the people." *New York Times Co. v. Sullivan*, 376 U.S. 254, 269 (1964). In *Pickering*, the Court held impermissible under the First Amendment the dismissal of a high school teacher for openly criticizing the Board of Education on its allocation of school funds between athletics and education and its methods of informing taxpayers about the need for additional revenue. Pickering's subject was "a matter of legitimate public concern" upon which "free and open debate is vital to informed decision-making by the electorate."

Pickering, its antecedents and progeny, lead us to conclude that if Myers' questionnaire cannot be fairly characterized as constituting speech on a matter of public concern, it is unnecessary for us to scrutinize the reasons for her discharge. When employee expression cannot be fairly considered as relating to any matter of political, social, or other concern to the community, government officials should enjoy wide latitude in managing their offices, without intrusive oversight by the judiciary in the name of the First Amendment. Ordinary dismissals from government service which violate no fixed tenure or applicable statute or regulation are not subject to judicial review even if the reasons for the dismissal are alleged to be mistaken or unreasonable.

We in no sense suggest that speech on private matters falls into one of the narrow and well-defined classes of expression which carries so little social value, such as obscenity, that the state can prohibit and punish such expression by all persons in its jurisdiction. We hold only that when a public employee speaks not as a citizen upon matters of public concern, but instead as an employee upon matters only of personal interest, absent the most unusual circumstances, a federal court is not the appropriate forum in which to review the wisdom of a personnel decision taken by a public agency allegedly in reaction to the employee's behavior. Our responsibility is to ensure that citizens are not deprived of fundamental rights by virtue of working for the government; this does not require a grant of immunity for employee grievances not afforded by the First Amendment to those who do not work for the state.

Whether an employee's speech addresses a matter of public concern must be determined by the content, form, and context of a given statement, as revealed by the whole record. In this case, with but one exception, the questions posed by Myers to her coworkers do not fall under the rubric of matters of "public concern." We view the questions pertaining to the confidence and trust that Myers' coworkers possess in various supervisors, the level of office morale, and the need for a grievance committee as mere extensions of Myers' dispute over her transfer to another section of the criminal court. We do not believe these questions are of public import in evaluating the performance of the District Attorney as an elected official. Myers did not seek to inform the public that the District Attorney's office was not discharging its governmental responsibilities in the investigation and prosecution of criminal cases. Nor did Myers seek to bring to light actual or potential wrongdoing or breach of public trust on the part of Connick and others. Indeed, the questionnaire, if released to the public, would convey no information at all other than the fact that a single employee is upset with the status quo. While discipline and morale in the workplace are related to an agency's efficient performance of its duties, the focus of Myers' questions is not to evaluate the performance of the office but rather to gather ammunition for another round of controversy with her superiors. These questions reflect one employee's dissatisfaction with a transfer and an attempt to turn that displeasure into a cause celebre.

To presume that all matters which transpire within a government office are of public concern would mean that virtually every remark—and certainly every criticism directed at a public official—would plant the seed of a constitutional case. While as a matter of good judgment, public officials should be receptive to constructive criticism offered by their employees, the First Amendment does not require a public office to be run as a roundtable for employee complaints over internal office affairs.

One question in Myers' questionnaire, however, does touch upon a matter of public concern. Question 11 inquires if assistant district attorneys "ever feel pressured to work in political campaigns on behalf of office supported candidates." Official pressure upon employees to work for political candidates not of the worker's own choice constitutes a coercion of belief in violation of fundamental constitutional rights. In addition, there is a demonstrated interest in this country that government service should depend upon meritorious performance rather than political service. Given this history, we believe it apparent that the issue of whether assistant district attorneys are pressured to work in political campaigns is a matter of interest to the community upon which it is essential that public employees be able to speak out freely without fear of retaliatory dismissal.

Because one of the questions in Myers' survey touched upon a matter of public concern, and contributed to her discharge we must determine whether Connick was justified in discharging Myers. The state's burden in justifying a particular discharge varies depending upon the nature of the employee's expression. Although such particularized balancing is difficult, the courts must reach the most appropriate possible balance of the competing interests.

The *Pickering* balance requires full consideration of the government's interest in the effective and efficient fulfillment of its responsibilities to the public. We agree that there is no demonstration here that the questionnaire impeded Myers' ability to perform her responsibilities. Connick, who characterized Myers' actions as causing a "mini-insurrection," viewed Myers' questionnaire as an act of insubordination which interfered with working relationships. When close working relationships are essential to fulfilling public responsibilities, a wide degree of deference to the employer's judgment is appropriate. We do not see the necessity for an employer to allow events to unfold to the extent that the disruption of the office and the destruction of working relationships is manifest before taking action. We caution that a stronger showing may be necessary if the employee's speech more substantially involved matters of public concern.

The District Court rejected Connick's position because "unlike a statement of fact which might be deemed critical of one's superiors, Myers' questionnaire was not a statement of fact, but the presentation and solicitation of ideas and opinions," which are entitled to greater constitutional protection because "under the First Amendment there is no such thing as a false idea." This approach, while perhaps relevant in weighing the value of Myers' speech, bears no logical relationship to the issue of whether the questionnaire undermined office relationships. Questions, no less than forcefully stated opinions and facts, carry messages and it requires no unusual insight to conclude that the purpose, if not the likely result, of the questionnaire is to seek to precipitate a vote of no confidence in Connick and his supervisors. Thus, Question 10, which asked whether or not the Assistants had confidence in and relied on the word of five named supervisors, is a statement that carries the clear potential for undermining office relations.

Also relevant is the manner, time, and place in which the questionnaire was distributed. The questionnaire was prepared, and distributed at the office; the manner of distribution required not only Myers to leave her work but for others to do the same in order that the questionnaire be completed. Although some latitude when official work is performed is to be allowed when professional employees are involved, and Myers did not violate announced office policy, the fact that Myers, unlike Pickering, exercised her rights to speech at the office supports Connick's fears that the functioning of his office was endangered.

Finally, the context in which the dispute arose is also significant. This is not a case where an employee, out of purely academic interest, circulated a questionnaire so as to obtain useful research. When employee speech concerning office policy arises from an employment dispute concerning the very application of that policy to the speaker, additional weight must be given to the supervisor's view that the employee has threatened the authority of the employer to run the office. Although we accept the finding that Myers' reluctance to accede to the transfer order was not a sufficient cause in itself for her dismissal, this does not render irrelevant the fact that the questionnaire emerged after a persistent dispute between Myers and Connick and his deputies over office transfer policy.

Myers' questionnaire touched upon matters of public concern in only a most limited sense; her survey, in our view, is most accurately characterized as an employee grievance concerning internal office policy. The limited First Amendment interest involved here does not require that Connick tolerate action which he reasonably believed would disrupt the office, undermine his authority, and destroy close working relationships. Myers' discharge therefore did not offend the First Amendment. We reiterate, however, one caveat: "Because of the enormous variety of fact situations in which critical statements by public employees may be thought by their superiors to furnish grounds for dismissal, we do not deem it either appropriate or feasible to lay down a general standard against which all such statements may be judged."

The First Amendment's primary aim is the full protection of speech upon issues of public concern, as well as the practical realities involved in the administration of a government office. Although today the balance is struck for the government, this is no defeat for the First Amendment. It would indeed be a Pyrrhic victory for the great principles of free expression if the Amendment's safeguarding of a public employee's right, as a citizen, to participate in discussions concerning public affairs were confused with the attempt to constitutionalize the employee grievance that we see presented here. The judgment of the Court of Appeals is

Reversed.

Justice BRENNAN, with whom Justice MARSHALL, Justice BLACKMUN, and Justice STEVENS join, *dissenting.*

Speech about "the manner in which government is operated or should be operated" is an essential part of the communications necessary for self-governance the protection of which was a central purpose of the First Amendment. Because the questionnaire addressed such matters and its distribution did not adversely affect the operations of the District Attorney's Office or interfere with Myers' working relationship with her fellow employees, I dissent.

Myers' questionnaire addressed matters of public concern because it discussed subjects that could reasonably be expected to be of interest to persons seeking to develop informed opinions about the manner in which the Orleans Parish District Attorney, an elected official charged with managing a vital governmental agency, discharges his responsibilities. The questionnaire sought primarily to obtain information about the impact of the recent transfers on morale in the District Attorney's Office. It is beyond doubt that personnel decisions that adversely affect discipline and morale may ultimately impair an agency's efficient performance of its duties. The Court does hold that one question — asking whether Assistants felt pressured to work in political campaigns on behalf of office-supported candidates — addressed a matter of public importance and concern. Having gone that far, the Court misapplies the *Pickering* test and holds that a public employer's mere apprehension that speech will be disruptive justifies suppression of that speech when all the objective evidence suggests that those fears are essentially unfounded.

The Court's decision today inevitably will deter public employees from making critical statements about the manner in which government agencies are operated for fear that doing so will provoke their dismissal. As a result, the public will be deprived of valuable information with which to evaluate the performance of elected officials. Because protecting the dissemination of such information is an essential function of the First Amendment, I dissent.

Note: Federal Employees, Private Honoraria

A federal statute prohibited federal employees from accepting any compensation for making speeches or writing articles. The law applied whether or not the subject of the speech or article or the person or group paying for it had any connection with the employee's official duties. Violations of the law were punishable by a fine of up to $10,000 or the amount of the honorarium. The law was challenged by various federal employees who received compensation for writing or speaking on various topics unrelated to their employment (e.g., a mail handler employed by the U.S. Postal Service who give lectures on the Quaker religion). The evidence showed that some famous authors (e.g., Nathaniel Hawthorne and Herman Melville) had been federal employees who wrote or spoke "on the side," and that a motivation for such activity was the compensation provided. In defense of the law, the government argued that Congress could "reasonably conclude that its interests in preventing impropriety and the appearance of impropriety in the federal work force outweigh the employees' interests in receiving compensation for expression that relates to their Government employment." In *United States v. National Treasury Employees Union*, 513 U.S. 454 (1995), the Court struck down the prohibition, concluding that it imposed a significant burden on expressive activity, and did not serve the government's interest in assuring that federal officers not misuse or appear to misuse power.

Rankin v. McPherson

483 U.S. 378 (1987)

Justice MARSHALL delivered the opinion of the Court.

On January 12, 1981, respondent Ardith McPherson was appointed a deputy in the office of the Constable of Harris County, Texas. The Constable is an elected official who functions as a law enforcement officer. At the time of her appointment, McPherson, a black woman, was 19 years old and had attended college for a year, studying secretarial science. Her appointment was conditional for a 90-day probationary period.

Although McPherson's title was "deputy constable," this was because all employees of the Constable's office, regardless of job function, were deputy constables. She was not a commissioned peace officer, did not wear a uniform, and was not authorized to make arrests or permitted to carry a gun. McPherson's duties were purely clerical. Her work station was a desk at which there was no telephone, in a room to which the public did not have ready access. Her job was to type data from court papers into a computer that maintained an automated record of the status of civil process in the county. Her training consisted of two days of instruction in the operation of her computer terminal.

On March 30, 1981, McPherson and some fellow employees heard on an office radio that there had been an attempt to assassinate the President of the United States. Upon hearing that report, McPherson engaged a co-worker, Lawrence Jackson, who was apparently her boyfriend, in a brief conversation, which according to McPherson's uncontroverted testimony went as follows: "*Q:* What did you say? *A:* I said I felt that that would happen sooner or later. *Q:* Okay. And what did Lawrence say? *A:* Lawrence said, yeah, agreeing with me. *Q:* Okay. Now, what was your next comment? *A:* Well, I felt like it would be a black person that did that, because I feel like most of my kind is on welfare and CETA, and they use medicaid. But then after I said that, he's cutting back medicaid and food stamps. And I said, yeah, welfare and CETA. I said, shoot, if they go for him again, I hope they get him."

McPherson's last remark was overheard by another Deputy Constable, who, unbeknownst to McPherson, was in the room. The remark was reported to Constable Rankin, who summoned McPherson. McPherson readily admitted that she had made the statement, but testified that she told Rankin, upon being asked if she made the statement, "Yes, but I didn't mean anything by it." After their discussion, Rankin fired McPherson.

McPherson brought suit under 42 U.S.C. §1983, alleging that petitioner Rankin, in discharging her, had violated her constitutional rights under color of state law. The District Court ruled that the statements were not protected speech. The Court of Appeals concluded that the Government's interest did not outweigh the First Amendment interest in protecting McPherson's speech. We granted certiorari and now affirm.

Even though McPherson was merely a probationary employee, and even if she could have been discharged for any reason or for no reason at all, she may nonetheless be entitled to reinstatement if she was discharged for exercising her constitutional right to freedom of expression. The determination whether a public employer has properly discharged an employee for engaging in speech requires "a balance between the interests of the employee, as a citizen, in commenting upon matters of public concern and the interest of the State, as an employer, in promoting the efficiency of the public services it performs through its employees." *Pickering v. Board of Education*, 391 U.S. 563, 568 (1968).

The threshold question in applying this balancing test is whether McPherson's speech may be "fairly characterized as constituting speech on a matter of public concern." "Whether an employee's speech addresses a matter of public concern must be determined by the content, form, and context of a given statement, as revealed by the whole record." Considering the statement in context, as *Connick* requires, discloses that it plainly dealt with a matter of public concern. The statement was made in the course of a conversation addressing the policies of the President's administration. It came on the heels of a news bulletin regarding what is certainly a matter of heightened public attention: an attempt on the life of the President. While a statement that amounted to a threat to kill the President would not be protected by the First Amendment, McPherson's statement did not amount to a threat punishable under 18 U.S.C. §871(a) or 18 U.S.C. §2385, or, indeed, that could properly be criminalized at all. The inappropriate or controversial character of a statement is irrelevant to whether it deals with a matter of public concern. "Debate on public issues should be uninhibited, robust, and wide-open, and may well include vehement, caustic, and sometimes unpleasantly sharp attacks on government and public officials." *New York Times Co. v. Sullivan*, 376 U.S. 254, 270 (1964).

Because McPherson's statement addressed a matter of public concern, *Pickering* next requires that we balance McPherson's interest in making her statement against "the interest of the State, as an employer, in promoting the efficiency of the public services it performs through its employees." The State bears a burden of justifying the discharge on legitimate grounds. The manner, time, and place of the employee's expression are relevant, as is the context in which the dispute arose. We have previously recognized as pertinent considerations whether the statement impairs discipline by superiors or harmony among co-workers, has a detrimental impact on close working relationships for which personal loyalty and confidence are necessary, or impedes the performance of the speaker's duties or interferes with the regular operation of the enterprise.

These considerations, and indeed the very nature of the balancing test, make apparent that the state interest element of the test focuses on the effective functioning of the public employer's enterprise. Interference with work, personnel relationships, or the speaker's job performance can detract from the public employer's function; avoiding such interference can be a strong state interest. From this perspective, however, petitioners fail to demonstrate a state interest that outweighs McPherson's First Amendment rights. While McPherson's statement was made at the workplace, there is no evidence that it interfered with the efficient functioning of the office. The Constable was evidently not afraid that McPherson had disturbed or interrupted other employees—he did not inquire to whom respondent had made the remark and testified that he "was not concerned who she had made it to." In fact, Constable Rankin testified that the possibility of interference with the functions of the Constable's office had *not* been a consideration in his discharge of respondent and that he did not even inquire whether the remark had disrupted the work of the office.

Nor was there any danger that McPherson had discredited the office by making her statement in public. McPherson's speech took place in an area to which there was ordinarily no public access; her remark was evidently made in a private conversation with another employee. Nor is there evidence that employees other than Jackson who worked in the room even heard the remark. Not only was McPherson's discharge unrelated to the functioning of the office, it was not based on any assessment by the Constable that the remark demonstrated a character trait that made respondent unfit to perform her work.

While the facts underlying Rankin's discharge of McPherson are somewhat unclear, it is undisputed that he fired McPherson based on the *content* of her speech. Evidently because McPherson had made the statement, and because the Constable believed that she "meant it," he decided that she was not a suitable employee to have in a law enforcement agency. But in weighing the State's interest in discharging an employee based on any claim that the content of a statement made by the employee somehow undermines the mission of the public employer, some attention must be paid to the responsibilities of the employee within the agency. The burden of caution employees bear with respect to the words they speak will vary with the extent of authority and public accountability the employee's role entails. Where, as here, an employee serves no confidential, policymaking, or public contact role, the danger to the agency's successful functioning from that employee's private speech is minimal. We cannot believe that every employee in Constable Rankin's office, whether computer operator, electrician, or file clerk, is equally required, on pain of discharge, to avoid any statement susceptible of being interpreted by the Constable as an indication that the employee may be unworthy of employment in his law enforcement agency. At some point, such concerns are so removed from the effective functioning of the public employer that they cannot prevail over the free speech rights of the public employee.

This is such a case. McPherson's employment-related interaction with the Constable was apparently negligible. Her duties were purely clerical and were limited solely to the civil process function of the Constable's office. There is no indication that she would ever be in a position to further—or indeed to have any involvement with—the minimal law enforcement activity engaged in by the Constable's office. Given the function of the agency, McPherson's position in the office, and the nature of her statement, we are not persuaded that Rankin's interest in discharging her outweighed her rights under the First Amendment.

Because we agree with the Court of Appeals that McPherson's discharge was improper, the judgment of the Court of Appeals is

Affirmed.

Justice POWELL, *concurring.*

McPherson's comment was made during a private conversation with a co-worker who happened to be her boyfriend. She had no intention or expectation that it would be overheard or acted on by others. If a statement is on a matter of public concern, it will be an unusual case where the employer's legitimate interests will be so great as to justify punishing an employee for this type of private speech that routinely takes place at all levels in the workplace.

Justice SCALIA, with whom THE CHIEF JUSTICE, Justice WHITE, and Justice O'CONNOR join, *dissenting.*

No law enforcement agency is required by the First Amendment to permit one of its employees to "ride with the cops and cheer for the robbers." McPherson's statement is only one step removed from statements that we have previously held entitled to no First Amendment protection even in the nonemployment context—including assassination threats against the President (which are illegal under 18 U.S.C. §871), "'fighting' words," epithets or personal abuse, and advocacy of force or violence. A statement lying so near the category of completely unprotected speech cannot fairly be viewed as lying within the "heart" of the First Amendment's protection; it lies within that category of speech that can neither be characterized as speech on matters of public concern nor properly subject to criminal penalties. Once McPherson stopped explicitly criticizing the President's policies and expressed a desire that he be assassinated, she crossed the line.

Statements by the Constable's employees to the effect that "if they go for the President again, I hope they get him" might also, to put it mildly, undermine public confidence in the Constable's office. A public employer has a strong interest in preserving its reputation with the public. The Court's sweeping assertion that where an employee "serves no confidential, policymaking, or public contact role, the danger to the agency's successful functioning from that employee's private speech is minimal," is simply contrary to reason and experience. Nonpolicymaking employees (the Assistant District Attorney in *Connick*, for example) can hurt working relationships and undermine public confidence in an organization every bit as much as policymaking employees. In sum, since Constable Rankin's interest in maintaining both an esprit de corps and a public image consistent with his office's law enforcement duties outweighs any interest his employees may have in expressing on the job a desire that the President be killed, even assuming that such an expression addresses a matter of public concern it is not protected by the First Amendment from suppression.

Notes

1. *The Principal's Memo.* In *Mt. Healthy City School District v. Doyle*, 429 U.S. 274 (1977), a teacher provided a copy of a principal's memo on teacher dress and appearance to a local disc jockey who announced it as a news item. Later, the principal recommended that Doyle not be rehired for the following year because of "a notable lack of tact in handling professional matters which leaves much doubt as to your sincerity in establishing good school relationships." That general statement was followed by references to the radio station incident and to an obscene-gesture incident. The Court held that, had the nonrenewal been based on Doyle's communication with the radio station, it would be actionable: "the burden was properly placed upon respondent to show that his conduct was constitutionally protected, and that this conduct was a 'substantial factor' or that it was a 'motivating factor' in the Board's decision not to rehire him. Respondent having carried that burden, the court should have determined whether the Board had shown by a preponderance of the evidence that it would have reached the same decision as to respondent's reemployment even in the absence of the protected conduct."

2. *The Exclusive Bargaining Representative.* In *Minnesota State Board for Community Colleges v. Knight*, 465 U.S. 271 (1984), although Minnesota authorized public employees to bargain collectively (regarding the terms and conditions of their employment), if professional employees (i.e., college faculty) have formed an appropriate bargaining unit and have selected an exclusive representative for mandatory bargaining, then their employer may exchange views on nonmandatory subjects only with that exclusive representative. The Court upheld the restriction: "Appellees' speech and associational rights have not been infringed by Minnesota's restriction of participation in 'meet and confer' sessions to the faculty's exclusive representative. The state has in no way restrained appellees' freedom to speak on any education-related issue or their freedom to associate or not to associate with whom they please, including the exclusive representative. Nor has the state attempted to suppress any ideas." Justice Stevens, joined by two other justices, dissented: "The First Amendment guarantees an open marketplace

for ideas—where divergent points of view can freely compete for the attention of those in power and of those to whom the powerful must account. The statute gives only one speaker a realistic opportunity to present its views to state officials."

3. *Circulating Petitions on Military Bases. Brown v. Glines,* 444 U.S. 348 (1980), involved Air Force regulations that required service members to obtain approval from their commanders before circulating petitions on Air Force bases. Under the regulations, commanders could deny permission if they determined that distribution of the material would result in "a clear danger to the loyalty, discipline, or morale of members of the Armed Forces, or material interference with the accomplishment of a military mission." Glines, a captain in the reserves, drafted petitions to members of Congress and the secretary of defense complaining about the Air Force's grooming standards. When Glines gave the petitions to a sergeant to solicit signatures, his commander punished him for violating the regulations by removing him from active duty and assigning him to the standby reserves. The Court upheld the regulations: "The unrestricted circulation of collective petitions could imperil discipline." Justice Stewart dissented: "It cannot conceivably be argued that a regulation requiring the preclearance of the content of all petitions to be circulated by servicemen in time of peace is 'necessary to the security of the United States.'"

∾ PROBLEMS ∾

1. *The History Professor and the Pistol.* A university history club asks faculty to pose with props related to their areas of interest. The plaintiff chose to pose wearing a coonskin cap and holding a .45-caliber pistol. Another plaintiff (who specialized in ancient Greece and Rome) chose to wear a cardboard laurel wreath and held a Roman short sword. A university official demanded that the photos be removed as "inappropriate," and the chancellor ordered the photos removed over the history department's objection. The professors sue, claiming a violation of their First Amendment rights. Should they prevail?

2. *The KKK Recruiter.* A sheriff's office employee (a clerical employee with responsibility for filing both public and confidential records) gave a television interview in which he discussed his work as a Ku Klux Klan recruiter. Even though he had an "outstanding" work record, he was dismissed because the sheriff claimed that the interview caused racial tension (the sheriff's office received more than 200 complaints about the interview, as well as a protest by the Klan and a counterprotest by an anti-Klan group), lowered esprit de corps in the sheriff's office, and damaged the office's credibility in the community (some argued that blacks should resist arrest by sheriff's office personnel because of a risk of death or serious bodily injury at the jail). Were the employee's association with the KKK and the interview protected by the First Amendment?

3. *The Pornographic Police Officer.* A police officer is fired for selling videotapes showing himself engaged in sexually explicit acts, sometimes in police uniform. One video shows him stripping off a police uniform (not the actual

city uniform) and masturbating. Another video shows him stopping a motorist to issue a citation, but ending up involved in sexual activity with the motorist. His website identified him "as employed in the field of law enforcement." The department concluded that the officer had violated specific police department policies, including conduct unbecoming of an officer, outside employment, and immoral conduct. Since all of the officer's activities were conducted during his "off-duty" hours, does the dismissal violate his First Amendment rights? How might *Pickering, Connick,* and *Rankin* apply to the dismissal? *See City of San Diego v. Roe,* 543 U.S. 77 (2004).

4. *More on the International Treaty Regulating the Internet.* Having read the various decisions discussing the ability of the U.S. government to restrict the speech of governmental employees, do you have a better sense of the type of treaty language that you might be able to agree to regarding limitations on the speech of public employees on the internet? If so, what language might be included in the treaty?

Garcetti v. Ceballos

547 U.S. 410 (2006)

Justice KENNEDY delivered the opinion of the Court.

Respondent Richard Ceballos has been employed since 1989 as a deputy district attorney for the Los Angeles County District Attorney's Office as a calendar deputy who exercised certain supervisory responsibilities over other lawyers. In February 2000, a defense attorney contacted Ceballos about a pending criminal case and said there were inaccuracies in an affidavit used to obtain a critical search warrant. After an investigation, Ceballos determined the affidavit contained serious misrepresentations. The affidavit called a long driveway what Ceballos thought should have been referred to as a separate roadway. Ceballos also questioned the affidavit's statement that tire tracks led from a stripped-down truck to the premises covered by the warrant because the roadway's composition made it difficult or impossible to leave visible tire tracks.

Ceballos spoke on the telephone to the warrant affiant, a deputy sheriff from the Los Angeles County Sheriff's Department, but he did not receive a satisfactory explanation for the perceived inaccuracies. He relayed his findings to his supervisors, petitioners Carol Najera and Frank Sundstedt, and followed up by preparing a disposition memorandum. The memo explained Ceballos' concerns and recommended dismissal of the case. On March 2, 2000, Ceballos submitted the memo to Sundstedt for his review. A few days later, Ceballos presented Sundstedt with another memo, this one describing a second telephone conversation between Ceballos and the warrant affiant. Based on Ceballos' statements, a meeting was held to discuss the affidavit. The meeting allegedly became heated, with one lieutenant sharply criticizing Ceballos for his handling of the case.

Despite Ceballos' concerns, Sundstedt decided to proceed with the prosecution, pending disposition of the defense motion to traverse. The trial court held a hearing on the motion. Ceballos was called by the defense and recounted his observations about the affidavit, but the trial court rejected the challenge to the warrant. Ceballos claims that in the aftermath of these events he was subjected to a series of retaliatory employment actions. The actions included reassignment from his calendar deputy position to a trial deputy position, transfer to another courthouse, and denial of a promotion. Ceballos' grievance was denied on the basis that he had not suffered any retaliation. Ceballos sued alleging that petitioners violated the First and Fourteenth Amendments by retaliating against him based on his memo of March 2. Petitioners claimed that no retaliatory actions were taken against Ceballos and that all the actions of which he complained were explained by legitimate reasons such as staffing needs. They further contended that Ceballos' memo was not protected speech under the First Amendment. The District Court granted petitioner's motion for summary judgment. The Court of Appeals for the Ninth Circuit reversed. We granted certiorari and we now reverse.

At one time, a public employee had "no right to object to conditions placed upon the terms of employment—including those which restricted the exercise of constitutional rights." *Connick v. Myers*, 461 U.S. 138 (1983). That dogma has been qualified in important respects. The Court has made clear that public employees do not surrender all their First Amendment rights by reason of their employment. Rather, the First Amendment protects a public employee's right, in certain circumstances, to speak as a citizen addressing matters of public concern. *See, e.g., Pickering v. Board of Ed. of Township High School Dist. 205, Will Cty.*, 391 U.S. 563 (1968); *Rankin v. McPherson*, 483 U.S. 378 (1987).

Pickering provides a useful starting point in explaining the Court's doctrine. There the relevant speech was a teacher's letter to a local newspaper addressing issues including the funding policies of his school board. "The problem in any case," the Court stated, "is to arrive at a balance between the interests of the teacher, as a citizen, in commenting upon matters of public concern and the interest of the State, as an employer, in promoting the efficiency of the public services it performs through its employees." The Court found the teacher's speech "neither was shown nor can be presumed to have in any way either impeded the teacher's proper performance of his daily duties in the classroom or to have interfered with the regular operation of the schools generally." Thus, the Court concluded that "the interest of the school administration in limiting teachers' opportunities to contribute to public debate is not significantly greater than its interest in limiting a similar contribution by any member of the general public."

Pickering and the cases decided in its wake identify two inquiries to guide interpretation of the constitutional protections accorded to public employee speech. The first requires determining whether the employee spoke as a citizen on a matter of public concern. If the answer is no, the employee has no First Amendment cause of action based on his or her employer's reaction to the speech. If the answer is yes, then the possibility of a First Amendment claim arises. The question becomes whether the relevant government entity had an adequate justification for treating the employee differently from any other member of the general public. This consideration reflects the importance of the relationship between the speaker's expressions and employment. A government entity has broader discretion to restrict speech when it acts in its role as employer, but the restrictions it imposes must be directed at speech that has some potential to affect the entity's operations.

To be sure, conducting these inquiries sometimes has proved difficult. This is the necessary product of "the enormous variety of fact situations in which critical statements by teachers and other public employees may be thought by their superiors to furnish grounds for dismissal." The Court's overarching objectives, though, are evident.

When a citizen enters government service, the citizen by necessity must accept certain limitations on his or her freedom. *See, e.g., Waters v. Churchill,* 511 U.S. 661 (1994) (plurality opinion). Government employers, like private employers, need a significant degree of control over their employees' words and actions; without it, there would be little chance for the efficient provision of public services. *Cf. Connick, supra,* at 143. Public employees, moreover, often occupy trusted positions in society. When they speak out, they can express views that contravene governmental policies or impair the proper performance of governmental functions.

At the same time, the Court has recognized that a citizen who works for the government is nonetheless a citizen. The First Amendment limits the ability of a public employer to leverage the employment relationship to restrict, incidentally or intentionally, the liberties employees enjoy in their capacities as private citizens. So long as employees are speaking as citizens about matters of public concern, they must face only those speech restrictions that are necessary for their employers to operate efficiently and effectively. *See, e.g., Connick, supra,* at 147.

The Court's employee-speech jurisprudence protects, of course, the constitutional rights of public employees. Yet the First Amendment interests at stake extend beyond the individual speaker. The Court has acknowledged the importance of promoting the public's interest in receiving the well-informed views of government employees engaging in civic discussion. In *Pickering,* the Court characterized its holding as rejecting the attempt of school administrators to "limit teachers' opportunities to contribute to public debate." It also noted that teachers are "the members of a community most likely to have informed and definite opinions" about school expenditures. The Court's approach acknowledged the necessity for informed, vibrant dialogue in a democratic society. It suggested, in addition, that widespread costs may arise when dialogue is repressed. *See, e.g., San Diego v. Roe,* 543 U.S. 77 (2004) (per curiam).

The Court's decisions, then, have sought both to promote the individual and societal interests that are served when employees speak as citizens on matters of public concern and to respect the needs of government employers attempting to perform their important public functions. Underlying our cases has been the premise that while the First Amendment invests public employees with certain rights, it does not empower them to "constitutionalize the employee grievance." *Connick,* 461 U.S., at 154.

Ceballos believed the affidavit used to obtain a search warrant contained serious misrepresentations. He conveyed his opinion and recommendation in a memo to his supervisor. That Ceballos expressed his views inside his office, rather than publicly, is not dispositive. Employees in some cases may receive First Amendment protection for expressions made at work. Many citizens do much of their talking inside their workplaces, and it would not serve the goal of treating public employees like "any member of the general public," *Pickering*, 391 U.S. at 573, to hold that all speech within the office is automatically exposed to restriction.

The memo concerned the subject matter of Ceballos' employment, but this, too, is nondispositive. The First Amendment protects some expressions related to the speaker's job. As the Court noted in *Pickering*: "Teachers are the members of a community most likely to have informed and definite opinions as to how funds allotted to the operation of the schools should be spent. Accordingly, it is essential that they be able to speak out freely on such questions without fear of retaliatory dismissal." The same is true of many other categories of public employees.

The controlling factor in Ceballos' case is that his expressions were made pursuant to his duties as a calendar deputy. That consideration—the fact that Ceballos spoke as a prosecutor fulfilling a responsibility to advise his supervisor about how best to proceed with a pending case—distinguishes Ceballos' case from those in which the First Amendment provides protection against discipline. We hold that when public employees make statements pursuant to their official duties, the employees are not speaking as citizens for First Amendment purposes, and the Constitution does not insulate their communications from employer discipline.

Ceballos wrote his disposition memo because that is part of what he, as a calendar deputy, was employed to do. It is immaterial whether he experienced some personal gratification from writing the memo; his First Amendment rights do not depend on his job satisfaction. The significant point is that the memo was written pursuant to Ceballos' official duties. Restricting speech that owes its existence to a public employee's professional responsibilities does not infringe any liberties the employee might have enjoyed as a private citizen. It simply reflects the exercise of employer control over what the employer itself has commissioned or created. Contrast, for example, the expressions made by the speaker in *Pickering*, whose letter to the newspaper had no official significance and bore similarities to letters submitted by numerous citizens every day.

Ceballos did not act as a citizen when he went about conducting his daily professional activities, such as supervising attorneys, investigating charges, and preparing filings. In the same way he did not speak as a citizen by writing a memo that addressed the proper disposition of a pending criminal case. When he went to work and performed the tasks he was paid to perform, Ceballos acted as a government employee. The fact that his duties sometimes required him to speak or write does not mean his supervisors were prohibited from evaluating his performance.

This result is consistent with our precedents' attention to the potential societal value of employee speech. Refusing to recognize First Amendment claims based on government employees' work product does not prevent them from participating in public debate. The employees retain the prospect of constitutional protection for their contributions to the civic discourse. This prospect of protection, however, does not invest them with a right to perform their jobs however they see fit.

Our holding is supported by the emphasis of our precedents on affording government employers sufficient discretion to manage their operations. Employers have heightened interests in controlling speech made by an employee in his or her professional capacity. Official communications have official consequences, creating a need for substantive consistency and clarity. Supervisors must ensure that their employees' official communications are accurate, demonstrate sound judgment, and promote the employer's mission. Ceballos' memo is illustrative. It demanded the attention of his supervisors and led to a heated meeting with employees from the sheriff's department. If Ceballos' superiors thought his memo was inflammatory or misguided, they had the authority to take proper corrective action.

Ceballos' proposed contrary rule would commit state and federal courts to a new, permanent, and intrusive role, mandating judicial oversight of communications between and among government employees and their superiors in the course of official business. This displacement of managerial discretion by judicial supervision finds no support in our precedents. To hold otherwise would be to demand permanent judicial intervention in the conduct of governmental operations to a degree inconsistent with sound principles of federalism and the separation of powers. Employees who make public statements outside the course of performing their official duties retain some possibility of First Amendment protection because that is the kind of activity engaged in by citizens who do not work for the government. The same goes for writing a letter to a local newspaper, or discussing politics with a co-worker. When a public employee speaks pursuant to employment responsibilities, however, there is no relevant analogue to speech by citizens who are not government employees. A public employer that wishes to encourage its employees to voice concerns privately retains the option of instituting internal policies and procedures that are receptive to employee criticism. Giving employees an internal forum for their speech will discourage them from concluding that the safest avenue of expression is to state their views in public.

The First Amendment does not prohibit managerial discipline based on an employee's expressions made pursuant to official responsibilities. Because Ceballos' memo falls into this category, his allegation of unconstitutional retaliation must fail. The parties do not dispute that Ceballos wrote his disposition memo pursuant to his employment duties. We thus have no occasion to articulate a comprehensive framework for defining the scope of an employee's duties in cases where there is room for serious debate. We reject, however, the suggestion that employers can restrict employees' rights by creating excessively broad job descriptions. Formal job descriptions often bear little resemblance to the duties an employee actually is expected to perform, and the listing of a given task in an employee's written job description is neither necessary nor sufficient to demonstrate that conducting the task is within the scope of the employee's professional duties for First Amendment purposes.

Justice Souter suggests today's decision may have important ramifications for academic freedom. There is some argument that expression related to academic scholarship or classroom instruction implicates additional constitutional interests that are not fully accounted for by this Court's customary employee-speech jurisprudence. We do not decide whether the analysis we conduct today would apply in the same manner to a case involving speech related to scholarship or teaching.

Exposing governmental inefficiency and misconduct is a matter of considerable significance. The dictates of sound judgment are reinforced by the powerful network of legislative enactments—such as whistle-blower protection laws and labor codes—available to those who seek to expose wrongdoing. *See, e.g.,* 5 U.S.C. §2302(b)(8). Cases involving government attorneys implicate additional safeguards in the form of, for example, rules of conduct and constitutional obligations apart from the First Amendment. *See, e.g.,* Cal. Rule Prof. Conduct 5-110 (2005). These imperatives, as well as obligations arising from any other applicable constitutional provisions and mandates of the criminal and civil laws, protect employees and provide checks on supervisors who would order unlawful or otherwise inappropriate actions.

We reject, however, the notion that the First Amendment shields from discipline the expressions employees make pursuant to their professional duties. Our precedents do not support the existence of a constitutional cause of action behind every statement a public employee makes in the course of doing his or her job.

The judgment of the Court of Appeals is reversed, and the case is remanded for proceedings consistent with this opinion.

It is so ordered.

Justice STEVENS, *dissenting.*

The notion that there is a categorical difference between speaking as a citizen and speaking in the course of one's employment is quite wrong. In *Givhan v. Western Line Consol. School Dist.,* 439 U.S. 410 (1979), we had no difficulty recognizing that the First Amendment applied when Bessie Givhan, an English teacher, raised concerns about the school's racist employment practices to the principal. It seems perverse to fashion a new rule that provides employees with an incentive to voice their concerns publicly before talking frankly to their superiors.

Justice SOUTER, with whom Justice STEVENS and Justice GINSBURG join, *dissenting.*

Private and public interests in addressing official wrongdoing and threats to health and safety can outweigh the government's stake in the efficient implementation of policy, and when they do public employees who speak on these matters in the course of their duties should be eligible to claim First Amendment protection.

A statement by a government employee complaining about nothing beyond treatment under personnel rules raises no greater claim to constitutional protection against retaliatory response than the remarks of a private employee. *See Connick v. Myers*, 461 U.S. 138 (1983). In between these points lies a public employee's speech unwelcome to the government but on a significant public issue. Such an employee speaking as a citizen with a citizen's interest, is protected from reprisal unless the statements are too damaging to the government's capacity to conduct public business to be justified by any individual or public benefit thought to flow from the statements. A government paycheck does nothing to eliminate the value to an individual of speaking on public matters, and there is no good reason for categorically discounting a speaker's interest in commenting on a matter of public concern just because the government employs him. The reason that protection of employee speech is qualified is that it can distract co-workers and supervisors from their tasks at hand and thwart the implementation of legitimate policy, the risks of which grow greater the closer the employee's speech gets to commenting on his own workplace and responsibilities.

The difference between a case like *Givhan* and this one is that the subject of Ceballos's speech fell within the scope of his job responsibilities, whereas choosing personnel was not what the teacher was hired to do. The effect of the majority's constitutional line between these two cases, then, is that a *Givhan* schoolteacher is protected when complaining to the principal about hiring policy, but a school personnel officer would not be if he protested that the principal disapproved of hiring minority job applicants. This is an odd place to draw a distinction, and while necessary judicial line-drawing sometimes looks arbitrary, any distinction obliges a court to justify its choice. Here, there is no adequate justification for the majority's line categorically denying *Pickering* protection to any speech uttered "pursuant to official duties."

The qualified speech protection embodied in *Pickering* balancing resolves the tension between individual and public interests in the speech, on the one hand, and the government's interest in operating efficiently without distraction or embarrassment by talkative or headline-grabbing employees. The need for a balance hardly disappears when an employee speaks on matters his job requires him to address; rather, the individual and public value of such speech is no less, and may well be greater, when the employee speaks pursuant to his duties in addressing a subject he knows intimately for the very reason that it falls within his duties. Would anyone deny that a prosecutor like Richard Ceballos may claim the interest of any citizen in speaking out against a rogue law enforcement officer, simply because his job requires him to express a judgment about the officer's performance?

The majority is rightly concerned that the employee who speaks out on matters relating to his own work has the greater leverage to create office uproars and fracture the government's authority to set policy to be carried out coherently through the ranks. But why do the majority's concerns, which we all share, require categorical exclusion of First Amendment protection against any official retaliation for things said on the job? The lesson of *Pickering* is still to the point: when constitutionally significant interests clash, resist the demand for winner-take-all; try to make adjustments that serve all of the values at stake.

The majority's position comes with no guarantee against factbound litigation over whether a public employee's statements were made "pursuant to official duties." Are prosecutors' discretionary statements about cases addressed to the press on the courthouse steps made "pursuant to their official duties"? Are government nuclear scientists' complaints to their supervisors about a colleague's improper handling of radioactive materials made "pursuant" to duties? The majority accepts the fallacy that any statement made within the scope of public employment is (or should be treated as) the government's own speech, and should thus be differentiated as a matter of law from the personal statements the First Amendment protects.

The majority argues that the First Amendment has little or no work to do here owing to an assertedly comprehensive complement of state and national statutes protecting government whistle-blowers from vindictive bosses. But "the applicability of a provision of the Constitution has never depended on the vagaries of state or federal law." *Board of Commrs., Wabaunsee Cty. v. Umbehr*, 518 U.S. 668 (1996). Speech addressing official wrongdoing may well fall outside protected whistle-blowing, defined in the classic sense of exposing an official's fault to a third party or to the public.

Justice BREYER, *dissenting*.

Where a government employee speaks "as an employee upon matters only of personal interest," the First Amendment does not offer protection. Where the employee speaks "as a citizen upon matters of public concern," the First Amendment offers protection but only where the speech survives a test, called "*Pickering* balancing." I believe that courts should apply the *Pickering* standard, even though the government employee speaks upon matters of public concern in the course of his ordinary duties.

Respondent complained of retaliation, in part, on the basis of speech contained in his disposition memorandum that he says fell within the scope of his obligations. The facts present two special circumstances that together justify First Amendment review. First, the speech at issue is professional speech — the speech of a lawyer. Second, a prosecutor has a constitutional obligation to learn of, to preserve, and to communicate with the defense about exculpatory and impeachment evidence in the government's possession, so that the need to protect the employee's speech is augmented, the need for broad government authority to control that speech is likely diminished, and administrable standards are quite likely available. Hence, I would find that the Constitution mandates special protection of employee speech in such circumstances.

Government administration typically involves matters of public concern. Why else would government be involved? And "public issues," indeed, matters of "unusual importance," are often daily bread-and-butter concerns for the police, the intelligence agencies, the military, and many whose jobs involve protecting the public's health, safety, and the environment. Moreover, the speech of vast numbers of public employees deal with wrongdoing, health, safety, and honesty: for example, police officers, firefighters, environmental protection agents, building inspectors, hospital workers, bank regulators, and so on.

The ability of a dissatisfied employee to file a complaint, engage in discovery, and insist that the court undertake a balancing of interests may interfere unreasonably with both the managerial function (the ability of the employer to control the way in which an employee performs his basic job) and with the use of other grievance-resolution mechanisms, such as arbitration, civil service review boards, and whistle-blower remedies, for which employees and employers may have bargained or which legislatures may have enacted. The list of categories substantially overlaps areas where the law already provides nonconstitutional protection through whistle-blower statutes and the like.

Notes

1. *Public Employees and the Petition Clause.* In *Borough of Duryea v. Guarnieri*, 564 U.S. 379 (2011), a police chief sought to characterize his employment grievance as involving the petition clause of the First Amendment ("the right of the people to petition the Government for a redress of grievances"), and argued that different rules apply to a claim under that clause. The case concerned the extent of the protection, if any, that the Petition Clause grants public employees in routine disputes with government employers. The Court concluded that the Petition Clause adds nothing to an employee's claim:

> When a public employee sues a government employer under the First Amendment's Speech Clause, the employee must show that he or she spoke as a citizen on a matter of public concern. *Connick v. Myers*, 461 U.S. 138 (1983). If an employee does not speak as a citizen, or does not address a matter of public concern, "a federal court is not the appropriate forum in which to review the wisdom of a personnel decision taken by a public agency allegedly in reaction to the employee's behavior." *Ibid.* Even if an employee does speak as a citizen on a matter of public concern, the employee's speech is not automatically privileged. Courts balance the First Amendment interest of the employee against "the interest of the State, as an employer, in promoting the efficiency of the public services it performs through its employees." *Pickering v. Board of Ed. of Township High School Dist. 205, Will Cty.*, 391 U.S. 563, 568 (1968). This framework "reconciles the employee's right to engage in speech and the government employer's right to protect its own legitimate interests in performing its mission." *San Diego v. Roe*, 543 U.S. 77, 82 (2004) (*per curiam*). A citizen who accepts public employment "must accept certain limitations on his or her freedom." *Garcetti v. Ceballos*, 547 U.S. 410, 418 (2006). The government has a substantial interest in ensuring that all of its operations are efficient and effective. That interest may require broad authority to supervise the conduct of public employees. "When someone who is paid a salary so that she will

contribute to an agency's effective operation begins to do or say things that detract from the agency's effective operation, the government employer must have some power to restrain her." *Waters v. Churchill*, 511 U.S. 661, 675 (1994) (plurality opinion). Restraints are justified by the consensual nature of the employment relationship and by the unique nature of the government's interest.

The Petition Clause protects the right of individuals to appeal to courts and other forums established by the government for resolution of legal disputes. Although retaliation by a government employer for a public employee's exercise of the right of access to the courts may implicate the protections of the Petition Clause, this case provides no necessity to consider the correct application of the Petition Clause beyond that context. Guarnieri just as easily could have alleged that his employer retaliated against him for the speech contained within his grievances and lawsuit. That claim would have been subject to the public concern test. Both speech and petition are integral to the democratic process, although not necessarily in the same way. The right to petition allows citizens to express their ideas, hopes, and concerns to their government and their elected representatives, whereas the right to speak fosters the public exchange of ideas that is integral to deliberative democracy as well as to the whole realm of ideas and human affairs. Both speech and petition advance personal expression, although the right to petition is generally concerned with expression directed to the government seeking redress of a grievance.

Courts should not presume there is always an essential equivalence in the two Clauses or that Speech Clause precedents necessarily and in every case resolve Petition Clause claims. Interpretation of the Petition Clause must be guided by the objectives and aspirations that underlie the right. A petition conveys the special concerns of its author to the government and, in its usual form, requests action by the government to address those concerns. *McDonald v. Smith*, 472 U.S. 479 (1985), has been interpreted to mean that the right to petition can extend no further than the right to speak. Claims of retaliation by public employees do not call for this divergence. The close connection between these rights has led Courts of Appeals other than the Third Circuit to apply the public concern test developed in Speech Clause cases to Petition Clause claims by public employees. This approach is justified by the common ground in the definition and delineation of these rights. The considerations that shape the application of the Speech Clause to public employees apply with equal force to claims by those employees under the Petition Clause.

2. Garcetti *and Subpoenaed Employees.* In *Lane v. Franks*, 573 U.S. 228 (2014), the Court held that the *Pickering* test protected an employee who provided truthful testimony in response to a subpoena regarding matters that he discovered in the course of his employment. According to the Court, the question is whether the government has "an adequate justification for treating the employee differently from any other member of the public" based on the government's needs as an employer. In particular, the Court cited the employer's legitimate "interests in the effective and efficient fulfillment of their responsibilities to the public," including "promoting efficiency and integrity in the discharge of official duties," and "maintaining proper discipline in public service." The Court noted that the employer's side of the *Pickering* scale was "entirely empty" because they did not "assert, and cannot demonstrate, any government interest that tips the balance in their favor. There is no evidence that Lane's testimony at Schmitz' trials was false or erroneous or that Lane unnecessarily disclosed any sensitive, confidential, or privileged information while testifying." As a result, the Court concluded that "Lane's speech is entitled to protection under the First Amendment."

1. *Other Employees.* As the dissents suggest, *Ceballos* might apply to an array of employee statements. Think about how the decision might apply to the following factual situations (some of which were suggested by Justices Stevens and Souter in their dissents): A) An internal police investigator brings the false testimony of a fellow officer to the attention of a city official, but is later demoted. *See Branton v. City of Dallas,* 272 F.3d 730 (5th Cir. 2001); B) A police officer is demoted after opposing the police chief's attempt to "use his official position to coerce a financially independent organization into a potentially ruinous merger." *See Miller v. Jones,* 444 F.3d 929, 936 (2006); C) A police officer is sanctioned for reporting criminal activity that implicates a local political figure, a good friend of the police chief, in official misconduct. *See Delgado v. Jones,* 282 F.3d 511 (7th Cir. 2002); D) A school district official's contract is not renewed after she gives frank (and negative) testimony about the district's desegregation efforts in a judicial proceeding. *See Herts v. Smith,* 345 F.3d 581 (8th Cir. 2003); E) An engineer is fired after reporting to his supervisors that contractors were failing to complete dam-related projects and that the resulting dam might be structurally unstable. *See Kincade v. City of Blue Springs,* 64 F.3d 389 (8th Cir. 1995); F) A state lottery board security officer is fired after informing the police about a theft made possible by "rather drastic managerial ineptitude." *See Fox v. District of Columbia,* 83 F.3d 1491, 1494 (D.C. Cir. 1996); G) A law professor is disciplined after publishing an article questioning the wisdom of state affirmative action policies.

2. *Kentucky's Anti-Blog Policy.* Kentucky's Republican governor faces criminal misdemeanor charges and is being repeatedly blasted on Democratic blog sites. Historically, in an attempt to preclude state employees from spending time on non-work-related internet sites, Kentucky has used blocking software to preclude state-owned computers from being used to access sites related to pornography, lingerie, computer games, hate sites, casinos, chat rooms, and illegal-activity sites. Is it permissible to extend the blocks to cover Web blogs? Can the ban be justified on the basis that visiting such sites, for non-work-related reasons, is not an "efficient" use of state employee time?

3. *Burning the U.S. Flag.* Suppose that a high school teacher, in an effort to teach students about the right to free speech, burns a small U.S. flag in class and then asks his students to write an essay about it. On learning about the incident, the school's principal decides to reassign the teacher to non-instructional duties. The principal, who was besieged by parents complaining about the burning of a U.S. flag, cited safety issues for his decision. A school board member suggested that the burning could have been offensive, especially to students with parents in the military. The teacher claimed academic freedom. Was it appropriate to discipline the teacher under these circumstances? Would you view the case differently if the teacher had left the children in the room, while the flag was still burning, in order to obtain some water to douse the flame? *See* Chris Kenning, *Teacher Burns U.S. Flag in Class,* Louisville Courier-J., Aug. 22, 2006, at A-1.

4. *More on Police Speech.* In Louisville, Kentucky, a police posted information related to his employment on his Facebook page. Following protests against the police in the African-American community, he posted: "If we really wanted you dead all we'd have to do is stop patrolling your neighborhoods. And wait." Later, he testified: "You take any neighbourhood in America and if they realize the police are not patrolling, crime would go through the roof." Regarding the Black Lives Matter movement, he posted the following: "Has it occurred to anyone that if you're able to organize this many people for a protest, you can organize this many people to clean up your community and get rid of the criminal element causing the problem." In another post, he stated: "It's NOT about color. It's about the law." The police department gives him a 30-day suspension on the theory that his statements demonstrated "blatant racial bias," and "hurt relationships within our community and damaged the image of the department." Did the officer have a First Amendment right to make the statements?

3. Associational Rights

Questions have arisen regarding whether public employees have special associational rights. Those issues are presented in the following case.

Elrod v. Burns

427 U.S. 347 (1976)

Mr. Justice BRENNAN announced the judgment of the Court and delivered an opinion in which Mr. Justice WHITE and Mr. Justice MARSHALL joined.

In December 1970, the Sheriff of Cook County, a Republican, was replaced by Richard Elrod, a Democrat. Respondents, all Republicans, were employees of the Cook County Sheriff's Office. They were non-civil-service employees and, therefore, not covered by any statute, ordinance, or regulation protecting them from arbitrary discharge. John Burns was Chief Deputy of the Process Division and supervised all departments of the Sheriff's Office working on the seventh floor of the building housing that office. Frank Vargas was a bailiff and security guard at the Juvenile Court. Fred L. Buckley was employed as a process server in the office. Joseph Dennard was an employee in the office.

It has been the practice of the Sheriff of Cook County, when he assumes office from a Sheriff of a different political party, to replace non-civil-service employees of the Sheriffs' Office with members of his own party when the existing employees lack or fail to obtain requisite support from, or fail to affiliate with, that party. Subsequent to Sheriff Elrod's assumption of office, respondents were discharged from their employment solely because they did not support and were not members of the Democratic Party and had failed to obtain the sponsorship of one of its leaders. Buckley is in imminent danger of being discharged solely for the same reasons. Respondents allege that the discharges were ordered by Sheriff Elrod under the direction of the codefendants in this suit.

Patronage practice is not new to American politics. It has existed at the federal level at least since the Presidency of Thomas Jefferson, although its popularization and legitimation primarily occurred later, in the Presidency of Andrew Jackson. The cost of the practice of patronage is the restraint it places on freedoms of belief and association. In order to maintain their jobs, respondents were required to pledge their political allegiance to the Democratic Party, work for the election of other candidates of the Democratic Party, contribute a portion of their wages to the Party, or obtain the sponsorship of a member of the Party, usually at the price of one of the first three alternatives. Regardless of the incumbent party's identity, Democratic or otherwise, the consequences for association and belief are the same. An individual who is a member of the out-party maintains affiliation with his own party at the risk of losing his job. He works for the election of his party's candidates and espouses its policies at the same risk. The financial and campaign assistance that he is induced to provide to another party furthers the advancement of that party's policies to the detriment of his party's views and ultimately his own beliefs, and any assessment of his salary is tantamount to coerced belief. Even a pledge of allegiance to another party, however ostensible, only serves to compromise the individual's true beliefs. Since the average public employee is hardly in the financial position to support his party and another, or to lend his time to two parties, the individual's ability to act according to his beliefs and to associate with others of his political persuasion is constrained, and support for his party is diminished.

It is not only belief and association which are restricted where political patronage is the practice. The free functioning of the electoral process also suffers. Conditioning public employment on partisan support prevents support of competing political interests. Existing employees are deterred from such support, as well as the multitude seeking jobs. As government employment, state or federal, becomes more pervasive, the greater the dependence on it becomes, and therefore the greater becomes the power to starve political opposition by commanding partisan support, financial and otherwise. Patronage thus tips the electoral process in favor of the incumbent party, and where the practice's scope is substantial relative to the size of the electorate, the impact on the process can be significant.

Our concern with the impact of patronage on political belief and association does not occur in the abstract, for political belief and association constitute the core of those activities protected by the First Amendment. "If there is any fixed star in our constitutional constellation, it is that no official, high or petty, can prescribe what shall be orthodox in politics, nationalism, religion, or other matters of opinion or force citizens to confess by word or act their faith therein." And, though freedom of belief is central, "the First Amendment protects political association as well as political expression." "There can no longer be any doubt that freedom to associate with others for the common advancement of political beliefs and ideas is a form of 'orderly group activity' protected by the First and Fourteenth Amendments. The right to associate with the political party of one's choice is an integral part of this basic constitutional freedom." *Kusper v. Pontikes,* 414 U.S. 51, 56-57 (1973). Patronage, to the extent it compels or restrains belief and association is inimical to the process which undergirds our system of government and is "at war with the deeper traditions of democracy embodied in the First Amendment." As such, the practice unavoidably confronts decisions by this Court either invalidating or recognizing as invalid government action that inhibits belief and association through the conditioning of public employment on political faith.

Wieman v. Updegraff, 344 U.S. 183 (1952), held that a State could not require its employees to establish their loyalty by extracting an oath denying past affiliation with Communists. Particularly pertinent to the constitutionality of the practice of patronage dismissals are *Keyishian v. Board of Regents,* 385 U.S. 589 (1967), and *Perry v. Sindermann,* 408 U.S. 593 (1972). In *Keyishian,* the Court invalidated New York statutes barring employment merely on the basis of membership in "subversive" organizations. *Keyishian* squarely held that political association alone could not, consistently with the First Amendment, constitute an adequate ground for denying public employment. In *Perry,* the Court broadly rejected the validity of limitations on First Amendment rights as a condition to the receipt of a governmental benefit, stating that the government "may not deny a benefit to a person on a basis that infringes his constitutionally protected interests especially, his interest in freedom of speech. For if the government could deny a benefit to a person because of his constitutionally protected speech or associations, his exercise of those freedoms would in effect be penalized and inhibited. This would allow the government to 'produce a result which it could not command directly.' Such interference with constitutional rights is impermissible."

Patronage practice falls squarely within the prohibitions of *Keyishian.* Under that practice, public employees hold their jobs on the condition that they provide, in some acceptable manner, support for the favored political party. The threat of dismissal for failure to provide that support unquestionably inhibits protected belief and association, and dismissal for failure to provide support only penalizes its exercise. The belief and association which government may not ordain directly are achieved by indirection. And regardless of how evenhandedly these restraints may operate in the long run, after political office has changed hands several times, protected interests are still infringed and thus the violation remains.

The prohibition on encroachment of First Amendment protections is not an absolute. If conditioning the retention of public employment on the employee's support of the in-party is to survive constitutional challenge, it must further some vital government end by a means that is least restrictive of freedom of belief and association in achieving that end, and the benefit gained must outweigh the loss of constitutionally protected rights.

One interest which has been offered in justification of patronage is the need to insure effective government and the efficiency of public employees. It is argued that employees of political persuasions not the same as that of the party in control of public office will not have the incentive to work effectively and may even be motivated to subvert the incumbent administration's efforts to govern effectively. We are not persuaded. The inefficiency resulting from the wholesale replacement of large numbers of public employees every time political office changes hands belies this justification. And the prospect of dismissal after an election in which the incumbent party has lost is only a disincentive to good work. Further, it is not clear that dismissal in order to make room for a patronage appointment will result in replacement by a person more qualified to do the job since appointment often occurs in exchange for the delivery of votes, or other party service, not job capability. More fundamentally, however, the argument does not succeed because it is doubtful that the mere difference of political persuasion motivates poor performance; nor do we think it legitimately may be used as a basis for imputing such behavior. At all events, less drastic means for insuring government effectiveness and employee efficiency are available to the State. Specifically, employees may always be discharged for good cause, such as insubordination or poor job performance, when those bases in fact exist.

It may be argued that patronage gives employees of an incumbent party the incentive to perform well in order to insure their party's incumbency and thereby their jobs. Patronage thus makes employees highly accountable to the public. But the ability of officials more directly accountable to the electorate to discharge employees for cause and the availability of merit systems, growth in the use of which has been quite significant, convince us that means less intrusive than patronage still exist for achieving accountability in the public work force and, thereby, effective and efficient government. The greater effectiveness of patronage over these less drastic means is at best marginal, a gain outweighed by the absence of intrusion on protected interests under the alternatives.

A second interest advanced in support of patronage is the need for political loyalty to the end that representative government not be undercut by tactics obstructing the implementation of policies of the new administration, policies presumably sanctioned by the electorate. The justification is inadequate to validate patronage wholesale. Limiting patronage dismissals to policymaking positions is sufficient to achieve this governmental end. Nonpolicymaking individuals usually have only limited responsibility and are therefore not in a position to thwart the goals of the in-party.

No clear line can be drawn between policymaking and nonpolicymaking positions. While nonpolicymaking individuals usually have limited responsibility, that is not to say that one with a number of responsibilities is necessarily in a policymaking position. The nature of the responsibilities is critical. Employee supervisors may have many responsibilities, but those responsibilities may have only limited and well-defined objectives. An employee with responsibilities that are not well defined or are of broad scope more likely functions in a policymaking position. In determining whether an employee occupies a policymaking position, consideration should also be given to whether the employee acts as an adviser or formulates plans for the implementation of broad goals. Since it is the government's burden to demonstrate an overriding interest in order to validate an encroachment on protected interests, the burden of establishing this justification as to any particular respondent will rest on the petitioners on remand, cases of doubt being resolved in favor of the particular respondent.

It is argued that a third interest supporting patronage dismissals is the preservation of the democratic process. "The party organization makes a democratic government work and charges a price for its services." The argument is thus premised on the centrality of partisan politics to the democratic process. Preservation of the democratic process is certainly an interest protection of which may in some instances justify limitations on First Amendment freedoms. But however important preservation of the two-party system or any system involving a fixed number of parties may or may not be, we are not persuaded that the elimination of patronage practice or the interdiction of patronage dismissals will bring about the demise of party politics. Political parties existed in the absence of active patronage practice prior to the administration of Andrew Jackson, and they have survived substantial reduction in their patronage power through the establishment of merit systems.

Patronage dismissals thus are not the least restrictive alternative to achieving the contribution they may make to the democratic process. The process functions as well without the practice, perhaps even better. Patronage can result in the entrenchment of one or a few parties to the exclusion of others and is a very effective impediment to the associational and speech freedoms which are essential to a meaningful system of democratic government. Thus, if patronage contributes at all to the elective process, that contribution is diminished by the practice's impairment of the same. The gain to representative government provided by the practice of patronage, if any, would be insufficient to justify its sacrifice of First Amendment rights.

We hold that subordination of other First Amendment activity, that is, patronage dismissals, not only is permissible, but also is mandated by the First Amendment. And since patronage dismissals fall within the category of political campaigning and management, this conclusion irresistibly flows from *Mitchell* and *Letter Carriers*. For if the First Amendment did not place individual belief and association above political campaigning and management, at least in the setting of public employment, the restraints on those latter activities could not have been judged permissible in *Mitchell* and *Letter Carriers*.

Patronage dismissals severely restrict political belief and association. Though there is a vital need for government efficiency and effectiveness, such dismissals are on balance not the least restrictive means for fostering that end. Any contribution of patronage dismissals to the democratic process does not suffice to override their severe encroachment on First Amendment freedoms. We hold, therefore, that the practice of patronage dismissals is unconstitutional under the First and Fourteenth Amendments, and that respondents thus stated a valid claim for relief.

The judgment of the Court of Appeals is *affirmed*.

Mr. Justice STEWART, with whom Mr. Justice BLACKMUN joins, *concurring in the judgment.*

The single substantive question involved in this case is whether a nonpolicymaking, nonconfidential government employee can be discharged or threatened with discharge from a job that he is satisfactorily performing upon the sole ground of his political beliefs. I agree with the plurality that he cannot.

Mr. Chief Justice BURGER, *dissenting.*

The Court strains the rational bounds of First Amendment doctrine and runs counter to longstanding practices that are part of the fabric of our democratic system to hold that the Constitution commands something it has not been thought to require for 185 years. For all that time our system has wisely left these matters to the States and Congress.

Mr. Justice POWELL, with whom THE CHIEF JUSTICE and Mr. Justice REHNQUIST join, *dissenting.*

Patronage practices of the sort under consideration here have a long history in America. Patronage in employment played a significant role in democratizing American politics. Patronage broadened the base of political participation by providing incentives to take part in the process, thereby increasing the volume of political discourse in society. Patronage also strengthened parties, and hence encouraged the development of institutional responsibility to the electorate on a permanent basis. The complaining employees who apparently accepted patronage jobs knowingly and willingly, while fully familiar with the "tenure" practices long prevailing in the Sheriff's Office. Such employees have benefited from their political beliefs and activities; they have not been penalized for them. In these circumstances, beneficiaries of a patronage system may not be heard to challenge it when it comes their turn to be replaced.

The plurality seriously underestimates the strength of the government interest especially at the local level in allowing some patronage hiring practices, and it exaggerates the perceived burden on First Amendment rights. Patronage hiring practices enable party organizations to persist and function at the local level. The dull periods between elections require ongoing activities: precinct organizations must be maintained; new voters registered; and minor political "chores" performed for citizens who otherwise may have no practical means of access to officeholders. It is naive to think that these types of political activities are motivated at these levels by some academic interest in "democracy" or other public service impulse. For the most part, the hope of some reward generates a major portion of the local political activity supporting parties. One would think that elected representatives of the people are better equipped than we to weigh the need for some continuation of patronage practices in light of the interests above identified, and particularly in view of local conditions. I thus conclude that patronage hiring practices sufficiently serve important state interests, including some interests sought to be advanced by the First Amendment, to justify a tolerable intrusion on the First Amendment interests of employees or potential employees.

The plurality asserts that patronage hiring practices contravene the fundamental principle that " 'no official, high or petty, can prescribe what shall be orthodox in politics, nationalism, religion, or other matters of opinion.' " But employees, regardless of affiliation, may vote freely and express themselves on some political issues. The principal intrusion of patronage hiring practices on First Amendment interests thus arises from the coercion on associational choices that may be created by one's desire initially to obtain employment. This intrusion, while not insignificant, must be measured in light of the limited role of patronage hiring in most government employment. The pressure to abandon one's beliefs and associations to obtain government employment especially employment of such uncertain duration does not seem to me to assume impermissible proportions in light of the interests to be served.

Notes

1. *Communist Party Affiliation.* In *Communist Party of U.S. v. Subversive Activities Control Board*, 367 U.S. 1 (1961), the Court sustained an order requiring the Communist Party of the United States to register as a Communist-action organization as required by federal law. The order became final in 1961. At that time, appellee, a member of the Communist Party, was employed as a machinist at a Seattle, Washington, shipyard that was designated as a "defense facility." Appellee was indicted under §5(a)(1)(D) of the Subversive Activities Control Act of 1950, under a complaint alleging that he had "unlawfully and willfully engaged in employment" at the shipyard with knowledge of the outstanding order against the party and with knowledge and notice of the shipyard's designation as a defense facility by the secretary of defense. In *United States v. Robel*, 389 U.S. 258 (1967), the Court concluded that the law violated the appellee's right of association: "The operative fact upon which the job disability depends is the exercise of an individual's right of association, which is protected by the provisions of the First Amendment."

2. *Assistant Public Defenders.* In *Branti v. Finkel*, 445 U.S. 507 (1980), defendant (a Democrat) terminated an assistant public defender because he was a Republican on the basis that an assistant public defender performs a "policy-making" function, and therefore the plaintiff could be dismissed because of his political beliefs. The Court overturned the dismissal: "Employment of an assistant public defender cannot properly be conditioned upon his allegiance to the political party in control of the county government. Whatever policymaking occurs in the public defender's office must relate to the needs of individual clients and not to any partisan political interests."

3. *Employment Consequences of Party Affiliation.* In *Rutan v. Republican Party of Illinois*, 497 U.S. 62 (1990), after the State of Illinois imposed a hiring freeze,

plaintiffs claimed that they were denied promotions, transfers and employment, or not recalled from layoffs, because of their political affiliation (they did not support the Republican Party). The Court held that the denials were unconstitutional: "Employees who do not compromise their beliefs stand to lose the considerable increases in pay and job satisfaction attendant to promotions, the hours and maintenance expenses that are consumed by long daily commutes, and even their jobs if they are not rehired after a 'temporary' layoff." Justice Scalia dissented: "The desirability of patronage is a policy question to be decided by the people's representatives."

∾ PROBLEM: PROTECTING POLITICAL AFFILIATION ∾

The executive secretary of the Illinois Civil Service Commission, a Republican, was fired when a Democratic administration was elected. The evidence shows that the executive secretary has broad authority to make policy, set priorities, interpret the law, and speak on behalf of the commission. Is the executive secretary the type of employee that a new administration can replace without violating the Constitution? *See Powers v. Richards,* 549 F.3d 505 (7th Cir. 2008).

I. GOVERNMENT SUPPORT OF SPEECH

This section involves decisions grouped together under the rubric of "government speech," but they actually involve several different categories of speech. One category of cases relates to the question of whether a government subsidy of particular speech, which comes with conditions attached, may be constitutional in particular contexts. A second category involves the question whether the government may limit the rights of students when it acts as an educator. The Court's cases in each category reveal changes in direction and doctrinal emphasis so the road to settled doctrine has not been smooth. Recently, special challenges to "government speech" doctrines have been presented by the development of the internet and the enactment of laws that seek to protect national security.

Legal Services Corp. v. Velazquez
531 U.S. 533 (2001)

Justice KENNEDY delivered the opinion of the Court.

In 1974, Congress enacted the Legal Services Corporation Act, which establishes the Legal Services Corporation (LSC) as a District of Columbia nonprofit corporation. LSC's mission is to distribute funds appropriated by Congress to eligible local grantee organizations "for the purpose of providing financial support for legal assistance in noncriminal proceedings or matters to persons financially unable to afford legal assistance."

LSC grantees consist of hundreds of local organizations governed, in the typical case, by local boards of directors. In many instances the grantees are funded by a combination of LSC funds and other public or private sources. The grantee organizations hire and supervise lawyers to provide free legal assistance to indigent clients. Each year LSC appropriates funds to grantees or recipients that hire and supervise lawyers for various professional activities, including representation of indigent clients seeking welfare benefits.

This suit requires us to decide whether one of the conditions imposed by Congress on the use of LSC funds violates the First Amendment rights of LSC grantees and their clients. The restriction prohibits legal representation funded by recipients of LSC moneys if the representation involves an effort to amend or otherwise challenge existing welfare law. As interpreted by the LSC and by the Government, the restriction prevents an attorney from arguing to a court that a state statute conflicts with a federal statute or that either a state or federal statute by its terms or in its application is violative of the United States Constitution.

Lawyers employed by New York City LSC grantees, together with private LSC contributors, LSC indigent clients, and various state and local public officials whose governments contribute to LSC grantees, brought suit seeking to declare the restriction, among other provisions of the Act, invalid. We agree that the restriction violates the First Amendment.

From the inception of the LSC, Congress has placed restrictions on its use of funds. For instance, the LSC Act prohibits recipients from making available LSC funds, program personnel, or equipment to any political party, to any political campaign, or for use in "advocating or opposing any ballot measures." The Act further proscribes use of funds in most criminal proceedings and in litigation involving nontherapeutic abortions, secondary school desegregation, military desertion, or violations of the Selective Service statute. Fund recipients are barred from bringing class-action suits unless express approval is obtained from LSC. The restrictions were part of a compromise set of restrictions enacted in the Omnibus Consolidated Rescissions and Appropriations Act of 1996 (1996 Act), §504, and continued in each subsequent annual appropriations Act. The relevant portion of §504(a)(16) prohibits funding of any organization

> that initiates legal representation or participates in any other way, in litigation, lobbying, or rulemaking, involving an effort to reform a Federal or State welfare system, except that this paragraph shall not be construed to preclude a recipient from representing an individual eligible client who is seeking specific relief from a welfare agency if such relief does not involve an effort to amend or otherwise challenge existing law in effect on the date of the initiation of the representation.

The prohibitions apply to all of the activities of an LSC grantee, including those paid for by non-LSC funds. We are concerned with the statutory provision which excludes LSC representation in cases which "involve an effort to amend or otherwise challenge existing law in effect on the date of the initiation of the representation."

The United States and LSC rely on *Rust v. Sullivan*, 500 U.S. 173 (1991), as support for the LSC program restrictions. In *Rust*, Congress established program clinics to provide subsidies for doctors to advise patients on a variety of family planning topics. Congress did not consider abortion to be within its family planning objectives, however, and it forbade doctors employed by the program from discussing abortion with their patients. Recipients of funds under Title X of the Public Health Service Act challenged the Act's restriction that provided that none of the Title X funds appropriated for family planning services could "be used in programs where abortion is a method of family planning." The recipients argued that the regulations constituted impermissible viewpoint discrimination favoring an antiabortion position over a proabortion approach in the sphere of family planning. They asserted as well that Congress had imposed an unconstitutional condition on recipients of federal funds by requiring them to relinquish their right to engage in abortion advocacy and counseling in exchange for the subsidy. We upheld the law, reasoning that Congress had not discriminated against viewpoints on abortion, but had "merely chosen to fund one activity to the exclusion of the other." The restrictions were considered necessary "to ensure that the limits of the federal program were observed." Title X did not single out a particular idea for suppression because it was dangerous or disfavored; rather, Congress prohibited Title X doctors from counseling that was outside the scope of the project.

The Court in *Rust* did not place explicit reliance on the rationale that the counseling activities of the doctors under Title X amounted to governmental speech; when interpreting the holding in later cases, however, we have explained *Rust* on this understanding. We have said that viewpoint-based funding decisions can be sustained in instances in which the government is itself the speaker, or instances, like *Rust*, in which the government "used private speakers to transmit specific information pertaining to its own program." *Rosenberger v. Rector and Visitors of Univ. of Va.*, 515 U.S. 819 (1995). As we said in *Rosenberger*, "when the government disburses public funds to private entities to convey a governmental message, it may take legitimate and appropriate steps to ensure that its message is neither garbled nor distorted by the grantee." The latitude which may exist for restrictions on speech where the government's own message is being delivered flows in part from our observation that, "when the government speaks, for instance to promote its own policies or to advance a particular idea, it is, in the end, accountable to the electorate and the political process for its advocacy. If the citizenry objects, newly elected officials later could espouse some different or contrary position."

Neither the latitude for government speech nor its rationale applies to subsidies for private speech in every instance, however. As we have pointed out, "it does not follow that viewpoint-based restrictions are proper when the government does not itself speak or subsidize transmittal of a message it favors but instead expends funds to encourage a diversity of views from private speakers."

Although the LSC program differs from the program at issue in *Rosenberger* in that its purpose is not to "encourage a diversity of views," the salient point is that, like the program in *Rosenberger*, the LSC program was designed to facilitate private speech, not to promote a governmental message. Congress funded LSC grantees to provide attorneys to represent the interests of indigent clients. In the specific context of §504(a)(16) suits for benefits, an LSC-funded attorney speaks on the behalf of the client in a claim against the government for welfare benefits. The lawyer is not the government's speaker. The attorney defending the decision to deny benefits will deliver the government's message in the litigation. The LSC lawyer, however, speaks on the behalf of his or her private, indigent client.

The Government has designed this program to use the legal profession and the established Judiciary of the States and the Federal Government to accomplish its end of assisting welfare claimants in determination or receipt of their benefits. The advice from the attorney to the client and the advocacy by the attorney to the courts cannot be classified as governmental speech even under a generous understanding of the concept. In this vital respect this suit is distinguishable from *Rust*.

The private nature of the speech involved here, and the extent of LSC's regulation of private expression, are indicated further by the circumstance that the Government seeks to use an existing medium of expression and to control it, in a class of cases, in ways which distort its usual functioning. Where the government uses or attempts to regulate a particular medium, we have been informed by its accepted usage in determining whether a particular restriction on speech is necessary for the program's purposes and limitations.

When the government creates a limited forum for speech, certain restrictions may be necessary to define the limits and purposes of the program. The same is true when the government establishes a subsidy for specified ends. As this suit involves a subsidy, limited forum cases may not be controlling in a strict sense, yet they do provide some instruction. Here the program presumes that private, nongovernmental speech is necessary, and a substantial restriction is placed upon that speech. The LSC advised us that lawyers funded in the Government program may not undertake representation in suits for benefits if they must advise clients respecting the questionable validity of a statute which defines benefit eligibility and the payment structure. The limitation forecloses advice or legal assistance to question the validity of statutes under the Constitution of the United States. It extends further so that state statutes inconsistent with federal law under the Supremacy Clause may be neither challenged nor questioned.

By providing subsidies to LSC, the Government seeks to facilitate suits for benefits by using the state and federal courts and the independent bar on which those courts depend for the proper performance of their duties and responsibilities. Restricting LSC attorneys in advising their clients and in presenting arguments and analyses to the courts distorts the legal system by altering the traditional role of the attorneys in much the same way broadcast systems or student publication networks were changed in the limited forum cases we have cited. Upon determining that a question of statutory validity is present in any anticipated or pending case or controversy, the LSC-funded attorney must cease the representation at once. This is true whether the validity issue becomes apparent during initial attorney-client consultations or in the midst of litigation proceedings. If, during litigation, a judge were to ask an LSC attorney whether there was a constitutional concern, the LSC attorney simply could not answer.

The restriction imposed by the statute here threatens severe impairment of the judicial function. Section 504(a)(16) sifts out cases presenting constitutional challenges in order to insulate the Government's laws from judicial inquiry. If the restriction on speech and legal advice were to stand, the result would be two tiers of cases. In cases where LSC counsel were attorneys of record, there would be lingering doubt whether the truncated representation had resulted in complete analysis of the case, full advice to the client, and proper presentation to the court. The courts and the public would come to question the adequacy and fairness of professional representations when the attorney, either consciously to comply with this statute or unconsciously to continue the representation despite the statute, avoided all reference to questions of statutory validity and constitutional authority. A scheme so inconsistent with accepted separation-of-powers principles is an insufficient basis to sustain or uphold the restriction on speech.

It is no answer to say the restriction on speech is harmless because, under LSC's interpretation of the Act, its attorneys can withdraw. This misses the point. The statute is an attempt to draw lines around the LSC program to exclude from litigation those arguments and theories Congress finds unacceptable but which by their nature are within the province of the courts to consider.

The restriction on speech is even more problematic because in cases where the attorney withdraws from a representation, the client is unlikely to find other counsel. Thus, with respect to the litigation services Congress has funded, there is no alternative channel for expression of the advocacy Congress seeks to restrict. This is in stark contrast to *Rust*. There, a patient could receive the approved Title X family planning counseling funded by the Government and later could consult an affiliate or independent organization to receive abortion counseling. Unlike indigent clients who seek LSC representation, the patient in *Rust* was not required to forfeit the Government-funded advice when she also received abortion counseling through alternative channels. Because LSC attorneys must withdraw whenever a question of a welfare statute's validity arises, an individual could not obtain joint representation so that the constitutional challenge would be presented by a non-LSC attorney, and other, permitted, arguments advanced by LSC counsel.

Congress was not required to fund an LSC attorney to represent indigent clients; and when it did so, it was not required to fund the whole range of legal representations or relationships. The LSC and the United States, however, in effect ask us to permit Congress to define the scope of the litigation it funds to exclude certain vital theories and ideas. The attempted restriction is designed to insulate the Government's interpretation of the Constitution from judicial challenge. The Constitution does not permit the Government to confine litigants and their attorneys in this manner. We must be vigilant when Congress imposes rules and conditions which in effect insulate its own laws from legitimate judicial challenge. Where private speech is involved, even Congress' antecedent funding decision cannot be aimed at the suppression of ideas thought inimical to the Government's own interest.

For the reasons we have set forth, the funding condition is invalid. Since the issue has not been briefed, we decline to address whether the language restricting LSC attorneys could be severed from the statute so that the remaining portions would remain operative.

The judgment of the Court of Appeals is

Affirmed.

Justice SCALIA, with whom THE CHIEF JUSTICE, Justice O'CONNOR, and Justice THOMAS join, *dissenting.*

The Court asserts that these cases are different from *Rust* because the welfare funding restriction "seeks to use an existing medium of expression and to control it in ways which distort its usual functioning." There is utterly no precedent for the proposition that the First Amendment has anything to do with government funding that—though it does not actually abridge anyone's speech—"distorts an existing medium of expression." None of the three cases cited by the Court mentions such an odd principle. The Court's "nondistortion" principle is also wrong on the facts, since there is no basis for believing that §504(a)(16) will distort the operation of the courts. It may well be that the bar of §504(a)(16) will cause LSC-funded attorneys to decline or to withdraw from cases that involve statutory validity. But that means at most that fewer statutory challenges to welfare laws will be presented to the courts because of the unavailability of free legal services for that purpose. So what? The same result would ensue from excluding LSC-funded lawyers from welfare litigation entirely. It is not the mandated, nondistortable function of the courts to inquire into all "serious questions of statutory validity" in all cases.

Finally, the Court is troubled "because in cases where the attorney withdraws from a representation, the client is unlikely to find other counsel." That is surely irrelevant, since it leaves the welfare recipient in no *worse* condition than he would have been in had the LSC program never been enacted. It is hard to see how providing free legal services to some welfare claimants (those whose claims do not challenge the applicable statutes) while not providing it to others is beyond the range of legitimate legislative choice. Rather than sponsor "truncated representation," Congress chose to subsidize only those cases in which the attorneys it subsidized could work freely. And it is impossible to see how this difference from *Rust* has any bearing upon the First Amendment question which is whether the funding scheme is "manipulated" to have a "coercive effect" on those who do not hold the subsidized position. It could be claimed to have such an effect if the client in a case ineligible for LSC representation could eliminate the ineligibility by waiving the claim that the statute is invalid; but he cannot. No *conceivable* coercive effect exists.

The LSC subsidy neither prevents anyone from speaking nor coerces anyone to change speech, and is indistinguishable in all relevant respects from the subsidy upheld in *Rust*. There is no legitimate basis for declaring §504(a)(16) facially unconstitutional.

Note

Review *Christian Legal Society Chapter of the University of California v. Martinez* in Section C, "Symbolic Speech," on page 1382.

∾ PROBLEM: MORE ON THE INTERNATIONAL TREATY REGULATING THE INTERNET ∾

Should the treaty contain any language either allowing or prohibiting (or, for that matter, saying anything about) the government's ability to provide financial support for speech?

United States v. American Library Association

539 U.S. 194 (2003)

Chief Justice Rehnquist announced the judgment of the Court and delivered an opinion, in which Justice O'Connor, Justice Scalia, and Justice Thomas joined.

To address the problems associated with the availability of Internet pornography in public libraries, Congress enacted the Children's Internet Protection Act (CIPA). Under CIPA, a public library may not receive federal assistance to provide Internet access unless it installs software to block images that constitute obscenity or child pornography, and to prevent minors from obtaining access to material that is harmful to them. The District Court held these provisions facially invalid on the ground that they induce public libraries to violate patrons' First Amendment rights. We reverse.

CIPA provides that a library may not receive E-rate or LSTA assistance unless it has "a policy of Internet safety for minors that includes the operation of a technology protection measure that protects against access" by all persons to "visual depictions" that constitute "obscenity" or "child pornography," and that protects against access by minors to "visual depictions" that are "harmful to minors." The statute defines a "technology protection measure" as "a specific technology that blocks or filters Internet access to material covered by" CIPA. CIPA also permits the library to "disable" the filter "to enable access for bona fide research or other lawful purposes." Under the E-rate program, disabling is permitted "during use by an adult." Under the LSTA program, disabling is permitted during use by any person.

Appellees are a group of libraries, library associations, library patrons, and Web site publishers, including the American Library Association (ALA) and the Multnomah County Public Library in Portland, Oregon (Multnomah). They sued the United States and the Government agencies and officials responsible for administering the E-rate and LSTA programs in District Court, challenging the constitutionality of CIPA's filtering provisions. The District Court held that the filtering software contemplated by CIPA was a content-based restriction on access to a public forum, and was therefore subject to strict scrutiny. Applying this standard, the District Court held that, although the Government has a compelling interest "in preventing the dissemination of obscenity, child pornography, or, in the case of minors, material harmful to minors," the use of software filters is not narrowly tailored to further those interests. We granted certiorari.

Congress has wide latitude to attach conditions to the receipt of federal assistance in order to further its policy objectives. *South Dakota v. Dole*, 483 U.S. 203 (1987). But Congress may not "induce" the recipient "to engage in activities that would themselves be unconstitutional." To determine whether libraries would violate the First Amendment by employing the filtering software that CIPA requires, we must first examine the role of libraries in our society.

CIPA does not directly regulate private conduct; rather, Congress has exercised its Spending Power by specifying conditions on the receipt of federal funds. Therefore, *Dole* provides the appropriate framework for assessing CIPA's constitutionality.

Public libraries pursue the worthy missions of facilitating learning and cultural enrichment. Appellee ALA's Library Bill of Rights states that libraries should provide "books and other resources for the interest, information, and enlightenment of all people of the community the library serves." To fulfill their traditional missions, public libraries must have broad discretion to decide what material to provide to their patrons. Although they seek to provide a wide array of information, their goal has never been to provide "universal coverage." Instead, public libraries seek to provide materials "that would be of the greatest direct benefit or interest to the community." To this end, libraries collect only those materials deemed to have "requisite and appropriate quality."

We have held in two analogous contexts that the government has broad discretion to make content-based judgments in deciding what private speech to make available to the public. In *Arkansas Ed. Television Commn. v. Forbes*, 523 U.S. 666 (1998), we held that public forum principles do not generally apply to a public television station's editorial judgments regarding the private speech it presents to its viewers. "Broad rights of access for outside speakers would be antithetical to the discretion that stations and their editorial staff must exercise to fulfill their journalistic purpose and statutory obligations." Recognizing a broad right of public access "would also risk implicating the courts in judgments that should be left to the exercise of journalistic discretion."

Similarly, in *National Endowment for Arts v. Finley,* 524 U.S. 569 (1998), we upheld an art funding program that required the National Endowment for the Arts (NEA) to use content-based criteria in making funding decisions. We explained that "any content-based considerations that may be taken into account in the grant-making process are a consequence of the nature of arts funding." In particular, "the very assumption of the NEA is that grants will be awarded according to the 'artistic worth of competing applicants,' and absolute neutrality is simply inconceivable." We expressly declined to apply forum analysis, reasoning that it would conflict with "NEA's mandate to make esthetic judgments, and the inherently content-based 'excellence' threshold for NEA support."

The principles underlying *Forbes* and *Finley* also apply to a public library's exercise of judgment in selecting the material it provides to its patrons. Just as forum analysis and heightened judicial scrutiny are incompatible with the role of public television stations and the role of the NEA, they are also incompatible with the discretion that public libraries must have to fulfill their traditional missions. Public library staffs necessarily consider content in making collection decisions and enjoy broad discretion in making them.

The public forum principles on which the District Court relied, are out of place in the context of this case. Internet access in public libraries is neither a "traditional" nor a "designated" public forum. First, this resource—which did not exist until quite recently—has not "immemorially been held in trust for the use of the public and, time out of mind, been used for purposes of assembly, communication of thoughts between citizens, and discussing public questions." We have "rejected the view that traditional public forum status extends beyond its historic confines." The doctrines surrounding traditional public forums may not be extended to situations where such history is lacking.

Nor does Internet access in a public library satisfy our definition of a "designated public forum." To create such a forum, the government must make an affirmative choice to open up its property for use as a public forum. "The government does not create a public forum by inaction or by permitting limited discourse, but only by intentionally opening a non-traditional forum for public discourse." The District Court likened public libraries' Internet terminals to the forum at issue in *Rosenberger v. Rector and Visitors of Univ. of Va.,* 515 U.S. 819 (1995). In *Rosenberger,* we considered the "Student Activity Fund" established by the University of Virginia that subsidized all manner of student publications except those based on religion. We held that the fund had created a limited public forum by giving public money to student groups who wished to publish, and therefore could not discriminate on the basis of viewpoint.

The situation here is very different. A public library does not acquire Internet terminals in order to create a public forum for Web publishers to express themselves, any more than it collects books in order to provide a public forum for the authors of books to speak. It provides Internet access, not to "encourage a diversity of views from private speakers," but for the same reasons it offers other library resources: to facilitate research, learning, and recreational pursuits by furnishing materials of requisite and appropriate quality. As Congress recognized, "the Internet is simply another method for making information available in a school or library." It is "no more than a technological extension of the book stack."

We require the Government to employ the least restrictive means only when the forum is a public one and strict scrutiny applies. Such is not the case here. In deciding not to collect pornographic material from the Internet, a public library need not satisfy a court that it has pursued the least restrictive means of implementing that decision.

In any case, the suggested alternatives have their own drawbacks. Close monitoring of computer users would be far more intrusive than the use of filtering software, and would risk transforming the role of a librarian from a professional to whom patrons turn for assistance into a compliance officer whom many patrons might wish to avoid. Moving terminals to places where their displays cannot easily be seen by other patrons, or installing privacy screens or recessed monitors, would not address a library's interest in preventing patrons from deliberately using its computers to view online pornography. To the contrary, these alternatives would make it *easier* for patrons to do so.

The District Court disagreed because, whereas a library reviews and affirmatively chooses to acquire every book in its collection, it does not review every Web site that it makes available. Based on this distinction, the court reasoned that a public library enjoys less discretion in deciding which Internet materials to make available than in making book selections. We do not find this distinction constitutionally relevant. A library's failure to make quality-based judgments about all the material it furnishes from the Web does not somehow taint the judgments it does make. A library's need to exercise judgment in making collection decisions depends on its traditional role in identifying suitable and worthwhile material; it is no less entitled to play that role when it collects material from the Internet than when it collects material from any other source. Most libraries already exclude pornography from their print collections because they deem it inappropriate for inclusion. We do not subject these decisions to heightened scrutiny; it would make little sense to treat libraries' judgments to block online pornography any differently, when these judgments are made for just the same reason.

Moreover, because of the vast quantity of material on the Internet and the rapid pace at which it changes, libraries cannot possibly segregate, item by item, all the Internet material that is appropriate for inclusion from all that is not. While a library could limit its Internet collection to just those sites it found worthwhile, it could do so only at the cost of excluding an enormous amount of valuable information that it lacks the capacity to review. Given that tradeoff, it is entirely reasonable for public libraries to reject that approach and instead exclude certain categories of content, without making individualized judgments that everything they do make available has requisite and appropriate quality.

The District Court faulted the tendency of filtering software to "over-block"—that is, to erroneously block access to constitutionally protected speech that falls outside the categories that software users intend to block. Due to the software's limitations, "many erroneously blocked Web pages contain content that is completely innocuous for both adults and minors, and that no rational person could conclude matches the filtering companies' category definitions, such as 'pornography' or 'sex.'" Any concerns are dispelled by the ease with which patrons may have the filtering software disabled. When a patron encounters a blocked site, he need only ask a librarian to unblock it or (at least in the case of adults) disable the filter. Libraries have the capacity to permanently unblock any erroneously blocked site, and the Solicitor General stated that a "library may eliminate the filtering with respect to specific sites at the request of a patron." With respect to adults, CIPA also expressly authorizes library officials to "disable" a filter altogether "to enable access for bona fide research or other lawful purposes." The Solicitor General confirmed that a "librarian can, in response to a request from a patron, unblock the filtering mechanism altogether," and that a patron would not "have to explain why he was asking a site to be unblocked or the filtering to be disabled." The District Court viewed unblocking and disabling as inadequate because some patrons may be too embarrassed to request them. But the Constitution does not guarantee the right to acquire information at a public library without any risk of embarrassment.

Appellees urge us to affirm the District Court's judgment on the alternative ground that CIPA imposes an unconstitutional condition on the receipt of federal assistance by requiring them, as a condition on their receipt of federal funds, to surrender their First Amendment right to provide the public with access to constitutionally protected speech. We rejected that claim in *Rust v. Sullivan*, 500 U.S. 173, 194 (1991), recognizing that "the Government was not denying a benefit to anyone, but was instead simply insisting that public funds be spent for the purposes for which they were authorized." The same is true here. The E-rate and LSTA programs were intended to help public libraries fulfill their traditional role of obtaining material of requisite and appropriate quality for educational and informational purposes. Congress may certainly insist that these "public funds be spent for the purposes for which they were authorized." Especially because public libraries have traditionally excluded pornographic material from their other collections, Congress could reasonably impose a parallel limitation on its Internet assistance programs. As the use of filtering software helps to carry out these programs, it is a permissible condition under *Rust*.

Appellees mistakenly contend, in reliance on *Legal Services Corp. v. Velazquez*, 531 U.S. 533 (2001), that CIPA's filtering conditions "distort the usual functioning of public libraries." In *Velazquez*, the Court concluded that a Government program of furnishing legal aid to the indigent differed from the program in *Rust* "in the vital respect" that the role of lawyers who represent clients in welfare disputes is to advocate against the Government, and there was thus an assumption that counsel would be free of state control. The Court concluded that the restriction on advocacy in such welfare disputes would distort the usual functioning of the legal profession and the federal and state courts before which the lawyers appeared. Public libraries, by contrast, have no comparable role that pits them against the Government, and there is no comparable assumption that they must be free of any conditions that their benefactors might attach to the use of donated funds or other assistance. Because public libraries' use of Internet filtering software does not violate their patrons' First Amendment rights, CIPA does not induce libraries to violate the Constitution, and is a valid exercise of Congress' spending power. Nor does CIPA impose an unconstitutional condition on public libraries. Therefore, the judgment of the District Court is

Reversed.

Justice KENNEDY, *concurring in the judgment.*

If, on the request of an adult user, a librarian will unblock filtered material or disable the Internet software filter without significant delay, there is little to this case. The Government represents this is indeed the fact. If some libraries do not have the capacity to unblock specific Web sites or to disable the filter or if it is shown that an adult user's election to view constitutionally protected Internet material is burdened in some other substantial way, that would be the subject for an as-applied challenge, not the facial challenge made in this case. There are, of course, substantial Government interests at stake here. The interest in protecting young library users from material inappropriate for minors is legitimate, and even compelling, as all Members of the Court appear to agree. Given this interest, and the failure to show that the ability of adult library users to have access to the material is burdened in any significant degree, the statute is not unconstitutional on its face.

Justice BREYER, *concurring in the judgment.*

Filtering technology, in its current form, does not function perfectly, for to some extent it also screens out constitutionally protected materials that fall outside the scope of the statute (i.e., "overblocks") and fails to prevent access to some materials that the statute deems harmful (i.e., "underblocks"). In determining whether the statute's conditions consequently violate the First Amendment, the plurality first finds the "public forum" doctrine inapplicable, and then holds that the statutory provisions are constitutional. I agree with both determinations. But I reach the plurality's ultimate conclusion in a different way.

I would apply a form of heightened scrutiny, examining the statutory requirements in question with special care. The Act directly restricts the public's receipt of information. And it does so through limitations imposed by outside bodies (here Congress) upon two critically important sources of information—the Internet as accessed via public libraries. For that reason, we should not examine the statute's constitutionality as if it raised no special First Amendment concern—as if, like tax or economic regulation, the First Amendment demanded only a "rational basis" for imposing a restriction. Nor should we accept the Government's suggestion that a presumption in favor of the statute's constitutionality applies.

At the same time, the First Amendment does not here demand application of the most limiting constitutional approach—that of "strict scrutiny." The statutory restriction in question is, in essence, a kind of "selection" restriction (a kind of editing). And libraries often properly engage in the selection of materials, either as a matter of necessity (i.e., due to the scarcity of resources) or by design (i.e., in accordance with collection development policies). To apply "strict scrutiny" to the "selection" of a library's collection (whether carried out by public libraries themselves or by other community bodies with a traditional legal right to engage in that function) would unreasonably interfere with the discretion necessary to create, maintain, or select a library's "collection" (broadly defined to include all the information the library makes available). That is to say, "strict scrutiny" implies too limiting and rigid a test for me to believe that the First Amendment requires it in this context.

Instead, I would examine the constitutionality of the Act's restrictions here as the Court has examined speech-related restrictions in other contexts where circumstances call for heightened, but not "strict," scrutiny—where, for example, complex, competing constitutional interests are potentially at issue or speech-related harm is potentially justified by unusually strong governmental interests. Typically the key question in such instances is one of proper fit.

In such cases the Court has asked whether the harm to speech-related interests is disproportionate in light of both the justifications and the potential alternatives. It has considered the legitimacy of the statute's objective, the extent to which the statute will tend to achieve that objective, whether there are other, less restrictive ways of achieving that objective, and ultimately whether the statute works speech-related harm that, in relation to that objective, is out of proportion.

The Act's restrictions satisfy these constitutional demands. The Act seeks to restrict access to obscenity, child pornography, and, in respect to access by minors, material that is comparably harmful. These objectives are "legitimate," and indeed often "compelling." Software filters "provide a relatively cheap and effective" means of furthering these goals. Due to present technological limitations, however, the software filters both "overblock," screening out some perfectly legitimate material, and "underblock," allowing some obscene material to escape detection by the filter. But no one has presented any clearly superior or better fitting alternatives.

At the same time, the Act allows libraries to permit any adult patron access to an "overblocked" Web site; the adult patron need only ask a librarian to unblock the specific Web site or disable the filter entirely. The Act does impose upon the patron the burden of making this request. But it is difficult to see how that burden (or any delay associated with compliance) could prove more onerous than traditional library practices associated with segregating library materials in, say, closed stacks, or with interlibrary lending practices that require patrons to make requests that are not anonymous and to wait while the librarian obtains the desired materials from elsewhere. Perhaps local library rules or practices could further restrict the ability of patrons to obtain "overblocked" Internet material. But we here consider only a facial challenge to the Act itself.

Given the comparatively small burden that the Act imposes upon the library patron seeking legitimate Internet materials, I cannot say that any speech-related harm that the Act may cause is disproportionate when considered in relation to the Act's legitimate objectives. I therefore agree with the plurality that the statute does not violate the First Amendment, and I concur in the judgment.

Justice STEVENS filed a dissenting opinion on the grounds that CIPA imposes an unconstitutional condition on government subsidies to local libraries; and Justice SOUTER filed a dissenting opinion in which Justice GINSBURG joined, agreeing with Justice Stevens's conclusion and arguing that CIPA is invalid in the exercise of the spending power under Article I.

Notes

1. *Public Library Computers.* Between 1994 and 2002 (the year before the decision in *American Library Association*), the internet connectivity of public libraries increased from 20.9 percent to 98.7 percent. One 2014 report found that 60 percent of urban libraries and 70 percent of rural libraries "are the only providers of free public access to computers and the internet in their communities." Also, 83 percent of adult library users regard the "computer access, training, and support provided by libraries" as "important or very important." Internet filters "are expensive to operate and maintain," and local libraries "have marginal control over the content that is filtered," because the filters are operated by entities such as "a state library, library consortium, or local or state government system." One study found that "half of all libraries with internet filters received requests from adult patrons to unblock the filters for legitimate purposes," such as Web-based e-mail and Web sites needed "to research prescription drugs and to complete school projects." *See* Kristen R. Batch, *Fencing Out Knowledge: Impacts of the Children's Internet Protection Act 10 Years Later,* Policy Brief No. 5, June 2014, ALA Library Association, http://www.ala.org/offices/sites/ala.org.offices/files/content/oitp/publications/issuebriefs/cipa_report.pdf.

2. *Speech Blocked Under CIPA.* The FCC website Guide for CIPA states that schools or libraries (that receive discounts for internet access through federal funding) must "certify that they have an internet safety policy that includes technology protection measures," which "must block or filter internet access to *pictures* that are (a) obscene; (b) child pornography; or (c) harmful to minors (for computers that are accessed by minors)." *See* Children's Internet Protection Act Guide, https://www.fcc.gov/guides/childrens-internet-protection-act. In 2008, Congress enacted an additional requirement that the internet safety policy "must include monitoring the online activities of minors and must provide for educating minors about appropriate online behavior including interacting with other individuals on social networking websites and in chatrooms and cyberbullying awareness and response." *See* Schools and Libraries Universal Service Support Mechanism, A National Broadband Plan for Our Future, https://www.fcc.gov/document/schools-and-libraries-universal-service-support-mechanism-national-broadband-plan-our-fut-1. However, CIPA does not "authorize any tracking of the internet use of anyone in an identifiable manner." The FCC also has not defined

"harmful to minors" to include online social media sites, such as Facebook. *See* Children's Internet Protection Act Guide, https://www.fcc.gov/guides/childrens-internet-protection-act. Notably, the FCC has not established "specific criteria for what constitutes effective filtering and has never found a school or library out of compliance since CIPA first went into effect in 2001." *See* Deborah Caldwell-Stone, *Filtering and the First Amendment: When Is It Okay to Block Speech Online?*, American Libraries Magazine, Apr. 2, 2013, http://americanlibrariesmagazine .org/2013/04/02/filtering-and-the-first-amendment/.

3. *Blocking Beyond CIPA Restrictions.* According to a 2014 report, "many libraries and schools filter well beyond the statutory requirements of the law." For example, "schools, in particular, do not limit filtering to visual images as CIPA mandates. In the name of CIPA's filtering mandate, schools increasingly block access to entire social media and social networking sites and to any site that is interactive or collaborative, such as blogs, wikis, or even Google Docs. The application of filters also is expanding as schools rely (mistakenly) on filtering to deal with issues of hacking, copyright infringement, and cyberbullying, denying access to certain websites and technologies." *See* Kristen R. Batch, *Fencing Out Knowledge: Impacts of the Children's Internet Protection Act 10 Years Later*, Policy Brief No. 5, June 2014, ALA Library Association, http://www.ala.org/offices/sites/ala .org.offices/files/content/oitp/publications/issuebriefs/cipa_report.pdf.

∼ PROBLEM: REFUSAL TO UNBLOCK WEBSITES ∼

The *American Library Association* opinion rejected a facial challenge to the CIPA. The plurality emphasized that any "concerns" about "erroneous overblocking" by software programs "are dispelled by the ease with which patrons may have the filtering software disabled." For adult users, CIPA "expressly authorizes library officials to 'disable' a filter altogether 'to enable access for bona fide research or other lawful purposes.'" During oral argument, the Solicitor General assured the Court that a patron would not "have to explain why he was asking a site to be unblocked or the filtering to be disabled." Assume that a regional library system with 30 branches decides to use the "FortiGuard Web Filtering Service," which "sorts web sites into 76 categories based on predominant content." These categories include (1) adult materials: mature content websites (18 years and over) that feature or promote sexuality, strip clubs, sex shops, etc., excluding sex education, without the intent to sexually arouse; (2) gambling: sites that cater to gambling activities such as betting, lotteries, and casinos, including gaming information, instruction, and statistics; (3) nudity: mature content websites (18 years and over) that depict the human body in full or partial nudity without the intent to sexually arouse; (4) web chat: websites that promote web chat services; (5) instant messaging: websites that allow users to communicate in "real time"; and (6) the "personals" section of craigslist.org. The library system also adopts a policy that internet filters will not be disabled at the request of an adult patron if it fits within one of the 76 categories. If a request is made and the library determines that the website does not fit one of these categories, then the library will treat the website as erroneously blocked and grant the request for unblocking. Can this policy be challenged on First Amendment grounds? What reasoning could be used to reject this challenge? *See Bradburn v. North Central Regional Library District*, 231 P.3d 166 (Wash. 2010) (en banc).

Matal v. Tam

137 S. Ct. 1744 (2017)

JUSTICE ALITO announced the judgment of the Court and delivered the opinion of the Court with respect to Parts I, II, and III–A, and an opinion with respect to Parts III–B, III–C, and IV, in which THE CHIEF JUSTICE, JUSTICE THOMAS, and JUSTICE BREYER join.

This case concerns a dance-rock band's application for federal trademark registration of the band's name, "The Slants." "Slants" is a derogatory term for persons of Asian descent, and members of the band are Asian-Americans. But the band members believe that by taking that slur as the name of their group, they will help to "reclaim" the term and drain its denigrating force. The Patent and Trademark Office (PTO) denied the application based on a provision of federal law prohibiting the registration of trademarks that may "disparage or bring into contempt or disrepute" any "persons, living or dead." 15 U. S. C. §1052(a). We hold that this provision violates the Free Speech Clause of the First Amendment. It offends a bedrock First Amendment principle: Speech may not be banned on the ground that it expresses ideas that offend.

I

"The principle underlying trademark protection is that distinctive marks—words, names, symbols, and the like—can help distinguish a particular artisan's goods from those of others." *B&B Hardware, Inc. v. Hargis Industries, Inc.*, 135 S. Ct. 1293, 1299 (2015). A trademark "designates the goods as the product of a particular trader" and "protects his good will against the sale of another's product as his." *United Drug Co. v. Theodore Rectanus Co.*, 248 U. S. 90, 97 (1918). It helps consumers identify goods and services that they wish to purchase, as well as those they want to avoid. Under the Lanham Act, trademarks that are "used in commerce" may be placed on the "principal register," that is, they may be federally registered. 15 U. S. C. §1051(a)(1). There are now more than two million marks that have active federal certificates of registration. This system of federal registration helps to ensure that trademarks are fully protected and supports the free flow of commerce. Without federal registration, a valid trademark may still be used in commerce. Even if a trademark is not federally registered, it may still be enforceable under

§43(a) of the Lanham Act, which creates a federal cause of action for trademark infringement. Unregistered trademarks may also be entitled to protection under other federal statutes, such as the Anticybersquatting Consumer Protection Act, 15 U. S. C. §1125(d). And an unregistered trademark can be enforced under state common law, or if it has been registered in a State, under that State's registration system. Federal registration, however, "confers important legal rights and benefits on trademark owners who register their marks." *B&B Hardware*, 135 S. Ct. at 1317. Registration on the principal register (1) "serves as 'constructive notice of the registrant's claim of ownership' of the mark" "is 'prima facie evidence of the validity of the registered mark and of the registration of the mark, of the owner's ownership of the mark, and of the owner's exclusive right to use the registered mark in commerce on or in connection with the goods or services specified in the certificate,'" *B & B Hardware*, 135 S. Ct. at 1200 (quoting §1057(b)); and (3) can make a mark "incontestable" once a mark has been registered for five years." Registration also enables the trademark holder "to stop the importation into the United States of articles bearing an infringing mark." 15 U. S. C. §1124.

The Lanham Act contains provisions that bar certain trademarks from the principal register. For example, a trademark cannot be registered if it is "merely descriptive or deceptively misdescriptive" of goods, §1052(e)(1), or if it is so similar to an already registered trademark or trade name that it is "likely to cause confusion, or to cause mistake, or to deceive," §1052(d). At issue is one such provision, which we will call "the disparagement clause." This provision prohibits the registration of a trademark "which may disparage persons, living or dead, institutions, beliefs, or national symbols, or bring them into contempt, or disrepute." §1052(a). This clause appeared in the original Lanham Act and has remained the same to this day. See §2(a), 60 Stat. 428. When deciding whether a trademark is disparaging, an examiner at the PTO generally applies a "two-part test." The examiner first considers "the likely meaning of the matter in question, taking into account not only dictionary definitions, but also the relationship of the matter to the other elements in the mark, the nature of the goods or services, and the manner in which the mark is used in the marketplace in connection with the goods or services." Trademark Manual of Examining Procedure §1203.03(b)(i) (Apr. 2017), p. 1200–150. "If that meaning is found to refer to identifiable persons, institutions, beliefs or national symbols," the examiner moves to the second step, asking "whether that meaning may be disparaging to a substantial composite of the referenced group." If the examiner finds that a "substantial composite, although not necessarily a majority, of the referenced group would find the proposed mark to be disparaging in the context of contemporary attitudes," a prima facie case of disparagement is made out, and the burden shifts to the applicant to prove that the trademark is not disparaging. Ibid. What is more, the PTO has specified that "the fact that an applicant may be a member of that group or has good intentions underlying its use of a term does not obviate the fact that a substantial composite of the referenced group would find the term objectionable."

Simon Tam is the lead singer of "The Slants." He chose this moniker in order to "reclaim" and "take ownership" of stereotypes about people of Asian ethnicity. The group "draws inspiration for its lyrics from childhood slurs and mocking nursery rhymes" and has given its albums names such as "The Yellow Album" and "Slanted Eyes, Slanted Hearts." Tam sought federal registration of "THE SLANTS," on the principal register, but an examining attorney at the PTO rejected the request, applying the PTO's two-part framework and finding that "there is a substantial composite of persons who find the term in the applied-for mark offensive." The examining attorney relied on the fact that "numerous dictionaries define 'slants' or 'slant-eyes' as a derogatory or offensive term." The examining attorney also relied on a finding that "the band's name has been found offensive numerous times"—citing a performance that was canceled because of the band's moniker and the fact that "several bloggers and commenters to articles on the band have indicated that they find the term and the applied-for mark offensive." Tam contested the denial of registration before the examining attorney and before the PTO's Trademark Trial and Appeal Board (TTAB) to no avail. Eventually, he took the case to court, where the en banc Federal Circuit found the disparagement clause facially unconstitutional under the First Amendment's Free Speech Clause. The Government filed a petition for certiorari, which we granted.

II

The clause prohibits the registration of marks that disparage "persons," and Tam claims that the term "persons" "includes only natural and juristic persons," not "non-juristic entities such as racial and ethnic groups." Tam's argument is refuted by the plain terms of the disparagement clause.

III

Because the disparagement clause applies to marks that disparage the members of a racial or ethnic group, we must decide whether the clause violates the Free Speech Clause of the First Amendment.

A

"The Free Speech Clause does not regulate government speech." *Pleasant Grove City v. Summum*, 555 U. S. 460, 467 (2009). When a government entity embarks on a course of action, it necessarily takes a particular viewpoint and rejects others. The Free Speech Clause does not require government to maintain viewpoint neutrality when its officers and employees speak about that venture. But while the government-speech doctrine is important—indeed, essential—it is a doctrine that is susceptible to dangerous misuse. If private speech could be passed off as government speech by simply affixing a government seal of approval, government could silence or muffle the expression of disfavored viewpoints. For this reason, we must exercise great caution before extending our government-speech precedents.

At issue is the content of trademarks registered by the PTO, an arm of the Federal Government. The Federal Government does not dream up these marks, and it does not edit marks. Except as required by statute, an examiner may not reject a mark based on the viewpoint that it appears to express. Thus, unless that section is thought to apply, an examiner does not inquire whether any viewpoint conveyed by a mark is consistent with Government policy or whether any such viewpoint is consistent with that expressed by other marks already on the principal register. If the mark meets the Lanham Act's viewpoint-neutral requirements, registration is mandatory. Moreover, once a mark is registered, the PTO is not authorized to remove it from the register unless a party moves for cancellation, the registration expires, or the Federal Trade Commission initiates proceedings based on certain grounds. In light of all this, it is far-fetched to suggest that the content of a registered mark is government speech. If the federal registration of a trademark makes the mark government speech, the Federal Government is babbling prodigiously and incoherently. For example, if trademarks represent government speech, what does the Government have in mind when it advises Americans to "make.believe" (Sony), "Think different" (Apple), "Just do it" (Nike), or "Have it your way" (Burger King)? Was the Government warning about a coming disaster when it registered the mark "EndTime Ministries"? The PTO has made it clear that registration does not constitute approval of a mark. See *In re Old Glory Condom Corp.*, 26 USPQ 2d 1216, 1220, n. 3 (TTAB 1993). In sum, the federal registration of trademarks is vastly different from the beef ads in *Johanns*, the monuments in *Summum*, and even the specialty license plates in *Walker*. Holding that the registration of a trademark converts the mark into government speech would constitute a huge and dangerous extension of the government-speech doctrine. Perhaps the most worrisome implication of the Government's argument concerns the system of copyright registration. If federal registration makes a trademark government speech and thus eliminates all First Amendment protection, would the registration of the copyright for a book produce a similar transformation? The Government attempts to distinguish copyright on the ground that it is "the engine of free expression," but trademarks often have an expressive content. Companies spend huge amounts to create and publicize trademarks that convey a message. It is true that the necessary brevity of trademarks limits what they can say. But powerful messages can sometimes be conveyed in just a few words. Trademarks are private, not government, speech.

B

We next address the Government's argument that this case is governed by cases in which this Court has upheld the constitutionality of government programs

that subsidized speech expressing a particular viewpoint. These cases implicate a notoriously tricky question of constitutional law. "We have held that the
Government 'may not deny a benefit to a person on a basis that infringes his
constitutionally protected freedom of speech even if he has no entitlement to
that benefit.'" *Agency for Int'l Development v. Alliance for Open Society Int'l, Inc.*,
570 U. S. 205, 214 (2013). But at the same time, government is not required to
subsidize activities that it does not wish to promote. Determining which of these
principles applies in a particular case "is not always self-evident," but no difficult question is presented here. Unlike the present case, the decisions on which
the Government relies all involved cash subsidies or their equivalent. In *Rust
v. Sullivan*, 500 U. S. 173 (1991), a federal law provided funds to private parties
for family planning services. In *National Endowment for Arts v. Finley*, 524 U. S. 569
(1998), cash grants were awarded to artists. The federal registration of a trademark is nothing like the programs at issue in these cases. The PTO does not pay
money to parties seeking registration of a mark. Quite the contrary is true: An
applicant for registration must pay the PTO a filing fee of $225–$600. And to
maintain federal registration, the holder of a mark must pay a fee of $300–$500
every 10 years.

The Government responds that registration provides valuable non-monetary
benefits that "are directly traceable to the resources devoted by the federal government to examining, publishing, and issuing certificates of registration for
those marks." But just about every government service requires the expenditure
of government funds. This is true of services that benefit everyone, like police
and fire protection, as well as services that are utilized by only some, e.g., the adjudication of private lawsuits and the use of public parks and highways. Trademark
registration is not the only government registration scheme. For example, the
Federal Government registers copyrights and patents. State governments and
their subdivisions register the title to real property and security interests; they
issue driver's licenses, motor vehicle registrations, and hunting, fishing, and boat-
ing licenses or permits. Cases like *Rust* and *Finley* are not instructive in analyzing
the constitutionality of restrictions on speech imposed in connection with such
services.

C

The Government urges us to sustain the disparagement clause under a new
doctrine that would apply to "government-program" cases. For the most part,
this argument simply merges our government-speech cases and the previously
discussed subsidy cases in an attempt to construct a broader doctrine that can
be applied to the registration of trademarks. The only new element consists
of two cases involving a public employer's collection of union dues from its
employees. But those cases occupy a special area of First Amendment case law,

and they are far removed from the registration of trademarks. Potentially more analogous are cases in which a unit of government creates a limited public forum for private speech. *See, e.g., Good News Club v. Milford Central School*, 533 U. S. 98 (2001). When government creates such a forum, in either a literal or "metaphysical" sense, some content- and speaker-based restrictions may be allowed. However, even in such cases, what we have termed "viewpoint discrimination" is forbidden. Our cases use the term "viewpoint" discrimination in a broad sense, and in that sense, the disparagement clause discriminates on the bases of "viewpoint." To be sure, the clause evenhandedly prohibits disparagement of all groups. It applies equally to marks that damn Democrats and Republicans, capitalists and socialists, and those arrayed on both sides of every possible issue. It denies registration to any mark that is offensive to a substantial percentage of the members of any group. But in the sense relevant here, that is viewpoint discrimination: Giving offense is a viewpoint. "The public expression of ideas may not be prohibited merely because the ideas are themselves offensive to some of their hearers." *Street v. New York*, 394 U. S. 576, 592 (1969). For this reason, the disparagement clause cannot be saved by analyzing it as a type of government program in which some content- and speaker-based restrictions are permitted.

IV

[In this section of the opinion, the Court rejected the argument that the law could be upheld as a regulation of commercial speech. That issue is discussed in Chapter 4, Section C.]

PROBLEM: "WANDERING DAGO" FOOD TRUCK

The operators of a food truck decided to use the "Wandering Dago" (WD) brand as a "nod to their Italian heritage" and to their immigrant ancestors. The sandwiches on their menu have names like "Goombah," "Guido," and "Polack." They say that the use of ethnic slurs in their business is meant to signal "an irreverent, blue collar solidarity" with their customers. When their application to participate as a food vendor in the Summer Outdoor Lunch Program in Albany's Empire State Plaza was denied by the New York State Office of General Services, the operators filed suit to challenge that decision as a violation of the First Amendment under *Matal*. The state official who denied the application found the WD branding to be "offensive" without reference to any law or regulation to justify her decision. The operators argued that the state official discriminated against their viewpoint, but counsel for the State argues that the operators' use of ethnic slurs "does not reflect any real viewpoint." How will the court resolve the First Amendment issue? *See Wandering Dago, Inc. v. Destito*, 879 F.3d 20 (2d Cir. 2018).

Agency for International Development v. Alliance for Open Society International, Inc.

570 U.S. 205 (2013)

Chief Justice ROBERTS delivered the opinion of the Court.

The United States Leadership Against HIV/AIDS, Tuberculosis, and Malaria Act of 2003 (Leadership Act), 22 U.S.C. §7601 *et seq.*, outlined a comprehensive strategy to combat the spread of HIV/AIDS around the world. As part of that strategy, Congress authorized the appropriation of billions of dollars to fund efforts by nongovernmental organizations to assist in the fight. Congress passed the Leadership Act after finding that HIV/AIDS had "assumed pandemic proportions, spreading from the most severely affected regions, sub-Saharan Africa and the Caribbean, to all corners of the world, and leaving an unprecedented path of death and devastation." According to congressional findings, more than 65 million people had been infected by HIV and more than 25 million had lost their lives, making HIV/AIDS the fourth highest cause of death worldwide. In sub-Saharan Africa alone, AIDS had claimed the lives of more than 19 million individuals and was projected to kill a full quarter of the population of that area over the next decade. The disease not only directly endangered those infected, but also increased the potential for social and political instability and economic devastation, posing a security issue for the entire international community. In the Leadership Act, Congress directed the President to establish a "comprehensive, integrated" strategy to combat HIV/AIDS around the world. The Act sets out 29 different objectives the President's strategy should seek to fulfill, reflecting a multitude of approaches to the problem. The strategy must include, among other things, plans to increase the availability of treatment for infected individuals, prevent new infections, support the care of those affected by the disease, promote training for physicians and other health care workers, and accelerate research on HIV/AIDS prevention methods, all while providing a framework for cooperation with international organizations and partner countries to further the goals of the program.

The Act "makes the reduction of HIV/AIDS behavioral risks a priority of all prevention efforts." The Act's approach to reducing behavioral risks is multifaceted. The President's strategy for addressing such risks must promote abstinence, encourage monogamy, increase the availability of condoms, promote voluntary counseling and treatment for drug users, and "educate men and boys about the risks of procuring sex commercially" as well as "promote alternative livelihoods, safety, and social reintegration strategies for commercial sex workers." Congress found that the "sex industry, the trafficking of individuals into such industry, and sexual violence" were factors in the spread of the HIV/AIDS epidemic, and determined that "it should be the policy of the United States to eradicate" prostitution and "other sexual victimization."

The United States has enlisted the assistance of nongovernmental organizations to help achieve the many goals of the program. Such organizations "with experience in health care and HIV/AIDS counseling," Congress found, "have proven effective in combating the HIV/AIDS pandemic and can be a resource in providing treatment and care for individuals infected with HIV/AIDS." Since 2003, Congress has authorized the appropriation of billions of dollars for funding these organizations' fight against HIV/AIDS around the world.

Those funds, however, come with two conditions: First, no funds made available to carry out the Leadership Act "may be used to promote or advocate the legalization or practice of prostitution or sex trafficking." §7631(e). Second, no funds made available may "provide assistance to any group or organization that does not have a policy explicitly opposing prostitution and sex trafficking, except to the Global Fund to Fight AIDS, Tuberculosis and Malaria, the World Health Organization, the International AIDS Vaccine Initiative or to any United Nations agency." §7631(f). It is this second condition—the Policy Requirement—that is at issue here.

The Department of Health and Human Services (HHS) and the United States Agency for International Development (USAID) are the federal agencies primarily responsible for overseeing implementation of the Leadership Act. To enforce the Policy Requirement, the agencies have directed that the recipient of any funding under the Act agree in the award document that it is opposed to "prostitution and sex trafficking because of the psychological and physical risks they pose for women, men, and children." 45 CFR §89.1(b) (2012).

Respondents are a group of domestic organizations engaged in combating HIV/AIDS overseas. In addition to substantial private funding, they receive billions annually in financial assistance from the United States, including under the Leadership Act. Their work includes programs aimed at limiting injection drug use in Uzbekistan, Tajikistan, and Kyrgyzstan, preventing mother-to-child HIV transmission in Kenya, and promoting safer sex practices in India. Respondents fear that adopting a policy explicitly opposing prostitution may alienate certain host governments, and may diminish the effectiveness of some of their programs by making it more difficult to work with prostitutes in the fight against HIV/AIDS. They are also concerned that the Policy Requirement may require them to censor their privately funded discussions in publications, at conferences, and in other forums about how best to prevent the spread of HIV/AIDS among prostitutes. Respondents Alliance for Open Society International and Pathfinder International commenced this litigation, seeking a declaratory judgment that the Government's implementation of the Policy Requirement violated their First Amendment rights. Respondents sought a preliminary injunction barring the Government from cutting off their funding under the Act for the duration of the litigation, from unilaterally terminating their cooperative agreements with the United States, or from otherwise taking action solely on the basis of respondents' own privately funded speech. The District Court granted such a preliminary injunction.

While the appeal was pending, HHS and USAID issued guidelines on how recipients of Leadership Act funds could retain funding while working with affiliated organizations not bound by the Policy Requirement. The guidelines permit funding recipients to work with affiliated organizations that "engage in activities inconsistent with the recipient's opposition to the practices of prostitution and sex trafficking" as long as the recipients retain "objective integrity and independence from any affiliated organization." 45 CFR §89.3. Whether sufficient separation exists is determined by the totality of the circumstances, including "but not limited to" (1) whether the organizations are legally separate; (2) whether they have separate personnel; (3) whether they keep separate accounting records; (4) the degree of separation in the organizations' facilities; and (5) the extent to which signs and other forms of identification distinguish the organizations. 45 CFR §§89.3(b)(1)-(5). The District Court continued its preliminary injunction. The Court of Appeals affirmed. We granted certiorari.

It is a basic First Amendment principle that "freedom of speech prohibits the government from telling people what they must say." *Rumsfeld v. Forum for Academic and Institutional Rights, Inc.*, 547 U.S. 47, 61 (2006). "At the heart of the First Amendment lies the principle that each person should decide for himself or herself the ideas and beliefs deserving of expression, consideration, and adherence." *Turner Broadcasting System, Inc. v. FCC*, 512 U.S. 622, 641 (1994). Were it enacted as a direct regulation of speech, the Policy Requirement would plainly violate the First Amendment. The question is whether the Government may nonetheless impose that requirement as a condition on the receipt of federal funds.

The Spending Clause of the Federal Constitution grants Congress the power "to lay and collect Taxes, Duties, Imposts and Excises, to pay the Debts and provide for the common Defence and general Welfare of the United States." Art. I, §8, cl. 1. The Clause provides Congress broad discretion to tax and spend for the "general Welfare," including by funding particular state or private programs or activities. That power includes the authority to impose limits on the use of such funds to ensure they are used in the manner Congress intends. *Rust v. Sullivan*, 500 U.S. 173 (1991). As a general matter, if a party objects to a condition on the receipt of federal funding, its recourse is to decline the funds. This remains true when the objection is that a condition may affect the recipient's exercise of its First Amendment rights. See, *e.g., United States v. American Library Assn., Inc.*, 539 U.S. 194 (2003) (plurality opinion); *Regan v. Taxation With Representation of Wash.*, 461 U.S. 540, 546 (1983). At the same time, we have held that the Government " 'may not deny a benefit to a person on a basis that infringes his constitutionally protected freedom of speech even if he has no entitlement to that benefit.' " *Forum for Academic and Institutional Rights, supra*, at 59 (quoting *American Library Assn., supra*, at 210). In some cases, a funding condition can result in an unconstitutional burden on First Amendment rights. See *Forum for Academic and Institutional Rights, supra*, at 59.

The dissent thinks that can only be true when the condition is not relevant to the objectives of the program, or when the condition is actually coercive, in the sense of an offer that cannot be refused. The relevant distinction is between conditions that define the limits of the government spending program—those that specify the activities Congress wants to subsidize—and conditions that seek to leverage funding to regulate speech outside the contours of the program itself. The line is hardly clear because the definition of a particular program can always be manipulated to subsume the challenged condition. We have held that "Congress cannot recast a condition on funding as a mere definition of its program in every case, lest the First Amendment be reduced to a simple semantic exercise." *Legal Services Corporation v. Velazquez,* 531 U.S. 533, 547 (2001).

Two cases help illustrate the distinction: In *Regan,* the Court upheld a requirement that nonprofit organizations seeking tax-exempt status under 26 U.S.C. §501(c)(3) not engage in substantial efforts to influence legislation. The tax-exempt status "had much the same effect as a cash grant to the organization." By limiting §501(c)(3) status to organizations that did not attempt to influence legislation, Congress had merely "chosen not to subsidize lobbying." In rejecting the nonprofit's First Amendment claim, the Court highlighted the fact that the condition did not prohibit that organization from lobbying Congress altogether. The nonprofit could continue to claim §501(c)(3) status for its nonlobbying activities, while attempting to influence legislation in its §501(c)(4) capacity with separate funds. Maintaining such a structure, the Court noted, was not "unduly burdensome." The condition thus did not deny the organization a government benefit "on account of its intention to lobby."

In *FCC v. League of Women Voters of California,* 468 U.S. 364 (1984), the Court struck down a condition on federal financial assistance to noncommercial broadcast television and radio stations that prohibited all editorializing, including with private funds. Even a station receiving only one percent of its overall budget from the Federal Government, the Court explained, was "barred absolutely from all editorializing." Unlike *Regan,* the law provided no way for a station to limit its use of federal funds to noneditorializing activities, while using private funds "to make known its views on matters of public importance." The prohibition thus went beyond ensuring that federal funds not be used to subsidize "public broadcasting station editorials," and instead leveraged the federal funding to regulate the stations' speech outside the scope of the program.

In *Rust,* we considered Title X of the Public Health Service Act, a Spending Clause program that issued grants to nonprofit health-care organizations "to assist in the establishment and operation of voluntary family planning projects to offer a broad range of acceptable and effective family planning methods and services." The organizations received funds from a variety of sources other than the Federal Government for a variety of purposes. The Act, however, prohibited the Title X federal funds from being "used in programs where abortion is a method of family planning." To enforce this provision, HHS regulations barred Title X projects from advocating abortion as a method of family planning, and required grantees to ensure that their Title X projects were "physically and financially separate" from their other projects that engaged in the prohibited activities. A group of Title X funding recipients brought suit, claiming the regulations imposed an unconstitutional condition on their First Amendment rights. We rejected their claim. Congress can, without offending the Constitution, selectively fund certain programs to address an issue of public concern, without funding alternative ways of addressing the same problem. In Title X, Congress had defined the federal program to encourage only particular family planning methods. The challenged regulations were simply "designed to ensure that the limits of the federal program are observed," and "that public funds are spent for the purposes for which they were authorized." "Title X expressly distinguishes between a Title X *grantee* and a Title X *project.*" The regulations governed only the scope of the grantee's Title X projects, leaving it "unfettered in its other activities." "The Title X *grantee* can continue to engage in abortion advocacy; it simply is required to conduct those activities through programs that are separate and independent from the project that receives Title X funds." Because the regulations did not "prohibit the recipient from engaging in the protected conduct outside the scope of the federally funded program," they did not run afoul of the First Amendment.

The distinction drawn in these cases—between conditions that define the federal program and those that reach outside it—is not self-evident. Here we are confident that the Policy Requirement falls on the unconstitutional side of the line. The Leadership Act has two conditions relevant here. The first—unchallenged in this litigation—prohibits Leadership Act funds from being used "to promote or advocate the legalization or practice of prostitution or sex trafficking." The Government concedes that §7631(e) by itself ensures that federal funds will not be used for the prohibited purposes. The Policy Requirement therefore must be doing something more. The dissent views the Requirement as simply a selection criterion by which the Government identifies organizations "who believe in its ideas to carry them to fruition." Whatever purpose the Policy Requirement serves in selecting funding recipients, its effects go beyond selection. The Policy Requirement is an ongoing condition on recipients' speech and activities, a ground for terminating a grant after selection is complete. The Government is not simply seeking organizations that oppose prostitution. Rather, "Congress has expressed its purpose 'to eradicate' prostitution and sex trafficking, and it wants recipients *to adopt* a similar stance." This case is not about the Government's ability to enlist the assistance of those with whom it already agrees. It is about compelling a grant recipient to adopt a particular belief as a condition of funding.

By demanding that funding recipients adopt the Government's view on an issue of public concern, the condition by its very nature affects "protected conduct outside the scope of the federally funded program." *Rust,* 500 U.S., at 197. A recipient cannot avow the belief dictated by the Policy Requirement when spending Leadership Act funds, and then turn around and assert a contrary belief, or claim neutrality, when participating in activities on its own time and dime. By requiring recipients to profess a specific belief, the Policy Requirement goes beyond defining the limits of the federally funded program to defining the recipient.

The Government contends that the affiliate guidelines, established while this litigation was pending, save the program. Under those guidelines, funding recipients are permitted to work with affiliated organizations that do not abide by the condition, as long as the recipients retain "objective integrity and independence" from the unfettered affiliates. The Government suggests the guidelines alleviate any unconstitutional burden on the respondents' First Amendment rights by allowing them to either: (1) accept Leadership Act funding and comply with Policy Requirement, but establish affiliates to communicate contrary views on prostitution; or (2) decline funding themselves (thus remaining free to express their own views or remain neutral), while creating affiliates whose sole purpose is to receive and administer Leadership Act funds, thereby "cabining the effects" of the Policy Requirement within the scope of the federal program.

Neither approach is sufficient. When we have noted the importance of affiliates in this context, it has been because they allow an organization bound by a funding condition to exercise its First Amendment rights outside the scope of the federal program. Affiliates cannot serve that purpose when the condition is that a funding recipient espouse a specific belief as its own. If the affiliate is distinct from the recipient, the arrangement does not afford a means for the *recipient* to express *its* beliefs. If the affiliate is more clearly identified with the recipient, the recipient can express those beliefs only at the price of evident hypocrisy. The guidelines themselves make that clear. See 45 CFR §89.3 (allowing funding recipients to work with affiliates whose conduct is "inconsistent with *the recipient's opposition* to the practices of prostitution and sex trafficking" (emphasis added)).

The Government suggests that the Policy Requirement is necessary because, without it, federal funds could free a recipient's private funds "to be used to promote prostitution or sex trafficking." That argument assumes that federal funding will supplant private funding, rather than pay for new programs or expand existing ones. The Government offers no support for that assumption, or any reason to believe it is true here. If the Government's argument were correct, *League of Women Voters* would have come out differently, and much of the reasoning of *Regan* and *Rust* would have been beside the point.

The Government contends that "if organizations awarded federal funds to implement Leadership Act programs could promote or affirmatively condone prostitution or sex trafficking, whether using public *or private* funds, it would undermine the government's program and confuse its message opposing prostitution and sex trafficking." But the Policy Requirement goes beyond preventing recipients from using private funds in a way that would undermine the federal program. It requires them to pledge allegiance to the Government's policy of eradicating prostitution. "If there is any fixed star in our constitutional constellation, it is that no official, high or petty, can prescribe what shall be orthodox in politics, nationalism, religion, or other matters of opinion or force citizens to confess by word or act their faith therein." *Barnette*, 319 U.S., at 642.

The Policy Requirement compels as a condition of federal funding the affirmation of a belief that by its nature cannot be confined within the scope of the Government program. In so doing, it violates the First Amendment and cannot be sustained. The judgment of the Court of Appeals is affirmed.

It is so ordered.

Justice SCALIA, with whom Justice THOMAS joins, *dissenting.*

This Policy Requirement is nothing more than a means of selecting suitable agents to implement the Government's chosen strategy to eradicate HIV/AIDS. That is perfectly permissible under the Constitution. The First Amendment does not mandate a viewpoint-neutral government. Government must choose between rival ideas and adopt some as its own: competition over cartels, solar energy over coal, weapon development over disarmament, and so forth. Moreover, the government may enlist the assistance of those who believe in its ideas to carry them to fruition; and it need not enlist for that purpose those who oppose or do not support the ideas. That seems to me a matter of the most common sense. If Hamas—reputed to have an efficient system for delivering welfare—were excluded from a program for the distribution of U.S. food assistance, no one could reasonably object. That would remain true if Hamas were an organization of United States citizens entitled to the protection of the Constitution. So long as the unfunded organization remains free to engage in its activities (including anti-American propaganda) "without federal assistance," *United States v. American Library Assn., Inc.*, 539 U.S. 194, 212 (2003) (plurality), refusing to make use of its assistance for an enterprise to which it is opposed does not abridge its speech. The constitutional prohibition at issue here is not a prohibition against discriminating against or injuring opposing points of view, but the First Amendment's prohibition against the coercing of speech. I am frankly dubious that a condition for eligibility to participate in a minor federal program such as this one runs afoul of that prohibition even when the condition is irrelevant to the goals of the program. Not every disadvantage is a coercion.

The views that the Government demands an applicant forswear are relevant to the program in question. The most obvious manner in which the admission to a program of an ideological opponent can frustrate the purpose of the program is by freeing up the opponent's funds for use in its ideological opposition. The economic reality is that when NGOs can conduct their AIDS work on the Government's dime, they can expend greater resources on policies that undercut the Leadership Act. To make it a valid consideration in determining participation in federal programs, it suffices that this is a real and obvious risk. The Court makes a head-fake at the unconstitutional conditions doctrine, but that doctrine is of no help. There is no case in which a condition that is relevant to a statute's valid purpose and that is not in itself unconstitutional (*e.g.*, a religious-affiliation condition that violates the Establishment Clause) has been held to violate the doctrine. Moreover, the contention that the condition here "coerces" respondents' speech is on its face implausible. Those organizations that wish to take a different tack with respect to prostitution "are as unconstrained now as they were before the enactment of the Leadership Act." *National Endowment for Arts v. Finley*, 524 U.S. 569, 595 (1998) (Scalia, J., concurring in judgment). "As a general matter, if a party objects to a condition on the receipt of federal funding, its recourse is to decline the funds," and to draw on its own coffers.

What Congress has done here — requiring an ideological commitment relevant to the Government task at hand — is approved by the Constitution itself. Americans need not support the Constitution; they may be Communists or anarchists. But "the Senators and Representatives, and the Members of the several State Legislatures, and all executive and judicial Officers, both of the United States and of the several States, shall be bound by Oath or Affirmation, to support the Constitution." U.S. Const., Art. VI, cl. 3. The Framers saw the wisdom of imposing affirmative ideological commitments prerequisite to assisting in the government's work. And so should we.

Notes

1. *Post-Decision Developments.* Following the holding in the prior case, the Court was confronted by follow-up litigation in *Agency for International Development v. Alliance for Open Society International, Inc.*, 140 S. Ct. 2082 (2020). That case dealt with the issue of whether participating foreign organizations were also exempt from having to articulate a "policy explicitly opposing prostitution and sex trafficking." §7631(f). The Court held that foreign organizations could be subjected to the requirement:

> Plaintiffs' position runs headlong into two bedrock principles of American law. *First*, it is long settled as a matter of American constitutional law that foreign citizens outside U. S. territory do not possess rights under the U. S. Constitution. See, *e.g.*, *Boumediene v. Bush*, 553 U. S. 723 (2008); *United States v. Verdugo-Urquidez*, 494 U. S. 259 (1990); U. S. Const., Preamble. If the rule were otherwise, actions by American military, intelligence, and law enforcement personnel against foreign organizations or foreign citizens in foreign countries would be constrained by the foreign citizens' purported rights under the U. S. Constitution. That has never been the law. See *Verdugo-Urquidez*, 494 U. S., at 2734. *Second*, it is long settled as a matter of American corporate law that separately incorporated organizations are separate legal units with distinct legal rights and obligations. See *Dole Food Co. v. Patrickson*, 538 U. S. 468 (2003). Plaintiffs' foreign affiliates were incorporated in other countries and are legally separate from plaintiffs' American organizations. Even though the foreign organizations have affiliated with the American organizations, the foreign organizations remain legally distinct from the American organizations.
>
> That conclusion corresponds to historical practice regarding American foreign aid. The United States supplies more foreign aid than any other nation in the world. Congress sometimes imposes conditions on foreign aid. Congress may condition funding on a foreign organization's ideological commitments — for example, pro-democracy, pro-women's rights, anti-terrorism, pro-religious freedom, anti-sex trafficking, or the like. Doing so helps ensure that U. S. foreign aid serves U. S. interests. By contrast, plaintiffs' approach would throw a constitutional wrench into American foreign policy. In particular, plaintiffs' approach would put Congress in the untenable position of either cutting off certain funding programs altogether, or instead funding foreign organizations that may not align with U. S. values. We see no constitutional justification for the Federal Judiciary to interfere with American foreign policy and American aid to foreign organizations. In short, plaintiffs' foreign affiliates are foreign organizations, and foreign organizations operating abroad have no First Amendment rights.

The Court also rejected the idea that a "foreign affiliates' statement of policy against prostitution and sex trafficking might be incorrectly attributed to the American organizations," and that "the American organizations themselves possess a First Amendment right against imposition of the Policy Requirement on their foreign affiliates": "Plaintiffs are free to choose whether to affiliate with foreign organizations and are free to disclaim agreement with the foreign affiliates' required statement of policy. Any alleged misattribution in this case and any effect on the American organizations' message of neutrality toward prostitution stems from their choice to affiliate with foreign organizations, not from U. S. Government compulsion. We appreciate that plaintiffs would prefer to affiliate with foreign organizations that do not oppose prostitution. But Congress required foreign organizations to oppose prostitution in return for American funding. And plaintiffs cannot export their own First Amendment rights to shield foreign organizations from Congress's funding conditions."

Justice Breyer, with whom Justice Ginsburg and Justice Sotomayor joined, dissented: "The question is whether American organizations enjoy that same constitutional protection against government-compelled distortion when they speak through clearly identified affiliates that have been incorporated overseas. The answer is yes. We have never before held that an American speaker forfeits First Amendment protection when it speaks though foreign affiliates to reach audiences overseas. Every respondent here is American. No foreign entities are party to this case, and respondents have never claimed that the Policy Requirement violates anyone's First Amendment rights apart from their own. I fear the Court's decision will seriously impede the countless American speakers who communicate overseas in a similar way. That weakens the marketplace of ideas at a time when the value of that marketplace for Americans, and for others, reaches well beyond our shores."

2. *Funding for the Arts.* In *National Endowment for the Arts v. Finley,* 524 U.S. 569 (1998), the Court upheld a provision of the National Foundation on the Arts and Humanities Act that required the National Endowment for the Arts (NEA) to make funding decisions based on "artistic excellence and artistic merit, taking into consideration general standards of decency and respect for the diverse beliefs and values of the American people." The Court reasoned that the NEA had limited resources and neutrality was not possible when employing "the inherently content-based 'excellence' threshold for NEA support." The facial challenge to the statute did not include an as-applied challenge by an artist alleging discrimination in a funding decision. Rather, plaintiffs argued that the funding criteria constituted viewpoint discrimination "because the criteria reject any artistic speech that either fails to respect mainstream values or offends standards of decency." But the Court rejected that argument, noting that the NEA interpreted the criteria as merely "hortatory" and did not preclude awards to controversial works, such as Robert Mapplethorpe's art that provoked the amendment of the Act by Congress.

J. GOVERNMENT AS EDUCATOR AND SPEECH RIGHTS OF STUDENTS

The Court's leading cases on the subject of the First Amendment rights of students are *Tinker v. Des Moines Independent Community School District*, 393 U.S. 503 (1969), and *Hazelwood School District v. Kuhlmeier*, 484 U.S. 260 (1988). In *Tinker*, when students wore black armbands to school to protest against the Vietnam war, they were suspended. The school's ban on armbands had been adopted when school administrators learned that the protest was planned. The Court rejected the school's argument that suspension of the students was necessary in order to avoid a potentially violent conflict. As Justice Fortas reasoned: "The school officials banned and sought to punish petitioners for a silent, passive, expression of opinion, unaccompanied by any disorder or disturbance on the part of the petitioners. There is here no evidence whatever of petitioners' interference, actual or nascent, with the schools' work or of collision with the rights of other students to be secure and to be let alone." He went on to note: "Only a few of the 18,000 students in the school system wore the black armbands. Only five students were suspended for wearing them. There is no indication that the work of the school or any class was disrupted. Outside the classrooms, a few students made hostile remarks to the children wearing armbands, but there were not threats or acts of violence on school premises." The Court concluded that there were no "finding and no showing that the exercise of the forbidden right would 'materially and substantially interfere with the requirements of appropriate discipline in the operation of the school.'"

In *Morse v. Frederick*, 551 U.S. 393 (2007), the Court held that a high school principal may restrict student speech at a school event when that speech is reasonably viewed as promoting illegal drug use. The school-sanctioned activity occurred during normal school hours when students were allowed to watch the Olympic Torch Relay from the sidewalk in front of their school. Frederick, a high school senior, was one of a group of students who unexpectedly unfurled a 14-foot banner that read, "BONG HiTS 4 JESUS." He was suspended because he did not immediately comply with the principal's demand to take down the banner. Her action was based on her belief that the message on the banner "encouraged illegal drug use, in violation of established school policy." When Frederick argued that the words on the banner "were just nonsense meant to attract the television cameras," the Court disagreed, finding the principal's pro-drug-use interpretation of the words to be plausible, "given the paucity of alternative meanings the banner might bear." In rejecting Frederick's claim that the speech on the banner was protected, the Court relied on *Fraser*'s reasoning that "school boards have the authority to determine 'what manner of speech in the classroom or in school assembly is inappropriate.'" The Court emphasized that deterring illegal drug use is an important interest, and perhaps even a compelling one. Thousands of school boards have adopted policies that seek to educate students about the dangers of illegal drug use, and the "special characteristics of the school environment" justify the restriction of student expression that school officials "reasonably regard as promoting illegal drug use." The three dissenters in *Morse* argued that the speech on the banner caused no disruption as required by *Tinker,* and objected to the acceptance of "special rules" for censorship of student speech about drug or alcohol use.

In *Hazelwood,* a high school principal withheld from a student newspaper two pages containing student-authored stories about pregnancy and divorce. The principal based his decision on his concern that the identity of pregnant students might be identifiable from the text, that references to sexual activity and birth control were inappropriate for some of the younger students, and that the parents of a student in the divorce story should be asked for consent to the publication of their daughter's comments about their divorce. The Court upheld the action of the principal and distinguished the case from *Tinker.* Although the Court recognized that students do not "shed their constitutional rights at the schoolhouse gate," it reasoned that "educators may exercise editorial control over the style and content of student speech in school-sponsored expressive activities so long as their actions are reasonably related to legitimate pedagogical concerns." The Court explained: "Activities such as school-sponsored publications, theatrical productions, and other expressive activities that students, parents, and members of the public might reasonably perceive to bear the imprimatur of the school may fairly be characterized as part of the school curriculum, whether or not they occur in a traditional classroom setting, so long as they are supervised by faculty members and designed to impart particular knowledge or skills to student participants and audiences." The Court also noted: "A school may in its capacity as publisher of a school newspaper or producer of a school play 'disassociate itself,' not only from speech that would 'substantially interfere with its work or impinge on the rights of other students,' but also from speech that is, for example, ungrammatical, poorly written, inadequately researched, biased or prejudiced, vulgar or profane, or unsuitable for immature audiences. A school must be able to set high standards for the student speech that is disseminated under its auspices."

Board of Education v. PICO, 457 U.S. 853 (1982), involved school board members who received a list of books labeled as "improper fare for students" from a politically conservative organization, and subsequently determined that 11 of the books were in the local high school library. The books included *Black Boy,* by Richard Wright; *Soul on Ice,* by Eldridge Cleaver; *Slaughterhouse-Five,* by Kurt Vonnegut, Jr.; and *Go Ask Alice* (by an anonymous author), as well as others. The board members notified the entire board that these books were in the library, and the board appointed a parent-teacher committee to make recommendations to the board concerning which books should be removed or retained in the library. When the committee recommended that only two of the books should be removed, the board overruled the committee and ordered that nine of the books be removed. Various students filed suit seeking injunctive relief to prevent removal of the books from the library, arguing that the board's decision to remove the books violated their First Amendment rights. A plurality of the

Court agreed, holding that the evidence raised a material fact as to whether the board's decision to remove nine books violated the First Amendment, and the Court therefore remanded for a trial on the merits of the students' claim. While the plurality recognized that the school board has discretion regarding curricular matters, it did not view this discretion as extending "beyond the compulsory environment of the classroom" into the school library. Although school boards retain "significant discretion" to control library content, they cannot "remove books from a library based on the partisan motivation or dislike for the ideas in the books." The plurality reasoned that the government may not prescribe official orthodoxy, noting that students have First Amendment rights in school, as well as a First Amendment right to receive ideas. As a result, the Court concluded that the school library is a unique site where freedom of voluntary inquiry by students "holds sway," which is why decisions to remove books for reasons of censorship of ideas interfere with that protected freedom of students. The Court concluded that an improper motive could be ascertained "by the origin of the Board's decision and its lack of procedural regularity." Accordingly, the Court remanded the case for trial. Nevertheless, the plurality recognized that a school board has the power to remove books that are "pervasively vulgar" or "educationally unsuitable," as long as the removal of such books is not based on partisan motives. The dissenters argued that students do not have a First Amendment right to access particular books in a school library, especially given their ability to obtain the books elsewhere. The dissenters also argued that no meaningful distinction could be drawn between removing books for vulgarity or unsuitability and removing books for political reasons. The dissenters predicted that the plurality's narrow recognition of students' right to prevent partisan-motivated removal of books would eventually lead to the Court playing "super censor" of school decisions.

Tinker dealt with student speech in the context of the school environment. Of course, student speech can also occur outside of the school grounds, but such speech may have an impact on those who work at or attend the school. For example, students may use social media to convey their ideas, or they may communicate via text message or e-mail. In a number of recent cases, schools have attempted to discipline students for these electronic communications. The cases have produced divergent results.

∾ PROBLEMS ∾

1. *The Confederate Flag.* The superintendent of schools decides to prohibit students from wearing any clothes that depict the Confederate battle flag. Some students and their parents challenge the ban, claiming that the clothing

constitutes symbolic speech protected under *Tinker.* However, the superintendent responds that the ban is justified by prior racial incidents, some of which had involved students displaying the Confederate flag. As a result, the superintendent believes that the ban is justified by the possibility of a substantial disruption or material interference with school activities. Is the prohibition valid under the First Amendment? *See B.W.A. v. Farmington R-7 School District,* 554 F.3d 734 (8th Cir. 2009).

2. *The Student Blog.* A high school student, a member of the student council, posted a blog entry when a "battle of the bands" concert (scheduled at the school) was cancelled. Although the entry was posted on an off-campus blog, it asked students to contact the superintendent of schools to urge that the concert be rescheduled. In her e-mail message, the student stated that the concert had been cancelled by "douchebags in the central office," and she provided students with a sample letter that they could send to the superintendent to "piss her off." The blog produced a number of calls to the superintendent's office. Because of the blog posting, the principal declined to endorse the plaintiff's candidacy for senior class secretary, thereby precluding her from running for that office. The principal based her decision on the fact that the student failed to accept the principal's counsel regarding the proper way to express and resolve disagreements, that the student included vulgar and inaccurate information in her blog post, and that the student had urged other students to contact the superintendent in order to "piss her off." Did the principal have the right to sanction the student for the content of speech that occurred on a non-school blog? Should it matter whether the speech was directed at the campus community and caused disruption? Would the school have the right to sanction a concerned citizen (e.g., a nonstudent) who posted a similar blog? *See Doninger v. Niehoff,* 527 F.3d 41 (2d Cir. 2008).

3. *The Threatening Blog.* Would you evaluate the blog in the above problem differently if the student had stated that she was "really angry" at school officials, and that "someone ought to take a gun and blow their heads off"? Would you reach a different result if the student were in college, rather than high school, and the college officials were equally alarmed?

4. *Bracelets and Sex Games.* Students at a middle school have started wearing "jelly" bracelets which correlate the color of the bracelet to the level of their sexual activity. School administrators have decided that the bracelets have become a distraction (in that students discuss the bracelets and their colors in class, in the hallways, and in e-mail messages) and have decided to ban them. Can school officials ban students from wearing jelly bracelets under these circumstances?

5. *The Anarchist Club.* Suppose that a public high school allows students to form clubs for a variety of purposes, and the school has a wide range of clubs for chess, fencing, 4-H, Republicans, and Democrats. However, when a student asks for permission to start an anarchist club designed to promote tolerance and to oppose the U.S. bombing of Afghanistan, the school denies the request on the basis that the club would "disrupt the educational process." When the student continues to push for the club and has fliers on her desk promoting the club,

she is suspended because "she was told that she could not in any way foster, try to advance, or try to start an anarchy club." Under *Tinker*, was the suspension constitutionally permissible? *See* Michelle Saxton, *Judge Prohibits School Anarchist Club*, Louisville Courier-J., Nov. 2, 2001, at C1-4.

6. *The Cinco de Mayo Event.* A school decides to ban students from wearing American flag T-shirts to its Cinco de Mayo celebration. In the past, there had been violent altercations at the school between Caucasian and Hispanic students, including at the most recent Cinco de Mayo celebration, and there had been threats of violence regarding this particular celebration. Even though the school banned American flag T-shirts, it allowed students to wear T-shirts promoting Cinco de Mayo. Did the school act permissibly? *See Dariano v. Morgan Hill Unified School District*, 745 F.3d 354 (9th Cir. 2014).

7. *The Horror Essay.* Students at a public middle school were asked to write "scary" or "horror" Halloween stories as part of a school project. Students were supposed to assume that they were "home alone" and heard "scary noises." One of the students refers to "busting out" a shotgun and accidentally shooting his teacher. Can the student be disciplined for the essay? *See* Associated Press, *Seventh-Grader Jailed over Violent Essay*, Louisville Courier-J., Nov. 4, 1999, at A-3.

8. *More on the International Treaty Regulating the Internet.* A number of countries believe that mandatory filters should be imposed on all newly manufactured computers as well as on all search engines. Delegates to the convention disagree about the types of information that should be targeted and excluded by filters. Some delegates want to filter out depictions of sexual activity. Others want to filter out any number of things, including child pornography, defamatory speech, subversive speech, and Nazi symbols. What language can you agree to regarding mandatory filters on computers and websites?

K. GOVERNMENT AS SPEAKER

Walker v. Texas Division, Sons of Confederate Veterans, Inc.

576 U.S. 200 (2015)

Justice BREYER delivered the opinion of the Court.

Texas requires all motor vehicles operating on the State's roads to display valid license plates. Drivers may choose to display the State's general-issue license plates which contain the word "Texas," a license plate number, a silhouette of the State, a graphic of the Lone Star, and the slogan "The Lone Star State." In the alternative, drivers may choose from an assortment of specialty license plates which contain the word "Texas," a license plate number, and one of a selection of designs prepared by the State. Finally, Texas law provides for personalized plates (also known as vanity plates). Pursuant to the personalization program, a vehicle owner may request a particular alphanumeric pattern for use as a plate number, such as "BOB" or "TEXPL8."

Here we are concerned with specialty license plates. Texas offers a variety of specialty plates, generally for an annual fee. Texas selects the designs for specialty plates through three processes. First, the state legislature may specifically call for the development of a specialty license plate. The legislature has enacted statutes authorizing plates that say "Keep Texas Beautiful" and "Mothers Against Drunk Driving," plates that "honor" the Texas citrus industry, and plates that feature an image of the World Trade Center towers and the words "Fight Terrorism." Second, the Board may approve a specialty plate design proposal that a state-designated private vendor has created at the request of an individual or organization. Among the plates created through the private-vendor process are plates promoting the "Keller Indians" and plates with the slogan "Get it Sold with RE/MAX." Third, the Board may create new specialty license plates on its own initiative or on receipt of an application from a nonprofit entity seeking to sponsor a specialty plate. A nonprofit must include in its application "a draft design of the specialty license plate." Texas law vests in the Board authority to approve or to disapprove an application. The Board "may refuse to create a new specialty license plate" for a number of reasons, for example "if the design might be offensive to any member of the public or for any other reason established by rule." Specialty plates that the Board has sanctioned through this process include plates featuring the words "The Gator Nation," together with the Florida Gators logo, and plates featuring the logo of Rotary International and the words "SERVICE ABOVE SELF."

In 2009, the Sons of Confederate Veterans, Texas Division (a nonprofit entity), applied to sponsor a specialty license plate through this last-mentioned process. SCV's application included a draft plate design. At the bottom of the proposed plate were the words "SONS OF CONFEDERATE VETERANS." At the side was the organization's logo, a square Confederate battle flag framed by the words "Sons of Confederate Veterans 1896." A faint Confederate battle flag appeared in the background on the lower portion of the plate. In the middle of the plate was the license plate number, and at the top was the State's name and silhouette. The Board's predecessor denied this application.

In 2010, SCV renewed its application. The Board invited public comment on its website and at an open meeting. After considering the responses, including a number of letters sent by elected officials who opposed the proposal, the Board voted unanimously against issuing the plate. The Board explained that it found "it necessary to deny the plate design application, specifically the confederate flag portion of the design, because public comments had shown that many members of the general public find the design offensive, and because such comments are reasonable." The Board added "that a significant portion of the public associate the confederate flag with organizations advocating expressions of hate directed toward people or groups that are demeaning to those people or groups."

SCV and two of its officers brought this lawsuit against the chairman and members of the Board. SCV argued that the Board's decision violated the Free Speech Clause of the First Amendment, and it sought an injunction requiring the Board to approve the proposed plate design. The District Court entered judgment for the Board. A divided panel of the Court of Appeals for the Fifth Circuit reversed. We granted the Board's petition for certiorari, and reverse.

When government speaks, it is not barred by the Free Speech Clause from determining the content of what it says. *Pleasant Grove City v. Summum*, 555 U. S. 460 (2009). That freedom reflects the fact that it is the democratic electoral process that first and foremost provides a check on government speech. See *Board of Regents of Univ. of Wis. System v. Southworth*, 529 U. S. 217 (2000). Thus, government statements (and government actions and programs that take the form of speech) do not normally trigger the First Amendment rules designed to protect the marketplace of ideas. See *Johanns v. Livestock Marketing Assn.*, 544 U. S. 550 (2005). Instead, the Free Speech Clause helps produce informed opinions among members of the public, who are then able to influence the choices of a government that, through words and deeds, will reflect its electoral mandate. See *Stromberg v. California*, 283 U. S. 359 (1931). Were the Free Speech Clause interpreted otherwise, government would not work. How could a city create a successful recycling program if officials, when writing householders asking them to recycle cans and bottles, had to include a plea from the local trash disposal enterprise demanding the contrary? How could a state government effectively develop programs designed to encourage and provide vaccinations, if officials also had to voice the perspective of those who oppose immunization? We have refused "to hold that the Government unconstitutionally discriminates on the basis of viewpoint when it chooses to fund a program dedicated to advance certain permissible goals, because the program in advancing those goals necessarily discourages alternative goals." *Rust v. Sullivan*, 500 U. S. 173 (1991). A contrary holding "would render numerous Government programs constitutionally suspect." Cf. *Keller v. State Bar of Cal.*, 496 U. S. 1, 12-13 (1990) ("If every citizen were to have a right to insist that no one paid by public funds express a view with which he disagreed, debate over issues of great concern to the public would be limited to those in the private sector, and the process of government as we know it radically transformed."). We have made clear that "the government can speak for itself." *Southworth, supra*, at 229.

That is not to say that a government's ability to express itself is without restriction. Constitutional and statutory provisions outside of the Free Speech Clause may limit government speech. The Free Speech Clause itself may constrain the government's speech if, for example, the government seeks to compel private persons to convey the government's speech. But, as a general matter, when the government speaks it is entitled to promote a program, to espouse a policy, or to take a position. In doing so, it represents its citizens and it carries out its duties on their behalf.

Specialty license plates issued pursuant to Texas's scheme convey government speech. Our precedents regarding government speech provide the appropriate

framework to approach the case. In *Summum*, we considered a religious organization's request to erect in a city park a monument setting forth the organization's
religious tenets. In the park were 15 other permanent displays. At least 11 of
these—including a wishing well, a September 11 monument, a historic granary,
the city's first fire station, and a Ten Commandments monument—had been
donated to the city by private entities. The religious organization argued that
the Free Speech Clause required the city to display the organization's proposed
monument because, by accepting a broad range of permanent exhibitions at the
park, the city had created a forum for private speech. We held that the city had
not "provided a forum for private speech" with respect to monuments. Rather,
the city had "engaged in expressive conduct." The speech was "best viewed as a
form of government speech" and "therefore was not subject to scrutiny under the
Free Speech Clause."

We based our conclusion on several factors. First, "governments have long
used monuments to speak to the public." Thus, "when a government arranges
for the construction of a monument, it does so because it wishes to convey some
thought or instill some feeling in those who see the structure." Second, it "is
not common for property owners to open their property for the installation of
permanent monuments that convey a message with which they do not wish to
be associated." "Persons who observe donated monuments routinely—and reasonably—interpret them as conveying some message on the property owner's
behalf." "Observers" of such monuments, as a consequence, ordinarily "appreciate
the identity of the speaker." Third, the city maintained control over the selection
of monuments. "Throughout our Nation's history, the government practice with
respect to donated monuments has been one of selective receptivity." The city government in *Summum* "'effectively controlled' the messages sent by the monuments
in the park by exercising 'final approval authority' over their selection." In light of
these and other relevant considerations, the Court concluded that the expression
was government speech. The Court rejected the premise that the involvement of
private parties in designing the monuments was sufficient to prevent the government from controlling which monuments it placed in its own public park.

Summum leads to the conclusion that here government speech is at issue.
First, insofar as license plates have conveyed more than state names and vehicle
identification numbers, they have communicated messages from the States. New
Hampshire plates have featured the "Old Man of the Mountain," Massachusetts
plates have included the codfish, and Wyoming plates have displayed a rider atop
a bucking bronco. State plates have included the phrases "North to the Future"
(Alaska), "Keep Florida Green" (Florida), "Green Mountains" (Vermont), and
"America's Dairyland" (Wisconsin). States have used license plate slogans to urge
action, to promote tourism, and to tout local industries. Texas, too, has selected
messages to communicate through its license plate designs. In 1995, Texas plates
celebrated "150 Years of Statehood." The Texas Legislature has authorized specialty plate designs stating, among other things, "Houston Livestock Show and
Rodeo," "Texans Conquer Cancer," and "Girl Scouts."

Second, Texas license plate designs "are often closely identified in the public mind with the State." Each Texas license plate is a government article serving the governmental purposes of vehicle registration and identification. The State places the name "TEXAS" in large letters at the top of every plate. Moreover, the State requires Texas vehicle owners to display license plates issued by the State. Texas also owns the designs on its license plates, including the designs that Texas adopts on the basis of proposals made by private individuals and organizations. Texas dictates the manner in which drivers may dispose of unused plates. Texas license plates are, essentially, government IDs. Issuers of ID "typically do not permit" the placement on their IDs of "messages with which they do not wish to be associated." "Persons who observe" designs on IDs "routinely—and reasonably—interpret them as conveying some message on the issuer's behalf." If not, the individual could simply display the message in larger letters on a bumper sticker. But the individual prefers a license plate design to the purely private speech expressed through bumper stickers. That may well be because Texas's license plate designs convey government agreement with the message displayed.

Third, Texas maintains control over the messages conveyed on its specialty plates. The State "has sole control over the design, typeface, color, and alphanumeric pattern for all license plates." The Board must approve every specialty plate design proposal. The State has rejected at least a dozen proposed designs. As in *Summum*, Texas "has 'controlled' the messages conveyed by exercising 'final approval authority' over their selection." This authority allows Texas to choose how to present itself and its constituency. Thus, Texas offers plates celebrating the educational institutions attended by its citizens. It need not issue plates deriding schooling. Texas offers plates that pay tribute to the Texas citrus industry. It need not issue plates praising Florida's oranges as better. Texas offers plates that say "Fight Terrorism." It need not issue plates promoting al Qaeda.

These considerations, taken together, convince us that specialty plates are similar enough to the monuments in *Summum* to call for the same result. That is not to say that every element of *Summum* is relevant here. *Summum* emphasized that monuments were "permanent" and that "public parks can accommodate only a limited number of permanent monuments." The speech was government speech in part because we found it "hard to imagine how a public park could be opened for the installation of permanent monuments by every person or group wishing to engage in that form of expression." A State could theoretically offer a much larger number of license plate designs, and those designs need not be available for time immemorial. But those characteristics of *Summum* were important because the government speech occurred in parks, which are traditional public forums for "the delivery of speeches and the holding of marches and demonstrations" by private citizens. By contrast, license plates are not traditional public forums for private speech. Other features of the designs on Texas's specialty plates indicate that the message conveyed is conveyed on behalf of the government. Texas selects each design featured on specialty license plates. Texas presents these designs on government-mandated, government-controlled, and government-issued IDs that have traditionally been used as a medium for government speech. It places the designs directly below the letters identifying "TEXAS" as the issuer of the IDs. "The designs are meant to convey and have the effect of conveying a government message, and thus constitute government speech."

SCV believes that Texas's specialty license plate designs are not government speech, at least with respect to the designs that were initially proposed by private parties. According to SCV, the State does not engage in expressive activity through such slogans and graphics, but rather provides a forum for private speech by making license plates available to display the private parties' designs. We cannot agree. We have used "forum analysis" to evaluate government restrictions on purely private speech that occurs on government property. But forum analysis is misplaced here. Because the State is speaking on its own behalf, First Amendment strictures that attend the various types of government-established forums do not apply. Texas's specialty license plates are not a "traditional public forum which has immemorially been held in trust for the use of the public and, time out of mind, has been used for purposes of assembly, communicating thoughts between citizens, and discussing public questions." *Perry Ed. Assn. v. Perry Local Educators' Assn.*, 460 U. S. 37, 45 (1983). "The Court has rejected the view that traditional public forum status extends beyond its historic confines." *Arkansas Ed. Television Comm'n v. Forbes*, 523 U. S. 666, 678 (1998). State-issued specialty license plates lie beyond those confines. Texas's specialty plates are neither a "designated public forum," which exists where "government property that has not traditionally been regarded as a public forum is intentionally opened up for that purpose," nor a "limited public forum," which exists where a government has "reserved a forum for certain groups or for the discussion of certain topics," *Rosenberger v. Rector and Visitors of Univ. of Va.*, 515 U. S. 819, 829 (1995). A government "does not create a public forum by inaction or by permitting limited discourse, but only by intentionally opening a nontraditional forum for public discourse." *Cornelius*, 473 U. S., at 802. In order "to ascertain whether a government intended to designate a place not traditionally open to assembly and debate as a public forum," this Court "has looked to the policy and practice of the government" and to "the nature of the property and its compatibility with expressive activity."

Texas's policies and the nature of its license plates indicate that the State did not intend its specialty license plates to serve as either a designated public forum or a limited public forum. First, the State exercises final authority over each specialty license plate design. Second, Texas takes ownership of each specialty plate design, making it untenable that the State intended specialty plates to serve as a forum for public discourse. Finally, Texas license plates have traditionally been used for government speech, are primarily used as a form of government ID, and bear the State's name. These features indicate that Texas explicitly associates itself with the speech on its plates.

For similar reasons, Texas's specialty license plates are not a "nonpublic forum," which exists "where the government is acting as a proprietor, managing its internal operations." *International Soc. for Krishna Consciousness, Inc. v. Lee*, 505

U. S. 672, 678 (1992). Texas is not simply managing government property, but instead is engaging in expressive conduct. We reach this conclusion based on the historical context, observers' reasonable interpretation of the messages conveyed by Texas specialty plates, and the effective control that the State exerts over the design selection process. The fact that private parties take part in the design and propagation of a message does not extinguish the governmental nature of the message or transform the government's role into that of a forum-provider. In *Summum*, private entities "financed and donated monuments that the government accepted and displayed." Here private parties propose designs that Texas may accept and display on its license plates. The "government may exercise its freedom to express its views" even "when it receives assistance from private sources for the purpose of delivering a government-controlled message." Forum analysis is inapposite.

Of course, Texas allows many more license plate designs than the city in *Summum* allowed monuments. But *Summum* was not dependent on the number of monuments found within the park. Further, there may well be many more messages that Texas wishes to convey through its license plates than there were messages that the city in *Summum* wished to convey through its monuments. Texas's desire to communicate numerous messages does not mean that the messages are not Texas's own. The fact that Texas vehicle owners pay annual fees in order to display specialty license plates does not imply that the designs are merely a forum for private speech. While some nonpublic forums provide governments the opportunity to profit from speech, the existence of government profit alone is insufficient to trigger forum analysis. Thus, if the city in *Summum* had established a rule that organizations wishing to donate monuments must also pay fees to assist in park maintenance, we do not believe that the result would have been different. Here, Texas is speaking through its specialty license plate designs, such that the existence of annual fees does not convince us that the specialty plates are a nonpublic forum.

This case is not like *Perry Ed. Assn.*, where we found a school district's internal mail system to be a nonpublic forum for private speech. There, a number of private organizations, including a teachers' union, had access to the mail system. Therefore private parties, and not only the government, used the system to communicate. Here, each specialty license plate design is formally approved by and stamped with the imprimatur of Texas. Nor is this case like *Lehman*, where we found the advertising space on city buses to be a nonpublic forum. There, the messages were located in a context (advertising space) that is traditionally available for private speech. The advertising space bore no indicia that the speech was owned or conveyed by the government. Nor is this case like *Cornelius*, where we determined that a charitable fundraising program directed at federal employees constituted a nonpublic forum. That forum lacked the kind of history present here. The fundraising drive had never been a medium for government speech. It was established "to bring order to a solicitation process" which had previously consisted of ad hoc solicitation by individual charitable organizations. The drive "was designed to minimize disruption to the federal workplace," not to communicate messages from the government.

Our determination that Texas's specialty license plate designs are government speech does not mean that the designs do not also implicate the free speech rights of private persons. Drivers who display a State's selected license plate designs convey the messages communicated through those designs. And the First Amendment stringently limits a State's authority to compel a private party to express a view with which the private party disagrees. See *West Virginia Bd. of Ed. v. Barnette*, 319 U. S. 624 (1943). But here, compelled private speech is not at issue. Just as Texas cannot require SCV to convey "the State's ideological message," SCV cannot force Texas to include a Confederate battle flag on its specialty license plates.

We hold that Texas's specialty license plate designs constitute government speech and that Texas was consequently entitled to refuse to issue plates featuring SCV's proposed design. Accordingly, the judgment of the United States Court of Appeals for the Fifth Circuit is

Reversed.

Justice ALITO, with whom THE CHIEF JUSTICE, Justice SCALIA, and Justice KENNEDY join, *dissenting.*

Under our First Amendment, the distinction between government speech and private speech is critical. When government speaks, it is free "to select the views that it wants to express." *Pleasant Grove City v. Summum*, 555 U. S. 460 (2009). By contrast, "in the realm of private speech or expression, government regulation may not favor one speaker over another." *Rosenberger v. Rector and Visitors of Univ. of Va.*, 515 U. S. 819, 828 (1995). The Court holds that all the privately created messages on specialty plates issued by the State of Texas convey a government message rather than the message of the motorist displaying the plate. Can this possibly be correct? Suppose you sat by a Texas highway and studied the license plates on the vehicles passing by. You would see, in addition to the standard Texas plates, an impressive array of specialty plates. You would likely observe plates that honor numerous colleges and universities. You might see plates bearing the name of a high school, a fraternity or sorority, the Masons, the Knights of Columbus, the Daughters of the American Revolution, a realty company, a favorite soft drink, a favorite burger restaurant, and a favorite NASCAR driver. Would you really think that the sentiments reflected in these plates are the views of the State of Texas and not those of the owners of the cars? If a car with a plate that says "Rather Be Golfing" passed by at 8:30 am on a Monday morning, would you think: "This is the official policy of the State—better to golf than to work?" If you saw Texas plates with the names of the University of Texas's out-of-state competitors in upcoming games—Notre Dame, Oklahoma State, the University of Oklahoma—would you assume that Texas was officially (and perhaps treasonously) rooting for the Longhorns' opponents? When a car zipped by with a plate that reads "NASCAR – 24 Jeff Gordon," would you think that Gordon (born in

California, raised in Indiana, resides in North Carolina) is the official favorite of the State government? The Court says that it is essential that government be able to express its own viewpoint, because otherwise, how would it promote its programs, like recycling and vaccinations? So when Texas issues a "Rather Be Golfing" plate, but not a "Rather Be Playing Tennis" or "Rather Be Bowling" plate, it is furthering a state policy to promote golf but not tennis or bowling. When Texas allows motorists to obtain a Notre Dame license plate but not a University of Southern California plate, it is taking sides in that long-time rivalry.

The precedent this case sets is dangerous. While all license plates contain *some* government speech (*e.g.*, the name of the State and the numbers and/or letters identifying the vehicle), Texas has converted the remaining space on its specialty plates into mobile billboards on which motorists can display messages. What Texas did was to reject one of the messages that members of a private group wanted to post because the State thought that many of its citizens would find the message offensive. That is blatant viewpoint discrimination. Suppose that a State erected electronic billboards along its highways. Suppose that the State posted some government messages on these billboards and then, to raise money, allowed private entities and individuals to purchase the right to post their own messages. Suppose that the State allowed only those messages that it liked or found not too controversial. Would that be constitutional? What if a state college or university did the same thing with a billboard or a campus bulletin board or dorm list serve? What if it allowed private messages that are consistent with prevailing views on campus but banned those that disturbed some students or faculty? Can there be any doubt that these examples of viewpoint discrimination would violate the First Amendment? I hope not.

Texas motorists can choose from more than 350 messages, including many designs proposed by nonprofit groups or by individuals and for-profit businesses through the State's third-party vendor. Drivers can select plates advertising organizations and causes like 4–H, the Boy Scouts, the American Legion, Be a Blood Donor, the Girl Scouts, Mothers Against Drunk Driving, Marine Mammal Recovery, Save Texas Ocelots, Texas Realtors ("I am a Texas Realtor"), the Texas Trophy Hunters Association, the World Wildlife Fund, the YMCA, and Young Lawyers. There are plates for fraternities and sororities and for in-state schools, both public (Texas A & M and Texas Tech) and private (Trinity University and Baylor). An even larger number of schools from out-of-state are honored: Arizona State, Brigham Young, Florida State, Michigan State, Alabama, and South Carolina. There are political slogans, like "Don't Tread on Me," and plates promoting the citrus industry and the "Cotton Boll." There are plates advertising Remax ("Get It Sold with Remax"), Dr. Pepper ("Always One of a Kind"), and Mighty Fine Burgers.

The SCV is composed of descendants of Confederate soldiers. Their proposed design featured a controversial symbol, the Confederate battle flag, surrounded by the words "Sons of Confederate Veterans 1896" and a gold border. The Texas Department of Motor Vehicles Board invited public comments and considered the plate design in April 2011. At that meeting, board members deadlocked on whether to approve the plate. The Board reconsidered the plate in November 2011. This time, many opponents of the plate turned out to voice objections. The Board voted unanimously against approval and issued an order stating: "A significant portion of the public associate the confederate flag with organizations advocating expressions of hate directed toward people or groups that are demeaning to those people or groups." The Board saw "a compelling public interest in protecting a conspicuous mechanism for identification, such as a license plate, from degrading into a possible public safety issue." It thought that the public interest required rejection of the plate design because the controversy surrounding the plate was so great that "the design could distract or disturb some drivers to the point of being unreasonably dangerous." At the same meeting, the Board approved a Buffalo Soldiers plate design by a 5-to-3 vote. Proceeds from fees paid by motorists who select that plate benefit the Buffalo Soldier National Museum in Houston, which is "dedicated to preserving the legacy and honor of the African American soldier." "Buffalo Soldiers" is a nickname that was originally given to black soldiers in the Army's 10th Cavalry Regiment, which was formed after the Civil War. The original Buffalo Soldiers fought with distinction in the Indian Wars, but the "Buffalo Soldiers" plate was opposed by some Native Americans. One leader commented that he felt "the same way about the Buffalo Soldiers" as African-Americans felt about the Confederate flag. "When we see the U. S. Cavalry uniform," he explained, "we are forced to relive an American holocaust."

Relying almost entirely on *Summum*, the Court holds that messages that private groups succeed in placing on Texas license plates are government messages. As we said in *Summum*, governments have used monuments since time immemorial to express important government messages, and there is no history of governments giving equal space to those wishing to express dissenting views. The history of messages on license plates is quite different. More than 70 years passed before the proliferation of specialty plates in Texas. It was not until the 1990's that motorists were allowed to choose from among 10 messages, such as "Read to Succeed" and "Keep Texas Beautiful." Up to this point, the words on the Texas plates can be considered government speech. The messages were created by the State, and they promoted state programs. When, within the last 20 years, the State began to allow private entities to secure plates conveying their own messages, Texas crossed the line. The contrast between the history of public monuments, which have been used to convey government messages for centuries, and the Texas license plate program could not be starker. Texas does not exhibit the "selective receptivity" present in *Summum*. The Board's chairman, who is charged with approving designs, explained that the program's purpose is "to encourage private plates" in order to "generate additional revenue for the state." Most of the time, the Board "bases its decisions on rules that primarily deal with reflectivity and readability."

Pressed to come up with any evidence that the State has exercised "selective receptivity," Texas (and the Court) rely primarily on sketchy information not contained in the record, specifically that the Board's predecessor (might have) rejected a "pro-life" plate and perhaps others on the ground that they contained messages that were offensive. But even if this happened, it shows only that the present case may not be the only one in which the State has exercised viewpoint discrimination. Texas's only other evidence of selectivity concerns a proposed plate that was thought to create a threat to the fair enforcement of the State's motor vehicle laws. This proposed plate was a Texas DPS Troopers Foundation plate. The Board rejected the plate due to apparent concern that the plate could give the impression that those displaying it would receive favored treatment from state troopers. The constitutionality of this action does not necessarily turn on whether approval of this plate would have made the message government speech. If the Texas specialty plate program created a limited public forum, private speech may be excluded if it is inconsistent with the purpose of the forum. *Rosenberger*, 515 U. S., at 829. Thus, the picture here is different from that in *Summum*. Texas does approve only proposed plates that convey messages that the State supports. Instead, it proclaims that it is open to all private messages — except those, like the SCV plate, that would offend some.

The Court believes that messages on privately created plates are government speech because motorists want a seal of state approval for their messages and therefore prefer plates over bumper stickers. This is dangerous. There is a big difference between government speech (speech by the government in further-ance of its programs) and governmental blessing (or condemnation) of private speech. Many private speakers would welcome a sign of government approval. But in the realm of private speech, government regulation may not favor one viewpoint over another.

A final factor that was important in *Summum* was space. A park can accommo-date only so many permanent monuments. The only absolute limit on the num-ber of specialty plates that a State could issue is the number of registered vehicles.

The Texas specialty plate program has none of the factors that were critical in *Summum*, and the program exhibits a characteristic that was missing in that case: Individuals who want to display a Texas specialty plate, instead of the stan-dard plate, must pay an increased annual registration fee. How many groups or individuals would clamor to pay $8,000 (the deposit required to create a new plate) in order to broadcast the government's message as opposed to their own? If Texas really wants to speak out in support of, say, Iowa State University (but not the University of Iowa) or "Young Lawyers" (but not old ones), why must it be paid to say things that it really wants to say? States have not adopted specialty license plate programs because they are bursting with things they want to say on their license plates. Those programs were adopted because they bring in many millions of dollars every year. Texas has space available on millions of little mobile billboards. Texas, in effect, sells that space to those who wish to use it to express a personal message — provided that the message does not express a viewpoint that the State finds unacceptable. That is not government speech; it is regulation of private speech.

What Texas has done is to create what we have called a limited public forum. It has allowed state property (*i.e.,* motor vehicle license plates) to be used by private speakers according to rules that the State prescribes. Under the First Amendment, those rules cannot discriminate on the basis of viewpoint. See *Rosenberger,* 515 U. S., at 829. But that is exactly what Texas did here. The Board rejected Texas SCV's design, "specifically the confederate flag portion of the design, because public comments have shown that many members of the general public find the design offensive, and because such comments are reasonable." These statements indisputably demonstrate that the Board denied Texas SCV's design because of its viewpoint. The Confederate battle flag is controversial. To the Texas Sons of Confederate Veterans, it is said to evoke the memory of their ancestors and other soldiers who fought for the South in the Civil War. To others, it symbolizes slavery, segregation, and hatred. Whatever it means to motorists who display that symbol and to those who see it, the flag expresses a viewpoint. The Board rejected the plate design because it concluded that many Texans would find the flag symbol offensive. That was pure viewpoint discrimination. If the Board's candid explanation of its reason for rejecting the SCV plate were not alone sufficient to establish this point, the Board's approval of the Buffalo Soldiers plate at the same meeting dispels any doubt. The proponents of both the SCV and Buffalo Soldiers plates saw them as honoring soldiers who served with bravery and honor in the past. To opponents, the images on the plates evoked painful memories. The Board rejected one plate and approved the other.

Many other specialty plates have the potential to irritate and perhaps even infuriate those who see them. Texas allows a plate with the words "Choose Life," but the State of New York rejected such a plate as "so incredibly divisive." Texas allows a specialty plate honoring the Boy Scouts, but the group's refusal to accept gay leaders angers some. Virginia issues plates for controversial organizations like the National Rifle Association, controversial commercial enterprises (raising tobacco and mining coal), controversial sports (fox hunting), and a professional sports team with a controversial name (the Washington Redskins). Allowing States to reject specialty plates based on their potential to offend is viewpoint discrimination.

The Board's decision cannot be saved by its suggestion that the plate "could distract or disturb some drivers to the point of being unreasonably dangerous." This rationale cannot withstand strict scrutiny. Other States allow specialty plates with the Confederate Battle Flag, and Texas has not pointed to evidence that these plates have led to incidents of road rage or accidents. Texas does not ban bumper stickers bearing the image of the Confederate battle flag. Nor does it ban any of the many other bumper stickers that convey political messages and other messages that are capable of exciting the ire of those who loathe the ideas they express.

Messages that are proposed by private parties and placed on Texas specialty plates are private speech, not government speech. Texas cannot forbid private speech based on its viewpoint. That is what it did here.

Notes

1. *Confederate Battle Flag Plates in Other States.* When *Walker* was decided, nine states offered specialty license plates honoring the Sons of Confederate Veterans that included an image of the Confederate Battle Flag. They included Alabama, Georgia, Louisiana, Maryland, Mississippi, North Carolina, South Carolina, Tennessee, and Virginia. The ruling in *Walker* was issued on the morning of June 18, 2015. On the night of June 17, nine African American parishioners at a Bible study group were shot and killed at the Emanuel African Methodist Episcopal Church in Charleston, South Carolina. The suspect, Dylann Roof, was arrested on June 18 and charged with nine counts of murder. On June 20, a photograph of Roof posing with a Confederate Battle Flag and handgun was discovered on a website registered to Roof, and the photograph was widely publicized by the media. *See* Frances Robles, *Dylann Roof Photos and a Manifesto Are Posted on Website,* N.Y. Times, June 20, 2015, http://www.nytimes.com/2015/06/21/us/dylann-storm-roof-photos-website-charleston-church-shooting.html. In the ensuing days, the governor of South Carolina called for the Confederate Battle Flag to be removed from the state capitol grounds. After an emotional debate, South Carolina's legislature voted to do just that. Alabama's governor ordered Confederate Battle Flags to be taken down from the state capitol, and in Mississippi, the Republican Speaker of the House and the two Republican Senators called for removal of the flag symbol from the Mississippi state flag. Calls for the removal of the flag and other symbols of the Confederacy were made across the country. *See* Jeremy Diamond & Eugene Scott, *Confederate Flag Debate Sweeps South,* CNN, June 25, 2015, http://www.cnn.com/2015/06/23/politics/confederate-flags-southern-states-debate-legislators.

In a matter of days, officials in five states announced their opposition to retaining the Confederate Battle Flag on license plates. Virginia's governor announced that such plates would be replaced "as quickly as possible" and Virginia's attorney general filed a motion seeking reversal of a Fourth Circuit decision that ordered issuance of the plates. Changes in the design of the plate were ordered in Georgia. The governors of North Carolina and Tennessee called for the flag to be removed from the license plates in their states, and legislation was introduced in Tennessee to remove the flag from the plates. The governor of Maryland announced that he would take action to pull the plates. *See, e.g.,* Jeremy Diamond & Eugene Scott, *Confederate Flag Debate Sweeps South,* CNN, June 25, 2015, http://www.cnn.com/2015/06/23/politics/confederate-flags-southern-states-debate-legislators.

2. *Choose Life Plates.* In terms of litigation, the two most controversial specialty plates have been the SCV plate and the "Choose Life" plate that is available in a majority of states. Before *Walker,* the federal circuit courts were divided on the constitutionality of a state's decision to approve a Choose Life plate, while failing to make a plate available with a pro-choice message. *See, e.g., Planned Parenthood of South Carolina, Inc. v. Rose,* 361 F.3d 786 (4th Cir. 2004) (finding First Amendment violation); *ACLU of Tennessee v. Bredesen,* 441 F.3d 370 (6th Cir. 2006) (finding no First Amendment violation). Over two dozen states issue a Choose Life plate and a handful of states issue pro-choice plates.

~ **PROBLEMS** ~

1. *Highway Billboards.* In describing the *Walker* ruling as a dangerous precedent, the dissent offered two hypotheticals. First, "suppose that a State erected electronic billboards along its highways. It posted some government messages on these billboards, and then, to raise money, allowed private entities and individuals to purchase the right to post their own messages. But the State allowed only those messages that it liked or found not too controversial." Second, "what if a state college or university did the same thing with a campus bulletin board or dorm list serve? What if it allowed private messages that are consistent with prevailing views on campus but banned those that disturbed some students or faculty?" The dissent opined that there was no doubt "that these examples of viewpoint discrimination would violate the First Amendment." Is that true after *Walker*?

2. *Alphanumeric Plates.* Consider the third license plate option in Texas, which provides for personalized plates for owners who request "a particular alphanumeric pattern for use as a plate number." The *Walker* dissent expressly noted that "this opinion does not address" whether the choice of these "patterns" by motorists would constitute "private speech." Assume that the Texas DMV Board rejected the request of one car owner who asked for the alphanumeric pattern of "HELL 666." How would the *Walker* majority analyze this case? How would the *Walker* dissent decide whether to treat this pattern as government speech or private speech?

L. BROADCAST REGULATION

Over time, as speech technology has expanded and developed, the courts have struggled to decide whether they should apply different media-specific rules to different types of technology. In this section, we examine the special rules that have developed relating to broadcast technology.

Red Lion Broadcasting Co. v. FCC

395 U.S. 367 (1969)

Mr. Justice WHITE delivered the opinion of the Court.

The Federal Communications Commission has for many years imposed on radio and television broadcasters the requirement that discussion of public issues be presented on broadcast stations, and that each side of those issues must be given fair coverage. This is known as the fairness doctrine, which originated very early in the history of broadcasting. It is an obligation whose content has been defined in a long series of FCC rulings in particular cases, and which is distinct from the statutory requirement of §315 of the Communications Act that equal time be allotted all qualified candidates for public office. Two aspects of the fairness doctrine, relating to personal attacks in the context of controversial public issues and to political editorializing, were codified more precisely in the form of FCC regulations in 1967.

There is a twofold duty. The broadcaster must give adequate coverage to public issues, and coverage must be fair in that it accurately reflects the opposing views. This must be done at the broadcaster's own expense if sponsorship is unavailable. Moreover, the duty must be met by programming obtained at the licensee's own initiative if available from no other source. The Federal Radio Commission had imposed these two basic duties on broadcasters since the outset, and in particular respects the personal attack rules and regulations at issue here have spelled them out in greater detail.

When a personal attack has been made on a figure involved in a public issue both the doctrine and also the 1967 regulations require that the individual attacked himself be offered an opportunity to respond. Likewise, where one candidate is endorsed in a political editorial, the other candidates must themselves be offered reply time to use personally or through a spokesman. These obligations differ from the general fairness requirement that issues be presented, and presented with coverage of competing views, in that the broadcaster does not have the option of presenting the attacked party's side himself or choosing a third party to represent that side. But insofar as there is an obligation of the broadcaster to see that both sides are presented, and insofar as that is an affirmative obligation, the personal attack doctrine and regulations do not differ from the preceding fairness doctrine.

Broadcasters challenge the fairness doctrine and its specific manifestations in the personal attack and political editorial rules on conventional First Amendment grounds, alleging that the rules abridge their freedom of speech and press. Their contention is that the First Amendment protects their desire to use their allotted frequencies continuously to broadcast whatever they choose, and to exclude whomever they choose from ever using that frequency.

Just as the Government may limit the use of sound-amplifying equipment potentially so noisy that it drowns out civilized private speech, so may the Government limit the use of broadcast equipment. The right of free speech of a broadcaster, the user of a sound truck, or any other individual does not embrace a right to snuff out the free speech of others.

When two people converse face to face, both should not speak at once if either is to be clearly understood. But the range of the human voice is so limited that there could be meaningful communications if half the people in the United States were talking and the other half listening. Just as clearly, half the people might publish and the other half read. But the reach of radio signals is incomparably greater than the range of the human voice and the problem of interference is a massive reality. The lack of know-how and equipment may keep many from the air, but only a tiny fraction of those with resources and intelligence can hope to communicate by radio at the same time if intelligible communication is to be had, even if the entire radio spectrum is utilized in the present state of commercially acceptable technology.

It was this fact, and the chaos which ensued from permitting anyone to use any frequency at whatever power level he wished, which made necessary the enactment of the Radio Act of 1927 and the Communications Act of 1934, as the Court has noted at length before. It was this reality which at the very least necessitated first the division of the radio spectrum into portions reserved respectively for public broadcasting and for other important radio uses such as amateur operation, aircraft, police, defense, and navigation; and then the subdivision of each portion, and assignment of specific frequencies to individual users or groups of users. Beyond this, however, because the frequencies reserved for public broadcasting were limited in number, it was essential for the Government to tell some applicants that they could not broadcast at all because there was room for only a few.

Where there are substantially more individuals who want to broadcast than there are frequencies to allocate, it is idle to posit an unabridgeable First Amendment right to broadcast comparable to the right of every individual to speak, write, or publish. If 100 persons want broadcast licenses but there are only 10 frequencies to allocate, all of them may have the same "right" to a license; but if there is to be any effective communication by radio, only a few can be licensed and the rest must be barred from the airwaves. It would be strange if the First Amendment, aimed at protecting and furthering communications, prevented the Government from making radio communication possible by requiring licenses to broadcast and by limiting the number of licenses so as not to overcrowd the spectrum. Congress unquestionably has the power to grant and deny licenses. No one has a First Amendment right to a license or to monopolize a radio frequency; to deny a station license because "the public interest" requires it "is not a denial of free speech."

By the same token, as far as the First Amendment is concerned those who are licensed stand no better than those to whom licenses are refused. A license permits broadcasting, but the licensee has no constitutional right to be the one who holds the license or to monopolize a radio frequency to the exclusion of his fellow citizens. There is nothing in the First Amendment which prevents the Government from requiring a licensee to share his frequency with others and to conduct himself as a proxy or fiduciary with obligations to present those views and voices which are representative of his community and which would otherwise, by necessity, be barred from the airwaves.

This is not to say that the First Amendment is irrelevant to public broadcasting. On the contrary, it has a major role to play. Because of the scarcity of radio frequencies, the Government is permitted to put restraints on licensees in favor of others whose views should be expressed on this unique medium. But the people as a whole retain their interest in free speech by radio and their collective right to have the medium function consistently with the ends and purposes of the First Amendment. It is the right of the viewers and listeners, not the right of the broadcasters, which is paramount. It is the purpose of the First Amendment to preserve an uninhibited marketplace of ideas in which truth will ultimately prevail, rather than to countenance monopolization of that market, whether it be by the Government itself or a private licensee. "Speech concerning public affairs is more than self-expression; it is the essence of self-government." *Garrison v. Louisiana,* 379 U.S. 64, 74-75 (1964). It is the right of the public to receive suitable access to social, political, esthetic, moral, and other ideas and experiences which is crucial here. That right may not constitutionally be abridged either by Congress or by the FCC.

Rather than confer frequency monopolies on a relatively small number of licensees, in a Nation of 200,000,000, the Government could surely have decreed that each frequency should be shared among all or some of those who wish to use it, each being assigned a portion of the broadcast day or the broadcast week. The ruling and regulations at issue here do not go quite so far. They assert that under specified circumstances, a licensee must offer to make available a reasonable amount of broadcast time to those who have a view different from that which has already been expressed on his station. The expression of a political endorsement, or of a personal attack while dealing with a controversial public issue, simply triggers this time sharing. The First Amendment confers no right on licensees to prevent others from broadcasting on "their" frequencies and no right to an unconditional monopoly of a scarce resource which the Government has denied others the right to use.

In terms of constitutional principle, and as enforced sharing of a scarce resource, the personal attack and political editorial rules are indistinguishable from the equal-time provision of §315, a specific enactment of Congress requiring stations to set aside reply time under specified circumstances and to which the fairness doctrine and these constituent regulations are important complements. That provision, which has been part of the law since 1927, has been held valid by this Court as an obligation of the licensee relieving him of any power in any way to prevent or censor the broadcast, and thus insulating him from liability for defamation. The constitutionality of the statute under the First Amendment was unquestioned.

Nor can we say that it is inconsistent with the First Amendment goal of producing an informed public capable of conducting its own affairs to require a broadcaster to permit answers to personal attacks occurring in the course of discussing controversial issues, or to require that the political opponents of those endorsed by the station be given a chance to communicate with the public. Otherwise, station owners and a few networks would have unfettered power to make time available only to the highest bidders, to communicate only their own views on public issues, people and candidates, and to permit on the air only those with whom they agreed.

It is strenuously argued, however, that if political editorials or personal attacks will trigger an obligation in broadcasters to afford the opportunity for expression to speakers who need not pay for time and whose views are unpalatable to the licensees, then broadcasters will be irresistibly forced to self-censorship and their coverage of controversial public issues will be eliminated or at least rendered wholly ineffective. Such a result would indeed be a serious matter, for should licensees actually eliminate their coverage of controversial issues, the purposes of the doctrine would be stifled.

At this point, however, that possibility is at best speculative. The communications industry, and in particular the networks, have taken pains to present controversial issues in the past, and even now they do not assert that they intend to abandon their efforts in this regard. If experience with the administration of those doctrines indicates that they have the net effect of reducing rather than enhancing the volume and quality of coverage, there will be time enough to reconsider the constitutional implications. The fairness doctrine in the past has had no such overall effect.

That this will occur now seems unlikely, however, since if present licensees should suddenly prove timorous, the Commission is not powerless to insist that they give adequate and fair attention to public issues. It does not violate the First Amendment to treat licensees given the privilege of using scarce radio frequencies as proxies for the entire community, obligated to give suitable time and attention to matters of great public concern. To condition the granting or renewal of licenses on a willingness to present representative community views on controversial issues is consistent with the ends and purposes of those constitutional provisions forbidding the abridgment of freedom of speech and freedom of the press. Congress need not stand idly by and permit those with licenses to ignore the problems which beset the people or to exclude from the airways anything but their own views of fundamental questions. The statute, long administrative practice, and cases are to this effect.

Licenses to broadcast do not confer ownership of designated frequencies, but only the temporary privilege of using them. Unless renewed, they expire within three years. The statute mandates the issuance of licenses if the "public convenience, interest, or necessity will be served thereby." In applying this standard the Commission for 40 years has been choosing licensees based in part on their program proposals. In determining how best to allocate frequencies, the Federal Radio Commission considered the needs of competing communities and the programs offered by competing stations to meet those needs; moreover, if needs or programs shifted, the Commission could alter its allocations to reflect those shifts.

We need not and do not now ratify every past and future decision by the FCC with regard to programming. There is no question here of the Commission's refusal to permit the broadcaster to carry a particular program or to publish his own views; of a discriminatory refusal to require the licensee to broadcast certain views which have been denied access to the airwaves; of government censorship of a particular program contrary to §326; or of the official government view dominating public broadcasting. Such questions would raise more serious First Amendment issues. But we do hold that the Congress and the Commission do not violate the First Amendment when they require a radio or television station to give reply time to answer personal attacks and political editorials.

In view of the scarcity of broadcast frequencies, the Government's role in allocating those frequencies, and the legitimate claims of those unable without governmental assistance to gain access to those frequencies for expression of their views, we hold the regulations and ruling at issue here are both authorized by statute and constitutional. The judgment of the Court of Appeals in *Red Lion* is affirmed and that in RTNDA reversed and the causes remanded for proceedings consistent with this opinion.

It is so ordered.

Notes and Questions

1. *Repeal of the Fairness Doctrine.* In 1987, the FCC repealed the fairness doctrine based on a 1985 report in which the FCC stated that it was "firmly convinced that the fairness doctrine, as a matter of policy, disserves the public interest" and raised questions about the doctrine's continuing constitutionality. Inquiry into Alternatives to the General Fairness Obligations of Broadcast Licensees, 102 F.C.C.2d 143 (1985).

2. *Political Advertisements.* The decision in *CBS, Inc. v. Democratic National Committee*, 412 U.S. 94 (1973), involved the Democratic National Committee (DNC) and the Business Executives' Move for Vietnam Peace (BEM), a national organization of businessmen opposed to U.S. involvement in the Vietnam conflict, who wanted to run paid ads on television. FCC orders provided that a broadcaster who meets its public obligation to provide full and fair coverage of public issues is not required to accept editorial advertisements. The Court sustained the orders, noting that Congress "opted for a system of private broadcasters licensed and regulated by Government." As a result, broadcast licensees have "a large measure of journalistic freedom," although they must "balance what they might prefer to do as a private entrepreneur with what they are required to do as a 'public trustee.'" This "journalistic freedom" gives broadcasters discretion about which ads to air. The Court expressed concern that, if the fairness doctrine were applied to editorial advertising, broadcasters might suffer financial hardship by being forced to "make regular programming time available to those holding a view different from that expressed in an editorial advertisement" and the "public interest would no longer be 'paramount' but, rather, subordinate to private whim." Justice Brennan dissented: "Licensees must respect the competing First Amendment rights of others. Broadcasters make such air time readily available to those 'commercial' advertisers who seek to peddle their goods and services to the public."

3. *Airing Private Documentaries.* In *CBS, Inc. v. FCC*, 453 U.S. 367 (1981), when the Carter-Mondale Presidential Committee requested time to air a documentary outlining the record of the Carter administration, and the networks declined

to make the requested time available, the FCC held that they had failed to provide "reasonable access." The Court upheld the FCC's determination: "Section 312(a)(7) creates a limited right to 'reasonable' access that pertains only to legally qualified federal candidates and may be invoked by them only for the purpose of advancing their candidacies once a campaign has commenced. We hold that the statutory right of access, as defined by the Commission and applied in these cases, properly balances the First Amendment rights of federal candidates, the public, and broadcasters."

4. *Should the Fairness Doctrine Be Reinstituted?* Although the FCC has now abandoned the fairness doctrine, does the rationale for that doctrine make sense today? Air waves may be as limited as before, but they are supplemented by cable and satellite television and radio stations (both over the air and online) in profusion. Given the modern environment, is the "scarcity" rationale still meaningful?

5. *Intermediate Standard of Review.* In *FCC v. League of Women Voters of California,* 468 U.S. 364 (1984), the Court considered the Public Broadcasting Act of 1967, which prohibited any noncommercial educational broadcasting station that receives grants from the Corporation for Public Broadcasting from "engaging in editorializing." The Court struck down the restriction: "Although the Government certainly has a substantial interest in ensuring that the audiences of noncommercial stations will not be led to think that the broadcaster's editorials reflect the official view of the government, this interest can be fully satisfied by less restrictive means that are readily available. Congress could simply require public broadcasting stations to broadcast a disclaimer every time they editorialize." Justice Rehnquist dissented: "It is plainly rational for Congress to have determined that taxpayer moneys should not be used to subsidize management's views or to pay for management's exercise of partisan politics." Justice Stevens also dissented: "The interest in keeping the Federal Government out of the propaganda arena is of overriding importance."

FCC v. Pacifica Foundation

438 U.S. 726 (1978)

Mr. Justice STEVENS delivered the opinion of the Court (Parts I, II, III, and IV-C) and an opinion in which THE CHIEF JUSTICE and Mr. Justice REHNQUIST joined (Parts IV-A and IV-B).

This case requires that we decide whether the Federal Communications Commission has any power to regulate a radio broadcast that is indecent but not obscene. A satiric humorist named George Carlin recorded a 12-minute monologue entitled "Filthy Words" before a live audience in a California theater. He began by referring to his thoughts about "the words you couldn't say on the public, ah, airwaves, um, the ones you definitely wouldn't say, ever." He proceeded to list those words and repeat them over and over again in a variety of colloquialisms. The recording indicates frequent laughter from the audience.

At about 2 o'clock in the afternoon on Tuesday, October 30, 1973, a New York radio station, owned by respondent Pacifica Foundation, broadcast the "Filthy Words" monologue. A few weeks later a man, who heard the broadcast while driving with his young son, wrote a letter complaining to the Commission. The complaint was forwarded to the station for comment. In its response, Pacifica explained that the monologue had been played during a program about contemporary society's attitude toward language and that, immediately before its broadcast, listeners had been advised that it included "sensitive language which might be regarded as offensive to some." Pacifica characterized George Carlin as "a significant social satirist" who "like Twain and Sahl before him, examines the language of ordinary people. Carlin is not mouthing obscenities, he is merely using words to satirize as harmless and essentially silly our attitudes towards those words." Pacifica stated that it was not aware of any other complaints about the broadcast.

The Commission issued a declaratory order holding that Pacifica "could have been the subject of administrative sanctions." The Commission did not impose formal sanctions, but it did state that the order would be "associated with the station's license file, and in the event that subsequent complaints are received, the Commission will then decide whether it should utilize any of the available sanctions it has been granted by Congress."

In its memorandum opinion the commission stated that it intended to "clarify the standards which will be utilized in considering" complaints about indecent speech on the airwaves. The Commission found a power to regulate indecent broadcasting in two statutes: 18 U.S.C. §1464, which forbids the use of "any obscene, indecent, or profane language by means of radio communications," and 47 U.S.C. §303(g), which requires the Commission to "encourage the larger and more effective use of radio in the public interest."

The Commission characterized the language used in the Carlin monologue as "patently offensive," though not necessarily obscene, and suggested that it should be regulated by principles analogous to the law of nuisance where the "law generally speaks to channeling behavior more than actually prohibiting it." "The concept of 'indecent' is intimately connected with the exposure of children to language that describes, in terms patently offensive as measured by contemporary community standards for the broadcast medium, sexual or excretory activities and organs at times of the day when there is a reasonable risk that children may be in the audience."

Applying these considerations to the language used in the monologue, the Commission concluded that certain words depicted sexual and excretory activities in a patently offensive manner, noted that they "were broadcast at a time when children were undoubtedly in the audience," and that the prerecorded language, with these offensive words "repeated over and over," was "deliberately broadcast." The Commission also issued another opinion in which it pointed out that it "never intended to place an absolute prohibition on the broadcast of this type of language, but rather sought to channel it to times of day when children most likely would not be exposed to it." The United States Court of Appeals for the District of Columbia Circuit reversed.

IV

The afternoon broadcast of the "Filthy Words" monologue was indecent within the meaning of §1464. At most, the Commission's definition of indecency will deter only the broadcasting of patently offensive references to excretory and sexual organs and activities.[18] While some of these references may be protected, they surely lie at the periphery of First Amendment concern and the question is whether the First Amendment denies government any power to restrict the public broadcast of indecent language in any circumstances. The words of the Carlin monologue are unquestionably "speech" within the meaning of the First Amendment. It is equally clear that the Commission's objections to the broadcast were based in part on its content. The order must therefore fall if the First Amendment prohibits all governmental regulation that depends on the content of speech. Our past cases demonstrate, however, that no such absolute rule is mandated by the Constitution.

Obscene materials have been denied the protection of the First Amendment because their content is so offensive to contemporary moral standards. *Roth v. United States*, 354 U.S. 476 (1957). But the fact that society may find speech offensive is not a sufficient reason for suppressing it. Indeed, if it is the speaker's opinion that gives offense, that consequence is a reason for according it constitutional protection. For it is a central tenet of the First Amendment that the government must remain neutral in the marketplace of ideas. If there were any reason to believe that the Commission's characterization of the Carlin monologue as offensive could be traced to its political content—or even to the fact that it satirized contemporary attitudes about four-letter words—First Amendment protection might be required. But that is simply not this case. These words offend for the same reasons that obscenity offends.

Although these words ordinarily lack literary, political, or scientific value, they are not entirely outside the protection of the First Amendment. Some uses of even the most offensive words are unquestionably protected. Nonetheless, the constitutional protection accorded to a communication containing such patently offensive sexual and excretory language need not be the same in every context. It is a characteristic of speech such as this that both its capacity to offend and its "social value" vary with the circumstances. Words that are commonplace in one setting are shocking in another. To paraphrase Mr. Justice Harlan, one occasion's lyric is another's vulgarity. *Cf. Cohen v. California*, 403 U.S. 15, 25 (1971).

---

18. A requirement that indecent language be avoided will have its primary effect on the form, rather than the content, of serious communication. There are few, if any, thoughts that cannot be expressed by the use of less offensive language.

In this case it is undisputed that the content of Pacifica's broadcast was "vulgar," "offensive," and "shocking." Because content of that character is not entitled to absolute constitutional protection under all circumstances, we must consider its context in order to determine whether the Commission's action was constitutionally permissible.

We have long recognized that each medium of expression presents special First Amendment problems. And of all forms of communication, it is broadcasting that has received the most limited First Amendment protection. Thus, although other speakers cannot be licensed except under laws that carefully define and narrow official discretion, a broadcaster may be deprived of his license and his forum if the Commission decides that such an action would serve "the public interest, convenience, and necessity." Similarly, although the First Amendment protects newspaper publishers from being required to print the replies of those whom they criticize, it affords no such protection to broadcasters; on the contrary, they must give free time to the victims of their criticism.

The reasons for these distinctions are complex, but two have relevance to the present case. First, the broadcast media have established a uniquely pervasive presence in the lives of all Americans. Patently offensive, indecent material presented over the airwaves confronts the citizen, not only in public, but also in the privacy of the home, where the individual's right to be left alone plainly outweighs the First Amendment rights of an intruder. Because the broadcast audience is constantly tuning in and out, prior warnings cannot completely protect the listener or viewer from unexpected program content. Second, broadcasting is uniquely accessible to children, even those too young to read. Although *Cohen's* written message might have been incomprehensible to a first grader, Pacifica's broadcast could have enlarged a child's vocabulary in an instant. Other forms of offensive expression may be withheld from the young without restricting the expression at its source. Bookstores and motion picture theaters, for example, may be prohibited from making indecent material available to children. We held in *Ginsberg v. New York,* 390 U.S. 629, that the government's interest in the "well-being of its youth" and in supporting "parents' claim to authority in their own household" justified the regulation of otherwise protected expression.[28] The ease with which children may obtain access to broadcast material, coupled with the concerns recognized in *Ginsberg,* amply justify special treatment of indecent broadcasting.

This case does not involve a two-way radio conversation between a cab driver and a dispatcher, or a telecast of an Elizabethan comedy. We have not decided that an occasional expletive in either setting would justify any sanction or, indeed, that this broadcast would justify a criminal prosecution. The Commission's decision rested entirely on a nuisance rationale under which

28. The Commission's action does not reduce adults to hearing only what is fit for children. Adults who feel the need may purchase tapes and records or go to theaters and nightclubs to hear these words. In fact, the Commission has not unequivocally closed even broadcasting to speech of this sort.

context is all-important. The time of day was emphasized by the Commission. The content of the program in which the language is used will also affect the composition of the audience, and differences between radio, television, and perhaps closed-circuit transmissions, may also be relevant. As Mr. Justice Sutherland wrote a "nuisance may be merely a right thing in the wrong place,—like a pig in the parlor instead of the barnyard." *Euclid v. Ambler Realty Co.,* 272 U.S. 365, 388. We simply hold that when the Commission finds that a pig has entered the parlor, the exercise of its regulatory power does not depend on proof that the pig is obscene.

The judgment of the Court of Appeals is reversed.

It is so ordered.

Appendix to Opinion of the Court

The following is the first part of a verbatim transcript of "Filthy Words" prepared by the Federal Communications Commission.

Aruba-du, ruba-tu, ruba-tu. I was thinking about the curse words and the swear words, the cuss words and the words that you can't say, that you're not supposed to say all the time, 'cause words or people into words want to hear your words. Some guys like to record your words and sell them back to you if they can, (laughter) listen in on the telephone, write down what words you say. A guy who used to be in Washington, knew that his phone was tapped, used to answer, Fuck Hoover, yes, go ahead. (laughter) Okay, I was thinking one night about the words you couldn't say on the public, ah, airwaves, um, the ones you definitely wouldn't say, ever, 'cause I heard a lady say bitch one night on television, and it was cool like she was talking about, you know, ah, well, the bitch is the first one to notice that in the litter Johnie right (murmur) Right. And, uh, bastard you can say, and hell and damn so I have to figure out which ones you couldn't and ever and it came down to seven but the list is open to amendment, and in fact, has been changed, uh, by now, ha, a lot of people pointed things out to me, and I noticed some myself. The original seven words were shit, piss, fuck, cunt, cocksucker, motherfucker, and tits. Those are the ones that will curve your spine, grow hair on your hands and (laughter) maybe, even bring us, God help us, peace without honor (laughter) um, and a bourbon. (laughter) And now the first thing that we noticed was that word fuck was really repeated in there because the word motherfucker is a compound word and it's another form of the word fuck. (laughter) You want to be a purist it doesn't really—it can't be on the list of basic words. Also, cocksucker is a compound word and neither half of that is really dirty. The word—the half sucker that's merely suggestive (laughter) and the word cock is a half-way dirty word, 50% dirty—dirty half the time, depending on what you mean by it. (laughter) Uh, remember when you first heard it, like in 6th grade, you used to giggle. And the cock crowed three times, heh (laughter) the cock—three times. It's in the Bible, cock in the Bible. (laughter) And the first time you heard about a cock-fight, remember—What? Huh? naw. It ain't that, are you stupid? man. (laughter, clapping) It's chickens, you know. (laughter) Then you have the four letter words from the old Angle-Saxon fame. Uh, shit and fuck. The word shit, uh, is an interesting kind of word in that the middle class has never really accepted it and approved it. They use it like, crazy but it's not really okay. It's still a rude, dirty, old kind of gushy word. (laughter) They don't like that, but they say it, like, they say it like, a lady now in a middle-class home, you'll hear most of the time she says it as an expletive, you know, it's out of her mouth before she knows. She says, Oh shit oh shit, (laughter) oh shit. If she drops something, Oh, the shit hurt the broccoli. Shit. Thank you.

Mr. Justice POWELL, with whom Mr. Justice BLACKMUN joins, *concurring in part* and *concurring in the judgment.*

Children may not be able to protect themselves from speech which, although shocking to most adults, generally may be avoided by the unwilling through the exercise of choice. At the same time, such speech may have a deeper and more lasting negative effect on a child than on an adult. For these reasons, society may prevent the general dissemination of such speech to children, leaving to parents the decision as to what speech of this kind their children shall hear and repeat. The Commission properly held that the speech from which society may attempt to shield its children is not limited to that which appeals to the youthful prurient interest. The language involved in this case is as potentially degrading and harmful to children as representations of many erotic acts.

In most instances, the dissemination of this kind of speech to children may be limited without also limiting willing adults' access to it. Sellers of printed and recorded matter and exhibitors of motion pictures and live performances may be required to shut their doors to children, but such a requirement has no effect on adults' access. The difficulty is that such a physical separation of the audience cannot be accomplished in the broadcast media. During most of the broadcast hours, both adults and unsupervised children are likely to be in the broadcast audience, and the broadcaster cannot reach willing adults without also reaching children. This is one of the distinctions that justifies a different treatment of the broadcast media for First Amendment purposes. The Commission was entitled to give substantial weight to this difference in reaching its decision.

The Commission's holding does not prevent willing adults from purchasing Carlin's record, from attending his performances, or, indeed, from reading the transcript. On its face, it does not prevent respondent Pacifica Foundation from broadcasting the monologue during late evening hours when fewer children are likely to be in the audience. The Commission's holding does not speak to cases involving the isolated use of a potentially offensive word in the course of a radio broadcast, as distinguished from the verbal shock treatment administered by respondent here. In short, I agree that on the facts of this case, the Commission's order did not violate respondent's First Amendment rights.

The result in this case does not turn on whether Carlin's monologue, viewed as a whole, or the words that constitute it, have more or less "value" than a candidate's campaign speech. The result turns instead on the unique characteristics of the broadcast media, combined with society's right to protect its children from speech generally agreed to be inappropriate for their years, and with the interest of unwilling adults in not being assaulted by such offensive speech in their homes.

Mr. Justice BRENNAN, with whom Mr. Justice MARSHALL joins, *dissenting.*

Although an individual's decision to allow public radio communications into his home undoubtedly does not abrogate all of his privacy interests, the residual privacy interests he retains vis-a-vis the communication he voluntarily admits into his home are surely no greater than those of the people present in the corridor of the Los Angeles courthouse in *Cohen* who bore witness to the words "Fuck the Draft" emblazoned across Cohen's jacket. Their privacy interests were held insufficient to justify punishing Cohen for his offensive communication.

Even if an individual who voluntarily opens his home to radio communications retains privacy interests of sufficient moment to justify a ban on protected speech if those interests are "invaded in an essentially intolerable manner," the "radio can be turned off"—and with a minimum of effort. It is surely worth the candle to preserve the broadcaster's right to send, and the right of those interested to receive, a message entitled to full First Amendment protection. To reach a contrary balance is "to burn the house to roast the pig." The Court's balance, of necessity, fails to accord proper weight to the interests of listeners who wish to hear broadcasts the FCC deems offensive. It permits majoritarian tastes completely to preclude a protected message from entering the homes of a receptive, unoffended minority. No decision of this Court supports such a result.

Although the government unquestionably has a special interest in the well-being of children and consequently "can adopt more stringent controls on communicative materials available to youths than on those available to adults," the Court has accounted for this societal interest by adopting a "variable obscenity" standard that permits the prurient appeal of material available to children to be assessed in terms of the sexual interests of minors. Because the Carlin monologue is obviously not an erotic appeal to the prurient interests of children, the Court, for the first time, allows the government to prevent minors from gaining access to materials that are not obscene, and are therefore protected, as to them.

My Brother Stevens finds solace in his conviction that "there are few, if any, thoughts that cannot be expressed by the use of less offensive language." The idea that the content of a message and its potential impact on any who might receive it can be divorced from the words that are the vehicle for its expression is transparently fallacious. A given word may have a unique capacity to capsule an idea, evoke an emotion, or conjure up an image.

Neither of the factors relied on by the opinion of my Brother Powell and the opinion of my Brother Stevens—the intrusive nature of radio and the presence of children in the listening audience can support the FCC's disapproval of the Carlin monologue. These two asserted justifications are further plagued by a lack of principled limits. Taken to their logical extreme, these rationales would support the cleansing of public radio of any "four-letter words" whatsoever, regardless of their context. The rationales could justify the banning from radio of a myriad of literary works, novels, poems, and plays by the likes of Shakespeare, Joyce, Hemingway, Ben Jonson, Henry Fielding, Robert Burns, and Chaucer; they could support the suppression of a good deal of political speech, such as the Nixon tapes; and they could even provide the basis for imposing sanctions for the broadcast of certain portions of the Bible. I would place the responsibility and the right to weed worthless and offensive communications from the public airways where it belongs and where, until today, it resided: in a public free to choose those communications worthy of its attention from a marketplace unsullied by the censor's hand.

My Brother Stevens also finds relevant to his First Amendment analysis the fact that "adults who feel the need may purchase tapes and records or go to theaters and nightclubs to hear the tabooed words." These alternatives involve the expenditure of money, time, and effort that many of those wishing to hear Mr. Carlin's message may not be able to afford, and a naive innocence of the reality that in many cases the medium may well be the message.

In our land of cultural pluralism, there are many who think, act, and talk differently from the Members of this Court, and who do not share their fragile sensibilities. It is only an acute ethnocentric myopia that enables the Court to approve the censorship of communications solely because of the words they contain. Today's decision will thus have its greatest impact on broadcasters desiring to reach, and listening audiences composed of, persons who do not share the Court's view as to which words or expressions are acceptable and who, for a variety of reasons, including a conscious desire to flout majoritarian conventions, express themselves using words that may be regarded as offensive by those from different socio-economic backgrounds.

Mr. Justice STEWART, with whom Mr. Justice BRENNAN, Mr. Justice WHITE, and Mr. Justice MARSHALL join, *dissenting*.

Since the Carlin monologue concededly was not "obscene," I believe that the Commission lacked statutory authority to ban it.

Notes

1. *Fleeting Expletives.* In 1960, Congress enacted a federal statute that authorized the FCC to impose civil penalties for "obscene language" or for "indecent or profane language" on network broadcasts on television or radio. However, it was not until the *Pacifica* case that the FCC first exercised the authority to issue sanctions for "indecent" language. When the FCC's interpretation of the undefined statutory term "indecent" was upheld by the *Pacifica* Court in the context of the sanction imposed upon the Carlin broadcast, Justice Powell's concurring opinion observed that "the Commission's holding does not prevent the radio station from broadcasting the monologue during late evening hours when fewer children are likely to be in the audience," and that neither the Commission's holding nor the Court's holding speaks to "cases involving the isolated use of a potentially offensive word in the course of a radio broadcast." Each of Justice Powell's comments proved to be significant. The FCC's "indecency" definition in *Pacifica* applied to broadcasts "at times of the day when there is a reasonable risk that children may be in the audience," and in later years, the FCC issued an order that the hours between 10:00 p.m. and 6:00 a.m. are a "safe harbor" time period when the broadcast of "indecent" language will not be sanctioned. Between 1987 and 2004, FCC rulings, in response to complaints by viewers and listeners, consistently took the position that "a single, non-literal use of an expletive was not actionably

indecent," and not subject to sanction when it was a "fleeting and isolated utterance within the context of live and spontaneous programming." This rule came to be known as the "fleeting expletive" exception.

2. *Industry Guidance.* In 2001, the FCC clarified the "indecency" definition by issuing a policy statement entitled *Industry Guidance,* which described two elements of an indecency determination: (1) whether the material "describes or depicts sexual or excretory organs or activities"; and (2) whether the broadcast is "*patently offensive* as measured by contemporary community standards for the broadcast medium." The FCC further explained that the key concept of being "patently offensive" would be determined by reference to three factors: 1) the "explicitness or graphic nature of the description or depiction"; and 2) "whether the material dwells on, or repeats at length"; and 3) "whether the material appears to pander or is used to titillate, or whether the material appears to have been presented for its shock value." However, the *Industry Guidance* statement reiterated the FCC's position that "fleeting and isolated" expletives were not actionably indecent.

3. *Change in FCC Enforcement Policy in 2004.* A dramatic change in the FCC's enforcement policy occurred in 2004. First, during the live broadcast of the 2003 Golden Globe Awards, U2 band member Bono exclaimed, upon receiving an award, "This is really, really, fucking brilliant. Really, really, great." The FCC responded to viewer complaints by issuing an order that overruled all its prior holdings that a "fleeting expletive" like Bono's was not *per se* "indecent." The FCC sanctioned NBC for Bono's comment in *Golden Globes,* although no fine was imposed. The *Golden Globes* order declared that the FCC's *Industry Guidance* "criteria" for the meaning of the term "patently offensive" would be applicable in the future to "fleeting expletives" as well as to other "indecent" speech. Additionally, the *Golden Globes* order declared that the use of the word "fuck" and its variants was presumptively indecent and profane, and a subsequent order reached the same determination concerning the word "shit" and its variants. Even so, the FCC recognized that these expletives might not be "indecent" if they occurred during a "*bona fide* news interview" or if they were "integral" to an artistic or educational work, or essential to informing viewers on a matter of public importance.

In 2004, the FCC decided to replace its former policy of issuing fines for "indecent" language on a "fine per program" basis with a new policy of issuing them for "each licensee's broadcast of the same program as a separate violation." Afterward, Congress amended the relevant federal statute to increase the maximum fine that could be imposed by the FCC from $32,000 to $325,000. As a result of these two developments, the cost of a fine for broadcasting any single fleeting expletive, assuming that it was determined to be "indecent", could amount to tens of millions of dollars. For example, in 2004, the FCC imposed $8 million in fines, compared to its imposition of $440,000 in fines in 2003. The Second Circuit's opinion in *FCC v. Fox Television Stations, Inc.,* 613 F.3d 317, 321-325 (2d Cir. 2011), described the preceding facts concerning the FCC's changes in enforcement policy, and notes that the new congressional and FCC policies concerning fines "were in large part caused by" viewer complaints about the 2004 Super Bowl broadcast, "during which Justin Timberlake exposed Janet Jackson's breast for a fraction of a second during their halftime show."

4. *The Fox and ABC Litigation.* Three events triggered the FCC's actions against Fox Television Stations, Inc. and ABC during 2003 that led to the Supreme Court's decision in 2012 to review the FCC's actions and invalidate them on due process grounds. At the 2002 Billboard Music Awards, Cher's acceptance speech included the comment "I've also had my critics for the last 40 years saying that I was on my way out every year. Right. So fuck 'em." At the 2003 Billboard Music Awards, Nicole Richie was presenting an award when she said, "Have you ever tried to get cow shit out of a Prada purse? It's not so fucking simple." Fox was the broadcaster for both shows. By contrast, ABC's broadcast attracted viewer complaints not because of language but because of nudity. In one episode of *NYPD Blue* broadcast in February 2003, a seven-second showing occurred of "the nude buttocks of an adult female character" and "for a moment the side of her breast." The character was "preparing to take a shower" during the scene, and a "moment of awkwardness" was portrayed when a child, playing the son of the female character's boyfriend, entered the bathroom. This "fleeting nudity" in the ABC broadcast, together with the "fleeting expletives" in the Fox broadcasts, were sanctioned by the FCC through the retroactive application of the 2004 *Golden Globes* ruling, even though the Fox and ABC broadcasts predated that ruling. After ABC and Fox challenged the FCC's decisions, the cases were consolidated in what became known as the *Fox I* litigation.

During the first round of litigation in *Fox I*, the Second Circuit ruled that the FCC's new policy was arbitrary and capricious, and it invoked the Administrative Procedure Act as the authority for setting aside the policy. The Court reversed this decision, holding that the FCC's new policy was rational and that the FCC's determination to "look at the patent offensiveness of even isolated uses of sexual and excretory words fits with the context-based approach" approved in *Pacifica*. The Court remanded the case to the Second Circuit to consider the constitutionality of the FCC's new policy. This time, in the *Fox II* litigation, the Second Circuit invalidated the policy on the grounds of vagueness, and emphasized the chilling effect on broadcasters that was produced by the inherent vagueness not only of the three criteria for "patent offensiveness," but also of the "bona fide news" exception and the "artistic integrity" exception.

5. *The 2012 Decision. In FCC v. Fox Television Stations, Inc.,* 567 U.S. 239 (2012) (Fox II), the Court issued a narrow ruling that the FCC had violated due process by its lack of fair notice to Fox and ABC "that a fleeting expletive or a brief shot of nudity could be actionably indecent." With regard to Fox, the FCC had imposed no fine for the two offending broadcasts, and therefore the FCC argued that Fox could not bring a vagueness challenge. However, the Court rejected that argument because the FCC possessed the authority to consider the violation in setting future penalties, and because the wide publicity

of FCC sanctions would cause reputational injury to Fox. As for ABC, which was penalized $1.4 million dollars for the fleeting nudity broadcast, the Court pointed to FCC rulings that found 30 seconds of nudity to be nonactionable, echoing the pre–*Golden Globes* rulings that treated Fox's type of fleeting expletives as nonactionable. The *Fox II* Court observed that because it "resolves these cases on fair notice grounds under the Due Process Clause, it need not address the First Amendment implications of the FCC's indecency policy." After noting the vagueness issue, the Court concluded by saying, "This opinion leaves the Commission free to modify its current indecency policy in light of its determination of the public interest and applicable legal requirements. And it leaves the courts free to review the current policy or any modified policy in light of its content and application."

∼ PROBLEM: ANTIABORTION ADVERTISING ∼

A candidate for Congress, an avid antiabortionist, wishes to run an antiabortion advertisement on evening telecasts. As part of the advertisement, he would show pictures of aborted fetuses alongside pictures of children singing antiabortion songs. A local television station declines to air the advertisement, fearing its effect on children. The station is willing to run the ads after 8:00 p.m. Does the candidate have the right to run the advertisements notwithstanding the station's objections? *See Becker v. Federal Communications Commission*, 95 F.3d 75 (D.C. Cir. 1996).

M. ADVANCING TECHNOLOGY

At the end of the twentieth century, "speech technology" began to change radically. In addition to cable television, which developed much earlier, there were significant developments in regard to the internet and satellite broadcasting. Some of these new technologies, particularly the internet, posed difficult challenges because they contained pornography, obscenity, and other forms of "indecent" material that were easy for children to access.

Courts have struggled with how to fit these new technologies into existing speech frameworks. As *Red Lion* and *Pacifica* demonstrate, the Court has historically distinguished between the printing press (which produces such items as newspapers and handbills), on the one hand, and broadcast technology (i.e., radio and television) on the other. While the courts have always provided strong protections for newspapers and handbills, they have sustained broader regulation of broadcast technology. "New" technologies, like the internet, have forced the Court to reconsider its precedents relating to technology.

Turner Broadcasting System, Inc. v. FCC

512 U.S. 622 (1994)

Justice KENNEDY announced the judgment of the Court and delivered the opinion of the Court, except as to Part III-B.

Sections 4 and 5 of the Cable Television Consumer Protection and Competition Act of 1992 require cable television systems to devote a portion of their channels to the transmission of local broadcast television stations. This case presents the question whether these provisions abridge the freedom of speech or of the press, in violation of the First Amendment.

I

The role of cable television in the Nation's communications system has undergone dramatic change over the past 45 years. With the capacity to carry dozens of channels and import distant programming signals via satellite or microwave relay, today's cable systems are in direct competition with over-the-air broadcasters as an independent source of television programming.

Broadcast and cable television are distinguished by different technologies. Broadcast stations radiate electromagnetic signals from a central transmitting antenna that can be captured by any television set within the antenna's range. Cable systems, by contrast, rely upon a physical, point-to-point connection between a transmission facility and the television sets of individual subscribers. Cable systems make this connection much like telephone companies, using cable or optical fibers strung above ground or buried in ducts to reach the homes or businesses of subscribers. The construction of this physical infrastructure entails the use of public rights-of-way and easements and often results in the disruption of traffic on streets and other public property. As a result, the cable medium may depend for its very existence upon express permission from local governing authorities.

Cable technology affords two principal benefits over broadcast. First, it eliminates the signal interference sometimes encountered in over-the-air broadcasting and thus gives viewers undistorted reception of broadcast stations. Second, it is capable of transmitting many more channels than are available through broadcasting, giving subscribers access to far greater programming variety. Newer systems can carry hundreds of channels.

The cable television industry includes both cable operators (those who own the physical cable network and transmit the cable signal to the viewer) and cable programmers (those who produce television programs and sell or license them to cable operators). Although cable operators may create some of their own programming, most of their programming is drawn from outside sources including not only local or distant broadcast stations, but also the many national and regional cable programming networks that have emerged in recent years, such as CNN, MTV, ESPN, TNT, C-SPAN, The Family Channel, Nickelodeon, Arts and Entertainment,

The Discovery Channel, American Movie Classics, The Learning Channel, and The Weather Channel. The cable system functions, in essence, as a conduit for the speech of others, transmitting it on a continuous and unedited basis to subscribers. In contrast to commercial broadcast stations, which transmit signals at no charge to viewers and generate revenues by selling time to advertisers, cable systems charge subscribers a monthly fee for the right to receive cable programming and rely to a lesser extent on advertising. Cable subscribers choose the stations they will receive by selecting among various plans, or "tiers," of cable service.

In 1992, Congress enacted the Cable Television Consumer Protection and Competition Act of 1992. Section 4 requires carriage of "local commercial television stations," defined to include all full power television broadcasters, other than those qualifying as "noncommercial educational" stations under §5, that operate within the same television market as the cable system. Subject to a few exceptions, a cable operator may not charge a fee for carrying broadcast signals in fulfillment of its must-carry obligations. Section 5 of the Act imposes similar requirements regarding the carriage of local public broadcast television stations, referred to in the Act as local "noncommercial educational television stations." Appellants are numerous cable programmers and cable operators. The District Court upheld the must-carry provisions. We noted probable jurisdiction.

II

Cable programmers and cable operators engage in and transmit speech, and they are entitled to the protection of the speech and press provisions of the First Amendment. Through "original programming or by exercising editorial discretion over which stations or programs to include in its repertoire," cable programmers and operators "seek to communicate messages on a wide variety of topics and in a wide variety of formats." *Los Angeles v. Preferred Communications, Inc.*, 476 U.S. 488 (1986). By requiring cable systems to set aside a portion of their channels for local broadcasters, the must-carry rules regulate cable speech in two respects: they reduce the number of channels over which cable operators exercise unfettered control, and they render it more difficult for cable programmers to compete for carriage on the remaining channels.

Cable television does not suffer from the inherent limitations that characterize the broadcast medium. Indeed, given the rapid advances in fiber optics and digital compression technology, soon there may be no practical limitation on the number of speakers who may use the cable medium. Nor is there any danger of physical interference between two cable speakers attempting to share the same channel. In light of these fundamental technological differences, application of the more relaxed standard of scrutiny adopted in *Red Lion* and the other broadcast cases is inapt when determining the First Amendment validity of cable regulation.

The must-carry rules, on their face, impose burdens and confer benefits without reference to the content of speech. The provisions interfere with cable operators' editorial discretion by compelling them to offer carriage to a certain minimum number of broadcast stations. The must-carry provisions also burden cable programmers by reducing the number of channels for which they can compete. But, again, this burden is unrelated to content, for it extends to all cable programmers irrespective of the programming they choose to offer viewers. And finally, the privileges conferred by the must-carry provisions are also unrelated to content. The rules benefit all full power broadcasters who request carriage — be they commercial or noncommercial, independent or network affiliated, English or Spanish language, religious or secular — provided only that the broadcaster operates within the same television market as a cable system.

The must-carry provisions distinguish between speakers in the television programming market based only upon the manner in which speakers transmit their messages to viewers, and not upon the messages they carry: Broadcasters, which transmit over the airwaves, are favored, while cable programmers, which do not, are disfavored.

Appellants contend that the must-carry regulations are content based because Congress' purpose in enacting them was to promote speech of a favored content. Our review of the Act and its various findings persuades us that Congress' overriding objective in enacting must-carry was not to favor programming of a particular subject matter, viewpoint, or format, but rather to preserve access to free television programming for the 40 percent of Americans without cable. Congress explained that because cable systems and broadcast stations compete for local advertising revenue, and because cable operators have a vested financial interest in favoring their affiliated programmers over broadcast stations, cable operators have a built-in "economic incentive to delete, reposition, or not carry local broadcast signals." Congress concluded that absent a requirement that cable systems carry the signals of local broadcast stations, the continued availability of free local broadcast television would be threatened. Congress sought to avoid the elimination of broadcast television because "there is a substantial governmental interest in promoting the continued availability of such free television programming, especially for viewers who are unable to afford other means of receiving programming."

Appellants maintain that the must-carry provisions trigger strict scrutiny because they compel cable operators to transmit speech not of their choosing. *See Miami Herald Publishing Co. v. Tornillo*, 418 U.S. 241 (1974); *Pacific Gas & Electric v. Public Utilities Commn.*, 475 U.S. 1 (1986). *Tornillo* and *Pacific Gas & Electric* do not control this case. First, unlike the access rules struck down in those cases, the must-carry rules are content neutral in application. Second, appellants do not suggest that must-carry will force cable operators to alter their own messages to respond to the broadcast programming they are required to carry. Finally, although a daily newspaper and a cable operator both may enjoy monopoly status in a given locale, the cable operator exercises far greater control over access to the relevant medium. Simply by virtue of its ownership of the essential pathway for cable speech, a cable operator can prevent its subscribers from obtaining access to programming it chooses to exclude. The First Amendment does not disable the government from taking steps to ensure that private interests not restrict, through physical control of a critical pathway of communication, the free flow of information and ideas. It would be error to conclude that the First Amendment mandates strict scrutiny for any speech regulation that applies to one medium (or a subset thereof) but not others. The must-carry provisions are justified by special characteristics of the cable medium: the bottleneck monopoly power exercised by cable operators and the dangers this power poses to the viability of broadcast television. Nor does it appear, that other media—in particular, media that transmit video programming such as MMDS multichannel multipoint distribution and SMATV satellite master antenna television—are subject to bottleneck monopoly control, or pose a demonstrable threat to the survival of broadcast television.

III

A

In sum, the must-carry provisions do not pose such inherent dangers to free expression, or present such potential for censorship or manipulation, as to justify application of the most exacting level of First Amendment scrutiny. The appropriate standard by which to evaluate the constitutionality of must-carry is the intermediate level of scrutiny applicable to content-neutral restrictions that impose an incidental burden on speech. To satisfy this standard, the requirement of narrow tailoring is satisfied "so long as the regulation promotes a substantial government interest that would be achieved less effectively absent the regulation." *Ward*, 491 U.S. at 799. Narrow tailoring in this context requires that the means chosen do not "burden substantially more speech than is necessary to further the government's legitimate interests."

Congress declared that the must-carry provisions serve three interrelated interests: (1) preserving the benefits of free, over-the-air local broadcast television, (2) promoting the widespread dissemination of information from a multiplicity of sources, and (3) promoting fair competition in the market for television programming. None of these interests is related to the "suppression of free expression," or to the content of any speakers' messages. We have no difficulty concluding that each of them is an important governmental interest. Nearly 40 percent of American households still rely on broadcast stations as their exclusive source of television programming. And as we said in *Capital Cities Cable, Inc. v. Crisp*, "protecting noncable households from loss of regular television broadcasting service due to competition from cable systems" is an important federal interest. 467 U.S. at 714. Likewise, assuring that the public has access to a multiplicity of information sources is a governmental purpose of the highest order, for it promotes values central to the First Amendment. Finally, the Government's interest in eliminating restraints on fair competition is always substantial, even when the individuals or entities subject to particular regulations are engaged in expressive activity protected by the First Amendment.

B

When the Government defends a regulation on speech as a means to redress past harms or prevent anticipated harms, it must demonstrate that the recited harms are real, not merely conjectural, and that the regulation will in fact alleviate these harms in a direct and material way. We are unable to conclude that the Government has satisfied either inquiry. Because there are genuine issues of material fact still to be resolved on this record, we hold that the District Court erred in granting summary judgment in favor of the Government.

The judgment below is vacated, and the case is remanded for further proceedings consistent with this opinion.

It is so ordered.

Justice STEVENS, *concurring in part* and *concurring in the judgment.*

Because I am in substantial agreement with Justice Kennedy's analysis of the case, I concur in the judgment.

Justice O'CONNOR, with whom Justice SCALIA and Justice GINSBURG join, and with whom Justice THOMAS joins as to Parts I and III, *concurring in part* and *dissenting in part.*

Under the First Amendment, it is normally not within the government's power to decide who may speak and who may not, at least on private property or in traditional public fora. Looking at the statute at issue, I cannot avoid the conclusion that its preference for broadcasters over cable programmers is justified with reference to content. Preferences for diversity of viewpoints, for localism, for educational programming, and for news and public affairs all make reference to content. Content-based speech restrictions are generally unconstitutional unless they are narrowly tailored to a compelling state interest. The interest in localism, either in the dissemination of opinions held by the listeners' neighbors or in the reporting of events that have to do with the local community, cannot be described as "compelling" for the purposes of the compelling state interest test. It is a legitimate interest, perhaps even an important one — certainly the government can foster it by providing subsidies from the public fisc — but it does not rise to the level necessary to justify content-based speech restrictions. It is for private speakers and listeners, not for the government, to decide what fraction of their news and entertainment ought to be of a local character and what fraction ought to be of a national (or international) one. The interests in public affairs programming and educational programming seem somewhat weightier, though it is a difficult question whether they are compelling enough to justify restricting other sorts of speech. Even assuming, arguendo, that the Government could set some channels aside for educational or news programming, the Act is insufficiently tailored to this goal. To benefit the educational broadcasters, the Act burdens more than just the cable entertainment programmers. It equally burdens CNN, C-SPAN, the Discovery Channel, the New Inspirational Network, and other channels with as much claim as PBS to being educational or related to public affairs. Even if the Government can restrict entertainment in order to benefit supposedly more valuable speech, I do not think the restriction can extend to other speech that is as valuable as the speech being benefited. My conclusion that the must-carry rules are content based leads me to conclude that they are an impermissible restraint on the cable operators' editorial discretion as well as on the cable programmers' speech.

Notes

1. *Following Remand.* When *Turner* came back from remand, the Court upheld the must-carry provisions. *Turner Broadcasting System, Inc. v. FCC,* 520 U.S. 180 (1997).

2. *Content Regulation of Cable Television. Denver Area Educational Telecommunications Consortium, Inc. v. FCC,* 518 U.S. 727 (1996), involved the Cable Television Consumer Protection and Competition Act of 1992, which regulated cable broadcasting of "patently offensive," sex-related material. The Act applied to programs known as "leased access channels" and "public, educational, or governmental channels" that carry programs prepared by those given special cable system access rights. Section 10(a) of the Act allowed cable system operators to prohibit the broadcasting of "programming" that the "operator reasonably believes describes or depicts sexual or excretory activities or organs in a patently offensive manner" over "leased access" channels. Section 10(c) allowed cable operators to impose similar restrictions on public access channels. The remaining provision required cable system operators to segregate certain "patently offensive" programming, to place it on a single channel, and to block that channel from viewer access unless the viewer requests access in advance and in writing. The Court upheld Section 10(a), but struck down the other two provisions:

> As for §10(a), the importance of the interest at stake here—protecting children from exposure to patently offensive depictions of sex; the accommodation of the interests of programmers in maintaining access channels and of cable operators in editing the contents of their channels; and the flexibility inherent in an approach that permits private cable operators to make editorial decisions, lead us to conclude that §10(a) is a sufficiently tailored response to an extraordinarily important problem. The permissive nature of the provision, coupled with its viewpoint-neutral application, is a constitutionally permissible way to protect children from the type of sexual material that concerned Congress.
>
> As for §10(c), there are four important differences. First, cable operators have traditionally agreed to reserve channel capacity for public, governmental, and educational channels as part of the consideration they give municipalities that award them cable

franchises. Unlike §10(a) therefore, §10(c) does not restore to cable operators editorial rights that they once had, and the countervailing First Amendment interest is nonexistent, or at least much diminished. Second, municipalities generally provide in their cable franchising agreements for an access channel manager who can set programming policy and approve or disapprove particular programming services. Third, the existence of a system aimed at encouraging and securing programming that the community considers valuable strongly suggests that a "cable operator's veto" is less likely necessary to achieve the statute's basic objective, protecting children. Finally, the public/nonprofit programming control systems now in place would normally avoid, minimize, or eliminate any child-related problems concerning "patently offensive" programming. The upshot, in respect to the public access channels, is a law that could radically change present programming-related relationships among local community and nonprofit supervising boards and access managers, which relationships are established through municipal law, regulation, and contract. In doing so, it would not significantly restore editorial rights of cable operators, but would greatly increase the risk that certain categories of programming (say, borderline offensive programs) will not appear.

As for the segregate/block/written-access provisions, the record does not explain why, under the new Act, blocking alone—without written access requests—adequately protects children from exposure to regular sex-dedicated channels, but cannot adequately protect those children from programming on similarly sex-dedicated channels that are leased. We cannot find that the "segregate and block" restrictions on speech are a narrowly, or reasonably, tailored effort to protect children. Rather, they are overly restrictive, "sacrificing" important First Amendment interests for too "speculative a gain." For that reason they are not consistent with the First Amendment.

Justice Kennedy, joined by Justice Ginsburg, argued that all three of the challenged sections were unconstitutional because they regulate a "public forum of unlimited character" and therefore are "subject to the highest scrutiny" and "survive only if they are narrowly drawn to achieve a compelling state interest." Although he agreed that Congress has a "compelling interest in protecting children from indecent speech," he concluded that the "Government has no legitimate interest in making access channels pristine," thereby depriving adults of access to the information. Chief Justice Rehnquist, Justice Scalia, and Justice Thomas would have upheld all three provisions. Justice O'Connor would have upheld §10(c).

3. *Dial-a-Porn. Sable Communications of California, Inc. v. FCC,* 492 U.S. 115 (1989), involved a challenge to the constitutionality of §223(b) of the Communications Act of 1934, which imposed a ban on indecent as well as obscene interstate commercial telephone messages. The challenge was brought by a company that offered sexually oriented, prerecorded telephone messages (also known as "dial-a-porn") for a fee. The Court struck down the law: "There is a compelling interest in protecting the physical and psychological well-being of minors. The FCC determined that its credit card, access code, and scrambling rules were a satisfactory solution to the problem of keeping indecent dial-a-porn messages out of the reach of minors. Because the statute's denial of adult access far exceeds that which is necessary to limit the access of minors to such messages, we hold that the ban does not survive constitutional scrutiny."

Reno v. American Civil Liberties Union

521 U.S. 844 (1997)

Justice STEVENS delivered the opinion of the Court.

At issue is the constitutionality of two statutory provisions enacted to protect minors from "indecent" and "patently offensive" communications on the Internet. Notwithstanding the legitimacy and importance of the congressional goal of protecting children from harmful materials, we agree with the three-judge District Court that the statute abridges "the freedom of speech" protected by the First Amendment.

I

The District Court made extensive findings of fact. The findings describe the character and the dimensions of the Internet, the availability of sexually explicit material in that medium, and the problems confronting age verification for recipients of Internet communications.

The Internet

The Internet is an international network of interconnected computers. It is the outgrowth of what began in 1969 as a military program called "ARPANET," which was designed to enable computers operated by the military, defense contractors, and universities conducting defense-related research to communicate with one another by redundant channels even if some portions of the network were damaged in a war. While the ARPANET no longer exists, it provided an example for the development of a number of civilian networks that, eventually linking with each other, now enable tens of millions of people to communicate with one another and to access vast amounts of information from around the world. The Internet is "a unique and wholly new medium of worldwide human communication."

The Internet has experienced "extraordinary growth." The number of "host" computers—those that store information and relay communications—increased from about 300 in 1981 to approximately 9,400,000 by the time of the trial in 1996. Roughly 60% of these hosts are located in the United States. About 40 million people used the Internet at the time of trial, a number that is expected to mushroom to 200 million by 1999. Individuals can obtain access to the Internet from many different sources, generally hosts themselves or entities with a host affiliation. Most colleges and universities provide access for their students and faculty; many corporations provide their employees access through an office network; many communities and local libraries provide free access; and an increasing number of "computer coffee shops" provide access for a small hourly fee. Several major national "online services" such as America Online, CompuServe, the Microsoft Network, and Prodigy offer access to their extensive proprietary networks as well as a link to the much larger resources of the Internet. These commercial online services had almost 12 million individual subscribers at the time of trial.

Anyone with access to the Internet may take advantage of a wide variety of communication and information retrieval methods. These methods are constantly evolving and difficult to categorize precisely. As presently constituted, those most relevant are e-mail, automatic mailing list services ("mail exploders," sometimes referred to as "listservs"), "newsgroups," "chat rooms," and the "World Wide Web." All of these methods can be used to transmit text; most can transmit sound, pictures, and moving video images. Taken together, these tools constitute a unique medium—known as "cyberspace"—located in no particular geographical location but available to anyone, anywhere in the world, with access to the Internet. E-mail enables an individual to send an electronic message—generally akin to a note or letter—to another individual or to a group of addressees. The message is generally stored electronically, sometimes waiting for the recipient to check her "mailbox" and sometimes making its receipt known through some type of prompt. A mail exploder is a sort of e-mail group. Subscribers can send messages to a common e-mail address, which then forwards the message to the group's subscribers. Newsgroups also serve groups of regular participants, but these postings may be read by others as well. There are thousands of such groups, each serving to foster an exchange of information or opinion on a particular topic running the gamut from, say, the music of Wagner to Balkan politics to AIDS prevention to the Chicago Bulls. About 100,000 new messages are posted every day. In most newsgroups, postings are automatically purged at regular intervals. Two or more individuals wishing to communicate more immediately can enter a chat room to engage in real-time dialogue—in other words, by typing messages to one another that appear almost immediately on the others' computer screens. At any given time "tens of thousands of users are engaging in conversations on a huge range of subjects." It is "no exaggeration to conclude that the content on the Internet is as diverse as human thought."

The best known category of communication over the Internet is the World Wide Web, which allows users to search for and retrieve information stored in remote computers, as well as to communicate back to designated sites. In concrete terms, the Web consists of a vast number of documents stored in different computers all over the world. Some of these documents are simply files containing information. However, more elaborate documents, known as Web "pages," are also prevalent. Each has its own address—"rather like a telephone number." webpages frequently contain information and sometimes allow the viewer to communicate with the page's (or "site's") author. They generally also contain "links" to other documents created by that site's author or to other related sites. Typically, the links are either blue or underlined text—sometimes images.

Navigating the Web is relatively straightforward. A user may either type the address of a known page or enter one or more keywords into a commercial "search engine" in an effort to locate sites on a subject of interest. A particular webpage may contain the information sought by the "surfer," or, through its links, it may be an avenue to other documents located anywhere on the Internet. Users generally explore a given webpage, or move to another, by clicking a computer "mouse" on one of the page's icons or links. Access to most webpages is freely available, but some allow access only to those who have purchased the right from a commercial provider. The Web is thus comparable, from the readers' viewpoint, to both a vast library including millions of readily available and indexed publications and a sprawling mall offering goods and services. From the publishers' point of view, it constitutes a vast platform from which to address and hear from a worldwide audience of millions of readers, viewers, researchers, and buyers. Any person or organization with a computer connected to the Internet can "publish" information. Publishers include government agencies, educational institutions, commercial entities, advocacy groups, and individuals. Publishers may either make their material available to the entire pool of Internet users, or confine access to a selected group, such as those willing to pay for the privilege. "No single organization controls membership in the Web, nor is there any centralized point from which individual Web sites or services can be blocked from the Web."

Sexually Explicit Material

Sexually explicit material on the Internet includes text, pictures, and chat and "extends from the modestly titillating to the hardest-core." These files are created, named, and posted in the same manner as material that is not sexually explicit, and may be accessed either deliberately or unintentionally during the course of an imprecise search. "Once a provider posts its content on the Internet, it cannot prevent that content from entering any community." Thus, for example, "when the UCR/California Museum of Photography posts to its Web site nudes by Edward Weston and Robert Mapplethorpe to announce that its new exhibit will travel to Baltimore and New York City, those images are available not only in Los Angeles, Baltimore, and New York City, but also in Cincinnati, Mobile, or Beijing—wherever Internet users live."

Some of the communications over the Internet that originate in foreign countries are also sexually explicit. Though such material is widely available, users seldom encounter such content accidentally. "A document's title or a description of the document will usually appear before the document itself and in many cases the user will receive detailed information about a site's content before he or she need take the step to access the document. Almost all sexually explicit images are preceded by warnings as to the content." For that reason, the "odds are slim" that a user would enter a sexually explicit site by accident. Unlike communications received by radio or television, "the receipt of information on the Internet requires a series of affirmative steps more deliberate and directed than merely turning a dial. A child requires some sophistication and some ability to read to retrieve material and thereby to use the Internet unattended."

Systems have been developed to help parents control the material that may be available on a home computer with Internet access. A system may either limit a computer's access to an approved list of sources that have been identified as containing no adult material, it may block designated inappropriate sites, or it may attempt to block messages containing identifiable objectionable features. "Although parental control software currently can screen for certain suggestive words or for known sexually explicit sites, it cannot now screen for sexually explicit images." Nevertheless, the evidence indicates that "a reasonably effective method by which parents can prevent their children from accessing sexually explicit and other material which parents may believe is inappropriate for their children will soon be available."

II

The Telecommunications Act of 1996 was an unusually important legislative enactment. Its primary purpose was to reduce regulation and encourage "the rapid deployment of new telecommunications technologies." The major components of the statute have nothing to do with the Internet; they were designed to promote competition in the local telephone service market, the multichannel video market, and the market for over-the-air broadcasting. The Act includes seven Titles, six of which are the product of extensive committee hearings and the subject of discussion in reports prepared by Committees of the Senate and the House of Representatives. By contrast, Title V—known as the "Communications Decency Act of 1996" (CDA)—contains provisions that were either added in executive committee after the hearings were concluded or as amendments offered during floor debate on the legislation. An amendment offered in the Senate was the source of the two statutory provisions challenged in this case. They are informally described as the "indecent transmission" provision and the "patently offensive display" provision.

The first, 47 U.S.C.A. §223(a) (Supp. 1997), prohibits the knowing transmission of obscene or indecent messages to any recipient under 18 years of age. It provides in pertinent part:

>   (a) Whoever—
>   (1) in interstate or foreign communications—
>   (B) by means of a telecommunications device knowingly—
>   (i) makes, creates, or solicits, and
>   (ii) initiates the transmission of,
>   any comment, request, suggestion, proposal, image, or other communication which is obscene or indecent, knowing that the recipient of the communication is under 18 years of age, regardless of whether the maker of such communication placed the call or initiated the communication;
>   (2) knowingly permits any telecommunications facility under his control to be used for any activity prohibited by paragraph (1) with the intent that it be used for such activity,
>   "shall be fined under Title 18, or imprisoned not more than two years, or both.

The second provision, §223(d), prohibits the knowing sending or displaying of patently offensive messages in a manner that is available to a person under 18 years of age. It provides:

> (d) Whoever—
>> (1) in interstate or foreign communications knowingly—
>>> (A) uses an interactive computer service to send to a specific person or persons under 18 years of age, or
>>> (B) uses any interactive computer service to display in a manner available to a person under 18 years of age,
>> any comment, request, suggestion, proposal, image, or other communication that, in context, depicts or describes, in terms patently offensive as measured by contemporary community standards, sexual or excretory activities or organs, regardless of whether the user of such service placed the call or initiated the communication; or
>> (2) knowingly permits any telecommunications facility under such person's control to be used for an activity prohibited by paragraph (1) with the intent that it be used for such activity, shall be fined under Title 18, or imprisoned not more than two years, or both.

The breadth of these prohibitions is qualified by two affirmative defenses. One covers those who take "good faith, reasonable, effective, and appropriate actions" to restrict access by minors to the prohibited communications. §223(e)(5)(A). The other covers those who restrict access to covered material by requiring certain designated forms of age proof, such as a verified credit card or an adult identification number or code. §223(e)(5)(B).

A three-judge district court entered a preliminary injunction against enforcement of both of the challenged provisions. In arguing for reversal, the Government contends that the CDA is plainly constitutional under three of our prior decisions: (1) *Ginsberg v. New York*, 390 U.S. 629 (1968); (2) *FCC v. Pacifica Foundation*, 438 U.S. 726 (1978); and (3) *Renton v. Playtime Theatres, Inc.*, 475 U.S. 41 (1986). A close look at these cases, however, raises doubts concerning the constitutionality of the CDA.

In *Ginsberg*, we upheld the constitutionality of a New York statute that prohibited selling to minors under 17 years of age material that was considered obscene as to them even if not obscene as to adults. We rejected defendant's broad submission that "the scope of the constitutional freedom of expression secured to a citizen to read or see material concerned with sex cannot be made to depend on whether the citizen is an adult or a minor." In rejecting that contention, we relied not only on the State's independent interest in the well-being of its youth, but also on our consistent recognition of the principle that "the parents' claim to authority in their own household to direct the rearing of their children is basic in the structure of our society." In four important respects, the statute upheld in *Ginsberg* was narrower than the CDA. First, we noted in *Ginsberg* that "the prohibition against sales to minors does not bar parents who so desire from purchasing the magazines for their children." Under the CDA, by contrast, neither the parents' consent—nor even their participation—in the communication would avoid application of the statute. Second, the New York statute applied only to commercial transactions, whereas the CDA contains no such limitation. Third, the New York statute cabined its definition of material that is harmful to minors with the requirement that it be "utterly without redeeming social importance for minors." The CDA fails to provide us with any definition of the term "indecent" as used in §223(a)(1) and, importantly, omits any requirement that the "patently offensive" material covered by §223(d) lack serious literary, artistic, political, or scientific value. Fourth, the New York statute defined a minor as a person under the age of 17, whereas the CDA, in applying to all those under 18 years, includes an additional year.

In *Pacifica*, we upheld a declaratory order of the Federal Communications Commission, holding that the broadcast of a recording of a 12-minute monologue entitled "Filthy Words" that had previously been delivered to a live audience "could have been the subject of administrative sanctions." The Commission found that the repetitive use of certain words referring to excretory or sexual activities or organs "in an afternoon broadcast when children are in the audience was patently offensive" and concluded that the monologue was indecent "as broadcast." Respondent did not quarrel with the finding that the afternoon broadcast was patently offensive, but contended that it was not "indecent" within the meaning of the relevant statutes. The plurality stated that the First Amendment does not prohibit all governmental regulation that depends on the content of speech. Accordingly, the availability of constitutional protection for a vulgar and offensive monologue that was not obscene depended on the context of the broadcast. Relying on the premise that "of all forms of communication" broadcasting had received the most limited First Amendment protection, the Court concluded that the ease with which children may obtain access to broadcasts, "coupled with the concerns recognized in *Ginsberg*," justified special treatment of indecent broadcasting. There are significant differences between the order upheld in *Pacifica* and the CDA. First, *Pacifica* targeted a specific broadcast that represented a rather dramatic departure from traditional program content in order to designate when — rather than whether — it would be permissible to air such a program in that particular medium. The CDA's broad categorical prohibitions are not limited to particular times and are not dependent on any evaluation by an agency familiar with the unique characteristics of the Internet. Second, unlike the CDA, the Commission's declaratory order was not punitive. Finally, the Commission's order applied to a medium which as a matter of history had "received the most limited First Amendment protection," in large part because warnings could not adequately protect the listener from unexpected program content. The Internet, however, has no comparable history. Moreover, the District Court found that the risk of encountering indecent material by accident is remote because a series of affirmative steps is required to access specific material.

In *Renton*, we upheld a zoning ordinance that kept adult movie theatres out of residential neighborhoods. The ordinance was aimed, not at the content of the films shown in the theaters, but rather at the "secondary effects" — such as crime and deteriorating property values — that these theaters fostered. According to the Government, the CDA is constitutional because it constitutes a sort of "cyberzoning" on the Internet. But the CDA applies broadly to the entire universe of cyberspace. And the purpose of the CDA is to protect children from the primary effects of "indecent" and "patently offensive" speech, rather than any "secondary" effect of such speech. Thus, the CDA is a content-based blanket restriction on speech, and, as such, cannot be "properly analyzed as a form of time, place, and manner regulation." *See Boos v. Barry*, 485 U.S. 312, 321 (1988).

These precedents, then, surely do not require us to uphold the CDA and are fully consistent with the application of the most stringent review of its provisions.

V

In *Southeastern Promotions, Ltd. v. Conrad*, 420 U.S. 546, 557 (1975), we observed that "each medium of expression may present its own problems." Thus, some of our cases have recognized special justifications for regulation of the broadcast media that are not applicable to other speakers. In these cases, the Court relied on the history of extensive government regulation of the broadcast medium, the scarcity of available frequencies at its inception, and its "invasive" nature.

Those factors are not present in cyberspace. Neither before nor after the enactment of the CDA have the vast democratic fora of the Internet been subject to the type of government supervision and regulation that has attended the broadcast industry.[17] Moreover, the Internet is not as "invasive" as radio or television. The District Court specifically found that "communications over the Internet do not 'invade' an individual's home or appear on one's computer screen unbidden. Users seldom encounter content 'by accident.'" It also found that "almost all sexually explicit images are preceded by warnings as to the content," and [the] "'odds are slim' that a user would come across a sexually explicit sight by accident."

We distinguished *Pacifica* in *Sable*, 492 U.S. at 128. In *Sable*, a company engaged in the business of offering sexually oriented prerecorded telephone messages (dial-a-porn") challenged the constitutionality of an amendment to the Communications Act that imposed a blanket prohibition on indecent as well as obscene interstate commercial telephone messages. We held that the statute was constitutional insofar as it applied to obscene messages but invalid as applied to indecent messages. In attempting to justify the complete ban and criminalization of indecent commercial telephone messages, the Government relied on *Pacifica*, arguing that the ban was necessary to prevent children from gaining access to such messages. We agreed that "there is a compelling interest in protecting the physical and psychological well-being of minors" which extended to shielding them from indecent messages that are not obscene by adult standards, but distinguished *Pacifica* because it did not involve a complete ban and involved a different medium of communication. We explained that "the dial-it medium requires the listener to take affirmative steps to receive the communication." "Placing a

---

17. When *Pacifica* was decided, given that radio stations were allowed to operate only pursuant to federal license, and that Congress had enacted legislation prohibiting licensees from broadcasting indecent speech, there was a risk that members of the radio audience might infer some sort of official or societal approval of whatever was heard over the radio. No such risk attends messages received through the Internet, which is not supervised by any federal agency.

telephone call," we continued, "is not the same as turning on a radio and being taken by surprise by an indecent message."

Finally, unlike the conditions that prevailed when Congress first authorized regulation of the broadcast spectrum, the Internet can hardly be considered a "scarce" expressive commodity. It provides relatively unlimited, low-cost capacity for communication of all kinds. The Government estimates that "as many as 40 million people use the Internet today, and that figure is expected to grow to 200 million by 1999." This dynamic, multifaceted category of communication includes not only traditional print and news services, but also audio, video, and still images, as well as interactive, real-time dialogue. Through the use of chat rooms, any person with a phone line can become a town crier with a voice that resonates farther than it could from any soapbox. Through the use of webpages, mail exploders, and newsgroups, the same individual can become a pamphleteer. As the District Court found, "the content on the Internet is as diverse as human thought." Our cases provide no basis for qualifying the level of First Amendment scrutiny that should be applied to this medium.

Regardless of whether the CDA is so vague that it violates the Fifth Amendment, the many ambiguities concerning the scope of its coverage render it problematic for purposes of the First Amendment. For instance, each of the two parts of the CDA uses a different linguistic form. The first uses the word "indecent" while the second speaks of material that "in context, depicts or describes, in terms patently offensive as measured by contemporary community standards, sexual or excretory activities or organs." Given the absence of a definition of either term, this difference in language will provoke uncertainty among speakers about how the two standards relate to each other and just what they mean. Could a speaker confidently assume that a serious discussion about birth control practices, homosexuality, the First Amendment issues raised by the Appendix to our *Pacifica* opinion, or the consequences of prison rape would not violate the CDA? This uncertainty undermines the likelihood that the CDA has been carefully tailored to the congressional goal of protecting minors from potentially harmful materials.

The vagueness of the CDA is a matter of special concern for two reasons. First, the CDA is a content-based regulation of speech. The vagueness of such a regulation raises special First Amendment concerns because of its obvious chilling effect on free speech. Second, the CDA is a criminal statute. In addition to the opprobrium and stigma of a criminal conviction, the CDA threatens violators with penalties including up to two years in prison for each act of violation. The severity of criminal sanctions may well cause speakers to remain silent rather than communicate even arguably unlawful words, ideas, and images. As a practical matter, this increased deterrent effect, coupled with the "risk of discriminatory enforcement" of vague regulations, poses greater First Amendment concerns than those implicated by the civil regulation reviewed in *Denver Area Ed. Telecommunications Consortium, Inc. v. FCC*, 518 U.S. 727 (1996).

The Government argues that the statute is no more vague than the obscenity standard established in *Miller v. California*, 413 U.S. 15 (1973). But that is not so.

Because the CDA's "patently offensive" standard (and, we assume arguendo, its synonymous "indecent" standard) is one part of the three-prong *Miller* test, the Government reasons, it cannot be unconstitutionally vague. The Government's assertion is incorrect. The second prong of the *Miller* test contains a critical requirement that is omitted from the CDA: that the proscribed material be "specifically defined by the applicable state law." This requirement reduces the vagueness inherent in the open-ended term "patently offensive" as used in the CDA. Moreover, the *Miller* definition is limited to "sexual conduct," whereas the CDA extends also to include (1) "excretory activities" as well as (2) "organs" of both a sexual and excretory nature.

The Government's reasoning is flawed. Just because a definition including three limitations is not vague, it does not follow that one of those limitations, standing by itself, is not vague. Each of *Miller*'s additional two prongs — (1) that, taken as a whole, the material appeal to the "prurient" interest, and (2) that it "lack serious literary, artistic, political, or scientific value" — critically limits the uncertain sweep of the obscenity definition. The second requirement is particularly important because, unlike the "patently offensive" and "prurient interest" criteria, it is not judged by contemporary community standards. This "societal value" requirement, absent in the CDA, allows appellate courts to impose some limitations and regularity on the definition by setting, as a matter of law, a national floor for socially redeeming value. The Government's contention that courts will be able to give such legal limitations to the CDA's standards is belied by *Miller*'s own rationale for having juries determine whether material is "patently offensive" according to community standards: that such questions are essentially ones of *fact*. In contrast to *Miller* and our other previous cases, the CDA thus presents a greater threat of censoring speech that, in fact, falls outside the statute's scope. Given the vague contours of the statute, it unquestionably silences some speakers whose messages would be entitled to constitutional protection. That danger provides further reason for insisting that the statute not be overly broad. The CDA's burden on protected speech cannot be justified if it could be avoided by a more carefully drafted statute. We are persuaded that the CDA lacks the precision that the First Amendment requires when a statute regulates the content of speech. In order to deny minors access to potentially harmful speech, the CDA effectively suppresses a large amount of speech that adults have a constitutional right to receive and to address to one another. That burden on adult speech is unacceptable if less restrictive alternatives would be as effective in achieving the legitimate purpose that the statute was enacted to serve.

In evaluating the free speech rights of adults, "sexual expression which is indecent but not obscene is protected by the First Amendment." *Pacifica* itself admonished that "the fact that society may find speech offensive is not a sufficient reason for suppressing it." It is true that we have repeatedly recognized the governmental interest in protecting children from harmful materials. But that interest does not justify an unnecessarily broad suppression of speech addressed to adults. The Government may not "reduce the adult population to only what is fit for children." *Denver*, 116 S.Ct. at 2393. "Regardless of the strength of the government's interest" in protecting children, "the level of discourse reaching a mailbox simply cannot be limited to that which would be suitable for a sandbox." *Bolger v. Youngs Drug Products Corp.*, 463 U.S. 60, 74 (1983).

The CDA effectively resembles the ban on "dial-a-porn" invalidated in *Sable*. In *Sable*, this Court rejected the argument that we should defer to the congressional judgment that nothing less than a total ban would be effective in preventing enterprising youngsters from gaining access to indecent communications. *Sable* thus made clear that the mere fact that a statutory regulation of speech was enacted for the important purpose of protecting children from exposure to sexually explicit material does not foreclose inquiry into its validity. That inquiry embodies an "over-arching commitment" to make sure that Congress has designed its statute to accomplish its purpose "without imposing an unnecessarily great restriction on speech." In arguing that the CDA does not so diminish adult communication, the Government relies on the incorrect factual premise that prohibiting a transmission whenever it is known that one of its recipients is a minor would not interfere with adult-to-adult communication. This premise is untenable. Given the size of the potential audience for most messages, in the absence of a viable age verification process, the sender must be charged with knowing that one or more minors will likely view it. Knowledge that, for instance, one or more members of a 100-person chat group will be minor—and therefore that it would be a crime to send the group an indecent message—would surely burden communication among adults.

At the time of trial existing technology did not include any effective method for a sender to prevent minors from obtaining access to its communications on the Internet without also denying access to adults. The Court found no effective way to determine the age of a user who is accessing material through e-mail, mail exploders, newsgroups, or chat rooms. The Court also found that it would be prohibitively expensive for noncommercial—as well as some commercial—speakers who have Web sites to verify that their users are adults. These limitations must inevitably curtail a significant amount of adult communication on the Internet. By contrast, the District Court found that "despite its limitations, currently available user-based software suggests that a reasonably effective method by which parents can prevent their children from accessing sexually explicit and other material which parents may believe is inappropriate for their children will soon be widely available."

The breadth of the CDA's coverage is wholly unprecedented. Unlike the regulations upheld in *Ginsberg* and *Pacifica*, the scope of the CDA is not limited to commercial speech or commercial entities. Its open-ended prohibitions embrace all nonprofit entities and individuals posting indecent messages or displaying them on their own computers in the presence of minors. The general, undefined terms "indecent" and "patently offensive" cover large amounts of nonpornographic material with serious educational or other value.[18] Moreover, the "community standards" criterion as applied to the Internet means that any communication available to a nation-wide audience will be judged by the standards of the community most likely to be offended by the message. The regulated subject matter includes any of the seven "dirty words" used in the *Pacifica* monologue, the use of which the Government's expert acknowledged could constitute a felony. It may also extend to discussions about prison rape or safe sexual practices, artistic images that include nude subjects, and arguably the card catalogue of the Carnegie Library.

We need neither accept nor reject the Government's submission that the First Amendment does not forbid a blanket prohibition on all "indecent" and "patently offensive" messages communicated to a 17-year-old—no matter how much value the message may contain and regardless of parental approval. It is clear that the strength of the Government's interest in protecting minors is not equally strong throughout the coverage of this broad statute. Under the CDA, a parent allowing her 17-year-old to use the family computer to obtain information on the Internet that she, in her parental judgment, deems appropriate could face a lengthy prison term. Similarly, a parent who sent his 17-year-old college freshman information on birth control via e-mail could be incarcerated even though neither he, his child, nor anyone in their home community, found the material "indecent" or "patently offensive," if the college town's community thought otherwise.

The breadth of this content-based restriction of speech imposes an especially heavy burden on the Government to explain why a less restrictive provision would not be as effective as the CDA. It has not done so. The arguments in this Court have referred to possible alternatives such as requiring that indecent material be "tagged" in a way that facilitates parental control of material coming into their homes, making exceptions for messages with artistic or educational value, providing some tolerance for parental choice, and regulating some portions of the Internet—such as commercial web sites—differently than others, such as chat rooms. In light of the absence of any detailed findings by the Congress, or even hearings addressing the special problems of the CDA, we are persuaded that the CDA is not narrowly tailored if that requirement has any meaning at all.

In an attempt to curtail the CDA's facial overbreadth, the Government advances three additional arguments for sustaining the Act's affirmative prohibitions. The Government first contends that, even though the CDA effectively censors discourse on many of the Internet's modalities—such as chat groups, newsgroups, and mail exploders—it is nonetheless constitutional because it provides a "reasonable opportunity" for speakers to engage in the restricted speech

---

18. Transmitting obscenity and child pornography, whether via the Internet or other means, is already illegal under federal law for both adults and juveniles. *See* 18 U.S.C. §§1464-1465 (criminalizing obscenity); §2251 (criminalizing child pornography).

on the World Wide Web. This argument is unpersuasive because the CDA regulates speech on the basis of its content. A "time, place, and manner" analysis is therefore inapplicable. It is thus immaterial whether such speech would be feasible on the Web (which, as the Government's own expert acknowledged, would cost up to $10,000 if the speaker's interests were not accommodated by an existing Web site, not including costs for database management and age verification). The Government's position is equivalent to arguing that a statute could ban leaflets on certain subjects as long as individuals are free to publish books. "One is not to have the exercise of his liberty of expression in appropriate places abridged on the plea that it may be exercised in some other place." The Government also asserts that the "knowledge" requirement of both §§223(a) and (d), especially when coupled with the "specific child" element found in §223(d), saves the CDA from overbreadth. Because both sections prohibit the dissemination of indecent messages only to persons known to be under 18, the Government argues, it does not require transmitters to "refrain from communicating indecent material to adults; they need only refrain from disseminating such materials to persons they know to be under 18." This argument ignores the fact that most Internet forums—including chat rooms, newsgroups, mail exploders, and the Web—are open to all comers. The Government's assertion that the knowledge requirement somehow protects the communications of adults is therefore untenable. It would confer broad powers of censorship, in the form of a "heckler's veto," upon any opponent of indecent speech who might simply log on and inform the would-be discoursers that his 17-year-old child—a "specific person under 18 years of age"—would be present. Finally, we find no textual support for the Government's submission that material having scientific, educational, or other redeeming social value will necessarily fall outside the CDA's "patently offensive" and "indecent" prohibitions.

The Government's three remaining arguments focus on the defenses provided in §223(e)(5). First, relying on the "good faith, reasonable, effective, and appropriate actions" provision, the Government suggests that "tagging" provides a defense that saves the constitutionality of the Act. The suggestion assumes that transmitters may encode their indecent communications in a way that would indicate their contents, thus permitting recipients to block their reception with appropriate software. It is the requirement that the good faith action must be "effective" that makes this defense illusory. The Government recognizes that its proposed screening software does not currently exist. Even if it did, there is no way to know whether a potential recipient will actually block the encoded material. Without the impossible knowledge that every guardian in America is screening for the "tag," the transmitter could not reasonably rely on its action to be "effective."

For its arguments concerning defenses, the Government relies on the latter half of §223(e)(5), which applies when the transmitter has restricted access by requiring use of a verified credit card or adult identification. Such verification is not only technologically available but actually is used by commercial providers of sexually explicit material. These providers, therefore, would be protected by the defense. Under the findings of the District Court, it is not economically feasible for most noncommercial speakers to employ such verification. Accordingly, this defense would not significantly narrow the statute's burden on noncommercial speech. Even with respect to the commercial pornographers that would be protected by the defense, the Government failed to adduce any evidence that these verification techniques actually preclude minors from posing as adults. Given that the risk of criminal sanctions "hovers over each content provider, like the proverbial sword of Damocles," the District Court correctly refused to rely on unproven future technology to save the statute. The Government thus failed to prove that the proffered defense would significantly reduce the heavy burden on adult speech produced by the prohibition on offensive displays. The CDA places an unacceptably heavy burden on protected speech, and that the defenses do not constitute the sort of "narrow tailoring" that will save an otherwise patently invalid unconstitutional provision. In *Sable,* we remarked that the speech restriction at issue there amounted to "burning the house to roast the pig." The CDA, casting a far darker shadow over free speech, threatens to torch a large segment of the Internet community.

Appellees do not challenge the application of the statute to obscene speech, which, they acknowledge, can be banned totally because it enjoys no First Amendment protection. Therefore, we will sever the term "or indecent" from the statute, leaving the rest of §223(a) standing. In no other respect, however, can §223(a) or §223(d) be saved by such a textual surgery.

In this Court, though not in the District Court, the Government asserts that—in addition to its interest in protecting children—its "equally significant" interest in fostering the growth of the Internet provides an independent basis for upholding the constitutionality of the CDA. The Government apparently assumes that the unregulated availability of "indecent" and "patently offensive" material on the Internet is driving countless citizens away from the medium because of the risk of exposing themselves or their children to harmful material. We find this argument unpersuasive. The dramatic expansion of this new marketplace of ideas contradicts the factual basis of this contention. The growth of the Internet has been and continues to be phenomenal. As a matter of constitutional tradition, in the absence of evidence to the contrary, we presume that governmental regulation of the content of speech is more likely to interfere with the free exchange of ideas than to encourage it. The interest in encouraging freedom of expression in a democratic society outweighs any theoretical but unproven benefit of censorship.

For the foregoing reasons, the judgment of the district court is affirmed.

It is so ordered.

Justice O'CONNOR, with whom THE CHIEF JUSTICE joins, *concurring in the judgment in part* and *dissenting in part.*

I view the Communications Decency Act of 1996 (CDA) as little more than an attempt by Congress to create "adult zones" on the Internet. Our precedent indicates that the creation of such zones can be constitutionally sound. It is possible to construct barriers in cyberspace and use them to screen for identity, making cyberspace more like the physical world and, consequently, more amenable to zoning laws. This transformation of cyberspace is already underway. Internet speakers have begun to zone cyberspace itself through the use of "gateway" technology. Such technology requires Internet users to enter information about themselves—perhaps an adult identification number or a credit card number—before they can access certain areas of cyberspace. Gateway technology is not available to all Web speakers, and is just now becoming technologically feasible for chat rooms and USENET newsgroups. Without such technology, cyberspace still remains largely unzoned—and unzoneable. Although the prospects for the eventual zoning of the Internet appear promising, we must evaluate the constitutionality of the CDA as it applies to the Internet as it exists today. Given the present state of cyberspace, I agree that the "display" provision cannot pass muster.

Notes and Questions

1. *The Section 230 Shield.* Section 230 of the Communications Decency Act draws a distinction between "publishers" (who are aware of the content that they are distributing and therefore potentially liable for that content) and "platforms" (which distribute information created by others). Section 230 was designed to insulate platforms from liability even if they engage in some content moderation on their websites. The bottom line is that social media platforms generally are not held liable, for example, for defamatory content that is posted by others on their platforms. After Twitter flagged some of President Trump's tweets for fact-checking, he issued an executive order questioning whether they were engaged in good faith moderation of content, and directed the Department of Commerce, the FCC and the Federal Trade Commission to look into these issues. He expressed concern that social media companies were flagging content as inappropriate, "making unannounced the unexplained changes to company policies that have the effect of disfavoring certain viewpoints; and deleting content and entire accounts with no warning, no rationale, and no recourse."

2. *The FCC and the Internet.* In March 2004, the Federal Communications Commission moved to crack down on offensive broadcasts, referring to the use of indecent curse words. Also, the FCC proposed fines against Howard Stern for his discussion of sexual practices with a couple who were allegedly having sex on the air. Would such communications be illegal on the internet?

3. *Is the FCC Becoming Irrelevant?* Since the decision in *Reno*, communications technology has continued to advance. For example, satellite radio networks have developed free of FCC control, and now have millions of subscribers. Following the FCC proposal, Howard Stern left broadcast radio for a satellite station. So, are the FCC and the Court's broadcast decisions (e.g., *Red Lion*) becoming

increasingly irrelevant? Does it continue to make sense to distinguish between internet and broadcast communications?

4. *The Child Online Protection Act.* After *Reno,* Congress enacted the Child Online Protection Act (COPA) in an effort to respond to the *Reno* Court's criticisms of the CDA. COPA made it illegal, "knowingly and with knowledge of the character of the material," to make "any communication for commercial purposes that is available to any minor and that includes any material that is harmful to minors." Congress adapted the three-part *Miller* obscenity test, but adapted it for minors.* Although *Ashcroft v. American Civil Liberties Union (Ashcroft I),* 535 U.S. 564 (2002), partially upheld COPA, the law was struck down in *American Civil Liberties Union v. Mukasey,* 534 F.3d 181 (3d Cir. 2008), *cert. denied,* 555 U.S. 1137 (2009). Noting that COPA criminalizes a category of speech that is harmful to minors but that is constitutionally protected for adults, the court applied strict scrutiny. Although the court held that the state has a compelling interest in protecting the physical and psychological well-being of minors, as well as in protecting minors from exposure to harmful material on the internet, it concluded that COPA was not narrowly tailored to effectuate its purpose. COPA defined the term *minor* so broadly as to encompass "an infant, a five-year old, or a person just shy of age seventeen." The fact that COPA limited liability to communications made for "commercial purposes" was deemed insufficient because liability could also be imposed if a Web site displayed information harmful to minors, even if the publisher does not make a profit from the publication and does not post such information as part of its business, but does accept advertising to help defray the expenses of the site. The court found that blocking and filtering software provided a less restrictive alternative to COPA, and offered a more effective means of restricting children's access to materials harmful to them. The court also upheld the district court's conclusions that the law was unduly vague and suffered from overbreadth.

5. *Super-Injunctions and Twitter.* New forms of social media are characterized by their immediate reach and global impact. These qualities create the potential for conflicts with the laws of nations that do not provide the same protections for free expression as does the U.S. One notable development in this regard is the United Kingdom's use of the so-called "super-injunction." This remedy prohibits reporting regarding the details of a court case, but also regarding the existence of the injunction. The remedy is traceable to a series of court rulings relating to legislation establishing a right to privacy and limiting the abridgment of this right to a handful of exigent circumstances. Given the United Kingdom's

---

* The statute defined "material that is harmful to minors" as a publication that "(A) the average person, applying contemporary community standards, would find, taking the material as a whole and with respect to minors, is designed to appeal to, or is designed to pander to, the prurient interest; (B) depicts, describes, or represents, in a manner patently offensive with respect to minors, an actual or simulated sexual act or sexual contact, an actual or simulated normal or perverted sexual act, or a lewd exhibition of the genitals or post-pubescent female breast; and (C) taken as a whole, lacks serious literary, artistic, political, or scientific value for minors."

strict defamation laws, and the global reach of social media, there is concern that the availability of super-injunctions may unduly limit speech. For example, a prominent British soccer player secured a super-injunction prohibiting the publication of a story concerning his extramarital affair with a woman, a "TV personality." However, his identity as the person who obtained the injunction was revealed in Parliament where parliamentary privilege protected the speech. Once disclosed, the information was reported in the press, and by thousands of Twitter users. Despite the widespread publication, the injunction remained in effect, and the player subsequently brought actions against Twitter and tweeters for disclosing his identity. *See* Adam Taylor, *What Is a Super-Injunction, and Why Does a UK Football Star Want to Sue Twitter?*, Business Insider, May 23, 2011, http://articles.businessinsider.com/2011-05-23/news/30085176_1_injunctions-british-parliament-number-of-twitter-users. To protest the censorship caused by super-injunctions, one Twitter user established an account to identify the names of celebrities who have obtained them. Of course, the rapid expansion of social networks has made it difficult to preserve and protect privacy interests. *See* Laura Roberts, *Twitter Account Naming Super-Injunction Celebrities Attracts 34,000 Followers*, Telegraph (London), May 9, 2011, http://www.telegraph.co.uk/technology/twitter/8502293/Twitter-account-naming-super-injunction-celebrities-attracts-34000-followers.html.

6. *The Internet and Social Protest.* The Internet has had a profound impact on the functioning of the democratic system. During the 2016 political campaign, candidate Donald Trump used Twitter to do an end run around traditional media and communicate directly with potential supporters. Following Trump's election victory, protestors used social media to organize and coordinate protests against President Trump's policies.

7. *Net Neutrality.* In recent years, there has been much controversy regarding so-called "net neutrality" which would prevent broadband providers from giving preferential treatment (e.g., a speed boost) to preferred content (e.g., a company that is willing to pay for the boost). In 2015, during the Obama Administration, the FCC voted to impose net neutrality rules. Essentially, this approach treated internet service providers as public utilities that provide telecommunication services, and therefore subjected them to "just and reasonable" regulation under Title II of the Communications Act. However, at the end of 2017, during the Trump Administration, the FCC voted to repeal its net neutrality rules. Of course, internet service providers remain subject to antitrust and anti-competition laws, and state consumer protection laws. Although the Senate voted to reverse the FCC's decision, the House failed to do so and the repeal took effect on June 11, 2018. However, over two dozen state legislatures are considering their own legislation and two states have enacted their own laws to replace the FCC's repealed policy. A handful of governors have issued executive orders to require broadband companies doing business with the state to observe net neutrality principles.

8. *Gatekeepers.* Historically, most advanced forms of communication have involved so-called "gatekeepers"—individuals (e.g., producers, editors, and

reporters) who exercise editorial control over the information that gets published or aired. With the internet, individuals can more easily communicate with one another without having to go through these editors, producers, and reporters. Indeed, ordinary people have a variety of methods for communicating, including blogs, listservs, Web sites, and other high-tech methods. Is this good? However, as internet and Web-based communications have assumed increased importance in society, private actors (particularly social media networks) have assumed increasing importance. Indeed, in some instances, internet service providers (ISPs) have chosen to delete controversial content from the Web. *See* Anick Jesdanun, *Free Speech Doesn't Always Extend to Web,* Louisville Courier-Journal, D-7, col. 2-6, July 13, 2008. For example, Facebook has been asked to remove Holocaust denial groups and hate speech from its service. Is this good? Should social media networks be controlling the content of speech and the viewpoints expressed?

9. *More on Gatekeepers.* Of course, there are "gatekeepers" on the internet. For example, following the violence in Charlottesville, Google cancelled the registration of a neo-Nazi website (Daily Stormer). GoDaddy also terminated its relationship with the Daily Stormer because of complaints about its "hate-filled stories." However, the Daily Stormer was able to remain online by moving to the so-called "Dark Web," which can only be seen using a special anonymous browsing tool Tor that hides the identity and location of its users. *See* Samuel Gibbs, *Daily Stormer jumps to dark web while Reddit and Facebook ban hate groups,* The Guardian, Aug. 16, 2017, https://www.theguardian.com/technology/2017/aug/16/daily-stormer-forced-dark-web-reddit-facebook-ban-hate-groups.

∾ PROBLEMS ∾

1. *Free Speech, the Internet, and Democracy.* How will the growth of the internet affect the democratic process? Because a significant percentage of advertising revenue has shifted from print media to the World Wide Web, a number of newspapers are in financial trouble. Not only have some papers had to furlough staff and make production cutbacks, but also many have been forced into bankruptcy. Indeed, some newspapers are now published entirely online. What are the ramifications of these changes for democracy? Historically, newspapers have served as a watchdog on government and have engaged in a certain level of investigative journalism. Will those watchdog/investigative functions continue if newspapers disappear? Or will those functions be assumed by internet sources such as online bloggers and newspapers? What do you make of evidence suggesting that, as the internet has flourished, individuals are increasingly inclined to express their complaints and gripes online? *See Neighborhood Gripes Hit Wire: Site Lets You Air Complaints,* Louisville Courier-Journal, A-9, c. 1-3, June 28, 2008.

2. *"Fake News" and Democratic Governance.* Of course, the great strength of the internet (the fact that it enables ordinary people to mass communicate) is also its greatest weakness. Speech can be used for good or for evil, and the so-called

"fake news" phenomenon illustrates the capacity for evil. Of course, "fake news" has been around for centuries in the sense that people have always disseminated false allegations. However, the circulation of fake news has been amplified by the internet which enables virtually everyone to engage in mass communication. The difficulty is that, if free speech provides the foundation for democratic governance, what happens if the "speech marketplace" is polluted by fake news? For example, a recent Pew Research Center poll suggested that 64% of Americans are confused about the basic facts of current issues and events. Does the inclusion of fake news pollute the political process? Moreover, the Pew poll showed that 62% of Americans get some of their news from social media, with 14% indicating that it is their "most important" source of news, and 20% indicating that they changed their positions on political issues, and 17% changed their views on political candidates, based on what they have read on social media.

3. *Distinguishing "Fake News" from "Biased Reporting."* Is there a clear line of demarcation between "fake news" and biased reporting? Some believe that the media (except, of course, for Fox News) has a generally left-leaning slant, and tends to tilt its reporting with a left-ward bias. Is it possible to create a meaningful distinction between "fake news" and "biased reporting?"

4. *Remedies for "Fake News."* If "fake news" is undermining the political process, is there an effective remedy? Can the government impose licensing requirements which require individuals to submit proposed content to the government, and obtain permission before publishing internet allegations? Can the government establish a "Federal Truth Commission" (FTC) which will criminally prosecute those who make false allegations? If so, how would the government decide what is "true" and what is "false?" For example, during the Obama Administration, could the FTC have prosecuted climate change deniers for circulating fake news? Conversely, during the Trump Administration, could the FTC have prosecuted climate change proponents? Is the existence of an FTC consistent with our constitutional structure? Is there a risk that biased journalists will also be prosecuted? Are the potential remedies for fake news likely to be ineffective if the false allegations are coming from foreign sources or from defendants who are judgment proof?

5. *Defamation Suits and "Fake News."* Do defamation law suits provide an effective remedy for fake news? During a presidential campaign, numerous misstatements are made regarding candidates. Indeed, candidates often hurl allegations against each other. But, after the decision in *New York Times Co. v. Sullivan*, are politicians likely to sue for defamation? During the 2017 presidential campaign, a false allegation was circulated to the effect that Hillary Clinton was running a child sex slave ring out of the basement of a pizzeria, Comet Ping Pong. In an effort to protect the children, a man entered the pizzeria with an AK-15 assault rifle and repeatedly fired the weapon. Is Clinton likely to be able to recover for defamation? What about the pizza parlor? Does it depend on who makes the false allegation and where they are located?

6. *Should Social Media Companies Remedy Fake News?* According to a recent Pew Research poll, a majority of Americans do not favor government restrictions

on false news, but a majority now favor such restrictions by social media companies. In the wake of allegations that the Russians tried to influence the 2017 presidential election, by trying to sow dissent or division through the deliberate dissemination of falsehoods, social media companies have been urged to take action to control or limit fake news. Some of this disinformation was circulated through bots or automated distributors. Of course, there is a federal law that prohibits foreign nationals from spending money to influence U.S. election. In regard to the social media companies, is there a risk that the companies will exercise undue control or censorship over the flow of information? Is that desirable? When publishing online political advertisements, should Facebook and Google be required to satisfy the same disclosure requirements as ads in the print, TV, and radio media?

7. *Google, Facebook, and Twitter Proposals.* Various proposals have been offered regarding how social media companies can control fake news. For example, Google has proposed that it will terminate advertising revenues for fake news sites. Other social media sites like Facebook have suggested that they will allow users to "flag" fake news, marking it as "false" or providing warnings to potential readers, or relegating to a less prominent position in search results. Is it desirable for social media companies to exercise this type of control over news items? Could a social media company show bias towards or against positions with which it agrees or disagrees (e.g., climate change proponents or climate change deniers)? Also, there has been an effort to create "fact checking" organizations which will identify fake news. Is a final proposal, from Twitter, less objectionable: to increase transparency regarding advertising by revealing the people and organizations who choose to advertise, and the details about their ads? Both Twitter and Facebook now endorse the Honest Ads Act.

8. *Fake Information During Election Campaigns.* The French government is likely to enact a law that "aims to identify and stop deliberately false information that is 'massively' spread online in the three-month period leading up to an election." One controversial provision would allow either a political party or a candidate to seek judicial review regarding online information that is "allegedly false or implausible," and obtain a ruling within 48 hours. A judge will be empowered to block publication of such information when it "has been massively and artificially spread online" and when "the allegedly false information could determine the course of an election." Other provisions of the law would require social media platforms to "clearly state who was sponsoring content," and the French media regulator would be empowered "to remove broadcasters' rights to air content in France if it is deemed to be deliberately fake or implausible." Is the law a desirable or necessary reform? Is it likely to be effective in suppressing what the law's supporters prefer to call the "manipulation of information" rather than "fake news"? Is the law likely to create a chilling effect on expressive freedoms? *See* Angelique Chrisafis, *French MP criticise 'hasty and inefective' fake news law,* The Guardian, June 8, 2018, https://www.theguardian.com/world/2018/jun/07/france-macron-fake-news-law-criticised-parliament

9. *Foreign Influences.* Of course, the nature of the internet is that it operates worldwide. As we saw in earlier chapters, different countries treat different categories of speech differently. For example, some European countries prohibit Holocaust denial, and also prohibit speech that "degrades human dignity," whereas the U.S. does not. To the extent that speech occurs over social media websites, is there a risk that regulators outside the U.S. (e.g., the European Union, France or Germany) will pressure social media companies to remove or block certain types of expression, thereby limiting the speech available to those outside those jurisdictions? How should social media companies in the U.S. respond to the European Union's new privacy law, the General Data Protection Regulation?

10. *Artificial Intelligence, Robotic Speech, and the First Amendment.* Are your views regarding "fake news" or the internet affected by the rise of so-called "bots" which are controlled by artificial intelligence rather than by humans? Some suggest that there are now 100 million online bots which can produce messages that recipients perceive as human generated but which are actually controlled by computers. Should bots be viewed as simply a free speech outlet for their human creators? Should it matter whether robotic speech is a direct reflection of the human's thoughts or has been altered by the bot? Should a bot be required to disclose that it is not human?

11. *More on the International Treaty Regulating the Internet.* In light of *Reno,* do you have further thoughts about the type of speech you might be able to agree to ban from the internet? What language could you agree to in the treaty?

Packingham v. North Carolina

137 S. Ct. 1730 (2017)

Justice Kennedy delivered the opinion of the Court.

A North Carolina law makes it a felony for a registered sex offender "to access a commercial social networking Web site where the sex offender knows that the site permits minor children to become members or to create or maintain personal Web pages." N. C. Gen. Stat. Ann. §§14–202.5(a), (e) (2015). A "commercial social networking Web site" is defined as a website that meets four criteria. First, it "is operated by a person who derives revenue from membership fees, advertising, or other sources related to the operation of the Web site." Second, it "facilitates the social introduction between two or more persons for the purposes of friendship, meeting other persons, or information exchanges." Third, it "allows users to create Web pages or personal profiles that contain information such as the name or nickname of the user, photographs placed on the personal Web page by the user, other personal information about the user, and links to other personal Web pages on the commercial social networking Web site of friends or associates of the user that may be accessed by other users or visitors to the Web site." Fourth, it "provides users or visitors mechanisms to communicate with other users, such as a message board, chat room, electronic mail, or instant messenger." The statute includes two express exemptions. The statutory bar does not extend to websites that "provide only one of the following discrete services: photo-sharing, electronic mail, instant messenger, or chat room or message board platform." The law also does not encompass websites that have as their "primary purpose the facilitation of commercial transactions involving goods or services between their members or visitors." §14–202.5 applies to about 20,000 people in North Carolina and the State has prosecuted over 1,000 people for violating it.

In 2002, petitioner Lester Packingham—then a 21-year-old college student—had sex with a 13-year-old girl. He pleaded guilty to taking indecent liberties with a child. Because this crime qualifies as "an offense against a minor," petitioner was required to register as a sex offender—a status that can endure for 30 years or more. As a registered sex offender, petitioner was barred under §14–202.5 from gaining access to commercial social networking sites. In 2010, a state court dismissed a traffic ticket against petitioner. In response, he logged on to Facebook.com and posted the following statement on his personal profile: "Man God is Good! How about I got so much favor they dismissed the ticket before court even started? No fine, no court cost, no nothing spent. Praise be to GOD, WOW! Thanks JESUS!" A member of the Durham Police Department was investigating registered sex offenders who were thought to be violating §14–202.5. The officer noticed that a "J. R. Gerrard" had posted the statement quoted above. By checking court records, the officer discovered that a traffic citation for petitioner had been dismissed around the time of the post. Evidence obtained by search warrant confirmed the officer's suspicions that petitioner was J. R. Gerrard. Petitioner was indicted by a grand jury for violating §14–202.5. The trial court denied his motion to dismiss. Petitioner was ultimately convicted and given a suspended prison sentence. At no point did the State allege that petitioner contacted a minor—or committed any other illicit act—on the Internet. The Court of Appeals of North Carolina struck down §14–202.5 on First Amendment grounds. The North Carolina Supreme Court reversed. The Court granted certiorari and reverses.

A fundamental principle of the First Amendment is that all persons have access to places where they can speak and listen, and then, after reflection, speak and listen once more. The Court has sought to protect the right to speak in this spatial context. A basic rule is that a street or a park is a quintessential forum for the exercise of First Amendment rights. *See Ward v. Rock Against Racism,* 491 U. S. 781 (1989). Even in the modern era, these places are still essential venues for public gatherings to celebrate some views, to protest others, or simply to learn and inquire. While in the past there may have been difficulty in identifying the most important places (in a spatial sense) for the exchange of views, today the answer is clear. It is cyberspace—the "vast democratic forums of the Internet" in general, *Reno v. American Civil Liberties Union,* 521 U. S. 844, 868 (1997), and social media in particular. Seven in ten American adults use at least one Internet social networking service. One of the most popular is Facebook, the site used by petitioner in this case. Facebook has 1.79 billion active users. This is about three times the population of North America. Social media offers "relatively unlimited, low-cost capacity for communication of all kinds." *Reno, supra*, at 870. On Facebook, for example, users can debate religion and politics with their friends and neighbors or share vacation photos. On LinkedIn, users can look for work, advertise for employees, or review tips on entrepreneurship. On Twitter, users can petition their elected representatives and otherwise engage with them in a direct manner. Indeed, Governors in all 50 States and almost every Member of Congress have set up accounts for this purpose. In short, social media users employ these websites to engage in a wide array of protected First Amendment activity on topics "as diverse as human thought." *Reno, supra*, at 870. While we may be coming to the realization that the Cyber Age is a revolution of historic proportions, we cannot appreciate its full dimensions and vast potential to alter how we think, express ourselves, and define who we want to be. This case is one of the first to address the relationship between the First Amendment and the modern Internet.

This background informs the analysis of the North Carolina statute at issue. Even making the assumption that the statute is content neutral and thus subject to intermediate scrutiny, the provision cannot stand. In order to survive intermediate scrutiny, a law must be "narrowly tailored to serve a significant governmental interest." *McCullen v. Coakley*, 134 S. Ct. 2518, 2529 (2014). In other words, the law must not "burden substantially more speech than is necessary to further the government's legitimate interests." Id. at 2535. For centuries now, inventions heralded as advances in human progress have been exploited by the criminal mind. New technologies, all too soon, can become instruments used to commit serious crimes. So it will be with the Internet and social media. There is also no doubt that "the sexual abuse of a child is a most serious crime and an act repugnant to the moral instincts of a decent people." *Ashcroft v. Free Speech Coalition*, 535 U. S. 234, 244 (2002). It is clear that a legislature "may pass valid laws to protect children" and other victims of sexual assault "from abuse." See id. at 245; *accord, New York v. Ferber*, 458 U. S. 747 (1982). The government, of course, need not simply stand by and allow these evils to occur. But the assertion of a valid governmental interest "cannot, in every context, be insulated from all constitutional protections." *Stanley v. Georgia*, 394 U. S. 557, 563 (1969).

It is necessary to make two assumptions to resolve this case. First, given the broad wording of the North Carolina statute, it might well bar access not only to commonplace social media websites but also to websites as varied as Amazon.com, Washingtonpost.com, and Webmd.com. The Court need not decide the precise scope of the statute. It is enough to assume that the law applies (as the State concedes it does) to social networking sites "as commonly understood"—that is, websites like Facebook, LinkedIn, and Twitter. Second, this opinion should not be interpreted as barring a State from enacting more specific laws than the one at issue. Specific criminal acts are not protected speech even if speech is the means for their commission. *See Brandenburg v. Ohio*, 395 U. S. 444 (1969) (per curiam). The First Amendment permits a State to enact specific, narrowly tailored laws that prohibit a sex offender from engaging in conduct that often presages a sexual crime, like contacting a minor or using a website to gather information about a minor. Specific laws of that type must be the State's first resort to ward off the serious harm that sexual crimes inflict. (The fact that the law imposes severe restrictions on persons who already have served their sentence and are no longer subject to the supervision of the criminal justice system is also not before the Court.)

Even with these assumptions about the scope of the law and the State's interest, the statute here enacts a prohibition unprecedented in the scope of First Amendment speech it burdens. Social media allows users to gain access to information and communicate with one another about it on any subject that might come to mind. By prohibiting sex offenders from using those websites, North Carolina with one broad stroke bars access to what for many are the principal sources for knowing current events, checking ads for employment, speaking and listening in the modern public square, and otherwise exploring the vast realms of human thought and knowledge. These websites can provide perhaps the most powerful mechanisms available to a private citizen to make his or her voice heard. They allow a person with an Internet connection to "become a town crier with a voice that resonates farther than it could from any soapbox." *Reno*, 521 U. S. at 870. To foreclose access to social media altogether is to prevent the user from engaging in the legitimate exercise of First Amendment rights. It is unsettling to suggest that only a limited set of websites can be used even by persons who have completed their sentences. Even convicted criminals—and in some instances especially convicted criminals—might receive legitimate benefits from these means for access to the world of ideas, in particular if they seek to reform and to pursue lawful and rewarding lives. The primary response from the State is that the law must be this broad to serve its preventative purpose of keeping convicted sex offenders away from vulnerable victims. The State has not, however, met its burden to show that this sweeping law is necessary or legitimate to serve that purpose. See *McCullen*, 134 S. Ct. At 2540. No case or holding of this Court has approved of a statute as broad in its reach.

The judgment of the North Carolina Supreme Court is reversed, and the case is remanded for further proceedings not inconsistent with this opinion.

It is so ordered.

JUSTICE ALITO, with whom THE CHIEF JUSTICE and JUSTICE THOMAS join, concurring in the judgment.

The North Carolina statute was enacted to serve an interest of "surpassing importance" but it has a staggering reach. It makes it a felony for a registered sex offender simply to visit a vast array of websites, including many that appear to provide no realistic opportunity for communications that could facilitate the abuse of children. Because of the law's extraordinary breadth, I agree that it violates the Free Speech Clause of the First Amendment. The fatal problem for §14–202.5 is that its wide sweep precludes access to a large number of websites that are most unlikely to facilitate the commission of a sex crime against a child.

∼ PROBLEMS ∼

1. *Rewriting the Statute.* After the holding in *Packingham,* is it possible to redraft the statute to restrict sex offender access without running afoul of the First Amendment? If so, how?

2. *Sex Offender Online Disclosure Rule.* A provision of the Illinois' Sex Offender Registration Act requires that convicted sex offenders must disclose their email addresses, internet identities, and websites to their local police department, and must update this information on an annual basis. Suppose that a convicted juvenile male fails to disclose his Facebook account as required and so is criminally charged under the statute. Does the disclosure provision violate the First Amendment? Is it a content-based or viewpoint-based restriction on speech? Should the restriction have been more narrowly tailored? *See People v. Minnis,* 2016 IL 119563, 67 N.E.3d 272 (Ill. 2016).

3. *Requiring Governmental Permission.* A man is convicted of producing child pornography, and is given a 40 year prison sentence along with 20 years of supervised release. One of the conditions of his release is that he must obtain the permission of probation authorities before accessing his computer or online services. In light of *Packingham,* is such a restriction valid? *See United States v. Perrin,* 926 F.3d 1044 (8th Cir. 2019).

N. FREEDOM OF ASSOCIATION

Although the First Amendment does not explicitly protect the right to associate, it does protect activities that are associational in nature (e.g., the right to peacefully assemble). In a number of cases, the Court has struggled to define the extent to which the First Amendment includes the right not only to associate but also to "disassociate."

1. The Right to Associate

The Constitution protects freedom of speech, which is inevitably more effective when groups of people can band together and speak with a common voice. In some instances, the gathering of individuals results in increased resources.

NAACP v. Alabama

357 U.S. 449 (1958)

Mr. Justice HARLAN delivered the opinion of the Court.

Alabama has a statute similar to those of many other States which requires a foreign corporation, except as exempted, to qualify before doing business by filing its corporate charter with the Secretary of State and designating a place of business and an agent to receive service of process. The National Association for the Advancement of Colored People is a nonprofit membership corporation organized under the laws of New York. Its purposes are those indicated by its name,* and it operates through chartered affiliates.

In 1956 the Attorney General of Alabama brought suit to enjoin the Association from conducting further activities within, and to oust it from, the State for violating the Alabama qualification law. The State then moved for production of the Association's records and papers, including the names and addresses of all Alabama "members" and "agents" of the Association. The court ordered the production of a substantial part of the requested records, including the membership lists. When the NAACP refused to produce the lists, the court held it in civil contempt and imposed a fine of $10,000, increasable to $100,000 for noncompliance.

Petitioner urges that it is constitutionally entitled to resist official inquiry into its membership lists, and that it may assert, on behalf of its members, a right personal to them to be protected from compelled disclosure of their affiliation with the Association. Petitioner argues that the effect of compelled disclosure of the membership lists will be to abridge the rights of its rank-and-file members to engage in lawful association in support of their common beliefs.

Effective advocacy of both public and private points of view, particularly controversial ones, is undeniably enhanced by group association, as this Court has more than once recognized by remarking upon the close nexus between the freedoms of speech and assembly. It is beyond debate that freedom to engage in association for the advancement of beliefs and ideas is an inseparable aspect of the "liberty" assured by the Due Process Clause of the Fourteenth Amendment, which embraces freedom of speech. *See Gitlow v. New York*, 268 U.S. 652 (1925). Of course, it is immaterial whether the beliefs sought to be advanced by association pertain to political, economic, religious or cultural matters, and state action which may have the effect of curtailing the freedom to associate is subject to the closest scrutiny.

The fact that Alabama has taken no direct action to restrict the right of petitioner's members to associate freely, does not end inquiry into the effect of the production order. In the domain of these indispensable liberties, whether of speech, press, or association, abridgement of such rights, even though unintended, may inevitably follow from varied forms of governmental action. Statutes imposing taxes upon rather than prohibiting particular activity have been struck down when perceived to have the consequence of unduly curtailing the liberty of freedom of press assured under the Fourteenth Amendment.

* The Certificate of Incorporation provides that its "principal objects are voluntarily to promote equality of rights and eradicate caste or race prejudice among the citizens of the United States; to advance the interest of colored citizens; to secure for them impartial suffrage; and to increase their opportunities for securing justice in the courts, education for their children, employment according to their ability, and complete equality before the law."

This Court has recognized the vital relationship between freedom to associate and privacy in one's associations. Inviolability of privacy in group association may in many circumstances be indispensable to preservation of freedom of association, particularly where a group espouses dissident beliefs.

We think that the production order must be regarded as entailing the likelihood of a substantial restraint upon the exercise by petitioner's members of their right to freedom of association. Petitioner has shown that on past occasions revelation of the identity of its rank-and-file members has exposed these members to economic reprisal, loss of employment, threat of physical coercion, and other manifestations of public hostility. Under these circumstances, compelled disclosure of petitioner's Alabama membership is likely to affect adversely the ability of petitioner and its members to pursue their collective effort to foster beliefs which they admittedly have the right to advocate, in that it may induce members to withdraw from the Association and dissuade others from joining it because of fear of exposure of their beliefs shown through their associations and of the consequences of this exposure.

It is not sufficient to answer that whatever repressive effect compulsory disclosure of names of petitioner's members may have upon participation by Alabama citizens in petitioner's activities follows not from state action but from private community pressures. The crucial factor is the interplay of governmental and private action, for it is only after the initial exertion of state power represented by the production order that private action takes hold.

We turn to the final question whether Alabama has demonstrated an interest in obtaining the disclosures it seeks from petitioner which is sufficient to justify the deterrent effect which we have concluded these disclosures may well have on the free exercise by petitioner's members of their constitutionally protected right of association. Such a "subordinating interest of the State must be compelling," *Sweezy v. New Hampshire*, 354 U.S. 234, 265 (concurring opinion). The State's purpose in requesting the membership lists was to determine whether petitioner was conducting intrastate business in violation of the Alabama foreign corporation registration statute. Petitioner (1) has admitted its presence and conduct of activities in Alabama since 1918; (2) has offered to comply in all respects with the state qualification statute; and (3) has apparently complied satisfactorily with the production order, except for the membership lists, by furnishing the Attorney General with varied business records, its charter and statement of purposes, the names of all of its directors and officers, and with the total number of its Alabama members and the amount of their dues. Whatever interest the State may have in obtaining names of ordinary members has not been shown to be sufficient to overcome petitioner's constitutional objections to the production order.

We hold that the immunity from state scrutiny of membership lists which the Association claims on behalf of its members is here so related to the right of the members to pursue their lawful private interests privately and to associate freely with others in so doing as to come within the protection of the Fourteenth Amendment. We conclude that Alabama has fallen short of showing a controlling justification for the deterrent effect on the free enjoyment of the right to associate which disclosure of membership lists is likely to have. Accordingly, the judgment of civil contempt and the $100,000 fine which resulted from petitioner's refusal to comply with the production order in this respect must fall.

For the reasons stated, the judgment of the Supreme Court of Alabama must be reversed and the case remanded for proceedings not inconsistent with this opinion.

Reversed.

Notes

1. *Boycotts and Civil Liability.* In *NAACP v. Claiborne Hardware Co.*, 458 U.S. 886 (1982), after the NAACP began a nonviolent boycott of white merchants in Mississippi, the merchants sought an injunction against future boycotts and damages for financial losses. The Court held that "encouragement to boycott" constitutes protected speech under the First and Fourteenth Amendments. Although the Court recognized that those who engage in violent activity could be held liable, the state could not hold nonviolent protestors liable merely because of their association with those who engage in violence.

2. *House Un-American Activities Committee.* In *Barenblatt v. United States*, 360 U.S. 109 (1959), during an inquiry concerning alleged Communist infiltration into the field of education held by a subcommittee of the House Un-American Activities Committee, the petitioner was charged with, and ultimately convicted of, *inter alia*, refusing to answer questions regarding his membership in the Community Party. The refusals were based on his privilege against self-incrimination. The Court rejected Barenblatt's First Amendment freedom of association, claiming: "First Amendment rights always involve a balancing by the courts of the competing private and public interests at stake. This Court has recognized the close nexus between the Communist Party and violent overthrow of government. The balance between the individual and the governmental interests here at stake must be struck in favor of the latter, and therefore the provisions of the First Amendment have not been offended." Justice Black dissented: "I cannot agree that this Nation's security hangs upon its power to punish people because of what they think, speak or write about, or because of those with whom they associate for political purposes. Members of the Communist Party who commit acts in violation of valid laws can be prosecuted."

3. *Fusion Candidates. Timmons v. Twin Cities Area New Party*, 520 U.S. 351 (1997), involved a Minnesota law that prohibited "fusion" candidates—those who appear on the ballot as the candidate of more than one party. The Court concluded that a ban on "fusion candidates" did not violate the right to associate: "The New Party and its members can endorse, support, or vote for anyone they like. The laws are silent on parties' internal structure, governance, and policy-making. Instead, these provisions reduce the universe of potential candidates who may appear on

the ballot as the Party's nominee only by ruling out those few individuals who both have already agreed to be another party's candidate and who prefer that other party. The burdens Minnesota imposes on the Party's First and Fourteenth Amendment associational rights—though not trivial—are not severe. States certainly have an interest in protecting the integrity, fairness, and efficiency of their ballots and election processes as means for electing public officials. The States' interest permits them to enact reasonable election regulations that may, in practice, favor the traditional two-party system, and that temper the destabilizing effects of party-splintering and excessive factionalism." Justice Stevens dissented: "Minnesota argues that the statutory restriction on the New Party's right to nominate the candidate of its choice is justified by the State's interests in avoiding voter confusion, preventing ballot clutter and manipulation, encouraging candidate competition, and minimizing intraparty factionalism. None of these rationales can support the fusion ban because the State has failed to explain how the ban actually serves the asserted interests."

4. *Closed Primaries.* In *Clingman v. Beaver*, 544 U.S. 581 (2005), the Court upheld a state's decision to adopt a "semiclosed" primary system under which only a party's members and independents may vote in party primaries. The Court rejected freedom-of-association claims.

5. *The IRS' Targeting of Political Groups.* In 2013, evidence came to light suggesting that the IRS was targeting Tea Party groups' applications for tax-exempt status for special scrutiny. *See* Editorial Board, *The IRS Plot Thickens*, Wash. Post, June 28, 2013, http://www.washingtonpost.com/opinions/the-irs-plot-thickens/ 2013/06/28/8f813a06-df72-11e2-b94a-452948b95ca8_story.html. As the story developed, it became clear that not just Tea Party groups had been singled out, but so had other groups, including some left-wing groups. *Id.*

∾ PROBLEMS ∾

1. NAACP *and the KKK.* How far does the *NAACP* ruling extend? After that decision, do all groups have the right to refuse to submit their membership lists to the government, or does the ruling apply only to persecuted groups? May the City of Louisville require unincorporated associations like the Ku Klux Klan to file their membership rosters with the city? Would it matter that the KKK claims that its members have been persecuted? What if the city could show that KKK members have engaged in acts of unlawful intimidation and violence? *See New York ex rel. Bryant v. Zimmerman*, 278 U.S. 63 (1928).

2. *More on the International Treaty Regulating the Internet.* In some countries, governments have the right to ban political parties that they regard as "subversive" or "dangerous." They also have the right to ban other groups. For example, in Germany and France, there are limitations on the Church of Scientology. Delegates from these countries have argued that banned political parties and

associations should be prohibited from communicating on the internet, and that this prohibition should be enforceable through fines and other criminal sanctions. Delegates from these countries would like the proposed treaty to contain language allowing them to extradite members of banned organizations who communicate on the internet in violation of the treaty. Can you agree to language authorizing the ban, the sanctions, and the extradition? Should you do so? Suppose that the foreign government attempts to "ban" a political party that is based primarily in the United States.

Roberts v. United States Jaycees

468 U.S. 609 (1984)

Justice BRENNAN delivered the opinion of the Court.

This case requires us to address a conflict between a State's efforts to eliminate gender-based discrimination against its citizens and the constitutional freedom of association asserted by members of a private organization.

The United States Jaycees (Jaycees), founded in 1920 as the Junior Chamber of Commerce, is a nonprofit membership corporation, incorporated in Missouri with national headquarters in Tulsa, Okla. The objective of the Jaycees, as set out in its bylaws, is to pursue "such educational and charitable purposes as will promote and foster the growth and development of young men's civic organizations in the United States, designed to inculcate in the individual membership of such organization a spirit of genuine Americanism and civic interest, and as a supplementary education institution to provide them with opportunity for personal development and achievement and an avenue for intelligent participation by young men in the affairs of their community, state and nation, and to develop true friendship and understanding among young men of all nations."

The organization's bylaws establish seven classes of membership, including individual or regular members, associate individual members, and local chapters. Regular membership is limited to young men between the ages of 18 and 35, while associate membership is available to individuals or groups ineligible for regular membership, principally women and older men. An associate member, whose dues are somewhat lower, may not vote, hold local or national office, or participate in certain leadership training and awards programs. Policymaking authority rests with an annual national convention, consisting of delegates from each chapter, with a national president and board of directors. At the time of trial, the Jaycees had approximately 295,000 members in 7,400 local chapters affiliated with 51 state organizations. There were 11,915 associate members. Women associate members make up about two percent of the Jaycees' total membership.

New members are recruited to the Jaycees through the local chapters, although the state and national organizations are actively involved in recruitment. A new regular member pays an initial fee followed by annual dues; in exchange, he is entitled to participate in all of the activities of the local, state, and national organizations. The national headquarters develop[s] "program kits" that are designed to enhance individual development, community development, and members' management skills. These materials include courses in public speaking and personal finances as well as community programs related to charity, sports, and public health. The national office also makes available to members a range of personal products, including travel accessories, casual wear, pins, awards, and other gifts. The programs, products, and other activities of the organization are all featured in publications made available to the membership, including a magazine entitled "Future."

In 1974 and 1975, the Minneapolis and St. Paul chapters of the Jaycees began admitting women as regular members. Currently, the memberships and boards of directors of both chapters include a substantial proportion of women. In 1978, the president of the national organization advised both chapters that a motion to revoke their charters would be considered at a forthcoming meeting of the national board. Shortly after, members of both chapters filed charges of discrimination with the Minnesota Department of Human Rights. The complaints alleged that the exclusion of women from full membership required by the national organization violated the Minnesota Human Rights Act (Act), which provides in part: "It is an unfair discriminatory practice: To deny any person the full and equal enjoyment of the goods, services, facilities, privileges, advantages, and accommodations of a place of public accommodation because of race, color, creed, religion, disability, national origin or sex." Minn. Stat. §363.03, subd. 3 (1982). The term "place of public accommodation" is defined in the Act as "a business, accommodation, refreshment, entertainment, recreation, or transportation facility of any kind, whether licensed or not, whose goods, services, facilities, privileges, advantages or accommodations are extended, offered, sold, or otherwise made available to the public." §363.01, subd. 18.

A state hearing examiner concluded that the Jaycees organization is a "place of public accommodation" within the Act and that it had engaged in an unfair discriminatory practice by excluding women from regular membership. He ordered the national organization to cease and desist from discriminating on the basis of sex and from imposing sanctions on any Minnesota affiliate for admitting women. In a separate proceeding, the Eighth Circuit held that application of the Minnesota statute to the Jaycees' membership policies would unconstitutionally interfere with the Jaycees' First Amendment right to freedom of association.

Our decisions have referred to constitutionally protected "freedom of association" in two distinct senses. In one line of decisions, the Court has concluded that choices to enter into and maintain certain intimate human relationships must be secured against undue intrusion by the State because of the role of such relationships in safeguarding the individual freedom that is central to our constitutional scheme. In this respect, freedom of association receives protection as a fundamental element of personal liberty. In another set of decisions, the Court has recognized a right to associate for the purpose of engaging in those activities protected by the First Amendment—speech, assembly, petition for the redress of grievances, and the exercise of religion. The Constitution guarantees freedom of association of this kind as an indispensable means of preserving other individual liberties. The intrinsic and instrumental features of constitutionally protected association may, of course, coincide. In particular, when the State interferes with individuals' selection of those with whom they wish to join in a common endeavor, freedom of association in both of its forms may be implicated. The Jaycees contend that this is such a case. Still, the nature and degree of constitutional protection afforded freedom of association may vary depending on the extent to which one or the other aspect of the constitutionally protected liberty is at stake in a given case.

The Court has long recognized that, because the Bill of Rights is designed to secure individual liberty, it must afford the formation and preservation of certain kinds of highly personal relationships a substantial measure of sanctuary from unjustified interference by the State. *E.g., Meyer v. Nebraska,* 262 U.S. 390 (1923). Without precisely identifying every consideration that may underlie this type of constitutional protection, certain personal bonds have played a critical role in the culture and traditions of the Nation by cultivating and transmitting shared ideals and beliefs; they thereby foster diversity and act as critical buffers between the individual and the power of the State. *See, e.g., Moore v. East Cleveland,* 431 U.S. 494 (1977) (plurality opinion). Moreover, the constitutional shelter afforded such relationships reflects the realization that individuals draw much of their emotional enrichment from close ties with others. Protecting these relationships from unwarranted state interference therefore safeguards the ability independently to define one's identity that is central to any concept of liberty. The personal affiliations that exemplify these considerations, and that therefore suggest some relevant limitations on the relationships that might be entitled to this sort of constitutional protection, are those that attend the creation and sustenance of a family — marriage, *e.g., Zablocki v. Redhail, supra;* childbirth, *e.g., Carey v. Population Services International,* 431 U.S. 678; the raising and education of children, *e.g., Smith v. Organization of Foster Families,* 431 U.S. 816 (1977); and cohabitation with one's relatives, *e.g., Moore v. East Cleveland, supra.* Family relationships, by their nature, involve deep attachments and commitments to the necessarily few other individuals with whom one shares not only a special community of thoughts, experiences, and beliefs but also distinctively personal aspects of one's life. Among other things, they are distinguished by such attributes as relative smallness, a high degree of selectivity in decisions to begin and maintain the affiliation, and seclusion from others in critical aspects of the relationship. As a general matter, only relationships with these sorts of qualities are likely to reflect the considerations that have led to an understanding of freedom of association as an intrinsic element of personal liberty. An association lacking these qualities — such as a large business enterprise — seems remote from the concerns giving rise to this constitutional protection. Accordingly, the Constitution undoubtedly imposes constraints on the State's power to control the selection of one's spouse that would not apply to regulations affecting the choice of one's fellow employees.

Between these poles lies a broad range of human relationships that may make greater or lesser claims to constitutional protection from particular incursions by the State. Determining the limits of state authority over an individual's freedom to enter into a particular association unavoidably entails a careful assessment of where that relationship's objective characteristics locate it on a spectrum from the most intimate to the most attenuated of personal attachments. Factors that may be relevant include size, purpose, policies, selectivity, congeniality, and other characteristics that in a particular case may be pertinent. Several features of the Jaycees clearly place the organization outside of the category of relationships worthy of this kind of constitutional protection.

The local chapters of the Jaycees are large and basically unselective groups. At the time of the hearing, the Minneapolis chapter had approximately 430 members, while the St. Paul chapter had about 400. Apart from age and sex, neither the national organization nor the local chapters employ any criteria for judging applicants for membership, and new members are routinely recruited and admitted with no inquiry into their backgrounds. A local officer could recall no instance in which an applicant had been denied membership on any basis other than age or sex. Furthermore, despite their inability to vote, hold office, or receive certain awards, women affiliated with the Jaycees attend various meetings, participate in selected projects, and engage in many of the organization's social functions. Indeed, numerous non-members of both genders regularly participate in a substantial portion of activities central to the decision of many members to associate with one another, including many of the organization's various community programs, awards ceremonies, and recruitment meetings. In short, the local chapters of the Jaycees are neither small nor selective. Moreover, much of the activity central to the formation and maintenance of the association involves the participation of strangers to that relationship. Accordingly, we conclude that the Jaycees chapters lack the distinctive characteristics that might afford constitutional protection to the decision of its members to exclude women.

An individual's freedom to speak, to worship, and to petition the government for the redress of grievances could not be vigorously protected from interference by the State unless a correlative freedom to engage in group effort toward those ends were not also guaranteed. According protection to collective effort on behalf of shared goals is especially important in preserving political and cultural diversity and in shielding dissident expression from suppression by the majority. *See, e.g., NAACP v. Button,* 371 U.S. 415 (1963). Consequently, we have long understood as implicit in the right to engage in activities protected by the First Amendment a corresponding right to associate with others in pursuit of a wide variety of political, social, economic, educational, religious, and cultural ends. In view of the various protected activities in which the Jaycees engages, that right is plainly implicated in this case.

Government actions that may unconstitutionally infringe upon this freedom can take a number of forms. Government may seek to impose penalties or withhold benefits from individuals because of their membership in a disfavored group, it may attempt to require disclosure of the fact of membership in a group seeking anonymity, and it may try to interfere with the internal organization or affairs of the group. By requiring the Jaycees to admit women as full voting members, the Minnesota Act works an infringement of the last type. There can be no clearer example of an intrusion into the internal structure or affairs of an association than a regulation that forces the group to accept members it does not desire. Such a regulation may impair the ability of the original members to express only those views that brought them together. Freedom of association therefore plainly presupposes a freedom not to associate. *See Abood v. Detroit Board of Education*, 431 U.S. at 234-235.

The right to associate for expressive purposes is not, however, absolute. Infringements on that right may be justified by regulations adopted to serve compelling state interests, unrelated to the suppression of ideas, that cannot be achieved through means significantly less restrictive of associational freedoms. We are persuaded that Minnesota's compelling interest in eradicating discrimination against its female citizens justifies the impact that application of the statute to the Jaycees may have on the male members' associational freedoms.

On its face, the Minnesota Act does not aim at the suppression of speech, does not distinguish between prohibited and permitted activity on the basis of viewpoint, and does not license enforcement authorities to administer the statute on the basis of such constitutionally impermissible criteria. Nor does the Jaycees contend that the Act has been applied in this case for the purpose of hampering the organization's ability to express its views. Instead, the Act reflects the State's strong historical commitment to eliminating discrimination and assuring its citizens equal access to publicly available goods and services. That goal, which is unrelated to the suppression of expression, plainly serves compelling state interests of the highest order.

The Minnesota Human Rights Act is an example of public accommodations laws that were adopted by some States beginning a decade before enactment of the federal Civil Rights Act of 1875. By prohibiting gender discrimination in places of public accommodation, the Minnesota Act protects the State's citizenry from a number of serious social and personal harms. Discrimination based on archaic and overbroad assumptions about the relative needs and capacities of the sexes forces individuals to labor under stereotypical notions that often bear no relationship to their actual abilities. It thereby both deprives persons of their individual dignity and denies society the benefits of wide participation in political, economic, and cultural life. These concerns are strongly implicated with respect to gender discrimination in the allocation of publicly available goods and services. Thus, in upholding Title II of the Civil Rights Act of 1964, which forbids race discrimination in public accommodations, we emphasized that its "fundamental object was to vindicate 'the deprivation of personal dignity that surely accompanies denials of equal access to public establishments.'" *Heart of Atlanta Motel, Inc. v. United States*, 379 U.S. 241 (1964). That stigmatizing injury, and the denial of equal opportunities that accompanies it, is surely felt as strongly by persons suffering discrimination on the basis of their sex as by those treated differently because of their race.

Nor is the state interest in assuring equal access limited to the provision of purely tangible goods and services. A State enjoys broad authority to create rights of public access on behalf of its citizens. Like many States and municipalities, Minnesota has adopted a functional definition of public accommodations that reaches various forms of public, quasi-commercial conduct. This expansive definition reflects a recognition of the changing nature of the American economy and of the importance, both to the individual and to society, of removing the barriers to economic advancement and political and social integration that have historically plagued certain disadvantaged groups, including women. Thus, in explaining its conclusion that the Jaycees local chapters are "places of public accommodations" within the meaning of the Act, the Minnesota court noted the various commercial programs and benefits offered to members and stated that "leadership skills are 'goods,' and business contacts and employment promotions are 'privileges' and 'advantages.'" Assuring women equal access to such goods, privileges, and advantages clearly furthers compelling state interests.

In applying the Act to the Jaycees, the State has advanced those interests through the least restrictive means of achieving its ends. Indeed, the Jaycees has failed to demonstrate that the Act imposes any serious burdens on the male members' freedom of expressive association. To be sure, a "not insubstantial part" of the Jaycees' activities constitutes protected expression on political, economic, cultural, and social affairs. Over the years, the national and local levels of the organization have taken public positions on a number of diverse issues, and members of the Jaycees regularly engage in a variety of civic, charitable, lobbying, fundraising, and other activities worthy of constitutional protection under the First Amendment. There is, however, no basis for concluding that admission of women as full voting members will impede the organization's ability to engage in these protected activities or to disseminate its preferred views. The Act requires no change in the Jaycees' creed of promoting the interests of young men, and it imposes no restrictions on the organization's ability to exclude individuals with ideologies or philosophies different from those of its existing members. Moreover, the Jaycees already invites women to share the group's views and philosophy and to participate in much of its training and community activities. Accordingly, any claim that admission of women as full voting members will impair a symbolic message conveyed by the very fact that women are not permitted to vote is attenuated at best.

While acknowledging that "the specific content of most of the resolutions adopted over the years by the Jaycees has nothing to do with sex," the Court of Appeals nonetheless entertained the hypothesis that women members might have a different view or agenda with respect to these matters so that, if they are allowed to vote, "some change in the Jaycees' philosophical cast can reasonably be expected." It is similarly arguable that, insofar as the Jaycees is organized to promote the views of young men whatever those views happen to be, admission of women as voting members will change the message communicated by the group's speech because of the gender-based assumptions of the audience. Neither supposition is supported by the record. In claiming that women might have a different attitude about such issues as the federal budget, school prayer, voting rights, and foreign relations, or that the organization's public positions would have a different effect if the group were not "a purely young men's association," the Jaycees relies solely on unsupported generalizations about the relative interests and perspectives of men and women. Although such generalizations may or may not have a statistical basis in fact, we have repeatedly condemned legal decisionmaking that relies uncritically on such assumptions. In the absence of a showing far more substantial than that attempted by the Jaycees, we decline to indulge in the sexual stereotyping that underlies appellee's contention that, by allowing women to vote, application of the Minnesota Act will change the content or impact of the organization's speech.

In any event, even if enforcement of the Act causes some incidental abridgment of the Jaycees' protected speech, that effect is no greater than is necessary to accomplish the State's legitimate purposes. Acts of invidious discrimination in the distribution of publicly available goods, services, and other advantages cause unique evils that government has a compelling interest to prevent—wholly apart from the point of view such conduct may transmit. Accordingly, like violence or other types of potentially expressive activities that produce special harms distinct from their communicative impact, such practices are entitled to no constitutional protection. In prohibiting such practices, the Minnesota Act therefore "responds precisely to the substantive problem which legitimately concerns" the State and abridges no more speech or associational freedom than is necessary to accomplish that purpose.

The judgment of the Court of Appeals is
Reversed.

Justice O'CONNOR, *concurring in part* and *concurring in the judgment.*

An association engaged exclusively in protected expression enjoys First Amendment protection of both the content of its message and the choice of its members. Protection of the association's right to define its membership derives from the recognition that the formation of an expressive association is the creation of a voice, and the selection of members is the definition of that voice. A ban on specific group voices on public affairs violates the most basic guarantee of the First Amendment—that citizens, not the government, control the content of public discussion. On the other hand, there is only minimal constitutional protection of the freedom of commercial association. While the Court has acknowledged a First Amendment right to engage in nondeceptive commercial advertising, governmental regulation of the commercial recruitment of new members, stockholders, customers, or employees is valid if rationally related to the government's ends.

Many associations cannot readily be described as purely expressive or purely commercial. No association is likely ever to be exclusively engaged in expressive activities. And innumerable commercial associations also engage in some incidental protected speech or advocacy. The standard for deciding just how much of an association's involvement in commercial activity is enough to suspend the association's First Amendment right to control its membership cannot, therefore, be articulated with simple precision.

An association should be characterized as commercial, and therefore subject to rationally related state regulation of its membership and other associational activities, when the association's activities are not predominantly of the type protected by the First Amendment. An association must choose its market. Once it enters the marketplace of commerce in any substantial degree it loses the complete control over its membership that it would otherwise enjoy if it confined its affairs to the marketplace of ideas. The purposes of an association, and the purposes of its members in adhering to it, are doubtless relevant in determining whether the association is primarily engaged in protected expression. Lawyering to advance social goals may be speech, but ordinary commercial law practice is not.

The Jaycees — otherwise known as the Junior Chamber of Commerce — is, first and foremost, an organization that, at both the national and local levels, promotes and practices the art of solicitation and management. The organization claims that the training it offers its members gives them an advantage in business, and business firms sometimes pay the dues for their employees. Recruitment and selling are commercial activities, even when conducted for training rather than for profit. The "not insubstantial" volume of protected Jaycees activity is simply not enough to preclude state regulation of the Jaycees' commercial activities. The State of Minnesota has a legitimate interest in ensuring nondiscriminatory access to the commercial opportunity presented by membership in the Jaycees. The Jaycees may not claim constitutional immunity by seeking to exercise their First Amendment rights through this commercial organization.

Note: More on Nondiscrimination Ordinances

New York State Club Association, Inc. v. City of New York, 487 U.S. 1 (1988), involved a law of the City of New York that prohibited discrimination in any "place of public accommodation, resort or amusement" on the basis of race, creed, color, national origin or sex. In upholding the law, the Court stated:

> The City has a compelling interest in providing all persons, regardless of race, creed, color, national origin or sex, a fair and equal opportunity to participate in the business and professional life of the city. One barrier to the advancement of women and minorities is the discriminatory practices of certain membership organizations where business deals are often made and personal contacts valuable for business purposes, employment and professional advancement are formed. While such organizations may avowedly be organized for social, cultural, civic or educational purposes, and while many perform valuable services to the community, the commercial nature of some of the activities occurring therein and the prejudicial impact of these activities on business, professional and employment opportunities of minorities and women cannot be ignored.

∾ PROBLEMS ∾

1. *Wendy Hills Political Club.* The Wendy Hills Political Club (WHPC) is a group that has come together to advocate on behalf of political causes (specifically, affirmative action) and to support political candidates who endorse the WHPC's position on those issues. WHPC discriminates on the basis of race (on the theory that whites oppose affirmative action) even though some whites tend to be supportive of affirmative action. May the City of Wendy Hills prohibit the WHPC from discriminating on the basis of race or sex? Does it matter whether the WHPC is successful or unsuccessful in its advocacy? For example, suppose that the WHPC holds a "preprimary" prior to the Democratic primary. The club unites behind the candidate who wins the "preprimary," and that candidate always wins the primary. Would you view the WHPC differently if it were anti–affirmative action and its members were white and excluded Blacks (on the theory that Blacks favor affirmative action)?

2. *More on the International Treaty Regulating the Internet.* Suppose that some delegates to the convention demand "equal treatment for women." They propose that the internet communications of any group (political or otherwise) be banned unless the group certifies (to a new international board) two things: 1) it does not discriminate on the basis of sex, and 2) it has taken affirmative steps to include women in its organization, including as officers and directors. They also propose that criminal sanctions be imposed on any group that makes an internet communication without obtaining the required certification. Can you agree to such a board and such a ban? What type of language might you be able to agree to?

2. The Right "Not to Speak"

The First Amendment right of association has been construed to protect not only the right to speak but also the right not to speak or to associate oneself with objectionable ideas or positions. In *Wooley v. Maynard*, 430 U.S. 705 (1977), Jehovah's Witnesses, who objected on religious and moral grounds to having the New Hampshire motto "Live Free or Die" on their license plates and covered it with tape, were prosecuted and convicted under a state law that made it a misdemeanor to knowingly obscure a license plate. The Court held that the state could not force the Maynards to associate themselves with this motto: "Freedom of thought includes both the right to speak freely and the right to refrain from speaking at all. We are faced with a state measure which forces an individual, as part of his daily life indeed constantly while his automobile is in public view to be an instrument for fostering public adherence to an ideological point of view he finds unacceptable." The Court rejected the state's first asserted interests (making it easier to determine whether passenger vehicles are carrying the proper plates) on the basis that New Hampshire plates "consist of a specific configuration of letters and numbers, which makes them readily distinguishable from other types of plates, even without reference to the state motto." The Court also rejected the argument that the plate communicates "an appreciation of history, state pride, and individualism" on the basis that "such interest cannot outweigh an individual's First Amendment right to avoid becoming the courier for such message." Justice Rehnquist, joined by Justice Blackmun, dissented: "The State has not forced appellees to 'say' anything. The State has simply required that all noncommercial automobiles bear license tags with the state motto. There is nothing in state law which precludes appellees from displaying their disagreement with the state motto as long as the methods used do not obscure the license plates."

Likewise, in *West Virginia State Board of Education v. Barnette*, 319 U.S. 624 (1943), the state adopted a resolution requiring all public school students and teachers to salute the U.S. flag on pain of insubordination. In an opinion by Justice Jackson, the Court held the law unconstitutional: "To sustain the compulsory flag salute we are required to say that a Bill of Rights which guards the individual's right to speak his own mind, left it open to public authorities to compel him to utter what is not in his mind. If there is any fixed star in our constitutional constellation, it is that no official, high or petty, can prescribe what shall be orthodox in politics, nationalism, religion, or other matters of opinion or force citizens to confess by word or act their faith therein."

Hurley v. Irish-American Gay, Lesbian and Bisexual Group of Boston

515 U.S. 557 (1995)

Justice SOUTER delivered the opinion of the Court.

The issue in this case is whether Massachusetts may require private citizens who organize a parade to include among the marchers a group imparting a message the organizers do not wish to convey. We hold that such a mandate violates the First Amendment.

March 17 is set aside for two celebrations in South Boston. As early as 1737, some people in Boston observed the feast of the apostle to Ireland, and since 1776 the day has marked the evacuation of royal troops and Loyalists from the city, prompted by the guns captured at Ticonderoga and set up on Dorchester Heights under General Washington's command. Washington himself reportedly drew on the earlier tradition in choosing "St. Patrick" as the response to "Boston," the password used in the colonial lines on evacuation day. Although the General Court of Massachusetts did not officially designate March 17 as Evacuation Day until 1938, the City Council of Boston had previously sponsored public celebrations of Evacuation Day, including notable commemorations on the centennial in 1876, and on the 125th anniversary in 1901, with its parade, salute, concert, and fireworks display.

The tradition of formal sponsorship by the city came to an end in 1947, however, when Mayor James Michael Curley himself granted authority to organize and conduct the St. Patrick's Day–Evacuation Day Parade to the petitioner South Boston Allied War Veterans Council, an unincorporated association of individuals elected from various South Boston veterans groups. Every year since, the Council has applied for and received a permit for the parade, which at times has included as many as 20,000 marchers and drawn up to 1 million watchers. No other applicant has ever applied for that permit. Through 1992, the city allowed the Council to use the city's official seal, and provided printing services as well as direct funding.

In 1992, a number of gay, lesbian, and bisexual descendants of the Irish immigrants joined together with other supporters to form the respondent organization, GLIB, to march in the parade as a way to express pride in their Irish heritage as openly gay, lesbian, and bisexual individuals, to demonstrate that there are such men and women among those so descended, and to express their solidarity with like individuals who sought to march in New York's St. Patrick's Day Parade. Although the Council denied GLIB's application to take part in the 1992 parade, GLIB obtained a state-court order to include its contingent, which marched "uneventfully" among that year's 10,000 participants and 750,000 spectators. In 1993, after the Council again refused to admit GLIB to the upcoming parade, the organization and some of its members filed this suit against the Council, the individual petitioner Hurley, and the city of Boston, alleging violations of the State and Federal Constitutions and of the state public accommodations law, which prohibits "any distinction, discrimination or restriction on account of sexual orientation relative to the admission of any person to, or treatment in any place of public accommodation, resort or amusement." Mass. Gen. Laws ch. 272, §98 (1992). We granted certiorari.

If there were no reason for a group of people to march from here to there except to reach a destination, they could make the trip without expressing any message beyond the fact of the march itself. Some people might call such a procession a parade, but it would not be much of one. Real "parades are public dramas of social relations, and in them performers define who can be a social actor and what subjects and ideas are available for communication and consideration." S. DAVIS, PARADES AND POWER: STREET THEATRE IN NINETEENTH-CENTURY PHILADELPHIA 6 (Temple University 1986). Hence, we use the word "parade" to indicate marchers who are making some sort of collective point, not just to each other but to bystanders along the way. Indeed, a parade's dependence on watchers is so extreme that "if a parade or demonstration receives no media coverage, it may as well not have happened." Parades are thus a form of expression, not just motion, and the inherent expressiveness of marching to make a point explains our cases involving protest marches. The protected expression that inheres in a parade is not limited to its banners and songs, however, for the Constitution looks beyond written or spoken words as mediums of expression. Noting that "symbolism is a primitive but effective way of communicating ideas," *West Virginia Bd. of Ed. v. Barnette*, 319 U.S. 624, 632 (1943), our cases have recognized that the First Amendment shields such acts as saluting a flag (and refusing to do so), wearing an armband to protest a war, displaying a red flag, and even "marching, walking or parading" in uniforms displaying the swastika. A narrow, succinctly articulable message is not a condition of constitutional protection, which if confined to expressions conveying a "particularized message," would never reach the unquestionably shielded painting of Jackson Pollock, music of Arnold Schoenberg, or Jabberwocky verse of Lewis Carroll.

Not many marches, then, are beyond the realm of expressive parades, and the South Boston celebration is not one of them. Spectators line the streets; people march in costumes and uniforms, carrying flags and banners with all sorts of messages (e.g., "England get out of Ireland," "Say no to drugs"); marching bands and pipers play; floats are pulled along; and the whole show is broadcast over Boston television. In spite of excluding some applicants, the Council is rather lenient in admitting participants. But a private speaker does not forfeit constitutional protection simply by combining multifarious voices, or by failing to edit their themes to isolate an exact message as the exclusive subject matter of the speech. Nor, does First Amendment protection require a speaker to generate, as an original matter, each item featured in the communication.

Respondents' participation as a unit in the parade was equally expressive. GLIB was formed for the very purpose of marching in order to celebrate its members' identity as openly gay, lesbian, and bisexual descendants of the Irish immigrants, to show that there are such individuals in the community, and to support the like men and women who sought to march in the New York parade. The organization distributed a fact sheet describing the members' intentions. In 1993, members of GLIB marched behind a shamrock-strewn banner with the simple inscription "Irish American Gay, Lesbian and Bisexual Group of Boston." GLIB understandably seeks to communicate its ideas as part of the existing parade, rather than staging one of its own.

The Massachusetts public accommodations law under which respondents brought suit has a venerable history. At common law, innkeepers, smiths, and others who "made profession of a public employment," were prohibited from refusing, without good reason, to serve a customer. The law today prohibits discrimination on the basis of "race, color, religious creed, national origin, sex, sexual orientation, deafness, blindness or any physical or mental disability or ancestry" in "the admission of any person to, or treatment in any place of public accommodation, resort or amusement." Mass. Gen. Laws ch. 272, §98 (1992). Provisions like these are well within the State's usual power to enact when a legislature has reason to believe that a given group is the target of discrimination, and they do not, as a general matter, violate the First or Fourteenth Amendments. *See, e.g., New York State Club Assn., Inc. v. City of New York*, 487 U.S. 1, 11-16 (1988).

Petitioners disclaim any intent to exclude homosexuals as such, and no individual member of GLIB claims to have been excluded from parading as a member of any group that the Council has approved to march. Instead, the disagreement goes to the admission of GLIB as its own parade unit carrying its own banner. Since every participating unit affects the message conveyed by the private organizers, the state courts' application of the statute produced an order essentially requiring petitioners to alter the expressive content of their parade. Although the state courts spoke of the parade as a place of public accommodation, once the expressive character of both the parade and the marching GLIB contingent is understood, it becomes apparent that the state courts' application of the statute had the effect of declaring the sponsors' speech itself to be the public accommodation. Under this approach any contingent of protected individuals with a message would have the right to participate in petitioners' speech, so that the communication produced by the private organizers would be shaped by all those protected by the law who wished to join in with some expressive demonstration of their own. But this use of the State's power violates the fundamental rule of protection under the First Amendment, that a speaker has the autonomy to choose the content of his own message.

"Since all speech inherently involves choices of what to say and what to leave unsaid," one important manifestation of the principle of free speech is that one who chooses to speak may also decide "what not to say." Although the State may at times "prescribe what shall be orthodox in commercial advertising" by requiring the dissemination of "purely factual and uncontroversial information," outside that context it may not compel affirmance of a belief with which the speaker disagrees. This general rule, that the speaker has the right to tailor the speech, applies not only to expressions of value, opinion, or endorsement, but equally to statements of fact the speaker would rather avoid, subject, perhaps, to the permissive law of defamation. Nor is the rule's benefit restricted to the press, being enjoyed by business corporations generally and by ordinary people engaged in unsophisticated expression as well as by professional publishers. Its point is to shield just those choices of content that in someone's eyes are misguided, or even hurtful.

Petitioners' claim to the benefit of this principle of autonomy to control one's own speech is as sound as the South Boston parade is expressive. Like a composer, the Council selects the expressive units of the parade from potential participants, and though the score may not produce a particularized message, each contingent's expression in the Council's eyes comports with what merits celebration on that day. Even if this view gives the Council credit for a more considered judgment than it actively made, the Council clearly decided to exclude a message it did not like from the communication it chose to make, and that is enough to invoke its right as a private speaker to shape its expression by speaking on one subject while remaining silent on another. The message it disfavored is not difficult to identify. Although GLIB's point is not wholly articulate, a contingent marching behind the organization's banner would at least bear witness to the fact that some Irish are gay, lesbian, or bisexual, and would suggest their view that people of their sexual orientations have as much claim to unqualified social acceptance as heterosexuals and indeed as members of parade units organized around other identifying characteristics. The parade's organizers may not believe these facts about Irish sexuality to be so, or they may object to unqualified social acceptance of gays and lesbians or have some other reason for wishing to keep GLIB's message out of the parade. But whatever the reason, it boils down to the choice of a speaker not to propound a particular point of view, and that choice is presumed to lie beyond the government's power to control.

Parades and demonstrations are not neutrally presented or selectively viewed. Unlike the programming offered on various channels by a cable network, the parade does not consist of individual, unrelated segments that happen to be transmitted together for individual selection by members of the audience. Although each parade unit generally identifies itself, each is understood to contribute something to a common theme, and accordingly there is no customary practice whereby private sponsors disavow "any identity of viewpoint" between themselves and the selected participants. Practice follows practicability here, for such disclaimers would be quite curious in a moving parade. Without deciding on the precise significance of the likelihood of misattribution, it nonetheless becomes clear that in the context of an expressive parade, as with a protest march, the parade's overall message is distilled from the individual presentations along the way, and each unit's expression is perceived by spectators as part of the whole.

The size and success of petitioners' parade makes it an enviable vehicle for the dissemination of GLIB's views, but that fact would fall far short of supporting a claim that petitioners enjoy an abiding monopoly of access to spectators. Considering that GLIB presumably would have had a fair shot (under neutral criteria developed by the city) at obtaining a parade permit of its own, respondents have not shown that petitioners enjoy the capacity to "silence the voice of competing speakers." Nor has any other legitimate interest been identified in support of applying the Massachusetts statute to expressive activity like the parade. The statute is a piece of protective legislation that announces no purpose beyond the object both expressed and apparent in its provisions, which is to prevent any denial of access to (or discriminatory treatment in) public accommodations on proscribed grounds, including sexual orientation. The object of the law is to ensure by statute for gays and lesbians desiring to make use of public accommodations what the old common law promised to any member of the public wanting a meal at the inn, that accepting the usual terms of service, they will not be turned away merely on the proprietor's exercise of personal preference. When the law is applied to expressive activity in the way it was done here, its apparent object is simply to require speakers to modify the content of their expression to whatever extent beneficiaries of the law choose to alter it with messages of their own. But in the absence of some further, legitimate end, this object is merely to allow exactly what the general rule of speaker's autonomy forbids.

It might have been argued that the point of forbidding acts of discrimination toward certain classes is to produce a society free of the corresponding biases. Requiring access to a speaker's message would thus be a means to produce speakers free of the biases, whose expressive conduct would be at least neutral toward the particular classes, obviating any future need for correction. But if this is the point of applying the state law to expressive conduct, it is decidedly fatal. Our tradition of free speech commands that a speaker who takes to the street corner to express his views should be free from interference by the State based on the content of what he says. The idea that a noncommercial speech restriction be used to produce thoughts and statements acceptable to some groups or, indeed, all, grates on the First Amendment, for it amounts to nothing less than a proposal to limit speech in the service of orthodox expression. While the law is free to promote all sorts of conduct in place of harmful behavior, it is not free to interfere with speech for no better reason than promoting an approved message or discouraging a disfavored one, however enlightened either purpose may strike the government.

Our holding today rests not on any particular view about the Council's message but on the Nation's commitment to protect freedom of speech. Disapproval of a private speaker's statement does not legitimize use of the Commonwealth's power to compel the speaker to alter the message by including one more acceptable to others. Accordingly, the judgment of the Supreme Judicial Court is reversed, and the case is remanded for proceedings not inconsistent with this opinion.

It is so ordered.

Notes

1. *Gay Scoutmasters. Boy Scouts of America v. Dale*, 530 U.S. 640 (2000), involved a private, not-for-profit, organization engaged in instilling values in young people. The organization asserted that homosexual conduct was inconsistent with the values it seeks to instill. Dale, a former Eagle Scout whose adult membership in the Boy Scouts was revoked when the Scouts learned that he was homosexual and a gay rights activist, sued, claiming a violation of New Jersey's public accommodations law. The Court held that the law could not be applied to the Boy Scouts: "A state requirement that the Boy Scouts retain Dale as an assistant scoutmaster would significantly burden the organization's right to oppose or disfavor homosexual conduct. The state interests do not justify such a severe intrusion on the Boy Scouts' rights to freedom of expressive association. The First Amendment prohibits the State from imposing such a requirement through the application of its public accommodations law." Four justices dissented. Justice Stevens stated: "Dale's participation sends no cognizable message to the Scouts or to the world. Dale did not carry a banner or a sign; and he expressed no intent to send any message. If there is any kind of message being sent, it is by the mere act of joining the Boy Scouts. Such an act does not constitute symbolic speech under the First Amendment."

2. *The Solomon Amendment.* During the era between 1993 and 2011, a federal law known as, "Don't Ask, Don't Tell," prohibited members of the military from identifying themselves as gays, lesbians, or bisexuals. The consequence of disclosure was discharge from the armed forces. During this era, the Association

of American Law Schools prohibited discrimination on the basis of sexual orientation by member schools. The AALS anti-discrimination policy effectively prohibited the U.S. military services from recruiting and interviewing law students at virtually all law schools. In response, Congress enacted the law known as the Solomon Amendment, which prohibited an institution of higher education, or any part of such an institution (such as a law school) from receiving federal funds if the institution "has a policy or practice that either prohibits or in effect prevents" military recruiters from having access to students on campus. When a group of law schools challenged the constitutionality of the Solomon Amendment on First Amendment grounds, the Court held that the law did not violate the law schools' freedom of association and did not compel the law schools to communicate the government's message. *See Rumsfeld v. Forum for Academic and Institutional Rights, Inc.*, 547 U.S. 47 (2006).

3. *The FACT Act.* In *National Institute of Family and Life Advocates v. Becerra*, 138 S. Ct. 2361 (2018), the Court struck down the California Reproductive Freedom, Accountability, Comprehensive Care and Transparency Act (FACT Act) which required crisis pregnancy centers, generally "pro-life" (largely Christian belief-based) organizations that are designed to offer women a range of options, besides abortions, and who offer a limited range of free pregnancy options, counseling, and other services to individuals that visit a center, to give clients the following government-mandated notice: "California has public programs that provide immediate free or low-cost access to comprehensive family planning services (including all FDA-approved methods of contraception), prenatal care, and abortion for eligible women. To determine whether you qualify, contact the county social services office at [insert the telephone number]." The Court struck down the notice on the ground, inter alia, that the law imposed a content-based restriction on speech.

∼ PROBLEMS ∼

1. *In God We Trust.* U.S. money bears the mottoes "In God We Trust" and "E Pluribus Unum." An atheist who objects to both mottoes paints over them on all money that comes into his possession. If the atheist is prosecuted under a federal law prohibiting the defacement of money, can he defend based on his right of association?

2. *Softball League.* Assume that a softball league organized by gay men decides to allow non-gay players as members, but limits the number of such players. When this limitation is challenged as a violation of a state anti-discrimination law, what reasoning could the court use to uphold the right of the league to establish this limitation? *See Apilado v. North American Gay Amateur Athlete Alliance*, 792 F.Supp. 2d 1151 (W.D. Wash. 2011).

3. *Promoting "Social Justice."* The University of Louisville's Louis D. Brandeis School of Law decides that its mission should include, among other things, the

promotion of "social justice." Suppose that the dean wishes to evaluate faculty for merit purposes based on the extent to which they help promote the law school's mission. Suppose that a conservative faculty member objects to the mission statement on the basis that the term "social justice" has no clearly defined meaning, and is likely to be construed by the dean as requiring faculty to promote a left-wing agenda (to which the faculty member objects). Can the faculty member be required, on pain of a lower annual raise, to promote social justice?

4. *The School Dress Code.* Suppose that a public elementary school adopts a mandatory dress code. However, rather than imposing a traditional dress code (e.g., plain-colored tops and bottoms), the school requires all students to wear T-shirts bearing the school's motto: Tomorrow's Leaders. One student objects to the T-shirt as "stupid" and "embarrassing." May a public school, consistently with the First Amendment, require a student to wear a T-shirt displaying its motto? *See Frudden v. Pilling*, 742 F.3d 1199 (9th Cir. 2014).

5. *Requiring Intercultural Competency.* According to media reports, a Clemson University administrator has proposed that student government candidates should be required to pass an "intercultural competency" test before being permitted to run for or hold office, and candidates/office holders can satisfy the requirement by showing that they have gone through training or workshops on intercultural competency. One student senator denounced the requirement as equivalent to "vetting candidates ideologically regarding their commitment to inclusivity and multiculturalism and brain washing. It reminds me of the kind of political totalitarianism that one sees in modern-day fascist and communist regimes." May a public university impose an "intercultural competency" test as a condition for running for or holding a student government office, and require candidates to go through "intercultural competency training"? *See Clemson official proposes 'intercultural' test for student government candidates*, Greenville Journal, April 26, 2017, https://greenvillejournal.com/2017/04/26/clemson-official-proposes-intercultural-test-student-government-candidates/.

Janus v. American Federation of State, County, and Municipal Employees

138 S. Ct. 2448 (2018)

Justice ALITO delivered the opinion of the Court.

Under the Illinois Public Labor Relations Act (IPLRA), employees of the State and its political subdivisions are permitted to unionize. If a majority of employees in a bargaining unit vote to be represented by a union, that union is designated as the exclusive representative of all the employees. Employees in the unit are not obligated to join the union, but whether they join or not, that union is their sole representative. Only the union may negotiate with the employer on matters relating to "pay, wages, hours, and other conditions of employment." This authority extends to the negotiation of what the IPLRA calls "policy matters," such as merit pay, the size of the work force, layoffs, privatization, promotion methods, and non-discrimination policies. This designation means that individual employees may not be represented by any agent other than the designated union; nor may individual employees negotiate directly with their employer. Protection of the employees' interests is in the hands of the union, and the union is required by law to provide fair representation for all employees in the unit, members and nonmembers alike.

Under *Abood v. Detroit Bd. of Ed.*, 431 U.S. 209 (1977), nonmembers may be charged for the portion of union dues attributable to activities that are "germane to the union's duties as collective-bargaining representative," but may not be required to fund the union's political and ideological projects. Outlays in the first category are known as "chargeable" expenditures, while those in the latter are labeled "nonchargeable." The IPLRA provides that an agency fee may compensate a union for costs incurred in "the collective bargaining process, contract administration, and pursuing matters affecting wages, hours, and conditions of employment." Excluded from the agency-fee calculation are union expenditures "related to the election or support of any candidate for political office." A union categorizes its expenditures as chargeable or nonchargeable and thus determines a nonmember's "proportionate share," this determination is then audited; the amount of the "proportionate share" is certified to the employer; and the employer automatically deducts that amount from the nonmembers' wages. Nonmembers need not be asked, and are not required to consent. After the agency fee is fixed, the union must send nonmembers a *Hudson* notice. *See Teachers v. Hudson*, 475 U.S. 292 (1986). This notice is supposed to provide nonmembers with "an adequate explanation of the basis for the agency fee." If nonmembers "suspect that a union has improperly put certain expenses in the chargeable category," they may challenge that determination. Unions charge nonmembers, not just for the cost of collective bargaining *per se*, but also for many other supposedly connected activities. Here, the nonmembers had to pay for "lobbying," "social and recreational activities," "advertising," "membership meetings and conventions," and "litigation," as well as other unspecified "services" that "may inure to the benefit of the members of the local bargaining unit." The total chargeable amount for nonmembers was 78.06% of full union dues.

Petitioner Janus is employed by the Illinois Department of Healthcare and Family Services as a child support specialist. Employees in his unit are among the 35,000 public employees who are represented by respondent American Federation of State, County, and Municipal Employees, Council 31. Janus refused to join the Union because he opposes "many of the public policy positions," including the positions it takes in collective bargaining. Janus believes that the Union's "bargaining does not appreciate the current fiscal crises in Illinois and does not reflect his best interests or the interests of Illinois citizens." Therefore, if he had the choice, he "would not pay any fees or otherwise subsidize the Union." Under the agreement, he was required to pay an agency fee of $44.58 per month. The Governor of the State commenced an action asking that the law be declared unconstitutional. The District Court [concluded] that the

Governor could not maintain the lawsuit, but that petitioner and other individuals had standing. The court [allowed] petitioner and others to file their own complaint. The amended complaint claims that all "nonmember fee deductions are coerced political speech" and that "the First Amendment forbids coercing money from nonmembers." Respondents moved to dismiss. The District Court granted the motion, and the Court of Appeals for the Seventh Circuit affirmed. We granted certiorari.

Abood upheld the constitutionality of an agency-shop arrangement like the one now before us, but this holding is "something of an anomaly," *Knox v. Service Employees*, 567 U.S. 298 (2012), and [its] "analysis is questionable." The First Amendment, applicable to the States by the Fourteenth Amendment, forbids abridgment of freedom of speech. We have held that freedom of speech "includes both the right to speak freely and the right to refrain from speaking at all." *Wooley v. Maynard*, 430 U.S. 705, 714 (1977). The right to eschew association for expressive purposes is likewise protected. *Roberts v. United States Jaycees*, 468 U.S. 609 (1984). As Justice Jackson put it: "If there is any fixed star in our constitutional constellation, it is that no official, high or petty, can prescribe what shall be orthodox in politics, nationalism, religion, or other matters of opinion or force citizens to confess by word or act their faith therein." *West Virginia Bd. of Ed. v. Barnette*, 319 U.S. 624, 642 (1943).

Compelling individuals to support views they find objectionable violates that cardinal constitutional command, and in most contexts, such effort would be universally condemned. Suppose that the State of Illinois required all residents to sign a document expressing support for a set of positions on controversial public issues—say, the platform of one of the political parties. No one would seriously argue that the First Amendment permits this. Perhaps because such compulsion plainly violates the Constitution, most of our free speech cases have involved restrictions on what can be said, rather than laws compelling speech. But measures compelling speech are as threatening. Free speech serves many ends. It is essential to our democratic form of government, and it furthers the search for truth, *see, e.g., Thornhill v. Alabama*, 310 U.S. 88 (1940). Whenever the Federal Government or a State prevents individuals from saying what they think on important matters or compels them to voice ideas with which they disagree, it undermines these ends. Individuals are coerced into betraying their convictions. Forcing free and independent individuals to endorse ideas they find objectionable is demeaning, and a law commanding "involuntary affirmation" of objected-to beliefs would require "even more immediate and urgent grounds" than a law demanding silence. *Barnette, supra*, at 633. Compelling a person to subsidize the speech of other private speakers raises similar First Amendment concerns. *Knox, supra*, at 309. As Jefferson famously put it, "to compel a man to furnish contributions of money for the propagation of opinions which he disbelieves and abhors is sinful and tyrannical." A Bill for Establishing Religious Freedom, in 2 PAPERS OF THOMAS JEFFERSON 545 (J. Boyd ed.1950). A "significant impingement on First Amendment rights" occurs when public employees are required to provide financial support for a union that "takes positions during collective bargaining that have powerful political and civic consequences." *Knox, supra,* at 310–311.

Because the compelled subsidization of private speech impinges on First Amendment rights, it cannot be casually allowed. In *Knox,* we found it sufficient to hold that the conduct in question was unconstitutional under even the test used for the compulsory subsidization of commercial speech. In *Harris,* an agency-fee requirement failed "exacting scrutiny." Petitioner contends that the Illinois law should be subjected to "strict scrutiny." The dissent proposes that we apply rational-basis review. This form of minimal scrutiny is foreign to our free-speech jurisprudence. We find it unnecessary to decide the issue because the Illinois scheme cannot survive under even the more permissive standard applied in *Knox* and *Harris.* In *Abood,* the main defense of the agency-fee arrangement was that it served the State's interest in "labor peace," *Abood* meant avoidance of the conflict and disruption that it envisioned would occur if the employees in a unit were represented by more than one union. We assume that "labor peace" is a compelling state interest, but *Abood* cited no evidence that pandemonium would result if agency fees were not allowed. *Abood* assumed that designation of a union as the exclusive representative of all the employees in a unit and the exaction of agency fees are inextricably linked, but that is not true. Under federal law, a union chosen by majority vote is the exclusive representative of all employees, but federal law does not permit agency fees. Nevertheless, nearly a million federal employees—27% of the work force—are union members. Likewise, millions of public employees in the 28 States that have laws prohibiting agency fees are represented by unions that serve as the exclusive representatives of all employees. "Labor peace" can be achieved "through means significantly less restrictive of associational freedoms" than the assessment of agency fees.

Abood cited "the risk of 'free riders'" as justification reasoning that agency fees are needed to prevent nonmembers from enjoying the benefits of union representation without shouldering the costs. Petitioner argues that he is more like a person shanghaied for an unwanted voyage. Avoiding free riders is not a compelling interest. Many private groups speak with the objective of obtaining government action that will benefit nonmembers. Suppose that a group lobbies or speaks out on behalf of senior citizens or veterans or physicians. Could the government require that all seniors, veterans, or doctors pay for that service even if they object? The First Amendment does not permit the government to compel a person to pay for another party's speech just because the government thinks that the speech furthers the interests of the person who does not want to pay. Those supporting agency fees contend that the situation here is different because unions are statutorily required to "represent the interests of all public employees in the unit," whether or not they are union members. It might be argued that a State has a compelling interest in requiring the payment of agency fees because (1) unions would otherwise be unwilling to represent nonmembers or (2) it would be fundamentally unfair to require unions to provide fair representation for nonmembers if nonmembers were not required to pay. Neither of these arguments is sound. First, unions represent millions of public employees in jurisdictions that do not permit agency fees. Designation as the exclusive representative confers many benefits. That status gives the union a privileged place in negotiations over wages, benefits, and working conditions. The employer is required by state law to listen to and to bargain in good faith with only that union. Designation as exclusive representative thus "results in a tremendous increase in the power" of the union. In addition, a union designated as exclusive representative is often granted special privileges, such as obtaining information about employees, and having dues and fees deducted directly from employee wages. The collective-bargaining agreement in this case guarantees a long list of additional privileges. These benefits greatly outweigh any extra burden imposed by the duty of providing fair representation for nonmembers. This duty entails an obligation not to "act solely in the interests of the union's own members." The union may not negotiate a collective-bargaining agreement that discriminates against nonmembers. Neither respondents nor any of the amicus briefs has explained why the duty of fair representation causes public-sector unions to incur significantly greater expenses.

What about the representation of nonmembers in grievance proceedings? Unions do not undertake this activity solely for the benefit of nonmembers. Representation of nonmembers furthers the union's interest in keeping control of the administration of the collective-bargaining agreement, since the resolution of one employee's grievance can affect others. When a union controls the process, it may subordinate "the interests of an individual employee to the collective interests of all employees in the bargaining unit." *Alexander v. Gardner–Denver Co.*, 415 U.S. 36, 58 (1974). Whatever unwanted burden is imposed by the representation of nonmembers in disciplinary matters can be eliminated "through means significantly less restrictive of associational freedoms" than the imposition of agency fees. Individual nonmembers could be required to pay for that service or could be denied union representation altogether.

Nor can fees be justified on the ground that it would be unfair to require a union to bear the duty of fair representation. That duty is a necessary concomitant of the authority that a union seeks when it chooses to serve as the exclusive representative of all the employees in a unit. Designating a union as the exclusive representative restricts the nonmembers' rights. Protection of their interests is in the hands of the union, and if the union were free to disregard or even work against those interests, these employees would be wholly unprotected. Serious "constitutional questions would arise" if the union were not subject to the duty to represent all employees fairly. Agency fees cannot be upheld on free-rider grounds.

Proponents of agency fees [claim that] *Abood* was correctly decided because the First Amendment was not originally understood to provide any protection for the free speech rights of public employees. We doubt that the Union—or its members want us to hold that public employees have "no free speech rights." Taking away free speech protection for public employees would mean overturning decades of landmark precedent. Under the Union's theory, *Pickering v. Board of Ed. of Township High School Dist. 205, Will Cty.*, 391 U.S. 563 (1968), and its progeny would fall. Indeed, *Abood* itself would go. Our political patronage cases would be doomed. *See, e.g., Rutan v. Republican Party of Ill.*, 497 U.S. 62 (1990). Also imperiled would be older precedents like *Wieman v. Updegraff*, 344 U.S. 183 (1952) (loyalty oaths), *Shelton v. Tucker*, 364 U.S. 479 (1960) (disclosure of memberships and contributions), and *Keyishian v. Board of Regents of Univ. of State of N. Y.*, 385 U.S. 589 (1967) (subversive speech). Respondents presumably want none of this. The Union offers no persuasive founding-era evidence that public employees were understood to lack free speech protections. Most of its historical examples involved limitations on public officials' outside business dealings, not on their speech. We do know that prominent members of the founding generation condemned laws requiring public employees to affirm or support beliefs with which they disagreed. Jefferson denounced compelled support for such beliefs as "sinful and tyrannical," and others expressed similar views.

The principal defense of *Abood* is based on *Pickering* which held that a school district violated the First Amendment by firing a teacher for writing a letter critical of the school administration. Under *Pickering* and later cases, employee speech is largely unprotected if it is part of what the employee is paid to do, or if it involved a matter of only private concern. When a public employee speaks as a citizen on a matter of public concern, the employee's speech is protected unless "the interest of the state, as an employer, in promoting the efficiency of the public services it performs through its employees' outweighs 'the interests of the employee, as a citizen, in commenting upon matters of public concern.'" *Harris*, 573 U.S., at —— (slip op., at 35).

Pickering was developed for use in a very different context—in cases that involve "one employee's speech and its impact on that employee's public responsibilities." *United States v. Treasury Employees*, 513 U.S. 454, 467 (1995). This case involves a blanket requirement that all employees subsidize speech with which they may not agree. [If] a single employee complains that he or she should have received a 5% raise. This individual complaint would constitute a matter of only private concern and would therefore be unprotected under *Pickering.* But a public-sector union's demand for a 5% raise for many thousands of employees could have a serious impact on the budget of the government unit, and denying a raise might have a significant effect on the performance of government services. When a large number of employees speak through their union, the category of speech that is of public concern is greatly enlarged, and the category of speech that is of only private concern is shrunk. Although both *Pickering* and *Abood* divided speech into two categories, the categorizations do not line up. Superimposing the *Pickering* scheme on *Abood* would significantly change *Abood.* Under *Abood,* a public employer is prohibited from permitting nonmembers to be charged for this speech, but under *Pickering,* the employees' free speech interests could be overcome if a court found that the employer's interests outweighed the employees'. A similar problem arises with respect to speech that is germane to collective bargaining. The parties dispute how much of this speech is of public concern, but respondents concede that much of it falls into that category. Under *Abood*, nonmembers may be required to pay for all this speech, but *Pickering* would permit that practice only if the employer's interests outweighed those of the employees. Thus, recasting *Abood* as an application of *Pickering* would substantially alter the *Abood* scheme. Even if we were to apply *Pickering*, Illinois' fee arrangement would not survive.

Respondents suggest that union speech in collective-bargaining and grievance proceedings should be treated like the employee speech in *Garcetti*, i.e., as speech "pursuant to an employee's official duties," In general when public employees are performing their duties, their speech may be controlled by their employer. Respondents suggest that the union speech funded by agency fees forms part of the official duties of the union officers who engage in the speech. When an employee engages in speech that is part of the employee's job duties, the employee is effectively the employer's spokesperson. But when a union negotiates with the employer or represents employees in disciplinary proceedings, the union speaks for the employees, not the employer. Otherwise, the employer would be negotiating with itself and disputing its own actions. If the union's speech is really the employer's speech, then the employer could dictate what the union says. Unions would be appalled by such a suggestion. *Garcetti* is totally inapposite.

The next step of *Pickering* [is] whether the speech is on a matter of public or only private concern. "It is impossible to argue that the level of state spending for employee benefits is not a matter of great public concern." Illinois, like other States suffers from severe budget problems. The Governor and public-sector unions disagree about what to do about these problems. The State claims that employment-related debt is "squeezing core programs in education, public safety, and human services, [and] limiting the State's ability to pay its bills." It "would address the financial crisis, in part, through collective bargaining." "The State's desire for savings" "drove its bargaining" positions on matters such as health-insurance benefits and holiday, overtime, and promotion policies. The Union countered with different suggestions. It advocated wage and tax increases, cutting spending "to Wall Street financial institutions," and reforms to "pension and tax systems (closing "corporate tax loopholes," "expanding the state sales tax," and "an income tax adjusted in accordance with ability to pay"). To suggest that speech on such matters is not of great public concern—or that it is not directed at the "public square,"—is to deny reality.

Unions express views on a wide range of subjects—education, child welfare, healthcare, and minority rights. What unions say on these matters in collective bargaining is of great public importance. Take education. The public importance of subsidized union speech is especially apparent in this field, since educators make up the largest category of state and local government employees, and education is typically the largest component of state and local expenditures. Speech in this area touches on fundamental questions of education policy. Should teacher pay be based on seniority to retain experienced teachers? Or should schools adopt merit-pay systems to encourage teachers to get the best results? Should districts transfer more experienced teachers to lower performing schools that may have the greatest need for their skills, or should teachers be allowed to stay where they have roots? Should teachers be given tenure protection and under what conditions? On what grounds and procedures should teachers be subject to discipline or dismissal? How should teacher performance and student progress be measured—by standardized tests or other means? Unions can also speak out in collective bargaining on controversial subjects such as climate change, the Confederacy, sexual orientation and gender identity, evolution, and minority religions. These are sensitive political topics, and they are of profound "value and concern to the public." *Snyder v. Phelps*, 562 U.S. 443 (2011). Such speech "occupies the highest rung of the hierarchy of First Amendment values" and merits "special protection." Even union speech in the handling of grievances may be of substantial public importance and may be directed at the "public square." For instance, respondent recently filed a grievance seeking to compel Illinois to appropriate $75 million to fund a 2% wage increase. The union speech in this case is overwhelmingly of substantial public concern.

Defenders of *Abood* have asserted a different state interest—the State's "interest in bargaining with an adequately funded exclusive bargaining agent." Although the dissent would accept the State's assertion that the absence of agency fees would cripple public-sector unions and thus impair the efficiency of government operations, ample experience shows that this is questionable. Especially in light of *Pickering*, the balance tips decisively in favor of employees' free speech rights. "The State has interests as an employer in regulating the speech of its employees that differ significantly from those it possesses in connection with regulation of the speech of the citizenry in general." The State may require that a union serve as exclusive bargaining agent for its employees—itself a significant impingement on associational freedoms that would not be tolerated in other contexts. We draw the line at allowing the government to go further and require all employees to support the union irrespective of whether they share its views. We conclude that public-sector agency-shop arrangements violate the First Amendment, and *Abood* erred in concluding otherwise.

"This Court has not hesitated to overrule decisions offensive to the First Amendment (a fixed star in our constitutional constellation, if there is one)." *Federal Election Comm'n v. Wisconsin Right to Life, Inc.*, 551 U.S. 449 (2007) (Scalia, J., concurring). Our cases identify factors that should be taken into account in deciding whether to overrule a past decision. States and public-sector unions may no longer extract agency fees from nonconsenting employees. Neither an agency fee nor any other payment to the union may be deducted from a nonmember's wages, nor may any other attempt be made to collect such a payment, unless the employee affirmatively consents to pay. *Abood* was wrongly decided and is now overruled. The judgment of the United States Court of Appeals for the Seventh Circuit is reversed, and the case is remanded for further proceedings consistent with this opinion.

It is so ordered.

Justice KAGAN, with whom Justice GINSBURG, Justice BREYER, and Justice SOTOMAYOR join, dissenting.

While protecting public employees' expression about non-workplace matters, *Abood* enabled government to advance important managerial interests—by ensuring the presence of an exclusive employee representative to bargain with. Today['s] decision will have large consequences. Public employee unions will lose a secure source of financial support. The relationships of public employees and employers will alter in wholly unexpected ways. The key question is whether unions without agency fees will be able to carry on as an effective exclusive representative. As more and more stop paying dues, those left must take up the financial slack (and feel like suckers)—so they too quit the union. When the vicious cycle ends, chances are that the union will lack the resources to effectively perform the responsibilities of an exclusive representative. The result is to frustrate the interests of every government entity that thinks a strong exclusive-representation scheme will promote stable labor relations.

A public employee must submit to "certain limitations on his or her freedom." *Garcetti v. Ceballos*, 547 U.S. 410 (2006). Government workers do not "lose their constitutional rights when they accept their positions." *Engquist*, 553 U.S., at 600. But their rights yield when weighed "against the realities of the employment context." *Ibid.* If it were otherwise—if every employment decision were "a constitutional matter"—"Government could not function." *NASA*, 562 U.S., at 149. When the government imposes speech restrictions relating to workplace operations, of the kind a private employer would, the Court upholds them. The Court has long applied a test originating in *Pickering*. The Court first asks whether the employee "spoke as a citizen on a matter of public concern." If not, a public employer can curtail her speech just as a private one could. But if she did speak as a citizen on a public matter, the employer must demonstrate "an adequate justification for treating the employee differently from any other member of the general public." The government needs to show that legitimate workplace interests lay behind the speech regulation. *Abood* drew the constitutional line by analyzing the connection between the government's managerial interests and different kinds of expression. The Court understood that expression as intimately tied to the workplace and employment relationship. The speech was about "working conditions, pay, discipline, promotions, leave, vacations, and terminations," *Borough of Duryea v. Guarnieri*, 564 U.S. 379, 391 (2011); the speech occurred in the workplace; and the speech was directed (mainly) to the employer. *Abood* allowed the government to mandate fees for collective bargaining. But the Court barred the use of fees for union speech supporting political candidates or "ideological causes." That speech was "unrelated to the union's duties as exclusive bargaining representative," but was directed at the broader public sphere. The Court saw no legitimate managerial interests in compelling its subsidization. *Abood* thus dovetailed with the Court's attitude in First Amendment cases toward the regulation of public employees' speech. Now, the government can constitutionally adopt all policies regulating core workplace speech in pursuit of managerial goals—save this one.

The majority's distinction between compelling and restricting speech lacks force. When a government mandates a speech subsidy from a public employee—a tax to support collective bargaining—it should get at least as much deference as when it restricts the employee's speech.

The question is not whether the public is, or should be, interested in a government employee's speech. The question is whether that speech is about and directed to the workplace—as contrasted with the broader public square. Speech about the terms and conditions of employment—the essential stuff of collective bargaining—has never survived *Pickering's* first step. The next question is whether the government has shown "an adequate justification for treating the employee differently from any other member of the general public." *Garcetti,* 547 U.S., at 418. This Court has reversed the government only when it has tried to "leverage the employment relationship" to achieve an outcome unrelated to the workplace's "effective functioning." *Garcetti,* 547 U.S., at 419. Many government entities have found agency fees the best way to ensure a stable and productive relationship with an exclusive bargaining agent. The Court has respected those interests. The Court allows a government entity to regulate expression in aid of managing its workforce to effectively provide public services.

Notes

1. *Janus' Aftermath. Janus* has turned out to be a very consequential decision. In 2018, the year the decision was rendered, nearly 210,000 individuals stopped paying agency fees to unions. The hardest hit was the American Federation of State, County and Municipal Employees (AFSCME) which saw a 98% drop in agency payers (leaving a total of 2,200 payers) followed by the Service Employees International Union (SEIU) which lost 94% of its agency payers (leaving a total of 5,800). Some teachers' unions were also hard hit. In terms of membership (members are required to pay dues), AFSCME showed a 9% increase in membership, but the SEIU showed a 0.3 decline. *Janus* also generated a series of other legal challenges, including requirements that all lawyers belong to state bar associations, and industry groups that require contributions to advertising for their products. Individuals have also challenged whether unions can act as the "exclusive representative" for workers or impose conditions on when individuals can stop paying dues.

2. *Home Health Care Workers.* In *Harris v. Quinn,* 573 U.S. 616 (2014), the Court held that the First Amendment precludes a state from compelling personal care providers to subsidize speech on matters of public concern by a union that they do not wish to join or support.

3. *Student Activity Fees. Board of Regents of the University of Wisconsin System v. Southworth,* 529 U.S. 217 (2000), involved the University of Wisconsin's student activity fee, which was used to fund student organizations (RSOs). The fee was imposed to facilitate the free and open exchange of ideas among students

on a viewpoint-neutral basis. Students sued, complaining that they were being required to subsidize speech that they found objectionable. While the Court recognized that it "all but inevitable that the fees will result in subsidies to speech which some students find objectionable and offensive to their personal beliefs," the Court refused to give each student the opportunity "to list those causes which he or she will or will not support." Not only would such a system be "disruptive and expensive," the Court held that the University was free to decide that "its mission is well served if students have the means to engage in dynamic discussions of philosophical, religious, scientific, social, and political subjects in their extra-curricular campus life outside the lecture hall," and that a mandatory student activity fee constituted a permissible way to achieve that objective provided that the system is viewpoint-neutral. However, the Court expressed concern about the fact that student referenda could result in either the funding, or defunding, of particular views. The Court remanded for review of this aspect of the program.

3. *Prohibition on Voluntary Deductions.* In *Ysura v. Pocatello Education Association,* 555 U.S. 353 (2009), the Court upheld an Idaho law that allowed a public employee to elect to have a portion of his wages deducted by his employer and remitted to his union to pay union dues, but that precluded an employee from having an amount deducted for the union's political action committee (because Idaho law prohibits payroll deductions for political activities). The Court upheld the law, noting that the "First Amendment prohibits government from 'abridging the freedom of speech'; it does not confer an affirmative right to use government payroll mechanisms for the purpose of obtaining funds for expression." The Court went on to note that "Idaho's law does not restrict political speech, but rather declines to promote that speech by allowing public employee checkoffs for political activities," and that "banning payroll deductions for political speech similarly furthers the government's interest in distinguishing between internal governmental operations and private speech." Justice Breyer concurred in part and dissented in part, arguing that the Court should inquire "whether the statute imposes a burden upon speech that is disproportionate in light of the other interests the government seeks to achieve," and expressed concerns about whether the particular exception had been applied "even handedly." Justice Stevens dissented, questioning whether the restriction was viewpoint-neutral because it was aimed at unions.

∾ PROBLEMS ∾

1. *Show Me State.* The State of Missouri erects billboards proclaiming its "Show Me State" motto, using general tax revenues to finance the billboards. May a citizen sue to prohibit the billboard message on associational grounds? May a taxpayer challenge the use of public funds to finance the message?

2. *Objections to Union Spending.* After *Abood,* a non–union member complains that he is ethically opposed to the union's decision to negotiate for the inclusion of abortion benefits in a medical insurance plan. Can an employee be required to finance these union activities?

Johanns v. Livestock Marketing Association

544 U.S. 550 (2005)

Justice SCALIA delivered the opinion of the Court.

The Beef Promotion and Research Act of 1985 announces a federal policy of promoting the marketing and consumption of "beef and beef products," using funds raised by an assessment on cattle sales and importation. 7 U.S.C. §2901(b). The statute directs the Secretary of Agriculture to implement this policy by issuing a Beef Promotion and Research Order, and specifies four key terms it must contain: The Secretary is to appoint a Cattlemen's Beef Promotion and Research Board (Beef Board or Board), whose members are to be a geographically representative group of beef producers and importers, nominated by trade associations. The Beef Board is to convene an Operating Committee, composed of 10 Beef Board members and 10 representatives named by a federation of state beef councils. The Secretary is to impose a $1-per-head assessment ("checkoff") on all sales or importation of cattle and a comparable assessment on imported beef products. The assessment is to be used to fund beef-related projects, including promotional campaigns, designed by the Operating Committee and approved by the Secretary.

The Secretary promulgated the Beef Order with the specified terms. The assessment is collected primarily by state beef councils, which then forward the proceeds to the Beef Board.[2] The Operating Committee proposes projects to be funded by the checkoff, including promotion and research. The Secretary or his designee approves each project and, in the case of promotional materials, the content of each communication. The Beef Order was promulgated on a temporary basis, subject to a referendum among beef producers. In 1988, a large majority voted to continue it. Since that time, more than $1 billion has been collected through the checkoff, and a large fraction of that sum has been spent on promotional projects authorized by the Beef Act—many using the familiar trademarked slogan "Beef. It's What's for Dinner." In 2000, the Beef Board collected over $48 million in assessments and spent over $29 million on domestic promotion. The Board also funds overseas marketing efforts; market and food-science research, such as evaluations of the nutritional value of beef; and informational campaigns for both consumers and beef producers. Many promotional

---

2. In most cases, only 50 cents per head is remitted to the Beef Board, because the Beef Act and Beef Order allow domestic producers to deduct from their $1 assessment up to 50 cents in voluntary contributions to their state beef councils.

messages funded by the checkoff bear the attribution "Funded by America's Beef Producers." Most print and television messages also bear a Beef Board logo, usually a check-mark with the word "BEEF."

Respondents are associations whose members collect and pay the checkoff, and several individuals who raise and sell cattle subject to the checkoff, who sued the Secretary, the Department of Agriculture, and the Board. While the litigation was pending, we held in *United States v. United Foods, Inc.*, 533 U.S. 405 (2001), that a mandatory checkoff for generic mushroom advertising violated the First Amendment. Respondents noted that the advertising promotes beef as a generic commodity, which impedes their efforts to promote the superiority of, *inter alia*, American beef, grain-fed beef, or certified Angus or Hereford beef. The District Court ruled for respondents and the Court of Appeals for the Eighth Circuit affirmed. We granted certiorari.

We have sustained First Amendment challenges to allegedly compelled expression in two categories of cases: true "compelled speech" cases, in which an individual is obliged personally to express a message he disagrees with, imposed by the government; and "compelled subsidy" cases, in which an individual is required by the government to subsidize a message he disagrees with, expressed by a private entity. We have not heretofore considered the First Amendment consequences of government-compelled subsidy of the government's own speech.

We first invalidated an outright compulsion of speech in *West Virginia Bd. of Ed. v. Barnette*, 319 U.S. 624 (1943); *see also Wooley v. Maynard*, 430 U.S. 705 (1977). The reasoning of these compelled-speech cases has been carried over to certain instances in which individuals are compelled not to speak, but to subsidize a private message with which they disagree. Thus, we have upheld state-imposed requirements that lawyers be members of the state bar and pay its annual dues[, but we have] invalidated the use of compulsory fees to fund speech on political matters. *See Keller v. State Bar of Cal.*, 496 U.S. 1 (1990). Bar or union speech with such content was not germane to the regulatory interests that justified compelled membership, and accordingly, making those who disagreed with it pay for it violated the First Amendment. These latter cases led us to sustain a compelled-subsidy challenge to an assessment very similar to the beef checkoff, imposed to fund mushroom advertising at issue in *United Foods*. Mushroom producers were obliged by "law or necessity" to pay the checkoff.

In all of the cases invalidating exactions to subsidize speech, the speech was, or was presumed to be, that of an entity other than the government itself. Our compelled-subsidy cases have consistently respected the principle that "compelled support of a private association is fundamentally different from compelled support of government." "Compelled support of government" — even those programs of government one does not approve — is of course perfectly constitutional. Some government programs involve, or entirely consist of, advocating a position. "The government, as a general rule, may support valid programs and policies by taxes or other exactions binding on protesting parties. Within this broader principle it seems inevitable that funds raised by the government will be spent for speech and other expression to advocate and defend its own policies." We have generally assumed, though not yet squarely held, that compelled funding of government speech does not alone raise First Amendment concerns.

Respondents do not seriously dispute these principles. They assert that the challenged promotional campaigns differ dispositively from the type of government speech that is not susceptible to First Amendment challenge. They point to the role of the Beef Board and its Operating Committee in designing the promotional campaigns, and to the use of a mandatory assessment on beef producers to fund the advertising. The Secretary of Agriculture does not write ad copy himself. Rather, the Beef Board's promotional campaigns are designed by the Beef Board's Operating Committee, only half of whose members are Beef Board members appointed by the Secretary. (All members of the Operating Committee are subject to *removal* by the Secretary.) Respondents contend that speech whose content is effectively controlled by a nongovernmental entity—the Operating Committee—cannot be considered "government speech." We reject this contention. The message set out in the beef promotions is from beginning to end the message established by the Federal Government. Congress has directed the implementation of a "coordinated program" of promotion, "including paid advertising, to advance the image and desirability of beef and beef products." Congress and the Secretary have also specified, in general terms, what the promotional campaigns shall contain and what they shall not. Thus, Congress and the Secretary have set out the overarching message and some of its elements, and they have left the development of the remaining details to an entity whose members are answerable to the Secretary (and in some cases appointed by him as well). Moreover, the Secretary exercises final approval authority over every word used in every promotional campaign. Nor is the Secretary's role limited to final approval or rejection: officials of the Department also attend and participate in the open meetings at which proposals are developed.

This degree of governmental control over the message funded by the checkoff distinguishes these cases from *Keller.* There the state bar's communicative activities to which the plaintiffs objected were not prescribed by law in their general outline and not developed under official government supervision. When, as here, the government sets the overall message to be communicated and approves every word that is disseminated, it is not precluded from relying on the government-speech doctrine merely because it solicits assistance from nongovernmental sources in developing specific messages.

Respondents also contend that the beef program does not qualify as "government speech" because it is funded by a targeted assessment on beef producers, rather than by general revenues. This funding mechanism, they argue, has two relevant effects: it gives control over the beef program not to politically accountable legislators, but to a narrow interest group that will pay no heed to respondents' dissenting views, and it creates the perception that the advertisements speak for beef producers such as respondents. The compelled-*subsidy* analysis is altogether unaffected by whether the funds for the promotions are raised by general taxes or through a targeted assessment. Here, the program is authorized and the basic message prescribed by federal statute, and specific requirements for the promotions' content are imposed by federal regulations promulgated after notice and comment. The Secretary of Agriculture, a politically accountable official, oversees the program, appoints and dismisses the key personnel, and retains absolute veto power over the advertisements' content, right down to the wording. And Congress, of course, retains oversight authority, not to mention the ability to reform the program at any time. No more is required. As to the second point, respondents' argument is that crediting the advertising to "America's Beef Producers" impermissibly uses not only their money but also their seeming endorsement to promote a message with which they do not agree. Whether the *individual* respondents who are beef producers would be associated with speech labeled as coming from "America's Beef Producers" is a question on which the record is silent. On the record before us an as-applied First Amendment challenge to the individual advertisements affords no basis on which to sustain the judgment.

The judgment of the Court of Appeals is vacated, and the cases are remanded for further proceedings consistent with this opinion.

It is so ordered.

Justice SOUTER, with whom Justice STEVENS and Justice KENNEDY join, *dissenting.*

The ranchers' complaint is on all fours with the objection of the mushroom growers in *United Foods* where a similar statutory exaction was struck down as a compelled subsidy of speech prohibited by the First Amendment absent a comprehensive regulatory scheme to which the speech was incidental. If government relies on the government-speech doctrine to compel specific groups to fund speech with targeted taxes, it must make itself politically accountable by indicating that the content actually is a government message, not just the statement of one self-interested group the government is currently willing to invest with power. The ads are not required to show any sign of being speech by the Government, and experience under the Act demonstrates how effectively the Government has masked its role in producing the ads. Many of them include the tag line, "funded by America's Beef Producers," which all but ensures that no one reading them will suspect that the message comes from the National Government. Readers would most naturally think that ads urging people to have beef for dinner were placed and paid for by the beef producers who stand to profit when beef is on the table. No one hearing a commercial for Pepsi or Levi's thinks Uncle Sam is the man talking behind the curtain. Why would a person reading a beef ad think Uncle Sam was trying to make him eat more steak?[7] Unless the government

---

7. Anyone who did draw such an unlikely connection would have to believe that Uncle Sam was having a hard time making his mind up, for other governmental messages take a different view of how much beef Americans should be eating. Dietary Guidelines for Americans 2005, a publication of the Departments of Agriculture and of Health and Human Services, suggests that Americans need to reduce their consumption of fats, and should get their fats from sources other than beef, namely fish, nuts, and vegetable oils.

speech appears to be coming from the government, its governmental origin cannot possibly justify the burden on the First Amendment interests of the dissenters targeted to pay for it.

∾ PROBLEM: GOVERNMENT SPEECH? ∾

Have you seen the ads at issue in the *Johann* case? Did you realize that they were being financed by a governmental program rather than by a private industry group? Or did you assume that they were being paid for and run by beef producers without governmental control and intervention? If the latter, how does that affect your assessment of the *Johann* decision?

O. CAMPAIGN FINANCE LAWS

[Important Note: The topic of campaign finance has grown dramatically in recent years, and few constitutional law teachers have the time to do an in-depth review. As a result, we have included only a brief textual discussion of the topic here.]

1. Modern Foundations

Modern First Amendment jurisprudence on campaign finance regulation begins with *Buckley v. Valeo*, which involved a challenge to the Federal Election Campaign Act of 1971 (FECA) and its 1974 Amendments. The Act contained provisions that operated to limit both expenditures and contributions, including the following restrictions during a calendar year: 1) a $1,000 limit on *expenditures* by an individual "relative to a clearly identified candidate" (and advocating either election or defeat); 2) a limit on *expenditures* by a candidate "from his personal funds, or the personal funds of his immediate family, in connection with his campaigns" ($50,000 limit for presidential or vice presidential candidates, $35,000 limit for Senate candidates, $25,000 limit for most House candidates); 3) a limit on campaign *expenditures* by candidates (for example, for a presidential candidate, a $10 million limit for the primary campaign and $20 million more for the general election campaign; for a House candidate, a $70,000 limit for each campaign); 4) a $1,000 limit on *contributions* by an individual to any single candidate; & 5) a $25,000 limit on total *contributions* by an individual to candidates.

The Court initially determined that campaign finance laws implicate First Amendment interests because they "operate" in the area of "discussions regarding public issues and debate on the qualifications of candidates," which discussions are essential in a free society. The Court emphasized that the "First Amendment protects political association as well as political expression." The Court found that "the giving and spending of money" produces communication that sometimes involves speech alone, sometimes involves conduct, and sometimes involves a combination of the two. Moreover, the Court found that even if such activities involve conduct rather than speech, the *O'Brien* test would not be satisfied because campaign finance laws suppress communication.

The Court invalidated each of the three expenditure limitations after holding that they should be subjected to "exacting scrutiny" because of their limitation "on core First Amendment rights of political expression." The Court held that the act's $1,000 ceiling on spending "relative to a clearly identified candidate" would exclude virtually all citizens and groups (except candidates, political parties, and the institutional press) "from any significant use of the most effective modes of communication." Given the cost of advertising, for example, the Court found that this section made it a federal crime "to place a single one-quarter page advertisement 'relative to a clearly identified candidate' in a major metropolitan newspaper." The Court concluded that the limitation on candidate expenditures from personal or family resources imposed a substantial restraint on the right of a candidate to "vigorously and tirelessly advocate his own election and the election of other candidates." Moreover, by relying on personal funds, candidates reduce their reliance on "outside contributions and thereby counteracts the coercive pressures and attendant risks of abuse to which the Act's contribution limitations are directed." In invalidating the limitation on overall campaign expenditures by candidates, the Court concluded that "the financial resources available to a candidate's campaign will normally vary with the size and intensity of the candidate's support" and "there is nothing invidious, improper, or unhealthy in permitting such funds to be spent to carry the candidate's message to the electorate."

None of the government interests offered in support of the three expenditure limits were deemed to be adequate to satisfy the exacting scrutiny standard. The Court rejected the argument that the government had an interest in "reducing the allegedly skyrocketing costs of political campaigns," reasoning that the First Amendment "denies government the power to determine that spending to promote one's political views is wasteful, excessive, or unwise." The Court also rejected the government's arguments that the expenditure limits could be justified by the government's right to "equalize" the resources and "relative ability of individuals and groups to influence the outcome of elections." The Court found that the "concept that government may restrict the speech of some elements of our society in order to enhance the relative voice of others is wholly foreign to the First Amendment." Finally, the Court rejected the government interest in preventing corruption and the appearance of corruption as a justification for the expenditure limits, reasoning that "the absence of prearrangement and coordination of an expenditure with the candidate alleviates the danger that expenditures will be given as a *quid pro quo* for improper commitments from the candidate."

By contrast, the Court viewed contribution limits as having a more limited impact on political expression than the expenditure limits. The Court noted that contribution limits involve less direct restraint on political communication because they allow some symbolic expression of support without infringing upon the contributor's right to publicly discuss candidates and issues. The Court also emphasized that, although a contribution "serves as a general expression of support for a candidate and his views," it "does not communicate the underlying basis for the support," and a contribution does not become speech without the need for communication by someone other than the contributor (that is, the candidate's campaign). The Court recognized that contributions play an "important role" in financing political campaigns and that "contribution restrictions can have a severe impact on political dialogue if the limitations prevented candidates from amassing the resources necessary for effective advocacy." Even so, the Court found that FECA's contribution limitations would not have a "dramatic adverse effect on the funding of campaigns and political associations." The only impact of the limits would be to require candidates to raise funds from a larger number of contributors, and any donor who wanted to exceed the contribution limits could make direct expenditures on behalf of the candidate instead.

Instead of adopting the exacting scrutiny standard for contribution limits, the Court imposed a less demanding burden on the government, holding that such limits could be sustained "if the State demonstrates a sufficiently important interest and employs means closely drawn to avoid unnecessary abridgment of associational freedoms." The Court identified one government interest that met the "sufficiently important" standard, which was its interest in preventing the "actuality and appearance of corruption" caused by large contributions to candidates made by individuals. The Court reasoned that "the integrity of our system of representative democracy is undermined" by such contributions when they are given to secure a "political *quid pro quo*," and "the appearance of corruption also may arise from public awareness of the opportunities for abuse inherent in a regime of large individual financial contributions." The Court rejected the argument that the government's interests could be satisfied adequately through the use of narrowly drawn disclosure requirements and bribery prosecutions, finding that such alternative means would deal with only the most blatant forms of corruption. In conclusion, the Court held that the First Amendment was not violated by the FECA limit of $1,000 for individual contributions to any single candidate because it was sufficiently "closely drawn" to achieve the government interests regarding corruption. The $25,000 aggregate limit, which restricted the total contributions to candidates that could be made by any individual, similarly met with the Court's approval. The Court noted that although the parties had not separately addressed this limit at length, it was a "modest restraint" that "serves to prevent evasion" of the $1,000 limit.

In *Randall v. Sorrell*, 548 U.S. 230 (2006), the Court invalidated contribution limits that were not only the lowest in the nation, but also well below the limits sustained in *Buckley*. The Court reasoned that the limits in a Vermont statute (1) significantly restricted the funding available for challengers to run competitive campaigns; and (2) severely limited the ability of political parties to assist candidates' campaigns by coordinating spending on advertising, candidate events, voter lists, mass mailings, and yard signs. The state did not advance a sufficient justification for enacting the low contribution limits that posed a serious threat to associational and expressive rights.

Almost 40 years after *Buckley*, the Court agreed that the "aggregate limits" on contributions in the Bipartisan Campaign Reform Act of 2002 (BCRA) should be invalidated in *McCutcheon v. Federal Election Committee*, 572 U.S. 185 (2014). The plaintiff contributor argued that *Buckley*'s deferential scrutiny standard for contribution limits should be overruled and replaced with the exacting scrutiny standard, but a plurality of justices saw no need "to revisit" *Buckley*'s standards of review because it was possible to invalidate BCRA's aggregate limits under the "closely drawn" level of scrutiny. Although the four *McCutcheon* dissenters characterized the plurality's opinion as overruling *Buckley*'s holding that upheld the validity of FECA's aggregate limits, the plurality determined more precisely that *Buckley*'s reasoning regarding those limits could "not control" the issue in *McCutcheon*. This was because the Court confronted "a different statute and different legal arguments, at a different point in the development of campaign finance regulation."

At the outset, the *McCutcheon* plurality emphasized that the Court had previously upheld the constitutionality of the "base" contribution limits under BCRA that restrict "how much money a donor may contribute to any particular candidate or committee." In an annual election cycle, those base limits restricted an individual's contribution to $2,600 per election for a candidate (or $5,200 for contributions to both the primary and general election); $10,000 per year to a state or local party committee; $32,400 per year to a national party committee; and $5,000 per year to a political action committee (PAC). The limits challenged in *McCutcheon* were the "aggregate" contribution limits for an annual election cycle that restricted "how many candidates or committees the donor may support, to the extent permitted by the base limits." Specifically, those limits restricted an individual to a total of $48,600 in contributions to federal candidates and a total of $74,600 to political committees; the latter limit was qualified by a further restriction that no more than $48,600 could be contributed to state or local party committees and PACs. The plaintiff in *McCutcheon* had complied with BCRA's base limits in his contributions to 16 federal candidates. But BCRA's aggregate limits prevented him from contributing similar sums to 12 additional candidates whose election he wished to support. He also wanted to contribute an amount that complied with base limits to three national party committees, but because of the size of his planned contributions, BCRA's aggregate limits allowed him to contribute to only one such committee.

The government's main argument in *McCutcheon* was that the aggregate limits satisfied *Buckley*'s scrutiny standard for contributions because (1) the government interest in deterring actual corruption and the appearance of corruption was "important," and (2) the aggregate limits were "closely drawn" to achieve this goal by preventing circumvention of the base limits. The plurality accepted the first proposition but rejected the second proposition for three reasons. First, the government could not demonstrate that the aggregate limits furthered its anti-circumvention goal, other than by means of hypotheticals based on conjecture that the plurality viewed as "divorced from reality." Second, the aggregate limits were not "narrowly tailored" to achieve the government's interest; instead, the plurality found that "the indiscriminate ban on all contributions above the aggregate limits is disproportionate" to the government's interest in preventing circumvention of the base limits. Moreover, the plurality identified "multiple alternative" regulations of a narrower kind that Congress could have employed to achieve a more "reasonable fit" between its means and ends. The plurality began its analysis with a description of the ways in which BCRA's aggregate limits imposed "significant First Amendment costs" upon individual citizens. By making a contribution to a candidate, an individual engages in the exercise of both the right of expression and the right of association, and the First Amendment equally protects individuals who make large or small contributions as participants in electoral debates. The plurality rejected *Buckley*'s characterization of aggregate limits as "modest" restraints upon protected political activity because the government "may no more restrict how many candidates or causes a donor may support than it may tell a newspaper how many candidates it may endorse." The most obvious constitutional harm caused by aggregate limits is that even when an individual complies with base limits in donations to a particular number of candidates, the aggregate limits "constitute an outright ban on further contributions to any other candidate." Thus, the limits force a donor to limit the number of candidates (and policy concerns) that he or she can support. Second, even though a donor can comply with the aggregate limits by giving less money to more people, this form of compliance effectively imposes "a special burden on broader participation in the democratic process." Third, the aggregate limits create an "especially great" burden upon individuals who "wish to support a wide variety of candidates or causes" but lack the time to express that support through avenues such as volunteer activities.

In considering the government's interest in preventing corruption or its appearance, the *McCutcheon* plurality emphasized that *Buckley* and subsequent precedents, require that "Congress may target only a specific type of corruption" or its appearance, namely *quid pro quo* corruption, and not the possibility that a contributor may garner "influence or access to" elected officials. The plurality characterized the base limits in BCRA as "the primary means of regulating campaign contributions" to achieve the goal of deterring *quid pro quo* corruption or its appearance. By contrast, the plurality explained that the aggregate limits "do not serve that goal in any meaningful way." The plurality began with the premise that when Congress established a base limit of $5,200 in contributions to both the primary and general election of a candidate, this decision reflected a judgment that this amount did not create "a cognizable risk of corruption." But it is not evident why Congress would find that such a risk is created when a donor contributes $5,200 to ten candidates (as prohibited under the aggregate limits) but not when a donor contributes to nine candidates (as allowed under those limits). Therefore, the plurality concluded that the government "must defend the aggregate limits by demonstrating that they prevent circumvention of the base limits," and this proved to be impossible for the government to do because each of the government's examples of potential circumvention was viewed by the plurality as implausible for different reasons.

One of the government's examples of potential circumvention was that a contributor might seek to evade base limits by channeling a lot of money to a favored candidate through "a series of contributions to PACs that have stated their intention to support" that candidate. However, the plurality emphasized that other regulations prohibit contributions to two types of PACs—those that support only the donor's candidate and those that the donor knows will route a "substantial portion" of his or her contribution to the candidate. Moreover, the plurality calculated that even if the donor makes a permissible contribution of the maximum base limit of $5,000 to a multicandidate PAC that is "likely" to route the money to the donor's candidate, the donor will be only one of 50 contributors and the PAC will be limited to giving $2,600 per election to the donor's candidate. Finally, the plurality found it difficult to believe that a rational contributor would engage in other hypothetical circumvention strategies, such as making contributions to a very large number of PACs. Other applicable regulations would limit that strategy and others, and a rational contributor would be more likely to engage in permissible unlimited "independent expenditures" on behalf of his or her favored candidate. After considering other government examples of potential circumvention, the plurality concluded that all of them suffered from varying degrees of implausibility, and that none of them were based on "real-world" examples of circumvention, but only on conjecture.

In rejecting BCRA's aggregate limits as not being sufficiently narrowly tailored to serve the anti-circumvention interest, the *McCutcheon* plurality relied on data from the 2012 election cycle to conclude that an "indiscriminate ban on all contributions" above those limits is "disproportionate" to that interest. The government argued that without the limits, an individual would be able to make contributions to "too many" initial recipients (including candidates, party committees, and PACs), and then circumvention of the base limits could occur because those initial recipients might subsequently recontribute a donation to other recipients. The plurality tested this argument by asking "whether experience under the present law confirms a serious threat of abuse," and found instead that experience supported the prediction that "the vast majority of contributions made in excess of the aggregate limits" would be likely to be retained and spent by their recipients. Finally, an important element of narrow tailoring analysis involves the inquiry whether narrower alternative measures could have been adopted by Congress to serve the anticircumvention interest effectively. On this point, the plurality identified a variety of such measures, including (1) targeted restrictions on the transfer of contributions among candidates and party committees; (2) the use of segregated, nontransferable accounts for contributions above aggregate limits, which accounts could be spent only by the recipients; and (3) additional earmarking regulations, such as prohibitions to prevent donors who contribute the maximum base limit to a candidate from also contributing to committees that support that candidate.

The government sought to offer an additional rationale to support the aggregate limits at oral argument in *McCutcheon,* but the plurality found that the acceptance of that new rationale would broaden "the circumscribed definition of *quid pro pro* corruption" in prior cases to an unacceptable degree. According to *Buckley* and other precedents, the "risk of corruption" that justifies base limits is the risk that arises when large contributions are made by an individual to a candidate. But according to the government's novel rationale for BCRA's aggregate limits, the same risk of corruption should be deemed to arise when an individual supplies a single large donation to a candidate to be divided "among numerous candidates and party committees." In the plurality's view, however, a "clear, administrable line" should be drawn between money funneled to a candidate, for which the candidate feels "obligated," and money "given widely to a candidate's party" for which the candidate would feel "grateful" like other members of the party. By erasing that line, the proffered rationale would impermissibly and "dramatically expand government regulation of the political process."

Justice Thomas, concurred, arguing that all contribution and expenditure limits should be subjected equally to strict scrutiny, and that none of *Buckley*'s distinctions between these two types of limits are persuasive. He emphasized that the Court's post-*Buckley* precedents have discarded three of *Buckley*'s four rationales for deferential treatment of contribution limits, namely: (1) that a contribution is transformed into "debate" through the speech of someone other than the contributor; (2) that a contribution does not communicate the basis for the contributor's expression of support; and (3) that the size of a contribution provides only a rough measure of the intensity of such support. Justice Thomas argued that *Buckley*'s one remaining rationale for deference to contribution limits was equally untenable: namely, that a contribution limit involves "little direct restraint" on political communication because it permits a contributor's "symbolic expression of support" and does not limit his or her "freedom to discuss candidates and issues."

Justice Breyer dissented, arguing that the plurality's holding was based on three flawed arguments. First, the plurality's definition of corruption was too narrow because it excluded the risk of corruption posed by contributions that represent efforts to obtain "influence over or access to" elected officials. Second, the plurality erred in concluding that in the absence of BCRA's aggregate limits, no realistic danger of circumvention of the base limits would arise. Justice Breyer provided examples of methods that party fundraisers can use after *McCutcheon* to evade the base limits, such as the creation of a "joint party committee" made up of national and state party committees, or the establishment of numerous new multicandidate PACs to take advantage of the ability of all donors, including rich ones, to make base limit contributions to an unlimited total of such PACs. Third,

Justice Breyer criticized the adequacy of the plurality's examples of alternate regulations, given the lack of evidence that any of them would be an effective replacement for the aggregate limits.

2. Corporate Speech

The most far-reaching and controversial modern ruling on campaign finance occurred in *Citizens United v. Federal Election Commission*, 558 U.S. 310 (2010), when the Court addressed the constitutionality of a provision in BCRA that prohibited corporations and unions from spending money from general treasury funds on speech expressly advocating the election or defeat of political candidates. This category of speech included "electioneering communications," which were defined to include any broadcast that "refers to a clearly identified candidate" in a federal election, and occurs within 30 days of a primary or 60 days of a general election.

Citizens United, a non-profit corporation, produced a film that expressly advocated the defeat of Senator Hillary Clinton when she was campaigning for the presidential nomination in 2008. In order to spend money to distribute the film as a video-on-demand during the 30-day period before the primary elections, Citizens United was required under BCRA to use money from its political action committee (PAC) that had been collected from the contributions of shareholders and employees. Instead of complying with BCRA, Citizens United filed suit to challenge BCRA's prohibition on the corporation's use of general treasury funds for the expenditure of money on the distribution of its film. In *McConnell v. Federal Election Commission*, 540 U.S. 93 (2003), the Court had upheld BCRA's prohibition, relying on the reasoning of *Austin v. Michigan Chamber of Commerce*, 494 U.S. 652 (1990), which upheld a state statutory ban on the use of corporate treasury funds for expenditures to support or oppose candidates in state elections. In *Citizens United*, the majority Court overruled *Austin* and that aspect of *McConnell* that relied on *Austin*, holding that BCRA's ban on the use of corporate treasury funds violated the First Amendment.

The Court began its analysis by emphasizing the broad scope and impact of BCRA's prohibition, which applied to the publication of books, the creation of Web sites, and the posting of blog messages. The Court characterized the BCRA-approved alternative of using PAC funds as a burdensome one, noting how the vast majority of corporations have not chosen to establish PACs for that purpose because they are expensive to administer and require compliance with extensive regulations. Next, the Court recognized the fact that even though FECA included a prohibition on expenditures by corporations using general treasury funds, the parties in *Buckley* did not challenge that prohibition. Notwithstanding that failure, the Court viewed *Buckley*'s reasoning as implicitly inconsistent with the preservation of the corporate-treasury ban that Congress reenacted in amendments to FECA, and later incorporated into BCRA electioneering provisions.

For example, *Buckley* dictated that as an expenditure limitation, the corporate-treasury ban could not be upheld unless it satisfied the strict scrutiny standard. Moreover, *Buckley* held that FECA's expenditure limits for individuals violated the First Amendment, reasoning that they "necessarily reduced" the quantity of political expression in three ways, by limiting the number of issues that could be discussed, the depth of such discussions, and the size of the audience that could be reached for such discussions. If *Buckley* found that the government could not reduce the impact of the voices of individual speakers through expenditure limits, then the corporate-treasury ban was vulnerable to challenge because of its reduction of the impact of the voice of corporate speakers.

In addition to support from *Buckley*, the *Citizens United* majority recognized that the corporate-treasury ban was inconsistent with the ruling in *National Bank of Boston v. Bellotti*, 435 U.S. 765 (1978), which invalidated a state law ban on corporate expenditures used to oppose the enactment of voter referenda on any issues that did not affect the " property, business or assets" of corporations, which category was defined to exclude taxation issues. The *Bellotti* opinion included broad reasoning that criticized the state's restriction of political speech based on the corporate identity of the speaker, and described the state as "constitutionally disqualified" from determining the subjects of permissible speech and the categories of speakers entitled "to address a public issue." For the *Citizens United* Court, *Bellotti*'s reasoning implicitly was inconsistent with the validity of the corporate-treasury restriction that was based upon the corporate identity of a speaker. The *Austin* decision had upheld such a restriction and sidestepped the implications of *Buckley* and *Bellotti*, but the *Citizens United* majority viewed *Austin* as an aberration. By overruling *Austin*, all of the government's arguments in *Citizens United* could be defeated on the grounds that they did not satisfy the strict scrutiny standard.

The government's first *Austin*-based argument was that BCRA's prohibition was based on the antidistortion rationale: that corporations must be prevented from using their unfair advantage of immense amassed wealth to distort the open marketplace of electoral debate with corporate ideas whose funding has little correlation to public support for those ideas. The Court found that this rationale was not compelling for three main reasons. First, *Buckley* rejected the validity of a government interest in "equalizing" the ability of speakers to influence elections. Second, although BCRA's prohibition included an exclusion for media corporations, the antidistortion rationale logically could be used to justify the same limitation on their speech expenditures. Therefore, its approval in *Austin* created a slippery slope that could lead to unprecedented government restriction of the impact of media voices. Third, the government's concern regarding immense amassed wealth was inapplicable to most corporations, including both nonprofits and small business corporations that lack large amounts of wealth. Moreover, the Court noted that the latter entities are arbitrarily disadvantaged by the BCRA prohibition, when compared to wealthy people and unincorporated associations that are allowed to make unlimited independent expenditures.

The government's second argument was based on the rationale that BCRA's limit was justified by the interest in deterring corruption or the appearance of corruption. The Court observed, however, that *Buckley* did not accept this interest as the basis for sustaining FECA's expenditure limits; instead *Buckley* invalidated those limits, reasoning that "the absence of prearrangement and coordination of an expenditure with the candidate" lessens the risk that expenditures will serve as a *quid pro quo* for "improper commitments" from a candidate. The Court emphasized that *Buckley*'s narrow corruption definition should be preserved and not be expanded to include the "influence over or access to" officials that speakers may obtain through expenditures, because that expanded definition has no inherently limiting principle. The Court cited the lengthy legislative record in *McConnell*, and its lack of examples of *quid pro quo* corruption, as confirmation of *Buckley*'s reasoning that independent expenditures do not produce this type of corruption or its appearance.

In rejecting the government's third rationale, that BCRA's prohibition served to protect dissenting shareholders who did not want the general treasury funds to be used for particular corporate speech, the Court reasoned that BCRA was both underinclusive and overinclusive in terms of its advancement of this interest. For example, the 30-day and 60-day limits on electioneering communications are unrelated to the protection of shareholders, and BCRA includes no exception for either nonprofits or for-profit corporations that have only one shareholder.

As the last step in its analysis, the Court turned to a consideration of the factors that are relevant in determining whether to depart from the principle of stare decisis that would dictate the preservation of *Austin* as precedent. First, given *Austin*'s inconsistency with *Buckley* and *Bellotti*, the *Citizens United* majority determined that *Austin* was not a well-reasoned decision. Similarly, no serious reliance issues appeared to exist. Third, in the light of experience, *Austin*'s ruling had been undermined by a variety of forces contributing to its circumvention, including rapid changes in the technology of communication that provide support for the argument that during an era when the "speech dynamic is changing," onerous restrictions like the BCRA prohibition should not be enforced to limit political speech "in certain media by certain speakers."

Soon after the ruling in *Citizens United*, the Montana Supreme Court upheld a statute that limited the expenditures of corporations to support candidates and political committees, reasoning that the record provided stronger support for this limitation than the *Citizens United* record had provided for the prohibition regarding corporate treasury funds. In *America Tradition Partnership, Inc. v. Bullock*, 567 U.S. 516 (2012), the Supreme Court promptly reversed the Montana decision on the grounds that *Citizens United* governed the case and required the invalidation of the state statute. The *Citizens United* dissenters disagreed with this reversal and supported the Montana court's position.

Chief Justice Roberts' concurring opinion emphasized that *Austin*'s toleration of speaker-based restrictions had been the subject of controversy for years,

and a majority of the justices had come to view *Austin* as based on "uniquely destabilizing" rationale whose logic could justify other similar restrictions in the name
of equality. Justice Scalia's concurrence criticized the dissent's argument that it
was implausible to believe that the Framers believed that "the freedom of speech"
in the First Amendment would extend equally to all corporate speakers. Justice
Scalia, who also concurred, observed that the Amendment is written in terms
"of speech, not speakers," and necessarily protects the freedom of individuals to
exercise their right to speak "in association with other individuals" through the
medium of an entity such as a newspaper, a political party, or a business corporation. He also noted that the Framers were familiar with a variety of incorporated
entities as well as unincorporated business associations that expressed their views
in the media of the founding era.

   Justice Stevens dissented, joined by four justices, emphasizing that "not a single for-profit corporation, union, or State" had sought the reversal of *Austin,* and
that recent changes in the composition of the Court accounted for its reversal by
a majority opinion that endorsed a recycled version of the *Austin* and *McConnell*
dissents. Justice Stevens characterized the BCRA regulation as analogous to an
acceptable time, place, and manner restriction that operated "in a viewpoint
neutral fashion." The congressional record that supported BCRA's restriction of
corporations persuaded the dissenters that the Court should defer to Congress's
findings, including the premise that corruption and the appearance of corruption needs to be deterred when it takes the form of "ingratiation and access" to
elected officials, especially given the virtual impossibility of obtaining proof of
quid pro quo exchanges of votes for dollars. Justice Stevens proposed that the government's antidiscrimination rationale should be understood as a type of anti-
corruption rationale, and concluded that the treasury resources of a corporation
make its electioneering "more likely to impair" compelling governmental interests, including each of the interests proffered by the government.

3. Disclosure Requirements

Buckley upheld the reporting and disclosure requirements of FECA. The provision
in Section 434(e) required "every person (other than a political committee or
candidate) who makes contributions or expenditures" aggregating over $100 in a
calendar year "other than by contribution to a political committee or candidate"
to file a statement with the Federal Election Commission. The Court decided that
the requirements must pass "exacting scrutiny" and that there must be a "substantial relation" between the governmental interest and the information required to
be disclosed. The Court identified three governmental interests: First, disclosure
provides the electorate with information "as to where political campaign money
comes from and how it is spent by the candidate" in order to aid the voters in
evaluating those who seek federal office. Second, disclosure requirements deter
actual corruption and avoid the appearance of corruption by exposing large

contributions and expenditures to the light of publicity. Third, and not least significant, record keeping, reporting, and disclosure requirements are an essential means of gathering the data necessary to detect violations of the contribution limitations.

After first finding that these "substantial governmental interests" supported the disclosure requirements, the Court then balanced those interests against the "burden" that disclosure requirements impose on individual rights. The Court recognized that by requiring public disclosure of contributions to candidates and political parties, the Act would "deter some individuals who otherwise might contribute" for fear of harassment or retaliation. Nevertheless, the Court found that the disclosure provisions constituted "the least restrictive means of curbing the evils of campaign ignorance and corruption that Congress found to exist." In addition, the Court found that the disclosure provisions increase "the fund of information concerning those who support the candidates" and that "informational interest can be as strong as it is in coordinated spending, for disclosure helps voters to define more of the candidates' constituencies."

In *Doe #1 v. Reed*, 565 U.S. 1048 (2011), the Court held that "as a general matter," the mandatory public disclosure of referendum petitions, as required by a Washington statute and the laws of other states, does not violate the First Amendment rights of the signers whose names and addresses are required to appear on such petitions. The Court recognized that when a person signs a referendum petition, his or her signature expresses the political view that a law "should be considered 'by the whole electorate,'" which expression therefore "implicates a First Amendment right." In the electoral context, challenges to disclosure requirements are reviewed with "exacting scrutiny," which requires, first, a "substantial relation between the disclosure requirement" and a "sufficiently important government interest." Also, the "strength of the government interest must reflect the seriousness of the actual burden on First Amendment rights."

The Court first determined that the state proffered a "sufficiently important interest" for requiring public disclosure, namely "preserving the integrity of the electoral process by combating fraud, detecting invalid signatures, and fostering government transparency and accountability." The Court noted that the job of verifying the validity of petition signatures was "large and difficult," so that the secretary of state can ordinarily check only between 3 percent and 5 percent of such signatures. This procedure "will not catch all invalid signatures" that are the product of either fraud or mistake. Thus, disclosure regulations "promote transparency and accountability in the electoral process" to an extent that "other measures cannot."

The Court also found that the strength of the government interest did "reflect the seriousness of the actual burden on First Amendment rights." Given the evidence that other petitions in Washington had been released in recent years "without incident," the Court found the state's argument to be "unrebutted" that "only modest burdens attend to the disclosure of a typical petition." Finally, however, the Court noted that if the petition signers in *Doe #1* could show "a reasonable probability that the compelled disclosure of personal information will subject them to threats, harassment, or reprisals from either Government officials or private parties," then they could prevail in their claim to resist disclosure. The signers in *Doe #1* objected to disclosure because they had signed a petition that sought to put a law extending "certain benefits to same-sex couples" to a popular vote, and the Court resolved to leave it to the lower courts "to consider in the first instance the signers' more focused claim concerning disclosure of the information on this particular petition."

Justice Sotomayor spoke for three justices in a concurring opinion that advocated a "heavy burden" for any party challenging disclosure because of the "minimal impact" of disclosure on their speech and associational rights. Justice Scalia's concurrence in the judgment went further, as he argued that a "long history of practice shows that the First Amendment does not prohibit public disclosure," so that case-specific relief should be available only if a state "selectively applies a facially neutral petition disclosure rule" in a discriminatory manner. By contrast, Justice Alito's concurring opinion advocated that petitioner signers should be able to obtain as-applied disclosure exemptions quickly and without making an "overly burdensome showing." Justice Thomas dissented on the grounds that the mandatory disclosure law was unconstitutional "because there will always be a less restrictive means" for vindicating the state's interest "in preserving the integrity of its referendum process."

4. Public Financing

Buckley upheld the provisions providing for public financing of presidential election campaigns. Section 9006 established a Presidential Election Campaign Fund, financed from general revenues based on designations by individual taxpayers, to finance (1) party nominating conventions, (2) general election campaigns, and (3) primary campaigns. The Court found that public financing provides a "means of eliminating the improper influence of large private contributions" and furthers a "significant governmental interest." In addition, the Court found that Congress could permissibly choose to relieve "major-party Presidential candidates from the rigors of soliciting private contributions."

In *Arizona Free Enterprise Club's Freedom Club PAC v. Bennett*, 564 U.S. 721 (2011), the Court invalidated the public financing system in the Arizona Citizens Clean Elections Act, and relied on *Davis v. Federal Election Commission*, 554 U.S. 724 (2008), which similarly invalidated the "millionaire's amendment" in the Bipartisan Campaign Reform Act of 2002 (BCRA). *Davis* held that a self-financing candidate's "unfettered" First Amendment right to make personal expenditures was violated by a provision that triggered extra financing for opponents (based on the raising of their contribution limits and coordinated party expenditures) when the candidate's expenditures from personal finances exceeded $350,000. This scheme of "discriminatory" limits imposed a "substantial burden" on the privately financed candidate, and was not supported by any compelling interest, such as the government interest in eliminating corruption or the appearance of corruption. The *Bennett* Court relied on similar reasoning to invalidate the Arizona scheme that granted publicly funded candidates "equalizing" or matching funds based on the amount of spending of personal funds by privately financed candidates. In both cases, the Court observed that "reliance on personal funds reduces the threat of corruption," and rejected the argument that the government had a compelling interest in "equalizing" the resources for all candidates. Justice Kagan's dissent was joined by three justices, and she argued that the Arizona law should be viewed not as a restriction of speech but as a law that "subsidizes" speech.

[Points to Remember for Chapter 11 is contained in online file.]

12

The Religion Clauses

[Roadmap for Chapter 12 is contained in online file.]

∿ PROBLEM: MORE ON THE EDUCATION FOR A BETTER AMERICA ACT ∿

Over the last half-century, schoolchildren in the United States have fallen farther and farther behind their counterparts in many other parts of the world, particularly Japan and western Europe. A bipartisan commission was appointed by Congress to study the problem, and it concluded that a variety of factors have contributed to the decline, including (and particularly) a lack of funding for buildings, equipment, supplies, and quality teachers. As a result, Congress is now considering legislation entitled the Education for a Better America Act that would dramatically increase federal funding for elementary and secondary education.

Suppose that you work for a member of the House of Representatives who has been charged with drafting the legislation and who has asked you to assist. Although Congress has the goal of improving the plight of all schoolchildren, including those in private and parochial schools, Congress is concerned about how the religion clauses of the First Amendment might (or should) affect the content of the proposed legislation. In particular, it is unclear whether (and to what extent) the Establishment Clause might preclude Congress from providing assistance to parochial schools. Congress is also uncertain about whether, if it decides to provide assistance to private school students, the Free Exercise Clause would require it to provide similar assistance to parochial school students.

As you work your way through this chapter, you will be asked to think about these issues in various contexts, and ultimately to reach conclusions regarding how you might construct the proposed legislation.

A. THE ESTABLISHMENT CLAUSE

The Establishment Clause is simply stated: "Congress shall make no law respecting an establishment of religion." Although the clause initially applied only to the federal government, its reach was extended to the states through the Fourteenth Amendment. *See Everson v. Board of Education*, 330 U.S. 1 (1947). It prohibits government from engaging in certain types of activities: establishing a national (or, for that matter, a state) church, passing laws that require individuals to go to or remain away from church against their will, and passing laws that force individuals to profess a belief or a disbelief in any religion. The difficulty is that few Establishment Clause cases have involved these types of activities. For example, there have been no attempts to declare a national religion and few (modern) attempts to force individuals to go to or remain away from church against their will or to force individuals to profess a belief or a disbelief in a particular religion. Most Establishment Clause litigation focuses on whether certain lesser acts (e.g., school prayer, financial aid to religious organizations, the posting of the Ten Commandments in public places) constitute an "establishment" of religion. Because these "lesser" acts do not clearly violate the First Amendment, the courts have struggled to define the term *establishment*. This has been done on a case-by-case basis.

1. Financial Aid to Religion

Although Establishment Clause issues can occur in a variety of contexts, they often arise in the context of governmental attempts to provide financial benefits to religion or religious organizations.

a. Early Cases

Everson v. Board of Education
330 U.S. 1 (1947)

Mr. Justice BLACK delivered the opinion of the Court.

Pursuant to New Jersey law, the board of education authorized reimbursement to parents of money expended for bus transportation of their children on regular busses operated by the public transportation system. Part of the money was for payment of transportation of children to Catholic parochial schools. These church schools give their students, in addition to secular education, religious instruction conforming to the religious tenets and modes of worship of the Catholic Faith.

Whether this New Jersey law is one respecting the "establishment of religion" requires an understanding of the meaning of that language, particularly with respect to the imposition of taxes. A large proportion of the early settlers of this country came here from Europe to escape the bondage of laws which compelled them to support and attend government favored churches. The centuries immediately before and contemporaneous with the colonization of America had been filled with turmoil, civil strife, and persecutions, generated in large part by established sects determined to maintain their absolute political and religious supremacy. With the power of government supporting them, at various times and places, Catholics had persecuted Protestants, Protestants had persecuted Catholics, Protestant sects had persecuted other Protestant sects, Catholics of one shade of belief had persecuted Catholics of another shade of belief, and all of these had from time to time persecuted Jews. In efforts to force loyalty to whatever religious group happened to be on top and in league with the government of a particular time and place, men and women had been fined, cast in jail, cruelly tortured, and killed. Among the offenses for which these punishments had been inflicted were such things as speaking disrespectfully of the views of ministers of government-established churches, nonattendance at those churches, expressions of non-belief in their doctrines, and failure to pay taxes and tithes to support them.

These practices were transplanted to and began to thrive in the soil of the new America. The charters granted by the English Crown authorized the individuals and companies designated to make the laws to erect religious establishments which all, whether believers or non-believers, would be required to support and attend. An exercise of this authority was accompanied by a repetition of many of the old world practices and persecutions. These practices became so commonplace as to shock the freedom-loving colonials into a feeling of abhorrence. The imposition of taxes to pay ministers' salaries and to build and maintain churches and church property aroused their indignation. It was these feelings which found expression in the First Amendment.

Prior to the adoption of the Fourteenth Amendment, the First Amendment did not apply as a restraint against the states. Most of them did soon provide similar constitutional protections for religious liberty. But some states persisted for about half a century in imposing restraints upon the free exercise of religion and in discriminating against particular religious groups. In recent years, so far as the provision against the establishment of a religion is concerned, the question has most frequently arisen in connection with proposed state aid to church schools and efforts to carry on religious teachings in the public schools in accordance with the tenets of a particular sect. Some churches have either sought or accepted state financial support for their schools. Here again the efforts to obtain state aid or acceptance of it have not been limited to any one particular faith. The state courts, in the main, have remained faithful to the language of their own constitutional provisions designed to protect religious freedom and to separate religious and governments. Their decisions, however, show the difficulty in drawing the line between tax legislation which provides funds for the welfare of the general public and that which is designed to support institutions which teach religion.

The "establishment of religion" clause of the First Amendment means at least this: Neither a state nor the Federal Government can set up a church. Neither can pass laws which aid one religion, aid all religions, or prefer one religion over another. Neither can force nor influence a person to go to or to remain away from church against his will or force him to profess a belief or disbelief in any religion. No person can be punished for entertaining or professing religious beliefs or disbeliefs, for church attendance or non-attendance. No tax in any amount, large or small, can be levied to support any religious activities or institutions, whatever they may be called, or whatever form they may adopt to teach or practice religion. Neither a state nor the Federal Government can, openly or secretly, participate in the affairs of any religious organizations or groups and vice versa. In the words of Jefferson, the clause against establishment of religion by law was intended to erect "a wall of separation between Church and State." *Reynolds v. United States*, 98 U.S. 145, 164 (1879).

The question has most frequently arisen in connection with proposed state aid to church schools and efforts to carry on religious teachings in the public schools in accordance with the tenets of a particular sect. Some churches have either sought or accepted state financial support for their schools.

New Jersey cannot consistently with the "establishment of religion" clause of the First Amendment contribute tax-raised funds to support an institution which teaches the tenets and faith of any church. On the other hand, the amendment commands that New Jersey cannot hamper its citizens in the free exercise of their own religion. Consequently, it cannot exclude individual Catholics, Lutherans, Mohammedans, Baptists, Jews, Methodists, Non-believers, Presbyterians, or the members of any other faith, *because of their faith, or lack of it,* from receiving the benefits of public welfare legislation. We must be careful that we do not prohibit New Jersey from extending its general State law benefits to all its citizens without regard to their religious belief.

We cannot say that the First Amendment prohibits New Jersey from spending tax-raised funds to pay the bus fares of parochial school pupils as a part of a general program under which it pays the fares of pupils attending public and other schools. It is true that children are helped to get to church schools. There is even a possibility that some children might not be sent to the church schools if the parents were compelled to pay their children's bus fares out of their own pockets. Similarly, parents might be reluctant to permit their children to attend schools which the state had cut off from such general government services as ordinary police and fire protection, connections for sewage disposal, public highways and sidewalks. Cutting off church schools from these services would make it far more difficult for the schools to operate. Such is not the purpose of the First Amendment. That Amendment requires the state to be neutral in its relations with groups of religious believers and non-believers; it does not require the state to be their adversary. State power is no more to be used so as to handicap religions, than it is to favor them.

Parents may send their children to a religious rather than a public school if the school meets the secular educational requirements which the state has power to impose. The State contributes no money to the schools. It does not support them. Its legislation does no more than provide a general program to help parents get their children, regardless of their religion, safely and expeditiously to and from accredited schools.

The First Amendment has erected a wall between church and state. That wall must be kept high and impregnable. We could not approve the slightest breach. New Jersey has not breached it here.

Affirmed.

BACKGROUND
The "Wall Between Church and State" Metaphor

Everson is famous for introducing this metaphor into the Court's Establishment Clause jurisprudence. As you go through this chapter, think about whether such a wall exists and whether the metaphor is accurate.

Mr. Justice JACKSON, *dissenting*.

This expenditure has no possible effect on the child's safety or expedition in transit. As passengers on the public busses they travel as fast and no faster, and are as safe and no safer, since their parents are reimbursed as before. The resolution which authorizes disbursement of this taxpayer's money limits reimbursement to those who attend public schools and Catholic schools. The Act prohibits payment to private schools operated in whole or in part for profit. The Court ignores the essentially religious test by which beneficiaries of this expenditure are selected. Could we sustain an Act that said police shall protect pupils on the way to or from public schools and Catholic schools but not while going to and coming from other schools, and firemen shall extinguish a blaze in public or Catholic school buildings but shall not put out a blaze in Protestant Church schools or private schools operated for profit? I should think it pretty plain that such a scheme would not be valid.

Mr. Justice RUTLEDGE, with whom Mr. Justice FRANKFURTER, Mr. Justice JACKSON, and Mr. Justice BURTON agree, *dissenting*.

Neither so high nor so impregnable today as yesterday is the wall raised between church and state by Virginia's great statute of religious freedom and the First Amendment. The First Amendment's purpose was not to strike merely at the official establishment of a single sect, creed or religion. It was to uproot all such relationships. It was to create a complete and permanent separation of the spheres of religious activity and civil authority by comprehensively forbidding every form of public aid or support for religion.

Does New Jersey's action furnish support for religion by use of the taxing power? Certainly it does. Believers of all faiths, and others who do not express their feeling toward ultimate issues of existence, pay the New Jersey tax. It is precisely because the instruction is religious and relates to a particular faith, whether one or another, that parents send their children to religious schools.

We are told that the New Jersey statute is valid because the appropriation is for a public, not a private purpose, namely, the promotion of education. If the fact alone be determinative, then I can see no basis for the state's refusal to make full appropriation for support of private, religious schools, just as is done for public instruction. Public money devoted to payment of religious costs, educational or other, brings the quest for more. It brings too the struggle of sect against sect for the larger share or for any. The end of such strife cannot be other than to destroy the cherished liberty.

This is not therefore just a little case over bus fares. Religious training and belief remains, as the Amendment made it, the kingdom of the individual man and his God. It should be kept inviolately private, not confounded with what legislatures legitimately may take over into the public domain. We have staked the very existence of our country on the faith that complete separation between state and religion is best for the state and for religion. That policy necessarily entails hardship upon persons who forgo the right to educational advantages the state can supply in order to secure others it is precluded from giving. But it does not make the state unneutral to withhold what the Constitution forbids it to give. The judgment should be reversed.

Note: Government Support for Religious Hospitals

In *Bradfield v. Roberts*, 175 U.S. 291 (1899), the Court held that the District of Columbia could pay to construct a building on the grounds of a religiously affiliated hospital. The Court emphasized that the payment had a secular purpose (to expand hospital facilities) and that the hospital did not discriminate on the basis of religion in its operation. The Court regarded the religious affiliation as "wholly immaterial."

∾ PROBLEMS ∾

1. *The Framers' Intent.* Jesse Choper argues that free public education "was virtually non-existent during the early years of Independence, and where it did occur it had a distinctly religious orientation." Jesse Choper, *The Establishment Clause and Aid to Parochial Schools*, 56 CAL. L. REV. 260, 263 (1968). What significance do you attach to these facts in interpreting the Establishment Clause as applied to public schools?

2. *A "Neutrality" Test?* Philip Kurland, in *Of Church and State and the Supreme Court*, 29 U. Chi. L. Rev. 1, 96 (1961), argues that the Free Exercise Clause and the Establishment Clause "should be read as stating a single precept: that government cannot utilize religion as a standard for action or inaction because these clauses, read together as they should be, prohibit classification in terms of religion either to confer a benefit or to impose a burden." Do you agree? Suppose that government decides to provide salary supplements to teachers in private schools. Under the Kurland test, can the government extend those benefits to religious schools? Indeed, must it extend those benefits to religious schools? Douglas Laycock, in *Formal, Substantive and Disaggregated Neutrality Toward Religion*, 39 DePaul L. Rev. 993, 1000-1003 (1990), argues that "Formal neutrality would produce results that many Americans find unacceptably favorable to religion" because it would allow government to give "unlimited amounts of unrestricted aid to religious schools" provided that it gives such aid to "all schools and not to religious schools alone." Indeed, he argues that any "aid to secular private schools *must* be given to religious schools, on exactly the same terms. To exclude religious schools from the aid program, or to impose restrictions on religious uses of the money, would be to classify on the basis of religion." Is a "neutrality" test desirable?

3. *More on the Education for a Better America Act.* Does *Everson* provide you with guidance about how to structure the Act? For example, if Congress is "neutral" toward all schools (public, private, and parochial), can it provide direct financial aid to religious schools? If Congress chooses to provide financial aid to private nonreligious schools, must it provide similar aid to private religious schools (or vice versa)?

b. The *Lemon* Test and Doctrinal Turmoil

The dominant Establishment Clause test for nearly 30 years was the so-called "*Lemon*" test, articulated in the following case.

Lemon v. Kurtzman

403 U.S. 602 (1971)

Mr. Chief Justice BURGER delivered the opinion of the Court.

Rhode Island found that the quality of education in nonpublic elementary schools was jeopardized by the rapidly rising salaries needed to attract competent and dedicated teachers. A statute authorized state officials to supplement the salaries of teachers of secular subjects by paying directly to a teacher an amount not in excess of 15% of his annual salary. The Act requires that teachers teach only those subjects and use "only teaching materials used in the public schools." Rhode Island's nonpublic elementary schools accommodated approximately 25% of the State's pupils. About 95% of these pupils attended schools affiliated with the Roman Catholic church. All teachers who applied for benefits under the Act are employed by Roman Catholic schools. The District Court held that the Act violated the Establishment Clause. We affirm.

The Pennsylvania Nonpublic Elementary and Secondary Education Act authorizes direct payments to nonpublic schools for actual expenditures for teachers' salaries, textbooks, and instructional materials. A school must identify the "separate" cost of the "secular educational service." Reimbursement is limited to courses "presented in the curricula of the public schools," and is further limited to courses in mathematics, modern foreign languages, physical science, and physical education. Textbooks and instructional materials must be approved by the state. The statute prohibits reimbursement for any course with "subject matter expressing religious teaching, or the morals or forms of worship of any sect." Some $5 million has been expended annually. Ninety-six percent of these pupils attend church-related schools, and most are affiliated with the Roman Catholic church. A three-judge federal court dismissed the complaint. We reverse.

We must draw lines with reference to the three main evils against which the Establishment Clause was intended to afford protection: "sponsorship, financial support, and active involvement of the sovereign in religious activity." *Walz v. Tax Commission*, 397 U.S. 664, 668 (1970). Every analysis in this area must begin with consideration of the cumulative criteria developed by the Court over many years. Three such tests may be gleaned from our cases. First, the statute must have a secular legislative purpose; second, its principal or primary effect must be one that neither advances nor inhibits religion; finally, the statute must not foster "an excessive government entanglement with religion."

The statutes clearly state that they are intended to enhance the quality of the secular education in all schools covered by the compulsory attendance laws. A State always has a legitimate concern for maintaining minimum standards in schools.

The legislatures have sought to create statutory restrictions designed to guarantee the separation between secular and religious educational functions and to ensure that State financial aid supports only the former. Our prior holdings do not call for total separation between church and state; total separation is not possible in an absolute sense. Some relationship between government and religious organizations is inevitable. Fire inspections, building and zoning regulations, and state requirements under compulsory school-attendance laws are examples of necessary and permissible contacts. The line of separation, far from being a "wall," is a blurred, indistinct, and variable barrier depending on all the circumstances of a particular relationship.

In order to determine whether the government entanglement with religion is excessive, we must examine the character and purposes of the institutions that are benefitted, the nature of the aid that the State provides, and the resulting relationship between the government and the religious authority. Here we find that both statutes foster an impermissible degree of entanglement.

The Rhode Island program gives rise to entangling church-state relationships of the kind the Religion Clauses sought to avoid. Teachers have a substantially different ideological character from books. A textbook's content is ascertainable, but a teacher's handling of a subject is not. We cannot ignore the danger that a teacher under religious control and discipline poses to the separation of the religious from the purely secular aspects of education. We do not assume that teachers will be guilty of bad faith or any conscious design to evade the limitations imposed by the statute and the First Amendment. We simply recognize that a dedicated religious person, teaching in a school affiliated with his or her faith and operated to inculcate its tenets, will experience great difficulty remaining religiously neutral. To ensure that no trespass occurs, the State carefully conditioned its aid with pervasive restrictions. A comprehensive, discriminating, and continuing state surveillance will inevitably be required to ensure that these restrictions are obeyed and the First Amendment otherwise respected.

The Pennsylvania statute involves an educational system that is very similar. The restrictions and surveillance necessary to ensure that teachers play a non-ideological role give rise to entanglements between church and state. The Pennsylvania statute has the further defect of providing state financial aid directly to the church-related schools. Such payments have almost always been accompanied by varying measures of control and surveillance. The government's power to determine which expenditures are religious and which are secular creates an intimate and continuing relationship between church and state.

A broader base of entanglement of yet a different character is presented by the divisive political potential of these state programs. In a community where such a large number of pupils are served by church-related schools, partisans of parochial schools, understandably concerned with rising costs and sincerely dedicated to both the religious and secular educational missions of their schools, will inevitably promote political action to achieve their goals. Those who oppose state aid, whether for constitutional, religious, or fiscal reasons, will inevitably respond and employ all of the usual political campaign techniques to prevail. Candidates will be forced to declare and voters to choose. Many people confronted with issues of this kind will find their votes aligned with their faith.

Ordinarily political debate and division, however vigorous or even partisan, are normal and healthy manifestations of our democratic system of government, but political division along religious lines was one of the principal evils against which the First Amendment was intended to protect. The potential divisiveness of such conflict is a threat to the normal political process. It conflicts with our history and tradition to permit questions of the Religion Clauses to assume such importance in our legislatures and in our elections. Here we are confronted with successive and very likely permanent annual appropriations that benefit relatively few religious groups. Political fragmentation and divisiveness on religious lines are thus likely to be intensified.

Nothing we have said can be construed to disparage the role of church-related elementary and secondary schools in our national life. Under our system government is to be entirely excluded from the area of religious instruction and churches excluded from the affairs of government. The Constitution decrees that religion must be a private matter for the individual, the family, and the institutions of private choice, and that while some involvement and entanglement are inevitable, lines must be drawn.

The judgment of the Rhode Island District Court in No. 569 and No. 570 is affirmed. The judgment of the Pennsylvania District Court in No. 89 is reversed, and the case is remanded for further proceedings consistent with this opinion.

Mr. Justice DOUGLAS, whom Mr. Justice BLACK joins, *concurring.*

Public financial support of parochial schools necessitates governmental suppression, surveillance, or meddling in church affairs. The constitutional mandate can in part be carried out by censoring the curricula. A sectarian course can be marked for deletion. But the problem only starts there. Sectarian instruction can take place in a course on Shakespeare or in one on mathematics. I would think that policing these grants to detect sectarian instruction would be insufferable to religious partisans and would breed division and dissension between church and state. If the government closed its eyes to the manner in which these grants are actually used it would be allowing public funds to promote sectarian education. If it did not close its eyes but undertook surveillance, it would intermeddle in parochial affairs in a way that would breed only rancor and dissension. A history class, a literature class, or a science class in a parochial school is not a separate institute; it is part of the organic whole living on one budget. What taxpayers give for salaries of those who teach only the humanities or science without any trace of proselytizing enables the school to use all of its own funds for religious training. Taxpayers' forced contribution to the parochial schools in the present cases violates the First Amendment.

Mr. Justice BRENNAN, *concurring.*

These statutes require "too close a proximity" of government to sectarian institutions and create real dangers of "the secularization of a creed." Rhode Island requires teachers to surrender their right to teach religion courses and to promise not to "inject" religious teaching into their secular courses. This led one teacher to stop praying with his classes, a testimonial to the self-censorship that inevitably accompanies state regulation. Both statutes prescribe extensive standardization of the content of secular courses, and of the teaching materials and textbooks used in the courses. Regulations implementing those requirements necessarily require policing of instruction in the schools. The picture of state inspectors prowling the halls of parochial schools and auditing classroom instruction raises more than an imagined specter of governmental "secularization of a creed." These cases involve direct subsidies of tax monies to the schools and the secular education those schools provide goes hand in hand with the religious mission that is the only reason for the schools' existence. These statutes do violence to the principle that "government may not employ religious means to serve secular interests, however legitimate, without a demonstration that nonreligious means will not suffice."

Mr. Justice WHITE, *concurring in the judgment in 89 and 153* and *dissenting in Nos. 569 and 570.*

It is enough for me that the States and the Federal Government are financing a separable secular function of overriding importance in order to sustain the legislation here challenged. There is no specific allegation that sectarian teaching does or would invade secular classes supported by state funds.

Notes

1. *The* Lemon *Test and Financial Aid to Parochial Schools.* The *Lemon* criterion has been used in a number of cases involving financial aid to parochial schools (some of which have been overruled): A) *Instructional materials: See Meek v. Pittenger,* 421 U.S. 349 (1975), and *Wolman v. Walter,* 443 U.S. w229 (1977) (the state may not loan "instructional material and equipment" i.e., maps, charts, periodicals, photographs, sound recordings, films, and laboratory equipment to parochial schools without impermissibly aiding "the sectarian school enterprise as a whole"); B) *Standardized testing: See Wolman, supra* (the state may pay for administering and scoring standardized testing if the tests are the same ones used in the public schools and nonpublic employees are not involved in the grading); *Levitt v. Committee for Public Education,* 413 U.S. 472 (1973) (the state may not reimburse for administering teacher-prepared tests); C) *Auxiliary services: See Meek, supra* (the state may not provide "auxiliary services" (remedial and accelerated instruction, guidance counseling and testing, speech and hearing services) directly to nonpublic special needs children without creating excessive surveillance, entanglement, and political divisiveness); and *Wolman, supra* (the state may provide speech and hearing diagnostic services and diagnostic psychological services to pupils attending nonpublic schools because they "have little or no educational content and are not closely associated with the educational mission of the nonpublic school"); D) *Remedial services: See Wolman, supra* (the state may pay for therapeutic, guidance, and remedial services for students who have been identified as having a need for specialized attention at neutral sites away from the parochial schools); E) *State-sponsored field trips: See Wolman, supra* (the state may not spend funds for student field trips "to governmental, industrial, cultural, and scientific centers designed to enrich the secular studies of students" without implicating "direct aid to sectarian education" and creating the need for "close supervision and excessive entanglement"); F) *Maintenance and repair: See Committee for Public Education and Religious Liberty v. Nyquist,* 413 U.S. 756 (1973) (the state may not provide direct money grants to "qualifying" nonpublic schools for the "maintenance and repair of school facilities and equipment to ensure the health, welfare and safety of enrolled pupils" when payments were not restricted to facilities used exclusively for secular purposes).

2. *Financial Aid to Higher Education.* Given that college students are older, and less impressionable, than elementary and secondary school students, the Court has always treated higher education funding somewhat differently than funding for lower level education. *See, e.g., Roemer v. Board of Public Works*, 426 U.S. 736 (1976) (Court upheld a Maryland law that provided annual grants of 15% per-pupil appropriation in the state system to private colleges subject to the restriction that the funds not be used for "sectarian purposes." Occasional audits would be "quick and non-judgmental."); *Hunt v. McNair*, 413 U.S. 734 (1973) (Court upheld a statute that authorized the issuance of revenue bonds for the benefit of a Baptist college, finding that the program's purpose was secular (education) and that "the College was not an instrument of religious indoctrination"); and *Tilton v. Richardson*, 403 U.S. 672 (1971) (Court upheld federal law providing construction grants to religious colleges for buildings and facilities used for secular educational purposes. "College students are less impressionable and less susceptible to religious indoctrination. Since religious indoctrination is not a substantial purpose, there is less likelihood that religion will permeate secular education and the necessity for intensive government surveillance is diminished." The Court did strike down a provision allowing religious use of the buildings after 20 years.).

Criticisms of the *Lemon* Test

Although the *Lemon* test attempted to provide a single unified criterion for evaluating Establishment Clause claims, that test has been much criticized, and some have argued that the test has not resulted in consistent or rational decision making. In a dissenting opinion in *Wallace v. Jaffree*, 472 U.S. 38 (1985), Chief Justice Rehnquist stated: "The *Lemon* test has simply not provided adequate standards for deciding Establishment Clause cases. For example, a State may lend geography textbooks that contain maps, but the State may not lend maps for use in geography class. A State may lend textbooks on American colonial history, but it may not lend a film on George Washington, or a film projector to show it. A State may lend classroom workbooks, but may not lend workbooks in which the parochial school children write, thus rendering them nonreusable. A State may pay for bus transportation to religious schools but may not pay for bus transportation from the parochial school to the public zoo or natural history museum. A State may pay for diagnostic services conducted in the parochial school but therapeutic services must be given in a different building; speech and hearing 'services' inside the sectarian school are forbidden, but the State may conduct speech and hearing diagnostic testing inside the sectarian school. Exceptional parochial school students may receive counseling, but it must take place outside of the parochial school. A State may give cash to a parochial school to pay for the administration of state-written tests, but it may not provide funds for teacher-prepared tests on secular subjects. Religious instruction may not be given in public school, but the public school may release students during the day for religion classes elsewhere, and may enforce attendance at those classes with its truancy laws." In a concurring opinion in *Board of Education of Kiryas Joel Village School District v. Grumet*, 512 U.S. 687 (1994), Justice O'Connor argued: It is always appealing to look for a Grand Unified Theory that would resolve all the cases under the Establishment Clause. But this may sometimes do more harm than good. Experience proves that the Establishment Clause, like the Free Speech Clause, cannot easily be reduced to a single test.

∼ PROBLEM: MORE ON THE EDUCATION FOR A BETTER AMERICA ACT ∼

Does *Lemon*'s analysis alter your views regarding the permissible content of the proposed Education for a Better America Act? Under the *Lemon* test, would it be permissible for Congress to provide direct financial aid to parochial schools? Would it be possible to do so without running afoul of *Lemon*'s three-part test? Would it matter that Congress's goal is to improve the quality of education in secular subjects, and that Congress believes that the grants would help achieve that objective?

c. *Agostini v. Felton*

In recent years, the Court has begun to back away from some of its earlier decisions and has also modified the *Lemon* test.

Agostini v. Felton

521 U.S. 203 (1997)

Justice O'CONNOR delivered the opinion of the Court.

In *Aguilar v. Felton*, 473 U.S. 402 (1985), this Court held that the Establishment Clause barred the city of New York from sending public school teachers into parochial schools to provide remedial education to disadvantaged children. On remand, the trial court entered a permanent injunction reflecting our ruling. Twelve years later, petitioners seek relief from its operation. Petitioners maintain that *Aguilar* cannot be squared with our intervening Establishment Clause jurisprudence and ask that we explicitly recognize that *Aguilar* is no longer good law.

Congress enacted Title I of the Elementary and Secondary Education Act of 1965 to "provide full educational opportunity to every child regardless of economic background." Toward that end, Title I channels federal funds, through the States, to "local educational agencies" (LEA's). The LEA's spend funds to provide remedial education, guidance, and job counseling to eligible students. An eligible student is one (i) who resides within the attendance boundaries of a public school located in a low-income area, and (ii) who is failing, or is at risk of failing, the State's student performance standards. Title I funds must be made available to *all* eligible children, regardless of whether they attend public schools, and the services provided to children attending private schools must be "equitable in comparison to services and other benefits for public school children."

Title I services may be provided only to those private school students eligible for aid, and cannot be used to provide services on a "school-wide" basis. In addition, the LEA must retain complete control over Title I funds; retain title to all materials used to provide Title I services; and provide those services through public employees or other persons independent of the private school and any religious institution. The Title I services themselves must be "secular, neutral, and nonideological," and must "supplement, and in no case supplant, the level of services" already provided by the private school.

Petitioner Board of Education of the City of New York (Board), an LEA, first applied for Title I funds in 1966. Approximately 10% of the total number of students eligible for Title I services are private school students. Recognizing that more than 90% of the private schools within the jurisdiction are sectarian, the Board initially arranged to transport children to public schools for after-school Title I instruction. Attendance was poor, teachers and children were tired, and parents were concerned for the safety of their children. The Board then moved the instruction onto private school campuses during school hours. Only public employees could serve as Title I instructors and counselors. Assignments to private schools were made on a voluntary basis and without regard to the religious affiliation of the employee or the wishes of the private school. A majority of Title I teachers worked in nonpublic schools with religious affiliations different from their own.

Title I employees were told that (i) they were employees of the Board and accountable only to their public school supervisors; (ii) they had exclusive responsibility for selecting students for the Title I program and could teach only those children who met the eligibility criteria for Title I; (iii) their materials and equipment would be used only in the Title I program; (iv) they could not engage in team-teaching or other cooperative instructional activities with private school teachers; and (v) they could not introduce any religious matter into their teaching or become involved in any way with the religious activities of the private schools. All religious symbols were to be removed from classrooms used for Title I services. Title I teachers could consult with a student's regular classroom teacher to assess the student's particular needs and progress, but were required to limit those consultations to mutual professional concerns regarding the student's education. To ensure compliance, a publicly employed field supervisor was to make at least one unannounced visit to each teacher's classroom every month.

Six federal taxpayers sued the Board seeking declaratory and injunctive relief. The District Court granted summary judgment for the Board, but the court of appeals reversed. In a 5-4 decision, this Court affirmed on the ground that the Board's Title I program necessitated an "excessive entanglement of church and state in the administration of Title I benefits." On remand, the District Court permanently enjoined the Board "from using public funds for any plan or program under Title I to the extent that it requires, authorizes or permits public school teachers and guidance counselors to provide teaching and counseling services on the premises of sectarian schools."

The Board then modified its Title I program to revert to its prior practice of providing instruction at public school sites, at leased sites, and in mobile instructional units (essentially vans converted into classrooms) parked near the sectarian school. The Board also offered computer-aided instruction, which could be provided "on premises" because it did not require public employees to be physically present on the premises of a religious school. Since the 1986-1987 school year, the Board has spent over $100 million providing computer-aided instruction, leasing sites and mobile instructional units, and transporting students to those sites. These "*Aguilar* costs" reduce the amount of money an LEA has available for remedial education, and LEA's have reduced the number of students who receive Title I benefits.

Petitioners filed motions seeking relief from the permanent injunction because the "decisional law had changed." Petitioners pointed to the statements of five Justices in *Board of Ed. of Kiryas Joel Village School Dist. v. Grumet*, 512 U.S. 687 (1994), calling for the overruling of *Aguilar*. The District Court denied the motion. We granted certiorari and now reverse.

In order to evaluate whether *Aguilar* has been eroded, it is necessary to understand the rationale upon which *Aguilar*, as well as its companion case, *School Dist. of Grand Rapids v. Ball*, 473 U.S. 373 (1985), rested. In *Ball*, the Court evaluated two programs implemented by the School District of Grand Rapids, Michigan. The Shared Time program provided remedial and "enrichment" classes, at public expense, to students attending nonpublic schools. The classes were taught during regular school hours by publicly employed teachers, using materials purchased with public funds, on the premises of nonpublic schools. The Shared Time courses were in subjects designed to supplement the "core curriculum" of the nonpublic schools. Of the 41 nonpublic schools eligible for the program, 40 were "pervasively sectarian."

The Court applied the so-called *Lemon* test. The Court's conclusion that the Shared Time program in *Ball* had the impermissible effect of advancing religion rested on three assumptions: (i) any public employee who works on the premises of a religious school is presumed to inculcate religion in her work; (ii) the presence of public employees on private school premises creates a symbolic union between church and state; and (iii) any and all public aid that directly aids the educational function of religious schools impermissibly finances religious indoctrination, even if the aid reaches such schools as a consequence of private decision making. Additionally, in *Aguilar* there was a fourth assumption: that New York City's Title I program necessitated an excessive government entanglement with religion because public employees who teach on the premises of religious schools must be closely monitored to ensure that they do not inculcate religion.

Our more recent cases have undermined the assumptions upon which *Ball* and *Aguilar* relied. We ask whether the government acted with the purpose of advancing or inhibiting religion. Likewise, we continue to explore whether the aid has the "effect" of advancing or inhibiting religion. What has changed is our understanding of the criteria used to assess whether aid to religion has an impermissible effect. Cases subsequent to *Aguilar* have modified the approach we use to assess indoctrination. First, we abandoned the presumption that the placement of public employees on parochial school grounds inevitably results in the impermissible effect of state-sponsored indoctrination or constitutes a symbolic union between government and religion. In *Zobrest v. Catalina Foothills School Dist.*, 509 U.S. 1 (1993)., we examined whether the IDEA, 20 U.S.C. §400 *et seq.*, was constitutional as applied to a deaf student who sought to bring his state-employed sign-language interpreter with him to his Roman Catholic high school. We held that this permissible and refused to presume that a publicly employed interpreter would be pressured by the pervasively sectarian surroundings to inculcate religion. We assumed that the interpreter would dutifully discharge her responsibilities as a public employee and comply with the ethical guidelines of her profession by accurately translating what was said.

Second, we departed from the rule that all government aid that directly aids the educational function of religious schools is invalid. In *Witters v. Washington Dept. of Servs. for Blind*, 474 U.S. 481 (1986), we held that the Establishment Clause did not bar a State from issuing a vocational tuition grant to a blind person who wished to use the grant to attend a Christian college and become a pastor, missionary, or youth director. Even though the grant recipient would use the money to obtain religious education, the tuition grants were " 'made available generally without regard to the sectarian-nonsectarian, or public- nonpublic nature of the institution benefitted.' " The grants were disbursed directly to students, who then used the money to pay for tuition at the educational institution of their choice. Any money that ultimately went to religious institutions did so "only as a result of the genuinely independent and private choices of" individuals. The same logic applied in *Zobrest*, where we allowed the State to provide an interpreter, even though she would be a mouthpiece for religious instruction, because the IDEA's neutral eligibility criteria ensured that the interpreter's presence in a sectarian school was a "result of the private decision of individual parents" and "could not be attributed to state decisionmaking."

Under current law, the Shared Time program in *Ball* and New York City's Title I program in *Aguilar* will not be deemed to have the effect of advancing religion through indoctrination. Each of the premises upon which we relied in *Ball* to reach a contrary conclusion is no longer valid. First, there is no reason to presume that, simply because she enters a parochial school classroom, a full-time public employee will depart from her assigned duties and instructions and embark on religious indoctrination. *Zobrest* also repudiates *Ball*'s assumption that the presence of Title I teachers in parochial school classrooms will, without more, create the impression of a "symbolic union" between church and state.

Nor under current law can we conclude that a program placing full-time public employees on parochial campuses to provide Title I instruction would impermissibly finance religious indoctrination. The provision of instructional services under Title I is indistinguishable from the provision of sign-language interpreters under the IDEA. As in *Zobrest*, Title I services are by law supplemental to the regular curricula. These services do not "relieve sectarian schools of costs they otherwise would have borne in educating their students."

Justice Souter finds our conclusion that the IDEA and Title I programs are similar to be "puzzling," and points to three differences he perceives between the programs: (i) Title I services are distributed by LEA's "directly to the religious schools" instead of to individual students pursuant to a formal application process; (ii) Title I services "necessarily relieve a religious school of 'an expense that it otherwise would have assumed' "; and (iii) Title I provides services to more students than did the programs in *Witters* and *Zobrest*. None of these distinctions is meaningful. While it is true that individual students may not directly apply for Title I services, it does not follow that those services are distributed "directly to the religious schools." They are not. No Title I funds ever reach the coffers of religious schools, and Title I services may not be provided to religious schools on a school-wide basis. Title I funds are instead distributed to a public agency (an LEA) that dispenses services directly to the eligible students within its boundaries, no matter where they choose to attend school. We fail to see how providing Title I services directly to eligible students results in a greater financing of religious indoctrination simply because those students are not first required to submit a formal application.

We are also not persuaded that Title I services supplant the remedial instruction and guidance counseling already provided in New York City's sectarian schools. We are unwilling to speculate that all sectarian schools provide remedial instruction and guidance counseling.

What is most fatal to the argument that New York City's Title I program directly subsidizes religion is that it applies with equal force when those services are provided off-campus, and *Aguilar* implied that providing the services off-campus is entirely consistent with the Establishment Clause. A financial incentive to undertake religious indoctrination is not present where the aid is allocated on the basis of neutral, secular criteria that neither favor nor disfavor religion, and is made available to both religious and secular beneficiaries on a nondiscriminatory basis.

Applying this reasoning to New York City's Title I program, it is clear that Title I services are allocated on the basis of criteria that neither favor nor disfavor religion. The services are available to all children who meet the Act's eligibility requirements, no matter what their religious beliefs or where they go to school. The Board's program does not, therefore, give aid recipients any incentive to modify their religious beliefs or practices in order to obtain those services.

We turn now to *Aguilar*'s conclusion that New York City's Title I program resulted in an excessive entanglement between church and state. The finding of "excessive" entanglement in *Aguilar* rested on three grounds: (i) the program would require "pervasive monitoring by public authorities" to ensure that Title

I employees did not inculcate religion; (ii) the program required "administrative cooperation" between the Board and parochial schools; and (iii) the program might increase the dangers of "political divisiveness." Under our current understanding of the Establishment Clause, the last two considerations are insufficient by themselves to create an "excessive" entanglement. They are present no matter where Title I services are offered. Further, the assumption underlying the first consideration has been undermined. We no longer presume that public employees will inculcate religion simply because they happen to be in a sectarian environment. Since we have abandoned the assumption that properly instructed public employees will fail to discharge their duties faithfully, we must also discard the assumption that pervasive monitoring of Title I teachers is required. There is no suggestion that unannounced monthly visits of public supervisors are insufficient to prevent or to detect inculcation of religion by public employees.

To summarize, New York City's Title I program does not run afoul of any of three primary criteria we currently use to evaluate whether government aid has the effect of advancing religion: it does not result in governmental indoctrination; define its recipients by reference to religion; or create an excessive entanglement. We therefore hold that a federally funded program providing supplemental, remedial instruction to disadvantaged children on a neutral basis is not invalid under the Establishment Clause when such instruction is given on the premises of sectarian schools by government employees pursuant to a program containing safeguards such as those present here. The same considerations that justify this holding require us to conclude that this carefully constrained program also cannot reasonably be viewed as an endorsement of religion. Accordingly, we must acknowledge that *Aguilar*, as well as the portion of *Ball* addressing Grand Rapids' Shared Time program, are no longer good law.

Our Establishment Clause jurisprudence has changed significantly since we decided *Ball* and *Aguilar*. We therefore overrule *Ball* and *Aguilar* to the extent those decisions are inconsistent with our current understanding of the Establishment Clause. We reverse the Court of Appeals and remand to the District Court with instructions to vacate its order.

It is so ordered.

Justice Souter, with whom Justice Stevens and Justice Ginsburg join, and with whom Justice Breyer joins as to Part II, *dissenting*.

Aguilar was a correct and sensible decision. The State is forbidden to subsidize religion directly and is just as surely forbidden to act in any way that could reasonably be viewed as religious endorsement. These principles were violated by the programs at issue in *Aguilar* and *Ball*, as a consequence of several significant features common to both Title I and the Grand Rapids Shared Time program: each provided classes on the premises of the religious schools; while their services were termed "supplemental," the programs and their instructors necessarily assumed responsibility for teaching subjects that the religious schools would otherwise have been obligated to provide, the public employees carrying out the programs had broad responsibilities involving the exercise of consider-able discretion, while the programs offered aid to nonpublic school students gen-erally, participation by religious school students in each program was extensive, and, finally, aid under Title I and Shared Time flowed directly to the schools in the form of classes and programs. What was significant in *Aguilar* and *Ball* was that the schemes assumed responsibilities indistinguishable from the responsibility of the schools themselves. The obligation to teach reading necessarily extends to teaching those who are having a hard time at it. Calling classes remedial does not distinguish them from basic subjects. If a State may constitutionally enter the schools to teach, it must be free to assume the entire cost of instruction in any secular subject in any religious school.

It may be objected that there is some subsidy in remedial education even when it takes place off the religious premises. If the aid is delivered outside of the schools, it is less likely to supplant some of what would otherwise go on inside them and to subsidize what remains. On top of that, sharing the teaching respon-sibilities within a school having religious objectives is far more likely to telegraph approval of the school's mission than keeping the State's distance would do. Minimal contact between state and church is the less likely to feed the resent-ment of other religions that would like access to public money for their own worthy projects. If a line is to be drawn short of barring all state aid to religious schools for teaching standard subjects, the *Aguilar-Ball* line was a sensible one capable of principled adherence.

Zobrest recognized that the Establishment Clause lays down no absolute bar to placing public employees in a sectarian school, but the rejection of such a *per se* rule was hinged expressly on the nature of the employee's job, sign-language interpretation. The signer could be seen as more like a hearing aid than a teacher, and the signing could not be understood as an opportunity to inject religious content in what was supposed to be secular instruction.

The Court claims that *Ball* rested on the assumption that "any and all public aid that directly aids the educational function of religious schools impermissibly finances religious indoctrination, even if the aid reaches such schools as a con-sequence of private decision-making." *Ball* held that the Shared Time program subsidized the religious functions of the parochial schools by taking over a sig-nificant portion of their responsibility for teaching secular subjects. The Court enquired whether the effect of the proffered aid was "direct and substantial" or merely "indirect and incidental," emphasizing that the question "is one of degree." *Witters* and *Zobrest* did nothing to repudiate the principle that religious institutions did not receive it directly from the State.

Notes

1. *A Return to Neutrality?* In *Mitchell v. Helms*, 530 U.S. 793 (2000), Justice Thomas authored a plurality opinion (joined by Chief Justice Rehnquist and

Justices Scalia and Kennedy) upholding Chapter 2 of the Education Consolidation and Improvement Act of 1981, which provided federal funds "for the acquisition and use of instructional and educational materials, including library services and materials (including media materials), assessments, reference materials, computer software and hardware for instructional use, and other curricular materials." Participating private schools received aid based on the number of children enrolled in each school, and they could use the funds to "supplement" but not supplant funds from nonfederal sources. The "services, materials, and equipment" provided to private schools must be "secular, neutral, and nonideological," and private schools could not acquire control of them. In upholding the Act, the plurality overruled *Meek* and *Wolman*, holding that it has "consistently turned to the principle of neutrality. If the government, seeking to further some legitimate secular purpose, offers aid on the same terms, without regard to religion, to all who adequately further that purpose, then it is fair to say that any aid going to a religious recipient only has the effect of furthering that secular purpose." The Court also focused on whether the governmental aid "defines its recipients by reference to religion" thereby creating "a financial incentive to undertake religious indoctrination." The Court concluded that this "incentive is not present where the aid is allocated on the basis of neutral, secular criteria that neither favor nor disfavor religion, and is made available to both religious and secular beneficiaries on a nondiscriminatory basis." The Court eschewed any distinction between "direct and indirect aid": "If aid to schools is neutrally available, and before reaching or benefiting any religious school, first passes through the hands (literally or figuratively) of numerous private citizens who are free to direct the aid elsewhere, the government has not provided any (support of religion)." Justice O'Connor, joined by Justice Breyer, concurred: "We have never held that a government-aid program passes constitutional muster *solely* because of the neutral criteria it employs as a basis for distributing aid and have long been concerned that secular government aid not be diverted to the advancement of religion." Justice Souter, joined by Justices Stevens and Ginsburg, dissented, noting that "neutrality" could lead to "government funding as massive as expenditures made for the benefit of their public school counterparts, and religious missions would thrive on public money." He also expressed concern that the aid was "divertible" to religious purposes.

2. *More on Standing*. In *Arizona Christian School Tuition Organization v. Winn*, 563 U.S. 125 (2011), the Court held that plaintiffs lacked standing to challenge an Arizona law that provided tax credits for contributions to school tuition organizations, or STOs, that use these contributions to provide scholarships to students attending private schools, many of which are religious. Plaintiffs could not show that their taxes would increase because of the credit, and they also could not establish standing under the *Flast* nexus: "The STO tax credit is not tantamount to a religious tax or to a tithe and does not visit the injury identified in *Flast*." Justice Scalia, joined by Justice Thomas, concurred, arguing that: "*Flast* is an anomaly in our jurisprudence, is irreconcilable with the Article III restrictions

on federal judicial power," and should be overruled. Justice Kagan, joined by Justices Ginsburg, Breyer, and Sotomayor, dissented, arguing that the Court broke from "precedent by refusing to hear taxpayers' claims that the government has unconstitutionally subsidized religion through its tax system."

∾ PROBLEMS ∾

1. *More on the Education for a Better America Act.* Does the holding in *Agostini* and the plurality opinion in *Mitchell* alter your views regarding how Congress might be permitted to structure financial aid to parochial schools under the proposed Act? If Congress has pure motives (e.g., its goal is to improve the education of schoolchildren rather than to promote religion), and if the aid is offered on equivalent terms to all schools (public, private, and parochial), would *Agostini* permit Congress to provide direct financial grants to all schools, including parochial schools? Could Congress extend the aid to such items as books, maps, field trips, and student performance testing? Could Congress also provide funding for educational buildings and athletic structures on the theory that a healthy body leads to a healthy mind?

2. *Charitable Choice.* Former President George W. Bush offered and implemented proposals for "charitable choice," allowing religious groups to receive government funds for antipoverty initiatives such as job training, high school equivalency, English as a second language, nutrition programs, homes for unmarried mothers, and alcohol treatment. After *Agostini* and *Mitchell*, are President Bush's proposals permissible?

3. *More on Charitable Choice.* Suppose that you were serving as White House counsel during the Bush administration, and you were asked to make recommendations regarding the structure of the charitable choice program. What criteria would you advise the President to consider in designing and implementing the program? For example, should the President consider such criteria as whether providers are chosen on neutral grounds, whether religious organizations can retain their identity in service areas by displaying religious symbols, whether they can use religious criteria in selecting employees (despite the fact that participating organizations are precluded from actively proselytizing as well as from discriminating against recipients of other faiths), and whether other "secular" organizations are available to serve those who object to receiving services from a religious organization?

4. *Historic Preservation.* May Congress provide funds to help restore and preserve historic buildings and allow religious organizations to receive funds to restore and preserve historic religious buildings (e.g., the Old North Church in Boston, Massachusetts)? Would it matter whether the religious buildings are in active use as religious structures?

d. School Vouchers

In recent years, much controversy has surrounded so-called "school vouchers"—vouchers that can be used to pay for tuition at both public and private schools. President George W. Bush promoted the concept of "school choice" as a way of dealing with educational problems in the public schools. Under a "choice" system, parents are provided with vouchers that they can use to pay for their children's schooling, and the parents can use the vouchers at schools of their choice. By bringing choice to the public school system, President Bush hoped to force schools to compete for students, with the goal of producing better schools and a better educational system.

Before the 2002 decision in *Zelman v. Simmons-Harris*, the Court's decisions on vouchers were seemingly contradictory. In *Committee for Public Education and Religious Liberty v. Nyquist*, 413 U.S. 756 (1973), applying the *Lemon* test, the Court invalidated a New York law that provided partial tuition reimbursements and tax benefits to the parents of children attending elementary or secondary nonpublic schools: "In the absence of an effective means of guaranteeing that the state aid derived from public funds will be used exclusively for secular, neutral, and non-ideological purposes, direct aid in whatever form is invalid." That same year, the Court decided *Sloan v. Lemon*, 413 U.S. 825 (1973), which involved a Pennsylvania law that reimbursed parents for a portion of tuition expenses incurred at nonpublic schools. The Court struck the law down, finding "no constitutionally significant distinctions" from *Nyquist*. However, in *Mueller v. Allen*, 463 U.S. 388 (1983), the Court upheld a Minnesota law that allowed taxpayers, in computing their state income tax, to deduct certain expenses incurred in providing for the education of their children. *Mueller* set the stage for the following decision.

Zelman v. Simmons-Harris

536 U.S. 639 (2002)

Chief Justice REHNQUIST delivered the opinion of the Court.

The State of Ohio has established a pilot program designed to provide educational choices to families with children who reside in the Cleveland City School District. The question presented is whether this program offends the Establishment Clause of the United States Constitution. We hold that it does not.

There are more than 75,000 children enrolled in the Cleveland City School District. The majority of these children are from low-income and minority families who do not enjoy the means to send their children to any school other than an inner-city public school. Cleveland's public schools have been among the worst performing public schools in the Nation. In 1995, a Federal District Court declared a "crisis of magnitude" and placed the entire Cleveland school district under state control. The district had failed to meet any of the 18 state standards for minimal acceptable performance. Only 1 in 10 ninth graders could pass a basic proficiency examination. More than two-thirds of high school students either dropped or failed out before graduation. Of those students who managed to reach their senior year, one of every four still failed to graduate. Of those students who did graduate, few could read, write, or compute at levels comparable to their counterparts in other cities.

Against this backdrop, Ohio enacted its Pilot Project Scholarship Program, Ohio Rev. Code Ann. §§3313.974-3313.979. The program provides financial assistance to families in any Ohio school district that is or has been "under federal court order requiring supervision and operational management of the district by the state superintendent." Cleveland is the only Ohio school district to fall within that category. The program provides two basic kinds of assistance to parents of children in a covered district. First, the program provides tuition aid for students in kindergarten through third grade, expanding each year through eighth grade, to attend a participating public or private school of their parent's choosing. Second, the program provides tutorial aid for students who choose to remain enrolled in public school.

The tuition aid portion of the program is designed to provide educational choices to parents who reside in a covered district. Any private school, whether religious or nonreligious, may participate in the program and accept program students so long as the school is located within the boundaries of a covered district and meets statewide educational standards. Participating private schools must agree not to discriminate on the basis of race, religion, or ethnic background, or to "advocate or foster unlawful behavior or teach hatred of any person or group on the basis of race, ethnicity, national origin, or religion." Adjacent public schools are eligible to receive a $2,250 tuition grant for each program student accepted in addition to the full amount of per-pupil state funding attributable to each additional student. All participating schools, whether public or private, are required to accept students in accordance with rules and procedures established by the state superintendent.

Tuition aid is distributed to parents according to financial need. Families with incomes below 200% of the poverty line are given priority and are eligible to receive 90% of private school tuition up to $2,250. For these lowest-income families, participating private schools may not charge a parental co-payment greater than $250. For all other families, the program pays 75% of tuition costs, up to $1,875, with no co-payment cap. These families receive tuition aid only if the number of available scholarships exceeds the number of low-income children who choose to participate. Where tuition aid is spent depends solely upon where parents who receive tuition aid choose to enroll their child. If parents choose a private school, checks are made payable to the parents who then endorse the checks over to the chosen school.

The tutorial aid portion of the program provides tutorial assistance through grants to any student in a covered district who chooses to remain in public school. Parents arrange for registered tutors to provide assistance to their children and then submit bills for those services to the State for payment. Students from low-income families receive 90% of the amount charged for such assistance up to $360. All other students receive 75% of that amount. The number of tutorial assistance grants offered to students in a covered district must equal the number of tuition aid scholarships provided to students enrolled at participating private or adjacent public schools.

In the 1999-2000 school year, 56 private schools participated in the program, 46 (or 82%) of which had a religious affiliation. None of the public schools in districts adjacent to Cleveland have elected to participate. More than 3,700 students participated in the scholarship program, most of whom (96%) enrolled in religiously affiliated schools. Sixty percent of these students were from families at or below the poverty line. In the 1998-1999 school year, approximately 1,400 Cleveland public school students received tutorial aid. This number was expected to double during the 1999-2000 school year.

The program is part of a broader undertaking by the State to enhance the educational options of Cleveland's schoolchildren that includes programs governing community and magnet schools. Community schools are funded under state law but are run by their own school boards, not by local school districts. These schools enjoy independence to hire their own teachers and to determine their own curriculum. They can have no religious affiliation and are required to accept students by lottery. During the 1999-2000 school year, there were 10 start-up community schools in Cleveland with more than 1,900 students enrolled. For each child enrolled in a community school, the school receives state funding of $4,518, twice the funding a participating program school may receive.

Magnet schools are public schools operated by a local school board that emphasize a particular subject area, teaching method, or service to students. For each student enrolled in a magnet school, the school district receives $7,746, including state funding of $4,167, the same amount received per student enrolled at a traditional public school. As of 1999, parents in Cleveland were able to choose from among 23 magnet schools, which together enrolled more than 13,000 students in kindergarten through eighth grade. These schools provide specialized teaching methods, such as Montessori, or a particularized curriculum focus, such as foreign language, computers, or the arts.

Respondents filed this action in United States District Court, seeking to enjoin the program on the ground that it violated the Establishment Clause of the United States Constitution. The District Court granted summary judgment for respondents. A divided panel of the Court of Appeals affirmed. We granted certiorari and now reverse.

The Establishment Clause of the First Amendment, applied to the States through the Fourteenth Amendment, prevents a State from enacting laws that have the "purpose" or "effect" of advancing or inhibiting religion. *Agostini v. Felton*, 521 U.S. 203 (1997). There is no dispute that the program challenged here was enacted for the valid secular purpose of providing educational assistance to poor children in a demonstrably failing public school system. The question is whether the Ohio program nonetheless has the forbidden "effect" of advancing or inhibiting religion.

Our decisions have drawn a consistent distinction between government programs that provide aid directly to religious schools and programs of true private choice, in which government aid reaches religious schools only as a result of the genuine and independent choices of private individuals, *Mueller v. Allen*, 463 U.S. 388 (1983); *Witters v. Washington Dept. of Servs. for Blind*, 474 U.S. 481 (1986); *Zobrest v. Catalina Foothills School Dist.*, 509 U.S. 1 (1993). While our jurisprudence with respect to the constitutionality of direct aid programs has "changed significantly" over the past two decades, our jurisprudence with respect to true private choice programs has remained consistent. Three times we have confronted Establishment Clause challenges to neutral government programs that provide aid directly to a broad class of individuals, who, in turn, direct the aid to religious schools or institutions of their own choosing. We have rejected such challenges. In *Mueller*, we rejected an Establishment Clause challenge to a Minnesota program authorizing tax deductions for various educational expenses, including private school tuition costs, even though the great majority of the program's beneficiaries (96%) were parents of children in religious schools. Viewing the program as a whole, we emphasized the principle of private choice, noting that public funds were made available to religious schools "only as a result of numerous, private choices of individual parents of school-age children." This, we said, ensured that "'no imprimatur of state approval' can be deemed to have been conferred on any particular religion, or on religion generally." We thus found it irrelevant that the vast majority of beneficiaries were parents of children in religious schools. That the program was one of true private choice, with no evidence that the State deliberately skewed incentives toward religious schools, was sufficient for the program to survive scrutiny under the Establishment Clause. In *Witters*, we used identical reasoning to reject an Establishment Clause challenge to a vocational scholarship program that provided tuition aid to a student studying at a religious institution to become a pastor. Finally, in *Zobrest*, we applied *Mueller* and *Witters* to reject an Establishment Clause challenge to a federal program that permitted sign-language interpreters to assist deaf children enrolled in religious schools.

Mueller, Witters, and *Zobrest* thus make clear that where a government aid program is neutral with respect to religion, and provides assistance directly to a broad class of citizens who, in turn, direct government aid to religious schools wholly as a result of their own genuine and independent private choice, the program is not readily subject to challenge under the Establishment Clause. A program that shares these features permits government aid to reach religious institutions only by way of the deliberate choices of numerous individual recipients. The incidental advancement of a religious mission, or the perceived endorsement of a religious message, is reasonably attributable to the individual recipient, not to the government, whose role ends with the disbursement of benefits. It is precisely for these reasons that we have never found a program of true private choice to offend the Establishment Clause.

We believe that the program challenged here is a program of true private choice, consistent with *Mueller, Witters,* and *Zobrest,* and thus constitutional. The Ohio program is neutral in all respects toward religion. It is part of a general and multifaceted undertaking by the State of Ohio to provide educational opportunities to the children of a failed school district. It confers educational assistance directly to a broad class of individuals defined without reference to religion, i.e., any parent of a school-age child who resides in the Cleveland City School District. The program permits the participation of *all* schools within the district, religious or nonreligious. Adjacent public schools also may participate and have a financial incentive to do so. Program benefits are available to participating families on neutral terms, with no reference to religion. The only preference stated anywhere in the program is a preference for low-income families, who receive greater assistance and are given priority for admission at participating schools.

There are no "financial incentives" that "skew" the program toward religious schools. Such incentives "are not present where the aid is allocated on the basis of neutral, secular criteria that neither favor nor disfavor religion, and is made available to both religious and secular beneficiaries on a nondiscriminatory basis." The program here in fact creates financial *dis*incentives for religious schools, with private schools receiving only half the government assistance given to community schools and one-third the assistance given to magnet schools. Adjacent public schools, should any choose to accept program students, are also eligible to receive two to three times the state funding of a private religious school. Families too have a financial disincentive to choose a private religious school because they must copay a portion of the school's tuition. Families that choose a community school, magnet school, or traditional public school pay nothing. Such features of the program clearly dispel the claim that the program "creates financial incentives for parents to choose a sectarian school."[3]

No reasonable observer would think a neutral program of private choice, where state aid reaches religious schools solely as a result of the numerous independent decisions of private individuals, carries with it the *imprimatur* of government endorsement. Any objective observer familiar with the full history and context of the Ohio program would reasonably view it as one aspect of a broader undertaking to assist poor children in failed schools, not as an endorsement of religious schooling in general.

There also is no evidence that the program fails to provide genuine opportunities for Cleveland parents to select secular educational options for their school-age children. Cleveland schoolchildren enjoy a range of educational choices: They may remain in public school, remain in public school with publicly funded tutoring aid, obtain a scholarship and choose a religious school, obtain a scholarship and choose a nonreligious private school, enroll in a community

---

3. Justice Souter suggests the program is not "neutral" because program students cannot spend scholarship vouchers at traditional public schools. This objection is mistaken: Public schools in Cleveland already receive $7,097 in public funding per pupil—$4,167 of which is attributable to the State.

school, or enroll in a magnet school. That 46 of the 56 private schools now participating in the program are religious schools does not condemn it as a violation of
the Establishment Clause. The question is whether Ohio is coercing parents into
sending their children to religious schools, and that question must be answered
by evaluating *all* options Ohio provides Cleveland schoolchildren.

Justice Souter speculates that because more private religious schools currently participate in the program, the program itself must somehow discourage
the participation of private nonreligious schools. But Cleveland's preponderance
of religiously affiliated private schools certainly did not arise as a result of the
program. By all accounts the program has captured a remarkable cross-section
of private schools, religious and nonreligious. It is true that 82% of Cleveland's
participating private schools are religious schools, but it is also true that 81% of
private schools in Ohio are religious schools. To attribute constitutional significance to this figure would lead to the absurd result that a neutral school-choice
program might be permissible where a lower percentage of private schools are
religious schools, but not in inner-city Cleveland, where Ohio has deemed such
programs most sorely needed, but where the preponderance of religious schools
happens to be greater. Likewise, an identical private choice program might be
constitutional in some States, such as Maine or Utah, where less than 45% of
private schools are religious schools, but not in other States where over 90% of
private schools are religious schools.

Respondents and Justice Souter claim that we should attach constitutional
significance to the fact that 96% of scholarship recipients have enrolled in religious schools. They claim that this alone proves parents lack genuine choice. This
argument was flatly rejected in *Mueller*, where we found it irrelevant that 96% of
parents taking deductions for tuition expenses paid tuition at religious schools.
The constitutionality of a neutral educational aid program simply does not turn
on whether and why, in a particular area, at a particular time, most private schools
are run by religious organizations, or most recipients choose to use the aid at a
religious school. "Such an approach would scarcely provide the certainty that this
field stands in need of, nor can we perceive principled standards by which such
statistical evidence might be evaluated."

This point is aptly illustrated here. The 96% figure upon which Justice Souter
relies discounts entirely (1) the more than 1,900 Cleveland children enrolled in
alternative community schools, (2) the more than 13,000 children enrolled in
alternative magnet schools, and (3) the more than 1,400 children enrolled in traditional public schools with tutorial assistance. Including some or all of these children in the denominator of children enrolled in nontraditional schools during
the 1999-2000 school year drops the percentage enrolled in religious schools from
96% to under 20%. The 96% figure also represents but a snapshot of one particular school year. In the 1997-1998 school year, by contrast, only 78% of scholarship recipients attended religious schools. The difference was attributable to
two private nonreligious schools that had accepted 15% of all scholarship students electing instead to register as community schools, in light of larger per-pupil

funding for community schools and the uncertain future of the scholarship program generated by this litigation. Many of the students enrolled in these schools
as scholarship students remained enrolled as community school students, thus
demonstrating the arbitrariness of counting one type of school but not the other
to assess primary effect.

Respondents finally claim that we should look to *Committee for Public Ed. &
Religious Liberty v. Nyquist*, 413 U.S. 756 (1973), to decide these cases. We disagree.
That program's "function" was "*unmistakably* to provide desired financial support
for nonpublic, sectarian institutions" and we expressly reserved judgment with
respect to "a case involving public assistance (e.g., scholarships) made available
without regard to the sectarian-nonsectarian, or public-nonpublic nature of the
institution benefitted."

In sum, the Ohio program is entirely neutral with respect to religion. It provides benefits directly to a wide spectrum of individuals, defined only by financial
need and residence in a particular school district. It permits such individuals to
exercise genuine choice among options public and private, secular and religious.
The program is therefore a program of true private choice. In keeping with an
unbroken line of decisions rejecting challenges to similar programs, we hold that
the program does not offend the Establishment Clause.

The judgment of the Court of Appeals is *reversed*.

Justice O'CONNOR, *concurring*.

These cases are different from prior indirect aid cases because a significant
portion of the funds reach religious schools without restrictions on the use of
these funds. $8.2 million of public funds flowed to religious schools under the
voucher program in 1999-2000. This amount pales in comparison to the amount
of funds that federal, state, and local governments already provide religious institutions. Religious organizations may qualify for exemptions from the federal corporate income tax, the corporate income tax in many States, and property taxes in
all 50 States. In addition, the Federal Government provides individuals, corporations, trusts, and estates a tax deduction for charitable contributions to qualified
religious groups. Finally, the Federal Government and certain state governments
provide tax credits for educational expenses, many of which are spent on education at religious schools. Religious hospitals rely on Medicare funds for 36 percent of their revenue. Against this background, the support that the Cleveland
voucher program provides religious institutions is neither substantial nor atypical
of existing government programs. Cleveland parents who use vouchers to send
their children to religious private schools do so as a result of true private choice.

Justice THOMAS, *concurring*.

Failing urban public schools disproportionately affect minority children most
in need of educational opportunity. Many blacks and other minorities support
school choice programs because they provide the greatest educational opportunities for their children in struggling communities. Poor urban families just want

the best education for their children, who will certainly need it to function in our high-tech and advanced society. If society cannot end racial discrimination, at least it can arm minorities with the education to defend themselves from some of discrimination's effects.

Justice STEVENS, *dissenting*.

The Court's decision is profoundly misguided. In reaching that conclusion I have been influenced by my understanding of the impact of religious strife on the decisions of our forbears to migrate to this continent. Whenever we remove a brick from the wall that was designed to separate religion and government, we increase the risk of religious strife and weaken the foundation of our democracy.

Justice SOUTER, with whom Justice STEVENS, Justice GINSBURG, and Justice BREYER join, *dissenting*.

The principle of nondivertibility has been enforced strictly, with its violation being presumed in most cases, even when state aid seemed secular on its face. It was not until today that substantiality of aid has clearly been rejected as irrelevant by a majority of this Court. Today's cases are notable for their stark illustration of the inadequacy of the majority's chosen formal analysis. In order to apply the neutrality test, it makes sense to focus on a category of aid that may be directed to religious as well as secular schools, and ask whether the scheme favors a religious direction. The majority looks not to the provisions for tuition vouchers, but to every provision for educational opportunity. The illogic is patent. If regular, public schools (which can get no voucher payments) "participate" in a voucher scheme, and public expenditure is still predominantly on public schools, then the majority's reasoning would find neutrality in a scheme of vouchers available for private tuition in districts with no secular private schools at all. "Neutrality" is literally, verbal and nothing more.

The majority's view that all educational choices are comparable for purposes of choice ignores the point of the choice test: it is a criterion for deciding whether indirect aid to a religious school is legitimate because it passes through private hands that can spend or use the aid in a secular school. The question is whether the private hand is genuinely free to send the money in either a secular direction or a religious one. When the choice test is transformed from where to spend the money to where to go to school, it is cut loose from its very purpose. Something is influencing choices in a way that aims the money in a religious direction: of 56 private schools in the district participating in the voucher program (only 53 of which accepted voucher students in 1999-2000), 46 of them are religious; 96.6% of all voucher recipients go to religious schools. There is no explanation that suggests the religious direction results simply from free choices by parents. One answer which would be consistent with the genuine choice claimed to be operating, might be that 96.6% of families choosing to avail themselves of vouchers choose to educate their children in schools of their own religion. This would not, in my view, render the scheme constitutional. Evidence shows, however, that almost two out of three families using vouchers to send their children to religious schools did not embrace the religion of those schools. The families had not chosen the schools because they wished their children to be proselytized in a religion not their own, or in any religion, but because of educational opportunity.

Even so, the fact that some 2,270 students chose to apply their vouchers to schools of other religions might be consistent with true choice if the students "chose" their religious schools over a wide array of private nonreligious options, or if it could be shown generally that Ohio's program had no effect on educational choices and thus no impermissible effect of advancing religious education. But both possibilities are contrary to fact. First, even if all existing nonreligious private schools in Cleveland were willing to accept large numbers of voucher students, only a few more than the 129 currently enrolled in such schools would be able to attend, as the total enrollment at all nonreligious private schools in Cleveland for kindergarten through eighth grade is only 510 children, and there is no indication that these schools have many open seats. Second, the $2,500 cap that the program places on tuition for participating low-income pupils has the effect of curtailing the participation of nonreligious schools: "nonreligious schools with higher tuition (about $4,000) stated that they could afford to accommodate just a few voucher students." By comparison, the average tuition at participating Catholic schools in Cleveland in 1999-2000 was $1,592, almost $1,000 below the cap. For the overwhelming number of children in the voucher scheme, the only alternative to the public schools is religious.

The scale of the aid to religious schools approved today is unprecedented, both in the number of dollars and in the proportion of systemic school expenditure supported. The matter before us involves considerable sums distributed through thousands of students attending religious elementary and middle schools in the city of Cleveland. The Cleveland voucher program has cost Ohio taxpayers $33 million. These tax-raised funds are on top of the textbooks, reading and math tutors, laboratory equipment, and the like that Ohio provides to private schools, worth roughly $600 per child. In paying for practically the full amount of tuition for thousands of qualifying students, the scholarships purchase everything that tuition purchases, be it instruction in math or indoctrination in faith. The consequences of "substantial" aid hypothesized in *Meek* are realized here: the majority makes no pretense that substantial amounts of tax money are not systematically underwriting religious practice and indoctrination.

Every objective underlying the prohibition of religious establishment is betrayed by this scheme. The first objective is respect for freedom of conscience. Madison thought it violated by any "'authority which can force a citizen to contribute three pence of his property for the support of any establishment.'" Memorial and Remonstrance & para. 3. Madison's objection to three pence has simply been lost in the majority's formalism. As for the second objective, to save religion from its own corruption, the risk is one of "corrosive secularism" to religious schools, and the specific threat is to the primacy of the schools' mission to educate the children of the faithful according to the unaltered precepts of their faith. In Ohio, a condition of receiving government money under the program is that participating religious schools may not "discriminate on the basis of religion," which means the school may not give admission preferences to children who are members of the patron faith. A participating religious school may well be forbidden to choose a member of its own clergy to serve as teacher or principal over a layperson of a different religion claiming equal qualification for the job and could be understood (or subsequently broadened) to prohibit religions from teaching traditionally legitimate articles of faith as to the error, sinfulness, or ignorance of others. It is well to remember that the money has barely begun to flow. Religious schools in Ohio are on the way to becoming bigger businesses with budgets enhanced to fit their new stream of tax-raised income. When government aid goes up, so does reliance on it; the only thing likely to go down is independence. Is there reason to wonder when dependence will become great enough to give the State of Ohio an effective veto over basic decisions on the content of curriculums? The third concern behind the ban on establishment is its inextricable link with social conflict. Not all taxpaying Protestant citizens, for example, will be content to underwrite the teaching of the Roman Catholic Church condemning the death penalty. Nor will all of America's Muslims acquiesce in paying for the endorsement of the religious Zionism taught in many religious Jewish schools, which combines "a nationalistic sentiment" in support of Israel with a "deeply religious" element. Nor will every secular taxpayer be content to support Muslim views on differential treatment of the sexes, or, for that matter, to fund the espousal of a wife's obligation of obedience to her husband, presumably taught in any schools adopting the articles of faith of the Southern Baptist Convention. Views like these have been safe in the sectarian pulpits and classrooms of this Nation not only because the Free Exercise Clause protects them directly, but because the ban on supporting religious establishment has protected free exercise. With the arrival of vouchers in religious schools, that privacy will go, and along with it will go confidence that religious disagreement will stay moderate. I hope that a future Court will reconsider today's dramatic departure from basic Establishment Clause principle.

Justice BREYER, with whom Justice STEVENS and Justice SOUTER join, *dissenting.*

The Religion Clauses embody an understanding, reached in the 17th century after decades of religious war, that liberty and social stability demand a religious tolerance that respects the religious views of all citizens, permits those citizens to "worship God in their own way," and allows all families to "teach their children and to form their characters" as they wish. C. Radcliffe, *The Law and Its Compass* 71 (Faber 1960). The Clauses reflect the Framers' vision of an American Nation free of the religious strife that had long plagued the nations of Europe. For this reason, the Court's 20th century Establishment Clause cases focused directly upon social conflict, potentially created when government becomes involved in religious education. The upshot is the development of constitutional doctrine that reads the Establishment Clause as avoiding religious strife, *not* by providing every religion with an *equal opportunity*, but by drawing fairly clear lines of *separation* between church and state—at least where the heartland of religious belief, such as primary religious education, is at issue. The principle underlying these cases—avoiding religiously based social conflict—remains of great concern. As religiously diverse as America had become when the Court decided its major 20th century Establishment Clause cases, we are exponentially more diverse today. America boasts more than 55 different religious groups and subgroups.

School voucher programs finance the religious education of the young. And, if widely adopted, they may well provide billions of dollars that will do so. Why will different religions not become concerned about, and seek to influence, the criteria used to channel this money to religious schools? Why will they not want to examine the implementation of the programs that provide this money—to determine, for example, whether implementation has biased a program toward or against particular sects, or whether recipient religious schools are adequately fulfilling a program's criteria? If so, just how is the State to resolve the resulting controversies without provoking legitimate fears of the kinds of religious favoritism that, in so religiously diverse a Nation, threaten social dissension?

Consider the voucher program here at issue. That program insists that the religious school accept students of all religions. Does that criterion treat fairly groups whose religion forbids them to do so? The program also insists that no participating school "advocate or foster unlawful behavior or teach hatred of any person or group on the basis of race, ethnicity, national origin, or religion." And it requires the State to "revoke the registration of any school" in violation of the program's rules. How are state officials to adjudicate claims that one religion or another is advocating, for example, civil disobedience in response to unjust laws, the use of illegal drugs in a religious ceremony, or resort to force to call attention to what it views as an immoral social practice? What kind of public hearing will there be in response to claims that one religion or another is continuing to teach a view of history that casts members of other religions in the worst possible light? How will the public react to government funding for schools that take controversial religious positions on topics that are of current popular interest—say, the conflict in the Middle East or the war on terrorism? Yet any major funding program for primary religious education will require criteria. And the selection of those criteria, as well as their application, inevitably pose problems that are divisive. Efforts to respond to these problems not only will seriously entangle church and state, but also will promote division among religious groups, as one group or another fears (often legitimately) that it will receive unfair treatment at the hands of the government.

I concede that the Establishment Clause currently permits States to channel various forms of assistance to religious schools, for example, transportation costs for students, computers, and secular texts. Yet the consequence has not been great turmoil. School voucher programs differ, however, in both *kind* and *degree* from aid programs upheld in the past. They differ in kind because they direct financing to a core function of the church: the teaching of religious truths to young children. Vouchers also differ in degree because they permit a considerable shift of taxpayer dollars from public secular schools to private religious schools.

I do not believe that the "parental choice" aspect of the voucher program sufficiently offsets the concerns I have mentioned. Parental choice cannot help the taxpayer who does not want to finance the religious education of children. It will not always help the parent who may see little real choice between inadequate nonsectarian public education and adequate education at a school whose religious teachings are contrary to his own. It will not satisfy religious minorities unable to participate because they are too few in number to support the creation of their own private schools. It will not satisfy groups whose religious beliefs preclude them from participating in a government-sponsored program, and who may well feel ignored as government funds primarily support the education of children in the doctrines of the dominant religions. And it does little to ameliorate the entanglement problems or the related problems of social division. Consequently, the fact that the parent may choose which school can cash the government's voucher check does not alleviate the Establishment Clause concerns associated with voucher programs. I dissent.

Note and Questions

1. *Charter Schools and the Conversion of Religious Schools.* Religious schools sometimes have compelling reasons for becoming public schools (e.g., so-called charter schools). For one thing, the conversion to a public school can help stabilize the school's finances and might bring about an increase in teacher salaries. On the other hand, the transition can sometimes be difficult. For example, the new school may be subject to more rigorous state-imposed requirements (e.g., mandates requiring grade tracking, testing, and data analysis). In addition, both teachers and students may struggle with the idea of how to function in a secular environment. How does a school teach values without impermissibly intruding into religious issues? *See* Javier C. Hernandez, *Upholding Catholic Values After Converting to Secular Education: Parish Schools in Fiscal Straits See a Test Case in Washington,* N.Y. Times, A-17, c. 1-6, Mar. 1, 2009.

2. In *Espinoza v. Montana Department of Revenue,* 140 S.Ct. 2246 (2020), the Court broke new ground. *Espinoza* involved a Montana law which sought to create parental and student choice through a scholarship program for students attending private schools. The program gave a tax credit of up to $150 to any taxpayer who donated to a participating "student scholarship organization" which, in turn, passed the money on as scholarships to students who attended private schools. However, the legislature directed that the aid program be administered consistently with Article X, section 6, of the Montana Constitution, which contains a "no-aid" provision barring direct or indirect governmental aid to sectarian schools. In order to comply with the no aid provision, the Montana

Supreme Court terminated the aid program for all students whether in sectarian or secular schools. The U.S. Supreme Court held that Montana acted improperly in terminating the program and in denying aid to sectarian schools:

> The Free Exercise Clause, which applies to the States under the Fourteenth Amendment, "protects religious observers against unequal treatment" and against "laws that impose special disabilities on the basis of religious status." *Trinity Lutheran*, 582 U. S., at ___. Montana's no-aid provision bars religious schools from public benefits solely because of the religious character of the schools. The provision also bars parents who wish to send their children to a religious school from those same benefits, again solely because of the religious character of the school. The provision bars aid to any school "controlled in whole or in part by any church, sect, or denomination." Mont. Const., Art. X, § 6(1). The provision's title—"Aid prohibited to sectarian schools"—confirms that the provision singles out schools based on their religious character. The provision plainly excludes schools from government aid solely because of religious status.
>
> The Montana Supreme Court applied the no-aid provision to hold that religious schools could not benefit from the scholarship program. So applied, the provision "imposes special disabilities on the basis of religious status" and "conditions the availability of benefits upon a recipient's willingness to surrender its religiously impelled status." *Trinity Lutheran*, 582 U. S., at ___ (quoting *Church of Lukumi Babalu Aye, Inc.* v. *Hialeah*, 508 U. S. 520, 533 (1993), and *McDaniel v. Paty*, 435 U. S. 618, 626 (1978) (plurality opinion)). To be eligible for government aid, a school must divorce itself from any religious control or affiliation. Placing such a condition on benefits or privileges "inevitably deters or discourages the exercise of First Amendment rights." *Trinity Lutheran*, 582 U. S., at ___ (slip op., at 11). The Free Exercise Clause protects against even "indirect coercion," and a State "punishes the free exercise of religion" by disqualifying the religious from government aid as Montana did here. *Trinity Lutheran*, 582 U. S., at ___ (slip op., at 10–11). Such status-based discrimination is subject to "the strictest scrutiny." *Id.*, at ___ (slip op., at 11). It is enough to conclude that strict scrutiny applies under *Trinity Lutheran* because Montana's no-aid provision discriminates based on religious status.

As a result, the Court reversed the Montana Supreme Court's decision to terminate the program for all recipients.

∽ PROBLEMS ∽

1. *Vouchers and the Education for a Better America Act.* Does *Zelman* suggest that Congress could include a general voucher program as part of the proposed Act? Suppose that Congress believes that school voucher programs will introduce competition into the educational system, and will thereby help foster improvements in both private and parochial schools. As a result, Congress is thinking about extending the benefits of vouchers to all school districts, not just those in crisis. Would such a voucher program be constitutional?

2. *More on Vouchers and the Education for a Better America Act.* Suppose that Congress has preliminarily decided to include vouchers in the proposed Act. Your boss has asked you for input regarding how to structure the voucher program to

ensure that it will withstand constitutional challenge. How will you advise Congress to structure the program? What components should be included? What, if anything, should be avoided?

3. *Extending the Act's Voucher Provisions to Religiously Homogeneous Areas.* In constructing the proposed Act, should you (must you?) take into account the fact that, in some states (e.g., Utah), the overwhelming majority of residents belong to a single religion (e.g., Mormonism)? What if, following adoption of the program, almost all Utah students who belong to the dominant religion withdraw from public schools, which are subsequently forced to close for lack of students, thereby leaving no public schools available for non-Mormons? Would the program be constitutional?

4. *The Creationist Museum.* The group Answers in Genesis seeks to build a "creationism" theme park ("Ark Encounter") in Northern Kentucky, which would include a massive wooden ark with educational attractions. *See* Stephanie Steitzer, *Theme Park for Creationism Proposed for Kentucky: Museum Operators Seek Tax Incentives,* Louisville Courier-Journal, A.1, c. 5-6, Dec. 1, 2010. The Commonwealth of Kentucky has a "Kentucky Tourism Development Act," which allows developers to recover up to 25% of the total cost of developing a new tourism-related business. The money comes in the form of a return of taxes paid by the developer on admission tickets, food, gift sales, and lodging costs. If the incentives are granted, would they be constitutional? Who would have standing to challenge the incentives?

2. School Prayer

Considerable debate and litigation have focused on the permissibility of prayer in public schools.

Engel v. Vitale

370 U.S. 421 (1962)

Mr. Justice BLACK delivered the opinion of the Court.

The respondent Board of Education of Union Free School District No. 9, New Hyde Park, New York, acting in its official capacity under state law, directed the School District's principal to cause the following prayer to be said aloud by each class in the presence of a teacher at the beginning of each school day:

> Almighty God, we acknowledge our dependence upon Thee, and we beg Thy blessings upon us, our parents, our teachers and our Country.

This procedure was adopted on the recommendation of the State Board of Regents to which the New York Legislature has granted broad supervisory powers over the State's public school system. These state officials composed the prayer which they recommended and published as a part of their "Statement on Moral and Spiritual Training in the Schools," saying: "We believe that this Statement will be subscribed to by all men and women of good will, and we call upon all of them to aid in giving life to our program." The parents of ten pupils challenged use of the official prayer. The New York Court of Appeals upheld the practice.

By using its public school system to encourage recitation of the Regents' prayer, the State of New York has adopted a practice wholly inconsistent with the Establishment Clause. Invocation of God's blessings as prescribed in the Regents' prayer is a religious activity. It is a solemn avowal of divine faith and supplication for the blessings of the Almighty. The constitutional prohibition against laws respecting an establishment of religion must at least mean that it is no part of the business of government to compose official prayers for any group of people to recite as part of a religious program carried on by government.

This very practice of establishing governmentally composed prayers for religious services was one of the reasons which caused many of our early colonists to leave England and seek religious freedom in America. By the time of the adoption of the Constitution, there was widespread awareness of the dangers of a union of Church and State. These people knew, some of them from bitter personal experience, that one of the greatest dangers to the freedom of the individual to worship in his own way lay in the Government's placing its official stamp of approval upon one particular kind of prayer or one particular form of religious services. Under the First Amendment, government is without power to prescribe any particular form of prayer to be used as an official prayer in any program of governmentally sponsored religious activity.

New York's state prayer program officially establishes the religious beliefs embodied in the Regents' prayer. Neither the fact that the prayer may be denominationally neutral nor the fact that its observance on the part of the students is voluntary can serve to free it from the limitations of the Establishment Clause. When the power, prestige and financial support of government is placed behind a particular religious belief, the indirect coercive pressure upon religious minorities to conform to the prevailing officially approved religion is plain. But the purposes underlying the Establishment Clause go much further than that. Its first and most immediate purpose rested on the belief that a union of government and religion tends to destroy government and to degrade religion. The history of governmentally established religion, both in England and in this country, showed that whenever government had allied itself with one particular form of religion, the inevitable result had been that it had incurred the hatred, disrespect and even contempt of those who held contrary beliefs. Religion is too personal, too sacred, too holy, to permit its "unhallowed perversion" by a civil magistrate. Another purpose of the Establishment Clause rested upon an awareness of the historical fact that governmentally established religions and religious persecutions go hand in hand. It was in large part to get completely away from systematic religious persecution that the Founders brought into being our Bill of Rights with its prohibition against any governmental establishment of religion. The New York laws officially prescribing the Regents' prayer are inconsistent both with the purposes of the Establishment Clause and with the Establishment Clause itself.

It has been argued that to apply the Constitution to prohibit state laws respecting an establishment of religious services in public schools is to indicate a hostility toward religion or toward prayer. Nothing could be more wrong. It is neither sacrilegious nor antireligious to say that government should stay out of the business of writing or sanctioning official prayers and leave that purely religious function to the people themselves and to those the people choose to look to for religious guidance.

The judgment of the Court of Appeals of New York is reversed and the cause remanded for further proceedings not inconsistent with this opinion.

Reversed and remanded.

Mr. Justice DOUGLAS, *concurring*.

The First Amendment leaves the Government in a position not of hostility to religion but of neutrality. The philosophy is that the atheist or agnostic—the nonbeliever—is entitled to go his own way. If government interferes in matters spiritual, it will be a divisive force.

Mr. Justice STEWART, *dissenting*.

I cannot see how an "official religion" is established by letting those who want to say a prayer say it. On the contrary, to deny the wish of these school children to join in this prayer is to deny them the opportunity of sharing in the spiritual heritage of our Nation.

At the opening of each day's Session of this Court we stand, while one of our officials invokes the protection of God. Since the days of John Marshall our Crier has said, "God save the United States and this Honorable Court." Both the Senate and the House of Representatives open their daily Sessions with prayer. Each of our Presidents, from George Washington to John F. Kennedy, has upon assuming his Office asked the protection and help of God.

The Court today says that the state and federal governments are without constitutional power to prescribe any particular form of words to be recited by any group of the American people on any subject touching religion. One of the stanzas of "The Star-Spangled Banner," made our National Anthem by Act of Congress in 1931, contains these verses:

> Blest with victory and peace, may the heav'n rescued land Praise the Pow'r that hath made and preserved us a nation! Then conquer we must, when our cause it is just, And this be our motto "In God is our Trust."

In 1954 Congress added a phrase to the Pledge of Allegiance to the Flag so that it now contains the words "one Nation under God, indivisible, with liberty and justice for all." In 1952 Congress enacted legislation calling upon the President each year to proclaim a National Day of Prayer. Since 1865 the words "IN GOD WE TRUST" have been impressed on our coins.

Countless similar examples could be listed, but there is no need to belabor the obvious. It was all summed up by this Court just ten years ago in a single sentence: "We are a religious people whose institutions presuppose a Supreme Being." *Zorach v. Clauson*, 343 U.S. 306, 313. I do not believe the State of New York has established a religion in this case. What it has done is recognize and follow the deeply entrenched and highly cherished spiritual traditions of our Nation. I dissent.

BACKGROUND
A Constitutional Amendment?

Following the decision in *Engel*, some have sought to amend the Constitution to permit prayer in public schools. Congressional proponents of such an amendment claim that court rulings have "attacked and twisted and warped" the First Amendment and have stifled religious expression "right and left all over the country." These amendments have failed to garner the votes necessary for passage.

Notes

1. *Legislative Prayer.* In *Marsh v. Chambers*, 463 U.S. 783 (1983), the Court held that the Nebraska legislature could begin its day with chaplain-led prayer. The Court upheld the practice: "From colonial times through the founding of the Republic and ever since, the practice of legislative prayer has coexisted with the principles of disestablishment and religious freedom. In this context, historical evidence sheds light not only on what the draftsmen intended the Establishment Clause to mean, but also on how they thought that Clause applied to the practice authorized by the First Congress." Justice Brennan dissented: "The 'primary effect' of legislative prayer is also clearly religious and there can be no doubt that the practice of legislative prayer leads to excessive 'entanglement' between the State and religion."

2. *Prayer at Monthly Town Council Meetings.* In *Town of Greece v. Galloway*, 572 U.S. 565 (2014), the Court extended *Marsh* to a case involving opening prayers at monthly town council meetings. The Court regarded the prayers as permissible because it "presumed that the reasonable observer understands that its purposes are to lend gravity to public proceedings and to acknowledge the place religion holds in the lives of many private citizens, not to afford government an opportunity to proselytize or force truant constituents into the pews." The Court rejected the argument that the prayers must be "generic" or "nonsectarian," noting that the "content of the prayer is not of concern to judges," provided "there is no indication that the prayer opportunity has been exploited to proselytize or advance any one, or to disparage any other, faith or belief." The invited chaplain is free "to address his or her own God or gods as conscience dictates, unfettered by what

an administrator or judge considers to be nonsectarian." The Court rejected the claim that the prayers were invalid because virtually all of the prayers had been given by Christian ministers. The town had shown a willingness to allow any faith to participate in the prayers. Justice Breyer dissented on this point, arguing that of "the more than 120 monthly meetings at which prayers were delivered during the record period, only four prayers were delivered by non-Christians." Despite this evidence, the Court concluded that the town had acted in a nondiscriminatory manner: "So long as the town maintains a policy of nondiscrimination, the Constitution does not require it to search beyond its borders for non-Christian prayer givers in an effort to achieve religious balancing." The Court suggested that it would invalidate town prayers if officials "directed the public to participate in the prayers, singled out dissidents for opprobrium, or indicated that their decisions might be influenced by a person's acquiescence in the prayer opportunity." The practice might also have been objectionable if "legislative prayer is alleged to be a means to coerce or intimidate others."

∾ PROBLEMS ∾

1. *School Prayer and the Education for a Better America Act.* In constructing the proposed legislation, what (if anything) should be said about school prayer? Can you (should you?) specifically allow or prohibit school prayer in schools that receive government funding? Should the prohibition extend to parochial schools as well? Is it permissible (appropriate?) to simply ignore the issue in constructing the legislation?

2. *Distinguishing Legislative Prayer from School Prayer.* If it is permissible for a legislature to employ a chaplain and begin its day with a prayer, then why is school prayer impermissible? In other words, what distinguishes school prayer from legislative prayer? Does it matter that there were virtually no public schools when the Constitution was adopted?

3. *The Atheist Chaplain.* Suppose that an atheist applies to the House of Representatives for permission to open a legislative session with a secular invocation. His request is refused on the basis that he is not an ordained minister. Just as the House may not discriminate between religions, is it also prohibited from discriminating against atheists? *See Barker v. Conroy,* 282 F.Supp.3d 346 (D.C. Cir. 2019).

Wallace v. Jaffree

472 U.S. 38 (1985)

Justice STEVENS delivered the opinion of the Court.

The constitutionality of three Alabama statutes is questioned: (1) §16-1-20, enacted in 1978, which authorized a 1-minute period of silence in all public schools "for meditation"; (2) §16-1-20.1, enacted in 1981, which authorized a period of silence "for meditation or voluntary prayer"; and (3) §16-1-20.2, enacted in 1982, which authorized teachers to lead "willing students" in a prescribed prayer to "Almighty God the Creator and Supreme Judge of the world." The Court of Appeals held both §16-1-20.1 and §16-1-20.2 unconstitutional. The question is whether §16-1-20.1, which authorizes a period of silence for "meditation or voluntary prayer," is a law respecting the establishment of religion within the meaning of the First Amendment.

When the Court has been called upon to construe the Establishment Clause, it has applied the *Lemon* criteria. It is the first of these three criteria that is most plainly implicated by this case. A statute must be invalidated if it is entirely motivated by a purpose to advance religion. The record reveals that §16-1-20.1 was not motivated by any clearly secular purpose.

The sponsor of the bill that became §16-1-20.1, Senator Donald Holmes, inserted into the legislative record—apparently without dissent—a statement that the legislation was an "effort to return voluntary prayer" to the public schools. Senator Holmes confirmed this purpose before the District Court. In response to the question whether he had any purpose for the legislation other than returning voluntary prayer to public schools, he stated: "No." The State did not present evidence of any secular purpose.

Unrebutted evidence of legislative intent is confirmed by a consideration of the relationship between this statute and the two other measures that were considered in this case. The earlier statute refers only to "meditation" whereas §16-1-20.1 refers to "meditation or voluntary prayer." The only significant textual difference is the addition of the words "or voluntary prayer."

The legislative intent to return prayer to the public schools is quite different from merely protecting every student's right to engage in voluntary prayer during an appropriate moment of silence during the school day. The 1978 statute already protected that right, containing nothing that prevented any student from engaging in voluntary prayer during a silent minute of meditation. Appellants have not identified any secular purpose that was not fully served by §16-1-20 before the enactment of §16-1-20.1. We must, therefore, conclude that the Alabama Legislature enacted §16-1-20.1 for the sole purpose of expressing the State's endorsement of prayer activities for one minute at the beginning of each schoolday. The addition of "or voluntary prayer" indicates that the State intended to characterize prayer as a favored practice. Such an endorsement is not consistent with the established principle that the government must pursue a course of complete neutrality toward religion. We conclude that §16-1-20.1 violates the First Amendment.

The judgment of the Court of Appeals is affirmed.

It is so ordered.

Justice POWELL, *concurring.*

The record makes clear that Alabama's purpose was solely religious in character.

Justice O'CONNOR, *concurring in the judgment.*

Nothing in the United States Constitution prohibits public school students from voluntarily praying at any time before, during, or after the school day. Alabama has facilitated voluntary silent prayers of students who are so inclined by enacting a statute which provides a moment of silence in schools each day. Twenty-five states permit or require public school teachers to have students observe a moment of silence in their classrooms. The typical statute calls for a moment of silence at the beginning of the schoolday during which students may meditate, pray, or reflect on the activities of the day. *See, e.g.,* Ark. Stat. Ann. §80-1607.1 (1980).

A state-sponsored moment of silence is different from state-sponsored vocal prayer or Bible reading. A moment of silence is not inherently religious. A pupil who participates in a moment of silence need not compromise his or her beliefs. A student who objects to prayer is left to his or her own thoughts, and is not compelled to listen to the prayers or thoughts of others.

By mandating a moment of silence, a State does not necessarily endorse any activity that might occur during the period. Even if a statute specifies that a student may choose to pray silently during a quiet moment, the State has not thereby encouraged prayer over other specified alternatives. A message of endorsement is inescapable if the teacher exhorts children to use the designated time to pray. Similarly, the face of the statute or its legislative history may clearly establish that it seeks to encourage or promote voluntary prayer over other alternatives, rather than merely provide a quiet moment that may be dedicated to prayer by those so inclined. The crucial question is whether the State has conveyed or attempted to convey the message that children should use the moment of silence for prayer. This question requires courts to examine the history, language, and administration of a particular statute to determine whether it operates as an endorsement of religion.

The inquiry into the purpose of the legislature in enacting a moment of silence law should be deferential and limited. If a legislature expresses a plausible secular purpose for a moment of silence statute in either the text or the legislative history, or if the statute disclaims an intent to encourage prayer over alternatives during a moment of silence, then courts should generally defer to that stated intent.

If we assume that the religious activity that Alabama seeks to protect is silent prayer, then it is difficult to discern any state-imposed burden on that activity that is lifted by §16-1-20.1. No law prevents a student who is so inclined from praying silently in public schools. Moreover, state law already provided a moment of silence to these appellees irrespective of §16-1-20.1.

Chief Justice BURGER, *dissenting.*

Some will find it ironic that on the very day we heard arguments in the cases, the Court's session opened with an invocation for Divine protection. The House of Representatives and the Senate regularly open each session with a prayer.

These legislative prayers are not just one minute in duration, but are extended, thoughtful invocations and prayers for Divine guidance. They are given, as they have been since 1789, by clergy appointed as official chaplains and paid from the Treasury of the United States. Congress has also provided chapels in the Capitol, at public expense, where Members and others may pause for prayer, meditation—or a moment of silence. Some wag is bound to say that the Court's holding today reflects a belief that members of the Judiciary and Congress are more in need of Divine guidance than are schoolchildren.

It makes no sense to say that Alabama has "endorsed prayer" by merely enacting a new statute "to specify expressly that voluntary prayer is *one* of the authorized activities during a moment of silence." All of the sponsor's statements were made after the legislature had passed the statute. There is not a shred of evidence that the legislature as a whole shared the sponsor's motive or was even aware of the sponsor's view of the bill when it was passed. The sole relevance of the sponsor's statements, therefore, is that they reflect the personal, subjective motives of a single legislator. No case supports the idea that post-enactment statements are relevant in determining the constitutionality of legislation. The sponsor also testified that one of his purposes in drafting and sponsoring the moment-of-silence bill was to clear up a widespread misunderstanding that a schoolchild is legally prohibited from engaging in silent, individual prayer once he steps inside a public school building.

The statute does not remotely threaten religious liberty; it affirmatively furthers the values of religious freedom and tolerance that the Establishment Clause was designed to protect.

Justice WHITE, *dissenting.*

The Court would approve statutes that provided for a moment of silence but did not mention prayer. But if a student asked whether he could pray during that moment, it is difficult to believe that the teacher could not answer in the affirmative. I would not invalidate a statute that provided the legislative answer to the question "May I pray?"

Justice REHNQUIST, *dissenting.*

It would come as a shock to those who drafted the Bill of Rights as it will to a large number of thoughtful Americans to learn that the Constitution prohibits the Alabama Legislature from "endorsing" prayer. George Washington himself, at the request of the very Congress which passed the Bill of Rights, proclaimed a day of "public thanksgiving and prayer, to be observed by acknowledging with grateful hearts the many and signal favors of Almighty God." History must judge whether it was the Father of his Country in 1789, or a majority of the Court today, which has strayed from the meaning of the Establishment Clause. Nothing in the Establishment Clause of the First Amendment prohibits any such generalized "endorsement" of prayer. I would therefore reverse.

⮞ PROBLEMS ⮜

1. *Other Moments of Prayer?* In a state without a history of school prayer, would a "religiously neutral" moment of silence statute pass constitutional muster? Suppose that the law was passed to "solemnize" the opening of the school day? Would it matter if the law specifically instructs teachers that students should not be encouraged to pray or to meditate (although students could do either)? Suppose that teachers are told that, if students ask whether they "may" pray during the meditation period, they should be told that they may. Does the answer render the moment of prayer invalid?

2. *Moments of Silence and Congressional Funding for Education.* In constructing the proposed legislation, would it be permissible for Congress to authorize or encourage schools to have a "moment of silence" at the beginning of the school day? Suppose that Congress makes it clear that the purpose of the moment of silence is to "settle schoolchildren down" and solemnize the opening of the school day, and that Congress also makes clear that school teachers are prohibited from encouraging (or, for that matter, discouraging) prayer. Should Congress address these issues in the legislation?

Lee v. Weisman

505 U.S. 577 (1992)

Justice KENNEDY delivered the opinion of the Court.

School principals in the public school system of Providence, Rhode Island, may invite members of the clergy to offer invocation and benediction prayers at graduation ceremonies for middle schools and for high schools. The lower courts held that the practice violated the Establishment Clause. We affirm.

The Constitution guarantees that government may not coerce anyone to support or participate in religion or its exercise, or otherwise act in a way which "establishes a state religion or religious faith, or tends to do so." The State's involvement in the school prayers challenged today violates these central principles. That involvement is as troubling as it is undenied. A school official, the principal, decided that an invocation and a benediction should be given, and chose the religious participant, here a rabbi.

The potential for divisiveness over the choice of a particular member of the clergy to conduct the ceremony is apparent. Divisiveness can attend any state decision respecting religions, and neither its existence nor its potential necessarily invalidates the State's attempts to accommodate religion in all cases. The potential for divisiveness is of particular relevance here because it centers around an overt religious exercise in a secondary school environment where subtle coercive pressures exist and where the student had no real alternative which would have allowed her to avoid the fact or appearance of participation.

The State's role did not end with the decision to include a prayer and with the choice of a clergyman. Principal Lee provided Rabbi Gutterman with a copy of the "Guidelines for Civic Occasions," and advised him that his prayers should be nonsectarian. Through these means the principal directed and controlled the content of the prayers. Even if the only sanction for ignoring the instructions were that the rabbi would not be invited back, no religious representative who valued his or her reputation would incur the State's displeasure. It is "no part of the business of government to compose official prayers for any group of American people to recite as a part of a religious program carried on by government," and that is what the school officials attempted to do.

Petitioners argue that directions for the content of the prayers were a good-faith attempt by the school to ensure that sectarianism which is so often the flashpoint for religious animosity be removed from the graduation ceremony. The concern is understandable, as a prayer which uses ideas or images identified with a particular religion may foster a different sort of sectarian rivalry than an invocation or benediction in terms more neutral. The question is not the good faith of the school in attempting to make the prayer acceptable to most persons, but the legitimacy of its undertaking that enterprise at all. We are asked to recognize the existence of a practice of nonsectarian prayer which is more acceptable than one which makes explicit references to the God of Israel, or to Jesus Christ, or to a patron saint. There may be some support that there has emerged a civic religion, one which is tolerated when sectarian exercises are not. Though the First Amendment does not allow the government to stifle prayers which aspire to these ends, neither does it permit the government to undertake that task for itself.

The First Amendment's Religion Clauses mean that religious beliefs and religious expression are too precious to be prescribed by the State. The design of the Constitution is that preservation and transmission of religious beliefs and worship is a responsibility and a choice committed to the private sphere, which itself is promised freedom to pursue that mission. It must not be forgotten that these same Clauses exist to protect religion from government interference. These concerns have particular application in the case of school officials, whose effort to monitor prayer will be perceived by the students as inducing a participation they might otherwise reject.

It is argued that our constitutional vision of a free society requires confidence in our own ability to accept or reject ideas of which we do not approve, and that prayer at a high school graduation does nothing more than offer a choice. Students may consider it an odd measure of justice to be subjected during the course of their educations to ideas deemed offensive and irreligious, but to be denied a brief, formal prayer ceremony that the school offers in return. This argument cannot prevail, however. It overlooks a fundamental dynamic of the Constitution.

There are heightened concerns with protecting freedom of conscience from subtle coercive pressure in the elementary and secondary public schools. Finding no violation under these circumstances would place objectors in the dilemma of participating, with all that implies, or protesting. Psychology supports the assumption that adolescents are susceptible to pressure from their peers towards conformity, and that the influence is strongest in matters of social convention. The government may no more use social pressure to enforce orthodoxy than it may use more direct means. There was a stipulation that attendance at graduation and promotional ceremonies is voluntary. To say a teenage student has a real choice not to attend her high school graduation is formalistic. In our society and in our culture high school graduation is one of life's most significant occasions.

The school district contends that the prayers are an essential part of these ceremonies because for many persons an occasion of this significance lacks meaning if there is no recognition, however brief, that human achievements cannot be understood apart from their spiritual essence. This position fails to acknowledge that what for many of Deborah's classmates and their parents was a spiritual imperative was for Daniel and Deborah Weisman religious conformance compelled by the State. While in some societies the wishes of the majority might prevail, the Constitution forbids the State to exact religious conformity from a student as the price of attending her own high school graduation.

Inherent differences distinguish this case from *Marsh v. Chambers*, 463 U.S. 783 (1983). At a high school graduation, teachers and principals must and do retain a high degree of control over the precise contents of the program. In this atmosphere the state-imposed character of an invocation and benediction by clergy selected by the school combine to make the prayer a state-sanctioned religious exercise in which the student was left with no alternative but to submit.

For the reasons we have stated, the judgment of the Court of Appeals is
Affirmed.

Justice BLACKMUN, with whom Justice STEVENS and Justice O'CONNOR join, *concurring.*

When the government "composes official prayers," selects the member of the clergy to deliver the prayer, has the prayer delivered at a public school event that is planned, supervised and given by school officials, and pressures students to attend and participate in the prayer, there can be no doubt that the government is advancing and promoting religion. It is not enough that the government restrain from compelling religious practices: It must not engage in them either.

Justice SOUTER, with whom Justice STEVENS and Justice O'CONNOR join, *concurring.*

Petitioners contend that because the early Presidents included religious messages in their inaugural and Thanksgiving Day addresses, the Framers could not have meant the Establishment Clause to forbid noncoercive state endorsement of religion. To be sure, the leaders of the young Republic engaged in some of the practices that separationists like Jefferson and Madison criticized. Those practices prove that the Framers simply did not share a common understanding of the Establishment Clause, and, at worst, that they, like other politicians, could raise constitutional ideals one day and turn their backs on them the next.

Religious students cannot complain that omitting prayers from their graduation ceremony would, in any realistic sense, "burden" their spiritual callings. They may express their religious feelings about it before and after the ceremony. They may even organize a privately sponsored baccalaureate if they desire the company of likeminded students.

Petitioners would deflect this conclusion by arguing that graduation prayers are no different from Presidential religious proclamations and similar official "acknowledgments" of religion in public life. But religious invocations in Thanksgiving Day addresses and the like, rarely noticed, ignored without effort, conveyed over an impersonal medium, and directed at no one in particular, inhabit a pallid zone worlds apart from official prayers delivered to a captive audience of public school students and their families.

Justice SCALIA, with whom THE CHIEF JUSTICE, Justice WHITE, and Justice THOMAS join, *dissenting*.

The history and tradition of our Nation are replete with public ceremonies featuring prayers of thanksgiving and petition. From our Nation's origin, prayer has been a prominent part of governmental ceremonies and proclamations. The Declaration of Independence, the document marking our birth as a separate people, "appealed to the Supreme Judge of the world for the rectitude of our intentions" and avowed "a firm reliance on the protection of divine Providence." In his first inaugural address, after swearing his oath of office on a Bible, George Washington deliberately made a prayer a part of his first official act as President. Such supplications have been a characteristic feature of inaugural addresses ever since. Our national celebration of Thanksgiving likewise dates back to President Washington. This tradition of Thanksgiving Proclamations—with their religious theme of prayerful gratitude to God—has been adhered to by almost every President. The other two branches of the Federal Government also have a long-established practice of prayer at public events. Congressional sessions have opened with a chaplain's prayer ever since the First Congress. And this Court's own sessions have opened with the invocation "God save the United States and this Honorable Court" since the days of Chief Justice Marshall. There exists a more specific tradition of invocations and benedictions at public school graduation exercises.

The notion that a student who simply sits in "respectful silence" during the invocation and benediction (when all others are standing) has somehow joined—or would somehow be perceived as having joined—in the prayers is nothing short of ludicrous. Maintaining respect for the religious observances of others is a fundamental civic virtue that government (including the public schools) can and should cultivate. The Court itself has not given careful consideration to its test of psychological coercion. For if it had, how could it observe, with no hint of concern or disapproval, that students stood for the Pledge of Allegiance, which immediately preceded Rabbi Gutterman's invocation? The government can, of course, no more coerce political orthodoxy than religious orthodoxy. Since the Pledge of Allegiance has been revised to include the phrase "under God," recital of the Pledge would appear to raise the same Establishment Clause issue as the invocation and benediction. Must the Pledge therefore be barred from the public schools (both from graduation ceremonies and from the classroom)?

I also find it odd that the Court concludes that high school graduates may not be subjected to this supposed psychological coercion. Graduation is significant because it is associated with transition from adolescence to young adulthood. Many graduating seniors are old enough to vote. Why, then, does the Court treat them as though they were first-graders? Beyond the fact that attendance at graduation is voluntary, there is nothing to indicate that failure of attending students to take part in the invocation or benediction was subject to any penalty or discipline.

The longstanding American tradition of prayer at official ceremonies displays with unmistakable clarity that the Establishment Clause does not forbid the government to accommodate it. The narrow context of the present case involves a community's celebration of one of the milestones in its young citizens' lives, and it is a bold step for this Court to seek to banish from that occasion the expression of gratitude to God that a majority of the community wishes to make. I dissent.

Notes and Questions

1. *Prayer at Football Games.* In *Santa Fe Independent School District v. Doe,* 530 U.S. 290 (2000), the Court struck down a school district policy that authorized nondenominational prayer at football games. Students were allowed to vote on whether to have a prayer and to select the student who would give it. The Court explained: "invocations are authorized by a government policy and take place on government property at government-sponsored school-related events. In addition, the only type of message that is expressly endorsed in the text is an 'invocation'—a term that primarily describes an appeal for divine assistance." Chief Justice Rehnquist, joined by Justices Scalia and Thomas, dissented: "The policy itself has plausible secular purposes: 'To solemnize the event, to promote good sportsmanship and student safety, and to establish the appropriate environment for the competition.' Where a governmental body 'expresses a plausible secular purpose' for an enactment, 'courts should generally defer to that stated intent.'"

2. *Does the Pledge of Allegiance Establish Religion?* In *Elk Grove Unified School District v. Newdow,* 542 U.S. 1 (2004), respondent, an atheist, challenged the fact that a school district began each day with a recitation of the Pledge of Allegiance. He contended that, because the pledge contains the words "under God," its recitation amounts to an establishment of religion. The Court refused to hear the case on grounds of nonjusticiability (the respondent, as a noncustodial parent, lacked standing). If the Court had heard the case, how should it have ruled? Justice O'Connor has argued that such recitations are permissible as a form of "ceremonial deism," which she defines broadly to encompass such things as the national motto ("In God We Trust"), religious references in traditional patriotic

songs i.e. such as "The Star-Spangled Banner"), and the words with which the marshal of this Court opens each of its sessions ("God save the United States and this honorable Court"). Do you agree with Justice O'Connor?

3. *The Scalia Proposal.* In his dissent in *Lee,* Justice Scalia suggested that invocations and benedictions would be permissible at graduation if the school announced (orally or in the program) that "while all are asked to rise for the invocation and benediction, none is compelled to join, nor will it be assumed, by rising, to have done so. That obvious fact recited, the graduates and their parents may proceed to thank God, as Americans have always done, for the blessings He has generously bestowed on them and on their country." Do you agree?

4. *Professional School Prayer?* Should *Lee's* holding apply to professional schools' graduation prayers? Are the factors that prompted the *Lee* decision applicable in that context?

∾ PROBLEMS ∾

1. *More on the Education for a Better America Act.* In constructing the proposed legislation, should you say anything at all about whether graduation prayers are allowed or prohibited? Would it be permissible for parochial schools that receive federal funding to have prayer at their graduation exercises?

2. *The Valedictorian's Thanks to God.* Suppose that a school has a policy of allowing four students to speak at graduation. The students are chosen based on their class standing, and they are allowed to deliver "an address, poem, reading, song, musical presentation, prayer, or any other pronouncement." School policy precludes school employees from censoring any presentation or requiring any content. In this situation, would it be constitutionally permissible for the valedictorian at a high school graduation to offer thanks to God—provided that the thanks is offered spontaneously, of the individual's own free will, and as a thanks for guidance and help in his or her own life?

3. Curricular Issues

There has been considerable litigation regarding whether schools may include religious teachings in the public school curriculum.

School District of Abington Township v. Schempp

374 U.S. 203 (1963)

Mr. Justice CLARK delivered the opinion of the Court.

Pennsylvania requires that "At least ten verses from the Holy Bible be read, without comment, at the opening of each public school on each school day." At

Abington Senior High School, opening exercises are broadcast through an inter-communications system under the supervision of a teacher by students in the school's radio and television workshop. Students read ten verses of the Holy Bible and then recite the Lord's Prayer. Other students are asked to stand and join in the prayer in unison. The exercises close with a salute to the flag and announcements. The student who reads the Bible verses may select the passages and read from any version he or she chooses, although the school furnishes only the King James version. The King James, the Douay, and the Revised Standard versions of the Bible have been used, as well as the Jewish Holy Scriptures. There are no prefatory statements, no questions asked or solicited, no comments or explanations, and no interpretations given during the exercises. A student may leave the classroom or elect not to participate in the exercises. In schools that do not have an intercommunications system, the Bible reading and the recitation were conducted by the homeroom teacher, who chose the verses and read them herself or had students read them. A Baltimore school board rule provided for opening exercises consisting primarily of the "reading, without comment, of a chapter in the Holy Bible and/or the use of the Lord's Prayer."

The State contends that the program has secular purposes including the promotion of moral values, the contradiction to the materialistic trends of our times, the perpetuation of our institutions and the teaching of literature. Even if its purpose is not strictly religious, the place of the Bible as an instrument of religion cannot be gainsaid, and the State's recognition of the pervading religious character of the ceremony is evident from the rule's specific permission of the alternative use of the Catholic Douay version as well as the recent amendment permitting nonattendance at the exercises. None of these factors is consistent with the contention that the Bible is used either as an instrument for nonreligious moral inspiration or as a reference for the teaching of secular subjects.

The exercises are being conducted in direct violation of the rights of the appellees and petitioners. The fact that individual students may absent themselves furnishes no defense to a claim of unconstitutionality.

It is insisted that unless these religious exercises are permitted a "religion of secularism" is established in the schools. We agree that the State may not establish a "religion of secularism" in the sense of affirmatively opposing or showing hostility to religion, thus "preferring those who believe in no religion over those who do believe." *Zorach v. Clauson*, 343 U.S. at 314. We do not agree that this decision has that effect. It might be said that one's education is not complete without a study of comparative religion or the history of religion and its relationship to the advancement of civilization. It certainly may be said that the Bible is worthy of study for its literary and historic qualities. Nothing we have said indicates that study of the Bible or religion, when presented objectively as part of a secular program of education, may not be effected consistently with the First Amendment. But the exercises violate the command that the Government maintain strict neutrality, neither aiding nor opposing religion.

We cannot accept that the concept of neutrality, which does not permit a State to require a religious exercise even with the consent of the majority of those affected, collides with the majority's right to free exercise of religion. While the Free Exercise Clause prohibits the use of state action to deny the rights of free exercise to anyone, it has never meant that a majority could use the machinery of the State to practice its beliefs.

Judgment in No. 142 *affirmed*; judgment in No. 119 *reversed and cause remanded with directions.*

Mr. Justice DOUGLAS, *concurring.*

The Establishment Clause precludes the State from conducting religious exercises and also forbids the State to employ its facilities or funds in a way that gives any church, or all churches, greater strength in our society than it would have by relying on its members alone. The present regimes must fall. Through the mechanism of the State, all people are being required to finance a religious exercise that only some of the people want and that violates the sensibilities of others.

Mr. Justice BRENNAN, *concurring.*

Religious exercises at the start of the school day may foster harmony and tolerance among the pupils, enhancing the authority of the teacher, and inspiring better discipline. To the extent that such benefits result not from the content of the readings and recitation, but simply from the holding of such a solemn exercise at the opening assembly or the first class of the day, it would seem that less sensitive materials might equally well serve the same purpose. It has not been shown that readings from the speeches and messages of great Americans, or from the documents of our heritage of liberty, daily recitation of the Pledge of Allegiance, or even the observance of a moment of reverent silence at the opening of class, may not adequately serve the solely secular purposes of the devotional activities without jeopardizing either religious liberties or the proper degree of separation between religion and government. The State acts unconstitutionally if it tries to attain religious ends by religious means, or if it uses religious means to serve secular ends where secular means would suffice.

It is argued that the particular practices before us are unobjectionable because they prefer no particular sect or sects at the expense of others. Any version of the Bible is inherently sectarian. The argument contains, however, a more basic flaw. There are persons in every community—often deeply devout—to whom any version of the Judaeo-Christian Bible is offensive. There are others whose reverence for the Holy Scriptures demands private study or reflection and to whom public reading or recitation is sacrilegious.

It has been suggested that a tentative solution to these problems may lie in the fashioning of a "common core" of theology tolerable to all creeds but preferential to none. But "history is not encouraging to" those who hope to fashion a "common denominator of religion detached from its manifestation in any organized church." Arthur Sutherland, *Establishment According to Engel,* 76 Harv. L. Rev. 25, 51 (1962).

The availability of excusal or exemption has no relevance to the establishment question, if it is once found that these practices are essentially religious exercises designed at least in part to achieve religious aims through the use of public school facilities during the school day. The State could not constitutionally require a student to profess publicly his disbelief as the prerequisite to the exercise of his constitutional right of abstention.

Mr. Justice STEWART, *dissenting.*

A compulsory state educational system so structures a child's life that if religious exercises are held to be an impermissible activity in schools, religion is placed at an artificial and state-created disadvantage. Permission of such exercises for those who want them is necessary if the schools are truly to be neutral in the matter of religion. And a refusal to permit religious exercises thus is seen, not as the realization of state neutrality, but rather as the establishment of a religion of secularism, or at the least, as government support of the beliefs of those who think that religious exercises should be conducted only in private.

The dangers both to government and to religion inherent in official support of instruction in the tenets of various religious sects are absent in the present cases, which involve only a reading from the Bible unaccompanied by comments which might otherwise constitute instruction. Since any teacher who does not wish to do so is free not to participate, it cannot be contended that some infinitesimal part of the salaries paid by the State are made contingent upon the performance of a religious function.

In these cases, what is involved is an attempt by the State to accommodate those differences which the existence in our society of a variety of religious beliefs makes inevitable. The Constitution requires that such efforts be struck down only if they entail the use of the secular authority of government to coerce a preference among such beliefs.

∾ PROBLEMS ∾

1. *More on the Education for a Better America Act.* In constructing the proposed legislation, should Congress say anything about whether schools are allowed to use (or, for that matter, prohibited from using) religious materials in their courses? Should Congress prohibit parochial schools that receive financial aid under the Act from using religious materials?

2. *University Courses on Religion.* May a public college, as part of its ordinary curriculum, offer a survey course designed to give students an overview of religion and religious concepts? Would it matter whether the course focused on only a particular religion?

Epperson v. Arkansas

393 U.S. 97 (1968)

Mr. Justice FORTAS delivered the opinion of the Court.

This appeal challenges the constitutionality of the Arkansas "anti-evolution" statute adopted in 1928. The statute was a product of the upsurge of "fundamentalist" religious fervor of the twenties. The Arkansas statute was an adaption of the famous Tennessee "monkey law" which that State adopted in 1925. The constitutionality of the Tennessee law was upheld by the Tennessee Supreme Court in the celebrated Scopes case in 1927.[2]

The Arkansas law makes it unlawful for a teacher in any state-supported school or university "to teach the theory or doctrine that mankind ascended or descended from a lower order of animals," or "to adopt or use in any such institution a textbook that teaches" this theory. Violation is a misdemeanor and subjects the violator to dismissal from his position.

The present case concerns the teaching of biology in a high school in Little Rock. Until the events here in litigation, the official textbook furnished for the high school biology course did not have a section on the Darwinian Theory. For the academic year 1965–1966, the school administration, on recommendation of the teachers of biology in the school system, adopted and prescribed a textbook which contained a chapter setting forth "the theory about the origin of man from a lower form of animal."

Susan Epperson was employed by the Little Rock school system in the fall of 1964 to teach 10th grade biology. At the start of the next academic year, 1965, she was confronted by the new textbook (which one surmises from the record was not unwelcome to her). She faced at least a literal dilemma because she was supposed to use the new textbook for classroom instruction and presumably to teach the statutorily condemned chapter; but to do so would be a criminal offense and subject her to dismissal.

She instituted the present action seeking a declaration that the Arkansas statute is void and enjoining officials of the Little Rock school system from dismissing her for violation of the statute's provisions. The trial court struck the statute down on First Amendment grounds.

Only Arkansas and Mississippi have "anti-evolution" or "monkey" laws on their books.[8] There is no record of any prosecutions in Arkansas and the statute may be more of a curiosity than a vital fact of life. Nevertheless, it is our duty to decide the issues presented.

Our precedents inevitably determine the result in the present case. The State's undoubted right to prescribe the curriculum for its public schools does

---

2. *Scopes v. State of Tennessee,* 154 Tenn. 105, 289 S.W. 363 (1927). The Tennessee court reversed Scopes' conviction on the ground that the jury and not the judge should have assessed the fine of $100.

8. Oklahoma enacted an anti-evolution law, but repealed it in 1926. The Florida and Texas Legislatures, between 1921 and 1929, adopted resolutions against teaching the doctrine of evolution.

not carry with it the right to prohibit, on pain of criminal penalty, the teaching of a scientific theory or doctrine where that prohibition is based upon reasons that violate the First Amendment.

There can be no doubt that Arkansas has sought to prevent its teachers from discussing the theory of evolution because it is contrary to the belief of some that the Book of Genesis must be the exclusive source of doctrine as to the origin of man. It is clear that fundamentalist sectarian conviction was and is the law's reason for existence. Its antecedent, Tennessee's "monkey law," candidly stated its purpose: to make it unlawful "to teach any theory that denies the story of the Divine Creation of man as taught in the Bible, and to teach instead that man has descended from a lower order of animals." Perhaps the sensational publicity attendant upon the Scopes trial induced Arkansas to adopt less explicit language. It eliminated Tennessee's reference to "the story of the Divine Creation of man" as taught in the Bible, but the motivation for the law was the same: to suppress the teaching of a theory which "denied" the divine creation of man.

Arkansas' law cannot be defended as an act of religious neutrality. Arkansas did not seek to excise from the curricula of its schools and universities all discussion of the origin of man. The law's effort was confined to an attempt to blot out a particular theory because of its supposed conflict with the Biblical account, literally read. Plainly, the law is contrary to the mandate of the First, and in violation of the Fourteenth, Amendment to the Constitution.

The judgment of the Supreme Court of Arkansas is reversed.

Reversed.

Mr. Justice BLACK, *concurring*.

I find it difficult to agree with the statement that "Arkansas sought to prevent its teachers from discussing evolution because it is contrary to the Book of Genesis." It may be that the people's motive was merely that it would be best to remove this controversial subject from its schools; there is no reason why a State cannot withdraw from its curriculum any subject deemed too emotional and controversial. It is not for us to invalidate a statute because of our views that the "motives" behind its passage were improper; it is simply too difficult to determine what those motives were. A second question that arises is whether this Court's decision infringes the religious freedom of those who consider evolution an anti-religious doctrine. How can the State be bound by the Federal Constitution to permit its teachers to advocate an "anti-religious" doctrine to schoolchildren?

Question: The Choper Analysis

Can it be argued that even though the Arkansas law may have been religiously motivated, it involved "none of the dangers the Establishment Clause was designed to prevent" because there was no "evidence that religious beliefs were either coerced, compromised or influenced"? Can it also be argued that there was no evidence that the law "(1) induced children of fundamentalist religions to accept the biblical theory of creation, or (2) conditioned other children for conversion to fundamentalism"? Can it be argued that there is (or is not) *"religious harm"* and a "threat to religious liberty"? *See* Jesse H. Choper, *The Religion Clauses of the First Amendment: Reconciling the Conflict,* 41 U. Pitt. L. Rev. 673, 687 (1980).

Edwards v. Aguillard

482 U.S. 578 (1987)

Justice Brennan delivered the opinion of the Court.[*]

The question for decision is whether Louisiana's "Balanced Treatment for Creation-Science and Evolution-Science in Public School Instruction" Act (Creationism Act), is facially invalid as violative of the Establishment Clause of the First Amendment.

The Creationism Act forbids the teaching of the theory of evolution in public schools unless accompanied by instruction in "creation science." No school is required to teach evolution or creation science. If either is taught, however, the other must also be taught. The theories of evolution and creation science are statutorily defined as "the scientific evidences for creation or evolution and inferences from those scientific evidences."

Appellees, who include parents of children attending Louisiana public schools, Louisiana teachers, and religious leaders, challenged the constitutionality of the Act. The District Court found no valid secular reason for prohibiting the teaching of evolution. The Court of Appeals affirmed. We affirm.

The Court has been particularly vigilant in monitoring compliance with the Establishment Clause in elementary and secondary schools. Families entrust public schools with the education of their children, but condition their trust on the understanding that the classroom will not purposely be used to advance religious views that may conflict with the private beliefs of the student and his or her family. Students in such institutions are impressionable and the State exerts great authority and coercive power through mandatory attendance requirements, and because of the students' emulation of teachers as role models and the children's susceptibility to peer pressure. We use the three-pronged *Lemon* test mindful of the particular concerns that arise in the context of public elementary and secondary schools.

Lemon's first prong focuses on the purpose that animated adoption of the Act. The Act's stated purpose is to protect academic freedom. This phrase might be understood as referring to enhancing the freedom of teachers to teach what they will. The Act was not designed to further that goal. While the Court is normally deferential to a State's articulation of a secular purpose, the statement of

---

* Justice O'Connor joins all but Part II of this opinion.

such purpose must be sincere and not a sham. It is clear that the purpose of the legislative sponsor was to narrow the science curriculum. During the legislative hearings, Senator Keith stated: "My preference would be that neither creationism nor evolution be taught." Such a ban on teaching does not promote—indeed, it undermines—the provision of a comprehensive scientific education.

It is clear that requiring schools to teach creation science with evolution does not advance academic freedom. The Act does not grant teachers flexibility that they did not already possess to supplant the present science curriculum with the presentation of theories, besides evolution, about the origin of life. No law prohibited Louisiana public school teachers from teaching any scientific theory. Thus the stated purpose is not furthered.

The goal of "fairness" is hardly furthered by the Act's discriminatory preference for the teaching of creation science and against the teaching of evolution. While requiring that curriculum guides be developed for creation science, the Act says nothing of comparable guides for evolution. Similarly, resource services are supplied for creation science but not for evolution. Only "creation scientists" can serve on the panel that supplies the resource services. The Act forbids school boards to discriminate against anyone who "chooses to be a creation-scientist" or to teach "creationism," but fails to protect those who teach evolution or any other non-creation science theory, or who refuse to teach creation science.

If the Louisiana Legislature's purpose was solely to maximize the comprehensiveness and effectiveness of science instruction, it would have encouraged the teaching of all scientific theories about the origins of humankind. But under the Act's requirements, teachers who were once free to teach any and all facets of this subject are now unable to do so. Moreover, the Act fails to ensure that creation science will be taught, but instead requires the teaching of this theory only when the theory of evolution is taught. Thus the Act does not protect academic freedom, but has the distinctly different purpose of discrediting "evolution by counterbalancing its teaching with the teaching of creationism."

There is a historic and contemporaneous link between the teachings of certain religious denominations and the teaching of evolution. The preeminent purpose of the Louisiana Legislature was to advance the religious viewpoint that a supernatural being created humankind. It is not happenstance that the legislature required the teaching of a theory that coincided with this religious view. The sponsor of the Act, Senator Keith, explained during legislative hearings his disdain for the theory of evolution resulted from the support that evolution supplied to views contrary to his own religious beliefs. According to Senator Keith, evolution was consonant with the "cardinal principles of religious humanism, secular humanism, theological liberalism, aetheistism *sic*." The senator repeatedly stated that scientific evidence supporting his religious views should be included in the public school curriculum to redress the fact that evolution coincided with religious beliefs antithetical to his own. The legislation therefore sought to alter the science curriculum to reflect endorsement of a religious view antagonistic to the theory of evolution.

We do not imply that a legislature could never require that scientific critiques of prevailing scientific theories be taught. Teaching a variety of scientific theories about the origins of humankind might be validly done with the clear secular intent of enhancing the effectiveness of science instruction. But because the primary purpose of the Creationism Act is to endorse a particular religious doctrine, the Act furthers religion in violation of the Establishment Clause.

The Louisiana Creationism Act advances religious doctrine by requiring either the banishment of the theory of evolution from public school classrooms or the presentation of a religious viewpoint that rejects evolution in its entirety. The Act violates the Establishment Clause because it seeks to employ the symbolic and financial support of government to achieve a religious purpose. The judgment therefore is
   Affirmed.

Justice SCALIA, with whom The CHIEF JUSTICE joins, *dissenting.*

"Legislative purpose" means the "actual" motives of those responsible for the challenged action. If those legislators acted with a "sincere" secular purpose, the Act survives the first component of the *Lemon* test. The Balanced Treatment Act did not fly through the Louisiana Legislature on wings of fundamentalist religious fervor—unlikely since only a small minority of the State's citizens belong to fundamentalist religious denominations. Most of the testimony in support of the bill came from Senator Keith himself and from scientists and educators, many of whom enjoyed academic credentials that may be regarded as quite impressive. Their testimony was devoted to lengthy, and seemingly expert scientific expositions on the origin of life. These scientific lectures touched upon biology, paleontology, genetics, astronomy, astrophysics, probability analysis, and biochemistry. The witnesses assured committee members that "hundreds" of highly respected, internationally renowned scientists believed in creation science.

Senator Keith and his witnesses testified essentially that:

1. There are two and only two scientific explanations for the beginning of life—evolution and creation science. Both posit a theory of the origin of life and subject that theory to empirical testing.
2. The body of scientific evidence supporting creation science is as strong as that supporting evolution and may be stronger. The evidence for evolution is far less compelling than we have been led to believe. Evolution is not a scientific "fact," since it cannot actually be observed in a laboratory. Rather, evolution is merely a scientific theory or "guess" and a very bad guess at that.
3. Creation science is educationally valuable. Students exposed to it better understand the current state of scientific evidence about the origin of life and evolution. Creation science can and should be presented to children without any religious content.
4. Although creation science is educationally valuable and strictly scientific, it is now being censored from or misrepresented in the public schools.

Teachers have been brainwashed by an entrenched scientific establishment composed almost exclusively of scientists to whom evolution is like a "religion." These scientists discriminate against creation scientists to prevent evolution's weaknesses from being exposed.

5. The censorship of creation science has at least two harmful effects. First, it deprives students of knowledge of one scientific explanation for the origin of life and leads them to believe that evolution is proven fact; thus, they are wrongly taught that science has proved their religious beliefs false. Second, it violates the Establishment Clause. The United States Supreme Court has held that secular humanism is a religion. Belief in evolution is a central tenet of that religion. By censoring creation science and instructing students that evolution is fact, public school teachers are advancing religion in violation of the Establishment Clause.

Senator Keith repeatedly and vehemently denied that his purpose was to advance a particular religious doctrine. We have no way of knowing how many legislators believed the testimony of Senator Keith and his witnesses. But we have to assume that many of them did. Given that assumption, the Court today plainly errs in holding that the Louisiana Legislature passed the Balanced Treatment Act for exclusively religious purposes.

Even with nothing more than this legislative history, it would be extraordinary to invalidate the Act for lack of a valid secular purpose. The Louisiana Legislature explicitly set forth its secular purpose ("protecting academic freedom") in the text of the Act. We have repeatedly relied upon or deferred to such expressions. The legislative history gives ample evidence of the sincerity of the articulated purpose. Witness after witness urged the legislators to support the Act so that students would not be "indoctrinated" but would instead be free to decide for themselves, based upon a fair presentation of the scientific evidence, about the origin of life. Other legislators made only a few statements, but those statements cast no doubt upon the sincerity of the articulated purpose.

It is undoubtedly true that what prompted the legislature to direct its attention to the misrepresentation of evolution in schools was its awareness of the tension between evolution and the religious beliefs of many children. But even appellees concede that a valid secular purpose is not rendered impermissible simply because its pursuit is prompted by concern for religious sensitivities. Because I believe that the Balanced Treatment Act had a secular purpose, which is all the first component of the *Lemon* test requires, I would *reverse the judgment* of the Court of Appeals *and remand for further consideration.*

∾ PROBLEMS ∾

1. *Secular Humanism.* Some critics of *Epperson* and *Edwards* have argued that "secular humanism" is a bona fide "religion" and that "evolution is the cornerstone

of that religion." These critics have argued that, by censoring creation science and instructing students that evolution theory is factually true, public school teachers are advancing religion in violation of the Establishment Clause. *See* Leonard Manning, *The Douglas Concept of God in Government*, 39 WASH. L. REV. 47, 63 (1964): "If we forbid the teaching of recognized religions in our public schools and forbid a prayer which simply acknowledges the existence of God and at the same time permit the teaching of some code of ethical conduct, some system of value norms, does not the system which the school then sponsors become the system of Secular Humanism or simply secular humanism?" Do you agree?

2. *Intelligent Design.* In recent years, a number of "creation theorists" have advanced an "intelligent design" theory. Basically, they argue that the structure of the earth and the universe provides evidence of an "intelligent design" suggesting the presence of a superior being that established the design. They argue that the "scientific evidence of intelligent design" should be taught in public schools alongside evolution. Do you agree? Suppose that a Pennsylvania school district requires that high school students be taught both the theory of evolution and the theory of intelligent design. The district justifies the requirement as a way to teach students critical thinking skills as well as to ensure that they are aware of all "scientific theories regarding the creation of life."

3. *Evolution, Creationism, and the Education for a Better America Act.* In the proposed legislation, should Congress attempt to address issues relating to the teaching of evolution or creationism? Does it matter that the proposed legislation would provide aid to all types of schools (private, public, and parochial)? Would it be permissible for Congress to simply ignore these issues altogether?

4. Official Acknowledgment

A continuing source of litigation under the Establishment Clause has been whether, and to what extent, government may "acknowledge" religion in public displays. This issue has arisen in numerous contexts, including Christmas and nativity displays and official monuments and displays of the Ten Commandments.

County of Allegheny v. American Civil Liberties Union

492 U.S. 573 (1989)

Justice BLACKMUN announced the judgment of the Court and delivered the opinion of the Court with respect to Parts III-A, IV, and V, an opinion with respect to Parts I and II, in which Justice STEVENS and Justice O'CONNOR join, an opinion with respect to Part III-B, in which Justice STEVENS joins, an opinion with respect to Part VII, in which Justice O'CONNOR join, and an opinion with respect to Part VI.

The county courthouse is Allegheny County's seat of government. It houses the offices of the county commissioners, controller, treasurer, sheriff, and clerk of court. Civil and criminal trials are held there. The "main," "most beautiful," and "most public" part of the courthouse is its Grand Staircase, set into one arch and surrounded by others, with arched windows serving as a backdrop.

Since 1981, the county has permitted a Roman Catholic group to display a creche in the county courthouse during the Christmas holiday season. The creche had a wooden fence on three sides and bore a plaque stating: "Donated by the Holy Name Society." The county placed poinsettia plants around the fence. The county also placed a small evergreen tree, decorated with a red bow, behind each of the two endposts of the fence. These trees stood alongside the manger and were slightly shorter. The angel thus was at the apex of the creche display. The entire display occupied a substantial amount of space on the Grand Staircase. No figures of Santa Claus or other decorations appeared on the Staircase. The county uses the creche as the setting for its annual Christmas-carole program. During the 1986 season, the county invited high school choirs and other musical groups to perform during weekday lunch hours. The county dedicated this program to world peace and to the families of prisoners-of-war and of persons missing in action in Southeast Asia.

The City-County Building is a block removed from the county courthouse and is jointly owned by the city of Pittsburgh and Allegheny County. For a number of years, the city has had a large Christmas tree under the middle arch outside the Grant Street entrance. The city placed at the foot of the tree a sign bearing the mayor's name and entitled "Salute to Liberty." Beneath the title, the sign stated:

> During this holiday season, the city of Pittsburgh salutes liberty. Let these festive lights remind us that we are the keepers of the flame of liberty and our legacy of freedom.

The city placed an 18-foot Chanukah menorah of an abstract tree-and-branch design. The menorah was placed next to the Christmas tree, against one of the columns that supports the arch into which the tree was set. The menorah is owned by Chabad, a Jewish group, but is stored, erected, and removed each year by the city. The tree, the sign, and the menorah were all removed on January 13.

III

In recent years, we have paid particularly close attention to whether the challenged governmental practice either has the purpose or effect of "endorsing" religion, a concern that has long had a place in our Establishment Clause jurisprudence. The prohibition against governmental endorsement of religion "precludes government from conveying or attempting to convey a message that religion or a particular religious belief is *favored* or *preferred*." *Wallace v. Jaffree*, 472 U.S. at 70 (O'Connor, J., concurring in judgment). Moreover, the term "endorsement" is closely linked to the term "promotion," and this Court long since has held that government "may not promote one religion or religious theory against another or even against the militant opposite." Whether the key word is "endorsement," "favoritism," or "promotion," the essential principle remains the same.

The Establishment Clause prohibits government from appearing to take a position on questions of religious belief or from "making adherence to a religion relevant in any way to a person's standing in the political community."

In *Lynch v. Donnelly*, we considered whether the city of Pawtucket, R.I., violated the Establishment Clause by including a creche in its annual Christmas display, located in a private park within the downtown shopping district. By a 5-to-4 decision, the Court upheld inclusion of the creche in the display, holding that inclusion of the creche did not have the impermissible effect of advancing or promoting religion. The opinion contained two strands. First, inclusion of the creche was "no more an advancement or endorsement of religion" than other "endorsements" this Court has approved in the past. Second, any benefit the government's display gave religion was no more than "indirect, remote, and incidental"—without saying how or why.

Justice O'Connor's concurrence differs in significant respects from the majority opinion. The main difference is that the concurrence provides a sound analytical framework for evaluating governmental use of religious symbols. First, the concurrence squarely rejects any notion that this Court will tolerate some government endorsement of religion. Endorsement of religion is "invalid," because it "sends a message to nonadherents that they are outsiders, not full members of the political community, and an accompanying message to adherents that they are insiders, favored members of the political community." Second, the concurrence articulates a method for determining whether an object with religious meaning has the effect of endorsing religion. The effect depends upon the message that the government's practice communicates based upon the context in which the contested object appears: "A typical museum setting, though not neutralizing the religious content of a religious painting, negates any message of endorsement of that content."

The concurrence applied this mode of analysis to the Pawtucket creche. In addition to the creche, the display contained: a Santa Claus house with a live Santa distributing candy; reindeer pulling Santa's sleigh; a live 40-foot Christmas tree strung with lights; statues of carolers in old-fashioned dress; candy-striped poles; a "talking" wishing well; a large banner proclaiming "SEASONS GREETINGS"; a miniature "village" with several houses and a church; and various "cut-out" figures, including those of a clown, a dancing elephant, a robot, and a teddy bear. The concurrence concluded that both because the creche is "a traditional symbol" of Christmas, a holiday with strong secular elements, and because the creche was "displayed along with purely secular symbols," the creche's setting "changes what viewers may fairly understand to be the purpose of the display" and "negates any message of endorsement" of "Christian beliefs."

The four *Lynch* dissenters agreed that the controlling question was "whether Pawtucket had endorsed religion through its display of the creche." The dissenters also agreed that context is relevant. They simply concluded that the other elements of the Pawtucket display did not negate the endorsement of Christian faith caused by the presence of the creche. They viewed the creche as placing "the government's imprimatur of approval on the particular religious beliefs exemplified by the creche." Thus, "the effect on minority religious groups was to convey the message that their views are not similarly worthy of public recognition nor entitled to public support."

Despite divergence, the five Justices in concurrence and dissent agreed that the government's use of religious symbolism is unconstitutional if it has the effect of endorsing religious beliefs. Our present task is to determine whether the display of the creche and the menorah, in their respective "particular physical settings," has the effect of endorsing or disapproving religious beliefs.

We turn first to the creche display. The creche uses words, as well as the picture of the Nativity scene, to make its religious meaning unmistakably clear. "Glory to God in the Highest!" says the angel in the creche—Glory to God because of the birth of Jesus. This praise to God in Christian terms is indisputably religious—indeed sectarian—just as it is when said in the Gospel or in a church service.

The effect of a creche display turns on its setting. Unlike *Lynch*, nothing in the context of the display detracts from the creche's religious message. The *Lynch* display composed a series of figures and objects, each group of which had its own focal point. Santa's house and his reindeer were objects of attention separate from the creche, and had their specific visual story to tell. Similarly, whatever a "talking" wishing well may be, it was a center of attention separate from the creche. Here, the creche stands alone: it is the single element of the display on the Grand Staircase. The floral decoration surrounding the creche cannot be viewed as somehow equivalent to the secular symbols in *Lynch*. The floral frame serves only to draw attention to the message inside the frame. The floral decoration surrounding the creche contributes to the endorsement message. It is as if the county had allowed the Holy Name Society to display a cross on the Grand Staircase at Easter, and the county had surrounded the cross with Easter lilies.

Furthermore, the creche sits on the Grand Staircase, the "main" and "most beautiful part" of the building that is the seat of county government. No viewer could reasonably think that it occupies this location without the support and approval of the government. By permitting the "display of the creche in this particular physical setting," the county sends an unmistakable message that it supports and promotes the Christian praise to God that is the creche's religious message. The fact that the creche bears a sign disclosing its ownership by a Roman Catholic organization does not alter this conclusion. The sign simply demonstrates that the government is endorsing the religious message of that organization, rather than communicating a message of its own.

Finally, the county argues that the display celebrates Christmas, and Christmas is a national holiday. This argument would allow the celebration of the Eucharist inside a courthouse on Christmas Eve. The government may acknowledge Christmas as a cultural phenomenon, but may not observe it as a Christian holy day by suggesting that people praise God for the birth of Jesus.

In sum, *Lynch* teaches that government may celebrate Christmas in some manner and form, but not in a way that endorses Christian doctrine. Allegheny

County has transgressed this line. It has celebrated Christmas in a way that has the effect of endorsing a patently Christian message: Glory to God for the birth of Jesus Christ. Under *Lynch*, nothing more is required to demonstrate a violation of the Establishment Clause. The display of the creche in this context must be permanently enjoined.

Justice Kennedy argues that *Marsh v. Chambers*, 463 U.S. 783 (1983) legitimates all "practices with no greater potential for establishment" than those "accepted traditions dating back to the Founding." Otherwise, the Justice asserts, such practices as our national motto ("In God We Trust") and our Pledge of Allegiance (with the phrase "under God," added in 1954), are in danger of invalidity. There is an obvious distinction between creche displays and references to God in the motto and the pledge. However history may affect the constitutionality of nonsectarian references to religion by the government, history cannot legitimate practices that demonstrate the government's allegiance to a particular sect or creed. We have expressly required "strict scrutiny" of practices suggesting "a denominational preference."

Although Justice Kennedy repeatedly accuses the Court of "latent hostility" toward religion, nothing could be further from the truth. Justice Kennedy misperceives respect for religious pluralism as hostility. Celebrating Christmas as a religious holiday necessarily entails proclaiming that Jesus is the Messiah, a specifically Christian belief. In contrast, confining the government's own celebration of Christmas to the holiday's secular aspects does not favor the religious beliefs of non-Christians over those of Christians. Rather, it simply permits the government to acknowledge the holiday without expressing an allegiance to Christian beliefs.

Not all religious celebrations of Christmas located on government property violate the Establishment Clause. It is not unconstitutional for a group of parishioners to go caroling through a city park on any Sunday in Advent or for a Christian club at a public university to sing carols during their Christmas meeting. These activities do not demonstrate the government's endorsement of the Christian faith. Once a proclamation has the effect of endorsing the Christian faith, then that practice must be enjoined to protect the constitutional rights of those citizens who follow some creed other than Christianity.

VI

The menorah is a religious symbol: it serves to commemorate the miracle of the oil as described in the Talmud. But the menorah's message is not exclusively religious. The menorah is the primary visual symbol for a holiday that, like Christmas, has both religious and secular dimensions.

The menorah here stands next to a Christmas tree and a sign saluting liberty. While no challenge has been made here to the tree and the sign, their presence is relevant in determining the effect of the menorah. The result is to create an "overall holiday setting" that represents both Christmas and Chanukah. Because government may celebrate Christmas as a secular holiday, government may also acknowledge Chanukah as a secular holiday. It would involve discrimination against Jews to celebrate Christmas as a cultural tradition while simultaneously disallowing the city's acknowledgment of Chanukah as a cultural tradition.

The question is whether the combined display has the effect of endorsing both Christian and Jewish faiths, or rather simply recognizes that both Christmas and Chanukah are part of the same winter-holiday season, which has attained a secular status in our society. The latter interpretation seems far more plausible. The Christmas tree, unlike the menorah, is not itself a religious symbol. Although Christmas trees once carried religious connotations, today they typify the secular celebration of Christmas. Numerous Americans place Christmas trees in their homes without subscribing to Christian religious beliefs, and when the city's tree stands alone in front of the City-County Building, it is not considered an endorsement of Christian faith. Indeed, a 40-foot Christmas tree was one of the objects that validated the creche in *Lynch*.

The tree, moreover, is clearly the predominant element in the city's display. The 45-foot tree occupies the central position in front of the entrance to the City-County Building; the 18-foot menorah is positioned to one side. Given this configuration, it is sensible to interpret the menorah in light of the tree.

In the shadow of the tree, the menorah is understood as simply a recognition that Christmas is not the only traditional way of observing the winter-holiday season. The combination of the tree and the menorah communicates a secular celebration of Christmas coupled with an acknowledgment of Chanukah as a contemporaneous alternative tradition.

Although the city has used a symbol with religious meaning as its representation of Chanukah, this is not a case in which the city has reasonable alternatives that are less religious in nature. It is difficult to imagine a predominantly secular symbol of Chanukah that the city could place next to its Christmas tree. The mayor's sign diminishes the possibility that the tree and the menorah will be interpreted as an endorsement of Christianity and Judaism. While no sign can disclaim a message of endorsement, an "explanatory plaque" may confirm that the government's association with a religious symbol does not represent government's sponsorship of religious beliefs. Given all these considerations, it is not "sufficiently likely" that residents of Pittsburgh will perceive the combined display of the tree, the sign, and the menorah as an "endorsement" or "disapproval of their individual religious choices." Constitutionality must be judged according to the standard of a "reasonable observer."

The conclusion that the menorah's display does not have an effect of endorsing religious faith does not foreclose the possibility that the display of the menorah might violate either the "purpose" or "entanglement" prong of the *Lemon* analysis. These issues were not addressed and may be considered on remand.

Lynch confirms, and in no way repudiates, the longstanding constitutional principle that government may not engage in a practice that has the effect of promoting or endorsing religious beliefs. The display of the creche in the county courthouse has this unconstitutional effect. The display of the menorah in front of the City-County Building, however, does not have this effect, given its "particular physical setting."

The judgment of the Court of Appeals is affirmed in part and reversed in part, and the cases are remanded for further proceedings.

It is so ordered.

Justice O'CONNOR, with whom Justice BRENNAN and Justice STEVENS join as to Part II, *concurring in part* and *concurring in the judgment.*

An Establishment Clause standard that prohibits only "coercive" practices or overt efforts at government proselytization, but fails to take account of the numerous more subtle ways that government can show favoritism to particular beliefs or convey a message of disapproval to others, would not adequately protect the religious liberty or respect the religious diversity of the members of our pluralistic political community.

Practices such as legislative prayers or opening Court sessions with "God save the United States and this honorable Court" serve the secular purposes of "solemnizing public occasions" and "expressing confidence in the future." These examples of ceremonial deism do not survive Establishment Clause scrutiny simply by virtue of their historical longevity alone. The "history and ubiquity" of a practice is relevant because it provides part of the context in which a reasonable observer evaluates whether a challenged governmental practice conveys a message of endorsement of religion. It is the combination of the longstanding existence of practices such as opening legislative sessions with legislative prayers or opening Court sessions with "God save the United States and this honorable Court," as well as their nonsectarian nature, that leads me to the conclusion that those practices, despite their religious roots, do not convey a message of endorsement of particular religious beliefs. Similarly, the celebration of Thanksgiving as a public holiday, despite its religious origins, is now generally understood as a celebration of patriotic values rather than particular religious beliefs. The question under endorsement analysis is whether a reasonable observer would view such longstanding practices as a disapproval of his or her particular religious choices, in light of the fact that they serve a secular purpose rather than a sectarian one and have largely lost their religious significance over time.

Neither the endorsement test nor its application in these cases reflects "an unjustified hostility toward religion." The government can *acknowledge* the role of religion in our society in numerous ways that do not amount to an endorsement. The city of Pittsburgh's combined holiday display had neither the purpose nor the effect of endorsing religion, but Allegheny County's creche display had such an effect.

Justice BRENNAN, with whom Justice MARSHALL and Justice STEVENS join, *concurring in part* and *dissenting in part.*

The display of an object that "retains a specifically Christian or other religious meaning," is incompatible with the separation of church and state demanded by our Constitution. The menorah is indisputably a religious symbol, used ritually in a celebration that has deep religious significance. That is all that need be said.

Justice STEVENS, with whom Justice BRENNAN and Justice MARSHALL join, *concurring in part* and *dissenting in part.*

The Establishment Clause creates a strong presumption against the display of religious symbols on public property. The presence of the Chanukah menorah, unquestionably a religious symbol, gives religious significance to the Christmas tree. The overall display thus manifests governmental approval of the Jewish and Christian religions. Although it conceivably might be interpreted as sending "a message of pluralism and freedom to choose one's own beliefs," the message is not sufficiently clear.

Justice KENNEDY, with whom THE CHIEF JUSTICE, Justice WHITE, and Justice SCALIA join, *concurring in the judgment in part* and *dissenting in part.*

The majority opinion reflects an unjustified hostility toward religion, a hostility inconsistent with our history and our precedents. The city and county sought to do no more than "celebrate the season," and to acknowledge, along with many of their citizens, the historical background and the religious, as well as secular, nature of the Chanukah and Christmas holidays. This interest falls well within the tradition of government accommodation and acknowledgment of religion that has marked our history from the beginning. Enforced recognition of only the secular aspect of the holiday would signify the callous indifference toward religious faith that our cases and traditions do not require.

There is no suggestion here that the government's power to coerce has been used to further the interests of Christianity or Judaism in any way. No one was compelled to observe or participate in any religious ceremony or activity. The creche and the menorah are purely passive symbols of religious holidays. Passersby who disagree with the message conveyed by these displays are free to ignore them. There is no realistic risk that the creche and the menorah represent an effort to proselytize or are otherwise the first step down the road to an establishment of religion.

The notion that cases arising under the Establishment Clause should be decided by an inquiry into whether a "reasonable observer" "may" "fairly understand" government action to "send a message to nonadherents that they are outsiders, not full members of the political community," is a most unwelcome addition to our tangled Establishment Clause jurisprudence. The endorsement test is flawed in its fundamentals and unworkable in practice.

The majority's approach threatens to trivialize constitutional adjudication by embracing a jurisprudence of minutiae. A reviewing court must consider whether the city has included Santas, talking wishing wells, reindeer, or other secular symbols as "a center of attention separate from the creche." After determining whether these centers of attention are sufficiently "separate" that each "had their specific visual story to tell," the court must then measure their proximity to the creche. Municipal greenery must be used with care.

Before studying these cases, I had not known the full history of the menorah. This history was likely unknown to the vast majority of people of all faiths who saw the symbol displayed in Pittsburgh and hardly informed the observers' view of the symbol.

BACKGROUND
Sabbath Day of Rest

There has also been litigation about whether states can compel a "uniform day of rest from worldly labor" and can choose Sunday as the day of rest. In *McGowan v. Maryland*, 366 U.S. 420 (1961), the Court held that, although Sunday closure laws were first enacted for religious reasons, their continued application is justified by "wholly secular" reasons—to provide a universal day of rest and ensure the health and tranquility of the community. Likewise, in *Estate of Thornton v. Caldor, Inc.*, 472 U.S. 703 (1985), the Court upheld a law that granted employees the right not to work on their sabbaths.

Notes: Requiring Swearing or Affirming a Belief in God

1. *Requiring Affirmation of God.* The states may not require, as a condition of holding office, that an applicant for the office of notary public swear or affirm his or her belief in God. *See Torcaso v. Watkins*, 367 U.S. 488 (1961).

2. *The French Principle of Laicité.* Under the French concept of liaicté, public authorities are required to 1) guarantee religious freedom, including freedom of worship; and 2) insure that public officials and public agencies remain neutral regarding the separation of church and state by avoiding public recognition or funding of religion. Under that principle, public officials are prohibited from displaying signs or symbols that show a public recognition or preference for a particular religion. In evaluating holiday displays, Laicité requires consideration of the entire context of the display in an effort to determine whether the display reflects a cultural, artistic or festive purpose rather than the purpose of recognizing or showing a preference for a religion. Exterior displays are presumptively permissible unless they reveal proselytism or the expression of a religious opinion. Inside public buildings, the reverse presumption applies and it must be show that the display reflects a cultural, artistic or festive purpose in order to be sustained.

〜 PROBLEMS 〜

1. *The Significance of Context.* In *County of Allegheny*, would it have been permissible to place a creche near the Christmas tree and the menorah? Suppose that, following the decision in *County of Allegheny*, the county decides to allow Roman Catholics to move the creche from the staircase to a place near the menorah. Regarding the display: a) Would it matter whether the creche was placed by itself or was surrounded by the same floral display as before and was accompanied by the same banner? b) Would the existence of the creche, surrounded by the floral display and the banner, affect the constitutionality of displaying the tree and the menorah? c) Would the same display be constitutional on the premises of an elementary school? In other words, might a display be constitutional in one setting but unconstitutional in another?

2. *The Living Nativity.* In LaGrange, Kentucky, members of the Grace Baptist Church annually erect a holiday creche on the courthouse lawn. Members of the church brave the cold each night to represent historical characters and thereby turn the display into a "living nativity." In evaluating the constitutionality of the display, what significance would you attach to each of these facts: a) the church (rather than the government) erects and pays for the display; b) the county judge executive and the pastor of Grace Baptist Church are present when the display is erected, and the pastor flatly states that the purpose of the display is to remind people that the holiday season is "all about Christ"; c) the government precludes all other groups from erecting displays; d) instead of prohibiting other groups from erecting displays (as in the preceding instance), the government treats the courthouse lawn as a public forum and invites all groups to erect displays (e.g., agnostics are allowed to place a large question mark next to the Baptist display over the objections of Christians, who claim that the question mark erodes the rights of Christians "to observe the birth of Christ"); e) the government imposes a permit requirement for displays but bans groups with objectionable ideas (e.g., the Ku Klux Klan) from erecting displays; and f) the government requires all groups that wish to erect displays to obtain a permit, but the requirements are "content-neutral" and seek information relating only to such things as how long the group would like to show the display and where it would like the display to be located.

3. *High School Choirs and Religious Music.* Can a high school choir sing and play religious music at its concerts? For example, may a high school choir put on an annual Christmas concert in which it sings music with religious lyrics (e.g., "Good Christian Men, Rejoice," "Joy to the World! The Savior Reigns," and "Come and Behold Him, Born the King of Angels") as well as "secular" Christmas songs (e.g., "Rudolph the Red-Nosed Reindeer")? Would it matter whether the concert is held on school premises or in a church? Is your analysis affected by the fact that 65% to 70% of all serious choral music is based on sacred themes or texts?

4. *The Jewish Eruv.* An "eruv" is a designated geographic area where Jews who subscribe to a certain interpretation of Jewish law can perform certain activities

that are otherwise prohibited on the Jewish Sabbath and on Yom Kippur. An eruv can be established simply by attaching plastic strips, known as "lechis," to utility poles. When a village allowed a Jewish group to attach the plastic strips to poles, and thereby create an eruv, the decision was challenged on Establishment Clause grounds. Unless one looked closely, the average person might not even have noticed the plastic strips. Should the creation of the eruv be viewed as an establishment of religion? What result under the *Lemon* test? Under the endorsement test? *See Jewish People for the Betterment of Westhampton Beach v. Village of Westhampton Beach,* 778 F.3d 390 (2d Cir. 2015).

5. *Christmas Displays and the Education for a Better America Act.* In the proposed legislation, should Congress say anything about whether schools can have Christmas or Chanukah displays, or about the content of those displays?

———

During the last 25 years, a number of cases have involved challenges to public displays of the Ten Commandments. The first case to come to the Court was *Stone v. Graham,* 449 U.S. 39 (1980). In that case, a Kentucky statute required that a copy of the Ten Commandments, purchased with private contributions, be placed on the wall of each public classroom. Applying *Lemon,* the Court struck down the law, noting that "Kentucky's statute had no secular legislative purpose, and is therefore unconstitutional." Over the next 25 years, litigation concerning the Ten Commandments continued to percolate in the federal courts.

Van Orden v. Perry

545 U.S. 677 (2005)

Chief Justice REHNQUIST announced the judgment of the Court and delivered an opinion, in which Justice SCALIA, Justice KENNEDY, and Justice THOMAS join.

The 22 acres surrounding the Texas State Capitol contain 17 monuments and 21 historical markers commemorating the "people, ideals, and events that compose Texan identity."[2] The monolith challenged here stands 6-feet high and 3-feet wide. It is located to the north of the Capitol building, between the Capitol and the Supreme Court building. Its primary content is the text of the Ten Commandments. An eagle grasping the American flag, an eye inside of a pyramid, and two small tablets with what appears to be an ancient script are carved above the text of the Ten Commandments. Below the text are two Stars of David and the superimposed Greek letters Chi and Rho, which represent Christ. The bottom of the monument bears the inscription "PRESENTED TO THE

———

2. The monuments are: Heroes of the Alamo, Hood's Brigade, Confederate Soldiers, Volunteer Fireman, Terry's Texas Rangers, Texas Cowboy, Spanish-American War, Texas National Guard, Ten Commandments, Tribute to Texas School Children, Texas Pioneer Woman, The Boy Scouts' Statue of Liberty Replica, Pearl Harbor Veterans, Korean War Veterans, Soldiers of World War I, Disabled Veterans, and Texas Peace Officers.

PEOPLE AND YOUTH OF TEXAS BY THE FRATERNAL ORDER OF EAGLES OF TEXAS 1961."

The State selected a site for the monument based on the recommendation of the state organization responsible for maintaining the Capitol grounds. The Eagles paid the cost of erecting the monument, the dedication of which was presided over by two state legislators.

Petitioner Thomas Van Orden is a native Texan and a resident of Austin. Since 1995, he has encountered the Ten Commandments monument during his frequent visits to the Capitol grounds. His visits are typically for the purpose of using the law library in the Supreme Court building. Forty years after the monument's erection and six years after Van Orden sued state officials seeking a declaration that the monument's placement violates the Establishment Clause, the District Court held that the monument did not contravene the Establishment Clause and the Court of Appeals affirmed.

Our cases, Januslike, point in two directions in applying the Establishment Clause. One face looks toward the strong role played by religion and religious traditions throughout our Nation's history. As we observed in *School Dist. of Abington Township v. Schempp*, 374 U.S. 203 (1963):

> It is true that religion has been closely identified with our history and government. The fact that the Founding Fathers believed devotedly that there was a God and that the unalienable rights of man were rooted in Him is clearly evidenced in their writings, from the Mayflower Compact to the Constitution itself. It can be truly said, therefore, that today, as in the beginning, our national life reflects a religious people who, in the words of Madison, are "earnestly praying, as in duty bound, that the Supreme Lawgiver of the Universe guide them into every measure which may be worthy of his blessing."

The other face looks toward the principle that governmental intervention in religious matters can itself endanger religious freedom.

This case, like all Establishment Clause challenges, presents us with the difficulty of respecting both faces. Our institutions presuppose a Supreme Being, yet these institutions must not press religious observances upon their citizens. One face looks to the past in acknowledgment of our Nation's heritage, while the other looks to the present in demanding a separation between church and state. Reconciling these two faces requires that we neither abdicate our responsibility to maintain a division between church and state nor evince a hostility to religion by disabling the government from in some ways recognizing our religious heritage:

> When the state encourages religious instruction or cooperates with religious authorities by adjusting the schedule of public events to sectarian needs, it follows the best of our traditions. For it then respects the religious nature of our people and accommodates the public service to their spiritual needs. To hold that it may not would be to find in the Constitution a requirement that the government show a callous indifference to religious groups. We find no constitutional requirement which makes it necessary for government to be hostile to religion and to throw its weight against efforts to widen the effective scope of religious influence. *Zorach v. Clauson*, 343 U.S. 306 (1952).

See also Rosenberger v. Rector and Visitors of Univ. of Va., 515 U.S. 819 (1995).

These two faces are evident in representative cases both upholding and invalidating laws under the Establishment Clause. Over the last 25 years, we have sometimes pointed to *Lemon v. Kurtzman,* 403 U.S. 602 (1971), as providing the governing test in Establishment Clause challenges.[3] Yet, just two years after *Lemon* was decided, we noted that the factors identified in *Lemon* serve as "no more than helpful signposts." *Hunt v. McNair,* 413 U.S. 734 (1973). Many recent cases simply have not applied the *Lemon* test. Others have applied it only after concluding that the challenged practice was invalid under a different Establishment Clause test. Whatever may be the fate of the *Lemon* test in the larger scheme of Establishment Clause jurisprudence, we think it not useful in dealing with the sort of passive monument that Texas has erected on its Capitol grounds. Instead, our analysis is driven both by the nature of the monument and by our Nation's history.

As we explained in *Lynch v. Donnelly,* 465 U.S. 668 (1984): "There is an unbroken history of official acknowledgment by all three branches of government of the role of religion in American life from at least 1789." For example, both Houses passed resolutions in 1789 asking President George Washington to issue a Thanksgiving Day Proclamation to "recommend to the people of the United States a day of public thanksgiving and prayer, to be observed by acknowledging, with grateful hearts, the many and signal favors of Almighty God." 1 *Annals of Cong.* 90, 914 (1798). President Washington's proclamation directly attributed to the Supreme Being the foundations and successes of our young Nation. 1 J. RICHARDSON, A COMPILATION OF THE MESSAGES AND PAPERS OF THE PRESIDENTS, 1789-1897 p. 64 (1899).

Recognition of the role of God in our Nation's heritage has been reflected in our decisions. We have acknowledged that "religion has been closely identified with our history and government," and that "the history of man is inseparable from the history of religion," *Engel v. Vitale,* 370 U.S. 421 (1962). This recognition led us to hold that the Establishment Clause permits a state legislature to open its daily sessions with a prayer by a chaplain paid by the State. *Marsh v. Chambers,* 463 U.S. at 792. Such a practice, was "deeply embedded in the history and tradition of this country" and "it would be incongruous to interpret the Establishment Clause as imposing more stringent First Amendment limits on the states than the draftsmen imposed on the Federal Government." We have upheld laws, which originated from one of the Ten Commandments, that prohibited the sale of merchandise on Sunday. *McGowan v. Maryland,* 366 U.S. 420 (1961).

In this case we are faced with a display of the Ten Commandments on government property outside the Texas State Capitol. Such acknowledgments of the role played by the Ten Commandments in our Nation's heritage are common throughout America. We need only look within our own Courtroom. Since 1935, Moses has

---

3. *Lemon* sets out a three-prong test: "First, the statute must have a secular legislative purpose; second, its principal or primary effect must be one that neither advances nor inhibits religion; finally, the statute must not foster 'an excessive government entanglement with religion.' "

stood, holding two tablets that reveal portions of the Ten Commandments written in Hebrew, among other lawgivers in the south frieze. Representations of the Ten Commandments adorn the metal gates lining the north and south sides of the Courtroom as well as the doors leading into the Courtroom. Moses also sits on the exterior east facade of the building holding the Ten Commandments tablets.

Similar acknowledgments can be seen throughout a visitor's tour of our Nation's Capital. For example, a large statue of Moses holding the Ten Commandments, alongside a statue of the Apostle Paul, has overlooked the rotunda of the Library of Congress' Jefferson Building since 1897. And the Jefferson Building's Great Reading Room contains a sculpture of a woman beside the Ten Commandments with a quote above her from the Old Testament. A medallion with two tablets depicting the Ten Commandments decorates the floor of the National Archives. Inside the Department of Justice, a statue entitled "The Spirit of Law" has two tablets representing the Ten Commandments lying at its feet. In front of the Ronald Reagan Building is another sculpture that includes a depiction of the Ten Commandments. So too a 24-foot-tall sculpture, depicting, among other things, the Ten Commandments and a cross, stands outside the federal courthouse that houses both the Court of Appeals and the District Court for the District of Columbia. Moses is also prominently featured in the Chamber of the United States House of Representatives.[9]

Our opinions, like our building, have recognized the role the Decalogue plays in America's heritage. (*See, e.g., McGowan v. Maryland*, 366 U.S. at 442.) The Executive and Legislative Branches have also acknowledged the historical role of the Ten Commandments. These displays and recognitions of the Ten Commandments bespeak the rich American tradition of religious acknowledgments.

The Ten Commandments are religious. According to Judeo-Christian belief, the Ten Commandments were given to Moses by God on Mt. Sinai. But Moses was a lawgiver as well as a religious leader. Simply having religious content or promoting a message consistent with a religious doctrine does not run afoul of the Establishment Clause. *See Lynch v. Donnelly*, 465 U.S. at 680. There are, of course, limits to the display of religious messages or symbols. For example, we held unconstitutional a Kentucky statute requiring the posting of the Ten Commandments in every public schoolroom. *Stone v. Graham*, 449 U.S. 39 (1980) (per curiam). In the classroom context, we found that the Kentucky statute had

---

9. Other examples of monuments and buildings reflecting the prominent role of religion abound. For example, the Washington, Jefferson, and Lincoln Memorials all contain explicit invocations of God's importance. The apex of the Washington Monument is inscribed "Laus Deo," which is translated to mean "Praise be to God," and multiple memorial stones in the monument contain Biblical citations. The Jefferson Memorial is engraved with three quotes from Jefferson that make God a central theme. Inscribed on the wall of the Lincoln Memorial are two of Lincoln's most famous speeches, the Gettysburg Address and his Second Inaugural Address. Both inscriptions include those speeches' extensive acknowledgments of God. The first federal monument, which was accepted by the United States in honor of sailors who died in Tripoli, noted the dates of the fallen sailors as "the year of our Lord, 1804, and in the 28th year of the independence of the United States."

an improper and plainly religious purpose and we have "been particularly vigilant in monitoring compliance with the Establishment Clause in elementary and secondary schools." *Edwards v. Aguillard,* 482 U.S. 578 (1987). Neither *Stone* itself nor subsequent opinions have indicated that *Stone*'s holding would extend to a legislative chamber or to capitol grounds.[11]

The placement of the Ten Commandments monument on the Texas State Capitol grounds is a far more passive use of those texts than was the case in *Stone,* where the text confronted elementary school students every day. Indeed, petitioner walked by the monument for a number of years before bringing this lawsuit. The monument is therefore quite different from the prayers involved in *Schempp* and *Lee v. Weisman.* Texas has treated her Capitol grounds monuments as representing the several strands in the State's political and legal history. Inclusion of the Ten Commandments monument has a dual significance, partaking of both religion and government. We cannot say that Texas' display of this monument violates the Establishment Clause of the First Amendment.

The judgment of the Court of Appeals is affirmed.

It is so ordered.

Justice SCALIA, *concurring.*

I would reach the same result by adopting an Establishment Clause jurisprudence that is in accord with our Nation's past and present practices, and that can be consistently applied — the central relevant feature of which is that there is nothing unconstitutional in a State's favoring religion generally, honoring God through public prayer and acknowledgment, or, in a nonproselytizing manner, venerating the Ten Commandments.

Justice THOMAS, *concurring.*

The Establishment Clause's text and history "resist incorporation" against the States. Even if incorporated, "establishment at the founding involved mandatory observance or mandatory payment of taxes supporting ministers." And "government practices that have nothing to do with creating or maintaining coercive state establishments" simply do not "implicate the possible liberty interest of being free from coercive state establishments." The Ten Commandments display at issue here is constitutional. In no sense does Texas compel petitioner Van Orden to do anything. The mere presence of the monument along his path involves no coercion and thus does not violate the Establishment Clause.

Justice BREYER, *concurring in the judgment.*

The First Amendment's Religion Clauses seek to "assure the fullest possible scope of religious liberty and tolerance for all." They seek to avoid that divisiveness

---

11. Nor does anything suggest that *Stone* would extend to displays of the Ten Commandments that lack a "plainly religious," "pre-eminent purpose."

based upon religion that promotes social conflict, sapping the strength of government and religion alike. The realization of these goals means that government must "neither engage in nor compel religious practices," that it must "effect no favoritism among sects or between religion and nonreligion," and that it must "work deterrence of no religious belief." *Schempp, supra,* at 305 (concurring opinion). The government must avoid excessive interference with, or promotion of, religion. But the Establishment Clause does not compel the government to purge from the public sphere all that in any way partakes of the religious. Such absolutism is not only inconsistent with our national traditions, but would also tend to promote the kind of social conflict the Establishment Clause seeks to avoid.

The Court has found no single mechanical formula that can accurately draw the constitutional line in every case. Tests designed to measure "neutrality" alone are insufficient. I see no test-related substitute for the exercise of legal judgment. It must reflect and remain faithful to the underlying purposes of the Clauses, and it must take account of context and consequences measured in light of those purposes.

A display of the tablets of the Ten Commandments can convey not simply a religious message but also a secular moral message (about proper standards of social conduct). And in certain contexts, a display of the tablets can also convey a historical message (about a historic relation between those standards and the law) — a fact that helps to explain the display of those tablets in dozens of courthouses throughout the Nation, including the Supreme Court of the United States. The circumstances surrounding the display's placement on the capitol grounds and its physical setting suggest that the State itself intended the non-religious aspects of the tablets' message to predominate. And the monument's 40-year history on the Texas state grounds indicates that that has been its effect. The Fraternal Order of Eagles, a private civic (and primarily secular) organization, while interested in the religious aspect of the Ten Commandments, sought to highlight the Commandments' role in shaping civic morality as part of that organization's efforts to combat juvenile delinquency. The tablets prominently acknowledge that the Eagles donated the display, a factor which thereby further distances the State itself from the religious aspect of the Commandments' message. The monument sits in a large park containing 17 monuments and 21 historical markers, all designed to illustrate the "ideals" of those who settled in Texas and of those who have lived there since that time. The setting, and the inscription about its origin, suggests that the State intended the display's moral message to predominate.

The display is not on the grounds of a public school, where, given the impressionability of the young, government must exercise particular care in separating church and state. To invalidate this monument would exhibit a hostility toward religion that has no place in our Establishment Clause traditions. Such a holding might well encourage disputes concerning the removal of longstanding depictions of the Ten Commandments from public buildings across the Nation. I concur in the judgment of the Court.

Justice STEVENS, with whom Justice GINSBURG joins, *dissenting.*

God's Commandments may seem like wise counsel. The question before this Court, however, is whether it is counsel that Texas may proclaim without violating the Establishment Clause of the Constitution. If any fragment of Jefferson's metaphorical "wall of separation between church and State" is to be preserved—if there remains any meaning to the "wholesome neutrality" of which this Court's Establishment Clause cases speak, a negative answer to that question is mandatory. The Establishment Clause has created a strong presumption against the display of religious symbols on public property. The practice runs the risk of "offending nonmembers of the faith being advertised as well as adherents who consider the particular advertisement disrespectful." *Allegheny County,* 492 U.S. at 651 (Stevens, J., concurring in part and dissenting in part).

The Establishment Clause demands religious neutrality. The wall that separates the church from the State does not prohibit the government from acknowledging the religious beliefs and practices of the American people, nor does it require governments to hide works of art or historic memorabilia from public view just because they also have religious significance. This Nation's resolute commitment to neutrality with respect to religion is flatly inconsistent with the plurality's wholehearted validation of an official state endorsement of the message that there is one, and only one, God.

The Fraternal Order of Eagles were motivated by a desire to "inspire the youth" and curb juvenile delinquency by providing children with a "code of conduct or standards by which to govern their actions." Achieving that goal through biblical teachings injects a religious purpose into an otherwise secular endeavor. The significant secular by-products are not the type of "secular" purposes that justify government promulgation of sacred religious messages. Moreover, despite the Eagles' best efforts, the Ten Commandments display projects not just a religious, but an inherently sectarian message. There are many distinctive versions of the Decalogue, ascribed to by different religions and even different denominations within a particular faith. In choosing to display this version of the Commandments, Texas tells the observer that the State supports this side of the doctrinal religious debate and prescribes a compelled code of conduct from one God, namely a Judeo-Christian God, that is rejected by prominent polytheistic sects, such as Hinduism, as well as nontheistic religions, such as Buddhism. Recognizing the diversity of religious and secular beliefs held by Texans and by all Americans, it seems beyond peradventure that allowing the seat of government to serve as a stage for the propagation of an unmistakably Judeo-Christian message of piety would have the tendency to make nonmonotheists and nonbelievers "feel like outsiders in matters of faith, and strangers in the political community."

The plurality relies heavily on the fact that our Republic was founded, and has been governed since its nascence, by leaders who spoke then (and speak still) in plainly religious rhetoric. When public officials deliver public speeches, we recognize that their words are not exclusively a transmission from *the* government because those oratories have embedded within them the inherently personal views of the speaker. The permanent placement of a textual religious display on state property is different in kind; it amalgamates otherwise discordant individual views into a collective statement of government approval. The plurality's reliance on early religious statements and proclamations made by the Founders is also problematic because those views were not espoused at the Constitutional Convention in 1787 nor enshrined in the Constitution's text. To constrict narrowly the reach of the Establishment Clause to the views of the Founders would leave us with an unincorporated constitutional provision. Not only could a State constitutionally adorn all of its public spaces with crucifixes or passages from the New Testament, it would also have full authority to prescribe the teachings of Martin Luther or Joseph Smith as *the* official state religion.

We serve our constitutional mandate by expounding the meaning of constitutional provisions with one eye towards our Nation's history and the other fixed on its democratic aspirations. The principle that guides my analysis is neutrality. The basis for that principle is firmly rooted in our Nation's history and our Constitution's text. I recognize that the requirement that government must remain neutral between religion and irreligion would have seemed foreign to some of the Framers; so too would a requirement of neutrality between Jews and Christians. Fortunately, we are not bound by the Framers' expectations—we are bound by the legal principles they enshrined in our Constitution. The judgment of the Court in this case stands for the proposition that the Constitution permits governmental displays of sacred religious texts. This makes a mockery of the constitutional ideal that government must remain neutral between religion and irreligion. I respectfully dissent.

Justice O'CONNOR, *dissenting.*

For essentially the reasons given by Justice Souter, as well as the reasons given in my concurrence in *McCreary County v. American Civil Liberties Union of Ky.*, I respectfully dissent.

Justice SOUTER, with whom Justice STEVENS and Justice GINSBURG join, *dissenting.*

A governmental display of an obviously religious text cannot be squared with neutrality, except in a setting that plausibly indicates that the statement is not placed with a predominant purpose on the part of government either to adopt the religious message or to urge its acceptance by others. A pedestrian happening upon the monument at issue here needs no training in religious doctrine to realize that the statement of the Commandments, quoting God himself, proclaims that the will of the divine being is the source of obligation to obey the rules, including the facially secular ones. In this case, the text is presented to give particular prominence to the Commandments' first sectarian reference, "I am the Lord thy God." That proclamation is centered on the stone and written in slightly larger letters than the subsequent recitation. To ensure that the religious nature of the monument is clear to even the most casual passerby, the word "Lord" appears in all capital letters (as does the word "am"), so that the most eye-catching segment of the quotation is the declaration "I AM the LORD thy God." What follows, of course, are the rules against other gods, graven images, vain swearing, and Sabbath breaking. And the full text of the fifth Commandment puts forward filial respect as a condition of long life in the land "which the Lord they God giveth thee." These "words make the religious meaning unmistakably clear." *County of Allegheny v. American Civil Liberties Union*, 492 U.S. 573 (1989). The engraved quotation is framed by religious symbols.[2] It would be difficult to miss the point that the government of Texas is telling everyone who sees the monument to live up to a moral code because God requires it, with both code and conception of God being understood as the inheritances specifically of Jews and Christians.

The monument's presentation of the Commandments with religious text emphasized and enhanced stands in contrast to any number of perfectly constitutional depictions of them, the frieze of our own Courtroom providing a good example, where the figure of Moses stands among history's great lawgivers. While Moses holds the tablets of the Commandments showing some Hebrew text, no one looking at the lines of figures in marble relief is likely to see a religious purpose behind the assemblage or take away a religious message from it. Only one other depiction represents a religious leader, and the historical personages are mixed with symbols of moral and intellectual abstractions like Equity and Authority. Since Moses enjoys no especial prominence on the frieze, viewers can readily take him to be there as a lawgiver in the company of other lawgivers; and the viewers may just as naturally see the tablets of the Commandments (showing the later ones, forbidding things like killing and theft, but without the divine preface) as background from which the concept of law emerged, ultimately having a secular influence in the history of the Nation. Government may, of course, constitutionally call attention to this influence, and may post displays or erect monuments recounting this aspect of our history no less than any other, so long as there is a context and that context is historical. Hence, a display of the Commandments accompanied by an exposition of how they have influenced modern law would most likely be constitutionally unobjectionable.[4] And the Decalogue could, as *Stone* suggested, be integrated constitutionally into a course of study in public schools.

---

2. That the monument also surrounds the text of the Commandments with various American symbols (notably the U.S. flag and a bald eagle) only underscores the impermissibility of Texas's actions: by juxtaposing these patriotic symbols with the Commandments and other religious signs, the monument sends the message that being American means being religious (and not just being religious but also subscribing to the Commandments, i.e., practicing a monotheistic religion).

4. For similar reasons, the other displays of the Commandments that the plurality mentions, do not run afoul of the Establishment Clause. The statues of Moses and St. Paul in the Main Reading Room of the Library of Congress are 2 of 16 set in close proximity, statues that "represent men illustrious in the various forms of thought and activity." Moses and St. Paul represent religion, while the other 14 (a group that includes Beethoven, Shakespeare, Michelangelo, Columbus, and Plato) represent the nonreligious categories of philosophy, art, history, commerce, science, law, and poetry. Similarly, the sculpture of the woman beside the Decalogue in the Main Reading Room is one of 8 such figures "representing eight characteristic features of civilized life and thought," the same 8 features (7 of them nonreligious) that Moses, St. Paul, and the rest of the 16 statues represent. The inlay on the floor of the National Archives Building is one of four such discs, the collective theme of which is not religious. Rather, the discs "symbolize the various types of Government records that were to come into the National Archive." The four categories are war and defense, history, justice, and

Texas argues that its monument (like Moses in the frieze) is not alone and ought to be viewed as only 1 among 17 placed on the 22 acres surrounding the state capitol. Texas says that the Capitol grounds are like a museum for a collection of exhibits. So, for example, the United States does not violate the Establishment Clause by hanging Giotto's Madonna on the wall of the National Gallery. But 17 monuments with no common appearance, history, or esthetic role scattered over 22 acres is not a museum, and anyone strolling around the lawn would surely take each memorial on its own terms. If neutrality in religion means something, any citizen should be able to visit that civic home without having to confront religious expressions clearly meant to convey an official religious position that may be at odds with his own religion, or with rejection of religion. *See County of Allegheny,* 492 U.S. at 626 (O'Connor, J., concurring).

I do not see a persuasive argument for constitutionality in the plurality's observation that Van Orden's lawsuit comes "forty years after the monument's erection." It is not that the passage of time is irrelevant in Establishment Clause analysis. We have approved framing-era practices because they must originally have been understood as constitutionally permissible, e.g., *Marsh v. Chambers,* 463 U.S. 783 (1983), and we have recognized that Sunday laws have grown recognizably secular over time, *McGowan v. Maryland,* 366 U.S. 420 (1961).

BACKGROUND
Justice Moore's Ten Commandments Display

Alabama Supreme Court Justice Roy Moore designed and displayed a 5,280-pound Ten Commandments monument at the Alabama Supreme Court. When a federal court held that the display constituted an establishment of religion and ordered its removal, Justice Moore defiantly ignored the court order and refused to move the monument. Ultimately, faced with contempt fines of $5,000 per day, the remaining justices of the court overruled Justice Moore and ordered the monument removed. In November 2003, Justice Moore was removed from the Alabama Supreme Court by an ethics panel for having "placed himself above the law." After the removal, he stated, "I have absolutely no regrets." He was elected to the Court again in 2012.

---

legislation. Each disc is paired with a winged figure; the disc containing the depiction of the Commandments, a depiction that, notably, omits the Commandments' text, is paired with a figure representing legislation. As for Moses's "prominent featuring in the Chamber of the United States House of Representatives," Moses is actually 1 of 23 portraits encircling the House Chamber, each approximately the same size, having no religious theme. The portraits depict "men noted in history for the part they played in the evolution of what has become American law." More importantly for purposes of this case, each portrait consists only of the subject's face; the Ten Commandments appear nowhere in Moses's portrait.

❧ PROBLEMS ❧

1. *Justice Moore's Alabama Display.* After *Van Orden*, are you clear about what aspects of the Texas State Capitol display render it constitutional? Is Justice Moore's Alabama Supreme Court monument more or less objectionable? Is the Alabama monument constitutionally distinguishable from the Texas display? Why? The trial court order requiring Justice Moore to remove the Ten Commandments monument from the Alabama Supreme Court provided that he could display the monument in his private chambers or in some other place at the court that was out of public view. Is this latter portion of the trial court order valid? Why is a display in the judge's office permissible when a public display is impermissible?

2. *The Anti-Blasphemy Law.* A Pennsylvania statute prohibits corporations from adopting names containing "words that constitute blasphemy, profane cursing or swearing or that profane the Lord's name." A newly formed corporation wants to adopt the name "I Choose Hell Productions LLC." The secretary of state rejects the name on the basis that it is blasphemous. Is the secretary of state's action consistent with the First Amendment? *See Kalman v. Cortes*, 723 F. Supp. 2d 766 (E.D. Pa. 2010).

As you read the following case, consider the effect of motive on Ten Commandments cases. Would *Van Orden* have been decided differently if both Texas and the Fraternal Order of Eagles had been religiously motivated in erecting the display? Is the "reasonable observer," who happens upon the Texas Ten Commandments display, necessarily going to be aware of the motives that prompted the display? Is the "reasonable observer's" reaction going to be affected by those motives if he or she is unaware of them? In addition, why is there a difference in result between this case and *Van Orden* (both of which were decided on the same day)?

McCreary County v. American Civil Liberties Union of Kentucky

545 U.S. 844 (2005)

Justice SOUTER delivered the opinion of the Court.

Petitioners McCreary County and Pulaski County, Kentucky (hereinafter Counties), put up in their respective courthouses large, gold-framed copies of an abridged text of the King James version of the Ten Commandments, including a citation to the Book of Exodus. In McCreary County, the legislative body required "the display to be posted in 'a very high traffic area' of the courthouse." In Pulaski County, the Commandments were hung in a ceremony presided over by the county Judge-Executive, who called them "good rules to live by" and who recounted the story of an astronaut who became convinced "there must be a divine God" after viewing the Earth from the moon. The Judge-Executive was accompanied by the pastor of his church, who called the Commandments "a creed of ethics" and told the press after the ceremony that displaying the Commandments was "one of the greatest things the judge could have done to close out the millennium." In both counties, this was the version of the Commandments posted:

> Thou shalt have no other gods before me.
>
> Thou shalt not make unto thee any graven images.
>
> Thou shalt not take the name of the Lord thy God in vain.
>
> Remember the sabbath day, to keep it holy.
>
> Honor thy father and thy mother.
>
> Thou shalt not kill.
>
> Thou shalt not commit adultery.
>
> Thou shalt not steal.
>
> Thou shalt not bear false witness.
>
> Thou shalt not covet.

Exodus 20:3-17.

In each county, the hallway display was "readily visible to county citizens who use the courthouse to conduct their civic business, to obtain or renew driver's licenses and permits, to register cars, to pay local taxes, and to register to vote."

Respondents American Civil Liberties Union of Kentucky et al. sued the Counties in Federal District Court under 42 U.S.C. §1983, and sought a preliminary injunction against the displays. The legislative body of each County authorized a second, expanded display, by nearly identical resolutions reciting that the Ten Commandments are "the precedent legal code upon which the civil and criminal codes of Kentucky are founded," and stating that "the Ten Commandments are codified in Kentucky's civil and criminal laws"; that the Kentucky House of Representatives had in 1993 "voted unanimously to adjourn in remembrance and honor of Jesus Christ, the Prince of Ethics"; that the "County Judge and magistrates agree with the arguments by Judge Roy Moore" in defense of his "display of the Ten Commandments in his courtroom"; and that the "Founding Fathers had an explicit understanding of the duty of elected officials to publicly acknowledge God as the source of America's strength and direction."

As directed by the resolutions, the Counties expanded the displays of the Ten Commandments in their locations along with copies of the resolution, which instructed that it, too, be posted. In addition to the first display's large framed copy of the edited King James version of the Commandments, the second included eight other documents in smaller frames, each either having a religious theme or excerpted to highlight a religious element. The documents were the "endowed by their Creator" passage from the Declaration of Independence; the Preamble to the Constitution of Kentucky; the national motto, "In God We Trust"; a page from the Congressional Record of February 2, 1983, proclaiming the Year of the Bible and including a statement of the Ten Commandments; a proclamation by President Abraham Lincoln designating April 30, 1863, a National Day of Prayer and Humiliation; an excerpt from President Lincoln's "Reply to Loyal Colored People of Baltimore upon Presentation of a Bible," reading that "the Bible is the best gift God has ever given to man"; a proclamation by President Reagan marking 1983 the Year of the Bible; and the Mayflower Compact.

The District Court entered a preliminary injunction ordering that the "display be removed from each County Courthouse IMMEDIATELY" and that no county official "erect or cause to be erected similar displays." The court's analysis followed the three-part formulation in *Lemon v. Kurtzman*, 403 U.S. 602 (1971). The Counties then installed another display in each courthouse, the third within a year. No new resolution authorized this one, nor did the Counties repeal the resolutions that preceded the second. The posting consists of nine framed documents of equal size, one of them setting out the Ten Commandments explicitly identified as the "King James Version" at Exodus 20:3-17 and quoted at greater length than before:

> Thou shalt have no other gods before me.
>
> Thou shalt not make unto thee any graven image, or any likeness of any thing that is in heaven above, or that is in the earth beneath, or that is in the water underneath the earth: Thou shalt not bow down thyself to them, nor serve them: for I the LORD thy God am a jealous God, visiting the iniquity of the fathers upon the children unto the third and fourth generation of them that hate me.
>
> Thou shalt not take the name of the LORD thy God in vain: for the LORD will not hold him guiltless that taketh his name in vain.
>
> Remember the sabbath day, to keep it holy.
>
> Honour thy father and thy mother: that thy days may be long upon the land which the LORD thy God giveth thee.
>
> Thou shalt not kill.
>
> Thou shalt not commit adultery.
>
> Thou shalt not steal.
>
> Thou shalt not bear false witness against thy neighbour.
>
> Thou shalt not covet thy neighbour's house, thou shalt not covet thy neighbor's wife, nor his manservant, nor his maidservant, nor his ox, nor his ass, nor anything that is thy neighbour's.

Assembled with the Commandments are framed copies of the Magna Carta, the Declaration of Independence, the Bill of Rights, the lyrics of the Star Spangled Banner, the Mayflower Compact, the National Motto, the Preamble to the Kentucky Constitution, and a picture of Lady Justice. The collection is entitled "The Foundations of American Law and Government Display" and each document comes with a statement about its historical and legal significance. The comment on the Ten Commandments reads:

> The Ten Commandments have profoundly influenced the formation of Western legal thought and the formation of our country. That influence is clearly seen in the Declaration of Independence, which declared that "We hold these truths to be self-evident, that all men are created equal, that they are endowed by their Creator with certain unalienable Rights, that among these are Life, Liberty, and the pursuit of Happiness." The Ten Commandments provide the moral background of the Declaration of Independence and the foundation of our legal tradition.

The ACLU moved to supplement the preliminary injunction to enjoin the Counties' third display,[6] and the Counties responded with several explanations for the new version, including desires "to demonstrate that the Ten Commandments were part of the foundation of American Law and Government" and "to educate the citizens of the county regarding some of the documents that played a significant role in the foundation of our system of law and government." The trial court supplemented the injunction, and the Court of Appeals for the Sixth Circuit affirmed. We granted certiorari and now affirm.

II

Twenty-five years ago in a case prompted by posting the Ten Commandments in Kentucky's public schools, this Court recognized that the Commandments "are undeniably a sacred text in the Jewish and Christian faiths" and held that their display in public classrooms violated the First Amendment's bar against establishment of religion. *Stone v. Graham*, 449 U.S. 39 (1980) (per curiam), found a predominantly religious purpose in the government's posting of the Commandments, given their prominence as "an instrument of religion." Since *Lemon*, looking to whether government action has "a secular legislative purpose" has been a common, albeit seldom dispositive, element of our cases. Though we have found government action motivated by an illegitimate purpose only four times since *Lemon*, "it nevertheless serves an important function." *Wallace v. Jaffree*, 472 U.S. 38 (1985) (O'Connor, J., concurring in judgment).

The touchstone for our analysis is the principle that the "First Amendment mandates governmental neutrality between religion and religion, and between religion and nonreligion." *Epperson v. Arkansas*, 393 U.S. 97 (1968). Manifesting a purpose to favor one faith over another, or adherence to religion generally, clashes with the "understanding, reached after decades of religious war, that liberty and social stability demand a religious tolerance that respects the religious views of all citizens." *Zelman v. Simmons-Harris*, 536 U.S. 639 (2002) (Breyer, J., dissenting). By showing a purpose to favor religion, the government "sends the

---

6. Before the District Court issued the modified injunction, the Counties removed the label of "King James Version" and the citation to Exodus.

message to nonadherents 'that they are outsiders, not full members of the political community, and an accompanying message to adherents that they are insiders, favored members.'" *Santa Fe Independent School Dist. v. Doe*, 530 U.S. 290 (2000) (quoting *Lynch v. Donnelly*, 465 U.S. 668 (1984) (O'Connor, J., concurring)).

The purpose apparent from government action can have an impact more significant than the result expressly decreed: when the government maintains Sunday closing laws, it advances religion only minimally because many working people would take the day as one of rest regardless, but if the government justified its decision with a stated desire for all Americans to honor Christ, the divisive thrust of the official action would be inescapable.

The Counties argue that true "purpose" is unknowable, and its search merely an excuse for courts to act selectively and unpredictably in picking out evidence of subjective intent. Examination of purpose is a staple of statutory interpretation and governmental purpose is a key element of a good deal of constitutional doctrine, e.g., *Church of Lukumi Babalu Aye, Inc. v. Hialeah*, 508 U.S. 520 (1993). Scrutinizing purpose does make practical sense where an understanding of official objective emerges from readily discoverable fact, without any judicial psychoanalysis. The eyes that look to purpose belong to an "objective observer," one who takes account of the traditional external signs that show up in the "text, legislative history, and implementation of the statute," or comparable official act. There is nothing hinting at an unpredictable or disingenuous exercise when a court enquires into purpose.

The cases point to the straightforward nature of the test. In *Wallace,* we inferred purpose from a change of wording from an earlier statute to a later one, each dealing with prayer in schools. In *Edwards v. Aguillard*, 482 U.S. 578 (1987), we relied on a statute's text and the detailed public comments of its sponsor, when we sought the purpose of a state law requiring creationism to be taught alongside evolution. In *Stone*, the Court held that the "posting of religious texts on the wall served no educational function." In each case, the openly available data supported a commonsense conclusion that a religious objective permeated the government's action. In some of the cases in which establishment complaints failed, savvy officials had disguised their religious intent so cleverly that the objective observer just missed it. But that is no reason for great constitutional concern. A secret motive stirs up no strife and does nothing to make outsiders of nonadherents, and it suffices to wait and see whether such government action has the illegitimate effect of advancing religion.

The Counties would read the cases as if the purpose enquiry were so naive that any transparent claim to secularity would satisfy it. The Court often does accept governmental statements of purpose, in keeping with the respect owed in the first instance to such official claims. But in those unusual cases where the claim was an apparent sham, or the secular purpose secondary, the unsurprising results have been findings of no adequate secular object. The Counties also argue that purpose in a case like this one should be inferred, if at all, only from the last in a series of governmental actions. Reasonable observers have reasonable

memories, and our precedents sensibly forbid an observer "to turn a blind eye
to the context in which the policy arose."[14] *Santa Fe Independent School Dist. v. Doe,
supra,* at 315.

III

On an appeal from a preliminary injunction, we review the District Court's legal
rulings *de novo,* and its ultimate conclusion for abuse of discretion. *Stone* recognized that the Commandments are an "instrument of religion" and could presumptively be understood as meant to advance religion. But *Stone* did not decide
the constitutionality of every possible way the Commandments might be set out
by the government, and under the Establishment Clause detail is key. *County of
Allegheny v. American Civil Liberties Union,* 492 U.S. 573 (1989). Hence, we look to
the progression leading up to the third display of the Commandments.

The display rejected in *Stone* had two obvious similarities to the first one
here: both set out a text of the Commandments as distinct from any traditionally
symbolic representation, and each stood alone, not part of an arguably secular
display. *Stone* stressed the significance of integrating the Commandments into a
secular scheme to forestall the broadcast of an otherwise clearly religious message, and for good reason, the Commandments being a central point of reference in the religious and moral history of Jews and Christians. They proclaim
the existence of a monotheistic god (no other gods). They regulate details of
religious obligation (no graven images, no sabbath breaking, no vain oath swearing). And they unmistakably rest even the universally accepted prohibitions (as
against murder, theft, and the like) on the sanction of the divinity proclaimed at
the beginning of the text. Displaying that text is thus different from a symbolic
depiction, like tablets with 10 roman numerals, which could be seen as alluding
to a general notion of law, not a sectarian conception of faith. Where the text is
set out, the insistence of the religious message is hard to avoid in the absence
of a context plausibly suggesting a message going beyond an excuse to promote
the religious point of view. The Counties' solo exhibit here did nothing more to
counter the sectarian implication than the postings at issue in *Stone.* The posting
by the Counties lacked even the *Stone* display's implausible disclaimer that the
Commandments were set out to show their effect on the civil law. What is more,
at the ceremony for posting the framed Commandments in Pulaski County, the
county executive was accompanied by his pastor, who testified to the certainty of
the existence of God. The reasonable observer could only think that the Counties
meant to emphasize and celebrate the Commandments' religious message. The
point is simply that the original text viewed in its entirety is an unmistakably
religious statement dealing with religious obligations and with morality subject

14. One consequence of taking account of purpose is that the same government action may be constitutional if taken in the first instance and unconstitutional if it has a sectarian heritage. This presents no incongruity. It will matter to objective observers whether posting the Commandments follows on the heels of displays
motivated by sectarianism, or whether it lacks a history demonstrating that purpose.

to religious sanction. When the government initiates an effort to place this statement alone in public view, a religious object is unmistakable.

Once the Counties were sued, they modified the exhibits to include a series of American historical documents with theistic and Christian references, which were to be posted in order to furnish a setting for displaying the Ten Commandments and any "other Kentucky and American historical document" without raising concern about "any Christian or religious references" in them. The resolutions expressed support for an Alabama judge who posted the Commandments in his courtroom, and cited the fact the Kentucky Legislature once adjourned a session in honor of "Jesus Christ, Prince of Ethics."

In this second display, the Commandments were not hung in isolation, merely leaving the Counties' purpose to emerge from the pervasively religious text of the Commandments themselves. Instead, the second version was required to include the statement of the government's purpose expressly set out in the county resolutions, and underscored it by juxtaposing the Commandments to other documents with highlighted references to God as their sole common element. The display's unstinting focus was on religious passages, showing that the Counties were posting the Commandments precisely because of their sectarian content. That demonstration of the government's objective was enhanced by serial religious references and the accompanying resolution's claim about the embodiment of ethics in Christ. Together, the display and resolution presented an indisputable, and undisputed, showing of an impermissible purpose. The Counties make no attempt to defend their undeniable objective, but instead hopefully describe version two as "dead and buried." Their refusal to defend the second display is understandable, but the reasonable observer could not forget it.

After the Counties changed lawyers, they mounted a third display, without a new resolution or repeal of the old one. The result was the "Foundations of American Law and Government" exhibit, which placed the Commandments in the company of other documents the Counties thought especially significant in the historical foundation of American government. The Counties cited several new purposes for the third version, including a desire "to educate the citizens of the county regarding some of the documents that played a significant role in the foundation of our system of law and government."[18] These new statements of purpose were presented only as a litigating position, there being no further authorizing action by the Counties' governing boards. The extraordinary resolutions for the second display were not repealed or otherwise repudiated. The sectarian spirit of the resolution found enhanced expression in the third display, which quoted more of the purely religious language of the Commandments than the first two displays had done; for additions ("I the LORD thy God am a jealous

---

18. The Counties' other purposes were: "to erect a display containing the Ten Commandments that is constitutional; to demonstrate that the Ten Commandments were part of the foundation of American Law and Government; to include the Ten Commandments as part of the display for their significance in providing the moral background of the Declaration of Independence and the foundation of our legal tradition."

God"); ("the LORD will not hold him guiltless that taketh his name in vain"); and ("that thy days may be long upon the land which the LORD thy God giveth thee"). No reasonable observer could swallow the claim that the Counties had cast off the objective so unmistakable in the earlier displays.

Nor did the selection of posted material suggest a clear theme that might prevail over evidence of the continuing religious object. In a collection of documents said to be "foundational" to American government, it is at least odd to include a patriotic anthem, but to omit the Fourteenth Amendment, the most significant structural provision adopted since the original Framing. And it is no less baffling to leave out the original Constitution of 1787 while quoting the 1215 Magna Carta. If an observer found these choices and omissions perplexing in isolation, he would be puzzled when he read the Declaration of Independence seeking confirmation for the Counties' posted explanation that the "Ten Commandments" influence is clearly seen in the Declaration; in fact the observer would find that the Commandments are sanctioned as divine imperatives, while the Declaration of Independence holds that the authority of government to enforce the law derives "from the consent of the governed." If the observer had not thrown up his hands, he would probably suspect that the Counties were simply reaching for any way to keep a religious document on the walls of courthouses.

In holding that the Counties' purpose had not changed at the third stage, we do not decide that the Counties' past actions forever taint any effort on their part to deal with the subject matter. We hold only that an implausible claim that governmental purpose has changed should not carry the day in a court of law. Nor do we have occasion here to hold that a sacred text can never be integrated constitutionally into a governmental display on the subject of law, or American history. Our own courtroom frieze was deliberately designed in the exercise of governmental authority so as to include the figure of Moses holding tablets exhibiting a portion of the Hebrew text of the later, secularly phrased Commandments; in the company of 17 other lawgivers, most of them secular figures, there is no risk that Moses would strike an observer as evidence that the National Government was violating neutrality in religion.

IV

The importance of neutrality as an interpretive guide is no less true now than it was when the Court broached the principle in *Everson v. Board of Ed. of Ewing*, 330 U.S. 1 (1947). The First Amendment contains no textual definition of "establishment," and the term is certainly not self-defining. No one contends that the prohibition of establishment stops at a designation of a national (or with Fourteenth Amendment incorporation, a state) church, but nothing in the text says just how much more it covers. The prohibition on establishment covers a variety of issues from prayer in widely varying government settings, to financial aid for religious individuals and institutions, to comment on religious questions. In these varied settings, issues of interpreting inexact Establishment Clause language, like difficult interpretative issues generally, arise from the tension of competing values, each constitutionally respectable, but none open to realization to the logical limit.

The First Amendment has not one but two clauses tied to "religion," the second forbidding any prohibition on the "the free exercise thereof," and sometimes, the two clauses compete. Limits on governmental action that might make sense as a way to avoid establishment could arguably limit freedom of speech when the speaking is done under government auspices. *Rosenberger v. Rector and Visitors of Univ. of Va.*, 515 U.S. 819 (1995). The principle of neutrality has provided a good sense of direction: the government may not favor one religion over another, or religion over irreligion, religious choice being the prerogative of individuals under the Free Exercise Clause. The Framers and the citizens of their time intended not only to protect the integrity of individual conscience in religious matters, but to guard against the civic divisiveness that follows when the Government weighs in on one side of religious debate; nothing does a better job of roiling society, a point that needed no explanation to the descendants of English Puritans and Cavaliers (or Massachusetts Puritans and Baptists). *E.g., Everson, supra,* at 8. To be sure, an appeal to neutrality alone cannot possibly lay every issue to rest, or tell us what issues on the margins are substantial enough for constitutional significance. But invoking neutrality is a prudent way of keeping sight of something the Framers of the First Amendment thought important.

The dissent puts forward a limitation on the application of the neutrality principle, with citations to historical evidence said to show that the Framers understood the ban on establishment of religion as sufficiently narrow to allow the government to espouse submission to the divine will. The dissent identifies God as the God of monotheism, all of whose three principal strains (Jewish, Christian, and Muslim) acknowledge the religious importance of the Ten Commandments. On the dissent's view, even rigorous espousal of a common element of this common monotheism, is consistent with the establishment ban. Some of the Framers thought some endorsement of religion was compatible with the establishment ban. There is also evidence supporting the proposition that the Framers intended the Establishment Clause to require governmental neutrality in matters of religion, including neutrality in statements acknowledging religion. The very language of the Establishment Clause represented a significant departure from early drafts that merely prohibited a single national religion, and, the final language instead "extended the prohibition to state support for 'religion' in general." *See Lee v. Weisman,* 505 U.S. 577 (1992) (Souter, J., concurring).

The historical record, moreover, is complicated beyond the dissent's account by the writings and practices of figures no less influential than Thomas Jefferson and James Madison. Jefferson, for example, refused to issue Thanksgiving Proclamations because he believed that they violated the Constitution. And Madison, whom the dissent claims as supporting its thesis, criticized Virginia's general assessment tax not just because it required people to donate "three pence" to religion, but because "it is itself a signal of persecution." There was no common understanding about the limits of the establishment prohibition, and the dissent's conclusion that its narrower view was the original understanding, stretches the evidence beyond tensile capacity. What the evidence does show is a group of statesmen who proposed a guarantee with contours not wholly worked out, leaving the Establishment Clause with edges still to be determined.

The dissent says that the deity the Framers had in mind was the God of monotheism, with the consequence that government may espouse a tenet of traditional monotheism. This is truly a remarkable view. History shows that the religion of concern to the Framers was not that of the monotheistic faiths generally, but Christianity in particular. The Framers would almost certainly object to the dissent's unstated reasoning that because Christianity was a monotheistic "religion," monotheism with Mosaic antecedents should be a touchstone of establishment interpretation. The divisiveness of religion in current public life is inescapable. This is no time to deny the prudence of understanding the Establishment Clause to require the Government to stay neutral on religious belief, which is reserved for the conscience of the individual.

V

Given the ample support for the District Court's finding of a predominantly religious purpose behind the Counties' third display, we affirm the Sixth Circuit in upholding the preliminary injunction.

It is so ordered.

Justice O'CONNOR, *concurring.*

The Court correctly finds an Establishment Clause violation. The purpose behind the counties' display conveys an unmistakable message of endorsement to the reasonable observer. Many Americans find the Commandments in accord with their personal beliefs. But we do not count heads before enforcing the First Amendment.

Justice SCALIA, with whom THE CHIEF JUSTICE and Justice THOMAS join, and with whom Justice KENNEDY joins as to Parts II and III, *dissenting.*

I would uphold the McCreary County and Pulaski County, Kentucky's displays of the Ten Commandments. George Washington added to the form of Presidential oath the concluding words "so help me God." The Supreme Court under John Marshall opened its sessions with the prayer, "God save the United States and this Honorable Court." The First Congress instituted the practice of beginning its legislative sessions with a prayer. The same week that Congress submitted the Establishment Clause as part of the Bill of Rights for ratification by the States, it enacted legislation providing for paid chaplains in the House and Senate. The day after the First Amendment was proposed, Congress requested the President to proclaim "a day of public thanksgiving and prayer, to be observed, by acknowledging, with grateful hearts, the many and signal favours of Almighty God." President Washington offered the first Thanksgiving Proclamation shortly thereafter on behalf of the American people "to the service of that great and glorious Being who is the beneficent author of all the good that is, that was, or that will be," thus beginning a tradition of offering gratitude to God that continues today. The same Congress also reenacted the Northwest Territory Ordinance of 1787 which provided: "Religion, morality, and knowledge, being necessary to good government and the happiness of mankind, schools and the means of education shall forever be encouraged." And of course the First Amendment itself accords religion (and no other manner of belief) special constitutional protection.

Those who wrote the Constitution believed that morality was essential to the well-being of society and that encouragement of religion was the best way to foster morality. President Washington opened his Presidency with a prayer, and reminded his fellow citizens that "reason and experience forbid us to expect that National morality can prevail in exclusion of religious principle." Farewell Address (1796), reprinted in 35 *Writings of George Washington* (J. Fitzpatrick ed. 1940). President John Adams wrote to the Massachusetts Militia, "our Constitution was made only for a moral and religious people." Thomas Jefferson concluded his second inaugural address by inviting his audience to pray. James Madison, in his first inaugural address, placed his confidence "in the guardianship and guidance of that Almighty Being whose power regulates the destiny of nations, whose blessings have been so conspicuously dispensed to this rising Republic, and to whom we are bound to address our devout gratitude for the past, as well as our fervent supplications and best hopes for the future."

Nor have the views of our people on this matter significantly changed. Presidents continue to conclude the Presidential oath with the words "so help me God." Our legislatures, state and national, continue to open their sessions with prayer led by official chaplains. The sessions of this Court continue to open with the prayer "God save the United States and this Honorable Court." Invocation of the Almighty by our public figures, at all levels of government, remains commonplace. Our coinage bears the motto "IN GOD WE TRUST." And our Pledge of Allegiance contains the acknowledgment that we are a Nation "under God." As one of our Supreme Court opinions rightly observed, "We are a religious people whose institutions presuppose a Supreme Being." *Zorach v. Clauson*, 343 U.S. 306 (1952).

With reality staring it in the face, how can the Court assert that "the First Amendment mandates governmental neutrality between religion and nonreligion," and that "manifesting a purpose to favor adherence to religion generally," is unconstitutional? Who says so? Surely not the words of the Constitution. Surely not the history and traditions that reflect our society's constant understanding of those words. Surely not even the current sense of our society. What distinguishes the rule of law from the dictatorship of a shifting Supreme Court majority is the absolutely indispensable requirement that judicial opinions be grounded in consistently applied principle. When the government relieves churches from the obligation to pay property taxes, when it allows students to absent themselves from public school to take religious classes, and when it exempts religious organizations from generally applicable prohibitions of religious discrimination, it surely means to bestow a benefit on religious practice—but we have approved it. Indeed, we have even approved (post-*Lemon*) government-led prayer to God. *See Marsh v. Chambers, supra.*

If religion in the public forum had to be entirely nondenominational, there could be no religion in the public forum at all. One cannot say the word "God," or "the Almighty," one cannot offer public supplication or thanksgiving, without contradicting the beliefs of some people that there are many gods, or that God or the gods pay no attention to human affairs. It is clear from our Nation's historical practices that the Establishment Clause permits this disregard of polytheists and believers in unconcerned deities, just as it permits the disregard of devout atheists. The Thanksgiving Proclamation issued by George Washington was nondenominational—but it was monotheistic. In *Marsh*, the fact the particular prayers offered in the Nebraska Legislature were "in the Judeo-Christian tradition," posed no additional problem, because "there is no indication that the prayer opportunity has been exploited to proselytize or advance any one, or to disparage any other, faith or belief."

Historical practices thus demonstrate that there is a distance between the acknowledgment of a single Creator and the establishment of a religion. The three most popular religions in the United States, Christianity, Judaism, and Islam—which account for 97.7% of all believers—are monotheistic. All of them, moreover (Islam included), believe that the Ten Commandments were given by God to Moses, and are divine prescriptions for a virtuous life. Publicly honoring the Ten Commandments is thus indistinguishable, insofar as discriminating against other religions is concerned, from publicly honoring God. Both practices are recognized across such a broad and diverse range of the population—from Christians to Muslims—that they cannot be reasonably understood as a government endorsement of a particular religious viewpoint.[4]

Justice Stevens argues that "reliance on early religious proclamations and statements made by the Founders is problematic," "because those views were not espoused at the Constitutional Convention in 1787 nor enshrined in the Constitution's text." I have relied primarily upon official acts and official proclamations of the United States or of the component branches of Government. What is more probative of the meaning of the Establishment Clause than the actions of the very Congress that proposed it, and of the first President charged with observing it?

Justice Stevens appeals to the undoubted fact that some in the founding generation thought that the Religion Clauses of the First Amendment should have a *narrower* meaning, protecting only the Christian religion or perhaps only Protestantism. *All* of the actions of Washington and the First Congress upon

4. This is not to say that a display of the Ten Commandments could never constitute an impermissible endorsement of a particular religious view. The Establishment Clause would prohibit, for example, governmental endorsement of a particular version of the Decalogue as authoritative.

which I have relied, virtually all Thanksgiving Proclamations throughout our history, and *all* the other examples of our Government's favoring religion that I have cited, have invoked God, but not Jesus Christ.

Justice Stevens says that if one is serious about following the original understanding of the Establishment Clause, he must repudiate its incorporation into the Fourteenth Amendment, and hold that it does not apply against the States. The notion that incorporation empties the incorporated provisions of their original meaning has no support in either reason or precedent.

Justice Stevens argues that original meaning should not be the touchstone anyway, but that we should "expound the meaning of constitutional provisions with one eye towards our Nation's history and the other fixed on its democratic aspirations." This is not the place to debate the merits of the "living Constitution." Even assuming that the meaning of the Constitution ought to change according to "democratic aspirations," why are those aspirations to be found in Justices' notions of what the Establishment Clause ought to mean, rather than in the democratically adopted dispositions of our current society?

Finally, I must respond to Justice Stevens' assertion that I would "marginalize the belief systems of more than 7 million Americans" who adhere to religions that are not monotheistic. The beliefs of those citizens are entirely protected by the Free Exercise Clause, and by those aspects of the Establishment Clause that do not relate to government acknowledgment of the Creator. In the context of public acknowledgments of God there are legitimate *competing* interests: On the one hand, the interest of that minority in not feeling "excluded"; but on the other, the interest of the overwhelming majority of religious believers in being able to give God thanks and supplication *as a people,* and with respect to our national endeavors. Our national tradition has resolved that conflict in favor of the majority.

As bad as the *Lemon* test is, its seemingly simple mandates have been manipulated to fit whatever result the Court aimed to achieve. Today's opinion is no different. Even accepting the Court's *Lemon*-based premises, the displays at issue here were constitutional. To any person who happened to walk down the hallway of the McCreary or Pulaski County Courthouse, the displays must have seemed unremarkable—if indeed they were noticed at all. The walls of both courthouses were already lined with historical documents and other assorted portraits. The frame holding the Ten Commandments was of the same size and had the same appearance as that which held each of the other documents. Posted with the documents was a plaque, identifying the display, and explaining that it "contains documents that played a significant role in the foundation of our system of law and government." The explanation related to the Ten Commandments was third in the list of nine and did not serve to distinguish it from the other documents.

The Foundations Displays manifested the purely secular purpose that the Counties asserted before the District Court: "to display documents that played a significant role in the foundation of our system of law and government." Even an isolated display of the Decalogue conveys, at worst, "an equivocal message, perhaps of respect for Judaism, for religion in general, or for law." But when the Ten Commandments appear alongside other documents of secular significance in a display devoted to the foundations of American law and government, the context communicates that the Ten Commandments are included, not to teach their binding nature as a religious text, but to show their unique contribution to the development of the legal system. The Supreme Court Building itself includes depictions of Moses with the Ten Commandments in the Courtroom and on the east pediment of the building, and symbols of the Ten Commandments "adorn the metal gates lining the north and south sides of the Courtroom as well as the doors leading into the Courtroom." Similar depictions of the Decalogue appear on public buildings and monuments throughout our Nation's Capital. The frequency of these displays testifies to the popular understanding that the Ten Commandments are a foundation of the rule of law, and a symbol of the role that religion played, and continues to play, in our system of government.

Displays erected in silence (and under the direction of good legal advice) are permissible, while those hung after discussion and debate are deemed unconstitutional. Reduction of the Establishment Clause to such minutiae trivializes the Clause's protection against religious establishment. If the Commandments have a proper place in our civic history, even placing them by themselves can be civically motivated—especially when they are placed, not in a school, but in a courthouse.

The Court has in the past prohibited government actions that "proselytize or advance any one, or disparage any other, faith or belief," or that apply some level of coercion. The passive display of the Ten Commandments, even standing alone, does not begin to do either. Nor is it the case that a solo display of the Ten Commandments advances any one faith. They are assuredly a religious symbol, but they are not so closely associated with a single religious belief that their display can reasonably be understood as preferring one religious sect over another. The Ten Commandments are recognized by Judaism, Christianity, and Islam alike as divinely given.

The Court points to the Counties' second displays, which featured a number of statements in historical documents reflecting a religious influence, and the resolutions that accompanied their erection, as evidence of an impermissible religious purpose. All it shows is that the exhibit was meant to focus upon the historic role of religious belief in our national life—which is entirely permissible. The same can be said of the resolution.

Turning to the displays, the Court faults the Counties for not *repealing* the resolution expressing what the Court believes to be an impermissible intent. It is unlikely that a reasonable observer *would even have been aware* of the resolutions. A plaque next to the documents informed all who passed by that each display "contains documents that played a significant role in the foundation of our system of law and government." There was no reason for the Counties to repeal or repudiate the resolutions adopted with the hanging of the second displays, since they related *only to the second displays*. I would reverse the judgment.

The American Legion v. American Humanist Association

139 S. Ct. 2067 (2019)

Justice ALITO announced the judgment of the Court and delivered the opinion of the Court with respect to Parts I, II–B, II–C, III, and IV, and an opinion with respect to Parts II–A and II–D, in which THE CHIEF JUSTICE, Justice BREYER, and Justice KAVANAUGH join.

The Bladensburg Peace Cross has stood as a tribute to 49 area soldiers who gave their lives in the First World War. Eighty-nine years after the dedication of the Cross, respondents filed this lawsuit, claiming that they are offended by the sight of the memorial on public land and the expenditure of public funds to maintain it violate the Establishment Clause of the First Amendment. They asked a federal court to order the relocation or demolition of the Cross or at least the removal of its arms. The Court of Appeals for the Fourth Circuit agreed that the memorial is unconstitutional. We reverse.

Although the cross has long been a preeminent Christian symbol, its use in the Bladensburg memorial has a special significance. After the First World War, the picture of row after row of plain white crosses marking the overseas graves of soldiers who had lost their lives in that horrible conflict was emblazoned on the minds of Americans, and the adoption of the cross at the Bladensburg memorial must be viewed in that historical context. For nearly a century, the Cross has expressed the community's grief at the loss of the young men who perished, its thanks for their sacrifice, and its dedication to the ideals for which they fought. It has become a prominent community landmark, and its removal or radical alteration at this date would be seen by many not as a neutral act but as the manifestation of "a hostility toward religion that has no place in our Establishment Clause traditions." *Van Orden v. Perry*, 545 U. S. 677, 704 (2005) (Breyer, J., concurring). There is no evidence of discriminatory intent in the selection of the design of the memorial or the decision to maintain it. The Religion Clauses of the Constitution aim to foster a society in which people of all beliefs can live together harmoniously, and the presence of the Cross on the land where it has stood for so many years is fully consistent with that aim.

I

The cross came into widespread use as a symbol of Christianity by the fourth century, and it retains that meaning today. But there are many contexts in which the symbol has also taken on a secular meaning. Indeed, there are instances in which its message is almost entirely secular. A cross appears as part of many registered trademarks held by businesses and secular organizations, including Blue Cross Blue Shield, the Bayer Group, and some Johnson & Johnson products. Many of these marks relate to health care, and it is likely that the association of the cross with healing had a religious origin. But the current use of these marks is indisputably secular. The familiar symbol of the Red Cross—a red cross on a white background—shows how the meaning of a symbol that was originally religious can be transformed. The International Committee of the Red Cross (ICRC) selected that symbol in 1863 because it was thought to call to mind the flag of Switzerland, a country widely known for its neutrality. The ICRC copied its design with the colors inverted. Thus, the ICRC selected this symbol for an essentially secular reason, and the current secular message of the symbol is shown by its use in nations with only tiny Christian populations.

The image used in the Bladensburg memorial—a plain Latin cross—took on new meaning after World War I. "During and immediately after the war, the army marked soldiers' graves with temporary wooden crosses or Stars of David"—a departure from the prior practice of marking graves in American military cemeteries with uniform rectangular slabs. As a result, the image of a simple white cross "developed into a 'central symbol'" of the conflict. Contemporary literature, poetry, and art reflected this powerful imagery. John McCrae's poem, In Flanders Fields, began with these memorable lines: "In Flanders fields the poppies blow Between the crosses, row on row." IN FLANDERS FIELDS AND OTHER POEMS 3 (G. P. Putnam's Sons ed. 1919). The poem was enormously popular. The image of "the crosses, row on row," stuck in people's minds, and even today for those who view World War I cemeteries in Europe, the image is arresting. After the 1918 armistice, the War Department announced plans to replace the wooden crosses and Stars of David with marble slabs like those previously used in American military cemeteries. But the public outcry against that proposal was swift and fierce. The American Battle Monuments Commission responded to this public sentiment by opting to replace the wooden crosses and Stars of David with marble versions of those symbols. This national debate confirmed the cross's widespread resonance as a symbol of sacrifice in the war. Recognition of the cross's symbolism extended to local communities across the country. In 1918, residents of Prince George's County, Maryland, formed a committee for the purpose of erecting a memorial for the county's fallen soldiers. Among the committee's members were the mothers of 10 deceased soldiers. The committee decided that the memorial should be a cross and hired sculptor and architect John Earley to design it. It is unsurprising that the committee—and many others commemorating World War I—adopted a symbol so widely associated with that wrenching event. The committee held fundraising events in the community.

The completed monument is a 32-foot tall Latin cross that sits on a large pedestal. The American Legion's emblem is displayed at its center, and the words "Valor," "Endurance," "Courage," and "Devotion" are inscribed at its base, one on each of the four faces. The pedestal also features a 9- by 2.5-foot bronze plaque explaining that the monument is "Dedicated to the heroes of Prince George's County, Maryland who lost their lives in the Great War for the liberty of the world." The plaque lists the names of 49 local men, both Black and White, who died in the war. It identifies the dates of American involvement, and quotes President Woodrow Wilson's request for a declaration of war: "The right is more precious than peace. We shall fight for the things we have always carried nearest our hearts.

To such a task we dedicate our lives." At the dedication ceremony, a local Catholic priest offered an invocation. United States Representative Stephen W. Gambrill delivered the keynote address, honoring the "men of Prince George's County" who "fought for the sacred right of all to live in peace and security." The ceremony closed with a benediction offered by a Baptist pastor.

Since its dedication, the Cross has served as the site of patriotic events honoring veterans, including gatherings on Veterans Day, Memorial Day, and Independence Day. These events have typically included an invocation, a keynote speaker, and a benediction. Over the years, memorials honoring the veterans of other conflicts have been added to the surrounding area, which is now known as Veterans Memorial Park. These include a World War II Honor Scroll; a Pearl Harbor memorial; a Korea-Vietnam veterans memorial; a September 11 garden; a War of 1812 memorial; and two recently added 38-foot-tall markers depicting British and American soldiers in the Battle of Bladensburg. Because the Cross is located on a traffic island with limited space, the closest of these other monuments is about 200 feet away in a park across the road.

As the area around the Cross developed, the monument came to be at the center of a busy intersection. In 1961, the Maryland-National Capital Park and Planning Commission acquired the Cross and the land on which it sits in order to preserve the monument and address traffic-safety concerns. The American Legion reserved the right to continue using the memorial to host ceremonies, including events in memory of departed veterans. Over the next five decades, the Commission spent approximately $117,000 to maintain and preserve the monument. In 2008, it budgeted an additional $100,000 for renovations and repairs to the Cross. Nearly 90 years after the Cross was dedicated and more than 50 years after the Commission acquired it, the American Humanist Association (AHA) lodged a complaint with the Commission. The complaint alleged that the Cross's presence on public land and the Commission's maintenance of the memorial violate the Establishment Clause of the First Amendment. The AHA sought declaratory and injunctive relief requiring "removal or demolition of the Cross, or removal of the arms from the Cross to form a non-religious slab or obelisk." The District Court granted summary judgment for the Commission and the American Legion. The Cross, the court held, satisfies both the three-pronged test announced in *Lemon v. Kurtzman*, 403 U. S. 602 (1971), and the analysis upholding the Ten Commandments monument at issue in *Van Orden v. Perry*, 545 U. S. 677. A panel of the Court of Appeals for the Fourth Circuit reversed. The Fourth Circuit denied rehearing en banc. We granted [certiorari].

II

A

The Establishment Clause of the First Amendment provides that "Congress shall make no law respecting an establishment of religion." While the concept of a formally established church is straightforward, pinning down the meaning of a "law respecting an establishment of religion" has proved to be a vexing problem. Prior to the Court's decision in *Everson v. Board of Ed. of Ewing*, 330 U. S. 1 (1947), the Establishment Clause was applied only to the Federal Government. After *Everson* recognized the incorporation of the Clause, the Court faced a steady stream of difficult and controversial Establishment Clause issues, ranging from Bible reading and prayer in the public schools, to Sunday closing laws, to state subsidies for church-related schools or the parents of students attending those schools. *Lemon* called on courts to examine the purposes and effects of a challenged government action, as well as any entanglement with religion that it might entail. The Court later elaborated that the "effects" of a challenged action should be assessed by asking whether a "reasonable observer" would conclude that the action constituted an "endorsement" of religion. *County of Allegheny v. American Civil Liberties Union, Greater Pittsburgh Chapter*, 492 U. S. 573 (1989). If the *Lemon* Court thought that its test would provide a framework for all future Establishment Clause decisions, its expectation has not been met. In many cases, this Court has either expressly declined to apply the test or has simply ignored it. As Establishment Clause cases involving a great array of laws and practices came to the Court, it became apparent that the *Lemon* test could not resolve them. It could not "explain the Establishment Clause's tolerance of the prayers that open legislative meetings, certain references to, and invocations of, the Deity in the public words of public officials; the public references to God on coins, decrees, and buildings; or the attention paid to the religious objectives of certain holidays, including Thanksgiving." *Van Orden, supra*, at 699 (Breyer, J.). The test has been harshly criticized by Members of this Court, lamented by lower court judges, and questioned by a diverse roster of scholars. The test presents particularly daunting problems in cases that involve the use, for ceremonial, celebratory, or commemorative purposes, of words or symbols with religious associations. These considerations counsel against efforts to evaluate such cases under *Lemon* and toward application of a presumption of constitutionality for longstanding monuments, symbols, and practices.

B

Cases often concern monuments, symbols, or practices that were established long ago, and in such cases, identifying their original purpose or purposes may be especially difficult. In *Salazar v. Buono*, 559 U. S. 700 (2010), we dealt with a cross that a group of World War I veterans had put up at a remote spot in the Mojave Desert more than seven decades earlier. The record contained virtually no direct evidence regarding the specific motivations of these men. We knew that they had selected a plain white cross, and that the man who looked after the monument for many years—"a miner who had served as a medic and had thus presumably witnessed the carnage of the war firsthand"—was not "particularly religious." The plurality thought that this particular cross was meant "to commemorate

American servicemen who had died in World War I" and was not intended "to promote a Christian message." The dissent "presumed" that the cross's purpose "was a Christian one for the simple reason that those who erected the cross chose to commemorate American veterans in an explicitly Christian manner." 70 years after the fact, there was no way to be certain about the motivations of the men who were responsible for the creation of the monument.

As time goes by, the purposes associated with an established monument, symbol, or practice often multiply. Take the example of Ten Commandments monuments, the subject we addressed in *Van Orden*, 545 U. S. 677, and *McCreary County v. American Civil Liberties Union of Ky.*, 545 U. S. 844 (2005). For believing Jews and Christians, the Ten Commandments are the word of God handed down to Moses on Mount Sinai, but the image of the Ten Commandments has also been used to convey other meanings. They have historical significance as one of the foundations of our legal system, and are depicted in the marble frieze in our courtroom and in other prominent public buildings in our Nation's capital. Just as depictions of the Ten Commandments in these public buildings were intended to serve secular purposes, the litigation in *Van Orden* and *McCreary* showed that secular motivations played a part in the proliferation of Ten Commandments monuments in the 1950s. As noted in *Pleasant Grove City v. Summum*, 555 U. S. 460, 476 (2009), "the thoughts or sentiments expressed by a government entity that accepts and displays a monument may be quite different from those of either its creator or its donor." Even if the original purpose of a monument was infused with religion, the passage of time may obscure that sentiment. As our society becomes more religiously diverse, a community may preserve such monuments, symbols, and practices for the sake of their historical significance or their place in a common cultural heritage.

Just as the purpose for maintaining a monument, symbol, or practice may evolve, "the 'message' conveyed may change over time." *Summum*, 555 U. S., at 477. Consider the message of the Statue of Liberty, which began as a monument to the solidarity and friendship between France and the United States and decades later came to be seen "as a beacon welcoming immigrants to a land of freedom." With time, religiously expressive monuments, symbols, and practices can become embedded features of a community's landscape and identity. The community may come to value them without necessarily embracing their religious roots. The recent tragic fire at Notre Dame in Paris provides a striking example. Although the French Republic rigorously enforces a secular public square, the cathedral remains a symbol of national importance to the religious and nonreligious alike. Notre Dame is fundamentally a place of worship and great religious importance, but its meaning has broadened. For many, it is inextricably linked with the very idea of Paris and France. Religion undoubtedly motivated those who named Bethlehem, Pennsylvania; Las Cruces, New Mexico; Providence, Rhode Island; Corpus Christi, Texas, and countless other places with names that are rooted in religion. Yet few would argue that this history requires that these names be erased from the map. Or take a motto like Arizona's, "Ditat Deus" ("God enriches"), adopted in 1864, or a flag like Maryland's, which has included two crosses since 1904. Familiarity itself can become a reason for preservation. When time's passage imbues a religiously expressive monument, symbol, or practice with this kind of familiarity and historical significance, removing it may no longer appear neutral, especially to the local community for which it has taken on particular meaning. A government that roams the land, tearing down monuments with religious symbolism and scrubbing away any reference to the divine will strike many as aggressively hostile to religion.

These considerations show that retaining established, religiously expressive monuments, symbols, and practices is quite different from erecting or adopting new ones. The passage of time gives rise to a strong presumption of constitutionality.

C

The role of the cross in World War I memorials is illustrative of each of the four preceding considerations. Immediately following the war, "communities across America built memorials to commemorate those who had served the nation in the struggle to make the world safe for democracy." Although not all communities included a cross in their memorials, the cross had become a symbol closely linked to the war. The fallen soldiers' final resting places abroad were marked by white crosses or Stars of David. The solemn image of endless rows of white crosses became inextricably linked with and symbolic of the ultimate price paid by 116,000 soldiers. This relationship between the cross and the war undoubtedly influenced the design of the many war memorials that sprang up.

This is not to say that the cross's association with the war was the sole or dominant motivation for the inclusion of the symbol in every World War I memorial. But the passage of time means that testimony from those actually involved in the decisionmaking process is generally unavailable, and attempting to uncover their motivations invites speculation. And no matter what the original purposes for the erection of a monument, a community may wish to preserve it for different reasons, such as historic preservation and traffic-safety concerns. In addition, the passage of time may have altered the area surrounding a monument in ways that change its meaning and provide new reasons for its preservation. Such changes are relevant here, since the Bladensburg Cross now sits at a busy traffic intersection, and numerous additional monuments are located nearby. Even the AHA is not offended by the sight of the Argonne Cross or the Canadian Cross of Sacrifice, both Latin crosses commemorating World War I that rest on public grounds in Arlington National Cemetery. The difference, according to the AHA, is that their location in a cemetery gives them a closer association with individual gravestones and interred soldiers. But a memorial's placement in a cemetery is not necessary to create such a connection. The parents and other relatives of many of the war dead lacked the means to travel to Europe to visit their graves, and the bodies of approximately 4,400 American soldiers were either never found or never identified. For many grieving relatives and friends, memorials took the place of gravestones. Whether in a cemetery or a city park, a World War I cross remains a memorial to the fallen.

Similar reasoning applies to other memorials and monuments honoring important figures in our Nation's history. When faith was important to the person whose life is commemorated, it is natural to include a symbolic reference to faith in the design of the memorial. For example, many memorials for Dr. Martin Luther King, Jr., make reference to his faith. National Statuary Hall in the Capitol honors a variety of religious figures: for example, Mother Joseph Pariseau kneeling in prayer; Po'Pay, a Pueblo religious leader with symbols of the Pueblo religion; Brigham Young, president of the Church of Jesus Christ of Latter-day Saints; and Father Eusebio Kino with a crucifix around his neck and his hand raised in blessing. These monuments honor men and women who have played an important role in the history of our country, and where religious symbols are included in the monuments, their presence acknowledges the centrality of faith to those whose lives are commemorated.

As World War I monuments have endured through the years and become a familiar part of the physical and cultural landscape, requiring their removal would not be viewed by many as a neutral act. An alteration like the one entertained by the Fourth Circuit—amputating the arms of the Cross—would be seen by many as profoundly disrespectful. A monument may express many purposes and convey many different messages, both secular and religious. Thus, a campaign to obliterate items with religious associations may evidence hostility to religion even if those religious associations are no longer in the forefront. Few would say that the State of California is attempting to convey a religious message by retaining the names given to many of the State's cities by their original Spanish settlers—San Diego, Los Angeles, Santa Barbara, San Jose, San Francisco. But it would be something else entirely if the State undertook to change all those names. The same is true about monuments to soldiers who sacrificed their lives for this country more than a century ago.

D

While *Lemon* ambitiously attempted to find a grand unified theory of the Establishment Clause, in later cases, we have taken a more modest approach that focuses on the particular issue at hand and looks to history for guidance. In *Marsh v. Chambers*, 463 U. S. 783 (1983), the Court upheld the Nebraska Legislature's practice of beginning each session with a prayer by an official chaplain, and in so holding, the Court conspicuously ignored *Lemon*. Instead, the Court found it highly persuasive that Congress for more than 200 years had opened its sessions with a prayer and that many state legislatures had followed suit. We took a similar approach recently in *Town of Greece*, 572 U. S., at 577. We reached these results even though it was clear that prayer is by definition religious. As the Court put it in *Town of Greece*: "*Marsh* must not be understood as permitting a practice that would amount to a constitutional violation if not for its historical foundation." "The case teaches that the Establishment Clause must be interpreted 'by reference to historical practices and understandings'" and the decision of the First Congress to "provide for the appointment of chaplains only days after approving language for the First Amendment demonstrates that the Framers considered legislative prayer a benign acknowledgment of religion's role in society."

The prevalence of this philosophy at the time of the founding is reflected in other prominent actions taken by the First Congress. It requested—and President Washington proclaimed—a national day of prayer, and it reenacted the Northwest Territory Ordinance, which provided that "religion, morality, and knowledge, being necessary to good government and the happiness of mankind, schools and the means of education shall forever be encouraged," 1 Stat. 52, n. (a). President Washington echoed this sentiment in his Farewell Address, calling religion and morality "indispensable supports" to "political prosperity." The First Congress looked to these "supports" when it chose to begin its sessions with a prayer. This practice was designed to solemnize congressional meetings, unifying those in attendance as they pursued a common goal of good governance. To achieve that purpose, legislative prayer needed to be inclusive rather than divisive, and that required a determined effort even in a society that was much more religiously homogeneous than ours today. Since then, Congress has welcomed guest chaplains from a variety of faiths, including Islam, Hinduism, Buddhism, and Native American religions. In *Town of Greece*, there was no disagreement that the Establishment Clause permits a nondiscriminatory practice of prayer at the beginning of a town council session. What mattered was that the town's practice "fit within the tradition long followed in Congress and the state legislatures." The practice begun by the First Congress stands out as an example of respect and tolerance for differing views, an honest endeavor to achieve inclusivity and nondiscrimination, and a recognition of the important role that religion plays in the lives of many Americans. Where categories of monuments, symbols, and practices with a longstanding history follow in that tradition, they are likewise constitutional.

III

The Bladensburg Cross does not violate the Establishment Clause. The Bladensburg Cross carries special significance in commemorating World War I. Due in large part to the image of the simple wooden crosses that originally marked the graves of American soldiers killed in the war, the cross became a symbol of their sacrifice, and the design of the Bladensburg Cross must be understood in light of that background. That the cross originated as a Christian symbol and retains that meaning in many contexts does not change the fact that the symbol took on an added secular meaning when used in World War I memorials. With the passage of time, it has acquired historical importance. It reminds the people of Bladensburg and surrounding areas of the deeds of their predecessors and of the sacrifices they made in a war fought in the name of democracy. As long as it is retained in its original place and form, it speaks as well of the community that erected the monument nearly a century ago and has maintained it ever since. The memorial represents what the relatives, friends, and neighbors of the fallen soldiers felt at the time and how they chose to express their sentiments. The monument has acquired additional layers of historical meaning in subsequent years. The Cross now stands among memorials to veterans of later wars. It has become part of the community. The monument would not serve that role if its design had deliberately disrespected area soldiers who perished in World War I. More than 3,500 Jewish soldiers gave their lives for the United States in that conflict, and some have wondered whether the names of any Jewish soldiers from the area were deliberately left off the list on the memorial or whether the names of any Jewish soldiers were included on the Cross against the wishes of their families. There is no evidence that either thing was done, and one of the local American Legion leaders responsible for the Cross's construction was a Jewish veteran.

The AHA's brief strains to connect the Bladensburg Cross and even the American Legion with anti-Semitism and the Ku Klux Klan, but the AHA's disparaging intimations have no evidentiary support. The monument was dedicated on July 12, 1925, during a period when the country was experiencing heightened racial and religious animosity. Membership in the Ku Klux Klan, which preached hatred of Blacks, Catholics, and Jews, was at its height. Just two weeks after the dedication of the Bladensburg Cross and less than 10 miles away, some 30,000 robed Klansmen marched down Pennsylvania Avenue in the Nation's Capital. But the Bladensburg Cross memorial included the names of both Black and White soldiers who had given their lives in the war; and despite the fact that Catholics and Baptists at that time were not exactly in the habit of participating together in ecumenical services, the ceremony dedicating the Cross began with an invocation by a Catholic priest and ended with a benediction by a Baptist pastor. We can never know for certain what was in the minds of those responsible for the memorial, but in light of what we know about this ceremony, we can make out a picture of a community that, at the moment, was united by grief and patriotism and rose above the divisions of the day. It is natural and appropriate for those seeking to honor the deceased to invoke the symbols that signify what death meant for those who are memorialized. In some circumstances, the exclusion of any such recognition would make a memorial incomplete. This explains why Holocaust memorials invariably include Stars of David or other symbols of Judaism. And this is why the memorial for soldiers from the Bladensburg community features the cross—the same symbol that marks the graves of so many of their comrades near the battlefields where they fell.

IV

The cross is undoubtedly a Christian symbol, but that fact should not blind us to everything else that the Bladensburg Cross has come to represent. For some, that monument is a symbolic resting place for ancestors who never returned home. For others, it is a place for the community to gather and honor all veterans and their sacrifices for our Nation. For others still, it is a historical landmark. For many of these people, destroying or defacing the Cross that has stood undisturbed for nearly a century would not be neutral and would not further the ideals of respect and tolerance embodied in the First Amendment. For all these reasons, the Cross does not offend the Constitution.

We reverse the judgment of the Court of Appeals for the Fourth Circuit and remand the cases for further proceedings.

It is so ordered.

Justice BREYER, with whom Justice KAGAN joins, concurring.

The Court must consider each case in light of the basic purposes that the Religion Clauses were meant to serve: assuring religious liberty and tolerance for all, avoiding religiously based social conflict, and maintaining that separation of church and state that allows each to flourish in its "separate sphere." Allowing the State of Maryland to display and maintain the Peace Cross poses no threat to those ends. In light of all these circumstances, the Peace Cross cannot reasonably be understood as "a government effort to favor a particular religious sect" or to "promote religion over nonreligion." And ordering its removal or alteration at this late date would signal "a hostility toward religion that has no place in our Establishment Clause traditions." The case would be different if there were evidence that the organizers had "deliberately disrespected" members of minority faiths or if the Cross had been erected only recently. But those are not the circumstances, and I see no reason to order this cross torn down simply because other crosses would raise constitutional concerns. The Court appropriately "looks to history for guidance," but it upholds the constitutionality of the Peace Cross only after considering its particular historical context and its long-held place in the community. A newer memorial, erected under different circumstances, would not necessarily be permissible under this approach.

Justice KAVANAUGH, concurring.

Each category of Establishment Clause cases has its own principles based on history, tradition, and precedent. If the challenged government practice is not coercive and if it (i) is rooted in history and tradition; or (ii) treats religious people, organizations, speech, or activity equally to comparable secular people, organizations, speech, or activity; or (iii) represents a permissible legislative accommodation or exemption from a generally applicable law, then there ordinarily is no Establishment Clause violation. The practice of displaying religious memorials, particularly religious war memorials, on public land is not coercive and is rooted in history and tradition. The Bladensburg Cross commemorates soldiers who gave their lives for America in World War I. The Bladensburg Cross is constitutional. At the same time, I have deep respect for the plaintiffs' sincere objections to seeing the cross on public land. I have great respect for the Jewish war veterans who say that the cross on public land sends a message of exclusion. I fully understand the deeply religious nature of the cross. A case like this is difficult because it represents a clash of genuine and important interests. Applying our precedents, we uphold the constitutionality of the cross.

Justice KAGAN, concurring in part.

I find much to admire in [the] emphasis on whether longstanding monuments, symbols, and practices reflect "respect and tolerance for differing views, an honest endeavor to achieve inclusivity and nondiscrimination, and a recognition of the important role that religion plays in the lives of many Americans." The opinion shows sensitivity to and respect for this Nation's pluralism, and the values of neutrality and inclusion that the First Amendment demands.

Justice THOMAS, concurring in the judgment.

The Establishment Clause resists incorporation against the States. Even if the Clause applied to state and local governments in some fashion, the *sine qua non* of an establishment of religion is "actual legal coercion." Respondents briefly suggest that the government's spending their tax dollars on maintaining the Bladensburg Cross represents coercion, but they have not demonstrated that maintaining a religious display on public property shares any of the historical characteristics of an establishment of religion. The local commission has not attempted to control religious doctrine or personnel, compel religious observance, single out a particular religious denomination for exclusive state subsidization, or punish dissenting worship. Lacking any characteristics of "the coercive state establishments that existed at the founding," the Bladensburg Cross is constitutional. I would overrule the *Lemon* test in all contexts. Because *Lemon* is not good law, we ought to say so.

Justice GORSUCH, with whom Justice THOMAS joins, concurring in the judgment.

Lemon is "flawed in its fundamentals," has proved "unworkable in practice," and is "inconsistent with our history and our precedents." In place of *Lemon*, Part II–D of the plurality opinion relies on a more modest, historically sensitive approach, recognizing that "the Establishment Clause must be interpreted by reference to historical practices and understandings." A practice consistent with our nation's traditions is just as permissible whether undertaken today or 94 years ago.

Justice GINSBURG, with whom Justice SOTOMAYOR joins, dissenting.

When a cross is displayed on public property, the government may be presumed to endorse its religious content. A display does not run afoul of the neutrality principle if its "setting plausibly indicates" that the government has not sought "either to adopt a religious message or to urge its acceptance by others." *Van Orden*, 545 U. S., at 737 (Souter, J., dissenting). The "typical museum setting," for example, "though not neutralizing the religious content of a religious painting, negates any message of endorsement of that content." *Lynch v. Donnelly*, 465 U. S. 668, 692 (1984) (O'Connor, J., concurring). "For nearly two millennia," the Latin cross has been the "defining symbol" of Christianity evoking the foundational claims of that faith. Christianity teaches that Jesus Christ was "a divine Savior" who "illuminated a path toward salvation and redemption." Central to the religion are the beliefs that "the son of God," Jesus Christ, "died on the cross," that "he rose from the dead," and that "his death and resurrection offer the possibility of eternal life." "From earliest times," Christianity was known as "the religion of the cross." Christians wear crosses, not as an ecumenical symbol, but to proclaim their adherence to Christianity. The principal symbol of Christianity should not loom over public thoroughfares, suggesting official recognition of that religion's paramountcy. The cross on a grave "says that a Christian is buried here," and "commemorates that person's death by evoking a conception of salvation and eternal life reserved for Christians." The cross affirms that, thanks to the soldier's embrace of Christianity, he will be rewarded with eternal life. "Making a Latin cross a war memorial does not make the cross secular," it "makes the war memorial sectarian." Recognizing that a Latin cross does not belong on a public highway or building does not mean the monument must be "torn down." The violation may be cured by relocating the monument to private land or by transferring ownership of the land and monument to a private party.

Notes and Questions

1. *The Church Veto.* In *Larkin v. Grendel's Den, Inc.*, 459 U.S. 116 (1982), a Massachusetts law vested in the governing bodies of churches and schools the power to veto applications for liquor licenses within a 500-foot radius of the church or school. The Court struck down the law: "§16C is not simply a legislative exercise of zoning power. The statute, by delegating a governmental power to religious institutions, inescapably implicates the Establishment Clause. The mere appearance of a joint exercise of legislative authority by Church and State provides a significant symbolic benefit to religion in the minds of some by reason of the power conferred. The Act substitutes the unilateral and absolute power of a church for the reasoned decisionmaking of a public legislative body acting on evidence and guided by standards." Justice Rehnquist dissented: "The state does not 'advance' religion by making provision for those who wish to engage in religious activities to be unmolested by activities at a neighboring bar or tavern."

2. *The Significance of Text.* Should it matter whether a Ten Commandments display includes an *English* version of the text of the Commandments? Would the frieze on the wall of the U.S. Supreme Court be unconstitutional if it included the actual words of the Ten Commandments in English rather than in Hebrew? What significance do you attach to the fact that *Van Orden* contained the words of the Ten Commandments but nonetheless was upheld?

∾ PROBLEMS ∾

1. *The Ten Commandments and the Education for a Better America Act.* What, if anything, should Congress say in the proposed legislation about whether schools may (or may not) erect displays of the Ten Commandments? Would it be permissible for the Act to allow parochial schools that receive federal funding to erect such displays?

2. *More on the Ten Commandments.* Suppose that, following the decision in *McCreary County,* the County decides to post a new display. Before doing so, the County specifically and unequivocally repudiates all religious motives in a proclamation. However, the display is the same display that was invalidated in the *McCreary County* case. *See* Peter Smith, *Commandments Case Back: 2 Counties Contend Motives Changed,* Louisville Courier-Journal, B-1, c. 2-5, Aug. 7, 2008. Is the new display permissible under the Establishment Clause?

3. *More on the Ten Commandments.* Suppose that another Kentucky county, Jefferson County (where Louisville is located), decides to erect a display that is similar to the third display in *McCreary County.* However, it makes no mention of the religious aspects of the display and otherwise expresses no religious purpose. Instead, Jefferson County focuses on the secular aspects of the Ten Commandments as reflected in the *Van Orden* and *McCreary County* opinions. Would the display be constitutional?

4. *Good Friday Closings.* Is it permissible for Jefferson County, Kentucky, to close all county offices on Good Friday? The county designates that day as a "spring holiday." Is such a closing permissible? What significance would you attach to the fact that a high percentage of residents are Christian, and absenteeism on Good Friday has been a recurring problem?

B. THE FREE EXERCISE CLAUSE

The American colonists demanded protections for religious freedom because of a history of religious persecution in Europe and in the American colonies. These demands led to the inclusion of the Free Exercise Clause in the First Amendment. *See Everson v. Board of Education,* 330 U.S. 1 (1947). Because there was such widespread agreement about the need for religious freedom, the Framers left little evidence of their intent regarding the meaning of the Free Exercise Clause. As a result, although there is widespread agreement that the clause protects religious thought, there is uncertainty about the extent to which it protects religious conduct. Even if it protects "conduct," the clause does not protect all conduct (e.g., the state can prohibit a religion that believes in human sacrifice from actually killing people). In this section, we explore the limits of the Free Exercise Clause.

1. Burdens on Religion

Free exercise cases usually arise when a law prohibits an individual from engaging in conduct required by religious beliefs, or requires conduct prohibited by religious beliefs (i.e., compulsory school attendance laws or laws denying unemployment compensation to those who refuse to work on Saturdays). Typically, in drafting these laws, the legislature was not trying to prohibit or burden a religious practice, but was instead trying to deal with some secular problem (e.g., parents who fail to educate their children or workers who unreasonably refuse to educate their children). A problem develops when the laws incidentally affect religious practices. At that point, a court must decide whether the individual interest in the free exercise of religion should prevail, or the state's interest in compliance prevails over the individual's religious interest.

a. Early Cases

Litigation about free exercise issues has arisen in a variety of contexts. In, for example, *Reynolds v. United States*, 98 U.S. (8 Otto) 145, 25 L.Ed. 244 (1878), a conflict arose between a federal law prohibiting polygamy and a Mormon who believed that his religion required him to engage in that practice. The Court upheld the federal law distinguishing between "belief" and "conduct," and concluding that the government has broad authority to prohibit religious "conduct." The Court stated that "laws are made for the government of actions, and while they cannot interfere with mere religious beliefs and opinions, they may with practices." *See also Davis v. Beason*, 133 U.S. 333 (1890).

Reynolds's "belief-conduct" distinction was modified and partially rejected in the Court's later decision in *Cantwell v. Connecticut*, 310 U.S. 296 (1940). In that case, a man (Cantwell) and his two sons, all Jehovah's Witnesses and ordained ministers, were arrested in Connecticut, and convicted of attempting to sell religious magazines without a permit and of disorderly conduct. The Court concluded that the statute prohibiting solicitation violated Cantwell's right to free exercise: "The First Amendment embraces two concepts,—freedom to believe and freedom to act. The first is absolute but, in the nature of things, the second cannot be. Conduct remains subject to regulation for the protection of society." However, the right to control religious conduct was not unfettered: "A state may not, by statute, wholly deny the right to preach or to disseminate religious views. It is equally clear that a state may by general and non-discriminatory legislation regulate the times, the places, and the manner of soliciting upon its streets, and of holding meetings thereon; and may in other respects safeguard the peace, good order and comfort of the community, without unconstitutionally invading the liberties protected by the Fourteenth Amendment." The Court struck down the solicitation statute because it gave local officials too much discretion to grant or deny permission. *Cantwell* is also important because it extended the Free Exercise Clause's protections to the states.

b. From *Sherbert* to *Smith*

For several decades, the Court was more accepting of free exercise claims and tended to impose heightened scrutiny on laws that infringed religious beliefs. The following case is illustrative.

Sherbert v. Verner

374 U.S. 398 (1963)

Mr. Justice BRENNAN delivered the opinion of the Court.

Appellant, a member of the Seventh-day Adventist Church, was discharged by her South Carolina employer because she would not work on Saturday, the Sabbath Day of her faith. When she was unable to obtain other employment because from conscientious scruples she would not take Saturday work, she filed a claim for unemployment compensation benefits under the South Carolina Unemployment Compensation Act. Appellee Employment Security Commission found that appellant's restriction upon her availability for Saturday work brought her within the provision disqualifying for benefits insured workers who fail, without good cause, to accept "suitable work when offered by the employment office or the employer." The Commission's finding was affirmed by the South Carolina courts.

Appellant's conscientious objection to Saturday work constitutes no conduct prompted by religious principles of a kind within the reach of state legislation. If, therefore, the decision of the South Carolina Supreme Court is to withstand appellant's constitutional challenge, it must be either because her disqualification as a beneficiary represents no infringement by the State of her constitutional rights of free exercise, or because any incidental burden on the free exercise of appellant's religion may be justified by a "compelling state interest in the regulation of a subject within the State's constitutional power to regulate." *NAACP v. Button*, 371 U.S. 415 (1963).

We turn first to the question whether the disqualification for benefits imposes any burden on the free exercise of appellant's religion. We think it is clear that it does. The consequences of such a disqualification to religious principles and practices may be only an indirect result of welfare legislation within the State's general competence to enact; it is true that no criminal sanctions directly compel appellant to work a six-day week. But here not only is it apparent that appellant's declared ineligibility for benefits derives solely from the practice of her religion, but the pressure upon her to forego that practice is unmistakable. The ruling forces her to choose between following the precepts of her religion and forfeiting benefits, and abandoning one of the precepts of her religion in order to accept work. Governmental imposition of such a choice puts the same kind of burden upon the free exercise of religion as would a fine imposed against appellant for her Saturday worship.

Nor may the South Carolina court's construction of the statute be saved from constitutional infirmity on the ground that unemployment compensation benefits are not appellant's "right" but merely a "privilege." It is too late in the day to doubt that the liberties of religion and expression may be infringed by the denial of or placing of conditions upon a benefit or privilege. South Carolina expressly saves the Sunday worshipper from having to make the kind of choice which we here hold infringes the Sabbatarian's religious liberty. When in times of "national emergency" the textile plants are authorized by the State Commissioner of Labor to operate on Sunday, "no employee shall be required to work on Sunday who is conscientiously opposed to Sunday work; and if any employee should refuse to work on Sunday on account of conscientious." S.C. Code, §64-4. The unconstitutionality of the disqualification of the Sabbatarian is thus compounded by the religious discrimination which South Carolina's general statutory scheme necessarily effects.

It is basic that no showing merely of a rational relationship to some colorable state interest would suffice in this highly sensitive constitutional area, "only the gravest abuses, endangering paramount interest, give occasion for permissible limitation." No such abuse or danger has been advanced in the present case. Appellees suggest no more than a possibility that the filing of fraudulent claims by unscrupulous claimants feigning religious objections to Saturday work might not only dilute the unemployment compensation fund but also hinder the scheduling by employers of necessary Saturday work. Even if the possibility of spurious claims did exist, it would plainly be incumbent upon the appellees to demonstrate that no alternative forms of regulation would combat such abuses without infringing First Amendment rights.

The state interest asserted in the present case is wholly dissimilar to the interests which were found to justify the less direct burden upon religious practices in *Braunfeld*. The Court recognized that the Sunday closing law which that decision sustained undoubtedly served "to make the practice of (the Orthodox Jewish merchants') religious beliefs more expensive." But the statute was nevertheless saved by a countervailing factor which finds no equivalent in the instant case — a strong state interest in providing one uniform day of rest for all workers. That secular objective could be achieved, the Court found, only by declaring Sunday to be that day of rest. Requiring exemptions for Sabbatarians, while theoretically possible, appeared to present an administrative problem of such magnitude, or to afford the exempted class so great a competitive advantage, that such a requirement would have rendered the entire statutory scheme unworkable. In the present case no such justifications underlie the determination of the state court that appellant's religion makes her ineligible to receive benefits.

In holding as we do, we are not fostering the "establishment" of the Seventh-day Adventist religion in South Carolina, for the extension of unemployment benefits to Sabbatarians in common with Sunday worshippers reflects nothing more than the governmental obligation of neutrality in the face of religious differences, and does not represent that involvement of religious with secular institutions which it is the object of the Establishment Clause to forestall. No State may "exclude individual Catholics, Lutherans, Mohammedans, Baptists, Jews, Methodists, Non-believers, Presbyterians, or the members of any other faith, because of their faith, or lack of it, from receiving the benefits of public welfare legislation." *Everson v. Board of Education*, 330 U.S. 1 (1947).

The judgment of the South Carolina Supreme Court is reversed and the case is remanded for further proceedings not inconsistent with this opinion. It is so ordered.

Reversed and remanded.

Mr. Justice DOUGLAS, *concurring.*

This case is resolvable solely in terms of what government may not do to an individual in violation of his religious scruples. If appellant is otherwise qualified for unemployment benefits, payments will be made to her not as a Seventh-day Adventist, but as an unemployed worker.

Mr. Justice HARLAN, whom Mr. Justice WHITE joins, *dissenting.*

This decision necessarily overrules *Braunfeld.* The meaning of today's holding is that the State must furnish unemployment benefits to one who is unavailable for work if the unavailability stems from the exercise of religious convictions. The State, in other words, must single out for financial assistance those whose behavior is religiously motivated, even though it denies such assistance to others whose identical behavior (in this case, inability to work no Saturdays) is not religiously motivated. Those situations in which the Constitution may require special treatment on account of religion are, in my view, few and far between. Such compulsion in the present case is particularly inappropriate in light of the indirect, remote, and insubstantial effect of the decision below on the exercise of appellant's religion and in light of the direct financial assistance to religion that today's decision requires.

BACKGROUND
Unemployment Compensation

Over the years, a number of free exercise cases have involved disputes about unemployment compensation. *See Frazee v. Illinois Department of Employment Security*, 489 U.S. 829 (1989) (Frazee, who refused employment because he would have been forced to work on his sabbath Sunday, was held to be entitled to unemployment benefits); *Hobbie v. Unemployment Appeals Commission*, 480 U.S. 136 (1987) (Hobbie, who was discharged because she refused to work on a Friday evening or Saturday because of her Seventh-day Adventist faith, was entitled to unemployment compensation).

Notes and Questions

1. *Child Labor Laws.* In *Prince v. Massachusetts,* 321 U.S. 158 (1944), Sarah Prince was charged under child labor laws with having her nine-year-old daughter help her sell religious magazines. Prince challenged the laws based on her free exercise rights (the duty to bring up the child in the tenets and practices of the faith) as well as the girl's free exercise rights (the girl believed that it was her religious duty to perform this work and that failure would bring condemnation "to everlasting destruction at Armageddon"). The Court upheld the child labor laws as applied to the mother: "The power of the state to control the conduct of children reaches beyond the scope of its authority over adults, as is true in the case of other freedoms, and the rightful boundary of its power has not been crossed in this case." Justice Murphy dissented: "Religious training and activity, whether performed by adult or child, are protected except insofar as they violate reasonable regulations adopted for the protection of the public health, morals and welfare."

2. *Free Exercise Losers?* Some argue that the free exercise "losers" have generally been minorities (e.g., Mormons and Jehovah's Witnesses). *See* Paul Marcus, *The Forum of Conscience: Applying Standards Under the Free Exercise Clause,* 1973 Duke L.J. 1217 ("These groups e.g., Mormons and Jehovah's Witnesses, as well as groups with more unusual views, have historically failed miserably in their free exercise arguments. While the courts had generally been tolerant toward religious minorities, the caveat must be added that the minority must not be too small or too eccentric."). If that is the case, how would you explain this tendency?

∾ PROBLEM: THE ATHEIST ∾

When an atheist is summoned for jury duty, she refuses to take an oath that contains a reference to God. She is then asked to raise her hand and take an oath that has no reference to God. She again refuses, claiming that she considers any affirmation to be religious. Under the Free Exercise Clause, can the court require an atheist to take at least the latter oath? Is there a suitable alternative? If so, what?

Wisconsin v. Yoder

406 U.S. 205 (1972)

Mr. Chief Justice Burger delivered the opinion of the Court.

Respondents are members of the Old Order Amish religion. Wisconsin's compulsory school-attendance law required them to send their children to school until reaching age 16 but respondents refused to send their children to school after the eighth grade. Respondents were convicted of violating the compulsory-attendance law and were fined the sum of $5 each. Respondents defended on the ground that the compulsory-attendance law violated their rights under the First and Fourteenth Amendments.

Old Order Amish communities are characterized by a fundamental belief that salvation requires life in a church community separate and apart from the world and worldly influence. This concept of life aloof from the world and its values is central to their faith. A related feature of Old Order Amish is their devotion to a life in harmony with nature and the soil. Amish beliefs require members of the community to make their living by farming or closely related activities. Amish objection to formal education beyond the eighth grade is grounded in these central religious concepts. They object to high school, and higher education generally, because the values are in marked variance with Amish values and the Amish way of life; they view secondary school education as an impermissible exposure of their children to a "worldly" influence in conflict with their beliefs. High school emphasizes intellectual and scientific accomplishments, self-distinction, competitiveness, worldly success, and social life with other students. Amish society emphasizes informal learning-through-doing; a life of "goodness," rather than a life of intellect; wisdom, rather than technical knowledge; community welfare, rather than competition; and separation from, rather than integration with, contemporary worldly society.

Formal high school education beyond the eighth grade is contrary to Amish beliefs, not only because it places Amish children in an environment hostile to Amish beliefs with increasing emphasis on competition in class work and sports and with pressure to conform to the styles, manners, and ways of the peer group, but also because it takes them away from their community, physically and emotionally, during the crucial and formative adolescent period of life. During this period, the children must acquire Amish attitudes favoring manual work and self-reliance and the specific skills needed to perform the adult role of an Amish farmer or housewife. They must learn to enjoy physical labor. Once a child has learned basic reading, writing, and elementary mathematics, these traits, skills, and attitudes admittedly fall within the category of those best learned through example and "doing" rather than in a classroom. At this time in life, the Amish child must also grow in his faith and his relationship to the Amish community if he is to be prepared to accept the heavy obligations imposed by adult baptism. High school attendance with teachers who are not of the Amish faith — and may even be hostile to it — interposes a serious barrier to the integration of the Amish child into the Amish religious community.

The Amish do not object to elementary education through the first eight grades because they agree that their children must have basic skills in the "three R's" in order to read the Bible, to be good farmers and citizens, and to be able to deal with non-Amish people in the course of daily affairs. They view such a basic education as acceptable because it does not significantly expose their children to worldly values or interfere with their development in the Amish community during the crucial adolescent period. Wherever possible they have established their own elementary schools in many respects like the small local schools of the past.

Compulsory high school attendance could not only result in great psychological harm to Amish children, because of the conflicts it would produce, but would also ultimately result in the destruction of the Old Order Amish church community. An expert stated that the Amish succeed in preparing their high school age children to be productive members of the Amish community. He described their system of learning through doing the skills directly relevant to their adult roles as "ideal" and perhaps superior to ordinary high school education. The Amish have an excellent record as law-abiding and generally self-sufficient members of society.

The Wisconsin Circuit Court affirmed the convictions. The Wisconsin Supreme Court reversed.

Providing public schools ranks at the very apex of the function of a State. Yet even this paramount responsibility must yield to the right of parents to provide an equivalent education in a privately operated system. In *Pierce v. Society of Sisters*, 268 U.S. 510 (1925), the Court held that Oregon's statute compelling attendance in a public school from age eight to age 16 unreasonably interfered with the interest of parents in directing the rearing of their off-spring, including their education in church-operated schools. The values of parental direction of the religious upbringing and education of their children in their early and formative years have a high place in our society. Thus, a State's interest in universal education, however highly we rank it, is not totally free from a balancing process when it impinges on fundamental rights and interests, such as those specifically protected by the Free Exercise Clause of the First Amendment, and the traditional interest of parents with respect to the religious upbringing of their children so long as they "prepare them for additional obligations."

In order for Wisconsin to compel school attendance beyond the eighth grade against a claim that such attendance interferes with the practice of a legitimate religious belief, it must appear either that the State does not deny the free exercise of religious belief by its requirement, or that there is a state interest of sufficient magnitude to override the interest claiming protection under the Free Exercise Clause. Only those interests of the highest order and those not otherwise served can overbalance legitimate claims to the free exercise of religion. However strong the State's interest in universal compulsory education, it is by no means absolute to the exclusion or subordination of all other interests.

If the Amish asserted their claims because of their subjective evaluation and rejection of the contemporary secular values accepted by the majority, much as Thoreau rejected the social values of his time and isolated himself at Walden Pond, their claims would not rest on a religious basis. Thoreau's choice was philosophical and personal rather than religious, and such belief does not rise to the demands of the Religion Clauses.

The traditional way of life of the Amish is not merely a matter of personal preference, but one of deep religious conviction, shared by an organized group, and intimately related to daily living. The Old Order Amish daily life and religious practice is a response to their literal interpretation of the Biblical injunction from the Epistle of Paul to the Romans, "be not conformed to this world." The Old Order Amish religion pervades and determines virtually their entire way of life, regulating it with the detail of the Talmudic diet through the strictly enforced rules of the church community.

Respondents' religious beliefs and attitude toward life, family, and home have remained constant—perhaps some would say static—in a period of unparalleled progress in human knowledge generally and great changes in education. Their church-oriented community, separated from the outside world and "worldly" influences, their attachment to nature and the soil, is a way inherently simple and uncomplicated, albeit difficult to preserve against the pressure to conform. Their rejection of telephones, automobiles, radios, and television, their mode of dress, of speech, their habits of manual work do indeed set them apart from much of contemporary society; these customs are both symbolic and practical.

As the society around the Amish has become more populous, urban, industrialized, and complex, particularly in this century, government regulation of human affairs has correspondingly become more detailed and pervasive. The Amish mode of life has thus come into conflict increasingly with requirements of contemporary society exerting a hydraulic insistence on conformity to majoritarian standards. So long as compulsory education laws were confined to eight grades of elementary basic education imparted in a nearby rural schoolhouse, with a large proportion of students of the Amish faith, the Old Order Amish had little basis to fear that school attendance would expose their children to the worldly influence they reject. But modern compulsory secondary education in rural areas is now largely carried on in a consolidated school, often remote from the student's home and alien to his daily home life. The values and programs of the modern secondary school are in sharp conflict with the fundamental mode of life mandated by the Amish religion; modern laws requiring compulsory secondary education have accordingly engendered great concern and conflict. Secondary schooling, by exposing Amish children to worldly influences in terms of attitudes, goals, and values contrary to beliefs, and by substantially interfering with the religious development of the Amish child and his integration into the way of life of the Amish faith community at the crucial adolescent stage of development, contravenes the basic religious tenets and practice of the Amish faith, both as to the parent and the child.

The impact of the compulsory-attendance law on respondents' practice of the Amish religion is not only severe, but inescapable, for the Wisconsin law affirmatively compels them, under threat of criminal sanction, to perform acts undeniably at odds with fundamental tenets of their religious beliefs. Nor is the impact of the compulsory-attendance law confined to grave interference with important Amish religious tenets from a subjective point of view. It carries with it precisely the kind of objective danger to the free exercise of religion that the First Amendment was designed to prevent. Compulsory school attendance to age 16 for Amish children carries with it a very real threat of undermining the Amish community and religious practice as they exist today; they must either abandon belief and be assimilated into society at large, or be forced to migrate to some other and more tolerant region. Enforcement of the State's requirement of compulsory formal education after the eighth grade would gravely endanger if not destroy the free exercise of respondents' religious beliefs.

Wisconsin argues that "actions," even though religiously grounded, are outside the protection of the First Amendment. But our decisions have rejected the idea that religiously grounded conduct is always outside the protection of the Free Exercise Clause. Nor can this case be disposed of on the grounds that Wisconsin's requirement for school attendance to age 16 applies uniformly to all citizens of the State and does not, on its face, discriminate against religions or a particular religion, or that it is motivated by legitimate secular concerns. A regulation neutral on its face may, in its application, nonetheless offend the constitutional requirement for governmental neutrality if it unduly burdens the free exercise of religion. The Court must not ignore the danger that an exception from a general obligation of citizenship on religious grounds may run afoul of the Establishment Clause, but that danger cannot be allowed to prevent any exception no matter how vital it may be to the protection of values promoted by the right of free exercise.

The State also argues that its interest in its system of compulsory education is so compelling that even the established religious practices of the Amish must give way. Where fundamental claims of religious freedom are at stake, we must searchingly examine the interests that the State seeks to promote by its requirement for compulsory education to age 16, and the impediment to those objectives that would flow from recognizing the claimed Amish exemption.

The State advances two primary arguments in support of its system of compulsory education. It notes that some degree of education is necessary to prepare citizens to participate effectively and intelligently in our open political system if we are to preserve freedom and independence. Further, education prepares individuals to be self-reliant and self-sufficient participants in society. We accept these propositions.

However, the evidence adduced by the Amish in this case is persuasively to the effect that an additional one or two years of formal high school for Amish children in place of their long-established program of informal vocational education would do little to serve those interests. It is one thing to say that compulsory education may be necessary when its goal is the preparation of the child for life in modern society as the majority live, but it is quite another if the goal of education be viewed as the preparation of the child for life in the separated agrarian community that is the keystone of the Amish faith.

The State attacks respondents' position as one fostering "ignorance" from which the child must be protected by the State. This argument does not square with the facts. The Amish community has been a highly successful social unit within our society, even if apart from the conventional "mainstream." Its members are productive and very law-abiding members of society; they reject public welfare in any of its usual modern forms. The Congress itself recognized their self-sufficiency by authorizing exemption of such groups as the Amish from the obligation to pay social security taxes.

It is neither fair nor correct to suggest that the Amish are opposed to education beyond the eighth grade level. They are opposed to conventional formal education of the type provided by a certified high school because it comes at the child's crucial adolescent period of religious development. An expert testified that their system of learning-by-doing was an "ideal system" of education in terms of preparing Amish children for life as adults in the Amish community. A way of life that is odd or even erratic is not to be condemned because it is different.

The State points to the possibility that some children will choose to leave the Amish community, and that if this occurs they will be ill-equipped for life. That argument is highly speculative. There is no evidence of the loss of Amish adherents by attrition, nor is there any showing that upon leaving the Amish community Amish children, with their practical agricultural training and habits of industry and self-reliance, would become burdens on society. There is nothing to suggest that the Amish qualities of reliability, self-reliance, and dedication to work would fail to find ready markets in today's society. Nor is there any basis for finding that an additional one or two years of formal school education beyond the eighth grade would serve to eliminate any such problem that might exist. The Amish alternative to formal secondary school education has enabled them to function effectively in their day-to-day life under self-imposed limitations on relations with the world, and to survive and prosper in contemporary society as a separate, sharply identifiable and highly self-sufficient community for more than 200 years in this country. This is strong evidence that they are capable of fulfilling the social and political responsibilities of citizenship without compelled attendance beyond the eighth grade at the price of jeopardizing their free exercise of religious belief.

Wisconsin's interest in compelling the school attendance of Amish children to age 16 emerges as somewhat less substantial than requiring such attendance for children generally. While agricultural employment is not totally outside the legitimate concerns of the child labor laws, employment of children under parental guidance and on the family farm from age 14 to age 16 is an ancient tradition that lies at the periphery of the objectives of such laws. There is no intimation that the Amish employment of their children on family farms is in any way deleterious to their health or that Amish parents exploit children at tender years. Our holding in no way determines the proper resolution of possible competing interests of parents, children, and the State in an appropriate state court proceeding in which the power of the State is asserted on the theory that Amish parents are preventing their minor children from attending high school despite their expressed desires to the contrary.

We hold that the First and Fourteenth Amendments prevent the State from compelling respondents to cause their children to attend formal high school to age 16.

Affirmed.

Mr. Justice WHITE, with whom Mr. Justice BRENNAN and Mr. Justice STEWART join, *concurring.*

Since the Amish children acquire the basic tools of literacy to survive in modern society by attending grades one through eight and since the deviation from the State's compulsory-education law is relatively slight, respondents must prevail, largely because "religious freedom is one of the highest values of our society." Cases like this inevitably involve the kind of close scrutiny of religious practices which the Court has been anxious to avoid. But such scrutiny is essential to implement free exercise values threatened by an otherwise neutral program instituted to foster some permissible, nonreligious state objective.

Mr. Justice DOUGLAS, *dissenting in part.*

If an Amish child desires to attend high school, and is mature enough, the State may override the parents' religiously motivated objections. The children themselves have constitutionally protectible interests. The emphasis on the "law and order" record of this Amish group of people is irrelevant. I am not at all sure how the Catholics, Episcopalians, the Baptists, Jehovah's Witnesses, the Unitarians, and my own Presbyterians would make out if subjected to such a test.

BACKGROUND
Old Order Amish and Social Security

In addition to *Yoder*, a number of other free exercise cases have involved the Old Order Amish. Illustrative is *United States v. Lee*, 455 U.S. 252 (1982), in which an Amish adherent objected to paying Social Security taxes on the basis that he was religiously precluded from receiving public insurance benefits, and he objected to the payment of taxes to support public insurance funds. The Court held that he was required to pay: "Because the social security system is nationwide, the governmental interest is apparent. Unlike the situation presented in *Yoder*, it would be difficult to accommodate the comprehensive social security system with myriad exceptions flowing from a wide variety of religious beliefs." In a similar vein, in *Jimmy Swaggart Ministries v. Board of Education*, 493 U.S. 378 (1990), the Court held that a religious organization was not entitled to an exemption from sales and use taxes on religious literature when the tax was applied to the sale of all goods and services.

∾ PROBLEMS ∾

1. *Old Order Amish and Buggy Reflectors.* Another area of disagreement between the Amish and the state involves traffic safety laws. For safety reasons,

some states require slow-moving vehicles to display fluorescent orange-red triangular emblems while traveling on state highways. The law is applied even to the Old Order Amish who drive horse-drawn buggies on public highways. The Amish object to the emblems because they believe that their religion prohibits them from displaying "loud colors" and "worldly symbols." The Amish do not object to lining the outside of their buggies with silver reflective tape or to adorning their buggies with lighted red lanterns. If the state deems these actions inadequate to protect the public interest in safety, can the state require the Amish to display the orange-red triangular emblem notwithstanding their religious beliefs?

2. *More on the Education for the Twenty-first Century Act.* In constructing the proposed legislation, should you (must you?) include any special accommodations for religion? If so, what accommodations?

Lyng v. Northwest Indian Cemetery Protective Association

485 U.S. 439 (1988)

Justice O'CONNOR delivered the opinion of the Court.

As part of a project to create a paved 75-mile road linking two California towns, the United States Forest Service upgraded 49 miles of previously unpaved roads on federal land. In order to complete this project (the G-O road), the Forest Service must build a 6-mile paved segment through the Chimney Rock section of the Six Rivers National Forest. In 1977, the Forest Service issued a draft environmental impact statement that discussed proposals for upgrading an existing unpaved road that runs through the Chimney Rock area. In response to comments on the draft statement, the Forest Service commissioned a study of American Indian cultural and religious sites in the area. The Hoopa Valley Indian Reservation adjoins the Six Rivers National Forest, and the Chimney Rock area has historically been used for religious purposes by Yurok, Karok, and Tolowa Indians. The study found that the entire area "is significant as an integral and indispensable part of Indian religious conceptualization and practice." Specific sites are used for certain rituals, and "successful use of the area is dependent upon and facilitated by certain qualities of the physical environment, the most important of which are privacy, silence, and an undisturbed natural setting." The study concluded that constructing a road along any of the available routes "would cause serious and irreparable damage to the sacred areas which are an integral and necessary part of the belief systems and lifeway of Northwest California Indian peoples." Accordingly, the report recommended that the G-O road not be completed.

In 1982, the Forest Service decided not to adopt this recommendation, and prepared a final environmental impact statement. The Regional Forester selected a route that avoided archeological sites and was removed as far as possible from the sites used by contemporary Indians for specific spiritual activities. Alternative routes that would have avoided the Chimney Rock area altogether were rejected because they would have required the acquisition of private land, had serious soil stability problems, and would in any event have traversed areas having ritualistic value to American Indians. At about the same time, the Forest Service adopted a management plan allowing for the harvesting of significant amounts of timber in this area of the forest. The management plan provided for one-half mile protective zones around all the religious sites identified in the report that had been commissioned in connection with the G-O road.

Respondents—an Indian organization, individual Indians, nature organizations and individual members of those organizations, and the State of California—challenged both the road-building and timber-harvesting decisions on Free Exercise grounds. The District Court issued a permanent injunction prohibiting the Government from constructing the Chimney Rock section of the G-O road or putting the timber-harvesting management plan into effect. The District Court's constitutional ruling was affirmed.

It is undisputed that the Indian respondents' beliefs are sincere and that the Government's proposed actions will have severe adverse effects on the practice of their religion. Those respondents contend that the burden on their religious practices is heavy enough to violate the Free Exercise Clause unless the Government can demonstrate a compelling need to complete the G-O road or to engage in timber harvesting in the Chimney Rock area. We disagree.

In *Bowen v. Roy*, 476 U.S. 693 (1986), we considered a challenge to a federal statute that required the States to use Social Security numbers in administering certain welfare programs. Two applicants contended that their religious beliefs prevented them from using a Social Security number for their 2-year-old daughter because the use of a numerical identifier would " 'rob the spirit' of their daughter and prevent her from attaining greater spiritual power." Similarly, in this case, it is said that disruption of the natural environment caused by the G-O road will diminish the sacredness of the area in question and create distractions that will interfere with "training and ongoing religious experience of individuals using sites within the area for personal medicine and growth and as integrated parts of a system of religious belief and practice which correlates ascending degrees of personal power with a geographic hierarchy of power." ("Scarred hills and mountains, and disturbed rocks destroy the purity of the sacred areas, and Indian consultants repeatedly stressed the need of a training doctor to be undistracted by such disturbance.") The Court rejected this kind of challenge in *Roy*:

> Just as the Government may not insist that the Roys engage in any set form of religious observance, they may not demand that the Government join in their chosen religious practices by refraining from using a number to identify their daughter. The Free Exercise Clause affords an individual protection from certain forms of governmental compulsion; it does not afford an individual a right to dictate the conduct of the Government's internal procedures.

The building of a road or the harvesting of timber on publicly owned land cannot meaningfully be distinguished from the use of a Social Security number in *Roy*. In both cases, the challenged Government action would interfere significantly with private persons' ability to pursue spiritual fulfillment according to their own religious beliefs. In neither case, however, would the affected individuals be coerced by the Government's action into violating their religious beliefs; nor would either governmental action penalize religious activity by denying any person an equal share of the rights, benefits, and privileges enjoyed by other citizens.

We are asked to distinguish *Roy* on the ground that the infringement on religious liberty here is "significantly greater," or on the ground that the Government practice in *Roy* was "purely mechanical" whereas this case involves "a case-by-case substantive determination as to how a particular unit of land will be managed." Similarly, we are told that this case can be distinguished from *Roy* because the proposed road will "physically destroy the environmental conditions and the privacy without which the religious practices cannot be conducted."

These efforts to distinguish *Roy* are unavailing. This Court cannot determine the truth of the underlying beliefs that led to the religious objections here or in *Roy*, and accordingly cannot weigh the adverse effects on the appellees in *Roy* and compare them with the adverse effects on the Indian respondents. Without the ability to make such comparisons, we cannot say that the one form of incidental interference with an individual's spiritual activities should be subjected to a different constitutional analysis than the other.

Respondents insist that that the courts below properly relied on a factual inquiry into the degree to which the Indians' spiritual practices would become ineffectual if the G-O road were built. Whatever may be the exact line between unconstitutional prohibitions on the free exercise of religion and the legitimate conduct by government of its own affairs, the location of the line cannot depend on measuring the effects of a governmental action on a religious objector's spiritual development. Government simply could not operate if it were required to satisfy every citizen's religious needs and desires. A broad range of government activities—from social welfare programs to foreign aid to conservation projects—will always be considered essential to the spiritual well-being of some citizens, often on the basis of sincerely held religious beliefs. Others will find the very same activities deeply offensive, and perhaps incompatible with their own search for spiritual fulfillment and with the tenets of their religion. The First Amendment must apply to all citizens alike, and it can give to none of them a veto over public programs that do not prohibit the free exercise of religion. The Constitution does not, and courts cannot, offer to reconcile the various competing demands on government, many of them rooted in sincere religious belief, that inevitably arise in so diverse a society as ours. That task, to the extent that it is feasible, is for the legislatures and other institutions.

Respondents stress the limits of the religious servitude that they are now seeking to impose on the Chimney Rock area of the Six Rivers National Forest. While defending an injunction against logging operations and the construction of a road, they apparently do not *at present* object to the area's being used by recreational visitors, other Indians, or forest rangers. Nothing in the principle for which they contend, however, would distinguish this case if they sought to exclude all human activity but their own from sacred areas of the public lands.

The Government's rights to the use of its own land need not and should not discourage it from accommodating religious practices like those engaged in by the Indian respondents. It is worth emphasizing that the Government has taken numerous steps in this very case to minimize the impact that construction of the G-O road will have on the Indians' religious activities. No sites where specific rituals take place were to be disturbed. In fact, a major factor in choosing among alternative routes for the road was the relation of the various routes to religious sites. Except for abandoning its project entirely, and thereby leaving the two existing segments of road to dead-end in the middle of a National Forest, it is difficult to see how the Government could have been more solicitous.

The dissent proposes a legal test under which it would decide which public lands are "central" or "indispensable" to which religions, and by implication which are "dispensable" or "peripheral," and would then decide which government programs are "compelling" enough to justify "infringement of those practices." The dissent thus offers us the prospect of this Court's holding that some sincerely held religious beliefs and practices are not "central" to certain religions, despite protestations to the contrary from the religious objectors who brought the lawsuit. We think such an approach cannot be squared with the Constitution or with our precedents, and that it would cast the Judiciary in a role that we were never intended to play.

The decision of the court below is reversed.

It is so ordered.

Justice BRENNAN, with whom Justice MARSHALL and Justice BLACKMUN join, *dissenting.*

Respondents have demonstrated that the Government's proposed activities will completely prevent them from practicing their religion, and such a showing entitles them to the protections of the Free Exercise Clause. The Court's refusal to recognize the constitutional dimension of respondents' injuries stems from its concern that acceptance of respondents' claim could potentially strip the Government of its ability to manage and use vast tracts of federal property. These concededly legitimate concerns represent yet another stress point in the longstanding conflict between two disparate cultures—the dominant Western culture, which views land in terms of ownership and use, and that of Native Americans, in which concepts of private property are not only alien, but contrary to a belief system that holds land sacred. The Court disclaims all responsibility for balancing these competing and potentially irreconcilable interests, choosing instead to turn this difficult task over to the Federal Legislature.

I believe it appropriate to require some showing of "centrality" before the Government can be required either to come forward with a compelling justification for its proposed use of federal land or to forego that use altogether. "Centrality," however, should not be equated with the survival or extinction of the religion itself. Native Americans consider all land sacred. Nevertheless, respondents deem certain lands more powerful and more directly related to their religious practices than others. It is not enough to allege simply that the land in question is held sacred. Adherents challenging a proposed use of federal land should be required to show that the decision poses a substantial and realistic threat of frustrating their religious practices. Once such a showing is made, the burden should shift to the Government to come forward with a compelling state interest sufficient to justify the infringement of those practices.

The Court today suggests that such an approach would place courts in the untenable position of deciding which practices and beliefs are "central" to a given faith and which are not. Courts need not undertake any such inquiries: like all other religious adherents, Native Americans would be the arbiters of which practices are central to their faith, subject only to the normal requirement that their claims be genuine and sincere. The Court's concern that the claims of Native Americans will place "religious servitudes" upon vast tracts of federal property cannot justify its refusal to recognize the constitutional injury respondents will suffer here. Should respondents or any other group seek to force the Government to protect their religious practices from the interference of private parties, such a demand would implicate not only the concerns of the Free Exercise Clause, but also those of the Establishment Clause as well. That case, however, is most assuredly not before us.

The Court holds that a federal land-use decision that promises to destroy an entire religion does not burden the practice of that faith in a manner recognized by the Free Exercise Clause. I *dissent.*

Notes

1. *The Army and the Yarmulke.* In *Goldman v. Weinberger,* 475 U.S. 503 (1986), a Jewish enlisted man in the U.S. Air Force wanted to wear a yarmulke in conjunction with his military uniform. He was prevented from doing so by an Air Force regulation mandating uniform dress by Air Force personnel. The Court concluded that "the military is, by necessity, a specialized society separate from civilian society" and that "the essence of military service is the subordination of the desires and interests of the individual to the needs of the service." Accordingly, the Court upheld the prohibition. Justice Brennan dissented: "It cannot be seriously contended that a serviceman in a yarmulke presents so extreme, so unusual, or so faddish an image that public confidence in his ability to perform his duties will be destroyed."

2. *Jumu'ah and Work Gangs. O'Lone v. Shabazz,* 482 U.S. 342 (1987), involved a challenge by members of the Islamic faith to prison policies requiring that prisoners who are transferred from maximum security to minimum security prisons be first assigned to labor groups that work outside the prison. The prison justified the regulation as a transitional rule designed to enable transferees to

adjust to a minimum security facility. The Muslim prisoners in the labor groups were thus precluded from attending Jumu'ah, a weekly Muslim service that was regularly held in the main prison building. Jumu'ah is mandatory under the Koran and must be held every Friday after the sun reaches its zenith and before the Asr, or afternoon prayer. Prison officials refused to allow "gang" workers to return to "the Farm" during the day because of security risks and administrative problems. Muslim prisoners sued, seeking an accommodation. The Court held that an accommodation was not required: "Lawful incarceration brings about the necessary withdrawal or limitation of many privileges and rights, a retraction justified by the considerations underlying our penal system. Evaluation of penological objectives is committed to the considered judgment of prison administrators." Justice Brennan dissented: "Jumu'ah is the central religious ceremony of Muslims."

c. Modern Cases

As *Sherbert* and *Yoder* reflect, the Court's early decisions balanced the governmental interest in imposing a requirement against the religious interest in an exemption, and often came down on the side of religion. The Court's approach began to shift with the following decision.

Employment Division v. Smith

494 U.S. 872 (1990)

Justice SCALIA delivered the opinion of the Court.

Oregon law prohibits the knowing or intentional possession of a "controlled substance" unless the substance has been prescribed by a medical practitioner. Persons who violate this provision by possessing a controlled substance listed on Schedule I are "guilty of a Class B felony." Included on the list of "controlled substances" is the drug peyote, a hallucinogen.

Respondents were fired from their jobs with a private drug rehabilitation organization because they ingested peyote for sacramental purposes at a ceremony of the Native American Church, of which both are members. When respondents applied for unemployment compensation, they were ineligible because they had been discharged for work-related "misconduct." The Oregon Court of Appeals. We granted certiorari.

Respondents' claim for relief rests on our decisions in *Sherbert v. Verner*, 374 U.S. 398 (1963), *Thomas v. Review Board*, 450 U.S. 707 (1981), and *Hobbie v. Unemployment Appeals Comm'n of Florida*, 480 U.S. 136 (1987), in which we held that a State could not condition the availability of unemployment insurance on an individual's willingness to forgo conduct required by his religion. But the conduct at issue in those cases was not prohibited by law.

Free exercise of religion means, first and foremost, the right to believe and profess whatever religious doctrine one desires. But the "exercise of religion" often involves not only belief and profession but the performance of (or abstention from) physical acts: assembling with others for a worship service, participating in sacramental use of bread and wine, proselytizing, abstaining from certain foods or certain modes of transportation. A State would be "prohibiting the free exercise of religion" if it sought to ban such acts or abstentions only when they are engaged in for religious reasons, or only because of the religious belief that they display. It would be unconstitutional, for example, to ban the casting of "statues that are to be used for worship purposes," or to prohibit bowing down before a golden calf.

Respondents contend that their religious motivation for using peyote places them beyond the reach of a criminal law that is not specifically directed at their religious practice, and that is concededly constitutional as applied to those who use the drug for other reasons. They assert that "prohibiting the free exercise of religion" includes requiring any individual to observe a generally applicable law that requires (or forbids) the performance of an act that his religious belief forbids (or requires). We do not think the words must be given that meaning. It is no more necessary to regard the collection of a general tax, for example, as "prohibiting the free exercise of religion" by those citizens who believe support of organized government to be sinful, than it is to regard the same tax as "abridging the freedom of the press" of those publishing companies that must pay the tax as a condition of staying in business. If prohibiting the exercise of religion (or burdening the activity of printing) is not the object of the tax but merely the incidental effect of a generally applicable and otherwise valid provision, the First Amendment has not been offended.

We have never held that an individual's religious beliefs excuse him from compliance with an otherwise valid law prohibiting conduct that the State is free to regulate. On the contrary, the record of more than a century of our free exercise jurisprudence contradicts that proposition. In *Reynolds v. United States*, 98 U.S. 145 (1879), we rejected the claim that criminal laws against polygamy could not be constitutionally applied to those whose religion commanded the practice. Subsequent decisions have held that the right of free exercise does not relieve an individual of the obligation to comply with a "valid and neutral law of general applicability on the ground that the law proscribes (or prescribes) conduct that his religion prescribes (or proscribes)." *United States v. Lee*, 455 U.S. 252, 263, n.3 (1982) (Stevens, J., concurring in judgment).

The only decisions in which we have held that the First Amendment bars application of a neutral, generally applicable law to religiously motivated action have involved not the Free Exercise Clause alone, but the Free Exercise Clause in conjunction with other constitutional protections, such as freedom of speech and of the press, *see Cantwell v. Connecticut*, 310 U.S. at 304-307 (invalidating a licensing system for religious and charitable solicitations under which the administrator had discretion to deny a license to any cause he deemed nonreligious), or the right of parents, acknowledged in *Pierce v. Society of Sisters*, 268 U.S. 510 (1925), to direct the education of their children. Some of our cases prohibiting compelled expression, decided exclusively upon free speech grounds, have also involved freedom of religion, *cf. Wooley v. Maynard*, 430 U.S. 705 (1977) (invalidating compelled display of a license plate slogan that offended individual religious beliefs); *West Virginia Bd. of Education v. Barnette*, 319 U.S. 624 (1943) (invalidating compulsory flag salute statute challenged by religious objectors). And it is easy to envision a case in which a challenge on freedom of association grounds would likewise be reinforced by Free Exercise Clause concerns.

The present case does not present such a hybrid situation, but a free exercise claim unconnected with any communicative activity or parental right. Respondents urge that when otherwise prohibitable conduct is accompanied by religious convictions, not only the convictions but the conduct itself must be free from governmental regulation. We have never held that, and decline to do so now. There being no contention that Oregon's drug law represents an attempt to regulate religious beliefs, the communication of religious beliefs, or the raising of one's children in those beliefs, the rule to which we have adhered ever since *Reynolds* plainly controls.

Respondents argue that even though exemption from generally applicable criminal laws need not automatically be extended to religiously motivated actors, at least the claim for a religious exemption must be evaluated under the balancing test set forth in *Sherbert*. Even if we were inclined to breathe into *Sherbert* some life beyond the unemployment compensation field, we would not apply it to require exemptions from a generally applicable criminal law. We conclude today that the sounder approach, and the approach in accord with the vast majority of our precedents, is to hold the test inapplicable to such challenges. The government's ability to enforce generally applicable prohibitions of socially harmful conduct, like its ability to carry out other aspects of public policy, "cannot depend on measuring the effects of a governmental action on a religious objector's spiritual development." To make an individual's obligation to obey such a law contingent upon the law's coincidence with his religious beliefs, except where the State's interest is "compelling"—permitting him, by virtue of his beliefs, "to become a law unto himself,"—contradicts both constitutional tradition and common sense.

The "compelling government interest" requirement seems benign, because it is familiar from other fields. But using it as the standard that must be met before the government may accord different treatment on the basis of race, or before the government may regulate the content of speech, is not remotely comparable to using it for the purpose asserted here. What it produces in those other fields—equality of treatment and an unrestricted flow of contending speech—are constitutional norms; what it would produce here—a private right to ignore generally applicable laws—is a constitutional anomaly.

Nor is it possible to limit the impact of respondents' proposal by requiring a "compelling state interest" only when the conduct prohibited is "central" to the individual's religion. It is no more appropriate for judges to determine the "centrality" of religious beliefs before applying a "compelling interest" test in the free exercise field, than it would be for them to determine the "importance" of ideas before applying the "compelling interest" test in the free speech field.

If the "compelling interest" test is to be applied at all, it must be applied across the board, to all actions thought to be religiously commanded. Moreover, if "compelling interest" really means what it says (and watering it down here would subvert its rigor in the other fields where it is applied), many laws will not meet the test. Any society adopting such a system would be courting anarchy, but that danger increases in direct proportion to the society's diversity of religious beliefs, and its determination to coerce or suppress none of them. The rule respondents favor would open the prospect of constitutionally required religious exemptions from civic obligations of almost every conceivable kind—ranging from compulsory military service, to the payment of taxes, to health and safety regulation such as manslaughter and child neglect laws, compulsory vaccination laws, drug laws, and traffic laws, to social welfare legislation such as minimum wage laws, child labor laws, animal cruelty laws, environmental protection laws, and laws providing for equality of opportunity for the races. The First Amendment's protection of religious liberty does not require this.

Values that are protected against government interference through enshrinement in the Bill of Rights are not thereby banished from the political process. A society that believes in the negative protection accorded to religious belief can be expected to be solicitous of that value in its legislation. It is therefore not surprising that a number of States have made an exception to their drug laws for sacramental peyote use. But to say that a nondiscriminatory religious-practice exemption is permitted, or even that it is desirable, is not to say that it is constitutionally required. Leaving accommodation to the political process will place at a relative disadvantage those religious practices that are not widely engaged in; but that unavoidable consequence of democratic government must be preferred to a system in which each conscience is a law unto itself or in which judges weigh the social importance of all laws against the centrality of all religious beliefs.

Because respondents' ingestion of peyote was prohibited under Oregon law, and because that prohibition is constitutional, Oregon may, consistent with the Free Exercise Clause, deny respondents unemployment compensation when their dismissal results from use of the drug. The decision of the Oregon Supreme Court is accordingly reversed.

It is so ordered.

Justice O'CONNOR, with whom Justice BRENNAN, Justice MARSHALL, and Justice BLACKMUN join as to Parts I and II, *concurring in the judgment.*[*]

---

[*] THE CHIEF JUSTICE, Justice SCALIA, and Justice THOMAS join all but Part II-A-2 of this opinion. Justice WHITE joins all but Part II-A of this opinion. Justice SOUTER joins only Parts I, III, and IV of this opinion.

Today's holding dramatically departs from well-settled First Amendment jurisprudence. Because the First Amendment does not distinguish between religious belief and religious conduct, conduct motivated by sincere religious belief, like the belief itself, must be at least presumptively protected by the Free Exercise Clause. A person who is barred from engaging in religiously motivated conduct is barred from freely exercising his religion.

The First Amendment does not distinguish between laws that are generally applicable and laws that target particular religious practices. Few States would be so naive as to enact a law directly prohibiting or burdening a religious practice as such. Our free exercise cases have all concerned generally applicable laws that had the effect of significantly burdening a religious practice.

The freedom to act, unlike the freedom to believe, cannot be absolute. We have required the government to justify any substantial burden on religiously motivated conduct by a compelling state interest and by means narrowly tailored to achieve that interest. The compelling interest test effectuates the First Amendment's command that religious liberty is an independent liberty, that it occupies a preferred position, and that the Court will not permit encroachments upon this liberty, whether direct or indirect, unless required by clear and compelling governmental interests "of the highest order."

In *Yoder* we expressly rejected the interpretation the Court now adopts. The essence of a free exercise claim is relief from a burden imposed by government on religious practices or beliefs, whether the burden is imposed directly through laws that prohibit or compel specific religious practices, or indirectly through laws that, in effect, make abandonment of one's own religion or conformity to the religious beliefs of others the price of an equal place in the civil community. A State that makes criminal an individual's religiously motivated conduct burdens that individual's free exercise of religion in the severest manner possible, for it "results in the choice to the individual of either abandoning his religious principle or facing criminal prosecution." I would have thought it beyond argument that such laws implicate free exercise concerns. We have never distinguished between cases in which a State conditions receipt of a benefit on conduct prohibited by religious beliefs and cases in which a State affirmatively prohibits such conduct. The *Sherbert* compelling interest test applies in both kinds of cases.

There is nothing talismanic about neutral laws of general applicability or general criminal prohibitions, for laws neutral toward religion can coerce a person to violate his religious conscience or intrude upon his religious duties just as effectively as laws aimed at religion.

The Court today suggests that the disfavoring of minority religions is an "unavoidable consequence" under our system of government and that accommodation of such religions must be left to the political process. However, the First Amendment was enacted precisely to protect the rights of those whose religious practices are not shared by the majority and may be viewed with hostility. The compelling interest test reflects the First Amendment's mandate of preserving religious liberty to the fullest extent possible in a pluralistic society.

There is no dispute that Oregon's criminal prohibition of peyote places a severe burden on the ability of respondents to freely exercise their religion. Peyote is a sacrament of the Native American Church and is regarded as vital to respondents' ability to practice their religion. There is also no dispute that Oregon has a significant interest in enforcing laws that control the possession and use of controlled substances by its citizens. I would hold that the State has a compelling interest in regulating peyote use by its citizens and that accommodating respondents' religiously motivated conduct "will unduly interfere with fulfillment of the governmental interest." Accordingly, I concur in the judgment of the Court.

Justice BLACKMUN, with whom Justice BRENNAN and Justice MARSHALL join, *dissenting*.

It is not the State's broad interest in fighting the critical "war on drugs" that must be weighed against respondents' claim, but the State's narrow interest in refusing to make an exception for the religious, ceremonial use of peyote. The State has not evinced any concrete interest in enforcing its drug laws against religious users of peyote.

The State proclaims an interest in protecting the health and safety of its citizens from the dangers of unlawful drugs. It offers, however, no evidence that the religious use of peyote has ever harmed anyone. The Federal Government does not find peyote so dangerous as to preclude an exemption for religious use. The Native American Church's internal restrictions on, and supervision of, its members' use of peyote substantially obviate the State's health and safety concerns. Not only does the church's doctrine forbid nonreligious use of peyote; it also generally advocates self-reliance, familial responsibility, and abstinence from alcohol.

The State also seeks to support its refusal to make an exception for religious use of peyote by invoking its interest in abolishing drug trafficking. There is, however, practically no illegal traffic in peyote. Peyote simply is not a popular drug; its distribution for use in religious rituals has nothing to do with the vast and violent traffic in illegal narcotics that plagues this country.

Finally, the State argues that granting an exception for religious peyote use would erode its interest in the uniform, fair, and certain enforcement of its drug laws. This Court, however, consistently has rejected similar arguments in past free exercise cases, and it should do so here as well.

The State's apprehension of a flood of other religious claims is purely speculative. Almost half the States, and the Federal Government, have maintained an exemption for religious peyote use for many years, and apparently have not found themselves overwhelmed by claims to other religious exemptions. The unusual circumstances that make the religious use of peyote compatible with the State's interests in health and safety and in preventing drug trafficking would not apply to other religious claims. Some religions, for example, might not restrict drug use to a limited ceremonial context, as does the Native American Church. Some religious claims involve drugs such as marijuana and heroin, in which there is significant illegal traffic, with its attendant greed and violence, so that it would be difficult to grant a religious exemption without seriously compromising law enforcement efforts. That the State might grant an exemption for religious peyote use, but deny other religious claims arising in different circumstances, would not violate the Establishment Clause. I *dissent.*

BACKGROUND
The Religious Freedom Restoration Act

After *Smith*, Congress passed the Religious Freedom Restoration Act (RFRA) in an effort to overrule that decision. RFRA provided that "Government shall not substantially burden a person's exercise of religion even if the burden results from a rule of general applicability" unless the government demonstrates that "application of the burden to the person — (1) is in furtherance of a compelling governmental interest; and (2) is the least restrictive means of furthering that compelling governmental interest." In *City of Boerne v. Flores*, 521 U.S. 507 (1997), the Court struck down RFRA, as applied to the states, concluding: "Broad as the power of Congress is under the Enforcement Clause of the Fourteenth Amendment, RFRA contradicts vital principles necessary to maintain separation of powers and the federal balance."

Notes

1. *Ministers and Antidiscrimination Laws.* In *Hosanna-Tabor Evangelical Lutheran Church and School v. EEOC*, 565 U.S. 171 (2012), plaintiff, a "called" teacher, sued, claiming employment discrimination when she was discharged from her employment. The Court rejected the claim, noting that the First Amendment bars such lawsuits when the employer is a religious group and the employee is one of the group's ministers: "The members of a religious group put their faith in the hands of their ministers. Requiring a church to accept or retain an unwanted minister, or punishing a church for failing to do so, intrudes upon more than a mere employment decision. Such action interferes with the internal governance of the church, depriving the church of control over the selection of those who will personify its beliefs. By imposing an unwanted minister, the state infringes the Free Exercise Clause, which protects a religious group's right to shape its own faith and mission through its appointments. According the state the power to determine which individuals will minister to the faithful also violates the Establishment Clause, which prohibits government involvement in ecclesiastical decisions." The Court also rejected the idea that *Smith* precluded application of the ministerial exception on the basis that

antidiscrimination laws are neutral and generally applicable: "The present case concerns government interference with an internal church decision that affects the faith and mission of the church itself. The contention that *Smith* forecloses recognition of a ministerial exception rooted in the Religion Clauses has no merit." Even though the Court did not precisely define the term *minister*, it concluded that a "called" teacher qualified because she held the title of "minister," had undergone theological training, and occasionally performed ministerial responsibilities "according to the Word of God and the confessional standards of the Evangelical Lutheran Church as drawn from the Sacred Scriptures." Also, the congregation was asked to bless her efforts, and the church periodically reviewed her ministry skills and provided for her "continuing education as a professional person in the ministry of the Gospel."

2. In *Our Lady of Guadalupe School v. Morrisey-Berru*, 140 S. Ct. 2049 (2020), the Court extended the ministerial exception to lay teachers who are entrusted with responsibility for instructing students in the faith: "Implicit in our decision in *Hosanna-Tabor* was a recognition that educating young people in their faith, inculcating its teachings, and training them to live their faith are responsibilities that lie at the very core of the mission of a private religious school. Morrissey-Berru and Biel both performed vital religious duties. Educating and forming students in the Catholic faith lay at the core of the mission of the schools where they taught, and their employment agreements and faculty handbooks specified in no uncertain terms that they were expected to help the schools carry out this mission and that their work would be evaluated to ensure that they were fulfilling that responsibility. As elementary school teachers responsible for providing instruction in all subjects, including religion, they were the members of the school staff who were entrusted most directly with the responsibility of educating their students in the faith. When a school with a religious mission entrusts a teacher with the responsibility of educating and forming students in the faith, judicial intervention into disputes between the school and the teacher threatens the school's independence in a way that the First Amendment does not allow." Justice Sotomayor, joined by Justice Ginsburg, dissented: "Neither school publicly represented that either teacher was a Catholic spiritual leader or 'minister.' Rather, the schools referred to both as 'lay' teachers. Neither teacher had a 'significant degree of religious training' or underwent a 'formal process of commissioning.' Nor did either school require such training or commissioning as a prerequisite to gaining (or keeping) employment. Neither held herself out as having a leadership role in the faith community. Both Biel and Morrissey-Berru had almost exclusively secular duties, making it especially improper to deprive them of all legal protection when their employers have not offered any religious reason for the alleged discrimination."

3. *Church Property.* *Hosanna-Tabor* was preceded by decisions holding that government has limited authority to intrude on church decisions. *Watson v. Jones*, 80 U.S. 679 (1871), involved a dispute between antislavery and pro-slavery factions over who controlled a church in Louisville, Kentucky. When the General

Assembly of the Presbyterian Church recognized the antislavery faction, the Court refused to question that decision: "Whenever the questions of discipline, or of faith, or ecclesiastical rule, custom, or law have been decided by the highest of the church judicatories, legal tribunals must accept such decisions as final, and as binding." In *Kedroff v. Saint Nicholas Cathedral of Russian Orthodox Church in North America*, 344 U.S. 94, 116 (1952), North American Russian Orthodox churches split from the Supreme Church Authority in Moscow, and tried to assert authority over a Russian Orthodox cathedral. A New York law required Russian Orthodox churches to recognize the governing body of the North American churches as authoritative. The Court held that the right to use the cathedral was "strictly a matter of ecclesiastical government," and that the courts could not impose their "power into the forbidden area of religious freedom." In *Serbian Eastern Orthodox Diocese for United States and Canada v. Milivojevich*, 426 U.S. 696 (1976), a bishop of the Serbian Orthodox Church sought reinstatement following his removal. The Court held that the First Amendment "permits hierarchical religious organizations to establish their own rules and regulations for internal discipline and government, and to create tribunals for adjudicating disputes over these matters." When ecclesiastical tribunals decide such disputes, "the Constitution requires that civil courts accept their decisions as binding."

4. *More on RFRA.* In *Gonzales v. O Centro Espirita Beneficente Uniao Do Vegetal*, 546 U.S. 428 (2006), the Court upheld RFRA as applied to the federal government. In that case, a religious sect with origins in the Amazon Rainforest had a practice of receiving communion by drinking a sacramental tea, brewed from plants unique to the region, that contains a hallucinogen regulated by the federal government under the Controlled Substances Act. The government sought to prohibit the small American branch of the sect from engaging in the practice, on the ground that the Controlled Substances Act bars all use of the hallucinogen. The Court held that RFRA required an accommodation because the government could not show that it had a compelling interest in refusing this limited accommodation.

5. *Religious Land Use and Institutionalized Persons Act.* After RFRA was struck down, Congress used its authority under the federal Spending and Commerce Clauses to pass the Religious Land Use and Institutionalized Persons Act of 2000 (RLUIPA), 42 U.S.C. §2000cc-1(a)(1)-(2), which provided in part: "No government shall impose a substantial burden on the religious exercise of a person residing in or confined to an institution," unless the burden furthers "a compelling governmental interest" and does so by "the least restrictive means." Current and former inmates of Ohio penal institutions sued, claiming that they were adherents of "non-mainstream" religions (Satanists, Wiccas, Asatrus, and the Church of Jesus Christ Christian) and that they were not being accommodated under RLUIPA. Prison officials claimed that RLUIPA impermissibly advanced religion in violation of the Establishment Clause. In *Cutter v. Wilkinson*, 544 U.S. 709 (2005), the Court disagreed, noting that government may accommodate religion without violating the Establishment Clause and that Section 3 of RLUIPA does

not, on its face, exceed the limits of permissible government accommodation of religious practices. On the contrary, the Act "alleviates exceptional government-created burdens on private religious exercise." The Court concluded that the Act allows institutions to maintain order and safety, and requires them only to "take adequate account of the burdens a requested accommodation may impose on nonbeneficiaries" and make sure that "the Act's prescriptions are and will be administered neutrally among different faiths." Even though the Act applied a "compelling governmental interest" standard, the Court noted that "context matters" in the application of that standard.

In *Sossamon v. Texas*, 563 U.S. 277 (2011), the Court held that a state that accepts federal funds does not (by virtue of the acceptance of federal funds) consent to waive its sovereign immunity to suits for money damages under the Religious Land Use and Institutionalized Persons Act of 2000 (RLUIPA), 114 Stat. 803, 42 U.S.C. §§2000cc *et seq.*

6. *Proliferating RFRA and RLUIPA Claims.* RFRA has led to a growing number of claims for religious exemptions. In *Holt v. Hobbs*, 574 U.S. 352 (2015), the Court held that the Arkansas Department of Corrections could not prohibit an inmate from wearing a short beard in accordance with the dictates of his religious faith. A number of other claims have also been asserted. For example, three Kentucky death row inmates claimed that they had the right to a sweat lodge, and to conduct powwows, and to consume buffalo meat. *See* Brett Barrouquere, *Prison Suit on Religion Revisited: Court Reinstates Cases over Indian Rites*, Louisville Courier-J., Aug. 16, 2014, at A-4; *see also Haight v. Thompson*, 763 F.3d 554 (6th Cir. 2014). Another inmate sued when he was denied the right to obtain Santeria beads, necklaces, and cowrie shells that had been dipped in the blood of animals. *See Davilla v. Gladden*, 777 F.3d 1198 (11th Cir. 2015). Individuals have also claimed the right to exemptions from bans on the possession of bald and gold eagle feathers. *See McAllen Grace Brethren Church v. Salazar*, 764 F.3d 465 (5th Cir. 2014). Under RLUIPA, a synagogue sued a local historic commission regarding denial of a proposed synagogue expansion. *See Chabad Lubavitch of Litchfield County, Inc. v. Litchfield Historic District Commission*, 768 F.3d 183 (2d Cir. 2014).

7. *RFRA and the Affordable Care Act (ACA).* In *Burwell v. Hobby Lobby Stores, Inc.*, 573 U.S. 682 (2014), the Court held that RFRA precluded the U.S. Department of Health and Human Services (HHS) from requiring three closely held corporations to provide health-insurance coverage for methods of contraception that violate the sincerely held religious beliefs of the companies' owners. In *Little Sisters of the Poor Saints Peter and Paul Home v. Pennsylvania*, 140 S. Ct. 2367 (2020), relying on RFRA, the Court held that the Government had created lawful exemptions from a regulatory requirement implementing the Patient Protection and Affordable Care Act of 2010 (ACA). The requirement at issue obligated certain employers to provide contraceptive coverage to their employees through their group health plans. Though contraceptive coverage was not required by (or even mentioned in) the ACA, the Government mandated such coverage

by promulgating interim final rules (IFRs) shortly after the ACA's passage. After six years of protracted litigation, the Departments of Health and Human Services, Labor, and the Treasury (Departments) — which jointly administer the relevant ACA provision — exempted certain employers who have religious and conscientious objections from this agency-created mandate. The Court held that the Departments had the authority to provide exemptions from the regulatory contraceptive requirements for employers with religious and conscientious objections.

8. *Trump's Health Care "Conscience Rule."* In 2019, the Trump Administration enacted a new regulation designed to protect workers who oppose abortion, sterilization or assisted suicide on religious or moral grounds from being forced to participate in those procedures. The rule is enforceable through the loss of federal funding to health care institutions. Opponents expressed concern that the rule might lead to discrimination against transgender or homosexual individuals. The rule was subsequently challenged in court.

∽ PROBLEMS ∽

1. *Prohibition and Sacramental Wine.* After *Smith*, one question that has arisen is whether government must accommodate other religious practices. For some religions, there is a history of accommodation. For example, during the Prohibition era, Congress decided to exempt the Roman Catholic Church's sacramental use of wine from the general ban on the possession and use of alcohol. *See* National Prohibition Act, Title II, §3, 41 Stat. 308. But is such an exemption constitutionally required? Suppose Congress re-imposes Prohibition (presumably after a constitutional amendment) but decides not to include an exemption for the sacramental use of wine. If Catholics challenge the law as an undue burden on their right to freely exercise their religion, does *Smith* require a holding that the Catholics are subject to this "neutral, generally applicable" law? Alternatively, does the Constitution require an accommodation?

2. *The Minister and the Occupational Tax.* Monty Bossard is a devout Baptist minister who firmly believes that the Bible commands him to "Render unto God what is God's, and unto Caesar what is Caesar's." Under Bossard's construction of the Bible, he does not have to pay the City of Louisville's occupational tax (which is imposed on everyone who works within the city). Is Bossard right? Does the Free Exercise Clause grant him an exemption from the city's occupational tax? Does *Smith* require an exemption?

3. *The Christian Scientist's Dying Son.* How does the Free Exercise Clause apply in the context of a Christian Scientist who does not believe in receiving medical care? Presumably, the Christian Scientist can make a decision for herself not to receive medical care. However, what if the adherent's minor son is in a diabetic coma and will likely die unless he immediately receives medical care? Does the

woman have a constitutional right to withhold medical care from her son? On the other hand, can the state charge her with the crime of criminal homicide if she withholds treatment and her son dies?

4. *The Collision Between Gay Rights and Religious Beliefs.* A number of state and local laws prohibit businesses from discriminating based on an individual's sexual preferences. Suppose that a woman who runs a small photography business objects on religious grounds to homosexuality. When a gay couple asks her to take pictures at the wedding, the woman refuses. She tells the gay couple that she is religiously opposed to homosexuality, would not feel comfortable taking pictures at a gay wedding, and is concerned that her work product would be of poor quality. The gay couple files a discrimination complaint against the photographer. Is the photographer entitled to a religious exemption from the discrimination law? *See Chelsey Nelson Photography LLC v. Louisville/Jefferson County Metro Government,* — F.Supp.3d —2020 WL 4745771 (W.D. KY. 2020); *Elaine Photography LLC v. Willock,* 309 P.3d 53 (N.M. 2013), *cert. denied,* 572 U.S. 1046 (2014). Could a large corporation also claim an exemption and exclude same-sex couples from patronizing its store? Is there a legitimate distinction between a photographer and a large corporation? Would you view the situation differently as applied to a religious official or a religious organization? In light of a local or state law prohibiting discrimination based on sexual preferences, could a minister who holds a religiously based belief that marriage can only be between a man and a woman refuse to perform marriages for same-sex couples? Could a religious college, whose underlying doctrine provides that marriage can only be between a man and a woman, treat same-sex couples differently than opposite-sex married couples regarding housing and other benefits? Of course, many religiously based colleges receive federal funding of various sorts for the construction of buildings, student financial aid, etc. If the state otherwise respects a college's decision to deny benefits to same-sex couples, can it withhold financial aid from colleges that do so?

5. *Religious Exemptions.* Could a state create an exemption from its antidiscrimination law for "sincerely held religious beliefs"? Should it create such an exemption? In Indiana, there was considerable controversy after the state passed a religious freedom law that some believed would have authorized discrimination against gays and lesbians. *See* Cara Anthony, *Thousands Protest "Religious Freedom" Law,* Louisville Courier-J., Mar. 29, 2015, at 2B. In response to the controversy, Indiana amended the law. However, comparable legislation was introduced in Congress, but has not been enacted.

6. *The Amish and Photo Drivers' Licenses.* Suppose that a sect of the Mennonite religion allows its members to drive motorized vehicles (unlike the Old Order Amish which do not allow it), but prohibits them from having their pictures taken (viewing pictures as "graven images" prohibited by the Bible). Louisiana law requires all drivers to carry a license and provides that all licenses must contain a picture of the driver. If a member of the Mennonite sect seeks an exemption from the picture requirement, is Louisiana required to grant the exemption?

7. *The Eagle Protection Act.* The Eagle Protection Act makes it illegal to kill or possess eagles. In enacting the Act, Congress expressed concern about a black market for eagles and eagle feathers, with single birds fetching as much as $10,000 and individual feathers bringing $35. Little Horse is a member of an American Indian tribe that uses eagle feathers in various religious rites, including funerals and burials, and he seeks an exemption from the law that will allow him to collect bird feathers. (Little Horse recognizes that many eagles are endangered and does not wish to kill them.) After *Smith*, must the state grant Little Horse an exemption? Alternatively, if Little Horse is prosecuted for possession of eagle feathers, can he defend based on the Free Exercise clause?

8. *The Ministerial Exception and Child Abuse.* Suppose that a religious organization ("Soldiers for God" or "Soldiers") believes that its ministers should maintain their distance from state officials and state processes. When state officials initiate a child sexual abuse investigation against the Soldiers, the organization dismisses a "minister" who gave testimony as part of the investigation. The minister sues, seeking damages and reinstatement, on the basis that the Soldiers' actions violate public policy. After *Hosanna-Tabor*, may a court order the Soldiers to pay damages or provide reinstatement on public policy grounds?

9. *The Dispute Over Vaccinations.* In the midst of outbreaks of measles, that some have described as a "public health emergency," New York has decided to eliminate its religious exemption to its requirement for mandatory measles vaccinations. If an individual has religious objections to vaccinations (on the basis that they were created using tissue from aborted fetuses), can the government override those objections in the interest of public safety?

10. *Controlling Teachings on Gender Identity.* Iowa's Civil Rights Commission interprets the state's Civil Rights Act as prohibiting anyone from expressing views that would "directly or indirectly" make "persons any particular . . . gender identity" feel "unwelcome," and as requiring organizations to make their bathrooms, locker rooms and shower facilities open based on "gender identity" rather than on "biological sex." The Commission takes the position that this law applies to any activities at churches that do not have "a bona fide religious purpose" which the Commission defines as including child care facilities at a church, or church services that are open to the public. Consistently with the First Amendment, could the Commission's interpretation be used to prevent a church from openly expressing its views on gender identity?

2. Discrimination Against Religion

Smith's analysis governs cases involving neutral, generally applicable, laws. But suppose that a law explicitly discriminates against religion or religious activity. In *McDaniel v. Paty*, 435 U.S. 618 (1978), the Court struck down a statute that prohibited ministers or members of religious orders from being members of state legislatures. Overt governmental discrimination against religion is relatively rare.

Church of the Lukumi Babalu Aye, Inc. v. City of Hialeah

508 U.S. 520 (1993)

Justice KENNEDY delivered the opinion of the Court, except as to Part II-A-2.

This case involves practices of the Santeria religion, which originated in the 19th century. When the Yoruba people were brought as slaves from western Africa to Cuba, their traditional African religion absorbed significant elements of Roman Catholicism. The resulting syncretion, or fusion, is Santeria, "the way of the saints." The Cuban Yoruba express their devotion to spirits, called orishas, through the iconography of Catholic saints, Catholic symbols are often present at Santeria rites, and Santeria devotees attend the Catholic sacraments.

The Santeria faith teaches that every individual has a destiny from God, a destiny fulfilled with the aid and energy of the orishas. The basis of the Santeria religion is the nurture of a personal relation with the orishas, and one of the principal forms of devotion is an animal sacrifice. According to Santeria teaching, the orishas are powerful but not immortal. They depend for survival on the sacrifice. Sacrifices are performed at birth, marriage, and death rites, for the cure of the sick, for the initiation of new members and priests, and during an annual celebration. Animals sacrificed in Santeria rituals include chickens, pigeons, doves, ducks, guinea pigs, goats, sheep, and turtles. The animals are killed by the cutting of the carotid arteries in the neck. The sacrificed animal is cooked and eaten, except after healing and death rituals. Santeria adherents faced widespread persecution in Cuba, so the religion and its rituals were practiced in secret. The religion was brought to this Nation most often by exiles from the Cuban revolution. There are at least 50,000 practitioners in South Florida today.

Petitioner Church of the Lukumi Babalu Aye, Inc. (Church), is a church that practices the Santeria religion. Ernesto Pichardov is the Church's priest and holds the religious title of Italero, the second highest in the Santeria faith. In April 1987, the Church leased land in the City of Hialeah, Florida, and announced plans to establish a house of worship as well as a school, cultural center, and museum. Pichardo indicated that the Church's goal was to bring the practice of the Santeria faith, including its ritual of animal sacrifice, into the open. The Church began the process of obtaining utility service and receiving the necessary licensing, inspection, and zoning approvals. Although the Church's efforts at obtaining the necessary licenses and permits were far from smooth, it appears that it received all needed approvals.

The prospect of a Santeria church in their midst was distressing to many members of the Hialeah community, and the announcement of the plans to open a Santeria church in Hialeah prompted the city council to hold an emergency public session on June 9, 1987. First, the city council adopted Resolution 87-66, which noted the "concern" expressed by residents of the city "that certain religions may propose to engage in practices which are inconsistent with public morals, peace or safety," and declared that "the City reiterates its commitment to a prohibition against any and all acts of any and all religious groups which are inconsistent with public morals, peace or safety." Next, the council approved an emergency ordinance, Ordinance 87-40, which incorporated in full, except as to penalty, Florida's animal cruelty laws. Among other things, the incorporated state law subjected to criminal punishment "whoever unnecessarily or cruelly kills any animal."

The city council desired to undertake further legislative action, but Florida law prohibited a municipality from enacting legislation relating to animal cruelty that conflicted with state law. Hialeah requested an opinion from the attorney general of Florida. The attorney general responded that the "ritual sacrifice of animals for purposes other than food consumption" was not a "necessary" killing and so was prohibited by §828.12. The attorney general defined "unnecessary" as "done without any useful motive, in a spirit of wanton cruelty or for the mere pleasure of destruction without being in any sense beneficial or useful to the person killing the animal." He advised that religious animal sacrifice was against state law, so that a city ordinance prohibiting it would not be in conflict.

The city council responded at first with a hortatory enactment, Resolution 87-90, that noted its residents' "great concern regarding the possibility of public ritualistic animal sacrifices" and the state-law prohibition. The resolution declared the city policy "to oppose the ritual sacrifices of animals" within Hialeah and announced that any person or organization practicing animal sacrifice "will be prosecuted."

In September 1987, the city council adopted three substantive ordinances addressing the issue of religious animal sacrifice. Ordinance 87-52 defined "sacrifice" as "to unnecessarily kill, torment, torture, or mutilate an animal in a public or private ritual or ceremony not for the primary purpose of food consumption," and prohibited owning or possessing an animal "intending to use such animal for food purposes." It restricted application of this prohibition, however, to any individual or group that "kills, slaughters or sacrifices animals for any type of ritual, regardless of whether or not the flesh or blood of the animal is to be consumed." The ordinance contained an exemption for slaughtering by "licensed establishments" of animals "specifically raised for food purposes." Declaring, moreover, that the city council "has determined that the sacrificing of animals within the city limits is contrary to the public health, safety, welfare and morals of the community," the city council adopted Ordinance 87-71. That ordinance defined sacrifice as had Ordinance 87-52, and then provided that "it shall be unlawful for any person, persons, corporations or associations to sacrifice any animal within the corporate limits of the City of Hialeah, Florida." The final Ordinance, 87-72, defined "slaughter" as "the killing of animals for food" and prohibited slaughter outside of areas zoned for slaughterhouse use. The ordinance provided an exemption, however, for the slaughter or processing for sale of "small numbers of hogs and/or cattle per week in accordance with an exemption provided by state law." All ordinances and resolutions passed the city council by unanimous vote. Violations of each of the four ordinances were punishable by fines not exceeding $500 or imprisonment not exceeding 60 days, or both.

Following enactment of these ordinances, the Church and Pichardo filed suit alleging violations of petitioners' rights under the Free Exercise Clause. The District Court ruled for the city and the Court of Appeals for the Eleventh Circuit affirmed.

II

The city does not argue that Santeria is not a "religion" within the meaning of the First Amendment. Nor could it. Although the practice of animal sacrifice may seem abhorrent to some, "religious beliefs need not be acceptable, logical, consistent, or comprehensible to others in order to merit First Amendment protection." Neither the city nor the courts below have questioned the sincerity of petitioners' professed desire to conduct animal sacrifices for religious reasons.

A law that is neutral and of general applicability need not be justified by a compelling governmental interest even if the law has the incidental effect of burdening a particular religious practice. A law failing to satisfy these requirements must be justified by a compelling governmental interest and must be narrowly tailored to advance that interest. These ordinances fail to satisfy the *Smith* requirements.

The First Amendment forbids an official purpose to disapprove of a particular religion or of religion in general. Petitioners allege an attempt to disfavor their religion because of the religious ceremonies it commands.

The protections of the Free Exercise Clause pertain if the law at issue discriminates against some or all religious beliefs or regulates or prohibits conduct because it is undertaken for religious reasons. Indeed, it was "historical instances of religious persecution and intolerance that gave concern to those who drafted the Free Exercise Clause." *Bowen v. Roy*, 476 U.S. 693 (1986) (opinion of Burger, C.J.). These principles, though not often at issue in our Free Exercise Clause cases, have played a role in some. In *McDaniel v. Paty*, 435 U.S. 618 (1978), for example, we invalidated a State law that disqualified members of the clergy from holding certain public offices, because it "imposed special disabilities on the basis of religious status." On the same principle, in *Fowler v. Rhode Island*, 345 U.S. 67 (1953), we found that a municipal ordinance was applied in an unconstitutional manner when interpreted to prohibit preaching in a public park by a Jehovah's Witness but to permit preaching during the course of a Catholic mass or Protestant church service.

Although a law targeting religious beliefs as such is never permissible, if the object of a law is to infringe upon or restrict practices because of their religious motivation, the law is not neutral, and it is invalid unless it is justified by a compelling interest and is narrowly tailored to advance that interest. There are, of course, many ways of demonstrating that the object or purpose of a law is the suppression of religion or religious conduct. To determine the object of a law, we must begin with its text, for the minimum requirement of neutrality is that a law not discriminate on its face. A law lacks facial neutrality if it refers to a religious practice without a secular meaning discernable from the language or context. Petitioners contend that three of the ordinances fail this test of facial neutrality because they use the words "sacrifice" and "ritual," words with strong religious connotations. We agree that these words are consistent with the claim of facial discrimination, but the argument is not conclusive. The words "sacrifice" and "ritual" have a religious origin, but current use admits also of secular meanings. The ordinances, furthermore, define "sacrifice" in secular terms, without referring to religious practices.

We reject the contention advanced by the city that our inquiry must end with the text of the laws at issue. Facial neutrality is not determinative. The Free Exercise Clause, like the Establishment Clause, "forbids subtle departures from neutrality," and "covert suppression of particular religious beliefs." Official action that targets religious conduct for distinctive treatment cannot be shielded by mere compliance with the requirement of facial neutrality. The Free Exercise Clause protects against governmental hostility which is masked, as well as overt.

The record compels the conclusion that suppression of the central element of the Santeria worship service was the object of the ordinances. First, though use of the words "sacrifice" and "ritual" does not compel a finding of improper targeting of the Santeria religion, the choice of these words is support for our conclusion. There are further respects in which the text of the city council's enactments discloses the improper attempt to target Santeria. Resolution 87-66, adopted June 9, 1987, recited that "residents and citizens of the City of Hialeah have expressed their concern that certain religions may propose to engage in practices which are inconsistent with public morals, peace or safety," and "reiterated" the city's commitment to prohibit "any and all such acts of any and all religious groups." No one suggests, and on this record it cannot be maintained, that city officials had in mind a religion other than Santeria.

Apart from the text, the effect of a law in its real operation is strong evidence of its object. To be sure, adverse impact will not always lead to a finding of impermissible targeting. For example, a social harm may have been a legitimate concern of government for reasons quite apart from discrimination. The subject at hand does implicate, of course, multiple concerns unrelated to religious animosity, for example, the suffering or mistreatment visited upon the sacrificed animals and health hazards from improper disposal. But the ordinances when considered together disclose an object remote from these legitimate concerns. The design of these laws accomplishes instead a "religious gerrymander," an impermissible attempt to target petitioners and their religious practices.

Almost the only conduct subject to Ordinances 87-40, 87-52, and 87-71 is the religious exercise of Santeria church members. The texts were drafted in tandem to achieve this result. Ordinance 87-71 prohibits the sacrifice of animals, but defines sacrifice as "to unnecessarily kill an animal in a public or private ritual or ceremony not for the primary purpose of food consumption." The definition excludes almost all killings of animals except for religious sacrifice, and the primary purpose requirement narrows the proscribed category even further, in particular by exempting kosher slaughter. We need not discuss whether this differential treatment of two religions is itself an independent constitutional violation. It suffices to recite that Santeria alone was the exclusive legislative concern. The net result is that few if any killings of animals are prohibited other than Santeria sacrifice, which is proscribed because it occurs during a ritual or ceremony and its primary purpose is to make an offering to the orishas, not food consumption. Indeed, careful drafting ensured that, although Santeria sacrifice is prohibited, killings that are no more necessary or humane in almost all other circumstances are unpunished.

Operating in similar fashion is Ordinance 87-52, which prohibits the "possession, sacrifice, or slaughter" of an animal with the "intent to use such animal for food purposes." This prohibition, extending to the keeping of an animal as well as the killing itself, applies if the animal is killed in "any type of ritual" and there is an intent to use the animal for food, whether or not it is in fact consumed for food. The ordinance exempts, however, "any licensed food establishment" with regard to "any animals which are specifically raised for food purposes," if the activity is permitted by zoning and other laws. This exception, too, seems intended to cover kosher slaughter. Again, the burden of the ordinance, in practical terms, falls on Santeria adherents but almost no others: If the killing is—unlike most Santeria sacrifices—unaccompanied by the intent to use the animal for food, then it is not prohibited by Ordinance 87-52; if the killing is specifically for food but does not occur during the course of "any type of ritual," it again falls outside the prohibition; and if the killing is for food and occurs during the course of a ritual, it is still exempted if it occurs in a properly zoned and licensed establishment and involves animals "specifically raised for food purposes." A pattern of exemptions parallels the pattern of narrow prohibitions. Each contributes to the gerrymander.

Ordinance 87-40 incorporates the Florida animal cruelty statute. Its prohibition is broad on its face, punishing "whoever unnecessarily kills any animal." The city claims that this ordinance is the epitome of a neutral prohibition. The problem, however, is the interpretation given to the ordinance by respondent and the Florida attorney general. Killings for religious reasons are deemed unnecessary, whereas most other killings fall outside the prohibition. The city, on what seems to be a *per se* basis, deems hunting, slaughter of animals for food, eradication of insects and pests, and euthanasia as necessary. There is no indication in the record that respondent has concluded that hunting or fishing for sport is unnecessary. Indeed, one of the few reported Florida cases decided under §828.12 concludes that the use of live rabbits to train greyhounds is not unnecessary. Further, because it requires an evaluation of the particular justification for the killing, this ordinance represents a system of "individualized governmental assessment of the reasons for the relevant conduct." In circumstances in which individualized exemptions from a general requirement are available, the government "may not refuse to extend that system to cases of 'religious hardship' without compelling reason." Respondent's application of the ordinance's test of necessity devalues religious reasons for killing by judging them to be of lesser import than nonreligious reasons. Thus, religious practice is being singled out for discriminatory treatment.

We also find significant evidence of the ordinances' improper targeting of Santeria sacrifice in the fact that they proscribe more religious conduct than is necessary to achieve their stated ends. It is not unreasonable to infer, at least when there are no persuasive indications to the contrary, that a law which visits "gratuitous restrictions" on religious conduct, seeks not to effectuate the stated governmental interests, but to suppress the conduct because of its religious motivation.

The legitimate governmental interests in protecting the public health and preventing cruelty to animals could be addressed by restrictions stopping far short of a flat prohibition of all Santeria sacrificial practice. If improper disposal is the harm to be prevented, the city could have imposed a general regulation on the disposal of organic garbage. It did not do so. Indeed, counsel for the city conceded that, under the ordinances, Santeria sacrifices would be illegal even if they occurred in licensed, inspected, and zoned slaughterhouses. Thus, these ordinances prohibit Santeria sacrifice even when it does not threaten the city's interest in the public health. The neutrality of a law is suspect if First Amendment freedoms are curtailed to prevent isolated collateral harms not themselves prohibited by direct regulation.

Narrower regulation would achieve the city's interest in preventing cruelty to animals. With regard to the city's interest in ensuring the adequate care of animals, regulation of conditions and treatment, regardless of why an animal is kept, is the logical response to the city's concern, not a prohibition on possession for the purpose of sacrifice. The same is true for the city's interest in prohibiting cruel methods of killing. Under federal and Florida law and Ordinance 87-40, which incorporates Florida law, killing an animal by the "simultaneous and instantaneous severance of the carotid arteries with a sharp instrument"—the method used in kosher slaughter—is approved as humane. Though Santeria sacrifice also results in severance of the carotid arteries, the method used during sacrifice is less reliable and therefore not humane. If the city has a real concern that other methods are less humane, the subject of the regulation should be the method of slaughter itself, not a religious classification that bears some general relation to it.

Ordinance 87-72—unlike the three other ordinances—does appear to apply to substantial nonreligious conduct and not to be overbroad. For our purposes here, the four substantive ordinances may be treated as a group for neutrality purposes. Ordinance 87-72 was passed the same day as Ordinance 87-71 and was enacted, as were the three others, in direct response to the opening of the Church. It would be implausible to suggest that the three other ordinances, but not Ordinance 87-72, had as their object the suppression of religion. We need not decide whether the Ordinance 87-72 could survive constitutional scrutiny if it existed separately; it must be invalidated because it functions, with the rest of the enactments in question, to suppress Santeria religious worship.

As in equal protection cases, we may determine the city council's object from both direct and circumstantial evidence. Relevant evidence includes, among other things, the historical background of the decision under challenge, the specific series of events leading to the enactment or official policy in question, and the legislative or administrative history, including contemporaneous statements made by members of the decisionmaking body. These objective factors bear on the question of discriminatory object. That the ordinances were enacted "because of, not merely in spite of," their suppression of Santeria religious practice, is revealed by the events preceding their enactment.

In sum, the neutrality inquiry leads to one conclusion: The ordinances had as their object the suppression of religion. The pattern we have recited discloses animosity to Santeria adherents and their religious practices; the ordinances by their own terms target this religious exercise; the texts of the ordinances were gerrymandered with care to proscribe religious killings of animals but to exclude almost all secular killings; and the ordinances suppress much more religious conduct than is necessary in order to achieve the legitimate ends asserted in their defense. These ordinances are not neutral.

We turn next to a second requirement of the Free Exercise Clause, the rule that laws burdening religious practice must be of general applicability. Respondent claims that Ordinances 87-40, 87-52, and 87-71 advance two interests: protecting the public health and preventing cruelty to animals. The ordinances are underinclusive for those ends. They fail to prohibit nonreligious conduct that endangers these interests in a similar or greater degree than Santeria sacrifice does. The underinclusion is substantial, not inconsequential. Despite the city's proffered interest in preventing cruelty to animals, the ordinances are drafted with care to forbid few killings but those occasioned by religious sacrifice. Many types of animal deaths or kills for nonreligious reasons are either not prohibited or approved by express provision. For example, fishing—which occurs in Hialeah—is legal. Extermination of mice and rats within a home is also permitted. Florida law incorporated by Ordinance 87-40 sanctions euthanasia of "stray, neglected, abandoned, or unwanted animals"; destruction of animals judicially removed from their owners "for humanitarian reasons" or when the animal "is of no commercial value"; the infliction of pain or suffering "in the interest of medical science"; the placing of poison in one's yard or enclosure; and the use of a live animal "to pursue or take wildlife or to participate in any hunting," and "to hunt wild hogs."

The city concedes that "neither the State of Florida nor the City has enacted a generally applicable ban on the killing of animals." It asserts, however, that animal sacrifice is "different" from the animal killings that are permitted by law. According to the city, it is "self-evident" that killing animals for food is "important"; the eradication of insects and pests is "obviously justified"; and the euthanasia of excess animals "makes sense." These *ipse dixits* do not explain why religion alone must bear the burden of the ordinances, when many of these secular killings fall within the city's interest in preventing the cruel treatment of animals.

The ordinances are also underinclusive with regard to the city's interest in public health, which is threatened by the disposal of animal carcasses in open public places and the consumption of uninspected meat. Neither interest is pursued by respondent with regard to conduct that is not motivated by religious conviction. The health risks posed by the improper disposal of animal carcasses are the same whether Santeria sacrifice or some nonreligious killing preceded it. The city does not, however, prohibit hunters from bringing their kill to their houses, nor does it regulate disposal after their activity. Despite substantial testimony at trial that the same public health hazards result from improper disposal of garbage by restaurants, restaurants are outside the scope of the ordinances. Improper disposal is a general problem that causes substantial health risks, but which respondent addresses only when it results from religious exercise.

The ordinances are underinclusive as well with regard to the health risk posed by consumption of uninspected meat. Under the city's ordinances, hunters may eat their kill and fishermen may eat their catch without undergoing governmental inspection. Likewise, state law requires inspection of meat that is sold but exempts meat from animals raised for the use of the owner and "members of his household and nonpaying guests and employees." The asserted interest in inspected meat is not pursued in contexts similar to that of religious animal sacrifice.

Ordinance 87-72, which prohibits the slaughter of animals outside of areas zoned for slaughterhouses, is underinclusive on its face. The ordinance includes an exemption for "any person, group, or organization" that "slaughters or processes for sale, small numbers of hogs and/or cattle per week in accordance with an exemption provided by state law." Respondent has not explained why commercial operations that slaughter "small numbers" of hogs and cattle do not implicate its professed desire to prevent cruelty to animals and preserve the public health. Although the city has classified Santeria sacrifice as slaughter, subjecting it to this ordinance, it does not regulate other killings for food in like manner.

We conclude that each of Hialeah's ordinances pursues the city's governmental interests only against conduct motivated by religious belief. The ordinances "have every appearance of a prohibition that society is prepared to impose upon Santeria worshippers but not upon itself." This precise evil is what the requirement of general applicability is designed to prevent.

III

A law burdening religious practice that is not neutral or not of general application must undergo the most rigorous of scrutiny. To satisfy the commands of the First Amendment, a law restrictive of religious practice must advance "interests of the highest order" and must be narrowly tailored in pursuit of those interests. A law that targets religious conduct for distinctive treatment or advances legitimate governmental interests only against conduct with a religious motivation will survive strict scrutiny only in rare cases. It follows from what we have already said that these ordinances cannot withstand this scrutiny.

First, even were the governmental interests compelling, the ordinances are not drawn in narrow terms to accomplish those interests. All four ordinances are overbroad or underinclusive in substantial respects. The proffered objectives are not pursued with respect to analogous non-religious conduct, and those interests could be achieved by narrower ordinances that burdened religion to a far lesser degree. The absence of narrow tailoring suffices to establish the invalidity of the ordinances.

Respondent has not demonstrated, moreover, that, in the context of these ordinances, its governmental interests are compelling. Where government restricts only conduct protected by the First Amendment and fails to enact feasible measures to restrict other conduct producing substantial harm or alleged harm of the same sort, the interest given in justification of the restriction is not compelling. "A law cannot be regarded as protecting an interest 'of the highest order' when it leaves appreciable damage to that supposedly vital interest unprohibited." The ordinances are underinclusive to a substantial extent with respect to each of the interests that respondent has asserted, and it is only conduct motivated by religious conviction that bears the weight of the governmental restrictions. There can be no serious claim that those interests justify the ordinances.

The Free Exercise Clause commits government itself to religious tolerance, and upon even slight suspicion that proposals for state intervention stem from animosity to religion or distrust of its practices, all officials must pause to remember their own high duty to the Constitution and to the rights it secures. Those in office must be resolute in resisting importunate demands and must ensure that the sole reasons for imposing the burdens of law and regulation are secular. Legislators may not devise mechanisms, overt or disguised, designed to persecute or oppress a religion or its practices. The laws here in question were enacted contrary to these constitutional principles, and they are void.

Reversed.

Justice SCALIA, with whom THE CHIEF JUSTICE joins, *concurring in part* and *concurring in the judgment.*

Perhaps there are contexts in which determination of legislative motive must be undertaken. But I do not think that is true of analysis under the First Amendment. The First Amendment does not refer to the purposes for which legislators enact laws, but to the effects of the laws enacted: "Congress shall make no law prohibiting the free exercise of religion." This does not put us in the business of invalidating laws by reason of the evil motives of their authors.

Note: The Buddhist Execution

In 2019, the Court stayed the execution of a Texas death row inmate on the basis that he had been denied a Buddhist spiritual adviser. Justice Kavanaugh argued that the state may not "allow Christian or Muslim inmates but not Buddhist inmates to have a religious adviser in the execution room." *See Murphy v. Collier,* 139 S. Ct. 1111 (2019) (Kavanaugh, J., concurring). However, in *Dunn v. Ray,* 139 S. Ct. 661 (2019), the Court denied a Muslim's claim that he should not have been denied access to an imam. In vacating a stay of execution, the Court emphasized the last minute nature of the application for a stay.

∾ PROBLEMS ∾

1. *Rewriting the Hialeah Law.* After the decision in *Lukumi,* the City of Hialeah remains adamant about prohibiting animal sacrifice. Is it possible to redraft the law in a way that will make it constitutionally neutral and generally applicable? How?

2. *Mormons and the Polygamy Ban.* At the beginning of the chapter, we examined the *Reynolds* decision which held that Mormons were not entitled to an exemption for polygamy. If *Reynolds* had arisen after *Lukumi,* should the Court have held that the ban on polygamy discriminated against Mormon beliefs and therefore is invalid? Why or why not?

3. *Church Services During the Coronavirus Pandemic.* A prior problem examined whether a ban on mass gatherings must give way to the religious rights of worshipers. Suppose that, instead of holding in-person services, On Fire wishes to hold "drive-up" services in which all worshipers must remain in their cars, and all cars must be at least six feet apart. Louisville's Mayor makes a public announcement to the effect that drive-up church services are also prohibited. Is there discrimination against religion? Would it matter that Louisville permits drive-up liquor purchases, but not drive-up church services?

4. *"Essential Services."* During the Coronavirus Pandemic. In imposing their lock down orders, most states distinguished between "essential" and "non-essential" services with essential services being allowed to continue. Does a state discriminate against religion by labeling such activities as liquor stores as "essential" services, but labeling religious services as "non-essential?"

5. *Rattlesnake Handlers.* Suppose that a fundamentalist congregation believes that it has a religious obligation to handle poisonous snakes. Its belief is based on the Bible — in particular, the Book of Mark, Chapter 16, which provides: "And these signs shall follow them that believe: In my name shall they cast out devils; they shall speak with new tongues; they shall take up serpents, and if they drink any deadly thing, it shall not hurt them." Suppose that Kentucky, concerned about deaths during fundamentalist services, decides to prohibit rattlesnake handling in church services. Under *Lukumi,* does the Kentucky law involve discrimination against religion? Would it matter whether the law also prohibits the handling of snakes in other contexts (e.g., live entertainment performance)?

6. *The Homophobic Landlord.* May the state prohibit a landlord, who finds homosexuality offensive on religious grounds, from discriminating in property rentals? Would he have a defense against a fair housing law that prohibits

discrimination against gays and lesbians? Is the landlord's refusal to rent protected under the Free Exercise Clause?

7. *The Anti-Sharia Constitutional Amendment.* In 2010, the Oklahoma legislature passed Joint Resolution 1056 which placed a proposed an amendment to the Oklahoma Constitution, known as the "Save Our State Amendment," on the ballot. The proposed amendment stated: "When exercising their judicial authority, Oklahoma courts shall uphold and adhere to the law as provided in the U.S. Constitution, the Oklahoma Constitution, the United States Code, federal regulations, established common law, the Oklahoma Statutes and rules promulgated pursuant thereto, and if necessary the law of another state of the United States *provided the law of the other state does not include Sharia Law.* The courts shall *not look to* the legal precepts of other nations or cultures. Specifically, the courts *shall not consider international law or Sharia Law.*" The amendment was approved by 70% of Oklahoma voters. Awad, an American citizen, and a Muslim who adheres to the religious principles of the Koran and the teachings of Mohammed, alleges that the amendment violates his First Amendment rights. He claims that the amendment singles out the Muslim faith, stigmatizes those who practice that faith, disallows a court from probating his last will and testament (which contains references to Sharia law), limits the relief Muslims can obtain from Oklahoma state courts, and fosters excessive entanglement between the government and his religion. Is the constitutional amendment valid? *See Awad v. Ziriax,* 670 F.3d 1111 (10th Cir. 2012). If the amendment is struck down as a violation of the Establishment Clause, can the amendment be rewritten in a way that would be constitutional?

8. *Muslim Dress in Public Schools.* May a public school prohibit Muslim girls from wearing the niqab (a full-face Muslim veil) in school? Suppose that a school offers the following justification for the ban: it makes non-Muslims feel "uncomfortable." *See* Alan Cowell, *Britain Proposes Allowing Schools to Forbid Full-Face Muslim Veils, N.Y. Times,* Mar. 21, 2015, at A-10. Would you view the ban differently if the schools claim that they have an interest in seeing the faces of all students so that they can determine a student's identity, and make sure that she has the right to be there? What if the schools claim that the wearing of the niqab is inconsistent with notions of equality for all because it seems to place girls in a subservient position?

9. *Prohibiting Oral Circumcision.* A city ordinance specifically prohibits the Jewish ritual act of direct oral suction on a circumcision wound on grounds of hygiene. The city believes that the act poses a risk of spreading the herpes simplex virus to the infant. Does the ordinance target religious beliefs and practices? If so, can it satisfy strict scrutiny? *See Central Rabbinical Congress of the United States & Canada v. N.Y.C. Department of Health & Mental Hygiene,* 763 F.3d 183 (2d Cir. 2014). Could the law be framed in a nondiscriminatory way?

10. *Humanist-Led Weddings.* Suppose that the State of Indiana allows certain elected officials to perform weddings, as well as certain religious clergy and certain enumerated religions that do not have clergy, but prohibits anyone else from doing so. Plaintiffs are secular humanists, a group that believes in ethical living

and has no belief in a deity. Under Indiana law, their leaders are prohibited from performing marriages. As a "secular humanist," can plaintiffs claim protection under the Free Exercise Clause? In other words, is their right to "freely exercise" a religion being impinged? *See Center for Inquiry, Inc. v. Marion Circuit Court Clerk*, 758 F.3d 869 (7th Cir. 2014).

11. *More on the Education for a Better America Act.* In constructing the proposed legislation, do you have any special concerns about discrimination against religion? Suppose, for example, that Congress proposes to prohibit schools from receiving federal funding if they segregate by sex. Could the Act prohibit discrimination by a religious school that believes in segregating children by sex or that believes in treating (and educating) girls differently from boys? Must Congress create an exception for such institutions?

Masterpiece Cakeshop, Ltd. v. Colorado Civil Rights Commission

138 S. Ct. 1719 (2018)

Justice KENNEDY delivered the opinion of the Court.

Masterpiece Cakeshop, Ltd., is a bakery in a suburb of Denver. The shop offers a variety of baked goods, ranging from cookies and brownies to elaborate custom-designed cakes for birthday parties, weddings, and other events. Jack Phillips is an expert baker who has owned and operated the shop for 24 years. Phillips is a devout Christian [whose] "main goal in life is to be obedient to" Jesus Christ and Christ's "teachings in all aspects of his life." He seeks to "honor God through his work at Masterpiece Cakeshop." One of Phillips' religious beliefs is that "God's intention for marriage is that it is and should be the union of one man and one woman." To Phillips, creating a wedding cake for a same-sex wedding would be equivalent to participating in a celebration that is contrary to his own most deeply held beliefs. [When] Charlie Craig and Dave Mullins [planned to marry in 2012, they] told Phillips that they were interested in ordering a cake for "our wedding." Phillips informed the couple that he does not "create" wedding cakes for same-sex weddings. He explained, "I'll make your birthday cakes, shower cakes, sell you cookies and brownies, I just don't make cakes for same sex weddings." [He] does not create wedding cakes for same-sex weddings because of his religious opposition to same-sex marriage. "To create a wedding cake for an event that celebrates something that directly goes against the teachings of the Bible, would have been a personal endorsement and participation in the ceremony and relationship."

The Colorado Anti-Discrimination Act (CADA) [prohibits] discrimination in places of public accommoda-tion, [including] discrimination on the basis of sexual orientation. Colo. Rev. Stat. §24–34–601(2)(a) (2017). The Act defines "public accommodation" broadly to include any "place of business engaged in any sales to the public and any place offering services to the public," but excludes "a church, synagogue, mosque, or other place that is principally used for religious purposes." Craig and Mullins filed a discrimination complaint against Masterpiece Cakeshop and Phillips [alleging] that they had been denied "full and equal service" at the bakery because of their sexual orientation. [An ALJ, appointed by the] Civil Rights Division determined that Phillips' actions constituted prohibited discrimination on the basis of sexual orientation, not simply opposition to same-sex marriage as Phillips contended. Phillips asserted that applying CADA in a way that would require him to create a cake for a same-sex wedding would violate his First Amendment right to free speech by compelling him to exercise his artistic talents to express a message with which he disagreed. Phillips also contended that requiring him to create cakes for same-sex weddings would violate his right to the free exercise of religion. The ALJ determined that CADA is a "valid and neutral law of general applicability" and therefore the ALJ ruled against Phillips and the cakeshop on both constitutional claims. The Commission affirmed and ordered Phillips to "cease and desist from discriminating against same-sex couples by refusing to sell them wedding cakes or any product they would sell to heterosexual couples." It also ordered additional remedial measures. The Colorado Court of Appeals affirmed. This Court granted certiorari.

Our society has come to the recognition that gay persons and gay couples cannot be treated as social out-casts or as inferior in dignity and worth. For that reason the laws and the Constitution can, and in some instances must, protect them in the exercise of their civil rights. The exercise of their freedom on terms equal to others must be given great weight and respect by the courts. At the same time, religious and philosophical objections to gay marriage are protected views and in some instances protected forms of expression. As this Court observed in *Obergefell v. Hodges*, 576 U. S. ___ (2015), "the First Amendment ensures that religious organizations and persons are given proper protection as they seek to teach the principles that are so fulfilling and so central to their lives and faiths." While those religious and philosophical objections are protected, it is a general rule that such objections do not allow business owners and other actors in the economy and in society to deny protected persons equal access to goods and services under a neutral and generally applicable public accommodations law.

When it comes to weddings, a member of the clergy who objects to gay marriage on moral and religious grounds could not be compelled to perform the ceremony without denial of his or her right to the free exercise of religion. This refusal would be well understood as an exercise of religion, an exercise that gay persons could recognize and accept without serious diminishment to their own dignity and worth. Yet if that exception were not confined, a long list of persons who provide goods and services for marriages and weddings might refuse to do so for gay persons, thus resulting in a community-wide stigma inconsistent with the history and dynamics of civil rights laws that ensure equal access to goods, services, and public accommodations. Colorado can protect gay persons, just as it can protect other classes of individuals, in acquiring whatever products and services they choose on the same terms and conditions offered to other members of the public. Petitioners conceded that if a baker refused to sell any goods or any cakes for gay weddings, the State would have a strong case under this Court's precedents that this would be a denial of goods and services that went beyond any protected rights of a baker who offers goods and services to the general public and is subject to a neutrally applied and generally applicable public accommodations law.

The neutral and respectful consideration to which Phillips was entitled was compromised here. The Civil Rights Commission's treatment of his case has elements of a clear and impermissible hostility toward the sincere religious beliefs that motivated his objection. That hostility surfaced at the Commission's formal, public hearings. At several points, commissioners endorsed the view that religious beliefs cannot legitimately be carried into the public sphere or commercial domain, implying that religious beliefs and persons are less than fully welcome in Colorado's business community. One commissioner suggested that Phillips can believe "what he wants to believe," but cannot act on his religious beliefs "if he decides to do business in the state." These statements might mean simply that a business cannot refuse to provide services based on sexual orientation, regardless of the proprietor's personal views. On the other hand, they might be seen as inappropriate and dismissive comments showing lack of due consideration for Phillips' free exercise rights and the dilemma he faced. The latter seems more likely. On July 25, 2014, another commissioner said far more to disparage Phillips' beliefs: "Freedom of religion and religion has been used to justify all kinds of discrimination throughout history, whether it be slavery, whether it be the holocaust, whether it be—we can list hundreds of situations where freedom of religion has been used to justify discrimination. To me it is one of the most despicable pieces of rhetoric that people can use to—to use their religion to hurt others." To describe a man's faith as "one of the most despicable pieces of rhetoric that people can use" is to disparage his religion by describing it as despicable, and also by characterizing it as merely rhetorical—something insubstantial and even insincere. The commissioner went so far as to compare Phillips' invocation of his sincerely held religious beliefs to defenses of slavery and the Holocaust. This sentiment is inappropriate for a Commission charged with the solemn responsibility of fair and neutral enforcement of Colorado's antidiscrimination law—a law that protects discrimination on the basis of religion as well as sexual orientation. The record shows no objection to these comments from other commissioners. The later state-court ruling reviewing the Commission's decision did not mention those comments, much less express concern. Nor were the comments disavowed in this Court. These statements cast doubt on the fairness and impartiality of the Commission's adjudication of Phillips' case. Members of the Court have disagreed on whether statements made by lawmakers may properly be taken into account in determining whether a law intentionally discriminates on the basis of religion. In this case, the remarks were made in a very different context—by an adjudicatory body deciding a particular case.

Another indication of hostility is the difference in treatment between Phillips' case and the cases of other bakers who objected to a requested cake on the basis of conscience and prevailed before the Commission. On at least three occasions the Civil Rights Division considered the refusal of bakers to create cakes with images that conveyed disapproval of same-sex marriage, along with religious text. Each time, the Division found that the baker acted lawfully in refusing service. It made these determinations because the requested cake included "wording and images the baker deemed derogatory," featured "language and images the baker deemed hateful," or displayed a message the baker "deemed as discriminatory." The treatment of the conscience-based objections in these cases contrasts with the Commission's treatment of Phillips. The Commission ruled against Phillips in part on the theory that any message the requested wedding cake would carry would be attributed to the customer, not to the baker. Yet the Division did not address this point in the other cases. The Division found no violation of CADA in the other cases in part because each bakery was willing to sell other products, including those depicting Christian themes, to the prospective customers. But the Commission dismissed Phillips' willingness to sell "birthday cakes, shower cakes, and cookies and brownies," to gay and lesbian customers as irrelevant. In short, the Commission's consideration of Phillips' religious objection did not accord with its treatment of these other objections.

Phillips protested that this disparity in treatment reflected hostility on the part of the Commission toward his beliefs. He argued that the Commission had treated the other bakers' conscience-based objections as legitimate, but treated his as illegitimate—thus sitting in judgment of his religious beliefs themselves. The Court of Appeals addressed the disparity only in a footnote. The court stated that "this case is distinguishable. [There was no impermissible discrimination because] the Division found that the bakeries refused the patron's request because of the offensive nature of the requested message." A principled rationale for the difference cannot be based on the government's own assessment of offensiveness. Just as "no official, high or petty, can prescribe what shall be orthodox in politics, nationalism, religion, or other matters of opinion," *West Virginia Bd. of Ed. v. Barnette*, 319 U. S. 624, 642 (1943), it is not the role of the State or its officials to prescribe what shall be offensive. The Colorado court's attempt to account for the difference in treatment elevates one view of what is offensive and sends a signal of official disapproval of Phillips' religious beliefs.

The Commission's treatment of [Phillips] violated the State's duty under the First Amendment not to base laws or regulations on hostility to a religion or religious viewpoint. In *Church of Lukumi Babalu Aye*, the Court made clear that the government, if it is to respect the Constitution's guarantee of free exercise, cannot impose regulations that are hostile to the religious beliefs of affected citizens and cannot act in a manner that passes judgment upon or presupposes the illegitimacy of religious beliefs and practices. The Free Exercise Clause bars even "subtle departures from neutrality" on matters of religion. Here, the Commission was obliged under the Free Exercise Clause to proceed in a manner neutral toward and tolerant of Phillips' religious beliefs. The Constitution "commits government itself to religious tolerance, and upon even slight suspicion that proposals for state intervention stem from animosity to religion or distrust of its practices, all officials must pause to remember their own high duty to the Constitution and to the rights it secures."

Factors relevant to the assessment of governmental neutrality include "the historical background of the decision under challenge, the specific series of events leading to the enactment or official policy, and the legislative or administrative history, including contemporaneous statements made by members of the decisionmaking body." The Commission's consideration of Phillips' case was neither tolerant nor respectful of Phillips' religious beliefs. The Commission gave "every appearance," of adjudicating Phillips' religious objection based on a negative "evaluation of the particular justification" for his objection and the religious grounds for it. Government has no role in deciding or even suggesting whether the religious ground for Phillips' conscience-based objection is legitimate or illegitimate. On these facts, Phillips' religious objection was not considered with the neutrality that the Free Exercise Clause requires. The official expressions of hostility to religion in some of the commissioners' comments—comments not disavowed at the Commission or by the State—were inconsistent with what the Free Exercise Clause requires. The Commission's disparate consideration of Phillips' case compared to the cases of the other bakers suggests the same. The order must be set aside.

The Commission's hostility was inconsistent with the First Amendments guarantee that our laws be applied in a manner that is neutral toward religion. Phillips was entitled to a neutral decisionmaker who would give full and fair consideration to his religious objection as this case was presented, considered, and decided. However later cases raising these or similar concerns are resolved in the future, the Commission's order must be invalidated. The outcome of cases like this in other circumstances must await further elaboration in the courts, all in the context of recognizing that these disputes must be resolved with tolerance, without undue disrespect to sincere religious beliefs, and without subjecting gay persons to indignities when they seek goods and services in an open market.

The judgment of the Colorado Court of Appeals is reversed.

It is so ordered.

Justice KAGAN, with whom Justice BREYER joins, concurring.

State actors cannot show hostility to religious views; rather, they must give those views "neutral and respectful consideration." The Colorado Civil Rights Commission did not satisfy that obligation. The Court partly relies on the "disparate consideration of Phillips' case compared to the cases of three other bakers" who "objected to a requested cake on the basis of conscience." A proper basis for distinguishing the cases was available. CADA makes it unlawful for a place of public accommodation to deny "the full and equal enjoyment" of goods and services to individuals based on certain characteristics, including sexual orientation and creed. The three bakers in the Jack cases did not violate that law. [The customer in the other cases] requested a cake (one denigrating gay people and same-sex marriage) that they would not have made for any customer. By contrast, the same-sex couple in this case requested a wedding cake that Phillips would have made for an opposite-sex couple. In refusing that request, Phillips contravened CADA's demand that customers receive "the full and equal enjoyment" of public accommodations irrespective of their sexual orientation.

Justice GORSUCH, with whom Justice ALITO joins, concurring.

When the government fails to act neutrally toward the free exercise of religion, the government can prevail only if it satisfies strict scrutiny, showing that its restrictions on religion serve a compelling interest and are narrowly tailored. [One customer] approached three bakers and asked them to prepare cakes with messages disapproving same-sex marriage on religious grounds. All three bakers refused, stating that they found his request offensive to their secular convictions. The Division declined to find a violation, reasoning that the bakers didn't deny him service because of his religious faith but because the cakes were offensive to their own moral convictions. The bakers were happy to provide religious persons with other cakes expressing other ideas. Craig and Mullins approached Phillips about creating a cake to celebrate their wedding. Phillips explained that he could not prepare a cake celebrating a same-sex wedding consistent with his religious faith. Phillips offered to make other baked goods for the couple, including cakes celebrating other occasions. Phillips would have refused to create a cake celebrating a same-sex marriage for any customer, regardless of his or her sexual orientation. The Commission held that Phillips's conduct violated the public accommodations law. In both cases, the effect was the same: bakers refused service to persons who bore a statutorily protected trait (religious faith or sexual orientation). But in both cases the bakers refused service only to honor a personal conviction. The bakers knew their conduct promised leaving a customer in a protected class unserved. But there's no indication the bakers actually intended to refuse service because of a customer's protected characteristic. All of the bakers would not sell the requested cakes to anyone, while they would sell other cakes to members of the protected class (as well as anyone else). The bakers in the first case were happy to sell to persons of faith, just as the baker in the second case was generally happy to sell to gay persons. In both cases, it was the kind of cake, not the kind of customer, that mattered to the bakers.

The Commission failed to act neutrally by applying a consistent legal rule. Even though the bakers knowingly denied service to someone in a protected class, the Commission found no violation because the bakers only intended to distance themselves from "the offensive nature of the requested message." Yet, in Phillips's case, the Commission dismissed this very same argument as resting on a "distinction without a difference." An "intent to disfavor" a protected class of persons should be "readily presumed" from the knowing failure to serve someone who belongs to that class. In its judgment, Phillips's intentions were "inextricably tied to the sexual orientation of the parties involved" and "irrational." If Phillips's objection is "inextricably tied" to a protected class, then [the other cases] must be "inextricably tied" to one as well. Just as cakes celebrating same-sex weddings are (usually) requested by persons of a particular sexual orientation, so too are cakes expressing religious opposition to same-sex weddings (usually) requested by persons of particular religious faiths. Both cases result in turning down customers who bear a protected characteristic. The Commission's decisions presumed that Phillip harbored an intent to discriminate against a protected class in light of the foreseeable effects of his conduct, but it declined to presume the same intent in [the other cases]. The Commission cannot apply a more generous legal test to secular objections than religious ones. That is anything but neutral treatment.

It appears the Commission wished to condemn Phillips for expressing just the kind of "irrational" or "offensive message" that the bakers in the first case refused to endorse. Many may consider Phillips's religious beliefs irrational or offensive. Some may believe he misinterprets the teachings of his faith. To be sure, this Court has held same-sex marriage a matter of constitutional right and various States have enacted laws that preclude discrimination on the basis of sexual orientation. But it is also true that no bureaucratic judgment condemning a sincerely held religious belief as "irrational" or "offensive" will survive strict scrutiny under the First Amendment. In this country, the place of secular officials isn't to sit in judgment of religious beliefs, but only to protect their free exercise. It must be the proudest boast of our free exercise jurisprudence that we protect religious beliefs that we find offensive.

It is no answer to observe that [one customer] requested a cake with text on it while Craig and Mullins sought a cake celebrating their wedding without discussing its decoration. These arguments fail to afford Phillips's faith neutral respect. Nor can anyone doubt that a wedding cake without words conveys a message. Words or not and whatever the design, it celebrates a wedding, and if the wedding cake is made for a same-sex couple it celebrates a same-sex wedding. The Commission denied Phillips that choice, even as it afforded the bakers in [the other cases] the choice to refuse to advance a message they deemed offensive to their secular commitments. That is not neutral. Nor would it be proper for this or any court to suggest that a person must be forced to write words rather than create a symbol before his religious faith is implicated. Civil authorities, whether "high or petty," bear no license to declare whether an adherent has "correctly perceived" the commands of his religion. It is our job to look beyond the formality of written words and afford legal protection to any sincere act of faith.

If "cakes that convey a message regarding same-sex marriage" were the relevant level of generality, the Commission would have to respect Phillips's refusal to make the requested cake just as it respected the bakers' refusal to make the cakes Jack requested. [Phillips'] religious beliefs are entitled to no less respectful treatment than the bakers' secular beliefs in [the other cases]. In *Thomas*, a faithful Jehovah's Witness and steel mill worker agreed to help manufacture sheet steel he knew might find its way into armaments, but he was unwilling to work on a fabrication line producing tank turrets. The Court didn't try to suggest that making steel is just making steel. Instead, it recognized that Thomas was entitled to define the nature of his religious commitments—and that those commitments, as defined by the faithful adherent, not a bureaucrat or judge, are entitled to protection under the First Amendment. It is no more appropriate for this Court to tell Phillips that a wedding cake is just like any other.

Phillips has conclusively proven a First Amendment violation and is entitled to judgment.

Justice THOMAS, with whom Justice GORSUCH joins, concurring in part and concurring in the judgment.

Once a court concludes that conduct is expressive, the Constitution limits the government's authority to restrict or compel it. Creating and designing custom wedding cakes is expressive. Phillips considers himself an artist. The logo for Masterpiece Cakeshop is an artist's paint palate with a paintbrush and baker's whisk. Phillips has a picture that depicts him as an artist painting on a canvas. Phillips takes exceptional care with each cake that he creates—sketching the design on paper, choosing the color scheme, creating the frosting and decorations, baking and sculpting the cake, decorating it, and delivering it to the wedding. Phillips sits down with each couple for a consultation before he creates their custom wedding cake. He discusses their preferences, their personalities, and the details of their wedding to ensure that each cake reflects the couple who ordered it. Phillips also sees symbolism in wedding cakes. To him, a wedding cake communicates that "a wedding has occurred, a marriage has begun, and the couple should be celebrated." Forcing Phillips to make custom wedding cakes for same-sex marriages requires him to acknowledge that same-sex weddings are "weddings" and suggest that they should be celebrated—the message he believes his faith forbids.

The First Amendment prohibits Colorado from requiring Phillips to "bear witness to these facts," or to "affirm a belief with which he disagrees." *Barnette*, 319 U. S., at 636. Phillips routinely sacrifices profits to ensure that Masterpiece operates in a way that represents his Christian faith. He is not open on Sundays. Phillips also refuses to bake cakes containing alcohol, cakes with racist or homophobic messages, cakes criticizing God, and cakes celebrating Halloween—even though Halloween is one of the most lucrative seasons for bakeries. The Court of Appeals erred by suggesting that Phillips could simply post a disclaimer, disassociating Masterpiece from any support for same-sex marriage. States cannot put individuals to the choice of "being compelled to affirm someone else's belief" or "being forced to speak when they would prefer to remain silent."

Our precedents demand "the most exacting scrutiny." According to respondents, Colorado can compel Phillips' speech to prevent him from "denigrating the dignity" of same-sex couples, "asserting their inferiority," and subjecting them to "humiliation, frustration, and embarrassment." These justifications are foreign to our free-speech jurisprudence. States cannot punish protected speech because some group finds it offensive, hurtful, stigmatic, unreasonable, or undignified. "If there is a bedrock principle underlying the First Amendment, it is that the government may not prohibit the expression of an idea simply because society finds the idea itself offensive or disagreeable." *Johnson, supra*, at 414. A contrary rule would allow the government to stamp out virtually any speech at will. "It is not the role of the State or its officials to prescribe what shall be offensive." "If it is the speaker's opinion that gives offense, that consequence is a reason for according it constitutional protection." *Hustler Magazine, Inc. v. Falwell*, 485 U. S. 46, 55 (1988). If the only reason a public-accommodations law regulates speech is "to produce a society free of biases" against the protected groups, that purpose is "decidedly fatal" to the law's constitutionality, "for it amounts to nothing less than a proposal to limit speech in the service of orthodox expression." *Hurley*, 515 U. S., at 578. "A speech burden based on audience reactions is simply government hostility in a different guise." *Matal v. Tam*, 582 U. S. ___, ___ (2017) (Kennedy, J., concurring) (slip op., at 4).

Phillips told the couple, "I'll make your birthday cakes, shower cakes, sell you cookies and brownies, I just don't make cakes for same sex weddings." It is hard to see how this statement stigmatizes gays and lesbians more than blocking them from marching in a city parade, dismissing them from the Boy Scouts, or subjecting them to signs that say "God Hates Fags" — all of which this Court has deemed protected by the First Amendment. Moreover, it is hard to see how Phillips' statement is worse than the racist, demeaning, and even threatening speech toward blacks that this Court has tolerated in previous decisions. Concerns about "dignity" and "stigma" did not carry the day when this Court affirmed the right of white supremacists to burn a 25-foot cross, *Virginia v. Black*, 538 U. S. 343 (2003); conduct a rally on Martin Luther King Jr.'s birthday, *Forsyth County v. Nationalist Movement*, 505 U. S. 123 (1992); or circulate a film featuring hooded Klan members who were brandishing weapons and threatening to "Bury the niggers," *Brandenburg v. Ohio*, 395 U. S. 444 (1969) (per curiam).

Nor does *Obergefell* diminish Phillips' right to free speech. "It is one thing to conclude that the Constitution protects a right to same-sex marriage; it is something else to portray everyone who does not share that view as bigoted" and unentitled to express a different view. The First Amendment gives individuals the right to disagree about the correctness of *Obergefell* and the morality of same-sex marriage. In *Obergefell*, I warned that the Court's decision would "inevitably come into conflict" with religious liberty, "as individuals are confronted with demands to participate in and endorse civil marriages between same-sex couples." The conflict has already emerged. In future cases, freedom of speech could be essential to preventing *Obergefell* from being used to "stamp out every vestige of dissent" and "vilify Americans who are unwilling to assent to the new orthodoxy."

Justice GINSBURG, with whom Justice SOTOMAYOR joins, dissenting.

When a couple contacts a bakery for a wedding cake, the product they are seeking is a cake celebrating their wedding — not a cake celebrating heterosexual weddings or same-sex weddings. Colorado prohibits precisely the discrimination Craig and Mullins encountered. Phillips declined to make a cake he found offensive where the offensiveness of the product was determined solely by the identity of the customer requesting it. The three other bakeries declined to make cakes where their objection to the product was due to the demeaning message the requested product would display. I see no reason why the comments of one or two Commissioners should be taken to overcome Phillips' refusal to sell a wedding cake. The proceedings involved several layers of independent decisionmaking, of which the Commission was but one. Phillips' case is thus far removed from *Church of Lukumi* where the government action that violated a principle of religious neutrality implicated a sole decisionmaking body, the city council. Sensible application of CADA to a refusal to sell any wedding cake to a gay couple should occasion affirmance.

Note: Phillips—Postscripts

Following the decision in the *Masterpiece Cakeshop* case, a second baker was sued for refusing to produce a custom cake for a same sex couple's wedding. The lower courts upheld a finding that the baker had discriminated in violation of Oregon's public accommodations law. The U.S. Supreme Court vacated the decision and remanded the case to the lower courts for further proceedings. *See Klein v. Oregon Bureau of Labor & Industry*, 139 S.Ct. 2713 (2019). There also arose other cases involving similar issues. In one, a transgender female requested a cake which would be pink on the inside and blue on the outside, and Phillips refused to make it. Phillips refused on the basis that preparation of the cake would violate his religious beliefs. The customer filed a complaint with the state's civil rights commission which found Phillips guilty of discriminating against LGBTQ people. In an unrelated case, the Washington Supreme Court refused to recognize that a florist's religious objections to same-sex weddings allowed him to refuse service for a same-sex wedding. The court concluded that the case had not been infected with the religious animus evident in the *Masterpiece* case. *See State of Washington v. Arlene's Flowers, Inc.*, 441 P.3d 1203 (2019).

∾ PROBLEMS ∾

1. *An Exception to Smith?* If another *Masterpiece Cakeshop* case comes up, but there is no discriminatory animus, how should the case be resolved? Will the Court simply declare that *Smith*'s neutral, generally applicable, standard applies? Might the Court create an exception for situations when "other fundamental rights" are involved? Might the Court create an exception for personal service situations? Which "other fundamental rights" might justify an exception?

2. *The Prohibition Against LGBT Bias.* Now, let's think a bit more about the Cleveland ordinance (enacted by the City of South Euclid) prohibiting discrimination based on sexual orientation, among other things. Suppose that a Catholic school (The Lyceum) sues, claiming that the ordinance reflects "hostility toward religion and religious beliefs," including Catholic doctrines opposing same-sex marriage and the concept of transgender identity. The school claims that it has the right to expel or deny admission to students who challenge its positions on marriage and sexuality, and to fire employees who do so. How would the school go about proving that enactment of the ordinance reflects hostility towards its religious beliefs?

3. *The Foster Care Policy.* The City of Philadelphia has a foster care contract with Catholic Social Services (CSS). The city adopts a non-discrimination policy that applies to all and prohibits discrimination against same-sex couples. Based on the non-discrimination policy, the City refuses to renew the contract of CSS. Should the non-renewal be regarded as hostility to religion, or simply as a general, neutrally applicable, law? *See Fulton v. Philadelphia,* 922 F.3d 140 (3rd Cir. 2019).

C. ESTABLISHMENT: FREE EXERCISE AND FREE SPEECH TENSION

Even though the Establishment Clause and the Free Exercise Clause are separately stated, they conflict in a number of different contexts. Consider the following case.

Board of Education of Kiryas Joel Village School District v. Grumet

512 U.S. 687 (1994)

Justice SOUTER delivered the opinion of the Court.

The Satmar Hasidic sect purchased an undeveloped subdivision. When a zoning dispute arose, the Satmars petitioned to form a new village, a right that New York law gives any group of residents who satisfy certain procedural niceties. The boundaries of the village of Kiryas Joel were drawn to include only the 320 acres owned and inhabited entirely by Satmars. The village has a population of 8,500 today.

The residents of Kiryas Joel are vigorously religious people who make few concessions to the modern world and go to great lengths to avoid assimilation. They interpret the Torah strictly; segregate the sexes outside the home; speak Yiddish as their primary language; eschew television, radio, and English-language publications; and dress in distinctive ways that include headcoverings and special garments for boys and modest dresses for girls. Children are educated in private religious schools, most boys at the United Talmudic Academy where they receive a grounding in the Torah and limited exposure to secular subjects, and girls at an affiliated school with a curriculum designed to prepare girls for their roles as wives and mothers.

These schools do not offer any distinctive services to handicapped children. In 1984 the Monroe-Woodbury Central School District provided such services for the children of Kiryas Joel at an annex, but ended that arrangement in response to our decisions in *Aguilar v. Felton* and *School Dist. of Grand Rapids v. Ball.* Children from Kiryas Joel who needed special education (including the deaf, the mentally retarded, and others suffering from a range of physical, mental, or emotional disorders) were then forced to attend public schools outside the village. Parents of these children withdrew them from the secular schools citing "the panic, fear and trauma suffered in being with people whose ways were so different." By 1989, only one child from Kiryas Joel was attending Monroe-Woodbury's public schools; the village's other handicapped children received privately funded special services or went without. It was then that the New York Legislature passed a statute which provided that the village of Kiryas Joel "is constituted a separate school district." 1989 N.Y. Laws, ch. 748. Governor Cuomo viewed the bill as "a good faith effort to solve the unique problem" associated with providing special education services to handicapped children in the village.

Although it enjoys plenary legal authority over the elementary and secondary education of all school-aged children in the village, the Kiryas Joel Village School District currently runs only a special education program for handicapped children. The other village children are in parochial schools, relying on the new school district only for transportation, remedial education, and health and welfare services. If any child without a handicap were to seek a public-school education, the district would pay tuition to send the child to another school district nearby. Several of the neighboring districts send their handicapped Hasidic children to Kiryas Joel. The district serves just over 40 full-time students, and two or three times that many on a part-time basis.

Respondents challenged Chapter 748 as an establishment of religion. Respondents won in the courts below. We granted certiorari.

"A proper respect for both the Free Exercise and the Establishment Clauses compels the State to pursue a course of 'neutrality' toward religion," *Committee for Public Ed. & Religious Liberty v. Nyquist,* 413 U.S. 756 (1973), favoring neither one religion over others nor religious adherents collectively over nonadherents. Chapter 748, the statute creating the Kiryas Joel Village School District, departs from this constitutional command by delegating the State's discretionary authority over public schools to a group defined by its character as a religious community, in a context that gives no assurance that governmental power has been or will be exercised neutrally.

In *Larkin v. Grendel's Den, Inc.,* 459 U.S. 116 (1982), the Court reviewed a Massachusetts statute granting religious bodies veto power over applications for liquor licenses. *Larkin* presented an example of united civic and religious authority, a violation of "the core rationale underlying the Establishment Clause." Chapter 748 resembles *Larkin* to the extent that the earlier case teaches that a State may not delegate its civic authority to a group chosen according to a religious criterion. Authority over public schools belongs to the State, and cannot be delegated to a religious group. What makes this litigation different from *Larkin* is the delegation of civic power to the "qualified voters of the village of Kiryas Joel," as distinct from a religious leader such as the village rov, or an institution of religious government like the parish council in *Larkin*. This distinction lacks constitutional significance.

Religious people cannot be denied the opportunity to exercise the rights of citizens simply because of their religious affiliations or commitments, for such a disability would violate the right to religious free exercise. *McDaniel v. Paty*, 435 U.S. 618 (1978) held that a religious individual could not, because of his religious activities, be denied the right to hold political office. If New York were to delegate civic authority to "the Grand Rebbe," *Larkin* would obviously require invalidation (even though under *McDaniel* the Grand Rebbe may run for, and serve on, his local school board). The difference lies in the distinction between a government's purposeful delegation on the basis of religion and a delegation on principles neutral to religion, to individuals whose religious identities are incidental to their receipt of civic authority.

Chapter 748 delegates power not by express reference to the religious belief of the Satmar community, but to residents of the "territory of the village of Kiryas Joel." But Chapter 748 effectively identifies these recipients of governmental authority by reference to doctrinal adherence. The boundary lines of the school district divide residents according to religious affiliation under the terms of an unusual and special legislative Act. Those who negotiated the village boundaries excluded all but Satmars, and the New York Legislature was well aware that the village remained exclusively Satmar when it adopted Chapter 748. The significance of this fact is that carving out the village school district ran counter to customary districting practices in the State. The trend in New York is not toward dividing school districts but toward consolidating them in order to provide a comprehensive education at affordable cost. The Kiryas Joel Village School District has only 13 local, full-time students, and in offering only special education and remedial programs it makes no pretense to be a full-service district.

The origin of the district in a special Act of the legislature, rather than the State's general laws governing school district reorganization, is likewise anomalous. Although the legislature has established some 20 existing school districts by special Act, all but one are districts in name only, designed to be run by private organizations serving institutionalized children. They have neither tax bases nor student populations of their own but serve children placed by other school districts or public agencies. The one school district that was formed by special Act of the legislature to serve a whole community is a district formed for a new town, much larger and more heterogeneous than this village. Thus the Kiryas Joel Village School District is exceptional to the point of singularity. This district "cannot be seen as the fulfillment of a village's destiny as an independent governmental entity."

Because the district's creation ran uniquely counter to state practice, following the lines of a religious community where the customary and neutral principles would not have dictated the same result, we have good reasons to treat this district as the reflection of a religious criterion for identifying the recipients of civil authority. We therefore find the legislature's Act to be substantially equivalent to defining a political subdivision and hence the qualification for its franchise by a religious test, resulting in a purposeful and forbidden "fusion of governmental and religious functions." The fact that this school district was created by a special and unusual Act of the legislature also gives reason for concern whether the benefit received by the Satmar community is one that the legislature will provide equally to other religious (and nonreligious) groups. The special Act in these cases stands alone.

The Constitution allows the State to accommodate religious needs by alleviating special burdens. But accommodation is not a principle without limits. Petitioners' proposed accommodation singles out a particular religious sect for special treatment. There are several alternatives here for providing bilingual and bicultural special education to Satmar children. Such services can be offered to village children through the Monroe-Woodbury Central School District. Since the Satmars do not claim that separatism is religiously mandated, their children may receive bilingual and bicultural instruction at a public school already run by the district. Or if the educationally appropriate offering should be a separate program of bilingual and bicultural education at a neutral site near one of the village's parochial schools, no Establishment Clause difficulty would inhere in such a scheme, administered in accordance with neutral principles that would not necessarily confine special treatment to Satmars.

We do not disable a religiously homogeneous group from exercising political power conferred on it without regard to religion. Unlike the States of Utah and New Mexico (which were laid out according to traditional political methodologies taking account of lines of latitude and longitude and topographical features), the reference line for the Kiryas Joel Village School District was drawn to separate Satmars from non-Satmars. The statute before us fails the test of neutrality. It delegates a power this Court has said "ranks at the very apex of the function of a State," to an electorate defined by common religious belief and practice, in a manner that fails to foreclose religious favoritism. It therefore crosses the line from permissible accommodation to impermissible establishment. The judgment of the Court of Appeals of the State of New York is accordingly

Affirmed.

Justice STEVENS, with whom Justice BLACKMUN and Justice GINSBURG join, *concurring.*

The isolation of these children unquestionably increased the likelihood that they would remain within the fold, faithful adherents of their parents' religious faith. Affirmative state action in aid of segregation of this character is fairly characterized as establishing, rather than merely accommodating, religion.

Justice O'CONNOR, *concurring in part* and *concurring in the judgment.*

What makes accommodation permissible, even praiseworthy, is that the government is accommodating a deeply held belief. But accommodations do not justify discriminations based on sect. A state law prohibiting the consumption of alcohol may exempt sacramental wines, but it may not exempt sacramental wine use by Catholics but not by Jews. Because this benefit was given to this group based on its religion, it seems proper to treat it as a legislatively drawn religious classification. The legislature may well be acting without any favoritism, so that if another group came to ask for a similar district, the group might get it on the same terms as the Satmars. But the nature of the legislative process makes it impossible to be sure of this. It seems dangerous to validate what appears to me a clear religious preference.

Our invalidation of this statute in no way means that the Satmars' needs cannot be accommodated. New York may allow all villages to operate their own school districts. If it does not want to act so broadly, it may set forth neutral criteria that a village must meet to have a school district of its own. A district created under a generally applicable scheme would be acceptable even though it coincides with a village that was consciously created by its voters as an enclave for their religious group. There is one other accommodation that would be permissible: the scheme which was discontinued because of our decision in *Aguilar.* If the government provides this education on-site at public schools and at nonsectarian private schools, it is only fair that it provide it on-site at sectarian schools as well.

Justice KENNEDY, *concurring in the judgment.*

There is more than a fine line between the voluntary association that leads to a political community comprised of people who share a common religious faith, and the forced separation that occurs when the government draws explicit political boundaries on the basis of peoples' faith. In creating the Kiryas Joel Village School District, New York crossed that line.

Justice SCALIA, with whom THE CHIEF JUSTICE and Justice THOMAS join, *dissenting.*

The Court today finds that the Powers That Be, up in Albany, have Conspired to effect an establishment of the Satmar Hasidim. I do not know who would be more surprised at this discovery: the Founders of our Nation or Grand Rebbe Joel Teitelbaum, founder of the Satmar. The Grand Rebbe would be astounded to learn that after escaping brutal persecution and coming to America with the modest hope of religious toleration for their ascetic form of Judaism, the Satmar had become so powerful, so closely allied with Mammon, as to have become an "establishment" of the Empire State.

These cases involve no public funding, however slight or indirect, to private religious schools. The school under scrutiny is a public school specifically designed to provide a public secular education to handicapped students. While the village's private schools are profoundly religious and strictly segregated by sex, classes at the public school are co-ed and the curriculum secular. The school building has the bland appearance of a public school, unadorned by religious symbols or markings; and the school complies with the laws and regulations governing all other New York State public schools. The only thing distinctive about the school is that all the students share the same religion. If a State can furnish services to a group of sectarian students on a neutral site adjacent to a private religious school, or even within such a school, how can there be any defect in educating those same students in a public school? The populating of North America is in no small measure the story of groups of people sharing a common religious and cultural heritage striking out to form their own communities. It is preposterous to suggest that the civil institutions of these communities, separate from their churches, were constitutionally suspect.

Justice Souter's position boils down to the novel proposition that any group of citizens can be invested with political power, but not if they all belong to the same religion. Of course such disfavoring of religion is positively antagonistic to the purposes of the Religion Clauses. Justice Souter's second justification for finding an establishment of religion is his facile conclusion that the New York Legislature's creation of the Kiryas Joel school district was religiously motivated. The handicapped children suffered sufficient emotional trauma from their predicament that their parents kept them home from school. Surely the legislature could provide a public education for these students. Justice Souter's case against the statute comes down to the fact that the residents of the Kiryas Joel Village School District are Satmars. But all its residents also wear unusual dress, have unusual civic customs, and have not much to do with people who are culturally different from them. On what basis does Justice Souter conclude that it is the theological distinctiveness rather than the cultural distinctiveness that was the basis for New York State's decision? The normal assumption would be that it was the latter. Justice Souter argues that the legislature must have been motivated by the desire to favor religion. There is no evidence of that. The special district was created to meet the special educational needs of distinctive handicapped children. When a legislature acts to accommodate religion, particularly a minority sect, "it follows the best of our traditions." I *dissent.*

BACKGROUND
Religious Exemptions

There has been considerable debate about whether government can, or should, exempt religious groups from the application of civil rights laws that conflict with their beliefs. Illustrative is *Corporation of Presiding Bishop v. Amos,* 483 U.S. 327 (1987), which involved Section 702 of the Civil Rights

Act of 1964, exempting religious organizations from Title VII's prohibition against discrimination in employment on the basis of religion as applied to a church's decision to discharge a nonmember from its employment. In upholding the exemption, the Court stated: "Where, as here, government acts with the proper purpose of lifting a regulation that burdens the exercise of religion, we see no reason to require that the exemption comes packaged with benefits to secular entities."

Note: Armed Forces Chaplains

Another context in which claims for religious exemption have surfaced involves military chaplains. The armed forces hire chaplains to meet the religious needs of soldiers. Although chaplains are given the status of commissioned officers and wear uniforms, they are not given commands. In *Katcoff v. Marsh*, 755 F.2d 223 (2d Cir. 1985), the court upheld the practice: "The problem of meeting the religious needs of Army personnel is compounded by the mobile, deployable nature of our armed forces, who must be ready on extremely short notice to be transported from bases to distant parts of the world for combat duty. Unless there were chaplains ready to move simultaneously with the troops and to tend to their spiritual needs as they face possible death, the soldiers would be left in the lurch, religiously speaking." The court emphasized that chaplains were not allowed to proselytize soldiers, and their "principal duties are to conduct religious services, to furnish religious education to soldiers and their families, and to counsel soldiers with respect to a wide variety of personal problems." The court questioned whether chaplains would be necessary in areas where civilian religious personnel are available.

∾ PROBLEMS ∾

1. *Accommodating the Satmars.* In *Kiryas Joel*, the Court invalidated New York's attempt to create a special school district. Does the holding in that case doom all further accommodations? Suppose that you are counsel to the legislature. Following the Court's holding, can you suggest ways that the legislature might accommodate the Satmars without violating the Establishment Clause?

2. *The Satmars and the Education for a Better America Act.* In constructing the proposed legislation, can you (should you?) attempt to accommodate religious groups like the Satmars? Can you provide financial aid to them on terms equivalent to those provided to other schools?

3. *Student Religious Music.* At times, officials have difficulty finding the dividing line between establishment and accommodation. For example, suppose that a choral teacher invites students to bring songs of their own choosing to class, and tells students that the class will collectively analyze the songs in terms of

tone, tempo, and dynamics. Suppose that one student decides to bring a recording that contains religious music. On establishment grounds, should the teacher refuse to play the music because of its religious content? Alternatively, should the teacher "accommodate" the student's desire to listen to religious music? How would you advise the school district? In that regard, consider the following case.

Rosenberger v. Rector and Visitors of the University of Virginia

515 U.S. 819 (1995)

Justice KENNEDY delivered the opinion of the Court.

In this case, the Student Activities Fund (SAF) at the University of Virginia denied funds for the printing of the student publication *Wide Awake: A Christian Perspective at the University of Virginia.* The Supreme Court first held that "the regulation invoked to deny SAF support, both in its terms and in its application to these petitioners is a denial of their right of free speech guaranteed by the First Amendment." The Court's description of the facts and the justices' opinions on the free speech issue are set forth in Chapter VIII. The Court then turned to the question of "whether the violation following from the University's action is excused by the necessity of complying with the Constitution's prohibition against state establishments of religion."

The University has argued that inclusion of WAP's contractors in SAF funding authorization would violate the Establishment Clause. The guarantee of neutrality is respected, not offended, when the government, following neutral criteria and evenhanded policies, extends benefits to recipients whose ideologies and viewpoints, including religious ones, are broad and diverse.

The governmental program here is neutral toward religion. There is no suggestion that the University created it to advance religion or adopted some ingenious device with the purpose of aiding a religious cause. The object of the SAF is to open a forum for speech and to support various student enterprises, including the publication of newspapers, in recognition of the diversity and creativity of student life. The University's SAF Guidelines have a separate classification for, and do not make third-party payments on behalf of, "religious organizations." The category of support here is for "student news, information, opinion, entertainment, or academic communications media groups," of which Wide Awake was 1 of 15 in the 1990 school year. WAP did not seek a subsidy because of its Christian editorial viewpoint; it sought funding as a student journal, which it was.

The neutrality of the program distinguishes the student fees from a tax levied for the direct support of a church or group of churches. A tax of that sort, of course, would run contrary to Establishment Clause concerns dating from the earliest days of the Republic. The exaction here, by contrast, is a student activity fee designed to reflect the reality that student life in its many dimensions includes the necessity of wide-ranging speech and inquiry and that student expression is an integral part of the University's educational mission.

Government neutrality is apparent in the State's overall scheme in a further meaningful respect. The University has taken pains to disassociate itself from the private speech involved in this case.

The University provides printing services to a broad spectrum of student newspapers qualified as CIOs by reason of their officers and membership. Any benefit to religion is incidental to the government's provision of secular services for secular purposes on a religion-neutral basis. To obey the Establishment Clause, it was not necessary for the University to deny eligibility to student publications because of their viewpoint.

The judgment of the Court of Appeals must be, and is, reversed.

It is so ordered.

Justice O'CONNOR, *concurring.*

Certain considerations specific to the program at issue lead me to conclude that by providing the same assistance to Wide Awake that it does to other publications, the University would not be endorsing the magazine's religious perspective. First, the student organizations, at the University's insistence, remain strictly independent of the University. And the agreement requires that student organizations include in every letter, contract, publication, or other written materials the following disclaimer:

> Although this organization has members who are University of Virginia students (faculty) (employees), the organization is independent of the corporation which is the University and which is not responsible for the organization's contracts, acts or omissions.

Any reader of Wide Awake would be on notice of the publication's independence from the University.

Second, financial assistance is distributed in a manner that ensures its use only for the University's purpose in maintaining a free and robust marketplace of ideas, from whatever perspective. Third, assistance is provided to the religious publication in a context that makes improbable any perception of government endorsement of the religious message. The University has provided support to The Yellow Journal, a humor magazine that has targeted Christianity as a subject of satire, and Al-Salam, a publication to "promote a better understanding of Islam to the University Community." By withholding from Wide Awake assistance that the University provides generally to all other student publications, the University has discriminated on the basis of the magazine's religious viewpoint in violation of the Free Speech Clause.

Justice SOUTER, with whom Justice STEVENS, Justice GINSBURG, and Justice BREYER join, *dissenting.*

The Court today, for the first time, approves direct funding of core religious activities by an arm of the State. I would hold that the University's refusal to support petitioners' religious activities is compelled by the Establishment Clause.

This writing is no merely descriptive examination of religious doctrine or even of ideal Christian practice in confronting life's social and personal problems. It is straightforward exhortation to enter into a relationship with God as revealed in Jesus Christ, and to satisfy a series of moral obligations derived from the teachings of Jesus Christ.

Using public funds for the direct subsidization of preaching the word is categorically forbidden under the Establishment Clause, and if the Clause was meant to accomplish nothing else, it was meant to bar this use of public money. The University exercises the power of the State to compel a student to pay a fee, and the use of any part of it for the direct support of religious activity thus strikes at what we have repeatedly held to be the heart of the prohibition on establishment. There should be no need to decide whether the University would violate the Free Speech Clause by limiting funding as it has done.

Notes and Questions

1. *Reconsidering the* Christian Legal Society *Decision.* In Chapter 11, we examined the *Christian Legal Society* case, which placed a gloss on *Rosenberger*'s holding. Are you clear about when universities can refuse to fund the speech of religious student organizations?

2. *Religious Instruction in Public Schools.* Another issue that has arisen is whether students can be provided with religious instruction during public school hours. Whether the instruction is regarded as an establishment or an accommodation depends on how it is structured. In *Illinois v. McCollum*, 333 U.S. 203 (1948), the Court held that Illinois could not allow privately employed religious teachers to enter public school buildings during regular school hours and substitute religious teaching for secular education. However, in *Zorach v. Clauson*, 343 U.S. 306 (1952), the Court held that students could be released from public school classes to attend religious classes off-site.

3. *Religious Use of Public School Facilities.* A number of cases have focused on whether religious groups may use public school facilities. In *Widmar v. Vincent*, 454 U.S. 263 (1981), when a state university opened its facilities to registered student groups, the Court held that it could not close those facilities to groups desiring to engage in religious worship and religious discussion. The Court held that the university was required to allow religious groups to use its facilities: "Having created a forum generally open to student groups, the University seeks to enforce a content-based exclusion of religious speech." Justice White, dissenting, argued that the case involved "religious worship only." In *Good News Club v. Milford Central School*, 533 U.S. 98 (2001), the Court confronted similar issues in the context of an elementary school. The Court found that Milford was operating a "limited public forum" and concluded that it had improperly excluded the Good News Club: "Milford engaged in viewpoint discrimination when it excluded the Club from the after school forum. The Club seeks to address a subject otherwise

permitted under the rule, the teaching of morals and character, from a religious standpoint. The only apparent difference is that the Club chooses to teach moral lessons from a Christian perspective through live storytelling and prayer." Justice Stevens dissented: "A school need not open its forum to religious proselytizing or worship." Justice Souter also dissented: "Good News's exercises blur the line between public classroom instruction and private religious indoctrination, leaving a reasonable elementary school pupil unable to appreciate that the former instruction is the business of the school while the latter evangelism is not."

4. *Vocational Assistance to the Handicapped.* Another context in which establishment–free exercise tension has been revealed is vocational assistance to the handicapped. In *Witters v. Washington Department of Services for the Blind*, 474 U.S. 481 (1986), a statute authorized payments "for special education and/or training in the professions, business or trades" to "assist visually handicapped persons to overcome vocational handicaps and to obtain the maximum degree of self-support and self-care." The Court held that the state could not deny assistance to a blind person who was studying at a Christian college to become a pastor, missionary, or youth director: "Any aid that flows to religious institutions does so only as a result of the independent and private choices of aid recipients. Washington's program is made available generally without regard to the sectarian-nonsectarian, or public-nonpublic nature of the institution benefitted, and is in no way skewed towards religion." Justice O'Connor concurred: "The aid to religion is the result of petitioner's private choice. No reasonable observer is likely to draw from the facts before us an inference that the State itself is endorsing a religious practice or belief."

5. *The Adolescent Family Life Act. Bowen v. Kendrick*, 487 U.S. 589 (1988), involved the Adolescent Family Life Act (AFLA), which provided funding to public or nonprofit private organizations addressing problems relating to pregnancy and childbirth among unmarried adolescents. The grants were intended to promote "self discipline and other prudent approaches to the problem of adolescent premarital sexual relations," to encourage adoption as an alternative for adolescent parents, to establish new approaches to the delivery of care services for pregnant adolescents, and to support research and demonstration projects "concerning the societal causes and consequences of adolescent premarital sexual relations, contraceptive use, pregnancy, and child rearing." The case focused on a congressionally imposed requirement that grant applicants describe how they would involve religious organizations in AFLA-funded programs. The Court rejected the challenge: "These provisions of the statute reflect at most Congress' considered judgment that religious organizations can help solve the problems to which the AFLA is addressed. Nothing in our previous cases prevents Congress from making such a judgment or from recognizing the important part that religion or religious organizations may play in resolving certain secular problems. Nothing indicates that a significant proportion of the federal funds will be disbursed to 'pervasively sectarian' institutions." The Court also rejected the argument that AFLA excessively entangled government with religion: "There is no reason to

fear that the less intensive monitoring involved here will cause the Government to intrude unduly in the day-to-day operation of the religiously affiliated AFLA grantees." Justice Blackmun dissented: "Congress enacted a statute that gave religious groups a pedagogical and counseling role without imposing any restraints on the sectarian quality of the participation."

∾ PROBLEMS ∾

1. *Withholding Student Activity Fees.* In two important decisions, *Keller v. State Bar of California,* 496 U.S. 1 (1990), and *Abood v. Detroit Board of Education,* 431 U.S. 209 (1977), the Court held that lawyers and laborers need not "associate" with the speech of state bar organizations and labor unions with which they disagreed. As a result, lawyers and laborers could withhold dues payments attributable to an objectionable message. After *Rosenberger,* may students at the University of Virginia withhold that portion of the student activity fee attributable to publications with which they disagree (i.e., WAP)?

2. *Prohibiting Religious Services.* Kentucky public schools maintain a limited public forum in which outside groups may use school facilities for meetings. The policy permits religious groups to use the facilities and allows any group "to discuss religious material or any material which contains a religious viewpoint." However, it prohibits religious services and instruction. After *Rosenberger,* is the policy valid?

3. *Student Murals.* A public high school allows art students to paint murals on the school's exterior walls and has established a contest to reward students who create the best murals. Under the contest rules, students may address any "political or social issue" in their murals, but they may not include "obscene" or otherwise "inappropriate" material. A student submits a mural proposal that depicts Jesus Christ, larger than life, and portrays him as instructing students. The school wants to reject the mural proposal on the basis that the Establishment Clause precludes the school from recognizing religion in this manner. If you are the school district's attorney, how would you advise it regarding the religious mural proposal?

Locke v. Davey

540 U.S. 712 (2004)

Chief Justice REHNQUIST delivered the opinion of the Court.

The Washington State Legislature found that "students who work hard and successfully complete high school with high academic marks may not have the financial ability to attend college because they cannot obtain financial aid or the financial aid is insufficient." To assist these high-achieving students, the legislature created the Promise Scholarship Program, which provides a scholarship, renewable for one year, to eligible students for postsecondary education expenses. Students may spend their funds on any education-related expense, including room and board. The scholarships are funded through the State's general fund, and their amount varies each year depending on the annual appropriation, which is evenly prorated among the eligible students. The scholarship was worth $1,125 for academic year 1999-2000 and $1,542 for 2000-2001.

To be eligible for the scholarship, a student must meet academic, income, and enrollment requirements. A student must graduate from a Washington public or private high school and either graduate in the top 15% of his graduating class, or attain on the first attempt a cumulative score of 1,200 or better on the Scholastic Assessment Test I or a score of 27 or better on the American College Test. The student's family income must be less than 135% of the State's median. Finally, the student must enroll "at least half time in an eligible postsecondary institution in the state of Washington," and may not pursue a degree in theology at that institution while receiving the scholarship. Private institutions, including those religiously affiliated, qualify as "eligible postsecondary institutions" if they are accredited by a nationally recognized accrediting body. A "degree in theology" is not defined in the statute, but the statute simply codifies the State's constitutional prohibition on providing funds to students to pursue degrees that are "devotional in nature or designed to induce religious faith." Wash. Const., Art. I, §11.

A student who applies for the scholarship and meets the academic and income requirements is notified that he is eligible for the scholarship. Once the student enrolls at an eligible institution, the institution must certify that the student is enrolled at least half time and that the student is not pursuing a degree in devotional theology. The institution, rather than the State, determines whether the student's major is devotional. If the student meets the enrollment requirements, the scholarship funds are sent to the institution for distribution to the student to pay for tuition or other educational expenses.

Respondent, Joshua Davey, was awarded a Promise Scholarship, and chose to attend Northwest College. Northwest is a private, Christian college affiliated with the Assemblies of God denomination, and is an eligible institution under the Promise Scholarship Program. Davey had "planned for many years to attend a Bible college and to prepare himself through that college training for a lifetime of ministry, specifically as a church pastor." When he enrolled in Northwest College, he decided to pursue a double major in pastoral ministries and business management/administration. The pastoral ministries degree is devotional and therefore excluded under the Promise Scholarship Program. When Davey learned that he could not use his scholarship to pursue a devotional theology degree, he brought an action under 42 U.S.C. §1983 arguing that the denial of his scholarship based on his decision to pursue a theology degree violated, *inter alia,* the Free Exercise, Establishment, and Free Speech Clauses of the First Amendment. The District Court rejected Davey's constitutional claims. A divided panel of the United States Court of Appeals for the Ninth Circuit reversed. We granted certiorari and now reverse.

The Establishment Clause and the Free Exercise Clause are frequently in tension. Yet we have long said that "there is room for play in the joints" between them. *Walz v. Tax Comm'n. of City of New York*, 397 U.S. 664 (1970). In other words, there are some state actions permitted by the Establishment Clause but not required by the Free Exercise Clause. This case involves that "play in the joints." The question before is whether Washington, pursuant to its own constitution, which has been authoritatively interpreted as prohibiting even indirectly funding religious instruction that will prepare students for the ministry, can deny them such funding without violating the Free Exercise Clause.

Davey contends that under the rule we enunciated in *Church of Lukumi Babalu Aye v. Hialeah*, 508 U.S. 520 (1993), the program is presumptively unconstitutional because it is not facially neutral with respect to religion.[1] We reject his claim of presumptive unconstitutionality. In the present case, the State's disfavor of religion (if it can be called that) is of a far milder kind. It imposes neither criminal nor civil sanctions on any type of religious service or rite. It does not deny to ministers the right to participate in the political affairs of the community. *See McDaniel v. Paty*, 435 U.S. 618 (1978). And it does not require students to choose between their religious beliefs and receiving a government benefit.[2] The State has merely chosen not to fund a distinct category of instruction.

Because the Promise Scholarship Program funds training for all secular professions, Justice Scalia contends the State must also fund training for religious professions. But training someone to lead a congregation is an essentially religious endeavor. Indeed, majoring in devotional theology is akin to a religious calling as well as an academic pursuit. And the subject of religion is one in which both the United States and state constitutions embody distinct views—in favor of free exercise, but opposed to establishment—that find no counterpart with respect to other callings or professions. That a State would deal differently with religious education for the ministry than with education for other callings is a product of these views, not evidence of hostility toward religion.

We can think of few areas in which a State's antiestablishment interests come more into play. Since the founding of our country, there have been popular uprisings against procuring taxpayer funds to support church leaders, which was one of the hallmarks of an "established" religion. J. Madison, *Memorial and Remonstrance Against Religious Assessments*. Most States that sought to avoid an establishment of religion around the time of the founding placed in their constitutions formal prohibitions against using tax funds to support the ministry. *E.g.*, Ga. Const., Art.

---

1. Promise Scholars may still use their scholarship to pursue a secular degree at a different institution from where they are studying devotional theology.
2. Davey, relying on *Rosenberger v. Rector and Visitors of Univ. of Va.*, 515 U.S. 819 (1995), contends that the Promise Scholarship Program is an unconstitutional viewpoint restriction on speech. But the Promise Scholarship Program is not a forum for speech.

IV, §5 (1789). That early state constitutions saw no problem in explicitly excluding *only* the ministry from receiving state dollars reinforces our conclusion that religious instruction is of a different ilk.

Far from evincing the hostility toward religion which was manifest in *Lukumi*, we believe that the entirety of the Promise Scholarship Program goes a long way toward including religion in its benefits. The program permits students to attend pervasively religious schools, so long as they are accredited. Students are still eligible to take devotional theology courses. Davey notes all students at Northwest are required to take at least four devotional courses, "Exploring the Bible," "Principles of Spiritual Development," "Evangelism in the Christian Life," and "Christian Doctrine," and some students may have additional religious requirements as part of their majors.

In short, we find neither in the history or text of Article I, §11 of the Washington Constitution, nor in the operation of the Promise Scholarship Program, anything that suggests animus towards religion. Given the historic and substantial state interest at issue, we therefore cannot conclude that the denial of funding for vocational religious instruction alone is inherently constitutionally suspect.

Without a presumption of unconstitutionality, Davey's claim must fail. The State's interest in not funding the pursuit of devotional degrees is substantial and the exclusion of such funding places a relatively minor burden on Promise Scholars. If any room exists between the two Religion Clauses, it must be here. We need not venture further into this difficult area in order to uphold the Promise Scholarship Program as currently operated by the State of Washington.

The judgment of the Court of Appeals is therefore

Reversed.

Justice SCALIA, with whom Justice THOMAS joins, *dissenting.*

In *Church of Lukumi Babalu Aye, Inc.*, the Court held that "a law burdening religious practice that is not neutral must undergo the most rigorous of scrutiny," and that "the minimum requirement of neutrality is that a law not discriminate on its face." The State of Washington has created a generally available public benefit, but has then carved out a solitary course of study for exclusion. No field of study but religion is singled out for disfavor in this fashion. Davey seeks only *equal* treatment—the right to direct his scholarship to his chosen course of study, a right every other Promise Scholar enjoys. One can concede the Framers' hostility to funding the clergy *specifically*, but that says nothing about whether the clergy had to be excluded from benefits the State made available to all. No one would seriously contend that the Framers would have barred ministers from using public roads on their way to church.

There are any number of ways that the state could respect both its unusually sensitive concern for the conscience of its taxpayers *and* the Federal Free Exercise Clause. It could make the scholarships redeemable only at public universities (where it sets the curriculum), or only for select courses of study. Either option would replace a program that facially discriminates against religion with one that just happens not to subsidize it. The State could also simply abandon the scholarship program altogether.

Justice THOMAS, *dissenting.*

Assuming that the State denies Promise Scholarships only to students who pursue a degree in devotional theology, I believe that Justice Scalia's application of our precedents is correct.

∽ PROBLEMS ∽

1. Rosenberger, Locke, *and the Education for the Twenty-first Century Act.* In constructing the proposed legislation, what (if any) conclusions do you draw from decisions like *Rosenberger* and *Locke?*

2. *Black Nativity.* Suppose that a theater arts professor at a state university wishes to present a play entitled *Black Nativity,* which is set in a Baptist church and celebrates the birth of Jesus. The director describes the play as being about "praising God for Jesus." The director states that "theater mirrors life. We teach that every day. God is a part of life. In my view, without Him there is no life." Does the presentation of the play constitute an establishment of religion? Or should it be regarded as an accommodation of the director's religious beliefs? Does the presentation violate the Establishment Clause?

3. *A Final Look at Congressional Funding of the Education for a Better America Act.* After reading this chapter on the religion clauses, have your views regarding the permissible scope of the legislation changed? What provisions would you include in the statute? Which would you exclude?

Trinity Lutheran Church of Columbia, Inc. v. Director

137 S. Ct. 2012 (2017).

Chief Justice ROBERTS delivered the opinion of the Court, except as to footnote 3.

The Trinity Lutheran Church Child Learning Center is a preschool and daycare center open to working families in Boone County, Missouri, and the surrounding area. The Center operates on church property. The Center admits students of any religion, and enrollment stands at about 90 children ranging from age two to five. The Center includes a playground that is equipped with slides, swings, jungle gyms, monkey bars, and sandboxes. The surface beneath and surrounding the play equipment is gravel. Youngsters, of course, fall on the playground or tumble [and] the gravel can be unforgiving. The Center sought to replace the gravel with a pour-in-place rubber surface by participating in Missouri's Scrap Tire Program. Run by the State's Department of Natural Resources to reduce the number of used tires destined for landfills and dump sites, the program offers grants to qualifying nonprofit organizations that purchase playground surfaces made from recycled tires. It is funded through a fee imposed on the sale of new tires.

The Department awards grants on a competitive basis based on several criteria, such as the poverty level and the applicant's plan to promote recycling. The Department had a strict policy of denying grants to any applicant owned or controlled by a church, sect, or other religious entity. In its application, the Center disclosed its status as a ministry of Trinity Lutheran Church and specified that the Center's mission was "to provide a safe, clean, and attractive school facility in conjunction with an educational program structured to allow a child to grow spiritually, physically, socially, and cognitively." After describing the playground and the safety hazards, the Center detailed the benefits of the proposed project: increasing access for all children, including those with disabilities, by providing a surface compliant with the Americans with Disabilities Act of 1990; providing a safe, long-lasting, and resilient surface under the play areas; and improving Missouri's environment by putting recycled tires to positive use. The benefits of a new surface would extend to the local community whose children often use the playground during non-school hours. The Center ranked fifth among 44 applicants in the 2012 Scrap Tire Program. Despite its score, the Center was ineligible to receive a grant. Under Article I, Section 7 of the Missouri Constitution, the Department could not provide financial assistance directly to a church. The Department awarded 14 grants. The Church alleged that the Department's policy of denying grants to religiously affiliated applicants violates the Free Exercise Clause of the First Amendment. The District Court [dismissed], relying on *Locke v. Davey,* 540 U.S. 712 (2004). The Eighth Circuit affirmed. We granted certiorari and reverse.

The First Amendment provides, in part, that "Congress shall make no law respecting an establishment of religion, or prohibiting the free exercise thereof." The Establishment Clause does not prevent Missouri from including Trinity Lutheran in the Program. Under the Free Exercise Clause, there is "play in the joints" between what the Establishment Clause permits and the Free Exercise Clause compels. The Free Exercise Clause "protects religious observers against unequal treatment" and subjects to the strictest scrutiny laws that target the religious for "special disabilities" based on their "religious status." *Church of Lukumi Babalu Aye, Inc. v. Hialeah,* 508 U.S. 520, 533 (1993). Denying a generally available benefit solely on account of religious identity imposes a penalty on the free exercise of religion that can be justified only by a state interest "of the highest order." *McDaniel v. Paty,* 435 U.S. 618 (1978) (plurality opinion). In *Everson v. Board of Education of Ewing,* 330 U.S. 1 (1947), we upheld against an Establishment Clause challenge a law enabling a school district to reimburse parents for the public transportation costs of sending their children to public and private schools, including parochial schools. In ruling that the Establishment Clause allowed New Jersey to extend that benefit to all its citizens regardless of their religious belief, we explained that a State "cannot hamper its citizens in the free exercise of their own religion. Consequently, it cannot exclude Catholics, Lutherans, Mohammedans, Baptists, Jews, Methodists, Non-believers, Presbyterians, or the members of any other faith, *because of their faith, or lack of it,* from receiving the benefits of public welfare legislation." In *McDaniel v. Paty,* the Court struck down under the Free Exercise Clause a Tennessee statute disqualifying ministers from serving as delegates to the State's constitutional convention. Said Chief Justice Burger, the Tennessee law "effectively penalizes the free exercise of McDaniel's constitutional liberties." Justice Brennan added that "because the challenged provision requires McDaniel to purchase his right to engage in the ministry by sacrificing his candidacy it impairs the free exercise of his religion."

In recent years, when this Court has rejected free exercise challenges, the laws in question have been neutral and generally applicable without regard to religion. We distinguish such laws from those that single out the religious for disfavored treatment. In *Employment Division, Department of Human Resources of Oregon v. Smith,* 494 U.S. 872 (1990), we rejected a free exercise claim by two members of a Native American church denied unemployment benefits. The Free Exercise Clause did not entitle the church members to a special dispensation from general criminal laws on account of their religion. The Free Exercise Clause *did* guard against the government's imposition of "special disabilities on the basis of religious views or religious status."[1] In *Church of Lukumi Babalu Aye, Inc. v. Hialeah,* we struck down facially neutral city ordinances that outlawed certain forms of animal slaughter. A law may not discriminate against "some or all religious beliefs." Nor may a law regulate or outlaw conduct because it is religiously motivated.

The Department's policy expressly discriminates against otherwise eligible recipients by disqualifying them from a public benefit solely because of their religious character. Trinity Lutheran is free to continue operating as a church, but at the cost of automatic exclusion from the benefits of a public program for which the Center is otherwise fully qualified. When the State conditions a benefit in this way, the State has punished the free exercise of religion. The Department contends that merely declining to extend funds to Trinity Lutheran does not *prohibit* the Church from engaging in any religious conduct or otherwise exercising its religious rights. The Department has simply declined to allocate to Trinity Lutheran a subsidy the State had no obligation to provide. But the Free Exercise Clause protects against "indirect coercion or penalties on the free exercise of religion, not just outright prohibitions." *Lyng,* 485 U.S., at 450. "The liberties of religion and expression may be infringed by the denial of or placing of conditions upon a benefit or privilege." *Sherbert,* 374 U.S., at 404. The express discrimination against religious exercise here is not the denial of a grant, but rather the refusal to allow the Church—solely because it is a church—to compete with secular organizations for a grant. The State's decision to exclude it for purposes of this public program must withstand the strictest scrutiny.

---

1. This is not to say that any application of a valid and neutral law of general applicability is necessarily constitutional under the Free Exercise Clause. *Hosanna–Tabor Evangelical Lutheran Church and School v. EEOC,* 565 U.S. 171 (2012), held that the Religion Clauses required a ministerial exception to the Americans with Disabilities Act.

The Department [argues] that the free exercise question is controlled by *Locke v. Davey* [which involved] a scholarship program [designed] to assist high-achieving students with the costs of postsecondary education. The scholarships were paid out of the State's general fund, and eligibility was based on criteria such as an applicant's score on college admission tests and family income. While scholarship recipients were free to use the money at accredited religious and non-religious schools alike, they were not permitted to use the funds to pursue a devotional theology degree — one "devotional in nature or designed to induce religious faith." Davey was selected for a scholarship but was denied funds when he refused to certify that he would not use them toward a devotional degree. He sued, arguing that the State's refusal to allow its scholarship money to go toward such degrees violated his free exercise rights. This Court disagreed. The State had "merely chosen not to fund a distinct category of instruction." Davey was not denied a scholarship because of who he *was*; he was denied a scholarship because of what he proposed *to do* — use the funds to prepare for the ministry. Here Trinity Lutheran was denied a grant simply because of what it is — a church. *Locke* also sought funding for an "essentially religious endeavor akin to a religious calling as well as an academic pursuit," and opposition to such funding "to support church leaders" lay at the historic core of the Religion Clauses. Here nothing of the sort can be said about a program to use recycled tires to resurface playgrounds.

The Department emphasizes Missouri's constitutional tradition of not furnishing taxpayer money directly to churches. But *Locke* took account of Washington's anti-establishment interest only after determining that the scholarship program did not "require students to choose between their religious beliefs and receiving a government benefit." Washington's scholarship program went "a long way toward including religion in its benefits." Students were free to use their scholarships at "pervasively religious schools." Davey could use his scholarship to pursue a secular degree at one institution while studying devotional theology at another. He could also use his scholarship money to attend a religious college and take devotional theology courses there. The only thing he could not do was use the scholarship to pursue a degree in that subject. In this case, Trinity Lutheran *is* put to the choice between being a church and receiving a government benefit. Such a condition imposes a penalty on the free exercise of religion that must be subjected to the "most rigorous" scrutiny. *Lukumi,* 508 U.S., at 546. Only a state interest "of the highest order" can justify the Department's discriminatory policy. *McDaniel,* 435 U.S., at 628. The Department offers nothing more than Missouri's policy preference for skating as far as possible from religious establishment concerns. In the face of the clear infringement on free exercise before us, that interest cannot qualify as compelling. "The state interest in achieving greater separation of church and State than is already ensured under the Establishment Clause of the Federal Constitution is limited by the Free Exercise Clause." *Widmar,* 454 U.S., at 276. The State has pursued its preferred policy [by] expressly denying a qualified religious entity a public benefit solely because of its religious character. Under our precedents, that goes too far. The Department's policy violates the Free Exercise Clause.

The judgment of the United States Court of Appeals for the Eighth Circuit is reversed, and the case is remanded for further proceedings consistent with this opinion.

It is so ordered.

Justice THOMAS, with whom Justice GORSUCH joins, concurring in part.

"Denying a generally available benefit solely on account of religious identity imposes a penalty on the free exercise of religion that can be justified," if at all, "only by a state interest 'of the highest order.'" This Court's endorsement in *Locke* of even a "mild kind" of discrimination against religion remains troubling. Because the Court today appropriately construes *Locke* narrowly, I join the Court's opinion.

Justice GORSUCH, with whom Justice THOMAS joins, concurring in part.

The Court leaves open the possibility a useful distinction might be drawn between laws that discriminate on the basis of religious *status* and religious *use*. I harbor doubts about the stability of such a line. The First Amendment's Free Exercise Clause guarantees the free *exercise* of religion, not just the right to inward belief (or status). The government may not force people to choose between participation in a public program and their right to free exercise of religion.

Justice BREYER, concurring in the judgment.

The State would cut Trinity Lutheran off from participation in a general program designed to secure or improve the health and safety of children. The sole reason is faith. It is that fact that calls the Free Exercise Clause into play. I would leave the application of the Free Exercise Clause to other kinds of public benefits for another day.

Justice SOTOMAYOR, with whom Justice GINSBURG joins, dissenting.

The Court [holds] that the Constitution requires the government to provide public funds directly to a church. Its decision slights our precedents and our history, and weakens this country's longstanding commitment to a separation of church and state. The Establishment Clause does not allow Missouri to grant the Church's funding request because the Church uses the Learning Center, including its playground, in conjunction with its religious mission. The government may not directly fund religious exercise. A house of worship exists to foster and further religious exercise. From its base, the faithful reach out to those not yet convinced of the group's beliefs. When a government funds a house of worship, it underwrites this religious exercise. The Church seeks state funds to improve the Learning Center's facilities, which are used to assist the spiritual growth of the children of its members and to spread the Church's faith to the children of nonmembers. The Church's playground surface are integrated with and integral to its religious mission.

This Court has found some direct government funding of religious institutions to be consistent with the Establishment Clause. But the funding came with assurances that public funds would not be used for religious activity, despite the religious nature of the institution. The Church cannot provide such assurances here. The Church has a religious mission. The playground surface cannot be confined to secular use any more than lumber used to frame the Church's walls, glass stained and used to form its windows, or nails used to build its altar. The Establishment Clause protects both religion and government from the dangers that result when the two become entwined, "*not* by providing every religion with an *equal opportunity* (to secure state funding or to pray in the public schools), but by drawing fairly clear lines of *separation* between church and state — at least where the heartland of religious belief, such as primary religious worship, is at issue." *Zelman v. Simmons–Harris*, 536 U.S. 639, 722 (2002) (Breyer, J., dissenting).

The Establishment Clause prohibits laws "respecting an establishment of religion" and the Free Exercise Clause prohibits laws "prohibiting the free exercise thereof." U.S. Const., Amdt. 1. "If expanded to a logical extreme," these prohibitions "would clash with the other." *Walz*, 397 U.S., at 668–669. Even in the absence of a violation of one of the Religion Clauses, the interaction of government and religion can raise concerns that sound in both Clauses. For that reason, the government may sometimes accommodate those concerns, even when not required to do so by the Free Exercise Clause, without violating the Establishment Clause. The government may sometimes accommodate those concerns, even when not required to do so by the Establishment Clause, without violating the Free Exercise Clause. "There is room for play in the joints productive of a benevolent neutrality which will permit religious exercise to exist without sponsorship and without interference." *Id.*, at 669. This space gives government room to recognize the unique status of religious entities and to single them out on that basis for exclusion from otherwise generally applicable laws.

This Court has held that the government may sometimes relieve religious entities from the requirements of government programs. A State need not, for example, require nonprofit houses of worship to pay property taxes. Nor must a State require nonprofit religious entities to abstain from making employment decisions on the basis of religion. But the government may not invoke the space between the Religion Clauses in a manner that "devolves into an unlawful fostering of religion." *Cutter v. Wilkinson*, 544 U.S. 709 (2005). The government may sometimes close off certain government aid programs to religious entities. The State need not fund the training of a religious group's leaders, those "who will preach their beliefs, teach their faith, and carry out their mission." *Locke v. Davey*, 540 U.S. 712, 722 (2004).

When reviewing a law that singles out religious entities for exclusion from its reach, we have not myopically focused on the fact that a law singles out religious entities, but on the reasons that it does so. Missouri has decided that the unique status of houses of worship requires a special rule when it comes to public funds. Missouri's decision, which has deep roots in our Nation's history, reflects a reasonable and constitutional judgment. In some [states,] a religious establishment never took hold. In others establishment varied in terms of the sect (or sects) supported, the nature and extent of that support, and the uniformity of support across the State. Every state establishment saw laws passed to raise public funds and direct them toward houses of worship and ministers. As the States disestablished, they undid those laws. Those who fought to end the public funding of religion based their opposition on the basic premise that the practice harmed both civil government and religion. The civil government could claim no authority over religious belief. Support for religion compelled by the State marked an overstep of authority that would only lead to more. Equally troubling, it risked divisiveness by giving religions reason to compete for the State's beneficence. Faith, they believed, was a personal matter, entirely between an individual and his god. Religion was best served when sects reached out on the basis of their tenets alone, unsullied by outside forces, allowing adherents to come to their faith voluntarily.

A state may not fund religious activities without violating the Establishment Clause. A state can reasonably use a "house of worship" as a stand-in for "religious activities." Today, thirty-eight States have a counterpart to Missouri's Article I, §7. The provisions date back to or before these States' original Constitutions. That so many States have for so long drawn a line that prohibits public funding for houses of worship, based on principles rooted in this Nation's understanding of how best to foster religious liberty, supports the conclusion that public funding of houses of worship "is of a different ilk."

Missouri's Article I, §7, is closely tied to the state interests it protects. A straightforward reading prohibits funding only for "any church, sect, or denomination of religion, or in aid of any priest, preacher, minister or teacher thereof, as such." Missouri will fund a religious organization not "owned or controlled by a church," if its "mission and activities are secular nature" and the funds "will be used for secular purposes rather than for sectarian purposes." Article I, §7, thus stops Missouri only from funding specific entities, ones that set and enforce religious doctrine for their adherents. These entities most acutely raise the establishment and free exercise concerns that arise when public funds flow to religion. The transfer of public funds to houses of worship raises concerns that sit exactly between the Religion Clauses. To avoid those concerns, it has prohibited such funding. In doing so, it made the same choice made by the earliest States centuries ago and many other States in the years since. The Constitution permits this choice.

The Court focuses on one aspect of Missouri's Article I, §7: that it denies funding to a house of worship, here the Church, "simply because of what it is—a church." The Court describes this as a constitutionally impermissible line based on religious "status" that requires strict scrutiny. The Constitution creates specific rules that control how the government may interact with religious entities. Of course a government may act based on a religious entity's "status" as such. It is that very status that implicates the interests protected by the Religion Clauses. Sometimes a religious entity's unique status requires the government to act. Other times, it merely permits the government to act. The dispositive issue is not whether religious "status" matters—it does, but whether the government must, or may, act on that basis.

Locke stands for the proposition that the government may, but need not, choose not to fund certain religious entities where doing so raises "historic and substantial" establishment and free exercise concerns. A decision to treat entities differently based on distinctions that the Religion Clauses make relevant does not amount to discrimination. We have instead focused on whether the government has provided a good enough reason, based in the values the Religion Clauses protect, for its decision. A State's decision not to fund houses of worship represents a valid choice to remain secular in the face of serious establishment and free exercise concerns. To fence out religious persons or entities from a truly generally available public benefit—one provided to all, no questions asked, such as police or fire protections—would violate the Free Exercise Clause. The Scrap Tire Program offers not a generally available benefit but a selective benefit for a few recipients each year.

The Court today dismantles a core protection for religious freedom. It holds not just that a government may support houses of worship with taxpayer funds, but that it must do so whenever it decides to create a funding program. The Religion Clauses separate the public treasury from religious coffers as one measure to secure the kind of freedom of conscience that benefits both religion and government. This separation means that the government cannot, or need not, tax its citizens and turn that money over to houses of worship. The Court today blinds itself to history and leads us to a place where separation of church and state is a constitutional slogan, not a constitutional commitment. I dissent.

Notes

1. *Discrimination and Voucher Programs.* In *Espinoza v. Montana Department of Revenue*, 140 S.Ct. 2246 (2020), the Court extended the *Trinity Lutheran* decision. *Espinoza* involved a Montana law which sought to create parental and student choice through the creation of a scholarship program for students attending private schools. The program involved a tax credit of up to $150 for any taxpayer who donates to a participating "student scholarship organization" which, in turn, passes the money on as scholarships to students who attend private schools. However, the legislature directed that the aid program be administered consistently with Article X, section 6, of the Montana Constitution, which contains a "no-aid" provision barring direct or indirect governmental aid to sectarian schools. In order to comply with the no aid provision, the Montana Supreme Court terminated the aid program for all students whether in sectarian or secular schools. The Court

held that Montana acted improperly in terminating the program and in denying
aid to sectarian schools:

> The Free Exercise Clause, which applies to the States under the Fourteenth Amendment,
> "protects religious observers against unequal treatment" and against "laws that impose spe-
> cial disabilities on the basis of religious status." *Trinity Lutheran*, 582 U. S., at ___. Montana's
> no-aid provision bars religious schools from public benefits solely because of the religious
> character of the schools. The provision also bars parents who wish to send their children
> to a religious school from those same benefits, again solely because of the religious char-
> acter of the school. The provision bars aid to any school "controlled in whole or in part by
> any church, sect, or denomination." Mont. Const., Art. X, §6(1). The provision's title — "Aid
> prohibited to sectarian schools" — confirms that the provision singles out schools based on
> their religious character. The provision plainly excludes schools from government aid solely
> because of religious status.
>
> The Montana Supreme Court applied the no-aid provision to hold that religious schools
> could not benefit from the scholarship program. So applied, the provision "imposes special
> disabilities on the basis of religious status" and "conditions the availability of benefits upon a
> recipient's willingness to surrender its religiously impelled status." *Trinity Lutheran*, 582 U. S.,
> at ___ (quoting *Church of Lukumi Babalu Aye, Inc. v. Hialeah*, 508 U. S. 520, 533 (1993), and
> *McDaniel v. Paty*, 435 U. S. 618, 626 (1978) (plurality opinion)). To be eligible for govern-
> ment aid, a school must divorce itself from any religious control or affiliation. Placing such
> a condition on benefits or privileges "inevitably deters or discourages the exercise of First
> Amendment rights." *Trinity Lutheran*, 582 U. S., at ___ (slip op., at 11). The Free Exercise
> Clause protects against even "indirect coercion," and a State "punishes the free exercise of
> religion" by disqualifying the religious from government aid as Montana did here. *Trinity
> Lutheran*, 582 U. S., at ___ (slip op., at 10–11). Such status-based discrimination is subject to
> "the strictest scrutiny." *Id.*, at ___ (slip op., at 11). It is enough to conclude that strict scrutiny
> applies under *Trinity Lutheran* because Montana's no-aid provision discriminates based on
> religious status.

The Court distinguished *Locke v. Davey*:

> The Department contends that this case is instead governed by *Locke* v. *Davey*, 540 U. S. 712
> (2004). *Locke* differs from this case in two critical ways. First, Washington had "merely cho-
> sen not to fund a distinct category of instruction": the "essentially religious endeavor" of
> training a minister "to lead a congregation." Thus, Davey "was denied a scholarship because
> of what he proposed *to do* — use the funds to prepare for the ministry." Apart from that
> narrow restriction, Washington's program allowed scholarships to be used at "pervasively
> religious schools" that incorporated religious instruction throughout their classes. By con-
> trast, Montana's Constitution does not zero in on any particular "essentially religious" course
> of instruction at a religious school. Rather, the no-aid provision bars all aid to a religious
> school "simply because of what it is," putting the school to a choice between being religious
> or receiving government benefits. At the same time, the provision puts families to a choice
> between sending their children to a religious school or receiving such benefits. Second,
> *Locke* invoked a "historic and substantial" state interest in not funding the training of clergy,
> explaining that "opposition to funding 'to support church leaders' lay at the historic core
> of the Religion Clauses," *Locke* emphasized that the propriety of state-supported clergy was a
> central subject of founding-era debates, and that most state constitutions from that era pro-
> hibited the expenditure of tax dollars to support the clergy.

As a result, the Court reversed the Montana Supreme Court's decision to terminate the program for all recipients.

2. *State Regulatory Requirements.* In *Illinois Bible Colleges Association v. Anderson,* 870 F.3d 631 (7th Cir. 2017), plaintiff sought an exemption from rules requiring state approval before offering degrees. The rules applied equally to secular and religious schools. In rejecting the exemption request, the court held that religious schools "may teach their faith without interference and use whatever faculty and methods they believe appropriate." The state's rules only apply when they "venture into the secular sphere" where "regulatory oversight" is required.

∿ PROBLEMS ∿

1. *Churches and Historic Preservation Funding.* How far does *Trinity Lutheran* extend? Suppose that a state offers historic preservation grants to help preserve old buildings, but prohibits grants to preserve churches. Under *Trinity Lutheran,* is this discrimination against churches permissible? Should the answer depend on the historical significance of the church (e.g., the Old North Church in Boston, which is Boston's oldest church, Boston's most visited historic site, and which played a role in the American Revolution)?

2. *Advising the University.* A state university theater professor wishes to present a play entitled "Black Christ" which is set in an African American protestant church and celebrates the Birth of Jesus. The director views the play as a tribute to Christ: "God is a part of life. In my view, without Him there is no life." When the university attempts to prevent the professor from going forward with the play, she states: "I think that there are a lot of things about African-Americans that predominately white universities don't understand, and church and God is one of them." If you are university counsel, how would you advise the University in terms of whether presentation will violate the Establishment Clause?

Note

Review *Christian Legal Society Chapter of the University of California v. Martinez,* 561 U.S. 661 (2010), in Chapter 11.

∿ PROBLEMS ∿

1. *Extending the All-Comers Policy.* Could Hastings decide to exclude CLS not only from the RSO program, but also from the use of the law school's facilities and all methods of internal communication unless it accepts all comers?

2. *The Takeover.* Suppose that, following this decision, a group of students decide to take over the CLS and change its bylaws and statement of beliefs to be accepting of gays, lesbians, and transgendered, and also to be accepting of premarital and nonmarital sex. The law school takes no action. If the ousted

members of CLS sue again, should their challenge to the all-comers policy now be accepted?

3. *More on the International Treaty on the Internet.* Suppose that the treaty negotiators discuss whether to include "religious speech" within the parameters of the treaty. In the United States, the courts have been very reluctant to decree that a purported religion is fraudulent or not really a religion. *See United States v. Ballard,* 322 U.S. 78 (1944). The same is not necessarily true in other countries. For example, France decided that the Jehovah's Witnesses should be subject to taxation, and a Russian court banned the distribution of writings on Scientology. What kind of language would be appropriate for such a treaty? What can you agree to, and what should you not agree to, consistent with the U.S. Constitution?

[Points to Remember for Chapter 12 is contained in online file.]

13

The Right to Keep and Bear Arms

[Roadmap for Chapter 13 is contained in online file.]

A. INTRODUCTION: NATURE OF THE SECOND AMENDMENT

Until recently, the Second Amendment was one of the least litigated provisions of the Bill of Rights. It provides: "A well regulated militia, being necessary to the security of a free state, the right of the people to keep and bear arms, shall not be infringed." The Second Amendment's preamble sets it apart from the rest of the Bill of Rights. The preamble—"*a well regulated militia, being necessary to the security of a free state*"—precedes the Amendment's operative clause—"*the right of the people to keep and bear arms, shall not be infringed.*" The question is whether the right of the people to keep and bear arms is conditioned upon some relationship to a "well regulated militia." Before 2008, most federal courts limited the Second Amendment's right to keep and bear arms to militia service—in some cases a right enforceable only by the states, and in other cases a right enforceable by individuals only in connection with their militia service. In 2008, the Supreme Court held for the first time that the Second Amendment guarantees an individual right to keep and bear arms unconnected to militia service, at least for the purpose of self-defense in the home. Two years later, the Court held that the Second Amendment applies to the states.

B. HISTORICAL BACKGROUND

Before 2008, the Supreme Court addressed the substantive meaning of the Second Amendment only once. There are two reasons for the scarcity of Second Amendment cases. First, Congress did not enact the first comprehensive federal firearms statute until the National Firearms Act of 1934. National Firearms Act of 1934, ch. 757, 48 Stat. 1236. Second, in the absence of federal firearms regulations, early Supreme Court cases necessarily dealt only with state firearms laws, and because these cases preceded the era of incorporation of the Bill of Rights and were decided based on *Barron v. City of Baltimore*, 32 U.S. (7 Pet.) 243 (1833), the Court held that the Amendment was a check only on the federal government and did not apply to the states.

For example, in *United States v. Cruikshank*, 92 U.S. 542 (1875), the Supreme Court sustained a challenge to the Enforcement Act of 1870, 16 Stat. 140, enacted by Congress under its newly established authority in Section Five of the Fourteenth Amendment. The Act made conspiracies to injure persons to prevent them from exercising their constitutional rights a felony. *Cruikshank* arose out of a Reconstruction-era dispute over control of a Louisiana Parish. Known as the Colfax Massacre, a group of whites attacked a group largely comprised of African Americans, killing between 80 and 150 people. One of the constitutional rights at issue in *Cruikshank* was the right of the African Americans to keep and bear arms. The Court held that—to the extent the Second Amendment declared that the right to bear arms shall not be infringed—it was only a check on Congress's power. *Cruikshank*, 92 U.S. at 553. *See also Presser v. Illinois*, 116 U.S. 252 (1886); *Miller v. Texas*, 153 U.S. 535 (1894).

Following the enactment of the National Firearms Act in 1934, the Supreme Court interpreted the meaning of the Second Amendment as it applied to the Act once—in *United States v. Miller*, 307 U.S. 174 (1939). In a rather enigmatic opinion, the Court upheld a provision prohibiting possession of a "short-barreled" shotgun because the weapon was unrelated to the "preservation or efficiency of a well regulated militia." *Id.* at 178. Until 2001, lower federal courts interpreted *Miller* to mean that the right to keep and bear arms is dependent upon a relationship to militia service. The courts' focus was the Amendment's preamble, and they found that the preamble defined the circumstances under which "the right of the people to keep and bear arms" could not be infringed.

The lower courts adopted two principal models for interpreting the Second Amendment. The first was the so-called collective rights model, under which the courts deemed the Second Amendment to apply only to the right of a state to maintain a militia, and not to an individual's right to keep and bear arms. *See Love v. Pepersack*, 47 F.3d 120 (4th Cir. 1995); *United States v. Warin*, 530 F.2d 103 (6th Cir. 1976); *United States v. Napier*, 233 F.3d 394 (6th Cir. 2000); *Gillespie v. City of Indianapolis*, 185 F.3d 693 (7th Cir. 1999); *Hickman v. Block*, 81 F.3d 98 (9th Cir. 1996); *Silveira v. Lockyear*, 312 F.3d 1052 (9th Cir. 2003). The second was the "limited individual rights" or "sophisticated collective rights" model, which limited the right to keep and bear arms to individuals in connection with their militia service. And because the Second Amendment refers not just to "a militia" but rather a "well regulated militia," the courts that adopted the "limited individual rights" model defined militia service to mean active participation in the "organized" (*i.e.*, the National Guard)—as opposed to the "unorganized"—militia. *See United States v. Rybar*, 103 F.3d 273 (3d Cir. 1996); *United States v. Hale*, 978 F.2d 1016 (8th Cir. 1992); *United States v. Parker*, 362 F.3d 1279 (10th Cir. 2004); *United States v. Haney*, 264 F.3d 1161 (10th Cir. 2001); *United States v. Wright*, 117 F.3d 1265 (11th Cir. 1997). Under either model, the Second Amendment did not seemingly prohibit federal or state governments from extensively regulating gun possession and use or—for that matter—disarming the American people altogether.

C. MODERN CASE LAW

1. *Individual Right to Keep and Bear Arms*

In 2001, the Court of Appeals for the Fifth Circuit broke with the other federal appellate courts, holding that the Second Amendment protects an individual's right to keep and bear arms unconnected with militia service, although refusing to overturn the application of the gun control measure before the court. *United States v. Emerson*, 270 F.3d 203 (5th Cir. 2001), *cert. denied*, 541 U.S. 1081 (2004). In 2007, the Court of Appeals for the District of Columbia Circuit became the second federal appellate court to adopt the "individual rights" model of the Second Amendment, and the first federal appellate court to overturn a gun control measure. *Parker v. District of Columbia*, 478 F.3d 370 (D.C. Cir. 2007), *cert. granted in part sub nom. District of Columbia v. Heller*, 552 U.S. 1035 (2007). The Supreme Court agreed to review the D.C. Circuit decision, and in the landmark case of *District of Columbia v. Heller*, 554 U.S. 570 (2008), the Court addressed the meaning of the Second Amendment for the first time in nearly 70 years.

At issue in *Heller* was a District of Columbia ordinance that prohibited the possession of handguns and required residents to keep their lawfully owned firearms, such as registered long guns, unloaded and dissembled or bound by a trigger lock or similar device unless they were located in a place of business or were being used for lawful recreational activities. The plaintiff was Dick Heller, a D.C. special police officer authorized to carry a handgun while on duty at the Federal Judicial Center. He applied for a registration certificate for a handgun that he wished to keep at home, but the District refused. *Id.* at 574-576.

The Supreme Court held the District's absolute ban on handgun possession in the home violated the Second Amendment, as did its prohibition against having operable lawful firearms in the home for self-defense. Writing for the majority, Justice Scalia centered the decision on the text and history of the Amendment. He cited the origins of gun rights in seventeenth-century England and traced them through the American Revolution and Reconstruction, determining that by the time of the nation's founding, "the right to have arms had become fundamental for English subjects." *Id.* at 593. Thus, the Court found that "the Second Amendment, like the First and Fourth Amendments, codified a pre-existing right." *Id.* at 592.

In a dissenting opinion, Justice Stevens, joined by Justices Souter, Ginsburg, and Breyer, acknowledged that the Second Amendment protects an individual right, but asserted that it does not curtail the legislature's "power to regulate the nonmilitary use and ownership of weapons." *Id.* at 637. Justice Breyer also wrote a dissenting opinion (joined by the other dissenting justices) arguing that the majority's conclusion is wrong for two reasons: (1) the Second Amendment protects militia-related, not self-defense-related, interests; and (2) the protection the Amendment provides is not absolute—it permits government to regulate the interests that it serves. *Id.* at 681. Justice Breyer advocated an "interest-balancing" test to assess the constitutionality of government regulation of firearms, which asks "whether the statute burdens a protected interest in a way or to an extent that is out of proportion to the statute's salutary effects upon other important governmental interests." *Id.* at 689.

2. *Application to the States*

Heller dealt with gun regulations in a federal enclave (the District of Columbia) and did not reach the question whether the Second Amendment applies to state and local governments. As noted above, early Supreme Court cases held that the Amendment applied only to the federal government; however, those cases were decided before the Court began the process of incorporating the Bill of Rights under the Fourteenth Amendment. Following *Heller*, lower federal and state courts were split over whether the Second Amendment restricts state governments. In *McDonald v. City of Chicago*, 561 U.S. 742 (2010), the Supreme Court held that the Amendment applies to the states.

At issue in *McDonald* was gun control laws in Chicago and Oak Park, Illinois, which were similar to the District of Columbia's ordinances in *Heller.* The plaintiffs were residents of the City of Chicago and Village of Oak Park who wanted to keep handguns in their homes for self-defense, but were prohibited from doing so by the municipalities' firearms laws. *Id.* at 750-751. Four justices found that the Fourteenth Amendment's Due Process Clause incorporates the Second Amendment right recognized in *Heller;* a fifth justice believed that the right applied to the states under the Fourteenth Amendment's Privileges and Immunities Clause.

Writing for the plurality (Chief Justice Roberts and Justices Scalia and Kennedy), Justice Alito declined the petitioners' invitation to overrule *The*

Slaughterhouse Cases, 83 U.S. (16 Wall.) 36 (1873) and incorporate the Second Amendment under the Fourteenth Amendment's Privileges and Immunities Clause. *Id.* at 758. Instead, the plurality opted for the traditional approach of using the Fourteenth Amendment's Due Process Clause as a vehicle for applying the right to keep and bear arms to the states. *Id.* at 759. Justice Alito noted that the question of incorporation turns on whether "the right to keep and bear arms is fundamental to *our* scheme of ordered liberty, or whether this right is 'deeply rooted in this Nation's history and tradition.'" *Id.* at 764 (emphasis in the original). Justice Alito concluded that, under *Heller*, citizens must be permitted to use handguns for the core lawful purpose of self-defense, and that *Heller* made it clear that the right to keep and bear arms is "deeply rooted in this Nation's history and tradition." *Id.* at 767-768. Dismissing the contention that the Second Amendment should be applied differently to the states, the plurality also held that "incorporated Bill of Rights protections are all to be enforced against the States under the Fourteenth Amendment according to the same standards that protect those personal rights against federal encroachment." *Id.* at 765, 784-785. Concurring in the judgment, Justice Thomas advocated overruling *The Slaughterhouse Cases*, and applying the Second Amendment to the states under the Privileges and Immunities Clause. *Id.* at 805.

3. Types of Arms Protected

After *Heller*, the Second Amendment clearly protects the right to possess handguns in the home for self-defense and extends to "other weapons typically possessed by law-abiding citizens for lawful purposes" (e.g., hunting). Moreover, while not explicitly mentioned in the Second Amendment, courts have found that "without bullets, the right to bear arms would be meaningless." *Jackson v. City and County of San Francisco*, 746 F.3d 953, 967 (9th Cir. 2014), *cert. denied*, 135 S. Ct. 2799 (2015) (but holding that the state could prohibit certain types of bullets). The *Heller* majority admitted, however, that the Amendment does not reach all weapons—specifically, the possession of "dangerous and unusual weapons." *Heller*, 554 U.S. at 627. The Court mentioned "M-16 rifles and the like," recognizing that while these weapons may be useful today for an effective militia, "modern developments have limited the degree of fit between the prefatory clause and the protected right." *Id.* at 627-628.

> *Heller* "distinguished between two classes of weapons: (1) those that are useful in the militia or military, and (2) those that are "possessed at home" and are in "common use at the time for lawful purposes like self-defense." The individual right protected by the Second Amendment *applies only to the second category of weapons*, though that category at times may overlap with the first. The Second Amendment does not create a right to possess a weapon solely because the weapon may be used in or is useful for militia or military service.

Hollis v. Lynch, 827 F.3d 436, 445 (5th Cir. 2016) (quoting *Heller* at 621-627) (emphasis in original).

Beyond the dicta in *Heller*, however, the Court did not further define the arms protected by the Second Amendment. Lower federal courts have categorized as "dangerous and unusual" such weapons as machine guns, *Hollis*, 827 F.3d at 451; *United States v. One (1) Palmetto Armory PA-15 Machinegun*, 822 F.3d 136, 141, 144 (3d Cir. 2016); *Hamblen v. United States*, 591 F.3d 471 (6th Cir. 2009), *cert. denied*, 559 U.S. 1115 (2010); short-barreled shotguns, *United States v. Fincher*, 538 F.3d 868 (8th Cir. 2008); *United States v. Hatfield*, 376 Fed. App'x. 706 (9th Cir. 2010); assault rifles, *Kolbe v. Hogan*, 849 F.3d 114, 135-136 (4th Cir. 2017) (en banc), *cert. denied*, 138 S. Ct. 469 (2017); *Friedman v. City of Highland Park*, 784 F.3d 406, 411 (7th Cir. 2015), *cert. denied*, 136 S. Ct. 447 (2015); *Wilson v. Cook County*, 937 F.3d 1028 (7th Cir. 2019); *Kampfer v. Cuomo*, 993 F. Supp. 2d 188, 195-196 (N.D.N.Y. 2014), *aff'd*, 643 Fed. Appx. 43 (2d Cir. 2016), *cert. denied*, 136 S. Ct. 2489 (2016); *Rupp v. Becerra*, 401 F. Supp. 3d 978, 988 (C.D. Cal. 2019); pipe bombs, *United States v. Tagg*, 572 F.3d 1320 (11th Cir. 2009); handguns not deemed safe under state law, *Pena v. Lindley*, 898 F.3d 969 (9th Cir. 2018), *cert. denied*, ___ S. Ct. ___, 2020 WL 3146680 (2020); and explosive grenades. *United States v. Musso*, 914 F.3d (1st Cir. 2019).

On the other hand, in *Caetano v. Massachusetts*, 136 S. Ct. 1027 (2016), the Supreme Court, in a per curiam decision, vacated and remanded a decision of the Massachusetts Supreme Judicial Court upholding a Massachusetts law prohibiting the possession of stun guns. The Court rejected the underlying bases for the Massachusetts decision that stun guns are not protected by the Second Amendment because they were not in common use at the time of the Amendment's enactment, that they are "dangerous per se at common law and unusual" inasmuch as they are "a thoroughly modern invention," and that nothing in the record suggests that stun guns "are readily adapted to use in the military." *Id.* at 1027-1028. Following its decision in *District of Columbia v. Heller*, 554 U.S. 570 (2008), the Court held that the Second Amendment "'extends to arms that were not in existence at the time of the founding,'" *Caetano*, 136 S. Ct. at 1027 (quoting *Heller*, 554 U.S. at 583), and that the Second Amendment protects more than just "'weapons useful in warfare.'" *Caetano*, 136 S. Ct. at 1028 (quoting *Heller*, 554 U.S. at 624-625). *See also Avitabile v. Beach*, 368 F. Supp. 3d 404 (N.D.N.Y. 2019) (holding that a state's total ban on stun guns and electronic dart guns violates the Second Amendment); *but cf. Teter v. Connors*, ___ F. Supp. 3d ___, 2020 WL 2476225 *15 (D. Haw. 2020) ("butterfly knives" are protected by the Second Amendment, but state prohibition against their sale, possession, and carrying sustained under intermediate scrutiny standard).

4. Standard of Review of Firearms Regulations

a. *Heller's* Limited Guidance

The only clear constitutional limit imposed by *Heller* on the regulation of firearms is that government may not completely ban the possession of a class of weapons commonly used by Americans in their homes for self-defense. Beyond this holding, the Court consciously did not enunciate a standard for reviewing the constitutionality of other types of regulations burdening the possession of arms. The Court did, however, explicitly reject the rational-basis test as a tool for assessing the legitimacy of gun-control measures, finding that "if all that was required to overcome the right to keep and bear arms was a rational basis, the Second Amendment would be redundant with the separate constitutional prohibitions on irrational laws, and would have no effect." *Heller,* 554 U.S. at 628 n.27. In dicta, the Court also outlined those regulatory measures it deemed to be presumptively constitutional, indicating that the list was not exhaustive. Specifically, the Court identified "longstanding prohibitions on the possession of firearms by felons and the mentally ill, or laws forbidding the carrying of firearms in sensitive places such as schools and government buildings, or laws imposing conditions and qualifications on the commercial sale of arms" as legitimate restraints on the right to keep and bear arms. *Heller,* 554 U.S. at 626-627.

b. Lower Courts' Standard of Review of Firearms Regulations

Most federal courts test gun-control measures under a heightened form of scrutiny. The Courts of Appeals for the First, Second, Third, Fourth, Fifth, Sixth, Seventh, Ninth, Tenth, Eleventh, and District of Columbia Circuits have adopted a two-pronged approach to Second Amendment challenges. *See, e.g., Gould v. Morgan,* 907 F.3d 659, 669 (1st Cir. 2018), *cert. denied,* __ S. Ct. ___, 2020 WL 3146683 (2020); *Kachalsky v. County of Westchester,* 701 F.3d 81, 90-93 (2d Cir. 2012), *cert. denied,* 569 U.S. 918 (2013); *United States v.* Marzzarella, 614 F.3d 85, 89 (3d Cir. 2010), *cert. denied,* 562 U.S. 1158 (2011); *United States v. Chester,* 628 F.3d 673, 682 (4th Cir. 2010); *National Rifle Ass'n v. Bureau of Alcohol, Tobacco, Firearms, & Explosives,* 700 F.3d 185, 194, 197 (5th Cir. 2012), *cert. denied,* 571 U.S. 1196 (2014); *United States v. Greeno,* 679 F.3d 510, 518 (6th Cir. 2012), *cert. denied,* 568 U.S. 922 (2012); *Ezell v. City of Chicago,* 651 F.3d 684, 701-704 (7th Cir. 2011); *United States v.* Chovan, 735 F.3d 1127, 1136 (9th Cir. 2013), *cert. denied,* 574 U.S. 878 (2014); *Peterson v. Martinez,* 707 F.3d 1197, 1209 (10th Cir. 2013); *Georgiacarry. org, Inc. v. State of Georgia,* 687 F.3d 1244, 1260 n.34 (11th Cir. 2012), *cert. denied,* 568 U.S. 1088 (2013); *Schrader v. Holder,* 704 F.3d 980, 988-989 (D.C. Cir.), *cert. denied,* 571 U.S. 989 (2013).

First, the courts determine whether the challenged law burdens conduct falling within the scope of the Second Amendment. If not, the inquiry is at an end. If so, the courts evaluate the law under some heightened form of means-end scrutiny. The courts generally conduct a textual and historical inquiry into the original meaning of the Second Amendment at the time of its ratification as well as how the right was understood at the time the Fourteenth Amendment was ratified. *Ezell,* 651 F.3d at 701-702. For example, courts will consider such factors as the nature of the weapons involved, noting that the Supreme Court in *Heller* acknowledged that the Second Amendment extends only to weapons "commonly owned by law-abiding citizens" and excluded "'dangerous and unusual weapons.'" *Marzzarella*, 614 F.3d at 90 (quoting *Heller v. District of Columbia*, 554 U.S. 570, 626 (2008)); *see* Joseph Blocher & Darrell A.H. Miller, *Lethality, Public Carry, and Adequate Alternatives*, 53 Harv. J. on Legis. 279, 283-291 (2016) (discussing the "historical" and "common-use" tests).

Courts that have adopted the two-pronged approach in Second Amendment challenges to firearms restrictions have, at times, avoided ruling on the first prong—whether the conduct falls within the scope of Second Amendment protections—and have decided cases on the second prong, finding that, even if the conduct falls within the scope of the Second Amendment, the challenged restriction passes muster under the appropriate standard of review. *See Woollard v. Gallagher*, 712 F.3d 865, 875 (4th Cir.), *cert. denied*, 571 U.S. 952 (2013); *NRA*, 700 F.3d at 204; *McGraw*, 719 F.3d at 347; *but cf. Kachalsky*, 701 F.3d at 89 (the Amendment must have some application to the context in which the right is being asserted). For challenges to presumptively lawful restrictions on firearm possession, some courts do not undertake an extensive historical inquiry to determine whether the conduct at issue was understood to be within the scope of the Second Amendment at the time of ratification; however, they "still conduct the traditional second step of applying an appropriate means-end scrutiny even for laws that receive a streamlined analysis." *Hamilton v. Pollozzi*, 848 F.3d 614, 624 (4th Cir. 2017), *cert. denied*, 138 S. Ct. 500 (2017) (sustaining statute prohibiting person convicted of felonies from possessing firearms); *see also Corcoran v. Sessions*, 261 F. Supp. 3d 579 (D. Md. 2017) (applying *Hamilton*); *compare Medina v. Sessions*, 279 F. Supp. 3d 246 (D.D.C. 2017) (convicted felon falls outside Second Amendment protections).

Second, if the challenged regulation burdens conduct protected by the Second Amendment, the courts determine the appropriate level of scrutiny, recognizing that the Supreme Court in *Heller* rejected the rational-basis test as an appropriate means of review. Instead, analogizing the standard of review applied in First Amendment cases, the courts have held that "the level of scrutiny depends upon the nature of the conduct being regulated and the degree to which the challenged law burdens the right." *Chester*, 628 F.3d at 682. The more severe the burden on the core right of "law-abiding, responsible citizens" to possess a firearm in the home for self-defense, the stricter the level of inquiry. *Ezell*, 651 F.3d at 708; *see also Jackson v. City and County of San Francisco*, 746 F.3d 953, 960-961 (9th Cir. 2014), *cert. denied*, 135 S.Ct. 2799 (2015).

Courts almost uniformly apply an intermediate standard of review to regulations that do not directly implicate the core right of law-abiding citizens to possess firearms in the home for self-defense. *E.g., Mai v. United States*, 952 F.3d 1106, 1115 (9th Cir. 2020) ("Strict scrutiny applies only to laws that both implicate a core Second Amendment right and place a substantial burden on that right.").

Where a gun-control measure implicates the core right of self-defense of law-abiding citizens in their homes, some courts have indicated a willingness to apply a more heightened standard of review, including strict scrutiny. *See United States v. McGinnis*, 956 F.3d 747, 754 (5th Cir. 2020); *Gould v. Morgan*, 907 F.3d 659, 669 (1st Cir. 2018), *cert. denied*, __ S. Ct. ___, 2020 WL 3146687 (2020); *Worman v. Healey*, 922 F.3d 26, 36-37 (1st Cir. 2019), *cert. denied*, __ S. Ct. ___, 2020 WL 3146687 (2020); *Chovan*, 735 F.3d at 1138; *Kachalsky*, 701 F.3d at 93-94; *Carter*, 669 F.3d at 416; *Ezell*, 651 F.3d at 708-709; *Masciandaro*, 638 F.3d at 471; *see also* Glenn Harlan Reynolds, Essay, *Second Amendment Penumbras: Some Preliminary Observations*, 85 S. Cal. L. Rev. 247, 248-249 (2012). Thus, for example, following the Supreme Court's decision in *McDonald v. City of Chicago*, 561 U.S. 742 (2010), the Chicago City Council lifted its law banning handgun possession and enacted the Responsible Gun Owners Ordinance in its place. *Ezell*, 651 F.3d at 689. Among other things, the ordinance required one hour of range training as a prerequisite to lawful gun ownership, yet at the same time prohibited firing ranges in the city. *Id.* In striking down the ordinance, the Court of Appeals for the Seventh Circuit suggested that, under the core right established by *Heller* and *McDonald*, laws that prohibit law-abiding citizens from possessing handguns in the home are categorically unconstitutional. Moreover, severe burdens on the ability to exercise the core constitutional right will require "an extremely strong public-interest justification and a close fit between the government's means and its ends." *Id.* at 708.

5. The Right Outside the Home

In both *District of Columbia v. Heller*, 554 U.S. 570 (2008), and *McDonald v. City of Chicago*, 561 U.S. 742 (2010), the Supreme Court was concerned only with the right to possess firearms for self-defense in the home. The Court did not address whether the right extends beyond the home. See *Dearth v. Lynch*, 791 F.3d 32, 40 (D.C. Cir. 2015) (Henderson, J., dissenting). The lower federal courts have not been consistent about the extent to which the Second Amendment protects the right of individuals to carry firearms outside the home. For example, some federal courts have sustained state laws requiring applicants for a permit to carry firearms to demonstrate a special need for self-protection distinguishable from that of the general community or of persons engaged in the same profession. *Kachalsky v. County of Westchester*, 701 F.3d 81 (2nd Cir. 2012), *cert. denied*, 569 U.S. 918 (2013); *Gould v. Morgan*, 907 F.3d 659 (1st Cir. 2018), *cert. denied*, __ S. Ct. ___, 2020 WL 3146683 (2020); *Woollard v. Gallagher*, 712 F.3d 865 (4th Cir.), *cert. denied*, 571 U.S. 952 (2013); *Drake v. Filko*, 724 F.3d 426 (3rd Cir. 2013), *cert. denied*, 569 U.S. 918 (2013). Other courts have rejected such requirements. *Wrenn v. District of Columbia*, 864 F.3d 650 (D.C. Cir. 2017); *Moore v. Madigan*, 702 F.3d 933 (7th Cir. 2012).

In *Heller*, the Supreme Court noted in dicta: "Like most rights, the right secured by the Second Amendment is not unlimited. . . . For example, the majority of the 19th-century courts to consider the question held that prohibitions on carrying concealed weapons were lawful under the Second Amendment or state analogues." *Heller*, 554 U.S. at 626 (emphasis added). Following *Heller*'s dicta, the Ninth Circuit, sitting en banc, sustained a California law requiring applicants for concealed carry of firearms licenses to show, inter alia, "good cause" as defined by the appropriate county sheriff. *Peruta v. County of San Diego*, 824 F.3d 919 (9th Cir. 2016) (en banc), *cert. denied*, 137 S. Ct. 1995 (2017). The San Diego County sheriff defined good cause as "a set of circumstances that distinguish the applicant from the mainstream and causes him or her to be placed in harm's way. Simply fearing for one's personal safety alone is not considered good cause." *Id.* at 926. The court stated that while "[t]he Second Amendment may or may not protect, to some degree, a right of a member of the general public to carry firearms in public . . . there is no Second Amendment right for members of the general public to carry concealed firearms in public." *Id.* at 939 (emphasis added). *See also United States v. Adams*, 914 F.3d 602, 605-606 (8th Cir. 2019) (rejecting under plain-error rule forfeited Second Amendment challenge for conviction of carrying a concealed weapon); *Peterson v. Martinez*, 707 F.3d 1197, 1211-1212 (10th Cir. 2013) (the Second Amendment does not protect concealed carry of firearms).

Moreover, the Supreme Court in *Heller* stated that "nothing in the decision should be taken to cast doubt on ... laws forbidding the carrying of firearms in sensitive places such as schools and government buildings." *Heller*, 554 U.S. at 626-627. The Court of Appeals for the Eleventh Circuit has held that the Second Amendment neither reaches a state law that prohibits possession of firearms in places of worship without the permission of the church, *Georgiacarry.org, Inc. v. State of Georgia*, 687 F.3d 1244, 1264-1265 (11th Cir. 2012), *cert. denied*, 568 U.S. 1088 (2013), nor an Army Corps of Engineers regulation that prohibits the possession of loaded firearms or ammunition on property managed by the Corps without the permission of the district commander. *Georgiacarry.org, Inc. v. U.S. Army Corps of Eng'rs*, 788 F.3d 1318, 1326 (11th Cir. 2015) (affirming denial of preliminary injunction). The Tenth Circuit, in *Bonidy v. United States Postal Service*, 790 F.3d 1121, 1125 (10th Cir. 2015), *cert. denied*, 136 S. Ct. 1486 (2016), upheld a regulation prohibiting storage and carriage of firearms on Postal Service property, including parking lots. And the District of Columbia Circuit in *United States v. Class*, 930 F.3d 460, 464 (D.C. Cir. 2019), upheld a conviction for possession of firearms located in a car parked in a lot on U.S. Capitol grounds.

The Supreme Court granted certiorari in a case involving the right to carry firearms outside the home. At issue was a New York City ordinance that prohibited licensed gun owners from transporting their firearms to shooting ranges, competitions, and second homes located outside of the city. The Court of Appeals for the Second Circuit rejected a Second Amendment challenge to the ordinance in *New York State Rifle & Pistol Ass'n v. City of New York*, 883 F.3d 45 (2d Cir. 2018), *cert. granted*, 139 S. Ct. 939 (2019). After the Supreme Court granted certiorari, the city amended the challenged regulation to enable holders of premises licenses to transport their handguns to additional locations, including second homes or shooting ranges outside of city limits, and the State of New York amended its handgun licensing statute to require localities to allow holders of premises licenses to engage in such transport. The Supreme Court held that the case was moot and vacated the decision of the appellate court. *New York State Rifle & Pistol Ass'n v. City of New York*, 140 S. Ct. 1525, 1526 (2020).

6. Commercial Firearms Sales

Heller and *MacDonald* only address the personal right to keep and bear arms; they say nothing about the right to manufacture and sell firearms. In both cases, the Court indicated, however, that laws imposing conditions on the commercial sale of arms are presumptively valid, *Heller*, 554 U.S. at 626-627; *MacDonald*, 561 U.S. at 786, and most courts have held that the Second Amendment does not protect a free-standing right to sell firearms. *Teixeira v. County of Alameda*, 873 F.3d 670 (9th Cir. 2017) (en banc), *cert. denied*, 138 S. Ct. 1988 (2017). On the other hand, courts have deemed categorical prohibitions on the commercial sale of firearms to be "untenable under *Heller*." *United States v. Marzzarella*, 614 F.3d 85, 92 n.8 (3d Cir. 2010), *cert. denied*, 562 U.S. 1158 (2011). Indeed, the Ninth Circuit in *Teixeira* acknowledged that the right to keep and bear arms would not mean much without the ability to acquire arms. *Teixeira*, 873 F.3d at 677-678.

Courts have upheld restrictions on commercial firearms sales, such as zoning ordinances dictating the location of firearms stores, *Teixeira*, 873 F.3d at 674-676; *Drummond v. Robinson Township*, 444 F. Supp. 3d 657 (W.D. Pa. 2020); *but cf. Association of Firearms Dealers v. City of Chicago*, 961 F. Supp. 2d 928 (N.D. Ill. 2014) (striking down ordinance prohibiting virtually all sales and transfers of firearms within city limits). Moreover, the courts have also upheld federal statutes restricting sales of firearms. *Mance v. Holder*, 896 F.3d 699 (5th Cir. 2018) (per curiam), *withdrawing and substituting* 880 F.3d 183 (5th Cir. 2018), *rev'g* 74 F. Supp. 3d 795 (N.D. Tex. 2015) (10 U.S.C. §922(3)); *see also United States v. Focia*, 869 F.3d 1269, 1286 (11th Cir. 2017) (18 U.S.C. §922(5)); *United States v. Hosford*, 843 F.3d 161 (4th Cir. 2016) (§922(a)(1)(A)).

[Points to Remember for Chapter 13 is contained in online file.]

TABLE OF CASES

Principal cases are indicated by bolded page numbers.

Los Angeles v. Preferred Commc'ns, Inc., 476 U.S. 488 (1986), 1655

Los Angeles, City of v. Lyons, 461 U.S. 95 (1983), 50, 88

Louisiana; United States v., 363 U.S. 1 (1960), 383

Louisville Joint Stock Land Bank v. Radford, 295 U.S. 555 (1935), 661

Lovell v. City of Griffin, 303 U.S. 444 (1938), 499, **1435–1436**, 1437, 1492

Loving v. Virginia, 388 U.S. 1 (1967), 793, 812–813, 822, 837, 839, 844, 846, **923–925**

Lubin v. Panish, 415 U.S. 709 (1974), 1110

Lucas v. Forty-fourth Gen. Assembly of Colo., 377 U.S. 713 (1964), 1072

Lucas v. South Carolina Coastal Council, 505 U.S. 1003 (1992), **624–632**, 633, 635, 636, 638–640, 644, 651

Lugar v. Edmondson Oil Co., 457 U.S. 922 (1982), 513, **536–538**

Lujan v. Defenders of Wildlife, 504 U.S. 555 (1992), 41, **96–97**, 106

Lunding v. New York Tax Appeals Tribunal, 522 U.S. 287 (1998), 465

Luther v. Borden, 48 U.S. 1 (1849), 35

Lynch v. Donnelly, 465 U.S. 668 (1984), 58, 1794–1797, 1804–1805, 1816, 1837

Lyng v. Northwest Indian Cemetery Protective Ass'n, 485 U.S. 439 (1988), **1850–1854**, 1906

MacCollum; United States v., 426 U.S. 317 (1976), 1047

Mai v. United States, 952 F.3d 1106, 1115 (9th Cir. 2020), 1922

Madigan, Illinois ex rel. v. Telemarketing Assocs., Inc. *See* Illinois ex rel. Madigan v. Telemarketing Assocs., Inc.

Madsen v. Women's Health Ctr., Inc., 512 U.S. 753 (1994), 1248, **1457–1453**, 1464

Magnano Co. v. Hamilton, 292 U.S. 40 (1934), 198

Mahan v. Howell, 410 U.S. 315 (1973), 1072, 1073

Maher v. Roe, 432 U.S. 464 (1977), 780

Mahoney v. Doe, 642 F.3d 1112 (D.C. Cir. 2011), 1437

Maine v. Taylor, 477 U.S. 131 (1986), 470, 482

Malloy v. Hogan, 378 U.S. 1 (1964), 749–750

Mance v. Holder, 896 F. 3d 699 (5th Cir. 2018), 1925

Manhattan Community Access Corp. v. Halleck, 139 S. Ct. 1921 (2019), 583–588, 1522–1523

Manigault v. Springs, 199 U.S. 473 (1905), 733

Manook, Estate of v. Research Triangle Inst., 759 F. Supp. 2d 674 (E.D.N.C. 2010), 566

Marbury v. Madison, 5 U.S. 137, (1 Cranch) 137, 2 L. Ed. 60 (1803), **3–7**, 12, 18, 19, 25, 33, 36, 53, 71, 76, 178, 185, 241, 341, 390, 394, 423, 748, 759, 1075, 1084, 1353

Marquan M.; People v., 24 N.Y.3d 1, 19 N.E.3d 480, 994 N.Y.S.2d 554 (N.Y. App. 2014), 1256

Marriage Cases, In re, 43 Cal. 4th 757, 183 P.3d 384 (2008), 834

Marsh v. Alabama, 326 U.S. 501 (1946), **563–564**, 565, 566, 570, 573, 585, 604, 623, 1529

Marsh v. Chambers, 463 U.S. 783 (1983), 1772, 1779, 1796, 1804, 1811, 1823, 1832, 1833

Martin v. Hunter's Lessee, 14 U.S. 304 (1816), **9–10**

Martin v. Struthers, City of, 319 U.S. 141 (1943), 1273

Martinez v. Bynum, 461 U.S. 321 (1983), 1126

Maryland v. Wirtz, 392 U.S. 183 (1968), 170, 188

Marzzarella; United States v., 614 F.3d 85 (3d Cir. 2010), *cert. denied*, 562 U.S. 1158, 131 S. Ct. 958 (2011), 1921, 1922, 1925

Masciandaro; United States v., 638 F.3d 458 (4th Cir.), *cert. denied*, 132 S. Ct. 756 (2011), 1923

Massachusetts v. Environmental Prot. Agency, 549 U.S. 497 (2007), **89–95**, 98, 103

Massachusetts v. Mellon, 262 U.S. 447 (1923), 51, 53, 54, 91, 210

Massachusetts v. United States, 435 U.S. 444 (1978), **408–412**

Massachusetts Bd. of Ret. v. Murgia, 427 U.S. 307 (1976), 893

Masson v. New Yorker Magazine, Inc., 501 U.S. 496 (1991), 1216

Masterpiece Cakeshop, Ltd. v. Colorado Civil Rights Commission, 138 S. Ct. 1719 (2018), 1879–1888

Matal v. Tam, 137 S. Ct. 1744 (2017), 1195, 1197, 1383, **1605–1610**, 1887

Mathews v. Diaz, 426 U.S. 67 (1976), 1021

Mathews v. Eldridge, 424 U.S. 319 (1976), 370, **641–648**, 648

Mathews v. Lucas, 427 U.S. 495 (1976), 1035

Matter of. *See name of party*

Mayer v. Chicago, 404 U.S. 189 (1971), 1047

Maynard v. Hill, 125 U.S. 190 (1888), 838, 844

Mazurek v. Armstrong, 520 U.S. 968 (1997), 796

McAllen Grace Brethren Church v. Salazar, 764 F.3d 465 (5th Cir. 2014), 1864

McBurney v. Young, 569 U.S. 201 (2013), 516–517, **527–530**

McCabe v. Atchison, Topeka & Santa Fe Ry. Co., 235 U.S. 151 (1914), 597

Principal coverage is indicated by bolded page numbers.